THE ROUGH GUIDE TO

SOUTH AMERICA
ON A BUDGET

This fifth edition updated by
Steph Dyson, Nick Edwards, Sara Humphreys, Daniel Jacobs, Anna Kaminski, Stephen Keeling, Shafik Meghji, Sorrel Moseley-Williams, Todd Obolsky, Daniel Schechter, Iain Stewart, Madelaine Triebe and Chris Wallace

ROUGH
GUIDES

Contents

Introduction to
South America

From the cloudforests of Ecuador to the pampas of Argentina, South America is a dizzying trove of landscapes, ancient ruins, giant rivers and dynamic, modern cities that have fuelled the imagination of adventurers for centuries. Trace Darwin's voyage through the Galápagos, Francisco de Orellana's fantastical journey along the Amazon or Che Guevara's route across the snowcapped peaks of the Andes. Discover Eva Perón's Buenos Aires, a truly beautiful, stylish metropolis, or pick up the trail of Bruce Chatwin across the lonely plains and ice-bound fjords of Patagonia. Whether exploring the elegant cities of Gabriel García Márquez's Colombia, soaking up Aymara culture in Bolivia, or just chilling on a white-sand Brazilian beach, options for budget travellers remain extensive and highly alluring.

Much of the continent's dynamism is a result of the collision of cultures here over the last five hundred years. South America's peoples were devastated by European invasion in the sixteenth and seventeenth centuries, not least by the introduction of diseases that killed thousands. Yet **indigenous culture** never entirely disappeared and is especially strong in Peru, Bolivia and Brazil to this day. Indeed, much of the continent's people are proud of their **mestizo heritage**; indigenous, Spanish and Portuguese cultures dominate, but West African, British, Italian, German, French and Dutch influences have also contributed over the years, supplemented more recently by waves of Japanese, Chinese and Middle Eastern settlers. As the Argentine saying goes, "Peruvians come from the Incas; Argentines come from the boats".

This blending of races and cultures across the continent means that South American nations have a lot in common. **Catholicism** has provided a foundation for spiritual life here for centuries – sometimes blurring with far more ancient indigenous beliefs, especially in the Andes, it has created a legacy of magnificent churches and exuberant fiestas. When it comes to natural wonders the continent is equally blessed, with just about every terrain – from deserts and glaciers, to grasslands, rainforests and wetlands

– and a range of **wildlife** found nowhere else: rheas, llamas, giant anteaters, jaguars and armadillos among them. The mighty Amazon River connects the Atlantic with the Brazilian jungle and the Peruvian Andes, while the lofty mountain chain itself runs from Colombia and Ecuador in the north, through Peru and Bolivia to the south of Chile and Argentina. This shared cultural and natural heritage is reflected in the ease of crossing borders, with multi-nation itineraries relatively simple to put together, whether traversing the River Plate between Argentina and Uruguay or the Atacama between Chile and Peru.

Today, South America is booming: Portuguese-speaking Brazil, the largest, richest and most populated country in South America, is a global power in the making, while Peru, Chile, Colombia and Argentina are important regional players. It's an exciting time to visit; backpackers will still find an extensive range of accommodation on offer, with plenty of options for the tight budget. South America also sports some of the best camping and hammock-slinging spots in the world, as well as many exhilarating **adventure tourism** destinations. Travelling within the continent varies wildly from country to country; sometimes it will require a little patience, initiative and navigating of red tape, but the colourful bus journeys, sunrise ferry crossings and people you'll meet along the way will be impossible to forget.

SOUTH AMERICA'S BEST BEACHES

1 Brazil: Copacabana and Ipanema, Rio
It's hard to beat the sand, cocktails and glamour at Brazil's most famous beaches, where you can sip on fresh coconuts, listen to samba or play volleyball, all in the shadow of one of the most dynamic cities on earth.

2 Brazil: South Atlantic beaches
The longest stretch of tropical beaches in the world? From the gorgeous tropical strands south of Salvador at Morro de São Paolo, a jumping resort of laidback lounges, bars and parties, all the way to Jericoacora, the land of giant dunes, celebrated for wind- and kite-surfing.

3 Colombia: Parque Nacional Tayrona
Colombia's Caribbean coast is lined with fine, white-sand beaches all the way to Panama, but some of the best (and least developed) can be found in this pristine national park, a short drive or boat ride from the city of Santa Marta.

4 Ecuador: Playa Los Frailes, Parque Nacional Machalilla
The most enticing of Ecuador's Pacific beaches, a blissfully untouched strand of chalky sand backed by jungle-smothered mountains. Visit during the week and you'll probably have it to yourself, especially in the early morning.

5 Peru: Huanchaco
Peru offers a string of relaxed backpacker resorts, from quiet retreats to party places such as Máncora, but the surfer hangout of Huanchaco just about tops the lot with its fine beaches and fishing-village appeal.

6 Uruguay: Cabo Polonio
Cabo Polonio is the place to really escape from civilization (it's only accessible by boat, 4WD jeep or a 7km hike over the rolling dunes). The main activities here are lounging in hammocks, strolling the dunes and visiting the nearby sea lions.

7 Venezuela: Playa El Agua, Isla de Margarita
Almost as glitzy as Copacabana (but much cheaper), El Agua is a 4km-long strip of golden sands, backed by huge palm trees, restaurants and jumping bars. Venezuela's current troubles seem very far away indeed.

SOUTH AMERICA

ATLANTIC OCEAN

Equator

CARIBBEAN SEA

PANAMÁ

COSTA RICA

NICARAGUA

Tobago

Trinidad

Cartagena

Maracaibo

CARACAS

Ciudad Bolívar

VENEZUELA

GEORGETOWN

PARAMARIBO

CAYENNE

GUYANA

SURINAME

FRENCH GUIANA

GRAN SABANA

Medellín

BOGOTÁ

COLOMBIA

Cali

QUITO

ECUADOR

Chimborazo (6310m)

Guayaquil

Cuenca

Gulf of Guayaquil

Galápagos Archipelago (Ecuador)

Iquitos

Leticia

Tabatinga

AMAZON BASIN

Macapá

Belém

São Luís

Manaus

Rio Amazonas

Porto Velho

Rio Branco

PERU

LIMA

Trujillo

Huascarán (6768m)

ANDES MOUNTAINS

Cusco

Lago Titicaca

Illimani (6402m)

LA PAZ

Arica

Iquique

BOLIVIA

Trinidad

Santa Cruz

Lago de Poopó

Sucre

Potosí

BRAZIL

BRASÍLIA

Cuiabá

Campo Grande

PARAGUAY

Fortaleza

Natal

Recife

Salvador

Belo Horizonte

Where to go

Brazil alone could occupy several months of travel, though many pan-continental itineraries also begin or end with **Rio de Janeiro**, one of South America's most alluring cities: with the world's most exuberant carnival, hip nightlife, trend-setting beaches and that mesmerizing skyline, it's hard to beat. South of Rio lie the wealthier parts of the country, from the colonial elegance of **Paraty**, the sprawling business and cultural hub of **São Paulo** and awe-inspiring **Iguaçu Falls** (also accessible from Argentina), to the golden beaches of **Florianópolis** and backpacker-friendly **Ilha do Mel**. Heading towards Uruguay, **Porto Alegre** is the home of belt-busting Brazilian churrasco (barbecue). In Northeast Brazil, the easy-going city of **Salvador** is one of the most energetic in the country and the home of tropical beaches and Afro-Brazilian culture. The interior of Brazil contains the enchanting colonial heartland of **Minas Gerais**, the unfairly maligned Modernist capital of **Brasília** and ultimately the **Amazonian Basin**, an unimaginably vast region of rivers and rainforest, rich in wildlife, best accessed from Belém or Manaus. It's possible to travel by boat from the mouth of the Amazon all the way to Peru, a spellbinding adventure.

Trips to **Chile** and **Argentina** are easily combined, often beginning with grand old **Buenos Aires**, Argentina's capital and the ravishing city of Evita, tango, Borges and Boca Juniors. To the west sits **Mendoza**, centre of Argentina's ever-improving wine regions, while across the pampas to the south lies **Patagonia**, divided from its Chilean

counterpart by the jagged peaks of the Andes. Slicing between the two countries are mind-boggling glaciers and ice-fields, shimmering mountain lakes, volcanoes and activity-based mountain towns, from **Bariloche** and the trekking centre of **El Chaltén** in Argentina, to **Pucón** and **Puerto Natales** across the Chilean border – the latter is the gateway to the jaw-dropping **Parque Nacional Torres del Paine**. These days **Tierra del Fuego** is more a land of penguins, sea lions and flamingos than a "land of fire", and is also split between the two countries, with isolated **Ushuaia** in Argentina the world's southernmost city. North of Chile's capital, **Santiago**, and the elegantly faded port city of **Valparaíso**, the **Atacama Desert** provides a dramatic, witheringly beautiful contrast. The sandy beaches of **Arica** in northern Chile make a pleasant stop en route to Peru or Bolivia.

Sandwiched between Argentina and Brazil, and easily tacked on to a trip to either, **Paraguay** and **Uruguay** lack major showstoppers, though landlocked Paraguay's Jesuit ruins and national parks offer a glimpse of a South America untrammelled by the twenty-first century. While adventure tourists may not flock to Uruguay, its relaxed, cultured capital **Montevideo** (an easy day-trip from Buenos Aires) sports crumbling churches and enlightening museums. **Punta del Este**'s upmarket beach resorts are only a couple of hours from here and are worth checking out, if only briefly, by those on a budget.

Bolivia is perhaps the continent's most intriguing destination, encompassing snaggle-toothed peaks, dense jungles and a dynamic indigenous culture, best absorbed in the capital **La Paz**, around **Lake Titicaca**, heartland of the Aymara and especially on the **Isla del Sol**, said to be the spiritual centre of the Andean world. The silver-mining city of **Potosí** funded the kings of Europe for centuries, while **Sucre** is one of the most captivating colonial cities on the continent.

Backpackers continue to flock to **Peru**, globally renowned for the great Inca ruins at **Cusco**, the **Valle Sagrado** and especially **Machu Picchu**, the jaw-dropping mountain hideout on which all images of "lost cities" are now based. Many travellers reach the city on foot via the **Inca Trail**, a truly magical experience. Yet Peru has a lot more to offer, from virgin Amazonian jungle protected in parks such as the **Pacaya Samiria National Reserve** and a long dry coastline where ceviche became an art form, to the booming nightlife and innovative culinary scene in **Lima**.

Ecuador has much in common with Peru and is easily combined with a trip to its larger southern neighbour. The highland capital, **Quito**, is crammed with absorbing museums and colonial architecture, while the rest of the country is littered with volcanoes, old Spanish towns and beguiling indigenous markets. Naturalists, however, should head straight for the extraordinary **Galápagos** islands, home to some of the world's most astonishing wildlife.

At the northern end of the continent, **Colombia** continues to be an up-and-coming travel destination, much safer after years of drug wars and guerrilla insurgencies. Immerse yourself in the salsa-soaked nightlife of **Bogotá**, the coffee-growing landscapes of the **Zona Cafetera** and the romantic colonial towns of **Cartagena** and **Popayán**. The mesmerizing scenery around **Villa de Leyva** is perfect for hiking, while **San Gil** is the base for adventure sports, especially white-water rafting. Far to the north, closer to Nicaragua than South America, the **Isla de Providencia** is part of the remote San Andrés chain, home of palm-fringed Caribbean beaches and a spectacular reef ideal for divers.

Neighbouring **Venezuela** remains a far more challenging country to visit (see page 860), but the rewards for doing so are considerable; experience untouched national parks, spectacular Caribbean beaches and the Amazon region of Guayana, which contains the **Angel Falls**, the world's tallest waterfall.

The **Guianas**, comprising the former British and Dutch colonies of **Guyana** and **Suriname** and the French overseas département of **French Guiana**, are often overlooked. However, their three capital cities, Georgetown, Paramaribo and Cayenne respectively, are home to cool bars and colonial wooden architecture in picturesque decay, while French Guiana has the added appeal of the **Centre Spatial Guyanais**, **Devil's Island** (immortalized in Papillon). English-speaking Guyana offers a taste of West Indian culture – with cricket, rum and rotis, it's more Barbados than Brazil.

When to go

With about two-thirds of South America near the equator or the Tropic of Capricorn, visitors to most destinations can expect a tropical or subtropical **climate** all year round. Temperatures rarely drop below 20°C, while rainforest regions average maximum temperatures of about 30°C. As you get further south (and don't forget the southern hemisphere reverses the seasons), you'll find colder winters from June to August and milder summers from December to February, with the extreme south of the continent freezing between April and October. It's important to plan around the **rainy season** in each country, particularly when travelling in the Andes.

Domestic tourism, especially in the richer countries of the south, is booming, meaning that hostels, hotels and transportation can become fully booked during the summer (December to March), especially on the coast, so book ahead if possible. Expect hordes of local tourists to hit the road in any country on major religious holidays, especially **Christmas** and **Semana Santa** (Easter).

Incredible Journeys

1 INCA TRAIL, PERU
See page 759
Tackle the four-day hike between Cusco and Machu Picchu, a spell-binding mountain trek into the Inca past.

2 CARRETERA AUSTRAL, CHILE
See page 444
Wend your way along this spectacular Patagonian highway, rounding ice-fields, vast glaciers and jagged fjords.

3 CYCLING THE DEATH ROAD, BOLIVIA
See page 171
A hair-raising adventure on two wheels in the mountains near La Paz.

4 RUTA 40, ARGENTINA
See page 134
Travel this epic 5000km highway along the Andes, from the Bolivian border to the bottom of Patagonia.

5 SERRA VERDE RAILWAY, BRAZIL
See page 347
This enchanting train ride winds around mountains and traverses one of the largest Atlantic Forest reserves in the country.

6 THE CIRCUIT, TORRES DEL PAINE, CHILE
See page 476
This seven- to ten-day hike is the best way to soak up the charms and wildlife of the rugged national park.

Architectural Wonders

1 VALPARAÍSO, CHILE
See page 390
Colourful half-painted houses cascade down the hills alongside distinctive *ascencores* (funiculars) in Chile's quirkiest city.

2 HISTORIC CENTRE, SALVADOR, BRAZIL
See page 277
Locals know it as Pelô and love this UNESCO World Heritage Site for its pastel-coloured buildings in their restored Renaissance glory.

3 CUSCO, PERU
See page 743
This former capital of the Inca empire charms with its colonial and Incan architectural treasures, which often battle it out on the same site.

4 NIEMEYER'S MASTERPIECES, BRAZIL
See page 315
Latin America's greatest architect, Oscar Niemeyer, designed the capital, Brasília, while his Museum of Modern Art, in Niterói near Rio, clings to the cliff like a recently landed flying-saucer.

5 CARTAGENA DE INDIAS, COLOMBIA
See page 515
The walled Old City is a beauty, its narrow old streets crammed with picturesque corners, while cool, new Afro-Colombian music blows in from Cartagena's neighbourhoods into the night.

6 LA COMPAÑÍA DE JESÚS, QUITO, ECUADOR
See page 573
Opulence? Try seven tonnes of gold to dress up this decadent wonder, which took 163 years to build.

Amazing Wildlife

1 THE PANTANAL, BRAZIL
See page 324

The world's largest wetland is home to thousands of animal species; giant river otters, giant anteaters, jaguars, pumas and capybaras among them.

2 GALÁPAGOS ISLANDS, ECUADOR
See page 632

Witness the giant tortoises, marine iguanas, penguins, sea lions and flightless cormorants that Charles Darwin observed, developing his theories on evolution here.

3 AMAZONIAN BASIN, BOLIVIA, BRAZIL, ECUADOR AND PERU
See pages 217, 302, 611 and 818

Explore the Amazon and you'll find everything from poison dart frogs to snapping piranhas.

4 CAÑÓN DEL COLCA, PERU
See page 783

The best place in the Andes to see condors rise up the sides of a mesmerizing canyon wall.

5 BEAGLE CHANNEL, ARGENTINA
See page 150

Take a thrilling boat trip to see the sea lions, penguins, whales and seabirds of Tierra del Fuego.

6 LOS LLANOS, VENEZUELA
See page 895

This tropical grassland supports hordes of capybaras, crocodiles, anaconda, armadillos, scarlet ibis and over sixty species of waterbirds.

Local Flavours

1 PISCO SOURS, CHILE AND PERU
See pages 403 and 772
There's a fierce rivalry between Chile and Peru about where the spirit pisco originates, but everyone agrees it's best drunk in a pisco sour. You can visit pisco distilleries in Chile's Elqui Valley and Ica in Peru.

2 ASUNCIÓN, PARAGUAY
See page 695
Eat fresh street food at Mercado 4, one of Latin America's great markets, or make for the neighbourhood of Loma San Jerénimo where local houses have been converted into homespun restaurants, and roof terraces into bars.

3 MENDOZA'S BODEGAS, ARGENTINA
See page 101
Splash out on a degustation – and a glass of wine, naturally – among the vineyards with views of the cordillera.

4 CÓRDOBA, ARGENTINA
See page 72
A wining and dining delight for everyone, the city offers fashionable restaurants in converted mansions, tasty empanadas on the go and edgy bars in revamped warehouses.

5 RIO DE JANEIRO'S NIGHTLIFE
See page 254
Head to the neighbourhood of Lapa on Friday night for its street parties and samba.

6 MIRAFLORES AND BARRANCO, LIMA, PERU
See page 735
These swanky neighbourhoods are Lima's sparkling coastal highlights; treat yourself to delicious lime-marinated ceviche and ocean views.

Itineraries

You can't expect to fit everything South America has to offer into one trip – or two or three or four, to be fair – and we don't suggest you try. This selection of itineraries will guide you through the different countries and regions, picking out a few of the best places and major attractions along the way. For those taking a big, extended trip around the continent you could join a few together, but remember that the distances you'll be covering can be vast. There is, of course, much to discover off the beaten track, so if you have the time it's worth exploring smaller towns, villages and wilderness areas further afield, finding your own perfect hill town, deserted beach or just a place you love to rest up and chill out.

SOUTHERN BRAZIL

❶ Rio de Janeiro The beaches, the samba, the towering statue of Christ the Redeemer looming over it all – Rio has every base covered to kick off your trip in style. See page 237

❷ Costa Verde Backed by forested mountain peaks, the coastline between Rio and São Paulo contains hidden gems like colonial Paraty and spectacular beaches at Ilha Grande. See page 256

❸ Minas Gerais This state inland from Rio offers some of Brazil's most stunning historic towns – none more attractive than Ouro Preto. See page 262

❹ Brasília Come see the vision of the future, circa 1960, courtesy of Oscar Niemeyer's Modernist architecture. See page 315

❺ The Pantanal If you're not going to make it out to the Galápagos during your travels, consider checking out the huge array of wildlife in this vast wetland. See page 324

❻ Ilha Santa Catarina Some of the best beaches in the country can be found on the coast near Florianópolis. See page 354

❼ Serra Gaúcha The mountain bases of Canela and Gramado serve two nearby parks with crashing falls and challenging climbs and hikes. See page 362

NORTHERN ARGENTINA, PARAGUAY AND URUGUAY

❶ **Buenos Aires** The most cosmopolitan of all South American cities, worth a few days of anyone's time. See page 54

❷ **Colonia del Sacramento** If you're just going to dip into Uruguay, you can't do better than the historic centre of this charming town. See page 846

❸ **Eastern beaches, Uruguay** Beach getaways to suit every budget, from quiet Cabo Polonio with no roads or electricity to the flashy surf resort of Punta del Este. See page 853

❹ **Rosario** The perfect spot to launch yourself into the Paraná Delta. See page 80

❺ **Córdoba** Wander from the colonial centre to Nuevo Córdoba, a neighbourhood chock-a-block with cool bars and restaurants in converted mansions. See page 72

❻ **Mendoza** Undoubtedly the best stop for wine-lovers, a sophisticated city with great restaurants and hundreds of nearby bodegas. See page 101

❼ **Cerro Aconcagua** Whether you take two weeks to scale the summit or just see a section on a day-hike, the tallest mountain in the western hemisphere will sear itself into your memory. See page 107

❽ **Salta** Its central plaza is a lovely place to begin an evening stroll. See page 92

❾ **Parque Nacional el Rey** The lush cloudforests here hold colourful toucans, as well as other exotic fauna and flora. See page 96

❿ **Iguazú Falls** Better to see the crashing waters from the trails and catwalks on the Argentina side. See page 88

⓫ **The Ruta Jesuítica** Visit Paraguay's famous Jesuit ruins; Trinidad and Jesús are a four- to five-hour coach ride from Iguazú Falls. See page 704

CHILE AND ARGENTINA: THE LAKE DISTRICTS AND PATAGONIA

❶ **Volcán Villarrica** Skiing, snowboarding, mountaineering – you can experience the smouldering volcano up close. See page 435

❷ **Lago Llanquihue** A sparkling blue lake with volcanoes, white-water rafting and waterfalls. See page 438

❸ **Western and southern Chiloé** The protected areas have some great coastal hiking through fishing villages, forests and beaches. See page 444

❹ **San Martín de los Andes** A lower-key version of Bariloche and a hub for getting out to the nearby lakes and Parque Lanín. See page 116

❺ **Parque Nacional Nahuel Huapi** Well-marked trails, plentiful campsites and huts, crystal-clear lakes and much more make this the most popular Patagonian park on the Argentine side. See page 123

❻ **Península Valdés** Consider an eastern detour here to see abundant birdlife, a sea-lion colony and – if you time it right – whales on their migration route. See page 131

❼ **Perito Moreno Glacier** The unquestioned highlight of Parque Nacional Los Glaciares, a calving glacier that provides theatrical drama for onlookers. See page 144

❽ **Parque Nacional Torres del Paine** The most famous destination on the Chilean side of Patagonia – and perhaps the best trekking in the entire region. See page 471

NORTHERN ARGENTINA, PARAGUAY AND URUGUAY

CHILE AND ARGENTINA:
THE LAKE DISTRICTS
AND PATAGONIA

PACIFIC OCEAN

CHILE

ARGENTINA

URUGUAY

ATLANTIC OCEAN

0   400
kilometres

⑤ San Pedro de Atacama An oasis town chock-full of natural attractions in the surrounding *altiplano* wilderness. See page 409

⑥ Salar de Uyuni You'll have to go on a tour, but it's worth the trip to see the flat, white salt "lake", perfectly reflective in summer when covered with water. See page 196

⑦ Potosí The colonial architecture and lively cafés make an uneasy contrast with the tragic legacy of the nearby silver mines at Cerro Rico. See page 191

NORTHERN CHILE AND
SOUTHERN BOLIVIA

BRAZIL

PERU

BOLIVIA

PARAGUAY

PACIFIC OCEAN

CHILE

ARGENTINA

ATLANTIC OCEAN

0   200
kilometres

⑨ Ushuaia If you've made it here you're practically at the end of the world – send a postcard, eat some seafood, ski in winter and dream of Antarctica, 1000km away. See page 146

NORTHERN CHILE AND SOUTHERN BOLIVIA

① Santiago Relatively developed Santiago is a gentle introduction to South America, with some interesting museums and neighbourhoods to explore. See page 378

② Valparaíso Ride the *ascensores* (funiculars) around the hilly streets by day, then eat, drink and carouse in the gritty port area at night. See page 390

③ Pisco Elqui This charming village, with views over the Elqui valley, is the perfect place to sample a pisco sour. See page 403

④ Parque Nacional Nevado de Tres Cruces Drive by arid salt flats, spot vicuñas and guanacos, and stay by a lake populated with colourful flamingos. See page 405

❽ Santa Cruz One of the rare places in Bolivia known for its excellent restaurant and club scene. See page 211

ECUADOR, PERU AND NORTHERN BOLIVIA

❶ Guayaquil An alternative introduction to Ecuador than more traditional Quito; the Malecón and nearby beaches make it seem like a different land entirely. See page 623

❷ Otavalo Few can resist the town's famous Saturday market, the ultimate place to purchase a hammock or woodcarving as a keepsake. See page 584

❸ Quito Base yourself in the old town, where plaza after plaza provides a vantage point for historic churches and narrow walkways. See page 571

❹ The Quilotoa Loop Hike for a few days around the peaceful waters of a volcanic crater lake. See page 591

❺ Nariz del Diablo train ride A five-hour journey starting in Riobamba and slicing its glorious way through the Andes. See page 599

❻ Cuenca Ecuador's third-largest city and possibly its most beautiful, with cobbled streets and the vibe of an Andean town. See page 601

❼ Huaraz This lively city, nestled in a valley, affords you an approach to trekking in both the Cordillera Blanca and Cordillera Huayhuash. See page 791

❽ Lima Love it or hate it, you can nevertheless find plenty to occupy you in the Peruvian capital, and the proximity to the sea makes it a great place to try out ceviche. See page 730

❾ Trails to Machu Picchu Discover less expensive and less crowded alternative Inca Trails deep in the imposing jungle. See page 768

❿ Cusco As much of a hub as Lima and closer to many of the country's highlights – though its plazas, museums, restaurants and nightlife certainly stand on their own. See page 743

⓫ Lago Titicaca Whether you visit the Uros islands on the Peru side or the sacred Isla del Sol in the Bolivian section, you're certain to be awed by the high-altitude lake. See pages 177 and 789

⓬ La Paz Now this is what an Andean capital city should be: delightfully situated high up in

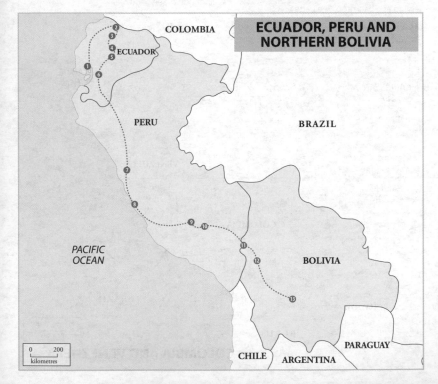

ECUADOR, PERU AND NORTHERN BOLIVIA

a canyon, full of interesting and inexpensive places to eat, drink and stay, and with an undeniable energy all its own. See page 166

⑬ Sucre The official capital's beautifully maintained colonial architecture accounts for the nickname "White City", but don't overlook this pretty town's excellent bars. See page 201

COLOMBIA AND VENEZUELA

Before undertaking this itinerary, note that Venezuela is in a state of crisis, that security (from crime) is a big problem in the country, that Western governments such as the UK's Foreign Office and US State Department were advising against all but essential travel there, and that you should therefore check out the latest situation before deciding whether to go there.

❶ Bogotá Colombia's densely packed, cosmopolitan capital divides opinion, but is a worthwhile first or last stop for its colonial architecture and raucous nightlife. See page 495

❷ San Agustín A crazy array of monolithic statues, with a lovely mountain landscape serving as a backdrop. See page 553

❸ Cali This might be Colombia's most fun and freewheeling city, with plenty of salsa clubs

and streetlife to balance out the sober array of churches. See page 546

❹ Medellín From Cali you can travel up to Medellín – an attractive, modern city that's had quite a makeover in the past decade – via Colombia's coffee country. See page 534

❺ Cartagena The jewel of the Caribbean coast, a gorgeous colonial city and a must on any Colombia trip. See page 515

❻ Parque Nacional Tayrona Beautiful beaches, lush flora and pre-Columbian ruins are the highlights of this pristine coastal park, accessed from Santa Marta. See page 526

❼ San Gil Colombia's best spot for adventure sports is known for its white-water rafting, but you can also try out paragliding, kayaking, abseiling and more in the mountains north of Bogotá. See page 508

❽ Villa de Leyva Under an hour from San Gil, this is a thoroughly unmodern and relaxed colonial town; from Villa de Leyva or San Gil you can loop back to Bucaramanga for buses to the border with Venezuela at Cúcuta, though don't linger here. See page 505

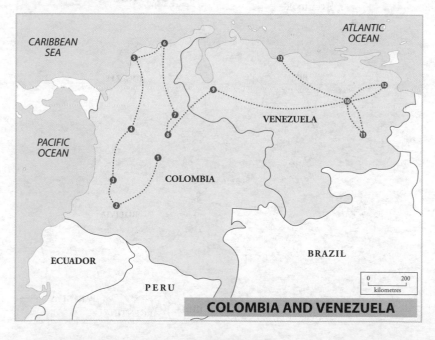

COLOMBIA AND VENEZUELA

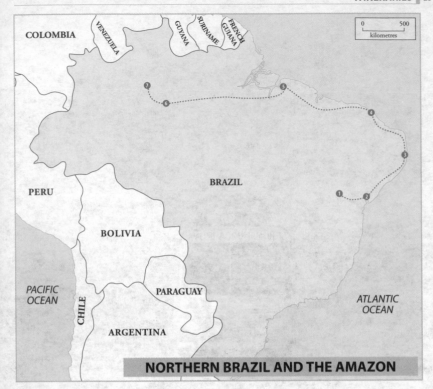

NORTHERN BRAZIL AND THE AMAZON

❾ Mérida Contemplate adventures to nearby mountains, a trip to wildlife-rich Los Llanos or just chill out in this laidback city. See page 889

❿ Ciudad Bolívar Venezuela's most lovely colonial town and the gateway to Angel Falls and the Orinoco Delta. See page 899

⓫ Angel Falls Journey by boat and on foot to reach this towering waterfall. See page 902

⓬ Orinoco Delta Visit the delta jungle region for a truly mind-blowing experience. See page 905

⓭ Parque Nacional Henri Pittier A great mix of beaches, wildlife and walking trails – and it's relatively near Caracas, which makes your exit or travel connections easier. See page 881

NORTHERN BRAZIL AND THE AMAZON

❶ Chapada Diamantina Some of the best hiking and waterfall hunting in the country is to be found in this canyon-filled national park. See page 287

❷ Salvador For candomblé, capoeira or Carnaval, Bahia's capital is practically the country's capital. Seek out fine beaches, diving and surf at nearby Morro de São Paulo. See page 277

❸ Olinda You won't find a prettier array of churches, plazas and houses anywhere in the north of the country. See page 295

❹ Fortaleza The central market is a sure bet to buy a hammock; take it with you to Jericoara, the best beach in the area. See page 298

❺ Belém Great restaurants and bars, but the main reason to come is its location at the mouth of the Amazon. See page 302

❻ Manaus After seeing the astounding Teatro Amazonas, grab some of the fine street food on offer and head to the lively port area. See page 309

❼ Amazon river trip Float along the Rio Negro to a jungle lodge or even just a clearing where you can string up a hammock – or head along the Amazon all the way to Iquitos in Peru. See page 313

HUMAHUACA TO IRUYA BUS, ARGENTINA

Basics

Getting there

The range of direct flights from Europe to South America – particularly Argentina, Brazil and Chile – is currently expanding. As well as European carriers like British Airways, Iberia and Air France, South American airlines, such as Aerolíneas Argentinas, Avianca and particularly LATAM (previously LAN and TAM), provide a choice of schedules and routes. Many people travel via the USA, usually through a hub such as Dallas-Fort Worth, Atlanta or Miami; these routes are particularly useful for northern South America. Note that many immigration departments in South America insist you have an onward or return ticket to enter the country, though the application of such rules is stricter in some countries than in others.

Airfares are seasonal, with the highest around July, August and mid-December to mid-January; you'll get the best prices during the dry winter (May, June and late Sept) and the wet summer (in most of the region Feb–April, excluding Carnaval and Easter). Flying on weekends is often more expensive. You can generally cut costs by going through a specialist flight agent, booking flights well in advance or taking advantage of online-only offers and (sometimes) airline frequent-flyer programmes. Another way to cut costs is to book with a tour operator that can put together a package deal including flights and accommodation, and tours as well.

Compare flight prices online with a site like Ⓦskyscanner.net.

Flights from the UK and Ireland

Book months, not weeks, in advance for cheaper flights to South America from the UK, unless you manage to get a last-minute deal – which you can't always bank on. If you're prepared to fly indirectly, you'll also get a cheaper price, but this could mean a long stopover. Return flights from the UK and Ireland start at around £450–500, though you should expect to pay more. British Airways has direct flights from Heathrow to Rio de Janeiro in Brazil, Buenos Aires in Argentina and Santiago in Chile, though fares tend to be more expensive than those of its European and South American rivals. In early 2018, Norwegian launched "low-cost" flights from Gatwick to Buenos Aires, and reportedly has plans for flights to further destinations in South America. There are also plenty of options to travel with a European airline such as Air Europa (which vies with Norwegian to provide the cheapest fares), Iberia, TAP or Air France, via their hub cities. US airlines like American Airlines sometimes offer competitive fares, too.

Flights from the US and Canada

American, Delta and United airlines have direct flights to most major South American capitals from US cities, with the cheapest fares generally from Dallas-Fort Worth, Atlanta and Miami. Several South American Airlines also serve the USA; Avianca often has good-value fares to northern South America, particularly its home base of Colombia. Direct flights from Canada are very limited; it's generally best to travel via the USA, though it is also possible to travel via Central America. Expect to pay from around US$500 for return flights from either the US or Canada.

Flights from Australia and NZ

The best deals to South America are offered by Aerolíneas Argentinas and LATAM in conjunction with Qantas and Air New Zealand. Aerolíneas Argentinas flies from Sydney to Buenos Aires, via Auckland, with connections across the continent; Qantas has code-shares with LATAM via Auckland to Santiago and beyond. There are also plenty of flights via the US, but these take longer and tend to cost more. From Australia and NZ expect to pay at least US$1400 – but you can sometimes pay much more. Often airlines will charge more if you wish to stay in South America for longer than a month.

ESTA CLEARANCE

The US government requires those travellers coming to or through the USA (even just transiting) on the **Visa Waiver Program** to apply for clearance via **ESTA** (Electronic System for Travel Authorization). This is not something to ignore – if you arrive at the airport without having done it, the airline won't allow you to check in. To apply, visit Ⓦcbp.gov/travel/international-visitors/esta. Make sure you do this at least 72 hours before travelling; you'll need your passport to hand, and the admin fee is US$14. Once a traveller has received clearance, it remains valid for two years for unlimited visits.

MAJOR BORDER CROSSINGS, OVERLAND AND SEA ROUTES

The following is an overview of the main land and sea crossings travellers can use to travel between the countries of South America. The information is fleshed out in the accounts of relevant border towns within this book.

TO ARGENTINA

From Brazil Most people use the easy road crossing to Puerto Iguazú from Foz do Iguaçu. See page 46.

From Bolivia There are three overland entry points: Villazón to La Quiaca, Bermejo to Aguas Blancas and Yacuiba to Pocitos. See page 46.

From Chile The most popular border crossing is the Santiago–Mendoza route via the Los Libertadores tunnel. If you're coming from the south, routes in the Lake District include Osorno–Bariloche, and Temuco–San Martín de Los Andes. Further south still are the Puerto Natales–El Calafate and Punta Arenas–Río Gallegos crossings. In the north, there is a popular crossing from San Pedro de Atacama to Jujuy/Salta. See page 46.

From Paraguay Popular road crossings include to Posadas from Encarnación, to Clorinda from Puerto Falcón, and to Puerto Iguazú from Ciudad del Este. See page 46.

From Uruguay Boats to Buenos Aires depart regularly from Colonia del Sacramento, and less frequently to Tigre from Carmelo. You can also cross by road to Gualeguaychú from Fray Bentos. See page 46.

TO BOLIVIA

From Argentina There are three overland entry points: La Quiaca to Villazón, Aguas Blancas to Bermejo, and Pocitos to Yacuiba. See page 157.

From Brazil The busiest crossing is from Corumbá to the railhead of Puerto Quijarro. There are also crossings in the Amazon, including from Guajará-Mirim to Guayaramerín. See page 157.

From Chile The most popular crossing is from San Pedro de Atacama to Uyuni via a three-/four-day salt flats tour. See page 160.

From Paraguay There's an arduous crossing via the trans-Chaco road. See page 160.

From Peru The most popular, and straight-forward, crossing is around Lake Titicaca, from Puno to Copacabana. See page 160.

TO BRAZIL

From Argentina Most people use the easy road crossing to Foz do Iguaçu from Puerto Iguazú. See page 227.

From Bolivia The busiest crossing is from the railhead of Puerto Quijarro to Corumbá. There are also crossings in the Amazon, including from Guayaramerín to Guajará-Mirim. See page 227.

From Colombia In the Amazon region it is possible to take a riverboat from Leticia to Manaus. See page 489.

From the Guianas Minibuses cross from the Guyanese town of Lethem to Boa Vista, 130km southwest. See page 230.

From Paraguay Most people cross over the Puente de la Amistad bridge from Ciudad del Este to Foz do Iguaçu. See page 230.

From Peru There is a land crossing to Assis Brasil from the Peruvian village of Iñapari. The small Amazonian port of Tabatinga can be reached from Iquitos, via the Santa Rosa border post. See page 561.

From Uruguay Many people use the overland crossing from Chuy to Chui; other options include from Rivera to Santana do Livramento, Bella Unión to Barra do Quarai, and Artigas to Quarai. See page 230.

From Venezuela From Santa Elena de Uairén buses cross to Boa Vista. See page 230.

TO CHILE

From Argentina One of the most popular border crossings is the Mendoza-Santiago route via the Los Libertadores tunnel. If you're coming from the south, routes in the Lake District include Bariloche-Osorno, and San Martín de Los Andes-Temuco. Further south still are the El Calafate-Puerto Natales and Río Gallegos-Punta Arenas crossings. In the north, there is a popular crossing from Jujuy/Salta to San Pedro de Atacama. See page 370.

From Bolivia The most popular crossing is from Uyuni to San Pedro de Atacama via a three-/four-day salt flats tour. See page 370.

From Peru Frequent buses, *colectivos* and taxis cross from Tacna to Arica. See page 370.

TO COLOMBIA

From Brazil In the Amazon region it is possible to take a riverboat from Manaus to Leticia. See page 489.

From Ecuador The Panamerican Highway runs north from Ecuador, with the Ipiales–Tulcán crossing the most popular and straightforward crossing. See page 489.

From Peru In the Amazon region travellers can take a riverboat from Iquitos to Leticia. See page 561.

From Venezuela There are three main overland border crossings: from San Cristóbal to Cúcuta, Maracaibo to Maicao, and Casuarito to Puerto Carreño. See page 489.

TO ECUADOR

From Colombia The Panamerican Highway runs south from Colombia, with the Ipiales–Tulcán crossing the most popular and straightforward crossing. See page 566.

From Peru There are three border crossings: Tumbes-Machala-Tumbes (the most popular, on the Panamericana); from Piura to Loja via La Tina; and (more difficult thanks to poorer roads and several bus changes) from Vilcabamba to Jaén. See page 566.

TO THE GUIANAS

From Brazil Minibuses cross from Boa Vista to the Guyanese town of Lethem, 130km northeast. See page 645.

TO PARAGUAY

From Argentina Popular road crossings include to Encarnación from Posadas, to Puerto Falcón from Clorinda, and to Ciudad del Este from Puerto Iguazú. See page 690.

From Bolivia There's an arduous crossing via the trans-Chaco road. See page 690.

From Brazil Most people cross over the Puente de la Amistad bridge from Foz do Iguaçu to Ciudad del Este. See page 690.

TO PERU

From Bolivia The most popular, and straight-forward, crossing is around Lake Titicaca, from Copacabana to Puno. See page 717.

From Brazil There is a land crossing from Assis Brasil to the Peruvian village of Iñapari, a three-hour bus ride from Puerto Maldonado. Inquitos can be reached from the small Amazonian port of Tabatinga via the Santa Rosa border post. See page 717.

From Chile Frequent buses, *colectivos* and taxis cross from Arica to Tacna. See page 720.

From Ecuador There are three border crossings: Machala-Tumbes (the most popular, on the Panamericana); from Loja to Piura via La Tina; and (more difficult thanks to poorer roads and several bus changes) from Jaén to Vilcabamba. See page 720.

TO URUGUAY

From Argentina Ferries head to Colonia del Sacramento from Buenos Aires, and less frequently to Carmelo from Tigre. There are buses from Colón. You can also cross by road to Fray Bentos from Gualeguaychú. See page 834.

From Brazil Many people use the overland crossing from Chui to Chuy; other options include from Santana do Livramento to Rivera, Barra do Quarai to Bella Unión, and Quarai to Artigas. See page 835.

TO VENEZUELA

From Brazil From Boa Vista, buses cross to Santa Elena de Uairén. See page 862.

From Colombia There are three main overland border crossings: from Cúcuta to San Cristóbal, Maicao to Maracaibo, and Puerto Carreño to Casuarito. See page 862.

ROUND-THE-WORLD TICKETS AND AIRPASSES

If South America is only one stop on a longer journey, consider buying a **round-the-world (RTW) ticket** – if your starting point is Australia or New Zealand, it may even be cheaper. An "off-the-shelf" ticket will have you touching down in about half a dozen cities. Alternatively, you can have a travel agent custom-make a RTW ticket for you, though this is more expensive. Fares depend on the month, point of origin and number of continents or distance travelled, and in general the more expensive options include South America, but they are worth exploring. Trailfinders (ⓦ trailfinders.com), STA Travel (ⓦ statravel.com) and Round The World Flights (ⓦ roundtheworldflights.com) all sell RTW tickets.

If you're planning to do a lot of travelling in South America, an alternative is to buy an **airpass**, for example, the Oneworld Visit South America Pass (ⓦ oneworld.com).

From Central America

Crossing overland from Panama into Colombia is not recommended as it entails traversing the Darién, a wild, lawless region occupied by guerrillas. The safest option is to fly – Bogotá and Caracas are the main points of entry – or take a boat from Panama to the Caribbean coast of Colombia. There is a ferry service from Colón in Panama to Cartagena, Colombia.

AIRLINES

Aerolíneas Argentinas ⓦ aerolineas.com.ar
Air Europa ⓦ aireuropa.com
Air France ⓦ airfrance.com
Air New Zealand ⓦ airnewzealand.com
Alitalia ⓦ alitalia.com
American Airlines ⓦ aa.com
Avianca ⓦ avianca.com
British Airways ⓦ ba.com
Delta Airlines ⓦ delta.com
Gol ⓦ voegol.com.br
Iberia Airlines ⓦ iberia.com
KLM ⓦ klm.com
LATAM ⓦ latam.com
Norwegian ⓦ norwegian.com
Qantas ⓦ qantas.com.au
TAP Air Portugal ⓦ flytap.com
United Airlines ⓦ united.com

A BETTER KIND OF TRAVEL

At **Rough Guides** we are passionately committed to travel. We believe it helps us understand the world we live in and the people we share it with – and of course tourism is vital to many developing economies. But the scale of modern tourism has also damaged some places irreparably, and climate change is accelerated by most forms of transport, especially flying. All Rough Guides' flights are carbon-offset.

AGENTS AND OPERATORS

Dragoman UK ☎ 01728 861133, ⓦ dragoman.com. A range of overland trips on a giant 4WD truck, with accommodation in hotels, hostels or tents.
Exodus UK ☎ 020 8675 5550, ⓦ exodus.co.uk. Walking and cycling – and everything in between across the continent.
HostelTrail ⓦ hosteltrail.com. A useful resource for hostels and budget tour companies in South America.
Hotwire ⓦ hotwire.com. Last-minute savings of up to forty percent on regular published fares. Travellers must be at least 18 and there are no refunds, transfers or changes allowed.
Intrepid Australia ⓦ intrepidtravel.com. Global company with almost three decades organizing adventure group travel – also has a "basix" option for those on a budget.
Journey Latin America UK ☎ 020 8747 8315, ⓦ journeylatinamerica.co.uk. Knowledgeable and helpful staff, good at sorting out stopovers, open-jaw flights and package tours.
REI Adventures US ☎ 1 800 622 2236, ⓦ rei.com/adventures. Climbing, cycling, hiking, cruising, paddling and multi-sport tours to many countries on the continent.
Round The World Flights ⓦ roundtheworldflights.com. Specialists in round-the-world flights, both tailored and off the shelf.
STA Travel UK ☎ 0333 321 0099, ⓦ statravel.co.uk. Low-cost flights and tours for students and under-26s, though other customers welcome. Good for round-the-world tickets.
Trailfinders UK ☎ 020 7368 1200, ⓦ trailfinders.com. One of the best-informed and most efficient agents for independent travellers.
Travel Cuts Canada ☎ 1 800 667 2887, ⓦ travelcuts.com. Canadian student-travel organization.
Tucan Travel Australia ☎ 029326 6633, ⓦ tucantravel.com. Specializing in adventure and backpacker holidays – and also has a budget option. Based in Australia but offices worldwide.
Wilderness Travel US ☎ 1 800 368 2794, ⓦ wildernesstravel.com. Adventure travel and wildlife tours throughout South America.

Getting around

Most South Americans travel by bus, and there is almost nowhere that you can't reach in this way. The major routes are

comfortable and reliable and always cost effective. Moreover, you will see more, and meet more people, if you travel by bus. Remember, though, that distances between towns can be huge, and that in more remote areas such as Patagonia there are few bus and no significant train services. If you have spare cash and limited time, you may want to fly occasionally, or rent a car. There are frequent flights within and between South American countries; the former are generally much cheaper. Public transport options vary within each country. Many places will have minibuses that depart when full and take set routes, as well as rickety local buses. There are also mototaxis in some places (similar to those in Thailand and India), which are good for covering short distances within towns.

By bus

This is by far the cheapest way to see the continent. While you can, technically, travel all the way from the tropical north to Tierra del Fuego by bus, there are relatively few direct international services and you often have to disembark at the border, cross it, then sometimes get on another bus to a large city in the new country. The best bet for an international service is in capital cities or major hubs near borders; in places with limited transport you may just have to buckle down and take what's on offer.

Terminals are often situated on the outskirts of towns – follow the signs to the *terminal* (in Spanish-speaking countries) or the *rodoviária* (in Brazil). Levels of comfort vary, so a quick visual check in the terminal will give you an idea of which company to go for. With better bus companies on long-distance routes, the **seating options** usually include normal seats, seats that partly recline (*semi-cama*) and seats that recline fully (*cama*) to become beds. They are priced according to the level of comfort, with the most expensive options including on-board meals, drinks, TV screens, and even games of bingo. Some of the cheapest companies only have one level of comfort and that can mean anything from wooden seats to standing in an aisle.

By car

In many parts of South America **roads**, especially outside the major cities, are notorious for their bumpy, potholed and generally poor conditions. Most car rental companies do not allow their vehicles to be driven across borders, making independent exploration of the continent by car difficult.

If you are determined to go it alone and drive around South America, you will find car rental companies at all airports and in most major cities. Hotels can advise you of better-value local places, but often it's better to book in advance online. Costs are high thanks to skyrocketing insurance rates, but the independence of a car may be worth it. An international driving licence is recommended although most of the time you will probably be able to use the one issued by your country of residence (and may not even be asked for the international one). Check your **insurance** carefully for exclusions, as car theft, vandalism and general security are renowned problems in many parts of South America, and you may not be covered for these. Damage to tyres or the underside of the car may also be excluded. Consider the state of the roads you'll drive on before choosing your vehicle type.

Rental charges vary from country to country and depend on the model of car. You will be required to present a credit card and valid driving licence. Most international rental companies won't allow crossing a border with a rental car. Buying can be an option, and with the industry booming in South America – and more cars on the road every day – most countries have competitive secondhand markets. If you want to buy a car, make sure you check the quality of vehicle (standards are lower than in Europe and the US) and your insurance cover. Driving standards are poor, so beware, especially at night. Honk your horn before going round any corner – the locals do this with great gusto, so no one will find you rude. South Americans drive on the right except in Suriname and Guyana. A useful website for driving in South America is Ⓦ driv-etheamericas.com.

By air

Given the distances involved in travelling South America, flying can save considerable time and energy. Budget airlines spring up (and often close down again) frequently in South America, thanks in part to the continent-wide dominance of major players like LATAM, and tend to be more expensive than their counterparts in Europe and North America. At the time of writing, budget airlines included: Argentina's Flybondi (Ⓦ flybondi.com), Brazil's Gol (Ⓦ voegol.com.br), Chile's Sky (Ⓦ skyairline.cl), Colombia's EasyFly (Ⓦ easyfly.com.co) and VivaColombia (Ⓦ vivacolombia.co), and Peru's VivaAir (Ⓦ vivaair.com).

ACCOMMODATION ALTERNATIVES

Useful websites that provide alternatives to standard hotel and hostel accommodation:
Airbnb ⓦairbnb.com
CouchSurfing ⓦcouchsurfing.org
Craigslist ⓦcraigslist.org
Homestay.com ⓦhomestay.com

By train

Trains are generally much less frequent and efficient than South American buses, but if you have a little time to spare they provide a wonderful way to see the countryside and wildlife, as they tend to travel more exotic routes. Typically, they are less expensive than buses, but services in popular tourist areas can be pricey. Two of the most famous routes are from Cusco to the start of the Inca Trail (see page 758) in Peru and the Serra Verde Express (see page 347) between Curitiba and Morretes in Brazil. There are several types of train, including the fast and efficient *ferrotren*, stopping at major stations only; the average *tren rápido*; the slower *expreso*, which stops at most stations; and the super-slow and amazingly cheap *mixto*, which stops for everyone – and their livestock too.

By boat

There are several ferry and catamaran services on South America's **lakes and rivers**, especially in Brazil, Chile, Argentina, Peru and Bolivia, providing unforgettable views, including the Southern Lakes Crossing (see page 440) between Argentina and Chile.

One of the finest ways to soak up the slow pace of South American life is to travel some of the continent's **rivers** by boat. Unfortunately, the riverboat industry is in decline, especially on the Amazon, with more passengers flying and cargo-only replacing many travel boats. However, several riverboat services survive, recommended for anyone with time and patience, particularly on the narrower, less-frequented rivers. Shop around, as boats vary hugely in quality. Your ticket will include hammock space and basic food, but drinks are extra and will probably be expensive on board – it's best to bring your own supplies. You should also bring a hammock, rope, insect repellent and a sleeping bag, and aim to be on board well before departure to ensure that you don't get put right next to the toilets.

By bicycle

If you're fit and hardy enough to consider cycling in South America, there are a few common-sense rules.

Given the terrain, a mountain bike is best, unless you stick to paved roads and well-travelled routes. Taking on some of the Andean roads, though, is an experience hard to rival. In adventure travel centres, especially in Argentina and Chile, bikes can be rented for short periods, but if you're doing serious cycling, bring your own. Bikes and bike parts tend to be of a lower quality in South America than in other parts of the world, so give your bike a thorough check before you go. Carry a basic repair kit and check the bike daily when you arrive. Weather can be a problem, especially in Patagonia, where winds can reach 80km/hr, and be aware that bicycle theft – particularly in larger towns – is common; bring a good bike lock. Finally, remember that South American drivers can be a hazard, so try to avoid major roads and motorways if at all possible.

Hitchhiking

While we don't recommend hitching as a safe way of getting about, there's no denying that it's fairly widely practised by South Americans in many rural areas. If you decide to hitch, set off early and be aware that many drivers expect to be paid – it's only in the Southern Cone (Argentina, Chile and Uruguay) that hitchhiking is generally understood to be free. Prices are usually around that of a bus fare, but if you head to the local truck park or refuelling station (most towns have one), ask around for the going rate. Hitchhiking in South America, like anywhere in the world, is a potentially dangerous enterprise – travellers should be aware that they do so at their own risk. Couples and groups are safest; women should never hitchhike alone.

Accommodation

The range of accommodation available in South America – and the variety of price and quality that goes with it – is enormous and, should you be embarking on a multi-country tour, you'll find that the US$10 that buys you a night's rest in Bolivia may not even stretch to breakfast in the Southern Cone or French Guiana.

Most local tourist offices provide a list of available accommodation, but bear in mind that establishments often pay to be included and that they may include little outside the main tourist hotspots. Generally, tourist boards will not recommend specific accommodation, nor book it.

Usually there is no shortage of places to stay, but use common sense if you plan to be somewhere at the time of a local festival, such as in Rio for Carnaval.

ALTITUDE SICKNESS

If you don't take care, altitude sickness, known locally as *soroche*, can seriously affect your trip. The most common symptoms are **headache**, **nausea** and **dizziness**, but when climbing at high altitude (above 2400m), symptoms can lead to more serious conditions such as **HAPE** (high altitude pulmonary oedema) or **HACE** (high altitude cerebral oedema), when medical attention should be sought immediately.

Soroche can affect anyone regardless of physical fitness. The key is to allow a few days to **acclimatize** when you arrive in a high-altitude region. When hiking, ascend slowly and follow the rule "sleep low and hike high" (sleep at a lower altitude than you ascended to that day), which allows your body time to recover. Drink plenty of water and eat light food, including carbs. Avoid alcohol and caffeine and, most importantly, pace yourself. Don't attempt to climb a mountain like Cotopaxi or Chimborazo after just a few days at 2800m in Quito – you need a couple of days above 2500m, then a couple more above 3500m before climbing over 4000m. If you are hiking as part of a tour and not dealing well with the altitude, alert your guide. Better to turn back than risk your health. In the Andes many locals swear by "*mate de coca*" – coca leaf tea – as a cure.

Obviously, accommodation fills up quickly at these times, prices skyrocket and it's best to book well in advance. While the types of lodging described below offer an overview of your options in South America, names, classifications and prices vary from country to country. Unless alternatives such as dorms or camping are specified, **prices** quoted for accommodation throughout the guide are for the **cheapest double room in high season** and include all taxes (where relevant). A handy resource for budget accommodation in South America is Ⓦ hosteltrail.com.

Hospedajes, residenciales, albergues and pensiones

These categories of accommodation are all used throughout South America and are largely interchangeable, although **pensiones** (known as *pensões* or *pousadas* in Portuguese) and **residenciales** are typically the most basic forms of accommodation. Generally, the Andean countries are the least expensive, and you should be able to find a decent room in a *residencial* or *pensión* for under US$15–20 (US$10 for dorms). For this price, you should expect a bed, shared bathroom and (generally) hot water. In Brazil, room costs usually include breakfast but most other places are room only. In southern Argentina and Chile, you can expect to spend around US$45–55 a night – check out the quality of the local *casas familiares* ("family houses", in which you stay with a local family in a room in their house), which are often good value for money in these areas.

Hostales, hosterías and haciendas

Hostales tend to fill the gap between the totally basic *pensión* and hotels, and come in many shapes, sizes and forms. Usually they include private bathrooms and hot water, clean towels and maybe a television, and cost US$15 to US$25 per night. In the southern countries, though, *hostale* sometimes means youth hostel.

Hosterías and **haciendas** are often old, sprawling estates or ranches converted into hotels, and are perhaps the grandest places to stay on the continent. They can be furnished in period style and offer excellent home cooking, log fires, maybe a swimming pool, and often horseriding and other country-style activities. Be aware that *hostería* can also refer to a family-style hotel complex out of town.

Camping

Camping is most popular in the southern region of Latin America, particularly in Argentina and Chile. It is wise to stick to official sites, which are usually well equipped, with hot water, toilets, fire pits and maybe even a self-service laundry. Camping is not really a popular or viable option in the northern countries unless as part of an organized tour, and is practically non-existent in Colombia, French Guiana and Paraguay, though French Guiana does offer *carbets*, shelters where you can hang a hammock.

Youth hostels

Youth hostels are not always the most viable option in South America, but in the more expensive countries like Argentina, Brazil and Chile, they are a more attractive choice: competition means that many have great facilities and offer extras, from free bike rental to barbecue nights. Prices average US$10–20 per night and most are open all year, although some only open in January and February for the South American summer. If you are planning on using hostels extensively, consider getting an official **HI card**, which will quickly pay for itself in discounted rates.

HOSTELLING ORGANIZATIONS

Argentina, Brazil, Chile, Peru and Uruguay Che Lagarto ⓦ chelagarto.com. Regional chain of hostels.

Brazil Federação Brasileira dos Albergues de Juventude ☎ 21 2531 1085, ⓦ hostel.org.br.

Chile Asociación Chilena de Albergues Turísticos Juveniles ☎ 02 577 1200, ⓦ hostelling.cl.

South America Hostelling International ⓦ hihostels.com. Membership cards and worldwide hostel booking.

Health

The potential health risks in South America read like a textbook of tropical diseases and the possibilities could easily deter nervous travellers before they even set out. But if you prepare for your trip carefully and take sensible precautions while travelling, you will probably face nothing worse than a mild case of diarrhoea as your system gets used to foreign germs and unhygienic conditions.

It is important to get the best health advice before you travel – prevention is always better than cure. Consult a medical specialist (see page 35) on each of the countries you wish to visit. About ten weeks before you travel, **vaccinations** can be arranged with your doctor or a specialized tropical diseases clinic. Bring your vaccination record when you travel. If you are taking any prescription drugs, your doctor can prescribe enough for the time you are away, and you should also take a list with you and a covering letter in case of emergencies. Good **medical insurance** (see page 39) is essential. It is important to declare any pre-existing conditions, and also to ensure that you have sufficient cover for all the extra activities you may undertake (particularly diving, extreme sports and hiking at high altitudes).

A common affliction is **heat stroke**, for which you should seek immediate treatment. Avoid dehydration by drinking bottled water and staying off alcohol, and stay out of the sun during the heat of the day (midday until around 4pm).

Pharmacies abound in every town but bringing a basic first-aid kit is sensible. Essentials in remote areas include insect repellent, bandages, painkillers, anti-diarrhoeal tablets and antiseptic cream.

Bites and stings

The general advice is to use an **insect repellent** containing at least 35 percent DEET, especially in rural areas or where malaria is endemic, and to wear light clothes that cover as much of your body as possible. It is wise to use a mosquito net or a mosquito coil containing permethrin at night, especially in the cheaper hotels.

Venomous **spiders and snakes** exist throughout the continent and bites from these, while rare, merit seeking medical advice as soon as possible. Most responsible tour companies carry antivenin, but in the absence of this, prompt medical attention is the only answer. A photo or description of the offending species may be useful, but never attempt to catch or kill it as this can provoke further bites, and don't listen to so-called local knowledge involving tourniquets, sucking venom or anything else – go to hospital.

If travelling to remote areas, consider a rabies vaccination – this will not make you immune to infection, but will buy you time to seek medical treatment after exposure. The majority of reported cases are from contact with dogs, and licks and scratches can be as dangerous as being bitten. If this happens, wash the area thoroughly with soap and water and disinfect it with alcohol or iodine solution. Always seek medical advice.

A much more likely nuisance when visiting wilder areas is the itchy **bites** given by tiny black sand flies or painful bites of ants and ticks. Hairy caterpillars are also capable of giving nasty stings similar to burns.

Mosquito-borne diseases

Malaria is present throughout the continent; check before travelling on current advice on the countries you plan to visit. Malaria prevention is two-fold; in addition to avoiding mosquito bites as detailed above, travellers should be sure to take a prescription anti-malarial drug, typically malarone (usually the best option), chloroquine or doxycycline – consult with a doctor before taking any. These should generally be started several weeks before you travel, and the full course must be completed which means continuing to take them after leaving a malaria zone. Symptoms can occur any time up to a year after travel, so it's important to inform your doctor about your travel history. Initial symptoms of malaria are a raging thirst and an aching upper back. Seek medical attention immediately if you think you may have picked it up.

Yellow fever is a serious disease carried by mosquitoes, which, like malaria, can be avoided by vaccination and taking sensible precautions against insect bites. It is present in most of South America except the far south. You'll need to show a certificate if travelling from one endemic country to another (although you won't always be asked for it, it's best to have one anyway). The following countries are considered the greatest risk areas: Bolivia, Brazil, Colombia, Ecuador, Peru and Venezuela.

Dengue fever is also mosquito-borne and there is no vaccine. The mosquitoes carrying the virus tend to live near stagnant water so it's more of a problem in poor areas. It has become a serious health issue in Brazil, Bolivia, Paraguay and Argentina, but is present in most countries in South America. Symptoms include high fever and aching limbs. Drink fluids, take paracetamol to reduce fever and seek medical attention immediately.

The **Zika virus** is spread by mosquitoes, too, and has been a problem in several parts of South America, notably Brazil. For most people it results in a mild infection and is not harmful; it can, however, be dangerous for pregnant women, as there is evidence that it causes birth defects. Symptoms include a rash, itching all over the body, fever, headache, joint and muscle pain, conjunctivitis, lower back pain, and pain behind the eyes. As with malaria, yellow fever and dengue fever, the best course of action is to avoid getting bitten by mosquitoes; cover up with long sleeves and long trousers, use insect repellents (containing DEET) on exposed skin and, where necessary, sleep under a mosquito net. If you do get ill, seek medical attention.

Intestinal problems

Common illnesses such as **diarrhoea** can be largely avoided by steps such as washing your hands before eating, and drinking bottled water. Unpasteurized dairy products and all un-refrigerated food should be avoided and fruit and vegetables should be washed and peeled. Take care with shellfish, lettuce and ice. If you do fall ill, rest and replace the fluids you have lost by drinking plenty of water and an oral rehydration solution. A home-made option is 1tsp salt and 8tsp of sugar in 1 litre of water. An anti-diarrhoeal tablet can usually alleviate symptoms.

Other than diarrhoea that usually lasts no more than a few days there are a number of more serious problems that you can encounter on your travels. **Cholera**, for example, is an acute infection with watery diarrhoea and vomiting; **dysentery** has similar symptoms but includes bleeding. If your diarrhoea persists for a week and your symptoms include a chill or fever or bleeding, or if you are too ill to drink, seek medical help. Typhoid is also a problem in the poorest, most rural areas and is transferred through food or water. Symptoms include fever, headache and occasionally a bleeding nose or spotty rash. Seek medical advice immediately – the fever can be easily treated with antibiotics but is serious if not caught early.

To avoid problems, always use bottled water, even for cleaning your teeth. Avoid buying food from street vendors unless the food is piping hot, and think carefully about swimming in lakes and rivers. If bottled water isn't available, there are various methods of treating water: boiling for a minimum of five minutes is the most effective method. Filtering alongside chemical sterilization is the next best option. Pregnant women or people with thyroid problems should consult their doctors about chemical sterilization formulae.

MEDICAL RESOURCES FOR TRAVELLERS

Canadian Society for International Health Canada ☎ 613 241 5785, ⓦ csih.org. Extensive list of travel health centres.
Centers for Disease Control and Prevention US ☎ 1 800 232 4636, ⓦ cdc.gov/travel. Official US government travel health site.
Hospital for Tropical Diseases Travel Clinic UK ☎ 0845 155 5000, ⓦ uclh.nhs.uk. Leading travel clinic and hospital.
International Society for Travel Medicine US ☎ 404 373 8282, ⓦ istm.org. Has a full list of travel health clinics.
MASTA (Medical Advisory Service for The Travel Doctor – TMVC Australia ☎ 1300 658 844, ⓦ traveldoctor.com.au. Lists travel clinics in Australia.
Travellers Abroad) UK ⓦ masta-travel-health.com for the nearest clinic.
Tropical Medical Bureau Ireland ☎ 1850 487 674, ⓦ tmb.ie. The TMB has 22 travel clinics across the country.

Culture and etiquette

South America is a vast continent and it's difficult to generalize about how to dress or behave; ultimately, you should try to behave unobtrusively and dress modestly if not at the beach.

Cultural hints

People usually shake hands upon introduction and women generally kiss acquaintances on one cheek or two (dependent on the country), although you can defer to a handshake if you prefer. It is common to wish people you meet on the street *"buenos días"* (*"bom dia"* in Brazil) or *"buenas tardes"* (*"boa tarde"* in Brazil). Politeness is a way of life in South America, and pleasantries are always exchanged before getting to any kind of business. Dress with respect in official or religious buildings.

Remember that in many South American countries, locals have a lax attitude to **time**, so expect people to arrive late in social situations and don't get annoyed if they do.

Tipping is generally common in restaurants and cafés but is lower than the norms in Europe and the USA. If in doubt, ask a local (and not a waiter!).

Shopping

Shops and markets in South America tend to offer a wide range of beautifully crafted goods and antiques for the visitor. Prices are usually reasonable; you can **bargain** in markets and outside the tourist drags, but only do so if you really think the item is worth less than its asking price. If you decide to buy something, be firm – ask the price and confirm it before offering cash. Be polite to street vendors, no matter how annoyed you get with them. Remember that this is their livelihood and smile, saying *"no, gracias"* or *"não, obrigado"*. Check that you are not purchasing objects plundered from the jungle or made from endangered species.

As a rule of thumb, native crafts are usually of the best quality and cheapest when bought close to the source. Buying such items, rather than mass-produced alternatives, is a good way to help local *artesania* and give something back to the communities you're visiting.

Public holidays and festivals

Travelling through South America entails negotiating a variety of **public holidays** (*feriados* in Spanish and Portuguese) that differ from country to country. Bear in mind as well that, particularly in more remote areas, some towns and villages celebrate saints' days and other local holidays that shut down businesses and make travel difficult. Check with local tourist information offices (where they exist) for more details. South Americans are not known for passing up an excuse to celebrate.

Every country in South America has a take on **Carnival** (known in Spanish and Portuguese as *Carnaval*); the exact time varies, but official celebrations usually take place on the days before Ash Wednesday and Lent. There are national variations, of course: in Ecuador, for instance, the festivities are most visibly represented by the water fights throughout the country. There are a couple of locations where Carnaval has become famous internationally, such

as Oruro in Bolivia and Encarnación in Paraguay. The most famous Carnaval of all, however, is in Rio de Janeiro, Brazil, which lasts for weeks before and after the "official" Carnaval time and is an extravagant mix of dance, sweat, drink, laughter and colour.

South America remains largely a devoutly Catholic continent, although Argentina and Uruguay are the most secular nations – expect lots of festivals around Semana Santa (Holy Week in Easter). Show respect and dress modestly when entering a church or religious site.

Work and study

Opportunities for volunteer and non-profit work abound, but be prepared to pay something towards your upkeep. Paid opportunities are few and far between, and some are likely to be illegal.

Teaching English

Qualified English teachers with a CELTA, TEFL or TESOL should be able to find work, but you are strongly advised to arrange a placement before you travel. Qualified schoolteachers from English-speaking countries can also find teaching opportunities, and if you have a Master's degree, you can teach at university. However, turning up and looking for work is likely to leave you frustrated and/or violating local laws – officially you will require a work permit. The British Council (Ⓦ britishcouncil.org) and the TEFL website (Ⓦ tefl.com) each has a list of English-teaching vacancies. Most jobs are in the larger cities.

Language study

South America has long been a hugely popular destination for people wishing to brush up on their **Spanish**: Cusco, Peru; Buenos Aires, Argentina; Sucre, Bolivia; and Quito, Ecuador, are the most popular destinations and a huge variety of courses and levels is available. In Brazil, most of the large cities are great locations for learning **Portuguese**. You can also learn **indigenous languages** such as Quechua in Bolivia or Guaraní in Paraguay. Typically, three types of course are on offer: a classroom-based course, a more active learning course through activities and excursions, or the live-in option with a host family.

LANGUAGE SCHOOLS

Academía Latinoamericana de Español Ⓦ latinoschools.com. Spanish classes in Quito, Cusco and Sucre.

Amerispan Ⓦ amerispan.com. Spanish courses and volunteer opportunities across Latin America.

Apple Languages Ⓦ applelanguages.com. High-quality Spanish schools throughout South America.

Bridge Linguatec Ⓦ bridge.edu. Spanish and Portuguese classes in Argentina, Chile and Brazil.

Don Quijote Ⓦ donquijote.org. High-quality, internationally recognized courses offered in Argentina, Bolivia, Chile, Colombia, Ecuador and Peru.

Escuela Runawasi Ⓦ runawasi.org. Quechua, Aymara and Spanish-language and literature lessons in Cochabamba, Bolivia.

Latin Immersion Ⓦ latinimmersion.com. Spanish immersion courses throughout the continent.

Simón Bolívar Spanish School Ⓦ bolivar2.com. Based in Cuenca, Ecuador, with courses based on a study of the country.

Spanish Study Holidays Ⓦ spanishstudyholidays.com. Courses from one week to nine months in Argentina, Bolivia, Chile, Ecuador and Peru.

Volunteering

Volunteer opportunities are available in social, environmental and conservation work in many South American countries, though you will be expected to pay for the privilege. You can easily **volunteer** in Chile, but you'll often have to pay for the privilege. Many organizations target people on gap years (at whatever stage in their lives) and offer placements on both inner city and environmental projects. For free or low-cost volunteer positions take a look at the excellent Ⓦ volunteersouthamerica.net.

VOLUNTEER ORGANIZATIONS

While many positions are organized prior to arrival, it's also possible to pick something up on the ground through word of mouth. Noticeboards in the more popular hostels are always good sources of information.

AFS Intercultural Programs Ⓦ afs.org. Intercultural exchange organization with programmes in more than fifty countries.

Amerispan Ⓦ amerispan.com. Highly rated educational travel company that specializes in language courses, but also runs volunteer programmes all over Latin America.

British Council Ⓦ britishcouncil.org. Produces a free leaflet which details study opportunities abroad. The website has a list of current job vacancies for recruiting TEFL teachers for posts worldwide.

Council on International Educational Exchange Ⓦ ciee.org. Leading NGO offering study programmes and volunteer projects around the world.

Earthwatch Institute Ⓦ earthwatch.org. Scientific expedition project that spans more than fifty countries with environmental and archeological ventures worldwide.

Rainforest Concern Ⓦ rainforestconcern.org. Volunteering opportunities protecting threatened habitats in Latin America.

Raleigh International Ⓦ raleighinternational.org. Volunteer projects across the world for young travellers.

Volunteer South America Ⓦ volunteersouthamerica.net. Free and low-cost volunteering opportunities across the continent.

Crime and personal safety

Many parts of South America suffer from high levels of poverty, which often goes hand in hand with crime problems. The risks in much of the continent are magnified by the international media, but shouldn't be ignored. Try not to be paranoid, though: the vast majority of people who visit South America do so safely.

In general, cities are more dangerous than rural areas, although the very deserted mountain plains can harbour bandits. Many of the working-class *barrios* of big cities are "no-go" areas for tourists, as are the marginal areas near them. One of the biggest problems in urban areas is **theft**, and bag snatching, handbag slitting and occasional armed robbery are problems in cities such as Buenos Aires, Caracas, Lima, Rio, Salvador, Recife, Georgetown, Quito and Cusco.

Take particular care on the street, in taxis and in restaurants and bars. Any unsolicited approach from a stranger should be treated with the utmost suspicion, no matter how well dressed or trustworthy they may look. There are obvious preventative measures you can take to avoid being mugged: avoid isolated and poorly lit areas, especially at night; never walk along a beach alone at night, or even in a pair if female.

Keep a particular eye out in busy areas and watch out on public transport and at bus stations, where **pickpocketing** is rife. If travelling by bus, keep your valuables in your carry-on luggage rather than stowing them below with your backpack. Make sure that you are given the numbered receipt corresponding to your bag. If you need to hail a taxi, get someone at your hotel to recommend one, or hail a moving one – never get into a "taxi" that just happens to be parked at the kerbside or which has two drivers. Avoid wearing expensive jewellery and watches, dress down, and keep cameras out of sight.

Car-jackings can also be a problem, particularly in certain areas of Brazil. When driving in the city, keep doors locked and windows closed, particularly at night, and be especially vigilant at traffic lights. Kidnapping of tourists in South America is extremely unlikely.

After decades of civil war, the security situation in **Colombia** has improved in recent times, though there are still flare-ups: in general the areas mentioned in this guide are safer than for many years. **Venezuela**, however, was extremely volatile at the time of research (see page 867); check the latest travel advice before planning a trip here.

Drugs

Ultimately, the key message is: just say no. In South America **drug trafficking** is a huge, ugly and complicated enterprise, and large-scale dealers love to prey on lost-looking foreigners. Don't let anyone else touch your luggage, be sure to pack it yourself and don't carry anything – no matter how innocuous it may seem – for anyone else. You will find that drugs, particularly marijuana and cocaine, are fairly ubiquitous in the region, but you should be aware that they are illegal and that punishments are severe. Uruguay has reformed its drugs laws (see page 838), but marijuana remains illegal for visitors to buy. Tourists are likely to come off much worse than locals at the hands of the South American police, something of which the dealers and pushers are very aware. If you happen to visit a region famed for drug trafficking, stay well away from anything that looks (or smells) like trouble.

The only **legal high** on sale to foreigners in South America is the leaves of coca (locals will be keen to point out it has nothing to do with chemically produced cocaine), which are particularly popular in Bolivia and Peru. They are usually used to make *mate de coca*, a hugely popular tea in the Andes, and one that's claimed to cure altitude sickness (among other things). Some people chew the leaves as this is meant to produce a mildly intoxicating state, but the taste and texture may well convince you that you can do without the alleged high. If you want to try *mate de coca* or chewing on coca leaves, be aware that there is a possibility that you could test positive for cocaine use in the weeks following your trip. Do not take any leaves out of the country as they may be illegal elsewhere.

Reporting crime

In case you are mugged or robbed, you should make sure that you have a photocopy of your passport and plane tickets in a safe place. Call the local police immediately and tell them what happened. It's likely that they won't do much more than take a statement, but you'll need it for insurance purposes. In some South American countries there is a special "tourist police" force, used to dealing with foreigners and, hopefully, able to speak English.

Women travellers

Though violent attacks against female travellers are uncommon, many women find that the barrage of hisses, hoots and comments in parts of South America comes close to spoiling their trip. On the whole, South American men are not renowned for their forward-thinking attitudes towards women's emancipation, and genuinely see nothing wrong with the heady sense of machismo that rules much of the continent.

There are some measures you can take to minimize how much you're hassled. Going to bars or nightclubs alone is often only undertaken by sex workers in the region, and you may be considered fair game if you do so. If you are approached and feel uncomfortable, try to calmly and politely make it clear you're not interested (in Spanish *"no estoy interesada"* or *"não estou interessada"* in Portuguese). It's sometimes easier to invent a boyfriend or husband than to get into a protracted dispute. Watch how the local women behave and where they go, and never be afraid to ask for help if you feel lost or threatened.

Going to remote locations alone may also increase the risks, and if you go as part of an organized visit,

---

BUDGET TIPS

- Take local transport, which means buses and *colectivos* instead of taxis or tourist shuttles.
- Avoid the most touristy destinations. Get off the beaten track and you'll notice the price difference.
- Eat and drink as the locals do. Eat street food from popular vendors and in restaurants choose local staples over the tourist menu; keep an eye out for good-value set lunches/dishes of the day. Buy from stores and markets rather than supermarkets or hostels/hotels.
- You can make big savings on bottled water, which many hostels will refill for free or a small fee.
- Be prepared to barter – bargaining can be fun. Don't be afraid to confront taxi drivers or chancers who you suspect are trying to rip you off. However, don't be too ruthless – bargaining over a few cents is not cool.

YOUTH AND STUDENT DISCOUNTS

Various official and quasi-official youth/student ID cards are available and are worth the effort to obtain: they soon pay for themselves in savings. Full-time students are eligible for the **International Student ID Card** (ISIC; ⊛ isiccard.com), which entitles the bearer (any student no matter their age) to special air, rail and bus fares and discounts at museums, theatres and other attractions. For Americans, there's also a health benefit, providing up to US$300,000 in emergency medical care, plus a 24hr hotline (☎ 1 800 353 1972).

You have to be 26 or younger to qualify for the International Youth Travel Card, which carries the same benefits. Teachers qualify for the International Teacher Card, offering similar discounts. All these cards are available from student travel specialists including STA.

check the credentials of the tour company. However, if you are attacked, you should not only get medical attention and go to the regular police, but also contact the tourist police and your country's embassy.

Travel essentials

Costs

South America is not as inexpensive as it used to be, but, if approached in the right way, you can still travel for less here than you would in many other parts of the world. French Guiana, Suriname, Argentina, Chile and Brazil are the most expensive countries, with prices often comparable to North America, Europe and Australia. Bolivia, Peru and Ecuador still remain budget destinations, but the highlights such as the Galápagos Islands, Easter Island, the Amazon and mountain climbing can add a lot of expense to the trip.

Electricity

The standard electrical current in most South American countries is 220V, 50/60Hz. The main exceptions are Colombia, Ecuador and Venezuela, where a 110/120V, 50/60Hz current is used, and Suriname, where 127V is standard. Some older buildings in some cities also use a 110V, 50Hz current, at odds with the rest of their country, including La Paz and Potosí in Bolivia and Rio de Janeiro and São Paulo in Brazil. For the most part **plug sockets** are flat two-pin (as in the US), but three-pin sockets are sometimes found. Your best bet if visiting several countries is to travel with a universal adaptor and make sure you check appliances' compatibility before plugging them in to South American sockets.

The South American attitude to safety can be lax and you may see plugs that obviously don't fit, forcibly pushed into sockets. Take particular care with electrical showers, which are common in many countries.

LGBTQ travellers

Rural, Catholic South America is not overly welcoming towards homosexuality but there is more acceptance in urban areas. You're probably safest following locals' example – public displays of affection between two men or two women could invite trouble on much of the continent.

Things are generally easier in the big cities, though, and there are a couple of major destinations where anything goes. Brazil boasts most of them – Rio de Janeiro, Salvador and São Paulo provide safe and welcoming havens for any sexual orientation, as do Buenos Aires, Montevideo and Santiago. If you are looking for thumping nightlife and a very "out" scene, then these cities are the best on the continent. A useful website for LGBTQ travel companies is ⊛ iglta. org/south-america.

Insurance

A typical **travel insurance policy** provides cover for the loss of baggage, tickets and – up to a certain limit – cash, as well as cancellation or curtailment of your journey. Most of them exclude so-called dangerous sports unless an extra premium is paid: this category can include scuba diving, white-water rafting, wind-surfing and trekking, though probably

PRICES

At the beginning of each country chapter you'll find a guide to "**rough costs**", including food, accommodation and travel. These costs are quoted in US$ to make comparison easy; within the chapter itself prices are quoted in local currency. Note that prices and exchange rates change all the time – they are particularly volatile in Venezuela (see page 869), where parallel black market rates operate – which may affect the accuracy of those figures we have quoted.

ROUGH GUIDES TRAVEL INSURANCE

Rough Guides has teamed up with Worldnomads.com to offer great **travel insurance** deals. Policies are available to residents of over 150 countries, with cover for a wide range of **adventure sports**, 24hr emergency assistance, high levels of medical and evacuation cover and a stream of **travel safety information**. Roughguides.com users can take advantage of their policies online 24/7, from anywhere in the world – even if you're already travelling. And since plans often change when you're on the road, you can extend your policy and even claim online. Roughguides.com users who buy travel insurance with Worldnomads.com can also leave a positive footprint and donate to a community development project. For more information go to ⓦ **roughguides.com/travel-insurance**.

not kayaking or jeep safaris. Many policies can be changed to exclude coverage you don't need. If you take medical coverage, ascertain whether benefits will be paid as treatment proceeds or only after your return home, and whether there is a 24-hour medical emergency number. When securing baggage cover, make sure that the per-article limit will cover your most valuable possession. If you need to make a claim, you should keep receipts for medicines and medical treatment and, in the event you have anything stolen, you must obtain an official statement from the police.

Internet

Internet/wi-fi access is virtually ubiquitous in cities and towns across South America, and only in rural areas is it difficult to come by. Connection speeds and costs vary from country to country, and in some cases from area to area. Most hostels and hotels, and many cafés, bars and restaurants, provide free wi-fi.

Mail

Post offices in cities and major towns offer a wide range of services; those in villages are much more basic, with shorter opening hours and slow service. It's often quicker and safer to use a courier service – although you'll pay much more. Hotels in capital cities may sell stamps and have a postbox – if you are staying in one, this can be the most convenient way

CALLING FROM ABROAD

To phone abroad, you must first dial the international access code of the country you are calling from, then the country code of the country you are calling to, then the area code (usually without the first zero) and then the phone number. In some South American countries there may be different international access codes for different providers. See below for details.

to send a letter home. Expect airmail to take from a week to a month to Western Europe and the US.

Maps

Excellent maps of South America, covering the region at a scale of 1:5,000,000 and individual countries, are produced by Canada's International Travel Maps and Books (ⓦ itmb.com); Stanfords (ⓦ stanfords.co.uk) in the UK is another good source. In South America, often the only source of accurate maps is the military – check at the local tourist offices on where to purchase them. If you'd rather be sure, buy maps at home and bring them with you.

Money

ATMs are widely available in most large cities, but in smaller towns and rural areas don't expect to rely solely on using international debit cards to access funds. Travellers' cheques have largely died out, but pre-paid **currency cards** are useful, though these, too, require access to an ATM. There is still nothing as easy to use as cash, preferably US dollars, and it makes sense always to carry at least a few small-denomination notes for when all else fails.

Credit card fraud is a problem on the continent, particularly in Brazil and Venezuela; be sure to keep an eye on your card and to retain your copy of the transaction slip. In many countries credit cards will only be accepted in the biggest hotels and shops, and banks will sometimes refuse to offer cash advances against them. Payments in plastic may also incur high surcharges when compared to cash payments.

When **exchanging money**, you should use only authorized bureaux de change, such as banks, cambios and tourist facilities, rather than deal with moneychangers on the streets. In remote and rural areas, and for shopping in local markets and stalls, **cash** is a necessity – preferably in small denominations of local currency. Some countries, including Venezuela (see page 869), have a flourishing black

INTERNATIONAL ACCESS CODES WHEN DIALLING FROM:

Argentina ☎ 00
Australia ☎ 0011
Bolivia ☎ 0010 (Entel), ☎ 0011 (AES),
☎ 0012 (Teledata), ☎ 0013 (Boliviatel)
Brazil ☎ 0014 (Brasil Telecom), ☎ 0015
(Telefónica), ☎ 0021 (Embratel), ☎ 0023
(Intelig), ☎ 0031 (Telemar)
Canada ☎ 011
Chile ☎ 00
Colombia ☎ 009 (Telecom), ☎ 007 (ETB/
Mundo), ☎ 005 (Orbitel)
Ecuador ☎ 00
French Guiana ☎ 00
Guyana ☎ 001
Ireland ☎ 00
New Zealand ☎ 00
Paraguay ☎ 002
Peru ☎ 00
Suriname ☎ 002
UK ☎ 00
Uruguay ☎ 00
US ☎ 011
Venezuela ☎ 00

COUNTRY CODES WHEN DIALLING TO:

Argentina ☎ 54
Australia ☎ 61
Bolivia ☎ 591
Brazil ☎ 55
Canada ☎ 1
Chile ☎ 56
Colombia ☎ 57
Ecuador ☎ 593
French Guiana ☎ 594
Guyana ☎ 592
Ireland ☎ 353
New Zealand ☎ 64
Paraguay ☎ 595
Peru ☎ 51
Suriname ☎ 597
UK ☎ 44
Uruguay ☎ 598
US ☎ 1
Venezuela ☎ 58

market with much better exchange rates, though this obviously carries risks.

Phones

The ubiquity of mobile phones means **public phone boxes** have all but disappeared in many South American countries. There are, however, plenty of *locutorios*, stores originally dedicated to telephone communications, most of which have now branched out into internet access as well. You can make direct-dial international calls from most South American phones, apart from remote areas, where calls must be made through an operator. International phone calls are, in general, expensive from South America, so you're best off trying to buy international calling cards where they exist or using web services such as Skype – most internet cafés are set up with webcams and headsets.

Mobile phones

If you want to use your **mobile phone** in South America, check with your phone provider whether it will work abroad, and what the call charges are (beware of amassing a fortune in data charges and use wi-fi wherever possible).

You are likely to be charged extra for incoming calls when abroad, as the people calling you will be paying the usual rate. If you're in the country for a while, and assuming your phone is unlocked (most contract phones are locked so that they can only be used on one network – your provider can usually unlock it for a fee), you can buy a **SIM card** from a local telephone company and use it in your phone. These are usually inexpensive and your calls will be charged at a local rate. If you don't have a mobile phone and are staying a few months in one country, consider buying a local phone, easily done for less than US$50.

Tourist information

The quantity and quality of tourist information varies from country to country, but in general, don't expect too much. While almost every city in Brazil, Argentina

---

TIME ZONES

Most of South America is spread across only two time zones, with the outlying islands spread across five:
GMT–6: Galápagos Islands and Easter Island
GMT–5: Colombia, Ecuador and Peru
GMT–4.5: Venezuela
GMT–4: Most of mainland Chile (GMT-3 Dec–March), Bolivia, Guyana, Paraguay, western Brazil and the Falklands
GMT–3: Argentina, Uruguay, French Guiana, Magallanes region of Chile, Suriname and most of Brazil
GMT–2: Fernando de Noronha (Brazil) and South Georgia

and Peru will have at least one well-equipped tourist office, they are much thinner on the ground in countries like Paraguay and the Guianas. We've listed websites wherever pertinent throughout the guide; the following is a general list of useful ones.

SOUTH AMERICA ONLINE

Many hotels, hostels, restaurants, bars, travel agencies and other places of interest to travellers have their own Facebook pages – we don't list these in the guide, but they are easy to track down and often contain useful info.

ⓦ **boliviabella.com** Useful English-language site with loads of info on Bolivia.

ⓦ **thebubble.com** Bueno Aires-based English-language site, with articles and a podcast on Argentina.

ⓦ **lab.org.uk** News, information and analysis from the UK-based charity and publisher the Latin America Bureau.

ⓦ **lapress.org** Non-profit news organization based in Lima, producing independent news and analysis.

ⓦ **planeta.com** Good selection of eco-tourism resources for South America (and beyond).

ⓦ **roughguides.com** Travel articles, videos, podcasts, and guides covering the whole of South America and beyond.

ⓦ **santiagotimes.cl** English-language Chilean newspaper, with news, analysis, culture and travel ravel articles

ⓦ **zonalatina.com/ZImusic** Regional music links and information, covering everything from Sertaneja to Shakira.

Travellers with disabilities

South America is not the friendliest of destinations for travellers with disabilities and many places are down-right inaccessible. The more modern the society, the more likely you are to find services for travellers with disabilities – this means that while Bolivia and Paraguay are pretty impenetrable, much of urban Chile and Argentina, as well as several cities in Brazil, is more accessible. Unfortunately, though, you may need to compromise over destination – big hotels in major cities that are very much on the tourist trail are much more likely to have facilities to cater to your needs than idyllic cabañas in the middle of nowhere. You might be limited as regards mobility, too, as local buses will probably prove difficult and you might need to settle for taxi services or internal flights. In any case, check with one of the agencies below before planning anything.

DisabledHolidays.com UK ☎ 0161 804 9898, ⓦ disabledholidays.com. The UK's largest operator in this field, offering holidays for people with restricted mobility across South America.

National Disability Services (NDS) Australia ☎ 02 6283 3200, ⓦ nds.org.au. Can supply lists of travel agencies and tour operators for people with disabilities.

PERITO MORENO GLACIER

Argentina

❶ **Buenos Aires** Tango and football rule in this European-style capital. See page 54

❷ **Iguazú Falls** The world's largest waterfalls are framed by lush, subtropical jungle. See page 88

❸ **Salta** This beautifully preserved colonial city is surrounded by epic mountain scenery. See page 92

❹ **Bariloche** An outdoor adventure hub in the Lake District with stunning mountain vistas. See page 119

❺ **Perito Moreno Glacier** A dramatic expanse of ice, deep in Patagonia. See page 144

❻ **Ushuaia** The end of the world (more or less) and just 1000km from Antarctica. See page 146

HIGHLIGHTS ARE MARKED ON THE MAP ON PAGE 45

ROUGH COSTS

Daily budget Basic US$50, occasional treat US$85
Drink Beer US$5
Food Steak and chips US$18–20
Camping/hostel/budget hotel US$9/15/35–40

FACT FILE

Population 44.5 million
Official language Spanish
Currency Argentine peso (AR$)
Capital Buenos Aires
International phone code ☏ 54
Time zone GMT -3hr

1

Introduction

Even without the titanic wedge of Antarctica that its cartographers include in the national territory, Argentina ranks as the world's eighth-largest country. Stretching from the Tropic of Capricorn to the most southerly reaches of the planet's landmass, it encompasses a staggering diversity of climates and landscapes: from hot and humid jungles in the northeast and bone-dry Andean plateaux in the northwest, through endless grasslands, to the windswept steppe of Patagonia and the end-of-the-world archipelago of Tierra del Fuego.

A country influenced by generations of immigration from Europe and elsewhere, Argentina offers a variety of attractions, not least the great spectacles of tango and football in the seductive European-style capital **Buenos Aires**. Moreover, the extent and diversity of the country's natural scenery are staggering. Due north of the capital stretches **El Litoral**, a subtropical region of riverine landscapes featuring the awe-inspiring **Iguazú** waterfalls. Highlights of the northwest are the spectacular, polychrome **Quebrada de Humahuaca** gorge and the **Valles Calchaquíes**, stunningly beautiful valleys where high-altitude vineyards produce the delightfully flowery *torrontés* wine.

West and immediately south of Buenos Aires are the seemingly endless grassy plains of the **Pampas**. This is where you'll still glimpse traces of traditional **gaucho** culture, most famously celebrated in **San Antonio de Areco**. Here, too, you'll find some of the country's best *estancias*. As you move west, the **Central Sierras** loom on the horizon: within reach of **Córdoba**, the country's vibrant second city, are some of the oldest resorts on the continent. In the lee of the Andes, the vibrant city of **Mendoza** is the country's wine capital, from where the scenic Alta Montaña route climbs steeply to the Chilean border, passing **Cerro Aconcagua**, the highest mountain in the Americas and a dream challenge for mountaineers from around the world.

To the north of Mendoza, San Juan and La Rioja provinces are relatively uncharted territory but their star attractions are **Parque Nacional Talampaya**, with its giant red cliffs, and the nearby **Parque Provincial Ischigualasto**, usually known as Valle de la Luna on account of its intriguing, moon-like landscapes.

Argentina claims the lion's share of the sparsely populated expanses of **Patagonia**, an enchanting place to explore, and the frigid isles of **Tierra del Fuego**. An almost unbroken chain of national parks hugs the mountains, making for some of the best trekking anywhere on the planet – certainly include the savage granite peaks of the **Parque Nacional Los Glaciares** in your itinerary. For wildlife enthusiasts the **Peninsula Valdés** is also essential viewing, famous as a breeding ground for southern right whales.

CHRONOLOGY

1516 The first Europeans reach the Río de la Plata and clash with Querandí natives.

1535 Pedro de Mendoza founds Buenos Aires.

1609 The first missions to the Guaraní people are established in the upper Paraná.

1806 The British storm Buenos Aires, only to be expelled within a few months.

1810 The first elected junta is sworn in to replace Spanish leaders.

1816 Independence is officially declared in the city of Tucumán.

1854 The country's first railways are built.

1912 Universal male suffrage is introduced.

1930 Radical Hipólito Yrigoyen is overthrown in a military coup.

1943 A coup led by Juan Domingo Perón results in the ousting of the constitutional government. Three years later he is elected president.

1952 Perón's wife Evita dies at the age of 33.

1955 Perón is overthrown in a military coup and exiled.

1973 Perón returns from exile in Spain and is re-elected.

ARGENTINA

HIGHLIGHTS

1. Buenos Aires
2. Iguazú Falls
3. Salta
4. Bariloche
5. Perito Moreno Glacier
6. Ushuaia

Metres

3000
1500
1000
400
200
0

BOLIVIA
La Quiaca
PARAGUAY
BRAZIL
Jujuy
RN-34
RN-9
Salta
RN-81
Cafayate
Puerto Iguazú
Tucumán
RN-16
Formosa
RN-12
Santiago del Estero
Resistencia
RN-11
Corrientes
Posadas
Catamarca
RN-9
RN-34
Río Paraná
RN-14
La Rioja
Laguna Mar Chiquita
BRAZIL
San Juan
Córdoba
Santa Fe
Concordia
URUGUAY
RN-9
Mendoza
Rosario
Río Uruguay
RN-7
San Luis
Gualeguaychú
RN-7
San Antonio de Areco
BUENOS AIRES
Colonia del Sacramento
San Rafael
RN-188
La Plata
RN-2
MONTEVIDEO
CORDILLERA DE LOS ANDES
RN-35
Santa Rosa
RN-3
CHILE
Bahía Blanca
Mar del Plata
PACIFIC OCEAN
Neuquén
RN-22
Río Negro
RN-3
Carmen de Patagones
San Martín de los Andes
N
Bariloche
El Bolsón
Península Valdés
Esquel
Río Chubut
Puerto Madryn
RN-25
Trelew
RN-3
ATLANTIC OCEAN
RN-40
Comodoro Rivadavia
RP-43
Perito Moreno
Puerto Deseado
Argentine Antarctic Territory
Puerto San Julián
El Calafate
Puerto Santa Cruz
Puerto Natales
Río Gallegos
Falkland Islands (Islas Malvinas)
Punta Arenas
RN-3
Straits of Magellan
Ushuaia
Cape Horn

0   200
kilometres

1

WHEN TO VISIT

Buenos Aires is at its best during spring (October and November), when purple jacaranda trees are in bloom all over the city and the weather is typically sunny and warm. For spectacular autumnal colours, visit **Mendoza** between April and May, or else in early March to witness its international harvest festival. Unless heading to **Bariloche** to ski, Patagonia is best avoided in the depths of winter. Instead, plan a visit between October and April, but if heading to **Peninsula Valdés**, be sure not to miss the southern right whale season, at its peak in early November.

1974 Perón dies and power defaults to his third wife "Isabelita".

1976 Videla leads a military coup against Isabel Perón, marking the beginning of the "Dirty War".

1978 Argentina hosts, and wins, the FIFA World Cup in the middle of a military dictatorship.

1982 A military force invades the Falkland Islands (Islas Malvinas) and is defeated by the British.

1983 Democracy is restored and Radical Raúl Alfonsín is elected president.

1989 Neoliberal Peronist Carlos Menem begins a decade as president during which most services are privatized.

2001 President De la Rúa is forced to resign in the midst of economic collapse and violent rioting.

2008 Cristina Fernández de Kirchner is inaugurated as the country's first elected female president, succeeding her husband, Néstor.

2010 The country celebrates two centuries of nationhood with parades and other festivities.

2012 The first year of Cristina Fernández de Kirchner's second term as president is marred by corruption scandals, rising inflation, mass demonstrations and urban riots.

2014 Argentina defaults on a debt with US "vulture" funds.

2015 Centre-right businessman Mauricio Macri is elected president.

ARRIVAL AND DEPARTURE

The majority of visitors to Argentina arrive at Buenos Aires' **Ezeiza International Airport**, although other major cities also have flight connections to countries within South America. There are no international **rail** links, but a plethora of **international bus routes** links Argentina with Chile, Brazil, Bolivia, Uruguay and Paraguay.

FROM BOLIVIA

There are three entry points into Argentina from Bolivia: Villazón, Bermejo and Yacuiba. You'll need to complete the requisite formalities at Bolivia's migration and customs office on the border and then register on the Argentina side.

FROM BRAZIL

Most people crossing from Brazil to Argentina do so at Foz do Iguaçu. If you're just going for the day you only need to get your passport stamped on the Argentine side, but if going for longer you must pass through both controls. The bus that takes you across the border stops at the Brazilian and Argentine passport controls and waits for passengers to get their passports stamped.

FROM CHILE

Travellers crossing via the high Andes should note that the passes sometimes close in winter. In the north, advance booking is recommended for the San Pedro de Atacama–Jujuy and Salta bus crossing. The most popular border crossing from Chile to Argentina is the Santiago–Mendoza route via the Los Libertadores tunnel. If you're coming from the south, routes in the Lake District include Osorno–Bariloche, and Temuco–San Martín de Los Andes. Further south still are the Puerto Natales–El Calafate and Punta Arenas–Río Gallegos crossings.

FROM PARAGUAY

Visitors can cross the Paraguayan border into Posadas (Argentina) from Encarnación (Paraguay). Travellers crossing here will have to go through migration control at both sides of the border, which are open 24 hours. Another popular option is the Puerto Falcón (Paraguay) to Clorinda (Argentina) crossing, but you can also cross into the Argentine cities of Formosa, Pocitos, Corrientes, Barranqueras and Iguazú.

FROM URUGUAY

From Colonia del Sacramento, the crossing is easy and quick with the Buquebus ferry service (❿buquebus.com), with a fast service taking an hour and the slower but cheaper service three hours. Otherwise opt for the more scenic route with Cacciola Viajes (⊛cacciolaviajes.com) from Carmelo to Tigre. If travelling by car, you can cross the border in Fray Bentos further north.

VISAS

Citizens of the EU, US, Canada, South Africa, Australia and New Zealand do not require visas, though Argentina charges reciprocal entry fees for nationals of countries that charge Argentine citizens to enter: the US, Canada and Australia are subject to **one-off arrival fees** that need to be paid in advance by signing up at ⊛reciprocidad.provincianet.com.ar. The rules do change frequently, so it's best to check the government website for the latest (⊛argentina.gob.ar). Tourists are routinely granted ninety-day entry permits – the easiest way to renew your tourist visa is to cross the border into a neighbouring country.

GETTING AROUND

Argentina is a huge country and you are likely to spend a considerable proportion of your budget on travel. Air travel is relatively expensive, so most people travel by bus (though that is increasingly pricey, too). Car rental is useful in places, but too expensive for most budget travellers, unless they can share the cost. Extra fees are charged for drivers under 25.

BY AIR

Argentina's most important domestic airport by far is Buenos Aires' **Aeroparque Jorge Newbery**. There are connections (mainly with Aerolíneas Argentinas, LAN and LADE) to most provincial capitals and major tourist centres. Some cut-price deals booked in advance can work out to be not much more than the bus. One of the best deals is the "Visite Argentina" airpass, sold by Aerolíneas Argentinas (⊛aerolineas.com.ar) and valid for domestic flights on Aerolíneas and its subsidiary, Austral, covering more than thirty destinations. This pass must be bought abroad; it is not sold in Argentina.

Many smaller airports are not served by public transport, though some airline companies run shuttle services to connect with flights; otherwise, you're stuck with taxis. When leaving certain airports, you have to pay a departure tax (usually AR\$20–30).

BY BUS

There are hundreds of private **bus companies**, most of which concentrate on one particular region, although a few, such as TAC, operate pretty much nationwide. Most buses are modern, plush models designed for long-distance travel, and your biggest worry will be what video the driver or conductor has chosen. On longer journeys, snacks and hot meals are served (included in the ticket price), although these vary considerably in quality. The more luxurious services are usually worth the extra money for long night-rides; some even have waiters and free alcoholic drinks. *Coche cama* services have wide, reclining seats, and *semi-cama* services are not far behind in terms of comfort. Most companies also offer *cama suite* or *cama ejecutivo* services, which have completely reclining seats and include an on-board meal.

Buying **tickets** is normally a simple on-the-spot matter, but plan in advance if travelling in peak summer season (mid-Dec to Feb), especially if you're taking a long-distance bus from Buenos Aires or any other major city to a popular holiday destination. In Buenos Aires look for kiosks advertising *venta de pasajes* – these are authorized ticket sellers and will save you having to visit the Retiro terminal before you leave.

BY CAR

You are unlikely to need a car for your whole stay in Argentina, but you'll find one useful if you hope to explore some of the more isolated areas of Patagonia, Tierra del Fuego, the Northwest, and Mendoza and San Juan provinces.

To **rent a car**, you need to be over 21 (25 with some agencies); most foreign licences are accepted for tourists. Bring your passport as well as a credit card for the deposit. Before you drive off, check that

1

you've been given insurance, tax and ownership papers. Check too for dents and paintwork damage, and get hold of a 24-hour emergency telephone number. Also, pay close attention to the small print, most notably what you're liable for in the event of an accident: excess normally doesn't cover you for the first AR$5000 or so, and you may not be covered for windscreens, headlights, tyres and more – all vulnerable on unsurfaced roads. Look for unlimited mileage deals, as the per-kilometre charge can otherwise exceed your daily rental cost many times over given the vast distance you're likely to be covering.

BY TRAIN

Argentina's **rail** network, developed with British investment from the late nineteenth century, collapsed in the 1990s with the withdrawal of government subsidies. The few remaining services are generally unsavoury, running on routes that are of limited use for visitors. However, the country's famous **tourist trains**, where the aim is simply to travel for the sheer fun of it, are a major attraction. There are two principal stars: *La Trochita*, the Old Patagonian Express from outside Esquel (see page 126); and the *Tren a las Nubes* (see page 95), one of the highest railways in the world, which climbs through the mountains from Salta towards the Chilean border.

ACCOMMODATION

You can often tell by a hotel's name what kind of place to expect: a **posada** for example suggests a slightly rustic feel, but generally comfortable or even luxurious. In a similar vein, **hostería** is often used for smallish, high-end hotels – oriented towards the tourist rather than the businessperson. **Hostal** is sometimes used too – but doesn't refer reliably to anything – there are youth hostels called *hostales* as well as high-rise modern hotels.

Residenciales and **hospedajes** are basically simple hotel-style accommodation. Most are reasonably clean and comfortable and a few stand out as some of Argentina's best budget

accommodation. Rooms start at around AR$400, but prices fluctuate.

A very different experience is provided by Argentina's *estancias*, as the country's large ranches are called. **Estancia** accommodation is generally luxurious, and with a lot more character than hotels of a similar price; from around US$200 per person a day you are provided with all meals, invariably including a traditional *asado* or barbecue. At working *estancias* you have the chance to observe or join in ranch activities such as cattle herding and branding, while almost all include activities such as horseriding and swimming. To book *estancia* accommodation, either approach individual establishments or try Estancias Argentinas (Diagonal Roque Sáenz Peña 616, 9th Floor; ☎011 4343 2366, ⓦestanciasargentinas.com) in Buenos Aires.

HOSTELS AND CAMPSITES

Youth hostels are known as *albergues juveniles*, *albergues de la juventud* or simply *hosteles* (you might wish to avoid *albergues transitorios* or motels, which are places that rent rooms by the hour). Accommodation is generally in dormitories (a dorm bed costing AR$140–350, depending on where you are and what time of year it is), though most places also have one or two double rooms, which are often good value. Facilities vary from next to nothing to internet access, washing machines, TVs and patios with barbecues.

There are plenty of **campsites** (*campings*) – most towns and villages having their own municipal site – but standards vary wildly. At the major resorts, there are usually privately owned, well-organized sites, with facilities ranging from provisions stores to volleyball courts and TV rooms. In less touristy towns, municipal sites can be rather desolate and not particularly secure: it's a good idea to check with locals before pitching your tent.

FOOD AND DRINK

Traditionally, Argentine food could be summed up in a single word: **beef**. Not just any beef, but succulent, cherry-red, healthy meat raised on some of the greenest, most extensive pastures known to cattle. The **barbecue** or *asado* remains a national institution, but it's not the whole story. An *asado* is prepared on a **parrilla** (grill), and is served everywhere, at restaurants also known as *parrillas*. Usually there's a set menu, but the establishments vary enormously. Traditionally, you start off by eating the offal before moving on to the choicer cuts, but you can choose to head straight for the steaks and fillets. The lightly salted meat is usually served with nothing on it, other than the traditional condiments of *chimichurri* – olive oil with salt, garlic, chilli pepper, vinegar and bay – and *salsa criolla*, similar but with chopped onion, tomato and red pepper added.

Alongside the *parrilla*, pizza and pasta are mainstays of Argentine cuisine, a reflection of the country's Italian heritage. Those staying in Argentina for a while may get frustrated by the lack of choice, particularly in rural areas, although the variety of restaurants in the cities, especially Buenos Aires, reflects a mosaic of communities who have migrated to Argentina: not just Italian and Spanish but Korean, Middle Eastern, German, Welsh, Japanese and Peruvian. **Vegetarians** will find that there are few options on most menus, but staples such as basic salads, *provoleta* (delicious melted cheese) and *tartas* (a kind of quiche) are almost always available, as well as pasta with meat-free sauces. In larger towns vegetarian restaurants are growing in popularity.

There are plenty of *minutas* or **snacks** to choose from. *Choripán*, a large sausage in a soft roll, is a national favourite, as is the ubiquitous *milanesa*, a breaded veal escalope. *Lomitos* are grilled steak sandwiches, the local answer to the hamburger. Excellent local-style fast food is also available in the form of *empanadas*, pasties that come with an array of fillings, from the traditional beef or mozzarella cheese to salami, Roquefort and chard. *Humitas* are made of steamed creamed sweetcorn, served in neat parcels made from the outer husk of corn cobs. *Tamales* are maize-flour balls, stuffed with minced beef and onion, wrapped in maize leaves and simmered. The typical main dish, *locro*, is a warming, substantial Andean stew based on maize, with onions, beans and meat thrown in.

WHERE TO EAT

Argentines love **dining out** and, in Buenos Aires especially, places stay open all day and till very late: in the evening hardly any restaurant starts serving dinner before 8.30pm, and in the hotter months – and all year round in Buenos Aires – very few people turn up before 10pm. By South American standards the quality of restaurants is high. You can keep costs down by taking advantage of restaurants' *menú del día* or *menú ejecutivo* – good-value set meals for as little as AR$150 served primarily, but not exclusively, at lunchtime. In the evening *tenedor libre* restaurants are just the place if your budget's tight. Here, you can eat as much as you like, they're usually self-service (cold and hot buffets plus grills) and the food is fresh and well prepared, if a little dull.

Cheaper hotels and more modest accommodation often skimp on **breakfast**: you'll be lucky to be given more than tea or coffee, and some bread, jam and butter, though *medialunas* (small, sticky croissants) are sometimes also served. The sacred national delicacy *dulce de leche* (a type of caramel spread) is often provided for piling onto toast or bread.

DRINK

Fizzy drinks (*gaseosas*) are popular with people of all ages and are often drunk to accompany a meal. Although few beans are grown in the country, good, if expensive, **coffee** is easy to come by in Argentina. In most towns and cities you can find a decent espresso or *café con leche* (milky coffee) for breakfast. *Mate*, the bitter national drink, prepared in a special gourd and drunk through a metal straw known as a *bombilla*, is a whole world unto itself, with rules of etiquette and ritual involved. It is drunk everywhere – at home, in parks, at the office, and always with friends.

Argentina's **beer** is more thirst-quenching than alcoholic and mostly

1

ARGENTINE WINE

Argentina is currently the world's ninth-largest producer of wine, and more than three-quarters of the stuff flows out of **Mendoza**. Enjoying around three hundred days of sunshine a year and a prime position at the foothills of the Andes, Mendoza's high-altitude vineyards produce premium vintages on a par with Chile's. The idyllic desert climate (cool nights, little rain and low humidity) works especially well for reds: **Malbec** – brought over from Cahors in southwest France – remains Argentina's star grape, producing rich fruity flavours that go down superbly well with the ubiquitous steak. For a dry yet fruity white alternative, give **Torrontés** a whirl. Others that are having an impact include **Bonarda** and **Cabernet Franc**, while many sparkling wines are well priced.

comes as fairly bland lager. The Quilmes brewery dominates the market with lagers such as Cristal; in Mendoza, the Andes brand crops up all over the place, while Salta's eponymous brand is also good. Most breweries also produce a *cerveza negra*, a kind of stout. More interesting microbreweries, however, are springing up all the time; the Lake District and Patagonia are particular craft beer hotspots. If you want draught beer ask for a *chopp*.

Argentine **wine** (see page 50) is excellent and reasonably priced – try the red Malbec grape variety. The locally distilled *aguardientes* or firewaters are often deliciously grapey. One national alcoholic spirit – an orange-flavour beverage called Hesperedina – is undergoing a comeback, while a number of Italian-style vermouths and digestifs are made in Argentina. **Fernet Branca** is the most popular, a demonic-looking brew the colour of molasses with a rather bitter, medicinal taste, invariably combined with cola, whose colour it matches, and consumed in huge quantities by students and young people.

CULTURE AND ETIQUETTE

Argentines are generally friendly, outgoing and incredibly welcoming to foreigners. In all but the most formal contexts, Argentines greet with one kiss on the cheek (men included), even on first meeting. In general, visitors are unlikely to find any huge culture shock in Argentine etiquette. Service in shops or restaurants is generally very courteous; conversations should be started with "*buen día*", "*buenas tardes*" or "*buenas noches*".

SPORTS AND OUTDOOR ACTIVITIES

Argentina is an exciting destination for outdoors enthusiasts, whether you're keen to tackle radical rock faces or prefer to appreciate the vast open spaces at a more gentle pace, hiking or on horseback. World-class fly-fishing, horseriding, trekking and rock-climbing options abound, as do opportunities for whitewater rafting, skiing, ice climbing, and even – for those with sufficient stamina and preparation – expeditions onto the Southern Patagonian Icecap. The Patagonian Andes provide the focus for most of these activities – particularly the area of the central Lake District around Bariloche and El Calafate/El Chaltén, but Mendoza and the far northwest of the country, around Salta and Jujuy, are also worth considering for their rugged mountain terrain. If you're planning on doing any of these, take out appropriate insurance cover before leaving home.

HIKING AND CLIMBING

Argentina offers some truly marvellous **hiking** possibilities, and it is still possible to find areas where you can trek for days without seeing a soul. Most of the best treks are found in the national parks – especially in Patagonia – but you can also find less well-known but equally superb options in the lands bordering the parks. Most people head for the savage granite spires of the Fitz Roy region around El Chaltén, an area whose fame has spread so rapidly over recent years that it now holds a similar status to Chile's renowned Torres del Paine and is packed in high season (late Dec to Feb). The other principal trekking destination is the mountainous area of Nahuel Huapi

National Park, which lies to the south of Bariloche, centring on the Cerro Catedral massif and Cerro Tronador.

For **climbers**, the Andes offer incredible variety – from volcanoes to shale summits, from the continent's loftiest giants to some of its fiercest technical walls. You do not have to be a technical expert to reach the summit of some of these and, though you must always take preparations seriously, you can often arrange your climb close to the date through local agencies – though it's best to bring as much high-quality gear with you as you can. The climbing season is fairly short – generally November to March, though December to February is the best time. The best known, if not the most technical, challenge is South America's highest peak, **Aconcagua** (6962m), accessed from Mendoza. In the far south are the Fitz Roy massif and Cerro Torre, which have few equals in terms of technical difficulty and grandeur of scenery. On all of these climbs, but especially those over 4000m, you must acclimatize thoroughly, and be fully aware of the dangers of altitude sickness (see page 33).

SKIING

The main **skiing** months are July and August (late July is peak season), although in some resorts it is possible to ski from late May to early October. Snow conditions vary wildly from year to year, but you can often find excellent powder. The most prestigious resort for downhill skiing is modern Las Leñas, which offers the most challenging slopes, followed by the Bariloche resorts of Cerro Catedral and Cerro Otto. These are the longest established in the country and are still the classic Patagonian ski centres, with their wonderful panoramas of the Nahuel

ARGENTINA ONLINE

ⓦ**turismo.gov.ar** The official tourist website for Argentina.
ⓦ**welcomeargentina.com** Information about accommodation and activities, and detailed transport advice.
ⓦ**buenosaires.gob.ar** City government site for Buenos Aires, with up-to-date details on cultural events.
ⓦ**bubblear.com** Satirical website poking fun at Argentina's news.
ⓦ**pickupthefork.com** Irreverent English-language blog about food and eating out.

Huapi region. It is also possible to ski in Ushuaia. Ski gear is widely available to rent. For updates on conditions and resorts, check out the Andesweb website (ⓦandesweb.com).

COMMUNICATIONS

Most hostels and guesthouses and many cafés and restaurants have free **wi-fi**, while inexpensive **internet** cafés are commonplace. In all but the most remote areas the connections are fairly fast.

Making **local phone calls** in Argentina is inexpensive and easy. In cities and towns, you are never far from a *locutorio*. It's worth asking about phone cards offering cheap minutes if you are planning to make a number of **national calls. Mobile calls** are expensive, but mildly cheaper if calling someone with the same phone company. The main ones are Claro, Personal and Movistar. If you're in Argentina for more than a couple of weeks, you may want to buy a pay-as-you-go SIM card to avoid extortionate roaming fees on your mobile.

There are Correo Argentino **post offices** throughout the country, and you will also come across *locutorios* offering postal

NATIONAL PARK INFORMATION

The **National Park Headquarters** at Santa Fe 690 in Buenos Aires (Mon–Fri 8am–8pm; ☏011 4311 0303, ⓦparquesnacionales.gob.ar) has an information office with introductory leaflets on the nation's parks. A wider range of free leaflets is available at each individual park, but these are of variable quality, and limited funding means that many parks give you only ones with a basic map and a brief park description. Contact the headquarters well in advance if you are interested in voluntary or scientific projects.

1

services and phone booths. International post is relatively expensive and not always reliable; use registered post if possible and try to avoid sending items of value.

CRIME AND SAFETY

Argentina is one of the continent's safer countries and, as long as you take a few basic precautions, you are unlikely to encounter any problems during your stay. Indeed, you'll find many of the more rural parts of the country pretty much risk-free: people often leave doors unlocked, windows open and bikes unchained. More care should be taken in large cities and some of the border towns, particularly the northeastern ones, where poverty and easily available arms and drugs make opportunistic crime a more common occurrence. Some potential pitfalls are outlined here, not to induce paranoia but on the principle that to be forewarned is to be forearmed.

The exception to this is **Buenos Aires**, where incidents of violence and armed robbery have increased in recent years, though the vast majority of travellers visit without problems. It's sometimes difficult to know how much local anxiety is due to a genuine increase in crime and how much to middle-class paranoia, a lot of it provoked by sensationalist news channels. In general, serious crime tends to affect locals more than tourists. Nevertheless, you should not take unmarked taxis; it's better to call a radio taxi (hotels and restaurants will do this for you), or flag one down, rather than take a waiting cab, particularly in affluent or tourist areas. Avoid walking around the quieter neighbourhoods after dark, and be especially wary near the main bus and train stations in Once, Retiro and Constitución; avoid carrying valuables around with you. In La Boca, stick to the main touristy areas such as Caminito – the non-touristy part is to be avoided and is considered dangerous. In the rare event of being held up at gunpoint, don't play the hero.

Theft from hotels is rare, but, as anywhere else in the world, do not leave valuables lying round the room (most have a safe). Some hostels have lockers; it's worth having a padlock of your own.

Drugs attract far more stigma than in most European countries, and Argentine society at large draws very little in the way of a line between "acceptable" soft drugs and "unacceptable" hard drugs. Although they are commonly found in clubs and bars, you're advised to steer clear of buying or partaking yourself – the penalties are stiff if you get caught.

HEALTH

Health issues are rarely a problem in Argentina, which has a generally good health service and clean drinking water. Vaccines are not really needed, but if you're planning on significant travel in rural areas within Salta, Jujuy or Misiones provinces, **malaria** tablets are recommended. **Yellow fever** vaccinations should be considered before visiting forested areas in the north of Argentina, including Iguazú Falls. All travellers over 1 year of age are advised to ensure they have the **hepatitis A** vaccination at least two weeks before arrival. If you're heading off the beaten track, vaccinations against typhoid and rabies are also recommended.

INFORMATION AND MAPS

Argentina's main **National Tourist Office** is at Santa Fe 883 in Buenos Aires (Mon–Fri 9am–5pm; ☎011 4312 2232, ⌖turismo. gov.ar) and offers maps of the country and general information about getting around. Every province maintains a *Casa de Provincia* in Buenos Aires too, where you can pick up information about what there is to see or do. The standard of information you'll glean from them varies wildly.

The clearest and most accurate **map** of the country is *Rutas de la Argentina*, which

---

EMERGENCY NUMBERS

Ambulance ☎ 107
Fire ☎ 100
Police ☎ 911/101
Tourist Police ☎ 011 4346 5748

1

STUDENT AND YOUTH DISCOUNTS

An **ISIC card** will entitle students of any age (over 12) to substantial discounts for many museums, travel and cultural events, as well as other services. See Ⓦ isic.com. ar for details. For travel discounts, contact Al Mundo ☎ 011 4345 7227, Ⓦ almundo. com.ar.

---

you can get free from the national tourist office; it has small but clear inset maps of twenty towns and cities as well as a 1:2,500,000 national map. Another useful resource for route planning is the website Ⓦ ruta0.com. The ACA (Automóvil Club; Ⓦ www.aca.org.ar) produces individual maps for each province, which vary enormously in detail and accuracy.

MONEY AND BANKS

The **Argentine peso** is divided into one hundred centavos. In Argentina, it's represented by the dollar sign ($), but to avoid confusion we have used the symbol AR$ throughout this section. Notes come in 2, 5, 10, 20, 50 and 100 peso denominations, and 1 and 2 peso and 5, 10, 25 and 50 centavo coins are also in circulation. Guard your loose change in Buenos Aires as you will need it for the buses. Try to cash large notes in hotels and supermarkets – never in taxis – and look out for counterfeit money. Check your notes for a watermark, and that the number is printed in shiny green.

Argentina has an unpredictable **economy**, with high inflation and periodic currency controls, so the peso can fluctuate dramatically against other currencies. The situation is fluid, and it's advisable to check the latest situation before you travel.

In recent years there have been two US dollar/peso exchange rates – an official one, used by **ATM**s (*cajeros automáticos*) and banks, and an (illegal) black market (confusingly known as the "blue") rate offered in *cuevas* ("caves"; essentially unmarked shops) or, more riskily, on the street. As currency controls are not currently in place, the difference between the two rates has narrowed, though this may change in the future.

ATMs (*cajeros automáticos*) are plentiful in Argentina, though you can sometimes be caught out in very remote places, especially in the northwest. They also frequently run out of money, especially on weekends, so it is wise to travel with a stash of US dollars. **Travellers' cheques** are not a viable option.

Argentina currently ranks as a fairly expensive destination by Latin American standards, though it's still cheaper than Brazil, Chile and Uruguay, and, if you travel outside the main tourist areas, you can still find some surprisingly good deals. At the time of writing, the official exchange rate was £1 = AR$24, US$1 = AR$18 and €1 = AR$21.

OPENING HOURS AND HOLIDAYS

Most **shops and services** are open Monday to Friday from 9am to 7pm, and Saturday till 2pm, although later in large towns, including Buenos Aires. In smaller towns they may close at some point during the afternoon for between one and five hours – sometimes offset by later closing times in the evening, especially in the summer. Supermarkets seldom close during the day and are generally open much later, often until 8 or 10pm, and on Saturday afternoons. Large shopping malls don't close before 10pm and their food and drink sections (*patios de comida*) may stay open as late as midnight. Most of them open on Sundays, too. **Banks** mostly open on weekdays only, from 10am to 5pm, while casas de cambio more or less follow shop hours. In the northeast, bank opening hours may be more like 7am to noon, to avoid the hot, steamy afternoons.

In addition to national **holidays**, some local anniversaries or saints' days are also public holidays when everything in a given city may close down. Festivals of all kinds, both religious and profane, celebrating local patrons such as Santa Catalina or the Virgin Mary, or showing off produce such as handicrafts, olives, goats or wine, are good excuses for much pomp and partying.

1

PUBLIC HOLIDAYS

January 1 New Year's Day (*Año Nuevo*)

Carnival (varies) Shrove Tuesday and the day before (usually in Feb)

March 24 Day of Truth and Justice

April 2 Malvinas Remembrance Day

Easter (varies) Easter Friday is a public holiday (Easter Thurs is optional)

May 1 Labour Day (*Día del Trabajo*)

May 25 May Revolution Day

June 20 Flag Day (*Día de la Bandera*)

July 9 Independence Day (*Día de la Independencia*)

August 18 Remembrance of General San Martín's death (*Día del Paso a la Inmortalidad del General José de San Martín*)

October 12 Columbus Day (*Día de la Raza*)

November 20 Day of National Sovereignty (fourth Monday of November; *Día de la soberanía nacional*)

December 8 Day of the Immaculate Virgin Mary

December 25 Christmas (*Navidad*)

Note that for some holidays the exact date may vary slightly from year to year.

FESTIVALS

Last week in January Festival de Cosquín. Large folk music festival.

February 2 Virgen de Candelaria, Humahuaca.

February 6 Pachamama festival, Purmamarca and Amaicha. Pachamama (Mother Earth) is celebrated across the Northwest.

First weekend in February Fiesta de la Manzana y la Semilla, Rodeo. A major folk festival.

Mid-February Feria Artesanal y Ganadera de la Puna, Antofagasta de la Sierra. Vibrant Northwest craft festival.

Five days before Ash Wednesday Carnaval, celebrated throughout Argentina, but most notably in Gualeguaychú.

Weekend after Shrove Tuesday Serenata Cafayateña, Cafayate. Popular folk jamboree.

First weekend in March Fiesta de la Vendimia, Mendoza. Grape harvest festival.

March 18 & 19 Pilgrimage of Puerta de San José, near Belén. A major pilgrimage.

March 19 St Joseph's Day, Cachi.

March/April Semana Santa (Holy Week), nationwide. Highlights include the pilgrimage to El Señor de la Peña, Aimogasta, La Rioja, the procession of the Virgen de Punta Corral, from Punta Corral to Tumbaya, and Maundy Thursday in Yavi.

June 10 Día de las Malvinas. Ceremonies to remember the Falklands/Malvinas conflict throughout Argentina.

June 24 St John's Day. A feast day in the Northwest.

July 25 St James' Day, Humahuaca.

Early August Fiesta Nacional de la Nieve, Bariloche. A five-day festival of snow.

August 15 Assumption, Casabindo. Festivities culminate in Argentina's only bullfight, a bloodless *corrida*.

Mid-August World Tango Festival, Buenos Aires, lasting around two weeks.

August 30 Santa Rosa de Lima, Purmamarca.

September 6–15 Fiesta del Milagro, Salta. Major Catholic fiesta climaxing in a huge procession.

Early October Oktoberfest. Ten days of drinking in the country's most German town, Villa General Belgrano.

First Sunday in October Our Lady of the Rosary, Iruya.

Around October 20 Fiesta de la Ollas, or "Manca Fiesta", La Quiaca. A crafts and music festival.

November 1 & 2 All Souls' Day and the Day of the Dead, Quebrada de Humahuaca and Antofagasta de la Sierra.

November 10 Fiesta de la Tradición, San Antonio de Areco. Gaucho festival.

December 24 Christmas Eve, Buenos Aires. Big fireworks displays in the capital.

Buenos Aires

With a huge variety of high-class restaurants, hotels and boutiques, as well as an eclectic mix of Neoclassical and modern architecture, **BUENOS AIRES** is deservedly – if tiredly – known as the "Paris of South America". The influence of immigrants from all over the world, Italian and Spanish above all, can be seen in its street names, restaurants, aesthetics and language. Sip a coffee in the famous *Café Tortoni*, visit a dark and romantic tango hall to watch the nation's famous sultry dance, or simply walk the streets of Recoleta and watch the ladies in fur coats walking tiny dogs on Chanel leads. If you grow weary of the people, noise and buses of the capital you can head out of the city to the waterways of the Paraná Delta, the quiet streets of La Plata or San Antonio de Areco, home of Argentina's gauchos.

WHAT TO SEE AND DO

The city's museums and sights are well distributed between the central areas of Recoleta, Retiro, Palermo and San Telmo, and the *microcentro* lies east of Avenida 9 de Julio between Retiro and San Telmo. The historic *barrio* (neighbourhood) of

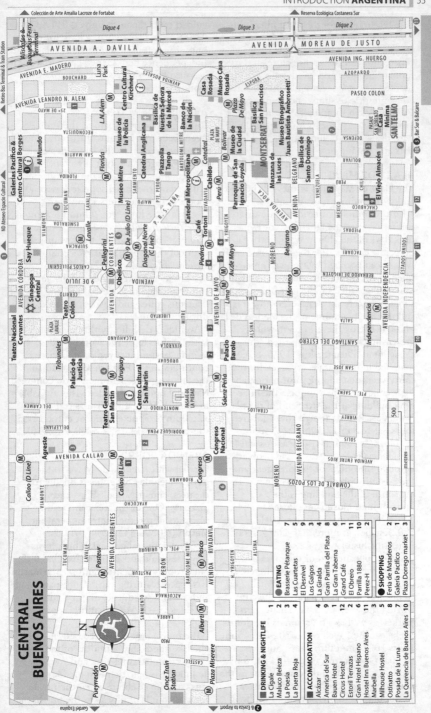

CENTRAL BUENOS AIRES

DRINKING & NIGHTLIFE	
La Cigale	1
Maluco Beleza	2
La Poesía	3
La Puerta Roja	4

ACCOMMODATION	
Alcázar	4
America del Sur	9
Bauen Hotel	1
Circus Hostel	12
Estoril Terrazas	2
Gran Hotel Hispano	6
Hostel Inn Buenos Aires	11
Marbella	3
Millhouse Hostel	8
Ostinatto	7
Posada de la Luna	5
La Querencia de Buenos Aires	10

● EATING	
Brasserie Pétanque	7
Las Cuartetas	5
El Desnivel	9
Los Galgos	3
La Giralda	4
Gran Parrilla del Plata	8
La Gran Taberna	6
Grand Café	12
El Obrero	2
Parrilla 1880	11
Perez-H	10

● SHOPPING	
Feria de Mataderos	2
Galería Pacífico	1
Plaza Dorrego market	3

1

San Telmo is one of the most interesting for visitors, on account of its atmospheric streets, surviving (if often faded) nineteenth-century architecture, and its Sunday antiques and handicrafts street market. The *microcentro* has the greatest concentration of shops and commerce, but Palermo Viejo should also be on every visitor's itinerary for its leafy streets lined with design and fashion shops, and hip bars and restaurants.

PLAZA DE MAYO

The **Plaza de Mayo** has witnessed the best and worst moments of Argentina's history – host to founding presidents, devastating military coups, the fanaticism of Evita, the dark days of the "Dirty War", and desperate crowds after the economic crisis. It has been bombed by its own military, filled to the brink with patriots, and left deserted, guarded by the federal police, in times of uncertainty, and even now it is still the spiritual home of the **Madres de la Plaza de Mayo**. These women, whose grown-up children "disappeared" during the Military Dictatorship (1976–83), marched in the plaza every week for over thirty years demanding information about their children's whereabouts. The huge pink building at the river end of the plaza is the **Casa Rosada** (email ahead for free tours Sat & Sun 12.30pm & 2.30pm; 011 4344 3804, visitascasarosada@ presidencia.gob.ar, casarosada.gob.ar) home to the offices of the president and the executive branch of government. To the south of the building is the underground **Museo Casa Rosada** (Wed–Sun 10am–6pm; free; 011 4344 3802), a look at more than 200 years of Argentine history.

At the opposite end of the plaza is the **Cabildo**, which, though much altered, is one of the few examples of colonial architecture left in this part of the city. During the week there is a small crafts market, as well as a **museum** of historical artefacts (Tues, Wed & Fri 10.30am–5pm, Thurs 10.30am–8pm, Sat & Sun 10.30am–6pm; free; 011 4334 1782); a pleasant café is open the same hours as the museum. The rather plain **Catedral Metropolitana** (daily 9am–6.45pm; free

guided tours, Spanish only; 011 4331 2845), close by, is worth a look for its imposing columns and the **mausoleum** to Independence hero General San Martín; it was also Pope Francis' previous place of work.

AVENIDA DE MAYO

Running west from behind the Cabildo, **Avenida de Mayo** is one of the city's most attractive streets. In the late nineteenth century, Argentina's first skyscrapers were erected along here, and an underground rail system (the *subte*) soon followed. Two blocks before the intersection with Avenida 9 de Julio, you'll find the famous *Café Tortoni* (daily 8am–1am), with over 150 years of service and the favourite of many of the capital's most successful writers, Jorge Luis Borges included. Within its mirrored golden walls, tango shows are held in the evenings, and delicious coffee and pastries are served during the day.

Avenida 9 de Julio (with sixteen busy lanes) claims to be the world's widest avenue: beyond it, Avenida de Mayo continues to the **Plaza de Congreso**, and the fabulous Greco-Roman-style **Congreso Nacional** building (guided visits available in English Mon, Tues, Thurs & Fri 12.30pm & 5pm; enquire at entrance on south side; 011 2822 3000 ext 2410).

AVENIDA CORRIENTES

Parallel with Avenida de Mayo to the north, **Avenida Corrientes** is lined with theatres, cinemas, bookshops and pizzerias. One of the most interesting places to stop is the **Teatro General San Martín** (0800 333 5254, complejoteatral.gob.ar), which hosts plays, festivals and exhibitions. Under the same roof is the **Centro Cultural San Martín** arts space, featuring exhibition spaces and auditoriums for music, drama and film (011 4374 1251, elculturalsanmartin. org).

The much-loved **Obelisco**, a 67m-tall obelisk, stands in the middle of the busy intersection of Corrientes and Avenida 9 de Julio. It is here that ecstatic football fans come to celebrate when their team wins. A couple of blocks to the north, the

1

huge French Renaissance **Teatro Colón** (☎011 4378 7100, ⓦteatrocolon.org.ar) still stands tall after more than one hundred years. Many opera and ballet greats have performed here, and the theatre triumphantly reopened in 2010 – during the national bicentenary celebrations – after extensive refurbishment works.

CALLE FLORIDA

Pedestrianized **Calle Florida**, packed throughout the week with shoppers, street vendors, buskers and performers, runs across the downtown area, heading north from Avenida de Mayo, close to the Plaza de Mayo, across Avenida Corrientes and ending at pleasant Parque San Martín. Towards the northern end the impressive **Galerías Pacífico** (ⓦgaleriaspacifico.com.ar) shopping centre, with its vaulted and frescoed ceiling, offers a welcome respite from the crowds outside. There is an inexpensive food court downstairs, and on the first floor is the entrance to the **Centro Cultural Borges** (Mon–Sat 10am–9pm, Sun noon–9pm; AR$150; ☎011 5555 5359, ⓦccborges.org.ar), with three floors of photography and art exhibitions.

PUERTO MADERO

Buenos Aires' nineteenth-century docks, neglected for decades, have been redeveloped over the past twenty years to become a pleasant, if somewhat sterile, residential area, **Puerto Madero**, where modern apartment blocks surround bright-red restored warehouses. These are now home to some of the city's most chic restaurants and hotels. One of the capital's best art galleries, the **Colección de Arte Amalia Lacroze de Fortabat**, Olga Cossettini 141 (Tues–Sun noon–9pm; AR$80; ☎011 4310 6600, ⓦcoleccionfortabat.org.ar), is housed in a peculiar hangar-style building on the waterfront. Within is an impressive private collection by both national and international artists, including works by Dalí, Warhol and Turner.

Also of note is the **Faena Arts Center**, at Aime Paine 1169 (Tues–Sun 11am–7pm; AR$100; ⓦfaenaartscenter.org), which frequently rotates contemporary exhibits and installations.

Nearby along the river's edge is the **Reserva Ecológica Costanera Sur** (entrance at Av Tristán Achával Rodríguez 1550; Tues–Sun 8am–6pm; free; ☎011 4893 1853), a large expanse of reclaimed and regenerated land. It makes a delightful afternoon stroll, and they hold full-moon tours once a month. In front of the entrance, a small craft market is held on weekends.

MONTSERRAT

Cobblestoned **Montserrat**, just south of Plaza de Mayo, is one of the oldest neighbourhoods of the city, and the most popular until a yellow fever outbreak in the nineteenth century forced wealthier families to move to Recoleta and Palermo. The *barrio*'s principal street is Calle Defensa, named after the event when residents trying to force back British invaders in the early 1800s poured boiling water and oil from their balconies onto the attacking soldiers.

The neo-Baroque **Basílica San Francisco** (Wed–Sun 11am–5pm; ☎011 4331 0625), at the corner of Alsina and Defensa, has an intricately decorated interior that can just about be made out through the atmospheric gloom. Nearby is the small **Museo de la Ciudad**, Defensa 223 (daily 11am–6pm; free; ☎011 4331 9855), which houses informative and well-presented changing exhibitions about the city. Two blocks west of Defensa is the collection of buildings known as the **Manzana de las Luces** (guided visits Mon–Fri at 3pm, Sat & Sun at 3pm, 4.30pm & 6pm in English; AR$65; info at Perú 272; ☎011 4342 9930), which dates back to 1686. Originally housing a Jesuit community, it has been home to numerous official institutions throughout its history, and today it accommodates the **Colegio Nacional**, an elite high school, and Buenos Aires' oldest church, **San Ignacio de Loyola** (daily 8am–8pm; ☎011 4331 2458), begun in 1675.

SAN TELMO

San Telmo begins further south along Defensa from Montserrat, on the far side of Avenida Belgrano. With its myriad antique stores and junk shops, as well as a

1

range of busy, late-opening restaurants and bars (especially around the intersection of Chile and Defensa), it's a great place to wander. For fresh food and eclectic antiques head to the **Mercado San Telmo** (daily 7am–7pm; ⓦmercadosantelmo. com.ar). The market takes up an entire city block, with an entrance on each side, including one on Defensa near the corner of Estados Unidos.

A few blocks further, **Plaza Dorrego** is a great place to pause for a coffee under the leafy trees, at least on weekdays when it's quieter. On Sundays the area is completely taken over by the **Feria de San Pedro Telmo** (10am–5pm; buses #8, #24, #86, #93 or #152 easily picked up downtown). Vintage watches, posters, clothes and jewellery are all on display at this huge open-air antiques market, enlivened by street performers and live tango acts. Another great place for antique-spotting is the **Pasaje Defensa**, Defensa 1179 (daily 10am–7pm), a converted mansion filled with hidden shops, cafés and workshops.

Calle Defensa continues, across the busy, ugly avenues of San Juan and Juan de Garay, to leafy **Parque Lezama**, home to the **Museo Histórico Nacional**, Defensa 1600 (Tues–Sun 11am–7pm, guided tours in English Thurs & Fri noon; free; ⓣ011 4300 7540, ⓦmuseohistoriconacional. cultura.gob.ar). This small museum has an interesting permanent exhibition on Argentina's history. The collection at the **Museo de Arte Moderno de Buenos Aires (MAMBA)**, Av San Juan 350 (Tues–Fri 11am–7pm, Sat & Sun 11am–8pm; AR$30, Tues free; ⓣ011 4342 9139, ⓦmuseomoderno.org), focuses mainly on Argentine art from the 1920s until the present day, and includes pieces by Xul Solar and Antonio Berni. Next door is sister museum **Museo de Arte Contemporáneo de Buenos Aires (MACBA)**, San Juan 328 (Mon & Wed–Fri 11am–7pm, Sat & Sun 11am–7.30pm; AR$60; ⓣ011 5263 9988, ⓦmacba.com.ar), which shows contemporary works.

LA BOCA

Easily accessible from Parque Lezama, the suburb of **La Boca** is known for the Caminito and as home to one of

Argentina's leading football clubs, **Boca Juniors**, arch-rivals of the River Plate team on the other side of town.

The **Caminito** is a small area of brightly coloured buildings along the river, created in the 1950s by the neighbourhood's most famous artist, **Benito Quinquela Martín**. These days the Caminito is a serious tourist trap, though it has an interesting open-air **arts and crafts fair** (daily 10.30am–6pm), street performers and cafés charging exorbitant prices.

A visit to the Boca Juniors' stadium, **La Bombonera** (Brandsen 805, three blocks west of Av Almirante Brown; ⓣ011 5777 1200), is definitely worthwhile even if you can't score tickets to a game. The starting point is the fascinating **Museo de la Pasión Boquense** (daily 10am–6pm; AR$200; ⓣ011 4362 1100, ⓦmuseoboquense. com), a must for football fans; guided tours of the stadium start from here (daily 11am–5pm hourly; AR$60 extra).

La Boca can be reached by **bus** #29 from Corrientes or Plaza de Mayo, #86 from Plaza de Mayo or #53 from Constitución. Note that La Boca has a bad reputation for **robberies**, so leave your valuables at home and do not stray from the touristy area around Caminito.

RECOLETA

Immediately north of the city centre, the wide streets of upper-class **Recoleta** are most famously home to the **Recoleta Cemetery** at Avenida Quintana and Junín (daily 7am–5pm; free), surrounded by café-lined streets and their designer-clad denizens. The cemetery is the resting place of some of Argentina's leading celebrities, including Evita herself, buried under her maiden name of Duarte. A map is available at the entrance to guide you around the great monuments of dark granite, white marble and bronze.

Next door are the white walls of the **Basílica de Nuestra Señora del Pilar** (Mon–Fri 8am–8pm, Sat 8am–7pm, Sun 8.30am–9pm; free; ⓣ011 4803 6793, ⓦbasilicadelpilar.org.ar). The eighteenth-century Jesuit building has been beautifully restored, and is much in demand for fashionable weddings: inside, the magnificent Baroque silver altarpiece,

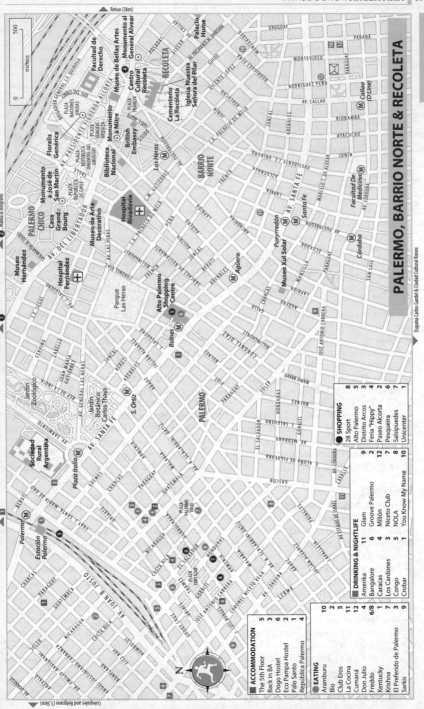

PALERMO, BARRIO NORTE & RECOLETA

Esquina Carlos Gardel & Ciudad Cultural Konex

ACCOMMODATION	
The 5th Floor	5
Back in BA	3
Dogo Hostel	6
Eco Pampa Hostel	2
Palo Santo	1
República Palermo	4

● EATING	
Aramburu	10
Bio	2
Club Eros	5
La Cocina	11
Cumaná	4
Don Julio	6/8
Freddo	7
Kentucky	7
Krishna	3
El Preferido de Palermo	9
Sarkis	1

■ DRINKING & NIGHTLIFE			
Amerika	11	Glam	8
Bangalore	6	Groove Palermo	5
Caracas	4	Millón	4
Los Cardones	7	Niceto Club	6
Congo	3	NOLA	7
Crobar	9	You Know My Name	1

● SHOPPING	
28 Sport	8
Alto Palermo	5
Distrito Arcos	9
Feria 'Hippy'	4
Paseo Alcorta	12
Pesqueira	6
Salsipuedes	7
Unicenter	10

1

embellished with an Inca sun and other pre-Hispanic details, was made by craftsmen from the north of Argentina. Adjacent, the **Centro Cultural de Recoleta** (Tues–Fri 1.30–10pm, Sat & Sun 11.30am–10pm; free; ☎011 4803 1040, ⓦcentroculturalrecoleta.org), at Junín 1930, is a fabulous art space with interesting temporary exhibitions.

If by now you're in need of a coffee or a shopping fix, head to **Buenos Aires Design**, a shopping centre focusing on chic design products and homeware, which adjoins the cultural centre. The large terrace upstairs overlooks a park, and is a great place for an afternoon drink.

Visible from the terrace of Buenos Aires Design, the **Museo Nacional de Bellas Artes** (Tues–Fri 11am–8pm, Sat & Sun 10am–8.30pm, tours in English Tues, Wed & Fri 1pm; free; ☎011 5288 9900, ⓦbellasartes.gob.ar) is at Av del Libertador 1473. Within the imposing, columned building is a traditional art gallery, primarily displaying European paintings but also with a small but valuable collection of colonial and modern Argentine work. For more local artworks, go to the **Museo Xul Solar** (Tues–Fri noon–8pm, Sat noon–7pm; AR$60; ☎011 4824 3302, ⓦxulsolar.org.ar), further to the southwest at Laprida 1212, near the corner of Calle Mansilla, which focuses on the bright and colourful Cubist paintings of twentieth-century Argentine artist Alejandro Xul Solar.

PALERMO

Expansive, middle-class **Palermo** stretches around Avenida del Libertador as it heads north from Recoleta, taking in the high-rise apartments near the north of Avenida Santa Fe, the chic cafés and hotels of Palermo Viejo, and the leafy streets and late-night bars of Palermo Hollywood. On or near tree-lined Libertador are three unmissable museums. The **Museo Nacional de Arte Decorativo**, Libertador 1902 (Tues–Sun 2–7pm; voluntary donation AR$25; ☎011 4801 8248, ⓦmnad.org), is housed in Palacio Errázuriz, one of the city's most original private mansions, with a lovely café in its patio. The collection is of mainly European sculpture, art and

furnishings, all beautifully displayed.

At Libertador 2373 you'll find the small and inviting **Museo de Arte Popular Hernández** (Tues–Fri 1–7pm, Sat & Sun 10am–8pm; AR$10, Wed free; ☎011 4802 9967), whose displays focus on local silverwork and textiles. A few blocks away, in a striking modern building at Av Figueroa Alcorta 3415, stands **Malba**, the **Museo de Arte Latinoamericano de Buenos Aires** (Mon & Thurs–Sun noon–8pm, Wed noon–9pm; AR$120, Wed half price; ☎011 4808 6500, ⓦmalba.org.ar). The permanent display of Latin American art from the early twentieth century onwards makes a refreshing break from stuffier museums. The art bookshop downstairs is one of the city's best, and the light and modern café *Ninina* (daily 9am–9pm) is recommended. In the foyer there is an excellent cinema.

The heart of trendy **Palermo Viejo** is Plaza Serrano, officially named **Plaza Cortázar** after the Argentine novelist Julio Cortázar, surrounded by cafés, bars and restaurants. Every Saturday and Sunday (10am–8pm) the plaza and one block of Honduras is host to markets full of locally designed clothes and crafts. Stroll along the connecting streets for fashion boutiques, bookshops and music shops. Even jazzier **Palermo Hollywood** is across the train tracks to the north. The busiest streets, Humboldt and Fitzroy, are home to excellent restaurants and bars, while late-night watering holes abound along Niceto Vega.

MATADEROS

Over an hour by bus from the centre, **Mataderos**, in the southwestern corner of the city, has a bloody past as home to the city's cattle slaughterhouses. Today, it is worth a visit for the **Feria de Mataderos**, held on Sunday for most of the year but on Saturday evenings in summer (Jan–March Sat 6pm–midnight, April–Dec Sun 11am–sunset; buses #36, #92 & #126; Mon–Fri ☎011 4323 9400 ext 2830, weekends ☎011 4687 5602). A celebration of all things gaucho, the Feria has stalls selling leatherwork, *mate*, gourds and silver, as well as folk music and displays of horseriding, plus some of the best *empanadas* in the city.

ARRIVAL AND DEPARTURE

By plane Nearly all international flights and a few domestic ones arrive at Ezeiza International Airport (☎ 011 5480 2500, ⓦ aa2000.com.ar), 35km southwest of the city centre. Manuel Tienda León runs express buses to and from the airport (every 30min; daily 6am–9pm, less frequent outside these times; AR$240 one-way; ☎ 011 4315 5115, ⓦ tiendaleon.com), which use its terminal at Av E. Madero 1299 (at San Martín) in the Retiro area. A taxi or *remis* (radio cab) will cost around AR$700 from Ezeiza to town. Buenos Aires has two domestic airports, the biggest being Aeroparque Jorge Newbery (☎ 011 5480 6111, ⓦ aa2000. com.ar) on the Costanera Norte, around 6km north of the city centre; it also serves some connections with Chile, Uruguay and Brazil. Military air base El Palomar (☎ 11 5480 6111, ⓦ aa2000.com.ar), 18km west of the city, opened to cater to budget airlines such as Andes (ⓦ andesonline.com), Fly Bondi (ⓦ flybondi.com) and Norwegian (ⓦ norwegian. com), the last of which was set to arrive in late 2018. Tienda Leon runs a bus service (200 pesos), to its Retiro terminal. Local buses #33 and #45 (AR$10) runs from the airport to Paseo Colón, on the fringe of the microcentro, while the #37 and #160 run to Plaza Italia in Palermo. Manuel Tienda León shuttles from Aeroparque to downtown are around AR$150.

Destinations Bariloche (up to 10 daily; 2hr 20min); Córdoba (10 daily; 1hr 15min); Corrientes (1 daily; 1hr 20min); El Calafate (10 daily; 3hr 20min); Jujuy (2 daily; 2hr 10min); La Rioja (1 daily; 3hr); Mar del Plata (up to 5 daily; 1hr 15min); Mendoza (up to 7–9 daily; 1hr 50min); Neuquén (4 daily; 1hr 40min); Puerto Iguazú (up to 10–12 daily; 1hr 50min); Rio Gallegos (3 daily; 3hr 15min); Salta (7 daily; 2hr); San Juan (1 daily; 1hr 50min); San Martín de los Andes (3 weekly; 2hr 20min); Santiago del Estero (1 daily; 1hr 40min); Trelew (4 daily; 2hr); Tucumán (5 daily; 1hr 50min); Ushuaia (6 daily; 3hr 40min).

By bus All domestic and international services use the Retiro bus terminal, at Av Antártida & Ramos Mejía. Taxis are plentiful and the Retiro *subte* (metro) station is just a block away, outside the adjoining train station. Be careful after dark; a vast shantytown, the Villa 31, is located behind the terminal and pickpockets operate around here. A variety of buses (around AR$10) leaves from outside, including #5 and #50, to Congreso, #106 to the edge of Palermo Viejo on the Av Córdoba side and #152 on the Av Santa Fe side, and #108 to Palermo Hollywood.

Destinations Frequent domestic services to Bariloche (19–25hr); Córdoba (9–11hr); Mendoza (14–16hr); Neuquén (14–19hr); Puerto Iguazú (17–18hr); Puerto Madryn (18–20hr); Rosario (4hr); Salta (20–22hr); Tucumán (16hr). Daily international services to La Paz (48hr); Montevideo (8–9hr); Santiago de Chile (19hr); São Paulo (34hr); Rio de Janeiro (40hr).

By ferry Ferries and catamarans cross the Río de la Plata from Montevideo and Colonia del Sacramento in Uruguay.

More convenient are services by Sea Cat (Av Antártida Argentina 821 ☎ 011 4314 5100, ⓦ seacatcolonia.com.ar) and Buquebus (Av Antártida Argentina 821; ☎ 011 4316 6530, ⓦ buquebus.com), which use the Terminal Dársena Norte (often just known as the Terminal Buquebús) at Viamonte & Costanera Sur, just a few blocks from the *microcentro*. Meanwhile, *Colonia Express* (☎ 011 4317 4100, ⓦ coloniaexpress.com) operates a third service from a terminal called Dársena Sur located at Pedro de Mendoza 330, close to La Boca.

Destinations Colonia (8 daily; 1–3hr); Montevideo (4 daily; 4hr).

By train The main stations are Retiro, Constitución and Once but are mostly used only for urban and provincial travel. Retiro station (Av Ramos Mejía, just to the east of Plaza San Martín) is the departure point for trains to Tigre and the northern suburbs. There are twice-weekly services from Retiro to Rosario, Córdoba and Tucumán (ⓦ sofse.gob. ar): see page 91.

GETTING AROUND

By subte The easiest part of the public transport system to get to grips with is the underground railway or *subte*, which serves the central neighbourhoods from 5.30am until 11.30pm (Mon–Sat) and from 8am to 10pm (Sun & public holidays) (ⓦ metrovias.com.ar). There are six lines – Lines A, B, D and E run from the city centre outwards, while lines C and H run respectively between Retiro and Constitución, and Las Heras and Hospitales, connecting them all. Tickets cost AR$7.50 for a single trip and are bought from booths at each station. It makes sense to invest in a pre-pay electronic SUBE card for AR$25, which will give cheaper subway fares at AR$6 if you use it more than twenty times in a month. Buy one (no photo card necessary) from any subway station as well as many *kioskos* (argentina.gob.ar/sube).

By bus Buses (ⓦ tucolectivo.info) are one of the most useful (and cheap) ways of getting around the city – and indeed the only way of reaching many outlying districts. Invest in a combined street and bus-route booklet, such as the Guía "T", widely available from street kiosks, to work out the routes. One-way tickets cost between AR$10 and AR$10.50 depending on the distance (announce your final stop to the driver) and can only be paid with a SUBE card. If you travel within 2hr of your first bus trip, the second ride receives fifty percent off, the third 75 percent. Many services run all night.

By remís These are radio cabs or minicabs, plain cars booked through an office (and therefore preferred by some wary locals). Not particularly economical for short journeys, they're cheaper than taxis for getting to the airport; try *Remises Uno* (☎ 011 4638 8318). It's safest to call a radio taxi at night, although there is an extra fee of AR$14 for the privilege. Ask your hostel for their preferred company or try *Taxi Alo* (☎ 011 4855 5555).

1

By taxi The city's black-and-yellow taxis are spectacularly plentiful. The meter starts at AR$27.70 (charges increase at night), and you should calculate on a ride costing around AR$55 per twenty blocks.

By bicycle Buenos Aires not only has an extensive cycle route known as the *bicisenda*, it also lends bikes for free (w ecobici.buenosaires.gob.ar). With more than a hundred stations dotted around the city, you can borrow a bike for a 4hr period. Visitors can take advantage of the scheme – sign up online with a scan of your passport and date of entry visa, and Ecobici will do the rest.

INFORMATION

Tourist information There are a number of *centros de informes* around the city run by the Secretaría de Turismo, including one at Av Alicia Moreau de Justo 200 in Puerto Madero (daily 9am–6pm; ☎011 4313 0187, w turismo. buenosaires.gob.ar). The best is on Florida 100, at Av Diagonal Roque Sáenz Peña (daily 9am–6pm, Sat & Sun until 7pm) where you can find information on more than fifty free tours. You can also pick up information from the well-organized National Tourist Office at Santa Fe 883 (Mon–Fri 9am–6pm; ☎011 4312 2232, w turismo.gov.ar), which has details of the provincial tourist offices within the capital.

TOUR OPERATORS

Walking tours are offered by the city government (free; in English and Spanish) around a given *barrio*, or with themes such as "Evita" or "Carlos Gardel". Ask at a tourism kiosk for the schedule.

Al Mundo Florida 825 ☎011 5199 7758, w almundo. com. Local travel agency offering help with cheap flight deals, city and international packages; student discounts available.

ANDA tours ☎011 3221 0833, w andatravel.com.ar. Organizes responsible tourist visits with a difference, such as its "La Boca Beyond Caminito" walking tour of Boca, which includes stop-offs at local art collectives and community organizations.

Buenos Aires Bus w buenosairesbus.com. City hop-on hop-off bus tours (daily 9am–5.30pm; every 20min) stopping at various points of interest, including Boca, the Reserva Ecológica and the Rosedal in Palermo. The price – AR$490/day or AR$1650/two days – represents good value compared to taxis if you're planning to cover a lot of ground.

MacDermott's Argentina Borges 2470, Office 1C ☎011 4773 2522, w macdermottsargentina.com. Organizes horseriding tours all around Argentina including Andes treks.

Say Hueque Thames 2062, ☎011 5258 8740, w sayhueque.com. A professional tour operator covering all of Argentina (and parts of Chile) including excursions to Iguazú waterfalls and five-day Patagonian hikes.

ACCOMMODATION

Finding accommodation in Buenos Aires shouldn't be a problem but advance planning is advised, especially for high season. Discounts can sometimes be negotiated, particularly if you are staying for more than a few days. Most backpackers head for San Telmo, where the hostels are concentrated, but you can also increasingly find good-value, pleasant accommodation in leafier Palermo.

HOSTELS

Most hostels have communal kitchens and offer free or cheap internet, breakfast and laundry.

CENTRAL BUENOS AIRES

★ **Estoril Terrazas** Av de Mayo 1385 (1st & 6th Floors), at Uruguay ☎011 4382 9684, w hostelestoril3. com; map p.55. Directly opposite the Palacio Barolo, one of Buenos Aires' most stunning buildings, *Estoril* has to be among the world's top hostels. Extremely comfortable and always impeccably clean, it offers all amenities and has a roof terrace with perfect views of Av de Mayo and Congreso. Ask for the rooftop dorm. Dorms <u>AR$280</u>, doubles <u>AR$900</u>

Milhouse Hostel Hipólito Yrigoyen 959, at Bernardo de Irigoyen ☎011 4345 9604, w milhousehostel.com; map p.55. A large, lively hostel in a colonial-style building with a huge range of activities on offer. One of the city's most popular, so book well in advance. *Milhouse Hostel* also has another outpost at Av de Mayo 1245. Dorms <u>AR$252</u>, doubles <u>AR$870</u>

PALERMO, RECOLETA AND RETIRO

Back in BA El Salvador 5115, at Uriarte ☎011 4774 2859, w backinba.com; map p.59. Small, friendly hostel with a low-key vibe, bar and a good-sized living area, as well as comfy beds and decent linen. Great location close to the heart of Palermo. Dorms <u>AR$290</u>, doubles <u>AR$720</u>

Dogo Hostel Cabrera 4716 ☎011 3968 7800, w dogohostel.com; map p.59. Intimate and colourful five-room Palermo hostel run by its owners. Some rooms have terraces and private bathrooms. Its ample terrace and *parrilla* barbecue area make this a great spot to meet other travellers. Dorms <u>AR$230</u>, doubles <u>AR$700</u>

Eco Pampa Hostel Guatemala 4778, at Borges ☎011 4831 2435, w hostelpampa.com; map p.59. Dubbing itself the city's first green hostel – the vibrant lime-hued facade sets the tone – *Eco Pampa Hostel* is comfortable as well as eco-friendly, with its leafy terrace and low-energy computers. Dorms <u>AR$234</u>, doubles <u>AR$850</u>

SAN TELMO

America del Sur Chacabuco 718, at Chile ☎011 4300 5525, w americahostel.com.ar; map p.55. A blockish new build, now a San Telmo classic; pop art and contemporary furnishing abound, giving it a hotel feel. That extends to the rooms too, as dorms are for a maximum of four. All rooms have private bathrooms, doubles include TV. Dorms AR$468, doubles AR$699

La Querencia de Buenos Aires Carlos Calvos 1328 ☎011 4304 2990, ⌨laquerenciadebuenosaires.com; map p.55. French-run four-room B&B set in a delightful renovated *casa chorizo* (long, sausage-shaped house) close to Constitución. Kitchen facilities available. AR$1100

Circus Hostel Chacabuco 1020, at Humberto Primo ☎011 4300 4983, ⌨hostelcircus.com; map p.55. Offering a variety of private rooms and four-bed dorms, and morning yoga classes are included at this smart hostel. When summer gets too steamy, slip into the outdoor swimming pool. Dorms AR$306, doubles AR$828

Hostel Inn Buenos Aires Humberto Primo 820, at Tacuarí ☎011 4300 7992, ⌨hostel-inn.com; map p.55. A restored mansion for a hostel could only be located in the heart of historical San Telmo. A plethora of activities is organized, such as free walking tours, movie nights and pizza parties. There's another hostel at Av de Mayo 1111. Dorms AR$250, doubles AR$690

Ostinatto Chile 680, at Perú ☎011 4362 9639, ⌨ostinatto.com; map p.55. Falls squarely in the category of "hip" hostel, with cool minimalist design, spacious dorms and friendly staff. Hosts free tango, yoga and Spanish classes as well as film and barbecue nights. Treat yourself to one of two self-contained apartments, the loft (AR$460) and penthouse (AR$480). Dorms AR$260, doubles AR$650

HOTELS AND B&BS

CENTRAL BUENOS AIRES

Alcázar Av de Mayo 935 ☎011 4345 0926, ⌨hotelalcazar.com.ar; map p.55. This old hotel with a lovely central staircase features basic rooms, all with heating, a fan and private bathroom. AR$1100

Bauen Hotel Av Callao 360 ☎011 4373 9009, ⌨bauenhotel.com.ar; p. 55. Taken over by staff made redundant in 2001's economic crisis, this co-operative hotel has an unbeatable central location though rooms are straight out of the 1980s. AR$850

Gran Hotel Hispano Av de Mayo 861, at Tacuarí ☎011 4345 2020, ⌨hhispano.com.ar; map p.55. Metres from the famous *Café Tortoni*, this family-run classic retains its original Spanish-style architecture. Most rooms are centred on a beautiful old courtyard, while some have balconies looking onto the street below. AR$1422

Marbella Av de Mayo 1261 ☎011 4383 8566, ⌨hotelmarbella.com.ar; map p.55. Calm, good-value lodgings (discounts for cash) in a central location. Rooms are modern with cable TV and decent-sized bathrooms, and there is also an economical restaurant. AR$990

Posada de la Luna Perú 565, at México ☎011 4343 0911, ⌨posadaluna.com; map p.55. Attractively decorated B&B set in a colonial townhouse on the cusp of San Telmo. Home-made bread and jam is served with breakfast and there's a jacuzzi and sun deck. No hotel sign outside the door means it's still a relatively well-kept secret. This corner can be a bit dodgy so keep your wits about you. AR$420

PALERMO, RECOLETA AND RETIRO

The 5th Floor Vidt, at Santa Fe ☎011 4827 0366, ⌨the5thfloorba.com; map p.59. Take the cramped lift to the fifth floor and step into a spacious Art Deco B&B that spans two floors. With terraces and shared spaces galore, this is a friendly option in a more residential part of Palermo, but still a stone's throw from the buzz. English breakfast included. AR$2160

Palo Santo Bonpland 2275, at Paraguay ☎011 5280 6100 ⌨palosantohotel.com; map p.59. Eco-friendly place in Palermo Hollywood with vertical gardens and a sustainable ethos. The chic rooms sport handcrafted furniture and splashes of colour, and there's a rooftop hot tub. AR$2100

República Palermo Costa Rica 4828, at Borges ☎011 4833 5834, ⌨republicapalermo.com; map p.59. Sleek twelve-room B&B, with designer features and a neat location in the heart of Palermo Soho. AR$1170

EATING

Buenos Aires has a busy, increasingly diverse, restaurant scene. Many restaurants offer a good-value *menú del día* on weekdays, usually including a drink, an excellent way to sample the best of BA's restaurants for less. It is wise to book ahead at the more popular places.

CENTRAL BUENOS AIRES

Las Cuartetas Av Corrientes 838 ☎011 4326 0171, ⌨lascuartetas.com; map p.55. Big, brightly lit theatre and pizzeria, opposite the Gran Rex theatre. Large pizzas from AR$200. Mon–Fri 11am–1.30am, Sat noon–1.30am, Sun 7pm–1.30am.

Los Galgos Callao 501 ☎011 43712 3561, ⌨barlosgalgos.com.ar; map p.55. Open since 1930 this notable bar was given a new lease of lifein 2015. Abundant pasta (AR$150), *picadas* (charcuterie plate; AR$200) and even frogs' legs (AR$400) are served under the watchful eyes of the ceramic namesake greyhounds. Mon–Wed 8am–11.45pm, Thurs–Sat 8–1am.

La Giralda Corrientes 1453 ☎011 4371 3846; map p.55. Brightly lit and austerely decorated Corrientes café, famous for its *chocolate espeso con churros* (thick hot chocolate with fritters; AR$90). A perennial hangout for students and intellectuals, and a good place to observe the *porteño* passion for conversation. Daily 8am–2am.

1

★ TREAT YOURSELF

Aramburu Vicente López 1661, Recoleta ☎011 4305 0439, ⓦarambururesto.com.ar; map p. 59. At this intimate and award-winning establishment, chef-owner Gonzalo Aramburu, who trained in Europe and the US before returning to Argentina, shows off his culinary wizardry. Splash out on the divine seventeen-course tasting menu with wine pairings – it will set you back around AR$2000 but will be worth every sip and bite. Book in advance. Tues–Sat 8.30–11.30pm.

La Gran Taberna Combate de los Pozos 95, Montserrat ☎011 4951 7586; map p.55. A popular, bustling and down-to-earth restaurant a block from the Congreso. The vast, reasonably priced menu offers a mixture of Spanish dishes, including a good selection of seafood, *porteño* staples and a sprinkling of more exotic dishes such as *ranas a la provenzal* (frogs' legs with parsley and garlic; AR$280). Many dishes are large enough to share. Mains AR$150–220. Daily noon–4pm & 8pm–2am.

Perez-H Maipú 618 ☎011 4328 8780, ⓦperez-h.com; map p.55. Burgers are extremely popular in BA, and this artisan chain grills up decent patties at great prices (AR$80). Mon–Wed & Sun noon–midnight, Thurs–Sat noon–1am.

PALERMO, RECOLETA AND RETIRO

Bio Humboldt 2192 ☎011 4774 3880 ⓦbiorestaurant.com.ar; map p.59. Vegetarian restaurant with lots of wholesome ingredients – wholemeal *empanadas*, quinoa risotto, tofu salad and so on –lunch (AR$170) comes with a drink. Organic wine and beer are also served. Daily 10am–midnight.

Club Eros Uriarte 1609, Palermo Viejo ☎011 4832 1313; map p.59. Fun, noisy cantina at a neighbourhood sports and social club, offering standard steak and chips at bargain prices. Daily noon–4pm & 8pm–midnight.

La Cocina Pueyrredón 1508, Recoleta ☎011 4825 3171; map p.59. Tiny budget place serving *locro* (a filling corn stew from the northeast of Argentina) and a selection of delicious Catamarca-style *empanadas*. Mon–Sat noon–1pm & 7pm–1am.

Cumaná Rodriguez Peña 1149, Retiro; map p.59. Popular with students and office workers, this is a good place to try *mate*, served from 4pm to 7.30pm with a basket of crackers. There's also a selection of provincial food, such as *empanadas* and *cazuelas* (casseroles). Daily from noon.

Don Julio Guatemala 4699, Palermo Viejo ☎011 4831 9564 ⓦparrilladonjulio.com.ar; map p.59. Excellent *parrilla* with choice cuts of meat, a superb wine list and smart, efficient service. *Lomo*, fries, salad and a glass of wine will set you back AR$500. Daily noon–5pm, 7pm–1am.

Freddo Branches throughout the city, including Alto Palermo Shopping and Armenia 1618, ⓦfreddo.com.ar; map p.59. Buenos Aires' best ice-cream chain. *Dulce de leche* fans will be in heaven, and the passionfruit mousse flavour (*mousse de maracuyá*) is superb. Prices from AR$50. Daily 10am–late.

Grand Café Basavilbaso 1340, Retiro ☎011 4893 9333, ⓦgrandcafe.com.ar; map p.55. Adorable, friendly café serving well-priced modern Argentine dishes. Kick back in an armchair with a daily lunch special such as fried chicken with mash and tartar sauce, a soft drink and dessert (AR$160). Also serves up a delectable croissant (AR$25) and large coffee (AR$65). Mon–Fri 8am–7pm & Sat 10am–4pm.

Kentucky Santa Fe 4602, Palermo Viejo ☎011 4773 7869, ⓦpizzeriaskentucky.com; map p.59. A Buenos Aires institution that's been around since 1942, serving excellent pizzas and *empanadas*. Expect old-school waiters in white shirts and bow ties, and a grungy clientele. The *empanadas* are abundant and worth the higher than normal price. Mon–Thurs & Sun 6am–2am, Fri & Sat 24hr.

Krishna Malabia 1833, Palermo Viejo ☎011 4833 4618, ⓦkrishnaveggie.com; map p.59. Tiny bohemian spot on Plaza Armenia run by the International Society for Krishna Consciousness and serving tasty vegetarian Indian food. Go for the mixed *thali* with a ginger lemonade. Mon 8pm–12.30am, Tues–Sun 12.30pm–12.30am.

El Preferido de Palermo Borges 2108, at Guatemala, Palermo Viejo ☎011 4774 6585; map p.59. Fun, *pulpería*-style diner with bottles and cans packing the shelves and hams hanging from the ceiling. Menu choices include a lentil and bacon stew and *milanesa* (breaded escalope) with potatoes. Mon–Sat 9am–11pm.

Sarkis Thames 1101, Villa Crespo ☎011 4772 4911; map p.59. Excellent tabbouleh, *keppe crudo* (raw meat with onion – much better than it sounds) and falafel at this popular restaurant serving a fusion of Armenian, Arab and Turkish cuisine. Close to Palermo Soho, and great value for money (very popular so expect long queues). Daily noon–3pm & 8pm–1am.

SAN TELMO AND AROUND

Brasserie Pétanque Defensa 595, San Telmo ☎011 4342 7930, ⓦbrasseriepetanque.com; map p.55. Authentic and chic French-owned brasserie, serving French classics (onion soup, steak tartare, crème brûlée and snails). Weekday lunch deal AR$280 (main course and drink). Tues–Sun 12.30–3.30pm & 8pm–midnight.

El Desnivel Defensa 855, San Telmo ☎011 4307 2481; map p.55. Classic San Telmo *parrilla* with accessible prices, great meat and a friendly, slightly rowdy atmosphere; popular with tourists and locals though quality has taken a hit in recent times. *Ojo de bife* steak AR$250. Mon 8pm–1am, Tues–Sun noon–4pm & 8pm–1am.

Gran Parrilla del Plata Chile 594, San Telmo ☎011 4300 8588, ⓦparrilladelplata.com; map p.55. Excellent-value steakhouse whose *asado de tira* ribs (AR$250) have to be one of the most tender cuts in town; Michelle Obama dined here in 2017. Mon–Sat noon–4pm & 8pm–1am, Sun noon–1am.

El Obrero Caffarena 64, La Boca ☎011 4362 9912; map p.55. With Boca Juniors souvenirs on the walls and tango musicians moving from table to table at weekends, the atmosphere at the hugely popular and moderately priced *El Obrero* is as much a part of the fun as the simple unfussy food (*lomo* steak AR$250, pasta dishes AR$180). Very popular, so prepare to queue at weekends. Take a taxi as the local area can be unsafe. Mon–Sat noon–10pm.

Parrilla 1880 Defensa 1665, San Telmo ☎011 4307 2746; map p.55. Extremely good *parrilla* joint, opposite Parque Lezama. Its walls are lined with photos and drawings from the restaurant's famous and mostly bohemian clients, and the friendly owner makes sure everyone is happy. Mains AR$150–300. Mon–Sat noon–4pm & 8pm–1am, Sun noon–4pm.

DRINKING AND NIGHTLIFE

Buenos Aires offers a lively nightlife every day of the week. The only exception is perhaps on Monday, when some venues, especially in the centre, tend to close. Wednesday is known as "After Office", when the city's bars and pubs start to fill from 6pm. Note that Buenos Aires starts – and finishes – late, so clubs don't fill up until around 2am. Check out *The Bubble* (ⓦthebubble.com) for articles on the city's cultural and nightlife happenings, or *Wipe* (ⓦwipe.com.ar; Spanish only) and *Aires de Bares* for bar reviews (ⓦairesdebares. com; Spanish only).

BARS AND PUBS

Bangalore Humboldt 1416, Palermo Hollywood ☎011 4779 2621; map p.59. Fine, traditional pub in Palermo Hollywood, popular with locals, expats and tourists. Happy hour until 10pm; pints and curries served. Mon, Tues & Sun 5pm–2am, Wed & Thurs 5pm–3.30am, Fri & Sat 5pm–4.30am.

Caracas Guatemala 4802, Palermo Soho ☎011 4776 8704, ⓦcaracasbar.com.ar; map p.59. Trendy Palermo

Soho venue attracting a cool crowd. Has a lovely roof terrace and serves Venezuelan food. Mon–Sat 6.30pm–3am.

Los Cardones Jorge Luis Borges 2180, Palermo Soho ☎011 4777 1112, ⓦcardones.com.ar; map p.59. One of the best *peñas* in town – a bar where traditional folk musicians play. Wed–Sat from 9pm.

La Cigale 25 de Mayo 597, Centro ☎011 4893 2332; map p.55. One of the most happening bars downtown, attracting an up-for-it crowd. Regularly hosts live music and DJs. Also hosts a monthly pub quiz in English. Mon–Fri from 6pm, Sat from 9.30pm.

Congo Honduras 5329, Palermo ☎011 4833 5857; map p.59. Sleek interiors and atmospheric lighting at this popular hang-out with *porteños* on the pull. Particularly heaving in summer thanks to the spacious outdoor patio. Wed–Sat 8pm–5am.

Milión Paraná 1048, Recoleta ☎011 4815 9925, ⓦmilion.com.ar; map p.59. Stunning bar that occupies an early twentieth-century townhouse. Packed with gringos and Argentines on the prowl for good times, this is a fun if pricey place to start the night and another venue with a superb garden. Mon–Fri noon–2am, Sat noon–4am, Sun 8pm–late.

NOLA Gorriti 4389, Palermo ⓦnolabuenosaires.com; map p.59. The original gastro-pub that kick-started the scene in 2015. The in-house craft beer, delectable fried chicken sandwiches (AR$130) and spicy dishes ensure hipsters pack the joint, even spilling out onto the street. Happy hour 12.30pm–8pm. Mon–Fri 5pm–midnight, Sat & Sun 1pm–midnight.

La Poesía Chile 502, San Telmo ☎011 4300 7340, ⓦcafelapoesia.com.ar; map p.55. Old-fashioned bar notable that feels like a Spanish tapas haunt. From the owners of the equally excellent *El Federal* (Carlos Calvo 599), *La Poesía* serves three types of artisan beer (AR$70–100) and does a wide range of *picada* (charcuterie) platters (AR$140–220). Mon–Thurs & Sun 8–2am, Fri & Sat 8–4am.

La Puerta Roja Chacabuco 733, San Telmo ☎011 4362 5649, ⓦpuertaroja.com.ar; map p.55. Hipsters and night owls while away the small hours in this first-floor bar that also dishes up well-priced curries and burgers. Daily noon–5.30am (happy hour noon–10pm).

MILONGAS

Milongas – regular dance clubs, usually starting with lessons (beginners welcome) – are popular with tango dancers young and old. They are a great way to try the moves for yourself and to get a feel for the scene, for a fraction of the price of a dinner show (entrance usually costs around AR$50). Among the city's best *milongas* are **La Viruta** (Armenia 1366, Palermo; ☎011 4775 0160, ⓦlavirutatango.com); **Salón Canning** (Scalabrini Ortiz 1331, Palermo; ☎011 4832 3224); **La Catedral** (Sarmiento 4006, Almagro; ☎011 5325 1630, ⓦlacatedralclub. com); and **Centro Cultural Torquato Tasso** (Defensa 1575, San Telmo; ☎011 4307 6506, ⓦtorquatotasso.com.ar).

1

NIGHTCLUBS

Amerika Gascón 1040, Villa Crespo ☎011 4865 4416, ⓦameri-k.com.ar; map p.59. Opening in 1999, it's still the city's biggest LGBTQ club, with three dancefloors playing mainly electro. Mon & Fri–Sun from midnight.

Crobar Marcelo Freyre s/n & Paseo de la Infanta, Palermo ☎011 4778 1500, ⓦcrobar.com.ar; map p.59. Glitzy club near the Hipódromo Argentino that plays commercial dance music and regularly welcomes international DJs such as Armin van Buuren. Fri & Sat from midnight.

Glam Cabrera 3046, Almagro ☎011 4963 2521, ⓦglambsas.com.ar; map p.59. One of the city's hottest gay bar-discos. Several lounge areas and dancefloors play everything from Latino beats to 1980s classics. Thurs & Sat from 1am.

Groove Palermo Av Santa Fe 4389, Palermo ⓦpalermogroove.com; map p.59. Club specializing in live music, often rock and international bands. Also a host venue of legendary alternative rock/reggae nights *Fiesta Clandestina*. Open Saturday night for club nights and for live music during the week.

Maluco Beleza Sarmiento 1728, Centro ☎011 4372 1737; map p.55. Long-running Brazilian club, playing a mix of *lambada*, afro-samba and reggae to a lively crowd of Brazilians and Brazilophiles. Wed–Sun from midnight.

Niceto Club Niceto Vega 5510, Palermo Hollywood ☎011 4779 9396, ⓦnicetoclub.com; map p.59. One of BA's best clubs, *Niceto Club* has a roster of live music during the week – local and international artists play here – mainly reggae and electronic music at weekends, with the outlandish Club 69 dance parties on Thursdays. Check website for hours.

You Know My Name Marcelo T de Alvear 1540, Recoleta ☎011 4811 4730; map p.59. Spread across a rambling old building with two bars, a coffee stand and a long, narrow dancefloor that packs out, *YKMN* plays a fun, danceable mix of funk, disco and rock music with Saturdays dedicated to 80s. Thurs from 7pm, Fri & Sat from 10pm.

ENTERTAINMENT

CULTURAL CENTRES

Buenos Aires has a number of excellent and popular cultural centres. Entry is free, although special temporary exhibitions occasionally charge a fee.

Centro Cultural Borges Viamonte 525 ☎011 5555 5359, ⓦccborges.org.ar. Named after Argentina's most famous writer; there's a permanent area dedicated to him, as well as exhibitions, a cinema and workshops. Mon–Sat 10am–9pm, Sun noon–9pm.

Centro Cultural Kirchner, Sarmiento 131, Microcentro ☎0800 333 9300, ⓦcck.gob.ar. After an extensive overhaul of the Belle Epoque former post office, the CCK opened in 2015 and is Latin America's largest cultural

centre, hosting exhibits, live music and dance classes, all for free. Tues–Sun 1–8pm.

Centro Cultural Recoleta Junín 1930 ☎011 4803 1040, ⓦcentroculturalrecoleta.org. Located next to the famous cemetery, this is an excellent centre with a particular focus on visual arts; it's also the occasional home of anarchic dance troupe Fuerza Bruta. Tues–Fri 1.30–8.30pm & Sat & Sun 11.30am–8.30pm.

Ciudad Cultural Konex Sarmiento 3131, Almagro ☎011 4864 3200, ⓦcckonex.org. Atmospheric cultural centre in converted warehouse. Hosts film and theatre productions as well as live music. Also the home of legendary drumming outfit La Bomba de Tiempo (shows on Mon at 7pm). Daily.

ND Ateneo Espacio Cultural Paraguay 918, Centro ☎011 4328 2888, ⓦndteatro.com.ar. Cultural space and theatre with an emphasis on live music. Shows from 9pm most evenings and there are also regular evening debates.

TANGO SHOWS

Tango shows are expensive, but they are the best way to see a series of top tango dancers in one evening, and most are well worth the splurge. All the following have nightly shows, and most include dinner. Prices range from around AR$800 (without food) to VIP treatment with haute cuisine for over AR$2000.

Bar Sur Estados Unidos 299, at Balcarce, San Telmo ☎011 4362 6086, ⓦbar-sur.com.ar; map p.55. This cosy little joint puts on fancy shows and encourages audience participation. From AR$900.

Café Tortoni Av de Mayo 825, Centre ☎011 4342 4328, ⓦcafetortoni.com.ar; map p.55. Buenos Aires' most famous café offers an affordable and rather theatrical tango show downstairs at AR$200.

Esquina Carlos Gardel Carlos Gardel 3200, Abasto ☎011 4867 6363, ⓦesquinacarlosgardel.com.ar; map p.59. Although very touristy, this smart venue, named after the king of tango, remains a classic. Nearest subway Carlos Gardel. Shows from AR$2300 (no dinner).

Piazzolla Tango Florida 165, Microcentro ☎011 4344 8200, ⓦpiazzollatango.com; map p.55. Housed in a grand old theatre in the centre, the show here is made up of two singers, an orchestra and a set of tango dancers, with prices starting at AR$955.

El Viejo Almacén Av Independencia 300, at Balcarce, San Telmo ☎011 4307 6689, ⓦviejoalmacen.com.ar; map p.55. Dinner and show from 8pm or show only from 10pm (from AR$1620).

SHOPPING

Buenos Aires offers some of the finest shopping in South America. Best buys include leather goods (handbags, belts, shoes), wine, home design and handicrafts (particularly handmade jewellery). Top shopping areas include Avenida Santa Fe, Palermo Viejo and San Telmo. Downtown Calle

PALERMO VIEJO

After the economic crash of the early noughties, this low-rise area became a hotbed of creative and design talent, and the streets have since been filled to bursting with tiny, beautifully presented boutiques. The area is perfect for browsing, but choice boutiques include: **Salsipuedes** (Honduras 4874; map p.59) for attractive local jewellery designs; **28 Sport** (Gurruchaga 1481; map p.59) for top-quality shoes for men and women; and **Pesqueira** (Gurruchaga 1750, map p.59), cool print heaven.

Florida is a famous shopping street from yesteryear but is a bit of a tourist trap today. Many Argentine clothing chains and designers have outlet stores in Villa Crespo, around Gurruchaga and Aguirre.

Malls The city's malls house Argentina's most successful brands, as well as big international names; they open every day of the week until 10pm. Try Alto Palermo (Santa Fé and Coronel Díaz, Palermo, ⊛altopalermo.com. ar; map p.59), Galerías Pacífico (Florida and Córdoba, Centre, ⊛galeriaspacifico.com.ar; map p.55), Distrito Arcos (Paraguay 4979, Palermo Soho ⊛distritoarcos. com; map p.59) or Paseo Alcorta (Salguero 3172 and Figueroa Alcorta, Palermo Chico, ⊛alcortashopping.com. ar; map p.59); the last has a large Carrefour hypermarket downstairs. The largest of all is Unicenter (⊛unicenter.com. ar; map p.59), north of the city in the outer suburbs, full of designer shops, a cinema, and with an IMAX close by. You can get there on the #60 bus from the centre, or by taxi.

Markets The city's ferias usually take place on weekends and are an excellent place to pick up inexpensive local handicrafts. The most extensive are: the Feria "Hippy" next to Recoleta cemetery (Sat & Sun, map p.59); Plaza Dorrego in San Telmo, spanning a dozen blocks along Defensa (Sun, map p.55); and on Sat or Sun depending on time of year, the Feria de Mataderos (see page 55). For locally made and designed clothes head to Plaza Serrano in Palermo Viejo, weekends from noon onwards, when the cafés surrounding the plaza are converted into indoor markets filled to the brim with affordable clothes and jewellery.

DIRECTORY

Banks and exchange Many casas de cambio closed down due to the double exchange rates that varied wildly during the Kirchner presidencies, and many people with dollars changed them at *cuevas* or unofficial exchanges to get more bang for their buck; while some have reopened following the change of government, ask your hotel or hostel about what is more convenient. Banks will change to or from dollars at the official rate.

Embassies and consulates Australia, Villanueva 1400 (☎011 4779 3500); Bolivia, Av Corrientes 545, 2nd Floor (☎011 4394 1463); Brazil, Cerrito 1350 (☎011 5246 7400); Canada, Tagle 2828 (☎011 4808 1000); Chile, Tagle 2762 (☎011 4808 8601); Ireland, Av del Libertador 1060, 6th Floor (☎011 4808 5700); New Zealand, Carlos Pellegrini 1427, 5th Floor (☎011 5070 0700); Paraguay, Las Heras 2545 (☎011 4802 3826); UK, Dr Luis Agote 2412 (☎011 4808 2200); United States, Av Colombia 4300 (☎011 5777 4533); Uruguay, Paraguay 1571 (☎011 6009 5040).

Hospitals Private hospitals: Hospital Británico (Pedriel 74 ☎011 4309 6400) has some English-speaking doctors and 24hr emergency care; for non-emergency visits there is also a more central location at Marcelo T de Alvear 1573 (☎011 4812 0040). Hospital Alemán (Av Pueyrredón 1640, between Beruti and Juncal ☎011 4827 7000), emergency (entrance on Beruti) and non-emergency care; English spoken. Public hospital: Hospital Juan A Fernández (Cerviño 3356, at Bulnes ☎011 4808 2600).

Laundry Laundries are plentiful and inexpensive (though not usually self-service). Expect to pay around AR$85 for a *valet* (wash and dry).

Pharmacies Farmacity (⊛farmacity.com.ar) has numerous branches, many open 24hr (for example, at Santa Fe 3880, and Vidt, Palermo ☎011 5778 3276).

Police In an emergency call ☎911. Tourist Police, Comisaría del Turista, Av Corrientes 436 ☎011 4346 5748 or ☎0800 999 5000 (24hr), English spoken.

Post office Correo Argentino has branches all over town (⊛www.correoargentino.com.ar). You can also send mail via OCA, a private postal service, found in many *librerías*.

Around Buenos Aires

Argentina's most spectacular scenery lies far from the capital but, thankfully, Buenos Aires province offers several rewarding and easily accessible destinations for a day-trip or a peaceful overnighter. The lush mini-Venice of **Tigre**, just north of Buenos Aires, is the gateway to the watery recreation of the Paraná Delta. A trip to the provincial capital, **La Plata**, is essential for natural history enthusiasts; the city's Museo de la Plata is home to an extraordinary array of megafauna skeletons. For a slice of gaucho life you can visit **San Antonio de Areco**, where late

1

nineteenth-century houses and cobbled streets combine with gaucho culture to charming effect. Taking the ferry across the Río de la Plata to **Colonia**, in Uruguay (see page 61), also makes a great day out.

TIGRE AND THE DELTA

A short train ride north of the city centre, the river port of **TIGRE** distributes the timber and fruit produced in the delta of the **Paraná River**. Originally a remote system of rivers dotted with inaccessible islands, the Delta is now crowded with weekend homes and riverside restaurants.

WHAT TO SEE AND DO

The river itself is the principal attraction; head for Tigre's **Estación Fluvial** from where inexpensive local wooden ferries leave every twenty minutes or so. Take one of these to "Tres Bocas" (AR$150) where there are two or three good restaurants and cafés with riverfront verandas, or simply enjoy a cruise. The tourist office at the Estación Fluvial can give you a map of the islands and details of the numerous boat companies serving them, among them Río Tur (☎011 4731 0280, ⍟rioturcatamaranes.com.ar), leaving from the Los Mimbreros dock; and Sturla (☎011 4731 1300, ⍟sturlaviajes.com.ar), from the Estación Fluvial. The town of Tigre also has some interesting places to visit. About eight blocks from the Estación Fluvial at Sarmiento 160 is the colourful **Puerto de Frutos** (daily 10am–8pm, ⍟puertodefrutos. gob.ar) where hundreds of baskets made from Delta plants, spices, wooden furniture and handicrafts are on sale. Across the bridge you'll find the ageing but well-thought-out **Museo Naval**, at Paseo

---

★ TREAT YOURSELF

Delta Eco Spa Río Carapachay Km6, Tigre ☎011 5236 0553, ⍟deltaecospa.com. A beautiful riverside setting with two swimming pools, this is an idyllic spot to kick back and unwind, especially during the week when it's quieter. Book a massage at the time of reservation for a ten-percent discount. AR$4590

Victorica 602 (Mon–Fri 8.30am–5.30pm, Sat & Sun 10am–6.30pm; AR$30), and if you keep walking up the river the spectacular **Tigre Club**, now the **Museo de Arte Tigre** (Wed–Fri 9am–6.30pm, Sat & Sun noon–6.30pm; AR$50; ⍟mat.gov.ar), will come into view. The carefully restored early twentieth-century building gives an idea of how the other half lived; there is a fine art collection inside and great views from the terrace.

ARRIVAL AND DEPARTURE

By train To get to Tigre you can either take a direct train from Retiro (Mitre line, every 10min; 1hr; AR$6.75 with a SUBE card, AR$12 without) or take the commuter train to Bartolomé Mitre (every 15min); walk across the bridge to Maipú station, and jump on the touristic *Tren de la Costa* (every 20min; AR$40 one-way for tourists), which runs through the leafy suburbs, stopping at scenic stations to the north of the city.

ACCOMMODATION

Delta Hostel Coronel Morales 1418, Tigre ☎011 5245 9776, ⍟tigredeltahostel.com.ar. This friendly hostel offers free massages and organizes a host of activities such as boat trips and kayaking on the Delta, as well as typical Argentine *asados*. Dorms AR$200, doubles AR$1500

EATING AND DRINKING

There are numerous cheap and cheerful *parrillas* on the mainland. A more romantic option, however, is to stop off by boat at one of the secluded riverside restaurants.
Alpenhaus Arroyo Rama Negra 100m from Río Capitán ☎011 4728 0422, ⍟alpenhaus.com.ar. Not only does *Alpenhaus* serve up home-made German food (including goulash and picadas (charcuterie), you can snooze it all off by the swimming pool in its peaceful garden or by its private beach. If you can't bear to tear yourself away, book yourself a room for the night (doubles AR$2000). Three-course lunch and pool days AR$990. Daily noon–3pm.
El Gato Blanco Río Capitán 80 ☎011 4728 0390, ⍟gato-blanco.com. A family favourite, *El Gato Blanco* has an attractive deck area and flower-filled garden, as well as a mini playground. Inside is an elegant tearoom. Three-course meal around AR$600. Daily noon–3pm.

SAN ANTONIO DE ARECO

The refined pampas town of **SAN ANTONIO DE ARECO**, set on the meandering Río Areco 110km northwest of Buenos Aires, is the spiritual home of the gaucho or

Córdoba

Mesopotamia

Rosario

ENTRE RÍOS PROVINCE

RN-14

AROUND BUENOS AIRES

SANTA FE PROVINCE

RN-9

URUGUAY

N

RN-8

Pergamino

San Pedro

RN-8

Zarate

Paraná Delta

Colonia del Sacramento

San Antonio de Areco

Tigre

Mendoza

Mercedes

BUENOS AIRES

MONTEVIDEO

Chivilcoy

La Plata

Lobos

RN-5

San Miguel del Monte

RN-205

Chascomús

RN-3

Las Flores

BUENOS AIRES PROVINCE

Dolores

Pta. Rasa
S. Clemente del Tuyú

RP-30

Cabo San Antonio

Azul

Pinamar

RP-76

RN-2

RP-11

Villa Gesell

Tandil

RN-226

Camet

Tres Arroyos

Mar del Plata

C. Corrientes
Pta. Mogotes

RN-228

Mar del Sud

Quequén

Necochea

Balneario Orense

Pehuén-Có

Bahía Blanca

SOUTH ATLANTIC OCEAN (MAR ARGENTINO)

0   100
kilometres

Argentine cowboy. A robust tourist industry has grown around the gaucho tradition: silver and leather handicraft workers peddle their wares in the town's shops, historic **estancias** (ranches) accommodate visitors in the surrounding countryside and an annual **gaucho festival** draws massive crowds every November. While bicycles rule the streets here, you'll also spot beret-clad *estancia* workers on horseback, trotting about the cobblestones.

WHAT TO SEE AND DO

The leafy town centre is laid out in a grid fashion around the main square, **Plaza Ruiz de Arellano**, and is full of genteel, slightly decaying, single-storey nineteenth-century buildings, many of them painted a blushing shade of pink. On the south side of the

1

ESTANCIAS

Reflecting Argentina's changing economic climate, many of the country's **estancias** – vast cattle and horse estates once lorded over by wealthy European settlers – have been converted into luxury accommodation. For anyone with latent aristocratic or cowboy aspirations, *estancias* offer the chance to milk cows, ride horses, go fly-fishing, play polo or simply tuck into a juicy slab of steak plucked straight off the *asado* while swanning poolside with a glass of Malbec.

Running the gamut from simple family farmhouses to Pampas dude ranches and ostentatious Italianate mansions, *estancias* are a character-filled throwback to the Argentina of yesteryear. For a list of *estancias* offering day trips and accommodation in and around San Antonio de Areco, see ⓦ sanantoniodeareco.com or ⓦ sanantoniodeareco.org. For more **information** on *estancias* in other parts of Argentina, visit ⓦ estanciasargentinas.com, ⓦ estanciastravel.com or ⓦ ranchweb.com.

square is the plain white **Iglesia Parroquial San Antonio de Padua**, the town's first chapel, dating from 1728. A sculpture of San Antonio graces the exterior. One block north, in a refurbished former power plant at Alsina 66, is the **Centro Cultural Usina Vieja** (Tues–Sun 11am–7pm; free), home to the **Museo de la Ciudad**, with nineteenth-century objects and temporary art exhibitions that depict life in rural Argentina.

Just north of town, across the Río Areco, lies **Parque Criollo**, home to the **Museo Gauchesco Ricardo Güiraldes** (daily 10am–5pm; guided visits daily 11.30am & 3pm; free). Just four of the nine rooms can be visited following a devastating flood in 2009, but the museum, set in a replica nineteenth-century *estancia*, has a collection of gaucho art and artefacts and pays homage to the life of author Ricardo Güiraldes, whose classic novel, *Don Segundo Sombra* (1926) – set in San Antonio de Areco – served to elevate the *mate*-sucking, horse-breaking, cow-herding gaucho from rebellious outlaw to respected and romantic national icon. Demonstrations of gaucho feats are held every year in the Parque Criollo during November's week-long **Fiesta de la Tradición** celebrations.

ARRIVAL AND INFORMATION

By bus The bus station (☎ 02326 453 904) is at General Paz and Av Dr Smith, a six-block walk from the town centre along C Segundo Sombra. There are buses to and from Buenos Aires (every 1–2hr; 2hr) and Rosario (6 daily; 4hr).
Tourist information The tourist office, which loans bicycles, is a short walk from the main square towards the river at Arellano and Zerboni (Mon–Fri 8am–7pm; Sat & Sun 8am–8pm; ☎ 02326 453 165, ⓦ areco.gob.ar).

ACCOMMODATION

While San Antonio de Areco can easily be visited on a day-trip from Buenos Aires, you might well be charmed into staying the night. Book ahead at weekends (the town is a popular destination for *porteños*) and well in advance for the Fiesta de la Tradición in November, or contact the tourist office, which can arrange homestays with families.
Hostal de Areco Zapiola 25 ☎ 02326 456 118, ⓦ hostaldeareco.com.ar. Centrally located in a pink colonial building, this B&B has a nice sunny garden and offers decent doubles with private bathrooms. **AR$600**
Club River Plate Areco ☎ 02326 453 590. This campsite is 1km west of town along Zerboni. The price is for two people. Camping **AR$400**
Hostel El Puesto Belgrano 270 ☎ 02326 15 402 159, ⓦ hostelelpuesto.com.ar. Located in a former stately home, just three blocks from the main square. Friendly staff, an outdoor swimming pool and free access to the barbecue equipment are all part of the attraction. Dorms **AR$350**, doubles **AR$1150**

EATING AND DRINKING

Many of San Antonio de Areco's restaurants and bars have been given Old World-style makeovers, and their continued patronage by weathered *estancia* workers gives them an air of authenticity.
Almacén de Ramos Generales Zapiola 143 ☎ 02326 456 376, ⓦ ramosgeneralesareco.com.ar. Old bottles and gaucho paraphernalia line the walls of this delightful *parrilla*; the rabbit and trout specials and waist-softening desserts ensure a steady stream of regulars. Mains around AR$200. Daily noon–3pm & 8–11pm.
La Esquina de Merti Arellano 147 ☎ 02326 456 705. Dolled up like a traditional corner store, this spacious and atmospheric plaza-side restaurant excels in fast and friendly service. *Parrilla* for two AR$400; pasta dishes around AR$160. Daily until 1am.
La Olla de Cobre Matheu 433 ☎ 02326 453 105, ⓦ laolladecobre.com.ar. A small chocolate factory and

sweet shop selling superb home-made *alfajores*. Sample before buying. 10am–1pm & 3–8pm; closed Tues.

LA PLATA

LA PLATA became the capital of the province of Buenos Aires in 1880, when the city of Buenos Aires was made the Federal Capital. Close enough to make an easy day-trip, it has a relaxed, small city feel. The geometric design, by French architect Pedro Benoît, and grid-numbered streets, were meant to make navigating the city easy but at times do exactly the opposite.

WHAT TO SEE AND DO

The most famous attractions can be found north of the city centre, next to the zoo, and in the middle of the pleasant lush parkland, **Paseo del Bosque**. The **Museo de la Plata** (Tues–Sun 10am–6pm; AR$6) was the first museum built in Latin America and has a wonderful collection of skeletons, stuffed animals and fossils, set in a crumbling building in the midst of the university. Though desperately in need of refurbishment, the museum is well worth visiting to see the vast whale bones and the models of prehistoric animals.

From the Paseo del Bosque (Av Iraola), avenidas 51 and 53 lead down through the historic centre to the **Plaza Moreno**. On its far side stands the colossal, neo-Gothic brick **Catedral**, with an impressive marble interior of thick columns and high vaulted ceilings. Roughly halfway between the two is **Plaza San Martín**, the lively heart of the city. On the western side, the **Centro Cultural Pasaje Dardo Rocha** (daily 8am–10pm; free) occupies the city's former train station, taking up an entire block between avenidas 49 and 50, 6 and 7. Behind the elegant, French- and Italian-influenced facade are housed a cinema and various exhibition spaces, including the excellent **Museo de Arte Contemporáneo Latinoamericano** (Tues–Fri 10am–8pm, Sat & Sun 2–9pm; free).

ARRIVAL AND INFORMATION

By bus Buses for La Plata leave from Retiro bus station every 30min (1hr 10min; AR$38 one-way). Destinations Mar del Plata (12 daily; 5hr); Puerto Madryn (4 daily; 18hr).

By train The train journey from Constitución station is much slower than travelling by bus. Trains leave approximately every 15min (1hr 15min; AR$4 with SUBE, AR$8 without one-way).

Tourist information There's a tourist office inside the Pasaje Dardo Rocha cultural centre (daily 10am–8pm; ☎0221 427 1535). Many of the best places to eat and drink are just south of here, around the junction of avenidas 10 & 47.

MAR DEL PLATA

Argentina's **beaches** are somewhat overshadowed by neighbouring Uruguay's golden sands, in particular glamorous Punta del Este (see page 853). Still, a seaside outing in summer is a quintessential Argentine experience – and **Mar del Plata**, boasting some 50km of beach 400km south of Buenos Aires, is the country's number one resort. In the summer season (mid-Dec to March), millions of city-dwellers descend on the place, generating vibrant eating, drinking and entertainment scenes (or overcrowding and overpricing, depending on your point of view).

Though Mar del Plata may have lost some of its lustre, glimpses of glamour still abound in the city's restored early twentieth-century mansions – check out French-style Villa Ortiz Basualdo, now the **Museo Municipal de Arte**, at Av Colón 1189, the **MAR Museo Municipal de Arte Contemporáneo**, Avenida F.U. Camet and Dardo Rocha, and the **Centro Cultural Victoria Ocampo**, Matheu 1851. The renowned **International Film Festival** is held in Mar del Plata in November, showing new Argentine and international films.

Nearby **Cariló** and **Mar de los Pampas** are both eco-resorts that provide a more laidback seaside experience, set within beautiful pine forests. Rent a house or stay in a luxury hotel and chill out for a few days – but be warned, these are boutique resorts for Argentina's rich and famous, so you won't find much in the way of mid-range or budget accommodation.

There are numerous daily **buses** from Buenos Aires to Mar del Plata (5hr), or (not recommended) you can make the journey less comfortably (from AR$500) by **train**, from Constitución station (1 daily, 6hr), or **fly** across in less than an hour (2–3 daily).

EATING AND DRINKING

Cervecería Modelo Diagonal 54, 496 ☎ 0221 421 1321, ⓦ cerveceriamodelo.com.ar. Old-school classic restaurant and café housed in a century-old building with legs of ham hanging from the ceiling. Serves excellent draught beer; paella and home-made *pan*

dulce (*panettone*) are the house specialities. Daily 8am–1am.

Cinco Sabios Brewing Co C 13 between 63 and 64 ☎ 0221 457 3333, ⓦ cincosabios.com. Brewer run by young handcraft-beer enthusiasts making waves in the city. Also tuck into home-made burgers and fries (AR$130). Daily 7pm–1am.

Córdoba Province

CÓRDOBA PROVINCE, 700km northwest of Buenos Aires, marks Argentina's geographical bull's-eye. Serene towns dot its undulating **Central Sierras**, the second-highest mountain range in Argentina after the Andes, and the region is one of the country's more affordable travel destinations, except perhaps in high season when many city-dwellers flock to its cool heights. Córdoba province is a relaxed place for exploring the great outdoors – via hikes, horserides or even **skydives** – or just hanging out sipping *mate* with the super-friendly locals.

Most of the action takes place in and around **Córdoba city**, which has the country's highest concentration of bars and clubs outside Buenos Aires. South of Córdoba city in the verdant **Calamuchita Valley**, towns such as **Alta Gracia** and Germanic, beer-brewing **Villa General Belgrano** have historically served as getaways for Argentina's elite. Northwest of the capital in the **Punilla Valley**, laidback towns such as **Capilla del Monte** are growing in popularity among bohemian *porteños* looking for a clean, green break from city life.

CÓRDOBA

Argentina's second-largest city, unpretentious **CÓRDOBA** boasts some beautifully restored colonial architecture, plentiful restaurants and a legendary nightlife at its best when the university students are around. It is a good base for exploring the province, though during the city's stiflingly hot summers you'll soon be lured west to the Sierras' cooler elevations.

PLAZA SAN MARTÍN AND AROUND

Once the bloody stage for bullfights, executions and military parades, **Plaza San**

Martín was converted into a civilized public square, replete with fountains and semi-tropical foliage, in the 1870s. Free tango events are hosted here most Saturday nights at 9pm.

On the square's western side, the two-storey, sixteenth-century **Cabildo** was once the city's colonial headquarters and has now been turned into the **Museo de la Ciudad** (Mon–Fri 9am–12.30pm & 3–5pm, Sat & Sun 9.30am–1pm & 3–7pm; free; ☎ 0351 433 2758). It also hosts concerts, art exhibitions and, in the summer, tango evenings.

Alongside the Cabildo is the **Catedral**, one of the oldest in the country. Construction began in 1577 but wasn't completed for another two hundred years, rendering the cathedral something of an architectural mongrel, with a mix of Neoclassical and Baroque styles and a Romanesque dome thrown in for good measure. Note the trumpeting angels in indigenous dress gracing the bell towers.

MANZANA JESUÍTICA

The seventeenth-century **Manzana Jesuítica** (Mon–Sat: summer 9am–1pm & 4–7pm, winter 9am–6.30pm; AR$15;

★ TREAT YOURSELF

Córdoba is the most affordable place in Argentina to jump out of a plane. Tumbling out of the door at 2500m, you get a bird's-eye view, after twenty seconds of face-flattening freefall, of city sprawl, a patchwork of green fields and the Central Sierras. **Paracaidismo Alta Gracia** (☎ 0351 15 348 7628, ⓦ paracaidismo-ag.com), thirty minutes' drive from downtown Córdoba, has fifteen years of skydiving experience and charges from AR$3650 for a tandem jump.

☎0351 433 2075), or Jesuit Block, a short walk southwest of the plaza, is Córdoba's top attraction. A testament to the missionaries who arrived hot on the heels of Córdoba's sixteenth-century colonizers, the **Templo de la Compañía de Jesús**, built in 1640, is Argentina's oldest surviving Jesuit temple. It has a striking Cusqueño altarpiece, and its barrel-shaped vaulted roof is made of Paraguayan cedar. The block also houses a private chapel, the **Capilla Doméstica**.

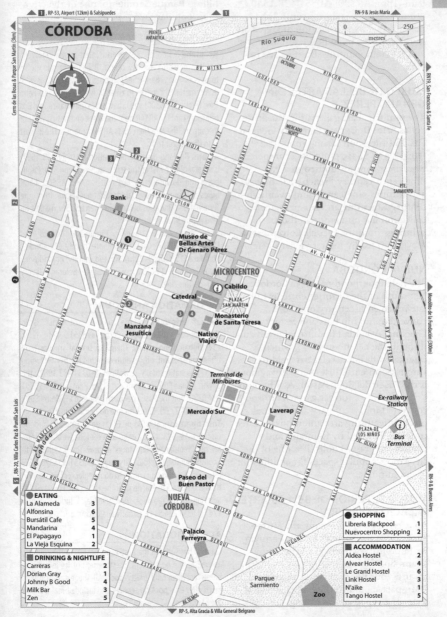

CÓRDOBA

RP-53, Airport (12km) & Salsipuedes | RN-9 & Jesús María

Cerro de las Rosas & Parque San Martín (3km)

RN19, San Francisco & Santa Fe

Monolito de la Fundación (300m)

RN-9 & Buenos Aires

RN-20, Villa Carlos Paz & Punilla San Luis

0 — 250
metres

PUENTE ANTÁRTICA

LAS HERAS

12 DE OCTUBRE

Río Suquía

BV. MITRE

IGUALDAD

RINCÓN

HUMBERTO Iº

TABLADA

LIBERTAD

LA RIOJA

MERCADO NORTE

ONCATIVO

SANTA ROSA

SARMIENTO

SUCRE

AVENIDA COLON

CATAMARCA

PTE. SARMIENTO

Bank

9 DE JULIO

LIMA

DEAN FUNES

Museo de Bellas Artes Dr Genaro Pérez

AV. OLMOS

MICROCENTRO

27 DE ABRIL

ⓘ **Cabildo**

25 DE MAYO

Catedral

PLAZA SAN MARTÍN

DE SANTA FE

Manzana Jesuítica

Monasterio de Santa Teresa

SAN JERÓNIMO

DUARTE QUIROS

Nativo Viajes

ENTRE RÍOS

Terminal de Minibuses

CORRIENTES

BV. SAN JUAN

Ex-railway Station

Mercado Sur

Laverap

BV. A. ILLIA

PLAZA DE LOS NIÑOS PTE. OLIVER

ⓘ **Bus Terminal**

RONDEAU

PARANÁ

Paseo del Buen Pastor

SAN LORENZO

NUEVA CÓRDOBA

OBISPO ORO

Palacio Ferreyra

DERQUI

D. LARRAÑAGA

AV. POETA LUGONES

J. M. ESTRADA

Parque Sarmiento

Zoo

AV. OLMOS

RP-5, Alta Gracia & Villa General Belgrano

● EATING
La Alameda	3
Alfonsina	6
Bursátil Cafe	5
Mandarina	4
El Papagayo	1
La Vieja Esquina	2

■ DRINKING & NIGHTLIFE
Carreras	2
Dorian Gray	1
Johnny B Good	4
Milk Bar	3
Zen	5

● SHOPPING
Librería Blackpool	1
Nuevocentro Shopping	2

■ ACCOMMODATION
Aldea Hostel	2
Alvear Hostel	4
Le Grand Hostel	6
Link Hostel	3
N'aike	1
Tango Hostel	5

1

MONASTERIO DE SANTA TERESA

Southwest of Plaza San Martín at Independencia 146 is the **Iglesia Santa Teresa**, part of a working convent that contains the **Museo de Arte Religioso Juan de Tejeda** (Independencia 122; Mon–Fri 9am–1pm; AR$20; ☎0351 428 1540, ⓦmuseotejeda.wordpress.com). It has perhaps the finest collection of sacred art in the country, including Jesuit artefacts and religious paintings from Cusco in Peru.

MUSEO DE BELLAS ARTES DR GENARO PÉREZ

The municipal art gallery, the **Museo de Bellas Artes Dr Genaro Pérez**, Av General Paz 33 (Tues–Sun 10am–8pm; free; ☎0351 434 1646, ⓦmuseogenaroperez. wordpress.com), is housed in a late nineteenth-century French-style mansion and features nineteenth- and twentieth-century Argentine art. The permanent collection has numerous landscape paintings from the **Escuela Cordobesa**, a movement led by master Genaro Pérez.

NUEVA CÓRDOBA

The neighbourhood of **Nueva Córdoba**, just south of the historic centre, is full of late nineteenth-century mansions converted into hip bars and restaurants. Diagonal Avenida Hipólito Yrigoyen cuts through the neighbourhood, which extends from Plaza Vélez Sarsfield to Parque Sarmiento. Just over halfway down is the **Paseo del Buen Pastor**, Av Hipólito Yrigoyen 325, a former women's prison converted into a culinary and cultural precinct featuring art exhibitions and free concerts. Flanked by fountains and landscaped grassy knolls, it is one of the city's most popular spaces for chilling out in the summer.

MUSEO SUPERIOR DE BELLAS ARTES PALACIO FERREYRA

An exemplary art museum, the **Museo Superior de Bellas Artes Palacio Ferreyra**, Av Hipólito Yrigoyen 511 (Tues–Sun 10am–8pm; AR$25; ☎0351 434 3636), features four floors of works in an opulent 1916 palace built in the French classical style. The top floor has rolling contemporary art exhibitions, while the basement level is devoted to photography. In between, some three hundred artists are represented, including Pablo Picasso and Argentina's Fernando Fader and Lino Enea Spilimbergo. A little further south is the hilltop **Parque Sarmiento**, one of the city's most popular green spaces.

ARRIVAL AND DEPARTURE

By plane Córdoba's Aeropuerto Internacional Taravella is 11km north of the city centre. It has domestic flights to Buenos Aires, Bariloche, Mendoza and Rosario, as well as international services to cities in Brazil, Chile and Peru. Taxis (around AR$300) and urban buses (purchase a Red Bus transport card for AR$40 from the kiosk on the first floor of the airport; the fare then costs AR$40) connect the airport with the city centre.

By bus The long-distance bus station (☎0351 433 1692) is several blocks east of the centre at Blvd Perón 380. Public buses run downtown; a taxi costs around AR$60. Local buses for some provincial destinations leave from the Terminal de Minibuses behind the Mercado Sur market on Blvd Arturo Illia.

Destinations Alta Gracia (every 15min; 1hr); Buenos Aires (frequent; 9–11hr); Capilla del Monte (hourly; 2hr 30min); Mendoza (15 daily; 9–10hr); Rosario (hourly; around 6hr); Salta (8 daily; 11–13hr); Villa General Belgrano (every 45min–1hr; 2hr).

INFORMATION AND TOURS

Tourist information The main tourist office is in the Cabildo (daily 8am–8pm; ☎0351 434 1200, ⓦcordobaturismo.gov.ar). There are several smaller (and often more helpful) offices dotted around the city, including at the bus station (daily 7am–9pm; ☎0351 433 1982), the airport (Mon–Fri 7am–9pm, Sat & Sun 8am–9pm; ☎0351 434 8390) and the Paseo del Buen Pastor (daily 8am–8pm; ☎0351 434 2727). Check for free guided walking tours.

Tour operators Servicio de Guías de Turismo de Córdoba (☎0351 15 593 1700, ⓦguiasdecordoba.webnode.com. ar) runs regular walking tours of downtown sights with English-language guides. City Tour (☎0351 15537 8687) offers sightseeing tours on a red double-decker bus starting from the Plaza San Martín near the cathedral. For day-trips and tours of the province, try Nativo Viajes, Independencia 174 (☎0351 424 5341, ⓦnativoviajes.com.ar).

ACCOMMODATION

Córdoba has some of the best-value hostels in the country, as well as the odd decent guesthouse, but its lower-cost hotels are generally pretty poor. All the establishments listed offer tour-booking services and include breakfast and use of kitchen.

★ **Aldea Hostel** Santa Rosa 447 ☎0351 426 1312, ⓦaldeahostelcordoba.com; map p.73. This bright, ambitious hostel has space for one hundred people and is bursting with extras including a café/bar serving lighter meals, a TV lounge, a leafy patio and a roof terrace. Discounts for extended stays. Dorms AR$250, doubles AR$750

Alvear Hostel Alvear 158 ☎0351 422 3977; map p.73. This popular hostel in a converted nineteenth-century townhouse has helpful staff and hosts weekly barbecues. The dorms sleep up to ten people. Dorms AR$230.

Le Grand Hostel Buenos Aires 547 ☎0351 422 7115, ⓦlegrandhostelcordoba.blogspot.com.ar; map p.73. The largest hostel on the scene, located in Nueva Córdoba, an area popular with students. There's a chill-out room with huge flat-screen TV, an excellently equipped kitchen and decent outside area. There are also smart private en-suite rooms with a/c. Dorms AR$200, doubles AR$700

Link Hostel Jujuy 267 ☎0351 421 6903, ⓦlinkcordobahostel.com; map p.73. Tour bookings, a roof terrace, patio with *parrilla* and TV room are just some of the perks of this bustling, modern hostel. Dorms AR$180, doubles AR$650

N'aike Fresnal 5048 ☎0351 589 0501, ⓦnaike.com.ar; map p.73. This friendly, well-run guesthouse is located in the quiet Villa Belgrano neighbourhood, a few kilometres northwest of the centre. There are six colourful rooms with a/c, and guests have access to a kitchen, a plunge pool and a jacuzzi. AR$1200

Tango Hostel Bolivar 613 ☎0351 425 6023, ⓦtangohostel.com.ar; map p.73. In a buzzing location, in Barrio Güemes, this hostel has a sociable atmosphere and a collection of decent, no-frills dorms, plus a few private rooms. Dorms AR$240

EATING

Córdoba is a real delight for winers and diners. There are restaurants for refined tastebuds, boisterous drinking holes serving pub grub, and plenty of eat-on-the-run *empanada* joints for lining your stomach before a night out on the town. The pick of the fashionable restaurants is in Nueva Córdoba.

La Alameda Obispo Trejo 170; map p.73. Savour inexpensive Argentine staples like *empanadas* and *humitas* for a few pesos, while sitting outside on wooden benches, or indoors where customers' poetry and art adorn the walls. Mains AR$60–150. Mon–Sat noon–2am.

★ **Alfonsina** Duarte Quiros 66 ☎0351 427 2847; map p.73. Antique typewriters, exposed brickwork and a jolly crowd of students are the hallmarks of this restaurant-bar, which offers a taste of Argentina's northwest (mains AR$100–200) and is popular for an evening *mate*. Other branches at Belgrano 763 and Viamonte, at Lima. Mon–Sat 8am–4am, Sun 8pm–2am.

Bursátil Cafe Ituzaingo, at San Jeronimo ☎0351 711 3333; map p.73. In Córdoba's small financial district, this café takes its name from the Spanish for "stock exchange". Food includes classics like *locro* (stew) and international dishes such as Caesar salad. Mains from AR$130. Mon–Fri 8am–7pm, Sat 9am–4/5pm.

★ **Mandarina** Obispo Trejo 171 ☎0351 426 4909; map p.73. This chilled-out crowd-pleaser is more inventive than the norm, with Chinese, Japanese and southeast Asian dishes, as well as plenty of veggie options. Mains from AR$65. Daily 7am–midnight.

El Papagayo Bas 69 ☎0351 425 8689, ⓦelpapagayo. com.ar; map p.73. While it holds the curious accolade of the narrowest restaurant in Argentina, this place has one of Córdoba's top chefs in charge, creating elaborate yet delicious tasting menus. Three-course lunch AR$400. Mon–Sat noon–3.30pm & 7.30–11.30pm.

La Vieja Esquina Caseros, at Belgrano ☎0351 424 7940; map p.73. This tiny local joint serves up excellent *empanadas* (around AR$15), *humitas* and *locro*; you can eat at one of the counters, take them away or even have them delivered to your room. Mon–Sat 11.30am–3pm & 7.30pm–midnight.

DRINKING AND NIGHTLIFE

Córdoba is no wallflower when it comes to partying, with Nueva Córdoba and Güemes the late-night destinations of choice. Hipsters gravitate to the revived warehouse district of El Abasto, just north of the centre, for its edgy bars and clubs. Further afield, in the Chateau Carreras neighbourhood, chic discos cater to a young crowd who love *cuarteto* music – a Córdoba speciality.

Carreras Av Cárcano, at del Piamonte, Chateau Carreras ☎0351 676 2342; map p.73. One of the city's biggest and liveliest clubs, *Carreras* focuses on house and electro, though early on in the evening the sounds are a bit more varied. Fri & Sat 11.30pm–5am.

Dorian Gray Blvd Las Heras, at Roque Sáenz Peña ☎0351 6205 025; map p.73. Bizarre decor and an alternative ambience draw an eclectic crowd who throw shapes well into the small hours to mostly electro music. Fri & Sat midnight–5am.

Johnny B Good Av Hipólito Yrigoyen 320, Nueva Córdoba ☎0351 424 3960, ⓦjbgood.com; map p.73. This busy, rather cheesy restaurant-bar serves up good US-style food (mains AR$200–300), a wide range of *tragos* (alcoholic drinks; from AR$100) and a rock-dominated soundtrack (live music most weekends). There's also another branch at Rafael Núñez 4791, Cerro de las Rosas. Mon–Wed 7.30pm–2am, Thurs 7.30pm–3am, Fri 7.30pm–4am, Sat 10am–5am, Sun 6.30pm–2am.

Milk Bar Laprida 139 ☎0351 208 6299 ⓦlovemilk.com. ar; map p.73. Put on some of your fancier rags, forget about Fernet and coke and order fine cocktails (around AR$60) at the trendiest bar in town. The big chandeliers in the ceiling and hipster bartenders give it an old-school,

1

although slightly pretentious, touch. Wed–Fri 9.30pm–5am, Sat & Sun 6.30pm–5am.

Zen Av Julio A Roca 730 ☏ 0351 613 4032, ⊚ zendisco.com; map p.73. This renowned LGBTQ-friendly club has two throbbing dancefloors and hosts kooky live shows. Fri & Sat midnight–5am.

SHOPPING

Bookshops Librería Blackpool, Deán Funes 395 (☏ 0351 423 7172; map p.73). Sells English-language novels and travel guides. Mon–Fri 9am–6.30pm, Sat 9am–1pm.

Markets On weekend evenings (5–9.30pm) there is an arts and crafts market at the Paseo de las Artes on the western edge of Nueva Córdoba in the bohemian Güemes neighbourhood, around Belgrano and Archaval Rodriguez streets.

Shopping centres Nuevocentro Shopping, Duarte Quirós 1400 (daily 10am–10pm; ☏ 0351 482 8193, ⊚ nuevocentro.com.ar; map p.73).

DIRECTORY

Banks and exchange Change money at Citibank, Rivadavia 104, or BBVA, 9 de Julio 450. ATMs are everywhere, especially around the Plaza San Martín.

Hospital Hospital Sanatorio Allende, Av Hipólito Yrigoyen 384 (☏ 0351 426 9200, ⊚ sanatorioallende.com).

Laundry Laverap, Chacabuco 313, at Belgrano 76.

Police Colón 1200, Independencia 300

Post office Av General Paz 201.

ALTA GRACIA

The pleasant colonial town of **ALTA GRACIA**, 38km south of Córdoba at the entrance of the Calamuchita Valley, was once a genteel summer refuge for the *porteño* bourgeoisie. Today it continues to bask in the reflected glory of its former residents: Jesuit missionaries, Spanish composer Manuel de Falla and Che Guevara have all left their mark here.

WHAT TO SEE AND DO

Easily walkable on foot, the town centre is dominated by an impressive Jesuit *estancia*, one of the finest examples in Argentina. But it's also a great springboard for walking in the nearby countryside or, for the more adventurous, skydiving.

PLAZA MANUEL SOLARES AND AROUND

Alta Gracia came into its own after 1643 when it was chosen as the site of a Jesuit *estancia*. When the Jesuits were expelled in

1767, the *estancia* was left to the elements, only briefly reinhabited in 1810 by Viceroy Liniers. The *estancia* buildings have been well preserved and overlook the town's main square, **Plaza Manuel Solares**. The **Iglesia Parroquial Nuestra Señora de la Merced**, dating from 1762, stands alongside the Jesuits' original living quarters, which have been converted into the UNESCO World Heritage-listed **Museo de la Estancia Jesuítica de Alta Gracia – Casa del Virrey Liniers** (summer Tues–Fri 9am–8pm, Sat & Sun 9.30am–8pm; winter Tues–Fri 9am–1pm & 3–7pm, Sat & Sun 9.30am–12.30pm & 3.30–6.30pm; free; free guided English-language tours on request; ☏ 03547 421303, ⊚ museoestanciaaltagracia.org). Here, a dramatic Baroque doorway leads to a cloistered courtyard and a motley collection of furniture and religious paintings.

ERNESTO "CHE" GUEVARA HOUSE AND MUSEUM

A twenty-minute walk uphill from the plaza brings you to the leafy residential neighbourhood of **Villa Carlos Pellegrini**, whose crumbling mansions once served as holiday homes and residences for moneyed socialites. The Guevara family moved within these circles after relocating from Rosario to Alta Gracia in the 1930s in the hope that the fresh mountain air would alleviate the asthma plaguing their 4-year-old son, **Ernesto "Che" Guevara**. The family's former home, Villa Beatriz, at Avellaneda 501, has been converted into the **Museo Casa de Ernesto "Che" Guevara** (Tues–Sun 9am–7pm; AR$200; ☏ 03547 428579), showcasing Che's personal effects as well as photographs charting his progression from carefree kid to revolutionary icon. Among the museum's highlights are video interviews with Che's childhood companions, a handwritten resignation letter to Fidel Castro, and photos from a visit Castro and Hugo Chávez made to the house in 2006.

ARRIVAL AND INFORMATION

By bus Regular buses from Córdoba (every 15min; 1hr) stop at the bus terminal on C.P. Butori, at Av Presidente Perón, around eight blocks west of the Tajamar reservoir; minibuses tend to stop nearer the centre on Lucas V.

Córdoba street. Buses to Villa General Belgrano (every 1hr; 1hr) stop on Ruta 5, at Av L.G. San Martín by the main entrance to town.

Tourist information The tourist office is in the clock tower alongside the Tajamar reservoir on Av Padre Viera, at C del Molino (Jan, Feb & July daily 8am–10pm; March–June & Aug–Dec Mon–Fri 7am–8pm, Sat & Sun 8am–8pm; ☎ 03547 428128, ⓦ altagracia.gov.ar).

ACCOMMODATION AND EATING

Alta Gracia Hostel Paraguay 218 ☎ 03547 428 810, ⓦ altagraciahostel.com.ar. A cosy little hostel, five blocks

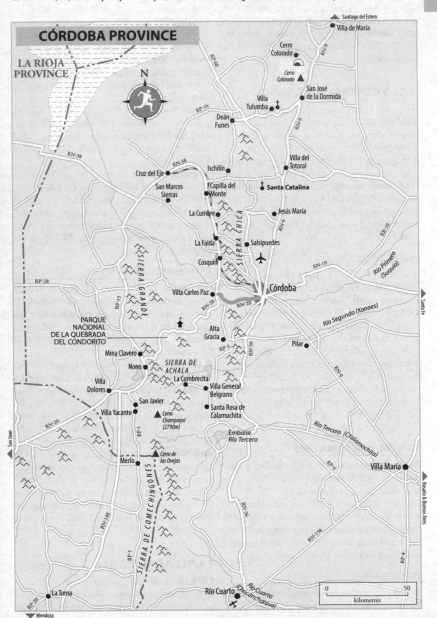

1

away from the main square, with a basic dorm, a couple of private rooms, a kitchen and a patio area at the back. There are bikes for rent. Dorms AR$280, doubles AR$790

Hispania Urquiza, at Mateo Beres ☎03547 426 555, ⓦhostalhispania.com.ar. Popular with locals and tourists, this Spanish seafood restaurant fills up fast at night. The extensive menu includes seafood *paella* (AR$190), king prawns in sherry sauce (AR$180), gazpacho (AR$110) and other Galician-styled dishes. Also offers up rooms from AR$1200. Tues–Sat noon–3pm & 8pm–midnight; Sun lunch only.

VILLA GENERAL BELGRANO

The twee resort town of **VILLA GENERAL BELGRANO**, 50km south of Alta Gracia, founded by the surviving seamen of the *Graf Spee*, which sank off the coast of Uruguay in 1939, unabashedly exploits its Germanic heritage with all kinds of kitsch. The town's main street, **Avenida Julio Roca**, comes over like an alpine theme park, with folksy German beer houses and restaurants resembling Swiss chalets. You'll either love it or hate it.

WHAT TO SEE AND DO

The best (and some might say only) reason to visit Villa General Belgrano is to sink steins of locally brewed beer at the annual **Oktoberfest**. Held during the first two weeks of October in Plaza José Hernández, it is considered the continent's best celebration of this German tradition. The most popular day-trip from Villa General Belgrano is 30km west to the alpine-flavoured village of **La Cumbrecita**, where there are good opportunities for hiking, abseiling and cooling off in the Río Almbach.

ARRIVAL AND DEPARTURE

By bus The bus terminal is on Av Vélez Sarsfield, a 10min walk northwest of the main street, although all buses make drop-offs and pick-ups in the town centre.
Destinations Alta Gracia (8 daily; 1hr) and Córdoba (every 45min–1hr; 2hr). Pájaro Blanco (☎03546 461709; call for the latest timetable) runs a minibus service several times a day to and from La Cumbrecita (7 daily; 1hr); its bus stop is on Av Ojo de Agua, in front of *Hotel Edelweiss*.

INFORMATION

Tourist information Av Julio Roca 168 (daily 8.30am–5pm; ☎03546 461215, ⓦvgb.gov.ar).

Mountain bike rental Cerro Negro Bikes, Av Champaqui 100 (☎03546 462785).

ACCOMMODATION

The hotels in town are generally overpriced, but cabañas (self-contained cabins) make a good alternative for groups of four or five – ask at the tourist office for suggestions.
Camping Rincón de Mirlos 9km west of the centre, off the RP-5 ☎0351 15 5164 254, ⓦrincondemirlos.com.ar. The best of several campsites around town, *Rincón de Mirlos* has a bucolic riverside setting, clean dorms, isolated camping pitches among the trees, a restaurant-bar, and long stretches of sandy beach. Camping/person AR$150, dorms AR$250
Posada Nehuen San Martín 17 ☎03546 461412, ⓦposadanehuen.com.ar. This central guesthouse has a selection of comfortable en-suite rooms with TVs, mini-fridges and phones, though the decor is a bit old-fashioned. AR$1180
★ **Hostel El Rincón** Alexander Fleming 347, 15min walk northwest of the bus station ☎03546 461323, ⓦhostelelrincon.com.ar. This laidback, HI-affiliated hostel offers dorms, en-suite private rooms, and a place to pitch your tent, as well as kitchen access and a small pool. Camping/person AR$210, dorms AR$300, doubles AR$1100

EATING AND DRINKING

Café Rissen Av Julio Roca 36 ☎03546 464100. Situated on the main strip, this kitsch café is probably the most popular in town. Excellent cakes (from AR$60) and sandwiches are on the menu: the Black Forest (*selva negra*) gateau, in particular, comes highly recommended. Daily 8am–around midnight.
El Ciervo Rojo Av Julio Roca 210 ☎03546 461345, ⓦconfiteriaelciervorojo.com. Dating back over fifty years, this appealing restaurant serves up an array of German and Central European dishes (mains AR$130–190) including smoked pork racks, goulash, *spätzle* (pork and pasta), sausages and sauerkraut. Live German music on Saturday nights. Daily 8am–midnight/1am.
Viejo Munich Av San Martín 362 ☎03546 463122, ⓦcervezaartesanal.com. The trout, goulash and venison mains aren't too bad, but the beer – eight different varieties, all brewed on-site – is the real star of the show. Free brewery tours (end Dec to early Feb: daily noon, rest of year no tours Thurs). Mon, Tues & Thurs 11am–3pm & 7–11.30pm, Fri–Sun 11am–midnight.

CAPILLA DEL MONTE

CAPILLA DEL MONTE attracts more alternative-lifestyle types in summer than you can shake an incense stick at. Situated 102km

THE TRUTH IS OUT THERE

Capilla del Monte hosts an international **UFO convention** every November, organized by local "research" group Centro de Informes OVNI, Juan Cabus 397 (☎03548 482485, ⓦciouritorco.org – OVNI is Spanish for UFO). **Mystical tourism** is gaining in popularity, with local tour operators jumping on the extra-terrestrial bandwagon by offering guided tours to sites of supposed UFO landings as well as night excursions to observe celestial happenings on remote mountaintops. You'll be in good hands with Angeluz (☎03548 482 768), Diagonal Buenos Aires 166, which does a (fairly) convincing range of otherworldly tours.

north of Córdoba city, the idyllic mountain town lies at the base of **Cerro Uriturco**, which, at 1979m, is the Sierra Chica's highest peak and is claimed by many locals to possess an inexplicable magnetic pull.

Set at the confluence of two (often dry) rivers on the northern edge of the Punilla Valley, Capilla del Monte's former glory can be glimpsed in its slowly decaying nineteenth-century mansions.

WHAT TO SEE AND DO

Capilla del Monte makes a good base for outdoor adventure sports, including **horseriding** in the surrounding countryside, **rock climbing** the strange sandstone formations around the hamlet of **Ongamira**, **hiking** to the summit of Cerro Uriturco (4hr or so to the top – register at the base of the mountain and start your return by 3.30pm; AR$300; ⓦcerrouritorcoam.com.ar), strolling through the multicoloured rock formations of **Los Terrones** (daily 9am–dusk; AR$150; ⓦlosterrones.com) or **paragliding** in the Sierras.

ARRIVAL AND INFORMATION

By bus The bus station is at Corrientes and Rivadavia. There are regular buses to and from Córdoba (hourly; 2–3hr).

Tourist information Pick up a map and information at the tourist office in the old railway station on Av Pueyrredón 552 (daily 8am–8pm; ☎03548 481913, ⓦcapilladelmonte. gov.ar). It can also provide information on the town's New Age healers.

ACCOMMODATION AND EATING

Calabalumba Calabalumba s/n ☎03548 489601. The closest campsite to town is the riverside *Calabalumba*, which has tent pitches and cabins sleeping up to six. Camping/person <u>AR$235</u>, cabins <u>AR$950</u>

★ **El Duende Azul** Chubut 75, at Aristóbulo del Valle ☎03548 15 569667, ⓦcordobaserrana.com.ar/elduendeazul.htm. A guesthouse in tune with the town's hippy vibe where you can frolic in the big garden or hang out in the common area overrun by pixie and elf figurines. The simple but pretty rooms are en-suite and the lovely owners arrange various detox programmes. <u>AR$300</u>

Maracaibo Buenos Aires 182 ☎03548 482 741. This unpretentious restaurant is a good all-rounder, serving fish, pasta and chicken mains, as well as lots of vegetarian options; the vegetable and corn lasagne is filling and tasty. Mains AR$120–220. Mon–Wed & Fri–Sun 11am–4pm & 7.45–11.45pm.

Los Tres Gómez 25 de Mayo 452 ☎03548 482 647, ⓦhostelencapilladelmonte.com. HI-affiliated joint with a lurid colour scheme in the communal areas – the dorms and private rooms, by contrast, are plain and a little bare. There's a kitchen, garden and a restaurant-bar; staff can also help plan excursions. Dorms <u>AR$300</u>, doubles <u>AR$900</u>

The Northeast

Sticky summers, *mate* tea and *chamamé* folk music characterize the sultry northeastern provinces of Entre Ríos, Corrientes, Misiones and Santa Fe, an area known as **El Litoral**. Most of the region is wedged between two awesome rivers, the Paraná and the Uruguay, which converge near Buenos Aires as the Río de la Plata. Eclipsing every other attraction in the region are the **Iguazú Falls**, the world's

most spectacular waterfalls, framed by lush subtropical forest. Located in the northeastern corner of Misiones Province, the falls straddle the border with Brazil. South of **Iguazú**, the well-preserved Jesuit Mission ruins at **San Ignacio Miní** make for the region's second-biggest draw.

Further afield, in Corrientes province, the sprawling wetlands of **Esteros del Iberá** offer prime wildlife-spotting opportunities. The

1

river-hugging, siesta-loving city of **Corrientes** is increasingly opening itself up to tourism, while Argentina's third-largest city (and the birthplace of Che Guevara), **Rosario**, in Santa Fe province, has some handsome historic buildings, arresting monuments and a lively weekend party atmosphere. The star of Entre Ríos province is the **Parque Nacional El Palmar**, with its forest of towering *yatay* palms, an easy

day-trip from the resort town of **Colón**.

If you have a problem with heat and humidity, steer clear of this region between December and March, when temperatures in the far north often creep above 40°C.

ROSARIO

Super-stylish **ROSARIO** is a cleaner, greener, less daunting version of Buenos

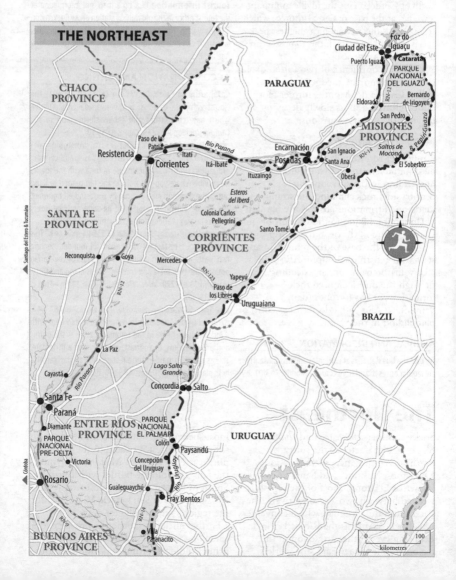

Aires. The city where Che Guevara learned to crawl and Lionel Messi learned to kick a ball is home to a handsome, academic and culturally inclined population of just over one million.

Sprawled on the banks of the **Río Paraná**, Rosario's assets are its riverside beaches, parks, restaurants, bars and museums. For an enjoyable day-trip, the sandy beaches of the subtropical **Alto Delta islands** are just a short boat or kayak ride away. Stylish shops line the streets of Rosario's pedestrianized centre, and there's free public wi-fi throughout the city. *Extranjeros* (foreigners) are still very much a novelty here, and whether you're in town to chill or to party, you'll be warmly received by the friendly locals.

WHAT TO SEE AND DO

The leafy parks and historic buildings make central Rosario a pleasant place to wander around at any time of year, while the riverfront and beaches are extremely appealing during the summer months. Start your stroll at the Plaza 25 de Mayo and be sure to check out the nearby Catedral de Rosario and Monumento a la Bandera, both postcard images of the city.

PLAZA 25 DE MAYO AND AROUND

The tree-lined **Plaza 25 de Mayo** lies three blocks west of the river. Here, at the heart of the city, you'll find some of the city's grandest buildings, including the late nineteenth-century **Catedral de Rosario** (daily 9am–12.30pm & 4.30–8.30pm; free), with its striking Italianate marble altar. On the southern side, the **Museo Municipal de Arte Decorativo Firma y Odilio Estévez** (Wed–Sun 9am–7pm; AR$15; ☎0341 480 2547) houses the lavish art collection of the Estévez family, Galician immigrants who struck it big cultivating *mate*. Pieces include a Goya painting, a Flemish tapestry and Greek sculptures.

MONUMENTO A LA BANDERA

Rising just east of the plaza, the **Monumento a la Bandera** (Monument to the Flag) is Rosario's most eye-catching landmark. A stark piece of nationalistic architecture, it marks the place where, in 1812, General Belgrano first raised the

Argentine flag. Take the **lift** up its 70m-high tower for panoramic city views (Mon 2–6pm, Tues–Sun 9am–7pm; AR$15; ☎0341 480 2238).

COSTANERA

Rosario's **Costanera** (riverfront) extends for around 20km from north to south, providing plenty of green space to sunbathe or sip *mate*, as well as waterfront restaurants, bars and museums. The central **Parque Nacional de la Bandera** – a narrow strip of parkland – is the main setting for regular markets and festivals. As you stroll north, the park merges with **Parque de España** and the large brick **Centro Cultural Parque de España** (Tues–Sun 3–8pm; free; ☎0341 426 0941, ⊛ccpe.org.ar), which hosts changing modern art exhibitions. Half a kilometre north at López Estanislao 2250 is the **Museo de Arte Contemporáneo de Rosario (MACRO)** (Tues–Sat 3–9pm, Sun 10am–1pm & 3–9pm; guided visits Fri 5pm; free but suggested donation AR$10; ☎0341 480 4981, ⊛castagninomacro.org), a kitsch temple to modern Argentine art housed inside a converted grain silo, its facade painted in pastel shades. The building – as well as the views from the top floor – outshines the displays, while the gallery's riverfront café-bar, *Davis*, is a great place to watch boats floating by over a drink or two. Also visit the Bellas Artes Castagnino, the original and sister museum in Parque de la Independencia, also dealing in contemporary art.

Most of the summer beach action happens 8km north of the centre at the **Balneario La Florida** (Dec–April; daily 9am–8pm; AR$40; ☎0341453 3491; bus #153). Just south of here is the Rambla Catalunya (with a free beach) and Avenida Carrasco, a strip of upmarket restaurants, bars and clubs that is the hub of Rosario's vibrant summer nightlife.

PARQUE DE LA INDEPENDENCIA

The **Parque de la Independencia**, 3km southwest of Plaza 25 de Mayo, is one of Argentina's largest urban green spaces. Within its extensive grounds are a football stadium, a racetrack, a theme park, a rose garden and two museums. The **Museo**

▲ Train Station, Balneario La Florida, Museo de Arte Contemporaneo & ❶

Río Paraná

Parque
de España

Centro Cultural
Parque de España

Parque Nacional
de la Bandera

Che Guevara's
house

Museo Municipal
de Arte Decorativo ⓘ Mercado de
Pulgas del Bajo

Palacio de los Leones

Monumento
a la Bandera

Palacio del Correo Catedral
de Rosario

Estación
Fluvial

Teatro
El Círculo

Parque
Urquiza

Complejo
Astronómico
Municipal

N

0   500
metres

ROSARIO

■ DRINKING & NIGHTLIFE	
Bar del Mar	3
Berlin	4
La Casa de Cristal	5
Fenicia	2
Willie Dixon	1

● EATING	
Comedor	3
Escauriza	1
La Estancia	4
Peña Bajada España	2
Via Apia	5

■ ACCOMMODATION	
La Casona de Don Jaime II	2
Euskadi Hotel	5
Mendoza Hotel	4
Posada Juan Ignacio	1
Rosario Inn	3

● SHOPPING	
Ameghino	3
Falabella	1
Mercado de Pulgas del Bajo	2

Municipal de Bellas Artes Juan B. Castagnino (Mon & Wed–Sun 2–8pm; free; ☎0341 480 2542, ⓦcastagninomacro.org), Av Pellegrini 2202, has an important collection of European and Argentine fine art. West of the lake, the **Museo Histórico Provincial Julio Marc** (Thurs–Sun 4–8pm; free; ☎0341 472 1457, ⓦmuseomarc.gob.ar) is strong on religious artefacts and indigenous ceramics from across Latin America.

CHE GUEVARA'S HOUSE

Though there's little of the fanfare about it that you might expect given his international icon status, **Ernesto "Che" Guevara** was born in Rosario in 1928. He lived in an apartment on the corner of Entre Ríos and Urquiza until the age of two, now an office not open to the public, although there's nothing to stop you gawking from the street. One block north and one block east, at the corner of Tucumán and Mitre, a **mural** of Che's intense and haggard-looking face dominates a small neighbourhood square, while there's a bronze **statue** of him on a rather forlorn

plaza on 27 de Febrero, at Laprida, twelve blocks east of Parque de la Independencia.

ALTO DELTA ISLANDS

Just across the river from Rosario, the predominantly uninhabited **Alto Delta islands** are linked to the mainland by regular passenger ferries in the summer (AR$130 return), while a weekend-only service runs in winter. **Ferries** leave from the Estación Fluvial. Some islands have underdeveloped beaches, camping facilities and restaurants. A good way to explore the delta is by taking a **kayak excursion**.

ARRIVAL AND DEPARTURE

By plane Rosario's airport (Islas Malvinas International Airport; ☎ 0341 451 1226) is 10km northwest of the centre. There are no buses into town; a taxi ride is around AR$300, or take a taxi to the Fisherton neighbourhood, from where buses #115, #116 and #133 run to the bus terminal.
Destinations Buenos Aires (5 daily; 55min); Córdoba (2 weekly; 1hr); Mendoza (2 daily; 3hr); São Paulo, Brazil (daily; 2hr 50min).
By bus The Terminal de Omnibus Mariano Moreno (ⓦterminalrosario.gov.ar) is twenty blocks west of the

centre, at Santa Fe and Cafferata (☎0341 437 3030). Buses #141 and #146 go to the centre. Fares cost AR$9.70 using a pre-paid MOVI pass (AR$30) available at kiosks where you see the MOVI sign, or AR$10.50 with exact change only.

Destinations Buenos Aires (every 30min; 4hr); Córdoba (every 30min; 6hr 30min); Corrientes (7 daily; 10–12hr); Montevideo, Uruguay (1 daily; 9hr); Puerto Iguazú (3 daily; 19hr); Salta (6 daily; 16hr).

By ferry The Estación Fluvial (☎0341 447 3838), in Parque Nacional de la Bandera, has ferries to the Delta islands (Dec–March daily; year-round Sat & Sun).

By train The train station (☎0800 333 3822) is 3km northwest of the centre.

Destinations Buenos Aires (1 daily; 7hr).

INFORMATION AND ACTIVITIES

Tourist information The riverside tourist office is on the corner of Av Belgrano and C Buenos Aires (Mon–Fri 8am–7pm, Sat 9am–7pm, Sun 9am–6pm; ☎0341 480 2230, ☯rosario.tur.ar). An information kiosk in the bus terminal has maps and hotel listings.

Activities Estación Fluvial ☎0341 447 3838, ☯estacionfluvial.com. The multi-function Estación Fluvial ferry terminal) offers an array of activities from boat cruises to city tours; you can also rent a bike here (AR$250/day). The city government Mi Bici Tu Bici scheme also provides bikes from 47 stations around the city from AR$14/day (☯mibicitubici.gob.ar).

ACCOMMODATION

Rosario has experienced a hostel boom in recent years and at weekends many fill up with party-hard *porteños*. The only time you need to book ahead is on weekends and public holidays, when prices go up.

HOSTELS

All hostels listed have kitchen facilities and breakfast.

La Casona de Don Jaime II San Lorenzo 1530 ☎0341 530 2020, ☯lacasonadedonjaime.com; map p.82. Hugely popular hostel for the range of excursions it provides (including boating, kayaking and cycling) – this must be one of the few hostels in Argentina to boast its own climbing wall. Spacious and clean with cool decor and themed private rooms. Dorms AR$250, doubles AR$800

Posada Juan Ignacio Tucuman 2534 ☎0341 439 1380, ☯posadajuanignacio.com.ar; map p.82. Ignacio's restored townhouse (complete with stained-glass windows) retains the feel of a private home, thanks in part to the friendliness of the staff. Rooms are basic but there's ample communal space including several roof terraces and garden equipped with a decent pool and *asado*. Dorms AR$300, doubles AR$1000

★ **Rosario Inn** Sargento Cabral 54 ☎0341 421 0358, ☯rosarioinn.com.ar; map p.82. With a fantastic

location near the river, this light-drenched hostel has two patios to hang out in and bikes for rent. Tango and theatre classes offered. Dorms AR$100, doubles AR$300

HOTELS

Euskadi Hotel 3 de Febrero 1255 ☎0341 421 3561, ☯hoteleseuskadi.com.ar; map p.82. This modern hotel is light and airy; the best of the budget options. Rooms have all the expected facilities. Breakfast included. AR$600

Mendoza Hotel Mendoza 1246 ☎0341 424 6544, ☯hotelmendozarosario.com; map p.82. Functional and comfortable, all rooms in this humble hotel feature private bathrooms, cable TV and a/c. Breakfast included. AR$900

ALTO DELTA ISLANDS

El Pimpollal ☎0341 549 4777, ☯elpimpollal.com. ar. Offers transport to and tours of the islands, including birdwatching, horseriding and boat trips. Overnight stay in a dorm can be included at AR$290

EATING

The bulk of Rosario's restaurants are clustered along Avenida Pellegrini, although in summer you'll want to take advantage of the waterfront aspect and pull up an outdoor chair at one of the many popular restaurants along the Costanera, many of which are open until the small hours (during winter most close by around 10pm, later at weekends).

Comedor Balcarce 1 ☎0341 425 6765, ☯comedorbalcarce.com.ar; map p.82. Popular with locals, this is the place for generous portions of traditional food (*empanadas, milanesas, parrilla*) at very affordable prices. Mon–Sat noon–3pm & 8.15pm–midnight.

Escauriza Escauriza 3162, at Paseo Ribereño ☎0341 454 1777, ☯escaurizaparrilla.com.ar; map p.82. Highly regarded *parrilla* specializing in fish, on the riverfront near the access to the Victoria road bridge. *Surubi* and *dorado* (river fish) are on the menu as well as more conventional meat, and the prices are reasonable. Daily noon–4pm & 8pm–midnight.

La Estancia Av Pellegrini 1510 ☎0341 449 8052; map p.82. Rosario's most popular restaurant is a (pricier) old-fashioned place with a vast menu. The emphasis is on – you guessed it – beef, and it's fun to watch the impeccably suited waiters rush around with tasty cuts of sizzling cow. Daily 12.30–3.40pm, 8.30pm–1am.

★ **Peña Bajada España** Av Italia, at España ☎0341 449 6801; map p.82. Restaurant with a tranquil wooden terrace overlooking the river and serving cheap barbecued fish feasts. Access is by elevator. Daily 10am–4pm, 7.30pm–1am.

Via Apia Av Pellegrini 961 ☎0341 481 3174; map p.82. It's easy to miss this small pizzeria among the vast neon-lit

1

food palaces of Av Pellegrini, but the crisp stone-baked pizzas are arguably the best in the city. Daily 7.30–11pm.

DRINKING AND NIGHTLIFE

Rosario's party spirit makes it a great place to go out. In summer, the clubs and bars in the riverfront Estación Fluvial attract a modish crowd. Summer fun also transfers to Rambla Catalunya, a waterfront avenue in the city's north. Nightlife in Rosario doesn't really get going until well after midnight, with some clubs not opening until after 2am.

Bar del Mar Balcarce 404, at Tucumán; map p.82. A restaurant-bar with an aquatic theme and colourful mosaics; good for people-watching before painting the town red. Wed–Sun 8.30pm–6am.

Berlin Pje Simeoni 1128, between the 300 block of Mitre & Sarmiento ⓦ elberlin.com.ar; map p.82. Regular events and a steady flow of German beer keep locals coming back to this trendy bar. Thurs–Sun 11pm–late.

La Casa de Cristal Av Pellegrini 1159 ☏ 0341 15 645 8601; map p.82. This LGBTQ-friendly nightclub is super-slick and stylish; the place to go for a break from the backpacker scene. Fri & Sat 10.30pm–5am.

Fenicia Av Francia 168 ☏ 0341 423 2376; map p.82. The first pub in Rosario with a brewery on site, their Californian draught beer is arguably the best in the city, if not Argentina. With excellent food to soak up all that extra liquid, this place gets very busy, especially at weekends. Tues–Thurs 6pm–2am, Fri & Sat 6pm–4am, Sun 7pm–2am.

Willie Dixon Suipacha, at Güemes ⓦ williedixonbluesclub.com; map p.82. Live music venue hosting quality Argentine acts; *the* place to watch (and partake in) *salsa* and *cumbia*. See website for schedule.

SHOPPING

Bookshop Ameghino, Corrientes 868 (☏ 0341 440 0417; map p.82), stocks English-language books.

Clothes The pedestrianized Av Córdoba is a busy shopping street flanked with handsome historic buildings, many of which now house chic boutiques. Falabella, at Cordoba and Sarmiento (map p.82), is a vast department store with good bargains to be found during end-of-season sales.

Markets The Mercado de Pulgas del Bajo flea market is on every weekend afternoon in the Parque Nacional de la Bandera (map p.82), near Av Belgrano 500. Handmade crafts, used books and antiques are on sale.

DIRECTORY

Banks and exchange Banco de la Nación Argentina, Córdoba 1026; many other options along Santa Fe 1064, San Martín 902 and Córdoba 1770/72. Rosario Transatlántica casa de cambio generally offers decent exchange rates and has branches at Rioja 1198 and Córdoba 1463.

Laundry 5àsec, at Maipú and Santa Fe.

Post office Buenos Aires, at Córdoba on Plaza 25 de Mayo.

PARQUE NACIONAL EL PALMAR

Only after ranching, farming and forestry had pushed the graceful *yatay* palm to the brink of extinction did it find salvation in the **PARQUE NACIONAL EL PALMAR** (☏ 03477 493 049, ⓦ parqueelpalmar.com. ar). The 85-square-kilometre park, on the banks of the Río Uruguay, lies 50km north of Colón at Km198 on the RN14, and is a stark, but beautiful, reminder of how large chunks of Entre Ríos province, Uruguay and southern Brazil once looked. Many of the **palms**, which can grow up to 18m tall, are over three hundred years old. Trails wind through the park, past palm savannah, streams and riverside beaches. Sunset is the perfect time to pull out the camera, when the palms look stunning silhouetted against a technicolour sky. El Palmar's creation in 1966 also did wonders for the habitat of local subtropical **wildlife**, including capybaras, viscachas, monitor lizards, raccoons and the venomous *yarará* pit viper. Parakeets, egrets, *ñandúes* (large, flightless birds similar to ostriches) and storks are some of the bird species that can

---

INTO URUGUAY

Colón, on the Río Uruguay 320km north of Buenos Aires, makes an inviting base for visiting the Parque Nacional El Palmar (see page 84), 50km to the north. Colón is also a prime gateway to Uruguay, and is linked to the city of Paysandú, 16km southeast, by the Puente Internacional General Artigas. It is 8km from Colón to the **Uruguayan border** (immigration office open 24hr; ⓦ aduanas.gub.uy) and a further 8km to Paysandú: approximately four buses daily make the journey. Colón's bus terminal is on the corner of Paysandú and 9 de Julio. There are frequent services to Concordia (5 daily; 1hr 45min), passing Parque Nacional El Palmar, and plenty of connections to Buenos Aires (14 daily; 5hr 30min). Colón's helpful tourist office is in the port area on the corner of Avenida Costanera and Calle Gouchón (Mon–Fri 6am–8pm, Sat & Sun 8am–8pm; ☏ 03447 421 233, ⓦ colonturismo.tur.ar).

> ### FEELING HOT, HOT, HOT!
> Despite the oppressive heat that strikes in summer, the city manages to muster up heroic levels of energy for the annual, Brazilian-style **Carnaval Correntino** (🌐atenticarnaval.com. ar), which takes place throughout January and February in the open-air Corsódromo at Av Centenario 2800. Raucous street parties, which frequently include bucketloads of iced water being thrown over the sweaty hordes, take place each weekend throughout Carnaval season.
> If you're in town over the second weekend in December, check out the **Festival del Chamamé** (🌐corrienteschamame.com), a celebration of regional folk dancing and music.

be spotted here. Local guide Valeria Olivella leads guided visits and hikes from AR$50 (✉valeriaolivella@yahoom.com.ar).

ARRIVAL AND INFORMATION

By bus To get to the park, catch any Concordia-bound bus from Colón (9 daily; 30min) along the RN14 to the entrance (where you pay AR$250 entry). From here it's a 12km walk, drive or hitchhike to the visitor centre and adjacent Los Loros campground.

ACCOMMODATION

Hostería del Puerto Peyret 158, Colón ☎03447 422 698, 🌐hosteriadecolon.com.ar. Simple en-suite rooms in a range of sizes at Colón's first hotel. AR$1500
Parque Nacional El Palmar campground ☎03447 423 378. This campsite in the park is well equipped with a store and restaurant and can organize horseback rides. Camping/person AR$120 plus AR$70 per tent

CORRIENTES

Subtropical **CORRIENTES** is one of the northeast's oldest cities (it was founded in 1588) but doesn't offer much in the way of conventional attractions. That said, its compact historic centre, elegantly crumbling buildings and shady riverside area make it an ideal place for a leg stretch between long bus rides. Party people will be at home here during the heat of summer – Corrientes has been dubbed Argentina's "Capital of Carnaval", and each January and February the city explodes in a riot of colourful costumes and thumping drums.

WHAT TO SEE AND DO

Corrientes' historic core fans out in grid fashion from the shady main square, **Plaza 25 de Mayo**. The square is framed by some of the city's most important nineteenth-century buildings, including the pink Italianate **Casa de Gobierno** and the plain **Iglesia de Nuestra Señora de la Merced**

(daily 7am–noon & 4–8pm; free). On the plaza's northeast corner, the **Museo de Artesanías Tradicionales Folclóricas de la Provincia** (Mon–Fri 7am–noon & 4–7pm; free) showcases regional basketwork, leather and ceramics within a whitewashed colonial residence.

One block south of the main square is Corrientes' 2.5km riverside avenue, the **Avenida Costanera General San Martín**, flanked by pretty jacaranda and native *lapacho* trees. It is the favoured haunt of fishermen, *mate*- and *tereré*-sippers, joggers, mosquitoes, daydreamers and courting couples. Locals flock to its promenades on summer evenings after emerging refreshed from siestas. There are a few small riverside **beaches** here, but swimming is not recommended, as the river's currents are notoriously strong.

ARRIVAL AND INFORMATION

By plane Corrientes' airport (☎03783 458 684) is 10km northeast of the city centre. Free shuttle services can take you from the airport to the centre. Aerolineas Argentinas (☎0800 222 86527) flies to Buenos Aires (2 daily; 1hr 30min).
By bus The bus terminal (☎03783 449 435) is 4km southeast of the city centre. Local buses run frequently between the terminal and the centre; a taxi will set you back around AR$100.
Destinations Buenos Aires (6 daily; 12hr); Posadas (9 daily; 5hr; change here for more regular services to Puerto Iguazú); Puerto Iguazú (10 daily; 9hr); Rosario (11 daily; 9hr).
Tourist information The provincial tourist office is at 25 de Mayo 1330 (Mon–Fri 7am–1pm & 3–9pm; ☎03783 427 200, 🌐turismocorrientes.com.ar); there is a municipal tourist office where the Costanera meets Pellegrini (daily 7am–9pm; ☎03783 474 702).

ESTEROS DEL IBERÁ

A vast area of marshy swampland, the **Esteros del Iberá** comprises a series of

1

lagoons, rivers, marshes and floating islands, much of which is protected in the **Reserva Natural del Iberá**. The islands are created by a build-up of soil on top of a mat of intertwined water lilies and other plants; these in turn choke the flow of water, creating what is in effect a vast, slow-flowing river, draining eventually into the Río Paraná. The wetlands make up nearly fifteen percent of Corrientes province – spreading annually in the rainy season and gradually contracting until the rains come again. With the protection of the natural reserve, the area's **wildlife** is thriving, and there's an extraordinary variety: three hundred species of birds, including storks, cormorants, egrets, ducks and around the edges of the lake the *chajá* (horned screamer), a large grey bird with a startling patch of red around the eyes; snakes (including the yellow anaconda) and caimans; and forty species of mammals, including capybara, marsh and pampas deer, otters and howler monkeys. The capybara, the world's largest rodent, makes an unlikely swimmer, but spends most of its time in the water – listen out for the splash as it enters. Take a trip out onto the water, and you can enjoy remarkably close encounters with many of them. Proyecto Iberá, a nature reserve set up by the late North American philanthropist Doug Tompkins, has worked ceaselessly to reintroduce the *yaguareté* (jaguar) back in the wild.

WHAT TO SEE AND DO

Access to the reserve is from the tranquil village of **Colonia Carlos Pellegrini**, on the banks of the Laguna del Iberá. At the approach to the village, immediately before the rickety wooden bridge that is the only way in, former poachers staff the Centro de Interpretación, the reserve's **visitor centre**, which has useful information as well as a fascinating photo display. A nearby forest trail is a good place to spot (and hear) howler monkeys. The **Laguna del Iberá** itself is covered in water lilies, especially the yellow-and-purple *aguapé*, and its floating islands teem with a rich microcosm of bird and aquatic life.

ARRIVAL AND DEPARTURE

Access to the reserve is from Colonia Carlos Pellegrini. The village has very little to it; a grid of sandy streets around the Plaza San Martín, with very few facilities – bring enough cash to cover your entire stay.

By bus Colonia Carlos Pellegrini is 120km from the village of Mercedes (3hr approx; departures from the bus terminal Mon–Sat at noon with Minibus Regular; AR$300 one-way; 11.30am daily with Rayo Bus ☎03773 420 184; AR$300 one-way). Eleven buses run daily from Corrientes to Mercedes (3hr).

INFORMATION AND TOURS

Tourist information Mercedes has a helpful tourist office (daily 7am–1pm & 2–8pm; ☎03773 15 438 8780) and you can also arrange private 4WD transfers from here, through your accommodation in Colonia Carlos or guide Mariana Fraga (☎03773 15 459 110). For more information on the reserve, visit ⊛ proyectoibera.org.

Tours Guided tours are highly recommended – and obligatory for visiting the lagoon and wetlands. Best organized through your accommodation, they are often included in the price. Trips on offer include by boat (you'll be poled through the marshier sections, where a motor is useless), on foot or on horseback. There are also moonlit night-time boat tours (Sat nights only) and walks to see nocturnal species.

ACCOMMODATION

Accommodation is provided by a handful of gorgeous posadas; they are more expensive than hostels but provide food (often as full-board) and organize tours.

Posada El Yacare Curupi y Yaguarete ☎03773 490 021, ⊛ posadaelyacare.com, ✉ ibertatours@hotmail.com. Posada built using natural materials. Rooms are spacious with all the expected amenities and there's a luscious garden at the front. AR$1000

Posada Ypa Sapukai Yacare at Mburucuya ☎03773 1551 4212, ⊛ posadadelibera.com. This charming lakeside place has a small pool, lookout tower, impeccable rooms and beautiful garden. Excursions can be organized for AR$300 upwards. Cost includes two nights' full board and two excursions. AR$4000

SAN IGNACIO

The riverside town of **SAN IGNACIO** is home to one of the major sights of northern Argentina – the dramatic remains of the Jesuit missions at **San Ignacio Miní**. There's little clue of that in the centre, though, where this is just another hot, sleepy town. If you time the buses right you can visit the missions and move on the same day, but there are a couple of other attractions worth visiting should you be staying longer.

WHAT TO SEE AND DO

The main street south will lead you past the **Casa de Horacio Quiroga** (daily 8am–6pm; AR$100; ☎0376 447 0130), a museum to the Uruguayan-born Argentine writer of Gothic short stories, who made his home here in the early twentieth century. The same road continues to **Puerto Nuevo** on the Río Parana, a couple of kilometres away, where a sandy beach offers wonderful views across the river to Paraguay.

SAN IGNACIO MINÍ

SAN IGNACIO MINÍ (daily 8am–6pm; AR$250; ticket valid for fifteen days; ☎0376 447 0186) was one of many Jesuit missions set up throughout Spanish America to convert the native population to Christianity. Originally established further north in what is now Brazil, the missionaries gradually moved south to avoid attack from Portuguese *bandeirantes* (piratical slave traders), eventually settling here in 1696. The mission became a thriving small town, inhabited by the local Guaraní, but, following the suppression of the Jesuits, was abandoned in the early nineteenth century. Rediscovered around a hundred years ago, the ruins are now among the best preserved of their kind in Latin America, a UNESCO World Heritage Site with some spectacular Baroque architecture.

At the entrance, at the northeastern end of the village, an excellent **Centro de Interpretación Regional** looks at the life of the mission and its Guaraní inhabitants. Rows of simple *viviendas* (stone-built, single-storey living quarters that once housed Guaraní families) lead down to a grassy Plaza de Armas, overlooked by the **church** that dominates the site. The roof and most of the interior have long since crumbled away, but much of the magnificent facade, designed by the Italian architect Brazanelli, still stands, and many fine details can be made out. Twin columns rise either side of the doorway, and the walls are decorated with exuberant bas-relief sculpture executed by Guaraní craftsmen.

ARRIVAL AND INFORMATION

By bus The bus station is located in town on RN12. Destinations Posadas (hourly; 1hr); Puerto Iguazú (hourly; 4–5hr).

Tourist information There's a small Centro de Informes on Av Sarmiento (☎0376 447 0186, ⓦmisiones.tur.ar), at RN12, at the entrance to town. Ask here, or at the ruins' entrance, about the musical and visual shows, held daily at 7pm at San Ignacio Miní.

ACCOMMODATION AND EATING

There's not a great deal of quality when it comes to food, but for budget eats, try one of the pizzerias and snack bars near the ruins. There is a decent supermarket on San Martín, between Av Sarmiento and Belgrano.

Adventure Hostel Independencia 469, ☎03752 470 955, ⓦsihostel.com. The general air of this HI hostel is one of tranquillity. Set in an expansive garden dotted with hammocks, facilities include a decent-sized swimming pool and barbecue. The high-ceilinged rooms are light and airy and it's a short walk to the ruins. Breakfast included. Dorms AR$270, doubles AR$880

La Carpa Azul Rivadavia 1295, ☎0376 4470 0096, ⓦlacarpaazul.com. Conveniently located just across from the ruins, it may be touristy but the traditional Argentine dishes are good quality and the prices reasonable. Daily 6am–4pm.

Residencial Yvy Pyta San Martin 1363 ☎03764 15 666 876, ⓦresidencial-yvypyta.com.ar. Rooms are simple but brightly decorated and there's a lovely outdoor seating area. Conveniently close to the ruins and there's an on-site tour desk. AR$700

PUERTO IGUAZÚ

PUERTO IGUAZÚ is an inevitable stop if you're visiting **Iguazú Falls** (see page 88) on a budget – it's a perfectly pleasant town with all the facilities you need, if a little dull. On the western edge of town, the **Hito Tres Fronteras** is an obelisk overlooking the rivers Iguazú and Paraná at the point where they meet and form the three-way border between Argentina, Brazil and Paraguay.

ARRIVAL AND DEPARTURE

By plane The airport is 25km southeast of Puerto Iguazú (☎03757 421 996). Buses meet flights and run to the bus terminal (AR$50; ☎03757 423 006).

Destinations Aerolineas Argentinas has several daily flights to Buenos Aires (1hr 45min); LATAM and Andes also fly there. For international destinations, LATAM (ⓦlatam.com) flies from the larger airport at Foz do Iguaçu on the Brazilian side of the border. Taxi drivers will take you from your hotel

1

INTO BRAZIL

To make your trip to Iguazú Falls complete you should really visit the **Brazilian side** (see page 351), where the view is more panoramic, and the photography opportunities are excellent. There are direct **buses** from Puerto Iguazú to the Foz do Iguaçu, as they known in Portuguese on the Brazilian side; services are run by Crucero del Norte or Rio Uruguay (AR$25). Get some Brazilian cash before you go, for bus fares and the like, and bear in mind that, from October to March, Brazil is one hour ahead of Argentina.

to the airport at Foz, allowing time for completing visa formalities, for around AR$700. Try Cataratas Taxi (☎ 03757 15 415 399, ⓦ cataratastaxi.com.ar).

By bus Rio Uruguay buses for the National Park depart from the obelisk at Hito Tres Fronteras every 20min (7am–5.30pm; 30min; AR$150 each way); you can also pick them up at intervals all the way along the main street, Av Victoria Aguirre. All other services use the bus terminal on Av Córdoba, at Av Misiones. For destinations in Brazil buses departing from Argentina are cheaper and more comfortable than those departing from across the border in Brazil, although it is often necessary to book well in advance. Crucero del Norte (ⓦ www.crucerodelnorte.com.ar) has regular departures to destinations across Argentina as well as to São Paulo and Rio de Janeiro in Brazil, and Asunción in Paraguay.

INFORMATION AND TOURS

National Park office Av Victoria Aguirre 66 (Tues–Sun: winter 8am–5pm, summer 8am–6pm; ☎ 03757 420 722, ⓦ iguazuargentina.com).

Tourist information Av Victoria Aguirre 311 (Mon–Fri 7am–9pm, Sat & Sun 8am–noon & 4–8pm; ☎ 03757 420 800). ⓦ iguazuturismo.gob.ar is a useful website and there are also a number of private information booths and travel agents at the bus terminal.

Tour operator Iguazú Jungle (☎ 03757 421 696, ⓦ iguazujungle.com) offer boat tours, from AR$400 for a gentle nature ride to AR$1000 for whitewater fun.

ACCOMMODATION

There are a number of big resort hotels near the falls, but budget travellers stay in Puerto Iguazú, where there are plenty of good hostels and inexpensive guesthouses. In high season, July and around Easter, reservations are recommended.

Lilian Fray Luis Beltrán 183 ☎ 03757 420 968, ✉ hotellilian@yahoo.com.ar. One of the slickest of the budget options, offering spotless modern rooms with good bathrooms. AR$900

Ma-Ri Cabañas y Camping Montecarlo, at Los Inmigrantes ☎ 03757 404 817, ⓦ argentinaturismo. com.ar/maricabanias. Popular campsite close to the centre of town that also offers wooden cabins. There's a swimming pool and large *quincho* (outdoor grill). Camping/person AR$400, cabañas AR$890

Noelia Residencial Fray Luis Beltrán 119, between Moreno and Belgrano ☎ 03757 420 729, ⓦ hostelnoelia. com. Excellent-value, family-run hotel not far from the bus station, with a/c, private baths and a lovely patio where breakfast is served. Dorms AR$200, doubles AR$300

Porämbá Hostel El Uru 120 ☎ 03757 423 041, ⓦ porambahostel.com. A quiet hostel surrounded by nature. Lovely pool, simple, clean rooms and an excellent breakfast. Dorms AR$270, doubles AR$450

EATING AND DRINKING

With a few exceptions, restaurants in Iguazú serve bland and touristy fare. At the falls there are several cafés, but the food is expensive and uninspiring, so consider packing a picnic.

Gustos del Litoral Av Misiones 209. This pocket-sized restaurant and bar serves lip-smacking dishes from neighbouring Paraguay. Try the *chipá guazú* – a warm, crumbly combination of fresh corn and white cheese; covered here in tangy tomato sauce. Good cocktails too. Mains AR$120–200. Daily 8.30am–midnight.

La Mamma Bompland 217 ☎ 03757 424 594. Tiny no-frills spot that produces home-made pasta, satisfying diners with vast and tempting bowls. Mains AR$90–150. Mon–Sat 6–11pm.

El Quincho del Tío Querido Perón 159, at Carafuatá ☎ 03757 420 151 ⓦ eltioquerido.com.ar. A relatively unexciting-looking *parrilla* on the main street, its grills of meat and river fish are decidedly more exciting, and are for sharing. Mains AR$150–300. Daily 11.30am–late.

La Rueda Córdoba 28 ☎ 03757 422 531, ⓦ larueda1975. com.ar. Pleasant restaurant with outdoor seating. Fish is a speciality (mains AR$150–250). Mon & Wed–Sun noon–midnight, Tues 5.30pm–midnight

IGUAZÚ FALLS

Around 275 individual cascades, the highest with a drop of over 80m, make up the stunning **IGUAZÚ FALLS** (*Cataratas de Iguazú*, or simply *Las Cataratas*). Strung out along the rim of a horseshoe-shaped cliff 2.7km long, their thunderous roaring can be heard from many kilometres away, while the mist rises 30m high in a series of dazzling rainbows. In the Guaraní language Iguazú means "great water", but clearly the Guaraní are not given to overstatement, for there's little doubt that these are the most spectacular falls in the world: only the Victoria Falls in Africa can compare in terms of size, but here the shape of the natural fault that created the falls means that you can stand with the water crashing almost all around you.

This section of the Río Iguazú makes up the border between Brazil and Argentina and the subtropical forests that surround the falls are protected on both sides: by the **Parque Nacional Iguazú** in Argentina, and the **Parque Nacional do Iguaçu** (see page 351) over the border. These parks are packed with wildlife, and even on the busy catwalks and paths that skirt the edges of the falls you've a good chance of seeing much of it. Orchids and serpentine creepers adorn the trees, among which flit vast, bright butterflies. You may also see toucans overhead and – if you're lucky – shy capuchin monkeys. Look out too for the swallow-like *vencejo*, a remarkable small bird, endemic to the area, which makes its nest behind the curtains of water.

PARQUE NACIONAL IGUAZÚ

Thanks to an extensive system of trails and boardwalks that lead around, above and below the falls, the Argentine side offers better close-up views of Iguazú, while the Brazilian side has sweeping panoramic views. Everything lies within the **Parque Nacional Iguazú** (daily 8am–6pm; AR$215, get your ticket stamped to receive half-price entry the next day; ⓦiguazuargentina.com), whose

entrance is 18km southeast of Puerto Iguazú along RN12. Buses drop passengers off here, and the visitor centre just inside can provide a map of the park and various leaflets. It's also the departure point of the **Tren de la Selva**, a natural-gas-fuelled train for Cataratas Station (daily every 30min 8.30am–4.30pm), which gives access to the walking trails and the Garganta del Diablo walkway.

Several well-signposted trails (most wheelchair-accessible) take you to the park's highlights. The **Paseo Superior**, a short trail that runs along the top of the first few waterfalls, makes a good introduction. For more drama, and a much wetter experience, the **Paseo Inferior** winds down through the forest before taking you to within metres of some of the smaller falls. At the bottom of this trail, a regular free boat service leaves for **Isla San Martín**, a rocky island in the middle of the river. Note that the boat doesn't run when water levels are high after heavy rains. The same jetty is also the departure point for more thrills-oriented boat rides, such as those offered by Iguazú Jungle (see page 88).

At the heart of the falls is the truly unforgettable **Garganta del Diablo** (The Devil's Throat), a powerhouse display of natural forces in which 1800 cubic metres of water per second hurtles over a semicircle of rock into the misty river canyon below. The 1km boardwalk takes you to a small viewing platform within just a few metres of the staggering, sheer drop of water. Often shrouded in mist during winter mornings and early afternoons, the Garganta del Diablo is best visited later in the day, when the views tend to be clearer.

The Northwest

Argentina's northwest is an area of deserts, red earth and whitewashed colonial churches, punctuated with pockets of cloudforest and lush green jungle. The bustling city of Tucumán is an assault on the senses and a must-see for anyone interested in the political history of Argentina, while its diversity gives it a contemporary edge. The pretty and inviting city of **Salta** is known for its well-preserved

colonial architecture and makes a great base for visiting the wonderful natural formations of the **Quebrada del Toro** and **Quebrada de Cafayate**, as well as the stylish wine-producing villages of the **Valles Calchaquíes**, such as **Cafayate**. To the north of Salta loom three jungle-clad **cloudforests** – El Rey above all is worth a visit – along with the busy market town of **San Salvador de Jujuy**, with its palm trees and wild

1

THE NORTHWEST

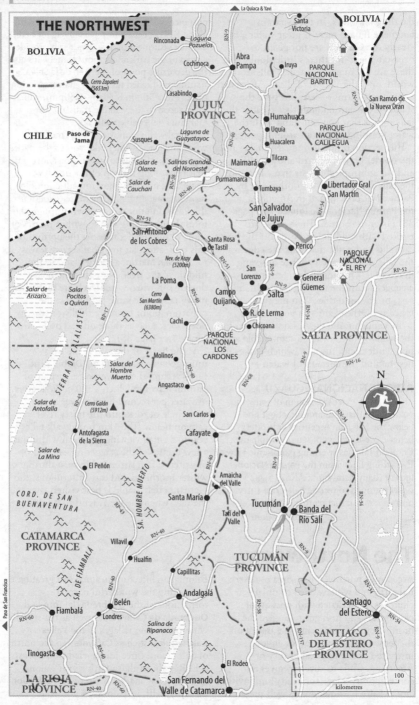

Andean feel. As you head further north, the seven-coloured **Quebrada de Humahuaca** ravine can be seen from the small mud-brick towns of **Tilcara** and **Humahuaca**.

SAN MIGUEL DE TUCUMÁN

Argentina's fifth-largest city and the seat of Argentine independence, **TUCUMÁN** (officially **San Miguel de Tucumán**) has a cosmopolitan air and lively cultural scene that attracts young people from across the country. By day, the energy can be overwhelming – it's noisier, dirtier and busier than neighbouring Salta – but the abundance of theatres, galleries, universities, bookshops and bars can't help but draw you in.

WHAT TO SEE AND DO

Walking is the best way to appreciate the city and its attractions, which can easily be explored in a day. The main sights surround **Plaza Independencia**, where Tucumán's rich heritage can be seen in the French and Italian architecture of the **Casa de Gobierno** (daily 8.30am–8.30pm; free; ☎0381 484 4000) and the adjacent **Museo Casa Padilla** (daily 9am–12.30pm & 3.30–7.30pm; free; ☎0381 431 9147), house of former governor José Frías (1792–1874). In the northwest corner of the square stands the Neoclassical **Iglesia San Francisco**, while the south is dominated by the impressive cathedral. It's particularly beautiful at night when the buildings are illuminated and locals relax among the lapacho and orange trees surrounding the marble Statue of Liberty.

A couple of blocks south of the plaza is the **Casa Histórica de la Independencia**, where congressmen signed the Declaration of Independence from Spain on July 9, 1816. It now serves as the **National Museum** (daily 10am–6pm; free; ☎0381 431 0826, ⓦcasadelaindependencia. cultura.gob.ar), where you can see the room in which the signing took place, lined with portraits of the signatories. Free English tours are available and there's a good sound-and-light show (daily except Thurs but temporarily suspended at time of writing; AR$10; tickets from the tourist office). Once you're up to speed on Tucumán's political history, head to the

Museo Folklórico (24 de Septiembre 565, daily 9am–1pm & 4–8pm; free; ☎0381 421 8250) for a lesson in indigenous and gaucho culture, including traditional instruments, pottery and weaving.

ARRIVAL AND INFORMATION

By plane Tucumán's airport (☎0381 426 5072) is 13km east of the city centre. A taxi should cost no more than AR$200.

Destinations Buenos Aires (8 daily; 1hr 45min) with Aerolíneas, LATAM and Andes. Norwegian is set to fly here from late 2018.

By bus All buses arrive at the mammoth bus terminal on Av Brígido Terán 250 (☎0381 430 0452, ⓦterminaltucuman. com).

Destinations Regular buses to Buenos Aires (16hr); Cafayate (6hr 30min); Córdoba (7hr); Jujuy (5hr); Mendoza (13hr); La Quiaca (11hr); Salta (4hr 30min).

By train Departs four times weekly to Buenos Aires (Mon, Wed, Thurs & Sat; 31hr; AR$700–2450 depending on class; ☎0381 430 9220). This is a scenic route with many stops along the way; book well in advance.

Tourist information The tourist office is opposite the Plaza Independencia at 24 de Septiembre 484 (☎0381 4303 644, ⓦtucuamnturismo.gob.ar).

ACCOMMODATION

A La Gurda Maipú 490, top floor ☎0381 497 6275, ⓦlagurdahostel.com.ar. Excellent downtown location in a beautiful colonial house with high ceilings and tiled floors. Homely but fresh, it's got ample communal space including a roof terrace, patio and courtyard. Dorms AR$300, doubles AR$700

Backpackers Tucuman Laprida 456 ☎0381 430 2716, ⓦbackpackerstucuman.com. The only HI-affiliated hostel in town, it's centrally located with amenities beyond standard hostel expectations (including a stereo system and PS2), making it a great place to meet fellow backpackers. Dorms AR$250, doubles AR$670

EATING, DRINKING AND NIGHTLIFE

Plaza de Almas Maipú 791. A lively "cultural eatery" in central Tucumán; fresh international dishes and traditional food at reasonable prices are served up with live music, independent cinema and theatrical performances. Nearby *El Arbol Galeano (at Virgen de la Merced 435)* and *Muna Muna* (vegetarian/vegan restaurant at Rivadavia 431) are part of the same cooperative. Tues–Fri 2.30pm–3am & 8pm–2am, Sat & Sun 8pm–3am

El Portal 24 de Septiembre 351 ☎0381 422 6024. Rustic restaurant with a cosy feel serving expertly cooked Argentine specialities including *empanadas*, *tamales* and *locro*. Daily noon–4pm & 8pm–midnight.

1

TAFÍ DEL VALLE

Lying 107km north of Tucumán in the Sierra de Aconquija, the hillside town **Tafí del Valle** is the gateway to the **Valles Calchaquíes** and a base from which to explore the surrounding scenery. The area is steeped in history, from ancient Tafí monoliths in the **Valles Calchaquíes Parque de los Menhires** to the eighteenth-century Jesuit ruins of **Capilla la Banda** (✆03867 421 685). The surrounding mountains, lakes and rivers mean it is also an excellent place for outdoor activities, including horseriding, fishing, trekking, paragliding and windsurfing. Don't miss the National Cheese Festival in February. For information see ⓦtafidelvalle.com. Aconquija is the only bus company from Tucumán (6–9 daily; 2hr 30min; ✆0381 422 7620, ⓦtransporteaconquija.com.ar).

La San Juan San Juan 1059 ✆0381 15 501 1942. *The* place to go for an evening of Latino fun; this vibrant resto-bar in a colonial building comes alive at night with *salsa, bachata, merenge* and *chachacha* dancers, as well as karaoke. Tues–Sun 9pm–3am.

SALTA

SALTA is one of Argentina's most elegant provincial capitals, with leafy plazas, well-preserved colonial architecture and, thanks to the altitude, a pleasantly balmy climate during the summer. In the winter months temperatures drop dramatically, and snow is not uncommon. Throughout the city, and in its hotels, restaurants and museums, there's a strong emphasis on the culture of the Andes, and you'll notice that the food is spicier than in the south of the country. Attractions include the cable-car ride to the top of **Cerro San Bernardo**; a peach-coloured Neoclassical church; and wonderful *peñas* that mix spicy food and live Andean music.

Salta is a great jumping-off point for the high passes of the **Quebrada del Toro** – ideally viewed from the **Tren a las Nubes** – and for the **Valles Calchaquíes**, where you can stay overnight among the vineyards of **Cafayate**. A less-visited option is the cloudforest national park of **El Rey**, to the east. Salta has scores of good backpacker hostels, but these tend to fill up quickly at weekends and during public holidays, making advance booking essential.

WHAT TO SEE AND DO

The verdant **Plaza 9 de Julio** lies at the heart of Salta, with scenic cafés nestled under its arches – in the evening the whole place is lit up, and half of Salta seems to descend on the square for an evening stroll.

PLAZA 9 DE JULIO

On the southern side of the leafy plaza, the whitewashed **Cabildo** houses the **Museo Histórico del Norte** (Mon–Fri 9am–1.30pm & 3–6.30pm, Sat 2.30–6.30pm, Sun 9.30am–1.30pm, free; ⓦmuseodelnorte. cultura.gob.ar), which displays an eclectic array of artefacts, from horse-drawn carriages to everyday objects. Facing the museum is the ornate Neoclassical **Catedral**, built in 1882, which has some interesting frescoes inside.

Just east of the plaza, Calle Caseros leads to two more interesting churches. The blood-red **Iglesia y Convento San Francisco**, designed by architect Luigi Giorgi, is one of the most impressive religious buildings in the country. Its exuberance makes a fascinating contrast with the whitewashed walls of the **Convento San Bernardo**, a lesson in simplicity and tranquillity of design.

MUSEO DE ARQUEOLOGÍA DE ALTA MONTAÑA (MAAM)

The **Museo de Arqueología de Alta Montaña (MAAM)**, on the west side of Plaza 9 de Julio (Tues–Sun 11am–7.30pm; AR$130; ⓦmaam.gob.ar), is a modern and controversial museum displaying the mummified remains of several high-mountain child sacrifices; many locals argue that the perfectly preserved remains should be laid to rest instead. The beautiful exhibits of Inca clothing and jewellery are well organized and have labels in English.

CERRO SAN BERNARDO

To the east of the *microcentro* a steep path leads you up **Cerro San Bernardo** hill (1458m; 45min), or you can take the easy option and hop on the **teleférico** (cable car; daily 10am–7pm; AR$85 return) from

Avenida Hipólito Yrigoyen, between Urquiza and Avenida San Martín, at the eastern end of Parque San Martín. At the top are gardens and a small café with sweeping views over Salta and out to the Lerma valley and Andes mountains beyond.

CALLE BALCARCE AND MUSEO DE ARTE ÉTNICO AMERICANO PAJCHA

The liveliest part of the city is the area around **Calle Balcarce**, especially the pedestrianized blocks north of Avenida Entre Ríos, about half a dozen blocks from

SALTA MICROCENTRO

DRINKING & NIGHTLIFE	
Boliche de Balderrama	2
La Casona del Molino	1

EATING	
Bartz	1
Heladería Fili	2
Ma Cuisine	3
Mercado Central	6
El Patio de las Empanadas	5
El Solar del Convento	4

ACCOMMODATION	
Backpacker's Hostel	6
Hostel Coloria	2
Munay	5
Hostal Prisamata	1
Prisamata Boutique	4
Las Rejas	3

1

the centre. Arts and crafts are on sale in the evenings and on weekends, and this is where you'll find the largest number of restaurants, bars, discos and folk-music venues. There is also an outstanding museum of American ethnic art, the **Museo de Arte Étnico Americano Pajcha**, 20 de Febrero 831 (Mon–Sat 10am–1pm & 4–8pm; AR$100, guided tour AR$20; ⓦmuseopajchasalta.com.ar), featuring handicrafts from Argentina and elsewhere in South America, with Mapuche silver jewellery and Andean ceramics the highlights.

ARRIVAL AND DEPARTURE

By plane Salta's airport (☎0387 424 7356) is 12km southwest of the city centre. A taxi should cost no more than AR$250.

Destinations Most parts of Argentina, including: Buenos Aires (2–3 daily; 2hr 30min); Córdoba (2–3 daily; 1hr 30min); Tucumán (2–3 daily; 40min). Also to La Paz in Bolivia (2 weekly).

By bus All buses arrive at the bus terminal (☎0387 401 1143, ⓦbuses.todowebsalta.com.ar) eight blocks east of the main plaza along Parque San Martín. It has luggage storage, cafés, chemists and bakeries but no internet.

Destinations Regular buses to Buenos Aires (20hr), Rosario (16hr), Córdoba (13hr), Tucumán (4hr), La Quiaca (7hr 30min) and Mendoza (19hr).

By train Bus #5 links the bus terminal with the train station, at Ameghino 690, via Plaza 9 de Julio. The only trains that serve Salta are the tourist *Tren a las Nubes*, which departs daily but from San Antonio de los Cobres (at time of writing), and infrequent goods and passenger trains to the Chilean border.

INFORMATION AND TOURS

Tourist information Salta city's tourist office is housed in a converted Neoclassical building at Caseros 711 (daily 8am–9pm; ☎0387 437 3341); it offers leaflets and a good city map. For information on Salta province there's an office at Buenos Aires 93 (daily 8am–9pm; ☎0387 431 0390).

Tour operators A wide variety of highly professional **tours, expeditions** and other **activities** all around the northwest region can be arranged from Salta city. Clark Expediciones, Mariano Moreno 1950 (☎0387 15 890 118, ⓦclarkexpediciones.com), is a small ecotourism company specializing in birdwatching tours. MoviTrack Safaris, Casero 468 (☎0387 431 1223, ⓦmovitrack.com.ar), runs lively one- to two-day overland safaris and sightseeing tours. Norte Trekking, Güemed 265, oficina 1 (☎0387 431 6616, ⓦnortetrekking.com), offers sightseeing, trekking and mountaineering adventures. Finally, Salta Rafting, Caseros 177 (☎0387 421 3216, ⓦsaltarafting.com), does fun whitewater rafting and zipwire excursions on the Río Juramento; it can also arrange horseriding and mountain-biking trips.

ACCOMMODATION

There are plenty of budget accommodation options within walking distance of the bus terminal and the central plaza.

HOSTELS

Backpacker's Hostel Buenos Aires 930 ☎0387 423 5910, ⓦbackpackerssalta.com; map p.93. One of three HI-affiliated hostels in Salta, this lively spot wins points for its free dinners, large pool, LCD TV and fun events such as five-a-side football. Doubles have TV and private bathroom. Dorms <u>AR$180</u>, doubles <u>AR$800</u>

Hostel Coloria General Güemes 333 ☎0387 431 3058, ⓦcoloriahostel.com; map p.93. Super stylish (rooms are colour themed) and clean, this modern hostel is conveniently located close to the historic centre. There's ample communal space – including a small pool – and a decent Argentine breakfast. Dorms <u>AR$200</u>, doubles <u>AR$800</u>

★ **Hostal Prisamata** Bartolomé Mitre 833 ☎0387 431 3900, ⓦhostalprisamata.com; map p.93. Located close to the nightlife in Balcarce, the large communal spaces and indoor hammocks in this restored colonial house make it perfect for socializing. Choose a room towards the back to avoid noise from the road. Dorms <u>AR$190</u>, doubles <u>AR$789</u>

Las Rejas General Güemes 569 ☎0387 422 7959, ⓦlasrejashostel.com; map p.93. Family-owned and run, this converted 1900 building offers hostel accommodation with dorms and doubles with breakfast,

---

INTO CHILE

One of the better Andean crossings – the RN9 to Jujuy, RN52 from Jujuy to the border and Ruta 27 on the Chilean side – is well maintained, given that it's an international route for lorries. At around 600km, it takes around seven and a half hours by car; be sure that your rental vehicle has the correct paperwork to cross into Chile. The highest point reaches 4750m above sea level so take the usual precautions for dealing with altitude. The Jama border (Chilean customs) is open daily 8am–11pm. Pullman leaves Salta bus terminal daily at 7am (9hr 30min). You can also reach La Quiaca, the Bolivian border, from Salta. Balut runs seven bus services daily (7hr 30min).

as well as more luxurious accommodation at the adjoining B&B, where rooms start at AR$475. Dorms AR$250, doubles AR$700

HOTELS

Munay Av San Martín 656 ☎0387 422 4936, ⓦmunayhotel.com.ar; map p.93. Good-quality budget hotel, with basic but clean rooms with private bathrooms. Breakfast included. AR$900 ★ **Prisamata Boutique** Vicente Lopéz 129 ☎0387 422 7449, ⓦhotel. prisamatagroup.com; map p.93. Five beautifully decorated rooms, with private bathrooms and a spectacular breakfast (there's an in-house pastry chef), which changes daily. AR$900

EATING

Salta has a good range of budget eating options, ranging from simple snack bars where you can enjoy delicious *empanadas* to atmospheric cafés and lively folk-music *peñas*, with the latter staying open well into the small hours at weekends and during peak tourist seasons; most charge extra for the entertainment.

Bartz Leguizamon 465 ☎0387 461 0160; map p.93. Excellent tapas restaurant serving delicious tasting plates from octopus to carpaccio at reasonable prices. Mon–Sat noon–12.45am.

Heladería Fili Av Sarmiento 229 ☎0387 422 3355; map p.93. This ice-cream parlour, housed in a natty Art Deco building, has been attracting locals for over sixty years with its vast selection of flavours, including a delicious *dulce de leche* with almonds, cinnamon or both. Daily 9am–10pm.

Ma Cuisine España 83 ☎0387 421 4376; map p.93. Fresh ingredients, crisp decor and a chalkboard menu of pasta, meat, seafood and vegetarian dishes which changes daily. Mon–Sat 8pm–midnight.

Mercado Central Av San Martín 750; map p.93. Good for lunch, with a range of inexpensive food stalls offering everything from *panchos* and fries to *locro* and *humitas* throughout the day.

El Patio de las Empanadas Caseros 117; map p.93. Pleasant place serving northwestern treats, with an outdoor patio. Try the famous *empanadas*, *humitas* and *tamales*. Mon–Fri 7am–midnight, Sat 7am–1am.

★ **El Solar del Convento** Caseros 444 ☎0387 421 5124; map p.93. Stylish decor, attentive service and thoughtfully prepared traditional dishes combine to make this restaurant a standout on Salta's dining scene (without being *too* expensive). The wine list is extensive, and local "champagne" is served on the house. Sometimes closed during low season but otherwise open daily for lunch and dinner.

DRINKING AND NIGHTLIFE

Boliche de Balderrama San Martín 1126 ☎0387 421 1542; map p.93. Somewhat pricey but popular *peña*

with local music – and sometimes dancing – while you eat. Mon–Sat noon–3pm & 9pm–4am.

★ **La Casona del Molino** Luis Burela 1, at Caseros ☎0387 434 2835; map p.93. It's a 30min walk or a quick taxi ride to this *peña* in a rambling old building, but well worth it for the delicious local food and lively atmosphere. The fairly priced menu includes *empanadas*, *locro*, *guaschalocro*, *tamales* and *humitas*. The house wine comes by the litre and is dangerously drinkable. Tues–Sun 12.15–3pm & 9pm–5am.

DIRECTORY

Banks and exchange There are several banks with ATMS at Plaza 9 de Julio, and Av España is lined with banks including HSBC, BBVA Francés and Santander. There are further cashpoints and exchange services on España, at Mitre.

Car rental Turismo Marina Semisa, Caseros 489 (☎0387 431 2097, ⓦmarina-semisa.com.ar).

Hospital San Bernado, Doctor Tobias 69

Internet Salta Internet, Florida 55.

Post office Deán Funes 170.

Tourist police Mitre 23.

LA QUEBRADA DEL TORO

There are several ways to experience the dramatic, ever-changing scenery of **La Quebrada del Toro** gorge and its surrounding town; you can rent a car, take an organized tour or hop on the **Tren a las Nubes** – a fabulous if expensive experience. Given that the complex railway line doesn't always receive the maintenance attention it deserves, it is prone to temporary closures. As of 2018, the train was only running from San Antonio de los Cobres to **Polvorilla Viaduct**. The company, however, runs bus services from Salta to San Antonio, or else you need to make your own way there, 159km on mostly dirt track. Check ahead. (Tues & Sat; bus and train return AR$2380, train only AR$1470 ⓦtrenalasnubes.com.ar). The rail tracks ascend to a dizzying 4200m above sea level, allowing you to experience this exceptional engineering achievement. There are 21 tunnels and more than thirteen viaducts, the highlight being the 64m-high, 224m-long **Polvorilla Viaduct**, almost at the top of the line. Along the way there are various stops and photo opportunities, usually including the town of **Santa Rosa de Tastil**, the pre-Incan site of **Tastil**, and the small mining town of **San**

1

Antonio de los Cobres, where local artists sell their jewellery, clothing and toys by the train station.

PARQUE NACIONAL EL REY

The spectacular cloudforests of the **PARQUE NACIONAL EL REY** (daily 9am–dusk; free) lie just under 200km from Salta. El Rey features an upland enclave covered in lush green vegetation, with high year-round humidity and precipitation but with very distinct seasons – very wet in summer, dry (or at least not so wet) in winter. The park is frequently covered in a low-lying mist, the signature feature of cloudforests, protecting the plants and animals beneath it. El Rey is particularly good for **birdwatching**: the giant toucan is the park's symbol, and is easily spotted, while at least 150 other bird species also live here, as well as jaguars and howler monkeys.

There is just one access road to the park (the RP20). The easiest way to discover the park is on an **organized trip** from Salta (see page 151), but if visiting independently you're advised to take a 4WD and check in with the **guardaparques** at the park entrance before you set off. The only option for an overnight stay at the park is to pitch a tent at the official **camping** spots, basic but with electricity, toilets and showers. Again, check with the *guardaparques* at the entrance for directions and prices.

VALLES CALCHAQUÍES

To the south of Salta lie the stunning **VALLES CALCHAQUÍES**, the valleys of the Río Calchaquí, fed by snowmelt from the Andes. Here you'll find some of the highest vineyards in the world. You can rent your own car from Salta to explore the area, which allows you to loop round via the amazing **Cuesta del Obispo mountain pass**, visit the wonderful cactus forests of the **Parque Nacional Los Cardones**, stop off in the little towns of **Cachi** and **Cafayate**, and return to Salta via the incredible rock formations of the Quebrada de Cafayate. There are also tours from both Cafayate and Salta, and Cachi and Cafayate are both

connected to Salta by bus (though not really to each other).

CACHI

CACHI lies around 160km southwest of Salta, along an incredibly scenic route with mountainous views across lush valleys. Small and still quite undiscovered, but what Cachi lacks in services, it makes up for in scenery and location. The permanently snow-covered **Nevado del Cachi** (6380m), 15km to the west, looms over the town.

WHAT TO SEE AND DO

Truth is, there's not a great deal to detain you in Cachi other than the picturesque nature of the place itself. A small **Plaza Mayor**, shaded by palms and orange trees, marks the centre of town and on the north side you'll find the well-restored **Iglesia San José**. Its bright white exterior gives way to an interior made almost entirely, from pews to confessional, of porous cactus wood. Not far away, the **Museo Arqueológico Pío Pablo Díaz** (Mon–Fri 10am–7pm, Sat & Sun 10am–6pm; AR$10) displays local archaeological finds in an attractive building with a wonderful patio. For the more energetic, a hiking track to the west of the village will lead you to **Cachi Adentro** (6km), where you'll have wonderful views of the surrounding landscape and may see the fields of drying paprika which line the route from March to May.

ARRIVAL AND DEPARTURE

By bus Buses drop passengers off at the main square. From there all services are within walking distance. There is at least one daily service and some days up to three with Ale Hermanos to Salta (4hr 15min) and more frequent services to local destinations.

ACCOMMODATION AND EATING

There are relatively few budget places to stay in Cachi.
ACA Hostería Cachi Av Automóvil Club Argentina ☎03868 491 904, ⌨ hosteriacachi.com.ar. The restaurant of the pricey *ACA Hostería Cachi* serves local food, including hearty soups and stews, as well as cakes, sandwiches and pastries at the adjoining café-bar. The setting is wonderful and the staff friendly.
Art Hostel Viracocha Federico Suarez at Ruiz de los Llanos ☎03868 491 713, ✉ viracocha.art.hostel@ gmail.com. Low-key little hostel with decent rooms at reasonable prices. The lack of kitchen might have something

to do to with the fact they have a (nice) restaurant just down
the road. Dorms **AR$350**, doubles **AR$1100**
Municipal Camping Av Automóvil Club Argentina
(at the end) ☎ 03868 491 902. Basic clean campsite,
with cabins that sleep up to five. Pool and shaded areas.
Camping/person **AR$65, cabins AR$900**
Pueblo Antiguo Ruíz de los Lanos s/n ☎ 03868 491
016, ⊜ puebloantiguocacho@outlook.com. Welcoming
inn that has made a concerted effort to respect local
building and decoration customs and techniques and offers
interesting tours of the immediate region. **AR$1320**

AROUND CACHI

The 157km drive from Cachi to Cafayate
takes you through some of Valles
Calchaquíes' most spectacular scenery and
some delightful little towns. A short stop
in **Molinos** (60km from Cachi) is
recommended to view the local crafts, see
the picturesque adobe houses and check
out a fabulous church, the eighteenth-
century **Iglesia de San Pedro Nolasco**.
Beyond the town of Angastaco, the red
sandstone **Quebrada de las Flechas** gorge is
filled with dangerous-looking arrowhead
formations. Shortly afterwards the road
passes through **El Ventisquero**, the
"wind-tunnel", and the natural stone walls
of **El Cañón**, over 20m high.

CAFAYATE

The largest town in the region, and the main
tourist base, is **CAFAYATE**. Set amid
apparently endless vineyards, it makes a
perfect place to hole up for a few days while
exploring the surrounding area on
horseback or sipping the local wines at
nearby *bodegas*. The town is lively, filled
with inviting plazas and popular restaurants.

WHAT TO SEE AND DO

The pleasure of your visit lies in getting out
into the countryside, though there are also
craft stalls and a couple of museums to fill

the hours. The sleek, modern **Museo de la
Vid y el Vino**, on Güemes Sur at Cesar
Fermin Perdiguero (Tues–Sun
10am–7.30pm; AR$70), uses poetry and
audiovisuals to bring to life the oenologist's
craft and explain why the climate in the
area is so good for the grapes. The **Museo
Arqueológico** (Mon–Fri 11.30am–9pm, Sat
11.30am–3pm; free; ☎ 03868 421 054), at
the corner of Colón and Calchaquí, is the
private collection of late collector Rodolfo
Bravo. On display alongside archeological
relics are local ceramics, and everyday items
from the colonial period.

ARRIVAL AND DEPARTURE

By bus Buses from Salta and nearby villages use the new
terminal on RN40 on the northern side of the Río Chuscha.
Destinations Salta (6 daily; 3hr30min); Tucumán (4 daily;
4hr).

INFORMATION AND TOURS

Tourist information An office at Nuestra Señora del
Rosario 9 opposite the plaza (daily 8am–9pm; ☎ 03868
480 038) dispenses information. Look for the helpful map
of the wineries.
Tour operators Ipuna Turismo, San Martín 81 (☎ 03868
421 808), can arrange horse rides, trekking, 4WD tours,
winery tours and mountain-bike adventures. Majo
Viajes, Nuestra Señora del Rosario 77 (☎ 03868 422 038,
ⓦ majoviajes.todowebsalta.com.ar), offers a huge variety
of tours and adventures across northern Argentina. Turismo
Cordillerano, next door to *Ruta 40* hostel at Camila Quintana
de Niño 59 (☎ 03868 422 137, ⓦ turismocordillerano.com.
ar), offers trekking and excursions in the valleys.

ACCOMMODATION

There is a range of options for budget accommodation; all
are within walking distance of the plaza and can advise on
winery visits.
Casa Arbol Calchaqui 84 ☎ 03868 422 238,
⊜ hostelcasaarbol@gmail.com. Centrally located hostel
in a small colonial house with a real home-from-home
vibe. Run by ex-backpackers who have lots of tips on the
surrounding area. Dorms **AR$300**, doubles **AR$850**
Rusty K Hostal Rivadavia 281 ☎ 03868 422 031,
ⓦ rustykhostal.todowebsalta.com.ar. Central, friendly
hostel with a pleasant garden to relax in. Dorms **AR$700**,
doubles **AR$1200**
Ruta 40 Güermes Sur 178 ☎ 03868 421 689, ⓦ hostel-
ruta40.com. The liveliest hostel in town, with clean dorms
and small doubles. Dorms **AR$350**, doubles **AR$1300**
Los Toneles Camila Quintana de Niño 38 ☎ 03868 422
301, ⓦ lostoneleshotel.com.ar. Friendly budget hotel half

1

a block from the plaza with barrels of character – literally, with giant beer barrels serving as decoration and as tables in the small patios off each room. A yard with benches that resembles an English pub garden completes the picture. __AR$1150__

★ **Hostal del Valle** San Martín 243 ☎ 03868 421 039, ✉ hostaldelvalle@infonoa.com.ar. Large, light spacious rooms, set around a luscious patio. Ask for a room upstairs. __AR$1000__

EATING AND DRINKING

Restaurants and cafés surround the main plaza, where in summer you can join crowds of locals strolling through the city at dusk with an ice cream.

Bad Brothers Camila Quintana de Niño 59, ☎ 03868 426 039 ⊛ badbrotherswe.com. This remodelled house and garden offers up a great wine experience with vinos from the eponymous label and the winemaker's side projects. Small plates for sharing include tasty braised beef rib (AR$170). Wine flights from AR$100. Mon–Wed & Sun 6.30pm–1am, Thurs–Sat noon–3pm & 6.30pm–1am.

Baco Güemes Norte, at Rivadavia, ☎ 03868 566 185. Simple decor and friendly staff make this corner restaurant popular, as do its pizzas, trout and local wines. Daily lunch & dinner.

Carreta de Don Olegario Güemes Sur 20, at Quintana de Niño on the east side of the plaza ☎ 03868 422 004. Popular for its reasonably priced local dishes, this well-located restaurant features live traditional music as well as hearty goat and lamb stews (AR$245), pasta dishes and delicious cheeses. There's a good selection of wines from local *bodegas* too. Daily noon–3pm & 7–11pm.

Las Dos Marias San Martín 27 ☎ 03868 422 463. A more intimate option than the other touristy restaurants on the plaza, serving high-quality Argentine fare at more reasonable prices. Daily lunch & dinner.

Miranda Av Güemes Norte 160, half a block north of the plaza. Gourmet ice creams in exotic flavours; try the famous wine sorbets (AR$40). Daily noon–8pm.

SAN SALVADOR DE JUJUY

Generally playing second fiddle to its prettier cousin Salta, **SAN SALVADOR DE JUJUY** (known as Jujuy) lies 90km to the north. Although it's the highest provincial capital in the country, at 1260m above sea level, Jujuy is set in a lush pocket of humidity and greenery. It's a busy place, with a frantic, market feel, where crumbling colonial buildings are juxtaposed with neon signs. Most travellers pass through for just one night on their way to **Tilcara** and **Humahuaca**, and, to the north, the spectacular colours of the **Quebrada de Humahuaca**.

WHAT TO SEE AND DO

If you have time to kill in Jujuy, head to the lively **Plaza General Belgrano**, east of the city centre. This large, green open space is generally crowded with young locals, checking out the craftsmen and market sellers who set up stalls here. On the west side of the plaza, the late eighteenth-century **Catedral** (daily 8am–1pm & 5–8pm; free) makes up for a plain facade with a wonderfully decorative interior, above all a spectacular pulpit decorated by local artists over two centuries ago. This has a rival in the intricate pulpit of the nearby **Iglesia San**

WINERY VISITS

There are some world-class wineries around Cafayate and most offer **tours** in English and Spanish with a tasting afterwards. Ask at the tourist office opposite the plaza in Cafayate for a winery map of the area.

Free tastings are now a thing of the past; regardless you can sample some mountain wines for a few quid. Two bodegas close to the main square are **El Porvenir de Cafayate**, at Córdoba 32 (Mon & Sun 9am–1pm, Wed–Sat 9am–1pm & 3–6pm; ☎ 03868 422 007, ⊛ elporvenirdecafayate.com; tasting AR$100) and the organic **Bodega Nanni**, on Silverio Chavarría 151 (Mon–Sat 10.30am–12.30pm & 2.30–6.30pm, Sun 11am–12.30pm & 2.30–5.30pm; ☎ 03868 421 527, ⊛ bodegananni.com; tasting AR$50). Slightly further afield, 2km south of town, is the nineteenth-century Finca Quara (Mon–Fri 9.30am–1pm & 2.15–4pm, Sat & Sun 9.30am–1pm, free guided tours every 30min; tasting AR$300; ☎ 03868, 421 709, ⊛ fincaquara.com). Wine aficionados will appreciate Estancia Los Cardones, whose oenologist Alejandro Sejanovich regularly tops critics' lists (Mon & Thurs–Sun 10am–6pm; RN40 south to Hualinchay km. 7, near Tolombón; ☎ 0387 486 3421, ⊛ estancialoscardones.com; tasting AR$150).

Francisco, whose tiny human figures, columns and scenes are thought to have been carved in Bolivia.

ARRIVAL AND DEPARTURE

By plane Jujuy's airport (Gobernador Horacio Guzmán International Airport; ☎ 0388 491 1102) is 32km southeast of the city. There are five flights daily between Buenos Aires and Córdoba. A taxi to the centre will cost around AR$800. You may want to consider flying to Salta and taking a bus to Jujuy from the city centre for AR$215.

By bus The new bus terminal (☎ 0388 498 3337) on Ruta 9 and Autopista 66, is 2km south of the centre, which serves all local, regional and national destinations, and also offers services to Chile and Bolivia. It replaced the Chico terminal, which only serves some local bus lines. Local buses accept the Buenos Aires SUBE electronic transport card; it costs AR$11 to the centre.

Destinations Buenos Aires (3 daily; 22hr); Córdoba (3 daily; 14–15hr); La Paz via Potosí (1 daily; 21hr); Salta (2 daily; 2hr); Tucumán (frequent; 5–6hr).

INFORMATION AND TOURS

Tourist information Secretaría de Turismo y Cultura, Canónigo Gorriti 295 (Mon–Fri 7am–10pm, Sat & Sun 9am–10pm; ☎ 0388 422 1325, ⓦ turismo.jujuy.gov.ar). There is also an office inside the bus terminal.

Tour operators Pasajes del Noroeste, San Martín 155 (☎ 0388 423 7565, ⓦ paisajesdelnoroeste.tur.ar), is a youth travel agency attached to *Club Hostel Jujuy*.

ACCOMMODATION

★ **Hostal Casa de Barro** Otero 294 ☎ 0388 423 5581, ⓦ casadebarro.com.ar. Wonderful and welcoming, with clean spacious dorms and private rooms, an excellent on-site restaurant and a pleasant common area. Dorms AR$200, doubles AR$750

Club Hostel Jujuy San Martín 132 ☎ 0388 423 7565, ⓦ clubhosteljujuy.com.ar. Busy, lively hostel with a small pool, within walking distance of the bus terminal and the centre. Dorms AR$250, doubles AR$700

Munay General Alvear 1230 ☎ 0388 422 8435, ⓦ munayhotel.com.ar. Just north of the centre, this friendly, budget hotel has clean, rather dark rooms with private bathrooms. AR$900

EATING AND DRINKING

The open-air market, next to the bus station, is a great place to fill up on *empanadas*, grilled meat sandwiches and coffee for just a few pesos.

La Candelaria Alvear 1346 ☎ 0388 421 9781. West of the city, this *parrilla* is a local institution, and a must for any meat-lover. Tues–Sat noon–3pm & 8.30pm–1am, Sun noon–3pm.

★ **TREAT YOURSELF**

Just 19km west of Jujuy are the thermal hot springs of the **Termas de Reyes** and the **Hotel Termas de Reyes** (☎ 0388 392 2522, ⓦ termasdereyes. com; double AR$2600, day pass AR$350). Sinking into a hot mineral spa bath, or relaxing with a mineral mud mask, is just the way to shake off a long bus ride. There are fourteen private thermal baths for three people, with stunning panoramic views, as well as two saunas. Bus #14 runs to Termas from the main bus terminal (4 daily; 20min).

★ **Macedonio** Lamadrid 524 ☎ 0388 431 0405. Wonderful cultural centre and café bar in an 1860s adobe house, with a palm-fringed patio where folk and jazz bands play (Wed–Sat). Inexpensive meals – hearty sandwiches, salads and pasta – are served. Mon–Fri 8am–9pm, Sat & Sun 8am–5pm.

Madre Tierra Belgrano 619 ☎ 0388 422 9578. Fresh salads, juices and vegetarian/vegan food. Mon–Sat 7.30am–2pm & 4–10pm, Sun 6–10pm.

DIRECTORY

Banks and exchange Alvear is lined with banks that accept foreign cards, including HSBC at Alvear 970.

Car rental Sudamerics, Belgrano 601 (☎ 0388 422 9002, ⓦ sudamerics.com).

Post office La Madrid, at Independencia.

QUEBRADA DE HUMAHUACA

The scintillating, multicoloured **QUEBRADA DE HUMAHUACA** gorge stretches 125km north of Jujuy, past the small village of **Purmamarca** (2324m above sea level) and the town of **Tilcara** (2324m), with its pre-Columbian archeological site, all the way to the busy village of **Humahuaca**. From there you can carry on to reach the border crossing with Bolivia at **La Quiaca**, 1000m higher and 150km further north. The region is popular with Argentine holidaymakers and backpackers, who come to hike and take in the extraordinary mountain scenery.

PURMAMARCA

As you head north, the first substantial settlement you reach along the RN9 is **PURMAMARCA** at Km61. This small town sits at the foot of the stunning **Cerro de los Siete Colores** (Hill of Seven Colours)

1

– best seen in the morning with the eastern sunlight – and is an ideal base for horseriding and hiking excursions. Walk up the south side past the cemetery and behind the hill for an equally colourful panorama. Purmamarca is home to an array of luxury hotels as well as more budget-friendly options, and retains plenty of rustic Andean charm, thanks to its traditional adobe buildings and colourfully dressed locals. The village has a fantastic seventeenth-century church, the **Iglesia Santa Rosa de Lima** – faithfully maintained and still in use today.

TILCARA

The busy tourist town of **TILCARA** is a favourite with holidaymakers for its fantastic restaurants, attractive hotels and a pre-Incan **pukará** or fortress (daily 9am–6pm; AR$80). Discovered in 1903 and heavily reconstructed in the 1950s, the site enjoys a wonderful, commanding location, covered in giant cacti. To get here, follow the signposted trail from the centre of town over the bridge across the Río Huasamayo. Keep your entrance ticket for admission to the **Museo Arqueológico** (same hours), on the south side of the square in a beautiful colonial house. The well-presented collection includes finds from the site and further afield, including anthropomorphic vases and a humanoid standing stone from another *pukará*.

HUMAHUACA

HUMAHUACA is a small, attractive place, originally founded in 1591 and popular with backpackers, with a wider spread of budget accommodation than elsewhere. Numerous shops, restaurants and craft stalls stand all around the leafy plaza. On the east side, the tiny **Iglesia de la Candelaria** (daily noon–1pm; free), constructed in 1631 and rebuilt in the

nineteenth century, has some interesting artworks. Beside the church, steps lead up to the base of the **Monumento a la Independencia**, a masculine and dramatic sculpture. There are awesome views from here, pocked by human-size cacti.

ARRIVAL AND DEPARTURE

By bus Buses leave every hour from Jujuy and run up the Quebrada to Purmamarca (1hr), Tilcara (1hr 30min–2hr) and Humahuaca (3hr), dropping off locals at farms and houses along the way. Only certain companies go all the way to La Quiaca – look for El Quiaqueño, Panamericano and Balut. Tilcara and Humahuaca have a central bus terminal that offers luggage storage; at other towns you will be dropped off at the main plaza.

INFORMATION AND TOURS

Tourist information The region's best tourist office is in Tilcara, Belgrano 590 (daily 8am–8pm; ☎0388 495 5720). It has lists of accommodation in the region and free maps. Otherwise there is a small tourist office in Humahuaca (daily 7am–9pm), in the white colonial *cabildo* building on the plaza.

Tour operators Tilcara Tours, Necochea 250 in Jujuy and Villafañe 369 in Tilcara (☎0388 422 6131, ⊛tilcaratours. tur.ar), organizes guided tours into the Quebrada de Humahuaca.

ACCOMMODATION

The best budget accommodation is in Tilcara and Humahuaca, although campsites can be found in nearly every town in the valley.

TILCARA

★ **Albahaca Hostel** Padilla, between Ambrosetti and Sarmiento ☎0388 155 855 194, ⊛albahacahostel. com.ar. The panoramic views of the gorge from the lovely sun terrace (where you can enjoy a breakfast of home-made bread) place this hostel above the rest, while the central location, cheerful furnishings and helpful staff (on hand to arrange tours and activities from dance classes to barbecues) do not disappoint. Dorms <u>AR$300</u>, doubles <u>AR$600</u>

INTO CHILE

The RN52 from SS de Jujuy to the border and Ruta 27 on the Chilean side are well maintained (see page 94). At 536km from Jujuy, it takes around six hours by car; be sure that your rental vehicle has the correct paperwork to cross into Chile. The highest point reaches 4750m above sea level so take the usual precautions for dealing with altitude. The Jama border (Chilean customs) is open daily from 8am–11pm. Andesmar leaves Jujuy bus terminal daily at 2.45am (8.45hr).

1

VISITING WINERIES

Barrel-loads of wineries near Mendoza offer free tours and tastings (some also have restaurants offering gourmet lunches), with the majority in the satellite towns of **Maipú** (15km southeast), **Luján de Cuyo** (7km south) and the eastern suburb of **Guaymallén**, all accessible by public transport from the city centre. Many Mendoza-based tour companies offer half- or full-day winery excursions, but if there are four of you, it can be more fun and cheaper to **rent a taxi** and hit the *bodegas* of your choice independently (call ahead for appointments; most closed Sun). Or if you want to exercise between swills (but maybe spit the wine out?), **rent a bike** in Maipú from Mr Hugo (AR$80/day; ☎0261 497 4067, ⊛mrhugobikes.com), arm yourself with their winery map, and cycle a 40km circuit, stopping at vineyards along the way. To reach Maipú from downtown Mendoza, catch *colectivos* #171, #172 or #173 from Rioja (between Catamarca and Garibaldi) and ask to get off at Plazoleta Rutini (45min).

If time only allows for one winery, walk around the corner to **Bodega La Rural** (Mon–Sat 9am–1pm & 2.30–5pm; ☎0261 497 2013) at Montecaseros 2625, which has an informative on-site wine museum. For expert advice on which wineries to visit, pick up a free copy of *Wine Republic* magazine from the tourist office or speak to the helpful staff at *Vines of Mendoza*.

Malka San Martín (at the top of the hill) ☎0388 495 5197, ⊛malkahostel.com.ar. It's a strenuous uphill walk to this hostel, which has comfortable cabañas for up to six people – great value if travelling in a group – as well as dorms and doubles. HI discounts. Dorms AR$400, cabins AR$2000
Piedra Mora Alverro 45 ☎0388 15 4752 054, ⊛piedramoratilcara.com.ar. Small complex of well-equipped cabañas that sleep up to five people. AR$800

HUMAHUACA

Hostal Humahuaca Buenos Aires 447 ☎0388 15 506 069, ⊛humahuacahostal.com.ar. Located just off the main plaza, this small hostel has slightly dark but cool dorm rooms set around a bright patio. Kitchen included. Dorms AR$200, doubles AR$800
Posada el Sol Barrio Medalla Milagrosa s/n (across the river) ☎0388 742 1466, ⊛elsolhosteldehumahuaca. com. Follow the signs from the bus station to this small rustic house on the outskirts of town. Small, comfortable dorms and doubles in peaceful surroundings at this HI hostel. Dorms AR$250, doubles AR$1000

EATING AND DRINKING

TILCARA

Makoka Belgrano 420 ☎0388 495 5237. Adorable café-bookstore that's perfect for a spot of afternoon tea with coca-leaf scones. Also serves up decent coffee. Daily 8am–9pm.

El Nuevo Progreso Lavalle 351 ☎0388 495 5237. This intimate, candle-lit spot serves delicious Andean cuisine in hearty portions. The llama steaks are good, salads using local produce are abundant, and there's a decent wine list sourced from local *bodegas*. Live music some evenings. Daily 6–11pm.
La Picadita Belgrano 672, ☎0388 419 3214. A breath of fresh culinary air at this cosy spot, updating traditional dishes from the Northwest. Try the *humita en olla* (corn mash) or *locro*. Mon–Sat 7–11.30pm.
Los Puestos Belgrano, at Padilla ☎0388 495 5100. For a meal in exceptionally beautiful surroundings, *Los Puestos* rules supreme: the varied menu features tender grilled llama, mouthwatering *empanadas*, juicy *humitas* and succulent pasta, all at reasonable prices. Daily 10am–3pm & 8.30pm–midnight.

HUMAHUACA

Pacha Manka Buenos Aires 276 ☎0388 742 1265. Charming café-restaurant serving home-cooked local food such as quinoa *empanadas* on terracotta plates. Sit outside on the back patio to enjoy the mountain sunshine. Daily 9am–midnight.
El Portillo Tucumán 69 ☎0388 742 1288. This hotel restaurant serves traditional food including llama meat, quinoa and Andean potatoes in a rustic environment. Daily 7pm–midnight.

Mendoza and San Juan

The vast midwestern provinces of **MENDOZA** and **SAN JUAN** are sparsely populated, sun-fried playgrounds for lovers of mountains and vineyards. The highest peaks outside the Himalayas rise to the west, capped by the formidable **Cerro Aconcagua**, whose icy volcanic summit punctures the sky at nearly 7000m, an irresistible magnet for experienced climbers. Further south down the Andean

1

cordillera is the see-and-be-seen resort of **Las Leñas**, whose powdery slopes deliver some of the best skiing in South America. Come summer, snowmelt rushes down the mountains, swelling rivers and creating ideal **whitewater rafting** conditions, especially along the Cañon de Atuel near the small city of **San Rafael**.

At the foothills of the mountains, the same sunshine that pummels the region's inhospitable, parched desertscapes also feeds its celebrated grapevines. Wine enthusiasts will feel right at home in the cultured city of **Mendoza**, the region's urban hub, which offers easy access to Argentina's best *bodegas*.

North of here, the provincial capital of **San Juan** and the village of **Valle Fértil** act as good bases for two of the country's most striking UNESCO World Heritage-listed parks: the bizarrely shaped rock formations of **Ischigualasto** (also known as Valle de la Luna), and, just over the border in the province of La Rioja, the wide-bottomed canyon, pre-Columbian petroglyphs and rich wildlife of **Talampaya**. For more arresting scenery, make for the tumbleweed town of **Malargüe**, which lies within easy reach of the cave network of **Caverna de las Brujas** and **La Payunia**, where guanacos roam across lava-strewn pampas.

MENDOZA

The sophisticated metropolis of **MENDOZA**, with a population of around a million, has the country's best wineries on its doorstep. Set in a valley less than 100km east of the Andes' loftiest snow-covered mountains, downtown is characterized by elegant, fountain-filled plazas and wide, sycamore-lined avenues. An earthquake in 1861 laid waste to Mendoza's former colonial glories, but the modern, low-rise city that rose in its wake is certainly no eyesore. *Mendocinos* know how to enjoy the good life, and, along with taking their siestas seriously (many businesses close between 1pm and 4pm), they enjoy dining at the city's many fine restaurants and alfresco drinking along the spacious pavements.

Mendoza makes an ideal base for exploring some of Argentina's undisputed highlights. Hundreds of *bodegas*, offering

wine-tasting tours (see page 104), lie within easy reach of downtown. Meanwhile, **tour operators** run a range of whitewater rafting, horseriding, paragliding and skydiving excursions, and those looming peaks offer skiing in winter and world-class mountain climbing in summer.

WHAT TO SEE AND DO

At the junction of the city's two principal thoroughfares – Avenida Sarmiento and Avenida Mitre – the spacious **Plaza Independencia** is the physical and cultural heart of Mendoza. Fountains and sycamore trees create an ideal space for chilling out or, over summer, taking in one of the regular outdoor concerts. One block east and south of here, **Plaza España** trumps Independencia in the beauty stakes, thanks to the Andalucian tilework gracing its stone benches, tree-lined paths, pretty fountains and monument to Spain's "discovery" of South America.

MUSEO DEL PASADO CUYANO

At Montevideo 544, the **Museo del Pasado Cuyano** (☎0261 423 6031; Tues–Sat 9.30am–1.30pm; AR$30) is the city's history museum, housed in a mansion dating back to 1873. The collection includes an exhibition on General San Martín, along with religious art, weaponry and period furniture.

PARQUE GENERAL SAN MARTÍN

A four-square-kilometre green space you could easily spend a day exploring, the forested **Parque General San Martín**, 1km west of Plaza Independencia, is one of the most impressive urban parks in the country.

Within it lie some fifty thousand trees, a rose garden, tennis courts, an observatory, swimming pool, lake, zoo, football stadium, amphitheatre and, in the southeastern corner, the **Museo de Ciencias Naturales y Antropológicas Juan Cornelio Moyano** (Tues–Fri 9am–6pm, Sat & Sun 3–6pm; free). This museum contains an intriguing collection of fossils and stuffed animals. Sweeping city views are to be had from the top of **Cerro de la Gloria** (Glory Hill), crowned by a bronze monument to San Martín's liberating army.

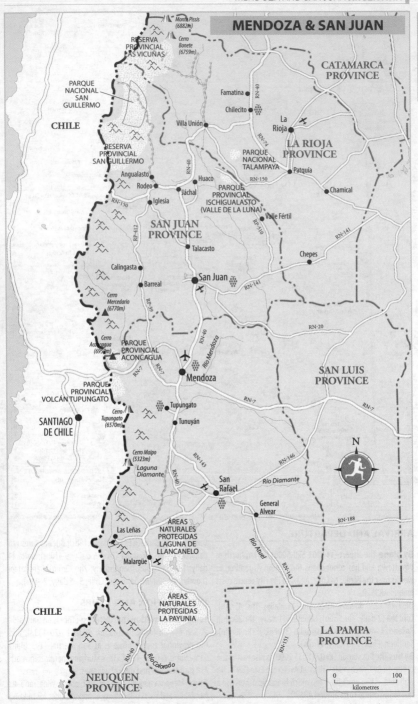

MENDOZA & SAN JUAN

1

Monte Pissis
(6882m)

Cerro
Bonete
(6759m)

RESERVA
PROVINCIAL
LAS VICUÑAS

CATAMARCA
PROVINCE

PARQUE
NACIONAL
SAN
GUILLERMO

Famatina

RN-40

Chilecito

La
Rioja

CHILE

Villa Unión

LA RIOJA
PROVINCE

RESERVA
PROVINCIAL
SAN GUILLERMO

RN-74

PARQUE
NACIONAL
TALAMPAYA

Patquía

Angualasto

RN-40

Huaco

RN-150

Rodeo

Jáchal

PARQUE
PROVINCIAL
ISCHIGUALASTO
(VALLE DE LA LUNA)

Chamical

RN-150

Iglesia

RP-412

SAN JUAN
PROVINCE

Valle Fértil

RP-510

RN-141

Calingasta

Talacasto

Chepes

Barreal

RP-39

San Juan

RN-141

Cerro
Mercedario
(6770m)

RN-20

Cerro
Aconcagua
(6950m)

PARQUE
PROVINCIAL
ACONCAGUA

RN-40

Río Mendoza

SAN LUIS
PROVINCE

RN-7

RN-7

Mendoza

PARQUE
PROVINCIAL
VOLCÁN TUPUNGATO

RN-7

RN-7

SANTIAGO
DE CHILE

Cerro
Tupungato
(6570m)

Tupungato

Tunuyán

Cerro Maipo
(5323m)

Laguna
Diamante

RN-143

RN-146

N

RN-40

San
Rafael

Río Diamante

General
Alvear

RN-188

Las Leñas

ÁREAS
NATURALES
PROTEGIDAS
LAGUNA DE
LLANCANELO

Río Atuel

RN-143

Malargüe

ÁREAS
NATURALES
PROTEGIDAS
LA PAYUNIA

LA PAMPA
PROVINCE

CHILE

RN-151

RN-40

Río Colorado

0   100
kilometres

NEUQUEN
PROVINCE

1

MENDOZA

RN-40, Airport (6km) & San Juan (185km)

N

Former
Railway
Station

LAS ORQUÍDEAS
LAS PETUNIAS

MAZA, J.

CNEL. PLAZA

BLANCO

BARCALA

AVENIDA GODOY CRUZ

GRAL. PAZ

AVENIDA LAS HERAS

NECOCHEA

PLAZA
CHILE

GÜTIERREZ

ESPEJO

PLAZA
INDEPENDENCIA

RIVADAVIA

Acomara

Museo del
Pasado Cuyano

PLAZA
ITALIA

MONTEVIDEO

SAN LORENZO

AVENIDA COLÓN

AVENIDA MOLINA P.

Centro de
Congresos y
Exposiciones

Centro
Cívico

Casa de
Gobierno

Zanjón Frías

SANTA CRUZ

GÜEMES

ESPAÑA

JUNÍN

MOYANO

San
Francisco

PLAZA PEDRO
DEL CASTILLO

BELTRÁN

ALBERDI

URQUIZA

CORRIENTES

CÓRDOBA

SAN LUIS

ENTRE RÍOS

BUENOS AIRES

LAVALLE

Museo
del Área
Fundacional

ÁREA
FUNDACIONAL

Parque
O'Higgins

Mercado
Central

Banco de
la Nación

Cambio Express

Campo
Base

SARMIENTO

Argentina
Rafting

GARIBALDI

AVENIDA ALEM

LÓPEZ, B.

DON BOSCO

PARDO

AVENIDA ZAPATA

RONDEAU

SIRIA

MORÓN

ZÁRATE

BARRAQUERO

FORMOSA

Aquarium

Serpentarium

Catedral

Hospital
Central

Bus
Terminal

FLORIDA

PRIORE

Banco de
la Nación
Aymara

PLAZA
ESPAÑA

PLAZA
SAN MARTÍN

■ ACCOMMODATION

Alamo	3
Campo Base	5
Chill Inn	8
Confluencia Hostal	2
Hostel Lao	7
Square Independencia	4
Quinta Rufino	6
El Suizo	1

● EATING

Anna Bistro	2
Azafrán	4
Bröd	6
Govinda	1
La Marchigiana	7
El Mercadito	7
Mercado Central	3
Tasca de la Plaza	5

■ DRINKING & NIGHTLIFE

Believe Irish Pub	2
Geo	4
Hangar 52	3
Wine Not?	1

0   300
metres

Inka Expediciones (1km), (3.5km) & Luján de Cuyo (15km)   RN-40, Chile (200km), San Rafael (230km) & Malargüe (350km)

ARRIVAL AND DEPARTURE

By plane The airport (☎0261 520 6000) is 7km north of downtown and has connections throughout Argentina, as well as over the border to Chile. A taxi to the city centre costs around AR$120.

Destinations Buenos Aires (10–14 daily; 1hr 45min); Córdoba (2 daily; 1hr 5min); Neuquen (1 daily; 1hr 20min); Rosario (3 weekly; 1hr 30min); Salta (3 weekly; 1hr 40min); Santiago (Chile; 2–3 daily; 45min).

By bus The bus station (☎0261 431 5000) is just east of the centre on Av Gobernador Videla, at Av Acceso Este (RN7). It's walkable, if you don't have too much luggage; otherwise a taxi to the centre costs around AR$70.

Destinations Bariloche (1–3 daily; 18hr); Buenos Aires (16 daily; 13–14hr); Córdoba (14–16 daily; 9–10hr); Salta (4 daily; 18–19hr); San Juan (hourly; 2hr 30min); San Rafael (hourly; 3hr 30min); Santiago (Chile; 5–6 daily; 7–8hr).

INFORMATION AND TOURS

Tourist information The city tourist office is on Garibaldi, at San Martín (daily 9am–9pm; ☎0261 420 1333), and the provincial tourist office is at San Martín 1143 (daily 9am–9pm; ☎0261 420 1333, ⊕turismo.mendoza.gov.ar). Ask staff for a list and map of wineries.

Tours Mendoza province is not just about wine, and its mountains and rivers offer plenty of opportunities for trekking and adventure sports, for which you'll need the services of the region's highly professional tour operators. Argentina Rafting (Amigorena 86; ☎ 0261 429 6325, ⓦ argentinarafting.com) runs whitewater rafting and kayaking trips down the Mendoza River, as well as ziplining, canyoning, mountain biking and horseriding excursions. Aymara (Av España 735; ☎ 0261 420 2064, ⓦ aymaramendoza.com.ar) has a range of both adventure and more traditional trips in and around Mendoza. Campo Base (Mitre 946; ☎ 0261 429 0707, ⓦ hostelcampobase. com.ar), attached to the hostel of the same name, offers adventure and wine tours, including a cycle-based vineyard excursion. El Rincón de los Oscuros (Av Los Cóndores s/n, Potrerillos ☎ 0262 448 3030, ⓦ rincondelososcuros.com.ar) specializes in horseriding and trekking trips.

ACCOMMODATION

Mendoza has dozens of good backpacker hostels, the best of which have gardens and swimming pools. Book well in advance if travelling in early March, as the city packs out for the *Fiesta de la Vendimia* wine festival.

HOSTELS
Alamo Necochea 740 ☎ 0261 429 5565, ⓦ hostelalamo. com; map p.104. On a quiet residential street, this attractive yellow mansion is a sociable and comfortable backpackers' retreat. There are four- to eight-bed dorms, private rooms and a glassed-in dining room facing the garden. Dorms AR$210, doubles AR$540

Campo Base Mitre 946 ☎ 0261 429 0707, ⓦ hostelcampobase.com.ar; map p.104. Although the four- to six-bed dorms are a bit cramped, this well-located hostel remains a hit with party people and Aconcagua climbers (treks and a variety of other tours are organized through the affiliated tour company; see above). Dorms AR$210, doubles AR$600

Chill Inn Aristides Villanueva 385 ☎ 0261 420 1744, ⓦ hostelchillinn.com; map p.104. A clean and modern hostel smack in the middle of the city's main bar/restaurant strip. The dorms are a bit sterile, but there's a communal kitchen, and a pleasant garden with swimming pool and barbecue area. The owners are also very friendly and helpful. Dorms AR$140, doubles AR$420

★ **Hostel Lao** Rioja 771 ☎ 0261 438 0454, ⓦ laohostel. com; map p.104. The most inviting of the city's many hostels, this British-run place is often full, so book in advance. Chilled-out but buzzing, it has plenty of common space, travel photography graces the walls, there's a large garden with a pool, a roof terrace, and clean four-bed dorms and private rooms. Regular communal meals, hammocks in the garden, and rescue dogs to pet are among the perks. Dorms AR$150, doubles AR$600

Square Independencia Mitre 1237 ☎ 0261 423 1806, ⓦ squareindependencia.com.ar; map p.104. Boisterous party hostel in a gorgeous mansion. The location

and common areas are among the best in the city; the bathrooms, sadly, are not. If you're sensitive to noise or alcohol, go elsewhere. Dorms AR$200, doubles AR$800

HOTELS
★ **Confluencia Hostal** Av España 1512 ☎ 0261 429 0430, ⓦ hostalconfluencia.com.ar; map p.104. If you want a bit more privacy, comfort and sophistication than the average hostel, head here. *Confluencia Hostal* has spacious and clean en-suite rooms, a TV lounge and large roof terrace with mountain views. AR$690

Quinta Rufino Rufino Ortega 142 ☎ 0261 420 4696, ⓦ quintarufino.com; map p.104. A B&B offering large rooms with private bathroom and TVs in a converted 1920s villa. The owners are adventure sports enthusiasts and can arrange tours. AR$800

CAMPING
El Suizo Av Champagnat in El Challao, 6km northwest of Mendoza ☎ 0261 444 1991, ⓦ campingsuizo.com.ar; map p.104. A shady spot for campers to pitch their tents, El Suizo has a swimming pool, restaurant and outdoor cinema. Bus #115 runs here from Av Alem, at San Martín. Camping/person AR$150

EATING

Mendoza has some exceptional restaurants, many specializing in local produce, Pacific seafood and regional wine. Prices aren't cheap, though many restaurants offer an economical set lunch during the week.

Anna Bistro Juan B. Justo 161 ☎ 0261 425 1818, ⓦ annabistro.com; map p.104. Cocktail-sipping diners lounge outside amid fragrant foliage and romantic lighting at this top-notch French-run restaurant with a globe-trotting menu (set lunch AR$180). Don't miss the delicious croissants, *pains au chocolat* and other delights from the nearby Brillat Savarin patisserie (Juan B. Justo 135). Daily 8am–11.45pm.

Bröd Chile 894 ☎ 0261 425 2993; map p.104. Superior bakery-café (though not as Swedish as its name may suggest) offering tasty sandwiches (AR$95–155), pastries, coffee and juices, which you can enjoy in the sunny courtyard. Mon–Sat 8am–9pm, Sun 9am–4pm.

★ **Govinda** Colón 424 ☎ 0261 429 3075, ⓦ govindavegetarian.com; map p.104. This highlight of this swish vegetarian restaurant is the gigantic buffet; you pay by the weight, and AR$120 or so will get you a hearty plateful. Plenty of vegan and gluten-free options, too. Mon–Sat 8.30am–midnight, Sun 9am–midnight.

La Marchigiana Patricias Mendocinas 1550 ☎ 0261 423 0751, ⓦ marchigiana.com.ar; map p.104. Widely considered the best Italian restaurant in the city, with quality food at reasonable prices (pasta mains AR$204–225). Daily noon–3pm & 8pm–12.30am.

El Mercadito Arístides Villanueva 521 ☎ 0261 463 8847, ⓦ elmercaditoar.com; map p.104. If you're all steaked out, this restaurant offers some welcome variety, with stir-fries and curries among the dishes on offer (mains around AR$200). Daily 11am–12.30am.

Mercado Central Las Heras between España and Patricias Mendocinas; map p.104. This bustling indoor market is full of inexpensive diners (and a mini food court) offering no-nonsense burgers, pizzas, *empanadas*, sandwiches and pasta dishes – you can get a decent feed for less than AR$100. Mon–Sat 8.30am–10pm, Sun 9.30am–1pm.

Tasca de la Plaza Montevideo 117 ☎ 0261 423 1403; map p.104. Flickering candles set off the wooden floorboards and bright-red walls covered with an eclectic array of art – pictures of bullfights, dogs playing poker, bottles of Jack Daniels, and so on – at this Spanish restaurant. As well as tasty tapas and paella, there's a good-value set lunch (AR$150). Mon–Sat 11am/noon–3pm & 8pm–midnight.

DRINKING AND NIGHTLIFE

Mendoza's bar scene is concentrated along bustling Aristides Villanueva, where pavement tables fill with drinkers on summer evenings. The best nightclubs are in outlying neighbourhoods like El Challao to the northwest, Las Heras to the north and Chacras de Coria to the south. Women generally get in free or for a reduced fee, and while *Mendocinos* like to party late, keep in mind that a city law stipulates that last entry is at 2.30am.

Believe Irish Pub Colón 241 ☎ 0261 429 5567; map p.104. Drawing travellers and locals alike, this joint shows international sport and has an economical happy hour (Tues–Fri 5–8pm) with offers such as two pints for AR$100. The burgers are highly rated, too, if you need something to soak up the alcohol. Mon, Sat & Sun 8.30pm–4.30am, Tues–Fri 12.30pm–4.30am.

Geo San Martín Sur 576 ☎ 0261 15 550 6042; map p.104. This club draws a cool crowd with a mix of EDM, reggaeton and rock DJs and groups. Fri & Sat 10pm–6.30am.

Hangar 52 Aristides Villanueva 168 ☎ 0261 666 1598; map p.104. This lively bar is often packed out with cool *Mendocino* kids drinking *cerveza artesenal* (from AR$80) from across the region and beyond, and mediocre cocktails. Mon–Thurs & Sun 6pm–2am, Fri & Sat 6pm–4am.

Wine Not? 25 de Mayo 917 ☎ 0261 565 8970, ⓦ winenotmendoza.com; map p.104. Forgive the pun: this centrally located wine bar is a fine place to sample some of the local vintages (glasses from AR$60; wine flights and snacks also available). Ring the buzzer to be let in. Daily 5–11pm.

SHOPPING

Handicraft Market Plaza Independencia. Craft stalls fill the square during the day every Fri, Sat & Sun.

Mendoza Plaza Av Acceso Este 3280 ⓦ mendozaplazashopping.com. This upscale shopping mall, to the east of the city centre, has around 200 shops and restaurants, plus a cinema. Daily 10am–10pm.

DIRECTORY

Banks and exchange Banco de la Nación Argentina accepts foreign cards and has branches across the city, including San Martín, at Gutierrez, and España 1275. Cambio Express, at Espejo 58, and Cambio Santiago, at Av San Martín 119, will exchange foreign cash.

Car rental Alamo Nacional Rent, Pvo de la Reta 928 (☎ 0261 429 3111, ⓦ alamo.com); Avis, Pvo de la Reta 914 (☎ 0261 420 3178, ⓦ avis.com); Hertz, Espejo 391 (☎ 0261 423 0225, ⓦ hertz.com.ar); Via Rent a Car, San Juan 931 (☎ 0261 429 0876, ⓦ viarentacar.com.ar).

Post office San Martín, at Colón.

Spanish school Intercultural, at Rep de Siria 241 (☎ 0261 429 0269, ⓦ spanishcourses.com.ar), offers a range of courses.

VISIT A VINEYARD

No trip to Mendoza is complete without visiting one or more of the region's **vineyards**. They are concentrated in Guaymallén, Maipú and in Luján de Cuyo, and dozens are open to the public. Some visits and tastings are free, but you're pointedly steered to a sales area at the end.

The easiest way to visit is on a tour with one of the city's travel agencies (see page 106), though you can also visit by car, by bus or even bike (note that the roads around Mendoza are very busy; ask in advance about the safest routes). Mendoza's tourist office (see page 104) has plenty of information.

Try and see different kinds of wineries, ranging from the old-fashioned, traditional *bodegas* to the highly mechanized, ultramodern producers; at the former you're more likely to receive personal attention and get a chance to taste finer wines.

CLIMBING ACONCAGUA

To trek or climb in the Parque Provincial Aconcagua between mid-November and mid-March, you need to obtain a **permit** (bring your passport) from the Dirección de Recursos Naturales Renovables (mid-March to mid-Nov Mon–Fri 8am–1pm; mid-Nov to mid-March Mon–Fri 8am–6pm, Sat & Sun 9am–1pm; ☎0261 425 8751), at San Martín 1143, 2nd floor, in Mendoza. Foreign trekkers pay between US$100 andch US$950 between December and March (depending on the date and length of trek). The rest of the year snow cover makes the climb extremely dangerous; the trekking/climbing fees at this time are US$500 to US$1200 plus a staggering US$30,000 deposit and climbers must apply for a special permit (for update see website ⓦaconcagua.mendoza.gov.ar).

ALTA MONTAÑA

The cathedral-like peaks of the Parque Provincial Aconcagua lie just three hours west of Mendoza, easily visited on a popular day-trip dubbed the **ALTA MONTAÑA ROUTE**. Leaving behind verdant vineyards and climbing into barren hills, this scenic excursion follows the RN7 (the highway to Santiago de Chile), following the former Trans-Andean railway and the Río Mendoza into the spectacular Uspallata Valley, where *Seven Years in Tibet* was filmed. From the crossroads village of Uspallata (105km west of Mendoza), it's a further 65km to **Los Penitentes**, a winter ski resort with 28 pistes (☎0261 429 9953, ⓦlospenitentes.com), and, in summer, a base for Aconcagua climbers (see page 107). Some 6km west of Los Penitentes is one of the area's most photographed landmarks, the **Puente del Inca**, a natural stone bridge traversing the Río de las Cuevas at 2700m. Beneath it, thermal waters seep among the ruins of an abandoned 1940s spa resort. The route passes Parque Provincial Aconcagua and ends at the Chilean border where a statue of **Cristo Redentor** (Christ the Redeemer) commemorates the 1902 peace pact between historic enemies.

PARQUE PROVINCIAL ACONCAGUA

At 6959m, **CERRO ACONCAGUA** – "the roof of the Americas" – lords it over the 710-square-kilometre Parque Provincial Aconcagua. The highest mountain in both the western and the southern hemispheres, Aconcagua's faces are ringed by five glistening glaciers. In 1985, the discovery of an **Inca mummy** at 5300m on Aconcagua's southwest face lent further weight to the theory that the Incas worshipped the mountain and offered it human sacrifices.

Inca worshippers have been replaced by ardent mountain climbers, who ascend in droves throughout summer. Only the most experienced attempt the **climb** without a professional guide. Taking into account acclimatization time, it should take at least thirteen days to reach the summit. There are three possible routes – south, west or east – with the least difficult being the western route, leaving from the Plaza de Mulas (4230m). For **route details** and advice, see ⓦaconcagua. mendoza.gov.ar. Easier **day hikes** are also possible in the park as well as multi-day treks to base camps and mountain *refugios*.

ARRIVAL AND TOURS

By bus Buttini (ⓦabuttini.com) operates three buses daily (around 4hr) from Mendoza to the base camps at Los Horcones and Punta de Vacas.

Tour operators Owing to the Cerro Aconcagua's unpredictable weather (storms claim lives every year), climbers are highly advised to go on organized trips with experienced local guides. The following are Mendoza-based operators that specialize in Aconcagua trips: Acomara (Rivadavia 430; ☎0261 425 1983, ⓦaconcaguaexpeditions. com); Aymara (see page 105); Fernando Grajales Expeditions (☎0261 428 3157, ⓦgrajales.net); and Inka Expediciones (Juan B. Justo 345 ☎0261 425 0871, ⓦinka. com.ar). Fernando Grajales Expeditions can arrange mule hire, if needed.

ACCOMMODATION

For accommodation at or near the base camps, there are several options at Puente del Inca (where many people spend a couple of days acclimatizing), Las Cuevas and Los Penitentes.

Hostel Campo Base Penitentes Los Penitentes ☎0261 425 5511, ⓦpenitentes.com.ar. This lively, 28-bed hostel, with well-equipped kitchen, is a jumping-off

1

point for organized ski trips in the winter and Aconcagua climbs in the summer. Half-board costs an extra AR$350. Dorms AR$300

Refugio El Nico Ruta 7 s/n Puente del Inca ☎0261 592 0736. A small and simple hostel just 1.5km from the Aconcagua park entrance. It has heated dorms and private twins/doubles communal bathrooms, plus a kitchen and lounge. Excursions can be arranged in summer and winter. Dorms AR$375, doubles AR$750

EATING AND DRINKING

Make the most of hostel kitchens, and bring plenty of food supplies with you, as refuelling opportunities are few and far between once inside the park itself. During ski season, the resort hotels of Penitentes offer decent, if unspectacular, food, while snacks and hot drinks can be found at Puente del Inca's outdoor market.

SAN RAFAEL AND AROUND

In the heart of wine country, the laidback city of **SAN RAFAEL**, 230km south of the provincial capital, likes to think of itself as a smaller, friendlier version of Mendoza; its wide, flat streets are filled with cyclists and its leafy plazas are squeaky clean. The city itself offers few distractions, beyond strolling around the main square, **Plaza San Martín**, and visiting the **Museo de Historia Natural** (daily 8am–7pm; AR$5), on Isla Diamante, 6km south of the centre, where the pre-Columbian displays include ceramics from Ecuador and a mummified child dating from 40 AD.

There are, however, worthwhile sights just beyond the city itself in the San Rafael department, including six hundred square kilometres of vineyards and around eighty **bodegas**. Most of the wineries are small, family-run affairs; the tourist office has a list of those open to the public. For **whitewater rafting** enthusiasts, the **Cañon del Atuel**, a short journey to the southwest, is one of the top destinations in the country for riding the rapids.

ARRIVAL AND DEPARTURE

By plane San Rafael Airport is 5km west of downtown, with one daily flight to/from Buenos Aires (1hr 30min). A taxi into town costs around AR$100.

By bus The centrally located bus terminal is at Géneral Paz, at Av Granaderos.

Destinations Buenos Aires (4 daily; 13hr); Las Leñas (June–Sept 1 daily, Dec–Feb 3 weekly on Tues, Thurs & Sat; 2hr

40min); Malargüe (8–9 daily; 2hr 40min); Mendoza (hourly; 3hr 30min).

INFORMATION AND TOURS

Tourist information The friendly tourist office is on Av Hipólito Yrigoyen, at Balloffet (daily 8am-9pm; ☎0260 442 4217, ⊚sanrafaelturismo.gov.ar).

Tour operator Risco Viajes (Av San Martin 261 ☎0260 443 6439) is a San Rafael-based tour operator for adventurous types. Offers wine-tasting, climbing and mountain-biking trips.

ACCOMMODATION

Sadly San Rafael's budget accommodation options lack the range and quality of Mendoza.

Camping El Parador Isla Río Diamante, 6km south of downtown, ☎0260 443 6756. The shady site offers both camping spot and simple apartments sleeping up to four, and a range of facilities. Camping/person AR$100, apartments AR$500

Tierrasoles Hostel Alsina 245 ☎0260 443 3449, ⊚tierrasoles.com.ar. An HI affiliated hostel offering up modest dorms and private rooms. You have to be a contortionist to use the toilets, though. Dorms AR$230, doubles AR$500

Trotamundos Hostel Barcala 298 ☎0260 443 2795, ⊚trotamundoshostel.com.ar. A cool hostel in a converted historical building with a four- to six-bed dorms, private rooms, large, open-plan kitchen and plenty of activities laid on. Dorms AR$180, doubles AR$420

EATING

San Rafael springs to life post-siesta, when locals pack out the restaurants, bars, nightclubs and ice-cream parlours along Hipólito Yrigoyen.

★ **El Antojo del Concinero** Balofet 173 ☎0260 442 3264. Easily the best restaurant in San Rafael, serving delicious humitas (savoury cakes of steamed corn) and hearty contemporary dishes (from AR$200). It's popular, so make sure you book ahead. Tues–Sat 9pm–midnight.

Jockey Club Belgrano 330 ☎0260 443 0237. With an appealing Old-World feel, this much-loved restaurant serves well-prepared, filling if not particularly exciting mains (AR$180–250) including good pasta, beef and chicken dishes. Daily 9–11pm.

Pettra Hipólito Yrigoyen 1750 ☎0260 443 9837. The most popular *parrilla* in the city, where you can tuck into a massive steak (from AR$200) straight from the *asado* and wash it down with local wine. Mon–Wed 8.45pm–12.30am, Thurs–Sun 12.30–3pm & 8.45pm–12.30am.

Tienda del Sol Hipólito Yrigoyen 1663 ☎0260 442 5022, ⊚tiendadelsol.net. A modern restaurant with outdoor tables, serving imaginative (for San Rafael) beef, chicken and fish mains (AR$180–270), along with a wide range of regional wines. Daily noon–2.30pm & 8.30pm–12.30am.

LAS LEÑAS

Some 180km southwest of San Rafael and 445km south of Mendoza, the exclusive ski resort of **LAS LEÑAS** is to winter what Uruguay's Punta del Este (see page 853) is to summer – a chic party playground for *porteño* socialites. Between June and September (snow permitting), they flock here on week-long packages. As well as après-ski glamour, the setting of Las Leñas is exquisite. The resort, which sits at 2240m, has the dramatic Cerro Las Leñas (4351m) towering over its 29 runs and 13 lifts. Pistes range in difficulty from nursery slopes to hair-raising black runs, with night-time and cross-country skiing also possible.

In summer, Las Leñas transforms into an outdoor action hub, offering horseriding, whitewater rafting, trekking, climbing, abseiling, 4WD tours, mountain biking, summer skiing and even scuba diving in high-altitude lakes.

ARRIVAL AND INFORMATION

By bus During the ski season there are daily buses from Mendoza (1 daily; 6hr), Malargüe (1 daily; 1hr 30min) and San Rafael (1 daily; 3hr); travel agencies in all three places also put on minibuses.

Tourist information The resort's office for booking ski packages and accommodation is in Buenos Aires at Bartolomé Mitre 401, 4th floor (Mon–Fri 9am–7pm; ☎011 4819 6060, ⓦlaslenas.com).

Lift ticket office Mid-June to late Sept daily 8.30am–5.30pm (☎0260 447 1100 ext 1130, ⓦlaslenas.com). Daily lift ticket prices range seasonally from AR$860 to AR$1270.

ACCOMMODATION AND EATING

Las Leñas accommodation needs to be booked through the resort's central Buenos Aires office (see page 62); there is only one low-priced lodging.

Innsbruck ☎02627 471100 ext. 1206. A log-cabin *confitería* in the ski village where you can buy fast food, pasta and stews (around AR$100–250) to enjoy over a beer from a terrace with piste views. Open for breakfast, lunch and dinner, as well as cocktails until the small hours. Daily 8am–late (winter only).

Leñas Hostel ☎0260 447 1172 ⊖hostel@laslenas. com. This modern 72-bed hostel is Las Leñas' only budget accommodation, so book ahead if you're tight on cash but not keen on commuting to get to the slopes. It has dorms with all the basic amenities: lockers, shared kitchen and communal bathrooms and showers. Dorms AR$410

UFO Point ☎02627 471100 ext. 1233. The appetizing pizzas served here have earned this restaurant a devoted

following, but they're not cheap (from AR$200). The restaurant is open for breakfast, lunch and dinner; at night it turns into a nightclub. Daily 10am–6am (winter only).

MALARGÜE

Set at the arid base of the Andes, 186km southwest of San Rafael, **MALARGÜE** is a small, nondescript town that's a jumping-off point for some of Argentina's most remarkable scenery. In winter its *raison d'être* is as an affordable base for **skiing** at the resort of Las Leñas (see page 109), while in summer the surrounding landscape offers ample opportunities for hiking, horseriding, fishing and whitewater rafting. Worthwhile day-trips from town are to the underground limestone caves of **Caverna de las Brujas** (73km southwest), the volcanic wonderland of **La Payunia** (208km south), and to **Laguna de Llancanelo** (see page 110).

WHAT TO SEE AND DO

Malargüe's flat, compact centre is easy to get your head around: the wide main drag is the RN40, known in town as **Avenida San Martín**. Here you'll find the tourist office, shops and the main square, **Plaza General San Martín**. Just south of the tourist office is the landscaped greenery of **Parque del Ayer** ("Park of Yesteryear"), filled with sculptures and native trees. Opposite, you can take a free guided tour at the **Observatorio Pierre Auger** (Mon–Fri 9am–12.30pm & 3–6.30pm, Sat & Sun 10am–12.30pm & 4–6.30pm; free; ☎0260 447 1562, ⓦauger.org.ar), an astrophysics centre that studies cosmic rays.

ARRIVAL AND DEPARTURE

By bus Malargüe's bus terminal (☎0260 447 0690) is on Av Gral Roca, at Esquibel Aldao, five blocks south and three west of Plaza San Martín.

Destinations Las Leñas (1 daily during ski season; 1hr 30min); Mendoza (3 daily; 6hr); San Rafael (8–9 daily; 2hr 40min).

INFORMATION AND TOURS

Tourist information The tourist office (daily 8am–9pm; ☎0260 447 1659, ⓦmalargue.tur.ar) is on the RN40 four blocks north of the plaza.

Tour operators Many local companies run tours to La Payunia, Laguna de Llancanelo (when not dried out) and

1

Caverna de las Brujas, as well as horseriding and other adventure activities. Check out the well-established Karen Travel at Av San Martín 54 (☎0260 447 2226, ⓦkarentravel.com.ar), where you can also rent 4WDs.

ACCOMMODATION AND EATING

Malargüe has plenty of affordable places to stay, including some well-run hostels. Prices rise significantly during winter, when it's wise to book ahead.

El Bodegón de Maria Rufino Ortega, at General Villegas ☎0260 447 1655. Trout, beef and chicken get all the attention at this welcoming rustic-style restaurant. Mains from AR$180 Daily noon–4pm & 8pm–midnight.

Cuyam-Co 8km west of Malargüe in El Dique ☎0260 15 466 1917. Catch your own meal (around AR$200) and have it cooked to perfection at this commercial trout farm. It's popular, so book ahead. Daily 12.30–2.30pm & 8pm–late.

EcoMalargüe Posada & Hostel Colonia Pehuenche I, Finca N. 65, 5km south of town (ask them for a taxi number for the transfer when booking) ☎0260 15 440 2439, ⓦhostelmalargue.com. There's some serious stargazing and R&R to be had at this rustic HI-affiliated hostel and guesthouse set on an organic farm. Home-made meals and horseriding excursions offered. Dorms AR$450, doubles AR$1500

Hostel La Caverna Cte Rodríguez 445 Este ☎0260 447 2569. This hostel has a spacious communal area and plenty of dorm beds. The self-catering apartment out back is ideal for groups. There is laundry service. Dorms AR$260, doubles AR$800

Hotel Rioma Fray Incalan 68 ☎0260 447 1065, ⓦhotelrioma.com.ar. Reasonable, if rather nondescript mid-range hotel in the town centre. There's an outdoor pool, and the owner lays on barbecues on request. AR$1100

AROUND MALARGÜE

Some 65km southeast of Malargüe is the nature reserve of **LAGUNA DE LLANCANELO**, a vast high-altitude lagoon famous for its abundant birdlife. Alongside the flamingos that flock here in their thousands, herons and black-neck swans can be easily spotted. Also look out for the *coipo*, a rodent similar in appearance to the capybara but a little smaller in size. The best way to visit the reserve is with a guided tour (see above); note, however, that it can become dried out, so check with operators on its condition.

The **CAVERNA DE LAS BRUJAS** ("Witches' Cave") is an incredible limestone cave filled with mesmerizing many-coloured rock formations, including **stalactites** and **stalagmites**. The cave, located 73km southwest of Malargüe and 8km along a dirt road off the RN40, is within a provincial park and is staffed by *guardaparques*. Guided visits (AR$150) are restricted to nine people at a time and are the only way to see the various underground chambers. The **temperature** inside the grotto can be 20°C lower than outside, so be sure to wrap up warm.

Continuing along the RN40, you'll reach the entrance to **LA PAYUNIA** at El Zampal. This expansive, wildlife-rich reserve spans 4500 square kilometres. Flaxen grasslands, black lava flows and eight hundred threatening-looking volcanoes (the highest concentration of volcanic cones in the world) provide a starkly wild backdrop for the guanaco, puma and condor that call it home. The best way to see La Payunia is on an organized **day-trip from Malargüe** (see page 109) that takes in the Caverna de las Brujas along the way.

SAN JUAN

SAN JUAN is a modern, low-rise provincial capital. In 1944, one of South America's most powerful earthquakes (8.5 on the Richter scale) razed the city, killing more than ten thousand people. Essentially a poorer, smaller and less attractive version of its southerly neighbour Mendoza, San Juan is unlikely to capture your imagination. It does, however, make a convenient base for sampling the fruits of nearby wineries as well as for excursions to the sculptural desert landscapes of **Parque Provincial Ischigualasto** and the surreal rock formations of **Parque Nacional Talampaya**. Try to avoid visiting in the summer, when *Sanjuaninos* cope with the midday heat by taking long, sluggish siestas.

WHAT TO SEE AND DO

The leafy Plaza 25 de Mayo, flanked by a couple of inviting cafés, marks the city centre. On its northwestern side, the modern cathedral's 50m-high brick campanile is a nod to St Mark's in Venice. If the mood takes, climb the **bell tower** (daily 9am–1pm & 5–9pm; AR$20) for great city and countryside vistas. Not far away at Sarmiento 21 Sur, opposite the tourist office, is the whitewashed childhood home of former Argentine president **Domingo Faustino Sarmiento** (1811–88), now a museum (Mon–Fri 9am–8.30pm, Sat & Sun 10.30am–4pm; free; guided tours every hour; ☎0264 422 4603, ⓦcasanatalsarmiento.cultura.gob.ar). Although damaged in the 1944 earthquake, the house has been lovingly restored and displays belongings and paraphernalia from Sarmiento's eventful life.

For a more artistic day head to **Museo Franklin Rawson**, Av Libertador 862 Oeste (Tues–Sun: summer noon–9pm, winter noon–8pm; guided tours: summer 7pm, winter 6pm; AR$30; ☎0264 420 0598, ⓦmuseofranklinrawson.org), where fine art and contemporary photography by local and national artists are displayed in an airy glass-walled building.

Finally, if all that has left your mouth dry, drop into the historic **Bodega Graffigna** (Thurs–Sat 11am–4pm; free; ☎0264 421 4227, ⓦgraffignawines.com), at Colón 1342 Norte, which houses the Museo de Vino Santiago Graffigna, and a wine bar where you can sample some provincial vintages.

ARRIVAL AND DEPARTURE

By plane Las Chacritas Airport (☎0264 425 4134) is 12km east of the city centre. A taxi downtown costs around AR$150.
Destinations Buenos Aires (3–4 daily; 1hr 50min); Santiago de Chile (3 weekly; 2hr 10min).
By bus The bus station (Estados Unidos 492 Sur; ☎0264 422 1604) is eight blocks east of Plaza 25 de Mayo. Most long-distance buses, including to Santiago de Chile, require a change in Mendoza.
Destinations Buenos Aires (10 daily; 16hr); Córdoba (5 daily; 8hr 30min–10hr); Mendoza (hourly; 2hr 30min); San Rafael (2 daily; 5hr 45min); Valle Fértil (3 daily; 4hr).

INFORMATION AND TOURS

Tourist information The tourist office at Sarmiento 24 Sur has good city and provincial information (daily 8am–8pm; ☎0264 421 0004, ⓦturismo.sanjuan.gov.ar).
Tour operators Companies offering trips to Ischigualasto and Talampaya include CH Travel, at Gral Acha 714 Sur (☎0264 427 4160, ⓦchtraveltur.com), and Yafar Destinos, at Rioja 428 Sur (☎0264 420 4052, ⓦyafardestinos.com.ar).

ACCOMMODATION

Camping Municipal Rivadavia RP-12 ☎0264 433 2374. Opposite the racetrack, this campsite has good facilities, including a swimming pool. Camping/person **AR$150**
Capital Hostel Ramón y Cajal 302 Norte ☎0264 421 0310, ⓦcapitalhostelsanjuan.com.ar. A friendly and well-run hostel, offering clean if compact bunk-bed dorms, though relatively little in the way of facilities. **AR$350**
Jardín Petit 25 de Mayo 345 Este ☎0264 421 1825, ⓦjardinpetithotel.com. A welcoming hotel with cosy, simple rooms (though they're much duller than the brightly coloured communal areas) and an inviting patio and pool. Discounts can sometimes be arranged. **AR$000**
San Juan Hostel Av Córdoba 317 Este ☎0264 4201 835. The plus points are helpful staff, a central location and a comfortable common area. The down sides are the basic, rather underwhelming four- to eight-bed dorms and private rooms, and the scruffy bathrooms. Dorms **AR$310**, doubles **AR$580**

EATING AND DRINKING

Antonio Gómez e Hijos Supermercado, General Acha at Córdoba. The heaving paellas (around AR$120) draw the lunchtime crowd at this Spanish-centric market stall. Mon–Sat noon–3.30pm.
★ **Ilinca** Morón 1301 Sur, Rivadavia, Marquesado ☎0264 416 2855. Located 10km west of the city centre, but well worth the journey, this outdoor bar-restaurant has a delightful atmosphere, with live music every evening and good pizzas. There are also several craft and art shops onsite, if you need to pick up a souvenir. Thurs–Sat 10am–1.30am.
Remolacha Av José Ignacio de la Roza Oeste, at Sarmiento ☎0264 422 7070. Traditional and hugely popular parrilla with a vast range of meaty treats to be enjoyed indoors or alfresco. Vegetarians won't starve either, thanks to some decent meat-free pasta dishes, mixed vegetable grills and interesting salads. Mains from AR$180. Daily noon–4pm & 8pm–3am.
El Rincón de Nápoli Rivadavia 175 Oeste ☎0264 422 7221. Noisy and cheerful fast-service restaurant serving up a steady supply of pizzas, pasta, burgers and grilled meat (mains from AR$120). Daily 7am–2am.
★ **Soychú** Av José Ignacio de la Roza 223 Oeste ☎0264 422 1939. Slip into something elasticated before gorging yourself on one of the continent's best vegetarian all-you-can-eat buffets, serving everything from bean burgers to pasta dishes (you can eat well for less than AR$150). The fresh juices are great too, and you can eat in or take away. Mon–Sat 8am–3pm & 4pm–1am, Sun 8am–3pm.

DIRECTORY

Banks and exchange HSBC at Gral Acha Sur 320; Banco de la Nación Argentina at Av Rioja Sur 218.

Car rental Avis, Sarmiento 164 Sur (☎0264 420 0571, ⓦavis.com).

Post office Av José Ignacio de la Roza 259 Este.

AROUND SAN JUAN

The UNESCO World Heritage-listed parks of **Ischigualasto** (better known as Valle de la Luna) and **Talampaya** lie in the provinces of San Juan and La Rioja respectively. The former is known for its other-worldly rock formations, the latter its red sandstone cliffs. Located close together, both can be visited on day-trips from San Juan, but the sleepy village of **San Agustín de Valle Fértil**, 250km northeast, is a much closer base. Some **tour operators** pack both parks into one day-long excursion, stopping off at Talampaya in the morning when the wind is low and the light best illuminates the red in the sandstone, before journeying 93km to visit Ischigualasto in the mid- to late afternoon.

SAN AGUSTÍN DE VALLE FÉRTIL

Set in a valley carved out by the Río San Juan and surrounded by olive groves and sheep and goat pasture, the town of **SAN AGUSTÍN DE VALLE FÉRTIL** is a verdant oasis amid desert-like terrain. Bring plenty of cash as the only ATM regularly runs dry and only a few places around town accept cards.

ARRIVAL AND INFORMATION

By bus The bus terminal is on Mitre, at Entre Rios; there are three daily services from San Juan (3hr 30min–4hr) and three weekly from La Rioja (4hr).

Tourist information The super-friendly tourist office (daily 7am–midnight; ☎02646 420 104, ⓦischigualastovallefertil.org) is at Plaza San Agustín, on General Acha, and can advise on tours and transport to the parks, as well as bicycle and horseriding excursions to view pre-Hispanic petroglyphs in the nearby mountains.

Tour operator Turismo Vesa, at Mitre s/n (☎02646 420 143), runs trips from Valle Fértil to Ischigualasto and Talampaya.

ACCOMMODATION

Altos del Valle Rivadavia 114 ☎02646 420 194, ⓦaltosdelvallesj.com.ar. A cosy and intimate apart-hotel with clean en-suite rooms, plus apartments sleeping up to four people. There is a peaceful garden with a small swimming pool in one corner. Doubles <u>AR$850</u>, apartments <u>AR$1550</u>

Camping Municipal Rivadavia, at Ischigualasto ☎0264 15 5172 411. Managed by a lovely couple, this campsite has the friendliest ambience in town. It is situated by the river and offers plenty of shade. Camping/person <u>AR$150</u>

Eco Hostel Mendoza 766 Norte ☎02646 420 147. A cooling swimming pool, an on-site bar and regular tango classes make this simple hostel, just two blocks from the bus station, a backpacker hit. Dorms <u>AR$180</u>, doubles <u>AR$430</u>

Hostería Valle Fértil Rivadavia 5400 ☎02646 420 015, ⓦalkazarhotel.com.ar. Seven blocks from the plaza on a breezy hillside overlooking the Dique San Agustín reservoir, this comfortable though slightly run-down complex has dorms, private rooms and pricey cabañas. There's a good restaurant (see below) and a pool. Dorms <u>AR$000</u>, doubles <u>AR$000</u>

EATING

Don't leave town without sampling the local cheese, or one of the roast-goat dishes.

La Cocina de Zulma Tucumán 1576 ☎0264 154 508 026. Steaks (from AR$190), *milanesas*, pastas and vast salads are the order of the day at this humble parrilla, opposite the petrol station on the edge of town. Daily noon–3pm & 8pm–late.

Hostería Valle Fértil Rivadavia 5400 ☎02646 420 015, ⓦalkazarhotel.com.ar. The restaurant here is open to non-guests in summer (for dinner only) and serves unpretentious dishes (AR$100–250) such as omelettes, salads and soups, as well as a tasty goat stew. Credit/debit cards accepted. Daily 8.30–11pm.

PARQUE PROVINCIAL ISCHIGUALASTO

Sculpted by more than two million years of erosion, wind and water, the **PARQUE PROVINCIAL ISCHIGUALASTO** (ⓦischigualasto.gob.ar), otherwise known as the Valle de la Luna (Moon Valley), is easily San Juan's most visited attraction. Set in a desert valley between two mountain ranges some 80km north of Valle Fértil, it is considered one of the most significant **dinosaur graveyards** on the planet. Skeletons dating from the Triassic era around two hundred million years ago have been unearthed here.

Given its size (150 square kilometres), you need a **car** to explore the park properly; rangers accompany visitors in convoy on a bumpy 45km circuit of the park's highlights (2–3hr), imparting explanations of its paleontological history, photogenic moonscapes and precarious sandstone rock formations. The southern section resembles the arid lunar landscapes of Cappadocia in Turkey, with surreally shaped rock formations dubbed El Submarino (the submarine), El Esfinge (the sphinx) and Cancha de Bolas (bowling alley); further north on the circuit lie stark white fields strewn with petrified tree trunks. If you're lucky, you might catch a glimpse of hares, red foxes, armadillos, lizards, guanacos, snakes and condors.

INFORMATION AND TOURS

Park information The park entrance, where there's a helpful *guardaparque* post, is along a signposted road off the RP510 at Los Baldecitos. Entrance (daily: April–Sept 9am–4pm; Oct–March 8am–5pm) is AR$300/person and includes a 3hr tour following a ranger in your own vehicle. An extra AR$200–300 buys you one of a range of special tours, including 2hr guided bicycle excursions, full-moon night tours and 3hr treks to the top of Cerro Morado (1748m), with tremendous views of the park. Make use of the toilet facilities and café at the entrance, as there are none within the park.

By bus The easiest way to visit the park is on an organized tour. To get there independently, Empresa Vallecito buses from San Juan to La Rioja run on Mon, Wed & Fri and pass the Los Baldecitos checkpoint, a 5km walk to the park entrance. It is sometimes possible to accompany rangers on a tour of the park, or hire a vehicle at the entrance, but always check this in advance before showing up.

ACCOMMODATION

Campers can pitch their tents for AR$150 next to the park visitors' centre, where there is also a bathroom and small café. Most people spend the night in nearby Valle Fértil (see page 112) and get a transfer to the park with one of the village's tour operators.

PARQUE NACIONAL TALAMPAYA

A familiar sight thanks to their regular appearances on posters promoting Argentine tourism, the smooth sandstone cliffs and surreal rock formations of

PARQUE NACIONAL TALAMPAYA

(w talampaya.gob.ar) are even more eye-boggling in reality. The centrepiece of the park is a 220-million-year-old **canyon**, with 180m-high rust-red sandstone cliffs rising on either side, rendering everything in between puny and insignificant. At the centre of the canyon, armadillos and grey foxes scurry among groves of cacti and native trees in a lush **botanical garden**. Elsewhere, erosion has carved out towering columns and gravity-defying **rock formations** where condors and eagles have found nesting sites. Other park highlights include a series of pre-Hispanic **petroglyphs** and **pictographs** etched onto gigantic rock faces. Thought to be around a thousand years old, the etchings depict llamas, pumas, hunters, stepped pyramids and phallic symbols.

INFORMATION AND TOURS

Park information The closest urban centre to the park is Villa Unión, an entirely forgettable town in La Rioja province, some 55km away along the RP26. Organized tours from San Juan, Valle Fértil or Villa Unión are the best option, as private vehicles are not allowed. If you want to visit the park independently, the *guardería* (daily: May–Oct 8.30am–4.30pm; Nov–April 8am–5pm; AR$250 entrance fee; ☎ 03825 470 397, w talampaya.com) is staffed year-round and you can explore on foot (not recommended) or take an excursion with an official guide in their truck (around AR$600); Talampaya (San Martin 80, Villa Unión, ☎ 0351 570 9909, w talampaya.com) offer tours from AR$595/person.

By bus Buses from Villa Unión to La Rioja and Valle Fértil can drop you off on the main road (check when the last bus goes past or you'll be stuck overnight).

ACCOMMODATION AND EATING

There is a basic, windswept campsite (free) next to the *guardería*; it can get brutally cold at night, and is not advised during the winter. A small kiosk here sells snacks and simple meals, but it's best to bring supplies with you.

The Lake District

The Argentine **LAKE DISTRICT** in northern Patagonia is an unspoiled region of azure glacial lakes, pristine rivers, snow-clad mountains, extinct volcanoes and verdant alpine forests. Dominated until the late nineteenth century by the indigenous Mapuche people, the Lake District is now Argentina's top year-round vacation destination – the place to go for hiking, camping, fishing, watersports, biking, climbing and skiing.

A series of spectacular national parks runs down the region's serrated Andean spine, providing easy access to the wilderness. The northernmost of Patagonia's national parks is **Parque Nacional Lanín** in Neuquén province, accessible from both the sleepy fishing town of **Junín de los Andes** or its dressier neighbour **San Martín de los Andes**. As you head south, the dazzling 110km route between San Martín de los Andes and the posh village of **Villa La Angostura** affords roadside vistas of snowcapped peaks reflected in picture-perfect lakes as well as the first glimpse of the gigantic **Parque Nacional Nahuel Huapi**.

The route continues south to the lakeside party city of **Bariloche**, the region's transport hub and base for hiking in **Nahuel Huapi** in summer, skiing in winter, and gorging on chocolate and craft beer all year round. Further south, in the province of Chubut, the dusty town of **Esquel** is within day-trip distance of the **Parque Nacional Los Alerces**, a dramatic wilderness area of lakes, rivers, glaciers and thousand-year-old alerce trees; it also boasts one of the world's most famous trains, the **Old Patagonian Express**.

PARQUE NACIONAL LANÍN

The imposing snow-clad cone of extinct Volcán Lanín rises 3776m at the centre of its namesake PARQUE NACIONAL LANÍN (☎0297 427233; AR$250). Lanín sits on the Chilean border, spanning 4120 square kilometres of varied Andean terrain. Fishing enthusiasts flock to its glacial lakes and trout-filled rivers, campers enjoy lakeside pitches at free or Mapuche-run campsites, while trekkers take advantage of the park's hiking trails. Forests of monkey-puzzle trees (also known as araucaria or *pehuén*) are the trademark of the northern section of the park. Volcano views are best from **Lago Huechulafquen**, 22km northwest of Junín de los Andes.

Lanín's southern sector is best explored from **San Martín de los Andes** (see page 116), set on the eastern shores of the park's **Lago Lácar**, or on the nearby section of the Seven Lakes Route (see page 118). Optimal visiting months are from October to mid-May, when there are organized excursions and regular buses.

JUNÍN DE LOS ANDES

It is impossible to avoid trout in pint-sized JUNÍN DE LOS ANDES; they not only populate the Río Chimehuín, but decorate every street sign and dominate every menu. Junín is well positioned for tours to the **Parque Nacional Lanín**, in particular the area around **Puerto Canoa**, the main base for treks around the volcano and boat trips on **Lago Huechulafquen**. Castelli (☎02972 491 557, ☯transportecastelli.com.ar) runs buses to Puerto Canoa from Junín twice daily in summer (1hr), skirting alongside the lake and passing campsites and fishing spots such as the **Boca del Chimehuin** along the way.

For something to do in town, take a stroll around the **Vía Christi** sculpture walkway, which starts at the base of Cerro de la Cruz, a fifteen-minute walk west of Plaza San Martín at the end of Avenida Antártida Argentina. A path winds through a pine-forested hillside dotted with sculptures and mosaics depicting the Stations of the Cross, which fuse Catholic and Mapuche symbolism. If you are thwarted by bad weather, check out the **Paseo Artesanal** instead. Behind the tourism office on the main square various cabins (generally daily 10am–1pm & 5–9pm) sell Mapuche crafts alongside woollen knits and handmade wooden crockery.

ARRIVAL AND INFORMATION

By plane Chapelco Airport (☎02972 428 388), which Junín shares with San Martín de los Andes, is 19km south of town. A taxi to the centre costs around AR$350; on your return, the hourly bus run by Castelli between Junín and San Martín will drop you off at the airport on request.
Destination Buenos Aires (1 daily; 1hr 55min).

By bus The bus station is three blocks from the main square at Olavarría and F.S. Martín.
Destinations Neuquén (7 daily; 6hr); San Martín de los Andes (hourly; 1hr).

Tourist information The tourist office is opposite Plaza San Martín (Padre Milanesio, at Coronel Suárez; daily 8am–9pm; ☎02972 491 160, ☯turismo.junindelosandes.gov.ar). Next door is the helpful Parque Nacional Lanín information office where you can register for hikes to Volcán Lanín (Mon–Fri 8am–3pm; ☎02972 492 748).

ACCOMMODATION AND EATING

Hotel prices hit Andean peaks in the summer, when advance bookings are recommended. Junín's culinary offerings

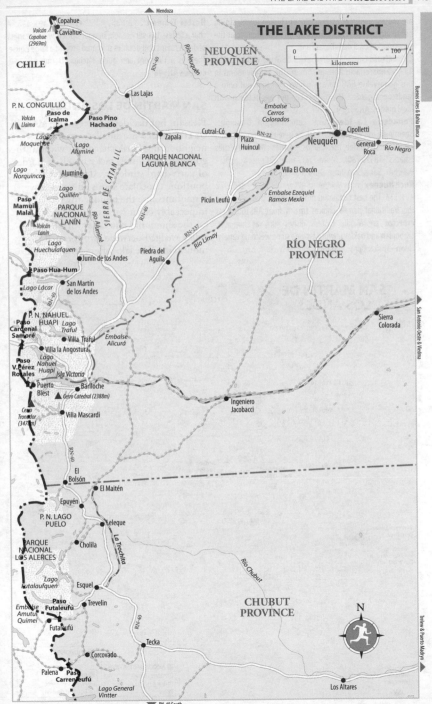

THE LAKE DISTRICT

NEUQUÉN PROVINCE

0   100
kilometres

CHILE

Volcán Copahue (2969m)
Copahue
Caviahue

Río Neuquén

RN-40

Embalse Cerros Colorados

P. N. CONGUILLÍO
Paso de Icalma
Volcán Llaima
Paso Pino Hachado

Las Lajas

Zapala
Cutral-Có
RN-22
Plaza Huincul
Neuquén
Cipolletti
General Roca
Río Negro

Lago Moquehue
Lago Aluminé

PARQUE NACIONAL LAGUNA BLANCA

Villa El Chocón

Lago Norquinco
Aluminé

Lago Quillén

Picún Leufú
Embalse Ezequiel Ramos Mexía

Paso Mamuil Malal
PARQUE NACIONAL LANÍN

RN-40

RÍO NEGRO PROVINCE

SIERRA DE CATAN LIL

RÍO ALUMINÉ

Volcán Lanín

Lago Huechulafquen

RN-237
Río Limay

Piedra del Aguila

Paso Hua-Hum
Junín de los Andes

Lago Lácar
San Martín de los Andes

Sierra Colorada

P. N. NAHUEL HUAPI
Lago Traful
Paso Cardenal Samoré
Villa Traful

Embalse Alicurá

Villa la Angostura
Lago Nahuel Huapi
Paso V. Pérez Rosales
Isla Victoria
Puerto Blest
Bariloche
Cerro Catedral (2388m)

Ingeniero Jacobacci

Cerro Tronador (3478m)
Villa Mascardi

RN-40

El Bolsón

El Maitén

Epuyén

P. N. LAGO PUELO
Leleque

PARQUE NACIONAL LOS ALERCES
Cholila

La Trochita

Río Chubut

Lago Futalaufquen

Esquel

Paso Futaleufú
Embalse Amutui Quimei
Trevelin

RN-40

CHUBUT PROVINCE

N

Futaleufú

Tecka

Corcovado

Palena
Paso Carrenleufú

Lago General Vintter

Los Altares

1

are mostly mediocre pizza, steak or chicken joints, strung out along the main road. Stock up on fresh produce at the supermarket on 9 de Julio, at Panil.

Chimehuín Coronel Suárez, at 25 de Mayo ☎02972 491 132, ⊗ hosteriachimehuin.com.ar. The homely rooms in this good-value B&B have windows that look out onto a landscaped garden. The owners can put you in touch with local guides. <u>ARS1350</u>

Panadería La Ideal Gral Lamadrid, at O'Higgins. Seemingly the whole town gathers here each morning and afternoon for coffee, *medialunas*, pastries and sandwiches (snacks ARS20–80). Mon–Fri 7am–1.30pm & 4.30–9.30pm, Sat & Sun 8am–1pm & 5–9.30pm.

Ruca Hueney Padre Milanesio, at Coronel Suárez ☎02972 491 113. The best restaurant in town serves trout alongside the traditional *parrilla* choices (mains from ARS160). Less expected are Middle Eastern dishes such as hummus, tabbouleh and baklava, which provide some welcome variety. Noon–3pm & 8pm–midnight; closed Wed.

Hostel Tromen Lonquimay 195 ☎02972 491 498. A characterless but serviceable budget option with a variety of dorm rooms and doubles scattered around a large house. There is a TV room and guest kitchen. Dorms <u>ARS150</u>, doubles <u>ARS480</u>

SAN MARTÍN DE LOS ANDES

Pleasant but decidedly pricey, **SAN MARTÍN DE LOS ANDES** is a smaller version of neighbouring Bariloche, albeit without the gobsmacking vistas, tacky hotels or hordes of party-hard students. Alpine-style chalets, boutique chocolate shops and expensive restaurants line the holiday town's impeccably clean streets. San Martín is set on the shores of **Lago Lácar**, in a peaceful valley wedged between two forested mountains. The lake offers great summer

SAN MARTÍN DE LOS ANDES

ACCOMMODATION
Camping Lolen   3
Laura   2
Puma   1

DRINKING
Downtown Matias   1

EATING
Corazón Contento   1
La Fondue de Betty 2

splashing, while hiking and biking trails lead off to lakeside viewpoints.

WHAT TO SEE AND DO

The **Museo de los Primeros Pobladores** (Tues–Sat 9am–1pm, Sun 7–9pm; free; ☎02972 428 676), set in a 1930s wooden house on the main plaza, puts the area in a historical context with changing exhibitions. If you're here in winter (June–Oct) and wondering where all the people are, your answer may lie 19km south on the slopes of **Cerro Chapelco** (☎02972 427 845, ⓦchapelco.com), where there are 29 ski runs, excellent options for beginners and a snowboard park and night skiing. San Martín is also the northern starting or finishing point for the **Seven Lakes Route** (see page 118).

ARRIVAL AND DEPARTURE

By plane Chapelco Airport (☎02972 428 388) is 25km from town, with minibus connections to the centre (around AR$100); a taxi costs around AR$350. If flying out of Chapelco, the hourly bus to Junín (run by Castelli) will drop you off at the airport on request.
Destinations Buenos Aires (1 daily; 1hr 55min).
By bus The bus terminal is on General Villegas between Juez del Valle and Coronel Diaz.
Destinations Bariloche (7 daily; 4hr); Junín de los Andes (hourly; 1hr); Villa La Angostura (7 daily; 2hr 30min).

INFORMATION AND TOURS

Tourist information The helpful tourist office is on San Martín, at J.M. de Rosas (daily 8am–9pm; ☎02972 427 347, ⓦsanmartindelosandes.gov.ar/turismo). For trekking and camping maps as well as general park information, head to the Intendencia del Parque Nacional Lanín, on Perito Moreno, at Eduardo Elordi (daily 8am–6pm; ☎02972 420 664).
Tour operator Pleasure boats run by Naviera Lacar Nonthue (☎02972 427 380), based at the lake pier, depart for excursions to Paso Hua-Hum near the Chilean border (1 daily; AR$900) and to the bay of Quila Quina on Lácar's southern shore (6 daily; AR$300).

ACCOMMODATION

San Martín's prices reflect its popularity with the Argentine elite. Advance reservations are recommended during the height of summer and in the ski season, when prices can double. Backpackers can choose from a handful of good hostels, although even here, prices are inflated.
Camping Lolen 4km southwest of town; map p.116. The pick of the town's three campsites is run by the Curruhuinca Mapuche community. The site is beautifully

positioned on the lake at Playa Catritre. Camping/person **AR$180**
Laura Misionero Mascardi 632 ☎02972 426 475; map p.116. If you want a little comfort and privacy without breaking the bank, the simple rooms in this unassuming wooden house are a good bet. **AR$900**
Puma Fosberry 535 ☎02972 422 443, ⓦpumahostel.com.ar; map p.116. A serviceable enough hostel with no-frills dorms, kitchen, laundry and plenty of party potential. Dorms **AR$350**, doubles **AR$900**

EATING

Dining out is an expensive pastime in San Martín, but generally worth every peso.
Corazón Contento San Martín 467 ☎02972 412 750; map p.116. Bustling café and takeaway offering a wide variety of filling sandwiches and burgers, though the generously stuffed veggie quiches are the biggest hits with locals (around AR$100). Jan–March & July–Oct 9am–midnight; April–June, Nov & Dec Mon–Sat 9am–midnight.
La Fondue de Betty Villegas 586 ☎02972 422 522; map p.116. Warm your hands on a fondue pot at this intimate restaurant. Cheese, meat and chocolate fondue are served up by the owners, alongside French favourites like beef bourguignon. Cheese fondue for two people from around AR$600. Daily 7.30–11pm.

DRINKING

Downtown Matias San Martín 598 ⓦdowntownmatias.com; map p.116. The owners have aimed for a "mountain Irish pub" feel, and pretty much succeeded. This is the location for the town's (fairly limited) nocturnal action. Daily 8pm–late.

VILLA LA ANGOSTURA

A hit with well-heeled Argentines, **VILLA LA ANGOSTURA** is a lovely little wooden village spread loosely along the northern shores of Lago Nahuel Huapi. It makes a tranquil alternative to Bariloche and is the obvious place to stay overnight before taking a stroll in the unique woodlands of **Parque Nacional Los Arrayanes**. Most of the village's shops and restaurants are in the commercial area known as **El Cruce**, spread along Avenida Arrayanes, a squeaky-clean main street with twee log-cabin buildings. Heading 3km downhill from here, along Boulevard Nahuel Huapi, you'll find a handful of pretty lakeside teahouses known as **La Villa**, as well as two jetties and the entrance to Parque Nacional Los Arrayanes.

1

Ten kilometres northeast of town is **Cerro Bayo** (Ⓦcerrobayoweb.com), a lovely small winter ski resort that caters for hikers and mountain bikers in the summer. Villa La Angostura is also the southern start (or end) point for the scenic Seven Lakes Route (see page 118), which heads north to San Martín de los Andes.

PARQUE NACIONAL DE LOS ARRAYANES

A mini-park nestled within the mammoth Parque Nacional Nahuel Huapi (see page 123), the **PARQUE NACIONAL DE LOS ARRAYANES** (daily: 9am–2pm if arriving by land, till 6pm if arriving by boat; AR$250) lies on Península Quetrihué, which dips into **Lago Nahuel Huapi** from Villa La Angostura. Its key feature is the **Bosque de los Arrayanes** at the peninsula's tip. The *bosque* (wood) hosts the world's last stand of rare *arrayán* myrtle woodland, where some of the trees are more than 650 years old. The myrtle's corkscrew-like trunks, terracotta-coloured bark and white flowers are a stunning contrast to blue sky or the shimmering lake.

To **get to Bosque de los Arrayanes**, you can either hike, bike or take a boat. To hike, follow the undulating trail (12km one-way) from the park entrance to the end of the peninsula; allow for a five- to six-hour round trip. Cycling is allowed on the trail; bikes can be rented at half-a-dozen places in Villa La Angostura. Leave early to get to the *bosque* before the catamarans full of tourists arrive at about 11.30am.

ARRIVAL AND INFORMATION

By bus The bus station is at Av Siete Lagos 35, just uphill from the main avenue.

Destinations Bariloche (10 daily; 1hr 30min); San Martín de los Andes (4 daily; 2hr 30min).

Tourist information You can pick up a map and organize accommodation at the tourist office (daily 8am–10pm; ☎0294 449 4124, Ⓦvillalaangostura.gov.ar), at Av Arrayanes 9, next to the bus terminal.

GETTING AROUND

By boat Catamarans depart for Bosque de los Arrayanes from the two jetties that are right across from each other in La Villa – Bahía Mansa and Bahía Brava. Futaleufú (☎0294 4494 405) runs three daily boat trips from Mansa (AR$280), and Patagonia Argentina (☎0294 4494 463) two daily trips from Brava. It's also possible to visit the *bosque* on a boat trip from Bariloche, usually stopping off at Isla Victoria on the way (Ⓦturisur.com.ar).

ACCOMMODATION AND EATING

Built solely to accommodate tourists, Villa La Angostura is luxury central, with the most exclusive hotels hugging the lakeshore. Nevertheless there are some reasonable budget options. Most restaurants in town are of the high-end variety.

SEVEN LAKES ROUTE

The **Ruta de los Siete Lagos** is one of South America's most picturesque drives. It winds for 110km between San Martín de Los Andes and Villa La Angostura along the RN40 traversing the dense alpine forests, snowcapped Andean peaks, brilliant blue lakes, trout-stuffed rivers and plunging waterfalls of two magnificent Patagonian national parks – **Lanín** and **Nahuel Huapi**. In summer the road is lined by purple and yellow wild flowers, and the dramatic snow-covered mountains make the view in winter.

Seven principal photogenic **alpine lakes** are visible or accessible from the roadside. From north to south they are: Machónico, Falkner, Villarino, Escondido, Correntoso, Espejo and Nahuel Huapi. You can spend the night en route at numerous free and serviced lakeside campsites as well as at *refugios* and lodges. *Camping Lago Falkner* (AR$18/person; ☎0294 154 411 607, ☎0294 154 411 772) has lots of facilities, including a restaurant and shop, and is popular with Argentine students and young families, who come to cool off in the lake, camp and party. The first half of the road is paved, while the final stretch, between Lago Villarino and Lago Espejo, is a bumpy dirt track, with vehicles spewing up walls of blinding dust in their wake, though tarmac is gradually being applied. Regular buses run the route, though check you are going on the "7 Lagos" route rather than the "Rinconada" alternative route that some buses take between San Martín and Villa Angostura. La Araucana (Ⓦaraucana.com.ar) runs two minibus trips daily, picking up and dropping off on request along the way. Despite obvious hazards from rip-roaring cars and buses, the route is also extremely popular with cyclists. Check in with the tourism office before setting out in winter, as parts of the road can be closed due to snow.

Hostel La Angostura Barbagelata 157 ☎ 0294 4494 834, ⊕ hostellaangostura.com.ar. It's a short uphill walk west of Plaza San Martín to this enormous green house fronted by wind chimes. The comfortable dorms are en suite and the front room is a huge chill-out space, with pool table, TV lounge and kitchen. HI members get a discount, and staff can help with bike rental. Dorms AR$480, doubles AR$1260

Camping Unquehué 0.5km west of the bus station on Av Siete Lagos ☎ 0294 4494 103, ⊕ campingunquehue. com.ar. This very lovely spot is the closest campsite to downtown. It also has cabins sleeping up to four people. Camping/person AR$200, cabins AR$2000

Gran Nevada Av Los Arrayanes 106 ☎ 0294 4494 512. This bare-bones eatery is always full, thanks to the gigantic and economical portions of steaks, *milanesas*, pasta, etc (mains from AR$130). Daily noon–3.30pm & 8.30–11.30pm.

La Luna Encantada Belvedere 69 ☎ 0294 4825 999. Skip the usual dinners; the draw here is the wood-fired pizza (from AR$160). The locally smoked trout and salmon make for tasty, if unusual, toppings. Good veggie options, too. Tues–Sun 1–3.30pm & 8.30pm–midnight.

Verenas Haus Los Taiques 268 ☎ 0294 4494 467, ⊕ verenas-haus.com.ar. The town's most affordable B&B-style option offers six impeccable if somewhat dark doubles/ twins (ask for discounts in low season). The living room has a selection of board games to keep you occupied. AR$1200

BARILOCHE

Set on the southeastern shores of sparkling Lago Nahuel Huapi and framed by magnificent snowcapped Andean peaks, **BARILOCHE** has its breathtaking setting to thank for its status as one of Argentina's top holiday destinations. Locals will tell you that it is the country's most European or Swiss-tinged city, but Bariloche itself is a rather ugly hotchpotch of high-rise hotels, garish souvenir stores and faux chalets. That said, the lake and surrounding landscape are undeniably stunning – snowy evergreens in winter and covered with purple and yellow wild flowers in summer. The lake is at its best when the sun is reflecting off a placid, cobalt-blue surface, but it can rapidly transform into a tempestuous sea, lashing icy wind through the streets and sending every warm-blooded being indoors to drink hot chocolate or huddle around a pot of cheese fondue.

Aside from lake views, Bariloche's forte is as an **outdoor adventure** hub. The town's proximity to the lakes, mountains, forests and rivers of Parque Nacional Nahuel Huapi makes it one of the top spots in the country for whitewater rafting, zip-lines, kayaking, paragliding, mountain biking, trekking and climbing. In winter, the fun shifts to the nearby pistes of Cerro Catedral (see page 123). To avoid the crowds, come in **spring** or **autumn**.

WHAT TO SEE AND DO

Bariloche's heart is its **Centro Cívico**, a spacious plaza dominated by an equestrian statue of a defeated-looking General Roca. Forming a horseshoe around the square is a set of attractive, mid-twentieth-century public buildings constructed of local timber and green-grey stone, a collaboration between Ernesto de Estrada and famed Argentine architect Alejandro Bustillo, who also built the **cathedral** a few blocks away. On Centro Cívico, the worthwhile **Museo de la Patagonia** (Tues–Fri 10am–12.30pm & 2–7pm, Sat 10am–5pm; AR$80) traces the area's indigenous and European history, and has displays on Patagonian flora and fauna. Bariloche's main drag, **Calle Mitre**, runs east of the plaza.

In the height of summer, you might be tempted to dip a toe beneath the lake's icy surface; the most popular **beach** is rocky Playa Bonita, 8km west of town (buses #10, #20, #21 or #22), or, for a warmer and more secluded dip, head 13km southeast to Villa Los Coihues on Lago Gutiérrez (buses #41 or #50). Pick up a map and schedule for the useful network of municipal buses at the tourism office.

ARRIVAL AND DEPARTURE

By plane Bariloche Airport (☎ 029 444 0516) lies 14km east of the centre. Local bus #72 runs into town every couple of hours; a taxi will set you back around AR$400.
Destinations Buenos Aires (8–12 daily; 2hr); Córdoba (4 weekly; 2hr); El Calafate (1 daily; 1hr 45min); Rosario (2 weekly; 2hr 5min); Viedma (3 weekly; 1hr 25min).
By bus The bus terminal (☎ 0294 443 2860) is a couple of kilometres east of the centre. Local buses #10, #20 and #21 run into town along C Moreno; a taxi to the Centro Cívico costs AR$80–90. Many intercity buses also drop off at the C Moreno stop in the city centre, so check with your driver.
Destinations El Bolsón (15 daily; 2hr); Buenos Aires (11 daily; 21–24hr); El Calafate (1 daily; 28hr); Esquel (7–8 daily; 5hr); Mendoza (1–3 daily; 18hr); Puerto Madryn (2

1

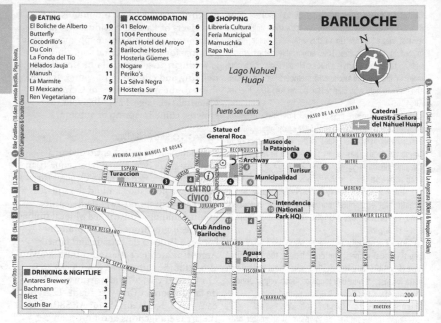

● EATING		■ ACCOMMODATION		● SHOPPING	
El Boliche de Alberto	10	41 Below	6	Librería Cultura	3
Butterfly	1	1004 Penthouse	4	Fería Municipal	4
Cocodrillo's	4	Apart Hotel del Arroyo	3	Mamuschka	2
Du Coin	2	Bariloche Hostel	5	Rapa Nui	1
La Fonda del Tío	3	Hosteria Güemes	9		
Helados Jauja	6	Nogare	7		
Manush	11	Periko's	8		
La Marmite	5	La Selva Negra	2		
El Mexicano	9	Hosteria Sur	1		
Ren Vegetariano	7/8				

BARILOCHE

Lago Nahuel Huapi

■ DRINKING & NIGHTLIFE	
Antares Brewery	4
Bachmann	3
Blest	1
South Bar	2

daily; 12–14hr); Puerto Montt in Chile (3 daily; 7–8hr); San Martín de Los Andes (7 daily; 4hr); Trelew (2 daily; 11hr 30min–13hr); Villa La Angostura (10 daily; 1hr 30min).

By boat Cruce de Lagos (☎ 011 5237 1246, ⚇ crucedelagos. com) organizes boat crossings (all year round; 12hr; US$491) from Bariloche to Puerto Varas in Chile (see page 438). The scenic journey cruises lakes Huapi, Frieas and Todos Los Santos, with the overland segments traversed by bus. Optional overnight stops at Puerto Blest and Peulla.

GETTING AROUND

By bus Annoyingly you need a Sube card (AR$45 for the card; you then need to top up with credit) to use the local buses (and those in Buenos Aires and Ushuaia). Local newsagents sell them.

INFORMATION AND TOURS

Club Andino Bariloche 20 de Febrero 30 (summer & winter daily 9am–9pm; rest of year Mon, Wed & Fri 9.30am–12.30pm & 5–8pm, Tues & Thurs 5–8pm; ☎ 0294 452 7966, ⚇ clubandino.org). The must-do stop before you set off hiking in Parque Nacional Nahuel Huapi (see page 123).

Intendencia del Parque Nacional Nahuel Huapi Av San Martín 24 (Mon–Fri 8am–5pm, Sat & Sun 10am–5pm; ☎ 0294 442 3111, ⚇ nahuelhuapi.gov.ar). Pick up official national park pamphlets here.

Tourist information The busy tourist office (daily 8am–9pm; ☎ 0294 442 9850, ⚇ barilocheturismo.go.ar) is in the

Centro Cívico; there's also a small booth in the bus station (same hours).

Tour operators Aguas Blancas, Morales 564 (☎ 0294 443 2799, ⚇ aguasblancas.com.ar) runs rafting excursions; Bike Cordillera at Av Bustillo Km18.6 (☎ 0294 452 4828, ⚇ apurabici.com) rents bicycles and runs half- and full-day cycling tours; Turaccion at San Martín 440 (☎ 0294 442 7507, ⚇ turaccion.com.ar) offers a range of backpacker-friendly excursions, including a four-day Ruta 40 trip to El Calafate in summer, and several horseriding excursions; Pura Vida (☎ 0294 441 4053, ⚇ puravidapatagonia.com. ar) offers kayaking and paddle-boarding trips on the lake; Turisur, at Mitre 219 (☎ 0294 442 6109, ⚇ turisur.com.ar), specializes in boat trips.

ACCOMMODATION

Bariloche's accommodation is among the most expensive in Argentina, and prices jump further in the high season (mid-Dec to Feb, July & Aug), when booking in advance is highly recommended. Many of the cabins and hotels that lie west of town along Av Bustillo offer great lake views and are a quieter alternative to staying in town. In the city itself there is a range of (generally) excellent and well-equipped hostels.

HOSTELS AND CAMPSITES

★**41 Below** Juramento 94 ☎ 0294 443 6433, ⚇ hostel41below.com; map p.120. A chilled-out, Kiwi-owned hostel with friendly staff and music grooving in its common area. Most dorms and doubles have partial lake views, as the hostel has a completely glass front. Ski/snowboard rental is available. Dorms AR$190, doubles AR$540

1004 Penthouse San Martín 127 ☎0294 443 2228, ⓦpenthouse1004.com.ar; map p.120. Despite the grandiose name, this is actually a hostel, albeit one offering panoramic mountain and lake vistas from the tenth floor of an apartment block. Travellers can hang out in the mellow living room, or watch the sunset – glass of *vino* in hand – from the balcony. The dorms and doubles, though, are not as stylish as the common area. Dorms AR$250, doubles AR$780

Bariloche Hostel Salta 528 ☎0294 442 5460, ⓦbarilochehostel.com.ar; map p.120. A nine-bedroom mountain-hut styled hostel with great lake views. A good place to come to relax in the small communal/kitchen area or on the wooden sun deck at the back. Dorms AR$200, doubles AR$800

Periko's Morales 555 ☎0294 452 2326, ⓦperikos.com; map p.120. Recharge your batteries at this rustic cabin with a big backyard swinging with hammocks. The four- and six-bed dorms are en suite and there are four bright doubles. Ski/snowboard hire and transfers are available. Dorms AR$250, doubles AR$850

La Selva Negra Av Bustillo, 3km west of town ☎0294 444 1013, ⓦcampingselvanegra.com.ar; map p.120. The *Black Forest* is the closest campsite to town, in an appropriately wooded location. Facilities include a wi-fi zone, bar/café and laundry. Discounts are available for multiple-night stays. Camping/person AR$260

HOTELS

Apart Hotel del Arroyo Av Bustillo Km4050 ☎0294 451 2391, ⓦdelarroyo.com.ar; map p.120. Located some 4km west of town, this is a good option for travellers with their own wheels. The spacious apartments are fully fitted, and sleep up to five people (the rate below is based on double occupancy). AR$1250

Hostería Güemes Güemes 715 ☎0294 442 4785, ⓦhosteriaguemes.com.ar; map p.120. A homely little guesthouse on a quiet residential street, with slightly cramped but comfortable enough en-suite rooms. AR$1150

Nogare Elflein 62 ☎0294 442 2438, ⓦhosterianogarebariloche.com; map p.120. A welcoming, centrally located budget hotel, with five pleasant blue-and-white rooms, all with private bathrooms and TVs. AR$1350

Hostería Sur Beschtedt 101 ☎0294 442 2677; map p.120. This two-star hotel, near the church, may not be the most beautiful, and desperately needs a spruce up, but is clean, comfortable and friendly. Good-value singles, too. AR$1100

EATING

Eating out in Bariloche can be an expensive exercise, though there are a few good-value options. Germanic and central European dishes such as goulash and apple strudel feature heavily on menus, as does venison.

El Boliche de Alberto Elflein 158 ☎0294 443 1433; map p.120. Make a glutton of yourself at this popular *parrilla* that serves massive portions; be prepared to wait for a table (they don't take reservations). Steaks, lamb and chicken cost AR$200–360 (the full portions are big enough to share), with sides costing AR$105–120. There are several other branches around town, but this is the pick of the bunch. Daily noon–3pm & 8pm–midnight.

Cocodrillo's Mitre 5 ☎0294 442 6640; map p.120. No-frills, local joint that, despite its central location offers inexpensive (at least for Bariloche) meals such as trout in butter sauce, *milanesas*, and venison in a mushroom sauce (AR$120–200), plus pizzas (AR$140–260). Daily 10am–12.30am.

Du Coin Mitre 594 ☎0294 460 8137; map p.120. Narrow coffee bar, with only four tables, seats fashioned from coffee sacks, and excellent cappuccinos, teas, filled bagels, cakes, biscuits, and even "cruffins" (a muffin crossed with a croissant). Drinks cost AR$43–99. Mon–Fri 8am–8pm, Sat 9am–1pm & 5–9pm.

La Fonda del Tío Mitre 1130 ☎0294 443 5011, ⓦlafondadeltio.com.ar; map p.120. Packed to the fluorescent-lit rafters with ravenous locals, this unpretentious, economical diner does outstanding versions of Argentine staples (steaks, huge *milanesas*, gnocchi and so on; most mains around AR$200). Mon–Sat noon–3.30pm & 8pm–midnight.

★**Helados Jauja** Moreno 48 ☎0294 443 7888, ⓦheladosjauja.com; map p.120. In a country known for its ice cream, *Helados Jauja* is widely considered the best. Try the ristretto, boysenberry or *dulce de leche* with blackberries. Not to be missed, however cold it might be outside. Cones/cups from AR$50. Mon–Sat 10am–12.30am, Sun 10.30am–12.30am.

Manush Elflein 10 ☎0294 442 8905, ⓦcervezamanush. com.ar; map p.120. Lively pub-restaurant with a range of crowd-pleasing favourites including twelve types of burger (AR$168–215), plus pizzas, nachos and chicken pot pie, as well as its own microbrews (daily happy hour 5.30–8pm). Daily 5.30pm–3am.

La Marmite Mitre 329 ☎0294 442 3685, ⓦlamarmite. com.ar; map p.120. This old-fashioned *café*-restaurant strung with antlers is a bit of a wallet-sapper; cheese or chocolate fondues for two to three people will set you back AR$490–620, while mains such as goulash cost AR$220–400. If that's too steep, opt for a slice of black forest gateau or apple strudel (AR$90). Mon–Sat noon–midnight, Sun 8pm–midnight.

El Mexicano Morales 362 ☎0294 442 3128; map p.120. This colourful Mexican restaurant serves mains (AR$275–395) such as quesadillas, enchiladas and tacos, as delicious as they are generous. Arrive between 7 and 9pm for two-for-one cocktails. Daily 7pm–1am.

Ren Vegetariano San Martín 298 & Moreno 307 ☎0294 442 1165; map p.120. Economical meat-free

1

★ TREAT YOURSELF

Butterfly Hua Huan 7831, Playa Bonita ☎0294 446 1441, ⓦbutterflypatagonia.com.ar; map p. 120. *Butterfly* has caused quite a stir by serving Michelin-quality meals. The creative tasting menus change regularly; past dishes include *sous-vide* steak with mango pepper sauce and "white truffle air", and raspberry gazpacho with "*criolla* prawns". Expect to pay around AR$1000/person. Reservations essential. Mon–Sat 7.45–9.30pm.

restaurant, where you select from pizza, quiches, stir fries, salads and so on, and then pay by the weight. A good plateful costs around AR$150. San Martín branch daily 11am–11pm; Moreno branch Mon–Sat 11am–10pm.

DRINKING AND NIGHTLIFE

Exhaustion after a day on the slopes/rapids/trails leaves many travellers tucked in bed by 10pm, but those with more energy can enjoy any number of bars and after-midnight action in lakeside clubs. The city also has a flourishing craft beer scene, which you can sample at the bars below, as well as at *Manush* (see page 121), which has an award-winning milk stout.

Antares Brewery Elflein 47 ☎0294 443 1454; map p.120. Sip the Antares microbrews (around AR$95 a pint) at a comfortable pub right at the source. Decent pub snacks and mains (many of which feature beer as an ingredient) are on offer as well. Happy hour 6.30–8.30pm. Daily 5.30pm–3am.

Bachmann Elflein 90 ☎0294 442 2249, ⓦ ceveceriabachmann.com.ar; map p.120. This microbrewery and pub has a great range of beers and lagers, from India and American pale ales to cream stouts and pilsners. Happy hour Mon–Thurs & Sun 5–8pm & 11.30pm–12.30am, Sat & Sun 5–8pm only (pints from AR$56 during these times). Daily noon–1am.

Blest Av Bustillo Km11.6 ☎0294 446 1026 ⓦ cervezablest.com.ar; map p.120. This out-of-town brewpub – reputedly the first of its kind in Argentina – has an excellent selection of beers (from AR$80), including a potent raspberry-flavoured one, as well as Germanic snacks and meals. Daily noon–midnight.

South Bar Juramento 30 ☎0294 445 8222; map p.120. Locals and tourists meet at this no-frills Irish bar to sip inexpensive pints and mixed drinks (around AR$70). Stay out late until the tables are pushed aside and the dancing commences. Mon–Sat 7pm–4am, Sun 8pm–4am.

SHOPPING

Books Librería Cultura, San Martín 243 ☎0294 442 0193; map p.120. Stocks a small selection of English-language books and travel guides. Mon–Sat 9am–9pm.

Chocolate Calle Mitre has numerous chocolate shops selling eye-wateringly expensive gourmet chocolate (though not nearly as good as you get in Europe). The local favourite is Mamuschka (☎0294 442 3294, ⓦmamuschka. com; daily 8.30am–11pm; map p.120), at Mitre 216. Rapa Nui (ⓦchocolatesrapanui.com.ar; Mon–Thurs & Sun 8am–10.30pm, Fri & Sat 8am–11.30pm; map p.120), at Mitre 202, is another popular choice.

Markets The bustling Fería Municipal (known colloquially as Mercado de Artesanias; daily 10am–8pm; see page 120) is behind the Centro Cívico on Urquiza between Mitre and Moreno, and sells locally made crafts.

DIRECTORY

Car rental Avis, at San Martín 162 (☎0294 443 1648, ⓦandesrentacar.com.ar); Budget, at Mitre 717 (☎0294 442 2482, ⓦbudgetbariloche.com.ar).

Hospital Moreno 601 (☎0294 442 6100).

Police Centro Cívico (☎0294 442 2772).

Post office Moreno 175.

DAY-TRIPS FROM BARILOCHE

Most day-trips from Argentina's outdoor adventure capital involve conquering – or at least ogling – the nearby mountains, rivers and lakes. Outside the winter months, when **skiing at Cerro Catedral** reigns supreme, the most popular excursions are cycling or driving the scenic **Circuito Chico** route (see page 123), **whitewater rafting** on the class III–IV Río Manson some 80km southwest of Bariloche, and hiking in **Parque Nacional Nahuel Huapi** (see page 123). Local tour operators also offer kayaking, kitesurfing, paddleboarding, windsurfing, scuba diving, horseriding, canyoning, rock climbing, mountain biking, parapenting (paraskiing), scenic flights, bus tours on the Seven Lakes Route (see page 118) and boating trips.

Shopaholics, beer-lovers and anyone who enjoys a new age vibe will find their spiritual home 123km south of Bariloche in the charming, hippy-ish town of **El Bolsón**, where the outstanding **fería artesanal** (Tues, Thurs, Sat & Sun 10am–dusk) sells locally crafted wares and food. Make sure you also pop in to Jauja (San Martín 2867; ☎0294 449 2448, ⓦheladosjauja.com; daily noon–midnight) for one of its outstanding ice creams. Afterwards, sample a pint of the local brew at *Cervecería El Bolsón*, at RN258 Km124 (☎0294 449 2595;

Mon–Sat 9am–midnight, Sun 10am–10pm). There are plenty of hiking opportunities in the surrounding mountains, which include Cerro Piltriquitron (2260m), considered by some to be one of the earth's "energy centres".

CIRCUITO CHICO

The **CIRCUITO CHICO**, a 65km road circuit heading west of Bariloche along the shores of Lago Nahuel Huapi, is a popular day excursion, with a variety of possible stop-offs. It can be explored by bike, rental car, minibus tour (4hr) or by catching a public bus and jumping on and off wherever you fancy. The first point of interest – and a decent half-day excursion on its own – is **Cerro Campanario** at Avenida Bustillo Km18. Take the chairlift (daily 9am–5.30pm, summer until 6.30pm); AR$220) or trail (a 30min steep walk) to the lookout for camera-battery-depleting 360-degree **views**; tours don't usually see here, so you'll need to come under your own steam. The next point of interest is the luxurious, mountain-framed **Llao Llao Hotel and Spa** at Km25 (☎0294 4448 530, ⓦllaollao.com), an alpine-style creation by architect Alejandro Bustillo. Non-guests can feast on pastries at the hotel's decadent afternoon tea (daily 4–7pm).

Just after the turn-off for the *Llao Llao* is **Puerto Pañuelo**, where boats leave for leisure trips to Puerto Blest, Isla Victoria and the Parque Nacional Los Arrayanes (see page 117). Beyond here the traffic dissipates and the circuit follows an undulating road flanked by thick forest. The scenery is superb, with worthwhile stops at **Villa Tacul**, **Lago Escondido**, **Bahia López** and **Punto Panorámico**, the last of these offering the most recognized postcard shot of the region. For a detour, the pretty Swiss village of **Colonia Suiza** offers an enjoyable opportunity for a lunch or afternoon tea break.

Cycling the circuit allows the flexibility to leave the main road and ride along forested trails to hidden beaches and lakes. As traffic is heavy along the first 20km stretch west of Bariloche, it's best to take a bus (#10, #11, #20 or #22) from downtown to Avenida Bustillo Km18.6, where Bike Cordillera (see page 120) rents **bicycles**. To see the circuit by **public bus**, take #20 along the lakeshore for *Llao Llao* and Puerto Pañuelo or #10 inland for Colonia Suiza. In summer, #11 does the entire circuit.

CERRO CATEDRAL

Named for a summit (2405m) that resembles the spires of a Gothic cathedral, **CERRO CATEDRAL** (☎0294 4409 000, ⓦcatedralaltapatagonia.com) is one of South America's top ski resorts from June to October, offering bedazzling lake and cordillera views, more than fifty runs, forty lifts and descents up to 9km long. **Villa Catedral**, a village just 20km south of Bariloche, lies at the base of the mountain and has hotels, restaurants and ski-rental shops. When the snow melts, Cerro Catedral stays open for trekking; a cable car (Mon–Fri 9am–4pm; AR$445) and chairlift (free) provide access to **Refugio Lynch** (1870m) and spectacular mountain vistas. A tough but worthwhile trail leads along the ridge and past glacial lakes to **Refugio Frey** (4hr); you can overnight there or push on to descend through spellbinding forest back to Villa Catedral (4hr). Mountain biking, abseiling and horseriding are other popular summertime activities on the mountain. Buses marked "Catedral" leave from Moreno 470 in Bariloche.

PARQUE NACIONAL NAHUEL HUAPI

Spanning a whopping 7050 square kilometres, the magnificent **PARQUE NACIONAL NAHUEL HUAPI** (daily 24hr; AR$150; ⓦnahuelhuapi.gov.ar) is deservedly one of Argentina's most visited national parks. It incorporates both Bariloche and **Lago Nahuel Huapi**, a sapphire-blue glacial lake flanked by forest-quilted slopes. In the park's wild heart lie forests of cypress and beech trees, crystal-clear rivers, cascading waterfalls, lupin-filled meadows, ancient craggy glaciers and formidable snowcapped summits. Nahuel Huapi's crown is **Cerro Tronador**, an extinct volcano whose three icy peaks (around 3500m) straddle the borders of Argentina and Chile. Wildlife includes Patagonian hares, guanacos and condors, although, in the height of summer, humans rule the roost.

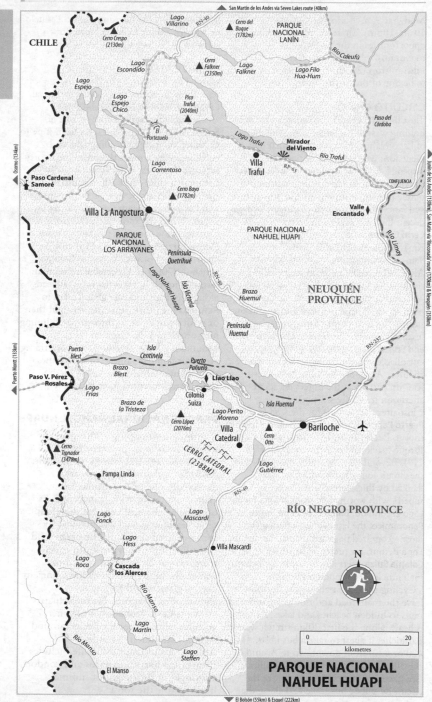

San Martín de los Andes via Seven Lakes route (40km)

CHILE

Osorno (134km)

Puerto Montt (133km)

Lago Villarino

Cerro Crespo (2130m)

Lago Escondido

Lago Espejo

Lago Espejo Chico

Cerro del Buque (1782m)

PARQUE NACIONAL LANÍN

Cerro Falkner (2350m)

Lago Falkner

Lago Filo Hua-Hum

Río Caleufú

Pico Traful (2040m)

El Portezuelo

Lago Correntoso

Lago Traful

Villa Traful

Mirador del Viento

Río Traful

RP-65

Paso del Córdoba

Junín de los Andes (130km), San Martín via 'Rinconada' route (170km) & Neuquén (350km)

CONFLUENCIA

Río Limay

Paso Cardenal Samoré

Villa La Angostura

Cerro Bayo (1782m)

PARQUE NACIONAL LOS ARRAYANES

Península Quetrihué

Isla Victoria

Lago Nahuel Huapi

RN-40

PARQUE NACIONAL NAHUEL HUAPI

Brazo Huemul

Valle Encantado

NEUQUÉN PROVINCE

Península Huemul

RN-237

Puerto Blest

Isla Centinela

Brazo Blest

Puerto Pañuelo

Llao Llao

Isla Huemul

Paso V. Pérez Rosales

Lago Frías

Brazo de la Tristeza

Colonia Suiza

Cerro López (2076m)

Lago Perito Moreno

Villa Catedral

Cerro Otto

Bariloche

Cerro Tronador (3478m)

CERRO CATEDRAL (2388M)

Lago Gutiérrez

Pampa Linda

RN-40

RÍO NEGRO PROVINCE

Lago Fonck

Lago Hess

Lago Mascardi

Lago Roca

Cascada los Alerces

Villa Mascardi

N

Río Manso

Lago Martín

Río Manso

El Manso

Lago Steffen

0   20
kilometres

PARQUE NACIONAL NAHUEL HUAPI

El Bolsón (55km) & Esquel (222km)

WHAT TO SEE AND DO

Nahuel Huapi has three distinct **zones** – northern, central and southern – and helpful *guardaparques* are stationed at key points to advise on trekking, fishing and camping.

THE NORTHERN ZONE

The park's **northern zone**, which lies just south of the town of San Martín de los Andes (see page 116), adjoins Parque Nacional Lanín (see page 114). This zone is defined by sky-blue **Lago Traful**, accessible from a turn-off on the Seven Lakes Route (see page 118). Also here is the **Paso Cardenal Samoré**, a popular overland pass into Chile.

THE CENTRAL AND SOUTHERN ZONES

The **central zone**, which incorporates the pretty Bosque de los Arrayanes (see page 118) and Isla Victoria, has **Lago Nahuel Huapi** as its centrepiece. In summer, this zone buzzes with tourists on boating, kayaking, cycling and hiking excursions. The southern zone has the best trails and facilities for hikers, and is focused around **Lago Mascardi**, ideal for swimming and diving in summer.

ESQUEL

Cowboys and urban sophisticates should feel equally at home in **ESQUEL**, the main town in the north of Chubut province. Some 340km south of Bariloche, Esquel means "bog" in the Mapuche language, a name that says nothing of the town's arresting mountainous backdrop. Although Esquel is often relegated to a pit stop en route to Bariloche or Chile, the town makes a perfect base to explore the lush **Parque Nacional Los Alerces** and for riding the historic **Old Patagonian Express** steam train (see page 126) on a touristic loop. Other local draws include the charming, tea-house-filled Welsh settlement of

---

TREKKING IN NAHUEL HUAPI

Parque Nacional Nahuel Huapi has an outstanding network of well-marked trails as well as numerous campsites and *refugios* (basic staffed mountain huts) to overnight in. Trails link many of these *refugios*, allowing hikers to embark on multi-day treks or return to Bariloche every couple of days for a hit of civilization.

The **hiking season** runs from December to March, although snow at high altitudes sometimes cuts off trails. January and February are the warmest and busiest hiking months, although this is also prime time for *tábanos* – intensely annoying biting horseflies that infest the lower altitudes. Spring in the park can be quite windy, while in autumn the leaves of the *ñire* and *lenga* trees turn a brilliant shade of red. Before heading for the hills, trekkers should visit **Club Andino Bariloche** (see page 120), where knowledgeable staff give out trekking maps and can answer questions about the status of trails, campsites and *refugios* as well as transport to trailheads. They also register solo hikers for safety reasons. Club Andino offers regular guided trekking tours to **Pampa Linda**, 90km southwest of Bariloche, from where you can hike to Refugio Otto Meiling, which cowers dramatically beneath Cerro Tronador, nestled between the Castaño Overa and Alerce glaciers.

ACCOMMODATION

All of the park's *refugios* (around AR$350) are spectacularly sited in the park's southern zone and have bathrooms with cold water and dorms (bring a sleeping bag, supplies and a torch). There are campsites at all major park locations, including *Lago Roca* (AR$260) near Cascada Los Alerces, *Los Rápidos* (☎0294 15441 6120, ⓦlosrapidos.com.ar; AR$550/person) at Lago Mascardi, and *Los Vuriloches* (AR$260/person) at Pampa Linda. *Hosterías* within the park are expensive; pleasant *Hostería Pampa Linda*, at the base of Cerro Tronador

(☎0294 4490 517, ⓦhosteriapampalinda.com.ar), costs AR$2250.

EATING AND DRINKING

River water is safe to drink untreated, as is the water from *refugio* taps. Fully equipped kitchens in the *refugios* can be used for a small fee, and hot meals, snacks and an impressive selection of alcohol can be purchased (although prices reflect the fact that everything has been lugged up the mountain by porters).

1

Trevelin, 23km south, and, in winter, the ski resort of **La Hoya** (☎02945 453 018, ⓦskilahoya.com), 12km northeast, where there are 22km of runs, plenty of off-piste skiing and a season that often extends into early October.

ARRIVAL AND DEPARTURE

By plane Esquel Airport is 21km east of town; a taxi into town will set you back around AR$250.

Destinations Buenos Aires (6 weekly; 2hr 10min).

By bus The bus terminal (☎02945 451 584) lies eight blocks from the town centre on the corner of A.P. Justo and Av Alvear, the main street.

Destinations Bariloche (7–8 daily; 5hr); El Bolsón (7–8 daily; 2hr 30min); El Calafate (1 daily; 24hr); El Chaltén (3–4 weekly; 18hr); Comodoro Rivadavia (3 daily; 9hr); Futaleufú in Chile (Jan & Feb 2 daily 3 times a week; rest of year 2 daily twice a week; 2hr); Mendoza (1 daily; 24hr).

By train The train station, used by *La Trochita* (aka the *Old Patagonian Express*), is on Roggero, at Brun, three blocks northwest of the bus terminal.

INFORMATION AND TOURS

Tourist information The town's tourist office is on Av Alvear, at Sarmiento (high season Mon–Fri 8am–10pm, Sat 9am–10pm; low season Mon–Fri 8am–8pm, Sat 9am–8pm; ☎02945 451 927, ⓦesquel.tur.ar).

Tour operator Tours of Parque Nacional Los Alerces can be booked through Gales al Sur (Av Alvear 1871, inside the bus terminal ☎02945 453 379, ⓦgalesalsur.tur.ar) and leave every day according to demand.

ACCOMMODATION, EATING AND DRINKING

La Barra Sarmiento 638 ☎02945 454 321. This popular *parrilla* serves big juicy slabs of beef (from AR$190) accompanied with chips, salad and home-made mayonnaise on lacy tablecloths. Mon–Sat 12.30–3pm & 8.30pm–midnight.

Fitzroya Pizza Rivadavia 1048 ☎02945 450 512. Inexpensive pizzas (most AR$130–250) loaded with unusual toppings such as broccoli, salmon and trout are delivered piping hot. Daily noon–3pm & 8pm–1am.

Hostel Sol Azul Rivadavia 2869 ☎02945 455 193, ⓦhostelsolazul.com.ar. The cosiest hostel in town boasts a wood-burning stove, heated floors and an all-stone bar. The four-bed dorms have bunk beds and lockers. Dorms __AR$350__

Moe Bar Rivadavia 873. Cocktails and classic rock are the orders of the night at this rowdy drinking hole (beer around AR$70) with half a yellow car protruding from its entrance. Tend to your hunger pangs with one of their tasty pizzas or *picadas*. Mon–Sat 10.30am–late.

Planeta Hostel & Suites Av Alvear 1021 ☎02945 456 846, ⓦplanetahostel.com. A central hostel with delightful owners, wacky artistic touches, an open kitchen area and a cosy living room with a flat-screen TV. The dorm beds are just what the chiropractor ordered and all rooms have en-suite bathrooms. Staff can arrange a range of tours/activities. Dorms __AR$310__, doubles __AR$1000__

THE OLD PATAGONIAN EXPRESS

Puffing and chugging its way across the arid Andean foothills at around 25km/hr, the **Old Patagonian Express** is both a museum on wheels and a classic South American train journey. Known as "*La Trochita*" ("little narrow gauge" in Spanish), the locomotive's tracks are a mere 75cm wide. Built in 1922 to connect sheep farmers in isolated, windswept communities with faraway markets for their goods, the train was put out of commission in 1993 when the railways were privatized. Immortalized in Paul Theroux's classic 1979 train-travel narrative, the express is today mostly involved in short, round-trip tourist jaunts. Passengers pile into antique wooden coaches, complete with wood-burning furnaces and dining cars, to puff from Esquel to a Mapuche community plus museum called **Nahuel Pan** and back (44km return; 3hr; AR$750). Peering out of the window, you might spot guanacos, rheas and hares – and you will certainly see cows. If you are really lucky, you may even see "bandits" that hold up the train on occasion – rest assured that it is an organized part of the experience and no one will be relieving you of your jewellery.

The train leaves throughout the year on Saturdays at 10am and then puts on extra trips depending on the season and demand – up to five departures a week in high season. Ask the tourist office for the latest schedule or call ☎02945 451 403. Renovations or strikes sometimes close the line completely, so check that it is running before you come to Esquel if the train ride is the main objective of your journey.

Occasionally, the train makes the 165km journey all the way from Esquel to El Maitén, where there is a museum and railway repair shops.

INTO CHILE

Esquel is well placed for crossing into Chilean Patagonia, with several buses weekly making the two-hour trip to the settlement of **Futaleufú**, (see page 454) where there is excellent white-water rafting. Feryval and Lago Espolón buses leave Esquel (travelling south via Trevelín) around four times a week. At the Chilean border (immigration 8am–8pm), passengers transfer to a minibus for the final 10km to Futaleufú.

PARQUE NACIONAL LOS ALERCES

PARQUE NACIONAL LOS ALERCES, 40km west of Esquel, encompasses 2630 square kilometres of gorgeous, glacier-carved Andean landscape (daily 9am–5pm; AR$250). Although far less visited than Parque Nacional Nahuel Huapi to the north, its network of richly coloured lakes and pristine rivers makes it a prime destination for anglers, while countless hiking trails through verdant forests attract summer walkers and campers. It's easily navigable on a day-trip from Esquel via the popular lake tour.

The *alerce* (or Patagonian cypress) that grows here is one of the oldest living species on the planet, with some examples surviving as long as 3000 years. In size, they're almost comparable to the grand sequoias of California, growing to 70m tall and 4m wide. Though the *alerce* gives the park its name, the flora is wildly varied: **Valdivian temperate rainforest** thrives in its luxuriant western zone near the Chilean border, which is deluged by around 3000mm of annual rainfall. Elsewhere, incense cedar, bamboo-like *caña colihue*, *arrayán*, *coihue*, *lenga* and southern beech thrive.

WHAT TO SEE AND DO

Most visitors gravitate towards the park's user-friendly and photogenic **northeast sector** where there is a network of four dazzling lakes – **Rivadavia**, **Verde**, **Menéndez** and **Futalaufquen**. The emerald-hued Lago Verde is often the first port of call for day-trekkers and campers.

Spilling over from Lago Verde is the **Río Arrayanes**, crossed by a suspension bridge that marks the start of an easy hour-long interpretive loop walk.

Some hikes, including the trek to the summit of **Cerro Alto El Dedal** (1916m), require registration with the park ranger's office (see below) first. The most popular day excursion is the **boat trip** run by Brazo Sur (Justo 982, Esquel; ☎02945 456359), which leaves from Puerto Chucao (halfway around the Lago Verde/Río Arrayanes loop trail, 11.15am departure, AR$680). The boats cross Lago Menéndez to visit **El Abuelo** (The Grandfather), a 57m-high *alerce* estimated to be more than 2600 years old.

ARRIVAL AND INFORMATION

By car One main dusty, bumpy road (the RP71) runs through Los Alerces and is usually accessible year-round, although it is occasionally blocked by snow in winter. There is no public transport outside of peak season, so a vehicle is recommended; otherwise, hikers need to walk along the road between trails, enduring clouds of body-coating dust from passing cars and trucks.

By bus Peak season is Jan–Feb, when Transportes Esquel (☎02945 453 529) runs two daily bus services to the park; it takes three bumpy hours to reach Lago Verde.

Tourist information The ranger's office (low season daily 9am–4pm; high season daily 8am–9pm; ☎02945 471 020) is at Villa Futalaufquen, a village on Lago Futalaufquen, 12km past the park entrance point, with a smattering of shops, public telephones and eating and accommodation options (which close in winter). It can provide information on camping, park accommodation, hiking and fishing, and sells fishing permits.

Patagonia

Vast, windswept and studded with glaciers, **PATAGONIA** has an undeniable mystique, a place where pioneers, outlaws, writers and naturalists have long come in

search of open space and wild adventure. While few corners have been left unexplored, there's still plenty of scope for adventure, whether you're watching a

1

southern right whale swim metres under your boat or strapping on crampons to hike across the Southern Patagonian Ice Cap.

For those short on time, flights allow you to hop between Patagonia's key attractions, but to appreciate the region's size, it's best to travel overland. After hundreds of kilometres of desolate steppe, nothing bedazzles quite like the sight of serrated Andean peaks rising up on the horizon.

Two main arteries traverse Patagonia. The RN40 runs parallel to the Andes and links some of Patagonia's major sights: the 10,000-year-old rock art of the **Cueva de las Manos**; the Fitz Roy sector of **Parque Nacional Los Glaciares** around the town of El Chaltén; and the **Perito Moreno** and **Upsala** glaciers in the park's southern sector, both easy day-trips from El Calafate. To the east, the RN3 loosely traces the Atlantic seaboard, passing the town of **Puerto Madryn**, a launching pad for the marine-wildlife-rich shores of **Península Valdés**, before heading south to the Welsh heartland of **Trelew** and **Gaiman**, a short jump to the continent's largest penguin colony, **Punta Tombo**.

December to February are the warmest months to visit Patagonia, but to avoid the crowds, inflated prices and high winds, March and April are better.

PUERTO MADRYN

Sprawling, windblown **PUERTO MADRYN**, an aluminium-producing fishing port, founded in 1865 by 153 intrepid Welsh families, that clings to the featureless coastal pampas of northern Patagonia, is an unlikely visitor destination at first sight. Its attractions lie more in its proximity to one of the world's most significant marine reserves – the **Reserva Faunística Península Valdés** – as well as to South America's biggest penguin colony. Scuba diving, snorkelling with sea lions and whale watching are among the area's draws. Puerto Madryn also makes a convenient base from which to explore the nearby Welsh towns of Trelew and Gaiman.

WHAT TO SEE AND DO

In the southern part of town, at Julio Verne 3784, is the excellent **Ecocentro** (daily 5–9pm; AR$2500; ℗ecocentro.org. ar), with interactive exhibitions on Patagonian ecosystems, breeding habits of southern right whales, sea-lion harems and more, as well as a changing art exhibition. Just outside is the skeleton of a whale that was beached nearby in 2001. Take bus #2 from the town centre to its last stop and walk another 1km south along the waterfront.

Around 20km north of town, and reachable via a fairly strenuous bike ride or shared taxi (AR$450 one-way), is **El Doradillo**, a pristine stretch of beach where between June and December you can spot whales swimming right near the shore.

Seventeen kilometres southwest of Puerto Madryn via a good gravel road is **Punta Loma**, with a viewpoint overlooking a sheltered beach that's home to a few hundred sea lions, plus a gulp of cormorants, best seen at low tide. Some agencies organize trips (2–3hr), but you can get here by bike or taxi.

ARRIVAL AND DEPARTURE

By plane Puerto Madryn's airport (Aeropuerto El Tehuelche; ℗0280 445 1909) is around 5km west of town (taxi about AR$900). There are several weekly flights to Buenos Aires, but nearby Trelew Airport serves more destinations.

By bus The bus terminal is at Avila and Independencia, on the northern edge of the centre. Bus timetables and accommodation details are displayed on the wall, and there are luggage lockers. Bus companies 28 de Julio (℗0280 447 2056) and Mar y Valle (℗0280 447 2056) serve Trelew; Andesmar (℗0280 447 3765) runs to Mendoza, Jujuy and Iguazú, Don Otto (℗0280 445 1675) serves Buenos Aires, Comodoro Rivadavia, Neuquén, Bariloche and Esquel; TAC (℗0280 445 7785) runs to Río Gallegos and Jujuy. Chaltén Travel sells bus tickets for Ruta 40 destinations.

Destinations Bariloche (daily at 9.30pm; 15hr); Buenos Aires (10–11 daily; 18–20hr); Comodoro Rivadavia (5–7 daily; 6–8hr); Esquel (2–3 daily; 9hr); Jujuy (5 daily; 36hr); Mendoza (2–3 daily; 24hr); Neuquén (2 daily; 12hr); Puerto Pirámides (1–2 daily; 1hr 15min); Río Gallegos (4–6 daily; 15–20hr); Trelew (every 30min–1hr; 1hr).

INFORMATION

Tourist information The tourist office is on Av Roca 223 (Dec–March daily 8am–9pm; shorter hours April–Nov; ℗0280 445 3504, ℗ madryn.gov.ar/turismo).

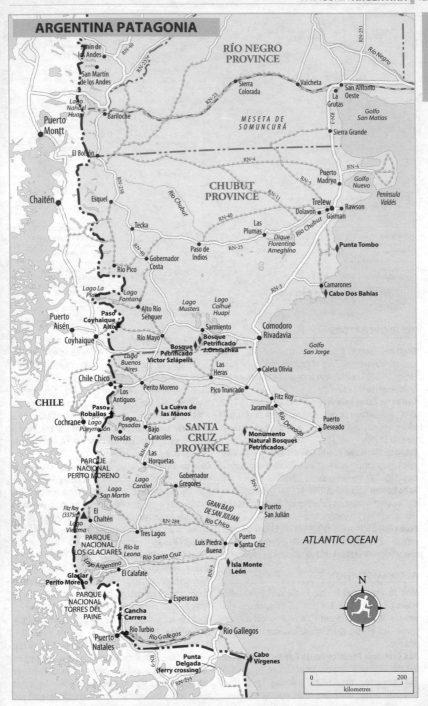

1

PUERTO MADRYN

DRINKING & NIGHTLIFE
Cervecería James Beer	1
Margarita	2
Mr Jones	3

EATING
El Almendro	5
Café Martínez	1
Lupita Taberna Mejicana	3
La Milonga	4
La Sandwichería	2

ACCOMMODATION
ACA Complejo Turístico Punta Cuevas	1
Casa Patagónica	2
Casa de Tounens	7
Chepatagonia Hostel	3
El Gualicho	5
Hi! Patagonia Hostel	4
Hotel Petit	8
La Tosca	6

TOUR OPERATORS

Chaltén Travel Roca 115 ☎0280 445 4906, ⓦ chaltentravel.com. Tours of Península Valdés and Punta Tombo (AR$1800 each). Also arranges onward travel and tours along the Ruta 40.

Costas de Patagonia Brown 893 ☎0280 15 472 1142, ⓦ costasdepatagonia.com. Recommended for mountain biking and trekking adventures, plus kayaking with sea lions (AR$1000).

Estación Marítima Puerto Rawson ☎0280 449 8508, ⓦ estacionmaritima.com.ar. Runs dolphin-watching boat trips (AR$1000) from Rawson.

Lobo Larsen Roca 885 ☎0280 447 0277, ⓦ lobolarsen. com.ar. Hugely popular snorkelling and diving with sea lion trips, as well as PADI courses.

Scuba Duba Brown 893 ☎0280 445 2699 ⓦ scubaduba. com.ar. PADI-affiliated, reputable diving operator; snorkelling with sea lions (AR$1000) is also on offer.

ACCOMMODATION

Most accommodation is close to the centre and within walking distance of the bus terminal (many hostels offer pick-ups if you call ahead). Prices drop outside high season (Jan–March). Rates include breakfast unless stated otherwise.

ACA Complejo Turístico Punta Cuevas Punta Cuevas ☎0280 445 2952, ⓦ acamadryn.com.ar; map p.130. This bare-bones complex has camping spots (tents provided), simple rooms and self-contained apartments

best for groups. Breakfast costs extra. Bus #2 runs within 500m of the complex; get off at the last stop. Camping/person AR$162, doubles AR$810, apartments AR$1620

Casa Patagónica Av Roca 2210 ☎0280 445 1540, ⓦ casa-patagonica.com.ar; map p.130. This homely, family-run B&B has four twins and triples which share a bathroom, plus one en suite. Guests have access to a microwave and fridge (though not a full kitchen), there is home-made cake for breakfast and owners are happy to help you plan your stay. AR$990

Casa de Tounens Pasaje 1ero de Marzo 432 ☎0280 447 2681, ⓦ lacasadetounens.com; map p.130. A block from the bus terminal, this friendly French-run place has a little patio, a compact living room, guest kitchen that's a magnet for socializing in the evenings, several spartan private rooms and a swing-a-cat dorm. Dorms AR$288, doubles AR$900

Chepatagonia Hostel A. Storni 16 ☎0280 445 5783, ⓦ chepatagoniahostel.com.ar; map p.130. Right on the waterfront, this compact hostel is run by a friendly local couple. Dorms have good mattresses and individual reading lights, there are bikes for rent (AR$350/day) and the owners throw the odd barbecue. Dorms AR$324, doubles AR$954

El Gualicho Marcos A Zar 480 ☎0280 445 4163, ⓦ elgualicho.com.ar; map p.130. The biggest, slickest hostel in town, *El Gualicho* welcomes a young backpacking clientele to a rock soundtrack. Dorms and doubles are large and spotless, the hammock-hung garden, beanbag-strewn lounge with guest computers and pool table are good and staff will book you in for every conceivable tour, but the sheer size (120 beds) makes it a little impersonal. Dorms AR$306, doubles AR$954

★ **Hi! Patagonia Hostel** Av Roca 1040 ☎ 0280 445 0155, ⓦ hipatagonia.com; map p.130. Small, sociable hostel run by young Argentine owner, Gaston. It attracts active travellers who make use of the climbing wall and bike rentals. Top-notch backpacker facilities include a hammock-festooned garden with a bar and a/c in the rooms, and there are occasional communal barbecues. Dorms AR$342, doubles AR$954

Hotel Petit Marceló T. de Alvear 845 ☎ 0280 445 1460, ⓦ hotel-petit.com.ar; map p.130. The rooms at this anonymous motel-style budget hotel are on the small side, but are all en suite with cable TV and some come with kitchen facilities. No fans, so avoid during hot weather. AR$720

★ **La Tosca** Sarmiento 437 ☎ 0280 445 6133, ⓦ latoscahostel.com; map p.130. Curving around a placid garden, this professionally run hostel caters to all backpacker needs. Pluses include two guest kitchens, a range of snug rooms with private and semi-private bathrooms, good beds and ample locker space. Well-travelled owners also bake cakes for their guests. Dorms AR$324, doubles AR$792

EATING

El Almendro Alvear 409, at 9 de Julio ☎ 0280 447 0525, ⓦ elalmendro.ucoz.com; map p.130. Simple, stylish decor, good service and an imaginative menu of Mediterranean-inspired dishes characterize this local favourite. The steaks are among the best in town, and the home-made pasta and gnocchi with imaginative sauces are good. Mains AR$130–270. Tues–Sun 8pm–midnight.

Café Martínez Roca 143; map p.130. The national chain's Chubut branch is Puerto Madryn's answer to Starbucks, serving sandwiches, wraps, salads, milkshakes and ample breakfasts involving fry-ups or granola. Coffee is not the cheapest but it's consistently good. Daily 8am–11pm.

Lupita Taberna Mejicana Av Gales 191; map p.130. With a psychedelic cactus mural and strategically placed sombreros, this is the Argentine take on Mexican food (so it's not particularly spicy), but the portions of burritos and quesadillas are generous and it makes a change. Mains AR$100–180. Daily 8pm–midnight.

La Milonga 9 de Julio 514; map p.130. The town's most popular pizzeria, with a clay oven and a vast range of toppings (pizzas AR$220–350). The *empanadas* are excellent as well. Tues–Sun 7pm–12.30am.

La Sandwichería Yrigoyen 128; map p.130. The Buena Onda Cartel runs this sandwich joint with ruthless efficiency (and plenty of good cheer). Choose between chunky sandwiches, a handful of mains (from AR$90) that

may include vegetable cannelloni and grilled chicken, and wash down your choice with Wynt and Antares craft beers while watching the game on the big screen. Mon–Sat 11.30am–2.45pm & 8–11.45pm.

DRINKING AND NIGHTLIFE

★ **Cervecería James Beer** Av Roca, at Roque Sáenz Peña ⓦ cerveceriajamesbeer.com; map p.130. Apart from serving microbrews from famous regional breweries such as Blest, La 40, Wynt and Kessel, this hip brewbar is both a decent restaurant – with a good mix of burgers, *tablas*, pizzas and pastas – and one of the most happening nightspots in town. Daily noon–4pm & 7pm–late.

Margarita Roque Sáenz Peña 15; map p.130. Visit this cosy, brick-walled pub to enjoy some good (and often live) music and rub shoulders with the locals over the long list of cocktails and a few local beers (from AR$70). Wednesday is sushi night. Mon–Sat 11am–4am.

Mr Jones 9 de Julio 116; map p.130. A bustling pub, popular with locals and young gringos alike, who fill up the wooden benches and spill out onto the streetside tables. The ambitious menu does best with items such as fish and chips, and you can't go wrong with a beer (from around AR$60) and a *picada* (cold meat and cheese platters). Mon–Sat 8pm–1am.

DIRECTORY

Banks and exchange Banco Galicia, at Mitre 25, changes money and has an ATM, one of dozens in the city.
Car rental Most rental company branches are along Av Roca. Rates start from AR$1500/day.
Laundry Servicios de Lavandería Morenas, Sarmiento, at Marcos Zar (Mon–Sat 8.30am–8.30pm).

DAY-TRIPS FROM PUERTO MADRYN

For animal lovers, it's hard to top the **Península Valdés** marine reserve, with its whale-watching boat trips and sightings of other marine fauna, though a trip to South America's biggest penguin colony at **Punta Tombo**, a little further afield, gives it a run for its money. South of Puerto Madryn is the excellent dinosaur museum in nearby **Trelew**. To delve into the region's Welsh heritage stop by tiny **Gaiman**, easily combined with Trelew on a single day-trip.

PENÍNSULA VALDÉS

PENÍNSULA VALDÉS is brimming with life. More than a million Magellanic penguins make their summer home here, along with numerous colonies of elephant seals and

1

sea lions, while the waters hide dolphins and orca (killer whales). Topping even that is a pod of southern right whales – vast, barnacled leviathans that come here to breed and raise their young, and that can be observed directly from the beach of **Puerto Pirámides**, the peninsula's tiny port surrounded by desert scrubland. If you're lucky, you can sometimes spot them from the beach, but you need to go on a boat trip to get close up.

ARRIVAL AND DEPARTURE

By bus There are daily Mar y Valle buses (Mon–Fri) from Puerto Madryn to Puerto Pirámides (6.40am & 4.30pm, returning 8.10am & 6pm; only the later bus runs on weekends; 1hr 30min; double check the frequently changing timetable at the bus terminal).

ACCOMMODATION AND EATING

If you prefer picturesque villages with a slow pace of life to cities, Puerto Pirámides has far greater appeal than Puerto Madryn. Dining options are either along Av Ballenas or in a cluster by the boat dock.

Hostal Bahía Ballenas Av de las Ballenas s/n ☎ 028015 4567104, ⊛ bahiaballenas.com. The only hostel in the village consists of two twelve-bed dorms, divided by gender. Don't expect peace and quiet, but it's a good place to meet travellers and the guest kitchen is a boon for self-caterers. Dorms **ARS306**

La Casa de La Tía Alicia Av de las Ballenas s/n ☎ 0280 449 5046, ⊛ hosteriatiaalicia.com.ar. This eye-catching pink house decked out with knick-knacks hides four compact en-suite rooms. Breakfast is basic,

but there's plenty of *buena onda* (good vibes) and the *Guanaco* pub/microbrewery next door is a welcome bonus. **ARS900**

TRELEW

An hour south of Puerto Madryn across some wind-blown pampas, **TRELEW** is a busy commercial centre, proud of its Welsh history – "Trelew" in Welsh means "village of Lewis", in honour of Lewis Jones, the town's founder. It's only worth staying here to cut down on travelling time to Punta Tombo and Gaiman.

It also has, at Fontana & Lewis Jones, the excellent **Museo Paleontológico Egidio Feruglio** (April–Aug Mon–Fri 10am–6pm, Sat & Sun 10am–7pm; Sept–March daily 9am–8pm; AR$120; ⊛ mef.org.ar), which houses Patagonia's most important paleontological finds. The newest (as of 2017) and most exciting discovery comprises the remains of the *Patagotitan*, the largest creature ever to have walked the earth. You can touch an enormous sauropod femur, wander among the skeletons of giant flightless birds and immense herbivores and predators, and check out the remains of a theropod predator, the *Tyrannotitan chubutensis*, discovered on a farm in Chubut in 1995.

ARRIVAL AND INFORMATION

By plane Almirante M.A. Zar International Airport (⊛ aeropuertotrelew.com), 5km northeast of the town,

---

VISITING PENÍNSULA VALDÉS

Most people visit Península Valdés on an organized tour (around AR$2000, 10–12hr round-trip; bring warm clothes), most of which follow the same itinerary, with minor variations according to the season and weather. The first stop, a short drive out of Puerto Madryn, is to pay the park entrance fee (AR$415) and visit the **information centre**, followed by an impressive look out over the Isla de los Pájaros (Bird Island). Next, across the isthmus on the peninsula proper, you'll stop off in Puerto Pirámides, where hugely worthwhile **sea-lion-** and **whale-watching** boat trips are offered (AR$1500); it's also possible to whale-watch from a custom-built semi-submergible Yellow Submarine (AR$1900). From Puerto Pirámides, most buses head east to Punta Cantor and Caleta Valdéz to see the **elephant seals** and their pups on the long gravel beach, with a brief stop at El Parador where there's a colony of **Magellanic penguins**. Some tours may instead head north to Punta Norte, to the huge colony of elephant seals and sea lions. **Orcas** are found here year-round, and between February and April they are most likely to stage stealth beach attacks on seal and sea-lion pups. Marine life is present year-round but some viewing stations close from Easter to June; optimal viewing is between September and February, but whales can be seen from June to December. Other than on day tours, the only other way to reach the viewpoints is by car, which can be good value if you are travelling in a group; most of the roads around the peninsula are dirt-and-gravel ones, so cautious driving is imperative.

has flights to Buenos Aires, Bariloche, Esquel, Ushuaia and El Calafate. A taxi to/from the centre costs about AR$130.

By bus The bus station is next to the Plaza Centenario. Destinations Bariloche (1 daily; 13–16hr); Buenos Aires (10–11 daily; 18–21hr); Esquel (daily; 8-9hr); Gaiman (every 30min; 25–35min; Puerto Madryn (every 30min–1hr; 1hr); Río Gallegos (4–5 daily; 14–17hr).

Tourist information The well-stocked tourist office is on San Martín, at Mitre (Mon–Fri 8am–8pm, Sat & Sun 9am–9pm; ☎ 0280 442 6819, ⓦ trelewpatagonia.gov.ar).

ACCOMMODATION AND EATING

Hostel El Ágora Edwin Roberts 33 ☎ 0280 442 6899, ⓦ hostelagora.com. Run by friendly young owners, this is the only hostel in town, with spacious, tiled rooms and spartan dorms with lockers and a kitchen. The owners sometimes throw a barbecue for guests and run bicycle tours. Dorms AR$360, doubles AR$936

Miguel Angel Trattoria Fontana 246. All dark wood and exposed brick, this is a stylish spot for thin-and-crispy pizza (the large is big enough for two) and home-made pasta. Mains AR$130–260. Tues–Sun noon–3pm & 8pm–midnight.

Touring Club Fontana 240, ⓦ touringpatagonia.com.ar. Antoine de Saint-Exupéry, author of *The Little Prince*, and (reportedly) Butch Cassidy and the Sundance Kid have stayed at this faded Art Deco hotel. Though the food's overpriced and mediocre, the imposing antique bar is worth lingering in with a drink for the atmosphere alone. Daily 7am–2am.

GAIMAN

Some 17km west of Trelew, **GAIMAN** is the most visitor-friendly of the region's Welsh settlements, an oasis of greenery thanks to the Río Chubut. Founded in 1874 by Welsh settlers – a third of its population still claims Welsh ancestry – and it's renowned for its immense **Welsh teas**; even the late Princess Diana stopped by for a cuppa in 1995. Served from 2 or 3pm every day in quaint cottages (or their gardens), they consist of tea, home-made cakes (including *torta negra*, a traditional Welsh fruitcake), scones, breads, tiny sandwiches and jams.

ARRIVAL AND INFORMATION

By bus There are regular 28 de Julio buses to and from Trelew (every 30min 7am–11pm; 25–35min); they arrive and depart from the central Plaza Roca.

Tourist information The tourist office is at Belgrano 574, a 5min walk from the main square (daily: Dec–March 9am–8pm, April–Nov 9am–6pm; ☎ 0280 449 1571, ⓦ gaiman.

gov.ar). You can pick up a map here to do a self-guided tour of Gaiman's historical buildings.

ACCOMMODATION AND EATING

Gwalia Lân Eugenio Tello, at Jones. Just off the main square, this well-loved local restaurant is run by a Welsh-speaking descendant of original settlers and serves excellent home-made pasta and fish dishes, washed down with the local Patagonia ale. Mains AR$200–380. Tues–Sat 12.30–3pm & 7.30pm–midnight, Sun 12.30–3pm.

Ty Gwyn 9 de Julio 147, ⓦ tygwyn.com.ar. A block from the main square, this spacious *casa de té* has tables set with blue-and-white china and serves an excellent afternoon tea (2–7pm; AR$360). It also has clean, compact rooms with wooden floors and partial views of the Río Chubut. AR$1050

Ty Nain Yrigoyen 283. The abundant tea (AR$350) is served by a descendant of the first Welsh woman born in Gaiman inside this gorgeous ivy-clad building that dates back to 1890. There's a tiny museum at the back. Tues–Fri 3–7pm, Sat & Sun, from 4pm.

★ **Yr Hen Ffordd** Michael Jones 342 ☎ 029 654 91394, ⓦ yrhenffordd.com.ar. Presided over by young, friendly owners, this appealing B&B with antique touches and tiled floors has just five rooms, all with a/c and TV and bathrooms. Breakfast includes delicious home-made scones. AR$990

PUNTA TOMBO

Around 180km south of Puerto Madryn and 110km south of Trelew, the **Reserva Provincial Punta Tombo** (Sept to late March daily 8am–6pm; AR$320) is the largest penguin-nesting site on the continent. Around a million Magellanic penguins come here to breed and raise their chicks, and wander freely across the paths (give them plenty of room). Penguins aside, you'll see a vast array of birds, from rock cormorants and kelp gulls to giant petrels. The reserve can be visited independently by car or on a long day tour (around AR$860) from Puerto Madryn or Trelew; tours often include stops at Rawson's Playa Unión for dolphin-spotting trips (AR$900) and Gaiman.

RUTA 40

Ruta 40 (or **RN40**) runs from the top to the bottom of Argentina, following the line of the Andes all the way to the far south from the border with Bolivia in the north. It covers 5000km and 11 provinces, crosses 18 important rivers on 236 bridges, and

1

connects 13 great lakes and salt flats, 20 national parks and hundreds of communities. The section between El Calafate/El Chaltén and Bariloche has long been popular with backpackers, with much of the route paved and buses running its length almost daily in season. It still retains a sense of isolation, however, thanks to the endless pampas scrubland, interrupted only by the occasional tiny settlement or *estancia*. The ancient **cave paintings** near the unappealing crossroads town of Perito Moreno are a worthwhile detour.

PERITO MORENO

Named after the explorer who rerouted the Río Fénix that provides the town with water, **PERITO MORENO** (not to be confused with the Perito Moreno glacier) is a small, unappealing, wind-blasted town roughly halfway between El Chaltén and Bariloche, and a convenient stopover along Ruta 40. Perito Moreno's main point of interest is as a base for excursions to the **Cueva de las Manos**.

ARRIVAL AND DEPARTURE

By bus The bus terminal is a 15min walk north of the centre. Sportman (☎02963 432303) passes through en route between Comodoro Rivadavia and Los Antiguos; buses are frequently late; Taqsa/Marga (☎02963 432675 ⓦtaqsa.com.ar) serves all destinations along Ruta 40, as does Chaltén Travel, leaving from Hotel Belgrano, San Martín 1001 (☎02963 432019, ⓦchaltentravel.com) on alternate days (mid-Nov to April).

Destinations Bariloche (5–6 weekly; 11hr); El Chaltén (5–6 weekly; 11hr); Comodoro Rivadavia (2–3 daily; 6hr); Los Antiguos (2–3 daily; 45min).

INFORMATION AND TOURS

Banks and exchange Banco de Santa Cruz on San Martín at Rivadavia has an ATM, but not always functioning; the nearest reliable sources of cash are El Calafate and Bariloche.
Tourist information The helpful tourist office on San Martín at Gendarmeria Nacional (mid-Dec to Feb daily 8am–9pm; shorter hours rest of year; ☎02963 432732 ⓦperitomoreno.gob.ar) has maps of the town and province.
Tour operators GuanaCóndor, Perito Moreno 1087 (☎02963 432303, ⓔjarinauta@yahoo.com.ar), run trips to the Cueva de las Manos, including an excellent hike. If you're heading to El Chaltén, you can combine a half-day tour of the Cueva de las Manos with a bus south from Bajo Caracoles with Chaltén Travel.

ACCOMMODATION AND EATING

There are a couple of small supermarkets along San Martín. Most lodgings double as basic restaurants. If arriving on a late bus, notify your lodgings in advance.
Hotel Americano San Martín 1327 ☎02963 432 074, ⓦhotelamericanoweb.com.ar. A decent place

---

TRAVELLING RUTA 40

The **best time to travel** Ruta 40 (ⓦturismoruta40.com.ar) from El Calafate/El Chaltén to Bariloche by public transport is from November to the end of March. Outside of these months, buses are infrequent and much accommodation shuts down. The Cueva de las Manos can only be visited from December to February.

Bus services between El Calafate and Bariloche, via Perito Moreno, are offered by the well-established **Chaltén Travel** (ⓦchaltentravel.com), which has offices in El Calafate, El Chaltén, Puerto Madryn and Bariloche, as well as Taqsa/Marga (ⓦtaqsa.com.ar); both run frequent services every other day between November and the end of March. Check the latest timetables before planning a trip.

If you have more time and money, plus a sense of adventure, the best way to see the region is to rent a **car** either in **Bariloche** or **El Calafate** and drive the route at your own speed (though one-way drop-off fees for rental cars can be as high as US$900).

It's a huge territory, and even though much of the route has been paved, some sections are still dirt-and-gravel and fuel stops are few and far between (so fill up at every opportunity). Watch out for wildlife in the road, carry spare tyres, food and water, and stop to help if you see anyone who's broken down, as there's no other roadside assistance. Two places to break for fuel are Bajo Caracoles, 130km south of Perito Moreno, and Gobernador Gregores, around 440km north, essential for petrol and food; Gobernador Gregores has better lodging options.

There is little in the way of budget **accommodation** along the route (especially as the windy, hard plains make camping virtually impossible), but there are a few *estancias*.

to stay in town, and one with the friendliest welcome, this budget hotel has compact, clean, warm rooms with small bathrooms (though some lack natural light) and a restaurant on-site. Book rooms in advance, particularly for Sundays. AR$1062

Camping Municipal Mariano Moreno, off San Martín ☎ 02963 432130. Next to the brackish Laguna de los Cisnes in the southern part of town, this campsite has little shelter from the wind, but there are hot showers, an indoor cooking/eating area and revamped four-person cabins. Camping/person AR$90, cabañas US$720

Salón Iturrioz Rivadavia at San Martín. Food at this atmospheric café is limited to toasted sandwiches and *empanadas*, but you can check out the beautiful antique tills and the collection of pioneer photos while sipping a coffee, fruit shake or a *submarino* (frothy hot milk with a melting chocolate bar). The place doubles as a social hub. Mains AR$50–180. Daily 8am–8pm.

LOS ANTIGUOS

West of Perito Moreno, the landscape changes and for much of the 57km journey to the border town of **LOS ANTIGUOS** the RN43 skirts the shore of the impossibly blue **Lago Buenos Aires** (the second-biggest lake in South America, after Lake Titicaca), with the Andes looming beyond.

Small, pretty and more cosmopolitan than Perito Moreno, Los Antiguos is the cherry capital of Argentina and home to a scattering of *chacras* (independent farms) where you can buy delicious fruits in season. Besides being an attractive stopover along Ruta 40, Los Antiguos is also the gateway to Chile via Chile Chico (see page 459), a mere 12km away.

ARRIVAL AND DEPARTURE

By bus The bus terminal is on Av Tehuelches, a 10min walk to the parallel Av 11 de Julio, the town's main street. Sportman (☎ 02963 491175) runs to Comodoro Rivadavia via Perito Moreno; Taqsa/Marga (☎ 0297 15419615, ⓦ taqsa.com.ar) serves Bariloche and El Chaltén, as does Chaltén Travel, the latter leaving from *Albergue Padilla* on alternate days (mid-Nov to April). Cross-border services to Chile Chico were suspended at research time, though it's possible to hike to the Argentine border (1.5km from Los Antiguos), then hike to the Chilean border post (an additional 1km) and either arrange for a taxi to pick you up on the Chilean side via your accommodation in Chile Chico, or hike the remaining 5km.

Destinations Bariloche (5–6 weekly; 12hr); El Chaltén (5–6 weekly; 12hr); Comodoro Rivadavia via Perito Moreno (1–2 daily; 7hr).

INFORMATION AND TOURS

Tourist information The tourist office on 11 de Julio at Lago Buenos Aires (daily 8am–8pm; ☎ 02963 491261) gives out maps of the town and surrounding farms; its Facebook page has helpful info.

Tour operators Chelenco Tours, Av 11 de Julio 584 (☎ 02963 491198 ⓦ chelencotours.com.ar), run daily trips to the Cueva de las Manos for a minimum of two (AR$900 each) from mid-Nov to mid-April.

ACCOMMODATION AND EATING

Albergue Padilla San Martín 44 ☎ 02963 491140. Family-run guesthouse that attends largely to the needs of Chaltén Travel passengers who get dropped off here in the wee hours. Owners can book onward Ruta 40 tickets. For dorms, bed linen costs extra. Dorms AR$252, doubles AR$630

Camping Municipal RP43 ☎ 02963 491265. On the approach to town, 1.5km away, this lakefront campsite is sheltered from the wind and has hot showers. The windowless cabins sleep up to four and get very hot in summer. Camping/person AR$108, cabañas AR$504

Viva el Viento Av. 11 de Julio 447 ⓦ vivaelviento. com. With its eclectic decor and a menu of steaks, pizzas, burgers and milkshakes, this bright Dutch-Argentine-run restaurant is the buzziest place on the strip. Dollars, Euros and Chilean pesos accepted. Mains AR$100-300. Oct–April daily 9am–9pm.

CUEVA DE LAS MANOS

A couple of hours south of Perito Moreno along Ruta 40 and a wonderfully scenic, steep gravel road that offers marvellous canyon views and plenty of wild animal sightings, the **CUEVA DE LAS MANOS** (daily 9am–7pm; guided tours AR$200) is an astonishing cave displaying 9000-year-old cave paintings depicting guanacos, hunters hurling bolos and, most famously, 829 hand stencils made by ancient local inhabitants using mineral pigments. The cave, a UNESCO World Heritage Site, is easily accessible from Perito Moreno or Los Antiguos via an organized day-trip (AR$900); you can also combine a tour with same-day travel south to El Chaltén with Chaltén Travel.

1

ACCOMMODATION

Hostería La Cueva de las Manos 7km off the RN40 📞 02963 432207, 🌐 cuevadelasmanos.net. The cave is actually located inside this *estancia's* perimeters and group tours approach it via a fairly tough guided trek that descends into the canyon. There are dorms, private rooms and a restaurant, and staff can organize transport, horse rides, hikes and trips to nearby Charcamata, another rock-art site. Book in advance through the Perito Moreno office, as there's no phone signal or internet at the *estancia*. Closed May–Oct. Dorms AR$450, doubles AR$1800

PARQUE NACIONAL PERITO MORENO

Consisting of over 1150 square kilometres of windy Patagonian steppe and the jagged peaks of the Sierra Colorado, **PARQUE NACIONAL PERITO MORENO** comes complete with herds of guanacos and condors wheeling overhead. Not to be confused with the glacier of the same name (see page 144), the remote national park is located along a rough dirt-and-gravel road that branches off Ruta 40 around halfway between Perito Moreno and El Chaltén; the closest town is Gobernador Gregores. You need a sturdy car to reach the park and you have to bring all your own supplies, including warm gear. Water in the park is drinkable. As the park receives few visitors, you may have it practically to yourself.

There's an information centre at the park entrance where you must register, and where guided hikes can be arranged. Trails include an easy hour's ramble to Pinturas Rupestres (cave paintings), a longer trail leading to Lago Belgrano, a 16km trek to Lago Burgmeister and a tough three-hour ascent of Cerro León (1434m) from *Estancia La Oriental*.

ACCOMMODATION

There are basic campgrounds with pit toilets and no showers: a wind-battered one at the information centre, a tree-shielded one at Lago Burgmeister and one at El Rincón; no fires permitted. There are two *estancias* bordering the park.

La Oriental 1km from Lago Belgrano 📞 011 4237 4043, 🌐 estanciasdesantacruz.com. This working *estancia* is beautifully situated, and makes a good base for trekking and horseriding. You can bed down in the triples or double in the main house or the triples and a four-bed dorm in the annexe; room rates include half board. Closed April–Oct. Dorms US$1260, doubles US$3150

PARQUE NACIONAL LOS GLACIARES

The **PARQUE NACIONAL LOS GLACIARES** hugs the eastern slopes of the Andes, extending for 170km along the border with Chile. A UNESCO World Heritage Site, nearly half of the park's 6000 square kilometres consists of virtually inaccessible continental ice fields. Elsewhere, thirteen glaciers sweep down from craggy mountains into two parallel turquoise lakes – Argentino and Viedma – while dry Patagonian steppe and sub-Antarctic forests of *ñire* (Antarctic beech) and *lenga* (lenga beech) trees provide exceptional trekking country and a home for endangered *huemul* deer, red fox and puma.

The park's northern section can be reached from the village of El Chaltén, where the jagged jaws of the Fitz Roy mountain range dominate a dramatic skyline. Tremendous glaciers, including the show-stopping **Glaciar Perito Moreno** (see page 144), are the stars of the park's southern sector, within easy reach of the town of El Calafate.

EL CHALTÉN

Argentina's self-proclaimed "national trekking capital" **EL CHALTÉN** lies within the boundaries of the Parque Nacional Los Glaciares, 217km northwest of El Calafate. It is set at the confluence of two pristine rivers, overlooked by the granite spires of Monte Fitz Roy (3405m) and Cerro Torre (3102m). El Chaltén means "smoking mountain", a name given to Monte Fitz Roy by the Tehuelche.

El Chaltén is Argentina's youngest town, officially created in 1985 as an outpost against Chilean encroachment. Since then it has experienced a tourist boom, and during the peak season of December to March, campers, hikers and climbers descend in large numbers, but there are enough trails in the immense park to keep them from getting crowded. From El Chaltén you can also cross over to Chile on foot and by boat (see page 140).

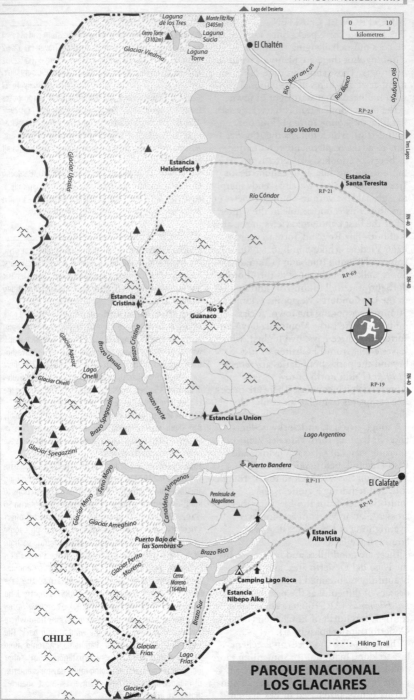

PARQUE NACIONAL
LOS GLACIARES

1

HIKES FROM EL CHALTÉN

Fitz Roy and Torre peaks offer some of the planet's most challenging technical climbing, but there are plenty of paths for beginners. Those short on time can enjoy a number of day-hikes in the national park with trailheads that start right in town.

The most popular trail is the relatively flat hike to **Laguna Torre** (11km; 6hr round-trip), which follows the Río Fitz Roy to a lake resplendent with floating icebergs, overlooked by Cerro Torre. A more strenuous hike is to **Laguna de los Tres** (12.5km; 8hr), which ascends sharply to a glacial lake with in-your-face views of Fitz Roy; this is impassable in the winter.

For the best panoramic views in the area – of both Fitz Roy and Torre as well as Lago Viedma – hike uphill to 1490m-high **Lomo del Pliegue Tumbado** (12km; 8hr). Short walks include those to the **Chorrillo del Salto** waterfall (4km; 2hr) and uphill to the **Los Condores** viewpoint (1km; 1hr 30min) overlooking the town. A classic multi-day hike is the **Monte Fitz Roy/Cerro Torre loop** (three days, two nights), which leaves either from El Chaltén or just beyond the park's boundaries at *Hostería El Pilar* (15km north of town; ⊛hosteriaelpilar.com.ar). There are three free **campsites** (with latrines only) along the route.

A tough five-day, anticlockwise loop takes in Laguna Toro, Paso del Viento, amazing views of Glaciar Viedma, and Paso Huemul, before skirting Lago Viedma on the way back to town. Tougher still, and requiring a guide, is the multi-day trek from Río Eléctrico that crosses Glaciar Marconi and involves overnighting at least twice on the Southern Ice Field.

There are good hikes and no crowds in the Lago del Desierto area, and three beautifully maintained trails of varying degrees of difficulty at the private *Reserva Los Huemules* (AR$100; ⊛loshuemules. com), 17km north of El Chaltén (Lago del Desierto transfers pass by it).

The park office produces an excellent **free trekking map**, but for something more detailed, the 1:50,000 *Monte Fitz Roy & Cerro Torre* map published by Zagier and Urruty can be purchased in El Chaltén.

ARRIVAL AND DEPARTURE

By bus The bus terminal is in the southeastern end of town on Güemes, at Perito Moreno. Chaltén Travel (☎02962 493092, ⊛chaltentravel.com), Taqsa/Marga (☎02962 493068, ⊛taqsa.com.ar) and Cal-tur (☎02962 493801, ⊛caltur.com.ar) all run up to three buses daily to El Calafate. Chaltén Travel and Taqsa/Marga also run buses up the Ruta 40 daily Nov–April. Las Lengas (☎02962 493023, ⊛transportelaslengas.com) runs shuttle services to El Calafate Airport, Lago del Desierto, Río Eléctrico and *Hostería El Pilar*. Buy tickets at least a day in advance for all services.

Destinations Los Antiguos (daily; 10hr 30min); Bariloche (1–2 daily; around 23hr); El Calafate (3–9 daily, typically at 8am, 1pm & 7.30pm; 3hr); El Calafate Airport (1–3 daily; 3hr); Perito Moreno (1–2 daily; 11hr 30min).

INFORMATION AND TOURS

A useful website is ⊛elchalten.com. Bring plenty of cash: the single ATM at the bus station is unreliable. Dollars, Euros and Chilean pesos are widely accepted. There's a basic *puesto sanitario* (health clinic) on Agostini, but for anything major, go to El Calafate.

Parque Nacional Los Glaciares office The excellent park office is at the entrance to town (daily: Dec–Feb 9am–8pm; March–Nov 9am–5pm; ☎02962 493004), with free maps, wildlife exhibits, video screenings and advice on leave-no-trace camping. All buses that arrive in El Chaltén stop here for an English- or Spanish-language introduction to the rules of the park. Climbers, multi-day trekkers and those using the Laguna Torre campsite must register here first.

Tourist information There's a helpful tourist office (daily 8am–8pm ☎0292 493370) in the bus station. Lists of accommodation options and info on local tour operators are posted on the bus station wall.

Tour operators El Chaltén Mountain Guides, San Martín 187 (☎02962 493320, ⊛ecmg.com.ar), run ice-climbing and rock-climbing trips – from half-day introductions to multi-day ventures. Fitz Roy Expediciones, San Martín 56 (☎02962 493110, ⊛fitzroyexpediciones.com.ar) offers a new, day-long trek to the Glaciar Cagliero, plus some ice trekking on the glacier itself and a via ferrata section. Fit, active travellers only (AR$4100). In the same office, Patagonia Aventura (☎02494 436424, ⊛patagonia-aventura.com) offers boat excursions across the lake to the snout of Glaciar Viedma (AR$1100), trekking on the Peninsula Viedma (AR$2100). *Patagonia Hostel* runs transfers to Lago del Desierto (37km) from where you bike back to town with the wind at your back. The Anglo-Argentine-run Walk Patagonia, Antonio Rojo 62 (☎02962 493275, ⊛walkpatagonia.com) offer logistical support to those doing multi-day treks and run all manner of guided treks themselves. Most agencies shut down in the winter.

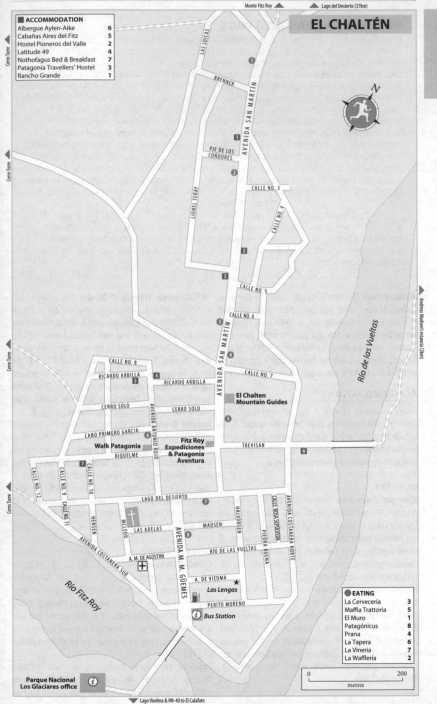

EL CHALTÉN

Monte Fitz Roy   Lago del Desierto (37km)

ACCOMMODATION
Albergue Aylen-Aike	6
Cabañas Aires del Fitz	5
Hostel Pioneros del Valle	2
Latitude 49	4
Nothofagus Bed & Breakfast	7
Patagonia Travellers' Hostel	3
Rancho Grande	1

EATING
La Cervecería	3
Maffia Trattoria	5
El Muro	1
Patagónicus	8
Prana	4
La Tapera	6
La Vineria	7
La Wafflería	2

El Chalten Mountain Guides

Walk Patagonia

Fitz Roy Expediciones & Patagonia Aventura

Las Lengas

Bus Station

Parque Nacional Los Glaciares office

Río Fitz Roy

Río de las Vueltas

Andreas Madsen's estancia (2km)

Cerro Torre

Lago Viedma & RN-40 to El Calafate

0   200
metres

1

HIKE, BIKE AND SAIL INTO CHILE

From El Chaltén, it's possible to cross to **Villa O'Higgins** (see page 463) in Chile (ⓦvillaohiggins.com) via an adventurous two-day trip by boat and foot (or bike) in the summer. Start by catching a morning bus from El Chaltén (1hr 30min; AR$500) in time to take the 10am **boat** across Lago del Desierto (late Dec to late Feb: Tues, Fri & Sun; early Dec & March to mid-April fewer departures; AR$500). The lake's northern shore can also be reached by **hiking** (16km; 5hr) along its eastern shore to a free campsite next to the Argentine border post, where you get an exit stamp from the police. From there, a narrow, hilly trail (you'll have to carry your bike part of the way) runs to Laguna Larga (2hr 30min) and beyond to no-man's-land in between. On the Chilean side, the trail turns into a wide dirt-and-gravel road that winds its way down to the Lago O'Higgins and the Chilean border post at Candelario Mancilla (4hr 30min), a handful of houses by the lake. There's one place to stay, *Hospedaje Candelario Mancilla* (ⓣ67 2567189) – a **campsite** with access to showers and two or three basic rooms available at owner Rodrigo's house (CH$8000/person); Rodrigo can provide meals on request. Bring plenty of food, as the ferry from Villa O'Higgins is weather-dependent and you may find yourself lingering here for an extra day or two.

There are boats to Villa O'Higgins (Dec–Feb Mon, Wed, Thurs & Sat; Nov & March Mon, Wed & Sat; one weekly boat Sept, Oct & April; CH$36,000), typically departing from Candelario Mancilla at 5.30pm; check ⓦvillaohiggins.com for up-to-date boat schedules and prices. Rodrigo can hire out pack horses to meet you at Lago del Desierto and help with luggage (CH$40,000 per horse).

Walking tour The first European settler to the area, Andreas Madsen, came here from Denmark in 1915 and built the Estancia Cerro Fitz Roy, a 40min walk along the Río de las Vueltas, on the side opposite town. Every day, Madsen's great-grandson Fitz Roy leads a walking tour in Spanish, English and German from the bridge (3hr; US$25; ⓣ02966 15 344540) to the restored *estancia*; book ahead.

ACCOMMODATION

Reserve a bed in advance if you are coming between December and March. Few places open year-round. Rates include breakfast, unless stated otherwise and all listed accommodation offers (painfully slow) wi-fi. Several basic campsites are scattered throughout the town.

HOSTELS

Albergue Aylen-Aike Trevisán 125 ⓣ02962 493311; map p.139. Particularly popular with those scaling Mt Fitz Roy (judging from a wall full of photos of climbers), this intimate hostel has plenty of *buena onda*, courtesy of knowledgeable owner Sebastian, the six-bed dorms are spacious enough so as not to be stuffy and guests can use the kitchen. Sept–April. Dorms AR$450

Hostel Pioneros del Valle San Martín 451 ⓣ02902 492217, ⓦcaltur.com.ar; map p.139. On the main street, the CalTur-affiliated behemoth offers professional if impersonal service, with a large range of backpacker amenities including currency exchange and bus pick-up/ drop-off, friendly staff and large, sparsely decorated en-suite and good-value private rooms. Dorms AR$350, doubles AR$1200

★ **Patagonia Travellers' Hostel** San Martín 493 ⓣ02962 493019, ⓦpatagoniahostel.com.ar; map p.139. With its slate walls, a beautiful, airy common space with plasma-screen TV and well-equipped guest kitchen, this chalet-like hiker refuge is the most appealing of the town's hostels. Downsides are lockers located outside the simple four-person dorms and school-gym-like communal bathrooms, though private rooms are en suite. Their biking tours from Lago del Desierto are justifiably popular. Mid-Sept to mid-April. Dorms US$306, doubles US$1350

Rancho Grande San Martín 520 ⓣ02962 493005, ⓦranchograndehostel.com; map p.139. This large Chaltén Travel-affiliated hostel is a backpacker factory, but they're good at what they do. Pluses include snug four-bed dorms, two-tiered dining/hangout area, on-site café/bar, small kitchen and a designated member of staff who helps you plan your stay. They also change currency, accept credit cards and sell onward bus tickets. Dorms AR$450, doubles AR$1920

GUESTHOUSES

Cabañas Aires del Fitz Ricardo Arbilla 124 ⓣ02962 493134, ⓦairesdelfitz.com.ar; map p.139. An effusive hostess runs four split-level cabañas sleeping either two/ three or six people; beautiful living spaces include a fully equipped kitchen and satellite TV in the common area, and nice touches such as blackout curtains and drying racks in bathrooms. Open year-round. No breakfast. Cabañas AR2160

Latitude 49 Ricardo Arbilla 145 ⓣ02962 493347, Wlatitud49.com.ar; map p.139. A justifiably popular place with spacious, self-contained apartments for two

1

or four people. The rooms are compact, but the hostess goes out of her way to help her guests. Closed June & July. **AR$2070**

★ **Nothofagus Bed & Breakfast** Hensen, at Riquelme ☎ 02962 493087, ⊛ nothofagusbb.com.ar; map p.139. A bright and homely B&B with wooden furnishing and a rustic feel; three rooms are en suites, while the other four share a bathroom; some have views of Fitz Roy. Besides the good breakfast, there's a small library and book exchange. Closed Easter–Oct. **AR$1170**

EATING

Opening times given are for high season; many places close Easter–Oct.

La Cervecería San Martín 564; map p.139. One of the most sociable spots in town, with locals and hikers perching on rough-hewn wooden seats to savour pints of bock or pilsner microbrews or tuck into ample portions of stew, pizza or pasta. There's a beer garden out back and you can visit the brewery during one of the daily tours. Daily 11am–midnight.

★ **Maffia Trattoria** Av San Martín 107 ☎ 02962 493069; map p.139. Decked out in bold crimsons and lime greens, and with some booths for privacy, *Maffia Trattoria* serves imaginative Italian fare, such as squid-ink pappardelle with seafood and gnocchi in saffron sauce. Mains AR$200320. Daily noon–11pm.

El Muro San Martín 948 ☎ 02962 493248; map p.139. Lasagne with lamb and mushrooms, trout in orange and almond sauce and sweet and sour ribs are just some of the tempting creations dished up at this hungry hiker haven. There's a climbing wall out back to help you work up an appetite. Mains from AR$250. Daily noon–midnight.

Patagónicus Güemes, at Madsen ☎ 02962 493025; map p.139. Consistently the best pizza in town (twenty types, including plenty of vegetarian ones), served at big wooden tables. The good range of beers includes their own Chaltén and Patagónicus brews. Small/large pizza from AR$100/200. Mon & Wed–Sun noon–11pm.

Prana San Martín; map p.139. Indian wall hangings decorate the salmon-pink walls of this snug vegetarian bistro, while delicious smells lure you in to try the likes of brown rice risotto, beetroot gnocchi stuffed with sheep's cheese and lentil stew. Fantastic selection of gourmet teas, too. Mains AR$140–180. Daily 9am–11pm.

La Tapera Av Antonio Rojo; map p.139. Adorable, split-level log cabin with a roaring fire, packed full of hungry punters tucking into pork shoulder cooked with beer, excellent steak, salmon with spring onion and ginger, a smattering of tapas and cold weather warmers: *locro* and lamb and lentil stew. Mains AR$97–192. Daily 12.30–11.30pm.

★ **La Vineria** Av Lago del Desierto 265 ☎ 02962 493301; map p.139. This busy, buzzy little joint is the place to sample a couple of dozen regional craft beers as well as wines from all over Argentina, accompanied by sharing platters (AR$360) of cold cuts (think smoked venison, trout, black pudding) and local and imported cheeses, as well as gourmet sandwiches (AR$150). Hugely popular, with a usually packed outdoor terrace. Daily 3pm–2am.

La Wafflería San Martín; map p.139. Colourful and snug, *La Wafflería* sates your cravings for waffles. Toppings vary from calafate ice cream with *dulce de leche* to blue cheese, black olives and nuts (AR$95–265), and tipples range from seven types of hot chocolate to El Chaltén's very own Supay brew. Daily 10.30am–10.30pm.

EL CALAFATE

If global warming were suddenly to lay waste to the Perito Moreno glacier, **EL CALAFATE** would promptly fizzle out in its wake. Settled by wool traders in the 1920s and named after the edible purple berry that pops up in summer, the town expanded rapidly following the creation of Parque Nacional Los Glaciares in 1937. Perito Moreno glacier remains the main draw for visitors, who flood the town particularly between December and March. The glacier aside, El Calafate makes an excellent base for boat trips, ice trekking and hiking into the remotest corners of this slice of wilderness.

WHAT TO SEE AND DO

The main drag, Avenida Libertador, is lined with tourism outfits and restaurants, with many lodgings located within a few blocks.

THE GLACIARIUM

The town's main attraction is the **Glaciarium** (daily: Sept–April 9am–8pm, May–Aug 11am–7pm; AR$360; ⊛ glaciarium.com), a superb interactive museum dedicated to glaciers. Displays recount the discovery of the two Patagonian ice fields and the tiny creatures that have adapted to live on the ice. The videos – a 3D documentary on the Parque Nacional Los Glaciares and one on environmental issues – are particularly worthwhile. Free shuttle buses to the Glaciarium depart from the car park on 1 de Mayo, between avenidas Libertador and Roca (hourly on the hour 9am–noon, then every 30min until 6pm; reduced service May–Aug).

1

ARRIVAL AND DEPARTURE

By plane El Calafate's airport (ⓦ aeropuertoelcalafate. com) is 22km east of town, served by taxis (AR$300) and minibuses run by Ves Patagonia (ⓣ 02902 494355 ⓦ vespatagonia.com.ar; AR$150). El Calafate is linked by frequent Aerolíneas Argentinas and LADE flights to numerous Argentine destinations. DAP (ⓦ dapairline.com) flies to Puerto Natales.

Destinations Daily to Bariloche, Buenos Aires, Trelew, Río Gallegos and Ushuaia; Puerto Natales (Thurs & Sun during high season; 35min)

By bus Buses arrive at the new Terminal de Omnibus (ⓣ 02902 491476) off Av Pluschow, a 10min walk east of the centre. Always Glaciers (Av Libertador 924, ⓣ 02902 493961, ⓦ alwaysglaciers.com) runs private bus transfers to Torres del Paine in Chile, as does South Road (Av Libertador 1215, ⓣ 02902 492393, ⓦ southroad.com. ar). Chaltén Travel (ⓣ 02962 493022, ⓦ chaltentravel. com), Taqsa/Marga (ⓣ 02966 4442 033, ⓦ taqsa.com.ar) and Cal-tur (ⓣ 02962 493150, ⓦ caltur.com.ar) all serve El Chaltén during high season, typically at 8am, 1pm and 6.30pm; Chaltén Travel and Taqsa/Marga also run buses up the Ruta 40 daily Nov–April. Taqsa/Marga also runs to Río Gallegos; change there for daily departures to Ushuaia. Cootra (ⓣ 02902 491444, ⓦ cootra.com.ar) and Turismo Zaahj (ⓣ 02902 491631, ⓦ turismozaahj.com) run daily services to Puerto Natales in peak season.

Destinations Bariloche (summer only; 1–2 daily; 27hr); El Chaltén (up to 9 daily; 3hr); Puerto Natales, Chile; 1–2 daily; 6hr); Río Gallegos (3 daily; 4hr–4hr 30min).

INFORMATION

Tourist information The poorly stocked tourist office is on the Anfiteatro del Bosque, off Av Libertador (daily: summer 8am–9pm; winter 9am–7pm; ⓣ 02902 491 090, ⓦ elcalafate.tur.ar); there's also a kiosk (same hours) inside the bus terminal. **Better is BAFT (Backpacking Free Travel),** Gregores at 9 de Julio (daily 9am–7pm; ⓦ baftravel.com), an excellent backpacker information centre that can book accommodation and onward travel.

Parque Nacional Los Glaciares office The national park office on Av Libertador 1302 has maps and can provide up-to-date information (Mon–Fri 8am–6pm, Sat & Sun 9am–6pm; ⓣ 02902 491005, ⓦ parquesnacionales.gov.ar).

TOUR OPERATORS

Cruceros MarPatag Av Libertador 1319 ⓣ 02902 492118, ⓦ crucerosmarpatag.com. Runs full-day boat trips aboard the luxurious *Crucero Maria Turquesa* that take in all three main glaciers – Upsala, Spegazzini and Perito Moreno (AR$3950).

Glaciar Sur 9 de Julio 57, Local 2 ⓣ 02902 495050, ⓦ glaciarsur.com. The only operator allowed to take small groups of visitors into the pristine, remote southwestern corner of Parque Nacional Los Glaciares (see page 136).

Hielo y Aventura Av Libertador 935 ⓣ 02902 492205, ⓦ hieloyaventura.com. Offers Mini Trekking (AR$2700) and Big Ice (AR$5200) ice-trekking trips on Glaciar Perito Moreno, as well as boat excursions to the glacier (AR$500).

Southern Spirit Av Libertador 1319 ⓣ 02902 491582, ⓦ southernspiritfte.com.ar. Runs a full-day boat cruise/ hike to the Glaciar Mayo (AR$2000).

Viva Patagonia Av Libertador 1037 ⓣ 02902 491133, ⓦ vivapatagonia.com. Offers half-day kayaking excursions along the Perito Moreno glacier (beginners welcome).

ACCOMMODATION

Reserve in advance for high season. Rates include breakfast and kitchen use.

★ **América del Sur** Puerto Deseado 153 ⓣ 02902 493525, ⓦ americahostel.com.ar; map p.143. A well-designed, spacious and friendly place with wonderful views of Lago Argentino and knowledgeable staff who can help you organize a wide range of trips. The four-bed dorms and private rooms are clean, bright and have under-floor heating. It's a 10min uphill walk from the centre. Dorms AR$415, doubles AR$1600

Hostel Cambalache Bed & Beer Moyano 1270 ⓣ 02902 492696; map p.143. The dorms at this centrally located hostel are very spartan, but there is plenty of *buena onda*, there are custom-made bamboo-frame electric bikes for rent and guests get discounts at the bistro/ craft beer bar next door. There are a few camping spots in the garden and owners are full of valuable local knowledge. Camping/ person AR$180, dorms AR$270

Hostel del Glaciar Libertador Av Libertador 587 ⓣ 02902 491792, ⓦ glaciar.com; map p.143. This enormous (and somewhat anonymous) wooden house sleeps more than a hundred, has spotless dorms with private bathrooms, and lovely private rooms. Walls are thin, so you may feel as if you're in bed with your neighbours, and the service is professional if impersonal. Dorms AR$350, doubles AR$1000

Hostel Nakel Yenu Puerto San Julián 244 ⓣ 02902 493711, ⓦ hostelnakelyenu.com; map p.143. This refurbished, bright-yellow hostel, with psychedelic mural, dreamcatchers and guitar for guest use, is one of the cosiest and most chilled-out in town. The kitchen/lounge are in a separate building next door so as not to disturb early sleepers, six- and four-bed dorms have lockers and the owners throw barbecues most weekends. A 10min uphill walk from the centre. Closed June–August. Dorms AR$450, doubles AR$1500

El Ovejero José Pantín 64 ⓣ 02902 493422; map p.143. Just a block from the main street, this clean campsite is protected from the wind by a row of trees and sits alongside a babbling brook and a *parilla* restaurant

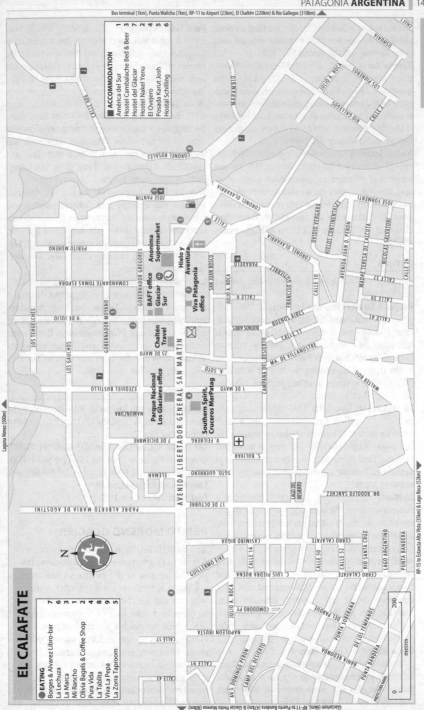

Bus terminal (1km), Punta Walichu (7km), RP-11 to Airport (23km), El Chaltén (220km) & Río Gallegos (310km) ▲

EL CALAFATE

● EATING
Borges & Álvarez Libro-bar	7
La Lechuza	6
La Marca	3
Mi Rancho	1
Olivia Bagels & Coffee Shop	2
Pura Vida	4
La Tablita	8
Viva La Pepa	9
La Zorra Taproom	5

■ ACCOMMODATION
América del Sur	1
Hostel Cambalache Bed & Beer	3
Hostel del Glaciar	7
Hostel Nakel Yenu	2
El Ovejero	4
Posada Karut Josh	5
Hostal Schilling	6

Laguna Nimez (500m) ◄

Anonima Supermarket

Hielo y Aventura

BAFT office
Glaciar Sur

Viva Patagonia office

Chaltén Travel

Parque Nacional Los Glaciares office

Southern Spirit, Cruceros MarPatag

AVENIDA LIBERTADOR GENERAL SAN MARTÍN

RP-15 to Estancia Alta Vista (35km) & Lago Roca (52km) ▶

metres
0   200

Glaciarium (6km), RP-11 to Puerto Bandera (47km) & Glaciar Perito Moreno (80km) ▲

1

and hostel. Price includes hot showers and there are picnic tables and *fogones* (fire pits for cooking; firewood costs extra). Camping AR$180, doubles AR$1300

Posada Karut Josh C 12 no. 1887 ☎02902 496444, ⓦcposadakarutjosh.com.ar; map p.143. This guesthouse, a short walk from the centre, has several things going for it: a peaceful location, spacious rooms decorated in bright colours and, above all, the warmth and hospitality of Claudia and Federico, who go out of their way to make their guests feel welcome. AR$1494

Hostal Schilling Gobernador Paradelo 141 ☎02902 491453, ⓦhostalschilling.com; map p.143. Its vast lounge wall decorated by globetrotting guests of all ages, this professionally run guesthouse offers spacious, comfortable but featureless en suite rooms and a single dorm. There's a bar on site, and the owner runs the excellent Glaciar Sur trips (see page 142). Dorms AR$324, doubles AR$738

EATING

Outside of the high season, most places have reduced opening hours.

Borges & Alvarez Libro-bar Av Libertador 1015; map p.143. This small, warm café-bar with a cave-like, book-covered lounge and elevated outdoor terrace attracts bibliophiles and cocktail lovers alike. There's an extensive range of Argentine and South American coffee-table books to flick through while perusing the long list of cocktails (AR$140–180), or sipping a regional craft beer or coffee. Daily 10am–3am.

La Lechuza Av Libertador 1301 ⓦlalechuzapizzas. com.ar; map p.143. This deservedly popular place serves up thirty or so varieties of what are arguably the best pizzas in town (AR$190–270) from its wood-fired oven, plus pasta dishes, make-your-own salads and huge sandwiches. There are a couple of other branches. Daily noon–11.30pm.

La Marca Jose Pantín 64; map p.143. Attached to a campsite and hostel, this is a budget favourite for all-you-can-eat *parilla*; AR$270 will get you your fill of lamb, steak, chicken, chorizo, morcilla (black pudding) and *chinchulines* (crispy lamb entrails). Daily noon–11pm.

★**Mi Rancho** Gobernador Moyano at 9 de Julio ☎02902 490540; map p.143. All exposed brick and homely touches, this intimate little restaurant offers some wonderfully creative and surprisingly affordable dishes. Your taste buds will thank you for the pork with apple chutney and lamb T-bone with calafate sauce. Mains AR$300–380. Daily noon–3pm & 8pm–midnight.

Olivia Bagels & Coffee Shop 9 de Julio 131; map p.143. The nicest of El Calafate's coffee shops, *Olivia Bagels & Coffee Shop* is the place to linger with one of its specialist brews, or enjoy a light lunch – they do filled bagels (AR$120), wraps and Caesar salad. Daily 10am–8pm.

Pura Vida Av Libertador 1876 ☎02902 493358; map p.143. A 10min walk from the centre, this A-frame cabin is a godsend for vegetarians, though meat eaters can enjoy the likes of "Granny's lentil stew", country chicken pie and lamb *empanadas*. Save room for dessert. Mains AR$200–260. 7.30–11.30pm; closed Wed.

★**La Tablita** Rosales 28 ⓦla-tablita.com.ar; map p.143. An El Calafate institution for almost thirty years, this large hall is popular with discerning carnivores who come for the spit-roasted Patagonian lamb, steak and traditional gaucho fare, such as lamb chitterlings and sweetbreads. If there are two of you, go for "Mix Carnes" (AR$550). Daily noon–3.30pm & 7pm–midnight.

Viva La Pepa Amado 833; map p.143. Cheerful, whimsical café decorated with children's paintings and specializing in sweet and savoury crepes (think lamb with honey and rosemary, chicken with blue cheese and pear, and *dulce de leche* with chocolate-covered banana (AR$120–160), as well as soups, sandwiches, fresh juices and coffee. Mon–Sat 11am–11pm.

La Zorra Taproom Av Libertador 832 ☎02902 488042, ⓦcervezazorra.com; map p.143. Its interior decked out with dozens of humorous beer-related posters, this wood-panelled taproom devoted to El Calafate's craft beer attracts a good mix of younger locals and travellers. There's a nice outdoor terrace, and the kitchen serves burgers, sandwiches and pizza to go with the dozen craft beers on tap. Mon 6pm–2am, Tues–Sun noon–2am.

DIRECTORY

Banks There are four banks with ATMs including at the Banco de la Nacion, Av Libertador 1133, and Banco de Santa Cruz, Av Libertador 1285.

Car rental Avis, Av Libertador 1078 (☎02902 492877, ⓦavis.com); Fiorasi, Av Libertador 1341 (☎02902 495330, ⓦfiorasirentacar.com). Prices start at around AR$1200/day.

Laundry Lava Andina, Espora 88.

Post office Av Libertador 1133.

PERITO MORENO GLACIER

The **PERITO MORENO GLACIER** is one of Argentina's greatest natural wonders. It's not the longest of the country's glaciers – Upsala is twice as long (60km) – and whereas the ice cliffs at its snout tower up to 60m high, the face of Spegazzini can reach heights double that. However, such comparisons prove irrelevant when you make your way along the extensive network of boardwalks facing the towering wall and seemingly endless field of immense white and blue spikes, and hear the muffled cracks as enormous chunks of ice cleave from the face of this immense glacier and drop into the lagoon. Afternoons are the better time to visit, as the majority of tours arrive in the morning.

Perito Moreno is considered to be "stable" in the sense that it is neither advancing nor retreating. It periodically pushes right across the channel, forming a massive dyke of ice that cuts off the Brazo Rico and Brazo Sur from the main body of Lago Argentino. Isolated from their natural outlet, the water in the *brazos* (arms) builds up against the flank of the glacier, flooding the surrounding area, until eventually the pressure forces open a passage into the canal once again. Occurring over the course of several hours, such a rupture is, for those lucky enough to witness it, one of nature's most awesome spectacles.

UPSALA AND OTHER GLACIERS

Although receding fast, **GLACIAR UPSALA** remains the longest glacier in the park and indeed in South America. The same height as Perito Moreno (60m), Upsala is twice as long (roughly 60km), 7km wide and known for calving huge translucent, blue-tinged icebergs that bob around Lago Argentino like surreal art sculptures. Tours (see page 142), usually called "All Glaciers", also take in the Spegazzini and Perito Moreno glaciers. Note that Upsala is occasionally inaccessible when icebergs block the channels. The Mayo glacier, reachable via the Brazo de Mayo, and closest to the Perito Moreno glacier, has recently become accessible to the public.

LAGO ROCA AND AROUND

The southern arm of Lago Argentino, and also known as Brazo Sur, **LAGO ROCA** is fringed by dense forest and hemmed in by mountains. This is the least visited and the most serene corner of the park, but to reach the most spectacular part – an unnamed glacial lagoon full of enormous chunks of ice, fed by two glaciers and with Glaciar Dickson peeping from the border of Chile's **Torres del Paine National Park** (see page 471) – you have to go via organized

tour. **Glaciar Sur** (see page 142) is currently the only company allowed to bring a group of up to fourteen people here daily. The tour involves a boat ride to the southern end of Brazo Sur, an hour's stiff hike to the smaller Lago Frías, a zodiac boat ride across and then a spectacular, mostly flat, hike along a dried riverbed to the lagoon, with waterfalls cascading down the mountains on one side.

RÍO GALLEGOS

The grim and windy oil refining port of **RÍO GALLEGOS** is an inevitable (but mercifully brief) stop for travellers travelling by bus between El Calafate and Ushuaia (if not heading to Punta Arenas in Chile) or between El Calafate, Ushuaia and destinations along the east coast of Argentina.

ARRIVAL AND DEPARTURE

By plane Río Gallegos Airport is 7km west of the city. A taxi to the centre costs around AR$250.

Destinations Daily flights with Aerolíneas Argentinas and LATAM to Buenos Aires and several weekly to Ushuaia and Río Grande. LATAM also flies to Punta Arenas, Chile, twice monthly.

By bus The bus terminal is 3km west of the city at the corner of Av Eva Perón and the RN3. Bus marked "B" or "terminal" connects the bus terminal with downtown; a taxi costs AR$120.

Destinations Buenos Aires (several daily, 36hr); El Calafate (4–5 daily; 4–5hr); Puerto Madryn (6 daily; 15–19hr); Ushuaia (daily; 12hr). In Chile: Punta Arenas (2 daily; 3hr 30min); Puerto Natales (4 weekly; 4hr).

INFORMATION

Tourist information There's a tourist information booth in the bus terminal (Mon–Fri 9am–8pm, Sat & Sun 9am–2pm & 4–8pm; ☎02966 442159).

ACCOMMODATION AND EATING

Accommodation caters mostly to business travellers, so budget options are thin on the ground.

British Club Roca 935 ☎02966 432668. A port of call for Bruce Chatwin, this atmospheric place has more than a hint of a gentleman's club about it. The weekday lunch menu (AR$100) is a bargain and the à la carte temps with the likes of Lancashire hotpot and black hake with vegetable risotto. Mains from AR$250. Daily noon–3pm & 8pm–midnight.

Hospedaje Elcira Pje Zuccarino 431 ☎02966 429856. Handy for the bus station, this guesthouse is adorned to

1

CROSSING INTO TIERRA DEL FUEGO

Reaching Argentine Tierra del Fuego or, specifically, Ushuaia, from the Argentine mainland requires travelling through Chilean territory. The journey, which takes the better part of a day (there are no night buses along this route and the border post in Tierra del Fuego is no longer open at night), involves crossing two borders, thus getting stamped in and out of Chile and Argentina twice, and a thirty-minute ferry ride across the Magellan Strait. If you book a bus ticket from Río Gallegos to Ushuaia, the ferry crossing is included in the ticket price and the bus driver will guide you through the border crossing formalities.

look like a stereotypical grandma's house, with a kitchen for guests but without any warmth or charm. Dorms AR$250, doubles AR$500

Laguanacazul Gob Lista, at Sarmiento ☎02966 444144. Chef Mirko Ionfrida doesn't shy from using locally sourced game in his Patagonian cuisine, so expect the likes of guanaco and rhea. At this waterfront restaurant, slow-cooked lamb is a worthy splurge; don't even think about turning up in backpacker gear. Mains from around AR$250. Tues–Sun noon–3pm & 8pm–midnight.

Sehuén Rawson 160 ☎02966 425683, ⓦhotelsehuen. com. An efficiently run little hotel with a range of decent rooms; each has a TV, phone and boxy private bathroom, and breakfast is served in a vaulted room. AR$650

Tierra del Fuego

A rugged and isolated archipelago at the extreme southern tip of the continent, **TIERRA DEL FUEGO** (Land of Fire) marks the finish line for South America. Here the Andes range marches into the chilly southern waters; deciduous forests and Ice Age glaciers lie a stone's throw from a wildlife-rich shoreline, penguins and sea lions huddle on rocky islets, salmon and trout thrash about in the rivers, and sheep and guanacos graze on arid windswept plains.

The archipelago is shared, with historic hostility, by Argentina and Chile, and only about a third of Isla Grande (Tierra del Fuego's main island) belongs to Argentina. This includes **Ushuaia**, however, the region's biggest city and top tourist destination. As locals will proudly point out, it is the planet's southernmost inhabited city (though the town of Puerto Williams in Chile is actually further south. It's a fantastic base for exploring the lakes and mountains of **Parque Nacional Tierra del Fuego**, wildlife-watching trips on the **Beagle Channel**, and, for luxury travellers, summer cruises to **Antarctica**.

High season is from December to March, when days are longest and warmest. Spring (Oct to mid-Nov) is beautiful and lush, but can be seriously windy. In autumn (late March to April) the countryside lights up in warm shades of red and orange. But Ushuaia's growing status as a winter-sports playground ensures it is now a year-round destination.

USHUAIA

Sandwiched between the Sierra Venciguerra range and the deep blue of the icy Beagle Channel, **USHUAIA** has one of the most dramatic locations of any South American city, its colourful houses tumbling down the hillside, and the bay protected from southwesterly winds and occasional thrashing storms.

The city lies 3500km south of Buenos Aires and just 1000km north of **Antarctica**, a fact you'll have no problem detecting: even in summer you may need to wrap up warm.

WHAT TO SEE AND DO

A former penal colony, Ushuaia is not the best-planned city, but it has a clutch of absorbing museums, and an excellent (though pricey) dining scene. Most of the tourist and commercial action is centred on **San Martín** and **Maipú** streets, while boats leave on wildlife-watching excursions from the Muelle Turístico. The post office issues end-of-the-world stamps, conveniently forgetting about Puerto Williams (see page 476). There's good **hiking** in Parque Nacional Tierra del

Fuego, plus ice climbing or trekking on nearby glaciers, horseriding in nature reserves, scuba diving in the chilly harbour, boating to penguin and sea-lion colonies and skiing and dog sledding in winter. You can also visit the historic *Estancia Harberton,* the oldest ranch in Tierra del Fuego and a fascinating place to explore.

MUSEO DEL FIN DEL MUNDO
The **Museo del Fin del Mundo**, Maipú, at Rivadavia (Mon–Fri 10am–5pm, Sat 2–6pm; free), has exhibits on the region's indigenous peoples – the Yámana, Selk'nam, Alakalúf – and the arrival of the Christian missionaries, including a rare example of the Selk'nam–Spanish dictionary written by the Salesian missionary José María Beauvoir. There's also a section on bird life, with stuffed

specimens, while the figurehead of the *Duchess of Albany*, a ship wrecked in 1893, looks on overhead.

MUSEO MARÍTIMO Y PRESIDIO
Housed inside the city's former prison, the excellent **Museo Marítimo y Presidio**, at Yaganes and Gobernador Paz (daily: Jan & Feb 9am–8pm, March–Dec 10am–8pm; AR$400; ⓦmuseomaritimo.com), is not to be missed, It displays exhibits that range from the maritime exploration of Antarctica and its wildlife to life in the prison and its most notorious inhabitants, arranged inside the cells. Most engaging are the scale models of famous ships from the island's history. The most celebrated prisoner to stay was early twentieth-century anarchist Simón Radowitzsky, whose miserable incarceration and brief escape in 1918 are recounted by Bruce

USHUAIA

EATING	
El Almacén Ramos Generales	8
Austral Modern	6
Bodegón Fueguino	3
Freddo	4
Kalma Restó	1
Maria Lola Resto	5
El Turco	2
El Vagón	7

DRINKING & NIGHTLIFE	
Dublin	1
Küar	2

ACCOMMODATION	
Antarctica Hostel	4
B&B Nahuel	2
La Casa en Ushuaia	3
Cruz del Sur	5
Galeazzi-Basily B&B	1
La Posta	7
Yakush	6

Bahía Encerrada

Causeway

Bahía Ushuaia

0 — 250 metres

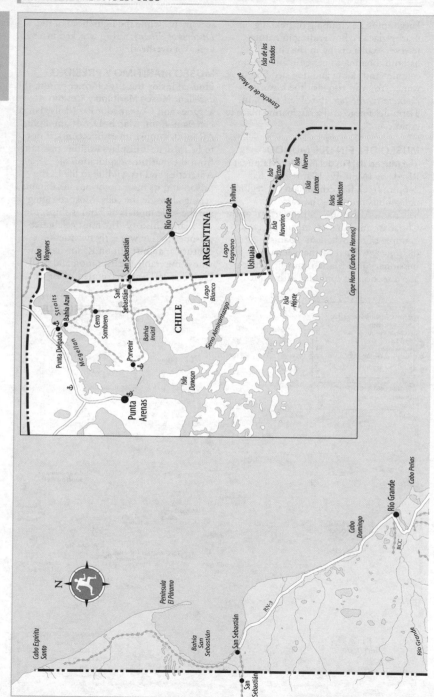

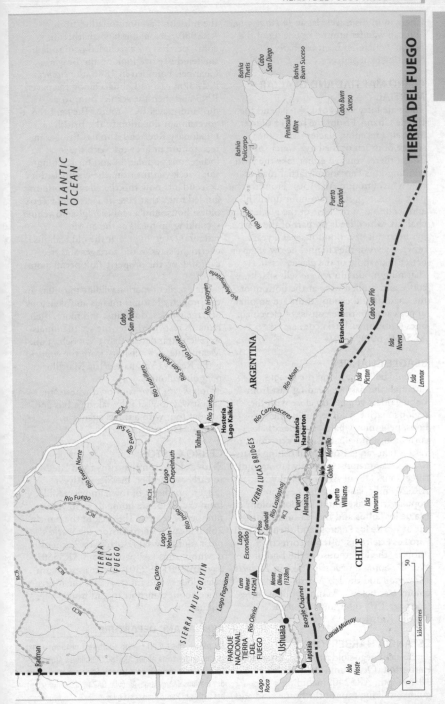

TIERRA DEL FUEGO

ATLANTIC OCEAN

ARGENTINA

CHILE

Bahía Thetis
Cabo San Diego
Bahía Buen Suceso
Cabo Buen Suceso
Península Mitre
Bahía Policarpo
Puerto Español
Río Leticia
Cabo San Pablo
Río Moneta
Río Irigoyen
Río Claro
Río San Pablo
Río Ladrillero
Río Turbio
Hostería Lago Kaikén
Tolhuin
Estancia Moat
Cabo San Pío
Isla Nuevo
Isla Picton
Isla Lennox
Río Moat
Río Cambaceres
Estancia Harberton
Isla Martillo
Isla Gable
SIERRA LUCAS BRIDGES
Río Lasifashaj
Río Gambeli
Paso Garibaldi
RC3
Puerto Almanza
Puerto Williams
Isla Navarino
Lago Chepelmuth
Lago Escondido
RCH
Río Ewan Norte
Río Ewan Sur
Río Fuego
Lago Yehuin
Río Indio
RCF
Cerro Alvear (1425m)
Monte Olivia (1328m)
Beagle Channel
Canal Murray
Río Olivia
Lago Fagnano
SIERRA INJU-GOIYIN
TIERRA DEL FUEGO
RCB
RCE
RCD
Radman
RCA
PARQUE NACIONAL TIERRA DEL FUEGO
Ushuaia
Lapataia
Lago Roca
Isla Hoste

0   kilometres   50

1

Chatwin in his travel classic *In Patagonia*. You can wander around one wing of the prison, which has been left bare, a haunting experience.

CERRO MARTIAL AND GLACIAR MARTIAL

There are lofty views of Ushuaia and the Beagle Channel from the base of **Glaciar Martial**, a receding glacier that is the source of much of the city's water supply. To get there, you can either take the 7km winding Luis Fernando Martial road or take a taxi (around AR$130). From the car park at the top, it's a two-hour uphill hike and scramble to the base of the glacier (the chairlift, which leads up part of the way, has been out of action for several years now). Views of the channel below are even better than those of the glacier itself. A charming mountain *refugio* sells snacks, coffee and mulled wine at the bottom of the chairlift and canopy tours are on offer in peak season: these consist of eleven zip lines (Ⓦcanopyushuaia.com.ar; AR$450–600).

BEAGLE CHANNEL

A scenic boat ride along the **Beagle Channel** (the passage heading east from Ushuaia) lets you get up close with the region's marine wildlife, including sea lions, penguins, whales, steamer ducks, cormorants and albatrosses. Excursions, in vessels that range from small fishing boats to large catamarans, generally last around three hours (about AR$1300, plus an AR$20 embarkation tax). The more popular trips take in the sea-lion colony at **Isla de los Lobos** and the sea-bird-nesting site at **Isla de los Pájaros**, and then sail past **Faro Les Eclaireurs**, often incorrectly dubbed "the Lighthouse at the End of the World". Some longer trips take in *Estancia Harberton* and the Isla Martillo penguin colony (see below). A number of agencies (see page 151) offer tours from the Muelle Turístico.

ESTANCIA HARBERTON

Tierra del Fuego's oldest ranch, **Estancia Harberton** (Oct to mid-April daily 10am–7pm; AR$240, including a 2hr guided walking tour of the homestead and

the museum; accommodation from AR$980/person; Ⓦestanciaharberton. com), perches on a secluded peninsula in a sheltered bay overlooking the Beagle Channel. Founded in 1886, the *estancia* lies 85km east of Ushuaia along the paved RN3 and then the scenic, bumpy, dirt-and-gravel RC-j route. The land was a government donation to the British missionary Reverend Thomas Bridges in recognition of his work with the local indigenous population and for rescuing shipwreck victims from the channels. His descendants now run the *estancia*, offering guided tours that take in Tierra del Fiego's oldest house and a replica Yaghan dwelling – cooking up meals at the on-site restaurant, serving tea at the old teahouse, overnight stays in the cottages and free camping on the property (ask permission first).

The excellent **marine wildlife museum** on the property features murals and skeletons of large whales, dolphins, and more, their remains recovered after the sea mammals were left stranded at Bahía San Sebastián. Meanwhile, just offshore from the *estancia* is the Reserva Yekapasela/Isla Martillo penguin colony.

Unless you have your own wheels, the easiest way to visit is by taking a bus and/ or boat tour with a travel agency in Ushuaia (see page 151).

CERRO CASTOR

With a ski season that runs from late May to early September, the Sierra Alvear ranges, northeast of town and accessible from the RN3, are home to a growing number of resorts. The pick of the bunch, 26km away, is **Cerro Castor**, the world's most southerly ski resort, with 22km of downhill runs (ski passes from AR$560/ day; ☏02901 499301, Ⓦcerrocastor.com), cafés, lodges and more. Ask at the tourist office about transport to and from Ushuaia.

ARRIVAL AND DEPARTURE

By plane The airport is 4km southwest of town; a taxi to the centre costs about AR$180. Aerolíneas Argentinas (Ⓦaerolineas.com.ar) and LATAM (Ⓦlatam.com) serve destinations in Argentina; Aerovías DAP (Ⓦdapairline.com) has flights to Punta Arenas in Chile.

Destinations Buenos Aires (4–8 daily; 3hr 20min); El Calafate (2–3 daily; 1hr 20min); Punta Arenas (Chile; 2 weekly Nov–March; 2hr); Trelew (1 daily; 2hr 10min).

By boat Companies like Piratour (☎02901 424834, ⓦpiratour.com.ar), Rumbo Sur (☎02901 421139, ⓦrumbosur.com.ar) and Ushuaia Boating (closed at the time of research but due to re-open; ☎02901 436193, ⓦushuaiaboating.com) run small boats between Ushuaia and Puerto Williams (Nov–April generally daily; 45min–1hr). All have offices in the Muelle Touristico. One-way tickets cost from US$120 and services are notoriously weather-dependent; crossings can be a rollercoaster ride and if it's too windy, they can be delayed for hours and sometimes days. Note that there's an ARS60 embarkation tax for international boat trips.

By bus There's no central bus terminal; instead buses depart from company offices around town. Frequent services run via Chile to both Argentine and Chilean destinations. All long-distance bus rides entail a short ferry ride at Primera Angostura. Buses Pacheco (book through Tolkeyen at San Martín 409; ☎02901 437073, ⓦtolkeyenpatagonia. com), Bus Sur (book through Tolkeyen) and Tecni Austral (book through Tolkar at Roca 157; ☎02901 431412, ⓦtolkarturismo.tur.ar) run to Punta Arenas, Bus Sur carries on to Puerto Natales; Río Gallegos is served by Taqsa (Fadul 126 (☎02901 435453, ⓦtaqsa.com.ar); change there for buses to El Calafate. These are high season schedules; services are more variable at other times of the year. The tourist office has up-to-date schedules.

Destinations Río Gallegos (3 daily; 12hr); Puerto Natales (1 daily via Punta Arenas; 15hr); Punta Arenas (2–3 daily; 12hr).

INFORMATION AND TOURS

Tourist information The main tourist office is at Av Prefectura Naval Argentina 470 (daily 9am–8pm; ☎02901 437666, ⓦturismoushuaia.com), by the passenger boat terminal: handily it has free wi-fi and toilets. There's also an information kiosk (☎02901 423970) at the airport that opens to meet incoming flights. Club Andino (Fadúl 50; ☎02901 422335, ⓦclubandinoushuaia.com.ar; Mon–Fri 10am–12.30 & 3–8.30pm) provides information on trekking, climbing and winter sports.

Tour operators Canal Fun, Roca 136 (☎02901 435777, ⓦcanalfun.com) runs a wide range of activities, including 4WD trips to Lago Fagnano, kayaking trips, horseriding, and much more; Compañía de Guías, San Martín 628 (☎02901 437753, ⓦcompaniadeguias.tur.ar) is an experienced agency that runs multi-day trekking trips in Tierra del Fuego and arranges ice- and rock-climbing, kayaking, and mountain-biking; Piratour, at Muelle Turístico (☎02901 424834, ⓦpiratour.net), is the only boat company authorized to offer a walk with the Magellanic penguins on Isla Martillo, which allows you to see the birds from up close; Tres Marías,

at Muelle Turístico (☎02901 436416, ⓦtresmariasweb.com), is the only boat company allowed to land on Isla H, taking only eight passengers at a time on hiking/birding excursions; Ushuaia Divers (☎02901 444701, ⓦtierradelfuego.org.ar/divers) operates diving trips in the frigid Beagle Channel to see shipwrecks, sea lions and king crabs.

ACCOMMODATION

Prices are higher in Ushuaia than most other parts of Argentina, so be prepared to stretch your budget. In the December to March high season, book accommodation well in advance.

HOSTELS

Antarctica Hostel Antártida Argentina 270 ☎02901 435774, ⓦantarcticahostel.com; map p.147. This hostel's best feature is the huge, light-drenched lounge with colourful wall hangings, mini-library, guitars for guest use and a bona fide bar serving a good range of drinks. However, the plain upstairs six-bed dorms are a bit of a hike from the downstairs bathrooms. Dorms ARS420, doubles ARS1600

Cruz del Sur Gob. Deloqui 242 T02901 434099; map p.147. Although it lags a bit behind the other hostels listed here, the "Southern Cross" is a reliable if unexciting budget choice. It has a well-equipped kitchen relaxed lounge area, and a small library. The four- to eight-bed dorms are warm and clean, but rather compact. Dorms ARS430

★**La Posta** Perón Sur 864 ☎02901 444650, ⓦlapostahostel.com.ar; map p.147. Located 3km southwest of downtown Ushuaia, this lovely, family-run hostel has facilities more akin to a hotel than a backpacker joint: two kitchens, free laundry, well-scrubbed dorms with five to eight beds, private rooms, and apartments with kitchenettes. There's a tangible sense of guest camaraderie and the owners are treasure troves of information. Dorms ARS420, doubles ARS1400, apartments ARS2150

Yakush Piedrabuena 118 ☎02901 435807; map p.147. One of the best hostels in Ushuaia, in a central location. It gets high marks for its good communal areas, sociable atmosphere, and economical four- to six-bed dorms and private rooms. Dorms US$28, doubles US$90

GUESTHOUSES

B&B Nahuel 25 de Mayo 440 ☎02901 423068, ⓦbybnahuel.com.ar; map p.147. A bright-green exterior makes this guesthouse easy to spot; inside are homely, rather frilly rooms (one of which has shocking-pink walls you'll either love or hate) with either shared or private bathrooms. There's also a TV lounge. ARS1700

La Casa en Ushuaia Gobernador Paz ☎02901 423202, ⓦlacasaenushuaia.com; map p.147. Run by the helpful, trilingual Silvia, this set of comfortable, cream-coloured doubles benefits from its central location, good breakfast and plenty of city-related information on hand. The only downside is the ratio of rooms to shared bathroom. **AR$1400**

★ **Galeazzi-Basily B&B** Gob Valdéz 323 ☎02901 423213, ⓦavesdelsur.com.ar; map p.147. This guesthouse, run by the warm and hospitable, English- and French-speaking Frances and Alejandro, is an excellent place to meet fellow travellers without sacrificing comfort or privacy. Besides the twin and a double there are two fully equipped cabañas which sleep up to four people. Doubles **US$80**, cabañas **US$140**

EATING

Seafood is king here, especially the local *centolla* (king crab), though *cordero al palo* (spit-roasted lamb), a Fuegian speciality, is also well represented. Many places operate restricted opening hours during the low season (May–Sept).

El Almacén Ramos Generales Av Maipú 749 T02901 424317; map p.147. At this half-museum, half-café/bakery, the antique-dotted surroundings are as much of a draw as the hearty soups, filled baguettes and mains (AR$260–450) like goulash, plus appealing croissants and pains au chocolat. Daily 9am–midnight.

Austral Modern 9 de Julio 74; map p.147. This café aims for a hip, Scandinavian aesthetic, with minimalist decor and a window filled with Fjällräven rucksacks, but thankfully also produces fine coffee (AR$45–85), plus a short but sweet range of sandwiches, cakes and snacks. Tasteful Tierra del Fuego-themed souvenirs are available, too. Mon–Sat 9am–1.30pm & 4–8.30pm.

★ **Bodegón Fueguino** San Martín 859 ☎02901 431972, ⓦtierradehumos.com; map p.147. Park yourself down on a sheepskin-draped wooden bench in this historic wooden house (built in 1896) and order the likes of lamb in a red wine sauce or pork leg with orange and honey sauce (mains AR$250–350). Good Tierra del Fuego-brewed beer (from AR$60) too. Mon 7.45–11.45pm, Tues–Sun noon–2.45pm & 7.45–11.45pm.

Freddo San Martín, at Rivadavia ⓦfreddo.com.ar; map p.147. This famous Argentine chain serves up excellent, and very moreish, ice cream (from AR$60): you can't go wrong with any of the various *dulce de leche* flavours. Hot drinks and snacks such as *medialunas* available too. Mon–Thurs & Sun 10am–12.30am, Fri 10am–1am, Sat 10am–1.30am.

Maria Lola Resto Deloqui 1048 ☎02901 421185, ⓦmarialolaresto.com.ar; map p.147. Besides its superlative views of the bay, this slick, professional restaurant delivers both creative and classic dishes: think linguine with king crab and scallops, or Fuegian lamb with sauteed vegetables (mains from AR$240); each dish is thoughtfully paired with a suggested wine. Mon–Sat 12.30–2.30pm & 8–11pm.

> ★ **TREAT YOURSELF**
>
> **Kalma Restó** Gob Valdez 293 ☎02901 425786, ⓦkalmaresto.com.ar; map p. 147. The menu changes depending on the season at this intimate restaurant, but you may be treated to the likes of king crab with apple, peppers and "sea air" foam and a "deconstructed" *chocotorta*. If you're going to splurge on a meal (five-course set menu AR$950) in Argentina, do it here. Reservations essential. Mon–Sat 7–11pm.

El Turco San Martín 1410 ☎02901 424711; map p.147. No-frills local restaurant that provides hearty (if not especially exciting meals) at relatively low (for Ushuaia at least) prices. The menu features milanesas, pizzas, pastas and steaks, plus a selection of fish dishes (mains AR$110–320). Mon–Sat noon–3pm & 8pm–midnight.

El Vagón Av Maipú 771 ☎02901 421480, ⓦelvagonushuaia.com.ar; map p.147. Decked out like an antique, wood-panelled train carriage, with glimpses of labouring convicts out of the "windows", this café offers "passengers'" a relatively economical menu of pizzas (from AR$120), pastas (AR$170–250), stir fries and snacks. Mon–Fri 8am–midnight, Sat 10am–midnight.

DRINKING AND NIGHTLIFE

In addition to the options listed below, *Bodegón Fueguino* is a good place for a drink.

Dublin 9 de Julio 168 ☎02901 430744; map p.147. This green-walled, red-roofed pub is a good place for a draught beer ($80 plus), with a buzzing atmosphere and occasional live music. Apart from the Guinness posters, however, there isn't much in the way of Hibernian trappings. Daily 7pm–4am.

★ **Küar** Perito Moreno 2232 ☎02901 437396, ⓦkuar.com.ar; map p.147. Set in an attractive stone-and-timber building right on the seafront, on the road towards Río Grande, this bar-restaurant has stupendous views and a blazing fire, as well as heaped *picadas* and a wide range of beers, cocktails and wine (alcoholic drinks from AR$80). It has another, less scenically located city centre branch (San Martín 471). Mon–Sat 12.30–3.30pm & 6.30pm–midnight.

DIRECTORY

Banks and exchange There are several ATMs in the city centre, including the HSBC at Maipú and Godoy.

Car rental Avis (☎02901 433323, ⓦavis.com) and Hertz (☎02901 432429, ⓦhertz.com) have offices at the airport.

Post office Gob. Godoy 118.

PARQUE NACIONAL TIERRA DEL FUEGO

Located 12km west of Ushuaia along RN3, **PARQUE NACIONAL TIERRA DEL FUEGO** (daily 8am–8pm, reduced hours in the winter; AR$350; if visiting the following day, let the park staff know, and you won't have to pay twice) stretches from the Beagle Channel in the south to Lago Fagnano in the north and the border with Chile in the west. Encompassing 630 square kilometres of mountains, waterfalls, glaciers, lakes, rivers, valleys, sub-Antarctic forest and peat bog, the park offers a number of good day hikes; the rest of the park is off-limits to the public. Guanacos, Patagonian grey foxes, Fuegian foxes, Southern river otters and some ninety bird species are among the park's fauna; introduced Canadian beavers and European rabbits also run amok, wreaking environmental havoc.

Highlights include the **Costera Trail** (8km; 3–4hr), which starts at the jetty and follows the shore of Bahía Ensenada through coastal forest of deciduous beech trees, meeting the RN3 near the Lapataiapark administration centre. It affords spectacular views of the Beagle Channel, passing grass-covered mounds that were former campsites of the indigenous Yámana and offering birdwatchers prime opportunities for spotting Magellanic woodpeckers, cormorants, gulls and oystercatchers.

For the park's best views, take the steep, picturesque route to the top of 973m-high **Cerro Guanaco Trail** (8km return; 7hr) from the car park at Lago Roca. Another popular route, **Hito XXIV Trail** (7km; 3hr), is a level path that starts from the same trailhead, traces the shores of Lago Roca and ends at a small obelisk that marks the border with Chile.

ARRIVAL AND DEPARTURE

By bus Regular high season private buses (hourly 9am–5pm; 20–30min; AR$500 return) depart from the small bus stand on the corner of Maipú and Fadúl in Ushuaia for various points in the park. Services are reduced during off-season.

PARQUE NACIONAL TIERRA DEL FUEGO

1

By train El Tren del Fin del Mundo is a scenic ride on the narrow-gauge train that used to transport wood in the days of the penal colony, departing from its main station, 8km west of Ushuaia (Daily: May-Aug 10am, 12.30pm — if there's enough demand — & 3pm; Sept— April 9.30am, noon & 3pm; 50min each way; AR$790 return; ☎02901 431600, ⓦtrendelfindelmundo.com. ar) and arriving at the park station, 2km from the main gate. A taxi from central Ushuaia to the main station costs AR$650.

By taxi It's only worth taking a taxi from Ushuaia (AR$930 to Lago Roca or AR$1115 to Bahia Lapataia, both one way; AR$2230 return with 3hr waiting time) if there are four of you.

ACCOMMODATION

There are four rudimentary free campsites which tend to get crowded and dirty; a couple are a bit of a hike from the nearest toilets. Take all your rubbish out of the park.

Camping Lago Roca ☎02901 433313. By the shores of the eponymous lake, this is the only serviced campsite (with hot showers, a café and an expensive shop). It also has a *refugio* with dorm beds. Camping/person **AR$150**, dorms **AR$300**

SALAR DE UYUNI

Bolivia

❶ **Death Road** Cycling the spectacular road between La Paz and Coroico. See page 171

❷ **Isla del Sol** The spiritual centre of the Andean world. See page 181

❸ **Cerro Rico** An unforgettable glimpse of the miners' life. See page 193

❹ **Salar de Uyuni** The world's largest salt flat. See page 196

❺ **Samaipata** Laidback town surrounded by lush cloudforest. See page 214

❻ **Parque Nacional Madidi** A pristine and diverse Amazonian rainforest. See page 219

HIGHLIGHTS ARE MARKED ON THE MAP ON PAGE 158

ROUGH COSTS

Daily budget Basic US$30, with the occasional treat US$45
Drink Small beer US$3
Food Fixed three-course lunch menu US$3.50–5.50
Hostel/budget hotel US$7–12/US$15–30
Travel Bus: La Paz–Copacabana (155km) US$3.70

FACT FILE

Population 11 million
Language Spanish (also more than thirty indigenous languages)
Currency Boliviano (B$)
Capital Sucre is the official capital; La Paz is the de facto capital
International phone code ☏591
Time zone GMT -4hr

Introduction

Surrounded by Brazil, Paraguay, Argentina, Chile and Peru, Bolivia lies at the heart of South America. Stretching from the majestic icebound peaks and bleak high-altitude deserts of the Andes to the exuberant rainforests and vast savannahs of the Amazon basin, it embraces an astonishing range of landscapes and climates, and encompasses everything outsiders find most exotic and mysterious about the continent.

Three centuries of Spanish colonial rule have left their mark, most obviously in some of the finest colonial architecture on the continent. Yet the European influence is essentially a thin veneer overlying indigenous cultural traditions that stretch back long before the Conquest: while Spanish is the language of business and government, more than thirty indigenous languages are still spoken.

Bolivia is dominated by the mighty **Andes**, which march through the west of the country along two parallel chains. In the north and east, they give way to the tropical rainforests and grasslands of the **Amazon and eastern lowlands**, in the southeast to the dry thornbrush and scrub of the **Chaco**. Yet, despite its extraordinary biodiversity and myriad attractions, Bolivia remains one of South America's least-visited countries.

Most visitors spend a few days in the fascinating city of **La Paz**, which combines a dizzying high-altitude setting with an intermingling of traditional indigenous and modern urban cultures. Close by is the magical **Lago Titicaca**, and the towns of **Coroico** and **Sorata**, good bases for trekking, climbing or mountain biking in the **Cordillera Real**, a range of high Andean peaks that plunge precipitously down into the Amazon basin through the dramatic, deep valleys of the **Yungas**. The best base for visiting the Bolivian Amazon further north is **Rurrenabaque**, the jumping-off point for exploring **Madidi National Park**.

South of La Paz, the southern **Altiplano** – the bleak, high plateau that stretches between the Andes – has historically been home to most of Bolivia's population. In **Potosí** you can experience underground life in the mines of **Cerro Rico**, while to the southwest, Uyuni is the gateway to the astonishing landscape of the **Salar de Uyuni** and the **Reserva de Fauna Andina Eduardo Avaroa**. Also well worth visiting are the towns of **Sucre**, with its fine colonial architecture, **Samaipata**, which has designs on Rurrenabaque's crown as the country's best ecotourism base, and **Santa Cruz**, a brash, lively tropical metropolis – and a good base for exploring the rainforests of the **Parque Nacional Amboró** and the immaculately restored Jesuit missions of **Chiquitos**.

CHRONOLOGY

1000 BC Founding of Tiwanaku on the shores of Lago Titicaca, centre of a colonial empire comprising much of modern Bolivia, southern Peru, northeast Argentina and northern Chile.

c.1000 AD Tiwanaku dramatically collapses, most likely as a result of a prolonged drought.

Eleventh to fifteenth centuries The Aymara take control of the Altiplano, maintaining a more localized culture and religion.

Mid-fifteenth century The Aymara are incorporated into the Inca Empire, albeit with a limited degree of autonomy.

1532 Francisco Pizarro leads his Spanish conquistadors to a swift and unlikely defeat of the Inca army in Cajamarca (Bajo), Peru.

1538 Pizarro sends Spanish troops south to aid the Aymaran Colla as they battle both the remnants of an Inca rebellion and their Aymara rivals the Lupaca. Spanish control of the territory known as Alto Peru is established.

1545 The continent's richest deposit of silver, Cerro Rico, is discovered, giving birth to the mining city of Potosí.

1691 San Javier is founded as the first of the Chiquitos Jesuit missions.

1767 The Spanish Crown expels the Jesuit order from the Americas.

1780–82 The last major indigenous uprising, the Great Rebellion, is led by a combined Inca-Aymara army of Túpact Amaru and pac Katari.

1809 La Paz becomes the first capital in the Americas to declare independence from Spain.

2

WHEN TO VISIT

Climate varies much more as a result of altitude and topography than it does between different seasons.

Winter (May–Oct) is the **dry season**, and in many ways the best time to visit Bolivia, with sunny, trek-friendly highland days and slightly lower temperatures in the generally hot and humid **lowlands**. While highland temperatures hover in the mid-teens most of the year (albeit with chilly winter nights), the summer **rainy season** (December into March and sometimes April) can see lowland temperatures reach 31°C. Rain affects the condition of roads throughout the country, especially in the Amazon, where river transport takes over from often impassable overland routes. The parched Altiplano and mountainsides nevertheless briefly transform into lush grassland, as wild flowers proliferate and the earth comes to life.

1824 The last Spanish army is destroyed at the battle of Ayacucho in (Bajo) Peru.

1825 The newly liberated Alto Peru rejects a union with either (Bajo) Peru or Argentina, and adopts a declaration of independence. Bolivia is born.

1879 Chile begins the War of the Pacific by occupying the entire Bolivian coastline and invading Peru.

1899 The Federal Revolution consolidates power of the new tin-mining barons and creates a new administrative capital in La Paz.

1904 Bolivia finally cedes its coastline to Chile, in addition to losing the Acre to Brazil.

1932–35 The Chaco War with Paraguay ends in stalemate and huge loss of life.

1952 The National Revolution sees armed civilians defeat the army in La Paz and the ascension to power of the Revolutionary Nationalist Movement (MNR).

1964 A resurgent army led by General René Barrientos seizes power, beginning eighteen years of military dictatorship.

1967 Che Guevara is captured and executed in the hamlet of La Higuera.

1970s General Hugo Banzer heads a brutal military regime, coinciding with an unprecedented period of economic growth.

1980–81 The most brutal and corrupt regime in modern Bolivian history is led by General Luis García Meza.

1985 Bolivia plunges into a recession as the bottom falls out of the tin market, and the economic vacuum is filled by the production and export of cocaine.

Late 1990s US-backed coca eradication policies provoke widespread resistance, led by indigenous activist Evo Morales.

2005 Morales is elected as Bolivia's first indigenous president with a programme of nationalization and agrarian reform.

2008 Morales suspends US Drug Enforcement programme, accusing agents of espionage. In retaliation, the US adds Bolivia to its drugs blacklist and suspends trade preferences.

2009 New constitution agreed, giving greater rights to indigenous people. Morales is elected for a second term.

2011 Mass demonstrations lead to a suspension of government plans to build a Brazil-funded highway through the TIPNIS reserve. Bolivia leaves UN Single Convention on Narcotics over its ban on coca leaf.

2013 Bolivia readmitted to Single Convention after UN agrees dispensation for traditional coca use. Constitutional Court rules Morales can run for a third presidential term.

2016 Referendum narrowly rejects (by 51.3 percent) a proposal to allow Morales to run for a fourth term. Morales announces that he will run for a fourth term in 2019 anyway.

ARRIVAL AND DEPARTURE

At present there are only **direct flights** to Bolivia from Washington DC and Miami in the US (including with American Airlines; ⓦaa.com), Madrid in Spain (with Air Europa; ⓦaireuropa.com) and neighbouring South American countries, the most frequent connections being from São Paulo in Brazil, Buenos Aires in Argentina, Santiago in Chile and Lima in Peru. The principal Bolivian international **airports** are El Alto in La Paz (see page 170) and Viru Viru in Santa Cruz (see page 211). International departure tax is nowadays included in ticket prices.

FROM ARGENTINA

The principal **border crossing** is from La Quiaca in Argentina to Villazón in the southern Altiplano (see page 199), with regular bus and train connections to the desert town of Tupiza. There's also a crossing between Pocitos in Argentina and Yacuiba in the Chaco (see page 216), from where it's possible to travel by bus or train to Santa Cruz.

FROM BRAZIL

The busiest crossing is the border at Puerto

2

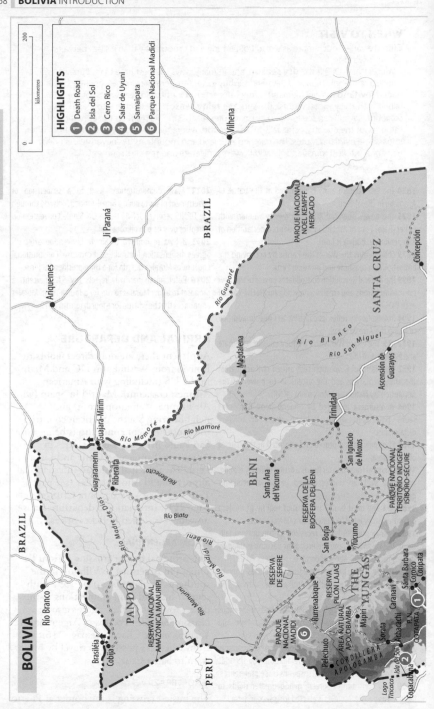

BOLIVIA

HIGHLIGHTS
1. Death Road
2. Isla del Sol
3. Cerro Rico
4. Salar de Uyuni
5. Samaipata
6. Parque Nacional Madidi

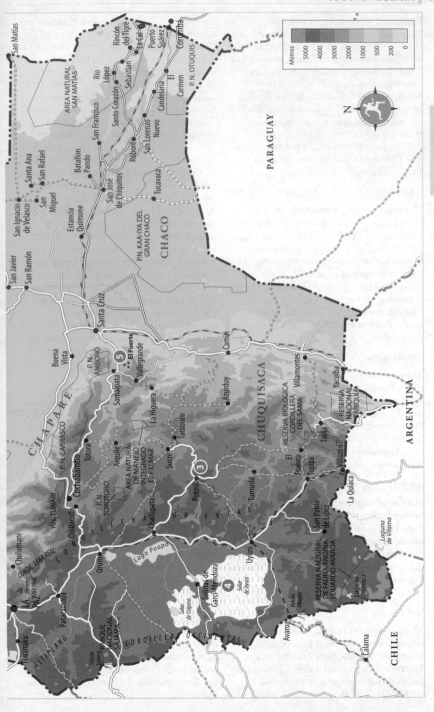

Metres
5000 4000 3000 2000 1000 500 200 0

N

2

PARAGUAY

San Matías

Rincón del Tigre

El Tal

Puerto Suárez

Corumbá

Río López

Sebastián

Candelaria

El Carmen

San Corazón

Santo Corazón

P. N. OTUQUIS

ÁREA NATURAL
SAN MATÍAS

San Francisco

Santa Ana

San Rafael

San Ignacio
de Velasco

San Miguel

Batallon
Pando

San José
de Chiquitos

Roboré

San Lorenzo
Nuevo

Tucavaca

CHACO

San Javier

San Ramón

Estancia
Quimone

San Matías

P.N. KAA-IYA DEL
GRAN CHACO

Santa Cruz

Buena
Vista

Camiri

P. N.
AMBORO

El Fuerte

Vallegrande

Villamontes

Yacuiba

Samaipata

Azurduy

RESERVA
NACIONAL
TARIQUIA

CHAPARE

P.N. CARRASCO

La Higuera

CHUQUISACA

ARGENTINA

Totora

Aiquile

Tarabuco

Sucre

RESERVA BIOLÓGICA
CORDILLERA
DEL SAMA

Tapia

P.N. TUNARI

Cochabamba

ÁREA NATURAL
DE MANEJO
INTEGRADO
EL PALMAR

El
Puente

Tupiza

Villazón

Quillacollo

P. N.
TOROTORO

Challapata

Potosí

Tumusla

La Quiaca

Chulumani

Oruro

CORDILLERA ORIENTAL

San Pablo
de Lipez

Laguna
de Vilama

LA PAZ

Illimani (6439m)

Patacamaya

Lago Poopó

Salinas de
Garci-Mendoza

Uyuni

Avaroa

RESERVA NACIONAL
DE FAUNA ANDINA
EDUARDO AVAROA

Laguna
Colorada

Tiwanaku

CORDILLERA REAL

ALTIPLANO

PARQUE
NACIONAL
SAJAMA

Volcán
Sajama

Solar
de Coipasa

Solar
de Uyuni

Volcán
Ollagüe

Calama

CHILE

CORDILLERA OCCIDENTAL

2

Quijarro (see page 213), near the Brazilian city of Corumbá, where the Bolivian Pantanal meets its more famous Brazilian counterpart. From Quijarro, it's a full day's train journey to Santa Cruz. There are also a couple of borders in **Amazonia**, from Guajará-Mirim (transit point Porto Velho) by boat across the Rio Mamoré to Guayaramerín, from where there are regular onward flights to Trinidad; and from Brasiléia (transit point Rio Branco) to Cobija, the capital of Pando province (see page 223).

FROM CHILE

The most popular **trans-Andean route** from Chile is the road up from Arica on the coast via Tambo Quemado (see page 189) to La Paz. A more adventurous option is the remote border crossing of **Laguna Verde** (see page 197), at the southern edge of Reserva Eduardo Avaroa, accessible via organized tours from the Chilean town of San Pedro de Atacama. Buses also run from Uyuni to Calama (see page 195).

FROM PERU

The most widely used land border of all is the **Yunguyo-Kasani crossing** (see page 180) at the southern tip of Lago Titicaca near Copacabana, easily accessible from Puno in southern Peru. Less busy but just as easy to get to from Puno is the crossing at **Desaguadero** (see page 170), with regular onward transport to La Paz.

FROM PARAGUAY

For the adventurous only, the **trans-Chaco** border between Bolivia and Paraguay (see page 160) is an arduous 26–28hr bus journey from Asunción to Santa Cruz, but buses may take longer, and may not run in the rainy season (Nov–May) if the road is flooded.

VISAS

Many visitors to Bolivia – including citizens of the **UK**, most European countries, **Canada**, **New Zealand** and **Australia** – don't need a visa. Citizens of **South Africa** do need a visa (around US$100); these are generally available on

entry (for cash only), but it is better to get one in advance if you can. Citizens of the **United States** can apply for a tourist visa in advance or on arrival (US$160/person, paid in cash). This is valid for ten years, and allows multiple entries of thirty days each up to ninety days total per year; check ⓦtravel.state.gov for further details.

For other nationalities, the situation changes periodically, so always **check** with your local embassy or consulate a month or two before travelling. On arrival, you'll be issued with a **tourist card** (*tarjeta de turismo*) valid for thirty or ninety days, depending on your nationality – check the number of days and make sure the border officials give you the stamp with the maximum number of days your nationality allows you. If they give you less than the maximum, you can request it on the spot (though there's no guarantee you'll get it) or go to the immigration office in La Paz or the nearest city to your border crossing and receive another stamp. The annual limit is currently restricted to ninety days, and, officially at least, you cannot just cross the border and get another ninety-day card.

GETTING AROUND

Bolivia's topography, size and lack of basic infrastructure mean that getting around can be a challenge, especially in the rainy season. However, buses are inexpensive and numerous, flying within the country is very affordable, and convenient, especially in rainy season, and trains follow some spectacular routes.

BY PLANE

La Paz, Santa Cruz, Sucre and Cochabamba are all connected by **daily flights**, and there are also frequent services to Tarija, Trinidad, Rurrenabaque and a number of remote towns in the Amazon and the eastern lowlands. State-run Boliviana de Aviación (ⓦboa.bo), Amazonas (ⓦamaszonas.com) and military-run TAM (ⓦtam.bo) are the main domestic carriers. Book at least several days in advance for busier routes. Flights are often cancelled or delayed, especially in the Amazon, where the weather can cause disruption.

BY TRAIN

FCA (Empresa Ferroviaria Andina; ⓦwww.
fca.com.bo) runs two passenger lines
– *Expreso del Sur* and *Wara Wara del Sur*
– from Oruro south across the Altiplano
via Uyuni and Tupiza to Villazón on the
Argentine border. **Ferroviaria Oriental**
(ⓦwww.fo.com.bo) runs two lines in the
lowlands: one from Santa Cruz east to the
Brazilian border at Quijarro (a service
known as the "death train" – a reference to
its speed, not its safety record); the other
from Santa Cruz south to Yacuiba in the
Chaco, on the Argentine border.

BY BUS

Bolivia's **buses** are run by a variety of
private companies and ply all the main
routes in the country. Road conditions
continue to improve greatly, but journey
times are still unpredictable, and you
should be prepared for major delays,
especially in the rainy season. In the
highlands, always bring warm clothing
and a blanket or sleeping bag, as journeys
can be bitterly cold.

Other forms of transport include:
minibuses (minivans that chug along fixed
routes in the bigger cities); *micros* (similar
to but bigger than minibuses); *trufis/
colectivos* (shared taxis that run along fixed
routes); and *mototaxis* (motorbike taxis).

BY BOAT

Although Bolivia is landlocked, there are
still several regions – particularly the
Amazon – where travelling by water is the
best way of getting around. There are two
main forms of **river transport** in the
Bolivian Amazon: dugout canoes, powered
by outboard motors, and more modern
motorboats, are used to visit protected
areas such as the Parque Nacional Madidi;
more economic but less comfortable cargo
boats ply the Río Mamoré, between
Trinidad and Guayaramerín on the
Brazilian frontier, and the Río Ichilo,
between Trinidad and Puerto Villaroel in
the Chapare.

BY CAR

Renting a car (from around US$35/day) is
an option, though it's often easier and not
much more expensive to hire a taxi to
drive you around for a day or longer.
Outside the main routes, many roads are
unpaved and in very poor condition, so a
four-wheel drive (4WD) is essential. Petrol
stations are scarce and breakdown services
even more so. A recommended car rental
company with offices at El Alto airport
and Santa Cruz (on the second ring road)
is Barbol (☎02 2820675, ⓦbarbolsrl.
com). You'll need to be over 25, and to
leave a major credit card or large cash
deposit as security; most rental companies
will include insurance cover with the hire
price, but it is worth checking.

ACCOMMODATION

While **accommodation** in Bolivia is
generally good value, the standard is not
particularly high, especially in smaller
towns. Room rates vary according to
season, rising during the high tourist
season (May–Sept) and on weekends in
popular resort towns, and doubling or
tripling during major fiestas. Even in the
coldest highland cities, heating is usually
non-existent; in the lowlands, heat, rather
than cold, is often a problem, though all
but the cheapest rooms are equipped with
a fan. Most places usually have **hot water**,
although it's generally intermittent and
often courtesy of individual electric
heaters that you'll find attached to the tops
of showers; don't touch the apparatus
while the water is running.

With few designated **campsites** and an
abundance of inexpensive
accommodation, few travellers camp in
Bolivia unless exploring the country's
wilderness areas. Beyond the cities and
towns, you can camp almost everywhere,
usually for free; make sure you ask for
permission from the nearest house first;
local villages may ask for a small fee of a
few bolivianos. In some **national parks**
you'll also find shelters where you can stay
for a minimal charge.

FOOD AND DRINK

The style of eating and drinking varies
considerably between Bolivia's three main
geographical regions – the Altiplano, the
highland valleys and the tropical lowlands.

2

Each region has *comidas típicas* (traditional dishes). Generally, be wary of street food and take recommendations before trying the real locals' restaurants – food hygiene can be an issue.

Restaurants almost all offer enormously filling good-value set lunches (*almuerzos*) usually costing between B$10 and B$40, while a smaller number offer a set dinner (*cena*) in the evening and also have a range of à la carte main dishes (*platos extras*), rarely costing more than B$30–40. For B$50–75 you should expect a substantial meal in more upmarket restaurants, while about B$75–130 will buy you most dishes even in the best restaurants in La Paz or Santa Cruz.

FOOD

While Altiplano cuisine is dominated by the humble **potato**, often served in hearty soups (llama and mutton are common), the valley regions cook with **corn**, often used as the basis for thick soups known as *laguas*, or boiled on the cob and served with fresh white cheese – a classic combination known as *choclo con queso*. Meat and chicken are often cooked in spicy sauces known as *picantes*: a valley mainstay is *pique a lo macho*, a massive plate of chopped beef and sausage fried with potatoes, onions, tomatoes and chillies. In the tropical lowlands, **plantains** and **cassava** (*yuca*) take the place of potatoes; beef is also plentiful – the lowlands are cattle-ranching regions, so beef is of good quality and relatively cheap.

Although Bolivia is obviously not the place to come for seafood, fish features regularly on menus, especially the succulent *trucha* (trout) and *pejerrey* (kingfish) around Lago Titicaca, and the juicy white river fish known as *surubí* and *pucú* in the lowlands. Ordinary restaurants rarely offer much in the way of **vegetarian food**, although you can almost always find eggs and potatoes of some description (usually fried), as well as the ubiquitous potato soup, often cooked without meat. The situation changes a great deal in cities and in popular travellers' haunts, where a cosmopolitan selection of vegetarian dishes, salads and pancakes is widely available, and there's a growing number of wholly vegetarian restaurants.

The most popular snack throughout Bolivia is the **salteña**, a pasty filled with a spicy, juicy stew of meat or chicken with chopped vegetables, olives and hard-boiled egg. It's usually eaten in the mid-morning accompanied by a cold drink and a little chilli sauce if desired.

DRINK

Mineral water is widely available – avoid the tap water – and a variety of delicious fresh juices is sold by market stalls and on the streets from handcarts across the country. **Coffee** is available almost everywhere, as well as tea and **mates**, or herbal teas – *mate de coca* is a good remedy for altitude sickness, but many others are usually available.

You can often find locally produced alcoholic drinks in Bolivia and drinking is a serious pastime. **Beer** (B$20–30) is available almost everywhere – Paceña, produced in La Paz, is the commonest, but good microbrewery beers are also easily found. Although not widely consumed, Bolivia also produces a growing variety of excellent high-altitude – and highly underrated – **wines** (*vinos*), mostly from the Tarija Valley; the best labels are Campos de Solana, Concepción and Kohlberg. A glass of red wine (*vino tinto*) costs B$20–30. While production is still a fraction of Argentina and Chile's, Bolivia's wines deserve a higher profile. One problem is that much cultivation is dedicated to muscat grapes, which, rather than being used for fine **wines**, are used to a produce a white grape brandy called *singani*, the beverage most Bolivians turn to when they really want to get drunk. It's usually mixed with Sprite or 7 Up, which creates a fast-acting combination known as *chuflay*. Finally, no visit to the Cochabamba is complete without a taste of *chicha*, a thick, mildly alcoholic yeasty-flavoured beer made of fermented maize and considered sacred by the Incas.

CULTURE AND ETIQUETTE

There isn't really such a thing as an all-encompassing Bolivian culture, as traditions vary widely according to different regions and climates, as well as according to social class and ethnic background. There are around forty official **ethnic groups** in the country, while a distinction is often made between the "camba" (people from the lowlands) and "colla" (those from the highlands). Tensions between the two regions have heightened as a result of sweeping reform on land distribution and nationalization introduced by President Evo Morales.

Spanish is the official language in Bolivia, and it's a great place to brush up on your language skills as Bolivians speak slowly and clearly compared with their Chilean or Argentine neighbours. **Indigenous languages** including Aymara, Quechua and Gurani are also widely spoken. **Catholicism** is the predominant religion, though many festivals and celebrations involve a mishmash of Catholic and indigenous beliefs with offerings made to both the Virgin Mary and Pachamama (mother earth).

Generally speaking, Bolivians are friendly and will go out of their way to help you. It's polite and common practice to pepper any requests with "por favor" and "gracias", and greet people with "buenos días" or "buenas tardes" before starting a conversation. There is little concept of personal space in Bolivia and people typically stand very close when speaking to you.

Chewing **coca leaves** is an integral part of daily life for many Bolivians. The controversial leaf is commonly chewed into a round ball, and kept in the side of the cheek, or used to make herbal tea. It is said to combat tiredness and altitude sickness, and to quell hunger, and is also used in ritual ceremonies.

When eating out at a restaurant, or taking part in a guided tour, a ten-percent **tip** is appreciated, and increasingly expected. Many museums and historical landmarks charge higher fees to foreigners, which some travellers find frustrating. If you are not sure of what you are being asked to pay, it is best to ask around to establish the going rate before assuming you are being ripped off. Haggling is not common.

SPORTS AND OUTDOOR ACTIVITIES

Dominated by the dramatic high mountain scenery of the Andes, Bolivia is ideal for **trekking**, **mountain biking** and **climbing**; whether you want to stroll for half a day, take a hardcore hike for two weeks over high passes down into remote Amazonian valleys, or climb one of the hundred peaks over 5000m, it's all possible. The best season for outdoor activity is between May and September, while the most pleasant and reliable weather is between June and August.

The easiest way to go trekking or climbing is with a tour operator. There are dozens of these in La Paz and in several other cities. Prices depend on group sizes.

Many travellers say one of the highlights of South America is a bike ride down the road from La Paz to Coroico in the Yungas, a thrilling 3500m descent along what was once dubbed the **world's most dangerous road**. There are plenty of tour companies and it's easy to organize as a day-trip from La Paz, but beware of cowboy operators (we recommend Gravity Assisted Mountain Biking; see page 171). You don't need any previous experience, but bear in mind that bikers have been killed on this route, and though the most dangerous stretch was bypassed in 2007, some vehicles still use it. Attempting the trip in the rainy season (Nov–March) is not recommended.

COMMUNICATIONS

Most hotels and some restaurants offer free (though generally far from fast) **wi-fi**. **Internet cafés** are ubiquitous but connections are often slow. Expect to pay about B$2–6/hr.

Calling internationally, the cheapest landline option is via an internet phone service such as Skype. Most mobile users in Bolivia have WhatsApp. There are **ENTEL** phone centres and Punto Cotel offices in most towns, where you can make local, national and international calls. It may be worth buying an inexpensive mobile phone, or bringing one with you, and getting a Bolivian pay-as-you-go SIM card (*chip*). If you're dialling long-distance within Bolivia, you'll need the respective **area code**, which for La Paz, Oruro and Potosí is ☎02; for Beni, Pando and Santa Cruz ☎03; and for Cochabamba, Chuquisaca and Tarija ☎04. Mobile phone numbers have eight digits wherever you are. Toll-free numbers begin ☎800.

Airmail (*por avión*) to Europe and North America tends to take one to two weeks; mail to places like Australia, New Zealand and South Africa takes longer. Letters cost B\$20 to North America, B\$23 to the UK or Europe, B\$26 to Australia or New Zealand. For a small extra charge, you can send letters certified (*certificado*), but even then don't send anything you can't afford to lose.

CRIME AND SAFETY

Despite being among the poorest countries in the region, Bolivia has lower levels of theft and violent crime than neighbouring Peru and Brazil, though in recent years levels have risen. The vast majority of crime against tourists is opportunistic theft, and **violence is rare**. One scam is for **fake policemen** to approach you in the street and ask to search you or see your documents (before making off with them), or ask you to go with them in a taxi to the "police station". Be aware that real policemen would never do this, so on no account hand over your documents or valuables and never accompany a stranger in a taxi.

Another trick is for **fake taxi drivers** or even minibus drivers to pick up unsuspecting passengers before either stopping in a deserted part of town where they and/or their associates rob the victims, or, in even worse scenarios, kidnap and seriously assault the victims to force them to reveal their PIN. Always check the ID of any taxi you take and only ever use official ones; better still, whenever possible ask your hotel to order one for you.

Another common means of theft starts with you being spat on or having some substance spilt on you; a "helpful passer-by" will stop you, point out the offending substance and attempt to clean it off you (while their partner in crime

quickly relieves you of your valuables). If this happens to you, don't stop, but walk on as quickly as possible before cleaning yourself up.

Political upheaval is a regular feature of everyday life in Bolivia. Keep an eye on the news and ask around before you make travel plans – road blockades are the go-to form of protest for many groups, and can easily disrupt your schedule. Street protests are also common.

HEALTH

Though levels of hygiene and sanitation are generally poor in Bolivia, you can reduce the risk of getting ill. Avoid drinking tap water and watch out for ice in drinks, as well as uncooked or unpeeled fruit and vegetables. Appreciate the risks of buying food from street vendors and always check that food has been properly cooked.

Altitude sickness is a common complaint in La Paz, Potosí and on the salt-flats tour. Mild symptoms include dizziness, headaches and breathlessness. Bolivians swear by coca tea (*mate de coca*), but resting and drinking plenty of non-alcoholic fluids should also help. You can buy small bags of coca leaf around the witches' market area of La Paz for a few bolivianos. Anyone with more severe symptoms should get immediate medical help.

It is advisable to get vaccinated against **yellow fever** before you travel to Bolivia; bring a doctor's certificate with you. Use mosquito repellent with a high DEET or PMD content and wear long sleeves and trousers to avoid insect-borne diseases such as malaria, Zika and dengue fever.

Bolivia is home to a wide range of venomous **snakes and spiders**. Watch where you step and seek medical advice if you are bitten or stung.

When looking for healthcare, it is always best to opt for **private clinics** (*clínica*) rather than state-run hospitals, which are often overcrowded and poorly equipped.

INFORMATION AND MAPS

Most major cities have a regional **tourist office**, run either by the city municipality or by the departmental prefecture. Tour operators, however, are often a better source of information, and are happy to answer queries, often in English, though obviously their main aim is to sell you one of their tours.

MONEY AND BANKS

The Bolivian currency is the **boliviano**. It's usually written "B$" or "B$" and is subdivided into 100 centavos. Notes come in denominations of 10, 20, 50, 100 and 200 bolivianos; coins in denominations of 1, 2 and 5 bolivianos, and of 5, 10, 20 and 50 centavos. At the time of writing, the **exchange rate** was roughly B$6.85 = US$1; B$8.40 = €1; B$9.50 = £1.

US dollars can be **withdrawn at some ATMs**, and changed at banks and some hotels, shops and by street moneychangers, so they're a good way of carrying emergency backup funds. Most day-to-day costs will be charged in B$, though tourist-based activities – especially the more upmarket kind – will often be quoted in US$. The easiest way to access funds in cities and larger towns is by using plastic; Visa and MasterCard are most widely accepted. In rural areas and smaller towns carry plenty of **cash**, as plastic is not widely accepted.

OPENING HOURS AND HOLIDAYS

Public offices in Bolivia have adopted the *horario continuo*, whereby they (theoretically at least) work Monday to Friday straight through from 8.30am to 4pm without closing for lunch.

Bank opening hours are generally Monday to Friday from 8.30am to noon and 2.30pm to 5pm; some branches are also open on Saturday mornings

Bolivians welcome any excuse for a party, and the country enjoys a huge number of national, regional and local **fiestas**, often involving lengthy preparation and substantial expense.

PUBLIC HOLIDAYS

January 1 New Year's Day (*Año Nuevo*).

January 22 Plurinational State Foundation Day.

February/March Carnaval (Shrove Monday and Tuesday), the last days before Lent. Oruro's Carnaval (see page 190) is the most famous, but Santa Cruz, Sucre and Tarija also stage massive fiestas.

Easter Semana Santa (Holy Week) is celebrated with religious processions throughout Bolivia. Good Friday is a public holiday.

May 1 Labour Day.

May/June Corpus Christi. La Paz stages the Señor del Gran Poder, its biggest and most colourful folkloric dance parade.

June 21 Aymara New Year (*Año Nuevo* or *Inti Raymi*). Crowds flock to the Tiwanaku ruins for a colourful ceremony of thanks to the sun and Pachamama (mother earth).

July 16 Virgen del Carmen (public holiday in La Paz department only). Processions and dances in honour of the Virgen del Carmen, the patron saint of many towns and villages across Bolivia.

August 6 Independence Day (*Día de la Patria*). Parades and parties throughout the country, notably in Copacabana.

November 1–2 All Saints (*Día de Todos los Santos*) and Day of the Dead (*Día de los Muertos*).

December 25 Christmas Day (*Navidad*).

FESTIVALS

Bolivian festivals include, but are not limited to, the public holidays listed on page 165. The big ones are Carnival, Easter and New Year. Others include the Feria de Alasitas (Jan 24) in La Paz, the Virgen del Carmen (July 16) in many towns and villages nationwide and a public holiday in La Paz *departamento*, the Fiesta Patronal (July 31) in San Ignacio de Moxos, and San Bartolomé (Aug 24) in Potosí.

BOLIVIA ONLINE

Ⓦ **bolivianexpress.org** Website of a free monthly English-language current affairs magazine.

Ⓦ **boliviabella.com** Fascinating website set up by a woman with detailed knowledge of the Santa Cruz region and a passion for everything related to the country.

Ⓦ **boliviaweb.com** Good general site with links to many other Bolivia-related pages and background information.

Ⓦ **lab.org.uk** The UK-based Latin America Bureau provides news, analysis and information on the continent, including Bolivia.

2

La Paz

Few cities have a setting as spectacular as **LA PAZ**, founded in 1548 as La Ciudad de Nuestra Señora de la Paz – the City of Our Lady of Peace – and now the political and commercial hub of Bolivia. Home to just under a million people, and sited at over 3500m above sea level, the sprawling city lies in a narrow, bowl-like canyon, its centre cradling a cluster of church spires and office blocks themselves dwarfed by the magnificent icebound peak of **Mount Illimani** (6439m) rising imperiously to the southeast. On either side, the steep slopes of the valley are covered by the ramshackle homes of the city's poorer inhabitants, which cling precariously to even the harshest gradients. From the lip of the canyon, the satellite city of **El Alto** sprawls in all directions across the Altiplano, a dirt-poor yet dynamic locus of urban Aymara culture and protest. The fact that its gridlocked main streets control access to La Paz below has often been exploited by the Aymara, with roadblocks used for political leverage.

WHAT TO SEE AND DO

There are still some fine colonial palaces and churches in the centre, with one of the main squares, **Plaza San Francisco**, bisected by the frantic thoroughfare of Avenida Mariscal Santa Cruz and its continuation, Avenida 16 de Julio, collectively known as **El Prado**. Though most of the surviving colonial buildings are in a poor state of repair, there's at least one street, **Calle Jaén**, where you can get a sense of how La Paz used to look. Many of the city's museums are also here. To the west of the Prado, lung-busting lanes sweep up to the travellers' enclave of **Calle Sagárnaga** and the Aymara bustle of the **market district** beyond. To the south lies the wealthy suburb of **Sopocachi**, where you'll find some of the city's best nightlife and restaurants.

Plaza Murillo

Though it remains the centre of Bolivia's political life, **Plaza Murillo** – the main square of the colonial city centre – has an endearingly provincial feel, busy with people feeding pigeons and eating ice cream in the shade. On the south side stands the **Catedral Metropolitana Nuestra Señora de La Paz** (Mon–Fri 9am–noon & 3–7pm, Sat & Sun 8am–noon; free), with its imposing facade but relatively unadorned interior, and the **Palacio de Gobierno** (Presidential Palace; closed to public), abutted by thin, elegant columns and ceremonial guards in red nineteenth-century uniforms.

Museo Nacional de Arte

On the southwest corner of Plaza Murillo at Calle Socabaya, the Palacio de Los Condes de Arana, one of La Paz's finest surviving colonial palaces, houses the **Museo Nacional de Arte** (Tues–Fri 9.30am–12.30pm & 3–7pm, Sat 10am–5.30pm, Sun 10am–1.30pm; B$20; @bit.ly/mnalapaz). The palace itself is a magnificent example of Baroque architecture, with a grand portico opening onto a central patio overlooked by three floors of arched walkways, all elaborately carved from pink granite in a rococo style with stylized shells, flowers and feathers.

Contemporary Bolivian artists are represented, but the museum's permanent collection is based firmly around colonial religious works, featuring several by the great master of Andean colonial painting, Melchor Pérez de Holguín. Look out for temporary exhibitions, which often stray from the colonial theme.

Templo de Santo Domingo

A block northwest from Plaza Murillo, the **Templo de Santo Domingo** (C Ingavi, at Yanacocha; Mon–Sat 8am–noon & 3.30–6pm, Sun 8am–noon; free) has a richly detailed eighteenth-century facade carved from soft white stone in Mestizo-Baroque style, exemplifying the combination of Spanish and indigenous symbolism characteristic of Andean colonial architecture.

Museo Nacional de Etnografía y Folklore

The small but rewarding **Museo Nacional de Etnografía y Folklore** (C Ingavi 916, at

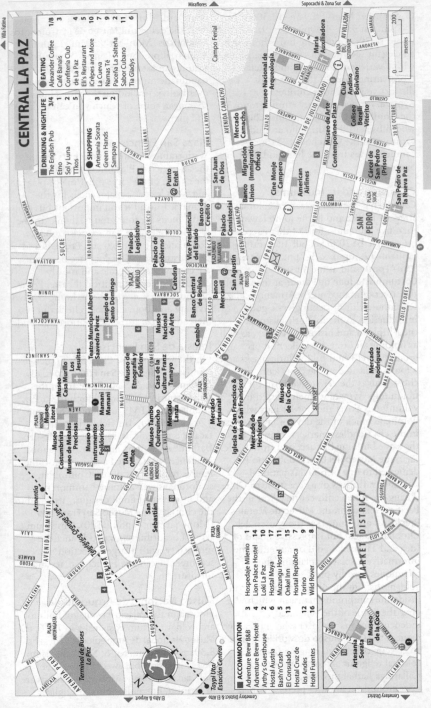

CENTRAL LA PAZ

● EATING
Alexander Coffee	1/8
Café Banaís	3
Confitería Club de La Paz	4
Elí's Restaurant	5
iCrepes and More	10
La Cueva	7
Namas Té	9
Paceña La Salteña	2
Sabor Cubano	11
Tía Gladys	6

■ DRINKING & NIGHTLIFE
The English Pub	3/4
Etno	1
Sol y Luna	2
TTkos	5

■ SHOPPING
Artesanía Sorata	3
Green Hands	1
Sampaya	2

■ ACCOMMODATION
Adventure Brew B&B	3
Adventure Brew Hostel	4
Arthy's Guesthouse	2
Hostal Austria	6
Bash'n'Crash	13
El Consulado	1
Hostal Cruz de los Andes	12
Hotel Fuentes	16
Hospedaje Milenio	14
Lion Palace Hostel	10
Loki La Paz	17
Hostal Maya	11
Muzungu Hostel	15
Onkel Inn	7
Hostal República	9
Torino	12
Wild Rover	8

2

G. Sanjinez; Mon–Fri 9am–12.30pm & 3–7pm, Sat 9am–4.30pm, Sun 9am–noon; B$20; ⓦmusef.org.bo) is housed in an elegant seventeenth-century mansion, with a variety of costumes and artefacts representing three of Bolivia's most distinctive indigenous cultures: the **Aymara**, formed of thirty ethnic groups in the Cordillera Oriental; the **Uru-Chipayas**, who subsist in the Altiplano around Oruro; and the Quechua-speaking **Tarabuqueños** from the highlands east of Sucre.

Calle Jaén and its museums

Calle Jaén is the best-preserved colonial street in La Paz and home to no fewer than five museums, four of them accessed on a single B$20 ticket (all Tues–Fri 9.30am–12.30pm & 3–7pm, Sat & Sun 9am–1pm), sold at the **Museo Costumbrista Juan de Vargas** at the top of the street (entrance on Av Armentia, Plaza Riosinho). This museum gives a good introduction to the folkloric customs of the Altiplano and history of La Paz, as well as holding an extensive collection of grotesque yet beautiful folkloric masks and a room dedicated to the city's icon, the **chola**. This is the vernacular term for the ubiquitous Aymara women dressed in voluminous skirts and bowler hats who dominate much of the day-to-day business in the city's endless markets. Housed in the same building but accessed from Calle Jaén, the **Museo del Litoral Boliviano** is dedicated to one of Bolivia's national obsessions: the loss of its coastline to Chile during the nineteenth-century War of the Pacific. Next door, the **Museo de Metales Preciosos**, also known as the Museo del Oro, has a small but impressive hoard of Inca and Tiwanaku gold ornaments, and informative displays explaining the techniques used by pre-Columbian goldsmiths. On the other side of the road, inside the sumptuous mansion which was once the home of the venerated independence martyr after whom it's now named, the **Casa Museo de Murillo** houses an eclectic collection, ranging from colonial religious art to artefacts used in Kallawaya herbal medicine.

Set around yet another pretty colonial courtyard a little further down at C Jaén 711, the delightful **Museo de Instrumentos Folkloricos** (Mon–Sat 9.30am–1.30pm & 4.30–6.30pm, Sun 10am–6.30pm; B$5) features an astonishing variety of handmade musical instruments from all over Bolivia, including the indigenous *charangos*, some of which you can pick up and play.

Plaza San Francisco

With traffic crawling through its centre, the all-concrete **Plaza San Francisco** lacks the charm of the city's other major plazas, and is no longer a major focus for the Aymara. Instead it's an important bus stop and a focus for tour groups, thanks to the looming Iglesia de San Francisco that dominates the whole space. **Protests** and demonstrations still take place here, but are generally small scale and mostly colourful pieces of political theatre. For a bewildering choice of cheap, home-cooked Aymara and Bolivian food, check out **Mercado Lanza** at the plaza's northern end.

Iglesia de San Francisco

On the south side of Plaza San Francisco stands the **Iglesia de San Francisco** (daily 6.30am–noon & 3.30–8pm; free), the most beautiful colonial church in La Paz, established in 1549 and rebuilt between 1743 and 1784. The richly decorated facade is a classic example of the Mestizo-Baroque style, showing clear indigenous influence, with carved anthropomorphic figures reminiscent of pre-Columbian sculpture as well as more common birds and intertwined floral designs. Attached to the church is the **Museo San Francisco** (Mon–Sat 9am–6pm; B$20), a museum set in a beautiful renovated Franciscan monastery, with a large collection of seventeenth-century Franciscan art and furniture.

Museo Nacional de Arqueología

Housed in the Palacio Tiwanaku, built for archeologist Arturo Posnansky in 1916, the **Museo Nacional de Arqueología** (Tues–Fri 8.30am–12.30pm, Sat & Sun 9am–1pm; B$14) is a short but sweet exhibition of Bolivian archeology. Most explanations are in Spanish, but audio-tours in English should be available by the time this book goes to press. The most impressive pieces are from the Tiwanaku culture (400–1000 AD), including an incense burner in the form of a jaguar, a llama jug that pours through the tail, and some macabre elongated skulls, one of which has been trepanned. There's also a superb jar in the form of a grim-faced man with plugs in his lip and ears.

Museo de Arte Contemporáneo Plaza

The **Museo de Arte Contemporáneo Plaza**, on the Prado at Av 16 de Julio 1698 (daily 10am–7pm; B$15), is housed in a gorgeous pale blue Art Nouveau mansion with Middle Eastern stained-glass windows and Gustave Eiffel iron staircases. The collection of paintings and sculptures is eclectic but compelling, including images of Che Guevara (one made of dominoes) and sculptures by Frederic Remington, nineteenth-century artist of the old American West.

Calle Sagárnaga and Witches' Market

Heading west from Iglesia San Francisco, **Calle Sagárnaga**, La Paz's main tourist street, is crowded with hotels, tour agencies, restaurants, handicraft shops and stalls. It's also the gateway to the main Aymara neighbourhoods of La Paz, one of the most distinctive parts of the city, with steep, winding lanes filled with lively markets. The **Mercado de Hechicería**, or Witches' Market – a cluster of stalls on calles Linares and Jiménez, leading off Santa Cruz – offers a fascinating window onto the world of Aymara mysticism and herbal medicine. The stalls are laden with a cornucopia of ritual and medicinal items, ranging from herbal cures for minor ailments like rheumatism or stomach pain to incense, coloured sweets, protective talismans and dried llama foetuses. The area offers plenty of great photo opportunities, but remember to ask permission or buy a memento.

Museo de la Coca

The small but enlightening **Museo de la Coca** (C Linares 906, a block south of C Sagárnaga; daily 10am–7pm; B$13; ⓦcocamuseum.com) is dedicated to the leaf that is both the central religious and cultural sacrament of the Andes and the raw material for the manufacture of cocaine. The museum gives a comprehensive overview of the history, chemistry, cultivation and uses of this most controversial of plants.

Market district

A few blocks west of the Witches' Market is the **market district**, a vast open-air bazaar sprawling over some thirty city blocks where La Paz's Aymara conduct their daily business. The market area goes by many names – locals tend to refer to specific streets where certain products are sold – but is generally known as **Mercado Negro** where Max Paredes meets Graneros (shoes and clothing), and **Huyustus** (or just "Uyustus"), further west around the street of the same name (clothing, bedding, toys, shoes and musical instruments). Street after street is lined with stalls piled high with sacks of sweet-smelling coca leaf, mounds of brightly coloured tropical fruit, enormous heaps of potatoes and piles of silver-scaled fish; there are also smuggled stereos and televisions, and endless racks of the latest imitation designer clothes. In the last week of January, the area, as well as most of the rest of the city, is taken over by stalls selling all manner of miniature items during the **Feria de las Alasitas**, which is centred on representations of Ekeko, the diminutive mustachioed household god of abundance.

Museo Tambo Quirquincho

Just northwest of Plaza San Francisco, **Plaza Alonso de Mendoza** is a pleasant square named after La Paz's founder, whose imperious statue stands at its centre. On the southern side of the square on Calle Evaristo Valle, the **Museo Tambo Quirquincho** (Tues–Fri 9am–12.30pm & 3–7pm, Sat & Sun 9am–1pm; B$8) is a showcase for Bolivian contemporary art. More interesting is the museum's setting: inside one of the largest examples of an eighteenth-century *tambo*, a compound that served during the colonial era both as accommodation and as marketplace for rural Aymaras.

2

2

THE FIGHTING CHOLITAS

One of the main reasons to visit La Paz's sister city of El Alto – other than for its airport – is to watch slightly kitsch, Mexican-style wrestling matches featuring the bowler hat-wearing indigenous women known as **cholitas**. The shows take place on Thursdays and Sundays (4–7pm) and can be booked through hostels or La Paz-based tour operators (all-inclusive trips including transport and tickets are typically B$90).

ARRIVAL AND DEPARTURE

By plane International and domestic flights use El Alto airport (✆ 02 2157300, ⓦ sabsa.aero/aeropuerto-el-alto), on the rim of the Altiplano, about 11km from La Paz and at over 4000m above sea level. The easiest way into town from here is by taxi; they wait right outside the terminal (30min; B$70–80). Cotranstur run shuttle minivans (*minibus*) down into the city and the length of the Prado to Plaza Isabella La Católica (Mon–Sat every 10–20min 6am–6.30pm, Sun every 30min; B$4 including baggage).

Destinations Cochabamba (13–18 daily; 35min; BoA, Ecojet, TAM); Puerto Suárez (15–21 daily; 1hr; BoA, Amaszonas); Rurrenabaque (4–6 daily; 40min; Amaszonas, TAM); Santa Cruz (11–20 daily; 1hr; BoA, Amaszonas, TAM); Sucre (1 daily; 50min; BoA); Tarija (1–2 daily; 1hr 5min; BoA, TAM); Trinidad (1 daily; 50min; BoA); Uyuni (4–5 daily; 50min; BoA, Amaszonas).

By bus Most international and inter-city buses arrive at and depart from the Terminal de Buses La Paz on Plaza Antofagasta, about 1km northwest of Plaza San Francisco. Minibuses and *micros* to the Lago Titicaca region, Copacabana, Sorata and Tiwanaku depart from the cemetery district, high up on the west side of the city. Plenty of minibuses and *micros* (marked "Cementerio") ply the route between the city centre and the cemetery, but the easiest way to get here is by Teleférico (red line), just one stop from Taypi Uta/Estación Central to Ajayuni/Cementerio. Buses and minibuses for Coroico and Chulumani in the Yungas, and one from Rurrenabaque and the Beni, use Terminal Puente Minasa in Villa Fatima, 2km from the centre in the northeast of the city; buses for Guayaramerín and Riberalta in the Beni depart from their offices around the intersection of Av de las Américas and C Virgen del Carmel, five blocks below the terminal. Plenty of *micros* and minibuses head to and from the city centre, but a taxi is preferable.

Destinations from Terminal de Buses La Paz Arica, Chile (4 daily; 9hr); Cochabamba (1–2 hourly; 7–8hr); Copacabana (6 daily; 3–4hr); Cusco, Peru (1 daily; 15hr); Lima, Peru (2 daily; 32hr); Oruro (1–3 hourly; 3hr 30min); Potosí (roughly hourly; 9–11hr); Puno, Peru (4 daily; 6hr–8hr); Santa Cruz (10 daily, leaving afternoons only; 16–18hr); Sucre (5 daily; 14–15hr); Tarija (17 daily; 16hr); Uyuni (5 daily; 9–12hr).

Destinations from Cemetery District Charazani (1 daily; 10hr); Copacabana (every 30min; 3hr 30min); Desaguadero (when full; 1hr 30min); Sorata (when full; 4hr 30min); Tiwanaku (when full; 1hr 30min).

Destinations from Villa Fátima Chulumani (7 daily buses, plus minibuses leaving when full; 4hr–4hr 30min); Cobija (1–2 daily; 48hr); Coroico (when full; 2hr–2hr 30min); Guayaramerín (2 daily; 32hr); Riberalta (2 daily; 30–40hr); Rurrenabaque (5 daily; 20hr).

GETTING AROUND

By minibus, micro and trufi There are two main forms of public transport in La Paz: rickety city buses, known as *micros*, and privately owned minivans, confusingly known as "minibuses" (even though they are smaller than *micros*). Minibus destinations are written on signs inside the windscreen and bellowed incessantly by the drivers' assistants. Your third option is a *trufi* – basically a car operating as a minibus with a maximum of four passengers and following fixed routes (mostly between Plaza del Estudiante and the wealthy suburbs of the Zona Sur). Trufis charge a flat rate of about B$3–3.50, *micros* about B$1–2 and minibuses B$2 for journeys in the city centre (B$2.60 for trips to the Zona Sur; fares increase to B$2.20 and B$2.80 respectively after 9pm). The city is currently developing a more integrated mass transit system dubbed "La Paz Bus", which includes the Teleférico cable car system (see page 172) and new "Pumakatari" buses, primarily aimed at commuters.

By taxis To reduce your chances of being robbed, assaulted or worse, it's advisable to only ever take a radio taxi: they're marked as such, usually with a telephone number painted on the side. Radio taxis charge a flat rate of B$15–20 to anywhere in the city centre regardless of the number of passengers (agree the price before you get in).

INFORMATION

Tourist information The municipal tourist office on Plaza del Estudiante (Mon–Fri 8.30am–noon & 2.30–7pm; ✆ 02 2371044) has information on La Paz and the surrounding area. InfoTur's office on the Prado at Av Mariscal Santa Cruz 1400 (at Colombia; Mon–Fri 9am–7pm, Sat & Sun 9am–1pm; ✆ 02 2651255) also offers city maps, and is better informed on destinations out of La Paz. Both are friendly and helpful, and usually have someone on hand who speaks English. There is also a very helpful kiosk in the bus terminal (Mon–Fri 6am–1pm & 2–9pm, Sat & Sun 7am–noon; ✆ 02 2285858), and a handy website at ⓦ turismolapaz.com.

TOUR OPERATORS

America Tours Ground-floor office 9, Edificio Avenida, Av 16 de Julio 1490 ✆ 02 2374204, ⓦ america-ecotours.

com. Efficient and reliable, they're the main booking agent for *Chalalán Ecolodge* in Parque Nacional Madidi, and a good place for booking internal flights.

Climbing South America C Linares 940, upper floor, La Paz ⓣ02 2971543, ⓦclimbingsouthamerica.com. Professional and dedicated mountaineering specialists, offering trips to all the Bolivian peaks, along with pioneering treks.

Fremen 10th floor, Edificio María Haydee, Av 20 de Octubre 2396 ⓣ02 2421258, ⓦandes-amazonia.com. Agency run by the sister of the owner of Fremen Tours in Cochabamba (see page 208), but otherwise unconnected to it, offering tailor-made tours throughout Bolivia, including river trips on the Río Mamoré on their own floating hotel.

Gravity Assisted Mountain Biking C Linares 940, upper floor ⓣ02 2310218, ⓦwww.gravitybolivia.com. The original and still the best downhill mountain-biking operator, offering daily Death Road trips (B$849) with excellent US-made bikes and experienced, enthusiastic English-speaking guides. They also offer a range of single-track options for more experienced bikers – their Chacaltaya–Zongo descent plummets 4300m. Gravity helped set up the lower-cost Barracuda (C Linares 971, ⓣ02 2310176, ⓦbarracudabiking.com), Red Cap Walking Tours (ⓣ7628 5738, ⓦredcapwalkingtours.com), Zzip (see page 185) and Urban Rush abseiling in central La Paz (ⓦurbanrushbolivia.com).

Huayna Potosí Travel Agency C Sagárnaga 398 ⓣ02 2317324, ⓦhuayna-potosi.com. Friendly and long-established family firm specializing in climbing and trekking expeditions in the Cordillera Real.

Kanoo Tours C Illampu 832 ⓣ02 2460003, ⓦkanootours.com. Englishman Phil is a top source of information for the budget traveller, with quality tours and bookings arranged across the country. Also has a branch in the *Adventure Brew Hostel*.

La Paz On Foot C Linares 882-B ⓣ7154 3918, ⓦlapazonfoot.com. Offers an interesting range of trips in the immediate vicinity of La Paz, not least the "Urban Trek", but also heads further afield with an ethos of responsible, rural community-supporting travel.

Topas Travel C Carlos Bravo 299, in Hotel El Consulado ⓣ02 2111082, ⓦtopas.bo. A wide-ranging, well-respected operator.

Travel Tracks C Sagárnaga 366 ⓣ02 2004513, ⓦtravel-tracks.com. Run by affable Dutch woman Aly Bakker and specializing in climbing, trekking and Salar de Uyuni tours.

Vertigo Biking C Jimenez 836, between calles Santa Cruz and Sagárnaga ⓣ02 2115220, ⓦvertigobiking.com. A recommended agency for cycling the "world's most dangerous road" (B$570), with top-of-the-range bikes, a good safety record and English-speaking guides.

Zig Zag C Illampu 867 ⓣ02 2453611, ⓦzigzagbolivia.com. Climbing and trekking specialist, including the Cordillera Real.

2

ACCOMMODATION

There's plenty of budget accommodation in La Paz. Most places are in the city centre within a few blocks of Plaza San Francisco, within walking distance of most of the city's main attractions.

NEAR THE BUS STATION

Adventure Brew B&B Av Montes 533 ⓣ02 2461614, ⓦtheadventurebrewhostel.com; map p.167. This B&B operation is a sister property to the hostel 50m down the road (see below), but don't confuse them – this place offers more comfortable private en-suite rooms as well as four- and eight-bed dorms, a roof restaurant for the buffet breakfast, and a free Saya beer included in the room rate. Doubles B$220, dorms B$80

★ **Adventure Brew Hostel** Av Montes 503 ⓣ02 2915896, ⓦtheadventurebrewhostel.com; map p.167. Popular hostel with a range of dorms, one free beer every day, an underground bar with pool table, a DVD lounge, top-floor restaurant and terrace with amazing views, Friday barbecues, and good food. Staff are incredibly friendly and the hostel is very popular so it's best to book online in advance, although they can usually find a bed. Access to the facilities of its associated B&B included. Dorms B$52

Arthy's Guesthouse Av Montes 693 ⓣ02 2281439, ⓦarthyshouse.tripod.com; map p.167. A cheap hotel rather than a hostel (no dorms, for example), this

CYCLING THE DEATH ROAD

One of the most popular trips in Bolivia, and some travellers' sole reason for crossing the border, is a chance to hurtle down the infamous **Death Road**. This exhilarating 3500m descent, along the old road from **La Paz to Coroico** in the Yungas, is easy to organize as a day-trip from La Paz. Cyclists have been killed or seriously injured on this rough, narrow track chiselled out of near-vertical mountainsides, and you must choose a tour operator with great care – some are truly unscrupulous. As well as the Death Road, there are many other excellent mountain-biking alternatives if you want to get off the beaten track. Recommended operators include Gravity Assisted Mountain Biking and Vertigo Biking (see page 171).

2

MI TELEFÉRICO – LA PAZ BY CABLE CAR

In 2014 the commute between El Alto and La Paz became a lot more serene with the opening of a Doppelmayr-built cable-car system that includes five colour-coded **Teleférico** routes running down the slopes of the city (with more lines planned). Though not billed as a tourist attraction – the red line (**Línea Roja**) connects the former train station (Taypi Uta/Estación Central on Av Maco Capac), the cemetery district (Av Entre Ríos) and El Alto (Zona 16 de Julio, Av Panorámica Norte) – for around B$3 each way this is a scintillating ride across the rim of the Altiplano. Each cabin seats ten passengers, leaving every twelve seconds, seventeen hours a day. The most central station is Armentia, near the bus terminal. See ⓦmiteleferico.bo for the latest information.

welcoming, pot-planted retreat offers carpeted rooms with bedside lamps, a TV room and communal kitchen. It's a bit worn round the edges, in a comfortable kind of way, but there's a midnight curfew, and breakfast is B$10 extra. B$90

Bash'n'Crash C Ingavi 681 ☎02 2280934, ⓦbashandcrashbackpackers.com; map p.167. Not for the fussy, this self-styled party hostel (the name says it all really) is rough and ready, rather raucous (and smoky), but very cheap and lots of fun. Accommodation consists largely of dorm beds, with a few private rooms, while the communal areas have enough bonhomie to take the chill off the coldest La Paz night. Residents get free entry to El Mural *peña* downstairs (see page 176). Dorms B$35, doubles B$115

PLAZA MURILLO AND EAST OF THE PRADO

Hostal Austria C Yanacocha 531, on the left at the top of the stairs ☎02 2408540, ⓔhotelaustria58@hotmail. com; map p.167. In a colonial building with lofty ceilings and a warren of wood and glass corridors, this place is both period and ramshackle at the same time. All bathrooms are shared and the gas-powered showers sometimes need a bit of help, and not all rooms have outside windows (although they're quieter). There's a TV room and a kitchen, but breakfast isn't included. Dorms B$42, doubles B$98

Loki La Paz Av América 120 ☎02 2457300, ⓦlokihostel.com; map p.167. The La Paz branch of this Peru-based party hostel chain is large, efficient and well run. The ground floor (shared with the Banco Ecofutura) is colonial but the upper floors are super-modern, with at least one bathroom to every dorm, and one dorm reserved for women. There's a seventh-floor bar with great views, a TV room, a smoking room, and pool and ping-pong tables. Dorms B$62, doubles B$205

Hospedaje Milenio C Yanacocha 860 ☎02 2281263, ⓦhospedajemilenio.blogspot.com; map p.167. Friendly family-run place on a cobbled street. Several rooms are comically tiny, most are without natural light and some bed frames still sport stickers, evidence of their past existence in a child's bedroom. Breakfast is B$9–15 extra. No en-suite bathrooms. Dorms B$40, doubles B$80

Hostal República C Comercio 1455 ☎02 2202742, ⓦhostalrepublica.com; map p.167. The former home of Bolivian president Jose M. Pando, this renovated pile is set around two cobbled courtyards. The downstairs rooms are fairly poky and noisy, but the upper rooms are brighter. B$190

Torino C Socabaya 457 ☎02 2406003, ⓦhoteltorino. com.bo; map p.167. Facing the crumbling north flank of the cathedral, the site includes a beautiful cloistered courtyard, which, unfortunately, the guest rooms are entirely apart from. Breakfast B$15 extra. Doubles (shared bathroom) B$90, (private bathroom) B$150

Wild Rover C Comercio 1476 ☎02 2116903, ⓦwildroverhostels.com; map p.167. One of La Paz's big gringo party hostels, centred on a pleasantly open-air, canary yellow-painted courtyard and an in-house bar that keeps the Guinness flowing till well into the wee hours (there's an Irish theme). They also claim to have "the comfiest beds in South America". Dorms B$59, doubles B$109

CALLE SAGÁRNAGA AND WEST OF THE PRADO

Hostal Cruz de los Andes C Aroma 216 ☎02 2451401, ⓔcruzdelosandes@hotmail.com; map p.167.This budget branch of the nearby (and also not unreasonably priced) *Hotel Estrella Andina*, has colourful rooms and indigenous art in the public areas, as well as an elegant wrought-iron stairwell and a sociable pool room. B$220

★ TREAT YOURSELF

El Consulado C Carlos Bravo 299 ☎02 2117706; map p.167. This place served as the Panamanian consulate in the mid-twentieth century and it retains a stately grandeur. Stay in one of their guest rooms if you can stretch to it (freestanding baths, original furniture and sky-high ceilings; doubles US$79 (B$535).

Hostal Maya C Sagárnaga 339 ☏ 02 2311970, ⓦ hostalmaya.com; map p.167. Tucked inside a little arcade, this is an old building that's been amateurishly redecorated, but has a certain charm for that, and the rooms are snug enough, if a bit worn round the edges. B$140

Hotel Fuentes C Linares 888, between Santa Cruz and Sagárnaga ☏ 02 2334145, ⓦ hotelfuentes.com.bo; map p.167. Nicely set back from the street, rooms lead onto a gallery that overlooks a (rather plain) inner courtyard. They're not particularly generous with the heating on cold days. Breakfast included, plus slow wi-fi (and terminals in the lobby). B$190

Lion Palace Hostel C Linares 1017 ☏ 02 2900454; map p.167. This budget hotel is a mini riot of Neoclassical-pillared, mock-colonial kitsch complete with plaster lion heads. Some of the paintwork's a bit scuffed but the rooms are comfortable and quite spacious, with parquet floors, and pretty good value all in all. B$160

Muzungu Hostel C Santa Cruz 441, at Av Illampu ☏ 02 2451640, ⓦ muzunguhostel.com; map p.167. A small, quiet hostel, with large, spacious dorms and double rooms (it's worth paying the B$20 more to get one with a private bathroom). The painted concrete floors make it feel a bit industrial, but otherwise there are all the facilities you need, friendly staff, and a top-floor bar and breakfast area with great city views. Dorms B$40, doubles B$140

Onkel Inn C Colombia 257 ☏ 02 2490456, ⓦ onkelinn.com; map p.167. Blessedly light and airy and not a shot glass in sight, this HI-affiliated hostel in an 1886 mansion is one to come to for R&R rather than partying, although it can be a bit of a squeeze, and of the private rooms, those with shared bathrooms are really not much of an improvement on being in a dorm. Dorms B$75, doubles B$200

CAMPING

Colibri Camping C 4, Jupapina, just beyond Mallasa (10km south of the city centre) ☏ 7629 5658, ⓦ colibricamping.com; map p.175. In a spectacular mountainside location overlooking the Valley of the Flowers and the Devil's Molar, this tranquil site is run by an extremely welcoming British-Bolivian family. It boasts A-frame cabins sleeping up to four, two teepees and several tent pitches (equipment available to rent), plus outdoor kitchen, hot tub and hammocks. Hiking, mountain biking and Spanish-language classes are offered, as well as volunteer opportunities through sister organization Up Close Bolivia (ⓦ upclosebolivia.org). A 30min drive south of La Paz; around B$70 by taxi. Camping/person B$50, teepees for two B$200, cabins for two B$200

EATING

La Paz has an excellent range of restaurants, cafés and street stalls, from traditional places that dish up local delicacies to tourist-orientated spots with international menus. The

cheapest places to eat are the city's markets, where you can get full meals for around B$12. Mercado Lanza, just up from Plaza San Francisco, is an initially uninviting concrete labyrinth but boasts an astounding range of excellent food stalls on the upper levels. Elsewhere, the ubiquitous *salteñas* and *tucumanas* (B$5–8) – delicious pastries filled with meat or chicken and vegetables – make excellent mid-morning snacks. Try *Tucumanas El Prado* (daily 8am–1.30pm), a series of street carts, just off the Prado on México (in front of the Coliseo Julio Borelli Viterito), known for their delicious fried *tucumanes* (B$6).

CAFÉS

Alexander Coffee Av 16 de Julio 1832, map p.167; C Potosí 1091, map p.167; Av 20 de Octubre 2463, Sopocachi, map p.175; ⓦ www.alexander-coffee.com. This Western-style mini chain ("the Bolivian Starbucks") offers decent cappuccinos (B$15) and generous breakfast plates. The C Potosí branch has plenty of atmosphere with a vaulted brick ceiling. Salads from B$20 – try the quinoa option, with broccoli, courgette, and alfalfa sprouts. Daily 8am–10.30pm.

Café Banaís Sagárnaga 161; map p.167. This elegant tourist-hub café has a pleasant central courtyard and tasty breakfasts, with huge bowls of muesli, cereal and fruit (from B$20), and very good-value buffets (B$38). Strong wi-fi. Daily 7am–10pm.

Confitería Club de La Paz Av Camacho 1202; map p.167. Though this café isn't quite as atmospheric as it once was, the coffee is usually good, and the breakfasts (B$22–30) cheaper than some of the nearby chains. They also serve beer, and a B$27 lunch menu. It was supposedly the haunt of Nazi war criminal Klaus Barbie before his 1983 extradition to France. Mon–Fri 8am–midnight, Sat 8am–6.30pm.

RESTAURANTS

CENTRAL LA PAZ

La Cueva C Tarija 210B ☏ 02 2147115, ⓦ 4cornerslapaz.com; map p.167. Colourful, authentic-feeling Mexican with a sense of humour (check out the Spiderman shrine), super-friendly management and a cosy orange glow. There are quesadillas (B$28–32), chicken enchiladas (B$40) and even chilli con carne (yes, we know, not really Mexican; B$40), not to mention a wide range of tequilas. Daily noon–midnight.

Eli's Restaurant Av 16 de Julio 1491, at Bueno ☏ 02 2335566; map p.167. This sweetly kitsch place has been cooking up Italian and South American food since 1942 (spaghetti with meatballs B$55, "baby beef" aka tenderloin B$69). Che Guevara is said to have worked or at least eaten here in the 1950s). The diner-style decor is a shrine to the silver screen, with a portrait of Humphrey Bogart in pride of place. Don't confuse the restaurant with the *Eli's Pizza Express* mini chain. Daily 8am–11pm.

iCrêpes and More Galeria Chuquiago, C Sagarnaga 217 ☎ 6993 0868; map p.167. As you might guess from the name, this place serves crêpes, both sweet and savoury, including *quattro formaggi* (B$30), vegetarian and prawn, and for dessert, Nutella or lemon cream crêpes, or a Bolivian crêpe Suzette (flambéed with *singani*; B$35). Mon–Fri 10am–7pm, Sat 10am–6pm.

★ **Namas Té** Zoilo C Flores 1334, at Almirante Grau ⓦ namastebolivia.com; map p.167. Run by Gonz Jove, an artist/sculptor responsible for several of the murals around La Paz, this bohemian enclave offers the best-value vegetarian (much of it vegan) *almuerzos* (B$29) in the city, prepared with healthy doses of quinoa and a flair for traditional adaptations. The fruity desserts are likewise imaginative, and they do delicious takes on the usual sandwiches, burritos, tacos, etc. Mon–Fri 8.30am–7pm, Sat 8.30am–4pm.

Paceña La Salteña Loayza 233 ⓦ pacenalasaltena. com; map p.167. A La Paz institution with several branches in the city (this is the most central), where a tasty pasty (meat, chicken or veg) will set you back the princely sum of B$6. Mon–Fri & Sun 8.30am–2pm, Sat 8.30am–3pm.

Sabor Cubano C Sagárnaga 357 ⓦ saborcubanobolivia. com; map p.167. Cheap, tasty and filling food in satisfyingly tattered surroundings, with graffiti-choked walls and vintage Cuban sounds. Various permutations of rice, beans, avocado and cassava as well as *almuerzos* (B$30) and the obligatory mojitos (B$25). Mon–Sat noon–midnight.

Tia Gladys C Illampu 809 ☎ 02 2452070; map p.167. A great little budget café-restaurant near the witches' market, handy for a set breakfast (B$13–30), a plate of pasta (B$35), or just a coffee and a cake (apple cake B$10, tiramisú B$12). Daily 8am–11pm.

SOPOCACHI

It's only a half-hour walk or ten-minute taxi ride from the Prado, but the middle-class neighbourhood of Sopocachi feels utterly cocooned from the hectic central area.

Café Beirut C Belisario Salinas 380 ☎ 02 2444486; map p.175. Though this cavernous café-restaurant lacks any Middle Eastern atmosphere and much of the food is in fact Mexican, it does have the best falafel in La Paz (B$26 for 4), not to mention further Lebanese-style meze delights such as *kebbi* (fried bulgur wheat balls stuffed with meat; B$15 each). Mon–Sat 9am–midnight, Sun 9am–10.30pm.

La Comédie Pasaje Medinacelli 2234 ☎ 02 2423561, ⓦ lacomedie-lapaz.com; map p.175. With expensive-looking art on the terracotta-coloured walls and wine glasses on tables, this Sopocachi restaurant is a notch up in class from almost everywhere else in the city. Mains

are upward of B$55, and the French-influenced cooking is generally exemplary. Mon–Fri noon–3pm & 7–11pm, Sat 5–11pm.

DRINKING AND NIGHTLIFE

Many travellers spend the majority of their partying time in the hostel bars, not moving on until *Loki*, *Wild Rover* and – to a lesser extent – *Adventure Brew* kick out in the small hours. The Sopocachi neighbourhood – a 30min walk or 10min cab ride – is a good target, with venues running the gamut from live jazz to raucous travellers' hangouts. Although La Paz's club scene isn't what it was, you can still find a busy dance floor heaving to just about any kind of music.

CENTRAL LA PAZ

The English Pub C Linares 189, at Tarija ☎ 02 2334717; map p.167. Well, the ale isn't English but the pints are imperial (0.57 litres, admittedly including the head), and the beer is decent enough (B$26 for a pint of Saya), while the pub grub includes such gourmet delights as fish and chips (B$60) or bangers and mash (B$55). There's also a branch at C Illampu 740. Daily 9am–1am.

Etno Jaén 722 ⓦ etnocafecultural.blogspot.com; map p.167. Artsy bar/café tucked away in La Paz's most charming street, with dimly lit wooden tables, good *café con leche*, Amazonian whisky and a relaxed vibe. Mojitos from B$20 (it's also the only place in La Paz serving absinthe). Mon–Sat 11am–3am.

Sol y Luna Murillo 999, at Cochabamba ⓦ solyluna-lapaz.com; map p.167. Dutch-owned institution serving hot coffee and cold beer in a mellow, stone-walled, candlelit atmosphere. There are pool tables, a book exchange, an excellent range of beers (including local microbrews), and food including Indonesian-style *gado gado* (B$48). Daily 9am–1am.

TTkos C Mexico 1555 ☎ 7011 5660; map p.167. Hot, dark, sweaty and often packed subterranean bolthole with a jumping local crowd losing themselves in some of the best live music, DJs and club nights in La Paz, notably reggae night (Tues) Bolivian bands Matamba and Chuquiago Reggae often perform here. Cover charge is usually around B$15–30. Wed–Sat 10pm–4am.

SOPOCACHI

Diesel Nacional Av 20 de Octubre 2271, between calles Rosendo Gutiérrez and Fernando Guachalla ☎ 02 2423477; map p.175. Industrial-chic bar with an extraordinary steampunk design, complete with aircraft engines (circa 1948) hanging from the ceiling (cocktails from B$30). Mon–Sat 7pm–3am.

Glam Av Sánchez Lima 2237 ☎ 7061 6000; map p.175. One of the city's most popular nightclubs, with a wide range of sounds – everything from salsa and bossa nova to retro rock, funk, house and techno. Saturday is the main night for electronic dance music, Friday (in principle, salsa night) tends to be more soulful, but that isn't hard and fast. Thurs–Sat 8pm–3am.

MagicK C Presbítero Medina 2526 ☏02 2910625, ⓦcafemagick.com; map p.175. This place calls itself a "cultural café", and it does indeed serve coffee, not to mention vegetarian food, but it's also a bar, with great beer and cocktails, not to mention regular music nights, when there's a B$20 cover charge and DJs spin dance sounds till past midnight. Tues–Sat 4–11pm.

Malegria Pasaje Medinacelli 2282 ☏02 2423700; map p.175. Tribal-themed nightclub with ethnic masks, stone walls and a middling music policy that runs between ska, Mexican and Argentine rock, and the usual generic stuff. The real reason to come here is the live Thursday-night Afro-Bolivian music (aka "Saya"), a veritable orgy of rhythm and colour. Thurs–Sat 10pm–3am.

Mongo's Rock-Bottom Café Hermanos Manchego 2444 ☏02 2440714; map p.175. Not quite the gringo rendezvous it once was, but its cocktail of televised sports, decent food, serious drinking, live music and raucous dancing still pulls a crowd at weekends. Live Cuban music on Tuesdays; it hosts salsa classes too. Daily 6pm–3.30am.

2

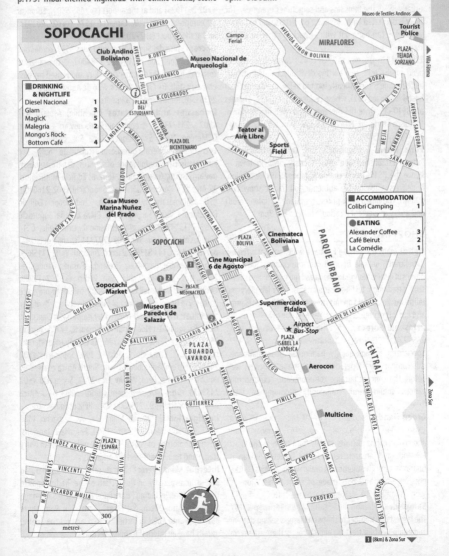

2

ENTERTAINMENT

La Paz has a few good **cinemas**. For more traditional entertainment, head to one of the folk music venues known as *peñas*, where – with varying degrees of authenticity – you can witness age-old Andean music and dance.

Cinemateca Boliviana C Oscar Soria 110, at Rosendo Gutiérrez ☎ 02 2444090, ⓦ cinematecaboliviana.org. An excellent arthouse cinema with a café that gives good views north towards Miraflores. Usually showing one or two blockbusters, too. Tickets B$10–30.

Cine Municipal Av 6 de Agosto 2284 ☎ 02 2440709. Cultural films and concerts at low rates (the concerts are usually B$50, the films less and sometimes even free). The foyer is decorated with old movie projectors, and has a café where you can hang out with a snack, a coffee or a juice. Daily 3–11pm.

El Mural C Ingavi 681 ☎ 02 0119458. Away off the regular *peña* tourist trail, this earthy, devilishly painted, mirror-balled venue is conveniently located below the *Bash'n'Crash* hostel (see page 172), whose residents get in free. Charges are B$10–15. Once the charangos and open fire die down, the disco starts up. Fri & Sat 8pm–3am (shows usually 11.30pm & 1.30am).

Peña Huari C Sagárnaga 339 ☎ 02 2316225. The longest-established and most touristy *peña* in town – hence the B$105 cover charge – tends to divide opinion. It delivers a reasonably authentic folk music show (2hr 30min), combined with pricey, traditional Altiplano food) and a very convenient location. Shows daily 8pm.

SHOPPING

With its many markets, La Paz has a wide range of *artesanía* (handicrafts) on sale from all over the country. You'll find dozens of outlets along Sagárnaga and the surrounding streets selling traditional textiles, leather items, silver jewellery and talismans. Fossils sold on this street are fake, though. Illampu also has lots of outlets selling fake big-name gear.

Artesanía Sorata C Sagárnaga 303, at Linares ☎ 02 2454728; ⓦ artesaniasorata.com; map p.167. Specializing in high-quality, handmade alpaca garments, this company was operating on fair-trade principles well before the concept became commonplace, and also runs various volunteer-run community programmes. Daily 10am–7pm.

Green Hands C Indaburo 710 (at Jaén) ☎ 7156 7306, ⓦ greenhandsbolivia.com; map p.167. Bolivian ethnic and ecological handicrafts, mostly from tribes in the Chaco lowlands and Amazon regions (the Ayoreos, Guaranies, Guarayos and Chiquitanos). Lovely woodcarvings, wicker pots, ceramics and pots made of plant fibres. Mon–Fri 9am–noon & 3.30–6.30pm, Sat 9am–1pm.

Sampaya C Illampu 803 ☎ 02 2000004; map p.167. The largest of a number of shops on Illampu selling clothing and equipment for trekking and climbing. There are several

others within spitting distance to compare prices and quality before buying. Daily 10am–8pm.

DIRECTORY

Banks and exchange There are plenty of ATMs in the centre of town. Banks include BNB on Av Camacho at C Colón, and Banco Mercantil Santa Cruz at Av Camacho 1448. Money changers are concentrated on the stretch of the Prado opposite the post office.

Car rental Barbol, Av Héroes 777 (Km7), opposite El Alto airport ☎ 02 2820675, ⓦ barbolsrl.com; Budget (ⓦ budget. bo), Capitán Ravelo 2130 (opposite the *Camino Real Hotel*; ☎ 02 2911925) and at the airport (☎ 7655 5509); Europcar (ⓦ europcar.com.bo), Av Camacho 1574 (☎☎ 02 2202933) and at the airport (☎ 7720 5118).

Doctor Clinica del Sur, Av Hernando Siles 3539, corner of C 7, Obrajes, Zona Sur, 2881 (☎ 02 2784001, ⓦ clinicadelsur. com.bo), has a 24hr emergency facility and is used by most embassy staff. Try Clinica Cemes, Av 6 de Agosto 2881 (☎ 02 2430350), for less serious ailments.

Embassies and consulates Argentina, Aspiazu 497 ☎ 02 2417737, ⓦ ebolv.cancilleria.gov.ar; Australia, C Moreno 1091, San Miguel, Zona Sur ☎ 7061 0626, ⓔ cristinafernandezm@gmail.com (consulate only; see embassy in Lima for full range of services, ⓦ peru.embassy. gov.au); Brazil, Ground Floor, Torre B, Edificio Multicentro, Av Arce at C Rosendo Gutiérrez, Sopocachi ☎ 02 2166400, ⓦ lapaz.itamaraty.gov.br; Canada, 2nd Floor, Edificio Barcelona, C Victor Sanjinés 2678, Plaza España, Sopocachi ☎ 02 2415141, ⓔ lapaz@international.gc.ca; Chile, C 14 #8024, Calacoto, Zona Sur ☎ 02 2797331, ⓦ chile.gob.cl/la-paz; Ecuador, C 14 #8136, Calacoto, Zona Sur ☎ 02 2115869, ⓦ bolivia.embajada.gob.ec; Ireland, Pasaje Gandarillas 2667 at C Macario Pinilla, San Pedro ☎ 02 2413949, ⓔ consulbolivia@gmail.com (honorary consulate only; see embassy in Buenos Aires for full range of services, ⓦ dfa.ie/argentina); New Zealand covered by embassy in Santiago, Chile; Paraguay, 1st Floor, Edificio Illimani II, Av 6 de Agosto 2512, Sopocachi ☎ 02 2433176, ⓔ embapar@acelerate. com; Peru, C Fernando Guachalla 300, Sopocachi ☎ 02 2441250, ⓦ embaperubolivia.com; South Africa covered by embassy in Lima, Peru; UK, Av Arce 2732, Sopocachi ☎ 02 2433424, ⓦ gov.uk/government/world/bolivia; US, Av Arce 2780, Sopocachi ☎ 02 2168000, ⓦ bolivia.usembassy.gov.

Immigration Oficina de Migración, Av Camacho 1480 ☎ 02 2110960 (Mon–Fri 7am–3pm). For visa extensions, bring a photocopy of your passport ID page, Bolivian entry stamp and tourist card, and the originals.

Internet Many internet cafés in central La Paz charging B$2–3/hr, especially on the section of the Prado opposite the post office, including Punto Entel opposite C Sagárnaga (Mon–Fri 8am–10pm, Sat 9am–10pm, Sun 9am–9pm; B$2/hr). Punto Cotel branches, dotted around the centre, usually have an internet terminal section.

Laundry Most hotels have a laundry service, and there are plenty of *lavanderías* around town. Try Lavandería Maya, C Sagárnaga 339, inside the same gallery as *Hostal Maya Inn*, or the friendly Fines, Ilampu 853.

Pharmacy Farmacias Bolivia (ⓦ www.farmaciasbolivia. com.bo) has branches all over town, including a 24hr branch at Av 16 de Julio 1473, by the Monje Campero cinema (☎ 02 2331838).

Post office Correo Central, Av Mariscal Santa Cruz 1228, at C Oruro (Mon–Fri 8am–7.30pm, Sat 8am–5pm, Sun 8–11am). There's also an endearing little office in the far corner of the *Angelo Colonial* courtyard, C Linares 922 (in principle daily 9am–4pm but often closed for no apparent reason).

Telephone centres One of the cheapest places to make international calls is Punto Entel on the Prado opposite C Sagárnaga (Mon–Fri 8am–10pm, Sat 9am–10pm, Sun 9am–9pm), which charges B$1/min to international landlines, B$3/min to mobiles.

Tourist police Edificio Olimpia, Plaza Tejada Sorzano, opposite the stadium in Miraflores (24hr; ☎ 02 2225016, toll-free ☎ 800 140081), also downtown on C Pando, at Chuquisaca (☎ 02 2462111 or ☎ 800 140071); you can report thefts (and get the necessary certificate for insurance claims) at either of these.

TIWANAKU

The most worthwhile attraction within a few hours of La Paz is the mysterious ruined city of **TIWANAKU** (also spelled Tiahuanaco), set on the Altiplano 71km to the west. It's Bolivia's most impressive archeological ruin, and was declared a World Heritage Site by UNESCO in 2000.

Founded some three millennia ago, Tiwanaku became the capital of a massive empire that lasted almost a thousand years, developing into a sophisticated urban-ceremonial complex that, at its peak, was home to some fifty thousand people. Tiwanaku remains a place of exceptional symbolic meaning for the Aymara of the Altiplano, who come here to make ceremonial offerings to the *achachilas*, the gods of the mountains. The most spectacular of these occasions, the **Aymara New Year**, takes place each year at the June winter solstice, when hundreds of *yatiris* (traditional priests) congregate to watch the sun rise and celebrate with music, dancing, rituals and copious quantities of coca and alcohol.

Though the city of Tiwanaku originally covered several square kilometres, only a fraction of the site has been excavated, and the main ruins (daily 9am–5pm, last entry 4pm; B$100) occupy a fairly small area that can easily be visited in half a day. Two **museums** by the entrance house many of the smaller archeological finds, as well as several large stone monoliths. The main ruins cover the area that was once the ceremonial centre of the city, a jumble of tumbled pyramids and ruined palaces and temples made from megalithic stone blocks, many weighing over a hundred tonnes. It requires a leap of the imagination to visualize Tiwanaku as it was at its peak: a thriving city whose great pyramids and opulent palaces were painted in bright colours and inlaid with gold, surrounded by extensive residential areas built largely from mud brick (of which little now remains) and set amid lush green fields, rather than the harsh, arid landscape you see today.

ARRIVAL AND INFORMATION

By minibus Minibuses to Tiwanaku depart from the corner of calles Aliaga and Eyzaguirre in the cemetery district in La Paz (every 30min; 1hr 30min; B$25–30); on the way back they leave from the square in Tiwanaku town, just under 1km walk away down Av Ferrocarril, though you can usually flag them down as they pass the entrance to the ruins.

Tour operators Most tour agencies in La Paz run full- or half-day trips to the site (B$100–140/person plus entry).

Guided tours It's worth investing in an English-speaking tour guide once you get to Tiwanaku. Official site guides (B$130/2hr in Spanish, or B$150/2hr in English) operate out of an office next to the ticket counter (*boletería*), and make a huge difference – there are very few signs or explanations on the site itself and it's easy to miss important objects. The same guides will also lead you around the museums, where all the labelling is in Spanish only.

Lago Titicaca

Some 75km northwest of La Paz, **Lago Titicaca**, an immense, sapphire-blue lake, easily the largest high-altitude body of water in the world, sits astride the border with Peru at the northern end of the Altiplano. The area around the lake is the heartland of the Aymara, whose distinct language and culture have survived centuries of domination, first by the Incas, then by the Spanish.

Titicaca has always played a dominant role in Andean religious conceptions. The

2

LAGO TITICACA, CORDILLERA REAL AND THE YUNGAS

San Borja

Rurrenabaque

RESERVA DE LA BIÓSFERA PILÓN LAJAS

PARQUE NACIONAL MADIDI

Caranavi

Río Coroico

Coroico

YUNGAS

Yolosa

Unduavi

Yanacachi

Coroico

Puente Villa

Chulumani

Río La Paz

Yunga (Cruz Trail)

Takesi Trail

Illimani (6439m)

REAL

Ventilla

Guanay

Río Zongo

PARQUE NACIONAL COTAPATA

CORDILLERA

Huayna Potosí (6088m)

Chacaltaya

LA PAZ

Oruno

Mapiri

Río Tipuani

Río Challana

RTE-19

RTE-2

Santa Rosa

Apolo

Consata

Sorata

Illampu (6427m)

Achacachi

Tiwanaku

Guaqui

RTE-1

PARQUE NACIONAL MADIDI

Charazani

Ancoraimes

Huatajata

Huarina

Isla Pariti

Isla Suriqui

Desaguadero

CORDILLERA APOLOBAMBA

AREA NATURAL DE MANEJO INTEGRADO NACIONAL APOLOBAMBA

Curva

Puerto Acosta

Escoma

San Pablo de Tiquina

San Pedro de Tiquina

Petchuco

Ulla Ulla

Isla de la Luna

Yunguyo

Isla del Sol

Copacabana

PERU

Lago Titicaca

Juliaca

Puno

0   50

kilometres

N

Incas, who believed the creator god Viracocha rose from its waters to call forth the sun and moon to light up the world, also claimed their own ancestors came from here. The remains of their shrines and temples can still be seen on the Isla del Sol and the Isla de la Luna, whose serene beauty is a highlight of any visit to the lake. Nor did Lago Titicaca lose its religious importance with the advent of Christianity: it's no coincidence that Bolivia's most important Catholic shrine can be found in Copacabana, the lakeside town closest to the Isla del Sol.

COPACABANA

The small town and backpacker hangout of **COPACABANA** overlooks the deep-blue waters of Lago Titicaca and is the jumping-off point for visiting Titicaca's sacred islands. The main drag, **Avenida 6 de Agosto**, is pleasant enough, lined with cafés, bars, cambios, tour agents and street entertainers. As home to Bolivia's most revered image, the Virgen de Copacabana, hordes of Catholic pilgrims descend on the city in early February and early August for its two main religious fiestas.

WHAT TO SEE AND DO

The spiritual heart of Copacabana is the imposing **Basílica de Nuestra Señora de Copacabana** (daily 7am–8pm; free), set on the Plaza 2 de Febrero six blocks east of the waterfront. Inside the bright, vaulted interior, the door to the left of the massive gold altarpiece leads to a staircase and a small chapel (*camarín*) housing the **Virgen de Copacabana** herself. Encased in glass, the lavishly dressed statue is never removed: locals believe this could trigger catastrophic floods (this section is often closed, however, since the shrine was robbed in 2013). You can see the replica used in festivals in a special room behind

COPACABANA

0 — 200 metres

Cerro Calvario

Kusijata & Yampupata

Capilla del Señor de la Cruz de Colquepata

PLAZA DE TOROS
Bullring

AVAROA

BALLIVIÁN

JUNÍN

3 DE MAYO

MICHEL PÉREZ

COCHABAMBA

SAN ANTONIO

AVENIDA GENERAL JAÚREGUI

BOLÍVAR

BENI

Museo Poncho

BAPTISTA

ZAPANA

PLAZA SUCRE ★ Buses to Kasani

ORURO

Mercado

MICHEL PÉREZ

Alcaldía Municipal   Police Station & Post Office

J. L. PÉREZ

Boats to Isla del Sol

AVENIDA 6 DE AGOSTO

PANDO

AVAROA

Banco Los Andes

LA PAZ

★ Buses to La Paz

PLAZA 2 DE FEBRERO

Prodem

EcoFuturo   Bank Bisa

Basílica de Nuestra Señora de Copacabana

JOSÉ MEJÍA

Lago Titicaca

BUSCH

AVENIDA 16 DE JULIO

BOLÍVAR

PANDO

JOSÉ BALLIVIÁN

Capilla de Velas

4

N

AVENIDA COSTANERA

Kioscos (Food Stalls)

MANUEL MEJÍA

JUNÍN

RIGOBERTO PAREDES

5

POTOSÍ

MURILLO

6

Intikala

PLAZUELA MANCO KAPAC

7

AVENIDA FÉLIX TEJADA

La Paz

▼ Kasani & Peru

▼ Horca del Inca

■ ACCOMMODATION
La Casa del Sol	4
Hostal La Cúpula	1
Hostal Emperador	6
Hostal Flores Del Lago	3
Hostal Las Olas del Titicaca	5
Hostal Sonia	7
Hotel Utama	2

■ DRINKING
Nemos	1

● EATING
Café Bistrot	2
El Condor and the Eagle	3
La Orilla	1

2

2

---

the altar. Try to catch a "vehicle blessing" ceremony (La Benedición de Movilidades), a ritual where car owners line up outside the cathedral with their vehicles decorated with flowers and ribbons and ask the Virgin to protect them. This usually takes place at about 10am, and usually on weekends.

Another enticing religious site is **Cerro Calvario**, the hill that rises steeply above the town to the north. It's a half-hour walk up to the top along a trail that begins beside the small church at the north end of Calle Bolívar, five or so blocks up from Plaza Sucre; it's a short but very steep ascent to 3973m, and the thin air can make the climb much longer than it looks. The trail follows the Stations of the Cross up to the summit and is dotted with ramshackle stone altars where pilgrims light candles, burn offerings and pour alcoholic libations to ensure their prayers are heard.

Though without the attractions of its more famous namesake in Brazil (which was named in honour of the shrine here), Copacabana's **beach** is a pleasant place for a lakeside stroll and a bite to eat; there are also plenty of pedal boats to rent.

ARRIVAL AND DEPARTURE

By tourist bus "Tourist buses" leaving La Paz in the morning (4hr, terminating at Plaza Sucre in Copacabana) will usually pick you up from your accommodation. Operators include: Milton Tours, Illampu 1123 (daily at 8am; ☎ 02 2368003, ⌨ hotelmiltonbolivia.com), which are more reliable than others; and Titicaca Bolivia, Illampu 773 (daily: 8am, pick-ups from 7am; & 2pm from Terminal de Buses La Paz; ☎ 02 2462655, ⌨ titicacabolivia.com).

By public bus Public buses depart most frequently from the Manco Kapac or 2 de Febrero offices on Plaza Tomás Katari in La Paz's cemetery district (roughly every 30min; 3hr 30min; B$20). Cooperativa 6 de Junio runs minivans

from the same place, but they are very cramped. Less frequent (but better regulated) buses leave from the main Terminal in La Paz. Remember that you must disembark when the bus crosses the Estrecho de Tiquina, and pay to cross over separately (B$2) before re-joining the bus, and that you may also need to show your passport there. The last departure from Copacabana (Plaza Sucre) to La Paz is at around 6.30pm.

INFORMATION

Tourist information There's a rudimentary tourist information office on Plaza Sucre (Mon–Fri 8am–noon & 2–6pm, Sat 8am–2pm, but the tour agencies are often better placed to answer questions.

Banks and exchange Three ATMs in town accept international cards (EcoFuturo on Av 6 de Agosto, Banco Fie on Plaza Sucre and, with higher charges, Banco Unión on Plaza Sucre), and Prodem on Av 6 de Agosto will pay out cash against plastic over the counter. Cambios along Av 6 de Agosto change dollars, euros and soles. Note that you get better rates changing soles to bolivianos or vice-versa here and at the border than you will elsewhere in Peru or Bolivia.

ACCOMMODATION

Owing to its role as a pilgrimage centre, Copacabana has an enormous number of places to stay, though they fill up fast and prices double or triple during the main fiestas.

La Casa del Sol C Ballivián ☎7010 3352; map p.179. Owned by Ligia and Samuel (a former mayor of Copacabana, who can impart insights into local life, should you so wish), this peaceful hotel on the edge of town upholds high standards and irrevocable cleanliness at budget prices. B$80

Hostal Emperador C Murillo 235 ☎02 8622083; map p.179. A cheap and basic budget option – the place is clean, but the narrow beds have seen far better days, and make sure they record your arrival date and any payments you make. Rarely has hot water. No breakfast. No English spoken. Doubles B$50

Hostal Flores Del Lago C Jáuregui (Final) ☎02 8622117, ✉floresdellago@hotmail.com; map p.179. Overlooking the ferry dock, this budget hotel option is fine if you just want somewhere to crash while passing

★ **TREAT YOURSELF**

Hostal La Cúpula Michel Pérez 1–3 ⓣ02 8622029, ⓦhotelcupula.com. A delightful hotel built in neo-Moorish style, overlooking the town and lake. It offers light and airy rooms, a nice garden overlooking the bay, plus hammocks, kitchen, laundry and a somewhat inconsistent restaurant. Breakfast not included. Reservations are recommended. **US$39 (B$265)**

through, with cheap, 1970s-style private rooms (some with lake views), the usual patchy but free wi-fi and a pleasant terrace. **B$120**

Hostal Las Olas del Titicaca Av 16 de Julio ⓣ02 8622205, ⓔolasdeltiticaca_@hotmail.com; map p.179. This is probably the best of Copacabana's bargain-basement traveller haunts, in a central location and with hot water. Spacious and clean en-suite doubles, but the staff can be tetchy on occasion. Breakfast (B$15) not included. Dorms **B$30**, doubles **B$120**

Hostal Sonia C Murillo 256 ⓣ02 8622019, ⓔhostalsoniacopacabana@gmail.com; map p.179. A notch up from nearby *Emperador*, this place has warm water (albeit sporadic), en-suite bathrooms and kitchen facilities. The rooftop terrace has lovely views. **B$140**

Hotel Utama C Michel Pérez 60, at San Antonio ⓣ02 8622013, ⓦutamahotel.com; map p.179. The modern central courtyard has an odd ambience, glowing yellow from the plastic corrugated roof and decorated with huge international flags. But this is a friendly place, with free tea and fruit, en-suite rooms, and breakfast included. **B$210**

EATING

There's no shortage of restaurants in Copacabana, most catering to travellers and pilgrims, and some doubling as bars and evening hangouts, though Copacabana is not a party town. Virtually all offer big plates of the delicious Titicaca trout (*trucha*), including a number of food stalls on the waterfront (B$25; most daily 10am–7pm). At the market you can get a coffee, plus a *pastel* (a bloated, bubbled morsel of fried dough) or *buñuelos* (a sort of doughnut) for around B$5.

Café Bistrot By Mirador Hotel on C Busch, at Av Costanera ⓣ7151 8310; map p.179. Backpacker favourite, mostly thanks to the Bolivian owner Fatima (who speaks French, English and Spanish) who is a fount of local information. Her tasty Bolivian-international fusion menu features decent espresso, plenty of veggie dishes, Thai curry and seasonal fresh fruit juices – there's even Marmite and Vegemite for hardcore fans. Chilled-out music. Mains B$60–90. Daily 7.30am–2.30pm & 5.30–9.30pm.

★ **El Condor and the Eagle** Inside Hostal Residencial Paris, Av 6 de Agosto; map p.179. A great vegetarian breakfast café (owned by an Irishman and his Bolivian wife) serving excellent organic coffee, hot chocolate and proper Irish Tea (all B$10–20), home-made dishes like baked beans on soda bread, and cakes and muffins. Mon–Fri 7am–1.30pm.

La Orilla Av 6 de Agosto ⓣ02 8622267; map p.179. Perennially popular restaurant, usually packed full by 6pm. *La Orilla* tends to divide opinion despite the hype, and it really depends on your expectations. It's not bad if you've been on the road for a while, but don't expect international standards of haute cuisine – the food is a bit hit and miss. The pizzas are usually solid choices (B$45–73), and the stuffed trout is good (B$58). Mon–Sat 5–10.30pm (last order 9.30pm).

DRINKING

Nemos Av 6 de Agosto; map p.179. A simple little bar run by a Brit and a Bolivian with a good playlist, and Bolivian microbrewery beers including Saya and Ted's Cervecería, plus international favourites such as Erdinger. Daily 5–11.30pm.

2

ISLA DEL SOL

Just off the northern tip of the Copacabana peninsula, about 12km northwest of Copacabana town, **ISLA DEL SOL** (Island of the Sun) is a world apart from the mainland, a beautifully preserved slice of old Bolivia. Now a quiet backwater, the island was one of the most important religious sites in the Andean world in the sixteenth century, revered as the place where the sun and moon were created and where the Inca dynasty was born. Scattered with **enigmatic ancient ruins** and populated by traditional Aymara communities, Isla del Sol is an enchanting place to spend some time hiking and contemplating the magnificent scenery. Measuring 9.5km long and 6.5km across at its widest point, it's the largest of the forty or so islands in Lago Titicaca, with three main settlements – Yumani, Ch'alla and Ch'allapampa. You can visit the island, along with nearby **Isla de la Luna** (see page 183), on a day- or even half-day trip from Copacabana, but it's really worth spending at least one night on the island to appreciate fully its serene beauty.

2

The best way to see the Isla del Sol is to walk the length of the island from Ch'allapampa in the north to Yumani in the south (or the other way round) – a three- to four-hour hike. You can do this on a day-trip or, much more comfortably, stay the night and depart Yumani the next day.

North Island (Parte Norte)

The island's northernmost settlement, **Ch'allapampa**, is a pleasant and peaceful village founded by the Incas as a centre for the nearby ceremonial complexes. At the dock you'll find public toilets (B\$2), and a couple of stalls selling sandwiches, water and snacks, while a short walk from the village lie several fascinating **Inca sites**. Note that local guides (free) meet the boats from Copacabana and try to shepherd day-trip visitors around these Inca sites at a healthy pace (worried they will miss the boat back) – you'll learn a lot (if you speak Spanish or someone translates), but this can also be a little restrictive, and you are not obliged to join them. The tiny **Museo del Oro** (daily 9am–noon & 2–5pm; B\$15 for museum and Inca ruins; buy your ticket here and keep hold of it, as there are a couple of checkpoints) has pre-Columbian artefacts found both on the island and at sites off the coast. From the village it's a forty-minute walk northwest along an easy-to-follow path to a cluster of Inca sights and ruins, including the **Roca Sagrada** or **Titikala**, the sacred rock where the creator god Viracocha is believed to have created the sun and moon. Nearby is the **Chincana** (daily 9am–5pm; included in ticket for Museo de Oro), an Inca complex of rambling interlinked rooms, plazas and passageways.

From Chincana you can return to Ch'allapampa for the boats or the trail south along the coast (see below), or take the much more scenic **Ruta Sagrada de la Eternidad del Sol (Willka Thaki)**, paved for most of the way to resemble an old Inca road. The trail runs along the central ridge of the island, with spectacular views throughout its 7km length (allow 3hr–4hr 30min). About halfway along there's a checkpoint where you pay a B\$15 fee. The path runs just below 4000m, so it can be a strenuous hike if you've just arrived in Bolivia. Just before Yumani you'll pass through another checkpoint to pay the B\$10 village entry fee.

South island (Parte Sur)

The coastal trail between Ch'allapampa and Yumani is a slightly easier route, running at a lower altitude than the ridge path, through small farms and villages. The main attractions along the way are the small village of Ch'alla (village admission B\$15) with its **Museo Arqueológico** (daily 9am–5pm, but often closed; free) and **Playa Ch'alla**, a picturesque stretch of sand.

Straggling up the slope from a small harbour about an hour and a half south of Ch'alla, **Yumani** (village admission B\$10) is the island's largest village and home to most of its accommodation. If you arrive by boat (as opposed to by trail from the north part of the island), the climb up to the best accommodation on the ridge (200m up) is a very steep, breathless hike. Yumani's only sight is the **Escalera del Inca** (222 steps), a stairway running steeply for 60m up from the dock through a natural amphitheatre covered by some of the island's finest Inca agricultural terracing, irrigated by bubbling stone canals. There's a small but evocative multi-roomed Inca site called **Pilko Kaina** (daily 9am–5.30pm; included in Yumani admission ticket) a thirty-minute walk from Yumani. Overlooking the lake, one room, whose small window is aligned with Isla de la Luna, floods with light at sunrise.

ARRIVAL AND DEPARTURE

By boat Boats leave from the waterfront in Copacabana at around 8.30am and 1.30pm, calling at "Parte Norte" (Challapampa; B\$25 there, B\$30 back) via "Parte Sur" (Yumani; B\$20 there, B\$25 back), though this sometimes depends on demand, returning to Copacabana from Challapampa at 8.30am, 10.30am and 1.30pm, and from Yumani at 10.30am and 4pm. If you are not staying the night, you get a boat to Challapampa, hike across the island and head back from Yumani (round trip B\$35), but you'll need to watch the time. If you're staying, you can mix and match any leg of these routes, paying one-way rates as you go. Note that it is very rare for any boat to leave Yumani after 4pm, so you'll have to hire a private boat if you get stuck (at least B$600 for a boat to Copacabana).

ACCOMMODATION

Yumani is home to the majority of the island's accommodation, most of which offers sporadic (and usually cold) water, and basic conditions. There are also a couple of simple but friendly places to stay in Ch'allapampa.

CH'ALLAPAMPA

Hostal Inca Uta Near the northern landing jetty at Ch'allapampa ☎7353 4990. Stone-walled *hostal* with en-suite rooms, but still very basic and, as everywhere on the island, the wi-fi comes and goes. No breakfast. B$80

Hostal Pachamama Just beyond the museum ☎7190 0272. A friendly place, overlooking the beach, with claustrophobic (but en-suite) ground-floor rooms and more spacious ones upstairs, mostly with shared bathrooms. There's solar-powered hot water, but no wi-fi and no breakfast. B$60

YUMANI

Hostal Inti Wayra Near the church, Yumani ☎7194 2015. A decent budget choice with sizeable, balconied rooms (with shared and private bathrooms) and excellent east-facing lake views. Those of a spiritual bent can avail themselves of the meditation room, and there's also a decent restaurant. B$140

Hostal Puerta del Sol At the top of the main street, on the left-hand side ☎7195 5181. The mustard-coloured *Hostal Puerta del Sol* has plain, clean rooms and fantastic views from its terrace. Breakfast, served in a rustic little dining room, is included if you take an en-suite room, but not if you take a room with shared bathroom. B$100

EATING

There are plenty of basic restaurants serving pizza, pasta and freshly caught Titicaca trout upon request.

Las Velas Yumani, high up near the eucalyptus forest ☎7123 5616. Run by a former chef at a top Bolivian resort, *The Candle* (it really is lit by candles, no electricity; bring a light) has a similar menu to the other restaurants in Yumani, but significantly higher standards: try the vegetable pizza or trout in wine sauce. Mains around B$50–70. Mon–Sat noon–2.30pm & 6–10pm.

ISLA DE LA LUNA

About 8km east of the Isla del Sol, the far smaller **Isla de la Luna** (Island of the Moon) was another important pre-Columbian religious site. For much of the twentieth century, the island was used as a prison for political detainees, yet for the Incas it was a place of great spiritual importance. Known as Coati ("Queen Island"), it was associated with the moon, considered the female counterpart of the sun, and a powerful deity in her own right. The main site on the island – and one of the best-preserved Inca complexes in Bolivia – is a temple on the east coast known as **Iñak Uyu** (daily 8am–6pm; B$10), the "Court of Women", probably dedicated to the moon and staffed entirely by women. From the beach a series of broad Inca agricultural terraces leads up to the temple complex, a collection of stone buildings with facades containing eleven massive external niches still covered in mud stucco, all around a broad central plaza.

ARRIVAL AND DEPARTURE

By boat Tour boats from Copacabana to Isla del Sol sometimes call at Isla de la Luna if there's enough demand (see page 183). Otherwise, you can charter a private boat from Copacabana or Yumani (around B$400).

ACCOMMODATION AND EATING

Although far fewer (and more basic) than the accommodation options on Isla del Sol, there is a handful of simple, locally run lodges dotted throughout the island; a double room costs around B$100. There are also a few shops to buy food, though you should bring some with you too.

THE CORDILLERA REAL

Stretching for about 160km along the northeastern edge of the Altiplano, the **Cordillera Real** is the loftiest and most dramatic section of the Andes in Bolivia, with six peaks over 6000m high and many more over 5000m forming a jagged wall of soaring, icebound peaks separating the Altiplano from the tropical lowlands of the Amazon Basin. Easily accessible from La Paz, the mountains are perfect for climbing and trekking (see page 184) – indeed, walking here is the only way to really appreciate the overwhelming splendour of the Andean landscape. Populated by isolated **Aymara communities** that cultivate the lower slopes and valleys and raise llamas and alpacas on the high pastures, the cordillera is a largely pristine natural environment. Here, the mighty **Andean**

2

TREKKING AND CLIMBING IN THE CORDILLERA REAL

The easiest base from which to explore the Cordillera Real is **La Paz**. Many of the best and most popular treks start close to the city, including the three so-called "Inca trails" which cross the Cordillera, connecting the Altiplano with the warm, forested valleys of the Yungas. Two of these ancient paved routes – the **Choro Trail** and the **Takesi Trail** – are relatively easy to follow without a guide; the third, the **Yunga Cruz Trail**, is more difficult – bring at least two days' worth of drinking water. You can do all of these treks, as well as many more challenging routes, with many of the adventure tour agencies based in La Paz (see page 170).

The other major starting point for trekking is **Sorata**. From here, numerous trekking routes take you high up among the glacial peaks, while others plunge down into the remote forested valleys of the Yungas. The **Sorata Guides and Porters Association** may possibly be able to help you find trekking guides, mules and porters.

With so many high peaks, the Cordillera Real is also obviously an excellent place for **mountain climbing**, for both serious and inexperienced climbers. **Huayna Potosí** (6088m), near La Paz, is one of the few peaks over 6000m in South America which can be ascended by climbers without mountaineering experience (albeit with the help of a specialist agency – check carefully that the guide they provide is qualified and experienced, and the equipment adequate).

condor is still a common sight, pumas, though rarely seen, still prowl the upper reaches, and the elusive Andean spectacled bear roams the high cloudforest that fringes the mountains' upper eastern slopes.

SORATA

Set at an altitude of 2695m, **SORATA** is an enchanting little town, and the most popular base for trekking and climbing in the Cordillera Real. Hemmed in on all sides by steep slopes, often shrouded in clouds and with a significantly warmer climate than La Paz, it was compared by Spanish explorers to the Garden of Eden. There's not a lot to do in Sorata itself except hang out and relax either side of some hard trekking or climbing, or less strenuous walks in the surrounding countryside.

ARRIVAL AND DEPARTURE

By bus Minibuses from the cemetery district in La Paz (Trans Unificada Sorata, C Manuel Bustillos 675, off Av Kollasuyo ☎ 02 2381693; 4am–6pm; leaving every 30min or when full; 3hr 30min–4hr; B$20) will drop you on Plaza Enrique Peñaranda. Going back to La Paz, buses leave from 14 de Septiembre, 300m south of Plaza Enrique Peñaranda, but note that some terminate in El Alto; Trans Unificada Sorata are the only ones which serve La Paz's cemetery district. The only way to reach Copacabana without going via La Paz is to take a La Paz-bound bus, change at Huarina, and hope that a Copacabana-bound bus or *combi* will

stop for you (which they should do if they have space); for Coroico you'll have to go via La Paz.

INFORMATION

Tourist information Sorata has no formal tourist office. The Asociación de Guías de Turismo Sorata at C Sucre 302 (☎ 7883 8808; often closed) should be able to help you find guides for the main trekking routes around Sorata (around B$200/day) as well as mules and some camping equipment. The *Casa Reggae* also dispenses tourist information.

Banks and exchange There's no ATM in Sorata, but Prodem, Plaza Enrique Peñaranda 136 (Mon 12.30–4.30pm, Tues–Fri 8.30am–4pm, Sat 8am–3pm) changes US dollars and gives cash advances against a credit (but not debit) card for a five-percent commission fee. For all these services, bring your passport.

ACCOMMODATION

★ **Altai Oasis** ☎ 7151 9856, ⊛ www.altaioasis.com. A series of imaginative cabins, rooms and dorms on the folds of the riverbank, including a tree-house-like hideaway, a conical yurt-like construction, as well as more humble abodes, all conceived with real love and dedication. There are also camping spots, a dorm, a pool and a great restaurant. It's 30min from town on foot via the road to the Gruta, so guests have access to a shortcut; alternatively, take a taxi for about B$20. Camping/person B$30, dorms B$84, doubles B$250

Hostal Mirador C Muñecas 400 (two blocks west of the plaza) ☎ 7350 5453, ✉ mirador_sorata@hotmail.com. Perched on the edge of a steep valley, the *Hostal Mirador* lives up to its name ("viewpoint") with the best views in town from its terrace. There's a shared kichen that you can use, and cosy rooms and an easy-going vibe. No wi-fi; breakfast not included. Dorms B$25, doubles B$60

Hostal Panchita Plaza Enrique Peñaranda ☎02 2134242. A welcoming, simple place with a sunny courtyard and clean rooms (though the "hot" shower doesn't quite live up to its name). There's a TV lounge and access to kitchen facilities. B$70

Hostal Las Piedras Villa Elisa C 2, near the football field ☎7191 6341, ✉soratalaspiedras@yahoo.com. A 10–15min walk out of town, *Las Piedras* offers spotless rooms (with or without bathrooms) with great views and styled with an attention to detail rare at budget level. Breakfasts (an additional B$35) are great, and may in season include home-made bread, yoghurt and marmalade from the *Café Illampu*. Good dinners are also available, but no wi-fi. B$100

Residencial Sorata Plaza Enrique Peñaranda ☎02 2136672. Set in the delightful, rambling nineteenth-century Casa Gunther, this *residencial* makes you feel you've stepped back in time by at least eighty years. There are cobbled courtyards, dusky rooms and a huge, wonderfully decorated drawing room. B$50

EATING AND DRINKING

Restaurant opening times are erratic: most places are open every day except Tuesday, from around 9/10am to 9/10pm. Some restaurants have shorter opening hours during the rainy season (Nov–March), and a few close completely.

Altai Oasis ✿www.altaioasis.com. You can dine to the peal of wind chimes and distant rattle of campground bongos on *Altai Oasis*'s idyllic outdoor deck. It's one of Sorata's best places to eat, with Eastern European dishes like goulash and *borsht*, vast T-bone steaks, veggie options and a wide range of breakfast choices. Mains B$30–80. Daily 8am–7.30pm.

Casa Reggae Just down the hill from Hostal El Mirador. A rather rustic outdoor bar, serving juices, wines or caipirinhas in the evening, with reggae music and a chilled out, hippyish feel. It also doubles as a backpackers' inn, with dorm beds at B$20. Daily 7pm–midnight or late.

La Casa del Turista Plaza Enrique Peñaranda ☎7326 6320. It calls itself a pizzeria, but skip the pizzas and pastas, and plump for one of the more interesting Mexican options: there are well-prepared tacos, enchiladas, quesadillas and nachos. Mains B$25–50. Daily 11am–10pm.

Restaurante Jalisco Plaza Enrique Peñaranda ☎7151 5801. This simple restaurant boasts a rather varied menu of Mexican and Italian food, as well as more traditional dishes. The enchiladas are surprisingly tasty (B$29). Daily 8am–10pm.

THE YUNGAS

East of La Paz, the Cordillera Real drops precipitously into the Amazon lowlands, plunging down through a region of

ZZIP THE FLYING FOX

Zip lines have made it to Bolivia, with this incarnation a 1555m beast in three sections, swooping 200m over the forest canopy at speeds of over 85km/hr. **Zzip the Flying Fox** (☎02 2313849, ✿ziplinebolivia.com), a Kiwi-Bolivian-run outfit, is located in Yolosa, 6km from Coroico, and most organized "Death Road" trips (see page 171) include a stop here as an optional extra. It's open daily 9am to 11am and 1pm to 5pm. Rides are around B$220.

rugged, forest-covered mountains and deep subtropical valleys known as the **Yungas**, abundant with crops of coffee, tropical fruit and coca. Three of the well-built stone roads that linked the agricultural outposts of the Yungas to the main population centres before the Spanish conquest, the so-called "Inca" trails – the **Takesi**, **Choro** and **Yunga Cruz** – are still in good condition, and make excellent three- to four-day hikes from La Paz. The most frequently visited Yungas town is the idyllic resort of **Coroico**, set amid spectacular scenery and tropical vegetation. From Coroico, the road continues north towards Rurrenabaque and the Bolivian Amazon (see page 218).

COROICO

Rightly considered one of the most beautiful spots in the Yungas, the peaceful little town of **COROICO** is perched on a steep mountain slope with panoramic views across the forest-covered Andean foothills to the icy peaks of the Cordillera Real beyond. It enjoys a warm and pleasantly humid climate, and this, combined with the dramatic scenery and good facilities, makes it an excellent place to relax and recuperate – especially if you've spent the day cycling the "Death Road" (see page 171). Many cafés and restaurants are closed on Monday mornings and Tuesdays.

WHAT TO SEE AND DO

Most visitors to Coroico spend much of their time relaxing on the peaceful **Plaza Principal**, lounging by a swimming pool and enjoying the fantastic views. However, there are some pleasant walks through the surrounding countryside, with forested mountain slopes covered in a lush patchwork of coffee and coca plantations, and banana and orange groves. If you're feeling adventurous, consider a canyoning trip with community ecotourism agency, El Vagante, based 9km out of town in Santa Rosa de Vagante (☎76018235, ⌨elvagante.com).

ARRIVAL AND DEPARTURE

By bus Minibuses (2hr 40min; B$20) and smaller but faster minivans (2hr; B$30) leave when full from Terminal Puente Minasa in La Paz's Villa Fatima district. They may drop you in Coroico's Plaza Municipal, but to go back to La Paz, you'll need to go to the bus station on the south side of Coroico (Av Manning; last departure around 6pm). Buses for most other destinations stop at Yolosita, connected with Coroico by regular minibuses (B$5, or B$7 if you've got heavy baggage; 15min), which stop in Coroico just above the Mercado Municipal on C Sagárnaga.

INFORMATION

Banks and exchange Banco Fie has an ATM on the main square, Banco Unión just off it. The Prodem ATM doesn't take foreign cards, but you can get cash with your card over the counter inside. Crecer IFD on the main square will change dollars; QA abogados on Zuazo Cuenca will change dollars and euros.

★ TREAT YOURSELF

La Senda Verde Animal Refuge & Eco Lodge ☎7472 2825, ⌨sendaverde.com. Situated 7km out of Coroico (Coroico–Yolosa minibuses will drop you off on the way; a taxi from Coroico will charge about B$40) and set in a beautiful valley next to a river that you can swim in, this animal sanctuary is the kind of gorgeous hideaway you won't ever want to leave – it's a home for animals rescued by illegal traffickers, including monkeys, toucans and parrots, ocelots and even spectacled bears (tours daily at 10am, 11am, noon & 3pm; 45min tours B$100, or B$130 including bears; no shorts, short skirts or children under 10). There are sprawling, lush grounds to wander around, pretty views and a restaurant that serves home-made pasta and salads. Accommodation is in two- to five-person cabins, which are dotted around the grounds. Prices include breakfast and monkey encounter. Basic huts B$320, treehouse B$380, doubles B$440

Tourist information There is a tourist office staffed by local guides on central Plaza García Lanza (daily 9am–1pm & 4–8pm; ☎7306 3696). The bus station also has a tourist office (daily 8am–noon & 2–6pm, but sometimes closed even within those hours).

ACCOMMODATION

For a small town Coroico has a good range of places to stay. At weekends and on public holidays everywhere gets very full and prices go up, so it's worth booking in advance.

Hostal Chawi In front of the petrol station, just off the road to La Paz ☎7355 5644, ⌨hostalchawi.com. The friendliest and cosiest budget option in town. Rooms are basic yet comfy, with dorms or private doubles with hot showers. Dizzying views, lush gardens, wonderful Bolivian hospitality and amazing home-cooked food and home-grown coffee add to the experience, but it sometimes closes up during the week if there are no customers. Dorms B$70, doubles B$180

Hotel Esmeralda Julio Zuazo Cuenca 725, 400m above the plaza ☎02 2136017, ⌨hotelesmeraldacoroico.com. This large hotel has great views, an attractive garden and pool, and a reasonable restaurant. There's a wide range of rooms, the best of which have private bathrooms and balconies with stunning vistas. There's also table football, wi-fi in the reception area, and a book exchange. Dorms B$120, doubles B$240

Hostal Kory Linares 3501 ☎7156 4050, ⌨hostalkory.com. The genuinely spectacular views of the valley are the real draw here – you can see Death Road winding its hair-raising way. A good-value choice with a huge pool (open to non-guests for B$10) and clean, parquet-floored en-suite rooms. There are also some cheaper options with shared bathrooms, plus a restaurant, communal kitchen and laundry service. B$160

★ Hostal Sol y Luna Just under 1.5km outside town, uphill on Julio Zuazo Cuenca, beyond the Hotel Esmeralda ☎7156 1626, ⌨solyluna-bolivia.com. Tranquil hideaway in beautiful hillside grounds that overlook the valley, with hammocks, fire pits, a yoga room and plunge pools. The restaurant does excellent, simple dishes too (daily 8am–10pm). Breakfast costs B$35–40 extra, and a taxi from town is around B$20–25. Wi-fi in the main building. Camping/person B$50, doubles B$160, cabins B$360

Villa Bonita C Héroes del Chaco, 100m past Hotel Bella Vista on the road to Caranavi ☎7191 8298, ✉Villa_Bonita05@yahoo.com. Amid the laidback, familial environs of their raspberry-coloured home and leafy garden – site, too, of a great café (see page 187) – friendly Bolivian-Swiss couple Ninfa and Gianni Pedetti have three lovely, wooden-shuttered rooms and a four-berth cabin. Cash only. Breakfast at the café included. Dorms B$80, doubles B$120

EATING AND DRINKING

El Cafetal C Miranda (near the hospital, 15min walk up from the plaza) ☎7193 3979. Great-value French-run hotel restaurant with panoramic views and delicious food (B$50–70), including trout lasagne, steak in Roquefort sauce, crêpes, soufflés and curries. All that's missing is the French wine, although Tarija supplies a fine substitute. 8am–8pm; closed Tues.

Carla's Garden Pub Pasaje Adalid Linares, 50m down the steps beyond Hostal Kory. Down a flight of steps that you won't relish climbing back up, *Carla's Garden Pub* is a cute, tucked-away little bar that does good simple food and a fine range of beers. It's also home to the Back-Stube Pasteleria Alemana, a German-style bakery offering excellent home-made cakes and pastries. Wed–Fri 4–10pm or later, Sat & Sun noon–10pm or later (a light at the top of the stairs tells you if it's still open).

La Casa Plaza Municipal (north side) ☎7328 1035. German/Bolivian-run restaurant where walls are adorned with an eclectic range of trinkets. Specializes in fondues (from B$50 per person, minimum two). The opening hours are one benefit in a town that shuts up shop once the weekending *paceños* have fled. Daily 6.30–10.30pm.

Pizza Italia Plaza Municipal (south side). A decent tourist restaurant on the main square, where you can get a variety of pizzas (B$38–86, depending on size and toppings), and veggie (but not vegan) dishes such as gnocchi in blue cheese sauce (B$40). Daily 8am–11pm.

Villa Bonita C Héroes del Chaco ☎7191 8298. It's a 10min walk from the plaza, but come for the friendly, boho atmosphere, shady garden, and delicious home-made ice cream (B$6/scoop) and vegetarian dishes. Wed–Sun 9am–5pm.

The Southern Altiplano

South of La Paz, the **Southern Altiplano** stretches 800km to the Chilean and Argentine borders. Set at an average altitude of around 3700m, this starkly beautiful landscape is the image most frequently associated with Bolivia: a barren and treeless expanse whose arid steppes stretch to the horizon, where snowcapped mountains shimmer under deep-blue skies.

The unavoidable transport nexus of the Altiplano is the tin-mining city of **Oruro**, 230km south of La Paz, a grim monument to industrial decline that nevertheless comes alive once a year during the **Carnaval**. Some 310km further southeast of Oruro is the legendary silver-mining city of **Potosí**, a city of sublime colonial architecture, marooned at 4100m above sea level and filled with monuments to a glorious but tragic past.

The Altiplano grows more desolate still as it stretches south towards the Argentine border. From the forlorn railway town of **Uyuni**, 323km due south of Oruro, you can venture into the dazzling white **Salar de Uyuni**, the world's largest salt lake. Beyond the Salar in the far southwestern corner of the country is the **Reserva de Fauna Andina Eduardo Avaroa**, a nature reserve of lunar landscapes, brightly coloured lakes and a surprising array of wildlife.

Southeast of Uyuni, the Altiplano changes character. The pleasant little mining town of **Tupiza** is surrounded by arid red mountains and cactus-strewn badlands eroded into deep gullies and rock pinnacles. In the far south of the country lies the provincial capital of **Tarija**, a remote yet welcoming city set in a fertile grape-growing valley that enjoys a much warmer climate than the Altiplano.

PARQUE NACIONAL SAJAMA

Southwest of La Paz, the road to Chile passes through a desert plain from the middle of which rises the perfect snowcapped cone of Volcán Sajama. At 6542m, Sajama is the tallest mountain in Bolivia and the centre of the country's oldest national park, **Parque Nacional Sajama**.

The mountain's slopes support the highest forest in the world while the surrounding desert is home to pumas, rare Andean deer and the rarely seen, flightless, ostrich-like rheas.

Mountain climbers are drawn by the peak's relative ease of ascent – only permitted between April and October, when the ice is sufficiently frozen. The lower slopes contain bubbling geysers and hot springs which make for excellent hiking.

2

THE SOUTHERN ALTIPLANO

The administrative centre, where you can register to climb the mountain and arrange guides, mules and porters, is **SAJAMA** village.

There is simple accommodation in the village (around B$100/person) and various places serving simple, inexpensive food. Bring warm clothing – it can get chilly.

ARRIVAL AND INFORMATION

Organized trips By far the easiest way to visit the park is on a tour from La Paz with firms such as America Tours, Kanoo or Topas (see page 1). Most of the hotels and lodgings in Sajama can arrange transport and trekking guides (around B$550/day) to places within the park.

By bus From the town of Patacamaya, a few kilometres off the La Paz–Oruro highway (reached by "*surubi*" minibus from Ceja terminal in El Alto or by *micro* from Oruro or Cochabamba) there's a single daily *micro* to Sajama village, operated by Sindicato Trans Sajama, leaving at 1pm Mon–Sat from Capitol Restaurant in the middle of town, or 1.30pm Sun from the marketplace six blocks west. Buses from La Paz to Arica (which also stop in Patacamaya) will leave you at the Sajama turn-off, 12km from the village. You can call ahead to the *Hostal Sajama* or to ☎ 7408 3873 or ☎ 7372 2394 to arrange for a vehicle to pick you up and bring you to the village (B$80), but a lot of people just walk (2hr 30min–3hr). **Park entrance fee** Buy your park entry ticket (B$100) at the office on the way into Sajama (1km from the turn-off; daily 9.30am–6pm). Keep your ticket with you in the park as you may need to show it.

ORURO

Huddled on the bleak Altiplano some 230km south of La Paz, the grim mining city of **ORURO** was the economic powerhouse of Bolivia for much of the twentieth century, thanks to the enormous mineral wealth in the surrounding mountains and tin mines established here in the late nineteenth century. Since the fall of world tin prices in 1985, Oruro's fortunes have plummeted and more than two decades of economic decline have made it a shadow of its former self – apart from during the epic Carnaval (see page 190).

2

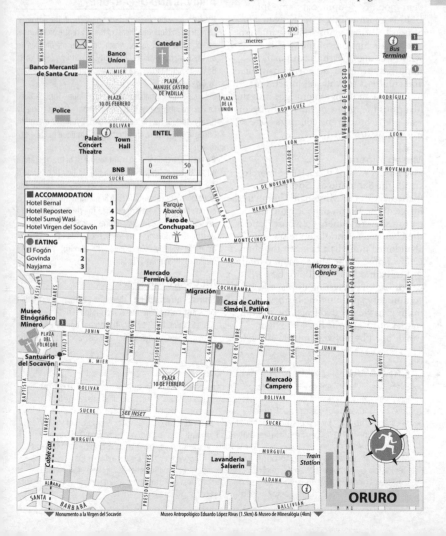

2

Oruro is a cold and rather sombre place, with the melancholic air of a city forever looking back on a golden age, and there's not much reason to stop here outside of Carnaval time.

Plaza 10 de Febrero and the Casa de Cultura

The town's main plaza, **Plaza 10 de Febrero**, is a pleasant square shaded by cypress trees. Two blocks east of the plaza, at Avenida Galvarro, the fascinating **Casa de Cultura** (guided tours Mon–Fri hourly 9am–noon & 3–6pm, Sat 9am–3pm; B$8) is a former home of "King of Tin" Simón I. Patiño, whose mining interests once made him one of the world's wealthiest men. With the original imported furniture, decadent chandeliers and children's toys all still intact, the museum is an intriguing insight into the luxurious life of one of the few Bolivians who got rich from the country's huge mineral wealth.

Museo Minero

Five blocks west of Plaza 10 de Febrero stands the **Santuario del Socavón** (Sanctuary of the Mineshaft), home to the image of the Virgin del Socavón, the patron saint of miners, in whose honour the Carnaval celebrations are staged. The abandoned mineshaft beneath the church is now home to the **Museo Minero** (daily 9–11.30am & 3.15–5.30pm; B$10), which has an interesting display of equipment explaining the history of mining, as well as two fearsome-looking statues of El Tío, the devil-like figure worshipped by Bolivian miners as the king of the underworld and owner of all minerals.

Museo Antropológico

In the south of the city, at the corner of Avenida España and Calle Urquidi, the **Museo Antropológico Eduardo López Rivas** (Mon–Fri 10am–6pm; B$5) has an extensive archeological and ethnographic collection from the region, with displays featuring arrowheads, stone tools, jewellery and a wonderful collection of traditional masks.

ARRIVAL AND DEPARTURE

By bus All long-distance buses pull in at the Terminal Terrestre, ten blocks northeast of the city centre on Villarroel except those from Tarija, which drop you off on Ejército on the eastern outskirts of the city. A taxi into town costs B$10–15; alternatively, take any *micro* heading south along Av 6 de Agosto.

Destinations Cochabamba (every 30min–1hr; 5–8hr); La Paz (roughly every 30min; 3hr 30min); Potosí (roughly hourly; 4hr); Sucre (17 daily; 8–10hr); Uyuni (12 overnight buses; 7–9hr). There are also buses to Iquique in Chile (17 daily; 8hr).

By train The train station is just southeast of the city centre on Av Galvarro (ⓦwww.fca.com.bo). To buy tickets you'll need to show your passport. Two services run south: the *Expreso del Sur* (departs Tues & Fri, returns Thurs & Sun) is quicker and more comfortable than the cheaper *Wara Wara del Sur* (departs Wed & Sun, returns Tues & Fri).

Destinations Tupiza (4 weekly; 12hr 30min–13hr 35min); Uyuni (4 weekly; 6hr 50min–7hr 20min); Villazón (4 weekly; 15hr 35min–17hr 5min).

INFORMATION

Tourist information There's a tourist information kiosk just outside the bus station (Mon–Fri 9am–noon & 2.30–6.30pm; ☏02 5287774), another opposite the train station (opens to meet train arrivals) and a third in the

---

CARNAVAL

Every year in late February or early March, Oruro explodes into life, celebrating its **Carnaval** in what is without doubt one of the most spectacular cultural events in all South America. Tens of thousands of visitors flock here to watch a sensational array of costumed dancers parading through the streets, and there's always a good deal of heavy drinking and chaotic water-fighting. At the centre of the festivities is the parade, starting with the **Entrada** on the Saturday before Ash Wednesday, with a massive procession of more than fifty different troupes of costumed dancers passing through the streets, followed by the **Diablada**, or Dance of the Devils, led by two lavishly costumed dancers representing Lucifer and St Michael, followed by hundreds of devil dancers who leap and prance through the streets. If you're coming to Oruro at this time of year, be sure to book accommodation in advance.

★ TREAT YOURSELF

Hotel Virgen del Socavón Junín 1179 ☏02 5282184; map p.189. Excellent hotel located across the street from the Plaza del Folklore, making it a perfect base for Carnaval. Although modern, there is a strong Christian theme to the decor, including crucifixes above the beds, which may surprise some guests. There's a sauna, and breakfast is included. B$420

Palais Concert Theatre on Plaza 10 de Febrero (Mon–Fri 9am–noon & 2.30–6.30pm; ☏02 5250144), but the official opening hours should be taken with a pinch of salt.

ACCOMMODATION

There are some reasonable places to stay in Oruro – though a lack of good budget choices. During Carnaval prices go up by as much as five times and most places will only rent rooms for the entire weekend.

Hotel Bernal Av Brasil 701 ☏02 5279468; map p.189. Near the bus station, this place has seen far better days, but is overall good value. Rooms (with shared or private bathrooms) at the front are noisy. B$120

Hotel Repostero Sucre 370 ☏02 5258001; map p.189. This once elegant nineteenth-century building has settled into being a decent mid-range hotel. The classier upstairs rooms (B$250) overlook a sunny courtyard, and have comfortable beds, private bathrooms and TVs; there are also some less comfortable economy rooms on the ground floor. B$200

Hotel Sumaj Wasi Av Brasil 232 ☏02 5276737, ⊕hotelessamaywasi.com; map p.189. Handily located just opposite the bus terminal, this good-value, mid-range option has clean and comfortable en-suite rooms with TVs. Road noise can be an issue, however. B$270

EATING

There are plenty of cheap roast-chicken restaurants and snack bars on Avenida 6 de Octubre between calles Montecinos and Junín, where late on Friday and Saturday night stalls serve the local speciality *rostro asado*, or roasted sheep's head.

El Fogón Av Brasil ☏02 5279456; map p.189. A convenient restaurant near the bus terminal, specializing in pork dishes (mains B$60–90) like *lechón* (roast pork) and *chicharrón* (deep-fried pork) and *charque* (dried llama meat, similar to jerky). Daily 7am–10pm.

Govinda Junín 533 ☏02 5255205; map p.189. This Hare Krishna-run vegetarian restaurant has a short menu featuring a few Indian dishes like samosas (B$5), plus pastas, pizzas, soya burgers and fresh juices. Set lunches B$13. Mon–Sat noon–2pm & 4–10pm.

Nayjama Pagador 1880, at Aldana ☏02 5277699; map p.189. One of Oruro's best restaurants, serving huge portions of delicious local food (mains from B$50), with specialities including sublime roast lamb and *criadillas* (bull testicles). Mon–Sat 11.30am–9pm, Sun 11.30am–3pm.

POTOSÍ

Set on a desolate, windswept plain amid barren mountains at almost 4100m above sea level, **POTOSÍ** is the highest city in the world, and at once the most fascinating and tragic place in Bolivia. Given its remote and inhospitable location, it's difficult to see at first glance why it was ever built here at all. The answer lies in **Cerro Rico** ("Rich Mountain"), the conical peak that rises imperiously above the city to the south and that was, quite simply, the richest source of silver the world had ever seen (see page 193).

The **silver rush** of Cerro Rico was triggered in 1545 by a llama herder who was caught out after dark on the mountain's slopes. He started a fire to keep warm, and was amazed to see a trickle of molten silver run out from the blaze. News of this discovery soon reached the Spaniards, the rush was soon under way, and the town's population mushroomed to more than 100,000 over the next twenty years, making it easily the largest metropolis in the Americas.

By the beginning of the seventeenth century, Potosí was home to more than 160,000 people and boasted dozens of magnificent churches, as well as theatres, gambling houses, brothels and dance halls. For the **indigenous workers and African slaves** who produced this wealth, however, the working conditions were appalling. Estimates of the total number who died over three centuries of colonial mining in Potosí run as high as nine million, making the mines of Potosí a central factor in the demographic collapse that swept the Andes under Spanish rule.

WHAT TO SEE AND DO

Potosí is a treasure-trove of colonial art and architecture, with hundreds of well-preserved buildings, including some of the finest churches in Bolivia.

2

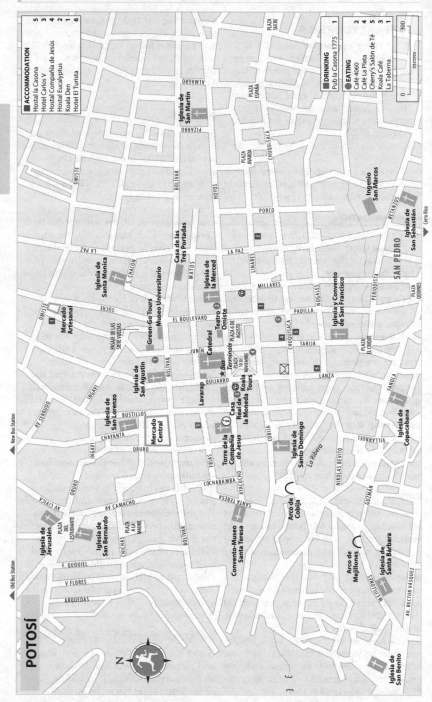

POTOSÍ

CERRO RICO

Immediately south of Potosí the near-perfect cone of **Cerro Rico** rises above the city, pockmarked with the entrances to the thousands of mines that lead deep into its entrails. Operators in town run regular tours of the **mines**, but be warned that this is an unpleasant and dangerous environment, where safety precautions are largely left to fate; anyone suffering from claustrophobia, heart or breathing problems is advised against entering. Some also question the ethics of making a tourist attraction of a workplace where conditions are so appalling. It is, however, also an extreme and unforgettable experience.

Tours of the mines begin with a visit to the **miners' market** on and around Plaza El Calvario. Here you can buy coca leaves, dynamite, black-tobacco cigarettes, pure cane alcohol and fizzy drinks as gifts for the miners you'll be visiting. Half-day tours cost around B$130 per person. Recommended operators include **Koala Tours** (Ayacucho 5, ☎02 6222092, ⍟koalabolivia. com.bo), with trips run by experienced multilingual guides, and **Green-Go Tours** (Junín 15–17; ☎02 6231362, ✉greengotours@hotmail.com).

Plaza 10 de Noviembre

The centre of the city is the **Plaza 10 de Noviembre**, a pleasant tree-shaded square with a small version of the Statue of Liberty, erected in 1926 to commemorate Bolivian independence. On the north side of the square, the site of the original church (which collapsed in 1807) is now occupied by the twin-towered **Catedral**, completed in Neoclassical style in 1836 (entrance at Matos 26; Mon–Sat 9am–noon & 2.30–6pm; B$20). To the east of the square lies the **Plaza 6 de Agosto**, at the centre of which is a column commemorating the Battle of Ayacucho in 1824, which secured Bolivian independence early the following year.

Casa Real de la Moneda

West of the Plaza 10 de Noviembre on Calle Ayacucho stands the unmissable **Casa Real de la Moneda**, or Royal Mint (by guided tour only, 1hr 30min–2hr; Mon–Sat 9am–noon, last tour 10.30am, & 2.30–6.30pm, last tour 4.30pm, Sun 9am–noon, last tour 10.30am; B$40, camera B$20, video B$40). One of the most outstanding examples of colonial civil architecture in all South America, it is now home to one of Bolivia's best museums. The collection includes the original minting machinery, some of the country's finest colonial religious art, militaria, archeological artefacts and a display of coins and banknotes.

Built between 1759 and 1773, La Moneda is a formidable construction, built as part of a concerted effort by the Spanish Crown to reform the economic and financial machinery of the empire to increase revenues. The rambling two-storey complex of about **two hundred rooms** is set around five internal courtyards, and housed troops, workers, African slaves and the senior royal officials responsible for overseeing operations. A vital nerve centre of Spanish imperial power in the Andes, it also served as a prison, treasury and near-impregnable stronghold in times of disorder.

La Torre de la Compañía de Jesus

On Calle Ayacucho, west of the Casa Real de la Moneda, stands **La Torre de la Compañía de Jesus** (Mon–Fri 9am–noon & 2–6pm, sometimes closes earlier; B$10), a bell tower which is all that now remains of a Jesuit church founded in 1581. Completed in 1707 and recently restored, the grandiose tower is one of the finest eighteenth-century religious monuments in Bolivia and a sublime example of the Mestizo-Baroque style. You can climb to the top, from where there are excellent views of the city and Cerro Rico.

Convento and Museo Santa Teresa

The **Convento-Museo Santa Teresa** (C Ayacucho; Mon–Sat 9am–12.30pm, last entry 11am & 2.30–6pm, last entry 4.30pm, Sun 3–6pm, last entry 4.30pm; B$30) is a beautiful colonial church and convent worth visiting both for its fine collection of colonial religious painting and sculpture, and for a somewhat disturbing insight into the bizarre lifestyle of nuns in the colonial era. Visits are by guided tour only, so you need to get here at least an hour before closing.

ARRIVAL AND DEPARTURE

By bus The new bus station is on Av Banderas, near the Centro Recreacional Los Pinos. All services depart from here apart from the Uyuni ones, which still use the old terminal on Av Universitario, on the way out of town towards Oruro. A taxi into the centre from either costs around B$10–15.

Destinations La Paz (roughly hourly; 9–11hr); Oruro (roughly hourly; 5hr); Sucre (roughly every 30min; 3hr); Tarija (9 daily, mostly at night); Uyuni (6–7 daily; 5hr).

By taxi A quicker and more comfortable way to get to Sucre is to take a collective taxi from the old bus terminal (leaving when full; 2hr 30min).

INFORMATION

Tourist information Infotur (Mon–Fri 8am–noon & 2.30–6.30pm, Sat 8am–noon; ☎02 6231021), in the modern mirrored building through the arch of Torre de la Compañía on C Ayacucho.

ACCOMMODATION

A primary consideration when choosing where to stay in Potosí is warmth – some places have central heating, but otherwise make sure there's adequate bedding.

Hotel Carlos V C Linares 42 ☎02 6231010; map p.192. This place feels clean and fresh and offers kitchen facilities to guests (breakfast is included in the price), plus there's a TV lounge, but wi-fi in public areas only. B$160

Hostal la Casona Chuquisaca 460 ☎02 6230523, ⓦ hotelpotosi.com; map p.192. They're not the friendliest bunch here, but there's an atmospheric feel to the place with its cloisters and dimly lit passageways. You can take your free breakfast in the pleasant courtyard. Dorms B$40, doubles B$100

Hostal Compañía de Jesús Chuquisaca 445 ☎02 6223173, ⓦ hostalcompania.galeon.com; map p.192. This economical hotel has a range of clean rooms (shared or private bathrooms) and a welcoming atmosphere. The wi-fi is rather iffy, and the rooms can get a bit chilly, but the beds are warm and the showers hot. B$90

Hostal Eucalyptus Linares 88A ☎7240 1884, ⓔ koalabolivia@hotmail.com; map p.192. Run by the Koala Tours agency (see page 193), this popular hostel has spick-and-span en-suite rooms, as well as a roof terrace with great views, and rates include a simple breakfast. B$230

Koala Den Junín 56 ☎02 6226467, ⓔ papaimilla@ hotmail.com; map p.192. A travellers' favourite, this charming, amicable hostelby Koala Tours, features decent dorms and inviting private rooms. Heating throughout means you won't feel the chill, and there are great showers,

a comfortable communal area, kitchen and large DVD collection. Breakfast is included. Dorms B$50, doubles B$150

Hotel El Turista C Lanza 19 ☎02 6222492, ⓔ hotelturista10nov@hotmail.com; map p.192. The rooms at this friendly old hotel are slightly musty but comfortable and come with private bath, heaters and TVs. For excellent views of Cerro Rico, ask for room 33 or 34 at the top of the building. B$240

EATING

Potosí's popularity with travellers is reflected in the city's growing variety of places to eat. The Mercado Central – on Bolívar, between Bustillos and Oruro – is your best bet for cheap local food.

Café 4060 C Hoyos 1 ☎02 6222623; map p.192. Named after Potosí's altitude, this popular café/pub has a pretty, stylish interior. Offers the dreaded "international" menu (a bit of everything from steaks to burgers to pizza; B$17–18), beer and good coffee. Mon–Sat 4–11.30pm.

Café La Plata Plaza 10 de Noviembre ☎02 6226085, ⓦ cafelaplata.com; map p.192. With its earthy tones, warm lighting and creaky floorboards, this elegant place screams hot chocolate and its spiced version is up to the task; fine coffee (B$10–24) and light meals are available too. Snooty service, however, lets the side down. Mon–Sat 9am–10pm.

Cherry's Salón de Té C Padilla 8 ☎02 6226753; map p.192. Appealing tearoom with orange walls, faux wrought-iron furnishings and plastic flowers. The economical menu features breakfasts (B$18–25), coffee, cakes, sandwiches and ice-cream sundaes, as well as a few more substantial meals. Daily 8am–10pm.

Koala Café C Ayacucho 5; map p.192. Those who appreciate shabby, higgledy-piggledy places will warm to *Koala Café*, spread across two creaky upper floors. At B$45 their *almuerzo* is not the cheapest, but it's generous, offering three courses (there's also a veggie alternative). Daily 8am–9pm.

La Taberna Junín 12 ☎02 6230123; map p.192. Smart, downstairs restaurant decked out with French posters, wine racks and antique typewriters. The excellent-value four-course lunch (B$20) is one of the best deals in town. Daily 8am–10pm.

DRINKING

★ **Pub la Casona 1775** C Frías 41 ☎02 6222954; map p.192. This is the liveliest bar in town (beer from B$22), housed in an eighteenth-century mansion with graffiti-covered walls, plus good food (mains B$30–50) and occasional live music. Mon–Sat 6pm–12.30am.

DIRECTORY

Banks and exchange Banks with ATMs include Banco Mercantil de Santa Cruz on C Padilla, at Matos, and BNB on

Junín at Bolívar (Casa de los Marqueses de Otavi). There are a couple of money changers at the rear of the central market, on Heroes del Chaco.

Internet There are plenty of cybercafés, including Pueblitos Net, 18-B Millares (daily 8am–10pm; B$2/hr).

Laundry Lavarap, Quijjaro at Matos (B$10/kg).

Post office Correo Central, a block south of Plaza 10 de Noviembre on Lanza, at Chuquisaca. Mon–Fri 8am–8pm, Sat 8am–6pm, Sun 9am–noon.

UYUNI

Set on the bleak southern Altiplano 212km southwest of Potosí, the chilly railway town of **UYUNI** is useful as a jumping-off point for expeditions into the beautiful and remote landscapes of the far southwest. In its heyday, the city was Bolivia's main gateway to the outside world and a symbol of modernity and industrial progress. Today, its railway heritage has left a rail museum (behind the station), a train graveyard (3km southwest of town), and a few old loco parts displayed on the central reservation of Avenida Ferroviaria. A small town, it holds everything you might need within a few blocks; the effective centre is the nineteenth-century clocktower at the intersection of avenidas Arce and Potosí. That Uyuni hasn't become a ghost town is thanks to the ever-growing number of travellers who come here to visit the spectacular scenery of the **Salar de Uyuni** and the **Reserva de Fauna Andina Eduardo Avaroa**, which are usually visited together on a three-day tour.

ARRIVAL AND DEPARTURE

By plane There's a small airport 1km north of Uyuni; a taxi to/from town costs around B$10. Amazonas and BoA fly to/from La Paz (5–7 daily; 50min).

By bus Buses from Potosí, Oruro and Tupiza pull up in front of the various bus company offices (an area optimistically described as "the terminal"), three blocks north of the train station along Av Arce. Todo Turismo (☎02 6933337, ⓦtodoturismosrl.com), at C Cabrera 208, has easily the most comfortable services to La Paz (around 10hr) via Oruro; its buses have heaters and a meal service, but cost significantly more than the competition. The journey to Tupiza is scenic but rough and you may have to changes buses midway at the town of Atocha; quicker and more comfortable jeeps sometimes run for part of the journey.

Destinations Calama, Chile (1–2 daily; 10hr including border formalities); La Paz (5 daily, usually departing

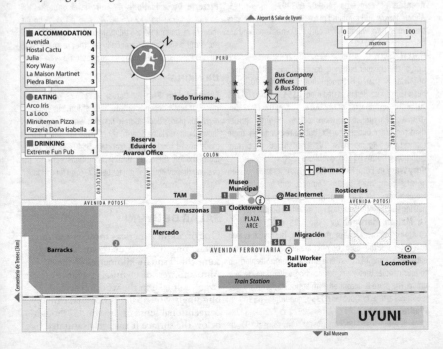

around 8pm; 10–12hr); Oruro (6–7 daily; 5hr); Potosí (hourly; 4hr); Tupiza (3 daily; 7hr).

By train Trains (ⓦ www.fca.com.bo) south to Villazón via Tupiza and north to Oruro depart from the train station on Av Ferroviaria, in the town centre. The *Expreso del Sur* is quicker and more comfortable than the cheaper *Wara Wara del Sur*. Note that the passenger service to Avaroa on the Chilean border no longer runs (but there are buses).

Destinations Oruro (4 weekly; 7hr 5min–7hr 25min); Tupiza (4 weekly; 5hr 20min–5hr 45min); Villazón (4 weekly; 8hr 25min–9hr 15min).

INFORMATION

Tourist information There is a small tourist office (officially Mon–Fri 8am–noon & 2.30–6pm, though it's often empty) in the clocktower on Av Potosí, though it's only really worth coming here if you want to complain about a tour agency – tourist police officers share the office. The numerous travel agencies are generally more helpful, though their main aim is to sell you a trip.

Internet Mac Internet on Av Potosí (B$5/hr).

Banks and exchange There are numerous ATMs, and a handful of money changers on Av Potosí around the junction with Av Arce.

ACCOMMODATION

There's a limited range of accommodation and most of it is fairly basic.

Avenida Av Ferroviaria 11 ☎02 6932078; map p.195. A vast, narrow and rambling place. Though rooms are very basic, most have windows out onto the central area and are bright enough. B$90

Hostal Cactu Av Arce 46 ☎02 6932043; map p.195. One of the cheaper but more basic options, with a choice of private or shared bathroom, hot water 7am–10.30pm, but no breakfast. Bed in shared room B$55, doubles B$110

Julia Av Ferroviaria, at Av Arce 314 ☎02 6932134, ⓦ juliahoteluyuni.com; map p.195. Slightly pricier than the other budget hotels, but correspondingly more comfortable. Rooms have TVs and shared or private bathrooms. Dorms B$100, doubles B$220

Kory Wasy Av Potosí 350 ☎02 6932670, ✉ kory_wasi@ hotmail.com; map p.195. Compact but bare en-suite rooms – some are a bit gloomy, so ask to see a few before making your choice. Breakfast not included. Doubles B$150

La Maison Martinet Av Potosí 16 ☎02 6932040, ⓦ lamaisonmartinet.com; map p.195. The layout is akin to a hotel, but the rooms on offer are actually apartments, each with a mini-kitchen and sitting room. Sleeping up to four people, they work out as good value if you're in a group. The place is decorated with antique apothecary and medicinal artefacts. Doubles B$350, quadruples B$500

Piedra Blanca Av Arce 27 ☎7222 3274, ⓦ piedrablancabackpackers.hostel.com; map p.195. In

a courtyard set back from the street, in a U-shaped building with stained-glass windows down one side. Guests get breakfast and can use the kitchen, and the showers are nice and hot. Wi-fi in public areas only and a bit iffy even then. Dorms B$75, doubles B$210

EATING

Tourist restaurants are centred on Plaza Arce. The mercado central on Av Potosí has cheap and decent local dishes. In the evenings, *rosticerías* on Av Potosí between Sucre and Camacho serve roasted meats for around B$20.

Arco Iris Arce 53 ☎02 6933177; map p.195. This central restaurant has decent pizza (portion B$23–30, individual B$38–45) and pasta (B$35–50), a cosy ambience and good background music. Mon–Sat 3–10pm.

La Loco Av Ferroviaria 13 ☎02 6933105; map p.195. This rustic, French-run restaurant-bar by the station has a railway theme and a French touch. Dishes include llama in blue cheese sauce (B$45) and chocolate crêpes (B$18), with drinks and a happy hour (7–8pm), and it does breakfast too. Mon–Sat 7am–1am.

Minuteman Pizza In the Toñito Hotel, Av Ferroviaria 60 ☎02 6933186, ⓦ bolivianexpeditions.com; map p.195. Oddly located directly outside the army barracks, this place is renowned for its buffet breakfast, which is expensive but bountiful (B$50), from porridge to pancakes with maple syrup. Their pizzas (from B$55) are equally good. Daily 8–10am & 5–9pm.

Pizzeria Doña Isabella Av Ferroviaria opposite the end of C Camacho ☎7375 9824; map p.195. A bright, modern restaurant whose thinnish-crust pizzas (B$60–90) are surprisingly good, especially as they're made with quinoa flour; each is enough for two people. Daily 6–10pm.

DRINKING

Extreme Fun Pub Av Potosí 9 ☎7573 4008; map p.195. It really depends on your idea of fun, but you can't deny this place's dedication to boozing with a wacky twist (how about a "Llama Sperm" shot?). One room has a floor made of salt blocks. Prices (cocktails B$40–80) are pretty high, though there are drinks promotions early in the evening (happy hour 2–7pm for beer, 7–9pm for cocktails). Daily 2pm–1am.

SALAR DE UYUNI

One of South America's most extraordinary attractions, the **Salar de Uyuni**, covering some 9000 square kilometres of the Altiplano west of Uyuni, is by far the largest salt lake in the world. The blindingly white Salar is not a lake in any conventional sense of the word – though below the surface it is largely saturated by

VISITING THE SALAR AND THE RESERVE

Pretty much the only way to visit the **Salar de Uyuni** and **Reserva de Fauna Andina Eduardo Avaroa** is on an organized tour, which can be easily arranged from Uyuni. The standard three-day tour price is usually B$800–1100 ($120–165) including food, accommodation, transport and a Spanish-speaking guide. You'll pay more if booking in La Paz, and often significantly more for an English-speaking guide. An additional B$30 is payable for the visit to Isla del Pescado and B$150 for entering the reserve. The tour is by 4WD around a circuit comprising the Salar de Uyuni and **lagunas Colorada** and **Verde** in the reserve; trips ending in San Pedro de Atacama in Chile (see page 409), starting or ending in Tupiza, and lasting four or more days, are also available. Note that wind-chill temperatures can drop to anything from -25°C to -40°C. You should bring high-factor sunblock and sunglasses to counter the possibility of snow blindness, as well as a good sleeping bag (available to buy or rent in Uyuni), a torch and plenty of warm clothing.

Late departures, inadequate accommodation and vehicle breakdowns are problems that may occur no matter which agency you choose, but it's definitely worth paying a little more to ensure good safety conditions. The cheaper agencies tend to have older cars, bad food and unfriendly, occasionally drunk drivers.

The best method of choosing an agency is to talk to travellers just returned from a tour. You should also visit several companies, ask for written itineraries, check the vehicles and confirm how many other people will be in the jeep with you: six or fewer is preferable; seven or eight can be very uncomfortable. Agencies regularly swap drivers, guides and vehicles, and many travellers find that they booked with one company only to be put on a tour run by another.

Despite all the hassles and potential pitfalls, however, these tours are well worth the trouble, and almost everyone who goes counts them among their best experiences in Bolivia.

water, its uppermost layer consists of a thick, hard crust of salt, easily capable of supporting the weight of a car. Tours will take you across the expanses, through the salt-processing village of **Colchani** and to the striking cactus-covered **Isla del Pescado** (also known as Inca Huasi), where a series of paths leads you on a short walk with breathtaking vistas of the vast Salar.

The surface is mostly covered by water between December and April, but even then it's rarely more than a metre deep, and usually much less. Driving across the perfectly flat white expanse of the Salar, with the unbroken chains of snowcapped mountains lining the far horizon, the terrain is so harsh and inhospitable it's like being on another planet.

RESERVA DE FAUNA ANDINA EDUARDO AVAROA

The southwesternmost corner of Bolivia is covered by the **Reserva de Fauna Andina Eduardo Avaroa**, a 7147-square-kilometre wildlife reserve, ranging between 4000m and 6000m in altitude and encompassing some of the most startling scenery in Bolivia. Like the Salar de Uyuni, the desolate landscapes possess an otherworldly beauty, with glacial salt lakes whose icy waters are stained bright red or emerald green, snowcapped volcanic peaks, high-altitude deserts and a wide range of rare **Andean wildlife** including the world's largest population of the James flamingo, the elusive **Andean fox** and herds of graceful **vicuñas**. There is an entrance fee (B$150), which is not usually included in the tour price and paid at a rangers' office at the point of entry. It is possible to cross into Chile at a **border crossing** near Laguna Verde in the far south of the reserve – inform your operator when booking if you wish to do this. Officials at the border post have been known to charge small unauthorized fees for letting you cross.

TUPIZA

Some 200km southeast of Uyuni, the isolated mining town of **Tupiza** nestles in a narrow, fertile valley that cuts through the harsh desert landscape with its cactus-strewn badlands, deep canyons and strangely shaped rock formations and pinnacles. In the late nineteenth and early twentieth centuries, Tupiza was the home of one of

2

ORGANIZED TOURS FROM TUPIZA

Tupiza's tour agencies all offer broadly similar guided excursions into the desert landscapes around the town. Often referred to as a "triathlon", they combine **4WD excursions**, **trekking**, **horseriding** and sometimes **mountain biking**. The full-day tours usually cost around B$400/person depending on numbers, and half-day tours are often offered for a little over half the price. You can also do longer but not terribly rewarding trips to **San Vicente**, where **Butch Cassidy and the Sundance Kid** are thought to have died. These same agencies organize trips to the Reserva de Fauna Andina Eduardo Avaroa and the Salar de Uyuni (see page 196), usually as a four-day circuit that should cost about B$1250–1600 (US$185–235), ending at Uyuni (though returning to Tupiza is usually possible). The advantage of doing the trip from Tupiza is that you hit the highlight of the salt flats on the last day.

TOUR OPERATORS

La Torre Tours Hotel La Torre ☎02 6942633, ⓦlatorretours-tupiza.com.

Tupiza Tours Hotel Mitru ☎02 6943003, ⓦtupizatours.com.

Valle Hermoso Tours Hostal Valle Hermoso ☎02 6942370, ⓦvallehermosotours.com.

Bolivia's biggest mining barons, Carlos Aramayo. His mines were rich enough to attract the attention of the infamous North American gunslingers **Butch Cassidy and the Sundance Kid**, who reputedly died in a shoot-out in the town of **San Vicente**, some 100km to the northwest. The town draws visitors largely because of the surrounding landscape, ideal for hiking, horseriding or just touring by jeep, activities that are easily arranged through local operators (see page 198), who also offer Butch-and-Sundance-related excursions.

ARRIVAL AND DEPARTURE

By bus The bus terminal is on Av Arraya, three blocks south and two east of the main square, Plaza Independencia. Several buses make the journey to and from Uyuni; you may have to change buses midway at Atocha; quicker and more comfortable jeeps sometimes run for the first part of the journey.
Destinations Tarija (5 daily; departing morning and evening; 6–7hr, sometimes longer in the rainy season); Uyuni (3 daily; 7hr); Villazón (12 daily; 2–3hr).
By train The train station is three blocks east of the main plaza on Av Serrudo. Trains (ⓦwww.fca.com.bo) head south to Villazón and north to Uyuni and Oruro. The *Expreso del Sur* is quicker and more comfortable than the cheaper *Wara Wara del Sur*. Buy tickets in advance.
Destinations Oruro (4 weekly; 12hr 45min–14hr 5min); Uyuni (4 weekly; 5hr 25min–6hr 10min); Villazón (4 weekly; 2hr 55min–3hr).

INFORMATION

Banks and exchange There are a couple of ATMs on the main plaza, and a couple of cambios on C Avaroa. Hotel *Mitru* and the *Hostal Valle Hermoso* will change dollars, and the latter will also change euros and Argentine pesos.
Tourist information There is no formal tourist office, but the tour operators (see page 198) can tell you what you need to know.

ACCOMMODATION

Mitru Av Chichas 187 ☎02 6943001, ⓦhotelmitru. com. A sunny central courtyard and swimming pool, clean, comfortable rooms and a buffet breakfast make this a popular choice, with prices depending on whether you're in the newer or older parts of the hotel (newer rooms, with attached bathrooms, cost B$280). Run by the same owners are *Anexo Mitru*, C Avaroa (☎02 6943002), and *Refugio del Turista*, Av Santa Cruz 244 (☎02 6943155), which has double rooms with use of a kitchen and *Mitru's* pool. *Mitru*: doubles B$160, *Anexo Mitru*: doubles B$165, *Refugio del Turista*: doubles B$100

La Torre Av Chichas 220 ☎02 6942633, ⓦlatorretours-tupiza.com. A friendly, family-run place with a handsome black-and-white tiled floor and a welcoming, family feel. There are potted plants galore, polished floors and a lovely roof terrace. Aside from a couple with shared facilities, all the rooms have private bathrooms and TVs. B$120

Hostal Valle Hermoso Av Pedro Arraya ☎02 694 2370, ⓦvallehermosotours.com. Split between two main buildings and a smaller "backpacker" annexe, the Hostelling International-affiliated *Valle Hermoso* has a range of clean and sunny dorms and private rooms, with shared or private bathrooms; most also have TVs. There's a book exchange, laundry service, common rooms with TVs, a DVD library and a roof terrace. Dorms B$40, doubles B$100

EATING AND DRINKING

There's a limited choice of places to eat and drink in Tupiza. As usual, the cheapest place is the market, on the first floor

2

INTO ARGENTINA

The main border crossing between **Bolivia** and **Argentina** is at the dusty ramshackle frontier town of **Villazón**, about 92km south of Tupiza by road or rail. Just walk south from the plaza down to the frontier along Avenida Internacional and get an exit stamp at the Bolivian *migración* office (open 6am–10pm Bolivian time), then walk across the bridge into Argentina, where immigration is open 7am–11pm Argentine time. From the Argentine border town of **La Quiaca** there are regular buses to the city of **Jujuy**, from where there are connections to the rest of the country.

of the corner of calles Chichas and Florida. Local specialities include *asado de cordero* (roast lamb), usually served at weekends, and *tamales* stuffed with dehydrated llama meat – the best are sold outside the Mercado Negro on Av Chichas.

Il Bambino C Florida, at Av Santa Cruz ☎7033 4542. Eating at this first-floor restaurant feels a little like dining in someone's house, and appropriately the food has a home-made touch. It's a good-value spot for a hearty lunch or supper, which is either way a set menu (B\$15). Mon–Sat noon–9pm.

El Buen Asador C Suipacha 14. The best food in town, popular with locals for its filling set *almuerzos* (B\$13–20), excellent meat dishes, including delicious Argentine-style steaks such as *bife chorizo* (B\$50), and special lamb roasts at the weekend. There's sometimes even live music. Mon–Sat 10am–9pm, Sun 10am–5pm.

La Torre de Italiana C Florida ☎7256 2488. As well as reasonable pizza and pasta (from B\$30), this touristy restaurant has decent Mexican food, Spanish omelettes and a good range of coffees, though service takes an age. Daily 8am–10pm.

TARIJA

In the far south of the country, the isolated city of **TARIJA** is a world apart from the rest of Bolivia. Set in a broad, fertile valley at an altitude of 1924m, Tarija is famous for its **wine** production, and the valley's rich soils and mild climate have historically attracted large numbers of Andalucian farmers. The surrounding countryside is beautiful, particularly in the spring (Jan–April), when the vineyards come to fruit and the whole valley blooms.

WHAT TO SEE AND DO

Tarija's tree-lined avenues and temperate climate give the city a laidback ambience. The two main squares, tranquil **Plaza Luis de Fuentes**, named after the city's founder, whose statue stands in the middle, and **Plaza Sucre**, two blocks southeast, are lined with excellent restaurants and cafés – perfect for a glass of the region's increasingly well-known wine. At nightfall, the streets around the Mercado Central, at the corner of Sucre and Bolívar, transform into a bustling street market, while Plaza Sucre is the centre for much of the town's nightlife.

Museo Paleontológico

A block south of the Plaza Sucre on the corner of calles Lema and Trigo, the **Museo Paleontológico** (Mon–Fri 8am–noon & 3–6pm, Sat 9am–noon & 3–6pm; free) offers a fantastic collection of fossils and skeletons from the Tarija Valley. Most of the specimens on display are of mammals from the Pleistocene era, between a million and 250,000 years ago, many of them from species similar to ones that still exist today, such as elephants, sloths and armadillos.

Casa Dorada

On the corner of Calle Ingavi and Calle Trigo is the **Casa Dorada** (visit by tour only, Mon–Fri 9am, 10am, 11am, 3pm, 4pm, 5pm; B\$5; ⓦcasadelaculturatarija. com), also known as Casa de la Cultura. Built in the nineteenth century in the Art Nouveau style by a wealthy merchant, the house has been restored and declared a national monument. You can wander through its rooms with photo displays depicting the history of Tarija, or check out one of the many cultural events hosted here, including concerts and dance performances.

ARRIVAL AND DEPARTURE

By plane The airport (☎04 6642399) is 3km southeast of the city centre along Av Jaime Paz Zamora. A taxi into the centre costs B\$20, or B\$8 if you walk out of the airport and catch one on the main road; there are also frequent *micros*.

2

To return to the airport catch a *micro* heading east along Av Domingo Paz. Airport tax is B$11.

Destinations Cochabamba (1–3 daily; 50min; BoA); La Paz (1 daily; 1hr 05min; BoA); Santa Cruz (1–2 daily; 55min; BoA, Ecojet); Sucre (4 weekly; 35min; BoA); Yacuiba (4 weekly; 20min; Amaszonas).

By bus The bus terminal is 7km southeast of the city centre, B$15 by taxi or B$1.50 by *micro* showing "Nueva Terminal" from Av Domingo Paz.

Destinations Bermejo (nearest Argentine border crossing; 20 daily; 4hr; plus minibuses from behind the terminal); La Paz (17 daily, generally departing in the late afternoon/ early evening; 16hr); Oruro (15 daily, mostly overnight; 12hr); Santa Cruz (6 daily; 13hr); Tupiza (5 daily, departing morning and evening; 6–7hr, sometimes longer in the rainy season); Villamontes (4 daily; 10–12hr; plus minibuses from behind the terminal); Villazón (5 daily; 8hr).

INFORMATION AND TOURS

Tourist information There's a tourist information office round the side (in C Sucre) of the municipal council building at the southeastern corner of Plaza Luis de Fuentes (Mon– Fri 8am–noon & 2.30–6.30pm, Sat & Sun 8am–noon; ☎04 6633581). There's also a tourist information desk at the bus station (Mon–Fri 7am–9pm, Sat & Sun 8am–2pm; ☎04 6636508). Both are helpful and give out a good town map, but don't speak much English. Viva Tours and VTB Tours (see below) are also good sources of information.

Tour operators VTB Tours (☎04 6643372, ⍟vtbtourtarija. com), inside *Hostal Carmen* at C Ingavi 784; and Viva Tours, C Bolívar 251 between calles Campos and Sucre (☎04 6638325, ✉vivatours.turismo@gmail.com), run half-day tours (around B$170) of the city and the vineyards and *bodegas* of the Tarija Valley.

ACCOMMODATION

★**Hostal Carmen** C Ingavi 784 ☎04 6643372, ⍟hostalcarmentarija.com. This rightly popular *hostal* has a range of well-decorated en-suite rooms; all have TVs and phones; there are also suites and semi-suites with a kitchenette (B$400–420). Perks include filtered water, tea and coffee. B$290

Grand Hotel Tarija C Sucre 762 ☎04 6642893, ⍟grandhoteltarija.com. Aimed predominantly at business travellers, the rooms here are very comfortable – each has a/c, TV, safe and minibar – though lacking in character. There's also a restaurant-bar and sauna. B$400

Hostal Miraflores C Sucre 920 ☎04 6643355, ✉leozurita@ yahoo.com. Converted colonial house with a sunny central courtyard, efficient staff and a choice between decent rooms with TVs and private bathrooms, as well as tiny, spartan rooms without. Wi-fi in lobby area only. No breakfast. B$100

Hostal Segovia C Angel Calabi ☎04 6675800, ⍟hotelsegoviatarija.com. Friendly hostel with clean

rooms, with or without bath and all with cable TV, conveniently located right by the bus terminal. B$190

Hostal Zeballos C Sucre 966 ☎04 6642068. Friendly budget *hostal* with a choice of plain, clean rooms with private bathrooms, or simple but still quite spacious ones with shared facilities, and a patio overflowing with grapevines and other plants. No breakfast however. B$120

EATING AND DRINKING

Nowhere is Tarija's strong Argentine influence more evident than in its restaurants. Good-quality grilled beef features strongly, ideally accompanied by a glass of local wine, while *Tarijeños* are also proud of their distinctive cuisine of meat dishes cooked in delicious spicy sauces – try *ranga-ranga*, *saice* or *chancho de pollo*.

Café Mokka Plaza Sucre ☎04 6650505. In a good people-watching spot, this busy café has a lengthy menu featuring over twenty types of coffee (from B$9), as well as Argentine-style *submarinos* (hot chocolate), cocktails and beer. Food-wise the breakfast and snacks are good, but the mains are a bit overpriced. Mon–Sat 8am–11pm, Sun 4–11pm.

Club Social Tarija Plaza Luis de Fuentes ☎04 6632473. Good-value traditional *almuerzos* (B$18–40) and more expensive à la carte options for dinner in a rather staid atmosphere. Daily 8.30am–11pm.

El Fogón del Gringo C Madrid 1051, five blocks west of the cathedral ☎04 6643399. In culinary terms this is as close as you'll get to Argentina without actually crossing the border. Succulent steaks (B$70–95) come with free access to a well-stocked salad bar, and there's a fine selection of wines. Mon 7–11pm, Tues–Sat noon–3pm & 7–11pm, Sun noon–3pm.

El Molino C Madrid 803, at Ramón Rojas ☎04 6643659. Vegetarian restaurant where lunch (B$20) consists of soup, salad bar and a choice of two main dishes, or come back later for just the main dish at B$17. 10am–3pm; closed Sat.

Pizza Pazza C Macondo Lazcano 317 ☎04 6654020. Eccentric, art centre open only two evenings a week, for art and music events accompanied by pizza (B$65). Thurs 8–11pm, Fri 8pm–3am.

★**Taberna Gattopardo** Plaza Luis de Fuentes ☎04 6630656. Vintage typewriters, radios and rifles, jazz paintings and discreet booths give this stylish restaurant-bar plenty of character. The vast menu includes sandwiches, pizzas, pasta, grilled meat and chicken, and the odd Mexican dish (tacos B$54), plus good coffee. Daily 8am–10pm.

DIRECTORY

Banks and exchange The Banco Nacional de Bolivia is on C Sucre at Ingavi, Banco Mercantil de Santa Cruz is on C Sucre at C 15 de Abril. There are money changers on C Bolívar between calles Sucre and Campos.

WINE IN THE TARIJA VALLEY

There are some worthwhile excursions close to Tarija in the warm and fertile Tarija valley, which is notable as Bolivia's prime **wine-producing region**. A visit to one of the **bodegas** (wineries) to see how the wines are produced and sample a few glasses makes an excellent half-day trip. Generally, you can only visit the closest *bodegas* on an organized trip with a Tarija-based agency (around B\$170 for half a day). To get to the La Concepción *bodega* take a minibus (every 30min or so; 30min) marked "V" from Corrado at Campero in Tarija to the village of Concepción, from where it's about a 10min walk along a track that heads out across a bridge to the right of the main road – ask the driver or anyone in the village for directions. You can taste the wine, wander around the pretty vineyards and eat lunch in the restaurant.

2

Internet Try Punto Entel at C Lema 144 on Plaza Sucre.
Laundry La Esmeralda, C Madrid 157 between calles Campos and Colón.

Post office Correo Central on C Lema, between calles Sucre and Trigo.

The central valleys

East of the Altiplano, the Andes march gradually down towards the eastern lowlands in a series of rugged mountain ranges, scarred with long, narrow valleys and blessed with rich alluvial soils. Both in climate and altitude, the **central valleys** are midway between the cold of the Altiplano and the tropical heat of the lowlands.

The administrative and political centre of Bolivia during Spanish rule, and still officially the capital of the republic, **Sucre** is a masterpiece of immaculately preserved colonial architecture, filled with elegant churches and mansions, and some of Bolivia's finest museums. The charms of **Cochabamba**, on the other hand, are more prosaic. Although lacking in tourist attractions, it's a pleasant and friendly city, with some great places to eat and drink. It is also the jumping-off point for **Parque Nacional Torotoro**, which boasts labyrinthine limestone caves, deep canyons and waterfalls, dinosaur footprints and ancient ruins.

East of Cochabamba, the main road to Santa Cruz passes through the **Chapare**, a beautiful region where the last foothills of the Andes plunge down into the Amazon basin. The area, though, is notoriously the source of most of Bolivia's coca crop.

SUCRE

Set in a broad highland valley on the eastern edge of the Altiplano, the UNESCO World Heritage Site of **SUCRE** is the most beautiful city in Bolivia, with some of the finest Spanish colonial architecture in South America and a spring-like climate all year round. Neon signs are banned, and municipal regulations require all buildings to be whitewashed annually, maintaining the characteristic that earned Sucre another of its many grandiose titles: "La Ciudad Blanca de Las Américas" – the White City of the Americas. It is also the administrative and market centre for a mountainous rural hinterland inhabited by Quechua-speaking communities renowned for their beautiful weavings. These can be seen – and bought – in the city itself or on a day-trip to **Tarabuco**, a rural town about 60km southeast of Sucre that hosts a colourful Sunday market.

Founded between 1538 and 1540 and initially named Chuquisaca, Sucre's official title subsequently changed to Villa de la Plata (City of Silver). After independence, it was made the capital of the new **Republic of Bolivia** and renamed **Sucre**, but the city's economic importance declined. When the seat of both congress and the presidency was moved to La Paz after the civil war between the two cities in 1899, the transfer merely confirmed long-established realities. Sucre remained the seat of the supreme court and was allowed to retain the title of official or constitutional capital, which it still holds today.

2

WHAT TO SEE AND DO

The extravagance of Sucre's past is evident in its beautifully preserved architecture. You can easily spend a few hours or days wandering the streets and admiring the grandeur of the city centre; the attractive **Plaza 25 de Mayo** is the best place to start.

Casa de la Libertad

On the northwest side of the Plaza 25 de Mayo stands the simple but well-preserved colonial facade of the original seventeenth-century Jesuit University. Now known as the **Casa de la Libertad** (Tues–Sat 9.15–11.45am & 2.45–5.45pm, Sun 9am–11.15am; B$15 including guided tours in Spanish, English and French; ☏04 6454200), this was where the **Bolivian act of independence** was signed on August 6, 1825, and it now houses a small but interesting museum dedicated to the birth of the republic. Inside, a copy of the document proclaiming a sovereign and independent state is on display in the assembly room (with the original displayed every August 6).

The Catedral and Iglesia de San Miguel

Sucre's sixteenth-century Catedral on Plaza 25 de Mayo is only open for Mass (Thurs & Sun 9am); next door is the **Museo Eclesiastico** (C Nicolás Ortiz 61; Mon–Fri 10am–noon & 3–5pm; B$20), which has a small collection of important religious relics.

Half a block northwest of Plaza 25 de Mayo along Calle Arenales, the modest whitewashed Baroque facade of the **Iglesia de San Miguel** (sporadic opening hours; best to visit during Sunday Mass, 6.30–8pm), completed in 1621, conceals one of the most lavish church interiors in Sucre, with glorious carved Baroque altarpieces covered in gold leaf and an exquisite panelled Mudéjar ceiling.

Museo de Arte Indígena

The fascinating **Museo de Arte Indígena** (Mon–Fri 9am–12.30pm & 2.30–6pm, Sat 9am–noon & 2.30–6pm; B$22 including tour; ☏04 6453841, ⓦasur.org.bo), at Pasaje Iturricha 314 in the Zona Recoleta, is dedicated to the distinctive weavings of two local Quechua-speaking indigenous groups, the Jalq'a and the Tarabuqueños, and provides an excellent insight into a distinctly Andean artistic expression.

Museo Universitario Charcas

On Bolívar, at Dalence, is the rambling but worthwhile **Museo Universitario Charcas** (Mon–Fri 9am–12.30pm & 2.30–6.30pm, Sat 9.30am–12.30pm; B$20; ☏04 6456100), housed in a delightful seventeenth-century mansion. It is four museums in one, combining archeological, anthropological, colonial and modern art collections. Visits are by guided tour only, generally in Spanish, and last around an hour.

Convento-Museo La Recoleta

On the southeast side of Plaza Pedro de Anzures stands the **Convento-Museo La Recoleta** (Mon–Fri 9–11.30am & 2.30–4.30pm, Sat 3–5pm; B$15; ☏04 645 1987), a peaceful Franciscan monastery that houses an interesting little

---

SUCRE TOUR OPERATORS

Candelaria Tours Plaza Cochabamba, at C Perez ☏04 6440340, ⓦcandelariatours.com. Excellent trips to Candelaria village, which has a long-standing textile tradition. It's far less touristy than Tarabuco. Volunteering opportunities also on offer.

Climb Sucre ☏7866 9637, ✉justmarsden@gmail. com, ⓦclimbsucre.com. Runs climbing tours in the mountains surrounding the city. There's no office, so get in touch by phone or email. If you need some practice, try out the indoor climbing wall at Condor Café (see page 204).

Condor Trekkers C Calvo 102 ☏7289 1740, ⓦcondortrekkers.org. Non-profit agency specializing in hikes (from B$70), plus trips to organic farms whose produce is used in the agency's café (see page 204).

Joy Ride Bolivia C Ortíz, at Audiencia ☏04 6425544, ⓦjoyridebol.com. Organizes mountain biking, hiking, horseriding, climbing, paragliding, quad-biking and motorcycling trips (from around B$250), as well as city tours and excursions to Tarabuco.

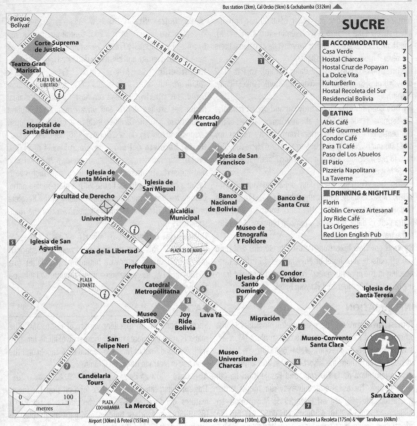

Bus station (2km), Cal Orcko (5km) & Cochabamba (332km)

SUCRE

■ ACCOMMODATION
Casa Verde	7
Hostal Charcas	3
Hostal Cruz de Popayan	5
La Dolce Vita	1
KulturBerlin	6
Hostal Recoleta del Sur	2
Residencial Bolivia	4

● EATING
Abis Café	3
Café Gourmet Mirador	8
Condor Café	5
Para Ti Café	6
Paso del Los Abuelos	7
El Patio	1
Pizzeria Napolitana	4
La Taverne	2

■ DRINKING & NIGHTLIFE
Florin	2
Goblin Cerveza Artesanal	4
Joy Ride Café	3
Las Orígenes	5
Red Lion English Pub	1

Airport (30km) & Potosí (155km)   Museo de Arte Indígena (100m), ⑥ (150m), Convento-Museo La Recoleta (175m) & Tarabuco (60km)

museum of colonial religious art and materials related to the missionary work of the Franciscan order. Visits are by guided tour in Spanish only.

The dinosaur footprints at Cal Orko

Five kilometres outside Sucre on the road to Cochabamba, the low mountain of **Cal Orko** is home to the world's largest collection of **dinosaur footprints**, discovered in 1994 by workers at a local cement works and limestone quarry. The site has become a major tourist attraction for its 5000 or so prints from at least 150 different types of dinosaur that cover an area of around 30,000 square metres of near-vertical rock face.

You can either gaze upon the tracks through a chain-link gate or pay a fee to enter the rather underwhelming **Parque Cretácico** (Mon–Fri 9am–5pm, Sat 10am–8pm, Sun 10am–5pm; B$30 includes guided tour, which run every 30min; cameras B$5; ☎04 645 7392), which has a better-positioned viewing platform. The fee includes a guided tour of the park: twice daily (noon & 1pm) these tours take you down into the quarry itself where you can view the footprints up close, and are well worth doing; the rest of the tours focus on the plaster replicas.

"Dino buses" run to the park from the cathedral (Tues–Fri 11am, noon, 2pm & 3pm, Sat & Sun 9.30am, 11am, noon, 2pm, 3pm & 4.30pm; B$15 return); alternatively take *micro* #4 (30min) from the city centre or a taxi (around B$50 return with waiting time).

ARRIVAL AND DEPARTURE

By plane Sucre's international airport is 30km south of the city. The departure tax is B$11. A taxi to/from the city

2

centre costs B\$50 for one passenger, B\$60 for two or more; alternatively take a *micro* (every 30min–1hr; 45min–1hr). The flights below are all direct; for most destinations, there are several more connecting flights.

Destinations Cochabamba (2 daily; 30min); La Paz (1–2 daily; 40min); Santa Cruz (5–6 daily; 30min); Tarija (1 daily; 40min).

By bus Long-distance buses arrive at and depart from the bus terminal (☎04 6456732), about 2.5km northeast of the city centre on Av Ostria Gutiérrez. From here it's a short taxi ride (around B\$20) into central Sucre, or take Micro A, which runs to the Mercado Central, a block north of the main Plaza 25 de Mayo.

Destinations Cochabamba (3 daily, departing early eve; 10–12hr); La Paz (3 daily, departing early eve; 12–14hr); Oruro (2 daily, departing early eve; 10–12hr); Potosí (hourly; 3hr) Santa Cruz (5 daily, from late afternoon onwards; 14–16hr; some travel via Samaipata).

By taxi *Colectivo* taxis from Potosí (2hr 30min) will drop you off outside your hotel or anywhere else in the centre; heading in the opposite direction, they can be caught from the bus station or organized via your hotel.

INFORMATION

Tourist information The most useful municipal tourist office is at Plaza Zudáñez, near the central plaza (Mon–Fri 8.30am–noon & 2.30 6pm; ☎04 6435240, ⓦdestino. sucre.travel/en); there are also booths at the airport, the bus station, Plaza de la Libertad, and Pasaje Iturricha (all same hours). There's also a university-run tourist office at C Estudiantes 49, just off Plaza 25 de Mayo (Mon–Fri 8.30am–12.30pm & 2.30–6.30pm; ☎04 6452283), but the information provided isn't always as accurate as it could be.

Websites Sucre Life (ⓦsucrelife.com) and Soy Sucre (ⓦsoysucre.info) are both handy.

ACCOMMODATION

Sucre has an excellent range of accommodation, mostly located in the heart of the old city centre.

Casa Verde C Potosí 374 ☎04 6458291, ⓦcasaverdesucre. com; map p.203. This friendly guesthouse has a wide range of rooms (including a good-value single; B\$145) with private bathrooms. There's a sun-trap patio, small pool, and a communal kitchen. B\$260

Hostal Charcas C Ravelo 62 ☎04 6453972, ⓔhostalcharcas@yahoo.com; map p.203. Accessed via a narrow hallway, this establishment has clean, but rather cramped rooms; those with private bathrooms (B\$130) lack ventilation. Breakfast costs extra. B\$80

Hostal Cruz de Popayan C Loa 881 ☎04 6440889, ⓦhotelsucre.com; map p.203. Popular place in a restored seventeenth-century townhouse. Rooms are a bit scruffy, but most are en suite and come with TVs. There is also an eight-bed dorm. Dorms B\$45, doubles B\$150

★**La Dolce Vita** C Urcullo 342 ☎04 6912014, ⓦdolcevitasucre.com; map p.203. Central guesthouse, run by a friendly, informative Franco-Swiss family, with good views from a relaxed terrace and big, nicely decorated rooms. B\$110

KulturBerlin C Avaroa 326 ☎04 6466854, ⓦkulturberlin.com; map p.203. Also known as *Hostal Berlin*, this attractive German-run hostel in an old colonial house has six-bed dorms and private rooms set around a courtyard garden. Facilities include a café-bar, Spanish lessons, and cookery classes. Dorms B\$80, doubles B\$230

Hostal Recoleta del Sur C Ravelo 205 ☎04 6454789, ⓔmariateresadalenz@gmail.com; map p.203. Reliable mid-range choice offering comfortable en-suite rooms with TVs in a converted colonial house with a glass-roofed patio. Despite the name, the hotel is not actually in the Recoleta district, but instead a 10min walk northwest of the main square. B\$180

Residencial Bolivia C San Alberto 42 ☎04 6454346; map p.203. This long-running *residencial* has spacious rooms with shared or private bathrooms (the latter cost B\$180) and TVs; there are some duds, though, so look at a few first. B\$100

EATING

Sucre is home to an excellent variety of restaurants. The markets are great places to find inexpensive, filling lunches: try the second floor of Mercado Central on C Zabelo and the food hall in Mercado Negro on C Junín.

Abis Café Plaza 25 de Mayo ☎04 6460222; map p.203. This appealing café is a great place for a pit stop. The menu features good coffee (B\$9–28), breakfasts, a set lunch (B\$40–50), sandwiches, burgers, and light meals, plus ice cream sundaes (B\$15–30). Mon–Fri 8.30am–10pm, Sat & Sun 8.30am–midnight.

★**Café Gourmet Mirador** Plaza Anzures ☎04 6452330; map p.203. Grab a deckchair in the garden of this outdoor café and enjoy fantastic city views. There are snacks (B\$10–30), pasta, crêpes and tiramisu, along with beer (B\$20–35), wine (glasses from B\$20), fresh juices and excellent iced cappuccinos. Daily 9.30am–7.30pm.

Condor Café C Calvo 102 ☎7343 3392, ⓦcondortrekkers. org; map p.203. Café-restaurant run by Condor Trekkers (see page 202). The menu features organic coffee (B\$10–18), breakfasts (B\$9–18), and pastries, snacks and light meals. From Thursday to Saturday evening it offers tapas and two-for-one drinks. Improbably, there's a small indoor climbing wall (B\$20). Mon–Sat 8.30am–10pm, Sun noon–8pm.

Para Ti Café C Audiencia 68 ☎04 6437901, ⓦchocolatesparati.net/en; map p.203. Sucre's finest chocolatier has several branches around Sucre, but this is the pick of the bunch, thanks to the attached café, which does hot chocolates, milkshakes, coffees and liqueurs. Daily 8.30am–8.30pm.

Paso del Los Abuelos C Bustillos 216 ☎04 6455173; map p.203. Smarter-than-average *salteñeria* where Sucre's wealthiest citizens go for their mid-morning snacks: at around B$8 each, the *salteñas* here are relatively expensive, but worth every cent. Mon–Sat 8am–1pm.

★ **El Patio** C San Alberto 18; map p.203. Widely considered the best *salteñeria* in town, popular with locals and tourists alike. Once you've got your rich, juicy *salteñas* (from B$8), grab a seat in the beautiful colonial patio. Get here early, as they sell out quickly. Daily 8am–1pm.

Pizzeria Napolitana Plaza 25 de Mayo 30 ☎04 6451934; map p.203. Sucre's longest-running Italian restaurant serves reasonable pizza (B$35–100) and pasta, as well as copious *copas* (ice-cream sundaes) and strong coffee. The lunch special costs B$35. Mon & Wed–Sun 8.30am–10.30pm.

La Taverne C Arce 35 ☎04 6455719, ⓦlataverne.com. bo; map p.203. The Alliance Française's restaurant mixes Gallic standards with international dishes (mains B$45–80), all presented with a certain flair. There's a good-value four-course set lunch (B$50). Mon–Sat 8.30am–11pm, Sun 7–10.30pm.

DRINKING AND NIGHTLIFE

A large student population and a steady stream of backpackers ensure a good range of bars and clubs.

Florin C Bolívar 567 ☎04 6451313; map p.203. This lively Dutch-run place has an authentic pub feel with excellent beer (including craft options; around B$25) and a daily happy hour (9.30–10.30pm). Mon–Fri noon–2am, Sat 8.30am–2am, Sun 8.30am–midnight.

Goblin Cerveza Artesanal C Grau 246 ☎7303 5722; map p.203. This small bar is run by a microbrewery, and offers everything from amber ales to stouts (from B$20), plus tasty meat and cheese platters. Live bands often play; at other times rock concerts are screened on the TVs. Thurs–Sat 8pm–2am.

Joy Ride Café C Ortiz 14 ☎04 6425544, ⓦjoyridebol. com; map p.203. This bar-restaurant serves an exhaustive range of dishes (mains B$35–85), but the drinks (cocktails and shots around B$30) and atmosphere are the real draw. There are film screenings, salsa classes, pool tables, a heated patio, and a book exchange. Mon–Fri 7am–late, Sat & Sun 9am–late.

Las Orígenes C Azurduy 473 ⓦespacioculturalorigenes. com; map p.203. An entertaining folkloric dance and music show (2hr). Most travel agencies sell tickets (B$150 with a decent dinner). Tues–Thurs 8.30–10.30pm, Fri–Sun 8–10pm.

Red Lion English Pub C Bolívar 490 ☎7612 6801; map p.203. This British-run joint lives up to expectations, with a good range of draught and bottled beers (from B$20), fish and chips and a full English breakfast on the menu, and live sport on the TV. Mon–Thurs 5pm–midnight, Fri 5pm–2am, Sat 7pm–2am. 11.30am–2pm, Sun 7pm–2am.

DIRECTORY

Banks and exchange Casa de cambios around the main square change foreign currencies at reasonable rates. There are plenty of ATMs, including at the Banco de Santa Cruz and Banco Nacional de Bolivia, C España, at San Alberto .

Hospital Hospital Santa Bárbara, Plaza de la Libertad (☎04 6451900).

Language courses Academia Latinoamericana de Español, C Dalence 109 at Ortiz (☎04 6439613, ⓦlatinoschools.com), offers private or group lessons, homestays and voluntary placements.

Laundry Lava Yá, C Audiencia 81.

TARABUCO

The most popular excursion from Sucre is to the small rural town of **TARABUCO**, set amid undulating mountains about 65km southeast of the city. The town's claim to fame is the Sunday market. This is the focus for the indigenous communities of the surrounding mountains, the Tarabuqueños, who come to sell the beautiful weavings for which they're famous throughout Bolivia. The market is a bit of a tourist trap, but the stalls selling weavings and other handicrafts to tourists are still far outnumbered by those selling basic supplies such as dried foodstuffs, agricultural tools, sandals made from tyres, big bundles of coca and pure alcohol in great steel drums.

THE CORDILLERA DE LOS FRAILES

The eastern section of the **Cordillera de los Frailes**, the mountain range that cuts across Potosí and Chuquisaca departments, is easy to explore from Sucre. Most travel agencies offer hikes, often following Inca trails. Highlights include the spectacular **Maragua Crater**, the pretty stone chapel at **Chataquila**, the **Garganta del Diablo** waterfall and **Boca del Diablo** cave, the dinosaur footprints and fossils at **Niñu Mayu** and **Mayu**, and the Jal'qa villages of **Potolo** and **Quila Quila**.

2

ARRIVAL AND DEPARTURE

By bus/truck Buses and trucks to Tarabuco (2hr) leave on Sunday morning (and most weekdays) from Plaza Huallpari-machi in the east of Sucre, returning in the afternoon.

By tourist bus It is much more convenient and only slightly more expensive to go on one of the tourist buses organized by hotels/tour agencies in Sucre, which will pick you up outside the Mercado Central on C Ravelo in the morning and bring you back in the afternoon – *Hostal Charcas* organizes a service every Sunday around 8.30am (B$40 return).

COCHABAMBA

At Bolivia's geographic centre, between the Altiplano and the eastern lowlands, **COCHABAMBA** is a vibrant, youthful city and the commercial hub of the rich agricultural region of the Cochabamba Valley, Bolivia's breadbasket. It is known as the "City of Eternal Spring" for its year-round sunny climate, and is perfect for relaxing in one of the cafés around Calle España.

WHAT TO SEE AND DO

Though Cochabamba isn't the place for colonial architecture, there are some historic sights. Shopaholics will enjoy the huge outdoor market of La Cancha, and there are also opportunities for exploring the understated attractions of the surrounding valleys.

Plaza 14 de Septiembre and the Museo Archeológico

The centre of Cochabamba is **Plaza 14 de Septiembre**, a placid and pleasant square with flower-filled ornamental gardens and plenty of benches. A block south of the plaza on the corner of calles Aguirre and Jordán is the **Museo Archeológico** (Mon–Fri 8am–6pm, Sat 8.30am–12.30pm; B$25; ☎04 4250010), which explains the evolution of pre-Hispanic culture in the region.

Convento de Santa Teresa

The lovely **Convento de Santa Teresa** (entrance at Baptista N-344; guided tours Mon–Fri 9am, 10am, 11am, 2.30pm, 3.30pm & 4.30pm, Sat 2.30pm, 3.30pm & 4.30pm; B$20; cameras B$5; ☎04 4525765) on Baptista, at Ecuador, is worth visiting. As well as the convent, this beautiful building houses a church built within a church (the original church was destroyed in the 1700s). The nuns still live on the site, though they are now housed in the complex next door.

La Cancha

The commercial heart of this market city is in the south, with its massive rambling street markets. An entire block between calles Tarata and Pulucayo is occupied by the covered street market known as **La Cancha** (Quechua for "walled enclosure"), where *campesinos* and merchants come to buy and sell their produce, in this sprawling labyrinth of stalls.

Palacio Portales

About 1km north of the city centre, with its entrance off Avenida Potosí, the opulent **Palacio Portales** (guided tours Tues–Fri 3pm, 3.30pm, 4.30pm, 5.30pm & 6pm (Spanish), 4pm, 5pm & 6.30pm (English/French), Sat & Sun 10am, 11am & noon (Spanish), 10.30am & 11.30am (English/French); B$20; ☎04 4489666, ⓦcentropatino.fundacionpatino.org) was built for the Cochabamba-born "King of Tin", Simón Patiño, though he never actually lived here. It features a bizarre mix of architectural styles, including French Neoclassical and Mudéjar. If anything, though, it's the magnificent **gardens** (Tues–Fri 3–6.30pm, Sat & Sun 9am–noon; free) that really impress.

Cristo de la Concordia

About 1.5km east of the city is the **Cristo de la Concordia** – a statue of Christ modelled on the one in Rio but just slightly taller. To reach the summit, the risk of muggings means you shouldn't walk: take the five-minute cable-car ride (Tues–Sat 10am–6pm, Sun 9am–6pm; B$10.50 return) for excellent views.

ARRIVAL AND DEPARTURE

By plane Jorge Wilsterman airport (☎04 4222846) is a few kilometres southwest of the city; a taxi into the centre costs B$30–40; alternatively, take *micro* #B. In addition to domestic flights there are a few services to neighbouring countries. The flights below are all direct; for most destinations, there are several more connecting flights.

COCHABAMBA

● **EATING**
Café Paris	3
Caféteria Ideal	2
Menta Restobar	1
Sucremanta	4

■ **DRINKING**
Casablanca	1

● **SHOPPING**
The Spitting Llama	1

■ **ACCOMMODATION**
Americana Hotel	4
City Hotel	3
Hotel Felipez	2
Running Chaski Hostel	1

Destinations La Paz (11–13 daily; 30min); Santa Cruz (10–12 daily; 45min); Sucre (2 daily; 30min); Tarija (2–3 daily; 1hr); Trinidad (1–2 daily; 50min).

By bus Most long-distance buses arrive at and depart from the bus terminal, in the south of the city on Av Ayacucho just south of Av Aroma. The surrounding area is rough, especially at night, so be very careful. A taxi to the centre costs about B$10–20 and is a much safer bet than walking. Buses and *trufis* to Villa Tunari (3hr–3hr 30min) depart when full from close to the junction of Av Oquendo and Av 9 de Abril, southeast of the city centre.

2

Destinations La Paz (hourly; 7–8hr); Oruro (6–7 daily; 5–8hr); Santa Cruz (10–12 daily; 10–12hr); Sucre (3 daily; 10–12hr).

INFORMATION

Tourist information The tourist office is on the eastern side of Plaza Colon (Mon–Fri 8am–noon & 2.30–6.30pm, Sat 8.30am–noon; ☎04 4662277, ⓦcochabamba.bo/turismo). There is also an information kiosk at the bus station (officially same hours, though not always kept to; ☎04 422 0550), and on Blvd de la Recoleta (officially same hours, though rarely staffed).

Tour operators Fremen Tours (C Tumulsa N-245 ☎04 4259392, ⓦandes-amazonia.com) runs trips into the Chapare, where it owns *Hotel de Selva El Puente*. Tusoco Viajes (C Sagarnaga 227, La Paz; ☎02 2140653, ⓦtusoco.com) is an umbrella organization representing community-based tourism projects. In the Cochabamba region, the Chocaya group offers camping in the Chocaya forest, north of Quillacollo. The Kawsay Wasi group, meanwhile, has a range of tours in the Chapare region). Contact via the website or by phone.

ACCOMMODATION

Budget accommodation in Cochabamba is underwhelming. The only time you really need to book ahead is in mid-August during the Fiesta de la Virgen de Urkupiña in nearby Quillacollo.

Americana Hotel C Arze S-788 ☎04 4250552, ⓦamericanahotel.com.bo; map p.207. A good-value high-rise hotel with attentive staff and comfortable, well-equipped en-suite rooms with TVs and city views (from rooms on the higher floors). The area isn't the safest, however, so be careful at night. $55 (B$374)

City Hotel C Jordan 341 ☎04 4222993, ⓦcityhotelbolivia.com; map p.207. Although frayed around the edges, this central hotel is an acceptable choice. Its en-suite rooms have TVs and faded decor – those at the back are the best bets. B$260

Hotel Felipez C España N-172 ☎04 4506393, ⓦfelipezhotel.com; map p.207. The orange-and-cream colour scheme may not be to everyone's taste, but this no-nonsense hotel does the basics well: clean and comfortable en-suite rooms, and a friendly welcome. While the doubles are a decent size, the singles are cramped. B$220

Running Chaski Hostel C España N-449 ☎04 4250559; map p.207. Cochabamba's top hostel has mixed and female-only dorms, with eight to ten beds in each, plus simple singles and doubles (with private bathrooms) and flashier suites sleeping up to four people (B$250 for double occupancy). Dorms B$49, doubles B$195

EATING

Café Paris C España, at Bolívar ☎04 4503561; map p.207. Sophisticated French-style café with Parisian posters, wrought-iron chairs and a stained-glass-covered bar. There's an extensive range of coffees (B$6–25), plus crêpes (B$13–28), ice-cream sundaes, and daily quiche and gâteau specials. Mon–Sat 8am–10pm.

Caféteria Ideal C General Acha, at Av Ayacucho ☎04 4251016; map p.207. Tucked away on a side street and lacking a sign, this tiny café would be easy to miss if it weren't for the enticing smell of fresh coffee. This lost-in-time place serves great *cortados*, cappuccinos, espressos and *cafés con leche* at rock-bottom prices (B$5–15). Mon–Sat 9am–6/7pm.

★ **Menta Restobar** C España N-356 ☎04 452 0113; map p.207. The best vegetarian restaurant in the city. For lunch, go for the set meal (B$21) or choose from one of the stacked bean, quinoa, chickpea or lentil burgers. The dinner menu expands to cover pizzas and mains (B$25–55) including lasagne and tacos. Mon–Sat noon–3pm & 6.30–10pm.

Sucremanta C Arze S-348 ☎04 4222839; map p.207. Popular restaurant specializing in traditional pork-based dishes from the Sucre region including delicious chorizo sausages, *fritanga* (a thick, spicy stew), *salteñas* and empanadas. There are other branches at Av N-510 and Hamiriya N-126. Mains B$22–50. Daily 9am–2pm.

DRINKING AND NIGHTLIFE

Boulevar Recolla, a pedestrianized strip on the right-hand turning from the roundabout before Av Pando, is a popular night-time spot. There are several bars and a few karaoke joints, too.

Casablanca C 25 de Mayo, at Ecuador ☎04 4521048; map p.207. A bohemian joint, decorated with classic film posters and photos of jazz legends, drawing students, young foreign volunteers, and (during the day at least) a few old timers. Although coffee and food is on offer, the beer (including some craft options; from B$18), wines (glass B$15), and cocktails (around B$35) are the best bets. There are often film screenings. Daily 9am–1/2am.

SHOPPING

The Spitting Llama C España, at Ecuador ☎04 4894540; map p.207. This excellent multilingual bookstore and exchange also stocks camping and hiking gear, as well as other travel supplies, and even a selection of craft beers. Mon–Fri 9am–1pm & 3–8pm, Sat 9am–1pm.

DIRECTORY

Banks and exchange There are exchange offices on the southwest side of Plaza 14 de Septiembre and street moneychangers in the centre of town. ATMs are common.

Hospitals Clínica Belga, C Antezana N-0457 ☎04 4231403.

Language classes Escuela Runawasi, C Maurice Lefebvre N-0470, Villa Juan XXIII (☎04 4248923, ⓦrunawasi.org),

offers Spanish and Quechua lessons (from B$1340/week), plus homestays (from B$665/week).
Laundry Limpieza Superior, C España N-616 (Mon–Sat 9am–6pm; B$12/kg; ☎ 04 4521307).

PARQUE NACIONAL TOROTORO

Some 139km south of Cochabamba, the **Parque Nacional Torotoro** covers just 165 square kilometres, making it Bolivia's smallest national park. But what it lacks in size it makes up for with its powerful scenery and varied attractions – high valleys and deep canyons, ringed by low mountains whose twisted geological formations are strewn with fossils, dinosaur footprints and labyrinthine limestone cave complexes. The park's cactus and scrubby woodland supports considerable wildlife – including flocks of parakeets and the rare and beautiful red-fronted macaw. The main attractions are the limestone caves of **Umajallanta**, the beautiful, waterfall-filled **Torotoro Canyon**, and hiking expeditions to the pre-Inca ruined fortress of **Llama Chaqui**.

ARRIVAL AND INFORMATION

By bus Buses to Torotoro leave Cochabamba from the corner of avenidas 6 de Agosto and Republica (Mon–Wed, Fri & Sat 6pm; Thurs & Sun 6am; they return from Torotoro Mon–Thurs & Sat 6am, Fri 6pm, Sun noon, 1pm & 3pm). The bus ride takes about 7hr in the dry season (May–Sept) – in the rainy season (Nov–March) it takes much longer and the route is sometimes impassable.
Tourist office The tourist office on the village main square (officially daily 8am–noon & 2–5pm, though opening hours are erratic; ☎ 7227 0968, ⊛ visitatorotoro.com.bo) is where you pay the B$30 park admission fee. It has basic information about the park and can find you a local guide for around B$100 a day.
Tours It's also possible to visit Torotoro on a tour – which is significantly easier but obviously more expensive. Try Fremen Tours (see page 208).

ACCOMMODATION

Hostal Las Hermanas C Cochabamba s/n ☎ 04 4135736. This simple, welcoming lodge is the best of the village's low-budget *alojamientos*. The rooms – shared or private bathrooms – are clean, basic and fine for a night or two. Good home cooking available. **B$100**
Villa Etelvina C Sucre s/n ☎ 7073 7807, ⊛ villaetelvina. com. Easily the best place to stay in Torotoro, *Villa Etelvina* has comfortable bungalows sleeping up to six people, rooms with shared bathrooms, and camping facilities.

There's a restaurant, and staff can organize hikes, mountain biking and rappelling. Doubles B$360, bungalows B$830, camping per person B$50

THE CHAPARE

Northeast of Cochabamba, the main road to Santa Cruz drops down into the **CHAPARE**, a broad, rainforest-covered plain in the Upper Amazon Basin and an area of great natural beauty. However, it's also Bolivia's largest provider of coca grown to make cocaine, so this is not the place for expeditions far off the beaten track. The peaceful towns along the main Cochabamba to Santa Cruz road are safe to visit, unless you go during one of the sporadic road blockades by protesting *cocaleros*; these are usually announced in advance, so ask around before your trip.

Villa Tunari

The laidback town of **Villa Tunari** is a good place to break a journey between Cochabamba and Santa Cruz and also to get a brief introduction to the Amazon lowlands.

ARRIVAL AND INFORMATION

By bus Buses (every 1–2hr; 3hr 30min) and *trufis* (leave when full; 3hr) to Villa Tunari leave from the intersection of avenidas Oquendo and 9 de Abril in Cochabamba. Heading back to Cochabamba from Villa Tunari, you can catch a bus or *trufi* from the office of Trans Tours 7 de Junio on the main road; alternatively flag down one of the services passing through town on their way to Cochabamba from elsewhere in the Chapare. Buses from Santa Cruz will drop you off at the police control *tranca* at the west end of town, and buses heading to Santa Cruz sometimes pick up passengers here if they have room, though most pass through in the middle of the night.

ACCOMMODATION

Hostal Habana Las Cocas A block north of the main road, opposite the church ☎ 04 413 6597. Probably the best budget option in town, with a range of clean rooms with shared or private bathrooms, fan or a/c, plus a plunge pool. **B$180**
★ **Hotel de Selva El Puente** About 4km east of town ☎ 04 4580085, ⊛ hotelelpuente.com.bo. Villa Tunari's best option is *Hotel de Selva El Puente*, which has simple *cabañas* with fans (a/c ones cost B$430) set amid a patch of rainforest. There's a swimming pool, fourteen delightful natural river pools and a restaurant. No wi-fi. A taxi from town costs around B$20. **B$365**

The eastern lowlands

Stretching from the last Andean foothills east to Brazil and south to Paraguay and Argentina, Bolivia's **eastern lowlands** have undergone rapid development in recent decades, fuelled by oil and gas, cattle-ranching and massive agricultural development. At the centre of this economic boom is **Santa Cruz**, a youthful,

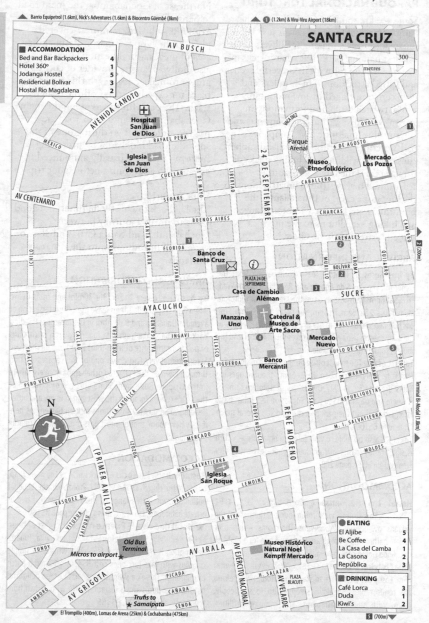

Barrio Equipetrol (1.6km), Nick's Adventures (1.6km) & Biocentro Güembé (8km)

(1.2km) & Viru-Viru Airport (18km)

SANTA CRUZ

0   300
metres

ACCOMMODATION
Bed and Bar Backpackers	4
Hotel 360°	1
Jodanga Hostel	5
Residencial Bolívar	3
Hostal Río Magdalena	2

AV BUSCH

AVENIDA CANOTO

MÉXICO

Hospital San Juan de Dios

RAFAEL PEÑA

Iglesia San Juan de Dios

CUÉLLAR

AV CENTENARIO

O(H)J(J)

SARAH

SANTA BÁRBARA

21 DE MAYO

LIBERTAD

SEOANE

BUENOS AIRES

FLORIDA

ESPAÑA

Banco de Santa Cruz

JUNÍN

AYACUCHO

CORDILLERA

VALLEGRANDE

INGAVI

VELASCO

COLÓN

S. DE FIGUEROA

CALLAO

YAPACANÍ

PERO VÉLEZ

LA CATÓLICA

PARÍ

N

(PRIMER ANILLO)

ISOZOG

MERCADO

MOS. SALVATIERRA

Iglesia San Roque

PARAPETÍ

VÁSQUEZ M.

VITUPIA

SALPURU

TUNDY

Old Bus Terminal
★ Micros to airport

AMBORÓ

AV GRIGOTA

PICADA

CAÑADA

SENDA

★ Trufis to Samaipata

El Trompillo (400m), Lomas de Arena (25km) & Cochabamba (475km)

24 DE SEPTIEMBRE

Parque Arenal

Museo Etno-folklórico

CABALLERO

BENI

CHARCAS

ARENALES

MURILLO

BOLÍVAR

AROMA

CASA DE CAMBIO
Aléman

PLAZA 24 DE SEPTIEMBRE

Casa de Cambio Aléman

Manzano Uno

Catedral & Museo de Arte Sacro

Mercado Nuevo

NUFLO DE CHAVEZ

Banco Mercantil

CHUQUISACA

LA PAZ

WARNES

REPUBLIQUETAS

RENE MORENO

M. I. SALVATIERRA

MOLDES

INDEPENDENCIA

LEMOINE

LA RIVA

Museo Histórico Natural Noel Kempff Mercado

H. SALAZAR

AV IRALA

AV EJÉRCITO NACIONAL

AV VELARDE

PLAZA BLACUTT

OYOLA

6 DE AGOSTO

Mercado Los Pozos

CAMPERO

QUIJARRO

SUCRE

BALLIVIÁN

COCHABAMBA

POTOSÍ

Terminal Bi-Modal (1.8km)

VACA DÍEZ

EATING
El Aljibe	5
Be Coffee	4
La Casa del Camba	1
La Casona	2
República	3

DRINKING
Café Lorca	3
Duda	1
Kiwi's	2

(700m)

lively city and gateway to the attractions of the surrounding area. West of the city are the pristine rainforests protected by the **Parque Nacional Amboró**; the beautiful cloudforest that covers the upper regions of the park can be visited from the idyllic town of **Samaipata**. From Samaipata, you can also head further southwest to the town of **Vallegrande** and the hamlet of **La Higuera**, where Argentine revolutionary, Ernesto "Che" Guevara, was killed in 1967. East of Santa Cruz, the railway to Brazil passes through the broad forested plains of **Chiquitos**, and its beautiful **Jesuit mission churches**. Finally, south of Santa Cruz, the vast and inhospitable **Chaco**, an arid wilderness of dense thorn and scrub, stretches south to Argentina and Paraguay.

SANTA CRUZ

Set among the steamy, tropical lowlands just beyond the last Andean foothills, **SANTA CRUZ** is Bolivia's economic powerhouse, with a fiercely independent-minded outlook. An isolated frontier town until the middle of the twentieth century, the city has grown in the past fifty years to become the biggest in the country. Its layout consists of a series of rings – called *anillos* – with the colonial city centre inside the Primer Anillo, and almost everything you need within the first two or three.

WHAT TO SEE AND DO

Santa Cruz can't match the colonial charm of highland cities like Sucre and Potosí, and has few conventional tourist sights beyond a handful of museums. While some travellers find its unapologetic modernity, commercialism and pseudo-Americanism unappealing, others enjoy its blend of dynamism and tropical insouciance. Be careful walking around the city centre at night as muggings do sometimes occur.

Plaza 24 de Septiembre

At the centre of Santa Cruz is **Plaza 24 de Septiembre**, a spacious, lively square with well-tended gardens shaded by tall trees. On the south side stands the salmon-pink **Catedral** (daily 7am–7pm;

free), or **Basílica Mayor de San Lorenzo**, a hulking brick structure with twin bell towers built between 1845 and 1915 on the site of an original church, which dated back to 1605. The cool, vaulted interior has some fine silverwork around the altar, but the best religious art is tucked away in the adjacent **Museo de Arte Sacro** (Mon–Fri 3–6pm; B$10). You can also climb up to a **mirador** (daily 8am–noon & 3–6pm; B$3) in the bell tower with good views.

Biocentro Güembé

About a thirty-minute taxi ride (about B$70) from the city centre, at Km7 Camino a Porongo, Zona Los Batos, **Biocentro Güembé** (daily 8.30am–6pm; adults B$180, children aged under 13 B$60, with a basic day package; ☏03 3700700, ⊛biocentroguembe.com) is a tranquil park retreat with numerous swimming pools, as well as opportunities for mountain biking, kayaking and beach volleyball. There's also a large butterfly house and orchid display.

Lomas de Arena

Some 25km southwest of the city is **Lomas de Arena**, a protected area of desert and tropical forest spanning around 130 square kilometres and containing a series of dramatic sand dunes. As well as sandboarding, there's the chance to spot sloths, capybaras, caymans, and over 250 species of bird. There's no public transport so it's best to visit on a tour; try those run by Nick's Adventures (see page 212); from B$245.

ARRIVAL AND DEPARTURE

By plane Aeropuerto El Trompillo, just south of the centre in the Segundo Anillo, is sometimes used by military airline TAM and some smaller carriers. But the vast majority of airlines use the modern Aeropuerto Viru-Viru (☏03 3852400), 17km north of the city centre. It is a B$70 taxi ride from the city centre; alternatively, catch a micro (every 20min; 30min) to the old bus terminal, seven blocks southwest of the city centre. In addition to the domestic flights listed here, there are also international connections. The flights below are all direct; for most destinations, there are several more connecting flights.

Destinations Cochabamba (13–17 daily; 45min); La Paz (13–17 daily; 1hr); Rurrenabaque (3 weekly; 1hr); Sucre

2

SANTA CRUZ TOUR OPERATORS

Amboró Tours C Libertad 417, 2nd floor 161 ☎7261 2515, ⓦamborotours.com. A well-established agency with friendly staff and a range of tours across the region, including to the eponymous national park.

Nick's Adventures C La Plata 8 este 11, Barrio Equipetrol ☎03 3441820, ⓦnicksadventuresbolivia.com. Another professional agency specializing in wildlife tours, including to

Amboró, Parque Nacional Kaa-Iya (see page 216), and the San Miguelito Jaguar Conservation Reserve, plus trips to see the spectacular Espejillos and Jardín de los Delicias waterfalls.

Ruta Verde C 21 de Mayo 318 T03 3396470, ⓦrutaverdebolivia.com. A well-run agency run by a very helpful Dutch-Bolivian couple, who have excellent local knowledge and speak Spanish, Dutch and English.

(5–7 daily; 40min); Tarija (1–2 daily; 50min); Trinidad (7 weekly; 50min).

By bus Long-distance buses and all trains use the Terminal Bi-Modal. For major routes there's generally no need to buy tickets in advance, but for all other destinations try to get one the day before.

Destinations Cochabamba (10–12 daily; 10–12hr); Concepción (around 8 daily; 6–7hr); La Paz (10 daily; 16–18hr); Oruro (1 daily; 12–14hr; or via Cochabamba); San Ignacio (around 3 daily, eves; 10–12hr); San Javier (around 7 daily, with departures in the morning and early eve; 4–5hr); Sucre (5 daily; 14–16hr); Tarija (6 daily; 16hr); Trinidad (18–22 daily; 9–10hr); Vallegrande (2–3 daily; 6–7hr).

By train Trains travel east to the Brazilian border at Quijarro, via San José de Chiquitos. There are two different trains: the *Expreso Oriental* and the quicker and more comfortable *Ferrobus*. There is also a weekly service (Thurs) south to the Argentine border at Yacuiba via Villamontes. Buy tickets for all services in advance.

Destinations Quijarro (6 weekly; 13hr–16hr 40min); San José de Chiquitos (6 weekly; 5hr 10min–6hr 10min); Villamontes (1 weekly; 13hr 45min); Yacuiba (1 weekly; 16hr 35min).

By trufi and micro The quickest, most comfortable way to reach Samaipata is by *trufi*, collective taxis/minivans that depart when full (most people travel in the morning). Trufis to Samaipata (2hr 30min–3hr) depart from two stops: two blocks south of the old bus terminal on Av Omar Chavez, at Solis de Olguín; and from Av Grigotá, at C Arumá in the second *anillo*.

INFORMATION

Tourist information The most central tourist office is in the Prefectura building on the north side of Plaza 24 de Septiembre (Mon–Fri 8am–noon & 2.30–6.30pm; ☎03 3368900). Other locations include the Terminal Bi-Modal (Mon–Fri 8am–noon & 3–7pm; ☎03 3218316).

ACCOMMODATION

Bed and Bar Backpackers C Velasco 480 ☎03 3536090; map p.210. The name of this hostel neatly

sums up its sociable ethos. There are colourful six- to ten-bed dorms and private rooms, a roof terrace, friendly staff and a well-stocked bar, though no breakfast. Dorms B$45, doubles B$150

Hotel 360° C Abaroa 548 ☎03 3264920; map p.210. In the heart of the Los Pozos market, this sparkling hostel has super-clean dorms and private rooms (the latter have their own bathrooms, TVs, and fan or a/c; note, though, that some only have internal windows), a roof terrace, communal kitchen, and a helpful owner. Dorms B$65, doubles B$215

★ **Jodanga Hostel** C El Fuerte 1380, near Parque Urbano ☎03 3396542, ⓦjodanga.com; map p.210. This excellent Hostelling International-affiliated hostel is a 20min walk from the plaza. It has private rooms and six- to ten-bed dorms, plus a swimming pool, jacuzzi, TV/DVD room, communal kitchen, laundry service and Spanish classes. Dorms B$75, doubles B$210

Residencial Bolívar C Sucre 131 ☎03 3342500, ⓦresidencialbolivar.com; map p.210. Based in a colonial-era building, this longstanding backpackers' haunt has helpful staff and small but clean rooms with fans and shared or private bathrooms around a cool, leafy patio with hammocks and several resident toucans. It's popular, so reserve in advance. Dorms $18 (B$122), doubles $35 (B$238)

Hostal Rio Magdalena C Arenales 653 ☎03 3393011, ⓦhostalriomagdalena.com; map p.210. A solid, mid-range choice with spick and span a/c rooms and a pool. It's a 10min walk from the main plaza. Doubles B$250

EATING

Santa Cruz's relative wealth and cosmopolitanism are reflected in the city's wide variety of restaurants.

El Aljibe C Potosí, at Ñuflo de Chávez ☎03 3352277, ⓦelaljibecomidatipica.com; map p.210. Charming family-run restaurant specializing in traditional, home-style *Cruceño* cooking. Expect dishes (B$25–50) like *sopa de mani* (peanut soup) and *picante de pollo* (a spicy chicken dish). Mon 11.30am–3pm, Tues–Sat 11.30am–11pm, Sun 11.30am–4pm.

Be Coffee C Ingavi, at Independencia ☎03 3329232; map p.210. A hip café that takes its coffee very seriously indeed, turning out excellent – though pricey – flat whites and the like (B$14–30) using an array of gadgets, including AreoPresses and Chemex filters. Daily 8.30am–10pm.

La Casa del Camba Av Cristóbal de Mendoza 1365 ☎03 3427864, ⓦcasadecamba.com; map p.210. The best of the many large, traditional *Cruceño* restaurants on this stretch of the second *anillo*, and a great place to enjoy a reasonably priced *parillada* (mixed grill) or *pacumutu* (a huge shish kebab), often to the accompaniment of live *camba* music. Mains B$35–120. Daily 11.30am–midnight.

La Casona C Arenales 222 ☎03 3378495, ⓦbistrolacasona.com; map p.210. German-run restaurant-bar with a lovely patio and mellow music (live bands on Thurs nights, and sometimes at the weekend). There's a strong German influence on the menu (schnitzel, *wurst*; mains B$62–150; two-course set lunch around B$40), and especially on the excellent range of beers (B$19–50). Mon–Sat 11.30am–late.

República C Bolívar 175 ☎03 3347050, ⓦrepublica.com.bo; map p.210. Contemporary photography and paper sculpture on the walls, well-chosen music, and just-so cooking, with excellent pasta and salads, plus pizzas, panini and steaks (mains B$45–80). The courtyard has a bar. Mon–Wed & Sun 10am–midnight, Thurs–Sat 10am–1am.

DRINKING AND NIGHTLIFE

The Equipetrol area, to the northwest of the city, is the main area for nightlife. After 10pm, the streets are lined with people going out and cars blaring loud music. Head to clubs on Av San Martín for dancing and drink deals, or, for a slightly calmer scene, check out Av Monseñor Rivero, between the first and second *anillos*. Dress up smart for clubs, as doormen will refuse scruffy-looking backpackers.

★ **Café Lorca** C Sucre 8 ☎03 3340562, ⓦlorcasantacruz.org; map p.210. This bohemian café-bar has a balcony perfect for people-watching. There are regular live jazz, blues and folk performances (Thurs–Sun nights), a strong list of drinks (beer B$25–40, glasses of wine B$25–33, cocktails B$30–60), and a creative menu.

Mon–Thurs 9am–11.45pm, Fri & Sat 9am–3am, Sun 6–11.45pm.

Duda Florida 228 ☎7760 0655; map p.210. Cool, idiosyncratic bar decked out with old photos, toys and other knick-knacks is one of the best nightspots in the city. The playlist is as varied as the decor, and there's a good range of drinks (from B$20). Tues–Thurs 9pm–2am, Fri & Sat 9.30pm–3am.

Kiwi's C Bolívar 208 T03 3301410, ⓦkiwiscafeteria.com; map p.210. The narrow front leads into a big, airy space with a slightly New Age vibe, offering good drinks, shisha pipes, and a menu ranging from salads to burgers, crêpes to fajitas (B$30–60). There are tango dances and classes every Saturday night. Mon–Fri noon–11.30pm, Sat 2.30pm–1.30am.

DIRECTORY

Banks and exchange You can change currency at any of the string of casas de cambio on the east side of Plaza 24 de Septiembre. ATMs are very common.

Cinema Cinecenter, second *anillo*, at C René Moreno (☎03 375456, ⓦcinecenter.com.bo), is the city's best cinema.

Hospital Clinica Lourdes, C Moreno 352 (☎03 3325518), is a good place to go if you need a doctor. For emergencies, head to Hospital Municipal San Juan de Dios, C Cuéllar 474, at España (☎03 3332222), or Hospital Japonés, third *anillo*, at C Conavi (☎03 3462031 or ☎03 3462031).

Spanish lessons *Jodanga Backpackers' Hostel* (see page 212) offers good-value language classes (B$80/hr guests, B$100 non-guests), as does *Residencial Bolívar* (see page 212).

PARQUE NACIONAL AMBORÓ

Forty kilometres west of Santa Cruz, the **Parque Nacional Amboró** spans 4300 square kilometres of a great forest-covered spur of the Andes jutting out into the eastern plains. Amboró's steep, densely forested slopes support an astonishing biodiversity, including more than 830 types of bird and pretty much the full range of rainforest mammals, including

---

INTO BRAZIL

From Santa Cruz, the railway line runs some 680km east to the **Brazilian border** across a seemingly endless expanse of forest and tangled scrub, gradually giving way to the vast swamplands of the **Pantanal** as the border draws near.

The last stop on the railway line in Bolivia is **Puerto Quijarro**, a dismal collection of shacks surrounding the station. If you're heading on to Brazil, you're better off pushing on to the border at Arroyo Concepción, 2km away and connected to Puerto Quijaro by *trufis*. The border town on the Brazilian side is Corumbá (see page 324).

jaguars, giant anteaters, tapirs and several species of monkey.

The northern gateway to the park is the peaceful town of **Buena Vista**, 100km northwest of Santa Cruz. You can arrange a tour into the park from there, or with one of the operators in Santa Cruz (see page 212) or Samaipata (see below). Day trips start at aound US$55/person.

SAMAIPATA

Some 120km west of Santa Cruz, the tranquil little town of **SAMAIPATA** is a popular tourist destination for both Bolivians and foreign travellers. Nestled in an idyllic valley surrounded by rugged, forest-covered mountains, it's the kind of place that's difficult to drag yourself away from. Just outside town stands one of Bolivia's most intriguing archeological sites – the mysterious pre-Hispanic ruins of **El Fuerte**.

WHAT TO SEE AND DO

At the centre of town lies the small **Plaza Principal**, the core of the grid of tranquil streets lined with whitewashed houses. A few blocks north on Bolívar, the **Museo Archeológico** (Mon–Fri 8am–noon & 2–6pm; Sat & Sun 8am–4pm; B$5; free with El Fuerte ticket) has a small collection of archeological finds from across Bolivia, including some beautiful Inca ceremonial *chicha*-drinking cups; Inca stone axes and mace heads; and pottery from various different cultures. Sadly there's relatively little on display related to El Fuerte.

Innumerable walking trails run through the surrounding countryside, the beautiful cloudforests of the Parque Nacional Amboró are within easy reach, and most tour companies offer **day-trips** to nearby valleys where you might spot condors, climb mountainous ridges for breathtaking vistas or enjoy an afternoon splashing around in some of the area's spectacular waterfalls.

ARRIVAL AND DEPARTURE

By micro/trufi *Micros* from Santa Cruz (3hr) arrive and depart from the plaza, but *trufis* (2hr 30min) are quicker, more comfortable and only a little more expensive. Coming from Santa Cruz, they stop at the plaza and can normally be persuaded to drop you at your hotel; heading back, they leave when full from the plaza and the petrol station.

INFORMATION AND TOURS

Tour agencies Samaipata's tour agencies make it easy to visit the area's less accessible attractions; they're also the best source of tourist information. One of the most popular excursions is along the Ruta del Che, a two-day, one-night trip that traces the last steps of Che Guevara (see page 215). One of the best treks in the region is the Elbow of the Andes, with spectacular scenery, waterfalls, and the chance to spot condors. Roadrunners (Bolívar; ☎03 9446193, ✉theroadrunners@hotmail.com) is a friendly, reliable and English-speaking agency. Julumari Tours (Av del Estudiante; ☎7576 0013) is another well-run agency. If you speak Spanish, contact the experienced Don Gilberto Aguilera (☎03 9446050, ☎7261 5523).

ACCOMMODATION

There's an excellent range of budget accommodation in Samaipata. Prices rise at weekends, particularly October–April, and on public holidays.

Hostal Andorina C Campero ☎03 9446333, ⊕andorinasamaipata.com. Top-class hostel with a hippyish vibe, comfortable and excellent-value private rooms and two- and three-bed dorms, a communal terrace and balcony with hammocks, guest kitchen, book exchange and plenty of information. No wi-fi. Dorms B$60, doubles B$130

EL FUERTE

Located 10km east of Samaipata, **El Fuerte** (daily 9am–4.30pm; B$50; guides B$75/hr) is a striking and enigmatic ancient site with a great sandstone rock at its centre, carved with a fantastic variety of abstract and figurative designs and surrounded by the remains of more than fifty **Inca buildings**. The easiest way to reach El Fuerte is by taxi from Samaipata (about B$100 return with waiting time; *moto-taxis* around half that), or to join a guided tour with one of the tour agencies in town. While it is possible to walk to the ruins in about two to three hours – follow the road out of town toward Santa Cruz for a few kilometres, then turn right up the marked side road that climbs to the site – it's a tiring, very hot walk, so it's advisable to take a taxi to the site and walk back, otherwise you might be too exhausted to appreciate the ruins.

Cabañas Traudi Outside town, 800m south of the plaza ☎ 03 9446094. A wide range of quirky en-suite rooms (shared or private bathrooms) and *cabañas* (sleeping 2–8 people, and with kitchens). There's a large pool, sauna and a talkative pet parrot. Doubles B$120, cabañas B$160

El Jardín C Arenales, two blocks east of the market ☎ 7310 1440, ⊛ eljardinsamaipata.blogspot.co.uk. This Belgian-Bolivian-run campsite and lodge is a great budget option. As well as sites to pitch your tent, there are simple three-bed dorms, private rooms, and cabins. Breakfast costs extra. Camping/person B$20, dorms B$35, doubles B$80, cabins B$130

★ **Finca La Víspera** Outside town, 1km south of the plaza ☎ 03 9446082, ⊛ lavispera.org. Sublime rural idyll with fantastic views, a beautiful herb garden and fields with horses, dogs and cats. There's a range of rooms and cabins, each thoughtfully decorated, as well as a campsite (gear is available to rent). They also have a superb café-restaurant (see below). Breakfast costs extra. Camping/person B$50, doubles and cabins B$230

EATING

As a resort town with a significant international community Samaipata has a varied range of restaurants and cafés.

Café 1900 Plaza Principal. *Café 1900* is a good spot at any time of the day with breakfasts, coffee, main meals (B$33–50) such as *coq au vin*, cakes and ice-cream sundaes. Daily 8am–10pm.

Café Jardin At Finca La Víspera. Don't miss out on a meal at this excellent outdoor café. Alongside breakfasts, there are huge omelettes and fresh bread, pasta dishes, tortillas, salads, and a few Southeast Asian stir fries and curries (mains B$45–60). Leave room for the rhubarb tart (B$25). Mon–Wed & Sun 8am–3pm, Thurs–Sat 8am–9pm.

La Cafette Plaza Principal ☎ 7857 5470. Cute little café serving Illy coffee (a cappuccino costs B$12) and hard-to-resist range of quiches, sandwiches, panini, pastries and cakes. Wed–Sat 9am–1pm & 4–8/9pm, Sun 9am–1pm & 4–6pm.

La Cocina C Sucre ☎ 6878 2105. Snazzy, super-popular joint with a handful of tables and seats at the counter, and a selection of high-quality burgers, burritos, falafel wraps and more, plus great chips (B$30 or so gets you a good feed). Tues–Sat 6–10pm.

DRINKING

★ **La Boheme** C Rubén Terrazas, at Sucre ☎ 6091 1243, ⊛ labohemebar.net. Easily the best bar in town, with a welcoming vibe, regular live music (cover charge around B$20), shisha pipes, book exchange and fine range of draught and bottled beer (from B$20) and cocktails. If you get peckish, you can order food (at no extra cost) from *La Cocina* (see above). Tues–Thurs 5pm–midnight, Fri & Sat 5pm–3am, Sun 5pm–1am.

DIRECTORY

Money There's a Banco Union (and a not especially reliable Visa-only ATM) on Campero, just east of the plaza; it's worth bringing some cash with you.

Laundry The nameless house opposite *Andoriña* offers a laundry service.

VALLEGRANDE AND LA HIGUERA

West of Samaipata on the old road from Santa Cruz to Cochabamba, a side road leads to the market town of **VALLEGRANDE**. Vallegrande leapt briefly to the world's attention in 1967, when it witnessed the end game of a doomed guerrilla campaign led by Cuban revolutionary hero, **Ernesto "Che" Guevara** (see below). A ten- to fifteen-minute walk northeast of Plaza 26 de Enero is the new **Centro Cultural Ernesto Che Guevara**,

---

REVOLUTIONARY CHE

Probably the most famous revolutionary of the twentieth century, Ernesto "Che" Guevara was executed in the hamlet of **La Higuera** about 50km south of Vallegrande on October 9, 1967. Visitors to the area may be surprised to learn that this iconic hero spent his final days hiding out in a remote ravine with only a few bedraggled followers. An Argentine-born doctor, Che became a close ally of Fidel Castro during the Cuban Revolution and then turned his sights to Bolivia, which he hoped would prove to be the kick-off point for a continent-wide revolution.

With a small band of rebel followers, Che tried to drum up support for change, but CIA-backed Bolivian troops were determined to quell any kind of revolution, and he was soon forced into hiding.

When Che was eventually captured, his last words, reportedly, were: "Shoot, coward, you are only going to kill a man". His body was flown to Vallegrande and put on display for the world's press in the town hospital. Today Che's mausoleum and the hamlet of La Higuera attract a steady trickle of pilgrims.

which features his mausoleum, a small museum, library, room for film screenings, snack bar and souvenir shop. The centre, the graves of some of Che's comrades, and the Hospital Señor de Malta (where Che's body was displayed) can only be visited on a Spanish-language guided tour (daily 8.30am, 11.30am, 2.30pm & 4.30pm; 1hr 30min–2hr 30min; B$40), which can be booked at the office opposite the Plaza 26 de Enero.

La Higuera

La Higuera, the hamlet where Che met his end, lies about 50km south of Vallegrande. It's a modest collection of simple adobe houses with tiled roofs and a one-room **Museo Histórico del Che** (no fixed opening hours, just ask around for the key; B$10) in the old school where Che was killed.

ARRIVAL AND INFORMATION

By bus A couple of daily buses run to Vallegrande from Samaipata (3hr 30min) and Santa Cruz (6–7hr). La Higuera can be reached by taxi or lorry from Vallegrande in 2–3hr, or by getting buses to Pucará from Vallegrande and getting local transport from there.

Tours Both Vallegrande and La Higuera can be visited on a tour (US$200–250); try agencies in Samaipata (see page 214) or Santa Cruz (see page 212).

ACCOMMODATION

Hostal Juanita Vallegrande ☎03 9422231, ✉hostaljuanita@cotas.net. A friendly place with reasonable rooms, though housekeeping standards aren't always as high as they should be. No breakfast. B$160
La Casa del Telegrafista La Higuera ☎7160 7893, ✉casadeltelegrafista@gmail.com. This French-run lodge has atmospheric stone-walled rooms. The owners offer hikes and can provide meals. Breakfast costs extra. Camping per person B$30, doubles B$180

CHIQUITOS: THE JESUIT MISSIONS

East of Santa Cruz stretches a vast, sparsely populated plain which gradually gives way to swamp as it approaches the border with Brazil. Named **CHIQUITOS** by the Spanish, this region was the scene of one of the most extraordinary episodes in Spanish colonial history. In the eighteenth century, a handful of Jesuit priests established a series of flourishing mission towns, where previously hostile indigenous Chiquitanos converted to Catholicism, adopting European agricultural techniques and building some of the most **magnificent colonial churches** in South America. This theocratic, socialist utopia ended in 1767, when the Spanish Crown expelled the Jesuits from the Americas. Six of the ten Jesuit mission churches have since been restored and are recognized as UNESCO World Heritage Sites. Their incongruous splendour in the midst of the wilderness is one of the most remarkable sights in Bolivia.

The six missions can be visited in a five- to seven-day loop by road and rail from Santa Cruz. A rough road runs northeast to **San Javier** and **Concepción**, then continues to **San Ignacio** (from where the churches of **San Miguel**, **San Rafael** and **Santa Ana** can all be visited by taxi in a day). From San Ignacio, the road heads south to **San José**. Buses connect all these mission towns as far as San José, from where you can get the train back to Santa Cruz or continue east to the Brazilian border. Alternatively, many agencies in Santa Cruz (see page 212) organize tours to the missions.

THE CHACO

South of the Santa Cruz–Quijarro railway line, the tropical dry forest gradually gives way to **the Chaco**, a vast and arid landscape that stretches beyond the **Paraguayan border**. The Chaco is one of the last great wildernesses of South America and supports plentiful wildlife, including jaguars, peccaries and deer – much of it protected by the 34,000-square-kilometre **Parque Nacional Kaa-Iya del Gran Chaco**, the largest protected area in South America. There are no organized tourist facilities in the Chaco, so your view of the region will likely be limited to what you can see from the window of a bus or train, either down the region's western edge to the towns of **Villamontes** and **Yacuiba**, which is on the Argentine border, or along the rough **trans-Chaco road** which makes for the Paraguayan border at **Hito Villazón**.

The Amazon Basin

About a third of Bolivia lies within the **Amazon Basin**, a sparsely populated and largely untamed lowland region of swamp, savannah and tropical rainforest, which supports a bewildering diversity of plant and animal life. Roads are poor in the best of conditions, and in the rainy season (Nov–April) often completely impassable; even in the dry season sudden downpours can quickly turn them into quagmires.

The small town of **Rurrenabaque**, on the banks of the Río Beni, is the region's key tourist destination, thanks to its proximity to the pristine forests of the **Parque Nacional Madidi**, one of Bolivia's most stunning protected areas.

The capital of the Beni – the northeastern lowlands region – is **Trinidad**, the starting point for slow boat journeys down the **Río Mamoré** to the Brazilian border or south into the **Chapare**. From Trinidad, a long and rough road heads west across the Llanos de Moxos, passing through the **Reserva del Biosfera del Beni** before joining the main road into the region from La Paz at Yucumo.

Meanwhile, from Rurrenabaque a dirt road continues north across a wide savannah-covered plain towards the remote backwater of the **Northern Amazon Frontier**, more than 500km away. As the road draws near to **Riberalta**, the largest city in the region, the savannah gives way to dense

THE AMAZON

0   100
kilometres

BRAZIL

Río Branco

Río Abuná

Río Acre

Río Madeira

Cachuela
Esperanza

Guajará-Mirim

Asis Brazil

Brasiléia

Río Orthon

Guayaramerín

Iñapari
Cobija

Riberalta

Río Tahuamanu

Porvenir

Río Manuripi

Río Madre de Dios

BRAZIL

San Silvestre

RESERVA NACIONAL
AMAZONICA
MANURIPI-HEATH

Río Itenez o Guaporé

Chivé

Puerto Heath

Río Madidi

Laguna
Ginebra

Río Mamoré

Río Itonamas

Bella Vista

Puerto
Maldonado

PERU

Magdalena

Río Beni

Santa Ana
de Yacuma

Río San Miguel

PARQUE
NACIONAL
MADIDI

Ixiamas

Tumupasa

Santa
Rosa

Yacuma

Río Maniqui

Río Bianco

Río Negro

Río Tuichi

Reyes

Río Beni

RESERVA DE
LA BIOSFERA
DEL BENI

L
L
A
N
O
S
   D
E

Río Heath

Rurrenabaque

RESERVA
PILON LAJAS

San
Borja

El Porvenir

Trinidad

Casarabé

M
O
X
O
S

Yacumo

San Ignacio
de Moxos

Caranavi

Río Sécure

Lago
Titicaca

Coroico

PARQUE NACIONAL Y
TERRITORIO INDIGENA
ISIBORO-SÉCURE

Copacabana

LA PAZ

N

2

Amazonian rainforest. East of Riberalta, the road continues 100km to **Guayaramerín**, on the banks of the Río Mamoré, which is the main border crossing point if you're heading north into Brazil.

RURRENABAQUE

Set on the banks of the Río Beni about 400km by road north of La Paz, the small town of **RURRENABAQUE** (or "Rurre") is the most popular ecotourism destination in the Bolivian Amazon. Popular targets from here include the spectacular rainforests of the **Parque Nacional Madidi** and the **Reserva de Biosfera y Territorio Indígena Pilón Lajas,** as well as the wildlife-rich pampas along the **Río Yacuma,** all of which are easily visited with one of Rurrenabaque's numerous tour agencies.

A fixture on the backpacker trail for many years, Rurre now has an **uncertain future** thanks to the devastating 2014 floods, falling tourist numbers (blamed by many on higher visa fees for some nationalities,

as well as flood disruption), and the plans for a major hydroelectric project nearby.

WHAT TO SEE AND DO

Surrounded by rainforest-covered hills, there is little in the way of formal sights in Rurre but it's an enjoyable town to watch the boats go by on the mighty Río Beni or just relax in a hammock. If you've an afternoon to spare, head up to one of the swimming pool miradors: **Oscar's** (daily 10.30am–1am; free entry after 6pm otherwise B$40), in the hills north of town, is the most popular choice. Ask a *mototaxi* to take you (around B$20).

ARRIVAL AND DEPARTURE

By plane Due to often impassable roads, many people choose to fly to Rurrenabaque. Amazonas (Comercio, at Santa Cruz; ☎03 8922472, ⓦamaszonas.com), has several daily flights in nineteen-seat, twin-prop planes that ensure a condor's-eye view of the Cordillera Real, the Yungas and the rainforest. Planes arrive at the tiny airport just north of the town, and are met by a shuttle bus (B$10; 10min) that will take you to the Amazonas office (this is also where you catch a bus back to the airport). In addition to Amazonas,

RURRENABAQUE

Airport (5km), Bus Station (5km), La Paz (415km) & Riberalta (510km)

18 DE NOVIEMBRE

JUNIN

COMERCIO

AYAROA

BOLIVAR

BUSCH

Migración

ANCIETO ARCE

ATM

Río Beni

PANDO

Mercado

Ferry to San Buenaventura (300m)

SANTA CRUZ

Bala Tours

TAM

Flecha

Amazonas

Villa Alcira Zipline Canopy Tours

Madidi Travel

Mapajo Ecoturismo Indígena

VACA DIEZ

ATM

San Miguel del Bala Ecolodge

Chalalán Office

CAMPERO

PLAZA 2 DE FEBRERO

Nra. Sra.de la Candelaria

LUIS F. PELLICIOLI

(200m) & (200m)

DRINKING	
Funky Monkey Bar	2
Luna Lounge	3
Moskkito Jungle Bar	4
El Nomádico	1

EATING	
Casa de Campo	4
Juliano's	2
Luz de Mar	1
Panadería Paris	3

ACCOMMODATION	
Hostal El Lobo	4
Hotel Los Tucanes de Rurre	1
Hotel Oriental	3
Hotel Rurrenabaque	2

0 — 500 metres

PARQUE NACIONAL MADIDI

On Rurre's doorstep, and spanning nearly nineteen thousand square kilometres, **Parque Nacional Madidi** (entry B$200) has some of the most diverse plant and animal life in the world. It encompasses a variety of Andean and Amazonian ecosystems and the wildlife is astonishing: more than seven hundred species of animal have been recorded, along with over a thousand species of bird (this represents a staggering eleven percent of the world's total bird species).

While you should treat viewing **wildlife** as a bonus rather than the main purpose of a visit, on a standard three- or four-day trip you should spot a fair amount of the local fauna, including monkeys, capybaras, caymans and a veritable cornucopia of birds, including toucans, macaws and parrots. If you're lucky you may also see larger animals like the jaguar or tapir.

It is also important to be aware of the dark clouds on the horizon for the park, as the Bolivian government continues to push ahead with a major **hydroelectric project** in the region. If it goes ahead, around two thousand square kilometres of land could be flooded, threatening the lives and livelihoods of thousands of indigenous people and the fragile ecosystem of one of the world's most significant protected areas.

2

military airline TAM (☎02 268111, ⍟tam.bo) also has three weekly flights to/from La Paz, and small-scale operator Alas (☎6938 6507) has three weekly flights to/from Trinidad. Flight cancellations are common during the rainy season.
Destinations La Paz (4–6 daily; 30–40min); Trinidad (3 weekly; 30min).
By bus/micro Buses and micros use the Terminal Terrestre, near the airport; a taxi to/from the town centre costs B$10. The times given below are for optimum dry season conditions – even a short cloudburst can extend them considerably. A new road now connects Rurrenabaque and Trinidad, though it's still an arduous journey.
Destinations La Paz (3 daily; 20–24hr); Riberalta (1–2 daily; 20–30hr); Trinidad (1–3 daily; 20–30hr); Yolosa (for connections to Coroico; 3 daily; 14–20hr).
By boat When the road is closed in the rainy season, motorized canoes occasionally carry passengers between Rurrenabaque and Guanay, a small town about 230km northwest of La Paz (6–8hr), and Riberalta (8–10 days).

INFORMATION

Tourist information The tourist office (C Comercio, at Campero; Mon–Sat 8am–noon & 2.30–6pm) has maps,

★ **TREAT YOURSELF**

A five-hour boat ride from Rurre, the spectacular **Chalalán Albergue Ecológico** is deep in Madidi beside the Río Tuichi. It overlooks a lagoon, the surrounding forest is covered by 25km of trails, and accommodation is in thatched wooden cabins. Tours cost from $399 (B$2713) per person; combined pampas trips also available. It has an office in Rurre on Calle Comercio, near the plaza (☎03 892 2419, ⍟chalalan.com).

limited materials on the parks, a list of authorized tour agencies, and detailed questionnaires filled in by previous travellers.
Banks Banco FIE (Comercio, at Aniceto Arce) and Banco Unión (Comercio, at Vaca Díez) both have ATMs, but bring sufficient cash with you in case they don't accept your card. You can obtain a cash advance at Prodem on the corner of Pando and Avaroa.

ACCOMMODATION

Hostal El Lobo C Comercio, at Ballivián ☎7012 5362, ⍟ellobohostel.com; map p.218. Around 500m south of Plaza 2 de Febrero, this solid choice has tidy dorms and rooms (with shared or private bathrooms, TVs, and communal balconies overlooking the river), a pool, restaurant and games' room. The mozzies, however, are ferocious. Dorms B$100, doubles B$180
Hotel Los Tucanes de Rurre C Aniceto Arce, at Bolívar ☎03 8922039, ⍟hotel-tucanes.com; map p.218. The thatched-roof reception suggests the rooms are slightly smarter than they are, but this is nevertheless one of the nicer budget options, and even if the rooms (with private or shared bathrooms) need a fresh lick of paint, they're clean and cool enough, and are grouped around a small bar. B$100
Hotel Oriental Plaza 2 de Febrero ☎03 8922401; map p.218. This ever-reputable, family-run hotel remains one of Rurre's better budget options, with cool, comfortable rooms (some with private bathrooms) set around a peaceful courtyard garden with hammocks. B$150
Hotel Rurrenabaque C Vaca Díez, at Bolívar ☎03 8922481, ✉hotelrurrenabaque@hotmail.com; map p.218. As the oldest two-storey house in town, this is the place to stay if you want some character, though the faded yellow-and-red sign indicates that it has seen better days. The rooms themselves are clean and – owing to the thickness of the old walls – slightly cooler than you'll find

2

TOUR AGENCIES IN RURRENABAQUE

A huge number of tour agencies offer trips to the rainforest and the pampas lowlands, generally lasting three nights. Most guides speak only Spanish, but agencies can usually arrange an English-speaking interpreter. Prices do not normally include the Parque Nacional Madidi or Pampas del Yacuma entry fees (B$200 and B$150, respectively). Beware super-cheap tours – corners will have been cut, both in your comfort and from a conservation point of view – and check the size of the group before booking. It's also a good idea to book a room for your return.

TOUR OPERATORS

Bala Tours Av Santa Cruz, at C Comercio ☎ 03 8922527, ⊛ balatours.com. Well-regarded operator offering three-day pampas and *selva* tours for around US$240 (B$1632), with jungle accommodation in their Río Tuichi lodge, plus a five-day option for around US$440 (B$2992) and specialist three- or five-day bird-watching tours from US$330 (B$2244).

Madidi Travel C Comercio, at Av Santa Cruz ☎ 03 8922153, ⊛ madidi-travel.com. Accommodation (three-day tours B$1899/person) at its private reserve, Serere, around 3hr by boat from Rurre, is in spartan yet stylish, two-storey cabañas. A healthy population of big cats such as pumas, jaguars and ocelots attests to the health of the area's ecosystem, and daily walks are led by excellent guides.

Mapajo Ecoturismo Indígena C Comercio ☎ 6801 0508, ✉ mapajo.ecoturismo.indigena@gmail.com. The *Albergue Ecológico Mapajo*, in the Reserva de Biosfera y Territorio Indígena Pilon Lajas, is 3hr from Rurre. A two- to six-day visit to the lodge – from $180(B$1224) per person – offers excellent opportunities for exploring the rainforest and spotting wildlife, as well as the chance to visit the local communities.

San Miguel del Bala Ecolodge C Comercio, at Vaca Díez ☎ 03 8922394, ⊛ sanmigueldelbala.com. Not the best option for spotting animals but excellent for a cultural experience of a Tacana community, and near enough to Rurre for a day-trip if you're in a rush (30min by motor canoe).

Villa Alcira Zip Line Canopy Tours C Comercio, at Av Santa Cruz ☎ 03 8923875, ⊛ tusoco.com/villa-alcira. Run by the Tacana community of Villa Alcira (15min from Rurre by boat) and offering two daily tours (8am & 2pm; B$300, plus B$35 "community entry fee") on 1200m of cable and across nine platforms. You can also stay overnight (doubles around B$680)

---

elsewhere, and some are en suite. There's a communal balcony, a sizeable garden, restaurant and laundry service. **B$130**

EATING

Time is an elastic concept at Rurre's **restaurants**; don't be surprised to find somewhere closed when it should be open, or, occasionally in the middle of the afternoon for the whole town to be minus any eating options at all (eat a decent breakfast). Most restaurants double up as bars (and vice versa).

★ **Casa de Campo** C Comercio, at Ballivián, by Hotel Lobo ☎ 7921 5612; map p.218. One of the best restaurants in Rurre, in a tranquil location around 500m south of Plaza 2 de Febrero. Perfect if you're lusting after something more healthy and wholesome than standard backpacker food, with a menu of natural fruit juices, quinoa and pumpkin soups, salads and delicious croissants (mains B$30–60). Daily 8am–2pm & 6–10pm.

Juliano's Av Santa Cruz, at C Bolívar ☎ 7392 0088; map p.218. A sophisticated spot (by Rurre standards at least) for a night out, *Juliano's* has a cosmopolitan menu and an easygoing atmosphere. As well as the usual fish, meat and pasta dishes (B$30–60), they also do thin-crust pizzas,

North African-style chicken and crispy calamari. Save room for the crème brulee. Daily 5–11pm.

Luz de Mar C Avaroa ☎ 7320 2501; map p.218. Rightly popular café-restaurant, this is one of the few in town that is (fairly) reliably open during the day. The menu ranges from pastries, cakes and sandwiches (try the cheese-and-chive empanadas; B$10) to standard mains (around B$40s), with drinks including juices, shakes, beer and cocktails. Tues–Sun 7.30am–10.30pm.

Panadería Paris C Avaroa, at Av Santa Cruz; map p.218. It might be a bit scruffy but this is a honeypot for tourists in the morning, who come for wonderful pastries (the *pain au chocolat* is particularly good) and rolls. Add a coffee, juice or *smoothie* for an excellent breakfast (B$12–20 in total). Mon–Fri 6.30am–12.30pm & 3.30–6.30pm, Sat 6.30am–12.30pm (or until they run out).

DRINKING

Funky Monkey Bar C Comercio, diagonally opposite the Amaszonas office ☎ 7255 9023; map p.218. The *Funky Monkey* is better as a bar than a restaurant, with friendly staff, a cache of cocktails (around B$30–50), and a raucous, rock-heavy soundtrack. Daily 5pm–midnight.

2

RAINFOREST TRIPS FROM TRINIDAD

Trinidad makes a great base for birdwatching excursions into the surrounding wilderness, boat trips or visits to remnants of the Moxos culture.

Paraíso Travel Av 6 de Agosto 138 ☎ 03 4620692, ✉ lyliamgonzalez@hotmail.com. Well-run agency with excellent guides offering trips in and around Trinidad, including bike tours (full-day B$250) and rental (B$100/day), and excursions to explore the nearby *lomas*.

Turismo Moxos Av 6 de Agosto 114 ☎ 03 4621141, ✉ moxosibc@hotmail.com. Offers a variety of one- to three-day trips into the rainforest by motorized canoe along the Río Ibare, a tributary of the Mamoré, with plenty of opportunity for seeing wildlife (including pink dolphins) and visiting indigenous communities. Horseriding also available.

Luna Lounge C Avaroa, at Av Santa Cruz ☎ 03 8922719; map p.218. Open during the day for decent thin-crust pizza and a variety of omelettes (mains B$40–60), this is also more of a bar than a restaurant, with bamboo walls and shell drapes. There's a pool table and book exchange. Happy hour 7–11pm daily. Mon–Sat 9am–3am, Sun 6pm–3am.

Moskkito Jungle Bar C Vaca Díez ☎ 03 8922267, ⓦ moskkito.com; map p.218. Dating back to 1999, and something of a Rurre legend, this convivial bar is popular with locals and travellers alike, with cold beer and suggestively named cocktails (from B$20; happy hour daily 7–9pm), a booming rock soundtrack, pool table and dartboard. Skip the mediocre food, though. Daily 4pm–3am.

★ **El Nomádico** C Avaroa ☎ 7284 3850; map p.218. Although it describes itself as the "best kept secret in Rurre", this bar-restaurant is far from in the shadows. As well as a fine selection of drinks (beer from B$20; daily happy hour 7–9pm), there's sport on TV, and good food. Mon–Thurs 6pm–12.30am, Fri 6pm–2.30am, Sat 4pm–2.30am, Sun noon–12.30am.

TRINIDAD

Close to the Río Mamoré, the city of **TRINIDAD** is the capital of the Beni and a modern commercial city dominated by a vigorous cattle-ranching culture and economy. Hot and humid, with few real attractions, Trinidad doesn't really merit a visit in its own right. It is, however, the jumping-off point for adventurous trips into the surrounding landscape.

WHAT TO SEE AND DO

Though most of its buildings are modern, Trinidad maintains the classic layout of a Spanish colonial town, its streets set out in a neat grid around a central square, the **Plaza Ballivián**, shaded by tall trees hiding three-toed sloths.

Some 1.8km north of the town centre, the illuminating **Museo Etnoarqueológico del Beni Kenneth Lee** (Mon–Fri 9am–12.30pm & 2.30-6pm, Sat & Sun by appointment; B$10; ☎ 03 462 4519) focuses on the emerging research that suggests a mighty and sophisticated civilization existed in the Amazon basin between 3000 and 1000 BC. It was the fruit of the labour of Texan engineer Kenneth Lee, who visited the area for work and became impassioned by the Moxos peoples and their highly advanced hydro-agricultural systems of raised fields and earth mounds (*lomas*).

ARRIVAL AND DEPARTURE

By plane The airport is 2km northwest of town; a *mototaxi* to the centre costs around B$10–12; regular taxis charge at least B$25.

Destinations Cochabamba (1–2 daily; 50min); Guayaramerín (5 weekly; 50min); La Paz (1–2 daily; 55min); Riberalta (1–2 daily; 50min); Rurrenabaque (3 weekly; 30min); Santa Cruz (6 weekly; 50min).

By bus The Terminal Terrestre is on Av Mendoza, at C Viador Pinto Saucedo, eight blocks east from the centre of town. Services from San Borja arrive just behind the terminal on Av Beni).

Destinations Guayaramerín (1–2 daily; 25–28hr); Rurrenabaque (1–3 daily; 20–30hr); Santa Cruz (18–22 daily; 9–10hr)

By boat Along the Río Mamoré arriving from, or departing for, Guayaramerín (2–3 weekly; 3–7 days) or Puerto Villarroel (2–3 weekly; 7 days), boats usually dock at Puerto Almacén, 9km southwest of Plaza Ballivián on the Río Ibare (a Mamoré tributary). *Moto-taxis* run back into town (around B$25).

INFORMATION

Tourist information The main tourist office is at C Felix Pinto Saucedo, at Nicolás Suárez (Mon–Fri 8.30am–

2

COMPLEJO TURÍSTICO ECOLÓGICO Y ARQUELÓGICO CHUCHINI

Some 14km northwest of Trinidad, the **Complejo Turístico Ecológico y Arqueológico Chuchini** (daily 8am–6pm; B$20; guided half-day tours B$100, one-day tours with accommodation, transfers and board B$600; transfers between Trinidad and Chuchini B$100 one-way; ☎ 7284 2200, ⓦchuchini.org) is based on a Moxos *loma*. Set on the edge of a glorious lagoon, the reserve has trails through the surrounding rainforest, home to toucans, monkeys, coatis and many other species. There's also a fascinating **museum** filled with exhibits from the Moxos culture and dinosaur fossils. Activities include boat trips, guided walks, swimming and fishing. Although you can visit for the day, it's well worth staying overnight (or longer) to make the most of the place; accommodation is in clean and spacious en-suite rooms, while meals are tasty and copious. Volunteering opportunities available too.

12.30pm & 2.30–6pm; ☎03 4621322). The local hotel association has a small, helpful office on Av 6 de Agosto, by *Hotel Campanario* (Mon–Fri 8.30am–12.30pm & 2.30–6pm; ☎03 4621141).
Money There are ATMs all over town, and cambios on Av 6 de Agosto between C Suárez and Av 18 de Noviembre.

ACCOMMODATION

Hostal Santa Anita C Antonio Vaca Díez 354 ☎03 4622257. This family-run hostel has bright, capacious and spotlessly clean rooms complete with private hammock and either fans or a/c, giving onto a slender, leafy patio. Masks and painted plant pots add some pizzazz. B$180
Hostal Sirari C Santa Cruz 526 ☎03 4624472, ✉hsirari@hotmail.com. Though they could do with a little sprucing up, the *Sirari*'s ageing, beamed-ceiling rooms complement what has to be the most verdant courtyard in Trinidad, with a trio of toucans. The lower rooms also come with white-painted, glass-panelled doors, while the upper rooms are more modern; a/c rooms cost around B$40 extra. B$170

EATING

La Casona Plaza Ballivián ☎03 4622437. This Trini institution is always busy, and a life-saver on Sunday evenings when everyone else has shut up shop. Along with *almuerzos*, they serve up relatively pricey (B$50–90) steak, fried river fish and kebabs. Daily 8am–11pm/midnight.

Club Social Plaza Ballivián, at C Suárez. A vast, elegant dining hall with a rather old-fashioned feel, serving up good-value, filling *almuerzos* and standard Bolivian dishes like *pique macho* (mains B$30–60). Daily 11am–2.30pm & 6–10pm.
La Estancia C Ibare, at Av Pedro Ignacio Muiba ☎03 4620022. The premier steakhouse in Trinidad, *La Estancia* offers prime cuts in gut-busting portions. If there are two or more of you, go for the *parrillada*, a mixed grill accompanied by an array of sides (from B$140). Mon & Wed–Sun 11am–3pm & 7–11.45pm.

RIBERALTA

Set on a bluff above a great sweep of the Río Madre de Dios, just after its silt-laden waters are joined by those of the Río Beni, sleepy, sun-baked RIBERALTA is the second-biggest town in the Amazon lowlands, with a population of about 80,000, largely employed in the brazil nut industry. There's no great reason to stop unless you're heading for Brazil (see page 213), though there's a certain charm to the place that makes it the most likeable of the Northern Amazon outposts.

INTO BRAZIL

From the port at the bottom of Av Federico Román, regular passenger boats (daily 6am–6pm; every 30min; additional services 6pm–6am at irregular times; B$10) make the 5min **crossing** to Guajará-Mirim in Brazil. The Bolivian (Mon–Fri 8am–8pm, Sat & Sun 8am–noon) is to the right of the port as you face the river: get an exit stamp here if you're continuing into Brazil but it's not necessary if you're just making a day-trip across the river. **From Guajará-Mirim** there are frequent buses to Porto Velho, from where there are connections to other destinations in Brazil.

If you need a **visa**, go to the Brazilian consulate (Mon–Fri 9am–noon & 3–5pm; ☎03 8553766) on the corner of calles Beni and 24 de Septiembre, four blocks south of the port. To enter Brazil you need to have an international certificate of **yellow fever vaccination**; if you don't, there's a clinic beside the immigration office in Guajará-Mirim.

2

ARRIVAL AND DEPARTURE

By plane The tiny airport is about 1km south of town (around B$5 by *mototaxi*). At the time of writing the only direct scheduled flights were with Ecojet to Trinidad (1–2 daily; 50min). An alternative is one of the daily *avionetas* (air taxis) that leave when full and fly direct to Guayaramerín.

By bus The potholed terminal is at the eastern edge of town, 2km from Plaza Principal (around B$5 on a *mototaxi*). Destinations Guayaramerín (5–6 daily; 2hr 30min–3hr); La Paz (1–2 daily; 35–40hr); Rurrenabaque (1–2 daily; 20–30hr); Trinidad (1 daily; 28hr).

By boat Occasional boats head up the Madre de Dios to Puerto Maldonado in Peru: departures are posted up outside the Capitanía del Puerto office at Puerto El Pila 1km east of town. Boats also occasionally travel to Rurrenabaque when the road is closed during the rainy season.

ACCOMMODATION AND EATING

★ **Hotel Colonial** C Plácido Méndez 745, just off the plaza ☎ 03 8523018, ⌨ hotelcolonialriberalta. boliviafull.com. One of the nicest surprises in this part of the Amazon, this tranquil hotel has whitewashed rooms hidden behind a curtain of tropical fronds. There's an elegant common area and an overflowing patio garden. B$280

Residencial Los Reyes C Sucre 781, at Oruro ☎ 03 8522628. If *bolivianos* are tight, try the *Residencial Los Reyes*, near the airport. As well as simple rooms, there are hammocks in the garden courtyard, and free coffee and chilled drinking water. B$80

★ **Restaurante Tropical** C Oruro 632, eight blocks south of the plaza ☎ 7293 0188. If you can get past the trophy skins and armadillo shells, this is an enjoyable restaurant, with huge portions (easily enough for two; B$50–110) of *pique a lo macho* (a pile of beef strips, French fries, eggs, peppers and onions) and fried river fish. Mon–Sat noon–3pm & 7pm–midnight, Sun noon–3pm.

GUAYARAMERÍN

On the banks of the Río Mamoré some 86km east of Riberalta, **GUAYARAMERÍN** is the main crossing point on Bolivia's northern border, a modern frontier town with a distinctly Brazilian flavour and a thriving economy based on duty-free sales. Most people only come here to cross into Brazil (see page 213).

ARRIVAL AND DEPARTURE

By plane The airport is four blocks east of the plaza. At the time of writing the only direct scheduled flights were with Ecojet to Trinidad (5 weekly; 50min). *Avionetas* (air taxis) serve other destinations on an ad-hoc basis.

By bus The Terminal de Buses is about 3km outside the town centre; a *mototaxi* costs about B$5–10. Buses to Riberalta leave throughout the day; only in the dry season services attempt the long journeys to Trinidad and Rurrenabaque.

Destinations La Paz (1–2 daily; 32hr); Riberalta (5–6 daily; 2hr 30min–3hr); Rurrenabaque (1daily; 26–48hr); Trinidad (1–2 daily; 25–28hr).

INFORMATION

Tourist information There's no tourist office but Mary Tours, on the north side of the main plaza (Oruro; ☎ 03 8553883, ✉ mary-tours@hotmail.com) is a good source of information.

Banks and exchange Cooperativa Jesús Nazareno on C Mariscal Santa Cruz, at Av 24 de Septiembre, on the northeast corner of the main plaza, has an ATM that should accept foreign cards; you can also obtain a cash advance on a credit card and change dollars and Brazilian reais. Prodem on Plaza Principal can also give cash advances on credit/ debit cards.

ACCOMMODATION

Hotel Santa Ana Av 25 de Mayo 611 ☎ 03 8553900. As the sole salubrious option on this street, *Hotel Santa Ana*'s timber-ceilinged rooms are best booked in advance, thus avoiding the gaggle of hopefuls that fill up reception after a flight. Relax in the cool courtyard garden instead, and look forward to some to some old-fashioned hospitality. B$150

IGUAÇU FALLS

Brazil

❶ **Rio de Janeiro** Sunbathing and samba in a stunning urban setting. See page 237

❷ **Cidades Históricas** Cobbled colonial streets, architectural gems and great food. See page 262

❸ **Salvador** Take in pulsating street life and the Afro-Brazilian martial art Capoeira. See page 277

❹ **Chapada Diamantina** Hike canyons and jump waterfalls in the Northeastern interior. See page 287

❺ **Iguaçu Falls** Straddling Argentina and Brazil is one of the planet's most impressive natural wonders. See page 351

HIGHLIGHTS ARE MARKED ON THE MAP ON PAGE 228

ROUGH COSTS

Daily budget Rio de Janeiro, São Paulo and Brasília: US$70/The North and Northeast: US$50
Drink Beer (600ml bottle) US$2.50
Food *Prato comercial/prato feito* (basic set meal) US$6–7
Hostel US$13–20
Travel Rio–São Paulo (352km) by bus, US$30

FACT FILE

Population 210 million (est. 2018)
Language Portuguese
Currency Real (R$)
Capital Brasília (population 3 million)
International phone code ☏55
Time zone GMT -2/-5hr

Introduction

Brazil has an energy like no other nation on earth. Unified through open-armed hospitality and the combined passions of football, the beach and all that's beautiful, even the glaring gap between rich and poor somehow fails to distract Brazilians from a determination to succeed – and party hard along the way. It's a huge country (larger than the United States excluding Alaska) with all the diverse scenic and cultural variety you'd expect, from Bahian beaches to Amazonian jungles. But Brazil is cosmopolitan too. You could as easily find yourself dancing samba until sunrise as you could eating sashimi amid a crowd of Japanese Brazilians. Rio and São Paulo are two of the world's great metropolises and fifteen other cities each have more than a million inhabitants.

3

Brazilians are one of the most **ethnically diverse** peoples in the world. In the south, German, Ukrainian and Italian immigration has left distinctive European features; São Paulo has the world's largest Japanese community outside Japan; while centred principally in Salvador and Rio is the largest black population outside Africa. Indigenous influence pervades the entire country but is especially evident in Amazonia and the northeastern interior. Enormous natural resources and rapid postwar industrialization have made it one of the world's ten largest economies, but **socio-economic contradictions** mean that this hasn't improved the lives of many of its citizens: there is a vast (and growing) middle class, yet all Brazil's cities are strewn with **favelas** (shantytowns) and slums.

Nowhere, however, do people know how to enjoy themselves more – most famously in the orgiastic annual four-day celebrations of **Carnaval**, but also reflected in the lively year-round nightlife you'll find almost everywhere. Brazil's vibrant arts, theatre and design scenes are accompanied by the most relaxed and tolerant attitude to **sexuality**, at any point on the spectrum, of anywhere in South America. And the country's hedonism also manifests itself in a highly developed **beach culture**, superb music and dancing, and rich regional cuisines.

CHRONOLOGY

1500 Off course, en route to India on behalf of Portugal, Pedro Álvares Cabral lands in Bahia.

1502 Amerigo Vespucci enters Guanabara Bay and calls it Rio de Janeiro.

1537 Olinda founded.

1549 King João unifies 15 hereditary captaincies under governor-general Tomé de Sousa, who founds Salvador, the first capital. Portuguese settlers begin to flow in.

1555 French take possession of Rio area and are finally expelled by the Portuguese in 1567.

1574 Jesuits given control of converted indigenous peoples.

1630 Dutch West India Company fleet captures Pernambuco.

1654 Brazilians, without Portuguese aid, defeat and expel the Dutch.

1695 *Bandeirantes* discover gold in Minas Gerais.

1757 Slavery of indigenous peoples abolished.

1759 Jesuits expelled from Brazil by prime minister Marquis de Pombal.

1763 Capital shifted from Salvador to Rio.

1789 First rebellion against Portuguese ends in defeat when José Joaquim da Silva Xavier, known as Tiradentes, is executed.

1807 Napoleon I invades Portugal. Portuguese prince regent Dom João evacuates to Brazil.

1808 Dom João declares Rio temporary capital of the empire, opens harbours to commerce and abolishes restrictions on Brazilian trade and manufacturing.

1822 With Dom João (King João IV) back in Portugal, his son, Dom Pedro I, declares Brazil independent and crowns himself emperor.

1825–28 Cisplatine War: Uruguay gains independence from Brazil.

1830 Slave trade abolished, but slavery continues.

1864–70 War of the Triple Alliance: Argentina, Brazil and Uruguay crush Paraguay.

1888 Princess Isabel, acting as regent, signs the "Golden Law" abolishing slavery. The following year Dom Pedro II overthrown and Brazil becomes a republic.

WHEN TO VISIT

If **Carnaval** is the main thing on your mind, then try to arrive in Rio, Salvador, Recife or Minas Gerais well before the action – dates change each year from February to early March. This is also the main tourist season and warmest part of the year for most of Brazil (Jan–March), with higher accommodation prices and crowded beaches and hostels. The other big draw is **Reveillon** (New Year), when beds in Rio are especially hard to find. As you go further south it gets noticeably **cooler**, so it's best to visit places like Foz do Iguaçu, Florianópolis and São Paulo between November and April. In the Amazon the less rainy and humid months are between May and October, while the Northeast has pretty good weather all year round.

1912–16 Contestado War; guerrilla revolt in the South.

1930 Great Depression leads to revolution. Getúlio Vargas rises to power.

1937 Vargas declares himself dictator, creates the "New State", the Estado Novo.

1944 Brazil accepts US aid in return for bases, joins Allies in World War II, and sends force to fight in Italy.

1954 Vargas commits suicide after military tells him to resign or be overthrown.

1956 Juscelino Kubitschek elected president with an ambitious economic programme. Construction of Brasília begins.

1958 Brazil wins its first World Cup – it wins again in 1962, 1970 and 1994.

1960 Brasília declared capital of Brazil.

1964 Massive population growth, disparity in wealth, economic inflation and fears of a rising proletariat lead to a military coup.

1968–73 Economy experiences spectacular growth.

1969 General Emilio Garrastazú Médici assumes presidency. Censorship and torture are routine and thousands are driven into exile.

1983–84 Mass campaign in Rio and São Paulo for direct elections.

1985 Tancredo Neves elected first civilian president in 21 years, but dies shortly afterwards. Military rule ends.

1994 Inflation peaks. President Cardoso introduces Real as new currency along with new economic plan.

2002 Liberal former trade union activist Luiz Inácio Lula da Silva elected on promises to curb hunger and create jobs; Brazil wins the World Cup for a fifth time.

2010 Lula succeeded by Dilma Rousseff, Brazil's first female president, on the promise of continuity assisted by discovery of vast new Atlantic oil reserves.

2014 Brazil hosts the World Cup – despite a humiliating 7–1 defeat to Germany in the semi-final, the tournament is considered a success.

2016 Rio de Janeiro hosts the Summer Olympics.

2016 Roussef impeached for corruption; replaced by Michel Temer.

2017 Brazil's economy starts to recover after three years of recession; Temer charged with taking bribes.

ARRIVAL AND DEPARTURE

There are direct **flights** to Rio and São Paulo from Europe, North America, Asia, South Africa, and from most major Latin American cities, while easy connections are available from Australia and New Zealand via Argentina or Chile. Brazil also has a well-developed network of domestic flights. **Direct crossings** are possible from most South American countries, with Colombia and Peru accessed **by boat**, and flights available from Chile, Ecuador and Suriname. If you enter Brazil **overland**, remember that crossing points can be very remote.

FROM ARGENTINA

Most people crossing between Argentina and Brazil do so at the frontier at **Foz do Iguaçu** (see page 351). Another handy crossing further south is at the Argentine city of Paso de los Libres, across the border from **Uruguaiana**, 694km west of Porto Alegre. There are daily **flights** from Buenos Aires to Brazil's main southern and central cities.

FROM BOLIVIA

You can reach Bolivia's southeastern border by train from the station a few kilometres out of Puerto Suárez or by hourly bus from Quijarro. From the border there's frequent transport to the *rodoviária* in **Corumbá**, where you'll find regular onward buses to Campo Grande (5–7hr), São Paulo (21hr) and Rio de Janeiro (26hr). In the north, passenger boats make the ten-minute crossing to **Guajará-Mirim** (see page 223) in Brazil, where there are frequent buses to Porto Velho, for connections to other destinations in Brazil. There are daily **flights** from La Paz to Rio, Salvador, São Paulo and other Brazilian cities.

3

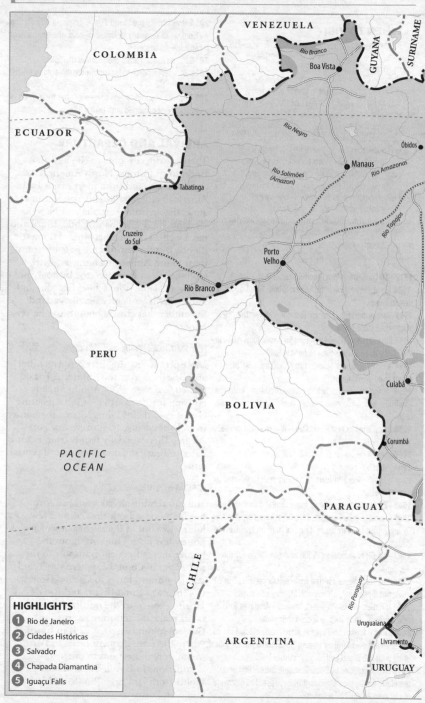

3

HIGHLIGHTS

1. Rio de Janeiro
2. Cidades Históricas
3. Salvador
4. Chapada Diamantina
5. Iguaçu Falls

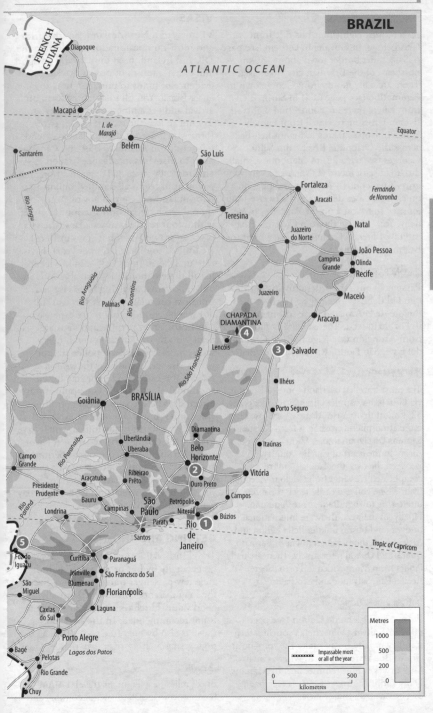

BRAZIL

ATLANTIC OCEAN

FRENCH GUIANA
Oiapoque
Macapá
Santarém
I. de Marajó
Belém
São Luis
Equator
Rio Xingu
Marabá
Teresina
Fortaleza
Aracati
Fernando de Noronha
Natal
Juazeiro do Norte
João Pessoa
Campina Grande
Olinda
Recife
Palmas
Rio Tocantins
Rio Araguaia
Juazeiro
Maceió
CHAPADA DIAMANTINA
Aracaju
Lençóis
Salvador
Rio São Francisco
Ilhéus
Goiânia
BRASÍLIA
Porto Seguro
Rio Paranaíba
Uberlândia
Uberaba
Diamantina
Itaúnas
Campo Grande
Araçatuba
Ribeirao Prêto
Belo Horizonte
Ouro Prêto
Vitória
Presidente Prudente
Bauru
Campinas
São Paulo
Petrópolis
Niterói
Campos
Rio Paraná
Londrina
Paraty
Santos
Rio de Janeiro
Búzios
Tropic of Capricorn
Foz do Iguaçu
Curitiba
Paranaguá
São Miguel
Joinville
Blumenau
São Francisco do Sul
Caxias do Sul
Florianópolis
Laguna
Porto Alegre
Bagé
Lagos dos Patos
Pelotas
Rio Grande
Chuy

1
2
3
4
5

3

Metres
1000
500
200
0

Impassable most or all of the year

0   500
kilometres

3

FROM THE GUIANAS

It's a bumpy eight-hour bus ride from Georgetown in Guyana to **Lethem** (see page 659), a quiet border town about 130km northeast of the Brazilian city Boa Vista. There are daily **flights** from Georgetown to **Paramaribo** (see page 664) in Suriname, from where there are connecting flights to Belém. Crossing to Brazil from French Guiana involves taking a dugout taxi-boat across the Oiapoque River from Saint Georges (see page 28) to **Oiapoque** a small dirt-road settlement. It's smarter to arrive in gritty Oiapoque by daylight and plan on a quick exit; buses depart for the twelve-hour journey to Macapá on the Amazon, twice daily. You can also **fly** from Cayenne (the capital of French Guiana; see page 676) to Belém and Fortaleza.

FROM PARAGUAY

Paraguay's busiest border crossing is from Ciudad del Este (see page 710) over the Puente de la Amistad (Friendship Bridge) to **Foz do Iguaçu**. There are daily **flights** from Asunción (see page 698) to Ciudad del Este, São Paulo, Rio and Porto Alegre.

FROM URUGUAY

The most travelled overland route to Brazil is via **Chuí** (Chuy on the Uruguayan side; p.28), 527km south of Porto Alegre. A less-used but more atmospheric crossing is from Rivera to **Santana Do Livramento**, 497km west of Porto Alegre in the heart of gaucho country. Between the two, there are also more complicated crossings from Melo to Aceguá, from where you can easily reach the more interesting town of **Bagé**, or to **Jaguarão**. Finally, in the west, there are international bridges (and buses) linking Bella Unión and Artigas with the Brazilian towns of **Barra do Quarai** and **Quarai** respectively. There are daily **flights** from Montevideo to Porto Alegre, Recife, Rio, Salvador and São Paulo.

FROM VENEZUELA

From Santa Elena de Uairén (see page 905) in Bolívar (Venezuela's southeastern state) two daily buses make the four-hour trip to **Boa Vista** in Brazil, where you'll find a twelve-hour connection to Manaus. Daily **flights** connect Caracas (see page 874) to Brazil's major cities.

VISAS

Visitors from New Zealand, South Africa and most European nations, including the UK and Ireland, need only a valid passport and either a return or onward ticket or evidence of funds to purchase one, to enter Brazil. You fill in an entry form on arrival and get a ninety-day tourist visa. Try not to lose the receipt of this entry form; you'll need it if you plan to extend. Citizens from **Australia**, **USA** and **Canada** need **tourist visas** in advance, **issued electronically** since 2018; application and payment of fees is all handled **online** at ⓦformulario-mre.serpro.gov.br. You should receive visa confirmation via email within four to five business days (the visa is valid for two years, but stays in Brazil are limited to ninety days per year). E-visa fees are US$40 (plus US$4.24 service fee) for all three nationalities (payable in US$ only); note that applying for a visa at a Brazilian consulate (which you can still do) will be considerably more expensive.

In Brazil, entry permits and visas are dealt with by the **Polícia Federal**. Every state capital has a federal police station with a visa section: ask for the *delagacia federal*. You can extend your stay for an additional ninety days if you apply at least fifteen days before your initial permit or visa expires, but it will only be extended once; if you want to stay longer, you'll have to leave the country and re-enter. A fee of around R$67 is made on tourist permit and **visa extensions**. If you stay past the permit date without having extended it you will be charged around R$8.50 per day before you leave the country.

GETTING AROUND

Travel in Brazil is usually straightforward: it's generally by bus or plane, though there are a few passenger trains, too, and given the long distances involved it's usually good value. Hitchhiking over any distance is not recommended. In the **Amazon**, travel is also by boat (see page 306), a slow yet fascinating river experience.

BY AIR

Brazil relies heavily on air travel. **LATAM** (ⓦlatam.com), **GOL** (ⓦvoegol.com.br) and

Azul (⊚voeazul.com.br) serve most domestic destinations, while **Avianca Brasil** (⊚avianca.com.br) also offers competitive fares. If you plan on flying within Brazil at least four times in thirty days, and don't mind sticking to an itinerary, it makes sense to buy an **airpass** with GOL. These need to be purchased from a travel agent before you depart (you can't buy them online yourself, or in Brazil); passes cost somewhere between US$505 and US$1980 for between four and nine flights. **Departure tax** is included in the price of your international ticket.

BY BUS

Hundreds of bus companies offer services that crisscross Brazil. **Bus travel** prices range from 25 to 75 percent of the cost of air travel, and this is usually the best-value option for journeys of under six hours – although in more remote areas buses tend to be packed and the roads in poor condition. Intercity buses leave from the **rodoviária**, a bus station usually built on city outskirts. **Prices** tend to be similar (though faster or all-night services may be more expensive), and there are often two levels of bus service: the perfectly comfortable *convencional* and marginally more expensive *executivo*; on the latter you're usually supplied with a blanket, newspaper and snack. **Leitos** are luxury buses that do nocturnal runs between major cities, with fully reclining seats in curtained partitions. All long-distance buses are comfortable enough to sleep in, however, and have on-board toilets. Bring water and a sweater for the often-cool air conditioning.

For most journeys it's best to buy your ticket at least a day in advance, from the *rodoviária* or some travel agents. An exception is the Rio–São Paulo route, with services every fifteen minutes. If you cross a state line, you may be asked for proof of ID (your passport is best) when you buy your ticket.

BY CAR

High accident rates, poor signposting, immense urban congestion and heavily potholed rural roads make driving in Brazil hardly a recommendation. Nonetheless, vehicle **rental** is easy, from about R$150/day for a compact car. International companies operate alongside local alternatives like Interlocadora, Localiza Hertz and Unidas – offices (*locadoras*) are at every airport and in most towns. An **international driving licence** is recommended: foreign licences are accepted for visits of up to six months but you may find it tough convincing police of this.

Be wary of driving at night as roads are poorly lit and lightly policed – specifically avoid the **Via Dutra**, linking Rio and São Paulo, due to the huge numbers of trucks at night and the treacherous ascent and descent of the Serra do Mar, and the **Belém–Brasília highway**, whose potholes and uneven asphalt make it difficult enough to drive even in daylight. Outside of big cities, service stations don't always accept international credit cards, so bring cash. If you're stopped by police, they can be intimidating, pointing to trumped-up contraventions when they're probably angling for a bribe. If such an on-the-spot **multa**, or fine, is suggested, it's your choice whether to stand your ground or pay up. Whatever you do, always appear polite. If your passport is confiscated, demand to call your consulate – there should always be a duty officer available.

BY TAXI

Metered **taxis** are easy to flag down and relatively inexpensive, though base fares vary from place to place and rates have risen a lot in recent years. An alternative is the radiotaxi, a metered cab you can call to pick you up. The app-based taxi service **Uber** is widely available in major cities across Brazil and is generally safe to use, though there have been cases of **express kidnappings** in the biggest cities – to be safe, don't get into a car alone.

ACCOMMODATION

Hostels (*albergues*) usually offer the best value, in most cases with dorms (*dormitórios*) and private rooms (*quartos*). There's an extensive network of Hostelling International-affiliated hostels, so it's worth taking out an HI membership (⊚hihostels.com). In most bigger cities and resorts you'll find numerous **private hostels** for R$35–75 a night per person. Slightly higher in price are small, family-run hotels called **pensão** (*pensões* in the plural) or *hotel* *familiar. Pensões* are often better in small towns than in large cities. You'll also find **pousadas**, which can be just like a *pensão*, or a small, luxurious or offbeat hotel. In the Amazon and the Pantanal pousadas tend to be purpose-built **fazenda** lodges geared towards upscale ecotourism.

Hotels run the gamut from cheap dives to ultra-luxe. The Brazilian star system (one to five) depends on bureaucratic requirements more than on standards – many perfectly good hotels don't have stars. A **quarto** is a room without a bathroom; an **apartamento** or suite is en suite (with private shower); an **apartamento de luxo** is an *apartamento* with a fridge/mini-bar. A **casal** is a double room, a **solteiro** a single. *Apartamentos* normally come with telephone, air-conditioning (*ar condicionado*), TV and fan (*ventilador*). Room **rates** vary tremendously by region and season. Generally, for R$80–150 a night you can stay in a reasonable hotel or pousada with private bathroom and fan or air-conditioning, though you can expect to pay a lot more in **São Paulo** and especially **Rio de Janeiro**, where rates have sky-rocketed in recent years: the cheapest one-stars charge R$120, while mid-range places are more likely to be R$300–350.

In many cases (especially smaller towns) the price of a double or twin room may be little more than two hostel beds – and the breakfast could be much better. During the off-season hotels in tourist areas offer hefty discounts of around 25 to 35 percent – and even in high season at hotels and pousadas it's worth asking "*tem desconto?*" ("is there a discount?").

Brazilian **campsites** are usually found on the coast near larger beaches. These have basic facilities – running water and toilets, a simple restaurant. Elsewhere camping is prohibited in most national parks, and is usually only undertaken on organized jungle treks or with local guides to ensure safety.

FOOD AND DRINK

Brazil has five main **regional cuisines**: **comida mineira**, from Minas Gerais, is based mainly on pork with imaginative use of vegetables and thick bean sauces; **comida baiana** (see page 283), from Bahia, has a rich seafood base and an abundance of West African ingredients; **comida do sertão**, from the interior of the Northeast, relies on rehydrated, dried or salted meat and regional fruits, beans and tubers; **comida amazônica**, based on river fish, manioc sauces and the many fruits and palm products of northern Brazil; and **comida gaúcha** from Rio Grande do Sul, the world's most carnivorous diet, revolves around *churrasco* – charcoal-grilling every meat imaginable. **Feijoada** is the closest Brazil comes to a national dish: a stew of pork, sausage and smoked meat cooked with black beans and garlic, garnished with slices of orange. Eating it is a national ritual at weekends, when restaurants serve *feijoada* all day.

Alongside regional restaurants, there are **standard meals** available everywhere for about R$12–15: **prato comercial** and **prato feito** (literally, pre-made dish) are two very budget-friendly phrases you'll see on (usually lunchtime) menus, consisting of *arroz e feijão* (rice and beans), a choice of steak (*bife*), chicken (*frango*) or fish (*peixe*), and often served with salad, fries and *farinha*, dried manioc (cassava) flour that you sprinkle over everything. *Farofa* is toasted *farinha*, and usually comes with onions and bits of bacon mixed in. The **prato do dia** (plate of the day) or set-menu **prato executivo** are similarly cheap and usually very filling (R$15–25). Also economical are **lanchonetes**, ubiquitous Brazilian snack bars where you eat at the counter. These serve *salgados* (savoury snacks) like *pão de queijo* (cheese profiteroles), *pastel* (fried pastry with meat or cheese filling) and *coxinha* (shredded chicken in corn dough, battered and fried), or cheap meals like a *bauru* – a basic filling steak meal with egg, fries and salad.

Restaurantes a quilo (or kilo) are the lunch choices of most Brazilian office workers, where you choose from (sometimes vast) buffets and pay by weight (*por kilo*); less lavish ones will cost you anything from R$12–25 for a decent plateful. **Rodizio** restaurants can be fantastic deals – specialized restaurants (such as pizza or sushi), where you pay a set fee and eat as much as you want of the endless supply food waiters bring around. The *churrascaria*, the classic Brazilian

steakhouse, operates similarly, with a constant supply of charcoal-grilled meat on huge spits brought to your table.

There are more **fruits** than there are English words for them. Some of the fruit is familiar – *manga* (mango), *maracujá* (passion fruit), *limão* (lime) – but most of it has only Brazilian names: *jaboticaba*, *fruta do conde*, *sapoti* and *jaca*. The most exotic fruits are Amazonian: try *bacuri*, *cupuaçu* and *açaí*. The last-named is often served *na tigela* with *guaraná*, crushed ice, sliced bananas and granola.

DRINK

Brazil is famous for **coffee** and you'll find decent espresso in many cafés, but in lots of local places the coffee comes ready loaded with copious amounts of sugar (Brazilians add it to *everything* and you'll draw looks if you don't follow suit; ask for it *sem açucar* to have them offer you a sugar substitute instead). **Tea** (*cha*) is surprisingly good: try **cha mate**, a strong green tea with a caffeine hit, or one of many herbal teas, most notably that made from *guaraná*. Fruit in Brazil is put to excellent use in **sucos**: fruit is popped into a liquidizer with sugar and crushed ice to make deliciously refreshing drinks. Made with milk rather than water, it becomes a **vitamina**.

Beer (*cerveja*) is mainly of the lager/pilsner type, though craft beers made in microbreweries are becoming popular in the South, São Paulo and Minas Gerais. Brazilians generally drink beer ice-cold, mostly from 600ml bottles. Draught beer is *chopp*. The regional beers of Pará and Maranhão, *Cerma* and *Cerpa*, are generally acknowledged as the best; of the nationally available brands, *Skol*, *Brahma*, *Antarctica* and *Bohemia* are all popular, though mild. Despite the undoubted improvement in the quality of Brazilian **wines**, those imported from Chile and Argentina remain more reliable.

As for spirits, stick to what Brazilians drink – **cachaça**, a sugar-cane liquor. The best way to drink it is in a **caipirinha** – *cachaça* mixed with fresh lime, sugar and crushed ice – one of Brazil's great gifts to the world. One thing to remember when enjoying Brazil's beverages: most clubs and some bars will give you an **individual card** when you enter upon which your drinks are tabulated. Don't lose it. Even if you have paid, unless you have the receipt at the door, you will have difficulty leaving and may even have to pay again.

CULTURE AND ETIQUETTE

The most widely spoken language in Brazil is **Portuguese**. Educated Brazilians often speak a little English, and there are plenty of Spanish-speakers, but knowing Spanish is of limited help in interpreting spoken Portuguese. You will do yourself a huge favour and likely make several new friends if you learn some Portuguese – even a little effort goes a long way.

On the whole, Brazilians are very friendly, open people (you'll be guided to your stop by passengers on public transport if you ask for help). The pace differs depending on the region. In major cities things operate fairly quickly and on a schedule. Things work in the Northeast too, but in their own special way – you're better off slowing to their pace.

Though attitudes vary regionally, in general Brazilians are remarkably open with their **sexuality**. Brazil's reputation as a sex destination is not completely without merit – prostitution is legal and you'll see love motels (hourly rates) everywhere. Also be aware that while Brazilians are very accepting of the LGBTQ community during Carnaval, more conservative views can prevail, especially in rural areas.

Restaurant bills in Brazil usually come with a ten-percent *taxa de serviço* included, in which case you don't have to **tip** – ten percent is about right if it is not included. Waiters and some hotel employees depend on tips. You don't have to tip taxi drivers (though they won't say no), but you are expected to tip barbers, hairdressers, shoeshine kids, self-appointed guides and porters. It's useful to keep change handy for them.

SPORTS AND OUTDOOR ACTIVITIES

Brazilian football (*futebol*) is globally revered and a privilege to watch, at its best reminding you why it's known as "the beautiful game" – despite being humiliated 7–1 by the Germans on home soil in the 2014 World Cup. Brazil have been **world**

champions a record five times, and **Pelé** – born in Minas Gerais – is still regarded as the best player of all time. Indeed, you won't really have experienced Brazil until you've attended a match. Stadiums are spectacular sights, games enthralling and crowds are wildly enthusiastic. **Tickets** are not expensive, ranging from R$20 to R$150 depending on whether you stand on the terraces (*geral*) or opt for stand seats (*arquibancada*) – major championship and international matches sometimes cost more. You can usually pay at the turnstile, though there are long last-minute queues. Regional rivalries are strong; fans are seated separately and given different exit routes to prevent fighting. In Rio, **Flamengo** and **Fluminense** have long had an intense rivalry; in São Paulo there are **São Paulo** and **Corinthians**.

The other major national sport is **volleyball** (*volei*), mostly played on the beach, though the hard-court game is also popular and sand is imported inland for beach volleyball championships elsewhere. In Rio especially, beach **foot-volleyball** (*futevolei*) has gained massive popularity in the last decade.

A full range of **outdoor activities** is available across the country, with regional highlights including hang-gliding in Rio, hiking and waterfall hunting in the coastal forests of the Serra do Mar or Bahia's marvellous Chapada Diamantina, river-based pursuits in the Amazon and Pantanal, and exploration of the lunar-like dune systems of Maranhão's Lençois Maranhenses.

COMMUNICATIONS

With **wi-fi** increasingly available across the country; **internet cafés** (here called *LAN houses*) are dwindling in number. Almost every hotel and hostel in Brazil (except in very remote locations) offers free wi-fi, as do most cafés.

If you have a compatible (and unlocked) **phone** and intend to use it a lot, it can be much cheaper to buy a Brazilian **SIM card** (R$10 or less) to use during your stay. Currently, **TIM Brasil** (⊛tim.com.br) is your best bet for a SIM card (look for TIM outlets or visit a branch of the Lojas Americanas chain store; bring your passport). Once the SIM is installed you should opt for a pre-pay plan ("*pré-pago*"); to add credit, just go to TIM shops, newspaper stalls or pharmacies and ask for TIM "*cargas*". Bear in mind that rates will apply only to calls within the same state – calling to and "roaming" within other states is charged at a hefty premium.

With the explosion of mobile/wireless communications, **public phones** are now hard to find in Brazil – aim to use a mobile phone if you can. Hostels are also usually happy to call ahead for reservations at your next stop.

Before making a national or **long-distance or international call** you must select the telephone company you wish to use by inserting a two-digit **carrier selection code** between the zero and the area code or country code of the number you are calling. To call Rio, for example, from anywhere else in the country, you would dial zero + phone company code + city code (21) followed by the eight-digit number. For **local calls**, you simply dial the seven- or eight-digit number. Assuming you have a choice, it doesn't matter which company you use, as costs are very similar (this goes for international calls too). Claro/Embratel, code 021, is reliable; from a TIM phone use 041.

Post offices (⊛correios.com.br) – *correios* – are identified by their bright yellow postbox signs. A postage stamp for either a postcard or a letter up to 20g to the USA costs R$1.80; R$2 to the UK, Ireland and most of Europe; and R$2.20 to Australia, New Zealand and South Africa. Airmail letters to Europe and North America take around two weeks, and, though generally reliable, it's better not to send valuables.

CRIME AND SAFETY

Brazil's reputation as a rather dangerous place is not entirely undeserved, but it is often overblown, and many visitors arrive with an exaggerated idea of the perils lying in wait. **Street crime** can be a problem, especially in the evenings and late at night (the targeting of tourists is worst in Rio, Salvador and Recife), but the key is to be sensible and not let fear grip you. Criminals are also getting more sophisticated – there has been an increase

BRAZIL ONLINE

Ⓦ**brasil.gov.br** Government site with information on Brazilian culture, environment and current affairs in English.
Ⓦ**visitbrasil.com** Official site of the Brazilian Ministério do Turismo.
Ⓦ**folha.uol.com.br/internacional/ en** São Paulo newspaper with a helpful English-language version.
Ⓦ**gringoes.com** Brazilian culture, arts, sports and travel in English.
Ⓦ**riotimesonline.com** Focused on news and entertainment in Rio, but with information for travellers across Brazil.
Ⓦ**buscaonibus.com.br** Useful bus timetables for long-distance travel.

in the **cloning of ATM cards**, so you should check your online account often.

PERSONAL SAFETY

Being a gringo attracts unwelcome attention but it also provides a measure of protection. The Brazilian police can be extremely violent to criminals, and law enforcement tends to take the form of periodic crackdowns. Therefore criminals know that injuries to foreign tourists mean a heavy clampdown, which in turn means slim pickings for a while.

Needless to say, avoid *favelas* in any city unless you are visiting with locals/tour guides who know the area – drug gang members shot a British tourist when her husband accidentally drove into a *favela* near Rio in 2017. Use GPS/SatNav devices with caution (double-checking routes with maps), as they can sometimes lead you through shady areas as the "fastest" or "shortest" route to a destination.

If you are unlucky enough to be the victim of an **assalto** (a mugging), remember, it's your possessions that are the targets. Don't resist: your money and anything you're carrying will be snatched, your watch yanked off, but within seconds it will all be over. Most *assaltos* happen at night, in backstreets and desolate areas of cities, so stick to busy, well-lit streets, and where possible take taxis; city buses generally run late too, though mind your belongings when it's crowded.

BUSES, BEACHES AND HOTELS

Long-distance **buses** are pretty secure, but it pays to keep an eye on your things. Get a **baggage check** on your luggage from the person loading it and keep an eye on your possessions until they are loaded. Overhead racks are less safe, especially during night journeys.

On city **beaches**, never leave things unattended; any beachside bar will stow things for you. In tourist areas and busy cities avoid walking on the beach at night. Shared **rooms** in pousadas and hostels usually have lockers (bring a padlock) and even many cheap hotels have **safes** (*caixas*).

POLICE AND DRUGS

If you are robbed or held up, it's best to immediately go to the **police**, even though, except with something like a theft from a hotel room, they're unlikely to be able to do much, and reporting something will likely take hours even without the language barrier. You may have to do it for insurance purposes, when you'll need a local police report; this could take a full and very frustrating day. If your passport is stolen in a city where there is a consulate, get in touch with the consulate first and take their lead.

Both **marijuana** (*maconha*) and **cocaine** (*cocaína*) are fairly common, but be warned: if the police find either on you, you will be in serious trouble. The following cannot be overstated: under no circumstances do you want to spend any time in a Brazilian jail.

HEALTH

Public healthcare in Brazil varies tremendously from poor to quite good, but private medical and dental treatment is generally more reliable; costs are significantly less than in North America (a

EMERGENCY NUMBERS

Ambulance ☎**192**
Fire ☎**193**
Police ☎**190**

TOURIST POLICE

Rio ☎**21 3399 7170**
São Paulo ☎**11 3214 0209**
Salvador ☎**71 3222 7155**

3

3

doctor's visit will cost on average R$120–160). Check directories at the end of each section for hospital information and refer to advice from your country's embassy or consulate. Standard drugs are available in *farmácias* (pharmacies) without prescriptions. Note that **malaria** is endemic in **northern Brazil**, and anyone intending to travel in Amazônia should take precautions very seriously. **Dengue fever**, another viral disease transmitted by mosquito bites (during the day), is increasingly common in all Brazilian cities (especially in the southeast). Since the major outbreak in 2015/2016, the risk of **Zika** (ZIKV) infection (also mosquito-borne) is now much lower in Brazil. Getting a **yellow fever vaccination**, which offers protection for ten years, is recommended if you're going to Amazônia, Goiás or Mato Grosso.

INFORMATION AND MAPS

Popular destinations in Brazil have friendly and helpful **tourist offices**, as do most state capitals, many of which distribute free city maps and booklets. Generally the airport information offices have the best English-speakers and are usually open the longest. They also have decent free maps but little else in English. EMBRATUR is the national tourist organization and has a useful website (ⓦvisitbrasil.com).

MONEY AND BANKS

The Brazilian currency is the **real** (pronounced "hey-al") and is made up of one hundred centavos. Its plural is **reais** (pronounced "hey-ice"), written R$. Notes are for 2, 5, 10, 20, 50 and 100 reais; coins are 1, 5, 10, 25 and 50 centavos, and 1 real. At the time of writing, US$1 = R$3.3, £1 = R$4.4 and €1 = R$3.9. **ATMs** are available all over Brazil, though not all accept foreign cards and many non-airport ATMs are inactive after 8pm or 10pm for security reasons. Banco do Brasil offer the most reliable machines; Bradesco and HSBC also accept foreign cards.

OPENING HOURS AND HOLIDAYS

Basic hours for most **shops** and **businesses** are from Monday to Saturday 8am to noon and 2pm to 6pm (with smaller shops tending to close Saturday afternoons). Shops in malls tend to stay open late Friday and Saturday nights (typically 9–10pm). Banks generally open weekdays from 10am to 4pm. **Museums** and historic **monuments** generally cost just a few reais and follow regular business hours, though many are closed on Mondays. In addition to the public holidays listed, there are plenty of local and state holidays when you'll also find everything closed.

PUBLIC HOLIDAYS

In addition to those below, between one and three further days are offered by each state; **Carnaval**, which takes place on the five days leading up to Ash Wednesday, is an "optional" rather than official national holiday (though almost every Brazilian takes at least one day off), as is **Corpus Christi** on June 11.

January 1 New Year's Day (Ano Novo)
March/April (varies) Good Friday
April 21 Tiradentes Day (Dia de Tiradentes)
May 1 Labour Day (Dia do Trabalhador)
September 7 Independence Day (Dia da Independência)
October 12 Feast Day of Nossa Senhora Aparecida (Our Lady of Aparecida, patron saint of Brazil)
November 2 Dia dos Finados (Day of the Dead)
November 15 Republic Day (Proclamação da República)
December 25 Christmas Day (Natal)

FESTIVALS AND CELEBRATIONS

Carnaval is by far the most important festival in Brazil, and when it comes, the country grinds to a halt as it gets down to some of the most serious partying in the world. The most familiar and most spectacular celebration is in **Rio** (see page 239), one of the world's great sights, televised live to the whole country. **Salvador**'s Carnaval (see page 277) is now almost as commercialized, with big headline performers, and a reputation for being even wilder than Rio's. **Olinda** and its winding colonial hilltop streets next to Recife make for a fun and perhaps less frenzied experience, while **Fortaleza**, and **Ouro Preto** and **Diamantina** in Minas Gerais, also host great parties.
Lavagem do Bonfim Second Thursday of January. Hundreds of women in traditional Bahian garb clean the steps of Salvador's beloved church with perfumed water (food and music follow).
Festa de Iemanjá February 2. Devotees make offerings on beaches along the coast to celebrate the goddess of the sea. Salvador's Praia Vermelha hosts one of the largest.
Bienal de São Paulo Biennial in March (next in 2020) ⓦ bienal.org.br. The largest arts event in Latin America.

Bienal de São Paulo Biennial in March (next in 2020) ⓦ bienal.org.br. The largest arts event in Latin America.

Paixão de Cristo (The Passion Play) Ten days leading up to Easter. Latin America's largest passion plays are enacted in Nova Jerusalém, outside Recife.

Festa de São João (Festa Junina) June 13–24. Celebrations of St John happen across Brazil, but Salvador, Pernambuco and cities in the Northeast are the most raucous, with *forró*, drinking and eating.

Bumba-meu-boi June 13–29. The people of São Luís re-enact the folk tale of a farmer who, having killed another farmer's ox, must resurrect it or face his own death. Costumes, dancing, capoeira, heckling and hilarity ensue.

Paraty International Literary Festival (FLIP) Early August ⓦ paraty.com.br/flip. Some of Brazil's and the world's best authors converge on Paraty, with events and talks in Portuguese and English, and performances by top Brazilian musicians.

Rio International Film Festival October ⓦ festivaldorio. com.br. The country's biggest film festival, showcasing 200 mainstream and independent releases.

Círio de Nazaré Second Sunday in October ⓦ ciriodenazare. com.br. An effigy of the Virgin of Nazaré is carried across the water from Vila de Icoaraci to the port of Belém.

Oktoberfest October 10–27 ⓦ oktoberfestblumenau. com.br. German-settled Blumenau has all the beer-swilling, German food and traditional garb you'd expect.

Grand Prix November. Brazil's Interlagos circuit near São Paulo is one of the most atmospheric Grand Prix venues.

Reveillon New Year's Eve. Major cities along the coast compete with fireworks displays. Rio's is nearly always the biggest.

3

Rio de Janeiro

The citizens of **RIO DE JANEIRO** call it the *cidade marvilhosa* – and there can't be much argument about that. It's a huge city with a stunning setting, extending along 40km of sandy coast and sandwiched between an azure sea and jungle-clad mountains. The city's unusual name has a curious history: Portuguese explorers arriving at the mouth of Guanabara Bay on January 1, 1502 thought they had discovered the mouth of an enormous river which they named the January River or Rio de Janeiro. By the time the first settlement was established and the error was realized, the name had already stuck.

Although riven by inequality, Rio has great style. Its international renown is bolstered by a series of symbols that rank as some of the greatest landmarks in the world: the **Corcovado** mountain supporting the great statue of Christ the Redeemer; the rounded incline of the **Sugarloaf mountain** standing at the entrance to the bay; the beaches of **Copacabana** and **Ipanema**, probably the most famous lengths of sand on the planet. Then there's the **Maracanã stadium**, a huge draw for football fans, which was renovated to host the 2104 World Cup and 2016 Olympic Games. It's a setting enhanced by a frenetic nightlife scene and the annual sensuality of **Carnaval**, an explosive celebration which – for many people – sums up Rio and her citizens, the Cariocas.

WHAT TO SEE AND DO

Rio's sights are scattered across three main sectors of the city, and improved metrô links make getting around fairly straightforward. **Centro** contains the last vestiges of the metropolis's colonial past, and its major sites are easily walkable in one day. The most obvious place to start is historic **Praça XV de Novembro**, while the other main focal point, Cinelândia, has numerous places of interest nearby. Just south of here are the lively *bairros* of **Lapa**, capital of Brazil's samba scene, and bohemian **Santa Teresa** sprawling across the hills above. It's the **Zona Sul** (south zone), however, where you're likely to spend most of your time – in no small part due to the 16km of sandy **beaches** that line its shores – though visits to the Corcovado and Sugarloaf mountains should not be missed. Many formerly run-down parts of the **Zona Norte** (north and west of Centro) were spruced up for the Olympics; fans of the "beautiful game" should make the pilgrimage to the **Maracanã football stadium**, while for the more culturally minded there's the **Museu Nacional**.

PRAÇA XV DE NOVEMBRO

Taking its name from the day in 1889 when Marechal Deodoro de Fonseca, the first president, proclaimed the Republic of Brazil, "**Praça Quinze**" (10min walk from Metrô Carioca) was once the hub of Rio's

RIO DE JANEIRO

Tom Jobim International Airport

PENHA

Baía de Guanabara

MADUREIRA

SÃO CRISTOVÃO

PONTE RIO-NITERÓI

SEE 'CENTRAL RIO' FOR DETAIL

NITERÓI

MÉIER   Feira Nordestina   Rodoviária Novo Rio   Santos Dumont Airport
Museu National   CENTRO
Maracaná Stadium   AVENIDA PRES. VARGAS   Museu de Arte Contemporânea

PARQUE NACIONAL DE TIJUCA   STA. TERESA

Pico do Papegaio   Pica da Tijuca   LARANJEIRAS   FLAMENGO

Corcovado   BOTAFOGO

ALTO DA BOA VISTA   LAGOA   Pão de Açúcar

Lagoa Rodrigo de Freitas   AVENIDA ATLANTICA

GÁVEA   COPACABANA   N

SÃO CONRADO   LEBLON   IPANEMA

SEE 'RIO: ZONA SUL' FOR DETAIL

BARRA DA TIJUCA

ATLANTIC OCEAN

■ ACCOMMODATION
Varandas do Vidigal   1

0   10
kilometres

social and political life. On the south side of the square is the striking **Paço Imperial** (Tues–Sun noon–6pm; free), which serves as an exhibition space. It was here in 1808 that the Portuguese monarch, Dom João VI, established his court in Brazil, and the building continued to be used for royal receptions and special occasions: on May 13, 1888, Princess Isabel proclaimed the end of slavery here. Just south is bold, Neoclassical **Palácio Tiradentes** (Mon–Sat 10am–5pm, Sun noon–5pm; free), the Rio state parliament, while to the north is the **Arco de Teles**, constructed on the site of the old *pelourinho* (pillory) in around 1755, and leading through to Rua do Mercado and Rua do Ouvidor, a lively street with restaurants, cafés, bookshops and bars.

On the Rua I de Março side of Praça Quinze, the **Antiga Sé** (Mon–Fri 7am–4.30pm, Sat 9.30am–12.30pm; free; guided tours Sat 9.30am, R$5) served until 1980 as Rio's cathedral. Inside, the high altar is detailed in silver and boasts a beautiful work by the painter Antônio Parreires. Below, in the **crypt**, rest the supposed remains of Pedro Álvares Cabral, Portuguese discoverer of Brazil – though

his final resting place is more likely to be Santarém in Portugal.

NORTH TO SÃO BENTO AND THE PORT

Heading north up **Rua 1 de Março** from the *praça*, you'll pass the church of **Santa Cruz dos Militares** (Mon–Fri 1.30–3.30pm; free), dating from 1628 and rebuilt in granite and marble by the army in 1780; a display of ecclesiastical and military oddments is to be found inside. North of here, the enormous **Candelária church** (Igreja de Nossa Senhora de Candelária; Mon–Fri 7.30am–4pm, Sat 8am–noon, Sun 9am–1pm; free) looms into view, luxuriously decorated inside in marble and bronze. Accessed by elevator from Rua Dom Gereardo 40, the hilltop **Igreja e Mosteiro de São Bento** (daily 7am–5pm, Sun Mass at 10am; free) was founded by Benedictine monks in 1633. The facade is pleasingly simple with twin pyramid-shaped spires, while the interior is richly adorned in gold designs and statues by Mestre Valentim. Further north again is Praça Mauá, part of a redevelopment featuring the new **Museu de Arte do Rio** (Tues–Sun 10am–5pm; R$20, Tues free;

CARNAVAL

Carnaval is celebrated in all of Brazil's cities, but Rio's is the biggest and most famous of all. From the Friday before Ash Wednesday to the following Thursday, the city shuts up shop and throws itself into the world's most famous manifestation of unbridled hedonism. Rio's carnival ranks as the most important celebration on the Brazilian calendar, easily outstripping either Christmas or Easter. In a poverty-stricken city, it represents a moment of release, when Cariocas unite to express their aspirations in music and song.

THE ACTION

Rio's street celebrations (known as *blocos* and *bandas)* happen all over town from the beaches to the distant suburbs, and you should keep your ears open for the biggest and best parties (Ⓦtodorio.com has listings). The processions feature loudspeaker-laden floats blasting out frenetic samba, and thousands of hyped-up revellers. **Avenida Rio Branco** (Metrô Carioca) is the most traditional spot, but Santa Teresa, Laranjeiras, and of course all the beach districts have loads going on. Many neighbourhoods also have their own **samba school**, competing in three leagues, each allowing promotion and relegation. It's a year-round occupation, with schools mobilizing thousands of supporters, choosing a theme, writing the music and learning the dances choreographed by the **carnavelesco** – the school's director. By December, rehearsals have begun and the sambas are released to record stores. From September to February a visit to a samba school is a must (see page 255), while you can check out the *Cidade do Samba* (Rua Rivadávia Correa, Gamboa, Centro Ⓦcidadedosambarj. com.br), a huge complex where carnival floats are constructed and touristic samba spectacles take place).

THE DESFILE

The main **procession** of *Grupo Especial* schools – known as the **Desfile** – takes place on the Sunday and Monday nights in the purpose-built **Sambódromo** at Rua Marques de Sapucaí (Metrô Praza Onze/Central do Brasil), a concrete structure 1.7km long that can accommodate ninety thousand spectators. Some schools may have thirty thousand participants; they compete for points awarded by judges according to the presentation of their song, story, dress, dance and rhythm. Each school must parade for between 85 and 95 minutes, with the **bateria**, or percussion section, sustaining the cadence that drives the school's song and dance. The **carros alegóricos** (decorated floats) carry prominent figures, and the **porta-bandeira** ("flag bearer") carries the school's symbol. The bulk of the procession behind is formed by the **alas** – each with hundreds of costumed individuals linked to a part of the school's theme.

The **parade** at the Sambódromo starts at 9pm, with six schools (see page 255) parading on each of the two nights, and it goes on till 4am. There are a number of different seating options, from grandstands, which are basically concrete steps where you sit where you like, to private chairs, boxes and luxury suites. Grandstand tickets start at R$91 for the main parades, with luxury seats costing up to R$1239 a go. **Tickets** are available from the organizers (Ⓦrio-carnival.net), or from agents such as Rio.com (☎1 800 260 2700 or ☎305 420 6900 in the US or Canada, ☎020 3129 3573 in the UK, ☎02 8015 5419 in Australia, Ⓦrio.com) or Bookers International (☎1 866 930 6020 in the US or Canada, Ⓦcarnivalbookers.com), or at premium prices from travel agents in Rio, and should be booked well in advance.

CARNIVAL BALLS

Carnival balls (*bailes de Carnaval*) and other live shows are a big feature of festivities before and during the main event. Check out Lapa's *Fundição Progresso* (Ⓦfundicaoprogresso.com.br) for appearances by top samba schools in the run-up, and Leblon's *Scala* (Ⓦscalario.com.br) for no-holds-barred affairs each night.

Ⓦmuseudeartedorio.org.br), a museum dedicated to the city's own art from colonial times to the present day. More impressive still is the futuristic **Museu do Amanhã** (Muesum of Tomorrow; Tues–Sun 10am–6pm; R$20, combined ticket with Museu de Arte do Rio R$35, Tues free; Ⓦmuseudoamanha.org.br). An amazing new science museum in a specially designed building, it focuses on humanity's place in

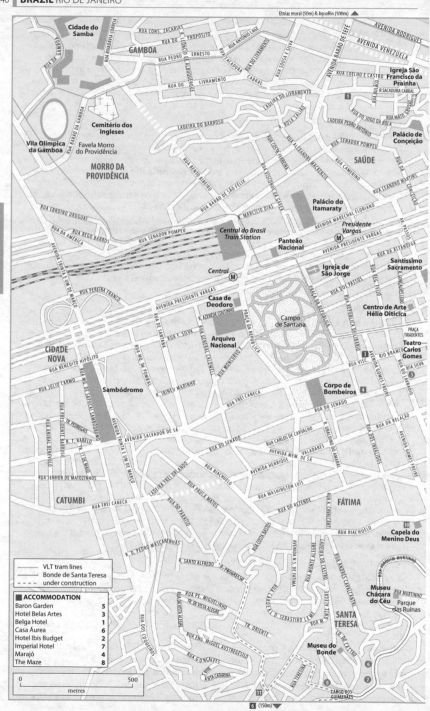

Etnias mural (50m) & AquaRio (500m)

ACCOMMODATION
Baron Garden	5
Hotel Belas Artes	3
Belga Hotel	1
Casa Áurea	6
Hotel Ibis Budget	2
Imperial Hotel	7
Marajó	4
The Maze	8

VLT tram lines
Bonde de Santa Teresa
under construction

0 — 500
metres

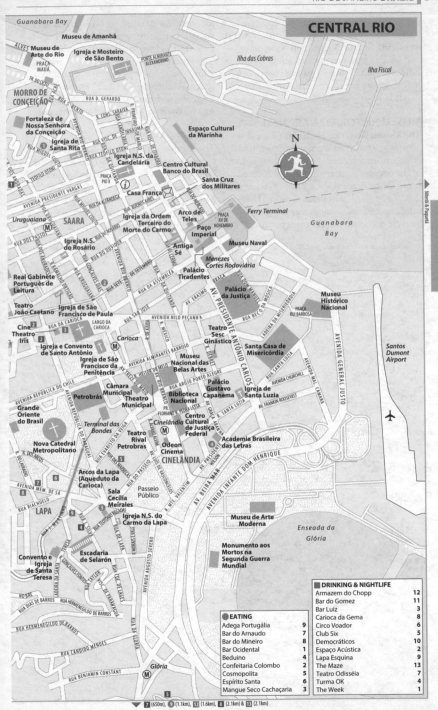

CENTRAL RIO

Guanabara Bay

Museu de Amanhã

Museu de Arte do Rio

Igreja e Mosteiro de São Bento

Ilha das Cobras

Ilha Fiscal

PRAÇA MAUÁ

MORRO DE CONCEIÇÃO

Fortaleza de Nossa Senhora da Conceição

Igreja de Santa Rita

Espaço Cultural da Marinha

Igreja N.S. da Candelária

Centro Cultural Banco do Brasil

Santa Cruz dos Militares

Casa França

Uruguaiana

SAARA

Igreja da Ordem Terceiro do Morte do Carmo

Arco de Teles

Paço Imperial

Ferry Terminal

Guanabara Bay

Igreja N.S. do Rosário

Antiga Sé

Museu Naval

Menezes Cortes Rodoviária

Real Gabinete Português de Leitura

Palácio Tiradentes

Palácio da Justiça

Museu Histórico Nacional

Teatro João Caetano

Igreja de São Francisco de Paula

LARGO DA CARIOCA

Teatro Sesc Ginástico

Cine Theatro Iris

Carioca

Igreja e Convento de Santo Antônio

Santa Casa de Misericórdia

Igreja de São Francisco da Penitência

Museu Nacional das Belas Artes

Santos Dumont Airport

Câmara Municipal

Petrobrás

Theatro Municipal

Palácio Gustavo Capanema

Igreja de Santa Luzia

Grande Oriente do Brasil

Biblioteca Nacional

Terminal das Bondes

Centro Cultural de Justiça Federal

Nova Catedral Metropolitano

Teatro Rival Petrobras

Cinelândia

Academia Brasileira das Letras

Odeon Cinema

CINELÂNDIA

Arcos da Lapa (Aqueduto da Carioca)

Passeio Público

Sala Cecília Meirales

LAPA

Igreja N.S. do Carmo da Lapa

Museu de Arte Moderna

Enseada da Glória

Convento e Igreja de Santa Teresa

Escadaria de Selarón

Monumento aos Mortos na Segunda Guerra Mundial

Glória

● EATING

Adega Portugália	9
Bar do Arnaudo	7
Bar do Mineiro	8
Bar Ocidental	1
Beduino	4
Confeitaria Colombo	2
Cosmopolita	5
Espírito Santa	6
Mangue Seco Cachaçaria	3

■ DRINKING & NIGHTLIFE

Armazem do Chopp	12
Bar do Gomez	11
Bar Luiz	3
Carioca da Gema	8
Circo Voador	6
Club Six	5
Democráticos	10
Espaço Acústica	2
Lapa Esquina	9
The Maze	13
Teatro Odisséia	7
Turma OK	4
The Week	1

▼ 7 (650m), 9 (1.1km), 12 (1.6km), 8 (2.1km) & 13 (2.1km)

Niterói & Paquetá

3

the history of the earth and the universe. Queues are long, especially on Tuesdays and weekends, and in August and September you have to buy your ticket online. Nearby, Eduardo Kobra's huge and impressive mural, **Etnias** is a three-block stroll down Avenida Rodrigues Alves.

MUSEU HISTÓRICO NACIONAL

The **Museu Histórico Nacional** (Tues–Fri 10am–5.30pm, Sat & Sun 1–5pm; R\$10; ⓦmuseuhistoriconacional.com.br), housed in the former military arsenal, is located south from Praça XV de Novembro in the shadow of the Kubitschek flyover. The exhibits contain some pieces of great interest, from furniture, firearms and

locomotives to displays on indigenous societies and the sugar, gold, coffee and beef trades. Information about slavery – so important to Brazil's history – is scarce, while the monarchy is granted ample space. Audio-guides (R\$8) are available in English, and the varied collection makes it one of Brazil's most important museums.

LARGO DA CARIOCA

The bustling square **Largo da Carioca** (Metrô Carioca) is dominated from above by the cloistered **Igreja e Convento de Santo Antônio** (Mon, Wed, Thurs & Fri 8am–7pm, Tues 6.30am–8pm, Sat 8–11am, Sun 9–11am; free; ⓦconventosantoantonio. org.br), though the square's other historical

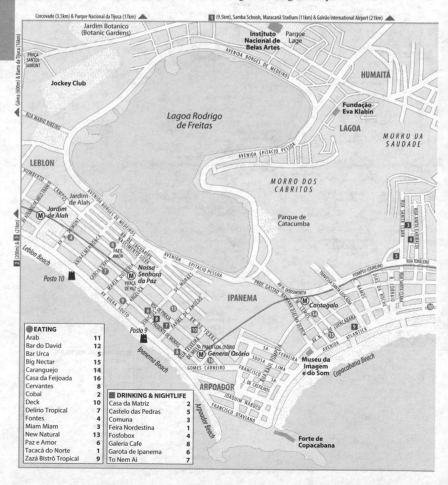

EATING	
Arab	11
Bar do David	12
Bar Urca	5
Big Nectar	15
Caranguejo	14
Casa da Feijoada	16
Cervantes	8
Cobal	2
Deck	10
Delírio Tropical	7
Fontes	4
Miam Miam	3
New Natural	13
Paz e Amor	6
Tacacá do Norte	1
Zazá Bistrô Tropical	9

DRINKING & NIGHTLIFE	
Casa da Matriz	2
Castelo das Pedras	5
Comuna	3
Feira Nordestina	1
Fosfobox	4
Galeria Cafe	8
Garota de Ipanema	6
To Nem Ai	7

buildings were, sadly, lost to ugly new high-rises. Built between 1608 and 1620, this is Rio's oldest church, a tranquil refuge decorated in marble and Portuguese tiling. Adjoining it, the striking **Igreja de São Francisco da Penitência** (Tues–Fri 9am–noon & 1–4pm; R$3) contains extensive gold and silver ornamentation. Lively shopping street Rua Uruguaiana heads north from here towards the Candelária.

SAARA AND CAMPO DE SANTANA

West from Metrô Uruguaiana ruas Alfândega and Passos run through Rio's best (and cheapest) market area, known as **Saara**, originally peopled by Jewish and Arab merchants.

A block south of Saara, the **Igreja de São Francisco de Paula** (Mon–Fri 8am–7pm, Sat 8am–5pm, Sun 9am–1pm; free), the site of the Mass to "swear in" the Brazilian Constitution in 1831, contains meticulous decoration by Valentim da Fonseca e Silva, known to Cariocas as Mestre Valentim, Brazil's most important eighteenth-century sculptor. One of Rio's most impressive ornate interiors is to be found two blocks west, however, at the **Real Gabinete Português de Leitura** (Mon–Fri 9am–6pm; free; ⓦwww.realgabinete.com.br), dating from 1887 and containing a library with 350,000 leather-bound volumes. At Saara's western end you come upon a surprisingly peaceful park, the

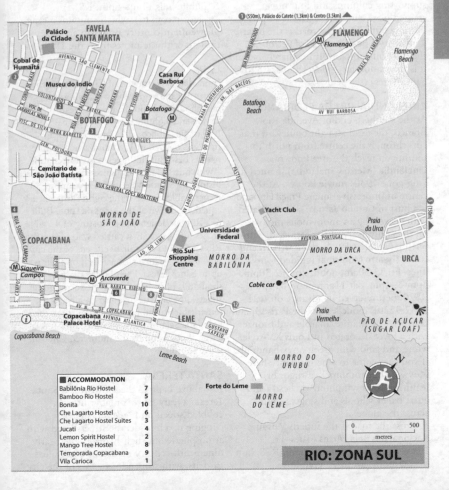

■ ACCOMMODATION	
Babilônia Rio Hostel	7
Bamboo Rio Hostel	5
Bonita	10
Che Lagarto Hostel	6
Che Lagarto Hostel Suites	3
Jucati	4
Lemon Spirit Hostel	2
Mango Tree Hostel	8
Temporada Copacabana	9
Vila Carioca	1

RIO: ZONA SUL

3

Campo de Santana (daily 7am–5pm; free), where Emperor Dom Pedro I proclaimed Brazil's independence from Portugal in 1822 – now complete with ponds, strutting peacocks and scuttling agoutis.

NOVA CATEDRAL AND AROUND

To the southwest of the Largo da Carioca, the unmistakeable form of the **Nova Catedral Metropolitana** (daily 7am–5pm) rises up like some futuristic tepee, 75m high and with a capacity of 20,000. Built between 1964 and 1976, it's an impressive piece of modern architecture, resembling the blunt-topped Maya pyramids of Mexico. It feels vast inside, its remarkable sense of space enhanced by the absence of supporting columns and four huge stained-glass windows, each measuring 20m by 60m. Over the road is the bizarre Cubist-style **headquarters of Petrobrás**, the state oil company. Immediately behind it is the station for *bondes* (trams) up to Santa Teresa (see below).

CINELÂNDIA: PRAÇA FLORIANO

At the southern end of Avenida Rio Branco, the dead-straight boulevard that cuts through the centre from north to south, you reach the area known as **Cinelândia** (Metrô Cinelândia), named for long-gone 1930s movie houses. At the centre of impressive square **Praça Floriano** is a bust of **Getúlio Vargas**, still decorated with flowers by an anonymous mourner on the anniversary of the former dictator's birthday, March 19. At the northern end is the **Theatro Municipal** (guided tours Tues–Fri 11.30am, noon, 2pm, 2.30pm, 3pm & 4pm, Sat 11am, noon & 1pm; R$20; best reserved in advance on ☎21 2332 9220), modelled on the Paris Opera Garnier – all granite, marble and bronze, with a foyer decorated in Louis XV-style white and gold with green onyx handrails. If you can, come to a performance here (ⓦwww. theatromunicipal.rj.gov.br) featuring Rio's symphony orchestra and guest ballet schools and singers from across the globe.

Across the road is the superb **Museu Nacional das Belas Artes** (Tues–Fri 10am–6pm, Sat & Sun 1–6pm; R$8, Sun free; ⓦmnba.gov.br), a grandiose construction imitating the Louvre in Paris. The European collection includes Boudin, Taunay and Frans Post, but the painting and sculpture by all the modern Brazilian masters are of much greater interest. Neighbouring **Biblioteca Nacional** (Mon–Fri 10am–5pm, Sat 10.30am–noon; guided tours in Portuguese hourly, and in English Mon–Fri 2pm; free but photo ID required; ⓦbn.gov.br) is also noteworthy, for the high Art Nouveau ceilings of its reading rooms and its stairway decorated by important artists like Visconti, Amoedo and Bernadelli. Ten minutes' walk southeast, at the edge of the Parque do Flamengo, is the **Museu de Arte Moderna** (Tues–Fri noon–6pm, Sat & Sun & public hols 11am–6pm; R$14; ⓦmamrio.com.br), which contains a range of twentieth-century Brazilian art. Start upstairs with the pieces from the 1920s.

LAPA

Immediately southwest of Cinelândia is the *bairro* of **Lapa**, a gracefully decaying neighbourhood and the beating heart of Rio's **samba and nightlife scenes** (see page 255). Its **Passeio Público** park (daily 9am–5pm; free) was opened in 1783 and is now a little past its best, but this green oasis still charms – with busts of famous figures from the city's history by Mestre Valentim. Lapa's most recognizable feature is the eighteenth-century aqueduct known as the **Arcos da Lapa**. Built to a Roman design and consisting of 42 wide arches, in its heyday it carried water from the Rio Carioca to the thirsty citizens of the city; now *bondes* (trams) pass across it on their way up to Santa Teresa. Each Friday night thousands of people throng the surrounding streets. Just off Rua Joaquim da Silva, a remarkable ascending tiled mosaic lines the **Escadaria Selarón** stairway into Santa Teresa, a feat of obsession by the murdered Chilean artist Selarón.

SANTA TERESA

Just above Lapa to the southwest is **Santa Teresa**, a leafy *bairro* of labyrinthine, cobbled streets and *ladeiras* (steps), clinging to a hillside, the streets lined with atmospheric but slightly dishevelled early nineteenth-century mansions and walled gardens, with stupendous views of the city and bay. Santa Teresa enjoys something of a bohemian reputation and is Rio's main artistic neighbourhood: in July or August around one hundred artists open their studios for **Portas Abertas**, offering the public an opportunity to look (as well as to enjoy an enormous street party) – though on any weekend the *bairro* is buzzing with visitors. The traditional and most picturesque way to get to Santa Teresa is to take the *bonde,* Rio's last remaining **electric tram** line, which recently reopened after a much-needed upgrade, and starts from a station near the Nova Catedral (see page 244).

Santa Teresa's tiny centre "square", **Largo do Guimarães**, is a great place to hang out for a drink or meal at any number of lively bars and restaurants nearby – every evening except Monday, but especially throughout the weekend. From here, more great bars are staggered along the bus/tram route westwards, while downhill to the east it's an enjoyable ten-minute walk to art gallery **Museu Chácara do Céu** at Rua Murtinho Nobre 93 (Mon & Wed–Sun noon–5pm; R$6, free Wed; ⓦmuseuscastromaya.com.br), in a modernist building surrounded by gardens. It holds a reasonable, eclectic collection of twentieth-century art, though its best works by Matisse, Picasso, Dalí and Monet were stolen in an audacious raid during Carnaval 2006, the culprits melting into the crowd in fancy dress.

Just up the street, the **Parque das Ruínas** (Tues–Sun 8am–6pm; free) is an attractive public garden with great views and containing the ruins of a mansion that was once home to a Brazilian heiress. Following her death, the mansion fell into disrepair, but reopened as a cultural and exhibition centre in the 1990s.

GLÓRIA AND CATETE

On your way to the Zona Sul from Centro, it's worth visiting the eighteenth-century **Igreja de Nossa Senhora da Glória do Outeiro** (Mon–Fri 9am–4pm, Sat, Sun & public hols 9am–noon; free), atop the Morro da Glória (5min walk from Metrô Glória). Notable for its innovative octagonal ground plan and domed roof, the latter decked with seventeenth-century blue-and-white *azulejos* and

nineteenth-century marble masonry, it's an architectural gem.

At Rua do Catete 153, adjacent to Metrô Catete station, the Palácio do Catete houses the **Museu da República** (Tues–Fri 10am–5pm, Sat & Sun 11am–6pm; R$6, free Wed & Sun). The displays begin with the period of the establishment of the first Republic in 1888 and end with Presidente Vargas's 1954 suicide, though it's the palace's spectacular Moorish Hall and opulent marble and stained glass that make a visit so worthwhile. Behind the palace is the Parque do Catete, a pleasing tranquil spot, while neighbouring to the south is the **Museu de Folclore Edison Carneiro** (Tues–Fri 10am–6pm, Sat & Sun 3–6pm; free), which holds a fascinating collection of traditional leatherwork, musical instruments, ceramics, toys and Afro-Brazilian religious paraphernalia.

FLAMENGO

Busy during the day, the tree-lined streets of **Flamengo** (Metrô Largo do Machado or Catete) are also lively after dark with residents eating in the local restaurants; it's tranquil enough to sit out on the pavements around large square **Largo do Machado**. The closest **beach** to the city centre is here, a superb place for walking, people-watching, volleyball and admiring the view across the bay to Niterói (see page 256) – though the sea here is not clean enough for swimming.

Skirting the beach as far as Botafogo Bay is the **Parque do Flamengo** (known locally as "Aterro"), the biggest land reclamation project in Brazil, designed by the great landscape architect Roberto Burle Marx and completed in 1960. The park comprises 1.2 square kilometres of prime seafront, and is extremely popular for sports – there are countless football pitches that operate 24hr.

BOTAFOGO

Botafogo (Metrô Botafogo) curves around the bay between Flamengo and the Sugarloaf, a *bairro* known as much for its lively arts scene, restaurants and hostels as its uncomfortably heavy traffic. The bay is dominated by yachts moored near Rio's yacht club, while seven blocks inland the

3

3

district's top attraction is the **Museu do Índio** (Tues–Fri 9am–5.30pm, Sat & Sun 1–5pm; free; ⓦmuseudoindio.gov.br) at Rua das Palmeiras. Housed in an old colonial building, the museum has broad and imaginative multi-sensory displays, as well as utensils, musical instruments, tribal costumes and ritual devices from many of Brazil's dwindling populations of indigenous peoples, plus an extensive library. A block north of here off Rua São Clemente, the bright colours of *favela* Santa Marta light up the Corcovado mountainside. The first of Rio's *favelas* to be pacified by police in 2008, it's now fine to walk around or to take the funicular elevator up to the summit, for fantastic views. In the *favela*'s upper west area you'll find a life-size bronze sculpture of Michael Jackson, a tribute to the late singer's (then controversial) shooting of the video *They Don't Care About Us* here in 1995, directed by Spike Lee.

To the south of the *bairro*, at the foot of Rua São João Batista, is the **Cemitério São João Batista**, the Zona Sul's largest resting place, with extravagant tombs for the Rio elite – Carmen Miranda and Bossa Nova master Tom Jobim are both near its central area. Botafogo's best bars and restaurants lie westwards around Rua Visconde de Caravelas. The **Cobal de Humaitá**, a partially covered complex of some twenty eateries, lies nearby on Rua Voluntários da Pátria.

URCA AND THE SUGARLOAF

The small, wealthy *bairro* of **Urca** stands on a promontory formed by a land reclamation project and flanked by golden beaches. Facing Flamengo, the **Praia da Urca**, only 100m long, is frequented almost exclusively by the *bairro*'s inhabitants, while in front of the cable-car station (see below) is **Praia Vermelha**, a gorgeous cove sheltered from the Atlantic and popular with swimmers.

The beaches aren't the main draw, however: a cable-car ride up the **Pão de Açúcar** is not to be missed. Rising where Guanabara Bay meets the Atlantic Ocean, **Sugarloaf** is so named because of its similarity in shape to the moulded loaves in which sugar was commonly sold in the days before granulated took over. The **cable-car**

station (daily 8am–8pm; every 20min, last car back down at 9pm; R$80; ⓦbondinho.com.br) is located at Praça General. Tibúrcio (bus "Urca" or "Praia Vermelha" from Centro, #581 from Ipanema and Copacabana). The 1325m journey is made in two stages, first to the summit of **Morro da Urca** (220m), then onwards to Pão de Açúcar itself (396m). It is possible to hike the first section and take the cable car for the second stage only, but it will not save you any money and you must first buy a ticket for the whole journey from the cable-car station, as tickets are not sold at the halfway stage. Aim to arrive well before sunset on a clear day and you'll find views as glorious as you could imagine right over the city.

COPACABANA AND LEME

Leme and **Copacabana** are different stretches of the same 4km beach. At the northeastern end of the Praia do Leme, the Morro do Leme rises up to the ruined **Forte do Leme** (Tues–Sun 9am–4.30pm, but closed in bad weather; R$4), a thirty-minute cobblestone walk from the army's sports club, great for more wonderful views of the Zona Sul and Guanabara Bay. Leme morphs into Copacabana at Avenida Princesa Isabel. The **Praia de Copacabana** runs a further 3km to the military-owned **Forte de Copacabana** (Tues–Sun 10am–7.30pm; museum 10am–6pm; R$6; ⓦfortedecopacabana.com), certainly worth a wander around and a drink at its branch of *Confeitaria Colombo*. The area's newest attraction is the **Museu da Imagem e do Som** (ⓦmis.rj.gov.br/nova-sede), which was due to open in 2014, but hasn't as yet. Covering the history of Brazil's film, recording and broadcast media, it will also house memorabilia from the now-defunct Carmen Miranda Museum, dedicated to Brazil's best-known Hollywood star. Copacabana's **beach** is stunning, right down to its over-the-top mosaic pavements, designed by Roberto Burle Marx to mimic rolling waves. The seafront is backed by a line of high-rise hotels and apartments that have sprung up since the 1940s, while a steady stream of noisy traffic clogs the two-lane **Avenida**

Atlântica. A strong undercurrent at Copacabana means that it is dangerous even for strong swimmers – don't do anything the locals don't do. Another problem is theft: take only the money and clothes that you will need.

ARPOADOR, IPANEMA AND LEBLON

On the other side of the point from Forte de Copacabana, the lively waters off **Arpoador** are popular with families and the elderly, as the ocean here is calmer than its neighbours – and the "Arpoador rock" often draws crowds to applaud the sunset. From here, as far as the unkempt and balding greenery of the **Jardim de Alah**, 3km away, you're in **Ipanema**; thereafter lies **Leblon**. The beaches here are stupendous and packed at weekends. Stalls sell fresh coconuts, while for bars and restaurants you'll need to walk a couple of blocks inland. Ipanema's beach is unofficially divided according to the particular interests of beach users; the "rainbow beach" between Rua Farme de Amoedo and Rua Teixeira de Melo is where gay men are concentrated, while posto 9 beyond is firmly for the party crowd; posto 10 is a little more low-key. On Sunday, the seafront road is closed to traffic, and given over to strollers, skateboarders and rollerbladers. At the far end of Leblon, the marvellously located Vidigal *favela*, "pacified" by police in 2011 along with neighbouring (and still sometimes violent) Rocinha, covers the hillside, and completes the sweep around the bay.

Since the 1960s, Ipanema and Leblon have developed a reputation as a fashion centre, and are now seen as among the most chic *bairros* in all of Brazil. Try to visit on a Friday for the **food and flower market** on the Praça de Paz, or on Sunday for the **Feira Hippie** bric-a-brac market at Praça General Osório. Bars and restaurants are scattered throughout the two *bairros*, though many of Rio's best restaurants are located around Leblon's Rua Dias Ferreira.

LAGOA, GÁVEA AND JARDIM BOTÂNICO

Inland from Ipanema's plush beaches is the Lagoa Rodrigo de Freitas, always referred to simply as **Lagoa**. A lagoon linked to the ocean by a narrow canal that passes through Ipanema's Jardim de Alah, Lagoa is fringed by wealthy apartment buildings. On Sundays, its 8km perimeter pathway comes alive with strollers, rollerbladers, joggers and cyclists. Summer evenings are especially popular, with food stalls and live music at parks on the southeastern and western shores of the lagoon.

North of Leblon, heading west from Lagoa's shores, is **Gávea**, home of the **Jockey Club**. Races usually take place four times a week (Mon 6.15–11pm, Fri 5–9.30pm, Sat & Sun 1.15–8pm; shorts not allowed; ⊕jcb.com.br). Any bus marked "via Jóquei" will get you here; get off at Praça Santos Dumont at the end of Rua Jardim Botânico. About 3km northwest of the Jockey Club, at Rua Marquês de São Vicente 476, is the **Instituto Moreira Salles** (Tues–Sun 11am–8pm; free; ⊕ims.com.br), one of Rio's most beautiful cultural centres. Completed in 1951, the house is one of the finest examples of modernist architecture in Brazil – and the gardens, landscaped by Roberto Burle Marx, are attractive too.

THE GIRL FROM IPANEMA

It was at a bar called **Veloso** in 1962 that master composer-musicians Tom Jobim and Vinicius de Moraes sat down and penned *Garota de Ipanema* – **The Girl from Ipanema** – which put both bossa nova and Ipanema on the global arts map. The song was inspired by 15-year-old local girl Heloisa Paez Pinto, who would pass each morning on her way to the beach. These days the bar has been renamed *A Garota de Ipanema*, and is located at Rua Vinicius de Moraes 49 – changed from Rua Montenegro in honour of the lyricist – while the song has been kept alive through numerous cover versions by the likes of Frank Sinatra and Shirley Bassey. Heloisa posed as a *Playboy* playmate in 1987 and 2003 – the latter at the age of 58 – and now runs a chain of fashion stores (one next door to the bar, at Rua Vinicius de Moraes 53). No prizes for guessing the name.

3

BARRA DA TIJUCA AND THE OLYMPICS

Rio's answer to Miami Beach, **Barra da Tijuca** occupies the coastal plain of the city's west zone (Zona Oeste) between an inland lagoon system and 23km of almost unbroken white sand. The natural setting is stupendous, but unless you have a love for skyscrapers and shopping malls (Barra Shopping offers a full kilometre of consumer therapy), not to mention your own wheels, you're unlikely to find a trip here very enlightening – or easy on the pocket.

Half the events of the **2016 Olympic Games** took place in Barra, mainly in a purpose-built Olympic village on the shores of picturesque Lagoa de Jacarepaguá (30km by road west of Leblon), a development which includes the vast RioCentro conference centre, famous for hosting the 1992 UN Earth Summit. Unusually, the main Olympic stadiums are located a good distance away: the Maracanã hosted the opening and closing ceremonies and much of the football, while the athletics competitions were at Engenhão stadium in the Zona Norte, an arrangement which had already been rehearsed at the 2007 Pan-American Games.

Controversy followed Barra's land speculation boom in advance of the games. Voracious **development** monopolized city resources for a quarter-century from the late 1960s, yet planners failed to account for the area's working-class builders, maids and other service personnel. As with other areas of Rio, *favelas* grew quickly, the most famous of which is just inland from Barra at Cidade de Deus (City of God), immortalized worldwide in the namesake Oscar-nominated film. While long-standing conflict ended with the implementation of a police "pacification" unit in 2009, removal of other irregular housing around Barra remains a matter of extreme contention – not least because many of their residents were forcibly removed from *favelas* in Rio's Zona Sul under the military dictatorship in the 1970s. New hotels, a golf course, bus routes and a metrô extension produced a mixed bag for a region not known for its social inclusion. Journalists and campaigners are eagerly following Olympic developments: check out the excellent sites ⓦrioblog.com and ⓦrioonwatch.org.

To the northwest of Lagoa lies the **Jardim Botânico** *bairro*, whose **Parque Lage** (daily 8am–5pm; free; ⓦeavparquelage. rj.gov.br), designed by the British landscape gardener John Tyndale in the early 1840s, consists of primary forest with a labyrinthine network of paths and ponds, as well as its artsy *Café do Lage* inside an Italianate mansion. A little further west is the **Jardim Botânico** itself (Mon noon–5pm, Tues–Sun 8am–5pm; R$15; ⓦjbrj.gov.br), half of it natural jungle, the other half laid out in impressive avenues lined with immense imperial palms that date from the garden's inauguration in 1808. A number of sculptures are dotted throughout, notably the Greek mythology-inspired *Ninfa do Eco* and *Caçador Narciso* (1783), the first two metal sculptures cast in Brazil.

CORCOVADO AND CHRIST THE REDEEMER

The unmistakeable Art Deco statue of **Cristo Redentor** (Christ the Redeemer), gazing across the bay from the **Corcovado** ("hunchback") hill with arms outstretched in welcome, or as if preparing for a dive into the waters below, is the city's most famous emblem. The immense statue – 30m high and weighing over 1000 metric tonnes – was scheduled for completion in 1922 as part of Brazil's centenary independence celebrations. In fact, it wasn't finished until 1931. In clear weather, it's every bit as awe-inspiring as you'd imagine – the journey up to the statue is breathtaking day or night – though what ought to be one of Rio's highlights can turn into a great disappointment if the Corcovado is hidden by cloud. By day the whole of Rio and Guanabara Bay is laid out magnificently before you; after dark, the flickering city lights of this vast metropolis create a stunning visual effect far more impressive than any artificial light show, enhanced by your position at Jesus's feet.

Most people reach the statue by the **Corcovado cog train** (daily every 30min 8am–7pm; tickets (R$61–74) are best obtained in advance, either online at ⓦcorcovado.com.br, or at post offices, or Rio Sul shopping mall in Botafogo, or the Riotur information kiosks on Praça Largo do Machado and on Avenida Atlántica in Copacabana opposite Rua Hilário de

PARQUE NACIONAL DA TIJUCA

The mountains running southwest from the Corcovado are covered with forest, representing the periphery of the **Parque Nacional da Tijuca** (daily: winter 8am–5pm; summer 8am–6pm; free; Ⓦ parquedatijuca.com.br). The park offers sixteen walking trails and some excellent views of Rio, and makes an appealing day retreat away from the city. The trails are steep and not for the unfit, but if you have the energy climb two to three hours for staggering views from coastal Pedra da Gávea (842m; guide essential), or in the far north of the forest, Pico da Tijuca (1021m) above popular picnic spot Bom Retiro. **Public transport** to the park is not especially convenient so it's most easily visited by car, taxi or on a tour. Alternatively, take #301 or #345 from Avenida Presidente Vargas in Centro or from Jardim Oceânico metrô station, asking to be let off at Alta de Boa Vista by the park entrance. Also accessible on foot from here is the Museu do Açude (Estrada do Açude 764; Wed–Mon 11am–5pm; R$6, Thurs free; Ⓦ museuscastromaya.com.br), built by the man responsible for the reforestation of the park, and containing wonderful Chinese bronze sculpture, painted vases and, outside, well-maintained forest trails interwoven with art installations.

Excellent small-group **hiking tours** are run by Rio Hiking (half a day from R$190/person; ☏ 21 2552 9204, Ⓦ riohiking.com.br). For a bird's-eye view take a tandem flight with a **hang-gliding** instructor; an experienced and reliable operator is Just Fly Rio (R$420; ☏ 21 99985 7540, Ⓦ justfly. com.br), with daily flights when weather permits. If you want to **cycle**, enter the park in the Zona Sul at Rua Pacheco Leão, which runs up the side of the Jardim Botânico to the Entrada dos Macacos and on to the Vista Chinesa, from where there's a marvellous view of Guanabara Bay and the Zona Sul.

3

Gouveia. The train leaves from the station at Rua Cosme Velho 513 (bus #180 from Centro or Catete, #570 from Ipanema, #583 from Copacabana, or a metrô feeder bus from Largo do Machado station with through metrô–bus tickets available) and proceeds slowly upwards through lush forest as it enters the **Parque Nacional da Tijuca** (see above). You still need to buy the same ticket in advance if you take a taxi to the top or if you walk from Parque Lage (see page 248), a steep and gruelling two- to three-hour climb on which, although there hasn't been a robbery for some years, it's still advisable to walk in a group.

MARACANÃ STADIUM

Sports fans will not want to miss the **Maracanã** (Metrô Maracanã; Linha 2) – the world's most famous football stadium, steeped in soccer history, which was refurbished before the 2014 World Cup, with a capacity of 78,800. The real name of this monumental arena is actually **Estadio Mario Filho**; *Maracanã* is a nickname derived from the Brazilian word for a macaw and given to a nearby river. But it's not just football that earns the stadium its place in the record books. In 1991 former Beatle Paul McCartney played to a crowd of 180,000 people here, the highest ever concert attendance. It's certainly worth

coming to a game, but if your visit doesn't coincide with a match, you can **tour** the stadium (hourly 9am–4pm, last tour on match days 7hr before kick-off; R$60; Ⓦ tourmaracana.com.br), visiting the dressing room, dug-out, press stand, and of course the hallowed turf itself.

QUINTA DA BOA VISTA

The area covered by the **Quinta da Boa Vista** (daily 9am–5pm; free; Metrô São Cristóvão) was once incorporated in a *sesmaria* (a colonial land grant) held by Jesuits in the seventeenth century, before it became the country seat of the Portuguese royal family in 1808. The park, with its wide expanses of greenery, tree-lined avenues, lakes and games areas, is an excellent place for a stroll, though it can get crowded at weekends. Looking out from a hilltop in the centre of the park is the imposing Neoclassical **Museu Nacional** (winter Mon noon–5pm, Tues–Sun 10am–4pm, summer Mon noon–6pm, Tues–Sun 10am–6pm; R$6; Ⓦ museunacional.ufrj.br). Its archeological section deals with the human history of Latin America; in the Brazilian room, exhibits of Tupi-Guarani and Marajó ceramics lead on to the indigenous ethnographical section, uniting pieces collected from the numerous tribes that once populated Brazil and with displays on

3

RIO DE JANEIRO TOURS

You can get around most of Rio's sights independently, but for off-the-beaten-track exploring such as to *favelas* and football matches, or for outdoor activities, experienced guides are on hand to help. All operators listed below speak English. Book tours personally rather than through commission-hungry hostels/hotels.

TOUR OPERATORS

Bike in Rio ☎ 21 98474 7740, ⓦ bikeinriotours.com. Four different bicycle tours of Rio and bike rentals.

Cruz the Coast ☎21 3251 5833, ⓦ cruzthecoastbrazil.com. Operates an excellent guided minibus trip to Salvador with a ten-day itinerary including accommodation and numerous excursions (from R$1190).

Favela Adventures ☎ 21 98221 5572, ⓦ favelatour. org. Offers a variety of tours of Rocinha, including opportunities to party with the locals.

Favela Tour ☎ 21 3322 2727, ⓦ favelatour.com.br. Responsible, community-approved trips to Rocinha by minibus for R$75.

Helisight ☎ 21 2511 2141, ⓦ helisight.com.br. Panoramic helicopter rides from Morro da Urca.

Jungle Me ☎ 21 4105 7533, ⓦ jungleme.com.br. Hikes in Parque Nacional da Tijuca (see page 249) and a Brazilian cooking class.

Rio Hiking ☎ 21 2552 9204, ⓦ riohiking.com.br. Offers a variety of trips around the city and state, as well as nightlife tours and adventure sports.

Brazilian folklore and Afro-Brazilian cults. The surprisingly spacious **Rio Zoo** (Tues–Sun 9am–5pm; R$15; ⓦ riozoo.com.br) is located next door.

ARRIVAL AND DEPARTURE

By plane Tom Jobim International Airport, known as Galeão (☎ 21 3398 5050, ⓦ aeroportogaleao.net), is 15km north of the centre and also handles many domestic flights. Santos Dumont Airport (☎ 21 3814 7070, ⓦ aeroportosantosdumont.net), southeast of (and walking distance from) Centro, handles mainly short-haul domestic services, including the São Paulo shuttle. Frequent executive buses (every 20min 5.30am–10.30pm; R$14) link the airports with the *rodoviária* (bus terminal), city centre and the Zona Sul beaches, passing through Flamengo, Botafogo, Copacabana, Ipanema and Leblon. To take a taxi at Galeão, buy a pre-paid ticket at one of the desks in arrival (R$74 to Copacabana); at Santos Dumont city taxis (yellow with a blue stripe) are on hand outside the terminal (R$33 to Copacabana, more at night).
Destinations São Paulo (approximately every 15min 6am–10.30pm; 1hr); Belo Horizonte (4–5 daily; 1hr 5min); Foz do Iguaçu (5–6 daily; 2hr 10min); Salvador (8–11 daily; 2hr 05min); Recife (7–9 daily; 2hr 50min).
By bus Buses arrive at the vast Rodoviária Novo Rio (☎ 21 3213 1800), 3km northwest of the centre at Av Francisco Bicalho. Late at night take a pre-paid taxi (R$25 to Centro, R$43 to Copacabana), otherwise take executive bus #2017 (R$14) to Flamengo, Botafogo, Copacabana, Ipanema and Leblon, or cross the street to Praça Hermes for city buses including TRO-8 to Centro and Cateche. Book intercity services a couple of days in advance at the *rodoviária* or from agencies such as Dantur in the Galeria do Condor mall on the south side of Largo do Machado (ⓦ dantur.com.br).

Destinations Belo Horizonte (17 daily, most overnight; 6hr 30min); Brasília (2 daily; 17hr); Foz do Iguaçu (5 daily; 23hr); Ouro Preto (3 daily; 7hr); Petrópolis (every 40min; 1hr 30min); Salvador (1 daily; 32hr); São Paulo (approximately every 15min; 6hr); Angra dos Reis (for Ilha Grande; approximately hourly; 3hr).

GETTING AROUND

By bus Buses are frequent and many run 24hr; numbers and destinations are clearly marked on the front. Get on at the front and pay the seated conductor; guard your valuables. Bus routes/numbers are available at ⓦ vadeonibus.com.br.
By ferry Frequent crossings from the terminal at Praça XV de Novembro to Niterói (see page 256) cost R$5.90 and take 20min.
By metrô Mon–Sat 5am–midnight, Sun 7am–11pm. *Linhas 1* and *4* (the same train) link Barra de Tijuca, Leblon, Ipanema, Copacabana, Botafogo and Flamengo with Centro (downtown) and several stations to the north; *Linha 2* runs from the northern suburbs to Centro and Botafogo. Tickets are R$4.30, with no discount for multiple journeys, but combined metrô and bus tickets (*superfície* or *integração*) are available for certain routes.
By tram The VLT tram system (ⓦ vltrio.rio) has two lines: line 1 from Santos Dumont airport and line 2 from Praça XV, both running, by different routes, through Centro to the Rodoviária Novo Rio. You can only pay VLT fares using a R$3 card available and chargeable at machines at all VLT stops, which you can also use on the metrô and on city buses in both Rio and Niterói.
By taxi Rio's taxis come in two varieties: yellow with a blue stripe, or white with a red-and-yellow stripe; the latter are pricier, more comfortable radio cabs, which you order by phone. Both have meters and you should insist that they are activated (except from the *rodoviária* or Galeão airport; pick up a ticket at the booth). Radio cabs include Santo Amaro Táxi in Glória (☎ 21 2252 0054) and Coopertramo in Bonsucesso (☎ 21 2209 9292).

INFORMATION

Tourist information Information about the city of Rio is from Riotur (W rio.rj.gov.br/riotur and W visit.rio), which distributes maps and brochures and has information booths at Rodoviária Novo Rio, both airports, Praça XV, Copacabana (O 21 2298 7890) and dotted about town.

ACCOMMODATION

Rio is by no means cheap, and during Carnaval and *Reveillon* (when you should book well in advance) you can expect to pay way over the odds. That said, there are numerous youth hostels, catering to a massive crowd of budget travellers. Accommodation is cheapest in Botafogo, Catete and Lapa, with Santa Teresa marginally more, Copacabana more still, and chic Ipanema/Leblon the most expensive. Most options include breakfast.

CENTRO, LAPA AND SANTA TERESA

Hotel Belas Artes Rua Visconde do Rio Branco 52, Centro O 21 2252 6336, W hotelbelasartes.com.br; map p.240. This small city-centre hotel in a pretty 1930s building has three types of simply furnished but impeccably clean rooms at slightly varying rates, but all are good value. R$140
Belga Hotel Rua Dos Andradas 129, Centro O 21 2263 9086, W belgahotel.com.br; map p.240. The rooms are small (standard rooms have double beds only) but they use their space economically at this well-designed, cool and modern city-centre hotel in a 1927 Art Deco building, where the bar and restaurant have a Belgian theme. R$207
Casa Áurea Rua Áurea 80, Santa Teresa O 21 3081 4652, W pousada-casa-aurea-rio.com; map p.240. Lovely pousada in a charming old house with an attractive courtyard garden and friendly, multilingual staff always on hand for local advice. Dorms R$70, doubles R$220
Hotel Ibis Budget Rua Silva Jardim 32, Centro O 21 3511 8500, W ibis.com; map p.240. The rooms here are triples, and the price is the same for one, two or three people. All are spotless, with their own bathrooms, and you can usually get reduced prices online. Breakfast is not included, and there's a three-day minimum stay. R$166
Marajó Rua São Joaquim da Silva 99, Lapa O 21 2224 4134, W hotelmarajorio.com; map p.240. Excellent choice for budget travellers not keen on the hostel scene. Modern facilities, clean, spacious rooms and friendly service in the heart of vibrant Lapa. Rooms at the front can be noisy at night. R$130

CATETE, FLAMENGO AND BOTAFOGO

Baron Garden Rua Barão de Guaratiba, Morro da Glória O 21 97293 1181, W barongarden.com; map p.240. A colonial house with grand views, pool and garden, a short walk from Flamengo beach and Metrô Catete, aimed at the 30-plus budget traveller. R$180
Imperial Hotel Rua do Catete 186, Catete O 21 2112 6000, W imperialhotel.com.br; map p.240. Spacious, modern rooms are housed in a distinguished-looking 1880s building well located near the *metrô* and the park. Parking is available and there's also a decent-sized pool, which is unusual for a hotel in this price category. R$186.90
Vila Carioca Rua Estacio Coimbra 84, Botafogo O 21 2535 3224, W vilacarioca.com.br; map p.242. Small and friendly hostel near Botafogo metrô station, with neat, balconied dorm rooms, patio and chill-out area. Has internet access and a/c. Dorms R$35, doubles $130

COPACABANA

Bamboo Rio Hostel Rua Lacerda Coutinho 45 O 21 2236 1117, W bamboorio.com; map p.242. Six blocks from the beach in a quiet, leafy suburb, *Bamboo Rio* is a hostel with refreshingly colourful, a/c rooms, a little plunge pool, great atmosphere, and a pleasant garden with wild monkeys. Excellent value. Dorms R$30, doubles R$100

STAY IN A FAVELA

Contrary to what the media would have you believe, Rio does have safe *favelas*, and staying in one can be an enjoyable, enlightening experience.

Babilônia Rio Hostel Ladeira Ari Barroso 50, Babilônia, Leme O 21 3873- 6826, W babiloniariohostel.com.br; map p.242. In a little favela just above Leme, bright and breezy with ocean views, a cool vibe and clean, airy dorms with three-storey bunks. Three quarters of their electricity is generated by their own solar panels. Breakfast is R$5 per person extra. Dorms R$30, doubles R$100
The Maze Rua Tavares Bastos 414, Casa 66, Catete O 21 2558 5547, W themazerio.com; map p.240. An eccentric, Gaudí-esque pousada with a truly inspirational view across Guanabara Bay. Offers a huge British-Brazilian breakfast and a weekly curry buffet lunch, and also hosts a popular monthly jazz night. R$140
Varandas do Vidigal Rua Madre Ana Coimbra, Casa 3 (off Av Goulart), Vidigal O 21 3114 3661, W varandasdovidigal.com.br; map p.238. Amazing sea views make the climb worthwhile at this super-friendly hostel in a vibrant community located to the west of Leblon. Buses #177, #521 and #522 and airport bus #2018 will take you to the entrance of the *favela*, from where there is transport up the hill. Dorms R$30, doubles R$125

3

3

(but R$48/R$240 on holidays other than Christmas and Carnival)

Che Lagarto Hostel Rua Barata Ribeiro 111 ☎21 3209 0348, ⓦchelagarto.com; map p.242. They pack them in here, but if big hostels are your thing and you don't mind the Copacabana price you won't regret staying here. Clean, with numerous facilities and the organization for which the name is known. Dorms R$75

Che Lagarto Hostel Suites Rua Santa Clara 305 ☎21 2257 3133, ⓦchelagarto.com; map p.242. This branch of the most established chain of hostels in Rio has gone upmarket, with smart, comfortable rooms and decent facilities, 10min walk from the beach. It costs less during the week. R$150

Jucati Rua Tenente Marones de Gusmão 85 ☎21 2547 5422, ⓦedificiojucati.com.br; map p.242. On an attractive residential square, this is a bargain if you're travelling in a group (always ask for a discount at booking). Apartments have a double and two bunks, TV and kitchenette. R$150 (four people R$210)

Temporada Copacabana Edificio Av Atlantica 3196 ☎21 2255 0681, ⓦtemporadacopacabana.com.br; map p.242. It won't win awards, but if you always dreamt of staying by the beach and can't afford the *Copacabana Palace*, this is your place. Note however that, even by Rio standards, the price goes crazy at Carnaval (R$2250!). No breakfast. R$160

IPANEMA AND LEBLON

Bonita Rua Barão da Torre 107 ☎21 2227 1703, ⓦbonitaipanema.com; map p.242. Bright candy-pink on the outside, this litle pousada was once the home of jazz and bossa nove legend Tom Jobim. It's quiet, it's pretty, and it even has a pool – all in all, pretty good value, with rates that beat most of Ipanema's hostels. Dorms R$70, doubles R$199

Lemon Spirit Hostel Rua Cupertino Durão 56, Leblon ☎21 2294 1853, ⓦlemonspirit.com; map p.242. It's difficult to believe that there's this hostel in the heart of Leblon, just one block from the beach and in one of the oldest buildings in this exclusive *bairro*. All rooms are a/c, there's a guest kitchen and a nice patio. Dorms R$70

Mango Tree Hostel Rua Prudente de Moraes 594 ☎21 3083 5031, ⓦmangotreehostel.com; map p.242. A block from posto 9 on the beach, this is easily Ipanema's best hostel option. Spacious dorms, grand bathrooms and an overgrown garden with hammocks. Dorms R$88, doubles R$208

EATING

Rio offers a huge variety of cuisines to discerning diners. In general, Cariocas eat well at lunch, so you'll find most restaurants in Centro and other office districts only open during the day. At night eating and drinking are always done together, whether in an informal bar with shared *petiscos* (tapas plates) or pricier fine dining. Santa Teresa, Botafogo and Leblon are the city's key districts for innovative options.

CENTRO AND LAPA

Bar Ocidental Rua Miguel Couto 124, Centro ☎21 2233 4042; map p.240. On a small pedestrianized street that runs alongside Rio Branco all the way up from Sete de Septembro, this is a cheap little bar where you can sit at a table outside and enjoy an early evening *chopp* (R$6) with a plate of fresh sardines (R$2.50 per fish). Mon–Sat 7am–10pm.

Beduino Av Presidente Wilson 123 ☎21 2524 5142, ⓦarabebeduino.com.br; map p.240. Popular and inexpensive Arabic restaurant, where a full meze spread (Lebanese hors d'oeuvres such as hummus or tabbouleh) will set you back R$62.90, or you can get just three *meze* dishes for R$32.76. A great option for vegetarians and carnivores alike. Mon–Sat 7am–11.15pm.

Cosmopolita Travessa do Mosqueira 4 ☎21 2224 7820; map p.240. An excellent Portuguese restaurant established in 1926 with a loyal and bohemian clientele. Fish dishes are firm favourites especially those based on saltfish (all R$120). Mon–Thurs 8am–10pm, Fri & Sat 8am–11pm.

Mangue Seco Cachaçaria Rua do Lavradio 23 ☎21 3852 1947, ⓦmanguesecocachacaria.com.br; map p.240. This great bar, offering the twin night-time pleasures of samba and *cachaça*, in the daytime also serves really good meals for a reasonable price. Specialities include *moqueca* (fish stew in coconut milk, R$106), with *pratos executivos* (cheap lunchtime dishes) from R$42, and seating indoors or on the pavment. Mon 11.30am–4pm, Tues–Sat 11.30am–2am.

SANTA TERESA

Bar do Arnaudo Rua Almirante Alexandrino 316 ☎21 2210 0817; map p.240. An excellent mid-priced place to sample traditional food from Brazil's northeast, such as

---

★ TREAT YOURSELF

Confeitaria Colombo Rua Gonçalves Dias 32, Centro ☎21 2505 1500, ⓦconfeitariacolombo.com.br; map p.240. Take the lift for a peek at the grand salão upstairs (after 4pm) or indulge in the excellent and huge teatime buffet, usually on Thursdays or Fridays at 5–7.30pm (R$69.50, check the website for dates). Otherwise relax over coffee or tea with pastries. An unmissable Rio institution. Mon–Fri 9am–7pm, Sat 9am–5pm.

Miam Miam Rua General Góes Monteiro 34, Botafogo ☎21 2244 0125, ⓦmiammiam.com.br; map p.242. Splashing out here is more than worthwhile, with creative international fusion dishes (palm heart tagliarini with prawns, for example, at R$78.90). They also plan to reintroduce their tasting menu (probably for around R$180). Tues–Fri noon–3.30pm & 7pm–midnight, Sat 1pm–midnight.

carne do sol (sun-dried meat, served with sweet manioc; R$58) and *caldinho de feijão de corda* (bean soup with pork scratchings; R$6). Daily 11.30am–8pm.

Bar do Mineiro Rua Paschoal Carlos Magno 99 ☎21 2221 9227, ⍵bardomineiro.net; map p.240. Inexpensive and authentic country-style food in an old bar that could be in any small town in Minas Gerais. Try the *carne seca abóbora* (dried meat in pumpkin purée; R$92), and there are also good beers and an excellent range of *cachaça*. Tues–Sun 11am–1am.

Espírito Santa Rua Almirante Alexandrino 264 ☎21 2507 4840; map p.240. Multi-regional Brazilian cuisine, the focus being on adaptations of flavoursome dishes from the Amazon, Bahia and Minas Gerais (seafood *bobó* R$68), with a fair few vegetarian versions (veg *moqueca* R$40.50). Daily noon–midnight.

FLAMENGO, BOTAFOGO AND URCA

Adega Portugália Largo do Machado 66a, Catete ☎21 2558 2821, ⍵adegaportugalia.com.br; map p.240. Don't miss out on the delicious house speciality at this popular bar/restaurant: casserole of tender roast goat (R$64.90), washed down with copious quantities of cold *chopp*. Daily 11am–midnight or later.

Bar Urca Rua Cândido Gaffrée 205, Urca ☎21 2295 8744, ⍵barurca.com.br; map p.242. Traditional neighbourhood gathering-point, with a bar on the street and a restaurant upstairs, where low-priced *pratos executivos* (Mon–Fri till 3pm) include prawn risotto (R$68). Restaurant: Mon–Sat 11.30am–11pm, Sun 11.30am–8pm; bar: Mon–Fri 6am–11pm, Sat 8am–11pm, Sun 8am–8pm.

Cobal Rua Voluntários da Pátria 446, Humaitá; map p.242. Humaitá's impressive indoor market, where you can take your pick of the moderately priced but excellent *lanchonetes* serving Brazilian Northeastern, Italian and Japanese food; this is a very popular lunch and evening meeting point for local residents. Daily 7am–11pm.

Tacacá do Norte Rua Barão do Flamengo 35-R, Flamengo ☎21 2205 7545; map p.242. A *lanchonete* with a difference: here you can try delights from the Amazon like the signature dish, *tacacá* (yellow shrimp and cassava hot pepper soup; R$27), and easily the best *açaí* in Rio, served with tapioca and granola (R$24). Mon–Sat 9am–11pm, Sun 9am–7pm.

COPACABANA

Arab Av Atlântica 1936 ☎21 2235 1884; map p.242. Reasonably priced Lebanese and North African restaurant, where you can enjoy meze at R$27 a portion, with main courses such as lamb couscous for R$62. Mon 5pm–1am, Tues–Sun 9am–1am.

Bar do David Ladeira Ari Barroso 66, Chapéu Mangueira ☎21 2542 4713; map p.242. Up in a little *favela* just above Leme, chef David has received press accolades for excellent shrimp bobó, seafood croquettes, and in particular

his signature seafood *feijoada* (R$45). It's also a great place for just a drink, but it does get quite rammed at weekends. Tues–Sun 11.30am–9pm.

Big Nectar Av Nossa Senhora de Copacabana 985, at Xavier Silveira ☎21 2522 1354; map p.242. A cut above the average *lanchonete* in Copa, serving pretty decent steak or chicken combo dishes for R$21, and quality juices. Daily 24hr.

Caranguejo Rua Barata Ribeiro 771, at Rua Xavier da Silveira ☎21 2235 1249; map p.242. Excellent street-corner seafood joint, where you can start with a dozen crab claws for R$39 before you tuck into a succulent prawn stroganoff (R$186). Daily 11am–1am.

Cervantes Av Prado do Júnior 335-B (restaurant) and Rua Barata Ribeiro 7 (bar) ☎21 2275 6147, ⍵restaurantecervantes.com.br; map p.242. Doing a roaring trade day and night, this restaurant/bar linked at the rear serves speciality thick-wedge meat sandwiches (steak with cheese and pineapple R$32). Tues–Sun noon–4am.

Deck Av Atlântica 2316, Copacabana, ⍵deckrestaurante. com.br; map p.242. This always-busy restaurant offers lunchtime buffets (R$20 Mon–Thurs, R$26 Fri–Sun) until 4.30pm. Daily noon–midnight.

IPANEMA AND LEBLON

Casa da Feijoada Rua Prudente de Morais 10, Ipanema ☎21 2247 2776, ⍵cozinhatipica.com.br; map p.242. *Feijoada*, traditionally served only on Saturdays, is offered here seven days a week (R$93), along with other traditional, moderately priced and extremely filling Brazilian dishes. Daily noon–midnight.

Delírio Tropical Rua Garcia D'Ávila 48, Ipanema ☎21 3624 8164, ⍵delirio.com.br; map p.242. Just a block from the beach and the best value for lunch you'll find anywhere near it, with lots of veggie options such as salads (R$16.50–25) and grilled trout (R$18.90), as well as light fish or meat options. Mon–Sat 11am–9pm, Sun in winter 11am–7pm, Sun in summer noon–8pm.

Fontes Galeria Astor, Rua Visconde de Pirajá 605 ☎21 2512 5900, ⍵fontesipanema.com.br; map p.242. Does inexpensive dishes made with only natural ingredients, mostly vegetarian. The menu changes daily but typical dishes include *aubergine au gratin* (R$14.60), and on Saturdays a hearty vegetarian *feijoada* is served (R$17). Mon–Fri 11am–9.20pm, Sat 11am–8pm.

New Natural Rua Barão de Torre 173, Ipanema ☎21 2287 0301; map p.242. Really good, mainly vegetarian, organic *por kilo* lunch place (R$49/kg) that always has a couple of meat choices too. Expect numerous salads, soya dishes and fresh juices. Daily 7am–10pm.

Paz e Amor Rua Garcia D'Ávila 173-I, Ipanema ☎21 2523 0496, ⍵restaurantepazeamor.com; map p.242. One end of this Brazilian bar/restaurant serves the best-value *prato feito* set-plate for miles around. R$18 will buy you a bargain pork steak or chicken escalope. Daily 10am–11pm.

3

Zazá Bistrô Tropical Rua Joana Angélica 40 ☎21 2247 9101, ⓦzazabistro.com.br; map p.242. Light-hearted, imaginative fusion cuisine, colourful decor and a terrace with a street-life view make this a popular spot with tourists and trendy locals alike. Dishes include chicken curry in coconut milk (R$72) or seared tuna with mash and wasabi (R$79). Mon–Thurs 6.30pm–12.30am, Fri noon–6pm & 7pm–12.30am, Sat 1–6pm & 7pm–1am, Sun 1–6pm & 7pm–midnight.

DRINKING AND NIGHTLIFE

BARS

Armazem do Chopp Rua Marquês de Abrantes 66, Flamengo, ⓦarmazemdochopp.com.br; map p.240. Beer hall serving decent-quality food in large quantities. The terrace overlooks the street, and the *bolinhas de bacalhau* (saltfish croquette balls; R$27.20 for five) are an excellent accompaniment to an icy glass of *chopp*. On Fridays in particular it tends to stay open late. Daily 11am–2am (or later).

Bar do Gomez (aka Armazém São Thiago) Rua Áurea, 26; map p.240. Santa Teresa's best bar, founded in 1919. The atmosphere's great, the sandwiches are filling, the beer's ice-cold, and there's a huge selection of *cachaças*. Mon–Sat noon–1am, Sun noon–10pm.

Bar Luiz Rua Carioca 39, ⓦbarluiz.com.br; map p.240. This hectic, but essentially run-of-the-mill, restaurant and bar, serving German-style food and chilled *chopp*, was founded in 1887 and is quite an institution. Still a popular meeting place for intellectuals, the food is good but a little overpriced; try the Kassler smoked sausage (R$55). Mon & Sat 11am–5pm, Tues–Fri 11am–9pm.

Garota de Ipanema Rua Vinícius de Morais 49, Ipanema; map p.242. Always busy, this bar entered the folk annals of Rio de Janeiro when the song *The Girl from Ipanema* was written here by Tom Jobim and Vinicius de Moraes (see page 247). While certainly touristy (with unexceptional food), there are few better places in Ipanema for a beer (R$9.50 for a 350ml *chopp*). Daily 11am–2am.

Lapa Esquina Rua Joaquim Silva 141, Lapa, ⓦlapaesquina.blogspot.com.br; map p.240. This little corner bar comes alive Monday, Tuesday and Sunday evenings with samba sounds, and in the daytime on weekdays it serves very low-priced lunch dishes such as salmon and mash, or veg with salad, all for R$20–22. Mon, Tues, Thurs & Fri noon–3am, Sat & Sun 9pm–3am.

LIVE MUSIC

Lapa is Rio's nightlife heart and the undisputed capital of samba: every Friday night around Avenida Mem de Sá and Rua do Lavradio one of the world's biggest street parties takes place, with numerous bars offering the real deal. Despite Lapa's obvious appeal, be careful walking around after dark; if in doubt, take a taxi. Other currently popular outdoor (free) parties include samba at Pedra do Sal (off Rua Sacadura Cabral, nr Praça Mauá, Centro; Mon from

8pm), and street jazz at Praça Tiradentes, Centro (Thurs from 10.30pm). During rehearsals for Carnaval (Sept–Jan), don't miss a trip to a Samba School (see page 255).

Carioca da Gema Av Mem de Sá 79, Lapa ⓦbarcariocadagema.com.br; map p.240. Samba and *choro* bar, this is a more upmarket but very fun place, especially lively on Monday and Friday nights. Mon–Fri 7pm–5am, Sat & Sun 8pm–5am.

Circo Voador Rua dos Arcos, Lapa ⓦcircovoador.com. br; map p.240. Rap, funk and fusion samba-punk-rock in a large circus tent, with a young crowd who come to dance and discover new bands. Fri, Sat and sometimes other days, usually from 10pm.

Democráticos Rua do Riachuelo 93, Lapa ⓦclubedosdemocraticos.com.br; map p.240. Never short on atmosphere, this traditional *gafieira* (dance hall) has been going since 1867, with popular live *forró* (Wed) and usually samba other nights. Wed 10pm–3am, Thurs–Sat 10pm–4am, Sun 8–11.45pm.

Feira Nordestina Campo de São Cristovão, São Cristovão (near Quinta da Boa Vista) ⓦfeiradesaocristovao.org. br; map.242. A 48hr non-stop party in a stadium every weekend might sound far-fetched, but exactly that has been hosted here for decades. *Forró*, funk and reggae for the Zona Norte and Northeastern Brazilian masses, with food and crafts stalls. Popular in the early hours post-clubbing. Tues–Thurs 10am–6pm, Fri 10am–Sun 9pm.

The Maze Rua Tavares Bastos 414, Casa 66, Catete ⓦthemazerio.com; map p.240. Jazz evenings on the first Friday of each month and sometimes other Fridays, in an unusual venue that also offers bed and breakfast (see page 251), run by a British jazz enthusiast and attracting solid local performers. 10pm–4am.

Teatro Odisséia Av Mem de Sá; map p.240. In an old theatre, featuring an eclectic mix of recorded and live Brazilian sounds from rock to samba. Wed–Fri 7.30pm–2am, Sat 7.30pm–6am, Sun 2pm–midnight.

NIGHTCLUBS

Rio's vibrant club scene offers a music mix from pop and rock to hip-hop and *funk Carioca*, as well as superb Brazilian electronica, samba and MPB (*Música Popular Brasileira*). Most places don't get going until midnight; entry fees R$30–60.

Casa da Matriz Rua Henrique Novaes 107, Botafogo ⓦcasadamatriz.com.br; map p.242. Stylish and perennially popular club with different music each night, from rock to reggae and samba to drum 'n' bass.

Castelo das Pedras Estrada de Jacarepaguá 3600, Favela Rio das Pedras, Jacarepaguá; map p.242. Rio's premier *funk Carioca* venue, with 3000-strong crowds of sweating, gyrating bodies. Fri–Sun 11pm–4am.

Club Six Rua das Marrecas 38, Lapa ⓦclubsix.com.br; map p.240. Three dancefloors featuring anything from reggae,

SAMBA

From September to February the ultimate highlight of Rio's nightlife is a visit to a **samba school**, when the emphasis is as much on raising funds for their extravagant Carnaval parade (see page 239) as it is on perfecting routines. Expect drummers and dancers en masse, and thousands of hyped-up revellers. There are many schools, of which a few are listed here; each has its own weekly programme. Check the websites and keep your ear to the ground.

SAMBA SCHOOLS

Beija-Flor Rua Pracinha Wallace Paes Leme 1652, Nilopolis ☎ 21 2247 4800, ⓦ beija-flor.com.br. Founded in 1948, their colours are blue and white; champions in 2003, 2004, 2005, 2007, 2008, 2011 and 2015.

Mangueira Rua Visconde de Niterói 1072, Mangueira ☎ 21 2567 3419, ⓦ mangueira.com.br. The largest and most famous school; weekend events attract many tour groups – so nights out here, while fun, sometimes lack a traditional feel.

Portela Rua Clara Nunes 81, Oswaldo Cruz ☎ 21 3256 9411, ⓦ gresportela.com.br. Thought of as a highly traditional school, with *feijoadas* (usually first Sat of the month), champions in 1984 and 2017.

Salgueiro Rua Silva Telles 104, Andaraí ☎ 21 2238 9226, ⓦ salgueiro.com.br. Most recently champions in 2009. Easily accessed from the Zona Sul and events here are often a great night out.

Unidos da Tijuca Clube dos Portuários, Av Francisco Bicalho 47, São Cristovão ☎ 21 2263 9679, ⓦ unidosdatijuca.com.br. Carnaval champions 2010, 2012 and 2014; has quite a big LGBTQ following.

trance or hip-hop to old-school Brazilian sounds such as *forró* and *zouk*, depending on the night. Fri & Sat 10pm–5am.

Comuna Rua Sorocaba 585, Botafogo ⓦ comuna.cc; map p.242. A split personality of electronica parties, art exhibitions, film screenings and even food makes this warehouse-style space a truly communal entertainment centre. Tues–Wed & Sun 6pm–1am, Thurs–Sat 6pm–2am.

Espaço Acústica Praça Tiradentes 2, Centro ⓦ espacoacustica.com.br; map p.240. Helping along the resurgence of one of Rio's most historic central squares, this is a hip yet unpretentious place to catch some of the best DJ talent in town. Electro/pop/rock/Brazilian mash-up. Fri & Sat from 10pm.

Fosfobox Rua Siquiera Campos 143, Copacabana ⓦ fosfobox.com.br; map p.242. This small, highly rated and long-standing basement club plays underground techno and alternative music for an animated crowd. Brazil's best DJs often pass through. Wed–Sat 11pm–5am.

LGBTQ RIO

Rio has one of the world's liveliest LGBTQ scenes, though you may be surprised that many venues are "GLS" ("gay, lesbian and sympathizers") with clubbers of all persuasions hanging out – for example, at *Fosfobox* (see above). Gay Pride takes place in Copacabana each September; the wildest weekend on the Gay Rio calendar. For up-to-date information check out ⓦ timeout.com.br/rio-de-janeiro/en/gay-lesbian.

Galeria Café Rua Teixeira de Melo 31-E, Ipanema ⓦ galeriacafe.com.br; map p.242. A bright little club catering to all branches of the LGBTQ community, and indeed anyone else who fancies coming along, and on Sundays it becomes a mini indoor market with fashion displays. Wed–Sat 11pm–5am, Sun 11am–8pm.

To Nem Ai Rua Farme de Amoedo 57, Ipanema ☎ 21 1224 7840; map p.242. This bar, done out darkly in black with blue lighting, is of course open to all, but Ipanema's LGBTQ community tend to meet up here for an afternoon drink, or to get in the mood before heading out clubbing of an evening. Mon–Fri 11.30am–3am, Sat & Sun noon–3am.

Turma OK Rua dos Inválidos 39, Centro ⓦ turmaok. com; map p.240. Run by the oldest LGBTQ group in town, this city-centre venue hosts excellent parties every weekend. Fri 9pm–Sun/Mon midnight.

The Week Rua Sacadura Cabral 154, Saúde ⓦ theweek. com.br; map p.240. The Rio branch of a São Paulo gay nightclub pumping out house music all night long. It's very popular so expect to queue. Sat 11.30pm–5am or later.

SHOPPING

Rio is replete with high-class shopping malls and designer stores. The main downtown area for budget shoppers is Saara (see page 243).

Ipanema Hippie Market Praça General Osório, Ipanema. Once it really was for hippies, but nowadays it's a touristy arts and crafts market with souvenirs, street shows and street food. Sun 7am–8pm.

La Vereda Rua Almirante Alexandrino 428, Largo dos Guimarães, Santa Teresa, ⓦ lavereda.com.br. One of the best handicraft shops in town, with a varied collection from all over Brazil, including work by local artists. Mon–Sat 10am–8pm, Sun 10.30am–8pm.

DIRECTORY

Banks and exchange You'll find a lot of banks with ATMs along Av Rio Branco in Centro.

Car rental Most agents are located along Av Princesa Isabel in Copacabana. Avis at no. 350 (☎0800 725 2847); Hertz at no. 500 (☎0800 701 7300); Unidas-at no. 168 (☎0800 771 5158).

Consulates Argentina, Praia de Botafogo 228 (☎21 2553 1646); Australia, Av Presidente Wilson 231, Centro (☎21 3824 4624); Canada, Av Atlantica 1130, Copacabana (☎21 2543 3004); UK, Praia do Flamengo 284, Flamengo (☎21 2555 9600); US, Av Presidente Wilson 147, Centro (☎21 3823 2000).

Hospitals Private hospitals with good reputations include Hospital Samaritano, Rua Bambina 98, Botafogo (☎21 3444 1000, ⓦhsamaritano.com.br), and Hospital Copa d'Or, Rua Figueiredo de Magalhães 875, Copacabana (☎21 2545 3600, ⓦcopador.com.br).

Police Emergency number ☎190. The beach areas have police posts at regular intervals. The efficient, English-speaking Tourist Police are at Av Afrânio de Melo Franco (opposite the Teatro Casa Grande), Leblon (☎21 2332 2924).

Post office Central branch on Rua 1 de Março (Mon–Fri 9am–5pm).

Visas Bring all necessary documents to the Polícia Federal's Registro de Estrangeiros at Galeão Airport, 3rd floor, Terminal 1, Sector A (Mon–Fri 8am–4pm; ☎21 3398 3182, ⓦdpf.gov.br).

Rio de Janeiro state

Though many travellers dash through the state in order to reach its glorious capital city, there are enough regional attractions to more than reward visitors. Either side of Rio lie two idyllic sections of coast. To the east beyond Rio's neighbouring city **Niterói** is the **Costa do Sol**, an area of gorgeous white beaches peppered with a string of low-key resort towns and three large **lakes**. The trendy and commercial resort town of **Búzios** is popular with the affluent but less of a draw for budget travellers, while nearby **Arraial do Cabo** offers a slice of beach paradise. To the south of Rio is one of Brazil's most magnificent landscapes, the **Costa Verde**, dotted with charming resort towns and blessed with dreamy stretches of deserted beach. The colonial town of **Paraty** is one of the region's highlights, while **Ilha Grande**'s verdant forests create a stunning unspoilt setting. The mountainous wooded landscape and relatively cool climate of the state's interior make a refreshing change from the coastal heat. Immediately to the north of Rio, high in mist-cloaked mountains, lies the imperial city of **Petrópolis**, with the magnificent **Parque Nacional Serra dos Orgãos** nearby. In the far west lies another breathtaking protected area, the **Parque Nacional Itatiaia**.

NITERÓI

Cariocas have a tendency to sneer at NITERÓI, typically commenting that the best thing about the city is the view back across Guanabara Bay to Rio. The vistas are undeniably gorgeous, but there are a few things to see too – without the need to stay overnight.

WHAT TO SEE AND DO

The Oscar Niemeyer-designed **Museu de Arte Contemporânea** (MAC; Tues–Sun10am–6pm, closing at 7pm on weekends in summer; R$10, free on Wed; ⓦculturaniteroi.com.br/macniteroi) is Niterói's biggest draw. Opened in 1996 and located just south of the centre on a promontory, the spaceship-like building offers breathtaking 360-degree views of the bay and a worthy, though hardly exciting, permanent display of Brazilian art from the 1950s to the 1990s, plus temporary exhibitions. But the real work of art is the building: trademark Niemeyer curves which even his most hardened critics find difficult to dismiss.

Beautiful **Praia de Icaraí** lies near the city's centre, but as the water in the bay is none too clean, take a bus to **Camboinhas** or **Itacoatiara**, long stretches of sand every bit as good as Rio's Zona Sul.

ARRIVAL AND INFORMATION

By bus Services from N.S. de Copacabana and Largo do Machado, via the 14km Rio–Niterói bridge, take you into the centre of Niterói; MAC and the Icaraí neighbourhood are a further bus journey (numerous services; look on front of bus) or a 30min walk.

By ferry The best way to get to Niterói is by ferry. MAC is just 1.5km from the ferry terminal; you pass the Universidade Federal Fluminense en route.

Tourist office By the Niterói ferry terminal (daily 9am–5pm; ☎0800 282 7755) and at the entrance to the Teatro Popular site just to its north (daily 9am–6pm; ☎21 2611 1462, ⓦniteroiturismo.com.br).

EATING

There are plenty of cheap eating places in the backstreets of central Niterói.

Da Carmine Rua Mariz e Barros 305, Icaraí ☎ 21 3602 4988, ⓦ dacarmine.com.br. Serves the city's best pizzas by far, and, though not cheap, offers cheap "executive lunches" weekdays until 4pm. Tues–Sun noon–4pm & 6–11.30pm, Mon 6–11.30pm.

Mercado de Peixe São Pedro Av Visconde do Rio Branco 55. This fish market, a 5min walk north from the ferry terminal, has some forty fish restaurants upstairs. Expect to pay around R$65–90 per head. Tues–Fri 6am–4pm, Sat & Sun 6am–noon.

BÚZIOS

The most famous resort on the Costa do Sol, a sandy stretch of coast east of Rio, "discovered" by Brigitte Bardot in 1964 and nicknamed "Brazil's St Tropez", is Armação dos Búzios, or **BÚZIOS** as it's commonly known. A former whaling town, it's now cashing in on the upscale tourist market. Bardot described the sea here as "foaming like blue champagne", and the seafront promenade, the **Orla Bardot**, now bears a statue of her in homage. From December to February the population swells from 20,000 to 150,000, and boats take pleasure-seekers island hopping and scuba diving along the very beautiful coastline. If a crowded 24-hour resort full of high-spending beautiful people and buzzing nightclubs is your thing then you're sure to fall for Búzios; if not, give it a miss – at least in high season.

ARRIVAL AND INFORMATION

By bus Direct buses from Rio (3hr) run eight times a day, arriving at the *rodoviária* on Estrada da Usina Velha.

Tourist information The kiosk in Armação's main square, Praça Santos Dumont (☎ 22 2623 2099) is supposed to open Mon–Thurs & Sun 8am–9pm, Fri & Sat 8am–10pm, but is often closed for no apparent reason.

ACCOMMODATION

Casa Yellow Rua de Mandrágora 13 (off Av José Bento Ribeiro Dantas, 1km southwest of central Armação) ☎ 22 2623 3419, ⓦ casayellowbuzioshostel.com. Here's where you can be a scruffy backpacker and stay cheaply in Búzios, although it's a bit of a walk to the beach. Still, the company's congenial, and there's even a small pool. Dorms R$50, doubles (available out-of-season only) R$130

Che Lagarto Rua da Paz 7 ☎ 22 2623 1173, ⓦ chelagarto.com. This little hostel opened by the Che Lagarto chain is extremely handy for bus departures (and indeed arrivals). There are only dorms here, but Che Lagarto have a separate place at Praça Santos Dumont 280 for those who want a private room. Both locales are basic and functional, nothing special, but clean and friendly. Prices are somewhat cheaper off-season and during the week. Dorms (Rua da Paz) R$40, doubles (Praça Santos Dumont) R$250

EATING, DRINKING AND NIGHTLIFE

Restaurants in Búzios are, predictably, expensive; cheaper options include the grilled fish stalls on the beaches and numerous pizza places in outlying parts of town.

Bananaland Rua Manoel Turíbio de Farias 50 ☎ 22 2623 2666, ⓦ restaurantebananaland.com.br. On a street parallel to Rua das Pedras, this is one of the best *por kilo* restaurants in Búzios (R$89.50/kg). The choice among the buffet of salads and hot dishes is outstanding. Daily 11.30am–11.30pm.

Chez Michou Crêperie Rua das Pedras 90 ☎ 22 2623 6137, ⓦ chezmichou.com.br. Thanks to its open-air bar, cheap drinks and imaginative crêpes (*doce de leite* crêpe R$18, chicken curry crêpe R$22), this has long been Armação's most popular hangout. Open until dawn, when it serves breakfast to the patrons pouring out of the nearby clubs. Daily 12.30pm–around 6am.

O Barco Rua José Bento Ribeiro Dantas 1054, Armação ☎ 22 2629 8307. An unpretentious little fish restaurant where you can tuck into some seriously tasty seafood without breaking the bank. There's fried fish for R$30, or garlic prawns for R$38, all served with a smile on a terrace by the seafront. Daily except Tues 10am–11pm.

Privilège Orla Bardot 500 ☎ 22 8819 0465, ⓦ privilegenet.com.br. A poppy, slightly glitzy resort disco favoured by bright young things from Rio, which plays upbeat housey sounds. *Luv*, next door, is rather similar. Thurs–Sat 11pm–late, sometimes also other days.

Zapata Orla Bardot 352 ☎ 22 2623 0973, ⓦ zapatabuzios.com. Rougher and readier than the more expensive nightclubs, with an often quite raucous atmosphere fuelled by the free beers included in the (after

---

★ TREAT YOURSELF

Hibiscus Beach Hotel Rua 1 No. 22, Quadra C. Praia de João Fernandes ☎ 22 2623 6221, ⓦ hibiscusbeach.com.br. Gorgeous bungalows, each with a small terrace and wonderful sea views, at this welcoming, British-owned pousada with a good-sized pool in a flower-filled garden. The area's best snorkelling beach is just seconds away. R$570

3

11pm) entrance fee of R$50 for men, R$30 for women. Bar Tues–Sun 5–11pm, club Wed–Sat 11pm–5am.

ARRAIAL DO CABO

Tipped by those in the know to have the best beaches east of Rio, the small fishing town of **ARRAIAL DO CABO** has many of the attractions of Búzios, 40km northeast, but without the crowds, nightlife and price tag. The draw here is relaxing on a stunning peninsula between sea, sand dune and lagoon, with beaches like the 23km **Praia Grande** and smaller turquoise gems **Praia do Forno** (for snorkelling), **Prainha da Pontal** and **Praia Brava** (for surfing). All have a rich marine life and excellent diving. Boat trips are available to the beaches of nearby **Ilha do Farol** and the aptly named **Grotto Azul** (Blue Grotto), a cavern famous for its deep blue water.

ARRIVAL AND DEPARTURE

By bus Direct buses leave Rio (daily every 1–2hr; 3hr 5min). Frequent buses also ply the route from Arraial do Cabo to neighbouring Cabo Frio (14km), where you can pick up buses to Búzios.

ACCOMMODATION

Marina dos Anjos Rua Bernardo Lens 145 ☎ 22 2622 4060, ⓦ marinadosanjos.com.br. Drawing Brazilians from Rio and Minas Gerais for the easy-going beach life, this HI hostel is pleasingly social with great communal areas. Dorms R$73, doubles R$220

ILHA GRANDE

ILHA GRANDE comprises 193 square kilometres of mountainous jungle, historic ruins and beautiful beaches, excellent for some scenic tropical rambling. The entire island, lying about 150km southwest of Rio, is a state park with limits on building development and a ban on motor vehicles.

WHAT TO SEE AND DO

Ilha Grande offers lots of beautiful **walks** along well-maintained and fairly well-signposted trails. As you approach the low-lying, whitewashed colonial port of **Vila do Abraão**, you'll see the mountains rise dramatically from the sea, and in the distance there's the curiously shaped summit of **Bico do Papagaio**

("Parrot's Beak"), which ascends to a height of 980m. There's little to see in Abraão itself, but it's a pleasant base from which to explore the island. A thirty-minute walk along the coast west are the ruins of the **Antigo Presídio**, a former prison for political prisoners that was dynamited in the early 1960s. Among the ruins you'll find the *cafofo*, the containment centre where prisoners who had failed in escape attempts were immersed in freezing water. Just fifteen minutes inland from Abraão, overgrown with vegetation, stands the **Antigo Aqueduto**, which used to channel the island's water supply. There's a fine view of the aqueduct from the **Pedra Mirante**, a hill near the centre of the island; close by, a waterfall provides the opportunity to cool off.

For the most part the **beaches** – **Aventureiro**, **Lopes Mendes**, **Canto**, **Júlia** and **Morcegoare**, to name a few – are wild, unspoilt and most easily reached by boat, though most have some basic accommodation or campsites. Araçatiba is home to a sizeable village, accessed by boat direct from Angra dos Reis on the mainland.

ARRIVAL AND INFORMATION

By bus A 5am bus from Rio connects with the 8am ferry from Mangaratiba, failing which there are buses roughly hourly from Rio's *rodoviária* connect to the ferry ports at Angra dos Reis (3hr).

By ferry CCR Barcas (ⓦ grupoccr.com.br/barcas) run ferries to Ilha Grande's Vila do Abraão from Mangaratiba (daily 8am, Fri also 10pm, returning daily 5.30pm; 80min; R$16.60) and Angra dos Reis (Mon–Fri 3.30pm, Sat & Sun 1.30pm, returning daily 10am; R$16.60). Private boats (R$25) also do the crossing to the island from Angra (6 daily; 90min) and Conceição de Jacarei (roughly hourly 8.30am–6pm; 90min).

Tourist information There are tourist information desks (daily 7am–7pm) at the ferry terminals on the island and in Angra dos Reis, and a tourist office in Angra on Av Ayrton Senna between the ferry terminal and the bus station (daily 8am–5pm; ☎ 24 3369 7704). Online try ⓦ ilhagrande.org. Bring plenty of cash: exchange facilities are limited (one travel agency, near the boat station, will sometimes change foreign currency) and most pousadas and restaurants do not accept credit cards. The Elite Dive Center (☎ 24 99936 4181, ⓦ elitedivecenter.com.br) is the only PADI-registered dive centre on the island.

ACCOMMODATION

There are some great pousadas all over Ilha Grande, though Abraão has the largest choice (generally mid-priced). Reservations are essential in the high season, but prices may be halved off-season. When you arrive you'll probably be approached by youths intent on taking you to a room in a private house (around R$80/person). Camping at a designated site is a decent alternative (R$25–75/person). Abraão has a number of basic campsites (ask at the jetty) while nearby Praia das Palmas is a more scenic alternative: Camping Florestinha De Palmas (ⓦcampingflorestinha.com.br]) has facilities including a restaurant and kitchen. For the more adventurous, try one of the tiny campsites at stunning and secluded Praia do Aventureiro on the island's southwest coast.

Holandês Rua do Assembléia, Abraão ☎ 24 3833 7979, ⓦ holandeshostel.com.br. Always popular, this trendy HI hostel is behind the beach next to the Assembléia de Deus. Accommodation in dorms or lovely chalets (which sleep up to 3) in lush gardens. Dorms R$60, chalets R$250

Lagamar Praia Grande de Araçatiba ☎ 24 9978 4569, ⓦ pousadalagamar.com.br. Superb-value pousada surrounded by lush jungle in a quiet fishing hamlet at the island's western end. Generous seafood dinners and large breakfast are included. Boat available direct from Angra. R$400

Marlin Hostel Rua Santana 11, Abraão ☎ 24 3021 4309, ⓦ marlinhostelilhagrande.com.br. A small hostel in the middle of Abraão, with four six-bed dorms, reasonably priced by Ilha Grande standards. Dorms R$120

EATING

Café do Mar Praia do Abraão. A great little bar and beach restaurant serving up the day's catch in various formats, notably with coconut or mango sauce (R$55). For those in need of a wake-up, they do a nice espresso too, but they're best known for their thrice-weekly barbecues (Mon, Wed & Sat 7pm). Daily 10am–11pm; closed Fri in winter.

Lua e Mar Rua Praia do Abraão ☎ 24 3361 5113. The best beachside restaurant on this stretch. Check out their seafood risotto (R$90) or seafood *moqueca* (R$93) Daily except Wed 11am–11pm.

PARATY AND AROUND

PARATY, 236km from Rio along the BR-101, is the Costa Verde's main attraction, and rightly so. Inhabited since 1650, Paraty remains much as it was in its heyday as a staging post for the eighteenth-century trade in Brazilian gold. Today, UNESCO considers the city one of the world's most important examples of Portuguese colonial architecture, with all the narrow cobbled streets and churches you'd imagine, and it has been named a national monument. Besides the town's charmingly relaxed atmosphere, the main draws are its great restaurants and bars, and stunning surrounding scenery, from rainforest and waterfalls to hidden coves, islands and **beaches**. Paraty really comes alive for its annual Literary Festival ("FLIP"; ⓦflip.org.br) in July or August, which in past years has drawn such figures as Tom Stoppard and Brazil's own Chico Buarque; book accommodation well in advance for this.

WHAT TO SEE AND DO

One of Brazil's first planned urban projects, Paraty's centre is a warren of narrow, pedestrianized cobbled streets bordered by houses built around quaint courtyards. The cobbles of the streets are arranged in channels to drain off storm water and allow the sea to enter and wash the streets at high tides.

CHURCHES

Paraty's **churches** traditionally each served a different sector of the population. **Nossa Senhora dos Remédios** (daily 9am–5pm), on the Praça da Matriz, is the town's most imposing building. Originally built on the site in 1668, the current construction dates from 1873 with building having begun 84 years earlier. Along Rua do Comércio is the smallest church, the **Igreja do Rosário** (Mon–Fri 9am–5pm), once used by slaves, while at the southern edge of the town, the Portuguese Baroque **Igreja de Santa Rita** (Mon–Fri 9.15am–noon & 2.15–5pm) served freed *mulattos* and dates from 1722. The oldest and most architecturally significant of the town's churches, it now houses the **Museu de Arte Sacra de Paraty**, with religious artefacts from all of the town's churches.

BEACHES AND ISLANDS

From the **Praia do Pontal**, across the Perequé-Açu River from town, and from the port quay, boats leave for the **beaches** of Parati-Mirim, Iririguaçu – known for its waterfalls – Lula and Conceição. In fact, there are 65 islands and about two hundred beaches to choose from – ask around for the current favourites. Hotels and travel agents sell tickets for trips out

3

PARQUE NACIONAL DO ITATIAIA

On the border with Minas Gerais, 167km west of Rio, the **Parque Nacional do Itatiaia** (☎ 24 3352 1292, ⓦ icmbio.gov.br/parnaitatiaia; R$32) takes its unusual name from a Tupi word meaning "rocks with sharp edges". Holding the distinction of being Brazil's first national park (1937), it's incredibly varied, from dense Atlantic forest in the foothills, through to treeless, grassy summits. The park's loftiest peak, **Agulhas-Negras**, is the second highest in Brazil, at 2789m. There are two separate entrances to the park: the lower area entrance (daily 8am–5pm) is accessible by bus from Itatiaia, but the plateau area entrance (daily 7am–6pm, last entry 2.30pm) is not served by public transport, so you will have to make your own arrangements for getting there; buses from Itatiaia to Caxambu will drop you at the state line, a 14km hike from the plateau area entrance.

There's no shortage of **walking trails**, as well as a couple of one- or two-day walks for serious hikers. Of those, the Tres Picos Trail can be covered in a day, but care should be taken as the path becomes narrow and slippery as it rises, and a **guide** is recommended (available from hotels within the park). Itatiaia is also a popular **birdwatching** destination, thanks to its varied terrain and flora: highland species present in the park include the Itatiaia spinetail – a small, brownish, skulking bird that occurs only in this range of mountains.

ARRIVAL AND INFORMATION

By bus Access to the park is via the town of Itatiaia, served by buses from Rio (6 daily; 3hr 10min) and São Paulo (12 daily; 4hr). Local buses serve Penedo (roughly hourly; 20min) and the lower park entrance (4 daily; 15min). Staying in the town of Itatiaia is the cheapest way to visit. Penedo offers alternative accommodation but is further away.

Visitors' centre 8.5km north of Itatiaia on the road to the lower park entrance (daily 8am–5pm; ☎ 24 3352 1461). Provides information and maps, and has a small Museu Regional da Fauna e da Flora.

ACCOMMODATION

Pequena Suécia Rua Toivo Suni 33 ☎ 24 3351 1275, ⓦ pequenasuecia.com.br. An excellent hotel in the middle of Penedo, with a choice of rooms or chalets, a pool and Finnish-style sauna, a Swedish restaurant and even its own jazz club. Breakfast included. The price is slightly lower during the week. **R$250**

---

to the islands, typically for around R$55 per person, leaving Paraty at 11am, stopping at three or four islands, giving time for a swim, and returning at 4pm. For a short **hike**, walk the trail to perfect **Praia do Sono**, 12km southwest of town.

Beyond Praia do Sono (21km from Paraty) and reached by a steep winding road is the village of **Trindade** (17 daily buses; 45min). Sandwiched between the ocean and Serra do Mar, it's crammed with backpackers and trippers in peak season, camping on the beaches or staying in one of numerous pousadas. Famed for its **beaches**, the best are across the rocky outcrops to **Praia Brava** and **Praia do Meio**, some of the most attractive mainland beaches on this stretch of coast, and completely unspoilt.

ARRIVAL AND INFORMATION

By bus The *rodoviária* is about 0.5km from the old town on Rua Jango de Padúa.

Destinations Angra dos Reis (19 daily; 2hr); Rio (12 daily; 5hr); São Paulo (5 daily; 5hr); Trindade (roughly hourly; 45min); Ubatuba (13 daily; 1hr 15min).

Tourist information Av Roberto Silveira 1 on Praça Chayariz (daily 9am–9pm; ☎ 24 3371 1222).

ACCOMMODATION, EATING AND DRINKING

Casa do Rio Hostel Rua Antonio Vidal 120 ☎ 24 3371 2223, ⓦ casadoriohostel.com.br. A well-organized HI hostel with a large communal area, social vibe and a variety of dorms – compare a couple before choosing. Helpful staff and tours on offer. Dorms **R$79**, doubles **R$212**

Che Lagarto Hostel Rua Benina Toledo do Prado 22 ☎ 24 3371 1564, ⓦ chelagarto.com. One of the better offerings from this popular hostel chain, fun and sociable with spacious communal areas, largely outside in the garden, although it's true that the dorms are rather less spacious. Dorms **R$72**, doubles **R$198**

Istanbul Rua Manuel Torres, Shopping Colonial ☎ 24 9974 9638. Great kebabs (R$22) as well as Turkish-style falafel (R$17) and Turkish coffee at this friendly and great-value snack bar with tables upstairs, just across from the bus station. Tues–Sat noon–10pm.

Marlim Eua da Floresta 395 ☎ 24 3371 5369. Cheap eats every lunchtime at the no-frills diner near the bus station. Fish or squid with beans, rice and a bit of salad are R$22, while fresh fried sardines are even cheaper. Daily 11am–10pm.

Sabor da Terra Av Roberto Silveira 180 ☎24 3371 2384, ⓦparaty.com.br/sabordaterra. Paraty's best *por kilo* restaurant (R$49.80/kg), offering a wide variety of inexpensive hot and cold dishes that include a choice of grilled meats. Daily 11am–10pm.

Solar dos Gerânios Praça da Matriz ☎24 3371 1550, ⓔs.geranio.s@hotmail.com. Beautiful and long-established pousada filled with rustic furniture and curios. Rooms are spartan but impeccable, most have a balcony and all are en suite. Great value. Reservations advised; request a room overlooking the *praça*. R$180

PETRÓPOLIS

Some 66km to the north of Rio, high in the mountains, stands the imperial city of **PETRÓPOLIS**, so named because in the nineteenth century Emperor Dom Pedro II had a summer palace built here, rapidly making the place a popular retreat for Brazilian aristocracy. En route the scenery is dramatic, climbing among forested slopes that suddenly give way to ravines and gullies, while clouds shroud the surrounding peaks. You can easily tour Petrópolis in a day – its cultural attractions and stunning setting make it well worth the trip.

WHAT TO SEE AND DO

The **Palácio Imperial** on Rua da Imperatriz (Tues–Sun 11am–5.30pm; R$10; ⓦmuseuimperial.gov.br) is a grandiose colonial structure, set in beautifully maintained gardens. Upon entry, you're given felt overshoes with which to slide around the polished floors of this royal residence, and inside there's everything from Dom Pedro II's crown to the regal commode. The cathedral of **São Pedro de Alcântara** (daily 8am–6pm) blends with the surrounding architecture, but is much more recent than its neo-Gothic style suggests – it was finished in 1939. Inside lie the tombs of Dom Pedro himself and several royal personages.

The town's most recognizable building is the **Palácio de Cristal** (Tues–Sun 9am–6pm) on Rua Alfredo Pachá, erected in 1884 to house local exhibitions, which it still does. The alpine chalet **Casa Santos Dumont** (Tues–Sun 9.30am–5pm; R$8) is worth a visit for its collection of the personal oddments of a famous local aviator.

ARRIVAL AND INFORMATION

By bus Buses leave Rio for Petrópolis every 30–40min (journey time 90min) – sit on the left side of the bus for best views – arriving at the *rodoviária* on Rua Dr Porciúncula, from where it's a further 10km by local bus into town.

Tourist information Rua da Imperatriz, opposite the entrance to the Museu Imperial (daily 9am–5pm; ☎0800 024 1516, ⓦdestinopetropolis.com.br), with another office (same hours) in Praça da Liberdade.

ACCOMMODATION AND EATING

There are a few reasonable options in town, though most are very classy former colonial mansions.

Restaurants are surprisingly lacklustre in Petrópolis, most of the best being some distance from town.

Albergue Quitandinha Rua Uruguai 570 ☎24 2247 9165, ⓦalberguequitandinha.com.br. Ten rooms and a dorm within wooden cabins, a bus ride from the Centro Historico. $140

Armazem 646 Rua Visconde de Itaboraí 646 ☎24 2243 1001, ⓦarmazem646.com.br. Welcoming bar-restaurant with live music most nights and a varied menu of meat and fish that will suit most tastes. Try *camarão com catupiry* (R$64.90). Daily 11am–midnight.

Bordeaux Rua Ipiranga 716 ☎24 2242 5711, ⓦbordeauxvinhos.com.br. In the converted stables of a stately home, moderately priced Italian- and French-influenced offerings include salmon carpaccio to start (R$36) with solid meat dishes such as steak au poivre (R$54) to complement the excellent wine list. Mon–Sat noon–midnight.

Casa d'Angelo Rua do Imperador 700 ☎24 2242 0888, ⓦcasadangelo.com.br. A *chopperia* (beer bar) and restaurant, slap-bang in the centre of town. Lunchtime *pratos executivos* (till 4pm) go for R$24.90, or you can tuck into a supper-time stroganoff for R$49, and of course wash it down with an ice-cold glass of *chopp*. Tues–Sun 11am–midnight.

Comércio Rua Dr Porciúncula 55 ☎24 2242 3500. One of the cheapest options in town, though by no means a bargain. Rooms without a bathroom are cheapest. R$100

Marowil Praca da Liberdade 27 ☎24 2243 0743, ⓦmarowill1.placeweb.site. Reasonably priced restaurant right on the square. The food is nothing to write home about but you'll struggle to find better value for money. At night it functions as a bar with food. Daily 8am–midnight.

Pousada 14 Bis Rua Buenos Aires 192 ☎24 2231 0946, ⓦpousada14bis.com.br. A themed pousada based on the life of aviator Santos Dumont. Rooms are nothing flashy, but decorated in attractive colonial style. R$220

3

PARQUE NACIONAL SERRA DOS ORGÃOS

The **Parque Nacional Serra dos Orgãos** (daily 8am–5pm; lower part R$33, upper part R$53; ⓦicmbio.gov.br/parnaso) is breathtakingly beautiful and refreshingly easy to visit from Petrópolis's plainer neighbour, **Teresópolis**. The park is dominated in its lower reaches by lush Atlantic forest, with bare mountain peaks emerging from the trees to create a stunning effect against the backdrop of a clear blue sky. It is these peaks that give the park its name, the rocks reminding the early Portuguese explorers of the pipes of cathedral organs.

There are a number of **walking trails** in the park, most of them short, easily accessible and suitable for people who like their hiking easy, though all have uphill stretches. Many of the park's most recognizable landmarks are visible on the horizon from Teresópolis. The most famous of all is the **Dedo de Deus** (Finger of God) – a bare, rocky pinnacle that points skyward – while arguably more picturesque is the **Cachoeira Véu da Noiva** waterfall. The longest and most challenging trail is the **Pedra do Sino** (Stone Bell), starting some distance from the park entrance, passing the bell-shaped rock formation (at 2263m the park's highest point) and emerging some 30km further on (close to the town of Petrópolis) – a guide is strongly recommended.

ARRIVAL AND INFORMATION

By bus Buses to Teresópolis run from Rio (hourly; 1hr 45min) and Petrópolis (7 daily; 1hr 30min), arriving at the *rodoviária* on Rua 1 de Maio. Teresópolis is located right at the edge of the park, the entrance being just to the south of town (served by hourly local buses, destination "Soberbo", heading south along Av Lúcio Meira, with more frequent buses to "Alto" leaving you a 15min walk away).

Tourist information Praça Olímpica, a square on Av Lúcio Meira (Mon–Sat 8am–6pm; ☎ 21 2742 5561).

ACCOMMODATION AND EATING

If you're not camping or walking to Petrópolis, you'll probably want to base yourself in Teresópolis, where there are a couple of reasonable accommodation options. There are plenty of *por kilo* lunch places.

Aventureiro Pousada Rua Padre Tintório 250 ☎ 21 2743 0388, ⓦaventureiropousadatere.com.br. A friendly little pousada, very neat and pretty central, but up a slightly steep hill. Your climb is rewarded, if you get the right room, with a balcony and good views of the Serra dos Orgãos. R$180

Várzea Palace Hotel Rua Sebastião Teixeira 41 ☎21 2742 0878, ⓦvarzea.palace.nafoto.net. Once the most elegant place in town to stay, only faint traces of its former luxury remain, but it's clean, welcoming and good value, with discounts midweek. R$140

Minas Gerais

Explorers flocked to **MINAS GERAIS** following the discovery of gold in 1693, and with the unearthing of diamonds and other gemstones the state has been exploited for these abundant natural resources ever since. For a hundred years the region was by far the wealthiest in Brazil, but as the gold reserves became exhausted so Minas Gerais declined, and by the mid-nineteenth century it was a backwater. Coffee in part served to stem the decline, and alongside extraction of workaday minerals like iron ore it continues to sustain much of the region today. Visitors flock here, too, enjoying a series of startlingly beautiful towns left behind by the boom.

Minas Gerais's **CIDADES HISTÓRICAS** started life as mining camps, as rough and basic as imagination can make them. But the wealth of the surrounding mountains transformed them, and today they are considered to be among the most beautiful cities in the Americas, with cobbled streets and alleyways, glorious churches encrusted in gold – built in the over-the-top local version of Baroque architecture *Barroco Mineiro* – and beautifully preserved colonial buildings. And all of this is set in an area of rugged natural beauty, with a few towns connected by historic trains.

Ouro Preto and **Diamantina** are both UNESCO World Heritage Sites and are the best places for budget travellers to base themselves; **Tiradentes** is pricier though barely less impressive, with attractive and affordable **São João del Rei** worth a brief visit nearby.

MINAS GERAIS

Montes Claros
Itaobim
Araçuaí
BAHIA
Diamantina
São Gonçalo do Rio das Pedras
MINAS GERAIS
Milho Verde
Serro
Itaúnas
Curvelo
Governador Valadares
São Mateus
Conceição da Barra
Sete Lagoas
Conceição do Mato Dentro
ESPÍRITO SANTO
Serra do Cipó
Itabira
Belo Horizonte
Sabará
Santa Maria de Jetibá
Linhares
Regência
Santa Teresa
Santa Bárbara
Santuário do Caraça
Barão de Cocais
Manhuaçu
Venda Nova
Santa Leopoldina
Brumadinho
Catas Altas
Vitória
Congonhas
Mariana
Pedra Azul
Parque Natural do Caraça
Tiradentes
Ouro Preto
Guarapari
São João del Rei
Anchieta
Domingos Martins
Barbacena
Três Corações
Cambuquira
Juiz de Fora
São Lourenço
Caxambu
Pouso Alegre
RIO DE JANEIRO
Rio de Janeiro
SÃO PAULO

N

0   250
kilometres

BELO HORIZONTE

Founded in 1893 and the first of Brazil's planned cities, **BELO HORIZONTE** is the booming capital of Minas Gerais. The third-largest urban area in Brazil may at first appear daunting and uninspired, but what this cosmopolitan metropolis lacks in aesthetics it makes up for in some eclectic architecture, enticing museums and superb food.

WHAT TO SEE AND DO

For all its size, the centre of Belo Horizonte is fairly easy to explore on foot. Heading south from the *rodoviária*, walk to Praça Raul Soares and then take Rua dos Guajajaras for the bustling **Mercado Central** (Mon–Sat 7am–6pm, Sun 7am–1pm), which has more than four hundred stalls and restaurants selling anything from cheeses to bamboo artefacts and bric-a-brac.

If you are in town on a Sunday morning (8am–2pm), don't miss the **Feira de Arte e Artesanato** (Arts and Crafts Fair) on Avenida Afonso Pena, the largest open-air fair in Latin America, with three thousand stalls.

PRAÇA DA LIBERDADE

At the traditional heart of the city lies park-like **Praça da Liberdade**, with its celebrated **Edifício Niemeyer**, designed by renowned Brazilian architect Oscar Niemeyer, the elegant Neoclassical-style **Palácio da Liberdade** and a fine ensemble of **museums**. The highly imaginative, entertaining galleries of the **Memorial Minas Gerais Vale** (Tues, Wed, Fri & Sat 10am–5.30pm, Thurs 10am–9.30pm, Sun 10am–3.30pm; free; ⓦmemorialvale.com.br) are more like artistic representations of various aspects of Minas Gerais culture and history than a typical museum, while the artfully designed **Museu das Minas e do Metal** (Tues–Sun noon–6pm, Thurs till 10pm; last entry 1hr before closing; free; ⓦmmgerdau.org.br) successfully makes the otherwise dry subjects of mining and minerals utterly absorbing.

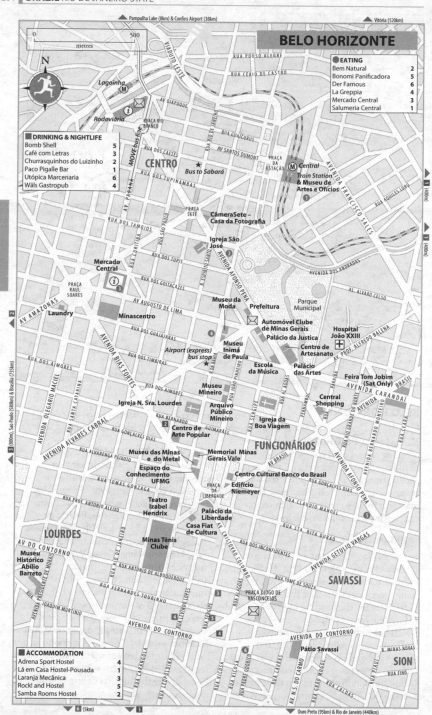

Pampulha Lake (8km) & Confins Airport (38km)

Vitória (520km)

BELO HORIZONTE

0   500
metres

N

Lagoinha

Rodoviária

RUA POUSO ALEGRE

RUA CÉRIO DE CASTRO

AV OIAPOQUE

VIADUTO LESTE

PRAÇA RIO BRANCO

● EATING
Bem Natural   2
Bonomi Panificadora   5
Der Famous   6
La Greppia   4
Mercado Central   3
Salumeria Central   1

■ DRINKING & NIGHTLIFE
Bomb Shell   5
Café com Letras   3
Churrasquinhos do Luizinho   2
Paco Pigalle Bar   1
Utópica Marcenaria   6
Wäls Gastropub   4

RUA GUAICURUS
AV SANTOS DUMONT

RUA DOS CAETÉS
MOVE bus line

CENTRO

Bus to Sabará

RUA DOS TUPINAMBÁS

PRAÇA DA ESTAÇÃO

Central Train Station & Museu de Artes e Ofícios

AVENIDA FRANCISCO SALES

RUA AQUILES LOBO

PRAÇA SETE

RUA DOS TAMOIOS

RUA CURITIBA

RUA SÃO PAULO

RUA DOS TUPIS

CâmeraSete – Casa da Fotografia

Igreja São José

AVENIDA AFONSO PENA

Mercado Central

PRAÇA RAUL SOARES

RUA DOS GOITACAZES

AV AUGUSTO DE LIMA

Museu da Moda

Prefeitura

Parque Municipal

AL. ÁLVARO CELSO

AVENIDA DOS ANDRADAS

Laundry

Minascentro

RUA DOS GUAJAJARAS

Automóvel Clube de Minas Gerais

Palácio da Justiça

Hospital João XXIII

AV AMAZONAS

RUA DOS TIMBIRAS

Airport (express) bus stop

Museu Inimá de Paula

Centro de Artesanato

AV PROF. ALFREDO BALENA

AVENIDA BIAS FORTES

RUA DOS AIMORÉS

Escola da Música

Palácio das Artes

RUA DOS AIMORÉS

Museu Mineiro

Feira Tom Jobim (Sat Only)

AVENIDA CARANDAÍ

Igreja N. Sra. Lourdes

Arquivo Público Mineiro

RUA BERNARDO

Igreja da Boa Viagem

Central Shopping

Centro de Arte Popular

RUA GUIMARÃES

Museu das Minas e do Metal

Memorial Minas Gerais Vale

FUNCIONÁRIOS

RUA GONÇALVES DIAS

RUA ALVARENGA PEIXOTO

Espaço do Conhecimento UFMG

AV BRASIL

Centro Cultural Banco do Brasil

RUA GONÇALVES DIAS

RUA TOMÁS GONZAGA

Edifício Niemeyer

PRAÇA DA LIBERDADE

RUA CLÁUDIO MANOEL

RUA PROF. ANTÔNIO ALEIXO

Teatro Izabel Hendrix

Palácio da Liberdade

Casa Fiat de Cultura

RUA STA. RITA DURÃO

LOURDES

AV DO CONTORNO

Museu Histórico Abílio Barreto

Minas Tênis Clube

RUA INCONFIDENTES

AVENIDA GETÚLIO VARGAS

SAVASSI

RUA ANTÔNIO DE ALBUQUERQUE

RUA TOMÉ DE SOUZA

RUA FERNANDES TOURINHO

PRAÇA DIOGO DE VASCONCELOS

AVENIDA DO CONTORNO

AVENIDA DO CONTORNO

Pátio Savassi

R. MINAS NOVAS

SION

RUA PIAUÍ

RUA FINO

■ ACCOMMODATION
Adrena Sport Hostel   4
Lá em Casa Hostel-Pousada   1
Laranja Mecânica   3
Rock! and Hostel   5
Samba Rooms Hostel   2

6 (5km)

5

Ouro Preto (95km) & Rio de Janeiro (440km)

3 (800m), São Paulo (580km) & Brasília (735km)

MUSEU DE ARTES E OFÍCIOS

On Praça Rui Barbosa, the **Museu de Artes e Ofícios** (Tues 9am–9pm, Wed–Sun 9am–5pm; free; ⓦmao.org.br) highlights traditional trades and industries within the wonderfully enigmatic premises of the renovated **train station**. Essentially this is a huge display of old machinery and tools from the nineteenth and twentieth centuries, but there are some truly intriguing exhibits, including a video of the process of traditional sugar refining, huge, antique sugar boiling vats, leather tanning drums and copper alambiques (distilleries).

MUSEU MINEIRO

The tiny but beautifully presented art collections in the **Museu Mineiro**, at Av João Pinheiro 342 (Tues, Wed & Fri 10am–7pm, Thurs noon–9pm, Sat, Sun & hols noon–7pm; free; ☎31 3269 1109), are enhanced by the elegant Neoclassical building it occupies, completed in 1897 as the state senate. Today its gorgeous rooms house a variety of religious statuary, the work of local painters from the twentieth century (mostly landscapes) and a small collection of six vibrant paintings by Minas Gerais Baroque master **Manuel da Costa Ataíde**.

PAMPULHA

Set around an artificial lake that is home to cormorants, grebes, ibis, egrets, herons and even large **capybara**, the surburb of **Pampulha**, 10km north of the city centre (MOVE buses #50 and #51 run direct to Estação Pampulha on the eastern side of the lake, in 40min), boasts some architectural gems, the work of great modern Brazilian designers Oscar Niemeyer and Roberto Burle Marx. The **Museu de Arte de Pampulha** (MAP; Tues–Sun 9am–6pm; free; ☎31 3277 7996), on a peninsula in the lake, is one of the finest, a work of art in itself (though also housing a small collection inside), which was built as a casino in 1942 before becoming a museum in 1957. Also on the lakeshore is the **Igreja de São Francisco de Assis** (Tues–Sat 9am–5pm, Sun 11am–2pm; R$3), among the finest works of Niemeyer, Burle Marx and Cândido Portinari, who created the beautiful *azulejo* tile facade in 1943.

Pampulha is also known for the **Mineirão** football stadium and its **Museu Brasileiro do Futebol** (Tues 9am–8pm, Wed–Fri 9am–5pm, Sat & Sun 9am–1pm; R$20; ☎31 3499 4312, ⓦestadiomineirao.com.br/museu-e-visita), at Av Coronel Oscar Paschoal 932. The museum, which has English labelling, chronicles the history of the stadium and its most famous matches (top team Cruzeiro play here), while one-hour guided tours (hourly, first-come, first-served; not available on public holidays or match days) take in the locker rooms, press room, stands and pitch where Brazil were crushed 7–1 by Germany in the semi-finals of the 2014 World Cup, dubbed "The biggest shame in history" by *Lance!*, the major Brazilian sports newspaper.

ARRIVAL AND DEPARTURE

By plane Confins Airport (☎31 3689 2700), officially called Aeroporto Internacional Tancredo Neves, is 38km north of the centre. Airport buses (1hr) run every 15–30min (24hr) to the main *rodoviária* in the centre (R$12.25; ⓦconexaoaeroporto.com.br), while posher *executivo* buses (every 15–30min, 24hr; R$26.75) drop you in the centre at Av Alvares Cabral 387, near the corner of Rua da Bahia. Taxis to the centre from Confins cost around R$120–130 on the meter, depending on traffic. Some domestic flights use Pampulha Airport (☎31 3490 2001), 9km from downtown; take a regular city bus to the *rodoviária* (4am–11.45pm; R$12.25).
Destinations Brasília (12 daily; 2hr); Rio de Janeiro (12 daily; 1hr); Salvador (5 daily; 3hr); São Paulo (20 daily; 1hr 30min).
By bus The *rodoviária* (☎31 3271 3000) is on Praça Rio Branco, at the northern end of the city centre. A new terminal is being built in the far less convenient northern suburb of São Gabriel (7.5km from the centre), but legal and funding problems have stalled the project for years; if it does finally open in 2018/2019, it will be connected to the metro and local bus system – taxis from here into the centre will be around R$45.
Destinations Brasília (9 daily; 10–11hr); Diamantina (8 daily; 5hr); Ouro Preto (hourly 6am–11pm; 1hr 55min); Rio de Janeiro (18 daily; 6–8hr); São João del Rei (7 daily; 3hr 30min); São Paulo (hourly; 8hr).
By train The train station (☎31 3273 5976) at Praça da Estação serves just one route, to Vitória on the coast (daily 7.30am, returning at 7am; 13hr; R$58; ☎0800 285 7000). You can buy tickets at the station or online; the Vitória station is "Cariacica" (ⓦtremdepassageiros.vale.com).
Car rental Numerous options at the airports, plus Localiza Hertz at Av Bernardo Monteiro 1567 (☎31 3247 7956), and Unidas at Av Bias Fortes 1019, near Praça Raul Soares (☎31 3586 5000).

3

ART IN THE JUNGLE

It comes as a bit of a shock to find the world's largest open-air art museum 60km from Belo Horizonte. But that's exactly what's on offer at **Inhotim Instituto Cultural** (Tues–Fri 9.30am–4.30pm, Sat & Sun 9.30am–5.30pm; Tues & Thurs R$20; Fri–Sun & hols R$44; free Wed; students pay half-price; ☎ 31 3571 9700, ⊚ inhotim.org.br), an exhibition of 400 pieces of contemporary art across **twelve pavilions** and set amid an incredible 500,000 acres of botanical reserve (though only 110 acres are accessible via walking trails). Opened in 2006, the collection includes paintings, sculpture, photos, videos and installations by Brazilians and international artists dating from the 1960s to the present. Inhotim's appeal goes beyond art, however, with **gardens** of orchids, palms and rare tropical species landscaped by Burle Marx.

You'll need a full day (or more) at Inhotim. Special **direct buses** (R$36.20 one-way; around 2hr) operated by Saritur leave from the *rodoviária* in Belo Horizonte (Sat, Sun & hols at 8.15am, returning at 5.30pm; ⊚ saritur.com.br). Converted golf carts whisk visitors around the park if walking gets too much (R$28/day). Cafés and restaurants on-site.

GETTING AROUND

By bus The city's bus system (⊚ bhtrans.pbh.gov.br) works along the same lines as elsewhere in Brazil (pay as you enter), with the exception of the MOVE bus rapid transit (BRT) system, which works like a subway, with dedicated bus lanes and stations – its main use for visitors is for travelling between the centre and Pampulha (p.265). You need to buy a BHBUS card or a stored value "Cartão Unitário" to go through the electronic turnstiles (buy them at kiosks outside the station), with single rides R$4.05. Other buses charge R$2.85 or R$4.05 depending on the route (fares are posted on the bus). Virtually all routes include a stretch along Av Afonso Pena, which is usually the most convenient place to catch a bus if you are staying in the centre.
By taxi The meter starts at R$4.70; budget for up to R$15 for most rides within the centre.

INFORMATION

Belotur Helpful offices at Mercado Central, Av Augusto de Lima 744 (Mon & Tues 8am–4.20pm, Wed–Sat 8am–5.20pm, Sun & hols 8am–1pm ☎ 31 3277 4691); Tancredo Neves (Confins) airport (Mon–Fri 8am–10pm, Sat & Sun 8am–5pm; ☎ 31 3689 2557); the *rodoviária*, Praça Rio Branco (daily 8am–6pm; ☎ 31 3277 6907), and at the tourist information centre on the lake at Av Otacílio Negrão de Lima 855, Pampulha (Tues–Sun 8am–5pm; ☎ 31 3277 9987).

ACCOMMODATION

★ **Adrena Sport Hostel** Av Getúlio Vargas 1635, Savassi ☎ 31 3657 9970, ⊚ adrenasporthostel.com.br; map p.264. Fun, chilled-out hostel in Savassi with an extreme sports theme; there's a full kitchen and bar on site and the dorms are clean and cosy (with fans). Also offers comfy "stand up" rooms for four people (one double and two bunks) and private bathroom. Cash only. Dorms R$50, doubles R$140
Lá em Casa Hostel-Pousada Rua Eurita 30, Santa Tereza ☎ 31 3653 9566, ⊚ laemcasahostel.com; map p.264. A well-maintained, attractive hostel in BH's bohemian quarter, a 10min bus ride from the centre. Dorms have five beds and an excellent breakfast is included. Discount for HI members. Dorms R$38, doubles R$120
Laranja Mecânica Rua Rodrigues Caldas 714, Santo Agostinho ☎ 31 3309 5881, ⊚ laranjamecanicahostelpousada.com; map p.264. Popular hostel (named after cult movie *A Clockwork Orange*), 2km southwest of the centre. Dorms are simple but stylish, while doubles come with or without bathrooms. Splashes of orange and murals inspired by the movie pay homage to the hostel's namesake. Dorms R$40, doubles R$140
Rock! and Hostel Rua Cristina 1185, São Pedro ☎ 31 2531 0579, ⊚ rockandhostelbh.com.br; map p.264. An excellent hostel in the Savassi neighbourhood, with clean, basic dorms (with hardwood floors, ceiling fans and private lockers) and simple doubles with fans and shared bathrooms; breakfast and free wi-fi. Dorms R$35, doubles R$100
Samba Rooms Hostel Av Bias Fortes 368 ☎ 31 3267 0740, ⊚ sambaroomshostel.com.br; map p.264. Popular hostel in the central Lourdes district, set in a pretty, canary-coloured 1930s mansion, offering bright double rooms (with private or shared bathrooms) and dorms with basic breakfast and ceiling fans. Communal kitchen, lounge and guest-use computer available. Laundry R$25 per 15kg/30 pounds. Dorms R$50, doubles R$110

EATING

There are plenty of cheap restaurants, *lanchonetes* and *churrascarias* – popular at lunchtime with city workers – on Rua Pernambuco, Rua dos Caetés and around Praça Sete.

★ **Bem Natural** Av Afonso Pena 941, Centro (inside a small plaza), and Rua Alagoas 911, at Rua dos Inconfidentes, Savassi; map p.264. Not the cheapest *por kilo* in town (around R$48.90 per kilo), but plenty of healthy and vegetarian offerings (meat dishes too) plus natural juices (R$3.20). Self-service only; Centro branch Mon–Fri 9am–6pm, Savassi also Sat & Sun 11.30am–3pm.

★ **Bonomi Panificadora** Av Afonso Pena 2600, Funcionários; map p.264. This upmarket café/bakery located in a rustic building is not strictly budget (salads, pasta and sandwiches from R$30), but the coffee is the best in town, the bread and pastries among the best in Brazil, and the sandwiches and soups tasty too. Tues–Sat 8am–10.30pm, Sun 8am–8pm.

Der Famous Av do Contorno 6399, São Pedro; map p.264. Justifiably popular gourmet hotdog joint – try the (try the "Karl Marx"; R$23.50) – featuring huge, German-style sausages. Tues–Thurs 5–11pm, Fri 6pm–1am, Sat 12.30pm–1am, Sun 12.30–11pm.

La Greppia Rua da Bahia 1196, Centro; map p.264. Classic 24hr spot for eating and drinking, with great-value tasty Brazilian and Italian meals and snacks. Try the R$25 unlimited lunchtime buffet, or evening pasta *rodizio* with dessert for R$25. Daily 24hr.

Mercado Central Av Augusto de Lima 744; map p.264. An atmospheric and popular place to grab lunch, a sandwich or a cold beer. There are several stand-up bars around the edges, but *Bar da Tia* and the classy *Botiquin do Antônio* have the most character. Mon–Sat 7am–6pm, Sun 7am–1pm.

★ **Salumeria Central** Rua Sapucaí 527, Floresta; map p.264. Right behind the train station, this Italian-Brazilian restaurant-bar serves salamis, hams, pasta, cheeses and the like from R$25 (try the meatballs with stout beer sauce), washed down with decent wine or beer. The outdoor seating's great for taking in views of the station square and the arches of the Santa Tereza viaduct. Mon–Sat 11.30am–3.30pm & 6.30pm–1am.

DRINKING AND NIGHTLIFE

The Savassi district is teeming with trendy – if expensive – bars and clubs, while Rua Pium-í continues the trend south of Av Contorno. For slightly more downmarket options, head to Rua da Bahia anywhere between Av Carandaí and Praça da Estação.

Bomb Shell Rua Sergipe 1395, Savassi; map p.264. Contemporary *boteco* with DJs spinning anything from *funk carioca* to jazz standards or rock/pop: check the schedule. Tasty eats for sharing, too. Mon & Sun 6pm–midnight, Tues–Fri 6pm–1am, Sat 1pm–1am.

Café com Letras Rua Antônio de Albuquerque 781, Savassi ⓦ cafecomletras.com.br; map p.264. Café, bar, bookshop and cultural space, with a calendar of live music (mostly jazz) and book launches throughout the year. DJs spin most nights. R$3.50–8 cover charge. Mon–Thurs noon–midnight, Fri & Sat noon–1am, Sun 5–11pm.

Churrasquinhos do Luizinho Av Francisco Sá 197, Prado ⓦ churrasquinhosdoluizinho.com.br; map p.264. Packed on Thursdays with up to 500 people, serving the usual drinks and delicious *espetos* (grilled beef on a skewer) – owner Luiz says the secret lies in the sauce, a recipe of his mother's. Free shot of *cachaça* with your *espetinho* on Mondays. Mon–Fri 5pm–midnight, Sat 11am–7pm.

Paco Pigalle Bar Av do Contorno 2314, Floresta (between Av dos Andradas and Av Assis Chateaubriand) ⓦ pacopigalle.com.br; map p.264. Plays a mix of hip-hop, reggae, salsa and disco to a high-spending, trendy crowd. Fri & Sat 10pm–5am.

★ **Utópica Marcenaria** Av Raja Gabáglia 4700, Santa Lúcia ⓦ utopica.com.br; map p.264. Popular live music venue, located a few kilometres south of Centro. Samba Thursdays, rock/MPB Friday, funk/soul on Saturday and *forró* on Sunday. Cover R$20–30. Fri & Sat 9pm–3am, Sun 7pm–1am.

★ **Wäls Gastropub** Rua Levindo Lopes 358, Savassi ⓦ walsgastropub.com.br; map p.264. Stylish bar

---

SERRA DO CIPÓ NATIONAL PARK

In a country of few mountain peaks the upland landscapes of the **Serra do Cipó** stand out as one of the finest places in the country for outdoor activities. This dazzling national park lies 100km northeast of Belo Horizonte, encompassing limestone hills, rugged valleys and grasslands, Atlantic forest and numerous pools and waterfalls. Rare bird species like the Cipó canastero and hyacinth visorbearer attract serious birders, while other fauna includes wolves, jaguars, monkeys and the *sapo de pijama* (pyjama frog).

Six **buses** daily (2hr 30min; R$25) ply the route from Belo Horizonte to the small town of **Serra do Cipó** (aka Cardeal Mota) at the edge of the reserve, spread out for several kilometres along MG-10 – an attractive place for backpackers with a low-key atmosphere, plus bars and pousadas. The main park office and entrance is 3km from the main road (the turning is around 2km south from the centre of the village), but there are also guides and **organized trips** available; for information contact Bela Geraes Turismo (☏ 31 3718 7394, ⓦ belageraes.com.br); Cipó Aventuras (☏ 31 9974 0878, ⓦ cipoaventuras.blogspot.com).

Entry to the park is free, and though at weekends the principal trails draw day-trippers in numbers, during the week it's often near-deserted. Check the websites ⓦ serradocipo.com and ⓦ serradocipo.com.br for details on accommodation.

dedicated to serving local Wäls craft beers, with a decent selection on tap from its session IPA to its "Petroleum", a Russian Imperial Stout. Mon–Wed 11.30am–midnight, Thurs 11.30am–1am, Fri 11.30am–2am, Sat noon–2am, Sun noon–11pm.

DIRECTORY

Banks and exchange Concentrated downtown on Av João Pinheiro, between Rua dos Timbiras and Av Afonso Pena. Bank ATMs throughout the city.

Consulates Canada, Av do Contorno 4520, 8th floor (☎31 3213 1651); US, Edifício Celta, Rua Maranhão 310, Santa Efigênia (☎31 3956 0800); UK, Rua Fernandes Tourinho 669/702 (☎21 2555 9600).

Hospital Ambulance ☎192. Pronto Socorro do Hospital João XXIII, Av Alfredo Balena 400, Santa Efigênia (☎31 3239 9200).

Laundry Lavanderia Just a Sec, Rua dos Guajajaras 1268, Centro (Mon–Fri 8am–6pm, Sat 8am–1pm).

Police ☎190. For visa extensions go to the Polícia Federal at Rua Nascimento Gurgel 30, Gutierrez (☎31 3330 5200).

Post office Main post office, Av Afonso Pena 1270 (Mon–Fri 8.30am–6pm, Sat 9am–noon); Savassi branch, Rua Pernambuco 1322 (Mon–Fri 9am–6pm, Sat 9am–noon); also a branch at the bus station (Mon–Fri 9am–7pm, Sat 9am–noon).

Taxis BH Táxi ☎31 3215 8081; Coopertramo ☎31 3454 5757.

OURO PRETO

The most enchanting of all the colonial towns in Minas Gerais, **OURO PRETO** ("Black Gold") lies 100km southeast of Belo Horizonte, its narrow, cobbled streets straddling impossibly steep hills topped with Baroque churches and lined with an assortment of candy-coloured eighteenth-century homes and mansions. The former capital of Minas Gerais (until 1897) was also the birthplace of renowned sculptor **Aleijadinho** and the focal point of the **Inconfidência Mineira**, a failed attempt in 1789 to end Portuguese rule and form a Brazilian republic. People flock to Ouro Preto from all over Brazil for **Semana Santa**, with its grand processions and Passion plays in open-air theatres, while **Carnaval** also attracts large crowds; book in advance at both these times.

WHAT TO SEE AND DO

The town is best explored on foot, taking in the cobbled passageways between its handful of stunning churches, excellent museums and numerous shopping and eating options – but be prepared for lots of uphill climbing.

PRAÇA TIRADENTES

Praça Tiradentes lies at the heart of Ouro Preto, with several sights right on the square. The **Museu da Inconfidência** (Tues–Sun 10am–6pm; R$10, students R$5; ⓦmuseudainconfidencia.gov.br), inside the old Paço Municipal and jail, chronicles the town's fascinating local history, though it is primarily a shrine to the doomed *Inconfidência Mineira* rebellion of 1789. The spiritual heart of the museum is a solemn room containing the tomb of Tiradentes, leader of the rebellion, and the remains of his fellow conspirators, marked with simple, flat tombstones. On the opposite side of the square, inside the vast **Escola de Minas**, the former governor's palace dating from the 1740s, the **Museu de Ciência e Técnica** (Tues–Sun noon–5pm; R$10) houses a large geological and mineralogical collection, though the main draw is the gallery containing gold, huge amethyst and quartz crystals, silver, diamonds and other precious stones.

MUSEU DO ORATÓRIO

Just behind the Igreja de Nossa Senhora do Carmo, off Praça Tiradentes, the intriguing **Museu do Oratório** (Mon & Wed–Sun 9.30am–5.30pm; R$5, students free; ⓦmuseudooratorio.org.br) displays a high-quality collection of eighteenth- and nineteenth-century oratorios (small Catholic altars or shrines) from throughout Brazil. Although there are some glittering examples featuring gold and silver (and even sea shells) on the top floor, including a fine example by Manoel da Costa Ataíde, the most touching shrines are the portable and "bullet" oratorios in the basement, carried by muleteers and other travellers to protect themselves from danger.

IGREJA DE SÃO FRANCISCO DE ASSIS

The most beautiful church in Ouro Preto, the **Igreja de São Francisco de Assis** (Tues–Sun 8.30am–noon & 1.30–5pm; R$10, including entry to the Museu Aleijadinho), east of Praça Tiradentes, was

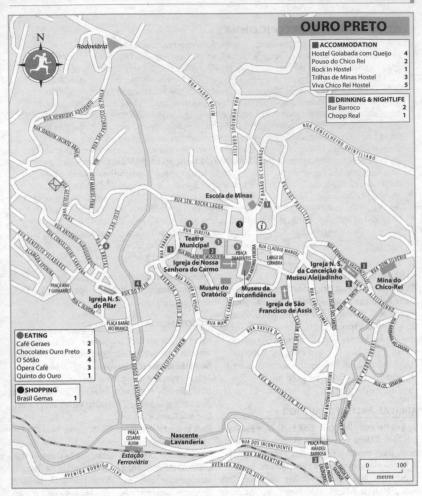

OURO PRETO

■ **ACCOMMODATION**
Hostel Goiabada com Queijo	4
Pouso do Chico Rei	2
Rock in Hostel	1
Trilhas de Minas Hostel	3
Viva Chico Rei Hostel	5

■ **DRINKING & NIGHTLIFE**
Bar Barroco	2
Chopp Real	1

● **EATING**
Café Geraes	2
Chocolates Ouro Preto	5
O Sótão	4
Ópera Café	3
Quinto do Ouro	1

● **SHOPPING**
Brasil Gemas	1

3

begun in 1765, and no other contains more works by Aleijadinho (see page 270). The exterior was entirely sculpted by the great master himself and the ceilings painted by his partner Manoel da Costa Ataíde. With the **Igreja Matriz de N.S. da Conceição** closed for renovation at the time of writing, precious artworks from the **Museu Aleijadinho** (same hours; ⟨w⟩museualeijadinho.com.br) are temporarily located inside São Francisco, in the side rooms and sacristy at the back.

MINA DO CHICO REI
Close to the Igreja Matriz de N.S. da Conceição, at Rua Dom Silvério 108, is the **Mina do Chico Rei** (daily 8am–5.30pm; R$25). Founded in 1702, the long-abandoned mine has claustrophobic tunnels to explore, and gives a good sense of the scale of the local mining operations. Constructed on five levels, it contains an astonishing eighty square kilometres of tunnels, vaults and passages. It's also an intriguing place to learn more about Chico Rei ("Little King") himself, a legendary figure said to have been an enslaved African king who bought himself and his people out of slavery and became fabulously wealthy.

3

ALEIJADINHO AND CONGONHAS

The most important sculptor in colonial Brazil, **Antônio Francisco Lisboa** (1738–1814), aka Aleijadinho, was born in Ouro Preto to a slave mother and a Portuguese architect father. Self-taught, Aleijadinho was exceptionally prolific, turning out scores of profoundly original works, an achievement made all the more remarkable by the fact that from his mid-30s he suffered from a degenerative disease (presumably leprosy) which led to loss of movement in his legs and hands, eventually forcing him to sculpt using chisels strapped to his wrists while apprentices moved him around on a trolley (the name **Aleijadinho** translates literally as "little cripple"). His extraordinary works reflect his Christian spirituality and abound in many of the *cidades históricas*, particularly Ouro Preto. His most famous works, sculpted towards the end of his life between 1796 and 1805, and credited with introducing greater realism into Baroque art, are the 76 life-size figures at the **Santuário do Bom Jesus de Matosinhos** (Tues–Sun 7am–6pm; free) in the otherwise utterly unremarkable town of **Congonhas**. Thankfully you don't have to stay there to visit them – Congonhas is a convenient stop-off between Ouro Preto (or Belo Horizonte) and São João del Rei: leave your baggage at the Congonhas *rodoviária*. To get to Bom Jesus, catch a local bus (every 30min–1hr; 15min; R$3.60) marked "Basílica", which takes you all the way up the hill to the church; it's impossible to miss. The bus to take you back to the *rodoviária* leaves from the parking bay behind the church. Taxis charge R$15–20.

IGREJA DO PILAR

At the foot of **Rua Brigador Mosqueira** stands the early eighteenth-century **Igreja Matriz N.S. do Pilar** (Tues–Sun 9–10.45am & noon–4.45pm; R$10), the most opulent church in Minas Gerais, as well as one of the oldest. Over the top even by Baroque standards, it's said to be the second richest in Brazil, with 434kg of gold and silver used in its decoration.

ARRIVAL AND INFORMATION

By bus The *rodoviária* (☎31 3559 3225) is on Rua Padre Rolim 661, a 15min steep uphill walk northwest of the city centre. Buses from Mariana stop right by Praça Tiradentes: alight here for accommodations and restaurants.
Destinations Belo Horizonte (hourly 6am–8pm; 2hr); Brasília (daily at 7.30pm; 13hr 30min); Mariana (every 30min; 30min); Rio (2 daily; 6hr 40min); São João del Rei (2 daily; 4–5hr).
By train The *Trem da Vale* tourist train links Ouro Preto with Mariana (see page 272), 12km to the east. Timetables can change, but trains usually depart Fri & Sat at 10am & 2.30pm, returning from Mariana at 1pm & 4pm (trips take 1hr); on Sundays trains depart Ouro Preto at 10am and 4pm, and from Mariana only at 2.30pm. Tickets are R$46 one-way or R$66 return (the "panoramic wagon" is R$70/R$90). The station is located south of the city centre at Praça Cesário Alvim (Wed–Sun 8.30am–5pm; ☎31 3551 7310).
To Mariana Heading to Mariana you can take the train (see above) or a local bus operated by Transcotta (daily 5.30am–11.30pm; every 30min; R$4.35), from Praça Tiradentes (no need to go to the *rodoviária*). Pay as you board. Taxis charge around R$60 one-way.

Tourist information The helpful Centro Cultural Turístico is at Praça Tiradentes 41 (daily 8am–5pm; ☎31 3559 3269, Ⓦouropreto.org.br).

ACCOMMODATION

Make sure that you book in advance in high season and at weekends. Expect substantial discounts midweek and off-season.
Hostel Goiabada com Queijo Rua do Pilar 44 ☎31 3552 3816, ✉goiabadacomqueijohostel@gmail.com; map p.269. No-frills hostel with super-helpful owners, clean dorms with parquet floors, communal kitchen and TV room. Cash only. Dorms __R$45__
Rock in Hostel Rua Brigadeiro Musqueira 14 ☎31 3551 3165, Ⓦrockinhostelouropreto.com.br; map p.269. Hostel with a rock music theme (posters and electric guitars on the walls, and a room dedicated to the Beatles), basic dorms, doubles with shared (and clean, modern) bathrooms, wonderful views and a big stereo system, used sparingly. Dorms __R$55__, doubles __R$130__

★ TREAT YOURSELF

Pouso do Chico Rei Rua Brigadeiro Musqueira 90, Centro ☎31 3551 1274, Ⓦpousodochicorei.com.br; map p.269. It's worth paying the extra to stay at this enchanting pousada, formerly graced by pre-eminent Brazilian singers Vinicius de Moraes and Dorival Caymmi. All rooms are individually furnished and some have commanding views of the Carmo church. A large breakfast is served in the dining room (amongst antiques and a fireplace), while complimentary tea and cake are available at any time. Cash only. __R$175__

★ **Trilhas de Minas Hostel** Praça Antonio Dias 21 ☎ 31 3551 6367, ⊛ trilhasdeminashostel.com; map p.269. Popular hostel on the edge of the historic centre (at the bottom of a steep slope), with compact but cosy dorms and doubles, all with wooden beds and parquet floors plus fine views of the city and a pleasant outdoor deck. Decent breakfast included. Incredibly helpful staff, though not many speak English. Can be cold in winter. Cash only. Dorms R$55, doubles R$150

Viva Chico Rei Hostel Praça Antônio Dias 14 ☎ 31 3552 3328, ⊛ vivachicoreihostel.com; map p.269. Wonderfully located hostel with heaps of charm, dorms (mixed and female only) with stylish bunks and spacious doubles (with fans), thoughtful owners and delicious buffet breakfast in the communal kitchen. Cash only. Dorms R$60, doubles R$170

EATING

Good cheap places to eat are scattered throughout Ouro Preto.

Café Geraes Rua Conde de Bobadela (Rua Direita) 122; map p.269. Café with fairly priced sandwiches and soups, delicious cakes and wine, as well as more extensive dinners, all served inside the gorgeous interior of an old townhouse (dinner mains R$40–59). Mon & Wed–Sun noon–midnight.

Chocolates Ouro Preto Praça Tiradentes 111; map p.269. Ouro Preto's most popular chocolatier offers excellent espresso (R$3.50) as well as hot chocolate (R$6–8), rich, tempting brownies and even local microbrews from Cervejaria Ouropretana in its casual café. Mon–Thurs & Sun 9am–7pm, Fri & Sat 9am–10pm.

Ópera Café Rua Conde de Bobadela 75 (inside the Pousada Solar da Ópera); map p.269. Stylish café serving superb local coffee, croissants, cakes (guava cheesecake) and pastries, but also more extensive menus of steaks and fish (mains R$25–75). Mon 1–8pm, Tues–Sun 10am–8pm.

O Sótão Rua São José 201; map p.269. Fun, colourful paintings decorate this student-friendly place with straw lightshades casting shadows on the walls. Cheap buffet at lunch and excellent rodízio (Tues–Sun from 5pm; R$27), as well as cachaças and light bites such as filled pancakes. Live and relaxing samba, MPB and bossa nova sets the mood from 8pm. Tues–Sun noon–2am.

Quinto do Ouro Rua Conde de Bobadela (aka Rua Direita) 76; map p.269. An attractive lanchonete with an excellent traditional mineira buffet (R$30) featuring several choices of meat, rich stews, vegetables and bean dishes. Tues–Sun 11am–3pm.

DRINKING AND NIGHTLIFE

Night-time action is centred on Rua Direita (aka Rua Conde de Bobadella) where students spill out of the bars, while there are a couple of options along Rua Barão de Carmargos.

★ **Bar Barroco** Praça Prefeito Amadeu Barbosa 81; map p.269. Hip student dive bar with wooden benches and graffiti-smothered walls. Live music (mostly MPB and jazz) and tasty coxhimba (fried chicken or cheese-filled pasteles). Mon–Sat noon–2am.

Chopp Real Rua Barão de Camargos 8; map p.269. A few psychedelic paintings decorate this popular joint with tables on the cobbled street in front, perfect for a chopp on a warm evening. Live bossa nova or MPB most nights from 8pm. Daily noon–2am.

SHOPPING

Ouro Preto is littered with jewellery stores selling the region's precious stones, notably tourmaline, emeralds, topaz and imperial topaz (the last is only found here). Quality is usually very good, and, despite the touristy focus, prices are much cheaper here than in the US or Europe and the trade is well regulated.

Brasil Gemas Praça Tiradentes 74 ☎ 31 3551 4448; map p.269. Sells various types of topaz, green tourmaline and amethyst, in made-to-order jewellery and designs.

DIRECTORY

Banks and exchange All the major banks with ATMs and exchange facilities are located along Rua São José. HSBC is at Rua São José 201.

Hospital Santa Casa de Misericórdia (24hr), Rua José Moringa 620, Bairro Bauxita (☎ 31 3551 1133).

Laundry Ask at your hotel/hostel as there are no laundries downtown. Nacente Lavanderia, at Rua dos Inconfidentes 5 (Mon–Fri 8am–5pm, Sat 8am–noon), picks up and drops off washing.

Post office Rua Conde de Bobadela 180 (Mon–Fri 9am–5pm; ☎ 31 3551 1855); also at Rua Getúlio Vargas 233 (near Rosário church; Mon–Fri 9am–5pm, Sat 9am–noon).

MARIANA

A thirty-minute bus ride from Ouro Preto, lovely **MARIANA**, founded in 1696 and named after King Dom João V's wife Maria Ana de Austria, is home to two of Minas's most elegant town squares and a beautifully preserved colonial centre. The town can be visited as a day-trip from Ouro Preto, but it's also a great place to stay should you wish to escape the hordes of tourists elsewhere.

WHAT TO SEE AND DO

Buses drop you at the base of the hill and colonial district along the main commercial drag, Avenida Salvador Furtado. Rua Padre Lopes leads one block south to Praça

Cláudio Manoel and the impressive, elaborate **Catedral de N.S. da Assunção** (Tues–Sun 7am–5pm; R$4). The church was designed by Aleijadinho's father in the early eighteenth century and contains many carvings by the man himself. The *tapa o vento* door, painted by Mariana native Ataíde, is considered by many to be the most beautiful in South America. Further riches include 365kg of gold leaf and a beautiful German organ with 1039 flutes and a keyboard made of elephants' teeth. **Organ concerts** are held on Friday at 11.30am and Sunday at 12.15pm (R$30).

Not far away, at Rua Frei Durão 49, the elegant former bishop's palace now houses the **Museu Arquidiocesano de Arte Sacra** (Tues–Fri 8.30am–noon & 1.30–5pm, Sat & Sun 9am–3pm; R$5), which displays religious treasures, paintings by Ataíde and sculptures by Aleijadinho. Two gorgeous Baroque churches stand on **Praça Minas Gerais**: the **Igreja de São Francisco de Assis** (Tues–Sun 8am–noon & 1–5pm; R$4), with yet more Aleijadinho carvings, is the final resting place of Ataíde; the relative restraint of the **Igreja de N.S. do Carmo** (Tues–Sun 9am–noon & 1.30–5pm; free) makes an interesting contrast.

MINAS DA PASSAGEM

Four kilometres from Mariana (on the road to Ouro Preto), **Minas da Passagem** (Mon & Tues 9am–5pm, Wed–Sun 9am–5.30pm, tours last 1hr; R$70; ⓦminasdapassagem.com.br) is one of the oldest and richest deep-shaft gold mines in the region. From 1719 to the mine's closure in 1985, 35 tonnes of gold were extracted from here. Once you've purchased tickets, walk to the mine head via the tiny museum (full of rusting equipment), and line up to board what for many tourists is the main attraction: a rickety open-seat railcar that trundles 315m down a steep slope into the main tunnel (be careful of bumping your head). At the bottom, guides lead you around the dripping, muddy but fairly spacious main tunnel, with smaller galleries branching off in all directions. Take the Ouro Preto–Mariana bus (R$4.35) and ask to get off at the stop opposite the mine; taxis from Ouro Preto charge R$40 one-way, and R$20/hr to wait for you.

ARRIVAL AND INFORMATION

By bus Transcotta buses from Ouro Preto (daily 5.30am–11.30pm; every 30min; R$4.35) stop right in the centre at Praça Tancredo Neves (Av Salvador Furtado). If you're coming from Belo Horizonte or São Paulo, you'll arrive at the *rodoviária* (ⓣ31 3557 1122), on the main road a couple of kilometres from the centre; if you don't wish to walk into the centre, catch one of the buses from Ouro Preto, which pass through the *rodoviária*.

By train The *Trem da Vale* (see page 270) connects Mariana with Ouro Preto. The train station is near the centre at Praça Juscelino Kubitschek (Wed–Sun 8.30am–5.30pm).

Tourist information The tourist information office is at Praça Tancredo Neves, opposite the bus stop (Tues–Sun 8am–noon & 1.30–5pm; ⓣ31 3557 1158). There's a smaller office at Rua Direita 91, a short walk into the old town, which can also supply maps (Mon–Fri 8am–5pm; ⓣ31 3558 2314). See also ⓦmariana.org.br.

ACCOMMODATION

Hotel Pousada das Gerais Av Nossa Senhora do Carmo 890 ⓣ31 3557 4146, ⓦhpdasgerais.com.br. One of the best deals in town (across the highway from the bus station, around 1km from the centre), with simple but comfy rooms, excellent breakfasts included and rates for single travellers from R$90. R$180

Minas Hotel Rodovia dos Inconfidentes 1650 ⓣ31 3557 1066, ⓦminashotelmg.com.br. Plain but clean and modern en-suite rooms (200m from the bus station, 1km from the centre), with rates for singles from R$110. R$185

EATING AND DRINKING

Chantilly Confeitaria Rua Frei Durão 32. The best café on Praça Gomes Freire, in a building completed in 1925, offering mouth-watering cakes, coffee, quiche and *empadas*. Daily 10am–9pm.

Rancho Praça Gomes Freire 108. Excellent local cuisine kept warm on a wood-fire stove, as well as a selection of pizzas (from R$30). Lunchtime buffet (R$26), soups and *petiscos* (from R$10) at night. Tues–Sun 11am–3pm & 6pm–midnight.

Scotch & Art Bar Praça Minas Gerais 57. Great location for an evening tipple, with a terrace overlooking the churches on the plaza and a menu of tasty bar snacks. Tues–Sun 6.30pm–2am.

SÃO JOÃO DEL REI

SÃO JOÃO DEL REI was one of the first settlements in the region, dating back to a mining camp established in 1704. Though its historic centre boasts several imposing Baroque churches, it is one of the few gold towns to have found a thriving place in the modern world. Given that São João's neighbour Tiradentes is the prettier town, you may wish to stay there and visit here for the day, even though it is the more economical option. On Fridays, weekends and public holidays you can ride between the two towns on the *Maria Fumaça* **steam train**.

WHAT TO SEE AND DO

Not far from the city's wide central artery (which has a rather fetid stream running through the middle), inside the old station at Hermílio Alves 366, the **Museu Ferroviário** (Railway Museum; Wed–Sun 9–11am & 1–4pm, Sun 9am–12.30pm; free), has interesting facts on the origins of the *Maria Fumaça* in the 1880s, and also houses the first engine to run on the track here.

On Rua Getúlio Vargas, the stunning 1721 Baroque **Catedral de Nossa Senhora de Pilar** (Mon 6–10.30am, Tues–Sun 6–10.30am & 1–8pm; free) has extensive gold gilding over the altar and attractive tiling. Virtually next door, housed in another sensitively restored building (a former jail), the **Museu de Arte Sacra** (Mon–Fri noon–5pm, Sat 9am–1pm; R$7) at Praça Embaixador Gastão da Cunha 8 boasts a small but enchanting collection of religious art: chalices, silver halos, carvings of saints, painted oratorios, crucifixes, huge silver processional crosses and so on.

Close by, the **Museu Regional**, Rua Marechal Deodoro 12 (Tues–Fri 9.30am–5.30pm, Sat & Sun 9am–1pm; free), has a rich collection of historical and artistic objects from furniture to paintings, housed in a beautifully restored mansion.

IGREJA DE SÃO FRANCISCO DE ASSIS AND TANCREDO NEVES

The most impressive and important of the city's churches, the 1774 Baroque **Igreja de São Francisco de Assis** (Mon 8am–4pm, Tues–Sat 8am–5pm, Sun after Mass from 9.15am–2.30pm; R$4) looks over the palm-filled Praça Frei Orlando. A deceptively large place with carvings by Aleijadinho and his pupils, the church has a graveyard to the rear where President Tancredo Neves is buried. Just around the corner at Rua Padre José Maria Xavier 7 is the **Memorial Tancredo Neves** (Thurs–Sat 9am–5.30pm, Sun & holidays 9am–3.30pm; R$2; ⓦ memorialtancredoneves.com.br), containing a collection of personal artefacts and documents relating to the former president's life. One of the nation's most revered politicians, Neves was born here in 1910, and is credited with masterminding Brazil's return to democracy in the 1980s.

ARRIVAL AND INFORMATION

By bus The *rodoviária* (☎ 32 3373 4700) is 2km northeast of town; outside and across Rua Cristovão Colombo, take a local bus (R$3) from in front of the *drogaria* and get off at Av Tancredo Neves (10min). Taxis (☎ 32 3371 2028) charge R$15–20.
Destinations Belo Horizonte (7–8 daily; 3hr 30min); Ouro Preto (2 daily; 4hr); Rio (3 daily; 5hr 30min); São Paulo (8 daily; 6hr–8hr 30min); Tiradentes (every 40min; 30min).
By train The *Maria Fumaça* leaves São João (Av Hermílo Alves 366; ticket office Thurs & Fri 9–11am & 1–4pm, Sat 9am–1pm & 2–4pm, Sun 9am–1pm; ☎ 32 3371 8485; ⓦ vli-logistica.com/pt-br/trem-turistico) for Tiradentes on Fri & Sat at 10am and 3pm, returning at 1pm and 5pm, and on Sun at 10am and 1pm, returning 11am & 2pm (R$50 single, R$60 return; 35min one-way).
Tourist information The tourist office (daily 8am–5pm; ☎ 32 3372 7388) lies across from the Catedral at Praça Frei Orlando 90.

ACCOMMODATION

★ **AZ Hostel** Rua Marechal Bitencourt 73 ☎ 32 98854 2842, ⓦ azhostel.com.br. Bright, spotless hostel with male- and female-only dorms, tiled floors, colourful artwork, simple but comfy en-suite doubles and extra-helpful owner. Sheets, towels and soaps included, plus free use of bikes. Breakfast is provided through vouchers for local cafés, including the highly rated *Taberna d'Omar* (p.274). Cash only. Dorms **R$65**, doubles **R$150**
Barroco Hostel Rua Marechal Bittencourt 61 ☎ 32 99937 1771, ⓦ barrocohostel.com.br. Set in one of the town's prettiest streets, this hostel offers bright and cheery dorms (male- and female-only, as well as mixed), with breakfast also offered at *Taberna d'Omar*. Dorms **R$50**, doubles **R$115**

EATING AND DRINKING

Biscoiteria Tradição Mineira Travessa Lopes Bahia 18. Seek out this small store in the commercial heart of town to load up on traditional *mineira* sweets and biscuits. Mon–Sat 9am–5pm.
Pelourinho Rua Hermílo Alves 276. A decent and cheap self-service place with a great variety of *mineira* food, near the train station; buffet by kilo, so you can stuff yourself for under R$30. Daily 11am–4pm and 6pm–midnight.
Restaurante Rex Av Hermílio Alves 146. Perfectly adequate and cheap *por kilo* restaurant, with a huge

3

selection of traditional items in a spacious, clean dining room (R$32–40/kilo). Try and get a table on the balcony. Daily 11am–3.30pm.

★ **Taberna d'Omar** Rua Getúlio Vargas 242. Small but superb coffee shop and artisanal bakery, selling all manner of breads, cookies and *pão de queijo* (from R$2), hot chocolate (R$4.50), plus more substantial dishes (such as quinoa-crusted sole; R$40). Mon & Tues 7am–7pm, Wed–Sat 7am–midnight, Sun 7am–4pm.

Villeiros Rua Padre José Maria Xavier 132, close to São Francisco church. The best *por kilo* restaurant in town, with a good range of typical *mineira* food (around R$36/kilo). Daily 11.30am–4pm; buffet served till 3pm.

DIRECTORY

Banks and exchange All banks and ATMs are on Av Tancredo Neves.

Post office Av Tiradentes 500 (Mon–Fri 9am–5pm, Sat 9am–noon).

Shopping The Feria do Artesanato, held every Sun on Av Presidente Tancredo Neves, sells local crafts.

TIRADENTES

With its quaint historic houses, cobblestone streets and horse-drawn carriages, TIRADENTES could be mistaken for a film set. Surrounded by mountains, the charming town is better appreciated during the week, as Brazilian tourists swarm in at weekends for a romantic break or to shop at the many little boutiques around town. Costs here are the most expensive in Minas, but despite this it's worth staying a night or two to fully appreciate the rich atmosphere, explore the town's cobbled alleyways – and, if you like the outdoors – go walking for an hour or two in the surrounding countryside.

WHAT TO SEE AND DO

Despite being described as a *cidade histórico*, modern Tiradentes is little more than a village, which at least ensures that everything is easily found.

The chief landmark, pretty much at the highest point in town, is the **Igreja Matriz de Santo Antônio** (daily 9am–5pm; R$5). Among the largest and most gold-laden of Minas Gerais' Baroque churches, it also features some of Aleijadinho's last works, and the classic view from the church steps is the most photographed in the state.

The **Museu da Liturgia** (Mon & Thurs–Sat 10am–5pm, Sun 10am–1.30pm; R$10) at Rua Jogo de Bola 15, a relatively new, stylish religious art museum, inside the shell of the old Casa Paroquial next to Santo Antônio, uses interactive exhibits, touchscreens and meditative background music to shed light on aspects of Catholic tradition, ceremonies and theology.

Nearby, at Rua Padre Toledo 190, in the former home of one of the heroes of the *Inconfidência Mineira*, where the conspirators first met in 1788, the **Museu Padre Toledo** (Tues–Sun 10am–5pm; R$10) has period furnishings, art and documents dating back to the eighteenth century, and a preserved slave quarters (now converted into toilets). The slaves themselves built, and worshipped at, the small, dignified and supremely attractive **Igreja da N.S. do Rosário dos Pretos** (Tues–Sun 9am–noon & 2–5pm; R$3), down the hill, which also contains three sculptures of black saints.

Housed in the old public jail (Cadeia Pública) at Rua Direita 93 (entrance on Rua da Cadeia), the **Museu de Sant'Ana** (Mon & Wed–Sun 10am–7pm; R$5) is another fascinating museum of religious art, focusing specifically on images of St Anne, the Catholic patron saint of home and family, and the mother of Mary.

ARRIVAL AND INFORMATION

By bus The *rodoviária* is in the centre of town off Rua Gabriel Passos. Buses leave regularly for São João del Rei (Mon–Fri 5.50am–7pm every 40min, Sat & Sun 7am–7pm every 1hr 30min–2hr; 30min; R$3.65), from where you can connect to other destinations. Taxis charge R$50 (one-way) for the trip.

By train The *Maria Fumaça* links Tiradentes with São João del Rei (see page 273). The train station is 1km southeast of the main square on Praça Estação.

Tourist information At Rua Resende Costa 71 (Mon–Thurs & Sun 9am–6pm, Fri & Sat 9am–8pm; ☎ 32 3355 1212).

ACCOMMODATION, EATING AND DRINKING

Tiradentes caters primarily for the well-to-do, but try visiting midweek when pousadas offer discounts – or stay in São João.

Most popular restaurants and bars are centred on Largo das Forras. Your best bet if in a small group is to share a *comida mineira*, usually large enough for two or three people.

Barouk Rua Gabriel Passos 23. Right by the square, the town's most popular lunch spot serves typical *mineira* food (buffet around $30, or *por kilo*) laid out on a raised hearth. Daily 9.30am–midnight.

Chico Doceiro Rua Francisco de Morais 74. Lauded local sweetshop, with all the traditional *mineira* treats inside handmade by octogenarian Chico "the candyman" since 1965 and now by his son; try the exquisite *doce de leite* or *doce de banana* (R$1 per piece). The open-front store has just one table inside. Daily 9am–6pm.

Confidências Mineiras Rua Gabriel Passos 26. Warm, candlelit place serving large (for three) portions of *mineira* delights such as mashed pork and bean Tutú cooked in *cachaça* (R$60), or *petiscos* to accompany your choice of their near-infinite range of *cachaças*. Wed–Fri 6–11pm, Sat noon–11pm, Sun noon–6pm.

Divino Sabor Rua Gabriel Passos 300. Popular lunch-only place in simple surroundings with wooden tables on a patio outside. *Mineira* buffet for R$28 or *por kilo* (R$45.50/kilo) Tues–Sun noon–3.30pm.

Odara Hostel Rua Custódio Gomes 286 ☎ 32 3355 1579, ⓦ odarahosteltiradentes.com.br. Excellent option a short walk from the centre, with clean mixed, male- and female-only dorms (all with just three bunks) with fans, plus two en-suite family rooms with kitchenettes (for up to five people). Friendly, English-speaking staff. Dorms R$40, doubles R$130

Hostel Raiz Rua Silvio Vasconcelos 141 ☎ 31 9170 6727, ⓦ hostelraiz.com. Simple but elegant rooms with tiled floors and shared bathrooms in the centre of town (100m from the bus station) – shared kitchen. Singles just R$70, doubles R$130

Torre Hostel Rua Herculano José dos Santos 92 ☎ 32 9993 20804, ⓦ torrehostel.com.br. One of the cheapest and friendliest places to stay, 1km from centre, with clean, simple rooms and newish dorms, shared kitchen and TV room, plus bike rentals. Free parking (reservation needed). Dorms R$40, doubles R$125

Virada's do Largo Rua do Moinho 11 ⓦ viradasdolargo. com.br. Beth Beltrão's restaurant is considered the best in town for *comida mineira*, with home-made linguiça sausage (smoke-cured pork), tutu (mashed cooked beans) and local *cachaça* (R$8.50; *caipirinha* R$18) especially outstanding. Choose single plates (mains R$38–48) or huge servings of pork, chicken, sausage and steaks for three people (R$97). Mon & Wed–Sun noon–10pm.

NIGHTLIFE AND ENTERTAINMENT

See ⓦ tiradentes.net for what's-on listings (in Portuguese).
★ **Centro Cultural Yves Alves** Rua Direita 168, ⓦ tiradentes.net. The town's cultural hub features theatrical performances, films, concerts and temporary exhibitions by local artists (free), as well as a tranquil, blossom-filled garden.

DIRECTORY

Banks and exchange All banks with ATMs are located off Rua Gabriel Passos, close to Largo das Forras.
Post office Rua Resende Costa 73 (Mon–Fri 9am–5pm).

DIAMANTINA

Six hours by bus from Belo Horizonte, **DIAMANTINA** is the most isolated of the historic towns yet well worth the trip. Nestled in the heart of the Serra do Espinhaço, it is surrounded by a breathtakingly wild and desolate landscape. Named after the abundant diamond reserves first exploited in the 1720s, the town is rich in history and was designated a UNESCO World Heritage Site in 1999. It retains a lively, friendly atmosphere and is the hometown of visionary 1950s president **Juscelino Kubitschek** who founded Brasília; a statue is dedicated to him on Rua Macau Meio. Diamantina justifies a couple of days' wandering around in its own right, but you should also try to follow a trail outside of town to take in the scenery and nearby waterfalls and rock pools – details of routes and guides can be found at the tourist office (see page 276).

(see page 276).

WHAT TO SEE AND DO

Diamantina's narrow streets are set on two exceptionally steep hills. Fortunately, almost everything of interest is tightly packed into the central area close to the main cathedral square, the Praça Conselheiro Mota. The **Museu do Diamante** (Tues–Sat 10am–5pm, Sun 9am–1pm; free; ⓦ museudiamante. blogspot.com) is right on the square at Rua Direita 14, bringing the colonial period vividly to life through an extraordinary variety of exhibits. They include real gold, real and fake diamonds, mining paraphernalia and a number of swords, pistols, guns and torture instruments that were used on enslaved indigenous people and Afro-Brazilians.

MERCADO VELHO

The **Mercado Velho** on Praça Barão de Guaicuí, just below the cathedral square, was once the focus of trade for the whole region, and is worth seeing for the building alone – an exceptional tiled wooden structure built in 1889, with a facade of rustic but very elegant shallow arches. The **market** (Fri 6–11pm, Sat 6am–3pm, Sun 8am–noon) itself has a very Northeastern feel, with its cheeses, *doces* made from sugar and fruit, blocks of salt and raw sugar, and *cachaça* sold by the shot as well as by the bottle – these days there are also cheap snack stalls and handicrafts for sale, as well as live music on Friday evenings.

CASA DA GLÓRIA

More worthwhile for the building than its contents is the eighteenth-century **Casa da Glória**, which is uphill from the tourist office at Rua da Glória 298 (daily 9am–5pm; R$1). Now owned by the Institute of Geology, sections of two buildings are open to visitors, with a modest collection of maps, gemstones and minerals. The main entrance is in the Casa da Glória itself, constructed between 1770 and 1780. In the nineteenth century the house became the residence of the town diamond inspectors, before reverting to the church in 1864 and later a school. The other building was constructed in 1850 and served as an orphanage. The premises span both sides of the street, linked by the Passadiço da Glória (1878), Diamantina's own "Bridge of Sighs".

CASA CHICA DA SILVA

Generally unknown outside of Brazil, Chica da Silva (1732–96) remains something of a legend inside the country, inspiring movies and telenovelas; the **Casa Chica da Silva** at Praça Lobo de Mesquita 266 (Tues–Sat noon–5.30pm, Sun 8.30am–noon; free) is dedicated to her story. Chica was born a slave, but grew rich and powerful nonetheless, becoming the mistress of her owner, João Fernandes de Oliveira, the government overseer of diamond mining in the region. She was eventually freed by him, and lived in this house and bore his thirteen children, though they were never married. The house itself is a beautiful example of colonial architecture, with wooden floors and garden courtyard, but the rooms are almost completely bare – IPHAN mostly uses the space to host revolving art exhibitions.

TWO CHURCHES

The **Igreja de N.S. Senhora do Carmo** on Rua do Carmo (Tues, Thurs & Fri 2.30–5pm, Sat 9am–noon & 2–5pm, Sun for Mass only; R$3), built between 1765 and 1784, is the most interesting of Diamantina's churches, with an exceptionally rich interior including an organ built in 1782 on which Lobo de Mesquita, considered the best composer of religious music of the Americas, performed many of his own works. Just downhill from here, the **Igreja de Nossa Senhora do Rosário dos Pretos** (same opening hours; R$3) was built in 1728 to serve local slaves and features an intricately painted ceiling.

ARRIVAL AND INFORMATION

By bus The *rodoviária* is on a steep hill, about a 10min walk above the centre of town (20min if walking uphill); a taxi costs around R$12–14. Pássaro Verde buses for Belo Horizonte leave at midnight, 6am, 10.45am, noon, 1pm, 3.30pm and 6pm daily (5–6hr). There is no service from Diamantina to Brasília, and usually just one bus a day to São Paulo (13–14hr).

Tourist information At Praça Antônio Eulálio 53 (Mon–Sat 9am–6pm, Sun 9am–2pm; ☎ 38 3531 9532, ⏎ diamantina.mg.gov.br).

ACCOMMODATION

Diamantina Hostel Rua do Bicame 988 ☎ 38 3531 5021, ⏎ diamantinahostel.com.br. This HI hostel is spotless and has a great view, yet the rooms are dark and not especially inviting. A 15min (uphill) walk from town and 10min from the *rodoviária*. There's a laundry. R$5 discount with HI card. Deposit required. Dorms R$59

★ **Pico do Itambé** Rua Professora Darcília Godoy 99 ☎ 38 3531 2392, ⏎ picodoitambe.com.br. Popular hostel with fairly compact but modern dorms, spotless bathrooms and fabulous views from the terrace. Dorms R$70, doubles R$140

Pousada Presidente Rua Oscar Batista 365 ☎ 38 3531 6369, ⏎ pousadapresidente.com.br. Basic but charming pousada a short walk from the centre, with cosy rooms equipped with fans, some with private bathrooms (R$170). Good breakfast included and singles pay just $60. R$140

EATING AND DRINKING

There's a decent variety of budget options around the town centre, most serving *comida mineira*. Bars around Rua da Quintanda such as *Café A Baiúca* have tables spilling onto the square – perfect to watch life go by as you sip a *chopp*.

Apocalípse Praça Barão do Guaicuí 78. A popular and classy *por kilo* (around R$54/kilo) restaurant across from the market; the menu includes Italian dishes and *comida*

mineira, plus sublime desserts. Daily 11am–3.30pm, Thurs–Sat also 7–11pm.
★ **Catedral Pub** Rua Direita 68. Stylish bar in an old house on the main plaza, with narrow interior, exposed wattle and daub walls, and a huge menu of craft beers (mostly local), ordered via tablet (R$16–25), including Cerveja Diamantina, Krug and Cerveja Wäls (from Belo Horizonte). Food served at the back (burgers R$28–36). Daily 10am–1am.

★ **Livraria Café Espaço B** Beco da Tecla 31. Just off the cathedral square, this is the place for good coffee (R$4.75) and cakes (R$9–10) late into the evening, in a dimly lit bookshop. Also does conventional main dishes (R$16–40). Mon–Sat 9am–midnight, Sun 10am–1pm.
Recanto do Antônio Beco da Tecla 39 (an alleyway off the Praça Barão do Guaicuí). Chilled-out spot with the appearance of a country tavern, serving beer, wine, sausage and *carne do sol*. Tues–Sun 11am–3pm & 6pm–midnight.

Bahia

Gateway to the Brazilian Northeast (see page 289) and, after Rio, the state drawing the most foreign visitors, **BAHIA** is a clear highlight of South America. Portuguese Brazil began here in the historic capital of **Salvador**, a legacy reflected today in its colonial architecture, political conservatism, and the significant population of Brazilians with African heritage. The syncretism of the African with the European in Brazilian culture is reflected in all aspects of daily life here – but especially in the city's food, music and religion.

Roughly the size of France, Bahia comprises an extraordinary natural landscape, from 1000km of stunning coastline to the vast semi-arid *sertão* of the interior. Rising up at the state's heart, the wide valleys and table mountains of the **Chapada Diamantina** provide some of the best trekking and climbing possibilities in the country – the perfect antidote to the resorts or laidback hideaways along the coast.

SALVADOR

High above the enormous bay of Todos os Santos (All Saints), **SALVADOR** has an electric feel from the moment you arrive. This is the great cultural and historical centre of Brazil, where Afro-Brazilian heritage is strongest and where capoeira, *candomblé* and *samba de roda* were created. The Centro Histórico is a magical place, a melange of narrow cobbled streets, peeling purple walls, grand Baroque churches, kids kicking footballs, rastas, locals sipping bottled beer on plastic chairs and the almost constant beating of drums, especially as the sun sets. Salvador was officially founded in 1549 by Portuguese conquistador **Tomé de Sousa**, who chose the city for its inaccessible perch high above the water. It was the scene of a great battle in 1624, when the Dutch destroyed the Portuguese fleet in the bay and stormed and captured the town, only to be forced out again within a year by a joint Spanish and

3

FESTIVE SALVADOR

Lavagem do Bonfim Second Thurs in Jan. The washing of the church steps by *baianas* (local Bahian women) in traditional dress is followed by food, music and dancing.

Carnaval Week preceding Lent. The largest street party in the world takes place in Salvador. There's an accepting atmosphere but it's worth bearing in mind that all-black *blocos* (street bands and groups) may be black culture groups who won't appreciate being joined by non-black Brazilians, let alone gringos; be sensitive or ask before leaping in.

Festa de Santo Antônio June 13. The main celebration of the patron saint of matrimony is held at Largo de Santo Antônio.

Dia de São João June 24. One of the other major holidays in Bahia outside Carnaval celebrates St John with *forró* (Northeastern Brazilian folk dance), straw hats and traditional food.

Independência da Bahia July 2. Celebrating the expulsion of the Portuguese and the province's independence since the year 1823.

Festa de Santa Barbara Dec 4. The other great day in the *candomblé* year, dedicated to the goddess Iansã and celebrated in São Félix, near Cachoeira.

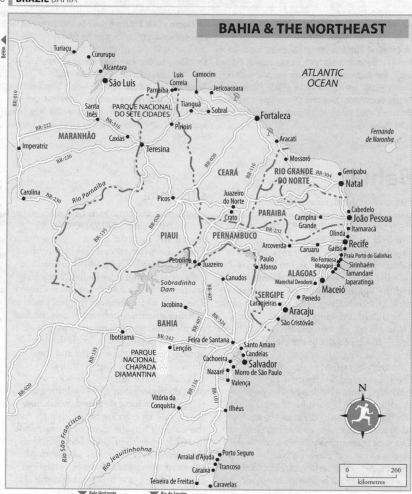

BAHIA & THE NORTHEAST

Portuguese force. For the first three hundred years of its existence, Salvador was the most important port and city in the South Atlantic – Rio only replaced it as capital in 1763.

If you tire of the city, go down to the pier and grab a boat for the choppy ride over to **Morro de São Paulo**, an island with beautiful beaches that's just two hours away.

WHAT TO SEE AND DO

Salvador is built around the craggy, 70m-high bluff that dominates the eastern side of the bay and splits the central area into upper and lower sections. The heart of the old city, **Cidade Alta** (upper city, or simply Centro), is strung along its top – this is the administrative and cultural centre of the city where you'll find most of the bars, restaurants, hostels and pousadas. This cliff-top area is linked to the old, shabby commercial district, **Cidade Baixa** (lower city), by precipitous streets, a funicular railway (daily 6am–10pm; R$0.15) and the towering Art Deco lift shaft of the **Carlos Lacerda elevator** (daily 24hr; R$0.15), the city's largest landmark. Stretching south along the coast are beaches, forts, expensive hotels, and **Barra**, where you will find more restaurants and pousadas. From Barra, a broken coastline of coves and beaches, large and small, runs east along the twisting **Avenida Oceânica**, which runs along the shore for 22km through the other main beach areas, **Ondina**, **Rio Vermelho** and **Itapuã** (near the airport).

PRAÇA MUNICIPAL

Praça Municipal, Cidade Alta's main square overlooking the bay, is the place to begin exploring. Dominating the *praça* is the **Palácio do Rio Branco** (Mon–Fri 9am–5pm, Sat & Sun 9am–1pm; free), the old governor's palace, burnt down and rebuilt during the Dutch wars. The fine interior is a blend of Rococo plasterwork, polished wooden floors, painted walls and ceilings. The exhibit inside, the **Memorial dos Governadores**, houses pieces from the colonial era and portraits of former governors. On the east side of the square is the **Memorial da Câmara Municipal** (Mon–Fri 8am–noon & 2–6pm; free), the seventeenth-century city hall, now a small, well-presented museum charting the history of the city.

Just north of the square is the **Museu da Misericórdia** (Tues–Fri 8am–5.30pm, Sat 9am–5pm, Sun noon–5pm; R$6), Brazil's first hospice and shelter for the sick and hungry. It's now a large colonial-period art museum with dazzling carved Baroque ceilings, mahogany panels and period furniture throughout. Head up to the mansion's upper rooms for stellar views across the bay.

PRAÇA DA SÉ

Rua da Misericórdia leads into the **Praça da Sé**, the heart of Cidade Alta. The square lies at the southern end of **Pelourinho** or **Pelô**, the area of Cidade Alta famed for its gorgeous architecture, shops, music, dining and nightlife, though less than twenty years ago it was decaying and run-down. At the end of the Praça da Sé, facing the adjoining square known as the **Terreiro de Jesus**, the **Catedral Basílica** (closed at the time of writing but usually Mon–Sat 8.30–11.30am & 1.30–5pm; R$3) was once the chapel of the largest Jesuit seminary outside Rome. To the left of its altar is the tomb of **Mem de Sá**, third governor general of Brazil (1556–70). You're likely to see some capoeira in full swing as you exit the cathedral, as groups often perform on the front steps. Be warned, they're going to want money if you take a picture of them.

MUSEU AFRO-BRASILEIRO

Next to the cathedral in what used to be the university medical faculty, the **Museu Afro-Brasileiro** (Mon–Fri 9am–5pm, usually open Sat mornings, but check in advance; R$6; ⓦmafro.ceao.ufba.br) is the city's best museum, offering an enthralling overview of

---

SALVADOR'S BEACHES

All of these beaches (apart from Aldeia Hippie) can be reached by bus (heading to either "Vilas do Atlântico" or "Praias do Flamengo") from Praça da Sé.

Praia da Onda This beach in Ondina is good for surfing (although watch the rocks) and even fishing.

Praia de Aleuluia The perfect spot to grab some lunch at one of the many bars or restaurants along the beach. Good waves for surfing too.

Praia de Itapuã One of the most scenic beaches, mainly because of its tall, lilting palm trees.

Praia de Jaguanibe Strong winds make this a perfect spot to surf, windsurf and kite-surf.

Praia de Stella Maris Good for long walks as well as surfing.

Praia do Farol da Barra Windswept palms and thatched huts punctuate this small, rocky beach near the lighthouse.

Praia do Porto da Barra The closest swimming beach to historic Salvador is calm and narrow, and just a short bus ride away.

Aldeia Hippie In Arembepe, about 50km from Salvador, the long beach here was made famous by Mick Jagger and Janis Joplin in the 1960s. Though often crowded, there are still peaceful spots to be found, and many people come to take a dip in the Capivara River. Frequent buses from the *rodoviária*.

Igreja do Bonfim (6km) & (7.8km)
Forte da Capoeira (1.6km)

SALVADOR

Santo Antônio

DRINKING & NIGHTLIFE

Bar Balaio de Gato	1
Casa do Amarelindo	2
Clube do Samba	4
O Cravinho Bar	3

EATING

Bar Zulu	7
Café Conosco	8
Casa da Gamboa	5
Conventual	2
Jardim das Delícias	6
Porto do Moreira	12
Ramma	9/11
Rango Vegan	3
Restaurante do SENAC	4
Sorvete da Ribeira	1
Tudo Azul	10

SHOPPING

Dinho	1

Convento do Carmo

CIDADE BAIXA

Citibank

Igreja da N. S. dos Pretos

Casa de Jorge Amado

Museu Abelardo Rodrigues

Instituto de Artesanato Visconde de Mauá

PELOURINHO

Museu Afro-Brasileiro

Catedral Basílica

Funicular Railway

TERREIRO DE JESUS

Central do Carnaval Bahia

Igreja da Ordem Terceira de São Francisco

Igreja de São Francisco

PRAÇA DA SÉ

Banco do Brasil

RUA DO BISPO

RUA TRES DE MAIO

Museu da Misericordia

RUA CUEDES DE BRITO

RUA DO TIJOLO

Laundry

CIDADE ALTA

Mercado Modelo

Terminal Marítimo Turístico

Elevador Carlos Lacerda

PRAÇA MUNICIPAL

Câmara Municipal

Palácio do Rio Branco

Bahia de Todos os Santos

PRAÇA CASTRO ALVES

0   100
metres

ACCOMMODATION

Acai Hostel	3
Âmbar Pousada	9
Casa do Amarelindo	4
Casa Inglesa	10
Che Lagarto	8
Hostel Galeria 13	5
Hit Hotel	7
Laranjeiras Hostel	6
Nega Maluca Guesthouse	1
Pestana Convento do Carmo	2

Terminal da Estação Marítima (2km)

Morro de São Paolo

Rio Vermelho (7km) & Rodoviária (7.2km)

10 (3.7km) 7 (3.7km) 11 (3.8km) 8 (4.3km) 9 (4.4km) 10 (4.5km), Barra, Beaches Forts & Airport (28.6km) 12 (600m), Museu da Arts Sacra (180m), MAM (300m) & Rio Vermelho (10km)

Brazil's (and especially Bahia's) African roots. The ground floor covers popular culture, including carnival, capoeira, religion and music, with special rooms dedicated to the famous **carved wood panels** by Carybé, Bahia's most famous artist, while the basement contains the **Museu Arqueológico e Etnológico**, given over to ceramics, basketware, textiles and artefacts from Afro-Brazilian burial sites, alongside coverage of the Jesuit conversion of indigenous people. Across all floors you'll see striking objects from ancient African civilizations, including jewellery, musical instruments, masks and sculptures of the *orixás* (African gods), widely worshipped today in the Brazilian *candomblé* religion.

LARGO DO CRUZEIRO DE SÃO FRANCISCO

On Largo do Cruzeiro de São Francisco, an extension of the **Terreiro de Jesus**, are the superb carved stone facades of two churches dedicated to St Francis: the **Igreja de São Francisco** (daily 9am–6.30pm; R$5), completed between 1708 and 1723, and the **Igreja da Ordem Terceira de São Francisco** (Tues–Sat 9am–6.30pm, Sun 10am–5pm; R$5). The former contains a small cloister decorated with one of the finest single pieces of *azulejo* (decorative glazed tiling) work in Brazil, while the latter, with an especially ostentatious sandstone facade, was completed in 1703 as a display of wealth and power by Portuguese colonizers keen to demonstrate to the world their imperial might in the Americas. Over 100kg of gold was

transported here and used to decorate the interior; the opulent walls display imperious paintings as well as *azulejos*.

LARGO DO PELOURINHO

The beautiful, cobbled **Largo do Pelourinho**, down narrow Rua Alfredo de Brito, has changed little since the eighteenth century and remains the heart of the Pelô. Lined with solid colonial mansions, it's topped by the oriental-looking towers of the **Igreja da Nossa Senhora do Rosário dos Pretos** (Mon–Sat 8am–noon & 1–5pm Sun 9.30am Mass only; R$3), built by and for slaves and still with a largely black congregation. Across from here is the **Casa de Jorge Amado** (Mon–Fri 10am–6pm, Sat 10am–4pm; R$5; free on Wed; ⓦjorgeamado.org.br), a museum given over to the life and work of the hugely popular modern novelist, author of 25 works including the critically acclaimed *Captains of the Sands* and *Gabriela, Clove and Cinnamon*; the displays here are devoted both to the author's life and to the contrasting (and controversial) themes of his books, from social realism to sexual mores.

MUSEU DA ARTE SACRA

Despite the concentration of riches in Cidade Alta, you'll have to leave the old city proper to find the **Museu da Arte Sacra** on Rua do Sodré 276 (20min walk south of Praça Municipal via Rua Chile and Carlos Gomez; Mon–Fri 11.30am–5.30pm; R$10; ⓔmas@ufba.br), one of the finest museums of Catholic art in Brazil. It's housed in a magnificent former convent with much of

3

CRIME AND SAFETY

Salvador (especially Centro) has more reported **robberies** and **muggings** of tourists than anywhere else in Bahia (and possibly Brazil). However, trouble is much easier to avoid than the statistics suggest. The vast majority of tourists who get mugged go exploring along pretty, but deserted, narrow streets. However enticing this might seem, never wander off the main drags or down ill-lit side streets in the day or at night, and don't use the **Elevador Lacerda** (see page 278) after early evening. Again, though it seems tempting (because it's so close), never walk up and down the winding roads that connect the Cidade Alta and the Cidade Baixa. Be careful using ordinary **city buses** on Sundays when there are few people around – and avoid wandering the backstreets of Barra at night.

If you stick to these rules you should have no problems: the main tourist area around **Pelourinho** is heavily policed and busy until quite late at night, and is therefore relatively safe. Needless to say, leave expensive jewellery, watches and electronics in the hotel while touring the old city, and if you are mugged, do not resist.

its original furniture and fittings still intact, and with a maze of small rooms stuffed with a remarkably rich collection of colonial art, primarily dating from the sixteenth to eighteenth centuries. The collection of Baroque work by **José Teófilo de Jesus** and **José Joaquim da Rocha**, founders of the Bahian school of painting, is especially good.

MERCADO MODELO

Cidade Baixa has few sights, but it is well worth the effort to get to the **Mercado Modelo** (Mon–Sat 9am–7pm, Sun 9am–2pm), which is full of Bahian handicrafts, trinkets and beachwear – great for gifts and souvenirs – though be prepared to haggle a little. You'll find it across the street from the bottom of the Lacerda elevator, behind a row of outdoor handicraft stalls.

MUSEU NÁUTICO DA BAHIA

The **Museu Náutico da Bahia** (Tues–Sun 9am–6pm, daily in Jan & July; R$15; ⓦ museunauticodabahia.org.br) sits within the picturesque **Forte de Santo Antônio** on the windy Barra point, where the Atlantic Ocean becomes the bay of Todos os Santos (local buses and the *executivo* service to Barra leave from the Praça da Sé). It houses a collection of seafaring instruments, maps, model boats, art and documents (all labelled in English). Founded in 1534 as a wattle-and-daub construction, this was the first European fort on the Brazilian coast (the current fortifications date from 1696–1702). Most people come for the views from the terrace above the museum; it's a popular place to have a cocktail as the sun sets.

IGREJA DO BONFIM

The **Igreja do Bonfim** (Mon 9am–5pm, Tues–Thurs & Sat 7am–5pm, Fri 6am–6.30pm; free), located at the top of the peninsula of Itapagipe, is worshipped at by *Candomblistas* (followers of the Afro-Brazilian religion, *candomblé*) and Catholics alike, an intriguing hotchpotch of city dwellers from *favelados* to wealthy matriarchs and rural *mestizos* to naval officers. The church houses the **Museu dos Ex-Votos do Senhor do Bonfim** (Tues–Sat 9am–noon & 2–5pm; free), lined with heart-wrenching photos of supplicants, written pleas for divine aid and thanks for wishes fulfilled. Hanging from the ceiling are a hundred body parts made of plastic and wood, offerings from the hopeful and the thankful. The church is a thirty-minute bus ride from the centre (take the buses marked "Bonfim" or "Ribeira" from the bottom of the Lacerda elevator).

ARRIVAL AND DEPARTURE

By plane Aeroporto Deputado Luis Eduardo do Magalhães (ⓣ 71 3204 1010, ⓦ aeroportosalvador.net) is around 30km northeast of the Cidade Alta, connected to the centre by an hourly shuttle express bus service (daily 7.30am–8pm; R$6.50), marked "Praça da Sé/Aeroporto", that leaves from directly in front of the terminal and takes you to Praça da Sé bus station via the beach districts. The length of the ride varies according to traffic, but if you're going back the other way make sure you allow two hours just to be safe. A taxi to the centre will cost around R$100 (fixed rate).

Destinations Daily flights to Miami, Buenos Aires, Lima, Madrid and Lisbon. Belo Horizonte (4 daily; 1hr 40min); Brasília (5 daily; 1hr 50min–2hr 10min); Recife (7 daily; 1hr 15min–1hr 30min); Rio (9 daily; 2hr 5min–2hr 35min); São Paulo (20 daily; 2hr 35min).

By bus Salvador's well-organized and large *rodoviária*, Av Antônio C. Magalhães 4362, Pituba (ⓣ 71 3616 8357, ⓦ rodoviariadesalvador.com.br), is 8km east of the centre. To get to/from the Cidade Alta an *executivo* bus runs between the Iguatemi shopping centre (across the busy road from the *rodoviária*) and Praça da Sé. The bus costs R$6 and makes stately progress via the beach districts of Pituba and Rio Vermelho. Alternatively, take a taxi (about R$40).

Destinations Belo Horizonte (1 daily; 23hr); Lençóis (3 daily; 6–7hr); Recife (1 daily; 12–16hr); Rio (1 daily; 28–30hr); São Paulo (1 daily; 33–35hr).

By boat Numerous launch services depart from the Terminal Marítimo Turístico, the blue building at the water's edge behind the Mercado Modelo. Popular destinations include the island of Itaparica, visible directly across the bay from Salvador, and Morro de São Paulo (see page 286) on Tinharé.

GETTING AROUND

By bus The bus system is efficient, cheap (R$3.10) and easy to use, running till 11pm on weekdays and 10pm on weekends. To reach the centre, any bus with "Sé", "C. Grande" or "Lapa" on the route card will do. Buses with route card "Flamengo" leave from Praça da Sé passing Barra, and stopping off at all the beaches to the north – the last stop is Ipitanga. Air-conditioned "*executivos*" buses run most of the same routes, though less frequently (R$6.50).

By taxi Taxis are metered and plentiful and are recommended at night, even for short distances within the

Cidade Alta. Meters start at R$4.80 and will quickly top R$50 for rides across the city. Radio Taxi Cometas (☎71 3377 6311); Chame Táxi (☎71 3241 2266, ⓦchametaxisalvador.com.br).

INFORMATION AND TOURS

Tourist information Helpful staff (most don't speak English) can be found at the tourist office at the Lacerda elevator on Praça Municipal (Mon 9am–6pm, Sat 9am–2pm; ☎71 3321 3127, ⓦbahia.com.br). There are also information desks at the airport (daily 7.30am–11pm; ☎71 3204 1244), in Cidade Alta at Rua das Laranjeiras 2 (daily 8.30am–6pm; ☎71 3321 2133) and at the *rodoviária* (daily 8.30am–6pm; ☎71 3450 3871). An additional source of information is the tourist hotline, "Disque Bahia Turismo" – call ☎71 3103 3103 (24hr) and you should be able to get an English-speaker.

Tour operators Salvador Bus (Mon–Sat; tickets from R$60; ☎71 3356 6425, ⓦsalvadorbus.com.br) operate double-decker buses for various city-tours with tickets available at hotels and travel agencies; Privé Tur, Rua Manuel Andrade 55, Sala 310, Pituba (☎71 3205 1400, ⓦprivetur.com.br), organizes city tours, beach trips and schooner cruises. Tours Bahia, Rua das Laranjeiras 05 sala 1, Pelourinho (☎71 3320 3280, ⓦtoursbahia.com.br), offers a range of good-quality services, covering city tours, airline tickets, transfers and money exchange.

ACCOMMODATION

The best area to head for is Cidade Alta, not least because of the spectacular view across the island-studded bay. The exception is if you want to be near the beach, in which case Barra offers great value for money and a good choice of party-vibe hostels. While pousada prices generally stay within reason, be aware that during Carnaval rates double or even triple. Out of season discounts are nearly always on offer, so make sure you ask for one ("*tem desconta?*").

CIDADE ALTA

Acai Hostel Rua do Passo 7, San Antonio ☎71 3241 1039 ⓦacaihostel.com; map p.280. Located just down from the Pelourinho and leading up into the San Antonio neighbourhood, this fun hostel touts its pod beds, which are a nice change from standard dorm bunks. There's a daily

caipirinha or shot, but no breakfast. There's also a lively bar next door. Dorms R$50

★ **Hostel Galeria 13** Rua da Ordem Terceira 23 ☎71 3266 5609, ⓦhostelgaleria13.com; map p.280. An interesting backpacker pad where English is spoken. Great breakfast buffet served until midday, plus luggage store. Have an afternoon dip in the pool or unwind in the dimly lit Moroccan chill-out room. Free (amazing) happy-hour *caipirinhas*. All rooms have a/c. Guests get a ten-percent discount at *Galeria 13*'s restaurant, *Zulu* (traditional cuisine with vegetarian options).Dorms R$50, doubles R$160

★ **Laranjeiras Hostel** Rua da Ordem Terceira (aka Rua Inácio Accioli) 13 ☎71 3321 1366, ⓦlaranjeirashostel.com.br; map p.280. This lively hostel in the heart of the historic centre has good security, relaxing hammocks and long thin dorms with high top bunks. The crêperie in the lobby and mezzanine chill-out area are great for mingling. Dorms R$55, doubles R$140

3

COMIDA BAIANA

The secret of Bahian cooking is twofold: a rich seafood base and the abundance of traditional West African **ingredients** like palm oil, nuts, coconut and ferociously strong peppers. **Vatapá**, a bright yellow porridge of palm oil, coconut, shrimp and garlic, looks vaguely unappetizing but is delicious. Other dishes to look out for are **moqueca**, seafood cooked in the inevitable palm-oil-based sauce; **caruru**, with many of the same ingredients as *vatapá* but with the vital addition of loads of okra; and **acarajé**, deep-fried bean cake stuffed with *vatapá*, salad and optional hot pepper. Bahian cuisine also has good **desserts**, which are less stickily sweet than elsewhere: **quindim** is a delicious small cake of coconut flavoured with vanilla, which often comes with a prune in the middle.

Nega Maluca Guesthouse Rua dos Marchantes 15 📞71 3242 9249, 🌐negamaluca.com; map p.280. This Israeli-owned hostel has winding, narrow corridors and dorms with deposit boxes for valuables, as well as sockets and lamps above each bed. There's a rooftop terrace with hammocks overlooking the upper part of Salvador, as well as a chill-out area at the back. Dorms R$45, doubles R$110

BARRA AND THE BEACHES

Âmbar Pousada Rua Afonso Celso 485 📞71 3264 6956, 🌐ambarpousada.com.br; map p.280. Friendly pousada with simple but neat, cosy rooms on two storeys, with or without bathrooms, set around an attractive courtyard. Good breakfast included, though the dining room has slightly dreary tablecloths and an old-fashioned feel. Staff are helpful and Barra beach is just a 10min walk away. Dorms R$40, doubles R$120

Casa Inglesa Rua Eng. Milton Olvieira 📞71 3022 0564 🌐casainglesasalvador.com; map p.280. Small guesthouse on a quiet residential street with seven bedrooms, each with a/c and minibar. Services include private Baian cuisine cooking classes and capoeira lessons. R$350.

Che Lagarto Av. Oceánica 84 📞71 3235 2404, 🌐chelagarto.com; map p.280. Part of the ubiquitous chain of party hostels throughout South America. The Salvador branch has a prime location on the waterfront, an upstairs terrace bar (happy hour 6–8pm), and a pizzeria downstairs. Can arrange tours and excursions. Dorms R$50, doubles R$165.

Hit Hotel Av Sete de Setembro 3691 📞71 3264 7433, 🌐hithotel.com.br; map p.280. A modern hotel with a cool, spacious lobby overlooking the beach, pretty good service, a restaurant and bright, contemporary style rooms with LCD TVs, fridge and sea views. R$189

EATING

Eating out is a pleasure in Salvador. There's a huge range of restaurants and the local cuisine (see page 283) is deservedly famous all over Brazil. Street food is fabulous too and readily available, with plenty of vendors selling local delicacies (try the *acarajé* stalls in Rio Vermelho district, including the celebrated *Acarajé da Dinha*). While the Cidade Alta has a growing number of stylish, expensive places, it's still relatively easy to eat well for under R$30.

CIDADE ALTA

Café Conosco Rua da Ordem Terceira do São Francisco 4, Pelourinho 📞71 8415 2332; map p.280. Attractive café set in an early eighteenth-century house; good coffee, quiche and cakes (R$11.50-12.50) made by owner Nilza Ribeiro, and a tranquil escape from the hubbub of the streets. Mon–Fri 10am–7pm, Sat 10am–4pm.

Casa da Gamboa Rua João de Deus 32, Pelourinho 📞71 3321 3393; map p.280. One of the district's top

restaurants, decorated with local paintings and worth a splurge. Serves mainly Bahian dishes; expect to pay about R$90 per head. Mon–Sat noon–4pm & 6–11pm.

Conventual Rua do Carmo 1, Santo Antônio 📞71 3329 3316, 🌐terezapaim.com.br; map p.280. Based in the cloisters of the exclusive *Convento do Carmo*, just a short stroll from the heart and heat of the Pelourinho, this is probably the city's most expensive restaurant. It has a mainly Portuguese menu, full of excellently prepared and presented dishes, plus there's a large and fancy bar. The best reason to eat here, however, is to enjoy the ambience of the leafy stone courtyard and cloisters. Daily 7am–11pm.

Jardim das Delícias Rua João de Deus 12 📞71 3321 1449; map p.280. A hidden tranquil world within the Pelourinho, this courtyard restaurant offers high-quality ingredients that are definitely worth splashing out for. Try the *badejo Jardim das Delícias* (white fish marinated with herbs and served with plantain). Mains R$40–60. Mon & Wed 4–11pm, Tues & Thurs–Sat noon–11pm.

★ **Porto do Moreira** Largo do Mocambinho 28 📞71 3322 4112; map p.280. Unassuming local spot with creative Bahian dishes and a long history – it was founded in 1938 by Portuguese immigrant José Moreira da Silva and is now managed by his two sons (the restaurant and the plaza featured in Jorge Amado's novel *Dona Flor and Her Two Husbands*). Dishes R$25–40. Daily 11am–3pm.

Rango Vegan Rua do Passo 62, San Antonio 📞71 3488 2756; map p.280. Herbivores will want to head straight to San Antonio and *Rango Vegan*, a quaint vegan spot on the hillside. Items on the daily-changing menu include lentil burgers, curries, rice dishes and tofu "fish" filets and fried corn nuggets with chickpeas. Mains R$20–40, Tues–Fri noon–8pm, Sat noon–11pm.

★ **Restaurante do SENAC** Largo do Pelourinho 📞71 3321 5502, 🌐ba.senac.br; map p.280. Municipal restaurant-school in a finely restored colonial mansion (once a legendary capoeira school). It looks very expensive from the outside, but it's good value for what you get. You pay a set charge for the lunch *buffet típico* upstairs – about R$56 – and take as much as you want from a choice of around forty dishes (and twelve desserts), all helpfully labelled so you know what you're eating. On street level is a simpler *"buffet à quilo"* option (R$34.90/kilo; Mon–Fri). Mon–Sat 11.30am–3.30pm & 6.30–10pm, Sun 11.30am–3.30pm.

Bar Zulu Rua de Laranjeiras 15, Pelourinho 📞71 98784 3172; map p.280. The owners of Hostel Galeria 13 opened this travellers' favourite in 2009. Fare includes Bahian-inspired burgers, great moquecas (you can learn how to make them at the cooking class offered by the hostel), homemade bread and a large selection of craft beers. R$30–90. Daily noon–11pm

BARRA

Ramma Rua Lord Cochrane 76 ☎71 3264 0044, ⓦ rammacozinhanatural.com.br; map p.280. This classic wholefood café (sister to the old town branch) provides an excellent range of tasty and healthy *comida por kilo* at lunchtimes. Get there well before 1pm to avoid the crowds. Figure on R$20–35. Daily 11.30am–3.30pm.

Tudo Azul Av Sete de Setembro 3717 ☎ 71 9104 8011; map p.280. This modest Swiss/Brazilian fusion place is great for a relatively cheap meal (mains R$30–55) and cold beer, with the names of customers scribbled on the walls. Think "Swiss" potatoes, *moqueca* and fresh shrimp. Staff hand out salted popcorn while you wait for a table. Mon–Fri 10am–10pm, Sat & Sun 9am–10pm.

RIBEIRA

★ **Sorveteria da Ribeira** Praça General Osório 87 Ribeira ☎71 3316 5451, ⓦ sorveteriadaribeira.com.br; map p.280. Salvador's most famous ice-cream shop lies on the waterfront a short taxi ride from Igreja da Bonfim. Founded by Italian immigrant Mario Tosta, it has been knocking out sweet icy treats since 1931, with flavours ranging from coconut and chocolate to tapioca and exotic Brazilian fruits such as *acai* and *biribiri* (scoops from R$7). Daily 9am–10pm.

DRINKING AND NIGHTLIFE

You'll find Salvador's most distinctive bars and nightlife in Pelourinho, though Barra also attracts the party crowd and other venues are scattered all over the city (Amaralina and Pituba are probably the liveliest areas to head for, and Friday and Saturday nights are best). Other than the weekend, Tuesday is a big night out, a tradition known as Terça da Benção ("blessed Tuesday").

Bar Balaio de Gato Rua do Passo 10; map p.280. Dive bar located adjacent to the *Acai Hostel* just down from Pelourinho. There's a big Tuesday party featuring live traditional samba music, which draws a fun crowd of locals and travellers. Free entry. Tues 10pm–2am.

Casa do Amarelindo Rua das Portas do Carmo 6, Pelourinho; map p.280. Smart, intimate hotel bar with a leafy indoor area serving superb *maracujá caipirinhas*. Wind your way up the spiral staircase to the terrace, where there's a small pool and lovely views across the bay. Daily 4–9pm.

Clube do Samba Largo do Terreiro de Jesus 5 ☎71 9361 1508, ⓦ clubedosamba.com.br; map p.280. Often hosts live samba acts on Saturdays and Sundays, and various local groups during the week. Cover R$10. Tues–Sat 5pm–midnight, Sun 4–10pm.

O Cravinho Bar Largo Terreiro de Jesus 3 ☎71 9314 6022, ⓦ ocravinho.com.br; map p.280. Traditional place

---

CAPOEIRA

The Brazilian martial art **capoeira** is widely considered to originate from ritual fights in Angola to gain the nuptial rights of young women, though in Brazil it developed into a technique of anticolonial resistance, disguised from slave masters as a dance. Although outlawed for much of the nineteenth century, capoeira is now practised across the country, a graceful, semi-balletic art form somewhere between fighting and dancing. Usually accompanied by the characteristic rhythmic twang of the *berimbau* (single-string percussion instrument), it takes the form of a pair of dancers/fighters leaping and whirling in stylized "combat" – which, with younger *capoeiristas*, occasionally slips into a genuine fight when one fails to evade a blow and tempers fly. There are regular displays on Terreiro de Jesus and near the entrances to the Mercado Modelo in Cidade Baixa, largely for the benefit of tourists and their financial contributions, but still interesting. The best capoeira, though, can be found in the *academias de capoeira*, organized schools with classes you can watch for free. If you want a really cool capoeira experience, leave the Pelourinho and head up to the Forte Santo Antônio, just a short walk up the hill. Inside the renovated white fort are several schools where the setting may make you feel more like a Shaolin monk in training.

CAPOEIRA SCHOOLS

Associação Brasileira de Capoeira Angola Rua Gregório de Matos 38 ☎71 9266 7881, ⓦ abca. portalcapoeira.com Runs biweekly classes (call to confirm times).

Associação de Capoeira Mestre Bimba Rua das Laranjeiras 1 (also known as Rua Francisco Muniz Barreto), Pelourinho ☎71 3322 0639, ⓦ capoeiramestrebimba.com.br. Named after the legendary pioneer of "Capoeira Regional", Mestre Bimba

(1899–1974). Visitors welcome to watch practices Mon–Fri 10am–noon 4–9pm, Sat 10am–noon; classes Tues–Fri 7.15pm & 8.15pm.

Capoeira Angola Irmões Gêmeos e Metre Curió Rua Gregório de Matos 9 (upstairs), Pelourinho ☎71 3321 0081, ✉ mestrecurio@yahoo.com.br. Established in 1982 by the great Mestre Curió, a student of legendary Mestre Pastinha (1889–1981), spiritual godfather of "Capoeira Angola". Call for times.

to start the evening, preferably with a glass of *infusões* (flavoured *cachaça*), the most popular – *cravinho* – made from essence of clove or ginger. This place gets busy on Tuesday evenings (the busiest weekday night in Pelourinho) and at weekends. Daily 11am–around 11pm.

ENTERTAINMENT

A soulful, foot-tapping weekly event worth heading to is the jazz concert at MAM, Av Contorno (Museum of Modern Art; Sat 7–9.30pm; R$8; ☎71 3117 6139, ⓦjamnomam. com.br), near the marina in the Cidade Baixa (take a taxi).
Balé Folclórico da Bahia Rua Gregório de Matos 49, Pelourinho ☎71 33221962, ⓦbalefolcloricodabahia. com.br. Frantic drumming as radiant dancers in colourful dresses spin around tapping their feet and moving their bodies to Afro-Brazilian music at the Teatro Miguel Santana. Performances Mon, Wed, Thurs, Fri 8–9.15pm; buy tickets (R$50) in advance from the box office (open from 2pm).
Show de Gerônimo Praca Pedro Arcanjo, Pelourinho. Don't miss this weekly live performance by Gerônimo (a veteran *Salvadorian* songwriter) supported by his band Mont'Serrat, renowned for its classy horn section. Sadly, the event only occurs during high season. Tues 7–10pm.

SHOPPING

Dinho Praca José Alencar 16, Pelourinho ☎71 3213 0416; map p.280. High-quality, handmade, traditional percussion instruments. Mon–Sat 9am–6pm.
Mercado Modelo Praça Visconde de Cayrú 250, ⓦmercadomodelobahia.com.br. Handicraft market in Cidade Baixa. Mon–Sat 9am–7pm, Sun 9am–2pm.
Shopping Barra Av Centenário 2992 ⓦshoppingbarra. com. Large mall that's handy for the Barra beaches. Mon–Sat 9am–10pm, Sun 12–9pm.

DIRECTORY

Banks and exchange There are several places to change money in the Pelourinho area, while Banco do Brasil has several branches, all with Visa ATMs, including one on the Terreiro de Jesus. Citibank has a branch at Av Estados Unidos 558, Cidade Baixa.
Consulates US, Av Tancredo Neves 1632, Room 1401, Salvador Trade Center, Torre Sul, Caminho das Árvores (☎71 3113 2090).
Hospitals Hospital Aliança, Av Juracy Magalhães Jr. 2096, Rio Vermelho (☎71 2108 5600, ⓦhospitalalianca.com.br); Hospital São Rafael, Av São Rafael 2152, São Marcos (☎71 3409 8000).
Internet Try Baiafrica Internet Café on the Praça da Sé (R$8/hr) or Lan House de Tega, Rua Alfonso Célso, 70, in Barra.
Laundries O Casal, Av Sete de Setembro 3564, Barra (☎71 3203 8000; $55 per load); Lavanderia Maria, Ladeira do Carmo 30, Pelourinho (☎71 4102 6405; R$50 per load).

Pharmacies Farmácia Sant'ana, Largo Porto da Barra, Barra (☎71 3267 8970); Drogaleve, Praça da Sé 6, Pelourinho (☎71 3322 6921).
Police The tourist police, DELTUR, are at Praça José de Anchieta 14, Cruzeiro de São Francisco, Pelourinho (☎71 3322 1188).
Post office Praca da Inglaterra s/n (Mon–Fri 9am–5pm; ⓦcorreios.com.br).

MORRO DE SÃO PAULO

Covering the tip of the island of **Tinharé**, some 60km south of Salvador by sea, the beach resort of **MORRO DE SÃO PAULO** is quite unlike anything else in Bahia. Safe, friendly, and with no cars and a string of gorgeous beaches lined with palm trees, reggae bars, hip pousadas and great seafood restaurants, it boasts a tropical, laidback beach scene reminiscent of Thailand or the Philippines – the main beaches are backed by jungle-clad mountains and you're as likely to hear Daft Punk as Sergio Mendes in the bars. However, this is no longer a backpacker haven. Brazil's middle class have been coming here for a while now, and though cheap hostels remain, more upmarket pousadas, lounge bars and restaurants are far more prevalent. Between November and March (especially at weekends, which are best avoided), Morro is swamped with visitors, though at other times it can still seem relatively peaceful and undeveloped.

WHAT TO SEE AND DO

There are four main beaches in Morro, known simply as **First**, **Second**, **Third** and **Fourth beaches**, with the first being the closest (and therefore most popular) to the village centre and the fourth being the furthest away and thus quietest.

On arrival, expect to be besieged by tenacious locals offering to be your "guide" – shake them off relatively easily by heading straight to the **Tiroleza do Morro Zipline** (daily 9am–5pm; R$50), a 70m-high and 340m-long zip-wire that will whizz you down to the First Beach in no time. To get to the zipline, head along the coastal path up the hill and make your way to the back of the lighthouse (Farol do Morro de São Paulo). Of course, you can just as easily, if less dramatically, walk to the beach in five minutes from the pier.

ARRIVAL AND INFORMATION

Though you can fly to Morro via chartered air taxi from Salvador, most people take the ferry. As of 2017, there is no longer an arrival tax. When you leave by ferry, you must pass through the Cais do Porto on the pier itself to pay the R$10 "Taxa de Embarque" but you can tack this fee onto your ferry ticket upon purchase.

By boat Several boats run back and forth between the Terminal Maritimo Turístico in Salvador and the ferry dock in Morro every day, beginning at 8am and usually running every hour or so till 2.30pm, with the last one at 3.30pm. Fares start at around R$95 for a one-way trip on a fast boat (*lancha*) or larger catamaran (usually a bit cheaper coming back); trips take about three hours, but be warned, the sea can be rough, even on a fine day. See Bio Tur (ⓦ biotur.com.br) or Passeios às Ilhas (ⓦ passeiosasilhas.com.br) for more information.

Tourist information There is currently no public tourist information point on Morro, but most hostels and pousadas can provide a wealth of info. Online help can be found at ⓦ morrodesaopaulo.com.br.

ACCOMMODATION

Accommodation on the island is generally expensive, particularly at holiday times. Most of the larger places are pousadas with their own restaurant and bar. Nearly all are within a stone's throw of the beaches.

Che Lagarto Hostel Rua Da Fonte Grande 11 ☏ 75 3652 1018, ⓦ chelagarto.com. Basic rooms and dorms, all with a/c, and a shared TV room, bar, table tennis and barbecue area – drinks are cheap and the owners lay on free popcorn. Dorms R$45, doubles R$320

Morro Hostel Travessa Prudente de Moraes ☏ 11 2302 3163, ⓦ thehostelmorro.com.br. Newer hostel with a good reputation. It's a little pricey, but the place is clean and the rooms bigger rooms than those in *Che Legarto*. Towels are provided too. There is a simple buffet breakfast and, like the other hostels, communal dinner nights. Dorms R$58, doubles R$165

Hostel Rosa dos Ventos Rua Chalon, Terceira Praia ☏ 75 3652 1529, ⓦ hostelrosadosventoshostel.com.br. Solid, clean budget choice 5min from Segundo Praia, with a communal kitchen (till 11pm) and a sociable bar. There are a/c doubles and larger rooms with two bunks that can function as dorms. Adequate breakfast included. Dorms R$90, doubles R$240

EATING

There are several good restaurants around the Praça Aureliano Lima and Caminho da Praia in town, with cheaper menus in the smaller, no-frills places towards the Fonte Grande.

★ **Marilyn Café** Segunda Praia ☏ 75 3652 1625. The place to be seen on the beachfront, with prime people-watching, quality cocktails and a surprisingly good menu for such a pretentious spot; try the *moqueca* (R$75 for two people), or fried fish ($80 for two people). Daily 9am–late.

Morena Bela Rua da Fonte Grande. This cheap joint knocks out stews, chicken, seafood and especially tasty *moquecas* for about R$25 per plate, with seating on plastic chairs and tables in a sleepy street. No sea views, but this is a real bargain. Daily 11.30am–midnight.

DRINKING AND NIGHTLIFE

Clubs, bars, beach and full moon parties – there's always something going on in Morro and you won't need much help in finding it. Most beach restaurants double as bars, and drinks prices are usually standardized – R$8 for a beer, R$10 for a *caipirinha* – but look out for happy-hour deals. Second Beach is the place to start (and often end) the evening, with dozens of caipirinha vendors and bars playing beats catering to all musical tastes – dancing goes on until the small hours. To get to the clubs, follow the path through the town centre and head up the hill.

Pulsar Disco Club Caminho do Fortaleza 1 (the path to the Fortaleza do Tapirandú) ⓦ pulsardisco.com.br. Surrounded by thick vegetation, Morro's party central is an Ibiza-style club that really gets going in the summer, with decent guest DJs from all over Brazil. Cover charge R$10–50. Fri & Sat midnight–8am.

Toca do Morcego Rua Caminho do Farol 11 (on the path up to the lighthouse) ⓦ tocadomorcego.com. Friday night is legendary at this club a 5min walk from the centre. Soak in the sea view as you sip on unbelievably potent *caipirinhas* and groove to dance tunes until the early morning. Cover R$80, but get flyers in advance for reductions. Sunset sessions Tues–Sun 4.30–10pm; club only Fri (five nights a week in summer) midnight–6am.

THE CHAPADA DIAMANTINA

One of Brazil's most exciting locations for hiking, climbing and rural sightseeing, the **PARQUE NACIONAL DA CHAPADA DIAMANTINA** offers 38,000 square kilometres of awe-inspiring table mountains, jagged rocky peaks and wide-open canyons interspersed with gigantic waterfalls, rivers, scrubland and forest. Once here, most visitors undertake a three- or six-day organized trek (guide essential; six days from R$1590), staying in local houses along the way with meals included. The experience is like no other in Brazil: you gain a glimpse of the slow *sertanejo* pace of life and rural northeastern hospitality while taking in stunning scenery. The challenge of a long hike is not for everyone, but guides tailor trips to your ability and fitness. It's advisable to come here in the cooler months between April and October – though conversely the region's waterfalls are at their most spectacular in rainy (and high) season, from December to March.

Though the sizeable and attractive ex-diamond-mining town of **Lençóis** provides the most obvious access to the northern half of the park – and offers consummate facilities – most independent/budget travellers choose to go directly on to the community of **Vale do Capão** within the park boundaries itself. Long a bohemian hangout, in recent years smarter pousadas have opened, adding a new level of alternative-chic with meditation, massage and saunas, and drawing a broader age group.

WHAT TO SEE AND DO

There is almost endless potential for hikes in the national park. Some of the most famous or accessible locations are not too far from Capão or Lençóis and can be visited on day or multi-day excursions. The (guided) hike between the two communities is usually undertaken over three days, though its most famous sight – Brazil's highest waterfall, the **Cachoeira da Fumaça** – can be visited on a circular hike from either location. Here, a stream tumbles 385m over a cliff face, vaporizing into a fine mist before it reaches the bottom. Jagged overhanging rocks provide dizzying viewing points. Hiking to the base of the waterfall is a somewhat more difficult trek than that of reaching the top, however, and in high season the caves that serve as overnight sleeping spots (camping gear provided or pre-arranged by guides) can get overrun with visitors.

Another celebrated sight is the **Morro do Pai Inácio**, a 1120m high mesa peak with fabulous views over the cactus-strewn tablelands, while the **Gruta do Lapão**, a 1km-long gorge formed from layered sandstone, lies just 5km north of Lençóis.

ARRIVAL AND DEPARTURE

By bus Real Expresso (☎0800 883 8830, ⓦrealexpresso. com.br) buses run between Salvador and Lençóis (3 daily; 6hr), all arriving at the main *rodoviária* in town and continuing on to Palmeiras (45min); *colectivos* shuttle between Palmeiras and Capão for around R$20 (30min); a taxi is R$60–70.

By plane Azul (ⓦvoeazul.com.br) operates one daily flight (1hr) between Salvador and the tiny airport outside Coronel Octaviano Alves (20km from Lençóis), where taxis will take you into town (R$100; agencies run transfers for $25) or to destinations inside the Parque Nacional da Chapada Diamantina.

INFORMATION AND TOURS

Guides are most often arranged by pousadas, but you can arrange your own. Standard rates for independent guides are R$150–200/day for a group of five or six people, though it can be tough to find someone that speaks good English. Information is available from the Associação dos Conductores de Visitantes at Rua 10 de Novembro 22 in Lençóis (daily 8am–noon & 2–8pm; ☎75 3334 1425). See also ⓦguiachapadadiamantina.com.br.

Chapada Adventure Daniel Praça Horácio de Matos 114, Lençóis ☎75 3334 1933, ⓦchapadaadventure. com.

Extreme Eco Adventure Av 7 de Setembro 15, Lençóis ☎75 3341 1727, ⓦextremeecoadventure.com.br.

H2O Travel Adventures Rua do Pires, Lençóis ☎75 3334 1229, ⓦh2otraveladventures.com.

ACCOMMODATION

Numerous pousadas are located in Lençóis and more are scattered throughout Vale do Capão. Book as far in advance as possible. Capão also offers a few basic restaurants, including a great pizzeria.

Hotel Canto das Águas Av Senhor dos Passos 1 ☎75 3334 1154, ⓦlencois.com.br. Expensive but excellent option, with luxurious rooms, well-kept gardens, a meditation and massage area and a beautiful riverside location; hearty breakfasts are included in the price and there's a pool. R$344

Hotel de Lençóis Rua Altina Alves 747 ☎75 3334 1102, ⓦhoteldelencois.com. Located mainly in a small mansion with spacious, modern rooms, this attractive place is set in the heart of sweet-smelling gardens with its own lauded restaurant. R$320

Pousada Safira Rua Miguel Calmon 124, Lençóis ☎75 3334 1443, ⓦpousadasafira.com. This is one of the friendliest budget options but with just a few small rooms, all with their own bathroom – singles pay R$70. Free wi-fi in public areas and breakfast is included. It's a little hard to find in the backstreets at the heart of town. R$100

★ **Viela Hostel** Travessa do Tamandaré s/n ☎75 3334 1271. Located in the centre, this is a very popular and economic place to stay in Lencois, with two kitchens and two TV rooms (one with Netflix), and a pool table. Breakfast is not served. Dorms R$50, doubles R$150

The Northeast

Long regarded as one of Brazil's poorest areas, **THE NORTHEAST** has benefited from the nation's economic boom and is now a region on the rise. Despite having the most dazzling coastline in South America, a buzzing beach scene and an exuberant culture that blends samba, reggae and African influences, the area, divided politically into eight separate states, has not been spoilt by tourism. There are major cities along the coast: some, such as **Recife**, **Olinda**, **São Luís** and **Fortaleza**, have deep colonial histories; others, such as **Natal**, have developed mostly in recent decades. All have their own city beaches plus more idyllic and deserted resorts hidden up and down the coast. The **Ilha de Fernando de Noronha**, hundreds of kilometres offshore, is one of the finest oceanic wildlife reserves in the world, an expensive destination but perfect for ecotourism.

RECIFE

The Northeast's largest metropolitan area, **RECIFE** ("her-see-fey") is a dynamic, sprawling city of over four million with a booming economy and two major ports. The city centre – the three islands of Santo Antônio, Boa Vista and Bairro do Recife – remains a chaotic place, where scrappy street vendors, markets, polluted drains and heavy traffic contrast with crumbling Art Nouveau buildings and a profusion of colonial churches. It's a compelling mix, once you get used to it, and the regenerated **Bairro do Recife** area in particular is a real gem, more akin to belle époque Europe than the rest of Brazil. Most of the money – and the middle class – lives in the beachside district of **Boa Viagem**, a forest of high-rise condos and beach hotels to the south. Just to the north lies **Olinda**, one of the highlights of Brazil (p.295).

WHAT TO SEE AND DO

Modern Recife sprawls over the mainland, but the broad **Avenida Dantas Barreto** forms the spine of the central island of **Santo Antônio**, lined with street markets almost its entire length, and crisscrossed with a web of crowded, narrow lanes lined with stalls and shops. It ends in the much quieter **Praça da República**, filled with majestic palms and surrounded by Recife's grandest public buildings.

CONVENTO DE SANTO ANTÔNIO AND THE CAPELA DOURADA

The most enticing attraction in central Recife is the **Capela Dourada** (Golden Chapel), housed inside the Franciscan complex known as the **Convento do Santo Antônio** on Rua do Imperador (Mon–Fri 8–11.30am & 2–5pm, Sat 8–11.30am; R$5). The convent, established in 1606, was incorporated by the Dutch into their fortress here in the 1630s, and it was largely rebuilt between 1702 and 1777. You enter via the **Museu Franciscano de Arte Sacra**, a small but precious collection of religious carvings and statuary (all with good English labelling), before walking through a quiet cloister to the Golden Chapel itself. Finished in 1724, the Baroque interior is smothered in lavish wall-to-ceiling ornamentation, everything covered with gold leaf, while its crowning glory is the series of ceiling panels by **Manuel de Jesus Pinto**, an *alforriado*, or freed slave, whose work graces many of the city's finest religious buildings.

PÁTIO DE SÃO PEDRO AND AROUND

Just off the Avenida Dantas Barreto, the impressive **Igreja São Pedro dos Clérigos** (closed for major renovation at the time of writing) stands on the graceful **Pátio de São Pedro**. Inside there's some exquisite woodcarving and a trompe l'oeil ceiling by Manuel de Jesus Pinto. The colonial buildings that line the square have been beautifully preserved, and in the evenings you can soak up the view over a beer at one of the many bars that set up tables outside. Browse the stalls lining the square's adjacent winding streets for crafts, or head west to the T-shaped **Casa da Cultura de Pernambuco**, a former prison turned crafts gallery, located on Rua Floriano Peixoto (Mon–Fri 9am–7pm, Sat 9am–6pm, Sun 9am–2pm; free; ⊛casadaculturape.com.br).

FORTE DAS CINCO PONTAS

The star-shaped **Forte das Cinco Pontas**, at

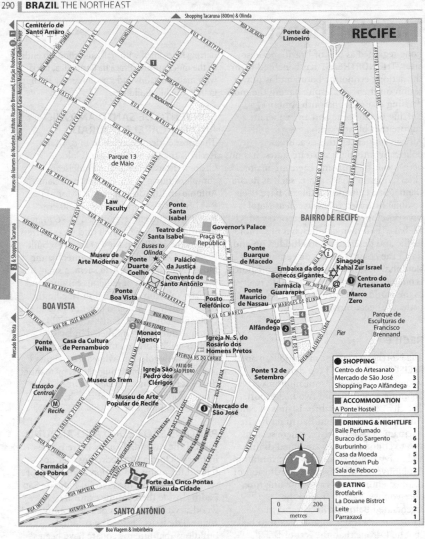

the southern end of Santo Antônio (built in 1630 by the Dutch, and the place they surrendered in 1654), currently houses the **Museu da Cidade** (Tues–Sun 9am–5pm; free; ☎81 3355 9540). Though the fort is worth visiting for its splendid sea views, the museum offers a window onto the city's myriad past lives with temporary exhibits, often with an architectural theme.

BAIRRO DO RECIFE
The once run-down district of **Bairro do Recife** (aka **Recife Antigo**) now has a thriving nightlife scene and is also a pleasant place during the day to explore, with grand, brightly painted belle époque buildings. Check out the **Sinagoga Kahal Zur Israel** or simply the **Centro Cultural Judaico**, Rua do Bom Jesus 197 (Tues–Fri 9am–5.30pm, Sun 2–5.30pm; R$10; ☎81 3224 2128), the site of the first synagogue built in the whole of the Americas; it dates back to 1639 when Jews started to coming to Dutch-controlled Brazil. When the rather less tolerant Portuguese resumed control of the city in 1654, the Jews were booted out and the

synagogue destroyed – today all that remains is the foundation, the excavated Mikvah (ritual bath) and some brick walls. Upstairs there's a re-creation of what it might have looked like in its heyday.

Nearby at Rua do Bom Jesus 183, the **Embaixada dos Bonecos Gigantes** (daily 8am–6pm; R$20; ⓦbonecosgigantesdeolinda.com.br) is a small, quirky museum displaying some of the giant **puppets** used in the Olinda Carnaval, many of them celebrities, from Lampião to a scary-looking Michael Jackson. At the heart of the Bairro do Recife's regeneration is Praça Barão Rio Branco, known simply as **Marco Zero** for the "Km 0" marker in the centre. On the other side of the plaza lies the **Centro do Artesanato** (see p.295), with views across the river to the totem-like 32m-high Torre de Cristal in the **Parque de Esculturas Francisco Brennand** (boats there daily 8am–5pm; R$5).

MUSEU DO HOMEM DO NORDESTE

Though it's a fair distance from the centre, it's worth making the trip to the fascinating **Museu do Homem do Nordeste** in Casa Forte, Av 17 de Agosto 2187 (Tues–Fri 8.30am–5pm, Sat & Sun 2–6pm; R$6; ⓦwww.fundaj.gov.br). Founded by Brazilian anthropologist Gilberto Freyre (see below) in 1979, the museum depicts everyday life and folk culture with more than twelve thousand exhibits ranging from carriages used by seventeenth-century sugar barons to present-day northeastern carnival costumes. To get here, take the "Dois Irmôes – Via Barbosa" bus from the post office or from Parque 13 de Maio, at the bottom of Rua do Hospício in Boa Vista, a thirty-minute drive through leafy northern suburbs. The museum is on the left, but hard to spot: ask the driver or conductor where to get off.

CASA MUSEU GILBERTO FREYRE

Anyone with even a passing interest in anthropology, or Brazil's cultural identity, shouldn't miss the chance to root around in the sugar-pink nineteenth-century **Casa Museu Gilberto Freyre**, whose 1933 book, *The Masters and the Slaves*, remains one of the most iconic texts ever written on the country. Located a shortish taxi ride away from the Museo do Homem do Nordeste

(or via bus #522 or #930 from Av Agamenon Magalhães), at Rua Dois Irmãos 320, Apipucos (Mon–Fri 9am–4.30pm, R$10; ☎81 3441 1733), the interior is stuffed with his collection of over forty thousand books and all manner of fascinating ethnic antiques and curios.

INSTITUTO RICARDO BRENNAND

One of Recife's most incongruous attractions is the **Instituto Ricardo Brennand** on Alameda Antônio Brennand in the outlying suburb of Várzea (Tues–Sun 1–5pm; R$30; ☎81 2121 0352, ⓦinstitutoricardobrennand.org.br). This mock-Tudor castle belongs to one of the sons of the city's renowned Brennand family, and is home to a fascinating gallery dedicated to the **Dutch occupation of Brazil** (including the world's largest collection of paintings by Frans Post), as well as Greco-Roman mythological figures, suits of armour and a collection of Swiss-army knives. To get here, catch bus #40 on Avenida Domingos Ferreira (in Boa Viagem) or Avenida Agamenon Magalhães (bordering Boa Vista) and take it to the end of the line. Continue on foot to the end of the road, and turn right onto Rua Isaac Buril. The institute is at the end of this road on the left. Taxis will charge at least R$150 round-trip from Boa Viagem.

OFICINA BRENNAND

A short walk south of the Instituto, on Propriedade Santos Cosme e Damião, you'll find the studio of the Brennand clan's most famous scion, sculptor Francisco (the cousin of entrepreneur Ricardo). A renovated ceramics factory-cum-Brazilian Parque Güell, **Oficina Brennand** (Mon–Thurs 8am–5pm, Fri 8am–4pm, Sat & Sun 10am–4pm; R$20; ⓦbrennand.com.br) displays thousands of his whimsical sculptures, decorated tiles, paintings and drawings in what is actually a vast open-air sculpture park surrounded by pristine *Mata Atlântica* forest.

BOA VIAGEM

Regular buses make it easy to get down to the district of **BOA VIAGEM** and the beach, an enormous skyscraper-lined arc of sand that constitutes the longest stretch of urbanized seafront in Brazil (over 7km), protected by the slim *arrecife* (reef) just offshore.

3

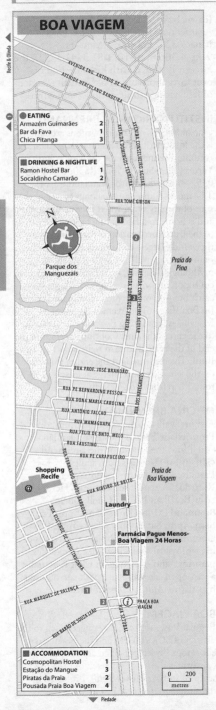

BOA VIAGEM

■ **EATING**
Armazém Guimarães 2
Bar da Fava 1
Chica Pitanga 3

■ **DRINKING & NIGHTLIFE**
Ramon Hostel Bar 1
Socaldinho Camarão 2

■ **ACCOMMODATION**
Cosmopolitan Hostel 1
Estação do Mangue 3
Piratas da Praia 2
Pousada Praia Boa Viagem 4

The narrow **beach** is packed at weekends and deserted during the week, with warm natural rock pools to wallow in just offshore when the tide is out. Pavilions punctuate the pavement along the noisy road, selling all sorts of refreshing drinks from coconut water to pre-mixed *batidas* (rum cocktails). If you want to swim, be aware that there have been a number of shark attacks over the years, but they usually involve surfers far offshore.

ARRIVAL AND DEPARTURE

By plane Recife's modern Aeroporto Internacional dos Guararapes is only 11km from the city centre, at the southern end of Boa Viagem; LATAM, Avianca, Azul and Gol connect it with the rest of the country. You can pay for fixed-rate taxis at the arrivals halls (COOPSETA; ☎ 81 3462 1584), which will cost R$20–30 to Boa Viagem, R$45 for Santo Antônio (city centre) and R$80 for Olinda, or opt for a pay-by-meter *taxi comum*, which are about the same, assuming it's not rush hour. Alternatively, for Boa Viagem take either the a/c bus #042 from outside the airport (every 20min, 5am–11.55pm; R$4), or bus #040 (every 20min, 5am–11.55pm; R$3.20) from nearby Praça Ministro Salgado Filho. For Boa Vista (city centre), take bus #163 (every 20min, 5am–11pm; R$3.20) from the same *praça*. The metrô (R$1.60) also runs from just south of the airport (connected by walkway) to Estação Central terminal (not the beach).
Destinations Fortaleza (7 daily; 1hr 15min–1hr 30min); Lisbon (1 daily; 7hr 25min); Panama City (4 weekly; 7hr 20min); Rio (23 daily; 2hr 50min); Salvador (12 daily; 1hr 20min); São Paulo (20 daily; 3hr 25min).
By bus The *rodoviária* is about 16km west of the centre at BR-232 km 15, Coqueiral (☎ 81 3207 1088), though this is not really a problem since the metrô whisks you very cheaply (R$1.60) and efficiently into the centre, gliding through various *favelas*. It will deposit you at the old train station, called Estação Central (or simply "Recife"). To get to your hotel from there, you're best off taking a taxi. Taxis from the bus station direct to Boa Viagem or the city centre should run R$60 on the meter.
Destinations Belo Horizonte (1 daily; 40hr); Brasília (2 daily; 48hr); Fortaleza (5 daily; 13hr); Natal (10 daily; 5hr); Porto de Galinhas (every 30min; 1hr); Rio (2 daily; 38–41hr); Salvador (2 daily; 12–16hr); São Paulo (1–3 daily; 45–50hr).

GETTING AROUND

By bus Most city buses originate and terminate on the central island of Santo Antônio, on Rua Cais de Santa Rita. They range in price from R$2.10 to R$4.40 (R$1.60–2.20 on Sun). To get from the city centre to Boa Viagem, take either bus #042, #039, #032 or #071. For up-to-date timetables see ⊛ granderecife.pe.gov.br.

By taxi Taxis use meters that start at R$4.85; reckon on R$25–30 between Boa Viagem and the city centre, and R$45–50 between Boa Viagem and Olinda.

INFORMATION AND TOURS

Tourist information The most helpful tourist information point is at the airport (daily 8am–6pm; ☎ 81 3182 8299, ⓦ www2.recife.pe.gov.br), where you may find English-speaking staff. There are also branches at the *rodoviária* (daily 7am–7pm; ☎ 81 3182 8298) and Praça de Boa Viagem (daily 8am–8pm; ☎ 81 3182 8297). There's the tourist hotline, the Apoio ao Turista (24hr; ☎ 81 3182 8299), on which you should be able to find someone who speaks English.

Tour operators Martur, Rua Dr Nilo Dornelas Câmara 90, Loja 02, Boa Viagem (☎ 81 3312 3666, ⓦ martur.com.br), organize flights, cruises and trips to Fernando de Noronha. There's also an office at the airport (☎ 81 3213 1404).

ACCOMMODATION

Boa Vista offers some excellent options in the city centre, though most of the city's hotels and hostels are located in Boa Viagem, near the beach. If you don't mind staying in a soulless high-rise, the beach may compensate for the steep prices. Olinda (see page 295) is also expensive, if offset by the charm of its colonial conversions. As ever, if you want to visit during Carnaval, you'll need to book months in advance.

BOA VISTA

A Ponte Hostel Rua Capitao Lima 410, Santo Amaro ☎ 81 3034 6603, ⓦ apontehostel.com.br; map p.290. Exceptionally clean and small hostel that offers dorms with very comfortable beds, as well lockers and a homemade breakfast cooked to order with couscous and tapioca. There are not many food outlets close to the hostel, but there's a decent and affordable Chinese restaurant around the corner. Dorms R$50, doubles R$150

BOA VIAGEM

Cosmopolitan Hostel Rua Paulo Setúbal 53 ☎ 81 3204 0321, ⓦ cosmopolitanhostel.com; map p292 Modern budget option, with basic en-suite doubles and spotless dorms, stylish TV lounge (cable TV and DVDs), shared kitchen and breakfast included. Dorms R$39, doubles R$109

Estação do Mangue Rua Raimundo Gomes Gondim 26 ☎ 81 3049 2626, ⓦ estacaodomangue.com.br; map p.292. Justly popular hostel, a short walk from the beach, with communal TV room and kitchen, simple dorms and private rooms. Buffet breakfast included. Dorms R$50, doubles R$150

Piratas da Praia Av Cons Aguiar 2034 (3rd floor), at Rua Prf. Osias Ribeiro ☎ 81 3326 1281, ⓦ piratasdapraia. com; map p.292. Neat pastel dorms with primary-coloured portraiture and a choice of fan or a/c. Lockers available. Also some rooms and small apartments. Breakfast included. Dorms R$46, doubles R$106

Pousada Praia Boa Viagem Rua Petrolina 81 ☎ 81 3039 5880, ⓦ pousadapraiaboaviagem.com; map p.292. A decent and more intimate option to the usual high-rise hotels in Boa Viagem, this pousada offers clean rooms with a/c LCD TV and minibar, 24hr reception and wi-fi in public areas. Just two blocks from the beach. R$180

EATING

BAIRRO DO RECIFE, BOA VISTA AND THE SUBURBS

Brotfabrik Rua da Moeda 87, Recife Antigo ☎ 81 3424 2250, ⓦ brotfabrik.com.br; map p.290. Bakery that almost pulls off the Dutch theme in a spacious old warehouse with espresso (from R$4.10), pastries, rye bread, *salgados*, sandwiches (R$9.70–12.90) and bite-sized pizzas (*brotinho*; R$10.90); popular, as the constant queue attests. Mon–Fri 7am–7pm.

Leite Praça Joaquim Nabuco 147, Santo Antônio ☎ 81 3224 7977; map p.290. Not really a budget option, this classy place serves tasty local and Portuguese dishes in a very stylish nineteenth-century interior (lots of cod, beef tongue in madeira sauce and the like). The restaurant was founded in 1882, but this building dates from around 1905. Mon–Fri & Sun 11.30am–4pm.

Parraxaxá Rua Igarassu 40, Casa Forte ☎ 81 3268 4169, ⓦ parraxaxa.com.br; map p.290. A little piece of the desert transplanted to the city, this celebrated *por kilo* place is themed around the talismanic *sertão* bandit, Lampião, with *cantina*-style tables and chairs, and a daily buffet featuring specialities such as *paçoca*, sun-dried beef and all manner of deliciously stodgy puddings (around R$63.90/kilo). A perfect lunch stop after the nearby Museu do Homem do Nordeste (see page 291). Daily 7am–10pm.

BOA VIAGEM

Armazém Guimarães Rua Baltazar Pereira 100 ☎ 81 3325 4011, ⓦ armazemguimaraes.com.br; map p.292. This is the place for authentic wood-fired pizza in Recife. What the barn-like interior lacks in romance, the food makes up in quality, with prices in the R$50–60 range. Mon–Sat 6pm–11.30pm, Sun 5pm–11.30pm.

★ TREAT YOURSELF

La Douane Bistrot Paço de Alfândega 35, Recife Antigo ☎ 81 3224 5799, ⓦ ladouane.com.br; map p.290. Located in the Alfândega shopping mall (see page 294), a beautifully renovated customs house. Waiting staff are immaculately turned out and the food is Mediterranean in flavour with a Brazilian bent – if you're feeling flush, splash out on the *bacalhau da restauraçao* with stuffed potato (R$78); if not, go for the set menu (R$50). Mon–Sat 9am–9pm, Sun noon–8pm.

3

3

Bar da Fava Rua Padre Oliveira Rolim 37A, Jardim Beira Rio, Pina ☎81 3463 8998, ⓦfacebook.com/bardafava; map p.292. Renowned for its exquisitely prepared *favas* (broad beans) that accompany virtually every meal. Most dishes are priced for two to three diners (R$69–86), though they do an *executivo individual* for R$24. Best take a taxi as it's difficult to locate. Mon & Tues 11am–6pm, Wed–Sat 11am–10pm, Sun 11am–7pm.

Chica Pitanga Rua Petrolina 19 ☎81 3465 2224, ⓦchicapitanga.com.br; map p.292. Long one of the most popular *por kilo* places in Recife, with a bright, stylish interior and tables that you'll likely have to wait patiently to snag. At R$75 per kilo (R$82 at weekends), it isn't cheap but you get what you pay for, with a dazzling buffet heavy on seafood. Mon–Fri 11.30am–3.30pm & 5.30–10pm, Sat & Sun 11.30am–4pm & 6–10pm.

DRINKING AND NIGHTLIFE

Recife lives and breathes live music. While Carnaval throbs to *frevo*, *afox* and *maracatu*, they've long been hybridized into the city's most famous musical export, *manguebeat*, a style that continues to exert a huge influence on acts you can either see for free, in the Pátio de São Pedro (see page 289), or on the big stage at Marco Zero or, for a modest fee, in the bars and clubs of Bairro do Recife. Look out, especially, for performances by Orquestra Contemporânea de Olinda, perhaps the most celebrated of the area's *manguebeat* inheritors.

BAIRRO DO RECIFE AND SUBURBS

Baile Perfumado Rua Carlos Gomes 390 ☎81 3033 4747; map p.290. Recife's newest live music venue, with a capacity of 5000 and an already impressive list of rock/pop performances including Céu, Arnoldo Antunes and Alceu Valença, as well as local heroes Otto and Mundo Livre S/A. Tickets are usually in the region of R$50. Located well out in the suburbs (5km west of the centre), so take a taxi. Opens according to show times.

Buraco do Sargento Pátio de São Pedro 33, Santo Antônio ☎81 3224 7522; map p.290. Classic old-school bar and café on the plaza since 1955, housed in the headquarters of the Batutas de São José (one of Recife's *blocos de carnaval*). Stand around the granite counter-top or sit on a table outside, sipping Brahma or *cachaça* and snacking on *galinha cozido* (chicken gizzards; R$20). Mon–Fri 9am–5pm.

Burburinho Rua Tomazina 106, Barrio do Recife (Recife Antigo) ☎81 3224 5854, ⓦbarburburinho.com.br; map p.290. Long *the* venue in Recife to hear local music in a sweaty nightclub setting, this place puts on everything from the new generation of local artists influenced by the '90s *manguebeat* explosion, to homages as diverse as The Cure and Creedence Clearwater Revival. Cover usually R$10–30; free on Tues. Hours vary; currently runs sessions with unsigned acts Tues and tribute nights Sat.

Casa da Moeda Rua da Moeda 150 Bairro do Recife (Recife Antigo) ☎81 3224 7095; map p.290. For a taster of Recife's bohemian side visit the bar run by local photographer and artist Sergio Altenkirch, decorated with his work. Join the alternative crowd to drink *cachaça* and snack, and to enjoy live music (from jazz and blues to rock). Mon–Wed & Sun 5pm–1am, Thurs 5pm–2am, Fri 5pm–3am, Sat 6pm–3am.

Downtown Pub Rua Vigário Tenório 105, Barrio do Recife (Recife Antigo) ☎81 3424 5731, ⓦdowntownpub.com.br; map p.290. Though the "casa do rock" – given a swanky makeover and definitely more of a club than a pub – lays it on thick with the Anglophone rock and tribute nights, you can sometimes land lucky with decent live reggae. Cover R$40. Fri & Sat 10pm–5am.

Sala de Reboco Rua Gregório Júnior 264, Cordeiro 264 ☎81 3228 7052, ⓦsaladereboco.com.br; map p.290. If you're really keen to pick up some authentic *forró pé-de-serra nordestino* (Northeastern Brazilian folk dance) skills, then it's worth your while heading out to the suburbs (bus #040 if you're not taking a taxi; ask the driver where to get off) to one of the country's best *casas de forró*, drawing a loyal crowd as well as some of Brazil's best *forrozeiros*. Thurs–Sat 10pm–late.

BOA VIAGEM

Ramon Hostel Bar Rua Olávo Bilac 20B 81 ☎3036 6930; map p.292. As a part of *Ramon Hostel*, this bar is a great budget option, has Spanish-speaking staff, serves ice-cold beers, as well as pizza Argentina style (with loads of cheese). The atmosphere is friendly and relaxed and the place is usually packed. Tues–Sun 6pm–late.

Socaldinho Camarão Av Visconde de Jequitinhonha 106 ☎81 3462 9500; map p.292. If you fancy some footie action, head here and join the locals for a beer over a gripping game of Brazilian *futebol* as you munch on some *peixe a móda* (R$50 for three people). Mon–Fri 11.30am–midnight, Sat 11am–2am, Sun 11am–midnight.

SHOPPING

Centro do Artesanato Av Alfredo Lisboa (Marco Zero), Armazém 11, Bairro do Recife (Recife Antigo) ☎81 3181 3451, ⓦartesanatodepernambuco.pe.gov.br; map p.290. Former warehouse on the waterfront that acts as a showcase for folk art and the traditional crafts of Pernambuco. Mon–Sat 8am–7pm, Sun 8am–4pm.

Mercado de São José Rua São José, Santo Antônio; map p.290. Opened in 1875, this is the oldest public market in Brazil. Stock up on some local crafts, or simply peruse the stacks of curious herbal medicines and everyday items as locals go about their daily shopping. Mon–Sat 6am–6pm, Sun 6am–noon.

Shopping Paço Alfândega Rua Alfândega 35, Bairro do Recife (Recife Antigo) ⓦpacoalfandega.com.br; map p.290. Chic, refurbished former customs building on Recife Island, housing the typical range of Brazilian chain stores and fast-food outlets as well as the swanky *La Douane Bistro* (see page 293). Mon–Sat 9am–9pm, Sun 11am–8pm.

DIRECTORY

Banks and exchange Most banks have ATMs. Banco do Brasil has branches at the airport (daily 10am–4pm), at Av Dantas Barreto 541, at Av Rio Branco 240. Shopping centres all have ATMs, banks and money-changing facilities that stay open until 9pm Monday to Saturday. The Bradesco bank on Conde de Boa Vista has an ATM that accepts most Visa cards.

Consulates UK, Av Agamenon Magalhães 4775, 8th floor (⊙ 81 2127 0200); US, Rua Gonçalves Maia 163, Boa Vista (⊙ 81 3416 3050).

Hospital Real Hospital Português de Beneficência, Av Agamenon Magalhães 4760, Boa Vista (⊙ 81 3416 1122).

Internet LAN Games Rua Waldemar Nery Carneiro Monteiro 104 (⊙ 81 3031 5104).

Laundry Prima Clean Rua Carlos Pereira Falcão 112, Boa Viagem (⊙ 81 3037 1249). A bit pricey (R$45 for one load), but same-day delivery.

Pharmacies Farmácia Pague Menos, Av Cons Aguiar 4635, Boa Viagem, 24hr (⊙ 81 3301 4220).

Post office The main post office is the Correio building at Av Guararapes 250 in Santo Antônio (Mon–Fri 9am–5pm). There's also a branch in the Bairro do Recife at Av Marquês de Olinda 262.

OLINDA

Founded in 1535, **OLINDA** is, quite simply, one of Brazil's most impressive examples of colonial architecture: a maze of cobbled streets, hills crowned with brilliant white churches, pastel-coloured houses, Baroque fountains and graceful squares. The city is also renowned for its street **Carnaval**, which attracts visitors from all over the world.

Despite its size, Olinda can effectively be considered a suburb of Recife: a high proportion of its residents commute to the city so **transport links** are good, with buses leaving every few minutes.

3

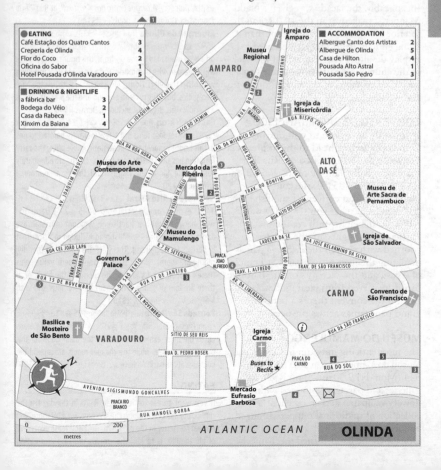

◼ EATING	
Café Estação dos Quatro Cantos	3
Creperia de Olinda	4
Flor do Coco	2
Oficina do Sabor	1
Hotel Pousada d'Olinda Varadouro	5

◼ DRINKING & NIGHTLIFE	
a fábrica bar	3
Bodega do Véio	2
Casa da Rabeca	1
Xinxim da Baiana	4

◼ ACCOMMODATION	
Albergue Canto dos Artistas	2
Albergue de Olinda	5
Casa de Hilton	4
Pousada Alto Astral	1
Pousada São Pedro	3

OLINDA

Olinda's colonial highlights include more churches than you could wish to see in an afternoon, and a curious puppet museum. Much of the appeal lies in wandering through the picturesque streets.

ALTO DA SÉ

A good spot to have a drink and plan your day is the **Alto da Sé**, the highest square in town, not least because of the stunning view of Recife's skyscrapers shimmering in the distance, framed in the foreground by Olinda's church towers, gardens and palm trees. The main attraction on the Alto da Sé is the **Igreja de São Salvador** (daily 9am–5pm; free), or just Igreja da Sé, reconstructed between 1656 and 1676 after the Dutch had destroyed the original. Inexplicably, the facade was given a bland Mannerist makeover in the 1970s, and the interior is now more of a museum than a living church, its former chapels used to display desultory religious art. At the back of the church is a patio from where you'll have the best views of the surrounding area and Recife.

CONVENTO DE SÃO FRANCISCO

If you only have time to visit one of Olinda's churches, head to the impressive **Convento de São Francisco** on Rua São Francisco (daily 9am–noon & 2–5.30pm; R$2; ☎81 3429 0517), the country's oldest Franciscan convent. Established in 1577, most of what you see today was rebuilt in the eighteenth century. Particular highlights are the cloister adorned with sixteen tiled *azulejo* panels depicting the lives of Jesus and St Francis of Assisi, and the sacristy's ornate Baroque furniture carved from jacaranda wood. Behind the convent there's a patio with grand panoramas across the ocean.

MUSEU DO MAMULENGO

The most enticing museum in Olinda is the **Museu do Mamulengo** at Rua São Bento 344 (Mon–Fri 9.30am–5pm; R$2), its galleries and passages festooned with flowery wallpaper and an excellent collection of traditional puppets arranged by theme and type (with English labelling). Don't miss the hand-turned mechanical diorama downstairs, and the depictions of bandit Lampião on the upper floor.

ARRIVAL AND INFORMATION

By bus From Recife, take bus #1983 or #1992 from Rua do Sol to Praça do Carmo, just by Olinda's main post office and a 2min walk up into the old city. From Boa Viagem, take bus #910 (every 30min).

Tourist information Information and maps are available from the Casa do Turista on Prudente do Morais 472 (Mon–Fri 8am–6pm, Sat & Sun 9am–6pm; ☎81 3305 1060, ⊛ olindaturismo.com.br). For all Carnaval-related information see ⊛ carnaval.olinda.pe.gov.br.

ACCOMMODATION

★**Albergue Canto dos Artistas** Rua Prudente de Moraes 351 ☎81 3493 2169; map p.295. Popular hostel in an old house in the centre, with bright, tastefully decorated dorms and rooms and a buffet breakfast. There's a sister property, *Albergue Canto dos Artistas II*, at Rua 27 de Janeiro 85. Dorms R$50, doubles R$140

Albergue de Olinda Rua do Sol 233, Carmo ☎81 3429 1592, ⊛ alberguedeolinda.com.br; map p.295. Located on a busy main road by the seafront, this bright HI hostel has a little garden with hammocks and a pool, ideal for mingling with other travellers. Dorms are a bit plain with just the bare necessities, but they're clean enough and the place itself has a friendly vibe. Breakfast included. Dorms R$60

Casa de Hilton Rua do Sol 77 ☎81 3494 2379; map p.295. Owner José rents out a few vibrantly painted rooms in this bright yellow house at an unbeatable price; the tatty furniture has seen better days but the rooms are adequately comfortable for a few nights, and there's a communal kitchen. R$120

★**Pousada Alto Astral** Rua 13 de Maio 305 ☎81 3439 3453, ⊛ pousadaaltoastral.com; map p.295. Decorated with naïve art with a handsome wrought-iron staircase and a breakfast area (lavish spread included in price) that is perfect for socializing. The staff are incredibly friendly, rooms are warm, wildly painted and superb value, plus there's a pool. Ask for any of the rooms at the back, or, if there are four of you, ask for room 8 – spacious and with leafy views over the city. R$150

Pousada São Pedro Rua 27 de Janeiro 95 ☎81 3439 9546, ⊛ pousadapedro.com; map p.295. A spiral staircase leads up to the more expensive rooms in the main house of this charming pousada, while the cheaper rooms are around the pool area at the back. All have a/c. Breakfast included. R$190

EATING

If you want to eat for less than R$20 in Olinda, try the *comida por kilo* places along the seafront. For a bit more, you can eat far better in the old town. Best and least expensive of all, though, is to join the crowds drinking and eating

3

★ TREAT YOURSELF

Oficina do Sabor Rua do Amparo 335 ☎81 3429 3331, ⓦoficinadosabor.com; map p.295. After two decades of supplying Recife and Olinda's chattering classes with exquisitely prepared Pernambucan cuisine, the reputation of this place precedes it. And with an interior that's hardly ostentatious, the emphasis is squarely on the food; blowing a day's budget on dishes such as their pumpkin stuffed with fish and shrimp in a passion fruit and coconut sauce serving two (R$144) is all too easy. Tues–Thurs 11.30am–4pm & 6pm–midnight, Fri & Sat 11.30am–1am, Sun 11.30am–5pm.

street food at the Alto da Sé. The charcoal-fired delights sold here include addictive Bahian *acarajé (around R$10)*.

Café Estação dos Quatro Cantos Rua Prudente de Moraes 440 ☎81 3429 7575; map p.295. Laidback café set in the backyard of an art gallery, handicrafts store and cultural space, with decent espresso, huge salads ($24–30), simple dishes like pasta bolognese (R$20) and snacks. Tues–Thurs & Sun 2–9pm, Fri & Sat 2–10pm.

Creperia de Olinda Praça João Alfredo 168 ☎81 3429 2935; map p.295. This agreeable crêperie is decorated with knick-knacks, local art and exposed brickwork, and has an open-air patio. The scrumptious crêpes come in both sweet and savoury (from R$9–41) varieties and they even do a curried version (R$32). Daily 11am–11pm.

Flor do Coco Rua do Amparo 199 ☎81 3429 6889, ⓦpousadadoamparo.com.br; map p.295. Pousada restaurant boasting excellent regional cuisine, including both local fish dishes and great pastas. Mains between R$54–69. Mon–Fri 6–11.30pm, Sat & Sun noon–5pm & 6–11.30pm.

Hotel Pousada d'Olinda Varadouro Rua 15 de Novembro 98 ☎81 3439 1163; map p.295. Tasty, unfussy and cheap *por kilo* food (R$32) at this small restaurant on the ground floor of *Pousada Varadouro*. Locals swarm in on their lunch break so get here early; if you'd rather not sit indoors, head to the back and eat by the pool. Mon–Fri 11.30am–3pm.

DRINKING AND NIGHTLIFE

a fábrica bar Praça do Fortim do Queijo ☎81 9872 7303; map p.295. This is Olinda's hippest bar and club, semi-alfresco with a great location close to several hostels on Rua do Sol and a busy schedule that includes live samba (Wed) and pop rock (Sat). Cover R$10 and under. Wed–Sun 5pm–5am.

★ **Bodega do Véio** Rua do Amparo 212 ☎81 3429 0185; map p.295. A convivial general store-cum-neighbourhood bar of the kind you still find in rural Brazil and Cape Verde, with brooms propped up against the walls and shelves stacked to the ceiling with everything from soap powder to packets of beans and, of course, booze. From mid-afternoon onwards, people are crammed up against the counter and spilling onto the cobbled streets, and there's usually some kind of live music at weekends. Mon–Sat 10am–11.30pm.

Casa da Rabeca Rua Curupira 340, Cidade Tabajara ☎81 3371 8197, ⓦcasadarabeca.com.br; map p.295. A legacy of the late Mestre Salustiano and a community focal point for the music that made his name, *forró da rabeca*, alongside *maracatu* and other traditional Pernambucan styles; the place comes into its own during Carnaval. It's a bit out of the way, so best take a taxi. Opening times and cover charge vary (some events are free), though there's usually always something happening. April–Sept Sat 9pm–late.

Xinxim da Baiana Av Sigismundo Gonçalves 742 ☎81 3439 8447; map p.295. Bahían-themed bar where local *forró de rabeca* stars, Quarteto Olinda, made their name. Still a good place for music new and old, as well as other myriad cultural happenings. Tues–Thurs & Sun 7pm–2am, Fri & Sat 7pm–4am.

DIRECTORY

Banks and exchange There are no ATMs in Olinda's historical centre, but there's a Banco24horas ATM at the gas station on Av Pres. Kennedy on the right-hand side coming from Recife.

Pharmacies Farmácia Bicentenária, Rua S Miguel 277, Novo Olinda (☎81 3429 2148).

Post office Praça João Pessoa s/n ☎81 3439 2203 (Mon–Fri 9am–5pm).

Shopping Built in the sixteenth century, Olinda's oldest market, Mercado da Ribeira on Rua Bernardo Vieira de Melo (daily 8am–6pm), offers a few shops selling craft goods; large festival puppets are displayed in the hall at the end.

FERNANDO DE NORONHA

Recife is one of the main launch points for this beautiful archipelago 545km off the coast of Pernambuco. It boasts pristine beaches and it's absolutely stunning for scuba diving; the water is clear for more than 30m in many places, with turtles, dolphins and a wide range of fish species to observe. Since 1988 much of the archipelago has been protected as a marine national park to maintain its ecological wonders (it's also the breeding territory for many tropical Atlantic birds). The main island, **ILHA DE FERNANDO DE NORONHA**, has plenty of gorgeous beaches. While you can no longer swim with the dolphins, you're likely to see quite a few should you visit, though you'll have to wake up early – they enter the bay every day between 5am and 6am.

It's not cheap to get here (one-way fares rarely dip below R$500; two daily flights from Recife with GOL or Azul), and you're also charged the **TPA** (Taxa de Preservaçao) **tax** at a *daily* rate of R$70.66 for the first four days, then increasing by varying amounts for each extra day (which goes towards protecting the archipelago), and a one-off park admission fee (R$162) – but this can be quite an experience. For more information, including restaurants and places to stay, check the government-run website, ⓦwww.noronha.pe.gov.br.

FORTALEZA

The languid state capital of Ceará, **FORTALEZA** is a sprawling city of over 2.5 million inhabitants, an oddly provincial place compared to Northeast rival Recife, despite its size. The city itself contains a smattering of sights, though there's nothing special to see, and it's the bar scene and shopping opportunities that make it an obvious pit stop on the road to the state's celebrated **beaches**: Cumbuco, Jericoacoara, Canoa Quebrada, Morro Branco and Lagoinha. Crystal-clear waters and palm-fringed sands are just one selling point – this is a kite- or windsurfer's paradise.

WHAT TO SEE AND DO

The nerve centre of the city is its largest square, **Praça José de Alencar**, home to the beautiful **Teatro José de Alencar**. Fortaleza's downtown streets are crowded with shops, with hawkers colonizing pavements and plazas, so much of the centre seems like one giant market. To the east is **Praia de Iracema**, home to the bulk of Fortaleza's nightlife, while further south is **Praia do Futuro**, the city's best beach. Downtown is fine to hang out in during the day, but it's deserted and unnerving at night. Wandering around the area on a Sunday by yourself is also best avoided.

CENTRO DE TURISMO

Housed in the city's old prison at Rua Senador Pompeu 350, the **Centro de Turismo** (Mon–Fri 8am–6pm, Sat 8am–4pm, Sun 8am–noon; free) is not a

tourist office but a shopping mall of arts and craft stalls, everything from local lace and tasty cashew nuts to hand-crafted dolls, toys and more standard souvenirs.

CATEDRAL METROPOLITANA AND MERCADO CENTRAL

Looming over Centro like a grimy Victorian throwback, Fortaleza's **Catedral Metropolitana** is a huge neo-Gothic oddity completed in 1978, though its interior is a surprisingly bright, open space enhanced by dazzling stained-glass windows. Next to it, on Rua Conde d'Eu, the **Mercado Central** (see page 302) dominates the skyline.

CENTRO DRAGÃO DO MAR

The vast **Centro Dragão do Mar** complex (museums Tues–Fri 9am–7pm, Sat & Sun 2–9pm; free; ⓦdragaodomar.org.br), a couple of blocks east of the market on Rua Dragão do Mar 81, contains a couple of small museums well worth a peek. The **Museu de Arte Contemporanea do Ceará** is a bright, well-curated gallery showing primarily local and Brazilian artists in a variety of media, while the **Memorial da Cultura Cearense** hosts changing exhibits on aspects of Ceará history, art and culture, but also houses a permanent exhibit on the lower levels dedicated to the **Vaqueiros**, the hardy cowboys of the state.

BEACHES IN TOWN

The main city beaches are **Praia de Iracema** and the adjacent **Praia do Meireles**, both focal points for Fortaleza's nightlife and broken up by a series of piers (*espigões*), though the boundary between the two beaches is blurry in practice. As beaches go, the Praia do Meireles wins hands down thanks to its greater expanse of sand, though the water is not as clean as the beaches out of town. Iracema is gradually receiving a long-overdue makeover (this is where a new **aquarium** will eventually open, but don't count on it). Cleaner water, higher rollers and better seafood are to be had further out at the 7km-long **Praia do Futuro**: take buses marked "Caça e Pesca" (#49) from Rua Castro e Silva in the centre or along Avendia Beira Mar. The beach *barracas* here are very good, and it's the only place where locals will actually swim. In terms of safety, by day

FORTALEZA

Ponte dos
Ingleses

Praia de
Iracema

Praia do
Mucuripe

RUA DOS TABAJARAS

AV. ALMIRANTE BARROSO

Estação Ferroviaria
& local bus terminal

Praia do
Meireles

AV. MONSENHOR TABOSA

RUA TENENTE BENÉVOLO

CENTRO

AV. BEIRA MAR

Praia do Futuro

AV. ABOLIÇÃO

Cyber Café

MEIRELES

RUA PEREIRA VALENTE

SEE MAP BELOW FOR DETAIL

Monte Klinikum Hospital

VARJOTA

AVENIDA SANTOS DUMONT

Droga
Nunes

PRAÇA
CORAÇÃO
DE JESUS

AVENIDA HERACLITO GRAÇA

Beach Park

Buses to
Aquiraz

AV. PADRE ANTÔNIO TOMAS

Shopping
Del Paseo

5à Sec

RUA JOÃO CORDEIRO

RUA ANTÔNIO SALES

ALDEOTA

AVENIDA BARÃO DE STUDART

AV. DESEMBARGADOR MOREIRA

AV. SENADOR VIRGÍLIO TÁVORA

AVENIDA COLUMBO SOUSA

3

ACCOMMODATION
Pousada 0031   2
Hotel Pousada
 Mundo Latino   1

FATIMA

AV. VISCONDE RIO BRANCO

RUA BARBOSA DE FREITAS

RUA ARAKEN SILVA

AV. ENG. SANTANA JUNIOR

Shopping
Iguatemi

Estação
Rodoviária

EATING
50 Sabores   3
Croco Beach   1
Neide do Camarão   2
Ponto do Guaraná   4
Real Sucos   5

AVENIDA PONTES VIEIRA

DRINKING & NIGHTLIFE
Café Pagliuca   1

Rio Cocó

Airport

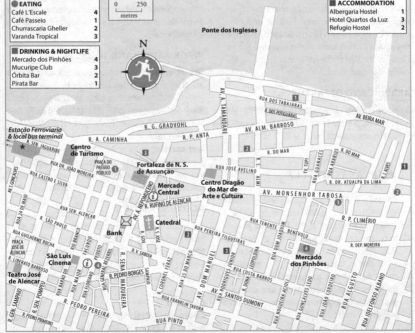

EATING
Café L'Escale   4
Café Passeio   1
Churrascaria Gheller 2
Varanda Tropical   3

0   250
metres

ACCOMMODATION
Albergaria Hostel 1
Hotel Quartos da Luz 3
Refugio Hostel   2

Ponte dos Ingleses

DRINKING & NIGHTLIFE
Mercado dos Pinhões 4
Mucuripe Club   3
Órbita Bar   2
Pirata Bar   1

N

RUA DOS TABAJARAS

R. DOS POTIGUARAS

AV. BEIRA MAR

AV. A. TAMANDARÉ

R. G. GRADVOHL

R. P. ANTA

AV. ALM. BARROSO

Estação Ferroviaria
& local bus terminal

R. A. CAMINHA

R. DO MAR

R. GUANACES

R. DO MAR

R. SEN. JAGUARIBE

Centro
de Turismo

PRAÇA DO
PASSEIO
PÚBLICO

RUA JOSÉ AVELINO

R. S.
ALMI.

TV. TUPI

RUA ARARIÚS

R. J. AIRES

RUA DR. JOÃO MOREIRA

Fortaleza de N. S.
de Assunçao

RUA CASTRO E SILVA

AV. GONÇALVES

RUA 24 DE MAIO

Mercado
Central

Centro Dragão
do Mar de
Arte e Cultura

R. DR. ATUALPA DA LIMA

AV. MONSENHOR TABOSA

R. SÃO PAULO

RUA SEN. ALENCAR

R. RUFINO DE ALENCAR

R. P. CLIMÉRIO

RUA GUILHERME ROCHA

RIO BRANCO

FACUNDO

Bank

Catedral

RUA PEREIRA FILGUEIRAS

R. DEP. MOREIRA

PRAÇA
JOSÉ DE
ALENCAR

R. SÃO JOSÉ

R. GOV.

RUA DOM JOAQUIM

Mercado
dos Pinhões

R. LIBERATO BARROSO

R. V. SABOIA

São Luis
Cinema

R. BARÃO DO RIO

R. SENA MADUREIRA

R. PEDRO BORGES

R. 23 DO MARÇO

RUA RODRIGUES JUNIOR

RUA COSTA BARROS

LEOPOLDINA

RUA NOGUEIRA ACIOLI

RUA JOÃO CORDEIRO

RUA ILDEFONSO ALBANO

Teatro José
de Alencar

R. GEN. SAMPAIO

R. SEN. POMPEU

R. MAJOR

R. GENERAL BEZERRIL

AV. DOM MANUEL

AV. SANTOS DUMONT

RUA GONÇALVES LEDO

RUA ALGUSTO

R. PEDRO PEREIRA

R. PEDRO PRIMEIRO

RUA FRANKLIN TÁVORA

RUA PINTO

the beaches are fine (though you should look out for **shark warnings**), but the area between Praia do Meireles and Praia do Futuro is unsafe at any time and should not be walked by night.

BEACHES OUT OF TOWN

The state of Ceará has plenty of incredible beaches on offer if you are prepared to travel a bit further. All can be reached on tours or by regular buses from the *rodoviária*. Ernahitur (☎85 3533 7700, ⓦernanitur.com.br) runs day trips to the beaches listed below.

With its emerald-green waters, **Cumbuco**, only 35km north of Fortaleza, is by far Brazil's best beach for kite-surfing. *Pousada 0031* (see below) can organize lessons. Make sure you go on a **dune-buggy ride** to check out the area's breathtaking scenery. Further up is the popular **Canoa Quebrada** (ⓦcanoa-quebrada.com), which has dramatic cliffs and fun nightlife that goes on until the early hours. Heading further north you come to Ceará's most famous beach, **Jericoacoara** (ⓦjeri-brazil.org), with fine white sands and high dunes, especially popular with wind- and kite-surfers. The second half of the trip up here is by 4WD, and it can take up to seven hours to make the 312km journey. Finally, in the opposite direction is **Morro Branco**, 80km to the south of Fortaleza and renowned for its beaches backed by maze-like cliffs of multicoloured sand.

ARRIVAL AND DEPARTURE

By plane Fortaleza's Aeroporto Internacional Pinto Martins is just 6km south of the centre. A fixed-rate taxi costs R$45 to Meireles, Iracema and Centro or R$32 to the *rodoviária*.

Pay first at the Coopaero desk in the terminal (higher rates apply Mon–Fri 8pm–6am, Sat after 1pm and all day Sun). You can also take a by-the-meter "Taxi Comum" that are nominally a little cheaper, but only if traffic is light. Buses with the route card Aeroporto/Benfica/Rodoviária (#404; R$3.50) run regularly to Praça José de Alencar in the centre via the *rodoviária* (daily 5.10am–10pm).

Destinations Belém (5 daily; 1hr 50min–3hr 40min); Recife (10 daily; 1hr 15min–1hr 35min); Rio (12–24 daily; 5hr 40min–8hr 15min); Salvador (7–9 daily; 1hr 40min–4hr 20min).

By bus The bus station, Rodoviária Engenheiro João Tomé, Av Borges de Melo 1630 (☎85 3230 1111), is about 3km from the centre, and served by the same Aeroporto/Benfica/Rodoviária bus. A taxi costs around R$25–30 from the *rodoviária* to most places.

Destinations Belém (3 daily; 24–26hr); Jijoca de Jericoacoara (16 daily; 5–6hr); Natal (7 daily; 8hr); Recife (6 daily; 12–13hr); Salvador (2 daily; 22hr); São Luís (3 daily; 18hr 30min).

GETTING AROUND

By bus Fortaleza has plenty of local buses (R$3.50). Useful routes that take you to the main beaches and back to the city centre are marked "Grande Circular I" and "Caça e Pesca/Centro/Beira Mar" or #49. The local bus station in the centre is known as Praça Da Estação, a large square by the old railway station.

By taxi Taxi meters start at R$4.85 – it's around R$25 between Meireles and the centre. Cooperativa Rádio Táxi de Fortaleza (☎85 3254 5744, ⓦradiotaxifortaleza.com.br) runs 24hr.

INFORMATION AND TOURS

Tourist information Fortaleza boasts a good range of tourist information outlets including a kiosk in the airport (daily 8am–8pm), as well as offices in the Mercado Central (Mon–Sat 9am–5pm; ☎85 3105 1475) and on Av Beira Mar near the Anfiteatro Flávio Ponte (Daily 9am–5pm; ☎85 3105 2670).

Tour operator Ernahitur Av. Barão de Studart 300, 17th floor, Meireles ☎85 3533 7700, ⓦernanitur.com.br. Arranges packages to Jericoacoara and day-trips to Canoa Quebrada and Lagoinha, in addition to all the other major beaches.

ACCOMMODATION

The budget hotels, as ever, tend to be downtown, which hums busily during the day but empties at night – it's best to stay elsewhere. Close by is Praia de Iracema, with a decent enough range of accommodation, while Praia do Meireles further along is home to more upmarket hotels.

CENTRO

Albergaria Hostel Rua Antônio Augusto 111, Praia de Iracema ☎85 3032 9005, ⓦalbergariahostel.com.

br; map p.299. Cheerful hostel close to the beach and nightlife and small clean dorms and doubles with tiled floors. Basic breakfast included, and there's a pool table and cold beers (for sale) at the bar. Dorms R$45, doubles R$170
Hotel Quartos da Luz Rua Rodrigues Junior 278 ☎ 85 3082 2260; map p.299. This hotel has a cosy atmosphere and an inviting backyard with bar stools and hanging chairs. The rooms are clean and colourful, equipped with both a/c and fan, and there's also a communal kitchen. Breakfast included. R$90
★ **Refugio Hostel** Rua Deputado João Lopes 31 ☎ 85 3393 4349, ⓦrefugiohostelfortaleza.com; map p.299. A German-owned and extremely well-run hostel with clean dorms and excellent service. The young staff are all English speaking and the shared bathrooms are spacious, and have hair dryers. Dorms R$30, doubles R$120

PRAIA DO MEIRELES
Hotel Pousada Mundo Latino Rua Ana Bilhar 507, Meireles ☎ 85 3088 3339, ⓦmundolatino.com.br; map p.299. The breakfast room and communal area are not exactly alluring with their PVC-covered sofas, but staff are helpful and the a/c rooms are spacious. Breakfast included. R$140

EATING

Downtown, Praça do Ferreira offers a few *por kilo lanchonetes* (self-service cafeterias), and Iracema has a few good restaurants, while the Centro Dragão do Mar is a popular spot, particularly in the evenings, with at least seven pavement cafés overflowing with people. The beaches all have a smattering of good restaurants as well as beach huts offering some of the best deals on seafood.

CENTRO
Café L'Escale Rua Floriano Peixoto 587 ☎ 85 3253 1976, ⓦlescale.com.br; map p.299. Excellent local pit stop right on Praça do Ferreira (in an Art Nouveau building dating from 1914), with the usual selection of *salgados*, drinks and self-service buffet options. Mon–Thurs 8am–9pm, Sat 8am–4pm.
★ **Café Passeio** Rua Dr. João Moreira, Praça do Passeio Público ☎ 84 3063 8782; map p.299. Elegant restaurant occupying the old-fashioned kiosks in the park with outdoor seating. It's a self-service Brazilian buffet during the week, with *feijoada* on Sat and a bigger buffet on Sun. Daily 9am–5pm.
Real Sucos Heráclito Graça 1709 ☎ 85 9 8509 3974, ⓦrealsucos.com.br; map p.299. Veteran chain serving renowned fresh fruit juices (R$9–17), including *açaí*, *graviola*, *carambola*, tamarind and papaya – the *cajú* juice is especially good – as well as lots of sandwich options (from R$8). Also at Shopping Aldeota ☎ 85 3458 1104, Shopping Benfica ☎ 85 3281 4029, and Center Um Shopping ☎ 85 3224 0121 (all 10am–10pm). Mon–Thurs 8am–1am, Fri & Sat 8am–4am, Sun 5pm–1am.

Varanda Tropical Av Monsenhor Tabosa 714, Praia de Iracema ☎ 85 3219 5195; map p.299. Open-fronted restaurant on the main road serving a solid range of meat, fish and seafood options, many of which will fill two bellies; if you're alone try the shrimps in garlic (R$29.90). Mains for two people around R$50–70. Mon–Sat 11am–11pm, Sun 11am–3pm.

PRAIA DO MEIRELES
50 Sabores Av Beira Mar 3958, Mucuripe ☎ 85 3077 9400, ⓦ50sabores.com.br; map p.299. This decades-old Fortaleza institution hides its light under a proverbial bush, with almost double the titular fifty flavours of ice cream, all of which change with the seasons, even if it feels like the weather never does. Try the plum, *caipirinha* or *maracujá* (R$12 one scoop). One of six branches spread around town. Mon–Sat 10am–10pm, Sun 2–8pm.
Churrascaria Gheller Av. Monsenhor Tabosa 825 ☎ 85 3219 3599; map p.299. No-nonsense steakhouse where the buffet is R$37.90 on weekdays (with salads, sushi, pasta and vegetables), though the *rodízio* is so-so. Drinks and desserts are extra. Daily 11am–11pm.
★ **Neide do Camarão** Av da Abolição 4772 Mucuripe ☎ 85 9 8892 8231; map p.299. You buy your shrimp at the door (R$39 *por kilo*), choose how you want it prepared, hand it to the waiter, then eat the crispy shrimp, shell and all, washed down with ice-cold beer. Local, authentic and awesome. Daily 5pm–midnight.
Ponto do Guaraná Av Beira Mar 3127-A Meireles ☎ 85 3086 5650; map p.299. *Guaraná* addicts should head here – there's plenty of flavours to choose from including lemon, *acerola* and *açaí* (drinks R$7–10). Sandwiches are also available (from R$10). Daily 6am–10pm.

PRAIA DO FUTURO
Croco Beach Av Zezé Diogo 3125 ☎ 85 3521 9600, ⓦcrocobeach.com.br; map p.299. Probably Futuro's most popular beach restaurant, serving huge sharing platters of seafood and a buffet for R$69.90/kilo, as well as salads (from R$26.90) and plenty of meat dishes (most mains for two R$62.90–88.90). Also lays on live local bands and MPB Tues & Thurs (R$25 cover) and DJs/live music at weekends (R$8 cover). Mon–Wed & Sun 8am–6pm, Thurs 8am–2am, Fri & Sat 8am–9pm.

DRINKING AND NIGHTLIFE

Fortaleza is justly famous for its *forró*. One of the busiest nightlife areas is the streets around the Ponte dos Ingleses. There's no better way to see what Cearenses do to have fun than to spend a night in a *dancetaria*, most of which open at 10pm but don't really get going until about midnight. Other nightlife is mainly out by the beaches: Praia Meireles appeals to a broad cross section of locals and tourists, whereas Praia Iracema is slightly younger.

Café Pagliuca Rua Barbosa de Freitas 1035 ☎85 3324 1903, ⓦcafepagliuca.com.br; map p.299. An arty, rustic-bohemian vibe makes this one of the mellowest spots in town for a quiet drink and live jazz, bossa and MPB. Food includes a range of authentic Italian risotto, and *feijoada* on Saturdays (R$44). R$20 cover. Tues–Thurs 5.30pm–midnight, Fri noon–midnight, Sat noon–1am.

Mercado dos Pinhões Praça Visconde 41 ☎85 3251 1299; map p.299. Perhaps the best place to get a sense of how locals take their *forró* and *chorinho* seriously, this old 1890s mercado is an arts and craft market by day (Mon–Fri 9am–noon & 2–5pm), but morphs into authentic *forró* dance hall three nights a week. Thurs, Fri & Sun 5pm–midnight.

Mucuripe Club Travessa Maranguape 108, Centro ☎85 3254 3020; map p.299. Veteran superclub hosting some of the country's biggest DJs, singers and bands in several themed areas including a film-set-like, colonial-style street, a huge "arena" for live shows and a hi-tech clubbing area, with a music policy covering everything from rock, funk and electronica to samba, *axé* and *forró*. No flip-flops or shorts. Cover varies (usually R$30–60). Fri & Sat 9.30pm–5am.

Órbita Bar Rua Dragão do Mar 207 ☎85 3453 1421, ⓦorbitabar.com.br; map p.299. A Fortaleza institution, with live Brazilian and international indie/alternative, blues, electronica and even – for those who like their twang – a night (Thurs) dedicated to the delights of surf-rock. Check out their radio station, ⓦorbitaradio.com.br. Cover R$10–30. Thurs–Sun 9pm–5am.

Pirata Bar Rua dos Tabajaras 325 ☎85 4011 6161, ⓦpirata.com.br; map p.299. The most famous place in Fortaleza (and Brazil) to get your fix of *forró*. By cannily cornering the club-less wilds of *segunda-feira*, this unashamed tourist trap has generated more than its fair share of publicity – the *New York Times* famously called it "the craziest place on earth on a Monday night". Cover is a hefty R$40. Mon 8pm–5am.

SHOPPING

Mercado Central Rua Alberto Nepomuceno 199, ⓦmercadocentraldefortaleza.com.br. Fortaleza's modern Mercado Central and the nearby shops diagonally across from the cathedral are the best places in the city to buy a hammock. This huge complex resembles a parking garage crowded with hundreds of small stores, most selling *artesanato* for which the city is famed. Mon–Fri 8am–6pm, Sat 8am–4pm, Sun 8am–2pm.

DIRECTORY

Banks and exchange Bradesco has an ATM in the city centre on Rua Senador Alencar 144. Banco24horas also has ATMs at Av Beira Mar 2982 and at **Av da Abolição 2900.**

Consulates UK, British Honorary Consulate, Rua Leonardo Mota 501, Meireles (☎85 242 0888); US, Torre Santos Dumont, Av Santos Dumont 2828, Suite 708, Aldeota (☎85 3021 5200).

Hospital Monte Klinikum Hospital, Rua República do Libano 747 (☎85 4012 0012, ⓦmonteklinikum.com.br).

Internet Cyber Café, Av da Abolição 2659, Meireles (Mon–Sat 8.30am–10pm.

Laundry Lavanderia São Luíz at Av da Abolição 2679 (Mon–Fri 8–11.30am & 12.30–6.30pm, Sat 8am–1pm) for drop-off service; the branch of Lav & Lev (ⓦlavelev.com.br) next door at Av da Abolição 2685 has self-service coin-operated machines (powder available).

Pharmacy Farmácia Santa Branca, Av da Universidade 3089, Benfica (☎85 3223 0000).

Police The tourist police are open 24hr and can be found at Av Almirante Barroso 805, Praia da Iracema (☎85 3101 2488).

Post office The central post office is at Rua Senador Alencar 38 (Mon–Fri 8am–5pm); in Mireles there is a branch at Av Monsenhor Tabosa 1561 (Mon–Fri 9am–5pm).

The Amazon

The Amazon is a vast forest – the largest on the planet – and a giant river system, covering over half of Brazil and a large portion of South America. The forest extends into Venezuela, Colombia, Peru and Bolivia, where the river itself begins life among thousands of different headwaters. In Brazil, only the stretch below Manaus, where the waters of the **Rio Solimões** and the **Rio Negro** meet, is actually known as the **Rio Amazonas**. The daily flow of the river is said to be enough to supply a city the size of New York with water for nearly ten years, and its power is such that the muddy Amazon waters stain the Atlantic a silty brown for over 200km out to sea.

BELÉM

Strategically placed on the Amazon River estuary, **BELÉM** was founded by the Portuguese in 1616 as the City of Our Lady of Bethlehem (Belém). Its original role was to protect the river mouth and establish the Portuguese claim to the region, but it rapidly became established as a slaving port

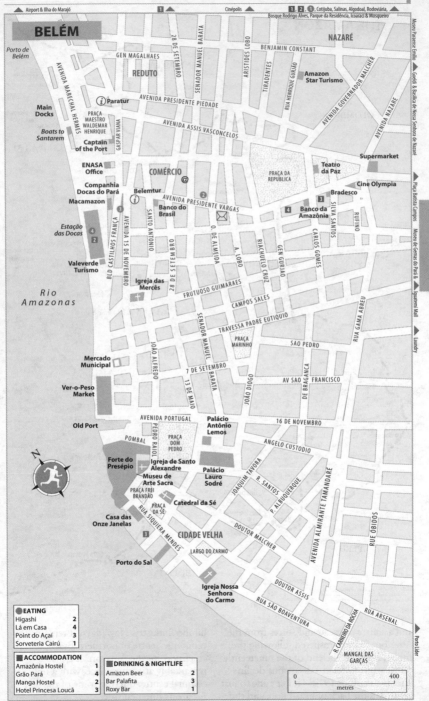

BELÉM

Porto de Belém

Rio Amazonas

Main Docks

Boats to Santarem

3

Museu Paraense Emílio · Godfil & Basílica de Nossa Senhora de Nazaré · Praça Batista Campos · Museu de Gemas do Pará & · Iguatemi Mall · Laundry · Porto Lider

● EATING	
Higashi	2
Lá em Casa	4
Point do Açaí	3
Sorveteria Cairú	1

■ ACCOMMODATION	
Amazônia Hostel	1
Grão Pará	4
Manga Hostel	2
Hotel Princesa Loucã	3

■ DRINKING & NIGHTLIFE	
Amazon Beer	2
Bar Palafita	3
Roxy Bar	1

0 — 400
metres

THE AMAZON

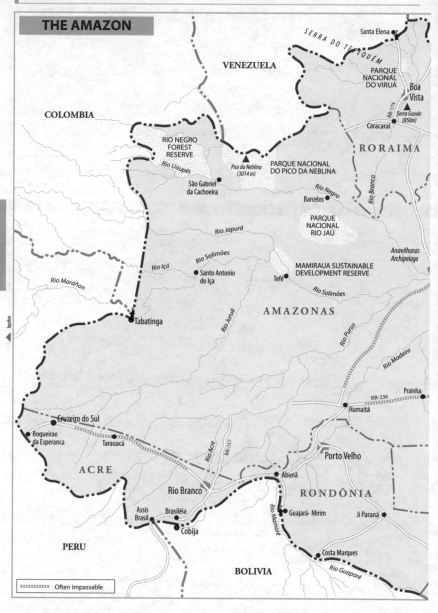

and a source of cacao and spices from the Amazon. Belém prospered following the rubber boom at the end of the nineteenth century but suffered a disastrous decline after the crash of 1914 – it kept afloat, just about, on the back of brazil nuts and the lumber industry. Nowadays, it remains the economic centre of northern Brazil, and the chief port for the Amazon. It is also a remarkably attractive place, with a fine colonial centre, offering some of the Amazon's finest cuisine.

3

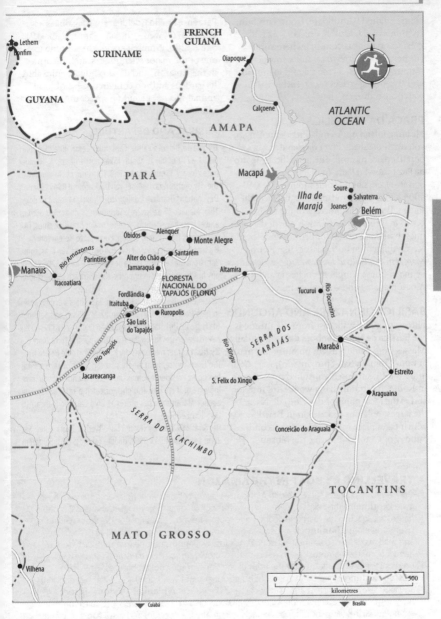

The old town or **Cidade Velha** is at the southern edge of the centre, where the cathedral and fort sit around the Praça da Sé. Immediately north on the waterfront lies one of the city's highlights, the **Ver-o-Peso** market, the largest open-air market in Latin America – visit in the morning when the market is bustling, its stalls overflowing with spices, potions, crafts, exotic fish and foodstuffs. Carrying on up the waterfront you reach the **Estação das Docas** cultural centre (daily 10amtill late, from 9am Sun; Av Boulevard Castilho s/n; ☎91 3212 5525, ⓦestacaodasdocas.com.br) where some (rather pricey) *artesanato* stalls compete with restaurants, cafés, a cinema and exhibition and live music spaces in a refurbished warehouse area.

PRAÇA DA REPUBLICA

Heading inland up Avenida Presidente Vargas, you reach the shady Praça da República, a popular place to stroll. The magnificent **Teatro da Paz** (Tues–Fri 9am–6pm, Sat 9am–noon, Sun 9–11am; hourly guided tours R$6; ☎91 4009 8750, ⓦtheatrodapaz.com.br) faces the square. Built on the proceeds of the rubber boom in Neoclassical style, it is one of the city's finest buildings; tickets for performances here – everything from opera classics like Pietro Mascagni's *Cavalleria Rusticana* to performances by the in-house symphony orchestra and the Amazônia Jazz Band – are often free.

BASÍLICA DE NAZARÉ AND AROUND

Fifteen minutes' walk east from the theatre is the **Basílica de Nossa Senhora de Nazaré** (daily Masses from 7am (6.30am on Sun); last mass at 6pm (5pm on Sat, 8pm on Sun); free; ☎91 4009 8400), supposedly inspired by St Peter's in Rome. It certainly has a wonderful interior, and is the focal point of the Cirio de Nazaré, the largest religious procession in Brazil, which takes place each year on the second Sunday of October. Nearby, the **Museu**

Paraense Emílio Goeldi at Av Magalhães Barata 376 (Wed–Sun 9am–5pm; R$3; ☎91 3182 3200, ⓦmuseu.goeldi.ru) is home to one of the major scientific research institutes in the Amazon, and it's also hugely enjoyable. Its gardens and zoo contain dozens of local animal species, including spider monkeys, caimans and macaws.

ARRIVAL AND DEPARTURE

By plane Belém's Val-de-Cans/Júlio Cesar Ribeiro Airport (☎91 3210 6000) is about 15km north of town. Regular buses (every 15min; 40min; R$3.10) connect the airport to the city centre. A taxi will set you back around R$45 (30min). Destinations Brasília (2 daily; 2hr 30min); Macapá (5 daily; 1hr); Manaus (5 daily; 2hr); Santarém (5 daily; 1hr 30min) and at least once daily to all other major Brazilian cities. TAP has weekly flights from Lisbon, Portugal to Belém (8hr).

By bus Belém's *rodoviária* is in the district of São Bras, some 3km from the centre at Praça de Operário (☎91 3266 2625); any bus from the stops opposite the entrance to the station will take you downtown (R$3.10; 20min).

Destinations Itapemirim (☎91 3226 3382) operates daily buses to Belo Horizonte (48hr) and São Paulo (49hr); and Salvador (daily 3pm; 31hr). Itapemirim and Guanabara (☎91 3323 1992) have daily services to Fortaleza (7.30am, noon & 1pm; 24hr).

By boat Larger riverboats dock at the Porto de Belém near the town centre, from where you can walk or take a local bus up Av Presidente Vargas (not recommended if you have luggage or if it's late at night), or catch a taxi (R$15). The agency Macamazon has offices at Blvd Castilho França 716 (☎91 3222 5604).

Destinations Macapá (Mon 11am, Wed & Thurs noon, Sat 2pm; 24hr; hammock R$60, double cabin R$225); Santarém

---

TRAVELLING BY BOAT IN THE AMAZON

On long river journeys there are different classes: avoid *cabine*, sweltering cabins, and choose instead **primeiro** (first class), sleeping in a hammock on deck. *Segundo* (second class) is often hammock space in the lower deck or engine room. The most essential item when travelling by boat is therefore a **hammock**, which can be bought cheaply (from about R$40 in the stores and markets of Manaus, Santarém or Belém), plus two lengths of rope (*armador de rede*) to hang it from. The hammock areas get extremely crowded, so arrive early and establish your position: the best spots are near the front or the sides for the cooling breezes.

Loose **clothing** is fine during daylight hours but at night you'll need some warmer garments and long sleeves to protect against the chill and the insects. A **blanket** and some **insect repellent** are also recommended. Virtually all boats now provide mineral water, although enough to **drink** (large bottles of mineral water are the best option) and extra **food** – cookies, fruit and the odd tin – to keep you happy for the duration of the voyage may also be a good idea. There are toilets on all boats, though even on the best they can get filthy within a few hours of leaving port – it's advisable to take your own roll of **toilet paper** just in case.

The most organized of the wooden riverboats are the larger **three-deck vessels**. All of these wooden vessels tend to let passengers stay aboard a night or two before departure and after arrival, which saves on hotel costs, and is handy for travellers on a low budget.

(Tues–Fri 7pm; 3 days; hammock R$200, double cabin R$800) and Manaus (Tues–Fri 6pm; 5 days; hammock R$250, double cabin R$1050). Tuesday departures to Santarém and Manaus leave from Porto Líder at Bernardo Sayão s/n), while Wed, Thurs & Fri departures leave from the Porto de Belém.

INFORMATION AND TOURS

Tourist information Paratur is at Praça Waldemar Henrique (Mon–Fri 8am–5pm ☎091 3110 8700); there is also a Paratur window at the airport (daily 8am–6pm; ☎91 3210 6330).

Tour operators Valeverde Turismo, in the Estação das Docas (☎91 3218 7333, ☒valeverdeturismo.com.br), organize good-value river tours around Belém, as well as city tours. Amazon Star Turismo, Rua Henrique Gurjão 210 (☎91 3212 6244 or 24hr line ☎9982 7911, ☒amazonstar.com.br), is an excellent French-run agency specializing in ecotours, including visits to Ilha de Marajó and half-day tours (R$170) through the streams of the Rio Guamá. Both offer excursions to Ilha dos Papagaios, an island near Belém where tens of thousands of parrots zoom out of the trees at dawn (R$180).

ACCOMMODATION

Amazônia Hostel Av Gov. José Malcher 592, ☒amazoniahostel.com.br; map p.303. Belém's first hostel features beautiful wooden floors and lovely high ceilings. Rooms are set on two floors, with separate male and female dorms; they're a bit small, but are comfortable, with sturdy bunks and personal lockers. Some dorms and doubles with a/c, others with fan. There's fast wi-fi in all areas and a communal chill-out area with TV. Ten-percent discount for HI members. Friendly, helpful staff; but don't expect anyone to respond to emails or social media messages. Standards have slipped in recent years. Dorms R$40, doubles R$80-100

Grão Pará Av Presidente Vargas 718 ☎91 3221 2121, ☒hotelgraopara.com.br; map p.303. A great-value mid-range hotel on the busy Vargas thoroughfare just a few steps from the Theatro da Paz, offering comfortable a/c rooms on fifteen floors, all with fridge, cable TV and private bath. R$130

★ **Manga Hostel** Av Ceará 290 ☎91 3347 2800, ☒mangahostelbelem.com.br; map p.303. New hostel founded in 2016 in a multi-storey home near the bus station. The facilities are stunning, with modern amenities such as flat-screen TVs, a/c, an expansive kitchen with bar, outdoor patio and best of all, a swimming pool (the only hostel in town that can claim one), perfect to beat Belém's often scorching heat. It's an oasis of calm in an otherwise hectic neighbourhood. Also near to Lider supermarket and ATMs. Dorms R$55, doubles R$125

Hotel Princesa Louçã Av Presidente Vargas 882 ☎91 4006 7000; map p.303. Formerly the *Belém Hilton*, this hotel dominates the Praça da República. It was built in the 1980s, and neither the Hilton nor the current owners have updated it much; it retains a bygone feel from days. There's a well-equipped gym and small outdoor pool. R$250

EATING AND DRINKING

Belém boasts plenty of excellent cheap restaurants, which have especially good deals at lunchtime. The stalls of Dona Miloca, in front of the Goeldi museum, and Maria do Carmo, in front of the Colégio Nazaré on Avenida Nazaré, just before the Basílica, serve excellent *tacacá* (shrimp soup with jambú leaves) and *açai*. In the evenings, head to the Estação das Docas where all places stay open till late.

Higashi Rua Ó de Almeida 509 ☎91 3230 5552; map p.303. An informal *por kilo* restaurant with a good range of dishes on offer, including shrimp, crab and salmon; the all-you-can-eat buffet on the first floor (daily excluding Sat; R$23.49) is a bargain. Daily 11am–3pm.

Lá em Casa Estaçao das Docas Av Castilhos França ☎91 3212 5588, ☒laemcasa.com; map p.303. One of the most popular restaurants in town, offering a lunchtime buffet (R$64) between noon and 3pm featuring all manner of regional dishes. In the evenings it's à la carte; try the *"menu Paraense"* (R$35 per person or R$69 for two) – a perfect introduction to Pará's cuisine – or the *corridinho de peixe* (R$55), featuring the very best fish from the Amazon. Mon–Thurs & Sun noon–midnight, Fri & Sat noon–3am.

Point do Açaí Blvd Castilho França 744 ☎91 3212 2168, ☒pointdoacai.net; map p.303. As the name suggests, this place has *açaí* aplenty – this refreshing Amazonian drink of crushed berries is served with most dishes – try the *chapa mista paraense* (serves three; R$135), a platter of local fish, meats and vegetables. Mon & Sun 10.30am–3.30pm, Tues–Sat 6–10.30pm.

Sorveteria Cairú Travessa 14 de Março at Gov José Malcher 1570 ☎91 3246 9129; map p.303. With over 65 exotic ice-cream favours on offer (R$5 per scoop), including an exciting selection of regional fruit flavours such as *cupuaçu*, *graviola* (soursop) and *acai*, this ice-cream chain is one of the best in town. There's another branch at the Estação das Docas. Daily 8am–11.45pm.

DRINKING AND NIGHTLIFE

Belém has some excellent nightlife, although most of the action takes place outside the centre of town; you'll find many bars along Av Almirante Wandekolk and in the Estação das Docas.

Amazon Beer In the Estação das Docas ☎91 3039 1456, ☒amazonbeer.com.br; map p.303. Beer-lovers will be in heaven at this bar with in-house brewery and a mouth-watering selection of artisan brews on tap (from R$6.60). Mon–Thurs 5pm–midnight, Fri 5pm–2am, Sat noon–2am, Sun noon–midnight.

★ **Bar Palafita** Rua Siqueira Mendes 264, Cidade Velha ☎91 3212 6302; map p.303. One of Belém's most famous treasures: an atmospheric bar on stilts right on the Amazon River with truly incredible views, especially at sunset. Drinks and grub (mains R$35) are served to the sound of live *carimbó*, *forró* and pop-rock bands on weekends. Tues–Sun noon–midnight.

3

Roxy Bar Av Senador Lemos 231 ☎ 91 3224 4514, ⓦ roxybar.com.br; map p.303. Attracting well-heeled Belenenses, the queue at this hugely popular joint forms way before the doors even open and you'll always see eager customers outside waiting to be seated. The trendy interior features bare-brick walls, funky paintings and a fun menu with dishes named after famous movie stars. Mains R$45. Also has a location at Shopping Bosque Grão-Pará near the airport. Daily 7.15pm–11.30pm.

DIRECTORY

Banks and exchange Banco da Amazônia, Av Presidente Vargas 800; Bradesco, Av Presidente Vargas 988; Banco do Brasil, 2nd floor, Av Presidente Vargas 248. There are also a number of ATMs in the Estação das Docas.

Hospital Hospital Guadalupe, Rua Arciprestes Manoel Teodoro 734 (☎ 91 4005 9877).

Internet Servicos E Solucões Av Presidente Vargas 144 (Mon–Sat 8am–6pm; R$5/hr; ☎ 91 3222 0350).

Laundry Lav & Lev Travessa Dr Moraes 576 (Mon–Sat 8am–6pm; wash R$15, dry R$15; ☎ 91 3223 7247).

Post office The central post office (Mon–Fri 9am–5pm) is at Av Presidente Vargas 498.

Shopping Belém is one of the best places in the world to buy hammocks (essential if you go upriver) – look in the street market hall Ver-o-Peso west of Av Presidente Vargas, starting in Rua Santo Antônio.

Taxi Cooperdoca Rádio Táxi ☎ 91 3241 3555; Águia Rádio Táxi ☎ 91 2764 4000.

ILHA DO MARAJÓ

The **ILHA DO MARAJÓ** is a vast island in the Amazon delta, opposite Belém, consisting of some forty thousand square kilometres of largely uninhabited mangrove swamps and spectacular freshwater beaches. Created by the accretion of silt and sand over millions of years, it's a wet and marshy area, the western half covered in thick jungle, the east flat savannah, swampy in the wet season (Jan–June), brown and firm in the dry season (June–Dec). It is home of the giant *pirarucu* fish, which, growing to over 180kg, is the largest freshwater breed in the world. The island is a popular resort for sun-seekers and ecotourists alike.

WHAT TO SEE AND DO

The main port of **Soure** is a growing resort offering pleasant beaches where you can relax under the shade of ancient mango trees. Magnificent empty **beaches** are scattered all around the island – the **Praia do Pesqueiro**, about 8km from Soure, is one of the more accessible. If you want to see the interior – or much of the wildlife – you have to camp or pay for a room at one of the *fazendas*: book with travel agents in Belém or take your chance on arrival. **Joanes**, with another tremendous wind-swept beach, is much quieter.

ARRIVAL

By boat From Belém's Terminal Hidroviário on Av Marechal Hermes there are daily fast (1hr 30min) and slow (3hr) boats to Ponto de Camará on Ilha do Marajó (slow boat 6.30am & 2.30pm, fast boat 2pm; slow boat returning 6.30am & 3pm, fast boat at 7am; R$25–35). At Ponto de Camará buses to Salvaterra (30min; R$8), Joanes (20min; R$10) and Soure (40min; R$12) meet the boats.

ACCOMMODATION AND EATING

Delícias da Nalva 4 Rua 1051 between Travessa 20 and 21 ☎ 91 8301 0110. Soure's best restaurant is not cheap, although the food is well worth the splurge. Chef Nalva serves plenty of buffalo meat dishes – the island's speciality – as well as chicken and fish mains (R$50). Daily 10am–10pm.

Casarão da Amazônia 4 Rua 626, at Travessa 9 ☎ 91 3741 1988. An Italian architect was flown in to restore this beautiful colonial building, which now houses five comfortable rooms of varying sizes. An additional five rooms are set in a separate building facing the yard; beds are sturdy and comfortable with amenities including TV, a/c and fridge. The restaurant looks onto the pool area, which makes a refreshing addition in Marajó's heat. R$200

★ **Hostel Tucupi** Rua Prolongamento 7, between streets 34 and 35, ☎ 91 98105 5264. This charming house sits on an expansive bit of property, and represents the island's only hostel. Rooms are shared with individual beds. Owners can help organize transfers through Edgar Transport. R$60

SANTARÉM AND ALTER DO CHÃO

The main reason to visit **SANTARÉM**, roughly halfway between Belém and Manaus and the first significant stop on the journey up the Amazon, is to visit the laidback beach resort of **ALTER DO CHÃO**. From July to November the bay is fringed by white-sand beaches, which combine with the deep blue of the Tapajós to give it a Mediterranean look. Alter do Chão sits at the shores of the beautiful **Lago Verde**, surrounded by verdant forest rich in fauna including monkeys, macaws, agoutis and armadillos. The town has a particularly mellow vibe to it, with friendly beach bars and laidback atmosphere – the perfect spot to while away a few days on your journey up or down river.

ARRIVAL AND DEPARTURE

By plane Santarém airport (☎93 3522 4328) is about 15km from the city centre. A taxi from here to Alter do Chão is R$100. LATAM, Azul and Gol have connections to Belém (4 daily; 1hr) and Manaus (3 daily; 1hr).

By boat Boats from Manaus and Belém dock at the Estação das Docas on Av Cuiabá to the west of Santarém.
Destinations Belém (Mon, Fri & Sat at noon; hammock R$200, cabin for two R$800); Manaus (Mon–Sat 11am; 42–50hr; hammock R$180, cabin for two R$600); Porto da Santana (for Macapá; daily at 6pm; 24hr; hammock R$120).

By bus The *rodoviária*, 3km from the city centre, is connected to Santarém by local buses (every 20min; 10min, R$3.25). From Praça Tiradentes in the centre you can catch a bus to Alter do Chão (hourly; 45min).
Destinations Cuiabá, Mato Grosso (daily, 6.30am, 3pm, 4pm & 9.30pm; 36hr); Campo Grande, Mato Grosso do Sul (daily 6.30am & 4pm; 48hr).

ACCOMMODATION

★ **Albergue da Floresta** Tv Antônio de Sousa Pedroso s/n ☎93 99209 5656, ✉alberguedafloresta@ hotmail.com. A laidback, welcoming place offering rustic accommodation that blends in with the jungle's environment: timber walkways lead to a series of cosy rooms, and there's an airy kitchen for guests' use. Bed sheets are an extra R$10. Hammocks R$25, dorms R$50, doubles R$150
Pousada do Tapajós Hostel Rua Lauro Sodré 100 ☎93 9210 2166, ⊚hosteltapajos.com.br. A friendly HI-affiliated hostel with clean tiled dorms equipped with

personal lockers and private baths. The leafy garden has hammocks and a barbecue area and there's also a kitchen for guests. Call ahead to organize airport pick-up (R$70). Lower rates for HI members. Dorms R$50, doubles R$180

EATING AND DRINKING

Farol da Ilha Rua Ladro Sodré s/n ☎93 99236 6704. This breezy restaurant on the riverfront features wooden tables and colourful paintings made by an Italian artist who used to live next door. There are some tasty dishes here; try the *Peixe Ilha dos Macacos*, fish grilled on a banana leaf with shrimp, *farofa* and banana (R$82). Thurs–Sun 10am–10pm.

Mae Natureza Praça 7 de Setembro s/n ☎93 3527 1264, ⊚maenaturezaecoturismo.com.br. This travel agency morphs into a happening bar at night, in particular on Thursday and Saturday evenings (and sometimes Tues) when live bands play *carimbó*, MPB and other Brazilian musical flavours, livening up the entire square. Tables spill onto the street, with drinking and dancing until closure. Tues–Sun 6pm–2am.

SHOPPING

Artesanato Rua Dom Macedo Costa ⊚araribah.com.br. This excellent Araríba arts and crafts shop displays beautiful pieces of indigenous art from ninety ethnic tribes. Mon–Thurs & Sun 9am–noon & 3–8pm, Fri & Sat 9am–noon & 3–9pm.

MANAUS

MANAUS is the capital of Amazonas, a tropical forest state covering around one-and-a-half-million square kilometres. The city actually lies on the Rio Negro, 6km from the point where that river meets

---

INTO FRENCH GUIANA

Travellers mainly only pass through **MACAPÁ**, capital of the state of Amapá, on the north side of the Amazon across from Ilha de Marajó, to get to French Guiana. You'll need to fly to Macapá from Belém. From Macapá's *rodoviária* catch a bus to **Oiapoque** (daily 5pm & 7pm; 10hr, up to 24hr in the rainy season; R$92); there are also 4WD services that shuttle passengers (7hr, can take longer in the rainy season; R$150). In Oiapoque you can catch a boat (every 5min; 10min; €10) across to Saint-Georges, although there is now a bridge linking the two. Brazilian **exit stamps** can be obtained from the Polícia Federal at the southern road entrance into Oiapoque; on the other side you have to check in with the *border police* (*Police des Frontiéres*) in Saint-Georges. From here you can hop on a bus to **Cayenne** (3hr; €35).

CROSSING THE BORDER

If you are not a citizen of a European Union country, the US or Canada, you will need a **visa** to enter French Guiana. It's best to try to arrange the visa before you leave home. If you're going to travel overland, buy **euros** in Belém or Macapá. You can get them in Oiapoque but the rates are worse, and you can't depend on changing either Brazilian currency or US dollars for euros in the border settlement of Saint-Georges in Guiana.

the Solimóes to form (as far as Brazilians are concerned) the Rio Amazonas. Arriving in Manaus may at first seem overwhelming given its near-two million inhabitants, noise and confusion, though it'll have you under its spell soon enough.

Towards the end of the nineteenth century, at the height of the rubber boom, architects were summoned from Europe to redesign the city, which rapidly acquired a Western feel – broad, Parisian-style avenues were laid down, interspersed with Italian piazzas centred on splendid fountains. Innovative Manaus was one of the first cities in Brazil to have electricity, trolley buses and sewage systems. However, by 1914 the rubber market was collapsing fast, leaving the city to slumber in past

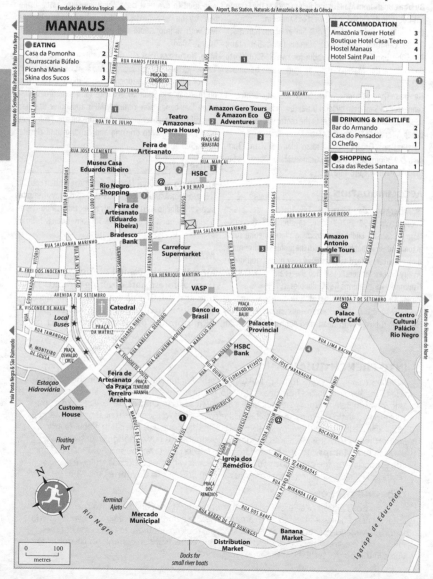

MANAUS

EATING
Casa da Pomonha	2
Churrascaria Búfalo	4
Picanha Mania	1
Skina dos Sucos	3

ACCOMMODATION
Amazônia Tower Hotel	3
Boutique Hotel Casa Teatro	2
Hostel Manaus	4
Hotel Saint Paul	1

DRINKING & NIGHTLIFE
Bar do Armando	2
Casa do Pensador	3
O Chefão	1

SHOPPING
Casas das Redes Santana	1

glories for much of the twentieth century. Today, however, Manaus is thriving again: an aggressive commercial and industrial centre for an enormous region.

WHAT TO SEE AND DO

To start with the real flavour of Manaus, head for the riverfront and the **docks**, a constant throng of chaotic activity set against the serenity of the moored ships as they bob gently up and down. During the day there's no problem wandering around the area (although watch your wallet), and it's easy enough to find out which boats are going where just by asking around. At night, however, the port is best avoided: many of the river men carry guns.

THE PORT AND THE MARKET

Known locally as the Alfândega, the impressive **Customs House** stands overlooking the floating docks. To cope with the river rising over a 14m range, the concrete pier is supported on pontoons that rise and fall to allow even the largest ships to dock all year round. Across the main road from the port is the **Praça Tenreiro Aranha**, where there are several craft stalls selling indigenous Amazon tribal *artesanato*. Along the riverfront is the covered **Mercado Municipal** (Mon–Sat 6am–6pm, Sun 6am–noon), displaying tropical fruits and vegetables, herbal remedies, and all manner of exotic freshwater fish, along with indigenous crafts.

TEATRO AMAZONAS AND AROUND

The sumptuous **Teatro Amazonas** (also known as the Opera House) on Avenida Eduardo Ribeiro (20min guided tours only, leaving every 30min; Tues–Sat 9.15am–5pm; R$20; ☎92 3232 1768) remains the architectural embodiment of Manaus's rubber boom: a belle époque extravagance built with materials brought from Europe and entirely decorated by European artists. Inaugurated in 1896, its main feature, the fantastic cupola, was created from 36,000 tiles imported from Alsace in France. In front of the theatre, the wavy black-and-white mosaic designs of the **Praça São Sebastião** represent the meeting of the waters. The beautiful little

Igreja de São Sebastião, on the same *praça*, was built in 1888 and only has one tower, the result of a nineteenth-century tax payable by churches with two towers.

MUSEU CASA EDUARDO RIBEIRO

This brightly painted rubber boom mansion, **Museu Casa Eduardo Ribeiro**, at Rua José Clemente 322 (Tues–Sun 9am–2pm; free; ☎92 3631 2938) was once home to the governor responsible for Manaus's neo-European spending spree. As such, it's a suitably opulent window on how the city's original other half lived, though pretty much everything that you see, apart from the walls, has been re-created, or, in the case of the antique furniture, brought in from elsewhere.

MUSEU DO HOMEM DO NORTE

The wonderful **Museu do Homem do Norte** at the Centro Cultural dos Povos da Amazônia on Praça Francisco Pereira da Silva (Mon–Fri 9am–2pm; free; ☎92 2125 5323; bus #611, #705, #706, #712, #713 or #715 from Praça da Matriz) houses a collection of over 2000 objects that offer an insight into the life and traditions of the Amazon's tribes. There are informative displays on pre-colonial societies, tribal rituals, medicinal herbs and exhibitions on rubber production.

PALACETE PROVINCIAL

Housed in the former military police headquarters, the **Palacete Provincial** on Praça Heliodoro Balbi, commonly known as Praça da Polícia (Tues–Sat 9am–2pm; free; ☎92 3631 6047), is a cultural and educational centre housing a number of curious museums and exhibition halls; among these are the Museum of Image and Sound, the Numismatic Museum and the Archeological Exhibition. The pleasant leafy square and the building itself are also worth checking out.

BOSQUE DA CIÊNCIA

Occupying an area of approximately 130,000 square metres, the **Bosque da Ciência** (Tues–Fri 9am–noon & 2–4pm, Sat & Sun 9am–4pm; R$5; ☎92 3643 3192, ⓦbosque.inpa.gov.br) on Avenida Otávio Cabral, Aleixo, is a plot of forest home to plenty of animals, including monkeys, manatees, otters and snakes. Don't miss the giant leaf of the coccolba plant that's on display in the museum within the grounds – measuring 250cm by 144cm, it's the largest ever found in the Amazon. To get here catch bus #125, #215, #515 or #517 from Praça da Matriz (1hr; R$3.10).

THE MEETING OF THE WATERS

The most popular and most widely touted day-trip from Manaus is to the **meeting of the waters**, some 10km downstream, where the Rio Negro and the Rio Solimões meet to form the Rio Amazonas. For several kilometres beyond the point where they join, the waters of the two rivers continue to flow separately, the muddy yellow of the Solimões contrasting sharply with the black of the Rio Negro, which is much warmer, and more acidic. Most one-day river trips stop here (see page 306).

PARQUE ECOLÓGICO DO JANAUARY

Most tours to the meeting of the waters stop in at the **Parque Ecológico do Januaury**, an ecological park some 7km from Manaus on one of the main local tributaries of the Rio Negro. Usually you'll be transferred to smaller motorized canoes to explore its creeks (*igarapés*), flooded forest lands (*igapós*) and abundant vegetation. One of the highlights of the area is the great quantity of *Victoria Amazonica*, the extraordinary giant floating lily for which Manaus is famous, and which reaches a diameter of two metres.

PRAIA PONTA NEGRA

At weekends, the river beach at **Praia Ponta Negra**, about 13km northwest of Manaus, is packed with locals. It's an enjoyable place to go for a swim, with plenty of bars and restaurants nearby serving freshly cooked river fish. The bus to Ponta Negra (#120) leaves from Praça da Matriz (every 30min; 40min).

MUSEU DO SERINGAL VILA PARAÍSO

The **Museu do Seringal Vila Paraíso** in Tarumã Mirim (daily 8am–4pm; R$12; ☎92 3631 3632) re-creates the living and working conditions of rubber barons and tappers from the beginning of the twentieth century. The rubber baron's

mansions displays antique pieces of furniture including a 1911 piano, while within the grounds you will also be able to see a rubber-smoking hut where liquid latex was solidified into rubber bales. To get here catch a boat from the Marina do David in Ponta Negra (hourly; 40min).

ARRIVAL AND INFORMATION

By plane The Aeroporto Internacional Eduardo Gomes (☎92 3652 1212) is at Av Santos Dumont 1350, Tarumã, 17km from the town centre. The airport is served by bus #059, #306 and #813; if travelling from the centre, catch a bus from Praça Matriz. A taxi to/from town is about R$75. Many tour operators offer airport pick-up if you're booked with them; Antônio Gomes of Amazon Antônio Jungle Tours (see page 313) offers airport pick-up for R$80 (up to four people), while Geraldo Mesquita of Amazon Gero Tours (see page 313) can organize a van pick-up for up to twelve people (R$120). There is also an express bus from the airport that runs between 3am and 11pm (R$20). Be warned that petty crime is an issue on city buses. When possible, you should take a taxi, uber or transfer service.
Destinations Belém (2 daily; 2hr); Brasília (5 daily; 3hr); Rio de Janeiro (2 daily; 4hr); São Paulo (3 daily; 4hr); Tabatinga (1 daily; 1hr 40min).
By bus The *rodoviária* (☎92 3642 5808) is at Rua Mário Ipiranga 2348, Florês, some 6km north of the centre; buses #201, #202, #203, #222, #214, #223, #227 and #228 connect the station to the city centre (40min; R$3.10).
Destinations Boa Vista (10 daily; 12hr); Porto La Cruz, Venezuela (with a change of bus in Boa Vista; Tues, Thurs & Sat at 7pm; 36hr); Puerto Ordaz, Venezuela (with a change of bus in Boa Vista; Tues, Thurs & Sat at 7pm; 30hr). For Santa Elena in Venezuela, grab a taxi from Boa Vista's *rodoviária* – it's actually cheaper and less time-consuming than the bus as there are plenty of Brazilian drivers keen to fill up with cheap fuel in Venezuela.
By slow boat Slow boats dock at the Estação Hidroviária where you also need to go to buy boat tickets to most destinations.
Destinations (via slow boat) Belém (Wed & Fri noon; 4 days; hammock R$200, double cabin R$1050); Porto Velho (Tues & Fri 6pm; 4 days; hammock R$250, double cabin R$600); Santarém (Mon–Sat 11am; 30hr; hammock R$100, double cabin R$400); Tabatinga (Wed & Fri 11.30am; 6 days; hammock R$350, double cabin R$1000).
By speedboat Speedboats depart from the Terminal Ajato (☎92 3622 6047, ⊕terminalajato.com.br) on the riverfront by the Estação Hidroviária.
Destinations (via speedboat) Tefé, for the Mamirauá Sustainable Development Reserve (daily except Tues 6am; 14hr; R$230); Tabatinga (Wed & Fri 7am; 9hr 30min; R$520).
Tourist information Amazonastur is at Rua Tapajós 174 (Mon–Fri 8am–2pm, Sat & Sun 8am–noon; ☎92 2123 3800,

ⓦvisitamazonas.am.gov.br). There's an information point at Mercado Municipal (Mon–Sat 8am–5pm, Sun 8am–1pm; ⓦmanauscult.manaus.am.gov.br), and an information desk at the airport (daily 7am–10pm; ☎92 3652 1656).

ACCOMMODATION

Amazônia Tower Hotel Av Getúlio Vargas 227 ☎92 3028 3891, ⓦamazoniatowerhotel.com.br; map p.310. This hotel doesn't have masses of character, but it's without a doubt among the best right in the city centre, featuring spotless a/c rooms with modern amenities, gym and pool. Staff are welcoming and helpful. R$140

Boutique Hotel Casa Teatro Rua 10 de Julho 632 ☎92 3633 8381, ⓦcasateatro.com.br; map p.310. A stone's throw from the Opera House, *Casa Teatro* is more of a doll's house than a hotel, with itsy-bitsy rooms and hallways decorated with the owner's little knick-knacks, all for sale, from teapots to old phones. The nine suites have private bathrooms, while the twins – all a serious squeeze – feature bunks and shared bathroom. There's a lounge area that's chock-a-block with curios, and a chill-out rooftop gazebo from where there are unobstructed views of the Opera House. R$310

Hostel Manaus Rua Lauro Cavalcante 231 ☎92 3233 4545, ⓦhihostelmanaus.com; map p.310. Aussie-owned, HI-affiliated hostel with firm comfortable dorm beds with lockers in lovely old high-ceilinged colonial rooms (some dorms with a/c) and a sweetly eccentric and eclectic bunch of staff. HI members get a ten-percent discount. Dorms R$40, doubles R$95

Hotel Saint Paul Rua Ramos Ferreira 1115 ☎92 2101 3800, ⓦhotelsaintpaul.tur.br; map p.310. At just 500m from the Opera House, this is one of the best options in the centre. The a/c rooms are comfortable with modern amenities, TV, minibar and safe. There's also a little pool, fitness centre and restaurant. R$180

EATING

There is plenty of cheap street food everywhere, especially around the docks, the Mercado Municipal and in busy downtown locations like Praça da Matriz, where a plate of rice and beans with a skewer of freshly grilled meat or fish costs about R$9.

Casa da Pamonha Rua Barroso 375 ☎92 3234 7086, ⓦcasadapamonha.com; map p.310. All the atmosphere of a doctor's waiting room yet a godsend for vegetarians who don't eat fish/seafood – though slightly pricey, the

---

JUNGLE TRIPS FROM MANAUS

The nature and quantity of the **wildlife** you get to see on a standard **jungle tour** depends mainly on how far away from Manaus you go and how long you can devote to the trip. Birds like macaws, jabiru and toucans can generally be spotted, and you might see alligators, snakes and a few species of monkey on a three-day trip. For a reasonable chance of glimpsing wild deer, tapirs, armadillos or wild cats, a more adventurous trip of a week or more is required.

There are scores of agencies offering jungle tours and lodge stays around Manaus, and competition is fierce. Touts roam the streets around the Opera House and pounce on tourists at the airport – just ignore them. Whatever you do, do not hand over money to someone who approaches you; always travel with a reputable tour operator. We have listed some of the most reliable operators below.

Amazon Antonio Jungle Tours Rua lauro Cavalcante 231, Centro ☎92 3234 1294, ☎92 9961 8314, ⓦantonio-jungletours.com. Experienced native tour guide Antonio Gomes runs this company, organizing jungle tours from two to ten days with stays at his pleasant ecolodge powered by solar panels 200km from Manaus along the Rio Urubu. Accommodation is in native-style chalets, bungalows and dorms; there's a canopy tower with wonderful views and a floating sundeck with loungers. The exciting activities include alligator spotting, piranha fishing, paddle canoeing and camping in the jungle. Price per day at the lodge from R$250 (full board). Antonio also runs the *Cumaru Pousada*, a smaller lodging option 240km downstream from Manaus along the Rio Urubu.

Amazon Eco Adventures Rua 10 de Julho 509 ☎92 8831 1011, ⓦamazonecoadventures.com. A one-man outfit run by experienced Pedro Neto. His tours are slightly pricier than the rest as he only works with small groups (max 10 people)– seeing the meeting of the waters from Pedro's very own speedboat instead of from a large boat packed with tourists is well worth it, though. He also runs a beautiful floating lodge, and is the only operator doing the Maruaga trail and cave. Tours from R$350 per person.

Amazon Gero Tours Dez de Julho 679, Centro ☎92 3232 4755, ☎92 9983 6273, ⓦamazongerotours. com. One of the most reliable and experienced operators, the owner Geraldo (Gero) Mesquita organizes tours mainly to the Mamori and Juma areas. Great rainforest accommodation is available in Gero's own *Ararinha Jungle Lodge*, located on the scenic and peaceful Lago Arara just off the Parana do Mamori. Tours from R$300 per person.

3

THE THREE-WAY FRONTIER: CROSSING INTO PERU AND COLOMBIA

From Manaus to **Iquitos** in Peru (see page 819), the river remains navigable by large ocean-going boats as well as the occasional smaller, more locally oriented riverboats. In spite of the discomforts, such as long delays and frequently broken-down boats, travellers still use this route as it's the cheapest way of travelling between Brazil and Peru.

The point where Brazil meets Peru and Colombia is known as the **three-way frontier**, and it's somewhere you may end up staying for a few days sorting out red tape or waiting for a boat. The best place to stay is in Leticia in Colombia, from where you can also head out on jungle trips.

If you want to break the journey before you reach the three-way border, you can do so at **Tefé**, around halfway. The main reason to call here is to visit the **Mamirauá Sustainable Development Reserve** (Ⓦ mamiraua.org.br), a beautiful and wild area of rainforest upstream from the town.

Staying at the rustic **Uakari Floating Lodge** (Ⓣ97 3343 4160, Ⓦ pousadauacari.com.br) makes it possible to explore the area from a comfortable base within the reserve.

---

lunchtime buffet (R$42.90 *por kilo*) includes regional dishes like *tapioca* with Brazilian nuts and *tucumã* (palm); the bread is home-made and the freshly squeezed juices (R$6–10) are well worth a try. There are a handful of vegan, sugar-free and gluten-free options too. Mon–Fri 7am–7pm.

★ **Churrascaria Búfalo** Rua Pará 490 Ⓣ92 3633 3773, Ⓦ churrascariabufalo.com.br; map p.310. With multiple locations in and around town, this is an absolute must for any foodie, and in particular meat lovers. This branch, in Vieiralves, offers a *por kilo* lunch buffet (R$89.90), and features 25 types of succulent meat served by waiters dressed in typical gaucho (cowboy) clothing; the buffet features paella, cod, salmon and a vast selection of salads. For dessert, try the *Petit Gateau*, an ice-cream/cake dish (R$25). Mon–Thurs 11.30am–3pm & 6.30–11pm, Fri & Sat 11.30am–3.30pm & 7–11pm, Sun 11.30am–4pm.

★ **Picanha Mania** Rua Ramos Ferreira 1684 Ⓣ92 3234 8054, Ⓦ picanhamania.com.br; map p.310. This large restaurant with impeccable, speedy service specializes in *picanha* (fillet steak), but also offers beef ribs (R$8.90/100g), pork ribs (R$21) and spring chicken (R$21), with individual sides starting at R$5 and up to R$25 for combos; the broccoli rice is particularly tasty. Mon–Thurs & Sun 11.30am–3pm & 6.30–11pm, Fri & Sat 11.30am–3pm & 6.30pm–midnight.

Skina dos Sucos Av Eduardo Ribeiro 629 Ⓣ92 3233 1970; map p.310. This no-frills café packed with fruits just south of the Opera House is the perfect spot to grab a freshly squeezed juice (R$10) on the go – there are plenty of exotic flavours on offer including energizing *guaraná*-based drinks and *açaí*. Mon–Sat 7am–6.30pm.

DRINKING AND NIGHTLIFE

The bulk of the action is outside the centre in Ponta Negra, Vieiralves and Adrianópolis, along with Avenida do Turismo in Tarumã, 18km north of the city centre, which is lined with restaurants and bars (taxi R$80). In the centre, the bars by the Praça do Teatro are frequented by tourists and locals alike – the rest of the centre can be unsafe, so don't head off anywhere on an evening stroll.

★ **Bar do Armando** Rua 10 de Julho 593 Ⓣ92 3232 1195; map p.310. As old-school as it gets, this local institution has beer crates stacked high against the back walls and ancient football strips dangling from the ceiling. For forty years now, it's where people have been heading for an ice-cold beer (Skol R$7), accompanied by exquisite *bolinhos de bacalhau* (*bacalhau* fritters; R$23). Mon & Tues 10am–1am, Wed–Sat 10am–2am, Sun 5–midnight.

Casa do Pensador Rua José Clemente 632, Centro Ⓣ92 9981 9556; map p.310. Formerly a school (it translates as "The House of the Thinker"), this bar and restaurant with tables spilling onto the square is a great spot for a sundowner as you soak in the views of the Opera House. Try the tasty *peixe à delícia* (R$30), grilled fish served with rice and potatoes. Daily 4–11pm.

O Chefão Av. Mário Ypiranga, 1300 Manauara Ⓣ92 3236 2605; map p.310. This longstanding Irish-style pub, set on two floors, has been redone with a *Godfather* theme (not clear why), with checkered wooden floors, a handful of comfy armchairs and plenty of curios dotted about. There are local and imported beers (R$8), bar snacks (from R$18) and burgers (R$20). There's an open-air courtyard at the back and live rock music on Fridays. Daily 10am–10pm

SHOPPING

Casa das Redes Santana Rua dos Andradas 106 Ⓣ95 3234 9814; map p.310. The best place to buy hammocks with a huge variety of all colours and sizes; prices for singles start at R$50, for doubles R$70. Mon–Fri 8am–5pm, Sat 8am–4pm.

Feira de Artesanato Praça Tenreiro Aranha. The best place to buy crafts at reasonable prices is at the Feira de Artesanato by the riverfront. (Mon–Sat 8am–6pm).

Feira de Artesanato Av Eduardo Ribeiro. The Sunday-morning street market that appears out of nowhere in the broad Av Eduardo Ribeira, behind the Teatro Amazonas, displays crafts, herbal remedies and food. Sun 7am–1pm.

DIRECTORY

Banks and exchange Bradesco, Av Eduardo Ribeiro 475; HSBC, Rua Dr Moreira 226 and Rua 24 de Maio 439; Banco do Brasil, Guilherme Moreira 315.

Consulates Colombia, Vereador Manoel Marçal, 651-A Parque 10 de Novembro (☎ 92 3234 6777); Peru, Av. Constelação 16 (☎ 92 3236 0585); UK, Rua Poraquê 240, Distrito Industrial (☎ 92 3613 1819); Venezuela, Rua Rio Jurai 10 (☎ 92 3584 3922).

Hospital The Fundação de Medicina Tropical, Av Pedro Teixeira 25 (☎ 92 2127 3555, ⊛ fmt.am.gov.br), also known as the Hospital de Doenças Tropicais, specializes in tropical illnesses.

Internet Palace Cyber Café, Av 7 de Setembro 1428 (daily 8am–11pm; R$5/hr); Top Cyber, Av Getúlio Vargas 821 (Mon–Sat 9am–10pm; R$5/hr; ☎ 92 9154 5815).

Laundry Lavandaria Brilhante, Rua Lima Bacuri 126 (Mon–Sat 7.30am–5pm, ☎ 92 3232 1214).

Police The tourist police is in the same building as the tourist office on Av Eduardo Ribeiro (☎ 92 98842 1786; or ☎ 190 works in emergencies).

Post office Praça do Congresso 90 and at Rua Barroso 226, at Rua Saldanha Marinho (both Mon–Fri 8am–4pm, Sat 8am–noon).

Brasília

Much of central Brazil, including most of the state of Goiás, the north and west of Minas Gerais and the east of Mato Grosso, is dominated by the Planalto Central (central highlands), a largely dry and savannah-like *cerrado*, once covered with low vegetation and now a centre for ranching and plantation agriculture. In this inhospitable landscape almost 1000km northwest of Rio lies **BRASÍLIA**, the largest and most fascinating of the world's "planned cities". Declared capital in 1960 and a UNESCO World Heritage Site in 1995, the futuristic city was the vision of **Juscelino Kubitschek**, who realized his election promise to build it if elected president in 1956. Designed by **Oscar Niemeyer**, South America's most famous modernist architect, it is located in its own federal zone – Brasília D.F. (Distrito Federal) – in the centre of Goiás state.

Intended for a population of half a million by 2000, today the city is Brazil's fastest growing, with close to three million inhabitants. At first glance the gleaming government buildings and excellent roads give you the impression that this is the modern heart of a new world superpower. Look closer and you'll see cracks in the concrete structures; drive ten minutes in any direction and you'll hit kilometres of low-income housing in the *cidades satélites* (poorer satellite cities). This is a city of diplomats, students, government workers and the people who serve them. Prices are high. Still, there are beautiful sunsets, two or three days' worth of things to see (more if you want to take in the best of Goiás), and an exuberant bar and restaurant scene.

WHAT TO SEE AND DO

Brasília's layout was designed to resemble an airplane (some say a bird, others a bow and arrow). At its centre is a sloped, grassy plain and two central traffic arteries, the **Eixo Monumental** (north/south) and the **Eixo Rodoviário** or **Eixão** (east/west), which neatly divide the centre into sectors: administrative, shopping, banking, commercial and embassy. These are the treeless (and thus shadeless) parts of Brasília where pavements are provided and you can actually walk between many of the sights. North and south of the centre are self-contained **residential areas** – each with its own shops, restaurants and nightlife; each one is spaced a long way from the next. The city is designed for the car, which means you can end up spending a lot of cash on taxis. To take advantage of better and cheaper food in the city's wings, pick an area with several restaurants and bars, take a bus there and walk between *quadras* (blocks).

ESPLANADA DOS MINISTÉRIOS

Brasília's *raison d'être* is the government complex known as the **Esplanada dos Ministérios**, focused on the iconic 28-storey twin towers of the **Congresso Nacional** (the nose of the plane or the

3

3

bird's "beak"). The buildings here, designed by Niemeyer, can all be seen in a day for free (though you'll need to plan carefully around their different opening hours) and are regarded as among the world's finest examples of modernist architecture. The white marble, water pools, reflecting glass and flying buttresses on the **Presidential Palace** and **Supreme Court** lend the buildings an elegance made more impressive at night by floodlights. A taxi or bus ride around the Esplanada in the early evening before the commuter traffic (6–8pm), when the buildings glow like Chinese lanterns, is a must.

PRAÇA DOS TRÊS PODERES

At the complex's centre is the **Praça dos Três Poderes** (Plaza of the Three Powers), representing the Congress, judiciary and presidency. Two large "bowls" on each side of the Congresso Nacional house the **Senate** (the smaller, inverted one) and the **House of Representatives**. There are free guided tours (weekdays every 30min 9am–5pm; English-speaking tours need to be booked in advance; ☎61 3216 1771, ⊕www2. congressonacional.leg.br/visite). You need to bring photo ID, and you cannot come wearing sandals, shorts or sleeveless T-shirts.

Behind the Congresso Nacional on the *praça's* northern side, the **Palácio do Planalto** houses the president's office (tours Sun only 9.30am–2pm; dress code as for Congress), whose stunning interior is dominated by sleek columns and a curved ramp. On weekdays, visitors must content themselves with a changing of the guard outside (Mon–Thurs, Sat & Sun 8am & 6pm, Fri 8am & 5pm).

Also on the *praça*, at its edge near the Avenida das Naçoes, is the **Panteão da Pátria Tancredo Neves** (daily 9am–6pm; free), dedicated to Brazil's national heroes, with murals and painted glass. Nearby, the **Museu Histórico de Brasília** (Mon–Sat 9am–6pm; free) is a curious and largely

empty oblong marble structure balanced on a plinth, originally intended to house a small exhibition on the city's history.

PALÁCIO DA JUSTIÇA AND PALÁCIO ITAMARATI

The **Palácio da Justiça** (interior not open to the public) is beside the Congresso on the northern side of the Esplanada dos Ministérios. The bare facade was covered with fancy – and, to many, elitist – marble tiles during the military dictatorship, but with the return to democracy they were removed, revealing the concrete pillars and waterfalls between them, cascading pleasantly into pools below.

A more worthwhile visit is the **Palácio Itamarati**, the vast foreign ministry building directly opposite (tours Mon–Fri 9am, 10am, 11am, 2pm, 3pm, 4pm & 5pm, Sat & Sun 9am, 11am, 2pm, 3pm & 5pm, must be booked in advance, dress code as for Congress; free; ☎61 2030 8051).

Combining modern and classical styles, it's built around elegant courtyards, gardens, and a surfeit of sculptures, including Bruno Giorgi's stunning marble *Meteor*. Inside, the building's spaciousness, set off by modern art and wall hangings, is breathtaking.

CATEDRAL METROPOLITANA, MUSEU NACIONAL AND TEATRO NACIONAL

Between the ministries and the downtown *rodoviária* (within walking distance of both), the striking **Catedral Metropolitana Nossa Senhora Aparecida** (Mon, Wed, Thurs, Sat & Sun 8am–5pm, Tues & Fri & Sun 10.30am–5pm, but no entry during Mass, and no shorts allowed) marks the spot where the city was inaugurated in 1960. Built in the form of an inverted chalice and crown of thorns, its sunken nave lies below ground level though is well lit, and the statues of St Peter and the angels suspended from the ceiling create a feeling of airiness and elevation.

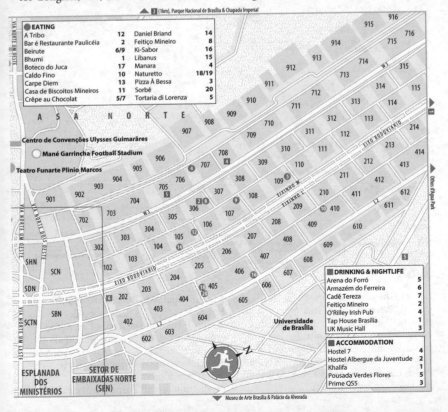

3

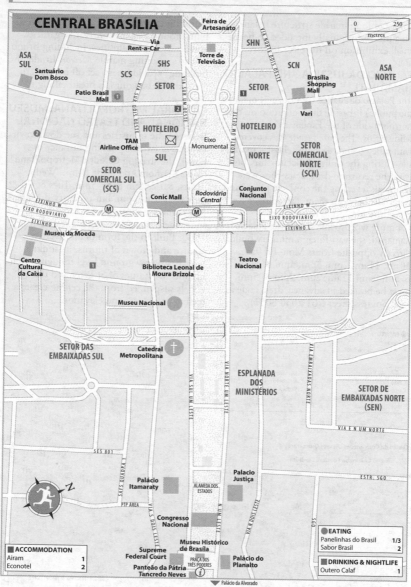

CENTRAL BRASÍLIA

ASA SUL

ASA NORTE

Santuário Dom Bosco

Feira de Artesanato

Via Rent-a-Car

SHS

SCS

SETOR

Torre de Televisão

SHN

SCN

Brasília Shopping Mall

SETOR

Patio Brasil Mall

HOTELEIRO

TAM Airline Office

SETOR COMERCIAL SUL (SCS)

SUL

Eixo Monumental

HOTELEIRO

NORTE

Vari

SETOR COMERCIAL NORTE (SCN)

Conic Mall

Rodoviária Central

Conjunto Nacional

EIXINHO W
EIXO RODOVIARIO
EIXINHO L

EIXINHO W
EIXO RODOVIARIO
EIXINHO L

Museu da Moeda

Centro Cultural da Caixa

Biblioteca Leonal de Moura Brizola

Teatro Nacional

Museu Nacional

SETOR DAS EMBAIXADAS SUL

Catedral Metropolitana

ESPLANADA DOS MINISTÉRIOS

VIA EMBAIXADAS NORTE

SETOR DE EMBAIXADAS NORTE (SEN)

VIA E N UM NORTE

SES 801

Palácio Itamaraty

ALAMEDA DOS ESTADOS

Palacio Justiça

ESTR. SGO

PTP AREA

Congresso Nacional

Supreme Federal Court

Museu Histórico de Brasília

PRAÇA DOS TRÊS PODERES

Palácio do Planalto

Panteão da Pátria Tancredo Neves

Palácio da Alvorada

0 250 metres

N

■ **ACCOMMODATION**
Airam 1
Econotel 2

● **EATING**
Panelinhas do Brasil 1/3
Sabor Brasil 2

■ **DRINKING & NIGHTLIFE**
Outero Calaf 1

Just to the north, also on the Esplanada, the domed **Museu Nacional** (Tues–Sun 9am–6.30pm; free), with its suspended curved walkway, looks something like a crashed, white Saturn half-submerged in concrete, and houses visiting art exhibitions.

Heading up towards the *rodoviária*, on the northern side of the Eixo

Monumental, you'll reach the **Teatro Nacional** (Mon–Sat 8am–noon & 2–6pm). Built in the form of an Aztec temple, this glass-covered pyramid allows light into the lobby, where there are often art exhibitions, while there are three performance halls inside. Most productions are in Portuguese but the venues are also used for classical and popular music **concerts**.

TORRE DE TELEVISÃO

The landmark TV Tower, the **Torre de Televisão**, makes a good place to start a city exploration, 1km northeast of the *rodoviária* (easily reached on foot or by bus #131). The viewing platform (daily 8am–8pm; free) atop the 218m-high tower puts Brasília into perspective, and there's no better spot to watch the sunset. On weekends the base of the tower is popular for its craft market, the **Feira de Artesanato** – great for clothing, souvenirs, and very cheap street food like tapioca, sugar-cane juice and *pasteis*.

JK MEMORIAL AND MEMORIAL DOS POVOS INDÍGENAS

For the **Juscelino Kubitschek (JK) Memorial** (Tues–Sun 9am–6pm; free; ☎61 3226 7860), 1.5km from the Torre de Televisão along the Eixo Monumental, you'll need to take the bus – dozens head up in this direction. Here, a Soviet-like statue of Brasília's founder stands inside a giant question mark, pointing towards the heart of government. The museum has many personal mementos and books of Kubitschek, the extraordinary force behind much of Brazil's twentieth-century

development, and features a fascinating display on the construction of the city. JK himself lies in state in a black marble sarcophagus, backlit by purple, violet and orange lights.

Across the road is another trademark white Niemeyer building, the **Memorial dos Povos Indígenas** (Tues–Fri 9am–5pm, Sat & Sun 10am–5pm; free; ☎61 3344 1154), which houses a good collection of Brazilian indigenous art, much of it from the inhabitants of the surrounding *planalto*. Highlights are the ceramic pots of the Warao, beautifully adorned with figures of birds and animals, and vivid, delicate featherwork.

PALÁCIO DA ALVORADA

To complete your Niemeyer tour take a short taxi or bus ride to the president's official residence, the **Palácio da Alvorada** (guided tours Wed only 2.30–4.50pm, but limited numbers, so turn up at least an hour early to get a ticket), about 3km away by the banks of Lake Paranoá (#0.104 or #104.2 from platform A16 at the *rodoviária*). Some consider this building, with its brilliant-white exterior nestled behind an emerald-green lawn and carefully sculpted gardens, to be Niemeyer's most beautiful – note the distinctive slender buttresses and

3

CRACKING THE ADDRESS CODES

While initially confusing, Brasília's **address system** does eventually make finding places easier than in cities with named streets. For example: 210 Norte (or SQN 210, or SHCN 210), Bloco B, Loja 10, means *superquadra* north no. 210, building B, shop no. 10. The *superquadra* number (210) is the location, the first digit the direction east or west of the Eixo Rodoviário, with odd numbers to the west and even numbers to the east; the numbers increase as you get further from the centre. The final two digits give the distance north or south of the Eixo Monumental. The logic also applies to roads: even numbers apply east of the Eixão, odd to the west; a letter in front indicates the side of the Eixão it runs, eg L for east (*leste*) or W for west. Some other helpful terms:

Asa Norte/Asa Sul The city's two "wings" (*asas*), north and south.

CLN/CLS or **SCLN/SCLS** *Comércio Local Norte/Sul*. Shopping blocks interspersed throughout the residential *superquadras* of Asa Norte and Asa Sul.

EQN/EQS *Entrequadras Norte/Sul*. An area between *superquadras*.

SBN/SBS *Setor Bancário Norte/Sul*. Two bank districts, either side of Eixo Monumental.

SCN/SCS *Setor Comercial Norte/Sul*. Two commercial office areas set back from the shopping centres.

SDN/SDS *Setor de Diversies Norte/Sul*. Two shopping centres (*conjuntos*) on either side of Eixo Monumental.

SEN/SES *Setor de Embaixadas Norte/Sul*. The embassy areas east of the bank sectors.

SHIN/SHIS *Setor de Habitaçies Individuais Norte/Sul*. Two peninsulas jutting into Lago Paranoá.

SQN/SQS or **SHCN/SHCS** *Superquadras Norte/Sul*. Individual *superquadras* in the residential wings Asa Norte and Asa Sul.

3

CLAIMING THE RIGHT OF WAY

Brasília has many cars, few traffic lights and an endless number of roundabouts. At most road crossings you'll see a yellow sign on the road near the kerb depicting an outstretched hand with the words, "*Dê sinal de vida*", a prompt to claim right of way. If you see approaching cars a fair distance away, do as the locals do and raise your hand with authority. As long as you don't do it at the last second, drivers are well trained to cede the road to you. Trying this elsewhere in Brazil may be your last act.

blue-tinted glass. If you go by taxi, make sure it waits for you.

SANTUÁRIO DOM BOSCO

Brasília attracts cults and New Agers of all sorts. One of the prime reasons for this is that in 1883 the canonized Italian priest **Don Bosco**, founder of the Salesians, foresaw the appearance of a "great civilization" here between "Parallels 15° and 20° South". Even if the doors of perception thing isn't for you, the **Santuário Dom Bosco** (easily walkable at 702 Sul, Bloco B, on W-3 South; daily 8am–6pm), built to honour him, is worth visiting for the atmosphere created by brilliant blue floor-to-ceiling stained glass.

ARRIVAL AND DEPARTURE

By plane Brasília International Airport is about 12km south of the city, served by bus #0.102 and #102.1 from platform A17 of the Rodoviária Central (R$5), with the #113 *executivo* service (every 30min 6.30am–7pm; R$12) following the same route and also going onwards to the Esplanada dos Ministérios and the Setor Hoteleiro Norte e Sul (hotel sectors north and south). A taxi from the airport to the hotel sector costs around R$50. From town to the airport try Unitáxi (☎61 3325 3030, ⌨unitaxidf.com.br; 24hr).
Destinations Belém (2–6 daily; 1hr 35min); Belo Horizonte (8–12 daily; 1hr 15min); Campo Grande (2–5 daily; 1hr 45min); Recife (5–7 daily; 2hr 30min); Rio (14–24 daily; 1hr 45min); Salvador (5–8 daily; 1hr 55min); São Paulo (1–4 hourly 5am–9.30pm; 1hr 45min).
By bus Inter-city buses use the new Rodoviária Interstadual at the far end of the Asa Sul (☎61 3234 2185), most easily reached by metrô (Metrô Shopping), but also served by bus #108.8 from platform A4 at the Rodoviária Central.
Destinations Belém (daily; 36hr); Belo Horizonte (6 daily; 11hr); Recife (2 daily; 36hr); Rio (3 daily; 20hr); Salvador (3 daily; 26hr); São Paulo (12 daily; 14hr).

GETTING AROUND

By bus City buses are based at the downtown Rodoviária Central. Useful services include the #131, which goes up Eixo Monumental past the TV Tower and JK Memorial,

and #108 and #104, which run frequently past the Museu Nacional, cathedral, ministries, Praça dos Três Poderes, Congresso Nacional, Palácio do Planalto and the Supremo Tribunal Federal.
By car Lúcio Costa didn't apparently design the city's layout with stoplights in mind; the incredible rush-hour traffic and getting the hang of roundabouts and tunnels may make renting a car more trouble than it's worth. If you do drive, be aware that there are speed cameras all over town.
By metrô The metrô (⌨www. metro.df.gov.br; R$5; system closes at 7pm on Sun) serves only the Rodoviária Central, Asa Sul, Rodoviária Interstadual and satellite cities of Guaráí, Águas Claras, Samambaia, Taguatinga and Ceilândia.
By taxi Metered and relatively expensive (especially at night and on Sun); expect to pay R$20–25 for quick trips and R$40–50 wing to wing.

INFORMATION

Tourist information The city's tourist office is in Praça dos Três Poderes (daily 8am–6pm; ☎61 3214 2764, ⌨turismo. df.gov.br), with a desk at the airport. They give out a free map with information about all the main sights. The *Correio Brasiliense* newspaper has a daily listings supplement.

ACCOMMODATION

There's a lack of centrally located hostels. The hotel sectors are aimed at diplomats and expense accounts, though many do offer discounts of up to fifty percent at weekends (be sure to ask). In general, the taller the hotel, the more expensive, so go for the squat, ugly ones. Cheaper pousadas (though often very poor quality or even semi-legal) are located in

ONLINE BRASÍLIA

⌨**aboutbrasilia.com** Facts and information along with city satellite maps.
⌨**vemviverbrasilia.df.gov.br** Decent what's on guide supported by the Distrito Federal's government.
⌨**vejabrasil.abril.com.br/brasilia** *Veja* magazine's online selection of the city's best restaurants and bars (in Portuguese).
⌨**soubrasilia.com** City listings, including restaurants and bars (in Portuguese).

the wings. The best-value accommodation in town is found through private B&B rentals like ⓦairbnb.com.

HOTELS

Airam SHN Q.5, Bloco A ☎61 2195 4000; map p.318. A good-value mid-range hotel midweek, with fine views from the upper floors, but no weekend discounts. It's seen better days, but it isn't bad value for the price. R$269

Econotel SHS Q.3, Bloco B ☎61 3204 7337, ⓦhoteleconotel.com.br; map p.318. The cheapest of the city-centre hotels. It's housed in a squat grey building that doesn't look too prepossessing, but it's actually fine inside: the rooms are cool and quite spacious, and all have TV, a/c and a fridge. R$239

Khalifa QS5, Lote 30, Taguatinga ☎61 3356 5011, ⓦhoteldiamantes.com.br; map p.316. Way out of town but only 400m from Taguatinga Sul metrô station, the rooms have TV and a fridge, although not all have outside windows, and there's a cheap bar-lancheonete next door and a small supermarket round the corner. R$80

Prime QS5 Rua 800, Lote 60, Taguatinga ☎61 3967 6006, ⓦhotelprime.com.br; map p.316. A good-value budget hotel in Taguatinga (300m from Taguatinga Sul metrô station). Rooms are surprisingly large, many with balconies, some with a/c. It's on a busy road, however, so you may prefer a room at the back. R$110

HOSTELS AND POUSADAS

Hostel 7 708 Norte, Bloco I, Loja 20 ☎61 3033 7707, ⓦhostel7.com.br; map p.316. Clean and modern, with mixed and girl-only dorms, in a residential area near some handy shops. Dorms R$55.90, doubles R$140

Hostel Albergue da Juventude Setor Recreativo Parque Norte (SRPN), Quadra 2, Lote 2, Camping de

3

ESCAPING THE CITY

There are parks and gardens on the outskirts of the city that can be reached on foot or by local bus. Wilder natural attractions and tourist towns a little further out require renting a car, hiring a taxi or taking a long-distance bus.

CITY PARKS AND GARDENS

Parque Sarah Kubitschek If you sicken of all the city concrete, visit this park sprawling west of the TV Tower, which has ponds and walking trails for a quick and easy escape. Daily 5am–midnight; free.

Olhos d'Água Park 414 Norte ☎61 3323 8099. Trails and playgrounds at this park within the residential wing. Take one of the buses running along Eixo Rodoviária Norte to Bloco 213 and walk one block to the park. Daily 6am–8pm; free.

Jardim Zoológico de Brasília Av das Nações, South Exit, Via L4 Sul ☎61 3445 7000, ⓦzoo.df.gov.br. The zoo has more than 250 species of birds, reptiles and mammals. Take one of the buses running along Av das Nações. Tues–Sun 8.30am–5pm; R$10.

Parque Nacional de Brasília SMAN, Zona Industrial,,Asa Norte ☎61 3233 6897. Trails and two swimming pools with running mineral water, about 6km northwest of the city centre. Take bus #128.1 or #128.3 from platform A at the Rodoviária Central. Daily 8am–5pm (last entry 4pm); R$26.

Botanical Garden Setor de Mansões Dom Bosco, Module 12 (entrance by QI-23 of South Lake) ☎61 3366 2141. Gardens with more than 100 species of native herbs, a 9km taxi-ride (R$35) southwest of the city centre. Tues–Sun 9am–5pm; R$5.

Pontão Lago Sul SHIS Quadra 10, Lote 1/30 ☎61 3364 0580, ⓦpontao.com.br. The beautiful people come to this lakeside area to eat, drink and be seen. Walk along the lake and check out the JK Bridge, a series of spectacular modernist arcs. There's no bus so take a taxi (20min; R$40); a line of waiting cabs is there for your return. Mon & Sun 7am–midnight, Tues–Thurs 7am–1am, Fri & Sat 7am–2am.

FURTHER AFIELD

Salto de Itiquira ☎61 3981 1234. A lovely park with a spectacular 168m waterfall 40km from Brasília, near the town of Formosa. There are hourly buses from Brasília to Formosa although buses from there to the park are less frequent. Daily 9am–5pm; R$10

Pirenópolis In the Serra dos Pireneus mountains, a five-hour drive from Brasília (regular buses ply the route). This attractive market town is a popular weekend retreat with cobbled streets, pousadas, river swimming, and numerous arts, crafts and hippy/alternative-lifestyle stores.

Goiás Velho One of the prettiest colonial towns in Brazil, entirely unhurried and almost completely surrounded by steep hillsides. To get there, you'll need to change buses at the state capital, Goiânia. Stay a night or two in a pousada to take in the cobbled streets and museums of this UNESCO World Heritage Site.

3

Brasília ☎ 61 3343 0531, ⊛ brasiliahostel.com.br; map p.316. Brasília's official HI hostel, though it's a bit of a trek from town (bus #134). HI cardholders get a discount. Dorms R$55, doubles R$180

Pousada Verdes Flores 705 Norte, Bloco A, Casa 40 ☎ 61 3447 8694, ✉ pousadaverdesflores@hotmail.com; map p.316. Not great value considering that discounts often bring the prices of city-centre hotels down to much the same level, but it has the advantage of being in a residential neighbourhood, and the rooms aren't at all bad, with a/c and bathroom, although not all have outside windows. R$149

EATING

There are great restaurants in Brasília, though they tend to be pricey. Asa Sul is especially popular, peppered with places ranging from Mexican and Chinese to Italian or fondue; a particularly good area is the restaurant complex in the commercial area of 404 and 406 Sul. Many malls of course have food courts.

RESTAURANTS

A Tribo 105 Norte, Bloco B, Lojas 52–9; map p.316. Excellent organic/vegetarian food including a *por kilo* buffet Tues–Sun lunch only, with a couple of fish/meat options thrown in. Prices are R$65.90 Tues–Fri, R$68.90 Sat & Sun. Tues–Sat 11.30am–3pm, Sun noon–4pm.

Bar é Restaurante Paulicéia 113 Sul, Bloco A, Loja 20 ☎ 61 3245 3031; map p.316. A cheap, local dive excellent for *picanha*, salty snacks and for sipping ice-cold beer as smoke from charring meats wafts over the patio. Patrons range from old men to students and office workers. On Fridays and Saturdays, theR$45/kg buffet includes *feijoada*. Mon–Thurs & Sat 2pm–midnight, Fri noon–midnight.

Beirute 109 Sul, Bloco A, Lojas 2–4 and 107 Norte, Bloco D, Lojas 19–29, ⊛ barbeirute.com.br; map p.316. Two branches of this all-ages institution where you often have to wait for a table; the Asa Sul branch has been open for 44 years. A selection of hot meze goes for R$45, a selection of cold ones for R$42. Daily 11am–1am.

Bhumi 113 Sul, Bloco C, Loja 34 ☎ 61 3345 0046; map p.316. The vegetarian lunchtime self-service is wonderful (R$52.90/kg), although the soups they serve in the evenings are pretty hearty too. Daily noon–3pm (self-service) & 6–10pm (soups).

Boteco do Juca 405 Sul, Bloco A, Loja 4 ☎ 61 3242 9415 ⊛ botecodojuca.com.br; map p.316. A great-value *a vontage* (ie, eat as much as you want) lunchtime buffet (noon–3pm) for just R$15.90, and come the evening (from 6.30pm), there's a low-priced pizza/pasta buffet instead,(R$21.90 weekdays, R$23.90 weekends). Daily noon–midnight.

Crêpe au Chocolat 109 Norte, Bloco C, Loja 5 ☎ 61 3340 7009; map p.316. Sweet crêpes of course, but savoury ones too – a carpaccio in mustard sauce crêpe for example

(R$28.70), with an "Afrodite" (passion fruit and white chocolate crêpe; R$22.80) for afters. Yum. There's a second branch at 210 Sul, Bloco B, Loja 24 (T61 3443 2050). Daily 11am–midnight.

Feitiço Mineiro 306 Norte, Bloco B, Lojas 45–51 ☎ 61 3272 3032, ⊛ feiticomineiro.com.br; map p.316. Even without the live music in the evenings (see page 323), this place would be worth patronizing for the food: a buffet of *comida mineira*, heavy on pork, beans and vegetables, served the traditional way on a wood-fired stove (lunch R$38.50/kg Mon–Thurs, R$44.50/kg Fri–Sun, supper R$82/kg). Mon–Sat noon–midnight, Sun noon–5pm.

Ki-Sabor 406 Norte, Bloco E, Lojas 20–34 ☎ 61 3036 8525; map p.316. Popular student self-service lunch buffet with patio seating. Salads, *feijoada*, grilled meats and decent desserts (R$42.90/kg). Mon–Sat 8am–4pm.

Libanus 206 Sul, Bloco C, Loja 36 ☎ 61 3244 9795, ⊛ libanus.com.br; map p.316. Perennially crowded spot serving up good-value, hearty Lebanese food daily (three meze with Middle Eastern bread R$45.90), with a young and buzzing scene at night. Mon–Thurs & Sun 11am–1am, Fri & Sat 11am–2am.

Manara 707 Norte, Bloco E, Loja 60 ☎ 61 98177 0584; map p.316. This is a simple self-service place with good-quality Brazilian and Lebanese food – hummus, *kibe* and the like (*rodizio* R$49.90 weekdays, R$59.90 Sat). Mon–Sat 11.30am–3pm.

Naturetto 405 Norte, Bloco C, Lojas 16–22 ☎ 61 3201 6223, ⊛ restaurantenaturetto.com.br; map p.316. You can eat well here, selecting from a large menu of largely vegetarian options, pastas, pizzas, with some meat and fish too (R$54.90/kg lunchtime, R$49.90 evenings). There's another, slightly pricier branch at 405 Sul, Bloco C, Lojas 16–22. Mon–Fri 11.30am–3pm & 6.30–10pm, Sat–Sun 11.30am–4pm.

Panelinhas do Brasil Pátio Brasil Shopping mall, Loja 03P ☎ 61 3037 2322, ⊛ panelinhasdobrasil.com.br; map p.318. A Brasília-based Brazilian-style fast food chain (and that's fast food, not junk food), serving, as its name suggests, *panelhinas* (little hot pots) of tasty Brazilian grub, mostly at R$18.30. There's another branch in the SCS at Quadra 3, Bloco A, Loja 10, and more around town (see the website for details). Mon–Sat 10am–10pm, Sun 2–8pm.

Pizza À Bessa 214 Sul, Bloco C, Loja 40 ☎ 61 3345 5252, ⊛ pizzaabessa.com.br; map p.316. This excellent pizza *rodizio* serves forty different slices including dessert pizza. It's all-you-can-eat for R$38.90 Mon–Thurs & Sun, R$42.90 Fri & Sat, so you can try each kind if you dare – though that would be some achievement. Daily 6pm–midnight.

Sabor Brasil 302 Sul, Bloco A, Lojas 1–5 ☎ 61 3226 5942; map p.318. A big, varied lunchtime buffet with lots of salads, fish, meat and good vegetarian options for R$54.90/kg Mon–Fri, R$69.90/kg at weekends. Mon–Fri 11.30am–2.30pm & 6pm–1am, Sat 11.30am–3pm & 6pm–1am, Sun 11.30am–3pm.

CAFÉS, SNACKS, ICE CREAM

Caldo Fino EQN 409/410; map p.316. Great soup (R$10) served nightly under an open tent that workers put up and take down each night. Try the pumpkin and gorgonzola or the *verde* (potato, leek and sausage). Mon–Sat 8pm–midnight.

Casa de Biscoitos Mineiros 106 Sul, Bloco A, Lojas 13–21 ☎61 3242 2922, ⓦcasadebiscoitosmineiros.com.br; map p.316. Decent bakery with bread, cakes, great biscuits and coffee served outside at the rear. Mon–Fri 8am–8pm, Sat 8am–6.30pm.

Daniel Briand 104 Norte, Bloco A, Loja 26, Asa Norte; map p.316. Upmarket French-owned patisserie and coffee-house serving Brasília's best quiche lorraine (R$65/kg). Great for coffee, cake, late weekend breakfast or afternoon tea. Tues–Fri 9am–10pm, Sat & Sun 8.30am–10pm.

Sorbê 405 Norte, Bloco C, Loja 41, Sudoeste ☎61 3447 4158, ⓦsorbe.com.br; map p.316. Artesanal *sorveteria* that has exotic fruit sorbets and unusual, enticing flavours like tapioca, coconut and jabuticaba (one scoop R$10, two scoops R$16). Daily 11am–7pm.

Tortaria di Lorenza 109 Norte, Bloco C, Loja 19 ☎61 3347 0474; map p.316. Gooey pastries (custard-filled éclair R$8) and espresso coffee (R$5) make this an ideal spot for some Continental-style elevenses or a sugar-and-caffeine pick-me-up. Daily 8am–10pm.

DRINKING AND NIGHTLIFE

Arena do Forró Setor de Clubes Sul, Trecho 3 ☎61 99982 0123; map p.316. *Arena do Forró* is the place for those who love swing from the Brazilian northeast. Every Thursday (and sometimes other nights) as advertised on their Facebook page (ⓦfacebook.com/forrodoarena); from 11pm.

Armazém do Ferreira 202 Norte, Bloco A, Loja 57 ☎61 3327 8342, ⓦarmazemdoferreira.com.br; map p.316. Popular with politicians, this place is best towards midnight, when it gets very crowded. The tables outside are very pleasant, huddled under trees. Tues–Thurs 4pm–1am, Fri & Sat noon–1am, Sun noon–4pm.

Cadê Tereza 201 Sul, Bloco B, Loja 1 ☎61 3225 0555; map p.316. Get down to some serious dancing at this popular joint for samba on Saturdays after 5pm, alongside the usual choice of food and *cerveja*. Mon–Sat 7.30am–midnight.

Feitiço Mineiro 306 Norte, Bloco B, Lojas 45–51 ☎61 3272 3032, ⓦfeiticomineiro.com.br; map p.316. A *mineiro* restaurant (see page 322) where you can see first-class live traditional Brazilian music while you dine or drink. Tues–Sat, usually from 10pm.

O'Rilley Irish Pub 409 Sul, Bloco C, Loja 36 ☎61 32442424, ⓦorilley.com.br; map p.316. Yes, rilley: an Irish-style pub in Brasila, and you can really get a Guinness here too (or Beamish stout, or German lager, or British ale). The music is rock, and the bands are live. All in all, a decent craic. Wed–Sat 8pm–2am.

Outero Calaf Edifício João Carlos Saad, SBS Quadra 2, Lojas 4–6 ☎61 3322 9581, ⓦcalaf.com.br; map p.318. Busy after work until late, this is *the* place in Brasília on Mondays for samba-rock, or samba on Tuesdays and Saturdays. Lunch Mon–Fri 11.30am–3pm, music Sun–Thurs 10pm–3am, Fri & Sat 6.30pm–3am.

Tap House Brasília 210 Norte, Bloco B, Lojas 53–75 ☎61 3033 6909, ⓦilovebeertaphouse.com.br; map p.316. With thirty craft beers on tap and loads more by the bottle, this is a place to come to if you care about your beer (although the bar snacks aren't bad either). Tues–Sun noon–midnight.

UK Music Hall 411 Sul, Bloco B, Loja 28 ☎61 3257 1993, ⓦukmusichall.com; map p.316. Known locally as the "UK-Brasil Pub", this smallish music venue spins a Brit-rock-leaning music selection with some reggae, blues and soul thrown in for good measure. Thurs–Sat 9pm–2am.

SHOPPING

Feira de Artesanato The market at the base of the TV Tower sells clothes and crafts, from hammocks to meticulously pin-pricked dried leaves and *capim dourado*, attractive golden-grass jewellery. Fri–Sun 7am–6pm.

DIRECTORY

Banks and exchange Most ATMs take foreign cards; try Banco do Brasil or Bradesco. Cambios are located at the airport, at Pátio Brasil shopping mall (unit 2, by the north entrance), and in the arcade in front of the *Hotel Nacional* behind Conic mall in the centre (indeed, they may give you better rates in the hotel itself – ask at reception).

Car rental Airport branches include: Avis (☎61 3664 9905); Hertz (☎61 3221 4400); Movida (☎0800 606 8686); Unidas (☎61 3365 2955). In town, Via Rent-a-Car (☎61 3322 3181, ⓦviadfrentacar.com.br).

Crime You'll feel pretty safe walking the streets by day, but at night the central area is mostly deserted, so take care. Remember, there are few traffic lights outside the centre and

---

★ TREAT YOURSELF

Carpe Diem 104 Sul, Bloco D, Loja 1 ☎61 3325 5301, ⓦcarpediem.com.br; map p.316. Deservedly the best-known bar/restaurant in town: great atmosphere, renowned politico hangout and reasonably priced. Famous among locals for the best lunch buffet (R$59.90) in the city, and for the Saturday *feijoada* (R$59.90). Mon–Sat noon–2am, Sun noon–11pm.

crossing main roads requires either entering dodgy tunnels or getting through gaps in traffic, so it's often safer to take a taxi instead of walking late at night. Lastly, beware of pickpockets in the *rodoviária* and on public transport at rush hour.

Embassies and consulates Argentina, SES Q.803, Lote 12 (☎ 61 3212 7600); Australia, SES Q.801, conj. K, Lote 7 (T61 3226 3111); Bolivia, SES, Q.809, Lote 34, (T61 3366 2238); Canada, SES Q.803, Lote 16 (☎ 61 3424 5400); Colombia, SES Q.803, Lote 10 (T61 3214 8900); Ecuador, SHIS Q.10, conj. 8, Casa 1 (☎ 61 3248 5560); Guyana, SHIS Q.5, conj. 19, Casa 24 (☎ 61 3248 0874); Ireland SHIS Q12, conj 5, Casa 9 (T61 3248 8800); New Zealand, SES Q.809, conj 16, Casa 1 (☎ 61 3248 9900); Paraguay, SES Q.811, Lote 42 (☎ 61 3242 3968); Peru, SES Q.811, Lote 43 (☎ 61 3242 9933); South Africa, SES Q.801, Lote 6 (☎ 61 3312 9500); Surinam, SHIS Q.9, conj. 8, Casa 24 (☎ 61 3248 3595); UK, SES Q.801, conj. K, Lote 8 (☎ 61 3329 2300); Uruguay, SES Q.803, Lote 14 (T61 3322 1200); US, SES Q.801, Lote 3 (☎ 61 3312 7000); Venezuela, SES Q.803, Lote 13 (☎ 61 2101 1010).

Hospital Hospital de Base do Distrito Federal, SMHS Q.101, Bloco A ☎ 61 3315 1280, ⓦ hospitaldebasedf.com.br.

Laundries There are *lavanderias* in residential *quadras*. Try the ubiquitous 5 à Sec (ⓦ 5asec.com.br), most centrally at 202 Norte, Bloco D, Loja 7.

Post office The main post office (Mon–Fri 9am–5pm) is a small, white building in the open grassy space behind the *Hotel Nacional*, with branch offices around town including 408 Sul and EQN 405/406.

The Pantanal

An open, seasonally flooded wetland larger than Spain, extending deep into the states of Mato Grosso and Mato Grosso do Sul, **THE PANTANAL** has some of the most diverse and abundant wildlife in Brazil. The word Pantanal is derived from the Brazilian word *pantano* (meaning marsh), reflecting its general appearance, but originally it was the site of a giant, prehistoric, inland sea. Today, with an area of 195,000 square kilometres, it represents the world's largest freshwater wetland and is one of the most ecologically important habitats in Brazil.

Travelling alone in the Pantanal is difficult, and the easiest way to experience it is by taking an economical **organized tour** or, if your budget stretches far enough, spending a night or two at a **fazenda-lodge** (called pousadas in the north). The *fazenda*-lodges are generally reached by jeep; those deeper in the interior require access by boat or plane. At least one night in the interior is essential if you want to see animals; three- or four-day excursions will greatly increase your chances of seeing the more elusive species. Most tours enter the Pantanal by road and spend a couple of days exploring in canoes, small motorboats or on horseback from a land base.

There are three main entry points: **Cuiabá** in the north, **Corumbá** in the west and **Campo Grande** in the east. You can visit the Pantanal any time of year, but you're more likely to see the biggest congregation of wildlife from April to October, during the dry season. Renting a car is not recommended unless you hire a local guide who knows the area well to accompany you – you will need a 4WD.

CORUMBÁ

CORUMBÁ was founded as a military outpost in 1778 and rose to prominence due to its strategic location on the Paraguay River. Located in the western Pantanal, today it dedicates itself to the more peaceful pursuits of ranching, mining and tourism (mainly fishing though). Of the three main Pantanal towns, **Corumbá** is best placed for getting into the Pantanal quickly by bus or jeep, and has a few good agencies to choose from, as well as boats for hire, though is more accessible from Bolivia than from Brazil. The town is not safe at night, so you do need to take care and avoid walking the streets after 10pm.

MUSEU DE HISTÓRIA DO PANTANAL

One of the city's highlights is undoubtedly the **Museu de História do Pantanal** on Rua Manoel Cavassa 275 (Tues–Sat 1–5.30pm; free; ☎ 67 3232 0303, ⓦ museumuhpan. blogspot.com.br). The museum, designated a national heritage building in 1992, was erected in 1876 when Corumbá was Latin America's third major river port; curiously, most of the materials used for its construction were imported from England. The museum covers over 8000 years of the region's human history in a highly interactive

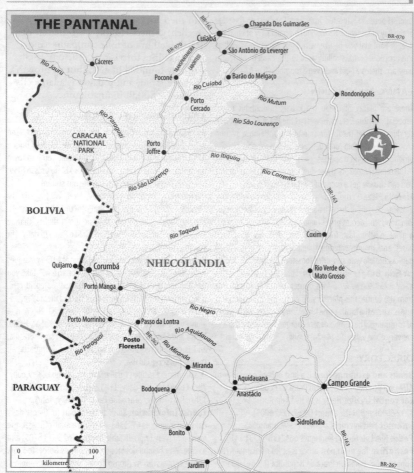

THE PANTANAL

manner, with a variety of archeological and ethnological artefacts complemented by modern resources in a high-tech setting.

ARRIVAL AND INFORMATION

By plane Aeroporto Internacional de Corumbá (☎67 3232 3023) is located 3km from the centre on Rua Santos Dumont. There are four flights a week (Azul) to São Paulo (see page 329). The bus with route card "Popular Nova" runs to and from Rua Antonio João in the centre.

By bus The small *rodoviária* is located at Rua Porto Carreiro 750 (☎67 3231 2033), a 10–15min walk south of the city centre. Destinations Andorinha (ⓦandorinha.com) serve Campo Grande (12 daily; 6–7hr).

Tourist information ⓦ corumba.com.br is a half-decent tourist web portal on the town and surrounding area.

ACCOMMODATION

Hostel Road Riders Rua Firmo de Matos 1 ☎67 3232 8143, ⓦhostelroadriders.com.br. Set in a beautiful villa in a quiet part of town, this hostel offers spacious dorms with a veranda looking out over the river. Most staff speak very little English, but owner Diego is a true traveller, knows all the best spots in the city and gladly chats with his guests when he is around. Dorms **R$50**

Laura Vicuna Rua Cuiabá 775 ☎67 3231 5874, ⓦhotellauravicuna.com.br. A peaceful and friendly place, very neat and tidy with clean rooms (all with TV and a/c), and a quirky line in sculpture (look out for the Don Quijote and Sancho Panza). Breakfast included. **R$150**

★ **Pousada do Cachimbo** Rua Alan Kardec 4, Bairro Dom Bosco ☎67 3231 4833, ⓦpousadadocachimbo. com.br. On the site of a former cattle farm, this delightful

3

colonial pousada is located 5min from Corumbá on the edge of the Bay of Tamengo. It's ideal for a small taster of what the deeper Pantanal will be like, with birds tweeting as well as the occasional duck strolling around the garden. All rooms have a/c, there's a pool and even a football pitch. **R$130**

EATING AND DRINKING

There are plenty of cheap snack bars throughout town, especially on Rua Delamare west of the Praça da República, serving good set meals for around R$20. Being a swamp city, fish is the main local delicacy, with *pacu* and *pintado* among the favoured species. You'll find bars all over town – the more relaxed are those down on the riverfront, where you can usually get a game of pool with your drink.

Fiorella Pizza On the eastern corner of Praça da República and Rua Delamare. In with a shout as the best pizzeria in the Pantanal, with decent prices (around R$30), alfresco tables in a quiet location, fast, friendly service, delicious wood-fired bases and mouth-watering toppings; try the wonderfully garlicky Buffalo with sun-dried tomatoes. Daily 6–11.30pm.

★ **Grill Burger** Rua Eugênio Cunha 11, Maria Leite ☎ 67 3232 9974. A no-frills burger joint a R$20 taxi ride from the centre, this place is well worth the transport cost, and is where the locals come for savoury burgers with plenty of trimmings. The combo deals – burger, fries and a drink – are very good value (R$14–24). Daily 6.30pm–midnight.

DIRECTORY

Banks and exchange There is a host of banks, some with ATMs, on Rua Delamare west of Praça da República.
Car rental Localiza/Hertz is at Rua Edu Rocha 969 (☎ 67 3232 6000) and at the airport (☎ 67 3232 6000).
Internet Nett Internet Café, Rua Frei Mariano 635.
Police Rua Luiz Feitosa Rodrigues 664 (☎ 67 3231 2413).
Post office The main post office is at Rua Delamare 708, opposite the church on Praça da República (Mon–Fri 9am–5pm, Sat 8am–11.30pm).

CAMPO GRANDE

Capital of the state of Mato Grosso do Sul, **CAMPO GRANDE** is a good gateway into the Pantanal on account of its excellent transport links with the rest of Brazil, plethora of tour companies and good facilities for visitors. The city itself was only founded in 1877 but its growth has been rapid, and today it is a large city with some 800,000 inhabitants.

ARRIVAL AND INFORMATION

By plane Campo Grande's international airport, the Aeroporto Antonio João (☎ 67 3368 6050), Is at Av Duque de Caxias. Local bus #409 (R$3.50) will take you into town via central Av Afonso Pena, while Expreso Mato Grosso (R$9; hourly) is the fastest way to get to the bus station.
Destinations Asunción (4 weekly; Mon, Wed & Fri; 1hr 10min); Cuiabá (2 daily; 1hr 10min); Curitiba (1 daily; 1h 25min); Rio de Janeiro (16 daily, no direct flights, change in São Paolo; 3hr 5min–15hr 10min); São Paulo (9 daily; 1hr 40min–2hr 10min).

By bus The *rodoviária* is 7km south of town at Av Gury Marques 1215 (☎ 67 3026 6789). Local bus #87 or #61 will take you into the centre (R$3.50) though you'll need a prepaid card, available from the central information kiosk in the station. Andorinha (ⓦ andorinha.com) serve Corumbá, Rio and – along with Viação Motta (ⓦ motta.com.br) – São Paulo. Motta and São Luiz (ⓦ viacaosaoluiz.com.br) serve Brasília, and Eucatur (ⓦ eucatur.com.br) serve Foz do Iguaçu. All companies serve Cuiabá.
Destinations Brasília (1 daily; 25hr); Corumbá (8–9 daily; 7hr); Cuiabá (15–17 daily; 11–12hr); Foz do Iguaçu (2 daily; 13hr); Rio (4 daily; 24hr); São Paulo (13 daily; 15hr).
Tourist information Kiosk at the airport (in theory daily 6am–midnight; ☎ 67 3363 3116), a small office at the *rodoviária* (very unpredictable hours; ☎ 67 3313 8705) and a large, very helpful downtown office at Av Noroeste 5140, on the corner with Av Afonso Pena (Tues–Sat 8am–6pm & Sun 9am–noon; ☎ 67 3314 9968).

ACCOMMODATION

Hauzz Hostel Rua Piratininga 1527 ☎ 67 3204 1511, ⓦ hauzzhostel.com. Located two blocks from Shopping Campo Grande, with an inviting garden, wooden floors,

INTO BOLIVIA

To get to the border crossing you take the **bus** from the Praça Independência on Rua Dom Aquino Corréa. Leaving Brazil, you should get an **exit stamp** from the Polícia Federal at the border (Mon–Fri 8–11am & 2–5pm, Sat & Sun 9am–1pm), before checking through Bolivian immigration and receiving your passport entry stamp. Most countries don't need a **visa** to enter Bolivia, but if you are from the US you should get one from abroad or pick up your Bolivian visa from the consulate at Rua Sete de Setembro 47 in Corumbá (☎ 67 3231 5605), before you make your way to the border crossing. Entering Brazil from Bolivia is essentially the same procedure in reverse, although US, Australian and Canadian citizens should remember to apply online for their visas at least 72 hours in advance (see page 160).

PANTANAL TOURS

Organized tours inevitably include at least some water-based transport and a guide who can tell you about what you see. Numerous tour companies are based out of the main access towns Corumbá, Campo Grande and Cuiabá; as ever, you get what you pay for, and the cheaper options don't always enjoy a good press.

TOUR OPERATORS

Águas do Pantanal Av Afonso Pena 367, Miranda ☎67 3242 1242, ⓦaguasdopantanal.com.br. This company, located about 200km southeast of Corumbá, organizes programmes in the southern Pantanal, as well as fishing trips and visits to traditional local farms where you can stay overnight. They also own a pleasant pousada offering both upscale and economical rooms in Miranda, between Corumbá and Campo Grande.

Brazil Nature Tours Rua Terenos 117 ☎67 3042 4659, ⓦbrazilnaturetours.com. Dutch/French-run company offering a wide range of activities and packages from one-week-long 4WD trips exploring the Nhecolândia region to cave diving in Lagoa Misteriosa and the Gruta do Lago Azul in Bonito.

Ecoverde Tours Pousada Ecoverde, Rua Pedro Celestino 391 ☎65 3624 1386 or ☎65 9638 1614, ⓦecoverdetours.com.br. Well-established company run by respected guide Joel Souza from his inimitable pousada (see page 329). Keen to foster sustainable ecotourism and offering a variety of nature tours, from birdwatching to jaguar treks deeper into the Pantanal. Stay at a *fazenda*-lodge or camp.

pool and even a piano, this is one of the better hostels in town. The clean, although slightly cramped and pricey dorms accommodate up to five people. Very affordable single room available. Breakfast included. Dorms R$70, doubles R$170

Internacional Rua Allan Kardec 223 ☎67 3384 4677, ⓦhotelinternacionalms.com.br. This is the largest and flashiest of the hotels around the old *rodoviária*, and it's surprisingly well appointed, with TVs and phones in all rooms and even a small pool. Well worth the extra few *reais*. R$145

Nacional Rua Dom Aquino 610 ☎67 3383 2461, ☻reservas@hotelnacionalms.com.br. One of the best value of the budget places around the old *rodoviária*, with a big breakfast featuring tropical fruit and freshly baked breads, cakes and pastries. Rooms come with TV and a choice of fan or a/c. R$85

EATING

Fogo Caipira Rua José Antônio 145 ☎67 3324 1641, ⓦfogocaipira.com.br. An inviting and intimate patio-garden is perfect for feasting on the likes of fried spaghetti with cubes of *carne do sol* (R$42), and, incredibly for a traditional restaurant in this part of the world, there are even a couple of vegetarian options, and imaginative ones at that. Tues–Thurs 11am–2pm & 7–11pm, Fri 11am–3pm & 7pm–midnight, Sat 11am–midnight, Sun 11am–4pm.

★ **Sabor En Quilo** Av Afonso Pena 2223 ☎67 3321 4726. An exceptionally hospitable, high-quality cross between a Japanese restaurant and a typical *por kilo* lunch joint, with eat-as-much-as-you-like prices held, at the time of writing, at an incredible R$20 on weekdays (slightly more on weekends). The spread features everything from freshly prepared sushi to various salads and four-cheese cannelloni. Mon–Fri 10.45am–2.30pm, Sat & Sun 10.45am–3pm.

★ **Yallah** Rua da Paz 95 ☎67 3305 1755. Small Syrian-run restaurant with an English-speaking owner. The menu is extensive and the restaurant serves everything from falafel with pitta bread (R$34) and tabbouleh to *kibbe* (fried bulgur and minced meat) and Moroccan rice with chicken and cashew nuts (R$27). The beef kofta (R$37) is good value for money, but avoid the overpriced starter *trio da pastas* (R$30) that is basically some hummus, yoghurt and baba ganoush with bread. Tues–Thurs 11am–10pm, Fri & Sat 11am–11pm, Sun 10.30am–5pm.

DIRECTORY

Banks and exchange There are ATMs that accept foreign cards at the airport and one at the corner of Rua 13 de Maio with Afonso Pena, opposite the main Praça Ari Coelho.

Car rental Localiza/Hertz, Av Afonso Pena 318 (☎67 3348 5500).

Consulates Paraguay, Rua 26 de Agosto 384 (☎67 3384 6610).

Hospital Hospital Santa Casa, Rua Eduardo Santos Pereira 88 (☎67 3322 4000).

Internet *Matrix Cyber Café*, Av Calogeras 2069 (☎67 3029 0206), has efficient a/c.

Pharmacy Drogasil, Av Afonso Pena 2940 (24hr).

Police Emergency number ☎190.

Post office Av Calógeras 2309, at Rua Dom Aquino (Mon–Fri 8.30am–5pm).

CUIABÁ

Capital of Mato Grosso and one of the hottest cities in Brazil, **CUIABÁ** is located at the dead centre of the South American continent, broiling home to over half a million people, many of whom speak with

3

one of the country's most distinctive local accents. The city's unusual name is of disputed origin but probably comes from an indigenous term meaning "arrow-fishing", a reference to the local Bororo hunting technique. The installation of Brasília as the nation's capital in 1960 revived Cuiabá's fortunes and its recent growth has been rapid. The city is the main gateway to the northern Pantanal.

ARRIVAL AND INFORMATION

By plane Marechal Rondon International Airport (☎65 3614 2500) is located 8km from the centre at Av João Ponce de Arruda, Varzea Grande. Bus #24 (R$3.10) runs between the airport and the small, turnstyle-controlled mini-terminal on the southeastern corner of Praça Ipiranga. Taxis to the centre cost around R$40. The construction of the new light-rail system from the airport had been stopped at the time of writing and doesn't look like it will be completed anytime soon.

By bus The *rodoviária* (☎65 3621 3629) lies 3km north of the centre on Av Marechal Rondon. Buses marked "Centro" (R$3.10) run between the station and can drop you off along Av Isaac Póvoas. Taxis to the centre cost around R$20. São Luiz (⊕viacaosaoluiz.com.br) serves Brasília; Andorinha (⊕andorinha.com) and Eucatur (⊕eucatur.com.br) serve São Paulo, with the latter also serving Porto Velho. Verde Transportes (⊕viagemverde.com.br) serves Cáceres, while Viação Util (⊕util.com.br) serves Rio. Most companies serve Campo Grande.

Destinations Brasília (4–8 daily; 20hr); Cáceres (1 daily; 3–4hr); Campo Grande (16–25 daily; 11hr); Porto Velho (9–13 daily; 23hr); Rio (2 daily; 31hr); São Paulo (2 daily; 24hr-plus).

Tourist information There's a Sedtur office at Rua Voluntários de Pátria 118 (Mon–Fri 9am–6pm; ☎65 3613 9300).

ACCOMMODATION AND EATING

Choppão Praça 8 de Abril ☎65 3623 9101. Traditional and hugely popular open-fronted restaurant-bar countering Cuiabá's ferocious heat with a frigid, turbo-charged fan and delicious pints of ice-fortified, hangover-free *chopp*. They serve traditional *escaldo* (egg- and fish-based soup) and have some fascinating historical photos on the walls. Mains cost around $100 and easily serve three people. Mon, Wed, Thurs & Sun 11am–2am, Tues 5.30pm–2am, Fri & Sat 11am–5am.

★ **Fundo de Quintal** Rua Estevão de Mendonça 1139 ☎65 99974 7742. This outdoor restaurant is beautifully set in a backyard and decorated with various memorabilia. The traditional local cuisine is served in pots, giving your meal a very home-away-from-home feeling. Try the *revirado de carne picadinha*, rice with beef and fried plantain (R$41). Mon–Sat 6pm–midnight.

Mato Grosso Rua Comandante Costa 643 ☎65 3614 7777. Within three blocks of Praça da República, this place has decent breakfasts and offers excellent-value rooms with private showers, TVs and a/c. R$130

O Regionalíssimo Av Manoel José de Arruda 1410, Museu do Rio ☎65 3623 6881. Excellent, moderately

---

PANTANAL WILDLIFE

First-time visitors to the Pantanal will be struck by the sheer quantity of **animals** that populate the region, allowing for some great photo opportunities. Undoubtedly the most visible inhabitants of the region are the **waterbirds**, vast flocks of egrets, cormorants and ibises that flush in the wake of your boat as you cruise the channels – an unforgettable spectacle. The most impressive of the region's waterbirds is the immense **jabiru**, a prehistoric-looking snow-white stork as tall as a man and the symbol of the Pantanal.

Another species that will undoubtedly catch your eye is the **spectacled caiman** (*jacaré*), a South American alligator whose regional populations are estimated at more than ten million. The mammal you'll see most of is the **capybara**, a rodent resembling a huge guinea pig that feeds in herds on the lush plant life, but you will need a bit more luck to see the rare **marsh deer** or the endangered **giant armadillo**. Listen out for the squeaky calls of the **giant otter**, a species that inhabits the more isolated parts of the Pantanal, but which is often overcome by its own curiosity when approached by a boat-load of tourists.

Jaguar and **puma** are present in the area but are active mainly at night; you will need a huge dose of luck to see either (unless you're on the river around Porto Jofre where it's not unusual to see three to four jaguar sightings a day during the dry season), and you shouldn't count on seeing **maned wolf** or **bush dog** either. **Lowland tapir**, looking something like a cross between a horse and a short-nosed elephant, are sometimes seen bathing in streams. You will likely be serenaded each morning by the far-carrying song of the **black howler monkey**, often observed lying prone on thick branches, while the gallery forests are the preserve of the **black spider monkey**, considerably more svelte and active as they swing acrobatically through the trees.

priced *rodízio* with regional dishes in one of Cuiabá's oldest restaurants near the port. In the evening they offer drinks and a buffet of different nibbles (R$30) including fried fish and there's sometimes live music at weekends. Mon 6–9.30pm, Tues–Sat 11am–2pm & 5.30–10pm, Sun 11am–2pm.

Hostel Pantanal Av Mal Deodoro 2301 ☎65 3624 8999, ⊚portaldopantanal.com.br. HI hostel painted in bright colours that organizes trips to the Pantanal. There's a half-decent kitchen and basic laundry facilities. Breakfast included. Dorms R$50, doubles R$140

★ **Pousada Ecoverde** Rua Pedro Celestino 391 ☎65 9638 1614, ⊚ecoverdetours.com.br. Very possibly unique in Brazil, at least at this price level: a tastefully rambling, shabby-chic, five-room pousada with hospitality and atmosphere to spare, crammed with bric-a-brac and antiques. Cats and hens roam freely around the communal library and book exchange to an original vinyl soundtrack of Herb Alpert, Frank Sinatra and Chico Buarque, while birds peck from feeders in a large, happily un-manicured garden with fruit trees and hammocks. Laundry and cooking facilities (free) are also available, as well as free airport and *rodoviária* transfers. Highly regarded tours (see page 327) to the Pantanal can be organized. R$80

DIRECTORY

Banks and exchange There are ATMs that accept foreign cards at the airport.

Car rental Localiza/Hertz, Av Dom Bosco 965 (☎65 3624 7979).

Internet LAN Phoenix, Av Tenente Coronel Duarte 07, close to the centre.

Police Av Tenente Coronel Duarte 1044 (☎65 3901 4839; 24hr).

Post office Praça da República (Mon–Fri 9am–6pm, Sat 9am–noon).

CHAPADA DOS GUIMARÃES AND AROUND

The mountain village of **CHAPADA DOS GUIMARÃES** is located bang on one of the oldest tectonic plates on the planet. It is on this plateau that the true geodesic centre of South America was pinpointed by satellite, much to the chagrin of the Cuiabanos who stick resolutely to their old 1909 mark; the actual spot, the Mirante da Geodésia, is located on the southern continuation of Rua Clariano Curvo from Praça Dom Wunibaldo, 8km away.

Mato Grosso's oldest church, the **Igreja de Nossa Senhora de Santana do Sacramento** (daily 8am–8pm; free), built in 1779, dominates the top end of leafy Praça Dom Wunibaldo. These days, the village has something of a reputation as a centre for the Brazilian "New Age" movement, with crystal shops, health food stores and hippy communities all springing up over the last years.

Over three hundred square kilometres of the stunning countryside around the village of Chapada dos Guimarães is protected as the **Parque Nacional da Chapada dos Guimarães** (daily 9am–4pm; free; ☎65 3301 1133); at 800m it's the highest land in Mato Grosso. Park highlights include the impressive and weird rock formations of Cidade da Pedra, the spectacular waterfalls of Cachoeira da Martinha, and a couple of interesting cave systems. The most spectacular sight of all is the Véu de Noiva waterfall, which drops over a sheer rock face for over 60m, pounding into the forested basin below. All visits must be accompanied by a guide – all of the operators based in Cuiabá, including Ecoverde Tours (see page 327), can arrange a guide and/or transport for a day-trip or excursions.

ARRIVAL AND DEPARTURE

By bus Expreso Rubi buses make the journey from Cuiabá's *rodoviária* to Chapada dos Guimarães (Mon–Sat 9 daily, Sun 8 daily; 1hr 30min).

ACCOMMODATION

Pousada Bom Jardim Praça Dom Wunibaldo 641 ☎65 3301 2668, ⊚pousadabomjardim.com.br. Right on the central square, this clean and very friendly hotel is good value for money and serves decent breakfasts; some rooms have a/c and are nicer than others. R$185

São Paulo

South America's largest city, **SÃO PAULO** – or "Sampa", as the locals call it – makes up for a lack of beach and leisure culture with all the urban buzz and modern grandeur that you would expect from a place that's home to a staggering half of Brazil's industrial output. With an exceptionally vibrant cultural scene, the city boasts 150 theatres and performance spaces, more than 250 cinemas, countless

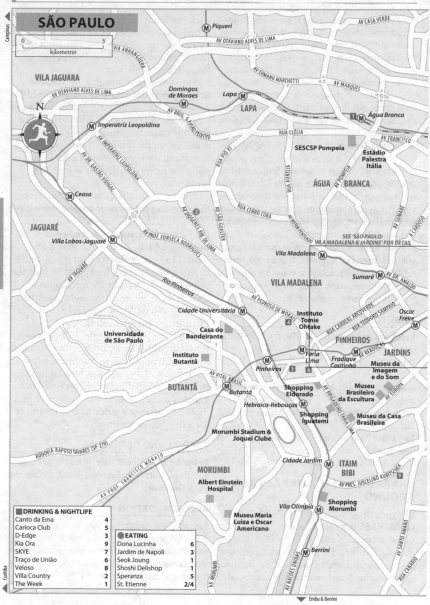

SÃO PAULO

0 — 3
kilometres

VILA JAGUARA

Domingos de Moraes
Lapa Ⓜ
LAPA

Piqueri Ⓜ

AV CASA VERDE
AV OTAVIANO ALVES DE LIMA
VIA ANHANGUERA
Campinas
AV OTAVIANO ALVES DE LIMA
AV ERMANO MARCHETTI
AV MARQUÊS

Imperatriz Leopoldina Ⓜ
AV BRIG. GAVIÃO PEIXOTO
AV IMPERATRIZ LEOPOLDINA
AV DR. GASTÃO VIDIGAL

Água Branca Ⓜ
AV FRANCISCO
RUA CLÉLIA
SESCSP Pompeia
Estádio Palestra Itália
ÁGUA BRANCA
RUA PIO XI
RUA AURÉLIA
AV POMPEIA

Ceasa Ⓜ
JAGUARÉ

Villa Lobos-Jaguaré Ⓜ
AV PROF. FONSECA RODRIGUES
AV DIOGENES RIB. DE LIMA
AV SÃO GUALTER
RUA CERRO CORÁ
AV HEITOR PENTEADO

SEE 'SÃO PAULO: VILA MADALENA & JARDINS' FOR DETAIL

Vila Madalena Ⓜ
AV SUMARÉ
R. CARDOSO
Sumaré Ⓜ AV DR. ARNALDO

AV JAGUARÉ
Rio Pinheiros

VILA MADALENA
AV PEDROSO DE MORAIS

Oscar Freire Ⓜ
RUA TEODORO SAMPAIO
RUA CARDEAL ARCOVERDE

Cidade Universitária Ⓜ
Instituto Tomie Ohtake

Universidade de São Paulo
Casa do Bandeirante
PINHEIROS
JARDINS

Instituto Butantã
Faria Lima Ⓜ
Fradique Coutinho
AV REBOUÇAS
Museu da Imagem e do Som

AV VITAL BRASIL
Pinheiros Ⓜ
Shopping Eldorado
Museu Brasileiro da Escultura
AV EUROPA

BUTANTÃ
Butantã Ⓜ
Hebraica-Rebouças
Shopping Iguatemi
AV BRIGADEIRO FARIA LIMA
Museu da Casa Brasileira

RODOVIA RAPOSO TAVARES (SP-270)
Morumbi Stadium & Joquei Clube

Cidade Jardim Ⓜ
ITAIM BIBI
AV PRES. JUSCELINO KUBITSCHEK

AV PROF. FRANCISCO MORATO
MORUMBI
Albert Einstein Hospital

Vila Olímpia Ⓜ
Shopping Morumbi
AV SANTO AMARO

AV MORUMBI
Museu Maria Luiza e Oscar Americano

Berrini Ⓜ
AV NAÇÕES UNIDAS
RUA CANÁRIO

Curitiba
Embu & Berrini

∎ DRINKING & NIGHTLIFE	
Canto da Ema	4
Carioca Club	5
D-Edge	3
Kia Ora	9
SKYE	7
Traço de União	6
Veloso	8
Villa Country	2
The Week	1

● EATING	
Dona Lucinha	6
Jardim de Napoli	3
Seok Joung	1
Shoshi Delishop	1
Speranza	1
St. Etienne	2/4

nightclubs and no fewer than 90 museums. São Paulo is Brazil's New York, and there are echoes of that city everywhere: in Avenida Paulista, it has South America's Park Avenue; in the Edifício Banespa its Empire State Building.

As a city of immigrants, with a heritage of Italian and Japanese influx – it has the largest Japanese population outside Japan – this is easily the best place to eat in Brazil. São Paulo's denizens, known as Paulistanos, like to live the good life and party hard at night. While many people will always want

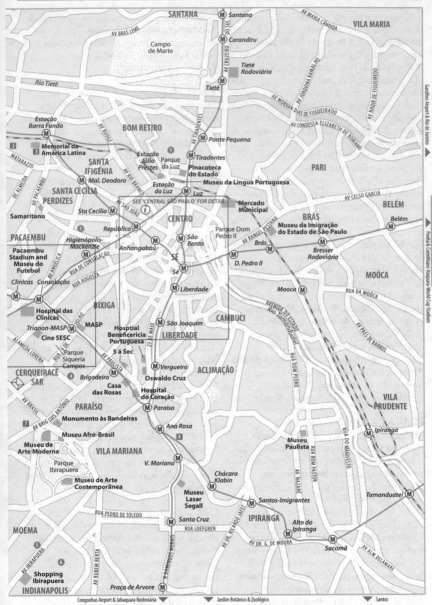

to contrast workhorse Sampa with the beauty of Rio, the city somehow manages its underdog status well, and its friendly population simply gets on with making money – and spending it. If you're someone who gets a thrill out of buzzing cosmopolitan streets and discovering the hottest bar, club or restaurant, then you'll love São Paulo – a city of both pure grit and sophisticated savoir-faire.

WHAT TO SEE AND DO

São Paulo is vast, but the central neighbourhoods and metrô lines are fairly

3

easy to get a handle on. The focal points downtown are the large squares of **Praça da Sé** and faded **Praça da República**, separated by the wide stretch of **Vale do Anhangabaú**. Just north of Praca da Sé is the seventeenth-century monastery of **São Bento**, and beyond lively shopping streets lead to the unmissable **Mercado Municipal** and the much cleaned-up red-light district of **Luz**. **Bixiga** (also called Bela Vista) and **Liberdade**, to the south, are home to a sizeable chunk of São Paulo's Italian and Japanese immigrants respectively. Rua Augusta is a key yet permanently down-at-heel nightlife district, leading southwards onto imposing commercial artery **Avenida Paulista**, with its sprawling upscale suburb gardens descending the hill on the far side. Heading back uphill west of here is **Vila Madalena**, another fashionable district with numerous bars and an artistic feel. Superb museums are scattered right across the city, including the palatial **Museu Paulista**, **Museu do Futebol**, **Museu Afro-Brasil**, **MASP art gallery**, and the Niemeyer-designed complex **Memorial América Latina**. A state-of-the-art stadium, the **Arena de São Paulo** at Itaquera in the east of the city, hosted the opening match and one semifinal of the 2014 football World Cup.

PRAÇA DA SÉ AND AROUND

The heart of the old part of São Paulo is **Praça da Sé**, a busy, palm-tree-lined square dominated by the large but unremarkable neo-Gothic **Catedral Metropolitana** (Mon–Fri 7.30am–7pm, Sat 7.30am–5pm, Sun 7.30am–6pm; free), completed in 1954. On the opposite side of the square, along Rua Boa Vista, is the whitewashed **Pátio do Colégio**, a replica of the chapel and college founded in 1554 by the Jesuit mission. Next door the run-of-the-mill collection of relics at the **Museu Anchieta** (Tues–Fri 9am–4.45pm, Sat & Sun 9am–4.30pm; R$8) is best bypassed in favour of its lovely patio café. Around the corner is São Paulo's sole remaining eighteenth-century manor house, the **Solar da Marquesa de Santos** (Rua Roberto Simonsen 136; Tues–Sun 9am–5pm; free), with a few displays telling the story of the city. Of the three colonial-era churches

near Sé, the seventeenth-century **Igreja de São Francisco** (daily 7.30am–7pm), two blocks west at Largo de São Francisco 133, is the best preserved and features an elaborate high altar.

SÃO BENTO

Heading northeast towards **São Bento** you'll meet the high-rises of the **Triângulo**, São Paulo's traditional banking district. The **Edifício Martinelli** (Av São João 35) was the city's first skyscraper at thirty storeys, although the views are best from atop the 36-floor **Edifício Banespa** (aka Farol Santander; Rua João Brícola 24; Tues–Sat 9am–7pm, Sun 9am–5pm; R$20; ID required), which was modelled after New York's Empire State Building.

A block away, the **Mosteiro São Bento** (Mon–Fri 6am–6.40pm, Sat & Sun 6am–noon & 4–6.40pm; free) has a church dating from 1598, though the impressive complex has been renovated multiple times, and is still home to a community of Benedictine monks who sing Gregorian chants early on Sundays. Take in busy market street Rua 25 de Março before moving on to Rua da Cantareira, where you'll find the city's **Mercado Municipal** (Mon–Sat 6am–6pm, Sun 6am–4pm), completed in 1933 and featuring stained-glass windows with rural plantation scenes. Countless food stalls sell exotic fruits plus trademark thick-wedge mortadella sandwiches and *pasteis de bacalhau* (saltfish pasties). Upstairs are some terrific bars and restaurants – a mob scene at weekends.

LUZ

From the Mercado Municipal it's five blocks' walk northwest to **Luz**, a red-light district now in the midst of a huge government renovation project. Close to the metrô at the head of Avenida Cásper Líbero you'll find São Paulo's grand train station, **Estação da Luz**, built by the British in 1901. Though gutted by fire in 1946, you can still appreciate much of its elegant original decoration. Behind the station, the startlingly tropical **Parque da Luz** (Tues–Sun 9am–6pm) was São Paulo's first public garden, dating from 1800. Its bandstands and ponds are proof of a ritzy

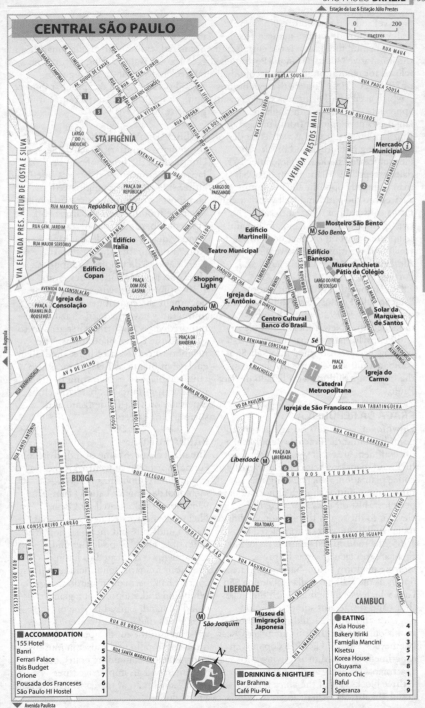

Estação da Luz & Estação Júlio Prestes

CENTRAL SÃO PAULO

0   200
metres

STA IFIGÊNIA

LARGO DO AROUCHE

PRAÇA DA REPÚBLICA

República

LARGO DO PAISSANDU

Mercado Municipal

Edifício Martinelli

Mosteiro São Bento

São Bento

Teatro Municipal

Edifício Banespa

Museu Anchieta
Pátio de Colégio

Edifício Italia

Edifício Copan

PRAÇA DOM JOSÉ GASPAR

Shopping Light

Igreja da S. Antônio

Solar da Marquesa de Santos

Igreja da Consolação

PRAÇA FRANKLIN D. ROOSEVELT

Anhangabau

Centro Cultural Banco do Brasil

PRAÇA DA BANDEIRA

Sé

PRAÇA DA SÉ

Igreja do Carmo

Catedral Metropolitana

Igreja de São Francisco

Liberdade

PRAÇA DA LIBERDADE

BIXIGA

LIBERDADE

São Joaquim

Museu da Imigração Japonesa

CAMBUCI

N

Avenida Paulista

■ ACCOMMODATION	
155 Hotel	4
Banri	5
Ferrari Palace	2
Ibis Budget	3
Orione	7
Pousada dos Franceses	6
São Paulo HI Hostel	1

■ DRINKING & NIGHTLIFE	
Bar Brahma	1
Café Piu-Piu	2

● EATING	
Asia House	4
Bakery Itiriki	6
Famiglia Mancini	3
Kisetsu	5
Korea House	7
Okuyama	8
Ponto Chic	1
Raful	2
Speranza	9

past, yet today the sculptures lining its walkways provide a more modern feel.

Back behind the station is the entrance to the innovative **Museu da Língua Portuguesa** (closed for renovation until the second half of 2019). A series of interactive exhibitions – which even non-Portuguese speakers will appreciate – guides you through the language's development from Portugal to Brazilian literary greats, as well as modern urban slang in football and music. The **Pinacoteca do Estado** (Av Tiradentes 141; daily except Tues 10am–6pm; R$6, Sat free) is directly opposite the museum, adjacent to the park, and well worth a visit for its collection of nineteenth- and twentieth-century Brazilian painting and sculpture – start on the first floor where you'll find the most impressive pieces by Almeida Junior, Cavalcanti, Segall and Portinari.

São Paulo's other great train station, **Estação Júlio Prestes**, lies two blocks west of Luz, built in 1926 and said to be modelled after New York's Grand Central and Pennsylvania stations. Its Great Hall has now been transformed into **Sala São Paulo**, a 1500-seat concert hall home to the Orquestra Sinfônica do Estado de São Paulo.

PRAÇA DA REPÚBLICA

Downtown São Paulo's other main focal point is around the **Praça da República**, a once-affluent area that was the site of high-end mansions belonging to wealthy coffee plantation owners during the nineteenth century, though almost all have been lost. Just off the *praça*, take the elevator to the top of the 42-storey **Edifício Italia** (Av Ipiranga 344), completed in 1965; the rooftop restaurant is tacky but there are spectacular vistas from the viewing platform (Mon–Sat 3–5pm; free). South of the Edifício Italia is **Avenida São Luis**, which was once lined with high-class shops and still retains some of its old elegance, though the building that most stands out is famed Brasília architect Oscar Niemeyer's S-shaped **Edifício Copan** – an experiment in mixed urban living with apartments available at all prices.

Three blocks east of the *praça* is the grand **Theatro Municipal**, an enticing mix of Art Nouveau and Renaissance styles and the city's premier venue for classical music, decorated with mirrors, Italian marble and gold leaf (viewable during performances or by free guided tour, in Portuguese Tues–Fri 11am, 3pm & 5pm, Sat 2pm & 3pm, in English Tues–Fri 11am, Sat noon; phone ☎ 11 3053 2092).

LIBERDADE AND BIXIGA

Immediately south of **Praça da Sé**, **Liberdade** is the home of São Paulo's Japanese community, its streets lined on either side with overhanging red lampposts. You'll find great traditional Japanese food here on the streets off **Praça da Liberdade** (site of a good Sunday market), as well as Chinese and Korean restaurants and stores. There is even a **Museu da Imigração Japonesa** (Rua São Joaquim 381; Tues–Sun 1.30–5pm; R$10), whose three floors document the contributions Japanese immigrants have made in Brazil in the hundred years since they first arrived to work on the coffee plantations. The neighbourhood west of here, the Italian enclave of **Bixiga** or Bela Vista, is also a fantastic place to eat, coming to life at night with restaurants, bars and clubs, especially on Rua 13 de Maio and surrounding streets.

BARRA FUNDA

The main claim to fame of industrial **Barra Funda** (northwest of Centro) is the extraordinary modernist complex **Memorial da América Latina** (Tues–Sun 9am–6pm; free), created by Oscar Niemeyer and located next to the giant Barra Funda bus and metrô station. The series of monolithic buildings and monuments is dedicated to Latin American solidarity, and includes a library, concert hall, permanent outdoor exhibition and sculpture of a giant bloodied hand. Linked by one of Niemeyer's trademark curvaceous walkways, to the south side of the highway is the anthropological museum **Museu Darcy Ribeiro**, containing crafts, bright costumes, and an impressive three-dimensional map of the continent beneath a glass floor.

ESTÁDIO DO PACAEMBU AND MUSEU DO FUTEBOL

A bus or taxi ride south from metrô Barra Funda along Avenida Pacaembu brings you to **Estádio do Pacaembu** (also reached by bus #917M from Av Paulista or #917H from Vila Madalena, or a 15min walk from metrô Paulista or Clínicas), former home to Corinthians football club, who now play at the Arena de São Paulo in Itaquera. The impressive 40,000-seat stadium was designed by Brasília's other great designer, Lúcio Costa; it stands at one end of a large square, Praça Charles Miller, that is named after the Englishman who introduced football to Brazil. The main reason for coming here, however, is the superb **Museu do Futebol** (Tues–Fri 9am–5pm, Sat, Sun & public holidays 9am–6pm, last entrance 5pm, closes early on match days; R$10; allow 3hr). Piecing together how football became Brazil's greatest national obsession through enthralling multimedia displays, the museum has an appeal far beyond the game itself, from the players, fans and commentators to the controversies of race and dictatorship in twentieth-century Brazil.

AVENIDA PAULISTA AND JARDINS

South of Bixiga, **Avenida Paulista** is central São Paulo's third major focal point, a 3km stretch that in the early 1900s was lined with Art Nouveau mansions owned by coffee barons. Redeveloped in the 1960s, it's now lined with skyscrapers topped by helipads and TV antennas dramatically lit by different colours at night. The **Casa das Rosas** (Av Paulista 35; Tues–Sat 10am–10pm, Sun 10am–6pm; free) gives some sense of what the avenue once looked like, a French-style mansion set in a walled garden that's a huge contrast to the surrounding steel-and-glass hulks, and now a state-run museum. Also worth a look is the **Museu de Arte de São Paulo** or **MASP** (Av Paulista 1578; Tues, Wed & Fri–Sun 10am–6pm, Thurs 10am–8pm; R$30, free Tues), standing on four red stilts floating above the ground and allowing a view of the city behind. Upstairs contains a large collection of Western art, while the basement below has a very enjoyable and reasonable buffet. Opposite MASP make sure you take a stroll along the trails of the eminently peaceful Parque Siqueira Campos, pure Atlantic forest landscaped by Roberto Burle Marx.

Separated from Bixiga by Avenida Paulista is **Jardins**, one of São Paulo's most expensive and fashionable neighbourhoods, modelled in 1915 according to the principles of the British Garden City movement, with cool, leafy streets leading down the hill. Actually a compendium of three smaller neighbourhoods – Jardim America, Jardim Europa and Jardim Paulista – it's home to swanky villas, top-end restaurants and bars. Have a walk on and around **Rua Oscar** and **Rua Augusta**, with their expensive shops and boutiques.

VILA MADALENA, PINHEIROS AND ITAIM BIBI

West of Jardins, the *bairro* of **Vila Madalena** is also chock-a-block with nightlife and restaurants, though with a younger, more bohemian feel than its neighbour. Southwards, **Pinheiros** is rougher around the edges but also home to some decent nightlife. Cutting through Pinheiros is Rua Teodoro Sampaio, a street lined with music stores, some of which feature free music performances on weekends.

Further south, **Itaim Bibi** is a chic neighbourhood with galleries, bars and more good restaurants. **Avenida Brig. Faria Lima** is the main drag here, while the nearby **Museu Brasileiro da Escultura** at Av Europa 218 (Tues–Sun 10am–6pm; free) is home to travelling exhibits of Brazilian artists and sculptors.

South of Itaim Bibi is the impressive new financial district, **Berrini**, within whose skyscrapers the largest sums of money in Latin America are now transferred. South again, and worth driving over (especially when dramatically lit at night), is the 138m-tall, cable-stayed **Octavio Frias de Oliveira Bridge**, a picture-postcard image with separate roadways passing under a giant concrete "X".

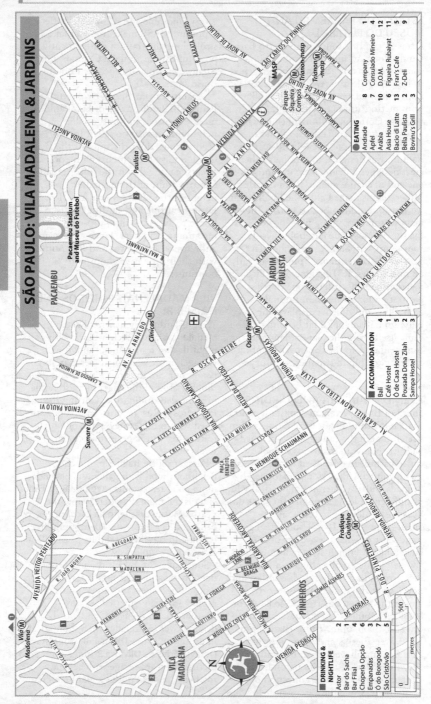

SÃO PAULO: VILA MADALENA & JARDINS

PACAEMBU

Pacaembu Stadium
and Museu do Futebol

MASP

VILA MADALENA

JARDIM PAULISTA

PINHEIROS

● EATING			
Andrade	8	Company	1
Apfel	7	Consulado Mineiro	4
Arábia	10	D.O.M.	12
Asia House	6	Figueira Rubaiyat	11
Bacio di Latte	13	Fran's Cafe	5
Bella Paulista	2	Z-Deli	9
Bovinu's Grill	3		

■ ACCOMMODATION	
Bali	4
Café Hostel	1
Ô de Casa Hostel	5
Pousada Dona Zilah	2
Sampa Hostel	3

■ DRINKING & NIGHTLIFE	
Astor	2
Bar do Sacha	4
Bar Filial	1
Choperia Opção	6
Empanadas	3
O do Borogodó	7
São Cristóvão	5

0 500 metres

PARQUE DO IBIRAPUERA

South of Jardins and sandwiched between Itaim Bibi and Vila Mariana, **Moema** is a wealthy district with some really good restaurants, although its main feature is the **Parque do Ibirapuera** (daily 5am–midnight; free; 10min walk from the bus stops on Av Brigadeiro Luís Antônio), opened in 1954 to celebrate the 400th anniversary of the founding of São Paulo. Outside its main north entrance is the **Monumento às Bandeiras**, a 1953 sculpture by Victor Brecheret that celebrates a *bandeirante* expedition. Inside the park, a triad of inspiring Niemeyer-designed buildings houses the **Museu de Arte Contemporânea** (Tues 10am–9pm, Wed–Sun 10am–6pm; free), with regularly rotated works by twentieth-century European and Brazilian artists; the **Museu de Arte Moderna** (Tues–Sun 10am–6pm; R$6; free Sat), a smaller museum featuring mostly temporary exhibits of Brazilian artists; and the **Auditório Ibirapuera** concert hall. The **Museu Afro-Brasil** in the northern part of the park (Gate 10, just off Av Pedro Álvares Cabral; Tues–Sun 10am–5pm; R$6) is an interesting collection exploring the African–Brazilian experience through paintings and artefacts, with sections on religion, slavery and oral history, as well as visiting exhibitions and occasional theatre.

VILA MARIANA AND IPIRANGA

East of the park is the **Museu Lasar Segall**, at Rua Berta 111 (daily except Tues 11am–7pm; free), which houses the work of the Latvian-born, naturalized-Brazilian painter, originally a member of the German Expressionist movement. The **Museu Paulista** (aka Museu do Ipiranga) in nearby Ipiranga is currently closed for repairs and is not expected to reopen until 2022.

ARRIVAL AND DEPARTURE

By plane São Paulo has two airports: Guarulhos, about 25km from downtown, serves international destinations and many domestic flights; and Congonhas, right in the city, for the shuttle (Ponte Aérea) to Rio and other relatively local domestic flights. From Congonhas taxis to downtown cost about R$39; from Guarulhos about R$120. An executive bus service (ⓦ www.airportbusservice.com.br) runs

CRIME
São Paulo has high crime. Keep valuables hidden and be careful at all times, especially in crowded areas like bus stations and markets. At night, much of downtown, including Luz and Praça da República through to São Bento, gets very seedy.

between the two airports, and from Guarulhos to Tietê bus station and Praça da República 343 (24hr; infrequent at night, with no buses from Praça Republica to the airport between 11.40pm and 5.40am), and from Guarulhos to the Paulista/Augusta hotel circuit and other central destinations (approximately hourly 6am–11pm); all services R$48.80. The cheapest option is local bus #257 from Guarulhos to Tatuape metrô station (5am–midnight; R$5.95; 1hr 30min). CPTM (metropolitan overground) line 13, due for completion in 2015 but delayed indefinitely due to technical problems, should eventually connect Guarulhos airport with Engenheiro Goulart station on line 12. Metrô monorail line 17 is due to serve Congonhas airport from 2018.
Destinations Belo Horizonte (27–42 daily; 1hr 15min); Foz do Iguaçu (10–11 daily; 1hr 40min); Salvador (20–25 daily; 2hr 20min); Recife (16–21 daily; 3hr 5min); Rio (2–7 hourly 6am–11pm).
By bus Almost all inter-state and international buses arrive at the vast Tietê Rodoviária north of the centre, served by metrô line 1. Rodoviária Barra Funda (on metrô line 3) serves towns in the west of São Paulo State and some inter-state services to the west, while Rodoviária Jabaquara (at the southern end of metrô line 1) serves Santos and much of the São Paulo coast.
Destinations Asunción (2 daily; 20hr); Belo Horizonte (30 daily, mostly overnight; 8hr 30min); Brasília (10 daily; 16hr); Buenos Aires (9 weekly; 36hr); Curitiba (1–2 hourly; 6hr 20min); Foz do Iguaçu (5 daily; 17hr); Montevideo (2 weekly; 30hr); Ouro Preto (6 daily; 12hr); Paraty (5 daily; 5hr); Rio (4–8 hourly; 6hr); Salvador (2 daily; 33hr); Santiago de Chile (2 weekly; 53hr).

GETTING AROUND

Avoid travelling around 4–7pm when the metrô and road network suffer from serious overcrowding.
By metrô Quiet, comfortable and fast, São Paulo's metrô (ⓦ www.metro.sp.gov.br) is by far the easiest way to move around the city. Although only five lines of the metropolitan train system are actually classed as metrô lines – there are also overground (CPTM) lines, plus an underground line run by an independent firm – it matters little because a R$3.80 ticket covers all twelve lines with free interchange between all of them. The metrô runs every day from 5am until midnight, although the ticket booths close at 10pm.

3

You can buy a bunch of tickets in one go to avoid having to queue each time, and there are integrated bus and metrô tickets too.

By bus Sampa's notoriously congested roads and 1500 bus routes make navigating the city above ground seem unduly complicated; it's best to use buses from metrô stations, where you can ask advice on which lines go to your destination. Standard fares are R$3.80. Buses run 4am–midnight.

By taxi Ordinary taxis are metered and start at R$4.50. You can also call the following radio-taxi companies: Coopertax (❶ 11 2095 6000, ⓦ coopertax.com.br); Ligue Táxi (❶ 11 2101 3030, ⓦ liguetaxi.com.br); Rádio-Táxi Vermelho e Branco (❶ 11 3146 4000, ⓦ radiotaxivermelhoebranco.com.br/).

INFORMATION AND TOURS

Tourist information São Paulo Turismo (❶ 11 2226 0400, ⓦ cidadedesaopaulo.com) maintains information booths, located in Praça República (daily 9am–6pm), on Av Paulista at Parque Siqueira Campos (mobile van, usually there Mon–Sat 9am–4pm), in Tietê bus terminal (daily 6am–10pm) and at Congonhas airport arrivals (daily 7am–10pm); there are also tourist information desks at Guarulhos airport, run by the airport authorities.

Tour operators São Paulo Free Walking Tour (ⓦ saopaulofreewalkingtour.com) offers walking tours in English (free but tips appreciated): on Mon, Wed and Sat a 4hr city-centre tour starts at 11.30am by the tourist information booth in Praça República; on Tues, Thurs & Sun a 3hr Vila Madalena tour starts at 11am outside Fradique Coutinho metrô station, and a 3hr Rua Augusta and Av Paulista tour begins at 3.30pm at the Banco do Brasil by Consolação metrô station. To join a tour, just turn up 15min before it starts. Linha Circular Turismo (❶ 0800 116566, ⓦ cidadedesaopaulo.com/sp/br/linha-circular-turismo/), is a hop-on hop-off circular bus tour of the city's main sights, with R$40 tickets valid for 24hr, but currently runs only three times a day.

ACCOMMODATION

All options serve breakfast unless otherwise indicated.

DOWNTOWN, LIBERDADE AND BIXIGA

155 Hotel 13 de Maio 731 ❶ 11 3150 1555, ⓦ 155hotel.com.br; map p.333. They bill this as "the most luxurious low-cost hotel in São Paulo", and that's what they try to be. The lower floors get a fair bit of street noise, so go for an upper floor if that bothers you. R$195

Banri Rua Galvão Bueno 209, Liberdade ❶ 11 3207 8877; map p.333. A friendly place with an East Asian feel. The rooms are small, but well kept (including some R$75 "economico" single rooms with outside bathroom), and it's handy for great Japanese dining nearby. R$154

Ferrari Palace Rua Conselheiro Nébias 445 ❶ 11 3224 8087, ⓦ ferraripalacehotel.com.br; map p.333. While not exactly a palace, this modest hotel, located on a side street near Praça da República that's full of motorbike repair shops, is clean and comfortable, with cheap eating places nearby. R$120

Ibis Budget Av São João, 1140, Centro ❶ 11 2878 6400, ⓦ ibis.com; map p.333. A couple of blocks from Praça da República, good value but the last word in characterlessness. Other Ibis Budget hotels are dotted around São Paulo, but the ordinary Ibis hotels (of which there are more) sometimes offer cheaper deals; all are cheaper if booked online. No breakfast. R$183.75

Orione Rua 13 de Mayo 731, Bela Vista ❶ 13 2769 3604, ⓦ orionehotel.com.br; map p.333. Nothing fancy but a simple budget hotel on the edge of Bixiga with a fan and fridge in each room, and lower rates during the week. R$149

Pousada dos Franceses Rua dos Franceses 100, Bixiga ❶ 11 3288 1592, ⓦ pousadadosfranceses.com.br; map p.333. More smart hostel than pousada, in an ideal spot in Bixiga, not far from Av Paulista and walking distance from downtown and Liberdade. Fresh rooms, small garden, guest kitchen and a mix of accommodation. Dorms R$55, doubles R$198

São Paulo HI Hostel Rua Barão de Campinas 94, Centro ❶ 11 3337 3305, ⓦ hostelsp.com.br; map p.333. The downtown area is grimy but this gigantic hostel is near the metrô, safe, friendly and with numerous facilities, including a roof terrace. HI discount available. Dorms R$67, doubles R$169

VILA MADALENA AND AROUND AVENIDA PAULISTA

Bali Rua Fradique Coutinho 740, Pinheiros ❶ 11 3812 8270, ⓦ hotelbali.com.br; map p.336. The mirrors behind the beds remind you that this is primarily a "love motel", and it's often fully booked, but if you can get a room, it'll be one of the cheapest in town. Near Vila Madalena. R$100

Café Hostel Rua Agissê 152, Vila Madalena ❶ 11 2649 7217, ⓦ cafehostel.com.br; map p.336. Small, low-priced hostel, very friendly, if a bit squashed together, with minimal breakfast, but handy for Vila Madalena's nightlife and metrô. Dorms R$32, doubles R$150

Ô de Casa Hostel Rua Inácio Pereira da Rocha 385, Vila Madalena ❶ 11 3063 5216, ⓦ odecasahostel.com; map p.336. A bar at the front with a hostel at the back, this is a fun place, handy for local nightlife, and very friendly, but not the quietest or most spacious. Breakfast not included. Dorms R$55, doubles R$160

Pousada Dona Zilah Rua Minas Gerais 112, Beka Vista ❶ 11 3062 1444, ⓦ zilah.com; map p.336. The only real pousada in town: it has a great location near Av Paulista, friendly, family touches and superb breakfast buffet, and there's always someone on hand to offer local advice. R$345

Sampa Hostel (Vila Madelena) Rua Girassol 519, Vila Madalena ☎11 3031 6779, ⌨hostelsampa.com.br; map p.336. A smart and cosy hostel, with consummate facilities and close to great bars. Breakfast not included. Dorms R$40, doubles R$140

EATING

With its profusion of immigrant communities – notably Japanese, Italian, Jewish and Arab – São Paulo hosts by far Brazil's best selection of restaurants, and you may well feel a need to splurge. Take advantage of the excellent Mercado Municipal at lunchtimes (its upstairs food court is good value, too). A range of cheap *por kilo* restaurants is located along Rua Augusta, north of Av Paulista. Also keep in mind that at night all bars serve food, with Vila Madalena known for high-quality options. Bixiga is the top *bairro* for Italian food, Liberdade for Japanese, with Korean restaurants concentrated in Bom Retiro.

DOWNTOWN, LIBERDADE AND BIXIGA

Asia House Rua da Glória 86, Liberdade ☎11 3106 1159; ⌨asiahouse.com.br; map p.333. Great-value *por kilo* lunch buffet (R$67/kg), with a range of Japanese soups, sushi and noodle dishes. There's another branch at Rua Augusta 1918 in Jardins. Mon–Sat 11am–3.30pm.

Bakery Itiriki Rua dos Estudantes 24, Liberdade ☎11 3277 4939, ⌨bakeryitiriki.com; map p.333. Brazilian and Japanese pastries and savoury snacks, with upstairs seating. Daily 8am–7pm.

Famiglia Mancini Rua Avanhandava 81 (off Rua Augusta) ☎11 3256 4320; map p.333. Established by a prominent local Italian-Brazilian family who bought up this run-down street and turned it into a popular eating venue, this is the flagship: an Italian restaurant specializing in pasta. There's a choice of pastas with a big choice of sauces (pesto, carbonara, *arrabiata* and *palermitana*, for example, all go for R$108), as well as lasagne, risotto and some meat dishes. Mon–Wed 11.30am–1am, Thurs–Sat 11.30am–2.30am, Sun 11.30am–midnight.

Kisetsu Rua da Glória 234, Liberdade ☎11 3101 1938; map p.333. The unlimited *rodizio* of wonderful sushi, sashimi, tempura and other delicious Japanese specialities served here is a bargain at R$56 on weekday lunchtimes (until 3pm), R$60.90 weekday evenings, and R$69.90 weekends. Daily 11am–9pm.

Korea House Rua Galvão Bueno 43, Liberdade ☎11 3208 3052; map p.333. One of the first Korean restaurants in São Paulo, where the inexpensive, often spicy, dishes are very different from the Japanese places in the same neighbourhood – try the Korean beef broth (R$52). Daily except Wed 11.30am–2.30pm & 6–10pm.

Okuyama Rua da Glória 553 ☎11 3341 0780, ⌨restauranteokuyama.com.br; map p.333. Great-value Japanese food and lots of it: the "festival de sushi" (R$62) – with vast amounts of sushi, sashimi and other dishes too – takes some getting through. Mon–Fri 11.30am–2pm & 6pm–2am, Sat noon–3pm & 6pm–3am, Sun noon–3pm & 6.30–11pm.

Ponto Chic Largo do Paissandú 27, Centro Novo ☎11 3222 6528, ⌨pontochic.com.br; map p.333. Established in 1922, this low-key sandwich bar is where they invented the traditional *baurú* sandwich (roast beef, tomato, pickle and a mix of melted cheeses in a baguette; R$24.90), and it's still the best place in town to try one. Mon–Sat 8am–2am.

Raful Rua Abdo Schahin 118, Centro ☎11 3229 8406, ⌨raful.com.br; map p.333. This bright Lebanese diner is a great spot for meze, or just a coffee, and in case you're hungrier than that, it also offers a big tasting menu for R$65. Mon–Fri 7am–6pm, Sat 7am–4pm.

VILA MADALENA AND AROUND AVENIDA PAULISTA

Andrade Rua Artur de Azevedo 874, Pinheiros ☎11 3085 0589, ⌨restauranteandrade.com.br; map p.336. Northeastern food is the speciality here, including *carne do sol* (sun-dried beef) served with pumpkin, sweet potato and manioc (R$90 for a full portion that'll serve two people, or R$81 for a half-portion). Live *forró* music Thurs–Sat evenings and Sun lunchtime. Tues–Thurs noon–3pm & 7pm–midnight, Fri & Sat noon–3pm & 7pm–4am, Sun noon–5pm.

Apfel Rua Bela Cintra 1343, Jardim Paulista ☎11 3062 3727; ⌨apfel.com.br; map p.336. An excellent and largely organic vegetarian buffet – a hundred-percent veggie, ninety-percent organic, they say – features hot and cold dishes, including salads, soups, sweets and savouries, for R$34.90 on weekdays, R$40.90 at weekends. Mon–Fri 11.30am–3pm, Sat & Sun 11.30am–4pm.

Arábia Rua Haddock Lobo 1397, Cerqueira César ☎11 3061 3234, ⌨arabia.com.br; map p.336. Excellent and moderately priced Middle Eastern food, with an emphasis on Lebanese cuisine. The mixed meze is a good way to sample a mixture of Middle Eastern hors d'oeuvres (R$122 for six dishes). Daily noon–midnight.

Bacio di Latte Rua Oscar Freire 136, Jardim Paulista ☎11 3062 0819, ⌨baciodilatte.com.br; map p.336. The flagship of São Paulo's very own chain of ice-cream parlours, based on the Italian tradition, but outdoing anything you'll find in Italy, with branches all over town. R$11.75 will get you three flavours. Mon–Fri & Sun 10am–midnight, Sat 10am–1am.

Bella Paulista Rua Haddock Lobo 354 ☎11 3214 3347, ⌨bellapaulista.com; map p.336. Handy for a drink, a meal, a coffee and cake or just an ice cream at any time of the day or night: it's a rare hour of a rare day that it isn't buzzing. Daily 24hr.

Bovinu's Grill Rua Augusta 1513, Consolação 1513 ⓣ11 3253 5440, ⓦbovinusaugusta.com.br; map p.336. Excellent-value *churrascaría* (branches around town, but this is the best), which has a huge selection of salads, Brazilian stews and other dishes, and, of course, lots of meat. At weekend lunchtimes there's an unlimited buffet (R$42.90 Sat, R$49.90 Sun). Mon–Fri 11.15am–3.30pm, Sat & Sun noon–4pm.

Company Av Paulista 2073 ⓣ11 3266 3250; map p.336. Popular with nearby office workers at lunchtime, this canteen-like diner offers good-value self-service buffet breakfasts (R$20) and lunches (R$39). Mon–Sat 6am–midnight, Sun 9am–8pm.

3

Consulado Mineiro Praça Benedito Calixto 74, Pinheiros ⓣ11 3064 3882, ⓦconsuladomineiro.com.br; map p.336. Satisfying fare from Minas Gerais at this popular choice in Jardins/Pinheiros. Crowded at weekends. Two can share one (huge) portion for around R$100. Tues–Sun 11.45am–midnight.

Fran's Cafe Rua Haddock Lobo 586, Jardim Paulista ⓣ11 3083 1019; ⓦfranscafe.com.br; map p.336. Excellent coffee. Part of a chain with branches around town and nationwide. Daily 24hr.

Z-Deli Alameda Lorena 1689, Cerqueira César ⓣ11 3064 3058; map p.336. A small Jewish deli-restaurant with an outstanding all-you-can-eat spread (available noon–4pm) of Ashkenazi Jewish specialities (R$49 weekdays, R$65 on Sat, when the selection's bigger). Mon–Fri 9am–5pm, Sat 10am–5pm.

ELSEWHERE IN THE CITY

Dona Lucinha Av Chibarás 399, Moema ⓣ11 5051 2050, ⓦdonalucinha.com.br; map p.330. Excellent unlimited lunch buffet (R$49 Mon–Fri, R$63 Sat & Sun) at the best *mineiro* restaurant in São Paulo. Try the full range of typical meat and vegetable dishes (vegetarians catered for), *cachaças* and desserts. Mon–Fri noon–3pm, Sat & Sun noon–4pm.

Jardim de Napoli Rua Dr Martinico Prado 463, Higienópolis ⓣ11 3666 3022, ⓦjardimdenapoli.com.br; map p.330. A simple cantina where some of São Paulo's best Italian food is served at moderate prices. Justifiably famous for its *polpettone* (giant meatballs; R$66), it also does excellent pasta. Mon noon–3pm & 7–11pm, Tues–Fri noon–3pm & 7pm–midnight, Sat noon–4pm & 7pm–midnight, Sun noon–5pm & 7–11pm.

Seok Joung Rua Correia de Melo 135, Bom Retiro ⓣ11 3338 0737, ⓦseokjoung.wordpress.com; map p.330. The most sophisticated of the numerous Korean restaurants in this *bairro*. Very authentic – and inexpensive – dishes (the speciality being *gogi gui*, or Korean barbecue; R$110) are served to largely Korean diners. Mon–Sat 11.30am–2.30pm & 5.30–9pm.

Shoshi Delishop Rua Correia de Melo 206, Bom Retiro ⓣ11 3228 4774, ⓦdelishoprestaurante.com.br; map p.330. In among the Korean eateries this inexpensive Jewish-Brazilian lunch and snack joint is super-friendly, and ideal if you're visiting museums in Luz. Mon–Sat 8.30am–3.30pm.

Speranza Av Sabiá 786, Moema ⓣ11 5051 1229, ⓦpizzaria.com.br; map p.330. This labyrinthine pizza house with balcony seating has been open since 1958, and successfully replicates genuine Neapolitan pizza (from R$47). Also delivers, and now has a branch at Rua 13 de Maio 1004, in Bixiga (map p.333). Mon–Thurs 6.30pm–midnight, Fri & Sat 6.30pm–1am, Sun noon–midnight (Bixiga branch Mon–Thurs & Sun 6.30pm–12.30am, Fri & Sat 6.30pm–1am).

St Etienne Alameda Joaquim Eugênio de Lima 1417, Jardins ⓣ11 3885 0691, & Av Diógenes Ribero de Lima 2555, Alto de Pinheiros ⓣ11 3021 1200, ⓦsantaetienne.com.br; map p.330. Busy, unpretentious 24hr cafés/bars with pavement seating, great sandwiches and, if you're really hungry, a variety of unlimited breakfast/lunch/tea buffets. Daily 24hr.

DRINKING AND NIGHTLIFE

São Paulo's nightlife is fantastic – a good enough reason alone for visiting the city. Options are scattered all over town, with things really getting going after midnight: Rua Augusta north of Av Paulista is the unofficial nightlife centre; Vila Madalena is good for more artsy and upscale locales. The São Paulo edition of the weekly magazine *Veja*

★ TREAT YOURSELF

D.O.M. Rua Barão de Capanema 549 ⓣ11 3088 0761, ⓦdomrestaurante.com.br; map p.336. One of Brazil's best restaurants, starring celebrated chef Alex Atala. There's no better way to do it than by working your way through the tasting menu (R$485 for four courses, R$645 for eight courses, vegetarian versions also available). Mon–Thurs noon–3pm & 7–11pm, Fri noon–3pm & 7– midnight, Sat 7pm–midnight.

Figueira Rubaiyat Rua Haddock Lobo 1738, Jardins ⓣ11 3063 3888, ⓦrubaiyat.com.br; map p.336. Built around a massive, golden-lit, 130-year-old majestic fig tree, this place serves the city's best steak, *feijoada* and Brazilian specialities. A chorizo (sirloin strip) steak goes for R$131, "baby beef" (super-tender heart of top sirloin) for R$141. Mon–Fri noon–4pm & 7–11pm, Sat & Sun 11am–midnight.

contains an excellent entertainment guide, and the daily newspaper *Folha de São Paulo* lists cultural and sporting events and, on Friday, contains an essential entertainment guide, the *Guia da Folha*. Great-value performances by famous Brazilian singers and dance troupes often take place at Auditório Ibarapuera: see ⓦ auditorioibirapuera.com.br.

BARS AND PUBS

Astor Rua Delfina 163, Vila Madalena ☎ 11 3815 1364, ⓦ barastor.com.br; map p.336. This well-established bar done out in Art Deco style, with an impressive stack of Johnny Walker bottles behind the bar, plus excellent beer and *petiscos* (snacks), is a great place to start a night out in Vila Madalena. Mon–6pm–midnight, Tues & Wed 6pm–2am, Thurs–Sat noon–3am, Sun noon–7pm.

Bar Brahma Av São João 677, Centro ☎ 11 3224 1250, ⓦ barbrahmacentro.com; map p.333. One of the city's oldest bars (opened 1948). Once a haunt for musicians, intellectuals and politicians, today it hosts musical acts most nights. Mon–Thurs 11am–1am, Fri & Sat 11pm–2am, Sun 11am–midnight.

Bar do Sacha Rua Original 45, Vila Madalena ☎ 11 3815 7665, ⓦ bardosacha.com; map p.336. Situated on a hillside opposite a pleasant grassy garden, this is a good spot to come for a *chopp* or a *caipirinha* on a sunny day or a warm evening. Daily 11.30am–1am.

Bar Filial Rua Fidalga 254, Vila Madalena ☎ 11 3813 9226, ⓦ www.barfilial.com.br; map p.336. Looks like a simple local bar, but is actually quite a sophisticated locale with a chequered floor, bow-tie-wearing waiters and a wide range of *cachaças*. Daily 5pm–late.

Café Piu-Piu Rua 13 de Maio 134, Bela Vista ☎ 11 3258 8066, ⓦ cafepiupiu.com.br; map p.333. Although this dance bar has a nice neighbourhood feel to it, the wide range of Brazilian music – including live samba and MPB – draws a mixed crowd into the early hours of the morning. Tues–Sun, hours vary but typically 9.30pm–late.

Choperia Opção Rua Carlos Comenale 97 ☎ 11 3288 7823, ⓦ choperiaopcao.com.br; map p.336. Just metres from Av Paulista and MASP, this is a really popular after-work place, with an outdoor terrace that's great for watching workhorse Sampa go by. Daily 5pm–2am.

Empanadas Rua Wisard 489, Vila Madalena ☎ 11 3032 2116; map p.336. The simple but effective selling-point of this busy bar is that, in addition to beer, it serves *empanadas* (savoury pasties_popular throughout South America but usually referred to as *empadas* in Brazil), with small ones at R$7 each or R$36.30 for half a dozen, big ones at R$8.90 apiece. Mon–Thurs noon–1am, Fri & Sat noon–3am, Sun 1pm–1am.

Kia Ora Rua Dr Eduardo de Souza Aranha 377, Itaim Bibi ☎ 11 3846 8300, ⓦ kiaora.com.br; map p.330. With its live rock bands, Kiwi-owned *Kia Ora* is a popular pub among expats and *Paulistanos* alike. On some nights there's a long

wait to get in, although you can reserve ahead. Be aware that there's a dress code – no shorts or football shirts, for example. Tues 6pm–1am, Wed & Thurs 6pm–3.30am, Fri 7pm–4am, Sat 8pm–4.30am.

São Cristóvão Rua Aspicuelta 533 ☎ 11 3097 9904; map p.336. This sports bar is a shrine to Brazilian football, and the walls here are completely covered with football memorabilia – scarves, flags, shirts, stickers, you name it. Daily noon–2am.

★ SKYE Hotel Unique, Av Brigadeiro Luis Antônio 4700, Jardim Paulista ☎ 11 3055 4702, ⓦ hotelunique.com.br; map p.330. This is the place to start your night, on the roof of the "watermelon hotel" sipping a cocktail along with the beautiful people and a 360-degree view of the skyline. Chic and luxurious. DJs from 9pm. Daily 6pm–12.30am.

Veloso Rua Conceição Veloso 56, Vila Mariana ☎ 11 5572 0254, ⓦ velosobar.com.br; map p.330. Perennially popular bar voted for serving Sampa's best *caipirinhas* and *coxinha* savouries. Inevitably neither comes cheap, but they are worth it. Tues–Fri 5.30pm–12.30am; Sat 12.30pm–12.30am, Sun 4–10.30pm.

CLUBS

Canto da Ema Av Brig. Faria Lima 364, Pinheiros ☎ 11 3813 4708, ⓦ cantodaema.com.br; map p.330. You can hear the *forró* outside despite the airlock entrance. Inside, it's all dancing fun and *cachaça*. Wed & Thurs 10.30pm–2am, Fri & Sat 10.30pm–5am, Sun 7pm–midnight.

Carioca Club Rua Cardeal Arcoverde 2899, Pinheiros ☎ 11 3813 8598, ⓦ cariocaclub.com.br; map p.330. This great dance hall features live *forró*, funk or samba nightly, with friendly people not averse to showing newcomers the ropes. Some acts start early (7–11pm), and others late (11pm–5am). The website has comprehensive details of what's on.

D-Edge Alameda Olga 170, Barra Funda ☎ 11 3665 9500, ⓦ d-edge.com.br; map p.330. Sampa's premier electronica club, with nightly DJs playing anything from techno to (*baile*) funk, and a mixed crowd ready to dance. Mon & Wed–Sat from midnight, with an afterparty on Sun 6am–noon.

Ó do Borogodó Rua Horácio Lane 21, Pinheiros ☎ 11 3814 4087; map p.336. This is the real Brazil: a gritty, authentic samba bar where everybody dances with everybody. Mon 8.15–11pm, Tues 9pm–2am, Wed–Sat 10pm–3am, Sun 7pm–12.30am.

Traço de União Rua Claudio Soares 73, Pinheiros ☎ 11 3031 8065, ⓦ tracodeuniao.com.br; map p.330. One of the city's top samba venues, especially busy on Friday nights, but also known for its Saturday *feijoadas* and always with a good vibe. Thurs & Fri 9pm–3am, Sat 1–9pm, Sun (sometimes) 3–10pm.

Villa Country Av Francisco Matarazzo 774, Barra Funda ☎ 11 3868 5858, ⓦ villacountry.com.br; map

3

p.330. *Serteneja* (Brazilian country music) has a big cult following, and this 1800-capacity venue needs to be seen to be believed. Expect crowds of cowboy hats and cowgirl hotpants. Thurs–Sun 8pm–5am, dancefloors Fri & Sat from 11pm.

The Week Rua Guaicurus 324, Lapa ☎ 11 3868 9944, ⓦ theweek.com.br; map p.330. São Paolo's biggest and most famous gay and lesbian club attracts top DJs and a fair few VIPs (not necessarily LGBTQ). Sat 11.30pm–8am, and sometimes other days.

DIRECTORY

Banks and exchange There are cambios at the airports and sprinkled throughout the city, with several banks and money changers along Av Paulista.

Car rental Avis, Rua Tito 66, Lapa ☎ 11 3594 4015; Hertz, Rua da Consolação 419, Centro ☎ 11 3231 3055; Movida, Rua da Consolação 293, Centro ☎ 0800 606 8686; Unidas Rua Cincinato Braga 388, Bela Vista ☎ 11 3155 4770.

Consulates Argentina, Av Paulista 2313 (☎ 11 3897 9522); Australia, Alameda Santos 700, 9th floor, suite 92, Cerqueira César (☎ 11 2112 6200); Bolivia, Rua Coronel Artur Godói 7, Vila Mariana (☎ 11 3289 0443); Canada, Av das Nações Unidas 12901, 16th floor, Itaim Bibi (☎ 11 5509 4321); Colombia, Rua Tenente Negrao 140, 7th floor, Itaim Bibi (☎ 11 3078 0262); Ireland (moving to permanent offices – check on ⓦ dfa.ie/irish-consulate/sao-paulo); New Zealand, Av Paulista, 2421 (Edifício Bela Paulista), 12th floor (☎ 11 3898 7400); Paraguay, Rua Bandeira Paulista 600, 8th floor (☎ 11 3167 7793); Peru, Av Paulista 2439 (☎ 11 3149 2525); South Africa, Av Paulista 1754, 12th floor (☎ 11 3265 0449); UK, Rua Ferreira de Araújo 741, 2nd floor, Pinheiros (☎ 11 3094 2700); Uruguay, Rua Estados Unidos 1284, Jardim America (☎ 11 2879 6600); US, Rua Henri Dunant 500, Campo Belo (☎ 11 3250 7000

Hospitals The private Hospital Albert Einstein, Av Albert Einstein 627, Morumbi (☎ 11 2151 1233, ⓦ einstein.br), is considered to be the best hospital in Brazil. For dentistry, Banatti, Av Paulista 925, 13th floor, Cerqueira César (☎ 11 3251 0228, ⓦ benattiodontologia.com.br), is central and English-speaking.

Laundries 5 à Sec: Rua Nestor Pestana 95, Loja A, Centro; Rua Frei Caneca 655, Bela Vista; Alameda Santos 1283, Cerqueira Cesar.

Left luggage Guarulhos, Congonhas and Tietê Rodoviária have 24hr lockers.

Police Emergencies ☎ 190. DEATUR, a special police unit for tourists (☎ 11 3257 4475), is located at Rua da Cantareira 390 by the Mercado Municipal and has posts at the two airports.

Post offices The main post office is downtown at Praça Correio, at the corner of Av São João (Mon–Fri 9am–6pm, Sat 9am–1pm). Smaller offices (Mon–Fri 9am–5pm), with their distinctive yellow signage, are scattered throughout the city.

Visas To extend your visa, visit the Polícia Federal, Rua Hugo D'Antola 95, 3rd floor, Lapa de Baixo (Mon–Fri 8am–2pm; ☎ 11 3538 5000; Metrô Lapa), and make sure you have all the necessary forms and receipts.

SANTOS

Half the world's coffee, oranges and sugar pass through **SANTOS**, Latin America's biggest port. Inevitably a big chunk of the city is given over to industrial complexes and shipyards, but the surprise beneath the grit is a charming historical centre that attests to its foundation by the Portuguese in 1535. Lying on the island of **São Vicente**, the city is surrounded by water and has some popular beaches that draw the crowds in from São Paulo at weekends (you may wish to give swimming a miss here, however, as the water is not especially clean).

WHAT TO SEE AND DO

You can see Santos's sights in a few hours, making it great for a day-trip from São Paulo or a stop-off if you're travelling from São Paulo along the coast to Paraty via São Sebastião.

The centre is easy to navigate on foot. Walk past the attractive colonial-era houses on Rua do Comércio towards the nineteenth-century train station. A **tourist tram** (hourly 11am–5pm; R$7) runs from from here on a forty-minute trip. Nearby, the grand **Bolsa de Café** (Rua XV de Novembro 95; Tues–Sat 9am–6pm, Sun 10am–6pm; R$10; ⓦ museudocafe.com.br) is Santos's main museum space. It hosts a remarkable permanent exhibition on the history of Brazil's coffee industry, partly responsible for the country's ethnic make-up given its enormous demand first for African slave labour, then for Italian, Japanese and other migrant workers in the late nineteenth and early twentieth centuries.

International football legend Pelé learnt his trade at **Santos Futebol Clube**, a legacy followed in part today by the club's more recent prodigy, Neymar. The stadium makes a worthwhile visit (Rua Princesa Isabel 77; Tues–Sun 9am–7pm except match days; R$8, guided tour R$15). There's a museum dedicated to Pelé opposite the old train station (Tues–Sun 10am–6pm; R$10).

ARRIVAL AND DEPARTURE

By bus The *rodoviária* is in the Centro on Praça dos Andradas. From São Paulo, Santos buses (every 15min; 1hr 15min) leave from the Jabaquara *rodoviária* and not from Tietê. Santos's *rodoviária* has left luggage and tourist information. Executive buses to São Sebastião depart daily at 7am, 1pm and 7pm (4hr; R$55.55; ⓦ litoranea.com.br).

ACCOMMODATION

HI Santos Hostel Rua Barão de Paranapiacaba 22 ❶ 13 2202 4566, ⓦ santoshostel.com.br. Smart, friendly and well organized, it's a 10min taxi ride south of the centre. Dorms R$50

THE SÃO PAULO COAST

Between São Paulo and Rio the coastline is fantastic, and while Paraty (see page 259) and Ilha Grande (see page 258) get all the credit, a couple of days along the São Paulo section is a really worthwhile diversion. Founded on sugar and fishing, **São Sebastião** is a pretty colonial town popular with Brazilian and Argentine backpackers and trippers. A calming place after the urban clamour of São Paulo, you can also visit the island of **Ilha Bela** from here, home to fantastic beaches and waterfalls – though it's on the radar of São Paulo's rich list and has no budget accommodation aside from camping. Stunning coves and Atlantic forest mark the route onwards to **Ubatuba**, an energetic yet plain town best known for its 72 beaches on nearby islands and inlets. Though some now resemble hotel resorts, they're still the state's best, and numerous secluded spots remain. A car or plenty of time on buses is needed to explore them, but you'll most probably find plenty of like-minded beach seekers to do it with.

ARRIVAL AND DEPARTURE

By bus 6 buses/day ply the route from São Paulo's Rodoviária Tietê (R$65) to São Sebastião, while there are 3/day from Santos (both 4hr). To get from São Sebastião to Ubatuba, change at Caraguatatuba. 2 buses daily go from Ubatuba direct to Rio (5hr), or 6 to Paraty (1hr 30min; R$12.50).

ACCOMMODATION

HI Tribo Hostel Rua Amoreira 71, Praia do Lázaro (15km southwest of Ubatuba) ❶ 12 3842 0585, ⓦ ubatubahostel.com. Consummate facilities include large buffet breakfast, games and book/DVD rental, while the lively party atmosphere is aided by the beach right on hand. Dorms R$70, doubles R$210

Pousada San Sebastian (Maresias Hostel) Rua Sebastião Romão Cesar 406, Maresias ❶ 12 3865 6612, ⓦ alberguemaresias.com.br. A great place to relax after the rigours of the big city, and also lively with Paulista and Argentine surfers in season. Dorms R$48, doubles R$110

Hotel Roma Praça Major João Fernandes, São Sebastião ❶ 12 3892 4622, ⓦ hotelroma.tur.br. A simple but handsome old hotel on São Sebastião's main square, where there's a range of rooms, sleeping one to four people, newer ones with a private bathroom around an attractive garden, and older ones without bathrooms in the main building. R$110

The South

Southern Brazil – the states of **Paraná**, **Santa Catarina** and **Rio Grande do Sul** – is a land of gauchos, barbecues and beaches. It's also generally considered to be the most developed region in the country and shows little of the obvious poverty found elsewhere. As a result the South can be an expensive place to travel, and hotel and restaurant prices are equivalent to those in Rio de Janeiro. Choose wisely, though, and you can still find good-value places to stay and eat out.

The spectacular **Iguaçu Falls** are deservedly the South's most visited attraction, though it's the subtropical southern coast that provides much of the region's allure in the summer (Nov–March). Building is virtually forbidden on the beautiful islands of the **Bay of Paranaguá** in Paraná – the most frequently visited being the gorgeous **Ilha do Mel**. By way of contrast, tourism has encroached along Santa Catarina's coast, but development has been restrained and resorts around **Florianópolis**, particularly in the south of the **Ilha Santa Catarina**, remain small and in tune with the region's natural beauty.

3

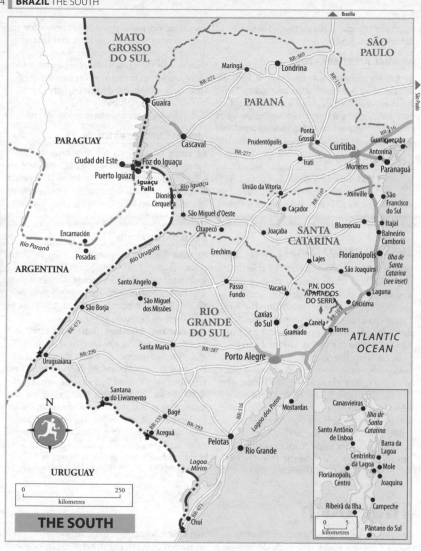

Beyond the pretty German enclaves of Gramado and Canela, the highland areas and the pampas of southern **Rio Grande do Sul** are largely given over to vast cattle ranches and latter-day **gauchos** – who share many cultural similarities with their Uruguayan and Argentine neighbours. The haunting remnants of **Catholic missions** pay homage to the brief but productive Jesuit occupation of the area.

CURITIBA

Founded by the Portuguese in 1693, **CURITIBA** was of little importance until 1853 when it was made capital of the newly created state of Paraná. Since then, the city's population has risen steadily from a few thousand to 1.8 million, its inhabitants largely descendants of Polish, German, Italian, Ukrainian and other immigrants. Home to a pristine old town and some enticing art museums, notably the eye-catching **Museu Oscar Niemeyer**, to visit Curitiba is to experience the wealthier side of Brazil: on average, *Curitibanos* enjoy the nation's highest standard of living, the city boasts facilities that are the envy of other parts of the country, and its eco-friendly design is a model that many urban planners try to emulate.

WHAT TO SEE AND DO

Most of Curitiba's attractions can be visited relatively easily in a day or so on foot, with the **Rua das Flores** – a pedestrianized section of the Rua XV de Novembro – the centre's main late afternoon and early evening meeting point. However, if you have limited time, take the Linha Turismo **bus tour**, which departs from Praça Tiradentes (Tues–Sun every 30min; first bus at 9am, last bus 5.30pm; R$45; cash only). Stopping at 25 attractions around the city centre and suburbs, it takes around three hours to complete the full circuit. Tickets allow passengers four hop-on hop-off stops.

PRAÇA TIRADENTES AND THE HISTORIC QUARTER

A couple of blocks north from Rua das Flores is **Praça Tiradentes**, home to the neo-Gothic **Catedral Basílica Menor de Nossa Senhora da Luz** (daily 6am–7pm; free). From here a pedestrian tunnel leads to Curitiba's **historic quarter**, an area of impeccably preserved eighteenth- and nineteenth-century buildings of Portuguese and central European design. The **Igreja da Ordem**, on Largo da Ordem, dates from 1737 and is the city's oldest surviving building. Plain outside, the church is also simple within, the only decoration being typically Portuguese blue and white tiling and Baroque altar and side chapels. Next door the **Museu de Arte Sacra** (Tues–Fri 9am–noon & 1–6pm, Sat & Sun 9am–2pm; free), with relics gathered from Curitiba's churches.

A short distance uphill from here, on the same street, is the **Igreja Nossa Senhora do Rosário** (Tues–Fri 1.30–5.30pm, Sat 2–6pm, Sun 8am–noon; free), built by and for Curitiba's slave population in 1737, though it was completely reconstructed in the 1940s. The **Museu Paranaense**, nearby at Rua Kellers 289 (Tues–Fri 9am–6pm, Sat & Sun 10am–4pm; free), contains paintings by twentieth-century Paranaense artists as well as arts and crafts made by the region's first indigenous population.

MODERN CURITIBA

The futuristic **Museu Oscar Niemeyer** (Tues–Sun 10am–6pm; R$16; ⓦ museuoscarniemeyer.org.br) lies about 3km to the north of **Curitiba**'s old town, on Rua Marechal Hermes. Designed by the Brazilian architect after whom it was named, the building's most notable feature resembles a giant eye. The galleries inside house primarily modernist art, including works by *paranaenses* Alfredo Andersen, Theodoro de Bona and Miguel Bakun, and many by Niemeyer himself, best known for designing much of Brasília (see page 315).

West of the *rodoferroviária* along Avenida Sete de Setembro is the city's converted former railway station, now the **Shopping Estação**, an atmospheric mall incorporating the small **Museu Ferroviário** (Tues–Sat 10am–6pm, Sun 11am–7pm; free), which houses relics from Paraná's railway era as well as temporary exhibits.

Finally, it's worth a trip out to Curitiba's most popular attraction, the **Torre Panorâmica** (Tues–Sun 10am–7pm; R$5) on Rua Lycio Grein de Castro Vellozo, the only telephone tower in Brazil with an observation deck (109m), offering sensational views across the city.

ARRIVAL AND INFORMATION

By plane The ultramodern Aeroporto Internacional Afonso Pena is about 18km from the city centre. Taxis to the centre charge about R$80 on the meter. Linha Aeroporto Executivo minibuses (every 15–20min; 45min; R$15; ☎41 3381 1326, ⓦ aeroportoexecutivo.com.br) connect the airport with the *rodoferroviária*, Rua Visconde de Nácar near Rua 24 Horas (which is the name of the stop) and Shopping Estação. The cheapest option isn't really worth the hassle; city bus #E32 (R$4.30) trundles between the airport and the Terminal do Boqueirão in the suburbs every 20–30min, where you'll have to change to reach the centre.

Destinations Frequent flights to all major cities in Brazil – including Florianópolis, Foz do Iguaçu, Porto Alegre and

3

São Paulo – and international flights to Paraguay and Argentina.

By bus The main bus station (☎41 3320 3232) – the *rodoferroviária* – is southeast of town, about ten blocks from the city centre on Av Pres. Affonso Camargo. It takes about 20min to walk to the centre, or there's a minibus from almost in front of the station: catch it at the intersection of Camargo and Av Sete de Setembro, to the left of the entrance to the station's driveway. Taxis should be around R$13–15 to the centre.

Destinations Camboriú (hourly; 2hr 30min); Florianópolis (hourly; 4–5hr); Foz do Iguaçu (9 daily; 10hr); Paranaguá (14 daily; 1hr 30min); Porto Alegre (8 daily; 12–13hr); Rio de Janeiro (4–5 daily; 13hr); São Paulo (hourly; 6–7hr).

By train The train station (☎041 3888 3488) is next to the bus station. The only passenger train from Curitiba is the Serra Verde Express (see page 347), which runs to Morretes.

Tourist information Go to the well-organized Visite Curitiba head office at Rua da Glória 362 (Mon–Fri 8am–noon & 2–6pm; ☎41 3352 8000, ⍵turismo.curitiba.pr.gov.br); there are more convenient branches in the *rodoferroviária* (daily 8am–6pm; ☎41 3320 3121); in Palacete Wolf, Praça Garibaldi 7 (Mon–Sat 9am–6pm, Sun 9am–4pm); ☎41 3321 3206; and at the Torre Panorâmica (Tues–Sun 10am–7pm; ☎41 3339 7613).

GETTING AROUND

Curitiba's centre is small enough to be able to walk to most places within the city centre.

By bus City buses (⍵urbs.curitiba.pr.gov.br) stop at the strange glass boarding tubes you see dotted around town. Pay at the turnstile on entering the tube, not on the bus (R$3–4.25).

ACCOMMODATION

There are numerous cheap and secure hotels near the *rodoferroviária*. Places in the city centre are within walking distance of most attractions and are generally excellent value.

Curitiba Hostel Rua Dr Claudino Santos 49, Largo da Ordem ☎41 3232 2005, ⍵curitibahostel.com.br. Fabulous location right in the heart of the old town, with clean dorms featuring triple bunks, cheap single rooms (R$70), buffet breakfast, hot showers and extra-friendly staff. Dorms R$45, doubles R$145

Knock Knock Hostel Rua Isaías Bevilácqua 262 ☎41 3152 6259, ⍵knockhostel.com. Stylish, modern hostel featuring six dorms, a fully equipped kitchen, laundry, barbecue area and terrace, a 10min walk from the centre. Free breakfast. Taxis from bus station R$15. Dorms R$50

★ **Motter Home Curitiba Hostel** Rua Desembargador Motta 3574 ☎41 3209 5649, ⍵motterhome.com.

br. This justly popular hostel a short stroll from the centre offers four clean dorms, three private rooms (with shared bathroom), communal kitchen, TV lounge and pool table. Breakfast included. Taxis from bus station R$15. Dorms R$53, doubles R$158

Pousada Betânia Monteiro Tourinho 1335 ☎41 2118 7900, ⍵pousadabetaniacuritiba.com.br. Cosy, tranquil accommodation, 20min from the bus station, with compact, modern en-suite rooms. Buffet breakfast included. R$136

Hostel Roma Rua Barão do Rio Branco 805 ☎41 3224 2117, ⍵hostelroma.com.br. A block from the Shopping Estação, midway between the *rodoferroviária* and the centre, this is an older, standard HI hostel (converted from an old 1909 hotel), with dorms, private rooms and an attractive courtyard and garden. Light breakfast included. Discount for HI members (R$3 off dorm beds). Dorms R$50, doubles R$134

EATING AND DRINKING

Curitiba boasts a good range of restaurants, with the most interesting located in the historic centre. For the cheapest eats check out the food court in Shopping Estação or the Mercado Municipal, Rua Sete de Setembro (Mon 7am–2pm, Tues–Sat 7am–6pm, Sun 7am–1pm).

★ **Bar Stuart** Praça General Osório 427 ☎41 3323 5504, ⍵barstuart.com.br. This old stalwart has been serving locals, artists and politicos since 1904 (it was a hangout of beloved local poet Paulo Leminski in the 1970s). Festooned with historical photos, it's a cosy place for a Brahma (R$12) or *cachaça*, to watch live football and try exotic bar snacks such as *carne de onça* (steak tartare served with onion and garlic) and *testículos de touro* (they are what they sound like). Mon–Fri 9am–11pm, Sat 9am–4pm, Sun 9am–3pm.

Bouquet Garni Alameda Doutor Carlos de Carvalho 271 ☎41 3223 8490. Excellent veggie restaurant offering lunch buffets of stroganoff chickpeas, spinach lasagne and *feijoada* with onion, turnip and coconut for R$25 Mon–

★ TREAT YOURSELF

Durski Rua Jaime Reis 254 ☎41 3225 7893, ⍵durski.com.br. This is Curitiba's renowned Ukrainian restaurant (from celebrity chef Junior Durski), located in a renovated house in the heart of the historic centre, looking onto Largo da Ordem. The food (including Polish and Brazilian dishes) is attractively presented and very tasty: try the delicious filet mignon with mash and sautéed mushrooms in Madeira wine. Mains R$70–130. Wed–Fri 7.30–10.30pm, Sat noon–3pm & 7.30–10.30pm, Sun noon–3pm.

Fri & R$35 Sat & Sun. Mon–Fri 11am–3pm, Sat & Sun 11am–3.30pm.

Caruso Empadas Rua Visconde do Rio Branco 877 ☎41 3029 5411. It's surprisingly rare to find a café with style and historic cachet in central Curitiba, but this tiny place delivers, with a few tables inside and on the street since 1954. It's best just for coffee (simple and strong, poured from an antique pot) and its signature treat, the *empada* (small pot pies made with filo pastry), stuffed with cod, sausage, shrimp, heart of palm or chicken, with boiled eggs and olives mixed in ($9–14). Mon–Fri 8.45am–8.30pm, Sat & Sun 8.45am–8pm.

Pastelaria Nakashima Praça General Osório 367 ☎41 9973 1204. This tiny, Japanese-Brazilian owned hole-in-the-wall (with just a row of stools at the counter) has garnered a loyal following thanks to its tasty fried *pastels* stuffed with meat, banana, heart of palm or cheese (R$4–8). Mon–Fri 8.30am–8.30pm, Sat 8.30am–1.30pm

Schwarzwald-Bar do Alemão Rua Claudino dos Santos 63 ☎41 3223 2585, ⍉bardoalemaocuritiba.com.br. This pub and restaurant has outdoor seating and a spacious, kitsch, Bavarian-themed interior. A popular evening meeting point for students in Largo da Ordem, at the heart of the old town, it serves excellent German food with cold beer. Lunch deals for around R$22; A plate of pork knuckle and sausages for two will set you back R$50. Daily 11am–2am.

DIRECTORY

Banks and exchange Main offices of banks are concentrated at the Praça Osório end of Rua das Flores.

Hospital In emergencies use the Nossa Senhora das Graças hospital at Rua Alcides Munhoz 433 in Mercês (24hr hotline: ☎41 3240 6555; ⍉hnsg.org.br).

Internet Try *Get On Lan House*, Rua Visconde de Nácar 1388, open 24hr (R$5/hr).

Laundry Premium Lavanderia at Rua Visconde de Nácar 1371 (Mon–Fri 8am–6.30pm, Sat 8am–noon; wash from R$15; ☎41 3322 0092), is a good central option.

Post office The most convenient central office is at Rua Marechal Deodoro 298 (Mon–Fri 9.30am–6pm; Sat 9.30am–1pm).

PARANAGUÁ

Brazil's second most important port for exports, **PARANAGUÁ**, 92km east of Curitiba, was founded in the 1550s on the banks of the Rio Itiberê, making it one of Brazil's oldest cities. Today it's also a departure point for ferries to Ilha do Mel (see page 348).

WHAT TO SEE AND DO

The appeal of Paranaguá lies in wandering around the cobbled streets and absorbing the faded colonial atmosphere of the town. Almost everything worth seeing is concentrated along **Rua XV de Novembro**, a block inland from the waterfront. At the corner of Rua Presciliano Correa is the very pretty **Igreja São Francisco das Chagas** (daily 9am–5.30pm; free), a small and simple church built in 1784 and still containing its Baroque altar and side chapels. Along the waterfront at Rua General Carneiro 458 is the **Mercado Municipal do Café** (Mon–Sat 7am–6pm, Sun 7am–3pm), an early twentieth-century building that used to serve as the city's coffee market. Today the Art Nouveau structure contains handicraft stalls. The handsome former fish market across the street, built in 1914, is now the **Mercado Artesanato** (Mon–Fri 9am–5pm, Sat & Sun 9am–3pm), home to arts and crafts shops.

SERRA VERDE EXPRESS

The **Serra Verde Express** (☎41 3323 4007, ⍉serraverdeexpress.com.br) is one of the most scenic train rides in Brazil, winding around mountainsides, slipping through tunnels and traversing one of the largest Atlantic Forest reserves in the country; make sure to sit on the left-hand side of the train for the best views (or on the right if you're not good with heights). Though the express used to go as far as Paranaguá, today the trains only go from **Curitiba** to **Morretes** (daily 8.15am, arriving 11.15am; Sat & Sun also 9.15am, arriving 12.15pm; return trains depart 3pm, arriving in Curitiba at 6pm), a lovely colonial town 16km inland from the Atlantic. A variety of tickets is available, from coach class (*economica*, R$94 one-way, R$72 extra return) to R$174 one-way for the special *executivo* service (which includes an English-speaking guide and local beer) and over R$360 for the weekend luxury train. For the cheaper tickets book several days in advance, as they are limited and sell out quickly. Morretes bus station lies just outside the centre; from here buses run to Paranaguá (hourly; 1hr; R$6.20), and back to Curitiba (9 daily; 1hr 30min; R$21).

Just beyond the market is Paranaguá's most imposing building, the fortress-like **Colégio dos Jesuítas**, the old Jesuit school, opened in 1755. Today it is home to the **Museu de Arqueologia e Etnologia**, Rua XV de Novembro 575 (Tues–Sun 8am–8pm; free; ⊛ proec.ufpr.br), with exhibits on prehistoric archeological finds, indigenous culture and popular art – the poor old Jesuits don't even get a mention. Three blocks inland from here on Largo Monsenhor Celso is the town's oldest church, **Igreja de Nossa Senhora do Rosário**, dating from 1578 (daily 8am–6pm; free).

ARRIVAL AND INFORMATION

By bus Buses arrive at the *rodoviária*, on the waterfront at Rua João Estevão 403. Buses depart for Curitiba hourly (1hr 30min).

By ferry Services depart from the Estação Nautica (Rua General Carneiro 258) to the bay islands, including Ilha do Mel (daily 8.30am, 9.30am, 11am, 1pm, 3pm, 4.30pm & 6pm in summer, with 9.30am & 3.30pm crossings in winter; R$53 return); the boats stop at Nova Brasília (1hr 30min) then Encantadas (2hr). See ⊛ abaline.com.br.

Tourist information There's a small but useful information kiosk just outside the bus station (daily 9am–6pm; ☎ 41 3425 4542).

ACCOMMODATION AND EATING

There is no real reason to hang around in Paranaguá, but should you need to, you can choose from a cluster of reasonably priced hotels within walking distance of the major transport terminals.

Cheap seafood and the local speciality, *barreado* (slow-cooked meat stew baked in clay pots), are the order of the day at most restaurants. There are some excellent inexpensive seafood places in the Mercado Municipal do Café (p.347), though they are open at lunchtimes only.

Casa do Barreado Rua Antonio da Cruz 78 ☎ 41 3423 1830, ⊛ casadobarreado.com.br. The best place to try the regional speciality *barreado* (R$40, with dessert included); the lunchtime buffet of Brazilian dishes is also good. Sat & Sun noon–4pm.

Hotel Palácio Rua Correia de Freitas 66 ☎ 41 3422 5655, ⊛ hotelpalacio.com.br. Centrally located hotel with clean but spartan rooms for up to four people. A good option for families on a budget. Breakfast and parking included. R$132

★ **Pastelaria Kubo** Mercado Municipal do Café ☎ 41 3423 2336. Tucked away in the old coffee market since 1950, this tiny Japanese-Brazilian stall knocks out delicious, crispy *pastels* in just four flavours: meat, cheese, shrimp and

banana with cinnamon (R$4–6). Wash them down with some potent black coffee. Tues–Sat 7am–noon & 2–6pm, Sun 7am–noon.

ILHA DO MEL

Famed for its golden beaches and tranquil setting, the idyllic **ILHA DO MEL** ("Island of Honey") in the Bay of Paranaguá is a hit with backpackers and surfers looking to enjoy the simpler things in life – and the island's waves. It's an unusually shaped island, to say the least. Its bulbous northern half, a protected Atlantic Forest ecological reserve (entry is prohibited), is joined to the slender south by a bridge of land where the lively main village of **Nova Brasília** is located. The island's other major settlement, **Encantadas**, near the southwest corner, has the atmosphere of a sleepy fishing port. It's little more than 12km from north to south, but given the hilly topography of the island most walks hug the coast. Bear in mind that there are no cars, no banks, no public transport and no shops on the island and electricity for only a short period each day – so come prepared.

WHAT TO SEE AND DO

Praia do Farol is the closest beach to Nova Brasília, curving in a wide arc around the "neck" of the island. It's a 4km walk north along these sands to the Portuguese fort of **Fortaleza Nossa Senhora dos Prazeres** (open daily; free), completed in 1769. Encantadas' nearest sandy beach is **Praia de Fora**. The entire stretch of coastline along the southeast side between Praia de Fora and Praia do Farol is dotted with enchanting coves, rocky promontories and small waterfalls. The rocks are slippery here, so take care, and the three-hour walk along the beach from Praia de Fora as far as the fort should only be attempted at low tide or you risk being stranded. The southern tip of the island, known as **Ponta Encantada**, is where you will find the **Gruta das Encantadas** (Enchanted Cave), focal point for a number of local legends.

ARRIVAL AND INFORMATION

By boat In summer seven daily ferries (1hr 45min; R$53 return) link Ilha do Mel with Paranaguá. You can also catch a bus from Curitiba (5 daily; 2hr 30min; R$40) to Pontal do Sul, from where boats leave every hour or so from the beach to the island (Mon–Thurs 8am–4pm, Fri & Sat 8am–6pm, Sun 8am–5pm; 20min; R$35 return; ⓦ abaline.com.br); all ferries usually serve Encantadas then Nova Brasília. There are fewer boats to the island in winter.

Tourist information There is a small tourist information booth at the dock in Nova Brasília (summer: daily 8am–8pm). See also the useful websites ⓦ ilhadomelonline.com. br and ⓦ visiteilhadomel.com.br.

ACCOMMODATION

If you plan to visit in the height of summer, it's best to arrive during the week and as early as possible, as accommodation books up quickly during the weekends. The island is always full to capacity over New Year and Carnaval, when reservations are essential and are accepted only for minimum stays of four or five nights. **Restaurants** on the island pretty much all offer an unsophisticated menu, based on fish, prawns, rice and beans. Summer evenings are always lively, with notices advertising live music and club nights.

Hostel Encantadas Ecologic Praia das Encantadas ☎ 41 99671 5030, ✉ hostelencantadasecologic@hotmail.com. Basic rooms and dorms in neat wooden cabañas near the beach, with modern shared and private bathrooms, decent breakfast and shared kitchen. Dorms R$45, doubles R$149

Pousadinha Caminho do Farol, Nova Brasília ☎ 41 3426 8026, ⓦ pousadinha.com.br. Popular backpacker hangout (180m inland from the dock) with leafy gardens and relaxing hammocks for chilling out. The en-suite rooms (for 3–4 people) are simple but good value, and multilingual staff can assist with booking activities. R$180

Pousada Lua Cheia Praia das Encantadas ☎ 41 3426 9010, ⓦ luacheiatur.com.br. Ten simple en-suite wood cabins that hold up to four people each, equipped with TV, fridge, fan and a/c. Breakfast included. Cabañas R$180

Pousada Toca da Ilha Praia das Encantadas ☎ 41 3426 9045, ✉ tocadailha@hotmail.com. Simple, rustic accommodation near the beach, with shared kitchen. Single (from just R$70), double, triple and quad rooms available. Doubles R$140

FOZ DO IGUAÇU

The city of **FOZ DO IGUAÇU** is the Brazilian gateway to the magnificent **Iguaçu Falls**, one of the world's greatest natural wonders, which lie 20km south. Much larger than its Argentine counterpart **Puerto Iguazú** (see page 87), it makes a livelier, if pricier, base for exploring the falls, with the advantage of decent restaurants and nightlife.

WHAT TO SEE AND DO

Foz do Iguaçu is a modern city with no real sights of its own, but on the road to the falls (Av de Cataratas), the parrots and showy toucans at **Parque das Aves**, Km17.1, just 300m from the falls entrance (daily 8.30am–5pm; R$40; ⓦ parquedasaves.com.br), are well worth the expense, with enormous walk-through aviaries in dramatic forested surroundings (all birds have been rescued from traffickers and would not survive alone in the wild). There is also a large walk-through butterfly cage – butterflies are bred throughout the year and released when mature. All the butterflies and eighty percent of the eight hundred bird species are Brazilian, many endemic to the Atlantic Forest.

ARRIVAL AND INFORMATION

By plane Foz do Iguaçu International Airport (☎ 45 3521 4200) is 12km southeast of town, halfway along the road to the falls (12km north of the falls themselves). It is served by flights from Curitiba, São Paulo, Rio de Janeiro, Brasília, Salvador and Belém. A taxi into town costs around R$50 (R$30 to the falls and R$85–95 to Puerto Iguazú), or take bus #120 (Mon–Sat 5.45am–12.40am, every 20min, Sun 5.30am–12.40am, every 45min; R$3.45), which shuttles between the falls and the local terminal in town on Av Juscelino Kubitschek.

By bus The *rodoviária* (☎ 45 3522 2590) is 4km north of the centre on Av Costa e Silva; buses #105 and #115 from here, marked "Rodoviária", can take you to the local bus terminal (TTU or Terminal de Transporte Urbano) on Av Juscelino Kubitschek in the city centre (R$3.45); taxis cost around R$25. At the TTU you can pick up bus #120 to the falls ("Aeroporto Parque Nacional"; R$3.45).

Destinations Buenos Aires (1 daily; 19hr); Curitiba (10 daily; 9hr); Florianópolis (9 daily; 16hr); Porto Alegre (6 daily; 14hr); Rio (3 daily; 24hr); São Paulo (5 daily; 14–15hr).

Tourist information There are tourist offices at the airport (daily 8am–10pm; ☎ 45 3521 4276) and at the *rodoviária* (daily 7am–6pm; ☎ 45 3522 1027). In town, there are offices at the Terminal de Transporte Urbano (daily 7.30am–6pm; ☎ 45 3523 7901), and the Centro Municipal de Turismo, Av das Cataratas 2330, Vila Yolanda (daily 7am–11pm; ☎ 0800 451516, ⓦ pmfi.pr.gov.br/turismo).

3

ACCOMMODATION

When choosing where to stay, your main decision is whether to pick a central option or to go for somewhere closer to the falls. Being central has the advantage of proximity to good restaurants and bars, while staying close to the falls, where there are a number of excellent hostels and a great campsite, cuts down your travelling time.

CENTRAL

★ **Concept Design Hostel** Rua Vereador Moacyr Pereira 337, Vila Yolanda ☎ 45 3029 3631, ⓦ conceptdesignhostel.com. This stylish, budget boutique hostel has spacious doubles with individual colour themes, slick dorms, each bed equipped with reading lights and power sockets, a central pool, bar and communal kitchen. Close to the bus stop for the falls. Dorms R$50, doubles R$155

Iguassu Guest House Rua Naipi 1019 ☎ 45 3029 0242, ⓦ iguassuguesthouse.com.br. A short walk from the bus station, this small hostel offers spotless dorms but also excellent private en-suite rooms with all the amenities – bar, book exchange, pool table, PC terminals. Dorms R$55, doubles R$130

Pousada Evelina Navarrete Rua Irlan Kalichewski 171 ☎ 45 3574 3817, ⓦ pousadaevelina.com.br. Extremely friendly place with a youth hostel atmosphere that mainly attracts foreign backpackers. Rooms are simple but spotless, breakfasts are adequate, and multilingual Evelina goes out of her way to be helpful. Well located for buses to the falls. Dorms R$45, doubles R$120

★ **Tetris Container Hostel** Av das Cataratas 639, Vila Yolanda ☎ 45 3132 0019, ⓦ tetrishostel.com.br. Quirky but very cool sustainable hostel primarily made out of brightly painted shipping containers (it has a green roof, water is solar-heated, rainwater is used for toilets and all the containers, and most of the furniture, is recycled). Choose from female-only or mixed a/c dorms (where the snappy colours continue), or compact doubles, with private bathroom and a/c. There's a bar (one free drink nightly), garden, shared kitchen and even a swimming pool built out of a shipping container. Dorms R$53, doubles R$150

ROAD TO THE FALLS

★ **Hostel Paudimar Campestre** Av das Cataratas Km12.5 ☎ 45 3529 6061, ⓦ paudimar.com.br. This excellent HI establishment has superb facilities, from basic shared dorms sleeping six to eight people and family apartments (with double bed, bunk bed, a/c and private bathroom) to pretty cabins for two. The extensive grounds include a swimming pool and bar. Kitchen facilities are available, and they also serve evening meals. The hostel organizes daily trips to the Argentine side of the falls. Camping R$30/pitch, dorms R$48, private cabin R$118

EATING AND DRINKING

While it's no gastronomic paradise, Foz do Iguaçu is a good place to eat cheaply, with a proliferation of buffet-style *por kilo* restaurants. The main drag for restaurants and bars is Av Jorge Schimmelpfeng, south of the city centre – taxis should be around R$10–15 (on the meter) from most hotels in town.

Búfalo Branco Rua Engenheiro Rebouças 530 ☎ 45 3523 9744, ⓦ bufalobranco.com.br. Top-notch *churrascaría* with the all-you-can-eat *rodízio* system and a vast, excellent salad bar. Normally R$79 per person, but look for lunchtime special offers. Free transfer from your hotel. Daily noon–11pm.

Capitão Bar Rua Jorge Schimmelpfeng 288 ☎ 45 3572 1512, ⓦ capitaobar.com. One of a series of lively bars on this stretch, playing loud music and serving "Torre de Chopp" (2.5 litre beer towers, R$36), mojitos (R$17.50) and affordable pizzas. Outdoor tables fill quickly so arrive early in summer if you want to sit outside. Daily 11.30am–2am.

IGUAÇU FALLS TOURS AND ACTIVITIES

The Iguaçu Falls has become a major adventure travel centre with a bewildering range of activities available. Every fifteen minutes the **Helisul helicopter** (☎ 45 3529 7474, ⓦ helisul. com) takes off just outside the park entrance, offering ten-minute flights over the falls for R$255 per person (minimum three people); sensational views, but controversial thanks to the noise pollution (which scares wildlife).

TOUR OPERATORS

Macuco Safari ☎ 45 3529 6262, ⓦ macucosafari. com.br. At its own dedicated bus stop in the park, Macuco operates a jet-boat ride through white water right up to and into the falls (daily 9am–5.30pm, every 15min; R$170/person). Macuco also operates Cânion Iguaçu (accessed at the Path of the Falls bus stop), which comprises a canopy trail – a series of ropes and ladders above the forest (R$80) – and a 55m cliff face that you can abseil down (R$70).

Martin Travel Travessa Goiás 200 ☎ 45 3523 4959, ⓦ martintravel.com.br. A reliable local travel agency that specializes in ecotourism and puts together groups to go canoeing, rafting or mountain biking along forest trails.

INTO PARAGUAY AND ARGENTINA

Buses bound for **Ciudad del Este** in **Paraguay** (see page 706) depart across Av Juscelino Kubitschek from the Terminal de Transporte Urbano (every 30min or so; 7am–8.50pm; around R$6); taxis charge R$40–50. You need to disembark at the Brazilian customs for your exit stamps – the bus will not wait but your ticket is valid for the next one. You will then cross the Friendship Bridge to the Paraguayan customs, where you will again be asked to disembark.

For **Puerto Iguazú** (see page 87) in **Argentina**, Crucero del Nord buses depart from Rua Mem de Sá, at Rua Tarobá, the street just north of the Terminal de Transporte Urbano (Mon–Fri every 40min 7am–7pm; Sat & Sun every hr, 45min past the hr; R$7/A$25); you can also flag them down at stops en route. They terminate at the bus terminal in the centre of Puerto Iguazú where there are regular buses to the Argentine falls. Taxis charge R$60–70 to the town, and R$120–150 to the Argentine falls return; you'll have to stop at both the Brazilian and Argentine immigration posts in both directions, but wait times are rarely more than a few minutes. Taxi drivers will wait for you while you clear immigration, but buses may not; keep your ticket and take the next one coming through. It's unlikely that your Brazilian reais will be accepted across either border, so change money as soon as you can.

3

Clube Maringá Rua Dourado 111, Porto Meira (6km south of the centre) ☏45 3527 3472, ⓦrestaurantemaringa.com.br. Justly popular for its superb *rodízio de peixe* lunch and stunning views of the Rio Paraná. As well as a vast selection of local freshwater fish – golden dorado, pacu, tilapia – mostly fried and battered but some soups and grilled fish, there's an excellent salad bar and desserts. The buffet operates lunch and dinner for R$60 per person (à la carte dishes are about the same). Take the "Porto Meira" bus and ask for directions, or take a taxi at night (R$25). Tues–Sat 11.30am–11pm, Sun till 4pm.

★ **Pop Art + Black Cat Café** Rua Edmundo de Barros 257 ☏45 3029 5939. Stylish coffee culture comes to Foz thanks to this cool T-shirt store-café, with really excellent espresso, plus gluten-free and vegan-friendly snacks (think beet panini, zesty bean soup and sublime carrot muffins; R$6–16). Mon 11.30am–6pm, Tues–Fri 11.30am–8pm, Sat 1.30–9pm, Sun 3–8pm.

Recanto Gaúcho Rua Oscar Genehr (800m off Av das Cataratas Km 15, near the airport) ☏45 3572 2358,

ⓦrecantogaucho.com. A favourite Sunday outing for locals and tourists, but the atmosphere's lively, the meat's excellent and good value (R$50/person for all you can eat), and the owner, who always dresses in full gaucho regalia, is a real character. Turn up early; food is served until 3pm. It's advisable to phone ahead. Sun 10.30am–6pm. Closed Dec & Jan.

DIRECTORY

Banks and exchange Dollars (cash or travellers' cheques) can be easily changed in travel agents and banks along Av Brasil; the banks have ATMs.

Consulates Argentina, Eduardo Bianchi 26 ☏45 3574 2969; Paraguay, Rua Marechal Deodoro 901 ☏45 3523 2898.

Hospital Ministro Costa Cavalcanti, Av Gramado 580, ☏45 3576 8000, is a good private hospital.

Police Tourist police ☏45 3523 3036.

Post office Praça Getúlio Vargas 72, near Rua Barão do Rio Branco (Mon–Fri 9am–5pm).

Taxi Coopertaxi Cataratas ☏45 3524 6464.

★ TREAT YOURSELF

Ipê Grill Parque Nacional do Iguaçu ☏45 2102 7000, ⓦbelmond.com. The only hotel restaurant worth a splurge. Located by the pool in the *Belmond Hotel das Cataratas* (overlooking the falls), it offers an extensive but very pricey buffet dinner of typical Brazilian dishes and "gaucho" style barbecue for around R$150 (lunch is a la carte, with mains R$65–89). Even if you can't afford to stay here (rooms start at around R$1005), you should take a wander around the hotel grounds just to have a look. Daily 6.30–10am, 12.30–3pm & 7.30–11pm.

IGUAÇU FALLS

The **IGUAÇU FALLS** are, unquestionably, one of the world's great natural phenomena. They form the centrepiece of the vast **Parque Nacional do Iguaçu (Iguaçu National Park)**, which was first designated in 1936 though the falls were discovered as early as 1542 by the Spanish explorer Alvar Nuñez Cabeza de Vaca. To describe their beauty and power is a tall order, but for starters cast out any ideas that Iguaçu is some kind of Niagara Falls transplanted south of the equator

3

– compared with Iguaçu, Niagara is a ripple. About 15km before joining the Rio Paraná, the Rio Iguaçu broadens out, then plunges precipitously over an 80m-high cliff in 275 separate cascades that extend nearly 3km across the river. To properly experience Iguaçu it is essential to visit both sides. The Brazilian side gives the best overall view and allows you to fully appreciate the scale of it; the Argentine side (see page 88) allows you to get up close to the major individual cascades.

The falls are mind-blowing whatever the season, but they are always more spectacular following a heavy rainstorm. Weekends and Easter are best avoided if you don't want to share your experience with thousands of Brazilian and Argentine holidaymakers.

WHAT TO SEE AND DO

At its best in the early morning, a 1.2km cliffside trail runs alongside the falls, offering predictably jaw-dropping photo opportunities. A stairway leads down from the bus stop to the start of the trail. The path ends by coming perilously close to the ferocious "**Garganta do Diabo**" (Devil's Throat), the point where fourteen separate falls combine to form the world's most powerful single cascade in terms of the volume of water flow per second. Depending on the force of the river, you could be in for a real soaking, so if you have a camera with you be sure to carry it in a plastic bag. From here, you can either walk back up the path or take the lift to the top of the cliff and the road leading to the *Belmond Hotel das Cataratas* (see page 351). You'll undoubtedly come across coatis on the trails (though raccoon-like, they are not raccoons, whatever the local guides may say) – don't be fooled by their cute and comical appearance; these little creatures are accomplished food thieves with long claws and sharp teeth.

ARRIVAL AND DEPARTURE

It costs foreigners R$63 to enter the park (concessions available for MERCOSUR and Brazilian residents), after which a shuttle bus (included) will deliver you to the trails. See ⊕ cataratasdoiguacu.com.br for more information.

By bus Bus #120 ("Aeroporto Parque Nacional"; $3.45) from Foz do Iguaçu terminates at the entrance to the falls (daily 9am–5pm).
By taxi Taxis (using the meter) will cost around R$50 from town.

ILHA DE SÃO FRANCISCO DO SUL

Travelling 135km south from Curitiba into the state of Santa Catarina, the coastline becomes the main attraction, with the beaches of **ILHA DE SÃO FRANCISCO DO SUL** well worth a diversion off the main highway. A low-lying island separated from the mainland by a narrow strait some 40km east of the industrial port city of Joinville and the site of a major Petrobras oil refinery, it might be reasonable to assume that São Francisco should be avoided, but this isn't the case. Both the port and refinery keep a discreet distance from the main town, **São Francisco do Sul**, and the beaches blend perfectly with the slightly dilapidated colonial setting. On the east coast, **Praia de Ubatuba**, 16km from the centre, and the adjoining **Praia de Enseada**, 20km from town, offer enough surf for you to have fun but not enough to be dangerous. A ten-minute walk across the peninsula from the eastern end of Enseada leads to **Praia da Saúdade** (or just Prainha), where the waves are suitable for only the most experienced surfers.

SÃO FRANCISCO DO SUL

One of the oldest settlements in the south, the gorgeous *centro histórico* of **SÃO FRANCISCO DO SUL** (aka "São Chico") is separated from the main commercial part of town by a ring of small hills, giving it a relaxed, languid air unusual in this part of Brazil – it's also one of the few places in Santa Catarina where a concentration of colonial and nineteenth-century buildings survives.

WHAT TO SEE AND DO

Dominating the city's skyline is the **Igreja Matriz Nossa Senhora da Graça**, the main church, originally built in 1699 by indigenous slaves, but completely reconstructed in 1926. The **Museu Nacional do Mar** on Rua Manoel Lourenço de Andrade in the historic centre

(Tues–Fri 9am–5.30pm, Sat & Sun 10am–5.30pm; R$5; ⓦmuseunacionaldomar.com.br) has a vast maritime collection with an emphasis on southern Brazil and its people. The prettiest beaches, **Paulas** and **Praia dos Ingleses**, are also the nearest to town, just a couple of kilometres to the east. Both are small, and have trees to provide shade. Surprisingly few people take advantage of the calm and shallow waters here, which are ideal for gentle swimming.

ARRIVAL AND INFORMATION

By bus The easiest way to reach São Francisco do Sul is by Verdes Mares (hourly; 1hr 30min; R$11.85; ⓦvmares. com.br) bus from Joinville's *rodoviária* (though there are less frequent direct buses from Curitiba); you can get to Joinville from Curitiba (hourly; 2hr) or Florianópolis (hourly; 2hr 30min). Buses from Joinville terminate at the *rodoviária*, inconveniently located outside São Francisco do Sul centre on Rua Dom Fernando Trejo y Sanabria (just off the main highway); most people get off the bus at the junction of Afonso dos Santos and Barão do Rio Branco in the commercial heart of town – from here it's a fairly straightforward 20min walk to the *centro histórico* (ask if you get lost), or R$5–10 by taxi (☎47 3444 2047). Similarly, heading back to Joinville you can pick up the bus from the bus stop in town (taxi drivers all know it). Local buses to the beaches (R$3.95) depart from the plaza near the church (Praça da Igreja); bus #5440 to Prainha; and numerous buses to Enseada along the coast road in both directions.
Destinations Curitiba (daily; 3hr); Joinville (hourly; 1hr 30min); São Paulo (daily; 8hr).
Tourist information The helpful local tourist office is on the waterfront at Rua Babitonga 62 (Mon–Fri 7.30am–1.30pm; ☎47 3444 5380, ⓦvisitesaofranciscodosul.com. br).

ACCOMMODATION

Most of the island's visitors bypass the town and head straight for the beaches to the east, so, even in midsummer, there's rarely any difficulty in finding a central hotel.
Kontiki Rua Babitonga 211 ☎47 3444 2232, ⓦhotelkontiki.com.br. Attractive hotel forged from two historic properties: the nineteenth-century Hospital de Caridade and the old police station, dating from 1920. Rooms are fairly basic (with fan or a/c) but clean and comfy, with cable TV. R$190
Pousada Farol da Ilha Praia da Enseada, just behind the beach at Rua Maceió 1156 ☎47 3449 1802, ⓦpousadafaroldailha.tur.br. This little family-run place, only 300m from the beach, also has its own pool. The rooms are decorated in a rustic style and it's particularly popular

with couples. There is a discount for rooms with a shared bathroom. R$180
Zibamba Rua Fernando Dias 27, São Francisco do Sul ☎47 3444 2020, ⓦhotelzibamba.com.br. The town's top digs is a gorgeous old property near the waterfront, with relatively plain rooms, pool and decent seafood restaurant – try and get a room with a balcony. R$206

EATING AND DRINKING

Eating out holds no great excitement, with the *Zibamba's* restaurant the best of a generally poor bunch serving up a seafood buffet at lunch and typical Brazilian dishes à la carte in the evenings. Enseada does have a lively nightlife, though.
Bar do Banana Av Brasília at João Pessoa, Prainha (18km from downtown São Francisco) ☎47 3444 0785, ⓦbardobanana.com.br. Popular with 20-somethings (and cruise-ship passengers) looking for reasonably priced drinks, food and fun by the sea. Daily 11am–11pm.
★ **Café do Museu** Rua Manoel Lourenço de Andrade 133 ☎47 3444 8071. Opposite the main entrance to Museu Nacional do Mar (and attached to the exit), this small café is by far the most atmospheric place to drink or grab a snack in town. It's a mellow, artsy space with old shed walls, part shop, part snack bar, with coffee, beers and light meals on offer. Tues–Fri 9am–6pm, Sat 10am–midnight, Sun 1–6pm.

BALNEÁRIO CAMBORIÚ

If you are travelling in search of the Santa Catarina party scene, look no further than **BALNEÁRIO CAMBORIÚ**, an effervescent resort town 112km south of São Francisco do Sul with a distinctly hedonistic approach to life often dismissed by Cariocas as the "poor man's Copacabana". Either way it's a popular summer destination with young Brazilians, Paraguayans and Argentines, and the town is packed out during the peak season with sunbathers and fun-seekers.

WHAT TO SEE AND DO

Camboriú has something of a Mediterranean holiday resort feel to it, with its high-rise buildings and pedestrian streets lined with artists peddling souvenirs; walking around town, you could be forgiven for thinking that you were on the Portuguese Algarve. The place is not without its charms – not least its 7km-long **Praia Central**, offering safe swimming and golden sand. **Praia do**

Pinho, on the other side of the peninsula west of town, is the site of Brazil's first nudist beach.

Camboriú even has its own 33m-high Rio-style Christ statue, the **Cristo Luz** (April & Sept Wed–Sat 4pm–midnight; May, June & Aug Thurs–Sat 4pm–midnight; July, Oct & Nov Tues–Sat 4pm–midnight; Dec–March Mon–Sat 4pm–midnight; year-round Sun 10am–midnight; R$15 10am–7pm, R$30 after 7pm; ⓦcristoluz.com.br), illuminated at night and casting a faint greenish glow over the town. The forested hillside of Morro da Aguada in the south of town is a nature reserve-cum-theme park, the **Parque Unipraias** (daily 9.30am–6pm; cable car R$39; ⓦunipraias.com.br). You can reach it via a 3.25km cable car (same hours) that starts at the Estação Barra Sul on the Praia Central before shooting up to the Estação Mata Atlântica on the summit (240m), offering glorious views over the town, beaches and out to sea. From here you can stroll the trails in the Parque Ambiental (same hours; included in price), enjoy the Zip Rider zipline (R$45) or the Youhooo! 60km/hr toboggan ride ($34). The cable car continues down to the beach at Praia Laranjeiras.

ARRIVAL AND INFORMATION

By bus Camboriú sits on the main Curitiba–Florianópolis highway (BR-101), and is just 80km north of Florianópolis. Buses arrive at the *rodoviária* (☎47 3367 2901) on Av Santa Catarina, at the edge of town close to the highway. Destinations Buenos Aires (1 daily; 28hr); Curitiba (22 daily; 2hr 30min); Florianópolis (38 daily; 1hr 30min); Joinville (26 daily; 1hr 30min); Porto Alegre (9 daily; 8–9hr); São Paulo (13 daily; 8–9hr).

Tourist information There is a tourist information office at Av do Estado 5041 (daily 7am–10pm; ☎47 3367 8005, ⓦvisitebalneariocamboriu.com.br), but inconveniently located some 2km inland from the beach, just off the main highway into the city.

ACCOMMODATION

You'd be wise to book ahead in the peak season when block bookings take up the majority of the more affordable hotels. If you're in a group, ask at the tourist office about renting a house – it's cheaper than you might think.

Hostel 325 Rua Panama 325 ☎47 99604 8718, ✉325hostel@gmail.com. Stylish modern hostel with comfy dorms (mixed, male or female), small outdoor courtyard (with barbecue) in a quiet residential block, a short walk from the beach. Shared kitchen, pool table and sociable clientele, though staff rarely speak English. Dorms R$60

Little Hostel Balneário Camboriú Rua 1500, no. 1555 ☎47 99927 4558, ⓦhostelbalneariocamboriu.com. Popular hostel, a 15min walk from the beach, with clean, cheap a/c dorms (mixed, male or female), decent breakfast and free cookies. Dorms R$45

EATING

In addition to the proliferation of fast-food joints and *lanchonetes*, there are some excellent restaurants around if you look hard enough, with seafood platters featuring heavily on most menus.

Guacamole Av Normando Tedesco 1122 ☎47 3366 0311, ⓦguacamolemex.com.br. Charismatic Mexican mini-chain with live music, mariachis and "tequileros" who are only too happy to wet your whistle. Latin dance shows every Tuesday night add to the experience. Spicy mains from R$45. Mon–Sat 7pm–3am, Sun 7pm–midnight.

O Pharol Av Atlântica 5740 ☎47 3367 3800, ⓦpharol. com.br. Classy seafood restaurant, well worth the extra reais. The seafood *rodizio* (R$87 per person) is something special and includes prawns, lobster, oysters and more; *feijoada* served Wed & Sat. Daily 11.30am–midnight.

DRINKING AND NIGHTLIFE

Camboriú has a vibrant, young nightlife scene. Most places are on or around Av Atlântica, especially at the southern end, the Barra Sul, where you'll find a huge array of beach bars and discos. Things don't start to get lively until well after midnight and the action continues until after the sun comes up.

Cachaçaria Uai Av Atlântica 2334 ☎47 3367 4978. Bar-style hangout on the beach, specializing in caipirinhas, the Brazilian cocktail made with *cachaça* and crushed limes, and food from Minas Gerais. Live music Tues–Sun. Daily 6pm–6am.

Woods Av Atlântica 4450, Barra Sul ☎47 7812 3475, ⓦwoodsbar.com.br. This popular *sertanejo* (country)-style pub and club chain features top live acts and cold beers served in a beachfront location. Cover usually ranges R$50–80. Fri & Sat 11pm–5am.

ILHA SANTA CATARINA

Joined to the mainland by suspension bridges, **ILHA SANTA CATARINA** is noted throughout Brazil for its gorgeous scenery and beaches, ideal climate, attractive fishing villages and the city of **Florianópolis**, the small and prosperous capital of Santa Catarina state (half of the city lies on the mainland and the other half on the island).

The island is peppered with resorts – the **north** of the island is the most developed while the extreme **south** remains the quietest and most unspoilt – while central **Lagoa da Conceição** is a great spot for budget accommodation and bar hopping. There are some 42 **beaches** around Ilha Santa Catarina, which means even the most crowded are rarely unbearably so. Anywhere on the island can be reached by bus within an hour or so from Florianópolis, although **renting a car** is a good idea if you have limited time, allowing you to explore the island more thoroughly. Note, however, that parts of Santa Catarina are notorious for bad traffic, especially on the weekends and in the summer. Also, locals often refer to the whole island as Florianópolis, with the city known simply as *centro*.

FLORIANÓPOLIS
Founded in 1675, **FLORIANÓPOLIS** (aka "Floripa") boomed 75 years later thanks to an influx of immigrants from the Azores. With the construction of the bridges linking the island with the mainland, Florianópolis as a port has all but died, and today it thrives as an administrative, commercial and tourist centre. It's a modern city, but the late nineteenth-century pastel-coloured, stuccoed buildings of the centre still have a whiff of old-world appeal, and it's worth taking time to have a look around. Few people visit Ilha Santa Catarina for the express purpose of seeing the city, however, and to see the natural beauty for which the island is renowned, you need to head out to the beaches.

WHAT TO SEE AND DO
On the former waterfront, you'll find two ochre-coloured buildings: the 1889 **Mercado Público** (Mon–Fri 7am–7pm, Sat 7am–2pm; bars can stay open until 10pm), which contains some excellent bars and small restaurants, and the **Alfândega** (Mon–Fri 9am–6.30pm, Sat 9am–1pm), a former customs house dating from 1875 that has been converted for use as a crafts market. Most sights of interest, however, are centred on the lush square **Praça XV de Novembro**, at the centre of which is the enormous, gnarled "**Centenary Fig**" tree. According to legend, walking three times around the tree will guarantee you fame and fortune. By the end of 2018 the old Casa de Câmara e Cadeia on the plaza's southeast corner should be open as the **Museu da Cidade**, chronicling the history of the city.

On one side of the square is the **Palácio Cruz e Souza**, an imposing pink building dating back to the eighteenth century, but largely built in its current form in the 1890s as the official governor's palace – it now houses the **Museu Histórico de Santa Catarina** (Tues–Fri 10am–6pm, Sat & Sun 10am–4pm; R$5, free on Sun; ⊕mhsc. sc.gov.br), whose nineteenth-century interior is more engaging than its collection of military memorabilia. The **Catedral Metropolitana** (Mon–Fri 6.15am–8pm, Sat 8am–noon & 4–8pm, Sun 7am–noon & 4–9pm), overlooking the square, dates back to the eighteenth century but has been modified many times since; the only church in the city centre virtually unchanged since the colonial era is the **Igreja de Nossa Senhora do Rosário**, built between 1787 and 1830 and approached by a flight of steps at Rua

BEER DRINKING IN BLUMENAU
Founded by German immigrants in 1850, the affluent city of Blumenau is best known today for its annual **Oktoberfest** (⊕oktoberfestblumenau.com.br), the biggest German festival in South America, attracting over 500,000 revellers annually to its vast beer tents, folk dancing, shooting matches and German singing contests. For accommodation options check out ⊕blumenau.sc.gov.br, but you'll need to book in advance; the cheapest option is usually the *Pousada e Hostel Vento Minuano* (Rua Lydia Zwicker 271; ☎47 9191 4422; dorms around R$40), 9km from the bus station (taxis are around R$20). Blumenau is just one hour thirty minutes from Camboriú, three hours by hourly bus from Florianópolis, and four hours from Curitiba.

Marechal Guilherme 60, two blocks north of the Praça.

ARRIVAL AND INFORMATION

By plane The airport (☎ 48 3331 4000) is 12km south of the city, with daily flights from Buenos Aires, São Paulo, Rio and Porto Alegre. You can get into the centre by taxi (around R$50 to the city centre or R$60 to Lagoa), or catch green bus #183 or #186 (every 10–30min and labelled "Corredor do Sudoeste"; R$3.90), which will end up at the Terminal de Integração Centro (TICEN) in the centre (around 45min).

By bus Buses arrive at the Terminal Rodoviária Rita María (☎ 48 3212 3100) at the foot of the road bridge that links the island to the mainland. Cross Av Paulo Fontes and it's a short walk to the centre; the local bus terminal (TICEN) is one long block east at Paulo Fontes 701.

Destinations Blumenau (hourly; 3hr); Buenos Aires (1 daily; 28hr); Curitiba (hourly; 4–5hr); Foz do Iguaçu (14 daily; 14hr 30min–15hr 40min); Joinville (hourly; 2hr 30min–3hr); Porto Alegre (12 daily; 5–7hr); Rio (1 daily; 14hr 40min); São Paulo (hourly; 11–12hr).

Tourist information There's a tourist information kiosk at the *rodoviária* (daily 8am–6pm; ☎ 48 3228 1095). Santa Catarina's state tourist board is based at Rua Felipe Schmidt 249, on the 8th floor (Mon–Fri 8am–7pm; ☎ 48 3212 6328, Ⓦ turismo.sc.gov.br).

GETTING AROUND

By bus The island has several local bus terminals, so be prepared to change if travelling by bus a lot (transfers are free). The central local bus terminal is Terminal de Integração Centro (or TICEN) at Paulo Fontes 701, which serves most of the island (fares R$3.90; R$3.71 with a *cartão magnético*, stored-value card). Faster, a/c yellow minibuses – *executivos* (R$6.50–8.50) – also zip between the main beaches.

Routes From Terminal de Integração Centro (TICEN): #311, #330 or #320 to Lagoa Da Conceição (TILAG); #231 or #233 to Canasvieiras (TICAN). From Lagoa da Conceição (TILAG): #360 to Barra da Lagoa; #363 to Joaquina via Praia Mole; #842 to Canasvieiras (TICAN). From Canasvieiras (TICAN): #276 to Balneário Canasvieiras.

ACCOMMODATION

Most tourists choose to stay at the island's beaches and resorts, but staying in Florianópolis itself has the benefit of direct bus services to other parts of the island. It's not cheap, though, and accommodation is snapped up quickly in high season.

Eco Box Hostel Rua Conselheiro Mafra 847 ☎ 48 3025 3945, Ⓦ ecoboxhostel.com.br. Hostel near the bus station that features tiny plywood a/c cubicles ensuring a modicum of privacy, and clean, modern bathrooms. The smallest singles are *very* small (two square metres for just R$43), but you can opt for bigger doubles (five square metres). R$100

Floripa Hostel Rua Duarte Schuttel 227 ☎ 48 3225 3781, Ⓦ floripahostel.com.br. Everything you would expect from an HI hostel (including linens and lockers), though more expensive than elsewhere on the island. It fills rapidly in summer, so get here early. It's R$10 discount for HI members. Dorms R$65, doubles R$145

Sumaré Hotel Rua Felipe Schmidt 423 ☎ 48 3733 4035, Ⓦ sumarehotel.com.br. The cheapest of the central hotels, in a secure area of town. The minimal rooms are nothing to write home about, but will do if you'd rather spend your money on enjoying yourself than on your digs. Rooms with private bathrooms from R$139, and cheaper single rates. R$95

EATING AND DRINKING

Getting a snack in Florianópolis is no problem, but finding a decent meal sometimes can be, and many of the better restaurants are some way from the centre along Av Beira Norte (take bus #134 from the local bus terminal) – expect prices similar to upmarket areas of Rio de Janeiro. The best place for cheap eats is the Mercado Público (see page 355).

Botequim Floripa Av Rio Branco 632 ☎ 48 3333 1234. Old-fashioned bar with a lively happy hour and cold beer on tap. Serves up great-value set lunch daily (R$15.90). Mon–Sat 11.30am–2.30pm & 5pm–1.30am.

Box 32 Mercado Público ☎ 48 3224 5588, Ⓦ box32.com.br. Seafood specialist and meeting place of the local glitterati who come to slurp oysters and munch prawns (try the *pastel de camarão*). That said, it's not as expensive as you might fear, with most meals setting you back R$30–35. Mon–Fri 10am–8pm, Sat 10am–3pm.

Cervejaria Devassa Rua Bocaiúva 2198 ☎ 48 3304 9800, Ⓦ cervejariadevassa.com.br. Buzzing local outpost of the national beer chain, serving all its prime pours on draught, plus a menu of Brazilian favourites. Wed–Sun 6pm–2am.

The Roof Lounge Av Beira Mar Norte 2746 (Majestic Palace Hotel) ☎ 48 3231 8000, Ⓦ theroof.com.br. Rooftop hotel lounge bar (with the *Black Sheep* sushi bar), with sensational views along the seafront, plush armchair and couch seating and an expensive cocktail list. Wed–Sat 7.30pm–4am.

DIRECTORY

Banks and exchange Banks are located on Rua Felipe Schmidt and by Praça XV de Novembro.

Car rental Avis, Av Deputado Diomicio Freitas s/n (☎ 48 3331 4176) and Localiza Hertz, Rua Henrique Valgas 112A (☎ 48 2107 6464), are also represented at the airport and can arrange delivery in the city centre. During the peak summer season advance reservations are essential.

CENTRINHO DA LAGOA

0   200
metres

N

Bus Terminal (TILAG)

Florianópolis Centro (11km)

AV. AFONSO DELAMBERT NETO

RUA CRISÓGONO VIEIRA DA CRUZ

RUA MANOEL ISIDORO DA SILVEIRA

RUA MANOEL SEVERINO DE OLIVEIRA

RUA JOSÉ HENRIQUE VERAS

RUA AFONSO LUIZ BORBA

RUA BENTO SILVEIRA

SRV. ANTÔNIO DA SILVEIRA

RUA JOÃO ANTÔNIO DA SILVEIRA

RUA ALTENOR VIEIRA

RUA DAS ARARAS

RUA RITA LOURENÇO DA SILVEIRA

RUA JOÃO OSNIO DA SILVA

LEOPOLDO JOÃO SANTOS

RUA NS. DA CONCEIÇÃO

RUA DAS PALMEIRAS

RUA HENRIQUE VERAS NASCIMENTO

R. ORLANDO CARIONI

AV. DAS RENDEIRAS

Lagoa da Conceição

DRINKING
The Black Swan   1
Books & Beers   2

EATING
DNA Natural   1
Querubim   2

ACCOMMODATION
Magic Monkey Hostel   3
Mama Africa Hostel   2
Pousada e Camping
  Lagoa da Conceição   5
Tucano House Backpackers   1
Hostel Way2Go   4

3

5 (1.1km), Praia Mole (3.3km), Joaquina (4.3km), Barra de Lagoa (7km), Campeche & South Coast (12km)

Pharmacies Farmacia Bela Vista, Rua Tenente Silveira 110. For homeopathic remedies try Farmacia Homeopática Jaqueline, Rua Felipe Schmidt 413.

Post office The main post office is at Praça XV de Novembro 242 (Mon–Fri 9am–5pm, Sat 8am–noon).

LAGOA DA CONCEIÇÃO

A large saltwater lagoon in the centre of the island, **Lagoa da Conceição** is popular for swimming, canoeing and windsurfing, with the bustling downtown area known as **Centrinho da Lagoa** (usually simply referred to as Lagoa) at the southern end. The town is both an attractive and convenient place to stay: there are good bus services from here into the centre of Florianópolis and to the east-coast beaches, and the main road is lined with restaurants and bars. This is arguably the liveliest place for nightlife on the island during the summer and at weekends throughout the year, with restaurants always crowded and people overflowing into the streets from the bars.

ACCOMMODATION

Magic Monkey Hostel Rua José Henrique Veras 469 ☎ 48 3065 0075, ⓦ magicmonkeyhostel.com; map p.357. Friendly hostel that's convenient for the local bus station (TILAG) in Centrinho and where staff make you feel part of the extended family. There's a sundeck, jacuzzi, pool table, huge widescreen TV, basic dorms and rooms with a/c. Dorms R$36, doubles R$130

Mama Africa Hostel Rua João Josino da Silva 196 ☎ 48 3030 0396; map p.357. Large modern doubles, shared terrace with hammocks and a/c dorms (mixed and female breakfasts), plus excellent breakfasts. Dorms R$75, doubles R$200

Pousada e Camping Lagoa da Conceição Av das Rendeiras 1480 ☎ 48 3232 5555, ⓦ pousadaecampinglagoadaconceicao.net; map p.357. Decent campsite shaded by trees, with hot showers and outdoor barbecues. Camping/person R$35

★ **Tucano House Backpackers** Rua das Araras 229 ☎ 48 3207 8287, ⓦ tucanohouse.com; map p.357. Popular place with six dorms and five doubles (all with a/c), some of which have lagoon views. Serves meals every night in an outside patio area, which makes a great place to meet fellow travellers. There are also half-price drinks at the bar between 5pm and 7pm. Other services include a pool, surfboard rental and bikes (R$40/day). Open Dec to mid-March only; cash only. Dorms R$55, doubles R$220

Hostel Way2Go Rua Rita Lourenço da Silveira 139 ☎ 48 3364 6004; map p.357. Well-located hostel near the bridge in Centrinho. Washing machines available for guests' use, TV room and excellent kitchen space. No curfew. Dorms R$60

EATING

DNA Natural Rua Manoel Severino de Oliveira 680 ☎ 48 3207 3441, ⓦ dnanatural.com.br; map p.357. Chain specializing in natural, healthy foods, including tasty wraps and huge mixed salads. There's also an exhaustive range of tropical juices and shakes (R$6–12). Daily 8am–midnight.

3

Querubim Av Henrique Veras do Nascimento 255 ☎ 48 3232 8743; map p.357. Arguably the best-value place to have lunch in Centrinho. The delicious buffet includes chicken, beef, shrimp and salads (around R$44/kilo or R$26 as much as you like). Lunch 11.30am–3.30pm; snacks until 4am.

DRINKING

The Black Swan Rua Manoel Severino de Oliveira 592 ☎ 48 3234 5682, ⓦ theblackswan.com.br; map p.357. Faux-English pub and sports bar run by a British expat, popular with Brazilians and an international crowd. Standard priced local beer on tap, plus a range of expensive imported beer from Europe. Happy hour 5–9.30pm and live music most nights (cover R$10–20). Mon–Fri 5pm–midnight, Sat & Sun 10.30am–2am.

Books & Beers Rua Senador Ivo D'Aquino 103 ☎ 48 3206 6664, ⓦ booksbeers.com.br; map p.357. Relaxed spot for a cold beer or seafood (mains R$31–60), with a cool terrace overlooking the lake and a cosy interior lined with books. Some of the craft beers are excellent but most are pricey (R$35–50); check before ordering. Tues–Fri 5pm–midnight, Sat 12.30pm–midnight, Sun 12.30–10.30pm.

THE EAST COAST

Just 4km from Centrinho da Lagoa, **PRAIA MOLE** is one of the most beautiful beaches in Brazil, slightly hidden beyond sand dunes and beneath low-lying cliffs.

Despite its popularity, commercial activity has remained low-key, probably because there's a deep drop-off right at the water's edge. The next beach as you head south, approached via a road passing between gigantic dunes, is at **JOAQUINA**, which attracts serious surfers. The water's cold, however, and the sea rough, only really suitable for strong swimmers. If you have the energy, climb to the top of the dunes where you'll be rewarded with the most spectacular views in all directions. The beaches of the east coast can be reached by bus from the terminal in Centrinho.

ACCOMMODATION

Sunset Backpackers Rodovia Jornalista Manoel de Menezes 631 ☎ 48 3232 0141, ⓦ sunsetbackpackers. com. Chilled-out hostel overlooking the bay from a ridge near Praia Mole, with a mix of private rooms and dorms equipped with fans and a/c, free *caipirinhas* for residents (daily 7.30–8.30pm), a hearty Brazilian barbecue on Sundays and the friendly *Elementum Temple* bar,

specializing in the microbrews of Cervejaria Elementum. Dorms R$40, doubles R$160

CANASVIEIRAS

The island's built-up **north coast** offers safe swimming in calm, warm seas and is popular with families. The long, gently curving bay of **CANASVIEIRAS** is the most crowded of the northern resorts (27km north of Floripa), largely geared towards Argentine families who own or rent houses near the beach. By walking away from the concentration of bars at the centre, towards **Ponta das Canas**, it's usually possible to find a relatively quiet spot.

Unless you're renting a house for a week or more (agencies abound, among them ⓦ aluguetemporada.com.br), finding accommodation is difficult, as the unappealing hotels are usually booked solid throughout the summer. The local **restaurants** mostly offer the same menu of prawn dishes, pizza and hamburgers.

ACCOMMODATION

Hostel Canasvieiras Rua Dr João de Oliveira 517 ☎ 48 3225 3781, ⓦ hostelcanasvieiras.com. Decent budget option, with shared kitchen, colour TV and eating area offering wonderful views across the coast. Dorms R$60, doubles R$180

World Hostel Rua Hipólito Gregório Pereira 464 ☎ 48 3307 3342, ⓦ worldhostel.com.br. Modern hostel with clean tiled floors two blocks back from the beach. Cheap dorms (mixed or male- and female-only), with small pool and a pool table. Dorms R$40

THE WEST COAST

The principal places of interest on the west coast are **SANTO ANTÔNIO DE LISBOA** to the north of Florianópolis and **RIBEIRÃO**

★ TREAT YOURSELF

Ostradamus Rodovia Baldicero Filomeno 7640, Ribeirão da Ilha ☎ 48 3337 5711, ⓦ ostradamus. com.br. Justly popular spot serving up creative dishes such as a dozen oysters with martini and lemon, as well as delicious mains – despite the high prices and long waits for tables, this is easily one of the island's best restaurants. Try the seafood risotto, washed down with local wine (mains R$110–140). Tues–Sat noon–11pm, Sun noon–4pm.

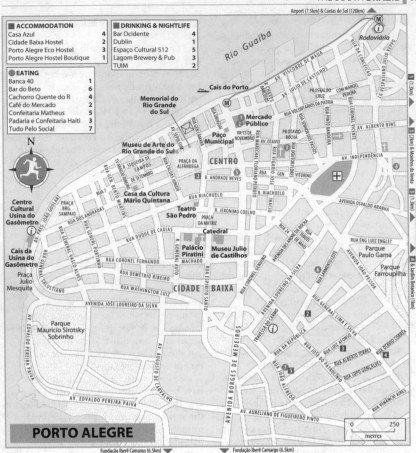

■ ACCOMMODATION

Casa Azul	4
Cidade Baixa Hostel	2
Porto Alegre Eco Hostel	3
Porto Alegre Hostel Boutique	1

■ DRINKING & NIGHTLIFE

Bar Ocidente	4
Dublin	1
Espaço Cultural 512	5
Lagom Brewery & Pub	3
TUIM	2

● EATING

Banca 40	1
Bar do Beto	6
Cachorro Quente do R	4
Café do Mercado	2
Confeitaria Matheus	5
Padaria e Confeitaria Haiti	3
Tudo Pelo Social	7

PORTO ALEGRE

Fundação Iberê Camargo (6.5km) ▼   ▼ Fundação Iberê Camargo (6.5km)

DA ILHA to the south. These are the
island's oldest and least developed
settlements, their houses almost all painted
white with dark blue sash windows, in
typical Azorean style, and both villages
have a simple colonial church. Fishing,
rather than catering to the needs of
tourists, remains the principal activity, and
the waters offshore from Santo Antônio
are used to farm mussels and oysters,
considered the best on the island. Because
the beaches are small and face the
mainland, tourism has remained low-key,
accommodation is limited and the few
visitors here tend to be on day-trips,
staying just long enough to sample oysters
at a local bar.

PORTO ALEGRE

The capital of Rio Grande do Sul, **PORTO
ALEGRE** lies on the eastern bank of the Rio
Guaíba, some 450km south of
Florianópolis. Settlers from the Azores
arrived here in 1752, but it wasn't until
Porto Alegre became the gateway for the
export of beef that it developed into
Brazil's leading commercial centre south of
São Paulo, with a population today of
some 4.5 million. Like most major
Brazilian cities it's not especially attractive,
with a skyline of primarily tired 1960s
high-rises, but the **Fundação Iberê
Camargo** is a must-see for art lovers
(assuming it's open), and the city remains
a fun place to eat and drink.

3

Everything in the centre worth seeing is within an easy walk, and a day or so is enough to visit most places of interest.

MERCADO PÚBLICO AND AROUND

The golden-coloured **Mercado Público** (Mon–Fri 7.30am–7.30pm, Sat 7.30am–6.30pm) stands at the heart of Porto Alegre's commercial district, located alongside Praça Rui Barbosa and Praça XV de Novembro. A replica of Lisbon's Mercado da Figueira, this imposing building contains an absorbing mix of stalls selling household goods, food and regional handicrafts. Upstairs are restaurants offering traditional Brazilian all-you-can-eat lunch buffets which stay open after the market stalls shut. Next to the market is the ochre **Paço Municipal**, the old *prefeitura* (town hall), built in Neoclassical style between 1898 and 1901, its impressive proportions an indication of civic pride and self-confidence during Porto Alegre's golden age.

West of here along Rua Sete de Setembro is the pleasantly verdant **Praça da Alfândega**, home of the grand **Museu de Arte do Rio Grande do Sul** (Tues–Sun 10am–7pm; free; ⓦmargs.rs.gov.br). You can spend an hour or so admiring the local modern art here, combined with a visit to the **Memorial do Rio Grande do Sul** next door (Tues–Sat 10am–6pm, Sun 1–5pm; free), which houses pictorial exhibitions on the history of the state.

PRAÇA DA MATRIZ

A short walk uphill from the Praça da Alfândega via Rua General Câmara leads to the **Praça da Matriz**, home to Porto Alegre's oldest buildings, though they have been so heavily altered over the last few centuries that few retain their original character (the Catedral Metropolitana was only completed in 1986). The **Palácio Piratini**, the state governor's residence (tours every 30min Mon–Fri 9.30–11.30am & 2–5pm; free), dates from 1909, while the **Teatro São Pedro** (ⓦteatrosaopedro.com.br) opposite was inaugurated in 1858.

CASA DE CULTURA MÁRIO QUINTANA

The **Casa de Cultura Mário Quintana**, Rua dos Andradas 736 (Tues–Fri 9am–9pm, Sat & Sun noon–9pm; free; ⓦccmq.com.br), a beautifully restored warren of art galleries, libraries and theatres, was a hotel between 1918 and 1980; the poet Mário Quintana was a long-time resident. Pride of place is given to his room on the second floor (no. 217, **Quarto do Poeta**), which is maintained in the state it was in when he lived here.

FUNDAÇÃO IBERÊ CAMARGO

Porto Alegre's under-visited crown jewel, the **Fundação Iberê Camargo** lies 5km south of the *centro histórico* at Av Padre Cacique 2000 (Sat & Sun 2–7pm; free; ⓦiberecamargo.org.br). The fascinating Modernist building is itself part of the attraction, vaguely reminiscent of the Guggenheim in New York, with a gleaming all-white interior and a spiral layout. The contemporary art exhibits here are usually impressive; displays revolve, but there's always work from Rio Grande do Sul artist **Iberê Camargo** (1914–94), whose unsettling Expressionist images have become some of Brazil's most revered art. The café here is the best place to **watch the sunset** over the Guaíba. Take any bus towards the Zona Sul (from Av Senador Salgado Filho to Juca Batista, Serraria, Padre Réus or Camaquã); to return you'll have to walk back along the highway to the bus stop, and then take any bus headed to town; a taxi from the bus station should be R$25.

Note that the foundation's **opening hours have been cut** drastically since Brazil's current economic crisis began (check the website for the latest).

By plane Aeroporto Internacional Salgado Filho, 6km northeast of downtown Porto Alegre, receives flights from all major national destinations and nearby capitals. Fixed-price Cootaero taxis (pay at the booth before you leave the terminal; ☎51 3342 5000) charge R$34–42 into the centre (reckon on R$40–55 heading back, when taxis use the meter); you can also take the monorail link (Aeromóvel) to the nearest metrô station (3min), the Estação Aeroporto, and catch trains into the city (5am–11.20pm; R$1.70; buy ticket before you board the Aeromóvel) in just 10min (the Mercado station).

By bus The *rodoviária* (☎51 3210 0101) is northeast of the centre at Largo Vespasiano Júlio Veppo 11, but within walking distance; after dark it's safer, and easier to ride the metrô to the Mercado Público or take a taxi (R$10–30; ☎51 3221 9371).

Destinations Canela (hourly; 2hr); Curitiba (8 daily; 11hr); Buenos Aires (1 daily; 18hr); Florianópolis (14 daily; 7–8hr); Foz do Iguaçu (8 daily; 14–16hr); Gramado (hourly; 2hr); Montevideo (1 daily; 11hr); Rio de Janeiro (1–2 daily; 24–25hr); Santo Ângelo (13 daily; 6–7hr); São Paulo (4 daily; 18hr).

INFORMATION AND TOURS

Tourist information The local Secretaria Municipal de Turismo (⊛portoalegre.travel) has very helpful branches at the airport, *rodoviária* (7am–10pm), the Centro Cultural Usina do Gasômetro (Tues–Sun 9am–6pm; ☎0800 517 686) and at the Mercado Público (Store 99, Ground Floor; Mon–Sat 8am–6pm; ☎0800 517 686).

Boat tours Excursions (1hr 30min) on the Rio Guaíba with Barco Cisne Branco leave from the tour-boat berth (Cais do Porto) on Av Mauá 1050, near the metro station (daily 10.30am, 3pm & 4.30pm; R$35; ☎51 3224 5222, ⊛barcocisnebranco.com.br).

ACCOMMODATION

Hostels are scattered all over the city centre, but it's a relatively small area and it's possible to walk to most places – though you should take a taxi after dark.

Casa Azul Rua Lima e Silva 912 ☎51 3084 5050, ⊛casaazulhostel.com; map p.359. Popular hostel in a house in Cidade Baixa with bar open to the public (Tues–Sun 6.30pm–1am). There's a spacious outside area, flatscreen TV, pool table and friendly staff who can organize excursions. Dorms R$42, doubles R$120

Cidade Baixa Hostel Rua Sarmento Leite 964, Cidade Baixa ☎51 3398 4648, ⊛cidadebaixahostel.com.br; map p.359. Friendly, bright hostel in a great area for nightlife, with a series of comfy but compact dorms (five mixed, one female-only) and spanking new bathrooms – the public spaces here (kitchen, TV room) are a bit cramped, but the staff are super-friendly and the breakfast is good. Dorms R$41

Porto Alegre Eco Hostel Rua Luiz Afonso 276, Cidade Baixa ☎51 3019 2449, ⊛portoalegreecohostel.com.br; map p.359. Justly the most popular hostel in the city, with excellent staff and comfy dorms right in Cidade Baixa. Extras include a swimming pool, games room, garden and bike rental. Breakfast included. Dorms R$40, doubles R$120

Porto Alegre Hostel Boutique Rua São Carlos 545 ☎51 3228 3802, ⊛hostel.tur.br; map p.359. Great location in a historic mansion, and though not really a "boutique", the rooms here are a step up from those of a normal HI hostel; all en suite with a/c and TVs. There's a buffet breakfast (usually R$9 extra), with laundry and communal kitchen on site too. Prices for HI members are given in brackets. Dorms R$60 (R$54), doubles, R$135 (R$125)

EATING

As the home of Brazilian *churrasco* (barbecue), Porto Alegre has some excellent places to eat, especially in the Cidade Baixa and Moinhos de Vento neighbourhoods. As always, the best-value places to eat are buffets (especially in the Mercado Público), serving a plentiful range of food and usually offering good lunchtime deals.

★ **Banca 40** Mercado Público Loja 40 ☎51 3226 3533; map p.359. Open since 1927 (it looks modern, however), this local institution is justly lauded for its *bomba royal* (R$15) ice-cream dessert; regular scoops of ice cream start at R$6, and you can also order sandwiches. Mon–Fri 8am–7.30pm, Sat 8am–6.30pm.

Bar do Beto Rua Sarmento Leite 811 ☎51 3332 9390, ⊛bardobeto.com.br; map p.359. Cidade Baixa restaurant that heaves at lunchtime due to its R$27 buffet special, when waiters walk round tables offering different cuts of beef and chicken. Dinner is à la carte only. Daily 11am–2am.

★ **Cachorro Quente do R** Praça Dom Sebastião; map p.359. This legendary cart has been cooking up hot dogs (*cachorro*) in front of Colégio Rosário since 1962 (several imitators have since emerged). Choose your sausage type (*salsicha* is typical hot dog; *linguiça* is a meatier, cured sausage), then what you want on it; mushy peas, parsley, ketchup, mustard and chilli. The gut-busting finished product (R$9.25–14.50) is smothered in their secret sauce and grated cheese. Daily 11am–midnight.

Café do Mercado Mercado Público Loja; map p.359. Best Brazilian coffee in the market (cappuccino R$7.70), with a few tables inside and outside on the plaza – you can also buy raw produce here. Mon–Fri 8.30am–7.30pm, Sat 9am–5pm.

Confeitaria Matheus Av Borges de Medeiros 421; map p.359. Classic downtown bakery and café founded in 1947, with a bustling interior and an amazing cake selection (R$5–9). Popular for breakfast (order the *dupla café cortado*, coffee with steamed milk, and the calorie-packed *sanduíche farroupilha*, a toasted sandwich with cheese and ham; R$5.20). Coffee from R$5. Mon–Fri 6am–10pm, Sat 7am–9pm.

Padaria e Confeitaria Haiti Av Otavio Rocha 421; map p.359. This 1955 diner oozes character, with a bar, huge cake selection and tightly packed eating area (get a coupon before you enter), serving classics such as "*a la minuta*" (stew; mains R$6.50–20), or you can walk up to the second floor for the lunch buffet (Mon–Sat 11am–3pm; R$19 eat as much as you like, or R$4.80/100g). Mon–Sat 6.30am–10pm, Sun 10am–6.30pm.

Tudo Pelo Social Rua João Alfredo 448 ☎ 51 3226 4405, ⓦ restaurantetudopelosocial.com.br; map p.359. Hugely popular restaurant that serves Brazilian classics like rice, beans and meat. Lunchtime buffet is a bargain at R$13 per person, while the à la carte *picanha* "for two" (R$23; with steak R$32) comes with huge portions of chips, rice and salad, and easily feeds three to four people. Mon–Sat 11am–2.45pm & 6–11.45pm, Sun 11am–2.45pm.

DRINKING AND NIGHTLIFE

Porto Alegre boasts a lively nocturnal scene, with two main centres: the more flashy action revolves around Moinhos de Vento, and the hub of Rua Padre Chagas, while the Cidade Baixa offers more traditional samba joints and bohemian bars in the streets around Rua da República and Av João Pessoa.

Bar Ocidente Av Osvaldo Aranha 960, at João Telles ☎ 51 3312 1347, ⓦ barocidente.com.br; map p.359. Legendary former meeting place of dissidents since 1980, now best known for good veggie lunches (R$10–17), its art gallery and lively party nights: Saturday is always a themed club night. Mon–Sat 11.45am–2.30pm & 6pm–2am.

Dublin Rua Padre Chagas 342, Moinhos de Vento ☎ 51 3268 8835, ⓦ dublinpub.com.br; map p.359. Every city must have one: this is your standard faux-Irish bar and the current place where well-to-do "gauchos" look to enjoy themselves. Live bands play daily and an entry fee is charged after 9pm (R$10–20). Mon–Wed & Sun 6pm–3am, Thurs–Sat 6pm–5am.

★ **Espaço Cultural 512** Rua João Alfredo 512 ☎ 51 3212 0229, ⓦ espaco512.com.br; map p.359. Popular live music bar with a busy weekly programme of performances and a popular house cocktail the *maracangalha* (cachaça, pineapple, ginger, passion fruit and red pepper). Cover R$10–15. Tues, Wed & Sun 7pm–midnight, Thurs 7pm–1am, Fri 7pm–2am, Sat 8pm–2am.

Lagom Brewery & Pub Rua Bento Figueiredo 72 ☎ 51 3062 5045, ⓦ lagom.com.br; map p.359. Porto Alegre's first brew pub serves a range of tasty ales, stouts and IPAs on a seasonal basis – top tipples include the amber ale and oatmeal stout. Tues & Wed 6pm–1am, Thurs–Sat 6pm–2am.

TUIM Rua General Câmara 333 ☎ 51 9962 8851; map p.359. Just off Praça de Alfândega, this pocket-sized pub in the centre is ideal for a cool, quiet beer. *TUIM* also has an impressive variety of spirits, including quality *cachaça*. Mon–Fri 10am–9pm.

DIRECTORY

Banks and exchange There are banks and casas de câmbio (Mon–Fri 10am–4.30pm) along Rua dos Andradas and Av Senador Salgado Filho near Praça da Alfândega, and there are ATMs everywhere. Citibank and HSBC have branches in Moinhos de Vento.

Consulates USA, Av Assis Brasil 1889, Passo d'Areia (by appointment only; Mon–Fri 9am–1pm; ☎ 51 3345 6000).

Hospital Hospital Municipal de Pronto Socorro (HPS), Largo Teodore Herzl (Av Osvaldo Aranha) ☎ 51 3289 7999.

Internet Free wi-fi is available at the Mercado Público, Praça da Alfândega and Usina do Gasômetro. Internet cafés can still be found in the centre. try *Dreams Lavanderia* at Rua dos Andradas 405 (Mon–Fri 7.30am–9pm, Sat 8am–2pm; R$5/hr), or *Office Lan House* at Galeria Edith, Rua dos Andradas 1273 (walk to the end of the passage; Mon–Fri 8am–7.30pm, Sat 9am–1pm; R$5/hr).

Post office In the *centro historico* at Rua Siqueira Campos 1100 ☎ 51 3220 8800 (Mon–Fri 9am–6pm, Sat 9am–noon), and inside the *rodoviária* (Mon–Fri 9am–6pm; ☎ 51 3225 1945).

GRAMADO AND CANELA

Some 120km north of Porto Alegre, **GRAMADO** is Brazil's best-known mountain resort – famous for its Natal Luz (Christmas lights) and its annual film festival (ⓦ festivaldegramado.net), held in August. Architecturally, Gramado tries hard to appear Swiss, with "Alpine" chalets and flower-filled window boxes the norm. It's a mere affectation, though, since hardly any of the inhabitants are of Swiss origin – the town was settled by the Portuguese in 1875 and only a small minority is of German extraction; most locals today are of Italian ancestry. The most pleasant time to visit the area is in spring (Oct & Nov) when the parks, gardens and roadsides are full of flowers. At 825m, Gramado is high enough to be refreshingly cool in summer and positively chilly in winter. Marginally cheaper than Gramado, but arranged very much along the same lines, **CANELA** (which means "cinnamon"), 8km further east, is another mountain retreat popular with holidaying Brazilians and better located for visits to the nearby national parks.

WHAT TO SEE AND DO

The chief appeal of both towns lies in their clear mountain air and generally relaxed way of life. There really isn't much to do in Gramado other than to admire the houses, enjoy the food and stroll around the large and very pretty flower-filled **Parque Knorr** (daily 10.30am–9.30pm; free; during the festive season the kitsch Santa Claus village is R$35). The surrounding region is magnificent, best appreciated at the **Ecoparque Sperry** (entrance just off Av das Hortênsias on the way to Canela; Tues–Sun 9am–5pm; R$15; ⍵ecoparquesperry.com.br). Here you can peruse the conservation park's **Centro de Interpretação** or stroll along forest trails and past waterfalls, taking in the local flora. Roads in the mountainous areas around Gramado are unpaved and can be treacherous after rain, so **guided tours** are a safer bet – ask at the tourist office for recommendations.

ARRIVAL AND INFORMATION

By bus Buses (⍵citral.tur.br) from Porto Alegre (every 30min–1hr; 2hr 30min) run to Gramado's *rodoviária* (☎54 3286 1302) on Av Borges de Medeiros 2100, a couple of minutes' walk south from the town centre. Buses between Porto Alegre and Canela (every 30min–1hr; 3hr) run to Canela's *rodoviária* (☎54 3282 1375), just behind the central main street, Av Júlio de Castilhos, a short walk from the main plaza. Buses between Canela and Gramado leave every 10–15min (20min). Citral runs buses to São Francisco de Paula from Canela for the Parque Nacional dos Aparados da Serra (8 daily; 1hr). Buses also depart here for the Parque Caracol.

Tourist information The Gramado tourist office is in the centre of town at Av Borges de Medeiros 1647 (Mon–Thurs 9am–6pm, Fri–Sun 9am–8pm; ☎54 3286 1475, ⍵visitgramado.com.br). The Canela tourist office, on Praça João Correa (daily 8am–7pm; ☎54 3282 2200, ⍵canelaturismo.com.br) in the town centre, can put you in touch with tour companies arranging trips to the national parks.

ACCOMMODATION

Accommodation is expensive and you should book ahead during peak periods. Outside busy times many hotels offer discounts during the week.

> ### ★ TREAT YOURSELF
>
> **La Caceria** Av Borges de Medeiros 3166, Gramado ☎54 3295 7575, ⍵casadamontanha.com.br. An intriguing but expensive restaurant in the classy *Hotel Casa da Montanha*, specializing in game dishes (mains R$98–129) with unusual tropical fruit sauces that complement the often strong-tasting meat. Tues–Sun 7.30–11.30pm.

Gramado Hostel Av das Hortênsias 3880, Gramado ☎54 3295 1020, ⍵gramadohostel.com.br. About 1.5km outside town on the road to Canela (20min walk or R$1.80 on the Canela bus), this HI hostel is decent value (R$10 discounts for members), with dorm rooms and some doubles. Dorms R$70, doubles R$200

Pousada Belluno Rua Nilo Dias 50, Gramado ☎54 3286 0820, ⍵pousadabelluno.com.br. The best of the cheaper hotels in downtown, with elegantly furnished, heated rooms, LCD TVs and floor-to-ceiling windows. The substantial buffet breakfast will set you up for the day. R$210

Hostel Viajante Rua Ernesto Urbani 132, Canela ☎54 3282 2017, ⍵pousadadoviajante.com.br. Right next to the *rodoviária*, this is the best budget choice, with economical doubles with shared bathroom and neat and tidy en-suite rooms – perfect for travellers winding down after a hard day's bungee jumping. R$160

EATING

Gramado is noted for its handmade chocolate and has some good restaurants (especially fondue places), but expect to pay through the nose for anything resembling a good meal; aim for the buffets or "café colonial" places to fill up for a reasonably good price; Canela is especially known for its apple strudel and other German-inspired sweet treats.

★ **Bela Vista Café Colonial** Av das Hortênsias 4665 (1.7km from central Gramado, on the right side of the highway heading to Canela) ☎54 3286 1608, ⍵belavista.tur.br. One of Gramado's classic Alpine-style cafés, offering fabulous "café colonial" spreads of cakes, pastries and meats for a hefty R$75. Mon–Fri 11am–11pm, Sat & Sun 10am–11pm.

ITA Brasil Av São Pedro 1005, Gramado (1km from the centre) ☎54 3286 3833. Off the main drag and very crowded, but well worth seeking out for the cheap lunch buffets (around R$26 or R$46/kilo) of classic Italian–Brazilian food, fresh juices, strong coffee and home-made *cachaça*. Daily 11.30am–2.30pm.

Lá em Casa Rua José Luiz Correa Pinto 346, Canela (1km from the centre) ☎54 3278 1049. Rustic, home-made Brazilian food served buffet style, where around R$50 gets you all the food you can eat. Leave room for the delicious *pudim de leite* (milk pudding). *Feijoada* on Saturday. Tues–Fri 11.30am–2pm, Sat & Sun 11.30am–3pm.

Restaurante da Torre (Cervejaria Farol) Rua Severino Inocente Zini 150, Canela ☎54 3282 7007, ⍵cervejariafarol.com.br. Excellent microbrewery (marked by a 32m "lighthouse"), offering the chance to tour the facilities (R$15 with tastings) before sampling the beers (the IPA is especially tasty) – also serves a decent menu of German dishes and snacks, and offers free lifts to and from your hotel. Has live music Tues, Fri & Sat. Tues–Fri 5pm–midnight, Sat 11am–midnight, Sun noon–3pm.

3

3

★ **Schnitzelstubb** Rua Baden Powell 246, Canela ☎ 54 3282 9562. This German-inspired restaurant is the place to sample that schnitzel, wurst and apple strudel. Mains R$40–60. Tues 7.30–11pm, Wed–Sat noon–3pm & 8–11pm, Sun 11.45am–3pm.

PARQUE ESTADUAL DO CARACOL

Just 7km outside Canela on RS-466 (aka Estrada do Caracol), the highlight of the **PARQUE ESTADUAL DO CARACOL** (daily 9am–5.30pm; R$20) is the spectacular **Cascata do Caracol**, a stunning waterfall on the Río Caracol that plunges dramatically over a 131m-high cliff of basaltic rock in the middle of dense forest. The main park area (near the entrance) essentially comprises a series of viewpoints on the lip of the canyon overlooking the falls, but you can also take a lift ("*elevador panorâmico*") up the 27m high **Observatorio Ecológico** (daily 9am–5.30pm; $12 in addition to park entry), which will give you a 360-degree bird's-eye view of the park and falls, across the park's distinctive araucaria pines. The **Centro Historico Ambiental**, a short walk from the car park, contains a small exhibit on the park, while trails fan out along the canyon rim and down to the falls themselves, though this involves over 700 exhausting steps. For even more scintillating views of the waterfall take the 830m **Teleférico de Canela** 500m further along the road from the park entrance, a nerve-jangling chair lift (daily 9am–5pm; 20min; R$42; ☎ 54 3504 1405).

Further along the main road (now the gravel-surfaced Caminho da Graces), at Km15 is the entrance to the **Parque Vale da Ferradura** (Tues–Sat 9am–5pm; R$12), where three viewpoints cover the dramatic 420m "horseshoe" canyon of the Río Caí and the Arroio Caçador waterfall.

Heading back to Canela you'll pass the araucaria wood **Castelinho** (RS-466 Km3; daily 9am–1pm & 2.20–5.40pm; R$10; ⊛ castelinhocaracol.com.br), a fairy-tale German-style mansion dating from 1915 and now a memorial to German immigration to the area (which serves incredible *apfelstrudel* in the tea rooms).

ARRIVAL AND DEPARTURE

By bus Buses run from the *rodoviária* in Canela to the park entrance (Mon–Sat 8.20am, 12.20pm & 5.30pm, returning at 8.35am, 12.25pm and 5.50pm; Sun 8.05am, 1.35pm & 5.35pm, returning 8.20am, 1.50pm & 5.50pm; R$3.25), or you can take a taxi (R$40 one-way).

PARQUE NACIONAL DOS APARADOS DA SERRA

Around 150 million years ago, lava slowly poured onto the surface of the Brazilian Shield, a vast **highland plateau**, developing into a thick layer of basalt rock. At the edge of the plateau, vast canyons puncture the basalt and the largest of these is protected within the predominantly untouched wilderness of the **Parque Nacional dos Aparados da Serra** (Tues–Sun 8am–5pm; R$17/person, plus R$15/car), some 100km east of Canela.

Approaching the park from any direction, you pass through rugged cattle pasture, occasionally interrupted by the distinctive umbrella-like araucaria pine trees and solitary farm buildings. As the dirt road enters the park itself, forest patches appear, suddenly and dramatically interrupted by a canyon of breathtaking proportions. Some 5.8km in length, between 600m and 2000m wide and 720m deep, **Itaimbézinho** is a dizzying sight. On the higher levels, with relatively little rainfall, but with fog banks moving in from the nearby Atlantic Ocean, vegetation is typical of a cloudforest, while

INTO URUGUAY AND ARGENTINA

Most overland travellers cross the southern Brazilian borders via long-distance bus – in this case formalities are fairly straightforward and you just need to know the entry requirements for Uruguay (see page 835) and Argentina (see page 47). The borders here are generally open, meaning anyone can just walk across – if you are a foreigner, however, you need to find the nearest immigration post to have passports stamped.

TO URUGUAY

Chuí/Chuy (340km northeast of Montevideo). By far the most travelled route, 527km south of Porto Alegre. Buses entering and leaving Brazil stop at an immigration office a short distance north of the town itself (Chuí/Chuy is actually divided by the border) on BR-471. The Uruguayan customs is 3km further south on Rte-9.

Santana do Livramento (497km west of Porto Alegre). There's no duty-free here or passport controls – the town simply merges into the Uruguayan city of Rivera (500km north of Montevideo). Before leaving Livramento you'll need a Brazilian exit (or entry) passport stamp from the Polícia Federal, at Rua Uruguai 1177, near the central park, and a stamp from Uruguay's Dirección Nacional de Inmigración, at Av Presidente Viera s/n. If you have any problems, head for the Uruguayan consulate in Livramento at Av Tamandaré 2101, 4th floor (☎ 55 3242 1416).

TO ARGENTINA

Most people heading to Argentina from Brazil cross the frontier at Foz do Iguaçu (see page 349), but if you find yourself in the south of the country, **Uruguaiana** (694km west of Porto Alegre) is the most convenient crossing – with Paso de los Libres on the other side (around 740km north of Buenos Aires). Customs formalities take place at either end of the 1400m-long road bridge across the Rio Uruguai. Accommodation and restaurant options are both better on the Argentine side of the border. The Argentine consulate is at Rua 13 de Mayo 1674 (☎ 55 3412 1925).

on the canyon's floor a mass of subtropical plants flourishes.

Three trails are open to visitors, the most difficult of which is the **Trilha do Rio do Boi** (8hr) – an option for experienced hikers that must only be attempted with a guide. It involves a 5m vertical descent of a rock face by rope and a complete descent to the rocky river in the canyon floor. Rather easier is the **Trilha do Vértice** (1.4km), which affords views of Itaimbézinho and two spectacular waterfalls **Véu da Noiva** and **Andorinhas**. If this isn't challenging enough for you, try the **Trilha do Mirante do Cotovelo** (6.3km return), which runs along the rim of the canyon and provides some glorious photo opportunities.

ARRIVAL AND DEPARTURE

By bus Getting to the park via public transport is tough – organized tours are worth considering here. First, take a bus (ⓦ citral.tur.br) from Gramado or Canela to São Francisco de Paula. From here take another bus 60km northeast to Cambará do Sul (Mon–Sat 9.15am & 5pm, Sun 11am; 1hr). Citral also has one bus to Cambará from Porto Alegre (Mon–

Sat 6am; 5hr 30min). From Cambará it's a further 18km to the park entrance along dirt road Estrada do Itaimbézinho (RS-427) towards Praia Grande (taxis charge at least R$100 return, but you'll need to negotiate pick-up in advance), and another 2km from there to the edge of the canyon. There is no bus service direct to the park.

By car If you intend to make the trip in your own vehicle it is imperative that you call ☎ 54 3251 1230 for up-to-date information on local road conditions.

INFORMATION AND TOURS

Tourist information There is a visitors' centre (☎ 54 3251 1262, ⓦ guiaaparadosdaserra.com.br) and a snack bar at the main entrance. Only a thousand visitors are permitted to enter the park each day, so it's advisable to phone the visitors' centre in advance to reserve a place.

Tour operators Trying to visit the park on your own is difficult and barely cheaper than doing it with a tour. Try ecotourism specialists Canyons do Sul (ⓦ canyonsdosul. com.br).

ACCOMMODATION

Camping is prohibited in the park, so if you decide to visit independently, you'll need accommodation – the most convenient place is Cambará do Sul, aka the "capital of honey" thanks to its numerous bee farms.

Pousada João de Barro Rua Padre João Francisco Ritter 631 ☎54 3251 1216, ⓦjoaodebarropousada. com.br. This cosy little hotel in the centre of Cambará is superb value, with just five en-suite rooms, TVs and delicious, wholesome breakfasts. The living room and fireplace is popular in winter. R$150

ROTA MISSÕES (MISSION ROUTE)

Though less well known than those in Argentina and Paraguay, Rio Grande do Sul is home to no fewer than seven **Jesuit Missions**, with four of the ruins in an excellent state of preservation and grouped together on what is called the **ROTA MISSÕES**. The Jesuits arrived here in 1626 determined to convert the local Guarani tribes, with the missions founded between 1682 and 1706 in nominal Spanish territory. In fact the region was virtually independent of both Spain and Portugal, a state of affairs ended by the 1750 Treaty of Madrid when the missions became definitively Portuguese; this led to the Guarani War of 1756, devastating the region (and dramatized in the film *The Mission*).

The best place to base yourself is the town of **SANTO ÂNGELO** in the far southwest of the state, where there is a cluster of accommodation options around Praça Rio Branco. The most accessible and best of the missions is **SÃO MIGUEL**

ARCANJO (Tues–Sun 9am–noon & 2–6pm, Oct–Feb till 8pm; R$5; ⓦmissoesturismo.com.br), founded in 1687 in the village of São Miguel da Missões. Guided tours are available, and the small Museu das Missões (same times) and a kitschy nightly light show (Feb–April & Aug–Oct 8pm; May–July 7pm; Nov–Jan 9.30pm; R$15) brings the story of the Jesuits to life.

ARRIVAL AND DEPARTURE

By bus The *rodoviária* at Santo Ângelo is 1km west of Praça Pinheiro Machado at Sete Povos das Missões 419. Antonello runs buses to and from São Miguel (Mon–Fri 7.15am, 11am, 3.30pm & 4.45pm; Sat 10am & 3.30pm; Sun 9.30am & 6.20pm; last bus returning Mon–Fri 5.45pm, Sat 5.30pm, Sun 5pm; 1hr 20min; R$10.50; ⓦturismoantonello.com. br). For Foz do Iguaçu you'll need to take a bus to Santa Rosa (1hr) and change there.

Destinations Curitiba (1 daily; 13hr); Porto Alegre (10 daily; 6–7hr); Rio (1 daily; 28hr).

ACCOMMODATION

There are also decent options in Santo Ângelo.

Pousada das Missões Rua São Nicolau 601, São Miguel da Missões ☎55 3381 1202, ⓦpousadadasmissoes. com.br. Right next to the São Miguel ruins, this is a smart choice if you intend to stay for the sound-and-light show, an excellent HI hostel (R$10 discount for members) that has clean dorm rooms as well as doubles (with a/c and TV) and a relaxing pool. Dorms R$80, doubles R$190

Chile

❶ **Valparaíso** Stunning setting, bohemian atmosphere and vibrant nightlife. See page 390

❷ **The Elqui Valley** Laidback villages, pisco tasting and stargazing. See page 402

❸ **San Pedro de Atacama** Gateway to spectacular high-altitude desert landscapes. See page 409

❹ **Pucón** Volcano climbing, white-water rafting and hot springs. See page 432

❺ **Parque Nacional Torres del Paine** World-class hiking amid majestic scenery. See page 471

❻ **Rapa Nui (Easter Island)** Wonderfully remote home to mysterious moai statues. See page 477

HIGHLIGHTS ARE MARKED ON THE MAP ON PAGE 369

ROUGH COSTS

Daily budget Basic US$55
Drink Pisco sour US$5
Food *Pastel de choclo* US$9
Camping/hostel/budget hotel US$10/20/50

FACT FILE

Population 17.9 million
Languages Spanish; indigenous languages Aymará, Huilliche, Kawéscar, Mapudungun, Quechua, Rapanui and Yámana
Currency Chilean Peso (CH$)
Capital Santiago region (population: 7 million)
International phone code ☎ 56
Time zone Mainland Chile except Magallanes region: -3hr GMT in summer, -4hr GMT in winter. Magallanes region: -3hr GMT year-round. Easter Island: -5hr GMT in summer, -6hr GMT in winter.

Introduction

Chileans often say that when God created the world, he had a little bit of everything left over, and put pieces of desert, rivers, lakes and glaciers together to make Chile. From the world's driest non-polar desert – the Atacama – in the north to the volcanic peaks and verdant landscapes of the Lake District and the icy wilderness of Patagonia and Tierra del Fuego in the south, it is perhaps the most geographically diverse and fascinating country in Latin America. Snaking between the Andes and the Pacific Ocean, Chile is a fantastic playground for lovers of the outdoors and adrenaline junkies, with world-class trekking, skiing, surfing, rafting, climbing and paragliding. The country's extensive national parks and nature reserves also boast an astounding array of plant and animal life.

Today, despite its troubled past under the brutal Pinochet dictatorship, Chile is among the most politically and economically stable countries in Latin America. For the most part, it is westernized and affluent, and its excellent bus network makes it an easy country to navigate.

Cosmopolitan **Santiago** is a very manageable starting point, with plenty of excellent hostels, restaurants and bars, as well as easy access to superb ski resorts and the vineyards of **Middle Chile**. Nearby, in the beguiling port of **Valparaiso**, you can ride the *ascensores* (funiculars), soak up the bohemian atmosphere, or relax on the sandy beaches of neighbouring **Viña del Mar**. Head further north to the **Norte Chico** to knock back a pisco sour in the tranquil **Elqui Valley**, or stargaze in some of the world's clearest skies. Further north still is the **Norte Grande**, where the strong breaks of the Pacific Ocean meet the moonscape

scenery of the Atacama Desert. Visit gleaming lagoons and steaming geysers in the backpacker oasis of **San Pedro de Atacama**, and get your fill of sun and surf in the beach towns of **Iquique** and **Arica**.

South of Santiago and Middle Chile, the **Lake District** – a region of lush forests and snowcapped volcanoes – exudes opportunities for hiking, rafting, cycling and mountaineering, while the fascinating archipelago of **Chiloé** has beautiful wooden churches and a distinct culture. Towering granite pillars and blue-tinged glaciers draw thousands of visitors to **Chilean Patagonia**, and the excellent trekking routes of **Parque Nacional Torres del Paine**, while a few head even further south to **Tierra del Fuego**. Last, but definitely not least, for serene beauty, ancient mystery and giant *moai* statues, head to the one of the world's most remote inhabited islands, **Rapa Nui** (Easter Island).

CHRONOLOGY

1520 Ferdinand Magellan is the first European to sail through what is now the Magellan Strait.
1536 Expedition from Peru to Chile by conquistador Diego de Almagro and his four hundred men ends in death for most of the party.
1541 Pedro de Valdivia, a lieutenant of Francisco Pizarro, founds Santiago; a feudal system in which Spanish landowners enslave the indigenous population is established.
1808 Napoleon invades Spain and replaces Spanish King Ferdinand VII with his own brother.
1810 The *criollo* elite of Santiago decide Chile will be self-governed until the Spanish king is restored to the throne.

WHEN TO VISIT

If you want to experience the whole of Chile in all its diversity you'll need to come prepared for both extreme cold and extreme heat. The *Lake District, Patagonia* and *Tierra del Fuego* are best explored from October through to April, since the Chilean winter effectively shuts down much of the south and transport can be very limited. *Norte Grande, Norte Chico, Middle Chile* and the *Pacific island* territories, however, can be accessed all year round.

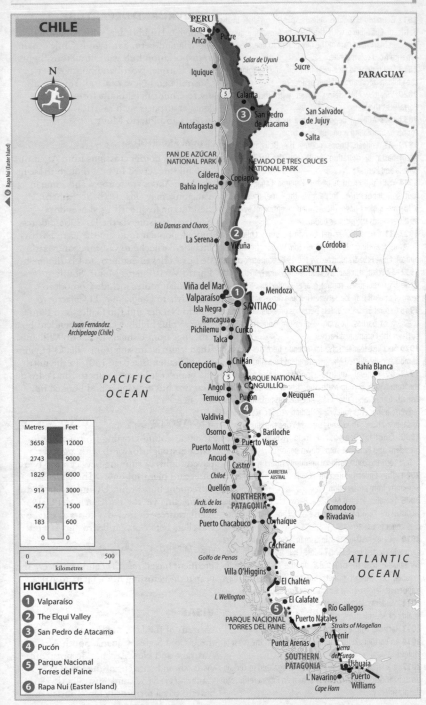

CHILE

N

◄ Rapa Nui (Easter Island)

PERU

Tacna
Arica
Putre

BOLIVIA

Salar de Uyuni

Sucre

PARAGUAY

Iquique

5
Calama

③ San Pedro
de Atacama

San Salvador
de Jujuy

Antofagasta

Salta

PAN DE AZÚCAR
NATIONAL PARK

NEVADO DE TRES CRUCES
NATIONAL PARK

Caldera
Bahía Inglesa

Copiapó

Isla Damas and Choros

La Serena

②

Vicuña

Córdoba

ARGENTINA

Viña del Mar
Valparaíso

①

Mendoza

*Juan Fernández
Archipelago (Chile)*

Isla Negra
Rancagua
Pichilemu
Talca

SANTIAGO

Curicó

Concepción

Chillán

Bahía Blanca

5

PARQUE NATIONAL
CONGUILLÍO

**PACIFIC
OCEAN**

Angol
Temuco

Pucón
④

Neuquén

Valdivia

Osorno

Bariloche

Puerto Montt

Puerto Varas

Ancud

Castro

Chiloé

CARRETERA
AUSTRAL

Quellón

*Arch. de los
Chonos*

NORTHERN
PATAGONIA

Comodoro
Rivadavia

Puerto Chacabuco

Coyhaique

Metres		Feet
3658		12000
2743		9000
1829		6000
914		3000
457		1500
183		600
0		0

0   500
kilometres

Cochrane

Golfo de Penas

**ATLANTIC
OCEAN**

Villa O'Higgins

El Chaltén

I. Wellington

El Calafate

Río Gallegos

⑤

Puerto Natales

HIGHLIGHTS

① Valparaíso

② The Elqui Valley

③ San Pedro de Atacama

④ Pucón

⑤ Parque Nacional
Torres del Paine

⑥ Rapa Nui (Easter Island)

PARQUE NACIONAL
TORRES DEL PAINE

Porvenir

Straits of Magellan

Punta Arenas

*Tierra
del Fuego*

Ushuaia

SOUTHERN
PATAGONIA

I. Navarino

Cape Horn

Puerto
Williams

4

1817 Bernardo O'Higgins defeats Spanish royalists in the Battle of Chacabuco with the help of Argentine general José San Martín, as part of the movement to liberate South America from colonial rule.

1818 Full independence won from Spain. O'Higgins signs the Chilean Declaration of Independence.

1829 Wealthy elite seizes power with dictator Diego Portales at the helm.

1832–60s Mineral deposits found in the north of the country, stimulating economic growth.

1879–83 Chilean troops occupy the Bolivian port of Antofagasta, precipitating the War of the Pacific against Bolivia and Peru.

1914 With the creation of the Panama Canal, shipping routes no longer need to pass via the Cape, thus ending Valparaíso's glory days. The German invention of synthetic fertilizers ends the nitrates boom.

1927–31 Carlos Ibáñez del Campo becomes Chile's first dictator, founding the corps of *carabineros* (militarized police); Chile is badly affected by the 1929 economic crash.

1932–52 Political instability: land belongs largely to the elite, while US corporations control copper production. Seeds are sewn of a political divide between left and conservative right.

1946 Gabriel González Videla becomes president of a broad coalition of parties; bowing to pressure from the US, he outlaws the Communist Party.

1970 Socialist leader Salvador Allende becomes the first democratically elected Marxist president by a slim margin.

1973–89 General Augusto Pinochet seizes control of the country in a coup with the support of the Chilean armed forces and the CIA. Intense repression of the regime's opponents follows, including arrests, torture and "disappearances"; thousands forced to flee the country.

1990 Christian Democrat Patricio Aylwin is elected president and Pinochet steps down peacefully, though not before securing constitutional immunity from prosecution.

2004 The Chilean Supreme Court strips Pinochet of immunity from prosecution.

2006 Socialist leader Michelle Bachelet, former torture victim of the Pinochet regime, is elected president. Pinochet dies under house arrest.

2010 Conservative businessman Sebastián Piñera narrowly elected president. Middle Chile is hit by a massive earthquake that measures 8.8 on the Richter scale. In October, 33 Chilean miners are rescued after 69 days trapped underground in a mine near Copiapó.

2011 Students launch massive protests over costs and quality of education.

2013 Bachelet wins a second presidential term.

2014 An earthquake measuring 8.2 strikes off the coast of Iquique.

2017 In a landmark move, abortion is legalized in certain circumstances. Later in the year Sebastián Piñera returns to the presidency.

ARRIVAL AND DEPARTURE

Chile has land borders with Argentina, Bolivia and Peru. Santiago is Chile's main transportation hub with numerous flights from Europe, North and South America, Australia and New Zealand. You can also fly to Chile's neighbours from several smaller airports such as Arica, Punta Arenas and Puerto Montt.

FROM ARGENTINA

Numerous **border crossings** from Argentina to Chile are served by bus, though those in the high Andes are seasonal and some in Patagonia may close for bad weather. Besides the frequently used Mendoza–Santiago crossing via the Los Libertadores tunnel, popular routes in the Lake District include Bariloche to Osorno, San Martín de Los Andes to Temuco, and Bariloche to Puerto Varas/Puerto Montt. Southern Patagonian routes include Comodoro Rivadavia to Coyhaique, El Calafate to Puerto Natales and Río Gallegos to Punta Arenas, plus highly weather-dependent boat crossings from Ushuaia to Puerto Williams. There's also a crossing from Villa O'Higgins to El Chaltén (see page 140). In the north, the popular Jujuy and Salta to San Pedro de Atacama bus crossing is best booked in advance.

FROM BOLIVIA

The year-round crossing from La Paz to Arica is straightforward, with a good paved highway running between the two cities and plentiful buses. There are infrequent buses from Uyuni to San Pedro de Atacama via the Portezuelo del Cajón; regular three- to four-day tours also take travellers between San Pedro and Uyuni.

FROM PERU

Frequent buses, *colectivos* and taxis serve the year-round crossing from Tacna to Arica.

VISAS

Citizens of the UK, the European Union, the United States, Canada, South Africa, Australia and New Zealand do not require **visas**, though citizens of the US (US$131), Canada (US$132) and Australia (US$61) have to pay a **reciprocity fee**. Tourists are routinely granted ninety-day entry permits and must surrender their tourist cards upon departure. In theory, visitors can be asked to produce an onward ticket and proof of sufficient funds, but this rarely happens. Ninety-day **visa extensions** can be granted by the Departamento de Extranjería, San Antonio 580, Piso 2, Santiago Centro (Mon–Fri 8.30am–2pm, calls taken 9am–4pm; ☎600 626 4222, ⊛www.extranjeria.gob.cl/ingles/), at a cost of US$100, although it may be cheaper and easier simply to cross the border into a neighbouring country and back again. If you lose your tourist card, you can get a replacement from the Policía Internacional, Morande 672, Santiago (☎2 2690 1010).

GETTING AROUND

Most Chileans travel by bus, and it's such a reliable and inexpensive option that you'll probably do the same. However, domestic flights are handy for covering long distances in a hurry.

BY PLANE

Several airlines offer frequent and reasonably priced flights within Chile. You'll often find better fares by booking locally, rather than in advance from home. **LATAM (formerly LAN;** ☎600 526 2000, ⊛latam.com) is easily the biggest airline, with efficient online booking, last-minute discounts and a good-value "Visit South America Airpass". **Sky Airline** (☎600 600 2828, ⊛skyairline. com) also has daily flights between Chile's major cities, and is generally cheaper. Punta Arenas-based **Aerovías DAP** (☎61 261 6100, ⊛dapairline.com) flies to various destinations in Chilean and Argentine Patagonia and Tierra del Fuego.

BY TRAIN

Chile has a very limited railway network. In Middle Chile, a reliable and comfortable service operated by Tren Central (⊛trencentral.cl) has services between Santiago and Chillán, with stops at stations such as Rancagua and Talca.

BY BUS

Bus travel is popular, affordable and convenient. The level of comfort depends on how much you are prepared to pay, with the *cama* buses generally being the plushest, their seats reclining almost horizontally. For example, the cheapest seats from Santiago to Arica cost from CH$50,000 to CH$55,000; shop around as there are often promotions.

Bus tickets are valid only for specified buses, and the major bus companies, such as **Tur Bus** (☎600 660 6600, ⊛turbus.cl) and **Pullman** (☎600 320 3200, ⊛pullman. cl), require you to buy your ticket before you board – though for many routes you'll have no trouble purchasing tickets at the bus station shortly before your departure. That said, south of Puerto Montt, and especially during the peak months, demand outstrips supply, so it is advisable to book in advance if you are on a tight schedule. Bus station kiosks are the easiest option – online booking services (such as ⊛recorrido.cl and ⊛voyhoy.cl) are available but cannot always process foreign credit/debit cards. If crossing **international** borders by bus, remember that it's prohibited to transport animal and plant matter to neighbouring countries, and luggage searches are frequent.

Smaller **local buses** and minibuses (*micros*) connect city centres with outlying neighbourhoods and smaller towns with villages. In some parts of Chile, especially in the north, *colectivos* (shared taxis with fixed fares) provide a faster and only slightly pricier service between towns than local buses.

BY FERRY

South of Puerto Montt, where Chile breaks up into a plethora of islands and fjords, you will have to take a **ferry**, whether to continue along the Carretera Austral or to work your way down to Southern Patagonia. Travelling south by boat is more expensive than going by bus, but it allows you access to some of the remotest and most beautiful parts of Chile. Popular routes include Puerto Montt to Puerto Natales, Puerto Montt to Chacabuco and Chacabuco to Laguna San Rafael.

BY CAR

Car rental is costly (around CH$30,000–45,000/day) and complicated, with

4

PACHAMAMA BY BUS

The hop-on, hop-off *Pachamama by Bus* service is aimed at backpackers and is designed to cover the most scenic spots in the Lake District and the Atacama Desert. You purchase a pass for the number of days you wish to travel – a seven-day pass costs CH$162,000 – and you can stay at any of the given stops. There are weekly departures on both routes (☎ 2 2688 8018, ⓦ pachamamabybus.com).

expensive insurance due to the varying condition of the dirt roads. Carrying spare tyres, a jack, extra petrol and plenty of drinking water is essential for driving around more remote parts of Chile, and punctures are frequent. Since public transport is perfectly adequate in most parts of the country, the only places where it may make sense to rent a **4WD vehicle** is on Easter Island, parts of Patagonia, and perhaps to some national parks. To rent a car, you need to be over 21 years old; take your passport as ID, and have a national driver's licence and major credit card on hand.

HITCHING

Hitchhiking remains popular in Chile, especially in rural areas, but it's not an entirely safe method of travel. If you decide to hitch, it's always best to do so at least in pairs.

BY BIKE

Cycling can be a good way of getting to the more remote national parks, some of which are inaccessible by public transport. It's a good idea to carry spare parts, although bike repair shops are found in most medium-sized towns. While in the south of Chile **drinking water** can typically be acquired from streams (though not in Tierra del Fuego, where giardia is widespread), in the northern half of the country it is highly advisable to carry your own, and essential if cycling anywhere in the arid Atacama region. There are few cycle lanes, and for the most part cyclists share the road with motorists; at least traffic outside cities tends to be light. Stray dogs can also be a nuisance in populated areas.

ACCOMMODATION

Chile has a good range of **budget accommodation**. Prices are highest during the peak season from December to February, when Chileans go on summer holiday; in shoulder seasons, they generally drop by around twenty percent. Many lodgings in the south of Chile close down during the winter months, so check ahead. Prices are normally listed inclusive of tax (or IVA: 19 percent) but it is best to establish this at the start of your stay; many hotels give foreigners the opportunity to pay in US dollars, which exempts you from paying IVA – they may need to be reminded of this.

RESIDENCIALES, CABAÑAS AND REFUGIOS

Residenciales are the most commonly available budget lodgings, found in both large cities and villages. Typically, they consist of furnished rooms in someone's home, often with breakfast included; not surprisingly, the quality varies enormously. A basic double room costs about CH$20,000; single rooms can cost as much as two-thirds the price of doubles.

Cabañas are usually found in well-visited spots, particularly by the ocean. They tend to come with a fully equipped kitchen, bathroom and bedrooms, and can be a great option for those travelling in groups. Depending on the time of year, a cabaña for two people typically costs from CH$30,000.

Refugios are inexpensive (except in Torres del Paine National Park), bare-bones lodgings in national parks, usually consisting of several bunk beds in a wooden hut. Most have clean bedding, showers and flushable toilets; some require you to bring your own sleeping bag. They cost around CH$5000–15,000 per person. Many *refugios* stay open year-round, but if you are planning on wilderness trekking, or on travelling in the south of Chile in the winter, try to arrange lodgings by calling the local **Conaf** office (ⓦ conaf.cl), Chile's national forestry service, in advance; individual offices are listed on its website.

HOSTELS AND CAMPING

Hostels are plentiful, especially in well-visited cities and popular outdoor destinations; dorm beds generally cost

CH$12,000-20,000. Some independent hostel groups compile booklets listing the best options, which are worth picking up. **Backpackers Chile**, for example (@backpackerschile.com), offer a reliable benchmark for high-quality hostels. The booklet is available from any of the hostels listed on the site, and at major information offices. Also worth picking up is the **Get South** booklet (@getsouth.com), which offers discounts for various hostels across Chile, as well as Argentina and Uruguay.

Most major cities and key tourist centres have a **Hostelling International**-affiliated hostel (@hihostels.com), for which member discounts are available. HI hostels are not necessarily better than independent hostels, though they do tend to meet basic standards, so can be preferable to some budget hotels.

Note that in some widely visited places, such as Pucón and San Pedro de Atacama, a **hostal** may not necessarily mean a bona fide youth hostel – in many cases they are simply family homes.

Chile offers marvellous opportunities for **camping**, with a proliferation of both fully equipped campsites (which can be somewhat pricey) and beautiful wilderness spots. There is ample free camping on empty beaches, although in most national parks you should only camp in designated spots.

FOOD AND DRINK

Chile has an abundance of fresh produce, but outside the bigger cities and tourist destinations **food** can be a bit bland, though *pebre* (a fairly spicy salsa served with bread) and *ají chileno*, served with barbecued meat, can liven things up. **Breakfast** (*desayuno*) consists of coffee and the ubiquitous pockmarked bread rolls with butter and jam. **Lunch** (*almuerzo*) is the main meal of the day, typically made up of three courses; most restaurants offer a good-value fixed-price lunch *menú del día*. **Dinner** (*cena*) is usually served late, rarely before 9pm, and in Chilean households is often replaced by a lighter **late afternoon-evening snack** (*once*). Restaurants generally open from around 7pm but don't start to fill up until around 9pm.

Beef and chicken are the commonest **meats**, the former often served grilled with a fried egg on top (*lomo a lo pobre*) or as part of a *parillada* (mixed grill). Two dishes found on menus across the country are *cazuela*, a hearty meat casserole, and *pastel de choclo*, a sweet-tasting corn and beef pie. When in Patagonia, do not miss the *asador patagónico*, spit-roasted lamb (*cordero*) and wild boar (*jabalí*) steaks, while llama and alpaca steaks and stew are a staple of *altiplano* cuisine in the north of Chile. Both Chiloé and Easter Island serve up *curanto*, a hearty meat and seafood dish.

There is a fantastic range of **fish and seafood**. Fish are typically served *frito* (battered and deep-fried), or *a la plancha* (grilled) with different sauces, and sushi bars are springing up everywhere. Don't miss the *ceviche* – raw fish marinated in lemon juice with coriander. Excellent seafood dishes include *machas a la parmesana*, baked razor clams covered with parmesan cheese, *chupe de locos*, creamy abalone casserole topped with breadcrumbs, and *paila marina*, seafood soup.

Some excellent vegetarian restaurants have appeared in recent years, but decent vegetarian cuisine may be hard to find outside major cities and tourist destinations. Delicious **fruit and vegetables** are abundant in most parts of Chile, barring Patagonia and Tierra del Fuego. The north of the country grows exotic delights like scaly green *chirimoya* (custard apple), papaya, *tuna* (cactus fruit) and melon-like *pepino dulce*. Easter Island cuisine incorporates Polynesian tubers such as the *camote* (sweet potato).

DRINK

Tap water is generally drinkable all over Chile, with the exception of the Atacama, though Santiago's high mineral content upsets some stomachs. **Mineral water** is inexpensive and comes *sin gas* (still) or *con gas* (carbonated). **Soft drinks** (*gaseosas* or *bebidas*) are plentiful and very popular, and freshly squeezed **fruit juices** (*jugos*) are abundant, especially in the fertile region of Middle Chile; most Chileans like their juice sweetened, so if you don't want a half-juice, half-sugar concoction, ask for it *sin azúcar* (without sugar). *Licuados* are fruit smoothies mixed with water or *leche* (milk). *Mote con huesillo*, a drink made from boiled, dried apricots, is popular, especially in Middle Chile.

4

Although things are improving, it can be surprisingly difficult to find real **coffee** (*café de grano*) in smaller towns, with Nescafé still unfathomably popular, but good coffee shops are springing up across Santiago and other cities. In the Lake District and Patagonia, thanks to the influence of Argentine culture, you will encounter *yerba mate*, an antioxidant-rich, energizing herb drunk from a gourd through a metal straw.

Chile has several generic lager **beers** including Escudo, Cristal and Austral; the best beers come from the rapidly expanding range of microbreweries. Chileans often start meals with a refreshing **pisco sour**, the national drink (see page 403).

Chilean **wine**, renowned worldwide, features on many restaurant menus. Wine tourism is very popular, with the Rutas del Vino (Wine Routes) in the Maule and Colchagua valleys giving visitors easy access to both the process of wine-making and the sampling of many different varieties.

CULTURE AND ETIQUETTE

Chilean city lifestyle, superficially at least, has more similarities with Europe than with neighbouring Bolivia or Peru. Bargaining is not common and rarely done, even in marketplaces, though Chileans are often excellent at seeking out bargain prices. When eating out, a ten-percent **tip** in restaurants is normal and appreciated.

Chileans are family- and **child-oriented**, and young people tend to live with their parents until they get married. The predominant religion is **Catholicism**, though the Church is not as influential as

it used to be. Machismo is not as prevalent here as in other parts of Latin America; **women** are more respected and a lone woman travelling around the country is not likely to encounter any trouble beyond catcalls. While **homosexuality** is still frowned upon, it is tolerated, and there is a thriving LGBTQ scene in larger cities.

Chileans are very **sociable** and will go out of their way to greet you in the street if they know you. If arranging to go out with Chileans, be aware that they may turn up later than the arranged time. When it comes to topics of conversation, Pinochet's brutal rule often provokes a heated discussion.

SPORTS AND OUTDOOR ACTIVITIES

While Chile is not quite in the same league as Argentina or Brazil when it comes to **football**, the game is taken very seriously and attending a live match in Santiago is worthwhile for the atmosphere alone. Be aware, though, that the passion for football can turn aggressive, and be ready to make an exit. Santiago team Colo Colo has the largest and most enthusiastic following.

Every year, more than three hundred **rodeos** are staged during the season (Sept–May) in Middle Chile and Aisén in particular. Evolved from the rural *huaso* (cowboy) culture, the rodeo is a spectacle worth going out of your way for.

La cueca, Chile's national **dance**, is also firmly rooted in *huaso* culture; it re-enacts the courting ritual between a rooster and a hen. Men and women clad in traditional outfits dance largely to guitar-led ballads,

---

EATING ON A BUDGET

Prices at some restaurants in places like Santiago and Valparaíso can give the impression that you have to break the bank to enjoy good food in Chile, but there are cheaper options.

In coastal towns, you can pick up superb fish at bargain prices at little *marisquerías*, rustic fish eateries usually found at the busiest point of the seafront. In most large cities, look out for the *market* area where you'll get excellent deals on fruit and vegetables.

Small *kiosks* along city streets and country roads will often sell delicious and filling snacks like *empanadas* (savoury pasties filled with meat or fish) and *humitas* (ground corn wrapped in leaves).

American-style *diners* and home-grown fast-food chains across Chile sell huge *completes*, hot dogs, and *italianos*, hot dogs covered in mayonnaise, ketchup and avocado, as well as a range of sandwiches, like *barros jarpa* (melted cheese and ham), as alternative cheap eats.

NEW PARKS AND RESERVES

In March 2017, **Tompkins Conservation** (see page 461) and President Michelle Bachelet signed an historic agreement to expand the area protected by national parks by more than 40,000 square kilometres – roughly the size of Switzerland. The private foundation donated more than 4000 square kilometres, the largest gift of its kind in South America, while the government committed almost 36,000 square kilometres of state-owned land. New parks will be created and existing ones expanded; eventually the government aims to develop a 1500km-long **Ruta de los Parques** (Route of Parks), a tourist trail through seventeen linked parks. In a separate move, later in 2017, the government also created a new marine reserve around Easter Island: the **Rapa Nui Rahui Marine Protected Area** spans some 740,000 square kilometres and protects dozens of endemic species.

though the tempo and the instruments vary from region to region. *La cueca* is most commonly seen during the Chilean independence celebrations in September, when troupes perform on streets and stages across the country, though Chileans often take little persuading to show off their beloved dance whatever the opportunity.

WATERSPORTS

The mighty rivers of the Lake District and Patagonia offer excellent **whitewater rafting** and **kayaking**, with Río Trancura, Río Petrohué and Río Futaleufú offering class V challenges. Futaleufú in particular is hailed as one of the top white-water runs in the world.

Sea kayakers can choose between multi-day paddling in the Patagonian fjords, shorter trips to small islands off the coast of Chiloé and wildlife-viewing on Isla Damas near La Serena.

Surfers head to Chile's top spot, Pichilemu, just south of Santiago, though there are excellent surfing and **windsurfing** opportunities all along the coast north of the capital, around Iquique in particular, and year-round swells on Easter Island.

In the northern half of the country, lack of rain makes for good visibility and abundant marine life for **divers** and **snorkellers**, while Easter Island has world-class dive spots.

HIKING, CLIMBING AND SKIING

Hiking in the Torres del Paine National Park, on Isla Navarino or anywhere in the south is limited to the summer, spring and autumn, but the rest of Chile can be visited at any time of year. There are currently 65 **Rutas Patrimoniales**

(ⓦ bienesnacionales.cl) covering the whole of Chile as part of a government initiative to preserve and develop land that has natural and historical value. These can all be explored on foot, by bike or on horseback. Another ambitious project, **Sendero de Chile** (ⓦ senderodechile.cl), consists of 35 trail sections intended to span the whole of Chile, including its Pacific islands. Once completed, it will become the longest trekking route in the world, but progress is currently slow.

Ice climbers will find excellent **climbing** routes in the Central and Patagonian Andes from November to March, with plenty of accessible glaciers, while the granite towers of Torres del Paine rank among the world's most challenging rock climbs. Middle Chile and the Lake District, however, have the greatest variety of climbing and mountaineering spots.

Along with Argentina, Chile has world-class powder snow, with some of the best **skiing** spots found within easy reach of Santiago (see page 389). The Lake District's Villarica-Pucón and Osorno give you the opportunity to whizz down the slopes of volcanoes.

CYCLING

Spectacular **cycling** terrain can be found from Norte Grande to Tierra del Fuego, though you will need a sturdy mountain bike to cope with the potholed trails. While the best time to cycle around much of Chile is between October and March, Norte Chico and Norte Grande can be explored year-round, though altitude is often a consideration, especially if you're planning on exploring Parque Nacional Lauca. Norte Chico offers easy and

4

enjoyable coastal rides, while the Lake District and Chiloé have the greatest variety of cycling routes, and the Carretera Austral is a challenging undertaking that rewards with amazing scenery.

COMMUNICATIONS

Internet/wi-fi is widely available across Chile and provided by virtually all hotels, hostels, and restaurants. Most towns and villages have **internet cafés**, where access costs around CH$300–600/hr, although on Isla Navarino and Easter Island it is considerably pricier (and slower).

Chile has a number of different telecoms operators, and in order to make an **international call**, you dial the three-digit carrier code of the telecom, followed by 0, then the country code and finally the phone number itself. Most local numbers consist of seven or eight digits, preceded by the city/area code; if dialling from the same area, drop the city or area code and dial the six or seven digits directly. In 2013, the government rolled out a new numbering system, adding a 2 to the start of every fixed-line number; some businesses have still not updated their details. Mobile phone numbers are eight digits and start with a 9, 8, 7, 6 or 5; if you're phoning from a landline, you need to use the prefix "09". Calls abroad from the numerous **centros de llamadas** to most European countries and North America cost around CH$150–250/min, although prices vary from area to area. Many internet cafés in Chile are Skype-equipped. Alternatively, get an inexpensive Chilean **SIM card** for an "unlocked" mobile phone; to do this,

annoyingly, you now need to register (for free) online – visit ⓦ multibanda.cl for more information.

Overseas mail sent from any part of Chile via Correos de Chile, the national **postal service**, generally takes two or three weeks to reach its destination. Important shipping to Chile is best sent via registered mail.

CRIME AND SAFETY

The risk of **violent crime** in Chile is very low; in larger cities pickpocketing and petty thievery are minor concerns, but assaults are practically unknown, and there is very little corruption among Chilean police.

HEALTH

There are no compulsory **vaccinations** for Chile, though there have been reported incidents of mosquito-borne **dengue fever** on Easter Island; use insect repellent. **Hantavirus**, caused by inhaling or ingesting rat droppings, is uncommon but deadly: when staying in rural buildings that could potentially have rodents, air them out thoroughly and do not sleep on the floor. Chile has two species of **spider** with a venomous and potentially dangerous bite: the black widow (found in parts of Torres del Paine National Park, among other areas) and the Chilean recluse spider (found throughout Chile). The recluse – or *araña del rincón*, literally "corner spider" – is commonly found in houses. Though bites from either spider are relatively rare, they can prove fatal – if you think you may have been bitten, seek medical help immediately.

INFORMATION AND MAPS

Official **Sernatur** tourist offices (Servicio Nacionalde Turismo; ⓦ sernatur.cl) are found in all the major cities and towns. They produce a plethora of brochures on local attractions, accommodation and outdoor activities, though some are better stocked than others. Some regions also have a **municipal tourism office** run by the regional authorities. For information on Chile's natural attractions, as well as maps and up-to-date trekking conditions for specific areas, you should head to the local **Conaf**

CHILE ONLINE

Chile Travel ⓦ chile.travel. Official government tourist site.

Latin America Bureau ⓦ lab.org.uk. Well-respected UK-based charity with news and analysis from across the region, including Chile.

Santiago Times ⓦ santiagotimes.cl. English-language newspaper, based in the capital.

Turismo Chile ⓦ chiletourism.travel. Info on Chile's major attractions, with some historical and cultural background.

EMERGENCY NUMBERS

Air rescue (for mountaineering accidents)
☎ 138
Ambulance ☎ 131
Coastguard ☎ 137
Fire ☎ 132
Investigaciónes (for serious crimes) ☎ 134
Police ☎ 133

---

office (Corporación Nacional Forestal; ⓦconaf.cl), again found in most towns.

JLM **Cartografía** maps are usually accurate and helpful, and can be found in most bookshops; they cover both cities and trekking routes in Chile. The Instituto Geográfico Militar (ⓦigm.cl) produces detailed topographic maps of the entire country, but they can be pricey.

MONEY AND BANKS

The **peso** is the basic unit of Chilean currency, and it comes in 1000, 5000, 10,000 and rare 20,000 denomination notes, and 10, 20, 50, 100 and 500 peso coins. It is usually represented with the $ sign, not to be confused with US$. Few places will accept US dollars or other foreign currencies, though some hostels and hotels may suggest you pay in dollars to avoid the nineteen percent IVA tax (value added tax) on accommodation, from which foreigners are exempted when paying in dollars (a small, though increasing, number allow you to do this by credit/debit card too). Chile is fairly expensive compared to most other Latin American countries, with prices comparable to those in North America and Europe.

At the time of writing, the exchange rate was £1 = CH$837; US$1 = CH$627 and €1 = CH$738.

Large and medium-sized cities have plentiful **banks** and **ATMs**; Banco de Chile and Santander are good bets for withdrawing cash with debit cards. Santiago and most of the more visited destinations have casas de cambio which can change travellers' cheques and foreign currencies at a reasonable rate. Some smaller towns only have Banco Estado ATMs, which generally accept only Cirrus and MasterCard. If you are heading to small towns off the beaten track, it's wise to carry enough cash to cover a few days as ATMs are not always reliable. **Credit cards** can also be used to pay for purchases, especially in larger towns, though budget lodgings and eating places rarely accept them.

OPENING HOURS AND HOLIDAYS

On weekdays, most services and **shops** tend to be open from 9 or 10am to 6 or 7pm; Saturday hours are usually 10 or 11am to 2pm. In smaller towns, **restaurants** are often closed in the afternoon between the lunchtime hours of 1 to 3pm and the dinnertime hours of 8 to 11pm. An increasing number of restaurants, bars and shops open on Sundays, but smaller places, particularly in more rural areas, generally remain closed.

Banks typically operate from 9am to 2pm on weekdays only, while post offices generally open Monday to Friday from 9am to 6pm; in larger towns, they also open Saturdays from 9am to 1pm. Monday is a day off for most **museums**; they are, however, usually open on Sundays, often with free entry. Shops and services are closed during national holidays, local festivals and on local and national election days.

PUBLIC HOLIDAYS

January 1 New Year's Day (*Año Nuevo*)
Easter (*Semana Santa*) national holidays on Good Friday, Holy Saturday and Easter Sunday
May 1 Labour Day (*Día del Trabajo*)

STUDENT AND YOUTH DISCOUNTS

ISIC International Student or **Youth cards** can get you reduced airfares to Chile with travel agencies such as STA Travel. Some museums offer reduced student rates. It may also be possible to get **reduced bus fares** with certain bus companies; enquire in advance. Having a **Hostelling International (HI) card** is very worthwhile, since you can get member discounts in a network of hostels around Chile.

May 21 Navy Day (*Día de las Glorias Navales*) marking Chile's naval victory at Iquique during the War of the Pacific

June 29 St Peter and St Paul (*San Pedro y San Pablo*)

July 16 Our Lady of Mount Carmel (*Solemnidad de la Virgen del Carmen, Reina y Patrona de Chile*)

August 15 Assumption of the Virgin Mary (*Asunción de la Virgen*)

September 17 If it falls on a Monday, an extension of Independence celebrations

September 18 National Independence Day (*Fiestas Patrias*) celebrates Chile's proclamation of independence from Spain in 1810

September 19 Armed Forces Day (*Día del Ejército*)

September 20 If it falls on a Friday, an extension of Independence celebrations

October 12 Columbus Day (*Día del Descubrimiento de Dos Mundos*) celebrates the European discovery of the Americas

November 1 All Saints' Day (*Día de Todos los Santos*)

December 8 Immaculate Conception (*Inmaculada Concepción*)

December 25 Christmas Day (*Navidad*)

FESTIVALS

January 20 San Sebastián. Spaniards brought the first wooden image of San Sebastián to Chile in the seventeenth century. After a Mapuche raid on Chillán, the image was buried in a field, and no one was able to raise it. The saint's feast day is now an important Mapuche festival.

February 1–3 La Candelaria. Celebrated since 1780, when a stone image of the Virgin and Child was discovered during a thunderstorm in the Atacama. Typical festivities include processions and traditional dances.

End of February Festival Internacional de la Canción. Popular five-day festival held in Viña del Mar, featuring performers from across Latin America.

Easter Semana Santa (Holy Week). Among the nationwide Easter celebrations, look out for Santiago's solemn procession of penitents dressed in black habits, carrying crosses.

May 13 Procesión del Cristo de Mayo. A huge parade through Santiago bearing the sixteenth-century *Cristo de Mayo* carving.

June 13 Noche de San Juan Bautista. An important feast celebrated by families with a giant stew, the *Estofado de San Juan*.

June 29 Fiesta de San Pedro. Fishermen decorate their boats and take the image of their patron saint out to sea to pray for good weather and large catches.

July 12–18 Virgen de la Tirana. Chile's largest religious festival, held in La Tirana in the far north, and attended by more than eighty thousand pilgrims and hundreds of costumed dancers.

August 21–31 Jesús Nazareno de Caguach. Thousands of Chilotes flock to the archipelago's tiny island of Caguach to worship at a 2m-high figure of Christ.

First Sunday of October Virgen de las Peñas. Dance groups and more than ten thousand pilgrims from Chile, Peru, Bolivia and Argentina visit a rock carving of the Virgin in the Azapa Valley, near Arica.

November 1 Todos los Santos (All Saints' Day). Traditionally the day when Chileans tend their family graves.

November 2 Día de los Muertos (All Souls' Day). A second vigil to the dead is held in cemeteries, with offerings of food and wine sprinkled on the graves.

December 8 La Purísima. Celebrated in many parts of Chile, the festival of the Immaculate Conception is at its liveliest in San Pedro de Atacama.

December 23–27 Fiesta Grande de la Virgen de Andacollo. More than 100,000 pilgrims come to Andacollo, in Norte Chico, to worship its Virgin and watch masked dancers.

Santiago

Towered over by the snow-streaked Andes, **SANTIAGO** has a distinctly European feel. Its rich pockets of culture and history are often overlooked by travellers frustrated by a lack of iconic sights, and put off by the smog that often hangs over the city. Yet those prepared to venture beyond the grid of central shopping streets will be rewarded with quirky, vibrant neighbourhoods filled with a huge variety of lively bars and excellent restaurants. The city is a microcosm of the country's contrasting ways of life, with ramshackle markets, smart office buildings, rough-and-ready bars and plush shopping malls all just a short metro ride from the main square.

Home to more than a quarter of Chile's population, the capital is crowded but easy to navigate with a clean and efficient metro system. And even if the city itself fails to impress, Santiago is an excellent base from which to explore, with world-class ski resorts, sun-kissed beaches and beautiful vineyards all within easy reach.

WHAT TO SEE AND DO

Downtown Santiago is loosely bordered by the **Río Mapocho** to the north, and the

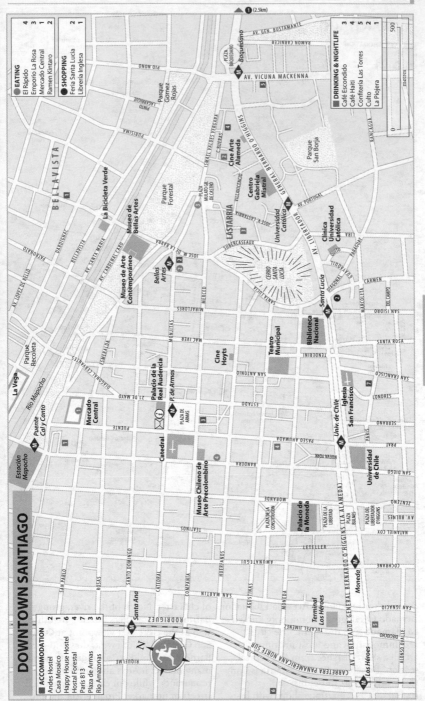

DOWNTOWN SANTIAGO

ACCOMMODATION	
Andes Hostel	2
Casa Mosaico	1
Happy House Hostel	6
Hostal Forestal	4
París 813	7
Plaza de Armas	3
Río Amazonas	5

● EATING	
El Rápido	4
Emporio La Rosa	3
Mercado Central	1
Ramen Kintaro	2

● SHOPPING	
Feria Santa Lucía	2
Librería Inglesa	1

■ DRINKING & NIGHTLIFE	
Café Escondido	3
Café Haití	4
Confitería Las Torres	5
Culto	2
La Piojera	1

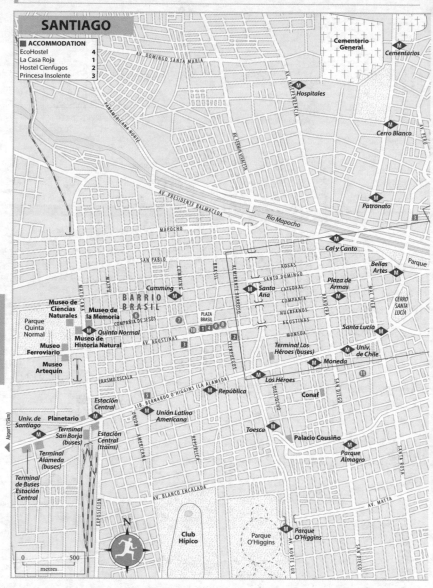

SANTIAGO

ACCOMMODATION	4
EcoHostel	4
La Casa Roja	1
Hostel Cienfugos	2
Princesa Insolente	3

central thoroughfare of Avenida Libertador Bernado O'Higgins – commonly known as **La Alameda** – to the south. The city's accommodation and most inviting *barrios* are all a short distance from this central section. Bohemian **Barrio Lastarria** is home to a wealth of art museums, cool restaurants and boutique shops with bags of character. North of the river, grungy **Barrio Bellavista** offers buzzing nightlife as well as the city's best viewpoint at **Cerro San Cristóbal**. In the west, down-to-earth **Barrio Brasil** and **Barrio Yungay** are home to many budget hostels and good-value restaurants, while out east, the tree-lined streets of upmarket **Providencia** and plush

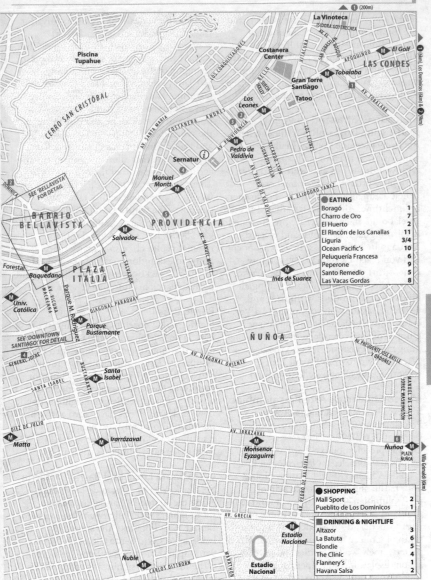

EATING

Boragó	1
Charro de Oro	7
El Huerto	2
El Rincón de los Canallas	11
Liguria	3/4
Ocean Pacific's	10
Peluquería Francesa	6
Peperone	9
Santo Remedio	5
Las Vacas Gordas	8

SHOPPING

Mall Sport	2
Pueblito de Los Dominicos	1

DRINKING & NIGHTLIFE

Altazor	3
La Batuta	6
Blondie	5
The Clinic	4
Flannery's	1
Havana Salsa	2

Las Condes are pocketed with luxury hotels and shopping malls.

Plaza de Armas

Pedro de Valdivia, the city's founder, intended the lush tree-studded **Plaza de Armas** to be a centrepiece for Chile, surrounding it with splendid colonial architecture. The oldest building is the **Catedral Metropolitana** (1748), on the west side of the plaza, its Neoclassical facade designed by the Italian architect Joaquín Toesca. To the north is the **Palacio de la Real Audiencia** (1804), housing the Museo Histórico Nacional, and the **Correo Central**. A lively gathering point since the mid-1800s, the plaza's flower gardens and the fountain in the centre honouring Simón Bolívar attract a multitude of chess players, street performers, vagrants, stray dogs, soap-box preachers and strolling families, making the square an ideal place to linger on a bench and people-watch.

Mercado Central and La Vega

By the south bank of Río Mapocho lies the lively **Mercado Central** (daily 6am–4pm), a mass of stalls spilling over with wondrous fish and seafood, dotted with busy little *marisquerías* whose delicious smells draw crowds of customers at lunchtime. All of this is gathered inside an elaborate metal structure prefabricated in Birmingham, England, and erected in Santiago in 1868. Cross the Río Mapocho and you reach **La Vega** (daily: roughly 6am–5pm), an enormous roofed market surrounded by outdoor stalls, selling all kinds of fresh produce, with fruit and vegetables at rock-bottom prices. La Vega is full of local character, giving you a glimpse of "real" Santiago: fragrant, pungent and chaotic. It's also the best place in town to grab a giant fruit smoothie, as well as excellent seafood.

Museo Chileno de Arte Precolombino

The excellent **Museo Chileno de Arte Precolombino** (Tues–Sun 10am–6pm; CH$4500; 2 2928 1500, museoprecolombino.cl), at Bandera 361, is housed in the elegant late-colonial Real Casa de Aduana (Royal Customs House, 1807). The unparalleled collection of pre-Columbian artefacts spans around ten thousand years and covers the whole of Latin America, from Mexico down to the south of Chile. More than 1500 examples of pottery, finely woven textiles and jewellery are on display, including permanent collections from the Andes, Mesoamerica, the Amazon and the Caribbean, and there are outstanding temporary exhibitions.

Palacio de la Moneda

The restored **Palacio de la Moneda**, (2 2690 4000) on the large **Plaza de la Constitución**, is the presidential palace and site of the dramatic siege that brought Pinochet to power on September 11, 1973, and led to the death of President Salvador Allende. A wide, squat Neoclassical construction, originally built to house the Royal Mint, the palace stages an elaborate **changing of the guard** on alternating days at 10am (weekdays) or 11am (weekends), featuring white-jacketed officers, cavalry and an inspired brass band. The palace's inner courtyards can be accessed through the North Gate (Mon–Fri 10am–6pm), and the basement features a huge relief map of Chile that allows visitors to get an accurate impression of the country's size. There are four free tours each day (visitas@presidencia.cl) – take your passport. The **Centro Cultural Palacio La Moneda** (daily 9am–8.30pm; exhibitions CH$5000, half-price Mon–Fri before noon; ccplm.cl), a smart, arty space, is home to exhibitions, craft shops and cafés and is accessed by steps to the left and right of the palace's main frontage.

Barrio Brasil

Starting half a dozen blocks northwest of Palacio de la Moneda, **Barrio Brasil** is centred around the nicely landscaped Plaza Brasil, with a surreal-looking playground and a tall monkey puzzle tree reaching for the sky. In the early twentieth century this was a prestigious residential neighbourhood; now its elegant streets have faded and it has morphed into a lively area with good restaurants and bars, popular with backpackers and Santiago's students.

Cerro Santa Lucía and Barrio Lastarria

Six blocks east of Palacio de la Moneda along the Alameda, Santiago's main thoroughfare (officially Avenida Libertador Bernardo O'Higgins), the splendidly landscaped **Cerro Santa Lucía** (Dec–Feb 9am–8pm, March–Nov 9am–7pm; free), is the historically significant promontory where Pedro de Valdivia defeated the indigenous forces (to whom it is known as Huelén – "the curse"), and where Santiago was officially founded on February 12, 1541. The barren hill was transformed into a lush retreat through the labour of 150 prisoners in the 1870s. The park's peaceful winding footpaths and the ornate Terraza Neptuno fountain draw amorous couples, while visitors take the steep footpaths to the top to be rewarded with **panoramic views** of the city. Immediately to the north and east, **Barrio Lastarria** is a haven for hip restaurants and bars.

Parque Forestal

It's hard to believe that the tranquil green space of the **Parque Forestal**, stretching along the Río Mapocho's south bank, was once a floodplain covered in rubbish dumps. Top attraction here is the grand and airy Neoclassical Palacio de Bellas Artes, housing the **Museo de Bellas Artes** (Tues–Sun 10am–6.45pm; free; ☏ 2 2499 1632, ⓦ mnba.cl), which features paintings,

sculptures, prints and drawings by predominantly Chilean artists. The **Museo de Arte Contemporáneo**, or **MAC** (same hours and price; ☏ 2 2977 1741, ⓦ mac. uchile.cl), on the other side of the building, offers temporary modern art exhibitions, some of them interactive, by cutting-edge national and international artists.

Barrio Bellavista

Crossing the Pío Nono bridge brings you to **Barrio Bellavista**, the trendy bohemian neighbourhood at the foot of **Cerro San Cristóbal**, the city's second-largest hill. Home to some of Santiago's best **bars**,

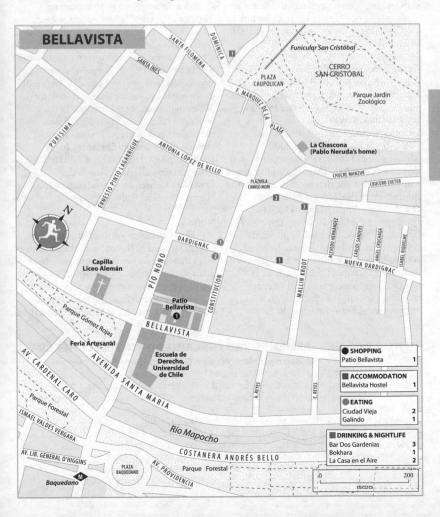

SHOPPING
Patio Bellavista 1

ACCOMMODATION
Bellavista Hostel 1

EATING
Ciudad Vieja 2
Galindo 1

DRINKING & NIGHTLIFE
Bar Dos Gardenias 3
Bokhara 1
La Casa en el Aire 2

Bellavista really comes into its own on weekends. There are also several good nightclubs and raucous beer-and-burger joints lining Pío Nono, the main street. You'll find **La Chascona**, one of the three residences of Chile's most famous poet, **Pablo Neruda**, down a little side street (Márquez de la Plata 0192; Tues–Sun: Jan & Feb 10am–7pm; March–Dec 10am–6pm; CH$7000; ☎ 2 2777 8712, ⓦfundacionneruda.org). Named after Neruda's wife Matilde, "the tangle-haired woman", the house is faithful to the nautical theme that characterizes all his residences, its creaking floorboards resembling those of a ship and strangely shaped rooms filled with a lifetime of curios. The ticket price includes a worthwhile self-guided audio tour, available in English.

Cerro San Cristóbal

A path winds up from Barrio Bellavista's Plaza Caupolicán to Terraza Bellavista or you can save some shoe leather by taking the **funicular railway** (Tues–Sun: Jan & Feb 10am–7.45pm, March–Dec 10am–6.45pm; return CH$2000 Mon–Fri, CH$2600 Sat & Sun), to reach **Cerro San Cristóbal**. There is also the newly reopened **cable car** that ascends to near the summit from Providencia (Tues–Sun: Jan & Feb 10am–8pm, March–Dec 10am–7pm; return CH$2510 Mon–Fri, CH$3010 Sat & Sun; ☎ 2 2730 1331, ⓦparquemet.cl). From Terraza Bellavista you walk up to the hill's summit, crowned with a huge statue of the Virgen de la Immaculada Concepción and offering excellent views of the city, though the outlying neighbourhoods might be clouded in a gentle haze of smog. The many dirt tracks running along the forested hillsides offer excellent mountain-biking opportunities, while walking down the spiralling road brings you to **Piscina Tupahue** (mid-Nov to mid-March Tues–Sun 10am–7.30pm; CH$6000), a popular open-air swimming pool and picnicking spot amid monkey puzzle trees. You can either return by the same route or continue down to Pedro de Valdivia metro station in Providencia.

Providencia

The attractive, tree-lined streets of chic **Providencia** are home to an increasing number of hotels, businesses and restaurants. At its eastern edge, where it morphs into the even more expensive **Las Condes**, you'll find a busy business and dining district known as Sanhattan, or El Golf. The shiny new skyscrapers here are symbolic of Chile's rapid development in recent years, particularly the 300m-high **Gran Torre Santiago**, Latin America's tallest building, which dominates the skyline and offers 360º vistas from its viewing platform, **Sky Costanera** (daily 10am–10pm; CH$15,000; ☎ 2 2916 9269, ⓦskycostanera.cl). At its base is the Costanera Center, one of the continent's biggest shopping malls.

Ñuñoa

Southeast of central Santiago, the laidback neighbourhood of **Ñuñoa**, with the attractive **Plaza Ñuñoa** at its heart, is overlooked by many visitors to the city, though it has a lively **nightlife** thanks to two nearby university campuses. Football fans also flock here to watch the matches at the **Estadio Nacional**, at

---

"NEVER AGAIN" – REMEMBERING THE CRIMES OF THE PINOCHET ERA

The large and excellent **Museo de la Memoria y los Derechos Humanos** at Matucana 501 (Tues–Sun: Jan & Feb 10am–8pm, March–Dec 10am–6pm; free; ☎ 2 2579 9600, ⓦmuseodelamemoria.cl; Metro Quinta Normal) documents the chilling human rights abuses, repression and censorship that occurred between 1973 and 1990 under the Pinochet dictatorship.

Another memorial to the victims of the regime is **Villa Grimaldi** at Av José Arrieta 8401, a former secret torture and extermination centre now transformed into a **Park for Peace** (daily 10am–6pm; free; guided tours Tues–Fri at 10.30am, noon & 3pm; ☎ 2 2292 5229, ⓦvillagrimaldi.cl). The buildings here were destroyed in an attempt to erase any evidence of the centre's existence, but among a series of memorials to its victims are explanations of the site's original layout. To get there, take bus #513, or #D09, or go to Metro Plaza Egaña and get a taxi (about CH$7500).

SANTIAGO TOUR OPERATORS

Attractions around Santiago include wineries, thermal baths, the outdoor enthusiast's paradise of the mountainous Cajón del Maipo valley, and more.

Andina del Sud Av El Golf 99, 2nd floor ☎ 2 2388 0101, ⓦ andinadelsud.com. This agency is good for booking inexpensive domestic and international flights, and also offers holidays and guided trips throughout Chile and neighbouring countries aimed at younger travellers. Four-night Easter Island package US$600.

La Bicicleta Verde Loreto 6, at Av Santa María, Bellavista ☎ 2 2570 9338, ⓦ labicicletaverde. com. See Santiago at a different pace with a range of bike tours in the city, and around nearby vineyards.

Also arranges bike rental. Afternoon tour of Santiago's highlights CH$25,000/person.

Monteagudo Aventura ☎ 2 2346 9069, ⓦ monteagudoaventura.cl. Experienced outfit running full-day horseriding and white-water rafting trips in the Cajón del Maipo, as well as treks to the San Francisco and Morado glaciers and night excursions to the Colina thermal baths. Full-day horseriding including an *asado* (barbecue) CH$90,000/person.

Avenida Grecia 2001. The stadium has a grim past – it was once used by Pinochet as a torture centre and prison.

ARRIVAL AND DEPARTURE

By plane Aeropuerto Arturo Merino Benítez (☎ 2 2690 1752, ⓦ aeropuertosantiago.cl), 30min from the city centre, has ATMs, currency exchange and a tourist information kiosk. The two airport bus services from just outside the terminal are the cheapest way to get to the city centre: Centropuerto (daily 6am–11.30pm, every 10min; CH$1800 one-way; ⓦ centropuerto.cl) terminates at Los Héroes metro station, while Tur Bus runs to Terminal Alameda (see below; daily 5am–midnight every 20min, midnight–5am hourly; CH$1800; ☎ 2 2822 7448). Both services also call at intermediate stops, including Pajaritos, useful for connections to Valparaíso and the coastal resorts. TransVip (☎ 2 2677 3000, ⓦ transvip.cl) charge from CH$10,000 to drop you off directly at your destination.

Destinations LATAM and Sky Airline have multiple daily flights to all major Chilean destinations: Arica (8–10 daily; 2hr 40min); Calama (12–15 daily; 2hr); Iquique (12–16 daily; 2hr 30min); La Serena (6–9 daily; 1hr); Puerto Montt (12–15 daily; 1hr 45min); Punta Arenas (8–12 daily; 3hr 30min).

By train The only train services run south from Santiago to the Central Valley, all departing from the Estación Central. For train information, call ☎ 600 585 5000 or check ⓦ efe.cl. Destinations Chillán (3 daily; 5hr 30min); Curicó (3 daily; 2hr 45min); Rancagua (10 daily; 1hr 30min); San Fernando (6 daily; 2hr); Talca (3 daily; 3hr 30min).

By bus The main bus station is Terminal Santiago, also known as Terminal de Estación Central (☎ 2 2376 1755), at Alameda 3850, near the Universidad de Santiago metro station, which handles international routes, and journeys to the west and south. The Terminal Alameda, next door at Alameda 3750 (☎ 2 2822 7400), is served by Pullman and Tur Bus, who also have some international departures. The two terminals have ATMs, snack shops and luggage storage,

as well as easy access to public transport along Alameda. Buses from northern and central Chile use Terminal San Borja (☎ 2 2776 0645), at San Borja 184, near the Estación Central metro station, while the smaller Terminal Los Héroes, at Tucapel Jiménez 21 (☎ 2 2420 0099), near Los Heroés metro station, serves a range of destinations in both northern and southern Chile.

Destinations Arica (hourly; 30hr); Chillán (every 30min–1hr; 5hr); Copiapó (4–6 daily; 10hr); Iquique (hourly; 24hr); La Serena (hourly; 6hr 30min); Pucón (every 30min; 12hr); Puerto Montt (every 30min; 14hr); Rancagua (every 15min; 1hr); Valparaíso and Viña del Mar (every 10–15min; 1hr 45min). Terminal Buses Estación Central has international departures to various South American countries including Argentina (Buenos Aires, Mendoza), Brazil (Saõ Paulo, Río de Janeiro) and Peru (Lima, Cusco, Tacna, Arequipa).

INFORMATION AND TOURS

Tourist information An excellent source of tourist information is the municipal tourism office on the north side of the Plaza de Armas (Mon–Fri 9am–6pm, Sat & Sun 10am–4pm; ☎ 2 2713 6745, ✉ turismo@munistgo.cl). The main Sernatur office is 3km east at Av Providencia 1550, near the Manuel Montt metro station, (Jan & Feb daily 9am–9pm; March–Dec Mon–Fri 9am–6pm, Sat 9am–2pm; ☎ 2 2731 8336, ⓦ sernatur.cl). It provides maps of the city and is well stocked with brochures on the surrounding area. Conaf has an office at Av Bulnes 265 (Mon–Thurs 9am–5.30pm, Fri 9am–4.30pm; ☎ 2 2663 0125, ⓦ conaf. cl), which provides information on national parks and reserves, as well as some pamphlets and inexpensive maps.

Listings For entertainment listings, check Friday's *El Mercurio* or *La Tercera*, Santiago's main newspapers.

Tours Free walking tours of the city's main sights are provided by the local authorities daily at 10am (enquire at the municipal tourist office). Bike tours are also a good option.

4

GETTING AROUND

By bus Fleets of "TranSantiago" (ⓦ www.transantiago. cl) buses run around the city. To use them, you need to purchase a "BIP" transit card (CH$1550), sold in most metro ticket booths, which you can then add credit to (at BIP centres across the city). Bus destinations are posted on window signs and at marked stops; fares start at CH$630, depending on the time of day and number of transfers (maximum two changes up to 2hr).

By colectivo Roughly the same price as buses, *colectivos* have their destinations displayed on their roofs and carry passengers on fixed itineraries, reaching their destination quicker than regular transport, though you need to know where you are going; useful for destinations outside the city centre.

By metro The metro (Mon–Fri 6am–11pm, Sat 6.30am–11pm, Sun 9am–10.30pm; ⓦ metrosantiago.cl) is the quickest way to get around the city, with just six lines that are easy to navigate, though it gets rather cramped during rush hour and does not serve all neighbourhoods. BIP cards (see above) are also the only way to use the metro, with each journey costing CH$610–740 depending on the time of day.

ACCOMMODATION

There are a number of accommodation options in Santiago to suit budget travellers although really cheap places are scarce. Good inexpensive lodgings are mostly to be found in the city centre and Barrio Brasil.

DOWNTOWN

EcoHostel General Jofré 349B, Metro Universidad Católica ☎ 2 2222 6833, ⓦ ecohostel.cl; map p.380. With its clean and spacious dorms, chilled-out common areas and fully equipped guest kitchen, this hostel and its environment-friendly ethic attracts mostly younger travellers. Lockers, good breakfast and knowledgeable, bilingual staff are a big plus. Dorms CH$10,000, doubles CH$27,000

París 813 París 813, Metro Universidad de Chile ☎ 2 2664 0921, ⓦ hotelparis813.com; map p.379. Decent low-cost hotel offering a range of slightly old-fashioned rooms, with TVs and private bathrooms; the older ones sometimes lack outside windows so unless pesos are really tight, opt for one in the newer annexe. CH$28,000

★ TREAT YOURSELF

Río Amazonas Vicuña Mackenna 47, Metro Baquedano ☎ 2 2635 1631, ⓦ hostalrioamazonas.cl; map p.379. Travellers of all ages flock to this charming *hostal*, next to the Argentine embassy. Each room has a private bathroom (and often a bath), colourful decor, phone, TV and plenty of space. The communal areas are attractive, and light meals are available. CH$58,000

★ **Plaza de Armas** Compañía 960, apartment 607, Metro Plaza de Armas ☎ 2 2671 4436, ⓦ plazadearmashostel. com; map p.379. This gem of a hostel, on the sixth floor of a building hidden within an alleyway filled with fast-food joints, has a prime location on the Plaza de Armas. There are bright dorms, colourful if compact private rooms, ample communal space and a terrace with fine views. Dorms CH$8,000, doubles CH$15,000

BARRIO BRASIL

La Casa Roja Agustinas 2113, Metro República ☎ 2 2695 0600, ⓦ lacasaroja.cl; map p.380. Sprawling, Aussie-owned converted mansion firmly established as backpacker party central, with spacious dorms and rooms. There's a jacuzzi, pool with swim-up bar, large common areas, free internet, kitchen and an on-site travel agency. A top budget choice, though not a place to catch up on your sleep; breakfast not included in dorms. Dorms CH$8000, doubles CH$27,000

Hostel Cienfuegos Cienfuegos 151, Metro Los Héroes ☎ 2 2671 8532, ⓦ hostelcienfuegos.cl; map p.380. Large, professionally run, HI-affiliated hostel with clean dorms, plush bunk beds, spacious dining room and bonuses including a book exchange, breakfast and laundry service. Dorms CH$10,500, doubles CH$25,000

★ **Happy House Hostel** Moneda 1829, Metro Los Héroes ☎ 2 2688 4849, ⓦ happyhousehostel.cl; map p.379. Travellers are made to feel really welcome at this beautifully decorated, spacious hostel, with large private rooms, attractive common areas, large kitchen, terrace bar and pool. Breakfast and internet included. Dorms CH$13,000, doubles CH$34,000

Princesa Insolente Moneda, Barrio Brasil, Metro República 2350 ☎ 2 2671 6551, ⓦ princesainsolentehostel. cl; map p.380. This popular and sociable hostel has clean and economical private rooms, three- to ten-bed dorms, a TV lounge and a patio. The cheerful staff members host regular barbecues. Dorms CH$8000, doubles CH$30,000

BARRIO LASTARRIA

Andes Hostel Monjitas 506, Metro Bellas Artes ☎ 2 2632 9990, ⓦ andeshostel.com; map p.379. Centrally located hostel with modern decor, bright dorms with individual lockers, and a whole range of facilities – guest kitchen, lounge with pool table and cable TV, free internet, laundry service and a fully stocked bar. Can get noisy. Dorms CH$13,000, doubles CH$48,000, apartments CH$50,000

Hostal Forestal Coronel Santiago Bueras 122, Metro Baquedano ☎ 2 2638 1347, ⓦ hostalforestal.cl; map p.379. Perpetually popular, *Hostal Forestal* throws impromptu barbecues and the bilingual staff can advise on sightseeing. Luggage storage, outdoor patio, guest kitchen and lounge with cable TV are some of the perks. Dorms CH$10,000, doubles CH$40,000

★ TREAT YOURSELF

Boragó Nueva Costanera 3467, Vitacura ☏2 2953 8893, ⓦborago.cl; map p.380. Considered one of Latin America's best restaurants, the chefs here use native ingredients to whip up an inventive and delicious multi-course tasting menu (from CH$43,000), pairing the dishes with appropriate local wines. Reservations required. Mon–Sat 8–11pm.

BELLAVISTA

Bellavista Hostel Dardignac 0184, Metro Baquedano ☏2 2899 7145, ⓦbellavistahostel.com; map p.383. It's easy to see why this hostel is extremely popular with younger travellers – a stone's throw from some of Santiago's best nightlife, it's cosy, colourful, run by helpful bilingual staff and has all the standard backpacker conveniences. Dorms C̲H̲$̲8̲0̲0̲0̲, doubles C̲H̲$̲2̲4̲,̲0̲0̲0̲

Casa Mosaico Loreto 109, Metro Bellas Artes ☏2 2671 2008, ⓦcasamosaicohostel.cl; map p.379. Just a few blocks from the nightlife action but quiet enough for a good night's sleep, this gaily painted hostel offers a range of six- or eight-bed dorms, plus en-suite singles and doubles. Activities include barbecues and dance classes. Dorms C̲H̲$̲1̲0̲,̲0̲0̲0̲, doubles C̲H̲$̲3̲0̲,̲0̲0̲0̲

EATING

Santiago has a proliferation of good restaurants. Most of the better ones are concentrated in Barrio Lastarria and Providencia, with some cheap options, popular with backpackers and students, in Bellavista, Barrio Brasil and up-and-coming Barrio Yungay.

DOWNTOWN AND BARRIO LASTARRIA

Emporio La Rosa Merced 291; map p.379. Coffee and ice-cream haven with tables out onto the street. The hot chocolate comes highly recommended. One ice-cream scoop from CH$2100. Mon–Thurs 8am–9pm, Fri 8am–10pm, Sat 9am–10pm, Sun 9am–9pm.

★**Mercado Central** Puente, at San Pablo; map p.379. The best place for large portions of inexpensive fish and seafood, the fish market's bustling eateries offer such delights as *pastel de jaiva* (creamy crab pie; CH$5000) and *machas a la Parmesana* (CH$4500); *Donde Augusto* is a popular spot. Daily; lunch only.

Ramen Kintaro Monjitas 460, ⓦkintaro.cl; map p.379. This clean, modern Japanese joint has reinvented itself as a ramen house, with meal deals for CH$6000–7000. Sit at the counter and watch the chefs at work. Mon–Fri 12.30–3pm & 7.30–11pm, Sat 7.30–11.30pm.

El Rápido Bandera 371; map p.379. Perfectly prepared *empanadas* and sandwiches, served at a snack counter rather than a restaurant. *Empanadas* from CH$1100. Mon–Fri 9am–9pm, Sat 9am–3.30pm.

BARRIO BRASIL AND BARRIO YUNGAY

Charro de Oro Av Ricardo Cumming 342A; map p.380. Spicy and inexpensive Mexican quesadillas (from CH$4500) and burritos served in an intimate, no-frills setting; happy hour until 9pm. Tues–Sat 5.30pm–late, Sun noon–late.

Ocean Pacific's Av Ricardo Cumming 221, ⓦoceanpacifics.cl; map p.380. Popular restaurant serving consistently good fish dishes (though not the cheapest), including an excellent salmon platter for two, with a backdrop of elaborate nautical decoration. Mains CH$7000–9000. Daily noon–11.30pm.

Peluquería Francesa Compañia de Jesús 2789 ☏2 2682 5243; map p.380. Take a trip back in time at this charming restaurant above a nineteenth-century hair salon, where each table literally bursts with quirky memorabilia. Excellent French cuisine (*coq au vin* CH$8500), and good cocktails. Mon–Fri 10am–8pm, Sat 10am–2pm, Sun 11am–5pm.

Peperone Huérfanos 1954; map p.380. Excellent *empanadería* dishing out baked *empanadas* with myriad fillings, including scallops. Cheese and crab *empanada* CH$1500. Mon–Sat lunch only.

★**Las Vacas Gordas** Cienfuegos 280 ☏2 2697 1066; map p.380. Probably the best restaurant for carnivores in the city, with steaks such as wagyu beef grilled to perfection at very reasonable prices (from CH$8000). Extremely popular, especially on weekends. Mon–Sat 12.30pm–12.30am, Sun 12.30–5pm.

BELLAVISTA

Ciudad Vieja Constitución 92; map p.383. This cool *sanguchería* turns sandwich-making into an art form: varieties (around CH$5000) include teriyaki chicken, suckling pig, fried *merluza* (hake) and the *chivito*, Uruguay's take on the steak sandwich. There's an extensive range of artisanal beers, too. Tues 12.30pm–1am, Wed 12.30pm–1.30am, Thurs 12.30pm–2am, Fri & Sat 12.30pm–2.30am, Sun 1–5pm.

Galindo Constitución, at Dardignac, ⓦgalindo.cl; map p.383. Perpetually packed spot serving traditional Chilean food, such as hearty *pastel de choclo*, *cazuela* and *lomo a la pobre*, along with beers until late, even on weekdays. If sitting outside, you will be entertained by street musicians. Mains from CH$5000. Mon–Sat 10am–2am.

PROVIDENCIA

El Huerto Orrego Luco 054, ⓦelhuerto.cl; map p.380. An excellent choice for a wide variety of lovingly prepared vegetarian dishes, such as hearty burritos or asparagus and ricotta strudel. Mains from around CH$7000. Mon–Sat noon–11pm, Sun 12.30–4.30pm.

4

TRAITORS' CORNER

For an unusual eating experience, try *El Rincón de los Canallas* ("Traitor's Corner"), at Tarapacá 810 (entry only by prior reservation on ☎ 2 2632 5491, ⓦ canallas.cl; map p.380). It was once a secret meeting place for the opposition during Pinochet's dictatorship, and though this is not the original site, you still need a password to enter. When asked, "*Quién vive, canalla?*", respond "*Chile libre, canalla.*" (Pinochet called his detractors "*canallas*", so the exchange roughly means: "Who's there, traitor?" "Free Chile, traitor.") Against a nostalgic backdrop including wall-to-wall rallying slogans, this intimate bar offers traditional Chilean grub served up under names like *Pernil Canalla* ("Traitor's Ham", a roasted leg of pork). Mains CH$6000–10,000.

★ **Liguria** Av Providencia 1373, ⓦ liguria.cl; map p.380. Portraits, film posters, flower designs and football pennants adorn the walls of this legendary Santiago restaurant-bar, which has ample pavement and indoor seating. Dishes include pot roast, pork ribs in mustard sauce and sea bass with capers. There are two other branches, but this one is the best. Mains CH$8000–9000. Mon–Sat 11am–2am.

Santo Remedio Roman Diaz 152, ⓦ santoremedio. cl; map p.380. The idiosyncratic decor has a surreal edge – including high-backed wooden chairs and a zebra-print sofa – and the food is billed as "an aphrodisiacal experience", with pastas, Thai curries, steaks and seafood all on the menu. It's also good for drinks and is *the* place for a Sunday night out. Mains and set lunches CH$5700–7900. Mon–Fri 1–3.30pm & 6.30pm–late, Sat & Sun 9pm–late.

DRINKING AND NIGHTLIFE

Santiago is not a 24-hour party town, and compared to other Latin capitals can seem rather tame. However, Thursdays, Fridays and Saturdays are lively, with crowds pouring into the streets and bars of the nightlife *zonas*.

DOWNTOWN AND BARRIO LASTARRIA

Café Escondido Rosal 346; map p.379. If you want cheap beer and bar snacks in a less than raucous environment, this intimate bar is the perfect spot. Mon–Sat 6pm–2.30am.

Café Haiti Ahumada 140; map p.379. A timewarp *café con piernas* (café with legs), where the mostly male clientele ogle waitresses in short skirts; dodgy gender politics aside, the coffee (from CH$1400) is excellent. Many branches around town. Mon–Fri 8am–9pm.

★ **Culto** Estados Unidos 246 ☎ 2 2632 3585, ⓦ cultobar. cl; map p.379. Laidback rock bar that specializes in theme days dedicated to bands from Pink Floyd to The Verve. Decent range of cocktails starting at CH$2700 and snacks from CH$4500. Mon–Thurs 5pm–1am, Fri & Sat 5pm–2am, Sun 5pm–midnight.

La Piojera Aillavilú 1030; map p.379. Carve your name into the wooden tables at this rough-and-ready bar with a loyal clientele, and knock back a *terremoto* (earthquake) – a powerful wine and ice-cream mix. Drinks from CH$2000. Daily noon–late.

BARRIO BRASIL

Blondie Alameda 2879 ⓦ blondie.cl; map p.380. Large and popular four-floor dance club featuring techno, goth, indie and other musical styles (depending on the night), as well as occasional live music. Thurs–Sat from midnight.

The Clinic Av Brasil 258 T2 2697 2578, ⓦ cerveceriatheclinic.cl; map p.380. Run by the people behind satirical magazine *The Clinic*, this restaurant-bar maintains an appealingly irreverent air with its cartoon menus. There are also inexpensive snacks and meals (CH$4000–10,000), plus a branch on Plaza Ñuñoa. Daily 12.30pm–2am.

Confitería Las Torres Alameda 1570 ☎ 2 2668 0751, ⓦ confiteriatorres.cl; map p.379. Elegant, nineteenth-century building hosting spellbinding live tango shows on weekends to accompany the expertly cooked traditional Chilean dishes (mains CH$6500–12,000). Mon–Sat 10.30am–midnight.

BELLAVISTA

Altazor Antonia López de Bello 0189 ☎ 2 2732 3934; map p.380. Popular bar packed on weekends, often featuring live folk music, jazz and blues. Cover CH$2500. Thurs–Sat from 10.30pm.

Bar Dos Gardenias Antonia López de Bello 199 ☎ 9 7757 2887, ⓦ bardosgardenias.cl; map p.383. A chilled-out and welcoming Cuban bar, with a faded red and yellow exterior, the obligatory Che picture, live Latin folk and rock and refreshing drinks (a mojito will set you back CH$3500). It's especially lively on Friday and Saturday nights. Mon & Tues 7pm–1am, Wed 7pm–2.30am, Thurs–Sat 7pm–3.30am.

La Casa en el Aire Antonia López de Bello 125 ☎ 2 2735 6680, ⓦ lacasaenelaire.cl; map p.383. Inviting candlelit venue offering poetry reading, contemporary theatre performances, film screenings and folk music; check the website for listings. Daily 8pm–2am.

PROVIDENCIA

Flannery's Tobalaba 379 ☎2 2303 0192, ⓦflannerys.cl; map p.380. The inevitable Irish pub, but a good choice for a night out in the Sanhattan area – large and busy, with a loyal local clientele and good number of expats, who come to sup Guinness and English ale, watch the football or rugby and eat Irish stew or fish and chips (CH$6800). Mon–Wed noon–1.30am, Thurs & Fri noon–2.30am, Sat 6pm–2.30am, Sun 6pm–12.30am.

Havana Salsa Dominica 142 ☎2 2737 1737, ⓦhavanasalsa.cl; map p.380. If you want to shake your hips to some salsa beats, this is the place. Cover and Cuban-style buffet dinner CH$13,990. Thurs–Sat 9pm–4am.

PLAZA ÑUÑOA

★ **La Batuta** J. Washington 52 ⓦbatuta.cl; map p.380. A thriving gem of Santiago nightlife, where Chilean and British rock music attract a dedicated following. Drinks around CH$4000. Wed–Thurs 10pm–2am, Fri & Sat 10pm–4.30am.

ENTERTAINMENT

Cine Arte Alameda Alameda 139, Metro Baquedano ⓦcentroartealameda.cl. An arts cinema showing independent and avant-garde films.

Cine Hoyts Moneda 835, Metro Santa Lucía ⓦcinehoyts.cl. Multiplex cinema showing the latest releases; English-language films are usually subtitled, although those of interest to young audiences may be dubbed (*doblada*).

Teatro Municipal Agustinas 794, Metro Universidad de Chile ☎2 2463 8888, ⓦmunicipal.cl. You can find the best of Chile's classical music, opera and ballet inside this magnificent historical building.

SHOPPING

In general, the prices of manufactured goods are expensive in Chile compared to Europe and the US, but cost and choice wise Chile compares well to other South American countries, so its capital is a good place to stock up on any essentials.

Feria Santa Lucia Santa Lucía, Cerro Santa Lucía; map p.379. Large crafts market stocking indigenous crafts, tie-dyed clothing and T-shirts featuring the Chilean flag. Daily 11am–9pm.

Librería Inglesa Huérfanos 669, downtown ⓦlibreriainglesa.cl; map p.379. Fairly good, expensive choice of Penguin paperbacks and other English-language books. Mon–Fri 10.10am–7.30pm, Sat 10.30am–1.50pm.

Mall Sport Av Las Condes 13451 ⓦmallsport.cl; map p.380. Mall dedicated to sports and outdoor pursuits, with mainly expensive and imported, but good-quality trekking and climbing gear as well as sleeping bags, backpacks etc. Daily 10am–9pm.

Patio Bellavista Between Constitución and Pío Nono, Barrio Bellavista ⓦpatiobellavista.cl; map p.383. Open-air space with a concentration of gift shops selling high-quality crafts and clothing, postcards, jewellery and home-made honey. Daily 10am–2/4am.

SKIING NEAR SANTIAGO

It's easy to arrange day-trips from Santiago to experience some world-class powder snow. The **ski season** lasts from mid-June to early October. All resorts rent ski equipment and clothing, and day lift passes cost CH$33,000–46,000. High in the Andes Mountains, 36km east of Santiago, three large ski resorts are clustered in the Tres Valles area: **El Colorado, La Parva** and **Valle Nevado**; all three can be accessed from *Farellones*, a village (2400m above sea level) at the foot of Cerro Colorado (3333m). The journey from Santiago takes about one hour thirty minutes along a winding road (don't attempt it with a hangover). A fourth resort, *Portillo*, is set on the banks of the stunning Laguna del Inca on the Argentine border, a two-hour drive from Santiago.

OPERATORS

Ski Total Av Apoquindo 4900, local 40-46 ☎2 2246 0156, ⓦskitotal.cl. Operates daily departures to all four resorts, and is a good choice for renting equipment and clothing.

Ski Van ☎9 7499 4509, ⓦskivan.cl. Daily departures to El Colorado, Valle Nevado and La Parva, from General Bustamante 10, just off Plaza Italia.

RESORTS

El Colorado ⓦelcolorado.cl. The most accessible and busiest resort houses 19 chairlifts and 21 runs, largely aimed at beginners to intermediate level.

La Parva ⓦlaparva.cl. The Cerro Franciscano (3608m) and Cerro La Falsa Parva here offer 30 runs for skiers of all abilities, with some excellent long advanced runs.

Portillo ⓦskiportillo.com. Chile's most exclusive resort is used for training by international ski teams and boasts 23 runs that cater to intermediates and experts alike, along with ample backcountry terrain and heli-skiing opportunities.

Valle Nevado ⓦvallenevado.com. With the best skiing conditions in Tres Valles and modern lifts, this resort has a good mixture of runs for all abilities, as well as a snow-board park and half-pipe.

Pueblito de Los Dominicos Apoquindo 9085, Las Condes; map p.380. Take the metro up to Los Dominicos to visit this large, pretty (if slightly pricey) crafts market next to the *barrio*'s copper-topped church. Daily around 10am–7pm.

DIRECTORY

Banks and exchange There are plenty of ATMs all over the city, including at the large bus terminals. There are exchange houses on Agustinas, between Ahumada and Bandera, which give a reasonable rate on foreign currencies (Mon–Fri 9am–2pm & 4–6pm, Sat 9am–2pm).

Embassies and consulates Argentina, Miraflores 285, downtown (☎2 2582 2606, ⍟ehile.mrecic.gov.ar); Australia, Isidora Goyenechea 3621, Las Condes (☎2 2550 3500, ⍟chile.embassy.gov.au); Bolivia, Av Santa María 2796, Providencia (☎2 2232 8180, ⍟consuladodebolivia.cl); Canada, Nueva Tajamar 481, 12th floor, Las Condes (☎2 2652 3800, ⍟canadainternational.gc.ca/chile-chili); New Zealand, Isidora Goyenechea 3000, 12th floor, Las Condes (☎2 2616 3000, ⍟nzembassy.com/chile); Peru, Av Andrés Bello 1751, Providencia (☎2 2339 2600, ⍟consulado.pe/es/santiago); South Africa, Apoquindo 2827, 4th floor, Las Condes (☎2 2820 0300, ⍟embajada-sudafrica.cl);

UK, Av El Bosque Norte 125, Las Condes (☎2 2370 4100, ⍟ukinchile.fco.gov.uk/en); US, Av Andrés Bello 2800, Las Condes (☎2 2330 3000, ⍟cl.usembassy.gov).

Hospitals Clínica Las Condes, Estoril 450, Las Condes (☎2 2210 4000, ⍟clinicalascondes.cl); UC Christus, Marcoleta 367, downtown (☎2 2222 9000, ⍟redsalud.uc.cl); Clínica Alemana, Av Vitacura 5951, Vitacura (☎2 2210 1111, ⍟alemana.cl).

Language schools BridgeChile, Los Leones 439, Providencia (☎2 2233 4356, ⍟bridgechile.com) and Natalislang, Arturo Bürhle 47, Providencia (☎9 9257 1436, ⍟natalislang.com) both offer intensive immersion Spanish courses, group tutorials and private lessons.

Laundry Try Lavandería Autoservicio, Monjitas 507, or Lavanderia Lolos, Moneda 2296, Barrio Brasil.

Pharmacies There are plenty of Farmacias Ahumada (⍟farmaciasahumada.cl) and Cruz Verde (⍟cruzverde.cl) pharmacies all over Santiago; Farmacia Ahumada at Av Portugal 125 is open 24hr.

Post offices Correo Central, Plaza de Armas 559 (Mon–Fri 8am–7pm, Sat 9am–2pm). Other branches are at Moneda 1170, near Morandé; Local 503, Exposición 51 Paseo Estación; and Av 11 de Septiembre 2092.

Valparaíso and Viña del Mar

Around 120km from Santiago, draped in a crescent around the Bahía de Valparaíso, the captivating city of **Valparaíso** is a UNESCO World Heritage Site. "Valpo" – as it's affectionately known – is Chile's principal port and naval base, and also the country's liveliest and most vibrant city. The bohemian **nightlife** and excellent cuisine attract much of Santiago to its bars and restaurants at the weekend, as does the nearby but starkly contrasting beach resort of **Viña del Mar**. Viña's attractions are wide, white beaches surrounded by expensive high-rise apartments, casinos and pricey, touristy restaurants. It has none of the character that distinguishes Valparaíso, but as they're so close together, it's easy enough to stay in Valparaíso and visit Viña's beaches for the day.

VALPARAÍSO

Few travellers fail to be inspired by the ramshackle beauty of **VALPARAÍSO**, with its mishmash patchwork of brightly coloured houses is built across a series of hills; steep stairways and the city's famous *ascensores* (elevators) link the hills to the port area. Still a major port today, the city came into its own during the California Gold Rush, and in the mid-nineteenth century was the main hub for ships crossing between the Atlantic and Pacific oceans. Valparaíso's narrow labyrinth of atmospheric alleyways offers glimpses of the city's decline from the grandeur of its former glories, and its more recent (partial) transformation into a bohemian, arty hub.

WHAT TO SEE AND DO

Valparaíso is effectively split into two halves: the hills (*cerros*), and the flat El Plan. Most restaurants and hostels can be found on the former, especially on touristy **Cerro Concepción** and **Cerro Alegre**. Visitors usually spend their time here meandering along the winding passageways, and enjoying the spectacular views from the rickety *ascensores*. **El Plan**, which includes the busy port area, is home to an extensive nightlife quarter as well as the shopping and administrative districts, all linked by traffic-choked narrow streets.

THE ASCENSORES OF VALPARAÍSO

Valparaíso's *ascensores*, or funiculars, were built between 1883 and 1916. As well as being one of the city's enduring attractions, they remain an essential way of getting about, and have recently been renovated. Most run daily from 7am to 11pm and cost CH$100–300 per journey. Below are some of the best. Note that they are periodically closed for renovation work.

Ascensor Polanco The only *ascensor* that is an actual elevator, Polanco is reached through a long underground tunnel from Calle Simpson, off Avenida Argentina. It rises vertically through the yellow tower to a *mirador* offering excellent views of the port; there's also some high-class graffiti, though bear in mind that the area is a bit sketchy.

Ascensor Concepción (also known as Ascensor Turri). The city's oldest funicular, built in 1883 and originally steam-powered, is one of the most popular. It climbs up to Paseo Gervasoni on Cerro Concepción, a delightful residential area and the start of many walking tours that cover Cerro Alegre as well. The lower entrance is opposite the Relój Turri clock tower.

Ascensor Artillería Extremely popular with visitors, this funicular should not be missed. It runs from Plaza Aduana up to Cerro Playa Ancha, and offers a beautiful panoramic view of the city and coastline, with Viña del Mar in the distance. The Museo Naval y Marítimo (see page 394) is nearby.

The cerros

Without a doubt, Valparaíso's biggest attraction is its **cerros** (hills). Few pastimes are as enjoyable as meandering up and down the area's winding narrow streets, or riding its antique funiculars. Visitors can stop to marvel at the impressive views of the city from a multitude of **miradores**

4

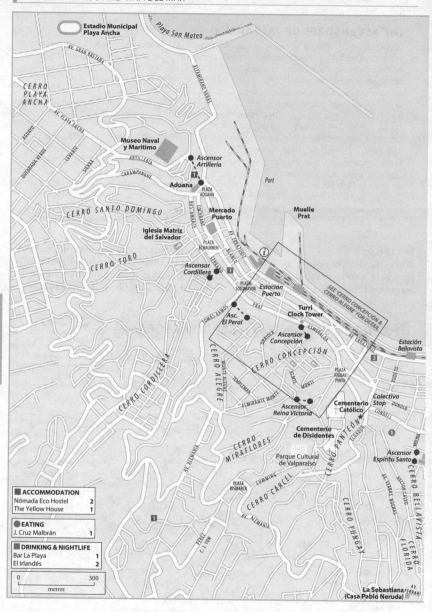

ACCOMMODATION
Nómada Eco Hostel	2
The Yellow House	1

EATING
J. Cruz Malbrán	1

DRINKING & NIGHTLIFE
Bar La Playa	1
El Irlandés	2

0 ——— 300
metres

(viewpoints), or duck into little shops and cafés to admire the colourful **murals** – a striking example of the city's bohemian culture. It is easy to see why Valparaíso has produced a string of notable writers, poets and artists.

Cerro Concepción and **Cerro Alegre** are the best known of the hills, with the highest concentration of churches and museums, but they are by no means the only gems. Nearby **Cerro Panteón**, reached by a network of winding paths, is home to three

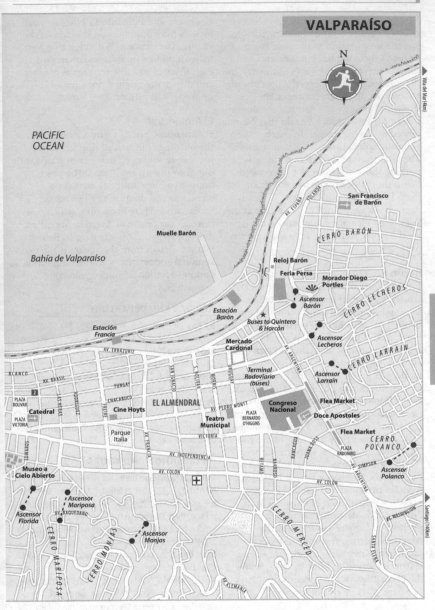

VALPARAÍSO

N

PACIFIC OCEAN

Bahía de Valparaíso

Muelle Barón

Viña del Mar (4km)

San Francisco de Barón

CERRO BARÓN

Reloj Barón
Feria Persa
Morador Diego Portles

Estación Barón

Ascensor Barón

CERRO LECHEROS

Buses to Quintero & Horcón

Ascensor Lecheros

Estación Francia

AV. ERRÁZURIZ

Mercado Cardonal

Ascensor Larraín

CERRO LARRAÍN

BLANCO
AV. BRASIL

YUNGAY

CHACABUCO

Terminal Rodoviario (buses)

AV. ARGENTINA

AV. URUGUAY

S. BOLIVAR

SAN IGNACIO

RODRIGUEZ

FREIRE

Flea Market

PLAZA BOLIVAR
Catedral

EL ALMENDRAL

AV. PEDRO MONTT

Congreso Nacional

Doce Apostoles

Cine Hoyts

PLAZA VICTORIA

Teatro Municipal

PLAZA BERNARDO O'HIGGINS

Flea Market

CERRO POLANCO

Parque Italia

VICTORIA

AV. FRANCIA

AV. INDEPENDENCIA

RETAMO

BARROSO

RANCAGUA

YUNA ROSS

PLAZA RADOMIRO

AV. SIMPSON

Ascensor Polanco

Museo a Cielo Abierto

AV. COLON

AV. COLON

AV. ARGENTINA

SANTA ELENA

Ascensor Mariposa

AV. BAQUEDANO

Ascensor Florida

CERRO MARIPOSA

CERRO MONJAS

Ascensor Monjas

CERRO MERCED

AV. ALEMANIA

AV. WASHINGTON

Santiago (140km)

4

colourful cemeteries, the most interesting of which is the **Cementerio de Disidentes**, resting place of non-Catholic European immigrants. Nearby **Cerro Cárcel** is the site of a former prison that has been turned into the **Parque Cultural de Valparaíso** (☏ 32 225 9400, ⓦparquecultural.cl), a vibrant, cultural hub.

La Sebastiana
La Sebastiana, Ferrari 692, off Alemania (Tues–Sun: Jan & Feb 10am–7pm;

March–Dec 10.10am–6pm; CH$7000; ☎32 225 6606, ⓦfundacionneruda.org), was the least lived-in of the poet **Pablo Neruda**'s three homes, but it offers incredibly picturesque views of the city and the interior design reflects the poet's quirky tastes. Like his other residences, the five-storey house has a nautical theme and is crammed with knick-knacks that Neruda picked up on his travels; unlike the others, you can explore this one without a guide. The vista from his bedroom window is nothing short of spectacular. To get here, take a short ride on *colectivo* #39 from Plaza Ecuador or bus #612 or "0" from Avenida Argentina or Plaza San Luis at the top of Templeman; if you stay on the latter for the whole route you get a low-cost city tour.

Barrio Puerto

El Plan consists of long east–west streets, crossed by shorter north–south streets leading into the hills, and is divided into two halves, with **Barrio Puerto** located northwest of Cerro Concepción. Its centrepiece, the pedestrianized **Plaza Sotomayor**, is lined with a mixture of modern concrete blocks and grand early twentieth-century buildings, and is home to the **Primera Zona Naval**, the country's naval headquarters. At the port end of the plaza, near the Estación Puerto, is **Muelle Prat**, the passenger pier, from where you can take boat trips out into the harbour (CH$3000/person; 30–45min). West of the pier, the five-block port-side stretch of Avenida Errázuriz and parallel Blanco make up Valparaíso's principal nightlife district, with **Mercado Puerto** and its plethora of fishy places to eat at the northwest corner. A couple of blocks south of the market is the elegant **Iglesia Matriz del Salvador**, built in 1842, while the **Plaza Aduana** and Ascensor Artillería (see page 391) lie two blocks west.

Museo Naval y Marítimo

The **Museo Naval y Marítimo** at Paseo 21 de Mayo 45 (Tues–Sun 10am–5.30pm; CH$1000; ☎32 243 7651, ⓦmuseonaval. cl) houses an extensive collection of artefacts related to Chile's famous military figures, including Arturo Prat, Lord Cochrane and Bernardo O'Higgins, and focuses most attention on the War of the Pacific. The museum is divided into four halls around an immaculate courtyard, each devoted to a different naval conflict and displaying original documents, uniforms and medals.

El Almendral

El Almendral, east of Cerro Concepción, is the bustling commercial district, where lively stalls selling all manner of goods spill out onto the streets. **Plaza O'Higgins** is home to a huge **antiques market** on weekends and doubles as a live music venue, while **Plaza Rodomiro**, which runs through the centre of Avenida Argentina, draws weekend shoppers with its **flea market**. Across from the square is the main **Terminal Rodoviario**, with the monolithic **Congreso National** building directly opposite it.

ARRIVAL AND DEPARTURE

By bus The Terminal Rodoviario (☎32 293 9646) is on the eastern end of Pedro Montt, opposite the Congreso Nacional; it's a 20min walk to the old town centre.
Destinations Isla Negra (every 15min; 1hr 30min); La Serena (every 1–2hr; 6hr); Santiago (every 15min; 1hr 30min–1hr 45min).

By train The Metro (ⓦmetro-valparaiso.cl) departs for Viña del Mar from several stations in Valpo (every 5–20min). Buy a plastic charge card (CH$1450) first, and top it up with credit before travelling.

INFORMATION AND TOURS

Tourist information The tourist office is at Muelle Prat by the port (☎32 223 6264, ⓦsernatur.cl; Mon–Fri 9am–2pm & 3–6pm, Sat 9am–2pm & 3–5pm). Note that (despite an old sign) there is no official tourist office at the bus station, which is filled with accommodation touts offering (at best) partial information.

Tours One of the best operators is Ruta Valparaíso (☎32 259 2520, ⓦrutavalparaiso.cl), which has half-day (CH$25,000) and full-day (from CH$35,000) city tours; it also offers excursions throughout the region. A good alternative for city tours is the appropriately named Tours for Tips (ⓦtours4tips.com), which leave from Plaza Sotomayor daily at 10am and 3pm and have several different routes; they are free but tips are welcomed. Wine Tours Valparaíso (☎09 8428 3502, ⓦwinetoursvalparaiso.cl) organizes wine-tasting trips in the Casablanca Valley and beyond. Chilean Cuisine (☎09 6621 4626, ⓦcookingclasseschile.cl) offers enjoyable cookery classes.

GETTING AROUND

By bus, colectivo and micro Frequent transport of all sorts runs to and from Viña del Mar; look for "Viña" displayed in the window. In El Plan, buses labelled "Aduana" run west towards the centre along Pedro Montt while "P. Montt" buses run back to the bus station.

By tram Antique trams offer limited but inexpensive service around El Plan; watch out the rails.

ACCOMMODATION

Casa Aventura Pasaje Gálvez 11, Cerro Alegre ☎32 275 5963, ⓦcasaventura.cl; map p.391. Well-established, friendly *Casa Aventura* has spotless dorms and private rooms (including good-value singles for CH$20,000), a sunny lounge and a communal kitchen. A reliable budget choice. Dorms CH$11,500, doubles CH$29,000

Hostal Jacaranda Urriola 636, Cerro Alegre ☎32 324 5077, ⓦhostaljacaranda.blogspot.co.uk; map p.391. Friendly, low-cost, no-frills hostel for travellers on a really tight budget. It's split over two nearby sites, within easy walking distance of the city's best restaurants and bars. No breakfast. Dorms CH$8,000, doubles CH$23,500

Hotel Ibis Errazuriz 811 ☎32 280 2300, ⓦibis.com; map p.391. In a downtown location, overlooking the port, this modern, mid-range hotel has a distinctive, multicoloured exterior, spick- and-span en-suite rooms (many with wonderful sea views), efficient staff, and an in-house restaurant-bar. CH$41,000

Nómada Eco Hostel Brasil 1822 ☎32 327 3081, ⓦnomadaecohostel.cl; map p.392. If you're not set on staying on one of the *cerros*, this downtown hostel is a great choice. The five- to ten-bed dorms and private rooms are cheerful and boast wooden floors, and there's plenty of artwork dotted around. It aims to be the first carbon-neutral hostel in Valpo. Dorms CH$11,000, doubles CH$33,000

Residencia en el Cerro Pasaje Pierre Loti 51, Cerro Concepción ☎32 249 5298, ⓦresidenciaenelcerro.cl; map p.391. Large, wonderfully friendly family-run place, with a good breakfast, and a number of cats to keep you company. Dorms CH$11,000, doubles CH$24,000

The Yellow House Capitán Muñoz Gamero 91, Cerro Artillería ☎32 233 9435, ⓦtheyellowhouse.cl; map

---

★ TREAT YOURSELF

Hotel De Vinci Urriola 426, Cerro Elegre ☎32 317 4494, ⓦhoteldavincivalparaiso.cl; map p.391. As the name suggests, there's an arty feel to this mid-range hotel, whose en suites, some split-level, are set around a light-filled central atrium, with photos and paintings covering the walls. Good value. US$83

---

p.392. Even by Valpo's high standards, the views from *The Yellow House*, a renovated 200-year-old building, are spectacular. Most of the rooms at this welcoming B&B are en suite, and there's also a comfortable apartment with a kitchenette. There's a book exchange, and a range of tours are available. Doubles CH$29,000, apartments CH$45,000

EATING

Alegretto Pilcomayo 529, Cerro Concepción ☎32 296 8839, ⓦallegretto.cl; map p.391. British–Chilean-run restaurant with colourful decor, draught beer, and live football on TV. The menu features thin-crust pizzas (CH$5800–9200), risottos, gnocchi and ravioli, and a good weekday lunch special (CH$5900). Mon–Thurs 1–3.30pm & 7–11pm, Fri 1–3.30pm & 7.30pm–1am, Sat 1–4.30pm & 7.30pm–1am, Sun 1–4.30pm & 7–11pm.

Amor Porteño Almirante Montt 418, Cerro Concepción ☎32 221 6253; map p.391. Charming ice-cream parlour/café, with a tiny dining area decorated with flowery murals and vintage mirrors. As well as real Argentine-style *helado* (from CH$1750), you can tuck into *churros* and *medialunas* (sweet, doughy croissants), and enjoy good coffee. Tues–Thurs & Sun 10.30am–9pm, Fri & Sat 10.30am–10pm.

Emporio La Rosa Plaza Aníbal Pinto 1189 ☎09 7516 4920, ⓦemporiolarosa.cl; map p.391. Pink-shirted waiting staff serve *onces* (CH$6900–8100), breakfasts, light meals and huge coffees at this cheerful café. The highlights, though, are the ice-cream sundaes (CH$3900–4200). Mon–Fri 8.30am–9.30pm, Sat 9am–9.30pm, Sun 11am–9.30pm.

Le Filou de Montpellier Almirante Montt 382, Cerro Concepción ☎32 222 4663; map p.391. A delightful little piece of France in Valpo: postcards of Montpellier and local paintings decorate the place, while the ever-changing set lunch (CH$8900) may include French onion soup, *moules mariniere*, and peach melba. Tues–Thurs 1–5pm, Fri 1–9pm, Sat 1–10.30pm, Sun 1–6.30pm.

Foto Cafe Av Esmeralda 1111 ☎32 223 1515, ⓦfotocafe.cl; map p.391. Something of a curiosity, combining a photography business with a classy café. There's a good-value three-course set lunch (around CH$8000), plenty of options for *onces*, coffee and alcoholic drinks (these last best enjoyed in the cosy upstairs nook, accessed via a spiral staircase). Mon–Fri 9.30am–7.30pm, Sat 10am–2pm.

J. Cruz Malbrán Condell 1466, up a side alley next to the Municipalidad ☎32 221 1225, ⓦjcruz.cl; map p.392. This extraordinary place is packed with kitsch trinkets. It also claims to have invented the *chorrillana* (a vast plate of steak strips, onions, eggs and French fries), which is not to be missed. Most mains CH$5500–7500. Mon–Thurs noon–2am, Fri & Sat noon–4.30am, Sun 1pm–2am.

4

DRINKING AND NIGHTLIFE

Bar La Playa Serrano 567 ☎ 32 225 9426; map p.392. The old sea dogs that once frequented *La Playa* have mostly departed, but it's still a characterful spot for a drink (from CH$2000; the food, though, is decidedly average), and there's frequently live music in the evenings. Mon–Wed 10am–10.30pm, Thurs–Sat 10am–late.

El Cinzano Plaza Aníbal Pinto 1182 ☎ 32 221 3043, ⓦ barcinzano.cl; map p.391. One of the oldest restaurant-bars in the city, offering a fantastic atmosphere, especially on Thursday, Friday and Saturday nights when it fills with locals and ageing crooners singing sentimental ballads. Beer from CH$1800; set lunch CH$5500. Mon–Wed 10am–1am, Thurs 10am–2am, Fri & Sat 10.30am–4.30am.

Fauna Dimalow 166, Cerro Alegre ☎ 32 327 0719, ⓦ faunahotel.cl; map p.391. The terrace at this restaurant-bar has panoramic views of Valpo's cerros and bay, making it an ideal spot for a sundowner, especially given the range of craft beers (from CH$3000). Good food, too. Daily 12.30–10.30pm.

El Irlandés Blanco 1279 ☎ 32 254 3592; map p.392. This Irish-run joint has an authentic pub-feel, with a long bar to prop yourself up at, an excellent range of imported

VIÑA DEL MAR

█ ACCOMMODATION
Casa Olga	2
My Father's House	3
Street Garden Hostel	1

● EATING
Cevasco	4
Entre Masas	2
Donde Willy	1
Panzoni	5
The Tea Pot	3

█ DRINKING & NIGHTLIFE
Café Journal	1

0 — 250 metres

PACIFIC OCEAN

and local beers, and a friendly, relaxed atmosphere. Tues & Wed 5pm–1.30am, Thurs 6.30pm–3am, Fri 4pm–3.30am, Sat 4pm–4.30am.

DIRECTORY

Banks and exchange The main financial street is Prat, with many banks, ATMs and *cambios*. Banco de Santiago is generally the best bet for currency exchange.

Hospital Try public hospital Carlos Van Buren, Colón, at San Ignacio (☎ 32 236 4000, ⓦ hospitalcarlosvanburen.cl), or private clinic Clínica Valparaíso, Av Brasil 2350 (☎ 600 411 2000, ⓦ clinicavalparaiso.cl).

Post office Prat 856 (Mon–Fri 9am–6pm, Sat 10am–1pm).

VIÑA DEL MAR

Though only fifteen minutes from Valparaíso, **VIÑA DEL MAR** could hardly be more different from its grittier neighbour. Purpose-built in the late nineteenth century as a weekend getaway for wealthy Santiago and Valparaíso residents, it draws thousands of holidaymakers during the summer and on weekends. Viña makes for an enjoyable day-trip to the beach, and is worth a visit during the week-long **Festival de la Canción** in the second or third week of February, which draws top Latino and international artists. The city also hosts spectacular Año Nuevo (New Year) celebrations. Other festivals include the two-week-long **Feria del Libro** (Jan), which attracts important literary figures and hosts live readings, and the acclaimed **Festival Cine Viña del Mar** film festival (Oct or Nov; ⓦ cinevina.cl).

WHAT TO SEE AND DO

The city is split in two by the broad, none-too-clean **Marga Marga** estuary, with a largely residential area to the south and most of the beaches in the northern half. **Avenida San Martín**, parallel to the beach, and the side streets off it feature numerous dining and nightlife options. At the heart of Viña lies the large, shady **Plaza Vergara**, a popular spot with the occasional busker or *capoeira* demonstration and horse-drawn carriages parked around it. Several blocks of **Avenida Valparaíso**, Viña's main thoroughfare, which runs from the square's southwest corner, have been pleasantly pedestrianized, with a number of shops and places to eat.

Museo Francisco Fonck

Museo Francisco Fonck (4 Norte 784; Mon 10am–2pm & 3–6pm, Tues–Sat 10am–6pm, Sun 10am–2pm; CH$2700; ☎ 32 268 6753, ⓦ museofonck.cl) has one of Chile's most important **Easter Island collections**, plus some fascinating pre-Hispanic exhibits. One of the museum's best pieces stands by the entrance in the garden: a giant *moai*, one of just six that exist outside Easter Island.

The beaches

Playa Caleta Abarca lies in a sandy cove south of **Castillo Wulff**, an impressive castle-like structure built on a rocky outcrop at the mouth of the estuary by a Valparaíso businessman in 1906. Located next to the large **Reloj de Flores** ("flower clock"), the beach draws a lively picnicking crowd on weekends. Just north of the estuary, Avenida Perú runs parallel to the sea, past the brash **Casino Viña del Mar**. Beyond you will find an almost unbroken line of sandy beaches, backed by high-rise apartment buildings, stretching all the way to the smaller resort of **Reñaca**, which itself has more good beaches and nightlife.

Quinta Vergara

The one spot besides the beaches where you might want to spend some time in Viña del Mar is the lovely **Quinta Vergara** park (daily: summer 7am–7pm; winter 7am–6pm), where the manicured grounds are home to a vast array of exotic imported plants. It's a couple of blocks south of Plaza Vergara behind the Estación Viña, with the futuristic-looking **Anfiteatro**, home to the annual music festival, its centrepiece.

ARRIVAL, INFORMATION AND TOURS

By bus The bus terminal is at the eastern end of Av Valparaíso. To go down the coast, your best bet is to catch a bus from Valparaíso (see page 390), reached by any *micro* (every 10min) marked "Puerto" or "Aduana" from Plaza Vergara or Arlegui; alternatively take the Metro (see below). Destinations Reñaca (every 15min; 25min); Santiago (every 15min; 1hr 30min–1hr 45min).

By train The Metro (ⓦ metro-valparaiso.cl) departs for Valparaíso from the centrally located Miramar and Viña del Mar stations (every 5–20min). Buy a plastic charge card (CH$1450) first, and then top it up with credit before travelling.

Tourist information The main office is off the northeast corner of Plaza Vergara, next to *Hotel O'Higgins* (Mon–Fri 9am–9pm, Sat 10am–9pm, Sun 10am–8pm; ☎32 218 5710, ⓦvisitevinadelmar.cl). There's also a smaller information booth at the bus station (daily 9am–6pm; ☎32 275 2000).

Tours Tours 4 Tips (☎2 2570 9338, ⓦtours4tips.com) runs daily English- and Spanish-language walking tours, departing from the Reloj de Flores at 10am and 3pm (free, but tips expected).

ACCOMMODATION

Casa Olga 18 de Septiembre 31 ☎32 318 2972, ⓦcasa-olga.com; map p.396. In a handsome 1930s townhouse this charming B&B is one of the best value options in town, with a handful of spick-and-span en-suite rooms, some with sea views. It's in the Recreo neighbourhood, a 20min walk from the Reloj de Flores. CH$40,000

My Father's House Gregorio Marañón 1210 ☎32 261 6136, ⓦmyfathershouse.cl; map p.396. Spacious, quiet single, double and triple rooms (with shared or private bathrooms), swimming pool and gracious owners. The only drawback is that it's about 2km from the centre of town; catch *colectivo* #31, #82 or #131. US$62

Street Garden Hostel 3 Poniente 379 ☎32 320 0208, ⓦstreetgardenhostel.cl; map p.396. Hostels open and close remarkably frequently in Viña: *Street Garden Hostel* is one of the current popular spots, with a lively (and noisy) atmosphere, four- to eight-bed dorms, basic private rooms, and a handy central location. Dorms CH$10,000, doubles CH$30,000

EATING

Cevasco Av Valparaíso 694–700 ☎32 271 4256, ⓦcevasco.cl; map p.396. Bustling *fuente de soda*, split between two locations, either side of an arcade, serving up tasty – if decidedly unhealthy – hot dogs, burgers and *barros lucos* (CH$1750–4750) to a steady stream of locals. Mon–Sat 8.30am–11pm, Sun 12.30–9.30pm.

Entre Masas 5 Norte 235 ☎32 297 9919; map p.396. Excellent little bakery, specializing in *empanadas* (CH$1500–2500): there are 49 varieties including crab and cheese, spinach and ricotta, and chicken, bacon and mushroom. Daily 10am–10pm.

Donde Willy 6 Norte 353 ☎32 342 1261; map p.396. Tucked away down a narrow alleyway, this little restaurant specializes in Chilean classics such as *pastel de jaiba* (crab pie) and *caldo de congrio* (conger eel soup). Mains CH$4900–9000. Daily noon-12.30pm

Panzoni Paseo Cousiño 12B ☎32 271 4134; map p.396. This charming Italian joint has a handful of tables, great service and inexpensive pastas and salads. You

may have to queue at lunchtime, but it's worth the wait (mains CH$5000–8000). Mon–Sat noon–4pm & 8pm–midnight.

The Tea Pot 5 Norte 475 ☎32 268 7671; map p.396. Kitsch wood panelling gives this café the feel of a Patagonian cabin. The menu features around fifty types of tea (from CH$1300) plus breakfast options, cakes, sandwiches and *onces*. Winter Mon–Sat 10am–9pm; summer Mon–Sat 10am–10pm, Sun 4.30–9pm.

DRINKING AND NIGHTLIFE

Café Journal Agua Santa 2 ☎32 266 6654; map p.396. Proximity to Viña's university ensures a healthy crowd of student drinkers, with pitchers of beer setting them up for a night dancing and carousing. It's busy throughout the week until the early hours, often featuring live music and/or DJs. Drinks CH$1500–4000. Mon–Wed noon–3.30am, Thurs 11.30am–3.30am, Fri & Sat 11.30am–4.30am, Sun 8pm–3.30am.

DIRECTORY

Banks and exchange Most banks and *cambios* are on Arlegui and Av Libertad, and there are innumerable ATMs scattered about town.

Post office Between Plaza Vergara and Puente Libertad (Mon–Fri 9am–7pm, Sat 10am–1pm).

ISLA NEGRA

The seaside village of **ISLA NEGRA** (not, incidentally, an island), about 80km south of Valparaíso, was the site of Pablo Neruda's favourite home. The **Casa Museo Isla Negra**, Poeta Neruda s/n (Tues–Sun: Jan & Feb 10am–7pm; March–Dec 10am–6pm; CH$7000, including audio tour in Spanish, English, French, German or Portuguese; the museum has limited capacity, so it's best to arrive in the morning; ☎2 2777 8741, ⓦfundacionneruda.org), lies down a wooded trail by the sea, a short walk from the main road. Larger than his other two homes, Isla Negra is fascinating for the sheer volume of **exotic objects** that Neruda accumulated here, and the consideration that went into every aspect of the design – from the arrangement of wooden ships' figureheads in the living room, to the positioning of blue glass bottles along the seaward side of the house. The poet's collection includes African wooden carvings, ships in bottles and an amazing array of seashells, housed in a purpose-built room that Neruda designed but never completed. A strong nautical theme runs throughout; there is even a small boat on the terrace so that the poet could be "a sailor on land".

ARRIVAL AND DEPARTURE

By bus Pullman (ⓦpullman.cl) and Tur Bus (ⓦturbus.cl) run buses from Santiago's Terminal Alameda (every 30min; 2hr). There are also services from Valparaíso (every 15min; 1hr 30min).

Norte Chico

Dominated by dry scrubland and sparse vegetation, the **Norte Chico** region, which stretches roughly from the northern tip of Santiago to the southern reaches of the Atacama, might seem unremarkable from a bus window. Visitors are, however, drawn here for its **stargazing**, long sandy beaches, and trips to its far-flung national parks. The biggest population centre is the relaxed seaside town of **La Serena** with its bustling market and colonial-style architecture, while the fertile **Elqui Valley**, which once inspired Nobel-Prize-winning poet Gabriela Mistral, is now the focal point for the country's favourite tipple, pisco. The islands of **Damas** and **Choros** brim over with seals, penguins and cormorants. Further north, the mining town of **Copiapó**, currently undergoing one of its regular copper-induced booms, is the jumping-off point for the stunning kaleidoscopic landscapes of **Parque Nacional Nevado de Tres Cruces** and **Parque Nacional Pan de Azúcar**. Horseriding, trekking and kayaking are all attractions which are likely to keep tourists in this region longer than they expected.

LA SERENA

LA SERENA, 474km north of Santiago, is one of Chile's prime **beach resorts**, though its charms also include an impressive number of churches and several worthwhile museums. It is also an excellent base for exploring the surrounding countryside. The city was founded in 1544, and during the following century it was the target of multiple raids by the French and British, including the pirate Francis Drake.

Downtown La Serena

With a tranquil vibe, La Serena's central streets are easy to wander around on foot.

The town's largest church is the Neoclassical **Iglesia Catedral**, at the corner of Los Carrera and Cordovez, off the Plaza de Armas, which has a beautiful, marble-decorated interior. **Iglesia de San Francisco**, Balmaceda 640, was the first church here to be built out of stone, and **Iglesia Santo Domingo**, Cordovez s/n, dates back to 1673.

The **Casa Gabriel González Videla**, Matta 495, on the west side of the Plaza de Armas (Mon–Fri 10am–6pm, Sat 10am–1pm; free), is well worth a visit. Originally the home of former president González Videla, who was born in the town, it is now a museum housing an impressive collection of fine art and contemporary painting.

At the junction of Cienfuegos with Cordovez, the **Museo Arqueológico** (Tues–Fri 9.30am–5.50pm, Sat 10am–1pm & 4–7pm, Sun 10am–1pm; free) displays elaborate Diaguita ceramics, as well as a 2.5m *moai* statue from Easter Island.

About two blocks west from Paza de Armas, the tranquil and beautifully sculpted Japanese-style **Jardín El Corazón** (Tues–Sun 10am–6pm; CH\$1000) is the perfect place to while away a sunny afternoon.

The beaches

While reasonably crowded in the summer, the **beaches** are quiet for the rest of the year. The nearest beach area is a half-hour walk west from the city centre from Jardín El Corazón along Francisco de Aguirre.

Between La Serena and the town of Coquimbo, a **cycle lane** runs beside a dozen or so wide, sandy beaches lined with pricey condominiums, hotels and restaurants – an easy and enjoyable day-trip. Many hostels and travel agencies have bikes to rent. Most of the beaches are suitable for swimming and windsurfing, although Playa Cuatro Esquinas is known to have strong rip currents.

4

ARRIVAL AND DEPARTURE

By plane Aeropuerto La Florida is 5km east of town along Ruta 41; catch a taxi (CH$6500), transfer (CH$2500) or *micro* to the centre.

Destinations Antofagasta (2 daily; 1hr 25min); Santiago (6 daily; 1hr).

By bus The main bus terminal is located on corner Amunátegui, at Av El Santo, a 20min walk south of the centre.

Destinations Antofagasta (20 daily; 12hr); Arica (5 daily; 24hr); Calama (11 daily; 15hr); Copiapó (every 30min–1hr; 5hr); Iquique (8 daily; 18hr); Montegrande (every 30min–1hr; 1hr 50min); Ovalle (every 15min; 1hr 20min); Pisco Elqui (every 30min–1hr; 2hr); Santiago (every 30min; 7hr); Valparaíso (6 daily; 5hr); Vicuña (every 30min–1hr; 1hr).

By colectivo Coquimbo (frequent daily departures from Av Francisco de Aguirre, between Los Carrera and Balmaceda; 20min); Elqui Valley (several departures daily from Domeyko in the centre; 1hr).

INFORMATION AND TOURS

From La Serena, a number of tour companies run excursions in the surrounding area. Popular tours (CH$15,000–50,000) of the *Elqui Valley* include pisco tasting, stargazing at the *Observatorio Mamalluca* and penguin-watching at **Reserva Nacional Pingüino de Humboldt**.

Tourist information Sernatur, Matta 461, Plaza de Armas (March–Nov Mon–Fri 9am–6pm, Sat 10am–4pm, Dec–Feb daily 9am–9pm; ☎ 51 222 5199).

Daniel Russ ☎ 09 9454 6000, ⓦ jeeptour-laserena.cl. An experienced and extremely knowledgeable man (with a jeep), who runs standard excursions for small groups, as well as trips to Paso del Agua Negra and tailor-made outings.

DOWNTOWN LA SERENA

RN Pinguino de Humboldt & Copiapó

Kayak Australis ☎2 3202 6850, ⓦkayakaustralis.cl. Specializes in multi-day sea-kayak trips around Chile, including one to Isla Damas. Book through the Santiago office at Barros Borgoño 71, Oficina 803, Providencia, or online.

Mundo Caballo Km27, along the road between La Serena and Vicuña ☎09 6191 0497, ⓦmundocaballo.cl. Stables 20km outside La Serena offering various horseriding trips, including one at night (CH$18,000–50,000). Best contacted by phone.

Turismo Delfines Matta 655 ☎51 222 3624, ⓦturismodelfines.cl. Established operator specializing in bilingual guided trips to Isla Damas.

ACCOMMODATION

Aji Verde Hostel Vicuña 415 ☎51 248 9016, ⓦajiverdehostel.cl; map p.400. A fun atmosphere pervades this central, HI-affiliated hostel with young staff, a roof terrace, kitchen and plenty of common areas for connecting with fellow travellers. Dorms CH$9000, doubles CH$33,000

Hostal Family Home Av El Santo 1056 ☎51 221 2099, ⓦfamilyhome.cl; map p.400. Good-value *hostal* that lives up to its name and is conveniently located close to the bus terminal (albeit on a busy road), with singles, doubles and triples (some en suite), plus use of a kitchen. CH$28,000

El Huerto Parcela 66, Peñuelas ☎51 231 2531; map p.400. Lovely, grassy campsite down at the quieter end of the beach, halfway between La Serena and Coquimbo (buses between the two stops nearby). Per person CH$25000

Hostal Maria Casa Las Rojas 18 ☎51 222 9282, ⓦhostalmariacasa.cl; map p.400. Small guesthouse with an effusive hostess, kitchen access, bikes to rent, and a relaxing garden; popular with backpackers. A 3min walk from the main bus station – ideal for late arrivals. Dorms CH$12,000, doubles CH$25,000

★ **Hostal El Punto** Andres Bello 979 ☎51 222 8474, ⓦhostalelpunto.cl; map p.400. German-run hostel with friendly and knowledgeable staff, daily excursions, an on-site café, laundry service and spotless rooms; popular with travellers of all ages. Call ahead if arriving later than 10pm. Dorms CH$10,000, doubles CH$21,000

EATING

La Casa del Guatón Brasil 750 ☎51 221 1519; map p.400. Lively, friendly and intimate, this colonial-style restaurant serves the town's best *parrilladas* (from CH$19,000). There's often live music. Mon–Sat 12.30pm–12.30am, Sun 1–6pm.

La Mia Pizza Av del Mar 2100; map p.400. Seafront pizzeria that offers excellent fish dishes as well as large portions of tasty pizza (from CH$7000). Mon–Sat 12.30pm–midnight, Sun 12.30–4.30pm.

DRINKING

La Biblioteca O'Higgins, at Av Francisco de Aguirre ☎09 8139 0449; map p.400. "*The Library*" is anything but: students congregate around small wooden tables, feeding the jukebox while downing *terremoto* cocktails (sweet white wine, pineapple ice cream and Amaretto). Drinks from CH$2000. Daily 2.30pm–3am.

Café Centenario Cordovez 391; map p.400. Lavazza coffee (CH$1500–3000), regional wines and local beer are served in this chic corner spot on the southeast corner of Plaza de Armas. Mon–Fri 8am–8pm.

COQUIMBO

A fifteen-minute *colectivo* ride south from La Serena lies its rougher, livelier twin: **Coquimbo**, the region's main port. The beautifully restored historical district of **Barrio Inglés** comprises several plazas with a far more exciting eating and nightlife scene than La Serena. Coquimbo's only real drawback is the lack of budget accommodation, though there is one exception.

The most striking landmark, looming over town, is a huge 93m cross, the **Cruz del Tercer Milenio** (ⓦcruzdeltercermilenio.cl). This slightly bizarre construction, the base of which provides a great viewpoint over town, was funded by the King of Morocco for the benefit of the town's Lebanese Muslim community.

ACCOMMODATION

Hostal Nomade C Regimento Coquimbo 5 ☎51 275 1161. HI-affiliated hostel in the large and rambling former residence of the French ambassador, which has a slightly haunted-house feel. It has informative staff, large rooms with exceptionally high ceilings, internet, kitchen facilities and other backpacker conveniences. Dorms CH$13,000, doubles CH$30,000

EATING, DRINKING AND NIGHTLIFE

With many fish restaurants, Coquimbo is a seafood-lover's paradise, and also comes alive at night with lively pubs and clubs – a popular drinking area is along Alduante between Freire and Argandoña.

Dolce Gelato Aldunate 862. If the ice-cream stand out front doesn't tempt you in, then live music wafting from the terrace will. Filling and reasonably priced Italian dishes (CH$5000–8000) such as seafood lasagne. Mon–Fri 10am–11pm, Sat 1–11pm.

Pub Aduana Argandoña 360. Cold beer, pisco-based cocktails and people-watching are the orders of the night

4

STARGAZING IN CHILE

With an average of 360 cloudless nights per year, northern Chile has some of the clearest skies in the world, so it's little wonder that it's home to some of the world's most powerful telescopes. The larger observatories allow public visits free of charge during the day, allowing you to view the equipment, though not to use it. There are an ever-increasing number of small centres offering nocturnal stargazing facilities expressly for tourists, though the best set up for visits are **Observatorio Cerro Mamalluca** (see page 403) and **Del Pangue Observatory** (see page 403) in the Elqui Valley.

The following places are the best of the big observatories; there is no public transport other than organized tours and you always need to reserve in advance.

OBSERVATORIES

ESO Paranal ☎55 243 5335, ✉visits@eso.org, ⌖eso.org. 130km south of Antofagasta, the observatory sports four VLTs (Very Large Telescopes), each with an 8m mirror. Tours Sat 10am & 2pm.

Cerro Tololo Office at Casilla 603, La Serena ☎51 220 5200, ⌖ctio.noao.edu Some 70km east of La Serena, this Inter-American observatory features an impressive 8.1m Gemini telescope. Tours Sat 9.15am–noon & 1.15–4pm.

La Silla Office near the airport at Panorámica 4461 ☎51 227 2601, ⌖eso.org. 147km northeast of La Serena, and home to fourteen telescopes. Tours Aug–May Sat 2–4pm.

---

at this popular bar with street-side tables and live music. Drinks from CH$2000. Thurs–Sat 10pm–5am.

ELQUI VALLEY

East of La Serena, the 62km journey to **Vicuña** is a scenic trip with breathtaking vistas of the tranquil **Elqui Valley**. Its fertile greenery contrasts with the valley's sandy sides, its slopes a spectrum of red, green and gold due to the mineral-rich soil. The ribbon of the highway, lined with pink peppercorn trees, runs along the valley floor, past vineyards and grapes drying on canvas sheets by the roadside. Tours of the valley typically take in the giant dam and man-made **Lago Puklara**, popular with windsurfers and kitesurfers, the historical village of **Vicuña**, the laidback community of **Pisco Elqui** and a pisco-tasting distillery, before finishing with stargazing at the **Observatorio Mamalluca**.

Vicuña

Sleepy **Vicuña** makes a convenient stopover for exploring the Elqui Valley. Formerly home to Nobel Prize-winner **Gabriela Mistral**, it has a **museum** at Gabriela Mistral 759 (Jan & Feb Mon–Fri 10am–7pm, Sat & Sun 10.30am–8pm; March–Dec Mon–Fri 10am–5.45pm, Sat 10.30am–6pm, Sun 10am–1pm; free), dedicated to her. **Planta Capel** (daily 10am–5pm; CH$4000–15,000; ☎51 255

4337, ⌖piscocapel.cl), the valley's largest **pisco distillery**, lies just south of town, and has half-hourly bilingual tours tracking the Muscatel grape's journey from the vine to the pisco bottle, culminating in a small free sample at the end.

ARRIVAL AND INFORMATION

By bus Vicuña's main terminal is one block south of the Plaza de Armas, on O'Higgins, at Prat (☎51 241 1348). For Santiago and other major cities, it is easiest to return to La Serena.

Destinations Coquimbo (20 daily; 1hr 30min); Pisco Elqui (every 30min–1hr; 1hr); La Serena (every 30min–1hr; 1hr).

By colectivo *Colectivos* to La Serena and Coquimbo leave from the bus station when full (daily 7am–9pm).

Tourist information Inside the Torre Bauer, San Martín s/n, in the northwest corner of the Plaza de Armas (Mon–Fri 8.30am–6pm, Sat 9am–6pm, Sun 9am–2pm; ☎51 267 0308).

ACCOMMODATION AND EATING

Chivato Negro Gabriela Mistral 565 ☎09 7862 9430, ⌖cafeovejanegra.com. Located in a 1920s heritage property, this literary-themed café offers up abundant sandwiches, veggie quiches and salads. The three-course lunch costs CH$4900. Daily 9am–10pm.

Hostal Donde Rita Condell 443 ☎51 241 9611, ⌖hostaldonderita.com. A comfortable set of rooms surrounded by a leafy garden, complete with pool and terrace area. Overseen by a charming German hostess, who prepares delicious breakfasts. Doubles CH$31,000

Soledad y Yo Carrera 320. A typical *picada* or family restaurant-bar, popular with locals, serving up substantial

PISCO

The climatic conditions in the Elqui Valley are ideal for growing the sweet Muscatel grapes from which the clear, brandy-like **pisco**, Chile's national drink, is derived. *Pisco* is a constant source of *dispute* between Chile and Peru. Peru claims that the drink originates from the Peruvian port of the same name, and some historical records demonstrate that pisco has been consumed in that area since the Spaniards introduced vineyards in the early 1600s.

Chileans claim that they have also been producing pisco for centuries, that their pisco is of better quality and that it plays a greater role in Chilean society. In both Chile and Peru, pisco is normally consumed in a *pisco sour* – a mix of pisco, lemon juice, sugar syrup, egg white, crushed ice and a drop of angostura bitters. It goes down deceptively smoothly, but packs a real punch.

servings of Chilean favourites, and decent drinks (from CH$1500). Mon–Thurs 11am–1am, Fri–Sun 11am–3am.

Hostal Valle Hermoso Gabriela Mistral 706 ☏ 51 241 1206, ⊕ hostalvallehermoso.com. Motherly Cecilia presides over this restored century-old adobe house with a bright central patio. Minimalist but sweet rooms have comfortable beds and private bathrooms complete with piping-hot showers. Doubles CH$36,000

Del Pangue Observatory

In a spectacular mountaintop setting 17km south of Vicuña, **Del Pangue Observatory** offers an intimate and personalized stargazing experience specifically designed for amateur astronomers. Two-hour tours (Jan & Feb 9pm & 11pm; June–Aug 6pm; rest of year 8pm; no tours five days around the full moon; tour times often change depending on planet positions; CH$24,000) are conducted by bona fide astronomers, and Del Pangue's state-of-the-art 63cm Obsession telescope is light years ahead of other public observatories. Book tours at the office at San Martin 233, Vicuña (daily 10am–7pm; ☏ 51 241 2584, ⊕ observatoriodelpangue.blogspot.com).

Observatorio Cerro Mamalluca

The **Observatorio Cerro Mamalluca** is located 9km northeast of Vicuña. Compared to other nearby observatories, its 30cm telescope is tiny, but it still offers magnification of 150 times – sufficient to look closely at the craters on the moon and to view nebulae, star clusters and Saturn. There are two tours offered (Oct–April 8.30pm, 10.30pm & 12.30am; May–Sept 6.30pm & 8.30pm; CH$7000): "Basic Astronomy" and "Andean Cosmovision", looking at the

night sky as seen by the pre-Columbian inhabitants of the area. Shuttles to and from the observatory (CH$3000 return) depart from the Cerro Mamalluca office in Vicuña (Gabriela Mistral 260, office 1; Mon–Fri 8.30am–8.30pm, Sat & Sun 10am–2pm & 4–8pm; ☏ 51 267 0330 or ☏ 51 267 0331) half an hour before the tour starts. Reserve tickets in advance, especially in the peak months from December to February.

Pisco Elqui

The green and laidback village of **PISCO ELQUI** boasts a beautiful hillside setting alongside the Río Clara, with unparalleled views of the Elqui Valley. The shaded **Plaza de Armas**, with its brightly painted Gothic church, hosts the **Mercado Artesanal** in the summer. A block away, the Destileria **Pisco Mistral** is Chile's oldest pisco distillery, and offers guided tours (O'Higgins 746; Jan–Feb daily 11am–5pm; March–Dec Tues–Sun 11am–5pm; CH$6000; ☏ 51 245 1358, ⊕ destileriapiscomistral.cl) complete with tastings. **Los Nichos** (tours daily: April–Nov 10am–6pm; Dec–March 11am–7pm; CH$1,000; ☏ 51 245 1085, ⊕ fundolosnichos.cl) is an old-fashioned distillery 3km south of Pisco Elqui, and worth visiting to see pisco processed by hand.

ARRIVAL, INFORMATION AND ACTIVITIES

There is just one ATM so bring plenty of cash.

By bus Buses stop in by the plaza and also go up into the village.

Destinations La Serena/Coquimbo (every 1–2hr; 2hr–2hr 30min); Vicuña (every 30min–1hr; 50min).

Tourist information Hostel owners will be able to help you with information, but an excellent option for

4

local knowledge of the area is the tour agency Turismo Migrantes, O'Higgins s/n (☎51 245 1917, ☎09 6667 3907, ⓦturismomigrantes.cl), where Bárbara and Pablo organize pisco tours, horseriding and bike rides in the surrounding area, and even stargazing tours at their own home.

ACCOMMODATION

Refugio del Angel El Condor s/n, 1km southeast of the plaza ☎51 245 1292, ⓦcampingrefugiodelangel.cl. This pretty riverside campground has shady camping spots, with picnic tables and hot showers. The "teahouse" provides breakfast, drinks and snacks. Per person CH$10,000

El Tesoro de Elqui Prat s/n ☎51 245 1069, ⓦtesoroelqui.cl. Cosy adobe dorms and rooms – one with a skylight for stargazing – and excellent food. The owners can help organize motorbike rental and tours. Dorms CH$16,000, doubles CH$57,000

Hostal Triskel Baquedano s/n ☎09 9418 8680, ⓦhostaltriskel.cl. Lovingly decorated rooms and decent breakfasts. They can arrange hiking, biking and horseriding too. Dorms CH$15,000 doubles CH$30,000

4 | RESERVA NACIONAL PINGÜINO DE HUMBOLDT

The **Reserva Nacional Pingüino de Humboldt** (April–Nov Wed–Sun 9am–5.30pm; Dec–March daily 9am–5.30pm; CH$12,000) is a remarkable marine wildlife reserve 110km north of La Serena, which comprises three islands jutting from the cold Pacific waters: Isla Chañaral, Isla Choros and Isla Damas. The islands are home to *chundungos* (sea otters), a noisy colony of **sea lions**, the **Humboldt penguin**, four species of cormorants, clamouring **Peruvian boobies** and countless seagulls.

Unless you plan to stay the night at Isla Chañaral (see below), it is much easier to visit as part of a tour from La Serena (see page 399). **Boats** sail (CH$8000/person; sailings dependent on conditions) from **Caleta de Choros**, the small fishing community closest to the islands, along the steep jagged coastline of **Isla Choros**. You get close enough to see the wildlife in great detail, and on the way to the island, pods of curious **bottlenose dolphins** often frolic around the boat; it's also possible to spot humpback, blue and killer **whales**. On the way back, visitors can take a short ramble on sandy **Isla Damas**, whose pristine beaches are home to a smaller penguin population.

INFORMATION AND TOURS

Tourist information There is a Conaf-run Centro de Información Ambiental (April–Nov Wed–Sun 9am–5.30pm; Dec–March daily 9am–5.30pm; ☎51 261 1555 or ☎09 9544 3052, ⓦconaf.cl) at Caleta de Choros, with informative displays on local flora and fauna, and another smaller one at Caleta Chañaral.

Tours Main full-day destinations are located east into the cordillera, taking in Parque Nacional Nevado de Tres Cruces and sometimes Laguna Verde and Ojos del Salado; and north to Parque Nacional Pan de Azúcar. Half-day trips go north into the Atacama dunes, west to the beaches around Bahía Inglesa, or east up the Copiapó River Valley. Operators include Atacama Chile (☎56 221 1191, ⓦatacamachile. com) and mountaineering outfit Aventurismo (☎09 9599 2184, ⓦaventurismo.cl), who specialize in multi-day ascents of the Ojos de Salado volcano between Nov and March.

ACCOMMODATION

Several people on Isla Chañaral rent out simple rooms in their homes (around CH$20,000 a double). There is a basic campsite at Caleta Chañaral, while camping is permitted on Isla Damas.

COPIAPÓ

The prosperous mining town of **COPIAPÓ**, 333km north of La Serena, was founded in 1744 and benefited greatly from the **silver boom** of the 1830s. Today, Copiapó still makes its living from mining, nowadays on **copper**. It will forever be linked in many people's minds with the 2010 rock collapse at the nearby San José mine, which left 33 miners ("Los 33") trapped underground for 69 days before the world cheered their safe rescue.

At the heart of Copiapó is the large **Plaza Prat**, dotted with pepper trees; handicraft stalls line the plaza's east side, facing the mall. The Neoclassical **Iglesia Catedral Nuestra Señora de Rosario** graces the southwest corner, while on the corner of Atacama and Rancagua, a ten-minute walk from the plaza, the **Museo Regional de Atacama** (Tues–Fri 9am–5.45pm, Sat 10am–12.45pm & 3–5.45pm, Sun 10am–12.45pm; free; ☎52 221 2313, ⓦmuseodeatacama.cl) has a display on the trapped miners of the San José mine, which includes their fateful hand-written note: "We are fine in the shelter – the 33". The other well-presented displays cover the exploration of the desert, the War of the Pacific, pre-Columbian peoples of the region and the Inca road system.

ARRIVAL AND DEPARTURE

By plane Aeropuerto Desierto de Atacama is around 50km northwest of the city; both the Manuel Flores Salinas minibus and Casther bus meet arriving planes and travel into town; taxis cost around CH$25,000.

Destinations Some of these routes require stopovers, which the travel times listed take into account. Calama (1–2 daily; 1hr 10min–4hr); Santiago (5–7 daily; 1hr 20min).

By bus Copiapó's main bus terminal is at Chañarcillo 655, two blocks south of Plaza Prat. Across the road, also on Chañarcillo, is the Tur Bus terminal; one block south, at Freire and Colipí, is the Pullman Bus terminal. For Caldera and Bahía Inglesa, Casther (☎52 221 8889), Expreso Caldera (☎09 6155 8048) and Trans Puma (☎52 223 5841) run a frequent service from the small bus station on the corner of Esperanza and Chacabuco, opposite the Líder Hypermarket (you can also catch a Casthar transfer to the airport here). Alternately you can catch one of the yellow *colectivos* that wait on the same corner opposite Líder.

Destinations Antofagasta (15 daily; 7hr); Arica (11 daily; 17hr); Calama (15 daily; 10hr); Caldera (every 30min; 1hr); Iquique (12 daily; 13hr); La Serena (every 30min–1hr; 5hr); Santiago (22 daily; 12hr); Valparaíso (6 daily; 12hr).

INFORMATION

Tourist information The well-organized Sernatur office is at Los Carrera 691 on Plaza Prat (Mon–Fri 8.30am–6pm, Sat 10am–2pm, ☎52 221 2838). Conaf is at Juan Martínez 56 (Mon–Thurs 8.30am–5.30pm & Fri 8.30am–4pm; ☎52 221 3404).

ACCOMMODATION AND EATING

Café Colombia Plaza Prat on Colipi, at Carrera. Pricey but excellent, this place serves good coffee (CH$1000–3000), plus cakes, ice-cream sundaes, sandwiches and pizzas. Mon–Sat 8am–10pm.

Flor de la Canela Chacabuco 710 ☎52 221 9570. This cheerful Peruvian joint offers a change from the Copiapó norm, with tasty dishes like *ceviche* and *lomo saltado* (mains CH$8300–11,000). Mon–Sat noon–4pm & 7pm–midnight, Sun noon–8pm.

Hotel Palace Atacama 741 ☎52 233 6427, ⌨palacehotel.cl. Copious wood-panelling gives *Hotel Palace* a vaguely 1970s feel. The carpeted rooms are comfortable enough, though overpriced (try haggling). __CH$38,000__

Residencial Benbow Rodriguez 541 ☎52 221 7634. Clean, no-frills rooms (CH$6000 extra for an en suite) around a narrow courtyard. Breakfast costs extra. Doubles __CH$22,000__

AROUND COPIAPÓ

The landscape surrounding Copiapó is astonishingly varied, with the salt flats of the **Parque Nacional Nevado de Tres Cruces**, mesmerizing **Laguna Verde**, active volcano **Ojos de Salado** and, to the west, the fine white sands of **Bahía Inglesa** and **Caldera**.

Parque Nacional Nevado de Tres Cruces

Remote and ruggedly beautiful **Parque Nacional Nevado de Tres Cruces** (daily 8.30am–6pm; CH$4000) is located east of Copiapó via Ruta 31, which winds through the mercilessly desolate desert landscape. The road climbs steeply before reaching the **Salar de Maricunga** – a great field of white crystals on the edge of the park, dotted with emerald-coloured salt pools – and continuing on towards **Paso San Francisco** on the Argentine border.

The park consists of two separate parts. The larger is the 490-square-kilometre **Laguna Santa Rosa** sector, 146km east of Copiapó at an altitude of 3700m, which comprises half of the salt flat and the namesake lake, with roaming herds of **vicuñas** and **guanacos** feeding on the abundant grasslands. The pale blue lagoon, dotted with flamingos and giant coots, is set against a backdrop of snow-streaked volcanoes, including the grand **Nevado Tres Cruces** (6749m). On the west side of the lake is a small and very rustic Conaf-run *refugio*, consisting of bare floorspace, basic cooking facilities and a privy out back.

Cutting across a vast expanse of parched brown land, dotted with hardy yellow *altiplano* plants, you reach the 120-square-kilometre **Laguna del Negro Francisco** sector, around 85km south. In summer it becomes a sea of pink and beige, thanks to the presence of eight thousand or so Andean, Chilean and James **flamingos** that migrate here from neighbouring Argentina, Bolivia and Peru. On the west side of the lake, Conaf's *Refugio Laguna del Negro Francisco* has beds and kitchen facilities; make reservations with Copiapó's Conaf office (CH$12,000/person).

4

Laguna Verde and Volcán Ojos de Salado

The magnificent spectacle of the misnamed **Laguna Verde** lies 65km beyond Laguna Santa Rosa, at a whopping altitude of 4325m. The first flash of its brilliant turquoise waters, around a bend in the road, is breathtaking. On the lake's salty white shore are some rustic and relaxing **hot springs** inside a little wooden shack. It's possible to camp here: you must bring all necessary supplies with you, including water, and remember that night-time temperatures drop well below freezing. Beyond the lake loom three volcanoes, including the second-highest peak in Latin America – **Ojos de Salado**. At an elevation of 6887m, it trails just behind Argentina's 6962m Aconcagua as the tallest mountain in the Americas. It is also the world's highest active volcano, with recent eruptions in 1937 and 1956.

Caldera and Bahía Inglesa

The towns of Caldera and Bahía Inglesa, 7km apart and 75km west of Copiapó, are both popular **beach resorts** famous for their large, delicious **scallops**. **CALDERA** itself is an unremarkable little town, though the Gothic **Iglesia San Vicente** (1862) on Plaza Condell is worth a look. Pedestrianized **Gana**, lined with craft stalls in the summer, makes for a nice stroll between the square and the waterfront **Costanera** (pier) – home to the oldest railway station in Chile, dating back to 1850, and now a museum (Tues–Sun 10am–2pm & 4–7pm; CH$600) and events centre. The pier is the best place to sample inexpensive seafood *empanadas* and other fishy delights.

Caldera's main beach, small seaweed-tinted Copiapina, is not the best in the area. For crystal-clear turquoise waters and long stretches of white sand, head to nearby **Bahía Inglesa**, either by *colectivo* or along the cycle path parallel to the road, which is immensely popular in summer for its laidback atmosphere, the proximity of the ocean and an abundance of cheap seafood *empanadas* vendors along the seafront. There are several small and sheltered beaches along the main Avenida El Morro, with the wide crescent of **Playa Las Machas** stretching into the distance.

ARRIVAL AND INFORMATION

By bus Buses to Copiapó leave from a small terminal at the corner of Cifuentes and Ossa Varas. Long-distance services to Chañaral and further north are provided by Pullman Bus and Tur Bus, from Caldera's main terminal at Gallo and Vallejos.
Destinations Chañaral (12 daily; 1hr); Copiapó (every 30min; 1hr).
By micro and colectivo Micros for Bahía Inglesa leave from the Plaza de Armas every 15min in Jan and Feb. The rest of the year, black taxi *colectivos* leave from the plaza.
Tourist information On Plaza de Armas in Caldera (daily 9am–2pm & 4–7pm; ☎52 253 5765, ⓦcaldera.cl).

ACCOMMODATION AND EATING

Most options are in Bahía, which has a greater selection of accommodation than Caldera, though it tends to be overpriced during peak season.
Camping Bahía Inglesa Off Playa Las Machas, just south of the town ☎52 231 6399 or ☎52 231 5424. An excellent place to camp, with hot showers, picnic tables and restaurants. Pitch for up to six people CH$26,000, cabin CH$40,000
Los Jardines de Bahía Inglesa Copiapó 100 ☎52 231 5359, ⓦjardinesbahia.cl. These smart cabañas sleep up to eleven people. There's a good-sized pool, a table-tennis table and a decent Italian restaurant. Cabins for two people CH$90,000
Hostel Qapaq Raymi Edwards 420, Caldera ☎09 7386 3041, ⓔhostel.qapaqraymi@gmail.com. Beds are comfy, the vibe relaxed and the spacious patio and bar make up for a cramped shared kitchen. Dorms CH$10,000, doubles CH$30,000
El Plateao El Morro 756 ☎09 6677 5174. Restaurant-bar with a terrace overlooking the beach, good service and an innovative menu offering exceptional seafood dishes (around CH$8000–10,000). Daily 1–5pm & 5pm–midnight.

PARQUE NACIONAL PAN DE AZÚCAR

About 180km north of Copiapó, **Parque Nacional Pan de Azúcar** entices visitors with its spectacular coastal desert landscape, which alternates between steep cliffs, studded with a multitude of cactus species, and pristine white beaches. A small gravel road leads into the park from the compact town of Chañaral and continues past Playa Blanca and Playa Los Piqueros to **Caleta Pan de Azúcar**, a small fishing village inside the park. **Isla Pan de Azúcar**, home to Humboldt penguins, sea lions, sea otters and a wealth of marine birds, lies a short distance offshore. Although landing on the island is forbidden, fishing boats (daily: March–Nov 9am–6pm; Dec–Feb 9am–7pm; CH$50,000 for up to ten people, or whatever deal you can strike) get visitors close enough to see (and smell) the wildlife. A 9km trail runs north from the village to the **Mirador Pan de Azúcar**, a lookout point offering staggering panoramic views of the coastline. Also heading north from the village, towards Ruta 5, is a dirt road with a 15km trail branching off to the west that leads you through the arid landscape to **Las Lomitas**, an outlook point often visited by inquisitive **desert foxes** and shrouded in rolling *camanchaca* (sea mist), the main water source for all the coastal vegetation.

ARRIVAL AND INFORMATION

By bus There are no public buses to the park, though northbound buses from Copiapó can drop you off in Chañaral, the nearest town. Ask around at the bus terminal in Chañaral, and you should be able to get someone to take

you to the park. Taxis cost CH$25,000 each way – worth it for a group. Alternatively, take a day-trip tour from Copiapó (see page 404).

Tourist information Conaf's Centro de Información Ambiental (daily 8.30am–12.30pm & 2–6pm) is opposite Playa Los Piqueros and has maps and information on the park, as well as a display of local cacti. The park fee of CH$5000 is payable here; no fee is charged if entering the park from the east.

ACCOMMODATION AND EATING

Rough camping is not allowed in the park, but there are a number of authorized camping areas. In Caleta Pan de Azúcar, a handful of restaurants on the water's edge serve fried fish, rice and *empanadas*.

Camping Los Pingüinos Just north of the Caleta Pan de Azúcar ☎52 248 1209. If you've got your own camping gear, this campsite has decent facilities. Per person CH$5000

Pan de Azúcar Lodge Playa Piqueros, south of Caleta Pan de Azúcar ☎09 9280 3483, ⓦpandeazucarlodge.cl. *Pan de Azúcar Lodge* has the national park's best camping facilities, with barbecues and picnic tables, as well as cabañas sleeping up to eight. Camping per person CH$5000, cabins CH$40,000

Norte Grande

In some parts of the vast Atacama Desert, which covers almost all of the Norte Grande region, there are areas where no rainfall has ever been recorded. With such an inhospitable landscape, it is no wonder that most of the population is squeezed into the more moderate climes along the coast. The sprawling port city of **Antofagasta** is the largest population centre, while other major towns include the beach resort of **Iquique** – popular with surfers and paragliders – and **Arica**, home to the iconic cliff of El Morro. The best base from which to enjoy the spectacular desert scenery is the laidback backpacker haven of **San Pedro de Atacama**, where visitors flock to whizz down dunes on sandboards, admire the steam rising from geysers in the early morning sun, and spot flamingos on Chile's largest salt flat.

ANTOFAGASTA

ANTOFAGASTA is the biggest city in northern Chile; a busy port and major

transport hub, it has few attractions to detain travellers, though it's a good place to stock up on necessities. James Bond fans may recognize flashes of the city from the film *Quantum of Solace*, part of which was filmed here.

WHAT TO SEE AND DO

Antofagasta's compact centre boasts the surprisingly lovely **Plaza Colón**, the apparent British influence accentuated by its centrepiece, the **Torre Reloj**, a small-scale Big Ben replica. To the southeast, three blocks of Arturo Prat are pedestrianized and feature shops and cafés; from here, walking three blocks southwest along Matta takes you to a large pedestrian square presided over by the impressive pink, grey and cream **Mercado Central**, with its evocative smells of fresh produce and frying fish.

At the port end of Bolívar, you'll find the oldest building in the city, the former **Aduana**, now housing the **Museo Regional** (Tues–Fri 9am–5pm, Sat & Sun 11am–2pm; free;

ⓦ museodeantofagasta.cl), with exhibitions on regional natural history, archeology and the War of the Pacific, and an outstanding mummified babies exhibit. *Colectivos* run along Matta to the often-crowded Balneario Municipal, and further south to the Balneario El Huáscar and Caleta Coloso. These are Antofagasta's better **beaches**, lined with places to eat, bars and discos, though not really suitable for swimming.

Ruinas de Huanchaca and the Museo Desierto de Atacama

On a hilltop a short distance inland, 3km south of the city centre near Universidad del Norte, the **Ruinas de Huanchaca** (no fixed opening hours; free; ⓦ ruinasdehuanchaca.cl) are the remains of an old Bolivian silver refinery. It was built to process the silver brought down from the Potosí mine, before being shipped out of Antofagasta. Looking at the square and circular walls of the complex from below, you'd be forgiven for thinking they were ruins of a pre-Columbian fortress. On the same site is the impressive **Museo Desierto de Atacama** (Tues–Sun 10am–1pm & 2.30–7pm; CH$2000).

La Portada

Much featured on postcards, the natural monument of **La Portada**, 15km north of Antofagasta, is a giant rock eroded into a natural arch. To get there, take a Mejillones-bound bus and ask to be dropped off at the junction (10min), from where it is a half-hour walk towards the ocean.

ARRIVAL AND INFORMATION

By plane Aeropuerto Cerro Moreno is 25km north of the city, right on the Tropic of Capricorn. Regular *colectivos* and infrequent *micros* head to the centre or you can take a minibus directly to your accommodation (they await every arrival).
Destinations Iquique (1–2 daily; 55min); La Serena (1–3 daily; 1hr 20min); Santiago (13–20 daily; 1hr 50min–3hr).
By bus The main Terminal Carlos Oviedo Cavada is on Pedro A. Cerda 5750, about a 15min drive from the centre – a taxi costs about CH$7000. A much cheaper option is to take *micro* #103 or #111 from right outside the terminal to the centre.
Destinations Arica (every 1–3hr; 10hr); Calama (hourly; 3hr); Caldera (hourly; 6hr); Copiapó (every 1–2hr; 7hr); La Serena (every 30min–1hr; 12hr); Santiago (hourly; 20hr).
Tourist information Prat 384 (Mon–Thurs 8.30am–5.30pm, Fri 8.30am–4.30pm; ☎55 245 1818, ⓔ infoantofagasta@sernatur.cl).

ACCOMMODATION, EATING AND DRINKING

El Arriero Condell 2644 ⓦ arrieroafta.cl. There is sometimes live jazz at this inviting spot. Try the excellent-value *parrilladas* (CH$10,900 for one person, CH$18,200 for two) or go for the good-value lunch menu (CH$4900). The attached *Fuente Alemana* is even cheaper. Mon–Sat 11.30am–4pm & 7.30pm–midnight, Sun 11.30am–4pm.
Hotel Colón San Martín 2434 ☎55 226 1851, ⓔ colonantofagasta@gmail.com. Decent option with clean, fairly comfortable and light en-suite rooms with TVs. Those facing the road can be rather noisy though. CH$35,000
Hotel Ibis Av Jose Miguel Carrera 1627 ☎55 245 8200, ⓦ ibis.com. This mid-range hotel is a reassuring, good-value choice: staff are professional and the en suites are well equipped. It's around 1.5km southwest of the main plaza. CH$39,900
Majuyen San Martín 2326 ⓦ majuyen.jimdo.com. Set back from the road in the Patio Alcántara, this tiny Japanese-Peruvian joint has tasty sushi, sashimi and *ceviche* (CH$4000–8000). Daily 1–4pm & 7–11pm.
Residencial El Cobre Arturo Prat 749 ☎55 222 5162. Centrally located option with a grubby-looking exterior and no-frills rooms, with shared bathrooms. CH$20,000

CALAMA

The busy city of **CALAMA**, at the heart of the Atacama **copper mining** industry, is a convenient transport hub and an almost inevitable stop for travellers heading to San Pedro de Atacama, although it is not worth staying unless you have to. While it's not overtly dangerous, you should watch your possessions here more vigilantly than is necessary in most of Chile.

WHAT TO SEE AND DO

Calama may lack the natural marvels of San Pedro de Atacama, but it does boast the giant Chuquicamata copper mine. State copper company Codelco offers tours, including views of the kilometre-deep open pit and the now abandoned company town. Free, bilingual English and Spanish tours leave from Calama (Mon–Fri 1.30pm, Jan & Feb also 3.30pm; 2hr; book in advance; call ☎55 232 2122 or email ⓔ visitas@codelco.cl).

ARRIVAL AND DEPARTURE

By plane Aeropuerto El Loa is 5km south of the centre; a taxi costs around CH$6500.

Destinations Copiapó (4 weekly; 1hr 10min); Santiago (12–18 daily; 2hr).

By bus Arriving by bus, you'll be dropped at your bus company's office, generally near the city centre. Pullman Bus and Tur Bus both have terminals of their own, the latter inconveniently situated nearly 2km north of town. Hail down *colectivo* #5 or #11 right outside the Tur Bus terminal to get to the centre, or take a taxi (around CH$4000).

Destinations Antofagasta (every 1–2hr; 3hr); Arica (5–6 daily; 10hr); Chuquicamata (every 30min; 30min); Copiapó (hourly; 10hr); Iquique (5–6 daily; 6hr); La Serena (10 daily; 12hr 30min–15hr); San Pedro de Atacama (every 30min–1hr; 1hr 30min); Santiago (hourly; 22hr 30min).

ACCOMMODATION AND EATING

Bavaria Sotomayor 2093 ⓦbavaria.cl. Decent if very predictable mid-price mains (CH$5000–11,000) and sandwiches from its downstairs café and upstairs restaurant. Restaurant daily noon–4.30pm & 7.30pm–midnight; café daily 8am–midnight.

Hostal Nativo Sotomayor 2215 ☎55 231 0377, ⓦnativo.cl. This centrally located, family-run hotel offers friendly service and plain, immaculately clean rooms with TVs. CH$33,000

Restaurant Paladar Vivar 1797 ☎55 292 6554. The swish *Paladar* has an imaginative menu (mains CH$7000–15,000), comprising sharing platters and international cuisine with a French twist. Mon–Sat 12.30–1.30am.

Hostal Toño Vivar 1970 ☎55 234 1185, ✉david6013@live.com. Secure and spacious rooms with TVs. The walls are thin so it can get noisy. CH$20,000

SAN PEDRO DE ATACAMA AND AROUND

SAN PEDRO DE ATACAMA, a little oasis town of single-storey adobe houses and unpaved streets, is situated 100km southeast of Calama, the nearest city.

No other northern destination can compete with the sheer number of natural attractions in the surrounding area: the stunning *altiplano* scenery draws hundreds of travellers year-round, while volcanoes, sand dunes, geysers and lagoons will keep any nature lover busy.

One of the oldest settlements in Chile, San Pedro was originally a stop on a pre-Columbian trade route between the highland and coastal communities; in 1547, the Spanish established their first mission here and subjugated the locals. The town later became an important rest stop for cattle drives from Salta, Argentina, when the nitrate industry took off in Chile and fresh meat was needed for the workers.

Despite getting extremely crowded during the peak season, San Pedro retains a friendly and relaxed vibe, and has an excellent assortment of budget accommodation and facilities for visitors, as well as the widest range of cuisine north of Santiago.

WHAT TO SEE AND DO

The centre of town is the cheery little **Plaza de Armas**, framed by *algarrobo* and pink peppercorn trees. The coffee-coloured **Iglesia de San Pedro** (1641) stands on the west side of the square, while most places to eat and other services are found along nearby Caracoles.

Museo Arqueológico Gustavo Le Paige

Unfortunately, the intriguing **Museo Arqueológico Gustavo Le Paige** was closed at the time of writing and not expected to reopen until late 2020. When it does, expect to see more than 380,000 clearly labelled pre-Columbian

4

INTO ARGENTINA AND BOLIVIA

Although not the most commonly used border crossing between the two countries, the bus ride between San Pedro de Atacama and *Jujuy* or *Salta* in Argentina is certainly a spectacular one, climbing up gradually into the Andes before a sharper descent on the eastern flank. Pullman offer a regular service, usually departing San Pedro at 9.30am on Wednesday, Friday and Sunday, with other companies sometimes operating the same route. The bus actually originates in Calama and can be boarded there a couple of hours earlier.

There is also a daily bus connection to *Uyuni* in Bolivia from Calama with Atacama 2000, departing at 6am, although many people prefer to take a three-day tour from San Pedro in a 4WD vehicle, so that they can really experience the salt flats.

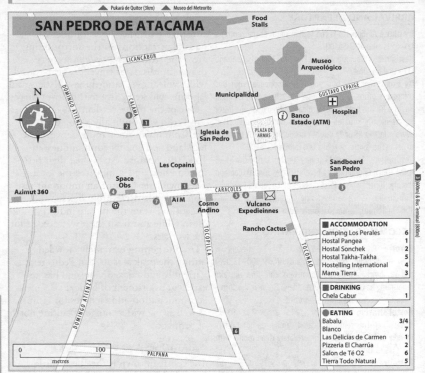

▲ Pukará de Quitor (3km)   ▲ Museo del Meteorito

SAN PEDRO DE ATACAMA

Food Stalls

LICANCÁBUR

DOMINGO ATIENZA

Museo Arqueológico

CALAMA

Municipalidad

GUSTAVO LE PAIGE

Banco Estado (ATM)

Hospital

Iglesia de San Pedro

PLAZA DE ARMAS

N

Les Copains

Sandboard San Pedro

Space Obs

CARACOLES

Azimut 360

@

AIM

Cosmo Andino

Vulcano Expedieinnes

TOCOPILLA

Rancho Cactus

TOCONAO

DOMINGO ATIENZA

0   100
metres

PALPANA

■ ACCOMMODATION	
Camping Los Perales	6
Hostal Pangea	1
Hostal Sonchek	2
Hostal Takha-Takha	5
Hostelling International	4
Mama Tierra	3

■ DRINKING	
Chela Cabur	1

◉ EATING	
Babalu	3/4
Blanco	7
Las Delicias de Carmen	1
Pizzeria El Charrúa	2
Salon de Té O2	6
Tierra Todo Natural	5

artefacts, perfectly preserved in the dry desert air.

Museo del Meteorito

A good way to complement some local star-gazing with a hands-on experience is to handle some of the 77 meteorites on display at the **Museo del Meteorito** (Tues–Sun 10am–1pm & 3–7pm; CH$3500; ⓦmuseodelmeteorito.cl), which is housed in several geodesic domes on the north side of the village. There are also numerous educational interactive displays and audio guides in English included in the entry fee.

ARRIVAL AND DEPARTURE

By bus Several companies have regular services from Calama to San Pedro; they all arrive at and depart from the bus terminal on Tumiza, a 10min walk southeast from the plaza. At most times of day you have to change at Calama (often with a delay) for major destinations, including Iquique, Arica and Santiago.

Destinations Antofagasta (5–6 daily; 5hr 30min); Arica (3 nightly; 12–13hr); Calama (every 30min–1hr; 1hr 30min); Iquique (1 nightly; 7hr).

INFORMATION

Bike rental Many places rent bikes, notably along Caracoles; most charge around CH$4000/half-day or CH$7000/day; try to get an emergency bike-repair kit too.

Exchange BCI bank on Caracoles and several ATMS dotted around the centre. Several casas de cambio, on Toconao and Caracoles; tour agencies running trips to Salar de Uyuni can often provide better rates for Bolivianos.

Tourist office Toconao, on the main plaza (Mon, Tues, Thurs & Fri 9.15am–8.15pm, Wed 9.15am–6pm, Sat & Sun 10am–8.15pm; ☎55 851 420, ✉sanpedrodeatacama@gmail.com). Hands out regional maps and lists of tour companies. Check ⓦsanpedroatacama.com for more information.

ACCOMMODATION

Camping Los Perales Tocopilla 481 ☎55 285 1114; map p.410. The best campsite in San Pedro, located a short distance south of the plaza, with lots of trees, hot water, a climbing wall and an outdoor kitchen. Per person CH$6000

★ **Hostal Pangea** Calama 375 ☎ 55 320 5080, ⓦ hostalpangea.cl; map p.410. An excellent, sociable *hostal* in a converted traditional building only minutes from the centre, with six- to ten-bed dorms and a range of rooms with shared or private bathrooms. Facilities include games, a shared kitchen and a nice leafy courtyard. Dorms CH$12,000, doubles CH$30,000

Hostal Sonchek Gustovo Le Paige 198 ☎ 55 285 1112, ⓦ hostalsonchek.cl; map p.410. With a welcoming and helpful English- and French-speaking hostess, this popular and conveniently located hostel has cosy rooms, kitchen use, a courtyard with table tennis and a laundry service. Dorms CH$16,000, doubles CH$27,000

Hostal Takha-Takha Caracoles 101a ☎ 55 285 1038, ⓦ takhatakha.cl; map p.410. Small but tidy and quiet rooms giving onto a pleasant garden. There's a lovely (but small) pool and you can also camp here. Also some good-value, though basic, singles (CH$20,000). Camping/person CH$13,000, doubles CH$41,000

Hostelling International Caracoles 360 ☎ 55 256 4683, ⓦ hostellingsanpedro.cl; map p.410. San Pedro's official YHI-affiliated hostel is rather cramped but offers some of the best prices in town, plus the chance to mix with other travellers. As well as six-bed dorms, there are a few private rooms, some en suite. Dorms CH$8000, doubles CH$16,000

Mama Tierra Pachamama 615 ☎ 55 285 1418, ⓦ hostalmamatierra.cl; map p.410. A 10min walk from the centre, this tidy hostel is popular with backpackers and offers dorms, singles and doubles with private or shared bathrooms. Extras include laundry service, and the congenial hostess can help organize volcano climbs in the area. Dorms CH$16,000, doubles CH$42,000

EATING

Prices are generally higher than in other parts of the country, though at least many competing restaurants offer evening set menus. For cheaper set meals, try one of the handful of restaurants at the top end of Licancabur or near the bus station. Note that food, albeit a small snack, must always be ordered with alcoholic drinks.

Babalu Caracoles 160; map p.410. Tiny *heladería* offering home-made ice creams (from CH$1900): try the pisco sour or chirimoya flavours. There's another branch at the other end of Caracoles (#419). Daily 10am–8pm.

Blanco Caracoles 195 ☎ 55 285 1164; map p.410. Conceived in white minimalist-chic adobe, this is one of the most stylish places in town (mains CH$8000–13,000). Try the caramelized salmon or the Thai chicken soup. Daily 6pm–12.30am.

★ **Las Delicias de Carmen** Calama 370B; map p.410. Owner Carmen serves up large helpings of hearty, home-

cooked food (mains CH$9000–15,000, set menu with wine CH$9000). Try the freshly baked *empanadas* and sweeter treats such as the lemon meringue pie. Daily 8am–10.30pm.

Pizzeria El Charrúa Tocopilla 442 ☎ 55 285 1443; map p.410. The wonderful aroma wafting out of this intimate pizzeria entices hungry punters inside (from CH$5000). Does delivery too. Daily 11am–11pm.

Salon de Té 02 Caracoles 295B; map p.410. This unpretentious café, right in the centre of town, serves up good-value, hearty breakfasts (from CH$2450), tasty quiches and home-made cakes. Daily 8am–10pm.

★ **Tierra Todo Natural** Caracoles 46; map p.410. Friendly restaurant specializing in wholesome home-made food (mains CH$5500–12,000; set menu CH$8500), including wholemeal bread, pizzas, *empanadas*, fish, fantastic salads and pancakes. Daily 8.30am–12.30am.

DRINKING

Chela Cabur Caracoles 211 ☎ 55 285 1576; map p.410. The name says it all: *Chela Cabur* translates as "mountain of beer" in Kunza-Chilean. Owned by a Finnish beer aficionado (beer CH$2500–3500), it's the only place you can drink without ordering food. Lively rock soundtrack. Mon–Thurs & Sun noon–1am, Fri & Sat noon–2am.

DAY-TRIPS FROM SAN PEDRO

Beyond San Pedro, the scenery is dramatic, dominated by large volcanic peaks, **Valle de la Luna**'s magnificent lunar landscape, the red rock of the **Valle de la Muerte**, the famous **El Tatio geysers**, Chile's largest salt flat **Salar de Atacama** and dazzling **lagoons**. With the exception of the village of **Toconao**, and Valle de la Muerte and Valle de la Luna, both of which can be visited by bike, these places are only accessible on a tour.

Valle de la Muerte

The easiest attraction to cycle to – only 3km from San Pedro – is the **Valle de la Muerte**, with its narrow gorges, peculiar **red rock formations** and 150m-high **sand dunes**. It is also a prime **sandboarding** destination, with scores of enthusiasts whizzing down the slopes in the early mornings and late afternoons. The rest of the time an exquisite silence reigns over the still sand and rocks, and you can often enjoy the views of the snow-peaked volcanoes in the distance entirely undisturbed.

4

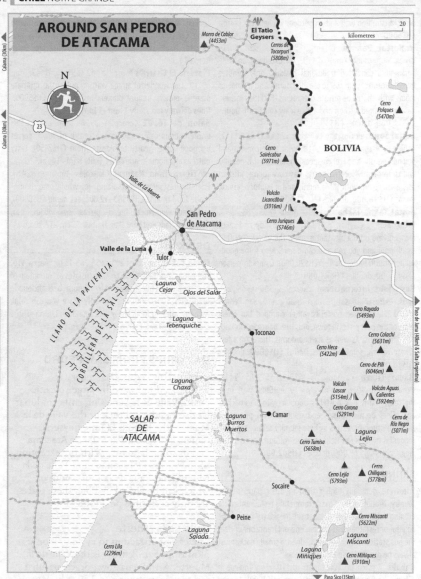

AROUND SAN PEDRO DE ATACAMA

Calama (50km)

Calama (30km)

23

N

Morro de Cablor (4453m)

El Tatio Geysers

Cerros de Tocorpuri (5808m)

BOLIVIA

Cerro Polques (5470m)

Cerro Sairécabur (5971m)

Volcán Licancábur (5916m)

Cerro Juriques (5746m)

Valle de La Muerte

San Pedro de Atacama

Valle de la Luna

Tulor

Laguna Cejar

Ojos del Salar

Laguna Tebenquiche

LLANO DE LA PACIENCIA

CORDILLERA DE LA SAL

Laguna Chaxa

Toconao

Paso de Jama (40km) & Salta (Argentina)

Cerro Rayado (5493m)

Cerro Colachi (5631m)

Cerro Heca (5422m)

Cerro de Pili (6046m)

Volcán Lascar (5154m)

Volcán Aguas Calientes (5924m)

Cerro Corona (5291m)

Cerro de Río Negro (5071m)

SALAR DE ATACAMA

Laguna Burros Muertos

Camar

Cerro Tumisa (5658m)

Laguna Lejía

Cerro Lejía (5793m)

Cerro Chiliques (5778m)

Socaire

Peine

Cerro Miscanti (5622m)

Laguna Miscanti

Cerro Lila (2296m)

Laguna Salada

Laguna Miñiques

Cerro Miñiques (5910m)

Paso Sico (35km)

0   kilometres   20

Valle de la Luna

Most people come here for the spectacular sunsets with one of a plethora of tour groups, but the lunar landscape of **Valle de la Luna** (summer 8.30am–7.30pm; rest of year 8.30am–5.30pm; morning CH$2500, afternoon CH$3000), at the heart of the Cordillera del Sal, is as impressive at sunrise, when the first rays of sunlight turn the surrounding jagged red peaks various shades of pink and gold. At dawn there are far fewer spectators, and after making your way up the giant sand dune along a marked trail, you can walk up the crest of the dune for a better vantage point. If cycling the 14km to the valley, go west

SAN PEDRO TOUR OPERATORS

Choosing a reputable **tour operator** in San Pedro can be difficult, but at least the competition keeps prices fairly stable. Talk to travellers who have done the tours recently, and look at the comments book in the tourist information office. Expect to pay around CH$15,000 to visit the Valle de la Luna, CH$25,000 for a tour to the Tatio geysers, and around CH$45,000 for a full-day tour of the lakes and oases (excluding entrance fees); three- to four-day tours (around US$200–250) that finish in Bolivia and take in the spectacular Salar de Uyuni are popular.

Cosmo Andino Caracoles s/n ☎55 285 1069, ⓦcosmoandino.cl. Well-established and respected company offering interesting variations on the most popular tours, as well as off-the-beaten track expeditions.

Rancho Cactus Tocanao 568 ☎55 285 1506, ⓦrancho-cactus.cl. For an alternative San Pedro experience, try the horse treks (from CH$22,000) run by Rancho Cactus. Treks last from a few hours to three days.

Sandboard San Pedro Caracoles 362H ☎55 298 3669, ⓦsandboardsanpedro.com. Run by an amiable bunch of hipsters, this is the only dedicated sandboarding operation. Trips of 3–4hr to the Death or Mars valleys leave at 9am and 4pm (CH$20,000). They also rent bikes.

Space Obs Caracoles 166 ☎55 256 6278, ⓦspaceobs.com. Excellent, highly memorable tours (in English, French, Spanish and German; CH$25,000/2hr 30min) of Northern Chile's night sky led by enthusiastic and personable astronomers. Book in advance.

Vulcano Expediciones Caracoles 317 ☎9 5363 6648, ⓦvulcanochile.com. The best operator for mountain and volcano ascents (from CH$60,000), plus they offer trekking, horseriding and bike tours.

along Caracoles out of town, turn left at the end and carry straight on; plenty of water, sunscreen and a torch are essential.

Salar de Atacama

The edge of Chile's largest salt flat, the **Salar de Atacama** (daily: summer 9am–7pm, winter 8am–6pm; CH$2500), lies a mere 10km south of San Pedro. It may disappoint those expecting a sparkling white field, but still makes an unforgettable spectacle: a jagged white crust, resembling dead coral, created by water flowing down from the mountains, stretches as far as the eye can see. Several shallow lakes dot the Salar, including **Laguna Chaxa**, made bright by the resident Andean, Chilean and James flamingos, which spend up to fourteen hours a day feeding on tiny saltwater shrimp. Many excursions will also take in **Laguna Cejar** – where salt content is so high that you can float on the surface – and gleaming **Laguna Tebenquiche**. Also look out for the **Ojos del Salar** – two small, and almost perfectly round, cold-water pools set amid the arid plain.

Toconao

Toconao, 38km from San Pedro, is a small village nestled in an idyllic spot surrounded by sandy hills, with houses built entirely of volcanic liparita stone. A cool stream runs through the valley and the surrounding fertile soil supports lush vegetation, including fig, pear and quince trees, as well as the hallucinogenic San Pedro cactus. The site has been inhabited since 11,000 BC, and its present population of around seven hundred villagers make traditional crafts. It is possible to stay in several rustic *hospedajes* here, and there are delicious *humitas* (corn paste wrapped in corn leaves) for sale. Buses Atacama and Buses Frontera each run twice-daily bus services to Toconao from San Pedro.

El Tatio geysers

The **El Tatio geysers** (CH$10,000), 95km north of town, are a morning attraction, with tours setting off at 4am in order to reach them by sunrise, when the fumaroles that spew steam and the jets of scalding water that shoot up from the geysers are at their most impressive. At dawn, there is a surreal quality to the plateau: dark shadowy figures move through the mist and the sunlight glints on patches of white ground frost. When walking around, stick to marked paths, since the ground crust can be very fragile – breaking it might result in a plunge into near-boiling water. The temperature here, at the world's highest geothermal field (4320m), is often below

4

freezing, so warm clothes are essential. A soak in the nearby thermal pool is a must.

Lagunas Miscanti and Miñiques

These two *altiplano* **lagoons** (CH$3000) lie 134km from town, at an elevation of around 4200m. Visitors here are left breathless not just by the altitude, but also by the first sight of the huge shimmering pools of deep blue, ringed with white ribbons of salt. There's abundant bird and animal life as well, and it is possible to see both flamingos and the inquisitive *zorro culpeo*, a type of **fox** that often approaches the area's picnic site to look for scraps.

IQUIQUE

The approach to the busy coastal city of **Iquique** is unforgettable, especially if coming from the east. The highway along the plateau suddenly gives way to a spectacular 600m drop, looking down onto the giant **Cerro Dragón** sand dune which in turn towers over the city. At sunset, the dune and the surrounding cliffs turn various shades of pink and red, giving the city an almost unearthly feel. Almost 500km north of Antofagasta, Iquique prospered in the nitrate era, between 1890 and 1920. Most of the grand buildings in the city's historical centre date back to that heyday. The town's biggest draws nowadays are its fine **beaches**, though the huge duty-free **Zofri** zone in the north of the city also attracts visitors. The city is also one of the top destinations in Latin America for **paragliders**.

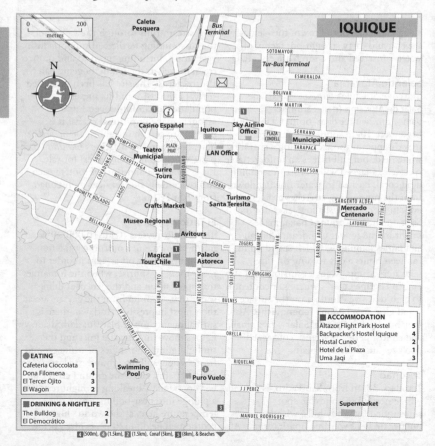

Plaza Prat

At the heart of Iquique's centre **Plaza Prat** is lined with banks and restaurants, with the tall white **Torre Reloj**, the city's symbol, built in 1877, as its centrepiece and the Neoclassical **Teatro Municipal** on the south side. The **Casino Español**, a 1904 Moorish-style wooden building with an opulent interior, graces the northeast corner of the square and is worth a visit both for the interior decorations and for the delicious pisco sours.

Calle Baquedano

Heading south from Plaza Prat towards Playa Bellavista, quiet pedestrianized **Calle Baquedano**, with its elevated boardwalks and grand wooden buildings, is strikingly different from the modern parts of Iquique, with a faded colonial feel about it. The **Museo Regional**, at no. 951 (Tues–Sat 9am–5.30pm, Sat 10am–2pm; free), is home to a number of curious pre-Columbian artefacts, the most impressive of which are the Chinchorro mummies and skulls, deliberately deformed by having bandages wrapped tightly around them. The natural history section features a sea-lion embryo pickled in formaldehyde and an informative exhibition on nitrate extraction in the area, along with a scale model of the ghost town of Humberstone.

The beaches

Iquique's most popular beach, **Playa Cavancha** is sheltered in a bay alongside the busy main thoroughfare of Avenida Arturo Prat, under 2km from the main plaza. It is particularly popular with sunbathers and boogie-boarders and is safe for swimming. The boardwalk, which winds along the beach amid the palm trees and giant cacti, is always teeming with bikers, rollerbladers and sun worshippers. At the north end of Playa Cavancha lies rocky **Playa Bellavista**, with several good surf breaks, while the large stretch of **Playa Brava**, lined by fun-fairs and themed restaurants, is south of the Peninsula de Cavancha, and is a popular landing spot for paragliders. The less crowded **Playa Huayquique** is located to the very south of the city; it also has good waves for surfers and can be reached by *colectivos* from the centre.

ARRIVAL AND INFORMATION

By plane Aeropuerto Diego Arecena lies 40km south of Iquique; you can get to the centre by transfer (CH$5500; ☎57 231 0800), regular taxi (CH$8000 shared, or CH$17,000 private) or *colectivo*.

Destinations Antofagasta (1–2 daily; 45min); Arica (1 daily; 40min); Santiago (13–18 daily; 2hr 10min).

By bus The main terminal is inconveniently located at the north end of Patricio Lynch; numerous *colectivos* run to the city centre and some bus companies pick up passengers at their central offices around Mercado Centenario. The Tur Bus terminal is slightly more central, on Esmeralda, at Ramírez.

Destinations Antofagasta (every 30min–1hr; 6hr); Arica (every 30min; 5hr); Calama (5–6 daily; 6hr); Caldera (12 daily; 12hr); Copiapó (12 daily; 13hr); La Serena (8–10 daily; 18hr); Pica (6 daily; 2hr); Santiago (hourly; 25hr).

Tourist information Aníbal Pinto 436 (Mon–Fri 9am–5pm, Sat & Sun 10am–2pm; ☎57 241 9241, ✉infoiquique@sernatur.cl). The Conaf office at Juan Antonio 2808 (Mon–Fri 8.30am–1.30pm & 3–5pm; ☎57 243 2085) can provide information on the Volcán Isluga National Park and arrange accommodation there.

ACCOMMODATION

Altazor Flight Park Hostel Via 6, Manzana Am Sitio 3, Bajo Molle, about a 15min bus ride from town ☎57 238 0110, ☎09 9886 2362, ⊛altazor.cl; map p.414. Built almost entirely of ship containers, the rooms at this international paragliding centre are surprisingly inviting, with shared kitchen, and chilled-out communal areas. Check their website for directions. Camping/person CH$5000, doubles CH$19,000, apartments CH$32,000

★ **Backpacker's Hostel Iquique** Amunátegui 2075, about 2km south of Plaza Prat ☎57 232 0223, ⊛hosteliquique.cl; map p.414. With English-speaking staff who help organize trips, a friendly atmosphere and a superb beachside location, this hostel remains a firm backpacker favourite. Kitchen facilities and frequent barbecues. Dorms CH$9000, doubles CH$27,000

Hostal Cuneo Baquedano 1175 ☎57 242 8654, ✉hostalcuneo@hotmail.com; map p.414. With a good location in an old timber building painted a striking turquoise on the historic stretch of Calle Baquedano, this hospitable and good-value *hostal* has small and neat if slightly dark rooms. CH$20,000

Hotel de la Plaza Paseo Baquedano 1025 ☎57 241 7172, ✉contacto@kilantur.cl; map p.414. An airy and light Georgian building on the main stretch with pictures of old Iquique adorning the walls and some racially dubious statues in the lobby. A leafy staircase leads up to pleasant, clean rooms, and there's a restaurant and bar. CH$35,000

4

PARAGLIDING IN IQUIQUE

Few things compare to the sheer rush of running off the cliff at **Alto Hospicio** on the plateau above Iquique. Once the butterflies settle, you find yourself soaring gently with white-headed eagles as tiny houses with minute turquoise swimming pools, ocean-side high-rises, beaches and the giant sand dune of Cerro Dragón spread out beneath you. You **paraglide** in tandem with an experienced instructor, who guides you through the entire procedure from take-off to landing.

The pros at **Puro Vuelo** (☎57 231 1127, ⊚purovuelo.cl) come highly recommended. A tandem flight will set you back CH$45,000 and includes a set of photos of you flying, which you can download from their website afterwards. **Altazor** (☎09 9886 2362, ⊚altazor.cl) also has a good reputation; if you want to enjoy a beer with some of the world's best paragliding talent, consider staying at their **Flight Park Altazor**. For the more faint of heart, tour companies will also help you organize a **sandboarding** trip on the dunes.

Uma Jaqi Obispo Labbé 1591 ☎09 8771 5768, ⊚umajaqi.cl; map p.414. This slightly ramshackle but friendly hostel has dorms of various sizes, plus doubles and triples, some with private bathrooms. There's a small bar and cushioned chill-out zone on the roof terrace. Dorms CH$7500, doubles CH$25,000

EATING

Cafeteria Cioccolata Av Anibal Pinto 487; map p.414. This sweet, old-fashioned tearoom opposite the tourist office serves up good coffee (CH$1500–3300) and obscenely huge slices of cake, waffles and pancakes. *Menu del día* CH$4900. Mon–Fri 8.45am–10pm, Sat 11am–10pm.

Dona Filomena Filomena Valenzuela 298; map p.414. Reliable *empanada*, beer and pizza joint, popular with a youngish crowd (dishes from CH$5000). Simple wooden decor and attractive outside seating. Mon–Sat 12.30pm–12.30am.

★ **El Tercer Ojito** Patricio Lynch 1420A ⊚eltercerojito.cl; map p.414. This peaceful garden oasis is the mellowest place to spend a shady afternoon or candle-lit evening. A healthy menu (mains CH$5500–12,000) darts from Chilean seafood to Thai curries, via salads, pasta and various veggie options. Tues–Sat 12.30–5pm & 7.30pm–1am, Sun 12.30–5pm.

El Wagon Thomson 85; map p.414. Nitrate-era paraphernalia lines the walls of this warm and friendly restaurant with imaginative fish and seafood dishes (CH$8000–12,000): the spicy *pescado a la Huara-Huara* is particularly good. Mon–Sat 1–4pm & 8pm–2am, Sun 1–4pm.

DRINKING AND NIGHTLIFE

The Bulldog Valenzuela 230; map p.414. Modern bar with big screens showing Premier League football and other sports by day and a decent sound system for the nights. Tasty bar meals available from CH$6000 and a well-stocked bar serving fine pisco sours and other drinks. Mon–Wed & Sun 11am–2am, Thurs–Sat 11am–4am.

El Democrático Obispo Labbé 466 ⊚bardemocratico.cl; map p.414. Quintessential scruffy 80-year-old local, with huge dried fish hanging from the walls. At the weekend, young locals replace the drunken fishermen and live bands join the party. Chilean beers start at CH$1500 and, if you're brave, try an old-school Chilean cocktail, "El Terremoto", made from pineapple ice cream, sweet white wine, whisky and grenadine. Daily 11.30am–late.

AROUND IQUIQUE

The nitrate pampas inland from Iquique is dotted with **ghost towns** left over from the area's mining heyday, with the biggest and best-preserved example being **Humberstone** (daily: Jan–March 9am–7pm; April–Dec 9am–6pm; CH$3000, also covers entry to Santa Laura), 45km to the east. Established in the middle of parched desert land in 1862, this once thriving mining town bears the name of Briton James Humberstone, a nitrate entrepreneur famous for introducing the "Shanks" ore-refining system to the industry. Visitors can wander the eerie streets where squalid and partially wrecked worker barracks contrast sharply with the faded glamour of the theatre and the well-maintained church. Workers here, mostly Chilean but some foreign, earned a pittance putting in long hours in a hot and dangerous environment.

Around 2km down the road is the much smaller **Santa Laura**, where you'll see a couple of remaining houses (one of which has been turned into a small museum), and an amazing processing plant, seeming to loom into the air like a

IQUIQUE TOUR OPERATORS

Apart from sandboarding and **paragliding** on Cerro Dragón, and **surfing** all along Iquique's coast, the area around the city has a wealth of attractions on offer, including trips to the **ghost town** of Humberstone, the Gigante de Atacama **geoglyph**, the **hot springs** of Mamiña and the Pica oasis, the **burial site** of an Inca princess at the village of La Tirana, and the sobering **mass graves** from the Pinochet era at the tiny settlement of Pisaqua. The cheapest – though perhaps not the most satisfying – tours combine a whistle-stop trip through all these attractions in a day (from CH$20,000). We recommend the following operators:

Avitours Baquedano 997 ⓣ 57 241 3334, ⓦ avitours.cl.

Iquitour Patricio Lynch 563, ⓣ 57 242 8772, ⓦ iquitour.cl.

Magical Tour Chile Baquedano 997 ⓣ 57 221 7290, ⓦ magicaltour.cl. Also offers cycling tours.

Surire Tours Baquedano 170 ⓣ 57 244 5440, ⓦ suriretours.cl.

Uma Jaqi Obispo Labbé 1591 ⓣ 09 8771 5768, ⓦ umajaqi.cl. Offers surfing lessons.

rusty old dinosaur. As you walk around the site, listening to the endless clanging of machinery banging in the wind, the sense of abandonment is nigh-on overwhelming.

The thermal springs at **Pica**, 114km southeast of Iquique, are well worth a visit for a relaxing splash around; the most popular is **Cocha Resbaladero** (daily 8am–8pm; CH$3000). The small, pre-Hispanic town is also famed for producing limes widely believed to make the perfect pisco sour, and the pretty **Iglesia de San Andrés**.

ARICA

ARICA, Chile's northernmost city, 316km from Iquique, benefits greatly from tourism, with foreign visitors flocking to its pleasant sandy beaches in the summer, and with a smattering of good museums. The city was the principal port exporting silver from Bolivia's Potosí mines until 1776, and only became part of Chile in the 1880s after the War of the Pacific. Aside from its own attractions, Arica makes a good base for the beautiful Parque Nacional Lauca (see page 421).

WHAT TO SEE AND DO

The compact city centre is easy to explore on foot, though a visit to Arica isn't complete without climbing **El Morro**, the dramatic cliff that looms high over the city.

El Morro

A steep path leads to the top of **El Morro** from the southern end of Calle Colón. From the clifftop, home to a number of turkey vultures and a giant Jesus statue that lights up at night, you can enjoy a magnificent panoramic view of the entire city. Also up here, with cannons stationed outside, is the **Museo Histórico y de Armas** (daily 8am–8pm; CH$1000), with displays of weaponry, uniforms and other artefacts from the War of the Pacific.

The city centre

Below El Morro is the large, palm-tree-lined **Plaza Vicuña Mackenna**, and alongside that lies Avenida Máximo Lira, the main coastal road. On the east side is the attractive **Plaza Colón**, decorated with pink flowers and ornate fountains. The plaza is home to one of Arica's most celebrated buildings, the Gothic **Iglesia de San Marcos**, designed by Gustave Eiffel (of Eiffel Tower fame), made entirely out of iron and shipped over from France in 1876. Eiffel was also responsible for the grand 1874 **Ex-Aduana** building nearby, alongside the Parque General Baquedano. This now houses the Casa de Cultura, which regularly hosts art and photo exhibitions.

The main thoroughfare, **21 de Mayo**, heads east from Plaza Colón before becoming a pedestrian strip, lined with restaurants and banks. South of the plaza, at Colón 10, the **Museo Sitio Colón** (Tues–Sun 10am–6pm; CH$2000)

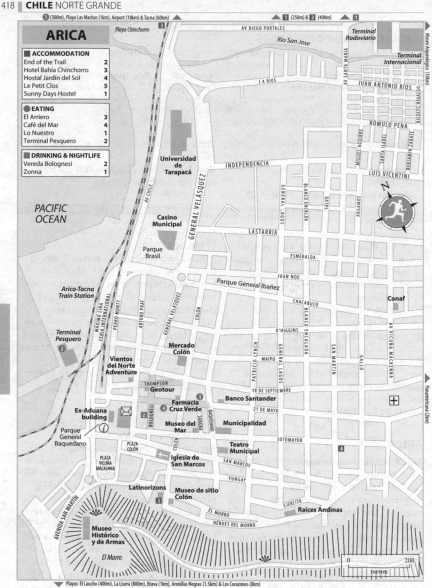

houses the extraordinary remains of 48 Chinchorro mummies, found in situ here during a planned building development and now enshrined under plate glass which you can walk over to view them.

The beaches

North of the centre and west of the bus terminals lies the popular **Playa Chinchorro**, which is ideal for swimming, sunbathing and body-boarding. The city's northernmost beach, **Playa Las Machas**, is not suitable for swimming because of the strong undertow but has some good surf breaks. A twenty-minute walk south of the centre will bring you to the sandy **Playa El Laucho** and **Playa La Lisera**, both popular and good for swimming, followed by the pretty **Playa Brava** and the dark-sand **Playa Arenillas Negra**, which has rougher waves. Finally, there's **Playa Los Corazones**, a beautiful expanse of clean sand flanked by cliffs 8km south of town. The southern beaches can be reached by *colectivo*, though these tend to run only during the summer season.

Museo Arqueológico

The excellent **Museo Arqueológico** (daily: Jan & Feb 10am–7pm; March–Dec 10am–6pm; CH$2000; ☎58 220 5551, ⓦmasma.uta.cl) lies 12km from Arica in the green **Azapa Valley**. The museum traces the history of the valley's inhabitants, from the earliest hunter-gatherers, via a remarkably thorough collection of regional pre-Hispanic artefacts. Most impressive of these are the four elaborately prepared **Chinchorro mummies** – a male, a female and two young children, which are believed to be around seven thousand years old, making them by far the oldest mummies in the world. To get there, catch one of the yellow *colectivos* labelled "Azapa" which run along Avenida Diego Portales past the bus terminals.

ARRIVAL AND DEPARTURE

By plane Aeropuerto Internacional Chacalluta is 18km north of Arica; a radio taxi downtown costs around CH$8000, or take a cheaper transfer for CH$4000.
Destinations Iquique (1 daily; 40min); Santiago (8–10 daily; 2hr 30min).

By bus Terminal Rodovario, at Diego Portales 948 northeast of the centre, is the main stop for domestic arrivals. Terminal Internacional is immediately adjacent, with connections to Bolivia and Peru (see page 419).
Destinations Antofagasta (every 1–3hr; 10hr); Calama (5–6 daily; 10hr); Chañaral (7 daily; 15hr); Copiapó (every 1–2hr; 17hr); Iquique (every 30min; 5hr); Putre (1 daily; 3hr); San Pedro de Atacama (3 nightly; 14hr); Santiago (10 daily; 29hr); Vallenar (10 daily; 20hr).

INFORMATION

Tourist information The tourist office is at San Marcos 101 (Dec–Feb Mon–Fri 9am–7pm; March–Nov Mon–Fri 9am–6pm; ☎58 225 4506, ⓔinfoarica@sernatur. cl). Helpful staff provide maps of town and a plethora of brochures on local attractions. Conaf has an office at Av Vicuña Mackenna 820 (☎58 220 1200) where staff provide information on, and maps of, local national parks; reserve beds at the few remaining regional Conaf *refugios* here.

ACCOMMODATION

You can camp for free at the Playa Las Machas.
End of the Trail Esteban Alvarado 117 ☎58 231 4316, ☎09 7786 3972, ⓦendofthetrail-arica.cl; map p.418. A congenial American owner runs this hostel, which has comfortable, quiet rooms around an indoor courtyard, amazing showers and a specially designed roof that keeps the house cool. Breakfast included. To get there from the bus station, walk two blocks west on Diego Portales, then four blocks north on Pedro de Valdivia. Dorms CH$11,000, doubles CH$26,000
Hotel Bahía Chinchorro Av Luis Beretta Porcel 2031 ☎58 226 5270, ⓔbahia_arica@latinmail.com; map p.418. A 20min walk from the centre, this place has direct access to Playa Chinchorro. The simple and rather shabby rooms – with attached bathrooms, a/c and TVs – are all glass-fronted, giving them superb ocean views. CH$35,000

INTO BOLIVIA AND PERU

There are two main routes from the far north of Chile across the Andes into Bolivia. The more southerly of the two is from Iquique to **Oruro** (for connections to Cochabamba or La Paz), served by a daily Jet Nort bus that usually departs at 6pm and takes 10–12hr. Far more frequently travelled is the busy road between Arica and **La Paz**, which has several daily buses operated by different companies. The journey of just under 500km takes 8–9hr, depending how long you have to wait at the border, and has the added bonus of going right through **Parque Nacional Lauca** (see page 421).

One of the busiest and easiest border crossings in all South America is the one on the Panamericana between Arica and **Tacna** in Peru, which lie less than 60km apart. Departing from Arica, you first pay the CH$350 terminal fee at the international terminal and then choose between the continuous stream of buses and *colectivos* that ply between the cities as soon as they are full. The journey can take little over an hour or well over two, depending how many vehicles coincide at the efficient border post.

TOUR OPERATORS AROUND ARICA

A number of tour companies offer trips into the *national parks* outside Arica. The standard three- to four-day trip takes in Parque Nacional Lauca, Reserva Nacional Las Vicuñas, Salar de Surire and Parque Nacional Volcán Isluga, with overnight stops in the *altiplano* villages of Putre and Colchane. Most tours either return to Arica or drop passengers off in Iquique. Tour operators do offer day-trips taking in Parque Nacional Lauca, and Putre, but this is not recommended as the altitude change is extreme, and is at best likely to make you feel queasy (see page 33).

Geotour Bolognesi 421 ☎ 58 225 3927, ⓦgeotour. cl. Slick, professional but fairly impersonal company offering mostly one-day tours around Arica, as well as trips further afield to Lauca, Matilla and Pica. There are two other branches in San Pedro de Atacama and Iquique.

★ **Latinorizons** Colón 7 ☎ 58 225 0007, ⓦlatinorizons.com. Friendly and extremely reliable Belgian-run company offering a wide range of altiplano tours, including overnight, with a more adventurous feel than most of the others on offer. French and English spoken. Charlie, the very knowledgeable owner, also owns the hostal next door (see page 420).

Hostal Jardín del Sol Sotomayor 848 ☎ 58 223 2795, ⓦhostaljardindelsol.cl; map p.418. Central *hostal* run by a very helpful and welcoming couple who organize all manner of outdoor activities for guests. Most rooms are en suite; shares arranged. Kitchen, lounge, TV, bike rental and a laundry service are some of the bonuses. Breakfast included. CH$36,500

Le Petit Clos Colón 9 ☎ 58 232 3746, ⓦlepetitclos.cl; map p.418. This elegantly converted old house is now the delightful hostal belonging to the owner of *Latinorizons* (see above). Some of the compact but comfortable rooms have private baths and there are great views of the ocean and nearby El Morro from the roof terrace. CH$27,000

★ **Sunny Days Hostel** Tomas Aravena 161 ☎ 58 224 1038, ⓦsunny-days-arica.cl; map p.418. Extremely friendly and knowledgeable Kiwi-Chilean hosts preside over travellers of all ages in this custom-built hostel. An excellent breakfast, kitchen and lounge facilities and a relaxed communal atmosphere all add to its appeal. Dorms CH$11,000, doubles CH$26,000

EATING

El Arriero 21 de Mayo 385 ☎ 58 223 2636, ⓦrestaurantelarriero.cl; map p.418. Recommended grill house serving tasty fillet steaks and other meat dishes (from CH$9000); often has live folk music at the weekends. Book ahead. Mon–Sat noon–4pm & 7–11pm.

Café del Mar 21 de Mayo 260; map p.418. Popular restaurant with a bargain *menú del día* at CH$4700, plus large salads and good quiches (from CH$2500). Mon–Sat 9.30am–midnight.

★ **Lo Nuestro** Raul Pey 2492; map p.418. Fine buffet restaurant behind Playa Chinchorro, where you can help yourself to as much tenderly grilled meat and food from the salad bar as you like. The price (lunch CH$9400, dinner CH$11,500) includes two desserts and a glass of wine. Tues–Sat 1–3pm & 9pm–midnight, Sun 1–3.30pm.

Terminal Pesquero Off Av Máximo Lira, across from entrance to C 21 de Mayo; map p.418. Several no-frills oceanside restaurants here cook up hearty portions of inexpensive fish dishes; *Mata Rangi*, in particular, stands out. Set lunches around CH$6000. Daily noon–5pm.

DRINKING AND NIGHTLIFE

Vereda Bolognesi Bolognesi 340 ⓦveredabolognesi. cl; map p.418. By night, from about 8pm, this smart little shopping gallery in town turns into a buzzing patio bar zone – several restaurant-bars compete with their happy hours so it's easy to get a good cocktail at a decent price. Mon–Sat 10am–11pm.

Zonna Av Argentina 2787 ☎ 58 222 1509, ⓦzonna.cl; map p.418. *Zonna*, the biggest, best-known and most popular nightclub in Arica, is really a collection of venues each playing different types of music ranging from salsa to 1980s hits. Ask about the weekly drink promotion. Thurs–Sun midnight–late.

PUTRE

The highland village of **PUTRE** sits at an altitude of 3500m and provides an ideal acclimatization point for venturing into the Parque Nacional Lauca. Populated by the indigenous Aymará people, Putre consists of basic stone houses centred around a square. It is a tranquil place to spend a few days, and is becoming an increasing must-see on the backpacker trail, with a growing number of accommodation options.

ARRIVAL AND INFORMATION

By bus Buses La Paloma, Germán Riesco 2071 (☎ 58 222 2710), has a daily bus to Putre from Arica (3hr).
Tourist information The tourist office is on the south side of the square (Mon–Fri 9am–6pm; ☎ 58 225 2803).

ACCOMMODATION AND EATING

★ **Canta Verdi** Arturo Perez Canto 339 ☎ 9 9890 7291. This welcoming place at the top of the square, decorated in warm earth colours, serves great alpaca steaks (CH$7500) and other local staples. Best wi-fi in town too. Daily noon–3pm & 6–11pm.

La Chakana A 20min walk from the plaza; head downhill past the church ☎ 09 9745 9519, ⓦ lachakana.com. On the western edge of town, about a 15min walk from the plaza, the large detached huts here stand on spacious grounds and are simply but pleasantly furnished. Breakfast in the owner's dining room. Doubles CH$33,000

★ **Hostal Pachamama** Centro s/n ☎ 9 6353 5187, ⓦ panchamamahosteltours.cl. By far the most backpacker-friendly place in Putre, with colourful but cramped four-bed dorms, doubles with shared bathrooms and one more spacious en-suite cabin. Large kitchen and lounge area. Dorms CH$15,000, doubles CH$25,000, cabin CH$60,000

Rosamel Latorre 400C ☎ 9 4164 2843. Simple L-shaped restaurant on the square serving good set menus made up of local dishes such as stews, spicy meat dishes and *papas rellenas* at affordable prices (CH$4500–6000). Daily 5.30am–10pm.

PARQUE NACIONAL LAUCA

From Putre, Ruta 11 leads up onto the *altiplano* to the **Parque Nacional Lauca**, a region of rich flora and fauna, shimmering lakes and snowcapped volcanoes 4300m above sea level. The most visited village at these dizzying heights and the only place with any accommodation is the little whitewashed settlement of **Parinacota**, accessible by public transport, though it's far easier to see the sights of Lauca on an organized tour.

Las Cuevas

The stony hillsides of **Las Cuevas**, 9km into the park, are the best place to see **viscachas**, the long-tailed, rabbit-like relatives of chinchillas, as they use their powerful hind legs to leap from boulder to boulder. The well-watered *bofedal* (alluvial depression) here provides permanent grazing for herds of **vicuñas**, the wild

relatives of llamas and alpacas, which are commonly seen. In addition, you'll find numerous examples of the *llareta* plant, which takes three hundred years to grow to full size; the plant looks like a pile of oddly shaped green cushions but is actually rock-hard. The local Aymará break up the dead plants with picks for use as firewood.

Parinacota

The **Conaf** headquarters (daily 9am–12.30pm & 1–5.30pm) are located in the tiny Aymará village of **Parinacota**, 19km east of Las Cuevas. Parinacota is worth a stop for its cheerful, whitewashed little **church**, reconstructed in 1789, and for the stalls opposite, selling colourful local **artesanía**. Besides a fetching bell tower with a tiny doorway, the church (ask around for the guardian of the key) has murals depicting scenes of Jesus being borne to the cross by soldiers resembling Spanish conquistadors, as well as sinners burning in hell. A small wooden table is tethered to the wall to the left of the altar; legend has it that the table wandered around the village, causing the death of a man by stopping in front of his house – the chain prevents the table from escaping again.

Parinacota can be reached by **public bus** from the Terminal Internacional in Arica (departs Tues–Fri at 11am, returning at 9am the following day). It may be possible to rent a very basic **room** from a villager, or stay in the basic hostel opposite the church.

Lago Chungará

Some 18km east of Parinacota, at a breathtaking altitude of 4600m, lies the stunning **Lago Chungará**. With its brilliant blue waters perfectly reflecting the towering snowcapped cone of **Volcán Parinacota** (6350m), this is undoubtedly one of the highlights of the national park. There is a short lakeside **nature trail**, which provides a good vantage point for viewing the giant coots, flamingos and Andean geese that nest here.

4

RESERVA NACIONAL LAS VICUÑAS AND SALAR DE SURIRE

A southbound turn-off from Ruta 11 by Lago Chungará heads through the 2091-square-kilometre **Reserva Nacional Las Vicuñas** towards the Salar de Surire salt lake. The *reserva* is made up of seemingly endless marshes and grasslands where herds of vicuñas can be seen grazing in the distance.

At an altitude of 4295m, the enormous, dirty-white **Salar de Surire** is home to up to ten thousand **flamingos** – mostly Chilean, but with a smattering of James and Andean species. Surire means "place of the rhea" in Aymará, and it's also possible to catch glimpses here of these swift, ostrich-like birds. On the southeast side of the salt flat are the **Termas de Polloquere**, several hot thermal pools amid a small geyser field, which are a good spot to soak and pamper yourself using the mud at the bottom of the pools. It is possible to **camp** at a rustic site near the pools.

There is no public transport to either the *reserva* or *salar*, and a tour is the easiest option.

PARQUE NACIONAL VOLCÁN ISLUGA

South of Las Vicuñas, the dirt track drifts eastwards, passing by large herds of **llamas** and their shorter and hairier **alpaca** cousins, as well as tiny, seemingly deserted Aymará hamlets. All these are overshadowed by the towering **Volcán Isluga** (5218m), from which the park takes its name. The little village of **Enquelga** is home to a small Conaf-run **refugio** with five beds and hot showers (CH$5500/person), as well as a free **campsite** (1km east of town) with Conaf-maintained shelters alongside a stream and some hot springs. One warm pool here, against the impressive backdrop of the volcano, is large enough for swimming.

Just outside the park, the small farming settlement of **COLCHANE**, surrounded by fields of bright red quinoa and *kiwicha* (a highly nutritious local staple), has several basic **guesthouses** providing simple home-cooked food. It is possible to get on a bus from Iquique to Colchane (daily 1pm & 9pm; 3hr), and get dropped off at the park, but it is best to contact Conaf in advance for advice. For drivers, the road condition is poor and requires a 4WD vehicle.

Middle Chile

As the southernmost reaches of Santiago's sprawling suburbs fade away, a vast expanse of fields, orchards and vineyards serves as a transition area between the bustling metropolitan borough and the natural landscapes of the Lake District. This is Chile's most fertile region, and home to the country's world-famous **wineries**, which are accessible by day-trip from Santiago but are much less rushed if taken from the quaint town of **Santa Cruz**. West of Santa Cruz is the country's surf capital of **Pichilemu**, where some of the world's biggest breaks crash along vast sandy beaches. Further south, **Concepción**, Chile's second-largest city and an important university town, has picked itself up after it was rocked by a massive **earthquake** in 2010 although the

surrounding area is likely to show the scars of the destructive quake for some years to come. **Talca** and **Chillán** are useful stop-offs along the long Panamericana – here, the Ruta 5 – as well as good bases for exploring the wineries, hot baths and natural attractions in the local area.

RANCAGUA

RANCAGUA is a busy agricultural city that lies 87km south of Santiago. The best time for a day-trip here is either in April, to witness the **National Rodeo Championships**, or the last weekend in March, during the **Fiesta Huasa**, a three-day celebration of cowboy culture held in the main square, involving traditional food and wine. Alternatively, if you are coming in November, try to catch the **Encuentro Internacional Criollo**, a demonstration of spectacular horse-breaking and lassoing skills from expert riders from all over Latin America.

ARRIVAL AND INFORMATION

By bus The Terminal O'Higgins (☎72 222 5425) hub for long-distance destinations lies northeast of town, just off Ruta 5. Tur Bus, at O'Carrol 1175, has a more convenient, central location. Expreso Santa Cruz and Pullman Del Sur run buses on to Santa Cruz.

By train The hourly Metrotrén from Santiago and the faster train to Chillán stop at the Estación Rancagua (☎600 585 5000), on Av Estación, between O'Carrol and Carrera Pinto, at the western edge of downtown.

Tourist information The helpful Sernatur office at Germán Riesco 277, 1st floor (Mon–Thurs 8.30am–5.30pm, Fri 8.30am–4.30pm; ☎72 223 0413, ⊛turismolibertador. cl), can provide plenty of information on the city and its festivals.

SANTA CRUZ

About 90km southwest of Rancagua, the attractive little town of **SANTA CRUZ** lies at the heart of the fertile Colchagua Valley, home to Chile's best-organized *Ruta de Vino*. The hot climate here has proved to be perfect for growing Carmenère, Cabernet, Malbec and Syrah grapes. The ideal time to visit is during the first weekend in March, when the **Fiesta de la Vendimia del Valle de Colchagua** (grape harvest festival) is held, allowing you to sample the best wines and the region's typical dishes.

WHAT TO SEE AND DO

The heart of Santa Cruz is the gorgeous **Plaza de Armas**, dotted with araucarias, conifers and palm trees, with an ornate fountain at its centre and drinking fountains around its periphery. Within a couple of blocks of the plaza are numerous places to eat and *hospedajes*.

The excellent, privately run **Museo de Colchagua**, at Errázuriz 145 (daily: Sept–Feb 10am–7pm; March–Aug 10am–7pm; CH$7000; ⊛museocolchagua.cl), displays the unmatched private collection of Carlos Cardoen, which includes pre-Columbian artefacts from around Latin America, conquistador weaponry, exquisite gold work, Mapuche weavings, a re-creation of the San José mine rescue and much more. Cardoen himself is a highly controversial figure: still wanted by the FBI for allegedly selling weapons to Iraq in the 1980s, the former arms dealer has transformed himself into a successful businessman and philanthropist with extensive interests in wine and tourism.

RUTA DEL VINO DE COLCHAGUA

The **Colchagua Valley** has some of the best red wines in the world, not to mention the most professionally run **wine route** in Chile. There are twelve **wineries i**n all, including both large, modern producers and small-scale, traditional *bodegas*; many of them can be visited on a drop-by basis or at short notice. The Ruta del Vino agency (☎72 282 3199, ⊛rutadelvino.cl) organizes full-day and half-day tours that take in two or three wineries with tastings and can include lunch, museum visits, and/or transfers from Santiago. Rates depend on the number of people and type of tour; a half-day tour will cost around CH$66,000. The agency can also book (mostly luxury) accommodation in the area.

WINERIES

Viña Casa Silva Hijuela Norte s/n Angostura, Km132, Ruta 5, San Fernando ☎72 291 3117, ⊛casasilva.cl. Award-winning winery with an excellent restaurant, set in a colonial-style hacienda, using modern technology to produce Carmenère, as well as the less common Viognier, Sauvignon Gris and Shiraz. Tours CH$20,000/person.

Viña Laura Hartwig Camino Barreales s/n ☎72 282 3179, ⊛laurahartwig.cl. Small, family-owned, boutique winery producing only reserve-quality wines; the owners directly oversee each stage of production. Book in advance. Tours CH$12,000–16,000/person.

Viña Viu Manent Carretera del Vino Km37 ☎72 285 8751, ⊛viumanent.cl. Family-owned winery close to Santa Cruz, famous for its excellent reds, especially Malbec, offering horse-drawn carriage tours as part of its attraction. Tours CH$13,000/person.

★ TREAT YOURSELF

Casa de Campo Los Pidenes, Km40 Ruta 50 ☎ 09 4496 9340, ⓦhotelcasadecampo.cl. If you're going to treat yourself anywhere, Santa Cruz is the place to do it, with a wealth of attractive lodgings, many in the vineyards themselves (the Ruta del Vino has a list). *Casa de Campo* is a wonderful family-run place just outside of town that won't blow the budget as much as some, with charming rural-chic rooms. Ask for one with a veranda or balcony overlooking the attractive gardens, vineyards and pool. CH$95,000

ARRIVAL AND INFORMATION

By bus Terminal Municipal is on Casanova 478, four blocks southwest of the Plaza de Armas.

Destinations Pichilemu (10 daily; 2hr); Santiago (frequent; 3hr).

Tourist information The tourist office is at Plaza de Armas 242 (Mon–Fri 8.30am–4pm). The Ruta de Vino headquarters on the east side of the Plaza de Armas 298 (Mon–Sat 9am–6pm, Sun 10am–5pm; ☎72 282 3199, ⓦrutadelvino.cl) is an excellent source of information on the Valle Colchagua.

ACCOMMODATION AND EATING

Café Sorbo Casanova 158, on the 2nd floor of a cultural centre. Extremely friendly café/restaurant with quality coffee, and great choice for vegetarians. Soya hamburger CH$7200. Daily 11am–8.30pm.

Gomero Capellania 327 ☎72 282 1436. Unremarkable hotel with clean but not particularly inviting rooms, and friendly staff. Breakfast included. Rooms CH$36,000

Pizzeria Refranes Diaz Besoain 176. Opposite the fire station. Traditional Chilean dishes combine with an excellent range of *empanadas* and divine slabs of pizza in a pleasant ambience. Large pizza CH$6300. Mon–Sat 1–4pm, 8pm–midnight, Sun 1–4pm.

Vino Bello Barreales s/n, 1.5km outside of town. Run by the nearby Laura Hartwig winery (see page 423), you can dine on decent Italian food including pasta, pizzas and salads on a candlelit terrace, with the impossibly romantic backdrop of the vineyards. Mains from around CH$8000. Mon–Sat 11.30am–11pm, Sun 11.30am–3.30pm.

PICHILEMU

The drive to the surfing magnet of **PICHILEMU**, 90km west of Santa Cruz, is particularly scenic. The Ruta 90 meanders past sun-drenched vineyards before snaking in and out of patches of pine forest. "Pichi", as it's known, was planned as an upmarket vacation spot by the local land baron Agustín Ross Edwards, though in recent years it's become ever more popular with a cool crew of **surfers** and local beach bums.

WHAT TO SEE AND DO

A spread-out town, Pichilemu has numerous guesthouses and places to eat concentrated along the east–west Avenida Ortúzar, and the north–south Aníbal Pinto, a couple of blocks from the sea. The water is always chilly (12–18°C) so you'll need a wetsuit if you want to do more than take a quick dip.

Playa Las Terrazas

Avenida Costanera Cardenal Caro runs alongside the black-sand expanse of **Playa Las Terrazas**, Pichilemu's principal beach. Good for both sunbathers and surfers, it has a cluster of places to eat and **surf schools** concentrated towards its southern end, at the rocky promontory of La Puntilla. Steps lead up to the meticulously landscaped **Parque Ross**, dotted with palm trees and boasting an excellent view of the coast.

SURF'S UP!

Budding surfers wanting to get in on the action can hone their skills with the help of a couple of surfing schools:

Lobillos Escuela de Surf Av Costanera 720 ☎ 09 9718 8391. Experienced surfing instructor charges CH$18,000 per lesson (2hr 30min), which includes board and wetsuit rental. Equipment rental alone costs CH$8000.

Manzana 54 Surf School Av Costanera, next to Waitara Restaurant ☎09 574 5984, ⓦmanzana54.cl. Professional surf school and equipment rental offering lessons for CH$18,000 (2hr), all equipment included. Equipment rental alone is CH$7000–8000 for a full day.

Punta de Lobos

Chile's most famous wave, **Punta de Lobos**, where the National Surfing Championships are held every winter, can be found 6km south of downtown Pichilemu; to get there, take a *colectivo* along Jorge Errázuriz (CH$3500), or cycle down Comercio until you reach the turn-off towards the coast and make your way to the end of the jutting, cactus-studded headland. At the tip of the promontory, intrepid surfers descend via a steep dirt path before swimming across the short churning stretch of water to **Las Tetas**, the distinctive sea stacks, and catching the powerful, consistent left break just beyond.

ARRIVAL AND INFORMATION

By bus The main Terminal Municipal is located on Millaco, at Los Alerces, though unless you're staying in Pichi's southeastern quarter it's more convenient to disembark at the bus stop on Angel Gaete. There are hourly departures to Santiago (daily 4.30am–6.40pm; about 3hr 30min; Buses Nilahue stop in Santa Cruz and Rancagua). Buy your ticket at the bus offices on Angel Gaete at Aníbal Pinto, and catch them at the bus stop on Santa María, four blocks northeast.

Spanish school Pichilemu Institute of Languages (☎72 284 2449, ⓦstudyspanishchile.com) offers short- and longer-term Spanish classes.

Tourist information There is a helpful booth on Angel Gaete, between Montt and Rodríguez (Mon–Fri 8am–1pm & 2.30–7pm; ⓦpichilemu.cl), which gives out maps of town and can help with accommodation.

ACCOMMODATION

Hostal Casa Verde Camino Vecinal 295, opposite Dunamar Cabanas, on Playa Hermosa Pasaje San Alfonso s/n; walk up the track opposite Verde Mar supermarket ☎09 9299 8866, ⓦhostalcasaverde.cl. About 3km from town, this small but popular hostel has good breakfasts, surfing classes, free bike rental, and a chilled-out vibe. Dorms CH$12,000, doubles CH$36,000

Hotel Chile España Av Ortúzar 255 ☎72 284 1270, ⓦchileespana.cl. Smart, central guesthouse with clean and comfortable rooms; breakfast is included and there's a pleasant patio area. Doubles CH$50,000

EATING, DRINKING AND NIGHTLIFE

El Balaustro Av Ortúzar 289 ☎09 8669 3401. Conveniently located, two-tiered pub which serves excellent lunchtime specials, both meat and fish, and has nightly drinks deals. Set lunch CH$3500. Daily lunch & dinner.

La Casa de las Empanadas Aníbal Pinto, between Aguirre & Acevedo. Takeaway with amazing range of excellent *empanadas* (CH$1500). Daily noon–midnight.

Loop Av Angel Gaete s/n. Pounding venue that acts as a magnet for Pichilemu's youth and surfing population. Doesn't kick off until after midnight.

Waitara Av Costanera 1039d ☎72 284 3004, ⓦwaitara. cl. The restaurant here is more appealing than the cabañas – its lunchtime menu features tasty and well-cooked fish dishes, and it turns into a party place later in the evening. Mains CH$5000.

TALCA

Some 250km south of Santiago, the agricultural city of **TALCA** has little in the way of its own attractions but makes a good stop-off along the long Ruta 5 between the capital and Patagonia. It also serves as a base for exploring the **Valle del Maule** and its **Ruta de Vino**, as well as for treks into the nearby sierra.

The city's streets are on a numbered grid, making it very easy to navigate. Most of the commercial activity revolves around the **Plaza de Armas**, dominated by the cathedral, between 1 Norte, 1 Sur, 1 Poniente and 1 Oriente. Banks and pharmacies line 1 Sur, and there are numerous inexpensive places to eat and *completo* stands within a couple of blocks of the square. Unfortunately, the Museo O'Higgiano, at 1 Norte 875, where the national hero Bernardo O'Higgins spent his childhood and signed the Declaration of Independence in 1818, remains closed due to severe damage suffered in the 2010 quake.

ARRIVAL AND DEPARTURE

By train The station (☎600 585 5000) is at 11 Oriente 1000; there is no luggage storage.
Destinations Santiago (2 daily; 3hr); Chillán (2 daily; 1hr 50min).

By bus Most long-distance and local buses arrive at the Terminal Rodoviario at 2 Sur 1920 (☎71 224 3270), ten blocks east of the Plaza de Armas; the Tur Bus terminal (☎71 231 0815) is at 13 Oriente 1962, at 3 Sur. Frequent *colectivos* go back and forth along 1 Sur to and from the train and bus stations.
Destinations Chillán (every 30min; 2hr); Puerto Montt (5 daily; 10hr); Santiago (hourly; 3hr 30min); Temuco (8 daily; 6hr).

INFORMATION

Tourist information The well-stocked and useful Sernatur office is in the Correos, on the east side of Plaza de Armas, at 1 Oriente 1150 (Mon–Fri 8.30am–5.30pm; ☎71 222 8029, ⓔinfomaule@sernatur.cl). The helpful

4

RUTA DEL VINO DEL MAULE

Valle del Maule is rapidly developing a **Ruta del Vino** involving nine wineries, most of which require reservations to visit. The Ruta del Vino del Maule headquarters at Av Circunvalacion Oriente 1055 in the lobby of Talca's casino (Mon–Sat 8.30am–2pm & 5–8pm; ☎09 8157 9951, ⊛valledelmaule.cl) can help to arrange full-day and half-day visits to the nearby wineries. Good options include:

Viña Balduzzi Av Balmaceda 1189, San Javier ☎73 232 2138, ⊛balduzzi.cl. Operating since the seventeenth century, this family winery runs interesting guided tours (CH$4500/person) and tastings in English, and is the easiest to visit by public transport: take the San Javier bus from Talca. No need to reserve. Mon–Sat 9.30am–6.30pm.

Viña Gillmore Camino a Constitución Km20, San Javier ☎73 197 5539, ⊛tabonko.cl. Also known as Tabonko, this boutique winery produces Cabernet Franc, Carignan, Malbec, Syrah, Carmenère and Merlot, with a fine on-site restaurant. Call to arrange a tour (CH$6000/person).

Conaf office, at 2 Poniente/3 Sur (☎71 222 8029), has information on the Reserva Nacional Altos de Lircay and Radal Siete Tazas.

ACCOMMODATION

Casa Chueca Camino Las Rastras s/n ☎71 197 0096, ☎09 9419 0625, ⊛trekkingchile.com. On the banks of the Río Lircay, a short distance out of Talca, this German/Austrian-run guesthouse is a peaceful retreat, with comfortable and charmingly decorated rooms, delicious, home-cooked, mainly vegetarian meals and a swimming pool set amid its lush gardens. Franz Schubert, its knowledgeable owner, also runs excellent guided excursions into the little-visited and under-appreciated protected areas nearby. To get here, take a "Taxutal A" bus from the bus stop at the southeast corner of the main bus terminal to the end of the route; if possible, call beforehand so they can pick you up. Otherwise, follow the dirt road from Taxutal for about 20min. Closed June–Aug. Dorms CH$15,000, doubles CH$48,000

Hostal del Puente 1 Sur 407 ☎71 222 0930. Small but elegant rooms set around a beautiful leafy courtyard, in a traditional adobe house just two blocks from the Plaza de Armas. Doubles CH$32,000

Refugio del Tricahue ✉refugio.tricahue@yahoo.fr, ⊛refugio-tricahue.cl. Run by French-Belgian couple Betty and Dimitri, this nature lover's retreat has simple wooden chalets set against a beautiful backdrop of tree-covered mountains, with opportunities for fishing, trekking and cycling. Take Bus Interbus towards Armerillo (5 buses daily; 1hr 30min). Camping/person CH$4000, dorms CH$7500, doubles CH$22,000

EATING

La Buena Carne 1 Norte 1305. Large restaurant specializing in grilled meat, owned by the butchers on the opposite corner. Excellent cuts at bargain prices. Humita CH$1000. Mon–Sat 9am–9.30pm.

Via Lactea 1 Sur 1339, local 10. Restaurant serving a range of meat and fish dishes and an excellent selection of ice cream. Tables fill up in the evenings. Mains CH$3500–CH$7000.

PARQUE NACIONAL ALTOS DEL LIRCAY

The **Parque Nacional Altos del Lircay** (daily 8.30am–5.30pm; CH$5000), about 70km east of Talca and 2km from the village of **Vilches Alto**, is one of the best trekking destinations in the central part of Chile, with hikes that snake through native forest before emerging above the tree line with spectacular views of snowcapped mountains and volcanoes. The area is also famous as a magnet for UFO sightings and enthusiasts. Multi-day trails around the area or linking Lircay with the nearby **Parque Nacional Radal Siete Tazas** – named for the "cups" (*tazas*) carved by a series of seven waterfalls out of the rock – are also possible; contact a local guide.

ARRIVAL AND INFORMATION

By bus Around 10–14 buses a day (☎09 5713 0436, ⊛vilchesalto.com) ply the route – in the process of being paved – between Talca and Vilches Alto.

Tourist information Staff at *Casa Chueca* and *Refugio Don Galo* can advise on treks in the park and help organize excursions.

ACCOMMODATION

Refugio Don Galo Hijuela R, Vilches Alto ☎71 251 9553, ⊛refugiodegalo.com. Simple but pleasant pine-walled refuge right by the reserve, with a restaurant and owners who are a good source of local information. CH$35,000

CHILLÁN

CHILLÁN lies 150km south of Talca in the middle of the green **Itata Valley**, a stopover on the Panamericana or launchpad for visiting the nearby skiing and hot-springs area of Nevados de Chillán. A nondescript town rebuilt time and time again after earthquake damage and Mapuche attacks, Chillán is famous as the birthplace of Chile's national hero and founding father, Bernardo O'Higgins. Its market is worth a visit, overflowing with an abundance of fresh produce and handicrafts. The centre of town is the **Plaza Bernardo O'Higgins**, featuring a towering 36m cross commemorating the thirty thousand victims of the 1939 earthquake, which largely destroyed the city. **Escuela Mexico**, a school built with Mexico's donations in the wake of the earthquake, draws visitors with its frescoes, painted by the famous **Mexican muralists** David Alfaro Siqueiros and Xavier Guerrero, and depicting famous figures from Latin American history.

ARRIVAL AND INFORMATION

By bus Most long-distance buses arrive at the Terminal María Teresa at Av O'Higgins 10 (📞42 227 2149), while the regional firm Linea Azul operates its own terminal at Constitución 1 (📞42 220 3800). Buses from local destinations, such as the Valle Las Trancas, arrive at the rural bus terminal at the market.

Destinations Concepción (8 daily; 1hr 30min); Santiago (every 50min; 6hr); Talca (8 daily; 3hr).

By train The station is at Av Brasil s/n (📞600 585 5000). Trains run a couple of times a day between Santiago and Chillán, stopping at several Central Valley towns.

Destinations Santiago (2 daily; 4hr 30min); Talca (2 daily; 2hr 20min).

Tourist information The helpful and well-stocked Sernatur office is located at 18 de Septiembre 455 (March–Nov Mon–Fri 8.30am–5pm; Dec–Feb Mon–Fri 8.30am–8pm, Sat 10am–8pm, Sun 10am–2pm; 📞42 222 3272).

ACCOMMODATION AND EATING

Arcoiris Roble 525. Excellent vegetarian restaurant specializing in delicious juices, crêpes and salads. Veggie burger CH$3500. Mon–Fri 8.30am–7pm, Sat 9am–5pm.

Mercado Municipal Bordered by Roble, Riquelme, Prat and 5 de Abril. Inexpensive, traditional Chilean dishes, such as *pastel de choclo* and *completos*, are served at the multitude of *cocinerías* here. *Longaniza y pure* (Chilean bangers and mash) CH$2500.

Sonia Itata 288 📞42 221 4879, 🌐hospedajesonia.cl. It doesn't get much cheaper than this *hospedaje*, with its friendly owners offering slightly tatty but clean rooms with basic shared facilities. Dorms CH$7000

NEVADOS DE CHILLÁN

The biggest attraction in the area is the hot-springs resort of **Nevados de Chillán** (📞42 243 4200, 🌐nevadosdechillan.com), which, with 29 runs, most of intermediate level, becomes a bona fide **ski resort** in the winter. There is also ample off-piste terrain, ideal for **snowboarders**, who are not allowed on some of the resort's runs. During the summer, in the valley overlooked by the looming **Volcán Chillán** (3212m), hiking, horseriding and downhill biking are all popular activities. The four open-air hot baths at the *Parque de Agua* in the resort are open to non-guests (CH$8000/person).

ARRIVAL AND DEPARTURE

By bus Regular Rem Bus (📞42 222 9377) services go to nearby Valle Las Trancas between 6.50am and 7.20pm from Chillán's rural bus terminal. For the 8km between Las Trancas and the resort you will need to hitchhike or pay for a private transfer (about CH$20,000).

ACCOMMODATION AND EATING

Staying in the resort itself is very expensive, so the majority of holidaymakers stay at the cheaper lodgings in Valle Las Trancas, which offers a scattering of *hospedajes*, campsites and restaurants, surrounded by immense mountains. Prices are considerably lower outside the ski season.

Chil'In Km72.5, Valle Las Trancas 📞42 224 7075, 🌐chil-in.com. Well-run hostel with its own pizzeria, attractive dorms and Skype-equipped free internet. Dorms CH$18,000, doubles CH$45,000

Ecobox Andino Camino Shangri-La Km 0.2, Valle Las Trancas 📞42 242 3134, 🌐ecoboxandino.cl. Four impeccably styled cabins made from recycled shipping containers are set within a magical *ñirres* forest. Plenty of natural light streams through the picture windows, which look onto snowcapped mountains; the pool and hot tub are pure Zen. CH$70,000

CONCEPCIÓN

CONCEPCIÓN is Chile's second-largest city, a bustling sprawl some 112km southwest of Chillán. It has little in the way of tourist sights, though its huge student

4

population ensures a high concentration of lively bars. Founded in 1550, the city was the administrative and military capital of colonial Chile. It suffered considerable structural damage in the huge 2010 earthquake.

The heart of Concepción's walkable city centre, lined with a mixture of elegant old buildings and modern concrete blocks, is the carefully landscaped **Plaza de la Independencia**. Partially pedestrianized Barros Arana, the main thoroughfare, has shops and places to eat, while at the western end lies the lively **Barrio Estación**, whose trendy bars and restaurants are centred on **Plaza España**. A four-block walk south from the Plaza de la Independencia along Aníbal Pinto brings you to the long green stretch of **Parque Ecuador**.

You can also catch a bus from Chacabuco street to Tomé and Dichato, small local coastal resorts with sandy beaches 30km or so north of the city.

Galería de la Historia

Three blocks west of the Parque Ecuador, at the corner of Lamas and Lincoyán, is the **Galería de la Historia** (Tues–Fri 10am–1.30pm & 3–6.30pm, Sat & Sun 10am–2pm & 3–7pm; free), which showcases the region's turbulent history through a series of interactive dioramas, with voice-overs dramatizing the scenes. There's also a large collection of ornate silver *mate* gourds.

Casa del Arte

Three blocks south of the Plaza de la Independencia, you can catch a *colectivo* or walk eastwards to the **Casa del Arte** (Tues–Fri 10am–6pm, Sat 10am–5pm, Sun 11am–2pm; free), just inside the grounds of the Universidad de Concepción. This museum displays a modest collection of Chilean art, but its highlight is the giant **mural**, *La Presencia de América Latina*, by Mexican muralist Jorge Gonzáles Camarena. Latin America – its conquest, its cultural and agricultural wealth – is captured in a series of densely packed images oriented

around the main figure of an *indígena* (a native woman). Interwoven throughout are colourful ribbons representing every Latin American flag and numerous national symbols.

By plane Aeropuerto Internacional Carriel Sur (☎41 273 2000) is 5km northwest of downtown; a door-to-door airport transfer service is available (CH$10,000; ☎09 8627 7607).

Destinations Santiago (10 daily, 1hr 5min) with LATAM (☎600 526 2000) and Sky Airline (☎41 221 8941).

By bus Most long-distance buses arrive at the Terminal de Buses Collao, Tegualda 860 (☎41 274 9000), from where numerous local buses run downtown.

Destinations Angol (6–8 daily; 2hr); Chillán (every 50min; 1hr 30min); Los Ángeles (hourly; 1hr 30min); Santiago (every 30min; 7hr); Talca (6–8 daily; 4hr).

Tourist information The Sernatur office is at Lincoyán 471 (Mon–Fri 10am–6pm; ☎41 262 4000, ⊚descubrebiobio. cl) and has plenty of information on the region surrounding Concepción. Conaf has an office at Barros Arano 215 (Mon–Thur 8.30am–5.30om, Fri 8.30am–4.30pm).

Apart Hotel Don Matías Colo Colo 155 ☎41 225 6846, ⊚aparthoteldonmatias.cl. An attractive B&B with friendly service, large rooms, some with private bathrooms, and a good breakfast. Doubles CH$55,000

San Sebastian Rengo 463 ☎41 295 6719, ⊚hotelsansebastian.cl. Somewhat flowery but perfectly adequate and clean budget hotel, with breakfast. Doubles CH$32,000

Hiper Lider on Prat/Freire is a massive supermarket with an excellent selection of fresh produce, as well as rare Thai and Chinese cooking ingredients.

Mercado Central Rengo, between Maipú and Freire. The informal *cocinerías* here are a good spot for inexpensive Chilean standards, such as *cazuela* (CH$3000).

Il Padrino Barros Arana, at Plaza España. Bustling Italian restaurant and bar, serving generous portions of pasta and pizza. Mains CH$6500–9000. Tues–Sat 6.30pm–late.

Banks and exchange There are numerous banks with ATMs on Barros Arana and O'Higgins; Afex, at Barros Arana 565, Local 57, changes foreign currencies.

Hospital Hospital Regional is on San Martín, at Av Roosevelt (☎41 272 2500).

Post office Colo Colo 417 (Mon–Fri 9am–7pm, Sat 9.30am–1pm).

The Lake District

Stretching south from the end of the Río Bío Bío to the large port of Puerto Montt, **THE LAKE DISTRICT** falls within the region of La Araucanía, one of the last parts of Chile to be colonized by Europeans thanks to fierce resistance by the Mapuche that lasted until 1880. While not as challenging as Patagonia, the area's multitude of snowcapped volcanoes, sparkling lakes and dense forest make it a vastly rewarding place to explore.

The Lake District's two biggest adventure sports hubs are **Pucón** and **Puerto Varas**, with numerous hiking, volcano-climbing, rafting, kayaking and horseriding options. From Pucón, you can explore the Mapuche culture of **Villarrica** and **Temuco**, and go trekking in Huerquehue, Conguillío and Villarrica national parks. Further south, the Spanish forts and excellent beer make lively university town **Valdivia** worth a visit, while the sparkling **Lago Llanquihue** by Puerto Varas beckons with its surrounding volcanoes and waterfalls. From the busy port of **Puerto Montt** it's easy to reach **Cochamó Valley** with its ancient trees and superb hiking, horseriding and rock climbing.

TEMUCO

The busy market city of **TEMUCO** was founded in 1881 towards the end of the "pacification" of the Mapuche, the indigenous people who still inhabit the area – Temuco remained a frontier town well into the early twentieth century, when poet Pablo Neruda grew up here.

WHAT TO SEE AND DO

A single compelling reason for visiting Temuco is the superb **Museo Regional de la Araucanía** (Mon–Fri 9.30am–5.30pm, Sat 11am–5pm, Sun 11am–2pm; CH$600; ⓦmuseoregionalaraucania.cl), which charts the history and migration of the Araucanían people. Beautifully presented exhibits include displays of asymmetric *metawe* pottery, funeral urns and sceptre-like sacred stones. Standout exhibits include an enormous seventeenth-century *wuampo* (hollow log canoe),

traditional weavings, ceremonial masks and drums and intricate Mapuche silverwork. The museum is a ten-minute walk along Avenida Alemana from the centre; most of the city's best restaurants are also located on Avenida Alemana.

If you love vintage trains, it's well worth taking a taxi to the **Museo Nacional Ferroviario Pablo Neruda** (Tues–Fri 9am–6pm, Sat & Sun 10am–6pm; CH$1000; taxi ride CH$1000; ⓦmuseoferroviariotemuco.cl), where you can climb aboard several of them and where retired locomotives stand proudly in the revamped roundhouse.

Museums aside, it's worth strolling through the lively and extensive **Feria Libre** (daily: summer 8.30am–6pm; winter 8.30am–5pm), a Mapuche fruit and veg **market** that stretches for several blocks of Aníbal Pinto between Lautaro/Barros Arana and Balmaceda.

ARRIVAL AND DEPARTURE

By plane Temuco's airport is 17km from the city, served by LATAM and Sky Airline flights to Santiago and Concepción, and connected to it by transfer minibuses (CH$6000). In peak season, there are direct transfers to Pucón.

By bus From Pucón or Villarica (you can visit on a day-trip), use Buses JAC as their bus terminal at Balmaceda 1005 is central and convenient. Most other long-distance buses use the Terminal Rodoviario, 5km north of the city centre on Vicente Pérez Rosales – taxis, buses and micros run every few minutes to the city centre. The Terminal Buses Rurales, near the market, at Aníbal Pinto 032, serves smaller destinations in the region.

Destinations Pucón (every 30min; 2hr); Puerto Varas (hourly; 5hr 15min); Santiago (every 30min; 9hr); Valdivia (every 30min; 3hr 15min); Villarrica (every 30min; 1hr 15min).

PARQUE NACIONAL CONGUILLÍO

A vast expanse of old lava fields, extending from the very active Llaima volcano, pristine lakes and araucaria forest, the **PARQUE NACIONAL CONGUILLÍO** (CH$6000; ⓦconaf.cl/parques/parque-nacional-conguillio) is all the more rewarding because of the relative remoteness and difficulty of access by pitted dirt road. The park offers a good

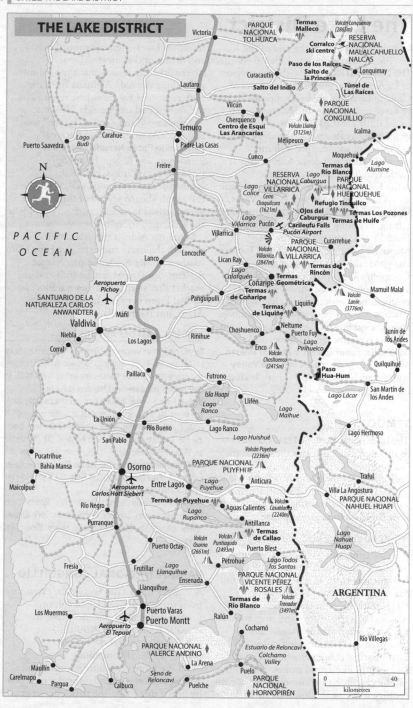

THE LAKE DISTRICT

Victoria

PARQUE
NACIONAL
TOLHUACA

Termas
Malleco

Volcán Lonquimay
(2865m)

RESERVA
NACIONAL
MALALCAHUELLO-
NALCAS

Corralco
ski centre

Paso de los Raíces
Salto de
la Princesa

Lonquimay

Curacautín

Túnel de
Las Raíces

Lautaro

Salto del Indio

Vilcún

Cherquenco

PARQUE
NACIONAL
CONGUILLIO

Centro de Esquí
Las Arancarías

Icalma

Temuco

Volcán Llaima
(3125m)

Padre Las Casas

Melipeuco

Moquehué

Lago
Alumine

Cunco

PACIFIC
OCEAN

Puerto Saavedra

Lago
Budi

Carahue

Freire

RESERVA
NACIONAL
VILLARRICA

Lago
Caburgua

Termas de
Río Blanco

PARQUE
NACIONAL
HUERQUEHUE

Lago
Colico

Refugio Tinquilco

Cerro
Chaquilcura
(1621m)

Ojos del
Caburgua

Termas Los Pozones

Lago
Villarrica

Pucón

Termas de Huife

Villarrica

Carileufu Falls
Pucón Airport

N

Lanco

Loncoche

Lican Ray

Lago
Calafquén

Volcán
Villarrica
(2847m)

PARQUE
NACIONAL
VILLARRICA

Curarrehue

Termas del
Rincón

Coñaripe

Termas
Geométricas

Aeropuerto
Pichoy

SANTUARIO DE LA
NATURALEZA CARLOS
ANWANDTER

Panguipulli

Termas
de Coñaripe

Volcán
Lanín
(3776m)

Mamuil Malal

Valdivia

Máfil

Termas
de Liquiñe

Liquiñe

Choshuenco

Neltume

Puerto Fuy

Junín de
los Andes

Niebla

Los Lagos

Riñihue

Enco

Volcán
Choshuenco
(2415m)

Lago
Pirihueico

Quilquihué

Corral

Paillaco

Futrono

Paso
Hua-Hum

San Martín de
los Andes

Isla Huapi

Llifén

Lago Lácar

Lago
Ranco

Lago
Maihue

La Unión

Río Bueno

Lago Ranco

Lago Hermoso

San Pablo

Lago Huishué

Pucatrihue

Bahía Mansa

Volcán Puyehue
(2236m)

PARQUE NACIONAL
PUYEHUE

Maicolpué

Osorno

Anticura

Traful

Entre Lagos

Lago
Puyehue

Villa La Angostura

Aeropuerto
Carlos Hott Siebert

Río Negro

Termas de Puyehue

Aguas Calientes

Volcán
Casablanca
(2240m)

PARQUE NACIONAL
NAHUEL HUAPI

Purranque

Lago
Rupanco

Antillanca

Volcán
Osorno
(2661m)

Volcán
Puntiagudo
(2493m)

Termas
de Callao

Lago
Nahuel
Huapi

Fresia

Puerto Octay

Puerto Blest

Petrohué

Lago Todos
los Santos

Frutillar

Lago
Llanquihue

PARQUE NACIONAL
VICENTE PÉREZ
ROSALES

Los Muermos

Ensenada

Llanquihue

ARGENTINA

Termas de
Río Blanco

Volcán
Tronador
(3491m)

Puerto Varas

Puerto Montt

Ralún

Aeropuerto
El Tepual

Cochamó

Río Villegas

PARQUE NACIONAL
ALERCE ANDINO

La Arena

Estuario de Reloncaví
Colchamo
Valley

Maullín

Seno de
Reloncaví

Puelo

Carelmapu

Pargua

Calbuco

Puelche

PARQUE
NACIONAL
HORNOPIRÉN

0   40
kilometres

4

selection of hikes for all abilities. For incredible views of the Sierra Nevada range through araucaria forest, take the 7km (2hr 30min) trail from Playa Linda, at the east end of Lago Conguillío, to the base of the Sierra Nevada. The challenging *Travesía Río Blanco* (5km; 5hr), which crosses a small glacier before continuing into the Sierra Nevada proper, is recommended only for very experienced trekkers only. From the western shores of Laguna Verde, the 11km (5hr) *Sendero Pastos Blancos* runs to the Laguna Captrén, traversing spectacular scenery and rewarding you with panoramic views of Sierra Nevada, Lago Conguillío and the Truful-Truful valley.

ARRIVAL AND DEPARTURE

By car It's possible to traverse the park by regular car (best from north to south), though you'll need a high-clearance vehicle outside the Dec–March season to cope with the snow.

By bus Nar Bus (❶ 45 240 7778, ⓦ narbus.cl) runs from Temuco to Melipeuco (Mon–Sat 8 daily, Sun 3 daily; 1hr 45min) – the southern gateway to the park, 91km east of Temuco and 30km from the park entrance. From here, you'll have to hitch or take a taxi. There are several daily Buses Erbuc (❶ 45 223 3958, ⓦ erbuc.cl) services from Temuco to Curacautín, the northern gateway to the park, 75km from Temuco and 30km from the administration (5 daily; 2hr). From Curacautín, Buses Curacautín Express (❶ 45 225 8125) run to the northern border of Parque Nacional Conguillío (Mon–Fri, daily; 1hr), from where it's a 12km hike to the park entrance.

INFORMATION

Tourist information The Conaf-run Centro de Información Ambiental (Oct–March daily 9am–1pm & 3–6.30pm; ❶ 65 297 2336) by Lago Conguillío has maps of the park.

ACCOMMODATION

La Baita 2.5km south of Laguna Verde, on the edge of a dense wood ❶ 45 258 1073, ⓦ labaitaconguillio. cl. Run by former singer Isabel, this complex consists of an attractive lodge (with hot tub) and six fully equipped, four- to six-person cabañas. Doubles C̲H̲$̲9̲0̲,̲0̲0̲0̲, cabañas C̲H̲$̲7̲5̲,̲0̲0̲0̲

Camping ❶ 45 229 8100. There are five campsites in all: two by the ranger stations inside the park, one along the south shore of Lago Conguillío and two along the El Contrabandista trail in the eastern section of the park, all run by concessionaires. Expect fire pits, toilets and cold-water showers. Nov–April. Camping/person C̲H̲$̲6̲0̲0̲0̲

VILLARRICA

Some 87km southeast of Temuco on the western shores of tranquil Lago Villarrica, the colonial town of **VILLARRICA** was destroyed several times by volcanic eruptions and abandoned after being captured by the Mapuche in 1603. What you see today has been built since the 1880s, when Swiss, German and Austrian immigrants resettled the area.

WHAT TO SEE AND DO

In the centre, the **Museo Histórico Municipal** (Mon–Fri 9am–1pm & 2.30–6.30pm; free), at Valdivia 1050, offers a crash course in Mapuche culture. You can acquaint yourself with *ñillawaka* (food storage bags), musical instruments such as the *trutruca*, silver jewellery and traditional weaving: you can tell a Mapuche woman's marital and social status just by looking at her embroidered belt. Next door to the museum on Valdivia, at Zegers, the stalls of the **Centro Cultural Mapuche** (daily 9am–5pm) sell some decent *raulí* woodcarvings and woollen goods, as well as Mapuche dishes, near a *ruka* – a traditional Mapuche dwelling with walls and roof tightly woven from reeds.

ARRIVAL AND INFORMATION

By bus Tur Bus at Muñoz 657 and Pullman (opposite) serve all major central Chile destinations on the way to Santiago. Buses JAC at Bilbao 610 serve all major Lake District destinations, while Igi Llaima at Valdivia 615 crosses the border to San Martín de Los Andes.

Destinations Pucón (every 20min; 45min); Puerto Montt (hourly; 5hr); Santiago (4 daily; 10hr); San Martín de Los Andes (Mon–Sat daily at 9am, Sun at 11.30am; 4hr 30min); Temuco (every 30min; 1hr 30min); Valdivia (7 daily; 2hr 30min).

Tourist information The helpful tourist office, at Pedro de Valdivia 1070 (Mon–Fri 8.30am–1pm & 2.30–6pm; Sat & Sun 9am–1pm & 3.30–5.30pm; ❶ 45 220 6619, ⓦ visitvillarrica.cl), offers free maps of the town.

ACCOMMODATION, EATING AND DRINKING

Hostal Don Juan Körner 770 ❶ 45 241 1833, ⓦ hostaldonjuan.cl. Boasting great views of Volcán Villarrica, this cosy hotel has an assortment of rooms and cabañas, plus table tennis and table football for the

4

MUSHER FOR A DAY

Based near Villarrica, **Aurora Austral Patagonia Husky** (☎09 8901 4518, ⦿novena-region. com), is home to a mix of Siberian and Alaskan huskies, and Konrad leads **multi-day husky sledding expeditions** that allow you to drive your own sled. You can choose either a day-trip in the vicinity of Volcán Villarrica (CH$80,000) or one of the multi-day expeditions – either to the Termas Geométricas hot springs or across the mountains into Argentina.

The sledding season runs from May to October, September being an excellent time to visit. Summer visitors (Dec–March) can test the half-tricycle, half-chariot contraptions (CH$33,000 per person, two-person minimum). They also rent out three beautiful two- to six-person cottages with skylights (CH$40,000–60,000) on their peaceful property, complete with wandering dogs and alpaca. Pickup from Villarrica arranged.

guests. Doubles (private bath) CH$45,000, shared bath CH$32,000

Fuego Patagón Montt 40 ☎45 241 2207, ⦿fuegopatagon.cl. From the lovely patio with faux-rustic decor to the expertly seared cuts of meat, this steakhouse means business. Try the signature dish of bacon-wrapped veal with quinoa and wild mushrooms. Mains from CH$9500. Daily 12.30–3.30pm & 7.30–11pm.

La Torre Suiza Bilbao 969 ☎45 241 1213. The wood-shingled interior of this legendary, biker-friendly hostel hides snug twins, doubles and quads with flowery bedspreads, a lounge where lingering is encouraged and a good ratio of guests per shared bathroom. Bikes available for rent. Dorms CH$15,000, doubles CH$30,000

Travellers Letelier 753. This aptly named watering hole attracts global wanderers with its diverse culinary range that spans India, China, Thailand and Mexico. There are regional craft beers, and the cocktails are amongst the best in the Lake District. Mains from CH$7500. Mon–Sat 9am–4am.

PUCÓN

On a clear day, you will spy the mesmerizing snowy cone of the **Volcán Villarrica** long before the bus pulls into **PUCÓN**, 25km east of Villarrica. This small lakeside resort town, awash with the smells of wood smoke and grilled meat, has firmly established itself as a top Chilean and backpacker destination in the last decade. Each November to April season brings scores of adventure sports fanatics looking to climb the volcano, brave the **rapids** on the Río Trancura and Río Liucura or explore the nearby Parque Nacional Huerquehue. A day outdoors is usually followed by eating, drinking and partying in the town's restaurants and bars, or by a soak in the nearby **thermal springs**.

ARRIVAL AND DEPARTURE

By bus The three main long-distance carriers have separate terminals: Buses JAC (and Condor), Palguín 505 (☎45 299 0880, ⦿jac.cl), serves Villarrica, Temuco, Valdivia and Puerto Montt; Pullman Bus, Palguín 555(☎45 244 3331, ⦿pullman.cl), and Tur Bus, O'Higgins 910 (☎45 244 3328, ⦿turbus.cl), are best for journeys to Santiago; Igi Llaima (Palguín 595, ⦿igillaima.cl) runs frequent services across the border to Junín de los Andes and San Martín de los Andes; Buses Caburgua (Uruguay 540, at Palguín) serves Parque Nacional Huerquehue (8.30am, 1pm & 4pm) and the Ojos de Caburgua.

Destinations Puerto Montt (hourly; 6hr); Puerto Varas (hourly; 5hr 45min); San Martín de los Andes (Mon–Sat daily at 9.20am; 5hr); Santiago (2–3 nightly; 10hr); Temuco (every 30min; 2hr); Valdivia (7 daily; 3hr 15min); Villarrica (every 30min; 45min).

INFORMATION

Tourist office O'Higgins, at Palguín (daily: March–Nov 8.30am–5pm; Dec–Feb 8.30am–10pm; ☎45 229 3002).

Travelaid Ansorena 425, Local 4 (Mon–Sat 10am–1.30pm & 3.30–7pm; ☎45 244 4040, ⦿travelaid. cl. Knowledgeable Swiss-run travel agency that sells guidebooks and detailed maps of different Chilean regions.

Bike rental Sierra Nevada at O'Higgins 524a ☎45 244 4210; mountain bikes CH$14,000/full day, CH$8000/5hr.

ACCOMMODATION

★ **Chili Kiwi Hostel** O'Higgins 20 ☎45 244 9540, ⦿chilikiwihostel.wixsite.com; map p.433. Right on the lakefront, and run by affable Kiwi James, this is Pucón's best backpacker hostel. Guests can bed down in cosy dorms, the "Harry Potter" room, tree house rooms, converted vans or "Hobbity Hollow" private cabins in the garden. The on-site bar serves excellent craft beer and gourmet dinners, the hostel employs own mountain guides for the volcano trek and there's a daily talk on what backpackers can do around Pucón that's worth their time and money. Dorms CH$12,000, doubles CH$42,000

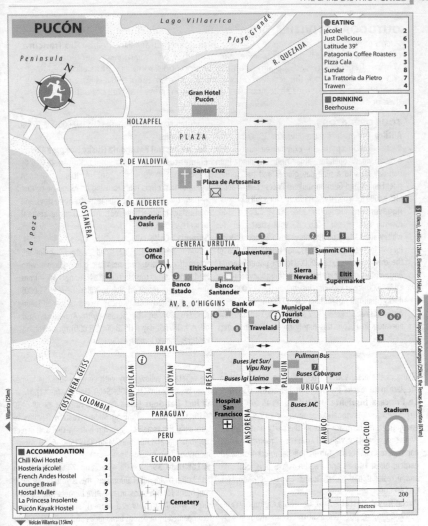

PUCÓN

Lago Villarrica

Playa Grande

R. QUEZADA

Peninsula

N

EATING
¡école!	2
Just Delicious	6
Latitude 39°	1
Patagonia Coffee Roasters	5
Pizza Cala	3
Sundar	8
La Trattoria da Pietro	7
Trawen	4

DRINKING
Beerhouse	1

Gran Hotel Pucón

HOLZAPFEL

PLAZA

P. DE VALDIVIA

Santa Cruz
Plaza de Artesanias

G. DE ALDERETE

COSTANERA

Lavandería Oasis

La Poza

Conaf Office

GENERAL URRUTIA

Aguaventura

Summit Chile

Eltit Supermarket

Sierra Nevada

Eltit Supermarket

Banco Estado

Banco Santander

AV. B. O'HIGGINS

Bank of Chile

Municipal Tourist Office

Travelaid

BRASIL

COSTANERA GEISS

CAUPOLICAN

LINCOYAN

FRESIA

Buses Jet Sur/ Vipu Ray

Buses Igi Llaima

PALGUIN

Pullman Bus

Buses Caburgua

URUGUAY

COLOMBIA

PARAGUAY

Hospital San Francisco

ANSORENA

Buses JAC

ARAUCO

COLO-COLO

Stadium

PERU

ECUADOR

Villarica (25km)

ACCOMMODATION
Chili Kiwi Hostel	4
Hostería ¡école!	2
French Andes Hostel	1
Lounge Brasil	6
Hostal Muller	7
La Princesa Insolente	3
Pucón Kayak Hostel	5

Cemetery

0		200
		metres

▼ Volcán Villarrica (15km)

S3 (10km), Antilco (12km), Elementos (16km) ▲ Tur Bus, Airport Lago Caburgua (25km), the Termas & Argentina (87km) ▲

4

Hostería ¡école! Urrutia 592 ☎ 45 244 1675, ⓦ ecole.cl; map p.433. Apart from some compact singles and doubles in the main building, there are new en suites in the tranquil garden out back. Perks include one of the town's best restaurants, info on outdoor activities and a wonderfully central location. **CH$45,000**

★ **French Andes Hostel** Pasaje Tinquilco 3 ☎ 45 244 3324, ⓦ french-andes.com; map p.433. Catering both to backpackers and budget travellers looking for a bit more privacy, this top-notch hostel offers Japanese-inspired capsule dorms and rooms, as well as regular doubles. Perks include rain showers, excellent kitchen facilities and a large garden for barbecues. Owner Vincent also rents compact

camper vans – ideal for touring the region on a budget. Dorms **CH$10,000**, doubles **CH$20,000**

Lounge Brasil Colo-Colo 281 ☎ 45 244 4035, ⓦ cafeloungebrasil.com; map p.433. Not only is there an adorable wood-fire-heated café on the premises, but prices at this intimate, super-central guesthouse, run by a friendly Brazilian proprietress, are an absolute steal for the six snug singles and doubles (all en suite). The on-site vegetarian café serves local craft beers. **CH$40,000**

Hostal Muller Arauco 560 ☎ 45 244 1735, ⓦ hostalmuller.cl; map p.433. In this homely, family-run guesthouse there are just six beautiful, wood-panelled rooms with sumptuous beds. The owners can advise on

OUTDOOR ACTIVITIES

Pucón operators offer a vast range of adventure tours and activities; the nearby **Río Trancura** offers a popular Class III run on the lower part of the river, with the more challenging Class VI upper Trancura run made up almost entirely of drop pools; some operators allow you to combine the two. Since the activities on offer involve an element of risk, it is important to use a reliable operator like those listed below. We don't recommend Trancura or Politur due to their poor safety records.

TOUR OPERATORS

Antilco Camino a Curarrehue, Km 15 ☏ 09 9713 9758, ⊛ antilco.com. An experienced and highly recommended operator organizing anything from half-day trips to a nine-day glacier and hot springs ride. English and German spoken. Prices start at about CH$30,000 for a half day, CH$50,000 for a full day.

Aguaventura Palguín 336 ☏ 45 244 4246, ⊛ aguaventura.com. This is your best bet for whitewater rafting on the nearby Río Trancura. Prices for two to three hours' rafting range from CH$20,000 for the lower Trancura to CH$28,000 for the upper Trancura. Aguaventura also offers hydrospeeding (bodyboarding; CH$30,000), river kayaking instruction (CH$25,000) and ducky (mini-rafting) outings (CH$30,000).

Air Skydive 336 ☏ 09 7477 3763. Of the two skydiving operators in Pucón, this highly professional one gets consistently stellar feedback. CH$180,000 for a 1hr tandem jump.

Aurora Austral Patagonia Husky (see page 432).

Elementos Camino a Caburgua, Km 16 ☏ 45 244 1750, ⊛ elementos-chile.com. A friendly German operator that offers tours focusing on Mapuche culture – from cooking with the Mapuche to homestays and multi-day, multi-activity options. Lafkenche cultural tour CH$95,500.

Summit Chile Urrutia 585 ☏ 45 244 3259, ⊛ summitchile.org. Headed by bilingual, internationally qualified mountain guide Claudio, who leads small group treks in Villarrica National Park – from the standard ascent of Volcán Villarrica (CH$55,000) to the more technical two-day ascent of Volcán Lanín (CH$220,000) on the border with Argentina. Also offers half-/full-day (CH$28,000/38,000) rock climbing ventures and ski touring excursions.

hiking in the area, you can relax by the volcanic stone fireplace in the lounge and there's kitchen access. US$70

La Princesa Insolente Urrutia 660 ☏ 45 244 1492, ⊛ princesainsolentehostel.cl; map p.433. Run by energetic staff, this place ticks all the party hostel boxes: two cosy, fireplace-warmed common rooms, on-site bar and restaurant, hot tub in the hammock-festooned garden, guest kitchen and free breakfast, plus local info and occasional barbecues. Dorms CH$10,000, doubles CH$30,000

Pucón Kayak Hostel Km 10, Camino a Caburgua ☏ 09 7545 9510, ⊛ puconkayakhostel.com; map p.433. Ideally located on the bank of Río Trancura, this place is geared towards kayak, ducky and SUP enthusiasts. Choose between a room in the main house, gypsy wagons, geodome glamping or basic bunkhouses. Equipment available for rent, and meals in the *quincho* (thatched barbecue area) and movie dome encourage socializing. Camping/person US$12, dorms US$20, doubles/gypsy wagon US$32, domes US$60

EATING

¡école! Urrutia 592 ☏ 45 244 1675; map p.433. Tasty, inexpensive and imaginative vegetarian dishes served either in the dining room or vine-covered courtyard. The vegetable lasagne has been superb for many years, as has the vegetable yellow curry with chutney and the home-made bread. Mains CH$4300–5400. Daily 8am–11pm.

★ **Just Delicious** Colo-Colo, at O'Higgins ☏ 09 7430 0016; map p.433. Bringing Middle Eastern flavours to Araucania, this Israeli-Chilean-run hole-in-the-wall serves superb falafel and hummus. Mains CH$1500–5000. Mon–Sat noon–4pm & 6.30–9pm.

★ **Latitude 39°** Urrutia 436 ☏ 09 7430 0016; map p.433. Run by friendly Californians, this is your home away from home for fish tacos, imaginative burgers (the Buddha Burger with Asian slaw is a winner), and other Tex-Mex, accompanied by generous lemonades and regional Chilean beers. Mains from CH$5500. Mon–Sat noon–11pm.

Patagonia Coffee Roasters Colo-Colo, at O'Higgins ☏ 09 9644 4831; map p.433. The American owner of the best coffee shop in Pucón roasts his own beans and focuses on brews from all over the world that no other local café serves. Daily 10am–7.30pm, Sat 10am–4pm.

Pizza Cala Lincoyán 361 ☏ 45 246 3024, ⊛ pizzacala.cl; map p.433. Pucón's best pizzeria serves excellent thin-crust pizza with some exotic and welcome toppings, baked in a clay oven in front of you. Mains CH$6500–7800. Daily 12.30pm–midnight.

Sundar Ansorena 438 ☏ 09 9281 0909; map p.433. Inside a little shopping centre, this no-nonsense place serves vast plates of wholesome vegetarian and vegan

EATING THE MAPUCHE WAY

An easy bus ride from Pucón (at least hourly; 45min), the highlight of the Mapuche town of Curarrehue is a meal at *Cocina Mapuche Mapu Lyagl*, Camino internacional s/n (☏ 09 8788 7188), with celebrated Mapuche chef Anita Epulef at the helm. You may taste roasted *piñónes* (fruit of the araucaria tree), roasted cornbread, quinoa creations and more. Dec–Feb daily noon–3pm (call ahead to confirm).

dishes, along with fresh fruit juices. Mains CH$5000. Mon–Fri noon–5pm.

La Trattoria da Pietro O'Higgins, at Colo-Colo ☏ 45 244 9024; map p.433. Handmade saffron-infused spaghetti, filled paninis, proper tiramisu and other Italian dishes are served with aplomb at this welcoming, authentically Italian joint. Mains from CH$8500. Tues–Sat 11am–10pm, Sun 11am–5.30pm.

★ **Trawen** O'Higgins 311 ☏ 45 244 2024, ⓦ trawen.cl; map p.433. This longstanding, offbeat restaurant serves imaginative, internationally inspired dishes such as goat's cheese gnocchi, bacon-wrapped venison with polenta and quinotto with trout. Ample fresh fruit juices too. Mains CH$5900–11,800. Daily 8am–11.30pm.

DRINKING

Beerhouse Urrutia 324; map p.433. A classic rock soundtrack accompanies nightly sessions at this craft beer bar with a covered outdoor terrace. Regional brews are its stars, from Pucón's very own Alasse to Villarrica's Crater and Valdivia's Cuello Negro, with a supporting cast of beer cocktails and burgers. Daily 5.30pm–2am.

VILLARRICA

The **Volcán Villarrica** (2847m) is the crown jewel of the **PARQUE NACIONAL**

VILLARRICA (daily 8.30am–6pm) and undoubtedly the biggest attraction from Pucón; in the winter it becomes a ski and snowboard destination. To do the climb, unless you have mountaineering experience, you should go with a guide (see page 434); they will provide all the necessary equipment and transportation. It's a fairly challenging four- to five-hour ascent (plus 3hr down), starting at the chairlift at the base of the volcano (at the end of the road), with much of the walking done on snow. If the chairlift (CH$10,000) is running, it cuts an hour off the climb. At the top, by the lip of the smoking crater, you'll be rewarded with unparalleled views across the Lake District, with lakes and distant volcanoes stretching out before you. The sulphuric fumes mean you cannot linger long over the spectacle though. Check the weather forecast before embarking on the climb, as some tour companies take groups out even in cloudy weather, only to turn back halfway.

Volcano ascent aside, the backcountry around the volcano makes for some superb multi-day hiking in January and February; register with the rangers and get a proper map of the park before setting off.

PARQUE NACIONAL HUERQUEHUE

The compact but dazzling 125-square-kilometre **PARQUE NACIONAL HUERQUEHUE** (daily 8.30am–8pm high season; CH$6000) comprises densely forested **precordillera** (foothills), highland araucaria groves, several waterfalls and many entrancing **lakes**, making it a perfect destination for day-hikes.

HOT SPRINGS IN THE LAKE DISTRICT

Most tour companies in Pucón run daily trips to these hot springs.

Termas Geométricas 16km northeast of Coñaripe towards Villarrica National Park ☏ 09 7477 1708, ⓦ termasgeometricas.cl. With a Japanese feel to the beautiful design, there are seventeen thermal pools here, connected by winding boardwalks around a ravine overflowing with greenery, as well as three cold plunge pools, two waterfalls and an excellent café. CH$20,000–28,000. Jan to late March 10am–11pm; shorter hours rest of year.

Termas Los Pozones Camino Km 34, Pucón-Huife ☏ 45 244 3059. The most rustic and natural of the hot springs in the area, these are simple, shallow pools dug out beside the river and dammed up with stones, with basic wooden changing huts above them. These *termas* (CH$9000) are extremely popular with backpackers, and there are evening tours from Pucón. Daily 11am–3am.

The prettiest of the lakes – Chico, Toro and Verde – are accessed via the popular **Sendero Los Lagos** trail, which climbs steeply to a height of 1300m from the park office at Lago Tinquilco, past two waterfalls (14km return) – expect sensational views back towards the **Volcán Villarrica** on a clear day. You can extend the loop by taking in the tiny Lago de los Patos and Lago Huerquehue (2hr extra) before re-joining the main path, or you can continue along the **Sendero Los Huerquenes** to Termas de San Sebastián and the stunning Renahue viewpoint overlooking the lakes below. It's possible to hike to the Termas in one day (23km; 8–9hr), since much of the Sendero Los Huerquenes is downhill (but only in Jan and Feb, when there's little snow on the trail), and stay at the excellent campsite here.

ARRIVAL AND INFORMATION

By bus Buses Caburgua (☎09 9641 5761) runs services from Pucón to the Conaf guardería at the park entrance during peak season (3–4 daily, 8.30am–7.30pm, last bus (Jan & Feb only) returning at 7.30pm; 45min). At the Conaf guardería at the Lago Tinquilco entrance, you'll find a trail map.

ACCOMMODATION

There's a basic, Conaf-run campsite at the entrance to the park.

Cabañas San Sebastián Termas San Sebastián ☎09 9231 8329, ⓦtermassansebastian.cl. Serene campsite and cabañas at the end of the Sendero Los Huerquenes; the rustic wood cabañas can accommodate up to seven people, and their bathrooms are fed by the hot springs (day use CH$7000). Cabañas CH$40,000, camping/person CH$10,000

Refugio Tinquilco Lago Tinquilco ☎09 9539 2728, ⓦtinquilco.cl. Excellent, airy wooden guesthouse in a beautiful stream-side location a 2km hike from the park entrance, with home-cooked meals, sauna, book exchange and an owner you'd want to split a bottle of wine with. Dorms CH$16,000, doubles CH$34,900

VALDIVIA

From 1848 onwards, thousands of German immigrants passed through the port of **VALDIVIA**, initiating an industrial boom that lasted well into the twentieth century. Founded in 1552 by Pedro de Valdivia, it is one of Chile's oldest cities, though it was razed by the Mapuche in the sixteenth century and largely destroyed by the devastating earthquake of 1960. Today Valdivia is an energetic university city that lies at the confluence of the Río Valdivia and Río Calle Calle.

Most of the action centres on the **waterfront**; you'll smell the fishy **Mercado Fluvial** and hear the noise before you reach it. The highlight here is the resident colony of enormous **sea lions**, which spend much of their day lounging behind the market. The waterfront is also a departure point for numerous boats offering entertaining half-day cruises up the river to the fort ruins for CH$25,000–40,000, though commentary is Spanish only.

WHAT TO SEE AND DO

Just on the other side of the Río Valdivia from the fish market, in a tranquil section of Isla Teja, the **Museo Histórico y Antropológico** (Jan & Feb daily 10am–8pm; March–Dec Tues–Sun 10am–1pm & 2–6pm; CH$1500, CH$2500 with Philippi museum; ⌨museosaustral.cl) offers a rare glimpse of nineteenth-century Chile. Built in 1861 as the Casa Anwandter for one of the city's wealthiest men (German-born Don Carl Anwandter established the brewing industry here in the 1850s), its period rooms contain an odd assortment of historic curios, while upstairs galleries are filled with Mapuche artefacts and prehistoric finds (some English labelling). Nearby is the **Museo R. A. Philippi de la Exploración** (same hours and admission) in Casa Schüller (dating from 1914), a tribute to German-born naturalist Rudolph Philippi, who worked here in the 1850s.

Las Fuertes (forts)

In 1645 the Spanish started building elaborate fortifications at **Corral**, **Niebla** and **Isla Mancera**, where the Río Valdivia and Río Tornagaleones meet the Pacific Ocean, to protect Valdivia from opportunistic attacks by British, French and Dutch privateers. A trip to the ruins is a fun day out; take the Niebla-bound bus #20 from Carampangue, at O'Higgins (25min; CH$700, frequent), and get off at the ferry pier 18km from the city. From here boats (Mon–Sat 5 daily, Sun 4 daily; CH$300) ply their way to Isla Mancera and the ruins of the **Castillo San Pedro de Alcántara** (Jan & Feb daily 10am–8pm; March–Dec Tues–Sun 10am–1pm & 2–6pm; CH$700).

You can also take a ferry (daily 9am–5.40pm; 30min; CH$650) across the Bahía de Corral to the **Castillo San Sebastián de la Cruz** (Nov–March daily 8.30am–7pm; April–Oct Tues–Sun 10am–5.30pm; CH$1700), reinforced in the 1760s.

To get an overview of the whole system visit **Fuerte Niebla**, 2km beyond the ferry pier, built between 1647 and 1672 and now the **Museo de Sitio Castillo de Niebla** (April–Oct Tues–Sun 10am–5.30pm; Nov–March Tues–Sun 10am–7pm; CH$1200; ⌨museodeniebla.cl). Only the battlements and a battery of rusty cannons remain, but the bay views are magnificent.

ARRIVAL AND INFORMATION

By plane Aeropuerto Pichoy (⌨aeropuertovaldivia.com) lies 32km northeast of the city; Transfer Aeropuerto Valdivia (☎63 222 5533 (⌨transfervaldivia.cl; CH$5000/person) runs a door-to-door minibus service; taxis cost around CH$25,000. Sky Airline and LATAM serve Santiago (2 daily; 1hr 30min).

By bus The Terminal de Buses (☎63 222 0498, ⌨terminalvaldivia.cl) is located at Anfión Muñoz 360, by Río Calle Calle.

Destinations Ancud (4 daily; 5hr); Bariloche, Argentina (1 daily at 8.15am; 8hr); Castro (4 daily; 7hr); Osorno (every 30min; 1hr 30min); Pucón (6 daily; 3hr 15min); Puerto Montt (every 30min; 3hr 45min); Puerto Varas (every 30min; 3hr); Santiago (every hour; 11hr); San Martín de Los Andes, Argentina (3 weekly on Wed, Fri & Sun at 7.30am; 7hr 30min).

Tourist information The helpful Sernatur office is at Arturo Prat s/n (on the Costanera, just north of the fish market; daily 9am–9pm; ☎63 223 9060, ⌨turismolosrios. cl).

ACCOMMODATION

★ **Hostal Aires Buenos** García Reyes 550 ☎63 222 2202, ⌨airesbuenos.cl; map p.436. Central, American-owned hostel with serious eco credentials. Colourful, secure

4

dorms and snug private rooms popular with international backpackers, the communal spaces include a guest kitchen (they'll even let you use herbs from their garden) and breakfast includes proper coffee and good bread. Dorms CH$12,000, doubles CH$32,000

Hostel Bosque Nativo Fresia 290 (off Janequeo) ☎63 243 3782, ⓦhostelnativo.cl; map p.436. Beautifully restored 1920s house with cosy wood-panelled rooms, kitchen, lounge and rooftop terrace; there's only one dorm, the rest are private rooms. Profits go towards the preservation of native Chilean forest. The staff couldn't be lovelier but don't speak English; continental breakfast included. Dorms CH$10,000, doubles CH$22,000

Kapai Hostel Prat 737 ☎09 9207 2616; map p.436. The rooftop terrace overlooking the river is one of the boons at this new hostel, just a few minutes' walk from the bus terminal. The capsule-style dorms offer more privacy (but less fresh air), and it's worth going for the four-bed dorm rather than the twelve-bedder. Bilingual owner Felipe is extremely helpful and the spacious kitchen and common area encourage lingering. Dorms US$23, doubles US$60

Hostal Totem Carlos Anwandter 425 ☎63 229 2849, ⓦturismototem.cl; map p.436. Quiet, welcoming guesthouse with squeaky wooden floors and spacious, en-suite doubles, triples and quads (some lacking in natural light) with cable TV. Breakfast includes home-made preserves and the helpful management speaks English and French. CH$33,000

EATING

The inexpensive eateries at the Mercado Municipal (on Prat) serve decent fish and seafood dishes.

★ **Café La Última Frontera** Pérez Rosales 787 ☎63 223 5264; map p.436. Everything about this café screams "bohemian", from the reggae on the stereo, mismatched colour scheme and photos of cats and tattoos gracing the walls to the grungy staff who serve you real coffee, sandwiches named after Etta James and Chairman Mao, and a selection of local microbrews. Mon–Sat 9am–2am.

Sombun Andwandter 288 ☎09 7659 2055; map p.436. A first in the Lake District, this low-key restaurant serves genuine Thai dishes such as *tom yum* (fragrant, spicy soup), *phad prik* (dry curry with meat), and *phad katit* (pork cooked in spiced coconut milk). The spice factor is toned down for local tastes, but genuine heat can be requested. Mains CH$3500–5000. Daily 11am–midnight.

Tilo Restobar Yungay 745 ☎63 243 4594; map p.436. The large riverside terrace here is ideal for a lazy afternoon beer or one of an extensive range of cocktails, while the bistro section serves terrific *ceviche*, palatable pizza and the likes of lamb and sage ravioli. Mains CH$7500–12,500. Mon–Fri 12.30–3pm & 6pm–midnight, Sat 7pm–midnight.

DRINKING

Cervecería Kunstmann 950 Ruta T350 ☎63 229 2969, ⓦcerveza-kunstmann.cl; map p.436. German-style beerhall serving monster portions of smoked meat, sauerkraut and potatoes to accompany its ten celebrated beers (from CH$2700). To get here, take bus #20 bound for Niebla. Daily noon–midnight.

★ **Growler** Saelzer 1 ☎63 222 9545 ⓦelgrowler.cl; map p.436. Not only is this Valdivia's premier craft beer brewery, it's also *the* nighttime gathering spot for locals and travellers alike. The Oregonian owner also provides delectable fish tacos, carpaccios and chunky sandwiches. Mains CH$6500–9000. Mon–Thurs noon–midnight, Fri & Sat noon–2am, Sun noon–11pm.

LAGO LLANQUIHUE

Some 170km south of Valdivia lies dazzling **LAGO LLANQUIHUE**, the second-largest lake in Chile, its shimmering blue waters framed by thick forest and the peaks of snow-tipped volcanoes. Travellers come for the ample natural attractions around the resort town of **Puerto Varas**, and to experience the laidback lifestyle of lakeside villages such as **Puerto Octay**, where the *Hostal Zapato Amarillo* (☎64 210 787, ⓦzapatoamarillo.cl; dorms CH$14,000, doubles CH$36,000) provides a welcoming place to stay amid stunning scenery with excursions around the area. Another great place to base yourself is *Quila Hostal* (Ruta 225, Km 37; 3km up the dirt road that branches off Ruta 225; ☎09 6760 7039, ⓦquilahostal.com; doubles CH$35,000). This rambling wooden house with large, spartan twins and doubles is run by an outdoor enthusiast who can arrange for you to hike up the surrounding volcanoes.

PUERTO VARAS

Dominating the southwestern corner of the lake, attractive **PUERTO VARAS** is a popular resort town and backpacker haunt, with unparalleled sunset views of the two nearby volcanoes, Osorno and Calbuco. Puerto Varas also makes an excellent base for volcano climbing, whitewater rafting, kayaking and cycling.

ARRIVAL AND INFORMATION

By plane Transfers to Puerto Montt airport cost CH$20,000.

PUERTO VARAS

● EATING

Café El Barista	1
La Costumbrista	3
Donde El Gordito	2
La Gringa	4

■ DRINKING

Bravo Cabrera	1

■ ACCOMMODATION

Casa Azul	5
Casa Margouya	2
Compass del Sur	1
Hospedaje Ellenhaus	3
Hostal Melmac	4

Puma Verde

Disused Train Station

Lago Llanquihue

Casa de Turista

Buses to Petrohué
Centro Médico
Lavandería Alba

Banco Santander

Casino

Buses to Petrohué
Centro Médico
Lavandería Alba

Buses to Frutillar & Llanquihue
LATAM

Buses to Puerto Octay
Banco Santander

Banco de Chile

Mercado

Buses to Puerto Montt

Supermarket Santa Isabel

Supermarket Express Líder

Iglesia del Sagrado Corazón de Jesús

Tur Bus/Tas Choapa/ Buses JAC terminal

0   300
metres

Panamericana, Cruz del Sur Bus Terminal, Osorno, Temuco (north) & Puerto Montt (south)

By bus Cruz del Sur (serving Chiloé and the Lake District up to Santiago) shares a bus terminal with Bus Norte (with services to Bariloche, Argentina) at San Francisco 1317. Tur Bus, Intersur, JAC, Tas Choapa, Andersmar and Cóndor Bus are all scattered about the outskirts of town.

Destinations Ancud (8 daily; 2hr 30min); Castro (8 daily; 4hr 30min); Puerto Montt (every 15min; 35min); Santiago (6 daily; 18hr); Valdivia (2–3 daily; 3hr).

By minibus Those for Ensenada (1hr), Frutillar (40min), Petrohué and the Saltos de Petrohué (45min) leave from San Bernardo 240, just north of Walker Martínez; frequent minibuses to Puerto Montt head up San Francisco.

Tourist information The Casa del Turista is at the foot of a pier (Muelle Piedraplan) on Av Costanera (Mon–Fri 9.30am–6.30pm, Sat & Sun 10am–6.30pm; ☎65 223 7956, ⓦpuertovaras.org).

ACCOMMODATION

Casa Azul Manzanal 66 at Rosario ☎65 223 2904, ⓦcasaazul.net; map p.439. Slightly uphill from the centre, this blue house has been hosting international travellers for years. The buffet breakfast (CH$3500) includes home-made muesli, the garden with the bonzai

trees is a lovely spot for relaxation and the owners organize tours to Parque Alerces, Volcán Osorno and the Saltos de Petrohué. Dorms CH$10,000, doubles CH$29,000

Casa Margouya Santa Rosa 318 ☎65 223 7640, ⓦmargouya.com; map p.439. This ever-popular hostel has a great downtown location, a smattering of dorms and a snug double branching off from the lounge area. There's a good ratio of guests per bathroom and the owner can help organize all manner of outdoor adventures. Dorms CH$10,000, double CH$22,000

★ Compass del Sur Klenner 467 ☎65 223 2044, ⓦcompassdelsur.cl; map p.439. This lovely three-storey hostel is popular with international travellers of all ages, who come to appreciate the creaky wooden floors, snug attic rooms, powerful showers and communal vibe. The helpful staff or the friendly Chilean-Swedish owners can help you organize your stay. Dorms CH$12,500, doubles CH$34,000

Hospedaje Ellenhaus Walker Martínez 239 ☎65 223 3577, ⓦellenhaus.cl; map p.439. This super-central labyrinth of compact rooms is your best bet for a cheap swing-a-cat single (facilities shared) or double (some en suite). Breakfast CH$3500 extra and wi-fi now works everywhere. CH$30,000

INTO ARGENTINA

Puerto Varas lies on the well-beaten path between Puerto Montt and Bariloche in Argentina (see page 119). If you're Argentina-bound, a **lake crossing** that allows you to experience the beauty of Chile's oldest national park – **Parque Nacional Vicente Pérez Rosales** – is an excellent alternative to a long bus journey. Starting out at 8am, you are first driven along the banks of Lago Llanquihue to **Petrohué**, before boarding the ferry that takes you across **Lago Todos Los Santos**, a spectacular expanse of clear blue-green water. As you sail along the densely forested shores, the volcanoes Osorno (2660m) and Puntiagudo (2190m) loom to the north, with the majestic Tronador (3491m) to the east. Bring a picnic lunch to have in Peulla as there's nowhere good to eat. After going through **Chilean customs** at Peulla, you then cross the Argentine border at Paso Pérez Rosales, and get stamped in at tiny Puerto Frías. At this point you'll board the ferry again for the short crossing of Laguna Frías, then transfer by bus to Puerto Blest and your final nautical leg of the journey, a boat across the stunningly beautiful **Lago Nahuel Huapi** (departing around 6pm), arriving at Puerto Pañuel. From here another bus should get you into Bariloche around 9pm. Cycling instead of busing it between lakes is possible. Book in advance, especially during the peak season, with Turistour (bus/cycle US$285/185; ☎65 243 7127, ⊛turistour.cl).

Hostal Melmac Santa Rosa 608 ☎65 223 0863, ⊛melmacpatagonia.com; map p.439. Up a steep staircase from the centre, this self-proclaimed "hostel from another world" features a snug three-bed dorm, two individually decorated doubles, a twin and plenty of *buena onda* (good vibes). The Argentinian-Colombian owner is good to share a beer with. Dorms <u>CH$14,000</u>, doubles <u>CH$45,000</u>

EATING

Café El Barista Walker Martínez 211 ☎65 223 3130, ⊛elbarista.cl; map p.439. A great spot for people-watching, this trendy café/bar serves some of the best coffee for miles around, with large slices of tasty *kuchen* and a good *menú del día* (CH$8500) that might involve vegetable risotto and palm heart salad. Daily 9am–late.

La Costumbrista Del Salvador 547 ☎09 6237 2801; map p.439. It's hard to beat this café for the sheer price/quality ratio. Frequently changing dishes on the succinct menu may include ossobucco, German-style pork chop, grilled hake and pasta of the day. The pisco sours are the cherry on the cake. Mains from CH$5000. Mon–Sat 1–4pm & 7–9.30pm.

Donde El Gordito San Bernardo 560 ☎65 223 3425; map p.439. Busy little local institution inside the market, its walls and ceilings covered in knick-knacks, and serving large portions of inexpensive fish and seafood to hungry locals. Squid in *pil-pil* sauce, clams baked with parmesan, grilled fish – it's all fresh and fantastic and Anthony Bourdain ate here. Mains from CH$6500. Daily 11am–10pm.

★ **La Gringa** Imperial 605 ☎65 223 1980; map p.439. *La Gringa*'s expat owner hails from Seattle and has recreated her home town's rainy-day café vibe that locals and travellers gravitate to. There are sticky, gooey cinnamon rolls and chocolate chip cookies to go with your coffee, and come noon the place fills up with ladies that lunch, with soups, salads and the likes of pulled pork sandwiches gracing the menu. *Menú del día* CH$9000. Mon–Sat 9am–8pm.

DRINKING

★ **Bravo Cabrera** Vicente Pérez Rosales 1071 ☎65 223 3441, ⊛bravocabrera.cl; map p.439. This is still one of the "it" places and justifiably so: "BC" has an incomparable selection of around fifty beers, including many mircobrews from around Chile, as well as excellent wood-fired pizzas, tablas (sharing plates of cold cuts) and vast platters of slow-cooked ribs. Occasional DJs liven up this already lively lakefront joint. Mon–Thurs 7pm–2am, Fri & Sat 12.30pm–3am, Sun 12.30–6pm.

SALTOS DE PETROHUÉ

Chile boasts hundreds of waterfalls, but none quite like the **Saltos de Petrohué** (daily: summer 8.30am–9pm; winter 9am–6pm; CH$4000). Some 50km from Puerto Varas, this series of boiling, churning rapids and falls shoots through eroded lava tubes and bizarrely shaped rocks. With the Osorno volcano as a backdrop, it's hard to imagine a more striking location. According to local legend, these rapids are the home of a monster, Cuchivilu, which resembles a giant puma with a claw on the end of its tail. Regular minibuses run here from Puerto Varas (every 30min; 45min) on the way to **Petrohué**.

PUERTO VARAS TOUR OPERATORS

The area around Puerto Varas offers a variety of outdoor adventures, from challenging climbs up the nearby volcanoes Osorno and Calbuco to rafting on the turbulent turquoise waters of the Río Petrohué and exploring the surrounding Parque Nacional Vicente Pérez Rosales on horseback. The operators listed below are reputable.

Alsur Expeditions Aconcagua, at Imperial ☎65 223 2300, ⓦalsurexpeditions.com. As well as offering standard trips, Alsur specialises in multi-day sea-kayaking to the northern part of Parque Nacional Pumalín (see page 453), rafting trips on the Ríos Petrohué, Puelo and Futaleufú, and hiking in Parque Nacional Vicente Pérez Rosales.

Ko'Kayak San Pedro 311 ☎65 223 3004, ⓦkokayak. cl. Excellent French-run multilingual rafting and kayaking specialists who run half- (CH$35,000) to four-day rafting trips in the Lake District, as well as one- or three-day sea kayaking trips, with more challenging twelve-day expeditions to the southern fjords. Adrenaline-filled options include rafting the Petrohué in smaller, four-person rafts and riding a whitewater kayak as a passenger.

Yak Expediciones ☎09 8332 0574, ⓦyakexpediciones.cl. Long-standing operator running multi-day sea-kayaking adventures to the northern part of Parque Nacional Pumalín (see page 453), Chepu valley in Chiloé, and the Reloncaví Fjord, as well as multi-day trekking and horseriding in Río Puelo valley and day kayaking on Todos Los Santos (CH$72,000).

PUERTO MONTT

Established in the 1850s by German settlers, **PUERTO MONTT** is beautifully situated on the **Seno de Reloncaví** (Strait of Reloncaví), with snowcapped mountains clearly visible beyond the sound on a good day. Pretty backdrop aside, Puerto Montt is a large, busy city – a place to stock up on provisions and equipment on the way south and a major transport hub.

The town stretches along the bay, with Avenida Diego Portales running east along the seafront towards the **Plaza de Armas** – the centre, surrounded by banks, cheap bars and restaurants. West of the main bus terminal, Avenida Costanera takes you to the busy passenger port with a **feria artesanal** (craft market) and the Angelmó fishing village.

ARRIVAL AND INFORMATION

By plane Aeropuerto El Tepual (ⓦaeropuertoeltepual. cl) is located 16km northwest of the city. Buses Andestur run to and from the airport hourly and meet flights. Daily LATAM and Sky Airline flights serve Santiago (up to 10 daily; 1hr 40min), Punta Arenas (2–4 daily; 2hr 10min) and Balmaceda/Coyhaique (2 daily; 1hr).

By bus Long-distance and local buses arrive at the large Terminal de Buses (ⓦterminalpm.cl), at Av Diego Portales 1001 on the waterfront. The bus station has an information office, ATMs, food stalls and luggage storage.

Destinations Ancud (every 30min; 2hr); Bariloche, Argentina (4 daily; 6hr); Castro (every 30min; 3hr 30min); Chaitén (2 daily at 7am & 11am; 9hr); Coyhaique via Osorno (4 weekly; 24hr); Futaleufú (2 weekly; 12hr); Hornopirén (3–4 daily; 4hr); Osorno (every 30min; 1hr 30min); Puerto Varas (every 15min; 30min); Santiago (every 30min; 14hr); Temuco (hourly; 5hr); Valdivia (every 30min; 3hr).

By ferry The Terminal Internacional de Pasajeros, 700m west of the bus terminal, Av Angelmó 1673, is home to Navimag (☎65 243 2360, ⓦnavimag.com) and Naviera Austral (☎65 227 0430, ⓦnavieraustral.cl. Navimag sails to Puerto Chacabuco (Wed & Sat at 11pm, 2 days; CH$51,000 for shared Class C cabin) and Puerto Natales (1–2 weekly at 4pm; 3-4 days; US$450 for shared Class CC cabin). Class CC accommodation consists of a bunk with bedding, a locker for storage and a curtain for privacy; bring your own towel. Naviera Austral serves Chaitén (Mon & Thurs at 11pm; 9hr; seat CH$17,300).

Tourist information There is a well-stocked Turismo Municipal office on the Plaza de Armas, on Varas at San Martín (Dec–March daily 9am–9pm; April–Nov Mon–Fri 9am–1pm & 2.30–6.30pm, Sat 9am–1pm; ☎65 225 4580).

ACCOMMODATION

Austral View Hostel Bellavista 620 ☎09 6284 0751, ⓦcasaperla.com; map p.442. Exuberant hellos from the two resident Bernese mountain dogs greet guests at this friendly guesthouse. Choose between a self-catering two-person cabaña, a dorm bed, or the snug doubles and take a drink out onto the terrace high above the city. Dorms CH$16,000, doubles CH$30,000, cabaña CH$40,000

Casa Perla Trigal 312 ☎65 226 2104, ⓦcasaperla. com; map p.442. Simple rooms and dorms with shared bathrooms in a yellow-shingled Chilean home, packed with antiques and knick-knacks and ruled over

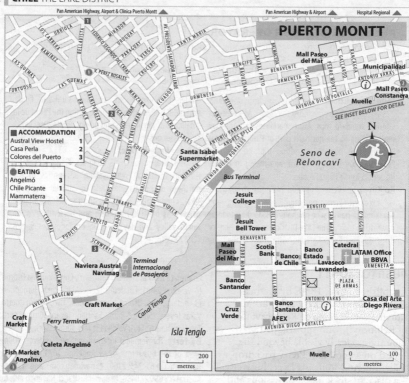

by Perla the matriarch. It's an uphill hike to the quiet residential neighbourhood, but pluses include a warm family atmosphere and camping out back; English and German spoken. Dorms **CH$11,500**, doubles **CH$27,000**, camping/person **CH$8000**

Colores del Puerto Schwerter 207 ☎ 65 248 9360, ⌨ coloresdelpuerto.cl; map p.442. Run by the wonderfully friendly and helpful Tomás, this informal hostel is only a 5min walk from the port and a 10min walk from the bus station, down a quiet street in Puerto Montt's historic neighbourhood. Three twin rooms share facilities and your host can fix up a simple breakfast. **CH$35,000**

EATING

There's a vast Unimarc supermarket in the basement of Paseo Costanera mall.

Angelmó Next to the fish market, Av Angelmó; map p.442. By far the best spot for an inexpensive seafood meal, this collection of no-frills eateries serves such goodies as *picorocos* (barnacles), *curanto* (see page 446), *almejas* (razor clams), *erizos* (sea urchins) and *chupe de locos* (abalone chowder). Mains from CH$5500. Daily noon–8pm.

★ **Chile Picante** Vicente Pérez Rosales ☎ 09 8454 8923, ⌨ chilepicanterestoran.cl; map p.442. All bright colours and bay views from its lofty location, the six tables at this compact restaurant fill up quickly. The ever-changing three-course daily menu is remarkably good value (CH$10,500) and you might be treated to such temptations as scallop *ceviche*, gnocchi with crab and calafate berry-flavoured *chapalele* (potato pancakes). Reservations a must. Mon–Sat 12.30–3.30pm & 7.30–11pm.

Mammaterra Illapel 10, Mall de Costanera, local 315B ⌨ mammaterral.cl; map p.442. Inside the Mall de Costanera, this place distinguishes itself by specializing in vegetarian "fast good". Expect quinoa burgers and falafel, beetroot- and carrot-infused burger baps and ample salads. Daily 10am–9.30pm.

COCHAMÓ

Sitting on the gorgeous Estuario de Reloncaví, against the backdrop of snow-tipped mountains 33km south of Lago Llanquihue and reachable by bus from Puerto Montt via Puerto Varas, the appealing fishing village of **COCHAMÓ** is

TREKKING IN THE RÍO COCHAMÓ VALLEY

With the temperate rainforest's gnarly trees clothed in lichen, towering *alerces* and granite mountains rising above the forest, it's easy to see how the **Río Cochamó valley** acquired its "Yosemite of the South" moniker. The valley is bisected by the remnants of a nineteenth-century logging road (little more than a muddy footpath in places) that now serves as a popular 13km hiking trail to the valley of **La Junta,** surrounded by mountains that are highly popular with rock climbers. The **trail to La Junta**, which takes 4–6hr to hike, is stunning and mostly easy to follow, but can be extremely muddy, as the horses bringing supplies to the two guesthouses churn up the path in rainy weather. Most visitors to the valley are trekkers; there is plenty of scope for day hikes in the valley and more adventurous travellers can even continue on foot to Argentina.

The trailhead for the Río Cochamó valley is at the end of an 8km dirt road that branches off the main road through Cochamó 4km south. Locals offer lifts up to the trailhead for CH$4000 in the summer months.

ACCOMMODATION

Campsites La Junta, ⓦreservasvallecochamo.org. There are five campsites in La Junta: La Junta, Vista Hermosa, Manzanas, Trawén and Campo Aventura. With the exception of Trawén, they are all well run. La Junta and Trawén are next to each other. Mazanas is 2km south of La Junta, reachable via a pulley system across the river. Campo Aventura is just before La Junta and across the river. Vista Hermosa, also reachable by pulley system, is just north of Refugio Cochamó. Expect solar-heated showers and quinchos for cooking. Advance bookings essential. Camping/person CH$5000

Campo Aventura Mountain Lodge & Camping La Junta, ⓦcampo-aventura.com. *Campo Aventura's* (see page 443) rustic outpost in the La Junta valley, this is a converted farmhouse with bunkrooms, simple rooms and camping spots; *asados* can be organized for guests. The Mountain Lodge is used as accommodation for horseback riding trips (4 people minimum). Camping/

person CH$5000, dorms CH$15,000, doubles CH$50,000

Cafe Escalada 300m before the La Junta trailhead ⓦcafeescalada.com. Run by Jonathan and Elizabeth from Cheltenham, this new café serves locally roasted coffee from Puerto Varas, Pudú artisanal ice cream, cakes and sausages in a bun. They'll store your luggage if you're heading to La Junta, and glamping is available in a star-lit meadow by the river. Daily 9am-5pm.

★ **Refugio Cochamó** La Junta ☎09 9289 4314 or 9289 4318, ⓦcochamo.com. This beautiful rustic lodge, run by a friendly American-Argentinian couple, sits amidst a vast riverside property across the river from La Junta, reachable via a pulley system. Climbers and hikers exchange stories in the cosy living area, and dinner (pizza or hearty vegetarian mains) has to be booked in advance. Choose between a 12-person dorm or two snug doubles. Dorm CH$17,000, doubles CH$48,000

---

the springboard for the popular hike to La Junta in the Río Cochamó valley – known as "the Yosemite of the South".

ARRIVAL, INFORMATION AND TOURS

By bus Buses Río Puelo (☎09 9323 0838) pass through Cochamó four times daily en route between Puerto Montt (2hr) and Río Puelo.

Tourist office There's a tourist information kiosk (Mon–Sat 9am–6pm) on the main street.

Tours Southern Trips (☎09 8407 2559 or ☎09 9919 8947, ⓦsouthern-trips.com) offer some fantastic horseriding in the area. Campo Aventura (see page 443) specialize in multi-day horse treks in the region.

ACCOMMODATION AND EATING

Campo Aventura Riverside Lodge B&B Around 4km south of Cochamó proper, near the turnoff for

Río Cochamó Valley ☎09 9289 4314 or 9289 4318, ⓦcampo-aventura.com. This rustic, American-run lodge accommodates adventurers in its cluster of rustic but comfortable rooms and lets them camp by the river. Specializes in horseriding adventures in the region, particularly multi-day explorations (see page 443). Nov to mid-April. Camping/person US10, doubles US$55

★ **Eco Hostal Las Bandurrias** Sector El Bosque s/n ☎09 9672 2590, ⓦhostalbandurrias.com. High up on a hill above Cochamó (arrange pickup in advance), this gorgeous little hostel consists of a single four-bed dorm, a twin and three doubles (shared bath), all with down duvets and run by a friendly and knowledgeable Swiss-Chilean couple. The excellent breakfast includes Sylvie's homemade bread. Dorms CH$14,000, doubles CH$32,000

La Bicicleta Hostel C Principal 179 ☎09 9402 9281, ⓦlabicicletahostel.cl. Friendly locals Sixto and his wife welcome backpackers and cyclists into their cosy little

"DOING" THE CARRETERA AUSTRAL

Though having your own wheels makes it easier to get around, and renting a car is reasonably inexpensive if you're travelling with others, the majority of the **Carretera Austral**'s attractions are reachable by public transport; all you need is a bit of time and some organizational skills, since not all buses run daily. Bear in mind that Coyhaique is the only place where you can reliably withdraw money, so bring plenty of cash. Be prepared for delays (landslides block the road during heavy rains) and keep in mind that transport can be less frequent outside the November to March high season. Book bus tickets in advance for routes less travelled, as buses tend to fill up.

bungalow. The four-bed dorms are simple but the mattresses are comfortable and the breakfast and warm welcome get rave reviews. Dorms CH$16,000, doubles CH$38,000
The Coffee House C Pueblo Hundido s/n ☎09 9919 8947. Cochamó's hottest gathering spot is this delightful café, owned by Tatiana from Southern Trips (see page 443).

Here you can find proper coffee, freshly squeezed juice, cakes, sandwiches and reliable wi-fi. Daily 11am–9pm Dec–April.
El Rincón Pirata C Principal s/n ☎09 9865 8075. Flying the Jolly Roger, this restaurant on the northern approach to the village has earned itself some loyal local and visiting fans with its stone-baked pizzas and grilled meats. Mains CH$7500–11,500. Daily 11am–11pm.

Chiloé

As the ferry ploughs through the grey waters of the Canal de Chacao that separates the **CHILOÉ** archipelago from the mainland, an island appears out of the mist. **Isla Grande de Chiloé** is the second-largest island in South America, a patchwork of forests and fields, with traditional villages nestling in sheltered inlets. Chiloé draws visitors to its two main towns, **Ancud** and **Castro**, lined with distinctive shingle houses and waterside *palafitos*, as well as its remote national parks with plenty of scope for trekking and its precious cache of uniquely constructed wooden **churches**, sixteen of which are UNESCO monuments.

Originally populated by the Huilliche (southern Mapuche), most of whom died from a smallpox epidemic shortly after European contact, Chiloé was colonized by the Spanish as early as 1567. Scores of refugees fled the fierce Mapuche on the mainland to the island, and Chiloé's very distinct culture evolved in relative isolation, resulting in a diverse and rich mythology that permeates people's lives to this day.

ANCUD

Tucked away on Chiloé's northern coast, **ANCUD** is the island's second-largest settlement and was the last stronghold of the Spanish, who held out against hostile forces for almost a decade after Chile's declaration of independence in 1818. Ancud's heart is the little **Plaza de Armas**, where there are craft and book stalls in the summer.

CHILOTE CHURCHES

It is impossible to visit Chiloé and not be struck by the sight of the archipelago's **wooden churches**, some of which have a vaguely Scandinavian rather than Spanish look. In 2001 UNESCO accepted sixteen of them onto its prestigious World Heritage list. The exterior is almost always bare, and the only thing that expresses anything but functionality is the three-tiered, **hexagonal bell tower** that rises up directly above an open-fronted portico. The facades, doors and windows are often brightly painted, and the walls clad with plain clapboard or wooden tiles. The roofs are built like traditional Chilote boats and then turned upside down. The ceilings are often painted too, with allegorical panels or golden constellations of stars painted on an electric blue background. Of the sixteen churches, fourteen are on mainland Chiloé; the other two are on remote islets.

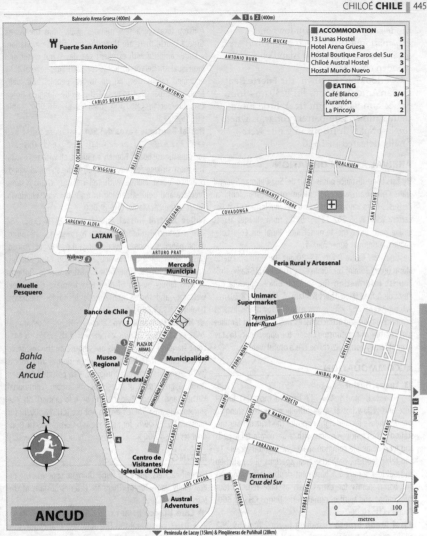

ACCOMMODATION

13 Lunas Hostel	5
Hotel Arena Gruesa	1
Hostal Boutique Faros del Sur	2
Chiloé Austral Hostel	3
Hostal Mundo Nuevo	4

EATING

Café Blanco	3/4
Kurantón	1
La Pincoya	2

ANCUD

Peninsula de Lacuy (15km) & Pinqüineras de Puñihuil (28km)

WHAT TO SEE AND DO

The small but illuminating **Museo Regional de Ancud** on the plaza (Jan & Feb Tues–Fri 10am–5pm, Sat & Sun 10.30am–3.30pm March-Dec Tues-Fri 10am–5pm, Sat & Sun 10.30am–1.30pm; free; ☎65 262 2413, ⓦmuseoancud.cl) consists of partly interactive Spanish-language exhibits, covering traditional Chilote industries such as fishing, crafts, Chiloé's environment and wildlife, European conquest, archeology and religious art, with striking photographs illustrating the impact of the 1960 earthquake which devastated much of the island. Don't miss the blue whale skeleton or the replica of the *Goleta Ancud* outside, the locally built ship that led the expedition to take control of the Strait of Magellan for Chile in 1843.

Make time also for the **Iglesias de Chiloé Centro de Visitantes** (Jan & Feb Mon–Fri 9am–7pm, Sat & Sun 10am–6pm; March–Dec Mon–Fri 9.30am–6pm; ⓦiglesiasdechiloe.cl; suggested donation CH$500) at Errázuriz 227. Intricate scale models, carved doors, windows and explanation boards (much in English) are a great introduction to the island's beloved wooden churches.

Overlooking the town, the **Fuerte Real de San Antonio** (Mon–Fri 8.30am–9pm, Sat & Sun 9am–8pm; free), little more than a ruined gun battery today, is where the last Spanish troops in Chile were finally defeated in 1826.

ARRIVAL AND INFORMATION

By bus Long-distance buses (Cruz del Sur, Pullman Sur and Trans Chiloé) arrive at the conveniently located Terminal de Buses (also known as the Cruz del Sur Terminal) at Los Carrera 850 (☎65 262 2249). Buses from villages across Chiloé pull up at the Terminal Inter-Rural on Colo Colo, above the Unimarc supermarket.

Destinations Castro (every 15–30min; 1hr 15min); Puerto Montt (every 30min; 1hr 30min–2hr); Quellón (16 daily; 4hr).

Tourist information The Sernatur office, opposite the Plaza de Armas (Mon–Thurs 8.30am–5.30pm, Fri 8.30am–4.30pm; ☎65 262 2800), has maps of town and lists of accommodation and attractions, as well as a list of families participating in Agroturismo Chiloé, the opportunity to stay in rural family homes. ⊚chiloe.cl is a useful website.

ACCOMMODATION

13 Lunas Hostel Los Carrera 855 ☎65 262 2106, ⊚13lunas.cl; map p.445. It's hard to miss this bright lime-and-yellow hostel, a beautifully renovated, shingled wooden house located right opposite the Cruz del Sur bus station. It has spacious rooms with large, comfortable beds and lockers, ample common spaces with guitars, cable TV and table football, barbecue area, spacious guest kitchen and outdoor terraces. A basement double lacks windows but bonus points for extras such as bike rentals, tour information and spirit of camaraderie. Dorms CH$10,500, doubles CH$30,000

Hotel Arena Gruesa Costanera Norte 290 ☎65 262 3428, ⊚hotelarenagruesa.cl; map p.445. At this great cliff-top location, a few minutes' walk from the Arena Gruesa beach, there are three choices of accommodation: a large campsite with excellent sea views, hot water and individual shelters with lights for each site; several fully equipped cabins sleeping up to ten people; and well-kept, wood-panelled rooms in the white-shingled hotel. Camping/person CH$7000, doubles CH$46,000, cabin CH$35,000

Hostal Boutique Faros del Sur Costanera Norte 320 ☎65 262 5799, ⊚farosdelsur.cl; map p.445. This cliff-top guesthouse boasts homely en suites, all with sea views. The most striking feature, however, is the splendid wood-panelled guest lounge with tall ceilings, chunky stone fireplace and light streaming in from the vast windows. Guest kitchen available. CH$49,000

Chiloé Austral Hostel Anibal Pinto 1318 ☎65 262 4847, ⊚ancudchiloechile.com; map p.445. Its snug, wood-panelled rooms overlooking the Bay of Ancud, this blue-shingled Chilote house has good value singles, doubles and triples. While little English is spoken, Roberto and his family go out of their way to make guests feel welcome, and there's home-made bread for breakfast. Doubles CH$23,000

★ **Hostal Mundo Nuevo** Salvador Allende (Costanera) 748 ☎65 262 8383, ⊚newworld.cl; map p.445. Long-standing favourite, this guesthouse on the *costanera* (waterfront) offers bright, top-notch dorms and rooms (with shared or private bathrooms) with polished wooden floors, a great ratio of guests per bathroom, communal kitchen and handy folders full of information on the surrounding area. There's even a hot tub (CH$12,000/hr for guests; CH$18,000/hr for non-guests). Dorms CH$14,000, doubles CH$41,000

EATING

For self-caterers, there's a huge Unimarc supermarket on Prat (daily 9am–10pm). There are eateries upstairs at the Mercado Municipal.

★ **Café Blanco** Ramirez 359 & Libertad 669 ☎65 262 0197; map p.445. The Ramirez branch of this mini chain (there's a smaller branch on the main square

---

CURANTO – WHAT'S IN A DISH?

Chiloé's signature dish, *curanto*, has been prepared for several centuries using cooking methods very similar to those used in Polynesia. First, extremely hot rocks are placed at the bottom of an earthen pit; then, a layer of shellfish is added, followed by chunks of meat, *longanisa* (sausage), potatoes, *chapaleles* (potato dumplings) and *milcaos* (fried potato pancakes). The pit is then covered with *nalca* (Chilean wild rhubarb) leaves, and, as the shellfish cooks, the shells spring open, releasing their juices onto the hot rocks, steaming the rest of the ingredients. *Curanto en hoyo* is slow-cooked in the ground for a day or two, but since traditional cooking methods are only used in the countryside, you will probably end up sampling *curanto en olla*, oven-baked in cast-iron pots. The dish comes with hot broth, known to the locals as "liquid Viagra", that you drink during the meal.

and a couple in Castro; see page 459) is a haven, particularly on a cold, wet day. As well as the town's best coffee (CH$1200–3300), there's a strong range of teas, cakes and snacks. Mon–Fri 9am–9.30pm, Sat 10am–9.30pm.

Kurantón Prat 94 ☎65 262 3090; map p.445. The legend reads: "Curanto: helping people to have good sex since 1826". Tuck into this veritable mountain of shellfish and potato dumplings amid photos of old Ancud, carvings of Chilote mythical creatures and nautical paraphernalia. Mains CH$6,000–10,000. Daily 12.30–3pm & 7–11.30pm.

La Pincoya Prat 61 ☎65 262 2613; map p.445. Overlooking the harbour, this faded, family-run restaurant with an old-school, bow-tie-clad waiter, is a good bet for fish and seafood dishes (CH$5000–10,000), such as *curanto en olla* and salmon *cancato*. Daily 11am–3pm & 7–10pm; erratic hours in the off-season.

PINGÜINERAS DE PUÑIHUIL

Pingüineras de Puñihuil is a large colony of Humboldt and Magellanic penguins spread over three tiny islands off the coast some 28km southwest of Ancud, and reachable via the beach of little fishing village **Puñihuil**. Monitored by Ecoturismo Puñihuil, a local organization dedicated to the protection of the penguins, the colony can be visited between December and March. The adults fish most of the day, so the optimum visiting time is either in the morning or mid- to late afternoon.

Three companies based in the guesthouse and restaurants on the beach pool their customers and run well-explained trips in twenty-person boats to see the penguins and other marine fauna, including the sleek *chungungos* (sea otters). The excursions depart directly from the beach at least once hourly and last around forty minutes; it's best to reserve in advance (☎09 8317 4302, ⓦpinguineraschiloe.cl) during peak season. Mar Brava (☎65 262 2312) runs daily buses (except Sun) from Ancud; share a taxi for around CH$20,000 one-way; or take a tour.

VALLE DE CHEPU

Around 25km south of Ancud, a turn-off leads to the **Valle de Chepu**, a large stretch of wetlands created during the 1960 tsunami, whose sunken forest provides a thriving habitat for hundreds of bird species and superb hiking trails as far as the Parque Nacional Chiloé.

ARRIVAL AND DEPARTURE

By bus Buses Peter (☎09 8383 1172) run from Ancud's Terminal Inter-Rural (generally Mon, Wed & Fri at 4pm, though check as they are subject to change; 1hr).

ACCOMMODATION

Chepu Adventures Camino a Chepu, Km13.2 ☎09 9227 4517 or 65 284 0543, ⓦchepu.cl. This wonderful, award-winning ecolodge is currently closed as the owners are looking to sell; check the website for updates.

CASTRO

The third-oldest continuously inhabited city in Chile, **CASTRO** was founded by the Spanish in 1567 and survived a number of calamities through the centuries: being pillaged by English and Dutch pirates, numerous fires and the great earthquake of 1960, which largely destroyed it, though these days it's the bustling capital of Chiloé.

WHAT TO SEE AND DO

A large **Plaza de Armas** surrounded by bars and restaurants is Castro's focal point. The UNESCO-listed, yellow-purple neo-Gothic **Iglesia San Francisco** (summer daily 9.30am–10pm; rest of year Mon–Sat 9.30am–12.30pm & 3.30–8.30pm, Sun 9am–12.30pm & 3–8.30pm; free) stands on the northeastern corner of the plaza and its all-wood interior is well worth admiring.

Now in a new location, northwest of the centre at Yumbel 863, the **Feria Yumbel** (Mon–Sat 8am–7pm) is a large covered market selling sweaters, wall hangings and other woolly goodies that the region is famous for (though not all are locally made). There are also produce stalls, and several inexpensive places to eat.

Palafitos

Chiloé's famous **palafitos** (stilt houses) are still found at several locations around Castro. Perched precariously above the water, these brightly painted, traditional wooden fishermen's dwellings are an unforgettable sight. The idea was that you could moor your boat at your back door

4

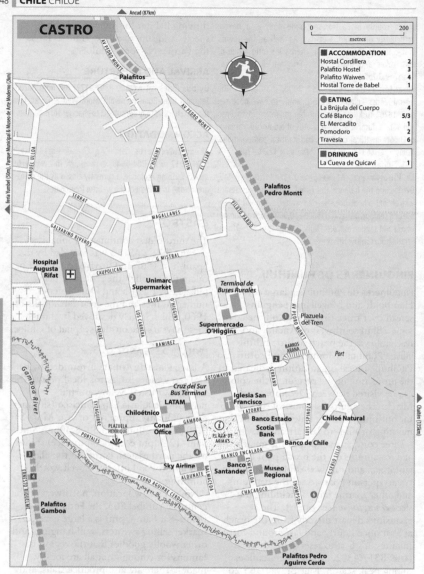

CASTRO

Ancud (87km)

Feria Yumbel (50m), Parque Municipal & Museo de Arte Moderno (2km)

Chaitén (135km)

ACCOMMODATION
Hostal Cordillera	2
Palafito Hostel	3
Palafito Waiwen	4
Hostal Torre de Babel	1

EATING
La Brújula del Cuerpo	4
Café Blanco	5/3
EL Mercadito	1
Pomodoro	2
Travesia	6

DRINKING
La Cueva de Quicaví	1

and walk out onto the street through the front one. Some impressive examples are found at the north end of town, off Pedro Montt, where they are perfectly reflected in the mini-lake by the roadside. More *palafitos* are found slightly south along the same street, while others at the southern end of town are used as restaurants. A final batch can be seen from the western end of Eusebio Lillo, across the Río Bamboa, and a number have been converted into guesthouses, restaurants and cafés.

ARRIVAL AND INFORMATION

By plane Castro is connected to Santiago and Puerto Montt by regular LATAM flights. Transfers to the airport can be organized by your accommodation (around CH$4000–4500).

By bus Cruz del Sur (ⓦ busescruzdelsur.cl) has its own bus terminal at San Martín 486 which serves numerous long-distance destinations up to and including Puerto Montt, Santiago, Punta Arenas and Ancud. The Terminal de Buses Municipal, at San Martín 667, has services to smaller destinations around Chiloé, including Cucao (Parque Nacional Chiloé), Dalcahue and Achao.

Destinations from Cruz del Sur terminal Ancud (hourly; 1hr 15min); Chonchi (every 30min; 30min); Puerto Montt (10–12 daily; 3hr); Quellón (every 30min–1hr; 1hr 30min).

Destinations from Terminal Municipal Achao (every 30min; fewer on Sun; 1hr 50min); Cucao and the Parque Nacional Chiloé, sector Anay (10–16 daily in peak season; 1hr 15min); Dalcahue (every 30min; 30min).

By ferry Naviera Austral (ⓦ navieraustral.cl) runs one weekly boat to Chaitén during the summer (time and day subject to change, so check in advance; 5hr 30min) from Castro's passenger terminal. Book tickets via Turismo Pehuén. From Chaitén you can connect with buses south along the Carretera Austral (see page 444).

Tourist office The tourist information centre is on the Plaza de Armas (officially daily 10am–8pm, though these times are not always kept; ⊖ turismo@municastro.cl).

Walking tours *Chiloé Natural* (see below) runs free walking tours around Castro, departing 10am from the Plaza de Armas.

TOUR OPERATORS

Altué Expeditions ⓣ 09 9419 6809, ⓦ seakayakchile. com. Offers multi-day trips around the Chiloé archipelago complete with lodging at their kayak centre near Dalcahue. Multi-activity combination trips in the Lake District and Patagonia are also on offer.

Chiloé Natural Blanco 100 ⓣ 65 253 4973, ⓦ chiloenatural.com. An experienced, English-speaking outfit offering day-trips and multi-day treks in Parque Tantauco, as well as horseriding trips to Parque Nacional Chiloé, *curanto*-eating outings to Chelín by catamaran, excellent kayaking adventures, and day visits to seven churches on the Ruta de las Iglesias. Tailor-made trips arranged and kayaks, mountain bikes and camping equipment available for rent, plus a detailed map of Chiloé in the attached shop.

Chiloétnico Los Carrera 435 ⓣ 65 263 0951, ⓦ chiloetnico.cl. Juan Pablo is an enthusiastic, English-speaking, experienced guide who arranges anything from trips to Parque Tantauco, Tepuhueico and Parque Nacional Chiloé to multi-day cultural immersion in traditional Chilote culture, half-day horseriding in Nercón and mountain bike, tent and sleeping bag rental.

Turismo Pehuén Chacabuco 498 ⓣ 65 263 5254, ⓦ turismopehuen.cl. Established company specializing in day-trips, from boat outings to Isla Mechuque, complete with *curanto*, to gastronomic tours, church tours and outings to the Pinguinera de Punihuil. Also offers car rental.

ACCOMMODATION

Hostal Cordillera Barros Arana 175 ⓣ 09 9512 2667, ⓦ hostalcordillera.cl; map p.448. Less atmospheric than many of its competitors, but still a solid choice, with a welcoming atmosphere, and reasonable rooms with shared or private bathrooms; solo travellers pay exactly half the price of a double. There's also a cabin sleeping up to seven people, and a rent-a-car service available. Doubles CH$36,000, cabins CH$100,000

★**Palafito Hostel** Riquelme 1210 ⓣ 65 253 1008, ⓦ palafitohostel.com; map p.448. Its curved wooden walls reminiscent of a ship, this revamped *palafito* has a selection of beautiful rooms (all en suite; two with sea-view balconies), a four-bed dorm, an appealing common space upstairs, adorned with contemporary art and woollen hangings, and an outdoor deck overlooking the water. Staff can organize a range of tours, including horseriding in Parque Nacional Chiloé. Dorms CH$17,000, doubles CH$58,000

Palafito Waiwen Riquelme 1236 ⓣ 65 253 3888, ⓦ palafitowaiwen.com; map p.448. Another palafito-based hostel in the pretty Gamboa neighbourhood, Waiwen has attractive wood-panelled en-suite rooms and slightly cramped four-bed dorms, some with wonderful views. Dorms CH$15,000, doubles CH$50,000

Hostal Torre de Babel O'Higgins 965 ⓣ 65 253 4569, ⓦ hostaltorredebabel.com; map p.448. Contrary to the name, travellers from all over the world are able to find a common language in the vast, wood-stove-heated, beanbag-strewn lounge of this welcoming hostel. Young, helpful owner Louis is happy to give advice, and the simple wood-panelled rooms are comfortable, though a bit gloomy. Dorms CH$18,000, doubles CH$36,000

EATING

There's a Unimarc supermarket on O'Higgins (Mon–Sat 9am–9.30pm, Sun 10am–9pm). In addition to the places listed below, the Feria Yumbel (see page 447) has a range of inexpensive places to eat.

La Brújula del Cuerpo O'Higgins 308 ⓣ 65 263 3229; map p.448. Travellers and locals alike gravitate to "The Body's Compass" – a busy café on the main square specializing in inexpensive burgers, salads, sandwiches, and ice-cream sundaes, plus a good value set lunch for around CH$5000. Mon–Thurs 9.30am–11pm, Fri 10am–midnight, Sat 11am–midnight, Sun 12.30–9pm.

Café Blanco Blanco 215 & 268 ⓣ 65 253 4636; map p.448. Part of a mini chain, with two branches on the same road in Castro and another pair in Ancud (see page 446), *Café Blanco* is a treat, with over a dozen coffees (CH$1200–3300), Twinings and Clipper tea, great cakes,

4

and light meals such as burgers, sandwiches and salads. Mon–Fri 9am–9.30pm, Sat 10am–9.30pm.

★ **El Mercadito** Montt 210 ☎65 253 3866, ⓦelmercaditodechiloe.cl; map p.448. Excellent, inventive restaurant, close to the dock. The imaginative menu includes fresh local oysters (CH$8000 for a dozen and a glass of wine) and a hearty chori burger that features chorizo in the patty (CH$7200). The decor is as whimsical as the food, with a colourful, shingle-covered bar, wacky light fixtures and knitted jellyfish. Mains from CH$6500. Daily 1–3.30pm & 7.30–10.30pm.

Pomodoro Sotomayor 520 ☎65 263 4141; map p.448. A standout Italian restaurant, offering everything from *vitello tonnato* to stonebaked pizzas, house-made pastas to tiramisu (mains CH$7000–10,000); make sure you ask about off-the-menu specials, which sometimes include king crab cannelloni. Tues–Sat 1–10pm, Sun 1–4pm.

Travesia Lillo 188 ☎65 263 0137; map p.448. An excellent place to sample traditional Chilote, fusion and global dishes (mains CH$8,000–10,000), all cooked and served with a contemporary flourish. The chef has also written a (Spanish-language) cookbook about Chilote cuisine and culture, *Chiloé Contado Desde La Cocina*, that's well worth picking up if you can find a copy. Mon–Sat 1–11pm, Sun 1–4pm.

DRINKING

La Cueva de Quicaví Encalada 55; map p.448. Despite a garish entrance guarded by a demon and a rough-and-ready interior, this is actually a pretty welcoming place for a drink (and sometimes a dance). Live music is luck of the draw – death metallers one night, reggae the next – but there's usually a lively crowd. Tues–Sat 7pm–2/3am.

EASTERN CHILOÉ

Eastern Chiloé remains a bastion of traditional village life, and the location of many of those famed wooden churches. **Dalcahue** is a good spot to base yourself, and **Achao** on Isla Quinchao makes an easy day-trip from Dalcahue or Castro.

Dalcahue

The bustling waterfront town of **DALCAHUE** lies 20km northeast of Castro via the turn-off at Llau-Llau. It is famous for its thriving traditional boat-building industry and the **Feria Artesanal**, open all week but busiest on Sundays, when artisans come from nearby islands to sell woollen crafts, wood-carvings and hand-woven baskets. The attractive Plaza de Armas features the imposing,

UNESCO-listed **Iglesia de Nuestra Señora De Los Dolores**, which boasts a unique nine-arched portico (under extensive renovation at research time).

Achao

Twenty-seven kilometres southeast of the ferry terminal on Isla Quinchao the fishing village of **ACHAO** boasts a scattering of houses, famous for their colourful *tejuelas* (shingles), and for its 1764 **Iglesia Santa Maria de Loreto** (Tues–Sun 11am–12.45pm & 2–4pm; free), the oldest Chilote church and a prime example. The other big draw is February's Muestra Gastronómica y Artesanal, which gives you a chance to both sample traditional Chilote cuisine and pick up local handiwork.

ARRIVAL AND DEPARTURE

By bus Buses Dalcahue Expreso run daily (Mon–Sat every 15min; Sun every 30min; 30min) from Castro to Dalcahue.

By ferry and bus for Achao Ferry services (every 30min 7am–11pm; foot passengers free) connect Dalcahue to Isla Quinchao. Achao's Terminal de Buses (Miraflores at Zañartu) has regular departures for Dalcahue (every 20–30min 7.15am–8.30pm; 40min).

ACCOMMODATION AND EATING

★ **Café Artesanías Casita de Piedra** Montt 144. Bringing urban sophistication to Dalcahue's *costanera*, at this split-level boutique/café you can purchase woollen goods downstairs (credit cards accepted) and then head up to the cheerful yellow café for a hit of espresso or a ristretto (coffee from CH$1400). Tues–Sat 10.30am–2pm & 3.30–8pm, Sun 10.30am–2pm.

Las Cocinera Dalcahue Next to the Feria Artesanal. This food stalls inside an establishment that resembles an upside-down boat is an excellent place to try inexpensive Chilote specialities. Shop around as local women dish up *curanto*, *empanadas*, *milcaos* (flat potato dumplings studded with smoked pork) and sweet baked twists known as *calzones rotos* (literally "torn underpants"). *Doña Lula*, Puesto 8, does fabulous *empanadas*; *Tenchita*, Puesto 2, is a favourite for *canacato*, while *La Nenita*, Puesto 4, offers very fresh salmon *ceviche*. You can have a good feed for less than CH$5000. Daily 9am–7/8pm.

Hostal Encanto Patagon Montt 146, Dalcahue ☎65 264 1651, ⓦhostalencantopatagon.blogspot.com. Sitting right on the *costanera* (waterfront), this venerable 120-year-old house with sloping wooden floors has a clutch of singles, doubles and triples named after locations on the Carretera Austral. The owners, Carlos and Cecilia, whip up delicious home-cooked meals and can help you if you're planning an adventurous getaway to some of the far-flung islands of the archipelago. CH$32,000

Hostal Lanita O'Higgins 50, Dalcahue ☏ 65 264 2020, ⓦ lanitahostal.blogspot.com. You'll be made to feel part of the family at this homely hostel. Besides the snug five-bed dorm there's a double and a triple. The only downside is the occasional queue to the two bathrooms. Dorms CH$13,000, doubles CH$32,000

PARQUE NACIONAL CHILOÉ

On the island's mountainous western coast, the **PARQUE NACIONAL CHILOÉ** comprises vast areas of native evergreen forest, covering the slopes and valleys of the **Cordillera de Piuchén**, as well as wide deserted beaches and long stretches of **rugged coastline**. The dense vegetation hides the elusive *pudú* (pygmy deer) and the shy Chilote fox. The park is divided into three sectors, though by far the most popular and accessible is Sector Anay.

Sector Anay

To reach Sector Anay, take a bus to the tumbledown village of **Cucao** from Castro's Terminal Municipal (10–16 daily in peak season; 1hr). Pay the park entrance fee at **Chanquín** (daily 9am–7pm; CH$2000), across the river from the village, where Conaf's **Centro de Visitantes** provides visitors with a detailed map of the park. Bring supplies with you if you plan to trek and camp rather than just do a day-trip.

Hike-wise, there's the circular, 770m "*El Tepual*" trail that runs through an area of *tepu* forest, a tree which thrives in this humid bogland; there are log walkways across the wetter sections of these enchanted-looking woods, with twisted moss-covered trunks intertwined with other native species. The second hike is the *Sendero La Playa*, which leads you through patches of *nalca* (native rhubarb) and tunnels of dense vegetation before emerging on the regenerating scrubland that takes you via sand dunes to the exposed Pacific coast. A little more taxing is the 3km (one-way) walk along the beach to Lago Huelde, where you pick up the 9km *Sendero Rancho Grande*, along the Río Deñal up to the edge of the tree line, revealing beautiful views below. The park's longest hike is the beautiful 25km (6hr) *Sendero Chanquín*, which alternates between stretches of coastline, pounded by the fierce Pacific surf, and dense, native evergreen forest, before finishing up at the Conaf *refugio* (bring own bedding) and campsite (CH$2000 per person) at Cole Cole.

Punta Pirulil

Reached via a rough, unpaved 45-minute drive south from Cucao, **Punta Piulil** is the stage for a beautiful, wind-whipped, two-hour walk over the hills and along wave-battered cliffs. Indigenous Huilliche tales have it that this part of the island acts as a bridge between this world and the next, with souls of the dead calling out to the boatman to ferry them across. A symbolic **Muelle de las Almas**, a bridge to nowhere that ends halfway, has been built here facing the bay. It's easiest to visit on a half-day tour with **Palafito Trip** (☏ 09 8849 5522, ⓦ palafitotrip.cl), based out of *Hostel Palafito Cucao*.

ACCOMMODATION AND EATING

El Arrayán Near the park entrance. This is the only reliable restaurant around, with rough-hewn wooden furniture, friendly service and a menu full of simple but well-executed meat and seafood dishes. Mains from CH$6500. Daily noon/1pm–10pm in high season.

Camping del Parque 200m past the Conaf visitors' centre ☏ 09 9507 2559, ⓦ parquechiloe.cl. This campsite offers 25 camping spots with fire pits, showers and picnic tables provided. There are also four fully equipped cabins sleeping up to six people. Camping/person CH$5000, cabin CH$50,000

★ **Hostel Palafito Cucao** ☏ 65 297 1164 or ☏ 09 8403 4728, ⓦ hostelpalafitocucao.cl. This shingled guesthouse is ideally situated 200m from the park entrance. It boasts views of Lago Cucao from its centrally heated rooms and dorm. Guests congregate in the cosy lounge, heated by a wood-burning stove, watch the sunset from the deck or simmer in the hot tub. Nab the corner room for the best views. Dorms CH$18,000, doubles CH$65,000

PARQUE TANTAUCO

At the very south of Chiloé, the remote 1200-square-kilometre private reserve of **PARQUE TANTAUCO** (ⓦ parquetantauco.cl) created by the current president of Chile, Sebastián Piñera, is completely

4

uninhabited apart from the fishing hamlet of **Caleta Inío** on the southern coast. The park consists of *Zona Norte*, accessible only by high-clearance vehicle, and *Zona Sur*, accessible by boat from port town Quellón, which is 93km south of Castro, with over 130km of well-signposted, meticulously maintained hiking trails of varying length and difficulty between the two, encompassing both the coastal areas and Chilote rainforest. It's possible to do some **day-hikes** in Zona Norte, 14km north of Quellón along a gravel road, basing yourself at Lago Chaiguata, 20km west of the Lago Yaldad ranger station on the road from Quellón (9am–5pm; CH$3500; get your map of the park here). Alternatively, you can tackle the two long trails in the park which form a T-shape: the east–west Ruta Caleta Zorra from Lago Chaiguata (41km one-way; seven-day return), and the north–south Ruta Transversal (52km; five days one-way) from Lago Chaiguata to Caleta Inío, which turns south halfway along to Caleta Zorra.

ARRIVAL AND INFORMATION

By bus Quellón is connected to Castro by bus (every 30min–1hr; 1hr 30min). In Jan and Feb, there are weekly buses between Quellón and Zona Norte; Chiloétnico or Chiloé Natural can book tickets.

By boat A private boat (around CH$60,000/person) can be chartered from Quellón either to drop people off at Caleta Inío or pick people up. It's sometimes possible to catch a ride from Caleta Inío to Quellón with one of the local fishing boats, but you have to have plenty of time to spare.

Park office Ruta 5 Sur 1826, Castro (Dec–March daily 9am–6pm; April–Nov Mon–Fri 9am–6pm; ☎ 65 263 3805, ⓦ parquetauco.cl). The main park office is just south of Castro, across the street from the casino.

Tours Chiloétnico and Chiloé Natural in Castro (see page 449) offer day- and multi-day tours of Parque Tantauco.

ACCOMMODATION

Refugios (CH$15,000; bring own bedding) are deliberately arranged with a day's hike between each site. Drinking water is found at every site apart from Refugio Mirador Inío, the highest of the sites. Accommodation at Lago Chaiguata and Caleta Inió – campsites (CH$15,000) and geothermal domes (from CH$84,000), plus a guesthouse (doubles from CH$60,000) at Caleta Inió – must be booked in advance at the park office or via the tour companies.

Northern Patagonia: Aysén

Comprising the northern half of Patagonia, **AYSÉN** is a land of spell-binding glaciers, soaring fjords and snowcapped mountains, still sufficiently remote to attract more adventurous travellers. The **Carretera Austral**, the partially paved, partly dirt-and-gravel "Southern Highway", stretches for 1240km down from Puerto Montt to tiny **Villa O'Higgins** – a popular destination for cyclists – interrupted in places by various bodies of water and supplemented by short ferry rides. This really is the end of the road – to get further south you'll need to fly, take a boat or travel through Argentina. The only town of any size is **Coyhaique**, roughly in the middle of the "Southern Highway" – a springboard for launching trips north and south.

HORNOPIRÉN

Perched on the northern shore of a wide fjord, at the foot of **Volcán Hornopirén**, the northernmost town on the Carretera Austral enjoys a spectacular location. Connected to Puerto Montt by a car ferry, this is also where you catch another ferry south to Caleta Gonzalo, where the Carretera Austral continues. It's worth hiking the short trails on the headland next to Ecocamping Patagonia El Cobre (below; CH$3000); one leads to a dolphin outlook (1hr return), while another one crests the steep hill (3hr return), leading to a viewpoint.

ARRIVAL AND DEPARTURE

By bus Kemel Bus (ⓦ kemelbus.cl) runs from the corner of the town's main square to Puerto Montt (3–4 daily; 3hr) and passes through en route to Chaitén at around 10am (1 daily; 5hr).

By ferry The La Arena–Caleta Puelche ferry to Puerto Montt is operated by Transportes del Estuario (every 30min, 6.30am–10.30pm; passengers free; ⓦ transportesdelestuario.cl). Transportes Austral (ⓦ taustral.cl) covers the two-stage ferry crossing between Hornopirén and Caleta Gonzalo, with daily ferries from Hornopirén departing for Leptepú at 10.30am, and ferries sailing from Caleta Gonzalo, at the north end of Parque Pumalín (see page 453), at 1pm. There's an extra daily departure from both ends in Jan and Feb. Rates are CH$5600 for passengers; book the Hornopirén–Caleta Gonzalo leg in advance in peak months online.

ACCOMMODATION AND EATING

★ **Ecocamping Patagonia El Cobre** Playa El Cobre ☎09 8227 5152, ✉patagoniaelcobre@gmail.com. Follow the beach round from the ferry ramp for 500m to reach this eco-campsite, partially hidden in woodland. Owner Roberto is serious about permaculture and recycling, and there's a café/hangout space for campers and visitors alike. There are bikes and kayaks for rent, too. Camping CH$5000 per person; dorm CH$14,000

Hotel Hornopirén Ignacio Carrera s/n ☎65 221 7256. Right on the waterfront, this is the town's oldest hotel, built over fifty years ago from alerce wood. It's a characterful place, with low ceilings and creaky floors; the largest doubles are en suite. Extensive breakfast includes homemade jams and other meals can be arranged on request. CH$35,000

El Pescadór Río Barceló s/n. ☎9 95089534. A short walk up from the ferry ramp, the best of the town's two restaurants is a reliable bet for *merluza a la plancha* (grilled hake) and other Chilean standards. Mains CH$5000–7500. Daily 10am–10pm.

CHAITÉN

On May 2, 2008, **Volcán Chaitén**, at the foot of which nestles its namesake town, **erupted** for the first time in over nine thousand years, taking the local residents completely by surprise. The town, and much of the surrounding area, had to be evacuated as the 30km plume of ash and steam from the volcano affected the local water sources and a mudslide caused floods which devastated the town. The town has been rebuilt since (though several eerie, wrecked houses have been left standing off Calle Río Blanco as a macabre outdoor museum) and is a useful transport hub and a good base for visiting Parque Nacional Pumalín (see page 453).

ARRIVAL, INFORMATION AND TOURS

By bus Buses Becker (☎67 223 2167, ✉busesbecker. com) run to Coyhaique via La Junta and Puyuhuapi (Fri at 11.30am; 8hr), Buses Cardenas (☎67 272 1214) and Buses Cumbres Nevadas (☎09 8597 6405) run to Futaleufú (Mon–Sat at 8am & 4pm; 2hr 30min), while Kemel Bus (☎65 225 3530 ✉kemelbus.cl) runs to Puerto Montt via

Hornopirén (daily at 8.30am & 2pm; 7hr). By the end of 2018, the Carretera Austral between Chaitén and Villa Santa Lucia that was destroyed by a deadly mudslide should be rebuilt.

By ferry Naviera Austral, Almirante Riveros at Todesco (✉navieraustral.cl) sells tickets for ferries to Quellón (Tues at 10am, Thurs at 1am; 5hr) and Puerto Montt (Thurs at noon, Sun at midnight; 9hr). In the same office, Transportes Austral (✉taustral.cl) sells tickets for the Caleta Gonzalo-Hornopirén car ferry north of Parque Nacional Pumalín.

Information and tours Chaitur, O'Higgins 67 (☎65 273 1429 ✉chaitur.com), run by informative American expat Nicolas La Penna, does day tours to Parque Pumalín and Termas de Amarillo from the town's bus station. Chaitén Nativo, Libertad 253 ☎65 273 1333 ✉chaitennativo.cl), runs outings to Termas de Amarillo, kayaking and mountain biking excursions and bilingual guided treks to different parts of Parque Pumalín.

ACCOMMODATION AND EATING

Hostel & Camping Las Nalcas Ercilla 342 ☎09 9619 9042. Run by a friendly couple, this hostel has camping spots in the garden out back, kitchen use and reliable hot showers, plus a handful of cosy rooms. Camping per person CH$4000, double CH$25,000

Hostería Llanos Corcovado 387 ☎65 273 1332. Spotless, family-run seafront residence with a clutch of wood-panelled rooms, some of them en suite, and a couple of swing-a-cat singles. CH$24,000

Natour Cafe O'Higgins s/n ☎09 4234 2803 ✉natour. cl. A block from the bus station, this green bus doubles as a popular café. Come here for your morning coffee or the breakfast of champions involving omelettes. Chilean-German owners run all manner of tours. Mon-Sat 9am-2pm.

Pizzeria Reconquista Portales at O'Higgins. The walls at this locally beloved pizzeria are hung with photos of Chaitén's spectacular eruption, and the bar serves Austral, Kunstmann and Kross beers. Pizzas are thin-and-crispy and sporting some exotic ingredients. Pizzas CH$6500–8800. Daily 12.30–3.30pm & 7–10pm.

★ **El Rincón del Mate** Libertad at Padre Juan Todesco ☎09 9195 8229. This ecodome is Base Camp meets gourmet restaurant. The *ceviche* is among the best we've had in Chile, and apart from the regional craft beers, there are also spectacular calafate sours, burgers and quesadillas. Mains CH$7000–10,000. Daily 12.30–11pm.

PARQUE NACIONAL PUMALÍN

Accessible from Hornopirén and Chaitén, **PARQUE NACIONAL PUMALÍN**, formerly the world's largest privately owned conservation area, became a national park

4

in January 2018 (see page 375). Covering 2900 square kilometres of land, it was founded by North American billionaire philanthropist Douglas Tompkins to protect one of the world's last strongholds of temperate rainforest. It's a place of overwhelming natural beauty, with pristine lakes reflecting stands of endangered, millennia-old *alerce* trees, ferocious waterfalls gushing through chasms of dark rock, and high, snowy-peaked mountains. Parque Nacional Pumalín consists of three sectors, with the southern sector the most visited.

Southern sector

The **southern section** has the most trails and campsites, all branching off the 58km of the Carretera Austral. Highlights include the **Sendero Cascadas** near **Caleta Gonzalo** (where the bus from Chaitén to Puerto Montt boards the ferry north), which climbs steeply through a canopy of overhanging foliage up to a 15m waterfall (3hr round-trip); the challenging **Sendero Laguna Tronador**, 12km south, taking you to a lookout point with fabulous views of Volcán Michinmahuida, ending at the pristine lake with a camping area alongside (4.8km, 3hr round-trip); the twenty-minute **Sendero Los Alerces** loop that runs through a grove of ancient, colossal *alerces*; and the **Sendero Cascadas Escondidas**, an two-hour round-trip that takes in three waterfalls.

Closer to Chaitén, the **Sendero Volcán Michimahuida** is a 12km (8-10hr round-trip) ramble to the base of the namesake volcano, and the 2.2km **Sendero Volcán Chaitén** is a steep, popular trail up to the rim of the eponymous volcano (3hr round-trip).

Sector El Amarillo

Next to the village of the same name, 24km south of Chaitén, the star of the **El Amarillo sector** is the flat 10km (6hr round-trip) **Sendero El Amarillo Ventisquero**, which runs to the base of the Michimahuida glacier from the Ventisquero campsite, with superb views en route, making it a really good, easy day hike. Starting from the road to the Ventisquero campground, the 2.2km (1hr) **Sendero El Mirador** climbs steeply along the slope of three volcanic cones before descending to the campground itself.

ARRIVAL AND INFORMATION

By bus Twice-daily buses between Chaitén and Puerto Montt can drop you off in the southern sector anywhere along that stretch of the Carretera Austral, including Caleta Gonzalo. Buses between Chaitén and any destination south can drop you off in El Amarillo; book onward bus tickets in Jan and Feb.

Information There are two Centros de Visitantes: one at Caleta Gonzalo and the other at El Amarillo (Mon–Sat: Dec–Feb 9am–7pm, March–Nov 10am–4pm; ⓦ parquepumalin.cl).

Tours Chaitur, Chaitén Nativo and Natour (see page 453) all offer guided treks in the park from Nov to March from Chaitén.

ACCOMMODATION AND EATING

SOUTHERN SECTOR

There are five well-equipped, beautifully sited campsites in the Southern sector and two in Amarillo.

Café Caleta Gonzalo At Caleta Gonzalo, this appealing restaurant serves Chilean dishes that use organic vegetables. There are also sandwiches to take away. Mon–Sat: Dec–Feb noon–10pm, March–Nov noon–4pm.

Camping Cascadas Escondidas 14km south of Caleta Gonzalo. Small campsite with showers and sheltered cooking area. Per site CH$8000

Camping Lago Blanco 36km north of Chaitén. This campsite has fantastic views of Lago Blanco from the covered sites, as well as hot showers and fire pits. Per site CH$8000

Camping El Volcán Halfway between Chaitén and Caleta Gonzalo. Large, tree-fringed campsite; each site comes with its own cooking area, barbecue and drinking water access. Per site CH$8000

EL AMARILLO SECTOR

Camping Grande Attractive campsite, 3.3km from the park entrance, with sites scattered around giant patches of native rhubarb and surrounded by trees. Per site CH$8000

Camping Ventisquero "The most beautiful campsite in Chile", 9km from the park entrance, comes with spectacular views of the hanging glacier. Per site CH$8000

FUTALEUFÚ

An attractive little town, **FUTALEUFÚ** serves as a popular summer base for rafting, kayaking, hiking and horseriding. Its proximity to the Argentine border also makes it handy for an easy transfer to Esquel (see page 125).

RAFTING OPERATORS

Futaleufú is a challenging river and tour operators take safety seriously. The most common trip for novices is the "Bridge to Bridge" section; it's wet, heart-stopping fun and occasionally people fall out of rafts and rafts flip; you are taught what to do in each situation. The following reputable operators offer half- (from CH$55,000) and full-day (from CH$90,000) rafting trips down the Futaleufú and the less challenging Río Espolón (from CH$30,000).

Bochinche Expediciones Cerda 697 ☎ 09 8847 6174, ⓦ bochinchex.com. The only operator offering full days on the Futa even if the water level is too high for others; they have catarafts, which are more stable than rafts, and double the safety personnel. Half-day CH$60,000. Also the only ones to offer riverbug and tandem kayaking.

Condorfu O'Higgins at Rodríguez ☎ 09 4213 9636, ⓦ condorfu.cl. Highly professional outfit, offering standard rafting excursions, as well as 2-hour canyoning outings both for beginners and those with experience (CH$25,000), as well as whitewater kayaking tuition (CH$25,000).

Patagonia Elements Cerda 549 ☎ 09 7499 0296, ⓦ patagoniaelements.com. Right on the plaza, this reputable, safety-conscious Chilean operator is an excellent bet for half- (CH$55,000) and full-day rafting on the Futa.

With its big "explosion waves" and massive "rodeo holes", the Río Futaleufú is regarded by many professional rafters and kayakers as one of the most challenging whitewater rivers in the world, with sections of the river known as "Hell" and "The Terminator". A number of Chilean and US operators offer **rafting** trips down the river, a body of water which runs through a basalt gorge known as the "Gates of Hell", and boasts over forty class IV–V rapids; rafting season is between November and March.

ARRIVAL AND INFORMATION

By bus All buses apart from those to Esquel depart from the corner of Prat and Balmaceda. Esquel-bound buses stop at the Chilean border; passengers then have to walk 400m and transfer to a connecting bus on the Argentinian side.
Destinations Chaitén (Mon–Sat 2 daily; 2hr 30min); Coyhaique (Wed & Sat at 10am; 8hr); Esquel, Argentina, leaving from Cerda between Prat and Aldea (Mon, Wed & Fri: 9am & 7pm; 30min; Buses Futaleufú); Puerto Montt via Argentina (daily except Wed & Sat at 7.30am).
Information The tourist office at O'Higgins 536, south side of the Plaza de Armas (summer only; daily 9am–9pm) is very helpful, with bus timetables, all accommodation options and tour operator info. The Banco Estado ATV on the Plaza de Armas doesn't accept some foreign cards so bring plenty of cash.

ACCOMMODATION

Camping Los Coihues Next to the bridge, just south of town ☎ 09 9326 8777, ⓦ campingfutaleufu.cl. With its own riverside beach, this large, well-located, tree-shaded campsite is the best in town. There are reliable hot showers, a *quincho* for cooking and even laundry service. Camping/person CH$7000

★ **La Gringa Carioca** Aldea 498 ☎ 65 272 1260 ⓦ hostallagringacarioca.cl. South African Adriana is the effusive hostess at this intimate cottage sitting in the middle of a large garden on the edge of Futa. The four light, bright, spacious doubles may all be individually decorated but have in common the high-quality beds and linens. An extensive breakfast seals the deal. Sept–April. CH$65,000

★ **Hostal Las Natalias** O'Higgins 302 ☎ 09 9631 1330, ⓦ hostallasnatalias.info. A 10min walk west of town along Calle Cerda, Futa's only bona fide hostel is run by hospitable American-Argentinian Nate, a fount of local knowledge who offers whitewater kayaking lessons. The huge open-plan communal area/kitchen is a very sociable place, and the dorms and private rooms are airy and spacious. Dorms CH$15,000, doubles CH$32,000

EATING

Cafe Mandala Cerda 545 ☎ 09 6168 4925. Decorated with colourful mandalas, this thimble-sized café right on the square is your best bet for proper coffee. Excellent *kuchen* of the calafate, blueberry and raspberry variety also. Mon–Fri 9am–8pm, Sat & Sun noon–9pm.

★ **Pizzas de Fabio** Carnicer 280 ☎ 09 8577 8334. Come to this diminutive takeaway for arguably the best pizza in Chile. The thin-and-crispy pizzas are cooked to perfection and the ingredients are top-notch. Daily noon–10pm.

Sur Andes Cerda 308 ☎ 65 272 1405. Real coffee and a long list of Chilean fast-food staples, made from quality local ingredients, contribute to the popularity of this tiny café. Come here for burgers and *completos* (hot dogs). Mains CH$5500. Daily 9am–11pm.

4

PUYUHUAPI

Sitting at the head of the narrow Ventisquero fjord, surrounded by steep, wooded hills and frequently shrouded in low-hanging mist, **PUYUHUAPI**, founded in 1935 by four young German immigrants, is a great place to break your journey along the Carretera Austral and to use as a base for visiting **Parque Queulat**. The main attraction here are the **Termas Ventisquero** (Dec–Feb daily 7am–9pm; shorter hours rest of year; CH$18,000, ☏ 09 7666 6862 ⊛ termasventisqueropuyuhuapi.cl), 6km south of town, which has two simple outdoor pools fed by thermal springs and an appealing café.

ARRIVAL, INFORMATION AND TOURS

By bus Puyuhuapi is connected to Coyhaique (daily 6am; 4hr 30min) and Futaleufú (Mon, Tues, Thurs & Fri at 7am; 4hr) by Buses Terra Austral (daily 6am; 4hr 30min; ☏ 67 225 4335); Buses Becker passes through en route from Coyhaique to Chaitén (Tues & Sat; 4hr 30min) and Futaleufú (Mon–Sat at noon; 4hr).

Information This well-stocked and helpful tourist office is located on Av Übel (daily 10.30am–1pm & 3–8pm; ⊛ puertopuyuhuapi.cl). There are no ATMs in Puyuhuapi; bring cash.

Tour operators Experiencia Austral, Av Übel (☏ 09 8744 8755, ⊛ puertopuyuhuapi.cl) offers kayaking both on the fjord and beneath the hanging glacier in Parque Nacional Queulat.

ACCOMMODATION AND EATING

★ **Casa Ludwig** Otto Uebel 202 ☏ 67 232 5220, ⊛ casaludwig.cl. The most popular option with international travellers, this rambling yellow chalet has comfortable singles and doubles (some en suite), polished wooden floors, excellent breakfast, a library and great views. It's run by English- and German-speaking Louisa, daughter of one of the original colonists and a wealth of information on the area. <u>US$42,000</u>

Hostal Augusto Grosse Camilo Henriquez 4 ☏ 67 232 5150, ⊛ hostalaugustogrosse.cl. This tiny hostel consists of a couple of dorms and doubles, all decked out with beautiful wooden furniture hand-carved by the owner. Guests gather in the tiny wood-stove-heated living area and are welcome to use the kitchen. Breakfast CH$1500. Dorms <u>CH$12,000</u>, doubles <u>CH$26,000</u>

El Muelle Otto Uebel s/n ☏ 09 7654 3598. This fjordside restaurant is the only place in the village that's reliably open for meals and its wonderfully fresh catch-of-the-day dishes do not disappoint. The grilled hake is a winner and the home-made *kuchen* with wild berries hits the spot. Mains CH$6000–9000. Daily 12.30–3.30pm & 7–10pm.

Mi Sur Otto Uebel 36 ☏ 09 7550 7656. With Bob Marley singing in the background and a generally mellow vibe, this new spot aspires to haute cuisine. The gravlax, risotto and the "creación del chef" are well worth a try, washed down with a local Hopperdietzel craft beer. Mains CH$7500. Daily 1–3pm & 6–10pm.

PARQUE NACIONAL QUEULAT

Consisting of rugged mountains, dense forest, raging glacial rivers and its namesake hanging glacier, the 1540-square-kilometre **PARQUE NACIONAL QUEULAT** is named after the incredible **Ventisquero Colgante**, or "hanging glacier". Wedged between two peaks, forming a V-shaped mass of blue-white ice, the glacier seems to hang suspended over a sheer rock face. From the parking area 2km beyond the *ranger post* (which is 2.5km from the Carretera Austral), cross the suspension bridge over the river, and turn right, taking the 600m **Sendero Laguna Témpanos** (15min one-way) through overgrown woods to the glacial emerald lagoon, fed by two thundering waterfalls plummeting 150m down from the glacier. Left of the bridge, the steep **Sendero Ventisquero Colgante** climbs 3.2km (2hr return) to a higher viewpoint overlooking the glacier.

Buses between Coyhaique and Puyuhuapi or destinations further north can drop you off by the entrance (45min from Puyuhuapi; 4hr from Coyhaique; book onward bus tickets in advance. You can also take a tour from Puyuhuapi (see page 456). Pay the park entrance fee (CH$5000) at the ranger post; the attractive camping spots near the trailheads (CH$6000 per site) come equipped with picnic tables, barbecue areas and icy showers.

COYHAIQUE

The town of **COYHAIQUE**, 634km south of Puerto Montt, sits roughly in the middle of the Carretera Austral, at the confluence of the Simpson and Coyhaique rivers. It is a welcome pocket of civilization if you've just passed through numerous little outposts along the Southern Highway, but beyond its services as a major transport hub, a place to withdraw money and eat out at a clutch of good restaurants, its charm is limited.

The heart of the city is the hexagonal **Plaza de Armas**, which resembles a wheel with ten spokes stretching out in various directions.

ARRIVAL AND INFORMATION

By plane Aeropuerto de Balmaceda is 55km south of town; all flights are met by three minibus companies that do door-to-door drop-offs (all CH$5000/person). Daily flights serve Puerto Montt (2 daily; 1hr 15min) and Santiago (2 daily; 3hr) with LATAM and Sky Airline, and there are also flights to Punta Arenas (Tues & Thurs; 1hr 45min) with Sky and DAP (ⓦdapairlines.com). Aeródromo Teniente Vidal, 7km out of town, handles Aerocord (General Parra 21 ☎67 224 6300, ⓦaerocord.cl) flights to Villa O'Higgins (Mon & Thurs at 10am; 1hr 15min), as well as charter flights to Laguna San Rafael.

By bus Most buses arrive at the main bus terminal on Lautaro at Magallanes, five blocks from the Plaza de Armas. Others depart from their own offices.

Destinations and operators Castro via Ancud, Puerto Montt and Osorno (Queilen Bus ☎67 224 0760; Mon, Wed & Fri at 2pm; 28hr); Chaitén via La Junta and Puyuhuapi (Buses Becker, General Parra 335 ☎09 8465 2959, ⓦbusesbecker.com; Tues & Sat at 8am); Cochrane via Villa Cerro Castillo, Puerto Río Tranquilo, Cruce El Maitén and Puerto Bertrand (Buses Acuario 13 ☎67 252 2143, Buses Don Carlos ☎67 252 2150 and Buses Sao Paulo ☎67 225 5726; 1–2 daily at 9am & 9.30am); Comodoro Rivadavia, Argentina (Transaustral ☎67 223 2067; Mon & Fri at 9am; 9hr); Futaleufú (Buses Becker; Sat at 8am; 12hr); Puerto Aysén and Puerto Chacabuco (Buses Suray, Prat 265, ☎67 223 8387, and Buses Ali, Dussen 283 ☎67 223 2788; every 30min;); Puyuhuapi (Buses Becker and Buses Terra Austral; 1–2 daily; 4hr 30min); Puerto Ibáñez (Miguel Acuña ☎67 225 1579; Buses Carolina ☎09 8952 1592 and Transporte Alonso ☎09 4247 1135 have schedules linked to ferry departure; 1–2 daily; 2hr 30min).

By ferry Navimag ferries to Puerto Montt (Tues & Fri; 20hr; Lillo 91; ⓦnavimag.cl); and Naviera Austral boats to Quellón on Chiloé (Mon & Fri; 28hr; Paseo Horn 40;

4

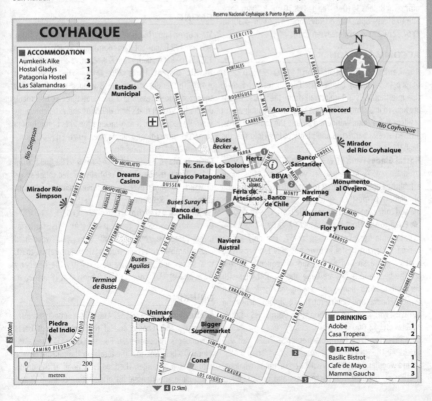

Reserva Nacional Coyhaique & Puerto Aysén ▲

COYHAIQUE

■ ACCOMMODATION
Aumkenk Aike	3
Hostal Gladys	1
Patagonia Hostel	2
Las Salamandras	4

N

Estadio Municipal

EJERCITO

PORTALES

RODRIGUEZ

Acuna Bus

Aerocord

Río Coyhaique

Buses Becker

Mirador del Río Coyhaique

PARRA

Hertz

Banco Santander

Nr. Snr. de Los Dolores

Lavasco Patagonia

BBVA

Dreams Casino

Feria de Artesanos

Banco de Chile

Buses Suray
Banco de Chile

Navimag office

Monumento al Ovejero

Mirador Río Simpson

Ahumart

Flor y Truco

Naviera Austral

Buses Aguilas

Terminal de Buses

Unimarc Supermarket

Bigger Supermarket

Piedra del Indio

CAMINO PIEDRA DEL INDIO

■ DRINKING
| Adobe | 1 |
| Casa Tropera | 2 |

● EATING
Basilic Bistrot	1
Cafe de Mayo	2
Mamma Gaucha	3

Conaf

0   200
metres

(2.5km)

VISITING LAGUNA SAN RAFAEL

If you only see one glacier in Latin America, make it **Laguna San Rafael,** 200km southeast of Coyhaique. It is estimated that in the next twenty years or so it will be completely gone.

As you pass through the tight squeeze of Río Témpanos ("Iceberg River"), and sail past the silent, densely forested shores of the long, narrow inner passage of **Estero Elefantes,** you catch numerous glimpses of marine wildlife. Nearing the impossibly huge glacier, over 4km in width and 60m in height, the boat dodges massive bobbing icebergs, some the size of small houses. Most boat trips allow the passengers to get close to the glacier in inflatable **Zodiacs,** and one of the trip's highlights is drinking whisky on the rocks – using the millennia-old ice, of course. Laguna San Rafael is accessible via the Valle Exporadores road from Puerto Río Tranquilo (see page 459); you need your own wheels to reach Bahía Exploradores, from where **Río Exploradores** (☎09 8259 4017, ✆ exploradores-sanrafael.cl) whisk you off in Zodiac boats on a three-hour journey to the glacier (CH$145,000). Alternatively, **Catamaranes del Sur** (CH$200,000; ☎2 2231 1902, ✆ catamaranesdelsur.cl) run high-speed catamaran day-trips (5hr each way) from Puerto Chacabuco; check website for departure dates. To reach Puerto Chacabuco from Coyhaique take buses by Buses Suray to Puerto Aisén (Prat 265; 2 hourly; 45min; ☎67 223 8387); from here the same company runs frequent buses to Puerto Chacabuco (25min).

✆ navieraustal.cl), sail from Puerto Chacabuco's Terminal de Transbordadores, 82km from Coyhaique, connected by frequent buses via Puerto Aysén.

Tourist office The well-stocked and super-helpful Sernatur office is at Bulnes 35 (Dec–Feb daily 8.30am–8.30pm, Sat & Sun 10.30am–6pm; March–Nov Mon–Fri 8.30am–5.30pm; ☎67 227 0290, ✆ exploreaysen.com).

ACCOMMODATION

Aumkenk Aike Hostel Simpson 1443 ☎09 9670 3853; map p.457. Run by enthusiastic English teacher Fareed, this guesthouse is a 15min walk from the plaza. Guests are housed in a clutch of spotless singles and doubles, with resident feline Pumi wandering around the common areas. Kitchen access, barbecues and plenty of local info seal the deal. US$34

Hostal Gladys Parra 65 ☎67 224 5488, ✆ hostalgladys. cl; map p.457. As central as you can get, this long-established guesthouse offers rooms with skylights (instead of windows), most en suite. Breakfast includes freshly brewed coffee, eggs and home-made jams. CH$40,000

★ **Patagonia Hostel** Lautaro 667 ☎09 6240 6974, ✆ patagonia-hostel.com; map p.457. The only proper backpacker/cyclist hostel in town has only ten beds (two doubles and a six-bed dorm), and is frequently booked up. The beds and bunks are large and comfortable, with personal reading lights; the young, energetic German owners, Thomas and Sandra, run their own tour agency and can assist with kayaking trips and more. Dorms CH$18,000, doubles CH$42,000

Las Salamandras Carretera Teniente Vidal, Km 2.5 ☎67 221 1865, ✆ hostalsalamandras.com; map p.457. Set in a woodland property by a river 2.5km from Coyhaique, this hostel, popular with backpackers and cyclists, offers kitchen use, ample common spaces, mountain-bike rental and a range of excursions, including one to Parque Nacional Queulat. Hot tub available (CH$20,000). Dorms CH$18,000, doubles CH$42,000, camping/person CH$10,000

EATING

Stock up on imported, hard-to-find groceries at Flor y Truco, Serrano 139 (Mon–Sat 9am–6pm); and Ahumart, Serrano 133 (Mon–Sat 9.30am–1pm & 3–8pm; ✆ ahumart.cl).

Basilic Bistrot Parra 220 ☎09 7766 2794; map p.457. This bright little bistro is a good spot for freshly squeezed juices, teas and a gourmet three-course menu del dia (CH$7000) that's both delicious and excellent value. Typically vegetarian, it may include the likes of mushroom carpaccio, gnocchi and apple pie. Tues–Fri 10.30am–7.30pm, Sat & Sun noon 9pm.

Cafe de Mayo 21 de Mayo 543 ☎09 9709 8632; map p.457. This is the best of the centrally located coffee shops in which to linger over an extensive menu of excellent coffees. Mon–Sat 9am–9pm.

★ **Mamma Gaucha** Horn 47 ☎67 221 0712 ✆ mammagaucha.cl; map p.457. At this trattoria-meets-Patagonia, efficient staff serve you wood-fired pizzas, lamb-filled ravioli, crudos (steak tartare) on toast, vast salads and imaginative desserts (try the blueberry crème brulée). Mains from CH$7000. Mon–Sat 10am–2am.

DRINKING

Adobe Baquedano 9 ☎67 224 0846 ✆ adobecoyhaique. cl; map p.457. Choose one of the regional craft beers (Puyuhuapi's Hopperdietzel, Puerto Cisnes' Finisterra, or a local D'olbek) and join the locals on the outside terrace with a tabla or burger. The food is as good as the drinks – including an extensive list of signature cocktails – and the *ceviche* stands out. Mains from CH$8000. Mon–Sat 12.45pm–2am.

★ **Casa Tropera** Camino Aeródromo Teniente Vidal, Km 1.5 ☎ 09 6597 0585 ⓦ tropera.cl; map p.457. *Tropera* brews eight beers, from the blond Bota Sucia and amber Horn 47 to the Crazy Juan brown ale and the Ranita de Darwin bitter double IPA. The beer terrace is often packed, and accompanying nibbles include truly excellent burgers (try the Annapurna). Mon–Sat noon–2am.

VILLA CERRO CASTILLO

Ninety-six kilometres south of Coyhaique, you pass through **VILLA CERRO CASTILLO**, a rather bleak pioneer settlement whose sole draw is the rugged hiking in the adjoining Reserva Cerro Castillo with its eponymous centrepiece, **Cerro Castillo** (2700m) whose needlepoint spires loom over the valley like the turrets of a Transylvanian castle.

The rewarding 40km **Sendero Cerro Castillo** hike, which takes four days to complete, starts at Villa Cerro Castillo before heading steeply up and passing the stunning **Laguna Cerro Castillo** at the foot of a glacier suspended from the mountainside before following Río La Lima upstream to a 1450m pass on the east side of Cerro Castillo (2300m) through *coigüe* and *ñire* forest. You eventually emerge at Km75, 6km south of the reserve's Conaf ranger station.

ARRIVAL AND INFORMATION

By bus Twice-daily buses pass through on the way between Coyhaique (1hr 30min) and Cochrane (3hr 30min).

ACCOMMODATION AND EATING

Cabañas El Tropero Carretera Austral 305 ☎ 09 7759 5766 ⓦ eltropero.cl. This friendly, family-run place offers two two-storey cabins for up to six people each, both with wood-burning stoves, cable TV and kitchenettes, as well as simple, wood-panelled rooms. Owners charge according to number of people. Cabins for 2/4 people CH$45,000/60,000

Camping & Hostel Senderos Patagonia Carretera Australs/n, ☎ 0962244725, ⓦ aysensenderospatagonia. com. At the southern approach to Cerro Castillo, mountain guides Mary and Christian run this appealing, sheltered campsite and hostel. Guides treks and horseback riding on offer, and there's an occasional *asado* (barbecue) as well. Camping/person CH$5000 dorm CH$10,000

El Puesto Huemul Camino Estero del Bosque ☎ 09 9218 3250. An unexpected treat in this small pioneer town, this Argentinian-run restaurant serves imaginative dishes such as lamb ravioli, barbecued lamb, freshly baked *empanadas* and gnocchi with wild mushrooms. Mains from CH$7500. Daily noon–11pm.

PUERTO RÍO TRANQUILO

Some 125km south of Cerro Castillo, **Puerto Río Tranquilo**, a picturesque village on the shore of Lago General Carrera, has long been a popular traveller stop thanks to its proximity to the **Capilla de Mármol** ("Marble Chapel"), an impressive limestone

4

TO THE RUTA 40 VIA CHILE CHICO

On the eastern shore of Lago General Carrera, the small agricultural town of **Chile Chico** sits only 11km west of the Argentine border and is the crossing point to Los Antiguos (see page 140), on the famous Ruta 40 (though you have to walk the 2km from the Chilean border to Argentina). Chile Chico's proximity to the **Sector Jeinemeni** lets you access the northernmost trail of **Parque Nacional Patagonia** (see page 460).

To reach Chile Chico you can either take a bus from Puerto Río Tranquilo (see page 459) or from Cochrane (see page 460), or else take **La Tehuelche** car ferry run by Sotramin (ⓦ sotramin.cl) across Lago General Carrera from Puerto Ibañez (daily departures; see website for schedule; 2hr 30min; passengers CH$2500). Puerto Ibañez is easily reachable from Coyhaique with Miguel Acuña (☎ 67 225 1579) and Buses Carolina (☎ 09 8952 1592), the minibuses timed to coincide with the ferries.

Accommodation options at Chile Chico include **Hospedaje & Camping Kon Aiken** (Rodríguez, at Burgos ☎ 67 241 1598), with a large garden for campers (CH$5000), tiny cheap rooms (CH$8000) and comfortable two-person cabañas (CH$30,000). Another alternative is **Hostería de la Patagonia** (Camino Internacional Chacra 3-A ☎ 09 8159 2146, ⓦ hosteriadelapatagonia.cl), a charming Belgian–Chilean-owned house with comfortable en-suite rooms (CH$62,000), sheltered camping spots (CH$5000) and good home-cooked food.

cliff streaked with blue-and-white patterns and gashed with caves, and **Cavernas de Mármol** ("Marble Caves"), further away by boat near the village of Puerto Sánchez. It can be visited by boat (CH$5000–8000/person; try any kiosk along the main road) or by kayaking or SUP excursion. The opening up of **Valle Exploradores**, a stupendously scenic road that snakes past glacial lakes and mountains for 82km to Bahía Exploradores, has made Laguna San Rafael considerably more accessible to visitors (see page 458). Some 55km west along the Valle Exploradores road is the starting point for the guided trek and ice hike run by El Puesto (see page 459) on the vast **Glaciar Exploradores**, the northern tongue of ice that extends from the Campo de Hielo San Valentín.

ARRIVAL AND DEPARTURE

By bus Buses Acuario 13 (☎ 67 252 2143), Buses Don Carlos (☎ 67 221 4507) and Buses Sao Paulo (☎ 67 252 2470) all stop along the Costanera en route between Coyhaique (5hr 30min) and Cochrane (2hr 30min) with at least two departures daily each way. Transportes Pia (☎ 09 9133 6363) and Transporte Martin Pescador (☎ 09 9786 5285) serve Chile Chico, with at least one daily departure in the early afternoon (4hr 30min).

ACCOMMODATION AND EATING

Camping Pudú 1km south of Puerto Río Tranquilo ☎ 67 257 3003, ⓦ puduexcursiones.cl. Attractive, sheltered lakeside campsite with hot showers, laundry service and sauna. The fully equipped six-person cabaña features terrific lake views. Owners are organize excursions to the Capilla de Mármol and into Valle Exploradores. Camping/person CH$5000, cabaña CH$50,000

Cervecería Río Tranquilo (Arisca) Carretera Austral s/n ☎ 09 9895 5577. Right on the waterfront, this microbrewery does a decent golden ale, amber ale and stout and complements it with massive *chorillana* plates to share (CH$10,000), chunky churrasco and chicken sandwiches and salmon tartar. Daily noon–midnight.

Hostería-Suite Los Pinos Godoy 51 ☎ 67 241 1572. Opposite the Copec petrol station, this basic guesthouse is popular with dusty motorcyclists and cyclists in search of a treat, with its clutch of compact, carpeted en-suite singles and doubles. No breakfast or wi-fi. CH$35,000

COCHRANE

The ranching settlement of **COCHRANE** lies 50km south of Puerto Bertrand. The town's paved, orderly grid of streets spreads out from the neat Plaza de Armas. There are limited services, which makes it a useful spot to rest up after the wildness of the Carretera Austral, or to pick up provisions if you're planning to hike into Parque Nacional Patagonia (see page 460).

ARRIVAL AND DEPARTURE

By bus Buses depart from the bus terminal off C Caucahues, two blocks north of the plaza. Buses Acuario 13, Buses Don Carlos, and Buses Sao Paulo run services to Coyhaique, while Buses Aguilas Patagonicas serve Villa O'Higgins as well as Coyhaique. Caleta Tortel is served by Buses Aldea, Buses Patagonia, Buses Katalina, Buses Cordillera and Buses Pachamama. Chile Chico via Puerto Bertrand and Puerto Guadal is served by Buses Marfer. Buses Marfer and Buses Katalina also run to Puerto Río Tranquilo.

Destinations Caleta Tortel (2–4 daily at 8am, 9.30am, 10am or 5.30pm; 3hr); Chile Chico via Puerto Bertrand and Puerto Guadal (Wed & Fri at 8am & Sun at 5pm; 5hr); Coyhaique (3–4 daily at 6.30, 7, 9am & 9.30am; 6–7hr); Puerto Río Tranquilo (daily at 8am & Mon-Fri at 3pm); Villa O'Higgins (Mon, Wed & Sat at 8.30am; 7hr).

ACCOMMODATION AND EATING

Café Tamango Esmeralda 464 ☎ 09 9158 4521. Just off the main square, this bright and wholesome café is a favourite gathering spot for cyclists. Lots of vegetarian options here, including quiches, soup and lentil burgers, plus good coffee and fresh juices to boot. Mon–Sat 9am–8pm.

★ **Cervecería Tehuelche** Teniente Merino 372 ☎ 09 6628 3961. Its walls decked out with prehistoric hunting scenes, Cochrane's best microbrewery has two own brews on tap, as well as a D'olbek from Coyhaique, and the food is great. The grilled fish (CH$8500) is super-fresh, and you can sip a fruit juice or a calafate sour on the outdoor terrace. Daily 12.30pm–late.

Hostal Lago Esmeralda San Valentín 141 ☎ 09 9718 6805. Particularly good for solo travellers (all but one of the seven rooms are singles, half the price of the double), this basic guesthouse has a decent restaurant downstairs and mostly functioning wi-fi. CH$30,000

Residencial Cero a Cero Lago Brown 464 ☎ 67 252 2158. This maze-like family home caters to backpackers and cyclists with their clutch of small, unheated twins and doubles. It's run by a friendly family, breakfast is basic and wi-fi works in the tiny lounge area. Per person CH$13,000

PARQUE NACIONAL PATAGONIA

Seventeen kilometres north of Cochrane and incorporating protected land 6km east

RUTA DE LOS PARQUES

On January 29, 2018, the Tompkins Foundation made the largest private land donation in history to the Chilean government. President Michelle Bachelet met with Kristine Tompkins to sign a historic agreement, according to which the Tomkins Foundation handed over one million acres of protected land, including their two flagship parks – Parque Pumalín and Parque Patagonia – and Bachelet added nine million acres of federal land, resulting in the creation of five new national parks (Pumalín, Patagonia, Melimoyu, Cerro Castillo and Kawéskar) and in the expansion of three more (Corcovado, Isla Magdalena and Hornopirén). These eight national parks are all part of the brand-new **Ruta de los Parques** – a chain of seventeen national parks that stretches down the spine of Chile for 1500 miles from Parque Nacional Alerce Andino to Parque Nacional Cabo de Hornos. "It's the culmination of our life's work," Kris Tompkins commented when asked about the historic handover. "This is what we've always intended."

of town, the newly created (as of Jan 2018) **Parque Nacional Patagonia** is the result of ten years of hard work by Conservacion Patagonica (ⓦconservacionpatagonica.org). Incorporating the former Reserva Tamango and Reserva Nacional Jeinimeni, this stunning national park comprises mountains, highland lagoons, Patagonian steppe and forest-covered hills. In the central section of the park, there are currently four trails. The 21km **Sendero Lagunas Altas** (6hr) starts by the *Westwinds Campsite* and climbs gently through scrubland and forest to a cluster of ten pristine highland lakes, with superb views of the valley en route and plentiful wildlife including guanacos. This trail is connected by another trail to Reserva Tamango. Parque Patagonia's second trail is **Sendero Los Áviles**, a 47km, three-day hike from Casa Piedra along the Áviles river valley to Sector Jeinimeni.

From the *Alto Valle Campsite*, 9km east of Casa Piedra along the road to Argentina, a 6km 4WD track ascends to the Mirador Douglas Tomkins that overlooks two gorgeous glacial lakes nestling between snow-peaked mountains – the landscape that the late conservationist loved deeply. The two new trails – **Sendero Los Gatos** and **Sendero Lago Chico** – branch off the 4WD track at 4.6km and 5.5km, respectively.

Sector Tamango

Sector Tamango (previously Reserva Tamango), 6km east of Cochrane, sits on the banks of **Lago Cochrane**. Of the eight trails within this part of the park, varying in length and difficulty, the longest trail leads to Laguna Tamanguito, seamlessly connecting Sector Tamango with Parque Nacional Patagonia's Lagunas Altas trail (see page 459). The reserve is notable for its population of around eighty *huemúl* (native deer); if you're lucky, you may spot one. There's no public transport, but it's possible to walk to the park entrance from Cochrane by taking Pasaje 1 north and then east from San Valentín and Colonia.

Sector Jeinimeni

Now the northern gateway to Parque Nacional Patagonia, created in January 2018 (see page 375), **Sector Jeinimeni** comprises Patagonian steppe, russet-coloured mountains and azure lakes. Most trails start from the main entrance, 52km from Chile Chico.

Twenty-five kilometres along the road is the entrance to a separate part of Sector Jeinimeni, with an excellent 6km loop trail, **Sendero Piedra Clavada** (3hr), that passes by the Cueva de los Manos – a cave with millennia-old Tehuelche cave paintings, as well as Valle Lunar – an arid moonscape of jagged red rock formations.

From the campsite beyond the main entrance to the park there's the Sendero El Miradór, an 800m-ascent to a viewpoint overlooking the lake via *lenga* forest, and the largely flat Sendero Lago Verde, a 5.2km, two-hour round-trip to the eponymous lake, skirting the cerulean Lago Jeinimeni.

The most ambitious hiking trail, however, is the three-day, 47km **Sendero**

4

La Leona, which starts at the Conaf ranger station, skirts the southern shore of Lago Jeinemeni, climbs up to the Cordón La Gloria and then follows Valle Hermoso and Valle Áviles to Casa Piedra in the central section of Parque National Patagonia (see page 460), Day excursions to the park are run by Patagoniaxpress in Chile Chico.

ARRIVAL AND INFORMATION

On foot There is no public transport to Parque Nacional Patagonia, but you can hike in from Cochrane via Sector Tamango (see page 461): a 7–8hr hike connects Sector Tamango to the Lagunas Altas trail from where it's another 2–3hr down to the park headquarters. From the Carretera Austral, it's a 17km hike to the Park Headquarters in the central sector.

Information There are Conaf ranger stations in the Jeinimeni and Tamango sectors. Check in at El Rincón Gaucho in the central sector (17km from the main entrance to the park; ☎ 65 297 0829) on arrival and pay for camping here.

ACCOMMODATION AND EATING

The campsites (first come, first served) in the central sector are open Oct–April. Sector Jeinimeni also has a basic campsite.

Camping Alto Valle 35km east of the park headquarters (see page 460). A sheltered campsite at the base of a hill. There are two large *quinchos* for large groups, six smaller ones for individual campers, plus solar-heated showers. Camping/person CH$8000

Camping Casa Piedra Around 25km east of the park headquarters along the X-83. Sheltered campsite in a splendid steppe location. Camping/person CH$8000

Camping Westwinds 2km from the park headquarters (see page 460). This tree-shaded campsite has cooking shelters and solar-heated showers. Oct to late April. Camping/person CH$8000

★ **El Rincón Gaucho** Park headquarters, 17km east of the park entrance. All high beams and stone, the park restaurant serves fantastic food, making full use of greens from the on-site greenhouses, local lamb, and more. Choose from set menu or à la carte. Lunch CH$16,000, dinner buffet CH$26,000. Daily 12.30–3pm & 7.30–10pm.

CALETA TORTEL

Located at the mouth of the Río Baker between the northern and southern ice fields and a logging spot for a lumber company, **CALETA TORTEL** is perhaps the most unusual village in Chile, with a

scattering of houses on forested slopes surrounding a pale emerald bay, linked by a network of walkways and bridges made of fragrant cypress. Tortel is a great detour from the Carretera Austral, and a jumping-off point for boat trips to the eerie Isla de Los Muertos and two glaciers: **Ventisquero Steffens**, which originates in the northern ice field (3hr north by boat; speedboat CH$240,000; *lancha* CH$250,000), and **Ventisquero Jorge Montt**, an enormous bluish ice wall that comes from the southern ice field (5hr by *lancha*; CH$280,000; 2hr by motorboat; CH$300,000), best done in a group of eight to ten people, as the trip is charged per vessel.

ARRIVAL AND INFORMATION

By boat Transbordadora Austral Broom (ⓦ tabsa.cl) sails weekly to Puerto Natales (Dec–Feb), and weekly three weeks out of four the rest of the year (passenger/bicycle CH$132,000/28,300).
Destinations Puerto Natales (Sat at 11pm; 40hr).
By bus Buses stop in the car park in Rincón Alto, the upper section of the village.
Destinations Cochrane (daily at 9.30am, some days also 8am, 10am, 2pm & 8.15pm; 3hr; Buses Aldea ☎ 67 263 8291, Buses Patagonia ☎ 67 252 2470, Buses Katalina ☎ 09 9932 4320, Buses Cordillera ☎ 09 8134 4990 and Buses Pachamama ☎ 09 9411 4811); Villa O'Higgins (Mon, Thurs & Sat at 4.30pm; 4hr; Buses VulTur Patagonia ☎ 09 9350 8156.
Information The very helpful kiosk with plenty of information on Tortel is in the car park (daily 10am–8pm in peak season).

ACCOMMODATION AND EATING

Hospedaje Brisas Del Sur Playa Ancha ☎ 09 9698 8244. Presided over by friendly Valeria, this budget option consists of basic but comfortable rooms, many with sea views. Valeria's brothers run boat tours to the graveyard and glaciers. CH$30,000

Hospedaje Costanera Rincón Base ☎ 09 6670 0236. Friendly Louisa Escobar houses her guests in a clutch of simple, carpeted rooms with wood-burning stoves. It's CH$15,000 per person, and some rooms lack natural light. CH$30,000

★ **Sabores Locales** Sectór Rincón Bajo. The indomitable Maritza serves up large portions of ultra-fresh fish dishes, hearty shellfish soup and vegetables from her own garden, as well as locally brewed craft beer. She's a great source of local info and has a guidebook of particular interest to cyclists. Mains around CH$9000. Daily 12.30–11pm.

VILLA O'HIGGINS

Continuing south from Cochrane to **VILLA O'HIGGINS**, a simple grid of wooden houses huddled against a sheer mountain face, the Carretera Austral winds its way around hairpin bends with sheer drops and spectacular vistas of glacial rivers cutting through endless forest. Once here, there are two choices: turn back, or cross **Lago O'Higgins** into Argentina.

A footpath off Calle Lago Cisnes runs through Parque Cerro Santiago up to a *mirador* overlooking the village; from there, the path continues on to a higher *mirador* and then towards the ice "tongue" of the **Ventisquero Mosco**, the nearest hanging glacier. It's a rugged 25km trail; you can camp wild halfway. There are several other tough hikes around the village; get the details from *El Mosco* (see page 463). Several glaciers, including the pristine **Ventisquero O'Higgins**, spill into Lago O'Higgins, but these can only be accessed via boat trips in the summer (Nov–April) with Robinson Crusoe (☎67 243 1821, ⍟hielosur.com), Carretera Austral Km1240.

ARRIVAL AND INFORMATION

By plane Aereocord (C Lago O'Higgins, between Río Pascua and Río Mayer, ⍟aerocord.cl) serves Coyhaique (CH$45,000 one way; 1hr) on Mon and Thurs.

By bus Buses Águilas Patagónicas (☎67 252 3730) serve Cochrane, departing from C Lago Christie at Río Bravo (Tues, Thurs & Sun at 8.30am, 7hr). Buses VulTur Patagonia (☎09 9350 8156) run to Tortel (Mon, Thu & Sat at 8.30am, 4hr) between November and April from Calle Lago Cisnes at Río Bravo. Buy tickets in advance.

Tourist information On the plaza (summer only; Mon–Fri 10am–2pm & 3–7pm; ⍟villaohiggins.com). The staff provide some info on the surrounding area, but El Mosco (see across) is a much better source of information. Since there are no banks or ATMs, bring plenty of cash. You can change a limited amount of cash on the *Quetru* boat (see page 465); if heading to Argentina, take plenty of US$.

ACCOMMODATION, EATING AND DRINKING

Several guesthouses offer basic rooms for CH$10,000 per person.

Eco Camping Tsonek Carretera Austral s/n, 1km north of Villa O'Higgins ☎09 7892 9695, ✉info@ tsonek.cl. Run by ornithologist Mauricio (who can arrange birdwatching and trekking tours), this ecologically sustainable campsite has wooden platforms for tents, a composting toilet, hot showers and a communal building for cooking. Camping/person CH$6000

★ **El Mosco** Carretera Austral Km 1240 ☎67 243 1819. With its hammock-festooned porch, the town's only hostel is a hiker and biker magnet. Friendly Orfelina offers plenty of info on travel around the Carretera Austral. Campers can use the hot showers, kitchen and lounge; the dorms are spacious, there are snug rooms upstairs (some with own bathroom) and a tower and cabin for groups. Splurge on a Finnish sauna (CH$15,000) or hot tub (CH$30,000). Sept–May. Dorms CH$10,000, doubles CH$30,000, camping/person CH$6000

Restaurante Entre Patagones Carretera Austral 1 ☎67 243 1810. The only proper restaurant in town fills up nightly with locals and travellers; food is simple and portions are large. Expect the likes of noodle soup and grilled hake; if you're lucky, you'll be there on *asador patagónico* (spit-roasted lamb) night. Meals around CH$10,000. Daily 12.30–3pm & 7.30–11pm.

Southern Patagonia

Enormous glaciers calving icebergs the size of houses, pristine fjords and dozens of islands make up the otherworldly vistas of Magallanes province, or **SOUTHERN PATAGONIA**. Add in forbidding craggy peaks, impossibly blue glacial lakes, a wealth of wildlife and the sheer size and majesty of the internationally renowned **Torres del Paine** national park, and it's easy to see why Patagonia captures the imagination. Cut off from the rest of Chile by the giant Campo de Hielo Sur

(Patagonian Ice Fields) to the northeast, the locals have a strong camaraderie with their counterparts across the Andes; many consider themselves to be Patagonians first, Chileans or Argentines second.

PUNTA ARENAS

On the shores of the Magellan Strait, Patagonia's largest city, **PUNTA ARENAS**, benefits from its proximity to penguins, glaciers and Tierra del Fuego. Established in 1843, nearby Fuerte Bulnes was Chile's first outpost in the region, but the city itself has its roots in a penal colony founded five years later. The port provided a convenient stopover for ships heading to California during the gold rush of 1849, and then grew in size and importance with the introduction of sheep from the Falkland Islands to the Patagonian plains. Punta Arenas emerged as a wool empire, drawing migrant workers from Croatia, Italy, Spain and especially Britain.

PUNTA ARENAS

Cemetery main enterance, Ferry Terminal (5km), Museo Nao Victoria (7km) & Airport (20km)

Hospital Regional (200m)

■ ACCOMMODATION	
Hospedaje Costanera	2
Hospedaje Magallanes	1
Hostal Independencia	6
Innata Patagonia	3
Patagonia B&B	5
La Petite Maison	4

Cementerio Municipal
ANGAMOS
AV MANUEL BULNES
MAIPÚ
Museo Salesiano Maggiorino Borgatello
Bulnes Statue
Santuario María Auxiliadora
SARMIENTO DE GAMBOA
H DE MAGALLANES
CROACIA
A SANHUEZA
CHILOE
BORIES
MEJICANA
SAMPAIO
JORGE MONTT
1
Unimarc Supermarket
3
2
Lavasco Josseau
CARRERA PINTO
Cruz Verde
O'HIGGINS
Buses Fernández/ Pinguino & Turibus
Pullman Bus
Río de las Minas
Central de Buses
Buses Pacheco
AV COLÓN
NAVARRO
AV ESPAÑA
Bus Sur
Unimarc Supermarket
LATAM
Aerovías DAP
4
JOSÉ MENÉNDEZ
Castillo Millward
St James
Museo Regional Magallanes
Buses Ghisoni, Queilen, Techni Austral
Hertz
Palacio Sara Braun
Club Militar
Banco Santander
WALDO SEGUEL
PEDRO MONTT
Residencia Blanchard
Palacio de la Gobernación
PLAZA MUÑOZ GAMERO
21 DE MAYO
Banco de Chile
Museo Naval y Marítimo
KÖRNER
3
4
5
PLAZA WILLIAMS
Catedral
FAGNANO
Banco Santander
ROCA
Palacio Montes Pello
ERRÁZURIZ
NOGUEIRA
6
COSTANERA DEL ESTRECHO
Casino Dreams del Estrecho
Solo Expediciones
BALMACEDA
O'HIGGINS
Port
Magellan Strait
AV INDEPENDENCIA

5 (50m) & Cerro de la Cruz Mirador

● EATING	
Café Inmigrantes	1
La Cuisine	4
History Coffee	5
La Marmita	2
La Mesita Grande	3
Wake Up	6

0   200
metres

4

TO ARGENTINA ON FOOT AND BY BOAT

Every year, a few dozen travellers tackle the boat-hike-boat route between **Villa O'Higgins** and Argentina's **El Chaltén**. At 7.50am, a minibus (CH$3000) run by Robinson Crusoe connects Villa O'Higgins to the dock at Bahía Bahamóndez, 7km east of town for Argentina. The sixty-passenger **Quetru** leaves here at 8.30am (Dec–Feb Mon, Wed, Thurs & Sat; Nov & March Mon, Wed & Sat; CH$46,000) and arrives at the hamlet of **Candelario Mancilla** at around 11am. The only accommodation option is *Hospedaje Candelario Mancilla* (☎67 256 7189) – a **campsite** with access to showers (US$2500) and two or three basic rooms available at owner Rodrigo's house (CH$8000/person); meals provided on request. Get your passport stamped by Chilean border control further up the road.

A gravel road winds uphill for 13km to the **international border**. Beyond the border, the 7.5km stretch of trail to the *Argentine Gendarmería* on the banks of the *Lago del Desierto* becomes a narrow, muddy footpath snaking its way through hilly forest and scrubland. After getting stamped into Argentina, you can either pitch a tent at *Camping Lago del Desierto* (US$8), or stay in the basic *cabaña* (US$20) run by the gendarmes. The next day, catch the motor launch **Huemul** across the lake (Nov–March daily at 11am & 5pm; 30–45min; CH$28,000/AR$950) or hike the remaining 16km (5hr) along a steep, thickly forested path on the left side of the lake, emerging by the pier on the south side.

Minibuses to **El Chaltén** meet the arriving motor launches (3–4 daily; AR$500). To book a guide and packhorses (CH$40,000 per packhorse, two-horse minimum), visit ⓦvillaohiggins.com.

4

Following the decline of the wool economy after World War II, the city was revitalized with the discovery of petroleum in Tierra del Fuego in the 1940s, and now makes its living from petroleum production, commercial fishing and tourism.

WHAT TO SEE AND DO

The heart of the city is the tranquil, shady square **Plaza Muñoz Gamero**, centred around a fierce-looking statue of **Ferdinand Magellan**, with a **Tehuelche** man at his feet. Local lore has it that if you touch the Tehuelche's big toe, you will one day return to Punta Arenas. The plaza is surrounded by several grand Art Nouveau mansions, evidence of the great wealth accumulated here in the 1890s.

Mirador Cerro La Cruz

A five-block walk along Calle Fagnano from the southeast corner of the plaza brings you up to the **Mirador Cerro La Cruz**, offering a stupendous view of the brightly coloured, galvanized metal rooftops of Punta Arenas and the deep blue Magellan Strait beyond.

Palacio Braun-Menéndez

Completed in 1906, the **Palacio Braun-Menéndez**, Magallanes 949, is the former family residence of Mauricio Braun, and Josefina Menéndez – a marriage that united the two wealthiest and most powerful families in Punta Arenas. Inside, the **Museo Regional de Magallanes** (Oct–April Mon & Wed–Sun 10.30am–5pm; May–Sept Mon & Wed–Sun 10.30am–2pm; CH1500; ⓦmuseodemagallanes.cl) showcases beautifully preserved private quarters, lavishly decorated with French Art Nouveau furnishings. Several rooms are devoted to a permanent exhibition detailing the colonization of Patagonia and Tierra del Fuego.

Museo Naval y Marítimo

Two blocks east of the plaza, at Pedro Montt 981, the small but illuminating **Museo Naval y Marítimo** (Tues–Sat 9.30am–12.30pm & 2–5pm; CH$1200) focuses on Punta Arenas's naval history and exploration of the southern oceans. The ground floor features scale models of famous ships, including Sir Ernest Shackleton's *Endurance*, as well as a block of Antarctic ice and maps of Cape Horn. Upstairs you can play around in the area decked out as a ship, complete with nautical equipment and interactive displays of sailing routes and Chile's southernmost lighthouses.

Museo Salesiano Maggiorino Borgatello

Located seven blocks north of the plaza, at Av Bulnes 336, absorbing **Museo Salesiano Maggiorino Borgatello** (Tues–Sun 10am–12.30pm & 3–5.30pm; CH$3000) focuses largely on the indigenous peoples of Southern Patagonia and Tierra del Fuego (Kawéshkar, Selk'nam, Yámana and Tehuelche) and the decimation of their population after the arrival of European missionaries. The unparalleled collection of photographs of the region taken by the Italian mountaineering priest Alberto de Agostini is particularly worth seeing.

Cementerio Municipal

The city's magnificent **Cementerio Municipal** (daily: Dec–March 8am–8pm; April–Nov 7.30am–6pm; free) extends over four city blocks to the northwest of the centre. Crisscrossed by a network of footpaths lined with immaculately clipped cypresses, it reflects the turbulent history of Patagonia. The monumental tombs of the city's ruling families – some made from Italian marble and elaborately engraved with the English and Spanish names – mingle with the Croatian and Scandinavian names of immigrant labourers, etched on more modest gravestones.

Museo Nao Victoria

Seven kilometres north of the centre, the interactive **Museo Nao Victoria** (daily 9am–7pm; CH4000; ⓦnaovictoria.cl) gives you the chance to scramble aboard Magellan's *Nao Victoria* carrack, which took him around Cape Horn, the HMS *Beagle* that carried Darwin to Tierra del Fuego, the *Goleta Ancud* that brought the original colonists to Punta Arenas, and to check out Shackleton's lifeboat that carried him and five crew members through the most violent stretch of ocean on earth after the *Endurance* was crushed by ice. Buses run to Río Seco, where the museum is, from the corner of Carrera Pinto and Chiloé.

ARRIVAL AND INFORMATION

By plane Aeropuerto Presidente Ibáñez is 20km north of town. Flights are met by taxis (CH$10,000), door-to-door minibuses (CH$5000) and Puerto-Natales-bound buses. LATAM and Sky Airline have flights to Santiago (4–5 daily; 3hr 20min); Puerto Montt (2 daily; 2hr); and Balmaceda/Coyhaique (Tues & Thurs; 1hr 30min). Aerovías DAP (ⓦdapairline.com) has flights to Puerto Williams (summer Mon–Sat at 10am; winter 3 weekly; 40min–1hr) and Porvenir (2–3 daily except Sun; 12min), while LATAM also flies to the Falkland Islands (weekly on Sat; 1hr 30min).

By bus Buses Tecni Austral, Navarro 975 (☎61 261 3420), Buses Pacheco, Av Colón 900 (ⓦbusespacheco.co.cl), Buses Barria, Av España 264 (☎61 224 0646) and Bus Sur, Av Colón 842 (ⓦbussur.com) serve Ushuaia via Río Grande; book ahead in peak season. Bus Sur, Buses Pacheco and Buses Fernández (Sanhueza 745; ⓦbusesfernandez.com) go to Puerto Natales. Bus El Pingüino, Sanhueza 745 (☎61 222 1812) and Buses Pacheco serve Río Gallegos. Buses Queilén, Navarro 975 (ⓦqueilenbus.cl), Turibus/Cruz del Sur, Sanhueza 745 (ⓦbusescruzdelsur.cl) and Pullman, Av Colón 568 (ⓦpullman.cl) run to Osorno, Puerto Montt, Ancud and Castro. Bus journeys to Ushuaia involve a 40min ferry crossing and don't always include a meal stop, so bring food.

Destinations Ancud and Castro via Puerto Montt and Osorno (Mon, Wed & Sat 9am; 27hr); Puerto Natales (16 daily; 3hr); Río Gallegos, Argentina (1–2 daily; 4hr); Ushuaia, Argentina, via Río Grande (daily 8.30am/9am; 12hr).

By ferry Ferries from Puerto Williams and Porvenir arrive at the Terminal Tres Puentes 5km north of the plaza; frequent *colectivos* (CH$1000) shuttle between the docks and the centre. Transbordadora Austral Broom, at Juan Williams 6450 (Mon–Fri 8.30am–12.15pm & 2–6.15pm; ⓦtabsa. cl), operates ferries to Puerto Williams (Nov–March weekly on Thurs at 6pm, also some Mondays; 32hr; Pullman seat CH$108,000, berth CH$151,000) and Porvenir (1 daily at 9am; 2hr 30min; CH$6200).

Tourist office The well-stocked Sernatur office is at Fagnano 643 (Mon–Fri 8.30am–8pm, Sat 10am–6pm; ☎61 224 3790, ⓦpatagonia-chile.com).

ACCOMMODATION

★ **Hospedaje Costanera** Correa 1221 ☎61 224 0175, ⓦhospedaje-costanera.hostel.com; map p.464. In a quiet, residential neighbourhood around a 20min walk from main attractions, this hostel gets rave reviews for its helpful owners and "home from home" vibe. Guest kitchen, luggage storage and a wealth of local info are some of the perks. Dorms CH$14,000, doubles CH$30,000

Hospedaje Magallanes Magallanes 570 ☎61 222 8616, ⓦhospedaje-magallanes.com; map p.464. There are five simple doubles (one windowless, one en suite) and a six-bed dorm on offer at this family home, which you'll share with gregarious owner Marisol and Emma the dog. Outdoor activities and tours of the surrounding area organized on request. Dorms CH$18,000, doubles CH$45,000

PUNTA ARENAS TOUR OPERATORS

Kayak Agua Fresca ☏09 9655 5073, Ⓦkayakaguafresca.com. Highly recommended outfit specializing in sea kayaking trips, including a half-day paddle along the Magellan Strait (CH$70,000) and a day-long outing around Cabo San Isidro (CH$230,000).
Solo Expediciones Nogueira 1255 ☏61 271 0219, Ⓦsoloexpediciones.com. With their fast, covered speedboat, these guys whisk passengers off on half-day trips to Isla Magdalena (CH$70,000), stopping at the sea lion colony of Isla Marta. They sail from Laredo pier, rather than Punta Arenas itself, which means far less time on the water than with Comapa (see below), though their boat is more weather-dependent.
Turismo Comapa Navarro 1112 ☏61 220 0200, Ⓦcomapa.com. This longstanding operator offers ferry excursions to Isla Magdalena (see page 467; CH$50,000) that involve four hours on the boat in total.

Hostal Independencia Independencia 374 ☏61 222 7572, Ⓦhostalindependencia.es.tl; map p.464. Friendly young owners allow cheek-by-jowl camping in the yard and can rent out equipment and organize tours of the area. Dorms and rooms are tiny, but the warmth of the owners and generous breakfast (CH$1500) make up for it. Camping CH$4000, dorms CH$8000, doubles CH$15,000
★ **Innata Patagonia** Magallanes 631 ☏9 6279 4254, Ⓦinnatapatagonia.com; map p.464. This brand-new B&B is within easy walking distance of most attractions, restaurants and bus stations, the helpful, bilingual staff can help you with onward travel and the whitewashed, spotless rooms are en suite and come with mini-kitchenettes, central heating and powerful showers. US$80
Patagonia B&B España 1048 ☏61 222 7243, Ⓦpatagoniabb.cl; map p.464. Set back from the main street, this is a beautiful, modern, hotel-like B&B; all twins and doubles are bright, spacious and en suite, with cable TV and bright splashes of colour. The CH$20,000 discount for solo travellers makes this a great bargain, but breakfast is lacklustre. CH$55,000
La Petite Maison Menéndez 1064 ☏61 232 3865; map p.464. The five rooms here are a bit threadbare, and a couple are windowless, but the location is super-central, the price is a bargain for budget travellers and owner Gloria is a helpful soul. CH$25,000

EATING

Unimarc supermarket at Bories 647 (Mon–Sat 9am–10pm, Sun 10am–9pm) is useful for self-caterers.
Café Inmigrantes Quillota 559 ☏61 222 2205, Ⓦinmigrante.cl; map p.464. Located on a corner in the quiet Croatian neighbourhood, this homely café is filled with sepia prints of historic Punta Arenas. Come here for chunky sandwiches overstuffed with locally smoked salmon, meats and the home-made cakes. Sandwiches from CH$6000. Mon–Sat 2.30–9pm.
★ **La Cuisine** O'Higgins 1037 ☏61 222 8641; map p.464. With his good-value lunch menu (CH$6500), French chef Eric has earned himself a loyal local clientele. While the set menu is not bad, the à la carte dinner choices shine, among them *boeuf bourguignon*, king crab lasagne and salmon in a red wine jus, served amid clichéd "French" decor – murals of the Eiffel Tower and ladies doing the cancan. Service is leisurely. Mains CH$7000–12,000. Mon–Sat 12.30–3pm & 7.30–11pm, Sun 1–3.30pm.
History Coffee Navarro 1065 ☏61 222 0000; map p.464. At this aptly named café you're surrounded by history (ye olde photos of Punta Arenas, antique coffee grinders) and coffee (beans embedded in your table). The brew is decent, there's a good selection of sweet and savoury crêpes, *churrascos* and burgers (CH$4000–5200). Mon–Sat 9am–9pm.
★ **La Marmita** Plaza Sampaio 678 ☏61 222 2056, Ⓦmarmitamaga.cl; map p.464. Among the eclectic decor you'll find some of the best flavours for miles around and attentive service from the young staff. The pisco (and berry) sours are the best in town, and you can feast on the likes of *ceviche*, vegetable risotto and hare casserole with black beer. The chef's signature dessert is the sublime chocolate pyramid with calafate berry mousse. Mains CH$8000–14,000. Mon–Sat 12.30–3pm & 7–11pm, Sun noon–midnight.
La Mesita Grande O'Higgins at Montt ☏61 224 4312, Ⓦmesitagrande.cl; map p.464. This Puerto Natales transplant has taken the city by storm, with its thin and crispy pizzas and lively, communal ambience, encouraged by the long wooden tables and benches. The *matavampiros* (mozzarella with roasted garlic) is excellent. Pizzas from CH$5300. Daily 12.30–11pm.
★ **Wake Up** Errázuriz 944 ☏61 237 1641; map p.464. A welcome new spot, *Wake Up* is the place to come for great coffee or an all-day breakfast. Choose from a stack of American pancakes, French toast, eggs Benedict and more. There's usually a lunchtime dish of the day, as well. Mains CH$4500–6000. Mon–Fri 7am–8pm, Sat 9am–4pm, Sun 10am–4pm.

ISLA MAGDALENA

In the middle of the stormy Magellan Strait lies **Isla Magdalena** – the largest Magellanic

4

penguin colony in all of Chile, with an estimated 100,000 nesting birds residing on a one-kilometre-square cliff by the old lighthouse. The monogamous birds spend the September-to-March breeding season here, living in burrows in the ground. The female lays two eggs in October, with both parents taking turns looking after the chicks once they've hatched in December, while the other fishes for food. In early February you'll find the grown chicks huddled near the sea, as large as their parents but still growing the adult feathers necessary for swimming. The **best time to visit** the colony is January, when the population is at its largest. Though you have to stick to the designated walking routes, the penguins don't fear humans and will come quite close to you. You can visit here with **Turismo Comapa** or with **Solo Expediciones** (see page 467).

4 PUERTO NATALES

Some 241km northwest of Punta Arenas, the town of **PUERTO NATALES** is situated in

relative isolation on the **Seno Última Esperanza** ("Last Hope Sound"). Officially founded in 1911, it was used primarily as a port for exporting wool and beef from the nearby Puerto Prat cattle *estancia*, built by German explorer **Hermann Eberhard** in 1893. The town's proximity to one of the continent's most gasp-inducing national parks – Torres del Paine – combined with the popular Navimag ferry from Puerto Montt, has firmly established Puerto Natales as one of Patagonia's top destinations for outdoor enthusiasts and backpackers.

Faced with a motley collection of tin and wooden houses, a visitor's first impression of Puerto Natales is invariably coloured by the weather. On a clear day, Seno Última Esperanza is a remarkably vivid, tranquil blue, with magnificent views of the snowcapped **Cordillera Sarmiento** and **Campo de Hielo Sur** visible across the bay.

WHAT TO SEE AND DO

The town is centred on the **Plaza de Armas**, with its main commercial

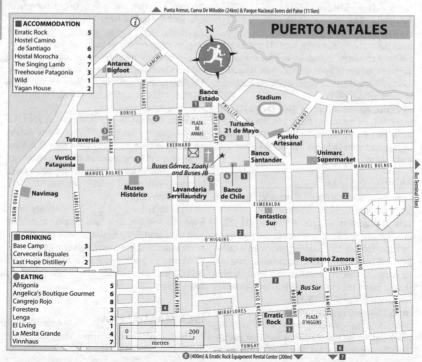

PUERTO NATALES

Punta Arenas, Cueva De Milodón (24km) & Parque Nacional Torres del Paine (111km)

■ **ACCOMMODATION**
Erratic Rock	5
Hostel Camino de Santiago	6
Hostal Morocha	4
The Singing Lamb	7
Treehouse Patagonia	3
Wild	1
Yagan House	2

■ **DRINKING**
Base Camp	3
Cervecería Baguales	1
Last Hope Distillery	2

● **EATING**
Afrigonia	5
Angelica's Boutique Gourmet	6
Cangrejo Rojo	8
Forestera	3
Lenga	2
El Living	1
La Mesita Grande	4
Vinnhaus	7

SANCHEZ
MAGALLANES
Antares/Bigfoot
Banco Estado
Stadium
BORIES
ROGERS
PLAZA DE ARMAS
ARTURO PRAT
PHILLIPI
Turismo 21 de Mayo
ANGAMOS
VALDIVIA
Pueblo Artesanal
Tutraversia
BARROS ARANA
EBERHARD
Vertice Patagonia
Buses Gómez, Zaahj and Buses JB
Banco Santander
Unimarc Supermarket
MANUEL BULNES
Navimag
LADRILLEROS
MANUEL BULNES
Museo Histórico
Lavandería Servilaundry
Banco de Chile
ESMERALDA
PEDRO MONTT
Fantastico Sur
O'HIGGINS
Baqueano Zamora
CHORRILLOS
GALVARINO
CARRERA PINTO
BLANCO ENCALADA
BAQUEDANO
E. RAMIREZ
B. ZAMORA
Bus Sur
MIRAFLORES
Erratic Rock
PLAZA O'HIGGINS
0 200 metres
YUNGAY
Bus Terminal (1km)

(400m) & Erratic Rock Equipment Rental Center (200m)

thoroughfares north–south Baquedano and east–west Bulnes. The worthwhile **Museo Histórico**, at Bulnes 285 (Mon–Fri 8am–7pm, Sat 10am–1pm & 3–7pm; CH$1000), has attractive bilingual exhibits on the region's **indigenous tribes**, illustrated with artefacts and black-and-white photos of Aónikenk and Kawéskar people, as well as on European settlement, the story of the Milodon's cave, and the region's first German settler, Hermann Eberhard; look out for his ingenious collapsible boat that turns into a suitcase.

ARRIVAL AND INFORMATION

By plane From the tiny airport some 6km north of Puerto Natales, in high season, LATAM serves Santiago (4 weekly; 3hr), while DAP flies to El Calafate (Nov–April Thurs & Sun; 35min).

By bus All buses depart from the main bus terminal, Rodoviario Puerto Natales, at Av España 1455. It's a 10–15min walk from the centre; taxis cost CH$1500 within town. Services to El Calafate (Argentina) and Torres del Paine only operate Oct–April.

Destinations El Calafate, Argentina (2–3 daily; 5hr); Coyhaique (Wed, noon; 17hr); Parque Nacional Torres del Paine (numerous daily; 2hr 30min; departures 7.30am & 2.30pm); Punta Arenas (hourly; 3hr); Río Gallegos, Argentina (3 weekly; 5hr); Ushuaia, Argentina (2 daily; 12hr).

By ferry From the Navimag ferry terminal (Pedro Montt 308; @61 241 2554, @navimag.cl) the MV *Edén* sails to Puerto Montt (Tues 6am; from US$450; around 70hr). Book a couple of weeks in advance in summer. Transbordadora Austral Broom at Montt 605 (@61 272 8100, @tabsa.cl) serves Caleta Tortel on the Carretera Austral (Thurs 5am; 41hr).

Tourist information Sernatur is at Pedro Montt 19 (Mon–Fri 8.30am–8pm, Sat & Sun 10am–6pm; @61 241 2125, @sernatur.cl), with very helpful staff.

Erratic Rock (@erraticrock.com) Visitors heading to the national park (see page 470) shouldn't miss the daily 11am and 3pm talks at the Erratic Rock Equipment Rental Center, Baquedano 955, where experienced trekkers give you the lowdown on how best to tackle the park and what gear you'll need.

ACCOMMODATION

★ **Erratic Rock** Baquedano 719 @erraticrock.com; map p.468. Run by congenial Oregonian Bill, this hostel is a Puerto Natales institution. The atmosphere is laidback – with hostel cat Clyde wandering in and out. Dorms and rooms are snug and there's a real sense of camaraderie among the guests. Besides the great breakfast, the daily "3 o'clock talk" gives you essential Torres del Paine tips; onward transport

and tours can now also be booked here. Dorms CH$12,000, doubles CH$30,000

Hostel Camino de Santiago Ramírez 952 @09 9304 1094, @hostalcaminodesantiago.cl; map p.468. One of the better additions to Natales' hostel scene, run by a Spanish/Chilean couple. There's a guest café and bar downstairs and mountain bikes for rent at the front. The quality bunks and beds in the four-bed dorms and bright twins and doubles make for a good night's rest. Dorms CH$21,000, doubles CH$60,000

Hostal Morocha Barros Luco 688 @09 9708 1250, @hostalmorocha.com; map p.468. With just five individually decorated rooms (expect James Dean quotes), a most satisfying breakfast spread and welcoming, knowledgeable owners (Pablo is a porter in Torres del Paine), this is an excellent choice for visitors who want some privacy without breaking the budget. Doubles have their own bathrooms; the twin and the singles share facilities. CH$40,000

The Singing Lamb Arauco 779 @61 241 0958, @thesinginglamb.com; map p.468. This well-designed hostel is a cut above in terms of facilities: nine-, six- and four-bed dorms with comfortable beds rather than bunks, homely common area, good showers and a block of private doubles with windows that open into the corridor. The breakfast is good, and staff can book onward transport and excursions. The downside is the hostel's large size and impersonal vibe. Dorms CH$18,000, doubles CH$60,000

★ **Treehouse Patagonia** Chorillos 653 @09 8417 4514; map p.468. Beautifully designed by its welcoming architect owner, Pancho, this intimate hostel has room for just ten guests. Choose between the snug four-bed dorm with large lockers or one of the three gorgeous en suites – a double and two twins – with high ceilings and woollen hangings. Closed June–Aug. Dorm CH$14,000, double CH$40,000

Wild Bulnes 555 @09 7715 2423, @wildhostel.com; map p.468. There's a lot to like about *Wild*, from its name spelled across a wall in tree branches and the eye-catching white, crimson and lime green decor to a plethora of amenities including an on-site bar and café. Bed down in one of the upstairs dorms or choose a garden double (or deluxe suite with kitchen). Equipment rental shop attached. Dorms CH$14,000, doubles CH$45,000

Yagan House O'Higgins 584 @61 241 4137, @yaganhouse.cl; map p.468. Excellent beds with down duvets, warm red-and-cream decor, eco-friendly practices and a guest lounge with a roaring fire distinguish this intimate hostel. Extras include gear rental, a small bar and laundry service. Dorms CH$15,000, doubles CH$45,000

EATING

★ **Afrigonia** Magallanes 247 @61 241 2877; map p.468. One of Natales's most imaginative restaurants

4

PUERTO NATALES TOUR OPERATORS AND TRIPS

Baqueano Zamora Baquedano 534 ☎ 61 261 3531, ⓦ baqueanozamora. Horse-trekking in Torres del Paine (CH$35,000/55,000 for half-/full-day) arranged by this longstanding operator. It operates out of the Estancia Tercera Barranca near Torres del Paine.

BigFoot Montt 161 ☎ 61 241 4611, ⓦ bigfootpatagonia.com. Operating out of *Refugio/ Campamento Grey* in Torres del Paine (p.475), and with an office in *Kau Patagonia*), this longstanding operator offers twice-daily (11am & 4pm) 5hr ice hikes on Glaciar Grey (CH$105,000) as well as kayaking (CH$66,000) amid the house-sized chunks of ice. Book in advance to get a discounted boat trip across Lago Grey/ice trekking combo (CH$130,000).

Erratic Rock Baquedano 719 ⓦ erraticrock.com. Experienced operator with an excellent reputation, running multi-day trekking trips to Cabo Froward and in Torres del Paine, as well as rock climbing ascents of Torre Norte and dog sledding jaunts in Ushuaia.

Estancia Travel Puerto Bories 13B ☎ 61 241 2221, ⓦ estanciatravel.com. Highly recommended horseriding trips, from half-day rides to the Cueva de Milodón to twelve-day *estancia* expeditions by an English/Chilean outfit.

Fantástico Sur Esmeralda 661 ☎ 61 261 4184, ⓦ fantasticosur.com. Makes bookings for the Torre Norte, Torre Central, Chileno and Los Cuernos *refugios* and campsites, as well as *Campamento Serón* and *Camping Francés*.

Tutravesia Barros Arana 176 ☎ 61 269 1196, ⓦ tutravesia.com. Established kayaking outfit offering multi-day trips for beginner and advanced kayakers alike – from a day-long paddle Río Grey and three-day trips to Glaciar Tundall to the spectacular four-day Ruta de Hielo, which ends in a lake filled with icebergs.

Vertice Patagonia Bulnes 100 ☎ 61 241 2742, ⓦ verticepatagonia.com. Bookings for Paine Grande, Lago Grey, Los Perros and Dickson *refugios*, as well as campsites in Torres del Paine.

serves delectable African/Patagonian fusion dishes. Standouts include *ceviche* with mango, melt-off-the-bone Patagonian lamb and spicy seafood curry with *wali* (rice with almonds and raisins). Be prepared for a leisurely dinner. Mains CH$10,000–14,000. Daily 1–10.30pm.

Angelica's Boutique Gourmet Bulnes 501; map p.468. This bakery-coffee shop serves good coffee, gooey brownies, home-made cheesecake and inexpensive daily specials, such as calzones, Greek salad and pizza with goat's cheese (from CH$6500). Also sells tiny wine bottles – ideal for taking to Torres del Paine. Daily 9am–4pm & 5–10pm.

Cangrejo Rojo Santiago Bueras 782 ☎ 61 241 2436; map p.468. Strategically strewn with nautical paraphernalia, this cute restaurant specializes in fish and seafood. Among the likes of *ceviche* and grilled conger eel with squid-ink rice you'll find more unusual items, such as grilled sheep's testicles. Mains from CH$8000. Mon–Sat 1–11pm.

Forestera Baquedano 699 ☎ 09 8295 2036; map p.468. This gourmet burger joint grills a devil's dozen of beef, lamb, chicken and vegetarian burgers (CH$7000) to your specifications. The Forestera – with caramelized onions and bacon – is a classic, while "del Puerto" comes topped with sheep's cheese and spinach. Regional Coirón and Fernando de Magallanes microbrews are a good accompaniment. Mon–Sat 1–3pm & 7.30–11pm.

★ **Lenga** Bories 221 ☎ 61 269 1187; map p.468. "Cook free or die" is the motto at this creative, intimate restaurant that makes the most of Patagonian ingredients. Presentation is striking, flavours are faultless, and you can expect scallop *ceviche* with edible flowers, slow-cooked

lamb shanks and chocolate brownie with calafate berry sorbet. Reservations recommended. Mains CH$10,000–14,000. Tues–Sun 6–11pm.

El Living Arturo Prat 156 ☎ 61 241 1140, ⓦ el-living. com; map p.468. An excellent vegetarian restaurant and lounge café, with chillout music in the background and comfortable sofas to sink into. Treats include three cheese and walnut ravioli, borscht, hummus and chunky sandwiches, such as avocado, camembert and olive. Their cakes and home-made honeycomb ice cream are equally good. Mains CH$5600–8200. Jan–March & Dec Mon–Sat 11am–10pm.

La Mesita Grande Eberhard 508 ☎ 61 241 1571, ⓦ mesitagrande.cl; map p.468. Hordes of hungry hikers stage a daily invasion of the best pizzeria in Patagonia, drawn by the generous portions of superb thin-crust pizzas (from CH$6800), home-made pasta and interesting desserts (including sweet pizza with *dulce de leche*). The two long wooden tables make for a communal dining experience. Daily 12.30–3.30pm & 7–11.30pm.

Vinnhaus Bulnes 499 ☎ 09 8269 2510, ⓦ vinnhaus. com; map p.468. Attached to the eponymous hostel, this cosy café and bar has become a travellers' haunt, whether you're after coffee, cake and quiche, or a craft beer from a regional brewery. Good wine selection, too. Daily 11am–10.30pm.

DRINKING

Base Camp Baquedano 731 ⓦ erraticrock.com; map p.468. Next door to the most popular hostel in town, this former brothel turned lively pub is usually full to the brim with pre- and post-Torres hikers, contentedly drinking local brews and eating thin and crispy pizzas. Expect occasional performances by local bands, themed nights and spontaneous barbecues. Daily 6pm–1am.

Cervecería Baguales Bories 430 ☎61 241 1920, ⓦcervezabaguales.cl; map p.468. If the one thing that would make your Patagonian hiking experience complete is returning to a cosy microbrewery serving ample platters of fiery buffalo wings, quesadillas, tacos and other Tex-Mex, accompanied by a home-made light, dark and amber brew, then you're in luck: look no further than this Californian/Chilean pub. Beers CH$2200; mains CH$6000–12,500. Mon–Sat 1pm–2.30am.

★ **Last Hope Distillery** Esmeralda 882 ☎09 7201 8585; map p.468. When Aussies Matt and Kiera couldn't find an après-trek beverage they wanted, they opened a gin and whisky distillery of their own. Choose from country-specific whisky flights – a selection unparalleled in Natales – or original cocktails including the signature G&T made with their own calafate berry gin. Snacks span the globe. *Last Hope* is the sort of place you find yourself lingering in until the wee hours. Wed–Sun 5pm–2am.

DIRECTORY

Banks and exchange Banco Santander, on Blanco Encalada, at Bulnes, and Banco de Chile, at Bulnes 544, both have ATMs.

Hospital Hospital Puerto Natales (☎61 241 1583), at Pinto and O'Higgins, handles basic medical emergencies.

Laundry Lavandería Servilaundy at Prat 332 (daily 9am–10pm).

Post office Eberhard 429, on the plaza.

PARQUE NACIONAL TORRES DEL PAINE

The great massif contained within the **PARQUE NACIONAL TORRES DEL PAINE**, 112km northwest of Puerto Natales, with the sheer granite towers of **Las Torres** to the east, and the multicoloured **Los Cuernos** to the west, is one of Patagonia's most jaw-dropping sights. The park offers incomparable opportunities for backcountry hiking, as well as animal spotting; you are likely to see **guanacos** – wild relatives of llamas – and *ñandú* or rhea (like a small ostrich). Pumas also live in the park, though they're shy, as well as foxes, the elusive *huemúl* deer and condors. There is also a host of other outdoor activities – from ice-trekking on Glacier Grey and kayaking in the icy Lago

HIKING THE "W"

Though Torres del Paine offers numerous hiking trails, the most popular is undoubtedly the **"W"**, a four- to five-day hike that takes in the park's highlights: the massive **Glacier Grey**, steep **Valle Francés** and, finally, the **mirador Las Torres**. It makes sense to hike the "W" from west to east, tackling the steepest ascent last, especially if you're carrying camping gear, as you will have eaten most of your provisions by the time you approach the challenging Las Torres *mirador*.

Grey to horseriding in the outlying hills.

Glacier Grey

From the pier at Pudeto where the catamaran drops you off at the *Paine Grande Lodge* (see page 474), a trail runs north through the scrubland, past a small lagoon and into the remnants of a *lenga* forest (damaged by a fire caused by human negligence in 2011). The trail emerges at the **Quebrada de los Vientos** ("Windy Gorge"), an hour or so into the hike, where your first glimpse of **Glacier Grey** – more than 7km wide at its largest point – stops you in your tracks. For the next couple of hours, you walk across exposed terrain, beside the pale water of Lago Grey and its house-sized chunks of blue ice. The glacier peeks from behind the dark rock of **La Isla Nunatak** on the lake's far side.

The trail then descends steeply through the *lenga* woods, crossing a wooden bridge over a gushing torrent, before arriving at the **Refugio y Campamento Grey**, which marks the end of the first leg of the "W".

Valle Francés

You need to double back on yourself for the second leg of the "W". Back at the *Paine Grande Lodge*, a two-and-a-half-hour-long, eastbound trail heads through scrubland and calafate bushes along Lago Pehoé before leading north with glimpses of **Lago Skottsberg** on your right-hand side. A hanging bridge brings you to the *Campamento Italiano*, where you can leave most of your gear before scrambling up the steep, rocky path leading up the **Valle Francés**, the middle part of the "W". The

Puerto Natales (116km)

Laguna Azul

Laguna Amarga

Laguna Goic

Laguna Azul

Laguna Amarga

Laguna Blanquillos

Laguna Smock

Laguna Escondida

Cascada Paine

4.5hrs (10km)

1.5hrs (7km)

Laguna Cebolla

Laguna Vega

Río Paine

Torre Norte

Torre Central

Serón

Hostería Las Torres

Valle y Río Ascencio

2hrs

Chileno

4hrs (9km)

Laguna Inge

Lago Paine

1.5hr (5km)

4.5hrs (11km)

Mirador las Torres

Cerro Almirante Nieto (2668m)

1hr (4km)

1hr

Río de los Calquenes

Río Paine

Japonés

Nido de Cóndor (2243m)

3hrs

Valle del Silencio

Torre Norte Monzino (2600m)

Torre Central (2600m)

Torre Sur Di Agostini (2650m)

Río Bader

Cuerno Este (2200m)

Lago Quemado

Horse trail

Río de los Perros

Cerro Fortaleza (3000m)

Mirador Valle de Francés

Cuerno Norte (2400m)

Cuerno Principal (2600m)

Dickson

0.5hr (2km)

2.5hrs (5.5km)

Valle y Río del Francés

Glacier Francés

Lago Dickson

4hrs (11km)

Glacier Los Perros

Cerro Paine Grande (3248m)

Los Perros

5hrs (12km)

Grey

1hr (4km)

John Gardner Pass (1241m)

Paso

2hrs (6km)

Lago Escondido

La Isla Nunatak

Glacier Grey

Serviced campsite
Unserviced campsite
Guardería (ranger station)
Refugio (mountain refuge)

4

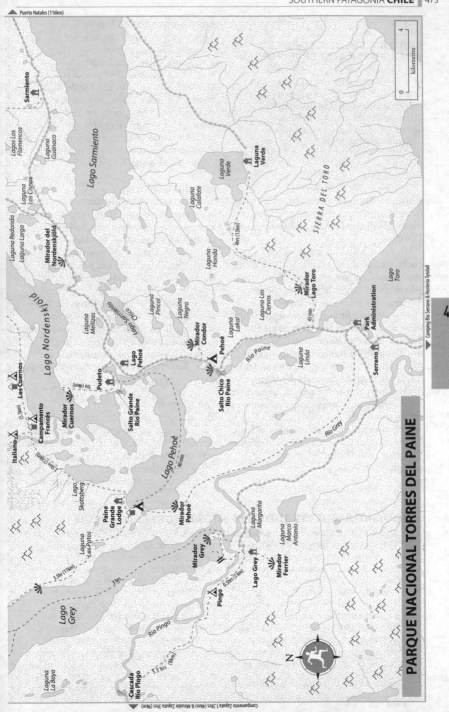

PARQUE NACIONAL TORRES DEL PAINE

4

▶ Camping Río Serrano & Hostería Tyndall

Sarmiento

Lagos Los Flamencos

Laguna Guanaco

Laguna Redonda

Laguna Larga

Lago Sarmiento

Laguna Los Cisnes

Laguna Verde

Laguna Calafate

Laguna Honda

SIERRA DEL TORO

4hrs (12km)

Mirador del Nordenskjöld

Lago Nordenskjöld

Laguna Mellizas

Lago Sarmiento Chico

Laguna Pincol

Laguna Negra

Mirador Condor

Pehoé

Laguna Lakal

Laguna Los Ciervos

Mirador Lago Toro

Lago Toro

45 min

Park Administration

Los Cuernos

(5.5km)

Mirador Cuernos

Lago Pehoé

Pudeto

1hr (4km)

Salto Grande Río Paine

Salto Chico Río Paine

Río Paine

Laguna Linda

Serrano

Italiano

Campamento Francés

2.5hrs (7.5km)

40 min

Lago Pehoé

Río Grey

Lago Skottsberg

Paine Grande Lodge

Mirador Pehoé

Laguna Marco Antonio

Laguna Les Patos

3.5hr (11km)

3 hrs

Mirador Grey

Pingo

0.5hrs (2 km)

Lago Grey

Laguna Margarita

Mirador Ferrier

Lago Grey

Río Pingo

Río Pingo

5.5 hrs (8km)

Cascada Río Pingo

Laguna La Boya

N

0 kilometres 4

LAGO AND GLACIER GREY BY BOAT, KAYAK AND CRAMPON

From the *Hostería Lago Grey* it's possible to take a spectacular three-hour *boat ride* up Lago Grey to Glacier Grey (4 daily; 3hr return; CH$75,000). If staying overnight (or taking the first boat in) at *Refugio y Campamento Grey*, you can go kayaking between icebergs on the icy lake or else go ice trekking on the glacier itself with BigFoot (see page 470).

Los Cuernos to Las Torres

From the *Refugio y Campamento Los Cuernos*, the trail runs through hilly scrubland, with Lago Nordenskjöld on your right. Shortly after you depart **Los Cuernos**, you cross to the **Río del Valle Bader**, a rushing glacial stream; the rest of the trail meanders gently up and down foothills. The hike takes around four and a half hours and you cross a bridge over the Río Asencio just before you reach the *Hostería Las Torres*.

Mirador Las Torres

The hike to the famous **Mirador Las Torres** is a steep, three-hour thirty-minute ascent alongside the Río Ascencio, followed by an hour-long scramble up boulders. Since the Torres campsite is now closed it's no longer possible to witness the spectacle of the sun's first rays colouring the magnificent Torres, perfectly reflected in the still waters of **Laguna Torres**, unless you start out in the wee hours of the morning from the *Refugio y Campamento Chileno*, halfway up the trail. The "W" ends with a short trek or minibus ride from *Torre Norte* and *Torre Central refugios* back to the park entrance.

The "Circuit"

The "Circuit" is an extended version of the "W", a seven- to ten-day hike that leads you around the back of the Torres and that may only be done anti-clockwise due to safety regulations.

Start from the *Paine Grande Lodge*, do

turbulent **Río del Francés** churns on your left-hand side and there are spectacular views of Glacier Francés and Glacier Los Perros.

After two hours hiking through enchanted-looking woods, you reach the very basic *Campamento Británico*, from where it's an hour's hike up to the steep lookout that gives you an excellent close-up view of the multicoloured Los Cuernos, as well as the aptly named 2800m-high **Fortaleza** ("fortress"), northeast of the *mirador*. From *Campamento Italiano*, allow two and a half hours for the hike through the forested backcountry to the *Refugio y Campamento Los Cuernos*; it's a long, steep descent on a scree-strewn trail followed by a brief stretch along the pale blue waters of Lago Nordenskjöld; you'll pass the turn-off for *Camping Francés* shortly after leaving *Campamento Italiano*.

BOOKING REFUGIOS AND CAMPSITES IN TORRES DEL PAINE

Most of the park's **campsites** and **refugios** (see page 475) are open only from October to April. Some basic campsites are run by Conaf, but the rest of the accommodation belong either to Vertice Patagonia or Fantástico Sur, both in Puerto Natales (see page 468). As of 2017, it is absolutely **essential to book** all your accommodation in the park in advance online, including all campsites, as reservations are checked by rangers en route and you may not proceed without them. Due to demand, it's best to book up to four months in advance. Some last-minute slots occasionally do come up and can be booked through the relevant offices in Natales (see page 469), but don't count on it. *Refugios* provide hot meals for around CH$13,000/19,000/25,000 for breakfast/lunch/dinner and most *refugios* no longer allow their guests to cook, meaning that you have no choice but go full board. You can rent (limited) camping equipment at most serviced sites (some readily put up for you on wooden platforms), but it's far cheaper to bring your own from Puerto Natales. There are several free, basic, Conaf-run campsites in the park which consist of a clearing with a fire pit; these include *Campamento Paso* and *Campamento Italiano* and must be booked via the Conaf website. Wild camping is not permitted.

the "W" and then carry on from *Hostería Las Torres* to *Campamento Serón* – an easy four-hour walk northwards up and down gentle inclines. From here, it's a five- or six-hour hike to *Refugio Dickson*. Finally, the trail descends steeply to *Refugio Lago Dickson* at the southern end of iceberg-flecked Lago Dickson.

Campamento Los Perros lies a four-hour hike from *Dickson* southwest along a largely uphill trail, with a fabulous view of Glaciar Los Perros above a round lagoon.

The weather has to be in your favour before you start on a three-hour climb to the top of **Paso John Gardner** (1241m) from *Campamento Los Perros*, as it's too dangerous to cross the pass in gale-force wind. Above the tree line, it's a straightforward uphill slog. The reward is the sudden, staggering view over the icy pinnacles of **Glaciar Grey** and **Campo del Hielo Sur**, over ten thousand square kilometres of icecap.

On the other side of the pass crude steps descend steeply into *lenga* forest. It takes a couple of hours to reach the small and unserviced *Campamento Paso* and around three hours to descend to *Refugio y Campamento Lago Grey*. In two places, you have to cross metal bridges.

ARRIVAL AND INFORMATION

By bus The only entrance to the park for visitors coming by bus from Puerto Natales (daily 7.30am & 2.30pm; 2hr 30min) is 117km from the town at Laguna Amarga, where you pay the park fee (CH$21,000) at the Conaf station. From here, minibuses meet bus arrivals from Natales for the transfer to *Hostería Las Torres* (see page 472; CH$3000). The buses from Natales continue along Lago Nordenskjöld for another 19km to the *guardería* at Pudeto, the departure point for the catamaran to *Paine Grande Lodge*; the morning buses arrive in time for the noon boat. The bus continues beyond here, past *Hostería Pehoé*, *Camping Pehoé* and *Explora*, opposite Salto Chico, to reach the Park Administration 18km further on, where there's a visitor centre, a *refugio*, a grocery store and a *hostería*. In peak months, book your bus tickets into the park at least a day in advance. From Argentina's El Calafate, Always Glaciers and South Road run day-trips and transfers to Torres del Paine.

By catamaran From the *guardería* at Pudeto, a Hielos Patagónicos catamaran (mid-Nov to mid-March daily 9.30am, noon & 6pm; early Nov & late March noon & 6pm; Oct & April noon; May–Aug 11am on the first and fifteenth of the month; 30min; CH$18,000 one-way, CH$28,000

return; tickets sold on board ☎61 241 1380) runs across Lago Pehoé. From Pudeto and Laguna Amarga there are two buses to Puerto Natales, leaving at 2pm and 7pm, and 2.30pm and 7.45pm, respectively. From the Las Torres visitor centre, transfers connect with the Puerto Natales buses at Laguna Amarga, leaving 45min before the bus departs.

Conaf The Conaf *guardería* at Laguna Amarga has basic information on the park's fauna and flora, as well as basic trekking maps. You must register and pay your CH$21,000/9000 peak/off-peak entrance fee here before watching the park safety video.

ACCOMMODATION

All prices quoted are per person.

Camping Los Perros (Vértice Patagonia) Last campsite before the John Gardner pass. Located in a wooded area, with a small food shop, cold showers and a cooking hut. CH$5000

Camping Serón (Fantástico Sur) Beside Río Paine. Partially shaded campsite with picnic tables, cooking hut, cold showers and a small shop in a pleasant meadow setting at the bottom of the massif's northeast corner. Camping US$13, camping *platforma* US$80, camping *platforma* full board US$240

Domos y Camping El Francés (Fantástico Sur) Overlooking Lago Nordenskjöld. A short, steep hike down from the trail between *Campamento Italiano* and *Refugio Los Cuernos*, with two multi-person geodomes (bring own bedding or rent it here). Camping US$13, camping *platforma* for US$80, camping *platforma* full board US$240, geodome without full board US$130, geodome full board US$210

Refugio y Campamento Dickson (Vertice Patagonia) On the shores of Lago Dickson. On the northern part of the Circuit, this is the most remote refuge in the park. There's a well-stocked shop and cooking facilities, plus a campsite with cold showers and toilets. Camping US$8, dorms US$32, dorms full board US$82

Refugio y Campamento Grey (Vertice Patagonia) Overlooking Lago and Glaciar Grey. A popular *refugio* with a beachside campsite, hot showers and a small on-site grocery store. Camping US$8, dorms with/without bedding US$80/US$32, full board US$50

Refugio y Campamento Paine Grande (Vertice Patagonia) by Lago Pehoe. This modern structure has a scenic location and a café, restaurant and small store within the lodge. You can camp in the adjoining grassy fields and there are separate toilets and hot showers, as well as a cooking hut for campers. Camping US$10, dorms with/without bedding US$80/US$50, full board US$50

Refugio y Camping Chileno (Fantástico Sur) Halfway along the Valle Ascencio. This small *refugio* offers just 32 beds and has a provisions shop as well as offering hot meals. Full board only. Dorms US$170, camping platform US$240.

Refugio y Camping Los Cuernos (Fantástico Sur) Northern shore of Lago Nordenskjöld. This *refugio* sits in a clearing beneath the Cuernos del Paine, with private cabañas as well as a cafeteria, cooking room for campers, tree-shaded campsite with platforms and hot showers.

Tierra del Fuego

The remotest and least visited of Chile's land territories, at the southern tip of the continent, **TIERRA DEL FUEGO** was named "Land of Fire" by Fernando Magellan, who sailed through the strait that now bears his name in 1520, and saw a multitude of cooking fires lit by the indigenous hunter-gatherers. From then on until the opening of the Panama Canal in 1914, the frigid waters around Cape Horn – the largest ship graveyard in the Americas – formed a link in the perilous yet lucrative trade route from Europe to the west coast of the Americas.

4

Tierra del Fuego's Isla Grande is split between Chile and Argentina; the Chilean half features the nondescript town of **Porvenir**, settled by a mixture of Chilote and Croatian immigrants in the late nineteenth century. The Argentine half includes the lively city of **Ushuaia** (see page 146), the base for Antarctic voyages. The region's biggest natural draw is southern Tierra del Fuego – a scattering of rocky islands, separated by labyrinthine fjords, home to the craggy Darwin Range and the southernmost permanently inhabited town in the world – Isla Navarino's **Puerto Williams**.

PUERTO WILLIAMS

PUERTO WILLIAMS is home to around three thousand people, including the last descendants of the **Yámana**. The windblown town has a desolate quality to it, though the community itself is warm and close-knit. Many travellers come to Puerto Williams to complete the challenging **Los Dientes de Navarino Circuit** – a strenuous four- to seven-day clockwise trek in the Isla Navarino wilderness for experienced hikers only (see below).

WHAT TO SEE AND DO

The worthwhile **Museo Antropológico Martin Gusinde**, Aragay, at Gusinde (Tues–Fri 9.30am–1pm & 3–6pm, Sat & Sun 2.30–6.30pm; free but donations welcomed), features informative and well-laid-out displays on the indigenous Kawéshkar, Selk'nam and Yámana groups, complete with a replica of a Selk'nam ritual hut, as well as exhibits on local geology, flora and fauna.

ARRIVAL AND INFORMATION

By plane The tiny airport is a 2.5km drive west of town; most guesthouses provide a pick-up/drop-off service. Aerovías DAP has its office at Centro Comercial Sur 151 (T 61 262 1114, W dapairline.com); confirm flight departure times here. Book well ahead for the Dec and Feb peak seasons.

Destinations Punta Arenas (Nov–March 1 daily Mon–Sat; otherwise 3 weekly; 45min–1hr 20min).

By boat From Punta Arenas, you'll arrive at the ferry ramp on Av Costanera. Boats from Ushuaia (see page 146) disembark at Puerto Navarino on the west side of the island, where you pass through Chilean customs before an hour's ride in a minibus to Puerto Williams. The Transbordadora

THE DIENTES DE NAVARINO CIRCUIT

Many travellers come to Puerto Williams to complete the **Dientes de Navarino Circuit**, a memorable, though strenuous four- to seven-day hike in the Isla Navarino wilderness. This is for experienced hikers only – the 53km route includes a particularly steep and treacherous descent at **Arroyo Virginia**.

Fuegia & Co, Partrullero Ortiz 49 (T 061 262 1251, E fuegia@usa.net), offer guided treks and logistical support in the Dientes de Navarino. The best map is the *Tierra del Fuego & Isla Navarino* satellite map by Zagier & Urruty Publications, available in Ushuaia, in conjunction with GPS. Make sure you have plentiful food and water supplies, sunscreen and warm and waterproof outdoor gear, and inform people in town of your plans.

Austral Broom office at Costanera 435 (📞61 262 1015, 🌐tabsa.cl) sells tickets for the Punta Arenas-bound ferry (CH$108,000/151,000 for *semi-cama/cama* [semi-reclining/ fully reclining] seats). A minibus picks up passengers at their *hospedaje* to take them to Puerto Navarino in time to catch a boat to Ushuaia (weather permitting).

Destinations Punta Arenas (1 weekly; 32hr); Ushuaia (Dec–Feb 1–3 daily, weather permitting; 45min–1hr).

Tourist information The tourist office (theoretically Mon–Fri 8.30am–1pm & 2–5pm, though it doesn't always keep these hours; 📞61 241 2125), next to the post office at Centro Comercial Sur s/n, has brochures on Puerto Williams and Cape Horn, though not maps of the Dientes de Navarino circuit. Banco de Chile, down a narrow passageway from the Centro Comercial towards the seafront, has an ATM, but it's best to bring plenty of cash to be on the safe side.

ACCOMMODATION

Hospedaje Akainij Austral 22 📞61 262 1173, 🌐turismoakainij.cl. Cosy en-suite rooms with down duvets, a cheerful living room filled with plants and friendly owners happy to arrange a plethora of excursions, make this an ideal mid-range guesthouse to base yourself. CH$50,000

Refugio El Padrino Av Costanera 276 📞09 8438 0843, ✉ceciliamancillao@yahoo.com.ar. A snug backpacker

haven, this colourful hostel has a sign on the door inviting you to let yourself in and decide if you wish to stay. Most do; Cecilia, the owner, may not speak much English, but her genuine warmth transcends language barriers. Dorms CH$12,000

Residencial Pusaki Piloto Pardo 222 📞61 262 1116, ✉pattypusaki@yahoo.es. A traveller favourite with a warm family atmosphere and excellent home-cooked food (the *centolla* dishes are particularly good). Even if you are not staying here, you can arrange to come for dinner, provided you give owner Patty a few hours' notice. Dorms CH$15,000, doubles CH$35,000

EATING AND DRINKING

Puerto Luisa Cafe Av Costanera 317 📞9934 0849. By the new ferry dock, in a bright orange building, this charming café offers views across the Beagle Channel, good coffee, cakes, toasted sandwiches, omelettes and breakfast options, plus a selection of souvenirs. Mon–Fri 10am–1pm & 4–9pm, Sat 8am–9pm.

El Resto del Sur Ricardo Maragano 146. The smartest restaurant in town, offering a short menu of pasta (CH$6500–10,000; try the *centolla* ravioli) and pizza (CH$9000–13,000), and a range of drinks, including a refreshing *calafate* sour. Daily 12.30–3.30pm & 8–11pm.

Easter Island

One of the most remote places on earth, over 2000km from the nearest inhabited part of the world, **EASTER ISLAND** entices visitors with the enduring mystery of its **lost culture**. A remarkable civilization arose here, far from outside influence on an island only 163 square kilometres in extent. It apparently declined rapidly and had all but disappeared by the time Europeans first arrived here. Once known as "Te Pito O Te Henua", or "the navel of the world", due to its isolation, and now called "Rapa Nui" by its inhabitants (*Pascuenses*), the island is home to a culture and people with strong Polynesian roots and a language of their own, which sets it well apart from mainland Chile. Archeological mysteries aside, the island has much to offer: year-round warm weather, excellent diving and surfing conditions and plenty of scope for leisurely exploration of the more out-of-the-way attractions, both on foot and on horseback. Welcoming people, excellent food and a

laidback atmosphere seal the deal.

HANGA ROA AND AROUND

The island's only settlement and home to around seven thousand people, **HANGA ROA** is a dusty village spread out along the Pacific coast. At night there is limited street lighting and the sky, lit with endless stars, is spectacular. North–south Atamu Tekena is the main road, lined with small supermarkets, cafés and tour agencies. Much of the action is centred on the pier, Caleta Hanga Roa, overlooked by **Ahu Tautira**, the only *moai* site in the town proper. Restaurants spread from here along oceanside Policarpo Toro and east–west Te Pito O Te Henua, which takes you past the small Plaza Policarpo Toro before ending at the Iglesia Hanga Roa, a Catholic **church** decorated with elaborate woodcarvings.

WHAT TO SEE AND DO

4

A BRIEF HISTORY OF EASTER ISLAND

500–800 AD Easter Island is settled by King Hotu Matu'a and his extended family, who come from either the Pitcairn Islands or the Cook or Marquesas Islands in Polynesia. The island is divided between *mata* (tribes), each led by a male descendant of the original king.

800–1600 Population grows to an estimated 20,000–30,000. Island culture evolves into a complex society and flourishes; *ahu* (ceremonial platforms) are built and *moai* (stone statues) are erected all over the island.

1600–1722 Natural resources are depleted and deforestation takes its toll. Two warring factions form: the Ko Tu'u Aro, who rule the island's western half, and the Hotu Iti, who populate its eastern half. *Moai* construction stops, the population declines and the Birdman cult develops.

1722 Dutch admiral Jacob Roggeveen lands and names the island after the day of his arrival – Easter Sunday.

1770 The expedition of Felipe Gonzáles de Haedo claims Easter Island for King Carlos III of Spain.

1774 Captain James Cook visits; he finds the *moai* in ruins and the population bedraggled.

1862 Nearly one thousand islanders are kidnapped to work as slaves in the guano mines of the Chincha Islands off the coast of Peru, including the island's king and all the priestly elite. Later, one hundred islanders are shipped back to Easter Island; the final fifteen survivors of this voyage infect the islanders with smallpox and the population is reduced to a few hundred.

1870 The island is purchased for a pittance by Frenchman Jean Baptiste Dutroux-Bornier, who wages war on missionaries. Most islanders agree to be shipped to Tahiti rather than work in indentured servitude.

1888–1953 Easter Island becomes part of Chile and is leased to the Compañía Explotadora de la Isla de Pascua, a subsidiary of the sheep-rearing Scottish-owned Williamson, Balfour and Company. Villagers are confined to Hanga Roa.

1953 Company's lease is revoked; Easter Island comes under the control of the Chilean Navy.

1967 Mataveri Airport is built. Islanders are given full rights as Chilean citizens.

1967–present day The island undergoes material improvement and the Rapa Nui language is no longer suppressed. Disputes with the Chilean government over political, economic and ancestral land rights, however, continue.

Just south of the pier and opposite the tourist office lies tiny **Playa Pea**, a rock pool safe for swimming, cordoned off from the stretch of ocean popular with surfers and bodyboarders. Avenida Policarpo Toro heads north, past the Hanga Roa **cemetery** with its colourful crosses, to three main sites, particularly spectacular at sunset. First is **Ahu Tahai**, with a single large *moai*, then **Ahu Vai Uri**, with five standing *moai* in various states of repair, and finally the much-photographed **Ahu Ko Te Riku**, a single *moai* with a *pukao* (topknot) and intact, pensive-looking coral eyes.

Museo Antropológico Padre Sebastían Englert

Amid gentle hills dotted with numerous *hare paenga* (boat-shaped foundations of traditional houses), off the coastal road just north of Ahu Tahai, lies the excellent **Museo Antropológico Padre Sebastián Englert** (Tues–Fri 9.30am–5.30pm, Sat & Sun 9.30am–12.30pm; free; ☎32 255 1020, ⊛museorapanui.cl). Not to be missed, it gives a thorough, informative introduction to the island's geography, history, society, Birdman cult (see page 482) and the origins and significance of the *moai*. The displays include a rare female *moai*, a wooden carving of a *moai kavakava* – a gaunt figure, believed to represent the spirits of dead ancestors – and replica *rongorongo* tablets (no original examples remain on the island). *Rongorongo* script is one of only four written languages in the world that developed independently of outside influence; the tablets were first mentioned in the nineteenth-century accounts of French missionary Eugene Eyraud, and their purpose remains unclear. It seems that only a small priestly elite was literate and that the knowledge perished with them during the slave raids and

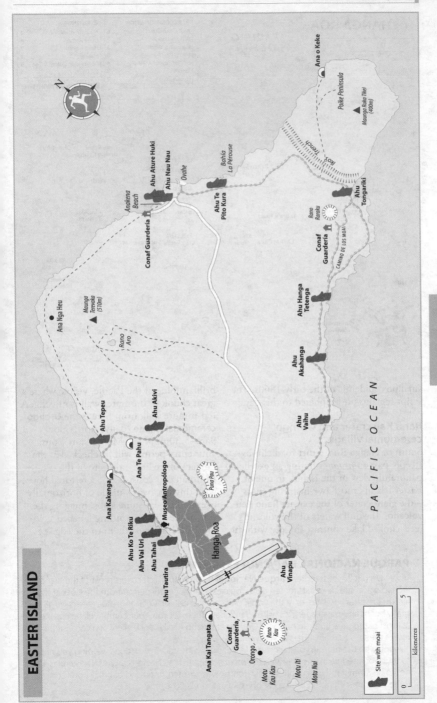

EASTER ISLAND

4

N

Ana o Keke

Poike Peninsula

Maunga Puka Tiketi (400m)

Ako's Trench

Ahu Ature Huki

Ovahe

Bahía La Pérouse

Ahu Nau Nau

Ahu Te Pito Kura

Anakena Beach

Conaf Guardería

Rano Raraku

Ahu Tongariki

Conaf Guardería

CAMINO DE LOS MOAI

Maunga Terevaka (510m)

Rano Aro

Ahu Hanga Tetenga

Ana Nga Heu

Ahu Akahanga

Ahu Tepeu

Ahu Akivi

Ahu Vaihu

Ana Te Pahu

PACIFIC OCEAN

Ana Kakenga

Museo Antropológico

Rana Pau

Ahu Ko Te Riku

Ahu Vai Uri

Ahu Tahai

Hanga Roa

Ahu Tautira

Ahu Vinapu

Ana Kai Tangata

Conaf Guardería

Rano Kau

Orongo

Motu Kau Kau

Motu Iti

Motu Nui

Site with moai

0   kilometres   5

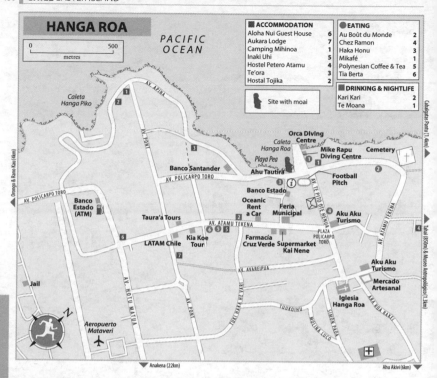

Map legend:

HANGA ROA

PACIFIC OCEAN

0 — 500 metres

■ ACCOMMODATION
Aloha Nui Guest House — 6
Aukara Lodge — 7
Camping Mihinoa — 1
Inaki Uhi — 5
Hostel Petero Atamu — 4
Te'ora — 3
Hostal Tojika — 2

● EATING
Au Boût du Monde — 2
Chez Ramon — 4
Haka Honu — 3
Mikafé — 1
Polynesian Coffee & Tea — 5
Tia Berta — 6

■ DRINKING & NIGHTLIFE
Kari Kari — 2
Te Moana — 1

Site with moai

smallpox epidemic of the early 1860s. The script remains undeciphered to this day.

Rano Kau crater and Orongo ceremonial village

South of Hanga Roa, a dirt road climbs steeply past a *mirador* offering an excellent panoramic view of the island, to one of Easter Island's most awe-inspiring spots – the giant crater of the extinct **Rano Kau volcano**. The dull waters of the volcano's reed-choked lake contrast sharply with the brilliant blue of the Pacific, visible where a great chunk of the crater wall is missing. A ten-minute walk from here is the **Orongo ceremonial village** (daily: April–Nov 9am–5.30pm; Dec–March 9am–7pm; your entry permit will be checked at the ranger's office here); the site of the Birdman cult consists of 53 restored houses with tiny doorways, made of horizontally overlapping flat stone slabs, hugging the side of the cliff. A winding labelled footpath leads past them to the edge of

---

PARQUE NACIONAL RAPA NUI ESSENTIALS

There is a US$80 fee to enter **Parque Nacional Rapa Nui**, which covers most of the island's archeological sites and lasts for ten days. You can buy your entry permit from the kiosk at the airport just after you land, or at the Conaf office on the outskirts of Hanga Roa (see page 483); many hotels and travel agencies will also purchase them for you. Your permit will be checked at most of the sites; you can only visit Orongo and Rano Raraku once each; you can visit the rest of the sites as many times as you want.

Along with the permit, you'll receive a leaflet map with strict instructions warning you not to touch or interfere in any way with the *moai* or the other archeological sites. These rules are not to be taken lightly: an idiotic Finnish tourist was arrested, fined and banned from Chile for three years after chipping off the earlobe of a *moai* in 2008.

THE RISE AND FALL OF THE MOAI OF EASTER ISLAND

The **giant stone statues**, around 887 of which litter the island, are a unique symbol of a lost civilization, whose existence raises many questions. Why were they made? By whom? How were they transported around the island and erected without the benefit of machinery? Why was their construction suddenly abandoned?

Believed to be representations of **ancestors**, the statues range from 2m to 10m in height, with an average weight of twelve tonnes. The majority of the **moai** share a similar appearance: elongated features and limbs, prominent noses, heavy brows and rounded bellies. Most are male, and some wear *pukao*, topknots carved of red stone in a separate quarry. Most *moai* once had coral-and-rock eyes, though now the only intact example is Ahu Ko Te Riku.

Carved from the slopes of the **Rano Raraku quarry**, the *moai* were buried upright in earthen pits so that their sculptors could shape their facial features with basalt *toki* (chisels), and then lowered down the volcano's slopes, presumably using ropes. Most archeologists believe that to transport them to the coastal *ahu* (platforms) the islanders used wooden rollers or sledges – a practice which resulted in complete **deforestation** – and that once at the foot of the *ahu*, the *moai* were lifted into place using wooden levers. All *moai*, apart from those at Ahu Akivi, were positioned around the coast facing inland, so as to direct their *mana* (life energy) towards their creators and to bless them with plentiful food and other bounties.

It is known that at the height of Easter Island's civilization (800–1500 AD), the tiny island supported a large and complex multi-tiered society, with a ruling class who worshipped *Make-Make*, the creator, and oversaw the construction of these statues. A phenomenal amount of energy must have gone into their creation and transportation, fatally depleting the island's resources and causing acute food shortages. Full-scale **warfare** erupted when farmers and fishermen couldn't or wouldn't support the *moai*-carving workforce any longer. The carving ceased and the *moai* were toppled from their pedestals. That which gave the civilization purpose was ultimately also its undoing.

Rano Kau, where a cluster of **petroglyphs** depicting the half-bird, half-human Birdman, as well as Make-Make, the creator, overlooks a sheer drop, with the islets Motu Kao Kao, Motu Iti and Motu Nui jutting out of the azure waters below.

THE SOUTHERN COAST

Heading east out of Hanga Roa, Hotu Matu'a leads you towards the **southern coast**. A right turn at the end, followed by an almost immediate left by the fuel storage tanks, takes you to **Vinapu**, an important site consisting of three *ahus* (stone platforms) with a number of broken *moai* scattered around. The *ahus* are made of overlapping stone slabs. Continuing east along this coast, you reach **Ahu Vaihu**, with its eight toppled *moai* and their scattered *pukao* (stone topknots). Up the road, the large **Ahu Akahanga** is widely believed to be the burial place of Hotu Matu'a, the first king of the island. The site features a dozen *moai*, lying face down, with petroglyphs carved into one of the platforms. There are also the remains of a village, consisting of *hare paenga*

outlines, as well as a number of *pukao*.

Another 3km east, the almost utterly ruined **Ahu Hanga Tetenga** consists of two toppled and shattered *moai*. Beyond, the road forks, the northern branch looping inland toward Rano Raraku, while the east-bound branch continues to **Ahu Tongariki**, one of the island's most enduring and awe-inspiring images. Consisting of fifteen *moai*, one significantly taller than the rest and another sporting a topknot, the island's largest *moai* site was destroyed by a tsunami in 1960, and re-erected by the Japanese company Tadano between 1992 and 1995.

Rano Raraku

Just inland of Ahu Tongariki lies the unforgettable spectacle of **Rano Raraku** (daily: April–Nov 9am–5.30pm; Dec–March 9am–7pm; your entry permit will be checked at the ranger's office here): the gigantic quarry where all of Easter Island's *moai* were chiselled out of the tuff (compressed volcanic ash) that makes up the sides of the crater. From the ranger station, a dirt path leads up to the volcano's slopes, littered with dozens of completed

---

THE CULT OF THE BIRDMAN

The Birdman cult venerating the creator *Make-Make* flourished in the eighteenth and nineteenth centuries, up until the 1860s. An important element of the religion was a brutal and dangerous **competition** staged each year between July and September to pick the Tangata Manu, or **Birdman**. Only military chiefs were allowed to compete; they would send their representatives, or *hopu*, on a swim through shark-infested waters to the *motu* (islets) off the coast. The *hopu* would often attempt to stab their rivals on the way. Once on the *motu* the competitors would wait for days to retrieve the first Manutara (sooty tern) egg of the season; the winner would then communicate his victory to those waiting in Orongo. The chosen Birdman then spent the year in complete seclusion, either in one of the houses in the Orongo village or in Anakena, attended to only by a priest, while his family enjoyed an elevated social status and special privileges.

---

moai, abandoned on the way to their *ahus*. The right branch meanders between the giant statues, buried in the ground up to their necks, their heads mournfully looking out to sea. You pass *moai* in various stages of completion, including the largest one ever carved, **El Gigante**, 21m tall and 4m wide, its back still joined to the stone from which it was carved. The east end of the path culminates in the kneeling, round-headed **Moai Tukuturi**, the only one of its kind, discovered by Thor Heyerdahl's expedition in 1955.

To the west, the trail winds its way up between wild guava trees into the crater itself, with a dirt path running through knee-high shrubbery alongside the large reed-strewn lake. You may take the footpath up to the crater's eastern rim for unparalleled views of the bay and Ahu Tongariki in the distance, but only if accompanied by a ranger or a guide. There has been increased concern regarding visitor behaviour ever since a Finnish tourist was caught in 2008 while trying to break an ear off a *moai* to take home as a souvenir.

Ovahe Beach

This small, sheltered **beach** is located off a dirt road just before Anakena Beach, on the other side of the Maunga Puha hillock. Backed by tall cliffs, its pristine sands are very popular with locals who come here to picnic, swim and snorkel. It's best earlier in the day, before the cliff blocks the afternoon sun.

Anakena Beach

Easter Island's largest and most popular beach is on the northeast side of the island, and can be reached directly by the paved, cross-island road. A white-sand beach dotted with coconut trees, it has picnic tables and fire pits, public toilets and showers, as well as food stands offering drinks and snacks. The beach is also home to the largest *hare paenga* (boat-shaped house) on the island and is believed to have been the landing point for the legendary King Hotu Matu'a. To the east stands the large, squat *moai* on **Ahu Ature Huki**, re-erected by Thor Heyerdahl's expedition of 1955 with the help of some islanders, while nearby stand the seven *moai* of **Ahu Nau Nau**, four sporting *pukaos* and two badly damaged. The best time for photographers to visit is in the mid-afternoon.

THE NORTHERN COAST AND THE INNER LOOP

Heading up the coast from the north end of Hanga Roa, a rutted dirt-and-gravel road takes you past **Ana Kakenga**, or Caverna Dos Ventanas – a cave set in the cliff with a spectacular view of the coast. Look for two offshore **islets**, Motu Ko Hepko and Motu Tautara; the cave is directly opposite them, with a cairn indicating the location. Bring a torch if you wish to explore. Further along, at the site of **Ahu Tepeu**, the road turns inland while a path carries on up to a copse of trees. The inland road leads you along fenced-off pasture land to **Ana Te Pahu** on your right-hand side – one of many underground **lava caves** on the island, used as a *manavai* (underground garden) to cultivate bananas, sweet potatoes, taro and other tropical plants due to its moisture and fertile soil.

At the southwestern base of **Maunga Terevaka**, the island's highest point (507m), is **Ahu Akivi**, with seven intact *moai*, the only ones on the island to be looking out to sea. As the road heads south to link up with the island's main thoroughfare, a dirt track to the west takes you to **Puna Pau**, the quarry where the *pukao* were carved.

ARRIVAL AND GETTING AROUND

By plane LATAM, the only airline serving Easter Island, has one or two daily flights to/from Santiago (4hr 50min–5hr 40min), and one weekly to/from Papeete, Tahiti (5hr 50min). Mataveri airport is on the southern edge of Hanga Roa, about 1km from the centre; most hotels will pick you up for free; if not, a taxi to the centre costs around US$10. The LATAM office is in Hanga Roa at the corner of Atamu Tekena and Pont (☎32 210 0279, ⓦlatam.com).

Car, scooter and bicycle rental Many travellers hire a car (from around CH$45,000/day), motorbike (from CH$25,000/day) or even a quad bike (around CH$40,000/day) to explore the island. Book a vehicle as soon as you can after arrival (or before). Outlets include Aku Aku Turismo (see page 483) and Oceanic Rent a Car, Atamu Tekena s/n (☎32 210 0985, ⓦrentacaroceanic.cl). Two things to note: there's no car insurance on the island; and the many free-roaming horses can be a hazard, especially at night. You can visit some of the sites closest to Hanga Roa on a mountain bike or on foot, though walking around the whole island would be quite a challenge. Several stores on Atamu Tekena, many hotels and Oceanic Rent a Car have bikes for rent (CH$10,000–15,000/day).

INFORMATION

Tourist office The Sernatur tourist office is at the corner of Tu'u Maheke and Policarpo Toro (Mon–Thurs 8.30am–5.30pm, Fri 9am–5pm; ☎32 210 0255, ⓦsernatur.cl).
Conaf Conaf has an office at Mataveri s/n on the outskirts of Hanga Roa (daily April–Nov 9am–6pm, Dec–March 9am–7pm; ☎32 210 0236, ⓦconaf.cl).
Website ⓦimaginaisladepascua.com is a handy Spanish-English website.

TOURS AND ACTIVITIES

Tours There are numerous tour operators in Hanga Roa, and touring the archeological sites with a knowledgeable guide, especially if you have limited time on Easter Island, can be very worthwhile. Aku Aku Turismo (☎32 210 0770, ⓦakuakuturismo.cl) and Kia Koe Tour (☎32 210 0282, ⓦkiakoetour.cl), both Av Atamu Tekena s/n, offer bilingual tours (from CH$26,000).
Horseriding Cabalgatas Pantu (*Pikerauri Eco Lodge*, Tekerera s/n; ☎32 210 0577, ⓦpikerauri.com) offers horseback tours (from US$55) of the west and north coasts,

including the ascent of Maunga Terevaka, the island's highest point, plus overnight camping trips.
Surfing and diving The well-established Orca Diving Center (☎32 255 0877 or ☎32 255 0375, ⓦorcadivingcenter.cl) and Mike Rapu Diving Centre (☎32 255 1055, ⓦmikerapu.cl), both with offices on the *caleta*, offer a range of scuba-diving (from CH$35,000) and snorkelling (CH$20,000-25,000) trips. The Hare Orca shop, next door and attached to the Orca Diving Center, rents out surfboards (CH$15,000/4hr), boogie boards (CH$10,000/4hr) and snorkelling gear (CH$10,000/8hr); the shop can put you in touch with surfing instructors.

ACCOMMODATION

Aloha Nui Guest House Av Atamu Tekena s/n ☎32 210 0274, ⓔhaumakatours@gmail.com; map p.480. Run by a charming couple, this tastefully decorated guesthouse has six clean and comfortable en suites, a tropical garden and a library filled with books, music and pieces of artwork. Excellent tours on offer, too. CH$80,000
Aukara Lodge Av Pont s/n ☎32 210 0539, ⓦaukara.cl; map p.480. Follow the signs for the Aukara art gallery, which showcases the owner's pieces, to this small guesthouse, surrounded by a lush garden. As well as simple but comfortable rooms, there's a small kitchen for guests, and tours are available. CH$85,000
Camping Mihinoa Pont s/n ☎32 255 1593, ⓦmihinoa.com; map p.480. Probably the best budget option on the island, this large campsite offers excellent ocean views and is run by a friendly family. Showers, kitchen facilities, dining room, and car, scooter and bike rental all available; the lack of shade is the only drawback. The adjoining guesthouse has simple rooms and a five-bed dorm. Camping/person CH$10,500, dorms CH$16,000, doubles CH$40,000
Hostel Petero Atamu Petero Atamu s/n ☎32 255 1823, ⓦhostalpeteroatamu.com; map p.480. Easter Island is a challenge for backpackers, but this hostel is a reasonable choice: the dorms and private rooms are tight, and the garish lime-green colour scheme won't be for everyone, but the rates are hard to beat. Dorms CH$16,000, doubles CH$25,000

4

Hostal Tojika Apina s/n ☎9 9215 2167, ⊚tojika.com; map p.480. An excellent, economical choice, *Hostal Tojika* has a collection of simple, clean en-suite rooms sleeping up to five people; the larger ones come with kitchenettes and are ideal for groups and families. CH$55,000

Inaki Uhi Av Atamu Tekena s/n ☎32 210 0231, ⊚inakiuhi.com; map p.480. As central as it gets, this guesthouse has sizeable, modern en suites with mini fridges and plenty of wood panelling, a guest kitchen if you want to prepare your own meals, a shady garden, and friendly staff. CH$85,000

Te'ora Apina s/n ☎32 255 1038, ⊚easterislandteora. bizland.com; map p.480. This friendly, good-value Canadian-run place has, amid its gardens, a trio of delightful, spotless *cabañas*; all come with kitchenettes, private patios and sea views. A laundry service (CH$5000/ load) is also available. CH$40,000

EATING

Chez Ramon Av Te Pito Te Henua s/n ☎32 210 0833; map p.480. This low-key restaurant has an overgrown garden, friendly service and a short, straightforward menu: think fish soup, tuna *ceviche*, and steak and chips. The dish of the day costs around $7000, which represents good value for Easter Island. Mon–Sat noon–3pm & 7.30–10pm.

Haka Honu Av Policarpo Toro ☎32 255 1677; map p.480. This super-friendly, open-fronted restaurant has a breezy location looking out to sea. Excellent fish and seafood is on offer, including *pastel de jaiba* (crab gratin), *ceviche*, and grilled fish with papaya chutney (mains CH$12,000–16,000). It's also a great place for a sundowner. Tues–Sun 12.30–11pm.

Mikafé Caleta Hanga Roa s/n; map p.480. This tiny café, with just a handful of tables outside, serves delicious home-made ice cream (from CH$2100) – banana split, blueberry, and beer are among the flavours – as well as cakes, muffins, pastries, and some of the best coffee on the island. Mon–Sat 9am–9pm.

Polynesian Coffee & Tea Caleta Hanga Roa s/n; map p.480. Delightful café, on the main strip, serving hot drinks (CH$1500–4000), breakfast options like yoghurt and granola, and cakes. If you've over-indulged, opt for a wheatgrass shot and a bowl of acai (an Amazonian super fruit), yoghurt and granola. Daily 7am–2pm & 5–9pm.

Tia Berta Av Atamu Tekena s/n ☎9 7979 6953; map p.480. Service may be a bit slack, but this popular local joint is a real hit. Steer past the standard mains, and go for one of the delicious – and huge – seafood empanadas (CH$3000–35000) and a cold Mahina beer (CH$4000). Mon–Sat noon–4pm.

DRINKING AND ENTERTAINMENT

Hanga Roa has a distinct shortage of genuine drinking spots; instead most restaurants double up as bars in the evening. Keep an eye out for the island's craft beer, Mahina: the IPA is particularly good.

Kari Kari Av Atamu Tekena s/n ☎32 210 0767; map p.480. The longest running traditional dance-and-music show (1hr) on the island, featuring talented young dancers and musicians in elaborate costumes. Entry US$25; with traditional *curanto* dinner US$60. Tues, Thurs & Sat 9pm.

Te Moana Av Policarpo Toro s/n, near the caleta ☎32 255 1578; map p.480. Smart restaurant-bar, right on the front and perfect for a sundowner: there's a good range of cocktails (CH$5000–8000) and beers (including the Tahitian lager, Hinano). The food (mains CH$14,000–18,000) is good too, but service can let the side down. Mon–Sat 12.30–11pm/midnight.

SHOPPING

There are two crafts markets: the Feria Municipal, at Tu'u Maheke at Atamu Tekena (daily 9am–1pm & 4–8pm), and the Mercado Artesanal, at Tu'u Koihu at Ara Roa Rakei (most stalls Mon–Sat 9am–1pm & 5–8pm; a few stalls also open on Sun on an ad-hoc basis); the latter is larger and better-stocked. Local crafts, and woodcarvings in particular, tend to be expensive; a cheaper option is to seek out the local jail (off Manutara, behind the airport), as local craftsmen sometimes outsource to inmates.

DIRECTORY

Honorary counsel British honorary counsel James Grant-Peterkin (☎09 8741 5166, ⊚easterislandspirit.com) can support travellers from the UK (and elsewhere) who get into trouble on Rapa Nui.

Hospital Hospital Hanga Roa on Simón Paoa s/n (☎32 210 0183), southeast of the church, has basic medical facilities.

Internet and wi-fi Getting online is a slow process, though most hotels and guesthouses do now offer wi-fi. There are also free wi-fi hotspots at various points around town, including by the Sernatour office and in the square at the corner of avenidas Atamu Tekena and Te Pito Ote Henua.

Banks and exchange There are a couple of ATMs: Banco Estado, Tu'u Maheke s/n, and Banco Santander, Policarpo Toro s/n; the latter is generally more reliable. Both also offer cash advances on credit cards. Several places change cash and travellers' cheques (generally at poor rates), and US dollars are widely accepted. Bring a stash of pesos/dollars with you from the mainland to be on the safe side.

Post office Av Te Pito Te Henua, opposite *Hotel O'Tai* (Mon–Fri 9am–6pm, Sat 10am–1pm). You can get a novelty Easter Island stamp in your passport here.

PARQUE NACIONAL TAYRONA

Colombia

❶ **San Gil** The best whitewater rafting in Colombia. See page 508

❷ **Cartagena's old city** Spain's most enduring architectural legacy in Latin America. See page 515

❸ **Parque Nacional Tayrona** A paradise of white sandy beaches and falling coconuts. See page 526

❹ **Providencía** Experience the unique Raizal culture on this tiny island. See page 530

❺ **La Zona Cafetera** Stay on an authentic coffee plantation and go hiking in the lovely Valle de Cócora. See pages 543 and 546.

❻ **San Agustín** Ponder the mystery behind the Parque Arqueológico's curious statues. See page 553

HIGHLIGHTS ARE MARKED ON THE MAP ON PAGE 487

ROUGH COSTS

Daily budget Basic US$40, occasional treat US$80
Drink Fresh fruit juice US$1.50
Food *Pargo frito con arroz con coco* (fried snapper with coconut rice) US$8
Hostel/budget hotel US$12/30
Travel Bogotá–Cartagena bus (663km; 19hr) US$70

FACT FILE

Population 50 million
Languages Spanish (official), plus various indigenous languages
Currency Colombian peso (C$ or C$)
Capital Bogotá (population: 8 million)
International phone code ☎57
Time zone GMT -5hr

5

Introduction

Home to a traumatic but rich history, stunning scenery and some of the continent's most welcoming and sophisticated people, Colombia is a natural draw for travellers to South America. Despite its four-decade-long civil war and reputation for violence, improved security conditions have led to a sharp increase in tourism. Foreigners and Colombians alike are now far more able to explore this thrilling paradise of cloudforested mountains, palm-fringed beaches and gorgeous colonial cities. The only country in South America to border both the Pacific and the Caribbean, Colombia offers a huge range of ecosystems, from the Amazon rainforest near Leticia to the snowcapped mountains of the Sierra Nevada de Santa Marta and the tropical islands of San Andrés and Providencia.

Cosmopolitan **Bogotá** is, like most capitals, a busy commercial centre, with a vibrant cultural scene and festive nightlife. The two other major cities, **Medellín** and **Cali**, are also lively but less overwhelming. Better still are the small towns scattered throughout the country that could turn out to be the highlight of your visit. **Popayán** and **Mompox**, for example, are famed for raucous Semana Santa (Easter week) celebrations, and Mompox has a timeless beauty to it. Colombia's coffee-growing region, the **Zona Cafetera**, offers breathtaking walks in the foothills where the bean is grown, accommodation in authentic *fincas* (coffee farms) and excellent trekking.

Most visitors make time – and rightfully so – to head north to the Caribbean for the sun. Just a stone's throw from the beach, the walled city of **Cartagena** is the biggest Spanish colonial port in South America. A few hours east, the less scenic **Santa Marta** and fishing village of **Taganga** are near **Parque Nacional Tayrona**, whose picturesque sandy beaches are unrivalled. The two are also great bases for a five-day trek to the archeological ruins of **La Ciudad Perdida**, the Lost City.

Almost un-Colombian in their feel, the remote Caribbean islands of **San Andrés** and **Providencia** both offer great diving, crystal-clear waters and – particularly in Providencia's case – a unique Raizal culture.

As you head north from Bogotá through the Andes to **Bucaramanga**, picturesque colonial villages like **Villa de Leyva** give way to more tropical, river-fed bastions of adventure tourism such as **San Gil**.

In the southeast, Colombia's stake of the Amazon, centred on **Leticia**, may not be as well known as Peru's or Brazil's but it offers a slice of jungle adventure and a gateway into the neighbouring countries. The southwest, near Popayán, boasts some wonderful scenery as well as the monumental stone statues and burial chambers of the forgotten cultures of **San Agustín** and **Tierradentro**.

WHEN TO VISIT

Colombia's proximity to the equator keeps regional **temperatures** stable throughout the year, around 24°C (75°F) along the coast and 7–17°C (45–63°F) as you move higher inland. However, **rainfall** does vary with the seasons. In the Andean region there are two dry and two wet seasons per year, the driest months being from December to March and July to August. In low-lying areas, especially southern Colombia, rainfall is more constant but showers never last very long. The Amazon climate is uniformly wet the entire year. Bear in mind that the most intense **tourist seasons**, with the highest prices, are from December to February and Semana Santa (Easter Week), the week before Easter.

CHRONOLOGY

10,000 BC Earliest evidence of human habitation at El Abra in present-day Bogotá.

1200 BC–1525 AD Indigenous cultures – including the Tayrona, Calima, Muisca, Quimbaya, Nariño and others – live scattered across the country.

700 AD The Tayrona build the Ciudad Perdida – their largest city.

1499 Alonso de Ojeda sets foot at Cabo de la Vela.

1525 Rodrigo de Bastidas establishes the first Spanish settlement in Santa Marta, kicking off the hunt for El Dorado.

1533 The Spanish found Cartagena.

1537–38 Spanish conquistador Gonzalo Jiménez de Quesada wrests power (and staggering amounts of gold and emeralds) from the native Chibchas and founds Santa Fe de Bogotá, now known simply as Bogotá.

1717 The Spanish consolidate their colonial holdings, creating the viceroyalty of Nueva Granada from the land now occupied by the independent nations of Colombia, Ecuador, Panama and Venezuela.

1819 Simón de Bolívar overthrows Spanish rule and founds Gran Colombia, comprised of Colombia, Ecuador, Venezuela and Panama. He becomes its first president, thus fulfilling his desire for a united, independent South America.

1830 Ecuador and Venezuela secede from Gran Colombia. Bolívar dies in self-imposed exile in Santa Marta.

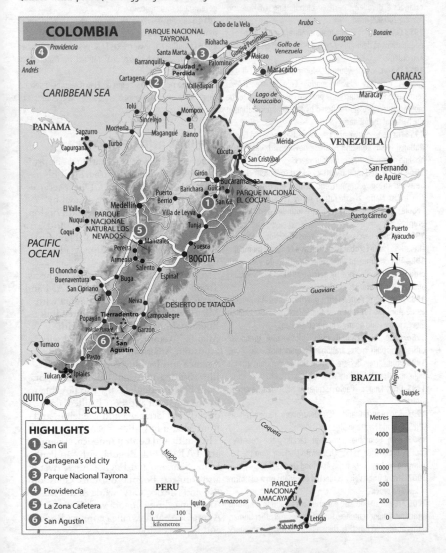

HIGHLIGHTS

1 San Gil

2 Cartagena's old city

3 Parque Nacional Tayrona

4 Providencia

5 La Zona Cafetera

6 San Agustín

5

1853 Colombia adopts a constitution that includes a prohibition against slavery.

1886 Nueva Granada becomes the Republic of Colombia, after Christopher Columbus.

1899–1902 The War of a Thousand Days, the bloody three-year-long civil war born of escalated antagonism between the Conservative and Liberal political parties.

1903 With the support of the US navy, Panama secedes from Colombia.

1948 The assassination of the working class's greatest advocate, Bogotá's populist mayor, Jorge Eliécer Gaitán, begins the massive rioting known as *El Bogotazo*, which catalyzes a decade of partisan bloodletting, *La Violencia*, leaving 200,000 dead.

1953 General Rojas Pinilla leads a military coup and begins negotiations to demobilize armed groups and restore peace and order.

1954 The group that would develop into Communist-linked Fuerzas Armadas Revolucionarios Colombianos (FARC) forms among the countryside peasants as a response to the violence and repression suffered by the rural population at the hands of the military.

1958 The Conservative and Liberal parties become a united National Front, agreeing to share power, with each party holding office alternately for four years.

1964 US-backed military attacks lead to violent clashes between the government and armed guerrilla groups. The leftist National Liberation Army (ELN) and Maoist People's Liberation Army (EPL) are founded and civil war erupts.

1982 Gabriel García Márquez wins the Nobel Prize in Literature. Pablo Escobar is elected as a Congress member.

1984 The government intensifies efforts to do away with drug cartels, as violence by narco-trafficker death squads and left-wing terrorists escalates.

1985 Members of radical leftist guerrilla group Movimiento 19 de Abril (M-19) take over the Palace of Justice, killing eleven judges and nearly a hundred civilians.

1986 Pope John Paul II visits Colombia. A grandiose cathedral is built in preparation in Chiquinquirá.

1990 Drug cartels declare war on the government after it signs an extradition treaty with the US.

1993 Drug kingpin Pablo Escobar is shot dead evading arrest.

1995 San Agustin and Tierradentro are recognized as UNESCO World Heritage Sites.

1999 Plan Colombia, aimed at tackling the country's cocaine production, is launched, with backing from the US. Spraying destroys coca fields and food crops alike.

2002 Álvaro Uribe Vélez is elected president on a platform of law and order.

2006 Around 20,000 AUC paramilitaries claim to disarm in return for lenient sentences for massacres and other human rights abuses. In practice, they reform as neo-paramilitary groups such as Los Rastrojos, and the drug trafficking, murders and land grabbing continues.

2008 The US and Venezuela assist in a government-orchestrated operation to free high-profile kidnapping victims. French-Colombian presidential candidate Ingrid Betancourt, held hostage for six years, and fifteen other captives are liberated. FARC founder Manuel Marulanda dies.

2010 Following Uribe's failed attempt to run for a third term, former Defence Minister Juan Manuel Santos is elected president.

2012 Peace negotiations between FARC and the Colombian government commence in Cuba.

2014 Santos narrowly re-elected president on platform of continuing negotiations with FARC.

2016 Colombia narrowly rejects FARC peace deal in October referendum; revised peace deal ratified by Congress in November.

2017 More peace talks begin as ELN (Colombia's second biggest guerrilla group) announce willingness to negotiate.

ARRIVAL AND DEPARTURE

Colombia's biggest international **airport** is Bogatá's Aeropuerto Internacional El Dorado (ⓦeldorado.aero). Direct services **from Europe** to Bogotá are offered by Avianca (Madrid, Barcelona and London), Iberia (Madrid), Air Europe (Madrid), Air France (Paris) and Lufthansa (Frankfurt). Avianca operates flights from Madrid to Cali and Medellín.

In **North America**, Air Canada connects Toronto to Bogotá, Avianca, LATAM and American Airlines connect Bogotá with Miami, while Avianca and United link Bogotá with New York, Delta with Atlanta, Avianca with LA, United with Houston, American with Dallas, and Avianca and Jet Blue with Orlando. Jet Blue, Spirit and Avianca all fly to Bogotá from Fort Lauderdale. It's also possible to fly from Miami and Fort Lauderdale directly to Cartagena and Medellín, and from Miami to Calí.

In **South and Central America**, Avianca and LATAM link Bogotá with São Paulo, Lima, Santiago and Buenos Aires; Avianca also connects Bogotá to Quito, Guayaquil, Rio and Mexico City; while Aerolineas Argentinas links Bogotá with Buenos Aires; Copa and Avianca connect Bogotá and Panama City.

OVERLAND FROM ECUADOR AND VENEZUELA

There are frequent bus services between Colombia and Ecuador, though there can be security issues, so check in advance. Firms such as Cruz del Sur (wcruzdelsur. com.pe) and Rutas de América (wrutasenbus.com) run direct buses from Lima and Quito.

There are two main overland **border crossings** with Venezuela (see page 513), the most popular being Cúcuta–San Antonio/San Cristóbal. The **Maicao– Maracaibo** crossing at Paraguachón is useful if you are travelling directly to or from Colombia's Caribbean coast. The Venezuelan authorities close the border from time to time, and at present you can only cross it on foot; always check the current situation before attempting to use Venezuelan border crossings.

The Panamerican Highway runs south into **Ecuador**, with the Ipiales–Tulcán crossing being the most popular and straightforward (see page 558).

There is no overland crossing between Colombia and Panama due to the presence of drug traffickers, paramilitaries and smugglers, and the threat of kidnapping in the Darién Gap.

BY BOAT TO/FROM BRAZIL, PERU AND PANAMA

From the Amazon region it's possible to travel by **riverboat** between Leticia, Colombia and Manaus, Brazil, or Iquitos, Peru, (see page 561).

The **ferry service** from Cartagena to Colón in Panama is currently suspended, but five-day boat journeys to Panama via the San Blas archipelago are possible; see wcasaviena.com/sanblasisland for the latest information.

VISAS

A passport and onward ticket are the sole entry requirements for nationals of most Western European countries, Canada, the US, Australia and New Zealand, but South Africans need a visa.

Upon arrival, all visitors receive an entry stamp in their passports, usually for **ninety days** if arriving by air, but sometimes only thirty or sixty days at land crossings. Double-check the stamp straightaway for errors. Make sure you get an entry stamp if coming in overland and that you get a departure stamp upon exiting to avoid trouble.

Ninety-day **extensions** cost C$85,000 (wmigracioncolombia.gov.co). You'll need two passport photos with a white background, copies of your passport and entry stamp as well as the original, and an onward ticket.

GETTING AROUND

Colombia's generally reliable and numerous **buses** are your best bet for intercity travel, though increased competition between domestic airlines means that **air travel** is frequently only slightly more expensive and far faster and more comfortable.

BY BUS, PICK-UP TRUCK AND JEEP

There's a wide range of options in comfort and quality for **buses**; it's a good idea to shop around at different companies' kiosks within larger stations. Generally, the larger, long-distance buses have reclining seats, toilets, loud cheesy music and videos; wear warm clothing as air conditioning can be arctic. Some recommended companies are: Expreso Bolívariano (wbolivariano.com.co), Expreso Brasilia (wexpresobrasilia.com), Expreso Palmira (wexpresopalmira.com. co), Berlinas (wberlinasdelfonce.com), Copetran (wcopetran.com.co) and Flota Magdalena (wflotamagdalena.com), though different companies cover different parts of the country. Long-distance buses sometimes stop at *requisas* (military checkpoints); the soldiers sometimes want to see ID, and very occasionally may check baggage. Each city has a *terminal de buses* (bus terminal) where the intercity buses arrive.

For shorter trips, you're better off sacrificing comfort and price for speed by buying a ticket on a *buseta*, *colectivo* or any similarly sized minibus or minivan that departs when full. If you want to be sure of getting the very next departure, don't hand over your luggage or pay unless you

5

can see that a bus is nearly full and ready to leave.

In rural areas you may get a **chiva**, something between a bus and an oversized pick-up; Colombia's most emblematic form of transport, they're usually brightly coloured, with seats in rows. In the coffee-growing areas, a common mode of transport is the hardy **Willys jeeps**, which tend to be inexpensive, although the ride can be bumpy.

BY PLANE

There are more than half a dozen domestic airlines. Avianca (ⓦavianca.com) serves the greatest number of domestic destinations. Copa (ⓦcopaair.com), the second-largest airline, covers largely the same destinations and flies to San Andres. LATAM (ⓦlatam.com) flies to all the major cities as well as smaller regional destinations. For flights out of Medellín the best airline is ADA (ⓦada-aero.com). Satena (ⓦsatena.com) offers flights to the Amazon, the Pacific coast and between San Andrés and Providencia. No-frills budget carriers include EasyFly (ⓦeasyfly. com.co), VivaColombia (ⓦvivacolombia. co) and Wingo (ⓦwingo.com).

A useful website to compare airline fares is ⓦlostiquetesmasbaratos.com.

The lowest-priced tickets are the first to sell out, so booking in advance if possible is wise. A one-way fare from Bogotá to Cartagena will usually cost around C$250,000–350,000 out of season, but with a promotional fare or a no-frills airline, you can sometimes pay as little as C$90,000–150,000.

ACCOMMODATION

Accommodation ranges considerably, but given the country's relative prosperity you'll be pleasantly surprised at the bargains available. **Backpacker hostels** are prolific, particularly in larger cities such as Bogotá, Medellín, Cali and Santa Marta, and prices start at around C$25,000 for dorms and C$70,000 for double rooms. Comfortable beds, shared kitchens, free wi-fi, book exchanges, laundry, cable TV and stacks of DVDs are common, and hostels are often the best places to find out

about local attractions; some rent bicycles and even horses. **Guesthouses** rarely cost more than C$150,000 for a double room with private bathroom.

Camping is an option in some rural areas and national parks, particularly Parque Nacional Tayrona on the Caribbean coast and Parque Nacional Cocuy in the highlands. Be aware that many campsites don't rent tents (or rent substandard ones), so it's best to bring your own if you plan to camp regularly. If you hike to the Ciudad Perdida (see page 528) you'll get to sleep in hammocks with mosquito nets.

In the coffee-growing region, you can stay on one of the stately **fincas**, coffee-growing plantations that have barely changed over the decades. Though these farms range from tiny to sleek, modernized operations, the majority are small estates that offer comfortable accommodation for a moderate price (around C$85,000 per room). Meals prepared from locally grown food as well as numerous outdoor activities, like farm tours and horseriding, are often included or available.

FOOD AND DRINK

Whether it's a platter full of starch or a suckling pig stuffed with rice, Colombian **food** is anything but light. Breakfast usually consists of *huevos pericos*, scrambled eggs with onion and tomatoes, accompanied by a corn pattie (*arepa*) and coffee or drinking chocolate. The midday *almuerzo* consists of soup, a main course and dessert. A cheap set lunch in a restaurant is called *almuerzo ejecutivo* or *comida corriente*. Dinners, after 6pm, also tend to involve meat or fish.

In Bogotá and other major cities there is an excellent array of Western and international cuisine.

LOCAL SPECIALITIES

Each region in Colombia has its own local speciality. The national dish is the *bandeja paisa* – an enormous platter of ground beef, chorizo, beans (*frijoles*), rice, fried banana (*plátano*), a fried egg, avocado and fried pork – usually found at inexpensive **market stalls** (*fondas*).

In rural areas, vegetarians will be hard-pressed for options, but in medium and large cities you can find a decent spread of vegetarian dishes.

Other Colombian favourites include *ajiaco* (a thick chicken stew replete with vegetables, maize, three types of potato, cream, capers and sometimes avocado), and *mazamorra* (a similar meat and vegetable soup but with beans and corn flour). Both are often served with *patacón*, squashed fried plantain.

More unusual regional specialities include *hormigas culonas* – fried giant ants, found in the Santander area. In Cali and southern Colombia, grilled guinea pig, known as *cuy* or *curí*, sometimes crops up on the menu. The coast is renowned for its fish and shellfish, served with aromatic *arroz con coco*, slightly sweet rice with caramelized coconut, while the Amazon is known for its unusual and delicious fish. The islands of San Andrés and Providencia specialize in locally caught crab dishes and lobster.

DRINKING

Though Colombia used to export its best **coffee**, demand from travellers has led to a proliferation of Juan Valdéz café branches; good coffee is now available in other establishments as well, though the majority of Colombians still drink heavily sugared, watered-down black coffee (*tinto*).

If there's one thing you'll pine for when you've returned home it's Colombia's exotic variety of **fresh fruit juices**. Worth trying are soursop, mango, passionfruit, *feijoa*, *lulo*, *mora* and guava.

Beer is reasonably inexpensive, with good craft beers produced by firms such as the Bogotá Beer Company (BBC), Tres Cordilleras and Apóstol. Also popular is the anise-flavoured *aguardiente*, pure grain alcohol, and rum (*ron*), both of which are drunk neat. Brave souls won't want to pass up any offer to try *chicha*, made from maize or yucca, which traditionally used the fermenting enzyme found in saliva (pieces of peeled root were chewed, spat into a bowl and left to ferment).

CULTURE AND ETIQUETTE

In Colombia you will notice a great disparity between the wealthiest members of society – who live a lifestyle akin to that of their counterparts in Europe's capitals – and the rest of the population: the poor city residents who live in dangerous neighbourhoods, and below them on the poverty scale the rural poor, particularly those who live in isolated areas where armed conflict still goes on.

When interacting with Colombians, Westerners will note that sincerity in expression, often expressed via good eye contact, is valued more highly than the typical steady stream of pleases and thank yous.

Tipping ten percent at mid-range restaurants is the norm; some establishments will ask you if you'd like for the tip to be included when you ask for the bill, while some add it on automatically. For short taxi trips, round up to the nearest thousand pesos.

TROPICAL FRUIT TREAT

Dotting the country's streets are vendors who will happily blend drinks for you from the juicy bounty in their baskets, either with milk (*con leche*), or the standard ice and sugar (*con agua*).

Corozo A round, maroon-skinned fruit, not unlike a cranberry in tartness.

Guanabaná Soursop, a big brother to the custard apple, with a slightly tarter flavour.

Lulo Resembling a vivid yellow persimmon, this tangy fruit is a perfect balance of sweetness and tartness.

Mora Close cousin of the blackberry.

Níspero Sapodilla or chicu, with a rich and musky pear-like flavour that goes really well with milk.

Tomate de árbol A tree tomato or tamarillo, this not very sweet orange-red fruit blurs the line between fruit and vegetable.

Zapote This luscious orange fruit's uncanny resemblance to sherbet is confirmed by the tendency of some locals to freeze its pulp to eat as dessert.

5

LOCAL SLANG

Colombians take much joy in their particular style of linguistic acrobatics and slang.

Un camello (n), **camellar** (v) A chore, to labour. A good way to refer to a particularly trying task.

Chimba (adj) Used to describe a situation or thing that is wonderful. Roughly synonymous with the youthful American usage of "awesome". Variations include "¡Qué chimba!" ("Nice!").

Elegante (adj) "Cool", loosely. Used to describe the subset of cool things – or happenings – that's particularly classy, well executed or elegant. Think football passes or a good outfit. *Chévere* and *bacán* are other words for "cool".

Paila (adj) "That sucks". Used in response to something that's bad luck or a nuisance.

Perico (n) Literally "parakeet", can mean cocaine, coffee with milk, or eggs scrambled with tomato and onion.

Al pelo (adj) Common response to a question like "How was your day?" that means "Good!" or "Perfect!"

Rumba (n), rumbiar (v) Party, a good way to describe a night out.

The **machismo** often ascribed to Latin American culture is present in Colombia, though a significant number (around thirty percent) of politicians and diplomats are female. The country's Catholic roots run quite deep and are apparent in sexual attitudes among both men and women, though there is some flexibility – and contradiction – in views toward gender and sexual orientation.

SPORTS AND OUTDOOR ACTIVITIES

Adrenaline junkies might hyperventilate when they discover Colombia. From almost every vantage point there's a snowcapped peak to climb, an untamed river to ride or some sunken coral reef to explore.

Colombia's waters are a good (and cheap) place to learn to **scuba dive**. All along its 3000km of coastline, but especially around Santa Marta and Taganga, and also on the islands of San Andres and Providencia – home to the world's third-largest barrier reef – operators offer week-long PADI certification courses for around C$900,000. Be sure to enquire about the reputation of dive operators before signing up, check their PADI or NAUI accreditation, the instructor-to-student ratio and ask for recommendations from other divers. Snorkelling is also particularly good on the islands.

There is a concentration of Class II–IV rapids among the many rivers in the *departamento* of Santander – three intersect near San Gil – that offer some spectacular challenges to **whitewater rafting** enthusiasts (see page 509), while the river near San Agustin gives you a somewhat tamer ride.

Hiking in Colombia is second to none: there are demanding week-long adventures in Parque Nacional de Cocuy (see page 512), jungle treks to the spectacular ruins of Ciudad Perdida (see page 528), and shorter but no less attractive rambles around Manizales and Salento in coffee country.

Football is the national sport and Colombians have a reputation for being some of South America's most skilled players. **Cycling** is also a common passion

---

TEJO

Colombia's own native sport is **tejo**, which involves throwing a hefty iron puck at a target embedded in a box of clay. In the middle is the bull's-eye (*balazo*), with four little packets of gunpowder (*mecha*) placed around it. The game works on a system of points – hitting the bull's-eye gets six points, exploding one of the *mechas* scores three, and getting closer to the bull's-eye than any other player nets one point. You'll find *tejo* bars in most towns and cities. Beginners are best off playing together rather than trying to pitch in with local *tejo* experts. Normally it's free to play and you just pay for your drinks.

– the mountainous land here is made for rugged biking – and Colombians regularly compete in the Tour de France.

COMMUNICATIONS

Internet cafés can be found even in small towns (from C$1500/hr), and free wi-fi spots are becoming easier to find.

The three major **mobile phone** networks are Movistar, Claro and Tigo, and it's inexpensive to purchase a local mobile phone: a basic handset will set you back around C$50,000–60,000; if you have an unlocked phone, a SIM card will set your back around C$12,000 with around C$5000 worth of credit, and top-up credits sold in every corner shop. However, it's cheapest to make **domestic long-distance calls** using the mobile phones in corner stores that buy minutes in bulk (look for the word "*minutos*"). Call centres (*telecentros*) allow you to make inexpensive calls both to local numbers and abroad, though Skype and WhatsApp are the cheapest way to go, given the proliferation of free wi-fi.

For **postal services**, packages are best sent via private companies such as Avianca (Ⓦaviancaexpress.com) and Deprisa (Ⓦdeprisa.com).

CRIME AND SAFETY

Colombia today is far safer and more accessible than it has been in decades. That said, pockets of guerrilla activity remain in remote parts of the country, particularly the jungle – a haven for drug-running activities – both by the rebels and particularly by the paramilitary groups who have the tacit support of the government, and who have been criticized for using techniques as dirty as those employed by the rebels. The FARC have made peace with the government, but ELN guerrillas, anti-guerrilla death squads, and *narcotraficantes* still control parts of the country. Tourists are not targeted specifically, but **certain areas should still be avoided**, including most of the Chocó, parts of Nariño, Putumayo, most of Meta, Arauca and rural parts of Cauca. Most guerrilla/paramilitary activity

COLOMBIA ONLINE

Ⓦ**colombiareports.com** Latest news, sports, culture and travel in English.
Ⓦ**colombia.travel** Colombia's official tourism site, with plenty of photos, good background and some practical information.
Ⓦ**hosteltrail.com/colombia** Budget accommodation and local attractions.
Ⓦ**parquesnacionales.gov.co** Portal to Colombia's national parks.

is confined to rural areas near the border with Panama and Venezuela. However, it's imperative that you stay abreast of current events: for up-to-date travel advice check Ⓦtravel.state.gov or Ⓦgov.uk/fco.

Violent crime does exist, particularly in poor neighbourhoods of the big cities, but visitors are far more likely to encounter pickpockets, so keep a sharp eye on your belongings. Beware of **scams** – such as criminals posing as plain-clothes policemen and asking to inspect your passport and money, allegedly in search of counterfeit notes, which they then confiscate. Counterfeit notes do exist, so ask locals how to identify them.

When out and about, take only as much cash as you need for the outing, and leave the rest (as well as your passport) in a safe in your lodgings. Always carry **a photocopy of your passport** with you – the main page and the page with your entry stamp. Local police have a mixed reputation for corruption.

Drugs are a sensitive subject in Colombia, and considering the harm it's done to their country, both in terms of criminal activity and environmental damage, it's no surprise that the majority of Colombians are strongly against cocaine use in particular. Even so, drugs are widely available, cocaine and marijuana especially. Possession of both is illegal and could result in a prison sentence, and being caught with drugs while trying to cross a border can have very serious consequences. Also be aware that cocaine in particular is much stronger than in Europe and the US.

Some tourists try the psychedelic jungle brew, *ayahuasca*, which is not illegal but can be potentially hazardous. While some

5

ayahuasca ceremonies are indeed conducted by genuine indigenous shamans, there are a lot of cowboys about, and going off with such people can be dangerous. Take this seriously: in 2014 a British tourist died after taking *ayahuasca* in Colombia, as did an American tourist in Peru in 2012.

Do not accept drinks, snacks or cigarettes from strangers as there have been reports of these being spiked with the tasteless and smell-free drug *burundanga*, or "zombie drug", that leaves victims conscious but incapacitated and susceptible to robbery and rape.

HEALTH

Vaccinations against hepatitis A, hepatitis B and typhoid are strongly recommended and rabies should also be considered; consult a travel health clinic weeks in advance. Vaccinations against **yellow fever** are necessary if visiting coastal national parks; some countries, such as Australia and Brazil, will not let you into the country without a yellow fever certificate if you're travelling directly from Colombia. Insect-borne diseases such as **malaria**, **dengue fever** and **Zika** are present, particularly in the Amazonas, Chocó, Antioquia, Córdoba, Bolívar, Putomayo and Atlántico departments. A new mosquito-borne illness **Chikungunya** has mostly affected the Caribbean region of Colombia. The illness is characterized by sudden onset of very high fever, rash, and severe joint pain usually lasting a week. Although non-fatal, the joint pain can be so severe it can be hard to walk. Victims are usually bed-bound. Seek medical help immediately to combat the fever and pain. Use mosquito repellent with fifty-percent DEET (repellants sold in Colombia have only up to 28 percent), or icaridin or PMD, and cover up with long sleeves and trousers.

Altitude sickness (*soroche*) may affect travellers at altitudes over 2500m, including those flying directly to Bogotá – take time to acclimatize before continuing your journey, drink plenty of water and avoid alcohol.

Colombia offers some of the best healthcare in South America; all major cities have **hospitals**, while in rural areas healthcare is more difficult to come by. In the case of serious health issues, you may be transferred to a larger hospital with more specialized doctors and facilities.

INFORMATION AND MAPS

Almost every town has a tourist office, although their staff often don't speak English, so hostels may be more helpful if you don't speak Spanish.

In Colombia, the annually updated (Spanish only) *Guía de Rutas*, sold at tollbooths and some tourist offices, has excellent maps, as well as potential road-trip routes and extensive local listings.

MONEY AND BANKS

Colombia's national currency is the **peso** (**COP**). Coins are for 50, 100, 200, 500 and 1000 pesos and notes for 1000, 2000, 5000, 10,000, 20,000 and 50,000 pesos. At the time of writing, rates were: US$1=C$2800; £1=C$4000; €1=C$3500.

Changing large notes can sometimes be problematic outside big cities.

ATMs are plentiful, with at least one even in small towns. For **changing money**, casas de cambio offer slightly better rates, have more flexible hours and provide quicker service than most banks.

OPENING HOURS

Shops are open 8am until 6pm, Monday to Friday. Many businesses also often open on Saturdays until mid-afternoon. Outside Bogotá many businesses close at noon for a two- or three-hour siesta. Commercial hours in cities in warmer areas such as Cali often get started and end earlier.

Government offices often follow the same pattern. Banks open around 9am and close at 4pm.

PUBLIC HOLIDAYS

January 1 New Year's Day (*Año Nuevo*)

January 6 Epiphany (*Día de los Reyes Magos*)

March 21 St Joseph's Day (Father's Day)

March or April Maundy Thursday and Good Friday (in *Semana Santa*, the week leading up to Easter)

May 1 Labour Day (*Día del Trabajo*)

May Ascension Day (six weeks after Easter Monday)

May/June Corpus Christi (nine weeks after Easter Monday)

May or June Sacred Heart (*Sagrado Corazón*, ten weeks after Easter Monday)

June 29 Saint Peter and Saint Paul (*San Pedro y San Pablo*)

July 20 Independence Day

August 7 Battle of Boyacá

August 15 Assumption of the Virgin Mary (*Asunción de la Virgen*)

October 12 Columbus Day (*Día de la Raza*)

November 1 All Saints' Day (*Día de Todos los Santos*)

November 11 Independence of Cartagena

December 8 Immaculate Conception (*Inmaculada Concepción*)

December 25 Christmas Day (*Navidad*)

FESTIVALS

January *Carnaval de Blancos y Negros*. Pasto's un-PC celebrations dating back to the days of slavery, with revellers with whitened and blackened faces throwing chalk and flour over each other.

February *Carnaval de Barranquilla*. Second-biggest carnival in South America, complete with parades, dancing, drinking and music, held forty days before Easter.

March or April *Semana Santa*. Holy Week celebrated with night-time processions by the faithful; particularly impressive in Popayán and Mompox.

Early July *Rock al Parque*. Massive free three-day pop/rock/funk/metal/reggae concert in Bogotá's Parque Simón Bolívar.

July/August *Feria de las Flores*. Medellín's big bash, culminating in a parade of peasants bearing flowers down from the mountains.

September *Festival Mundial de Salsa*. Cali's salsa festival, with the hottest moves on show at the Teatro al Aire Libre Los Cristales.

November *Reinado Nacional de Belleza*. Cartagena crowns Miss Colombia amid parades, street dancing and music

December *Feria de Cali*. Epic street parties.

Bogotá and around

Colombia's capital, **BOGOTÁ**, is a city that divides opinion. Its detractors cite poverty, gridlock traffic and crime, as well as depressingly regular rain, and with over eight million tightly packed inhabitants and some decidedly drab neighbourhoods, Bogotá rarely elicits love at first sight. Given a day or two, however, most people do fall for this cosmopolitan place with its colonial architecture, numerous restaurants and raucous nightlife. Besides, love it or hate it, odds are you'll have to pass through it at some stage during your travels in Colombia.

Situated on the **Sabana de Bogotá**, Colombia's highest plateau at 2600m, the city was founded on August 6, 1538 by Gonzalo Jiménez de Quesada in what was a former citadel belonging to the Muisca king **Bacatá**, from whom the city's name is derived. For many years, Bogotá's population did not expand in step with its political influence, and even in the 1940s the city had just 300,000 inhabitants. That all changed in the second half of the twentieth century, thanks to industrialization and civil war, which prompted a mass exodus of peasants from rural areas who live in dire conditions in the slums on the southern approach to the city – in marked contrast to the affluent neighbourhoods in the northern part

A WORD ON GETTING AROUND

Getting around Bogotá – and all Colombian cities for that matter – is facilitated by a foolproof **numbering system**, derived from the original Spanish grid layout, which makes finding an address virtually arithmetic. The names of the streets indicate their direction: **calles** (abbreviated C) run at right angles to the hills, from east to west, while **carreras** (abbreviated Cra) run from north to south. Addresses are a function of both, with the prefix indicating the cross street. For example, the address Cra 73 no. 12–20 can be found on Carrera 73 at number 20, between calles 12 and 12B. To make matters a little confusing, in La Candelaria, C 13 doesn't follow C 12; there are streets labelled 12 A–12 D in between.

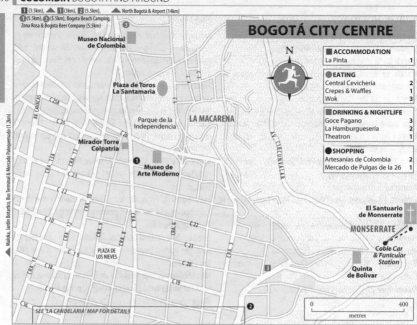

BOGOTÁ CITY CENTRE

Museo Nacional
de Colombia

Plaza de Toros
La Santamaria

Parque de la
Independencia

LA MACARENA

Mirador Torre
Colpatria

Museo de
Arte Moderno

El Santuario
de Monserrate

MONSERRATE

Cable Car
& Funicular
Station

PLAZA DE
LOS NIEVES

Quinta
de Bolívar

Maloka, Jardín Botanico, Bus Terminal & Mercado Paloquemado (1.2km)

SEE 'LA CANDELARIA' MAP FOR DETAILS

■ ACCOMMODATION	
La Pinta	1

● EATING	
Central Cevicheria	2
Crepes & Waffles	1
Wok	3

■ DRINKING & NIGHTLIFE	
Goce Pagano	3
La Hamburguesería	2
Theatron	1

● SHOPPING	
Artesanías de Colombia	2
Mercado de Pulgas de la 26	1

0   400
metres

of town. Today, Bogotá is South America's fourth-largest city and home to one of the continent's most vibrant cultural scenes.

WHAT TO SEE AND DO

The city's historic centre, **La Candelaria**, is full of colourfully painted colonial residences. It begins at Plaza de Bolívar and stretches northward to Avenida Jiménez de Quesada, and is bordered by Cra 10 to the west and the mountains to the east. **Downtown Bogotá** is the commercial centre, with office buildings and several museums, while **North Bogotá**, a catch-all term for the wealthier neighbourhoods to the north of the centre, offers stylish shopping districts and enough dining options to suit most palates and wallets.

Plaza de Bolívar

The heart of La Candelaria is the **Plaza de Bolívar**, awhirl with street vendors, llamas, pigeons and visitors; in the evenings, street-food carts set up shop by the cathedral. A pigeon-defiled statue of El Libertadór stands at its centre, surrounded by monumental buildings in disparate

architectural styles spanning more than four centuries, most covered with political graffiti.

On the south side stands the Neoclassical **Capitol**, where the Congress meets, with its imposing, colonnaded stone facade. On the plaza's north side is the modern **Palacio de Justicia**, which was reconstructed in 1999 after the original was damaged during the army's much-criticized storming of the building in 1985, in response to the M-19 guerrilla takeover, with more than a hundred people killed in the raid.

Catedral

Looming over the Plaza de Bolívar, Bogotá's Neoclassical **Catedral** (Tues–Fri 9am–5pm, Sat & Sun 9am–6pm ; free; ⓦcatedraldebogota.org) supposedly stands on the site where the first Mass was celebrated in 1538. Rebuilt over the centuries after several collapses, it was completed in 1823, and while its interior is gold-laced, it's still relatively austere compared to the capital's other churches. You'll find the tomb of Jiménez de Quesada, Bogotá's founder, in the largest chapel.

5

Casa de Nariño

A couple of blocks south of Plaza de Bolívar, between Cra 7 and 8, is the heavily fortified presidential palace and compound, **Casa de Nariño**, done in the style of Versailles. This is where President Santos currently lives and works. To take part in a guided visit (2–4 visits daily; ID required; ⓦpresidencia.gov.co), book online – look for "Casa de Nariño" on the website. It's also possible to watch the ceremonial changing of the guard three times a week (Wed, Fri & Sun at 4pm) – best viewed from the east side of the palace.

Museo Botero

Housed in a fine colonial mansion surrounding a lush courtyard, the **Museo Botero** (C 11 no. 4–41; Mon & Wed–Sat 9am–7pm, Sun 10am–5pm; free; ⓦbanrepcultural.org/bogota/museo-botero) contains one of Latin America's largest collections of modern and Impressionist art, donated in 2000 by Colombia's most celebrated artist, Fernando Botero. There are no fewer than 123 paintings and sculptures by Medellín-born Botero himself, which rather upset the residents of his home city. Botero's trademark is the often satirical depiction of plumpness – he claims to find curvy models more attractive than slim ones – and here you will find fatness in all its forms, from a chubby Mother Superior to rotund guerrilla fighters.

Also on display are works by Picasso, Miró, Monet, Renoir and Dalí, as well as a sculpture room featuring works by Henry Moore and Max Ernst.

Casa de Moneda

The stone-built **Casa de Moneda**, or mint (C 11 no. 4–93; Mon & Wed–Sat 9am–7pm, Sun 10am–5pm; free; ⓦbanrepcultural.org/bogota/casa-de-moneda), is home to the **Colección Numismática**, its displays chronicling the history of money in Colombia from the barter systems of indigenous communities to the design and production of modern banknotes and coins. Ramps lead to the **Colección de Arte**, featuring a permanent exhibition of works owned by the Banco de la República. The focus here is on contemporary Colombian artists, but the pieces on display range from seventeenth-century religious art through to works by twentieth-century painters. Behind the permanent collection is the **Museo de Arte**, a modern, airy building that houses free, temporary exhibitions of contemporary art, photography and challenging installations.

Museo Colonial

Set around a beautiful leafy courtyard, the **Museo Colonial** (Cra 6 no. 9–77; Tues–Fri 9am–5pm, Sat & Sun 10am–4pm; C$3000, free on Sun; ⓦmuseocolonial.gov.co) displays fine colonial-era religious and portrait art, as well as sculptures and furniture.

Museo Histórico Policía

Friendly young English-speaking police officers provide free guided tours of the **Museo Histórica Policía** (C 9 no. 9–27; Tues–Sun 9am–5pm; free; ⓦpolicia.gov.co/historia/museo), which are really worthwhile just to hear about their experiences. The basement is largely given over to a display on the notorious 499-day police hunt for drug lord Pablo Escobar, and includes his Bernadelli pistol, also known as his "second wife", and there's a great view across the city from the roof.

Museo Militar

Run by the military, the **Museo Militar** (C 10 no. 4–92; Tues–Sun 8.30am–4.30pm; free; ID required; ⓦbit.ly/1BaVJNE) showcases weaponry through the ages, jaunty military uniforms, model battleships, anti-aircraft guns and other articles relating to the art of war.

Plazoleta del Chorro de Quevedo

Nowhere is La Candelaria's grittier, bohemian side better captured than on the streets surrounding the **Plazoleta del Chorro de Quevedo** (C 12 B and Cra 2). The tiny plaza is said to be the site of the first Spanish settlement, though the tiled-roof colonial chapel on the southwest corner is a modern reconstruction.

Cerro de Monserrate

Perched above La Candelaria is the rocky outcrop that is one of Bogotá's most

5

recognizable landmarks: **Cerro de Monserrate**. The hilltop, crowned by **El Santuario de Monserrate** church, offers spectacular views back down on the seemingly endless urban sprawl that is Bogotá. It is easily reached by the frequent *teleférico* cable car (Mon–Sat noon–midnight, Sun 10am–4.30pm; return prices: C$19,000 before 5.30pm, C$20,000 after, Sun C$11,000; Ⓦcerromonserrate.com) or by funicular railway (Mon & Wed–Fri 6.30–11.45am, Sat 6.30am–4pm, Sun 6.30am–5.30pm; prices same as *teleférico*). Alternatively, it's a ninety-minute trek up the 1500-step stone path that begins at the base of the hill and leads to the summit 600m above.

Be aware that there have been a few reports of **robberies** both on the way up the hill and on the walk between the Quinta and its base. The safest (and cheapest) time to go is before 4pm, or

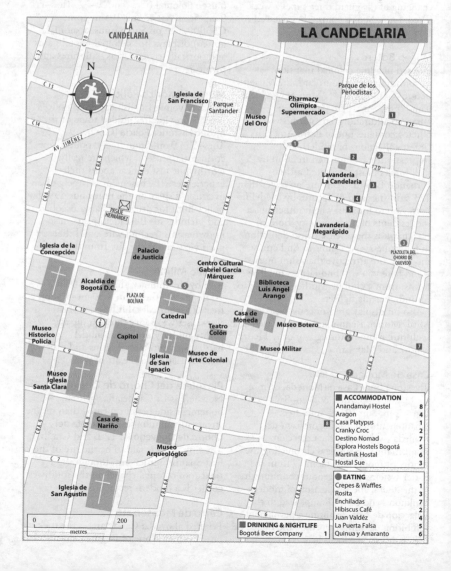

LA CANDELARIA

■ ACCOMMODATION	
Anandamayi Hostel	8
Aragon	4
Casa Platypus	1
Cranky Croc	2
Destino Nomad	7
Explora Hostels Bogotá	5
Martinik Hostal	6
Hostal Sue	3

● EATING	
Crepes & Waffles	1
Rosita	3
Enchiladas	7
Hibiscus Café	2
Juan Valdéz	4
La Puerta Falsa	5
Quinua y Amaranto	6

■ DRINKING & NIGHTLIFE	
Bogotá Beer Company	1

5

THE CHURCHES OF LA CANDELARIA

In addition to its cathedral, La Candelaria is teeming with some of the best-preserved colonial-era **churches and convents** found in Latin America:

Museo Iglesia de Santa Clara Cra 8 no. 8–91 (Tues–Fri 9am–4.30pm, Sat & Sun 10am–3.30pm; same ticket as Museo Colonial). Overlooking Casa de Nariño, the austere exterior, built in the early part of the seventeenth century and formerly part of the convent of Clarissa nuns, contrasts sharply with its opulent gold-plated interior and Day of the Dead-looking anaemic Christ.

Iglesia de San Francisco Cra 7, at Av Jiménez (Mon–Fri 6.30am–6.30pm, Sat 6.30am–12.30pm & 4–6.30pm, Sun 7.30am–2pm & 4.30–7.30pm; free; ⓦ templodesanfrancisco. com). Across from the Gold Museum, San Francisco is appropriately noted for its particularly splendid golden altar.

Iglesia de la Concepción C 10 no. 9–50 (daily 7am–5pm; free). The soaring vault here is a fine example of the Moorish-influenced Mudéjar style popular in the sixteenth century.

Iglesia de San Ignacio C 10 no. 6–35 (closed for restoration at the time of writing). The largest and most impressive of the colonial-era churches is the domed San Ignacio, founded in 1610 as the first Jesuit church in Nueva Grenada.

Sunday, when you'll be accompanied by thousands of pilgrims hoping for miracles from the church's dark-skinned Christ.

Quinta de Bolívar

At the foot of Monserrate is the **Quinta de Bolívar** (C 20 no. 2–91 Este; Tues–Fri 9am–5pm, Sat & Sun 10am–4pm; English guided tour Wed 11am; C$3000; ⓦ quintadebolivar.gov.co), a spacious colonial mansion with beautiful gardens where Simón Bolívar lived sporadically between 1820 and 1829. The informative museum retells the story of Bolívar's final, desperate days in power before being banished by his political rivals, in a collection that includes a plethora of Bolívar paraphernalia including his military medals, billiard table and bedpan. One object you won't see here is the sword El Libertadór used to free the continent from four centuries of Spanish rule. It was stolen in 1974 from the collection in the now legendary debut of urban guerrilla group **M-19**. When they handed in their arsenal in 1991, the sword was quickly shuttled into the vaults of the Banco República.

Museo del Oro

On the northeastern corner of Parque de Santander, at Cra 6 and C 16, is Bogotá's must-see **Museo del Oro**, or Gold Museum (Tues–Sat 9am–6pm, Sun 10am–4pm; C$4000, Sun free; ⓦ banrepcultural.org/ bogota/museo-del-oro). The world's largest collection of gold ornaments, some 55,000 pieces strong, is spread out over three floors, with extensive displays on Colombia's indigenous cultures, cosmology and symbolism, techniques used in working with gold, and a region-by-region breakdown of the use of various pieces. Note the recurring symbolism of animals (jaguars, birds, monkeys, human/animal hybrids), the very fine filigree earrings, gold offerings used in rituals and elaborate ornamentation worn by chieftains and those who communed with deities. Free one-hour tours are available (in English Tues–Sat 11am & 4pm; in Spanish Tues–Fri 11am, 3pm & 4pm, Sat 10am, 11am, 3pm & 4pm).

Museo Nacional de Colombia

Inside a fortress-like building, the **Museo Nacional de Colombia** (Cra 7, at C 28; Tues–Sat 10am–6pm, Sun 10am–5pm; C$4000, Sun and after 4pm Wed free; ⓦ museonacional.gov.co) provides a detailed chronological look at the country's tumultuous history. The converted jailhouse's most impressive exhibits relate to the conquest and the origins of the beguiling El Dorado myth that so obsessed Europe. The second floor houses an extensive collection of paintings by modern Colombian artists, including Fernando Botero, while on the third floor,

5

don't miss the exhibit on Jorge Gaitán, the populist leader assassinated in 1948. Descriptions are in Spanish only, but you can pick up English-language placards. There's an on-site restaurant and a Juan Valdez café.

Mirador Torre Colpatria

Fantastic 360-degree views can be had from the **Mirador Torre Colpatria** (Cra 7 no. 24–89; Fri 6–9pm, Sat 2–8pm, Sun 11am–5pm; C$7000), Colombia's tallest skyscraper (162m). Here you can catch a glimpse of the **Plaza de Toros La Santamaría**, the Moorish-style bullring.

Museo de Arte Moderno

The **Museo de Arte Moderno** (C 24, at Cra 6; Mon–Sat 10am–6pm, Sun noon–5pm; C$10,000; ⓦmambogota.com) has the largest collection of contemporary Colombian art in the country, running the gamut from photography and painting to sculpture and graffiti. Frequently changing exhibits tend to focus on Latin American artists, such as the psychedelic works of Jairo Maldonado.

ARRIVAL AND DEPARTURE

By plane Most international flights land at El Dorado International Airport (ⓦeldorado.aero), 14km northwest of the city centre, though some domestic flights use the Puente Aéreo terminal, 500m from the international one. A taxi downtown costs around C$30,000. Make sure the taxi meter is turned on. You can buy TransMilenio bus cards at gate 5, and take TransMilenio bus #M86 to Portal del Dorado, where you can change for route #1 to Universidades station near Candelaria (#M86 itself continues to the Museo Nacional and up Cra 7 through Chapinero). Destinations There are multiple flights daily to Bucaramanga (1hr 05min); Cali (1hr 05min); Cartagena (1hr 30min); Leticia

(2hr 05min); Manizales (1hr 05min); Medellín (1hr); Pasto (1hr 20min); Pereira (1hr); Popayán (1hr 30min); San Andres (2hr 10min); Santa Marta (1hr 30min). International routes include: Buenos Aires (6hr 20min); Caracas (1hr 50min); Guayaquil (1hr 55min); La Paz (3hr 40min); Lima (3hr); Quito (1hr 40min); Rio (8hr 15min); Santiago (5hr 50min); São Paulo (6hr 10min).

By bus The huge long-distance bus terminal, Terminal de Transporte (Diagonal 23 no. 69–60, off Av de la Constitución; ☎1 423 3600, ⓦterminaldetransporte. gov.co), is around 5km southwest of the city centre. It's divided into five colour-coded modules, roughly serving destinations north (No.3; red), south (No. 1; yellow), east and west of the city and international departures (No. 2; blue). A taxi to the centre costs about C$20,000. El Tiemp TransMilenio station is ten blocks away.
Destinations from No. 1 (yellow) Cali (4–5 hourly; 10hr); Pasto (8 daily; 22hr); Pereira (2–4 hourly; 9hr); Popayán (5 daily; 12hr); San Agustin (7 daily; 12hr).
Destinations from No. 2 (blue) Domestic: Manizales (24 daily; 8hr); Medellín (5–6 hourly; 9–10hr); Popayán (1 daily; 12hr). International: Lima (3 weekly; 72hr); Quito (3 weekly; 28hr).
Destinations from No. 3 (red) Cartagena (19 daily; 21hr); Cúcuta (10–12 daily; 15hr); San Gil (3–4 hourly; 7hr 30min); Santa Marta (11 daily; 18hr); Villa de Leyva (15 daily; 4hr).

GETTING AROUND

Most of Bogotá's attractions are in or near La Candelaria and can be reached on foot from there. The area west of Cra 10 below Av Jiménez is best avoided.
Buses As well as minibuses, Bogotá is covered by a "Bus Rapid Transit" system with dedicated lanes called TransMilenio (daily 5am–11pm; ⓦ www.transmilenio.gov. co), with a flat fare of C$2200 per journey; to use it, buy a card (C$3000) which you can load up with credit at any station. Bus lines are a little confusing, with all-stops and limited-stop services, and bus routes have different letter prefixes for each direction. It's possible to plan a route at ⓦtullaveplus.com – find "Planea tu viaje", open the map, and right-click on your origin and destination.

BOGOTÁ TOURS

The cheapest way to tour the city is to devise a self-guided **bus** tour. For the price of a single Transmilenio ticket, you can ride the buses for as long as you like, as long as you don't leave the stations.

Bogotá Graffiti Tour ☎321 297 4075, ⓦbogotagraffiti.com. This excellent three-hour walking tour takes in Bogotá's not inconsiderable collection of street art (daily 10am & 2pm; free, but suggested donation of C$20,000–30,000); reserve ahead.

Cycling Every Sunday morning (until 2pm), there is much good-natured fun to be had as many of Bogotá's main roads close to traffic in a civic attempt to get people cycling, known as *Ciclovía*. Bogotá Bike Tours runs informative guided tours of the city (C$40,000, 10.30am & 1.30pm daily, 4hr).

BOGOTÁ FESTIVALS

Colombia's capital has no shortage of festivals. **Semana Santa** (Holy Week; March or April) brings processions, re-enactments and religious pomp. In even-numbered years, around Holy Week the city also hosts the **Ibero-American Theater Festival**, one of the continent's biggest festivals of theatre, a fortnight of international performing art and street processions. In April/May, there's the **Feria Internacional del Libro** (international book fair). A highlight of the annual calendar is **Rock al Parque** (Rock in the Park; June/July; ⍵ rockalparque.gov. co), South America's biggest rock music festival, which lasts three days, before the **Festival de Verano** (summer festival; early Aug) to commemorate Bogotá's founding. September heralds **Jazz al Parque** mainly in Usaquén's Parque el Country, followed by the **Festival de Cine** (film festival; Oct), which includes open-air screenings, and **Salsa al Parque** (Salsa in the Park; Nov), a weekend of free salsa in Parque Simón Bolívar. Soon after that, the city begins gearing up for a truly South American **Christmas**.

Taxis Taxis in Bogotá are yellow, small and relatively inexpensive. Fares correspond to the number of units on the taxi meter, with a small surcharge levied between 8pm and 5am, on Sundays and holidays; ask the driver to turn the taxi meter on and check the fare table as some drivers overcharge. It's safer to call a taxi company rather than grab one off the street; you'll need to give the driver the passcode, usually the last two digits of the phone number you call from. Try TaxExpress (☎ 1 411 1111), Taxis Ya (☎ 1 333 3333) or Taxis Libres (☎ 1 211 1111).

INFORMATION

Tourist information Bogotá's tourist bureau produces city maps. The most useful Puntos de Información Turística are at the airport, bus station and the southwest corner of Plaza Bolívar at Cra 8 no. 9–85 (Mon–Sat 8am–6pm, Sun 8am–4pm; ☎ 01 8000 127 400, ⍵ bogotaturismo. gov.co).

Publications On Fridays, Bogotá's leading newspaper, *El Tiempo*, has entertainment listings (⍵ eltiempo.com/cultura/entretenimiento). The monthly free English-language *The City Paper* (⍵ thecitypaperbogota.com) is also a useful resource.

ACCOMMODATION

Most budget accommodation is concentrated in La Candelaria. Most have private rooms with either shared or private bathrooms; prices below are for doubles with shared bathroom in high season (single rooms are often around two-thirds the price of a double).

Anandamayi Hostel C 9 no. 2–81 ☎ 1 341 7208, ⍵ anandamayihostel.com; map p.498. This hostel is pure Zen, set in a restored colonial house around three flower-filled, hammock-strung courtyards frequented by hummingbirds. Rustic dorms and private rooms come with lockers, and shared bathrooms have spacious stone showers. At night, guests gather around the wood-fire stove in the communal kitchen. Basic breakfast included. Dorms C̲$̲4̲0̲,̲5̲0̲0̲, doubles C̲$̲1̲4̲0̲,̲5̲0̲0̲

Aragon Cra 3 no. 12C–13, La Candelaria ☎ 1 342 5239; map p.498. While this bare-bones hotel has zero atmosphere, the warm rooms with shared bathrooms are clean and cost far less than their youth hostel equivalent. Singles C̲$̲2̲7̲,̲0̲0̲0̲, doubles C̲$̲4̲6̲,̲0̲0̲0̲

★ **Cranky Croc** C 12D no. 3–46 ☎ 1 342 2438, ⍵ crankycroc.com; map p.498. A friendly, Australian-owned place with sparklingly clean dorms and private rooms (those with bathrooms being actually quite deluxe), a well-equipped shared kitchen, regular barbecues and daily group outings. Dorms C̲$̲3̲5̲,̲0̲0̲0̲, doubles C̲$̲1̲0̲0̲,̲0̲0̲0̲

Destino Nomada C 11 no. 00–38 ☎ 1 352 0932, ⍵ destinonomada.com; map p.498. This hostel is guaranteed to leave you breathless (thanks to the uphill walk). It's a compact place with guest kitchen, small bar (offering a daily happy hour), TV lounge, and a small but sweet inner courtyard. Breakfast included. Dorms C̲$̲2̲4̲,̲0̲0̲0̲, doubles C̲$̲6̲5̲,̲5̲0̲0̲

Explora Hostels Bogotá C 12C no. 3–19 ☎ 1 282 9320, ⍵ explorahostels.com; map p.498. An

---

★ TREAT YOURSELF

Casa Platypus C 12F no. 28, La Candelaria ☎ 1 281 1801, ⍵ casaplatypusbogota.com; map p.498. Located in a beautiful colonial house overlooking Parque de los Periodistas, *Casa Platypus* combines many of the comforts of a boutique hotel with backpacker-friendly facilities. Rooms are compact but stylish and there's a huge dining room/lounge where a hefty breakfast including fresh fruit and juice, eggs, granola and yoghurt is served up (included in room rate). Add to this a roof terrace, communal kitchen, free coffee, public computers, cold beers on an honour system plus information and friendly advice from super-knowledgeable owner Germán, and you really do have the best of both worlds. C̲$̲1̲7̲3̲,̲0̲0̲0̲

5

unassuming exterior hides this appealing hostel with an indoor hammock-festooned common space. The kitchen is minuscule but there's a café that cooks up breakfast (C$5000). Some of the rooms face the covered courtyard and dorms feature nice touches such as large lockers and individual reading lights. Dorms C$25,000, doubles C$70,000

La Pinta C 65 no. 5–67 ☎1 211 9526, ⓦlapinta.com. co in; map p.496. and while the hostel is a 15min walk from the main Transmilenio route, regular minibuses along Cra 7 connect it to La Candelaria and the airport. Dorms C$33,000, doubles C$61,000

Martinik Hostal Cra 4 No. 11–88, La Candelaria ☎1 283 3180, ⓦhostalmartinik.com; map p.498. Formerly Swiss- but now Canadian-run, *Martinik Hostal* retains its reputation for being one of the cleanest, best-kept and best-value hostels in town, but those with an aversion to street sounds should opt for a room upstairs or at the back. Breakfast included. Dorms C$22,000, doubles C$65,000

Hostal Sue Cra 3 no. 12C–18 ☎1 341 2647, ⓦsuecandelaria.com; map p.498. This well-maintained hostel with a party vibe has neat dorms, three doubles with TVs, on-site bar, bean-bag-stacked TV lounge, kitchen, free coffee, laundry service, ping-pong table and regular pub crawls. Breakfast included. Dorms C$27,000, doubles C$60,000

EATING

While the traditional highlander diet consists of meat and starch, middle-class *Cachacos* prefer the same cosmopolitan cuisine as their counterparts in London or New York. Bogotá has four main restaurant zones, from south to north: gritty La Candelaria; trendy La Macarena (Cra 4 between calles 23 & 28); LGBTQ-friendly Chapinero, including the "G-Zone" (between calles 58 & 72 and carreras 3 & 7); and upmarket Zona Rosa (concentrated in the "T Zone" at C 82 and Cra 12). The prime area for **budget eating** is around the junction of Cra 5 with C 18 in the city centre, where, come lunchtime, you'll find no shortage of diners offering *comidas corridas* at C$6000–9000. Another good area for cheap eats is Pasaje Hernández, on C 12A at Cra 8.

Central Cevicheria Cra 13 No. 85–14, Zona Rosa; map p.496. Look no further to sate your cravings for fish and seafood – be it laced with spicy sauce or cut into thin *tiradito* slices. Busy and popular, it also serves cooked mains such as prawn curry. Expensive, but worth it. *Ceviche* from C$19,900. Mon–Wed noon–11pm, Thurs–Sat noon–midnight, Sun noon–10pm.

Crepes & Waffles Av Jiménez no. 4–55; map p.500; Cra 11 no. 85–75 in the Zona Rosa; map p.498; and more than thirty other city outlets ⓦcrepesywaffles.com; map p.496. A hugely popular chain restaurant that fulfils every savoury and sweet craving with a monster menu of crêpes and waffles (veg crêpe C$10,500, *arequipe* waffle;

C$8400) plus great ice cream. Mon–Thurs 11.45am–8.30pm, Fri & Sat 11.45am–9pm, Sun 11.45am–5pm.

Rosita C 12B bis no. 1A–26, La Candelaria; map p.498. Aimed unashamedly at students and backpackers, this is one of the few La Candelaria restaurants open late seven days a week. The food is well priced and not at all bad, especially if you stick to Colombian dishes (such as *ajiaco santandereño*; C$21,000), or pasta (spag bol C$21,000). The top floor has live music in the evenings. On the downside, service can be rather slow. Mon–Thurs 8am–11pm, Fri & Sat 8am–1am, Sun 8am–10pm.

Enchiladas C 10 no. 2–12, La Candelaria; map p.498. Tuck into enchiladas, burritos and other Mexican staples at this colourful spot festooned with Day of the Dead paraphernalia and black-and-white film photos. The home-made salsas have a real kick to them and the *sopa de tortilla* really hits the spot. Mains include *pollo en mole poblano* (chicken in chocolate and chilli sauce; C$32,000). Tues, Wed & Sun noon–5pm, Thurs–Sat noon–8pm.

Hibiscus Café C 12D bis no. 2–21, La Macarena; map p.498. A spot-on little place for a low-priced breakfast or lunch; nothing fancy but filling, staple dishes, well cooked, with set breakfasts from C$4000 (continental) to C$6300 (full Colombian) and set lunches for C$9000. Mon–Sat 7am–3pm.

Juan Valdéz Cra 7, at C 11, La Candelaria; map p.498. Colombia's answer to Starbucks, with good hot and cold caffeine drinks, muffins, sandwiches and more. Be prepared to pay top dollar for it, though. Branches across town. Espresso C$3400. Mon–Sat 9am–8pm, Sun 9am–5pm.

La Puerta Falsa C 11 no. 6–50, La Candelaria; map p.498. This 1816 establishment is where the good citizens of Bogotá come a traditional *chocolate completo* breakfast (hot chocolate with cheese, bread and cheesy cornbread, C$7500), and colourful sweets beckon in the window. Mon–Sat 7am–10pm, Sun 8am–8pm.

★ **Quinua y Amaranto** C 11 no. 2–95, La Candelaria; map p.498. A tiny place with an open kitchen and delicious, largely organic and vegetarian set lunches (C$16,000). Sample dishes include black bean soup and mushroom risotto. Also sells wholewheat *empanadas*, bread, eggs and coffee. Mon & Sat 8.30am–4pm, Tues–Fri 8.30am–7pm.

Wok Cra 13 no. 82–74, Zona Rosa, also next to the Museo Nacional ⓦwok.com.co; map p.496. This chain of trendy restaurants has all-white modern decor and a menu that was clearly constructed by someone who knows about Asian food. Choose from heaped noodle salads, Thai curry, sushi, tempura and much more. The shrimp speared on sugar-cane stalks with Vietnamese dipping sauce are seriously tasty, and the lemonade is among the best in town. Spice fans should ask for extra chilli. Mains start around C$19,000. Mon–Sat noon–10.30pm, Sun noon–9pm.

5

DRINKING AND NIGHTLIFE

Rumbear, literally to dance the rumba, is how locals refer to a night's partying, which invariably involves heavy doses of dancing. Bars and discos in La Candelaria attract a somewhat bohemian, often studenty, crowd, while their fluorescent-lit counterparts in the Zona Rosa in North Bogotá (around C 83 and Cra 13) appeal to the city's beautiful people. Virtually everywhere shuts down at 3am. Take taxis to and from your destination.

Bogotá Beer Company C 12D no. 4–02, La Candelaria; C 85 no. 13–06, Zona Rosa ⓦbogotabeercompany. com; map p.498. Artisan brews including stout and wheat beer, served in bottles and on tap, fourteen seasonal microbrews, plus excellent pub grub to soak them up. One of the few places that's busy even on a Monday night. Daily 12.30pm–1am.

Goce Pagano Diagonal 20A no. 0–82 Downtown; map p.496. Less is more in this divey watering hole, which has a simple dancefloor and Bogotá's largest rack of golden-era salsa LPs. Owner Gustavo is a throwback to the era when the revolution was fought listening to salsa. Fri 6pm–3am, Sat 7pm–3am.

★ TREAT YOURSELF

Andrés Carne de Res C 3 no. 11A–56, Chía ⓦandrescarnederes.com. Suburban legend *Andrés Carne de Res* must be seen to be believed. A 1000-capacity restaurant and salsa club that looks like something from a Tim Burton film, it is the biggest all-singing, all-dancing party in the Colombian capital. The four floors (Hell, Earth, Purgatory and Heaven, the last with large roof terrace) are decked out in a kind of gothic burlesque, with live salsa music and staff dressed as circus performers and coquettish chambermaids who parade around dragging non-dancers to their feet. The menu is 62 pages long and features no fewer than nine pages of alcoholic drinks as well as countless eating options, such as the steaks they are famous for. There's live music, and the party runs until 3am Fri & Sat (cover C$12,000 after 7pm Fri, C$21,000 after 6pm Sat). The location is far out – 23km north of the city, and if you don't want to splurge on a taxi (around C$180,000 return, including waiting time), many hostels run party buses to *Andrés* on Saturday nights; for C$70,000, you get the transport there and back and booze along the way. For those who can't make it to the original and best, there's a more sedate version at C 82 no. 12–21, Zona Rosa. Wed, Thurs & Sun noon–11pm, Fri & Sat noon–3am.

La Hamburguesería C 85 No. 12–49, Zona Rosa; map p.496. A burger bar, part of a city-wide chain, but also a live music venue, and a good one. This is where a lot of local bands launch their new releases, and it's an important venue so far as Bogotano rock is concerned. Entry for concerts is usually around C$10,000–15,000 on Saturdays, free on Fridays. Mon–Thurs & Sun noon–11pm, Fri & Sat noon–3am, music Fri & Sat from 9pm.

Theatron C 58 no. 10–18, Chapinero ⓦtheatron.co; map p.496. A neon-lit wonderland, this colossal gay club is spread over three floors and six rooms, some of which are men only. Also hosts live shows, which attract a mixed audience. The C$35,000 cover charge on Saturday night gets you a cup and access to an open bar (until 2am). Thurs 9pm–3am, Fri 9pm–4am, Sat and eve of public holidays 9pm–5am.

SHOPPING

Artesanías de Colombia Cra 2 no. 18A–58, ⓦartesaniasdecolombia.com.co; map p.496. Not cheap, but has beautiful, high-quality handicrafts and jewellery all over Colombia that's far nicer than the tat you'll find in the tourist traps around the Museo del Oro. Theres another branch at C 86A no. 13A–10, Zona Rosa. Mon–Sat 10am–7pm, Sun 11am–5pm.

Mercado de Pulgas de la 26 Cra 7, at C 24 and around; map p.496. Bogotá's biggest and most interesting flea market. There's plenty of junk and bric-a-brac of course, bargains of all sorts, books and records, things that are more like proper antiques, food, crafts and jewellery. Sun 7am–5pm.

Paloquemao C 19 no. 25–02. The largest and most bustling market in the city, where you can stock up on supplies to cook at your hostel. Fantastic veg and tropical fruit, a somewhat gory meat section and plenty of dry goods. Tuesdays and Fridays are when the flower-sellers show up: get there by about 8am to catch the best of their displays. It's safe enough to take a camera if you are sensible with it: be discreet and ask permission before taking photos of people. Mon–Sat 4.30am–4.30pm, Sun 5am–2.30pm.

DIRECTORY

Banks and exchange A number of moneychangers can be found around the junction of Av Jiménez with Cra 6; rates vary so ask around before choosing. There are concentrations of banks with ATMs on Cra 7 immediately north of Parque de Santander and at C 16–C 17 and C 19–C 20.

Embassies Australia, Edificio Tierra Firme, Cra 9 no. 115–06/30, suite 2002 (ⓣ1 657 0800); Brazil, C 93 no. 14–20, 8th floor (ⓣ1 635 1694); Canada, Cra 7 no. 114–33, 14th floor (ⓣ1 657 9800); Ecuador, C 89 no. 13–07 (ⓣ1 212 6512); Peru, C 80A no. 6–50 (ⓣ1 746 2360); UK, Cra 9 no. 76–49, 8th floor (ⓣ1 326 8300); US, Cra 45 no. 24B–27

5

(☎1 275 2000); Venezuela, Cra 11 no. 87–51 (☎1 644 5555).

Hospital Clínica Marly, C 50 no. 9–67 (☎1 343 6600, ⓦmarly.com.co), and San Ignacio, Cra 7 no. 40–62 (☎1 594 6161, ⓦwww.husi.org.co), are well-equipped medical facilities accustomed to attending foreigners.

Immigration Migración Colombia, C 26 No. 59–51 (Edificio Argos), Torre 3, 4th floor; Mon–Fri 7am–4pm.

Laundry Lavandería La Candelaria, C 12D no. 3–75 (Mon–Sat 8.30am–7pm, Sun 8.30am–1pm); Lavandería Megarápido, Cra 3 no. 12C–23 (Mon–Sat 7.30am–7.30pm; also has a great clothes repair service.

Pharmacy In the Olímpica supermarket on Av Jiménez at C 13 no. 4–74 (daily 7am–9pm).

Police Tourist Police, C 28 no. 13A–24 (☎1 337 4413 or ☎1 243 1175).

Post office Cra 8, at C 12 (Mon–Fri 8am–6pm, Sat 9am–noon). Típicos Muzo de Colombia, C 13 (Av Jiménez) No. 4–76, sells stamps (and a big variety of postcards) and has a postbox (Mon–Sat 9am–7pm, Sun 10am–5pm).

DAY-TRIPS FROM BOGOTÁ

The **Zipaquirá salt cathedral** and the up-and-coming adventure sports town of **Suesca** are both within easy day-trip distance of the capital.

The Zipaquirá salt cathedral

The most popular day-trip from Bogotá is a visit to the salt cathedral of **ZIPAQUIRÁ** (daily 9am–5.30pm; C$50,000; ⓦcatedraldesal.gov.co), some 50km north of the city. Inaugurated in 1995 to great fanfare – having replaced an earlier one that closed because of collapse – the cathedral lies completely underground, topped by a hill that was mined by local indigenous communities before the Spanish arrived in the seventeenth century. As you descend 180m into the earth, you'll pass fourteen minimalist chapels built entirely of salt that glow like marble in the soft light, each a different combination of colours. The main nave is

a feat of engineering, complete with the world's largest subterranean cross, and the vast salty cavern is impressive, though the changing lighting is very gimmicky.

Above ground, there's a **museum** (same hours as cathedral) explaining the history of salt extraction; more expensive ticket combinations include museum entry. You must enter the salt cathedral with a **guided tour** that's included in the entrance fee, but once inside, you're free to escape. To get there from Bogotá, take the TransMilenio to the Portal del Norte station at the end of the B line and from here a *buseta* (C$5100) to Zipa or Zipaquirá. From the centre of Zipaquirá, it's a short taxi ride or fifteen minute walk to the entrance.

Suesca

Some 65km north of Bogotá, the small town of **SUESCA** is one of Colombia's top rock-climbing destinations. Adventure-sports enthusiasts of all persuasions will feel at home here, but it is the sandstone cliffs on the town's doorstep that steal the show, offering traditional and sport rock-climbing with more than six hundred routes including multi-pitch.

The gateway for the rocks is Vereda Cacicazgo, half a kilometre short of the town itself, which is where you'll find the hostels and adventure sports companies.

ARRIVAL AND DEPARTURE

By bus To get to Suesca from Bogotá, take the TransMilenio to the northern terminus at Portal del Norte and then jump on one of the regular buses (1hr). You'll probably want to get off at Vereda Cacicazgo rather than in the town centre.

ACCOMMODATION

El Nómada Cacicazgo, on the main road (Cra 4) no. 105 ☎320 431 4606, ⓦelnomadahostel.com. Fifteen minutes on from the rocks, this hostel and adventure activities agency also has a good café. Tents C$15,000, dorms C$30,000, doubles C$85,000

North of Bogotá

Away from Bogotá, the smog and busy streets give way to the bucolic countryside of Colombia's central Andean departments Boyacá, Cundimarca and Santander, which mark the geographical heart of the

country. First inhabited centuries ago by the gold-worshipping Muisca people, these mountainous highlands played a pivotal role in forging Colombia's national identity. **Tunja**, one of Colombia's oldest cities, is famous for its architecture, while an hour further northwest is one of Colombia's best-preserved colonial towns, **Villa de Leyva**, its surrounding countryside studded with archeological treasures.

Tiny **Barichara**, just a steep 22km from the burgeoning adventure centre of **San Gil**, is a compact colonial beauty. Further north again, the modern city of **Bucaramanga** or the colonial town of **Girón** are both decent midway points if you're heading to Venezuela or the coast. Follow a different road from Bogotá, and eight hours later you arrive at the high-altitude splendours of **Parque Nacional El Cocuy**, with its glacial lakes and snowcapped peaks.

TUNJA

Founded in 1539 on the ruins of the ancient Muisca capital of Hunza, **TUNJA** is not the region's most exciting city, though its historic centre is one of the foremost preserves of the country's colonial heritage, and is worth a quick stop on the way to Villa de Leyva.

WHAT TO SEE AND DO

The mansions around the Plaza de Bolívar are particularly splendid. The **Casa del Fundador Suárez Rendón** (Cra 9 no. 19–68; Tues–Sun 9am–11.30am & 2–4.30pm; free), home of the town's founder, was built in the Moorish Mudéjar style in 1540 and features interesting scenes on its ceiling, while the **Casa de Don Juan de Vargas** (C 20 no. 8–52; Mon–Fri 9am–noon & 2–5pm, Sat & Sun 9.30am–noon & 2–4pm; C$3000) also stands out for its eighteenth-century ceiling frescoes. The motifs are a curious mishmash of imagery – from Greek gods to exotic animals and coats of arms, combined in unusual settings.

The town's churches are no less interesting, with **Iglesia de Santo Domingo** (Cra 11 no. 19–55; open for Mass, including most evenings at 6pm) known for its Rosario Chapel, richly decorated with religious paintings and magnificent gilded woodcarving by Gregorio Vásquez de Arce y Ceballos. **Iglesia y Convento de Santa Clara de Real** (Cra 7 no. 19–58;

Mon–Fri 9am–4.30pm, Sat & Sun 10am–4pm; free) was the first convent in Nueva Granada, and combines indigenous and Catholic imagery in its elaborate decor; note the sun on the ceiling, the main god of the Muisca.

About 16km south of Tunja on the main road back to Bogotá is a reconstructed colonial-era bridge, **El Puente de Boyacá**, commemorating the Battle of Boyacá of August 7, 1819, which cleared the way for Bolívar and his freedom fighters to march triumphantly into Bogotá. Any Bogotá–Tunja bus will drop you off/pick you up (provided there's room).

ARRIVAL AND DEPARTURE

By bus The bus terminal is on Av Oriental, several blocks uphill from Plaza de Bolívar. Buses north to Bucaramanga (every 30min; 7hr), the main jumping-off point for the Caribbean coast, travel via San Gil (4hr 30min). Small buses to Villa de Leyva leave about every 15min (45min), with 5–6 Bogotá departures every hour.

ACCOMMODATION

Hotel Casa Real C 19 no. 7–65 ☎ 8 743 1764, ⓦ hotelcasarealtunja.com. Atmospheric place with attractive en-suite rooms in an old colonial building between the bus station and Plaza de Bolívar. C$80,000

VILLA DE LEYVA

Tucked against the foot of spectacular mountains, scenic **VILLA DE LEYVA**, founded in 1572, is a must-see showcase of colonial architecture. The untroubled ambience and mild, dry climate make it a perfect place to relax – sitting in the 400-year-old plaza drinking sangria, you'll be able to appreciate why many describe it as Colombia's most beautiful town. In the mountains around (see page 508), you can go hunting for fossils, bathe in waterfalls or enjoy the countryside on horseback. The narrow streets throng with day-trippers from Bogotá on weekends, but the rest of the time, this lovely town reverts to its former tranquil, timeless self.

WHAT TO SEE AND DO

Villa de Leyva looks and feels immaculately preserved, right down to hand-painted tiles prohibiting horseriding and car traffic along the main plaza. A lively **market**,

mostly featuring fruit, veg and clothing, is held in the Plaza de Mercado on Saturday morning. There's a smaller, organic food market on Thursday mornings.

Plaza Mayor

The impressive **Plaza Mayor** is one of the largest in the Americas, paved with large cobblestones, centred on a stone Mudéjar well and surrounded by attractive colonial buildings. Dominating the plaza is the huge stone portal of the seventeenth-century **Catedral**, rebuilt after an 1845 earthquake.

Casa-Museo Luis Alberto Acuña

Facing the Plaza Mayor is the **Casa-Museo Luis Alberto Acuña** (daily 10am–6pm; C$6000), which houses the most comprehensive collection of sculptures and other artwork by influential, avant-garde twentieth-century artist Luis Alberto Acuña, who lived here for the last fifteen years of his life. The large, colourful murals in the courtyard, depicting Muisca mythological figures, are a highlight.

Museo del Carmen

Facing the imposing **Monasterio de las Carmelitas** and its attached church is the

Museo del Carmen (Plazuela del Carmen; Sat, Sun & hols only 9am–5pm; C$7000), justifiably famous for its collection of religious art. Here you'll find large numbers of wooden icons from the Church's early years of proselytizing in the New World, as well as altarpieces and paintings that date back to the sixteenth century.

Casa de Antonio Ricaurte

Once home to a national hero who fought for Bolívar, and operated by the Colombian armed forces since 1970, the house where **Antonio Ricaurte** was born (Wed–Fri 9am–noon & 2–5pm; free) contains some personal objects and documents (in Spanish only), plus modern military paraphernalia, but the best reason for coming here is the beautiful garden.

ARRIVAL AND DEPARTURE

By bus The bus station is three blocks southwest of the Plaza Mayor, towards the road to Tunja. Direct buses run to Bogotá (15 daily; 4–5hr) between 5am and 5pm, and plentiful minibuses connect Villa de Leyva with Tunja (about every 15min; 1hr). To continue north to San Gil or Bucaramanga, it's possible to go via Arcabuco or Chiquinquirá, but better to backtrack to Tunja and catch a bus from there as they are more frequent and more certain.

GETTING AROUND

Taxis You can hire a taxi for the day to drive you from site to site around the city (approx. C$25,000 per site, but negotiate). Alternatively, you can travel by horseback or walk to some sites, though the winding roads can be dangerous for unwary pedestrians.

INFORMATION AND TOURS

Tourist information The tourist office is at Cra 9 no. 13–04 (Mon–Sat 8am–noon & 2–6pm, Sun 9am–5pm; ☎ 8 732 0232). There's also an office at the bus station (daily 7am–8pm).

Tours Colombian Highlands, based at the *Renacer* hostel (ⓦcolombianhighlands.com), is an excellent stop to pick up information on outdoor excursions. They can organize hiking, abseiling and horseriding, and they offer ten percent discounts to those who stay at their hostel.

ACCOMMODATION

There are several campsites around town, but you'll need your own tent. Discounts of up to thirty percent are often available during the week; book early for weekends and holidays.

Casa Viena Cra 10 no. 19–114 ☎ 8 732 0711, ⓦhostel-villadeleyva.com; map p.506. Friendly little hostel – two doubles, a single and a three-bed dorm – run by Hans and his family. It's on the same road as *Hostal Renacer* and they'll refund you the taxi fare from the bus station (except in high season) if staying for more than one night (C$4000). Dorms <u>C$45,000</u>

Hospedería La Roca C 13 no. 9–54, Plaza Mayor ☎ 8 732 0331, ⓦlarocavilladeleyva.com; map p.506. This place has a fantastic location on the main square, plus a pretty courtyard and 23 rooms (including one for up to six people) with private bathrooms and TV. <u>C$140,00</u>

★ **Hostal Renacer** Cra 10 no.21–Finca Renacer (up path by no. 21–26) ☎ 8 732 1201, ⓦrenacerhostel.com; map p.506. Owned by Oscar Gilède, the English-speaking biologist behind Colombian Highlands tour operators, *Hostal Renacer* is a haven surrounded by trees and mountain views. A TV room, hammocks, free hot drinks, a fridge full of beer and heaps of information, plus rooms with huge windows and comfortable beds, make it popular with backpackers who aren't precious about the odd creepy-crawly. You can also camp. The location, about 1km uphill from the centre,

is a bit of a pain, but if you call when you arrive in town they'll pay for your taxi. Camping per person with own tent <u>C$18,000</u>, dorms <u>C$38,000</u>, doubles <u>C$120,000</u>

Zona de Camping C 11, at Cra 10 ☎311 530 7687; map p.506. No-frills camping, with a wall set up around a large patch of grass and a basic toilet/shower block. Great mountain views. Per person <u>C$15,000</u>

EATING

If you can spare the pesos, you will eat very well here, as the food scene is very diverse; the best gourmet food courts are Casona La Guaca (Cra 9 between C 13 & C 14) and Casa Quintero (Cra 9, at C 12). You can find information about the town's culinary options on ⓦvilladeleyva.net.

Carnes y Olivas Cra 10 no. 11–55 ☎8 732 1368; map p.506. Offers a fantastic-value, three-course *menu del día* (C$12,500), including traditional dishes such as tender braised *sobrebarriga* (flank steak), cooked with considerable skill and flair. Also international dishes such as pizza and hamburgers. Daily 9.30am–8pm.

Casa Blanca C 13 no. 7–02 ☎8 732 0821, ⓦbit.ly/cablaleyva; map p.506. Refined, posh eating, with tablecloths, where the specialities include *bagre criollo* (catfish with tomatoes and onions; C$29,000) or chicken *ajiaco* (C$23,000), all well presented, and served up by waiters dressed in claret-coloured aprons. Daily 8.30am–8pm.

Savia Local 20, C 10 no. 6–67 ☎322 474 9859, ⓢrestaurantesavia.com; map p.506. The organic dishes at this fantastic little spot will delight vegetarians, vegans and fish-eaters alike. Huge mains (big enough for two) include the likes of vegetable and lentil quinoa and mega salads. Mains from C$14,600. Daily noon–8pm.

La Waffleria La Casona de Arroyo, Cra 9 no. 14–14; map p.506. Cute little café dishing up all the crêpes and waffles your heart may desire – sweet and savoury. Waffles from C$11,500. Mon–Thurs 12.30–9pm, Fri 12.30–10pm, Sat & Sun 9am–11pm.

DRINKING

Nightlife is centred on Plaza Mayor.

Dortkneipe Cra 9, Plaza Mayor, no. 12–88; map p.506. The nicest bar on the main square draws beer connoisseurs with its selection of unusual (mostly German) beers on tap, as well as the ubiquitous Aguila. Mon–Wed 4pm–

LOCAL FIESTAS

The town plays host to two spectacular annual festivals. The larger is the **Festival de Luces** (Festival of Lights; Dec 7–9), a fireworks extravaganza that gathers the best of the region's pyrotechnicians. During Semana Santa (the week leading up to Easter), an acoustic music festival, the **Encuentra de Música Antigua**, is held in the town's churches while the popular **Festival de las Cometas** (Kite Festival; Aug) sees the country's finest kite-flyers compete in a variety of categories as spectators shout encouragement.

5

midnight, Thurs & Sun 10.30am–midnight, Fri & Sat 10.30am–2am.

AROUND VILLA DE LEYVA

Attractions surrounding Villa de Leyva include giant fossils, archeological sites, nature reserves and a town specializing in local crafts. They can be reached on horseback, by bicycle, bus or taxi or via a tour. If making an arrangement with a taxi, make sure the driver knows exactly which sites you want to see, and agree on the price beforehand.

Centro de Investigaciones Paleontológicas

About 5km from Villa de Leyva and just down the road from El Fósil on Km4, this interactive museum and centre of palaeontology research (Tues–Thurs 8am–noon & 2–5pm, Fri–Sun 8am–5pm; C$9000), Centro de Investigaciones Paleontológicas exhibits wonderfully preserved fossils of species that inhabited the area 110 million years ago, among them the marine ichthyosaurs, kronosaurus and pliosaurus. The sabre tooth tiger fossil is a highlight, and a camera link to the lab shows palaeontologists hard at work.

El Fósil

The arid desert highlands surrounding Villa de Leyva attract trekkers, but 120 million years ago the huge flood plain would have been better suited to scuba diving. The ocean waters have since retreated, leaving the country's largest repository of fossils. Five kilometres out of town along the road to Santa Sofía, the star of the El Fósil museum (daily 9am–5pm; C$8000) is the most complete fossil of a 120-million-year-old baby kronosaurus, a prehistoric marine lizard found by a *campesino* here in 1977. The 12.8m-long lizard is one of only two in the world excavated in its entirety, but on display you'll find it without the 5m tail, which was lost.

Estación Astronómica Muisca

Also known as El Infernito, this Muisca observatory (Tues–Sun 9am–5pm; C$8000), dating back to early centuries

AD and located around 2km on from El Fósil, is Colombia's answer to Stonehenge. Pathways run between the 115-odd stone monoliths, the larger ones strongly resembling enormous stone phalluses. The Muisca used to decide when to start planting crops by measuring the length of the shadows between the stones.

El Santuario de Iguaque

Around 15km north of town, the large nature reserve of El Santuario de Iguaque has excellent hiking. It's named after the park's most sacred lake, Laguna de Iguaque – believed by the native Muiscas to be the birthplace of humanity – which can be visited as a day-trip; there are eight lakes altogether in the park at an altitude between 3550m and 3700m, and it can be cold and wet (the best time to come is Jan, Feb, July & Aug), so come equipped accordingly.

A visitor centre, 12km northeast out of Villa de Leyva, offers basic shared accommodation (C$50,000 per person) and food. The entrance fee for the reserve is C$44,500 for foreigners. Take one of the buses that leave for Arcabuco (up to 7 daily) and ask to be dropped off at Casa de Piedra (aka Los Naranjos) at Km12; from here it's a 3km walk to the visitor centre.

Ráquira

Tiny Ráquira, 25km from Villa de Leyva to the west, is famous countrywide for its pottery. If you're looking for crafts to take home, besides perusing the many pottery workshops, you can raid the craft shops around the main square for hammocks, jewellery, woodcarvings and ponchos. Sunday is market day and a particularly good time to visit. Ráquira can be reached by bus from Villa de Leyva (4 daily; 45min; or take a Chiquinquirá bus and get off at Tres Esquinas, 4km from Ráquira with frequent transport). A taxi costs around C$35,000 one-way.

SAN GIL

An adventure-sports hotspot, SAN GIL is one of the biggest backpacker draws in northern Colombia. The compact town is a premier destination for white-water

5

ADVENTURE SPORTS

Adrenaline junkies are spoilt for choice by the array of **adventure sports** on offer in San Gil. There are two main **whitewater rafting** routes: a hair-raising day-trip down the Class IV/V (depends on the season) Río Suarez costs about C$130,000, while a more sedate half-day on the Río Fonce is C$45,000. **Abseiling** down the Juan Curí waterfalls will set you back C$60,000, or you can take flight with a tandem **paraglide** (C$80,000). **Spelunkers** have the choice of several caves to explore (around C$35,000). Other sporty options include kayaking, horseriding and extreme mountain biking.

Most accommodation can arrange any of the above, and you should pay the same as if you book direct. The staff at *Macondo Guesthouse* are particularly helpful if you're trying to decide what to opt for. Alternatively, **recommended operators** are:

Colombian Bike Junkies ☎316 327 6101, ⓦcolombianbikejunkies.com.

Colombia Rafting Expediciones Cra 10 no. 7–83 ☎7 724 5800, ⓦcolombiarafting.com.

Nativox C 7 no. 10–25 ☎7 723 9999, ⓦnativoxsangil. com.

Páramo Santander Extremo Via principal, Entrada al Municipio, Páramo (19km south of San Gil) ☎7 725 8944, ⓦparamosantanderextremo.com.

rafting and paragliding, as well as hiking and other outdoorsy activities that take place in the surrounding countryside, and for day-trips to quiet colonial Barichara. For those craving a spot of culinary adventure, fried *hormigas culonas*, or fat-bottomed ants, a Santander delicacy, can be bought from a few places around town including the market and the street by the river.

San Gil's main attractions lie outside town, but if you want a quiet moment in between adventures, make your way to the large riverside **Parque El Gallineral** (daily 8am–5.30pm; C$6000), its trees atmospherically festooned with tendrils of "old man's beard" moss. There's a natural spring-fed swimming pool, and the entrance fee gets you a wristband that means you can go in and out of the park all day. To get here, head to the river and turn left along the Malecón to its end.

ARRIVAL AND DEPARTURE

By bus The main terminal is around 2km southwest of town. with departures to Bucaramanga (every 30min; 2hr 30min) and Bogotá (3–4 hourly; 7hr 30min); a taxi to the centre costs around C$5000, or there are local buses. Buses to Barichara (every 30min; 45min) leave from the "*Terminalito*" at C 15 and Cra 10.

ACCOMMODATION

★ **Macondo Guesthouse** C 8 no. 10–35 ☎7 724 8001, ⓦmacondohostel.com. Australian-owned *Macondo Guesthouse* has a homey, laidback atmosphere, with guests relaxing in the jacuzzi after an adrenaline-packed day. An excellent place to organize your outdoor adventures. Dorms C$22,000, C$60,000

Mansión Hostel C 12 no. 8–71 T7 724 6044, ⓦmansionhotel.com. There's no stopping Sam of *Sam's VIP*: this colonial mansion on the corner of Parque Central features attractive rooms around a central courtyard. There's a decent gastropub downstairs too. Dorms C$25,000, doubles C$110,000

Sam's VIP Cra 10 no. 12–33 ☎7 724 2746, ⓦsamshostel. com. This lively hostel with particularly attractive decor has a balcony overlooking the main square, poker table and even a small swimming pool. Dorms are on the small side, but there's a superb guest kitchen and the double rooms downstairs are great value. Dorms C$25,000, doubles C$110,000

Santander Alemán Terrace Vista Cra 10 No. 15–07, ⓔhostelsantanderaleman@gmail.com. A slightly sedate, family-friendly hostel near the *Terminalito* (local bus station), modern, fresh and clean, where each four-bed dorm and private room has its own bathroom. And there's a terrace with a view over the rooftops, as promised. Reductions for longer stays. Dorms C$25,000, doubles C$60,000

EATING AND DRINKING

By far the liveliest place to drink on most evenings is the main plaza, where vendors grill meat skewers and corn on the cob. The central market between calles 13 and 14 is the best bet for ses, as well as fresh fruit juice, and is open until 2pm daily. By the riverside park, vendors sell a local speciality – fried giant ants.

Donde Betty Cra 9 no. 11–96. The best place for fruit juices (C$3000) and superb scrambled eggs, each portion cooked and served in its own miniature frying pan; try the *huevos rancheros* (with fresh tomato, chorizo and coriander) for the *huevos Israeelis* (with onions and spinach). Mains C$4000. Daily 7am–midnight.

5

★ **Gringo Mike's** C 12 no. 8–35. Sooner or later, everyone makes their way to this candlelit courtyard for the mega breakfast burritos, brie-and-bacon burgers the size of your head, doorstop sandwiches and that old gringo dessert favourite, brownie with ice cream. Mains C$23,500. Daily 8am–11pm.

El Maná C 10 no. 9–49. Ask a local for advice on restaurants and you'll probably be directed here: *El Maná* is extremely popular for its dependable set meals (C$14,000), which come with a choice of dishes such as grilled trout and *carne asado* (grilled meat). You won't leave hungry. Daily 11am–3pm & 6–9pm.

AROUND SAN GIL

Cascadas de Juan Curí

For a spectacular swim in a natural pool at the base of a 180m-high waterfall, or to abseil down its face, take a trip out of town to the **Cascadas de Juan Curí** (daily 8am–4pm; C$9000). Take a bus to Charalá (35min) from Calle 10 on the east side of the bridge, and ask to be let off at the *Las Cascadas* sign. From here it's a 25-minute walk to the waterfalls along either of the two trails.

Parque Nacional del Chichamocha

About an hour from San Gil on the road to Bucaramanga, Colombia's newest **national park** (Wed–Fri 10am–6pm, Sat, Sun & public hols 9am–7pm; C$25,000, or C$38,000 including entrance to the waterpark; ⊕parquenacionaldelchicamocha.com), **Parque Nacional del Chichamocha**, holds a collection of tacky, forgettable attractions situated next to a beautiful canyon. The *teleférico*, a cable car which runs down into the canyon and over to the other side, is the best way to get sweeping views (Wed–Fri 10.30–11am, 12.30–1pm, 2.30–3pm & 4.30–5.30pm, Sat & Sun 9am–6pm; park entrance with *teleférico* C$50,000). You can also watch the scenery whizz by at much higher speed while hurtling along a zipline (C$25,000), or get a bird's-eye view by paragliding above the valley (C$180,000).

BARICHARA

With its undulating stone-slab roads,

clay-tiled *tejas* roofs draped in bougainvillea blossoms and single-storey adobe homes, the sedate colonial town of **BARICHARA** looks like it hasn't changed much in its 250 years. So well kept is the town that it was declared a national monument in 1978 and, with its historical buildings restored, it now makes a popular set for Spanish-language films. Barichara is considerably less crowded than similarly picturesque Villa de Leyva, making it a peaceful, if expensive, resting spot for travellers. Indeed, the town's name comes from a Guane word, *Barachala*, meaning "a good place to rest". Alternatively, it makes for a great day-trip from San Gil.

WHAT TO SEE AND DO

Barichara's quiet streets, lined with beautiful architecture, and tranquil vibe are its biggest attraction. Once you've checked out the striking **Catedral de la Inmaculada Concepción**, take a look at the elaborate marble tombs at the **Capilla de Jesús Resucitado cemetery**. Surrounding an attractive patio at **Casa de la Cultura** (Mon & Wed–Sat 8am–noon & 2–6pm, Sun 8am–noon; C$2000) is a collection of regional photos, Guane pottery, fossils and various early twentieth-century paraphernalia.

Very popular with hikers is the 9km **Camino Real**, an ancient stone-paved trail used by the indigenous Guane people, leading down through a cactus-filled valley with great mountain views to the tiny village of **Guane** (2hr one-way). To join the path, head uphill along C 5 from the cathedral before taking a left along Cra 10 to the edge of Barichara. From Guane, there are five buses daily back to Barichara, the last leaving at 6pm; bring plenty of water and wear sturdy footwear.

ARRIVAL AND DEPARTURE

By bus Buses run between Barichara's Parque Central and San Gil's *Terminalito* (every 30min 5am–6.30pm; 45min).

ACCOMMODATION

There is far more choice for budget accommodation in San Gil than there is in Barichara.

Casa de Hercilia C 3 no. 5–33 ☏7 726 7450. A light and airy guesthouse that oozes tranquillity, with hammocks, beanbags and leafy pot plants liberally scattered throughout. Also has a well-equipped communal kitchen. No dorms, but in low season it's worth asking about renting a single bed in one of their bigger rooms. **C$120,000**

Tinto Hostel Cra 4 no. 5–39 ☏7 726 7725, ⓦtintohostel.com. There's quite a rustic feel to this hostel with wooden fittings and tiled floors. It offers a lush garden, good views, hammocks and even a small pool. Dorms **C$25,000**, doubles **C$80,000**

EATING

El Cabrito al la Brasa C 6 no. 5–03 ☏7 726 7074. A good-value small restaurant where they have a C$9000 set menu and good breakfasts. They also serve *chicha* (a traditional alcoholic corn brew). Daily 11am–5pm.

Panadería Central Cra 6, no. 5–82. This bright bakery on the main square doubles as a café, with espresso-based coffee, juices and cakes – *churros* stuffed with *arequipe* even. Daily 6.30am–9pm.

BUCARAMANGA

Founded in 1622, **BUCARAMANGA** has shed much of its colonial heritage and evolved into one of Colombia's largest, most modern cities. The centre might be low on attractions, but it makes a great jumping-off point for visits to nearby Girón, the mountains surrounding the city are superb for paragliding and it is a convenient stopover for anyone travelling to the coast or Venezuela.

WHAT TO SEE AND DO

Simón Bolívar (El Libertadór) spent seventy days living in Bucaramanga in 1828, enough for the locals to rename the house where he stayed, at C 37 no. 12–15, **Casa de Bolívar** (Mon–Fri 8am–noon & 2–6pm, Sat 8am–noon; C$2000). It contains a small historical museum, the highlight of which is the Guane mummies and artefacts. Across the street another colonial mansion houses the **Casa de la Cultura** (Mon–Fri 8am–noon & 2–6pm, Sat 8am–noon; free), which holds displays of regional art. Also of interest to art lovers is the **Museo de Arte Moderno** (C37 no. 26–16; Tues–Fri 9am–noon & 2.30–7pm, Sat 10am–6pm; free), featuring temporary exhibitions of contemporary painting and sculpture.

Bucaramanga is justifiably taking off as a **paragliding** destination, thanks to Colombia Paragliding (☏312 432 6266, ⓦcolombiaparagliding.com), which offers everything from one-off fifteen-minute tandem flights (C$80,000) to ten-day courses for those who want their international licence (C$3,400,000). The owners, who run *Kasa Guane*, also have a hostel at their flight site outside town, which means you can be airborne within about ten minutes of getting out of bed.

ARRIVAL AND DEPARTURE

By plane Palonegro International Airport lies about 25km west of the downtown area. The taxi fare to downtown is around C$35,000. You can also take one of the *colectivos* that run to and from C 35 no. 20–23, just off Parque Santander (☏7 642 5250; C$11,000). Alternatively, your accommodation can arrange a lift in a shared taxi. There are twelve flights daily to Bogotá (1hr).

By bus The Terminal de Transportes (ⓦterminalbucaramanga.com) is about 5km southwest of the city, and is accessible by city bus marked "Terminal" from Cra 15, or by taxi (C$8000).

Destinations Bogotá (2–3 hourly; 10hr); Cartagena (20 daily; 12hr); Cúcuta (2–3 hourly; 5hr); Santa Marta (10 daily; 10hr).

ACCOMMODATION

Balmoral Cra 21 no. 34–75 ☏7 630 4136. Lacking in style, but has very cheap double rooms which are clean, secure and have private baths and TVs. . The rooms are compact but fully equipped, with private bathroom, a/c and minibar. **C$65,000**

★ **Kasa Guane** C 11 no. 26–50 ☏7 657 6960, ⓦkasaguane.com. Airy dorms, a great vibe, a cool top-floor bar, and a restaurant that makes a decent stab at Middle Eastern veg grub. It's the best place to stay if you want to find out about activities such as paragliding or rock climbing, and the owners run a volunteering project helping local kids learn English and other skills. Breakfast included. Dorms **C$35,000**, doubles **C$90,000**

EATING

Keep an eye out for regional specialities such as *cabra* (goat). You'll find a few places serving cheap set lunches in the area north of Parque de Santander.

Donde Lety Cra 29 no. 40–34. This popular fish restaurant serves up a range of succulent dishes, and a good-value C$13,000 *menu ejecutivo*. Daily 11am–4pm.

La Patata Cra 34 no. 35–18. Fast food restaurant made from transport containers, with open-air (but covered) seating, upstairs or downstairs, a good vibe, and decent burgers (C$17,000), fries, ribs and beers. Tues–Sun 6–11pm.

El Viejo Chiflas Cra 33 no. 34–10. *Comida típica* including *cabra en salsa* (goat in sauce; C$37,200) and nibbles such

5

as chorizo or *papas criollos*. Open 24hr from Thursday to Sunday, so very handy if you're coming back from a night out. Mon–Wed 7am–midnight, Thurs 7am–Sun midnight.

DRINKING AND NIGHTLIFE

Calison C 33 no. 31–35. A salsa club where there's no entry fee – you just pay for drinks, and the music is solid salsa, much of it from the collection of vinyl and CDs that they keep behind the mixing desk. Mon–Wed & Sun 5.30pm–1am, Thurs–Sat 5.30pm–2am.

GIRÓN

With its whitewashed colonial buildings, leafy main square, stone bridges and elegant churches, pretty **GIRÓN** makes for a great day-trip from nearby Bucaramanga, and is particularly worthwhile for those who don't have time to visit other colonial gems like Villa de Leyva and Barichara. The pace of life here is extremely relaxed, and the narrow cobbled streets are perfect for a wander. Keep an eye out for the main **Catedral del Señor de los Milagros** and the attractive eighteenth-century **capilla de las Nieves** on the tiny namesake square.

ARRIVAL AND DEPARTURE

By bus You can pick up buses for Girón on Cra 33 in Bucaramanga. For the return journey, pick them up on C 27 in Girón.

By taxi A taxi from Bucaramanga's bus terminal to Girón costs C$12,000; from the airport it's around C$30,000.

ACCOMMODATION AND EATING

Girón Chill Out Cra 25 no. 32–06 ☎7 646 1119, ⓦgironchillout.com. The Italian-run hotel offers cosy rooms and an in-house restaurant. Breakfast included. C$140,000

Restaurante La Casona C 28 no. 28–05. Just off the Plazuela de los Nieves, this rustic-style restaurant in a colonial house specializes in regional dishes such as *cabro con pepitoria* (goat with a side dish of black pudding made from its blood and offal; C$34,900). Daily noon–8pm.

PARQUE NACIONAL EL COCUY

PARQUE NACIONAL EL COCUY (C$58,500 plus compulsory rescue insurance C$7000/day or show proof of adequate travel insurance coverage) rises to a high point of 5330m above sea level, taking in 32 glacial lakes and 22 snowcapped peaks, and is a hiker's dream but local concerns over water supplies and sacred land have limited the areas you are allowed to visit – check ⓦparquesnacionales.gov.co and ⓦpnncocuy.com for updates before visiting. Be prepared for any climatic conditions and be aware that at night it gets bitterly cold, so pack plenty of warm gear and a four-season sleeping bag (you can rent sleeping bags from tour companies, but they may not be as warm as you need). By far the best weather is from December to February.

WHAT TO SEE AND DO

Visits to the park are now limited to three one-day trails, each stopping short of the snowline. The starting points for any trip to the park are the towns of **El Cocuy** and **Güicán**, where you should stop a day to acclimatize before continuing. You can then hike up to *cabañas* just inside the park which are bases for the one-day treks. The first two are best accessed from El Cocuy, the third from Güicán. It is obligatory to engage a local guide, which will cost around C$120,000–150,000 per group per day for one with a guides' qualification, or C$100,000–120,000 for a locally registered *interprete local*. Guides can be engaged from the Asociación de Guías de Güican y Cocuy (Aseguicoc; see page 513). You should register at the park office in El Cocuy or Güicán the day before you set off (both open daily 7–11.45am & 1–4.45pm).

The most popular of the three permitted hiking trails is the **Lagunillas Pulpito Trail**, the base for which is *Cabañas Sisuma* (☎311 255 1034, ⓔaseguicoc@gmail.com; C$50,000 per person). From here you can hike 12km towards El Pulpito del Diablo (The Devil's Pulpit), a column of rock that sits dramatically in the middle of a glacier. You should be able to get there and back in around ten to twelve hours.

The base for the **Laguna Grande Trail** (Sendero Laguna Grande de la Sierra) is *Hacienda la Esperanza* (☎314 221 2473; C$40,000 per person including breakfast), a homely old *finca* near the village of La

Capilla. The hike from here to the edge of the Pico Cóncavo glacier is 9.6km long and takes nine to ten hours for the round trip.

For the **Ritacuba Trail**, the base is *Cabañas Kanwara* (☎ 311 231 6004; C$50,000 per person by advance reservation only), from where the trail runs for 5km towards Ritacuba Blanco, the Eastern Cordillera's highest peak (5330m), stopping just short of the snowline.

ARRIVAL AND DEPARTURE

By bus There are six daily buses to El Cocuy and Güicán from Bogotá (14hr) and Tunja (11hr) – two in the morning and four overnight. Going back, the first departure is at 3am from Güicán, 4am from El Cocuy, with two buses later in the morning and three overnight. Note that it can get pretty cold on the overnight buses – be sure to take enough warm clothing or blankets. To get between Cocuy and Bucaramanga, change at Capitanejo (3 daily; 3hr 30min, then 11hr to Bucaramanga; you may have to change again at Málaga).

To the park From Güicán or El Cocuy it takes five hours to hike to the park entrance. Hiring a vehicle to take you up there costs around C$80,000, but will take up to six people. Milk trucks (*lecheros*) no longer take passengers.

GUIDES

Asociación de Guías de Güican y Cocuy (Asegecoc) ✉ aseguicoc@gmail.com; in El Cocuy c/o Wilson Torres ☎ 311 255 1034); in Güicán c/o Alejandro López ☎ 314 252 8977. This is the local guides' association. Contact them to arrange a guide or *interprete local*.

Colombia Trek ☎ 320 339 3839, ⊛ colombiatrek.com. This agency, run by bilingual climber Rodrigo Arias, can organize a trip if you don't want to do it independently.

ACCOMMODATION

Most visitors use El Cocuy as a base for the Lagunillas Pulpito and Laguna Grande trains, Güicán for the Ritacuba Trail.

EL COCUY

Hotel Casa Muñoz Cra 5 no. 7–26 ☎ 8 789 0328, ⊛ hotelcasamunoz.com. Modern, not terribly memorable hotel on the main square, with functional, clean rooms around a flower-filled courtyard and reliable hot showers. Rooms per person C$30,000

La Posada del Molino Cra 3 no. 7–51 ☎ 8 789 0377, ⊛ elcocuycasamuseo.blogspot.com. An allegedly haunted colonial mansion featuring patios, a handful of en-suite rooms with some period furniture and unusual bathrooms. Per person C$35,000

GÜICÁN

Brisas del Nevado Cra 5 no. 4–5 ☎ 8 789 7028, ⊛ brisasdelnevado.com. This is the best hotel in town, with private baths in most rooms and complete with a restaurant serving delicious takes on local specialities. Per person C$35,000

El Eden Transversal 2 no. 9–58 ☎ 311 808 8334, ⊛ hotel-eleden.com. Family-run guesthouse popular with travellers, with assorted wildlife in the garden and (mostly) en-suite rooms filled with the smell of pine. It's a 10min walk from the main square; turn right onto the dirt road from Cra 4 past the basketball court, then first right and second left. Per person C$25,000

CROSSING INTO VENEZUELA: CÚCUTA

The main reason to visit the border town of **Cúcuta** is if you're heading by land to Venezuela. The city is hot and grimy, with a dodgy bus station, so exercise caution.

There were previously buses and *colectivos* across the border from Cúcuta's bus terminal to San Cristóbal, but at last check the border was open to pedestrians only (daily 6am–7pm), and the Venezuelan government sometimes closes it altogether. To get to the border town of San Antonio del Táchira, take a local bus from the terminal or along Diagonal Santander (for example at C 8 or at Ventura Plaza mall), or to take a cab (about C$12,000) and then walk across or take a *mototaxi* (around C$3000) to the Venezuelan immigration office (four blocks to the right after the bridge). When crossing the border between Cúcuta in Colombia and San Antonio del Táchira in Venezuela, you must complete border formalities on both sides: get an exit stamp from the country you are leaving and an entry stamp for the country you are entering. Make sure you stop at both border posts to do this. If you don't, you may be turned back, you may be fined, and you may have problems if you ever come back to either country.

To get to Caracas from San Antonio, you will probably need to take a bus or *colectivo* to San Cristóbal, the capital of Venezuela's Táchira state, and get a bus from there.

5

Cartagena and the Caribbean

Ever since Rodrigo de Bastidas became the first European to set foot on Colombian soil in Santa Marta in 1525, there's been a long history of foreigner fascination with the country's Caribbean coastline, and hundreds of thousands – Colombian

holidaymakers chief among them – follow in his footsteps annually. In addition to hot weather and cool breezes, **Cartagena** boasts splendours from the town's past role as the main conduit for the Spanish Crown's imperial plundering. For its

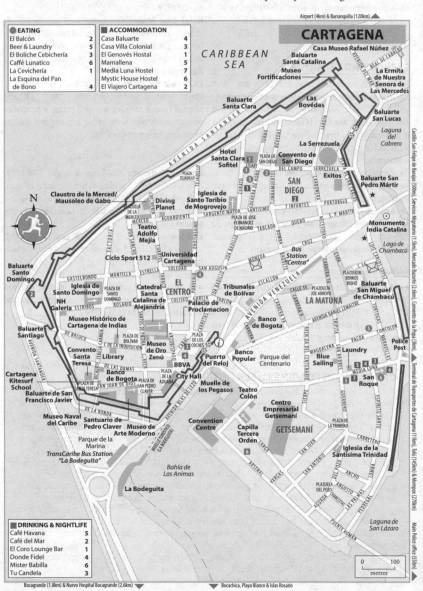

Airport (4km) & Barranquilla (120km)

CARTAGENA

CARIBBEAN SEA

● EATING	
El Balcón	2
Beer & Laundry	5
El Boliche Cebichería	3
Caffé Lunatico	6
La Cevichería	1
La Esquina del Pan de Bono	4

■ ACCOMMODATION	
Casa Baluarte	4
Casa Villa Colonial	3
El Genovés Hostal	1
Mamallena	5
Media Luna Hostel	7
Mystic House Hostel	6
El Viajero Cartagena	2

■ DRINKING & NIGHTLIFE	
Café Havana	5
Café del Mar	2
El Coro Lounge Bar	1
Donde Fidel	4
Mister Babilla	3
Tu Candela	3

Map labels:
Casa Museo Rafael Núñez; Baluarte Santa Catalina; Museo Fortificaciones; La Ermita de Nuestra Senora de Las Mercedes; Baluarte Santa Clara; Las Bóvedas; Baluarte San Lucas; Laguna del Cabrero; La Serrezuela; Hotel Santa Clara Sofitel; Convento de San Diego; SAN DIEGO; Exitos; Baluarte San Pedro Mártir; Claustro de la Merced/Mausoleo de Gabo; Diving Planet; Iglesia de Santo Toribio de Mogrovejo; Monumento India Catalina; Lago de Chambacú; Teatro Adolfo Mejía; Ciclo Sport 512; Universidad Cartagena; Bus Station "Centro"; Baluarte Santo Domingo; Iglesia de Santo Domingo; NH Galeria; EL CENTRO; Tribunales de Bolívar; Baluarte San Miguel de Chambacú; LA MATUNA; Museo Histórico de Cartagena de Indias; Catedral Santa Catalina de Alejandría; Palacio de Proclamacion; Banco de Bogota; Baluarte Santiago; Convento Santa Teresa; Museo de Oro Zenú; Banco de Bogota; BBVA; Puerto del Reloj; Banco Popular; Parque del Centenario; Blue Sailing; Laundry; Police Post; San Roque; Cartagena Kitesurf School; Baluarte de San Francisco Javier; City Hall; Muelle de los Pegasos; Teatro Colón; Museo Naval del Caribe; Santuario de Pedro Claver; Museo de Arte Moderno; Parque de la Marina; Convention Centre; Centro Empresarial Getsemaní; Capilla Tercera Orden; GETSEMANÍ; Iglesia de la Santisima Trinidad; TransCaribe Bus Station "La Bodeguita"; La Bodeguita; Bahía de Las Animas; Laguna de San Lázaro

Castillo San Felipe de Barajas (500m); Servicios Migratorios (1.5km); Mercado Bazurto (2.6km); Convento de la Popa (3km); Terminal de Transportes de Cartagena (11km); Tolú (145km) & Monpox (270km); Main Police Station (550m)

0 — 100 metres

extensive fortifications and colonial legacy, the walled city was declared a UNESCO World Heritage Site in 1984.

The 1600km coast holds a wide variety of landscapes from the inaccessible dense jungles of the **Darién Gap** on the border with Panama to the arid salt plains of **La Guajira Peninsula**. If it's a tropical paradise you're after, try the white, jungle-fringed beaches of **Tayrona National Park** and **Palomino** near **Santa Marta**. The translucent waters around the fishing village of **Taganga** number among the most inexpensive places in the world to learn to scuba dive. Inland, travel back to the sixteenth century in sleepy **Mompox** and cross paths with coca-chewing Kogis on a mesmerizing five-day trek to the **Ciudad Perdida**.

While the vast majority of travellers come straight to Cartagena by night bus from Medellín, it's possible to break your journey in the appealing beach town of **Tolú** and do a day-trip to the Islas de **San Bernardo archipelago**.

CARTAGENA DE INDIAS

Without a doubt the Caribbean's most beautiful city, **CARTAGENA DE INDIAS** offers stunning colonial architecture, gourmet dining, all-night partying and beaches. Cartagena literally embodies Colombia's Caribbean coast, with many of the city's colourful, weathered buildings built using coral from the surrounding reefs.

Founded in 1533, Cartagena was one of the first Spanish cities in the New World and served as the main port through which the continent's riches were shipped off to the mother country. Not surprisingly, the city proved an appetizing target for English pirates prowling the Caribbean, and it suffered several sieges in the sixteenth century, the most infamous led by Sir Francis Drake in 1586, during which he held the town hostage for more than a hundred days. After "the Dragon" was paid a hefty ransom to withdraw, the Spaniards began constructing the elaborate fortifications that are now the city's hallmark. Cartagena's monopoly on the Caribbean slave trade in the early seventeenth century is evident in its

diverse population, the rhythms of its music, its songs, dances and traditions.

WHAT TO SEE AND DO

Bursting with history, Cartagena's supremely photogenic walled **Old City** is a colourful assault on the senses and where the bulk of the sightseeing is. The greatest pleasure here is wandering the narrow streets, lined with colonial buildings painted in bold colours with their wrought-iron detail, bougainvillea tumbling down from balconies, peddlers trying to sell you all manner of tat, and horse-drawn carriages passing by. You might get a little lost, but the city's many **plazas** can guide you, acting not only as convenient landmarks but also as distinct social hangouts. You can take in the city by strolling the 11km of stone **ramparts** that encircle it, though it's best to avoid this late at night.

San Diego, home to a good number of mid-priced *hostals* and several hostels, offers a more mellow, though still lively, version of the Old City. Grittier **Getsemaní**, where *cumbia* music blasts out in the plazas, lacks some of the architectural grandeur of the walled city but offers a better taste of local life. The most raucous nightlife and nearly all budget accommodation are found here. South of the Old City is **Bocagrande**, Cartagena's modern tourist sector, a thin isthmus dotted with high-rise hotels.

Plaza de los Coches and around

The city's main entranceway is the triple-arched **Puerta del Reloj**, which gives way to the **Plaza de los Coches**, a triangular former slave-trading square. In the centre stands a statue of the city's founder, **Pedro de Heredia**, while in the plaza's covered arcade, **Portal de los Dulces**, vendors adeptly pluck sweets of your choice out of a sea of huge glass jars. In the evening, several lively bars open up above the arcade.

Plaza de la Aduana and around

The largest and oldest square, the **Plaza de la Aduana**, once used as a parade ground, features the restored Royal Customs House, now the City Hall, and a statue of Columbus.

5

Convento and Iglesia de San Pedro Claver

Standing on the quiet plaza of the same name, the imposing **Convento de San Pedro Claver** (daily 8am–6pm; C$12,000) was founded by Jesuits in 1603, and is where Spanish-born priest Pedro Claver lived (and died, in 1654). Called the "slave of the slaves" for his lifelong ministering to the city's slaves, aghast at the conditions in which they lived, the ascetic monk was canonized two centuries after his death. His skull and bones are guarded in a glass coffin at the altar of the adjacent **church** (9.30am–noon & 3–5pm; free). The convent itself is a grand three-storey building surrounding a large courtyard bursting with greenery; besides exhibits of religious art and pre-Columbian ceramics, there's the humble cell in which San Pedro Claver spent his nights, the infirmary where he died and the old slave dormitory.

Museo de Arte Moderno

Housed in the seventeenth-century Almacén de Galeras (warehouses), the **Museo de Arte Moderno** (Mon–Fri 9am–noon & 3–7pm, Sat 10am–1pm, Sun 4–9pm; C$8000) offers a refreshing break from Spanish colonial with a respectable collection of Colombian and Latin American art since the 1950s. Highlights include work from locals **Enrique Grau** and **Cecilia Porras**, as well as acclaimed artist **Alejandro Obregón**.

Museo Naval del Caribe

The extensive **Museo Naval del Caribe** (daily 10am–5pm; C$16,000) is perhaps the best history museum in the city, though almost everything is labelled in Spanish only; hire a guide at the entrance (C$30,000) to get the most out of it. The museum chronicles the history of Cartagena, and also of Colombia's navy since 1810.

Plaza de Bolívar

Locals and tourists alike come to find respite from the heat in this leafy, shaded square, with a statue of **Simón Bolívar** as its centrepiece. Formerly the Plaza de Inquisición, the square is surrounded by some of Cartagena's most opulent buildings.

Museu Historico de Cartagena (MUHCA)

On the west side of Plaza de Bolívar stands **Museu Historico de Cartagena,** formerly known as the **Palacio de la Inquisición** (Mon–Sat 9am–6pm, Sun 10am–4pm; C$19,000), a splendid block-long example of late colonial architecture. The seat of the dreaded Inquisition for two hundred years from 1611 onwards, it wasn't completed until 1776, and is believed to be the site where at least eight hundred people were sentenced to death. Heretics were denounced at the small window topped with a cross, around the corner from the entrance, and culprits found guilty of witchcraft and blasphemy were sentenced to public *autos-da-fé* (executions) until independence in 1821. The museum within features a particularly grisly display of torture implements favoured by the Inquisition, as well as scale models of Cartagena, pre-Columbian pottery and displays on the city's history.

Museo de Oro Zenú

If you're haven't yet visited Bogotá's larger counterpart, this excellent **gold museum** (Tues–Fri 10am–1pm & 3–7pm, Sat 10am–1pm & 2–5pm, Sun 11am–4pm; free), off the Plaza de Bolívar, will whet your appetite. The displays feature the intricate gold creations of pre-Columbian cultures, particularly the Zenú. Look out for their intricate "woven" earrings and mammal-bird hybrids, as well as the elaborate gold and copper figures of the Tayrona and the schematic representations of shamans from the San Jacinto range.

Catedral

Looming above the northeast corner of the Plaza de Bolívar is the fortress-like **Catedral** (Mon–Sat 10.30–11.30am & 12.30–7.30pm; Sun 9–11.30am & 12.30–6pm), whose construction began in 1575, but which wasn't completed until 1612 due to setbacks such as its partial destruction by cannon fire in 1586 by Sir Francis Drake. The interior is airy and immaculate after a massive renovation (work will continue on and off until 2019).

Iglesia de Santo Toribio de Mangrovejo

The compact church of **Iglesia de Santo Toribio de Mangrovejo** (Mass only: Mon–Fri 6.30am, noon & 6.15pm) on Calle del Sargento Major, built between 1666 and 1732, has a particularly attractive interior, with splendid Mudéjar panelling and a striking altar. During the failed attack on the city by Vernon in 1741 a cannonball landed inside the church but didn't cause casualties; you can see it in a glass display case on the left wall.

Iglesia de Santo Domingo

On the lively **Plaza de Santo Domingo** and fronted by Fernando Botero's voluptuous *La Gorda* sculpture, the church of **Santo Domingo** (Tues–Sat 9am–7pm, Sun noon–8pm) constitutes the plaza's main draw. Completed in 1579, the fortress-like structure's austere interior belies its status as Cartagena's oldest church. To the right of the Baroque altar, in its own niche, there's a venerated sixteenth-century calvary known as *Cristo de la Expiración*.

Las Bóvedas

In the northeast corner of the walled city, these mustard-coloured dungeons, built into the city walls between 1792 and 1796, have been used variously as munitions storage, a jail and – their current incarnation – as craft shops.

Getsemaní

The focal point of **Getsemaní** is languid Plaza de la Trinidad, one of the oldest squares in the city, though the humble **Iglesia de la Santísima Trinidad** is rarely open (Mass Mon–Sat 7pm, Sun 9am & 6pm) – the plaza is especially lively at night, with food stalls and street performers. From here peruse the increasingly prominent murals and street art in the neighbourhood (especially along Calle San Juan), or wander down gorgeous Calle del Poz, especially busy on Sundays and holidays with locals playing dominoes in the side streets; it ends at the small Plazuela del Pozo and the old well (*pozo*) for which it is named.

Convento de la Popa

For a bird's-eye view of Cartagena, take a taxi (30–45min; around C$50,000 return; haggle) up the hill 2km northeast of the Castillo de San Felipe to the **Convento de la Popa** (Mon–Fri 8.45am–5pm; C$15,000), outside the city's walls. Alternatively, take a city tour (C$50,000) on one of the brightly coloured buses known as *chivas* leaving daily from the Torre del Reloj. Don't walk: robberies have been reported along that zigzagging road. The restored whitewashed chapel, built in 1608, is clearly visible from almost anywhere in the city. On February 2, when the city celebrates the day of its patron saint, the **Virgin of Candelaria**, protector against pirates and the plague, a candle-lit procession of pilgrims storms the hill.

Castillo de San Felipe de Barajas

More than a single, uniform wall, Cartagena is surrounded by a series of impressive fortresses, most of which are still standing. The largest and most important was **Castillo de San Felipe de Barajas** (daily 8am–6pm; C$25,000), a towering stone fort just east of the walled city along Avenida Pedro de Heredia. The sacking of the city by Sir Frances Drake highlighted the need for protection, and so this mighty fort was built between 1656 and 1798 with plans from a Dutch engineer. The fort is an ideal spot from which to watch the sunset, and getting the audioguide (C$15,000) is well worth it while you walk around the fort walls and underground passages, learning about its important landmarks, such as the leper hospital. Alternatively, you can hire one of the guides who hang around at the entrance (C$60,000).

Islas del Rosario

At least fifty minutes out to sea from Cartagena, 35km southwest of the city lies an archipelago of small coral islands known as the **Islas del Rosario**, in transparent turquoise waters. In total there are 27 islands, many of them private islets barely large enough for a bungalow. Not technically part of the chain, **Playa Blanca**,

5

on Barú island, is one of the more popular beach spots.

For **day-trips by boat**, all of which depart in the morning around 8–9.30am and return around 4–5pm, you can either book through your accommodation or head straight to the **Muelle Turístico** (better known as "**La Bodeguita**"), the wharf across from the Convention Center. For C$60,000 you can get a round-trip ride on a boat to Playa Blanca with about twenty others, including a lunch of fried fish, *patacones* (smashed, fried plantains), rice and salad.

The boats sail through Bocachica Strait, and usually stop for lunch on Playa Blanca where you're let loose for a couple of hours. If you're short of time, ask if there's a boat heading straight to Playa Blanca and missing out the "panoramic tour" on the way.

There are a few basic **accommodation** options on Playa Blanca, with hammocks available for around C$15,000 and rustic huts for around C$70,000. Snorkelling costs C$5000 if you bring your own gear – and entrance to the open-water **Oceanario** aquarium that's a stop on some trips (ask ahead) is an additional C$50,000. A C$15,500 park fee applies to all those leaving from the port.

Volcán de Lodo El Totumo

The small, mud-blowing **Volcán de Lodo El Totumo**, 50km northeast of Cartagena, makes for another popular day-trip. You can clamber down into the crater for a refreshing wallow in the mud (C$5000) that allegedly has therapeutic properties, while helpful locals gather nearby, offering to photograph you in your *Creature From the Black Lagoon* guise, and to give you an energetic but not terribly professional massage (another C$5000). Most hostels arrange this trip (around C$50,000 to C$70,000 including lunch at La Boquillo beach), but note that it can get very crowded since all the tours arrive at the same time.

ARRIVAL AND DEPARTURE

By plane Cartagena's Rafael Nuñez International Airport is 10min by taxi (C$13,500) or a slightly longer bus ride (C$2100) from the city centre.

Destinations Multiple flights daily to Bogotá (1hr 25min); Cali (3 weekly; 1hr 30min); and Medellín (6 daily; 1hr 10min). Twice-daily flights to San Andrés (2hr).

By bus The city's large bus terminal is 12km west from the Centro Histórico. Take any local bus (C$2100) 2km to the Portal El Gallo TransCaribe bus stop, then change to the #T100 express (another C$2100) to the Centro bus stop. A taxi between Portal El Gallo and the bus terminal should be around C$7000. From the bus terminal, taxis charge set rates of around C$23,000–25,000 into the centre.

Destinations Barranquilla (every 30min 5am–10pm; 2hr); Bogotá (every 30min; 20hr); Medellín (6 daily 5am–9pm; 13hr); Mompox (1 daily at 7.30am; 6hr 30min); Riohacha (every 2hr 5am–8pm; 7hr); Santa Marta (every 1–2hr 4.30am–8pm; 4hr); Tolú (hourly; 2hr 30min).

By sailboat to Panama/San Blas Sailboats run between Cartagena and Panama via the remote islands of the San Blas archipelago (5–6 days) through Blue Sailing, C San Andrés no. 30–47 (☎ 5 668 6485, ✆ bluesailing.net); prices vary but range US$500–650 one-way (including bunk, three meals a day and snorkel gear).

GETTING AROUND AND INFORMATION

Most visitors will get around by foot, though the streams of available taxis make a trip to the other end of town after a long night out easy.

Tourist information The most convenient information point lies outside the Puerta del Reloj in the Plaza de la Paz, open Mon–Sat 9am–noon & 1–6pm, Sun 9am–5pm.

ACCOMMODATION

Budget lodgings are spread out equally over the attractive San Diego neighbourhood in the heart of the historical centre, as well as grittier Getsemaní, a short walk from the Old City. Prices during the high season (Dec–Feb) usually surge ten to twenty percent.

Casa Baluarte C Media Luna no. 10–86, Getsemaní ☎ 5 664 2208, ✆ hostalcasabaluarte.co; map p.514. One of the more airy and upmarket guesthouses in the area, housed in an attractive colonial building. The 24 a/c rooms with terracotta floors are well kept and breakfast is served on the roof terrace. **C$164,000**

Casa Villa Colonial C Media Luna no. 10–89, Getsemaní ☎ 5 664 5421, ✆ casavillacolonial.co; map p.514. Quiet colonial house with spacious en-suite rooms (all have a/c), friendly staff and attractive communal areas. The small kitchen dispenses free coffee all day long (no breakfast, though). Doubles **C$204,000**

El Genovés Hostal C Cochera del Hobo no. 38–27, San Diego ☎ 5 646 0972, ✆ genoves.mr-websolutions.com; map p.514. Gorgeous colonial property offering dorms with lockers (bunks in timber-beamed rooms) and plain but spotless private rooms (all a/c) with simple breakfast included. Guests can use a shared kitchen and a small pool. No children permitted. Dorms C$50,000, doubles C$150,000

Mamallena C Media Luna no. 10–47, Getsemaní ☎5 670 0499, ⓦhostelmamallenacartagena.com; map p.514. One of the best hostels in town, with wood bunks in clean dorms and simple private rooms (all with a/c), sunny bar/patio (things can get loud till 1am), shared kitchen, big lockers and pancake breakfast included; laundry C$15,000 for full load. Recommended place to arrange tours and onward transport. Dorms C$47,600, doubles C$143,000

★ **Media Luna Hostel** C Media Luna no. 10–46, Getsemaní ☎5 664 3423, ⓦmedialunahostel.com; map p.514. This super-hostel (with 160 beds) has rooms and dorms all overlooking the central courtyard with pool. There are plenty of tours on offer, and bicycles for rent. Frequent parties on the enormous roof terrace – with a bar open until 4am. Dorms C$57,000, doubles C$115,000

Mystic House Hostel C Media Luna 10C–36, Getsemaní ☎5 660 7773; map p.514. One of the brighter and more stylish of the hostels on backpacker row, with simple, neat bunks in dorms (a/c or fan) and solid value en-suite doubles (with a/c) adorned with contemporary art. Dorms C$40,000, doubles C$120,000

El Viajero Cartagena C 7 Infantes no. 9–45, San Diego ☎5 660 2598, ⓦelviajerohostels.com; map p.514. At this sociable hostel, the a/c rooms and dorms are clustered around a couple of inner courtyards with colourful murals where everyone meets to socialize and, on some nights, learn salsa. There's a small bar on-site as well as a tour agency. Don't count on getting much sleep on weekends. Simple breakfast included. Dorms C$57,000, doubles C$216,000

EATING

Among Cartagena's greatest charms is its array of fine restaurants catering to all palates, though most are expensive.

El Balcón Plaza de San Diego (entry C de Tumbamuertos no. 38–85), San Diego; map p.514. Owned by a Colombian-British couple, this is a solid spot for budget-friendly meals (C$28,000–44,000) as well as early evening drinks (beers C$10,000) with the second-floor balcony (above La Tumbamuertos Burger Bar) lined with stools the perfect place for plaza-watching. Mon–Sat noon–11pm, Sun 4–11pm.

★ **Beer & Laundry** C 31 No. 10–101 Local 2, Getsemaní; map p.514. This small laundry has developed a cult following for serving cold beers and cheap pizzas (C$18,000) while you wait for your washing (there are just a couple of tables inside). It's a great idea, and the friendly owners are a font of local information. Mon–Fri 8am–6pm, Sat 8pm–4pm.

★ **El Boliche Cebichería** Cra 8 no. 38–17, San Diego; map p.514. Although not cheap, this thimble-sized

cevichería with an open kitchen dishes out delicious crabmeat empanadas. The Costeño ceviche made with octopus, shrimp, squid and white fish served with sour cream and a crispy cassava roll are highly recommended. Figure on at least C$100,000/person for a full meal. Mon–Fri 12.30–3pm & 7–11pm, Sat & Sun 6–11pm.

Caffé Lunatico C Espíritu Santo no. 29-184, Getsemaní; map p.514. Small, chilled-out café and restaurant with relaxed atmosphere, open for brunch (Colombian breakfasts for C$24,000), coffee, pre-dinner tapas (C$8,000–19,000) and drinks (cocktails C$20,000–24,000). Daily 11am–10.30pm.

La Cevichería C Stuart no. 7–14, San Diego; map p.514. Small, smart cevichería with lively outdoor seating, with music from passing street musicians filling the air. Innovative takes on ceviche – including shrimp, octopus and squid combos in coconut-lime and mango sauces. The Vietnamese-style grilled seafood on brown rice is nothing short of inspired. Mains C$40,000–70,000. Daily 1–11pm.

La Esquina del Pan de Bono C Agustín Chiquita no. 35–78, El Centro; map p.514. Popular with students from the Universidad de Cartagena across the street, this is a rare find in the old centre, a local bakery and snack shop selling cubanos, airy pan de bono (cheesy buns; C$1600), pasteles (from C$2400) and jugos (C$3500). Daily 7am–7pm.

DRINKING AND NIGHTLIFE

Getsemaní tends to be a better bet for late-night partying, with Calle del Arsenal and Calle Media Luna the liveliest strips – "Visa por un Sueño" is a wildly popular party held on the roof of Media Luna Hostel every Wednesday from 10pm. Another option for a night out is a chiva ride – essentially a party bus in an old-fashioned, luridly decorated trolley that takes you on a late-night city tour fuelled by rum, fried finger foods, and vallenato music. Chivas tend to depart at 8–8.30pm and return at midnight; any tour agency and most hotels can hook you up with a tour (C$45,000).

★ **Café Havana** C de la Media Luna, at C del Guerrero, Getsemaní; map p.514. You'll be transported to Old Havana at this packed club, where black-and-white photos of Cuban music legends line the walls and thumping live Cuban beats get the crowd's hips swinging. Cover around C$30,000. Wed–Sun 8.30pm–4am.

Café del Mar Baluarte de Santo Dominigo, El Centro; map p.514. Perched on the city's stone fortress walls, with spectacular 360-degree views of the Caribbean and the Old City's elegant colonial buildings, this is the perfect spot to lounge on an open-air couch with a sunset martini (C$27,000) surrounded by cool locals. Food is served until 1am and DJs take over from 10pm. Dress nicely. Daily 5pm–2am.

Donde Fidel Portal de los Dulces no. 32–09, El Centro; map p.514. These outdoor tables, between the city wall and the Plaza de los Coches, are the place to people-watch

5

over a beer. Inside, every centimetre of the walls is covered with pictures of owner Fidel and friends. Pounding Cuban music from an extensive salsa collection is the soundtrack to which couples get romantic. Daily 11am–2am.

Mister Babilla Av del Arsenal no. 8B–137, Getsemaní; map p.514. The tacky jungle-themed decor aside, this massive multi-floor club will get you dancing to at least one of its music genres, be it salsa, rock or house. The party usually extends until the wee hours of the morning. Entry usually C$20,000. Thurs–Sun 9pm–3.45am.

Tu Candela Above the Portal de los Dulces no. 32–25, El Centro; map p.514. One of Cartagena's wildest and most popular clubs, frequented by tourists and Colombian jet-setters, who dance the night away predominantly to salsa, though reggaeton, *merengue* and other genres creep on to the playlist. Daily 8.45pm–4am.

DIRECTORY

Banks and exchange Several banks with 24hr ATMs and casas de cambio are on the Plaza de la Aduana and adjoining streets.

Immigration For visa extensions, DAS has an office in the airport and at Cra 20b No. 29–18, Pie de la Popa (Mon–Fri 8am–noon & 2–5pm; ☎5 670 0555).

Medical Nuevo Hospital Bocagrande at C 5 No. 6–49 at Cra 6 (☎5 665 5270, ⓦnhbg.com.co).

TOLÚ

Popular with holidaying Colombians but practically undiscovered by overseas travellers, the seaside town of **TOLÚ** is a pleasant, laidback spot to break your journey from Medellín to Cartagena. Bicycles rather than than cars fill the streets, though the brightly decorated *bicitaxis*, each one blaring its own choice of upbeat music, make up in volume for the lack of motorized traffic. While Tolú's beaches are nondescript in comparison to the ones in Parque Nacional Tayrona (see page 526), you can reach those 20km south, near Coveñas, by *colectivos* from the corner of Cra 2 and C 17 in Tolú. The town's malecón, lined with restaurants, craft stalls and bars, makes for a nice stroll, but Tolú's main attraction – the Islas de San Bernardo – lies off the coast.

ARRIVAL AND DEPARTURE

By bus Most buses terminate or drop off at the petrol station (aka "Bomba") on the eastern edge of town (where C 16 meets the main road between Sincelejo and Coveñas). From here *mototaxis* will be waiting to whisk you to where you want to go, or it's around a 15–20min walk to the malecón.

Destinations Bogotá (2 daily; 20hr); Cartagena (hourly; 3hr); Medellín (4 daily; 10–12hr); Montería for Necoclí (hourly; 2–3hr); Santa Marta (5 daily; 7hr).

ACCOMMODATION AND EATING

There are plenty of informal places to eat along the malecón, most serving fried fish and *ceviche*, while around the main plaza there are several bakeries and *arepa* stalls.

Hostel V&A Villa Alejandra Cra 2 no. 10–80 ☎301 597 9969. With a great location near the waterfront, this relatively new hostel offers cheap, spotless rooms (with a/c and balcony access) and dorms, free drinking water and coffee all day, shared kitchen and TV room. Dorms C$20,000, doubles C$50,000

MOMPOX

Marooned on a freshwater island in the vast low-lying wetlands of the Río Magdalena's eastern branch, **MOMPOX** (also spelt Mompós) was founded in 1537 by Don Alonso de Heredia (brother of Cartagena's founder). It served as the lynchpin for the mighty river's trade network between coastal Cartagena and the country's interior, and remained one of Colombia's most prosperous commercial centres until the silt-heavy river changed its course in the late nineteenth century and Mompox was left to languish as a forgotten backwater. Simón Bolívar raised an army here and Mompox was the first town in Colombia to declare complete independence from Spain in 1810.

LAS ISLAS DE SAN BERNARDO

An archipelago of ten islands, the **Islas de San Bernardo** are wonderfully tranquil (when not overrun by Colombian holidaymakers), and their teal waters and blinding-white beaches make for a great day-trip. Boats leave Tolú's Muelle Turístico at around 8.30/9am, returning around 4pm. Tours (C$60,000–75,000) loop around **Santa Cruz del Islote** – a tiny island smothered with shacks populated by fishermen and their families – **Isla Tintípan**, the largest of the islands, and mangrove-fringed **Isla Múcura**, where you get to linger the longest – around three hours – to have lunch, sip a cold beer or go snorkelling. Tours often finish on **Isla Palma**, which is the best of the lot when it comes to snorkelling, with greater visibility and an abundance of fish. Some 60km south of the main archipelago (but only 11km off the coast), the lesser-visited **Isla Fuerte** is gaining popularity for those looking to get off the beaten path; take a bus to Lorica, then a taxi (C$30,000) to the fishing village of Paso Nuevo (30–45min). From here boats zip across to the island (30–45min) every few hours (or when full; C$15,000–20,000 per person).

ACCOMMODATION

Casa en El Agua 🕿 304 537 1560, 🌐 casaenelagua. com. True to its name, *Casa en El Agua* ("house in the water") is a rustic hostel on stilts just off Isla Tintípan. Surrounded by coral reef, you can spend your days snorkelling, sunbathing, and dodging scuttling crabs. The hostel offers trips out to nearby beaches, and night swims with the plankton. Delicious lobster dinners can be whipped up on demand, although it's best to bring at least some food supplies, along with water and cash. To get here, a public boat leaves Tolú daily around 8am for Tintípan and *Casa en El Agua* (C$15,000–20,000) or splash out on a speedboat (daily 9am; C$100,000 one-way) from La Bodeguita in Cartagena (2hr). Wayyu hammocks **C$70,000**, dorms **C$80,000**, doubles **C$180,000**

Its beauty has remained practically untouched ever since, and **UNESCO** declared it a World Heritage Site in 1995 in recognition of its outstanding colonial architecture. It was also the setting for **Gabriel García Márquez**'s classic novella *Chronicle of a Death Foretold*. Time seems to stand still here: locals unhurriedly putter around the unpaved streets and fishing boats ply the network of rivers and lakes. The town's remoteness has kept it out of mainstream travel but its appeal as the "anti-Cartagena" – architecture to rival the coastal city but none of the hustle – has seen a recent influx of visitors.

WHAT TO SEE AND DO

Mompox's grid of streets stretches out alongside the river and is easy to explore on foot. Its sprawl of grand Catholic churches and elaborate colonial mansions is a constant reminder of the town's faded glory and wealth. The town is also famous for its **wooden rocking chairs**, which residents drag on to the streets in the evenings to watch the world go by, as well as **filigree silver and gold** work sold around Calle Real del Medio, and **Vinimompox** – fruit wines made from banana, guava, orange and tamarind.

The best way to explore is to wander the streets, peeking at the whitewashed colonial houses with wrought-iron grilles, intricately carved doorways, clay-tile roofs and fragrant flower-draped balconies.

The churches

Of its six churches, the finest is **Iglesia de Santa Bárbara**, at the end of Calle 14 on the riverfront plaza of the same name. With its Baroque octagonal bell tower and Moorish balcony adorned with ornate mouldings of flowers and lions, it resembles a fancy cake. **Iglesia de San Agustín**, on Calle Real del Medio, houses several richly gilded religious objects, most notably the Santo Sepulcro, used in the traditional Semana Santa processions.

Cementerio Municipal

Hiding behind Mompox's most attractive leafy square, the atmospheric **cemetery** (C 18; daily 8am–noon & 2–5pm), where elaborate white marble tombs stand alongside more modest graves in the unkempt grass, will appeal to those with a taste for the macabre.

5

Museo de Arte Religioso

The **Museo de Arte Religioso**, at Cra 2 no. 17–07 (Mon–Fri 9am–noon & 2–5pm, Sat 9am–noon; C$5000), where Simón Bolívar once stayed, has a small collection of religious art. Bolívar's statue graces the small namesake square nearby (Plaza Bolívar), while the inscription on the plinth of another Bolívar-related statue in tiny Plaza del Libertad reads (in Spanish): "To Caracas I owe my life but to Mompox I owe my glory."

Boat tours

Particularly worthwhile if you're interested in local birds and wildlife, **boat trips** are a great way to spend an afternoon and are easily booked through your accommodation. Tours leave around 3pm, generally take four hours and cost C$30,000–50,000, depending on the number of people. Your guide will point out numerous animals and birds that live alongside the river, such as giant iguanas, howler monkeys, herons, fishing eagles and kingfishers, and there's usually an opportunity for a swim in one of the lakes, such as the **Ciénaga de Pijino**, reachable by narrow channels from the main waterway. Returning by boat to Mompox after a quick sunset dip, you'll be greeted by a sixteenth-century vision of how the town would have appeared to new arrivals, with all six of its imposing churches facing the river to welcome you. A popular new tour, **La Valerosa** (☎312 618 8435), departs Plaza de la Concepción at 4.30pm daily (C$30,000; 2hr), turning into a party boat (especially in high season), with music, bar and dancing.

ARRIVAL AND INFORMATION

By bus By 2019 a new 12km highway should link Magangué and Mompox, slashing bus travel times between Cartagena and Mompox to 3hr 30min. The Copetran bus terminal is at Cra 5 (behind the Cementerio, between calles 17 and 18), offering direct bus services from Bogotá (4 daily; 15–17hr), Medellín (daily 8pm; 10–12hr), Bucaramanga (daily 9.45pm; 7–8hr), San Gil (daily 6.15pm; 11–12hr) and Santa Marta (daily 2.30pm; 6hr). Unitransco runs from its terminal on Cra 3 just south of Callejón de Santa Bárbara (C 14) to Cartagena (daily 7.30am; 6hr 30min–7hr) and Barranquilla (2 daily; 7hr). Cootracegua runs a convenient minibus route between Mompox and Maicao (3–4 daily;

7–8hr), via Valledupar, with onward connections to La Guajira (p.530). These usually depart/drop off 400m south of Plaza Santa Bárbara on Cra 1.

By van A door-to-door van ("puerta-a-puerta") can be arranged from Cartagena with Toto Express (☎310 707 0838; C$80,000; around 6–7hr) departing at 4.30am; Omaira de la Hoz (☎311 414 8967) runs a similar service from Santa Marta (6–7hr; C$90,000) with 3am or 11am pick-up. Heading back, call *La Casa Amarilla* to book, or ask for more information at your hostel.

Tourist information There is no tourist office but Richard McColl at *La Casa Amarilla* is very knowledgeable. The three ATMs on Plaza Bolívar often run out of money, so arrive with plenty.

ACCOMMODATION

★ **La Casa Amarilla** Cra 1 no. 13–59 ☎5 685 6326, ⊕lacasaamarillamompos.com. This beautifully restored, riverfront colonial building has ten stylish rooms, all en suite with a/c, cable TV and colourful murals. The bright, plant-filled courtyard is great for an afternoon hammock snooze, and the open-air shared kitchen, rooftop terrace, bike rental and book exchange make backpackers feel welcome. The owner – British journalist Richard McColl – is an excellent source of information and can arrange transport and tours. **C$175,000**

Casa Roberto Nieto Albaradda (Cra 1) no. 16–43 ☎311 714 3145, ✉martin@bignieto.com. Hostel in one of the oldest houses in town, with eight spacious rooms with high ceilings (all have fans or a/c, some with private bathroom) and a dorm with ceiling fan. There's also an apartment with kitchen and space for 4–6 people. Dorms **C$30,000**, doubles **C$120,000**, apartment **C$300,000**

Hostal Doña Mebi Cra 4 no. 21b–56 ☎313 692 8116. One of the newer budget options, just outside the centre, with a clean six-bed dorm and private doubles (all with a/c) managed by the congenial Dimas and his family. Dorms **C$30,000**, doubles **C$70,000**

EATING AND DRINKING

In the evenings, Plaza de Concepción is the best place to people-watch while sitting in one of the rocking chairs next to the huddle of open-air restaurants and sipping an ice-cold beer, while Plaza Santo Domingo bustles with popular food stands after 5pm.

Beraca Plaza de la Concepción. Bar and restaurant famed for its rocking chairs set up over the plaza and overlooking the river each evening, with a selection of local beers and music (and often blaring TV) that ranges from classical to more upbeat salsa at the weekend. Mon–Thurs 5pm–midnight, Fri & Sat 5pm–3am.

★ **Comedor Costeño** Cra 1 (C de la Albarrada). Informal outdoor eatery on the breezy riverfront serving excellent-value set meals. Try the mouthwatering *bagre* (catfish) with coconut rice, fried plantain and yucca, which comes with a fish soup starter and drink (C$22,000). Daily noon–4pm.

BARRANQUILLA

Despite being Colombia's fourth-largest city and main port, **BARRANQUILLA**, on the mouth of the Río Magdalena, would be all but overlooked if it were not for its annual **Carnaval** (ⓦcarnavaldebarranquilla.org) – Colombia's biggest street party. For four days, this swelteringly hot, industrial city drapes itself in a riot of vibrant colours, playful costumes and pulsating music: salsa, *cumbia*, *vallenato* and African drumming. Preparations begin much earlier, in mid-January, and once the festivities begin, the town converts into one huge street party, kicked off by traditional parades like the "Battle of the Flowers" and "Dance of the Caiman". Parallel to the festivities, the city-sponsored LGBTQ Carnaval, though less publicized, is equally bacchanalian. Although barely known outside Latin America, Barranquilla's festivities are second only to Rio's Carnaval in size. Outside festival time, you'll only want to pass through on the way to either Cartagena or Santa Marta without stopping.

ARRIVAL AND DEPARTURE

By bus The bus terminal is 7km out of the city centre (C$25,000 by taxi; 30min).
Destinations Bogotá (1–2 hourly; 17hr); Cartagena (every 30min; 2hr); Santa Marta (every 30min; 2hr).

ACCOMMODATION AND EATING

Arrange accommodation well in advance if you visit during Carnaval.
Meeting Point Hostel Cra 61 no. 68–100, El Prado ⓣ 318 2599. Backpacker hub in a family house with four- to eight- bed dorms and a/c singles and doubles in a busy, safe area, plus terrace with hammocks and shared TV room. Cash only. Dorms C$65,000, doubles C$90,000
Narcobollo Cra 43 no. 84–188. This iconic canteen chain is celebrated for its delicious *bollo costeño* (a traditional bun) in various flavours (sweet potato, coconut and corn; C$2000–3000), as well as various *fritos*, *pasteles* and *quibbe* (Lebanese kibbeh). Daily 7am–9pm.

SANTA MARTA AND AROUND

Although Colombia's oldest city, founded in 1525, **SANTA MARTA**'s colonial heritage was all but swept away by a massive earthquake in 1834. The result is a busy beach city geared to middle-class Colombians on holiday and international backpackers in search of jungle adventure. Though its narrow streets are clogged with traffic, restoration in the city centre over the past few years has created attractive public spaces, such as the Parque de los Novios, a pedestrian area surrounded with bustling restaurants, and an international marina full of yachts.

Not far away are some of the country's best beaches, particularly in and near **Parque Nacional Tayrona**, Colombia's most popular national park. Also close by is the fishing/party village of **Taganga**, ultra-popular with backpackers, hippies and holidaying Colombians. Santa Marta also acts as the hub for organizing hikes (see page 528) to the **Ciudad Perdida**.

WHAT TO SEE AND DO

Although better known as the jumping-off point for the region's attractions, Santa Marta does have several sights of its own.

Museo del Oro Tairona

A striking building with wooden garrets underneath a pitched tile roof, the

---

MAGICAL MACONDO

Before you came to Colombia, you may have read about the town of **Macondo** in *One Hundred Years of Solitude* by Gabriel García Márquez. Now you can visit it. Yes, officially it's called **Aracataca**, but the birthplace of the author seems to blur the lines between reality and magical realism. The **Casa Museo Gabriel García Márquez** (C 5 no. 6–35; Tues–Sat 8am–1pm & 2–5pm, Sun 9am–2pm; free) is a recreation of the house in which the author was born and grew up the 1930s, while the **Casa del Telegrafista** (Tues–Sun 9am–1pm & 4–8pm; free) was where Gabo's father worked in the late 1920s. The old **Estación del Tren de Aracataca** (Tues–Sun 9am–1pm & 4–8pm; free) at C 3 and Cra 1, also reopened as a museum in 2017.

Regular **buses** run to Aracataca from Santa Marta's bus terminal (every 30min; 1hr 30min).

5

enlightening **Museo del Oro Tairona** is set inside the magnificently restored Casa de la Aduana (Customs House; C 14 no. 2–7, Plaza de Bolívar; Tues–Sat 9am–5pm, Sun 10am–3pm; free), the city's oldest building, dating from 1531. Simón Bolívar stayed here briefly, and his body lay in state in an upstairs gallery after his death. The museum has extensive displays on ancient Tairona culture and its modern-day descendants – the Wintukua (Arhuaco), Kogi, Wiwa (Arsanio) and Kankuamo.

Quinta de San Pedro Alejandrino

Whether or not you have a particular interest in Colombia's liberation hero, the hacienda and sugar plantation of **Quinta de San Pedro Alejandrino**, 5km south of town where Simón Bolívar spent his last agonizing days makes for a great visit (daily 9am–5.30pm; C$21,000; guided tours in Spanish included in the price). The lush grounds, with an enchanting forest of twisted trees and creeping vines, are a pleasure to wander. Peek into the mustard-coloured buildings for a glimpse of the Libertadór's personal effects – an Italian marble bathtub, miniature portraits of the Bolívar family and military badges. Just to the right of the imposing Altar de la Patria memorial, the **Museo Bolívariano** features contemporary works by artists from countries liberated by Bolívar – Colombia, Peru, Bolivia, Ecuador, Panama and Venezuela. Buses leaving the waterfront main drag (Cra 1) for the Mamatoco suburb will drop you off at the Quinta if you ask the driver (C$1600), or take a taxi for C$8000.

Catedral

The large whitewashed **catedral** (Cra 5 no. 16–30, Plaza de Catedral) is the oldest church in Colombia, though the current structure, with its bulky bell tower and stone portico, dates mostly from the seventeenth century. Just to the left of the entrance are the ashes of Rodrigo de Bastidas, the town's founder. Simón Bolívar's remains were kept here until 1842, when they were repatriated to his native Caracas.

ARRIVAL AND INFORMATION

By plane Santa Marta's Simón Bolívar airport is 16km south of the city centre. Taking a taxi to the airport costs C$30,000.

MINCA

Just 20km southeast of Santa Marta, the small mountain town of **Minca** awaits with its cool climate, hundreds of exotic bird species and yoga classes – it's rapidly becoming one of Colombia's most popular backpacker hangouts. Other than soaking up the languid atmosphere, most visitors head out to **waterfalls** or **coffee farms** in the surrounding hills. Minibuses (45min) depart Santa Marta Cra 9, at C 12, and cost C$8000.

Destinations Bogotá (12 daily; 1hr 30min); Medellín (3 daily; 1hr 30min).

By bus The Terminal de Transportes (main bus station) lies 5km to the southeast of the city centre and taxis cost around C$8000.

Destinations Barranquilla (hourly; 2hr); Bogotá (hourly 2–8pm; 17hr); Bucaramanga (3 daily; 10hr); Cartagena (hourly 5am–8pm; 4hr); Medellín (11 daily; 15hr). Buses run between Taganga and Cra 5 in Santa Marta (every 10min 5am–10pm; C$1600); buses for Minca (Cra 9, at C 12), Tayrona and Palomino (both Cra 9, at C 11) depart near the market.

Taxis A taxi to Taganga from central Santa Marta costs C$12,000.

Tourist information Fontur operates a tourist office in the bus station (daily 7am–7pm), small kiosks at the airport (nominally daily 7am–10pm) and on the malecón (nominally Mon–Sat 9am–noon & 2–5pm). Several tour operators (see page 528) in Santa Marta arrange trips to Ciudad Perdida and La Guajira.

ACCOMMODATION

Hostels are numerous, but book in advance in December and January. Prices can double in peak season.

Aluna C 21 no. 5–72 ☎ 5 432 4916, ⓦ alunahotel.com. Feel well looked after and rested at this peaceful hostel, beautifully designed by Dublin-born architect and owner Patrick Flemming. Paintings by local artists line the walls, rooms are spotless and fresh, thanks to wooden slats that allow air to circulate, and a bamboo roof offers welcome shade from the blazing midday sun. Excellent book exchange and a great little café on the premises. Pricier rooms have a/c (C$130,000). Dorms C$35,000, doubles C$107,000

La Brisa Loca C 14 no. 3–58 ☎ 5 431 6121, ⓦ labrisaloca. com. This sprawling converted mansion is owned by two party-loving Californian dudes and has firmly established itself as a backpacker haven, with spacious dorms, a roof terrace, lively late-night bar, billiards and a well-used pool. The helpful bilingual staff are a plus. Dorms C$35,000, doubles C$140,000

> ## DIVING IN TAGANGA
>
> One of the cheapest spots in the world for **scuba** certification, both PADI and NAUI, Taganga has so many dive shops that the prices and services offered by each are pretty competitive. A three-day certification course costs about C$850,000 and often includes English- or Spanish-speaking dive masters, and six open water dives. Try Oceano Scuba (ⓦoceanoscuba.com. co) or Poseidon (ⓦposeidondivecenter.com). Always check the dive school's PADI or NAUI accreditation, your instructor's credentials, the instructor-to-student ratio, and ensure that equipment is well maintained.

★ **Dreamer Hostel** C 51 no. 26D–161, Magdalena ⓣ5 433 3264, ⓦthedreamerhostel.com. Some 5km out of town but closer to Tayrona and more than worth it for the atmosphere, this backpacker favourite has a pool in a hammock-bedecked courtyard, Italian and Mexican food on the menu and a plethora of day-trips. Dorms C$56,000, doubles C$153,000

★ **La Villana Hostel** C 17 No. 3–70 ⓣ5 420 9566, ⓦlavillana.co. Justly popular hostel, a small, cosy and artful renovation of a 1720 colonial house, with bright, Ikea-like dorms, small pool and one simple en-suite double ("the pink room"). Dorms C$41,600, doubles C$170,000

EATING, DRINKING AND NIGHTLIFE

★ **Charlie's Bar and Grill** C 19 no. 4–12. Delicious mojitos are a speciality at this congenial pub just off the Parque de los Novios, with a blend of antique and new furnishings, a breezy terrace and the indomitable Charlie (originally from Chicago) himself usually in attendance. Addictive buffalo wings served to accompany the booze. Tues & Wed 6pm–12.30am, Thurs–Sat 6pm–2.30am.

Crab's Bar C 18 no. 3–69. If you like old-school music videos, this is the bar for you. Owner Oscar takes rock and blues very seriously – and likes a bit of kitsch too. Signed vintage albums and plastic crabs hang on the walls, and there's a bathtub in the middle of the bar. Live blues band on Wednesday evenings. Wed 8pm–1am, Thurs–Sat 8pm–3am.

Ikaro Café C 19 no. 3–60. Huge backpacker hangout for good reason – it's a spacious café with vegan-vegetarian-gluten free dishes (mostly Thai and Vietnamese) and excellent coffee (with almond, coconut or soy milk). Lounge on re-cycled furniture or pallet couches. Mains C$15,000–28,000. Daily 8am–9pm.

Lulo Cra 3 no. 16–34. Friendly owners Melissa and David whip up fantastic breakfasts at this excellent café. Try the delicious "Lula la Ranchera" arepa made from natural corn, served with egg, beans, cheese and chorizo (C$12,000). Great smoothies from C$6000. Mon–Fri 8am–10pm, Sat & Sun 9am–10pm.

Ouzo Cra 3 no. 19–29, Parque de los Novios. Quality Mediterranean-style cuisine with a focus, naturally, on Greek specialities like gyros, keftedes (meatballs) and meze (mains C$18,000–43,000), but also crispy wood-fired pizzas

(from C$23,000–26,000). Ideal location on the square, with indoor or outdoor tables shaded by the palms. Mon–Thurs noon–10.30pm, Fri & Sat noon–11pm.

La Puerta C 17 no. 2–29. Local students and foreign backpackers in their 20s and 30s frequent this jam-packed, sexy club. Salsa, electronica and international club hits will have you sweating on the narrow dancefloor that snakes into one of the club's many nooks and crannies. Cool off on the outdoor patio if the crowd gets too much. Tues & Wed 6pm–1am, Thurs–Sat 6pm–3am.

TAGANGA

Once upon a time a pristine fishing village, lively **TAGANGA**, 4km north of Santa Marta (between it and Parque Nacional Tayrona), is where backpackers come to party. Built on the side of a mountain, the town has unpaved dirt streets, a busy beach, and arid hills surrounding the horseshoe-shaped bay. For budget travellers, it's an alternative to Santa Marta before or after tackling the Ciudad Perdida hike (see page 528) and other surrounding attractions.

WHAT TO SEE AND DO

Everything here is pretty much water-related, whether diving or hitting the beach. Fishermen ply an easy alternative access route to Tayrona National Park's southern beaches, the most popular being the crystalline waters of **Bahia Concha**, about an hour away by boat. Costing at least C$60,000 (one-way), this is a good excursion for small groups. Accessible by boat (5min; C$7000) and foot (20min) is the much closer **Playa Grande**, which is modestly sized, heavily touristed and a bit pebbly, but still has the makings for a day of sun and sea. Taganga's main beach is awash with small boats, many available for hire, though you'll find people swimming at the southern end.

5

Conveniently, Ciudad Perdida treks and a whole manner of adventure travel options are on offer too at bigger shops on the main drag, along the beach.

ARRIVAL AND INFORMATION

By boat A daily speedboat runs to Cabo de San Juan in Parque Nacional Tayrona from the waterfront by the tourist information kiosk at 10.30am (1hr; C$100,000); book in advance at your hostel as spaces are limited.

By bus Frequent buses (every 10min 6am–9pm; 15min; C$1600, C$1700 on Sun) head north along Cra 5 in Santa Marta; on arrival in Taganga they pass along Cra 2 and terminate at the waterfront (Cra 1, at C 11). Daily minibus transfers to Parque Nacional Tayrona are best arranged through your accommodation.

By taxi A taxi between the centre of Santa Marta and Taganga costs C$12,000. If you're coming from the bus terminal, it will be around C$15,000.

Tourist information There's a tourist information kiosk on the waterfront (9am–7pm) where you can pick up maps of Taganga. The only ATM, on Cra 2 next to the police station, often runs out of money, so it's best to load up in Santa Marta.

ACCOMMODATION

Casa de Felipe Cra 5A no. 19–13 ☎5 421 9101, ⓦlacasadefelipe.com. Three blocks uphill from the beach, with beautiful views of the bay and a lush, greenery-filled garden, the rustic rooms at this long-time backpacker favourite fill up quickly so book in advance. Plenty of information on exploring the area available. Dorms C$38,500, rooms C$98,000, private apartments for up to five people C$340,000

Hostel Divanga B&B C 12 no. 4–07 ☎5 421 9092, ⓦdivanga.com. This French-run hostel has a small pool surrounded with hammocks, an upstairs bar, a sociable vibe and wonderfully friendly staff. Rooms are compact but spotless and the restaurant is one of the best in town. There's another branch a block away. Dorms C$42,000, doubles COP110,000

Hostal Techos Azules Sector Dunkarinca, cabaña no. 1–100 ☎5 421 9141, ⓦtechosazules.com. Sitting high above Taganga, just off the main road to Santa Marta, this rambling blue-roofed guesthouse offers a plethora of rooms for individuals and groups and great views of the town. Some rooms have kitchenettes, some share bathrooms, and all have access to the airy, hammock-festooned patio. The road leads steeply down to the beach. More expensive with a/c. Dorms C$30,000, doubles C$90,000

EATING, DRINKING AND NIGHTLIFE

The waterfront is lined with fruit juice and fried snack sellers, as well as *palapas* specializing in fish-heavy lunches. The menus (*ceviche*, fried fish, *arroz de coco*) are comparable.

Babaganoush Cra 1 no. 18–22. Huge diner overlooking the sea serving culinary creations from Thai green curries to Mediterranean-inspired dishes. Mon & Wed–Sun 1–11.30pm.

★ **Café Bonsai** C 13 no. 1–7. This cool Swedish-run café serves delicious home-made treats (around C$3000–6500), including brownies in chocolate sauce, fresh sandwiches on crusty home-baked bread, healthy muesli breakfasts with yogurt and blackberry jam, organic local coffee and an array of over twenty teas. Mains are around C$18,000. Mon–Sat 9am–4pm.

El Mirador Cra 1 no. 18–107. The frisson sparked by the mix of locals and backpackers that fill this club favourite makes this place taxi-worthy even if you're staying in Santa Marta. A disco with a great view, this spot throbs with mainstream pop. Wed–Sat 8.30pm–4am.

El Reef Cra 1 no. 15–09 (malecón). Relaxed café right on the waterfront, with outdoor tables under a *palapa*, popular for breakfast (from C$12,000), sandwiches (C$15,000) and local fruit flavours of ice cream (like *maracuyá* and *arequipe*). Daily 7am–midnight.

★ **Pachamama** C 16 no. 1C–18. Off a quiet backstreet, this Tiki bar-tapas bar serves some of the most imaginative offerings in town. The tapas plates (C$7,000–20,000) are small, so you can have quite a few. Choose from the likes of *kefta* (spiced lamb meatballs), prawns wrapped in bacon, fish in passionfruit sauce and grilled Camembert. Mains range C$15,000–38,000. Mon–Sat 6pm–1am.

PARQUE NACIONAL TAYRONA

Colombia's most unspoilt tropical area, **PARQUE NACIONAL TAYRONA**, a 45-minute drive east of Santa Marta, is a wilderness of beaches, with lush jungle running right down to the sand. The laidback attitude of the place makes it feel like a paradisiacal summer camp, though it does get overcrowded during the holidays so it's best to avoid coming in peak season if you can.

Tayrona stretches over 120 square kilometres on land, with an additional 30 square kilometres of marine reserve, but since much of the park isn't easily accessible, visitors find themselves sticking largely to the string of beaches that stretch for around 8km from the entrance of the park, bounded by **Cañaveral** to the east and with **Cabo San Juan** to the west.

Beaches

Tayrona's beaches and the jungle that edges them are the irrefutable stars of the park. If arriving by boat, you'll get dropped off at **Cabo San Juan**, an attractive palm-fringed beach where many budget visitors stay; further west into the park from here are two more beaches, the second being a **nudist beach** (30min). Twenty minutes' walk east of Cabo San Juan brings you to **La Piscina**, a beach good for swimming and snorkelling, with calm, deep water. From there, it's another twenty-minute stroll east to **La Aranilla**, a narrow strip of sand framed by huge boulders, fine for swimming, followed almost immediately by the long, beautiful, wave-lashed stretch of **Arrecifes** where signs warn you that over two hundred tourists have drowned here; rip tides and strong currents make swimming extremely dangerous. Another forty minutes or so east along a wooded, muddy trail takes you to **Cañaveral** and eventually the entrance to the park **El Zaíno**. The beach at Cañaveral is good for sunbathing but the rip tides make it unsuitable for swimming.

Pueblito

A clear and physically demanding uphill path from Cabo San Juan (3–4hr return) brings you to the archeological site of **Pueblito**, a former Tairona village with a large number of terrace dwellings, sometimes called a mini Ciudad Perdida. Although it's possible to complete an Arrecifes–Cabo San Juan–Pueblito circuit in one long, strenuous day, the trip is better made as part of a multi-day stay on the beaches in the park. From Pueblito, you can also hike two hours through the jungle down to the alternative park entrance at **Calabazo** and catch a bus back to Santa Marta from that park exit point, instead of returning along your original route to Cabo San Juan.

ARRIVAL AND INFORMATION

By boat Regular speedboats run from Taganga to Cabo San Juan, arriving at around 11am and departing at around 4pm (see page 525). Rangers collect the park entrance fee (C$54,000, cash only) when you disembark. From Cabo San Juan it's around a 4hr walk east to the El Zaíno park entrance via various beaches.

By bus Buses run from Santa Marta (every 30min; 1hr; C$7000) from the market at the corner of Cra 9 and C 11 in El Zaino, 35km away, which is the main entrance to Tayrona,

where your passport will be checked, and entrance fee (C$54,000) collected. From here, take one of the jeeps that regularly traverse the 4km to the end of the paved road at Cañaveral for C$3000. From Cañaveral to Cabo San Juan the walk takes around 4hr, but make sure you start off in the morning to avoid the midday heat.

Park information Opening times are 8am–5pm. Bring plenty of cash – only the Aviatur-run restaurant and accommodation accept credit cards – and lots of insect repellent. Bring as little as possible to the park to avoid trekking in the heat with a heavy load. Most hostels in Santa Marta/Taganga will let you leave your backpack for a few days.

ACCOMMODATION AND EATING

The two main beaches offering budget accommodation are Arrecifes and Cabo San Juan; both offer the option of renting tents and hammocks, and cabañas are a good alternative for medium to large groups at Arrecifes. Lockers are available too. There are basic restaurants at Cabo San Juan, Cañaveral (this is the only place in the park with wi-fi) and Arrecifes. You can bring in your own food (no alcohol however), but there are no cooking facilities anywhere in the park.

CABO SAN JUAN

Cabo San Juan del Guía 📞 323 356 9912, 🌐 cecabosanjuandelguia.com.co. The downside to the hammocks here – both on the beach and in a gazebo on a small hillock – is that they offer no mosquito netting, so bring your own, and it can get quite chilly at night. Seek out the information hut next door to the restaurant (mains from C$17,000–35,000), the only real building in sight. Camping (own tent, per person) **C$20,000**, hammock on the beach **C$25,000**, "VIP" hammock in gazebo **C$30,000**, camping (rented tent per person) **C$30,000**, cabañas **C$200,000**

ARRECIFES

Camping Don Pedro 📞 2 550 3933. At the time of writing a major reorganization of Arrecifes accommodation by the park authorities was underway, but this looks set to remain the cheapest option, with hammocks, simple en-suite cabañas and tents 10–15min walk inland from the beach, with a no-frills restaurant (breakfast usually included, dinner around C$20,000). Camping (own tent, per person) **C$18,000**, hammocks **C$20,000**, camping (rented tent per person) **C$25,000**, cabañas **C$200,000**

PALOMINO

Located 70km from Santa Marta past the Parque Tayrona entrance towards Riohacha, the small town of **PALOMINO** has in recent years become popular with travellers craving Caribbean beach time.

5

Once associated with paramilitary action, Palomino is now safe, with a number of beachfront hostels and cabins, while retaining the atmosphere of a perfect peaceful haven, much like Taganga once was. The town itself is not much more than a few dusty roads just off the highway, lined with basic restaurants and homes, but it's the stunning palm-fringed beach and jungle backdrop just behind the town that's responsible for Palomino's speedy rise to fame. It affords fantastic views of the Sierra Nevada de Santa Marta mountain range: on a clear day you can see Colombia's highest peaks, the snowcapped Pico Cristóbal Colón and Pico Simón Bolívar, both over 5700m high. Things to do include **tubing** on the Palomino River (which most hostels can arrange for C$20,000–35,000) and excursions to **Quebrada de Valencia**, a waterfall, and several natural swimming holes in the middle of the jungle, thirty minutes away by bus. If you want to visit a traditional Kogi or Arhuaco village, hostels such as the *Dreamer* can arrange trips to the Sierra Nevada de Santa Marta national park (horseriding optional). Note that the sea current can be strong, particularly where the Palomino River meets the Caribbean, so be cautious – on certain days, it's best to avoid swimming in the sea altogether – or stick to a dip in one of the two rivers.

ARRIVAL AND DEPARTURE

By bus Minibuses run from Santa Marta (every 30min; 1hr 30min; C$9000) from the corner of Cra 9 and C 11 to Palomino. It's a 20min walk down to the beach, or take a *mototaxi* for C$3000.

ACCOMMODATION AND EATING

There's no ATM in Palomino, although many accommodation options accept credit cards. There are basic restaurants dotted around town serving typical Colombian fare (cash only), or eat at one one of the hostels or cabins along the beach.

★ **Dreamer Hostel** Playa Donaires s/n ☎ 300 609 7229, ⓦ thedreamerhostel.com. No frills but modern and spacious en-suite rooms with terraces as well as four small, basic dorms and decent pool just off the beach – tends to be more of a party place thanks to its popular bar (which closes at midnight) and dependable satellite wi-fi. The excellent buffet breakfast is open to non-guests (extra C$11,000). Dorms C$65,000, doubles C$175,000

CIUDAD PERDIDA

The "Lost City" of the Taironas, **CIUDAD PERDIDA** ranks among South America's most magical spots. More than a lost city, it's a lost world. Although its ruins are more understated than Machu Picchu in Peru, thanks to its geographic isolation the once-teeming city perched high in the Sierra Nevada de Santa Marta manages to preserve the natural allure that the overrun Inca capital has lost. While climbing the sierra's luxuriant foothills, you'll get a

---

CIUDAD PERDIDA: TOUR GUIDES AND TIPS

Since 2008 the area has been safe from paramilitaries, but you can only do the hike as part of an **organized group**. There are four tour companies authorized to lead tours, all with offices in Santa Marta, the most reputable being **Magic Tour** (C 16 no. 4–41, Santa Marta; ☎ 5 421 5820, ⓦ magictourcolombia.com) and **Expotur** (C 3 no. 17–27, Santa Marta; ☎ 5 420 7739, ⓦ expotur-eco.com), though you may find that guides from different companies swap clients to accommodate those who wish to do the tour in more or fewer days, and during low season the four companies pool clients. The official **price** of the tour is set at C$950,000 (for 4–6 days) and includes all meals, accommodation along the trail, the entrance fee to the ruins and transport to and from the trailhead. Guides generally don't speak English. Groups consist of four to twelve hikers.

The hike can be done all year; the driest period is between late December and March, while during the wet months from May to November the trail can get exceedingly muddy. It's a reasonably challenging trek and a reasonable level of **physical fitness** is required.

Expect to get wet at any time of the year and pack everything you'll need, especially: **sturdy footwear** suitable for river crossings (either waterproof trekking sandals or hiking boots and flip-flops); fifty percent DEET **insect repellent** (not available in Colombia); **water-purifying tablets**; **anti-malarial prophylactics** (there's low risk of malaria but if you want to err on the side of caution); **waterproof bag** and **poncho**, and **sunscreen**.

THE KOGI

Although now uninhabited, Ciudad Perdida is in many respects a living monument. It's surrounded by villages of **Kogi** people, who call the revered site Teyuna. You may be able to interact with the Kogis as they drift on and off the main trail you'll traverse as part of the trek, though as it comprises only a fraction of the wilderness they call home, and they are increasingly less present. The men are recognizable by their long, black hair, white (or off-white) smocks and trousers, a woven purse worn across one shoulder and trusty *póporo*, the saliva-coated gourd holding the lime that activates the coca leaves they constantly chew. Women also dress in white, and both women and girls wear necklaces; only the men own *póporo*. About nine thousand Kogis are believed to inhabit the Sierra Nevada.

In the 1970s, the Sierra Nevada became a major marijuana factory, and an estimated seventy percent of its native forests were burned to clear the way for untold amounts of the lucrative Santa Marta Gold strand. As the forest's prime inhabitants, the Kogis suffered dearly from the arrival of so many fast-buck farmers, one of the reasons why they're sceptical of the outside world; while Kogi children may well approach you, asking for sweets, don't take pictures of adults without their permission.

chance to bathe in idyllic rivers, visit inhabited indigenous villages and marvel at the swarms of monarch butterflies and beautiful jungle scenery.

Founded around 660 AD, the Tairona capital is less than 50km southeast of Santa Marta and is believed to have been home to around four thousand people before the Spanish wiped the Tairona out – the city was abandoned between 1550 and 1660. The ruins weren't "discovered" until the early 1970s, when a few *guaqueros* (tomb raiders) from Santa Marta chanced upon the city while scavenging for antiquities. Perched atop a steep slope 1300m high in the vast jungle, the site consists of more than 1350 circular stone **terraces** – with more still being uncovered – that once served as foundations for Tairona homes. Running throughout the city and down to the Buritaca river valley is a complex network of paved footpaths and steep stone steps – more than 1350 – purportedly added later to obstruct the advance of Spanish horsemen.

The hike

The trek covers 40km, with most hikers opting for the five-day version. You get picked up in Santa Marta for the three-hour drive to **El Mamey**, the village where the hike begins after lunch. From here it's four to five hours to **Camp 1** – mostly a steep uphill slog with a long, steep descent towards the camp. There's a swimming hole close to the start of the trail and another at

Camp 1, where there are hammocks with mosquito nets. **Day two**'s four- to five-hour hike to Camp 2 is an hour's ascent, a steep hour's descent, and an attractive flat stretch that takes you past a Kogi village. At the camp there's good swimming in the river and relatively comfortable bunks with mosquito nets. **Day three** consists of a four-hour hike that includes a narrow path overlooking a sheer drop and ups and downs along a narrow jungle trail, and a bridge across the main river. Camp 3, Paraíso Teyuna, tends to be the most crowded, and has hammocks, bunks and musty tents with mattresses. Weather permitting, some groups press on to the Ciudad Perdida in the afternoon (four-hour round trip), an hour's ascent from Camp 3, most of it up a very steep bunch of uneven and slippery stone steps – particularly challenging on the way down. And then it's there – your prize – stone terrace upon stone terrace, tranquil and overgrown with jungle, with splendid views of the main terrace from the military outpost. The alternative is to hike to Ciudad Perdida on the morning of day four. On your return, you either stay overnight in Camp 2 at the end of **day four** or, if you made it to Ciudad Perdida on day three, you make the eight- to nine-hour hike from Camp 3 back to Camp 1. **Day five** is then either a very early start and a gruelling seven-hour hike from Camp 2 back to El Mamey before lunch, or – if you're already at Camp 1 – a somewhat less gruelling four-hour slog,

5

with the steepest part at the very beginning. Hearty victory lunch follows, and a transfer back to Santa Marta.

LA GUAJIRA

Colombia's northernmost region, **La Guajira** has a hostile desert climate that has kept it largely isolated since colonial times. As a result it's one of those places where independent travellers can still feel as if they're leaving fresh tracks. Some 240km long and no more than 50km wide, the barren peninsula is empty except for the semi-nomadic Wayuu. More challenging to explore than the rest of the Caribbean coast, the Guajira Peninsula rewards those who make the effort with the end-of-the-world feel of **Cabo de la Vela** and **Punta Gallinas**. Cabo de la Vela is a remote Wayuu fishing village, 180km northwest of **Riohacha**, the capital of La Guajira, which is 175km northeast of Santa Marta. On the journey to Cabo you pass through a landscape of sand, baked mud huts and goats grazing under the sparse shade of the acacia trees.

Cabo de la Vela

A dusty one-street settlement strung out along an aquamarine bay, **CABO DE LA VELA**'s main draw is the spectacular landscape: a long sliver of beach, rocky cliffs and cactus-studded arid plains. In December and January the village is inundated with holidaying Colombians, but the rest of the year it's a tranquil spot for sunset viewing, particularly from the westernmost hill at the far end of the bay, El Faro, kitesurfing and lazing on the sand.

ARRIVAL AND INFORMATION

It's easiest to go with a tour company such as Expotur or Magictour from Santa Marta (see page 528).

By bus Catch an early morning bus from Santa Marta's Terminal de Transportes to Riohacha (3hr); from Riohacha, Cootrauri (C 15 no. 5–39; ☎ 5 728 0000) runs shared cars to Uribia (1hr; C$17,000) where the driver will drop you off at the pick-up truck departure point. The last trucks head for Cabo at 3pm at the latest (1hr 30min–2hr; C$15,000–20,000). Coming back, trucks leave Cabo between 4 and 4.30am.

ACCOMMODATION AND EATING

There's plentiful accommodation consisting of hammocks (C$15,000), traditional Wayuu *chinchorros* (warmer hammocks; C$25,000), Wayuu huts made of *yotojoro* (the inner core of the cactus) and basic concrete rooms (around C$60,000–80,000). Showers tend to be bucket-style affairs. Most guesthouses have generators that only work between 6 and 10pm, and many double as restaurants serving goat and locally caught fish and lobster.

Punta Gallinas

If Cabo is insufficiently remote, then perhaps **Punta Gallinas** will suffice – intrepid travellers who make it to this otherworldly spot are unlikely to regret their efforts. What awaits is a turquoise bay fringed by what is arguably Colombia's most beautiful beach, and a series of giant sand dunes simply folding into the sea. Colombia's northernmost tip is most comfortably visited by organized tour – it's difficult to attempt the journey solo, even in a 4WD. Contact **Kaí Ecotravel** in Riohacha (☎ 311 436 2830, ✆ kaiecotravel.com). Hostels in Cabo can also help arrange very bumpy jeep rides, departing around 5am (3hr 30min), for around C$120,000 (return).

San Andrés and Providencia

A world apart from the rest of Colombia, both geographically and culturally, the islands of San Andrés and Providencia sit in the Caribbean sea near Nicaragua, with Providencia atop the third-largest barrier reef in the world. Visitors come all this way for the fantastic beaches, the best diving in Colombia, and the unique Raizal culture; the Afro-Caribbean residents of **Providencia** in particular speak an English-based Creole with a Caribbean lilt. On larger, busier **San** Andrés the Raizal culture is much more diluted, and for many Colombians, one of the island's draws is its duty-free status, making it a much cheaper place to shop than the mainland.

SAN ANDRÉS

Seahorse-shaped **SAN ANDRÉS** is a full-on Colombian resort island with gorgeous (if often crowded) white-sand beaches, surrounding azure waters and fantastic diving (see page 532). Budget accommodation is concentrated in **San Andrés Town**, the capital – a busy whirl of unattractive concrete buildings, duty-free shops and careering scooters.

WHAT TO SEE AND DO

Though San Andrés Town has a main beach of its own, the best beach is on **Johnny Cay**, the palm-shaded, iguana-inhabited island visible directly across the water. Numerous boats depart from San Andrés beach for Johnny Cay in the mornings around 9am; a return trip costs around C$20,000–25,000, with the last boats returning around 4pm (make sure you remember on which boat you came). Visits to Johnny Cay can be combined with a stop at **Acuario** – a sliver of sand off the east coast of the island next to Haynes Cay, where the water is swimming-pool clear – though on busy days you'll find yourself fighting for space – and its three shacks poking out of the water (one for snacks and drinks, one for lockers and one for toilets); trips to both places cost around C$30,000.

If you rent a bicycle or scooter, you can do an easy loop around the island, following the coastal road. Along the west coast, south of El Cove, you'll pass **West View** (daily 9am–6pm), a beachside restaurant and snorkelling combo: for C$5000 entry, you can swim with the many fishes who'll eat out of your hand (further south is the similar **Piscinita**). At the southern tip of the island is **Hoyo Soplador** (free) – a natural blowhole surrounded by makeshift bars, gift shops and restaurants; when the tide and wind conditions are right, a jet of water shoots up to 20m up out of the hole in the rock. On the east side of the island, you're often likely to have the white-sand, windswept beaches of **San Luis** all to yourself.

ARRIVAL AND DEPARTURE

By plane San Andrés airport, a short walk from San Andrés Town, is served by numerous daily Avianca and Copa flights from the mainland and is connected to neighbouring Providencia by SATENA flights. You have to buy a tourist card (C$105,000; cash only) on the mainland when you check in for your San Andrés flight. Taxis from the airport to the heart

of San Andrés Town cost C$15,000, or else you can walk in 15min.

Destinations Bogotá (4–5 daily; 2hr); Cali (1 daily; 2hr); Cartagena (1 daily; 1hr 25min); Medellín (1 daily; 1hr 45min); Panama City (2 daily; 1hr 20min); Providencia (2–4 daily; 15–20min).

By boat Weather permitting, a catamaran service to Providencia runs several times a week (Mon, Wed, Thurs, Fri & Sun) at 8am; 3hr 30min; C$185,000–195,000 one-way; ☎ 318 347 2336 or ⓦ conocemosnavegando.com). Boats return at 2.30pm from Providencia.

GETTING AROUND AND INFORMATION

By bus Local buses leave every 20–30min (7.30am–8.30pm) from near the *Hotel Hernando Henry* in San Andrés Town and cost C$2200 per ride; there are basically two routes: the "San Luis" bus and the "Loma/Cove" bus that runs all the way along the coast road to the Hoyo Soplador.

Bicycle/scooter/golf carts Several outlets in San Andrés Town rent bicycles (C$25,000/day) and scooters (C$80,000/day). Souped-up golf carts are C$120,000/day. Cycling is a good way to explore the rest of the island, as the roads are paved and there's not much traffic. Most scooter rental places won't ask you for your licence and they won't provide you with a helmet, either; be prepared for some erratic local driving.

Tourist information On Av Newball, almost directly opposite *Restaurante La Regatta* (Mon–Fri 8am–noon & 2–6pm; ☎ 8 513 0801).

ACCOMMODATION

★ **Blue Almond Hostel** Los Almendros, Manzana 4, Casa 3 ☎ 8 512 3746, ⓦ bluealmondhostel.com. Small, charming hostel run by the amicable Juan Velasquez (who speaks English) and Jennifer Muñoz, around a 15min walk from the town centre, with functional kitchen, four simple but clean rooms and dorms (no a/c, fans only) with shared bathroom, communal computer and TV room. Free lockers and surfboards; bike rentals for C$25,000/day. Dorms C$49,500, doubles C$102,000

The Rock House Hostel C 8 no. 18A–59, Cabañas Altamar ☎ 316 579 1342, ✉ therockhouse1@hotmail.com. In a quiet residential area behind the airport, a 25min walk to town, Doña Luz and her family greet you with open arms for a bit of homely comfort. The en-suite rooms are spotless and the atmosphere just wonderful. Doubles C$100,600

El Viajero San Andrés Av 20 de Julio no. 3A–12 ☎ 8 512 7497, ⓦ elviajerohostels.com. Thoughtfully designed, this upscale hostel occupies an entire multi-storey building. Expect a/c dorms and doubles, and all the perks you can think of – daily tours organized, a movie room, chill-out bar area, large guest kitchen and balconies to hang out on. Dorms C$65,000, doubles C$300,000

5

EATING AND DRINKING

Fisherman Place Av Colombia, just behind the airport. Aka "El Pescadero", this is a large, casual, open-air restaurant, founded by local fishermen in 1975, and still serving the best of the local catch every lunchtime. The grilled fish in garlic sauce with all the trimmings comes in a heaped platter, and the *rondón* (local seafood stew with coconut milk) is flavourful and filling. Mains from C$25,000. Daily noon–4pm.

★ **Kella Reggae Bar** Carretera Circunvalar, Sector San Luis. This long-running favourite (run by Kella Williams since 1980) is an old-style beach shack and reggae bar offering a real taste of the Caribbean with authentic reggae, dance-hall music and a Rastafari vibe right on the shoreline. Things don't really get going till after midnight. Daily 6pm–4am.

Miss Celia Av Colombia, at C 2. This friendly wooden seafood shack, with fishing nets hanging from the ceiling, nautical memorabilia and plastic fish aplenty, is the best place in town to sample the local dish *rondón* (a seafood stew cooked in coconut milk; C$36,000), though they often run out and service can be hit-or-miss. If you're prepared to wait, you can't go wrong with the stewed crab or conch (C$42,000) or curried seafood (fish C$60,000). Daily noon–10pm.

PROVIDENCIA

Tiny **PROVIDENCIA** is the antithesis of its sister island: a sleepier, friendlier place with a population of around five thousand, where everyone knows everyone else, and where most speak an English-based Creole; with a mountainous interior covered with lush vegetation, and the world's third-largest barrier reef beckoning divers from all over the world.

WHAT TO SEE AND DO

Providencia is circled by a 16km loop of a coastal road, so it's easy to see all the sights along it. At the north tip of the island is **Santa Isabel**, the main "town", with ATMs and other services. A pedestrian bridge takes you across to the minute **Santa Catalina Island** – from late afternoon, it's possible to see manta rays swimming under the bridge. On Santa Catalina Island, a footpath leads past the mangroves and a ramshackle village to Morgan's Cannon on the right, while a slightly longer walk to the left leads you up to the ruins of Fort Warwick and down to **Fort Beach** where it's possible to snorkel. A narrower path leads on from here (15min or so) to **Morgan's Head**, a jagged outcrop that is said to resemble the infamous pirate's head.

Back on Providencia and heading clockwise, a road loops off from the main coastal road through Maracaibo, where the pricey but good seafront restaurant *Deep Blue* is a fantastic spot for an oceanside

---

THE BEST OF ISLAND DIVING

The islands' biggest attractions are to be found under the sea, and both Providencia and San Andrés have several reputable diving outfits that can introduce you to a whole new world, even if you're a first-time diver.

GREAT DIVE SITES

Cantil de Villa Erica Turtles, manta rays and eagle rays to be found around this reef southwest of San Andrés; 12–45m depths.

Manta's Place Southern stingrays (rather than mantas) congregate at this Providencia spot.

Palacio de la Cherna Exciting wall dive that drops from 12m to over 300m, with reef and nurse sharks, lobster and king crab among its denizens; southeast of San Andrés.

Piramide Large numbers of morays, octopus and shoals of fish make this shallow reef dive in San Andrés one of the most exciting.

Tete's Place An abundance of schoolmasters, goat fish, parrotfish and more makes you feel as if you're swimming in a giant aquarium southwest of Providencia.

DIVE OPERATORS ON SAN ANDRÉS

Banda Dive Shop Av Colombia, San Andrés Town ☎8 513 1080, ⌨bandadiveshop.com. A friendly, central choice.

San Andrés Divers Av Circunvalar Km 10 ☎312 448 7230, ⌨sanandresdivers.com. Particularly recommended for their professional approach.

DIVE OPERATORS ON PROVIDENCIA

Felipe Diving Center in Freshwater Bay ☎8 514 8775, ⌨felipediving.com.

Sirius Dive Center Southwest Bay, next to Sirius Hotel ☎314 370 2566.

drink. Directly across the water is **Crab Cay**, a tiny island with some superb snorkelling and a great view of Providencia from the top (boat trips to Crab Cay are easily arranged through your accommodation for C$90,000; admission is another C$19,000).

In the south of the island, a hiking trail leads from **Casabaja** village up **El Pico** (360m), the island's only mountain, with superb 360-degree views from the top. The hike takes around ninety minutes one-way; be sure to ask for directions and bring plenty of water.

From Casabaja, another road leads south to **Manchineel Bay** (Bahía Manzanillo), a rustic, unspoiled stretch of palm-backed sand, home to *Roland's* bar (see page 533). Further west long the coastal road, you pass the turn-off to **Southwest Bay** (Bahía Suroeste), the island's best beach, with a couple of hotels and places to eat. On the west side of the island, **Freshwater Bay** (Aguadulce) is the main hotel strip (though still low-key), with just a small beach at the southern end.

ARRIVAL AND DEPARTURE

By plane Several Satena (ⓦsatena.com) flights daily (15–20min) connect Providencia with San Andrés only; there are no flights from the mainland. Luggage allowance is 10kg. Pick-up trucks meet flights and will drop you off anywhere on the island for a non-negotiable C$25,000 per vehicle; if there are several people going to the same place, costs are shared.

GETTING AROUND AND INFORMATION

By bus *Colectivos* (basically pick-up trucks) do make circuits around the island (flat fare C$2500), but are not very reliable (they are supposed to run hourly); you can also flag down passing vehicles who might give you a lift (confirm the price first).
By bike/scooter You can rent bicycles (around C$40,000/day) or a scooter (C$60,000–70,000/day) from operators in Freshwater Bay and Santa Isabel.

Tourist information There's a helpful tourist booth in Santa Isabel by the bridge to Santa Catalina island (daily 8am–noon & 2–5pm).

ACCOMMODATION

Blue Almond Hostel (inside Cabañas Agua Dulce), Freshwater Bay ☏317 654 7117, ⓦbluealmondhostel.com. Solid budget option, with one mixed dorm (one double bed and single beds, for a maximum of six people) with two full bathrooms in one of the Cabañas Agua Dulce cabins; no lockers, no wi-fi, and no kitchen. Breakfast is C$15,000. Dorm C$45,000
Old Providence Hotel Santa Isabel ☏8 514 8691. Decent budget option, with no-frills, modern rooms in the centre of town (some with balconies), with a/c and small flat-screen TVs. There is a laundry on site, and mopeds are easy to rent here (no breakfast). Single rooms available for C$85,000. C$155,000
Posada Mr Mac Freshwater Bay ☏8 514 8366, ⓔposadamistermack@hotmail.com. Large, simple rooms right by the water. Ideal for self-caterers, as rooms come with kitchenettes; discounts for solo travellers. No wi-fi. Doubles C$180,000

EATING AND DRINKING

The liveliest part of the island is Freshwater Bay, though the best beach restaurants and bars can be found down the road at Southwest Bay.

★ **Café Studio** Maroon Hill (200m along the main road from Southwest Bay to Freshwater Bay) ☏8 514 9076. The best restaurant on the island, run by a Canadian-Raizal couple; try anything in Creole sauce and don't leave without sampling either the cappuccino pie or the lemon pie. Mon–Sat 11am–10pm.
El Divino Niño Southwest Bay ☏316 827 7489. This local beach shack institution is best known for its awesome mixed plate (*plato mixto para dos*), with enough lobster, conch, shrimp, crab and fish to sink a ship (C$60,000), but also does fried fresh fish, amazing seafood stews, and local lobsters/langoustines (mains C$22,000–60,000). Daily 11am–4pm.
Roland Roots Bar Manchineel Bay ☏8 514 8417. This Rasta-themed bar rocks to a thumping reggae soundtrack and there are even swings from which to fling yourself into the sea. Mon–Thurs & Sun 10am–midnight, Fri & Sat 10am–2am.

Tierra Paisa

Nominally a slang term to describe anyone from the mountainous region of Antioquia, **paisas** are alternately the butt of jokes and the object of envy for many Colombians. What makes them stand out is their rugged individualism and reputation for industriousness. Their fame dates back to the early nineteenth century,

5

when they cleared Colombia's hinterland for farming in exchange for the government's carrot of free land. Perhaps the biggest *paisa* contribution to Colombia is its role in the spread of coffee.

The heart of *paisa* country is the metropolis of **Medellín**, which has made a remarkable turnaround since its days as Colombia's murder capital in the early 1990s, and is now thriving and attractive cosmopolitan city. The picturesque coffee-growing *fincas* near the modern cities of **Manizales** and **Pereira** were almost all established by *paisa* homesteaders and some growers have opened their estates to tourists, who during harvest time can partake in the picking process. Easily accessible from Pereira, the incredibly photogenic village of **Salento** is the gateway to some great hiking in the misty **Valle de Cócoro**. The so-called **Zona Cafetera**, or "Coffee Zone", is the base for exploring one of Colombia's most postcard-perfect national parks, **Parque Nacional Natural Los Nevados**.

MEDELLÍN

It's hard to think of a city that was more in need of a public relations makeover than **MEDELLÍN**. When turf wars between rival drug gangs became public in the 1980s and 1990s, Colombia's second-largest city was rampaged by teenage hitmen, called *sicarios*, who, for as little as US$30, could be hired to settle old scores.

But when cocaine kingpin **Pablo Escobar** was snuffed out in 1993, Medellín began to bury its sordid past, though the notorious Mr Escobar remains an infamous attraction (see page 537). These days, the increasing number of travellers who come here find an inviting, modern city with one of the country's best climates – year-round temperatures average 24°C.

WHAT TO SEE AND DO

Pleasant green spaces, interesting museums, a bustling centre and thriving commercial areas make Medellín an exciting place to explore, while top-notch restaurants, vibrant bars and a pumping club scene provide non-stop fun until the early hours. The reliable metro makes it

easy to get around. **El Poblado**, an upmarket area in the southeastern part of Medellín, has the highest concentration of lodgings, restaurants and nightlife.

Museo de Antioquia

Medellín is the birthplace of sculptor and painter **Fernando Botero**, known for his satirical representation of all things fat – oranges, priests, even a chubby Mona Lisa. Although Medellín residents felt miffed by Botero's donation of his extensive European art collection to the Museo Botero in Bogotá (see page 497), the highlight of the **Museo de Antioquia** (Cra 52 no. 52–43; Mon–Sat 10am–5.30pm, Sun 10am–4.30pm; C$18,000; Ⓦmuseodeantioquia.co) is the largest collection of his works, including paintings, sculptures and sketches. Another twenty Botero sculptures are on display outside the museum in the busy **Plaza Botero**, including a rotund Roman legionary.

Basílica Nuestra Señora de la Candelaria

A few churches from the late colonial era survive. The most important is the **Basílica Nuestra Señora de la Candelaria** (Cra 50, at C51 Boyacá), whose Baroque interior dates from 1776. Its most impressive feature is a German pipe organ that made its way here on the backs of long-suffering horses.

Catedral Metropolitana

The fortress-like **Catedral Metropolitana** at **Plaza Bolívar** (between Cra 48 & 49), four blocks from Basílica de la Candelaria along a pedestrian walkway, was constructed between 1875 and 1931 and claims to be the largest church in the world built entirely of bricks – 1.2 million of them. A large **handicraft fair** is held on the first Saturday of every month in the plaza.

Parque San Antonio

If your appetite for Botero isn't sated, check out his *Pájaro de Paz* (Bird of Peace) sculpture at **Parque San Antonio**, on Carrera 46 between calles 44 and 46. When a guerrilla bomb destroyed the bronze sculpture in 1996, Botero ordered the skeleton to be left in its shattered state and a replica of the original was placed alongside it as an eloquent protest against violence.

Museo de Arte Moderno de Medellín

Housed in an attractively restored industrial warehouse in the Ciudad del Río neighbourhood, the **Museo de Arte Moderno de Medellín** (Cra 44 no. 19A–100; Tues–Fri 9am–6pm, Sat 10am–6pm, Sun 10am–5pm, last Fri of the month 9am–10pm; C$10,000;

MEDELLÍN: CENTRE

ACCOMMODATION	
Black Sheep Hostel	5
Casa Kiwi	7
Conquistadores	1
Enso Hostel	3
Pit Stop Hostel	6
Tiger Hostel	4
Wandering Paisa	2

DRINKING & NIGHTLIFE	
3 Cordilleras	2
El Blue	3
Eslabón Prendido	1
Luxury	4

EATING	
The Flip Flop Sandwich Shop	3
Hummus	4
Il Forno	6
Royal Thai	5
Señor Itto	2
Verdeo	1

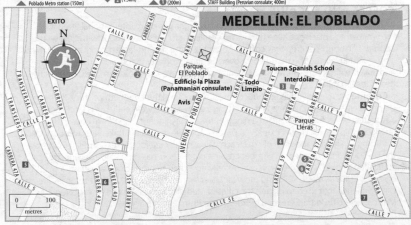

MEDELLÍN: EL POBLADO

5

ⓦelmamm.org; metro Poblado) features an impressive selection of contemporary art by international and national artists, including prolific Medellín painter Débora Arango.

Pueblito Paisa

The geographical limitations of so many people living in a narrow valley mean that many residents live in overcrowded conditions, with homes running up 45-degree slopes. Within the city centre itself there's a huge shortage of open recreational spaces. An exception is **Pueblito Paisa** at C 30A no. 55–64 (daily 7am–midnight, restaurants open from 10am; free), a replica of a typical Antioquian village that's situated atop Cerro Nutibara, a hilly outcrop downtown that offers fabulous panoramic views of the city. At the bottom of the hill is the **Parque de las Esculturas**, a sculpture park where the imagination of South American artists takes on abstract form. The closest metro station is Industriales, from where it's a ten-minute walk up Cerro Nutibara.

Jardín Botánico de Medellín Joaquín Antonio Uribe

The **Jardín Botánico de Medellín Joaquín Antonio Uribe** (C 73 no. 51D–14; daily 9am–4.30pm; free; ⓦbotanicomedellin. org; metro Universidad) is one of Colombia's oldest, dating from 1913 and home to over six hundred plant species as

well as a butterfly enclosure. Don't miss a visit to the stunning Orchideorama – a weaving structure of steel trunks and towering wooden petals – where plants are showcased and the garden's annual orchid exhibition is held in August during the Feria de las Flores flower festival.

Parque Arví

On the eastern slopes of the Aburrá Valley, **Parque Arví** (Tues–Sun 9am–6pm; free; ⓦparquearvi.org) is an ecological nature reserve and archeological site. It forms part of the network of pre-Hispanic trails of Parque Ecológico Piedras Blancas (see page 539), which can be reached from the park in an hour on foot. Other attractions include canopy ziplines and a butterfly enclosure, and you can easily spend the day exploring this welcome bit of wilderness. The park is connected to downtown Medellín via the Cable Arví Metrocable (Linea L; closed for maintenance on Mon) from the Metro Santo Domingo interchange; the fifteen-minute ride up glides over the mountain ridge and into the park, affording spectacular views of the city.

ARRIVAL AND INFORMATION

By plane Medellín's futuristic José María Córdova Airport (ⓦaeropuertojosemariacordova.com) lies a hilly 28km from the city along a scenic highway; it services all international and most domestic flights. Taxis to the city cost around C$70,000. Conbuses, at Cra 50a no. 53–13, run between the

---

COFFEE AND COCAINE

It's hard to say which of Colombia's two cash crops garners more international attention, the white or the black one. One thing is for certain: both are synonymous with quality. The country's first bumper crop was **coffee**. Colombia is the second-largest producer of Arabica coffee after Brazil and the third-largest overall coffee producer in the world (behind Vietnam and Brazil). High temperatures, heavy rainfall and cool evening breezes make Colombia the bean's ideal habitat.

   Cocaine was perceived as an innocuous stimulant until the twentieth century. Two US presidents, several European monarchs and even a pope were early users (and vocal advocates) of Vin Tonique Mariani, a nineteenth-century liqueur made from coca extract. Sherlock Holmes was partial to a seven percent solution of cocaine (taken intravenously), and for Sigmund Freud, a spoonful of coke each day was the cure for depression. Plan Colombia, the US-backed programme to combat cocaine production, has seen some decline in coca cultivation, though coca growers have merely moved on to producing hardier coca crops that give four times as much yield and grow far faster than old crops. However, the cocaine-related cartel violence that used to plague the cities of Medellín and Cali has been "exported" to Mexico, where drug trade-related murders have risen dramatically.

5

ESCOBAR'S LEGACY

Few individuals have had as great (and negative) an impact on Medellín in recent history as **Pablo Escobar Gaviria**, the most successful of the cocaine barons. After years of inflicting violence on the city's civilians because of the Medellín cartel's rivalry with the Cali cartels – his brutality included a willingness to blow up a plane just to get at a single passenger – Escobar was unceremoniously shot down on the roof of a house on December 2, 1993, while on the run from the police.

ESCOBAR TOURS

Though many Medellín citizens find the idea of this godfather of crime posthumously becoming a major tourist attraction distasteful, a number of **tours** have sprung up that take you around the city to various Escobar-associated sights. You get to see the building he lived in, apartment blocks he built, the rooftop on which he was shot, and, finally, his gravestone at the Jardines de Montesacro cemetery. Tours cost around C$55,000 per person; the original operator is **Paisa Road** (☎317 489 2629, ⊛paisaroad.com), known for its sensitive and balanced tours.

ESCOBAR'S HIPPOS

Escobar is also the reason why there are feral hippos in the mountains of Antioquia. To find out why, you can visit **Hacienda Nápoles** (Tues–Sun 9am–5pm; C$42,000; ☎1800 510 344, ⊛haciendanapoles.com), the huge farm that was once Escobar's private kingdom, complete with mansions, menagerie of exotic animals, bullring and more. Once Escobar was on the run, the abandoned hippos broke out of their enclosure, fled into the wild and bred. Today you can see them in a hippo park. Unfortunately, the mansion where Escobar used to live has now been pulled down, making this a rather less interesting excursion than it was.

Nutibara Hotel, across the street from Plaza Botero, and the airport (every 20min roughly 4am–9pm; 1hr; C$9500; ☎4 311 4023). The city's smaller second airport is Olaya Herrera (☎4 403 6780, ⊛aeropuertoolayaherrera.gov.co), located beside the southern bus terminal and serving domestic destinations; taxis to El Poblado cost around C$6000.

Domestic destinations Barranquilla (10 weekly; 1hr 10min); Bogotá (roughly hourly; 50min); Bucaramanga (1 weekly; 55min); Cali (2–3 daily; 1hr 10min); Cartagena (1–3 daily; 1hr 05min); Pereira (3 weekly; 40min); San Andrés (1 daily; 1hr 45min).

International destinations Caracas (6 weekly; 1hr 50min); Lima (5 weekly; 2hr 55min).

By bus Depending on which part of the country you're coming from, long-distance buses arrive either at the Terminal del Norte (Metro Caribe) or Terminal del Sur. Terminal del Norte handles traffic from the north, east and southeast, while Terminal del Sur has departures for destinations south and west. A taxi from the northern terminal to El Poblado, where most of the hostels are, costs about C$15,000, but it is cheap and easy to get the metro (station: metro Polado). A taxi from the southern terminal to El Poblado is C$6000.

Terminal del Norte destinations Bogotá (5–6 hourly; 9–10hr); Cartagena (10 daily; 13hr); Magangué for Mompox (7 daily; 12hr); Santa Marta (9 daily; 15hr).

Terminal del Sur destinations Cali (24 daily; 9hr); Ipiales (4 daily; 20–22hr); Manizales (2–4 hourly; 5hr); Pasto (5 daily; 18hr); Pereira (1–2 hourly; 6hr); Popayán (3 daily; 10hr).

Tourist information There are information stands at both airports and bus terminals, Parque de las Luces, Pueblito Paisa and Parque Arví. The main office is at Alpujarras, piso 10 (daily 9am–5pm; ☎4 385 6966).

GETTING AROUND

Metro The city's excellent metro system (Mon–Sat 4.30am–11pm, Sun 5am–10pm; C$2300; ⊛www.metrodemedellin. gov.co) is clean and efficient; included in the price of a metro ride are cable cars that leave from Acevedo, Santo Domingo and San Javier metro stations, carrying passengers high above the city for remarkable views of the city and close-up views of the hilltop shanty towns. Ticket booth queues

---

★ TREAT YOURSELF

Medellín's cool mornings and warm days create thermal updraughts that are ideal for **paragliding**. A number of gliding schools offer short tandem flights 45 minutes from the city centre over the Aburrá Valley with sensational views back to Medellín. Recommended operator Zona de Vuelo offers tandem flights (from C$130,000 for 15min; ☎4 388 1556, ⊛zonadevuelo.com). Buses leave Medellín's northern bus terminal (metro Caribe) every half-hour for the town of San Felix. Ask the driver to let you off at "parapente".

5

can be long, so if you're in the city for a few days, it's worth buying several journeys at once (all on one card, valid from any station to any station).

Buses The safety and efficiency of the metro means that you're far less likely to use buses, but at C$2000 a ride they're cheap. Bus #133 runs between Parque Berrío and C 10 in El Poblado, and to get from the Zona Rosa to Metro Poblado, just hop on any bus running along C 10A.

Taxi Taxis are cheap and plentiful and there is no surcharge for journeys to the bus terminal, airports or at night.

ACCOMMODATION

Most of the good budget accommodation is close to the night-time action in El Poblado and Patio Bonito.

HOSTELS

★ **Black Sheep Hostel** Transversal 5A no. 45–133, Patio Bonito ☎ 4 311 1589, ⓦ blacksheepmedellin. com; map p.535. This sociable backpackers' pad has all bases covered, including Spanish classes, high-pressure showers and weekly barbecues. The Kiwi owner has travelled extensively in Colombia and is happy to share his knowledge. Single rooms available. Dorms C$34,000, doubles C$95,000

Casa Kiwi Cra 36 no. 7–10 ☎ 4 268 2668, ⓦ casakiwi. net; map p.535. Done out in the style of a bamboo beach hut, this popular party hostel has clean dorms, a DVD room, pool table and small pool, bar, kitchen, laundry service, and an adjoining luxury wing with fancy doubles, some en suite. Dorms C$40,000, doubles C$100,000

Conquistadores Cra 54 no. 49–31 ☎ 4 512 3232, ⓦ hotel-conquistadores.com.co; map p.535. A slightly drab but clean, friendly and respectable budget hotel on a grimy downtown street that's just a couple of blocks from the city's main sights. If you like a bit of daylight, it's worth asking for a room with an outside window. C$48,000

Enso Hostel C 47 no. 70A–73, Laureles ☎ 310 378 8743, ⓦ ensohostelen.wordpress.com; map p.535. A small, low-priced hostel that's handy for the football stadium and public swimming pool, and just a block from the metro. Facilities include a kitchen, and bicycle and motorbike rental. Breakfast included. Dorms C$20,000, doubles C$70,000

Pit Stop Hostel Cra 43E no. 5–110 ☎ 4 352 1176, ⓦ pitstophostel.com; map p.535. In a quiet street in a residential part of El Poblado, this low-key little hostel is surprisingly well equipped, with a good pool and a basketball court complemented by the chillout areas – one with steam room, another with hammocks. Dorms C$30,000, doubles C$70,000

Tiger Hostel Cra 36 no. 10–49 ☎ 4 311 6079, ⓦ tigerhostelmedellin.com; map p.535. Right in the middle of the Zona Rosa, this lively hostel has its own bar, lounge and pool table. The rooms are colourful but a bit

basic – not that it matters, since you won't be spending much time sleeping. Dorms C$28,000, doubles C$79,000

Wandering Paisa C 44A no. 68A–76 ☎ 4 436 6759, ⓦ wanderingpaisahostel.com; map p.535. A little out of the way, this hostel goes the extra mile when it comes to arranging social events for its guests. There's an on-site bar to assist with the social lubrication. Dorms C$24,000, doubles C$70,000

EATING

Paisa cuisine, among Colombia's most distinctive, is heavy on the *frijoles* (black beans), grilled meat, plantains and rice. Perhaps no dish is more characteristic of the region than the *bandeja paisa*, a large bowl filled with ground beef, chorizo sausage, *frijoles*, rice, fried green bananas, a fried egg, avocado and fried pork. The city's trendiest restaurants are around leafy Parque Lleras in El Poblado, also known as the Zona Rosa.

★ **The Flip Flop Sandwich Shop** Cra 36 no. 8A–92; map p.535. An excellent sandwich joint which does lunches and breakfasts all day. Sandwiches include a BLT with proper bacon (C$12,000) or a "buffalo chicken" (C$16,000), containing chicken with a hot sauce. Sun–Fri 9.30am–6pm.

Il Forno Cra 37A no. 8–9; map p.535. A modern, open-air Italian place and El Poblado institution with plenty of mood lighting and satisfying pizza (five cheeses; C$14,500), home-made pasta (*spaghetti alla carbonara;* C$18,000) and salads (house salad; C$5,500). Mon & Tues noon–9pm, Wed noon–9.30pm, Thurs noon–10pm, Fri & Sat noon–11pm, Sun noon–8.30pm.

★ **Hummus** C 6 no. 43C–16; map p.535. Not only are there plenty of vegetarian options at this classy Lebanese restaurant, their *limonada de coco* is also easily the best in town, and if you're extra hungry, go for the *mixto platter* – complete with *kofta, tabbouleh, shawarma, kibbeh* and rice (C$28,000). Mon–Sat noon–10pm, Sun noon–8pm.

Royal Thai C 8A no. 37A–05; map p.535. Though there are Japanese elements to the decor upstairs, the food here is authentic Thai. The curries, though not cheap, are beautifully flavoured and hit that spice spot, and the dessert menu features the classic sticky rice with mango. Mains C$39,000. Mon–Wed 6–10pm, Thurs & Fri noon–3pm & 6–11pm, Sat 2.30–11pm, Sun 6.30–10pm.

Señor Itto C 9 no. 43B–115; map p.535. For a taste of beautifully prepared raw fish, try what is considered to be the best sushi joint in town. The "Dinamita Especial" deserves applause and there are plenty of noodle and teriyaki dishes. Lunch *menú* C$15,000, mains C$33,000–47,000. Mon–Sat noon–3pm & 7–10pm, Fri & Sat till 11.30pm.

Verdeo C 12 no. 43D–77; ☎ 4 268 5321; map p.535. A good and inventive vegetarian restaurant, with a C$14,900 lunchtime set menu, and a variety of veggie burgers starting at C$18000. Mon–Thurs noon–9pm, Fri & Sat noon–11pm.

DRINKING AND NIGHTLIFE

A cluster of thumping bars and clubs – most of them catering to a young clientele – is in El Poblado. If you fancy something a bit more authentic, start with a beer on C 70 (Metro El Estadio) and listen to local musicians playing *vallenato* before heading on to C 33 (Metro Floresta) for a dance. Bars usually close around 2am Mon–Wed and 4am Thurs–Sat.

3 Cordilleras C 30 no. 44–176 ☎4 444 2337; map p.535. If you take beer seriously and want to learn a thing or two about how it's made, this brewery offers two weekly tours (C$23,000 Thurs. C$28,000 Fri), including five free beers, to help you appreciate Medellín's finest. Thurs 5.30–9pm, Fri 6.30–11pm.

El Blue C 10 no. 40–20; map p.535. Giant speakers pump hard "alternative" sounds (which mostly means rock) to a student and backpacker-centric crowd who wave along to flashing green laser lights. Entry C$10,000. Fri & Sat 9pm–4am.

★ **Eslabón Prendido** C 53 no. 42–55; map p.535. Renowned for its live music on Tuesday nights, when the tightly packed crowd goes wild to Colombia salsa. Entry C$5000. Tues, Thurs, Fri & Sat 7.30pm–2am.

Luxury Cra 39 No. 8–45, Poblado; map p.535. This is where a young, tipsy crowd gets down and dirty to reggaeton, hip-hop and more. Luxury it ain't, but it sure is lively. Entry C$10,000. Thurs–Sun 10pm–4am.

DAY-TRIPS FROM MEDELLÍN

A few nearby parks make good if not absolutely essential stops within range of Medellín.

Parque Ecológico Piedras Blancas

The **Parque Ecológico Piedras Blancas** (daily 8am–5pm; C$18,000), 26km east of the city, serves as the lungs of Medellín. Set at the cool height of 2500m, much of this nature reserve has been reforested with native species, attracting butterflies and birds such as the brilliant blue soledad and the toucanet. Well-preserved pre-Columbian stone trails constructed between 100 BC and 700 AD weave through the park, while there is a butterfly gallery and a slick **insect museum** close to the official entrance.

To **get to the park**, board a bus from the corner of Calle 50 and Carrera 52 in the city centre (leaves hourly) to the village of Santa Elena (30min), where another bus runs to the park. The metro cable car that runs from Santo Domingo to Parque Arví (see page 536) also connects the city to the park.

Piedra del Peñol and Guatapé

Bearing a freakish resemblance to Rio de Janeiro's Sugar Loaf Mountain, **Piedra del Peñol**, or simply "the rock", rises spectacularly from the edge of Embalse del Peñol, an artificial lake some 70km east of Medellín, studded with islands. Locals may tell you that the 200m granite and quartz monolith is a meteorite. Whatever geological or intergalactic anomaly brought it here, it's well worth climbing the 649 stone steps to the rock's peak for phenomenal 360-degree views of emerald-green peninsulas jutting into the azure Embalse del Peñol – a hydroelectric dam that submerged the original town of El Peñol in the 1970s.

There are a handful of restaurants and tourist stalls at the base of the rock, but it's better to walk or take a bus or moto-taxi to the delightful lakeside village of **Guatapé**, 3km away, which is full of restaurants serving trout fresh from the lake. The palm-lined main square, Plaza Simón Bolívar, is well preserved, with its crowning glory the Iglesia La Inmaculada Concepción; throughout you'll find colourful colonial houses adorned with intricate artistic motifs.

The best places to eat are along the lakefront Avenida Malecón (also known as Calle 32), all serving more or less the same menu. You'll get tasty trout mains with a salad, plantain and fries for C$17,000, or opt for the three-course lunch menus for around C$12,000. **Buses** leave for Guatapé roughly every half-hour from Medellín's northern bus terminal (2hr; C$14,000). Ask the driver to let you off at "La Piedra".

ACCOMMODATION

Lake View Hostel Cra 22 No. 29B–29, Guatapé ☎4 861 0023, ⊛lakeviewhostel.com.This British/American-run hostel by the lake (which also claims to be a "boutique hotel") has all sorts of activities on offer, including kayaking, cycling, visits to swimming spots and Pablo Escobar's old *finca*, as well as dorms and private rooms, a roof terrace, and a good Thai restaurant on the roof. Dorms ‾C$23,000‾, doubles ‾C$75,000‾

5

MANIZALES AND AROUND

Founded in 1849 by migrating *paisas*, **MANIZALES** developed in the late nineteenth century with the growth of the coffee industry. One legacy is the numerous Neoclassical buildings in the city centre, which has been declared a national monument. This high-mountain city (altitude 2150m) sits at the base of the snowcapped Nevado del Ruiz volcano, which on a clear day you can sometimes see burping vapour, from the bridge in front of the Teatro Los Fundadores. Manizales owes its hilly topography to the geologically volatile earth beneath it, and small earthquakes occur with some frequency.

WHAT TO SEE AND DO

Much of the town's charm lies in its large student population, who helps create a festive atmosphere, with night-time entertainment centred mostly on the Zona Rosa district, also known as El Cable. The party comes to a head in the first weeks of January during the **Fería de Manizales**, when there are colourful parades, a beauty pageant in search of a new Coffee Queen and bloody bullfights staged in the Plaza de Toros (C 10 and Cra 27). Manizales also makes an excellent base for exploring the surrounding **coffee farms** (see page 543) and the **Parque Nacional Natural Los Nevados** (see page 541).

Plaza de Bolívar

In the centre of the city, the **Plaza de Bolívar** is dominated by the vast **Catedral de Manizales** (tower: daily 9am–8pm; C$10,000), made of reinforced concrete and featuring a vertigo-inducing, 106m-tall tower that you can ascend with a guide; tours start on the hour, and there's also a coffee shop inside the cathedral. In the centre of the plaza stands an obligatory **statue of Simón Bolívar**, but with a twist – *Bolívar-Cóndor*, the creation of Rodrigo Arenas Betancur, is half-man, half-condor.

Torre Mirador

In the northwest suburb of Chipre, on a high bluff at the end of Avenida 12 de Octubre, the 45m-tall **Torre Mirador** (daily 10am–9pm; C$5000) is the town's best lookout. On a clear day you can see seven *departamentos* and three mountain ranges. Buses run to Chipre from the Cable Plaza along Avenida Santander every minute or so.

Reserva Ecológica Río Blanco

Around 3km northeast of Manizales, the **Reserva Ecológica Río Blanco** (daily 11am–4pm, by appointment only; C$65,000 plus guide fee) is home to 380 bird species, 180 butterfly species and around 60 mammals. Tranquil orchid-lined uphill hikes through impressive cloudforest reveal dense jungle flora entwined in a battle for a place in the sun; if you are lucky, you may catch a glimpse of the reserve's endangered spectacled bear. There is also a hummingbird farm. You'll need to request permission to enter the reserve from Aguas de Manizales (☎6 875 3950, ⊕reservarioblanco@ aguasdemanizales.com.co). They will book the compulsory guides (C$35,000 for up to ten people). A taxi to the entrance costs around C$35,000 (20min); arrange a return trip.

Recinto del Pensamiento

Butterflies and birds are the main attraction at this nature park (Tues–Sun 9am–4pm; C$16,000; ☎6 889 7073, ⊛recintodelpensamiento.com), 14km from Manizales. As well as visiting the colourful butterfly enclosure, you can also wander through a medicinal herb garden, have lunch at the restaurant, enjoy a stroll through the orchid forest and marvel at the gigantic *guadua* bamboo gazebo, used for conventions and wedding ceremonies. Guides are compulsory and included in the admission price. Buses (marked Sera Maltería; 40min; C$1850) leave from along Avenida Santander, or you can catch a taxi (20min; C$15,000).

ARRIVAL AND DEPARTURE

By plane La Nubia Airport is about 9km southeast of the city centre. A taxi costs around C$15,000 or you can jump on one of the frequent buses for C$1850 from three blocks from the airport to the centre.

Destinations Bogotá (3–6 daily; 1hr 05min); Medellín (10 weekly; 40min).

By bus The bus terminal (☎6 878 5641, ⊛terminaldemanizales.com.co) is at Cra 43 no. 65–100.

Ride the cable car to the centre of town from where regular buses (C$1550) run to Cable Plaza, or jump in a taxi (around C$7000).

Destinations Bogotá (24 daily; 8hr); Cali (2 hourly; 5hr); Medellín (2–4 hourly; 5hr); Pereira (every 15min, 1hr 15min).

GETTING AROUND AND INFORMATION

Cable car The city's cable-car line runs from the bus station (Cambulos stop) to Cra 23 in the centre of town (Fundadores stop) in less than 10min and costs C$1800. You can also ride the cable car to Villa Maria.

Tourist information Parque Benjamin López on the corner of Cra 22 and C 31 (8am–noon & 2–6pm; ☎6 873 3901) dishes out maps.

ACCOMMODATION

Kaleidoscopio C 20 no. 21–15 ☎6 890 1702, ⓦhostalkaleidoscopio.com. Just two blocks from the cathedral, the location of this simple and central *hostal* is its main selling point. It might not offer any social activities or tours, but the rooms are clean (two have balconies), and breakfast is included. Dorms C$30,000, doubles C$70,000

★ **Mirador Andino** Cra 23 no. 32–20 ☎6 882 1699, ⓦmiradorandino-hostel.com. Just steps from the cable car's Fundadores stop, this spacious hostel is a great city-centre option, immaculately clean and with a stylish retro design. The roof terrace has stunning views across the city and is perfect for a sunset beer. They can also organize multiple-day hikes to Los Nevados. Dorms C$28,000, doubles C$70,000

Hostal Palogrande C 62 No. 23–36 ☎6 890 9000, ⓦhostalpalogrande.com.co. More like a homestay than a hostel, as you're sharing the family home and there are single and double rooms but no dorms. It's clean, friendly and quiet, bright and modern, and it's well located for the Zona Rosa bars and the football stadium. Breakfast included. C$60,000

EATING

The city centre clears out at night and most eating is done in the Zona Rosa.

El Zaguán Paisa Cra 23 no. 31–27. Enter through a long bamboo corridor for a hearty *menú del día* (C$7000); it's conveniently located for the cable car to the bus station. Daily 11.30am–8.15pm.

La Cantera Paisa Cra 23 no. 58–40. A good but basic diner where you can get a filling breakfast, a solid lunch or early supper (set menu; C$8000), Nothing fancy but cheap and cheerful. Mon–Sat 7am–6.30pm, Sun 7am–5pm.

★ **La Clave del Mar** C 69A no. 27–100, Barrio Palermo ☎6 887 5528. Excellent fresh seafood delivered from Tumaco or Buenaventura on the Pacific coast. Try the delicious *cazuela de mariscos* seafood casserole (C$26,500) or the *sancocho del bagre* (C$21,500), a potato, cassava and catfish soup. Mon–Sat 11am–9pm, Sun 11am–4pm.

Spago C 59 no. 24A–10 ☎6 885 3328. A stylish Italian restaurant that offers great home-made pasta (*fettuccine alla putanesca*; C$22,000) and wood-fired pizza (vegetarian; C$20,000). Mon–Sat noon–3pm & 6–11pm, Sun noon–3.30pm.

La Suiza Cra 23 no. 26–57 & Cra 23B no. 64–06. Two branches of a superb bakery where you can grab breakfast or a light lunch – crêpes, sandwiches – or treat yourself to home-made chocolates and sweet pastries. Mon–Sat 9am–8pm, Sun 9.30am–7pm.

DRINKING AND NIGHTLIFE

Most drinking is done around Cable Plaza in the Zona Rosa. In the city centre, the main nightlife attraction is La Calle del Tango ("Tango Street"), on C 24 between Cra 22 and Cra 23.

Bar la Plaza Cra 23B no. 64–80. Heaving with students who down cocktails (such as martinis or mojitos; C$16,500), then dance the night away between the tables. Mon–Thurs 11.30am–1am, Fri & Sat 11am–2am.

Juan Sebastian-Bar Cra 23 no. 63–66. Charismatic owner Elmer Vargas has a passion for jazz and an awesome CD collection. Popular with artists, writers and university lecturers, this intimate spot has great views of the city and fine cocktails. Mon–Thurs 5.30pm–1 am, Fri & Sat 5.30pm–2am.

PARQUE NACIONAL NATURAL LOS NEVADOS

The **PARQUE NACIONAL NATURAL LOS NEVADOS** (entry C$28,500 plus guide fee), 40km southeast of Manizales, protects some of the last surviving snowcapped peaks in the tropics. Three of the five volcanoes are now dormant, but **Nevado del Ruiz** – the tallest at 5321m – remains an active threat, having killed 22,000 people and buried the now extinct town of Armero when it erupted in 1985. Sadly, though, for a park whose name, Nevado, implies perpetual snow, climate change has lifted the snow line to almost 5000m on most peaks. Note that the most spectacular part of the park, the Nevado del Ruiz, has been closed since 2012 because of volcanic activity. Information about the current situation can be found (in Spanish) on the Colombian National Parks website at ⓦbit.ly/pnnevados.

The best months to visit are January and February – clear days make for spectacular views of the volcanic peaks. March, July,

5

August and December can also be ideal, while the rest of the year sees a fair amount of rain.

WHAT TO SEE AND DO

Since 2012, the Nevado del Ruiz volcano has been off-limits due to a resurgence of volcanic activity. Tours go as high as Valle de las Tumbas at 4350m, but hikers will be disappointed as much of it is by 4WD. Instead, alternative tours to **Volcano Santa Isabel** have become far more popular, stopping off at waterfalls, and to admire condors and other birds and mammals, before finally reaching the glaciers at the 4800m summit. Day visits are 7.30am–3pm (last entry at 9am) for the southern part of the park, 8am–3.30pm (last entry 2pm) in the northern sector. You can also do two- and three-day treks, staying overnight with a local family in a mountain cabin, or camping. As there is no public transport to the park, most visitors come with a tour company. In low season, tours don't run every day so check beforehand.

The dramatic **southern sector**, where a dense wax-palm forest slowly metamorphoses into *páramo* near the cobalt-blue **Laguna del Otún** (3950m), can only be accessed on foot – many people make a single trip, taking in both this and Volcano Santa Isabel. You can reach the trout-stuffed Laguna del Otún from Villamaria (10min from Manizales), taking in Laguna Verde and Volcano Santa Isabel on the way. You can also approach from Salento (see page 544).

At 5220m, the park's second-highest peak is **Nevado de Tolima**, rated its most beautiful, in the southeast corner, which can be accessed from Salento or Ibagué. Climbing it is no mean feat and would involve a four-day expedition with the right equipment and permits.

No longer a *nevado* (snowcapped peak), the **Paramillo del Quindio** has been demoted thanks to global warming, but is a relately easy climb at 4750m, and affords views of the park's three white-topped volcanoes: Nevado del Ruiz, Nevado de Santa Isabel and Nevado de Tolima. It can be reached on a three-day excursion from Salento. Contact a tour operator as all visits must be accompanied by guides.

TOUR OPERATORS

Asdeguias Caldas C 25 no. 20–25, Manizales ☎ 312 829 5426, ⓦ asdeguiascaldas.com. A local guides' association, useful for those going independently who need a guide.
Ecosistemas C 20 no. 20–10, Manizales ☎ 6 880 8300, ⓦ ecosistemastravel.com.co. Offers a variety of routes, including one-day trips to Nevado Santa Isabel for C$180,000/person.
Kumanday C 66 no. 23B–40, Manizales ☎ 6 887 2682, ⓦ kumanday.com. One-day tours on foot or by mountain bike, or a three-day trek. They have a hostel in Manizales.
★ **Páramo Trek** Cra 5 no. 9–33, Salento ☎ 311 745 3761, ⓦ paramotrek.com. Friendly and well-informed operator offering easy two-day visits to the southern part of the park along with the Valle de Cócora for C$550,000 per person (somewhat less in groups of more than two). They also offer more challenging three-day visits including the peak of the Paramillo del Quindio.

PEREIRA

Just 56km south of Manizales, **PEREIRA** makes an equally suitable base for exploring the Zona Cafetera. The region's largest city, it shares Manizales' history as a centre for the coffee industry, and though its historic centre has been repeatedly destroyed by earthquakes, the most recent striking in 1999, it's closer to many of the region's coffee *fincas* and thermal springs.

Pereira's **Plaza de Bolívar** is unique among the uniformly named central plazas of Colombia for Rodrigo Arenas Betancourt's modern sculpture of *Bolívar Desnudo* – El Libertadór nude on horseback, a controversial pose when it was unveiled in 1963 but now a beloved city symbol. Also on the plaza is the town's magnificent **Catedral**, built in 1875. Nondescript from the outside, the Catedral's single-nave interior is supported by an elaborate latticework of twelve thousand wooden beams forming a canopy like a spider's web.

ARRIVAL AND INFORMATION

By plane Pereira's international Aeropuerto Matecaña (☎ 6 314 8151) is 5km west of the city centre. A taxi downtown costs around C$65000, or jump on one of the frequent buses for C$2300.
Destinations Bogotá (14–19 daily; 50min); Medellín (2 weekly; 40min).
By bus The bus terminal (☎ 6 315 2323, ⓦ terminalpereira. com) lies 1.5km south of the city centre at C 17 no. 23–157.

STAYING ON A COFFEE FARM

Coffee is the planet's most-traded commodity after oil and Colombia is one of its largest producers, with 500,000-plus growers and the unique benefit of two annual harvests. Recognized for producing world-class coffee, **coffee fincas** in the Zona Cafetera are now following in the footsteps of the wine industry and opening their doors to curious tourists.

Fincas range from traditional estates still attended by their owner to deceptively modern rural hotels where the only coffee you'll find comes served with breakfast. Scenically, the farms look out on lush slopes, overgrown with the shiny-leaved coffee shrubs and interspersed with banana plants and bamboo-like *guadua* forests. Many will also arrange horseriding and walks, and they make an ideal base to explore the region's many attractions.

To locate the best *fincas* for your needs, ask other travellers; you can also enquire at the local tourist offices or hostels in Manizales (see page 540) or Pereira (see page 542).

FINCAS

Hacienda Guayabal Cra 3 no. 15–72 Chinchiná ☎314 772 4856, ⓦwww.haciendaguayabal.com. Runs tours, in English, of their postcard-perfect coffee farm (C$40,000). Guests can stay in the main house, and the price includes breakfast, a tour and use of the swimming pool. To get there, take a bus from Manizales or Pereira to Chinchiná (30min) and then travel the last 3km by taxi or catch a bus from in front of the church to the farm. C$150,000

★**Hacienda Venecia** Vereda el Rosario ☎320 636 5719, ⓦhaciendavenecia.com. This fourth-generation, family-owned working coffee farm is an essential stop for anyone who wants to learn more about coffee production. Tours (C$45,000 including pick-up from Manizales) allow visitors to observe the production process from start to finish. Spend a night at the guesthouse or *hostal*, swinging in a hammock on the veranda, firefly-spotting and listening to the croaks of happy frogs. Breakfast included. To get there from Medellín, ask the bus to drop you off at Puente San Pellegrino. Someone from the farm can pick you up from the restaurant by the bridge (they can make the call for you). Dorms C$35,700, doubles C$83,000

A taxi to the centre is C$6000; a bus will set you back C$2300.

Destinations Armenia (every 10min; 45min); Bogotá (2–4 hourly; 9hr); Cali (5–6 hourly; 4hr); Manizales (every 15min, 1hr 15min); Medellín (1–2 hourly; 6hr); Salento (9 daily; 1hr); Santa Rosa de Cabal (every 5min; 25min).

Tourist information The friendly and helpful tourist office (Mon–Fri 8am–6pm) is on the bottom floor of the Centro Cultural Lucy Tejada on C 17, at Cra 10. They also have a desk at the airport (Mon–Sat 7am–7pm).

ACCOMMODATION

Pereira has few accommodation options for budget travellers, so it's worth staying at one of the converted *fincas*, many of them former coffee plantations, between 5km and 35km from the city (see page 543).

Hotel Cumanday Cra 5 no. 22–54 ☎6 324 0416. Solid downtown option, with reliable hot showers, cable TV and a place to wash your dirty togs. The rooms are nice and fresh, but with a slightly chintzy touch. C$50,000

Kolibrí Hostel C 4 no. 16–35 ☎6 331 3955, ⓦkolibrihostel.com. Hostel run by a wonderfully friendly Dutch–Colombian couple. The rooms are bright, the atmosphere sociable and the location is great for going out in the Sector Circunvalar. Dorms C$22,000, doubles C$55,000

Hotel Mi Casita C 25 no. 6–20 ☎6 333 9995, ⓦhotelmicasita.amawebs.com. Close to Parque El Lago Uribe and used to dealing with travellers, this no-frills option is one of the better budget spots in town, with cable TV and rather kitschly decorated. C$65,000

EATING

The majority of good eating and drinking options are located in the Sector Circunvalar, on or near the Av Circunvalar.

Crepes & Waffles Centro Comercial Victoria mall (bottom floor), Cra 11 bis no. 17–56. Branch of the ubiquitous chain where the myriad sweet and savoury offerings are always a crowd-pleaser. Waffles from C$8400. Daily 11am–8pm.

Govinda C 15 no. 6–58, upstairs. Vegetarians and anyone in need of a break from the meat and stodge will find this Indian-ish lunchtime veg restaurant (meal C$10,000) something of an oasis – also offers vegan dishes. Mon–Sat noon–2.30pm.

★**Leños y Parilla** Cra 12 no. 2–78. This Argentine-style steakhouse specializes in what is possibly the best grilled meat in Colombia. A beautifully cooked cut of your choice with all the trimmings is served by smartly attired waiters, and is amazing value for the quality and quantity. *Bife chorizo* (sirloin strip, a favourite Argentine cut) C$26,900. Mon–Sat noon–3pm & 6–10.30pm, Sun noon–5.30pm.

5

DAY-TRIPS FROM PEREIRA

Pereira makes a good base for striking out on numerous ventures to the nearby hot springs, hiking trails and coffee *fincas*.

Termales Santa Rosa

Sitting at the foot of a 25m-high waterfall and surrounded by lush greenery, these attractive **hot springs** (daily 9am–11.30pm; C$38,000 [C$23,000 Mon–Thurs outside of holiday time]) consist of four thermal pools and a visitor centre with cafeteria and massages on offer, and you can also take a dip in the natural pool directly beneath the waterfall. Just a little further down the dirt road are the **thermal springs** (daily 9am–11.30pm; C$52,000 (C$34,000 Mon–Thurs outside of holiday time]; ⓦtermales.com. co) attached to the *Hotel Termales*, which resembles an alpine chalet, with one large pool and two thimble-sized hot tubs available to non-guests, set against a spectacular backdrop of three tall waterfalls. There's also a lavish spa on site.

The springs are easily reachable from Santa Rosa de Cabal, 9km west. Frequent buses run from Pereira to Santa Rosa de Cabal (C$2300; 45min). From the corner of Santa Rosa's *la galería* (marketplace), opposite the police station, *chivas* and buses (try to catch a *chiva* if possible) leave for the hot springs (5 daily; 45min; check timetables before departure), coming back pretty much straight after. If you miss the bus, one of the Willys Jeeps parked by the market will take you there for around C$30,000.

Termales San Vicente

These lavishly landscaped **hot springs** (daily 8am–midnight; C$50,000 [C$30,000 after 5pm Mon–Fri except public holidays]; ☎6 333 6157, ⓦsanvicente.com.co), 35km northeast of Pereira via the town of Santa Rosa de Cabal, feature a selection of steaming medicinal thermal pools scattered across some five square kilometres of cloudforest, river, waterfalls and luxuriant countryside. At 2330m, it gets pretty chilly up here, so it helps that the average pool temperature is 38°C. A variety of spa treatments is offered, including massage (C$70,000)

and mud therapy (C$30,000). If you want to **spend the night** at the springs, the most cost-effective option is camping (C$85,000 including entrance fee and breakfast). Further up the accommodation ladder are four- to six-person cabañas (from C$144,000 per person), or rooms (doubles C$372,000).

There's no public transport to the spa but you can make your own way by catching a bus to Santa Rosa from the bus terminal in Pereira and grabbing a seat on a Willys Jeep (ex-US military 4WD) from *la galería* (market) for Termales San Vicente (C$100,000 each way for four people).

SALENTO

In the heart of coffee country, the adorable village of **SALENTO** is one of the region's earliest settlements, and its slow development means the original lifestyle and buildings of the *paisa* journeymen who settled here in 1842 have barely been altered since.

Rural workers clad in cowboy hats and *ruanas* (Colombian ponchos) are a common sight. The colourful, wonderfully photogenic one-storey homes of thick adobe and clay-tile roofs that surround the plaza are as authentic as it gets.

WHAT TO SEE AND DO

Salento is a popular destination for weary backpackers who linger here to soak up the town's unpretentious charms and hike in the spectacular Valle de Cócora or to use the town as a base to explore the rest of the Zona Cafetera. The town is also the second most popular weekend destination in the country for Colombians, and on Saturdays and Sundays the main plaza hosts a **food and handicrafts fair**. Salento's annual fiesta falls in the first week of January, when the town kicks up its heels for a week of horse processions, mock bullfighting and folk dancing.

From the top of Calle Real, steps lead to **Alto de la Cruz**, a hilltop *mirador* offering unbeatable vistas of the Valle de Cócora and, on a clear day, the peaks of snow-clad volcanoes in Parque Nacional Natural Los Nevados (see page 509).

ARRIVAL AND INFORMATION

By bus The bus station is on C 6 at the entrance to town. Willys

Jeeps (daily at 6.10am, 7.30am, 9.30am, 11.30am; 20min) run to Cócora. They return when full at around 3 or 4pm.

Destinations Armenia (roughly every 15min 6am–8pm; 45min); Pereira (9 daily, but every 30min on Sun and public hols; 45min). Going to/from Pereira, you can also take an Armenia-bound bus to the Las Flores junction and then catch one of the frequent buses from Armenia to Salento or Pereira.

Information The *Punto de Información Turística* (PiT) is in the town hall on the main square (Mon–Sat 8am–noon & 2–6pm, Sun 9am–1pm & 2–6pm).

ACCOMMODATION

Book ahead if you plan to visit during the annual fiesta at the start of January.

Hostal Ciudad de Segorbe C 5 no. 4–06 ☎6 759 3794, ⓦ hostalciudaddesegorbe.com; map p.545. Stylish rooms offer stunning views of the Valle de Cócora and balconies overlook the spacious flower-filled central courtyard, which is a great place to unwind with a book. **C$160,000**

Hostal Tralala C 7 no. 6–45 ☎314 850 5543, ⓦ hostaltralalasalento.com; map p.545. Friendly Dutch owner, Hemmo Misker, has worked hard to convert this traditional *paisa*-style house into a beautiful, modern hostel. The spotless rooms with ultra-comfortable beds and smart bathrooms retain original features, like the wooden floors with furnishings made by local artisans. Bonus features include a fully equipped guest kitchen, DVD lounge, library and sun terrace. Dorms **C$30,000**, doubles **C$55,000**

La Serrana Via Palestina Km1.5 ☎316 296 1890, ⓦ laserrana.com.co; map p.545. Eco-friendly working farm and hostel with faux-rustic rooms, 1.5km from Salento, with spectacular views of the surrounding Cócora mountains and valleys. Horseriding and mountain biking are offered and there's a campfire every night. End your day on a comfy sofa enjoying the great music selection. Dorms **C$22,000**, doubles **C$96,000**, camping (if you bring your own tent) **C$10,000**

★ **The Plantation House** C 7 no. 1–04 ☎316 285 2603, ⓦ theplantationhousesalento.com; map p.545. Amid gardens and trees, with access to a fantastic viewpoint at the owner's house close by, and the option to stay down in the valley on the hostel's working coffee farm, this is Salento's first backpackers' hostel and the best place to stay in town if you want local information, of which the British owner has loads that he's happy to share. The hostel also runs tours, and daily coffee farm tours, on which guests get big discounts. Dorms **C$30,000**, doubles **C$70,000**

EATING

Fresh trout is on the menu in most of the town's restaurants and is usually served with big crunchy *patacones* (fried plantains).

★ **Brunch** C 6 no. 3–25; map p.545. This American-run spot has been winning rave reviews from an international crowd for its burgers, fajitas and delectable peanut butter brownies, among other things. They'll whip up packed lunches for Cócora-bound hikers and there's even a little cinema room for nightly screenings. Daily 6.30am–9pm.

La Eliania Cra 2 no. 6–65; map p.545. If you're pining for a curry, look no further: choices include chicken tikka masala, chicken jalfrezi or even a Thai green curry (chicken or veg), all for C$20,000. Mon–Sat 1.30–9pm.

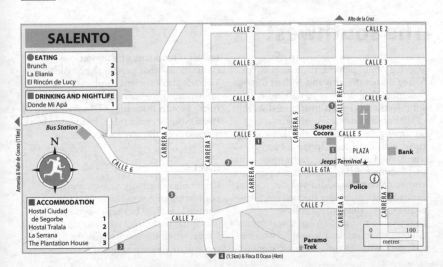

5

El Rincón de Lucy Cra 6 no. 4–02; map p.545. A whizz in the kitchen, Lucy serves the best set lunches in town. For C$8000 you get juice, soup and a heaped plate of beans, vegetables and fish or meat. Daily 7am–4pm & 6–9pm.

DRINKING

The main square has several lively bars with outside tables. Or meet locals to play *tejo* (see page 492) at Cra 4, C 3–32.

★ **Donde Mi Apá** Cra 6 no. 5–24, main square; map p.545. The town's most atmospheric watering hole, chock-a-block with bric-a-brac, the main illumination being a neon sign reading *"música vieja"*, which fairly describes the 18,000-odd rare and classic vinyl records of Colombian and South American tunes they keep behind the bar and play (usually now from their digitized recordings of them). Mon–Thurs & Sun 4pm–midnight, Fri & Sat 4pm–2am.

DAY-TRIP FROM SALENTO: VALLE DE CÓCORA

Salento sits atop the **VALLE DE CÓCORA**, which contains a thick forest of the skyscraper wax palm, Colombia's national plant, which grows up to 60m high. The valley, which offers picturesque hikes, is easily explored in a day-trip from Salento. The hamlet of **Cócora**, with a handful of restaurants, small shops and hotels, lies 11km east of Salento. From Cócora a well-trodden path leads into misty, pristine cloudforest, scattered with the remains of pre-Columbian tombs and dwellings. Orchids, bromeliads and heliconias are just some of the plant species that thrive

here, and the fauna includes spectacled bear, native deer and puma, along with hundreds of bird species such as toucans, eagles and motmots.

A five- to six-hour **loop walk** starts from the blue gate in Cócora; the muddy track passes a trout farm and runs through farmland for around 45 minutes before reaching the park entrance, after which you're following an uneven, slippery trail through cloudforest. The trail eventually branches, with one track leading up to the extremely worthwhile **Reserva Acaime** (entrance C$5000), home to eighteen species of hummingbirds that flock to its bird feeders. The price includes a large mug of revitalizing hot chocolate and a chunk of locally produced cheese. You then retrace your steps to the main trail that crosses nine rickety wooden Indiana Jones-style bridges over the Río Quindío before the Finca La Montaña branch culminates at a mountain-top viewing platform with exhilarating valley views. The way down along a wide gravel road takes you past a cluster of wax palms.

To **get to Cócora**, take one of the four Willys Jeeps (ex-US military 4WDs) that leave daily from Salento's main plaza (daily at 6.10am, 7.30am, 9.30am, 11.30am & 4pm; 20min; C$4000 one-way). They return when full at around 3 or 4pm. Jeeps can also be hired for C$31,000 one-way.

The southwest

Leaving the snowy white caps of the "Coffee Zone" behind, the Cauca River Valley descends south and widens until you reach **Cali**, gateway to Colombia's southwest and the self-proclaimed world capital of salsa music. A knuckle-whitening detour from Cali takes you to the tiny town of **San Cipriano**. Further south, the Panamerican Highway stretches past steamy fields of sugar cane to the serene, colonial town of **Popayán**, known for its blindingly white Rococo colonial architecture. The verdant rolling countryside around **San Agustín** is some of Colombia's finest, and would be worth a visit even without the enigmatic stone

statues – remnants of a mysterious civilization – that pepper the hillsides. **Tierradentro**'s ancient tombs are less well known but no less fascinating. Heading further south from the overlooked town of **Pasto**, you ascend a ridge dominated by volcanoes all the way to Ecuador.

CALI

Colombia's third-largest city, with a population of 2.4 million, **CALI** was founded in 1536 but only shed its provincial backwater status in the early 1900s, when the profits brought in by its sugar plantations prompted industrialization. Today it's one of Colombia's most prosperous cities, in part because of its central role in the drug trade since the dismantling of the rival Medellín cartel in the early 1990s; however, Cali is now more famous for salsa dancers than white powder.

The low-lying and extremely hot city (with temperatures routinely surpassing 40°C) straddles the **Río Cali**, a tributary of the Río Cauca, surrounded by the sugar plantations of the marshy Cauca Valley. The large numbers of African slaves brought to work the sugar mills left a

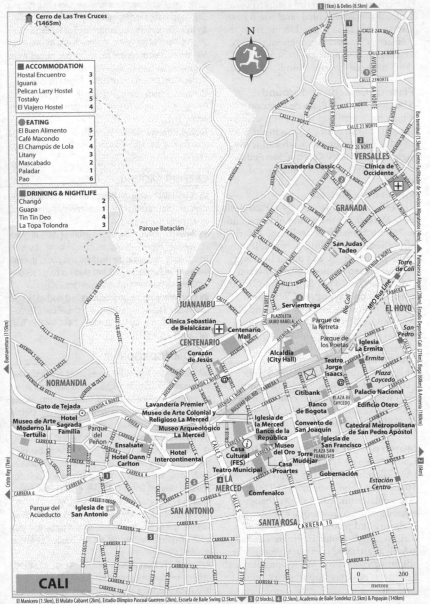

CALI

ACCOMMODATION	
Hostal Encuentro	3
Iguana	1
Pelican Larry Hostel	2
Tostaky	5
El Viajero Hostel	4

EATING	
El Buen Alimento	5
Café Macondo	7
El Champús de Lola	4
Litany	3
Mascabado	2
Paladar	1
Pao	6

DRINKING & NIGHTLIFE	
Changó	2
Guapa	1
Tin Tin Deo	4
La Topa Tolondra	3

Cerro de Las Tres Cruces (1465m)

Parque Bataclán

VERSALLES

Lavandería Classic

Clínica de Occidente

GRANADA

San Judas Tadeo

Torre de Cali

EL HOYO

JUANAMBU

Servientrega

Río Cali

San Pedro

Clínica Sebastián de Belalcázar

Centenario Mall

Parque de la Retreta

CENTENARIO

Corazón de Jesús

Alcaldía (City Hall)

Parque de los Poetas

Iglesia La Ermita

Ermita

Teatro Jorge Isaacs

Plaza Caycedo

NORMANDIA

Citibank

Banco de Bogotá

Palacio Nacional

Edificio Otero

Gato de Tejada

Lavandería Premier
Museo de Arte Colonial y Religioso La Merced

Museo de Arte Moderno la Tertulia

Hotel Sagrada Familia

Parque del Peñon

Museo Arqueológico La Merced

Iglesia de la Merced
Banco de la República

Convento de San Joaquín

Catedral Metropolitana de San Pedro Apóstol

Ensalsate

Hotel Dann Carlton

Hotel Intercontinental

Casa Cultural (FES)
Teatro Municipal

Museo del Oro

Iglesia de San Francisco

Torre Mudéjar

Casa Proartes

Gobernación

Estación Centro

Parque del Acueducto

Iglesia de San Antonio

SAN ANTONIO

LA MERCED

Comfenalco

SANTA ROSA

Buenaventura (115km)

Cristo Rey (7km)

Bus terminal (1.5km), Centro Facilitador de Servicios Migratorios (4km)

Palmaseca Airport (20km), Estadio Deportivo Cali (21km), Buga (68km) & Armenia (180km)

(1km) & Deliro (8.5km)

0   200
metres

El Manicero (1.5km), El Mulato Cabaret (2km), Estadio Olímpico Pascual Guerrero (2km), Escuela de Baile Swing (2.5km), 3 (2 blocks), 4 (2.5km), Academia de Baile Sondeluz (2.5km) & Popayán (140km)

5

notable impact on Cali's culture, nowhere more so than in its music.

Parts of central Cali are **unsafe** to walk around; be sure to get up-to-date advice on where not to go.

WHAT TO SEE AND DO

The city stakes a powerful claim to being Colombia's party capital, and you'll hear Cuban-style **salsa** music blaring from the numerous *salsatecas* throughout the day and night. If you're here in September, don't miss the Festival Mundial de Salsa.

Plaza de Caycedo and around

The city's centre is **Plaza de Caycedo**, which has a statue of independence hero Joaquín de Caycedo y Cuero in the middle. On the plaza's south end is the eighteenth-century **Catedral San Pedro**, with its elaborate stained-glass windows.

Iglesia de la Merced

The oldest church in the city is the **Iglesia de la Merced**, on the corner of Cra 4 and C 7, built from adobe and stone shortly after the city's founding. In the adjoining former convent – Cali's oldest building – is the **Museo Arqueológico la Merced** (Mon–Sat 9am–1pm & 2–6pm; C$4000), which has displays of pre-Columbian pottery including funerary urns and religious objects unearthed throughout central and southern Colombia.

Museo del Oro

This small museum at C 7 no. 4–69 (Tues–Fri 9am–5pm, Sat 10am–5pm; free) has a well-presented collection of gold and ceramics from the Calima culture from the region northwest of Cali.

Museo de Arte Moderno La Tertulia

Cali's **Museo de Arte Moderno La Tertulia** (Av Colombia no. 5–105 Oeste; Tues–Sat 10am–8pm, Sun 2–6pm; C$10,000; ⓦmuseolatertulia.com) shows changing exhibitions of contemporary photography, sculpture and painting, sometimes featuring high-profile international names, as well as arthouse film screenings in the adjoining *cinemateca*. Walk along Río Cali for fifteen minutes from the city centre to get here.

ARRIVAL AND INFORMATION

By plane The best way to and from Cali's Aeropuerto Palmaseca (☎ 2 666 3200), 16km northeast of the city, is to catch one of the regular minibuses that run to and from the bus terminal (40min; C$6500). A taxi is C$52,000.

Destinations Bogotá (daily; 50min); Cartagena (2–3 weekly; 1hr 25min); Medellín (4 daily; 40min); Pasto (2 daily; 1hr). Also international departures for Lima, Panama City, Quito, Madrid and Miami.

By bus The city's gigantic bus terminal at C 30N no. 2AN-29, 2km north of the centre, is connected to downtown by MIO, the efficient integrated bus system (see below). A taxi into downtown costs C$6000–7000 on the meter.

Destinations Armenia (hourly; 4hr); Bogotá (hourly; 12hr); Manizales (hourly; 5hr); Medellín (8 daily; 9hr); Pasto (hourly; 9hr); Pereira (several daily; 4hr); Popayán (every 30min; 3hr).

Tourist information The Secretaria de Cultura y Turismo is on Cra 4, at C 6 (Mon–Fri 8am–noon & 2–5pm; ☎ 2 885 6173).

GETTING AROUND

Much local sightseeing can be done on foot, provided you're staying in the Granada or San Antonio neighbourhoods and are prepared to walk a lot.

By bus The main route of the efficient MIO network of electric buses (ⓦmio.com.co), akin to Bogotá's TransMilenio, runs along the river, and also passes through the centre and along the Av Quinta (Av 5). It costs C$2000–2200 per ride; you need to buy a swipecard.

By taxi Some outlying attractions are best reached by taxi. Always take a taxi at night (most rides should cost C$6000–8000 in the centre). Try Taxi Libres (☎ 2 444 4444) or Taxis Val Cali (☎ 2 333 3333).

ACCOMMODATION

Cali's backpacker hostels are concentrated in two clusters, one around the Granada neighbourhood with good access to nightlife on Avenida 6N and the restaurants around Avenida 8N, and the other in the characterful (but slightly less secure at night) colonial neighbourhood of San Antonio.

★ **Hostal Encuentro** C 2 Oeste no.4–16 ☎ 2 890 2464, ⓦhostalencuentro.com; map p.547. One of the city's best hostels, with helpful staff, stylish dorms and doubles (with comfy beds) plus a tranquil terrace and delicious breakfast included. Dorms C$23,500, doubles C$80,000

Iguana Av 9N no. 22N-46 ☎ 2 660 8937, ⓦiguana.com.co; map p.547. A friendly, Swiss-run youth hostel with all facilities spread over two houses: garden barbecues, plus loads of information on the region. Dorms C$24,000, doubles C$99,000

Pelican Larry Hostel C 20N no. 6AN-44 ☎ 2 382 7226, ⓦhostelpelicanlarry.com; map p.547. The big beds, DVD room and twice-weekly barbecues at this fabulous location in Granada make this hostel popular with younger backpackers who are in Cali to party. Dorms C$27,500, doubles C$66,000

Tostaky Cra 10 no. 1–76 ☎2 893 0651, ⊛tostakycali.com; map p.547. There's a refined atmosphere at this French-run hostel in San Antonio, which probably has something to do with the coffee bar complete with chess sets in the front room. Guest kitchen for self-caterers is a bonus. Dorms C$30,000, doubles C$95,000

El Viajero Hostel Cra 5 no. 4–56 ☎2 893 8342, ⊛elviajerohostels.com; map p.547. If you're looking to dance, chill and have a good time, then this hostel's for you: they offer free salsa classes (Mon–Sat), a lovely pool and happy hour at the bar (7–9pm). There's also a genuine attempt at sustainability (solar-powered hot water, recycled rainwater and recycled trash). Dorms C$37,000, doubles C$115,000

EATING

El Buen Alimento Cra 5 no. 3–23, San Antonio; map p.547. Elegant colonial property with a pretty courtyard, housing one of the best vegetarian restaurants on the continent. Feast on lasagne with plantains and corn, spiced apples, tasty soups and falafel sandwiches all for around C$18,000, plus large fresh juices (C$5000) and breakfast plates (C$5000–9500). Tues–Sat 11.30am–10pm, Sun 11.30am–5pm.

Café Macondo Cra 6 no. 3–03, San Antonio; map p.547. This cosy café with a jazz and blues soundtrack offers sandwiches, salads and veggie burgers (from C$18,000) plus delicious cakes (C$7000–14,000) and a decent list of coffees and stronger tipples. Mon–Thurs 11am–11pm, Fri & Sat 11am–midnight, Sun 4.30–11pm.

El Champús de Lola Av 2N no. 10–129, El Centro; map p.547. Come to this no-frills local place to try a local speciality: *champús* (12-ounce cups C$3500), the refreshing meal-in-a-drink made with brown sugar syrup, crushed maize, marinated pineapple, cinnamon bark and cloves, best accompanied with an *empanada* or plantains with *chicharrón* (fried pig skin). Daily 8am–7pm.

★**Litany** C 15AN no. 9N–35, Granada ☎2 661 3736, ⊛restaurantelitany.com; map p.547. Flavour-starved foodies should make a beeline for this acclaimed Lebanese restaurant, which serves up mouthwatering platters featuring *tabouli*, falafel, vine leaves and top-notch *shawarma* (mains C$25,000–35,000). Mon–Thurs noon–3pm & 6–10pm, Fri & Sat noon–3pm & 6–11pm, Sun noon–4pm.

★**Mascabado** C 17N No. 8N–30, Granada; map p.547. Popular with backpackers and anyone seeking quality, healthy meals – traditional home-made breads and cakes, fresh fruits, salads and sandwiches (C$20,000–22,000). English menus and friendly service (most mains C$19,000–30,000), and even pots of Early Grey tea for

C$6500. Mon–Thurs 8.30am–9.30pm, Fri 8.30am–10.30pm, Sat 8am–10.30pm, Sun 9am–4pm.

Paladar Av 6AN no. 23–27; map p.547. This is an excellent, relatively upscale cafeteria (go upstairs for a/c), where you choose your dishes on trays – delicious plates of home-made lasagna, stews, seafood rice and shrimp. You get a small bowl of salad or guacamole with bread included for around C$56,000; meat sets range C$26,000–34,000 (check the price first). The desserts (C$11,000) are well worth sampling, from guava tarts to *tres dulce* puddings. Mon–Sat 9.30am–8pm.

★**Pao** C 2 No. 4–128, San Antonio; map p.547. Tiny café serving excellent coffee, refreshing lemonade flavoured with ginger and cucumber/mint (C$5000) and tasty breakfasts (French toast from C$11,000), plus *pan de bono* and brownies. Mon & Wed–Sat 9am–9pm, Sun 9am–3pm.

DRINKING AND NIGHTLIFE

Much of the late-night action is just beyond the city limits. Cover charges, where they exist, are usually converted into drinks vouchers. The clubs around Avenida 6N are liveliest at the weekends. Single male travellers should find themselves a mixed group to go out with or risk being refused entry.

★**Changó** Km 3 Vía a Cavas, ⊛chango.com.co; map p.547. Legendary club named after the African god of virility and leisure, overlooking the Río Cauca at the entrance to Juanchito. Skilled salsa dancers regularly fill its two dancefloors, and so the clientele are less forgiving of gringos with two left feet than at some other places. Taxi around C$25,000. Thurs–Sat 8am–6am.

Guapa C 28N no. 2bis–97; map p.547. There's rock, pop and electronica at this large, rowdy disco, but the live bands, who usually blast out salsa, are the biggest draw. Cover C$10,000–15,000. Fri & Sat 9pm–4am.

★**Tin Tin Deo** C 5 no. 38–71 ⊛tintindeo.com; map p.547. Unpretentious salsa temple where the odd reggae tune also sneaks onto the playlist and dancers sing along to the music. Particularly popular with foreigners on Thursdays. Entrance is usually C$10,000 for women, C$15,000 for men (though C$13,000 of that can be used for drinks). Thurs–Sat 8pm–4am.

La Topa Tolondra C 5 no. 13–27; map p.547. Frequented by tourists and locals young and old, this lively little salsa spot draws in the dancing crowds every night of the week with predominantly old-school salsa by the likes of Willie Colón and Rubén Blades. Tuesdays are bolero nights, while Thursday is a mix of Boogaloo, mambos and Cuban salsa. Mon–Wed 7pm–1am, Thurs–Sat 8pm–4am.

SAN CIPRIANO

Set in the sweltering tropical jungle 128km northwest of Cali, the straggly

5

jungle community of **SAN CIPRIANO** offers an entertaining change of pace for those who need time out from city life. The crystalline river here provides plentiful secluded cooling-off opportunities, but it is the unique journey to the 300-strong community of African slave descendants that has put San Cipriano on the traveller's map. There's no road and only a forest-flanked railway line linking San Cipriano with the town of Córdoba, 6km away, and since it sees very little train action, to bring visitors from Córdoba, inventive locals have attached motorcycle-powered wooden carts (*brujitas*) to the tracks. The journey down is nothing short of hair-raising and exhilarating; since it's a single-track railway, and there might be traffic coming the other way, be prepared to leap off in case of emergency.

San Cipriano lies at the confluence of the Escalarete and San Cipriano rivers and there are nine sites for safe **river swimming**, as well as opportunities for **tubing** (C$10,00). Follow the only road out of the settlement (the river will be on your right); well-signed tracks positioned every few hundred metres lead down to the river.

ARRIVAL AND DEPARTURE

To reach San Cipriano, catch any Buenaventura bus from Cali's bus terminal and ask to be let out at the junction to Córdoba (2–3hr). Walk down the hill (10min) to the train tracks from where carts leave roughly every hour. The carts leave when they are full; agree the price of your cart trip before setting off (around C$12,000 return). San Cipriano is just inland from the port city of Buenaventura (45min by bus), making it a convenient stopover for adventurous souls heading to the Pacific coast.

ACCOMMODATION AND EATING

A number of restaurants serve meals and many also offer basic accommodation. If you do plan to spend the night here, bring a mosquito net.

Hotel David ⊕ 312 815 4051. The basic rooms here come with fans, and shared or private bathrooms with cold water only; the food is hearty and tasty. Per person C$30,000

POPAYÁN

Although less illustrious than Cartagena, Colombia's other open-air colonial museum, **POPAYÁN**, has little reason to envy its more celebrated rival. Founded in 1537 by Sebastián de Belálcazar on his march northward from Quito, the "White City" was a powerful counterweight to Bogotá's dominance during the colonial era and a bastion of Spanish loyalty during the wars of independence. Unlike Cartagena, which saw its influence wane after independence, Popayán's aristocrats remained very active in politics, and no fewer than eleven presidents have emerged from their ranks.

When a disastrous earthquake destroyed most of the historic centre in 1983, collapsing the cathedral's roof onto the worshippers just before the Maundy Thursday celebrations, residents banded together to rebuild. The result is one of the most attractive cities in Colombia, its streets flanked by single-storey houses and whitewashed mansions and its churches lit up beautifully at night. During Easter week the city is cordoned off to make way for thousands of parading worshippers brandishing candles and colourful flowers. Popayán's Semana Santa celebrations are the second largest in the world, after Seville in Spain.

WHAT TO SEE AND DO

Besides its attractive architecture and leafy main square, most of Popayán's attractions lie outside the city. The museums are of limited interest to visitors, though you can kill a couple of hours on a rainy day there.

The churches

The town's leafy main square, Parque Caldas, is overlooked by the whitewashed **Catedral**. Although the biggest and most frequently used of the churches, architecturally it's the least important, built around 1900 on the site where two earlier structures stood. Four blocks east, on C 5 and Cra 2, is the city's oldest standing church, **La Ermita**, which features an austere single-naved chapel comprised of wooden ribbing and a golden altar dating from 1564.

On C 4 and Cra 5, the **Iglesia de Santo Domingo**'s Baroque stone portal is an excellent example of Spanish New World architecture. Equally ornate is the

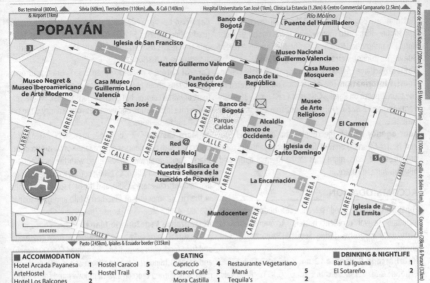

Map labels: Bus terminal (800m) & Airport (1km) | Silvia (60km), Tierradentro (110km) & Cali (140km) | Hospital Universitario San José (1km), Clínica La Estancia (1.2km) & Centro Commercial Campanario (2.5km)

POPAYÁN

Museo de Historia Natural (200m) & Cerro El Morro (270m) & (100m) & Capilla de Belén (1km) & Coconuco (28km) & Puracé (32km)

5

Banco de Bogotá
Río Molino
Puente del Humilladero
Iglesia de San Francisco
CALLE 3
Museo Nacional Guillermo Valencia
Teatro Guillermo Valencia
Casa Museo Mosquera
CALLE 4
Museo Negret & Museo Iberoamericano de Arte Moderno
Casa Museo Guillermo Leon Valencia
Panteón de los Próceres
Banco de la República
San José
Banco de Bogotá
Museo de Arte Religioso
CARRERA 10
CARRERA 11
CARRERA 9
Parque Caldas
Alcaldía
El Carmen
CALLE 3
CARRERA 8
Banco de Occidente
CALLE 4
N
Red
Torre del Reloj
CALLE 5
Iglesia de Santo Domingo
CARRERA 7
CARRERA 2
CARRERA 1
CALLE 6
Catedral Basílica de Nuestra Señora de la Asunción de Popayán
La Encarnación
Iglesia de La Ermita
CARRERA 6
CARRERA 5
CARRERA 4
CARRERA 3
0   100   metres
CALLE 7
Mundocenter
CALLE 8
San Agustín

Pasto (245km), Ipiales & Ecuador border (335km)

■ ACCOMMODATION			● EATING			■ DRINKING & NIGHTLIFE	
Hotel Arcada Payanesa	1	Hostel Caracol 5	Capriccio	4	Restaurante Vegetariano	Bar La Iguana	1
ArteHostel	4	Hostel Trail 3	Caracol Café	3	Maná 5	El Sotareño	2
Hotel Los Balcones	2		Mora Castilla	1	Tequila's 2		

staircased pulpit of **Iglesia de San Francisco**, situated on a quiet plaza on C 4 and Cra 9, where several of Popayán's patrician families are buried. La Ermita and Iglesia de Santo Domingo are beautifully lit up at night.

Cerro de Morro, El Cerro de las Tres Cruces and Capilla de Belén

For a tremendous view of the town, follow Carrera 2 north to the **Cerro de Morro**. Once thought to be a pre-Hispanic pyramid, excavations since the 1950s have proved that it is a natural feature used and developed by indigenous tribes as a sacred ritual site. Today it's capped by an equestrian statue of Sebastián de Belalcázar. From the top of El Morro, a path continues to the three crosses of **El Cerro de las Tres Cruces** and on to the hilltop chapel of **Capilla de Belén**, also accessible via a steep cobbled path from the eastern end of C4; the entire walk takes a couple of hours. There are usually people on El Morro, whereas the Capilla de Belén is more isolated; leave valuables behind if visiting either.

Casa Museo Mosquera

If you're interested in a glimpse of the salon society of the colonial and early independence era, the **Casa Museo Mosquera**, C 3 no. 5–14 (Tues–Sat 9am–noon & 2–6pm; C$3000), the childhood residence of Tomás Cipriano de Mosquera, four times Colombia's president, offers just that. On a macabre note, Mosquera's heart is kept in an urn in the wall.

Museo Negret and Museo Iberoamericano de Arte Moderno

The former home of Modernist sculptor Edgar Negret, **Museo Negret** (C 5 no. 10–23; Mon & Wed–Fri 8am–noon & 2–6pm, Sat & Sun 9am–noon & 2–5pm; C$3000) is now a museum exhibiting his work. The museum annexe contains the **Museo Iberoamericano de Arte Moderno** (same opening hours; included in entry to Museo Negret), which exhibits Negret's private collection of works by Picasso and other important artists from Spain and Latin America.

ARRIVAL AND INFORMATION

By plane Popayán's airport is just a 20min walk north of the centre of town on C 4N, opposite the bus terminal.

By bus Popayán's bus station is just off the Pan-American Highway, a 20min walk from the historic centre (walk over the footbridge across the Pan-American, and continue straight along Cra 11).

5

Destinations Bogotá (5 daily; 12hr); Cali (every 15min; 2hr 30min–3hr); Pasto (hourly; 6hr; travel during daylight hours); San Agustín (6 daily; 4hr–4hr 30min); Silvia (every 30min; 1hr 30min); Tierradentro (2–4 daily; 4hr).

Taxis Taxis charge C$4000–4500 to anywhere in the centre.

Tourist information The information office operated by the tourist police on Parque Caldas at Cra 7 no. 4–36 (daily 9am–6pm; ☎ 2 822 0916) hands out free city maps but little else.

Tour agency Run by the couple who own *Hostel Trail* and *Hostel Caracol*, Popayan Tours (ⓦ popayantours.com) organizes bike tours, night trips to the thermal baths and hikes up Volcano Puracé.

ACCOMMODATION

Popayán boasts a good selection of budget options, including several excellent hostels. Accommodation is particularly expensive during Semana Santa; book well ahead.

Hotel Arcada Payanesa C2 no. 4–62 ☎2 832 1717, ⓦ hotelarcadapayanesa.com; map p.551. Relatively new option, with stylish rooms blending modern furnishings and antique fittings. Excellent breakfast included. C$126,000

ArteHostel C 3 no. 1–32 ☎2 832 4323; map p.551. Cosy, spotless centrally-located hostel with small dorms and modern, bright private rooms (with shared bathroom), a shared kitchen and lounge. Dorms C$25,000, doubles C$55,000

Hotel Los Balcones Cra 7 No. 2–75 T2 824 2030, ⓦ hotellosbalconespopayan.com; map p.551. Shabby-chic option, with plenty of historic charm – the property was built in 1798 for former president Joaquín Mosquera – but could do with a renovation. Decent breakfast included. C$146,000

Hostel Caracol C 4 no. 2–21 ☎2 820 7335, ⓦ hostelcaracol.com; map p.551. *Hostel Trail*'s offshoot, popular with travellers who like a quiet place to retreat to at the end of the day, offers cosy rooms clustered around a covered courtyard and all the information you need on the area, courtesy of the helpful staff. Dorms C$27,000, doubles C$62,000

★ **Hostel Trail** Cra 11 no. 4–16 ☎2 831 7871, ⓦ hosteltrailpopayan.com; map p.551. Friendly Scottish owners Tony and Kim run an excellent hostel with clean, bright rooms, free coffee, DVD room and a sociable atmosphere. There's heaps of information on the walls about Popayán and the region, and free bike rentals. Breakfast C$7000, laundry C$15,000 (with express 4hr turnaround). Dorms C$27,000, doubles C$62,000

EATING

For self-caterers, there's an enormous *Exito* supermarket next door to the bus station.

Capriccio C 5 no. 5–63; map p.551. Fabulous *granisados* (iced coffee drinks; C$4500–7000) and more at this little café that roasts its own coffee beans. Mon–Sat 8.30am–12.30pm & 2–8.30pm.

Caracol Café C 4 no. 2–21; map p.551. Grind your own coffee beans on an antique machine at this travellers' hub (part of *Hostel Caracol*, but open to non-guests), where you can peruse information and even get your laundry done (in 4hr). Daily 8am–8pm.

★ **Mora Castilla** C 2 no. 4–44; map p.551. Gem of a restaurant with two floors serving a range of classic Popayán snacks: *tamal de pipián* (*tamale* filled with the local potato, tomato and peanut filling; C$2500), *patacón con queso* (fried plantain with cheese; C$3500), and the best *salpicón payanés* in the city (a smoothie of blackberry, lulo and guanabaná; C$3500–4700). Mon–Sat 10am–7pm, Sun 1–7pm.

Restaurante Vegetariano Maná C 7 No. 9–56; map p.551. Great value and a welcome break from red meat and fried food, with seven items for around C$6000 (lunch) and C$9000 (dinner) – choose from soups, salads, lentil meatballs, curried broccoli and cauliflower and fresh juices (listed on the white board – write down what you want on slips of paper provided). Mon–Sat 7am–8pm.

Tequila's C 5 no. 9–25; map p.551. A jaunty Tex-Mex café that is not going to win any fine-dining awards, but does get a prize for its burritos and quesadillas (from C$8000), cheap beer, good cocktails, lively music and very friendly service. Mon–Thurs 5–10pm, Fri & Sat 5pm–midnight.

DRINKING AND NIGHTLIFE

Bar La Iguana C 4 no. 9–67; map p.551. This dimly lit bar has a good cocktail list (from C$10,000), funky salsa soundtrack, projector screen for showing videos, and trendy clientele. Live music on Wednesdays. Mon–Wed 7pm–1am, Thurs–Sat 7pm–3am.

★ **El Sotareño** C 6 no. 8–05; map p.551. Frozen in time since the 1960s, this old bar is renowned for owner Agustín Sarria's huge vinyl collection of vintage salsa, tango and other Latin music (the man himself is usually working behind the bar). Order a cold beer, bag one of the booths then sit back and listen as the tunes are spun. Mon–Sat 7pm–1am.

AROUND POPAYÁN

The colourful market village of **Silvia**, an outstanding **natural park** and some invigorating **thermal springs** are all within 60km of Popayán.

Silvia

Well worth a detour is the rural village of **SILVIA**, 60km northeast of Popayán, which fills up with members of the Guambiano indigenous group, with the men in blue skirts with fuchsia trim and bowler hats (don't take photos as they can become aggressive), every Tuesday morning for market day. The market focuses on fruit, veg and basic household goods rather than handicrafts, but the Guambiano, who arrive from their homes in the mountain villages above Silvia, make it a great opportunity for people-watching. **Buses** (every 30min; 1hr 15min) leave for Silvia from Popayán's bus terminal. If coming from Cali, take a Popayán-bound bus to Piendamó (2hr), then grab a bus to Silvia (30min). Once here, it's possible to hire horses (C$6000–8000/hr) by the small lake and ride up to the village of Guambía (1hr) where the Guambiano cook up fried trout, plucked fresh from nearby trout farms.

Parque Nacional Natural Puracé

The high-altitude **Parque Nacional Natural Puracé** (Mon–Fri C$40,000, Sat & Sun C$50,000; guides C$35,000 per trip), 58km east of Popayán, encompasses 860 square kilometres of volcanoes, snowcapped mountains, sulphurous springs, waterfalls, canyons, trout-stuffed lagoons and grasslands. The park's literal high point is **Volcán Puracé** (4650m), which last blew its top in 1956. It's a lung-straining four-hour climb to the steaming crater where, on a clear day, there are sensational views of Cadena Volcánica de Los Coconucos – a chain of forty volcanoes. There are also less strenuous trails, including an orchid walk, and thermal baths. The local Kokonuko community now runs much of the park; you must stop at the entrance (**Puente Tierra**) to pay the entrance fee and hire a guide (mandatory). The weather is best for climbing the volcano in December and January; it is worst from June to August.

At the time of research only one Sotracauca bus departed Popayán for La Plata daily, passing Puente Tierra (2hr; C$15,000; other La Plata buses take a faster route) and other locations along the main national park road (C$18,000 to San Juan Termales; 2hr 30min). This leaves the bus station at 5am, making this a tough trip to do independently. The bus

back to Popayán passes El Cruce between 4.30pm and 5pm. Popayán Tours (see page 552) offer guided hikes up the volcano with private transport.

Thermal springs at Coconuco

The village of **Coconuco**, 26km from Popayán, is near to some rudimentary outdoor thermal baths. With the once-popular **Termales Agua Tibia** closed indefinitely due to disputes with the local Kokonuko community, the indigenous-run **Agua Hirviendo** (Tues–Sun 24hr; C$12,000), 3km east of Coconuco, is your best bet. It's less picturesque than Agua Tibia but it's open around the clock, its sulphur-reeking pools are far toastier, and the on-site waterfall is a refreshing shock to the system. Basic cabins are available for rent and a restaurant serves meals until late.

To **get to the baths**, take the bus from Popayán to Coconuco (hourly, more frequently on weekends; 45min; C$5000 one-way), from where it's a 4km walk (or C$4000 *mototaxi* ride, C$8000 by jeep, both one-way) to the springs (on a side road to the left, just out of the village). The owners of *Hostel Trail* in Popayán organize cycling trips that involve driving you and a rented bicycle to the thermal baths from C$60,000. Having enjoyed the waters, you can then pedal your way back to town, mostly downhill.

SAN AGUSTÍN

The thoroughly laidback little town of **SAN AGUSTÍN**, 140km southeast of Popayán, has everything a budget traveller could want: awesome landscape, cryptic remains of a forgotten civilization, bargain-basement prices and a plethora of outdoor activities. Some 3300 years ago the jagged landscape around the town was inhabited by masons, whose singular legacy is the hundreds of monumental fanged stone statues, many of them in the **archeological park**, comparable in detail to the more famous Moai statues found on Chile's Easter Island.

Much mystery still surrounds the civilization that built the monoliths, though the surreal imagery of sex-crazed

5

monkeys, serpent-headed humans and other disturbing zoomorphic glyphs suggests that the hallucinogenic San Isidro mushroom may have been working its magic when the statues were first created. What is known is that the priestly culture disappeared before the Spanish arrived, probably at the hands of the Inca, whose empire stretched into southern Colombia. The statues weren't discovered until the middle of the eighteenth century.

To see San Agustín and its surroundings properly, you ideally need three days: one for the archeological park, one for a day-long jeep tour of the outlying sights, such as the Alto de los Idolos, and one for a horseback tour of El Tablón, La Chaquira, El Purutal and La Pelota.

Parque Arqueológico Nacional de San Agustín

Unmissable for its wealth of statues, the **Parque Arqueológico Nacional de San Agustín**, which was declared a UNESCO World Heritage Site in 1995 (Mon & Wed–Sun 8am–5pm; C$25,000, valid for two days), lies 2.5km west of San Agustín town. The park contains over a hundred stone creations, the largest concentration of statues in the area. Many of them are left as they were found, linked by trails A, B and C, while others, like the ones in the wooded sector known as the **Bosque de las Estatuas**, are rearranged and linked by an interpretative trail. The statues are beguiling – their fanged faces, the animal-human hybrids, the stylized animal carvings – and they are all very much intact, though their purpose remains a mystery. Don't miss the **Fuente de Lavapatas**, a maze of terraced pools, covered with clearly visible images of reptiles and human figures, thought to have been used for ritual ablutions. Further along, and up, is the furthest point of the park, **Alto de Lavapatas**, the oldest of the sites, with statues sitting forlornly on a hilltop, their brooding gaze sweeping over the countryside.

There's also a **Museo Arqueológico** (daily 8am–5pm; included with park admission) featuring pottery, jewellery, smaller statues and background information on the San Agustín culture; visit it before hitting the statue sites if possible.

El Tablón, La Chaquira, La Pelota and El Purutal

Hundreds more statues are littered across the colourful hillside on either side of the Río Magdalena. Some of the most popular destinations are **El Tablón**, **La Chaquira**, **La Pelota** and **El Purutal**, which most visitors see as part of a four-hour horseriding tour. While the four sites are also doable as part of a day-long hike from town, riding through spectacular scenery is one of the highlights of San Agustín, and knowledgeable guides can shed some light on what you are seeing. Of the four sites, La Chaquira is the most impressive, with deities carved into the sheer rock above the beautiful Río Magdalena gorge. Horses and guides can be booked through your accommodation, or try Pacho Muñoz (☎ 311 827 7972), Abay Menezes (☎ 311 453 3959), or Chaska Tours (☎ 311 271 4802); around C$70,000/person plus C$80,000 per guide.

Alto de los Ídolos, Alto de las Piedras and around

Alto de los Ídolos (Mon, Tues & Thurs–Sun 8am–4pm; admission with Parque Arqueológico ticket C$25,000) is the area's second most important site after the Parque Arqueológico, and its two hills lined with tombs are home to the region's tallest statue, 4m high. Four kilometres southwest of the village of San José de Isnos (26km northeast of San Agustín), it can be reached by joining a day-long **jeep tour** (around C$45,000/person), which is easily arranged through your accommodation. Jeep tours also take in the **Alto de las Piedras**, another important archeological site, its highlight being *Doble Yo*, a statue that is half-man, half-beast. If you look closely, you'll see that there are four figures carved on that rock. Other stops include Colombia's tallest waterfall, the **Salto de Bordones**, and a smaller viewpoint over the **Salto de Mortiño**.

Whitewater rafting

Though they play second fiddle to the archeological attractions, **whitewater rafting** and **kayaking** are also popular in San Agustín, thanks to ready access to the Class II–IV Río Magdalena. Viajes Colombia/Magdalena Rafting offers excursions (C$58,000/half-day; ☎311 271 5333, ⓦviajes-colombia.com); trips can also be arranged via your guesthouse.

ARRIVAL AND INFORMATION

By bus Buses depart in the centre of town near the corner of C 3 and Cra 11, where there is a cluster of bus company offices. Most buses from Popayán are bound for Pitalito and drop off at the Cruce de Isnos (aka "Kilometro 5") – from here pick-up truck *camionetas* shuttle passengers the 5km into San Agustín itself (cost included in your ticket).

Destinations Bogotá (5 daily; 10–12hr; afternoon and evening only); Neiva (5 daily; 4–5hr); Pitalito (several daily; 45min); Popayán (at least 7 daily; 4hr 30min). The once notorious road to Popayán is now safe and much improved, though work has stopped indefinitely on the final 40km gravel section. Getting to Tierradentro from San Agustín involves two bus transfers, which can extend the journey time to around 7hr. The first transfer is at Pitalito, then at La Plata (after 3hr). From La Plata it's 1hr 30min to El Cruce de San Andrés (or directly to the museum). There are many more buses to destinations (including Bogotá) from Pitalito.

Tourist information The helpful tourist office (C 3, at Cra 12; Mon–Fri 8am–noon & 2–5pm; ☎8 837 3062) is inside the town hall.

ACCOMMODATION AND EATING

There is an abundance of budget accommodation in San Agustín, including some fantastic-value *fincas* in stunning locations just outside town.

La Casa de Francois 250m along Vía Estrecho (Cra 13) ☎8 837 3847, ⓦlacasadefrancois.com. Situated on a bluff over-looking the city, this ecologically friendly and sociable place offers airy dorms (one with fantastic views), an excellent communal kitchen and a couple of private doubles. The enthusiastic owner offers home-made bread, jam and other goodies, plus hearty breakfasts (C$8000). Dorms C$32,000, doubles C$85,000

DESIERTO DE TATACOA

The bizarre **Tatacoa Desert** makes for a worthwhile detour en route from Bogotá to San Agustín or Tierradentro. Measuring just 300 square kilometres, tiny Tatacoa's arid topography – cracked earth, giant cacti, orange-and-grey soil and towering red rock sculptures – is all the more astonishing because it lies only 37km northeast of Neiva, a city encircled by fertile coffee plantations. Scorpions, spiders, snakes, lizards, weasels and eagles have all found a home here, while fossils indicate that the area was an ancient stomping ground for monkeys, turtles, armadillos and giant sloths.

Some of the fossils are on display at the paleontology museum (Mon–Fri 7.30am–12.30pm & 2–5.30pm, Sat & Sun 7am–12.30pm & 1.30pm–6pm; C$2500), on the main plaza in the village of **Villavieja**, 4km from the desert. Villavieja has a few basic hotels and restaurants, but since one of Tatacoa's chief attractions is the amazing night sky, it pays to stump up for one of the basic four-walls-and-a-corrugated-iron-roof deals in the desert itself; accommodation is scattered along the road just past the **observatory**, the desert's focal point. In the evenings, don't miss local astronomer Javier Fernando Rua Restrepo's star show, where you get to observe the night sky from his three powerful telescopes (weekends 7–9.30pm; by appointment on weekdays; C$10,000; ☎310 465 6765). Across the road from the observatory, there's a lookout point over the Laberintos de Cusco – the maze of otherworldly red rock formations. A 45-minute trail runs down from the red-roofed bar through this labyrinth to the main road; a number of locals also offer guided **desert tours** by car, *mototaxi* or horseback (C$80,000–100,000). The best time to explore the desert is early morning before the heat becomes intolerable (temperatures frequently reach 43°C).

Villavieja is an hour **by bus** from Neiva, which in turn is 6hr by bus from Bogotá and 5hr from San Agustín on the main Bogotá–San Agustín road. Buses and vans from Neiva (C$8000; 1hr) run frequently early in the morning and late in the afternoon; A *motocarro* (tuk tuk) from Villavieja to the observatory costs C$25,000 each for up to three people.

ACCOMMODATION

Accommodation tends to be basic and overpriced for what it is, though with some negotiation you can bring the prices down.

Noches de Saturno ☎313 305 5898. A little further up the road from the observatory, with very basic rooms and camping; there's a small swimming pool for C$5000 per use. Doubles C$60,000, camping/person (with own tent) C$18,000

Sol de Verano Doña Lilia ☎313 311 8828. This place is 400m past the observatory; basic camping is also possible and meals are available on request. Camping (per person, with own tent) C$10,000, hammocks C$12,000, dorms C$28,000, cabins C$60,000

5

Casa de Nelly Vía la Estrella 1.5km along Av 2 ☎310 215 9057. Tricky to find, as the route along a poorly lit dirt track from town is not brilliantly signposted, but lovely once you've made it. Romantic cabins surrounded by trees make this a great spot for those who want to hide away and relax for a couple of days. Has a restaurant serving breakfasts (C$8000) and "whatever's available" for dinner. Dorms C$23,000, doubles C$60,000

★ **Finca El Maco** 750m along the road to the Parque Arqueológico and then 500m up a rough road ☎8 837 3437, ⊛elmaco.ch. This working organic farm with a gaggle of friendly dogs offers a range of sleeping options from camping and simple dorms to luxurious *casitas* (literally "small houses"). The restaurant serves up good-value Thai curries, great crêpes and massive breakfasts (C$10,000). Alternatively, you can buy home-made bread, cheese, pasta sauces and yoghurt and make your own meals in the basic communal kitchen, then retire to a hammock and admire the surrounding hills. Dorms C$25,000, doubles C$90,000

EATING

The town's fruit-and-veg market on the corner of C 2 and Cra 11, where self-caterers can stock up, is open daily but liveliest Sat, Sun & Mon when the *campesinos* come to sell their wares.

★ **Donde Richard** 750m along the road to the Parque Arqueológico at C 5 no. 23–45. The best spot to chow down in town serves high-quality, carnivore-friendly food such as barbecued pork, chicken, beef and fish, all cooked on a big grill at the front of the restaurant (mains from C$22,000). Don't miss the Sunday special of *asado huilense* (slow-cooked pork marinated overnight). Daily noon–8pm.

El Fogón C 5 no. 14–30. Extremely popular restaurant that serves up a better-than-average *menú del día* (C$11,000) to scores of hungry locals every day of the week. Mon–Sat 11.45am–10pm.

Restaurante Italiano da Ugo Vereda el Tablón. A short taxi ride out of town (C$5000), this authentic Italian spot delivers consistently good dishes, including home-made pasta, that have earned the praise of Italian and non-Italian travellers alike. Mains from C$20,000. Mon–Sat noon–10pm.

TIERRADENTRO

After San Agustín, **Tierradentro** is Colombia's most treasured archeological complex, though far less visited. Its circular tombs, some as deep as 9m and reachable by steep, smooth original steps through trapdoors, are decorated with elaborate geometric iconography. Monumental statues have also been found here, indicating a cultural influence from San Agustín, though again little is known about the tomb-building civilization other than that it flourished around 600–900 AD, with the statue phase occurring around 500 years later and the sites abandoned before the thirteenth century.

No large population centres have been discovered, lending credence to the belief that the original inhabitants belonged to a dispersed group of loosely related farmers. The modern **Nasa (Páez)** population, 25,000 of whom live in the surrounding hillside, is not thought to be related to the creators of the tombs.

Tierradentro means "Inner Land", an appropriate nickname to describe the rugged countryside of narrow valley and jagged summits. The area receives far fewer visitors than San Agustín, thanks to the poor quality of the road from Popayán, though that's likely to change, given the ongoing road improvements and with the area currently safe from guerrillas.

WHAT TO SEE AND DO

The main village is tiny **San Andrés de Pisimbalá**, 4km from El Cruce de San Andrés, the junction on the main Popayán–La Plata road. San Andrés had a picturesque thatched-roof **chapel** that dated from the seventeenth century – this was tragically burnt to the ground by arsonists in 2013, and may, eventually, be restored (at the time of research a temporary zinc roof covered the nave). Two kilometres along the road to San Andrés lies the entrance to the **Parque Arqueológico Tierradentro** (daily 8am–4pm; closed first Tues of every month; C$25,000), which comprises the five burial sites. The trail begins behind the **Museo Etnográfico** (daily 8am–4pm), where you pay the park entry fee and receive a wristband, valid for two days. The well-presented displays in the museum focus on the history and customs of the indigenous Nasa, while the **Museo Arqueológico** (daily 8am–4pm; free) across the road has an archeological display including funeral urns, some statuary and

5

CROSSING INTO ECUADOR: PASTO

Pasto is the commercial hub of southern Colombia – a bustling town devoid of major sights and likely to be visited only in passing on the way to Ecuador, 88km further south along the Panamerican Highway, unless you happen to be travelling through during the Carnaval de Blancos y Negros (see page 495).

The Colombian town of **Ipiales**, a 2hr bus ride from Pasto, is 2km from the **Rumichaca Bridge**, which has Colombian and Ecuadorian border control offices on either side. From Ipiales bus terminal, you can catch *colectivo* (shared) taxis to the Ecuador border (labelled "Rumichaca") for around C$2500/person (C$10,000/whole vehicle; US dollars usually accepted). The border is normally open open 24hr.

You will need to cross into Ecuador on foot and take a new *colectivo* from there; the town of **Tulcán** is 7km from the bridge (shared taxis charge US$1/person; see page 588), and from there you can connect to Quito, Otavalo and elsewhere. Check the **safety** situation on the Ecuadorian side before travelling. There are moneychangers on both sides of the border on and close to the bridge

ACCOMMODATION IN PASTO

Casa Hospedaje La Bohemia Cra 18 no. 16–2 ☎ 301 390 3408. If you have to stay overnight in Pasto, try this friendly hostel near the centre, with one small dorm (five beds) and six basic but spotless private rooms, shared bathrooms (with hot showers), common kitchen and TV room. Dorms C̲$̲3̲0̲,̲0̲0̲0̲, doubles C̲$̲8̲0̲,̲0̲0̲0̲,

---

information about the park's tombs; both are worth visiting before you visit the sites.

It's possible to visit all five sites, spread out over a sublime landscape, on a full-day, 14km walk that runs in a loop from the Museo Etnográfico and the Museo Arqueológico, with San Andrés making a convenient lunch stop. Be sure to bring your own torch to explore the tombs, as some are unlit, as well as plenty of water, and wear sturdy footwear. The guards at each site who open the tombs for you can answer most questions (in Spanish). It's best to do the loop anticlockwise, since a clockwise route would mean tackling a long, tough uphill climb first thing.

Start with **Segovia** (20min walk uphill), the most important of the tomb sights. There are 29 of them; you descend into the trapdoors and down large, steep stone steps to peer into the gloom; note the black, red and white patterns that have survived the centuries. From here, it's fifteen minutes up to **El Duende**, a smaller site with five open tombs and very little colour on the walls. It's then a 25-minute walk to **El Tablón** – where you'll fine nine weather-worn stone statues which look similar to the ones found in San Agustín. To get here, go up to the main road and head left; El Tablón will be well signposted on your left. From here you can either take the main road into the village or else descend down the muddy trail that joins the other road that runs up into San Andrés from the two museums.

The best place for lunch is *La Portada*, after which you can pick up the trail again along the side of the restaurant. A ten-minute walk gets you to **Alto de San Andrés**, its seven open tombs boasting well-preserved wall paintings. From here, it's a good hour and a half uphill to the last and most remote site, **El Aguacate**, a ridge with spectacular views of the valley and a style of tomb painting not found in the others. Allow plenty of daylight time for the hour-and-a-half walk down to the museums as in the past there have been several robberies along this isolated trail.

ARRIVAL AND DEPARTURE

By bus Tierradentro is 113km from Popayán along a rough mountain road that's currently undergoing improvement. There is one direct bus at 10.30am daily (5hr 30min) from Popayán (C$18,000) and three daily (5am, 8am & 1pm) that pass El Cruce de San Andrés – a road junction. From here it's a 2km walk to the museums and a further 2km uphill to San Andrés de Pisimbalá. There's a direct bus to Popayán daily from San Andrés at 6am, and from El Cruce de San Andrés at 9am, 11am & 1pm. Buses and pick-ups run from San Andrés to La Plata (6.30am, 8.30am, 1pm; 2hr) where you can pick up connections to San Agustín and Bogotá via Neiva (and Tatacoa).

ACCOMMODATION AND EATING

There are several basic guesthouses of comparable standards right near the two museums; meals available on request in most places.

★ **La Portada** ☎ 311 601 7884. Located along the main road in the village, *La Portada* has attractive, clean rooms with reliably hot showers. The excellent, home-cooked food on offer in the pretty restaurant (breakfast C$6000, lunch and dinner C$12,000) is the best in town and the gregarious owner is a treasure trove of local knowledge. C$70,000

Hospedaje Ricabet ☎ 312 795 4636. A short walk up from the museums, with small, basic rooms with shared or private bath, set around a pretty cobbled courtyard. C$42,000

Hotel El Refugio ☎ 312 811 2395. A 2min walk from the museums, this hotel with a pool and somewhat musty rooms is the swishest option besides *La Portada*. No wi-fi. Camping/person C$13,000, doubles C$84,000

The Pacific coast

One of the least-visited parts of the country, and a ruggedly beautiful one at that, the Pacific coast is where the jungle and ocean meet alongside grey-sand beaches, where you can go whale- and dolphin-spotting, or stay in small villages, the majority of whose residents are of African descent. You will need plenty of time and patience to explore this region, as the majority of the settlements are reachable only by boat from the main port of **Buenaventura**.

BUENAVENTURA

A busy, gritty and charmless port city, **BUENAVENTURA** is the major gateway to the region, so you will end up overnighting here. The boats to various coastal destinations run from the *muelle turístico* (tourist wharf); the area around it is reasonably safe (which is more than can be said for much of the rest of town), and you'll find a number of guesthouses and eateries nearby.

Buenaventura doesn't lend itself to sightseeing, though if you're a surfer it's well worth visiting **Ladrilleros**, an hour's boat ride north, where enormous 2–3m waves lash the shore during the August–November rainy season and where you can stay in a number of basic digs. To reach Ladrilleros, take a boat to Juanchaco, from where you can either walk the 2.5km or get a ride on the back of someone's motorbike.

ARRIVAL AND DEPARTURE

By bus Numerous buses run between Buenaventura and Cali (3–4hr) and you can stop in San Cipriano (see page 549) on the way.

By boat Speedboats for various coastal destinations leave from the *muelle turístico*.

ACCOMMODATION AND EATING

In Buenaventura, as the cheapest digs are downright unsavoury, it's worth paying a little more for comfort. Cheap eats are to be had at *la galería* (market) in Pueblo Nuevo; the stalls on the second floor serve the likes of fish stewed in coconut milk and other coastal specialities. A taxi here costs around C$4000–5000.

Hotel Cordillera Diagonal 3 no.. 3B–51 ☎ 2 242 2008, ⓦ hotelcordillera.com. Huge, excellent-value hotel in the centre of town, with clean, modern rooms (some with sea views) equipped with flat-screen cable TV (there's also a gym). Breakfast included. C$45,000

EL VALLE AND AROUND

Way north up the coast, 14km by road southwest of **Bahía Solano**, a town famous for sports-fishing and whale-watching, compact **EL VALLE** is a good spot for surfing, as well as visiting **Parque Nacional Natural Ensenada de Utría**, where it's possible to see whales close to the shore during calving season. Entry to the park costs C$44,500 and you can stay overnight in one of the cabins in the park (C$820,000/two people); group trips can be arranged from El Valle, with boats costing around C$80,000 per person (minimum three people per boat).

In En Valle, there's some good **surfing**, and between September and December it's possible to see **turtles** nesting at Estación Septiembre, a sanctuary (donation requested) 5km south along the coast. You can also do a day hike through the jungle to the **Cascada del Tigre** (entry C$5000), a splendid waterfall with a refreshing waterhole (guide necessary).

5

ARRIVAL AND DEPARTURE

By plane To reach El Valle, you can fly from Medellín with Satena into Bahía Solano's tiny airport, with flights very much weather-dependent, and then take a Jeep from opposite the school (around C$20,000; 1hr).

By boat Cargo boats leave Buenaventura every Tuesday (24hr; around C$150,000 including three meals and a bed) to Bahía Solano and then take a Jeep. Return journey from Bahia Solano leave on Saturday.

ACCOMMODATION

Humpback Turtle on Playa Almejal, El Valle ☎312 756 3439, ⓦhumpbackturtle.com. Complete with beach bar, hammock room, rustic camping, a plethora of tours, surfboard rental, on-site restaurant and even an organic farm. Owner Tyler is a fount of knowledge on the area. To get there, take a Jeep from Bahia Solano and tell them to take you to "Donde Tyler". Camping/hammocks C$25,000, dorms C$39,000, doubles C$120,000

Amazonas

Accounting for around a third of Colombia in size and largely inaccessible to visitors, the **Amazon basin** feels unlike any other part of the country, with its pristine rainforest, fantastic wildlife and indigenous groups living deep in the jungle, their cultures still preserved intact. The capital of the Amazonas province, the bustling jungle town of **Leticia**, is only accessible by air and river, and thus retains a somewhat isolated feel. Travellers come to Leticia for a taste of jungle adventure and also to cross over into Brazil or Peru, as this is where the three countries meet.

LETICIA

This compact riverside town, its partially unpaved streets abuzz with a fleet of scooters and motorcycles – the local transport of choice – has worn many hats during its lifetime. Founded in 1867, **LETICIA** was part of Peru until it was awarded to Colombia in 1933 in a ceasefire agreement following a war between the two countries in 1932. A den of iniquity and sin (well, drug trafficking) in the 1970s, Leticia had to clean up its act when the Colombian army moved in, though visitors are still warned not to wander out into the outskirts of Leticia after dark. Today it's a hot, humid, yet relatively tranquil place, with a lively waterfront and houses hidden amid the greenery. It makes a good base for short trips up the Amazon and for crossing over into Brazil or Peru.

WHAT TO SEE AND DO

The main attractions lie outside the town, but in Leticia proper you can stop by the

Museo Etnográfico Amazónico (Cra 11 no. 9–43; Mon–Fri 8am–noon & 2–5pm, Sat 9–1pm; free) to check out the collection of indigenous weaponry, splendid (and scary) ceremonial masks, pottery and more. For high-quality crafts made by local indigenous tribes, the best selection is at the **Galería Arte Uirapuru** (C 8 no. 10–35; Mon–Sat 8.30am–noon & 3–7pm).

ARRIVAL AND INFORMATION

By plane Leticia is served by several flights daily from Bogotá (2hr) with LAN and Avianca. All visitors must pay C$30,000 tourist tax upon landing at the tiny Aeropuerto Nacional Alfredo Vásquez Cobo. From the airport, you can walk (20min) or catch a taxi (C$8000) into town. Tabatinga International Airport, 4km south of Tabatinga (only some Tabatinga *colectivos* from Leticia will reach this far – you'll need to ask the driver), has daily flights to Manaus with Azul.

Tourist information The helpful tourist office (C 8 no. 9–75; Mon–Fri 8am–noon & 2–5pm; ☎8 592 5066) can provide onward transport info and maps.

Visas Both locals and foreigners are allowed to move between Leticia, adjoining Tabatinga, and Peru's Isla Santa Rosa without visas or passport control (though you should keep your passport on you). If heading further into Brazil or Peru, you'll need to get a Colombian exit stamp from the immigration office at Leticia Airport (daily 8am–6pm) or at the port (daily 8am–noon & 2.30–6pm), and then an entry stamp from the Brazilian Policía Federal in Tabatinga (Av de Amizade 26; 8am–noon & 2–6pm; ☎97 3 412 2180 in Brazil) or the Peruvian immigration office on Isla Santa Rosa (daily 8am–noon & 2–6pm). Some nationalities need a visa to enter Brazil; try to get it before coming to Leticia; otherwise, visit the Brazilian consulate (C 11 no. 8–104; Mon–Fri 8am–3pm; ☎320 846 0637). You'll also need a yellow fever certificate to enter Brazil.

INTO BRAZIL AND PERU BY BOAT

Many travellers come to Leticia en route to Brazil or Peru. To get to the former, you need only head to the port of **Tabatinga**, just across the border, which has virtually fused with the Colombian town; there are no checkpoints between the two and all you have to do is walk south along Av Internacional.

Boats leave for **Manaus** from Tabatinga's port on Tuesdays, Wednesdays, Fridays and Saturdays at around noon (double-check times in advance and remember that the time in Brazil's Amazonas state is 1hr ahead of Colombia time), taking three days and four nights and costing around R$220 if you have your own hammock, or around R$1000–1500 for a double cabin. The reverse journey (upstream) takes around six days and is more expensive. Faster boats leave Tuesday, Thursday, Saturday and Sunday mornings, taking 34hr, and costing R$470–490.

High-speed passenger boats connect Leticia and **Iquitos** in Peru, leaving from Isla Santa Rosa; since the boats depart early in the morning, it's easiest to stay in Santa Rosa the night before; at the very least you'll need to arrange a ferry over to Santa Rosa in advance (they don't otherwise run from Leticia at night, and may not be able to in the dry season, when you may have to take one from Tabatinga instead). Boats depart around 3am (double-check departure times), with Transportes Golfinho (Tues, Thurs & Sat; ☎97 3412 3186, ⓦtransportegolfinho.com) and Amazonas I (Wed, Fri & Sun; ☎T97 99150 6898). Price includes breakfast and lunch. Don't forget to get an exit stamp and relevant visa (see pages 230 and 720) before departing Leticia.

ACCOMMODATION

★**Amazon B&B** C 12 no. 9–30 ☎8 592 4981, ⓦamazonbb.com. If you have just got off the boat from Brazil or Peru, this lovely hotel will seem like paradise. Think minimalist chic, ceiling fans, crisp white sheets and plenty of space in both rooms and bungalows to throw your gear about. Doubles C$225,000

Anaira Hostel C 7 no. 1–40 ☎316 320 5009, ⓔreservas@anairahostel.com. A small hostel with a big dorm opening onto a small garden, with a handful of private rooms and a pool. Dorms C$23,000, doubles C$65,000

La Jangada Cra 10 no. 7–16 ☎311 498 5447, ⓔlajangadaleticia@gmail.com. This hostel wins extra points for friendliness and helpfulness; the fan-cooled rooms and dorms are clean and airy, you can book your jungle adventures here and the kitchen whips up a simple breakfast, which is included. Dorms C$27,000, doubles C$55,000

EATING

In Leticia you'll find culinary delicacies you won't encounter elsewhere in Colombia – an abundance of river fish and a vast variety of fruit juices. The most delicious fish include *gamitana* and *pirarucú*, though you should avoid eating the latter during its breeding season (mid-Nov to mid-March), when fishing it is banned to conserve stocks. Places to eat are concentrated along C 8 and Cra 10, off C 8.

★**Tierras Amazónicas** C 8 no. 7–50. Cool, open-fronted restaurant serving huge slabs of perfectly cooked *pescado a la pupeca* (fish steamed in a banana leaf) for C$30,500. Wash it down with *borojó* or *copoazú* juice (C$4300). Tues–Sun 11.30am–10.30pm.

AROUND LETICIA

Amazonas' biggest attractions are found outside Leticia. These include the abundant wildlife of Parque Nacional Natural Amacayacu, jungle hikes and stays in Puerto Nariño, upstream of Leticia – a great base for dolphin-spotting trips.

Jungle trips

There are numerous tour agencies in Leticia that can organize **jungle and river trips** of virtually any length, taking in flora, fauna and the area's indigenous communities. However, that also means that there are a number of unscrupulous operators, so make sure you've agreed on exactly what's included and avoid pushy "guides" who approach you in the street. Since the Amazon is such a vast area, odds are, you won't see any big mammals, but you're very likely to see monkeys and numerous bird species, and a three-day stint in the jungle is great exposure to a unique environment. Recommended operators include Amazon Jungle Trips (Av Internacional no. 6–25; ☎8 592 7377, ⓦamazonjungletrips.com.co), going strong after more than 25 years, and Tanimboca (Cra 10 no. 11–69; ☎8 592 7470, ⓦtanimboca.org), with English-speaking guides.

5

Parque Nacional Natural Amacayacu

Around ninety minutes upstream from Leticia, the 3000-square-kilometre **Parque Nacional Natural Amacayacu** is a spectacular slice of wilderness, home to five hundred bird species, plenty of crocodiles, anacondas and other reptiles and 150 mammal species, including big cats. The park is officially closed at present due to flooding, but it is still possible to enter with guides from the neighbouring villages of San Martín and Mocagua; come prepared for squadrons of mosquitoes. A particularly worthwhile visit is to the Fundación Maikuchiga, a project for rehabilitating monkeys – visits can be arranged through *La Jangada* hostel (see page 561) for C$1000,000 per person for transport, food and guide, plus C$120,000 for up to six people for entrance to the monkey sanctuary.

Puerto Nariño

Eco-friendly **PUERTO NARIÑO** sits around 75km upstream of Leticia and makes a great base for spotting the Amazon's pink dolphins; half-day excursions to Lago Tarapoto cost around C$70,000 for up to six people. You can learn more about the endangered creatures at the riverfront Fundación Natütama (🌐 natutama.org), located near the dock. The town itself, peopled mostly by the indigenous Yagua, Tikuna and Cocoma, is a shining example of recycling, organic waste management and rainwater collection; other Colombian towns could learn a great deal here, and this may well be the only Colombian settlement with zero motorized traffic.

ARRIVAL AND DEPARTURE

By boat Three high-speed boats run daily from Leticia at 8am, 10am and 1.30pm (C$30,000; 2hr), returning at 7.30am, 11am and 3.30pm. Bring enough cash, as there are no banks here. Visitors have to pay a C$10,000 tax on arrival.

ACCOMMODATION AND EATING

Las Margaritas C 6 no. 6–80. This thatch-roofed place does a great home-cooked lunchtime buffet.

Paraíso Ayahuasca C 4 no. 5–71 ☎ 320 244 0187, ✉ paraisoayahuasca@gmail.com. A friendly place to stay, where the walls on four sides are mainly just mosquito netting, and the common space upstairs affords great views. Dorms C$25,000, doubles C$70,000

MUSEO SOLAR INTI ÑAN, QUITO

Ecuador

❶ **Quito** Explore the capital's historic centre, Baroque churches and museums. See page 571

❷ **Avenue of the Volcanoes** Experience the bustle of indigenous markets under soaring ice-covered summits. See page 584

❸ **Páramo del Angel** Hike off the beaten track amid a bizarre landscape that looks straight out of Star Wars. See page 588

❹ **Cuenca** Quito's southern rival is one of Latin America's best-preserved colonial cities. See page 601

❺ **Amazon lodges** A fine base for seeking out exotic wildlife and ancient rainforest cultures. See page 616

❻ **Galápagos Islands** Witness the miracle of evolution. See page 632

HIGHLIGHTS ARE MARKED ON THE MAP ON PAGE 565

ROUGH COSTS

Daily budget Basic $25, occasional treat $45

Drink Cerveza Pilsener $1.50

Food Set menu two-course lunch $2.50

Hostel/budget hotel $6–15

Travel Quito–Otavalo: 2hr, $2

FACT FILE

Population 16.6 million

Languages Spanish, Kichwa, Shuar

Currency US dollar ($)

Capital Quito (population: 2,680,000)

International phone code ☏ 593

Time zone GMT -5hr

6

Introduction

In Ecuador it's possible to wake up on the Pacific coast, drive through the snowcapped Andes and reach the edge of the Amazon jungle by sundown. Although Ecuador is only slightly larger than the UK (or Michigan), its diversity is astonishing, with some 25,000 species of plants and around 1600 species of birds. It's entirely fitting, therefore, that the Galápagos Islands, where Charles Darwin developed his theory of evolution, belong to Ecuador.

Mainland Ecuador is divided into three geographically distinct regions: Pacific coast, Andean highlands and Amazon jungle. The highlands are utterly captivating, with **Quito** a convenient starting point. The capital's historic sights, range of day-trips and excellent facilities can keep you busy for several days.

Northwest of Quito are the cloudforest reserves around **Mindo.** Head north and you'll find the indigenous market town of **Otavalo**, whose woven crafts are a shopper's dream.

Ecuador's most dramatic mountain scenery rises up to the south of Quito, including **Volcán Cotopaxi**, the highest active volcano in the world, and the volcanic lake **Laguna Quilotoa**. Further south is the popular spa town of **Baños**, and **Riobamba**, a base for exploring Ecuador's highest mountain, **Chimborazo** (6310m), and the **Nariz del Diablo** train ride. In the southern highlands are Ecuador's best-preserved Inca ruins, **Ingapirca**, its beautiful third city, **Cuenca**, and the relaxing "Valley of Longevity", **Vilcabamba**.

Excursions can take you deep into wildernesses of primary jungle, including **Cuyabeno Natural Reserve** and **Yasuní National Park**, along the majestic Napo River, while shorter trips and stays with Amazon indigenous communities are best via **Puyo** and **Tena**, Ecuador's white-water-rafting capital and the most appealing jungle town.

On the coast is Ecuador's largest city, **Guayaquil**, and a succession of fine Pacific beaches: surfer hangouts **Montañita** and **Canoa** and the unspoilt coastline of **Parque Nacional Machalilla** and **Mompiche**.

Some 1000km west of mainland Ecuador lie the country's crown jewels, **the Galápagos Islands**, which remain among the world's top destinations for watching wildlife and are easy to explore independently.

CHRONOLOGY

8000 BC The oldest archeological evidence of human settlement found in today's Ecuador dates from around 8000 BC.

4000 BC The Valdivia culture develops one of the earliest ceramic techniques in the Americas.

1460 AD Tupac Yupanqui leads the first Inca invasion of Ecuador.

1495 Huayna Capac conquers territory up to Pasto, now in Colombia, despite violent resistance. He dies in Quito.

1532 Atahualpa defeats his half-brother Huascar in an Inca civil war, but is captured and executed by Spanish conqueror Francisco Pizarro.

WHEN TO VISIT

Ecuador's climate is incredibly varied. Because of the country's diverse landscapes, the best time to visit varies by region. On the **coast**, temperatures are typically 25–35°C. The rainy season is dramatic, with downpours between January and April. This is the hottest time of the year, at times uncomfortably humid, but also the best months for the beach. It's cooler and cloudier between June and December. In the **highlands**, the temperature is on average 15°C, but due to the altitude it gets hot at midday and cold at night, particularly above 2500m. The driest, warmest season is June to September. In the **Oriente** the temperature is generally 20–30°C with high levels of rainfall and humidity. The driest season is December to March. In the **Galápagos**, the temperature peaks at over 30°C in March and cools to the low 20s in August. It's best to avoid the rough seas and cold between June and September.

1541 Francisco de Orellana journeys down the Amazon and reaches the Atlantic.

1809 On August 10, Quito declares independence from Napoleonic Spain.

1822 On May 24, Quito wins independence at the Battle of Pichincha. Bolívar's dream of a united continent dies and Ecuador secedes from Colombia in 1830.

1861 Ultramontane Gabriel García Moreno gains power, quashes rebellions and makes Catholicism a prerequisite for all citizens. He is assassinated in Quito in 1875.

1895 Liberal Eloy Alfaro becomes president and introduces sweeping reforms, ending the connection between Church and state. He is assassinated in 1912.

1941 Peru invades Ecuador and forces it to recognize as Peruvian 200,000 square kilometres of jungle, almost half its claimed territory.

1967 Oil is discovered in the Ecuadorian Oriente, ushering in an oil boom.

1979 Left-winger Jaime Roldós is elected president, ending military rule. He emphasizes human rights and dies in a mysterious plane crash two years later.

1996 Self-styled *loco* (crazy) Abdalá Bucharam wins the presidency but quickly becomes engulfed in corruption scandals. Protests lead to his ouster by Congress, ushering in a decade of instability.

1998 After a brief war, President Jamil Mahuad and Peruvian President Fujimori sign a peace treaty, which ends the long-running border dispute.

2000 A bank crisis and hyperinflation leads Mahuad to move to replace the sucre with the dollar. He is ousted in a coup but his successor Vice President Gustavo Noboa presses ahead with dollarization.

6

6

2002 Former coup leader Lucio Gutiérrez wins the presidency but is toppled in 2005 after infuriating his left-wing base with neo-liberal policies and attempts to increase presidential powers.

2007 Rafael Correa becomes Ecuador's seventh president in ten years. He refuses to pay part of Ecuador's national debt, engages in left-wing populism, replaces Congress with a new Assembly and introduces a new constitution that centralizes power in the president's hands.

2011 Correa wins a narrow victory in a referendum that hands him control over the judiciary.

2012 Work begins on a metro in Quito and huge infrastructure projects commence.

2014 Correa blocks environmentalist efforts to force a vote on oil development.

2017 Lenín Moreno, the world's only disabled head of state, is elected president with a mandate to tackle corruption.

ARRIVAL AND DEPARTURE

Arriving by **air**, most travellers enter Ecuador via Quito's airport (see page 574), though Guayaquil's José Joaquín de Olmedo (see page 625) is more convenient for the Galápagos and the beach. There are only flights to/from Europe with Iberia (to Madrid) and KLM (to Amsterdam). From North America, American Airlines, Delta, JetBlue, TAME and United are the main airlines.

FROM PERU

You can reach Ecuador by **bus** from Peru via Tumbes and Huaquillas on the coast, with frequent bus connections. It's also possible to cross via Macará or Zumba in the highlands.

FROM COLOMBIA

Travelling to and from Colombia overland is possible via Tulcán in the northern highlands. There's another crossing north of Lago Agrio in the Oriente which is not recommended as the region is a drug-smuggling hotbed.

PASSPORTS AND VISAS

Visitors to Ecuador from most Western countries (including the EU, US, Canada, Australia and New Zealand) can stay for **ninety days** providing your passport is valid for six months. On entry you'll receive a T3 tourist card, which must be kept until departure. Officially, you should bring proof of sufficient funds to support yourself and a return ticket or proof of onward travel, but it's rarely demanded. To stay more than ninety days you'll need a visa, consult ⓦcancilleria.gob.ec.

GETTING AROUND

BY BUS

Ecuador's cheap **buses** are the easiest form of public transport, reaching just about everywhere there's a road. Major routes are in good shape. However, poor driving conditions, particularly in the rainy season, often result in **delays**; the worst roads tend to be around Esmeraldas and the Oriente.

Public buses cost about $1–1.50 per hour of travel. Quality varies considerably, but the main inter-city routes are frequented by fairly comfortable services. Local buses tend to stop frequently en route and journeys can be slow. For longer bus rides at peak periods, buy tickets in advance. Avoid bus travel at night if possible as **crime** and accidents are more common. Pickpocketing is rife on public buses, especially popular tourist routes out of Quito; always keep a watch on your valuables.

Another option is **van services**, which are more expensive (around $3 per hour), but quicker as they do not stop en route. Some van companies offer a pick-up and drop-off service, saving on taxi fares. Others operate from private terminals.

BY TAXI, CAR & MOTORCYCLE

Taxis are widely available and relatively inexpensive, with short trips costing $2–3. In bigger cities they are the best way to get around, but as few drivers use meters (except in Quito) negotiate the fare in advance. The safest option is to book a cab from a reputable company (hotels and restaurants can help) or use a taxi app: Uber and Easy Taxi are recommended. Taxi drivers in tourist towns will often offer longer trips, but daily hire rates are around $75.

Renting a car is possible ($300–500/ week) but beware the excess ($1000 or more) in case of damage. For **motorbike** rental contact Quito-based Freedom Bikes (wfreedombikerental.com) which offers well-maintained scooters and bikes, riding gear and also offer self-guided trips (using GPS devices) from $45 per day and superb guided tours.

BY AIR

Ecuador has a good choice of internal flight connections: Quito to Cuenca typically costs $50 to $85 one-way. Flights are necessary to reach the Galápagos, and often convenient to the Amazon. The main domestic airlines include Avianca (◉1 800 003434, wavianca.com); LATAM (◉1 800 842526, wlatam.com) and TAME (◉02 2397 7100, wtame.com. ec). Small planes serve jungle hamlets from Mera.

ACCOMMODATION

Ecuador has a wide variety of **accommodation**, from dirt-cheap rickety shacks to comfortable mid-range hotels and luxury high-rise options. A dorm bed in a cheap *pensión*, *residencial* or *hostal* can cost just $5. The mid-range is where Ecuador offers best value. In most destinations $25–50 gets you a good-sized double room with comfortable beds, private bathroom, hot water and cable TV. Above $75 you're looking at swanky international city hotels, colonial haciendas and jungle lodges.

Cities such as Quito, Guayaquil and Cuenca are slightly more expensive but competition keeps the prices down. The Galapagos are undoubtedly the most expensive part of the country, with hotel rooms roughly fifty percent higher than on the mainland. Air-conditioning is not necessary in highland regions, but often costs extra on the humid coast and in the Oriente. Consider bringing your own mosquito net if you plan to spend time in the jungle or on the coast during the rainy season. Deep in the jungle, budget options are harder to find so expect to pay more as part of a tour. **Camping** is not widely available but possible in some areas for $5 per person.

FOOD AND DRINK

There's a lot more to Ecuadorian cuisine than roasted guinea pig. Rice and potatoes are staples, and rice is often served with everything. Budget travellers can enjoy cheap set menu *almuerzos* (lunches) and *meriendas* (dinners), which serve a soup, main course and drink for $2–3 ($5 in the Galapagos). *Sopa* (soup), *caldo* (broth) and *seco* (stew) are cheap ways to stay full. *Locro de papa* is a hearty potato soup with cheese and avocado; *chupe de pescado* is a thick fish-and-vegetable soup. *Seco de pollo* (chicken stew with coriander) or *lomo salteado* (salted beef steak) are common main courses, whereas *caldo de pata* (cow's foot soup) is for the more adventurous. In the highlands and Oriente the fish of choice are tilapia and river trout. The famous *cuy* (guinea pig) and *hornado* (roast pork) are Andean delicacies and are often roasted whole on a spit.

On the coast, the **seafood** is among the best in the world. *Ceviche*, seafood marinated with lemon and onion, is excellent, but often only served until mid-afternoon. *Encebollado*, a fish and onion soup, is often eaten to stave off a hangover. Another interesting option is *cazuela*, a seafood and vegetable broth made with plantains and peanut. In Manabí try *biche*, a sweeter fish soup with corn and *maduros* (sautéed plantains). The best white fish is *corvina* (sea bass), which can be *frito* (fried), *apanado* (breaded), *a la plancha* (grilled) or *al vapor* (steamed). Note that shellfish is a common cause of illness, so take care.

If you're on a tight budget, **snacks** come in handy, but it's probably best to avoid meat cooked on the street and all snacks sold on public transport. Popular treats from bakeries include *empanadas* (meat- or cheese-filled pastries), *tortillas de verde* (fried mashed green bananas) or *yuca* (cassava, a starchy tropical root) and delicious *humitas* (mashed corn with cheese wrapped in a corn husk and steamed). *Pan de yuca* (cassava bread), eaten with cheese, is a common snack.

Always buy **bottled water** and never drink from the tap. Avoid ice in cheaper places. Abundant tropical fruits make fresh *jugos* (juices) and *batidos*

6

6

(milkshakes) great breakfast options. Alongside pineapple, melon, papaya and banana are more unusual fruits such as *naranjilla* (a sour orange) and *granadillas* (egg-shaped passion fruit).

Sodas (fizzy drinks) are everywhere. Coffee is of variable quality; locals tend to favour a weak brew but you'll find cafés with espresso machines in all of the main tourism centres. The most common beers are the standard local Pilsener and slightly more expensive Club Verde, but Ecuador's craft beer scene is growing quickly – there's even a craft beer (Endémica) made in the Galápagos. Domestic rum and the local firewater *aguardiente* are cheap and strong enough to give you a stonking hangover. *Chicha*, made from fermented corn or potato, is drunk by indigenous people in the Andes. The Amazon version is made from chewed cassava, and it's impolite to refuse it.

CULTURE AND ETIQUETTE

A highlight of Ecuador is the hospitable, relaxed people. For travellers, Ecuadorians are very easy to get along with: most are kind and polite towards visitors and there's little in the way of hustle and hassle. On the road, drivers are relatively considerate and there's little or no tooting and honking of horns.

Ecuador's population of more than sixteen million is divided almost equally between the coast and highlands, with five percent in the Oriente. Some 65 percent are *mestizo* (mixed race), 25 percent indigenous, three percent Afro-Ecuadorian and seven percent white. While many indigenous people hold on to traditional customs and dress, the rest of the population uses Western dress. The 1998–2000 crisis led many to emigrate, while around 500,000 Colombians live in Ecuador.

More than eighty percent of Ecuadorians are Roman Catholic, although evangelical Christianity is increasing. Rivalry between the mountains and coast is strong, and regional accents are completely different and immediately distinguishable. Stereotypes prevail: many *Costeños* consider *Serranos* (mountain people) to be conservative and uptight. *Serranos* can label *Costeños* as uncultured, immoral gossips. Rivalry ranges from banter to deep resentment.

Ecuadorians' lax attitude to time is notorious. At social gatherings, add at least an hour to the agreed meeting time. However, scheduled departures such as buses and tours are usually punctual, so don't be caught out.

Greetings are essential for Ecuadorians – a kiss on each cheek for women and a handshake between men. If you don't know any Spanish, it's worth learning basic greetings and pleasantries.

Tipping is not essential in most situations but advisable in higher-end restaurants. If your guide is good, show your appreciation.

SPORTS AND OUTDOOR ACTIVITIES

TEAM SPORTS

Football is the number one sport in Ecuador and watching a major local match at a stadium in Quito or Guayaquil is unforgettable. Quito has three major teams: Liga, Nacional and Deportivo Quito, while Guayaquil has two: Emelec and Barcelona. Football, volleyball and basketball can be played in many parks, while other sports include rugby and hockey (on ice only in Quito).

HIKING AND CLIMBING

The highlands' open spaces offer a vast range of **hiking** – the Quilotoa Loop, Parque Nacional Cotopaxi, the hills around Baños, lake country around Otavalo, Parque Nacional Cajas and Vilcabamba are but a few. On the coast, Parque Nacional Machalilla near Montañita offers good hiking. The most demanding **climbing** is on Cotopaxi and Chimborazo, although ensure you are fit, acclimatized and with a qualified guide.

WATERSPORTS

For watersports, including **rafting** and **kayaking**, Tena and Baños are best for trips on fast-flowing rapids and gentler tributaries. Some of the most rewarding

surfing is around Montañita, which holds a famous surfing competition around Carnaval, and Canoa and Mompiche. For kitesurfing head to Santa Marianita beach near Manta where there's a good new school. **Scuba-diving** and **snorkelling** opportunities are limited on the mainland. Parque Nacional Machalilla has a few operators but the best place by far is the Galápagos Islands, whose amazing marine life makes it one of the world's top underwater destinations.

WILDLIFE

Birdwatching enthusiasts should head to the cloudforests of Mindo, which have more than 400 bird species and 250 species of butterfly. Hummingbirds are a highlight, commonly seen in the cloudforests and the jungle. The Andean condor is a rare but unforgettable sight, occasionally seen in Parque Nacional Cotopaxi. For other **wildlife-watching**, the Oriente offers opportunities to observe sloths, otters, caymans, tapirs, many species of monkey and even perhaps an anaconda. The Galápagos is of course unbeatable for wildlife, with giant land tortoises and sea turtles, marine iguanas and outstanding birdlife.

COMMUNICATIONS

In towns and cities virtually all hotels and hostels have free, fairly reliable **wi-fi**, as do many cafés and restaurants. In the high Andes and remote parts of the Oriente connections can be very slow or non-existent though. A few **internet cafés** still survive (rates are $1–1.50/hr). Obviously wi-fi can be used for international Skype/Viber/WhatsApp calls.

To make **phone** calls in Ecuador it's cheapest to buy a local SIM card and use your own phone: Claro and Movistar are the two main providers. You'll need to register the SIM, for which a passport is officially needed; some phone stores will do this for you.

Loading your card with a dollar or so per day will enable to make a domestic call or two and access 3G and 4G for short periods of internet use.

The **postal** system in Ecuador is adequate in major towns, but can be unreliable in rural areas.

CRIME AND SAFETY

Sneak theft is common for travellers across Ecuador. Expert pickpockets target tourists, particularly in Quito. Be vigilant in crowded areas and on public transport, keep your money out of sight and be wary of strangers engaging you in conversation, a common diversionary tactic. Don't carry large amounts of cash. **Armed robbery** is rare but a possibility. Transport terminals are a notorious hangout for thieves. The tourist district of Mariscal Sucre in Quito is now well patrolled by police and security guards, but avoid its dark side lanes late at night. It's best to take a licensed taxi back to your hotel at night. Other crime hot spots in Quito include parts of the Old Town, the walk up to El Panecillo (take a taxi) and Parque Carolina.

In Guayaquil, be extra vigilant at night, particularly downtown. Esmeraldas and Atacames also have problems with theft and robbery; avoid the northern coastal town of San Lorenzo completely. Drug smuggling, Colombian guerrilla activity and risk of kidnappings in the northern border areas have made areas of Sucumbíos (capital Lago Agrio), Carchi (capital Tulcán) and Esmeraldas (capital Esmeraldas) provinces unsafe. On the southern border, the Cordillera del Cóndor, southeast of Zamora, contains landmines from the conflicts with Peru.

By law you must carry **identification** – this means your passport. If you can't produce it, you may be detained by the police. Carry **drugs** in Ecuador and you may end up in jail for up to fifteen years, so avoid contact with drug dealers. Foreigners are occasionally vulnerable to drug set-ups and a bail-out is an easy way for corrupt police officials to make money.

> ### EMERGENCY NUMBERS
> Police/fire/ambulance ☎**911**
> Report crimes via the efficiently managed
> ✉ denuncias@turismo.gob.ec.

6

HEALTH

Vaccinations that are recommended include typhoid, hepatitis A and yellow fever. Others to consider are hepatitis B and rabies. **Malaria** is present (but rare) in the Oriente and on the northern coast. Wear long sleeves, light-coloured clothes and use repellent to avoid mosquito bites. **Dengue fever** is spread by day-biting mosquitoes, mainly during the rainy season, and is an increasing problem in urban areas on the coast. There is no vaccine, so seek medical help immediately if you show symptoms (high fever, aching limbs, vomiting and diarrhoea).

The most common problem is **travellers' diarrhoea**. Minimize risks of bacterial and parasitic infections by avoiding bus vendor/street food; also try to eat in clean restaurants. Tap water, ice, salad, ice cream, unpeeled fruit and seafood are common culprits. Eat plenty of carbohydrates, drink water and pack oral rehydration and Imodium.

Another common problem is **altitude sickness**, which can be dangerous. When arriving at altitudes over 2000m (most of the highlands), don't over-exert yourself, avoid alcohol and don't attempt to climb mountains without sufficient time to adjust to the altitude.

Sunburn and **sunstroke** are also very common because the equatorial sun is fiercely strong.

Ecuador's public health system is poor and **emergency care** particularly bad. Travelling with valid insurance is essential. If you have an emergency, try to head for a private hospital. In Quito, Hospital Metropolitano (ⓦhospitalmetropolitano. org) is good, and in Guayaquil, Clínica Kennedy (ⓦhospikennedy.med.ec) has several branches. Pharmacies dish out some medicines without prescription, so you are responsible for knowing what you're taking – opt for brand names rather than generic drugs and bring essential medicine from home.

INFORMATION AND MAPS

Ministry of Tourism iTur offices (ⓦecuador.travel), in provincial capitals and the main tourist centres, supply maps, lists of hotels, restaurants and sights, and the website is a good source of information. Quito's main tourist office is the best in Ecuador.

The Instituto Geográfico Militar in Quito, Seniergues E4-676 y Gral. Telmo Paz y Miño, sells topographical maps for $3 (bring your passport as ID to enter the institute). For tablets and smartphones, apps using OpenStreetMap (ⓦopenstreetmap.org) tend to be slightly superior to Google Maps. Waze (ⓦwaze. com) is excellent for finding your way.

MONEY AND BANKS

Ecuador uses the **US dollar** as its currency. There are 1, 5, 10, 25, 50 cent and 1 dollar coins. Notes come in 1, 5, 10, 20, 50 and 100 dollars, though avoid the last two if you can as they're tough to change.

Carry enough cash for a few days; a credit card is recommended as backup. Visa, MasterCard, Cirrus and Maestro are commonly accepted at ATMs. In larger agencies, you can pay for tours with a credit card but you may be charged five to ten percent more. Note rates of exchange for currencies outside South America (eg British pounds) are often poor, so bring cash in US dollars wherever possible. Travellers' cheques are serious hassle to use.

OPENING HOURS AND HOLIDAYS

Most shops and public offices are open Monday to Saturday 9am to 5pm or 6pm, but family-owned businesses open at the owner's discretion. Most banks are open 8 or 9am to 4pm Monday to Friday and until noon weekends in shopping malls. Call centres open 8am to 10pm. Restaurant and bar opening hours vary and museums are usually open weekends and closed Mondays. On weekends and public holidays government offices and some shops are closed.

The majority of national holidays mark famous historical events as well as Catholic festivals. Ecuadorians love to party with lots of food, drink and late nights, so it's a great experience. Tourist resorts, especially beach towns, are extremely busy on national holidays, with sky-high prices. Note the government habitually changes the dates of national holidays to tag them onto the weekend.

PUBLIC HOLIDAYS

January 1 New Year's Day (*Año Nuevo*).

January 6 Epiphany (*Reyes Magos*). Celebrated mainly in the highlands.

February/March Carnival (*Carnaval*). The week before Lent is Ecuador's biggest party. Monday and Tuesday are holidays. Beaches are packed and in the highlands Ambato and Guaranda are famous for celebrations. Don't be surprised to get wet, as throwing water is part of the fun.

March/April Holy Week (*Semana Santa*). The big processions in Quito are on Good Friday, a public holiday.

May 1 Labour Day (*Día del Trabajo*).

July 24 Birthday of Simón Bolívar, the man who dreamed of a united South America and helped liberate Ecuador.

August 10 Quito Independence Day (*Día de la independencia*).

October 12 Columbus Day (*Día de la Raza*).

November 2 All Souls' Day or Day of the Dead (*Día de los Muertos*).

December 25 Christmas Day (*Navidad*). Most Ecuadorians celebrate Christmas on Christmas Eve night and relax on Christmas Day.

December 31 New Year's Eve (*Nochevieja* or *Años viejos*). New Year rivals Carnaval as the country's biggest party. Locals burn effigies of well-known characters. Note that safe use of fireworks is absent.

FESTIVALS

May 24 Battle of Pichincha (*La Batalla del Pichincha*). Celebrating the decisive battle for independence in 1822 (highlands only).

June 21/22 Festival of the Sun (Inti Raymi), an indigenous celebration in Otavalo featuring indigenous dances.

October 9 Independence of Guayaquil (Guayaquil only).

November 3 Independence of Cuenca (Cuenca only).

December 6 Foundation of Quito. Bullfights are the order of the day (Quito only).

Quito

At a dizzying elevation of 2850m, **QUITO** is the second-highest capital in the world after Bolivia's La Paz. It has a dramatic location, with active Volcán Pichincha, which covered the city in ash in 1999, looming to the west and two valleys descending east separated by the snowcapped Antisana from the Amazon basin. If the altitude doesn't leave you breathless then the architecture will. Founded by the Spanish in 1534, Quito rapidly became a major colonial centre, and its churches, monasteries, cobbled streets and wide plazas have been beautifully preserved. The warmest, driest time is June to September, but the rest of the year can be chilly, especially at night, with frequent rain in the afternoons.

WHAT TO SEE AND DO

Although most visitors stay in the centre-north, the **Old Town**, mostly known as "El Centro Histórico", is what makes Quito special. Highlights include the two main squares **Plaza Grande** and **Plaza San Francisco**, the **Palacio de Carondelet**, the **Catedral**, the gaudy gold church **La Compañia** and the **Church of San Francisco**. For great views, take a taxi up to the top of

El Panecillo or climb the stairs of the neo-Gothic **Basílica del Voto Nacional**, the earlier, the better.

The **centre-north** has a generous range of accommodation, restaurants and bars. Cheaper options abound in the area dubbed "La Mariscal" and neighbouring La Floresta.

Modern Quito has plenty of attractions, but they are spread out. Cultural highlights include Ecuador's biggest art museum, **El Museo Nacional**, Oswaldo Guayasamín's extraordinary work of art **La Capilla del Hombre** and the excellent **Centro de Arte Contemporáneo**. A trip up to 4100m on the **Teleférico** should not be missed either.

Plaza Grande and around

This picture-perfect sixteenth-century plaza forms the political and religious focal point of Quito, linking the cathedral, Presidential Palace, Archbishop's Palace and city hall. You can visit the **Palacio de Carondelet** (Presidential Palace; 45min tours Tues–Sun 8.30am–5pm, except when the cabinet is in session; free) on a guided tour to see the staterooms, a stunning mosaic and various indigenous

6

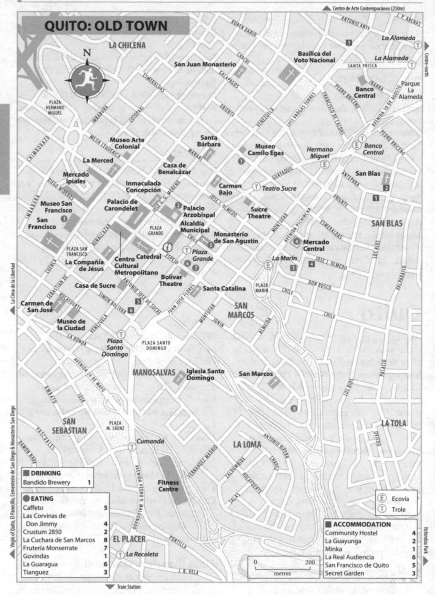

QUITO: OLD TOWN

Centro de Arte Contemporáneo (250m)

DRINKING
Bandido Brewery   1

EATING
Caffeto   5
Las Corvinas de
Don Jimmy   4
Crustum 2850   2
La Cuchara de San Marcos   8
Frutería Monserrate   7
Govindas   1
La Guaragua   6
Tianguez   3

E Ecovía
T Trole

ACCOMMODATION
Community Hostel   4
La Guayunga   2
Minka   1
La Real Audiencia   6
San Francisco de Quito   5
Secret Garden   3

0 ———— 200
metres

artefacts. To enter the palace you must present your passport. On the south side of the square is the **Catedral**, entered through the museum (entrance on Venezuela; Mon–Sat 9.30am–5pm; $2, Sun services free). Its interior features seventeenth- and eighteenth-century religious art, the tombs of liberator Mariscal José Antonio Sucre and ultramontane president Gabriel García Moreno, who was hacked to death under here (an inscription marks the spot).

On the corner of García Moreno and Espejo is the **Centro Cultural Metropolitano**

(Tues–Sat 9am–5.30pm, Sun 10am–pm; free), with regular exhibitions and performances in its courtyard.

Walk half a block south from Plaza Grande along Calle García Moreno to reach Quito's most extravagant church, **La Compañía de Jesús** (Mon–Fri 9.30am–6pm, Sat 9.30am–4.30pm, Sun 12.30–4pm; $5), built by Jesuits in the seventeenth and eighteenth centuries. It took 163 years to construct, with many kilos of gold to cover the interior. It's a wonder to behold, despite bordering on opulence gone mad.

Continue south down García Moreno to reach the **Museo de la Ciudad** (Tues–Sun 9.30am–5.30pm; $3; free last Sat of every month). Aside from a confusing layout, it's rewarding, depicting life in Quito through the centuries.

Plaza San Francisco
From La Compañía head northwest to **Plaza San Francisco**, one of Ecuador's most beautiful squares (though there's ongoing metro station construction here). The sixteenth-century **Iglesia de San Francisco** is Quito's oldest church and its twin bell tower is one of the city's most famous sights. Recent painstaking restoration has left the interior nearly as resplendent as that of La Compañía. Behind the impressive facade is one of the largest religious complexes in South America. The **Museo Fray Pedro Gocial/San Francisco** (Mon–Sat 9am–5.30pm, Sun 9am–1pm; $2; ⓦmuseofraypedrogocial.com) is housed in the cloisters and has an impressive collection of religious

sculptures, paintings and furniture. Through the museum, you can enter the choral room of the church with a statue of the "dancing virgin" and depictions of planets on the ceiling.

Plaza Santo Domingo and La Ronda
Follow Simón Bolívar east of Plaza San Francisco to reach Quito's third impressive square, **Plaza Santo Domingo**, dominated by the sixteenth-century **Iglesia Santo Domingo**. From this square take Guayaquil south to reach the winding alley of **La Ronda**, one of Quito's oldest streets. This atmospheric cobbled lane is lined with restaurants, bars and cave-like art galleries. It's a popular spot at night to listen to live music or have a *canelazo* (a hot mix of *naranjilla*, cinnamon water and *aguardiente*).

El Panecillo
Old Quito's southern skyline is dominated by the 40m-high aluminium statue of the **Virgin de Quito** (daily 9am–5pm; $1) on the hill known as **El Panecillo** ("little bread loaf"). From the top, the city vistas are spectacular. It's not considered safe to walk here, so take a taxi (about $3 one-way from the Old Town or $8 return including waiting time).

Basílica del Voto Nacional
Take Calle Venezuela uphill from Plaza Grande to admire the neo-Gothic grandeur of the **Basílica del Voto Nacional** (daily 9am–5pm; $2, free Sun). Construction took place over the past century, beginning in 1892. Instead of gargoyles, the church has iguanas and Galápagos tortoises protruding from its sides. Climbing the steep stairs (extra $2) and ladders up the 115m towers is unnerving, so take the lift if you're afraid of heights. The views are fantastic.

Centro de Arte Contemporáneo
Around 500m north of the Basílica, the city's fine **Centro de Arte Contemporáneo** (Tues–Fri 10.30am–5.30pm, Sat & Sun 9am–5.30pm; free; ⓦcentrodeartecontemporaneo.gob.ec) is housed in a colossal neo-colonial structure; once a military hospital, today it hosts

> **SIX SCENIC VIEWS OF QUITO**
>
> Quito's stunning location in a valley surrounded by volcanoes means you are spoilt for choice for the finest views of the city. Here are six of the best. All are most easily accessed by taxi (La Basílica can be reached on foot from Plaza Grande).
> 1. El Teleférico, Volcán Pichincha
> 2. El Panecillo, Old Town
> 3. La Basílica, Old Town
> 4. Parque Itchimbía, Old Town
> 5. Guápulo, centre-north
> 6. Parque Metropolitano, Northeast

6

impressive contemporary art and sculpture (as well as performing arts, including gigs). Well-briefed art students (most speak good English) guide you around the exhibits.

Itchimbía Park and Cultural Centre

Perched high on a hill east of the Old Town, the glass-and-steel **Cultural Centre** inside the park hosts occasional exhibitions, but the main draw is the view and a chance to escape the city on footpaths winding through the extensive natural landscape. A taxi from the Old Town costs $2–3.

La Casa de la Cultura

To the northeast of Parque El Ejido, the modern oval building of **La Casa de la Cultura** (Patria between 6 de Diciembre and 12 de Octubre; ☎02 222 0967, ⓦcasadelacultura.gob.ec) contains cinemas, theatres, auditoriums and the **Museo Nacional** (closed for renovation), which when it reopens will showcase an astonishing collection of pre-Columbian, colonial, early republican and modern art.

Museo Fundación Guayasamín and the Capilla del Hombre

Oswaldo Guayasamín is Ecuador's most famous modern artist, and Quito's Bellavista district, where he used to live, houses two collections of his art (both Tues–Sun 10am–5.30pm; $8 ticket includes brief guided tour and entrance to both sites). The **Museo Fundación Guayasamín** (Mariano Calvache E18-94; ⓦguayasamin.org) exhibits many paintings as well as his enormous collection of pre-Columbian ceramics and colonial religious art. This landmark building, which has a café, was designed by Guayasamín's son. A further ten-minute walk up the hill is the even more impressive **Capilla del Hombre** (Lorenzo Chávez EA18-143; ⓦcapilladelhombre. com), one of South America's most important works of art. This was Guayasamín's final great project, initiated in his last years and not fully completed until after his death in 1999. From the museum you can walk up to the garden of Guayasamín. Just up from the Capilla del Hombre is the **Parque Metropolitano**,

Quito's largest park, with forested trails, picnic areas and sweeping views. There are occasional buses up to Bellavista but it's best to take a taxi ($2).

Parque Carolina

Quito's modern mid-town central park is **Parque Carolina**. This is where locals come to walk and play sports. The park contains a beautiful set of **Botanical Gardens** (Tues–Sun 8am–4.45pm; $3), which showcases Ecuador's array of flowers and trees, including more than five hundred orchid species. Check out the excellent farmers' market next door if you're here on a Sunday (8am–2pm) and the **Vivarium** (Tues–Sun 9.30am–5.30pm; $3), which features reptiles including caimans, turtles and snakes. Across the park, the **Museo de Ciencias Naturales** (Mon–Fri 8.30am–1pm & 1.45–4.45pm; $2) has a huge collection of dead insects and arachnids.

Guápulo

On an eastern slope of the centre-north, this pretty neighbourhood is a world away from downtown. With steep cobbled streets, historic houses and pleasant cafés, it's a relaxing place with squares and a major park. The focal point is the beautiful seventeenth-century Iglésia de Guápulo, a jewel box of Baroque colonial sculpture.

The Teleférico

Quito's most dizzying tourist attraction is the **Teleférico** (daily 8am–8pm; $8.50; ⓦteleferico.com.ec), a cable car ride high above the city. The main attraction is the twenty-minute ride up to 4100m, from where the views are stunning (on a clear day). At the top, take in the views, relax in the café or tackle the hike to Rucu Pichincha, 3km away (do not attempt this walk alone as robberies have been reported). Bring warm clothes and take care not to over-exert yourself at this altitude. Teleférico shuttles run from Rio Coca, at 6 Diciembre (Ecovía) and Estación Norte (Trole); or take a taxi ($3.50).

ARRIVAL AND DEPARTURE

By plane Aeropuerto Internacional Mariscal Sucre (☎02 395 4200, ⓦaeropuertoquito.aero) is 38km northwest of the centre. The airport has regular flights to North America, Central America and other South American cities, plus a daily flight or two to Europe. The journey to/from Quito (45–100min) costs $25–30 by taxi. Shuttle buses (every 30min; $8) connect it to old airport terminal on Av Amazonas, where there's a taxi rank. Cheap but slower local buses are also available for $2, heading to Quitumbe bus terminal (and also Río Coco in the centre-north of the city, but the latter is not considered a secure area).

By train Trains from Quito leave from Chimbacalle station, 2km south of the old town, which can be reached on the trolleybus or via a taxi from La Mariscal District ($4–5). These trains are leisure excursions not run as regular passenger services; advanced booking is advised, as services are popular. One route (Fri–Sun 8am–5.30pm) passes through Machachi and Boliche before returning to Quito; see W trenecuador.com.

By bus Quito has three main bus terminals. All destinations from the south, including the coast and jungle, use the largest terminal, Quitumbe, in the far south of Quito. It's complicated, involves changes and takes over an hour to reach central Quito by trolleybus, so consider a taxi (around $10). From Otavalo and the northern highlands, you arrive at Carcelén terminal, at the northern end of the Metrobus line. From Mindo, you arrive at Ofelia in the far north on the Metrobus line. It takes an hour to get to the centre from these stations by Metrobus or taxi ($7–9).

Destinations from Quitumbe Ambato (hourly; 2hr 30min); Atacames (daily; 7hr); Baños (hourly; 3hr); Coca (daily; 9hr); Cuenca (hourly; 10hr); Guaranda (daily; 5hr); Guayaquil (hourly; 8hr); Lago Agrio (daily; 8hr); Latacunga (hourly; 1hr 45min); Riobamba (hourly; 4hr); Santo Domingo (hourly; 3hr); Tena (hourly; 5hr).

Destinations from Carcelén Norte Atacames (6 daily; 7hr); Esmeraldas (8 daily; 6hr); Ibarra (hourly; 2hr 30min); Los Bancos (indirect to Mindo, daily; 2hr); Otavalo (every 45min; 2hr); Tulcán (hourly; 5hr).

Destinations from Ofelia Cayambe (hourly; 1hr 30min); Mindo (direct, daily; 2hr); Mitad del Mundo (via Metrobus line, hourly; 1hr).

By van Door-to-door van services include Taxi Lagos (Otavalo and Ibarra $12; ☎02 256 5992); Guaytambos, (Ambato $12; Riobamba, $15; ☎098 710 0679); Grey (Guayaquil, $30; ☎098 402 8211).

GETTING AROUND

By bus These cost only $0.25 per trip and while hit and miss are useful for travelling short distances up main avenues such as 12 de Octubre, 6 de Diciembre, 10 de Agosto, and Colón.

By electric bus There are three main electric bus routes running north to south, with designated stations and car-free lanes, making them the most efficient way to get around. All charge $0.25 flat fare (bought at kiosks or machines in advance). The three services rarely link up, so changing routes often involves walking several blocks. They generally run every 10min Mon–Fri 6am–midnight, Sat & Sun 6am–10pm. El Trole is the trolleybus system that runs down 10 de Agosto to the Old Town; stops are easy to spot because of their distinctive green raised platforms. In the Old Town buses travel south along Guayaquil and return north on Flores and Montúfar. Ecovía are buses that run mainly along 6 de Diciembre from Río Coca in the north to Plaza la Marín in the Old Town. Metrobus runs from Carcelén bus terminal down Avenida América to Universidad Central. Pickpocketing is a chronic problem on Quito's trolleybuses so be vigilant and don't carry valuables.

By car Rental companies with offices outside the international terminal of the airport include Avis (☎02 244 0270; avis.com.ec) and Hertz (☎02 225 4258; hertzecuador. com.ec).

By taxi Taxi are very convenient, inexpensive and recommended at night. Check that the meter is reset when you get in. From the Old Town to La Mariscal is only $2–3. Fares increase at night, when most drivers don't use the meter (in which case, agree the price beforehand). Most hoteliers and bars have numbers of trusted companies. Reliable 24hr services include Central Radio Taxis (☎02 250 0600) and Teletaxi (☎02 222 2222). App cabs including Easy Taxi and Uber cost less than conventional taxis and work well in Quito.

INFORMATION

Tourist information The Quito Visitors Bureau (W quito. com.ec) has several offices in the city with brochures, maps and information on Ecuador. The main office is on the east side of Plaza Grande (Mon–Fri 9am–6pm, Sat 9am–8pm, Sun 9am–5pm; ☎02 257 2445); other offices are in the Casa de La Cultura Ecuatoriana (6 de Diciembre, at Patria; Mon–Fri 9am–5pm, Sat & Sun 10am–4pm; ☎02 222 1116) and in La Mariscal (Reina Victoria, at Luis Cordero; ☎02 255 1566).

ACCOMMODATION

Many visitors stay in La Mariscal in the centre-north, which is geared up for tourists with a wide selection of hostels and hotels, restaurants, bars and tour operators. The area gets noisy on weekends and until recently was considered somewhat dodgy at night, but increased security has really improved things. Quieter alternatives include La Floresta and the Centro Histórico.

CENTRE-NORTH

Hostal El Arupo Juan Rodríguez E7-22, at Reina Victoria ☎02 255 7423, W hostalelarupo.com; map p.576. A renovated family-run place with TV lounge and brightly painted rooms (singles are $27.50). Free storage, and breakfast is included. **$49**

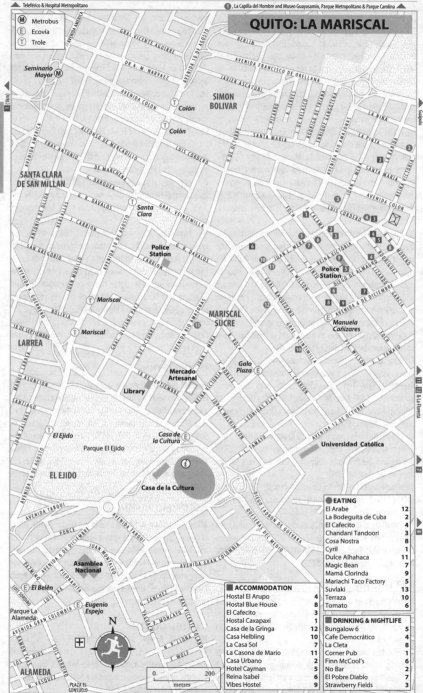

Teleférico & Hospital Metropolitano

La Capilla del Hombre and Museo Guayasamin, Parque Metropolitano & Parque Carolina

QUITO: LA MARISCAL

M Metrobus
E Ecovía
T Trole

Seminario Mayor

SIMON BOLIVAR

Colón

Colón

SANTA CLARA DE SAN MILLAN

Santa Clara

Police Station

Mariscal

Mariscal

MARISCAL SUCRE

Police Station

LARREA

Manuela Cañizares

Galo Plaza

Mercado Artesanal

Library

El Ejido

Parque El Ejido

Casa de la Cultura

Universidad Católica

EL EJIDO

Casa de la Cultura

Asamblea Nacional

El Belén

Eugenio Espejo

Parque La Alameda

ALAMEDA

N

0	200
metres	

● EATING

El Arabe	12
La Bodeguita de Cuba	2
El Cafecito	4
Chandani Tandoori	3
Cosa Nostra	8
Cyril	1
Dulce Alhahaca	11
Magic Bean	7
Mamá Clorinda	9
Mariachi Taco Factory	5
Suvlaki	13
Terraza	10
Tomato	6

■ ACCOMMODATION

Hostal El Arupo	4
Hostal Blue House	8
El Cafecito	3
Hostal Caxapaxi	1
Casa de la Gringa	12
Casa Helbling	10
La Casa Sol	7
La Casona de Mario	11
Casa Urbano	2
Hotel Cayman	5
Reina Isabel	6
Vibes Hostel	9

■ DRINKING & NIGHTLIFE

Bungalow 6	5
Cafe Democrático	4
La Cleta	8
Corner Pub	1
Finn McCool's	6
No Bar	2
El Pobre Diablo	7
Strawberry Fields	3

Hostal Blue House Pinto, at Diego de Almagro ☎02 222 3480, ⓦbluehousequito.com; map p.576. In the thick of things, this popular, cheap backpacker hostel has a kitchen, bar with pool table and is a good place to meet others and socialize. Dorms $\overline{\underline{\$7}}$, doubles $\overline{\underline{\$25}}$

El Cafecito Luís Cordero 1124 ☎02 223 0922, ⓦelcafecitohostel.wixsite.com; map p.576. On the northern fringes of Mariscal, this hostel has lots of charm with vintage furnishings and the ground floor café-resto is a great place to chill. Dorms $\overline{\underline{\$10}}$, doubles $\overline{\underline{\$25}}$

Hostal Caxapaxi Pasaje Navarro 364, ☎02 254 2663, ⓦhostal-casapaxi.com; map p.576. On the west side of the city, 3km from Mariscal, this excellent, inexpensive guesthouse has lots of character with high-beamed ceilings, artwork and a guests' kitchen. Breakfast included. $\overline{\underline{\$18}}$

Casa de la Gringa Guipuzcoa E16-55 ☎02 223 7298, ⓦhostal.lacasadelagringa.com; map p.576. If La Mariscal is not for you, stay in the quieter neighbourhood of La Floresta. A small and welcoming budget place run by a hospitable couple in a traditional house with just three rooms. Cafés and restaurants are close by, and the Old Town is $2.50 in a taxi. $\overline{\underline{\$22}}$

Casa Helbling Vientimilla E8-152 ☎02 222 6013, ⓦcasahelbling.de; map p.576. A well set up Swiss/ Ecuadorian-owned place with excellent service that has a guests' lounge with fireplace and a small library, sun terraces, kitchen, laundry room and café (breakfasts from $3.80). $\overline{\underline{\$33}}$

La Casa Sol Calama 127 ☎02 223 0798, ⓦlacasasol. com; map p.576. Decorated in warm colours and featuring traditional Andean textiles this guesthouse has a cosy feel. An excellent breakfast is included. $\overline{\underline{\$55}}$

La Casona de Mario Andalucia 213, at Galicia ☎02 254 4036, ⓦcasonademario.com; map p.576. This welcoming home away from home in La Floresta, run by an Argentine, has a communal kitchen and comfortable lounge area. $\overline{\underline{\$24}}$

★ **Casa Urbano** La Rábida N26-25 ☎02 222 9964, ⓦcasaurbanahostal.com; map p.576. This fine new hostel, in a historic structure, has an artistic feel and a choice of dorms (mixed or female) and private rooms (with shared bathrooms). Expect reliable hot showers, good cleanliness and comfort, a handy location and fine roof terrace. Dorms $\overline{\underline{\$13}}$, doubles $\overline{\underline{\$35}}$

Hotel Cayman Juan Rodríguez 270, at Reina Victoria ☎02 256 7616, ⓦhotelcaymanquito.com; map p.576. Attractive renovated old house with a large leafy garden, quiet location and good restaurant. Most rooms are light and airy, and simply but quite stylishly presented. Free breakfast. $\overline{\underline{\$57}}$

Vibes Hostel Joaquín Pinto 132 ☎02 255 5154; ⓦvibesquito.com/hostel; map p.576. Very popular with young travellers, this hostel is a good base for those in search of a social vibe as it has a bar-café and is right by

★ **TREAT YOURSELF**

Reina Isabel ☎02 255 5156, ⓦhotelreinaisabel. com; map p.576. If you're just off a long flight, this modern midrange hotel makes a comfortable first base, with inviting, very spacious rooms (bathrooms are dated though have tubs), a first-class gym and superb complimentary breakfast. Located on the fringe of La Mariscal. $\overline{\underline{\$82}}$

Plaza Foch. It's also a key hangout for volunteer workers in Quito. Dorms $\overline{\underline{\$8}}$

OLD TOWN

★ **Community Hostel** Pedro Fermín Cevallos N6-78, across from the Mercado Central ☎09 5904 9658, ⓦcommunityhostel.com; map p.572. With free yoga classes, a strong social ethos, communal feel and well-presented and -kept accommodation, this Old Town option is an excellent choice. Dorms $\overline{\underline{\$9}}$, doubles $\overline{\underline{\$25}}$

La Guayunga Antepara E4-27 ☎02 228 8544, ⓦguayunga.com; map p.572. Cheery family-run hostel in the central La Tola neighbourhood, with gorgeous views of the centre from the glass-topped rooftop terrace. Dorms range from three to twelve beds. Dorms $\overline{\underline{\$10}}$, doubles $\overline{\underline{\$35}}$

Minka Matovelle 219 ☎02 255 3953, ⓦminkahostel. com; map p.572. Well-run hostel that boasts a great café-lounge with pool table for hanging out, drinks and meals. Near the basilica, so very convenient. Dorms $\overline{\underline{\$10}}$, doubles $\overline{\underline{\$30}}$

La Real Audiencia Bolívar 220, at Guayaquil ☎02 295 0590, ⓦrealaudiencia.com; map p.572. For a classy atmosphere, try this upmarket option with stylish rooms, arty photography and a fabulous view of Plaza Santo Domingo from the restaurant (open to non-guests). Breakfast included. $\overline{\underline{\$76.50}}$

★ **San Francisco de Quito** Sucre 217, at Guayaquil ☎02 228 7758, ⓦsanfranciscodequito.com.ec; map p.572. Fine Old Town option with impressive rooms set around a courtyard, a fountain, rooftop patio and great views. Breakfast included. $\overline{\underline{\$65}}$

Secret Garden Antepara E4-60, at Los Rios ☎099 602 3709, ⓦsecretgardenquito.com; map p.572. Southeast of the Old Town, this is a great Aussie-run budget hostel set on five floors with basic rooms and a rooftop terrace where big breakfasts are served up. Pub crawls and quiz nights mean there's a good social scene. Dorms $\overline{\underline{\$10}}$, doubles $\overline{\underline{\$28}}$

EATING

Quito boasts the best selection of international restaurants in Ecuador – from Asian to Middle Eastern and Mediterranean. Most are in the centre-north, with Old Town eating options restricted. For those on a budget, fill yourself

6

6

up at lunch, as most restaurants offer specials for $2–4. Many places are closed Sunday evenings.

CENTRE-NORTH

El Arabe Reina Victoria 627 between Veintimilla and Carrión ☎ 02 254 9414; map p.576. Authentic kebabs, falafel, salads and flatbreads. Mon–Sat 11am–10pm, Sun 11am–5pm.

La Bodeguita de Cuba Reina Victoria N26-105; map p.576. Cuban specialities here include *ropa vieja* (shredded, slow-cooked meat) and there's live Latin music some nights, when drinking and dancing continues into the early hours. Mon, Tues & Sun noon–10pm, Wed & Thurs noon–midnight, Fri & Sat noon–2am.

El Cafecito Luís Cordero 1124 ; map p.576. Highly atmospheric café, with vintage decor, front terrace and a boho vibe. Serves fine espresso, breakfasts, soups, home-made cakes, crêpes and vegetarian meals ($3–5). Daily 8am–11pm.

Chandani Tandoori Juan León Mera, at Luis Cordero; map p.576. Offers authentic Indian food at low prices. Masala, korma, dupiaza, balti and hot vindaloo – all the classics are done well for only $3–6. Daily 9am–9.30pm.

Cosa Nostra Moreno, at Diego de Almagro; map p.576. Italian-owned restaurant with some of the best pizzas in town ($6–18) and good pasta made with imported ingredients; there are two other branches in Quito. Tues–Sun 12.30–3pm & 6.30–10.30pm.

Dulce Alhahaca Juan Leon Mera N23-66; p.576. This cool café-bar-health food store makes a modish setting for a nutritious meal, with a good choice of vegan and veggie dishes including wholesome soups and creative salads. Ingredients, including organic produce, are sourced locally. Mon–Fri 9am–9pm, Sat & Sun 10am–7pm.

Magic Bean Foch, at Juan León Mera ⓦ magicbeanquito. com; map p.576. Reliable, long-running café on a busy corner plot popular for breakfasts, paninis, pancakes and grilled meats (try the rosemary chicken kebabs); most mains are $8–14). Café branch also at Portugal E9-106. Daily 8am–10pm.

Mamá Clorinda Reina Victoria 1144; ⓦ mamaclorinda. webs.com; map p.576. Well-prepared if pricey

---

Ecuadorian specialities including guinea pig (*cuy*) and cow foot soup (caldo de patas); mains are $10–15. Mon–Sat 11am–10pm.

Mariachi Taco Factory Foch, at Juan León Mera; map p.576. Lively Mexican place serving up a decent selection of tacos, burritos, chimichangas and the like for $6–9, and the colour scheme, Mexican blanket tablecloths and decor adds ambience. Daily noon–11pm.

Suvlaki Av Río Amazonas, at Robles; map p.576. A casual place serving trad Greek favourites including moussaka, salads and a wide choice of souvlaki ($2.50–8). Espresso coffee is inexpensive and packs a punch. Mon–Sat 8.30am–7.30pm.

Terraza Juan León Mera, map p.576. An unpretentious place that's wildly popular with local office workers and students at lunchtime for its filling, flavoursome three-course set menus ($2.50). Mon–Sat noon–3pm & 7–9pm.

Tomato Juan León Mera, at Calama; map p.576. A casual spot good for inexpensive pizza ($5–8) and pasta; try the *calzone*. Daily 9–3.30pm & 5–midnight.

OLD TOWN

Caffeto Chile, at Guayaquil; map 572. At the entrance to San Agustín Monastery, this café serves good breakfasts, *tamales*, *empanadas*, soups and cakes for $3–6. Mon–Sat 7.30am–10pm, Sun 7.30am–2pm.

Las Corvinas de Don Jimmy Mercado Central, Esmeraldas; map p.572. On the second floor of the central market, this ever-popular food stand serves up dishes such as *corvina* fish and great *ceviche* (a full meal is around $5). Grab a fresh juice from one of the neighbouring stalls and you're set. Daily 9am–3pm.

Crustum 2850 Mejía; map 572. On the pretty square of Plaza San Agustín, this attractive café serves "slow food" with an Ecuadorian twist (from $8) and great sandwiches from bread baked on the premises. Daily 8am–9.30pm

★ **La Cuchara de San Marcos** Junín E3-121 ⓦ lacucharadesanmarcos.blogspot.co.uk; map p.572. Occupying the upstairs and courtyard of a large old-town house, this veggie restaurant features flavoursome meals (around $8) and craft beers. Try the handmade organic chocolate. Tues–Sat noon–10pm, Sun 11am–5pm.

Frutería Montserrate Espejo Oe2-12; map p.572. Famous for its great fruit salads, which locals devour with ice cream ($2–5). Cheap *almuerzos* and sandwiches also available. Mon–Sat 7am–7.30pm, Sun 9am–3pm.

Govindas Esmeraldas 853; map p.572. A reliable vegetarian option in the Old Town offering healthy breakfasts and a $3 set lunch. Mains $2–4. Mon–Sat 9am–3pm.

La Guaragua Espejo Oe2-40; map p.572. A traditional place that's worth trying for Ecuadorian dishes like *seco de pollo* (chicken stew) and great-value set lunches ($3). Mon–Sat 11.30am–7pm.

Tianguez Plaza de San Francisco; map p.572. This restaurant enjoys a perfect setting, with a large terrace facing a historic square. It's a little pricey (meals around $12–16), and perhaps a little touristy, but the Ecuadorian dishes, including specialities from the Andes, coast and Amazon are well prepared. There's often live music in the evenings and it's also home to a huge craft store. Mon & Tues 9.30am–6pm, Wed–Sun 9.30am–11.30pm.

DRINKING AND NIGHTLIFE

MODERN QUITO

La Mariscal has a vibrant nightlife and gets packed Thursday to Saturday evenings. Plaza Foch, and the lanes around the square, are the hub of the action. Bars are busy from 7pm onwards with the clubs filling up towards midnight and winding down around 3am. La Mariscal is well policed around Plaza Foch but it's probably best to avoid dark side roads late at night and take a taxi home.

Bungalow 6 Calama, at Diego Almagro; w bungalow6ecuador.com; map.576. DJs spin EDM and chart sounds in this busy bar-club, which draws a good mix of locals and tourists. Wednesday is Ladies Night, Thursday is Latin night. Entrance is free for girls, guys pay $5 including one drink on weekends. Wed–Sat 8pm–2am.

Cafe Democrático, Lizardo García, w cafedemocratico. wordpress.com; map p.576. Always lively, this buzzing venue hosts live gigs (from funk bands to indie acts) and club nights with house and electro DJs. There's a second branch at the Centro de Arte Contemporáneo. Tues–Sat 6pm–2.30am.

★ **La Cleta** Lugo N24-250, at Guipuzcoa; map p.576. Bicycle-themed bar with outdoor terrace in La Floresta. They've a fine selection of craft beers and serve good stone-baked pizzas. Mon–Sat 11.30–11pm.

Corner Pub Amazonas, at Calama; map p.576. A small bar on the corner of La Mariscal's main drag, popular with expats and locals alike. Mon–Wed 3pm–midnight, Fri & Sat noon–midnight.

Finn McCool's Almagro, at Pinto; w irishpubquito. com; map p.576. Popular expat pub, with draught beer,

---

ACTIVITIES IN AND AROUND QUITO

City tours are offered by several outfits, with options including walking (some are free), cycling (from $15) and motorcycling tours (self-drive $40). And, after a few days of sightseeing and acclimatization, you will be ready to take advantage of the huge range of activities in the mountains near the city. The most popular one-day tours are cycling and horseriding. For **cycling**, Cotopaxi National Park and Ilinizas are firm favourites (average cost $70/day). There are numerous locations south of Quito offering **horseriding** (average cost $55/day). For **rafting and kayaking**, day tours in valleys north and west of Quito cost $70–90. The most popular **trekking** route is around Lake Quilotoa (see page 591). One- and two-day tours can be booked from Quito. If you fancy **climbing**, the easier peaks include Pasochoa (4199m), El Corazón (4788m) and the more challenging Iliniza Norte (5126m). All cost around $70 for a one-day tour. Cotopaxi (5897m), Cayambe (5790m), Antisana (5755m) and Chimborazo (6310m) are tough and can all be climbed by well-prepared, fit people on two-day tours (from $180).

TOUR OPERATORS

Alta Montaña Jorge Washington 8–20 ☎02 255 8380, w climbing-ecuador.com. High-summit climbing and trekking trips.

Biking Dutchman La Pinta E731☎02 254 2806, w bikingdutchman.com. Mountain-biking tours.

Ecuadorian Alpine Institute Ramírez Dávalos 136, at Amazonas ☎02 256 5465, w volcanoclimbing. com. Top-class climbing tours; also trekking and biking.

Enchanted Expeditions De las Alondras N45–102, at Los Lirios ☎023340525, w enchantedexpeditions. com. Specialists in Galápagos yachts and haciendas in the highlands.

★ **Freedom Bikes, C Finlandia N35-06,** ☎02 600 4459, w freedombikerental.com. Self-guided motorbike trips (using GPS devices) and superb cross-country guided tours on motorbikes and 4WDs.

Free Walking Tour Contact Community Hostel, Pedro Fermin Cevallos N6-78, ☎02 228 5108, w freewalkingtourecuador.com. Informative, free 3hr city walking tours; be sure to tip!

Gulliver JL Mera, at Calama ☎02 252 9297, w gulliver.com.ec. Climbing, hiking, biking and jungle tours as well as Galápagos visits.

★ **Royal Galapagos** Sonelsa Tower, 265 Foch, at 6 de Diciembre ☎02 602 4568 w royalgalapagos.com. A range of high-quality Galápagos trips on fine boats led by expert naturalists.

Surtrek Reina Victoria N24–151 ☎02 255 3658, w surtrek-adventures.com. Quality tours throughout Ecuador including hiking, biking, and birdwatching.

Yacu Amu Amazonas N25-23, at Colon ☎02 255 0558, w yacuamu.com. White-water rafting and kayaking specialist.

6

pool, quiz nights, movie nights and live TV sport coverage including football, rugby and NFL. Mon–Wed noon–1am, Thurs–Sat 11am–3am, Sun 11am–7pm.

No Bar Calama 380; map p.576. Raucous Mariscal disco with a large dancefloor, themed nights and good drinks promos. No cover charge before 11pm, entrance $5 including one drink) after. Wed–Sat 8pm–3am.

El Pobre Diablo Isabel La Católica, at Galavis ⓦelpobrediablo.com; map p.576. Bohemian hangout in La Florista that draws an older crowd. There's a good restaurant, live music (jazz, Latin, acoustic) and art exhibitions. Mon & Tues 12.30–3pm & 6.30pm–midnight, Wed–Sat 12.30–3pm & 6.30pm–1.30am.

Strawberry Fields González Suárez ⓦstrawberryf.bar; map p.576. Dedicated to the Fab Four, this upscale bar is brimming with Beatles memorabilia. You'll find a classic rock playlist and casual bites. Tues–Thurs 6pm–midnight, Fri & Sat 6pm–2am.

OLD TOWN

★ **Bandido Brewery** Olmedo E1-136 ⓦbandidobrewing.com; map p.572. Microbrewery extraordinaire, with seven craft beers on tap, right across from the Mercado Central. Expect a warm atmosphere, pizzas and tacos in historic premises, which contain a chapel. Pints are $3 in happy hour (weekdays 4–7pm). Mon–Fri 4–11pm, Sat 2–11pm.

DIRECTORY

Banks and exchange There are ample banks and ATMs, most open Mon–Fri 8.30am–4pm and Sat am. Try Banco de Guayaquil, Reina Victoria, at Colón, or Banco del Pacífico, 12 de Octubre, at Cordero.

Books The English Bookshop, Venezuela at Manabi (daily 10am–6.30pm) is the best place to buy, sell or borrow fiction and travel books. Confederate Books Amazonas N24-155 at Mariscal Foch (Mon–Sat 10am–6pm) is very good for secondhand books.

Embassies and consulates Canada, Amazonas 4153, Edificio Eurocenter (ⓣ02 245 5499, ⓦcanadainternational.gc.ca); Colombia, 12 de Octubre N24-528 World Trade Centre Torre B (ⓣ02 222 2486, ⓦ.ecuador.embajada.gov.co); Peru, República de El Salvador 495, at Irlanda (ⓣ02 246 8410, ⓦconsulado.pe); UK, Naciones Unidas, at República de El Salvador, Edificio Citiplaza, 14th floor (ⓣ02 297 0801, ⓦukinecuador.fco.gov.uk); US, Avigiras E12-170 (ⓣ02 398 5000, ⓦecuador.usembassy.gov).

Hospital Hospital Metropolitano, Av Mariana de Jesús, at Av Occidental ⓣ02 226 1520, emergency and ambulance ⓣ02 226 5020, ⓦhospitalmetropolitano.org.

Police Tourist Police at Reina Victoria, at Roca ⓣ02 254 3983.

Post offices Reina Victoria, at Colón (Mon–Fri 8am–7pm, Sat & Sun 8am–noon; ⓣ02 250 8890).

Shopping Mercado Artesanal (Juan León Mera, at Jorge Washington, La Mariscal), weekend market at Parque El Ejido, and Mercado Ipiales (Chile, at Imbabura, Old Town).

QUITO EXCURSIONS

Visitors can reach many attractive sites within a few hours from central Quito: Papallacta, Mindo and Cotopaxi are all less than three hours from the city.

Pululahua and Mitad del Mundo

Best visited early mornings for spectacular views, the extinct volcanic crater of **Pululahua** forms a 32-square-kilometre nature reserve, with small farms at the bottom, making this one of the very few inhabited craters on the planet. Excellent for hiking, biking or horseriding, it takes about three hours for the steep climb down and back from the most easily accessible scenic overlook on its east side. Near the rim, the **Museo Templo del Sol** (daily 9am–6pm; $3), a museum of contemporary indigenous art is housed in a massive stone building reminiscent of Inca and medieval fortresses. The temple doubles as a holistic centre selling essential oils, coco leaf tea and the like too. There are no direct buses from Quito; local buses along the highway connect Pululahua with the touristy **Mitad del Mundo** ("The Middle of the World"; daily 9am–6pm; $3, ⓦmitaddelmundo.com). Its 30m-high equator **monument** (entrance $3.50), topped by a brass globe, can be climbed and also includes an **Ethnographic Museum**. There are various other small exhibitions dotted around the complex, the highlight being the France building with a good exhibition on the measurement of the equator by Charles Marie de La Condamine. Although everybody wants to get a photo straddling the equator in front of the monument, this is not actually the real equator, which lies approximately 300m along the main road to the east at the **Museo Solar Inti Ñan** (daily 9.30am–5pm; $4; ⓦmuseointinan.com.ec). Here you use experiments to prove you are standing on the equator (though

Ecuador's best equatorial site is Quitsato near Cayambe). It's worth taking a short taxi ride to the nearby fifteenth-century ruins of the small Inca fortress of **Rumicucho**, overlooking the Guayllabamba River as it heads north.

To get to Mitad del Mundo, take the Metrobus on Avenida America north to the Ofelia terminal and then a green Mitad del Mundo **bus** ($0.50). The trip from north-central Quito takes about an hour. Numerous tours from Quito also drop by the attraction.

Volcán Pichincha

Two summits crown the active **Volcán Pichincha** overlooking Quito. **Rucu**, meaning Elder in Kichwa, and **Guagua** (baby) make good hikes, but each has its problems (both are over 4700m). Rucu, which is easily accessed from the top of the *Teleférico*, has suffered from muggings, but a beefed-up police presence on the trail has improved security. Guagua is badly behaved and a violent eruption showered Quito in ash in 1999. It's still officially active and harder to climb. Ask at a tour operator in Quito for the latest situation.

Papallacta

About 65km (2hr) from Quito, the road to Lago Agrio and Tena passes through the high-altitude (3300m) village of **Papallacta**, home to the best thermal baths in Ecuador. The entrance to **Las Termas de Papallacta** (daily 6am–10.30pm; $8.50; ☎02 232 0040, ⚲termaspapallacta.com) is a thirty-minute walk up a dirt road, so consider a $2 taxi. The complex is impressive, with 25 baths of different temperatures, spa and (very pricey) wooden cabins. On clear days there are great views of snowcapped Volcán Artisana. Avoid weekends if possible.

ACCOMMODATION

Hostal Coturpa ☎06 289 5000, ⚲hostalcoturpa.com. Don't let the ugly concrete exterior put you off: this place has a cosy wooden interior and is run by a gracious couple. Breakfast included. Singles $22, doubles $30, with jacuzzi $56

The Northern Highlands and Western Andean slopes

North of Quito lie two dramatically different regions. To the northwest are verdant **cloudforests**, filled with birdlife. The small town of **Mindo** is the best base to explore the forest's biodiversity and indulge in adrenaline-pumping adventure sports. To the north, magnificent Andean scenery populated by vibrant indigenous cultures extends to the Colombian border. The most popular destination is **Otavalo**, whose colourful Saturday market is one of the largest in South America and heaven for lovers of indigenous crafts and clothing. Some 30km from here is the stately Ciudad Blanca, **Ibarra**, the largest city in the region. Between Ibarra and **Tulcán** on the border with Colombia are Afro-Ecuadorian villages and **Páramo del Ángel**, an extraordinary, otherworldly landscape.

MINDO

Snuggled in a cloudforest at a pleasant elevation of 1200m, the overgrown village of **MINDO** is a wonderfully relaxing destination. Its pint-sized high street, lined with traditional stores and cafés, has a pleasingly rustic character while the evergreen hills around town are home to over 400 species of birds, gushing rivers perfect for tubing, zip-lines, hiking trails and waterfalls. Many attractions are a one- or two-hour walk from town; to save time, share a taxi for $5–10.

Mariposas de Mindo

The dirt road leading south out of town forks after about 1km. To the left, 2.5km from Mindo's centre, is the butterfly farm **Mariposas de Mindo** (daily 9am–5pm; $7.50; ⚲mariposasdemindo.com), which breeds 25 species, including the Brown Owl Eye and the Peleides Blue Morpho, the latter with a wingspan of 20cm. Come in the early morning and you may be lucky and see them hatch.

Mindo Canopy Adventure
If you take a right when the dirt road out of town forks you reach **Mindo Canopy Adventure** ($10; ☎098 542 8758, ⓦmindocanopy.com); 2.8km from central Mindo. Adrenaline lovers can get their fix by zinging along cables from 20m to 400m in length, high above the forest, either solo or accompanied by a guide. The thirteen-line circuit takes about one hour thirty minutes ($20), or do three lines for $8.

Continuing about 1km up the hill is a more relaxed way to traverse the treetops.

La Tarabita cable car ($3/person) cruises 150m above a densely forested river valley. On the other side are trails to seven waterfalls. The paths are confusing in places but you can't really get lost as there is only one exit – wear boots as it's muddy. The entire circuit takes two hours and goes deep inside the cloudforest; hiring a birdwatching guide is a great way to learn more. Most charge $50/half-day and $100/full-day.

Tubing and canyoning
For adventure-sports lovers, there's plenty in Mindo. Many tour companies offer **tubing** (from $8 for a couple of hours including transport) and **canyoning** is also available (around $55/full-day).

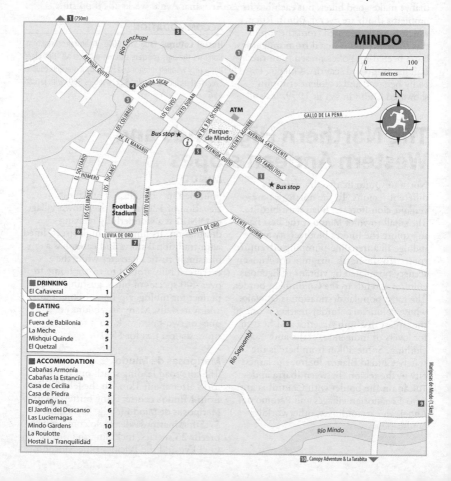

MINDO

Birdwatching

There's excellent birding all around the Mindo region, though many private reserves are costly. At *El Jardín del Descanso* (see page 583) owner Rodney Garrido will enthusiastically point out the birds (including tangaras, toucans, mot-mots and many types of hummingbird) which frequent his hotel garden for $3/person.

ARRIVAL AND DEPARTURE

By bus Cooperativa Flor del Valle (☎02 252 7495, ⓦflordelvalle.com.ec) runs buses from Quito's Ofelia bus station (daily 8am, 9am, 11am, 1pm & 4pm, returning 6.30am, 11am, 1.45pm, 3pm & 5pm; Sat & Sun more frequent; 2hr). If you miss the morning bus from Quito, go to Carcelén terminal and take any bus heading to Los Bancos and ask the driver to let you off at the turn-off to Mindo, from where taxis cost $2 or so).

INFORMATION AND TOURS

Information The helpful Centro de Información is on the main drag, Av Quito (Wed–Sun 8.30am–12.30pm & 1.30–5pm). It has lists of recommended guides.

Tours Recommended tour operators include *La Isla Mindo* (☎0993 272190, ⓦlaislamindo.com) and *Mindo Bird* (☎0 987 597806, ⓦmindobirdtours.com), both on Av Quito.

ACCOMMODATION

Mindo has a wide selection of accommodation but it's more enjoyable to stay in one of the lodges on the edge of town, surrounded by cloudforest.

Cabañas Armonía Lluvia de Oro ☎0999 435098, ⓦbirdingmindo.com; map p.582. On the outskirts of town, this peaceful place has well-constructed wooden cabins, all with balconies and hammocks, in a shady orchid garden full of hummingbirds. Breakfast included. $28

Cabañas la Estancia ☎099 878 3272; map p.582. Cross the rickety bridge to these spacious cabins, set in landscaped gardens with outdoor restaurant, a swimming pool and even a waterslide. Cabins $20, camping/person $4

Casa de Cecilia End of 9 de Octubre ☎0993 345393, ⓦlacasadececilia.com; map p.582. This popular riverside lodge has inexpensive, if small, rustic cabins and chillout zones. Meals are available. Dorms $10, doubles $22

Casa de Piedra C Julio Goetche ☎02 217 0436, ⓦcasadepiedramindo.com; map p.582. Just off the main drag, this pleasant, affordable place has leafy grounds, pool and a selection of well-presented rooms Dorms $15, doubles $30

Dragonfly Inn Quito, at Sucre ☎02 217 0426, ⓦmindo.biz; map p.582. An impressively built timber lodge with nine atmospheric rooms, some with balconies overlooking

★ **TREAT YOURSELF**

Mindo Gardens ☎099 7223260, ⓦmindogarden.com.ec; map p.582. Set in a private forested reserve, this attractive midrange lodge has brightly coloured cabins located by a river, guests' lounge and pool table. Breakfast included. $87

La Roulotte ☎098 976 4484, ⓦhosterialaroulottemindo.com; map p.582. These gypsy-style wagons with double bunk beds are a quirky option in Mindo. Bread is baked on-site and the restaurant is excellent. It also has a roofed pétanque court, so you can play in the rain. $75

the river and forest. Also home to a good restaurant. Breakfast included. $29

El Jardín del Descanso Los Colibríes ☎099 482 9587; map p.582. Near the southern edge of town owned by birdwatcher Rodney Garrido. The garden here is a mecca for birds and the four rustic rooms are comfortable and well kept. $40

★ **Las Luciernagas** Vía Cunuco ☎02 316 1690, ⓦmindoluciernagas.galeon.com; map p.582. A tranquil retreat 1km northwest of the centre with cute cabins in spacious shady grounds. It's run by Willy, a welcoming owner who really looks after his guests and prepares gut-busting breakfasts. $30

Hostal La Tranquilidad C El Progresso ☎099 947 6512; map p.582. Perfect for those on a tight budget, this little guesthouse has small, neat timber rooms, attentive owners and a guests' kitchen. Book direct for the best rates. $20

EATING

You'll find plenty of restaurants on the main street offering Ecuadorian standards for $5 or so. International dishes, including Mexican and Mediterranean are also available.

El Chef Quito; map p.582. Deservedly one of the busiest places in Mindo and famous for its meat dishes including great *lomo a la piedra* (grilled steak served on a hot stone). Portions are generous and prices moderate (mains $6–10). Mon–Fri 7am–7.30pm.

Fuera de Babilonia 9 de Octubre; map p.582. A rustic restaurant with misshapen tables and a wide-ranging menu (pizza, trout; most dishes $6–9). There's live music at weekends. Daily 7am–7.30pm.

La Meche Quito; map p.582. On the eastern edge of town, this is the best place to fill up on carefully prepared pizza and pasta dishes (most $6–10). Mon–Thurs 8am–9pm, Fri & Sat 8am–10pm, Sun 8am–5pm.

★ **Mishqui Quinde** Aguirre; map p.582. This boho veggie mecca specializes in inexpensive quinoa dishes (burgers, soups and Chinese-style meals); mains are

6

6

$2.75–6. They also serve craft beers and great home-made ice cream. Daily except Tues 11.30am–10pm.
El Quetzal 9 de Octubre, ⓦelquetzaldemindo.com; map p.582. Head to this temple of chocolate for terrific desserts, brownies and fine coffee. Daily 8am–9pm.

DRINKING

Mindo has very little nightlife, but there are a few haunts where bar hounds gather.
El Cañaveral Quito; map p.582. This little bar-resto is a great spot to quaff a beer, with streetside terrace tables and a welcoming vibe. There's live music on some weekend nights. Daily 10am–11pm.

CAYAMBE

Between Quito and Otavalo, the little town of **CAYAMBE** is the centre of Ecuador's important flower industry. It's a quieter base than Otavalo to explore surrounding peaks, notably the eponymous volcano. **Quitsato**, Ecuador's best and most precise equatorial monument, is a $6 round-trip taxi ride away. Cayambe celebrates the festival of Inti Raymi fervently in late June.

ARRIVAL AND DEPARTURE

By bus There are direct buses to Cayambe from Quito's Ofelia terminal (hourly; 1hr 20min) and regular buses from Otavalo (hourly; 30min).

ACCOMMODATION

Hotel La Gran Colombia Av Natalia Jarrín S3-74 ☎02 236 1238. Mid-range comfort just south of the centre; back rooms are quieter. There's a popular restaurant. **$32**
Hostal Cayambe Bolívar 107 ☎02 236 3042. A modern, centrally located place with neat, comfortable and good-value singles, doubles and triples. **$16**

CAYAMBE COCA RESERVE AND VOLCÁN CAYAMBE

Ecuador's second-largest Andean **reserve** ranges in altitude from 600m to 5790m at the top of **Cayambe** itself – the highest point in the world that straddles the equator. It's a tough climb, possibly the most difficult in the country, so is for advanced climbers only. From the mountain refuge it's a seven-hour trek through constantly changing terrain and frequent snowstorms. Contact Alta Montaña in Quito (☎02 252 4422) to arrange a trek. Highlights of the surrounding reserve include more than eighty lakes and 900 species of birds, among them condors and toucans.

OTAVALO

A highland town with a strong indigenous identity, **OTAVALO** is famous for its huge Saturday *artesano* market which draws traders from across the Andes.

WHAT TO SEE AND DO

The Saturday market is concentrated in the Plaza de Ponchos, and there's a terrific range of handicrafts, clothing, hammocks, weavings, carvings, jewellery, ceramics and oddities such as fake shrunken heads. You'll find *Otavaleño* traders are not too pushy, though obviously eager for trade.

During the week the town is quieter but the market remains open. Otavalo's other impressive square, the graceful Parque Central is framed by colonial structures and a good place to mingle with locals.

Otavalo's surroundings are also impressive – the town is nestled between the extinct volcanic peaks of Imbabura and Cotacachi on opposite ends of town. Some 4km out of town is the well-run **Parque Cóndor** (Wed–Sun 9.30am–5pm; $4.50; ☎06 304 9399, ⓦparquecondor. org), which rehabilitates owls, eagles, falcons and condors and has popular raptor- flying demonstrations twice daily.

Located in the remains of 200-year old hacienda on the edge of town, the excellent Museo Viviente Otavalango (Mon–Sat 9am–5pm; ☎06 290 3879; $5; ⓦotavalango. wordpress.com) is dedicated to local craft traditions, particularly textiles, with local weavers demonstrating techniques. There are also regular art exhibitions.

ARRIVAL AND INFORMATION

By bus Buses to Otavalo leave from Quito's Carcelén terminal about every 30min (2hr). There are also services from Ibarra (hourly; 40min). The bus station is on Atahualpa, at Neptali Ordoñez, a couple of blocks northeast of the central Plaza de Ponchos market.
Tourist office For information and maps, try the Cámara de Turismo office (Quiroga, at Modesto Jaramillo; Mon–Fri 8am–1pm & 2–5pm, Sat 8am–4pm; ☎06 292 7230, ⓦotavalo.travel).

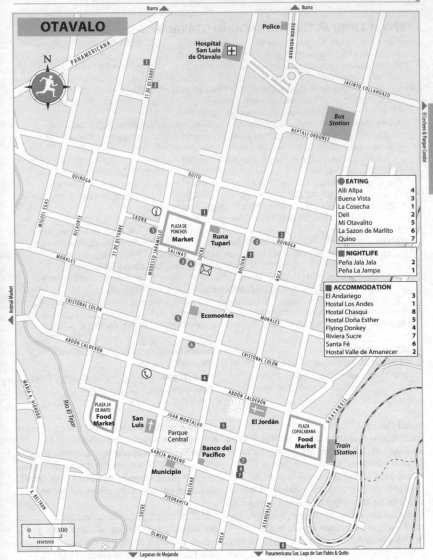

GETTING AROUND

Otavalo is small enough to walk around, but a taxi across town costs just $1 and is recommended at night. Taxis to surrounding attractions like Peguche and Parque El Cóndor cost $3–4.

ACCOMMODATION

Otavalo has a lot of hotels for such a small town, most of which have low weekday occupation rates but fill up at weekends (book ahead for Fri & Sat). The area near the market can be noisy.

★ **El Andariego** Otavalo Bolívar 12-10, at Quiroga ☎099 860 7987; map p.585. A very tastefully presented and welcoming budget place in a convenient location close to the Parque Central. The large, inviting rooms (some with shared bath) have attractive pine furniture and bright bedspreads and there's a kitchen. Dorms $12, doubles $20

Hostal Los Andes Quiroga, at Sucre ☎06 292 1057; map p.585. Overlooking the market, with great views and 25 simply-furnished rooms with private bathrooms. Quads are available. $23

6

SPORTS AND ACTIVITIES AROUND OTAVALO

While most travellers come to Otavalo for a day or two, you could easily fill a week exploring the stunning mountains and valleys that surround it.

The lonely, brooding high Andes terrain around the three **Lagunas de Mojanda**, 16km south of town, offers some of the best hiking and scenery in the region. Well-maintained trails loop around the lakes and up to the peak of **Fuya Fuya** (4275m). There's no public transport here, a round-trip taxi from Otavalo costs $25 (arrange a time for your return); maps are available from many mountain lodges including *La Luna*.

Of the many indigenous communities near Otavalo, the best known is **Peguche**, a five-minute journey by bus (Coop Imbaburapac at the terminal does this route). The town is famed for its weavers and musicians, and for a 20m-high waterfall.

Another popular trip is the stunning **Laguna Cuicocha**, a 3km-wide extinct volcanic crater lake with steep forested islands in the middle. It sits at the foot of Cotacachi Volcano and can be reached by taxi from the leatherworking town of Cotacachi (a 30min bus ride from the Otavalo terminal). Hiking trips to Mojanda and Cuicocha can be organized with tour operators in Otavalo (from $30). Cycling tours (from $45) are also available.

The valleys and rivers around Otavalo offer great adventure-sports opportunities. **Canyoning** is possible in Peguche and in Taxopamba (from $40). There is class III–IV **white-water rafting** in Río Chota, Río Mira and Río Intag (from $40). The best **mountain-biking** tour descends into the Intag Valley to the west ($50). For those well acclimatized and fit, the mountains around Otavalo offer unforgettable climbing. **Imbabura** (4690m; $70) is the easiest climb, **Cotacachi** (4944m; $90) has technical climbing at the summit, and **Cayambe** (5789m; $210) is Ecuador's third-highest peak and takes a minimum of two days.

For a less strenuous excursion, consider the spectacular train ride to Salinas. This route only operates at 8am Friday to Sunday ($53, 10hr) and is organized as a daytrip by Tren Ecuador (Ⓦtrenecuador.com), taking in craft villages en route. The train station is on Calle Guayaquil.

TOUR OPERATORS

All About EQ Los Corazas Av 433, ☎062 923633, Ⓦall-about-ecuador.com.

Ecomontes Juan León Mera N24-91 ☎02 290 3629, Ⓦecomontestour.com.

Runa Tupari Sucre at Quito ☎0999 590646, Ⓦrunatupari.com.

Hostal Chasqui Piedrahita 141 ☎06 292 1826; map p.585. A huge three-storey place with clean, rustically decorated rooms that represent good value. There are fine city vistas from the rooftop and a guests' kitchen. $28

Hostal Doña Esther Montalvo 4-44 ☎06 292 0739, Ⓦotavalohotel.com; map p.585. This small colonial-style hotel has friendly service, a verdant courtyard and a great restaurant with Mediterranean specialities. It's a shade overpriced but does have atmosphere. $58

★ **Flying Donkey** Abdón Calderón 510 ☎06 292 8122, Ⓦflyingdonkeyotavalo.com; map p.585. Spacious, light dorm rooms and, the highlight of this hostel, a rooftop terrace with great views of the town and surrounding mountains. There's a kitchen and the location is very convenient. Dorms $10, doubles $22

Riviera Sucre Roca, at Garcia Moreno ☎06 292 0241, Ⓦrivierasucre.com; map p.585. Rooms here boast plenty of character thanks to attention to detail (exposed stone walls, highland blankets and art) and there's a relaxing lounge area and beautiful garden. $40

Santa Fé 1 Roca, at Garcia Moreno ☎06 292 3640, Ⓦhotelsantafeotavalo.com; map p.585. A great deal, with a quiet location, excellent-quality rooms furnished in pine and good restaurant. Includes breakfast. $16

Hostal Valle del Amanecer Roca, at Quiroga ☎06 292 0990; map p.585. A wide selection of cosy budget rooms, some with shared bathrooms, set around a lovely cobbled, shady courtyard. There's an outdoor fireplace and café. $24

EATING

Alli Allpa Plaza de Ponchos, at Salinas; map p.585. Endearing little café serving generous portions of great-value Ecuadorian meals. Three-course set lunch $4. Daily 9am–9pm.

Buena Vista Plaza de Ponchos, at Salinas Ⓦbuenavistaotavalo.com; map p.585. Popular restaurant with a terrific view from its balcony over the market. There's a wide-ranging menu and a well-stocked bar. Mains $5–8. Mon & Sun 1–10pm, Wed–Fri 10am–10pm, Sat 8am–10pm.

★ **La Cosecha** Modesto Jaramillo, at Salinas; map p.585. This immaculately designed café of whitewashed walls and exposed wooden beams has large windows overlooking the market and a short menu of bagels (from

$2) and hearty sandwiches (from $4). Serves the best coffee in town and good craft beers. Daily 9am–8pm.

Deli Quiroga, at Bolívar; map p.585. Little gem of a café a block from the market specializing in Tex-Mex and Italian (main dishes $5–8), with vegetarian options available. The set lunch is just $2.50. Mon–Thurs & Sun 9.30am–9pm, Fri & Sat 9.30am–11pm.

Mi Otavalito Sucre, at Morales; map p.585. A farmhouse-style restaurant where you can enjoy well-presented Ecuadorian dishes (most $7.50–10), like trout in seafood sauce and grilled meats, in a traditional setting. Live Andean music at weekends. Daily 10am–10pm.

La Sazon de Marlito Cristóbal Colón, at Sucre; map p.585. A superb family-run *comedor* with an unbeatable lunchtime set menu ($2.50 for three courses) as well as good breakfasts and dinners. Mon–Sat 8am–10am, noon–3pm & 6–9pm.

Quino Roca, at García Moreno; map p.585. If you're craving seafood you won't be disappointed at family-run *Quino*: try the *ceviche* or calamari. Juices, cocktails and mulled wines are also good. Mains $6–15. Tues–Sun noon–10pm.

NIGHTLIFE

Peña Jala Jala 31 de Octubre, at Quito; map p.585. Showcases live Latin music and DJs spin a mix of local and international tunes. Fri & Sat 7pm–2am.

Peña La Jampa 31 de Octubre near Panamericana; map p.585. Three blocks north of the market, this is the place in town for live performances from traditional Andean bands. Fri & Sat 9pm–2am.

IBARRA

Forty minutes by bus northeast of Otavalo lies **IBARRA**, the largest town in the northern highlands. Known as La Ciudad Blanca (white city), Ibarra is famous for its attractive architecture, including beautiful squares, as well as the quality of its *helados de paila* (fruit sorbets).

WHAT TO SEE AND DO

Parque La Merced is impressive, fronted by the nineteenth-century Basílica La Merced, but eclipsed in terms of beauty by **Parque Pedro Moncayo**, dominated by the Baroque-influenced **cathedral** adorned with a golden altar. The recently renovated **Museo y Centro Cultural Ibarra** on the corner of Sucre and Oviedo (Tues–Sun 9.30am–5.30pm; free) has a fine exhibition of archeology from prehistory to colonial times including a gold funeral

mask from nearby Pimampiro and some outstanding ceramics.

A popular excursion is to **Laguna Yahuarcocha**, which means Lake of Blood, a reference to its violent history (tens of thousands of dead Cara soldiers were dumped into the lake after an Incan victory in 1495). You can rent boats or just walk around and enjoy the beautiful setting. Buses run regularly at weekends from the obelisk on Sánchez and Cifuentes. A **train service** that used to run all the way to San Lorenzo now does a 26km excursion from Ibarra's train station to Salinas (Thurs–Sun 11.25am–4.40pm; $30; ☎ 06 295 0390, ⓦ trenecuador.com).

ARRIVAL AND INFORMATION

By bus Aerotaxi and Expreso Turismo have regular services to and from Quito's Carcelén terminal (every 45min; 2hr 30min) and Atacames (2 daily; 9hr); Trans Otavalo goes to and from Otavalo (every 30min; 30min); buses head to and from Tulcán for the Colombian border (hourly; 2hr 30min) and also to Baños (2 daily; 6hr) and Esmeraldas (6 daily; 8hr). Services depart from the terminal 1km out of town, so to/from the centre take a bus ($0.25) or a taxi ($1).

Tourist information García Moreno on Parque La Merced (Mon–Fri 8.30am–5pm; ☎ 06 260 8489).

ACCOMMODATION

While Ibarra beats Otavalo for beauty, Otavalo has better hotel options, so many travellers prefer a day-trip. You'll find attractive haciendas away from the centre.

Hostería Cananvalle Línea Ferrea Km167 ☎ 098 260 9132, ⓦ hosteria-cananvalle.com. This lovely family-run, solar-powered farmstay is a 10min taxi ride west of town. It offers traditionally styled rooms, an outdoor whirlpool and fine meals, and many exotic birds frequent its delightful grounds. $60, extra beds $15

Casa Aída La Esperanza ☎ 06 266 0221, ⓦ casaaida. com. Rustic hippie hangout just south of Ibarra (taxi $5), which has been hosting travellers since the 1970s. Excellent home-cooked meals are available and it''s a good base to explore the scenic region east of Mount Imbabura. Dorms $10, doubles $20

Hotel Madrid Pedro Moncayo 7-41, at Olmedo ☎ 06 295 6177. Quiet, basic and inexpensive downtown hotel with decent rooms, though some lack windows. $20

Hostel Refugio Terra Esperanza Galo Plaza Lasso, La Esperanza ☎ 06 266 0228, ⓦ hostelterraesperanza.com. A good base for hikers, this boho, basic lodge is run by an amiable mother-and-son team (Emerson leads hikes in the mountains and Inés looks after meals and rooms). Located

6

CROSSING INTO COLOMBIA

Seven kilometres east of the town of **Tulcán** is the Rumichaca Bridge border crossing (open 24hr), which is 2–3hr by bus from Otavalo and Ibarra. This region has a bad rep as a narco trafficking centre and though plenty of travellers do use the border post, it's best not to linger. Carry your passport at all times. **Buses to the border** leave from Parque Isidro Ayora (15min; $1), while a taxi costs $3.50. In early 2018 travellers were reporting long waits to get through immigration on both sides of the border.

From the border, **Ipiales** is the nearest town with decent hotels. It is 3km away and you can take a taxi shuttle ($1), bus ($0.50) or taxi (around $2.50). Official **moneychangers** abound on both sides of the border, but check the calculations before handing money over. There are ample ATMs in Tulcán.

6km south of Ibarra (served by buses or $5 in a taxi). Dorms $12, doubles $22

EATING AND DRINKING

There are plenty of cheap restaurants serving filling *almuerzos* (from $2.50).

La Casa De Frida Rocafuerte, at Flores. A quirky little café dedicated to Mexico's Frida with good books to browse, great coffee to drink and light meals including veggie burgers and tortilla wraps. Mon–Thurs 10am–9pm, Fri & Sat 10am–11pm, Sun noon–7pm

Café Arte Salinas 5-43, at Oviedo. Owned by a local artist, this café-gallery serves a wide variety of international food – from tacos to filet mignon – in a vibrant setting, with live music (reggae, Latin, acoustic). Mains $5–7. Thurs–Sat 5.30pm–late.

La Hacienda Sucre, at Oviedo. This hacienda-themed deli-restaurant has good crepes, pizzas, sandwiches and large salads. Sells craft beer and wine by the glass. Mon–Sat 2–11.30pm.

★ **Heladería Rosalía Suárez** Oviedo, at Olmedo. Founded in 1897, this is the best place to try Ibarra's famous sorbet. Ice creams $0.50–3. Mon–Sat 7am–6.30pm, Sun 7.30am–6.30pm.

PÁRAMO DEL ÁNGEL

Near the border with Colombia, giant furry flower-like plants (actually sub-shrubs) called *Frailejónes* create an alien landscape, the **Páramo del Ángel** (Angel Steppe), amid soaring peaks above 4000m and lagoons in the mist. When the sun breaks through the clouds, hikers can see all the way to Imbabura and Cayambe. Polylepis trees, with twisted branches and soft brown bark that peels away like paper, create fairy-tale forests in ravines sheltered from the wind.

These unique areas are protected by the 15,700-hectare **Reserva Ecológica El Ángel**, a cold, high-altitude area just south of the Colombian border.

ARRIVAL AND INFORMATION

By bus Access via El Ángel 15 km away costs $16 one-way in a hired *camioneta*. Day-trips are possible from Otavalo or Ibarra, with several buses daily from each city but most easily done on a tour.

The Central Highlands

South of Quito lies Ecuador's most dramatic Andean scenery, where the Panamericana winds between two parallel mountain chains. Ecuador's highest peaks are here so it's unsurprising that nineteenth-century German explorer Alexander von Humboldt named the region "**the Avenue of the Volcanoes**". On the eastern side, the most popular peak to visit (and climb if you're fit enough) is **Cotopaxi** (5897m), which dominates the surrounding valley. To the southwest lies the turquoise luminescence of **Lake** **Quilotoa**, one of Ecuador's most stunning natural sights. The region's principal towns are **Latacunga**, **Ambato** and **Riobamba**, all of which are at altitudes similar to Quito and provide convenient bases. The spa town of **Baños**, with its ideal climate, beautiful setting, thermal baths and adventure sports, is a highlight. Nearby **Volcán Tungurahua** has been erupting regularly for the past decade and is an attraction in itself. South of Riobamba, the **Nariz del Diablo train ride** is a terrific excursion.

PARQUE NACIONAL COTOPAXI

About 60km south of Quito, **Volcán Cotopaxi** (5897m) is everybody's idea of a picture-perfect volcano, its symmetrical cone-shaped peak dominating the landscape. But Cotopaxi's beauty belies its destructive heritage – it has erupted on eleven occasions since 1742, destroying Latacunga several times. After decades of relative slumber the volcano erupted again in 2015 and the national park was closed to visitors. Visitors were gradually allowed to return in the following months but access to the summit was only reopened in October 2017.

Thanks to its proximity to Quito, **Parque Nacional Cotopaxi** (daily 8am–5pm, last entrance 2pm) is also Ecuador's most-visited park. The volcano offers a spectacular climb (see below), but for a more relaxed experience, the surrounding *páramo* (Andean grasslands) offers great opportunities for trekking and cycling. Inhabitants of the park include deer, rabbits, foxes, wild horses, pumas and ninety species of birds, among them the endangered Andean condor. Several ancient haciendas dot the countryside and San Agustín de Callo, a former monastery, has small but well-preserved Inca remains, and a chapel open to visitors ($4).

INFORMATION AND TOURS

Most people take a guided tour from Quito, although they are possible from other locations. A one-day hiking and cycling tour costs $50–60, taking in the museum, Limpiopungo Lake and going up to the edge of the ice. A two-day climbing tour costs from $180 and the better three-day tour about $220–270. In Quito, try Gulliver (see page 579), while in Latacunga Volcan Route (see page 592) is recommended. All of the accommodation options listed below can also arrange tours.

ACCOMMODATION

Cuello de Luna El Chasqui, Panamerican Highway South Km44 ☎ 099 970 0300, ⓦ cuellodeluna. com. Lovely hacienda setting, just 6km from the park entrance, this place offers decent dorms or homely private rooms with fireplaces. Cash only. Dorms $22, doubles $67

Secret Garden Cotopaxi ☎ 099 357 2714, ⓦ secretgardencotopaxi.com. An ecolodge set in the foothills of Pasochoa, near the village of Pedregal, overlooking the national park. Many rooms have their own fireplace to keep warm. Full-board package deals are also available. Dorms $10, doubles $28

Hostelería Tambopaxi 2km from Control Norte ☎ 02 222 0241, ⓦ tambopaxi.com. High, high in the *altiplano* this stunning lodge enjoys spellbinding views of Cotopaxi from its 3750m perch. Great guided hikes and horseriding are offered. Dorms $24, doubles $117

CLIMBING COTOPAXI

Climbing Cotopaxi can be done with little technical mountaineering experience. However, as it's an active volcano it's essential to first check its current status (try the website ⓦ www. igepn.edu.ec). Access to the summit was prohibited between August 2015 and October 2017 due to volcanic activity.

It's certainly not a climb to be taken lightly. You must be in good physical shape, acclimatized and travel with a qualified guide, preferably certified by ASEGUIM (Asociación Ecuatoriana de Guías de Montaña) and arranged through a tour operator (see page 579).

The importance of **acclimatization** cannot be stressed enough. If you're pushed for time it's tempting to think: "let's climb a volcano today". Unscrupulous guides won't hesitate in taking your money and going to the high-altitude refuge. But above 3000m you need to ascend slowly over a few days. A couple of days in Quito (2800m) is not enough to tackle Cotopaxi (5897m). Lake Quilotoa (3800m) is good preparation and a three-day, rather than two-day, climbing tour of Cotopaxi is recommended.

The best preparation is to climb lower peaks first. The most popular option is Rumiñahui (4712m), mainly a steep hike. You can also try Corazón (4788m) or the more challenging Illiniza Norte (5126m).

When climbing Cotopaxi itself, beginning from the José Rivas refuge at 4800m, it's six to eight strenuous hours to the top, negotiating snow, ice and several crevices. The views of Ecuador's other major peaks are breathtaking, as is the view down into the steaming crater. The descent takes three to four hours. December to April is usually the best time to climb Cotopaxi, when the snow is hardest, but it can be climbed year-round.

6

SAQUISILÍ

SAQUISILÍ holds a popular Thursday market, a less known but more authentic indigenous market than Otavalo. On market day the centre is flooded with tradespeople selling food, herbal remedies, household goods and live animals. It's also a social gathering for the locals, many of whom arrive in their best traditional dress and felt hats. You'll find a good selection of handicrafts for sale and there are also plenty of tasty *tortillas de maíz* to snack on.

Saquisilí is a few kilometres off the Panamericana, two hours south of Quito. Ask the bus driver to drop you at the junction and hop on another bus – or catch a regular bus from Latacunga (30min).

LATACUNGA

Some 30km south of Cotopaxi National Park, **LATACUNGA** doesn't look inviting from the highway, but venture towards the town centre and you'll find quaint cobbled streets and friendly locals. There's not a huge amount to do, but the town serves as a good base to explore **Quilotoa** and **Cotopaxi**, with several tour operators (see page 588) and decent accommodation.

WHAT TO SEE AND DO

The town has been rebuilt in colonial style after being destroyed several times by Cotopaxi's eruptions. The main square – **Parque Vicente León** – forms the town's focal point, flanked by the cathedral and town hall. A few blocks to the west, next to the river Cutuchi, is **Museo de la Casa de la Cultura** (Vela, at Salcedo; Tues–Fri 8am–noon & 2–6pm, Sat 8am–2pm; $0.50), which has a small ethnography and art museum. In late September and again in early November (usually the Saturday before November 11) Latacunga parties hard for **La Fiesta de la Mama Negra**, which features a parade of colourful costumed characters and culminates in the arrival of the Mama Negra, a man dressed up as a black woman in honour of the liberation of African slaves in the nineteenth century. The November celebration is secular and more raucous.

ARRIVAL AND INFORMATION

By bus Latacunga's bus station is on the Panamericana, five blocks west of town. If Latacunga is not the final destination of your bus, you'll be dropped off 400m further west. There are very regular services from the bus station to Quito's Quitumbe terminal (every 20min; 1hr 20min), Ambato (every 20min; 1hr) and Saquisilí (every 15min; 25min). To get to Quilotoa, there is only one direct bus per day (around noon); if you miss it, take a bus to Zumbahua and a taxi from there.

Tourist information Captur is at Orellana, at Guayaquil (Mon–Fri 8am–1pm & 2–5pm; ☎ 03 280 8494).

ACCOMMODATION

Hotel Central Orellana, at Salcedo ☎ 03 280 2912, ✉ hotelcentrallatacunga@hotmail.com. A decent if slightly dated budget option: rooms have private bathrooms and cable TV, some have a great view of the main square. They'll let you store your bags here for no charge if you're off hiking the Loop. $27

Hotel Rodelu Quito 16-49 ☎ 03 280 2172, ⓦ rodelu.com.ec A quieter option than the *hostals* on the main square, where the rooms have wooden floors and high ceilings. $28

Hostal Tiana Vivero, at Ordoñez ☎ 03 281 0147, ⓦ hostaltiana.com. The most atmospheric option in town, this friendly place has a range of colourful rooms and a fine roof terrace with Cotopaxi views. Breakfast included. Dorms $10.50, doubles $25

Cabañas los Volcanes Ciudadela Estrella Pamba in Lasso, 20km north of Latacunga ☎ 03 271 9524, ✉ maexpediciones@yahoo.com. A family-run budget option with a beautiful garden. It makes a good base camp to explore Cotopaxi and the Illinizas, and the owner's son Marcelo acts a mountain guide. $28

EATING

El Gringo y La Gorda Padre Salcedo, at Quito. Charming colonial setting in the middle of Latacunga, with Ecuadorian, Louisianan and vegetarian cuisine ($6–9). Doubles as a bar, so try a cocktail. Tues–Sat 2–10pm.

La Mama Negra Ordoñez, at Rumiñahui. The best place to try the local speciality *chugchucara* (fried pork with fried potatoes, plantains and corn). $6–8. Tues–Sun 10am–6pm.

Pizzería Buon Giorno Orellana, at Maldonado. A friendly place to escape the pork and rice highland staples, with great pasta, salads and pizzas (mains $5–8). Portions are generous. Mon–Sat 3–11pm, Sun 5–11pm.

El Submarino Café Orellana, at Tarquí. Cool café for all your espresso needs, and, as the name suggests, serves good subs and burgers ($2.50–4.50). Mon–Sat 9am–9pm.

LAKE QUILOTOA AND THE QUILOTOA LOOP

The luminous turquoise water of volcanic crater lake **Laguna Quilotoa** is one of Ecuador's most awe-inspiring sights. The lake was formed 800 years ago by a massive eruption and subsequent collapse of the volcano. The caldera is 3.2km wide and the lake 250m deep. You can visit from Latacunga on a day-trip but it's better to at least stay overnight or spend a couple of days hiking parts of the **Quilotoa Loop**.

WHAT TO SEE AND DO

The second town after leaving Latacunga is **Tigua** (3500m), famous for indigenous arts and handicrafts. Another 30km further is **Zumbahua**, a small village that gets boisterous at the weekend with its busy Saturday market and accompanying merriment. A further 14km north is the somewhat touristy village of **Quilotoa** (3800m), perched high above the lake. A good base for exploring, you can hike down the crater to the waterside in forty minutes. The water's high sulphurous content makes it unsuitable for swimming, and it's quite cold, but there are canoes for rent. For a longer walk to appreciate the lake from all angles, allow four hours to walk around the perimeter. The most popular hike on the Quilotoa Loop is the dramatic route from Quilotoa to Chugchilán. It takes about five hours, but don't attempt it alone and do not set off after 1pm.

GETTING AROUND

Until recently the biggest problem in this region was getting around because public transport was so infrequent. But as virtually all the entire loop is now paved bus links have really improved. Consult the *Black Sheep Inn's* website (see page 592) for updated transport information.

By bus Latacunga–Zumbahua–Quilotoa–Chugchilán buses leave Latacunga daily at 7am, 11.45am and 3pm. It is around 1hr 45min to Quilotoa and a further 45min to Chugchilán. There's also a daily 11.30am Latacunga–Sigchos–Chugchilán bus. Coming back, Chugchilán–Quilotoa–Zumbahua–Latacunga buses leave Chugchilán daily at 5am, 6am and 1pm, with an additional service on Fridays at 2pm. There's also a return Chugchilán–Sigchos–Latacunga bus at 4am.

ACCOMMODATION

The Quilotoa Loop has limited accommodation options.

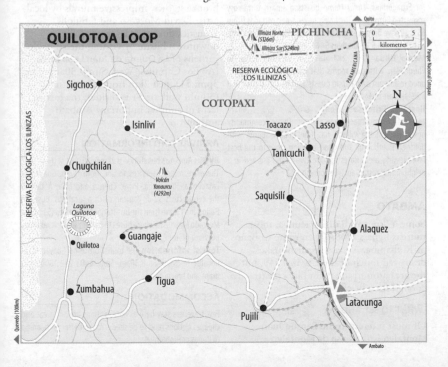

6

TOURS TO QUILOTOA

If you're travelling alone or want to see Quilotoa without the inconvenience of relying on public transport, take a **guided tour** from Latacunga. A one-day tour to the lake costs $40–50, or three days to do the entire loop costs from $140. These Latacunga operators also offer hiking and climbing tours to Cotopaxi.

TOUR OPERATORS

Neiges Guayaquil 6–25 at Quito ☎03 281 1199, ⓦneigestours.wixsite.com/neiges.
Tierra Zero Padre Salcedo, at Quito ☎099 953 7846, ⓔtierrazerotours@hotmail.com.

Tovar Expeditions Guayaquil 5-38, at Quito ☎03 281 1333,. ⓦtovarexpeditions.com.
Volcan Route Quevedo, at Guayaquil ☎03 281 2452, ⓦvolcanroute.com.

Black Sheep Inn Chugchilán, ☎03 270 8077, ⓦblacksheepinn.com. Rustic lodge with cosy fireplace-equipped rooms and a great ten-bed bunkhouse. There's a sauna, hot tub, small gym and yoga studio. Rates include three substantial meals. Dorms $35, doubles $120
Hostal Cabañas Quilotoa ☎099 212 5962. A good budget option, owned by local artist Humberto Latacunga, with comfortable rooms, hot showers and woodburners. $20
Hostal Cloud Forest ☎03 281 4808, ⓦcloudforesthostal.com. A backpacker favourite in Chugchilán, with simple rooms and a common room with fireplace to warm up. Rates include two meals. Dorms $15, doubles $40
★ **Llullu Llama** ☎099 292 8559, ⓦllullullama.com. In the village of Isinliví, and a tongue-twister to say even for Ecuadorians, *Llullu Llama* boasts a smart, ultra-cosy converted farmhouse. The lovely new garden cottages (from $55) all have fireplaces and balconies. There's also a spa with jacuzzi. Dorms $19, doubles $46
Mama Hilda ☎03 281 4814. A well-run lodge in Chugchilán, with cosy rooms that have pine trimmings. A good restaurant and a snug guests' lounge too. Dinner and breakfast are included. $44
Hostal Princesa Toa ☎098 075 4418, ⓔhostalprincesatoa@gmail.com. This community hostal in Quilotoa village has fine quality rooms with polished floorboards and good bedding close to the best lake-viewing area. Rates include two meals (served in a neighbouring restaurant). Per person $37

AMBATO

Some 47km south of Latacunga, most tourists bypass **AMBATO** en route to Baños or Riobamba. A massive earthquake destroyed much of the city in 1949, but the area around the main plaza is attractive enough for a brief visit.

WHAT TO SEE AND DO

Of most interest in the **Parque Juan Montalvo** is the **Casa de Montalvo**

(ⓦcasademontalvo.gob.ec; Mon–Fri 9.30am–5pm, Sat 10am–3pm; $1), the former residence of Juan Montalvo, Ambato's most famous literary son. A liberal, he was forced into exile by conservative president Gabriel García Moreno in 1869. The house has a collection of photos, manuscripts, clothing and a life-size portrait. Unnervingly, Montalvo's body is on display in the mausoleum. Across the square is the city's modern **cathedral**, rebuilt after the 1949 earthquake, one of Ecuador's leading Art Deco constructions. The interior has huge bronze statues, impressive murals by local artist David Moscoso and fabulous acoustics during Mass. Escape the downtown bustle by visiting the riverside gardens of **La Quinta de Juan León Mera** (Av Los Capulíes; Wed–Sun 9.30am–5pm; $1), just 2km from the centre (30min walk or $1 taxi ride), the former farm of another important Ambato author.

ARRIVAL AND INFORMATION

By bus Ambato's bus station is 2km northeast of the centre. There are regular services to and from Quito, Guayaquil, Latacunga, Riobamba, Puyo, Cuenca and Loja. A taxi to the centre costs $2 or you can catch a local bus. Buses to Baños don't leave from the bus station: take a taxi ($1.50) to Mercado Mayorista where buses to Baños pass several times per hour (45min).
Tourist information The tourist office on Guayaquil, at Rocafuerte (Mon–Fri 8.30am–5pm; ☎03 282 1800), has maps and brochures.

ACCOMMODATION

Few travellers stay here as hotel options are not great and cheaper options tend to be seedy. You're better off heading to Baños or Riobamba.

BACK ON TRACK

Ecuador's **rail network** took nearly forty years of toil before completion in 1908, when President Eloy Alfaro rode triumphantly from Guayaquil to Quito. But as the twentieth century rolled on, Ecuador's train service rolled backwards; by the 1990s one of the few lines still running was the short section along the famous Nariz del Diablo (Devil's Nose) south of Riobamba (see page 597).

Ex-president Rafael Correa, who idolized Alfaro, revitalized the entire rail network. Around $240 million was ploughed into the service, resulting in a luxury train linking Durán (across from Guayaquil) with Latacunga.

Much cheaper, popular **tourist trips** are available along short stretches of restored railway. Note that these are round-trip tours rather than point-to-point transport options. For information visit ⓦtrenecuador.com. Nearest to Cotopaxi is the **Quito–El Boliche–Quito (via Machachi)** trip (Fri–Sun; 8am–5.30pm; $41).

6

Hotel City Park Sucre 432, at Quito ☎03 282 7266, ✉cityparkhotel@hotmail.com. Just south of the Parque Juan Montalvo, this hotel has good-value rooms with firm beds and a fine location. **$36**

La Florida Av Miraflores in front of Inmaculada school ☎03 242 2007. Worth considering, this place has well-appointed, carpeted rooms with cable TV. **$38**

EATING AND DRINKING

Comedores inside the Mercado Central (on 12 de Noviembre, 500m northeast of the Parque Juan Montalvo) serve filling highland-style meals for $2–3.

Café la Catedral Bolívar. Head to this café, in a small mall opposite the cathedral entrance for good-value lunches ($2.50–4). Morphs into more of a bar in the evening, when there's sometimes live music. Mon–Sat noon–late.

La Fornace Av Cevallos 17–28. One of the city's best restaurants, serving delicious pizza (baked in a massive brick oven) as well as great pasta and seafood dishes ($4–8). Daily noon–10.30pm.

Marcelos Kfetería Castillo, at Rocafuerte ☎03 282 8208. Renowned locally as one of the best places to eat in town. Choose from a wide range of gourmet sandwiches, grilled meats and delicious ice cream. $6–11. Mon–Sat 9am–10pm.

SALASACA

On the road between Ambato and Baños, it's worth stopping briefly at **SALASACA**, famous for its tapestries. The indigenous people who live here look noticeably different, dressed in black ponchos and white hats. They originate from Bolivia, forced here by the Incas in the fifteenth century. There is a craft market every Sunday; on other days, it's best to browse the tapestry stores. About 6km from Salasaca is **Pelileo**, with surely more

cut-price jeans per square metre than anywhere else in South America. To visit Pelileo and Salasaca, hop off the bus from Ambato to Baños. There are several buses per hour.

BAÑOS

In the shadow of lava- and ash-spewing **Volcán Tungurahua** (see page 588), **BAÑOS DE AGUA SANTA** has grown from a sleepy spa town into something of a tourism hotspot in the last decade or so. It's easy to understand the town's appeal: a mild climate, stunning location in a verdant valley surrounded by steep hills plus, of course, the thermal baths that give the town its name. However the recent tourism boom has led to a somewhat tacky ambience, especially on weekends when young Ecuadorians flock here to swill beer and party hard – if you can, visit during the week.

For travellers, Baños is ideally located between the Avenue of the Volcanoes and Amazonia and is the base of numerous adventure sports operators offering fine mountain biking, hiking, canyoning, rafting and horseriding excursions.

WHAT TO SEE AND DO

In town, don't miss the **Basílica de Nuestra Señora de Agua Santa** on the main Ambato street. This massive church is dedicated to the Virgin Mary, credited with several miracles including saving the town from Tungurahua's eruption in 1773. The facade is attractive when lit up at night, dominating the town's skyline.

6

Inside are ten huge, amusing naive paintings depicting the Virgin saving the town and its citizens from various calamities, while upstairs a small **museum** (daily 8am–noon & 2–4pm; $1) houses a collection of the Virgin's processional clothes, religious art and a bizarre collection of stuffed animals.

Piscinas de la Virgen

The most popular baths are the **Piscinas de la Virgen** (daily 5am–4pm & 6–10pm; $2 daytime, $3 at night) at the foot of a small waterfall to the eastern end of Avenida Martínez. The cloudy yellow waters are high in minerals. There are three pools – freezing cold, warm and hot (45°C: just a little too hot to linger for more than a few minutes). The baths get very busy so it's best to go either early morning or early evening to avoid the crowds.

Piscinas El Salado

About 2km out of town, **Piscinas El Salado** (daily 5am–5pm; $4) consist of five concrete pools, ranging from 16 to 42°C, fed by hot spring water. They're not exactly pristine, more public baths than spa. A taxi here costs $1.50.

Around Baños

The best way to take in the town's stunning setting is to walk to **Bellavista**, high above the town. It's a steep forty-minute climb up a rocky, muddy path, rewarded with spectacular panoramic views over Baños and the Pastaza valley leading down to the Oriente. There are a couple of cafés at the top selling light lunches and drinks. You can continue on the path uphill for a further hour to the hamlet of **Runtún** at 2600m, then loop around to the other side of Baños, passing the statue of La Virgen del Agua Santa and

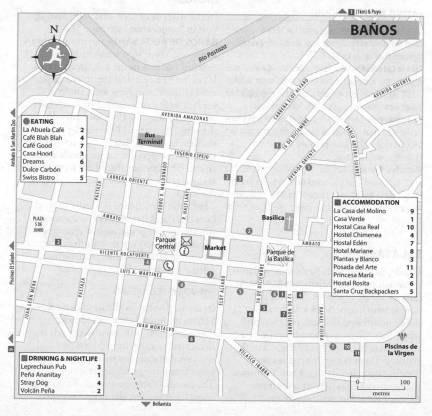

BAÑOS

EATING
La Abuela Café	2
Café Blah Blah	4
Café Good	7
Casa Hood	3
Dreams	6
Dulce Carbón	1
Swiss Bistro	5

ACCOMMODATION
La Casa del Molino	9
Casa Verde	1
Hostal Casa Real	10
Hostel Chimenea	4
Hostal Edén	7
Hotel Mariane	8
Plantas y Blanco	3
Posada del Arte	11
Princesa María	2
Hostal Rosita	6
Santa Cruz Backpackers	5

DRINKING & NIGHTLIFE
Leprechaun Pub	3
Peña Ananitay	1
Stray Dog	4
Volcán Peña	2

THE ROAD FROM BAÑOS TO PUYO

One of Ecuador's most beautiful routes, the road from Baños to Puyo, drops nearly 1000m following the Río Pastaza down from lush Andean foothills, through cloudforest to the edges of the tropical jungle. It's best admired from the saddle, and good bikes can be rented from agencies in Baños for $10/day, including helmet, map and repair kit. A guided tour costs $40. Leaving Baños, you cross the Agoyan hydroelectric project and it's about forty minutes until the impressive **Manto de La Novia** (Bride's Veil) waterfall. You can take the cable car ($2) 500m across the river gorge for a closer look. The second waterfall in the same location was caused by a landslide here in 2010. A 25-minute ride then brings you to the village of Río Verde, where you can lock your bike and hike 15 minutes downhill to see the even more spectacular **Pailón del Diablo** (Devil's Cauldron) waterfall. View it from a rickety suspension bridge or pay a small charge to get a closer look from the panoramic balcony. There is also a path cut into the rock so you can go inside the cave behind the waterfall. Cycling half an hour uphill from Río Verde, you reach **Machay**. From here, hike a 2.5km trail into the cloudforest past eight waterfalls, the most beautiful of which is Manantial del Dorado. From Machay, it's downhill to **Río Negro** where the surroundings begin to feel tropical with bromeliads, giant tree ferns and colourful orchids. The final highlight is the spectacular view of the Pastaza as it broadens out into Amazonia. Start early if you want to cover the entire 61km but bear in mind the route is far more scenic than the end destination of **Puyo**. Most people hop on a bus back to Baños from Río Verde or Río Negro or Mera if you ride down into the Oriente proper.

Ride defensively along the entire route and exercise caution during the rainy season due to the (rare but possible) risk of landslides.

back to town. The entire walk takes about four hours, or you can **hire horses** ($15/2hr, $26/4hr, including guide). Uphill at Runtún, small meets stunning in the form of the Casa del Árbol (daily 9am–5pm; $1), or tree house, where an enterprising local has built a small tree house at a spectacular scenic overlook. You can watch eruptions from there while enjoying (if you're unafraid of heights) a spectacular swing over a steep slope.

When Tungurahua blows its lid, it becomes a star attraction. **Las Antenas** up the mountain just north of Baños has spectacular night viewing during eruptive activity. Tour operators offer viewing tours in open chiva buses.

ARRIVAL AND INFORMATION

By bus Baños's bus terminal is a few blocks northwest of the main square; many bus companies here offer computerized ticketing so you can book seats ahead. Central Baños is so compact that you can walk everywhere, or a taxi across town costs just $1.

Destinations Ambato (every 30min; 1hr); Cuenca (3 daily; 7hr); Guayaquil (12–14 daily; 7hr); Puyo (every 30min; 1hr 30min); Quito (20 daily; 4hr); Riobamba (every 30min; 2hr); Tena (11 daily; 3hr 30min). Note the direct road to Riobamba is often closed due to Tungurahua's eruptions.

Tourist information Free maps are on offer at the municipal tourist office (Mon–Fri 8am–5pm; ☎03 274

0483, ⓦ banos-ecuador.com) on the east side of the Parque Central.

ACCOMMODATION

★ **La Casa del Molino** Blanco Barrio San José ☎03 274 1138, ⓦ casamolinoblanco.com; map p.594. This eco hostel (powered by wind and sun) has rooms and dorms of a very high standard considering the modest rates. There's a courtyard with hammocks and it enjoys a quiet location 600m west of the Parque Central. A free continental breakfast is included. Dorms $10, doubles $24

Casa Verde Santa Ana, off the road to Puyo, 1.5km from the town centre ☎098 659 4189, ⓦ lacasaverde. com.ec; map p.594. Right on the banks of the Río Pastaza, this ecolodge has balconies and decks from which to admire the stunning scenery. Rooms are simple yet very elegant, with polished pine floors and lots of natural light. Breakfast is an amazing spread featuring homemade jams and freshly pressed juices. $50

Hostal Casa Real Montalvo, at Pasaje Ibarra ☎03 274 2338, ⓦ hostalcasareal.com; map p.594. A well-run, fine-value hotel located close to the waterfall and thermal baths. Rooms are simple but brightened up by murals of wildlife. Breakfast included. $48

Hostel Chimenea Martínez, at Veira ☎03 274 2725, ⓦ hostelchimenea.com; map p.594. This efficient, friendly, good-value hostel has good rooms and dorms (four to six beds), clean bathrooms, plus a great rooftop terrace. There's a small pool, jacuzzi and a chilled vibe. Dorms $8.50, doubles $24

6

Hostal Edén 12 de Noviembre ☎03 274 1046; map p.594. Among the cheapest options, the *Edén* has basic rooms with cable TV set on a small garden courtyard. $20

Hotel Mariane Montalvo, at Halflants ☎03 274 1947, ⓦhotelmariane.com; map p.594. A characterful long-running little hotel where many spacious rooms have balconies and there's a quiet, leafy courtyard. Try the excellent French food in the restaurant while you're here. $30

Plantas y Blanco Martínez, at 12 de Noviembre ☎03 274 0044, ⓦplantasyblanco.com; map p.594. Very popular party hostel offering clean dorms and tidy en-suite rooms. Highlights include the great rooftop terrace, luggage storage, massages and a kitchen. Dorms $8, doubles $26

Posada del Arte Pasaje Ibarra ☎03 274 0083, ⓦposadadelarte.com; map p.594. In a tranquil location on the edge of town, this comfortable North American-owned place has invitingly colourful rooms, many with fireplaces. The good restaurant has craft beers and there's an attractive guests' lounge where you can enjoy reading a book. $72

Princesa María Mera, at Rocafuerte ☎03 274 1035, ⓦhostalprincesamaria.com; map p.594. A very welcoming family-run hostel in a quiet residential area with clean, bright en-suite rooms and firm beds. There's a kitchen and living room with DVD player too. $24

Hostal Rosita 16 de Diciembre, at Martínez ☎03 274 0396, ⓦhostalrosita-banios-ec.blogspot.co.uk; map p.594. This centrally located place is a good budget option, and there are two larger apartments for longer stays. $20

Santa Cruz Backpackers 16 de Diciembre ☎03 274 3527, ⓦsantacruzbackpackers.com; map p.594. Popular with young travellers this funky little place has simple, colourfully decorated rooms and a kitchen. Dorms $8, doubles $22

EATING

Baños offers some of the finest international cuisine outside Quito, with most of the best places away from the centre. The town is also famous for dozens of stalls selling *membrillo* (a gelatinous red block made with guayaba) and *milcocha*, chewy sugar-cane bars that you can watch being made, swung over wooden pegs. Outside the market, *cuy* (guinea pig) are roasted on spits.

La Abuela Café Ambato, at 16 de Diciembre ☎099 965 4365; map p.594. Offers a wide-ranging menu and a balcony to watch the world go by. Mains $6–8. Hours vary.

Café Blah Blah Martínez, at Halflants ☎098 305 9111; map p.594. A fine bet for breakfast, this intimate, inexpensive café serves good breakfasts, salads, sandwiches, omelettes and pancakes. Meals $4–6. Daily 8am–8pm; closes one day a week Mon–Wed.

Café Good 16 de Diciembre ☎03 274 0592, ⓦcafegoodbanos.com; map p.594. Specializes in vegetarian food including fresh salads and Asian dishes – the curries are worth trying, though not really authentic. Mains $4–8. Daily 8am–10pm.

Café Hood Montalvo ☎03 250 5097; map p.594. This relaxed, stylish café-restaurant has good salads, filled baguettes, Mexican and Italian dishes and espresso coffee. Enjoy your meal or drink on the pretty street terrace. Mains $6–8. Daily 10am–10pm.

★**Casa Hood** Martínez ☎03 274 2668; map p.594. Attractive café-bar with a vibrant atmosphere and tempting menu of international dishes including falafel, Mexican and Asian dishes and lots of vegan choices. There's a fine book exchange, daily lunch special ($3.75) and live music some weekend nights. Mains $5–8. Mon & Wed–Sun 10am–10pm.

Dreams Martínez ☎03 274 0044; map p.594. Offering a new dining concept for Baños, *Dreams* is all about sharing plates around low tables, while the subdued lighting creates an atmospheric mood. The (mainly) Middle Eastern and Mexican food is good; leave those shoes at the door. Mains $6–9. Daily 6–11pm.

Dulce Carbón 12 de Noviembre, at Oriente ☎03 2740353; map p.594. Serving cheap, succulent spit-roasted and chargrilled poultry and meat dishes, this friendly, efficient place is understandably popular. Mains $6–9. Mon, Tues & Thurs–Sun 6pm–midnight.

★**Swiss Bistro** Martínez, at Alfaro ☎03 274 2262, ⓦswiss-bistro.com; map p.594. One of the best-regarded restaurants in Ecuador, this alpine delight is kitted out with cow skins on the walls and even cow-patterned lampshades. The cheese and meat fondues ($19–21) and *rostis* ($10.50) are fabulous, and there's a good wine list. Daily 7.30am–midnight.

NIGHTLIFE

Nightlife in Baños is rather sleepy during the week, but gets very busy at weekends, particularly on Saturday night. There are over a dozen bars on Alfaro north of Ambato.

Leprechaun Pub Alfaro; map p.594. This double-decker of a pub is a great spot to hang out, with a pool table and lively vibe most nights. Mon–Sat 9am–2am, Sun 9am–11pm.

Peña Ananitay 16 de Diciembre, at Espejo; map p.594. The best place in town to catch some traditional folk music. Tues & Wed 5pm–midnight, Thurs–Sat 5pm–1am.

Stray Dog Rocafuerte, at Maldonado; map p.594. This fine brewpub has all bases covered, with IPA and stouts, wheat beers and pilsners. Mon & Wed–Sat 3–11pm, Sun 11am–7pm.

Volcan Peña Alfaro; map p.594. Offering more of a Latin vibe than most on this strip, with DJs spinning reggaeton and merengue. Mon–Thurs 6pm–1am, Fri & Sat 6pm–2am.

VOLCÁN TUNGURAHUA

Tungurahua, which means "throat of fire", has a troubled relationship with Baños.

ACTIVITIES AND TOURS

Adventure sports are popular in the Pastaza valley between Baños and Puyo. **Rafting** is particularly good. A half-day on the Río Pastaza (grade II to IV depending on the time of year) costs from $30 including transport, equipment, licensed guide and lunch. Other adrenaline-filled activities include **bridge jumping** (rather like bungee except you swing like a pendulum) off the 100m Puente San Francisco for $20, as well as zipping across the valley on **canopy lines** ($20). Canyoning trips start at $30 for a half-day trip. Climbing (from $45) and paragliding ($60) are also possible. Exact prices depend on numbers. You can book tours to many jungle destinations including Coca and Lago Agrio, but these generally go through Quito so it's better booking there (see page 579). For a more accessible jungle experience, there are good trips via Puyo.

TOUR OPERATORS

Geotours Ambato, at Thomas Halflants ☎ 03 274 1344, ⓦ geotoursbanios.com. Highly recommended; activities include paragliding and rafting.

Pailon Travel 12 de Diciembre, at Montalvo ☎ 03 274 0899, ⓦ pailontravel.com Tours include canyoning and rafting.

Rainforestur Ambato, at Maldonado ☎ 098 446 9884, ⓦ rainforestur.com. Jungle and rafting tour specialist.

El Topo Turismo El Topo ☎ 098 685 0757, ⓦ eltopoturismo.wixsite.com/eltopoturismo.

Community tourism venture offering horse riding, fishing and farm visits.

MASSAGE

Baños has many skilled professionals and you can get all types of massage treatments here. Most charge around $20 per hour. For a real treat head to El Refugio (ⓦ elrefugiospa.com), 1km east of town, a lovely spa complex where numerous treatments are available.

Chakra Alfaro, at Luis Martínez ☎ 03 271 2027.

Stay in Touch Montalvo ☎ 03 274 0973.

The volcano supplies the **hot springs** that make the town famous, but eruptions have caused regular alerts in recent years. The volcano awoke from years of dormancy in October 1999 with a spectacular eruption that covered Baños in ash. However, because the crater is on the opposite side, the town escaped further damage. Subsequent eruptions have occurred regular intervals, and in 2016 a large explosion of ash and smoke blew over the district. The volcano remains highly active at the time of writing.

Bañenos have been living in Tungurahua's shadow for centuries, and it's now constantly monitored. Check the national press, Instituto Geofísico's Spanish website (ⓦ igepn.edu.ec) or the Smithsonian Institution's English site (ⓦ volcano.si.edu). Only in extreme cases will authorities – and then with good reason – warn against visiting Baños.

RIOBAMBA

Near the centre of Ecuador, the sprawling city of **RIOBAMBA** lies almost in the shadow of mighty **Volcán**

Chimborazo, Ecuador's highest mountain and is the best base from which to climb the giant peak. Riobamba is one of Ecuador's coldest towns, and night temperatures can drop near freezing in cold snaps. Though restoration has spruced up much many nineteenth-century buildings in the centre, it offers few facilities geared towards foreign travellers.

WHAT TO SEE AND DO

The best sightseeing is centred around **Parque Maldonado**. The facade of the **Catedral** is all that remains of the original building after a 1797 earthquake and was painstakingly moved and reconstructed when the town was rebuilt at a new location (the old spot is nearby Cajabamba). Inside the Monasterio de las Conceptas, the **Museo de Arte Religioso** has a large collection of religious art (entrance on Argentinos; Mon–Sat 9am–12.30pm & 3–5pm; $4). On Saturdays, Riobamba has one of the largest **markets** in the region, spreading out northeast of Parque de la Concepción. Twenty kilometres southwest on the

6

RIOBAMBA

ACCOMMODATION
Inti Sisa	6
El Libertador	2
Montecarlo	4
Oasis	5
Rincón Alemán	1
Tren Dorado	3

EATING
Bonny	4
El Delirio	3
Pizzería d'Baggio	2
El Rey de Burrito	1

Panamericana, **Colta** on the eponymous lagoon features the charming Balbanera church, Ecuador's oldest, dating back to 1534. On clear days, the walk along the south shore of the lagoon offers beautiful views of Chimborazo.

On weekends there's a government-run **train tour** to Urbina, dubbed the "Ice Train" tour as it goes to the highest spot on the railway (Sat & Sun 8am–2.30pm; $28).

ARRIVAL AND DEPARTURE

By bus Riobamba's main bus terminal is 2km northwest of the centre. From the Oriente you arrive at the Terminal Oriental (Espejo, at Luz Elisa Borja); take a regular bus ($0.25) to the centrally located train station. A taxi into town from the terminal costs $1.

Destinations Ambato (every 20min; 1hr); Baños (every 30min via Ambato; 2hr); Cuenca (every 40min; 5hr); Guayaquil (every 30min; 4hr 30min); Quito (every 15min; 3hr 30min).

ACCOMMODATION

Most accommodation is situated close to the train station.
Inti Sisa Vargas Torres, at García Moreno, Guamote, between Riobamba and Alausí ☎ 03 291 6529, ⓦ intisisa.com; map p.598. A charming rustic guesthouse, part of a community tourism initiative deeply involved with the local Kichwa. Tours available (including Chimborazo) and breakfast is included. Dorms $25, doubles $65

El Libertador Av Daniel León Borja 29–22 ☎ 03 294 7393, ⓦ hotelellibertador.com; map p.598. Offering good value, this colonial-style hotel has spacious, tastefully furnished rooms with cable TV. $30

Montecarlo 10 de Agosto 25–41 ☎ 03 296 1557, ⓦ hotelmontecarlo-riobamba.com; map p.598. A restored historic house around a pleasant flower-filled courtyard. Breakfast included. $33

★ **Oasis** Veloz, at Almagro ☎ 03 296 1210, ⓦ oasishostelriobamba.com; map p.598. South of the Basílica in a quiet area of town, this guesthouse has a pretty garden and guests' kitchen. Rooms (including triples and quads) are tastefully decorated. Book ahead. Singles $18, doubles $30

Rincón Alemán Remigio Romero Mz H, Casa 9 at Alfredo Pareja ☎ 03 260 3540, ⓦ hostalrinconaleman. com; map p.598. In a leafy location around 3km west of the centre, this comfortable European-style guesthouse has rooftop terrace views of Chimborazo. Singles $42, doubles $64

Tren Dorado Carabobo 22–35, at 10 de Agosto ☎ 03 296 4890, ⓦ hoteltrendorado.com; map p.598. Right across from the station, with compact but perfectly adequate rooms; try to get one at the back. $32

EATING

Bonny Primera Constituyente; map p.598. For a real treat, this elegant formal restaurant is just the ticket, serving expertly grilled meats and fine fish dishes. Prices are quite moderate given the surrounds. Mains $8–12. Tues–Sat 11am–10pm, Sun 11am–3pm.

Pizzeria d'Baggio Av León Borja 33–24 ☎ 03 296 1832; map p.598. Unbeatable for sumptuous pizzas and

---

★ TREAT YOURSELF

El Delirio Primera Constituyente 28–16 ☎ 03 296 6441, ⓦ eldeliriorestaurant.wordpress. com; map p.598. Visited by Bolívar himself, this traditional colonial house is the perfect place for a atmospheric meal, set inside a pretty courtyard with a log fire to ward off the chills. Mains ($8–12) include fine steaks and seafood.

calzone hand-made in front of you. Pizzas $4–8. Daily noon–10pm.

El Rey de Burrito Brasil 16–31 ☎03 295 3230; map p.598. Perfect for a dose of Mexican fare, this likeable place offers good burritos and enchiladas with plenty of vegetarian options. $6–8. Daily 11am–11pm.

VOLCÁN CHIMBORAZO

Just 30km northwest of Riobamba, the extinct **Volcán Chimborazo** looms large. At 6268m, it's Ecuador's highest peak and the furthest point from the centre of the Earth due to the equatorial bulge. The nature reserve has good roads so it can be easily visited from Riobamba. On a day-trip you can walk from the lower refuge (4800m) to the second refuge (5000m), but bear in mind that the climb in altitude from Riobamba could leave you suffering, and only experienced mountaineers should tackle the summit. For this, there are several tour operators in Riobamba charging $240 for a two-day tour. Recommended operators include: Alta Montaña, Posada La Estación, Urbina (☎099 869 6710, ⊛altamontanaecuador. com), which also offers a five-day hike around Chimborazo and expert mountaineers Expediciones Andinas, Urb. Las Abras (☎03 236 4278, ⊛expediciones-andinas.com).

For non-climbers, enjoy the unworldly moonscapes and sweeping *páramo* that are home to thousands of vicuñas, brought back from the brink of extinction, and other wildlife. This enormous reserve stretches over 580 square kilometres in three provinces. It also contains Carihuairazo (5020m), a summit often tackled as a preparation climb. One-day hiking tours to Chimborazo National Park cost from $50 per person with tour operators in Riobamba. Alternatively, take a bus to Guaranda and ask to be let off near the refuge (8km from the main road) or take a taxi from Riobamba ($35).

If cycling is more your thing, Biking Spirit at the corner of Ilapo and Tixán (☎03 261 2263, ⊛bikingspirit.com) runs a range of day-tours down and around Chimborazo.

ALAUSÍ

The regeneration of the train line has brought some sparkle back to the small Andean town of **ALAUSÍ**. Situated in a verdant valley with steep hills rising up on all sides, Alausí is a pleasant starting point for the most exhilarating train ride in Ecuador: the **Devil's Nose train ride** (see below). Many of the old houses lining the rail line as well as the old metal bridge and main squares have been restored. The walk up to the huge statue of Saint Peter ten minutes from the centre offers excellent views over the town and valley. For even better views, head to *Hostería Pircapamba* and hire horses to ride around the hills.

ARRIVAL AND DEPARTURE

By bus There are regular bus services to Alausí from Riobamba (every 30min; 2hr); Cuenca (10 daily; 4hr); Quito (10 daily; 5hr); and Guayaquil (4 daily; 5hr).

By truck or taxi To begin the Inca Trail to the south, occasional trucks head to Achupallas from 5 de Junio, or you can take a taxi.

THE DEVIL'S NOSE TRAIN RIDE

Not quite as adventurous as it used to be after a complete modernization, the **Devil's Nose Train Ride** still offers fabulous mountain views. The 12km ride takes you down from Alausí to Sibambe in the valley. The main event is a hair-raising 800m descent through a series of tight switchbacks carved out of the steep mountainside, viewable through panoramic windows from inside the modern rail cars.

Tickets can be purchased online at ⊛trenecuador.com or at Alausí's train station (arrive 30min early and you'll need your passport. Book ahead if you plan to travel on weekends or holidays.

The tour (Tues–Sun 8am & 11am; 2hr 30min; $33) includes a stop at the restored Sibambe station on the Guasuntos River, featuring folkloric dances and friendly llamas, before returning up the Devil's Nose to Alausí.

6

ACCOMMODATION

★ **Community Hostel Alausí** Alfaro 172 ☏ 098 563 7714, ⊛ communityalausi.com. This wonderful new hostel opened in late 2017 and offers a superb base, with lovely clean rooms fitted with quality pine furniture and fab dorms (with en-suites). There's a good restaurant (breakfast is included) and super-helpful staff can advise about local hikes and excursions. Dorms $12.50, doubles $30

Panamericana 5 de Junio, at 9 de Octubre ☏ 03 293 0156. It's seen better days but this old timer is one of the few decent budget choices in town. Its adequate rooms have shared or private bath; cash only. $18

Hostal San Pedro 5 de Junio ☏ 03 293 0089. Inexpensive hotel in the centre with well-lit, plain, comfortable rooms with private bath and cable TV. $28

EATING

Alausí has plenty of budget places to eat but few stand out. If money is tight, choose from various set menus on Av 5 de Junio.

Chifa Pekín 5 de Junio. Good-value Chinese serving tasty noodles, fried rice and a range of soups. Mains $4–6.

El Trigal 5 de Junio, at Pedro de Loza. A bustling *comedor* serving inexpensive *comida típica*, including $3 *almuerzos*.

The Southern Highlands

South of Riobamba, the snowcapped summits of the Andes fade from you, replaced by undulating green mountains. The hub of the region is **Cuenca**, Ecuador's third-largest city and one of Latin America's best-preserved colonial cities. Cuenca is also the most convenient base to explore the Inca archeological site **Ingapirca**, and the rugged moors and lakes of **Parque Nacional El Cajas**.

South of Cuenca, distances between towns lengthen and the climate warms up. The historic plazas and award-winning parks of the provincial capital of **Loja** are worth visiting before heading to the relaxing backpacker favourite of **Vilcabamba**, nicknamed the "Valley of Longevity". Recharge your batteries and take advantage of great hiking and horseriding trails in the surrounding hills.

INGAPIRCA

Between Riobamba and Cuenca lies the site of **Ingapirca** (daily 8am–6pm; $2 including 45min guided tour in English or Spanish), Ecuador's only major Inca ruins. Those who've already visited Peru may be disappointed by this more modest site; however, the complex boasts the Inca Empire's sole remaining sun temple. The site's strategic position is impressive, at a height of over 3200m with panoramic views over the surrounding countryside.

Ingapirca was built at the end of the fifteenth century by Huayna Capac on top of the ruins of a Cañari site. The stone of the Cañari moon temple, which the Inca preserved from its earlier construction, is still visible. Sadly, much of the site is now little more than stone foundations and it takes imagination and a guided tour to bring it to life.

WHAT TO SEE AND DO

Points of interest include the **calendar stone** and sacrificial site, but the highlight is the well-preserved **Temple of the Sun**, constructed with more than three thousand intricately carved blocks. It's captivating to stand in the sentry posts of the temple and hear your whispers reverberate through the walls. Just outside the complex is a **museum** (included in the

THE INCA TRAIL TO INGAPIRCA

Though by no means as famous or impressive as the trail in Peru, keen hikers can tackle the three-day trail from near Alausí to Ingapirca. The start of the trail is at **Achupallas**. To get there, take a bus from Riobamba towards Cuenca and get off at La Moya, 10km south of Alausí. From there, it's a steep climb on foot.

Alternatively, *colectivo* trucks and pick-ups connect Alausí and Achupallas (11am–4pm; $1) or it's $16 to hire one. There's a small hostal, *Ingañan* (☎03 293 0663; $24), in Achupallas which also serves meals.

The hike takes you south down the Río Cadrul valley and through a narrow gap between two hills, Cerro Mapahuiña and Cerro Callana Pucará. Continue towards Laguna Tres Cruces and camp nearby. This hike is about six hours in total through parts of Sangay National Park.

On day two, continue southwest and up along Cuchilla Tres Cruces, which commands great views of the Quebrada Espíndola valley. Descend into the valley to the left of the final peak, Quillo Loma. There are remains of an Inca road, protected as a UNESCO site, and the foundations of an Inca bridge. You'll also find a trail to Laguna Culebrillas and more ruins at **Paredones**.

On day three, head southwest from Paredones on the 7m-wide Inca road. After the village of **San José** turn right to **El Rodeo**, then follow the road to **Ingapirca**. It takes nearly five hours in total. Take plenty of food, water and camping equipment and ensure you are prepared as the entire trail is not well marked. Alternatively, take a guided tour. Several operators based in Riobamba and Cuenca (see page 603) operate tours.

6

entrance fee), which houses a small collection of objects found at the site.

ARRIVAL

By bus To get to Ingapirca, take a Transportes Cañar bus from Cuenca's bus terminal (9am & 12.20pm; 2hr). The return service is at 1pm a& 4.30pm (weekends 9am only, returning at 1pm). Guided tours from Cuenca cost $55/person. If you're travelling south from Alausí, get off the bus at El Tambo.

ACCOMMODATION

Options to stay overnight are limited and a day-trip is most common.

Cabañas El Castillo ☎07 221 7002, ✉cab.castillo@hotmail.com. Basic, clean rooms 100m from the ruins, offering comfortable beds and fine views. Also has a small restaurant. **$30**

Hostal Inti Huasi ☎07 229 2940. Very basic rooms in Ingapirca village, 5min from the site. Bring warm clothes, as it gets cold at night. **$16**

CUENCA

CUENCA is Ecuador's third-largest city, with a population of 340,000, but it doesn't feel that way, retaining the atmosphere of a traditional Andean town. The Incas established **Tomebamba** in the late fifteenth century, one of the most important cities in the Inca Empire. It was destroyed shortly afterwards in the civil war between brothers Atahualpa and

Huascar, and the Spanish later founded Cuenca in 1557. Little remains of the city's Inca past, although ruins have been excavated behind the **Museo Pumapungo**. Most museums and restaurants are closed on Sundays, which is the best day to take a trip outside the city to **Cajas** or **Ingapirca**.

WHAT TO SEE AND DO

The cobbled streets, charming squares, traditional architecture and tree-lined paths along the banks of the Río Tomebamba are delightful. However the city urgently needs a pedestrianization programme as heavy traffic and fumes curse the centre.

The historic city centre

Cuenca was declared a UNESCO World Heritage Site in 1996. The focal point of its historic centre is **Parque Calderón**, an elegant square filled with flower beds and palm trees, dominated by the towering nineteenth-century **Catedral Nueva**. Its interior is relatively bare except for the stunning gold-leaf altar and the massive sky-blue domes, best viewed from the side or rear. Just north of the cathedral a walled courtyard operates as a handicraft and foodstuff market. Southwest of the cathedral, along Calle Sucre, is a flower market presided over by Chola women. Five blocks west on an elegant, quiet square is the handsome

CUENCA

Bus Terminal & Airport

Baños (Cuenca)

Museo Pumapungo & 13

EATING

Cacao y Canela	5
Café Nucallacta	7
Moliendo Café	8
Restaurante La Esquina	10
El Pedregal Azteca	2
Pizzeria Marea/ El Mentidero Cafe	9
La Quinua	1
Raymipamba	3
Taj Mahal	6
Tiestos	4

DRINKING & NIGHTLIFE

Far Out	2
Jodoco	1
Monday Blue	4
Verde Pintón y Maduro	3
Wunderbar	5

ACCOMMODATION

Alternative Hostel	13
Casa del Águila	6
El Cafécito	4
La Casa Cuencana	10
Hostal Casa del Barranco	9
Hostal Casa Naranja	2
La Cigale	7
Hostal Colonial	5
Hotel de la Culturas	8
Hotel Forum	3
Macondo	1
Posada del Río	11
Posada Todos Santos	12

seventeenth-century **Iglesia San Sebastián**. Opposite is the **Museo de Arte Moderno** (Mon–Fri 9am–5.30pm, Sat 9am–1pm; free), which houses temporary exhibitions of Latin American modern art. For refreshments, there's a cool café or two worth investigating in this emerging boho area.

Along the Río Tomebamba

Busy Calle Larga forms the southern fringe of the historic centre. At the western end is the large concrete Mercado 10 de Agosto, which has an amazing selection of tropical fruit sold on its ground floor and Andean food stalls on its upper. A short walk away along Larga is the **Museo del Sombrero** (Mon–Fri 9am–6pm, Sat 9.30am–5pm, Sun 9.30am–1.30pm; free) where you can learn about the process of making Panama hats, which are actually

from Ecuador. Continuing along Larga, the stunning **Museo Remigio Crespo Toral** (Mon–Fri 10am–1pm & 3–6pm, Sat & Sun 10am–2pm; free) exhibits pre-Columbian ceramics, colonial and modern art in a remarkable, immaculately restored nineteenth-century mansion. A couple of blocks further east, the excellent **Museo de las Culturas Aborígenes** (Mon–Fri 9am–6pm; $4, ⊚www. museodelasculturasaborigenes.com) has an enormous collection of pre-Hispanic artefacts – from Stone Age tools to Inca ceramics.

Calle Larga has three staircases, the largest of which is **La Escalinata**, which drop down to the lovely shady riverbank of the Río Tomebamba, pleasant for walking or biking between El Vado (the ford) in the west and Pumapungo and beyond in the east.

Museo Pumapungo

Museo Pumapungo (C Larga, at Huayna Capac; Tues–Fri 8am–5.30pm, Sat & Sun 10am–4pm; free; ☎07 283 1255) is Cuenca's biggest museum and worth the twenty-minute walk east of the centre (taxi $1.50). The three floors include a large collection of colonial art, an archeology room and an exhibition of indigenous costumes and masks. The highlight is the **ethnographic** exhibition of Ecuador's indigenous cultures with animated dioramas, re-created dwellings and a stunning display of five *tsantsas* (shrunken heads) from the Shuar culture. Entrance includes access to the **Pumapungo archeological site** behind the museum, where the most important buildings of the Inca city of Tomebamba were located, although little more than foundations remain. Below the ruins are landscaped gardens and a bird rescue centre.

Mirador de Turi

For great views over Cuenca, take a taxi ($3) or a bus from 12 de Abril, at Solano ($0.25), to the **Mirador de Turi**, a lookout point on a hill 4km south of the centre. Views are particularly good in the evening when the churches are lit up.

ARRIVAL AND DEPARTURE

By plane Cuenca's airport (Mariscal Lamar; ☎07 286 7120) is 2km northeast of the centre. There are daily flights to and from Quito by Tame (Av Florencia Astudillo; ☎07 288 9581, ⓦtame.com.ec), LATAM (Bolívar 9–18, at Benigno Malo; ☎07 282 2783) and Avianca (Av España 1114; ☎07 286 1041From the airport buses run along Av España to the northern edge of central Cuenca or it's a 10min walk to the main bus terminal.

By bus The bus terminal is near the airport, 1.5km northeast of the centre.

Destinations Ambato (hourly; 7hr); Baños, Central Sierra (3 daily; 7hr); Guayaquil (hourly; 5hr); Loja (hourly; 4hr); Piura, Peru (4 daily; around 10hr, via Machala); Quito (every 30min 10hr); Riobamba (hourly; 6hr).

By minibus Private companies offer speedy non-stop connections to Guayaquil (over 20 daily; 4hr) and other destinations. Most are grouped together on Remigio Crespo, 3km west of the centre. OperAzuay Tur (☎07 420 3537, ⓦoperazuaytur.com) is a reliable operator.

By taxi Taxis cost $2 from the bus station or airport to the centre. Minimum charges around town are $1.50.

By tram A long-delayed 10km tram line running through the centre, passing the bus and airport terminals is due to start operating in 2018 or 2019; there will be stops on Av España.

INFORMATION

Tourist information The iTur office on the main square (Mariscal Sucre; Mon–Fri 8am–8pm, Sat 9am–1pm; ☎07 282 135, ⓦcuencaecuador.com.ec) has helpful staff providing maps and regional information; free guided 2hr walks leave from here Tues–Sat 10am (guides speak limited English). It also has an office at the airport, which opens for flight arrivals. Good-value $8 double-decker city bus tours leave from Parque Calderón (hourly: Mon–Sat 9am–7pm except 1pm & 2pm, Sun 10am, 11am, noon & 3pm), covering the centre and the Mirador de Turi.

TOUR OPERATORS

The following offer tours to Ingapirca, Cajas and elsewhere. Trips to Cajas and Ingapirca cost $40–55/person.

Expediciones Apullacta Gran Colombia 11-02, at General Torres ☎07 283 7815, ⓦapullacta.com.

Kushi Waira at Carolina Bookstore, Hermano Miguel 4–36, ⓦkushiwaira.com. Community-based tourism.

Monodedo Av 12 de Abril, at Guayas ☎07 288 5909, ⓦmonodedoecuador.com. Rock-climbing and canyoning pioneers.

Terra Diversa Travel and Adventure Hermano Miguel 5-42, at Honorato Vásquez ☎07 282 3782, ⓦterradiversa.com.

ACCOMMODATION

Cuenca has a wide range of hotels in charming colonial buildings. Book ahead at weekends and on national holidays.

Alternative Hostel Huayna Capac, at Cacique Duma ☎07 408 4101, ⓦalternativehostal.com; map p.602. Excellent-value modern hostel with cool on-site café, reading lounge, good kitchen-dining facilities, small patio terrace and luggage storage. It's 1.5km southeast of the centre next to Pumapungo museum; expect some traffic noise. Dorms $9, doubles $20

★ TREAT YOURSELF

Casa del Águila Sucre 13–56 ☎07 283 6498, ⓦhotelcasadelaguila.com; map p.602. Lovingly restored nineteenth-century mansion, with gorgeous individually decorated rooms, painted in warm, natural colours with distinctive flourishes. Staff are friendly and efficient, and rates include a full buffet breakfast. $80

6

El Cafécito Honorato Vasquez 7-36, at Cordero ☎07 283 2337, ⓦelcafecitohostel.wixsite.com; map p.602. Northeast of the main square, this place has simple, clean, well-presented rooms, some with private bathroom; dorms have four to six beds. Dorms $\overline{\$10}$, doubles $\overline{\$30}$

La Casa Cuencana Hermano Miguel 4-45 ☎07 282 6009, ⓦlacasacuencana.wordpress.com; map p.602. Close to the river, with ample cafés and bars close by, this popular spot is spread over three buildings. Offers simple rooms (some with private bathrooms) and decent dorms. Dorms $\overline{\$11}$, doubles $\overline{\$27}$

Hostal Casa del Barranco C Larga 8-41, at Cordero ☎07 283 9763, ⓦcasadelbarranco.com; map p.602. This family-run place occupies a historic house displaying paintings by local artists and has an unbeatable location. Some rooms have river views. Breakfast included. $\overline{\$30}$

Hostal Casa Naranja Lamar 10-38, at Padre Aguirre ☎07 282 5415; map p.602. Inside a traditional house, the modern decor and spacious bathrooms put this centrally located place somewhere between hostel and cheap boutique hotel. $\overline{\$39}$

La Cigale Vásquez 7-80 ☎07 2835308, ⓦhostallacigale. com; map p.602. Appealing French-owned hostel in a lovely restored old building set around a courtyard café-restaurant, which has live music most weekends, so it can get noisy. En-suite doubles are neat but small. Breakfast included for rooms. Dorms $\overline{\$7}$, doubles $\overline{\$27}$

Hostal Colonial Gran Colombia 10-13, at Padre Aguirre ☎07 2841 644; map p.602. Offering fine value, this *hostal* has well-presented rooms in an eighteenth-century house set around a small courtyard. It's on a quiet lane and breakfast is included. $\overline{\$32}$

★ **Hotel de la Culturas** Vázquez 7-36, ☎07 283 2337, ⓦhoteldelasculturas.com; map p.602. Enjoys an excellent location between the river and Parque Calderón and has a wide choice of spacious, very clean rooms with modern decor. The owners are welcoming and speak good English; a substantial breakfast is included. $\overline{\$58}$

Hotel Forum 10-91, at Lamar ☎07 282 8801; map p.602. A beautifully restored, centrally located mansion full of understated elegance. The twelve rooms are very competitively priced, include buffet breakfast, and there's a fine restaurant. $\overline{\$74}$

★ **Macondo** Tarqui 11-64, at Mariscal Lamar ☎07 284 0697, ⓦhostalmacondo.com; map p.602. Colonial-style favourite with artwork on the walls, a spacious lawn in the back garden and a choice of private or shared bathrooms Good prices for solo travellers. Breakfast included. $\overline{\$45}$

Posada del Río Hermano Miguel 4-18; map p.602. Situated in an atmospheric colonial building, this place has lots of character. Rooms are clean, if spartan, and there are kitchen facilities and a TV lounge stocked with DVDs. Dorms $\overline{\$9}$, doubles $\overline{\$25}$

★ **TREAT YOURSELF**

Restaurante La Esquina Largo ☎07 284 5344; map p.602. La Esquina ("The Corner") is on busy Calle Largo but you'll love the accomplished Argentinian and Latin American cooking here, with perfectly executed meat and fish dishes, try the *costilla tomahawk* (ribs) or *corvina al limón* (sea bass in lemon sauce). The desserts are simply epic and the wine selection terrific. Mains $10–18

Posada Todos Santos C Larga 3-42, at Ordóñez ☎07 282 4247, ⓔposadatodossantoscue@latinmail.com; map p.602. Well-maintained place with pleasant, carpeted rooms and good en-suite showers. The owners are friendly and knowledgeable about Cuenca. $\overline{\$38}$

EATING

Cuenca has a good variety of international and local cuisine. *Membrillo* (a sweet gelatinous red block made with guayaba) is a local speciality. For inexpensive meals and fruit shakes head to the Mercado 10 de Agosto, on C Larga.

Cacao y Canela Jaramillo, at Borrero; map p.602. Snug little café serving a huge selection of hot chocolate drinks ($2–3) – rum, cinnamon, almonds and mozzarella are just a few of the flavours available. Great cakes and snacks too. Mon–Sat 4pm–late.

Café Nucallacta Hermano Miguel 5–62 ☎098 619 0490, ⓦcafenucallacta.com; map p.602. One of the hottest cafés in town; though the top-notch beans are the main draw, it also offers tasty breakfasts, brunches and light lunches. Mon–Sat 9am–7pm, Sun 9am–3pm.

Moliendo Café Honorato Vásquez 6–24; map p.602. Deservedly popular casual Colombian place offering fine *arepas* (maize buns) and filling *almuerzos* ($2.50) and *cenas* ($3.50). Mon–Sat 9am–9pm.

★ **El Pedregal Azteca** Estévez de Toral 860 ☎07 282 3652; map p.602. A classy, upmarket little Mexican place serving interesting, creative dishes such as *chile en nogada* (stuffed pepper with nut sauce) and delicious *pollo mole poblano* (chicken with spiced chocolate sauce). Mains $6–11. Tues–Sat noon–3pm & 6.30–10.30pm, Sun noon–3pm.

Pizzeria Marea/El Mentidero Cafe Hermano Miguel ⓦ pizzeriamarea.com.ec; map p.602. This boho bakery has all bases covered, its wood-fired oven pumping out great thin-crust pizza (from $6) while the café side of the operation offers fine breakfasts, cakes and pastries and espresso coffee ($1.60).

★ **La Quinua** Beningo Malo 12-73, at Vega Muñoz; map p.602. Excellent, mainly vegan breakfast and lunchtime menus – choose from soups, salads and veggie burgers or more traditional *motepillo* or guatita (stew) – to be enjoyed in a delightful interior courtyard. Modestly priced dishes ($3–8) and *almuerzos*. Mon–Fri 10am–4pm.

Raymipamba Benigno Malo, Parque Calderón; map p.602. A local institution, this bustling café is under the colonnaded arches of the Catedral Nueva, offering large portions of filling Ecuadorian staples and sweet and savoury crêpes for $4–6. Mon–Fri 8.30am–11pm, Sat & Sun 9.30am–10pm.

Taj Mahal C Larga, at Benigno Malo; map p.602. Yes the decor is a a tad tired, but the curries and *biryani* are authentic, delicious and inexpensive. They also do good kebabs. Main $4–6. Daily 8am–11pm

Tiestos Jaramillo 4-89 ☎07 283 5310, ⓦtiestosrestaurante.com; map p.602. Perhaps Cuenca's hottest dining ticket – evening reservations a must – offering casual, family-style dining with an open kitchen and dishes to share. Generous portions of creative Ecuadorian and fusion cuisine come in rich sauces. Around $30 a head. Tues–Sat 12.30–3pm & 6.30–10pm, Sun 12.30–3pm.

DRINKING AND NIGHTLIFE

There's everything from brewpubs to wine bars in central Cuenca. Many places are south of downtown and along C Larga.

Far Out Jaramillo 7-36, at Borrero; map p.602. This tiny rock music café boasts Ecuador's baddest stereo speakers per square metre. Huge high-sampling music collection and German-made craft beers on tap. Tues–Sat 7pm–late.

★ **Jodoco** Plaza San Sebastián ☎098 857 0082; map p.602. A gorgeous café-bar serving Belgian craft brews, accompanied by tapas-style snacks. There are outside tables on one of the town's most delightful squares, and a classy, arty interior. Also works as a café for an espresso hit. Mon–Sat 11am–late.

Monday Blue C Larga, at Cordero; map p.602. Atmospheric little bar with walls covered in art and eclectic memorabilia, serving cheap TexMex food. Thurs–Sat 8pm–late.

Verde Pintón y Maduro Presidente Borrero ☎099 474 8081; map p.602. Great bar-disco that's big on salsa on Thursday nights, though other tropical beats feature too – merengue, bachata, kizomba and even the ubiquitous reggaeton creeps in later on. National and international artists perform live at weekends. Variable cover charge. Tues–Thurs 6pm–midnight, Fri & Sat 6pm–3am.

Wunderbar Escalinata 3–43, off C Larga ☎07 2831274; map p.602. By day it's a relaxed café, by night it's a vibey bar. There's a stylish interior, large wooden tables, international bottled beers and occasional live music. Mon–Sat noon–midnight.

DIRECTORY

Banks and exchange Banco de Guayaquil on Mariscal Sucre, at Hermano Miguel; Banco de Austro on M. Sucre, at Borrero; Banco de Pacifico on Benigno Malo 9-75.

Hospitals Hospital Santa Inés on Av Daniel Cordova Toral 2-113, at Augustian Cueva (☎07 281 7888); Hospital Monte Sinai at Miguel Cordero 6-111, at Av Solano (☎07 288 5595).

Police Benigno Malo & Antonio Muñoz (☎07 281 0068).

Post office On Presidente Borrero, at Gran Colombia.

BAÑOS (CUENCA)

The ideal way to relax after sightseeing is to visit **BAÑOS** (not to be confused with its namesake between Ambato and Puyo), once a hamlet and now a suburb of Cuenca, a fifteen-minute uphill drive from the centre. A number of baths and spas have been established here, two of which are head and shoulders above the rest.

Hostería Durán (Av Ricardo Durán; $6; ☎07 289 2301, ⓦhosteriaduran.com), founded in the 1920s, sprawls over ten acres, with a hotel and large pool in the middle of an Andalucian-style colonnade, and a modern spa, Novaqua. This is rivalled by *Piedra de Agua* (Paseo de la Guadalupana; pool $12, spa circuit $35, spa packages from $65, ☎07 289 2496, ⓦpiedradeagua.com.ec), a more modern set-up with mud pools, Turkish baths and several mid-sized pools.

ARRIVAL

By bus Buses #12 and #200 (every 10min; 15 min) depart from Vega Muñoz, at Padre Aguirre or the bus terminal for Baños.

By taxi A taxi from Cuenca to Baños costs $5.

PARQUE NACIONAL EL CAJAS

Just 30km northwest of Cuenca, the enormous **PARQUE NACIONAL EL CAJAS** (daily 6am–5pm) spans nearly 300 square kilometres of spectacular moor-like *páramo*. With two hundred lakes shining beneath rugged hillsides, this is one of Ecuador's most compelling wildernesses, offering great hiking and trout-fishing opportunities. Highlights include wild llamas, which were introduced to the park in the late 1990s. There are ten hiking trails, ranging from a couple of hours to three days.

6

The short hike around Laguna Toreadora is the most popular, while the trail to Laguna Totoras takes six hours. However, the wind, rain and fog can often make visits uncomfortable so come prepared with rainproof gear, snacks, warm clothing and walking boots. Most of the park lies above 4000m so ensure you are properly acclimatized before tackling long hikes.

It's easy to visit independently by taking a Guayaquíl-bound bus and walking 100m to the Laguna Toreadora refuge station, which has maps and information on popular hiking trails. The station also has a few beds, or you can camp in the recreation area for about $5 per person, but it gets very cold. Cuenca-based tour operators (see page 588) offer guided tours costing from $35 per person.

The privately operated website ⓦ parque-nacional-cajas.org has useful information, or the tourist office in Cuenca can also help plan a trip.

VILLAGES AROUND CUENCA

There are several interesting indigenous villages close to Cuenca, famous for handicrafts. **Gualaceo** (45min east of Cuenca; bus from the terminal) has the largest indigenous market in the area on Sundays with a range of woven textiles – from shawls to tapestries. **Chordeleg** is 5km further and renowned for jewellery. A further fifteen minutes by bus is **Sigsig**, well known for the Panama hat factory on the edge of town. On a separate route, southeast of Cuenca, the village of **San Bartolomé** (30min by bus) is famous for handmade guitars.

LOJA

South of Cuenca, the road winds through varied Andean dry-and-warm or cold-and-wet microclimates until **LOJA**, some 215km away. Loja was founded in 1548 and today boasts a well-preserved historic centre, thriving music scene and spectacular parks.

WHAT TO SEE AND DO

Begin at the **Parque Central**, dominated by the towering yellow and white **Catedral**.

On the south side, the Museo de la Cultura Lojano (Mon–Fri 9am–5pm, Sat 9am–1pm; free) has a small collection of pre-Columbian ceramics and religious art. Walk south on Bolívar, and you reach the beautiful **Iglesia Santo Domingo**, which houses more than one hundred oil paintings. A couple of blocks further is the highlight of central Loja, the **Plaza de la Independencia** (also known as Plaza San Sebastián) with its brightly coloured colonial buildings. On the southwest corner is the **Iglesia San Sebastián**, while the square's focal point is an impressive clock tower with stone depictions of the battles for Ecuador's independence. Don't miss charming Calle Lourdes, which runs past San Sebastián and is lined with historic houses.

Loja's delightful parks are easily reached by a short taxi ride ($2). The best is the **Parque La Argelia** (daily 8am–6pm; $1), which has trails up through the forest and impressive views. Across the road is the **Jardín Botánico Reynaldo Espinosa** (daily 8am–6pm; $1), which has more than two hundred species of orchids.

ARRIVAL AND DEPARTURE

By plane Daily flights from Quito and Guayaquil arrive at the Aeropuerto Ciudad de Catamayo, 33km to the west. A shared taxi (about $6/person) is the only way to get directly to Loja from the airport, or take a taxi to the town of Catamayo ($2) and a bus from there to Loja.

By bus Loja's bus terminal is 2km north of the centre on Av Cuxibamba, with plenty of taxis ($1.50) and buses ($0.30) into town. Buses to Vilcabamba (75min; $1.25) leave about every 20–30 min.

By taxi The quickest way to reach Vilcabamba is in a shared taxi (40min; $2.50, or $10 for the whole taxi). The taxi company, 11 de Mayo (ⓣ 07 257 0956), has an office in the street of the same name, near Mercadillo.

INFORMATION

Tourist information iTur office, on Bolívar at Eguiguren (Mon–Fri 8am–6pm, Sat 9am–2pm; ⓣ 07 257 0407).

ACCOMMODATION

Hostal Londres Sucre 07-51 ⓣ 07 256 1936; map p.607. Perfect for real dollar watchers with very basic rooms, somewhat creaky beds, shared bathrooms and spotty wi-fi. A block west of the Parque Central. **$12**

Hostal Los Lirios Peña 09-59 ⓣ 07 258 8563; map p.607. This well-run little place, a 10min walk from the

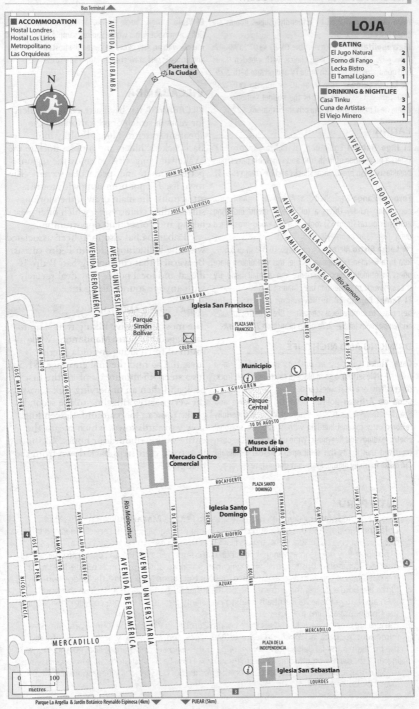

Bus Terminal

■ ACCOMMODATION
Hostal Londres	2
Hostal Los Lirios	4
Metropolitano	1
Las Orquideas	3

LOJA

● EATING
El Jugo Natural	2
Forno di Fango	4
Lecka Bistro	3
El Tamal Lojano	1

■ DRINKING & NIGHTLIFE
Casa Tinku	3
Cuna de Artistas	2
El Viejo Minero	1

6

N

Puerta de
la Ciudad

AVENIDA CUXIBAMBA

JUAN DE SALINAS

AVENIDA TOILO RODRIGUEZ

18 DE NOVIEMBRE

JOSÉ F. VALDIVIESO

SUCRE

BOLÍVAR

QUITO

AVENIDA ORILLAS DEL ZAMORA

AVENIDA AMILIANO ORTEGA

Río Zamora

AVENIDA IBEROAMERICA

AVENIDA UNIVERSITARIA

IMBABURA

BERNARDO VALDIVIESO

Iglesia San Francisco

Parque
Simón
Bolívar

PLAZA SAN
FRANCISCO

OLMEDO

JUAN JOSÉ PEÑA

COLÓN

RAMÓN PINTO

AVENIDA LAURO GUERRERO

JOSÉ MARÍA PEÑA

Municipio

J. A. EGUIGUREN

Parque
Central

Catedral

10 DE AGOSTO

**Museo de la
Cultura Lojano**

**Mercado Centro
Comercial**

ROCAFUERTE

PLAZA SANTO
DOMINGO

BERNARDO VALDIVIESO

OLMEDO

JUAN JOSÉ PEÑA

PASAJE SINCHINA

24 DE MAYO

Río Malacatus

18 DE NOVIEMBRE

**Iglesia Santo
Domingo**

SUCRE

MIGUEL RIOFRÍO

AVENIDA LAURO GUERRERO

RAMÓN PINTO

JOSÉ MARÍA PEÑA

NICOLÁS GARCIA

AZUAY

BOLÍVAR

AVENIDA IBEROAMERICA

AVENIDA UNIVERSITARIA

MERCADILLO

MERCADILLO

PLAZA DE LA
INDEPENDENCIA

Iglesia San Sebastian

LOURDES

0   100
metres

Parque La Argelia & Jardín Botánico Reynaldo Espinosa (4km)   PUEAR (5km)

main plaza, is managed by a friendly couple. Rooms are small but neat. **$22**

Metropolitano 18 de Noviembre 06-31 ☎ 07 257 0007; map p.607. Solid mid-range choice, with wooden floors and good-sized rooms with cable TV and private bath. **$25**

★ **Las Orquideas** Bolívar, at 10 de Agosto ☎ 07 258 7008; map p.607. The best of the budget options, with clean, neat rooms with TV and private bathroom. **$22**

EATING

El Jugo Natural Eguiguren, at Bolívar; map p.607. Offers a huge range of fresh fruit and vegetable juices, plus breakfasts, fresh bread, local snacks and ice cream ($2–3). Daily 7am–7.30pm.

Forno di Fango 24 de Mayo, at Azuay ⓦ fornodifango. com; map p.607. Offers a full Italian menu including authentic pizzas (from $5) cooked up in a wood-fire domed oven. Tues–Sun noon–10pm.

★ **Lecka Bistro** Alemán 24 de Mayo 10-51; map p.607. Run by a German-Ecuadorian couple, this welcoming place offers an intimate dining experience from a small menu. Try the *currywurst* and a German beer. Mains $5–8

El Tamal Lojano 18 de Noviembre; map p.607. The best place to sample local specialities like *humitas*, *tamales* and *empanadas* for $1–2. Another branch on 24 de Mayo.

DRINKING AND NIGHTLIFE

Casa Tinku Lourdes, at Bolívar; map p.607. In a colonial-style setting, a good place to catch live music (rock, cover bands) or a DJ at weekends.

Cuna de Artistas Bolívar, between Rocafuerte and Riofrío ☎ 0994 280390; map p.607. Wonderfully restored, arty colonial building with exhibitions, seasonal poetry readings and live music. Wrap up warm, as the open courtyard that fronts this semi-open café-bar-restaurant can make for chilly dining. Mon–Sat noon–late.

El Viejo Minero Sucre 10-76, at Riofrío; map p.607. Boho, atmospheric bar where you can sample craft beer and mingle with an arty crowd. Occasionally hosts live rock gigs and acoustic sets at weekends. Mon–Sat 5pm–late.

VILCABAMBA

VILCABAMBA has been attracting travellers for years in search of relaxation and the apparent secret to a long, healthy life. Backpackers, hikers and hippies flock to the "Valley of Longevity" to enjoy the region's perfect climate and spectacular scenery. The town itself is not brimming with tourist attractions; the main draw is the glorious surrounding countryside, which offer great **hiking** and **horseriding** opportunities.

Vilcabamba has also long been associated with the hallucinogenic San Pedro cactus. Be warned that consuming San Pedro is illegal and local police may deal severely with anyone found taking it.

WHAT TO SEE AND DO

The most impressive hiking trail is up to the jagged hill **Cerro Mandango**. Walk south of town along Avenida Eterna Juventud to find the trail entrance ($1.50). It's a steep 45-minute climb to the first peak and then an unnerving trek across the very narrow ridgeline to the second peak. You can loop around, descending slowly towards town, which means the entire walk is about four hours. To shorten it, retrace your steps back down from the first peak.

INTO PERU

If you're in the southern sierra, it's better to cross to Peru via **Macará**, 190km southeast of **Loja**, than go down to the coast and cross via frenetic Huaquillas. A bus service operated by Cooperativa Loja (☎ 07 257 9014) travels from Loja to Piura in Peru via Macará (7am, 1pm & 11pm; 6hr). Buy tickets in advance if possible. The company has offices in Loja bus terminal and next to Vilcabamba's bus terminal. From Vilcabamba take a bus to Loja and change. In Macará the bus stops at the 24hr Migración office for your exit stamp. Walk across the bridge, which forms the border, to get the entry stamp on the other side, and then get back on the bus.

An alternative route via Zumba is gaining popularity because it is more convenient if visiting the Chachapoyas ruins in Peru.

There are eight scheduled buses from Loja to Zumba via Vilcabamba (6hr). From Zumba, infrequent trucks called *rancheras* leave at (8am, 2pm, and, less reliably, 5pm; 1hr 30min) to the border post at La Balsa. However sections of this road are only partially paved and rough in parts; there may be closures in the rainy season. From La Balsa shared-taxi *camionetas* leave for San Ignacio (2hr; $7–15 depending on the number of passengers) where there are decent guesthouses and an ATM.

Easier trails are found at Rumi Wilco Nature Reserve (ⓦrumiwilco.com), just ten minutes east of town. There are half a dozen trails through the protected forest beside the river Chamba.

Many hotels have excellent **massage** facilities attached, try Massage Beauty Care (Diego Vaca de Vega, at Bolívar; $15/hr; ⓣ07 264 0359). For yoga head to Izhcayluma (see page 610) where there are daily sessions. The well-regarded Mindfulness Meditation, Bolívar (ⓣ08 959 2880, ⓦmindfulnessmeditationinecuador. org) is dedicated to meditation.

ARRIVAL AND DEPARTURE

By bus Buses run to and from Loja (every 20–30min; 75min) from the corner of Av de la Eterna Juventud and C Jaramillo. To go to Peru, buses to Zumba pass through Vilcabamba. To cross via Macará, take a bus from Loja.

By taxi Pick-up trucks act as taxis and charge $1– 1.50 to most of the accommodation in and around Vilcabamba.

INFORMATION AND TOURS

Banks and exchange There are a couple of ATMs on the Parque Central but no bank; the nearest is in Loja. Machines frequently run out of money at weekends.

Tourist information The tourist office, on the Parque Central (daily 8am–1pm & 2–6pm; ⓣ07 264 0090), provides maps and information on hikes and excursions around Vilcabamba.

Tour operators Caballos Gavilán (Sucre, at Diego Vaca; ⓣ07 264 0281) organizes fine horseriding tours ($50/day) to the Podocarpus cloudforest and hiking trips; La Tasca Tours, Parque Central (ⓣ07 264 0404, ⓔlatascatours@ yahoo.com) offers a variety of tours: biking, horse riding and/or hiking to a waterfall and private reserve (where they have cabins).

6

★ TREAT YOURSELF

Madre Tierra ☎07 264 0269, ⓦmadretierra. com.ec; map p.609. A lovely, award-winning spa hotel with a wide range of stone and timber rooms and stylish suites. There are fabulous views of the valley and also a popular patio restaurant and small pool. Breakfast and soft drinks included. Located 1km north of town. Doubles $39, family suites $79

ACCOMMODATION

Expect to pay a little more for accommodation in Vilcabamba than in other parts of Ecuador.

★ **Izhcayluma** ☎07 264 0095, ⓦizhcayluma.com; map p.609. About 2km south of town, this friendly German-owned *hostería* has a good choice of rustic accommodation, daily (free) yoga sessions, a small spa, lovely pool, table tennis and great views. The owners have mapped out trails around Vilcabamba for hikers. Don't miss the Bavarian specialities in the restaurant. Breakfast included. Dorms $9.50, doubles $26

Jardín Escondido Sucre, at Diego Vaca ☎07 264 0281; map p.609. Simple but spacious rooms around a garden with lemon trees, a small pool and jacuzzi. The hotel's Mexican restaurant is excellent. Dorms $14, doubles $35

Las Margaritas Sucre, at C Jaramillo ☎07 264 0051; map p.609. This B&B feels like a family residence, with a cosy atmosphere and well-maintained rooms, all with en suites. Breakfast is included. $32

Le Rendez-Vous Diego Vaca de la Vega ☎093 948 5087; ⓦrendezvousecuador.wixsite.com; map p.609. A peaceful, French-owned guesthouse, located a short walk from the centre with charming cottages set in lush gardens. Breakfast included. $35

Rumi Wilco Ecolodge 1km northeast of the centre ☎07 264 0186, ⓦrumiwilco.com; map p.609. Fine ecolodge set in a large private reserve with good hiking trails. Offers a wide a variety of self-catering accommodation: wooden cabins, adobe buildings and camping ($5/person). Dorms $10, doubles $23

EATING

Many hotels have good restaurants attached, particularly the Mexican food at *Jardín Escondido* and German food at *Izhcayluma*.

La Cocina de Carolina Diega Vaca de Vega; map p.609. Specializes in delicious home-baked pies, with personal portions at just $2.50 and large pot pies (try the sliced beef) starting at $6. Also good soups, salad and iced tea. Mon–Sat 8am–4pm.

Katherine Sucre, at Jaramillo; map p.609. Inexpensive Ecuadorian food and friendly service are offered by this simple local restaurant, with *seco de chivo* (goat stew) at weekends. Mains $3–6. Daily 8am–10pm.

Natural Yoghurt Bolívar, at Diego Vaca; map p.609. Tiny café serving excellent-value fresh, organic food: healthy breakfasts, and lots of vegetarian and vegan choices including good soups and quesadillas with tasty guacamole. Dishes $1.50–3.50. Daily 8am–10pm.

Shantas Diego Vaca de la Vega; map p.609. This casual place offers a fine selection of dishes, including trout and frog's legs and very popular pizzas ($7–10). Tues–Sun noon–9pm.

La Terraza Parque Central; map p.609. Serves good *almuerzos* as well as tasty Mexican, Italian and Chinese dishes ($5–7). The set lunch ($2.50) is great value. Daily 9am–10pm.

DRINKING

Nightlife is almost non-existent in Vilcabamba but there are some spots for a brew or two.

Donde Bava Vía Yamburara; map p.609. Atmospheric microbrewery where three craft beers (lager, red and dark) are served and there's a small menu of (mainly) vegetarian food. Fri & Sat 6–11pm, Sun 1–9pm.

PODOCARPUS AND YACURI

Ecuador's southernmost national parks contain remarkable diversity from high *páramo* to tropical jungle. The parks are comparatively remote, but visitors are rewarded with pristine lakes, hillsides covered in cloudforest, waterfalls, and thousands of species of plants. There are six hundred species of birds, including 61 species of hummingbirds, as well as spectacled bear, tapirs and deer, although you will be very lucky to see them.

ARRIVAL AND TOURS

Cajanuma ranger station between Loja and Vilcabamba is the most popular and accessible entrance to Podocarpus.
By bus Buses from Vilcabamba drop you on the main road 9km from the entrance (tell the driver you are going to Podocarpus).
By taxi A taxi from Vilcabamba is approximately $15.
Tours There are hikes ranging from one hour to several days. If you are planning to stay longer, you are better off arranging a tour in Vilcabamba.

The Oriente

East of Quito, the Andes drop dramatically and snowcapped mountains give way to verdant swathes of tropical rainforest stretching 250km to the Colombian and Peruvian borders. Ecuador's chunk of the Amazon basin, known as the **Oriente** ("The East"), constitutes almost half of the country's territory, although only five percent of the population lives here, in oil towns and remote indigenous communities. However, with oil exploration increasing and roads improving, new villages and towns are expanding. Sadly, areas of

pristine jungle remain under threat here with one of the continent's highest rates of deforestation.

The **Eastern Oriente** offers the most spectacular opportunities for visitors to encounter an array of flora and fauna in primary rainforest. The highlights are huge protected areas – **Parque Nacional Yasuní** and the **Reserva Faunística Cuyabeno** and lodges in indigenous communities to the south. Reaching these unforgettable wildernesses usually involves travelling through the forgettable hubs of **Lago Agrio** or **Coca**. For those with limited time

JUNGLE TOURS

If you dream of striking out on your own and hacking through dense jungle like a hardcore explorer, dream on. Unguided travel is strongly discouraged by the government and not advisable, considering how inhospitable and inaccessible parts of the Oriente remain. **Guided tours** are the best option, starting at around $45 per person per day for daytrips. Multiday trips begin at around $85/day. Always check that your guide has a **permit** from the Ministry of Tourism. Generally the larger the number of people in your group, the lower the price. Solo travellers usually have to share a cabin or pay a higher rate for a separate room. Tours range from two to eight days and can often be booked at the last minute. For tours around Puyo and Tena, a couple of days will give you an insight into life in the Oriente, but if you are travelling deep into the jungle, more than four days is recommended, because nearly two days will be spent travelling.

You must prepare thoroughly and pack **essentials** before heading into the jungle. Take plenty of insect repellent, long-sleeved tops, trousers, waterproofs, a torch and boots. A first-aid kit is also advisable, although the guide will carry one. Anti-malarials and yellow fever vaccinations are recommended (see page 34). You must carry your original **passport**, as copies are not sufficient at military checkpoints.

TOUR OPERATORS

It's easiest to book your tour in Quito, particularly for those going via Coca and Lago Agrio. For shorter tours to secondary jungle, operators in Tena (see page 615) and Baños (see page 597) are also useful. Booking locally in Coca and Lago Agrio is more difficult so it's better to make arrangements beforehand. The following Quito operators are recommended:

Cuyabeno River Lodge Juan León Mera N24-91 ☎02 290 3629, ⓦcuyabenoriver.com. Economical tours of the Cuyabeno reserve exploring its various black- and white-water river systems by canoe, and visiting local communities. Four-day tours cost $260.

Dracaena J Pinto E4-453, at Amazonas ☎02 254 6590, ⓦamazondracaena.com. Offers four- to eight-day tours (starting at $280) of Cuyabeno staying at campsite and lodges.

Magic River Tours 18 de Diciembre, at C Primera, Pacayacu ☎02 262 9303, ⓦmagicrivertours.com. German-owned company specializing in canoe trips in the Cuyabeno reserve. Four days from $360.

Neotropic Turis J Pinto E4-340 near Amazonas and Wilson ☎02 252 121, ⓦneotropicturis.com. Four-day tours to Cuyabeno Reserve, staying in *Cuyabeno Lodge*, from $380.

Rainforestur Amazonas 410, at Robles ☎02 223 9822, ⓦrainforestur.com. Wide range of jungle tours throughout the Oriente via Lago Agrio, Coca, Puyo and Tena. English, French- and German-speaking guides available; four days from $260.

Tropic Journeys in Nature Pasaje Sánchez Melo OE 1-37 and Galo, Plaza Lasso ☎02 240 8741, ⓦtropiceco.com. Ecologically minded agency that works alongside community-based ecotourism projects. Two-day tours to Kichwa communities near Tena cost $760.

seeking an accessible experience, much more pleasant towns of **Tena** and **Macas** (and perhaps Puyo) are surrounded by secondary rainforest with chances to stay with **indigenous communities**. The higher elevation of these towns makes **whitewater rafting** and **kayaking** popular activities in rapids tumbling down to the Amazon basin. From **Mera** near Puyo, small aircraft provide short flights to remote indigenous villages.

THE ROAD TO LAGO AGRIO

The bus ride from Quito to Lago Agrio (7hr) is long and arduous and you might consider flying. If you take the bus, it makes sense to break the journey up with visits to **Papallacta** (see page 581) and **San Rafael Falls**, Ecuador's largest waterfalls. The latter are located three hours after Baeza, 2.5km along a trail from the main road (ask the bus driver). You should allow yourself about one hour thirty minutes to walk down to the falls and back.

LAGO AGRIO

The gritty frontier town of **LAGO AGRIO** was used by Texaco in the 1960s as a base for oil exploration in the Oriente and takes its name (meaning "sour lake") from the company's original headquarters in Texas. Today it epitomizes the power struggle between oil companies keen to get their hands on the "black gold" underneath the jungle and tour operators keen to preserve the once pristine forests of the nearby **Cuyabeno Reserve**. Now that the Colombian FARC guerrilla group (who infiltrated the region until recently) has disbanded, security issues have eased, though "Lago" (as it's known locally) remains a somewhat edgy place.

ARRIVAL AND DEPARTURE

By plane The airport is 4km east of Lago Agrio. TAME (9 de Octubre, at Orellana; ☎06 283 0113) has six to seven weekly flights from Quito. Taxi cost $3 to the town centre.
By bus The bus station is 2km northeast of the centre. Destinations Coca (every 45min; 2hr); Puyo (3 daily; 8hr 30min); Quito (every 30–60min; 7hr); Tena (3 daily; 7hr).

ACCOMMODATION AND EATING

Gran Colombia Av Quito 265 ☎06 283 1032. Well-equipped but rather characterless rooms with fans (a/c extra) and cable TV. $30
Hotel D'Mario Quito 2-63 ☎06 2830172, ⓦhoteldmario.com. Ignore the mustier downstairs rooms and go for the rooms and suites on the middle or top floors, which are fresher and cleaner, with a/c, cable TV, fridge and phone. Continental breakfast included. The restaurant here does filling local dishes. $25
★ **Hostal Platinum Class** Amazonas ☎06 236 6797. Fine new hotel run by a hospitable couple, offering good-value, en-suite rooms. Located on the edge of town, $1.50 in a taxi from the centre. $35

Pedacito de Colombia Quito, at Colombia. Offers cheap Colombian specialities such as *arepas* (stuffed corn pancakes) and *tamales* on Sundays. Daily 6am–8pm.

RESERVA FAUNÍSTICA CUYABENO

This beautiful reserve (admission $20) of unique **flooded rainforest** spreads out over 6000 square kilometres east of Lago Agrio, extending to the Peruvian border. It contains an astonishing biodiversity of plants, trees, mammals and aquatic wildlife. Meandering down the Río Aguarico through huge areas of inundated forest and passing countless lagoons is unforgettable. Pink freshwater **dolphins**, white and black **caiman**, **anacondas**, **giant otters** and many species of **monkeys** are commonly seen, while jaguars will likely prove elusive.

The borders of the reserve were expanded in the early 1990s, partly in response to damaging oil exploration. Sadly, areas of Cuyabeno have been badly polluted, but vocal indigenous protest has improved the situation and there remain areas of unspoilt jungle. You need a guided tour (see page 579) to explore this remote region.

COCA

The booming capital of Orellana province, **COCA** has grown rapidly since the 1970s into a sprawling oil town. It's not somewhere to linger long, but does boast an attractive riverfront malecón. The fine new **Museo Arqueológico Central Cultural Orellana** on Avenida 6 de Diciembre (Mon–Fri 8am–noon & 2–6pm, Sat 9am–1pm; $5) has a small collection of fascinating artefacts from pre-Columbian riverine communities; don't miss the black and white "magic axes". Coca is the last major town on the Río Napo, the gateway to the enormous **Parque Nacional Yasuní**, and is also a possible gateway to Peru via **Nuevo Rocafuerte**, though it's an arduous trip involving many river boats.

Wildlife Amazon, at *Hotel San Fermín*, Bolívar and Quito (☎06 288 0802, ⓦamazonwildlife.ec), is a reliable outfit offering a wide range of jungle tours (around $380 for four days). Otherwise, most travellers organize tours from Quito (see page 579).

ARRIVAL AND DEPARTURE

By plane Tame flies to Quito, Guayaquil and Latacunga while Avianca flies to Quito daily. The terminal is 2km from the central riverfront on the Napo (taxi $1).

By boat Coop de Transportes Fluviales Orellana (☎06 288 0087) has an office on the riverside and operates boat services to Nuevo Rocafuerte on the Peruvian border (daily at 7.30am; 10–12hr; $18). Advance booking advised. The office doubles as a tourist information point.

By bus Coca's modern bus terminal is 3.5km north of town. Destinations Baños (3 daily; 7hr); Quito (14 daily; 8–10hr); Tena (every 30min–1hr; 4hr);.

By taxi Taxis will transport you to/from the bus terminal ($2) or around town for $1.

ACCOMMODATION AND EATING

El Auca Napo, at Rocafuerte. The best upscale place in town, with a varied menu – from shrimps in garlic to pork chops with pineapple. $8–12.

La Casa de Maito Espejo. Best place in town for *maito*, a delicious traditional fish dish, usually tilapia, which is folded in leaves and chargrilled. Mon & Wed–Sun 7am–10pm.

La Misión Camilo de Torrano ☎06 288 0260, ⓔhotelamision@hotmail.com. Next to the river, this long-running place has a choice of somewhat dated but decent rooms, swimming pools and steam baths. Squirrel monkeys roam the grounds. $55

Hotel San Fermín Bolívar, at Quito ☎06 288 0802, ⓦamazonwildlife.ec. Attractive budget hotel featuring lots of natural wood. Rooms have fans and shared or private bathroom; a/c costs $7 extra. $20

Oasis Camilo de Torrano ☎06 288 0206. Simple, small rooms that don't face the river, but the terrace does. $15

PARQUE NACIONAL YASUNÍ

YASUNÍ is one of Ecuador's last great wildernesses and the country's largest mainland national park. The terrain of nearly 10,000 square kilometres ranges from upland tropical forest to seasonally flooded forest, marshes, swamps, lakes and rivers. This region remained jungle through the last Ice Age and therefore has staggering biodiversity – more than five hundred species of **birds** and sixty percent of Ecuador's **mammals**, including jaguar, puma and tapir. A highlight is the spectacle at the clay licks where dozens of parrots and parakeets congregate daily to feed.

UNESCO declared it an International Biosphere Reserve in 1979 but this didn't prevent oil exploration. The construction of a road, Vía Maxus, through parts of the park and pollution from irresponsible oil companies has damaged some areas. However, large sections remain unscathed and Yasuní still offers the best opportunity in Ecuador to experience pristine

---

CROSSING INTO PERU: NUEVO ROCAFUERTE

For adventurers wanting to emulate Francisco de Orellana and float deeper down the Río Napo into the Amazon Basin, improved relations between Ecuador and Peru in the past decade have made it easier to cross the border via Nuevo Rocafuerte. There are even plans afoot to make the trip possible all the way to Brazil's Atlantic coast, although this remains to be seen. This is not a trip for those who like comfort, as it's around ten hours downstream from Coca. Boats leave Coca daily at 7.30am ($18 one-way), usually stopping off at Pañacocha. Come prepared with adequate supplies of food, water purification tablets and insect repellent. In Nuevo Rocafuerte there are a few basic, cheap places to stay but nowhere good enough to linger long. From Nuevo Rocafuerte you receive an **exit stamp** and boats cross the border to Pantoja, where you get an **entry stamp**. Pantoja also has a small amount of basic accommodation. Slow boats leave to Iquitos (Peru) from Coca via Nuevo Rocafuerte only once or twice a month, a trip that takes a minimum of six days. For a far speedier trip, contact Luis Duarte (ⓔecocaselva@hotmail.com) who runs two-day trips to Iquitos in Peru in a twin-engine boat (minimum ten passengers). Wildlife Amazon (see page 613) also offers boat tours to Iquitos.

6

rainforest. Most tours coming through Coca include a visit to the park.

TENA

TENA is the most pleasant town in the Oriente to be based for a few days. Rather than being merely a gateway to the jungle, it's a destination in itself, with a slightly cooler climate, good hotels and restaurants, and an impressive setting on the river surrounded by lush forest. Nearby **Misahuallí** also offers a convenient place to dip into the jungle experience.

Aside from exploring the lanes around the cathedral and relaxing in a riverside

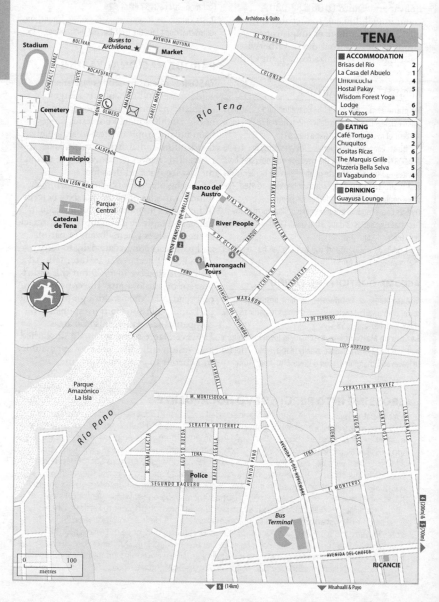

▲ Archidona & Quito

TENA

■ **ACCOMMODATION**
Brisas del Rio	2
La Casa del Abuelo	1
Limoncocha	4
Hostal Pakay	5
Wisdom Forest Yoga Lodge	6
Los Yutzos	3

● **EATING**
Café Tortuga	3
Chuquitos	2
Cositas Ricas	6
The Marquis Grille	1
Pizzería Bella Selva	5
El Vagabundo	4

■ **DRINKING**
Guayusa Lounge	1

Stadium

Buses to Archidona ★

Market

Cemetery

Municipio

Parque Central

Catedral de Tena

N

Banco del Austro

River People

Amarongachi Tours

Parque Amazónico La Isla

Río Pano

Police

Bus Terminal

RICANCIE

0   100
metres

▼ **6** (14km)   ▼ Misahuallí & Puyo

TOUR OPERATORS

Tena-based operators offer jungle tours, most of which are all-inclusive of transport, accommodation, food and guides. Tena is also the best place in Ecuador for **whitewater rafting** and **kayaking** on the countless tributaries surrounded by spectacular jungle scenery. There are plenty of local tour operators, but ensure you book with an experienced, well-equipped organization, ideally accredited by AGAR. The most famous stretches of river are the Jondachi and Jatunyacu or Upper Napo (both class III) and the wilder Misahuallí and Hollín (class IV). Day-trips are typically $50–75, and longer trips with overnight accommodation are from $140

Agency Limoncocha Sangay 533 ☎06 288 7583, ⓦ hostallimoncocha.com. Based in the *hostal* of the same name; offers good jungle tours, two-day trips cost $110–130.

Pakay Tours Urb. 30 de Diciembre ☎06 284 7449, ⓦ en.ecuadorpakaytours.com. A variety of personalized, informative and ethical tours, from tubing to investigating petroglyphs. $40–75/day.

Ricancie Av El Chofer, at Pullurcu ☎06 284 6262, ⓦ ricancie.nativeweb.org. Coordinates ten indigenous community ecotourism projects in the upper Napo

region. Rafting on the Jatun Yaku river costs from $60/ person.

Rios Ecuador Tarqui 230 ☎06 288 6727 or Quito ☎02 260 5828, ⓦ riosecuador.com. Runs rafting and kayaking excursions and jungle adventure trips combining horse riding, hiking and rafting. Expect to pay $65–95/day.

River People 15 de Noviembre, at 9 de Octubre ☎0995 440234, ⓦ riverpeopleecuador.com. Professional, English-run outfit offering a range of river-based tours (most $70–90 for day-trips).

restaurant, the main attraction is **Parque Amazónico La Isla** (daily 8am–6pm; $2) connected to town via a sleek new pedestrian bridge. This park has several self-guided forested trails, diverse plants and wildlife.

ARRIVAL AND INFORMATION

By bus The terminal is 1km south of the centre. A taxi from here or anywhere around town costs $1.

Destinations Baños (hourly; 4hr); Coca (hourly; 4hr 30min); Puyo (every 30–45min; 2hr 30min); Quito via Baeza (every 45min; 5hr); Riobamba (7 daily; 6hr).

Tourist information Agusto Rueda (Mon–Fri 8am–12.30pm & 2–5pm; ☎06 288 8046). Helpful, and has maps.

ACCOMMODATION

Brisas del Río Av Francisco de Orellana 248 ☎06 288 6208; map p.614. One of the best-located budget hotels on the river, and with friendly owners. Single rooms are available while pricier options have a/c, cable TV and private bath. $18

La Casa del Abuelo Sucre 432 ☎06 288 6318; map p.614. An inviting place which offers well-furnished rooms with high ceilings and a pleasant rooftop terrace. $38

Limoncocha Av del Chofer ☎06 288 7583, ⓦ hostallimoncocha.com; map p.614. German-Ecuadorian-run *hostal* on the southeast edge of town with a travel agency, guests' kitchen and lovely terrace with hammocks. Dorms $7, doubles $16

★ **Hostal Pakay** Urb. 30 de Diciembre, ☎06 284 7449, ⓦ en.ecuadorpakaytours.com; map p.614. Eco-hostel set in lush, tropical forest with well-constructed accommodation and terraces ideal for birdwatching. They

run a wide range of ethical tours. Breakfast included. Located 2km or so from the centre. Dorms $13, doubles $34

Wisdom Forest Yoga Lodge ☎098 368 8467, ⓦ wisdomforest.org; map p.614. Some 15km southwest of Tena this remote yoga lodge could be the perfect off-grid experience you're seeking. Expect fine, structured yoga classes in a spectacular shala overlooking the rainforest, wonderful veggie food and a clean-living ethos: no alcohol, drugs, meat (or wi-fi!). $30/person full board

★ **Los Yutzos** Agusto Rueda 190, at 15 de Noviembre ☎06 288 6717, ⓔ yutzos@outlook.com; map p.614. Enjoys a riverside location and its spacious, tastefully decorated rooms make this a fine choice. Lounge on the terrace overlooking the river or relax in the gardens. Breakfast included. $42

EATING

Café Tortuga Francisco de Orellana; map p.614. Travellers' favourite with friendly service, an ideal location on the river and great coffee, juices and shakes, breakfasts, snacks and desserts. Meals $3–6. Mon–Sat 7am–7.30pm, Sun 7am–1pm.

Chuquitos Off Parque Central; map p.614. An excellent riverside position, with a wide-ranging menu and attentive service. The fish is particularly good. Mains $7–10.

Cositas Ricas Av 15 de Noviembre, at 9 de Octubre; map p.614. Serves tasty Ecuadorian staples (most $4–7) and is a good option for the cheap set lunch. Daily 12.30–9.30pm.

★ **The Marquis Grille** Amazonas, at Olmedo; map p.614. One of Tena's few upmarket restaurants, this formal, stylish restaurant offers specialities including paella and *parrilladas*, try the grilled corvina ($17) Mains $10–28. Mon–Sat noon–3pm & 6–11pm, Sun noon–3pm.

6

Pizzeria Bella Selva Francisco de Orellana; map p.614. Bustling waterside place serving pizza and large plates of pasta. Pizza from $7. Daily noon–10pm.
El Vagabundo 9 de Octubre, at Tarqui; map p.614. Popular, atmospheric bar-restaurant offering a varied, well-priced menu at cosy candlelit tables. Choose from German, Italian, Mexican and Ecuadorian favourites; try the goulash. Daily 5pm–late.

DRINKING

Guayusa Lounge Olmedo, at Juan Montalvo; map p.614. As hip as it gets in the Oriente, this stylish lounge has house and electronic DJs on weekends and occasionally live music. There's a devilish cocktail list (most under $4) as well as bar food. Tues–Sat 4pm–late.

PUYO

If you're arriving from Baños or even Tena, **PUYO** will at first sight be a disappointment, as the centre is less than attractive. But 3km southeast of town is the **Jardín Botánico Las Orquídeas** (daily 8.30am–4.30pm; $5 book in advance; ☏03 253 0305, ⊛ jardinbotanicolasorquideas.com). These botanical gardens, set among lush hills, boast more than two hundred species of native Amazonian orchids. Also worth visiting is **Parque Pedagógico Etno-Botánico Omaere** (daily 9am–5pm; $3; ⊛ omaere.wordpress. com), a ten-minute walk north from the city centre, which has guided tours along forested paths past indigenous dwellings. Part of the park is primary jungle and it offers an interesting glimpse for those not planning to venture further into the rainforest.

ARRIVAL AND DEPARTURE

By bus The bus station is 1km west of the centre, $1.50 by taxi.
Destinations Baños (every 30min; 1hr 15min); Quito (every 45min; 5hr); Tena (hourly; 2hr 30min).

INFORMATION AND TOURS

Tourist information Inside the *municipio*, 9 de Octubre (Mon–Fri 8.30am–6pm; closes for lunch; ☏03 288 5122). Staff are friendly and can provide a map.
Tour operators Most travellers book tours from Quito or Baños but there are a few good tour operators in Puyo. Tribal communities, such as the Huaorani, are only reachable by

THE BEST JUNGLE LODGES

Prices include all accommodation, food, guides and tours. Transfers are extra. Contact details given are for the Quito offices of each operator. Most lodges do last-minute deals when you can save up to thirty percent, but you risk coming up empty-handed.

Cabañas Shiripuno Comunidad de Shiripuno ☏06 289 0203, ⊛ shiripuno.weebly.com. Just 2km from Misahuallí these rustic cabins are run by the Shiripuno community, who also share cultural activities, including cooking and hunting, with guests. All-inclusive tour cost for two sharing $70/day.
Cotococha Lodge Amazonas, at Wilson ☏02 223 4336, ⊛ cotococha.com. Located on the Napo River between Tena and Puyo, with 22 thatched cabañas and a lounge area. Three days from $295.
Cuyabeno Lodge Pinto, at Amazonas ☏02 252 121, ⊛ cuyabenolodge.com.ec. The first lodge in Cuyabeno Reserve, these simple eco-cabins are still one of the cheapest ways to experience primary jungle. Transport from Lago Agrio is included; four days from $380.
Itamandi Eco Lodge Tamayo N24-96, at Foch ☏02 222 0827, ⊛ itamandi.com. Elegant lodge near Tena

with swimming pool, but reachable by river only. The best quick jungle experience, starting from two days/one night from $133 (ten-percent discount for cash).
Jamu Lodge Calama, at Reina Victoria ☏02 222 0614, ⊛ jamulodge.com. Fine-value jungle lodges, with nine thatched cabins in the Cuyabeno Reserve. Three days from $262.
Liana Lodge ☏0999 800463, ⊛ lianalodge.ec. Simple but nicely crafted cabins on the Río Arajuno, a tributary of the Napo. Activities include guided walks, birding, visits to a Kichwa family and shaman, fishing and visiting AmaZOOnico, which the profits help support. Three-night inclusive packages $291
La Selva Jungle Lodge San Salvador E7-85, at Carrión ☏02 255 0995, ⊛ laselvajunglelodge.com. Deep in primary jungle next to Yasuní National Park this luxe lodge enjoys a spectacular lakeside location. Four days from $1215.

OIL AND THE ENVIRONMENT

Oil has provided lifeblood for Ecuador's economy since 1972, when the military dictatorship paraded around the first barrel of oil to herald the country's future prosperity. But today, the Oriente, which produces almost all of Ecuador's oil, has some of the poorest areas of Ecuador and the environmental impact has been devastating in places.

The sad legacy of the industry's first two decades can be seen on the road between Lago Agrio and Coca in the form of open pits and numerous spills that continue to happen with depressing regularity. Between courtroom battles and street protests, the struggle over responsibility has dragged on. In 2007, Rafael Correa floated an idea to keep the oil in the northeastern part of Yasuní National Park underground as an anti climate-change initiative. Named after the Ishpingo, Tambococha and Tiputini (ITT) oilfields, Correa sought $3.6 billion in international donations in exchange for leaving the oil *in situ*. But design flaws and doubts about Ecuador's reliability kept the money to a trickle. Blaming stingy foreigners, Correa U-turned in 2013 and pressed ahead with oil development.

In 2018, Ecuador's state oil company Petroamazonas started drilling the first of 97 planned wells inside the Yasuní, provoking outrage and protests from environmental groups.

light aircraft from the Shell-Mera airport 10km west of town; information about Huaorani communities can be obtained from the political body ONHAE (☎03 288 6148). Amazonía (Atahualpa, at 9 de Octubre; ☎03 288 3219) offers a range of tours to indigenous communities close to Puyo from $30/day depending on numbers. Papangu (27 de Febrero, at Sucre; ☎03 288 7684, ⑩papangutours. com.ec) is an indigenous-run agency offering tours to nearby indigenous communities and further afield to Misahualli and Kapawy (some destinations involve travel by light aircraft). Tours start at $75/day not including flights. Selva Vida (Ceslao Marín, at Villamil; ☎03 288 9729, ⑩selvavidatravel.com) offers jungle trips plus five-day trips to Yasuní for $450.

ACCOMMODATION

Puyo has decent-enough hotels and guesthouses but if you can afford it head straight to a jungle lodge.

Hostal Araucano Ceslao Marín, at 27 de Febrero ☎03 288 5686. Worn, weathered rooms but very friendly service in this cosy budget option in town. Breakfast included. $18

Las Palmas 20 de Julio, at 4 de Enero ☎03 288 4832. A flashpackers' stronghold on the edge of town with fine-value rooms and a lush garden to enjoy; breakfast included. $35

Posada Real 4 de Enero ☎03 288 5887, ⑩posadarealpuyo.com. This well-run colonial-style guesthouse has a convenient central location and its rooms are well presented, some with balconies. A filling breakfast is included . $50

EATING

★ **EscoBar-Cafe** Ceslao Marín. This rustic-chic bar-restaurant is Puyo's coolest place to chill, a landmark bamboo structure decorated with tribal art. Upstairs, tuck into healthy, tasty breakfasts, salads and grilled meats (most mains $5–8), or laze in the café-bar below, sipping fresh juice, craft beer or a cappuccino. Daily 9am–midnight.

El Jardín Barrio Obrero. In the lodge of the same name, this is the best restaurant in the region, with specialities including *pollo Ishpingo* (chicken with cinnamon). Most mains $10–12. Daily 9am–midnight.

MACAS

MACAS, the attractive and tranquil capital of the strongly Shuar province of Morona-Santiago, lies 129km south of Puyo. Indigenous pride burns strongly and there have been confrontations with the government. Tourists can only visit the traditional villages that surround Macas with approved guides. Local tour agencies also arrange jungle treks.

WHAT TO SEE AND DO

In the centre of Macas, the main attraction is the large modern **Catedral** on Parque Central, which commands good views of the town. Five blocks to the north is the **Parque Recreacional Campo Alegre**, which has even better views.

ARRIVAL AND INFORMATION

By bus The new bus terminal is 2km from the centre; a taxi is $1.50.

Destinations Very frequent daily buses to Cuenca (7hr 30min), Puyo (3hr) and Quito (8hr 30min).

By taxi Taxis around town cost $1.

Tourist information There is a tourist office on Comin (Mon–Fri 8am–8pm; ☎07 270 0143).

6

ACCOMMODATION

Casa Blanca Soasti, at Sucre ☎07 270 0195. Offers spacious, well-furnished rooms with private bath, cable TV and breakfast included set around a small pool and garden. **$36**

Hostal Los Helechos Tarqui ☎07 270 2964, ✉ hostalloshelechos@hotmail.com. A welcoming, spotless guesthouse, with selection of rooms including family-friendly suites. **$28**

EATING AND DRINKING

Guayusa Bar La Maravilla Soasti, at Sucre. This atmospheric bar-restaurant serves good meat and fish mains (most $4–8) with delicious yuca chips and salad. Occasional live music at weekends. Mon–Sat 6pm–late.

La Napolitana Amazonas, at Tarqui. Serves pizza, pasta and barbecue as well as great fish dishes, including tilapia and trout. Mains $4–8. Daily 8am–10pm.

The northern coast and lowlands

Travelling up the Ecuadorian coast, the scenery gets greener and the vibe more Caribbean. The Afro-Ecuadorians who make up a large part of the population of **Esmeraldas** province give the region a different cultural feel to the rest of the country. Locals are exuberant, extrovert and talkative, a refreshing change from the mountains.

The main route from the Sierra descends dramatically via **Santo Domingo de los Colorados**, an unattractive transport hub. Avoid the dangers of grim **Esmeraldas** town and head south to a string of beach resorts. **Atacames** is the most popular party town. Further south, the beautiful beach at **Mompiche** is emerging as a popular spot for budget travellers. In the province of **Manabí**, head to **Canoa**, a haven for surfers and sunseekers. Nearby, the elegant resort **Bahía de Caráquez** juts out dramatically on a slim peninsula, close to mangroves and tropical forest. Further south is Ecuador's second-largest port, **Manta** which holds nothing of interest for travellers but nearby beaches are a mecca for kitesurfers.

The north coast of Ecuador suffered a 7.8 magnitude earthquake in April 2016, which caused hundreds of deaths and widespread damage. Fast forward a couple of years and the area has bounced back remarkably well.

SANTO DOMINGO DE LOS COLORADOS

This inland transport hub is the most convenient route from the Sierra to the coast. From here you can head north to Esmeraldas and Pedernales or south to

Bahía de Caráquez, Manta and Guayaquil. Parts of town are plagued by street crime, so take care at night (when you should travel by taxi). Santo Domingo has little to offer other than nearby Tsáchila communities, but as most places on the coast are connected by direct buses an overnight stay here is usually unnecessary.

ARRIVAL

By bus The bus terminal is 1.5km north of the town centre (take a taxi for $1 or a public bus).

ACCOMMODATION AND EATING

Hotel Diana Real 29 de Mayo, at Loja ☎02 275 1380, ✉ hugo_loaiza@hotmail.com. A reasonable mid-range option in the centre, with spacious rooms and a restaurant attached. **$30**

Timoneiro Av Quito, at Tsátchila. Just one of the good restaurants east of the centre serving chicken, soups and filling set meals ($3–6). Daily 8am-10pm.

ATACAMES

ATACAMES is the busiest, brashest beach resort on the north coast. It's not really a natural habitat for travellers but wildly popular with city dwellers on weekends when the beachfront **Malecón** strip bounces with bars booming out reggaetón. Beware the Pacific undertow which can make swimming dangerous. Also note women have been reported being hassled here and street crime is an issue.

ARRIVAL AND INFORMATION

By bus There are buses to and from Quito (roughly hourly; 7hr) and Guayaquil (hourly; 8hr). Use Trans Esmeraldas, Aerotaxi or Trans Occidentales (offices across the footbridge) in the town. Trans La Costeñita and Trans Pacífico buses run several times an hour to Súa, Same and Muisne (1hr 30min).

For Mompiche (2hr 30min), there are four direct buses a day, or you can catch a bus heading to Pedernales and be dropped off nearby.

By tricycle taxi Motorized tricycle taxis cost $1–2 a ride.

Tourist information iTur Av Las Acacias, by the road bridge (Mon–Fri 2–6pm; ☎06 273 1912).

ACCOMMODATION AND EATING

It can be surprisingly hard to find anything decent during peak periods, when prices rise, so book ahead. Unless otherwise indicated, all restaurants are on the Malecón, where you're spoilt for choice for seafood.

Andy Internacional Malecón, at Los Ostiones ☎06 276 0221. Concrete beachfront hotel with decent well-kept rooms with fans and TV, although it gets noisy. $28

Delicias del Mar Malecón. Always rammed on weekends this is the spot for a seafood feast; try the fish soup or breaded shrimps. The set lunch menu is a steal.

Jennifer Malecón, at C La Tolita ☎06 273 1055, ⓦhostaljennifer.com. A fine budget choice just off the Malecón, with light, airy clean rooms equipped with fans and en-suites. There's a pool too. $22

★ **La Pérgola** Tonsupa. In the resort of Tonsupa, in a rustic garden setting, this is the best restaurant in the region. Besides the fresh seafood, La Pérgola specializes in Italian cuisine (the chef is from Genoa) – from stone-baked pizzas to house speciality steak in gorgonzola sauce. Mains $7–15.

★ **Via Via** Tonsupa ☎06 246 5014, ⓦelflamenco.ec. Some 4km up the coast in Tonsupa, this likeable, good-value hostel has eight rooms (singles are $14) all with en-suite bathrooms. There's a welcoming vibe, bar-restaurant and it's two blocks inland from the beach. $24

MOMPICHE

The tiny little village of **MOMPICHE** is home to one of the most beautiful sandy bays in Ecuador. This, combined with great surfing conditions, has made it increasingly popular with backpackers, though erosion has affected the coastline in recent years.

There's an excellent left point break at Punta Suspiro, at the south end of the bay (best in Dec & Jan), and other good possibilities nearby. Most hotels offer surfboard rental ($15/day) and organize whale-watching tours in season (June–Sept) and boat trips. Horseriding and long beach walks are other options.

Cash up before you head here – there's no ATM in Mompiche, and the nearest are in Atacames.

ARRIVAL AND DEPARTURE

By bus Five daily buses connect Esmeraldas with Mompiche. Otherwise, hourly buses passing up and down the coast between Chamanga and Esmeraldas drop off and pick up passengers at the main road, 6km east of Mompiche. *Mototaxis* can take passengers to Mompiche ($5 private; $1/person *colectivo*) from the junction. From the south, travel via Pedernales and then Chamanga.

ACCOMMODATION

Mompiche has limited accommodation options, so book well ahead during busy periods.

DMCA Surf Hostal Beachside ☎06 244 8022, ⓦhosteltrail.com/dmca. Funky surfers' hangout with rock-bottom rates, featuring basic rooms with private or shared cold-water bathrooms. Lounge, kitchen, and hammock terrace. Camping/person $3, dorms $6, doubles $12

La Facha One block back from beach ☎06 244 8024. This place is a good spot for socializing, as it draws young party-minded crowd. Accommodation is fine value and the owners rustle up decent pizza and barbecues in the small restaurant. $25

Kiwi Hostel A block inland from beach ☎099 882 4223. Welcoming place run by a hospitable family with smallish rooms (some with a/c) and ample hammocks. $25

Gabeal Beachside ☎06 244 8060, ⓦhosteriagabeal.wixsite.com/turismoecuador. This attractive lodge has huge bamboo cabins, each with a private bathroom and more spacious mid-range options. $40

Maracumbo ☎0987 408 887, ⓦmaracumbo.com. Occupying a large plot 400m inland from the beach, this new Swiss-owned place is steadily developing and offers a welcoming base for backpackers. There are raised platforms for campers, clean cabañas and a comfy dorm. You'll find surfboards for rent and excellent travel information. Camping $5/person, dorms $7, cabañas $15

★ **Mud House** 300m inland from the beach ☎06 244 8080, ⓦthe-mud-house.com. A lot of thought has gone into creating this wonderful eco-hostel with thatched bungalows and an eight-bed dorm set in a small tropical garden. There's a tiny bamboo kitchen and yoga deck and inexpensive nature hikes, surf lessons and horseriding are offered. Dorms $8, cabañas $25

EATING

Restaurante El Sol de Oro Beachside. Nice hanging lanterns and a raised deck give this place ambience to match the tasty seafood. Mains $6–16. Daily 8am–9.30pm.

La Chocolata A block inland from the beach. Terrific café serving up some of the best cakes and desserts on the coast, plus wonderful crepes, salads and gourmet sandwiches (from homemade bread) and fine coffee. $2–6. Mon–Sat 8am–10.30pm.

6

La Langosta A block inland to the south of the main road, this is renowned as the best place in town for lobster, *ceviche* and fried fish. $5–9. Daily noon–9.30pm.

★ **Suly's** One block back from the beach. Expect tasty, freshly made food in this nicely decorated, open-sided bamboo-and-thatch bar-restaurant, where you can dine by candlelight or enjoy a quiet drink. Choose from burgers, pastas and daily specials, from $8. Daily 6–10pm.

CANOA

CANOA is a fishing village that has developed into a laidback resort by virtue of its beautiful beach and great surfing conditions. It has a dramatic setting, with waves crashing upon long stretches of sand flanked by steep cliffs. At present, it's probably Ecuador's best beach resort for budget travellers but it's changing fast and can get pretty crowded on high season weekends.

An interesting excursion from Canoa is **Río Muchacho Organic Farm** (ⓦriomuchacho.com), where you can see sustainable farming in practice and learn about the culture of the *Montubios* (lowland farmers). Guided hikes, horseriding and birdwatching are available.

Canoa, a village of 2500 people, was hit very hard by the 2016 earthquake. More than fifty inhabitants and tourists died here including several worshippers who were inside an evangelical church when the structure collapsed.

ARRIVAL AND DEPARTURE

By bus From Quito there are direct buses with Transvencedores and Reina del Camino from Quitumbe bus station (daily; 7hr). There are more regular buses from Quito to Bahía de Caráquez; from there take a bus to Canoa (twice hourly; 20min). From Pedernales, there are buses to Canoa every 30min.

INFORMATION, TOURS AND ACTIVITIES

Tourist information There's no iTur. Staff at the Muchacho office on Av 3 de Noviembre can help out or you can chat to the guys at Surf Shak for advice.

Tours and activities Many hotels including Surf Shak (ⓦcanoathrills.com) rent surfboards ($15/day) and/or offer lessons ($20–25 for 2hr). Fishing, mountain biking, sea kayaking or birdwatching are other possibilities. Paragliding is another option – ask at Surf Shak. Betty Surf and Yoga (ⓦbettysurfandyoga.com) provides instruction as the name suggests, including yoga and surfing packages.

ACCOMMODATION

Accommodation prices are seasonal in Canoa. The prices given are for high season (Dec–April & national holidays). They can drop by 25 percent out of season.

Amalur Hostal San Andrés, overlooking the Plaza Cívica ☎0983 035038, ⓦamalurcanoa.com. Great-value hostel with excellent on-site restaurant (see page 620), boasting bright, spacious rooms with hot-water showers. From the rooftop hammocks there are mesmerizing sea views. Surf, salsa and Spanish lessons are offered. Dorms $10, doubles $25

Bambú Beachfront, on north side of bay. ☎05 258 8017, ⓦhotelbambuecuador.com. One of Canoa's most happening places, with small rooms but beautiful beachfront gardens. The restaurant is worth visiting even if you don't stay. Camping $5/person, doubles $50

Casa Shangri La 200m north of the park by the old road ☎05 258 8076, ⓔcasashangrilacanoa@gmail.com. Secluded Dutch-owned hotel with a walled tropical garden, pool, bar, BBQ and thatched bar. Rooms are clean and homely. $28

Coco Loco Malecón ☎099 243 6508, ⓦhostelcocoloco.com Two blocks left of the junction with the beach is this expanding place. There are new dorms (female only and mixed) and attractive private rooms with shared or private bathrooms. Factor in the numerous hammocks, kitchen, bar and a friendly atmosphere and it's a sound choice. Dorms $10, doubles $30

País Libre Filomeno Hernández at San Andrés ☎05 258 8187, ⓦhotelpaislibre.webnode.es. Run by friendly local surfer Favio Coello this place has well-kept rooms, plenty of artwork and a small pool set in leafy gardens. Dorms $8, doubles $25

Posada Olmito Javier Santos ☎099 553 3341, ⓦolmito.org. An endearing place with basic fan-cooled rooms in an intricately constructed, somewhat ramshackle wooden building. $26

Sundown Beach Hotel Km2 Via San Vicente ☎099 364 5470, ⓦecuadorbeach.com. A 20min walk from town, this quiet beachfront place is a good spot to get away from it all, with private patio, garden and communal atmosphere. $20

La Vista Hotel ☎098 647 0222, ⓦlavistacanoa.com. Mid-range beachfront hotel offering comfortable, airy rooms, all with sea view and private bathroom. There's a café-restaurant here too. $35

EATING AND NIGHTLIFE

Canoa has plenty of restaurants – mainly informal beachfront places offering fresh seafood. Nightlife is restricted but quite busy in the bars on the main street at weekends and on national holidays.

★ **Amalur** C San Andrés. Highly atmospheric, upmarket restaurant with daily specials chalked up on a board. Specializes in Spanish food including lots of seafood and fish, tortilla and salads (dishes $5–8). Daily 8am–3pm & 5–11pm.

Cevichería Saboréame Malecón. The best seafood in town according to locals – and they should know. Seafood soups and *encocado*, all delicious. Mains $4–6. Daily 7.30am–9pm.

Koraimar Beachfront. Locally owned beach shack serving superb soups, *ceviches* and other seafood mains (most $6–8), accompanied by great patacones. Wed–Sun 7am–5.30pm.

Surf Shak Malecón, ⓦ canoathrills.com/surf-shak. This American-owned place is the centre of the expat community in Canoa. Choose from big breakfasts, big burgers, pizzas and fresh coffee. Hosts a popular quiz night on Tuesdays, screens American and European sports and Pete (the owner) offers tours and travel advice. Mains $5–13. Daily 7.30am–midnight.

BAHÍA DE CARÁQUEZ AND AROUND

The most dramatic location of Ecuador's coastal resorts, **BAHÍA DE CARÁQUEZ** sits on a slim sand peninsula jutting out from the mouth of the River Chone into the Pacific. The town, known simply as Bahía to locals, has endured multiple recent disasters including massive landslides in 1998 and two earthquakes but the city is still standing and welcoming visitors (mainly domestic tourists).

Commendable and wide-ranging environmental programmes (recycling, sustainable development, reforestation and environmental education) have lead to Bahía declaring itself an "eco city". The result is that, unlike many of Ecuador's resorts, Bahía is a clean and pleasant place to stroll around.

WHAT TO SEE AND DO

The **Museo Bahía de Caraquez** (Tues–Fri 10am–5pm, Sat & Sun 10am–4pm; free) suffered damage from the 2016 earthquake but still has a very good collection of pre-Columbian artefacts including tools, gold pectorals and ceramics. The **Mirador La Cruz**, a large cross above the south end of town, offers wonderful views over the city and surrounding bay. Some 15km south of town is the **Chirije archeological site**, which has countless ancient artefacts such as ceramics and burial sites dating from 500 BC. Inland from Bahía, the River

Chone has some excellent unspoilt mangroves inhabited by abundant birdlife, including a colony of frigate birds to rival those found in the Galápagos.

ARRIVAL, INFORMATION AND TOURS

By bus Buses to the terminal (4km south of town) run up and down Malecón. There are regular services to and from Canoa, Portoviejo, Manta and Guayaquil, and five a day to Quito (or travel via Pedernales).

Tourist information The tourist information office is on Bolívar, at Malecón (☎ 05 269 1044).

Tours The Chirije archeological site can be visited through Bahía Dolphin Tours (Bolívar 1004; ☎ 05 269 0257), which manages the site. This company also offers wildlife-watching and cultural excursions (from $30/person).

ACCOMMODATION

Most budget travellers prefer to stay in Canoa, but Bahía is a pleasant alternative. Hotels fill up quickly during high season (Dec–April) and on national holidays.

Bahía Bed and Breakfast Inn Ascazubi 316, at Morales ☎ 05 269 0146. Rock-bottom budget option with basic rooms with fans and cable TV in the lounge. Not to be confused with the more upscale *Hotel Bahía B&B*. $16

Hotel Bahía B&B Puente los Caros ☎ 05 269 1880, ⓦ ecuavacation.com. This conveniently situated and efficiently run Canadian-Colombian-owned guesthouse has tidy, tiled en-suite rooms with large sliding glass doors. Breakfast included. $40

★ **Villa Kite Resort** ⓦ hotelvillakite.com. Located 14km southwest of Manta in the fishing village of Santa Marianita, this fine beachfront Dutch hotel is a very well-equipped kitesurfers' stronghold. There are two pools, panoramic ocean views, a bar-resto and excellent kitesurfing instruction, plus boards and SUPs to rent. Breakfast included. $60

EATING

Colombius Bolívar. A cheap place for set lunches of chicken and fish ($2–4). Daily 7am–10pm.

Muelle Uno Malecón. One of a string of restaurants on the pier near the docks, serving huge barbecue platters and seafood dishes – try the *ceviche*. $4–8.

Puerto Amistad Malecón. Jutting out into the bay, the waterside deck here is a fine spot for shrimp salads and grilled meat and fish dishes ($5–12). Daily 9am–10.30pm.

MANTA

Ecuador's second port used to be a pleasant expat haven, but a deteriorating security situation means that the city is best avoided. There are far better beaches elsewhere too. However, you may need to pass through

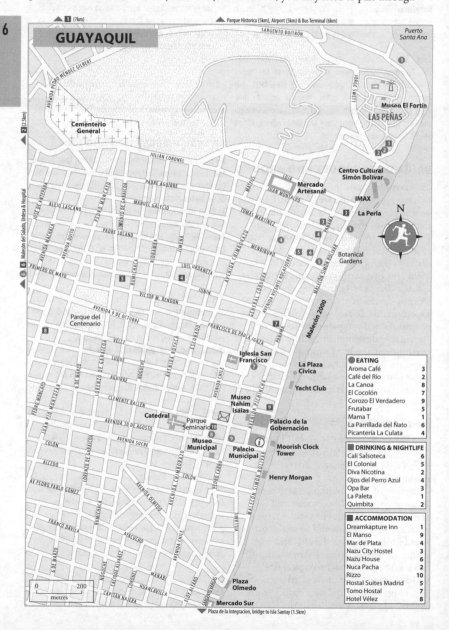

GUAYAQUIL

● EATING	
Aroma Café	3
Café del Río	2
La Canoa	8
El Cocolón	7
Corozo El Verdadero	9
Frutabar	5
Mama T	1
La Parrillada del Ñato	6
Picantería La Culata	4

■ DRINKING & NIGHTLIFE	
Cali Salsoteca	6
El Colonial	5
Diva Nicotina	2
Ojos del Perro Azul	4
Opa Bar	3
La Paleta	1
Quimbita	2

■ ACCOMMODATION	
Dreamkapture Inn	1
El Manso	9
Mar de Plata	4
Nazu City Hostel	3
Nazu House	6
Nuca Pacha	2
Rizzo	10
Hostal Suites Madrid	5
Tomo Hostal	7
Hotel Vélez	8

Manta on your way up or down the coast. If stuck for a few hours, head for the seafood promenade at Playa Murciélagos.

ARRIVAL AND DEPARTURE

By plane The airport is 4.5km east of the city centre; taxis charge $3–4. TAME and Avianca operate daily flights to and from Quito.

By bus Manta's new bus terminal is 3.5km east of the centre.

Destinations Bahía de Caráquez (hourly; 2hr 30min); Esmeraldas (5 daily, 10hr); Guayaquil (every 40min; 4hr); Montañita (daily; 3hr 30min); Puerto López (hourly; 2hr); Quito (hourly; 8hr).

Guayaquil

GUAYAQUIL is Ecuador's largest city and handles most of the country's imports and exports. The heat, dirt and danger used to be reasons enough to stay away, but the city has undergone quite a facelift in the past two decades and the waterfront and city centre have enough to keep visitors occupied for a day or two.

Arriving from the mountains, the contrast is striking between Quito's cool colonial charms and Guayaquil's hot, humid vivacity. *Guayaquileños* (or *Guayacos*) are fiercely proud of their city. Guayaquil's 3km-long **Malecón** and renovated artistic district of **Las Peñas** are great achievements, as are the new airport, bus terminal and museums.

WHAT TO SEE AND DO

Be aware that the heat and traffic pollution can make sightseeing an uncomfortable experience. Outside the centre and Urdesa, Guayaquil is not picturesque and remains dangerous, particularly at night.

El Malecón

The **Malecón** (daily 7am–midnight) running alongside the river is a public space that is easily the highlight of the city – enclosed, pedestrianized and patrolled by security guards. The best point to enter is **La Plaza Cívica** at the end of 9 de Octubre. Start at **La Rotonda**, a statue of South America's liberators, José de San Martín and Simón Bolívar, shaking hands in front of a semicircle of marble columns. Past the plush Guayaquil Yacht Club is the 23m-high Moorish Clock Tower, and further south **The Henry Morgan**, a replica of a seventeenth-century pirate ship, is docked. A one-hour trip on the river costs $5 (hourly departures afternoons and evenings).

Further south is **Plaza Olmedo**, with its contemplative monument of José Joaquín de Olmedo (1780–1847), the first mayor of Guayaquil. The southern end of Malecón reaches La Plaza de la Integración and an artisans' market, selling indigenous clothing and crafts.

Botanical gardens

North from La Rotonda is a large children's play area, then you'll pass some **botanical gardens** with more than three hundred species of coastal vegetation. The gardens are divided into four zones: ornamental trees, humid forest, palms and conifers. Above the gardens is a set of 32 transparent panels with the names of some 48,000 citizens who contributed to the construction of the Malecón.

IMAX and Museo Guayaquil en La Historia

At the far north end of Malecón is an **IMAX cinema** (☎04 256 3078, ⓦcinemamalecon.com) with a 180-degree screen. Below the cinema is **Museo Guayaquil en La Historia** (Tues–Sun 9am–1.30pm & 4–8pm; $3), which condenses a compact history of the city in English and Spanish, from prehistory to the present day, into fourteen dioramas.

La Perla

Right on the riverbank at the north end of the Malecón, the **La Perla** sightseeing wheel (Mon–Thurs & Sun 10am–10pm, Fri & Sat 10am–midnight, ⓦlaperladeguayaquil.com) soars over the city, up to a height of 57m with stunning views over La Peña and Isla Santay.

6

Centro Cultural Simón Bolívar

The Malecón culminates in the spacious **Centro Cultural Simón Bolívar** (Tues–Fri 8.30am–5pm, Sat & Sun 10am–4pm; free), which includes a cinema and cultural space. Regular exhibitions are held here and there's a huge collection of pre-Columbian ceramics and first-rate modern art.

Mercado Artesanal (artisans' market)

A few blocks inland along Calle Loja from the IMAX is the huge, enclosed **Mercado Artesanal** (Mon–Sat 9am–7pm, Sun 10am–4pm), which has a wide selection of traditional handicrafts and clothing. Haggle hard.

Malecón del Salado

At the opposite end of 9 de Octubre (a 20min walk or short taxi ride) is the **Malecón del Salado**, next to the Estero Salado, a tributary of the River Guayas. It's a picturesque place to stroll, and for great views of the river you can cross the bridges (which tower over 9 de Octubre). Otherwise, take a boat trip or relax in one of the seafood restaurants.

Las Peñas

Rising above the north end of Malecón is the colourful artistic district of **Las Peñas**, formerly a run-down area, which has been revamped. Like the Malecón, it's patrolled by security guards. Round the corner to the right of the steps is the historic, cobbled street of Numa Pompilio Llona, named after the *Guayaco* lawyer and poet. The street leads from old to new, reaching **Puerto Santa Ana**, the city's latest grand project with waterfront shops, restaurants, luxury apartments and an extensive marina. There are a couple of interesting museums, the best of which is **Museo de la Música Popular Julio Jaramillo** (Wed–Sat, 10am–5pm, Sun 10am–3pm; free; Ⓦmuseomunicipaldelamusicapopular. com), dedicated to the city's most famous singer. Next door is **Museo Pilsener** (Wed–Sat, 10am–1pm & 2–5pm, Sun 10am–3pm; free) for everything on Ecuador's most popular beer.

For spectacular views of Guayaquil, climb the 444 steps up Las Peñas to the peak of **Cerro Santa Ana** (en route, there's a wide selection of bars). At the top of the hill in the Plaza de Honores is a new colonial-style chapel and the **Lighthouse** (free), based on Guayaquil's first, built in 1841. Also here is the open-air **Museo El Fortín del Santa Ana** (free), which holds the foundations of the Fortress of San Carlos. The fortress, which defended the city from pirates, has original cannons and replicas of Spanish galleons. The highlight is the sweeping panoramic view over the rivers Daule and Babahoyo, downtown Guayaquil and, across the river, the reserve of Santay Island, reachable via footbridge from the south end of the Malecón.

Parque Seminario and Catedral

Three blocks behind the grand **Palacio Municipal** (town hall) is the small **Parque Seminario**, also known as Parque Bolívar or, more aptly given that dozens of urban iguanas reside here, Parque de las Iguanas. At the centre of the park is an imposing monument of liberator Simón Bolívar on horseback. The huge white neo-Gothic **Catedral**, reconstructed in 1948 after a fire, towers over the west side of the square.

Museo Municipal

One block southeast from the park is the **Museo Municipal** (Sucre, at Chile; Tues–Fri 8.30am–4.30pm; Sat & Sun 10am–2pm; free). This is the oldest museum in Ecuador and the city's best. The pre-Hispanic room has fossils, including the tooth of a mastodon, as well as sculptures created by the Valdivia – Ecuador's oldest civilization – and a huge Manteña funeral urn. Upstairs is a room of portraits of Ecuadorian presidents, nicknamed "the room of thieves", plus a small exhibition of modern art. Free tours in English are recommended.

Parque Histórico Guayaquil

Across the bridge in the wealthy district of Entre Rios is the **Parque Histórico** (daily 9am–5pm; free; ☏04 283 2958). The park is divided into three zones. Created out of the natural mangroves of the River Daule, the **wildlife zone** provides a snapshot of the Ecuadorian jungle with deer, tapirs, monkeys, sloths, ocelots, tortoises, parrots, toucans, caimans and fermenting termite mounds. The **traditions zone** depicts the rural way of life via haciendas, "peasant" houses and crops. In the **urban architecture zone**, some of Guayaquil's late nineteenth-century buildings are reproduced. To **get there**, catch bus #81 from the terminal or get a taxi from downtown (around $5).

Isla Santay

A new bridge 1.5km south of the Malecón has opened up mangrove-covered **Isla Santay** (daily 6am–5pm; ⊚islasantay.info) to pedestrians and cyclists. This island has 1.8km of raised paths through wetlands to the former impoverished fishing village of Santay, now turned eco-community. There's a locally run restaurant, a small sanctuary for endangered crocodiles and guided boat trips along the river are possible. These internationally recognized wetlands boast over one hundred avian species – so are great for morning birdwatching – and some rare mammals: crab-eating raccoons, anteaters and white-tailed deer.

Bikes ($4 with helmets) are available for rent on the city side of the bridge – but avoid weekend crowds if possible.

ARRIVAL AND DEPARTURE

By plane Guayaquil's very modern José Joaquín de Olmedo airport, about 5km north of downtown (☎04 216 9000, ⊚tagsa.aero), has international flights to destinations including Miami, New York, Madrid, Panama City and Santiago and domestic connections to Quito, the Galápagos, Cuenca, Loja and Latacunga. There's an exchange bureau and ATM. Take a taxi ($6) to your hotel, as Metrovía and public buses are not best tackled with luggage.

By bus The new Terrestre bus terminal is 7km north of downtown, 1.4km from the airport, with many food courts and shops. Taxis ($4–5 to downtown) are the safest option but buses do operate: catch the Metrovía ($0.30), a rapid transit bus system, from Terminal Río Daule (opposite the bus station) through downtown to the south. Get off at La Catedral stop for the main tourist sights. Watch your belongings as pickpockets are common.

Destinations Bahía de Caráquez (hourly; 7hr); Baños (12–14 daily 7hr); Canoa (3 daily; 7hr); Lima, Peru (3 weekly, 28hr); Puerto López (8 daily; 4hr); Montañita (3 daily; 3hr 30min); Quito (every 30min; 9hr); Piura, Peru (3 daily; 12hr) Salinas (hourly; 2hr).

By taxi Few taxi drivers use meters and overcharging is common, so negotiate the price first or consider using Easy Taxi or Uber (both operate in Guayaquil). Do not take

unmarked or informal cabs. Short taxi rides around the city centre should cost about $2–3.

INFORMATION AND TOURS

Tourist information The Dirección Municipal de Turismo office at 10 de Agosto and the Malecón (Mon–Fri 9am–5pm; ☎04 259 9100, ⊚guayaquilesmidestino.com) has friendly staff, maps and brochures. The tourist site also produces a dozen downloadable guidebooks.

Tour operators Ecoventura (Miraflores Av Central 300A ☎04 283 9390, ⊚ecoventura.com); El Manso (Malecón 1406, ☎04 252 6644, ⊚http://manso.ec); Metropolitan Touring (Francisco de Orellana, World Trade Centre Millennium Gallery, ground floor; ☎04 263 0000, ⊚metropolitan-touring.com).

ACCOMMODATION

Guayaquil has plenty of hotels but is still not well geared up for the backpacker market. Many budget hotels are of a very poor standard in unappealing areas. It's best to stay near to Parque Bolívar or Parque Centenario. The lanes off the Malecón also have good places.

CITY CENTRE

El Manso Malecón 1406, at Aguirre ☎04 252 6644, ⊚manso.ec; map p.622. A slice of Arabia in Guayaquil with arty, individually designed rooms; dorms have a/c. There are regular music performances in the lounge area and bike rental. Dorms **$15**, doubles **$38**

Mar de Plata Junín 718, at Boyacá ☎04 230 7610; map p.622. Six blocks from the Malecón, this place has basic but clean rooms with fans, cable TV and private bathrooms (a/c $5 extra). **$35**

Nazu City Hostel Juan Montalvo 102, at Malecón ☎099 9115 1587, ⊚nazucityhostel.com; map p.622. At the northern end of the Malecón, this fine modern hostel enjoys an excellent location and has a selection of bright, artistically decorated rooms and dorms. Breakfast included. Dorms **$15**, doubles **$50**

Rizzo Clemente Ballén 319, at Chile ☎04 601 7500; map p.622. Adequate rooms, some with small balconies, ideally situated next to Parque Bolívar. **$48**

Hostal Suites Madrid Quisquis 305, at Rumicacha ☎04 230 7804, ⊚hostalsuitesmadrid.com; map p.622. The location, 1km inland from the Malecón, is not that great, but this is a fine-value option, with colourful decor, spacious rooms, a feast of artwork and very friendly service. $30

Tomo Hostal Rendon 212 ☎ 04 256 2683, ⊛ tomohostel. com; map p.622. Only a block from the Malecón, this place successfully combines chic minimalism with a relaxed vibe: lots of sofas for lounging and the semi-open walled rooftop terrace is superb. Dorms have eight beds, lockers and reading lights. Breakfast included. Dorms $15, doubles $49

Hotel Vélez Vélez 1021, at Quito ☎ 04 253 0292; map p.622. Very simple but clean cell-like singles, doubles and triples (with fan or a/c) with cold-water en-suite bathrooms. It's worth paying the extra $5 for a window and a/c. Cash only. $14

OTHER AREAS

Dreamkapture Inn Alborada Doceava Etapa ☎ 04 224 2909, ⊛ dreamkapture.com; map p.622. A few kilometres from the centre, this is one of the city's few backpacker haunts. Secure, well maintained and friendly, the comfortable rooms have a/c and there's a small pool and luggage storage. The hostel also owns its own travel agency. Breakfast included. Dorms $9, doubles $23

Nuca Pacha Bálsamos Sur 308, ☎ 04 261 0553, ⊛ nucapacha.com; map p.622. This popular hostel has a good selection of spacious rooms and a lovely pool and garden with hammocks for chilling. It's in Urdesa Central, a residential location 4km northwest of the Malecón. Dorms $12, doubles $29

EATING

Guayaquil has a wide range of restaurants spread around the city. Downtown, there are plenty of cheap, basic places. Las Peñas is the most pleasant area to eat, with a cluster of cafés. Riverfront places are to the north in Puerto Santa Ana. An alternative is to take a taxi ($3) to the fashionable neighbourhood of Urdesa, where there's a wide range of restaurants.

Aroma Café Jardines del Malecón; map p.622. Right on the Malecón, with a selection of Ecuadorian specialities ($6–8) served overlooking the botanical gardens. Daily noon–midnight.

Café del Río Llona; map p.622. Simple little café at the base of Las Penas that's good for a pastry, portion of *tarta espinaca* (spinach pie), cupcake or coffee (a cappuccino is $1.50). Snacks $2–3. Daily 8am–8pm.

La Canoa At Hotel Continental, 10 de Agosto, at Chile; map p.622. Serves authentic coastal and Andean staples to around a thousand people a day, along with sandwiches and *humitas*. Mains $12. Daily 24hr.

El Cocolón Pedro Carbo, at 9 de Octubre; also Plaza Orellana in Urdesa Norte; map p.622. Named for crusty rice, this is where you can taste imaginative Pacific Lowlands specialities, with plenty of *bolón*, *maduro*, *secos* and *verde*

dishes. However service can be distracted. Mains $7–12. Mon–Fri & Sun 11am–6pm, Sat 11.30am–10pm.

Corozo El Verdadero Av Pedro Carbo 103, at Roca; map p.622. Fabled canteen-style Afro-Ecuadorian seafood restaurant, with a 40-year track record. Mains $5–9. Mon–Sat 7.30am–4pm.

Frutabar Malecón, at Martínez, ⊛ frutabar.com; map p.622. Funky, boho hangout with mismatched furnishings, tropical murals, a huge selection of *batidos* (fruit shakes) and imaginative burgers, sandwiches and *piqueos* (deep-fried pork balls). Cocktails too. $4–6. Daily 9am–11pm.

Mama T Puerto Santa Ana ⊛ mami-t.com; map p.622. On the north side of Las Peñas, this smart restaurant serves up fine Latin American food, try the *chupe de camarón* (a rich shrimp soup with avocado and potatoes) or a burrito. Daily 12.30–10pm.

La Parillada del Ñato Estrada, at Laureles, Urdesa, ⊛ parilladelnato.com; map p.622. Huge plates of barbecued meats are the speciality in this enormously popular Urdesa institution. Seafood and pizza are also offered. There's a branch in the centre at Luque, at Pichincha. Mains $6–12. Mon–Sat 11am–1am, Sun noon–11pm.

Picantería La Culata Córdova; map p.622. This small, bohemian street café-resto attracts an arty crowd, enticed by its delicious *encocados*, *ceviches*, *encebollados* and the like with rice or *patacones* (from $6). Also snacks to share. Mon–Sat 8am–late, Sun 8am–4pm.

DRINKING AND NIGHTLIFE

Guayaquileños love to party, and the city has nightlife to rival Quito's. Las Peñas is bursting with café-bars and Urdesa is also a good place for a few drinks. To hit the dancefloor, go to the Zona Rosa, between downtown and Las Peñas, around Rocafuerte and Panamá. Bars tend to open around 6pm while clubs (most open Thurs–Sat only) start up around 10pm. Check out ⊛ farras.com for nightlife information.

Cali Salsoteca Panamá, at Martínez; map p.622. Legendary salsa club in the Zona Rosa, attracting national and international artists. Cover charges vary; women often free. Thurs–Sat usually 8pm–late.

El Colonial Rocafuerte, at Imbabura, Zona Rosa; map p.622. Traditional Peñas bar with drinks specials most weeknights and live music at weekends. Mon–Thurs 4pm–midnight, Fri & Sat 4pm–2am.

Diva Nicotina La Escalinata, Las Peñas; map p.622. At the bottom of the steps of Las Peñas, you can catch some great live music here – from Cuban Habanera to jazz – accompanied by whisky and cigars. Tues–Thurs 7pm–midnight, Fri & Sat 7pm–2am.

Ojos del Perro Azul Panamá, at Padre Aguirre; map p.622. A bohemian bar that's a good place to catch live rock, folk, ska, reggae and Latin music at weekends. Wed & Thurs 8pm–midnight, Fri & Sat 8pm–2am.

Opa Bar Panamá 209; map p.622. A block from the north end of the Malecón, this intimate bar draws an arty crowd and hosts photographic exhibitions and live music on weekends. Wed 1pm–midnight, Thurs 7pm–midnight Fri & Sat 7pm–2am.

★ **La Paleta** Llona, Las Peñas; map p.622. Atmospheric, dimly lit bar with cosy corners, a good wine and cocktail list and bars on two floors. Tues–Sat 8pm–2am.

Quimbita Galeria La Escalinata, Las Peñas; map p.622. This art gallery doubles as a café-bar with live folk music at weekends. Wed & Sun 5pm–1am, Thurs–Sat 5pm–3am.

DIRECTORY

Banks and exchange Banco del Pacífico, Banco de Guayaquil and Banco Pichincha are all on Icaza and Pichincha.

Consulates Australia, Rocafuerte 20, at Tomás Martínez (☎04 601 7529, ✉ ausconsulate@unidas.com.ec); Brazil, Av San Jorge 312 (☎04 229 3046); Canada, Blue Towers 6th floor office 604, Av Francisco de Orellana 234 (☎04 263 1109); Colombia, World Trade Center, Torre B, Av Francisco de Orellana (☎04 263 0674, ⊛ guayaquil.consulado.gov.co);

Peru, Edif. Centrum, 14th floor, Av Francisco de Orellana 234 (☎04 263 1109); UK, General Córdova 623, at Padre Solano (☎04 256 0400); US, Santa Ana, at Rodríguez Bonín (☎04 232 3570, ⊛ ec.usembassy.gov/embassy-consulate/guayaquil).

Hospital Clínica Kennedy, Av del Periodista, Kennedy (☎04 224 7900).

Post office The main office is at Aguirre 301 and Pedro Carbo.

The south coast beaches

At weekends, *Guayacos* flee the city's heat in droves and head west to the cooler Pacific beaches of the **Ruta del Sol**. It gets very crowded in peak season between Christmas and Easter, when the weather is hottest. Among the beach resorts, **Playas** is the closest to Guayaquil, **Salinas** is the playground of wealthy *Guayacos*, and surfer hangout **Montañita** draws in backpackers. Further north is the beautiful province of Manabí, which contains the coastal **Parque Nacional Machalilla**. The port of **Puerto López** is the most convenient base to explore the park and Isla de la Plata, billed as the "poor man's Galápagos" because of its birdlife. **Whale-watching** is a highlight between June and September.

PLAYAS AND PUERTO EL MORRO

PLAYAS, one hour thirty minutes from Guayaquil by bus, attracts beach-starved *Guayacos*. Like all south-coast resorts, it's jammed in high season and quiet the rest of the year. The beach is very long but not sheltered and currents are strong.

A few kilometres east of Playas is the small port of **Puerto El Morro**, which makes a great day-trip. To get here from Guayaquil, change at Playas. The main attractions are mangroves, birdlife and dolphins in the estuary, as well as Islas de los Pájaros, which has a large population of magnificent frigatebirds and pelicans.

TOUR OPERATOR

Ecoclub Los Delfines ☎04 252 9496. Arranges tours of Puerto El Morro (1hr 30min, $7; 3hr, $10). A short tour takes in the mangroves, lets you see dolphins and even do a spot of fishing, and a longer tour includes an extended boat trip and a walk on the Isla de los Pájaros to see frigate birds and blue-footed boobies.

ACCOMMODATION AND EATING

Cabins line the beach selling great fresh seafood.

La Cabaña Típica Malecón. A cosier alternative to the beach, serving seafood specialities at $4–6. Daily noon–9.30pm.

Hostal Cattan Malecón ☎04 276 0179. Cheapie budget hotel, right by the Parque Municipal, with twelve very simple rooms. $15

Hotel Dorado Malecón ☎04 276 0402. A good mid-range choice with a/c, private bath and cable TV. $38

Posada del Sueco Km2 on the road to Data ☎099 020 7629, ⊛ posadadelsueco.com. Just off the beach, this green, shady Swedish-Ecuadorian retreat has homely rooms, ocean-view suites and a family cabin arranged round a delightful shady tropical garden and small pool. $65

La Sason del Cholito#1 Paquisha, at Roldos. Very popular cevichería and restaurant offering mains from around $8. Daily 8am–8pm; May–Nov closed Wed.

SALINAS

To new arrivals **SALINAS** looks like a wannabe Miami Beach with high-rise apartment blocks and expensive yachts. Inland from the

6

ACTIVITIES IN MONTAÑITA

Montañita has a growing choice of activities other than surfing.

SURFING

Lessons cost around $25 for a 1hr 30min class, boards cost $15/day. Recommended instructors can be found at Balsa Surf Camp (w balsasurfcamp.com); Montañita Surf School at Casa del Sol (w casadelsolmontanita. com; see page 629) and Montañita Surf Club (w facebook.com/MontanitaSurfClub).

TOURS & TRIPS

Mountain biking, horseriding and trekking as well as whale-watching excursions (June–Sept) are popular. Good operators include Montañitours, Rocafuerte at Chiriboga (☎ 04 2060043, w montanitours.com).

STUDYING SPANISH

Both schools charge $180–240 for one-to-one tuition and offer after-class activities. Montañita Spanish School, El Tigrillo (☎ 04 206 0116, w montanitaspanishschool.com) is well established and has its own hostel.
Marazul Spanish School (☎ 098 251 1853, w facebook.com/Mar-Azul-Spanish-School) can organize homestay accommodation.

YOGA

Yoga Montañita (☎ 098 251 1853, w yogamontanita.com) at the Casa del Sol has an ocean-facing studio and good instruction, classes are $8.

---

waterfront, Salinas is rather ugly.

But it's worth stopping here to walk along the attractive prom. West of the Malecón is a second beach, **Chipipe**, which is quieter and has a plaza, church and park.

You should also drop by the informative **Museo de Ballenas** (General Enríquez Gallo; daily 8am–5pm by appointment; W museodeballenas.org; free) attached to the *Oystercatcher* restaurant which features a 12m skeleton of a humpback whale and skulls and bones of other cetaceans. Whale-watching trips (June–Oct) are another big draw; staff at the museum can set up tours.

ARRIVAL AND INFORMATION

By bus Comfortable CLP buses run to and from Guayaquil (every 15min; 2hr 30min). Change at Santa Elena for Montañita.
Tourist information The tourist information office (Enriquez Gallo, at C 30) is open sporadically.

ACCOMMODATION

Book hotels well ahead in high season, particularly at weekends and on national holidays.
Chescos Malecón, near the western end of the main beach, ☎ 04 277 0875, w chescos.com The best backpacker option, with the most international flavour. It's bang on the beach with a hammock-hung zone overlooking the action. The blue-and-white rooms are light and airy while the dorm has five wooden bunks; all options have a/c. Dorms $\overline{\$15}$, doubles $\overline{\$40}$
Cocos Malecón, at Fidón Tomalá ☎ 04 277 0361, w hostal-cocos.com. Economical if faded seafront hotel with a restaurant, bar, disco and games room. Quads are available. $\overline{\$48}$
Yulee Eloy Alfaro, at Mercedes Molina ☎ 04 277 4325. In Chipipe, this brightly painted colonial-style hotel is a break from the high-rise concrete. It has three levels of rooms and you won't find a cheaper option. $\overline{\$18}$

EATING

You're spoilt for choice on where to eat, particularly seafood. Avoid the seafood stalls, nicknamed "Cevichelandia", as sanitation is a problem. Salinas' nightlife heats up in high season.
La Bella Italia Malecón ☎ 04 277 1361. Mouth-watering pasta and pizza is prepared in front of you in this comfortable restaurant. Mains $4–7.
La Ostra Nostra Eloy Alfaro, at Las Almendras A popular place with a wide range of seafood, soups and meat dishes (mains $6–10); it's out towards Chipipe.
Oystercatcher Gallo. Has limited (weekend-only) opening hours but the oysters are the best in town in this intimate bar-restaurant. Also serves delectable seafood and fish dishes. Mains from $8. Fri & Sat 9am–9pm, Sun 9am–6pm.

MONTAÑITA

Perhaps there should be a sign at the entrance to surf hangout **MONTAÑITA** that reads: "You are now leaving Ecuador". Such is the international vibe that you could be anywhere. At first sight, the town feels like countless backpacker havens, but whether you love it or hate it, you can't deny the place's infectious energy. The surfing contingent has been joined in recent years by hippies and partygoers, making it the coast's most buzzing resort for budget travellers. Many people stay for months, while others get out after a couple of excessive nights. Surfers can enjoy rideable breaks most of the year, frequently 2–3m on good days. There are plenty of experienced teachers and there's a renowned annual international surf competition around Carnaval (Feb/March).

ARRIVAL

By bus The bus stop is a couple of blocks inland from the beach on the corner of Rocafuerte. Comfortable CLP buses leave Guayaquil almost hourly (3hr 30min). Buses north to Puerto López pass hourly (1hr). For Quito, go to Manta or Puerto López and change.

ACCOMMODATION

Montañita has a huge amount of accommodation. Bear in mind the centre is often very noisy and at weekends partying continues until after dawn. The north end is quieter with the best-quality mid-range places. Prices double on high season weekends.

Abad Lounge Av Costanera, at Malecón ☎099 386 4688. This popular beachside hotel has tidy, clean a/c rooms, many with sea views and balconies. $30

★ **Casa del Sol** ☎099 248 8581, ⓦcasadelsolmontanita. com. Very popular hangout run by a Californian surfer with timber-and-thatch rooms set around a verdant garden. There's a great restaurant and bar area, yoga studio and surf instruction. Bike rental and breakfast are included. Dorms $15, doubles $50

El Centro de Mundo Malecón, at Rocafuerte ☎099 728 2831. Cheap, basic rooms in a three-storey, wooden beachfront building. Expect a lot of Noise on weekends, though. Dorms $5, doubles $18

Charos Malecón between 15 de Mayo and Rocafuerte ☎04 206 0044, ⓦcharoshostal.com. Just inland to the left of the beachfront. One of the most comfortable places to stay in the centre, with a/c rooms, a bar, restaurant and small pool. $48

Funky Babylon Backpackers 43 Ruta del Spondylus ☎098 267 0029. Very popular with young backpackers, this lively place has a busy bar, kitchen, garden, hammocks and table tennis. However dorms and shared bathrooms could be cleaner. Dorms $8

★ **Kamala Hostería** ☎099 813 2693. Aussie-owned travellers' stronghold just north of Manglaralto where thatched cabins are set around a small swimming pool. It's

just off the beach and there's also a bar, restaurant, pool table, volleyball, ping pong and dive school. Dorms $7, doubles $30

Tiki Limbo Chiriboga, at Segunda ☎04 206 0019, ⓦtikilimbo.com. A stylish, sociable choice, this place is centred on a bamboo-and-thatch structure with lounge-around sofas, hammocks to chill in, pool table, buzzing restaurant and surf school. Rooms (all a/c) are very inviting and well presented too. Dorms $20, doubles $50

EATING

Hola Ola 10 de Agosto. Two blocks inland, *Hola Ola* is the centre of the town's social scene. Big breakfasts in the morning, cappuccinos and international food in the day, a wide range of cocktails in the evening and parties at weekends. Mains $7–12. Daily 8am–late.

Karukera Guido Chiriboga. A great choice for breakfast, this place specializes in crêpes and also serves up Caribbean cuisine. Mains $5–8. Daily 7.30am–9pm.

★ **Tambo Sabores** Peruanos Primera, opposite Hola Ola. Intimate, simple-looking Peruvian place offering authentic and beautifully presented seafood and meat dishes. Jugs of sangría ($15) and pisco sours go down a treat too. Mains $6–10. Daily 11am–11pm.

Tiburón Chiriboga, at Rocafuerte. Serves excellent Asian and Ecuadorian dishes (mains from $7) including delicious Thai curries, salads and huge lunchtime *empanadas*. Daily 11am–11pm.

Tiki Limbo Guido Chiriboga. This backpackers' favourite takes pride in its food (most $6–10); Asian, Mexican and vegetarian dishes are particular specialities. Daily 8am–11pm.

DRINKING AND NIGHTLIFE

Montañita throws quite a party at weekends, particularly in high season (Dec–April). Most bars on the main street, Guido Chiriboga, offer two-for-one happy hours on cocktails ($3).

Caña Grill Av Costanera. The town's busiest disco, with two dancefloors playing a mix of electronic and Latin music. The partying continues until after dawn; entrance $5. From 10pm at weekends.

Nativa Bambú Malecón, at Primera. Multistorey bar-restaurant-club with breezy top-floor dancefloor offering stellar sea views. Generally plays electrónica on the first floor and Latin on the top deck. Variable cover charge. Tues–Sat 5pm–late.

DOS MANGAS

DOS MANGAS is the best base to explore the tropical dry forest of the Cordillera Chongón. This tiny community makes a living from crafts and agriculture. It has a small information centre, and two paths

6

through the forest to waterfalls and natural pools. Trucks from the main coast road head to Dos Mangas every hour and you can hire guides and horses (around $10/ person). The park entrance fee is $1. Alternatively, book a tour in Montañita.

6 OLÓN

This tranquil village on the north side of the point is developing as a quiet alternative to Montañita; it has a long beach and a few good hotels and restaurants. The sea isn't suitable for surfing but you could just about swim in it.

ACCOMMODATION

Hostería N&J ☎ 04 278 8091, ⓦ hosterianj.com. This friendly place on the beachfront has eleven well-kept simple rooms. Breakfast included. $27

Quimbita ☎ 04 278 8019, ⓦ quimbita.com. Charming, colourful hotel with a permanent art exhibition two blocks from the beach. $35

MONTAÑITA TO PUERTO LÓPEZ

Head north from Montañita and cross into the province of **Manabí**. This is probably the most beautiful stretch of Ecuador's coastline – so if you prefer peace to partying head here. On the road to Parque Nacional Machalilla, you pass a succession of fishing villages – **Ayampe**, **Las Tunas**, **Puerto Rico** and **Salango**. Tourist facilities are still developing, and the beaches are often deserted.

ACCOMMODATION

Between Montañita and Puerto López there are several highly recommended *hosterías*.

★ **La Barquita** ☎ 05 274 7051, ⓦ hosterialabarquita. com. Near Puerto Rico. These rooms are set in idyllic gardens with a swimming pool. There's a wooden, boat-shaped restaurant for meals. $38

Cabañas La Tortuga ☎ 05 257 5163, ⓦ latortuga.com. ec. The well-constructed, attractive accommodation here is the only beachfront option in Ayampe. Breakfast included. $50

Viejamar Hostel 12 de Octubre, Las Tunas ☎ 05 234 7032. Right on the beach, 13km south of Puerto López, this relaxed hostel is a really peaceful retreat. There are panoramic ocean views, good surf and inexpensive Isla de la Plata tours. Dorms $10, doubles $30

Hostería Mandala Malecón ☎ 05 230 0181, ⓦ hosteriamandala.info. Deservedly popular, this welcoming place has spacious thatched-roof cabins set in lush tropical gardens. The main building has a pool table, board games and books, and a lovely wraparound veranda – the perfect place to linger over the restaurant's excellent international cuisine. Breakfast included. $65

PUERTO LÓPEZ

PUERTO LÓPEZ is the tourism hub for the Machalilla area and the best base to explore **Parque Nacional Machalilla** and **Isla de la Plata**. The town isn't pretty but boasts one of the most attractive locations on the coast, set in a wide bay surrounded by green hills of Ecuador's largest protected coastal forest. The dusty Malecón has a certain beaten-down charm, with fishermen heading out from the bay every morning. The town gets very busy on weekends during the whale-watching season (June–Sept).

ARRIVAL AND INFORMATION

By bus The new terminal is 2.5km north of the centre; *mototaxis* charge $1.

Destinations Guayaquil (9 daily, 3hr 30min); Manta (every 30min; 2hr). Quito (6 daily; 10hr);

Tourist information iTur, Av Machalilla, at Atahualpa (daily 8am–noon & 1–4.30pm; ☎ 099 199 5390).

ACCOMMODATION

★ **Hostal Itapoa** Malecón ☎ 05 230 0071, ⓦ hosteriaitapoa.com. North of town, just off the beach, this charming Brazilian-run place has fine rustic cabins and rooms. There's a pretty garden and bike trips, snorkelling excursions and surfing lessons are offered. Profits fund the owners' environmental projects, including locally produced organic chocolate. Breakfast included. Dorms $15, doubles $40

Hostal Máxima Suárez, at Machalilla ☎ 099 953 4282, ⓦ hotelmaxima.org. Excellent-value Ecuadorian–US hostel set around a nice garden with airy accommodation (single to family-sized). There's also an open kitchen, café, and TV area with a free DVD library. Camping $5/person, doubles $18

Maremonti Bed & Breakfast C San Francisco, ☎ 099 173 1325, ⓦ maremonti.info. Almost all the rustic rooms at this B&B enjoy spectacular views, with hammocks slung on their individual balconies. There's a pool too, and very

CROSSING THE PERUVIAN BORDER

The only significant coastal town between Guayaquil and the Peruvian border is the banana hub, **Machala**. Some 75km south of here is the grubby border town of **Huaquillas**, the busiest crossing point from Ecuador to Peru. Spend as little time as possible here; Cuenca and Guayaquil are both at an easy distance by bus so there should be no need to stay overnight.

ACCOMMODATION AND EATING IN HUAQUILLAS

Grand Hotel Hernancor 1 de Mayo 323, at Hualtaco ☎ 07 299 5467. With modern, well-presented a/c rooms this hotel is a good option. **$36**

La Habana Hotel Restaurant T. Córdovez, at Santa Rosa ☎ 07 299 5832, ⓦ lahabanahotel.com.ec. A popular choice for Ecuadorian breakfasts and filling meat and fish dishes; mains from $6. Above the restaurant are midrange hotel rooms, many with fine views. **$40**

INTO PERU

What was once one of the worst border crossings in South America is now hugely improved, thanks to a new "CEBAF Huaquillas-Aguas Verdes" integrated Ecuadorian-Peruvian migration, open 24hr. The main road bypasses the grubby border towns entirely. Cross-border buses stop and handle their paperwork separately while travellers exit through the building, first getting Ecuadorian exit stamps and then Peruvian entry stamps, or of course vice versa. Lines are long, however, and it can take 2hr or more to clear on a normal day.

INTO ECUADOR

For those arriving in Ecuador, **buses** from Huaquillas leave from private depots a few blocks from the international bridge.

For Cuenca use Transportes Azuay (6 daily; 5hr). Heading to Machala, CIFA operates buses (every 10min until 8pm; 1hr 30min) and there are also express buses (every 20min; 1hr). For Guayaquil use CIFA, Ecuatoriano Pullman, Rutas Orenses or Transfrosur minivans (every 20–30min; 4hr–4hr 30min). Travelling up to Quito there's Panamericana (10 daily) and Transportes Occidentales (5 daily); the trip is about 12hr.

If you intend to go to Loja, it's better to cross from Peru at Macará but Transportes Loja has two daily buses (11.30am & 6pm; 5hr).

---

good rates for single travellers but it's a 10–15min walk down to the beach. **$30**

Hostería Nantu Malecón ☎ 05 230 0040, ⓦ hosteriananantu.com. Excellent value, offering very inviting rooms at moderate rates. Firm beds, hot water, as well as a small pool and games room to keep you busy. **$42**

Sol Inn Juan Montalvo, at Eloy Alfaro ☎ 05 230 0248, ⓦ hostalsolinn.machalillatours.org. Somewhat ramshackle place with basic wooden cabins and laidback vibe. Lots of tours are offered. Dorms **$6**, doubles **$15**

EATING AND DRINKING

Doña Elsie's Montalvo, at Córdova. Modestly priced Esmeraldeñan cuisine – *encocados*, *ceviches* and rice and plantain (most dishes $5–6) – served in no-nonsense fashion on plastic tables. Daily 8am–9pm.

Patacón Pisa'o General Córdova. Head here for Colombian specialities such as *arepas*. Mains $4–5. Daily 1–9.30pm; Oct–May closed Sun.

Restaurante Carmita Stands out from the cluster of restaurants along the Malecón with a great selection of seafood (mains $6–8) in a polished setting. Daily 8am–9.30pm.

PARQUE NACIONAL MACHALILLA

Ecuador's only coastal national park was set up in 1979 to preserve the rapidly disappearing tropical dry forest that once stretched north all the way to Costa Rica. It's a dramatic setting with thickly forested hills crowned by candelabra cacti, dropping down to pristine, peaceful beaches. The park headquarters (daily 8am–5pm; ☎ 05 230 0102) is based in Puerto López, opposite the market on Alfaro, where you pay your entrance fee (valid for five days; mainland only $12; Isla de la Plata only $15; combined ticket $20).

WHAT TO SEE AND DO

The best place to explore the park's dry forest is **Agua Blanca**, a village inhabited by some 300 indigenous people and an important archeological site of the Manteño culture that lived here from 800 to 1500 AD. Getting to Agua Blanca involves either taking a bus north from Puerto López and then walking the unpleasant 5km trail up a dirt track, or hiring a *mototaxi* ($5 one-way from town, $10 return). The museum houses an interesting collection of sculptures, funeral urns and pickled snakes. A guided tour ($5) includes museum entry followed by a two-hour forest walk. Highlights include the towering ceibos, barbasco and fragrant Palo Santo trees whose wood is burnt as incense and to repel mosquitoes. Take in the spectacular views up to San Sebastián before a refreshing soak in a pungent but relaxing sulphur pool, considered sacred by local indigenous people.

San Sebastián

The landscape rises to 800m inland, where the dry forest turns into the cloudforest of **San Sebastián**, with lush vegetation including orchids, bamboo and wildlife such as howler monkeys, anteaters and 350 species of birds. This virgin forest can be explored on a 20km hike with a mandatory guide hired in Agua Blanca ($20). You can camp overnight or stay with local villagers.

Playa Los Frailes

A few kilometres further north is the entrance to **Playa Los Frailes**, a stunning virgin beach, often deserted in early mornings. Present your park ticket or pay the entrance fee at the kiosk, then either head straight for Los Frailes on a thirty-minute hike or take the 4km circular trail via the black-sand cove of La Payita and Playa La Tortiguita. To get straight to the beach, take a taxi from Puerto López ($5 one-way).

ISLA DE LA PLATA

The tongue-in-cheek tag of "poor man's Galápagos" refers to the fantastic amount of wildlife visitors can find on the small island of **ISLA DE LA PLATA**. Just 37km from Puerto López, it's by all means worth a day-trip to see its birdlife, which is easy to combine with whale-watching in the summer months. The island is home to numerous blue-footed boobies, masked boobies and frigate birds. Red-footed boobies and waved albatrosses are also seen from April to October. The island has a small colony of sea lions, though it's rare to see them. You can only visit the island with a tour operator.

WHAT TO SEE AND DO

There are two circular **footpaths** around the island, the 3.5km Sendero Machete and the 5km Sendero Punta Escaleras. There's no shade, so bring sunscreen, water and a hat. Close encounters with boobies are the main highlight. Cool off after the hike with some snorkelling among an array of marine life. Peak season is June to September (particularly July & Aug) when humpback whales arrive for the mating season, which is an awesome spectacle.

TOUR OPERATORS

Day-trips to Isla de la Plata cost $35–40/person including guide and light lunch. Recommended companies include:

Cercapez González Suárez and Malecón ☎ 05 230 0173, ✉ operadoracercapez@gmail.com. Whale-watching and Isla de la Plata tours.

Exploramar Diving Malecón, Puerto López, ☎ 099 950 0910, ⊛ exploradiving.com. Specializes in diving trips along the coast.

Naturis Cordova, at Montalvo, Puerto López ☎ 05 230 0218, ⊛ machalillatours.com. Offers community tourism and multi-activity trips including kayaking, fishing and snorkelling.

Palo Santo Malecón, at Calderón ☎ 099 230 9366, ⊛ whalewatching-ecuador.com. Environmentally conscious operator offering bilingual whale-watching trips.

The Galápagos

Charles Darwin developed his monumental theory of evolution after travelling to the **GALÁPAGOS** in the 1830s, and it's no exaggeration to say that the creatures of these unworldly volcanic islands, 1000km west of the Ecuadorian coast, were fundamental in changing the way we view ourselves.

The array of **wildlife** in the Galápagos is spellbinding. From giant tortoises to marine iguanas, sea lions to sharks and blue-footed boobies to magnificent frigate birds, it's hard to know which way to turn. Nowhere else on earth can you view wild mammals, reptiles and birds that are utterly unconcerned by human presence – a legacy of there being few natural predators on the islands.

Visiting the Galápagos independently is now relatively easy and last-minute deals are better than ever. However, a week in the Galápagos will cost much more than one on the mainland. The **low season** is May/June and September/October, while December to mid-April and July/August is **high season**, though cheap deals can still be found.

Weather conditions are highly unusual considering that the islands bestride the equator. Between December and April, the balmy influence of the Panama current brings warm seas and sunny weather. From June to October the temperature dips considerably, as the cool Humboldt current sweeps past the islands bringing mist, drizzle and rougher seas. Whenever you choose to visit, you can only see a tiny percentage of the islands because 97 percent of the area is protected by the national park and the seventy registered visitor sites comprise only 0.01 percent of the landmass, a comforting fact for environmentalists.

ARRIVAL AND DEPARTURE

By plane Return flights to San Cristóbal or Baltra start at about $360 with TAME, Avianca or LATAM. If booking online, you must indicate your nationality; if you mistakenly book as an Ecuadorian resident, you will have to pay surcharges. In San Cristóbal it's a $1.50 taxi ride to town, i.e. Puerto Baquerizo Moreno. If arriving on Baltra, it's more complicated. To get to the main port Puerto Ayora involves a free 10min bus ride south, a $1, 5min ferry crossing and then a $3 bus (50min) or $20 taxi (35min).

INFORMATION

Tourist information The Ministry of Tourism (☎05 252 6174, ⓦturismo.gob.ec) has iTur offices in Puerto Ayora, Puerto Baquerizo Moreno and Puerto Villamil. The Galápagos National Park entrance fee is $100 for foreign adults, payable in cash on arrival. There is also a $20 transit card, which must be purchased before check-in at Quito or Guayaquil airport counters.

TOUR OPERATORS

The price of tours, accommodation and cruises varies hugely. When booking from abroad, tours cost $2000–5000 for a week. Booking last-minute in Quito and Guayaquil brings the prices down to $700–2200 (not including flights). Most backpackers now travel independently and book day-trips ($50–150/day) or short cruises (from $400) on arrival. Doing it this way, it's possible to spend a week on the islands for perhaps $1500 total, including flights.

In Quito Aida Maria Travel (Amazonas N23-31 and Veintimilla, Quito ☎02 254 6028, ⓦaidamariatravel.com); Galápagos Tours (Amazonas N23-71, at Wilson; ☎02 254 6028, ⓦgalapagostours.net); Metropolitan Touring (Av de las Palmeras N45-74, at De las Orquídeas ☎02 298 8312); Ninfa Tour (Av Amazonas N24-62, at Pinto ☎02 222 3124, ⓦgalapagosninfatour.com); Nuevo Mundo Expeditions (Vicente Ramón Roca N21-293, at Leonidas Plaza ☎02 450

WHERE TO SEE WILDLIFE IN THE GALÁPAGOS

Blue-footed boobies Most easily viewed on North Seymour, Punta Pitt (San Cristóbal), Española or Genovesa.

Frigate birds Try Seymour Norte, Punta Pitt or Española.

Galápagos penguins Colonies on Floreana, Bartolomé, Fernandina and Isabela.

Giant tortoises See them in the wild in the Santa Cruz highlands or at the breeding centres in Puerto Ayora and on Isabela and San Cristóbal.

Green sea turtles Encountered by divers all round the islands. The best-known nesting sites are Bartolomé, Tortuga Bay (Santa Cruz) and Gardner Bay (Española).

Iguanas The marine variety is found on all major islands; see their land cousins on Seymour Norte, South Plaza or Santa Fé.

Sea lions Found on numerous beaches, large numbers hang around the dock and bays in Puerto Baquerizo Moreno. To see them underwater, the best snorkelling spots are Champion Island (Floreana) and La Isla de los Lobos (San Cristóbal). Males are territorial, so keep your distance.

Sharks Docile white-tipped and black-tipped reef sharks are best viewed off Floreana, North Seymour, Bartolomé and León Dormido (San Cristóbal), while hammerhead sharks are mainly seen by divers (also at León Dormido).

Waved albatross Exclusively found on Española from April to November.

6

5412, ⓦnuevomundoexpeditions.com); Royal Galapágos (Sonelsa Tower, 265 Foch, at 6 de Diciembre ⓣ02 602 4568, ⓦroyalgalapagos.com).

In Guayaquil Ecoventura (Edificio Samborondon, Torre ⓣ04 283 9390, ⓦecoventura.com); Via Natura (Junín 114, at Malecón, Ed. Torres del Rio, Floor 7 ⓣ04 256 9052, ⓦvianatura.com).

In Puerto Ayora Galapatour (Av Rodríguez Lara; ⓣ05 252 6088); Moonrise Travel (Av Charles Darwin 160; ⓣ05 252 6348, ⓦgalapagosmoonrise.com); Scuba Iguana (Av Charles Darwin; ⓣ05 252 6497, ⓦscubaiguana. com); Galapagos Sub-Aqua (Av Charles Darwin; ⓣ099 919 8798, ⓦgalapagos-sub-aqua.com); We are the Champions Tours (Av Charles Darwin; ⓣ05 252 6951, ⓦwearethechampionstours.com).

GETTING AROUND

By plane TAME connects Baltra with Cristóbal several times a week and EMETEBE (Galápagos ⓣ05 252 1183, Guayaquil ⓣ04 230 9209, ⓦemetebe.com.ec) operates small eight-seater planes on a charter basis between Baltra, Isabela and San Cristóbal.

By boat Daily services on small launches connecting Santa Cruz with San Cristóbal and Isabela (all routes $30 one-way; 2hr–2hr 30min). There are usually at least two boats (morning and afternoon) on all routes, but you should book one day in advance via an agent in the main ports. There's also a public boat link (2–3 weekly; 2hr; $30) between Floreana and Santa Cruz. Expect a bumpy ride; pharmacies sell anti sea-sickness pills.

ISLA SANTA CRUZ

This is the most developed island in the Galápagos and its capital **PUERTO AYORA** is the central tourism hub. It's by no means the highlight of the archipelago, but the central location and wide range of hotels, restaurants and tour operators make it a convenient base to explore surrounding islands.

Puerto Ayora

In this somewhat functional town you can arrange tours and pick up last-minute deals. A visit to the Charles Darwin Research Station to see the tortoises is worth it, and there are some interesting short hikes out of town.

WHAT TO SEE AND DO

There are various attractions close to Puerto Ayora, but for some you need to take the **Bay Tour** ($35 from most local operators).

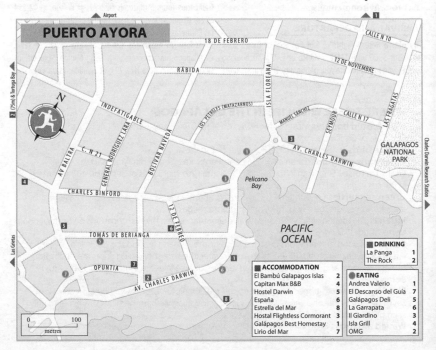

PUERTO AYORA

DRINKING
La Panga ... 1
The Rock ... 2

ACCOMMODATION
El Bambú Galapagos Islas ... 2
Capitan Max B&B ... 4
Hostel Darwin ... 5
España ... 6
Estrella del Mar ... 8
Hostal Flightless Cormorant ... 3
Galápagos Best Homestay ... 1
Lirio del Mar ... 7

EATING
Andrea Valerio ... 1
El Descanso del Guía ... 7
Galápagos Deli ... 5
La Garrapata ... 6
Il Giardino ... 3
Isla Grill ... 4
OMG ... 2

The tour takes in La Lobería, where you can snorkel with sea lions, Playa de los Perros, where marine iguanas and various birds are seen, Las Tintoreras, channels where sharks are often found, and Las Grietas.

A fifteen-minute walk east of town is the **Charles Darwin Research Station** (daily 7am–6pm; free; ☏05 252 6146, ⌖darwinfoundation.org), which contains an information centre and a museum. The highlight is the giant tortoise enclosure where you can view the Galápagos giants close-up. Of the original fourteen subspecies, eleven have survived. "Lonesome George" was the most famous resident until his death in 2012 meant the extinction of his Pinta island subspecies. Today you can view an embalmed George, (nowadays not so lonely – he's a key tourist attraction) in a totally over-the-top air-conditioned monument (which cost $500,000) to construct.

If you're in Puerto Ayora and want to hit the beach, then the best option is **Tortuga Bay**. Follow the trail from the western edge of town along a paved path through cactus forest (a 30min walk with some shade). The first exposed bay you reach is not actually Tortuga Bay, but one of the longest beaches in the archipelago, popular with surfers but dangerous to swim. Walk to the end of the shoreline and cross over to a lagoon to find the bay where marine turtles, in their hundreds some nights, come to lay their eggs. The beach officially closes at 5pm, but if you want to linger, waiting excursion boat captains will usually take you back to Ayora for $10.

Las Grietas

Another side trip from the port with a relaxing dip at the end is the walk to **Las Grietas**, a crevice in the rocks that supplies the port with much of its fresh water. Take a water taxi ($0.60) across the bay towards Playa de Los Alemanes, then venture along rocky trails for a further twenty minutes to reach Las Grietas. Fissures in the lava rocks have created two layers of brackish water – saline and fresh. It's a beautiful, sheltered place for a swim. Be aware that the rocky trails are a bit tricky; walking shoes will come in handy.

The highlands

The highlands offer a very different experience to the beaches on Santa Cruz and it's worth venturing inland to see the diversity of the island. At El Chato, you can observe giant tortoises in their natural habitat in the reserve (entrance $3 including guide). Nearby are the lava tunnels, which are naturally formed and

6

THE GALÁPAGOS IN DANGER

From the 1980s onwards, Galápagos tourism has experienced explosive growth. But the influx of humans, both transient and permanent, has done huge damage to parts of the fragile ecosystem and the islands were placed on the **UNESCO Danger List** in April 2007. The key problems included: uncontrolled immigration; high traffic levels; an inadequate sewage system; invasive species such as livestock, pets and fruits; and overfishing.

The Ecuadorian government took action by deporting hundreds of illegal Ecuadorian immigrants back to the mainland and using satellite technology to stop illegal fishing. Recycling and renewable energy are being rolled out. Isabela, Floreana and Santiago have seen goat extermination programmes, with more than 250,000 killed since 2006. Other harmful invasive species are fruit flies, fire ants and rats, the last of which have proved the most difficult to exterminate.

Emergency measures were deemed successful, and, to the dismay of scientists and environmentalists, the Galápagos Islands were removed from the UNESCO Danger List in July 2010. The islands' problems are far from over and tourists can help by following the strict rules on waste disposal and recycling. Sadly, in 2014, the government lifted restrictions on hotel construction again, without comment on environmental impact.

Overfishing has affected the Galápagos, despite conservation laws. Organizations including UNESCO and WWF have funded coastguard equipment to monitor the Galápagos Marine Reserve, introducing satellite and radar technology. Yet just outside the reserve are fleets of trawlers, from as far afield as Korea and China, lying in wait just inside international waters.

have lighting so you can walk through them. Either side of the main road which cuts through Santa Cruz are the Gemelos (twins), collapsed 30m-deep craters. The sheer drop into the craters, covered in vegetation, makes them an impressive sight. All of the attractions above can be seen on a guided tour with any of the tour operators in Puerto Ayora ($70/person).

Las Bachas

On the north coast, **Las Bachas**, once a base for the US military, is a long white-sand beach often covered in Sally Lightfoot crabs. Flamingos frequent in the lagoons inland and marine turtles are abundant in the bay's waters. Tour operators often combine a visit here with other excursions such as North Seymour (see page 638).

ACCOMMODATION

Santa Cruz has the largest selection of accommodation on the islands and it's even possible to find a budget room in peak periods. Book in advance as places fill up fast.

El Bambú Galapagos Islas Duncan ☎099 567 2234; map p.634. Owned by a friendly couple, with spacious doubles, suites and apartments (with kitchens) at moderate rates. Limited English spoken. $45

Capitán Max B&B ☎05 252 4412; ⓦcapitanmax. com; map p.634. Run by a very friendly and helpful local guy, the spacious rooms here are grouped around a pleasant lounge area where a generous breakfast is served. $73

Hostal Flightless Cormorant Av Darwin, at 12 de Febrero ☎05 252 4343; ⓔhostalcomorant2016@ outlook.com; map p.634. Centrally located and with great views of the bay from the top-floor terrace. All rooms are a/c and en suite and there's cheap bike rental. $34

Hostel Darwin Av Herrera, at Tomás de Berlanga ☎05 252 6193; map p.634. This pleasant hotel has a collection of clean, no-frills rooms with private bathrooms (with hot water) set around a small courtyard. Staff are friendly and breakfast is included. $33

España Thomas de Berlanga, at 12 de Febrero ☎05 252 6108, ⓦhotelespanagalapagos.com; map p.634. Popular budget hotel, with neat en-suite rooms around a colourful courtyard. Singles, triples and quads are available. Doubles $40

Estrella del Mar 12 de Febrero, next to police station ☎05 252 6427; map p.634. The cheapest hotel on the waterfront has great views and simple rooms with a/c and cable TV. Book early to get a view of Academy Bay. $72

Galápagos Best Homestay Piqueros, Barrio Escalesia ☎05 301 5345, ⓦgalapagosbesthomestay.com; map p.634. Excellent hostel, smoothly operated by Kevin, a hospitable local who offers guests a free walking tour. Rooms are well equipped with microwaves, small fridges and a/c. Dorms $20, doubles $45

Lirio del Mar Islas Plaza, at Thomas de Berlanga ☎05 252 6212; map p.634. Dependable budget option with a small terrace and basic, no-frills rooms. A/c extra. Dorms $18, doubles $45

EATING

Puerto Ayora has a wide range of restaurants, though mostly in the slightly higher range ($15–25 for dinner). For an inexpensive feed head to the *kioskos* along Charles Binford (pedestrianized in evenings) where you can get a meal for $5–7.

★ **Andrea Valerio** Av Darwin; map p.634. This stylish new place has a wonderful upper deck overlooking the fish market and excellent Ecuadorean dishes like *corviche* (mashed green plantain with seafood) and *chupe de pescado* (fish soup). Mains $9–19. Mon & Wed–Sun 9am–10pm.

El Descanso del Guía Av Darwin (next to the church); map p.634. A popular option for locals to fill up on Ecuadorian staples such as *bolón* (fried plantain ball) for breakfast and a variety of white fish for lunch. Two-course set meals are well above average and cost just $4. Daily 8am–9pm.

Galápagos Deli Tomás de Berlanga, between Baltra and Islas Plaza; map p.634. Modern, open-plan café-restaurant featuring Puerto Ayora's best thin-crust pizza (from $6.50), gourmet sandwiches (from $4.70), excellent home-made ice cream, yummy cakes and espresso coffee. Tues–Sun 7am–9.45pm.

La Garrapata Av Darwin, near Berlanga; map p.634. Laidback local favourite with a varied menu including excellent seafood, as well as good-value set lunches. Mains $6–16. Mon–Sat 9am–4pm & 6.30–10pm.

Il Giardino Av Darwin, at Binford; map p.634. Boasts a prime spot on the waterfront and offers a garden setting for well-prepared meat and fish dishes and panini. There's always a daily special ($12 or so). Mains $9–17. Tues–Sun 8am–10.30pm.

Isla Grill Av Darwin, ⓦislagrillgalapagos.com; map p.634. Excellent grilled seafood and meats including steaks and barbecued ribs. Mains $9–16. Daily noon–10pm.

OMG Av Darwin ⓦomg.ec; map p.634. Simply the best coffee in town, organic and sourced in the Galápagos, with a lovely street-facing terrace to sip it. Snacks including *empanadas* and cakes also available. Mon–Sat 8.30am–7.30pm, Sun 3–7.30pm.

CRUISES

Although many budget travellers now choose to travel independently and stay in hotels, in many ways the best way to see the Galápagos is on a **cruise**. If you can deal with the seasickness, which is likely on all but the most luxurious boats, then you'll be rewarded with more quality time at sites and be spared the daily return journey to a port. There are also many sites only accessible to cruise boats.

Vessels that tour the Galápagos range from small boats to luxury cruise yachts carrying ninety passengers. Longer tours can access the more remote islands. Single-cabin supplements are usually very high. If you have some flexibility, you can make substantial **savings** on cruises by booking last-minute in Puerto Ayora or Guayaquil. Prices are even lower booking last-minute in Puerto Ayora and you could be lucky enough to get the higher-level cruises on the cheap. Always check the official grading of the boat before booking. Prices below are full prices for eight days based on two sharing (last-minute discounts can be as little as fifty percent of these prices). The rock-bottom economy-class boats have all but disappeared as budget travellers increasingly opt for land-based tours.

Tourist class boats cost from $2000 for eight days and offer a basic level of comfort. They have Class II guides with a good level of knowledge and English-language skills.

Tourist-superior boats start at around $3000 for eight days and have more comfortable cabins, better food and Class II guides.

First-class yachts cost $3750 to over $5000 for eight days, can travel faster and have a decent level of comfort, high-quality food and Class III guides, the highest level of accreditation.

Deluxe vessels start around $5000 for eight days. These are the largest yachts and ships with the most stability and have extra facilities such as jacuzzis and more spacious social areas.

Rates are very flexible, according to demand and season. All the main cruise companies offer last-minute specials.

DRINKING AND NIGHTLIFE

La Panga Darwin, at Thomas de Berlanga; map p.634. The town's main club, which pumps out Latin and international dance hits until 2am. *Bongo*, the archipelago's most elegant late-night bar, is upstairs. Wed–Sat 7pm–2am.

The Rock Darwin, at Islas Plaza; map p.634. Named after the first Galápagos bar set up on Baltra in the 1940s, this endearing place offers a wide variety of juices, shakes and cocktails plus Mexican and international dishes *(mains $8–13).* Tues–Sun 2pm–midnight.

AROUND ISLA SANTA CRUZ

Isla North Seymour

Off the north coast of Santa Cruz is the tiny island of **NORTH SEYMOUR**, which offers some of the best opportunities in the archipelago to watch frigate birds and get close to blue-footed boobies. Follow the 2.5km circular trail around the island to see frigates nesting and the amusing courtship of the boobies. Sea lions and iguanas are also common. A day tour is comparatively pricey ($125/person with Puerto Ayora tour operators) due to restricted access.

Islas Plazas

Off the east coast of Santa Cruz are the two tiny islands of **Plazas**, home to a large sea-lion colony and a great place to observe these animals up close on land. You can only visit the south island, where a 1km trail around the cliffs offers good views of birdlife including pelicans and frigate birds. There's also a sea-lion bachelor colony. Like North Seymour, day tours cost around $125/person, combined with Punta Carrión.

Isla Santa Fé

Southeast of Puerto Ayora, the small island of **SANTA FÉ** has great snorkelling as well as opportunities to see white-tipped reef sharks, marine iguanas, sea lions and stingrays. Santa Fé land iguanas laze around the trails that wind through a forest of 10m-high *Opuntia* cacti. Access to the island's land sites is restricted to cruise boats, but there are day-trips from Puerto Ayora (around $60), which are of limited appeal because you can only visit selected offshore sites.

Centros de Interpretación & Playa Cabo de Horno

6

La Lobería & Airport

PUERTO BAQUERIZO MORENO

DRINKING
Iguana Rock	1
Midori	2

EATING
Coffee Shop by Calypso	5
Cri's	2
Mi Grande	4
Miconia	1
Tongo Reef Bar	3

ACCOMMODATION
Gosen Guest House	1
Hostal Casa de Nelly	2
Hostal León Dormido	4
Hotel Mar Azul	5
Hostal San Francisco	3

ISLA SAN CRISTÓBAL

The most easterly island of the archipelago, this is the administrative centre of the islands. It's quieter than Santa Cruz, which may appeal, and the large population of sea lions in the main port is a particular highlight.

WHAT TO SEE AND DO

The most popular boat trip (from $125) is the "360 Tour" which zips you right around the coast of San Cristóbal in a speedboat, a full day out. Stops usually include the pristine bay of Rosa Blanca and Punta Pitt, where three species of boobies can be seen, then on to the offshore islands of León Dormido (also known as Kicker Rock) which is one of the best snorkelling and diving sites in the archipelago, with great opportunities to see reef and

Galápagos sharks, turtles and stingrays.

Inland, highlights include El Junco Lagoon, one of the few freshwater lakes in the islands, with abundant birdlife. Nearby is the Galapaguera, a giant-tortoise reserve set in dry forest. To visit these two attractions as well as nearby beach Puerto Chino, either take a guided tour (from $50) or hire a taxi.

Puerto Baquerizo Moreno

The islands' capital is smaller and calmer than Puerto Ayora. It has its share of tourism infrastructure, however, with hotels, restaurants, tour operators, a smart waterfront promenade and beaches usually covered in sea lions.

A fifteen-minute walk north of town past the small, popular Mann Beach is the impressive **Centro de Interpretación** (daily 6am–6pm; free), which provides an in-depth overview of the islands' history, development and current environmental problems, split into three galleries. Continue walking past the centre and you will find a forked path that leads to Cerro Tijeretas (Frigatebird Hill) to observe the birds and enjoy sweeping views over the bay below. Then take the other path down to Playa Cabo de Horno, which has good snorkelling. On the opposite end of town, it's a hot, thirty-minute walk to La Lobería, a large sea-lion colony. There's also good surfing nearby (taxi from port $2).

TOUR OPERATORS

Tours to León Dormido and the highlands can be arranged with most tour operators in town, including Sharksky (Española, at Darwin; ☎099 954 0596, ⓦsharksky.com) and Galakiwi (Darwin at Malecón; ☎05 252 1562, ⓦgalakiwi.com). Good dive schools include Dive and Surf Club (Melville; ☎098 087 7122, ⓦdivesurfclub.com) and Galapagos Blue Evolution (☎05 301 0264, ⓦgalapagosblueevolution.com.ec). A two-dive trip to León Dormido costs $160 including all equipment.

ACCOMMODATION

Gosen Guest House Carlos Mora, at Northia ☎05 252 0328; map p.639. Attractive murals of Galápagos wildlife distinguish this small, friendly place. There's a large kitchen and fan-cooled rooms. **$48**
Hostal Casa de Nelly Carrer Playa de Mann ☎05 252 0112, ⓦcasadenellygalapagos.com.ec; map p.639. On a quiet side street between the centre and the western beaches, this popular *hostal* has a fine garden for chilling and spacious rooms, many with large balconies. **$44**
Hostal León Dormido José de Villamil, at Malecón ☎05 252 0169, ⓦleondormidogalapagos.com.ec; map p.639. Offering decent value, this budget option has sixteen clean, somewhat perfunctory rooms with private bath, fans and TV. Wi-fi is spotty. **$40**
Hotel Mar Azul Alsacio Northia, at Esmeraldas ☎05 252 0139, ⓦhotelmarazulgalapagos.com; map p.639. Cheap clean rooms with a/c and cable TV and a breezy covered seating area. Located a short walk inland from the Malecón. **$48**
Hostal San Francisco Malecón ☎05 252 0304; map p.639. Cheap and fairly cheerful, this option has simple, basic a/c rooms, and breakfast is included. **$25**

EATING

Inexpensive places are dotted along the streets off the Malecón.
Coffee Shop by Calypso Off the Malecón; map p.639. One of the nicest settings in town for a meal (seafood, pizza, pasta, salads) in an atmospheric old dining room decorated with monochrome photographs. Also serves espresso coffee. Mains $9–21.
Cri's Teodoro Wolf; map p.639. Always busy, this excellent burger joint is the most popular place in town thanks to its moderate prices and tasty grub. They also serve tacos, fried chicken and Endémica craft beer. Mains $7–12.
Mi Grande Villamil; map p.639. Head up the stairs to this no-nonsense diner-style restaurant for filling meals ($4–6) including burgers, breakfasts, *empanadas* and *bistec con bolon*.
Miconia Malecón; map p.639.The first-floor dining area here overlooks the bay and specializes in fresh seafood and pasta (most mains $10–21), or there's a separate healthy-eating café on the ground floor for snacks like *arepas* ($3.50–4.50) and excellent cold-pressed juices.
Tongo Reef Bar Malecón; map p.639. A simple snack bar along the waterfront, *Tongo* serves breakfasts, burgers, sandwiches and fruit juices for $4–8.

DRINKING

Iguana Rock J José Flores, at Av Quito; map p.639. Shoot pool, catch a band, have a few beers and dance until the early hours at the town's most popular bar.
Midori Malecón; map p.639. The balcony of this waterfront bar offers a mighty fine perspective of the San Cristóbal bay. Craft beer and cocktails are served.

ISLA ISABELA

This is by far the largest island in the Galápagos and the most westerly of the populated islands. It also has the most dramatic landscapes because of its recent volcanic activity. **Puerto Villamil** is the only town with accommodation on the island.

Puerto Villamil

This overgrown village has a sleepy atmosphere, charming sandy streets and is an ideal place to really relax. There's a $5 municipal dock fee on arrival. You'll find plenty of attractions to keep you busy.

Five minutes' walk west of the centre is a set of pozas (lagoons), where flamingos are often seen. Continue walking along the trail for twenty minutes to reach the **Centro de Crianza de Tortugas** (Tortoise Breeding Centre; daily 9am–5pm; free), which has hundreds of tortoises in eight separate enclosures. An information centre has details of the giant tortoise's life cycle and the programme to boost the populations of the five subspecies endemic to Isabela.

Continuing along the coast to the west, it's a pleasant but longer walk (a further two hours) to reach the Muro de las Lágrimas ("Wall of Tears"), a former penal colony built in the 1940s. The story of the convicts who were forced to build their own prison in the 1940s is compelling. You can cycle here by mountain bike (available for $10/day in town) or the wall is included on many guided tours.

Southeast of town is a set of islets called **Las Tintoreras**, named after the reef sharks that frequent them. This is a very good snorkelling spot, with opportunities to watch sea lions, turtles, penguins and white-tipped sharks, which sometimes rest in the canals. There's also a short trail around the islets.

Volcán Sierra Negra
A trek around the volcano is the highlight of a trip to Isabela. You can trek there yourself, but it's far safer to take a guided tour. There are two routes – the shorter, known as **Volcán Chico**, takes four to five hours, usually on foot and horseback. You can see small lava cones and impressive views over the north of the island and Fernandina. The visibility tends to be better on this side. The longer trek to **Las Minas de Azufre** (Sulphur Mines) takes around seven hours and is tougher, especially in the rainy season. However, the extra effort is rewarded with a more spectacular experience. The walk around the crater is followed by a descent into the yellow hills of the sulphur mines, which spew out pungent sulphuric gas. Note that the longer trek is less popular so you may need to book ahead.

TOUR OPERATORS
Tours of the Villamil area cost around $30. A good tour operator is Nautilus (Antonio Gil, at Las Fragatas; ☎ 05 252 9076). Tours of Volcán Sierra Negra are around $35, the sealife marvel Los Tuneles snorkelling site costs $75.

ACCOMMODATION
There is quite a large accommodation offering for such a small town. Accommodation on the beach tends to be a bit more expensive than inland.
Caleta Iguana Antonio Gil, western end of town ☎ 05 252 0484. A key surfers' hangout with seven pleasant white or colourful rooms right on a beach frequented by marine iguanas. $45

Hospedaje Las Gardenias Las Escalecias ☎ 05 252 9115. With helpful owners, this place has three en-suite rooms and a triple with shared facilities, plus a kitchen and a TV lounge. Meals are available on request. $40

Posada del Caminante Near Cormorant ☎ 05 252 9407, ⓦ posadadelcaminante.com. This sociable, inexpensive place consists of a low-rise compound and a three-storey building nearby. Most clean, bright rooms have a kitchen and there's free laundry. $40

EATING AND DRINKING
Bar Beto Antonio Gil. At the far end of the main road, one of the few open-air bars in town; a place where you can soak up beach vistas with a beer or cocktail in hand. Mon–Sat 5pm–1.30am.

El Encanto de la Pepa Antonio Gil. Renowned for its seafood including grilled fish with garlic sauce, *ceviche*, crispy squid and breaded shrimps. There's an attractive terrace setting and a $8 set menu. Mains $8–21. Mon–Sat noon–9.30pm.

NORTHERN ISLANDS

Isla Santiago
Northwest of Santa Cruz are the blackened lava fields of **ISLA SANTIAGO**, also known as San Salvador, only accessible to cruises. Highlights of the island include the lava trails of **Sullivan Bay**. On the western side is **Puerto Egas**, the best landing point to hike along the lava flow and watch countless crabs and marine iguanas. On the southeastern tip of Santiago, the waters around the volcanic cone of **Sombrero Chino** are also excellent for snorkelling.

Bartolomé, just off the east coast, is available on day-trips. It contains the Galápagos's most famous landmark, **Pinnacle Rock**, a partially eroded lava formation. Climb up 108m to a viewpoint commanding spectacular views over the 40m-high rock with two horseshoe-shaped beaches in the foreground and the blackened lava of Santiago's Sullivan Bay beyond. There's very good snorkelling below and opportunities to see Galápagos penguins and marine turtles. Bartolomé can be visited on a day-trip from Puerto Ayora (around $135/person with Puerto Ayora tour operators).

6

Genovesa

This is one of the remotest northern islands, only included on cruises. However, it is worth the eight-hour overnight trip to see the largest red-footed booby population in the archipelago. The two visitor sites are Darwin Bay Beach, with a trail to see boobies and frigates, and a boat trip along the cliffs at Prince Philip steps, named after a royal visit in the 1960s. There's fine snorkelling in Darwin Bay, where you may encounter large stingrays.

SOUTHERN ISLANDS

Isla Floreana

The southern island of **FLOREANA** has a hamlet at Puerto Velasco Ibarra. It was actually the first island to be populated thanks to its freshwater supply, and a descendant of the German Wittmer family runs the beachside *Hotel Wittmer* (☎05 252 0150; $65), but the infrequent transportation and strict regulations mean that the most practical way to visit is on a cruise or a day tour. Post Office Bay is the most common landing point for cruises, with its quirky post office barrel – leave a postcard, hoping a fellow tourist will post it, and take letters to post in your country. In the highlands, there is a small tortoise-breeding centre and caves that were inhabited by pirates in the sixteenth century. Punta Cormorant is a good place to observe flamingos and various wading birds. The islands of Enderby and Champion are excellent spots for snorkelling, while nearby Devil's Crown, a half-submerged volcanic cone, is one of

the top snorkelling and diving sites in the archipelago, with reef sharks, turtles and rays. A day-trip from Puerto Ayora costs about $85, but only includes the highlands, Enderby and Champion. The tour misses out many of the most famous sites, which are restricted to cruises.

Isla Española

ISLA ESPAÑOLA is the southernmost island and can only be visited via a cruise. The island is the sole place in the Galápagos with a colony of waved albatrosses, which flock here between April and November. Seeing them land at one of the "albatross airports" is quite a sight. As well as sea lions, iguanas and boobies, there are opportunities to see the rare hood mockingbird and the finches made famous by Charles Darwin's studies. Punta Suárez is the most popular landing point, and there is excellent snorkelling at Turtle Island.

ISLA FERNANDINA AND OUTLYING ISLANDS

West of Isabela is the volcanic **FERNANDINA**, which can only be visited on a cruise. The highlight is the huge population of marine iguanas sunning themselves on the rocks of **Punta Espinoza**, the only visitor site; there are also trails through the recently formed lava fields. Fernandina's volcano La Cumbre erupted as recently as September 2017. Further north are the tiny, remote islands of **Darwin** and **Wolf**. These are restricted to specialist diving trips to see large populations of hammerhead and whale sharks.

The Guianas

❶ **Kaieteur Falls** One of the world's highest single-drop waterfalls. See page 656

❷ **Rupununi Savannah** Friendly indigenous villages and fantastic wildlife viewing. See page 656

❸ **Upper Suriname** River Unique Saramaccan culture and jungle walks. See page 670

❹ **Galibi Nature Reserve** Watch baby turtles hatch on the beach. See page 671

❺ **Centre Spatial Guyanais** View a space rocket being launched into orbit. See page 680

❻ **Îles du Salut** Spot fearless wildlife and learn about the history of these former French prison islands. See page 681

HIGHLIGHTS ARE MARKED ON THE MAP ON PAGE 646

ROUGH COSTS

Daily budget Basic G: US$60; S: US$50; FG: US$100
Drink Beer G: US$2; S: US$2; FG: US$5
Food G: *Pepperpot* (stew) US$6; S: Saoto soep US$3.50; FG: Blaff (soup) US$12
Guesthouse/budget hotel G: US$30–50; S: US$15–35; FG: US$60–90
Travel Georgetown–Lethem, bus: 18hr, US$60

FACT FILE

Population G: 747,884; S: 591,919; FG: 250,109
Official languages G: English; S: Dutch; FG: French
Currencies G: Guyanese dollar (G$); S: Suriname dollar (SRD); FG: euro (€)
Capitals G: Georgetown; S: Paramaribo; FG: Cayenne
International phone codes G: ☎592; S: ☎597; FG: ☎594
Time zones GMT -3hr (-4hr in Guyana)

Introduction

The Guianas, which comprise the independent nations of Guyana and Suriname and the French overseas département of French Guiana, feel more Caribbean than South American. As a result of colonial legacies the official languages are English (Guyana), Dutch (Suriname) and French (French Guiana), and each has an ethnically diverse population, a mix of indigenous peoples, descendants of European colonizers and their slaves, East Indians, Indonesians, Brazilians, Southeast Asian refugees and Haitians.

Tucked between Brazil's Amazonian region and the continent's northeast coast, the verdant Guianas are criss-crossed by rivers; indeed, the native word *guiana* means "land of many waters". Between eighty and ninety percent of the geological region known as the Guiana Shield (which also includes parts of Brazil and Venezuela) is covered by dense tropical forests – some of the oldest and most pristine on earth. Jaguars, pumas, caimans, iguanas, ocelots, tapirs and other diverse wildlife thrive in this environment, making the Guianas an ecotourism haven. Sparse development and a dearth of tourists mean that getting to certain destinations may entail considerable expense but the thrill of staying in a **jungle lodge**, cruising down majestic **rivers**, or witnessing **sea turtles** laying their eggs more than justifies it.

The towns take a back seat to nature in the Guianas, but the capital cities of **Georgetown** (Guyana), **Paramaribo** (Suriname) and **Cayenne** (French Guiana)

have a certain charm and are worth exploring for a day or two. Paramaribo is the best preserved, Georgetown is the most lively and dynamic, and edgy Cayenne offers an authentic taste of colonial-era life. These three capitals comprise the main international gateways from the Caribbean, North America and Europe.

Borders between the Guianas are marked by rivers, and crossing involves taking scheduled ferries or go-when-full motorized boats. From Guyana to Suriname, you'll need to cross the Corentyne River from Moleson Creek to South Drain near Nieuw Nickerie (see page 670); and from Suriname to French Guiana, the Maroni River from Albina to Saint-Laurent du Maroni (see page 662).

Guyana

GUYANA, the largest and most populous nation of the three Guianas, is a rum-drinking and cricket-loving country, and the only English-speaking nation in South America. **Georgetown**, the capital, typifies this with its cosmopolitan mix of black, white, East Indian, Asian and indigenous ethnicities and a laidback Caribbean attitude.

Guyana's principal attractions are its rainforests, its wildlife and its indigenous culture. Its natural wonder par excellence is the majestic Kaieteur Falls – among the tallest and most powerful in the world

---

WHEN TO VISIT

Temperatures in the Guianas vary little from one month to the next: generally 20°C to 33°C, with a mean temperature of around 27°C (slightly hotter in the interior owing to the absence of the cooling coastal trade winds). Travel plans should be based around the region's two annual **wet seasons**, which pummel the region from May to July and, to a lesser extent, December to January. While the tropical forest is lush and green during the wet season, navigating the many unsealed roads that govern land access to the interior can be difficult (if not impossible). As such, late summer/early autumn and late winter/early spring are the optimum times for a visit – the latter particularly, as this is when many carnival celebrations take place.

– made all the more dramatic by their isolated location at the end of an immense jungle gorge.

Going down the middle of the country from north to south is the **Iwokrama Rainforest**. Gold and diamond mining are very common throughout the interior and independent travel within the region is easiest along "pork-knocker" (Guyanese term for freelance gold miner) routes. Further southwest, the jungle gives way to the wide-open spaces of the **Rupununi Savannah**, dotted with indigenous villages. Here you can immerse yourself in indigenous culture and go in search of caimans, giant anteaters and giant river otters.

CHRONOLOGY

10,000 BC First settlers arrive, having crossed a land bridge from Asia.

1492 Christopher Columbus sets foot in the region. Unsuccessful Spanish exploration in search of the Lost City of Gold.

1595 Sir Walter Raleigh visits Guyana and publishes The Discoverie of the Large, Rich and Bewtiful Empyre of Guiana, igniting European interest in the region.

1613–21 The Dutch found Fort Kyk Over Al, build trading posts, and establish sugar-cane plantations.

1650s African slaves replace indigenous ones, who in turn help the Dutch capture runaways.

1763 A slave revolt is led by Guyana's national hero, Cuffy, though quelled in 1764; 125 slaves executed.

1796 Dutch lose control of colony to the British.

1802 Dutch regain control of Guyana.

1814 Treaty of Paris grants the British control of the area.

1823 Demerara slave revolt brutally suppressed.

1834 Slavery abolished. Thousands of indentured labourers from India, China, England, Ireland, Portugal and Africa are brought to Guyana to work the sugar-cane plantations.

1870s Charles Barrington Brown is the first European to find Kaieteur Falls. Gold found in Guyana's interior.

1950 The People's Progressive Party (PPP) is established.

1953 PPP wins first elections allowed by British. Cheddi Jagan becomes leader. Britain suspends constitution and sends in troops, fearing plans to establish Guyana as a communist state.

1955 PPP splits and Forbes Burnham forms the People's National Congress (PNC).

1957 Elections permitted and PPP wins. Jagan becomes first premier in 1961.

1966 Guyana achieves independence.

1978 More than 900 members of Rev. Jim Jones' People's Temple religious sect commit mass suicide in northwestern Guyana (see page 651).

SURFING, SWINGING AND SLEEPING

The Guianas are not a traditional budget destination so traveller hospitality websites such as ⓦcouchsurfing.com (see page 32) are a good option for those on tight budgets. It's also well worth investing in a hammock (easily available in any of the three capital cities) and accompanying mosquito net.

1980 Guyana gets a controversial new constitution and Burnham becomes president.

1985 Burnham dies; Prime Minister Hugh Desmond Hoyte becomes president.

1992 Cheddi Jagan's PPP wins election.

1997 Jagan dies. His American widow, Janet, is elected president.

1999 Janet Jagan resigns and is succeeded by Bharrat Jagdeo.

2009 Norway agrees to invest US$250m to preserve Guyana's rainforests.

2015 After 23 years in power, the PPP is defeated in elections by the opposition APNU-AFC alliance, with Brigadier David A. Granger elected to the presidency.

2017 Major oil and natural gas deposits discovered offshore by Exxon Mobil.

ARRIVAL AND DEPARTURE

Guyana's **Cheddi Jagan International Airport** (Wcjairport-gy.com), 41km from Georgetown, receives **direct flights** from Suriname, Trinidad, Panama, New York, Miami, and Toronto. Some flights from Suriname, Barbados and domestic flights arrive at the smaller **Eugene F. Correia International Airport** (formerly Ogle and often still called that), twenty minutes east of Georgetown's centre.

A G$5000 (or US$25) exit tax is included in the ticket price for those departing the country by air.

FROM BRAZIL

Travellers arriving overland from Brazil enter Guyana at the town of **Lethem**, about 130km northeast of Boa Vista, Brazil. It is a cramped and bone-jarring eighteen-hour **minibus** ride (see page 659) from Lethem to Georgetown along a dirt logging road that slices the country

7

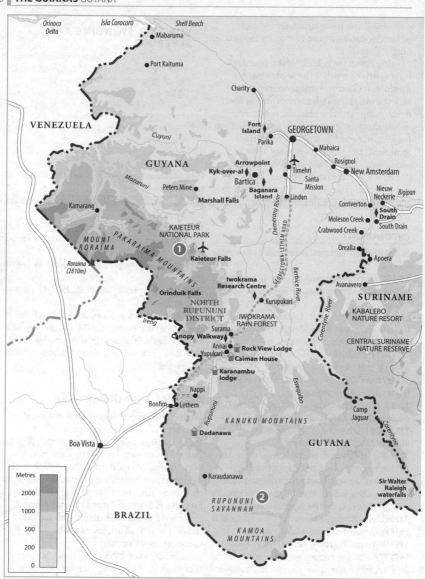

in half. Two small airlines also run daily flights from Lethem to Georgetown, and tickets can be bought in their offices beside the town's airstrip.

FROM SURINAME

Travellers from Suriname must board a **ferry** at South Drain, near Nieuw Nickerie, and make the thirty-minute journey across the Corentyne River to Moleson Creek on the Guyana border before taking a local minibus to Georgetown (see page 662). It's possible to arrange direct transport from Paramaribo to Georgetown (total travel time 10hr).

THE GUIANAS

HIGHLIGHTS

1 Kaieteur Falls
2 Rupununi Savannah
3 Upper Suriname
4 Galibi Nature Reserve
5 Centre Spatial Guyanais
6 Îles du Salut

VISAS

You must have a passport with six months' validity and an onward ticket if arriving by air. Guyanese immigration grants visitors stays of up to thirty days. To extend your stay, contact the Department of Citizenship & Immigration Services (164 Waterloo St; ☎226 2221, ✉ministryofcitizenship.gy@gmail.com) or the Central Office of Immigration (Camp St), both in Georgetown.

Visas are required for all visitors except those from the USA, Commonwealth, most European and CARICOM (Caribbean community) countries. Contact your nearest Guyanese embassy/consulate for more details.

GETTING AROUND

Privately owned **minibuses** operate to nearly all destinations accessible by road, including Lethem close to the Brazilian border (US$60). Roads are paved from Georgetown to towns along the coast and inland as far as Linden; beyond, it's dirt roads only, which sometimes become impassable during rainy season.

Hitchhiking is common outside of the capital. Independent travel in the interior requires cash (no ATMs) to pay for boats, minibuses and 4WD vehicles with a driver. Motorcycle rides are often given freely (see page 657). Daily **flights** in small aircraft connect Georgetown to settlements in the Rupununi and elsewhere; these are reliable and relatively cheap.

Travel along Guyana's main rivers involves **river taxis** (speedboats), whereas locals tend to use dugout canoes and motorboats when travelling along the smaller rivers.

ACCOMMODATION

Decent budget options are scarce in Georgetown, and it can be a challenge to find a decent room for under G$10,000. Prices are a bit lower outside the capital. In the Rupununi Savannah there are several excellent **ecolodges** and **ranches** that offer an introduction to traditional savannah life as well as outdoor pursuits such as wildlife-watching and fishing. Rates usually include meals and transport, as there may be no alternatives. Most villages will have a *benab* (wooden shelter with thatched roof) where you can hang your hammock (bring your own and make sure you invest in a mosquito net, cost/night US$10); in the absence of a *benab*, you may well be able to hang it on someone's porch.

Not all establishments accept foreign credit cards, so check when making a booking. Call rather than email.

FOOD AND DRINK

Curries, cassava, rice and coconut milk reign over **Guyanese cuisine**. Chicken, pork and beef are fried Creole-style, and then curried with East Indian spices. **Rice** is ubiquitous, boiled with coconut milk, black-eyed peas, lentils, *channa* (chickpeas), okra or *callaloo* (spinach); such medleys are referred to as *cookup*. Other staples include roti and *dhal puri* (akin to a tortilla wrap).

Bakes, a fried and puffed-up bread of Trinidadian origin are also cut open and stuffed with all manner of Creole fillings.

Saltfish (codfish fillets salted for preservation) is common in the interior, often served with bakes for breakfast.

The indigenous contribution to Guyanese cuisine is *pepperpot* – made with stewed meat (or fish), coloured, preserved and flavoured with *cassareep* (a thick dark sauce made from cassava juice), cinnamon and hot peppers.

Locals consider **wild meat** a delicacy and adventurous eaters will have the opportunity to try deer, capybara, iguana, wild pig, *manicou* (opossum) and *labba* or *agouti* (jungle rat).

Snacks such as patties, buns, egg balls (boiled eggs wrapped in mashed potatoes, deep-fried and served with mango sauce), *pholouri* (seasoned flour and lentil balls), pineapple tarts, *salara* (red coconut rolls) and cassava pone (like bread pudding but made with coconut and cassava) are sold in bakeries (G$200–300 each).

In Georgetown you'll also find Brazilian and Chinese restaurants as well as Western-style international cafés. A hot meal costs G$500–600 from a market *cook shop*; in local cafés it costs twice that, and in upmarket restaurants you'll spend over G$2000. A fourteen-percent tax is added to the bill in some restaurants.

DRINK

Alcoholic drinks worth trying include local award-winning **Banks Beer** (G$400) and Demerara Distillers' El Dorado fifteen-year-old, reputedly the best rum in the world.

Fizzy soft drinks (many from Brazil) are sold everywhere, along with regional brands such as I-Cee. "Local juices" like mauby (a tree bark-based beverage), cherry and sorrel (each flavoured with their eponymous ingredient) are very refreshing, as are coconut water and ginger juice. Drinking tap water is inadvisable.

CULTURE AND ETIQUETTE

English is the national **language** but locals tend to converse in *Creolese* (as the locals refer to their dialect), an English-based Creole influenced by the indigenous, African, Dutch and Indian languages.

The nine native communities speak several dialects including Arawak, Macushi and Warao, while the prominent Brazilian population speaks Portuguese. The three dominant **religions** are Christianity, Hinduism and Islam.

Women can expect to get plenty of loud comments and persistent kissing noises. Guyanese dress stylishly for work, church, visiting government offices and dining out. **Tipping** is not compulsory though it is appreciated.

SPORTS AND OUTDOOR ACTIVITIES

The country's national sport is cricket, though visitors are more likely to come for the outdoor activities such as canoeing, birdwatching, wildlife-spotting and mountain climbing in the interior. **Horseriding** in the Rupununi Savannah is easily accessible and a visit to the annual **Rupununi Rodeo** in Lethem is recommended.

COMMUNICATIONS

Internet and/or **wi-fi** is available in most hotels and guesthouses (mostly for free) and some cafés, both within and outside the capital.

Guyana's country code is 592. To use your unlocked **mobile phone**, buy a local SIM card (G$500) from either GT&T or Digicel outlets. Mobile internet plans are available, although you don't get much for your money.

Sending letters and postcards from Guyana is cheap (G$200) but slow.

CRIME AND SAFETY

Most visits to Guyana are trouble-free. Still, locals warn that opportunistic **petty crime** is not uncommon, particularly in Georgetown, so avoid displaying valuable items. Take taxis if going more than a few

---

GUYANA ONLINE

ⓦ**exploreguyana.org** Directory of accommodation, restaurants, airlines and travel agencies run by the Tourism and Hospitality Association of Guyana.
ⓦ**visitrupununi.com** Site focusing on natural attractions of the vast Rupununi Savannah, with an emphasis on community-based tourism.

---

blocks after dark and avoid walking alone down deserted, sparsely lit streets.

HEALTH

There is one public and several private **hospitals** in Georgetown. Rural and outlying areas are served by municipal hospitals and health centres; Medivac services (emergency air ambulance) are also available in emergencies. Medical facilities at Georgetown public hospital (see page 655) are rather limited; serious injury or illness may require an airlift to Port of Spain, Trinidad.

Avoid drinking tap water, and pack sunscreen and a broad-rimmed hat, as well as rehydration mix for severe cases of travellers' diarrhoea.

Consult your doctor regarding vaccinations; advice currently includes hepatitis A and B, typhoid, tetanus-diphtheria and rabies. Although cases of malaria have been reported in remote areas of the interior, it is seldom an issue in tourism destinations and seasoned Guyana travellers say prophylaxis is unnecessary; mosquito nets, repellent and long-sleeved clothing remain effective precautions.

INFORMATION AND MAPS

The **Tourism and Hospitality Association of Guyana** (THAG; 157 Waterloo St; Mon–Fri 8am–4pm; ☏ 225 0807, ⓦexploreguyana.org) serves as the

---

EMERGENCY NUMBERS

Police ☏911
Fire service ☏912
Ambulance ☏913

7

country's chief tourism info provider and produces the informative annual magazine, *Explore Guyana*. Also useful is the pocket-sized guide called *Guyana: where & what*. Both are available at hotels and tourism agents around the city. **Permits** are required to visit indigenous villages, arranged by tour operators for organized trips. Independent travellers should contact the Ministry of Indigenous People's Affairs, at 251–252 Quamina, at Thomas (☏ 227 5067, ⓦ moipa.gov.gy).

MONEY AND BANKS

The unit of **currency** is the Guyanese dollar (G$), available in 20, 50, 100, 500, 1000 and 5000 notes. Most businesses and hotels accept US$, while fewer accept euros. While major **credit cards** such as MasterCard, Visa and American Express are accepted in some restaurants and hotels, take plenty of Guyanese dollars if travelling in the interior. Scotiabank ATMs accept foreign cards. The currency fluctuates with the US dollar. At the time of writing, US$1=G$208, €1=G$254, £1=G$288.

OPENING HOURS

Banks operate Monday to Thursday 8am to 2pm, Friday 8am to 2.30pm. Government offices are open Monday to Thursday 8am to noon and 1 to 4.30pm, Friday 8am–noon and 1 to 3.30pm. Shops and businesses open Monday to Friday 8.30am to 4pm and Saturday 8.30am to noon.

PUBLIC HOLIDAYS

January 1 New Year's Day
February 23 Republic Day (Mashramani carnival)
March Phagwah (Hindu festival of colours; date varies)
March/April (varies) Good Friday
March/April (varies) Easter Monday
May 1 Labour Day
May 5 Indian Arrival Day
May 26 Independence Day
July Caricom Day (first Mon)
August 1 Emancipation Day
October Diwali (Hindu festival of lights)
December 25 Christmas Day
December 26 Boxing Day
Eid ul Adha (Muslim festival; date varies)

FESTIVALS AND CELEBRATIONS

National celebrations are often marked with spectacular float parades, masquerade bands and dancing in the streets. Christmas season is an excellent time to sample traditional festive food and experience the Boxing Day Main Big Lime (street party) and New Year's Eve parties.

GEORGETOWN

GEORGETOWN is the colourful, gritty, commercial and administrative heart of Guyana. Set on the east bank of the Demerara estuary, the capital is a grid city designed largely by the Dutch in the eighteenth century, originally nicknamed "The Garden City" because of its parks, tree-lined boulevards and abundance of flowers. Though its charm may be somewhat blemished by the relentless traffic and rubbish-strewn streets, Georgetown remains the gateway to Guyana's true attractions and is likely to be your base for several days.

WHAT TO SEE AND DO

The capital is worth exploring for its diverse cultural, religious and historical landmarks.

Main Street and around

One of downtown's most distinctive buildings, the towering **St George's Cathedral** on Church Street is one of the world's tallest freestanding wooden structures at 44m, with an attractive, airy interior (daily 9am–5pm, except public hols). A couple of blocks south along the Avenue of the Republic is the turreted City Hall, built in the Victorian Gothic style.

The **Walter Roth Museum of Anthropology** (61 Main St; Mon–Thurs 8am–4.30pm, Fri 8am–3.30pm, Sat 9am–2pm; entry by donation) is a good introduction to the culture of Guyana's nine indigenous tribes, showcasing everything from cassava-processing, traditional fishing and hammock-making to the medicinal use of plants and ceremonial wear, which includes some splendid macaw-feather headgear.

The **Guyana National Museum** (North Rd; Mon–Fri 9am–4.30pm, Sat 9am–2.30pm; entry by donation)

JONESTOWN MASSACRE

The chilling events of November 18, 1978, when hundreds of members of a sect died in an apparent mass suicide in northwestern Guyana, about 80km southwest of the town of Mabaruma, have been the subject of many books. In 1974, American **Reverend Jim Jones**, the leader of a sect called **The People's Temple**, chose Guyana to establish a self-sufficient community of about 1100 based on utopian socialist ideals, which he humbly named Jonestown. Referring to an unnamed enemy that would come to destroy Jonestown, he told his flock that "revolutionary suicide" was the only way to combat this threat. When US Congressman Leo Ryan and a party of journalists and concerned family members visited Jonestown in November 1978 to investigate alleged human rights abuses, the enemy had apparently arrived. Ryan and others were shot and killed at Port Kaituma airstrip as they tried to leave, while back at Jonestown the men, women and children were instructed to drink cyanide-spiked Kool-Aid. A total of 913 people died, although a coroner's report suggested that many were forcibly killed, including at least 200 children. A few managed to escape and later wrote about their experiences. Today the Jonestown site is overrun by bush and there is no monument or other reminders of its existence.

7

showcases the history of slavery in Guyana, the gold-mining industry, including a demonic-looking (and pretty accurate) statue of a "pork-knocker", and an enormous replica of the extinct giant sloth that once roamed the Guyanese bush.

Stabroek Market and around

The busy-as-bedlam focal point for higglers (fruit and vegetable sellers), moneychangers, beggars and jewellers, **Stabroek Market** on Water Street is dominated by its four-faced clock tower. Originally the site of the slave market where the exhausted survivors of the Middle Passage first faced a hostile New World, Stabroek now spills over with shoes, fabrics and gold jewellery. It's also a great place for a cheap lunch at a snackette. To climb the clock tower, go to the rear of the market and find the office of the Constable, who'll escort you there. East of Stabroek, off North Street, is the small but lively **Bourda Market**, a colourful shantytown filled with 24-hour fruit and vegetable vendors.

The National Art Gallery and around

Located in Castellani House on Vlissengen Road – once the official residence of the prime minister of Guyana – is the **National Art Gallery** (Mon–Fri 10am–5pm, Sat 2–6pm; free), a well-lit space hosting changing exhibitions by contemporary Guyanese artists. Just south of the gallery

is the **1763 Monument**, a 5m-high bronze memorial to Cuffy, an African slave who led an unsuccessful slave rebellion in 1763. Behind the art gallery are the **botanical gardens** (daily 9.30am–5.30pm; free), whose collection includes the national flower, the Victoria Regia Lily, and the **Zoo** (daily 9.30am–5.30pm; $G200), where Guyana's formidable birds, mammals and snakes are loosely arranged by geographical zone.

The seawall

Despite being on the coast, Georgetown is a few metres below sea level. The Dutch-built **seawall**, which keeps the Atlantic at bay, produces a bizarre sight at high tide, when you can stand on the wall and look at the water at a higher level than the town on the other side. On Sunday nights the whole town turns out to drink, flirt and strut their stuff along the promenade. On any other day the safest time to go is around 4.30–6pm.

ARRIVAL AND DEPARTURE

By plane Cheddi Jagan International Airport (w cjairport-gy.com) is located at Timehri, 41km south of the centre. International carriers currently serving CJIA include Delta Airlines, Caribbean Airlines, Fly Jamaica Airlines and Suriname Airways. Domestic airlines include Air Guyana (w airguyana.biz), Air Services Ltd (w aslgy.com), Roraima Airways (w roraimaairways.com) and Trans Guyana Airways (w transguyana.net). Minibus #42 runs from Lombard St, two blocks south of Georgetown's main market to the airport (45min; G$280); taxis cost G$6000. Some flights to

7

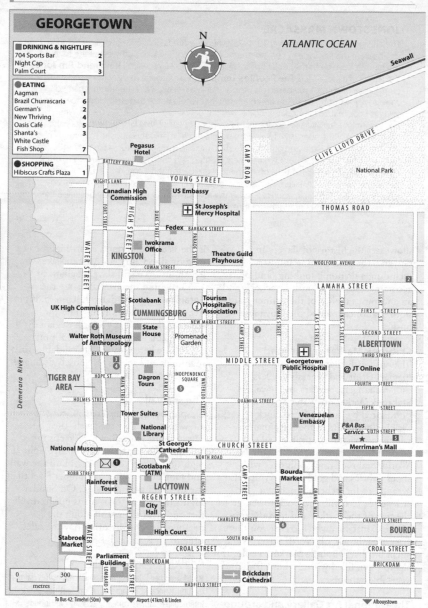

GEORGETOWN

DRINKING & NIGHTLIFE
704 Sports Bar	2
Night Cap	1
Palm Court	3

EATING
Aagman	1
Brazil Churrascaria	6
German's	2
New Thriving	4
Oasis Café	5
Shanta's	3
White Castle Fish Shop	7

SHOPPING
Hibiscus Crafts Plaza	1

ATLANTIC OCEAN

Seawall

National Park

CLIVE LLOYD DRIVE

THOMAS ROAD

WOOLFORD AVENUE

LAMAHA STREET

Pegasus Hotel
BATTERY ROAD
WIGHTS LANE
YOUNG STREET
Canadian High Commission
US Embassy
St Joseph's Mercy Hospital
Fedex
BARRACK STREET
Iwokrama Office
Theatre Guild Playhouse
KINGSTON
COWAN STREET

UK High Commission
Scotiabank
CUMMINGSBURG
Tourism Hospitality Association
State House
Promenade Garden
NEW MARKET STREET
Walter Roth Museum of Anthropology
BENTICK
Dagron Tours
INDEPENDENCE SQUARE
MIDDLE STREET
Georgetown Public Hospital
FIRST STREET
SECOND STREET
ALBERTTOWN
THIRD STREET
JT Online
FOURTH STREET
FIFTH STREET
ALBERTTOWN
TIGER BAY AREA
HOPE ST
HOLMES STREET
QUAMINA STREET
Venezuelan Embassy
P&A Bus Service
SIXTH STREET
Tower Suites
National Library
St George's Cathedral
CHURCH STREET
Merriman's Mall
National Museum
ROBB STREET
Scotiabank (ATM)
NORTH ROAD
Rainforest Tours
LACYTOWN
REGENT STREET
City Hall
High Court
CHARLOTTE STREET
Bourda Market
BOURDA
CHARLOTTE STREET
Stabroek Market
Parliament Building
BRICKDAM
CROAL STREET
SOUTH ROAD
CROAL STREET
BRICKDAM
Brickdam Cathedral
HADFIELD STREET

Demerara River
WATER STREET
MAIN STREET
HIGH STREET
FORT STREET
DUKE STREET
SIDE STREET
CAMP ROAD
PARADE STREET
CARMICHAEL ST
WATERLOO STREET
CAMP STREET
THOMAS STREET
EAST STREET
CUMMINGS STREET
LIGHT STREET
ALBERT STREET
WELLINGTON ST
KING STREET
AVENUE OF THE REPUBLIC
LOMBARD ST
ALEXANDER STREET
BOURDA STREET
ORANGE WALK
CUMMINGS STREET
LIGHT STREET
ALBERT STREET

N

0   300
metres

To Bus 42: Timehri (50m)   Airport (41km) & Linden   Albouystown

Suriname and Barbados and internal flights depart from Eugene F. Correia (formerly called Ogle) airstrip, 8km from Georgetown; taxis cost G$1200.

Destinations Lethem (3–4 daily; 1hr 30min). For points en route – Iwokrama, Surama, Annai or Karanambu– you must notify the airline in advance that you want to alight here. A diversion fee is charged unless there are six passengers to pick up or drop off.

By minibus The interior is served by several minibus companies, including Carly's (57 Robb St ☏ 616 5984) and P&A (75 Church St ☏ 225 5058); buy a ticket the day before if possible. Minibuses from Georgetown to Lethem leave around 6pm, while those travelling in the opposite direction

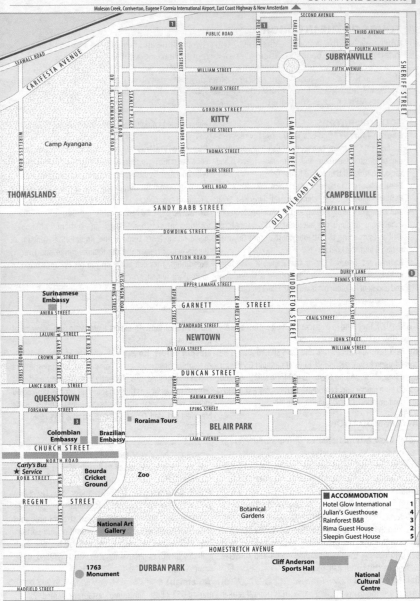

Moleson Creek, Corriverton, Eugene F Correia International Airport, East Coast Highway & New Amsterdam

SEAWALL ROAD
CARIFESTA AVENUE
WIRELESS ROAD
Camp Ayangana
THOMASLANDS

DR J LACHMANSINGH ROAD
VLISSENGEN ROAD
STANLEY PLACE
QUEEN STREET
ALEXANDER STREET

PUBLIC ROAD
WILLIAM STREET
DAVID STREET
GORDON STREET
KITTY
PIKE STREET
THOMAS STREET
BARR STREET
SHELL ROAD
SANDY BABB STREET

SECOND AVENUE
PEEL STREET
EARLE AVENUE
CHURCH ROAD
THIRD AVENUE
FOURTH AVENUE
SUBRYANVILLE
FIFTH AVENUE
SHERIFF STREET

LAMAHA STREET

OLD RAILROAD LINE

CAMPBELLVILLE
CAMPBELL AVENUE
AUSTIN STREET
DELPH STREET
SEAFORD STREET

DOWDING STREET
RAILWAY STREET
STATION ROAD

IRVING STREET
VLISSENGEN ROAD

UPPER LAMAHA STREET
REPUBLIC STREET
GARNETT STREET
DE ABREU STREET
D'ANDRADE STREET
NEWTOWN
DA SILVA STREET
DUNCAN STREET

MIDDLETON STREET

DUREY LANE
DENNIS STREET
CRAIG STREET
DELPH STREET
JOHN STREET
WILLIAM STREET

Surinamese Embassy
ANIRA STREET
NEW GARDEN STREET
PETER ROSE STREET
LALUNI STREET
CROWN STREET
LANCE GIBBS STREET
QUEENSTOWN
FORSHAW STREET
Colombian Embassy
Brazilian Embassy
CHURCH STREET
NORTH ROAD
Carly's Bus Service
ROBB STREET
REGENT STREET
NEW GARDEN STREET

ORONOQUE STREET

ABARY STREET
BARIMA AVENUE
EPING STREET
Roraima Tours
BEL AIR PARK
LAMA AVENUE
ELUM STREET
RUPUNUNI ST
OLEANDER AVENUE

Bourda Cricket Ground
Zoo
National Art Gallery

Botanical Gardens

HOMESTRETCH AVENUE
1763 Monument
DURBAN PARK
Cliff Anderson Sports Hall
National Cultural Centre
HADFIELD STREET

■ ACCOMMODATION
Hotel Glow International — 1
Julian's Guesthouse — 4
Rainforest B&B — 3
Rima Guest House — 2
Sleepin Guest House — 5

depart at around 5pm (G$12,000/US$60). Several private minibus services offer pick-ups from your accommodation in Georgetown and take you to Moleson Creek by the Surinamese border with a reciprocal arrangement with a Surinamese operator on the other side of the river, so you only need to buy one ticket. These include Dugla (☎622 0203) and Champ's (☎629 6735).

Destinations Moleson Creek (3hr); Lethem (18hr); Timehri for CJ Airport (bus #42; 45min).

GETTING AROUND

By minibus Privately owned minibuses run all over Georgetown and its outlying towns from Stabroek Market

TOURS OF THE INTERIOR

While travels in the interior are cheapest if you have the time and flexibility to arrange it all independently (see page 657), there are several reputable tour operators in Georgetown who specialize in nature and adventure tours throughout Guyana's hinterland and who can also arrange day-trips to Kaieteur Falls and other destinations within easy reach of the capital. Prices are roughly as follows: tour of the city (US$30–50); day-trip to Bartica (US$120); day-trip to Santa Mission (US$120); flight to Kaieteur Falls (US$175–275).

TOUR OPERATORS

Dagron Tours 91 Middle St ☎ 223 7921, ⓦ dagron-tours.com. City tours, two types of Kaieteur Falls trips, day-trips up Essequibo and Demerara Rivers, and various cultural and historical tours.

Leon Moore Nature Experience ☎ 444 2167, ⓦ journeyguyana.com. Linden-based naturalist Leon and crew offer birdwatching and wildlife photography expeditions through the rainforest and savannah, as well as tours along the Atlantic coast to spot Guyana's national bird, the hoatzin.

Rainforest Tours 5 Av of the Republic, 1st floor ☎ 231 5661, ⓦ rftours.com. Proprietor of the original and excellent Kaieteur overland tour, Frank Singh's office above a fried chicken shop can customize tours to suit you.

Rupununi Trails ☎ 593 663 8888, ⓦ rupununitrails.com. Specializing in tours of the South Rupununi region with an extensive network among native communities. Canoe trips on the Rupununi and upper Essequibo, savannah experiences with expert naturalists.

Untamed Adventures ☎ 648 7570, ⓦ utadventures.com. Based in Lethem, offering horse-riding tours through the Rupununi Savannah, jungle walks, trekking in the Kanuku range and river expeditions. They can also help you set up unescorted tours of the region.

(G$80–100). They tend to be packed, drive very fast and are impossible to board during rush hour.

By taxi Taxis are unmetered, and fares should always be agreed upon before getting in. Fares are around G$300 for up to four blocks around town, G$400 for a short hop and G$500 for a longer one. Legitimate cabs display a company logo and number plates beginning with "H".

ACCOMMODATION

Hotel Glow International 23 Queen St, Kitty ☎ 227 0863; map p.652. Right across from the seawall, this classic wooden house has broad verandas, freshly painted rooms and an attached bar/restaurant serving Creole fare. US$45

Julian's Guesthouse 33 Cummings St, South Cummingsburg ☎ 226 3552, ⓔ julian-restaurant-bar@hotmail.com; map p.652. Near the vegetable market, this friendly corner spot has compact, window-screened rooms with fridge. The bar's breezy veranda makes a good perch to observe the lively neighbourhood and converse with gregarious host Julian. US$40

Rainforest B&B 272 Forshaw St ☎ 227 7800, ⓦ rainforestbbguy.com; map p.652. This tropical retreat is in the serene Queenstown district, east of the centre. It contains five en-suite rooms, and the lush front garden feels like a patch of rainforest. Owner Sayeeda is involved in wildlife rescue efforts, and pets are allowed of course. US$90

Rima Guest House 92 Middle St ☎ 225 7401, ⓔ rima@networksgy.com; map p.652. For budget travellers, the obvious choice: central and homely, with vintage furniture and powerful fans. An expert team whips up economical lunches at the rear. US$30

Sleepin Guest House 151 Church St ☎ 223 0991, ⓦ sleepinguesthouse.com; map p.652. Opposite the cricket club ground, this efficiently run guesthouse attracts self-caterers as well as those in search of simple, fan-cooled rooms, with several kitchenette-equipped studios. Basic breakfast included. Doubles US$45, studios US$75

EATING

Georgetown has a wide range of bakeries, snackettes and *cook shops* – many attached to Bourda Market and inside Stabroek Market.

Brazil Churrascaria 208 Alexander St, Lacytown ☎ 231 1268; map p.652. At this hangar-like space, the pitmaster slices unlimited sizzling meat straight onto your plate from his skewer – pay by the weight of your portion. Round off your meal from the copious salad bar, and wash it all down with caipirinhas (G$500). Meals G$2500. Daily noon–10pm.

★ **German's** 8 New Market, at Mundy St ☎ 227 0079; map p.652. Busy lunchtime restaurant famed for its legendary cow-heel soup (G$1500) and Creole dishes. Located in a reputedly sketchy part of town. Mon–Sat 10am–5.30pm, Sun 9.30am–3pm.

New Thriving 32 Main St ☎ 225 0868; map p.652. Palace of authentic Chinese cuisine with two sections: a posh dining room with boulevard-view terrace upstairs and a fast-food section below, site of the popular lunchtime buffet (G$2900). Daily 10am–10pm.

map p.652

> ★ **TREAT YOURSELF**
>
> **Aagman** 28A Sheriff St ☎ 219 0161; map p.652. The first-generation Indian management here operate a real tandoor oven, make desserts the traditional way and take obvious pride in their business. They specialize in Mughlai cuisine, both vegetarian and with chicken, lamb or fish. Mains from G$2500–3000 but big enough for two.

Oasis Café 125 Carmichael St ☎ 681 1648; map p.652. A/c enclave where local office workers linger over iced caramel lattes (G$700), quiches and inventive lunchtime mains (from G$2000). Mon–Fri 7.30am–6.30pm, Sat & Sun 9am–6pm (also open for dinner on Fri).

★ **Shanta's** 225 New Market St; map p.652. Serving up fresh rotis, dhal and curries for cheap, this corner location is a must for fans of Creole Indian food. Puris, filled with such items as mango curry, calaloo and pumpkin, are their speciality. Meals around G$900. Mon–Sat 7am–6pm.

White Castle Fish Shop Hadfield St, at John St; map p.652. Popular neighbourhood hangout, as much for the lip-smacking fish & chips (G$1200) as the Banks beers, which pile up on the terrace tables as the evening progresses. Order at the booth – the cashier doubles as DJ. Mon–Sat 9am–1am, Sun 4–11pm.

DRINKING AND NIGHTLIFE

Bars and clubs are mostly concentrated along Main Street in the vicinity of the Tower Hotel. The real action starts around midnight on weekends. On Sunday nights the seawall is the place to be, with stands selling drinks and food all along the road.

704 Sports Bar 1 Lamaha St ☎ 225 0251; map p.652. Casual club built around a circular bar. The ambience is dominated by cricket, soccer and basketball action beamed to a youthful crowd. Daily 4.30pm–2am.

★ **Night Cap** 8 Pere St, Kitty ☎ 231 8466; map p.652. A lush tropical garden bedecked with twinkly lights, nestling beside the walls of the Russian embassy. Swing in a hammock, lounge on the patio, or sit in the wi-fi-enabled a/c cool of the café. Sip a classic rum punch, or try out the odder peanut butter frappes and espresso martinis. Tues–Sun 5–11pm.

Palm Court 35 Main St ☎ 231 8144; map p.652. Popular restaurant/nightspot with electric palms lining its breezy courtyard. Makes a good rum punch and stays open as long as the clients are having fun. Daily 11 am– 2am.

SHOPPING

The bustle in and around Stabroek Market spills eastward, especially along Robb St.

Hibiscus Crafts Plaza North Rd; map p.652. Opposite the National Museum, this row of stalls is the place to look for handmade leather sandals, baskets, hammocks, hardwood walking sticks and other souvenirs.

DIRECTORY

Banks and exchange Scotiabank at 104 Carmichael St, Pegasus Hotel and along Robb St. Trustco (62–63 Middle St) is a reliable exchange service.

Embassies and consulates Brazil, 308 Church St (☎ 225 7970); Canada, High St, at Young St (☎ 227 2081); Suriname, 171 Peter Rose St, at Crown St (☎ 226 7844); UK, 44 Main St (☎ 226 5881); US, 100 Young St, at Duke St (☎ 225 4900); Venezuela, 296 Thomas St (☎ 226 1543).

Hospital St Joseph Mercy Hospital, 130–132 Parade St (☎ 227 2072). Private hospital with 24hr emergency room.

Internet JT Online Internet Café at 38 Cummings St.

Pharmacies Medicare Pharmacy at 16 Hinck St or Medicine Chest at 316 Middle St.

Post office Robb St (Mon–Fri 7am–4pm, Sat 7–11am).

DAY-TRIPS FROM GEORGETOWN

Georgetown makes a good base for ventures into the interior to visit **Kaieteur Falls** (see page 656) as well as trips up Essequibo River for an appreciation of the country's colonial past and mining present, and to Santa Mission, for a taste of indigenous life.

Essequibo and Mazaruni rivers

West of Georgetown via the market town of Parika, the **Essequibo River**, third largest river in South America, is dotted with islands and remnants of colonial occupation, such as **Kyk Over Al**, a seventeenth-century Dutch fort. About an hour's cruise upriver, at the confluence of the Cuyuni and **Mazaruni rivers** is **Bartica**, a gritty gold-mining town near several riverside resorts, notably the island of Baganara. Day tours by Dagron, among others, take in Bara Cara Falls or else Marshall Falls – both great spots for a dip – and a short hike through the jungle for a chance to see some of the country's fabled wildlife. It's also possible to reach Bartica independently by catching a bus from in front of Stabroek Market to Parika (G$500), where public motorboats depart as they fill (G$2500). If you'd rather overnight in Bartica, *'D' Factor 2 Interior Guest House* (☎ 455 2544, ✉ cutienadira@ hotmail.com) offers sparkling rooms with a terrific wraparound balcony and tours of villages on the Mazaruni and Cuyuni rivers.

7

KAIETEUR FALLS

The region's most popular attraction, 226m **Kaieteur Falls** are in a cavernous gorge surrounded by the dense rainforest of the **Kaieteur National Park**. Their isolation, power and pristine surroundings make them a heart-stopping sight.

Operators (see page 654) offer flights to Kaieteur Falls in twelve-seater planes from Georgetown's Ogle airport (from US$175). A day-trip usually involves a brief guided tour of the three viewpoints from which you can admire the sight of 30,000 gallons of water per second crashing down into the valley below (with the more intrepid visitors crawling to the cliff edge to watch the rainbows play on the water spray). Your guide will point out interesting animal life, such as the tiny golden frogs, the toxins from which are used in Haitian voodoo ceremonies.

Alternatively, you can take a five-day/four-night overland journey involving a 4WD drive, boat trip and a fairly strenuous hike, with rustic accommodation thrown in along the way (from US$900). If you want to visit independently, the only overnight accommodation is a rustic lodge near the falls (G$3000/person), booked through the Protected Areas Commission (☎ 227 1888, ext 157, ✉ reservations.pac@gmail.com). You will be rewarded with views of the falls at dusk and dawn without the crowds. Air Services Ltd (🌐 aslgy.com), together with Roraima Airways (🌐 roraimaairways.com), offer flights year-round on weekends, with one to three flights during the week depending on the season.

THE INTERIOR: IWOKRAMA RAINFOREST AND THE RUPUNUNI SAVANNAH

Visitors come to Guyana for two things: pristine nature and indigenous culture. Both are found in the interior, reachable either by Guyana's north–south highway that runs all the way to the Brazilian border, or by frequent flights made by small aircraft. The road passes through some of the oldest and most pristine jungle on earth, home to jaguar, tapir, ocelot, puma, peccary and anaconda. In the heart of the country lies Guyana's only official nature reserve: the vast **IWOKRAMA RAINFOREST**, known for its incredibly diverse plant, bird and animal species. Beyond Iwokrama, dense jungle dramatically gives way to the **RUPUNUNI SAVANNAH**, Guyana's cowboy country – scrubland and grassland that stretches as far as the eye can see, punctuated with giant anthills, the odd cattle ranch and a smattering of thatched roofs, which announce the presence of an indigenous village. Here you can sling your hammock in the hospitable villages of Annai and Yupukari, linger in the friendly frontier town of Lethem or go wildlife-spotting from one of the local ecolodges. The savannah's grasslands abound with giant anteaters and storks, while the many rivers are home to the black caiman, giant river otter and arapaima, the world's biggest scaled freshwater fish.

The office of Visit Rupununi in Lethem (☎ 772 2227, 🌐 visitrupununi.com) provides copious information about the vast region's myriad tours and lodgings.

Iwokrama Research Centre and Canopy Walkway

The largely intact, 400-square-kilometre **Iwokrama Rainforest** contains three-quarters of the animal species in Guyana, with extraordinary biodiversity. An internationally funded project to study forest management and sustainable development, with participation from local indigenous communities, the **Research Centre** (☎ 225 1504, 🌐 iwokrama.org) also has a tourism component. Besides the eight deluxe solar-powered riverside cabins (rooms US$178; meals US$58/day), more economical options include en-suite cabins for visiting biologists, botanists and journalists (US$74) and barracks with shared bath for trainees (US$54). Meals are served on the open-air upper level of the circular central building with magnificent views of the Essequibo River. Visits to nearby indigenous villages, night-time caiman spotting, and multi-day excursions into the jungle and up Turtle Mountain are all offered. Note that although rates for tours are reduced as group size increases, you must get approval to join a pre-arranged group.

A one-hour drive from the Research Centre is the **Canopy Walkway** (Ⓦiwokramacanopywalkway.com), a 154m network of aluminium suspension bridges set amid the treetops, 30m from the forest floor. Its three observation platforms provide excellent vantage points to spot birds, howler monkeys and other fauna within the forest canopy – preferably at dusk or dawn, when animal life is at its most active. An overnight stay at the luxurious *Atta Lodge*, at the foot of the canopy walk trail, costs US$360 for a double room, including all meals, the canopy user fee and a trained guide (not including a "forest user fee" of US$15 per person). Day visitors pay G$5050. Booking in advance is vital. Alternatively, tours can be arranged from the Research Centre.

Surama Village and Ecolodge

An ecotourism success story, **Surama Village** (Ⓣ548 9262, Ⓦsuramaecolodge.com) is a Makushi settlement of some 300 people and thatch-roofed huts connected by dusty paths at the foot of the Pakaraimas range, 45 minutes' drive west of the Canopy Walkway. Located on the outskirts of the village, the ecolodge consists of four traditional *benabs* with windows screens and private bath (rooms G$3500/person), a new thatched cabin with four rooms, and the central *benab*/ dining hall with an upper-level lounge where you can sway the night away in a hammock (G$1800), learn about medicinal plants from knowledgeable local guides, or hike up Surama Mountain (230m) and go wildlife-watching along the Burro Burro River. Alternatively, stay in one of the two basic camps along the river (G$1800) and go jungle trekking. A village tax of G$1500 is charged.

Annai

The first significant place you reach after emerging from the jungle is **Annai**, around 2km off the main road – a compact hilltop

---

INDEPENDENT TRAVEL IN THE INTERIOR

Independent travel in Guyana's interior requires forward planning, time and flexibility, but it's possible to visit all main attractions without having to go with a tour operator. Overland travel away from the Lethem–Georgetown highway is along Guyana's many rivers, and boatmen need to be negotiated with over prices. If you can't give them a specific date to be collected from where they drop you, it's advisable to take a mobile phone for communication. To visit most native villages (barring Annai and Rupertee), you first have to get permission from either the Ministry of Indigenous People's Affairs office (see page 650) in Georgetown or its equivalent in Lethem. Book accommodation there in advance instead of just rocking up. If travelling overland, it is essential that you have your **passport** (or at least a photocopy) with you, as there are several police checkpoints in the interior.

GETTING AROUND

By plane See page 651.

By minibus Georgetown–Lethem minibuses can stop en route at Annai or drop you at the turn-offs to Surama or the Iwokrama Research Centre and Canopy Walkway (make arrangements to be picked up from the turn-off or walk in). Since minibuses tend to overflow with passengers and luggage, to board a bus from a location in between Lethem and Georgetown, reserve a seat in advance, if possible, by calling the minibus company directly or through your lodgings. In most cases you can get a seat to the next point but you may have to pay full fare regardless of distance travelled, since passengers generally ride the entire length of the journey. That said, movement is seasonal so buses tend to fill up in one direction or the other.

By 4WD and boat There is no public transport from the main "highway" to remote lodges and villages, but all lodges can help you make arrangements to reach them. Otherwise, you may hire a 4WD with driver for around US$200/day –check with Rupununi Eco-Hotel or Hotel Amazonas in Lethem. In the rainy season, you will find yourself travelling more by motorboat.

By motorbike The least expensive way of getting around the Rupununi is on the back of someone's motorbike. It's usually possible to arrange onward transport by motorbike just by asking around. Several hours' ride or hiring someone to take you around for a day will set you back no more than US$40. Keep in mind, though, that insurance won't generally cover this option.

Makushi community of around six hundred people in the foothills of the Pakaraima mountain range. Dotted with giant shady trees, the lively village features several schools, a café where you can sample farine (a sort of cassava cereal), Radio Paiwomak (97.1 FM), which serving fifty communities throughout the North Rupununi, and a craft shop with carvings of local hardwoods as well as intricate woven goods and bows and arrows (still used for hunting in these parts).

Across the main road from the bus stop/gas station known as the Oasis is the start of the Panorama Nature Trail, which snakes up a forested hill with tree identification signs and plenty of benches; from the top there's a splendid view of the savannah.

ACCOMMODATION

Oasis ☎645 7750. The budget-friendly sister to Rock View Lodge is a 10min walk away. Just off the main road–though still peaceful – it's a popular stop for minibuses. Comprises spacious, cheerily decorated en-suite rooms with mosquito nets, a hammock *benab* and simple, inexpensive meals. Their *pepperpot* is justly renowned. Doubles G$10000, hammocks G$1000

Rock View Lodge ☎645 9675 ⓦrockviewlodge.com. One of the North Rupununi's original lodges, the *Rock View* has eight clean and comfortable en-suite rooms with hammock-laden verandas and is set in spacious grounds with spreading trees and a swimming pool. It is the creation of local hero Colin Edwards, who'll show you his sustainable agriculture endeavours and arrange horse-riding and birding tours, including visits to nearby Wowetta to spot the rare cock-of-the-rock. Toothsome regional fare and local juices are served buffet-style in the cosy clubhouse. Ask about community rates. Doubles US$120, triples US$145

Yupukari and Caiman House

Yupukari is a hilltop village of around 500 mostly Makushi inhabitants, a couple of hours' drive along a rutted dirt track from Annai; it's also possible to reach it by boat along the Rupununi River from Ginep Landing, 21km west of Annai (2hr; US$120). The main attraction here is the **Caiman House Field Station**, whose purpose is to study the black caiman. If you're lucky, you will join the local research crew in the evening when they go out to capture, weigh, measure and tag the fearsome creatures.

ACCOMMODATION

Caiman House ☎772 9291, ⓦrupununilearners.org. This guesthouse has en-suite rooms with mosquito nets, a hammock *benab* and some of the best home-cooked food in the savannah (meals are included). The place is a constant hub of activity, with knowledgeable Fernando to talk to and a lively learning centre for the local children next door (book donations welcome). Doubles US$95, hammocks US$60

LETHEM AND AROUND

With its wide dirt streets, unhurried pace of life and an everybody-knows-everybody feel, **LETHEM** is a fine place to linger en route to Brazil or Venezuela and a good base from which to launch your exploration of the southern **Rupununi Savannah**. Moco Moco and Kumu Falls (30min drive each) are both great for swimming, and you can live out your cowboy fantasy at the remote Dadanawa Ranch.

Lethem really comes alive during Easter weekend, when cowboys from all around (including Brazilian vaqueros) gather in town for bull-riding, calf-roping and stallion-taming competitions (book accommodation weeks in advance). February sees the Rupununi Music & Arts Festival with performances by indigenous artists and international guests.

★ TREAT YOURSELF

Karanambu Lodge ⓦ karanambutrustandlodge. org. Sitting in a clearing near the Rupununi River, this one-of-a-kind lodge consists of six luxurious cabins. Started by Diane McTurk—renowned for her work with orphaned giant river otters until her death in 2016, it is now managed by her nephew Edward and wife Melanie. Thanks to Diane's efforts, the 110-square-mile area of savannah, wetlands and rainforest around the lodge has been conserved, and there's a good chance of seeing jaguars, giant anteaters, tapirs and caimans during guided walks and river trips, not to mention the evening opening of giant water lilies. The meals are excellent, the rate is inclusive of everything and the staff are wonderful. *Karanambu* is 30min by boat from *Caiman House*, and many travellers combine visits to both places. Lethem-bound flights will land at the local airstrip with a minimum of five passengers. Cabañas US$225

INTO BRAZIL

To get from Lethem to the Brazilian town of Bonfim, cross the Takutu River Bridge about 5km north of Lethem by taxi. Pick-ups from the airstrip to the crossing cost around G$1500. Taxis will stop at the Lethem immigration office for **Guyanese immigration formalities**, then take you across the border to the Brazilian town of **Bonfim**. Stamp in with the Federal Police, on the left as you come off the bridge. Beyond is a lot with the Customs office on the right. Across the way, buses pick up passengers for the ride to **Boa Vista** (4 daily; R$22), some 150km away, with connections to Manaus (Brazil) and Caracas (Venezuela).

GBTI **bank** in Lethem (Lot 121; Mon–Fri 8am–2pm) offers foreign currency exchange but may not have any reais available. Otherwise try the Hotel Amazonas (Lot 22, Barack Retreat Rd).

ARRIVAL AND INFORMATION

By plane Two airlines fly between Lethem and Georgetown (4 departures daily, more during rainy season; 1hr to 1hr 30min), and their offices are located next to the airstrip. ASL will stop at Iwokrama, Surama and Annai on request (minimum five passengers). Ticket prices (one-way) cost around US$130–150. Check-in two hours before the flight. During the rainy season, when sections of the route become impassable, flying is sometimes the only mode of travel between Georgetown and Lethem.

By minibus Several minibus companies make the long, rough-and-tumble journey to Lethem (departing Georgetown 6pm, Lethem at 5pm; 18–20hr). Depending on the season, you may have to pay full fare to points in between. The Georgetown terminal of Carly's Bus Service (☎699 1339) is at 57 Robb St; P&A (☎225 5058) is at 75 Church St. Aside from the paved stretch between Georgetown and Linden, the rest of the "highway" is unpaved and rutted, and the car ferry at Kurupukari runs only between 6am and 6pm; minibuses break their journey near the ferry dock; in the reverse direction, at Surama junction. Passengers may rent a hammock at either place (G$500) to get a few hours' sleep before proceeding. Another service runs buses between Lethem and Annai (2hr 30min; G$2500) four days per week, departing from Betty's Creole Corner.

Tourist information In Lethem, head for Visit Rupununi (Lot 164, ☎772 2227, ☻visitrupununi.com), which shares its office/mission of sustainable tourism development with Conservation International. It's in the roundabout with Andy's General Store, which anyone can point you to.

ACCOMMODATION AND EATING

Dadanawa Ranch ☎663 8888, ☻rupununitrails.com. Situated against the dramatic backdrop of the Kanuku Mountains, this is the largest and most isolated ranch in Guyana, a 3hr drive southeast of Lethem. Grab a lasso and work the cattle with the ranch hands the traditional way. Other options include trekking, horseriding, nature walks, birdwatching, swimming and fishing. Meals included. __US$240__

Manari Ranch Eco-Lodge ☎668 2006. Nearest of the local ranches, a 15min drive north of Lethem, this makes a convenient option to experience the Rupununi, with ten comfortable rooms in the lodge. Otters splash around nearby Manari Creek, and such endemic rarities as the hoary-throated spinetail attract birders. __US$220__

Ori Hotel ☎772 2124 ☻orihotel@yahoo.com The loveliest hotel in town, with friendly, indigenous staff and en-suite rooms (with fan or a/c) in tranquil gardens. The restaurant serves delicious Creole dishes. It's a 15min walk west of the airstrip. __G$5000__

Takutu Hotel ☎772 2034. ☻takutuhotel@gmail.com. Modern, central place, 5min from the airstrip, with spick-and-span, tiled en-suite rooms with a/c. It's attached to a popular *benab*/bar beneath a spreading flame tree. __G$6000__

Three Sisters Snackette School St. Popular and welcoming cook shack serving Creole fare (cookup rice, saltfish, dal and so on) at tables out front (meals G$600–800). Mon–Fri & Sun 7.30am–8.30pm.

Wayka's Barack Retreat Rd. Join Lethem's Brazilian community at this churrascaria on the main road into town, featuring spit-grilled steaks and sausage (pay by weight) and a salad bar. Daily 11.30am–3.30pm

Suriname

SURINAME, formerly Dutch Guiana, is South America's smallest independent nation and has a lot in common with its neighbours – a brutal history of slavery, for one, but also of robust rebellion. Though it predominantly attracts tourists and volunteers from Holland, English-speaking travellers are also made to feel welcome. The capital, **Paramaribo**, is the most attractive city in the Guianas, with much of its eighteenth- and nineteenth-century wooden architecture still intact; it also makes a good base for visiting the former plantations nearby and river dolphin-watching on the Commewijne River.

While ecotourism is still in its fledgling state, and facing constant challenges (thirteen percent of Suriname's land surface area is under official environmental protection but that hasn't stopped illegal gold mining), there are dozens of excellent ecolodges along the Upper Suriname River that act as springboards for exploration of the unique indigenous and Saramaccan (Maroon) communities. There are great opportunities for hiking and wildlife watching at the Central Suriname Nature Reserve, while on the coast Galibi Nature Reserve offers the chance to observe giant sea turtles laying their eggs. If you're short of time, Brownsberg Nature Park, near Paramaribo, gives you a taste of Suriname's wilderness.

CHRONOLOGY

10,000 BC Suriname's earliest inhabitants are thought to be the Surinen, after whom the country is named.

1498 Columbus sights Surinamese coast.

1602 Dutch begin to settle the land.

1651 England's Lord Willoughby establishes first permanent settlement – Willoughbyland, with 1000 white settlers and 2000 slaves.

1654 Jews from Holland expelled from Brazil arrive, establishing plantations at Jodensavanne.

1667 Suriname becomes Dutch Guiana with the Treaty of Breda, after conquest of Willoughbyfort (now Fort Zeelandia) by Dutch Admiral Crynssen.

1700s–1800s Slavery under the Dutch particularly harsh, with rape, maiming and killing of slaves common. Many flee into the interior and form Maroon communities, conducting occasional murderous raids on the plantations and their owners.

1799 Suriname reconquered by the British.

1814 Suriname given back to Holland as part of the Treaty of Paris.

1853 Chinese plantation labourers arrive.

1863 Formal abolition of slavery (though slaves not released for another ten years as part of transition period).

1873 Labourers from India, and later Indonesia, arrive.

1941 US troops occupy Suriname to protect bauxite mines.

1949 First elections based on universal suffrage held.

1975 Suriname wins independence. 40,000 Surinamese emigrate to the Netherlands.

1980 Military coup led by Sergeant Major Dési Bouterse topples government. Socialist republic declared.

1982 Fifteen prominent leaders of re-democratization movement executed.

1986 Civil war begins between military government and Maroons, led by Bouterse's former bodyguard, Ronnie Brunswijk. At least 39 unarmed inhabitants of the N'Dyuka Maroon village, Moiwana, mostly women and children, are murdered by military.

1987 Civilian government installed with new constitution for Republic of Suriname, but Bouterse remains in charge of army.

1990 Bouterse dismisses civilian government with phone call in "telephone coup".

1991 Bouterse holds elections under international pressure. The New Front coalition wins; Ronald Venetiaan is elected president.

1996 National Democratic Party (founded by Bouterse in 1987) wins election.

1999 Bouterse convicted of drug smuggling in Holland in absentia.

2000 Venetiaan and the New Front coalition regain presidency (and again in 2006).

2004 Surinamese dollar introduced as currency.

2007 UN maritime border tribunal awards both Guyana and Suriname a share of the potentially oil-rich offshore basin under dispute.

2008 Trial begins of Bouterse and others accused of involvement in executions of opponents of military regime in 1982.

2010 Bouterse elected president.

2012 National Assembly clears president of charges for December '82 executions.

2015 Bouterse re-elected unopposed.

ARRIVAL AND DEPARTURE

Johan Adolf Pengel International Airport (also known as Zanderij), two hours south of Paramaribo, receives direct **flights** from Aruba, Amsterdam, Belém (Brazil), Cayenne (French Guiana), Curaçao, Georgetown, Miami and Port of Spain (Trinidad). **Zorg en Hoop**, a smaller airport about fifteen minutes west of the capital, receives small domestic aircraft, as well as daily flights to and from Guyana.

FROM GUYANA

From Georgetown it's a three-hour bus ride to the **ferry** port at Moleson Creek, with one crossing per day (10am), then a three-hour bus to South Drain to Paramaribo (see page 664).

FROM FRENCH GUIANA

Travellers from French Guiana must cross the Maroni River from St Laurent du Maroni to Albina by **ferry** or motorized canoe, before continuing the two-and-a-half-hour drive by **minibus** or **taxi** to Paramaribo (see page 664).

VISAS

Visas are required for all visitors except nationals from CARICOM countries, and a few Asian and South American countries. Visitors may apply for a Tourist Card, valid for thirty days, single entry only (US$35). Tourist Cards may be obtained at Paramaribo airport (Johan Adolf Pengel International Airport) on arrival, whereas overland travellers need to secure theirs in advance at the consulates in Guyana (see page 655) and French Guiana (see page 678); processing takes around twenty minutes. For stays of longer than thirty days or multiple entry, visas must be obtained (from US$45), which may not be processed on the same day for certain nationalities. For updated information on visa requirements, check ⓦsurinameembassy.org.

GETTING AROUND

While commuting around the capital and outlying areas is reasonably easy, there are no major highways in Suriname except for the Oost–Westverbinding (East–West Highway) that runs between Albina and Nieuw Nickerie. Scheduled state-run buses and private minibuses run to most destinations on or near this conduit, though for the remote interior you'll need to travel by 4WD, small plane or motorized dugout canoe (or a combination of all three); it's often cheaper and easier to go as part of a tour.

BY PLANE

There are some **scheduled internal flights** to such destinations as Botopasie and Djumu, but tour operators tend to charter planes to visit parks and reserves, and this limits their frequency to the number of tourists wishing to make a trip.

BY BUS

Brightly decorated, crowded **private minibuses** are numbered and run along assigned routes both between the capital and smaller cities near the coast, and to Paramaribo's neighbourhoods. These don't leave until they are full, but are more frequent than the scheduled state-run services and stop wherever you want along the road. Journeys may be of the sardine-tin variety; shared taxis are a more comfortable option. The plainer NVB **state-run buses** (*staatsbus*; ⓦnvbnv.sr) have a dedicated bus station, follow a schedule and use bus stops.

BY SHARED TAXI

Shared taxis (generally private minivans) run to Albina and Nickerie. Your guesthouse can recommend a reliable operator.

BY BOAT

Navigating the Suriname and Commewijne rivers around Paramaribo is done by public ferry. They cross the water at specific points, and fees for journeys to other towns along the rivers' banks can be negotiated at the docks, where boatmen wait for customers. NVB also runs boat services, notably along the Upper Suriname, recognisable by their yellow flags.

ACCOMMODATION

Accommodation in Paramaribo consists of **guesthouses** and mid-range hotels, some in historic wooden buildings. Almost all rooms will come equipped with running water, fans and mosquito nets.

If you travel into the interior, you're likely to stay in **lodges** in Suriname's nature parks and reserves, which vary from rustic (a place to hang your hammock and shared facilities) to the more luxurious (en-suite rooms with mosquito nets). This is usually on an all-inclusive basis and bookings are best made through tour operators.

STINASU, Suriname's nature conservation organization (see page 667), maintains basic lodges at Brownsberg, Raleighvallen and Galibi.

7

7

CROSSING BETWEEN SURINAME AND GUYANA

Getting to Guyana involves crossing the Corantijn (Corentyne) River on the Canawaima ferry, with daily departures at 10am (SRD113 single) from **South Drain**, an hour west of Nickerie. The gate closes an hour before departure. Taxis will collect you from your Nickerie hotel and take you to the ferry (SRD150). Numerous minibuses make the early morning journey from Paramaribo to catch the 10am boat (3hr; SRD100); some minibus companies work in partnership with Guyanese tour companies (see page 654). You will need time to clear customs and a valid passport. Once you arrive at **Moleson Creek, Guyana**, you must clear customs again and get your passport stamped before taking one of the waiting minibuses for the three-hour journey to Georgetown (G$2500). There is no currency exchange or ATM at South Drain or Moleson Creek, but euros or US$ (preferably the latter) can be easily exchanged at either location with unofficial (and costly) moneychangers for Suriname/Guyanese dollars, respectively. If going from Guyana to Suriname, most minibus companies pick up passengers at around 4–4.30am in order to arrive an hour before the 10am ferry to Suriname. Note: Guyana is an hour behind Suriname.

FOOD AND DRINK

Food in Suriname is inexpensive, tasty and influenced by its ethnically diverse population. Informal Javanese (Indonesian) eateries known as **warungs** (notably in the Blauwgrond district of Paramaribo), and Hindustani **roti shops** sit alongside Chinese, sushi, European-style and Creole restaurants. Meals cost around SRD25–35.

Kip (chicken) is very popular and typical Surinamese dishes include *moksie alesie* (rice, beans, chicken and vegetables) and *pom* (chicken baked with a root vegetable). Indonesian specialities include *saoto* (chicken soup, beansprouts, potatoes and a boiled egg), *bami* (fried noodles) and *nasi goreng* (fried rice). Two tasty peanut-based dishes are *pindasoep*, made with *tom-tom* (plantain noodles), and *petjil*, a salad of greens and sprouts topped with a rich peanut sauce. *Bakabanna* (plantain slices, dipped in a pancake batter and fried) is an established crowd-pleaser. Traditional Dutch favourites like *bitterballen* (breaded and fried minced meat balls) and *poffertjes* (sugared pancakes) are plentiful. If travelling in the interior, you may well get to try various game dishes.

DRINK

Suriname produces some of the Caribbean's best **rum**, and both Borgoe and Black Cat brands are worth a try; the lethal 90 percent proof stuff is usually used to mix cocktails. Imported and local beer (Parbo is the very drinkable local tipple of choice), soft drinks and bottled water are widely available, as is **dawet**, a very sweet, pink concoction of coconut milk and lemongrass.

CULTURE AND ETIQUETTE

Suriname's diverse population is 27 percent Hindustani (the local term for East Indian); eighteen percent Creole (people of mixed European and African origin); fifteen percent Javanese (Indonesian); fifteen percent Maroon (Bush Negro). Various indigenous groups comprise around three percent of the population. The main **religions** are Hinduism, Christianity and Islam.

The official **language** in Suriname is Dutch but the common language is Sranan Tongo (Surinamese Creole), also known as Taki-Taki. Several Maroon languages, including Saramaccan and Aukan, are spoken, as are indigenous languages such as Carib. A reasonable number of people speak some English, particularly in Paramaribo. Always ask permission before taking pictures of people, buildings and sacrificial areas when visiting Maroon villages. For tipping, ten percent is the norm if a service charge hasn't been included.

COMMUNICATIONS

Internet/**wi-fi** is available in many hotels/ guesthouses, mostly free of charge.

The country code is 597. To use your **mobile phone**, get it unlocked, then purchase a Telesur or Digicel SIM card (SRD30) and request top-ups at outlets or stores.

Postal services are provided by the Central Post Office, Surpost, near at Kerkplein.

CRIME AND SAFETY

Locals are proud of saying that tourists can walk safely from one end of Paramaribo to the other at night. Take this with a pinch of salt; as in most cities, burglary, armed robbery and other **petty crime** does take place. Avoid flaunting valuables and don't walk down inadequately lit streets after dark.

Travel to the interior is usually without incident. Be careful on the **roads**, as drivers can be reckless, and mopeds, scooters and motorcycles always have the right of way. Pedestrians are marginalized and, pavements, where they exist, often become parking lots.

HEALTH

Medical care is limited, though most communities you're likely to visit have a clinic or hospital. In Paramaribo, **St Vincentius Ziekenhuis** (Koninginnestraat 4; ☏ 471 212, ⓦ svzsuriname.org) has 24-hour emergency room service as well as general practitioners who speak English. Drink bottled water where possible. Insect repellent is essential as there are reported cases of mosquito-borne dengue and Zika fever. Consult your doctor regarding the various **vaccinations** required, which include hepatitis A, hepatitis B, yellow fever, typhoid, tetanus-diphtheria and rabies.

SURINAME ONLINE

ⓦ **surinametourism.sr** The Suriname Tourism Foundation has information on what to do, where to stay and how to get around in Suriname.

ⓦ **planktonik.com/ birdingsuriname** Authoritative guide for birdwatchers, with details on prime destinations.

ⓦ **stinasu.sr** The site of Suriname's conservation organization lists and describes the country's protected areas.

EMERGENCY NUMBERS

Fire services ☏ 110
Ambulance ☏ 113
Police ☏ 115

INFORMATION AND MAPS

For information and to pick up a copy of *Suriname's Destination Guide*, visit the Toeristen Informatie Centrum in Paramaribo (see page 666). Vaco bookstore (see page 668) in Paramaribo offers a good selection of city and regional maps.

MONEY AND BANKS

The unit of **currency** is the Suriname dollar (SRD), which comes in 5, 10, 20, 50 and (rare) 100 notes and 5, 10, 25, 100 and 250 cent coins. Prices are often given in euros, which are readily accepted (as are US$), and cambios (money exchanges) offer better exchange rates than banks. Major **credit cards** are accepted by most tour operators and in some restaurants and hotels in Paramaribo. Some ATMs in Paramaribo accept foreign bankcards; elsewhere ATMs are sparse, so carry extra cash. At the time of writing, €1=SRD9.25, US$1=SRD7.47 and £1=SRD10.62.

OPENING HOURS AND HOLIDAYS

Banks are open Monday to Friday 7am to 2.30pm. Government institutions operate Monday to Friday 7am to 3pm. Shops and other businesses open Monday to Friday 8am–4.30pm, Saturday 8am–1pm.

PUBLIC HOLIDAYS

January 1 New Year's Day
February (date varies) Chinese New Year
February 25 Day of Liberation and Innovation
March Holi Phagwa (Hindu festival; date varies)
March/April (varies) Good Friday
March/April (varies) Easter Monday
May 1 Labour Day
July 1 Keti Koti (Emancipation Day)
August 9 Indigenous People's Day; Javanese Immigration Day
October 10 Day of the Maroons

Mid-October to mid-November Diwali (Hindi festival of lights; date varies)
November 25 Srefidensi. Independence Day
December 25 Christmas Day
December 26 Boxing Day
Eid-al-Fitre (Muslim festival; date varies)

FESTIVALS AND CELEBRATIONS

Other festivities include the Brazilian carnival (Feb); Suriname Heritage Festival (March); Suriname Jazz Festival (Oct); and Surifesta, the end of year festival (Dec). On New Year's Eve (Oase Owru Yari Dyugu Dyugu) there is a spectacular fireworks display in the capital.

7 PARAMARIBO

PARAMARIBO ("Parbo" to the locals) is arguably the most appealing of the three Guyanese capitals. Reflecting its role as the administrative, much fought-over capital of the Guianas during the colonial era, the streets in Parbo's core are lined with attractive eighteenth- and nineteenth-century colonial Dutch, British, Spanish and French wooden buildings, earning it UNESCO World Heritage status in 2002. Brave the bustle and chaos of the market, then take refuge from the heat in the beautiful palm tree grove that is Palmentuin, and at sunset head for the riverfront near historic **Fort Zeelandia**.

WHAT TO SEE AND DO

Paramaribo's Old Town is best explored at an unhurried pace. Some of the finest examples of classic wooden buildings, whether restored or delapidated, stand along the Waterkant, Mr De Mirandastraat and Mr F.H.R. Lim A Postraat. It's easy to organize cycling tours of nearby plantations, as well as river dolphin-spotting on the Commewijne River.

Onafhankelijkheidsplein and around

The centrepiece of the historic inner city is **Onafhankelijkheidsplein (Independence Square)**, an expanse of lawn near the Waterkant overlooked by a statue of a rather rotund Johan Adolf Pengel (former prime minister), behind him the atypically brick Ministry of Finance, and on its north side by the grand **Presidential Palace**.

Early on Sunday mornings (around 7–8am) Independence Square plays host to competitive **bird-singing contests**, weather permitting. Here, picolets and twatwas are persuaded to sing in turns, the winning bird earning a payout for its owner.

Fort Zeelandia

The tree-shaded colonial buildings of **Fort Zeelandia** overlook the Suriname River. One of the darkest spots in the fort's recent history was the 1982 "December murders", when fifteen prominent Surinamese citizens were executed by the military. Today it houses the **Surinaams Museum** (Tues–Fri 9am–2pm, Sun 10am–2pm; SRD25; tours Sun at 10.30am & noon; ⓦsurinaamsmuseum.net), its exhibits ranging from displays on the coffee and sugar trade and old potion bottles and other medical memorabilia, to original Hindi, Javanese and Jewish artefacts and relics of slavery such as metal punishment collars. Upstairs exhibits highlight Suriname's indigenous cultures with displays of traditional weaving and weaponry (the only section labelled in English).

Surinaamsch Rumhuis

Making rum has been a Surinamese tradition for centuries, and at the **Surinaamsch Rumhuis**, Cornelis Jongbawstraat 18 (Tues–Fri 9.30am–2.30pm, free; tours at 10am & 2.30pm, US$15; ☎473 344, ⓦrumhuis. sr), you can visit its well-designed interactive museum then sample the product at the attractive, barrel-shaped bar. The rum brands produced at the distillery next door are Borgoe, Black Cat and Mariënburg, and tastings usually include a good mix – from the lethal ninety-percent proof white rum to the venerable 15-year-old Borgoe. Mixology classes are offered, too.

Religious sites

An imposing yellow and cobalt-blue edifice made entirely of wood, the neo-Gothic, twin-towered **St Peter and Paul Cathedral** on Henck Arronstraat (Mon–Fri 6am–1.30pm, Sat & Sun 8.30am–noon, tours in English by request) was elevated to the status of basilica by Pope Francis in 2014. The airy

Leonsburg & Nieuw Amsterdam ferry (10km)

PARAMARIBO

N

Suriname River

■ ACCOMMODATION	
Albergo Alberga	6
Greenheart Hotel	2
Guesthouse TwenTy4	3
De Kleine Historie	7
Guesthouse	1
Un Pied-A-Terre	4
Zin Resort	5
Zus & Zo	

● EATING	
Anthony's Corner	9
La Cuisine	1
Eetcafé de Gadri	10
Grand Roopram Roti	7/8
Jiji's	11
Jomax	5
Souposo	4
Spice Quest	3
Warung Renah	2
Zus & Zo	6

● SHOPPING	
Jeruzalem Bazaar	3
Readytex Art Gallery	2
Vaco	1

■ DRINKING & NIGHTLIFE	
D'Bar	3
Euphoria	1
't Vat	2

Surinaamsch Rumhuis

STINASU

Fort Zeelandia

Stichting Surinaams Museum

Palmentuin

Presidential Palace

Ministry of Finance

Canadian Consulate

Dutch Embassy

Fletsen in Suriname

French Embassy

St. Peter and Paul's Cathedral

Republique Bank (Blue Machine)

Riverfront Food Stalls

SMS Pier

Plattebrug (ferries to Meerzorg)

Maroon Market

Central Market

Guyanese Embassy

Suriname Rainforest & Cultural Experience

Suriname Tourism Foundation

METS

Mosque

Neveh Shalom Synagogue

Vaillantsplein

NVB Bus Terminal

Knuffels Gracht

Times Mall

HEERTOGSTRAAT
MAURICIUSSTRAAT
CORNELIS JONGBAWSTRAAT
WILHELMINASTRAAT
ROOSTEDE CRULL'LAAN
CROMMELIN
VAN SOMMELSDIJCK STRAAT
KLEINE DWARSSTRAAT
GROTE COMBEWEG
LOUISELAAN
JULIANASTRAAT
PRINS HENDRIKSTRAAT
VAN ROOSEVELTKADE
KLEINE WATERSTRAAT
WICHERSSTRAAT
PRESIDENT DA COSTALAAN
TAMARINDELAAN
INDEPENDENCE SQUARE
WATERKANT
KEIZERSTRAAT
COSTERSTRAAT
KONINGINNESTRAAT
JESSURUNSTRAAT
TOURTONNELAAN
HENCK ARRONSTRAAT
M.G.R. WULFINGHSTRAAT
M.C.F.H.R. LIM A POSTRAAT
MR. DE MIRANDASTRAAT
KROMMEELEBOOG STRAAT
WATERMOLENSTRAAT
KERKPLEIN
GROTOROT STRAAT
KERKSTRAAT
KLIPSTENENSTRAAT
HEILIGENWEG
HEERENSTRAAT
NEUMANPAD
WAGENWEGSTRAAT
DOMINEESTRAAT
STEENBAKKERIJSTRAAT
JODENBREESTRAAT
MAAGDESTRAAT
ZWARTENHOVENBRUGSTRAAT
DR. SOPHIE REDMONDSTRAAT
SAMSON STRAAT
LADESMASTRAAT
GRAVENSTRAAT
HOFSTEDE CRULLLAAN
SWALMBERG STRAAT
DR. J.F. NASSYLAAN
STOELMAN STRAAT
PRINSESSESTRAAT
MATEGBAUMSTRAAT

& Apotheek MacDonald
(150m)
US Embassy
Zorg En Hoop

0   150
metres

7

interior is beautiful, with intricately carved columns and scenes of the Passion of the Christ and the Resurrection. A couple of blocks west, on Keizerstraat, a **mosque** and **synagogue** stand happily side by side.

ARRIVAL AND DEPARTURE

By plane Johan Adolf Pengel International Airport (Zanderij) receives flights from the Netherlands, Brazil, Aruba and the US, as well as thrice-weekly flights from French Guiana. The smaller Zorg en Hoop Airport is for domestic and Guyana flights. Airport transfers with Ashruf (w garage-ashruf.com) and De Paarl (w garagedepaarl.com) take around 2hr and cost SRD90; book in advance. Taxis from JAPI into town cost SRD200. From Zorg en Hoop, minibus line #9 passes near the airport and drops you at Steenbakkerijstraat (SRD1.85). Taxis from Zorg en Hoop cost SRD30 and take about 15min.

Destinations Scheduled domestic flights operated by Blue Wing (w bluewingairlines.com) depart to destinations on the Upper Suriname (Botopasie, Djumu, Kajana three times weekly provided there are at least four passengers; while Gum Air (w gumair.com) flies to Drietabbetje (on the Tapanhony River near the border with French Guiana) on Wednesdays. Trans Guyana Airways (w transguyana.net) flies from Zorg en Hoop to Guyana (2 daily Mon–Fri, 1 daily Sat & Sun; 1hr 20min).

By minibus State-run NVB buses (w nvbnv.sr) operate out of a terminal between Heiligenweg and Knuffelsgracht. Arrive at least an hour in advance to get a number from the ticket office; you then present the number to the minibus driver and pay for your seat when you board. NVB offers service to/from Nieuw Nickerie (2 daily except Sun; 3hr; SRD12.50), Albina (3 daily, 1 Sun 3–4hr; SRD8.50), Lelydorp (frequent or hourly; 1 hr) and Atjoni (various operators depart around 9am; 2hr). In addition, #PN minibuses to/from South Drain (Guyana river crossing) and Nieuw Nickerie (3hr; SRD70) depart when they're full from Dr Sophie Redmondstraat (the spot is known locally as "Ondrobon"); to Albina (2hr 30min; SRD50). #PA buses use a lot on Drambrandersgracht at F Derbystraat, west of the centre. Various operators to Atjoni (linked to boats on the Upper Suriname) depart around 9am from Saramaccastraat (2hr; SRD60). Private minibuses such as Skyline (t 331 117) have a reciprocal arrangement with minibus companies in Guyana, so you can buy a ticket all the way to Georgetown. Destinations Albina (3–4hr); Atjoni (2hr); Nieuw Nickerie and South Drain (3hr).

By taxi To and from South Drain shared taxis cost SRD65–200 depending on passenger numbers (3hr). Taxis to Albina (for the French Guiana border crossing) cost SRD70–200 depending on passenger numbers (3hr). Fany's (t 891 1600) is one reliable operator to Nickerie, the women-driven Femaleline (t 862 7495, e femalelinevoyages@gmail.com) to Albina.

GETTING AROUND

By bicycle Fietsen in Suriname, at Grote Combeweg 13a (t 520 781, w fietseninsuriname.com), rents Gazelle bicycles from Holland, both fixed and multi-gear, from SRD45/day (plus €50 deposit). Keep in mind that, although a handful of Dutch cyclists ply the streets with gusto, cycling is not especially popular among the locals and can be hazardous. Watch out for ditches along the sides of roads.

By bus The larger, cheaper but less frequent scheduled state buses (staatsbus) leave from the bus station at Knuffelsgracht 10. Fares in and around Paramaribo cost SRD1.30.

By taxi Taxis wait for passengers along Heiligenweg, near the Central Market (Waterkant). A spate of reliable metered taxi services can be summoned by dialling their four-digit numbers: 1660, 1689, 1690. Trips within the city should cost SRD10–12.

INFORMATION

Tourist information The Toeristen Informatie Centrum is at Fort Zeelandia Complex, Waterkant 1 (Mon–Fri 8am–3.30pm; t 479 200). Staff are very helpful, speak English and provide free maps.

ACCOMMODATION

Albergo Alberga Mr F.H.R. Lim A Postraat 13 t 520 050, w guesthousealbergoalberga.com; map p.665. Lovely nineteenth-century wooden house in the city centre with a button-sized swimming pool. Rooms (some with a/c) vary in size and fragrance; sniff around before checking in. €26

Greenheart Hotel Costerstraat 68 t 521 360, w greenheart-hotel.com; map p.665. This excellent-value guesthouse was resurrected from an abandoned structure by its Dutch owner, who used tropical hardwoods for the broad verandas and high-ceilinged rooms. The restaurant/bar, attached to a sweet little pool, makes a good retreat for locally inspired cuisine. SRD606

Guesthouse TwenTy4 Jessurunstraat 24 t 420 751, w twenty4suriname.com; map p.665. One of the best deals around, this comfortable, smartly designed guesthouse stands beside a creek on a peaceful street. Rooms (most en-suite) are neat and spacious, and some have terrific balconies. Friendly staff can help arrange tours, and breakfast is served. €27.50

De Kleine Historie Guesthouse Dr J.C. De Mirandastraat 8 t 521 007, w dekleinehistorieguesthouse.com; map p.665. Half a block from the riverfront in the heart of the historic district, this vintage wooden house has spiffy

SURINAME TOURS

Unless you have a lot of time to spare, you'll need a tour operator for excursions into the interior. In the off-season, tour operators work together and share customers in order to make up minimum group numbers.

TOUR OPERATORS

Fietsen in Suriname Grote Combéweg 13a ☎520 781, ⊕fietseninsuriname.nl. Cycling tours of the Commewijne plantations, mountain biking and cycling/canoeing expeditions.

METS Dr J. F. Nassylaan 2 ☎477 088, ⊕mets.sr. One of the longest-running, reputable operators; specializes in visits to the interior and manages jungle lodges in Awarradam, Kasikasima and Palumeu, but also does day-trips around Parbo.

STINASU Cornelis Jongbawstraat 14 ☎476 597, ⊕stinasu.sr. National conservation authority leads budget-priced overnight tours to Central Suriname Nature Reserve, Galibi and Brownsberg, where it maintains lodges. They can also inform you about the soonest available tours to those destinations by other operators.

Suriname Rainforest & Cultural Experience Dr J. F. Nassylaan 38 ☎866 40 30 ⊕upper-suriname.com. Organizes "lodge-hopping" tours on the Upper Suriname.

Waterproof Tours Venusstraat 26 ☎454 434 ⊕waterproofsuriname.com. Renowned for its sunset dolphin-spotting cruises and "Sugar Trail" tours of Commewijne plantations.

7

compact rooms (shared bath) and broad balconies, plus an attached café. €30

★ **Un Pied-À-Terre Guesthouse** Costerstraat 59 ☎470 488, ⊕guesthouse-un-pied-a-terre.com; map p.665. Just down the street from, and related to, *Greenheart Hotel*, this finely restored old house run by a Dutch-French Caribbean couple has a homely, low-key ambience. Breezy verandas, four-poster beds, beers on the honour system and breakfast from €4. Alternatively, hang a hammock (don't forget your mosquito net) in the tranquil rear garden; lockers are provided for your belongings. Rooms €27, hammocks €10

Zin Resort Van Rooseveltkade 20 ☎472 224, ⊕zinresort.sr; map p.665. Suitably across the way from Embassy of the Netherlands, this off-street resort is frequented by a youthful Dutch clientele, who lounge around its sizeable pool. The 21 rooms are classed as "basic" or "deluxe" but all have Euro-standard comforts. €30

Zus & Zo Grote Combéweg 13a ☎520 905, ⊕zusenzosuriname.com; map p.665. Opposite the Palementuin, the traveller hub of Parbo comprises several compact, brightly painted rooms with shared bath, helpful staff, tour agency, and one of the best chillout spots in town. Book in advance as it fills up quickly. €30

EATING

You can eat well in Parbo, its mix of cultures reflected in the capital's diverse cuisine. The cheapest options are the *warungs* (Javanese restaurants) on the lower level of the Central Market – ten in a row – extremely simple places where a plate of chicken, rice, greens and brown beans will get you change from SRD20.

Anthony's Corner Domineestraat 44; map p.665. Downtown shoppers crowd this high-volume sandwich maker, with a daily lunch menu (SRD12). Mon–Fri 7am–3pm, Sat 7am–1pm.

La Cuisine Tourtonnelaan 50 ☎425 656; map p.665. Tasty home-cooked Creole fare is served with a variety of local greens. The dining terrace is shielded from the traffic by a wall of ferns. Meals around SRD45. Mon–Sat 11am–10pm.

Eetcafé de Gadri Zeelandiaweg 1 ☎420 688; map p.665. Generous portions of Creole and Indonesian food (SRD29–45), served at tables overlooking the Suriname River. Mon–Fri 7am–10pm & Sat 11am–10pm.

★ **Grand Roopram Roti** Zwartehovenbrugstraat 23; map p.665. Visit for generous portions of *roti* (Indian pancake) stuffed with various curried meats (or vegetables) with all the trimmings for SRD23. Daily 8am–11pm. Another location at Watermolenstraat 37 (daily 8am–3pm).

Jiji's SMS Pier Waterkant ☎887 1555; map p.665. This upper-level dining spot at the west end of the Waterkant drinking stalls enjoys a supremely romantic location overlooking the river. The food is a melange of Surinamese and international dishes. Meals around SRD80 with some SRD50 combos. Daily 6–11pm.

★ **TREAT YOURSELF**

Spice Quest Dr J.F. Nassylaan 107 ☎520 747; map p.665. Stylish restaurant set in a tropical garden with a lovely ambience. You'll find yourself paying over the odds for Vietnamese spring rolls, crispy Chinese duck and various fusion dishes, but it's all delicious and beautifully presented. Mains around US$25. Mon 6–11pm, Tues–Sun 11am–3pm & 6–11pm.

Jomax Tourtonnelaan 32 ☎ 890 8767; map p.665. A Dutch-style *eetcafe* with eclectic decor and Dutch snacks (*bitterballen, frikandel*), great quesadillas and some vegan dishes, served on a beachy terrace. The invariably festive vibe is perhaps due to the original cocktail mixology classes offered. Meals SRD60–80. Daily 5pm–midnight.

Souposo Costerstraat 20a; map p.665. Soup takes centre stage here with Creole, Dutch, Indian and Chinese variations daily, plus eclectic salads and terrific natural juice combos. All sorts of characters gather in the rear garden. Soups around SRD30. Mon–Sat 10am–11pm.

Zus & Zo Grote Combéweg 13a ☎ 520 905; map p.665. This garden café serves international tapas (grilled plantain, *sate, patatas bravas*) as well as more substantial mains (SRD60) – noodles, grilled meats and more, accompanied by tangy ginger juice and Parbo beer. The little stage hosts live music at weekends. Daily 9am–11pm.

DRINKING AND NIGHTLIFE

Join the beer guzzlers at the stalls along along the riverfront, open round the clock. The ones on the west end prepare grilled meats and Javanese snacks. Nightlife action focuses on the strip of Kleine Waterstraat opposite the Torarica Hotel.

D'Bar Kleine Dwarsstraat 1 ⓦ dbarsuriname.com; map p.665. With a sleek bar and copious rum selection, the narrow space is a magnet for Parbo youth. Daily 8pm–2am.

Euphoria Kleine Waterstraat 5 ⓦ euphoria-nightclub.com; map p.665. Strobe-lit dancehall over a popular restaurant, major DJ events. Mon–Fri 7am–3pm, Sat 7am–1pm.

't Vat Kleine Waterstraat 1a; map p.665. Anchor of the nightlife zone, the sprawling hall buzzes round the clock, fuelled by cocktails and reasonably priced snacks. Daily 24hr.

SHOPPING

The main downtown shopping zone is along Domineestraat and parallel Maagdenstraat. Times Mall is the main downtown shopping centre. On Sundays, it's worth checking out the flea market (8am–1pm) along Tourtonnelaan – as much for the people-watching as for the merchandise, mostly clothing being hawked from backs of cars.

Jerusalem Bazaar Saramacca St 42; map p.665. Huge shop stocking all kinds of hammocks (including mosquito nets).

Markets On Waterkant, west of the SMS pier, is the vast Central Market (Mon–Fri 6am–4pm, Sat 6am–2pm), where you can shop for all manner of fresh produce in the pungent semi-gloom. The upper level is dominated by Hindi vendors of household goods, clothing and fabrics. At an adjacent building to the left, Maroon women sell all manner of herbs, leaves and barks as cleansing remedies.

Readytex Art Gallery Steenbakkerijstraat 30 ⓦ readytexartgallery.com; map p.665. Four stories of locally produced art in a historic building.

Vaco Domineestraat 26; map p.665. Good selection of English popular fiction and Suriname maps.

DIRECTORY

Banks and exchange Republique Bank's "Blue Machines" accept most foreign cards; they can be found around town, notably on Kerkplein. A reliable cambio is Surora Exchange, at Henck Arronstraat 57.

Embassies and consulates Brazil, Maratakastraat 2 (☎ 400 200); Canada, Grote Combéweg 37 (☎ 424 575); France, Henck Arronstraat 82 (☎ 475 222); Guyana, Gravenstraat 82 (☎ 477 895); Netherlands, Van Roosveltkade 5 (☎ 477 211); US, Kristalstraat 165 (☎ 475 222).

Pharmacies Apotheek MacDonald, at Tourtonnelaan 29.

DAY-TRIPS FROM PARAMARIBO

From Paramaribo you can do numerous interesting day-trips; some destinations are reachable by public transport or by bike, whereas others are more easily accomplished by organized tours (see page 667).

Brownsberg Nature Park

About 130km south of Paramaribo on the Mazaroni Plateau, **BROWNSBERG NATURE PARK** (SRD35) can be visited from Paramaribo as a very long day-trip. On a lucky day, you might see howler and spider monkeys, deer, agouti, and birds such as woodpeckers, macaws and parrots. There are also fine views from the plateau of the rainforest and the vast **Van Blommestein Lake** (aka Brokopondo), created to provide electricity for the Alcoa aluminium industry (which resulted in the displacement of several Maroon villages). All the tour companies offer day-trips to the reserve (US$60), with transport, lunch and a hike to one of the three waterfalls included (bring your bathing suit); contact STINASU (see page 667) to find out who's going next.

If you'd rather go independently, STINASU can arrange transport (SRD250 per person return with a minimum of five). STINASU operates a lodge on the plateau comprised of several buildings with shared kitchens (rooms from SRD200 for up to four), as well as

CYCLING NEAR PARIMARIBO

The region around Parbo, once packed with highly profitable sugar-cane plantations and rum distilleries, is navigable by bicycle and makes for a great day-trip. Fietsen in Suriname (p.666) can help with maps and independent trip planning and produces a route booklet (Dutch only). Cycle northeast along the river road (Anton Drachtenweg) to Leonsburg (10km) and put your bike on a motorboat to **Nieuw Amsterdam** (SRD30). Picnic on the riverfront (Chinese supermarkets and roadside smoked fish vendors can provide supplies) or cycle on to **Marienburg** (5km) where a guide will show you around a plantation that produced sugar and rum until as recently as 1998 – the abandoned, rusted machinery (made in Liverpool) looks far older. From Marienburg take a ferry to the north bank of the Commewijne River, where there are functioning plantations, notably at Rust en Werk, and the resort at Frederiksdorp where you can get lunch. Returning you might take the east bank of the Suriname River by following Commissaris Thurkoweg to Meerzorg. From the rotunda follow Weg Naar Peperpot west to the ferry, which carries you and your bike back to Waterkant. The complete route is around 30km of cycling.

7

primitive hammock facilities (SRD50), and there's a restaurant.

Suriname and Commewijne rivers

Paramaribo stands on the banks of the Suriname River, which joins Commewijne River a short distance east. The area is littered with the remnants of plantations (alongside a few working ones) and colonial architecture. **Peperpot** is an old coffee and cocoa plantation that's great for birdwatching, and includes a small **museum** (daily 8am–5pm; SRD20). The Mopentibo Trail cuts right through the cool, moist interior of the plantation with interpretive signs – a delight to cycle (no need to backtrack as there are entrances at either end). Across the Commewijne from Mariënburg, **Frederiksdorp** (SRD25 to tour the grounds), founded in 1747 as a coffee plantation, has stone and wooden buildings that have been fully renovated and converted into a delightful hotel and restaurant, the **Plantage Resort** (☎424 522, wplantagefrederiksdorp.com). The star-shaped **Fort Nieuw Amsterdam** (Mon–Fri 9am–5pm, Sat & Sun 10am–6pm; SRD15) is located at the meeting point of the Commewijne and Suriname rivers. An entertaining open-air museum occupies the southern half of the fort, with exhibitions held in the former jail cells and the impressive American World War II cannons. The top of the star (free entry) commands views of the confluence with some rickety observation posts, highly suitable for birdwatching.

North of Fort Nieuw Amsterdam, near the mouth of Suriname River, is **Matapica Beach**, a reserve to protect the nesting places of the sea turtles. Nowadays, much of the beach has eroded and the sands shifted west to Braamspunt, where green turtles visit the shores to lay their eggs between February and May, leatherbacks between April and July. It is also the habitat of many species of waterfowl.

Plantage Resort at Frederiksdorp offers reasonably priced tours, whether you're staying there or not, including cycling to Rust & Werk, moonlight turtle-watching and cruises along the Suriname River to spot pink dolphins. Otherwise you can go by **bike** (see above), either as a group tour or solo, or by public transport, most easily from the bus terminal at Meerzorg, with frequent departures to Peperpot, Nieuw Amsterdam and Mariënburg. To get there from Parbo, catch one of the frequent **motorboats** from Plattebrug.

Neotropical Butterfly Park

Located east of Lelydorp, the **Neioptropical Butterfly Park** (Mon–Sat 8.30am–3.30pm, Sun 9am–2pm; SRD80; ⓦbutterflyparksuriname.com) is part of a farm that breeds butterflies (and turtles and snakes) for export. Plan on spending the day: besides the elaborately landscaped butterfly garden, which contains the twenty species bred here including the owl butterfly and blue morphos, there's an outstanding insect museum and a panoramic painting of Suriname's environments. A tour takes you through the butterfly breeding process. To get to the park, take a PL bus from Zwartenhovenbrugstraat in Paramaribo to Lelydorp centre, from where it's a 2km walk or taxi ride along Lelydorperweg.

NIEUW NICKERIE AND BIGIPAN

Though easily bypassed if you're taking a direct minibus between the border and Paramaribo, **Nieuw Nickerie**, with its orderly grid of palm tree-lined canals, is worth an overnight stay, if only to visit **Bigipan**, a coastal lagoon known for its abundance of birds, particularly the scarlet ibis. Various tours depart from the Longmay dock on the Nickerie River east of town and ply an 8km mangrove-lined channel to reach Bigipan. It's best to spend the night at one of the lodges that stand on stilts in the lagoon and provide dusk tours to observe the incredible birdlife. At Mantje's (☎868 4809; SRD500 per person), the rate includes accommodation in ramshackle rooms or on a hammock platform, meals, transport to and from the lagoon and evening tour.

ARRIVAL AND DEPARTURE

Nickerie is reachable by NVB state buses and private minibuses from Paramaribo (3hr) and by minibus from South Drain (1hr). Taxis to South Drain cost SRD150 and will pick you up early from your hotel to catch the morning ferry to Guyana.

ACCOMMODATION

Hotel Concorde R. B. Wilhelminastrat 3 ☎232 345, ✉hotelconcordmhf@yahoo.com. A great deal, this hotel opposite the port boasts old-fashioned style and comforts. Go for one of the upper-level rooms, some with balconies. **SRD165**

UPPER SURINAME

One of Suriname's highlights is a tour up the **Suriname River**, leading deep into the forested interior. A journey there combines traditional African culture with natural wonders, and it's relatively easy and affordable to access independently.
The river winds almost 100km from Atjoni, the end of the road below the Brokopondo Reservoir, to the jungle lodge at Awarradam. Along its length it is dotted with dozens of villages populated by **Saramaccan Maroons**,

descendants of runaway plantation slaves who fled deep into the jungle in the early eighteenth century. Long boats convey passengers along a succession of bends, interrupted at points by treacherous rapids which may test the navigational skills of the boatmen, particularly when going upriver. Scenes of village life unfold along the banks between stretches of wilderness – a slice of Africa in the depths of the Surinamese jungle. Women still carry large loads on their heads, and the Saramaccan tongue spoken is based on the dialects spoken in Ghana over three hundred years ago; though Christianity has made inroads, most of the villages still follow ancestral animist religions and practise traditional dance, which you may be able to see – and participate in. A museum devoted to Saramaccan culture is located at **Pikin Slee**, a two-and-a-half-hour boat ride upriver from Atjoni. Many settlements are linked by good footpaths that are ideal for nature walks and birdwatching.

There are more than twenty low-key **ecolodges** of varying degrees of cost and comfort up the river. Most lodges can arrange guides to take you wildlife-spotting along the river, swimming in the nearby rapids and to the Saramaccan villages. With daily public boat transport, it is entirely possible to "lodge hop", though it's essential to contact the lodges beforehand. All of the lodges are catalogued on the website of the Association of Saramaccan Lodge Holders (℗upper-suriname.com). Better still, visit the office of Suriname Rainforest & Cultural Experience in Paramaribo (see page 667) beforehand and they can help you make arrangements.

An **information booth** at Atjoni (☎861 7409), the river port at the end of the road, can give you up-to-date details on lodge availability and river transport. Note that supplies are sparse and expensive up the river; those planning to do self-catering should stock up in Atjoni.

ARRIVAL AND TOURS

The cheapest way to approach the Upper Suriname is to take a bus to Atjoni (SRD60, 2hr), departing around 9am from Saramacca Street in Parbo, then get rides on public boats up the river.

By plane There are airstrips at Botopasie, Nieuw Aurora, Djumu and Kajana. Blue Wing (w bluewingairlines.com) has scheduled flights three times weekly provided there are at least four passengers.

By boat Boat departures, both private and NVB (recognizable by their yellow flags), are generally linked to bus arrivals, with most boats departing upriver around or before 2pm. Going as far as Djumu, they stop by request at villages and lodges along the way, including Gunsi (SRD70; 1hr) and Pikin Slee (SRD100, 2hr 30min).

Tour operators Trips to Awarradam are booked through METS (see page 667), which offers four-/five-day stays, departing Mon & Fri. Suriname Rainforest & Cultural Experience, linked to the lodge-holders association, sets up river tours and accommodations based on your time/budget/interests.

ACCOMMODATION

Awarradam Jungle Lodge ☎ 477 088, w mets.sr. Located on an island in the Gran Rio, about 20km upriver from Djumu, the lodge consists of a number of self-contained huts with mosquito nets owned by and run by members of a local Saramaccan village. It generally accommodates visitors on four- or five-day tours (US$645) organized by METS.

Hotel Botopassei ☎ 896 8157, w botopasi.com. On the wilder east bank, Dutch-run slightly upmarket *Botopassie* is at a picturesque bend in the river, and it's one of the few spots on the Upper Suriname where you can get a cappuccino. Paths lead through a patch of jungle behind the lodge. You can stay in the main house or one of the cabins, set slightly back from the river. With meals. €80

Koto Hati Lodge Foetoenakaba ☎ 878 2879, w kotohati.com. Near the neat, Christianized village of Foetoenakaba, this serene spot has lovingly kept thatched-roof en-suite cabins facing a serene stretch of the river. A broad path leads to the nearby village of Pikin Slee with the Saramacca Museum. With meals per person SRD125

Kumalu Dream Island ☎ 866 40 30, e marcel. chandoesing@gmail.com. One of the river's original lodges, *Kumalu* occupies an islet across the river from the village of Djumu, on the Pikin Rio at its confluence with the Gran Rio. It's an appealing spot for lounging and appreciating the river views, with en-suite cabins and hammock huts. Tours are offered to the waterfalls and natural pools at Tapawutra by the mouth of the Gran Rio. Rooms with meals SRD250, hammocks SRD75

Tei Wei Gunsi ☎ 882 8998, w gunsiteiwei.wordpress. com. Just downriver from the fearsome Felulasidan rapids, *Tei Wei* has simple stilted huts with porches on a hillside overlooking a placid stretch of the river. One of the best-value places on the Upper Suriname, it is near the village of Gunsi, about an hour upriver from Atjoni. Rooms with meals SRD275

THE CENTRAL SURINAME NATURE RESERVE

Occupying nine percent of Suriname, the **Central Suriname Nature Reserve** is a diverse and popular destination for single- to multi-day trips into the interior. Though illegal gold-mining is rife and poorly controlled, it is nevertheless a staggeringly beautiful part of the country, home to diverse fauna such as spider monkeys, ocelot and the world's largest-known species of the cock-of-the-rock bird. Highlights include Ralleighvallen (Raleigh Falls) and Voltzberg mountain.

Visitors stay at the basic lodge on Foengoe Island next to Ralleighvallen, reachable either by short flight (50min) or five hours overland. Tours can be organized through STINASU, which runs the lodge, or Waterproof Tours (see page 676), among others.

GALIBI NATURE RESERVE

Situated in the northeastern corner of Suriname at the mouth of the Maroni River, the **GALIBI NATURE RESERVE** is a major nesting ground for leatherback and green **turtles** between February and July. Several tour operators, including METS (see page 667), run two- to three-day trips to Galibi (€180–295), which involve a bus ride to Albina, followed by a three-hour boat ride down the Marowijne river to the indigenous village of Christiankondre, beyond which STINASU maintains a lodge, Baboensanti, for overnight stays (under renovation at time of writing). The visit to the Galibi site itself is at night, when the newly hatched baby turtles make a break for the water. Outside turtle season there are full moon beach parties or simply beachcombing and village life. To arrive independently by boat, contact John Tokoe (☎ 859 5863), who has a lodge in the village.

7

French Guiana

FRENCH GUIANA is a strange beast. It's a tropical corner of France that is staunchly proud of its connection to the old country, despite few French mainlanders paying it much attention. The country speaks, eats and thinks French, though the majority of its population hail from African-Caribbean stock.

One of the most expensive countries in South America, it's nevertheless worth visiting for **Cayenne** – a colonial outpost masquerading as a French seaside town. The country also has significant Laotian, Chinese, Haitian and Brazilian populations, which is evident in the capital's varied cuisine.

A notorious penal colony for much of its existence, French Guiana's muggy, oppressive climate, malaria-ridden forests and inhospitable terrain were considered an ideal way to punish French criminals (as well as World War II prisoners of war). French Guiana next came to international attention in the 1960s, when the European Space Agency cleared a patch of jungle and built a **space centre** to launch satellites into orbit from the town of **Kourou**. A rocket launch is one of the country's biggest attractions, along with the **Îles du Salut**, rocky islets that were once home to French criminal deportees.

French Guiana is perfect for adventurous travellers; it helps to have your own transport and to speak a little French. You'll find the three towns of Cayenne, Kourou and St Laurent fairly straightforward to visit. The attractions of the Hmong village of Cacao and the turtle-watching beach, Plage Les Hattes, lie in the interior or somewhat off the beaten path. Finally, there are expeditions down the country's rivers deep into the jungle and visits to remote indigenous communities – which means flights by tiny plane, nights in hammocks and long boat journeys into the unknown.

CHRONOLOGY

10,000 BC Originally settled by various groups such as the Arawak and the Caribs.

1498 AD Columbus briefly sets foot in Guiana and dubs it "the land of pariahs".

1604 First attempts at French settlement made difficult by tropical diseases and native resistance.

1643 Cayenne founded but French soon forced out by hostile indigenous communities.

1664 Cayenne finally established as a permanent settlement.

1665 Dutch occupy Cayenne.

1667 Colony awarded to France under the Treaty of Breda. All inhabitants now French citizens.

1676 Brief Dutch occupation and expulsion.

1763–65 France sends around 12,000 immigrants as part of the Kourou Expedition to develop the region, but 10,000 die of yellow fever and typhoid.

1809 Combined Anglo-Portuguese naval force captures the colony for Portugal.

1814 Guiana restored to France as part of the Treaty of Paris but Portuguese remain until 1917.

1848 Slavery is abolished. The colony's fragile plantation economy collapses. Ex-slaves establish Maroon communities in the jungle.

1852 Region designated a penal colony by Napoleon; more than 70,000 French convicts transported to the area.

1853 Gold discovered in the interior.

1946 French Guiana becomes an overseas département of France.

1947 Penal colony abolished but the last convicts only leave in 1952.

1964–68 ESA (European Space Agency) establishes space station in Kourou to launch communications satellites.

1974 French Guiana gains own Conseil Régional with some autonomy in social and economic matters.

1997 Independence leader Jean-Victor Castor arrested by police, leading to civil violence in Cayenne.

2000 Riots occur in Cayenne following an organized march calling for greater autonomy.

2008 President Sarkozy dedicates 1000 troops to combat growing immigration problems.

2009 The largest space telescope yet created is launched from Kourou.

2010 The option of increased autonomy rejected in referendum.

2011 Russian rocket "Soyuz" launched from Kourou.

2013 The False-Form Beetle, a new species which coexists with fire ants, is discovered in interior.

2017 Strikes, led by the Collective of 500 Brothers, over rising crime, lack of funding for education and health, and general neglect on the part of France, paralyze the nation.

ARRIVAL AND DEPARTURE

French Guiana's main international airport, **Aéroport de Félix Eboué**, is some

17km south of Cayenne, near the town of Matoury. It receives direct flights from France, Martinique, Brazil (Belem and Fortaleza) and Suriname.

FROM BRAZIL

Travellers arriving from Brazil enter French Guiana via a boat or by bridge across the Oyapok River to the town of **Saint-Georges** (see page 680).

FROM SURINAME

Travellers from Suriname must take a ferry or dugout canoe across the Maroni River to **St Laurent du Maroni** (see page 682) then continue via road by bus or car.

VISAS

As French Guiana is an overseas *département* of France, **visas** are only required for those travellers who would also need a visa for France. Non-EU nationals unsure of their visa requirements should check ⓦdiplomatie.gouv.fr/en.

GETTING AROUND

Shared taxis or minibuses are the best and most economic way to move around the country. **Minibuses** will pick up and drop off passengers at their hotels around town. Reservation numbers change periodically, although hotels and guesthouses are kept up to date.

Both government-run TIG (Transport Interurbain Guyanais and private operators run passenger vans along the main highway routes. TIG vehicles run on fixed schedules with lower fares.

Hitchhiking is widely practised by locals outside Cayenne; common-sense precautions apply.

Renting a car is relatively inexpensive – in some cases cheaper than the bus not counting fuel costs – and pretty much essential if you wish to travel beyond the coastal towns or even around Cayenne and Kourou. Prices start at around €25 per day and you can rent cars in Cayenne, Saint Laurent and at Félix Eboué Airport. The main roads are paved and well signed. Keep your passport with you, as there are occasional *gendarme* checkpoints.

Travel into and within the interior involves taking tiny planes and motorized *pirogues* (dugout canoes).

ACCOMMODATION

Accommodation in French Guiana is limited and very expensive, with the budget end geared towards independent travellers with their own transport. In large towns, you're likely to be confined to unremarkable business-oriented hotels (from €60/double). On the outskirts of towns and in rural areas you'll find gîtes (family-run lodgings), which range from simple to fairly luxurious (from €30/ double). Adventurous and budget-conscious travellers may opt for **carbets** – wooden shelters for hammocks. Check the excellent wescapade-carbet.com for a definitive guide to the country's swinging accommodation. Many are unmanned and free of charge, located by the sides of roads or on beaches, and have no facilities attached; for these you'll need your own hammock and two lengths of rope to hang it (easily purchased in Cayenne). Others are found in villages and even in some towns; some come with an attached shower/toilet block and provide hammocks at extra cost (€10–15/night).

FOOD AND DRINK

Those on a tight budget will look to street vendors, markets, well-stocked supermarkets (in Cayenne) and small takeaway joints. The preferred fast foods are Chinese and pizza, as well as proper coffee, baguettes with Caribbean Creole fillings, crêpes and croissants in cafés and bakeries. Cayenne offers the best variety of cuisines, with French, Laotian, Chinese, Indonesian, Vietnamese, Brazilian and Creole options, some of which you'll also find in St Laurent and Kourou. The best Laotian food is found in the Hmong village of Cacao (see page 679).

Fish dishes are plentiful, one of the more typical being *blaff*: a stock heavily seasoned with onion, garlic, celery, basil and spices. Another popular stock, used mostly at Easter and the Pentecost, is *bouillon d'awara*, made from the *awara* palm tree

7

fruit and cooked with chicken, shrimp, crab and vegetables. *Fricassée* and *colombo* are typical Creole stews, the latter a meat- and vegetable-based curry stew. Wild game like capybara, peccary, paca, agouti and armadillo can also be found on the menu, often incorporated into curries.

DRINK

The authentic drink here is the sweet French aperitif **Ti' punch**: lime, sugar-cane syrup and rum, without ice, downed in one. Fresh fruit juices (*jus locaux*) are popular and found at the Cayenne market, in Cacao and in some restaurants, or mixed with rum to create the ubiquitous fruit punch.

You can find an excellent selection of French wines, and French beer is a popular import, expats appreciating the presence of Kronenbourg 1664.

CULTURE AND ETIQUETTE

Indigenous communities and Maroons largely maintain their own cultural traditions, as does the immigrant population of Hmong from Laos in villages such as Cacao and Javouhey. The majority of the population is **Creole**, and mixed-Creole culture is dominant in the metropolitan areas; there is also an increasing number of immigrants from Brazil, Colombia and other South American countries, whose presence is evident in Cayenne and St Laurent. All teachers, police, *gendarmes* and other civil functionaries are recruited in mainland France. Note that the French generally don't tip.

> ### LANGUAGE
>
> French is the most widely spoken language, though a significant proportion of the population also speaks a French-based patois or Creole, with Chinese, *Neg Maron* (Bush Negro or Maroon), Portuguese and native languages spoken in certain areas. In St Laurent, due to the number of Surinamese and Guyanese immigrants, some English is also spoken, and the one language common to all three Guianas – Taki-Taki – is heard along the rivers.

> ### EMERGENCY NUMBERS
>
> Ambulance ☎ 15
> Police ☎ 17
> Fire service ☎ 18

COMMUNICATIONS

The efficient postal system is integrated with that of metropolitan France, so deliveries to Europe are quick and cheap. Digicel or Orange SIM cards can be purchased for unblocked mobile phones in any of the three major towns. When calling French Guiana from abroad, you must dial 594 (country code) followed by a nine-digit number also beginning 594 (or 694 for mobiles). For international calls, opt for Skype or WhatsApp; most hotels offer wi-fi and there are internet cafés in both Cayenne and St Laurent.

CRIME AND SAFETY

Certain areas of Cayenne are best avoided, such as immediately south of the Canal Laussat. At night it's best to stick to Place des Palmistes and the better-lit main streets of the centre. If spending the night in a carbet on a deserted beach, keep your valuables in the hammock with you.

HEALTH

Malaria prophylactics are recommended for the border rivers, though the risk is thought to be low along the coast. A number of vaccinations, including hepatitis A, hepatitis B, typhoid, yellow fever, tetanus-diphtheria and rabies, are also strongly recommended. Vaccination against yellow fever is compulsory if you're arriving from certain South American countries. There have also been recent outbreaks of dengue fever and Zika virus, so mosquito repellent is essential.

Locals claim that the coastal **tap water** is safer to drink than that of Paris.

European-standard **medical care** is available in Cayenne, Kourou and St Laurent du Maroni. The European Health Insurance Card (ⓦehic.org.uk) that allows travellers to receive free medical treatment in participating member states works in French Guiana.

May 8 WWII Victory (VE) Day
May/June (varies) Ascension Day
May/June (varies) Whit Monday
June 10 Abolition of Slavery Day
July 14 Bastille Day
August 15 Assumption Day
November 1 All Saints' Day
October (varies) Cayenne festival
November 11 Armistice (Remembrance Day)
December 25 Christmas Day

INFORMATION AND MAPS

Printed information (mostly in French) is readily available in tourist offices in Cayenne and St Laurent, where you will also find good city maps. Ask for a copy of *Vakans an Nou Koté*, a handy annual guide, which lists hotels, restaurants, bars and clubs throughout French Guiana (in French). Those who read French might pick up the *Guide Guyane* by Philippe Boré – a detailed guidebook to French Guiana.

MONEY AND BANKS

The currency of French Guiana is the **euro** (€), and credit/debit cards are widely accepted in the urban centres. **ATMs** generally accept Visa, MasterCard or Eurocard, and hotels usually take American Express. Few banks have foreign exchange facilities; Cayenne has several bureaux de change but St Laurent has none. At the time of writing, US$1.24=€1, £0.88=€1.

OPENING HOURS AND HOLIDAYS

Many businesses and shops shut for two to three hours over lunch. Most shops are open Monday to Saturday 8/9am to 1pm and 3/4 to 6.30/7pm. Supermarkets remain open until around 9pm, on Sunday till lunchtime. Banks open Monday to Friday 7.30am to noon & 2 to 4pm; some open on Saturday morning as well.

PUBLIC HOLIDAYS

January 1 New Year's Day
February (varies) Ash Wednesday
March/April (varies) Good Friday
March/April (varies) Easter Monday
May 1 Labour Day

FESTIVALS AND NATIONAL CELEBRATIONS

The major festival in French Guiana is Carnaval, which begins after Epiphany in the first week of January and goes on for about two months until Ash Wednesday – locals claim it is the longest in the world. On Friday and Saturday nights during Carnaval you can witness the tradition of Touloulou balls, when women (Touloulou), heavily disguised and wearing masks, are given the sole, non-reciprocal right to ask men to dance; men may not refuse. Women disguise their faces, bodies and voices to become unrecognisable even to their own husbands. Mardi Gras (Carnaval Monday and Tuesday) takes place during the last five days of Carnaval, which ends on Ash Wednesday. It features colourful street parades with music, dancing, exotic costumes and merriment.

CAYENNE

In your travels around French Guiana **CAYENNE** is likely to be your base for exploration of the surrounding sights. This sprawling city has a compact centre with an attractive main square which becomes the focal point of community activity in the evenings. Eighteenth-century colonial buildings, French mainlanders on overseas postings and a lively market add up to the most European experience on the South American continent and well worth a visit.

WHAT TO SEE AND DO

Place des Palmistes and around

Place des Palmistes, on Avenue du Général de Gaulle, is a refreshing green space sparsely covered with palms, where you can catch an impromptu football game or live music performance some weekends. A statue of Felix Éboué (1884–1944), a black French Guianese who governed various French territories in Africa and the Caribbean, stands at the lower end. Just

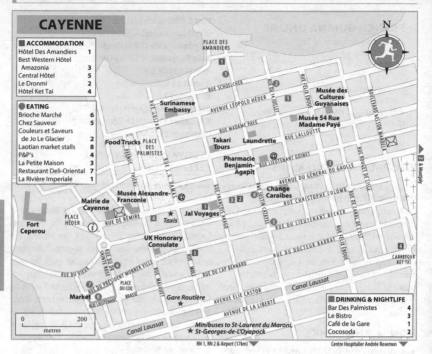

CAYENNE

ACCOMMODATION
Hôtel Des Amandiers	1
Best Western Hôtel Amazonia	3
Central Hôtel	5
Le Dronmi	2
Hôtel Ket Tai	4

EATING
Brioche Marché	6
Chez Sauveur	5
Couleurs et Saveurs de Jo Le Glacier	2
Laotian market stalls	8
P&P's	4
La Petite Maison	3
Restaurant Deli-Oriental	7
La Rivière Imperiale	1

DRINKING & NIGHTLIFE
Bar Des Palmistes	4
Le Bistro	3
Café de la Gare	1
Cocosoda	2

RN 1, RN 2 & Airport (17km)

Centre Hospitalier Andrée Rosemon

---

off the square, the **Musée Alexandre-Franconie**, 1 Av du Général de Gaulle (Mon 10am–2pm & 3–6pm, Wed–Fri 8am–2pm & 3–6pm, Sat 9am–1.30pm; €3, under 18s free; ☎ 594 295 913), in one of the original wooden Creole mansions, contains an extensive entomological collection and, in the upstairs gallery, a series of paintings of the hardships of penal colony life by inmate Francis Lagrange. You might also drop into the adjacent public library with a comfy reading lounge.

Fort Céperou

For a sweeping view of Cayenne, climb up the hill at the end of Rue de Rémire to the crumbling remains of **Fort Céperou**, the first building to appear in Cayenne after the Compagnie de Rouen purchased the hill from a Galibi chief named Céperou in 1643.

Musée des Cultures Guyanaises and around

The **Musée des Cultures Guyanaises** at 78 Rue Madame-Payé (Mon–Fri 8am–1pm & 3–5.45pm, Sat 8–11.45am, closed Wed afternoon & Sun; €2, under 18s free) stages temporary exhibits curated from its vast collection of artefacts, crafts, costume and art to highlight the diverse cultures of French Guiana. A new component, located in a traditional Creole home on the next block at Rue Madame Payé 54, is dedicated to its nineteenth-century inhabitant, Herménégilde Tell, former director of the prison network, and other personalities and events of that period.

ARRIVAL AND DEPARTURE

By plane Félix Eboué International Airport (⊕ guyane.cci.fr) is in Matoury, 17km south of Cayenne. Taxis to Cayenne cost €35 (€50 after 7pm).
Destinations Air France (⊕ airfrance.com) has regular flights to Paris and Martinique; Air Caraïbes (⊕ aircaraibes.com) flies to Brazil and France and connects French Guiana with Martinique and Guadeloupe; Surinam Airways (⊕ flyslm.com) connects Belem in Brazil to Paramaribo three times a week with an optional stop in Cayenne. Air Guyane (⊕ airguyane.com) provides domestic services to Maripasoula, Saül and St Laurent du Maroni.
By minibus TIG has scheduled services to St-Georges de l'Oyapock (Ligne 9; 7 daily; €30) and Kourou (Ligne 5; 8

daily, fewer on weekends; €10), departing from the south side of Canal Laussat. Private buses leave when full and charge more.

Destinations Saint-Georges de l'Oyapock via Régina (2hr 30min); Saint Laurent du Maroni via Iracoubo (4hr).

GETTING AROUND AND INFORMATION

By bus Agglobus (ⓦodm973.com) provides service in and around Cayenne (Mon–Sat). Buses and minivans leave from the Gare Routière on the north side of Canal Laussat, near the market. Useful routes include Ligne 7 to Matoury (€2; 35min) and Ligne B to Remire-Montjoly(€2; 25min). To get to Roura, take a bus to Matoury Eglise, then catch a Ligne D bus. There is no service to the airport but you can reduce costs by travelling to nearby Matoury and getting a taxi from there.

By taxi Taxis in Cayenne are metered; there's a taxi stand just off the Place de Coq in front of the market. Rates are around €7.10 to hire, plus €1.80/km (€2.75 on Sun & 7pm–6am).

Tourist information Office de Tourisme Ville de Cayenne, 12 Rue Louis Blanc (Mon–Fri 8.30am–noon & 2–5pm, Sat 8.30am–1pm; ☎594 39 68 83, ⓔtourisme@ville-cayenne.fr) has helpful staff, some of whom may speak English, and a plethora of maps and brochures.

ACCOMMODATION

Budget accommodation is limited. All accommodation below has a/c and en-suite bathrooms.

Hôtel Des Amandiers Place Auguste-Horth ☎594 28 97 28 ⓦhoteldesamandiers.com; map p.676. Rambling colonial house facing a lovely seafront park shaded by almond trees, with a popular terrace café for a sunset Ti' Punch. Functional rooms and frosty service though. **€80**

Best Western Hôtel Amazonia 28 Av du Général de Gaulle ☎594 28 83 00, ⓦbestwestern.fr; map p.676. Right in the centre of town, this business-oriented hotel offers stylishly furnished a/c rooms with balconies, and there's a pool beside the lobby. **€120**

Central Hôtel Rue Molé, at Becker ☎594 256 565, ⓦcentralhotel-cayenne.fr; map p.676. It is indeed central – a few blocks from the market – and the multilingual staff aim to please. Kitchenettes in some rooms are a bonus for self-caterers. **€91**

Le Dronmi 42 Av du Général de Gaulle ☎594 31 77 70, ⓦledronmi.com; map p.676. A brothel in a previous incarnation, this trendy and central hotel is just a few staggers from a lively watering hole. It has flat-screen TVs and kitchenette; breakfast included. **€95**

Hôtel Ket Tai 72 Blvd Nelson Mandela ☎594 28 97 77, ⓔg.chang@wanadoo.fr; map p.676. Brazilian telenovelas in the lobby, friendly service and compact, featureless, tiled rooms with struggling a/c. If every other hotel in town is full, there's a good chance you can still find a bed here. **€60**

EATING

Self-caterers will find fresh produce at the market on Av du Président Monnerville (Wed, Fri & Sat 4am–2pm), fresh bread in the boulangerie around the corner from the market, and pretty much everything else at the enormous Carrefour on the southern approach to town. Food trucks producing burgers, crepes and Chinese fast food set up nightly from 6pm along the Place des Palmistes.

Brioche Marché Rue du Ste Rose; map p.676. Popular little bakery offering chocolate croissants, sardine-filled pastries and superb baguette sandwiches, plus coffee. Mon–Sat 7.30am–1.30pm.

Chez Saveur 67 Rue J. Catayée ☎594 385 839; map p.676. Corner joint turning out tasty home-cooked dishes such as *blaff* and *pimentade de crevettes* (spicy shrimp stew, €9) without the slightest pretension. Mon–Sat 9am–2.30pm & 6.30–9pm.

Couleurs et Saveurs de Jo Le Glacier Rue du 14 Juillet at Rue Scholcher; map p.676. Exotic flavours at this old-fashioned ice cream parlour include *prune de cythère* (ambarella) and guava. For a more substantial dessert, get several scoops atop a *guafre* (waffle). Daily 2–9pm.

FRENCH GUIANA TOURS

If you wish to explore Guiana's jungle and rivers, virtually the only way to do so is to join an **organized excursion**, although it's cheaper to hire local guides by asking around. High season is from July to November, outside of which time you can generally show up at the travel agent on spec.

TOUR OPERATORS

Le Morpho ☎06 94 23 82 55, ⓦlemorpho.com. Highly recommended for tours of Kaw marshes aboard floating lodges (day/overnight €71/139).

Riché & Kaw ☎694 287 950, ⓦricheandkaw.fr. Night caiman-spotting excursions on the Kaw River (€55), plus Cacao village tours (€45).

Takari Amazonie CC Family Plaza, Matoury ☎594 28 70 00, ⓦtakari-amazonie.com. All-purpose operator, offering everything from a 3hr history tour of Cayenne (from €20) to multi-day adventures on the Oyapock and Maroni rivers (from €570).

7

★**Laotian market stalls** Av du Président Monnerville; map p.676. Feast on nems (spring rolls), *phô* soup and other Laotian dishes at the market. Portions are generous and the dishes are full of flavour, with plenty of fresh herbs. Meals from €5. Other stalls offer various fresh juice concoctions. Wed, Fri & Sat 6.30am–1pm.

P & P's 56 Av du Général de Gaulle ☎ 594 25 16 74; map p.676. Quality thick-crust pizzas (from €5) and galettes (wholewheat crepes) with a few tables for dining in. Mon–Sat noon–2pm & 6–10pm, Sun 6–10pm.

Restaurant Deli-Oriental 7 Av Gaston Monnerville ☎ 594 31 90 17; map p.676. Outside market hours, you can still find southeast Asian fare across the street, this being the best of four locales there. Enjoy huge bowls of phô (from €6.50) and *bo bun* – salad on a bed of vermicelli noodles with bits of spring rolls – in a/c bliss. Meals from €7. Mon–Sat 7am–3.30pm & 6.30–9.30pm, Sun 9am–2.30pm.

La Rivière Imperiale 10 Rue J. Catayée ☎ 594 28 62 51; map p.676. Crispy *nems* (spring rolls), noodles, *fricassée* and conch stew are all on the menu at this inviting bistro specializing in Vietnamese, Creole and Haitian dishes. Meals €8–13. Mon, Tues & Thurs–Sat noon–2.30pm & 7–10pm, Sun noon–2.30pm.

DRINKING AND NIGHTLIFE

Bar Des Palmistes 12 Av du Général de Gaulle; map p.676. A popular spot for both locals and Metros to meet, morning or evening, the long terrace of this colonial mansion faces the palms of Cayenne's signature square. Daily 6.30am–midnight.

Le Bistro 42 Av du Général de Gaulle; map p.676. Perch on the terrace of this perennial hangout for an afternoon beer, a pre-dinner short drink, or even a liquid breakfast (coffee, that is). Daily 8.30am–1am.

Cafe de La Gare 42 Av Leopold Héder ☎ 594 28 53 20; map p.676. Whatever is programmed for the evening at this egalitarian nightspot – mazurka dancing, karaoke or DJ sets – it usually involves the roomy dance floor. Cover of €5–10 for live music events. Daily from 8.30pm.

★**TREAT YOURSELF**

La Petite Maison 23 Rue Félix Eboué ☎ 594 385 839; map p.676. In a renovated Creole house, this bistro serves unpretentious and affordable food with gastronomical flair. Vegetarians won't eat, but meat eaters will be pleased with duck breasts or *confit*, succulent lamb, local fish and home-made fries. Desserts are arranged artfully and birthdays are specially honoured. Meals around €25, prix fixe at lunchtime €16. Mon, Tues, Thurs & Fri noon–3pm & 7–10pm, Wed & Sat 7–10pm.

Cocosoda 493 Plage de Montabo ☎ 694 45 35 04; map p.676. Beach party tonight! A volunteer-run *carbet*-bar with stiff caipirinhas, grilled snacks and DJs, this stretch of sands turns festive most Friday nights, as Cayenne's slacker set gather beneath the palms. Starts kicking quite late, and shuts when they feel like it. It's a 15min ride from the centre to Montabo beach. Fri 9pm–1am (check Facebook page for next event).

DIRECTORY

Banks and exchange ATMs along Av du Général de Gaulle; there are half a dozen at the post office at the avenue's east end. Change Caraïbes offers good exchange rates at 68 Av du Général de Gaulle (Mon–Fri 7.30am–12.30pm & 3–5.45pm, Sat 8am 11.45pm).

Car rental Avis, 68 Blvd Nelson Mandela (☎ 594 30 25 22); Budget, 55 Zone Artisanale Galmot (☎ 594 35 10 20).

Embassies and consulates Brazil, 444 Chemin Saint-Antoine (☎ 594 296 010); Suriname, 3 Av Leopold Héder (☎ 594 282 160); UK, Honorary British Consul, 16 Av du Président Monnerville (☎ 594 311 034).

Hospital Centre Hospitalier de Cayenne Andrée Rosemon, 3 Av des Flamboyants (☎ 594 395 050, ⊛ ch-cayenne.fr).

Internet PC Yuan Yuan, southeast corner of Place des Palmistes, itself a free-wifi zone.

Laundry Laverie, 31 Rue J. Catayée, 8am–8pm, self-service.

Pharmacies Pharmacie Du Centre, 67 Av du Général de Gaulle.

Post office East end of Av du Général de Gaulle (Mon–Fri 8am–3pm, Sat 8am–noon).

DAY-TRIPS FROM CAYENNE

There are a number of varied attractions outside Cayenne that make for easy day-trips though you need to have your own wheels to reach most of them.

Plage de Montjoly

The wildest stretch of the 4km **Plage de Montjoly** beach, east of Cayenne, is **Les Salines**, backing up on a 63-hectare nature reserve around a lagoon. It takes about an hour and a half to hike the loop trail along its eastern edge, which traverses three environments – forest, salt marsh and shoreline, where you can spot numerous endemic birds and amphibians, and in the spring, turtles which nest along the beach here. Catch an Agglobus Ligne B from the Gare Routière.

Îlet la Mère

One of a set of four islets 13km from the

coast and reachable from Cayenne's Marina de Degrad-des-Cannes at Monjoly, east of the city centre, **Îlet la Mère** (⊕ilet-la-mere. com) is home to an abundance of squirrel monkeys, iguanas, caimans and red ibis. You can either walk around the island's perimeter (3.5km; 1hr 30min), with its various viewpoints and picnic spots, or else hike up to the old semaphore tower to admire the environs. Or both. Count on making this a day-trip, since the boat (€34; ☏594 28 01 04) departs the marina at 8.30am, 9.15am, 10.30am and 2.30pm, returning four to six hours later (departures and returns are fixed per boat; times may vary with tides).

Overnight stays on this wild islet are forbidden (bring sunscreen, water and food for the day, as there are no shops).

Cacao

A slice of Asia in Guyana's interior, about 75km southwest of Cayenne, **CACAO** was settled in 1977 by refugees from Laos. Since then, this small Hmong community has become the fruit and vegetable basket of the département because of the extensive cultivation of Cacao's steep hillsides. It's best visited on Sunday, market day, when you can chow down on large bowls of phô, porc caramel, spring rolls and other outstanding Laotian dishes in and around the central market building. Next door is **Le Planeur Bleu** (Sun 9am–1pm & 2–4pm; other days by appointment; €4; ☏594 27 00 34), a museum that contains a wealth of insects and a butterfly garden, along with old coins, artefacts from penal colonies and other bric-a-brac from French Guiana's history. Demonstrations by resident naturalists give you the chance to hold live tarantulas.

ARRIVAL AND DEPARTURE

By car Take the RN2 towards the airport and continue south toward St-Georges before turning off along the beautiful, winding 12km road to Cacao.

ACCOMMODATION

Quimbe Kio ☏594 270 122, ✉infos@quimbekio.com. Overnight stays on a wooded hill near the centre, either in a *carbet* (€5 discount if you bring your own hammock) or in one of the en-suite rooms (breakfast included). Kayaking, boat and quad tours available. With demi-pension (obligatory) doubles €100, *carbets* €40

ROURA AND KAW

Some 75km east of Cacao, across the heavily forested Kaw Hills, the Everglades-style swamp Marais De Kaw covers around one thousand square kilometres, an excellent place to spot water birds, including flamingos. Tour operators such as Le Morpho and Riché & Kaw (see page 677) offer wildlife-spotting boat trips along the river, after-dark *pirogue* trips to spot black caiman and overnight stays in a floating carbet. When driving to Kaw, you pass through the pleasant village of **Roura**, where it's possible to arrange kayak rentals and boat trips to Îlet la Mère (see page 684). At the Reserve Naturelle Tresor, about midway between Roura and Kaw, two well-maintained interpretive trails wind through protected forest, habitat for red howler monkeys, scarlet macaws and dyeing dart frogs.

ARRIVAL AND DEPARTURE

Visitors to Kaw arrive as part of an organized tour or by rented car. In addition, Agglobus Ligne D has daily departures from Montoury Eglise (reachable from Cayenne on Ligne 7) to/ from Roura (€5).

ACCOMMODATION AND EATING

If you're planning to stay overnight, arrangements should be made in advance.
Auberge de Camp Caïman PK 36, Route de Kaw ☏594 307 277. In between Roura and Kaw, this eco-friendly large wooden hostel with a library offers neatly kept doubles and several *carbets*. Butterfly-catching, marsh walks and other activities on demand. Meals available on request. Closed Wed. Doubles €40, *carbets* (including hammock rental) €15
Habitation Rour' Attitude 6 rue Edgard Yago, Roura ☏594 37 04 07, ⊕ location-guyane.fr. These finely crafted split-level *carbets* and bungalows with fully equipped kitchens descend the hillside to the Roura River. Kayak rentals offered. Bungalows €115, *carbets* €20
★ **Malou & Son Verger** Route de Kaw ☏694 21 07 12 ⊕malou-et-son-verger.fr. 3km east of Roura, this roadside lodge has a pair of Zen-simple a/c rooms and dining area opening on a breezy terrace that overlooks the orchard. It's a favourite with serious birdwatchers. Malou prepares superb Creole cuisine and juices (three-course *prix fixe* €25) for lodge guests or by reservation. Doubles €60, *carbets* €15

KOUROU

There's not much to **KOUROU**, a seaside town built mainly to service the **Centre Spatial Guyanais** – the space station that

7

INTO BRAZIL

From the south side of Canal Laussat in Cayenne, minibuses to Régina and Saint-Georges run from 5am to 6pm by both private operators (€40) and TIG (€30). *Do not* drive between Cayenne and Saint-Georges at night or pick up hitchhikers along the Régina/Saint-Georges road; French authorities periodically clamp down on those seen to assist illegal immigrants. Saint-Georges is a small border town with a lively Brazilian feel, used as the jumping-off point for Brazil and tours of local indigenous villages along the Oyapok River.

To cross over to **Brazil**, non-EU passport holders must get their passport stamped at the Police aux Frontières (Rue du Commandant Kodji, four blocks from river; daily 8am–6pm; closed for lunch). Then take one of the motorized canoes across the river to **Oiapoque** in Brazil (15min; €5). The Pont Sur l'Oyapock opened in 2017 (Mon–Fri 8am–6pm, Sat 8am–noon); there's an immigration post on the approach ramp where you may stamp out.

Once in Brazil, get your passport stamped by the **Policia Federal**; from the boat dock go right to Avenida Barão do Rio Branco, then left until a small church. The office is on the right side, 250m past the church. Currency exchange houses and ATMs in both Saint-Georges and Oiapoque can change your euros into reais and vice-versa.

If travelling further into Brazil, there are noon and 5 or 6pm buses daily from Oiapoque to Macapá (10–24hr; R$100). The terminal is 3km east of the centre along the main road.

ACCOMMODATION IN SAINT-GEORGES

Chez Modestine Rue Elie Elfort ☎ 594 37 00 13. Functional a/c en-suite rooms in a traditional house on the main square. The wi-fi-ready café functions as the town's nerve centre. **€60**

Ilha do Sol ☎ 694 407 311. Take a *pirogue* (5min; €2) to this Brazilian-run psychedelic shack on an island in the river to swing a hammock or stay in a basic double. Meals are served on the delightful veranda. Doubles **€30**, *carbets* **€12**

---

employs the majority of its residents. But if your timing is right, you can witness one of the most impressive spectacles you're ever likely to see: the fiery launching of a rocket into space.

The town is also the departure point for French Guiana's next biggest tourist attraction – the Îles du Salut.

Centre Spatial Guyanais

Like something out of a Bond film, the launch towers at the **CENTRE SPATIAL GUYANAIS** stand amid tropical forest. The CSG (3hr guided tours Mon–Thurs 8.15am & 1pm, Fri 8.15am; free but advance reservation essential, visitors must be over 8 years old and provide ID; ☎ 594 326 123, ⊕cnes-csg.fr) occupies an area of 690 square kilometres and has sent more than five hundred rockets (most carrying satellites) into orbit since Véronique blasted off on April 9, 1968. **Tours** take in all three rocket sites, and include a film charting the site's history and a visit to the Jupiter Control Centre. No tours take place on launch days, or the days before and after.

The partially interactive, state-of-the-art **Musée de l'Espace** (Mon–Fri 8am–6pm, Sat 2–6pm; €7 or €4 if on a guided tour of the CSG), next to the CSG welcome centre, introduces visitors to space exploration, with exhibitions on human space flight, the history of the base, the universe and more, through multimedia animations, space-related artefacts and temporary exhibits. The museum is sometimes closed on launch days.

Unless visiting the CSG via a tour operator, make your own way by car, or else take a bus (see below) from Cayenne to Kourou and then a taxi to the site.

ARRIVAL AND INFORMATION

With no public transport to speak of, carless travellers must navigate Kourou on foot.

By minibus TIG Ligne 5 (⊕tig5.info) runs eight minibuses to/from Cayenne Mon–Fri (fewer on weekends) with a stop at the Médiathèque (1hr, €10), while Ligne 7 goes to/from St-Laurent thrice daily (€25). Various private services such as Transport Antoinette (☎ 694 16 73 54) pick up/drop off at your lodging.

Tourist information Av de L'Anse (Mon–Fri 9am–1pm & 3–4.30 or 6pm, Sat 9am–noon; ☎ 594 32 98 33, ✉ot-kourou@orange.fr). Impressive collection of information in French and English on the space centre, Îles du Salut and Kourou.

ACCOMMODATION

Budget travellers can pitch a hammock at the *carbets* at the lower end of the beach at Plage de la Cocoteraie (no facilities). Accommodation tends to be booked up weeks in advance if there's a rocket launch due.

Hôtel Le Ballahou 1–3 Rue Amet-Martial ☎ 594 22 00 22, ⍟ hotel-ballahou.com. The stucco structure is in a quiet backstreet near the beach's western end, about 3km from the jetty to the islands. Some of the bright, colourful en-suite rooms feature kitchenettes. Studios €69, doubles €56

Résidence le Gros Bec 56 Rue D. Floch ☎ 594 32 91 91, ☎ hotel.legrosbec@orange.fr. Only three blocks from the catamaran dock for the Îles du Salut, this gated compound has English-speaking staff and offers studios with kitchenettes around a relaxing garden. Studios €89

EATING AND DRINKING

You'll find a few places to eat, drink and be reasonably merry on the seafront Av de l'Anse and along Av du Général de Gaulle.

Bar Le 13 60 Av Gaston-Monnerville. Metros gather nightly under the ceiling fans of this tropical hall for the continental beers on tap. It's in the district of Monnerville, west of the centre. Daily 6.30pm–1am.

L'orchidée 6 Allée de L'Europe, off Av F. Kennedy, opposite the post office. Heaped portions of delicious Vietnamese food – it's difficult to go wrong with the phô or any of the noodle dishes. Mains from €8. Daily noon–10.30pm.

Restaurant le Flamengo 42 Rue du Général de Gaulle ☎ 594 32 00 34. Wild game (*paca*, *agouti*) is the basis for various Creole stews, served with plenty of rice, brown beans and fiery pepper at this soulful kitchen. There's an open-air pavilion out front. Mains €15–18. 9am–2.30pm & 7–10pm; closed Thurs.

ÎLES DU SALUT

The **ÎLES DU SALUT**, 15km off the coast, comprise three beautiful islands shaded with coconut trees and surrounded by azure waters: **Île Royale**, **Île Saint-Joseph** and **Île du Diable**. Their English name – Salvation Islands – is an ironic misnomer, given their use as a penal colony responsible for the deaths of over 50,000 of its 70,000 prisoners between 1852 and 1953. Thanks to Henri Charrière's book, *Papillon*, which recounts the horrors of life in the colony and his various attempts at escape, the islands are the country's most popular attraction.

WHAT TO SEE AND DO

Île Royale, the main and most-visited island, was originally used for administration and housing common-law criminals. You can peer at the ruins of old buildings and go swimming in the small bay sheltered from the sea by rocks. The fearless wildlife is another attraction and you're certain to spot monkeys and agouti.

Île Royale is home to the islands' only hotel and rather pricey restaurant – consider picnicking on the beach instead. The small **Musée du Bagne** (daily 10am–noon & 2.30–4pm; free), in the old colony administrator's mansion beside the jetty, covers the grim history of the islands, all of it translated into readable English.

BLAST OFF! VISITING A ROCKET LAUNCH

Few spectacles compare to the sight of a rocket leaving the atmosphere for outer space. There's a launch pretty much every month, usually scheduled on a weekday night, and the one you're most likely to see is Ariane 5 – the French rocket that frequently launches satellites into orbit. The Centre Spatial Guyanais has six official observation sites from which you can watch the rocket launch: Agami, Venus, Ibis, Jupiter, Colibri and Toucan; access is limited and by invitation only. To obtain an **invitation** (you must be over 16), go to the Centre's website (wcnes-csg.fr) and click on "Assistez a un lancement". Your ticket will be emailed to you. Delays are possible, so it helps if your schedule is flexible. On the day of the launch, visitors assemble at the Médiathèque du Kourou, from where they are taken to the assigned observation sites by a convoy of coaches (free). You'll most likely end up at Agami, Toucan or Colibri (5.5–7.5km from the launch site), where you'll watch the countdown on the giant screen and have an unobstructed view of the rocket itself for a spectacle lasting between seven and thirty minutes. Even without an invitation, it's possible to drive up to Carapa, 5km west of Kourou, to view the launch, or otherwise from Pointe de Roches, at the south end of the beach. Or even from Cayenne: crowds gather at Place des Amandiers, where a closed-circuit broadcast is customarily set up, to watch the blastoff.

ÎLES DU SALUT TOURS

Various catamaran operators run day tours, departing between 7 and 8 am from Kourou's *appontement des pêcheurs* (fishermen's jetty) at the end of Avenue du Général de Gaulle (€48–51). It takes a little more than an hour over choppy waters to reach Île Royale, with complimentary drinks and a bit of background (in French). You're free to roam the island till after lunch, then transported to nearby Île Saint-Joseph for an afternoon wander (some opt to swim to the island's shores rather than ride the raft from the anchor point). Finally you are taken back to Kourou at 5pm. Should you wish to spend the night, Pro Maritime (☎ 594 28 42 36, ⊛ promaritimeguyane.fr), connected to the island's lodgings, charges €43 for the round-trip journey; it will cost you an additional €5 to hop over to Saint-Joseph.

TOUR OPERATORS
La Hulotte ☎ 594 323 381, ⊛ www.lahulotte-guyane.fr.

Tropic Alizes ☎ 694 40 20 20, ⊛ ilesdusalut-guyane.com.

7

"Incorrigible" convicts and those who tried to escape were sent to **Île Saint-Joseph**. Today it's home to a small naval base, and visitors can take the tranquil, coconut-tree-lined path around the perimeter of the island, or climb up to explore the ruins of the penal colony, now overgrown with vegetation.

The Île du Diable is off-limits to visitors, although the swimming area on the northeast side of the Île Royale offers views of its wrecked prison buildings.

ACCOMMODATION

Auberge des Îles Île Royale ☎ 594 321 100, ⊜ comercial@aubergedesiles.fr. Choices at the isles' only lodgings range from bright and breezy rooms in the main building to more modern studios with fantastic private balconies behind it, to cheaper digs in the old guards' barracks to the former prison block for hammock owners, with access to bathroom facilities. During high season (July–Nov) reserve ahead of arrival, outside these months you can show up on spec. Suite with obligatory meals €272, guards' quarter €70, hammocks €12.50

SAINT LAURENT DU MARONI

Outside **SAINT LAURENT DU MARONI**'s tourist office is a statue of a convict with his head in his hands – an apt monument to despair, given that this town was a transportation camp for prisoners until the middle of the twentieth century. Saint Laurent is less homogeneous than the capital, thanks to the porous border between French Guiana and Suriname; the large number of illegal Surinamese, Brazilian and Guyanese residents

accounts for the melange of languages spoken and the laidback feel of this riverside frontier town. The town is the best base for excursions up the **Maroni River**, visits to the **indignous** and **Maroon** communities or the beautiful **Voltaire Falls**.

WHAT TO SEE AND DO

Saint Laurent has some fine colonial architecture in the triangular "Petit Paris" area north of Rue du Lieutenant-Colonel Chandon, such as the old bank and town hall.

Camp de la Transportation

The **Camp de la Transportation**, where prisoners were processed before their final destinations, is an imposing complex. You can walk around the grounds, with some interpretive signs, but access to the cells is by guided tour only and not to be missed (Mon 3pm & 4.30pm, Tues–Sat 9.30am, 11am, 3pm & 4.30pm, Sun 9.30am & 11am; 1hr 15min; €6; tours in English available; tickets sold at the tourist office). An informed peek into the horrors of French transportation puts everything into chilling context. Cell no. 47 supposedly once held Papillon.

A recent addition to the complex, Le Centre de L'Architecture et du Patromonie (Tues–Sat 9am–noon & 2.30–5.30pm, Sun 9am–12.30pm; €6, credit card only) features exhibits, creatively installed in some of the camp's old administrative buildings, on the lives of the convicts, the town's architectural styles, the ethnically varied population of present-day St-Laurent, and contemporary photography.

ARRIVAL AND DEPARTURE

By plane There are daily flights to/from Cayenne with Air Guyane (ⓦairguyane.com), as well as up the Maroni River to Maripasoula and Grand Santi.

By minibus From 4am to 5pm, minibuses to Kourou/ Cayenne (€25/35) depart as they fill from La Glacière, a lot at the bottom of Blvd du Général de Gaulle. From the same place, TIG Ligne 7/Transport Antoinette (ⓣ694 23 15 06) has three scheduled departures daily to Kourou. In addition, Transport Best (ⓣ694 28 11 50) offers a service to Awala-Yalimapo (€10) from the *gare routière*, three blocks north of the market.

Destinations Awala-Yalimapo (1hr 10min); Cayenne (4hr); Kourou (2hr 30min).

SAINT LAURENT FESTIVALS

Saint Laurent has a festival or three happening pretty much every month, all celebrated in the sandy Place de la Republique. Festivities not to miss include January's **Carnaval**; **Nereid's Ralleye**, a regatta heralding the arrival of sailboats from Trinidad in early October; and **Les Journées de la Culture Bushinengué** (a celebration of traditional Maroon culture), in late October.

INFORMATION

Tourist information The Office du Tourisme at 1 Esplanade Laurent Baudin (Mon 2.30–6pm, Tues–Sat 8am–12.30pm & 2.30–6pm, Sun 8.30am–12.30pm; ⓣ594 342 398, ⓦot-saintlaurentdumaroni.fr) provides

SAINT-LAURENT DU MARONI

ACCOMMODATION
Amazonie Accueil — 3
Hôtel la Tentiaire — 1
Star Hôtel — 2

EATING
Café Kaho Melho — 3
Chez Felicia — 1
La Goëlette — 4
Tipic Kréol's — 2

Maroni River

PLACE DE LA RÉPUBLIQUE

ALBERT SARRAUT
AVENUE LÉON GONTRAND DAMAS
AVE DÉSIRÉE TIMAUT
BOULEVARD MALOUET
AVENUE DU PRÉSIDENT F. ROOSEVELT
AVENUE CARNOT
AVENUE DANTON
RUE GASTON DARQUITAIN
RUE EUGENE NONNON
RUE JEANNE GARRE
ESPLANADE LAURENT BAUDIN
Town Hall
The Old Bank
RUE DU LIEUTENANT-COLONEL CHANDON
AV FÉLIX ÉBOUÉ
RUE LÉA CHAPELAIN
Pharmacie Forum Santé
LCL
RUE MORTRAVEL
Gare Routière
RUE ANDRÉ TANON
RUE DE L'HÔPITAL
Camp de la Transportation
RUE VICTOR HUGO
RUE S. RAYNARD
Stadium
RUE SCHOELCHER
AVENUE FÉLIX ÉBOUÉ
Market
RUE J.J. ROUSSEAU
RUE LAURENT BAUDIN
AVENUE GASTON MONNERVILLE
Economink
St-Laurent-du-Maroni Cemetery
RUE MARCEAU
AVENUE DE GENERAL DE GAULLE
Stadium
RUE THIERS
AVENUE JOSEPH SYMPHORIEN
RUE DU LIEUTENANT COLONEL TOURTET
RUE SIMON
RUE GUYNEMER
RUE H. RIVIEREZ
RUE JUSTIN CATAYEE
VILLAGE CHINOIS
RUE ROLAND BARRAT

0 — 250
metres

⓸ ,Minibuses to Kourou and Cayenne, ▼ Immigration, Ferries to Suriname, Airport & Saint-Maurice   ▼ Airport, Apatou & Voltaire Falls

Budget, N1, Awala-Yalimapo & Kourou

7

EXCURSIONS FROM SAINT LAURENT

The **Maroni River** lends itself to a variety of activities – from visits to indigenous and Maroon villages by pirogue to swimming, fishing, wildlife-spotting and jungle trekking. Trips range from two-hour to multi-day adventures.

Apatou is an Aluku Maroon village, about 70km upriver from Saint Laurent, and is a great place to experience Maroon culture and food. It's at the end of the road, and Taxi Fabrice ☎ 694 24 09 00 can take you there. Otherwise, Maroni Tours arranges visits to the village, as well as longer stays.

A visit to the secluded **Voltaire Falls**, about 73km south of St Laurent, is very rewarding. Getting there involves a 4WD journey through dense forest via the Route de Paul Isnard and Route d'Apatou forest roads, followed by a one-hour-thirty-minute hike. Tour operators including Nature de Guyane (see below) follow this up with a climb up to **L'Inselberg**, a peak with views over the jungle canopy, and set up camp there. Otherwise, you can stay at **L'Auberge des Chutes Voltaire** (ⓦ aubergechutesvoltaire.com; with *demi-pension* doubles €100, *carbets* €80; advance bookings only), on the banks of the Voltaire River, close to the Falls.

TOUR OPERATORS

Amazonie Accueil 3 Rue Barrat, Saint Laurent ☎ 594 34 36 12, ⓔ am.ac@orange.fr.

Maroni Tours Village de Saint-Jean ☎ 594 30 70 80, ⓦ maronitours.com.

Nature de Guyane ☎ 594 27 97 16, ⓦ naturedeguyane.com.

the excellent *Discover Saint-Laurent du Maroni* booklet, as well as other useful information, and also rents Velo-Style bicycles at €10/20 per half/whole day.

ACCOMMODATION

Amazonie Accueil 3 Rue R. Barrat ☎ 594 34 36 12; map p.683. Hang your hammock along with up to eight other backpackers at this in-town carbet, with adequate bathroom facilities. Knowledgeable owner Gilbert leads pirogue tours up the Maroni and prepares breakfast. Also known as La Boîte à Cheveux, for the adjacent hair salon. *Carbets* **€15**

Star Hôtel 26 Rue Thiers ☎ 594 34 10 84; map p.683. This central hotel is where the *gendarmes* stay on tour, with functional tiled rooms around an ovate swimming pool. Conveniently located opposite the soccer field and beside a lively bar terrace. **€68**

Hôtel la Tentiaire 12 Av du President F. Roosevelt ☎ 594 34 26 00, ⓔ tentiaire@wanadoo.fr; map p.683. The nicest hotel in the centre of town, complete with stylish rooms (some with balconies), friendly service and swimming pool. Advance booking advised, as this place is the first to fill up. **€65**

EATING

Try to be in town on a Wednesday or Saturday, when the Central Market is taken over by the Hmong community and people share long central tables for hearty bowls of *phô* (€5–8) and *nems* (spring rolls). Other stalls squeeze up tropical fruit beverages.

Café Kaho Melho 1 bis Av Hector Rivierez; map p.683. Catch up on the local word at this busy bakery/café with

pavement tables, offering fresh croissants and pastries from very early. Mon–Sat 5.30am–1pm.

Chez Felicia 23 Av du Général de Gaulle; map p.683. A low-key, family-run bistro going strong after three decades, *Felicia's* menu focuses on generous portions of Creole dishes. Mains €9–12. Generally Mon–Thurs & Sat noon–2.30pm & 7.30–10pm.

La Goëlette 17 Rue des Amazone ☎ 594 34 28 97; map p.683. This boat-restaurant is the most atmospheric place for a meal for miles around. The quality of the Creole and French dishes matches the ambience and there are music sessions on Sunday nights. It's at Balaté beach, 3km south of the centre. Mains €18–20. Tues–Sun noon–2pm & 7–9pm.

★ **Tipic Kreol's** 24 Rue Thiers ☎ 594 34 09 83; map p.683. An invariably lively spot with open-air dining under a big thatched roof, this temple of Creole cuisine is a good place to sample wild game like agouti, armadillo and paca, the basis for *fricassées*, and the locally fished "*jamais goûtée*", which you've certainly never tasted before. Mains €14–18.

DIRECTORY

Banks and post office The post office at the north end of Av du Général du Gaulle (Mon–Fri 8am–4pm, Sat 8am–noon, closed Sun) has a pair of reliable ATMs. There is no currency exchange.

Car rental Budget (328 Av Gaston Monnerville ☎ 594 34 02 94, wbudget-guyane.com) has an office by a petrol station (closed noon–3pm).

Internet Economink Cyber, at 25 Av Félix Eboué.

Pharmacy Pharmacie Forum Santé, 36 Rue du Lieutenant-Colonel Chandon.

PLAGE LES HATTES

From roughly March to July, the wide, clean stretch of sand that is **Plage Les Hattes**, at the mouth of the Maroni River a few kilometres from the Suriname border, is French Guiana's best place to view endangered **leatherback turtles** laying their eggs. Leatherbacks are massive – they can grow up to 1.6m in length and weigh up to 750kg. During peak egg-laying season, an estimated 200 turtles crawl up onto the beach each night to lay their eggs. In August and September thousands of baby turtles can be seen hatching at night and dashing towards the water to escape predators.

The indigenous twin village of **Awala-Yalimapo** is 4km from the beach. Unless you are part of an organized tour, it's best to rent a car and base yourself here, or in the pleasant town of Mana 20km away. You can also stay on the beach itself (in which case bring food, water, a hammock and mosquito protection).

In early December, Yalimapo is the scene of **Les Jeux Kali'na** (wawala-yalimapo.fr), a sort of Guianan Olympics in which athletes compete at such ancient skills as harpoon throwing, coconut palm climbing and Le Jeu de Diable, a devilishly difficult puzzle challenge. There

CONVICT ART

If you happen to be driving between Saint Laurent and Cayenne, you'll invariably pass through Iracoubo. The **Eglise Saint Joseph d'Iracoubo** by the roadside is famed for its interior, covered with wildly colourful fresco paintings that sprang from the imagination of Pierre Huguet, a convict and untrained artist who painted them between 1892 and 1898.

are musical performances by regional artists too.

ARRIVAL AND DEPARTURE

By minibus Transport Best (☎ 694 28 11 50) has a 6am departure to Awala-Yalimapo (€10) from the gare routière, three blocks north of Saint Laurent's central market.

By car Plage Les Hattes is some 60km from Saint Laurent. Take the N1 toward Cayenne and about 5km east, turn left onto the D9 to Mana, from where it's a 20km ride over a good paved road to Awala-Yalimapo. Plage Les Hattes is less than 1km from Yalimapo, the westernmost of the two villages.

ACCOMMODATION AND EATING

Gite Yalimalé ☎ 594 34 71 05, ✉ yalimale@hotmail. com. Attached to a snack bar in the village of Yalimapo, with hammocks in four thatched huts. Carbets with hammock €20

Kudawyada 260 Av du 31 Décembre 1988 ☎ 594 34 20 60, ✉ kydawyada.sk@gmail.com. About 1km east of Yalimapo, this retreat has three mosquito-proofed thatch-roofed *carbets* for hammock slingers, each with toilets and

CROSSING BETWEEN FRENCH GUIANA AND SURINAME

The **ferry** runs between Saint Laurent and **Albina** in Suriname (3–6 daily; 7am–5.30pm; €4 one-way for foot passengers; motorbike/car €15.50/€34; euros only). Unless you have a vehicle (and rental vehicles may not cross borders), the quickest way to cross the Maroni River is to take one of the many **motorized dugout canoes** (10–15min; €3 or SRD27). When crossing the river, ask to be dropped off either at the **Surinamese Immigration office** (daily 7am–7pm) or the **French Immigration office** (daily 6am–6pm) – both located at the ferry piers – to get your visa checked and passport stamped. For Suriname, most passport holders require either a visa or a Tourist Card (see page 661).

There is a **cambio** near the Albina ferry terminal, which gives good rates when exchanging Suriname and US dollars for euros: change your money here, as in Saint Laurent there are no money-changing services. The French Immigration office is around 2km south of the centre of Saint Laurent; taxis charge €5 for the five-minute ride downtown; otherwise it's a twenty-minute walk. Unlike Saint Laurent, Albina is not a town to linger in; minibuses (SRD80–100) and taxis (SRD150–200) meet the ferries and take passengers to Paramaribo (2–3hr). State buses between Albina and Paramaribo run from the centre of Albina; take a taxi (SRD5) to and from the pier.

showers, all set in a woodsy patch near the beach. *Carbets with hammock* €20

Le Samana Hôtel 18 Rue bruno Aubert ☎ 594 27 87 73, ✉ hotellesamana@orange.fr. This sleek self-contained modern hotel with attached café stands by the bank of the Mana River, on the outskirts of the town of the same name, 20km from Plage Les Hattes. *Studios* €70, *doubles* €60

Simili Youth Hostel ☎ 594 34 16 25, ✉ ajs.simili@ wanadoo.fr. Some 2.5km east of Yalimapo village, this beachside complex has accommodation to suit all tastes, from basic bungalows sleeping two to six people to a large *carbet* with mosquito-netted hammocks (bring your own for €8 discount); meals provided on request. Leatherbacks nest on the beach here, and it's beside the Reserve Naturelle de l'Amana, a protected forest with a well-marked interpretive nature trail. Outside turtle season, advance reservations are a must. *Bungalow/person* €5, *carbets* €15

CENTRAL ASUNCIÓN

Paraguay

❶ **The Paraguayan Pantanal** Spot a wealth of birds and mammals, including giant otters, anteaters and armadillos. See page 692

❷ **Asunción** Learn about Paraguay's history by day and bar-hop by night. See page 695

❸ **San Bernardino** Watch the sunset over the great lake in this tranquil holiday town. See page 701

❹ **The Ruta Jesuítica** Stargaze at remote Jesuit missions and explore under-threat Atlantic Forest. See page 704

❺ **The Chaco Mennonites** The Mennonites share this immense wilderness with indigenous tribes and jaguars. See page 712

HIGHLIGHTS ARE MARKED ON THE MAP ON PAGE 689

ROUGH COSTS

Daily budget basic US$30, occasional treat US$50
Drink 1 litre Pilsen beer US$4
Food *Sopa paraguaya* US$0.75, *asado* US$10
Hostel/budget hotel US$12–15/US$25–40
Travel Asunción–Encarnación (365km): bus US$11

FACT FILE

Population 6.8 million
Language Guaraní and Castellano (Spanish). The blending of the two languages is known as *Jopará*.
Currency Guaraní (Gs)
Capital Asunción (population: 2.3 million)
International phone code ☎ 595
Time zone GMT -4hr

Introduction

Paraguay is billed as the "Heart of South America", but perhaps "South America's forgotten corner" is more appropriate. Despite being one of the most traditional countries on the continent, with an indigenous tongue as its official language (Guaraní) and the vast majority of the population proudly bilingual, Paraguay is far too often passed over by travellers. Those who do stop here find themselves pleasantly surprised by the rich culture, host of under-promoted natural attractions, fascinating and bloodthirsty history and real feeling of being "off the beaten track".

Paraguay combines the scorching, arid wilderness of the **Chaco** – one of the best places in South America to see large mammals – with the wet and humid **Atlantic Forest** of eastern Paraguay; the rampant commercialism of **Ciudad del Este** with the muted, backwater feel of colonial towns like **Concepción**. Paraguay is difficult to pin down, in part due to its mixed immigrant intake over the past century; you're as likely to stumble across a colony of Japanese migrants, Mennonites or Australian socialists as you are to meet an indigenous tribe. The small country is not lacking in attractions – it is part-owner of the second-largest hydroelectric dam in the world and home to superbly preserved **Jesuit-Guaraní missions** – but tourism is undeveloped. Don't let this deter you, though; if you've a sense of adventure and crave a real, uncommercialized South American experience, you'll definitely find it here in Paraguay.

CHRONOLOGY

1537 The Spanish found the city of Nuestra Señora de Asunción.

1609 Jesuit missionaries arrive with the aim of converting indigenous tribes.

1767 The Jesuits are expelled from Paraguay by King Charles III of Spain.

1811 Paraguay declares its independence from Spain in a bloodless revolution.

1814 Dr José Gáspar Rodríguez de Francia is chosen as the first president and takes Paraguay into a period of isolation and industrialization.

1816 Rodríguez de Francia declares himself "El Supremo" – dictator for life, becoming progressively more arbitrary through his reign, suppressing the Church, isolating the country and taking to torturing opposition.

1844 Rodríguez de Francia is succeeded by Carlos Antonio López and Paraguay enters its period of greatest prosperity.

1862 Francisco Solano "Mariscal" López takes over as president from his ailing father, who leaves him with the deathbed advice that the pen is mightier than the sword.

1865–70 López launches Paraguay into the disastrous War of the Triple Alliance against Brazil, Argentina and Uruguay, which sees the country lose vast sections of its territory and more than seventy percent of its adult male population.

1927 The first Mennonites arrive in Paraguay, part of a campaign to colonize the Chaco.

1932–37 The Chaco War breaks out after rumours of undiscovered oil reserves provoke a violent reaction from the Paraguayan government at Bolivian army presence in the Paraguayan Chaco.

1954 After 22 presidents in 31 years, General Alfredo Stroessner seizes power and goes on to become the longest-lasting dictator in South American history, holding power for 34 years.

1989 Stroessner is driven into exile and Paraguay declares itself a Republic.

WHEN TO VISIT

Paraguay is an extremely hot country for most of the year. Eastern Paraguay can be very humid, while the Dry Chaco (northwest) is arid. The hottest time is November to February, when daytime temperatures peak at around 45°C (or hotter in the Chaco) and high atmospheric pressure makes simply walking along the street a tough task. Winter (June–Aug) is often pleasantly warm during the day (around 20–25°C), generally sunny and dry, though can get as cold as 5°C. Between September and November spectacular electric storms are frequent and travelling off-road can be difficult.

1993 The first democratic elections are held, and are won by the quasi-liberal Colorados, effectively returning Stroessner's political party to power.

1999 Eight protesters are shot dead by snipers during pro-democracy protests during a month of unrest now referred to as the Marzo Paraguayo.

2008 Fernando Lugo, an ex-Catholic priest with a socialist agenda, defeats the Colorado Party candidate, ending 61 years of Colorado party rule.

2012 Lugo is impeached in a 24hr period in what many consider a "parliamentary" coup d'état. His vice president, Federico Franco, continues the presidency until the 2013 general elections.

2013 The leader of the Colorado Party, Horacio Cartes, wins the general election and becomes president.

2017 The Congress building is partially burned down and one protestor shot dead by police in protests against a secret vote in the Senate to change the constitution and allow sitting president Horacio Cartes to stand for re-election. Following the riots, Cartes confirms he won't stand in the 2018 elections.

ARRIVAL AND DEPARTURE

If you're **arriving by land**, be aware that buses frequently cross the border without stopping at the customs post. It is your responsibility to get exit stamps from Bolivia, Brazil and Argentina and the required entry stamp for Paraguay or you risk a substantial fine – inform your driver that you need stamps and take your bags with you as buses won't always wait.

The entry stamp entitles you to a ninety-day stay in Paraguay and this can be renewed once at a cost of Gs340,185 at the Immigration Office (Caballero, at Ayala) in Asunción. A **yellow fever certificate** may also be demanded at border control.

BY PLANE

Those arriving on international flights will land at Aeropuerto Internacional Silvio

HIGHLIGHTS
1. The Paraguayan Pantanal
2. Asunción
3. San Bernardino
4. The Ruta Jesuítica
5. The Chaco Mennonites

Pettirossi (☎021 688 2000, ⓦdinac.gov. py), 15km northeast of Asunción in the suburb of Luque. The main **airlines** operating in and out of Paraguay are: LATAM (to Brazil, Bolivia, Peru, Argentina and Chile; ⓦlatam.com); Amaszonas (internally to Ciudad del Este and externally to Bolivia, Argentina and Uruguay; ⓦamaszonas.com); Aerolineas Argentinas (to Buenos Aires, Cordoba and Madrid; ⓦaerolineas.com.ar); Avianca (to Lima; ⓦavianca.com); GOL (to various Brazilian cities; ⓦvoegol.com.br); Air Europa (to Madrid; ⓦaireuropa.com). It's a good idea to confirm your flight 24 hours in advance, as there are often cancellations. You are no longer required to pay a departure tax. In the military airbase next door, SETAM, (☎021 645 885) has Wednesday flights to Bahía Negra, via Concepción.

FROM ARGENTINA

Argentina wraps around all of southern Paraguay and is easily accessible. From Asunción many international buses make a quick exit out of Paraguay across the river headed towards Formosa, Resistencia and Corrientes in Argentina. The border city of Encarnación sits across the River Paraná from **Posadas**; international buses connect the terminals on each side of the border. Similar buses run from Ciudad del Este in Paraguay to **Puerto Iguazú**, making day-trips to the falls – or onwards into Argentina – easy (see page 710).

FROM BOLIVIA

Land crossings from Bolivia are fairly straightforward in good weather, less so during heavy rains. A paved but potholed road branches off from the Trans-Chaco to cross the border at **Fortín Infante Rivarola**; international buses stop here en route from Santa Cruz to Asunción. There's no passport control, so border formalities must be done elsewhere (see page 713).

FROM BRAZIL

The busiest border crossing with Brazil is the **Puente de la Amistad** ("friendship bridge") linking Ciudad del Este with Foz do Iguaçu. Regular buses make the short crossing, and it is also possible by taxi, motorcycle-taxi (much cheaper) or even on foot (see page 710). Many other border crossings with Brazil, such as that at Pedro Juan Caballero, are popular smuggling routes and considered unsafe.

PASSPORT AND VISAS

A **passport** valid for the period of stay is required by all visitors, except residents of Argentina or Brazil who can use their national identity cards. Australian, Canadian and US citizens need to get an **entry visa** before travelling; Western European and UK citizens do not (see ⓦworldtravelguide.net for a list of countries not requiring visas).

GETTING AROUND

Buses in Paraguay are cheap and easy, although they may stop short of national parks, *estancias* or other isolated attractions. Renting a car is extremely expensive and not recommended if driving alone or for non-Spanish speakers.

BY BUS

The easiest and cheapest way to get around Paraguay is by **bus**; there are frequent, affordable and reliable services between the major cities. Visiting areas away from these is more difficult and bus services – when they exist – are uncomfortable. Journey durations and departure times tend to be erratic, as buses leave when full and may pick further passengers up en route.

Asunción is the country's major transport hub and there are so many companies at the main "Terminal" (see page 698) that, outside of the holiday seasons, there is no need to book tickets in advance. The quality of service varies greatly: in general, you get what you pay for. Pluma (ⓦpluma.com.br) has services to Brazil, NSA (ⓦnsa.com.py) offers national bus services as well as international routes to Argentina, while Crucero del Norte (ⓦcrucerodelnorte. com.ar) is an Argentine company whose buses link up most of the southern half of the continent.

BY CAR

Renting a **car** is possible only in Asunción, Ciudad del Este or Encarnación, and a 4WD is necessary for the dirt roads that crisscross the country away from the national highway system. Rental is expensive (around Gs1,100,000 per day or more for a 4WD with unlimited mileage), making it difficult to see more remote areas of the country cheaply, though petrol costs are low (around Gs5000 a litre for unleaded). An **international driving licence** is required.

Heading off the Ruta Trans-Chaco on your own is strongly discouraged. If you plan on going deeper into the Chaco than the Mennonite colonies, you should take a guided tour (see page 713) – many tourists come to grief by embarking on poorly planned journeys in an effort to save money. Once past the Mennonite colonies there is nowhere to stay or buy food, and very few places to refuel.

There are rental agencies at the airport in Asunción, including international chains, but the only company that currently serves all three of the main cities is Localiza (☏0800 979 2000, ⓦlocaliza.com); 24hr breakdown cover is provided by the Touring y Automovil Club Paraguayo (TACPy; ☏021 210 550, ⓦtacpy.com.py).

BY TAXI

Taxis are well organized in Paraguay and there is not much need to barter. *Taxistas* are assigned a rank to wait at, and these are clearly marked in towns by a yellow shelter saying "Taxi". Ask for the meter (*contadora*) to be switched on (*prendida*), or at least agree on a price before embarking. Journeys in small towns or around central Asunción will cost around Gs10,000–25,000, while trips out of towns or to airports may be up to Gs100,000.

BY BOAT

Most of the **boats for tourists** in Paraguay are very expensive, but ferries do run to Brazil, Argentina and Bolivia. For the adventurous traveller there is a boat trip from Concepción up the Río Paraguay to Bahía Negra and the Paraguayan Pantanal (see page 692) – or the reverse.

ACCOMMODATION

Accommodation in Paraguay is surprisingly expensive, although you'll usually get air-conditioning, TV, en-suite bathroom and breakfast included. It's not necessary to book in advance, except in Caacupé during the weeks surrounding the Immaculate Conception (Dec 8), during the Carnaval in Encarnación (Feb) and in the Mennonite colonies during the Trans-Chaco Rally (last weekend in Sept), when prices rise dramatically.

In Asunción there are ten or so **youth/ backpacker hostels** that have opened in recent years. Don't bank on **camping** in Paraguay as campsites are few and far between and in rural areas, most land is in private hands so you risk being accused of trespassing if you do not have the permission of the landowner. Times are changing, however, and SENATUR is trying to develop a camping culture to attract tourists; it's worth asking them for updates if you're determined.

FOOD AND DRINK

At first glance, **Paraguayan cuisine** may appear to be based entirely on junk-food joints selling hamburgers, *milanesas* (schnitzels) and pizza. However, a little exploring will uncover a number of excellent restaurants, at least in the major cities. The mainstay of the Paraguayan diet is **asado** – essentially barbecue – almost always accompanied by *mandioca* (manioc, also known as cassava or yucca). The best cuts are *tapa de cuadril*, *corte Americano* and *colita de cuadril*. Those with a weak stomach should avoid *mondongo* (tripe), *lengua* (tongue), *chinchulín* (small intestine) and *tripa gorda* (large intestine). *Morcilla* is black pudding and *chorizo* is sausage – but no relation to Spanish chorizo. *Pollo asado* (grilled chicken) is often sold on roadside grills, and don't forget to try *corazoncitos* (chicken hearts).

Fish is generally expensive and at least twice the price of beef, *surubí* being the most frequently available. For a cheap, tasty snack, *empanadas* (pasties) are widely available and there is almost always somebody selling **chipa** (cheese bread made with manioc flour) – it is best when

8

PARAGUAY'S HARD-TO-REACH NATURAL WONDERS

The immense range of **flora and fauna** in Paraguay should be drawing tourists in their droves; the Chaco is one of the best places in South America to see large mammals, while the Atlantic Forests of eastern Paraguay are some of the most threatened natural habitats on the planet. Paraguay also has a sizeable slice of the mighty Pantanal, a wildlife wonderland normally associated with Brazil. Paraguay suffers from aggressive deforestation and encroaching agrarian interests, but luckily, people are starting to catch on that the country needs protecting. All of the options below are worth investigating, but many – in the Chaco in particular – are notoriously difficult to access. **Fauna Paraguay** (ⓦfaunaparaguay.com) provide an impressive number of ecologically sensitive tours with extremely knowledgeable English-speaking guides (including all of the below). Many of the Asunción-based tour companies (see page 699) will also arrange tours.

Central Chaco Lagoons Correctly the Cuenca del Riacho Yacaré Sur, they are a series of temporal saline lakes east of the Mennonite colonies, whose presence depends on rainfall in previous months. In winter they can be occupied by ducks and Chilean flamingos; from September to December, huge flocks of sandpipers and plovers are attracted to the water. To visit without a tour agency, get in touch with the Mennonites (see page 713) who may be able to provide transport, accommodation and food (upwards of US$250/day).

The Lower Chaco South of Asunción and composed of grassland, marshes and corridors of forest along the rivers, the humid part of the Chaco is also rich in wildlife and best appreciated by volunteering with conservation group Para la Tierra (ⓦparalatierra.org) based in Pilar. They also receive people at Ideal-Eco Hostel (☎098 526 0074, ⓦecohostelideal.wixsite.com/idealeco-hostel; dorms Gs70,000, doubles Gs170,000).

Laguna Blanca One of the most beautiful and peaceful places in Paraguay with its crystal-clear water and much-needed "beaches". Activities such as birdwatching (with a chance of seeing one of the world's rarest birds, the white-winged nightjar), kayaking, snorkelling, fishing and horseriding are available. Unfortunately, the main accommodation (☎021 424 760, ⓦlagunablanca.com.py) temporarily suspended services in 2017; it's worth contacting them directly to check if they're back up and running.

Bosque Mbaracayú This forest reserve, consisting of over 640 square kilometres of Atlantic Forest and *cerrado* habitat, is accessible to tourists thanks to the Fundación Moises Bertoni (Prócer Carlos Argüello 208, Asunción; ☎021 608 740, ⓦaidev.in/fmb; doubles Gs475,000, camping/person Gs35,000). It's home to over 400 bird species, and 89 different mammals, including pumas and jaguars. FMB run a lodge for tourists, and you can hike, canoe, birdwatch or mountain bike with guides. Buses from Asunción go to Villa Ygatimi, 25km from the forest, where FMB can pick you up (Gs250,000 return).

The Pantanal Paraguay's slice of the enormous wetlands spanning Brazil and Bolivia is difficult to reach (a more accessible route is from Corumba, Brazil), and largely not tourist-friendly. However, thanks to its remoteness, people who do make it here are rewarded with many of nature's giants, including giant otters, giant armadillos, giant tegus and giant anteaters. For those short on time, it's best to visit with Fauna Paraguay (see page 692) between April and September – the roads are impassable and flights often cancelled outside of these months. Those with a sense of adventure can visit independently by staying at Tres Gigantes, a research centre run by NGO Guyra Paraguay (ⓦguyra.org.py) 16km from Bahía Negra. Accommodation is at their lodge (Gs240,000, camping/person Gs50,000) and you can join photography safaris, fishing excursions or hike their three self-guided trails. They can also help with transportation logistics, including boat transfers to and from Bahía Negra from where onward travel is available in the form of the Aquidabán (see page 711) or weekly flights to Asunción with SETAM.

Parque Nacional San Rafael Set in 730 square kilometres of Atlantic Forest, this national park contains some 300 species of bird, big mammals such as pumas, ocelots and tapirs, within a unique ecosystem where you'll also find rare orchids. Pro Cosara (☎098 571 0900, ⓦprocosara. org) are the main NGO working here and they can provide food and accommodation with kitchen (Gs180,000/day or full board Gs340,000 in cabins, camping/person Gs25,000 plus Gs40,000 transportation into the park from nearest town Ynambu; minimum two-day stay) and hiking trails. You can organize an English-speaking guide through Fauna Paraguay.

hot (*caliente*). Oddly, *chipa* in Asunción is frequently disappointing, so don't let it put you off trying it elsewhere. *Sopa Paraguaya* is not soup, but a savoury cheese cornmeal cake, delicious when warm. *Chipa Guazu* is similar, but made with fresh corn and egg. Both come as accompaniments to meals.

Ask around for unmarked eating houses, which local people always know about, where you may be able to find home-cooked Paraguayan food such as *bori-bori* (soup with corn balls), *guiso de arroz* (a sort of Paraguayan paella) and *so'o apu'á* (meatball soup).

Paraguayan **desserts** include *ensalada de frutas* (fruit salad), which you can buy from street sellers after lunch, the sandwich spreads *dulce de leche* and *dulce de guayaba*, as well as *dulce de batata con queso paraguayo* (a candied sweet potato accompanied with cheese).

DRINK

Wondering what those wildly decorated thermos flasks contain? It's *tereré*, or ice-cold *yerba mate*, a refreshing and addictive herbal tea, undoubtedly the most widely consumed drink in Paraguay. It is sometimes drunk mixed with fruit juice (*tereré Ruso*) or with milk and desiccated coconut (*tereré dulce*). Look out for street vendors with baskets of **yu-yos**: native plants with medicinal properties. Whether you have a hangover or want to lose weight, let the vendor know and he'll add the appropriate plant mix to your *tereré*. Ask a "*yuyero/a*" if they sell the *tereré por el vaso* (by the cup) if you want to try some.

The preferred **local beer** is Pilsen. *Chopp* is a generic term for draught beer, although beer is more widely available in returnable litre bottles.

CULTURE AND ETIQUETTE

Paraguay is generally an informal and laidback country. Men greet each other with a shake of the hand and women are greeted with a kiss on each cheek. The main **religion** is Roman Catholicism. As in many Latin American countries, there is a typically macho attitude to **women**, who may be seen as "fair game" when travelling

alone; try to avoid any behaviour or clothing that may be misconstrued as "flirty", especially away from the major cities. Equally, it's not considered appropriate for women to be drunk in public. If you wish to take a photo of somebody, ask permission and don't offer payment if it's not asked for.

Tipping is not expected but is always appreciated. A tip of Gs2000–3000 is appropriate for a meal; as most museums are free, a tip to the guide is always welcome.

SPORTS AND OUTDOOR ACTIVITIES

As in most South American countries, **soccer**, or *fútbol*, is the main sporting obsession and Paraguay's special claim is that it now houses the **Museo del Fútbol Sudamericano**, near Asunción's airport (Av Sudamericana 595, Autopista Aeropuerto Internacional Km12, Luque; Mon–Fri, call in advance; free; ☎021 645 781; bus #30 from Oliva/Cerro Corá). For football fans this museum is a pilgrimage to see the trophy room containing all the most important cups South American teams play for. Regular matches are played on Sundays and the two biggest clubs are Olimpia and Cerro Porteño. Tickets are bought at the stadium upon entry. **Motor racing** fans will want to look into the **Trans-Chaco Rally**, one of the most demanding motor races on earth (see page 712).

COMMUNICATIONS

Internet access is ubiquitous in the major cities and very cheap (around Gs4000/hr), with generally good connections; most hotels and hostels offer wi-fi.

For **public telephones** you need to look out for *cabinas telefónicas*, telephone booths inside a shop. Copaco (ⓦcopaco. com.py) are the national phone company and have an office in most towns with *cabinas* that generally open between 8am and 8pm. If you are going to be in the country a while, consider buying a local *chip* (sim card). Tigo (ⓦtigo.com.py) have the best country-wide reception and sims

8

are free; take along a photocopy of your passport.

Postal services, run by Correo Paraguayo (🌐correoparaguayo.gov.py), are unreliable, so important mail should always be sent registered (*certificado*) or by international courier. There are no post boxes – you have to go into the post office.

CRIME AND SAFETY

Paraguay is generally a safe country to visit; with so few tourists around they are rarely targeted by thieves. The usual precautions regarding personal safety and protecting your belongings should be taken, and it's unwise to wander alone after dark in unpopulated areas of the capital. If you report a crime, don't expect the **police** to offer more assistance than the taking of your statement for insurance purposes. Tourist police can be identified by their light blue shirts and chequered hats.

The border area in **Ciudad del Este** is occasionally unsafe and you should take a taxi if you have all your belongings with you; it's also not recommended to wander the city's streets after dark. Although the area around Tacuati, east of Concepción, sometimes hits the news for reasons of narco-trafficking, the region remains safe for tourists. Further afield, the vast, largely unpopulated wilderness of the **Chaco** is an extremely desolate and hostile environment, and you should not go off the beaten track without a local guide and substantial preparation and supplies.

HEALTH

Travellers coming to Paraguay should be **vaccinated** against diphtheria, yellow fever, hepatitis A and typhoid. Your doctor may also recommend malaria, rabies and hepatitis B vaccines, depending on your travel plans. Take the usual precautions against mosquitoes; while malaria is uncommon, dengue fever is on the rise here, particularly in the capital and around Filadelfia. Zika has also been reported across the country so pregnant women are advised not to travel here. The tourist board says all running **tap water** is safe; however, bottled or sterilized water is preferable and essential in more rural areas, where you may also want to avoid eating prepared salads.

Bed bugs are an increasing problem internationally, so scour mattresses for signs of them; they hide in the seams and you might notice blood spots from bites.

INFORMATION AND MAPS

The tourist board is run by **SENATUR** (Secretaría Nacional de Turismo; 🌐senatur. gov.py). They produce good leaflets and maps; be sure to drop into their Asunción office (see page 699). ASATUR (🌐asatur. org.py) lists all tour agents in Paraguay. Fauna Paraguay (see page 692) provides lists and image galleries of the majority of the species present in the country.

For detailed **maps**, try the Touring y Automovil Club Paraguayo (TACPy; C 25 de Mayo 1086, at Brasil, Asunción; ☎021 210 550, 🌐tacpy.com.py). Most Paraguayans locate places by landmarks, so addresses are often vague. Paraguayans know places by being "almost at" a crossroad (usually indicated by the word *casi*, shortened to c/), or, if they are at a street corner, the address will say *esquina* (or esq).

MONEY AND BANKS

The **guaraní** has been relatively stable in recent years. Notes are issued in denominations of 1000, 5000, 10,000, 20,000, 50,000 and 100,000. Coins come in denominations of 50, 100, 500 and 1000. Note that the Gs2000 note is plastic currency, while other notes are paper. It is almost impossible to change the guaraní outside Paraguay. **Credit cards** are not widely accepted outside the capital and incur a charge of five to ten percent – plan on paying in cash wherever you go. There are 24hr **ATMs** which will accept international cards in all sizeable towns and cities, though an administration charge of Gs25,000 is usually applied.

You'll get the best exchange rates if you **exchange money** midweek at a casa de cambio; prices tend to rise at weekends. Do not use street moneychangers – when you are dealing with hundreds of thousands of guaraníes you can be easily tricked. The chain MaxiCambios (ⓦmaxicambios.com.py) has branches in Asunción and Ciudad del Este and is reliable for exchanging money.

OPENING HOURS AND HOLIDAYS

Opening hours for shops are generally Monday to Friday 8am until 6pm, plus Saturday until early afternoon. Restaurants are open around 11am to 2.30pm and 6.30pm to midnight. Banks are typically open Monday to Friday 8am to 6pm and closed at weekends, though ATMs can be used at any time. Many **museums** are only open in the mornings, or not at all unless you find the guide or guardian, but persevere.

In addition to the national holidays listed below, some local anniversaries or saints' days are also public holidays, when everything in a given town may close down.

PUBLIC HOLIDAYS

January 1 New Year's Day (*Año Nuevo*)
February 3 Day of San Blas, patron saint of Paraguay (*Día de San Blas*)
March 1 Heroes' Day (*Día de los Héroes*)
March/April Easter and Holy Week (*Pascua y Semana Santa*)

May 1 Labour Day (*Día del Trabajador*)
May 15 Independence Day (*Día de la Independencia Patria*)
June 12 Commemoration of the end of the Chaco War (*Paz del Chaco*)
August15 Founding of Asunción (*Fundación de Asunción*)
December 8 The Immaculate Conception and the Virgin of Caacupé (*La Immaculada Concepción y la Virgen de Caacupé*)
December 25 Christmas Day (*Navidad*)

FESTIVALS

Last week Jan until February 2 La Virgen de Candelaria. A religious affair held in Areguá, with a focus on local *artesanía*, music and dance, culminating in a liturgical parade through the town's streets.
February 3 San Blas. In honour of the patron saint of Paraguay, festivities are biggest at the Catedral de San Blas in Ciudad del Este, but expect lively celebrations across the country.
February Carnaval. Like most South American countries, **Carnaval** is one of the country's most important festivals, with Encarnación Paraguay's self-proclaimed "Capital of Carnival" erupting into parades of music and dance for the month of February.
December 8 La Immaculada Concepción. Up to 200,000 pilgrims from across the country arrive in Caacupé to worship the Virgén de Caacupé, through various masses and religious processions.
June 24 San Juan. Combining festivities in celebration of San Juan Buatista and the summer solstice, this event sees the main squares of villages in the Misiones department fill will food and locals playing traditional games, including the somewhat dangerous "Pelota Tatá", where a cloth football is set on fire and kicked into the crowd.
Last weekend in July Nanduti. Named after the typical Paraguyan lace and held in Itagua where it's made, this festival celebrates the region's arts and crafts through the medium of food, drink and plenty of dancing.

Asunción

Less intimidating than many South American capital cities, **ASUNCIÓN** sits astride a broad bay on the Río Paraguay. Once the historic centre of government for the Spanish colonies of Río de la Plata, the city declined in importance with the founding of Buenos Aires, while the impenetrable Chaco prevented it from becoming the envisioned gateway to the riches of Peru. This quirky city brims with the history of its despots and dictators, but the real stars are its friendly and

accommodating citizens, whom you'll meet if you take advantage of the city's increasingly hip nightlife.

WHAT TO SEE AND DO

While Asunción offers the usual Latin American urban dichotomy of a crumbling historical centre and modern, wealthy suburbs, its personality shines through once you start delving into the country's crazy history. The **historic centre**, or *casco histórico*, is spookily deserted in the evenings and at weekends, but provides enough cultural attractions for at least a couple of days. The action is centred on **Plaza Uruguaya**, **Plaza de los Héroes** and the **waterfront**. Many of the city's high-end restaurants are in the area around the mammoth **Shopping del Sol** complex in the suburb of **Villa Mora**, but the old centre is still the best place to look for cheap accommodation and cutting-edge nightlife. A visit to the multi-coloured *barrio* of **Loma San Jerónimo**, with its cobbled streets and lively markets, is also not to be missed.

Those seeking more tranquil surroundings will find solace in the arty towns around the peaceful **Lago Ypacaraí**, easily reached as a day-trip from the city.

Note that in the centre, the street names running east–west change after Independencia Nacional, which cuts them north–south, so Cerro Corá and Oliva, for example, are the same street.

Plaza de los Héroes

The *casco histórico* is easy to explore on foot and a good starting point is the main square, **Plaza de los Héroes**. A lively place, filled with *lapacho* trees that bloom a dramatic pink in July and August, it's a frequent concert venue and attracts tourists, protesters and pedlars alike. Made up of four squares, each with its own name, it's generally referred to as a whole as the Heroes' Square thanks to the redoubtable **Panteón de los Héroes** (daily 8am–6pm; free) in its northwestern corner. In a country lacking in postcard-perfect moments, it's Paraguay's most instantly recognizable monument and it contains the remains of former presidents: Carlos Antonio López, his son Francisco Solano López and the dictator Dr Rodríguez de Francia.

The Costanera

Northwest of Plaza de los Héroes the **Costanera** (waterfront) runs along the banks of the Río Paraguay. As you walk here from the centre, you'll pass the squat yet overblown pastel pink **Palacio de Gobierno, which** will come as something of a shock. Often referred to as the Palacio de los López, the seat of government was

started in the 1850s by the elder of the López dictators who wanted to bring a touch of Europe to Paraguay. He hired an English contractor to whip up a palace with a touch of Versailles, the White House and Westminster, but for all its grand pretensions, the resulting building now looks a bit faded and mildly ridiculous. Thanks to the lack of fencing, you can walk almost right up to it.

Walking a few blocks west of the Palace, down El Paraguauo Independiente, brings you to the **puerto** (port; at Colón), where you can catch boats across the Río Paraguay (daily 6.30am–5pm; 20min; Gs3500 one-way; ☎0983 127 965) to the small town of Chaco'í from where you'll get lovely views of Asunción, as well as respite from its smog. Immediately opposite the palace is a terrace of old buildings with Italianate facades which are known collectively as the **Centro Cultural Manzana de la Rivera** (C Ayolas 129; Mon–Sat 8am–7pm, Sun 9am–6pm; free; ☎021 442 448, ⓦcentroculturalmanzanarivera.blogspot. com), a series of restored houses dating from 1750, housing the **Museo Memoria de la Ciudad**, with artefacts from the city, a gallery space with temporary exhibitions, a library and a bar that fills with after-work drinkers and overlooks the beautifully lit palace.

Plaza de Armas

A two-block walk east along El Paraguayo Independiente from Palacio de Gobierno will bring you to the unofficially named **Plaza de Armas** (also known as Plaza Mayor, Plaza de la Independencia, Parque de la República or Plaza del Marzo Paraguayo). The square, home to some of the most important buildings in the city, feels sleepy and almost forgotten. It's dominated by the **Cabildo**, which housed the national congress until 2004 when a modern building was completed just off the northwestern corner of the square along Avenida República. Built in the 1840s, the Cabildo now houses the **Centro Cultural de la República** (Mon–Fri 9am–8pm, Sat & Sun 10am–6pm; free; ☎021 441 826, ⓦcabildoccr.gov.py), which exhibits artwork by Paraguayan artists and has a series of rooms charting immigration to Paraguay. Free concerts and talks are often held here in the evening. On the plaza's southeastern corner stands the Neoclassical **Catedral** (daily 8am–noon & 2–8pm), built in the same decade as the Cabildo. It's not safe for tourists to walk in the slums that lead from this plaza to the bay.

A few blocks away, the **Casa de la Independencia** (C 14 de Mayo, at Pte Franco; Mon–Fri 7am–6pm, Sat 8am–1pm; free; ☎021 493 918, ⓦcasadelaindependencia.org.py), dating back to 1811, is one of the oldest and most important buildings in the country. It was here that the architects of Paraguayan independence secretly met to discuss their plans. Today it houses a museum with artefacts from the time of the declaration of independence.

Plaza Uruguaya

With several bookshops in the middle, leafy **Plaza Uruguaya** has an appealingly gentle pace, encapsulated by the nostalgic and elegant **Estación de Ferrocarril** (C México 145, entrance on C Eligio Ayala; Mon–Fri 8am–4pm; Gs10,000; ☎021 447 848, ⓦfepasa.com.py), the city's old railway station, which dates back to 1861. It now serves as a museum to Paraguay's historic railway, with grand old carriages in the station hall to wander around. At night, things get a bit seedy here, but the streets surrounding the square become the centre of the city's nightlife.

Other museums in the centre

Five blocks east along Eligio Ayala from the Plaza Uruguaya is the modest **Museo Nacional de Bellas Artes** (C Eligio Ayala 1345, at Curupayty; Tues–Fri 7am–6pm,

CENTRAL ASUNCIÓN

8

ACCOMMODATION
Arandú Hostal	2
Black Cat Hostel	1
El Jardín Hostal	4
El Nómada	5
Urbanian Hostel	3

SHOPPING
El Lector	1

DRINKING & NIGHTLIFE
Britannia Pub	5
La Cachamba	3
La Casa del Mojito	1
El Poniente	2
Sacramento Brewing Co.	4

EATING
Bar La Esquina	5
Bar San Roque	8
Bolsi	4
Café Consulado	1
Koggi	7
Lido Bar	2
La Piccola Trattoria	6
Taberna Española	3

Sat 7am–2pm; free; ☎021 211 578), which primarily displays artworks collected by Paraguayan intellectual Juan Silviano Godoy (1850–1926). It includes some European art, but the real draw is the selection of national art evoking a bygone Paraguay.

A little further out of the centre, in an unassuming terraced house, sits the former torture centre of the Stroessner dictatorship, now accommodating the moving **Museo de las Memorias** (C Chile 1066, between calles Manduvirá and Jejuí; Mon–Fri 9am–4pm; free; ☎021 493 873). The museum's displays are based on the "terror archives" discovered in 1992 detailing the human rights abuses carried out under the 35-year dictatorship. You'll see cells where up to a hundred people at a time were kept, plus a bathtub used for water torture and other gruesome implements used by the regime.

Loma San Jerónimo

A lookout point for ships during the nineteenth-century Spanish occupation, the colourful little neighbourhood of **Loma San Jerónimo** lies to the west of the centre and towards the port at avenidas Republica, Diaz de Pefaur and Oliva, and is reminiscent of La Boca in Buenos Aires. Once a poor and run-down *barrio*, a government incentive saw houses painted bright colours, streets strung with bunting and many homespun businesses popping up (often in locals' front rooms), attracting tourism and turning the area into one of Asunción's gems. Wander through the winding cobbled alleyways and ask a local for directions to the church, which you can climb to the top of for the best views of the city (the neighbouring mirador is more expensive, whereas the church only asks for a donation). On weekends, the area buzzes with craft and food stands.

Mercado Cuatro

One of those sprawling Latin American markets where you can buy anything and everything (not to mention delicious and dirt-cheap street food), **Mercado Cuatro** (4) is a warren of seemingly endless passageways where it's easy to get lost in the bustle. In 2012, a film based entirely in the market, *7 Cajas* (Maneglia & Schémboli), or "7 Boxes" as it's known in English, brought Paraguay's great market to the world's attention. As with any market, keep your wits about you and belongings close (or leave them in the hostel). It's a twenty-minute uphill trudge from the centre via Calle Pettirossi, or hop on any bus going southwest with "Mercado" in the window.

Villa Mora and the Museo del Barro

Like many Latin American countries, Paraguay's elite have left the crumbling splendour of the historic centre for flashy modernity at arm's length from their past. Most buses going away from the centre up Avenida España will pass through the neighbourhood of **Villa Mora** and its beating heart, the vast, American-style **Shopping del Sol** mall, and Paseo Carmelitas, which has restaurants and bars popular in the evening.

If you're not a shopaholic, the best reason to make the trip here is to visit arguably Paraguay's best museum, the **Museo del Barro** (C Grabadores del Kabichu'i 2716; free; Wed–Sat 9am–noon & 3.30–8pm; ☎021 607 996, ⊛museodelbarro.org; bus #28, #30 or #56 from any corner of C Oliva, which becomes C Cerro Corá). Dedicated to Paraguay's indigenous, folk and urban/ contemporary visual arts, it also has a good shop selling folk art. Don't miss the eighteenth-century *ñandutí* (spiderweb lace specific to Paraguay).

ARRIVAL AND DEPARTURE

By plane Aeropuerto Internacional Silvio Pettirossi (☎021 646 094) is 15km northeast of the city along Av España and its continuation Aviadores del Chaco. Taxis from the airport are extremely expensive (Gs100,000 to central Asunción); if you arrive by day, walk to the avenue outside the airport and take a taxi there (approx. Gs60,000 to city centre), or even better, get the bus from the stop on the roundabout (#30; 45min–1hr depending on traffic; Gs2000), which takes you directly into the centre.

By bus The two-tiered intercity bus terminal (☎021 551 740/1, ⊛toa.asuncion.gov.py), at the junction of Av Fernando de la Mora and Av República de Argentina, is in the southeast of the city. A taxi from the terminal to the centre will cost around Gs40,000.

International destinations Buenos Aires (several daily; 21hr); Córdoba (daily; 20hr); Salta (weekly; 20hr); Santa Cruz, (daily; 20hr); Santiago (weekly; 30hr); Rio de Janeiro (weekly; 26hr); São Paulo (daily; 22hr); Montevideo (2 weekly; 20hr).

Domestic destinations Ciudad del Este (every 15min; 4–5hr); Concepción (several daily; 7hr); Encarnación (hourly; 6hr); Filadelfia (3 daily; 7hr); San Bernardino (every 1–2hr; 2hr); San Ignacio (5 daily; 4hr).

GETTING AROUND

The city centre is compact and easily walkable, as is Mercado 4. You'll want to take a bus to the Villa Mora area.

Buses You can flag down buses at all street corners. Destinations are advertised on the front (better to go by this than the number) and there is a flat fare of Gs2000; those with a/c cost Gs3300. From the centre, buses to most parts of town run along C Oliva, which becomes C Cerro Corá. Buses #31, #8 and #15.4 go to the bus terminal; #30A goes to the airport via Villa Mora; #28, #30, #37B and #56 all go to Villa Mora from the centre; #13, #14, #33, #38 and #15.2 go from C Herrera/C Haedo in the centre to Mercado 4.

Taxis A journey within the centre shouldn't cost more than Gs25,000; there are ranks every few streets in the centre and in Plaza de los Héroes. After 10pm and on Sundays, a 30% levy is added. The radio taxi number is ☎ 021 311 080.

INFORMATION AND TOURS

Tourist information The Turista Róga (C Palma 468, at C 14 de Mayo; daily 7am–7pm; ☎ 021 494 110, ⊛ visitparaguay.travel), run by SENATUR, is packed with maps, information and high-quality handicrafts. Staff are extremely helpful and there are computers with internet access to use free of charge. There's also a booth at the airport (Mon–Fri 7am–10pm, Sat & Sun 7am–7pm; ☎ 021 645 600).

Tour operators DTP, Gral. Brúguez 353, at C 25 de Mayo (☎ 021 221 816, ⊛ dtp.com.py) offer some of the best tours to destinations across the country, as well as around Asunción and Lago Ypacaraí. They also have offices in Ciudad del Este and Encarnación.

ACCOMMODATION

For people on a budget, there is far more choice and quality in the historic centre than Villa Mora. Breakfast, a/c and hot water are included unless otherwise stated.

Arandú Hostal C 15 de Agosto 783, at Humaitá ☎ 021 449 712, ⊛ aranduhostal.com; map p.697. A bright, airy hostel in the owner's refurbished family home, with lovely facilities including robust, generous bunks each with locker, a roof terrace with great views west over the city and cosy communal areas. Dorms Gs65,000, doubles Gs185,000

Black Cat Hostel C Eligio Ayala 129, between calles Yegros and Independencia Nacional ☎ 021 449 827,

⊛ hostelblackcat.com; map p.697. The *Black Cat* – Paraguay's first backpacker hostel – boasts all the features backpackers love, including a roof terrace with barbecue and a/c in every room; there's even a small pool. The mother–daughter team running the place speak good English. Dorms Gs56,000, doubles Gs220,000

★ **El Jardín Hostal** C Azara 941, between calles EEUU and Tacuari ☎ 984 860 340, ⊛ eljardinhostal.com; map p.697. Rooms are a bit cramped but bathrooms have some of the best showers around, and the garden is convivial. Run by a Paraguayan–Swedish couple, whose friendly policies, such as no checkout time, set this place apart. Dorms Gs50,000, doubles Gs180,000

★ **El Nómada** C Iturbe 1156, between Av Rodriguez de Francia and C Colombia ☎ 098 410 5050; map p.697. With its huge dorms, wide, sunny garden with pool, and sociable feel, this hostel attracts a young crowd. It's a bit of a stroll into town but its bar and knowledgeable staff make this a top budget choice. Dorms Gs56,000, doubles Gs215,000

Urbanian Hostel Montevideo 1029, between calles Jejuí and Manduvira ☎ 021 441 209, ⊛ urbanianhostel. com; map p.697. Modern, Scandinavian-style decor, custom-built beds with room to sit up on the bottom bunk, and a pool are the main attractions here. There's no kitchen, but a good restaurant-bar. Dorms Gs90,000

EATING

At lunchtime it is easy to find cheap filling food – simply look out for the barbecues outside restaurants all over the centre, chalk boards displaying the *menú del día*, or head over to Mercado 4.

Bar La Esquina C Gral. Díaz, at C 14 de Mayo ☎ 021 492 918; map p.697. Popular among office workers for a cheap and speedy lunch, this buffet restaurant allows you to sample a range of Paraguayan dishes – although the lack of labelling can leave you with little idea as to what you're eating. Buffet starts at Gs15,000. Mon–Sat 8–4pm.

Bar San Roque C Eligio Ayala 792, at Tacuari ☎ 021 446 015; map p.697. Classic Paraguayan food in a classic Paraguayan restaurant – it claims to be the oldest in the country. Service by the bow-tied waiters is slow, but sometimes the best things are worth waiting for. Mains from Gs35,000. Mon–Fri 9am–3pm & 6pm–midnight, Sat 9am–3pm & 7pm–12.30am, Sun 10am–3.30pm.

★ **Bolsi** C Estrella 339, at Alberdi ☎ 021 491 841, ⊛ bolsi.com.py; map p.697. Heralded as Asunción's best restaurant, this lively bistro serves traditional Paraguayan dishes alongside a range of fresh salads and international dishes. Don't miss the sensational *Parisienne*-style pastry counter. Mains Gs50,000. Daily 24hr.

★ **Café Consulado** C O'Leary 1210, at Franco ☎ 097 175 3756; map p.697. Nestled on a downtown side street, this New York-inspired, Paraguayan-owned and

8

unashamedly hipster coffee house is where all the cool kids come to sip cappuccinos or beer. They've got the city's best bagels, while the decor showcases cartoons by local artists. Mon–Fri 9am–9pm, Sat 10am–10pm.

★ **Koggi** C Padre Cardozo 533, between calles Espinosa and Núñez ☎098 497 1721; map p.697. Walkable from the centre, this trendy Korean food truck manages to combine a tiny but authentic menu with an effortlessly cool ambience and some of the best food in Asunción. Mains G̲s̲2̲0̲,̲0̲0̲0̲. Wed–Sun 7pm–midnight.

★ **Lido Bar** C Palma, at Chile ☎021 447 232; map p.697. Make this your first stop in Asunción to get a taste for Paraguayan food and the locals. It's as central as you can get – right in front of the Panteón de los Héroes – and packed day and night. It has a diner-style interior with everyone sitting around the bar; waitresses in matching coffee-coloured outfits yell orders into the kitchen. Mains G̲s̲4̲0̲,̲0̲0̲0̲. Daily 7.30am–1am.

La Piccola Trattoria Av Boggiani 5737, at Nudelman ☎983 211 932; map p.697. In a new location but still with its trademark gingham tablecloths, this tiny restaurant serves fresh pasta, with simple but exquisitely flavoured sauces, finished off with a shot of *Limoncello*. Mains G̲s̲4̲0̲,̲0̲0̲0̲. Mon & Thurs–Sun 7pm–midnight.

Taberna Española C Ayolas 631, at Gral. Díaz ☎021 441 743; map p.697. Excellent tapas, hearty portions of paella and flowing sangría at this cosy and eccentrically decorated Spanish restaurant. Plate of mixed tapas G̲s̲7̲5̲,̲0̲0̲0̲. Daily noon–2.30pm & 7pm–12.30am.

DRINKING AND NIGHTLIFE

Asunción has a thriving nightlife, especially at weekends, though things only really get going after midnight. The centre offers the coolest and most exciting places while Villa Mora is more upmarket. Asuncioning (ⓦasuncioning.com.py) has live music listings; Juhu (ⓦjuhu.com.py) information about cultural events.

Britannia Pub C Cerro Corá 851, between calles EEUU and Tacuari ☎021 443 990; map p.697. There are two other good bars on this block of Cerro Corá, but *Britannia* is the best; despite being over twenty years old, this British-themed pub still heaves with Asunceños. Unlike most bars it's busy on weeknights and the action starts earlier than elsewhere. Tues–Fri 6pm–2am, Sat 7pm–4am, Sun 7pm–midnight.

La Cachamba C Manuel Gondra, at Av Mcal. López ☎021 441 000; map p.697. Set in a train graveyard adorned with fairy lights and mismatched furniture, the "wagon bar" serves imaginative cocktails and is a firm favourite among Asunción's cool cats. Head down at the weekend to party on the open-air dancefloor. Wed–Sun 7pm–3am.

La Casa del Mojito Loma San Jerónimo ☎098 513 2806; map p.697. Watch the sunset from the roof terrace while sipping on exquisite herb-infused cocktails. Mon–Fri 8pm–1am, Sat & Sun noon–2am.

El Poniente C Palma, at Montevideo ☎097 178 0643; map p.697. This downtown dive wouldn't look out of place in Berlin. Set in a colonial townhouse, exposed brickwork and industrial lighting are softened by the palatial beauty of the house's former glory. Local DJs play modern house music at the weekend, making it *the* place to be seen. Thurs & Sun 7pm–2am, Fri & Sat 7pm–5am.

★ **Sacramento Brewing Co.** C Sacramento 655 ☎098 515 4261; map p.697. This Paraguayan take on a gastro pub has eight beers on tap – all made in the adjoining brewery. Watch the sport on the huge screen or quaff a beer alongside a classic Paraguayan burger (*mandioca* features heavily on the menu). At the rear of El Parque Taller car park. Wed, Thurs & Sun 6pm–2am, Fri & Sat 6pm–3am.

SHOPPING

Artesanía The website ⓦartesania.gov.py has a rundown of arts and crafts by department. There's a good and high-quality selection sold at the Turista Róga (see page 698) while the Paseo Artesanal on the western side of Plaza de los Heroés and continuing onto C Palma has the cheapest, widest range.

Bookshops Many in and around the Plaza Uruguaya, but not much in English except El Lector (25 de Mayo, at Antequera; map p.697); its outlet on Av San Martino, at Austria, a few blocks from the Shopping del Sol mall, has a larger selection.

DIRECTORY

Banks and exchange Branches of all major banks in Shopping del Sol. In the centre there's 24hr ATMs at BBVA, C Yegros 435, at C 25 de Mayo; Banco GNB, C O'Leary 302, at Palma; Sudameris Bank, C Independencia Nacional, at Cerro Corá. Casas de cambio are clustered around calles Palma and Aberdi, with MaxiCambios in Shopping Asunción Super Centro at C 14 de Mayo, at Oliva, and in Shopping del Sol.

Embassies and consulates Argentina Av España esq Perú (☎021 212 320); Bolivia C Israel 309 (☎021 211 430); Australia, C Procer Arguello 208 (☎021 608 740); Brazil C Coronel Irrazábal Casi Eligio Ayala (☎021 248 4000); Canada, Av Mcal. López 3794 (☎021 227 207); New Zealand, C Dr Maciel, at Ntra. Sra. del Carmen – Duplex 5 (☎021 608 648); South Africa, C Fulgencio R. Moreno 509 – Piso 8 (☎021 441 971); UK, Av Mcal. López 3794, at Cruz del Chaco – Piso 5 (☎021 614 588); USA, Av Mcal. López 1776 (☎021 213 715).

Hospital Centro Medico Bautista, Av República de Argentina, at Campos Cervera (☎021 688 9000, ⓦcmb.org.py).

Internet Easy Internet on Plaza Uruguaya, C 25 de Mayo, at Antequera, has internet and telephone *cabinas* (Gs5,000/hr; closed Sat afternoon & all day Sun). There is free wi-fi in any plaza where you see the wi-fi/Tigo sign.

Language school Idipar, C Manduvira 963, at Colón (☎021 447 896, ⓦ idipar.com.py), provide lessons in Spanish and Guaraní.

Laundry Lavandería de Mahily, C Montevideo 324, at Palma.

Pharmacy Farmacenter is a slick chain with 24hr delivery service (☎021 438 8000, ⓦfarmacenter.com.py), and many stores open 24hr. Central branch: C Estrella 526, at C 14 de Mayo (24hr).

Phone Copaco, 14 de Mayo, at Oliva.

Police Tourist police, C Independiente, between calles Chile and Ntra. Sra. de la Asunción (☎021 446 608).

Post office C 25 de Mayo, at Yegros (Mon–Fri 7am–6pm, Sat 7am–noon).

DAY-TRIPS FROM ASUNCIÓN

Respite from Asunción's oppressive heat is easier than you might imagine, and just a short distance from the city limits the buildings clear and the pace of life slows to a more typically Paraguayan tempo. Two of the most interesting nearby towns are situated on the cool (but contaminated) waters of **Lago Ypacaraí**, a huge lake with attached national park. Although it's easy (and cheap) to hop on local buses between the towns (you can see them both in a day), tours are available (see page 699). Weekends are the best times to visit; Mondays and Tuesdays see most things closed.

Areguá

A pleasant town full of big old houses located among the lush hills above the lake, arty **AREGUÁ** is noted for its ceramics, but has drawn all kinds of artists and literary types over the years. It has a small "**beach**" by the lake (a 10min walk down Calle Mcal. Estigarribia) with a picturesque pier, which becomes crowded from December to February with Asunceños escaping the city. The town is also known for its huge strawberry (*frutilla*) crops, and every September it holds the Festival de las Frutillas. Don't miss the outstanding **craft shops** El Cántaro (C Mcal. Estigarribia 102, at Martinez de Irala; ⓦel-cantaro.com; daily 10am–6pm) and the Centro Cultural del Lago (C Ruta Areguá 855, at Av Mcal. López; Thurs–Sun 10am–6pm). There is **tourist information** at Av La Candelaria 515 (☎0291 433 500; daily 7am–6pm.) To get there, catch bus #113 (Aregueña) from Mercado 4 (Gs3300; 1hr 45min).

San Bernardino

From Areguá you can get two buses (change at the main crossroads in Ypacaraí; takes 30min) to the shady town of **SAN BERNARDINO** (or "SanBer"), on the eastern shore of the lake. Founded in the 1880s by five German families, the town has retained an orderly feel. In the winter it is a ghost town full of exotic birdsong, bromeliads, and sprinklers maintaining the perfect lawns of Asunción's elite's second homes, but in summer it springs to life, although prices soar. Outside town there's fantastic walking, while in town there are rowing boats and pedalos for rent, as well as craft stalls at Playa la Rotonda near the main square. **Tourist information** is at Casa Hassler on Calle 14 de Mayo, at Luís F. Vaché, one block from the plaza (Mon–Fri 7am–2pm, Sat 8am–1pm; ☎051 223 2212, ⓦsanbernardino.gov.py). Aventura Xtrema (C Ntra. Sra. de la Asunción, at Hassler; ☎098 168 2243, ⓦaventuraxtrema.com. py) can sort out all your extreme sporting needs, including waterskiing and quad-biking. Buses depart every one to two hours from Asunción's main terminal (see page 698).

ACCOMMODATION AND EATING

Brisas del Mediterraneo ☎051 223 2459, ⓦparaguay-hostel.com. A space to camp 2km north of town, still on the shores of the lake. Doubles G̲s̲1̲8̲0̲,̲0̲0̲0̲, camping/person G̲s̲7̲0̲,̲0̲0̲0̲

El Café Francés C Santiviago, at Independencia Nacional ☎051 223 2295. Lovely little French restaurant serving everything from crêpes to fondue, or meat to cook on your own hotplate. Possibly the best crème brûlée outside France. Mains Gs50,000. Tues–Sun 10am–10pm.

★ TREAT YOURSELF

Hotel del Lago C Tte. Weiler 401, San Bernadino ☎512 232 201, ⓦhoteldellago.org. Built in 1888, the *Hotel del Lago* boasts a formidable history tinged with dark Nazi associations. Tastefully restored to its full Victorian glory, it now includes a museum and treetop adventure circuit, plus resident squirrel monkeys. Watching the sunset from its fern-laden terrace overlooking the lake will be a highlight of any trip to Paraguay. G̲s̲3̲4̲0̲,̲0̲0̲0̲

8

East of the Río Paraguay

The Río Paraguay slices the country into two distinct landscapes. The wild west of the Chaco couldn't be more different to the populous, diverse east. Some 97 percent of the population live on this side of the river, and it holds the majority of Paraguay's tourist draws. Whether you experience the human influence of the **Jesuit missions**, the **Itaipú hydroelectric dam**, Encarnación's fabulous **Carnaval**, or the under-promoted and under-explored wildlife of the Atlantic Forest, in either the **Parque Nacional San Rafael** or **Bosque Mbaracayú** (see page 692), you'll leave wondering why more people don't come to Paraguay. The exquisite **Laguna Blanca** (see page 692), and the tranquil town labelled the "Pearl of the North", **Concepción**, will only confirm the feeling that you've stumbled across some of the world's last secret spots.

ENCARNACIÓN

Known as the "Perla del Sur" (Pearl of the South), **ENCARNACIÓN** is Paraguay's third-largest, but second-wealthiest, city outside of the capital, and you'll notice some extraordinary houses as you walk around its streets. However, unlike its commerce-hungry fellow border town of Ciudad del Este, Encarnación has a laidback modernity that makes it much more likeable.

WHAT TO SEE AND DO

Although it's a pleasant, cosmopolitan town, there's not much to do here outside of **Carnaval** but enjoy the benefits of the town's immigrant populations – which include Germans, Eastern Europeans and Japanese – in the city's **restaurants**, and become a river-beach bum lazing on the

8

ENCARNACIÓN

DRINKING & NIGHTLIFE
Galway Irish Pub 1

EATING
Hiroshima 3
Las Papas Belgas 1
Piccola Italia 2

ACCOMMODATION
Casa de la Y 3
Colonial Hostel and Camping ... 2
Germano 1

INTO ARGENTINA

Buses between **Encarnación** and **Posadas** in Argentina start from Ruta 1 at the junction with Caballero and go down Mallorquín through the centre where you can catch the bus on most corners every 10min (5am–11pm; 1hr; Gs9000). Make sure to get off the bus at both ends of the bridge for **customs** formalities. The bus won't wait for you to get your stamps, but your ticket remains valid for the next service. You can also cross via the 8min train service from the Estación de Tren, C Maria de Lara (7am–7pm; Gs7000), which is vastly quicker than the bus during peak traffic hours.

sandy **beach** looking over to Posadas in Argentina. If you're visiting in winter, you're probably better off staying in the countryside near the reductions (see page 705), but it's worth stopping by to get some good food and to visit the tourist information, which specializes in the Jesuit missions.

ARRIVAL AND DEPARTURE

By bus Most visitors arrive at the bus terminal on C General Cabañas at C Mcal. Estigarribia, six blocks downhill from the Plaza de Armas. If you're coming from Argentina you'll arrive at the San Roque González International Bridge in the south of the city.

Destinations Asunción (hourly; 5–6hr); Buenos Aires, Argentina (3 daily; 17hr); Ciudad del Este (9 daily; 4–5hr); Posadas (every 15min; 1hr); San Cosme (2 daily; 2hr).

INFORMATION AND TOURS

Tourist information Good English is spoken at the tourist office run by SENATUR, Ruta 1, at Av Padre Bolik (daily 7am–7pm; ☎071 202 889, ⍟sienteitapua.com). They can help with booking Carnaval tickets, reserving posadas and luggage storage. The Ruta Jesuítica office (☎098 581 3030) doesn't currently have a fixed location but can assist with information There's another office at customs at Puente San Roque González de Santa Cruz (daily 7am–7pm). Good road maps can be bought at Touring and Automovil Club Paraguayo (C Gral. Artigas, at Villarrica).

Tour operators Most of the tour operators in Asunción will do one- or two-day tours to the Jesuit ruins, but they tend to be prohibitively expensive unless you are in a large group. The tourist office can provide an English-speaking guide to take you to them on public transport, for a fee.

Taxi Central Encarnación is easily walkable, but there are taxi ranks every few streets; no journey within the city should cost more than Gs20,000. For a return trip to Jesús and Trinidad with local guide (Gs500,000) contact Castorina Obregon (☎098 575 3997), who is based in Trinidad.

ACCOMMODATION

Book well ahead for Carnaval, when prices rise considerably. Avoid the hotels around the bus terminal (except *Germano*)

and those along Tómas Romero Pereira in the centre. The former attract an undesirable clientele, the latter have serious noise issues at weekends.

Casa de la Y C Carmen de Lara Castro, at Yegros ☎098 577 8198, ⍟casadelay.wix.com/casa-de-la-y; map p.702. Doña Yolanda will make you feel like part of the family in this cosy homestay. Space is tight, and booking ahead is essential, but a good choice for a bed with breakfast in the city. Doubles Gs180,000

Colonial Hostel and Camping C Gral. Artigas 762, at Gral. Cabañas ☎071 201 500, ⍟colonialhostelcamping. com map p.702. With beautiful views of the Rio Parana and excellent transport links to the sights, this bright and airy hostel is a favourite among budget travellers. Dorms Gs100,000, camping/person Gs40,000

Germano C Gral. Cabañas, at C.A. López ☎071 203 346 map p.702. Conveniently located right in front of the bus station, this is the city's best-value budget option. It is basic (fans only, breakfast not included, en-suite extra), but it's a good place to get your head down for the night. Doubles G130,000

EATING

There are surprisingly good eating options in Encarnación, thanks to its multicultural population. For cheap food fast, the *comedor* (dining hall) behind the bus station has lots of little restaurants, as does La Placita indoor market

★ **Hiroshima** C 25 de Mayo, at Lomas Valentinas ☎071 206 288; map p.702. What this place lacks in character, it makes up for with good service, fresh ingredients and excellent sushi. Mains Gs45,000. Also runs a pop-up restaurant by the beach in summer. Tues–Sun 11.30am–2pm & 6.30pm–11.30pm.

Las Papas Belgas C Angel R. Samudio, at Ruta 1 ☎097 511 6425; map p.702. Set within a charming garden, expertly cooked fries and other classic Belgian dishes and beers are on the menu in this Belgian-run restaurant. Mains Gs30,000. Tues–Sun 7–11pm.

Piccola Italia Ruta 1, at Caballero ☎071 202 344; map p.702. Faux Mediterranean surroundings and a cheery Paraguayan/Italian host at this popular trattoria. Pig out on huge portions of pizza and pasta – one plate is easily enough for two. Mains Gs40,000. Mon, Tues, Thurs & Fri 6.30–11.45pm, Sat & Sun 10am–2pm & 6–11.45pm.

8

CARNAVAL

For most Paraguayans, Encarnación is synonymous with **Carnaval** (🌐 carnavalencarnaceno. com), a spectacular celebration transforming the city into a whirlpool of frivolity during four weekends from January to February. Some claim the Carnaval here is better than Rio's thanks to the crowd and community participation. Things begin to hot up during the week with bands of children roaming the streets armed with spray-snow and water balloons, looking to make fools out of the unwary, but the main events are the weekend *corsos* (parades) in the Sambodromo on Av. Rodriguez de Francia. The action begins around 9pm each night in the Sambódromo on the Costanera, and lasts through to the early hours. Tickets (Gs20,000–200,000, some with after-party entrance) sell out rapidly, so book ahead online or in person at the pop-up ticket booths outside the Sambódromo.

DRINKING AND NIGHTLIFE

Encarnación's nightlife revolves around one or two bars for most of the year, but in summer everything moves to the beach, with pop-up bars and restaurants.

Galway Irish Pub C Mallorquín, at Pereira ☎ 094 851 310; p.702. There's little that's Irish about this bar but the beer and cocktail selection is extensive and it gets lively here, particularly at weekends. Gs10,000 entry. Mon–Thurs 7pm–1am, Fri & Sat 7pm–4am.

DIRECTORY

Banks and exchange Itaú, Regional and Itapúa on the Plaza de Armas all have ATMs.

Hospital Hospital Regional Memmel, at C Independencia Nacional.

Laundry Anabella C Curupayty, at González.

Post office Nuevo Circuito on the Ruta Internacional, at San José.

Tourist police Av Rodriguez de Francia, at Constitución Nacional (☎ 071 204 420).

THE RUTA JESUÍTICA

No trip to Paraguay is complete without visiting at least a few of the seven towns that make up the **RUTA JESUÍTICA** (Jesuit route; ☎ 071 205 021; see 🌐 rutajesuitica. com.py for details of museums, ruins and accommodation; see also 🌐 misiones.gov. py), so dubbed by SENATUR to promote the route between Asunción and Encarnación. There are four towns with Jesuit connections in the department of **Misiones** (see page 705), while in neighbouring Itapúa, there are the remains of three **Jesuit-Guaraní missions**. While **Trinidad** is the most well-known, neglecting its neighbour **Jesús**, or the further-afield **San Cosme**, the other side of Encarnación, would be a great loss. It's worth timing trips to Trinidad and San Cosme for an evening, as both have special events. There is a **joint ticket** (Gs25,000) for all three as long as you go within 72 hours. The best places to stay are in posadas (see page 706), or one of the fancy or unusual hotels (see page 705) along the way. There are no ATMs in any of the villages, so carry cash.

Trinidad

The mission of **Trinidad**, or **La Santísima Trinidad del Paraná** to give it its full unwieldy name (daily 7am–9.15pm, Luz y Sonido show daily; 7.30pm May–Oct; 8.30pm Nov–April; Gs25,000 joint ticket; ☎ 098 577 2803, ✉ trinidad@senatur.gov. py), is the most complete and important of all the *Treinta Pueblos*, and retains its magic (despite being just 700m from Ruta 6) thanks to its hilltop location. It provides a sense of how life would have been for the inhabitants of the missions. The most impressive structure is the **Iglesia Mayor**, filled with fantastically ornate stone carvings, the most famous being the **frieze of angels** stretching around the altar (look up). Try and time your visit to see the *Luz y Sonido* which, at nightfall, provides – you've guessed it – lights and sounds re-creating daily life in the mission.

Trinidad is easily reached on **public transport** travelling in either direction on Ruta 6 (ask to be dropped at Trinidad at Km31, clearly signposted next to an incongruous power plant). Buses and *colectivos* to Trinidad leave the Terminal in Encarnación regularly (hourly; 30min–1hr). It's 250km from here to Ciudad del Este and you can flag down any of the larger buses, which will probably be heading there.

THE ENTRANCE AND EXIT OF THE JESUITS

The **Jesuits**, a religious order of Catholic missionaries, came to Paraguay in 1607 and based seven of their *Treinta Pueblos* (the thirty towns they built in South America between Brazil, Argentina, Bolivia and Paraguay) within the modern borders of the country. In the missions (also known as reductions), isolated from the colonial world, the arts flourished and the Jesuit-Guaraní partnership produced music, a printing press (the first in South America), sculpture and architecture. The missions survived and grew for 160 years, but the Jesuits were finally expelled in 1768, having plagued the colonial rulers for too long with their insular governance and protection of the indigenous community from exploitation. The Oscar-winning film *The Mission* (Roland Joffe; 1986), starring Robert De Niro, explores many of the reasons for their expulsion.

ACCOMMODATION AND EATING

Posada Maria Trinidad ☎098 576 9812. Just a few hundred metres from the entrance to the ruins, this cosy posada offers a warm welcome, comfortable rooms and excellent home cooking. Gs160,000

Jesús

Some 13km from the ruins at Trinidad lie those of **Jesús** (Jesús del Tavarangüe; daily 7am–7pm, until 6pm May–Oct; ☎098 663 3651, ✉jesus@senatur.gov.py), in rolling agricultural lands punctuated by palm trees and simple wooden houses painted in shades of blue and green. The mission is, again, set on a hill above the modern village and has enough original buildings to give visitors a feel for how the inhabitants lived. Although there would have been a great workforce living here, it was not completed before the expulsion of the Jesuits, and the church is unfinished, but it was on track to be the greatest.

To get between the sites, get the ticket office to call you a taxi (15min; Gs60,000 round trip), or there are *colectivos* that leave from the petrol station on Ruta 1, at the turning to Jesús, every two to three hours (Mon–Fri 8.30am–5pm & Sat 8.30am–1pm; Gs5000).

San Cosme

Accessed from the turn-off about 12km west of Coronel Bogado, **SAN COSME Y SAN DAMIÁN** (to give it its full name) is a worthy detour. The **mission** here (buy tickets from the astronomical observatory; there is usually a peace corps volunteer in town who can help translate into English if you let the staff know in advance; on the main plaza; daily 7am–9pm; ☎073 275

315, ✉sancosme@senatur.gov.py) has two unique draws. Firstly, it is the only working mission from that period: the main building, dating to 1760, is still used as the town's main church. A restored doorway (don't miss the cheeky bat guarding the top) and the original structure of most of the mission still stands. You'll see original painted wooden ceilings, as well as the only ironwork left in any of the missions on one of the windows.

The second attraction here is the **Centro Astronómico Buenaventura Suárez** (daily 7am–9pm; included in joint ticket; ☎073 275 315), which promotes the work of the eponymous Jesuit astronomer who worked from this mission and developed the incredibly accurate sundial in the mission's plaza, among other celestial discoveries; he was the first person to document the Paraguayan sky. You'll be shown a documentary on the Guaraní understanding of the stratosphere and then taken to a little **planetarium**. Spending time in San Cosme's plaza or

---

★ TREAT YOURSELF

There's a cluster of good hotels in Bella Vista, on the road between Encarnación and Ciudad del Este, after Jesús and Trinidad; all buses heading between the two cities pass through this town.

Papillon Ruta 6, Km 45 ☎076 724 0235, ⓦwww. papillon.com.py. With modern facilities, a lovely pool and pretty grounds, locals prefer this spotless choice. There's also an on-site restaurant with *à la carte* and buffet-style dining. Doubles Gs465,000

STAYING IN A POSADA

To help local communities and tourists alike, the **posadas** scheme was established as a way of integrating the two. To open as a posada, the homeowner must have an en-suite guestroom, sometimes away from the rest of the house. Rooms cost Gs40,000–120,000, and SENATUR provides details (☏021 494 110, ⓦvisitparaguay.travel). There are posadas in Jesús, Trinidad and San Cosme. It's always best to call ahead to book; if you can't speak Spanish, call or email the Encarnación tourist office (see page 703), who can help.

---

down by the river, experiencing the enormity of the sky here, is an unforgettable Paraguayan experience.

There are direct **buses** from Encarnación (2 daily; Gs20,000; 2hr), or catch a *colectivo* (3 daily; Gs10,000; 1hr) to San Cosme from Coronel Bogado's bus terminal (any bus passing along Ruta 1 between Asunción and Encarnación will stop in Coronel Bogado).

Coronel Bogado is a sizeable town with ATM and money-changing facilities. San Cosme's only **accommodation** options are its posadas (see above).

CIUDAD DEL ESTE

Commercial, tacky, frequently intimidating and occasionally sordid, **CIUDAD DEL ESTE** ("city of the east") is a shock to the system for many entering Paraguay for the first time; you'd be forgiven if your first instinct is to escape across the Puente de la Amistad into Brazil. Paraguay's second city, with a population of some 320,000 is hard to love, but do stick around and explore the sights: it does get better. Founded in 1957 as a garden city named Puerto Presidente Stroessner, it grew rapidly as people flocked to the jobs and homes created by the **Itaipú Dam**. Capitalizing on its position on the triple frontier, the town provides cheap duty-free – and frequently contraband – goods to Brazilians and Argentines hungry for bargains; almost everything is priced in US dollars.

WHAT TO SEE AND DO

The city's relative modernity means that it has little in the way of sights, but don't miss the **Museo de la Tierra Guaraní** (Hernandarias; Tues–Sun 8am–5pm; ☏061 599 8638), an excellent new museum charting 200 years of indigenous Guaraní culture through interactive multimedia displays.

CDE's **malls** (or *shoppings*) provide the real entertainment, with shops, bars, clubs, arcades and cinemas. **Shopping Zuni** and **SAX Department Store**, on Avenida San Blas, and Ramirez Rolon alongside the Ruta Internacional, are two of the best for entertainment (Corazón has better eating and drinking; Zuni has one of Paraguay's few cinemas out of the capital). The real attractions, however, lie in the surrounding area, including the dam and numerous nature reserves.

ARRIVAL AND INFORMATION

By plane Aeropuerto Internacional Guaraní, 30km west of town on Ruta 7, has regular flights to Asunción with Sol de Paraguay (ⓦviajaconsol.com). A taxi to most points in the city costs Gs150,000.

By bus The bus terminal is some way south of the centre on C Chaco Boreal, adjacent to the Estadio P. Sarubi on C Gral. Bernadino Caballero. There are *colectivos*, but if you arrive with luggage it's safer to take a taxi (Gs25,000 to Centro).

Destinations Asunción (hourly; 6hr); Encarnación (every 2hr; 5hr); Foz do Iguaçu (every 15min, 45min if no traffic); Puerto Iguazú (every 30min–1hr, 1hr if no traffic); Rio de Janeiro (2 weekly; 25hr); Sao Paulo (4 weekly; 18hr).

Tourist information SENATUR's office (daily 7am–7pm; ☏061 508 810, ✉senaturcde@senatur.gov.py) is at Av Jara, at C Mcal. Estigarribia, just off Ruta Internacional down Av del Lago next to the bus stands. They have free maps of the city. Good road maps can be bought at Touring and Automovil Club Paraguayo (Av San Blas Km 1.5 in petrol station).

Tours Mariza Martinez (☏098 365 4619, ✉mariza@cosmos.com.py) organizes tours for two agencies and can arrange English-speaking guides to most of the surrounding places if you write in advance. You could also try Mavani, who work in CDE with Exchange Tours (offices next to each other in Edificio Saba, Av Nanawa 90, at Av Jara, ☏061 509 5866, ⓦmavani.com.py).

LA SANTÍSIMA TRINIDAD DE PARANÁ,

ACCOMMODATION

Mid-range accommodation in Ciudad del Este is widely available, but cheap options are thin on the ground and seedy. Avoid the area around the bus station and head for the cluster of decent hotels that line C E. R. Fernández, two blocks north of the Ruta Internacional or those found within the Boquerón neighbourhood. All prices include breakfast, TV and a/c unless stated.

Austria C Fernández 165 T098 316 1026 Whotelaustriarestaurante.com. Excellent rooms with TV and a spacious terrace with majestic views out over the river. The restaurant is also recommended, even if you do not plan to stay, for its pleasant faux-alpine ambience and good range of food. Doubles Gs245,000

★ **Casa Alta Hostel** C Tacuru Pucu 20, at Av del Lago ☎ 098 310 0349, ✉ casaaltahostel@gmail.com. Its location outside the city centre (25min walk) means this hostel has plenty of space for a swimming pool, barbecue area, several chill rooms and a sunset terrace with hammocks: a welcome oasis of calm after a hectic day in the city. Dorms Gs75,000, doubles Gs165,000

Teko Arte Hostel Av Benítez, between calles Picuiba and Acá Caraya ☎ 099 328 5905. Bang on the main stretch of bars and restaurants in Boquerón, this small hostel without a/c makes up for its lack of character with large rooms, a garden with terrace bar, hammocks and swimming pool. Staff speak excellent English and can give information about border crossings and visiting Iguazú Falls. Dorms Gs75,000

EATING

Food tends to be pricier here than elsewhere in Paraguay. For cheap food, try the *comedor* for workers between the southbound Ruta Internacional and Av Monseñor Rodríguez.

Gouranga C Pampliega, at Av Ayala, behind the Municipalidad complex ☎ 061 510 362. An Indian vegetarian restaurant with bargain set lunches (Gs20,000) including veggie takes on Paraguayan classics and inventive fresh juices. Mon–Sat 7am–3pm.

Ña Morocha Av Choferes del Chaco, at Av Campo Vía ☎ 061 500 005. Best place in the city for *empanadas* (Gs5000) and other traditional snacks. Mon & Sun 7.30am–3pm, Tues–Sat 7.30am–9pm.

Top Lomitos C Almada, at Garay ☎ 061 505 933. Look beyond the tacky sign outside; this shabby-chic restaurant has some of the best kebabs you'll eat in South America, at rock-bottom prices (Gs17,000). It's a local favourite for a light dinner. Daily 5pm–1am.

DRINKING AND NIGHTLIFE

Época Av Rogelio Benítez 439, approx 700m up Av Bernardino Caballero from the Centro ☎ 097 353 0913. Not cheap, but this 1950s Americana-themed bar/restaurant is a stand-out in distinctly uncool Paraguay. There's a dancefloor with mirror-ball, stage and live music (with small entrance fee). Worth booking a table if you want to go for the music. Mon–Thurs & Sun 5pm–midnight, Fri & Sat 5pm–1am.

SHOPPING

CDE is known as the "Supermarket of South America", and just about everything you can think of can be purchased here at prices well below market rates. Electronics, alcohol and perfumes provide the best deals, but beware of substandard goods and don't be afraid to haggle. Compare prices beforehand and ask for products to be tested; not all dealers are honest. Most bargains are found in the maze of shops and stalls on either side of Ruta Internacional, though the area attracts thieves – do not carry valuables with you.

DIRECTORY

Banks and exchange Many on Av Jara.

CIUDAD DEL ESTE ORIENTATION

The **Ruta Internacional**, running east–west through the centre of town, leads to the rest of Paraguay one-way, and Brazil via the bridge over the Río Paraná the other. It is flanked by **Av San Blas** going east and **Av Monseñor Rodríguez** going west. Nearly all the malls, markets and shops are along this mammoth avenue and south, in the **Centro district**. At the roundabout, just before the Ruta leads down to the bridge, **Pioneros del Este** runs south and splits around one of the parks into Avenida Alejo García and Calle Gral. Bernadino Caballero (which goes to the bus station). There are plenty of restaurants along Avenida Jara in Centro, but this part of the city becomes deserted in the evenings as trading stops, and nightlife moves to the **Boquerón** neighbourhood, southwest of the centre and concentrated on **Avenida Rogelio Benítez** southwards. There's a sizeable proportion of hotels here too; this residential area is one of the safest zones to stay in.

In the **San Blas** neighbourhood, immediately north of Centro across the Ruta Internacional, **Calle E.R. Fernández** is packed with hotels with stunning views over the Río Acaray at its juncture with the Paraná. It's not recommended to walk around this area at night.

THE MUSEUMS OF MISIONES

It's all well and good roaming the ruins of Itapúa department, but if these have piqued your interest there is a lot more to see in the neighbouring Misiones department with its four **museums** containing some of the finest remaining Jesuit-Guaraní art of all the *Treinta Pueblos*. There are five designated buses daily to San Ignacio, or any bus heading south along Ruta 1 will drop you there (4hr from Asunción). From here it's easy to hop on local *colectivos* to some towns; taxis will cost upwards of Gs75,000.

Museo Diocesano del Arte Jesuítico Guaraní Three blocks from Ruta 1 South at C Iturbe 870, San Ignacio ☎098 518 7824, ✉museoartejesuitico@hotmail.com. San Ignacio was the first Jesuit-Guaraní mission established in Paraguay. The museum here contains art and history from this mission (it's the best place to see carved woodwork from the Jesuit period) and is housed in a seventeenth-century adobe building, which was the Jesuit college then and, amazingly, now. Daily 8–11.30am & 2–5pm. Gs10,000.

Museo de Santa María de Fe To the right of the church in Santa María. The unrivalled collection of carved wooden statues displays the Guaraní Baroque style at its best, and you can see the differences between the carvings done by the Italian–Jesuit masters and those done by their indigenous pupils. Contact the guide, Irma (☎097 661 8461) for the key or ask at Santa María Hotel for access. Gs10,000.

Loreto Chapel On Santa Rosa's main square ☎0858 285 221. The village of Santa Rosa has the only remaining Jesuit Loreto Chapel, with beautiful frescoes and fine carved pieces, as well as a full terrace of *casas de indios* from the original mission and a surviving high bell tower. Mon–Sat 7.30–11.30am; ask at the parochial office next door for access. Gs10,000.

Museo Tesoros Jesuíticos In Santiago, 18km south of Ruta 1 on the road to Ayolas next to the church on the main plaza ☎097 762 008. Museum where the only remaining wooden altarpiece of any of the Jesuit ruins is displayed, along with other Jesuit treasures. Opening hours are erratic. Gs15,000 for entry with a guide.

ACCOMMODATION

★ **Santa María Hotel** Across the plaza from the museum in Santa María ☎0781 283 311, ⊛santamariahotel.org. The best place to stay in Misiones department, started by a Brit (Margaret, a travel writer with extensive knowledge of Paraguay) with the aim of generating employment for locals, this pint-size hotel has great food, excellent English is spoken, and country-wide tours are offered. They can also take you to the nearby weaving cooperative. Includes American breakfast. Gs180,000

Car rental Various options at the airport, or Localiza (☎061 572 456) inside Shopping Arena on C Cadete Pando.
Hospital Fundación Tesai (⊛tesai.org.py) on Av Caballero behind the bus terminal.
Internet *Shopping Mirage* Gs5000/hr.
Laundry Lavya Garay, at C Valentina.
Post office Correo Paraguayo, Av Alejo Garcia, at C Centro Democrático.

AROUND CIUDAD DEL ESTE

The main reasons for staying in CDE are to visit **Iguazú Falls** – both the Brazilian (see page 351) and Argentine (see page 88) sides are an easy day-trip from here – and the **Itaipú Dam**, the second-largest in the world (and the largest producer of hydroelectric power), an extraordinary engineering feat. The Itaipú Dam company oversees eight small nature reserves, but if you have time, head straight for the **Reserva Bosque Mbaracayú** (see page 692).

Itaipú Dam

Sited 20km north of Ciudad del Este, **ITAIPÚ** (in Hernandarias 10km from CDE; ☎061 599 8069, ⊛itaipu.gov.py) was once referred to as one of the seven wonders of the modern world. With a maximum height of 195m and generating up to 75,000GWh of energy per year (and fulfilling 87 percent of Paraguay's energy needs), it's still something to behold. Visits are by **guided tour only** (on the hour: Mon–Fri 8am–4pm; free, passport required; 1hr 30min), with a short documentary shown first. There are tours from the Brazilian side where you can pay to see the inner workings of the colossal

8

1km-long machine room, which is fantastic, but as tours from the Paraguay side are free, those on a budget will be more than satisfied with the enormous vistas outside. There are also spectacular light shows on Friday and Saturday nights at 9pm (free, but reserve in advance with passport details).

The project's backers had to invest heavily in ecological damage-limitation projects, establishing the **Centro Ambiental** (Tues–Sun 8am–11am & 2–4pm; tours of the zoo every hour; free), a few kilometres south of the dam's entrance (back towards CDE) and easily reached by taxi. It contains a good museum about the Guaraní peoples, as well as an excellent zoo by South American standards, set up to house animals rescued from the flooding. The Dam also runs several **nature reserves** in this area, but these are really only worth looking into if you won't have time to make it to Mbaracayú or San Rafael (see page 692).

The Dam is easily accessed by **public transport**; simply jump on any bus marked "Hernandarias" from Avenida San Blás north of the SENATUR office (Gs3500; 20min) and get off at Km17 where you'll see the entrance on your right. Buses pick up from the petrol station opposite.

CONCEPCIÓN

From CDE it's possible to catch a connecting bus from transport hub Coronel Oviedo up to **CONCEPCIÓN**, although it's a comfier journey from Asunción. A peaceful and historic port town on the bank of the Río Paraguay, Concepción is the main trading centre in the northeast of the country. It has a wealth of **museums** for a town of its size and is becoming popular with tourists as a departure point for rustic but picturesque **river trips** along the Río Paraguay to the Paraguayan **Pantanal** (see page 692).

WHAT TO SEE AND DO

Concepción is best known by Paraguayans for its graceful Italianate and Art Deco turn-of-the-twentieth-century **mansions**, with Villa Heyn (set back from Calle C.A. López between calles Brasil and Otaño), housing the regional government and the tourism office, arguably the finest example. The bulk of the tourist sights are in the centre, concentrated on the main street Avenida Pinedo, which runs north–south, with east–west streets running from Calle Pinedo to the river. Calle Presidente Franco goes from Avenida Pinedo to the port and is mainly commercial, calles Mariscal Estigarribia

---

INTO BRAZIL AND ARGENTINA

The Puente de la Amistad (Ponte da Amizade in Portuguese, or Friendship Bridge), across the Río Paraná, marks the border with the Brazilian town of **Foz do Iguaçu**. Immigration formalities take place at either end of the bridge. This is Paraguay's busiest border crossing, and there are frequently huge queues in either direction (if crossing by bus, try to go before midday and return after 2pm). A local bus runs from the bus terminal along Av Gral. C Bernardino Caballero, C Pioneros del Este, then to the Ruta Internacional to the terminal in "Foz", as it's known locally (every 15min; duration depends on bridge traffic; Gs8000). Often crossing on foot is quicker, but be sure to obtain all necessary entrance and exit stamps; you need them even if you are just visiting the waterfalls. A taxi will cost around Gs100,000, while a cheaper (and certainly more hair-raising) option is a motorcycle-taxi (Gs45,00).

The companies Río Uruguay and Risa run buses daily between CDE and **Puerto Iguazú** in Argentina (every 30min–1hr, 7am–5pm, duration depends on bridge traffic; Gs13,000 or AR$40). It starts from the Terminal, but you can catch it anywhere along C Gral. Bernardino Caballero or Ruta Internacional. You need to get stamps at the Migración office before crossing the bridge to leave Paraguay, and again at the Argentine border, some 20min later. You do not need to get stamps to go in and out of Brazil if you do not plan to get off the bus before Argentina. Buses won't wait around for you to sort out your stamps at the Paraguayan Migración office; to avoid paying twice (the next bus is likely a different company and so won't accept your original ticket) walk to this office (about 20min from centre of town) to get your paperwork in order and then flag down the next bus; all buses pass in front of this immigration checkpoint.

and Mariscal López run parallel to the south of Franco, and have three plazas between them, containing the bulk of the museums with beautiful nineteenth-century mansions between. While here, don't miss hanging out at the port at sunset with a *termo* of *tereré*, watching locals swimming in the river and the sun setting over the Chaco.

The museums

The town's small but high-quality museums are mostly only open in the morning. The ones not to miss include the **Museo del Cuartel de Villa Real** (C Mcal. Estigarribia, at C.A. López; Mon–Sat 8am–noon; free), with a motley collection of historical artefacts housed in a refurbished part of the army barracks dating back to the Triple Alliance war. Nearby is the stately pink and white **Palacio Municipal** dating from 1898 (pop in in the morning to see two enormous murals in the main hall), while one block south of the palace, on C Mcal. López between calles Cerro Corá and Gral. Garay, the **Museo Cívico Municipal** within the Casa de Cultura (☎ 033 124 2079; Mon–Fri 7am–5pm; free) houses a fascinating haul of furniture, musical instruments and electronic items and has occasional evening music recitals.

ARRIVAL AND INFORMATION

By boat The Aquidabán (☎ 097 267 8695) goes upriver to Bahía Negra in the Paraguayan Pantanal once a week. It leaves Concepción every Tuesday around 11am, arriving at dawn on Friday and returning to Concepción the same day. It costs Gs120,000, or Gs220,000 with a bed (you'll need to rent a hammock for Gs30,000 or settle for a wooden seat if not). Boats are uncomfortable, and while there are meals for sale, it's best to take your own food and water.

By bus Buses arrive at the terminal on C Asunción, between calles Gral. Garay and Andrés Miancoff, eight blocks north of the town centre. NSA (☎ 021 289 1000, ⓦ nsa.com.py) and La Santaniana (☎ 021 238 1111, ⓦ lasantaniana.com.py) are the best companies, offering national and international routes.

Destinations Asunción (hourly; 7hr); Buenos Aires (3 daily; 24hr); Campo Grande, Brazil (2 daily; 7–10hr); Ciudad del Este (2 daily; 10hr); Coronel Oviedo (2 daily; 6–7hr); Filadelfia (2 daily; 6hr); Pedro Juan Caballero (6 daily; 4–5hr); Vallemí (3 daily; 3–4hr); São Paulo, Brazil (daily; 24hr).

Tourist information The local tourist office, at Villa Heyn, is enthusiastic if not hugely knowledgeable (☎ 098 156 2161; Mon–Fri 7am–2pm).

ACCOMMODATION

There isn't a vast range of accommodation in town but there's a great *estancia* in the countryside. Hotels listed below are en-suite and include breakfast, TV and a/c.

IN TOWN

★ **Colonial Hotel** C Franco, at Gral. Diaz ☎ 033 124 2956. Brand-spanking new rooms, access to a sizeable terrace with views across town and a substantial breakfast make this Concepción's best-value choice. <u>Gs120,000</u>.

Victoria C Franco, at Pedro Caballero ☎ 033 124 2256, ⓔ hotelvictoria@hotmail.es. The hotel has seen better days, but the rooms have comfortable beds and there's a patio with orchids and ferns for relaxing in. Doubles with fan <u>Gs90,000</u>, with a/c <u>Gs140,000</u>

ESTANCIAS NEAR CONCEPCIÓN

Granja El Roble Km16 towards Belén ☎ 098 589 8446, ⓦ paraguay.ch. This farm offers treehouses, camping space or cabins. The owner can organize excursions – including the Chaco – as well as rafting and fishing, while the English-language website has excellent information about travel in the region. Cabins <u>Gs150,000</u>, camping/person <u>Gs40,000</u>,

EATING AND DRINKING

There are numerous *copetíns* (snack bars) in town serving juices, *empanadas* and sandwiches for next to nothing, and a market two blocks east of Av Pinedo on C Don Bosco (extension of C Franco), plus a supermarket at the corner of calles Brasil and Perez.

Brasil Sabor C Mcal. Estigarribia between calles Iturbe and Cerro Corá, in front of the Municipalidad ☎ 033 124 1415. At this excellent Brazilian restaurant, choose from a range of beef or fish accompanied with a feast of rice, beans and five types of salads and vegetables. One portion is more than enough for two people. Mains Gs50,000. Tues–Sun 7pm–1am.

Colonial Restobar C Franco, at Gral. Diaz ☎ 033 124 2956. This relaxed, music-themed bar – with a particular focus on British musicians through the ages – has a wide selection of cocktails, beers and light bites. It gets busy Thursdays through Saturdays when live bands play. Daily 7pm–midnight.

Tagatiyá Av Mcal. López, at C Cerro Corá ☎ 033 124 1858. Within the swanky *Palace Hotel*, smartly dressed waiters serve up posh takes on Paraguayan cuisine, with fish caught from the river a particular treat. Mains Gs60,000. Daily noon–3pm & 7pm–midnight.

Hotel Victoria & La Quincha de Victoria C Franco, at Pedro Caballero. The lunchtime restaurant is in the hotel itself and is a pleasant place for a Gs20,000 set lunch. The evening restaurant is right across the street, and is a popular outdoor spot to have a grill, steak, burger or beer, and listen to Paraguayan music. Mains Gs40,000. Mon–Sat 11am–3pm & 7pm–midnight, Sun 11am–3pm.

DIRECTORY

Banks and exchange Avenidas Franco and Pinedo are lined with casas de cambio and banks, most of which have 24hr ATMs.

Hospital State-run hospital Colombia, at C Dr Marcial Roig.

Internet Franco, at Yegros; look for the doorway with signs for "*fotocopias*" and "*impressiones*". Gs4000/hr.

Laundry Available in *Hotel Victoria*.

Phone Copaco office on C Franco between calles Pinedo and C Yegros (Mon–Sat 8am–8pm)

Post office Correo Paraguayo, 485 C Mcal. Estigarribia, at Cerro Corá.

West of the Río Paraguay

West of the Río Paraguay lies the area of the country that accounts for over sixty percent of the land, but just two to three percent of the population: **THE CHACO**. The main route north from the capital is Ruta 9 – the "Trans-Chaco" – which takes you straight up through this "inferno verde", or "green inferno", as it is popularly known, and beyond to Bolivia. It is split into three departments, Presidente Hayes, Alto Paraguay and Boquerón, but it is more helpful to think of it as two climate zones – the **lower Chaco** being humid, and the **upper Chaco** being dry. Where they meet in the central Chaco there is a cluster of fascinating **Mennonite colonies** which provide the only real urban tourism in the whole place.

Vast swathes of the Chaco are uninhabited, and this, along with the extreme heat, makes it very dangerous to travel around, even for those who live here; locals always travel in groups. **Guided tours** are the easiest (and safest) way to see the highlights, which include stunning birdlife at the **Central Chaco Lagoons** (see page 692); however, these can be cripplingly expensive and difficult to organize. Exploring independently is not recommended.

THE MENNONITE COLONIES

While indigenous tribes still make up just over fifty percent of the Chaco's denizens (some 28,000 people), the German **Mennonites**, who first came to Paraguay in 1927 as a group of just 1700 or so to escape persecution or enforced

participation in national service (Mennonites are pacifists), are now the largest minority group here. Despite their early struggles, today the Mennonites are some of the most prosperous people in Paraguay. They are the major dairy producers in the country and their three colonies operate with an efficiency that belies their isolated location, with beautifully kept gardens, ruler-straight streets and solidly made brick houses, interspersed with parks and pavements. The Mennonites here are relatively liberal, modern and open, and have embraced tourism and relish the opportunity to show off their achievements to the few visitors who pass through.

WHAT TO SEE AND DO

The **three Mennonite colonies** who settled here each established one of the central Chaco towns, and the only thing to do in the towns, other than seeing how the Mennonites, indigenous peoples and *mestizo* Paraguayans rub along together, is to visit the interesting **Mennonite museums**, monuments and co-operative supermarkets in each.

Unless you are a motor-racing fanatic, the area is best avoided in the last week of September when it is gripped by **Trans-Chaco Rally** fever (Ⓦ rally.com.py). Billed as one of the toughest motorized events on earth, it is accompanied by a considerable hike in hotel prices and a need to book well in advance.

Filadelfia

Thanks to its proximity to the Ruta Trans-Chaco, **FILADELFIA**, home to the

Fernheim Colony, has grown to be the capital of the Boquerón department and receives all the long-distance buses, as well as being the hub for "local" buses for the Chaco. Of all the colonies, it also has the most to do, with several museums, on or around the main Avenida Hindenburg. In a prim park at the corner of Calle Unruh sit the **Museo Jakob Unger**, which houses taxidermy of Chaco wildlife, and the **Museo de la Colonia** (both Mon–Fri & Sun 7–11.30am & 2–4pm, Sat 7–11.30am; free), based in the only surviving building from the original pioneers. In the same park is a **tourist information** office run by the very helpful Gati Harder, who speaks perfect English (opening hours as above; ☎049 141 7380, ☎098 582 0746, ✉turismo@fernheim.com.py) and will happily give talks on Mennonite history, and her other speciality, the trees of the Chaco. Arrange with her a half-day guided tour of different departments of the Cooperative Fernheim (Ⓦfernheim.com. py), at a cost of Gs150,000.

Loma Plata and Neu Halbstadt

The largest of the Mennonite towns is **LOMA PLATA**, home to the Menno Colony, whose Chortitzer Cooperative makes Paraguay's largest dairy brand, Trébol. Other than the small **Museo de Historia Mennonita** (next to the co-operative on the main street; daily 7–11.30am), it's the least interesting of the colonies. Its one redeeming feature is Patrick Friesen, an excellent local guide (☎098 120 0535, ✉turismo@chortitzer.com.py) who can organize tours of the colony and the Chaco lagoons.

The Neuland Colony's main town, **NEU HALBSTADT** (locally known as Neuland; Ⓦneuland.com.py), has tourist information next to the co-op (☎098 316 9393).

ARRIVAL AND INFORMATION

The three Mennonite cities are populous, with wide streets and huge blocks making them tiring to walk around. ATMs accepting foreign cards are on the principal avenue in each town, and each has a post office and a supermarket.

By bus There is a bus terminal in Filadelfia run by NASA, on C Chaco Boreal, one block west of Hindenburg. Most services from Filadelfia pass through Loma Plata en route to the capital.

Destinations Asunción (5 daily; 7hr); Concepción (2 daily; 4–5hr); Mariscal Estigarribia (3 daily; 1hr–1hr 30min).

Taxi There is a taxi rank on Hindenburg in Filadelfia of 4WDs charging Gs150,000 to Loma Plata, Gs250,000 to Neuland, or Gs30,000 within Filadelfia.

Tours Other than the guides mentioned, it's worth looking at Ⓦgranchacoturismo.net or contacting Heinz Wiebe at ✉hwiebe@neuland.com.py. Give him advance warning and he can arrange a translator for his tours of Neuland and Fortín Boquerón, the latter the main battlefield of the Chaco War.

ACCOMMODATION

The Mennonites run mid-range, spotless, efficient hotels in all three colonies. All are en-suite, with TV, a/c, excellent buffet breakfasts and dining options.

Boquerón Opposite the co-op on main street Av 1 de Febrero, Neu Halbstadt ☎049 324 0311, ✉hotel@ neuland.com.py. Recently refurbished, this lovely Mennonite hotel has lawns and flanking spacious rooms with pine beds. Gs150,000

Estancia Iparoma ☎098 194 0050, Ⓦestanciaiparoma. com. Worth investigating if you want to stay out in the Chaco without putting yourself in danger, this Mennonite-run working farm, 19km from Filadelfia, provides

8

INTO BOLIVIA

At the small town of **La Patria**, a fully paved but still potholed road (formerly Picada 108) branches off the Trans-Chaco to the border crossing of **Fortín Infante Rivarola**. There is a small guard post here that does not have exit stamps; you have to stop in Mariscal Estigarribia en route to do immigration formalities, all buses stop here and at the border with Bolivia. This border point is extremely isolated and a popular smuggling route, so you are not advised to attempt to cross by yourself. The only bus from Filadelfia to Santa Cruz in Bolivia is with Stel Turismo (Unruh, at Miller), but you still have to go via Mariscal Estigarribia. This bus will drive into Filadelfia if there are enough people waiting, otherwise it will pick up from the main road outside the town. Alternatively, buses from Asunción (1–2 daily; 30hr) are run by the companies Yacyretá, Stel Turismo and Río Paraguay. Bus tickets from Filadelfia and Asunción are the same price.

accommodation, food, horseriding and other activities. Marilyn can also organize tours into the Chaco. Doubles Gs200,000, full board Gs400,000, camping/person Gs20,000

Hotel Florida Av Hindenburg 165–S, Filadelfia ☎ 049 143 2151, ⓦ hotelfloridachaco.com. The smartest hotel in the colonies, rooms are well-sized and set around a large patio. Unusually, there's also a swimming pool. Don't miss the restaurant with its international buffet of meats and salads (Gs58.000/kg) alongside traditional dishes. Gs280,000

Hotel Golondrina Av Hindenburg 635-Sur, at C Palo Santo, Filadelfia ☎ 049 143 3111, ⓦ hotelgolondrina. com. Laid out in a motel style with clean but soulless rooms, it's one of the cheaper B&Bs in Filadelfia. Make sure to ask for a room with a/c. They've also got marginally more expensive – and larger – rooms at their centrally located hotel of the same name (C Industrial 157-Este, at Miller, ☎ 049 143 2218). Gs182,000

EATING AND DRINKING

Boquerón Boquerón, at C Miller, Filadelfia. A big and bright restaurant with a good choice of food including everything from Mexican to pizza and buffet (Gs60,000/kg) to barbecue. Daily 9am–2pm & 6–10pm.

Girasol Unruh 122, at Av Hindenburg, Filadelfia ☎ 049 143 2078. Regarded as the best restaurant in the colonies, this place does a great range of grills, as well as a buffet (Gs68,000/kg). It has a lovely patio for drinks, too. Mon–Sat 11.30am–1.30pm & 6–11pm, Sun 11.30am–1.30pm.

MACHU PICCHU

Peru

❶ **Machu Picchu** Walk the Inca Trail to these legendary ruins. See page 760

❷ **Líneas de Nazca** Dazzling geometric designs etched into the desert. See page 775

❸ **Cañón del Colca** At its deepest point the canyon reaches 4km. See page 783

❹ **Huaraz** Trek the stunning snowcapped peaks of the Andes. See page 790

❺ **Cajamarca** Outstanding architecture, great food and access to the Northern Highlands. See page 810

❻ **Reserva Nacional Tambopata** Lush Amazonian rainforest, colourful macaw clay licks, and mammals galore. See page 826

HIGHLIGHTS ARE MARKED ON THE MAP ON PAGE 718

ROUGH COSTS

Daily budget Basic US$25, occasional treat US$40
Drink Cristal beer US$2
Food Lunchtime menu US$3–5
Hostel/budget hotel US$3–10
Travel Tumbes–Lima: 18hr, US$30–40, Lima–Cusco: 22hr, US$30–65

FACT FILE

Population 31.8 million
Language Spanish, Quechua, Aymara
Currency Nuevo Sol (S/)
Capital Lima (population: 9.7 million)
International phone code ☎51
Time zone GMT -5hr

9

Introduction

Peru is the most varied and exciting of all the South American nations, with a combination of Inca relics, immense desert coastline and vast tracts of tropical rainforest, divided by the Andes, its chain of breathtaking peaks, over 6km high and 400km wide in places, rippling the length of the nation. So distinct are these regions that it is very difficult to generalize about the country, but one thing for sure is that Peru offers a unique opportunity to experience an incredibly wide range of spectacular scenery, a wealth of heritage and a vibrant living culture.

Hedonists will head for the beaches of **Máncora**, the nightclubs of **Lima** and the bars of **Cusco** – the latter a city where a cosmopolitan lifestyle coexists alongside pre-Columbian buildings and ancient festivals. Just as easily, you can retreat from civilization, travelling deep into the remote parts of the **Peruvian Amazon** or walking in the footsteps of the Incas, taking on the challenge of the **Inca Trail** to reach the ancient citadel of **Machu Picchu**. You can take flight over the **Nazca Lines** to ponder the meaning of the giant figures etched into the desert and hike the canyons and snow-tipped peaks around **Arequipa** and **Trujillo**.

In the more rural parts of Peru, local life has changed little in the last four centuries, though roads and tracks now connect almost every corner of the country, making travel quite straightforward. Nevertheless, you should be prepared to accept the occasional episode of social unrest or travel delays caused by natural disasters as part and parcel of the travel experience.

CHRONOLOGY

c.40,000–15,000 BC The first Peruvians, descendants of nomadic tribes, cross into the Americas from Asia during the last ice age.

2600 BC The complex civilization at the site of Caral develops, lasting for an estimated 500 years.

200–600 AD Emergence and growth of the Moche and Nazca cultures.

1200 The Inca Empire begins to emerge.

1438–70 Pachacutec becomes ruler of the Inca Empire. Machu Picchu and the Inca capital of Cusco are constructed.

1500–30 The Inca Empire stretches over 5500km, from southern Colombia right down to northern Chile.

1532 Francisco Pizarro leads his band of 170 Conquistadors from Tumbes to Cajamarca, capturing the Inca ruler Atahualpa and massacring thousands of Inca warriors.

1533 Atahualpa is executed and the Spaniards install a puppet Inca ruler, Manco Inca.

1535 Lima is founded by Pizarro as the "City of Kings".

1538–41 Conquistadors fight for control of the colony. Diego de Almagro is executed by Pizarro, who in turn is assassinated by Almagro's son.

WHEN TO VISIT

The best time to visit Peru will depend upon which areas of the country you intend to visit, and what activities you plan on doing. **The coast** tends to be mostly dry year-round, but sits under a blanket of fog from April to November each year (especially in Lima); the driest, sunniest months here (Dec–March) tend to coincide with the rainiest weather elsewhere.

In the **Andes** the seasons are more clearly marked, with heavy rains from December to April and a relatively dry period from June to September, which, although it can be cold at night, is certainly the best time for trekking and most outdoor activities. In much of the **jungle**, rainfall is heavier and more frequent, and it's hot and humid all year. In the lowland rainforest areas around Iquitos water levels are higher between December and January, which offers distinct advantages for spotting wildlife and accessing remote creeks by canoe.

Those wishing to avoid the crowds will prefer to visit during the shoulder seasons of May and September to November, as from May to August many popular tourist attractions are packed with tour groups.

1542 The Viceroyalty of Peru is established by Spain's King Charles I, with Lima as its capital.

1571 Unsuccessful rebellion by the last Inca, Túpac Amaru, results in his execution.

1821 Argentine general José de San Martín declares Peruvian Independence on July 28.

1824 The last of the Spanish forces are defeated at the battles of Junín and Ayacucho. Peru becomes an independent state.

1879–1883 The War of the Pacific with Chile. Chile is victorious, annexing a large chunk of southern Peru, including the nitrate-rich northern Atacama desert.

1911 Hiram Bingham discovers Machu Picchu.

1948–56 The economy spirals into ruin and a military junta takes control.

1969–75 Massive economic crisis occurs after General Juan Velasco nationalizes foreign-owned businesses, bans foreign investors and gives all the hacienda land to workers' cooperatives.

1980–92 The Maoist Sendero Luminoso ("Shining Path"), led by Abimael Guzman, carries out terrorist attacks against the government. The conflict causes 69,000 deaths and "disappearances", at least 75 percent of them Quechua-speaking highlanders.

1985 Socialist Alan García comes to power. Financial reforms cause massive hyperinflation and trigger the worst economic crisis Peru has ever experienced.

1990 Surprise presidential victory by Alberto Fujimori over renowned author Mario Vargas Llosa. Privatization of state-owned companies improves economic conditions.

1994 Amnesty offered to Shining Path members; more than 6000 surrender.

2000 Fujimori re-elected amid allegations of electoral fraud, but flees to Japan shortly after due to revelations of corruption, extortion, arms trafficking and human rights abuses.

2001–06 Alejandro Toledo becomes Peru's first full-blooded indigenous president. Protests against the US-backed eradication of coca plantations and nationwide strikes ensue, but the economy remains stable.

2007 Massive earthquake devastates the coastal province of Ica, killing 520 people.

2007–09 Fujimori extradited to Peru. After a lengthy public trial he is convicted and sentenced to 25 years in prison for authorizing death squad killings in 1991–92.

2010 Mario Vargas Llosa wins the Nobel Prize for Literature.

2011 Ollanta Humala wins the presidential election in a run-off vote.

2013 Original Shining Path faction leader Comerade Artemio is captured, charged with terrorism and drug trafficking, and sentenced to life in prison.

2017 The country is outraged as Fujimori is granted a medical pardon and released from prison.

ARRIVAL AND DEPARTURE

Peru has land borders with Chile, Ecuador, Bolivia, Brazil and Colombia. While the borders with Chile, Ecuador and Bolivia are easily negotiated, the borders with Brazil and Colombia are deep in the jungle and less easily reached. Lima is a major transport hub with international flights from the US and Europe; there are also good connections from Lima to other South American countries. International flights within South America tend to be expensive, while national flights within Peru average around US$90 to any destination. Save money by crossing borders by land and only flying within Peru.

Major operators include LATAM and CopaAir and Avianca; also American Airlines from the US, Iberia from Europe via Madrid, and KLM from Europe via Amsterdam. Local airlines include Star Perú, Andes Air and Peruvian Airlines. US citizens are required to show a return ticket if flying in.

If crossing land borders from Chile, Bolivia or Ecuador, aim to take a long-distance bus that goes directly to your destination across the border – it may be a little pricier, but that way you avoid hanging around dodgy border crossing areas and the drivers can assist you with border formalities.

FROM BOLIVIA

The southern cities of Puno, Cusco and Arequipa are easily reached overland from Bolivia. There are two main crossings: **Yungayo** from Copacabana on Lago Titicaca, and **Desaguadero** from La Paz; Yungayo is marginally less chaotic. Regular buses run direct to Puno (and some to Cusco) from both destinations. It's possible, though difficult, to take a boat to Puerto Maldonado from Bolivia's Puerto Heath via Puerto Pardo. As there is no scheduled transport, you may be hanging around for several days for a ride. You should also check the security situation before travel, since the illegal mining in the area means men with guns.

FROM BRAZIL

It's a simple bus journey along the Carretera Interoceánica (Interoceanic

9

PERU

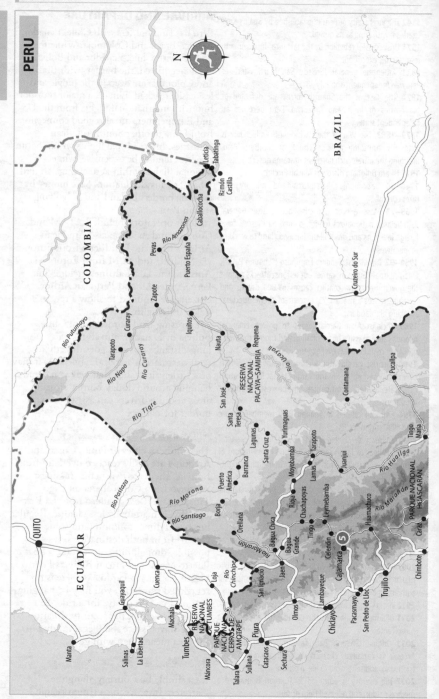

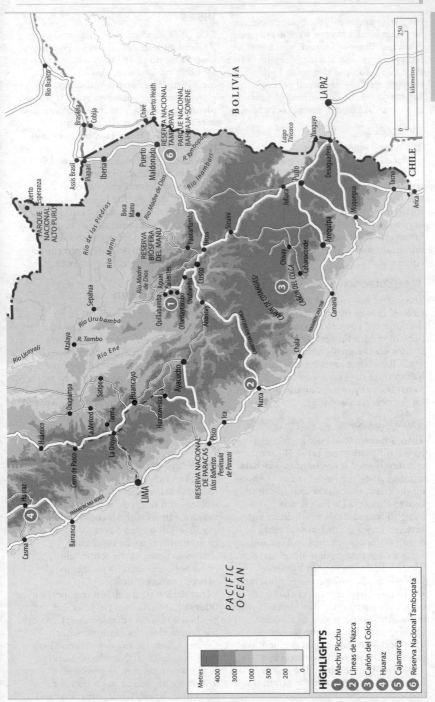

BOLIVIA

CHILE

LA PAZ

Lago Titicaca

PACIFIC OCEAN

250

kilometres

0

Río Branco

Brasiléia

Cobija

Chivé   Puerto Heath

RESERVA NACIONAL TAMBOPATA

PARQUE NACIONAL BAHUAJA-SONENE

Assis Brasil   Iñapari   Iberia

Puerto   Puerto Maldonado

R. Tambopata

R. Inambari

Río Madre de Dios

Yunguyo

Puno

Juliaca

Desaguadero

Tacna

Arica

Puerto Esperanza

PARQUE NACIONAL ALTO PURÚS

Río de las Piedras

Boca Manu

Río Manu

RESERVA BIÓSFERA DEL MANU

Río Madre de Dios

Pilcopata   Aguas Calientes

Quillabamba   Ollantaytambo

Sicuani

Urcos

Cusco

Abancay

CAÑÓN DE COTAHUASI

Chivay   Cabanaconde

CAÑÓN DEL COLCA

Arequipa

Moquegua

Camaná

Sepahua

Atalaya   R. Tambo

Río Urubamba

Río Ucayali

Río Ene

Oxapampa   Satipo

Huánuco   La Merced   Tarma

Cerro de Pasco   La Oroya

Huancayo

Huancavelica

Ayacucho

Ica

Pisco

Nazca

Chala

Camaná

Huaraz

Casma

Barranca

PANAMERICANA NORTE

LIMA

RESERVA NACIONAL DE PARACAS

Islas Ballestas   Península de Paracas

PANAMERICANA SUR

CORDILLERA VILCABAMBA

Metres

4000

3000

1000

500

200

0

HIGHLIGHTS

1 Machu Picchu
2 Líneas de Nazca
3 Cañón del Colca
4 Huaraz
5 Cajamarca
6 Reserva Nacional Tambopata

9

Highway) and across the bridge from the Brazilian border post of **Assis Brasil** to the Peruvian village of Iñapari, which is three hours by bus from Puerto Maldonado (see page 828). You can also reach Iquitos via the Amazon from the small port of **Tabatinga** via the border post of Santa Rosa, just like from Colombia's Leticia.

FROM CHILE

The **Arica–Tacna** border (see page 782) in the far south of Peru causes few problems for travellers. Buses and taxi *colectivos* run regularly across the border and the driver will help with border formalities for a small tip. You can also make the journey between Arica and Tacna by train, with immigration formalities conducted with minimum fuss at the train stations at either end.

FROM COLOMBIA

The easiest way to reach Peru from Colombia is by bus via Ecuador, but if in the Amazon, you can also take a boat from the Colombian border town of Leticia to Iquitos via the small immigration post of Santa Rosa; river journeys take two and a half to three days on a slow boat, but nine to ten hours by *rápido*, or around fifteen on the new ferry service.

FROM ECUADOR

There are three road border crossings open between Ecuador and Peru. The most commonly used is the **Tumbes–Machala** crossing along the Panamerican Highway on the coast, though the crossing from **Loja** to Piura via La Tina is also straightforward, as there are direct buses between major destinations in each country, stopping at the Peruvian and Ecuadorian immigration offices en route. The third crossing – from Vilcabamba to Jaén – is further inland where roads are not so good, and it involves changing basic transportation several times. If you're in the Amazonian region in Ecuador, you can also enter Peru via the **Nuevo Rocafuerte–Pantoja** border on the Rio Napo, which joins the Amazon just downriver from Iquitos. The journey from Iquitos takes at least two days from the border.

VISAS

EU, US, Canadian, Australian and New Zealand citizens can all stay in Peru as tourists for up to 183 days without a visa; for other nationalities, check with your local Peruvian embassy. You're typically given ninety days upon entry, so if you're planning to stay a long time in Peru, make sure to ask for the maximum time allowance, as it is not possible to extend tourist visas.

Previously, all nationalities needed a **tourist or embarkation card** (*tarjeta de embarque*) to enter Peru, issued at the border or on the plane before landing, but this has been mostly phased out. In smaller places or in remote areas, they may ask for it, but your passport should suffice to avoid paying the eighteen-percent tax that national citizens are subject to.

GETTING AROUND

Given the size of the country, many Peruvians and holiday-makers fly to their destinations, as all Peruvian cities are within a two-hour flight from Lima. Most budget travellers get around the country by bus, as these go just about everywhere and are extremely good value. There is a limited rail service along some routes, and though often picturesque they are considerably slower and more expensive than the equivalent bus journey.

BY BUS

Peru's privately operated buses offer remarkably low fares. They range from the efficient and relatively luxurious *cama* or *semicama* buses with air conditioning, snacks/meals included and on-board entertainment, to the more basic *económico* buses, to the scruffy old ex-school buses used on local runs between remote villages.

Cruz del Sur (⊚cruzdelsur.com.pe) and **Oltursa** (⊚oltursa.com.pe) offer the plushest and most reliable buses; Cruz del Sur covers most destinations, while Oltursa is best for any destination along the Panamericana. **Ormeño** (⊚grupo-ormeno.com.pe; note the website frequently has issues) has routes as far as Colombia, Brazil, Chile, Argentina and

Bolivia, though it also has a reputation for lateness, and the condition of the buses has declined over the years. Other reliable companies that have countrywide coverage include **Civa** (wciva.com.pe), **Movil Tours** (wmoviltours.com.pe) and **TEPSA** (wtepsa.com.pe). **Línea** (wlinea.pe) offers routes across northern Peru while **Flores** (wfloreshnos.net), **TransMar** (wtransmar.com.pe) and **Soyuz** (wsoyuz.com.pe) are cheaper options for the south. For intercity rides, it's best to buy tickets in advance direct from the bus company offices; for local trips, you can buy tickets on the bus itself.

If storing main luggage in the hold, you should get a receipt, which you'll need to hand in at the end of your journey to claim your bags. Keep your hand luggage with you at all times, particularly if travelling on cheaper buses like Soyuz/PerúBus.

BY TAXI, MOTOTAXI AND COLECTIVO

Taxis are easily found at any time in almost every town. Any car can become a taxi simply by sticking a taxi sign up in the front window; a lot of people take advantage of this to supplement their income. However, this has led to an increase in crime, so if possible call a radio taxi from a recommended company. Always fix the price in advance, since few taxis have meters. Relatively short journeys in Lima generally cost around S/7 after a bit of haggling, but it's cheaper elsewhere. Taxi drivers in Peru do not expect tips.

In many towns, you'll find small cars and *mototaxis* (**motorcycle rickshaws**). The latter are always cheaper than taxis, if slightly more dangerous and not that comfortable. Outside Lima, you will almost never pay more than S/5 for a ride within a town.

Colectivos (shared taxis) are a very useful way of getting around. They look like private cars or taxis but run a fixed route; each has a small sign in the window with the destination and can squeeze in up to six passengers. They connect all the coastal towns, and many of the larger centres in the mountains, and tend to be faster – sometimes dangerously so – than the bus, though they often charge twice as much. What's more, because they are unregulated, and cars in rural areas in particular can be in poor condition, they have a poor safety record, especially on mountainous routes. *Colectivos* can be found in the centre of a town or at major stopping places along the main roads. The price is generally double that of *combis*, depending on distance travelled. *Colectivo* minibuses, also known as **combis**, or **minivans**, can squeeze in twice as many people, or often more. They cost on average S/5 per person, per hour travelled. Do keep in mind that in the cities, particularly in Lima, *colectivos* (especially *combis*) have a poor reputation for safety. They frequently crash, turn over and knock down pedestrians.

BY TRAIN

Peru's spectacular train journeys are in themselves a major attraction. **Peru Rail** (wperurail.com) runs passenger services from Puno to Cusco, from where another line heads down the magnificent Valle de Urubamba as far as Machu Picchu. **Inca Rail** (wincarail.com) also operates the Cusco–Machu Picchu route. The world's second-highest railway route, from Lima to Huancayo, is considered to be among the most scenic in the world, but it only runs once a month or so; check departure dates and times at wwww.ferrocarrilcentral.com.pe.

Trains tend to be slower than buses and considerably more expensive, but they do allow ample time to take in the scenery and are quite comfortable. If you're planning on visiting Machu Picchu but don't intend to hike the Inca Trail, or walk the back route along the railway tracks, you have no option but to take a tourist train priced in US dollars.

At the time of writing, the Cusco–Puno service costs $192, while a bus costs S/55; the cheapest train fare from Ollantaytambo in the Valle Sagrado to Machu Picchu usually costs from US$65 one way – though it is possible to find a $57 round trip, albeit rarely – while from Cusco's Poroy station it is US$80. If possible, tickets should be bought at least a day in advance, and a week in advance on the Cusco–Machu Picchu route.

9

Tickets can be purchased online, but rates vary widely.

BY AIR

Peru is so vast that the odd flight can save a lot of time, and flights between major towns are frequent and relatively inexpensive. The most popular routes usually need to be booked at least a few days in advance (more at the time of major fiestas). For the best fares to popular destinations, either book your flights in advance with Chilean-owned LATAM (wlatam.com), the main airline, or with the smaller Peruvian subsidiaries of Star Perú (wstarperu.com), Peruvian Airlines (wperuvianairlines.pe) or LC Perú (wlcperu.pe).

Some places in the jungle, such as Iquitos, are more easily accessible by plane, as there is no land access and river routes take much longer and can cost as much as a plane ticket.

Flights are sometimes cancelled, delayed or leave earlier than scheduled, especially in the rainy season, so it is important to reconfirm your flight 48 hours before departure. If a passenger hasn't shown up twenty minutes before the flight, the company can give the seat to someone on the waiting list.

BY BOAT

There are no coastal boat services in Peru. In the jungle, river travel is of enormous importance, and cargo boats are an excellent way of travelling along the Amazon – though you have to have plenty of time at your disposal. The facilities are basic (bring your own hammock to hang on deck or rent a cabin), as is the food. The most popular routes are either from Pucallpa or Yurimaguas to Iquitos, from where you can then go on to Colombia or Brazil. Faster and more expensive covered motorized boats also cover these routes. On smaller rivers, motorized dugout canoes are the preferred local mode of transport and come in two basic forms: those with a large outboard motor, and slow and noisy *peke-peke* (the name describes the sound of the engine).

ACCOMMODATION

Peru has the typical range of Latin American accommodation, from top-class international hotels to tiny rooms at the back of someone's house for around ten soles a night. Virtually all upmarket accommodation will call itself a hotel or, in the countryside regions, a posada. Lodges in the jungle can be anything from quite luxurious to an open-sided, palm-thatched hut with space for slinging a hammock. *Pensiones* or *residenciales* tend to specialize in longer-term accommodation and may offer discounts for stays of a week or more.

GUESTHOUSES AND HOTELS

Budget **guesthouses** (usually called *hospedajes* or *hostales* and not to be confused with youth hostels) are generally old – sometimes beautifully so, converted from colonial mansions with rooms grouped around a courtyard – and tend to be quite central. At the low end of the scale, which can be basic with shared rooms and a communal bathroom, you can usually find a bed for S/20–30, the price often including breakfast. Rooms with private bath tend to cost about S/20 more. *Hostales* can be great value if you're travelling with one other person or more; you can often get a good, clean en-suite room for less than two or three bunk beds in a backpackers' hostel. A little haggling is often worth a try, particularly in the low season.

HOSTELS AND CAMPING

There are many cheap and reliable hostels in the major tourist centres across Peru,

---

TAX HOAX

If any restaurant tries to add an extra "tax" to your bill, be aware that in Peru, the 18 percent VAT is automatically added to the cost of the dishes and that you shouldn't have to pay anything extra. Also, for a bill to be legal, it has to be either a *boleto de venta* or a *factura*, with the name and address of the restaurant on it. Should any establishment insist that you pay an illegal bill or tax, you have the right to report them to SUNAT, the local regulating board (wsunat.gob.pe).

including several hostel chains such as
Flying Dog and Mamá Simona. Some of
these establishments have their own online
booking facility; otherwise try ⓦhostels.
com, ⓦhostelbookers.com or
ⓦhostelworld.com). **Camping** is possible
all over Peru. In towns and cities you may
be charged the same amount to put up a
tent in the grounds of a hostel as for a
dorm bed. Organized campsites are
gradually being established on the
outskirts of popular tourist destinations,
though these are still few and far between.
Outside urban areas, apart from some
restricted natural reserves, it's possible to
camp amid some stunning scenery along
Peru's vast coast, in the mountains and in
the jungle. It's best not to camp alone, and
if you are setting up camp anywhere near a
village or settlement, ask permission or
advice from the nearest farm or house first.

FOOD AND DRINK

Peruvian cuisine is wonderfully diverse,
and essentially a *mestizo* creation, merging
indigenous cooking with Spanish, African,
Chinese, Italian and Japanese influences.
Along the coast, *ceviche* is the classic
Peruvian seafood dish, consisting of raw
fish, assorted seafood or a mixture of the
two, marinated in lime juice and chilli and
served with corn, sweet potato and onions.
You'll also find *arroz con mariscos* (rice
with seafood), *tiradito* (like sashimi, served
with a sweet or tangy sauce), *conchitas a la
parmesana* (scallops baked with cheese)
and fish prepared a dozen different ways.
In coastal areas you'll also find numerous
chifas (Chinese restaurants) serving ample
portions of inexpensive Chinese dishes,
including vegetarian options.

Food in the Andes includes delicious,
hearty soups, such as *sopa de quinoa*
(quinoa soup), *chupe de camarones* (shrimp
chowder) and *sopa criolla* (beef noodle
soup with vegetables). Peru is home to
hundreds of potato varieties, the standout
dishes from which include *ocopa* (potato
with spicy peanut sauce), *papa a la
Huancaína* (potato in a spicy cheese sauce)
and *causa* (layers of mashed potato with
countless fillings). Other popular dishes
include *lomo saltado* (stir-fried beef), *ají de
gallina* (chicken in a mild chilli sauce),
arroz con pato (rice with duck, simmered
in dark beer with coriander) and the
ubiquitous *cuy* (seared or fried guinea pig).

In the jungle, the succulent local fish,
such as *dorado* and *paiche*, comes grilled,
as *patarashka* (spiced, wrapped in banana
leaves and baked on coals) or as *paca*
(steamed in a banana tube). Fried and
mashed plantain figures highly, along with
yuca (a starchy tuber rather like a yam)
and *juanes* (banana leaves stuffed with
chicken, rice and spices). There is often
game on the menu, but beware of eating
turtle or other endangered species. It is
best not to eat fish along the River
Tambopata (unless it's farmed) due to the
high levels of mercury used extensively in
river mining activities.

In big cities, there are often a handful of
vegetarian restaurants, though vegetarian
food may be quite difficult to find
elsewhere. If you ask for your dish *sin
carne* (without meat), that may only
exclude red meat, but not chicken or fish.

Dessert-wise, Peru offers a wide array of
tropical fruit, such as *lúcuma*, *chirimoya*
(custard apple) and *grenadilla* (a less
vibrant passion fruit), as well as
mazamorra morada (purple corn pudding
with cloves and pineapple) and *suspiro
limeño* (caramelized condensed milk
topped with meringue).

In Peru, lunch is the main meal of the
day, and the time to grab the best food
bargains. In coastal areas, some of the best
food is found in *cevicherías*, simple seafood
restaurants usually open at lunchtime only.
Ask for the *menú marino* – a lunchtime
seafood menu that typically consists of
two courses, such as *ceviche* and *arroz con
mariscos*, and costs around S/15–20.
Elsewhere, most restaurants will offer a
menu (del día) – a three-course set lunch
from S/10 upwards; some places offer a
similar set menu for dinner.

DRINK

In Peru you can find all the popular soft
drink brands, though Peruvians prefer the
neon-yellow Inca Kola, which tastes like
liquid bubblegum. Fresh fruit juices (*jugos*)
are abundant, with *jugerías* (juice stalls) in
markets and elsewhere offering a variety of

9

flavours, such as papaya, *maracuyá* (passion fruit), *plátano* (banana), *piña* (pineapple) and *naranja* (orange); specify whether you want yours *con or sin azúcar* (with or without sugar). Another excellent non-alcoholic drink is *chicha morada*, made from purple corn – not to be confused with *chicha*, home-made corn beer popular in the Andes (look out for a red flag outside homes).

Surprisingly for a coffee-growing country, Peruvians tend to drink either *café pasado* (previously percolated coffee mixed with hot water to serve) or simple powdered Nescafé, though it is possible to find good coffee in the big cities. A wide variety of herbal teas is also available, such as *muña* (Andean mint), *manzanilla* (camomile) and the extremely popular *mate de coca* – tea brewed from coca leaves that helps one acclimatize to high altitude.

Peru brews some excellent beer, the most popular brands being *Cristal*, *Pilsen* and *Cusqueña* – all light lagers, though you can also get Pilsen and Cusqueña *cerveza negra* (dark beer). Good regional brews include *Arequipeña* and *Trujillana* (named after the cities they're brewed in). Most Peruvian wine tends to be sweet and almost like sherry. Among brands more attuned to the Western palate are *Tabanero*, *Tacama* and *Vista Alegre*. The national beverage and a source of great pride is **pisco**, a potent grape brandy with a unique and powerful flavour. Pisco sour – a potent mix of pisco, lime juice, ice and sugar – is a very palatable and extremely popular cocktail found on menus everywhere.

Bars and pubs tend to be open from 11am until midnight and later on weekends. Clubs typically open at 8pm or 9pm, though things don't kick off until after midnight, and the revelry continues until 4am or 5am.

CULTURE AND ETIQUETTE

Due to the huge variety of geographical conditions found within Peruvian territory, culture and traditions tend to vary between regions. On the whole, coastal people tend to be more outgoing and vivacious, while the mountain people of Quechua descent are more reserved and modest. The jungle is still home to many indigenous groups who keep their ancestral traditions and way of life. All Peruvians are family-oriented and tend to be close to large extended families. Machismo is alive and well in Peru, though women travelling alone are not likely to encounter much trouble. Note that whistling in the north of Peru can be a greeting rather than an attempt at harassment.

One of the most common things travellers do that offends local people is to take their picture without asking – so always ask first, and respect a negative answer. At tourist sites all over Peru, you'll encounter women and children in stunning traditional dress who expect a tip for having their photo taken (one or two soles is a reasonable amount). In the highlands in particular there is a strong culture of exchange, meaning that if you receive something, you are expected to give in return. This can be as simple as giving someone coca leaves in exchange for directions on a trail.

Tipping is the norm in more upmarket restaurants, where a ten-percent gratuity is expected and sometimes automatically added to the bill; in cheap local joints tips are received with surprise and gratitude. It's worth bearing in mind that some unscrupulous travel agencies pay their

---

PERU'S CULINARY WONDERS

No foodie should come to Peru without sampling the gastronomic delights of **Gastón Acurio**, the chef who put Peruvian cuisine on the world map. His restaurants include *ChiCha* in both Cusco and Arequipa, *La Trattoria del Monasterio* in Arequipa, *Tanta*, *Mangos* and *La Mar* in Lima and his flagship restaurant, *Astríd y Gastón*, also in the capital. The food ranges from superb takes on regional cuisine to original and innovative fusion creations. Lima has a ton of other spots to blow the budget, including the top-rated *Central*, chef Virgilio Martínez' deep reflection on the origins of Peruvian ingredients, and Pedro Miguel Schiaffino at *amaZ* and *Malabar*.

LGBTQ TRAVEL IN PERU

Being gay in Peru is still very much frowned upon due to a culture infused with machismo and fervent Catholicism, though tolerance is slowly improving. **Epicentro** (Jr Jaén 250A, Barranco, Lima; ☏ 01 247 2755, Ⓦ epicentro.org.pe) is a not-for-profit community centre that organizes a range of events including dances, theatre and cinema outings and more.

guides and drivers very low wages, meaning that they rely on tips, as do freelance guides in museums (agree on a fee before a tour). You should always tip your guide and porters on the Inca Trail (see page 760).

SPORTS AND OUTDOOR ACTIVITIES

When it comes to exploring the wilderness, few of the world's countries can offer anything as varied, rugged and colourful as Peru.

TREKKING AND HIKING

Peru offers a spectacular variety of trekking routes; the main hiking centres are Cusco and Arequipa in the south and Huaraz in the north. The most popular trekking route is, of course, the famous Inca Trail, but other trails in and around the Valle Segrado are rapidly gaining popularity, partly because you get to experience fantastic Andean scenery without being overrun by hordes of tourists. From Arequipa, you can descend into two of the world's deepest canyons – Cañón de Colca and the more remote Cañón de Cotahuasi – which are accessible all year, unlike the Valle Segrado. The Cordillera Blanca near Huaraz lures hikers and climbers alike with its challenging peaks, many of them over 5000m high.

Guides are required for some trekking routes, such as the Inca Trail, and for some challenging routes you'll need to hire mules and *arrieros* (muleteers). You can rent trekking gear or join guided treks at all the major hiking centres; good topographic maps are available from the Instituto Geográfico Nacional (IGN).

Always make sure you're properly equipped, as the weather is renowned for its dramatic changeability, and properly acclimatized.

MOUNTAIN BIKING

Bike shops and bicycle repair workshops are easy to find throughout Peru, though you should bring your own bike if you're planning on some major cycle touring, as mountain-bike rental in some places is pretty basic. Various tour companies (see page 738) offer guided cycling tours, which can be an excellent way to see the best of Peru. Huaraz and Cusco are both popular and challenging destinations for experienced bikers, while the Cañón del Colca is a better bet for novices although it also has its fair share of advanced biking activities too.

WATERSPORTS

Cusco is one of the top white-water rafting and kayaking centres in South America, with easy access to a whole range of river grades, from Class II to V on the Río Urubamba (shifting up grades in the rainy season) to the most dangerous white water on the Río Apurímac, only safe for rafting during the dry season. Río Chili near Arequipa offers good rafting for beginners, with half-day trips passing through Class II and III rapids. A superb multi-day rafting expedition from Cusco goes right down into the Amazon Basin on the Tambopata River. Kayaking along the Río Utcubamba near Chachapoyas, with class I to IV rapids, is also becoming popular.

Bear in mind that rafting is still not a regulated sport in Peru, so it's very important to go with a responsible and eco-friendly operator (see page 738). Also see Ⓦ peruwhitewater.com.

SURFING

Surfing is a popular sport in Peru, with annual national and international championships held in Punta Rocas, south of Lima. You can find good breaks even in Lima itself, particularly in the Miraflores area, though Punta Hermosa, further south, is less crowded. Peru's north coast offers some world-class breaks, with Puerto Chicano boasting the world's

9

longest left-hand wave, whereas Lobitos is an up-and-comer for the surfing set and Pacasmayo outside Chiclayo also has excellent waves. Equipment rental is abundant and it's possible to take surfing lessons. Check out ⓦvivamancora.com for more information.

SANDBOARDING AND DUNE BUGGYING

The best places to ride the sand are in Nazca (see page 776), home of the world's largest dune, Cerro Blanco, and Huacachina, near Ica (see page 772). You can either rent a board from the numerous agencies or go out on the dunes with one of them; snowboarding experience is helpful but not necessary. Also in Huacachina, you can experience the stomach-churning adrenaline rush of dune-buggy rides. While in Nazca they can also be used as the most efficient means of reaching distant desert sites, in Huacachina they are just for thrill-seekers.

COMMUNICATIONS

Peru has good internet connections. Though internet cafés, once abundant in big cities, are in decline, they can still be found in the most unlikely of small towns (though the connection may be slow). The general rate is S/1 per hour, though in touristy places you may end up paying as much as S/5. Virtually all hotels, hostels and cafés have free wi-fi.

All public **phones** are operated by coins or phone cards (*tarjetas telefónicas*), which are available in 3, 5, 10, 15, 20, 40 and 50 sol denominations. You can buy cards at little *tiendas* (corner shops) or at *farmacias* (pharmacies) or on the street from cigarette stalls in the centres of most towns and cities. Both 147 and Hola Peru cards are good for local, national and international landline calls. A number of shops, restaurants and corner shops in Peru have a phone available for public use, which you can use for calls within Peru only. If you need to contact the international operator, dial ☎103. Collect calls are known either simply as *collect* or *al cobro revertido*.

If you have an unlocked **mobile** phone, it's cheap and easy to get a Peruvian SIM

PERU ONLINE

ⓦ**andeantravelweb.com/peru** Links to a whole range of travel-related features and listings.
ⓦ**howtoperu.com**/ⓦ**newperuvian. com** Up-to-date practical travel-related websites written by ex-pats living in Peru.
ⓦ**peru.travel** The official promotional site for Peru, with information on every area of the country.
ⓦ**visitperu.com** Holds similarly comprehensive information.
ⓦ**worldtravelguide.net** English-language pages on art, entertainment and travel.

card with data good for thirty days (S/15–25), in Lima and other major cities, on presentation of your passport at the chosen service provider's main office; alternatively, you can buy a cheap mobile for the duration of your stay (S/80). The networks with the most extensive coverage of the country are Telefonica Movistar and Claro; the latter allows you to send free text messages via their website.

Postal services are slow and very expensive but quite acceptable for normal letters and postcards.

CRIME AND SAFETY

Perhaps the most common irritants are the persistent **touts** found at bus stations and other tourist spots, offering anything from discount accommodation to tours; be very wary of accepting their services, and don't give them money up front. Also don't take **unlicensed taxis** if possible.

You're most likely to come into contact with **police** at the border posts. While they have a reputation for being corrupt, they will mostly leave tourists alone, though some travellers may experience petty harassment aimed at procuring a bribe. If they search your luggage, be scrupulously polite and be aware that possession of any drugs is considered an extremely serious offence in Peru – usually leading to at least a ten-year jail sentence.

Violent crime, such as muggings, is relatively rare. Robberies occasionally occur on overnight buses and there have

EMERGENCY NUMBERS

All services ☎ **105**

been isolated attacks on hikers in the area around Huaraz, so it's best not to hike alone. It's not advisable to travel at night between Abancay and Ayacucho, around the Valle de Apurímac near Ayacucho or in the Río Huallaga area in the north, between Tingo María and Juanjui, as those areas are notorious for drug trafficking. If you're unlucky enough to have anything stolen, your first port of call should be the **tourist police** (*policía de turismo*), from whom you should get a written report. Bear in mind that the police in popular tourist spots, such as Cusco, have become much stricter about investigating reported thefts, after a spate of false claims by dishonest tourists. This means that genuine victims may be grilled more severely than expected, and the police may even come and search your hotel room for the "stolen" items.

HEALTH

In most cities there are **private clinics** (*clínicas*) with better medical facilities than general hospitals, and if given the choice in a medical emergency, opt for a *clínica*. The EsSalud national hospitals have undergone drastic improvements in the last few years, and although they are supposed to be for Peruvians who pay into an insurance scheme with them, they can take independent patients (who pay a higher price). Even in relatively small villages there is a *posta médica* where you can get basic medical attention and assistance in getting to a larger medical facility. iPerú offices can provide you with a list of recommended doctors and clinics.

INFORMATION AND MAPS

The government iPerú offices present in every large city are useful for basic information and advice (in English), as well as free local maps and leaflets (24hr hotline: ☎01 574 8000, Ⓦperu.info); they are also the place to go if you need to make a formal complaint about dishonest guides, tour companies not meeting their obligations, and so on.

Good bookshops stock the Lima 2000 series, which includes the best maps of the major cities as well as the best road map of Peru. For excellent topographic maps of remote places, try Lima's Instituto Geográfico Nacional (Ⓦign.es).

MONEY AND BANKS

The current Peruvian currency, the **nuevo sol**, whose symbol is S/ (or S), is simply called a "sol" on the streets and has so far remained relatively steady against the US dollar. The bills come in denominations of 10, 20, 50, 100 and 200 soles; there are coins of 1, 2 and 5 soles, and the sol is divided into céntimos, in values of 5, 10, 20 and 50. Beware of counterfeit bills, which feel smooth and glossy to the touch, rather than crisp and coarse; genuine bills should have watermarks and thin ribbons when held up against a light source, and when tilted from side to side, the reflective ink on the number denomination should change colour.

Changing foreign currencies is easy in all major cities; you will find casas de cambio around the Plaza de Armas or along the main commercial streets. They readily change euros and British pounds, though the preferred currency is US dollars. You'll find that some tour companies and hotels still quote prices in US dollars, and happily accept them as long as the notes are new; few places will accept US$100 bills.

Banks and ATMs are numerous in cities; if travelling to remote villages, take plenty of cash in small denomination bills and coins with you. BCP (Banco de Crédito) accepts all major credit cards and is the best bank for cash withdrawals, as it doesn't charge a fee for the transaction; Scotiabank also offers free ATM withdrawals to cards from banks that belong to the Global ATM Alliance, which includes Barclays and Bank of America. The Global Net network, on the other hand, can charge up to US$2.50 per withdrawal.

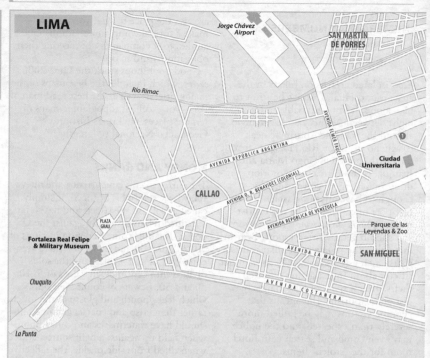

LIMA

Jorge Chávez
Airport

SAN MARTÍN
DE PORRES

Río Rimac

AVENIDA ELMER FAUCETT

AVENIDA REPÚBLICA ARGENTINA

Ciudad
Universitaria

CALLAO

AVENIDA O. R. BENAVIDES (COLONIAL)

AVENIDA REPÚBLICA DE VENEZUELA

PLAZA
GRAU

Parque de las
Leyendas & Zoo

Fortaleza Real Felipe
& Military Museum

AVENIDA LA MARINA

SAN MIGUEL

Chuquito

AVENIDA COSTANERA

La Punta

N

PACIFIC

■ ACCOMMODATION	
Hostal Barranco	2
Domeyer	3
The Point	1

■ DRINKING & NIGHTLIFE	
Ayahuasca	2
La Candelaria	4
La Noche	1
Wahio's Bar	3

● EATING	
Anticuchos Tío Jhony	2
El Grifo	1
Café Cultural Expreso	
Virgen de Guadalupe	3
Mi Carcochita	4

0   2
kilometres

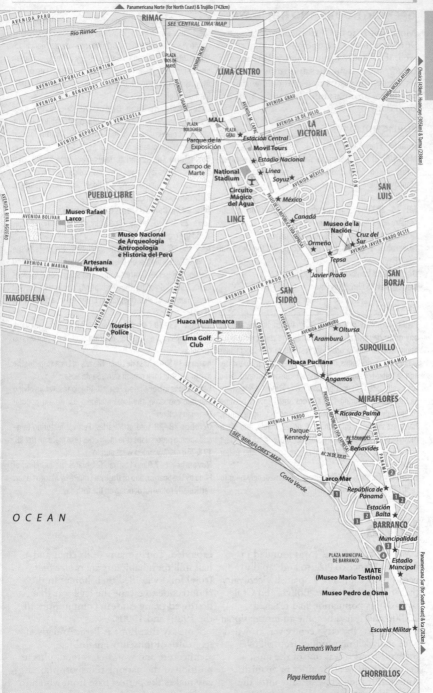

Panamericana Norte (for North Coast) & Trujillo (742km)

AVENIDA PERÚ

RIMAC

Río Rímac

SEE 'CENTRAL LIMA' MAP

PLAZA DOS DE MAYO

AVENIDA REPÚBLICA ARGENTINA

AVENIDA O. R. BENAVIDES (COLONIAL)

AVENIDA TACNA

AVENIDA A. UGARTE

LIMA CENTRO

AVENIDA GRAU

AVENIDA A. CÁPAC

AVENIDA 28 DE JULIO

AVENIDA NICOLÁS AYLLÓN

Chosica (43km), Huancayo (305km) & Tarma (238km)

AVENIDA REPÚBLICA DE VENEZUELA

PLAZA BOLOGNESI

MALI

PLAZA GRAU

★ *Estación Central*

Parque de la Exposición

★ **Movil Tours**

LA VICTORIA

AVENIDA AVIACIÓN

SAN LUIS

AVENIDA BRASIL

Campo de Marte

National Stadium

★ *Estadio Nacional*

★ *Línea Soyuz* ★

AVENIDA MÉXICO

PUEBLO LIBRE

AVENIDA RIVA AGÜERO

AVENIDA BOLÍVAR

Museo Rafael Larco

Museo Nacional de Arqueología Antropología e Historia del Perú

Circuito Mágico del Agua

LINCE

★ *México*

PASEO DE LA REPÚBLICA (VÍA EXPRESA)

★ *Canadá*

★ *Ormeño*

Museo de la Nación

Cruz del Sur

AVENIDA JAVIER PRADO OESTE

AVENIDA LA MARINA

Artesanía Markets

AVENIDA SALAVERRY

AVENIDA BRASIL

Tepsa ★

SAN BORJA

MAGDALENA

Huaca Huallamarca

Tourist Police

Lima Golf Club

COMANDANTE ESPINAR

AVENIDA JAVIER PRADO ESTE

SAN ISIDRO

AVENIDA AREQUIPA

★ *Javier Prado*

AVENIDA ARAMBURÚ

★ *Oltursa*

★ *Aramburú*

SURQUILLO

AVENIDA ANGAMOS

Huaca Pucllana

★ *Angamós*

AVENIDA EJÉRCITO

AVENIDA LARCO

PASEO DE LA REPÚBLICA (VÍA EXPRESA)

★ *Ricardo Palma*

MIRAFLORES

AVENIDA PANAMÁ

SEE 'MIRAFLORES' MAP

AVENIDA J. PARDO

Parque Kennedy

AV. BENAVIDES

★ *Benavides*

AV. 26 DE JULIO

2

Costa Verde

Larco Mar

1

República de Panamá ★

1 **2**

Estación Balta ★

2 **3**

BARRANCO

Muncipalidad

OCEAN

PLAZA MUNICIPAL DE BARRANCO

3 **3**

4

Estadio Muncipal

Panamericana Sur (for South Coast) & Ica (283km)

MATE (Museo Mario Testino)

Museo Pedro de Osma

4

Escuela Militar ★

Fisherman's Wharf

Playa Herradura

CHORRILLOS

9

OPENING HOURS AND HOLIDAYS

Most shops are open from around 9am to 9pm, and many are open on Sunday as well, if for more limited hours. Peru's more important ancient sites and ruins usually have opening hours that coincide with daylight – from around 7am until 5pm or 6pm daily.

PUBLIC HOLIDAYS

January 1 New Year's Day.
March/April Easter; Semana Santa (Holy Week). Maundy Thursday and Good Friday are national holidays, Easter Monday is not.
May 1 Labour Day.
July 28–29 National Independence Day. Public holiday with military and school processions.
October 8 Anniversary of Battle of Angamos.
November 1–2 All Saints' Day, and Day of the Dead (All Souls' Day).
December 8 Immaculate Conception.
December 25 Christmas Day.

FESTIVALS

Peru is a country rich with culture and traditions, and on any given day there is a town or village celebrating their anniversary or similar occasion. Festivals can be spectacular events with processions, usually with live music and dancing, and a proud usage of traditional dress. Carnaval time (generally late Feb) is especially lively almost everywhere in the country. During fiesta times small towns become completely booked up, hotel prices go up significantly, transport services stop running or prices double, and often most people will stop work and celebrate for a few days either side of the festival. Below are some of the major events.

February Carnaval. Wildly celebrated immediately prior to Lent, throughout the whole country.

February 2 Virgen de la Candelaria. Celebrated in the most spectacular way in Puno (known as the folklore capital of the country) with a week of colourful processions and dancing.
March/April Semana Santa (Holy Week). Superb processions all over Peru (the best are in Cusco and Ayacucho), the biggest being on Good Friday and Easter Saturday night.
Late May/early June Q'oyllor Riti. One of the most breathtaking festivals in Peru; thousands of people make the overnight pilgrimage up to Apu Ausangate, a shrine located on a glacier just outside of Cusco.
Early June Corpus Christi. Takes place nine weeks after Maundy Thursday and involves colourful processions with saints carried around on floats and much feasting. Particularly lively in Cusco.
June 24 Inti Raymi is Cusco's main Inca festival.
June 29 St Peter's Day. Fiestas in all the fishing villages along the coast.
July 15–18 Virgen del Carmen. Celebrated in style in the town of Paucartambo, on the road between Cusco and Manu Biosphere Reserve. Dancers come from surrounding villages in traditional dress for the celebration, which lasts several days. There's a smaller celebration in the Valle Sagrado town of Pisac.
August 13–19 Arequipa Week. Processions, firework displays, plenty of folklore dancing and craft markets in Arequipa.
August 30 Santa Rosa de Lima. The city of Lima stops for the day to worship their patron saint, Santa Rosa.
Late September Spring Festival. Trujillo festival involving dancing, especially the local marinera dance and popular Peruvian waltzes.
October 18–28 Lord of Miracles. Festival featuring large and solemn processions (the main ones take place on Oct 18, 19 & 28); many women wear purple.
November 1–7 Puno Festival. Celebrates the founding of Puno by the Spanish and of the Inca Empire by Manco Capac. Particularly colourful dancing on the fifth day.

Lima

LIMA, "City of Kings", was founded in 1535 by **Francisco Pizarro** and rapidly became the capital of a Spanish viceroyalty that included Ecuador, Bolivia and Chile. By 1610 its population had reached 26,000 and it had become an international trading port, the city's centre was crowded with stalls selling produce from all over the world and it was one of the most beautiful and wealthy cities in Spanish America. It then grew steadily until the twentieth century, when the population exploded. Today, many of its eight and a half million inhabitants are *campesinos* (rural folk) who fled their homes in the countryside to escape the civil war that destroyed many Andean communities in the 1980s and 1990s.

Some say that Lima is Peru. And given its wealth of museums, nightlife, architecture and world-class food, plus its position as the nation's transport hub, the city makes the perfect base from which to explore the rest of the country. Ignore

Lima's grey and polluted facade, ride the *combis* and get comfortable – no visit to Peru is complete without time well spent in Lima.

WHAT TO SEE AND DO

Lima is very much a city of neighbourhoods, and it's worth visiting several before making up your mind about this huge capital. You can't beat **Central Lima** for sights or architecture, while up-and-coming neighbourhood **Pueblo Libre** to the southwest has some excellent museums loaded with pre-Hispanic artefacts. Coast-hugging **Miraflores** and

neighbouring **San Isidro** are certainly the most modern and commercial areas of the city and you'll find many designer stores, gourmet restaurants and sophisticated lounge bars here, as well as some of the best tourist attractions and nightlife. Arty and colourful **Barranco** feels like a sleepy seaside town by day, and is fantastic for escaping the chaos of central Lima, but at night comes alive and is packed with bars and clubs.

Plaza Mayor

Lima's main square, known as the **Plaza Mayor** or the Plaza de Armas, boasts

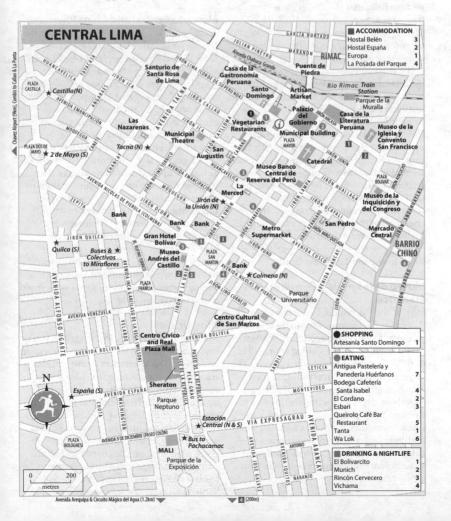

9

UNESCO World Heritage status due to its former colonial importance – Lima was capital of the Spanish Empire in South America – and its colours and famous wooden balconies are kept in beautiful condition accordingly. It is one of the largest squares in South America and has some of the most important government and religious buildings in Peru.

On the eastern corner of the plaza stands the austere Renaissance-style **Catedral** (open for Mass Sat 9am & Sun 11am). The interior retains some of its appealing Churrigueresque (highly elaborate Baroque) decor and it houses the **Museo de Arte Religioso** (Mon–Fri 9am–5pm, Sat 9am–1pm, Sun 1–5pm; S/10; ☎01 427 9647), which contains paintings from the seventeenth century as well as the remains of Francisco Pizarro.

The original **Palacio del Gobierno** was built on the site of Pizarro's adobe house, where he spent the last few years of his life until his assassination in 1541. The present building was only built in 1938 (the older palace was destroyed by an earthquake). It's possible to arrange a free tour, on Saturdays only, although this can take a few days to sort out (contact the Jefatura de Turismo, English spoken, on ☎01 311 3900, extension 523, ✉scuadros@presidencia.gob.pe). The **changing of the guard** takes place outside (daily 11.45am), which always draws a crowd to watch the marching soldiers and listen to the military brass band.

Museo de la Iglesia y Convento San Francisco

East of the Palacio del Gobierno along Jr Ancash is the majestic **Museo de la Iglesia y Convento San Francisco** (daily 9.30am–5pm; S/10 for 40min guided tour; ☎01 426 7377, ⓦmuseocatacumbas.com). The large seventeenth-century church has an attached **monastery**, which contains a superb library, a room of paintings by (or finished by) Rubens, Jordaens and Van Dyck, some pretty cloisters and, the main highlight, the vast crypts with gruesome **catacombs**, which contain the skeletons of some seventy thousand people – all of it well worth the visit.

Museo de la Inquisición

A couple of blocks southeast of San Francisco, the **Museo de la Inquisición y del Congreso**, Jr Junín 548 (daily 9am–5pm; free, by regular guided tours only, available in English; ☎01 311 7777, ⓦcongreso. gob.pe/museo.htm), was the headquarters of the Inquisition for the whole of Spanish America from 1570 until 1820. The museum includes the original tribunal room, with its beautifully carved mahogany ceiling, and beneath the building you can look round the dungeons and torture chambers, which contain a few gory, life-sized human models.

Mercado Central and Chinatown

Walk south on Avenida Abancay from the Museo de la Inquisición, take a left on Ucayali and after a couple of blocks you'll see the fascinating **Mercado Central** on your left, where you can buy almost anything (keeping one eye open for pickpockets). A little further east, an ornate Chinese gateway ushers visitors into Lima's **Barrio Chino**. This pedestrianized section of the street is, rather graphically, commonly referred to as Calle Capón (Castration Street) after some of the practices the Chinese used to fatten up their animals. As you'd expect, this is where many of Lima's best (from cheap to super-swanky) Chinese restaurants are, crammed into a few bustling streets. There's also an indoor mall selling Asian goods, and don't forget to look down at the modest walk of fame paying tribute to many *Limeños* who could afford to pay for a tile.

Jirón Ucayali

Walking back towards Plaza Mayor, you'll find that **Jirón Ucayali** has a few interesting buildings. The **Iglesia San Pedro**, on the corner with Jirón Azángaro (Mon–Sat 8.30am–1pm & 2–4pm; free), was built by the Jesuits in 1636 and the plain exterior is completely at odds with its richly decorated interior, a world of gold leaf, ornate tiles and impressive altars. A short walk west on the corner with Jirón Lampa is the excellent **Museo Banco Central de Reserva del Perú** (Tues–Sat 9am–5pm; free; ⓦwww.bcrp.gob.pe), whose permanent collection includes textiles, ceramics and a security-heavy room full of gold and precious artefacts, as well as a short history of Peruvian painting, with good information in English.

Santa Rosa de Lima and Las Nazarenas

Heading west down Jirón Lima from the Plaza Mayor you'll pass the **Iglesia y Convento Santo Domingo** on the corner with Camaná (Mon–Sat 9.30am–noon & 3–6pm, Sun 9am–1pm; monastery S/7, church free; ⓦconventosantodomingo.pe). It's here that you can see the skull and other remains of the first saint canonized in the Americas, Santa Rosa de Lima, along with those of another Peruvian saint, Martín de Porres.

If you continue on to Avenida Tacna, you'll come to the terracotta **Santuario de Santa Rosa de Lima** (Mon–Sat 9am–1pm & 3–6pm ; free), birthplace of the saint. Directly behind the church, a small garden offers a pleasant escape from the chaos of Lima, and many Peruvians come here to drop cards with their wishes on down the well.

A few blocks south on Tacna, at the junction with Huancavelica, is the **Iglesia de Las Nazarenas** (daily 6am–noon & 4–8.30pm; free), small and outwardly undistinguished but with an interesting history. After the 1655 earthquake, a mural of the crucifixion, painted by an Angolan slave on the wall of his hut, was apparently the only object left standing in the district. Its survival was deemed a miracle – the cause of popular processions ever since – and it was on this site that the church was founded. The widespread and popular processions for the **Lord of Miracles**, to save Lima from another earthquake, take place every autumn (Oct 6, 7, 18, 19, 28 & Nov 1). ·

Jirón de la Unión

The stretch of **Jirón de la Unión** between Plaza Mayor and Plaza San Martín is the main shopping street, with everything from designer brands to thrift stores. Nestled among the modern shops is perhaps the most noted of all religious buildings in Lima, the **Iglesia de La**

Merced, on the corner with Jirón Miro Quesada (daily 8am–noon & 5–8pm; free). Built on the site where the first Latin Mass in Lima was celebrated, the original church was demolished in 1628 to make way for the present building. Much of its beautiful colonial facade is not original, but look out for the **cross of Padre Urraca**, whose silver staff is smothered by hundreds of kisses every hour and witness to the fervent prayers of a constantly shifting congregation.

Plaza San Martín and around

Plaza San Martín is virtually always busy, with traffic tooting its way around the square and buskers, mime artists and soapbox *políticos* attracting small circles of interested faces. It has been (and continues to be) the site of most of Lima's political rallies. Of note is the huge **Gran Hotel Bolívar**, not for its rooms but for its streetside bar *El Bolivarcito*, which serves arguably the best pisco sour in Lima.

One block east of the Plaza, Avenida Nicolás de Piérola runs towards the **Parque Universitario**, with the grand old buildings of the first university in the Americas, San Marcos. The buildings now house the **Centro Cultural de San Marcos** (Mon–Sat 9am–5pm; free or S/5 with guided visit of historic building; ⓦcentrocultural.unmsm. edu.pe), the cultural centre of the modern university, now sited in Pueblo Libre. It hosts many interesting talks and events and also contains a gallery, focusing on Peruvian folk and contemporary art, and an archeological and anthropology museum with rotating exhibits on Peruvian history, as well as a permanent collection of textiles and ceramics.

Plaza Grau and around

The Jirón de la Unión becomes Jirón Belén and leads down to the **Plaza Grau** and the **Paseo de la República** (also known as the Vía Expresa), an enormous dual carriageway that cleaves through the city. Underneath the plaza is the Estación Central of the Metropolitano bus service (see page 737).

Just south of the plaza at Paseo Colón 125 is the **Museo de Arte Lima** (MALI; Tues–Fri & Sun 10am–7pm, Sat

9

FOOD, GLORIOUS FOOD

The ever-popular **La Mistura** gastronomy festival (ⓦmistura.pe) is held in September on **Campo de Marte** parkland. Created by Gastón Acurio (see page 724), this five-day food fest with more than two thousand stalls showcases the best of Peru's food and drink, from haute cuisine to street stalls, and is not to be missed. Go during the week if you can, to avoid the crowds.

10am–5pm; S/30; English-speaking guides available 10.30am–4pm; S/3; minimum two people; ⓦmali.pe), housed in the former International Exhibition Palace built in 1868 and designed by Eiffel. It contains interesting collections of colonial art and many fine crafts from pre-Columbian times, and also hosts frequent temporary exhibitions of modern photography and other art forms, as well as lectures and film screenings. MALI sits in the **Parque de la Exposición** (daily 8am–10pm; free), a pleasant green space with duck ponds and some pretty bandstands.

Through the park is the **Estadio Nacional** (National Stadium), and just beyond that lies Lima's most eccentric attraction, the **Circuito Mágico del Agua**, Av Petit

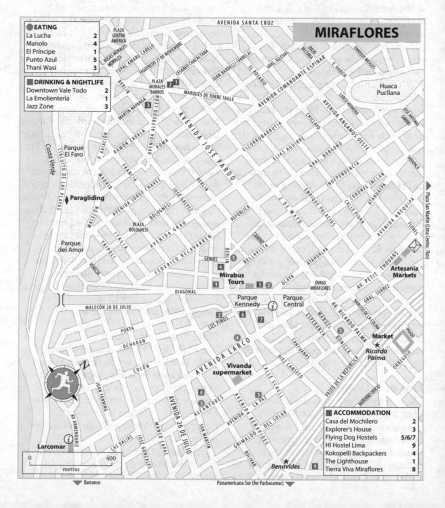

● **EATING**
La Lucha	2
Manolo	4
El Príncipe	1
Punto Azul	5
Thani Wasi	3

■ **DRINKING & NIGHTLIFE**
Downtown Vale Todo	2
La Emolientería	1
Jazz Zone	3

MIRAFLORES

■ **ACCOMMODATION**
Casa del Mochilero	2
Explorer's House	3
Flying Dog Hostels	5/6/7
HI Hostel Lima	9
Kokopelli Backpackers	4
The Lighthouse	1
Tierra Viva Miraflores	8

Thouars, at Jr Madre de Dios (Tues–Sun & holidays 3–10.30pm; S/4; ⓦparquedelareserva.com.pe). It's a park showcasing thirteen different fountains, including one over 80m tall and one sprouting arches you can walk under, all choreographed to pop music and coloured lights.

Museo de la Nación

The **Museo de la Nación**, Av Javier Prado Este 2466 (daily 9am–5pm; free; ☎01 476 9878, ⓦcultura.gob.pe), in San Borja, a district southeast of the centre, is one of the country's largest and most important museums and has an outstanding and very moving exhibition about the devastation caused by the Sendero Luminoso group, which terrorized the country in the 1980s and 1990s (see page 717).

To **get here**, take the Metropolitano bus from the centre or from Miraflores to the huge intersecting Avenida Javier Prado. Then take any bus east marked "todo Javier Prado" and ask for the museum.

Miraflores

Miraflores, its streets lined with cafés and flashy shops, is the major focus of Lima's gastronomy and nightlife as far as affluent locals and most tourists are concerned – along with San Isidro, further north, which has even more exclusive boutiques and lounge bars. To get here from the centre, either take the Metropolitano at Jr de la Unión and Avenida Emancipación and get off at Puente Ricardo Palma, or take a *combi* (line A; purple and white coloured) on Avenida Tacna.

The attractive **Parque Kennedy** at the end of Avenida Arequipa has a small craft and antiques market every evening (6–10pm). Avenida Larco, which runs along the eastern side of the park, leads to the ocean and to **Larcomar** (ⓦlarcomar.com), a popular clifftop mall with fantastic sea and coastline views. From here you can walk north along the Malecón through the small parks and flower gardens, as many others do at weekends. At the **Parque Raimondi** you can take tandem paraglides (daily 10am–6pm; S/260 for 10min; ☎01 495 3396) from the clifftop down to the beach, and a little farther on, the romantic

Parque del Amor holds a series of winding mosaic benches beneath a huge sculpture of a pair of embracing lovers.

Barranco

Barranco, scattered with old mansions as well as colourful smaller homes, was the capital's seaside resort during the nineteenth century and is now a kind of *limeño* Left Bank, with young artists and intellectuals taking over many of the older properties. To get here, take any *combi* along the Diagonal beside Parque Kennedy (about 10min), or take the Metropolitano to the Municipalidad stop.

The best museum here is the pleasant **Museo Pedro de Osma**, Av Pedro de Osma 421 (Tues–Sun 10am–6pm; S/20; ☎01 467 0141, ⓦmuseopedrodeosma.org), which houses a good collection of religious art, silver and antique furniture in a stunning French-style mansion with stained-glass windows designed by the eponymous collector. Another highlight is the **Museo Mario Testino**, or MATE, Av Pedro de Osma 409 (Tues–Sun 10am–7pm; S/10; ☎01 200 5400, ⓦmate.pe), housed in another beautifully restored colonial town house and the first permanent exhibition to the UK-based fashion photographer in his home town.

A walk across the **Puente de Suspiros** (The Bridge of Sighs) to the cliffside bars and cafés is a favourite pastime for locals – as well as checking out some of the colourful houses, often daubed with graffiti, on streets such as Calle Cajamarca – but otherwise there's little else to see specifically; besides the two museums, the main draws of Barranco are its bars, clubs and cafés clustered around the attractive **Plaza Municipal**.

Pueblo Libre

This upcoming neighbourhood, southwest of the centre, hosts two world-class museums. The **Museo Nacional de Arqueología, Antropología e Historia del Perú** (Plaza Bolívar s/n; daily 8.45am–5pm; S/10) has an extensive collection of pre-Hispanic and colonial artefacts, helpfully laid out in chronological order. It also houses the two most important relics from the Chavín de Huántar site near

9

HUACAS

There are reminders of Lima's pre-Columbian past all over the capital in the form of adobe **huacas** – sacred places – also referred to as pyramids. They are mostly associated with the Lima culture, which dominated in the area from 200 to 700 AD. Two of the most impressive sit wonderfully at odds with the modern monstrosities around them. The **Huaca Pucllana**, at General Borgoño block 8, Miraflores (Mon & Wed–Sun 9am–4.30pm; S/12; ☎01 617 7138, ⓦhuacapucllanamiraflores.pe/english), the larger of the two, was thought to have been a major administrative centre. It's a short walk from Av Arequipa at block 44 (off to the right if you're coming from central Lima). **Huaca Huallamarca**, Nicolás de Ribera 201, San Isidro (Tues–Sun 9am–5pm; S/5), is three blocks from Camino Real along Choquehuanca. It's thought to be a little older than Pucllana and pertains to the Hualla tribe. The spaceship-like ramp can be scaled to get great views of the neighbourhood. Both tickets include entrance to small site museums.

The most wonderful of all Lima's *huacas*, **Pachacamac**, lies outside the city at Km31.5 off the Antigua Panamericana Sur, Lurín (Mon–Sat 9am–5pm, Sun 9am–4pm; S/15; ☎01 430 0168, ⓦpachacamac.cultura.pe). It's easily reached by public transport – you can do it in half a day. Get there from Lima centro by catching the brown *combi* marked San Bartolo from outside MALI and double-check that it's going to Lurín. Alternatively, you can get this same *combi* nearer Miraflores by taking any bus marked "todo Benavides" from Miraflores to the Panamericana; go down the steps to the busy motorway and wait at the stop under the bridge. From here it's about 30min away and you can be dropped off right outside the Museo de Sitio (site museum).

Huaraz: the Raimondi Stela, a 2m-tall piece of granite with intricate carvings, and the Tello Obelisk, which once lurked underground, worshipped by priests of the Chavín cult. Part of the museum is in a mansion once inhabited by the liberators Simón Bolívar and José de San Martín.

Follow the (sometimes worn) blue line outside the museum for a pleasant 25-minute walk to the expensive but excellent **Museo Rafael Larco** at Av Bolívar 1515 (daily 9am–10pm; S/30; guided tour in English S/25, reserve in advance; ☎01 461 1312, ⓦmuseolarco.org). Situated in a viceroy's mansion, which in turn was built on a pre-Columbian pyramid, it displays the enormous private collection of Peruvian archeologist Rafael Larco, which includes textiles, jewellery, gold, silver and ceramics. Best of all, you can explore the vast storage rooms, packed to the rafters with more than 45,000 pre-Columbian objects. It's also famous for its extensive collection of erotic ceramics.

These museums are close to both the **artisan stalls** on blocks 6–8 of Avenida La Marina known as the Mercado Inca (9am–8.30pm) and the **Parque de las Leyendas**, Av Las Leyendas 580 (daily 9am–6pm; S/10; ⓦleyendas.gob.pe), a family-orientated zoo landscaped to represent the three zones in Peru – coast,

mountains and jungle. The site also contains more than thirty pre-Columbian *huacas* (see page 736), all in differing stages of excavation, as well as a botanical garden and boating lake.

ARRIVAL AND DEPARTURE

BY PLANE

All flights leave and depart from Jorge Chávez Airport (ⓦwww.lap.com.pe) in Callao, 10km northwest of the city centre – departure and arrival taxes are included in the price of tickets. The two main carriers serving the rest of the country are LATAM (ⓦlatam.com) and the cheaper StarPerú (ⓦstarperu.com).

FROM THE AIRPORT INTO TOWN

By taxi The quickest and safest way to get into central Lima (45min) is to take an official taxi from one of the companies with desks at the airport on street level – pay there and you'll be assigned a driver. Taxi Green is the cheapest (S/45–55 to downtown; ☎01 484 4001, ⓦwww.taxigreen.com. pe). Taxi Directo is another reliable option (☎01 711 1111, ⓦtaxidirecto.com).

Destinations Arequipa (10 daily; 1hr 20min); Cajamarca (5 daily; 1hr 20min); Cusco (15 daily; 1hr 15min); Iquitos (8 daily; 1hr 45min); Tumbes (daily; 1hr 50min).

BY BUS

Unfortunately Peru doesn't have central terminals – each bus company has its own private terminal. Buses to Lima usually arrive and depart in the district of La Victoria, near central Lima, or at the other end of La Victoria on Av

Javier Prado. Whichever terminal, it's best to hail the first decent-looking taxi you see and fix a price – about S/12–15 from or to anywhere in the centre, or S/15–18 from or to anywhere else in Lima. Many buses can't be booked online, so you'll have to visit the office in person – it's worth booking in advance if you want the best seats (ie *cama*, with fully reclining seats). A good option is to find a decent travel agent – the in-house agency in the *Hotel España* is recommended and they can advise you about different companies, hours and prices.

BUS COMPANIES

The following bus companies have the best fleets and services.

Cruz del Sur Av Javier Prado 1109 (☎01 311 5050, ⊛cruzdelsur.com.pe)

Línea Av Paseo de la República 941–959 (☎01 424 0836, ⊛linea.pe)

Movil Tours Paseo de la República 749, (☎01 716 8000, ⊛moviltours.com.pe)

Oltursa Av Aramburu 1160, San Isidro (☎01 708 5000, ⊛oltursa.pe)

Ormeño Av Javier Prado Oeste 1057 (☎01 472 1710)

Soyuz Perú Av México 333 (☎01 266 1515, ⊛soyuz.com.pe)

Tepsa Av Javier Prado Este 1091 (☎01 617 9000, ⊛tepsa.com.pe)

DESTINATIONS

Ayacucho (9hr 30min): Cruz del Sur (3 daily)

Arequipa (15hr): Cruz del Sur (7 daily), Oltursa (6 daily), Ormeño (1 daily), TEPSA (2 daily)

Cajamarca (14hr): Cruz del Sur (1 daily), Línea (2 daily), TEPSA (1 daily)

Chachapoyas (20hr): Movil Tours (1 daily)

Chiclayo (12hr): Cruz del Sur (4 daily), Línea (2 daily), Movil Tours (2 daily), Oltursa (4 daily), TEPSA (3 daily)

Cusco (22hr): Cruz del Sur (2 daily), Oltursa (1 daily), Movil Tours (1 daily), TEPSA (2 daily)

Puno (20hr): Ormeño (1 daily)

Huaraz (7hr 30min): Cruz del Sur (4 daily), Oltursa (4 daily), Movil Tours (5 daily)

Nazca (7hr 30min): Cruz del Sur (5 daily), Oltursa (3 daily), Ormeño (2 daily), Soyuz Perú (hourly), TEPSA (3 daily)

Tacna (19hr): Cruz del Sur (2 daily), Oltursa (2 daily), TEPSA (1 daily)

Trujillo (9hr): Cruz del Sur (4 daily), Oltursa (3 daily), Línea (9 daily), Movil Tours (1 daily), TEPSA (2 daily)

Tumbes via Máncora (18–20hr): Cruz del Sur, Línea, Oltursa, Ormeño, TEPSA (all 1 daily).

BY TRAIN

Apart from a small local service, the only train from Lima goes to Huancayo once a month (⊛ferrocarrilcentral.com.pe). It departs from Desamparados station (Jr Ancash 207).

GETTING AROUND

By bus *Combis* race from one street corner to another along all the major arterial city roads. Wave one down and pay the flat fare (S/1–1.50 within Lima, depending on distance) to the driver or *cobrador* (conductor). A fantastic unofficial map of Lima's most useful and safe *combis* (many are more than a little ropey) can be purchased for US$2.50 at ⊛rutasrecomendables.com.

By colectivo A useful form of transport for getting to outer districts of the capital such as Chosica and Comas, mostly leaving from Plaza Bolognesi (S/4–8).

By taxi Taxis should not cost more than S/20 within the city (except to/from the airport). Most are unofficial, although the yellow ones with a licence plate number on the side are, in theory, regulated. It is, perhaps, better to look at the condition of the car and always agree on a price beforehand as they don't have meters. As a guide, taxis within a district (such as anywhere within central Lima) should be S/6–12, while Miraflores to the centre should be S/12–15. Private companies are few and far between, change numbers regularly and charge a lot more.

By shared taxi Uber (⊛uber.com) operates In Lima, and is both convenient and quite user-friendly, at perhaps a sole or two more than a regular taxi, without the haggling.

INFORMATION

Tourist information The municipal tourist office is just off the Plaza Mayor behind the Palacio Municipal (Pasaje Los Escribanos 145; daily 9am–5pm; ☎01 315 1300,

---

METROPOLITANO

Lima may be one of the largest cities in the world without an underground metro, but it does have the very modern **Metropolitano** bus service (daily 6am–9.50pm, express service during rush hours 7–9.30am & 5–8.30pm; ⊛www.metropolitano.com.pe). This bus runs through the city north to south and connects the main tourist areas of Barranco, Miraflores and San Isidro along the Paseo de la República with central Lima. It uses a rechargeable card which subtracts S/2.50 per ride, and it's the quickest, easiest and certainly the safest way to get around Lima as the buses use special lanes and the fleet is new. Check the website (under "rutas") for any changes before you use the service.

9

ext 1542). iPerú is the national tourist info provider, and can also help if you need to make a complaint, visit the police or simply book accommodation. iPerú has desks in Lima airport (open 24hr; ☎01 574 8000) and Miraflores (Larcomar, stand 10; daily 11am–2pm & 3–8pm; ☎01 445 9400), as well as San Isidro (Jorge Basadre 610; Mon–Fri 8.30am–6pm; ☎01 421 1627). Callao has a basic tourist information booth on the road between Plaza Grau and Chuquito (daily 10am–5pm), which has information about the museums in the area. There's also a fairly helpful tourist office in Barranco's Parque Municipal (Mon–Sat 9am–6.30pm & Sun 2–6.30pm; ☎01 719 2046).

TOUR OPERATORS

Bike Tours of Lima C Bolívar 150, Miraflores ☎01 445 3172, ⓦbiketoursoflima.com. Does what it says on the tin, as well as bike rentals.

Ecocruceros Av Arequipa 4960, Miraflores, and a stand by the port in Callao ☎01 226 8530, ⓦislaspalomino. com. Runs trips to the Islas Palominos ($49).

Fertur Peru Jr Junín 211, Central Lima ☎01 427 2626, ⓦfertur-travel.com. Offers nationwide package tours and some local tours.

Kolibri Expeditions C Schreiber 192, Miraflores ☎988 555 938, ⓦkolibriexpeditions.com. Recommended for birdwatching tours locally and across Peru.

Lima Vision Jr Chiclayo 444, Miraflores ☎01 447 7710, ⓦlimavision.com. The best choice for Lima tours, including Pachacamac and the museums.

Mirabús Stalls in both Parque Kennedy and Plaza Mayor ☎01 242 6699, ⓦmirabusperu.com. Runs open-top bus tours of Lima by day/night, as well as to Pachacamac. Also connects for boat trips to the Islas Palominos (bi-monthly) and a land and sea excursion (Thurs, Fri & Sat 2pm).

ACCOMMODATION

There are good budget options throughout the city, although Central Lima works out slightly cheaper and offers hostels within walking distance of some of the most important tourist sights. Barranco has a relaxed bohemian atmosphere and is close to the sea, but the most popular district for tourists is still Miraflores; with bright lights and fast-food joints on every corner, it has a cosmopolitan feel, plus plenty of chain backpacker hostels providing mainly dorm-style accommodation. There are no campsites, official or otherwise.

CENTRAL LIMA

Hostal Belén Nicolás de Piérola 953, Plaza San Martín ☎01 427 8995; map p.731. One of the best-value budget options in Central Lima – a well-maintained colonial gem with a restaurant (Mon–Sat) serving bargain set lunches. Try to get a room with views of the plaza. S/85

★ **Hostal España** Jr Azángaro 105 ☎01 428 5546, ⓦhotelespanaperu.com; map p.731. The main courtyard, filled with antique oil paintings, marble statues and trailing pot plants, is quite stunning. There's also a verdant rooftop patio where breakfast is served (S/6–6.50) – look out for peacocks strutting about. *España* is perhaps a little old-school, but it's secure and has a book exchange and a tour operator service for onward travel anywhere in the country. Dorms S/25, doubles S/65

Europa Jr Ancash 376 ☎01 427 3351; map p.731. A very basic and slightly run-down building opposite the San Francisco church, with a pretty internal courtyard. The rooms are worthy of a monastery in their simplicity (most have shared bathroom), but it's good value (although can be cold in winter). Dorms S/25, doubles S/38

La Posada del Parque Parque Hernan Velarde 60, Santa Beatriz ☎01 433 2412, ⓦlaposadadelparque. com; map p.731. A wonderful boutique hotel in a large, quiet and stylish house close to Lima Centro and the Parque de la Exposición, but south of the city's busiest sectors. The rooms are excellently kept and well furnished, with super breakfasts. S/150

MIRAFLORES

Casa del Mochilero Jr Cesareo Chacaltana 130A, upstairs ☎01 444 9089, ⓔpilaryv@hotmail.com; map p.734. This safe place is remarkably good for the price, with hot water, cable TV and a stainless-steel kitchen. It's not right at the centre of Miraflores's action, but it's close enough. Don't confuse it with the similarly named and decorated hostel next door; ask for Pilar or Juan to be sure you're in the right place (it's the green building). Dorms S/17, doubles S/50

Explorer's House Av Alfredo Leon 158 ☎01 241 5002, ⓦexplorershouselima.com; map p.734. Out of the centre of Miraflores but close to the sea, *Explorer's House* is a good old-fashioned hostel. Breakfast is included, and hot water and a rooftop terrace add to the charm; there's also a small kitchen for guests to use. Book ahead as it is small and popular. Dorms S/28, doubles S/80

Flying Dog Hostels ⓦflyingdogperu.com; map p.734. The *Flying Dog* is the most established backpacker joint in the city, with several outlets: *Backpackers*, Diez Canseco 117 (includes breakfast); *Bed and Breakfast*, C Lima 457; *Hostel*, Olaya 280. All locations offer cheap accommodation, kitchen use, TV room, storage service and breakfast, as well as being hugely popular and therefore a great place to meet people. Dorms S/40, doubles S/110

HI Hostel Lima C Casimiro Ulloa 328 ☎01 446 5488, ⓦlimahostell.com; map p.734. East of the Paseo de la Republica highway, the big, fairly modern house sports a pool, and a restaurant and bar with views to a pleasant garden. A great deal. Airport pick-up available. Dorms S/51, doubles S/185

★ TREAT YOURSELF

Tierra Viva Miraflores Larco C Bolivar 176 ☎01 637 1003, ⓦtierravivahoteles.com; map p.734. A good-value spot worth a little splurge, the medium-sized rooms are sleek and splashed with bright multicolour accents. Great location off Av Larco, and breakfast is served adjacent to an airy terrace overlooking the city. S/260

Kokopelli Backpackers C Berlin 259 ☎01 242 5665, ⓦhostelkokopelli.com; map p.734. Another top spot for meeting people, with the social life revolving around a rooftop bar that is always buzzing. Dorms S/41, doubles S/115

★ The Lighthouse Jr Cesareo Chacaltana 162 ☎01 446 8397, ⓦthelighthouseperu.com; map p.734. Spacious, comfortable rooms in this B&B (one with a balcony) with cable TV – good for those looking for a more tranquil stay. A patio with barbecue plus a communal area with DVDs, books and wi-fi offer the budget traveller some real creature comforts. Kitchen use and a generous breakfast all add to the experience. Book in advance as there are only eight rooms. $33

BARRANCO

Hostal Barranco Jr Ignacio Mariategui 105 ☎01 252 6666, ⓦhostalbarranco.com; map p.728. You won't be hanging out with other travellers here, but there are plenty of bars nearby. The clean rooms and en-suite bathrooms, and 24hr security, make up for the thin walls and slight street noise. Off Av Bolognesi, northeast of the Plaza de Armas. S/70

Domeyer C Domeyer 296 ☎01 247 1413; map p.728. This hostel has a bohemian feel (there's normally one or two long-stayers here), shared kitchen and living room plus laundry service (and a decent breakfast included with room price). Rooms include cable, and there is a cheaper dorm room. LGBTQ friendly. Dorms S/50, doubles S/150

The Point Malecón Junín 300 ☎01 247 7997, ⓦthepointhostels.com; map p.728. Boasts lots of facilities including TV room and kitchen, as well as the on-site *Pointless Bar*, a great place to meet other travellers and have a good time. Relaxed garden with hammocks is a boon. Dorms S/34, doubles S/90

EATING

Lima has seen its gastronomy boom in the past few years, partly thanks to Peruvian celebrity chefs Gastón Acurio and Virgilio Martinez (see page 724); the swell in national pride surrounding Peruvian cuisine is palpable, nowhere more so than in Lima. Many of the more upmarket restaurants fill up very quickly, so it's advisable to reserve in advance.

CENTRAL LIMA

There is a Metro supermarket on Jr Cusco 245 (between Lampa and Augusto Wiese) and other locations, as well as several large and nicely stocked Vivanda markets around the city. Most *chifas* (Chinese restaurants) in Chinatown are good and very cheap. There is also a whole street full of vegetarian restaurants one block from the Plaza de Armas on Camaná.

★ Antigua Pastelería y Panedería Huérfanos Azángaro 700 ☎01 428 6273; map p.731. This cake shop has been here for over one hundred years – and is easily the best place in central Lima for bread. It also makes its own fresh pasta and you can buy pastries and biscuits by weight. Also has a small restaurant. Plate of lasagne with wine and bread S/20. Daily 6.40am–8.50pm.

★ Bodega Cafetería Santa Isabel Jr Carabaya 520 ☎01 426 0058; map p.731. Recharge after sightseeing in this tiny *huarique* that serves some of the best coffee in Lima. Excellent chocolates and drinks are available, and they also specialize in regional cheeses and hams – their sandwiches and *empanadas* (S/3) are excellent. Mon–Sat 8am–9pm.

El Cordano Jr Ancash 202 ☎01 427 0181, ⓦrestaurantecordano.com; map p.731. Beside the Palacio del Gobierno, this is one of the city's last surviving traditional bar-restaurants, open since 1905. The food is overpriced, but go for a drink, soak up the atmosphere and feel yourself slip back in time. Does a roaring trade in local ham sandwiches (S/10). Mon–Sat 8am–9pm.

Esbari Jr de la Unión 574; map p.731. Primarily an ice-cream parlour with fabulous flavours and sundaes (S/15), good coffee and cheap food – look for the *"ofertas"* section in the back of the menu where everything is less than S/10. Mon–Sat 9am–11.30pm, Sun 9am–9pm.

Queirolo Café Bar Restaurant Camaná 900; map p.731. Arguably there is no place that better represents old bohemian Lima; this bar has seen every artist and writer in the city come through its doors for lunch or drinks since 1880. They serve a good set lunch (S/10), as well as sandwiches and the usual *criolla* favourites. Mon–Fri 9am–2am.

Tanta Pj Nicolás de Rivera 142 ☎01 428 3115; map p.731. If you can't afford a whole Gastón Acurio meal, his café chain *Tanta* can give you a taste of what he has to offer. This one, opposite the tourist information office, is a very pleasant place to refuel while sightseeing. Serves breakfasts, sandwiches, soups, salads and mains. Try the *ají de gallina* (S/30) or *lomo saltado* (S/43) and one of the fruit juice mixes (S/12–16). There's another location inside Larco Mar mall. Mon–Sat 9am–10pm, Sun 9am–6pm.

Wa Lok Jr Paruro 864, Chinatown ☎01 427 2656; map p.731. An excellent and traditional Chinese restaurant, consistently recommended by many Peruvians. It offers a range of authentic *chifa* dishes, and although it's not

9

the cheapest (mains S/38–60 and up), there are good vegetarian and dim sum options under S/20. Mon–Sat 9am–11pm, Sun 9am–10pm.

MIRAFLORES

Eating options tend to be a little more expensive out of the centre, but there are a lot of good set menus for S/8–12 on Los Pinos (even at dinner) and in the small passage connecting Manuel Bonilla to Esperanza (go for the ones that are full of locals). Both streets are off Parque Kennedy. There is also a huge food market between the Ovalo Parque Kennedy and Paseo de la Republica at Jr Eledoro Romero, and supermarkets everywhere.

La Lucha Av Diagonal, at C Olaya, plus other locations in the city; map p.734. This sandwich joint may be diminutive, but its oversized sandwiches with a variety of meaty fillings and sauces certainly aren't – the *chicharrón* (deep-fried pork) is particularly delicious at S/14.10 for a large portion. You can also pick up a variety of juices and shakes, too. Mon–Thurs & Sun 8am–1am, Fri & Sat 8am–3am.

Manolo Av Larco 608 ☎01 44 2244, ⊛manolochurros. com; map p.734. This Miraflores institution is all about the Spanish-style *churros con chocolate* – a thin doughnut that comes with hot chocolate for dipping; heaven for just S/12.80. Also does breakfasts, mains, burgers and the like. Daily 7am–1am.

El Príncipe Berlín 250 ☎01 241 4332; map p.734. A standout weekday lunchtime menu (S/9) with Peruvian fish and meat dishes tastier and more generous than similar deals on the same street. Many wash it all down with a stein of beer and return at night for a pisco sour. Mon, Wed, Thurs & Sun 11am–1am, Tues 11am–5pm, Fri & Sat 11am–3am.

★ **Punto Azul** Benavides 2711 and San Martín 595, Miraflores ☎01 445 8078, ⊛puntoazulrestaurante.

★ **TREAT YOURSELF**

El Grifo Av Oscar R. Benavides (ex-colonial) 2703, near the crossroad with Universitaria ☎01 564 7789, ✉jefatura.colonial@elgrifo.pe; map p.728. Literally called "the petrol station", this chic Lima restaurant is on an old petrol forecourt. It serves some of the best versions of classic Peruvian dishes in Lima, including mouth-watering *lomo saltado* (S/26) – marinated steak, their speciality – and original fusions such as the delicious *fettuccini a la Huancaína con lomo* (S/29), as well as stunning desserts. The standard of food and service is impeccable, more than worth the price. Take a taxi. Breakfasts S/10–20, Mains S/20–40. Daily 9am–10pm.

---

com; map p.734. This *cevichería* is a real gem. As well as *ceviche* (S/25) it serves other Peruvian classics involving fish or seafood, such as *causas* (tuna with mashed potato and lime) and *chupes* (chowder). The original site, a *huarique* on the busy Javier Prado in San Isidro, has you sitting on stools outside, while those in Miraflores are more restaurant-like. Tues–Sun 11am–4pm.

Thani Wasi C Manuel Bonilla 176; map p.734. Locals pack out the small wooden tables here at lunchtime for the tasty and healthy food on good-value menus (S/8–12), featuring everything from *bistec a la pobre* (steak, egg and chips) to *trucha* (trout). Daily 11am–4pm.

BARRANCO AND OTHER SUBURBS

Anticuchos Tio Jhony Catalina Miranda 101, at Av Paseo de la República; map p.728. This authentic *huarique* serves some of the best *anticuchos* (beef heart kebabs) in the capital. Don't be put off by the unusual meat – *anticuchos* are the most flavourful beef you'll ever try, especially here (S/20–30). "Uncle" Jhony's special chilli sauce is spectacular. Daily 5pm–1am.

Café Cultural Expreso Virgen de Guadalupe Av San Martín 15A, next to the Municipalidad ☎01 252 8907; map p.728. A unique vegetarian restaurant in an old tram car right on the main square. Lunchtime buffet S/21 (S/23 at weekends) for a great selection of meat-free and some vegan dishes. Daily 5pm–midnight (live music weekends from 10pm).

Mi Carochita Av Pedro de Osma, at Malecón Castilla ☎01 248 7826; map p.728. Friendly corner bar and café that does a good range of snacks, sandwiches and juices – but the main draw is the fact that it's open 24hr. Lunch menu S/15 (S/17 at weekends).

DRINKING AND NIGHTLIFE

The daily newspaper *El Comercio* provides good entertainment listings and its Friday edition carries a comprehensive supplement on Lima's nightlife. The Plaza San Martín is a frenetic nightlife spot, with enough bars and clubs there to take you through until dawn. Barranco is also trendy and the liveliest place to hang out at weekends, while Miraflores has the highest concentration of cheap bars around the Parque Kennedy. There are good places for live music in all three areas. As you would expect, Friday and Saturday nights are the most popular, and many bars and clubs only open on those days. Most bars have Facebook pages to check what's on.

BARS AND CLUBS

The distinction between a bar and a club in Lima is often blurred, as bars become dancefloors and stay open all night. A good guide as to which is which is the opening times – many of the clubs only open at weekends. Lima also has a fun and rapidly growing gay and lesbian scene; see ⊛lima. gaycities.com for current information about what's on.

Ayahuasca Av Prol San Martín 130, Barranco ☎01 247 6751; map p.728. A fantastic venue, this place is based in a lovingly restored mansion with several interesting bar areas; it's not cheap but the drinks are inventive and there are some great bites as well. Very busy after 11pm on weekends. Mon–Sat 8pm–3am.

El Bolivarcito Jr de la Unión 926, Central Lima ⓦ granhotelbolivar.com.pe; map p.731. Come to the "catedral" of pisco sour, part of the *Gran Hotel Bolívar*, for probably the best in Lima (the classic house pisco will set you back S/28). Also does an excellent set lunch (S/17; except Sun). Mon–Sat noon–midnight, Sun noon–11pm.

Downtown Vale Todo Pasaje Los Pinos 168, Miraflores ☎01 444 6433, ⓦ mundovaletodo.com; map p.734. The name means "everything's allowed downtown" and it certainly is here at Lima's most established LGBTQ club. Often has live drag or strip shows. Usually free Mon–Thurs, entrance fee at weekends. Mon–Thurs & Sun 8pm–1am, Fri & Sat 8pm–3am.

La Emollentería JC Diagonal 598, Miraflores ☎01 444 5579; map p.734. Very spare but hip ambiance, with lots of glass, a science-lab inspired bar, and two floors of colour and artwork, with a wide variety of flavoured pisco cocktails made to order from S/25. Mon–Fri noon–1am, Sat noon–2.30am, Sun 5.30pm–1am.

Munich Jr de la Unión 1044, Central Lima; map p.731. German-themed underground piano bar with a barrel for a doorway, plus bar food, a live pianist and nostalgic European landscapes on the walls. Mon–Sat 5pm–midnight.

Rincón Cervecero Jr de la Unión 1045A, Central Lima ☎01 428 8866, ⓦ rinconcervecero.com.pe; map p.731. Another German-themed bar opposite *Munich*, where you can order beer in containers of all forms, including a 5-litre barrel (S/80), from Peruvian waiters in lederhosen. Mon–Thurs noon–midnight, Fri & Sat noon–3am, Sun noon–9pm.

Vichama Jr Carabaya 945, Central Lima; map p.731. A seriously cool rock bar/club in a huge colonial space, with many small art-filled rooms containing a mix of shabby-chic furniture. Free entry. Thurs–Sat 7pm–6am.

Wahio's Bar Pasaje Espinoza 111 on the Plaza de Bomberos ☎987 555 422; map p.728. Cosy bar club with several rooms playing different sounds, though you'll mostly hear reggae and electronic pop. Walls are packed with photos and artwork, there's comfy seating and bar food is served. Free entry. Thurs–Sat from around 9.30pm until the last people leave.

LIVE MUSIC

The great variety of traditional and hybrid sounds is one of the most enduring reasons for visiting the capital. The best place to go for an evening's entertainment is a *peña* – a live music spectacular featuring many styles of national song and dance with an MC, live band, some audience participation and much dancing. *Peñas* are great fun for all ages – they start late and the dancing can last all night. The Lima versions are very expensive compared to the rest of the country (you can pay up to S/60 just to enter) – so if you can't go here, be sure to seek one out elsewhere.

La Candelaria Av Bolognesi 292, Barranco ☎01 247 1314, ⓦ lacandelariaperu.com; map p.728. Impressive costumes, choreography and plenty of audience participation mark this place out as one of Barranco's most popular *peñas*. The amazingly decorated room adds to the atmosphere. Entrance fee (depending on the show) S/35–45, including a pisco sour. Shows Thurs & Sat starting at 9.30pm.

Jazz Zone Av La Paz 646, Pasaje El Suche, Miraflores ☎01 241 8139, ⓦ jazzzoneperu.com; map p.734. Live music (most often rock, jazz and *música criolla*) from local and international groups in this atmospheric joint upstairs. Entrance fee varies depending on the show. Tues–Sat from 8pm.

★ **La Noche** Psj Sanchez Carrión 199A, Barranco ⓦ lanoche.com.pe; map p.728. At the top end of the Boulevard, this bar is really packed at weekends and is the top nightspot in the neighbourhood. There's a section with a stage for live music, with free jazz sessions on Monday. Free entry to bar, cover charge for live music. Mon–Sat 7.30pm–3am.

SHOPPING

Artesanía All types of Peruvian *artesanía* are available in Lima, including woollen goods, crafts and gemstones. Some of the best in Peru are on Av Petit Thouars, which is home to a handful of markets between Av Ricardo Palma and Av Angamos, all within easy walking distance of Miraflores centre. Often considerably cheaper are the artisan markets on blocks 9 and 10 of Av La Marina in Pueblo Libre, as well as the good craft and antique market in the Miraflores Park between Diagonal and Av Larco, which takes place every evening (6–9pm; map p.731). In central Lima the Artesanía Santo Domingo, opposite the church of the same name, houses a range of suppliers to suit all budgets, just a stone's throw from the Plaza Mayor; it is especially good for loose beads.

DIRECTORY

Banks and exchange Central Lima, Miraflores, Barranco and San Isidro all have several casas de cambio, and Interbank will change money. Moneychangers on the streets will often give a slightly better rate but will try all sorts of tricks, from doctored calculators to fake money. Official moneychangers on the streets around Parque Kennedy offer good rates. Ensure that they are wearing the official blue vests and laminated badges. Often the best way to change money in Lima is by buying things in supermarkets with large US$ notes and asking them for the change in soles – they usually give good rates.

9

Embassies and consulates Australia, Av La Paz 1049, 10th floor, Miraflores (☎ 01 630 0500); Bolivia, Los Castaños 235 (☎ 01 440 2095); Brazil, Av José Pardo 850, Miraflores (☎ 01 512 0830); Canada, Bolognesi 228, Miraflores (☎ 01 319 3200); Chile, Av Javier Prado Oeste 790 (☎ 01 710 2211); Colombia, Av Víctor Andrés Belaúnde, Office 602 (☎ 01 201 9830); Ireland, Av Paseo de la Republica 5757b, Miraflores (☎ 01 242 9516); Ecuador, Las Palmeras, San Isidro (☎ 01 212 4161); South Africa, Av Víctor Andrés Belaúnde, Edificio Real 3, Office 801, San Isidro (☎ 01 440 9996); UK, Torre Parque Mar, Av Larco 1301, 22nd floor, Miraflores (☎ 01 617 3000); USA, Av La Encalada, block 17, Surco (☎ 01 618 2000).

Postal services Not overly reliable, the principal postal company is SERPOST whose main office is on Pasaje Piura s/n off Jr de la Unión, one block from the Plaza de Armas (8am–8.30pm; ☎ 01 511 5110). SERPOST also has an office in Miraflores at Petit Thouars 5201.

Tourist police Jr Moore 268, Magdalena del Mar (☎ 01 460 1060 or ☎ 980 121 462, ✉ divtur@pnp.gob.pe). English spoken.

CALLAO

Still the country's main commercial harbour, and one of the most modern ports in South America, **Callao** lies about 14km west of central Lima. Its main attraction is the pentagonal **Fortaleza del Real Felipe**, on Plaza Independencia, which houses the **Museo del Ejército** (Military Museum; Tues–Sun 9.30am–4pm; S/15 by 1hr 30min guided tour in Spanish or English; ☎ 01 429 0532). The collection of eighteenth-century arms and rooms dedicated to Peruvian heroes are interesting, but the real star is the fort itself, a superb example of the military architecture of its age. A short walk from the fort, at the dock on Plaza Grau, you can take **boat tours** (see page 820) out around local islands. Book ahead for trips further out to the **Islas Palomino** (4hr; around S/115), where you'll see sea birds, dolphins and sometimes whales.

ARRIVAL

By bus or colectivo To get to Callao from central Lima, take a *colectivo* from Plaza Dos de Mayo running down Av Oscar R. Benavides, or a bus from Av Tacna (line Roma 1). Note that Callao can be dangerous in the evening, and even in the daytime, so exercise caution.

Ayacucho

Beautiful **AYACUCHO** (2761m) played a vital role for the fifteenth-century Spanish Conquistadors, thanks to its strategic location between Lima and Cusco and between Potosí (Bolivia) and Antofagasta (Chile), both home to gold, silver and mercury mines. Ayacucho attracted rich miners and landowners who financed the construction of the beautiful churches and colonial buildings that are still standing today. More recently, the region was one of the worst hit in the 1980s when the Maoist revolutionary movement Sendero Luminoso, or Shining Path, launched mass internal conflict leading to the death of thousands. The city's isolation and its turbulent history mean that the area has mostly remained off the backpacker trail. Nonetheless, since the late 1990s, the region has become as safe as the rest of Peru and travellers have begun to explore the city's treasures and enjoy the surrounding Andean landscape.

WHAT TO SEE AND DO

The heart of the city is the Plaza Mayor, with its sixteenth- and seventeenth-century buildings characterized by stone arches, pillars with balustrades and red-brick clay roofs. The plaza is home to the seventeenth-century **Catedral**, which combines Renaissance and Baroque elements. Despite its somewhat sombre facade, its rich interior comprises ten beautiful gold-leaf altarpieces.

Visitors should not miss the **Museo de la Memoria** (Prolongación Libertad 1229; Mon–Fri 9am–1pm & 3–6pm, Sat 9am–1pm; S/2; ☎ 066 317 170), which focuses on the socio-political violence inflicted by the Shining Path revolutionary movement in the 1980s and 90s, with photographs of the dead and missing, as well as a replica of a torture cell.

ARRIVAL AND DEPARTURE

By plane The airport (☎ 066 527 092) is 4km east of town, a 10–15min taxi ride (S/6). *Combis* (every 15min; 10min) connect the airport to Puente Nuevo on Jr Vivanco. LATAM, at Jr 9 de Diciembre 107 (☎ 066 310 998), and LC Perú, at Jr 9 de Diciembre 139 (☎ 066 312 151) (4 daily; 1hr 5min) have offices in the city.

By bus Most buses use the Terminal Municipal Los Libertadores de America on Av Pérez de Cuellar s/n (☎ 066 312 666), although many companies have ticket offices on Manoc Copac, four blocks north of the Plaza de Armas. Cruz del Sur, with buses to Lima, has its own terminal at Jr Mariscal Cáceres 1264 (☎ 066 312 813).

Destinations Cusco (2 daily; 12–16hr); Ica (1 daily; 6hr); Lima (several daily; 8–9hr).

INFORMATION

Tourist information The friendly and helpful iPerú office is at Jr Cusco 108, just off the Plaza de Armas (Mon–Sat 9am–6pm, Sun 9am–1pm; ☎ 066 318 305, ✉ iperuayacucho@promperu.gob.pe).

ACCOMMODATION AND EATING

La Casona Jr Bellido 463 ☎ 066 312 733. This place gets busy at lunchtime for its good-value set lunch of local dishes (S/13); à la carte mains start at S/15. Service can be slow. Mon–Sat 11am–5pm & 6.30–9.30pm, Sun 11am–5pm.

Club La Posada San José Mz P Lote 17 ☎ 970 219 308. High above the city in the Santa Ana neighbourhood, a 20min walk from the plaza, this small hotel has spectacular views of the valley from its two shady terraces. Large, en-suite rooms are decorated with textiles and furniture made in Ayacucho. Wi-fi only in communal areas. Good deals on four-bed rooms. **S/80**

★ **Tres Máscaras** Jr Tres Máscaras 194 ☎ 066 312 921, ⟨w⟩ hoteltresmascaras.galeon.com. Two friendly dogs supervise the premises of this welcoming hostel with a lush courtyard area with prickly pears, cacti and orange trees. Rooms are spacious and all have TV and private bath; breakfast S/8–10. Dorm-style accommodation on request. Dorms <u>S/30,</u> doubles <u>S/55</u>

Via Via Café Portal Constitución 4. This welcoming Belgian-owned restaurant/café with great views over the square serves excellent grub, including quinoa risotto (S/18) and alpaca-based mains (S/25). Prices are at least S/5 cheaper at their other locale on Alameda Bolognesi, a 15min walk south. Daily 7am–11pm.

SHOPPING

Ayacucho is renowned throughout Peru for its thriving craft industry, with its best-known items including intricately woven rugs and *retablos* (wooden boxes containing elaborate three-dimensional religious and domestic scenes made from potato mixed with plaster of Paris).

Mercado Artesanal Shosaku Nagase Av Maravillas 101. Great for textiles, alabaster carvings (known in Peru as Huamanga stone carving) and *retablos*. Daily 9am–7.30pm.

Casa del Retablo Los Artesanos Mz F Lote 1 ☎ 980 249 255 ⟨w⟩ casadelretablo.strikingly.com. See how retablos are made at this workshop-cum-museum, run by renowned artisan Silvestre Ataucusi Flores. Daily, call ahead.

DIRECTORY

Banks and exchange BCP and Banco Continental are on the northern side of the square. Casas de cambio and moneychangers are on the western edge.

Laundry LHL, C Garcilazo de la Vega 265.

Post office C Asamblea 293.

Tourist police Jr Sol 280 (daily 8am–9pm; ☎ 066 315 845).

Cusco and around

The former capital of the Inca empire, modern **CUSCO** is an exciting and colourful city, enclosed between high hills and dominated by the imposing ceremonial centre and temple of **Sacsayhuamán**. It's one of South America's biggest tourist destinations, thanks to its narrow whitewashed streets, thriving culture, lively nightlife, substantial Inca ruins and architectural treasures from the colonial era.

Once you've acclimatized to the 3400m altitude, there are dozens of enticing destinations within easy reach. For most people the **Valle Sagrado** is the obvious first choice, with the citadel of Machu Picchu as the ultimate goal. The mountainous region around Cusco boasts some of the country's finest trekking, and beyond the **Inca Trail** to

WHEN TO VISIT

The best time to visit the area around Cusco is during the dry season (May–Sept), when it's warm with clear skies during the day but relatively cold at night. During the wet season (Oct–April) it rarely rains every day or all week, but the heavy downpours trigger landslides, making it difficult and dangerous to travel in the nearby mountains.

9

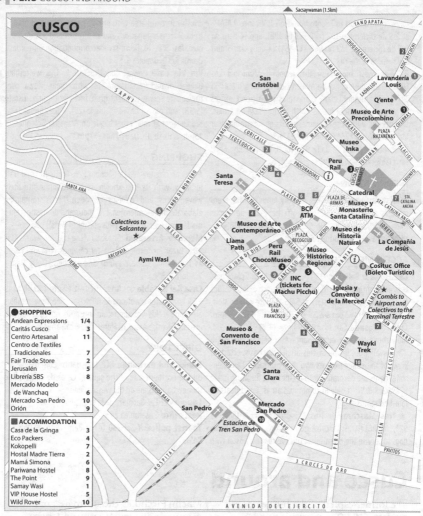

CUSCO

▲ Sacsaywaman (1.5km)

● SHOPPING

Andean Expressions	1/4
Caritás Cusco	3
Centro Artesanal	11
Centro de Textiles Tradicionales	7
Fair Trade Store	2
Jerusalén	5
Librería SBS	8
Mercado Modelo de Wanchaq	6
Mercado San Pedro	10
Orión	9

■ ACCOMMODATION

Casa de la Gringa	3
Eco Packers	4
Kokopelli	7
Hostal Madre Tierra	2
Mamá Simona	6
Pariwana Hostel	8
The Point	9
Samay Wasi	1
VIP House Hostel	5
Wild Rover	10

Machu Picchu are hundreds of lesser-known paths into the mountains, including the **Salcantay** and **Ausungate** treks, which are even more stunning and challenging, though the current budget favourite is the **Jungle Trek**. Cusco is also a convenient jumping-off point for the exploration of the lowland **Amazon rainforest** in Madre de Dios, such as the Reserva Nacional Tambopata, or the Reserva Biósfera del Manu, among the most biodiverse wildernesses on Earth.

BRIEF HISTORY

Legend has it that Cusco was founded by **Manco Capac** and his sister **Mama Occlo** in around 1100 AD. Over the next two centuries, the **Valle de Cusco** was home to the Inca people, but it wasn't until **Pachacutec** assumed power in 1438 that Cusco became the centre of an expanding empire. The new ruler designed the city in the shape of a puma, with its head incorporating some of its most important sites. Of all the Inca rulers, only **Atahualpa**, the last, never actually resided in Cusco, and even he was

DRINKING & NIGHTLIFE	
El Duende	3
Indigo	4
Km 0	1
Mama Africa	5
Paddy Flaherty's	7
Los Perros	2
Ukuku's Bar	6

EATING	
La Bodega 138	5
Bojosan	7
Jack's Café	3
Juanito's	1
Korma Sutra	2
Maikhana	8
Organika	4
Q'ori Sara	9
Vida Vegan	6

en route there when the Conquistadors captured him at Cajamarca. **Francisco Pizarro** reached the native capital on November 15, 1533, after holding Atahualpa to ransom, then killing him anyway. The city's beauty surpassed anything the Spaniards had seen before in the New World; the stonework was better than any in Spain and precious metals were used in a sacred context throughout the city. As usual, the Conquistadors lost no time in looting it.

Like its renowned art, the Cusco of today is dark yet vibrantly coloured,

reflecting its turbulent legacy. It's a politically active, left-of-centre city where the streets are often alive with fiestas and demonstrations.

WHAT TO SEE AND DO

The city divides into several distinct zones, with the **Plaza de Armas** at the heart of it all.

The **Boleto Turístico** (Tourist Ticket; see page 746) will give you an idea of some of the most popular city and Valle Sagrado sites, but it does not include entry to the one unmissable Cusco site, the Inca

9

THE CUSCO TOURIST TICKET AND BOLETO INTEGRAL

The **Boleto Turístico** (S/130 for ten days, students with ISIC card S/70) is a vital purchase for most visitors, as you can't visit most important sites without it. It covers the Sacsayhuamán, Q'enqo, Pukapukara and Tambomachay ruins near the city, as well as those in Ollantaytambo, Chinchero, Pisac, Moray, Tipón and Pikillacta, plus the optional extras of the Museo Histórico Regional, Museo de Arte Contemporáneo, Museo de Arte Popular, Centro Qosqo de Arte Nativo, the Pachacutec monument and the Q'orikancha site museum (though not Q'orikancha itself). It's available from all of the sites on the ticket, or from the issuing COSITUC offices at Av Sol 103 (daily 8am–6pm; ☎084 261 465, ⓦcosituc.gob.pe). You can also buy three *boletos parciales*, valid for two days (S/70): one covers the ruins immediately outside Cusco, another the above museums, and the third, the Valle Sagrado ruins. The **Boleto Religioso** (S/30, or S/15 for students; valid for ten days; ⓦcra.org.pe), which must be purchased at one of the following sites, covers the star attraction of the Catedral, as well as the Iglesia de San Blas, the Templo de San Cristóbal and the Museo de Arte Religioso.

Templo del Sol (Sun Temple) at **Q'orikancha**. Around the city there are opportunities for tours, hikes and extreme sports, as well as the fascinating Inca sites of **Sacsayhuamán** and **Tambomachay**.

Plaza de Armas

Cusco's ancient and modern centre, **Plaza de Armas** corresponds roughly to the ceremonial *Huacaypata*, the Incas' ancient central plaza, and is a constant hub of activity, its northern and western sides filled with shops and restaurants. Here you'll be approached by touts, waiters and shoe-shine boys, and here is where you'll come to watch the parades during Cusco's festivities. You'll see two flags flying here – the Peruvian one and the rainbow flag of Tuhuantinsuyo, which represents the four corners of the Inca empire (not to be confused with the gay pride flag). On the northeastern side stands the imposing cathedral, flanked by the Jesús María and El Triunfo churches, with the Compañía de Jesús church on the eastern side.

La Catedral

The plaza's exposed northeastern edge is dominated by the fortress-like Baroque-style **Catedral** (daily 10am–6pm; S/25, or with the Boleto Religioso; see page 746). Inside you'll find some of the best examples of art from the *Escuela Cusqueña* (Cusco School): look out for *The Last Supper*, with Christ sitting down to a feast of *cuy* (guinea pig), and the portrayals of the Virgin Mary as Pachamama (Mother Earth). Also check out the cathedral's finely carved granite altar and oldest surviving painting in Cusco, depicting the terrible 1650 earthquake, as well as a Neoclassical high altar made entirely of finely beaten embossed silver. Ten smaller chapels surround the nave, including the Capilla del Señor de los Temblores (Chapel of the Lord of Earthquakes), which houses a 26kg crucifix made of solid gold and encrusted with precious stones.

Iglesia de la Compañía de Jesús

As you look downhill from the centre of the plaza, the **Iglesia de la Compañía de Jesús** (Mon–Sat 9am–5pm, Sun 9–11am & 1–5pm; S/15, S/10 with ISIC card) dominates the skyline, and is often confused with the cathedral on first glance due to the splendour of its highly ornate facade. First built in the late 1570s, it was resurrected after the earthquake of 1650 in a Latin cross shape, over the foundations of Amara Cancha – originally Huayna Capac's Amaru Kancha (Palace of the Serpents). Cool and dark inside, with a grand gold-leaf altarpiece and a fine wooden pulpit displaying a relief of Christ, its transept ends in a stylish Baroque cupola.

Museo Inka

North of the cathedral, slightly uphill, you'll find one of the city's most beautiful colonial mansions, **El Palacio del Almirante** (The Admiral's Palace), which now houses the **Museo Inka** (Mon–Fri 8am–6pm, Sat & public holidays 9am–4pm; S/10). The museum itself is the best place in Cusco to see exhibits of Inca pottery, textiles, trepanned skulls, mummies, finely crafted metalwork (including miniature metal llamas given as offerings to the gods) and the largest range of wooden *quero* vases in the world.

Q'orikancha

If you visit one site in Cusco it should be **Q'orikancha**. The Convento de Santo Domingo at the intersection of Avenida El Sol and Calle Santa Domingo rises imposingly but rudely from the impressive walls of the Q'orikancha complex (Mon–Sat 8.30am–5.30pm, Sun 2–5pm; S/15; S/5 with ISIC card), which the Conquistadors laid low to make way for their uninspiring Baroque seventeenth-century church. Before the Spanish set their gold-hungry eyes on it, the temple must have been even more breathtaking, consisting of four small sanctuaries and a larger temple set around the existing courtyard, which was encircled by a cornice of gold made of seven hundred solid gold sheets (Q'orikancha means "golden enclosure"). Below the temple was an artificial garden in which everything was made of gold or silver and encrusted with precious jewels, from llamas and shepherds to the tiniest details of clumps of earth and weeds, including snails and butterflies. The Incas used the Q'orikancha as a solar observatory to study celestial activities, and archeologists believe that the mummies of the previous Incas were brought here and ritually burned.

Visitors need to use their imagination when they enter the courtyard inside the site, although surviving sections of the original Inca wall, made of tightly interlocking blocks of polished andesite, stand as firmly rooted as ever, completely unshaken by the powerful earthquakes that have devastated colonial buildings.

Museo de Sitio del Q'orikancha

The underground and rather uninspiring **Museo de Sitio del Q'orikancha**, Santo Domingo s/n (daily 9am–6pm; entry with Boleto Turístico) consists of five dimly lit rooms, containing various relics such as pottery shards, Inca weaponry, mummies and a section on the practice of trepanning, complete with medical instruments and several examples of trepanned skulls from the Paracas area.

Museo Machu Picchu

A number of artefacts including beautiful Inca ceramics that Hiram Bingham unearthed during the 1911 expedition to Machu Picchu – and that were only returned to Peru in 2011 – are now on display at the fascinating **Museo Machu Picchu** (Mon–Sat 9am–5pm; S/20) at C Santa Catalina Ancha 320. There are a number of informative videos too – it's worth visiting before travelling to the ruins to get a clearer idea of what lies behind the Incan marvel that is Machu Picchu.

Iglesia y Convento de La Merced

Just southwest from the Plaza de Armas along Calle Mantas is the **Iglesia y Convento de La Merced** (Mon–Sat 8am–noon & 2–5pm; S/10). Founded in 1536, it was rebuilt after the 1650 earthquake in a rich combination of Baroque and Renaissance styles. While its facade is exceptional, the highlight is a breathtaking 1720s **monstrance** standing a metre high; it was crafted by a Spanish jeweller using more than six hundred pearls, 1500 diamonds and 22kg of solid gold. The monastery also possesses a fine collection of *Escuela Cusqueña* paintings, and entombed in the church on the far side of the cloisters are the bodies of the two Diegos de Almagro, father and son, the former executed for rebelling against Francisco Pizarro and the latter for killing Pizarro in revenge.

Plaza San Francisco

Continue on another block and you'll come to the **Plaza San Francisco**, which comes alive on Sundays with street performers and food stalls selling traditional favourites. The square's southwestern side is dominated by the simply decorated **Convento de San Francisco** (daily 5–8pm; free), completed in 1652. The two large cloisters inside have a large collection of colonial

9

paintings, while the attached **museum** (Mon–Sat 9am–6pm; S/15; S/5 for the belltower) features a work by local master Juan Espinosa de los Monteros, responsible for the massive oil canvas measuring 12m by 9m – allegedly the largest in South America. Look out also for an unusual candelabra made out of human bones.

ChocoMuseo

Hidden away in a courtyard off Garcilaso, around the corner from pretty Plaza Regocijo, the **ChocoMuseo** (daily 9am–7pm; free; workshops S/75 for 2hr) has a range of interpretative displays on the history of cacao, starting with the ancient Maya's love of this plant. The museum also organizes **workshops** on chocolate making and tours to cacao plantations in the Cusco region, and allows you to see artisanal chocolate production first-hand in the on-site **factory**, from cacao bean to chocolate bar. More chocolate in various forms can be sampled in the **café**, or purchased in the **shop**.

Mercado San Pedro

Stop in at the **Mercado San Pedro** southwest of the city centre just off Calle Santa Clara (daily 6am–6pm) to enjoy a freshly squeezed juice, or to stock up on anything from llama toenail ornaments to herbal potions. Although it is principally a food market, there are several stalls selling traditional costumes. Leave your valuables behind, as pickpockets are rife here.

Museo Histórico Regional y Casa Garcilaso

At the southern corner of Plaza Regocijo, the **Museo Histórico Regional y Casa Garcilaso** (daily 8am–5pm; entry with Boleto Turístico) is home to fascinating pre-Inca ceramics and a number of Inca artefacts such as bolas, maces, and square water dishes that functioned as spirit levels. The museum also displays some gold and silver llama statuettes found in 1996 in the Plaza de Armas when the central fountain was being reconstructed, golden figurines from Sacsayhuamán, and wooden *quero* drinking vessels and dancing masks from the colonial era.

Museo de Arte Precolombino (MAP)

On the western side of the small, quiet Plaza Nazarenas, the **Museo de Arte Precolumbino**, housed in the Casa Cabrera (daily 8am–10pm; S/20), has an open courtyard that's home to *MAP Café*, one of Cusco's finest restaurants, and elegant exhibition rooms displaying some exquisite pre-Columbian works of art; these include a fine collection of Nazca and Mochica pottery, ornately carved Mochica ceremonial staffs, and the highlight: several rooms of exquisite gold and silver ornaments.

San Blas

Just around the corner from Plaza Nazarenas you come to the narrow alley of **Hathun Rumiyoq**, the most famous Inca passageway of all. Within its impressive walls lies the celebrated **Inca stone**; the twelve-cornered block fits perfectly into the original lower wall of what used to be the Inca Roca's old imperial palace.

From here, walk north up the Cuesta de San Blas, and you come to the Plazoleta de San Blas, which hosts a Saturday (and sometimes Sunday) handicrafts market (9am–4pm). Also on the tiny square is the small **Templo de San Blas** (daily 8am–6pm; S/10 or free with Boleto Religioso). The highlight here is an incredibly intricate pulpit, carved from a single block of cedar wood in a complicated Churrigueresque style by an indigenous man who allegedly devoted his life to the task and whose skull – some believe – rests in the topmost part of the carving.

Museo de la Coca

Just up Calle Suytuqatu from Plazoleta San Blas lies the fascinating little **Museo de la Coca** (daily 9am–7pm; S/10), devoted to the history of the coca leaf through the ages. The exhibits explore the significance of the plant in Peru from its first known ceremonial use by the Andean people to the present day through a series of displays, from ancient ceramic figures with cheeks bulging from chewing coca leaves to nineteenth-century texts on research into the medical use of cocaine. The curator is happy to answer any questions you may have.

ALTITUDE SICKNESS

Located at 3400m above sea level, Cusco is, for most travellers, the highest point on their trip. *Soroche*, or **acute mountain sickness** (see page 33), is a reality for many people arriving by plane from sea level. Cusco's mountainous location also means that a number of the city's steep streets, in particular high up in San Blas, will quickly leave you breathless as you explore town. Make sure to take it easy for the first couple of days, even sleeping a whole day just to assist acclimatization. Although Cusco's lively nightlife is an obvious draw, stay away from bars at least on the first night. Virtually all guesthouses offer complimentary *mate de coca* (coca tea), a traditional remedy for altitude sickness.

ARRIVAL AND DEPARTURE

By plane Cusco Airport (Alejandro Velasco Astete International Airport; ☎084 222 611) is 4km south of the city centre. You can either take a taxi from outside the arrivals hall (S/20–30 to the city centre), or hop on a Correcaminos *colectivo* (S0.80) from outside the airport car park, which goes along Av Sol to C Ayacucho, two blocks from the Plaza de Armas.

Destinations LATAM, Peruvian Airlines, Star Perú, Andes and Avianca have regular flights to major national destinations, including Lima (every 30min–1hr; 1hr 20min), Puerto Maldonado (3–4 daily; 55min), Arequipa (2 daily; 1hr) and Juliaca (for Puno; 1 daily; 50min). Peruvian Airlines flies to La Paz (daily; 1hr 55min) in Bolivia.

By bus Most international and inter-regional buses use the Terminal Terrestre (☎084 224 471) at Vía de Evitamiento 429, 2km southeast of the centre. *Colectivos* (S0.80) marked "Correcaminos" run from one block north of the station dropping passengers off at C Almagro between Sol and Bernardo. To get to the bus station catch the same *colectivo* from Ayacucho between Sol and Andrés; a taxi will set you back S/7–8. Recommended bus companies include: Cruz del Sur, which has its own bus depot at Av Industrial 121 (☎084 243 261) and at the Terminal Terrestre (☎084 248 255); Ormeño (☎084 227 501); Inka Express (☎084 247 887); Tour Peru (☎084 236 463); Litoral (☎084 281 920); Movil Tours (☎084 262 526); San Martín (☎097 970 9615); Transzela (☎084 238 223).

Destinations Arequipa (several each night; 10hr); Ayacucho (2 daily; 13hr); Copacabana, Bolivia (several daily; 10hr); La Paz, Bolivia (daily several at around 10pm; 12–14hr); Lima (14 a day; 20hr); Puerto Maldonado (12 overnight; 9hr); Puno (6 daily; 7–8hr); Rio Branco, Brazil (2 weekly; 20hr).

By train The train between Cusco and Machu Picchu actually leaves from Poroy, a 15min taxi ride west of the city centre; however, given the high cost of the train fare on this route (from around US$200 one-way) travellers are far more likely to travel by bus/minivan to Ollantaytambo, much further down the line, and take the train from there (see page 757). Peru Rail has offices in town at Plaza Regocijo 202 and Plaza de Armas (both daily 7am–10pm), though it's also easy to buy tickets directly through ⓦperurail.com. For Machu Picchu, it's best to buy at least a week in advance

in peak season, but only after you have booked your tickets for Machua Picchu.

INFORMATION

Tourist information iPerú is at Portal de Harinas 177 on the Plaza de Armas (Mon–Fri 9am–7pm, Sat & Sun 9am–1pm; ☎084 252 974, ⓔiperucusco@promperu.gob. pe); they also have a couple of kiosks in the main hall of the airport as well as at arrivals (daily 6am–5pm; ☎084 237 364). As well as providing maps, they have contact lists and can help arrange homestays in local villages involved in turismo vivencial (community-based tourism).

GETTING AROUND

On foot Most of the main sights lie within the centro histórico, within a 10–15min walk of the Plaza de Armas.
By bus and colectivo The city bus and *colectivo* networks are incredibly complicated, though cheap and fast once you learn your way around, and charge S0.80 per person. Taking buses up and down Av Sol are the most straightforward and to/from the bus station and airport (see page 746).
By taxi Rides within Cusco cost around S/5–6 or S/10 for trips to the suburbs or up to Sacsayhuamán and Q'enqo (some *taxistas* may charge S/20 and wait for you, in which case give them half in advance and half later).

ACCOMMODATION

There are numerous budget options around the Plaza de Armas and in the quieter artists' quarter of San Blas uphill from the square. All include breakfast unless stated.
Casa de la Gringa Tandapata, at Pasnapacana 148 ☎084 241 168, ⓦcasadelagringa.com; map p.744. Cactus pots and colourful murals decorate this pleasant guesthouse focused on spiritual healing. Try and stay in the main building as the annexe has darkish rooms. There's a kitchen for guests' use and a communal area with TV. **S/99**
Eco Packers Santa Teresa 375 ☎084 231 800, ⓦecopackersperu.com; map p.744. This fun and colourful hostel has clean dorms (for up to 18) set around a leafy interior courtyard. There is table football and billiards to unwind, as well as a laid-back bar with live rock music on Saturday evenings. Dorms **S/45**, doubles **S/156**

9

TOURS IN AND AROUND CUSCO

Tours in and around Cusco range from a half-day city tour to a full-on adventure down to the Amazon. Service and facilities vary considerably, so check exactly what's provided. A good introduction to the city is to take a free **walking tour** (W freewalkingtourcusco.com): guides can speak English and work on a tips-only basis. **Standard tours** around the city, Valle Sagrado and to Machu Picchu range from a basic bus service with fixed stops and little in the way of a guide, to luxury packages including guide, food and hotel transfers. The "Classic" four-day **Inca Trail** is by far the most popular (and most regulated) of the **mountain treks**, and needs to be booked months in advance with a licensed operator; research carefully well in advance (see page 759).

Other popular **alternative Inca trails** (see page 766) are around the snowcapped mountains of Salcantay (6264m) to the north and Ausangate (6372m) to the south, a more remote trek, which needs at least a week plus guides and mules. The current backpacker craze is the gruelling one-day haul up Vinicunca – aka "Rainbow Mountain".

You can also rent out **mountain bikes** for trips to the Valle Sagrado and around, and some operators arrange biking tours. Horseriding, ziplining and rafting can also be organized from Cusco. Many **jungle trip** operators – are also based in the city (see pages 829 and 772).

TOUR OPERATORS

The Cusco area is an adrenaline junkie's paradise, with a huge range of adventure sports on offer. As well as trekking expeditions in the Valle Sagrado, there's world-class river rafting on the Río Apurimac – and thrilling enough rafting on the Río Urubamba – as well as climbing and canyoning in the nearby mountains, and mountain biking.

Andina Travel Plazoleta Santa Catalina 219 ☎084 251892, W andinatravel.com. Andina are the pioneers in real alternative treks and are constantly working at opening and developing new alternatives to remote areas, including Quillatambo. Part of the profits goes towards community projects including building new schools, reforestation projects and the reintroduction of native Andean alpacas and llamas.

Llama Path San Juan de Dios 250 ☎084 223 448, W llamapath.com. One of the newer Inca Trail trekking operators in town, Llama Path has quickly established itself as a more affordable, high-quality, responsible outfit.

Peru Treks Av Pardo 540 ☎084 222 722, W perutreks.com. Experienced and responsible family-run business that only offers the classic four-day Inca Trail (US$650), in groups of four to sixteen on set dates. The company is committed to ethical and sustainable practices, taking porter welfare seriously and supporting community projects.

Q'ente Choquechaca 229 ☎084 222 535, W qente.com. Responsible adventure travel company specializing in alternative treks as well as the traditional Inca Trail.

Wayki Trek Quera 239 ☎084 224 092, W waykitrek.net. Professional company supporting many community projects in the area and offering some off-the-beaten-trail treks. Also offers a "wayki option" on the Inca Trail whereby groups spend the night in a porter community prior to starting the trail.

★ **Kokopelli** San Andrés 260 ☎084 315 224, W hostelkokopelli.com; map p.744. Set in a beautiful colonial house, this place has female only and mixed dorms, including pod-style (with private curtains) beds, as well as en-suite doubles. There's table tennis, mini-football, a TV lounge, billiards and a cosy wooden bar-restaurant. Dorms S/36, doubles S/170

★ **Hostal Madre Tierra** Atoqsaycuchi 647 ☎084 248 452, W hostalmadretierra.com; map p.744. A wonderful little guesthouse offering brightly coloured en-suite doubles, set on two floors. The interiors are decked out in local wood and the fireplace adds a homely feel. Breakfast is served communally. S/183

Mamá Simona Ceniza 364 ☎084 260 408, W mamasimona.com; map p.744. Laidback place with an internal patio featuring armchairs, fun murals and colourful beanbags and masks. Dorms and good-value doubles with lovely parquet floors and pine beds are kept spick and span. There's a bright red kitchen for guests' use, too. Dorms S/36, doubles S/100

Pariwana Hostel Mesón de la Estrella 136 ☎084 233 751, W pariwana-hostel.com; map p.744. A long-standing favourite among backpackers, *Pariwana* has dorms – boasting beds with two pillows – and doubles set around a lovely interior courtyard dotted with colourful beanbags. Table tennis, mini-football, TV lounge, book exchange and drinking games are sure to keep you busy. Dorms S/36, doubles S/159

The Point Mesón de la Estrella 172 ☎084 252 266, W thepointhostels.com; map p.744. Cusco's party hostel hits it hard every night at the lively bar upstairs. Luckily there's a verdant garden at the back to get some air and come back to your senses in the morning. Dorms are mostly dark and the premises could do with a bit more of a clean. Dorms S/22

Samay Wasi C Atoqsaycuchi 416, San Blas ☎084 253 108, ⓦsamaywasiperu.com; map p.744. High up in San Blas, this place boasts spectacular city views from the breakfast patio and second-floor rooms. Tidy en-suite doubles and dorms are set into the rock and spread over two storeys. There's a kitchen for guests' use and all-day coca tea. Dorms S/33, doubles S/82

VIP House Hostel Meloc 422 ☎084 238 688, ⓔviphousecusco@outlook.com; map p.744. Run by chilled, friendly guys, this unlikely hostel – long corridors and dark rooms with heavy, rather dated furniture – is a real find. Dorms are spacious with warm bedding and lockers, while the lounge areas are relaxing places and the free informative tour of Cusco is a star extra. Shared and private bathrooms. Dorms S/30, doubles S/100

Wild Rover C Matará 261 ☎084 221 515, ⓦwildroverhostels.com; map p.744. Another lively party hostel with a fiesta every night. Rooms at the back are slightly quieter although lack sunlight; on the plus side, this makes them the perfect spot to kick that hangover. Dorms S/28, doubles S/120

EATING

There are dozens of stalls at the Mercado San Pedro where you can get hearty dishes for a bargain S/5, though eating is less frenetic at the Mercado San Blas. Self-caterers can stock up on fresh produce here too, as well as at Orión Supermarket, just opposite the Mercado San Pedro. Sunday food stalls in the Plaza San Francisco are another good bet, while hostel restaurants also serve inexpensive comfort food.

La Bodega 138 Herrajes 138; map p.744. This welcoming restaurant attracts a young, laidback crowd who enjoy superior pizzas and pastas (from S/30) in a couple of dining areas. The salads (S/26) are made with organic ingredients from the Valle Sagrado, and the delicious Nutella cheesecake is large enough to share. Daily noon–10.30pm.

Bojosan C San Agustín 275 ☎084 246 502; map p.744. This little udon bar with an open kitchen that aims to re-create Japanese ambience and cuisine is the perfect spot for a warming bowl of noodles on a cold Cusco evening. Choose from beef, duck, curry, chicken, seaweed and pork udon (S/20–25) accompanied by Japanese green tea, beer or sake. 12.30–3.30pm & 6.30–10.30pm; closed Wed.

★ **Jack's Cafe** Choquechaca 509; map p.744. A real backpacker hangout – don't be surprised to see customers standing in line. The ingredients here come from local suppliers and the coffee is family grown. Plenty on offer, from big tasty sandwiches to hearty home-made soups (both under S/20). Mon–Sat 1–10pm.

Juanito's Qanchipata 596; map p.744. This tiny sandwich joint serves the best pick 'n' mix sandwiches (S/12–25) in town. It's the perfect spot to grab a bun (or a burger) before a long bus journey. Mon–Sat noon–10.30pm, Sun noon–9pm.

Korma Sutra Teatro 382, 2nd floor; map p.744. Cusco's main Indian restaurant attracts crowds of Brits itching for generous portions of onion bhajis (S/12) and chicken tikka masala (S/29), all to be washed down with a refreshing mango lassi (S/8). More adventurous types can go for the crispy tandoori guinea pig (S/24). Mon–Sat 6–10pm.

Maikhana Av Sol 106; map p.744. It's the price than brings in the punters here: all-you-can eat Indian buffet (noon–2pm) for a mere S/15. Get here early to catch the food at its hottest. It's not gourmet, but is decent enough and great value. Daily noon–10pm.

Organika Resbalosa 410; map p.744. A small, cheery café dishing up nicely presented, healthy sandwiches, salads and soups (S/10–20) alongside more substantial mains (from S/22) such as trout with pineapple, using organic ingredients. Daily 9am–9.30pm.

Q'ori Sara Garcilaso 290; map p.744. Hole-in-the-wall joint aimed squarely at the local market: expect vast, filling plates laden with rice or noodles plus some protein for very little: three-course set menus for lunch and dinner (S/10) plus a glass of *chicha morada*. Mon–Sat 7am–9.30pm, Sun 11am–4pm.

★ **Vida Vegan Bistro** Tambo de Montero 508, Santa Ana; map p.744. This intimate, buzzing bistro is not to be missed. The kitchen turns out delicious, creative veggie and vegan dishes (S/15–25) – try the quinoa mushroom risotto in yellow hot pepper sauce; everything is beautifully presented – topped with a fresh flower – and served by upbeat, efficient staff. Noon–10pm; closed Wed.

DRINKING AND NIGHTLIFE

Apart from Lima, no Peruvian town has as varied a nightlife as Cusco. Clubs open early, around 9pm, but don't start getting lively before 11pm, and close in the wee hours. Pubs and clubs alike often offer 2-for-1 drink deals during happy hour. Beware of your drink being spiked in crowded nightspots.

PUBS AND BARS

El Duende Tecsecocha 429; map p.744. A local joint, this dimly lit bar is crammed with folk drinking and chatting. Try the fiery house speciality *té macho* (hot tea with pisco) *and té piteado* (more of the same plus aniseed liqueur) designed to stave off the cold nights. Daily 5pm–late.

Indigo Tecsecocha 415; map p.744. It's always happy hour at this laidback, cosmopolitan bar. The Thai food (S/25–35), hookahs, board games, background classics and friendly staff will ensure you linger for a while. Daily 3pm–late.

9

★ **Paddy Flaherty's** Triunfo 124; map p.744. At 3347m, *Paddy's* proudly boasts that it is the highest 100-percent Irish owned pub on the planet. The pub attracts a melting pot of Peruvians and tourists alike and the menu offers all sorts of British home favourites, such as shepherd's pie and cheeseburgers (all under S/20). Daily 10am–late.

Los Perros Tecsecocha 436; map p.744. This relaxed "couch wine bar" with dark red undertones, hanging lamps – including a chic chandelier – and comfortable sofas is the perfect spot to linger over a beer (S/7) or cocktail (S/22). The spicy snacks are delicious too, including chilli rolls and spicy wonton (around S/24). Daily 11am–midnight.

CLUBS AND LIVE MUSIC

Km 0 Tandapata 100, San Blas; map p.744. This chilled-out bar with a relaxed lounge area upstairs hosts live bands (daily 10.30pm–midnight) playing an eclectic mix – of variable quality – from reggae to funk. Hookahs (S/18), darts, tapas (from S/8) and more substantial mains including Thai curry (S/27). Daily 6pm–late.

Mama Africa Portal de Panes 109, 3rd floor, Plaza de Armas; map p.744. Right on the main square, the dancefloor of this popular backpacker hangout is often heaving. The main musical flavour is Latino pop, including reggaeton, mixed with US club music, though salsa classes are offered – often informally – 9–11pm. Fri & Sat cover charge S/10–20. Happy hour until 11pm. Daily 9pm–late.

Ukuku's Bar Plateros 316; map p.744. This is one of the oldest and largest bars in town, with psychedelic murals and a world collection of liqueur bottles dating back over one hundred years. It really gets going at 10.30pm, with loud live music and dance shows. Profits go towards preserving the Andes by planting native trees, as well as helping children in local communities. Happy hour 7–10pm. Drinks start at S/10. Daily 7pm–late.

SHOPPING

The best shopping area is around Plazoleta San Blas – Tandapata, Cuesta San Blas and Carmen Alto.

Books The best bookshops with extensive English-language sections are Jerusalén at Heladeros 143 (map p.744), with a large book exchange (if you give two books you can take one) and guidebooks, and the smaller Librería SBS on Av El Sol 781A (map p.744), which also sells topographical maps – essential for hikers.

Clothing Buy quality T-shirts with unique designs at Andean Expressions on Choquechaca 213 (map p.744).

Crafts Mercado Modelo de Wanchaq on Av Garcilaso, at Huascar (daily 6am–6pm; map p.744) stocks a good range of crafts and you can find quirky gifts at Mercado San Pedro (map p.744).

Food Self-caterers can stock up on fruit and veg at the Mercado Modelo de Wanchaq. The best supermarket is

Orión (daily 8am–10.30pm; map p.744), just opposite the Mercado San Pedro.

Textiles Centro de Textiles Tradicionales del Cusco, on Av El Sol 603A (daily 7.30am–8.30pm; map p.744), promotes traditional weaving techniques, so not only can you purchase textiles of excellent quality – though their prices tend to be higher, but you may also watch weavers demonstrate their skill. The Centro Artesanal on Av Tullumayo (daily 8am–9pm; map p.744) is home to dozens of stalls selling similar products, including blankets, jumpers and colourful woolly hats. Inexpensive textile shops, where most profits go directly to the artisans, include the Fair Trade and Cáritas shops at calles Chiwampata 515 and Cuesta del Almirante 211, respectively (both open Mon–Sat 8am–7pm; map p.744).

DIRECTORY

Banks and exchange BCP has a global ATM (Plateros, at Espaderos on the Plaza de Armas), and there are ATMs in the BCP and BBVA bank branches along Av El Sol, which also has places to change money. The small Scotiabank branch on the Plaza de Armas allows you to use a credit card to withdraw up to S/4000 at a time (upon presentation of your passport).

Camping equipment Most tour agencies rent out tents, sleeping bags, sleeping mats and cooking equipment. There are also several shops on Procuradores and Plateros. Try Camping Equipment Rosly, C Procuradores 394 (☎084 248 042). Make sure to thoroughly check the equipment before renting.

Consulates Embassies are in Lima, though there are several consulates and honorary consul representatives in Cusco; a list of consulates and contact details can be found at ⒲ embassypages.com/city/cusco.

Hospital and pharmacies Clínica Peruana Suiza (☎084 242 114, ⒲ cps.com.pe) on Av Perú K-3, Urbanización Quispicanchis, is well equipped to deal with 24hr emergencies. There are pharmacies along Av El Sol.

Laundry The cheapest laundry places are along C Choquechaca. Try Lavandería Louis at Choquechaca 264 (Mon–Sat 8am–8pm; S/3/kg).

Post office The post office is at Av Sol 800 (Mon–Sat 8am–8pm, Sun 9am–4pm).

Taxis Reliable companies include AloCusco (☎084 222 222).

Tourist police On Plaza Tupac Amaru s/n (24hr; ☎084 235 123).

INCA SITES OUTSIDE CUSCO

There are four major Inca sites, all an energetic day's **walk** from Cusco: the megalithic fortress of **Sacsayhuamán**, which looms high above the city, the great *huaca* of **Q'enqo**, the fortified hunting lodge of **Pukapukara** and the nearby imperial baths of **Tambomachay**. To start from the top and work your way downhill, take one of the regular **buses** to Pisac leaving from Avenida Tullumayo or Calle Puputi every twenty minutes throughout the day and ask to be dropped off at the highest of the sites, Tambomachay, from where it's an easy two-hour walk back into the centre of Cusco, visiting the above sites in reverse order. The **opening times** for all the sites are daily 7am–6pm and entry is by Boleto Turístico only (see page 746).

Sacsayhuamán

From central Cusco, it's quite a steep 2km climb up to the ruins of **SACSAYHUAMÁN** from the Plaza de Armas. Take Calle Suecia, then the first right along Huaynapata until it meets the even narrower Pumacurco going steeply up (left) to a small café-bar. From there, follow the signposted steps all the way up to the ruins.

Because Sacsayhuamán was protected by such a steep approach from the town, it only needed defensive walls on one side, and three massive parallel walls zigzag together for some 600m. Little of the inner structures remains, yet these enormous ramparts stand 20m high, unperturbed by past battles, earthquakes and the passage of time. The strength of the mortar-less stonework – one block weighs more than 300 tonnes – is matched by the brilliance of its design: the zigzags expose the flanks of any attackers trying to clamber up. The Inca Pachacutec began work on Sacsayhuamán in the 1440s, although it took the labour of some twenty thousand men and nearly a century of work to finish it.

A flat expanse of grassy ground divides the temple from a large outcrop of volcanic rock, called the **Rodadero** ("precipice"), which is used today during the colourful – and now highly commercialized –spectacle of the **Inti Raymi festival** held annually during the summer solstice in June.

Q'enqo

From the warden's hut on the northeastern edge of Sacsayhuamán, take the track towards the Cusco–Pisac road; **Q'ENQO** is just across this road.

This great stone or *huaca* revered by the Inca is carved with a complex pattern of steps, seats, geometric reliefs and puma designs, and illustrates the critical role of the Rock Cult in the realm of Inca cosmological beliefs; the name of the temple means "zigzag" and refers to the patterns carved into the upper western edge of the stone. At an annual festival priests would pour *chicha* or sacrificial llama blood into a bowl at the serpent-like top of the main channel; if it flowed out through the left-hand fork, this was a bad omen for the fertility of the year to come. If, on the other hand, it continued the full length of the zigzag and poured onto the rocks below, this was a good omen.

Pukapukara

A relatively small ruin named **PUKAPUKARA** ("Red Fort", due to the pinkish hue of the rock) is situated right beside the main Cusco–Pisac road, a two-hour cross-country walk uphill from Q'enqo. Although in many ways reminiscent of a small European castle, Pukapukara is more likely to have been a hunting lodge, or out-of-town lodgings for the emperor, than simply a defensive position. Thought to have been built by the Emperor Pachacutec, it commands views towards glaciers to the south of the Valle de Cusco.

Tambomachay

TAMBOMACHAY, otherwise known as "El Baño del Inca" ("The Bath of the Inca"), less than fifteen minutes' walk away along a signposted track from Pukapukara, is an impressive temple, evidently a place for ritual as well as physical cleansing and purification.

The ruins consist of three tiered platforms. The top one holds four trapezoidal niches that may have been used as seats; on the next level, underground water emerges directly from a hole at the base of the stonework, and from here cascades down to the bottom platform, creating a cold shower just about high enough for an Inca to stand under.

9

On this platform the spring water splits into two channels, both pouring the last metre down to ground level. The superb quality of the stonework suggests that its use was restricted to the higher nobility, who perhaps used the baths only on ceremonial occasions.

Tipón

Around 25km east out of Cusco, the town of **TIPÓN** is famous for its Sunday lunches, featuring oven-roasted *cuy* (guinea pig), and its ruins – a large structure made up of several terraces and one of the few working examples of Inca irrigation systems, with fountains and water channels covering the area. From the town, it's a steep 45-minute climb (or 10min taxi ride; S/10 each way) to the ruins. To get here take an Urcos-bound *colectivo* from Avenida de la Cultura, one block west of the Hospital Regional, or from the corner of Tullumayo and Garcilaso de la Vega, and ask to be let out at the Tipón turn-off (45min). For S/50

you can get a taxi to take you both to the ruins of Tipón and Pikillaqta (see below), then drop you back at the main road, where you squeeze onto a passing bus to get back to Cusco.

Pikillaqta and Rumicolca

One of the few well-preserved pre-Inca sites in the area, **Pikillaqta** was built by the Huari culture and comprises a sprawling residential compound surrounded by a defensive wall in the midst of rolling grasslands. It is the earliest example in the region of two-storey buildings. Further on, on the opposite side of the road, is **Rumicolca**, the huge Inca gateway to Cusco, built on top of what used to be a massive Huari aqueduct. The contrast between the fine Inca stonework and the cruder earlier constructions of the Huari is quite striking. You can easily visit this site together with Tipón in a day-trip from Cusco; otherwise, stay on an Urcos-bound bus for an extra 5km; the site is 1km from the main road.

El Valle Sagrado and Machu Picchu

The Río Urubamba valley, also known as **El Valle Sagrado** or the **Sacred Valley,** traces its winding, astonishingly beautiful course to the northwest of Cusco. Standing guard over the two extremes of the Valle Segrado road, the ancient **Inca citadels** of Pisac and Ollantaytambo are among the most evocative ruins in Peru, while the small Andean towns of Pisac and Chinchero

really come into their own on Tuesdays, Thursdays and especially Sundays – market days – when villagers in colourful regional dress gather to sell their crafts and produce.

Beyond Ollantaytambo the route becomes too tortuous for any road to follow, the valley closes in around the rail tracks, and the Río Urubamba begins to

race and twist below **Machu Picchu** itself, the most famous ruin in South America and a place that – no matter how jaded you are or how commercial it seems – stops you in your tracks.

Unless you're walking the Inca Trail, you will probably spend at least one night in Machu Picchu town, commonly referred to as **Machu Picchu Pueblo**, or even Aguas Calientes (its former name). Given the town's brutalist architecture and overpriced accommodation and eating establishments, it's best not to linger here for too long.

A plethora of tour companies runs day-trips to Machu Picchu (which have to be booked in advance), as well as whirlwind day tours of the Valle Sagrado (from S/60 upwards, plus entry to the sites). While guiding standards vary, it's a good way of seeing sights that are far apart, especially if you don't have much time, though it's more rewarding to linger and explore the valley at your leisure.

PISAC

A vital Inca road once snaked its way up the canyon that enters the Valle Sagrado at **PISAC**, and the ruined citadel that sits at the entrance to the gorge controlled a route connecting the Inca Empire with Paucartambo, on the borders of the eastern jungle. Nowadays, the village is best known for its Tuesday, Thursday and – above all – Sunday craft **market**, held on the town's main square, the Plaza Constitución, though most stalls are open all week, with fewer crowds on non-market days. The main local **fiesta** – Virgen del Carmen (July 15–18) – is a good alternative to the simultaneous but more remote and raucous Paucartambo festival of the same name, with processions, music, dance groups, the usual fire-cracking celebrations, and food stalls around the plaza.

WHAT TO SEE AND DO

It takes roughly two hours to climb directly to the **citadel** (daily 8am–4pm; entry by Boleto Turístico), heading up through the agricultural terraces still in use at the back of Plaza Constitución. Alternatively, take a taxi to the top of the ruins (20min; S/20–25 one-way, or negotiate a return fare with waiting time) and then walk back down, visiting all four archeological complexes on the way. The budget option is to take a combi from the market bound for the village of Maska, high up the valley, alighting at the turn-off (*desvio*) to the ruins, after about 15min, from where it's a five-minute walk to the entrance, and another ten minutes to reach the lower terraces of the site.

Set high above a valley floor patchworked by patterned fields and rimmed by centuries of terracing amid giant landslides, the stonework and panoramas at the citadel are magnificent. On a large natural balcony, a semicircle of buildings is gracefully positioned under row upon row of fine stone terraces thought to represent a partridge's wing (*pisac* means "partridge"). In the upper

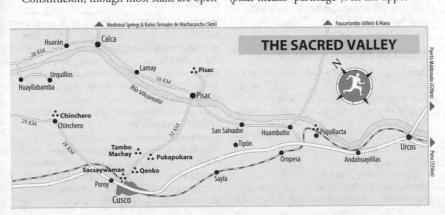

9

sector of the ruins, the main **Templo del Sol** (Sun Temple) is the equal of anything at Machu Picchu. Above the temple lie still more ruins, largely unexcavated, and the honeycombed cliff wall opposite the fortress is the handiwork of agile grave robbers who desecrated the cliff tombs.

ARRIVAL AND DEPARTURE

By colectivo From Cusco, catch a *colectivo* throughout the day from C Puputi (every 15min; 45min); they drop you off and you can pick a returning one up on Pisac's main street.

ACCOMMODATION AND EATING

Horno Pumachayoc Av Federico Zamalloa s/n ☎ 984 012 575. Tasty sweet or savoury hand-made empanadas (S/6) are the order of the day here made with natural local ingredients. The dough is proudly made from seven types of flour, including quinoa and coca; fillings include, cheese, tomato or tropical fruits. Enjoy your selection with glass of chicha morada (S/4). Daily 6am–6pm.

Hospedaje Chaska Wasi Av Amazonas s/n ☎ 985 903 868, ⓦpisachotel.com. A great backpacker pad a short walk from the main square with warm and welcoming rooms set around a large garden. There's a kitchen for guests' use and a palapa with cushioned seating. Dorms S/30, doubles S/120

Intikilla Backpacker Av Amazonas 153 ☎ 984 992 424. Bare-bones bunkhouse at rock-bottom rates, with shared or private rooms – all with shared bathrooms – and a communal sofa and TV on each floor. Breakfast extra. Dorms S/15, doubles S/45

Ulrike's Café C Pardo 613. Set over two floors and a rooftop terrace, this German-run restaurant is a pleasant place to hang out and produces consistent fare. Breakfasts (S/12–20) run until noon, starring quinoa and banana pancakes and chai-spiced oatmeal, while the main menu (from S/15) includes curries, salads, and home-made carrot cake (S/8), their bestselling dessert. Set menu S/28. Daily 8am–9pm.

URUBAMBA AND AROUND

Spread-out **URUBAMBA** lies about 80km from Cusco via Pisac or around 60km via Chinchero. Although it has little in the way of obvious historic interest, the town has numerous connections to other parts of the Valle Segrado and is situated in the shadow of the beautiful Chicon and Pumahuanca glaciers.

The attractive Plaza de Armas, dominated by the red sandstone **Iglesia San Pedro**, is laidback and attractive, with palm trees, a couple of pines and surrounded by interesting topiary, while at its heart is a small fountain topped by a maize corn. At weekends there's a large **market** on Jirón Palacio, which serves the local villages.

WHAT TO SEE AND DO

Urubamba makes an ideal base from which to explore the mountains and lower hills around the Valle Segrado, which are filled with sites. The eastern side of the valley is formed by the **Cordillera Urubamba**, a range of snowcapped peaks dominated by the summits of Chicon and Veronica. Many of the ravines can be hiked, and on the trek up from the town you'll have stupendous views of Chicon. **Moray**, a stunning Inca site, lies about 6km north of Maras village on the Chinchero side of the river, within a two- to three-hour walk from Urubamba. Make a circuit to include the spectacular **Maras salt flats**.

ARRIVAL AND INFORMATION

By bus *Colectivos* leave from C Pavitos in Cusco (every 20min from about 5–6am; 1hr 30min). Minibuses also connect Urubamba with Pisac (every 20min; 1hr) via Calca (40min); Ollantaytambo (every 15–20min; 30min); for Chinchero (40min) catch a Cusco-bound bus. Buses and colectivos use the Urubamba Terminal Terrestre on the main highway, 1km west of town. A *mototaxi* into town will set you back S/2–3.

Tourist information The Municipalidad, on the main square, has a small tourist office round the side which provides limited tourist information (in Spanish).

ACCOMMODATION

★ **Flying Dog Hostel** On the road to Cotahuincho s/n ☎ 977 743 011, ⓦflyingdogperu.com. A mere 10min walk from the bus station, this converted old house has bags of character, set in a lovely garden with fabulous mountain views. Whitewashed en-suite rooms (including the four-bed dorms) boast wooden floors and beams, plus large windows. There is space to chill – inside and out – plus all the usual hostel amenities. Buffet breakfast included. Dorms S/35, doubles S/135

Hostal Los Jardines Av Convención 459 ☎ 084 201 331, ⓦlosjardines.weebly.com. A very pleasant budget choice a few blocks east of the main square with rooms giving onto a verdant garden area dotted with chairs and parasols. En-suite rooms are simply furnished but welcoming, with hot-water showers. Breakfast is an extra S/12. S/80

Tres Keros Av Sr de Torrechayoc ☎ 084 201 701. This superb restaurant is one of the very best in the Valle Sagrado and is not to be missed. The warm atmospheric interior features candle-lit tables and a fireplace, while beautiful ceramic plates adorn the walls. The food is all home-made – the *lomo saltado* (S/42) is exceptional, as is the trout (S/38), while veggie options include home-made pastas with pesto and curries. 12.30–3.30pm & 6.30–9.30pm; closed Tues.

Hostal Los Perales Pasaje Arenales 102 ☎ 084 201 151, ⓦ ecolodgeurubamba.com. This pleasant guesthouse features neat rooms set around a large overgrown garden. There's table tennis and a billiards table, too. The congenial owner, who speaks some English, also offers apartments sleeping six, all fully equipped with kitchen. **S/70**

EATING

Kachi Wasi Av Mariscal Castilla 921 ☎ 084 214 989. Enthusiastically run local café-restaurant, offering a ridiculously inexpensive *menu del día* (S/8) and a small selection of well-prepared popular local mains, such as the ubiquitous *lomo saltado* and various *chicharrones* (S/22–30). Also does drink offers. Daily 8am–10pm.

OLLANTAYTAMBO

On the approach to **OLLANTAYTAMBO** from Urubamba, the river runs smoothly between a series of fine Inca terraces that gradually diminish in size as the slopes get steeper and rockier. Built as an Inca administrative centre rather than a town, it's hard not to be impressed by the two huge Inca ruins that loom above the village, or by the foundations that abound in the cobbled backstreets radiating up from the plaza, especially in Calle del Medio. Laid out in the form of a maize corncob – and one of the few surviving examples of an Inca grid system – the plan can be seen from vantage points high above it, especially from the hill opposite the fortress. Ollanta is an attractive, laidback village, and a wonderful place in which to linger.

WHAT TO SEE AND DO

The hubs of activity in town are the main **plaza** – the heart of civic life and the scene of traditional folk dancing during festive occasions – and the Inca fortress.

Downhill from the plaza, just across the Río Patacancha, is the old Inca Plaza Mañya Raquy, dominated by the town's star attraction – the astonishing Inca ruins atop some steep terraces. Climbing up through the **fortress** (daily 7am–5pm; entrance with Boleto Turístico), the solid stone terraces, jammed against the natural contours of the cliff, remain frighteningly impressive and the view of the valley from the top is stupendous. Not only was this the site of a major battle in 1536 between the Spaniards and the rebellious Manco Inca, who fought them off before being forced to retreat to the jungle stronghold in Vilcabamba, but this was also a ceremonial centre; note the particularly fine stonework towards the top of the ruins.

Directly across, above the town, are rows of **ruined buildings** originally thought to have been prisons but now believed to have been granaries. It's a stiff forty-minute climb to the viewpoint; follow the signpost from Waqta, off the Plaza de Armas.

ARRIVAL AND DEPARTURE

By bus and colectivo From Cusco, several buses daily go via Urubamba from Av Grau 525, as well as numerous *colectivos* and *combis* from C Pavitos (6am–5pm; 1hr 30min–2hr); minibuses from Urubamba leave from the bus station (every 10–15min; 30min). From Ollanta, Cusco-bound tourist buses and minivans (1hr 30min –2hr) leave from the small yard just outside the train station. For Urubamba catch a *combi* or *colectivo* from the Mercado Central, off the southeastern corner of the plaza (every 15min; 30min).

By bus/minivan You can also book a seat in one of the daily **private minivans** from Cusco which pick up passengers in the main plaza (8.30–9.30am), heading directly for the hidroeléctrica (hydroelectric power station; see page 768). Bookings can be made in Cusco, or in the *artesanía* shop on the northwest corner of the main plaza in Ollanta.

By train The train station is just under 1km from town, or a 10min walk down Av Ferrocarril from the centre of the village. A *mototaxi* into town is S/1 per person. There are up to twenty trains daily each way between Cusco and Machu Picchu via Ollanta during high season (check ⓦ perurail. com and ⓦ incarail.com for the schedule); book tickets in advance online, or at the station, or at one of the Peru Rail offices in Cusco, particularly the return, since return trains fill up with hikers coming off the Inca Trail.

9

INFORMATION AND TOURS

Tourist information The Municipalidad on the main plaza has an office providing tourist information (Mon–Fri 8am–1pm & 2–5pm and Sat in peak season).

Tour operators Soto Adventure & Travel (☎ 9844555841, ⓦ sotaadventure.com) does rafting (from US$45), trekking, horseriding and mountain biking tours.

Banks and exchange There are three ATMs in the town centre.

ACCOMMODATION

Hostal Iskay Patacalle 722 ☎ 084 434 109, ⓦ hostaliskay.com. Tucked away in a quiet alleyway, this welcoming place offers a series of rustic rooms on an old Inca site, all with private bathrooms and some with bare stone walls. Some of the single rooms are a bit of a squeeze. The buffet breakfast is another plus. S/120

Hostal Mamá Simona Av Ocobamba s/n ☎ 084 436 383, ⓦ mamasimona.com. A 10min walk up the valley, this little oasis boasts a pretty riverside garden and offers comfortable four- and six-bed dorms and doubles – some have balconies – with sturdy beds and colourful blankets. There's a fully equipped kitchen, hammocks and a barbecue set for guests, along with all-day coca tea and luggage storage facilities. Dorms S/45, doubles S/125

Hostal El Tambo C del Horno s/n ☎ 084 385 770, ⓦ hostaleltambo.com. The rooms at this wonderful place are set on two floors overlooking a pleasant garden with hammocks. Local fabrics and paintings decorate the whitewashed interiors of rooms that have beautiful hardwood floors. S/80

EATING

Alma Amor Av Principal s/n. Part of a new wellness and yoga centre with a veggie and vegan menu that also caters for ayahuasca and huachuma diets. Tasty dishes include chickpea curry and a stir-fry bowl (S/22–28) and a S/25 lunch special consists of soup plus a light bite. Mon–Wed & Fri–Sun 12.30–9pm.

Hearts Café Av Ventiderio s/n. This wonderful little café serves chunky home-made soups, huge salads, and a range of Peruvian and international dishes (mains from S/16), including plenty of veggie options. The afternoon tea with home-made scones is an unexpected treat. Some of the profits go to local community projects and a local NGO. Daily 7am–8.45pm.

Tutti Amore Av Estación s/n. This little ice-cream joint produces over eighty flavours a year, solely using local produce including all manner of seasonal fruits. S/5/scoop or two for S/8. Daily 9am–7pm.

THE INCA TRAIL

The world-famous **Inca Trail** is set in the **Santuario Histórico de Machu Picchu**, an area set apart by the Peruvian state for the protection of its flora, fauna and natural beauty. Acting as a bio-corridor between the Cusco Andes, the Valle Segrado and the lowland Amazon forest, the reserve has outstanding biodiversity, with species including the cock-of-the-rock (known as *tunkis* in Peru), spectacled bear (*tremarctos ornatus*) and condor (*vultur gryphus*). Although just one of a multitude of paths across remote areas of the Andes, what makes the 33km Inca Trail so popular is the fabulous treasure of **Machu Picchu** at the end.

SETTING OFF AND DAY ONE

An early departure from Cusco (around 5am) is followed by a three-hour drive to Ollantaytambo (where you can buy last-minute supplies, including recycled walking sticks). The trail begins at **Piscacucho**, at Km82, where you cross the Río Urubamba after signing in at the first checkpoint on the trail. The first day consists of a 12km stretch, beginning at an elevation of 2600m and gains 400m during the course of the day. The gentle incline of the trail first follows the river and passes a viewpoint with the terraced Inca ruins of the **Llaqtapata** fortress below, before it descends past rock formations to the first night's campsite at **Huayllabamba**. Along the way you pass the villages of Miskay and Hatunchaca, where you can buy (overpriced) snacks and water, as well as *chicha* (traditional fermented corn beer).

If you haven't acclimatized and don't feel well, then Huayllabamba is the last place from which it's fairly easy to return to Cusco; beyond, it's nearly impossible.

DAY TWO

The second day is the toughest part of the hike – an ascent of 1100m to the Abra Huarmihuañusca, or **Dead Woman's Pass** (4200m), the highest point on the trail, followed by a steep descent to the second night's campsite at Paq'aymayo. There is little shade or shelter, so prepare for diverse weather conditions, as cold mist sometimes descends quickly, obscuring visibility.

After an hour or so, you reach the campsite of Ayapata (where some groups

THE INCA TRAIL: WHEN AND HOW TO DO IT

Consider the **season** when booking your Inca Trail. The dry season runs approximately from May to October – expect blistering sun during the daytime and sub-zero temperatures at night. During the rainy season of November to April the temperature is more constant but, naturally, the path is muddier and can be slippery, and afternoon thunderstorms are the norm. The trail is closed for maintenance throughout February.

In recent years, due to the growing popularity of the Inca Trail, a **limit has been imposed of 500 people a day** on the Inca Trail, including the guides and porters of the certified tour operator whose services you are required to engage. By law, permits must be purchased thirty days before departure on the trail with the name and passport number of each trekker. In practice, however, it is usually necessary to **book six to nine months in advance** to make sure you get a space on the trail. Currently permits cost just over US$100 per person, including entrance to Machu Picchu – this permit should always be included in the price of your trek. Check the government website ⓦ machupicchu.gob.pe for permit availability. Always carefully research the **tour company** (see page 761) that you choose, and make sure you know exactly what you are paying for, as well as what conditions your porters will be working under (see page 760). Make sure you enquire about the toilets used on the trek, as more reliable companies use portable toilets, thereby avoiding the facilities at the campsites that are used by hundreds of people every day, though bear in mind that your porters will be cleaning those out too.

Prices vary considerably, most between US$600 and US$800; although a higher price doesn't always reflect genuine added value, usually the better and more responsible companies will have higher expenses to cover (for better food, equipment, fair wages, and so on). Check what's included in the price: train tickets, quality of tent, roll mat, sleeping bag, porter to carry rucksack and sleeping bag (or if not, how much a personal porter will cost), bus down from ruins, exactly which meals, drinking water for the first two days, and what transport to the start of the trail.

As far as **preparations** go, the most important thing is to acclimatize, preferably allowing at least three days in Cusco if you've flown straight from sea level, because altitude sickness will ruin your travel plans. Other than that you'll need layers of clothing to put on/take off (as temperatures fluctuate between night and day), sun cream and repellent, since the mosquitoes can be vicious.

If you don't want to hike for four days, or camp, the **two-day Inca Trail** is a good option. It starts at Km104 some 8km from Machu Picchu; the footbridge here leads to a steep climb (3–4hr) past Chachabamba to reach Wiñay Wayna (see page 760), where you join the remainder of the Inca Trail to Intipunku ("The Sun Gate"; 2hr) After taking in the classic view of Machu Picchu, you descend to Machu Picchu Pueblo to spend the night before returning to explore the ruins themselves on the second day.

camp on the first night), where there are bathrooms and a snack stall. Another one hour thirty minutes to two hours along a combination of dirt path and steep stone steps through mossy forest takes you up to the second campsite of Llulluchapampa, your last chance to purchase water or snacks.

The views from the pass itself are stupendous, but it gets cold rapidly. From here the trail drops down into the Valle de Paq'aymayo. The descent takes up to two hours, but you're rewarded by sight of the attractive **campsite** by the river (3600m), complete with showers (cold water only).

DAY THREE

This is the longest day but also the most enjoyable, with some of the loveliest scenery. It takes forty minutes up the steep, exposed trail to reach the ruins of the Inca fortress of **Runkurakay**, then another twenty minutes of stone steps and steep dirt track before you pass the false summit with a small lake before arriving at the **second pass** – Abra de Runkuracay (3950m), from which you can see the snow-covered mountains of the Cordillera Vilcabamba.

About an hour's descent along some steep stone steps leads to the Inca ruins of **Sayaqmarka**, a compact fortress perched

PORTER WELFARE

Even though the Peruvian government has introduced regulations, stipulating that the Inca Trail porters must be paid a minimum wage (S/43 per day) and carry no more than 20kg, abuses of staff by unscrupulous tour agencies still occur, especially on the alternative trails, where you may find your porters eating leftovers, carrying huge weights and sleeping without adequate cold-weather gear. Avoid doing the Inca Trail for the cheapest price possible, and be prepared to pay more by going with a reputable company that treats its staff well (see page 761). When trekking, keep an eye on the working conditions of the porters, offer to share your snacks and water, ask the porters about how they are treated, and don't forget to **tip** them at the end of the trek (around US$20 per porter is fair; a bit more if you had a personal porter). If you find evidence of abuse, don't hesitate to report it at your nearest iPerú office.

on a mountain spur, overlooking the valley below. From Sayaqmarka you make your way down into increasingly dense cloudforest where delicate orchids begin to appear among the trees, and then up to the Chaquicocha campsite, where some groups break for lunch. The one-hour hike between Chaquicocha and the **third pass** – Abra de Phuyupatamarka (3650m) – is the most scenic bit of the hike; the trail runs through stretches of cloudforest, with hummingbirds flitting from flower to flower and stupendous views of the valley. The trail then winds down to the impressive ruin of **Phuyupatamarca** – "Town Above the Clouds" – where there are five small ceremonial baths and, in the wet season, fresh running water. Some groups camp here on the third night and wake to a starry milky way at 4am, followed by breathtaking views of the surrounding range of glaciers at sunset.

It's a rough two- to three-hour descent to the final campsite. The first section comprises steep stone steps for forty minutes, followed by gentler stretches of dirt track. Most groups will spend their last night at **Wiñay Wayna** ("Forever Young"), the trail's most impressive citadel after Machu Picchu.

DAY FOUR

To reach **Intipunku** ("The Sun Gate") for sunrise the next day, most groups form a bottleneck at the Wiñay Wayna guard post long before it opens at 5.30am; groups aren't allowed to leave the campsite any earlier. A well-marked track from Wiñay Wayna skirts the mountain, leading you along some gentle ups and downs for about an hour before you reach a

spectacularly steep set of stone steps – the last ascent of the hike – which leads to a pathway paved by the Inca. This in turn culminates in a large stone archway, Intipunku, where you catch your first sight of Machu Picchu – a stupendous moment, however exhausted you might be. From Intipunku, to reach the main ruins, it's an easy thirty- to forty-minute descent.

MACHU PICCHU

The most dramatic and enchanting of the Inca citadels lies suspended on an extravagantly terraced saddle between two prominent peaks. **MACHU PICCHU** is one of the greatest of all South American tourist attractions, set against a vast, scenic backdrop of forested mountains that spike up from the deep valleys of the Urubamba and its tributaries.

With many legends and theories surrounding the position of Machu Picchu (meaning "ancient mountain"), most archeologists agree that the sacred geography of the site helped the Inca Pachacutec decide where to build it. Its intactness owes much to the fact that it was never discovered by the Spaniards, and the atmosphere, as you wander around, drinking it all in, is second to none.

BRIEF HISTORY

Unknown to the outside world, for many centuries the site of Machu Picchu lay forgotten, except by local Quechua people. In the 1860s it was first looted by a pair of German adventurers and then rediscovered by the US explorer **Hiram Bingham**, who came upon it on July 24, 1911.

It was a fantastic find, not least because it was still relatively intact, without the usual ravages of either Conquistadors or tomb robbers. Bingham was led to the site by an 11-year-old local boy, and it didn't take long for him to see that he had come across some important ancient Inca terraces. After a little more exploration Bingham found the fine white stonework, which led him to believe (incorrectly, as it transpired) that Machu Picchu was the lost city of Vilcabamba, the site of the Incas' last refuge from the Spanish Conquistadors. Bingham returned in 1912 and 1915 to clear the thick forest from the site and in the process made off with thousands of artefacts; the Peruvian government is currently trying to reclaim the remainder from Yale University, where some are still kept.

While archeologists are still not clear as to what Machu Picchu's purpose was, there is a general consensus that it was an important religious and ceremonial centre,

VISITING MACHU PICCHU

Since July 2017, in an attempt to alleviate the stress on the archaeological site, a **two-shift entry** system has been operating at Machu Picchu. Just over 3000 entries are allowed for each shift – 6am–noon and noon–5.30pm – including hikers coming off the Inca Trail. In addition, only 400 tickets are allocated per day to climb Huayna Picchu – the famous sugarloaf mountain you can see in the background of most photos of Machu Picchu. Here too visitors enter in two waves, the first 200 at 7–8am, the second 10–11am; for the lengthier, more demanding hike up Montaña Machu Picchu, 800 tickets are available daily, allowing visitors up between 7–8am and 9–10am.

The website Ⓦmachupicchu.gob.pe allows you to check availability and prices for all ticket permutations, and you can purchase tickets online using a Visa credit card, though the English version of the website can be temperamental. Alternatively, book via a travel agency or in person in Cusco at the INC office on C Garcilaso s/n (cash and cards accepted; ☎084 236 061; Mon–Sat 7am–8pm) or – in low season – at the INC office in Machu Picchu Pueblo (cash only; ☎084 582 030).

No tickets are sold at the entrance to the ruins, where you will need to present your **passport**. Note also that once tickets have been purchased for a specific date and time, they cannot be changed. At the time of going to press, only an official **student ID** card with an expiry date after your intended visit to the citadel (as well as a passport) qualifies you for a student discount, though following a number of cases of fraud, many applications for student discounts are being rejected. ISIC cards are no longer valid for Machu Picchu, though check in advance as regulations are constantly changing.

Another new regulation introduced in 2017 is that all visitors to the ruins need to be accompanied by a **guide**; however, at the time of going to press, this was not being enforced since there are insufficient certified guides (rates around S/150–180 for a small group) to go round. Guides can usually be hired just outside the main entrance.

Bear in mind that food and drink are not allowed to be taken into the ruins – though most people manage to smuggle a few snacks and a bottle of water in their day sack. Large backpacks or bags have to be deposited at **left luggage** by the entrance (S/5). Tickets only allow for one re-entry into the site during the period of their validity; since the only **toilet** (expect a long queue) and (overpriced) restaurant facilities are outside the site entrance, plan your one exit carefully.

If you're arriving from Machu Picchu Pueblo, you can choose between taking a **bus** up the 8km of hairpin bends to the citadel (US$12 each way, payable in Soles) or **hiking up** a much shorter, but steeper clearly marked footpath (1hr 30min–3hr, depending on how fit you are). Expect **long queues** (up to 2hr) in high season for the early morning buses, and for the mid-afternoon buses back down from the ruins.

When walking around the ruins, you have to stick to the designated trails, or the zealous wardens will blow their whistles at you.

There is no **accommodation** near Machu Picchu itself apart from the hideously overpriced *Machu Picchu Sanctuary Lodge*, located right at the entrance to the ruins. You will have to spend the night down in the valley at Machu Picchu Pueblo (see page 764).

9

given the layout and quantity of temples, as well as the quality of the stonework. The citadel may have been built as an administrative, political and agricultural centre, while the existence of numerous access routes to Machu Picchu has led others to believe that it was a trading post between the Andes and the Amazon. Conflicting theories aside, there is no denying Machu Picchu's great importance to the Inca culture.

WHAT TO SEE AND DO

Though more than 1000m lower than Cusco, Machu Picchu seems much higher, constructed as it is on dizzying slopes overlooking a U-curve in the Río Urubamba. More than a hundred flights of stone steps interconnect its palaces, temples, storehouses and terraces, and the outstanding views command not only the valley below in both directions but also extend to the snowy peaks around Salcantay. Wherever you stand in the ruins, spectacular terraces (some of which are once again being cultivated) can be seen slicing across ridiculously steep cliffs, transforming mountains into suspended gardens.

Unless you're coming off the Inca Trail, you'll be following the footpath from the main entrance to the ruins proper. For a superb view of the ruins, take the staircase up to the thatched **Casa del Guardián** (Guardhouse) and the **Roca Funeraria** (Funerary Rock) behind it; this is thought to have been a place where mummified nobility were laid due to its association with a nearby graveyard where Bingham found evidence of burials, some of which were obviously royal.

Templo del Sol and the Tumba Real

Entering the main ruins through the ancient doorway, you soon come across the **Templo del Sol** (Temple of the Sun) on your right, also known as the *Torreón* – a wonderful, semicircular, tower-like temple displaying some of Machu Picchu's finest stonework and built for astronomical purposes. Its carved steps and smoothly joined stone blocks fit neatly into the existing relief of a natural boulder, which served as some kind of altar. During the

June and December solstices, the first rays of the sun shine directly into the eastern and western windows respectively, illuminating the tower perfectly. The temple is cordoned off, but you can appreciate it from above.

Below the Templo del Sol is a cave with a stepped altar and tall niches, known as the **Tumba Real** (Royal Tomb), despite the fact that neither graves nor mummies have ever been found here. Along the staircase leading up to the Templo del Sol, you'll find sixteen small **fountains**, the most beautiful at the top.

La Plaza Sagrada

Another staircase ascends to the old quarry, past the **Royal Area**, so-called due to the imperial-style Inca stonework. Turn right and cross the quarry to reach the **Plaza Sagrada** (Sacred Square) flanked by an important temple complex. Dominating the southeastern edge of the plaza, the attractive **Templo de las Tres Ventanas** (Three-windowed Temple) has unusually large windows, perfectly framing the mountains beyond the Valle de Urubamba. Next to it is the **Templo Principal** (Principal Temple), so-called because of the fine stonework of its three high main walls; the damage to the rear right corner was caused by the ground sinking. Directly opposite the Templo Principal, you'll find the **Casa del Gran Sacerdote** (House of the High Priest).

Intihuatana

An elaborately carved stone stairway leads up from the Templo Principal to one of the jewels of the site, the **Intihuatana**, loosely translated from Quechua as the "hitching post of the sun". This fascinating carved rock, sometimes mistakenly referred to as a sundial, is one of the very few not to have been discovered and destroyed by the Conquistadors in their attempt to eradicate sun worship. Its shape resembles Huayna Picchu and it appears to be aligned with the nearby mountains. Inca astronomers are thought to have used it as an astro-agricultural clock for viewing the complex interrelationships between the movements of the stars and constellations.

La Roca Sagrada

Following the steps down from the Intihuatana and passing through the Plaza Sagrada towards the northern terraces brings you in a few minutes to the **Roca Sagrada** (Sacred Rock), below the access point to Huayna Picchu. A great lozenge of granite sticking out of the earth like a sculptured wall, little is known for sure about the Roca Sagrada – though its outline is strikingly similar to the Inca's sacred mountain of Putukusi, which towers to the east.

Eastern side of the ruins

On the other side of the Plaza Sagrada lies the secular area, consisting largely of workers' dwellings and the industrial sector. At the back of this area lie some shallow circular depressions, dubbed the **Espejos de Agua** ("Water Mirrors" or Mortars), possibly used for astronomy, though their real purpose remains unknown. On the other side of the passageway from the Espejos de Agua lie **Las Cárceles** (Prison Quarters) – a maze of cells, the centrepiece of which is the **Templo del Cóndor** (Temple of the Condor), named after a carving on the floor that resembles the head and neck of the sacred bird. The rocks behind it bear a resemblance to a condor's outstretched wings.

Huayna Picchu

Huayna Picchu is the prominent peak at the northern end of the Machu Picchu site that looms behind the ruins in every photo you see. It is easily scaled by anyone reasonably energetic and with no trace of vertigo but entries are restricted and you need to buy the separate entry ticket when you purchase your general entry ticket (see page 761). From the summit, there's a great view of the ruins suspended between the mountains among stupendous forested Andean scenery.

Templo de la Luna

From Huayna Picchu, two trails signposted "Gran Caverna" lead down to the stunning **Templo de la Luna** (Temple of the Moon), hidden in a grotto hanging magically above the Río Urubamba. Few visitors make it this far (45min one-way); besides, only those who have a ticket for Huayna Picchu will have access to the trails. If you make it to the temple, you'll be rewarded with some of the best stonework in the entire site, the level of craftsmanship hinting at the site's importance to the Inca. The temple is set in the mouth of a dark cave and there is a flowing, natural feel to the stonework and the beautifully recessed doorway. Its name comes from the fact that it is often lit by moonlight, but some archeologists believe the temple was most likely dedicated to the spirit of the mountain.

Intipunku

If you don't get to climb Huayna Picchu or visit the Templo de la Luna, for spectacular views of the ruins, simply head back to the Casa del Guardián on the other side of the site and take the path below it, which climbs gently for forty minutes or so up to **Intipunku**, the main entrance to Machu Picchu from the Inca Trail. This offers an incredible view over the entire site, with the unmistakeable shape of Huayna Picchu in the background.

Montaña Machu Picchu

Montaña Machu Picchu, which towers above the ruins opposite Huayna Picchu and offers a 360-degree view of the surrounding valleys, as well as of the ruins and Huayna Picchu also requires an advance purchase ticket (see page 761) and is a longer climb; most people take one hour twenty minutes to two hours to reach the top, but the trail is not as vertigo-inducing as Huayna Picchu. Take the path towards Intipunku and then follow the signpost to the right before leaving the ruins.

El Puente Inca

If you don't suffer from vertigo, there's an excellent scenic and level twenty-minute walk that you can take from the Casa del Guardián through the cemetery to the **Puente Inca** (Inca Drawbridge). Follow the narrow path along the tops of the southern terraces, along the side of the cliff, and over an artificial ledge until you reach the barrier several hundred metres above the bridge, which spans the gap in the Inca road that was built on a sheer cliff face. You're not allowed to get close to it, as someone fell to their death from it a few years ago, but it's certainly an impressive sight.

MACHU PICCHU PUEBLO

Anyone wishing to come to Machu Picchu will invariably pass through the settlement of **MACHU PICCHU PUEBLO** (often referred to as Aguas Calientes), which is connected to the ruins by bus, though the town itself is only really accessible by train from Ollantaytambo (or Cusco) via the Valle Segrado. Its warm, humid climate and surrounding landscape of towering mountains covered in cloudforest make it a welcome change to Cusco, though it has even more of a touristy feel to it: every other building in this little town seems to be either a hotel, restaurant or a souvenir shop and you constantly run the gauntlet of touts. If you wish to see Machu Picchu at sunrise and enjoy the surrounding scenery when it is not overrun by day-trippers, you'll need to stay here for at least one night.

WHAT TO SEE AND DO

The town's main attraction (besides Machu Picchu) is the natural **thermal baths** east of town (daily 5am–8pm; S/20), which are particularly welcome after a few days on the Inca Trail. Several shops rent/sell towels, swimming caps and bathing suits near the entrance.

There is also a **hiking trail** (around 90min each way; closed on rainy days) up the sacred mountain of Putukusi, starting just outside of town, a couple of hundred metres down on the left if you follow the railway track towards the ruins. The walk offers stupendous views of the town and across to Machu Picchu, but watch out for the small, venomous snakes. It is also not for the faint-hearted as the trail is very steep in parts (some sections have been replaced by rock ladders) and very narrow.

ARRIVAL AND DEPARTURE

By train You are most likely to arrive in Machu Picchu Pueblo by train. Peru Rail (ⓦperurail.com) and Inca Rail (ⓦincarail.com) trains connect Ollantaytambo to Machu

MACHU PICCHU PUEBLO

ACCOMMODATION	
Camping Municipal	5
Eco Packers	4
Hostal El Místico	1
Mamá Simona	6
Pirwa	3
Rupa Wasi Lodge	2
Super Tramp Hostel	7

● EATING	
La Boulangerie de Paris	2
Palate	4
Toto's House	3
Tree House	1

Picchu Pueblo, with Peru Rail offering the more frequent and generally the cheapest tickets (from US$110 return), which can be booked online or at ticket offices in Lima, Cusco or at the stations in Ollantaytambo or Machu Picchu Pueblo. In high season, do not buy a train ticket until you have confirmed the date and time of your entry ticket to Machu Picchu.

On foot Budget travellers taking the *hidroeléctrica* route (see page 768) will probably have walked along the railway tracks (10–11km; 2–3hr), arriving at Machu Picchu Pueblo from the western end of town.

INFORMATION

Tourist information iPerú is at Av Pachacutec s/n just by the main square (daily 9am–6pm; ☎084 211 104, ✉iperumachupicchu@promperu.gov.pe), with a small kiosk on the square itself that stays open until 9pm.

Machu Picchu Tickets The INC (Instituto Nacional de Cultura) office, just off the main square at Av Pachacutec 123 (daily 5.20am–8.40pm; ☎084 211 067), sells tickets for Machu Picchu (S/126, students S/63). If you stay overnight in Machu Picchu Pueblo before visiting the site, buy your ticket as soon as you arrive in town as this will save you time in the morning; if visiting in high season (June–Sept) you'll need to buy your tickets even earlier.

Banks and exchange The BCP, Av Los Incas 600, next to *Toto's*, Banco de la Nación, Av Los Incas 540 by the police station, and Caja Municipal by the Mercado Artesanal all have ATMs, but sometimes run out of money, especially at weekends.

ACCOMMODATION

Although there is an overwhelming choice of accommodation, most hostels in Machu Picchu Pueblo lack charm; there can be a lot of competition for lodgings during high season (June–Sept) and the better places need booking a week or two in advance. The cheapest hotels tend to line Avenida Pachacuteq, the main pedestrian street.

Camping Municipal Just before the bridge over the Río Urubamba, a 20min walk from Machu Picchu Pueblo, towards the ruins; map p.764. The municipal campsite has toilets, showers with intermittent hot water, and cooking facilities. An idyllic oasis – bar the Machu Picchu buses rumbling past – away from the commercial maelstrom. Camping/person **S/15**

Eco Packers Av Imperio de los Incas 136 ☎084 211 121, ✉ecopackersperu.com; map p.764. A popular place with dorms and doubles off narrow corridors that wind their way up to the rooftop terrace with billiards table and cable TV. Dorms are rather cramped, while the more comfortable doubles feature en-suite bathrooms – rooms at the back are quieter. Dorms **S/43**, doubles **S/150**

Hostal El Místico Av Pachacutec 814 ☎084 011 107, ✉elmisticomachupicchu.com; map p.764. This

pleasant guesthouse decorated with psychedelic paintings has twelve rooms (singles to quads) spread over three floors, each with a lounge area. The friendly owner organizes free mystical tours around town. **S/145**

Mamá Simona Amuraypa Tikan 104, Las Orquideas ☎084 436 757, ✉mamasimona.com; map p.764. Sparkling new hostel decked out in the chain's characteristic bright colours, and with all the essentials: activity desk, laundry, shared kitchen, board games, TV room and great staff. Superior dorm beds enjoy reading lights and power points. Dorms **S/45**, doubles **S/150**

Pirwa Tupuc Yupanqui 103 ☎084 244 315, ✉pirwahostelscusco.com; map p.764. No-frills hostel with dorms and doubles, some with private baths. There's a kitchen for guests' use. Call ahead and a staff member will pick you up from the train station. Dorms **S/35**, doubles **S/105**

Super Tramp Hostel C Chaska Tika, Plaza de la Cultura ☎084 435 830, ✉supertramphostel.com; map p.764. This friendly, brightly painted hostel offers a range of dorm rooms sleeping eight to twelve. Doubles, all with shared bathrooms, are small but comfortable. There's a communal kitchen, a lounge area with cable TV, book exchange, all-day coffee and tea and an attached burger joint, but the vibey rooftop bar is the biggest draw. Dorms **S/36**, doubles **S/100**

EATING

A combination of a captive audience and the need to import a lot of produce into the town results in generally overpriced restaurants, though some of the food is first rate. Budget dining, beyond the stalls upstairs at the municipal market, is virtually non-existent.

La Boulangerie de Paris Jr Sinchi Roca; map p.764. This French-run bakery serves superb freshly baked sweet and savoury pastries, including quiche (S/13), croissants (S/3.50) and exquisite cakes (S/10–15); there's superb

---

★ TREAT YOURSELF

Rupa Wasi Lodge C Huanacaure 180 ☎084 211 101, ✉rupawasi.net; map p.764. The young conservationist owners here have tried to preserve the original design of the house and maintain the surrounding natural environment; the result is a beautiful eco-friendly lodge avocado, walnut and native trees. En-suite rooms are small and cosy with light, wooden interiors and large windows; the pricier suites have private balconies with lovely views over the surrounding cloudforest. The rustic **Tree House** restaurant is one of the best in town, featuring *novoandina* cuisine, which combines local ingredients with international influences to great effect. They also offer cooking lessons (S/210). **S/242**

9

hot chocolate (S/12) too. It's a good spot to buy a packed lunch for Machu Picchu or the journey back to Cusco. Daily 4am–9pm.

Palate Chaska Tika, Plaza de la Cultura; map p.764. With furniture made from recycled pallets, this cosy joint by *Super Tramp* hostel serves excellent and affordable meat and veggie burgers with crisp fries, as well as pizzas, salads and snacks at affordable prices (S/20–24). Machu Picchu lunch boxes cost S/30. Tues–Sun noon–10pm.

Toto's House Imperio de los Incas s/n; map p.764. This warm, rustic restaurant with a crackling open fire to grill meats and views over the Río Urubamba offers a huge buffet lunch (noon–4pm; S/60) and wide-ranging à-la-carte menu (from S/48) at tourist prices. Daily noon–10pm.

ALTERNATIVES TO THE INCA TRAIL

As permits to walk the famous Inca Trail become more expensive and the Trail more crowded, many tour operators and individuals have started exploring **alternative Inca Trails**. Many of these offer stunning scenery to rival that of the Inca Trail, as well as ecological biodiversity and, in the case of **Choquequirao**, an archeological site larger than Machu Picchu itself. Of the several established alternative trails, only one (**Salcantay**) takes you close to the site of Machu Picchu. Rates from around US$100 per day for all of these treks, though very experienced hikers can do them unaccompanied with the relevant equipment and topographical maps, and/or by engaging a local guide.

Salcantay

The most popular of the alternatives, this five- to seven-day hike takes you either as far as the *hidroeléctrica* or to the village of Huayllabamba, where you can join the regular Inca Trail. Beginning in Mollepata, the **first day** is a gentle climb through winding cloudforest trails to Soraypampa. On the **second day** there's a steep climb up to the only high pass on the trail (4750m), at the foot of the Salcantay glacier; the landscape here is sparse and dry. From the pass you descend into cloudforest with views of the verdant canyon below, camping that evening at Colcapampa. On the **third day** a five-hour walk takes you to the jungle town of La Playa, and then it's either an hour's bus ride to the town of Santa Teresa, or a six- to seven-hour walk.

From Santa Teresa, you walk along the valley to the hydroelectric plant, from where there are trains to Machu Picchu Pueblo (check for the latest schedules).

Alternatively, on the second day you'll descend along the right-hand side of the pass into the valley towards the village of Huayllabamba, and join the Inca Trail there. Buses run from Cusco's Avenida Arcopata to Mollepata every morning (hourly from 5.30am; 3hr).

Choquequirao

A trek to the archeological site of **Choquequirao** and back is very demanding and will take four or five days. Believed to be much larger than Machu Picchu, Choquequirao is only forty percent uncovered, and is a much more authentic experience as it still receives few visitors and you can find yourself wandering alone among huge ruined walls covered with cacti and exotic flowers. There are four trekking options, starting either at **Cachora** (a bus ride from Abancay), or at the trailhead itself (10km further along the road at Capuliyoc), by crossing the canyon through which the Río Apurímac runs. Day one is a steep descent of around 2000m, and day two a steep climb up the other side. It is recommended to spend one whole day (day three) at the ruins, and then either return on the same route, or via Huanipaca. It is also possible to link this trail to the last day of the Salcantay via Yanama, or to Hancacalle, returning to Cusco via Quillabamba (allow at least eight days for these options).

Hiring *arrieros* and mules is highly recommended for the above treks, as the area is very remote. To **get to Cachora**, take an Abancay-bound bus from Cusco and ask to be dropped off at the Cachora turn-off (4hr); here you can catch a taxi to the village, where there is basic accommodation, *arrieros* and mules for hire.

Ausangate

This incredible high-altitude trek takes five to six days, plus two more days for travel, and provides the chance to see herds of vicuña wander among glacial lakes with the imposing snowcapped **Ausangate**

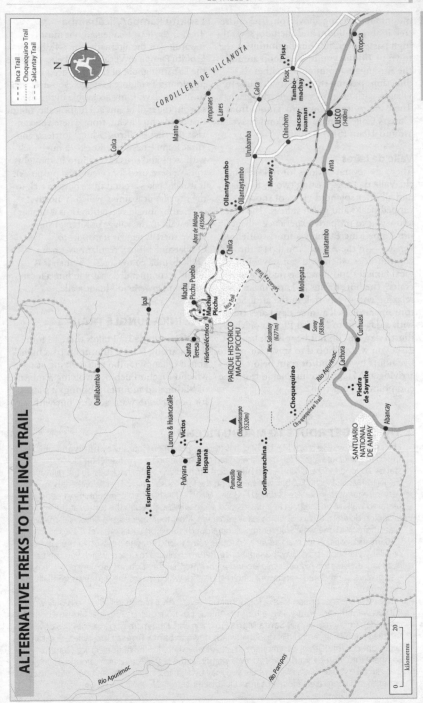

ALTERNATIVE TREKS TO THE INCA TRAIL

- - - - Inca Trail
.... Choquequirao Trail
- - - Salcantay Trail

N

CORDILLERA DE VILCANOTA

Oropesa
Pisac
Pisac
Tambo-machay
Calca
Amparaes
Lares
Manto
Chinchero
Sacsay-huaman
CUSCO (3400m)
Colca
Urubamba
Anta
Ollantaytambo
Ollantaytambo
Moray
Abra de Málaga (4350m)
Limatambo
Chica
Salcantay Trail
Mollepata
Inca Trail
Ipal
Machu Picchu Pueblo
Machu Picchu
Nev. Salcantay (6271m)
Soray (5838m)
Curhuasi
Santa Teresa
Hidroeléctrica
PARQUE HISTÓRICO MACHU PICCHU
Río Apurímac
Cachora
Quillabamba
Choquequirao
Piedra de Saywite
Choquetacarpo (5320m)
Lucma & Huancacalle
Víctos
Choquequirao Trail
Abancay
Nusta Hispana
Pukyara
SANTUARIO NATIONAL DE AMPAY
Pumasillo (6246m)
Corihuayrachina
Espíritu Pampa

Río Apurímac

Río Pampas

0   20
kilometres

9

mountain towering above you. The entire trek is above 4000m and includes several high passes over 5000m. Beginning at the town of **Tinqui**, you make a loop around the Ausangate mountain, in either direction, passing through small Andean villages with great views of nearby glaciers. There are morning buses to Tinqui from Cusco's Calle Tomaso Tito Condemayta at around 10am (5hr).

Valle de Lares

There are several options for trekking in the **Valle de Lares**, lasting two to five days, and all offer splendid views of snow-capped peaks and green valleys. The hikes allow you to properly experience village life – albeit increasingly a tourist-oriented version – in the Andes. You'll pass through communities where you can stay with local families and purchase traditional crafts. The hot springs in Lares make for a relaxing end to any trek in the area. Some tour operators sell a three-day Lares trek with a day-trip to Machu Picchu on the fourth day, but do not be misled; in most cases you will still need to travel for two to five hours by bus and/or train before arriving at Machu Picchu Pueblo from the end point of your trail.

Espíritu Pampa/Vilcabamba

To visit the least frequented but most rewarding of the alternative Inca Trails, **Espíritu Pampa** or **Vilcabamba**, believed to be the last stronghold of the Inca, deep in the jungle and as remote as it gets, you need ten to sixteen days. Only accessible in the dry season, the trail begins at Huancacalle, 60km east of Machu Picchu, from where you can visit the sites of **Vitcos** (a huge fortress) and **Yurac Rumi** (the White Rock – a huge rock with steps and seats carved into it, thought to have been used for ceremonial purposes). It usually takes around three days to trek to the site of Vilcabamba, which is mostly covered by jungle vegetation. It is a further day's walk to the village of **Kiteni**, from where there is regular transport to Quillabamba (6hr); regular buses from Quillabamba go to Cusco (7–9hr). It is highly recommended that you hire a local guide and *arrieros* in Huancacalle.

THE INKA JUNGLE TRAIL

The **Inka Jungle Trail** takes three to four days starting from a mountain pass high above Ollantaytambo and arriving at Machu Picchu Pueblo, involving a mixture of hiking and mountain biking; it's ideal for people who want activity but without

---

THE BUDGET ROUTE TO MACHU PICCHU

The cheapest way to reach Machu Picchu is to take a circuitous journey by **minivan** from Cusco to the *hidroeléctrica* (6–7hr) – a glorified railway siding by a hydroelectric power station beyond Machu Picchu – and **hike** the flattish 10km (2–3hr) back beside the railway tracks to Machu Picchu Pueblo, while enjoying the fabulous scenery. That said, there is a very infrequent train service (3 daily; US/33) to Macchu Picchu Pueblo, though most people prefer to walk. Mind the train as it passes, and avoid walking through the tunnel at the end by dropping down to the road, which leads into town. Most tour operators in Cusco sell minivan seats (from S/40 one-way; S/80 return – shop around); transport usually leaves Cusco around 7.30am and stops off for snacks/lunch en route; you can also arrange a pickup in Urubamba or Ollantaytambo but will pay the same price. Return minivans to Cusco (which you can book in advance) leave the *hidroeléctrica* around 2pm. Note that these drivers are very poorly paid – so tips are appreciated – and work long (14hr) shifts, which makes the journey potentially dangerous.

The even cheaper option takes a lot longer but saves only a handful of soles, so is only worth it if you want the adventure. Take a Turismo Ampay bus from Cusco's Terminal Terrestre bound for Quillabamba, alighting at **Santa María** (10 daily; 8hr). From here hop in a *colectivo* down the precipitous hair-raising dirt road that winds down to **Santa Teresa** (1hr), where you can overnight cheaply. Other, less frequent *colectivos* leave here for the hidroeléctrica (20min). For the return journey, you'll find *colectivos* waiting at the *hidroeléctrica* from around midday that can take you to Santa María, where you may be able to catch a minivan bound for Cusco, rather than having to wait for a bus from Quillabamba.

spending too much money – rates from around US$300 – and would rather avoid the train fare to Machu Picchu. It takes the "back route" to Machu Picchu, through spectacular changing scenery via the untouristy small settlements of Santa María and Santa Teresa. There are optional side-activities available en route, such as ziplining and/or rafting. Accommodation can involve a combination of homestays, camping and cheap local hostels.

On the first day of the tour you'll go by private bus to Abra Málaga (4300m), the high mountain pass between Ollantaytambo and Santa María, before going on an exhilarating four-hour (60km) downhill **bike ride** to Santa María. This can be cancelled in the rainy season if conditions are dangerous; even in the dry months, make sure your company provides

helmets, breakdown support, high-visibility vests etc. Day two usually involves a **long hike** through sub-tropical forest – or sometimes rafting – to Santa Teresa, via a dip in the superb **hot springs** of Cocalmayo (daily 5am–11pm; S/10), 4km outside Santa Teresa. The third day often includes an optional **adventure activity** at Cola de Mono (w colodemonoperu.com), usually a two- to three-hour zipline adventure. Day three involves **hiking** to Machu Picchu Pueblo via the *hidroeléctrica* and along the railway line (see page 768) while the final day takes you to the ruins themselves.

Independent travellers should note that Cola de Mono also offers great camping (in your own or a rented tent) and tree-house accommodation while Santa Teresa also has some basic inexpensive lodgings and restaurants.

Nazca and the South Coast

The south has been populated as long as anywhere in Peru and for at least nine thousand years in some places. With the discovery and subsequent study, beginning in 1901, of ancient sites throughout the coastal zone, it now seems clear that this was home to at least three major cultures: the **Paracas** (500 BC–400 AD), the influential **Nazca** (500–800 AD) and finally, the **Ica** or **Chincha Empire** (1000–1450 AD), which was overrun by and absorbed into Pachacutec's mushrooming Inca Empire in the fifteenth century.

The area has a lot to offer the modern traveller: the enduring mystery of the enigmatic **Líneas de Nazca**, the desert beauty of the **Parque National Paracas** and wildlife haven of the **Islas Ballestas**, as well as the fading oasis of **Huacachina** – the essential stop on the gringo trail around Peru for **dune-buggying** and **sandboarding** trips on the immense dunes that surround it.

PISCO, PARACAS AND THE ISLAS BALLESTAS

The town of **Pisco**, devastated by a powerful earthquake in 2007, has little of interest for tourists, as it is largely

industrial. Most travellers choose to stay in the seaside village of **El Chaco** (often simply known as Paracas), 15km south of Pisco, and the launching point for tours to the **Isla Ballestas** and the **Reserva Nacional de Paracas** – the entrance to the latter is located 4km south of El Chaco.

Reserva Nacional de Paracas

Founded in 1975, the **RESERVA NACIONAL DE PARACAS** covers approximately 3350 square kilometres; with a large area of ocean within its boundaries, it also includes red-sand beaches, stunning cliffs and islands. The reserve is Peru's principal centre for marine conservation and is home to dolphins, whales and sea lions, as well as masses of seabirds. The name Paracas comes from the Quechua "raining sand", and the reserve is constantly battered by strong winds and sandstorms. Despite the harsh climate, the area has been inhabited for around nine thousand years, most notably by the pre-Inca culture known as the Paracas.

Islas Ballestas

Around twenty minutes offshore, the **Islas Ballestas**, one of the most impressive marine reserves in Latin America, are

9

TOURS OF THE RESERVA NACIONAL DE PARACAS AND ISLAS BALLESTAS

There are several local **tour operators** running standard speedboat **tours** to the Islas Ballestas (departures at 8am, and at 10am and noon provided there is sufficient demand) returning a couple of hours later. Many people choose to do an afternoon tour of the Reserva Nacional de Paracas with the same operator (often with a S/5–10 discount), making a whole-day trip. The boat trips to the **Islas Ballestas** cost S/35, not including the S/11 entrance fee (S/17 combined with the reserve entry) to be paid at the pier. They take in the giant trident-shaped Candelabro de Paracas **geoglyph** on the northern part of the Paracas Peninsula, 124m tall and 78m wide, before bobbing very close to the islands to give you the full measure of the impressive stench, the rocks alive with wildlife and the sky dark with birds. You can sometimes see sea lions, penguins and bottlenose dolphins.

Excursions into the **Reserva Nacional de Paracas** typically cost S/40, not including the S/11 entry fee or lunch. Tours begin at around 11am to coincide with the return of the boats from the islands tour, and take in a stretch of desert with 40-million-year-old fossils, two attractive beaches, the popular "La Catedral" rock formation just off the shore, which collapsed after the 2007 earthquake, and a couple of fantastic viewpoints overlooking the desert scenery. Tours often include a lunch stop (not included) at the tiny fishing village of Lagunillas (*menú marino* S/30). They sometimes stop at the fascinating interpretive centre close to the reserve entrance (free), which is more interesting than the adjacent archeological museum (S/6), since the best exhibits are now in Ica (see page 771).

It's best to buy **tickets** the day before; you can arrange to be picked up at your lodgings if you already have tickets, or arrange to meet at the jetty.

You can also **rent a bike** for the day (S/25–40) and do the reserve's well-signed 30km tourist circuit on both tarred and unsealed roads, though be prepared for brutal heat, sand and sun.

TOUR OPERATORS

Most companies also organize cycling and camping trips into the reserve, tours to other nearby attractions, such as Tambo Colorado – adobe ruins built by the Chinca culture – and dune-buggy excursions into the desert. Note that this last activity is unregulated and may be harmful to the desert ecology. Kite-surfing is also taking off in the sheltered, though rather algae-prone bay.

Paracas Overland San Francisco 111, Pisco (☎056 533 855, ⓦparacasoverland.com.pe), or El Chaco, just as you enter the village (☎056 545 141).

Paracas Explorer Av Paracas MzD L5, El Chaco (☎056 531 487, ⓦparacasexplorer.com).

PeruKite based at the Hilton Hotel, 2km south of El Chaco, towards the reserve (☎994 567 802, ⓦperukite.com)

protected nesting grounds for vast numbers of sea birds. They are sometimes referred to as the Guano Islands, because of the intensive guano mining that took place here in the 1800s, and because they remain completely covered in guano or bird droppings. Today these rocky islets are alive with a mass of sea lions soaking up the sun, and birds, including pelicans, Humboldt penguins, Inca terns, Peruvian boobies and cormorants.

ARRIVAL AND DEPARTURE

Under 4hr south of Lima, the Reserva Nacional de Paracas is easily reached via the Panamericana highway.

By bus Only two bus companies, Oltursa and Cruz del Sur, run directly to El Chaco. Most drop you at El Cruce de Pisco, in the middle of the Panamericana, from where you can take a *colectivo* to Pisco (S/3) or to El Chaco (S/5); taxis to El Chaco will cost (S/15). The only bus terminal in Pisco itself is shared by Flores and Cetur, two blocks west of the main square. If travelling from Ayacucho, buses drop you off at San Clemente, from where you will need to catch a *colectivo* to El Cruce. Oltursa (☎994 616 492) operates one northbound (9.50am) and one southbound (10.15am) bus a day; both stop outside the *Refugio del Pirata* in El Chaco. Cruz del Sur has its own bus station at the north end of the village (☎056 536 636).

Destinations Oltursa to: Nazca (daily at 10.15am; 3hr); Arequipa (daily at 10.15am; 12hr); Lima (daily at 9.50am; 4hr). Cruz del Sur to: Lima (7 daily; 4hr); Nazca (7 daily; 4hr); via Ica (7 daily; 1hr 30min); Arequipa (daily at 10.30am; 12hr).

By colectivo *Colectivos* to Paracas leave from outside Pisco's central market when full, throughout the day (15min; S/3). *Colectivos* to the Panamericana leave from Pisco, just off the main square. To head back into Pisco, grab a *colectivo* (*combi* or car) anywhere along the main avenue in El Chaco.

STAY IN THE RESERVA NACIONAL DE PARACAS

You can **camp** on some of the beaches inside the reserve (S/20 for three nights including entry fee) and it is a wonderful way to experience the peace and the wildlife around you. Be warned that the sun and wind can be quite harsh, and come prepared with food and water; the occasional toilet facilities – no showers – may not have water, and are often locked. Don't expect solitude on holiday weekends when the camping turns into a beach party.

ACCOMMODATION

As Pisco is a rather unattractive dusty town, it is best to base yourself in the laidback fishing village of El Chaco. All guesthouses here can arrange trips to the Islas Ballestas and the Reserva Nacional de Paracas.

Atenas Backpacker Hospedaje Av Los Libertadores Mz G, Lote 2 ☏ 971 148 201, ⍟ bhwj6aix.preview.suite. booking.com. Simple, spotless and cheerfully decorated dorms, double and triples – all with shared bathrooms – at rock-bottom rates. Add to that a sheltered patio common area, a small kitchen complete with Welsh dresser, plus lockers, bike rental and a breakfast for S/8. Dorms S/25, doubles S/85

Kokopelli Hostel Paracas Av Paracas 128 ☏ 056 311 824, ⍟ hostelkokopelli.com. Clean, cool common areas with colourfully painted walls, a lively bar and a beachfront location make this the most popular backpackers' in town. The beds are comfortable in the dorms (4 to 8 beds & 14-bed pods), and the private rooms (S/35 more for your own bathroom) are light, spacious and welcoming. Dorms S/30, doubles S/115

Paracas Backpackers House Av Los Libertadores MzJ–1 ☏ 056 773 131, ⍟ paracasbackpackershouse. com.pe. Cheaper accommodation here is in little wooden huts with clean, shared bathrooms, while the tiled en suites with marine-themed blankets are at the back in a concrete block. There's a sandy chill-out area with deckchairs plus a communal kitchen and laundry area. Room only. Dorms S/20, doubles S/55

EATING AND DRINKING

Brisa Marina Malecón El Chaco (boardwalk). The most Peruvian and the pick of all the touristy restaurants along the seafront, this place serves a variety of fish and seafood options *pescados a la plancha* (grilled fish; S/27–35. A *menú marino* will set you back S/25. Daily 11am–3pm.

Cevicherías Off the southern end of the Malecón El Chaco. This row of no-frills fish and seafood eateries offers the cheapest set menus in town and they usually include *ceviche* followed by a fish or seafood main (*menú marino*; S/20–25).

Hideout Grill At Kokopelli's. Well-prepared, inexpensive backpacker fare: steak and chips, pizza, pasta, burgers and burritos (S/16–24), with beer to wash it down. Daily from 6pm.

Misk'i Opposite the jetty at El Chaco. With a mellow backpacker vibe aided by a suitably chilled reggae soundtrack, this casual, cosy bar is *the* place to hang out. Though the wood-fired pizzas, burritos and salads are nothing special (from S/18), the strong cocktails really hit the spot. Daily 5.30pm–late.

Pukasoncco Av Libertadores s/n ☏ 949 052 610. A veritable Aladdin's cave of pre-Columbian-style crafts, this unpromising bamboo hut set back from the road also houses a small restaurant. Artist-chef Sanson lovingly prepares healthy local cuisine with lots of noodles or rice dishes aimed at vegetarians (such as *papas a la huancaina*) for around S/20. Daily 8am–8pm.

ICA

The city of **ICA** lies 50km inland, in a fertile valley surrounded by impressive sand dunes. It suffered considerable damage in the 2007 earthquake and several buildings were completely destroyed, including almost one entire side of the Plaza de Armas. In the city itself, the **Museo Regional** is excellent, and the surrounding area offers **vineyard tours** to wineries and pisco *bodegas*. It's better to stay in nearby Huacachina.

WHAT TO SEE AND DO

Ica's busy streets do not lend themselves to leisurely strolls; however, it is easy to get around using the numerous *mototaxis* that will take you anywhere in the city for around S/3–5.

Museo Regional de Ica

Located in an Ica suburb, the superb **Museo Regional** (Av Ayabaca, block 8; Tues–Fri 8am–7pm, Sat & Sun 9am–6pm; S/15) is one of the best in Peru, housing important Nazca, Ica and Paracas cultural artefacts. The exhibits range from mummies (including those of children and parrots), trophy heads and trepanned skulls to examples of Nazca pottery and stunning Paracas weavings; a scale model of the Líneas de Nazca is out

9

ICA AND HUACACHINA TOURS

Most hostels in Huacachina rent out **sandboards** and run morning (8am) and late-afternoon (4pm) **dune-buggy tours**, which finish off with some sandboarding. Those looking to cut costs may want to rent a board (S/10) and go it alone, but make sure it is waxed – else you won't move far on the sand – and note that following a fatality, it is now forbidden to sandboard down the very steep dunes that immediately surround the oasis.

TOUR OPERATORS

Irresponsible dune-buggy drivers are known to drive quite recklessly, and serious accidents do sometimes occur, so check out the buggy (and driver) before you commit and talk to other travellers. Reputable agencies include:

Curasi Balneario de Huacachina 197 ☎ 056 216 989, ⓦ huacachinacurasi.com. A reliable outfit running sandboarding and dune-buggy tours (S/40 plus S/4 entry tax payable as you enter the dunes).

Desert Adventures Hospedaje Desert Nights By the lagoon ☎ 056 228 458, ⓦ desertadventure.net. An established Huacachina-based tour company, offering the standard two-hour dune-buggy tours of the dunes (S/65), with sandboarding included. Also runs bodega excursions (S/65) and overnight camping in the desert (S/210).

back. To get here, take a *mototaxi* from the centre of Ica (S/3).

Bodega and vineyard tours

Ica's main tourist attraction and principal industry is the many pisco *bodegas* and vineyards nearby, which can be visited on tours, both from the city and from Huacachina, and which usually involve a look around the vineyard followed by a pisco tasting and the chance to buy. The most commonly visited are: Bodega Vista Alegre (ⓦ vistaalegre.com.pe), Bodega Tacama (ⓦ tacama.com) – which also produces decent red wine, Bodega Lazo (ⓦ bodega.lazotur.com) and Bodega El Catador (☎ 056 403 427, ⓦ elcatador.pe), where the visitors are allowed to join in the stomping of the grapes in February and March. On the same road as El Catador is Tres Generaciones (☎ 056 403 565,) which offers great pisco and a good explanation of how pisco is made plus an excellent restaurant.

You can reach most *bodegas* by local bus; alternatively, visit two to three by hiring a local taxi driver for around S/40; half-day tours cost US$20–35.

ARRIVAL AND DEPARTURE

By bus Most bus companies have their own terminals at or around the intersection between Manzanilla and Lambayeque; there are numerous departures in both directions along the Panamericana during the day. Recommended companies include Ormeño, (☎ 056 215 600); Cruz del Sur, (☎ 056 223 333); Oltursa (☎ 056 211 960) and Civa (☎ 056 523 019). If travelling with Soyuz/Perúbus (☎ 056 224 138) or Flores (☎ 056 212 266), go with the quicker, direct busses.

Destinations Arequipa (frequent daily; 10–12hr); Lima (frequent daily; 4hr); Nazca (frequent daily; 2–3hr); Paracas (several daily; 2hr).

By mototaxi A *mototaxi* to Huacachina will set you back S/6.

HUACACHINA

Since Ica itself is not terribly attractive, most people prefer to base themselves at the nearby oasis of **HUACACHINA**, 5km outside Ica, as it's just as easy to do *bodega* tours from here. This once peaceful oasis, nestled among huge sand dunes, and boasting a dwindling lagoon that once had curative properties – water has now been diverted to sustain it – has been overrun with travellers, eager for adrenaline-packed adventures (in particular **sandboarding** and **dune-buggying**) and all-night parties around dimly lit pools.

ARRIVAL AND DEPARTURE

By taxi/mototaxi A taxi from town should be around S/10, a mototaxi S/6

By colectivo *Colectivos* leave when full, from near the kiosks at the entrance of the lagoon in Huacachina to the Plaza de Armas in Ica (S/2).

ACCOMMODATION

Most hostels either run their own sandboarding, dune-buggy and *bodega* (vineyard) tours, or they can organize them for you. Much of the nightlife in Huacachina revolves around the hostels, which usually have their own restaurants and bars, and throw wild parties in the evenings.

★ **La Casa de Bamboo** Av Perotti behind the Hostería Suiza ☏ 056 776 649. Small family place where you can escape the party, but not pay a fortune. Rooms are small and simple, but light and cool, some with a balcony. The owners are great and the garden restaurant/café is a treat. Room only. Dorms S/30, doubles S/90

Hospedaje Desert Nights By the lagoon ☏ 056 228 458, ⊛ desertadventure.net. In a brand-new building, this popular backpacker choice has six-bunk dorms and doubles with shared or private bathrooms. Best of all, you get fabulous views of Huacachina from the roof terrace. Room only. Dorms S/25, doubles S/80

★ **Upcycled Hostel** Road to Huacachina, 800m before the oasis ☏ 982 054 725. A short hop from Huacachina, this secluded walled property with a chilled vibe is full of superlatives: friendly, helpful staff, spotless facilities – much is made from recycled materials – comfy dorms and doubles with fans, plenty of space to lounge round the garden and pool, in the sun or shade. Add to that bike rental, well-priced tasty comfort food, and a generous breakfast. Dorms S/57, doubles S/110

EATING

La Casa de Bamboo Av Perotti s/n, behind the Hostería Suiza. This laidback family-run restaurant with tables dotted around the garden offers superb espresso and delicious vegetarian dishes, including a Thai curry (S/22) that everybody loves – all at comfortable prices (S/15–30). The go-to spot for the sweet tooth. Daily 8am–10pm.

Desert Nights Balneario de Huacachina ☏ 056 228 458. A simple place with a great terrace overlooking the lagoon that serves a full breakfast for S/15, and bit of everything else at a good price (S/18–28) at other times – you can't really go wrong. Daily 8am–10pm.

NAZCA AND AROUND

The small, sun-baked town of **NAZCA** spreads along the margin of a small coastal valley. Although the river is invariably dry, Nazca's valley remains green and fertile through the continued use of ancient subterranean aqueducts. The town is one of Peru's major attractions, and though most travellers come here solely to take a flight over the enigma that is the **Líneas de Nazca** (Nazca Lines; see page 771), other local attractions include the excellent **Museo Didáctico Antonini**, the adobe Inca ruins of **Los Paredones** on the outskirts, and the popular (if somewhat macabre) outlying archeological sites, such as the

nearby **Necrópolis de Chauchilla** and the **Pirámides de Cahuachi**, an hour's drive into the desert.

WHAT TO SEE AND DO

Plaza de Armas is the heart of Nazca, with main street Jr Bolognesi connecting it to Plaza Bolognesi three blocks to the west. Numerous restaurants, bars and hostels are all within a couple of blocks of the two plazas.

Museo Didáctico Antonini

Heading east five blocks from the Plaza de Armas along Bolognesi you will find the fascinating **Museo Didáctico Antonini** (daily 9am–7pm; S/15). The museum stretches over six blocks and presents interpretative exhibits covering the evolution of Nazca culture, with superb examples of pottery, household tools and trophy skulls with pierced foreheads. There's a good audiovisual show and scale-model reconstructions of local ruins such as the Templo del Escalonado at Cahuachi. The museum complex includes an archeological park that contains the Bisambra aqueduct (once fed by the Bisambra reservoir higher up the valley) and some burial reconstructions. The exhibit labels are in Spanish but you can pick up translation booklets at the front desk.

María Reiche Planetarium

For those with a particular interest in the Líneas de Nazca, a trip to the **María Reiche Planetarium** in the *Nazca Lines Hotel* (Bolognesi 147; showings in English daily at 7.30pm and in Spanish at 8.30pm; S/20) is a good idea. The shows last about 45 minutes and focus primarily on María Reiche's theories about the Lines, and their correspondence to various constellations, followed by a quick look through a powerful telescope.

ARRIVAL AND DEPARTURE

By bus There's no central bus terminal, but most bus companies cluster around the óvalo (roundabout) at the western end of Jr Lima where it meets Bolívar. Persistent touts meet all buses, trying to sell you anything from accommodation to flights; ignore them, as well as any taxi drivers who tell you that your hostel is dirty/too far/has

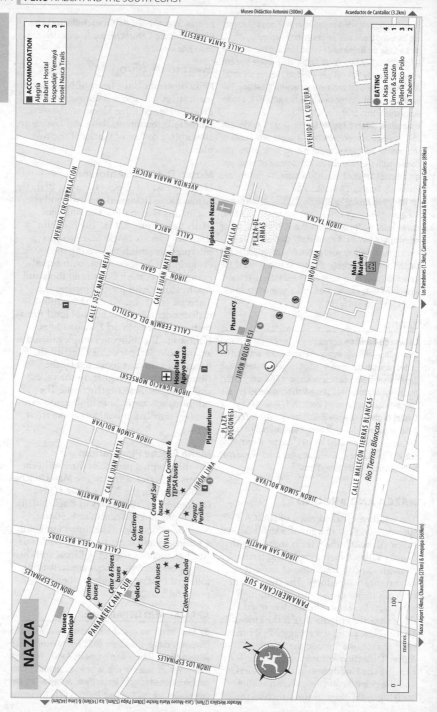

NAZCA

■ **ACCOMMODATION**
Alegría   4
Brabant Hostal   2
Hospedaje Yemayá   3
Hostel Nasca Trails   1

● **EATING**
La Kasa Rústika   4
Limón & Sazón   1
Pollería Rico Pollo   3
La Taberna   2

CALLE SANTA TERESITA

TARAPACÁ

AVENIDA DE LA CULTURA

AVENIDA MARÍA REICHE

AVENIDA CIRCUNVALACIÓN

CALLE ARICA

JIRÓN CALLAO

PLAZA DE ARMAS

JIRÓN TACNA

Iglesia de Nazca

GRAU

CALLE JUAN MATTA

JIRÓN LIMA

CALLE JOSÉ MARÍA MEJÍA

CALLE FERMÍN DEL CASTILLO

Pharmacy

Main Market

JIRÓN IGNACIO MORESKI

Hospital de Apoyo Nazca

JIRÓN BOLOGNESI

JIRÓN SIMÓN BOLÍVAR

Planetarium

PLAZA BOLOGNESI

CALLE JUAN MATTA

CALLE MALECÓN TIERRAS BLANCAS

Río Tierras Blancas

Cruz del Sur buses

Oltursa, Cromotex & TEPSA buses

JIRÓN LIMA

JIRÓN SIMÓN BOLÍVAR

Colectivos to Ica

Soyuz/ PerúBus

JIRÓN SAN MARTÍN

JIRÓN SAN MARTÍN

PANAMERICANA SUR

CALLE MICAELA BASTIDAS

Ormeño buses

Getur & Flores buses

CIVA buses

Policía

Colectivos to Chala

PANAMERICANA SUR

JIRÓN LOS ESPINALES

Museo Municipal

ÓVALO

JIRÓN LOS ESPINALES

0   100   metres

N

Los Paredones (1.3km), Carretera Interoceánica & Reserva Pampa Galeras (89km) ▲

Nazca Airport (4km), Chauchilla (27km) & Arequipa (569km) ▲

Mirador Metálico (27km), Casa-Museo María Reiche (30km) Palpa (52km), Ica (143km) & Lima (442km) ▲

closed down. Companies include: Civa (☎ 056 524390); Cruz del Sur (☎ 056 720 440); Oltursa (☎ 056 522 265); Soyuz/ PerúBus (☎ 056 521 464).

Destinations Arequipa (frequent daily; 10–11hr); Cusco (several daily; 11–12hr; Ica (frequent daily; 2hr30min); Lima (frequent daily; 7–8hr); Paracas (several daily; 3hr 30min).

INFORMATION

Tourist information The best choice for information is the iPerú office at the airport (☎ 979 980 622). The main municipal tourist office, located on the eastern end of Plaza de Armas (Mon–Fri 8am–4pm, Sat 8am–noon), has maps and limited information on the town.

ACCOMMODATION

Alegría Lima 166 ☎ 056 522 702, ⦿ hotelalegria.net; map p.774. An upmarket option, this popular hotel has clean en-suite rooms set around a verdant pool; service is friendly yet professional and the hotel's well-established agency next door can organize all manner of tours, including flights over the Lines. **S/180**

Brabant Hostal C Juan Matta 878 ☎ 056 524 127, ⦿ brabanthostal.com; map p.774. One of the very few places in town offering a dorm, this hostel has five simple rooms, all with cable TV, set on two floors; ask for a pad on the second floor as those downstairs are a bit dark. There's a book exchange, luggage storage, and a rooftop terrace. Room only. Dorms **S/20**, doubles **S/45**

Hospedaje Yemayá Callao 578 ☎ 056 523 146, ⦿ hospedajeyemaya.com; map p.774. Rooms are en suite, compact, clean and cool – with fans for warm nights – and the staff are friendly. Centrally located, there's a large shaded rooftop terrace. Breakfast S/12. **S/50**

Hostel Nasca Trails Fermín del Castillo 637 ☎ 056 522 858, ⦿ nascatrailsperu.com; map p.774. The rooms at this family-run hostel are en suite with cable TV; set around a pleasant outdoor area with sofas, armchairs and hammocks, it's perfect for an afternoon siesta. There's also table football, a book exchange and home-cooked dinners. The friendly, multilingual owner runs good local tours. Room only. **S/52**

EATING

★**La Kasa Rustika** Bolognesi 372; map p.774. Currently the top culinary spot in town, offering an extensive menu of delicious international and Peruvian dishes to suit all wallets: from S/18 for a juicy lasagne, S/28 for *lomo saltado* to S/48 for a succulent marinated *lomo al pobre* with plantain, egg and *tacu-tacu* (beans and rice). Plenty of seafood too, excellent service and a lively bar. Mon 11.30am–11pm, Tues–Sun 7am–11pm.

Limón & Sazón Av Los Incas s/n; map p.774. Great *ceviche* as well as Creole dishes (most S/20–30) are rustled

up at this airy restaurant with *peña* shows at lunchtime (Sat & Sun). Daily 9am–6pm.

Pollería Rico Pollo Lima 190; map p.774. Join the locals and dig into some generous portions of fried chicken and fries (quarter chicken S/16), chorizo (S/14) or *salchipapas* (S/12) at one of Nazca's most popular *pollerías*. Daily 10am–1am.

La Taberna Lima 321; map p.774. The scribbled walls here are testament to the numerous travellers and locals who have stopped by this family-run place; what it lacks in decor, it makes up for with a great-value *menú de casa* (S/12), washed down nicely with a *chicha morada* and accompanied by live folk music some nights. There's a veggie menu too (S/14). Daily 11am–midnight.

LAS LÍNEAS DE NAZCA

One of the great mysteries of South America, the **LÍNEAS DE NAZCA (Nazca Lines)** are a series of animal figures and geometric shapes, none of them repeated and some up to 200m in length, drawn across some 500 square kilometres of the bleak, stony Pampa de San José. Each one, even such sophisticated motifs as a spider monkey or a hummingbird, is executed in a single continuous line, most created by clearing away the brush and hard stones of the plain to reveal the fine dust beneath. Theories abound as to what their purpose was – from landing strips for alien spaceships to some kind of agricultural calendar, aligned with the constellations above, to help regulate the planting and harvesting of crops. Perhaps at the same time some of the straight lines served as ancient sacred paths connecting *huacas*, or power spots. Regardless of why they were made, the Lines are among the strangest and most unforgettable sights in the country.

At Km420 of the Panamericana, 27km north of Nazca, the tall **Mirador Metálico** (or metal viewing tower; S/3) has been built above the plain, from which you get a partial view of a giant tree, a pair of hands and half a lizard; going with a good guide, you'll learn more about the geoglyphs than you will on a **flight** over the Lines (see page 777). Some tours travel another half an hour north on the Panamericana to the **Mirador de Palpa** (S/2) where you can see a series of even older, human-like petroglyphs from the Paracus culture.

9

Around 5km south along the Panamericana from the *mirador*, you'll find the **Museo María Reiche** (Mon–Sat 9am–15pm; S/15), the former home of the German mathematician who made research into the Lines her life's work. Here you can see her possessions and sketches and visit her tomb.

AROUND NAZCA

Chauchilla and **Cahuachi**, after the Lines the most important Nazca sites, are both difficult to reach by public transport, so you may want to consider a tour (see page 776).

Cerro Blanco

You can easily see **Cerro Blanco**, reputedly the world's largest sand dune, from anywhere in the city. Formerly used as a religious centre, it's now the site for extreme dune-buggy rides and sandboarding. Several tour agencies (see page 776) run morning trips here, typically leaving at 5am and returning at lunchtime.

Necrópolis de Chauchilla

Roughly 30km south of Nazca, the **Necrópolis de Chauchilla** is an atmospheric sight. Scattered about the dusty ground are thousands of graves, dating back to the Nazca culture (400 BC–800 AD), which have been cleaned up in recent years and organized for visitors, though bits of

human bone and broken pottery shards still litter the ground, left there by grave robbers from decades ago.

There are clear walkways from which you must not stray, and open graves have roofs built over them to save the mummies, skeletons, shroud fabric and lengths of braided hair from the desert sun. The mummies with the longest hair are the chiefs, and the Nazca mummified animals as well; look for a child's pet parrot. It is an impressive experience, intensified by the curator's decision to arrange the mummies into positions intended to represent their daily lives. Tours of the cemetery last around three hours and take in a pottery workshop and a gold-processing centre on the way back to town.

Cahuachi

Currently being excavated by an Italian archeological team, **Cahuachi** is an enormous ceremonial centre of great importance to the Nazca culture, consisting of 44 pyramids, only one of which has been renovated; the rest are still hidden under the sand. There is also a llama cemetery and a site called Estaquería – a possible place of mummification. It lies in the middle of the desert, 25km west of Nazca along a dirt track; on the way, you pass ransacked ancient graveyards with scattered human remains. Tours normally take place in the morning, as sandstorms can pick up in the afternoon.

TOURS AROUND NAZCA

Some well-established companies arrange **tours** to the major sites around Nazca, all offering similar trips to one or more of the following sights: Los Paredones, the Acueductos de Cantalloc, Cahuachi, Chauchilla and the Lines. Costs can be as low as S/40–60 if you book with a local tour operator in Nazca. Tours around the Necrópolis de Chauchilla last 2hr 30min, while a trip to the Mirador Metálico (viewing tower) and the Casa Museo María Reiche also takes 2hr 30min. Since these last two sights are on or near the Panamericana, they can also be visited independently by taking a local Ica-bound *combi* and asking to be dropped off. Tours out to the ruined temple complex in the desert at Cahuachi (see page 776) are 4hr and cost around S/160–225 for four people; these need to be arranged in advance.

TOUR OPERATORS
Alegría Tours Lima 166 ☎056 522 497, ⓦalegriatoursperu.com. Well-established company. Cultural tours from US$/30.

Edunastours Bolognesi 307 ☎056 523 189, ⓔedunastours@hotmail.com. For sandboarding, Cerro Blanco, buggy rides, ATV and bike rental.
Perú Nasca Tours Bolognesi 449 ☎056 523 300, ⓦperunascatours.com. Well-respected cultural tours from US$20.

FLYING OVER LAS LÍNEAS DE NAZCA

A spectacular way of seeing the Lines is to **fly** over them. Flights leave from Nazca airstrip, about 3km south of Nazca, and cost US$50–250 per person (depending on the season and demand), lasting around thirty minutes. Note that flights only take off when the skies are clear; this can sometimes mean a delay at the airport until the weather conditions improve. Depending on the time of day, the Lines appear different due to the angle of the sun, although both morning and afternoon departures have their own particular charm. Generally, though, early morning is best to have a calmer flight, as the winds tend to get up in the afternoons and the air gets hazier. Those who suffer from motion sickness may want to skip breakfast as it is not unlike being on a roller coaster when the small plane zips around the sky, turning tight circles around each giant figure so that people on both sides of the plane get a good look. While you can't beat the view from the air, there's precious little time for any background information, and it can feel a bit like a conveyor belt in high season, being quickly squeezed in and out of the planes.

TOUR OPERATORS

You will be assaulted with offers of flights the moment you arrive in Nazca, but there are plenty of options and it's worth taking the time to choose a good one. It's best to ask at the iPerú office at the airport and book directly with the company there – this helps avoid any possible fraud. Otherwise any hotel/hostel will help you organize your flight. The airline will usually pick you up and drop you off at your lodgings after the flight.

Before boarding, you will need to pay the S/30 airport tax and present your passport. The three preferred airlines, all with excellent safety records and well-maintained planes, are:
Aero Nasca (☎ 056 522688 ⓦ aeronasca.com); AeroParacas (☎ 01 641 7000, ⓦ aeroparacas.com); and Movil Air (☎ 01 7168005, ⓦ movilair.com.pe).

Los Paredones and Acueductos de Cantalloc

These two sites are normally seen as part of one tour as they are close together. The **Paredones ruins**, 2km southeast of town, are the crumbling remains of an Inca fortress and administrative centre (and now home to desert owls). The **Acueductos de Cantalloc** lie 5km further on; constructed by the Nazca, these aquaducts consist of stone spirals going deep into the ground, thought to be air vents for a vast underground system of aqueducts bringing water from higher in the valley, or, some theorize, from a large underground well in Cerro Blanco. They are still used to irrigate the nearby fields. It is possible to circle down to the openings at the bottom and dip your fingers in this cool, well-travelled water.

Arequipa and around

The country's second-biggest and arguably, after Cusco, most attractive city, **AREQUIPA** sits some 2400m above sea level with **El Misti**, the dormant volcano poised above, giving the place a rather dramatic appearance. An elegant yet modern city, with a relatively wealthy population of more than a million, it has a relaxed feel and maintains a rather aloof attitude towards the rest of Peru.

The spectacular countryside around Arequipa rewards a few days' exploration, with some exciting trekking and rafting possibilities (best in the dry season, May–Sept). Around 200km to the north of the city is the **Cañón del Colca**: called the "valley of marvels" by the Peruvian novelist Mario Vargas Llosa, it is nearly twice the size of Arizona's Grand Canyon and one of the country's most extraordinary natural sights. Further north, the remote **Cañón de Cotahuasi** offers even more remote and challenging treks for those with plenty of time. Around 120km west of Arequipa, you can see the amazing petroglyphs of **Toro Muerto**, perhaps continuing on to hike amid the craters and cones of the **Valle de los Volcanes**.

9

WHAT TO SEE AND DO

The city centre is compact and walkable, spreading out in a grid shape from the Plaza de Armas. Arequipa's architectural beauty comes mainly from the colonial period, characterized here by white *sillar* stone, which perhaps gives the city the name "Ciudad Blanca" ("White City"). Of the huge number of religious buildings spread about the old colonial centre, the **Monasterio de Santa Catalina** is the most outstanding. Within a few blocks of the Plaza de Armas

are half a dozen churches that merit a brief visit, and a couple of superb old mansions. You can walk to the attractive suburb of **Yanahuara**, renowned for its dramatic views of the valley with the volcanoes.

The Plaza de Armas and Catedral

The **Plaza de Armas**, one of South America's grandest, comprises a particularly striking array of colonial architecture, dotted with palms, flowers and gardens, and looks particularly

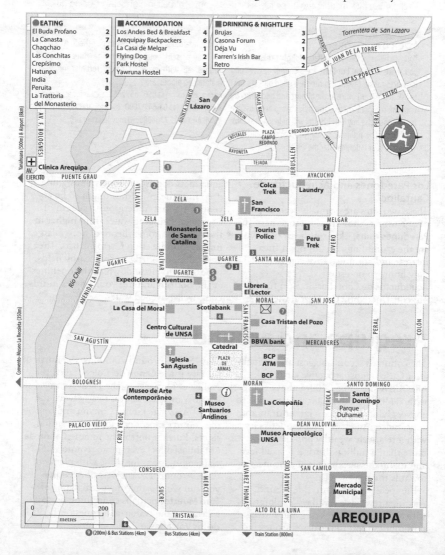

● EATING		■ ACCOMMODATION		■ DRINKING & NIGHTLIFE	
El Buda Profano	2	Los Andes Bed & Breakfast	4	Brujas	3
La Canasta	7	Arequipay Backpackers	6	Casona Forum	2
Chaqchao	6	La Casa de Melgar	1	Déja Vu	2
Las Conchitas	9	Flying Dog	2	Farren's Irish Bar	4
Crepísimo	5	Park Hostel	5	Retro	2
Hatunpa	4	Yawruna Hostel	3		
India	1				
Peruita	8				
La Trattoria del Monasterio	3				

AREQUIPA

splendid when illuminated at night. It is dominated by the arcades and elegant white facade of the seventeenth-century **Catedral** (Mon–Sat 7–10am & 5–7pm, Sun 9am–1pm; free), which has one of the largest organs in South America, imported from Belgium. Note the serpent-tailed devil supporting the wooden pulpit. Entry to the adjacent **Museo de la Catedral** (Mon–Sat 10am–4.10pm; S/10), which houses religious artefacts, also grants access to the belltower from where there are wonderful views of the city and beyond.

Iglesia de la Compañía

On the southeast corner of the plaza lies the elaborate **Iglesia de la Compañía** (Mon–Fri 9am–12.30pm & 3–7.30pm, Sat 9am–12.30pm & Sun 10am–12.30pm; free), founded in 1573 and rebuilt in 1650, with its magnificently sculpted doorway, and a locally inspired Mestizo-Baroque relief. Next door to the Iglesia La Compañía are two fine **Jesuit Cloisters**, their pillars supporting stone arches covered with intricate reliefs showing more angels, local fruits and vegetables, seashells and stylized puma heads, and today home to crafts and clothes shops. The second cloister grants access to the stunning **Capilla de San Ignacio de Loyola** (Mon–Sat 9am–1pm & 3–6pm, Sun 9am–1pm; S/5), whose cupola depicts jungle imagery alongside warriors, angels and the Evangelists.

Other churches

Other notable churches within a few blocks of the Plaza include **Santo Domingo** (daily 7.30–9.30am & 3.30–6.30pm; free), two blocks east of La Compañía, built in 1553 by Gaspar Vaez, with the oldest surviving Mestizo-style facade in the city; and the imposing **Iglesia de San Francisco** (Mon–Sat 7.15am–9am & 4–8pm, Sun 7.15am–12.45pm & 6.15–8pm; free), at the top of its namesake street, built in the sixteenth century and featuring an unusual brick entranceway.

Monasterio de Santa Catalina

Just two blocks north of the Plaza de Armas, the **Monasterio de Santa Catalina** (daily 9am–5pm, Tues & Thurs until 8pm; S/40, multilingual guides available for about S/20) is the most important and prestigious religious building in Peru – a citadel within a city – and its enormous complex of rooms, cloisters, streets and tiny plazas is perfect to explore at a leisurely pace.

The monastery was founded in 1580 by the wealthy María de Guzmán, and its vast protective walls once sheltered almost two hundred secluded nuns – daughters of wealthy Spanish families – and three hundred servants until it opened to the public in 1970. Some twenty nuns still live here today; though restricted to their own quarter, they are no longer completely shut off from the world.

The most striking feature of the architecture is its predominantly Mudéjar style, adapted by the Spanish from the Moors, and the quality of the design is emphasized and harmonized by a superb interplay between the strong sunlight, white stone and brilliant colours in the ceilings and walls and the deep blue sky above the maze of narrow streets.

Convento-Museo La Recoleta

Over the Río Chili, a ten-minute walk west from the Plaza de Armas, is the beautiful Franciscan **Convento-Museo La Recoleta** (Mon–Sat 9am–noon & 3–5pm; S/10), founded in 1648 by Franciscan friars. If you duck into the rooms leading off the cloisters, you will come across a collection of art and ceramics made by pre-Inca cultures, as well as trepanned skulls and several mummies.

Bibliophiles will appreciate the impressive **library** on the second floor, housing more than 23,000 antique books and maps, which are only used by researchers with special permission from the Father.

The **Amazonian section** of the museum is a must-see; one room houses jewellery collected by the Franciscan monks from indigenous groups in their early missions, as well as photographs of their first encounters with the "natives". The second room displays a large variety of stuffed birds and animals from the Amazon, as well as traditional weapons, some still used today,

9

TOURS, TREKKING AND CLIMBING AROUND AREQUIPA

Most companies offer trips of one to three days out to the **Cañón del Colca** for S/100–350 or more (sometimes with *very* early morning starts) or to the petroglyphs at **Toro Muerto** for from around S/14. Both these are easy places to visit on your own by bus – and a lot cheaper; if necessary, you can hire a local guide at Cabanaconde (see page 784). Trips to the **Valle de los Volcanes**, as well as specialist adventure activities (such as rafting, mountaineering or multi-day trekking) are best done with a tour operator, and can cost anything from S/150 (rafting) to S/350 (to climb El Misti) or over S/2000 for a six-day trek.

SPECIALIST TOUR OPERATORS

Colca Trek Jerusalén 401b ☎054 206 217, ⓦcolcatrek.com.pe. An excellent trekking, climbing, mountain-biking and canoeing operator that specializes in customized tours permitting a mix of these, as well as three-day tours of the Cañón del Colca (US$296) Also sells maps and has equipment rental for independent trekkers.

Expediciones y Aventuras Santa Catalina 219 ☎054 221 653, ⓦexpedicionesyaventuras.com. Specialists in rafting and kayaking trips along the ríos Chili and Majes River (from S/100), they also arrange downhill and cross-country mountain-biking trips, including to El Misti (from S/100) and Volcán Chachani.

---

and maps of early exploration of the Manú and Madre de Dios areas. Make sure to head up to the belfry, from where there are wonderful views of Arequipa and beyond.

Museo Santuarios Andinos

Often referred to as the "Juanita" or "Ice Princess" museum after its most famous exhibit – the immaculately preserved mummy of a 12- to 14-year-old girl sacrificed to a mountain deity around five hundred years ago – the superb little **Museo Santuarios Andinos** lies just off the plaza at Calle La Merced 110 (Mon–Sat 9am–6pm, Sun 9am–3pm; S/20). After a dramatic twenty-minute National Geographic video about the discovery of Juanita, a multilingual guide can talk you through the exhibits related to the sacrificial and burial practices of the Incas before finally unveiling the museum's star attraction. The intricate tiny offerings to the gods, made of gold and precious stones, are particularly fine, and ice-covered Juanita is very well preserved, although note that her body is on display for only six months of the year. At other times "Sarita" takes her place. Bring warm clothes, as it's rather cold inside, and don't forget to tip the guide (S/10).

Museo Arqueológico UNSA

A block and a half south of the plaza along Álvarez Thomas, you'll find the small yet fascinating **archeological museum** (Mon–Fri 9am–4pm; S/2), which gives a

glimpse into the local pre-Inca culture. The displays, labelled in Spanish only, feature Nazca, Chiribaya and Huari pottery; Nazca mummies and ritually deformed skulls; fine cloaks adorned with parrot feathers; and Inca and Spanish weaponry.

Mercado Municipal

For a taste of local life, check out the covered **market** (daily 6am–6pm), which takes up an entire block between San Camilo and Alto de la Luna. Lose yourself amid the stalls piled high with local produce, the smells of cooking, *juguerías*, the vendors of jungle potions and wandering musicians. Just leave your valuables behind.

The views: Yanahuara and Mirador de Carmen Alto

A jaunt across the Río Chili via Puente Grau followed by a fifteen-minute uphill stroll brings you to the attractive plaza of the Yanahuara neighbourhood. It features a **viewing point** (*mirador*), with a postcard panorama of Misti framed behind by the white stone arches. The elaborately carved facade of the small eighteenth-century **Iglesia San Juan Bautista** nearby is a superb example of Mestizo art.

From here, a five-minute taxi ride (S/5–8) takes you to the **Mirador del Carmen Alto**, which features a stupendous view of the city and all the volcanoes surrounding it.

ARRIVAL AND DEPARTURE

By plane Flights land at Arequipa airport (☎054 443 464), 8km northwest of the town. A taxi to downtown Arequipa will set you back S/30 (30min).

By bus There are two main bus terminals in Arequipa: the Terminal Terrestre (☎054 427 798), Av Cáceres, at Arturo Ivañez, which mainly receives buses from the highlands; and the newer Terrapuerto (☎054 348 810), just next door at Av Arturo Ivañez, with buses travelling mainly to coastal destinations such as Lima, Nazca, or Tacna, but there are various exceptions and some companies have counters in both bus stations. Leaving from the Terrapuerto for destinations including Lima, Nazca and Cusco are Cruz del Sur (☎054 427 375) and Cial (☎054 429 090). Flores (☎054 431 717) has numerous services to Puno and to Lima via Nazca and Ica. If you're going to the Cañon del Colca, use Andalucía (☎054 445 089), Milagros (☎054 298 090) or Reyna (☎054 430 612); for the Cañon de Cotahuasi take Reyna or Cromotex (☎054 451 555). Both terminals are around 4km from the centre of town; there are regular buses from outside the station to Av La Marina west of the city centre (30–40min); a taxi to the Plaza de Armas is S/10–15. Destinations Chivay, for the Cañon del Colca (8 daily; 4hr); Cotahuasi (4 nightly; 9–10hr); Cusco (frequent, mostly with night-time departures; 9–11hr); Desaguadero (4 daily; 8–10hr); La Paz, Bolivia (daily; 12–14hr); Lima (hourly; 16hr) via Nazca (9hr 30min) and Ica (12hr); Puno (7 daily; 6–7hr); Tacna (hourly; 6–7hr).

INFORMATION AND GETTING AROUND

Tourist information iPerú is on the Plaza de Armas (Mon–Sat 9am–6pm, Sun 9am–1pm; ☎054 223 265, with ✉iperuarequipa@promperu.gov.pe). There is also a branch at the airport that meets incoming flights (daily 6am–3pm). For topographic maps of the Cañon del Colca, try Colca Trek (see page 819), while Librería El Lector on San Francisco 213 (Mon–Sat 9am–8pm) has an extensive English-language book section, as well as detailed city maps.

Taxis While it is generally safe to hail a cab during daylight hours (provided you check that it has an official sign on the roof and licence number painted both sides), it's safer to call a cab – many drivers are illegal and robberies have taken place in the past. To call a taxi, there's Aló Cayma (☎054 458 282), Aló 45 (☎054 454 545) or Taxi Plus (☎054 438 070).

ACCOMMODATION

Los Andes Bed & Breakfast La Merced 123 ☎054 330 015, ⓦlosandesarequipa.com; map p.778. This welcoming place has spacious rooms with parquet flooring and a rooftop terrace with views over town. Self-caterers will delight at the huge open-plan kitchen with a large outdoor seating area, complete with TV lounge. Dorms **S/26**, doubles **S/65**

La Casa de Melgar Melgar 108 ☎054 222 459, ⓦlacasademelgar.com; map p.778. Formerly the home of a nineteenth-century bishop and thereafter of the well-known independence poet Melgar, this welcoming hotel has spacious rooms, most with brick-vaulted ceilings and beautiful antique furnishings, giving off several leafy colonial courtyards. **S/160**

Arequipay Backpackers Pasaje O'Higgins 224 ☎054 234 560, ⓦarequipaybackpackers.com; map p.778. A fun hostel with brightly painted walls featuring two movie rooms with flatscreen TVs and PlayStation, a pool room and a pleasant patio with hammocks and barbecue set. Dorms are comfortable if a bit cramped, with sturdy beds, lockers and shared bathrooms. Dorms **S/25**, doubles **S/72**

★ **Flying Dog** Melgar 116 ☎054 231 163, ⓦflyingdogperu.com; map p.778. Misti the dog and Chacani the cat patrol the premises of this pleasant hostel located in a colonial building just a couple of blocks east of the Monastery of Santa Catalina. Rooms are warm and clean, there's a kitchen for guests' use and a lounge area with a pool table, as well as a bar for evening drinks. Dorms **S/30**, doubles **S/75**

Park Hostel Deán Valdivia 238a ☎04 212275, ⓦparkhostel.net; map p.778. With more of a hotel than a backpacker vibe, this popular converted house serves both local and international travellers in a central yet non-touristy street. Basically furnished rooms have snug duvets, plus there's a roof terrace with chairs, tables and sun-loungers, a kitchen and small games/DVD room. Avoid the noisy rooms round reception. Dorms **S/30**, doubles **S/85**

Yawruna Hostel Ugarte 202 ☎941 312 69, ⓦjawrunahostel.com; map p.778. This recently renovated first-floor hostel has kept its colonial charm – moulded high ceilings, decorative tiled floors and wooden balustrades – but with modern arty touches too, especially on the fabulous plant-filled roof-terrace and bar. Both private and dorm rooms are en suite, with flat-screen TVs. Room only. Dorms **S/25**, doubles **S/100**

EATING

El Buda Profano C Bolívar 425 ☎997 228 590; map p.778. This vegan sushi restaurant is such a hit – with vegans and carnivores alike – that you may have to wait to claim one of only a handful of small wooden tables. Try the tasting menu for two (S/50), or a *ceviche serrano*, made with beans and mushrooms (S/13). If that all sounds too healthy, indulge yourself with a choco-maki dessert. Daily noon–9pm.

★ TREAT YOURSELF

La Trattoria del Monasterio Santa Catalina 309 ☎ 054 204 062; map p.778. Three intimate dining areas located in the grounds of the Santa Catalina Monastery, offering sumptuous fusion dishes with the best of *arequipeño* and Italian flavours. As is to be expected, the exquisite pasta here is all home-made; try the *Arequipa risotto*, with lima beans, peas and shrimp (S/46). Daily noon–3pm & 7–11pm; closed Sun dinner.

La Canasta Jerusalén 115 ☎ 054 211 820; map p.778. This popular bakery tucked away off C Jerusalén offers a range of artisanal, organic goodies, including *empanadas*, sandwiches, cakes and quinoa and cheese croissants (S/14–13), which can be enjoyed in the peaceful courtyard. Mon–Sat 8.30am–8pm.

★ **Chaqchao** Santa Catalina 204 ☎ 054 234 572, ⓦ chaqchao.com; map p.778. A chocolate lover's paradise specializing in chocolate every which way. Feast on home-made brownies, double chocolate cake and exquisite hot chocolate (S/8) as you people-watch from the balcony overlooking C Santa Catalina. Daily chocolate-making classes (S/65), too. Daily 9.30am–9pm.

★ **Las Conchitas** Av San Martín 200 ☎ 054 223 672; map p.778. This small and friendly local hangout serves excellent fresh fish and seafood dishes at very reasonable prices. The crab *empanadas* (S/6) are delicious, as are the *ceviche* (S/24) and steamed fish with yucca or rice (mains from S/20). Tues–Sun 11am–4pm.

★ **Crepísimo** Santa Catalina 208; map p.778. This Swiss-run café serves one hundred varieties of sweet and savoury crêpes; the *crepísimo* with ham, cheese and egg (S/17) remains their bestseller, and they have a great lunch deal for S/32, which includes salad, crêpe, dessert and drink. Daily 8am–11pm.

Hatunpa Ugarte 208 ☎ 054 212 918; map p.778. This cheap and cheerful restaurant attracts a young foreign crowd for its potato-exclusive menu: spuds smothered in a meat or veggie topping of choice, rustled up in front of your eyes in the little open-plan kitchen. Mon–Sat 12.30–9.30pm.

India Bolívar 502 ☎ 958 095 318; map p.778. Winning no awards for ambiance, this Indian-Peruvian enterprise scores highly on spice – and it can be hot – and flavour. Curries, masalas, vindaloos and kormas are all there (S/15–28) but the jalfrezis in particular hit the sensory spots. Mon–Sat 1–9pm.

Peruita Palacio Viejo 321A; map p.778. One of southern Peru's very few Italian-run pizzerias; here you will see the *pizzaiolo* spinning all sorts of exotically flavoured pizzas (from S/22), while there's an excellent-value set lunch for only S/10–15. Mon–Sat 1–3pm & 5.30–10.30pm.

DRINKING AND NIGHTLIFE

Brujas San Francisco 300; map p.778. On Arequipa's busy nightlife strip, this laidback bar with wooden interiors and low lighting is a great spot for those wanting to enjoy a beer and a chat without their voices being drowned by pumping music. Daily 6pm–3am.

Casona Forum San Francisco 317; map p.778. This three-storey complex houses some of Arequipa's best nightspots, such as *Zero Pub & Pool*, with pool tables, and the *Terrasse* lounge restaurant, offering fine dining and stunning views of the city through 360-degree windows. The jewel in the crown – the basement *Forum* disco – is the place to see and be seen among young *Arequipeños*, with a lively tropical decor including palm trees, pools and a large artificial waterfall.

★ **Déja Vu** San Francisco 319B ☎ 054 221 904, ⓦ dejavuaqp.com; map p.778. This popular place gets particularly busy in the evening, on its appealing terrace with sofas and views over town – a top spot for a sundowner. It morphs into a club at night, mainly playing an eclectic mix of salsa and dance music on the ground floor and electronica on the first floor. Free dance classes Thurs and Fri. There's a S/10 entry charge on weekends after 11.30pm. Daily 11am until late.

Farren's Irish Bar Pasaje Catedral 107; map p.778. Just behind the plaza, this little Irish bar/pub with outdoor

INTO CHILE

The **border with Chile** (Mon–Fri 8am–midnight, Sat & Sun 24hr) is about 40km south of Tacna (a 6hr bus ride from Arequipa, and a surprisingly pleasant place to spend a night). Regular buses and *colectivos* to **Arica** (see page 417) leave from the modern international bus terminal on Hipólito Unanue in Tacna; the *colectivos* (S/20) are a particularly quick and easy way to cross the border. For a small tip, the drivers will assist you with border formalities. **Coming into Peru** from Arica is as simple as getting there; *colectivos* run throughout the day from the Terminal Internacional de Buses on Diego Portales 1002. Even cheaper, and less hassle, is to cross the border by train along the newly restored line between Tacna and Arica (2 daily; 1hr 15min; S/18); immigration formalities are carried out in the waiting room before embarkation.

seating provides predictable comforts: Guiness, imported beers, including Old Speckled Hen and Abbot Ale (S/20), and football match screenings. Happy hour 6–10pm. Tues–Sat 10am–midnight.

Retro San Francisco 317; map p.778. Located in the Casona Forum, this is Arequipa's only bar hosting bands early on in the week. Rock groups hit the stage Tuesday through to Saturday at 10pm, occasionally backed up by some salsa, reggaeton, and 1970s, 80s and 90s tunes. Mon–Sat 7pm–2am.

DIRECTORY

Banks and exchange BCP at San Juan de Dios 125 and Scotia Bank on Mercaderes, have ATMs and can change/dispense US dollars. There are *cambios* on the Plaza de Armas, on Jerusalén and on San Juan de Dios.

Hospital Clínica Arequipa, Av Bolognesi con Puente Grau (☎054 599 000, ⓦclinicarequipa.com.pe).

Laundry There are plenty of laundry places on Jerusalén to the north of the plaza. Try Kaely, Jerusalén 412 (Mon–Sat 8am–8pm, Sun 8am–5pm; S/5/kg; ☎054 691 777).

Post office Moral 118 (Mon–Fri 8am–8pm, Sat 8am–7pm).

Tourist police Jerusalén 315A (☎054 201 258).

LA CAÑÓN DEL COLCA

The sharp terraces of the **CAÑÓN DEL COLCA**, one of the world's deepest at more than 4km from cliff edge to river bottom, are still home to Andean villages that have maintained much of their traditional way of life, despite the canyon's growth into Peru's second most popular tourist attraction (after Machu Picchu). The **Mirador Cruz del Cóndor** is the most popular viewing point – the canyon is around 1600m deep here – from where you can almost guarantee seeing condors circling up from the depths against breathtaking scenery (best spotted 7–9am; in May, June and July sightings are best 9–11am).

The entry point for the Cañón del Colca is the market town of **Chivay**, 150km north of Arequipa (3–4hr by bus), though the smaller, less touristy town of **Cabanaconde** (3300m), about 10km further down the road, serves as a much better base for descending into the canyon.

You'll need a couple of days to begin exploring the area and three or four to do it any justice, but several tour companies offer punishing one-day tours as well as extended trips with overnight stops. When you enter the canyon, you need to purchase the Boleto Turístico (Tourist Ticket; S/70) from the control point just before the entrance to Chivay, or at an Autocolca office (see page 783). Only buy tickets from Autocolca authorities, as counterfeit tickets do exist.

Chivay

This is the largest village in the Valle del Colca, although note it is not in the canyon itself. Its attractions include the hot springs, 3km northeast of town (daily 4am–7pm; S/15), with a zip-line (ⓦcolcaziplining.com) next to it. *Colectivos* run from the Plaza de Armas (daily every 20min; 10min). There are also several hiking trails here, although as **CHIVAY** is not so attractive, many visitors continue on to the laidback village of Cabanaconde.

ARRIVAL AND DEPARTURE

By bus Regular buses connect Chivay with Arequipa (8 daily; 3hr) and Cabanaconde (6 daily; 1hr 30min). Private minivans to Chivay also leave from outside the main bus terminal in Arequipa.

The bus companies 4MM (ⓦ4m-express.com) and Rutas del Sur (ⓦtoursrutasdelsur.com) have daily connections with Puno (6hr); both leave Puno for Chivay around 6am, returning from Chivay at around lunchtime; these are pricier tourist buses (US$35–50), which include bi-lingual guiding and a few photo stops en route.

INFORMATION

Tourist information Autocolca (ⓦautocolca.pe) operates several tourist offices, where you can purchase your Tourist Ticket (see page 746): in Arequipa at Puente Grau 116, and on the main square in Chivay, Picolle and Cabanaconde. The offices can also provide information about the area (in Spanish), and can help arrange village homestays.

Money There's a BCP ATM on the main plaza in Chivay and another ATM just opposite the market, although it's probably wise to bring some spare cash from Arequipa

ACCOMMODATION AND EATING

Aromas Caffee Plaza de Armas 301 ☎054 796 512. This small coffee joint is a great spot to grab a refreshing frappuccino (S/8) on a hot day or a warming hot chocolate (S/6) on a nippy evening. Seating is at little wooden tables – just enough space to fit your slab of cake or toasted sandwich (S/4–5). Mon–Sat 8am–10pm, Sun 9am–10pm.

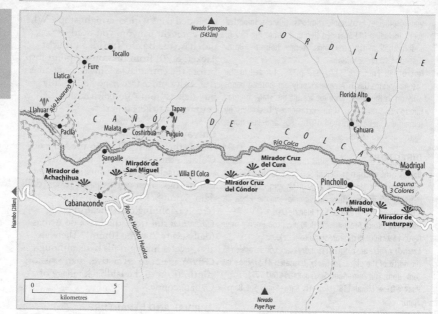

Hostal La Pascana Siglo XX 106 ☎054 531 001, ⓦ hostal-lapascana.com. A pleasant respite from the endless concrete blocks, *La Pascana* has recently refurbished rooms giving onto a central flowering courtyard. The triple room, at S/160, is really good value. **S/126**

Q'anka Salaverry 105, 3rd floor ☎958 296 914. This atmospheric little place specializes in hot stone steaks, with a particularly tasty *lomito de alpaca* (S/35), and pizzas (S/20), also served sizzling on hot stones. The walls are decorated with masks and mud vases adorn the tables. Daily 11am–9pm.

Hostal Rumi Wasi Sucre 714 ☎054 480 091. Friendly place with a six-bed dorm and modest en-suite rooms of various sizes with Cable TV. Plenty of blankets provided but no heating. The semi-open roof-top terrace is good for lounging on, and a popular pancake breakfast is served. Use of kitchen, bike rental & horse riding. Dorms **S/25**; doubles **S/80**

Cabanaconde

Perched on the southern rim of the canyon, surrounded by Inca terracing, the laidback village of **CABANACONDE** makes an excellent base for hiking down into the canyon, with the lodgings listed below able to set you up with advice, equipment and a guide, if necessary.

The "classic" trek is the hike into the canyon to the **Oasis de Sangalle** – a splotch of blue and green amid parched scenery – where many hikers choose to stay the night. The trail starts at the end of Calle Grau, just beyond La Casa de Santiago, descending very steeply to the oasis below. The trek takes about three hours, and, while it's possible (and exhausting) to ascend on the same day, it's far more rewarding to either camp or stay in one of the basic huts at Sangalle.

Another popular route is Cabanaconde–San Juan de Chuccho–Coshñirhua–Malata–Oasis de Sangalle, or one that takes in a bubbling **geyser** and some hot pools in Llahuar.

It is strongly advised to tackle most routes with a guide, given that there has been the very occasional accident and even death of tourists who have ventured off unaccompanied into the canyon. Check the websites of the lodgings listed below for more information, and details of other activities such as **mountain biking**.

ARRIVAL AND DEPARTURE

By bus There are several daily departures to Arequipa (6hr) via Chivay (1hr 30min).

ACCOMMODATION AND EATING

All the lodgings in Cabanaconde listed below have bags of knowledge about hiking in the area; they can also arrange

CAÑÓN DEL COLCA

N

Nevado Quehuisha (5318)

Cahotota

Sibayo (28km) & Cailloma (90km)

Lari

Coporaque

Planetario y Observatorio Colca

La Calera

Uyo Uyo

Soccaro

Maca

Ichupampa

Río Colca

Chivay

Oroya

Achoma

Yanque

Arequipa (143km)

guides, mules and muleteers and rent out mountain bikes, but advance notice is preferred, and is essential in high season (June–Sept).

La Casa de Santiago ☎054 203 737, ⓦlacasadesantiago.com. This calm little oasis with clean and tidy rooms has a verdant garden with hammocks and wonderful views over the surrounding mountains. **S̶/120**

★**Oasis Paraíso Camping Lodge** Sangalle Oasis ☎054 398 439, ⓦoasisparaisoecolodge.com. Deep in the canyon in the lush Oasis de Sangalle, this rustic place has a lush garden area with a very inviting pool that will make sure you linger here for longer than planned. Simple meals are served in the open-fronted restaurant; it's happy hour 4–6pm. **S̶/82**

Pachamama ☎054 767 277, ⓦpachamamahome. com. The main area of this hostel is warm and welcoming with a wood-fire pizza oven that keeps the room toasty and plenty of board games and a book exchange to keep travellers happy. Rooms here are rather plain but pleasant enough; those with a private bath will set you back a bit more. Dorms **S̶/32**, doubles **S̶/70**

★**Valle del Fuego** ☎054 668 910, ⓦvalledelfuego. com. Laidback and friendly owner Yamil will welcome you with a potent pisco sour. The en-suite brick and stone rooms are warm and welcoming and command lovely views over the surrounding mountains. Their rustic family-run restaurant and bar just a few doors down serves pizzas and sandwiches (from S/14) with mains at about S/25. Camping **S̶/10**, doubles **S̶/80**

CAÑÓN DE COTAHUASI

The magnificent and remote **CAÑÓN DE COTAHUASI**, like its better-known neighbour the Cañón del Colca, is one of the world's deepest canyons; but it's blissfully free of tour buses and tourists. This is mainly because it's much further from Arequipa – accessible only by overnight bus – and the road there has yet to be fully paved. Those that make it here base themselves at **Cotahuasi**, the valley's attractive main settlement, which has quaint narrow streets and a few simple lodgings and restaurants.

It's a wonderful area to spend several days, wandering through traditional hamlets made from adobe and thatch, taking in Huari and Inca **ruins**, waterfalls – the **Catarata de Sipia** is particularly impressive – spectacular panoramic vistas of snow-capped peaks, sightings of **condors** and **thermal baths**, to soothe the aching limbs. Other attractions include a **cactus forest** and pockets of puya raimondii, the world's largest **bromeliad** – an imposing phallus of up to 15m in height. Sporadic battered combis from Cotahuasi's surprisingly modern bus station will help you to bump along the

9

dirt roads to reach the various small settlements across the valley.

ARRIVAL AND INFORMATION

By bus Cromotex and Reyna each offers an overnight bus service (9–11hr) to Cotahausi from Arequipa's Terminal Terrestre; buses back to Arequipa are also overnight.

Tourist information The municipal office on C Centenario can supply you with tourist information (in Spanish) and a good tourist map of the valley.

Money There is no ATM in Cotahuasi – so bring cash – though the Banco de la Nación on the main street will change US dollars.

ACCOMMODATION

Hatunhuasi Hotel Centenario 307–309, Cotahuasi ☎ 054 581 054, ⓦ hatunhuasi.com. This small, family-run hotel features eleven simple, clean tiled-floor rooms giving onto a garden area (grab an upstairs room). The owner can cook meals upon request. **S/60**

★ **Hotel Valle Hermoso** Tacna 106, Cotahuasi ☎ 054 581 057, ⓦ hotelvallehermoso.com. A very pleasant guesthouse with rooms set around a lovely garden area – some with a balcony, overlooking avocado, orange and fig trees and a couple of grazing llamas. The rooms have individual touches, such as lamps with old irons as stands, and breakfast includes home-made jams and bread, as well as freshly squeezed juice. **S/100**

Puno and Lago Titicaca

An immense region both in terms of its history and the breadth of its magical landscape, the **Titicaca Basin** makes most people feel as if they are on top of the world. The skies are vast and the horizons appear to blend away below you. With a dry, cold climate – frequently falling below freezing in the winter nights of July and August – **Puno** is a breathless place (at 3870m above sea level), with a burning daytime sun in stark contrast to the icy evenings. On the edge of the town spreads the vast **Lago Titicaca** – overlooked by distant snow-capped peaksand dotted with unusual **floating islands**. The lake is home to the Uros culture, as it is to the island communities of **Amantani** and **Taquile**, which can all be visited by boat from Puno.

PUNO

The first Spanish settlement at **PUNO** sprang up around a silver mine discovered by the infamous Salcedo brothers in 1657, a camp that forged such a wild and violent reputation that the Lima viceroy moved in with soldiers to crush the Salcedos before things got too out of hand. In 1668 he established Puno as the capital of the region and from then on it developed into Lago Titicaca's main port and an important town on the silver trail from Potosí. Rich in traditions, Puno is also famed as the folklore capital of Peru. During the first two weeks of February, fiestas are held in honour of the **Virgen de**

la **Candelaria** – a great spectacle, with incredible dancers wearing devil masks, which climaxes on the second Sunday of February.

WHAT TO SEE AND DO

Puno is a congested, chaotic but friendly town, compact enough to walk around. Most travellers use it as a stopover on their way to see the islands, but there are a couple of sites of interest in the town itself. There are three main points of reference in Puno: the spacious **Plaza de Armas**, the cosmopolitan, pedestrianized strip of **Jirón Lima**, on which most restaurants and bars can be found, and the bustling **port** area, which lies eight blocks (1.2km) down Avenida Titicaca from the main square.

The Plaza de Armas and around

The seventeenth-century **Catedral** on the Plaza de Armas (daily 7am–noon & 3–6pm; free) is surprisingly large, with an exquisite Baroque facade and, unusually for Peru, a very simple interior, in line with the local Aymaras' austere attitude to religion. High up, overlooking the town and the Plaza de Armas, **Mirador Kunur Wasi** – topped by a large, unmissable condor (Kuntur in Quechua) – sits on a prominent hill, a steep fifteen-minute climb up around six hundred steps from the end of Jirón Llave – head left at the top end of the Plaza de Armas. The viewpoint offers stupendous views across the bustle of Puno to the serene blue of Titicaca and its unique skyline, though there have been some reported muggings here, so be careful.

If you have time, it's worth checking out Puno's two small museums: opposite the cathedral the **Museo Carlos Dreyer** (Mon–Sat 9am–7pm; S/15) contains interesting archeological pieces from the Inca and earlier Pukara periods; two blocks off the main square on Calle Llave, the informative **Museo de la Coca y Costumbres** (Mon–Sat 9am–7pm; free)

chronicles the history, cultural significance and multiple uses of the coca plant in Andean societies, though the real treat is the top-floor exhibition of some of the wonderfully extravagant costumes that are worn for the annual Fiesta de la Virgen de la Candelaria.

The Yavari
An unlikely museum, and an even more unlikely bed and breakfast, is the nineteenth-century British-built steamship **Yavari** (☎051 369 329; ⊛yavari.org).

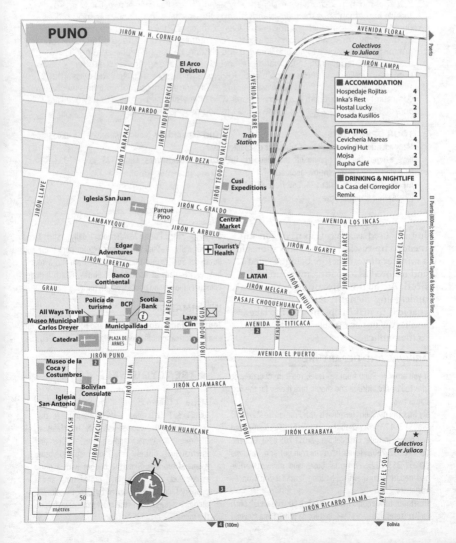

PUNO

JIRÓN M. H. CORNEJO

AVENIDA FLORAL

Colectivos to Juliaca ★

JIRÓN LAMPA

El Arco Deústua

■ ACCOMMODATION
Hospedaje Rojitas · 4
Inka's Rest · 1
Hostal Lucky · 2
Posada Kusillos · 3

● EATING
Cevichería Mareas · 4
Loving Hut · 1
Mojsa · 2
Rupha Café · 3

■ DRINKING & NIGHTLIFE
La Casa del Corregidor · 1
Remix · 2

JIRÓN PARDO

AVENIDA LA TORRE

JIRÓN INDEPENDENCIA

JIRÓN TARAPACÁ

Train Station

JIRÓN DEZA

JIRÓN TEODORO VALCÁRCEL

Cusi Expeditions

JIRÓN LLAVE

Iglesia San Juan

Parque Pino

JIRÓN C. GRALDO

LAMBAYEQUE

JIRÓN F. ARBULU

Central Market

AVENIDA LOS INCAS

Edgar Adventures

JIRÓN LIBERTAD

Tourist's Health

JIRÓN A. UGARTE

JIRÓN PINEDA ARCE

AVENIDA EL SOL

GRAU

Banco Continental

LATAM

JIRÓN MELGAR

Policía de turismo

BCP

Scotia Bank

JIRÓN AREQUIPA

PASAJE CHOQUEHUANCA

JIRÓN CAHUIDE

WENDORE

All Ways Travel

Museo Municipal Carlos Dreyer

Municipalidad

Lava Clin

JIRÓN MOQUEGUA

AVENIDA TITICACA

Catedral

PLAZA DE ARMES

Museo de la Coca y Costumbres

JIRÓN PUNO

AVENIDA EL PUERTO

Bolivian Consulate

JIRÓN LIMA

JIRÓN CAJAMARCA

Iglesia San Antonio

JIRÓN AYACUCHO

JIRÓN HUANCANE

JIRÓN TACNA

JIRÓN CARABAYA

JIRÓN ANCASH

Colectivos for Juliaca ★

AVENIDA EL SOL

N

0 — 50 metres

JIRÓN RICARDO PALMA

4 (100m)

Bolivia

Puerto · El Puerto (800m); boats to Amantaní, Taquile & Islas de los Uros

9

TOURS AROUND PUNO

There are four main tours on offer in Puno, all of which can potentially reward you with abundant bird and animal life, immense landscapes and insights into indigenous traditions. The trip to the ancient burial towers or *chullpas* at **Sillustani** normally involves a three- to four-hour trip by minibus and costs from S/60 including the entrance fee (S/15) and guide. This can easily be done independently by taking a Juliaca-bound *combi* (20min) getting out at the turn-off to Sillustani, where there are usually *colectivo* cars that can take you to the ruins (20min), though you may have to wait a while in low season.

The other tours generally involve a combination of visits to the floating Islas de los **Uros** and to **Taquile and Amantani**. Many of these visits result in an unsatisfactory, voyeuristic experience for the tourist and an exploitative one for the community concerned. If you have the time (and a little Spanish), it's better for all concerned – and cheaper – to organize a visit directly with the communities/families involved so they get more of the money. You'll get much more from the experience by staying at least a night or two. The Islas Uros, Taquile and Amantani – the main islands tourists visit– all have community transport offices down by Puno's tourist jetty, at the end of Avenida Titicaca. They can also help organize accommodation. Amantani now has a hostel (W kantutalodge.com) and six other homestay options; Taquile, known for its fine weaving and knitting, has a high-profile community association (W taquile.net) that organizes all-inclusive visits, and several families offer homestays; individual islands of the Islas de los Uros also organize activities and overnight stays. The iPerú office in Puno has a list of contacts of various families/communities involved in community-based tourism (*turismo vivencial*), who offer visitors the chance to stay overnight and/or join in activities such as guided walks, fishing or agricultural tasks.

TOUR OPERATORS

Many agencies run formulaic tours and some companies have a reputation for ripping off the islanders. The following show a more sensitive approach:
All Ways Travel Deustua 576, 2nd floor ☎ 051 353 979, W titicacaperu.com.

Cusi Expeditions Teodoro Valcarcel 155 ☎ 051 369 072.
Edgar Adventures Lima 328 ☎ 051 353 444, W edgaradventures.com.

Initially used as a Peruvian navy gunship, it ended up rusting on the lake's shores for a number of years before being rescued and restored as a floating museum and B&B. At the time of writing it was still undergoing a lengthy refurbishment to enable it to make trips around the lake and it was unclear when it would reopen to the public.

ARRIVAL AND DEPARTURE

If you arrive in Puno from sea level, you'll immediately be affected by the altitude and should take it easy for the first day or two.
By bus The main bus terminal is at Jr Primero de Mayo 703 (☎ 051 364 733). A taxi to the centre is S/5. Recommended companies include: Cruz del Sur (☎ 051 205 824), Ormeño (☎ 051 352 780), Reyna (W reyna.com.pe) and Transzela (☎ 051 353 822). Provincial buses and minivans arrive and depart from the neighbouring Terminal Zonal on Av Costanera.
Destinations Arequipa (frequent; 6hr); Cusco (several; 6hr); La Paz (several; 6–7hr) via Copacabana (3hr); Lima (several

daily; 18–21hr); Puerto Maldonado, 1 daily; 15hr); Tacna (several daily; 8–9hr) 4M Express (W 4m-peru.com) and Rutas del Sur (W tourrutasdelsur.com) both run a tourist bus service (daily at 6am; 6hr) to Chivay, which includes bilingual guiding and photo stops en route.

INFORMATION

Tourist information The helpful and friendly staff at the tourist information office on the Plaza de Armas (Deustua,

★ TREAT YOURSELF

Mojsa Jr Lima 635, 2nd floor, Plaza de Armas ☎ 051 363 182; map p.787. This popular, cosy restaurant with wooden interiors translates as "delicious" in Aymara and so it is – local and international dishes here are prepared using highland produce. Blow the budget with a *causa escabechada* (mashed potato, grilled trout and a peppery sauce; S/20) followed by alpaca steak with quinoa *pesque* (S/38) – the most expensive dish on the menu. Daily noon–9.30pm.

at Lima; Mon–Sat 9am–6pm, Sun 9am–1pm; ☎051 365 088, ✉iperupuno@promperu.gob.pe) can provide maps, leaflets and other information. iPerú also operates a kiosk at the Terminal Terrestre (daily 6am–8pm).

ACCOMMODATION

Hospedaje Rojitas Chucuito 252 ☎948 035 125, ✉kenyr486@hotmail.com; map p.787. Unpromising exterior but this friendly shoestring place does the basic job of providing a bed – mattresses variable – for the night in a clean room with shared bathroom possessing hot water. Room only. S̲/̲2̲5̲ per person

Inka's Rest Psje San Carlos 158 ☎051 368 720, ⓦinkas-rest-pe.book.direct; map p.787. This welcoming place has spacious, comfortable dorms and doubles, all with individual communal areas with sofas, TV, kitchen, computers and all-day coca tea. There's a billiards table, and shared kitchen too. Dorms S̲/̲2̲6̲, doubles S̲/̲6̲5̲

Hostal Lucky Av Titicaca 144 ☎051 353 552, ⓦluckyyourhouse.com; map p.787. The simply furnished rooms at this cosy guesthouse are clean and welcoming, and guests have access to the kitchen. The living area is adorned with a few trinkets and an old wooden bar where guests are encouraged to mingle. Inexpensive single rooms too. No breakfast. S̲/̲9̲0̲

Posada Kusillos Jr Federico More 162 ☎051 364 579; map p.787. This small homely place has ten rooms, all with en-suite facilities, and two little patios with pot plants. The walls of the common area are decorated with the owner's international collection of masks. Room only. S̲/̲1̲1̲0̲

EATING

Cevichería Mareas Cajamarca 448 ☎051 777 000; map p.787. A popular open-fronted *cevichería* that gets packed at lunchtime for its tasty *ceviche* (S/15) and other fish-based dishes including rice with seafood (S/17). Daily 9am–4pm.

Loving Hut Choquehuanca 188 ☎051 353 523; map p.787. Offering tasty vegan cuisine at extremely reasonable prices, this place understandably gets very busy at lunchtime. The lunch menu will set you back S/15, or you can choose individual dishes for about S/8. Mon–Fri 11am–8pm, Sat 11am–6pm.

Rupha Café Moquegua 338 ☎051 354 179; map p.787. Pleasant upstairs spot – perfect for breakfast (until noon), all-day waffles (S/10), *empanadas*, baguettes (S/9–13) or a slice of cake, or more substantial burger and chips. Service is brisk and reliable. Mon–Sat 7am–9.30pm, Sun noon–9.30pm.

DRINKING AND NIGHTLIFE

La Casa del Corregidor Deustua 576 ☎051 351 921, ⓦcafebar.casadelcorregidor.pe; map p.787. A welcoming café and bar with a quirky room with upturned funnels as lampshades and walls plastered with vinyl discs. The food is average, but the sunny courtyard is a pleasant spot to kick back with a freshly squeezed juice (S/8) or a beer (S/10). Mon–Sat 9am–9pm.

Remix Puno 517, Plaza de Armas; map p.787. This snug two-storey pizza-bar is simple in its tastes: rock music and pizza – oven-fired (which keeps the place warm) by the slice or the whole thing (from S/12). Mon–Sat 5–9.30pm.

LAGO TITICACA

An undeniably impressive sight, **Lago Titicaca**'s skies are vast, almost infinite, and deep, deep hues of blue; below this sits a usually placid mirror-like lake, reflecting the big sky back on itself. A national reserve since 1978, the lake has more than sixty varieties of birds, fourteen species of native fish and eighteen types of amphibians. It's also the world's largest high-altitude body of water, at 284m deep and more than 8500 square kilometres in area, though threatened by global warming, the lake is gradually shrinking.

The unique, artificial **floating islands**, which have been inhabited since their construction centuries ago by the indigenous **Uros** people, are an impressive sight. Tour groups only visit a couple of the forty or so islands where the people are used to tourism; they will greet you, offer

---

CROSSING INTO BOLIVIA

The most popular routes to Bolivia involve overland road travel, crossing the frontier either at **Yunguyo/Kasani** (best for Copacabana) or at the principal border of **Desaguadero** (best for La Paz). En route to either you'll pass by some of Titicaca's more interesting colonial settlements, each with its own individual styles of architecture. By far the easiest way is to take a direct bus from Puno to either Copacabana or La Paz, which will stop for the formalities at the border. Otherwise, from Puno you can take a *combi* to Yunguyo, then another to Kasani, then walk across the border and take a Bolivian *combi* for the ten-minute ride to Copacabana. From Copacabana it is approximately four hours to La Paz.

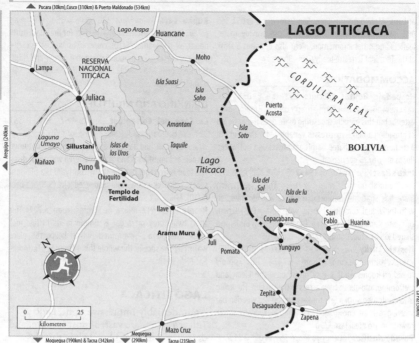

you handicrafts for sale and possibly suggest a tour on one of their boats, made from the same **totora** reeds as their island homes, for a small fee. For a more rewarding experience, visit the communities who live on the fixed islands of **Taquile** and **Amantaní**, who still wear traditional clothes and follow ancient local customs, though are adapting to the challenges of modernization more on their own terms. There are, in fact, more than seventy islands in the lake, the largest and most sacred being the **Isla del Sol** (see page 181), an ancient Inca temple site on the Bolivian side of the border that divides the lake's southern shore. Titicaca is an Aymara word meaning "Puma's Rock", which refers to an unusual boulder on the Island of the Sun. The Bolivian islands can

only be visited from Copacabana.

ARRIVAL AND DEPARTURE

Community-operated boats leave from Puno's tourist jetty at the end of Av Titicaca to the various islands. Check with the relevant island transport office at the jetty a day in advance to confirm.

To Amantaní Daily departures at around 8am, sometimes via the Islas Uros, returning from Amantaní at 3.30pm –sometimes via Taquile (4hr; S/30 return, including S/8 island fee).

To Taquile Daily departures at 7.20am, returning from Taquile at 2pm (2hr 30min; S/25 return, including S/8 island fee).

To Islas de los Uros Hourly departures from around 8am (15min; S/10 return). The community transport office also runs its own tours to the islands (2hr 30min; S/25–30) usually stopping off at two islands.

Huaraz and the Cordillera Blanca

Sliced north to south by the parallel **Cordillera Blanca** and **Cordillera Negra** (the white and black mountain ranges), the department of Ancash offers some of

the best hiking and mountaineering in the Americas. Its capital **Huaraz** – eight hours by bus from Lima – is tourist-friendly, has a lively atmosphere and makes an ideal base for exploring some nearby lagoons, ruins, glaciers and remote trails. Through the valley known as the Callejón de Huaylas is the pretty town of **Caraz**, which offers a taste of traditional Andean life.

HUARAZ

With glaciated peaks and excellent trekking nearby, **HUARAZ** is a place to stock up, hire guides and equipment, and relax with great food and drink after a breathtaking expedition. While there are only a couple of tourist attractions to visit in the city itself, the spectacular scenery and great cafés make it a pleasant stop for even non-adventurous spirits. Make sure to acclimatize before trying any hikes; Huaraz is 3090m above sea level.

WHAT TO SEE AND DO

Huaraz was levelled by an earthquake in 1970 and today most of the houses are single-storey modern structures topped with gleaming tin roofs. The one surviving pre-earthquake street, **Jiron José Olaya**, serves as a sad reminder of Huaraz's colonial past and is worth a stroll down to see what this city was once like. The **Museo Arqueologico de Ancash**, at Av Luzuriaga 762 on Plaza de Armas (daily 9am–5pm; S/5.50; ☎043 721 551), is worth a look for its attractive landscaped gardens and superb collection of ceramics, as well as some trepanned skulls. On the other side of the Plaza de Armas is the **Catedral** (daily 7am–7pm); the vast blue-tiled roof makes a good landmark and, if you look closely, appears to mirror the glaciated Nevado Huanstán to the east.

9

There's an easy day trek (7km; 3hr) from Huaraz to the remains of a Huari mausoleum, **Wilcahuaín** (Mon–Sat 9am–5pm & Sun 9am–2pm; S/5). An option for a relaxing afternoon is the half-hour taxi ride (S/10) to the nearby thermal springs at **Monterrey**, or the ones 2km further at **La Reserva** . It's not advisable to walk, as attacks on tourists have been reported on this route.

ARRIVAL AND DEPARTURE

By plane LC Perú operates daily flights from Lima. The small airstrip is close to the village of Anta, some 23km north of Huaraz; a 30min ride into the city from the side of the road by *combi* (S/2.50) or taxi (S/40).

By bus Most bus companies have terminals a street or two from the main drag of Av Luzuriaga on Jr Comercio which becomes Jr Lucar y Torre.

Destinations Chimbote (4–6 daily; 7hr); Lima (6 daily; 8hr); Trujillo (7–9 daily; 9hr).

GETTING AROUND

Av Luzuriaga is the north–south axis of the town centre, where most of the restaurants, nightlife and tour operators are based. Much of Huaraz town can be negotiated on foot once you've acclimatized to the altitude; however, some of the more remote sectors around the urban area should not be walked alone at night.

By taxi For short journeys within the city, the best option is to use one of the regular *taxi colectivos* that run on fixed routes along Av Luzuriaga and Av Centenario (S0.80). A taxi ride anywhere in the city should not cost more than S/3. Companies include Phono Taxi (☎043 428 800) and Taxi Plus (☎043 792 111).

INFORMATION

Tourist information iPerú, at Pasaje Atusparia just off the Plaza de Armas (Mon–Sat 9am–6pm, Sun 9am–1pm;

TOURS AND ACTIVITIES IN AND AROUND HUARAZ

Most of the tour operators in Huaraz can be found along Avenida Luzuriaga, or the two small squares that join it to the Plaza de Armas, and are open from 7am until late, closing between 1pm and 4pm. Most specialize in hiking and mountaineering. Popular excursions include the 8hr **Llanganuco Lakes** (see page 794), the 9–11hr **Chavín de Huantar** (see page 794) and the edge of the **Pastoruri Glacier** at 5240m (8hr). Most operators can also arrange trips to the Monterrey **thermal baths** (2hr) and some offer **adventure activities** in the area. Costs usually exclude entrance fees and food; make sure your guide can speak English if you need them to. If you're hiring your own guide, always check for certification and that they're registered at the Casa de Guías (see below). iPerú can help with any complaints.

TREKKING

If you're organizing your own trek in Huascarán National Park, register beforehand with the Park Office (see page 793), where you should buy your permit (S/65; valid for six days) to enter the park; if you're trekking with an agency then they should sort all of this for you. In theory you're not meant to enter the park without one of these agencies – unless you're a professional. Also visit the Casa de Guías (Parque Ginebra 28-G; ☎043 421 811) for the best information about local trails, current climatic conditions and advice on hiring guides, equipment and mules – they also organize rock- and ice-climbing courses. They have a useful noticeboard, worth checking to see if there are any groups about to leave on treks that you might want to join, and they sell detailed trekking maps.

TOUR OPERATORS

★ **Andean Kingdom** Parque Ginebre 120 ☎944 913 011, ☜andeankingdom.com. Argentine-run tour operator specializing in climbing and trekking. Has its own centre out in the Cordillera Negra, where they offer lodging and rock-climbing courses.

Galaxia Expeditions Parque del Periodista, Mza. Unica, Lote 36 ☎043 425 355, ☜galaxia-expeditions.com. The biggest and most popular tour office in town offers a variety of treks, mountaineering trips and day tours as well as horsebackriding, mountain

biking and canyoning. Also owns a guesthouse (*Aldo*; see Galaxia website). Four-day Santa Cruz trail US$120 all-inclusive; a day trek to Laguna 69 costs US$45–55. Daily 6am–10pm.

Mountain Bike Adventures Jr Lucar y Torre 530, 2nd floor (one block east of Av Luzuriaga) ☎043 424 259, ☜chakinaniperu.com. Customizable guided bike tours and hikes, with English-speaking guides. Also rents bikes and sells local *artesanía* in the office. Good reputation for safety.

☎ 043 428 812). Make sure to pick up the free mini-booklet *Map Guide Huaraz-Peru*, produced by ⓦ andeanexplorer. com, with excellent information on local treks and lots of maps; it's also available in many of the tourist restaurants in Huaraz.

Huascarán National Park office Jr Federico Sal y Rosas 555 (Mon–Fri 8.30am–6pm, Sat & Sun 7–11am; ☎ 043 422 086).

Tourist police Av Luzuriaga 724, at the Plaza de Armas (daily 8am–8pm; ☎ 043 421 341). Some English spoken.

ACCOMMODATION

Even in high season, around August, it's rarely difficult to find accommodation at a reasonable price, and except during high season it's definitely worth bargaining.

Albergue Churup Jr Amadeo Figueroa 1257 ☎ 043 424 200, ⓦ churup.com; map p.791. A good base for trekkers, with luggage storage as well as reference maps and a book exchange. Although it's an uphill walk from the centre, they'll pick you up from the bus station for free and the views from the terrace are great. Breakfast included. Dorms **S/55**, doubles **S/180**

B & B Mi Casa Av 27 de Noviembre 773 ☎ 043 423 375, ⓦ micasahuaraz.jimdo.com; map p.791. A pleasant, family-run B&B with a flower-filled courtyard and bright dining room. **S/850**

★ **Benkawasi Albergue** Parque Santa Rosa 928 ☎ 043 423 150, ⓦ huarazbenkawasi.com; map p.791. This hostel is run by a friendly Huaraz family who have done a lot for the area – the owners built Huaraz's first hotel after the 1970 earthquake (now *Andino Club Hotel*). The communal areas are pleasant, with table tennis and games, and there's a shared kitchen. If you're into adventure sports, owner Benquelo Morales is the man to see. Dorms **S/5**, doubles **S/20**

★ **El Jacal Guest House** Jr José de Sucre 1044 ☎ 043 424 612; map p.791. This place is amazing value, with friendly owners and lots of extras like laundry, kitchen use and cable TV. But above everything (literally) there's a terrace with unbelievable 360-degree views. Breakfast included. **S/75**

Jo's Place Jr Daniel Villaizan 276 ☎ 043 425 505, ✉ josplacehuaraz@hotmail.com; map p.791. Although ramshackle and somewhat chaotically managed, *Jo's Place* is a die-hard backpacker joint, with functional rooms and dorms, some with wonderful views. It's always popular and there's a common room with TV and a terrace with hammocks. Full English breakfast (S/10), thanks to the British owner. Dorms **S/18**, doubles **S/45**

Olaza's Guest House Jr Julio Arguedas 1242, La Soledad ☎ 043 422 529, ⓦ olazas.com; map p.791. Nice large rooms here, very clean and all with private baths, and access to kitchen and laundry. It's also a great source of information, with fellow travellers exchanging tips in the communal living room or on the roof terrace with super views. **S/120**

EATING

There's no shortage of restaurants in Huaraz, with a huge number of budget options, but the places aimed at tourists tend to be better (albeit pricier). Mercado Central is good for cheap fresh food and there are a few mini-marts on Luzuriaga.

Bistro de Los Andes Jr Julian de Morales 823 ☎ 043 426 249; map p.791. A gem for breakfast, with seats outside, good yoghurt, coffee and pancakes (S/10); also popular during the evening. Features a book exchange too. Mon–Sat 7.30am–9pm, Sun noon–9pm.

La Brasa Roja Av Luzuriaga 915 ☎ 043 427 738; map p.791. Very popular and always busy, serving cheap and generous plates of chicken, pizza, grills and hamburgers. Pasta dishes from S/15; chicken and chips with salad S/21. Daily noon–midnight.

★ **Café Andino** Jr Lucar y Torre 530 915 ☎ 043 421 203, ⓦ cafeandino.com; map p.791. This top-floor café with amazing views is a true gem. It serves a range of international dishes and great breakfasts with pizza-sized pancakes. There's not only a book exchange, but a substantial library of guides on the area, as well as maps. Try the *shara shara* herbal tea for altitude sickness; mains S/8–25. Daily 11am–10pm.

★ **California Café** Jr 28 de Julio 562 915 ☎ 043 428 354; map p.791. One of several very pleasant cafés in town, this one predictably has West Coast vibes, which makes it a relaxing spot to refuel at any time. The food, including American breakfasts, soups, salads and sandwiches (mains S/12–18; American-style pancakes S/13), is great, and they also have a good book exchange as well as games and maps. Mon–Sat 7am–10.30pm, Sun 7am–2pm.

Chilli Heaven Parque Ginebra ☎ 043 396 085; map p.791. Fun, popular place, run by a Peruvian/British couple, that draws an international crowd. Spicy dishes from around the world are on the menu, including Indian and Thai curries (mains around S/30). Owner Simon is also a motorbike fanatic and organizes tours. Daily 8am–9.30pm.

El Horno Parque Ginebra ☎ 043 424 617; map p.791. The best wood-fired pizzas in town, as well as charcoal grills and a mean pasta carbonara. Pizzas S/18–25. Daily 5–11pm.

DRINKING AND NIGHTLIFE

13 Buhos Parque Ginebra; map p.791. A popular bar with a chill, lowdown vibe; note that the cocktails are on the expensive side. Also serves food. Daily 9pm–2am.

Bonus Track Parque del Bombero, Jr Morales 767 ☎ 955 918 069; map p.791. There's a party-like scene at this bar, with walls plastered in album sleeves, photos and country flags. Live music on weekends. Daily 5.30pm–2am.

9

El Tambo Jr José de la Mar 776 ☎043 423 417, ⓦeltambo.negocio.site; map p.791. One of Huaraz's best nightspots, spinning Western music with Latino beats and occasional live music. Food also served. Mon–Thurs 10pm–2am, Fri & Sat 10pm–4am.

CHAVÍN DE HUANTAR

One of the most popular day-trips from Huaraz is to **Chavín de Huantar** (Tues–Sun 9am–4pm; S/15; ☎043 454 042), a mysterious stone temple complex that was at the centre of a puma-worshipping religious movement some 2500 years ago. The pretty village of **Chavín**, with its whitewashed walls and traditional tiled roofs, is a gruelling but stunning drive from Huaraz; from here the complex is a few hundred metres away. The same distance in the other direction is the accompanying **museum** (same hours; free), which displays some of the most important finds from the site, including most of the famous tenon heads that originally adorned the walls of the temple.

Most people arrive on a **full-day tour** (S/50 excluding lunch and entrance), although the distance can make visits feel rushed and many agencies only provide

Spanish-speaking guides. To visit independently, take one of the buses that leave Huaraz for Chavín daily around 6am (3–4hr; S/10–15 one way) from small terminals on Jr Andres Avelino Cáceres. Buses return from Chavín more or less on the hour from 3–6pm. It's a small village, but there are a couple of hostels, and you can camp by the Baños Quercos thermal springs, a twenty-minute stroll from the village.

THE CORDILLERA BLANCA

The highest range in the tropical world, the **Cordillera Blanca** consists of around 35 peaks poking their snowy heads over the 6000m mark, and until early in the twentieth century, when the glaciers began to recede, this white crest could be seen from the Pacific. Above Yungay, and against the sensational backdrop of Peru's highest peak, **Huascarán** (6768m), are the magnificent **Llanganuco Lakes**, whose waters change colour according to the time of year and the movement of the sun.

Fortunately, most of the Cordillera Blanca falls under the auspices of the **Huascarán National Park**, and the habitat

---

HIKING IN THE HUARAZ REGION

Given the scope of the mountain ranges and the passion of mountaineers, it's not surprising that there is an enormous range of **hikes** and guides in the area. Anyone interested in really getting stuck in should arm themselves with good maps and detailed guidebooks, and talk to everyone in town, from hostel owners to expats. Wherever you end up, be sure to pay heed to the rules of **responsible trekking**: carry away your waste, particularly above the snow line, where even organic waste does not decompose. And always carry a camping stove – campfires are strictly prohibited in Huascarán National Park. It's also vital to be fit, particularly if you are going it alone.

It's essential to spend at least a couple of days **acclimatizing** to the altitude before attempting a hike; if you intend high mountain climbing, this should be extended to at least five days. Although Huaraz itself is 3060m above sea level, most of the Cordilleras' more impressive peaks are over 6000m.

HIRING A GUIDE

Going hiking alone without an agency is possible, but not recommended to anyone but the most experienced hikers and climbers, and you'll likely end up paying a lot more as you'll be shouldering the costs alone. Be very careful when hiring an independent guide and always check them out with the Casa de Guías (see page 792), which has a list of qualified guides. On top of the national park fee (S/30 for one day, S/60 for two or three days, S/150 for longer) and guide's fee (around US$60 per day for someone certified), you'll be expected to foot the bill for return transport, accommodation and food for everyone hired to help. Auxiliary porters, mule drivers (*arrieros*) and cooks will each cost you around US$10 a day, plus an additional US$10 per day per pack-carrying mule or llama.

has been left relatively unspoiled. Among the more exotic **wildlife** are viscacha (Andean rabbit-like creatures), vicuña, grey deer, pumas, foxes, the rare spectacled bear and several species of hummingbirds.

To get here without an organized trek, take a *combi* along the valley to Yungay or Caraz and ask around for recommended guides (check them out first with the Casa de Guías in Huaraz).

CARAZ

Further along the valley north from Huaraz are the distinct settlements of **Yungay** and the much prettier and friendly **CARAZ**. The town sits at an altitude of 2285m, making it much warmer than Huaraz, and palm trees and flowers adorn a classic colonial **Plaza de Armas**. While most people come for the hiking or cycling trails around the town, there's enough here to divert you for a day or so, most notably the pre-Chavín era remains of **Tumshukayko** (daily 8am–5pm; free; a taxi here costs S/5–8 each way), an archeological structure about 1km uphill from the Plaza de Armas (turn right once you hit Av 28 de Julio). This impressive series of stone walls, stairways and terraces (the layers have been dated to between 2500 BC and 300 AD) needs a huge amount more excavation to make greater sense of it, but is nevertheless fascinating to wander around. Finally, no stay in Caraz would be complete without careful consideration of the dessert menu: Caraz is famous for its **manjar blanco** – a caramel-like substance similar to *dulce de leche*; all bakeries in town sell it.

ARRIVAL AND DEPARTURE

By plane Anta Airport is 45km from Caraz and has a daily flight to and from Lima (50min). There's a regular bus service to town (S/5) or Pony Exhibitions can organize a minibus (for groups).

By bus Most of the bus terminals are along Daniel Villar and Córdova, within a block or two of the Plaza de Armas. From anywhere in the Callejón de Huaylas, it's best to go back through Huaraz and down the main road to the coast. The only other alternative is to take the longer, more difficult road north from Caraz via the Cañon del Pato down to Chimbote on the coast, where you'll have to change buses.

Destinations The main routes are Chimbote via Cañon del Pato (2 daily; 7–10hr); Lima (7 daily; 8hr); Trujillo (5 daily; 8–10hr).

INFORMATION AND TOURS

Tourist office In the municipality building on the Plaza de Armas (sporadic hours but often Mon–Sat 7.45am–1pm & 2.30–5.30pm; ⓣ 043 391 029), but try it for maps and brochures covering the attractions and hikes in the area.

Pony Expeditions Jr Sucre 1266, at Plaza de Armas ⓣ 043 391 642, ⓦ ponyexpeditions.com. A professional and knowledgeable organization good for local information. Offers tours of the area (including the stunning Cañón del Pato) as well as guides for trekking. Prices get cheaper the larger the groups.

GETTING AROUND

By mototaxi Everywhere in Caraz is walkable; don't let the *mototaxis* charge you more than S/1 for anywhere in town (S/2 to bus terminals outside the centre).

By combi *Combis* pull in at Av Sucre, three blocks south of the Plaza de Armas.

ACCOMMODATION

Apu EcoLodge C Jabon Rumi ⓣ 995 194 288. About 2km north of downtown, the eight bungalows and apartments here have room for four, amongst an oasis that includes an organic garden, a patio with stone oven and firepit, a climbing wall and a menagerie of small animals. S/150

★ **Los Pinos Lodge** Psj 9 #116 Parque Plazuela La Merced, Barrio Yanachaca ⓣ 043 391 130, ⓦ lospinoslodge.pe. This hostel on a little plaza a 5min walk from the centre has colourful and tastefully decorated common areas with a retro feel. The bedrooms are not as impressive, but offer basic accommodation at reasonable rates. Also offers camping space. Breakfast included. Camping/person S/10, doubles S/50

San Marco Jr San Martín 1133 ⓣ 956 997 170. Just off the plaza, this hostel in a pretty colonial building has quiet, light-filled rooms at the back around gorgeous courtyards. Even cheaper dark, front rooms lack private bathrooms and TVs. Breakfast not included. S/50

EATING

Eating in Caraz is basic. The small daily market, three blocks north of the plaza, is good for fresh food and traditional Andean goods.

Café de Rat Above Pony Expeditions on Jr Sucre 1266 ⓣ 043 391 642. It may sound unsanitary, but this place has the joint appeal of cheap, good food (including vegetarian) and a cosy feeling like that of being in someone's kitchen. The little balcony overlooks the main square. Best for pizza (S/15–34) and breakfasts (S/5–10). Mon–Sat 8.30am–9pm.

9

Café La Terraza Jr Sucre 1107 ☎ 043 301 226. Probably the best place in town to grab a cappuccino or espresso. Also does excellent artisan ice cream (S/2) using regional fruits. Daily 8.30am–9pm.

La Pizza del Abuelo Jr Antonio Raimondi 425 ☎ 968 752 971. Close to the main plaza, this Italian café is a solid choice for snacks and pasta, and of course, flavourful pies (S/4 a slice, S/28 whole pizza). Daily 6am–11pm.

Trujillo and the North

Pizarro, on his second voyage to Peru in 1528, sailed by the ancient Moche site of **Chan Chan**, then still a major city and an important regional centre of Inca rule. He returned to establish a Spanish colony in the same valley, naming it **Trujillo** after his birthplace in Extremadura. Despite two Inca rebellions, the Spanish hold was lasting and Trujillo grew to become the main port of call for the Spanish treasure fleets. It still boasts one of the most impressive colonial centres in Peru, as well as some of the grandest pre-Inca remains with day-tripping distance.

North of Trujillo, the vast desert stretches all the way to the Ecuadorian frontier just beyond **Tumbes**, passing the modern, hectic city of **Chiclayo** as well as Peru's liveliest beach town, **Máncora** – plus some genuinely unspoilt stretches of terrain. This area has an incredible wealth of pre-Inca pyramids, tombs and temple sites to explore, as well as world-class museums, many of which can be easily visited in day-trips from the main cities. From here you can travel on to the Northern Highlands (see page 810), which offers a vastly different perspective of Peru's ancient

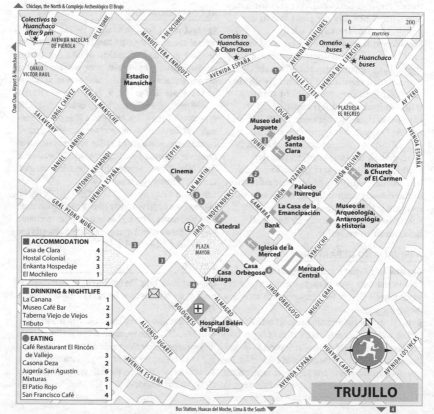

ACCOMMODATION
Casa de Clara	4
Hostal Colonial	2
Enkanta Hospedaje	3
El Mochilero	1

DRINKING & NIGHTLIFE
La Canana	1
Museo Café Bar	2
Taberna Viejo de Viejos	3
Tributo	4

EATING
Café Restaurant El Rincón de Vallejo	3
Casona Deza	2
Jugería San Agustín	6
Mixturas	5
El Patio Rojo	1
San Francisco Café	4

TRUJILLO

history than the one seen by travellers who stick to the classic gringo trail.

TRUJILLO

Traditionally a trading point for coastal and jungle goods, **TRUJILLO** retains a cosmopolitan atmosphere and a welcoming attitude towards visitors. The climate is usually pleasant all year, although in winter it can be grey and sometimes fresh and the past few years have seen the city and nearby coastal towns ravaged by freak El Niño rains.

WHAT TO SEE AND DO

From the graceful colonial mansions and Baroque churches at its heart, Trujillo's commercial buildings, light industry and shantytown suburbs give way to rich sugar-cane fields that stretch far into the neighbouring Valle de Chicama. Everything within the circular **Avenida España** is considered the centre and this is where most of the colonial buildings and museums lie. **Jirón Gamarra** is the main commercial street, dominated by modern buildings, shops, hotels and restaurants. The other main street, older and more attractive, is **Jirón Pizarro**, which has been pedestrianized from the pleasant **Plazuela El Recreo**, to the elegant **Plaza Mayor**, the heart of the city.

The city also has the largest mural in Latin America; it runs along the walls of the Universidad de la Nación, where avenidas Jesús de Nazareth and Juan Pablo II meet (worth seeing at night when lit up).

Around Plaza Mayor

Trujillo's **Plaza Mayor** (Plaza de Armas) is often packed with street vendors and entertainers. The city's **Catedral** (daily 7–11.45am & 4–7pm; free), built in the mid-seventeenth century and then rebuilt the following century after earthquake damage, sits in one corner of the plaza. Beside the cathedral is its **museum** (Mon–Fri 9am–1pm & 4–7pm, Sat 9am–1pm; S/4), which exhibits a sombre range of mainly eighteenth- and nineteenth-century religious paintings and sculptures.

Also on the square at Jr Pizarro 313 is the **Casa Urquiaga** (Mon–Fri 9.15am–3.15pm & Sat 10am–1pm; free; take your passport), a colonial mansion worth a visit for its well-kept interiors and historical importance. Simón Bolívar stayed here while he organized his final push for liberation.

East of Plaza Mayor

East of the plaza, on the corner of Jr Pizarro and Gamarra, stands another of Trujillo's impressive mansions, **La Casa de la Emancipación**, Jr Pizarro 610 (Mon–Fri 9am–1pm & 4–8pm; free). The building is now head office of the Banco Continental but hosts contemporary art displays in its colonial rooms, plus the occasional music concert.

At the eastern end of Jr Pizarro, five blocks from the Plaza Mayor, there's a small but attractive square known as the **Plazuela El Recreo**, a shady square with vast 135-year-old fig trees. Colonial Trujillo's waterworks can be seen beneath scratched glass panels on the ground; the Spaniards extended Moche and Chimu irrigation channels to provide running water to the city.

Museo de Arqueología, Antropología e Historia

The **Museo de Arqueología, Antropología e Historia**, at Jr Junín 682 (Mon 9am–2.30pm, Tues–Sat 9am–4.30pm; S/5; ☎044 474 850), is housed in a colonial mansion; among the highlights are beautiful anthropomorphic ceramics. It's well worth visiting for solid background information before going on any tours in the area. Entry fee includes a guide (some speak English).

Museo del Juguete

The delightfully quirky toy museum, **Museo del Juguete**, Jr Independencia 705 (Mon– Sat 10am–6pm, Sun 10am–1pm; S/7; ☎044 208 181), is the brainchild of one of Peru's most successful artists, Gerardo Chávez, and is crammed with antique toys from all over the world. The most fascinating are undoubtedly those in the pre-Hispanic room, with Moche ceramic rattles dating back to 100–800 AD.

9

ARRIVAL AND INFORMATION

By plane Flights land at Carlos Martínez de Pinillos Airport, near Huanchaco (☎ 044 464 224). LATAM, Jr Almagro 490 (☎ 044 221 469), Avianca, inside Real Plaza, Av. César Vallejo Oeste 1345, and LC Perú, Jr Almagro 305 (☎ 044 290 299) have flights to Lima. Taxis into the city will cost around S/15–20, or you can get a bus, which leaves every 20min from Av Del Aeropuerto at a stop called "El Cruce" (10–15min walk from airport), for around S/1.50. You can also take a taxi to Huanchaco for S/10.

By bus Most buses arrive from the south at the *Terrapuerto* on the Panamericana Norte Km 558; a taxi to town is the only option, and will cost around S/8. Heading north, most bus companies have terminals close to Av España in the southwest, or east along avenidas America Norte or Ejercito. If you decide to stay in Huanchaco you'll have to return to Trujillo to get an onward connection.

Destinations Cajamarca (several daily; 6–8hr); Chachapoyas (1 daily; 13hr); Chiclayo (12 daily; 3hr); Guayaquil (1 daily except Tues; 18hr); Huamanchuco (5 daily; 5hr); Lima (20 daily; 9hr); Piura, via Chiclayo (8 daily; 6hr); Máncora (several daily; 6hr); Tarapoto (1 daily; 18hr); Tumbes (1 daily; 10hr). Cruz del Sur, Amazonas 437 (☎ 044 261 801) has buses to Guayaquil (daily, except Tues, at 11.55pm; 18hr; S/130)

By combi and taxi *Combis* cannot enter within Av España, but if you walk to this boundary you can find one to most places. If you're arriving by day it's fine to walk to the city centre, though at night it's best to take a taxi (around S/5 for a ride within Trujillo). Navy-blue and white coloured *combis*, and a special red and yellow bus, go to Huanchaco (S/1.50). Of the taxi companies, Sonrisa (☎ 044 233 000) and New Takci (☎ 044 290 494) are recommended by iPerú.

Tourist information iPerú office is inside Casona Minka, Jr Independencia 467 (Mon–Sat 9am–6pm, Sun 9am–1pm; ☎ 044 294 561, ✉ iperutrujillo@promperu.gob.pe) on the Plaza Mayor.

ACCOMMODATION

The majority of Trujillo's hotels are within a few blocks of the central Plaza Mayor; however, there are surprisingly few good-value hotels for a city this size. Many people prefer to stay in the nearby (12km northwest) surf town of Huanchaco (see page 799), which has a much wider variety, including some good budget options.

Casa de Clara C Cahuide 495 ☎ 044 243 347; map p.796. About a 10min walk south from the centre, this small guesthouse with a family feel has hot showers and spacious rooms. It's run by archeologist Clara who organizes tours to local sites. **S/60**

Hotel Colonial Jr Independencia 618 ☎ 044 258 261, ⓦ hotelcolonial.com.pe; map p.796. A central place, the highlight here is the stunning colonial building. Rooms are cosy and come with TV, plus there's a patio and a decent breakfast. Also has a cheap tour agency and taxi service. **S/120**

Enkanta Hospedaje Jr Independencia 341 ☎ 992 534 141; map p.796. A real budget favourite, this place has tired decoration and furniture, but a sociable vibe. Shared kitchen and large common area at the front; dorms at the back of the building are quieter. No breakfast. Dorms **S/35**, doubles **S/50**

El Mochilero Jr Independencia 887 ☎ 044 297 842; map p.796. Rooms are scruffy and lack natural light, but the staff are friendly and there's a pleasant open-air courtyard, snack bar and hammock area; no breakfast. Dorms **S/20**, doubles **S/40**

EATING

There's no shortage of restaurants in Trujillo. Jr Pizarro has a huge assortment of cafés and a Metro supermarket at no. 700. A speciality of the area is seafood, which is best appreciated on the beach at nearby Huanchaco.

Café Restaurant El Rincón de Vallejo Jr Orbegoso 313 ☎ 044 226 232; map p.796. Cesar Vallejo, Peru's most famous poet, was brought up in the house that now hosts this café. Really good, well-priced *criollo* food, so predictably this place gets packed and rushed at lunch. Set menu S/6.90–8.90. Mon–Sat 7am–11pm, Sun 7am–3pm.

Casona Deza Jr Independencia 630 ☎ 044 474 756; map p.796. A first-rate Italian restaurant set in a 1635 building. Two gorgeous open-air patios to dine in, and the walls are decorated with impressive artwork. Pizzas from S/27. Mon–Sat noon–11pm.

Jugería San Agustín Jr Bolívar 522 ☎ 044 245 653; map p.796. Trujillo's most famous juice bar, a few blocks from the plaza. Best known for its unmissable *sandwich de pavo* (turkey sandwich) for S/7. The original, pint-sized shop serves takeaway downstairs; the new spacious café is around the corner at San Agustín 104. Daily 8am–1pm & 4.15–8.30pm.

Mixturas Jr de Orbegoso 319 ☎ 044 205 946; map p.796. This café-bar serves good Peruvian snacks – try the fried yuca (S/4) – and is decorated with colourful local artwork. There's a relaxing garden to escape from Trujillo's busy centre. Set lunch S/15. Mon & Tues 9am–10.30pm, Wed–Sat 9am–11pm.

★ El Patio Rojo Jr San Martín 883 ☎ 044 242 339; map p.796. There's vegetarian *ceviche* (S/20), hearty quinoa dishes (S/20–28) and vegan cakes (S/5–8), plus a S/9 lunch menu at this hip café. Popular with an alternative crowd for its Thursday pizza nights and occasional live music at weekends. Mon–Thurs 8am–11pm, Fri–Sat 8am–1am, Sun 10am–4pm.

San Francisco Café Jr Gamarra 433 ☎ 044 252 195; map p.796. Offers light bites, such as *papas rellenas* (deep-fried potatoes stuffed with meat; S/5), as well as a good lunch menu for S/12.50. Friendly service in a magnificent hall with wooden rafters and large chandeliers that must have once hung in a grand colonial home. Mon–Sat 7am–10pm.

DRINKING AND NIGHTLIFE

★ **La Canana** Jr San Martín 791 ☎ 044 295 422; map p.796. A highly popular restaurant-*peña* serving excellent meals, with a great atmosphere and shows with bands and dancing, usually culminating in a disco. The music and dances are fantastic and you'll be amazed at Peruvian stamina. Meals from S/16, cocktails S/20. Thurs–Sat from 8pm for food, from 10pm for show until the last people leave.

★ **Museo Café Bar** Jr Independencia 701 ☎ 044 346 741; map p.796. Next door to the Museo del Juguete, this plush café-bar with an old-world vibe is cluttered with posters and features a saloon bar. The menu is limited to sandwiches (S/12–16), coffee, juices and alcohol but it's worth it for the atmosphere alone (expect an ever-so-cool jazz soundtrack, and live jazz on Fridays and Saturdays). Mon–Thurs 9am–midnight, Fri & Sat 9am–1am.

Taberna Viejo de Viejos Jr San Martín 323; map p.796. This rustically decorated place is a truly Peruvian experience; a specialist pisco bar serving cocktails and local wines. Try the "Viejo" deals: from S/50 you get a whole bottle of pisco and everything else you need to make various cocktails, and you'll be shown how to make them at your table. Great for groups. Tues–Thurs 8pm–2am, Fri & Sat 8pm–3am.

Tributo Jr Pizarro 389 ☎ 989 969 050; map p.796. Featuring live music nightly with regular drinks specials, this is one of the most happening places in Trujillo. Thurs–Sat 10pm–5am.

DIRECTORY

Banks and exchange BBVA, Jr Pizarro 620; BCP, Jr Gamarra 562; Scotiabank, Jr Pizarro 699. There are also several casas de cambio on the Pizarro side of the Plaza Mayor, and on block 6 of Pizarro.

Consulate UK, Jr Alfonso Ugarte 310 (☎ 044 245 935).

Hospital Hospital Belén de Trujillo, at Jr Bolívar 350 (☎ 044 245 748). Open 24hr.

Laundry Lavandería El Olivo, Jr Orbegoso 270

Post office SERPOST, Jr Independencia 286.

Tourist police Jr Almagro 442 (☎ 044 291 705).

HUANCHACO

A traditional fishing village turned popular surfing resort, **HUANCHACO** is the perfect base for exploring nearby ruins while relaxing by the beach and enjoying excellent seafood. Just fifteen minutes from the centre of Trujillo, Huanchaco has exploded in terms of popularity and growth in the last thirty years. While prices do rise in summer, it's nowhere near as overpriced as some other beach towns.

WHAT TO SEE AND DO

There is a multitude of **surf and language schools** in town; Espaanglisch (ⓦespaanglisch.com) has Spanish classes (English spoken), while the excellent Otra Cosa network has well-priced classes as preparation for volunteer work with them (ⓦotracosa.org). For surfing, check out Muchik Surf School at Independencia 100 (☎ 044 633 487, ⓦescueladetablamuchik. com), Huanchaco's most established. If you're not a surfer, catch some waves with a local fisherman in their traditional *caballitos de mar* – hand-made reed fishing boats first used by the Moche culture; you'll see them lined up along the front. There is a long beachfront promenade and a rickety pier. Reggae parties on the beach are commonplace, and Latino music blasts from the many beachfront restaurants.

ARRIVAL AND DEPARTURE

By taxi or combi Taxis to and from Trujillo should cost no more than S/15–17, or it's easy enough to take any one of the frequent *combis* (yellow & orange) from Av España on the corner with Jr Junín, or at Av Juan Pablo II and Jesus Nazereth near the university (S/1.50). *Combis* come in along Av La Rivera, by the sea.

ACCOMMODATION

Every other house in Huanchaco seems to offer lodging of some sort. For those on a really tight budget, there are many no-frills places that charge S/10 per person for small and often dark rooms with shared bath. Los Pinos, the street that all the buses turn down away from the sea, has a few hostels and many signs saying *alquilo habitaciones* ("I rent rooms"). Prices drop outside high season. Many places do not have hot water – fine in summer but miserable in winter.

★ **ATMA** Palma 442 ☎ 044 664 507, ⓦ atmahuanchaco. com. The polar opposite of the party hostels on this side of town, *ATMA* oozes serenity with daily yoga classes, large dorms and ample relaxed communal space, including a sea-facing terrace. There's a kitchen and staff are exceptionally knowledgeable. Dorms S̲/̲2̲2̲, doubles S̲/̲7̲0̲

Casa Fresh Av La Rivera 322 ☎ 044 462 700, ⓦcasafresh.pe. A small hostel with the friendliest vibe in town and a great terrace overlooking a quieter part of the beach near the beginning of Rivera – less traffic noise and

9

more sound of the sea, with access to the biggest waves. Dorms S/20, doubles S/60

Moksha Yoga & Surf Hostel Av La Rivera 224 ☏ 973 713 628. Accommodation is a bit on the scruffy side, but the vibe's good and it's right next to the main strip of bars. Out the back, there's a small kitchen and larger patio with a fire pit. Within the hostel but open to the public, they serve great veggie and vegan food and guests get a discount on breakfast. Dorms S/30, doubles S/60

★ **Naylamp** Av Victor Larco 1420 ☏ 044 461 022, ⓦ hostalnaylamp.com. Set over two distinct areas, with a shady patio with hammocks in the first and, across the road, a communal kitchen and grassy area for camping and socializing. Dorms are large with private baths; doubles are on the small side. Dorms S/20, doubles S/60, camping/person S/15

Oceanus Los Cerezos 105 ☏ 044 461 653. The blue-fronted, family-run *Oceanus* is a block away from the beachfront, which can be a blessing on busier days. There is a shared kitchen and the rooms are spacious, well lit, have private baths and are spotless thanks to daily cleaning. Don't miss the *cremoladas*, a rough fruity sorbet) downstairs; the *lúcuma* and *coco* are spectacular. S/50

EATING

There are restaurants all along the front in Huanchaco, many of them with balconies overlooking the beach. Not surprisingly, seafood is the local speciality, including excellent crab; *ceviche* is traditionally only served at lunch and a handful of restaurants make it fresh daily.

★ **Chocolate Café** Av La Rivera 752 ☏ 044 626 973. Great Peruvian hot chocolate for the low season when Huanchaco gets pretty cold. Breakfasts, soups, wraps and inventive sandwiches are served up in a cheerful incense-scented café. Daily 8.30am–6pm.

Restaurant El Caribe Atahualpa 100. Just around the corner from the seafront avenue to the north of the pier, this restaurant has good *ceviche* (S/34) and is popular with locals. Mon–Sat 10.30am–5pm.

Menu Land C Los Pinos 250. Run by a friendly German-Peruvian couple, the name refers to the set lunch *menú* (S/8–10) you get all over Peru. Food is basic, but you won't find bigger or cheaper portions anywhere else; great for refuelling on a very tight budget. Daily 8.30am–10.30pm.

DRINKING AND NIGHTLIFE

Huanchaco has a buzzing nightlife, with many bars and clubs. Always ask around to see if there's a pop-up party on the beach going on, or to find the coolest bar (these can open and close quickly). Outside of peak season, nightlife is calmer.

Jan Pix Av La Rivera 305. With free salsa classes Thursdays at 10pm and live DJs the rest of the weekend, this is a reliable option for great night out; it's at its liveliest Thursdays and Saturdays but doesn't get going until late. Wed–Sun 10pm–3am.

My Friend C Los Pinos 533 ☏ 044 639 853. A good restaurant, with dishes for S/12, as well as a cheap hostel, but it is definitely the most well-known meeting spot in town and serves cheap pizza and drinks; happy hour 4.30–10.30pm (Thurs evening, all cocktails are two for S/8). Daily 8am–10.30pm.

Sabes? Av Larco 1230 ⓦ sabesbar.com. This place is either great fun or fairly quiet, as it's right down at the end of the main drag past *Big Ben* restaurant. When it's the former, it's a fantastic place to meet people, relax on the outdoor terrace with a happy-hour cocktail and munch on a pizza (S/25–35). Mon–Sat 7pm–1am.

ANCIENT SITES AROUND TRUJILLO

One of the main reasons for coming to Trujillo is to visit the numerous **archeological sites** dotted around the nearby Moche and Chicama valleys, fascinating for those with even a passing interest in Peruvian.

Huacas del Moche

Five kilometres south of Trujillo, beside the Río Moche in a barren desert landscape, are two temples that bring ancient Peru to life. The stunning complex known as the **HUACAS DEL MOCHE** (daily 9am–4pm; S/10 including guided tour in English or Spanish, tip expected; ⓦ huacasdemoche.pe) is believed to have been the capital, or most important ceremonial and urban centre, for the **Moche** (Mochica) culture at its peak between 400 and 600 AD. It contains two temples: the **Huaca del Sol** (Temple of the Sun), set over 12,000 square metres, is perhaps the most impressive in scale of the many pyramids on the Peruvian coast, although it's still being excavated and remains closed to tourists. Its twin, **Huaca de la Luna** (Temple of the Moon), is thought to have been a ceremonial centre. It's smaller, but more complex and brilliantly frescoed: don't miss the sophisticated mural *The Myths*, with its chaotic assimilation of warriors in scenes of combat, fishermen with reed boats and even a hairless dog. In between the two you can see the remains of a town in the midst of excavation, and there's also an excellent **museum** across from the site,

ANCIENT SITES

Most companies offer tours to **Chan Chan** (see page 801) and to the **Huacas del Moche** (see page 800), the Huaca del Sol and Huaca de la Luna. These cost around S/30 each (half-day), or S/50 for both (full day), but prices vary depending on the season; expect to pay more for an English-speaking guide. All operators have slightly different programmes, so shop around. Tours can also be organized from Trujillo for Chiclayo sites, and even sites as far away as Kuelap near Chachapoyas.

TOUR OPERATORS
Clara Brava's Tours At Casa de Clara (see page 798).
Colonial Tours Jr Independencia 616 ☎044 291 034, ⓦcolonialtoursnorteperu.com.

Muchik Tours C Santa Teresa 146 depto. 203, La Merced ☎044 243 022, ⓦmuchiktours.com.

displaying a host of pottery and other objects found in the temples.

To **get here** from Trujillo, walk down Avenida Almagro from the centre, which turns into Avenida Moche once you cross Avenida España (a 20min walk), and take the small "CM" or "SD" *combis* from Ovalo Grau, which will should take you all the way to the car park of the Huacas (20min; S/1.50), although some drop you off on the road, within sight, but still a ten- to fifteen-minute walk away. From Huanchaco, take the larger *combi* "H Corazón" all the way to Ovalo Grau (30min; S/1.50) and change. A taxi from Trujillo costs around S/15 (20min).

The Chan Chan complex
It's possible to see the Moche influence in the motifs around **CHAN CHAN**, the huge, stunningly beautiful ruined capital city of the **Chimú Empire**, located across the other side of Trujillo from the Huacas. Just as impressive as the Huacas, if not more so, the site stretches almost the whole way between Trujillo and Huanchaco and represents the largest pre-Columbian ruins in the whole of South America. While most of the area is little more than melted mud walls, there are a few remarkably well-preserved areas - while others have been vigorously, if not sensitively, restored - that give a great insight as to what the city may have looked like. The main ones to see are spread out and comprise the Tschudi (Nik An) temple complex, a site museum, the Huaca El Dragon and the Huaca La Esmeralda (all daily 9am–4pm; S/10 for 2-day pass to all sites; ☎044 206 304, ⓦchanchan.gob.pe).

It's best to start at the **museum**, which you'll find about halfway to Huanchaco on the main road; you can buy tickets at any of the sites. It has some good background information, but most importantly it has an enormous model of what the city would once have looked like, which helps as you tour the site proper. From here, try to catch a *combi* outside or take a taxi (they wait in the car park) to the **Nik An Palace**, a series of open-air temples and passageways with some extraordinarily beautiful restored patterns and lattice-work. Not far away, the **Huaca Arco Iris** (The Rainbow Temple; also referred to as Huaca El Dragón, or Dragon Temple) was a ceremonial or ritual pyramid rather than a citadel, and sports more geometric and zoomorphic designs, with debate continuing over whether they depict a dragon or rainbow, which have been restored with relish if not historical perfection. On the other side of this enormous city, Huaca La Esmeralda was similar in function to Arco Iris but is much older (around 1100 years old) and while its adobe walls were damaged in the freak rains of 1925 and 1983, you can still make out intricate, original designs including friezes of fishing nets, a flying pelican, a sea otter and repetitive patterns of geometrical arabesques.

To **get here**, take any *combi* going between Trujillo and Huanchaco and ask the driver to drop you at the Museo de Chan Chan. There is no public transport between the different sites, so hire a taxi from Trujillo (see page 797) to take you round and wait (depending on sites visited and distance covered, expect to pay S/30

AROUND TRUJILLO

▲ Aeropuerto Internacional Capitán FAP Carlos Martínez de Pinillos (3.5km)   ▲ Complejo Archeológico El Brujo, Chicama, Chiclayo, Piura & Tumbes

▼ Panamerican Highway to Lima

per hour), or take a hat and lots of water if you plan to walk; the sun is unforgiving.

Complejo Archeológico El Brujo

Equally impressive but less visited (perhaps because it's 60km northwest of Trujillo) lies another fascinating Moche ruin, the **COMPLEJO ARQUELÓGICO EL BRUJO**, which means "The Wizard" and is home to the impressive Huaca Cao Viejo. Only discovered in 2006, the huaca contained a mausoleum in which an extremely well-preserved woman was found, buried with enough pomp to suggest that she was an important Moche leader (the first female discovery of this type in Peru). The heavily tattooed *Señora de Cao* as she is now known is on display in the excellent adjoining museum, along with the dazzling array of treasures uncovered in

her tomb. There's also a full replica of her face, made using cutting-edge forensic technology and drawing on the facial structures of Moche descendants still living in the region, in another room (daily 9am–5pm; S/10; ⊛elbrujo.pe).

To **get here** from Trujillo, it's easiest to visit on a tour. Otherwise, take a bus from the Santa Cruz stop to Chocope (45min; S/3). From Chocope take a *colectivo* to Magdalena de Cao (20min; S/1.50); from there, a *mototaxi* will take you and wait for S/15.

CHICLAYO

Apart from building a few convents, the Spanish never really bothered with **CHICLAYO**, and tourists, too, would be forgiven for missing out Peru's fourth-largest city if it were only for the city itself.

Though not an unpleasant place to spend a day or so, it's full of casinos, banks and bus stations and pressing, noisy traffic. The attractions here are the remarkable **archeological finds** in the nearby countryside, which are of huge importance to Peruvian culture and identity. It's well worth spending at least a few days in the area getting to grips with the different groups that formed part of the pre-Inca landscape here, and seeing their intriguing tombs, temples and pyramids, most still in the process of being uncovered.

WHAT TO SEE AND DO

The Plaza de Armas, or **Parque Principal**, is still very much the centre of Chiclayan life, with the huge commercial Avenue Balta running north to the fascinating witches' market and south to the main bus stations.

The only real point of interest in town is the **Mercado Modelo** – a good general

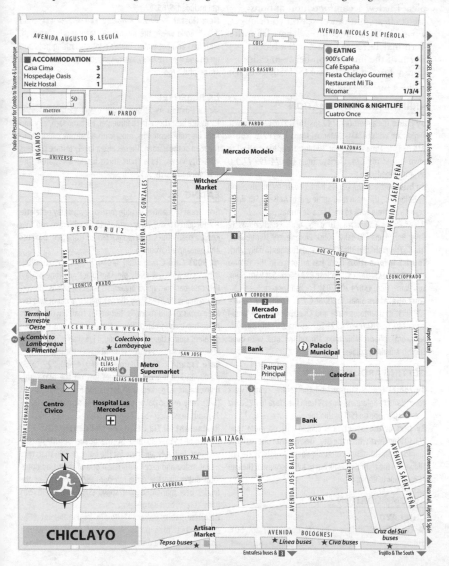

ACCOMMODATION
Casa Cima	3
Hospedaje Oasis	2
Neiz Hostal	1

● EATING
900's Café	6
Café España	7
Fiesta Chiclayo Gourmet	2
Restaurant Mi Tía	5
Ricomar	1/3/4

■ DRINKING & NIGHTLIFE
Cuatro Once	1

CHICLAYO

9

market – but if you turn left on Arica, walk another block and enter where you see the plants, you'll reach the **witches' market**. Here the stalls sell shaman's tools, elixirs, swords, taxidermied snakes and voodoo aids. Avoid the northern end of the market as it's seedy, and watch out for pickpockets; don't walk here after dark.

A good place to stay overnight in Chiclayo is nearby **La Pimentel**, a soothing seaside village with a long boardwalk and pier. The few accommodation options aren't cheap, but out of season you can get a bargain. Regular combis depart from the Terminal Terrestre Oeste, half a block north of the intersection between calles Lora y Lora and San José (S/1.50; 20min), while a taxi costs S/15.

ARRIVAL AND INFORMATION

By plane The airport (☎ 074 236 016) is 2km east of town. Flights are with LATAM, C Manuel María Izaga 770 (☎ 074 274 875) to Lima (daily; 1hr 30min). From here, a taxi to town should cost S/4. Chiclayo Tours (☎ 074 799 772) is recommended.

By bus Most bus companies have private terminals along Av Bolognesi, the main road at the end of Av Balta Sur. From here it's a 10min walk to the Plaza de Armas.

Destinations Cajamarca (10 daily; 6hr); Chachapoyas (2 daily; 9hr); Lima (10 daily; 10hr); Piura (every 30min; 3hr); Trujillo (several daily; 3hr 30min–4hr); Tumbes (8 daily; 7hr).

Tourist information iPerú has an office in the Palacio Municipal de Chiclayo, C San José 823 (Mon–Sat 9am-6pm, Sun 9am–1pm; ☎ 074 205 703); English spoken.

Tour operators Sipán Tours, at C 7 de Enero 772 (☎ 074 229 053, ⊛ sipantours.com) and Chaskiventura, C Manuel Izaga 740, Of. 207 (☎ 074 221 282, ⊛ chaskiventura-travel-peru.com), offer reliable tours around the area, with good English-speaking guides.

GETTING AROUND

By combi Combis skirt around the centre; simply walk down Balta to Bolognesi, or east from the Plaza to Av Sáenz Peña, to pick one up (S/1 within town).

By taxi or mototaxi Taxis should cost no more than S/3.50 anywhere within the city. Always go for one with the municipal shield stencilled on the doors. Mototaxis are not allowed in the centre, so walk out to Av Bolognesi at the end of Balta Sur to find one.

ACCOMMODATION

CHICLAYO

★ **Casa Cima** Chiclayo C Los Mangos 161, apt 501, Urb Santa Victoria ☎ 074 617 862, ⊖ infocima.ingles.

cix@gmail.com; map p.803. Rooms are in the owner's penthouse with a terrace that has great views over the city. Hosts Liam and Teòfila are great company and eager to help you get the best out of your time in the region. The two rooms (one with en-suite bathroom) are comfortable and there is a kitchen you can use. Cheap laundry and a solid breakfast. **S/120**

Hospedaje Oasis C Lora y Cordero 858 ☎ 074 626 490; map p.803. Everything's a bit yellow and the private bathrooms are titchy but it's clean, reasonably priced, rooms have fans and its only two blocks from the plaza. Breakfast not included. **S/65**

Neiz Hostal Av Pedro Ruiz 756 ☎ 074 229 441; map p.803. Solid value, the rooms are clean and big enough, with fans and hot water. There's a lot of clashing gold and green and if you're lucky, swan-shaped towels, but the staff are helpful. **S/65**

LA PIMENTEL

★ **La Posada** Av Alfonso Ugarte 491 ☎ 074 484 894. Easily the best choice in La Pimentel, with modern, airy and light en-suite bedrooms, most with a balcony overlooking the road or the garden. There's also a lovely terrace upstairs with city views. It's a short three blocks away from the seafront and beach. **S/120**

EATING

Good local specialities include *tortilla de raya* (ray omelette – an acquired taste), *arroz con pato* (duck with rice) and *King Kong*, a pastry thick with *manjar blanco* (caramel), peanuts and pineapple flavouring.

★ **900's Café** C Izaga 900 ☎ 074 209 268, ⊛ cafe900. com; map p.803. A really pleasant place any time of day, this café-bar does good breakfasts, snacks, salads, pastas, criollo mains (S/20–35; try the *spaguetti a la huancaina con lomo al pisco*) and cocktails. But better than anything, this place has truly great coffee – there are around eighteen different concoctions on the menu. Live music Thurs–Sat. Mon–Thurs 8am–11pm, Fri & Sat 8am–1am.

Café España C 7 de Enero 502 ☎ 074 491 722; map p.803. Tucked down a side street just off the plaza, this relaxed café is packed with locals for a cheap breakfast (S/8). They've also got an ample range of sandwiches (S/8–10) and juices. Mon–Sat 7am–11.30pm.

Restaurant Mi Tía C Elías Aguirre 662 ☎ 074 205 712; map p.803. Easy to find by the queue outside in the evenings, but they are there for the burgers; skip that, take a seat inside and order with relish one of their traditional local dishes like the *arroz con pato* (S/23) or any of the tender beer-marinated goat stews (S/32–40). Mon–Sat 8am–11pm, Sun 8am–4pm.

Ricomar Saenz Peña 841, Pedro Ruiz 1059, at Elias Aguirre 241; map p.803. A chain of *cevicherías* with a good range of little dishes, ideal for trying different classic

9

Peruvian starters like *papa rellena* (stuffed potato), *tamales* and of course *ceviche*. Lunch from S/7. Daily 9am–4pm.

DRINKING AND NIGHTLIFE

★ **Cuatro Once** C Juan Cuglievan 411; map p.803. This slick restobar, popular with Chiclayo's younger crowd, serves craft beer from eight Peruvian breweries, with pairing suggestions for regional nibbles on its menu, including *conchas negras ceviche* (S/25) and *yuquitas con queso* (deep-fried yuca oozing cheese; S/20). Mon–Thurs 5pm–midnight, Fri–Sat 5pm–2am.

DIRECTORY

Banks and exchange You'll find all the banks and moneychangers by walking south on Balta from the Plaza de Armas.
Hospital Hospital Clínica del Pacífico at Av José Leonardo Ortiz 420 ☎074 228 585 ⓦclinicadelpacifico.com.pe (24hr).
Laundry Lavandería Diamante, at C 7 de Enero 639.
Post office Jr Elías Aguirre 140.
Tourist police Av Saenz Peña 830 (Mon–Sat 8am–6pm; ☎074 238 658).

AROUND CHICLAYO

There are several sites around Chiclayo that are definitely worth seeing, all offered on organized tours, though it can get confusing as some sites have several names, while different places have similar names.

★ TREAT YOURSELF

Fiesta Chiclayo Gourmet Av Salaverry 1820 ☎ 074 201 970; map p.803. This is where celebrity chef Hector Solís started his empire, and it remains the best place to eat refined, creative versions of the best local dishes. He breeds his own ducks and goats at his nearby farm and serves up stunning food in a fine-dining atmosphere. Don't miss the *ceviche caliente*, a grouper *ceviche* flash-grilled in its own juices in an open banana leaf (S/65). Daily 10am–10pm.

The most easily confused are **Sipán**, where remains from the **Moche** culture were discovered, and the **Sicán** (or Lambayeque) culture. Add to the mix the fact that several Sipán sites are located in the town of Lambayeque and it all becomes too much. The sights below are essential viewing, but there are many, many more. You can visit them independently, but it is easier, quicker and cheaper to go with a tour company.

Huaca Rajada

The Moche culture (100–800 AD) was based all along the coast in northern Peru. The tombs found at the **Huaca Rajada** (also known as the **Temple of Sipán**) in Sipán (site museum daily 9am–5pm; S/8;

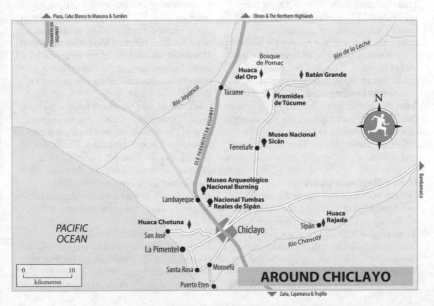

AROUND CHICLAYO

9

☎074 434 616) are vital to Moche history, as, unlike the *huacas* near Trujillo, they were never plundered by treasure hunters. Excavation began in 1987, with the extraordinary treasures now mostly displayed at the Museo Nacional Tumbas Reales de Sipán in Lambayeque. There's a small museum documenting the digs, but it is best combined with a visit to the larger museum. It's fascinating to think how much more is still to be found.

To **get to Sipán**, take a *combi* from the Terminal EPSEL on Avenida Nicolás de Piérola in Chiclayo (25min; S/2–3).

Lambayeque museums

The treasures from the Huaca Rajada's multiple tombs are displayed at the world-class **Museo Nacional Tumbas Reales de Sipán** in Lambayeque (Av Juan Pablo Vizcardo y Guzmán; Tues–Sun 9am–5pm; S/10; ☎074 283 978). The hauls from the various digs are laid out as they were discovered, and there are an overwhelming number of sacred objects all intricately made from precious metals, shells and stones, the most impressive being those from the tomb of **El Señor de Sipán**, an important Moche noble.

The **Museo Arqueológico Nacional Bruning**, also in Lambayeque (Block 7, Av Huamachuco; daily 9am–5.30pm; S/8; ☎074 282 110), contains displays on all Peru's ancient cultures and spans five millennia. Housed in a modernist building, the collection is displayed over four floors and even has a "Sala de Oro" (room of gold), full of Sipán and Sicán treasures.

To **get to Lambayeque**, take a *colectivo* from the corner of Calle San José opposite the Plazuela Elías Aguirre, six blocks west of Parque Principal (15min; S/2). The museums are within walking distance of each other.

Museo Nacional Sicán

Little is known about the Sicán, or Lambayeque, culture, even though it existed as recently as the fourteenth century AD. Some suggest Sicán culture was simply an extension of Moche culture, which makes it fascinating to compare the haul at the **Museo Nacional Sicán** in Ferreñafe (Tues–Sun 9am–5pm; S/8; ☎074 286 469)

with its counterpart in Lambayeque, as it's clear there are similarities between the two in terms of their belief and adornment. Although this museum is the less well-presented of the two and the treasures fewer, the metalwork here is finer and the use of semi-precious stones just as remarkable. There's also a reconstruction of the surreal tomb of the Señor de Sicán; his body was discovered decapitated, upside down and with huge gauntlets laid out beside him.

To **get to the museum**, take a *colectivo* from the corner of Avenida Sáenz Peña and Calle Leoncio Prado in Chiclayo (approx 25min; S/2.50) or a *combi* from the EPSEL terminal to the town of Ferreñafe and then a *mototaxi* to the museum (approx 10min; S/2).

Bosque de Pómac

The major treasures from the Sicán culture on display in Ferreñafe were discovered in the Huaca del Oro (Temple of Gold) in the **Bosque de Pómac** (Pomac Forest) in Batán Grande. This is considered to be the seat of the Sicán empire, with a host of other *huacas* rising majestically out of the verdant forest – it's worth scaling the **Huaca las Ventanas** (Temple of the Windows) to get a wonderful view of them.

The forest is a great place for a picnic, birdwatching or horseriding – Rancho Santana (☎979 712 145, ⊕cabalgatasperu. com) offers different riding tours from S/75 for four hours. Don't miss the **Árbol Milenario**, an ancient carob tree which locals believe has magic and religious powers; it's situated along the main road through the forest.

Tours will take you here from Chiclayo, usually combined with a visit to one or two of the museums, but if you want to go alone, get a *combi* from the Terminal EPSEL in Chiclayo for Batán Grande (45min; S/4) and ask to be dropped off at the Centro de Interpretación, at the entrance to the forest on the main road from Chiclayo, for information.

Valle de los Pirámides

The Sicán culture was also responsible for the extraordinary **Valle de los Pirámides** (Valley of the Pyramids) at Túcume (museum daily 8am–4.30pm; two sites

S/8, or S/12 for a full tour). This site comprises a cluster of a few of the 26 trapezoidal structures that fan out from here – you can see many of them for miles around if you scale the tallest in the complex and many are still being excavated by archeologists. There's a small but excellent museum with rooms dedicated to ceramics, as well as the tomb of Señor de Túcume, a nobleman found buried with 130 human sacrifices and extensive funerary offerings including tiny metal panpipes and trumpets.

Combis to Túcume cost S/2.50 and leave from the Terminal Leguía at the Ovalo del Pescador in Chiclayo (take a taxi there, as it's a 30min walk from the centre and in a rough neighbourhood). Ask for "los pirámides" and the *combi* will drop you on the main road about 1km from the site. A *mototaxi* from there will cost S/1.50 per person.

MÁNCORA AND AROUND

Just a small fishing village until about twenty years ago, **MÁNCORA** has become Peru's most popular beach resort – justifiably so, as the sea is warm most of the year, the beaches are white and the waves near perfect. It's definitely worth a stop to relax on the beach, eat to your heart's content at the great restaurants and try the outdoor sports. Máncora's **nightlife** is also famous, but can definitely make you feel that sleep is for the weak. Between the loud music and the busy main road, *la bulla* (the ruckus) puts many off, but there are more peaceful resorts along the coast between here and Tumbes – such as Pocitas, Vichayito, Cabo Blanco, Canoas de Punta Sal and Zorritos – where you'll find quieter, unspoilt stretches of coastline.

WHAT TO SEE AND DO

Máncora itself is a small settlement based along Avenida Piura (the stretch of the Panamericana that passes through) and the few side roads and passageways (many without an official name) that lead to the beach. There are no real **sights** other than some small mud baths about forty minutes away by *mototaxi*; hit the waves, wander around the *artesanía* stalls along the main avenue, have a cocktail and watch the spectacular sunsets.

Outdoor activities

Long famed for its **surf**, the area is now also a world-class destination for **kite-surfing**, and regularly hosts national and international competitions. The long beach and warm water make for a great place to learn and there's no shortage of teachers. You can rent gear and take lessons from several places along the beach from around S/60 per hour for surfing lessons or US$65/hr for kite-surfing (cheaper if you buy package deals).

Horseriding is also popular, and you'll see touts along the beach offering ragged-looking ponies for S/20–30 per hour; it's preferable to go through your hostel or use a tour agency listed with the tourist office, as the animals may be better treated. It's also possible to arrange tours to see marine wildlife, including **humpback whale spotting** from August to October.

ARRIVAL AND DEPARTURE

By plane Piura Airport is 3hr 30min by bus, or 2hr 30min in a minivan, which is more expensive (S/30) and leaves directly from the airport or from a terminal on Av Sánchez Cerro. (While Tumbes is closer, flights are considerably cheaper to Piura.)

By bus The bus companies have terminals all over town, but rarely more than a S/5 *mototaxi* ride from the centre.

THE TURTLES AT EL ÑURO

A great day-trip when the surf is flat is the fishing village of **El Ñuro** 7km past Los Organos. Here, around the pier you can usually see numerous turtles lazing around in the clear aquamarine water, waiting for scraps from the fishermen. You can jump in off the pier and swim with them – just don't get too close; these are wild animals, and you may get a deserved nip. There is a S/5 entrance fee to the beach. Go early for best visibility and to avoid crowds. Get there with an EPPO bus south to Los Organos (15min; S/2.50) and then a *mototaxi* to the beach (S/5).

9

Destinations Most buses to Lima (8 daily; 17–19hr) leave Tumbes in the afternoon and may stop at Máncora (2hr), Piura (6hr), Chiclayo (8hr), Trujillo (10hr), or go straight there. Cifa, Grau 313 (☎ 941 816 863), goes direct to Machala (1 daily, 9pm; 1hr 30min once through immigration) and Guayaquil (5–6 daily; 8hr). EPPO buses leave hourly to Piura, stopping along the way at Los Organos, El Cruce (for Cabo Blanca) and Talara (for Lobitos), without a/c.

By colectivo and combi Combis drive up and down Av Piura or leave from the layby half a block north of the Cruz del Sur office on Av Piura, picking up passengers until they are full for the trip to Tumbes (2hr; S/12–15). *Colectivos* to Punta Sal leave from directly outside the same office (30min; S/5).

INFORMATION AND TOURS

Check ⓦ vivamancora.com for up-to-date information about the area, including upcoming surfing events.

Tourist information There's a small office on Av Piura 534 (daily 8am–1pm & 2.45–9pm). The main iPerú office in Piura can supply information (☎ 073 320 249; ⓔ iperupiura@promperu.gob.pe.

Tour operators Spondylous Dive School (☎ 999 891 268, ⓦ buceaenperu.com) also offers half-day snorkel (US$45) and scuba diving (US$100) tours in the waters near Máncora.

GETTING AROUND

By mototaxi *Mototaxis* are a standard S/2–4 in town (look for those with the official jacket), although many will try to charge you more – fix a price before riding. Don't take one of the taxis without an official-looking sticker on the front, especially if you are going out of town, as there have been incidences of tourists getting robbed.

ACCOMMODATION

Those looking for peace and quiet will do better staying on the edges of town, although take care when returning late at night, as attacks on tourists are not unheard of. Note that prices are given for high season (Nov–March); out of season you can get a great deal. Avoid peak public holidays.

Laguna Surf Camp Acceso Veraniego s/n ☎ 994 015 628, ⓦ lagunasurfcamp.insta-hostel.com. Half a block from the beach and a short stroll into town (but far enough to escape the noise), this is unbeatable value and location for the price. Bamboo-roofed bungalows surround a small pool and lounging area. Energetic and friendly owner Pilar offers quality surf lessons. Dorms S̲/̲4̲0̲, doubles S̲/̲1̲5̲0̲

Misfit Hostel Playa del Amor ☎ 969 173 750, ⓦ hostelmisfitsmancora.com. Four friends from different parts of the world built four wood and bamboo A-frame bungalows on the isolated Playa del Amor. Each is distinct, with rather trippy murals inside, and sat right on the sand.

Hugely popular with a great, social atmosphere; book well in advance. Dorms S̲/̲2̲6̲, doubles S̲/̲8̲5̲

Psygon Surf Camp Playa El Amor 124 ☎ 994 142 389. With a more relaxed vibe than many of the other party-focused backpacker hostels, this shoestring hostel has large rooms and some camping spots located around a palm-thatched patio, and bar that's open daily until midnight with live music on Fridays. They organize surfing class and bike rental. Dorms S̲/̲2̲5̲, doubles S̲/̲9̲5̲, camping/person S̲/̲1̲5̲

EATING

Many of the restaurants aimed at gringos are along the Panamericana and serve excellent international cuisine, but none is cheap. Better-priced grub can be found towards the market at the north end of town, where Av Piura becomes Av Prolongación Grau. Here there are S/7 menus, *pollo a la brasa* (spit-roast chicken) joints, *ceviche* for S/15, and fresh fruit and veg.

El Ají Grill & Bar Pasaje 8 de Noviembre s/n (between Papa Mo's & Del Wawa) ☎ 998 488 325. Down a little passageway that leads to the sea – from the beach looking back towards the main drag it's to the right of *The Birdhouse*. A tiny little Mexican restaurant that serves great burritos, tacos and quesadillas, not forgetting some mean cocktails with "happy life" (aka "happy hour") for S/20. Mains S/20–35. Daily noon–11pm.

La Bajadita Av Piura 424 ☎ 073 258 385. For a decent espresso and a huge selection of home-made cakes and desserts (S/7.50–9), this place can't be beaten. Also serves reasonably priced sandwiches and cocktail deals. Tues–Sun 11am–10pm.

The Birdhouse On a balcony overlooking the sea next to *Hostal Sol y Mar* is this colourful three-in-one restaurant. *Green Eggs and Ham* does the best breakfasts in town, including waffles and fantastic American pancakes (S/12); *Papa Mo's* has milkshakes and nothing but milkshakes; and *Surf & Turf* is open for lunch and dinner and does, as the name suggests, fish and steak plates and a lunch menu for S/15. Daily 7am–8pm.

Bonaire Beach Acceso Veraniego 80. This restaurant is the best for very large portions of seafood such as *ceviche* and *parihuela espada* (stew) and chicharrón. Mains average S/28–30, lunch menu S/15. Daily 8am–11pm.

★ **Café del Mundo** Av Piura 246. This French-themed café oozes charm and serves up delicious plates of both French and local cuisine. Goat features heavily on the menu: try the *bourguinon de cabrito* (goat stew) or *lasagne de cabrito* (goat lasagne). Lunch and dinner menu is a steal at S/15. Daily 8am–11pm.

DRINKING AND NIGHTLIFE

Eating might be expensive in Máncora, but drinking certainly is not. Every bar in town has a very flexible "happy hour", which usually runs all night; you can get two cocktails or beers for S/10 in many bars. The most happening bars change regularly; after-hours nightlife tends to take place in the hostels, especially *Sol y Mar*, *Loki* and *The Point*, whose monthly full-moon party has become a town fixture.

La Balsa Av Piura 245. This pint- (well, pisco-) sized bar has thumping music and a great selection of home-infused piscos, in flavours from blackberry to green chilli, making their signature sour a lot less sweet than normal mixes. Happy hour 7–11pm. Daily 5.30pm–2am.

DIRECTORY

Banks and exchange Banco de la Nación, Av Piura 525–527; Globalnet ATM outside Minimarket Marlon, Av Piura 520.
Health Clínica San Pedro, C Grau 636 (☎073 258 513).
Laundry Laundry Service, Av Piura 314.
Tourist police Av Piura 330 (☎073 496 925).

TUMBES

Unlike most border settlements, tropical **TUMBES**, about 30km from the Ecuadorian border, is a surprisingly friendly place, but away from the plaza the city is shabby and chaotic. Tumbes is close to some of Peru's finest **beaches** and three national parks of astounding ecological variety: the arid **Cerros de Amotape**, the mangrove swamps of the **Santuario Nacional Manglares de Tumbes** and the tropical rainforest of the **Zona Reservada de Tumbes**. Unfortunately, as so few tourists explore this part of Peru, tours are infrequent and expensive.

WHAT TO SEE AND DO

Tumbes is good for a stroll to see the bright, almost gaudy, modern architecture around its centre. The large **Plaza de Armas** feels very tropical, with sausage trees, a huge rainbow archway and a stripy cathedral. Next to the plaza runs the pedestrianized **Paseo de la Concordia** (also known as Av San Martín), which has huge sculptures and more colourful architecture.

Getting to the parks is almost impossible without a tour company or car, but you can ask at the tourist information office.

ARRIVAL AND INFORMATION

By plane There are three daily flights to and from Lima with LATAM (1hr 45min). Note that Tumbes Airport is often very quiet, particularly at night, when there's no access to food or drink. A taxi into town is around S/20; it's a 15min journey.
By bus or colectivo Most buses and *colectivos* coming to Tumbes arrive at offices along Av Tumbes Norte. From here it's a couple of blocks to the Plaza de Armas. You can reach Tumbes from Lima (20–22hr) and many of the major coastal cities. From Máncora, there are buses, but it is a quicker and more pleasant journey in a *combi*. Buses from Guayaquil, Ecuador are also an option.
Tourist information iPerú, Jr Bolognesi 194 (Mon–Sat 9am–6pm, Sun 9am–1pm; ☎016 167 300 ext 3049; ✉iperutumbes@promperu.gob.pe).
Tour operators Mayte Tours, Jr Bolognesi 196 (☎072 523 219, ⓦmaytetours.com), run English-speaking tours to Puerto Pizarro mangrove swamp (S/40) and to local beaches (S/80). They also visit Parque Nacional Cerros de Amotape and the Santuario Nacional los Manglares de Tumbes (both S/70).

ACCOMMODATION

While there are many budget hotels in Tumbes, few are recommendable. If you don't have mosquito repellent, go for places with windows that close and fans.
Hospedaje Amazonas Av Tumbes Norte 317, at Plaza de Armas ☎072 525 266 or ☎972 683 780. One of the more pleasant of the budget places, with cable TV, fans and light en-suite rooms. S̄/10 extra for hot water. S̄/40
Hospedaje Franco Paseo la Concordia 105 ☎072 525 295. On the pedestrian avenue off the Plaza de Armas, it is considerably quieter here. Big rooms with ceiling fans but no breakfast; S/5 more for hot water. S̄/70

EATING AND DRINKING

Tumbes is the best place in Peru to try *conchas negras* – the black clams found only in these coastal waters, where they grow on the roots of mangroves.
Acuarelas Av Grau 401 ☎072 522 490. A popular, smart little restaurant with superb three-course lunch menu of salad or soup starters followed by dishes of chicken and lentils or beef stews, followed by dessert, all for S/10. They've got a menu with fish dishes and *ceviches* too (S/15–30). Mon–Sat 7am–11pm.
★ **Eduardo El Brujo** Jr Malecón Benavides 850 ☎972 634 456, ⓦeduardoelbrujo.com. One of the

9

INTO ECUADOR

Crossing the border from Tumbes can be complicated and has caught many tourists, especially non-Spanish-speaking ones, adrift in a no-man's land with a lot of canny locals trying to fleece you for as much as possible. Make sure you get some US dollars for Ecuador in Tumbes, as exchange rates in **Aguas Verdes** (the closest town to the border) can be extortionate. There is an iPerú office at the border (☎ 016 167 300).

By far the easiest, and in the end, the cheapest way to cross the border is to take an **international bus service** from Tumbes, such as Cruz del Sur or the Ecuadorian company Cifa, which take you straight through to Machala (S/20–65) or Guayaquil (S/114), waiting at the new CEBAF border control while you get your exit and entry stamps (in the same building, located on the Ecuadorian side). If you can't do this, you'll have to go it alone.

Colectivos (S/5) for the border leave Tumbes from block four of Av Mariscal Castillo, just past the market, and drop you in Aguas Verdes. Once here, it is a short stroll across the Puente Internacional (international bridge) and on the other side you take one of the yellow taxis to the CEBAF control point (10min; US$3–5). Get your stamps and return to Huaquillas (the Ecuadorian equivalent of Aguas Verdes) and choose a bus for any Ecuadorian destination. If you're coming into Peru from Ecuador, it's simply a reversal of the above procedure – note that Tumbes is a much nicer place to stay than Aguas Verdes – and in both directions the authorities occasionally require that you show an onward ticket out of their respective countries. **Do not take photographs** anywhere near the border or immigration offices.

best restaurants in this part of the world, this place serves exquisite seafood in a light, open restaurant spanning two floors, including a rooftop terrace with river views. Try the fantastic *sudado de conchas negras*, a thick seafood stew served with rice, with supposedly aphrodisiac properties. A little pricey (mains S/30–50), but portions are big enough to share. Mon–Sat 10.30am–11.30pm, Sun 11am–5pm.

The Northern Highlands

The **Northern Highlands** offers some of the least-explored areas in Peru. The two main cities, **Cajamarca** and **Chachapoyas**, are welcoming and steadily growing in terms of tourism. Each makes a fantastic springboard for exploring the wealth of archeological sites in the surrounding countryside.

CAJAMARCA

Nestling in a fertile rolling valley of eucalyptus and pine, 2720m above sea level, **CAJAMARCA** is a charming colonial town shrouded in legend, most famously – or infamously – known as the place of Inca ruler **Atahualpa's last stand** against Pizarro in 1532, signalling the end of the Inca Empire. While its Spanish colonial ambience, along with its one remaining Inca building and Andean location, have earned it the title "the Cusco of the north", Cajamarca has a character all of its own. Relatively small until Peru's largest gold mine (within driving distance) was discovered, the city's population has grown

rapidly in the last decade to around 220,000. Despite this, Cajamarca is still surprisingly low-key; the liveliest time to visit is during the week-long Carnaval, complete with parades, music and water fights.

WHAT TO SEE AND DO

Cajamarca's sights lie in the centre around the **Plaza de Armas**, in the swish suburb of **Baños del Inca** and **outside the city**, where the attractions are all accessible on half-day tours.

Around the Plaza de Armas

The **Plaza de Armas** is at the heart of the city, with most places of interest in the easy-to-navigate surrounding streets. On the plaza sit the **Catedral** (Mon 4–6pm, Tues–Fri 8–11am & 4–6pm, Sat 9–11am) and **Iglesia San Francisco** (Mon–Sat 7–11am & 4–7pm, Sun 4–8pm). The adjoining **Museo de Arte Religioso** in the **Convento San Francisco** (Mon–Sat 10am–noon & 4–6pm; S/5), whose entrance is on Amalia Puga, houses an interesting selection of religious art in a rambling run of rooms, crypts and cloisters in a working monastery.

Cerro Santa Apolonia

South from the Plaza de Armas, a steep walk up Jr Dos de Mayo takes you past sellers flogging crafts, children playing, gussied-up llamas and Quechua ladies in their ten-gallon hats up to the pretty white church on the hill of **Cerro Santa Apolonia**. Next to the church, pay S/1 (daily 7am–6.30pm) to go right to the top through pretty gardens, and see the rock formation known as the **Silla del Inca** (Inca chair), reputed to be a place where the Inca ruler would sit and gaze out over his empire.

El Cuarto del Rescate (Atahualpa's Ransom Room)

One **joint ticket** (S/5, available from all sites) gives you entrance to several sights. The most famous is the only surviving Inca structure in Cajamarca – a modest stone room known as **El Cuarto del Rescate** (the ransom room), at Jr Amalia Puga 722 (Tues–Sat 9am–1pm & 3–8pm, Sun 9am–1pm). Legend has it that it was this very room that Atahualpa offered to fill with gold for the Conquistadors in order to save his life, although in reality it is probably just the room in which he was held prisoner.

Compejo Belén

The gorgeous Baroque **Compejo Belén** (Tues–Sat 9am–1pm & 3–8pm, Sun 9am–1pm; same ticket as El Cuarto del Rescate) includes two former hospitals on either side of the Iglesia Belén, on the corner of Calle Belén and Jr Junín. One is now an archeology and ethnography museum, displaying ceramics and weavings from pre-Inca civilizations (don't miss the two four-breasted women flanking the gate,

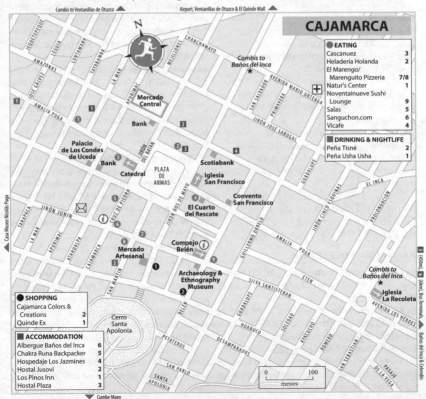

CAJAMARCA

EATING
Cascanuez	3
Heladería Holanda	2
El Marengo/ Marenguito Pizzeria	7/8
Natur's Center	1
Noventainueve Sushi Lounge	9
Salas	5
Sanguchon.com	6
Vicafe	4

DRINKING & NIGHTLIFE
Peña Tisné	2
Peña Usha Usha	1

SHOPPING
Cajamarca Colors & Creations	2
Quinde Ex	1

ACCOMMODATION
Albergue Baños del Inca	6
Chakra Runa Backpacker	5
Hospedaje Los Jazmines	4
Hostal Jusovi	2
Los Pinos Inn	1
Hostal Plaza	3

9

allegedly symbols of fertility). The other is a vaulted space with small alcoves that would have held patients, with a room dedicated to the colourful Andean scenes painted by Cajamarcan artist Andrés Zevallos. The church is worth seeing for its ornate carved interiors and particularly graphic portrayal of the Crucifixion.

Casa Museo Nicolás Puga

The privately owned collection in the **Casa Museo Nicolás Puga**, at Av José Gálvez 634 (by appointment only; S/20; ☎976 234 433) has a superb collection of pre-Hispanic textiles, some dating back 2000 years to the Nazca and Paracas cultures, plus an incredible display of Mochica tumbaga armour (made from a metal alloy of copper mixed with gold) and Chavín stone statues, including a seated mummy and a musician playing the flute.

Baños del Inca

The hugely popular and thoroughly relaxing **Baños del Inca** (daily 5am–4.45pm, final entrance 3pm; public pool S/3, private bath S/6–25, massage S/20/30min; ⓦctbinca.com.pe) are 6km east of the centre. As you walk around the area you'll see steam rising from the streams – the water reaches up to 72°C. At the tourist complex this water is channelled into private and communal baths, a pool, jacuzzis and even an aromatic sauna filled with orange peel and eucalyptus.

Combis to the baths depart from of the corner of Jr Dos de Mayo and Jr Chanchamayo, four blocks northeast of the Plaza de Armas (15min; S0.80).

ARRIVAL AND DEPARTURE

By plane The airport, 4km out of town, has four flights a day to Lima (1hr 20min) with LATAM (ⓦlatam.com) and LC Perú (ⓦlcperu.pe).

By bus Most bus terminals are located around the third block of Av Atahualpa. Civa (☎076 368 186) and Línea (☎076 507 690) have the most comfortable services to Lima. Móvil Tours (☎076 280 093) runs a night service to Chicalyo, with good onward connections to Tumbes via Máncora. For Chachapoyas via Leymebamba, Virgen del Carmen (☎076 606 966) has two daily departures.

Destinations Chachapoyas (2 daily at 5am & 5pm; 11–12hr); Chiclayo (7 daily; 6hr); Lima (at least 10 daily; 16hr); Trujillo (5 daily; 6hr).

INFORMATION AND TOURS

Tourist information iPerú, Jr Cruz de Piedra 601 (Mon–Sat 9am–6pm, Sun 9am–1pm; ☎076 365 166) are happy to explain how to reach outlying attractions independently. Some English spoken.

Tour operators All the companies offer pretty much the same array of tours. Catequil Tours (☎076 363 958, ⓦcatequiltours.com) organizes everything from guided city tours to community tourism in the nearby countryside; Cumbe Mayo Tours (Ir Amalia Puga 635 ☎076 362 938) has excursions to all the main sights.

GETTING AROUND

By taxi or mototaxi Taxis should cost no more than S/4 in the city centre and as far as the bus stations. Baños del Inca or the airport will cost S/10–15. *Mototaxis* are a standard S/4 per journey within the city.

ACCOMMODATION

A few families in Cajamarca offer cheap homestays (*turismo vivencial*), which the tourist board has information about. They are mostly outside the city with local communities – most notably in Huayanay (1hr from town) and Namora (40min from town).

Albergue Baños del Inca Located behind the Baños del Inca ☎076 348 249, ⓦctbinca.com.pe; map p.811. This place has doubles and family rooms, as well as two-person bungalows, all very comfortable and with their own built-in thermal bathrooms, and TV. Free access to the main thermal pool at the baths complex. S/60, bungalows S/150

★ **Chakra Runa Backpacker** Psje Cutervo 129 ☎971 096 916; map p.811. Comfortable and homely, this backpackers' hostel is well located for both the bus station and the plaza (it's a 10min walk to each). The Peruvian and French hosts are experts on activities in the local area and can advise on reaching nearby cave paintings and waterfalls. Dorms S/25, doubles S/52

★ **Hospedaje Los Jazmines** Jr Amazonas 775 ☎076 361 812, ⓦhospedajelosjazmines.com.pe; map p.811. A comfortable hostel in a converted colonial house surrounds a leafy courtyard, and the excellent café on the premises serves some of the best coffee in town. Rooms are simple en-suites. This place is associated with a charity that supports patients who can't afford cancer treatment. S/90

Hostal Jusovi Jr Amazonas 637 ☎076 362 920; map p.811. Looks like a concrete monstrosity from the outside and breakfast isn't included, but inside the singles, doubles and triples are small but spotless and come with cable TV. S/60

Los Pinos Inn Jr La Mar 521 ☎076 365 992, ⓦlospinosinn.com; map p.811. This mansion combines Old World elegance in the form of gilded mirrors and antique furniture, a touch of kitsch (the suits of armour) and modern amenities (including cable TV). Bed down in the cheaper old wing or the more elaborate new wing; suites are great value for groups of three to four. Doubles S̲/̲1̲2̲0̲, suites S̲/̲2̲8̲0̲

Hostal Plaza Amalia Puga 669 ☎076 362 058; map p.811. At this House of Chintz, rooms are basic but generous and come with plastic flowers and teddy bears. Some of the rooms look out over the plaza from the little balconies. No breakfast. S̲/̲5̲0̲

EATING

Cajamarca is famous for its dairy products – including some of the best cheese in Peru. It's often served as *choclo con queso*, a slab of cheese with a big cob of corn. Other dishes include *caldo verde* (green broth made from potato, egg, herbs and *quesillo* cheese) and *picante de papas con cuy* (potatoes with peanut and chilli sauce with fried guinea pig). There is a mall housing a supermarket, El Quinde, at Av Hoyos Rubios blocks 6 and 7, a 20min walk from the Plaza de Armas.

★ **Cascanuez** Jr Amalia Puga 548 ☎076 366 089; map p.811. Some of the best coffee and cake in town, in a refined café. Also good for lunchtime sandwiches, *humitas* and four types of breakfast (S/15–17). Daily 7.30am–midnight.

Heladería Holanda Jr Amalia Puga 657, on the plaza; map p.811. There's a real artisan at work here preparing some excellent ice cream using local milk and fresh tropical fruit. It's hard to go wrong with *maracuyá* or *lucuma*. Cones from S/3. Daily 9am–7pm.

El Marengo/Marenguito Pizzeria Jr Junín 1201 ☎076 368 045, & Junín 1184 ☎076 344 251; map p.811. This tiny pizzeria is so popular it has two locales around the corner from each other; both get packed with locals after the best pizza in town (around S/16), washed down with sangria. Daily 5.30–11pm.

Natur's Center Jr Amalia Puga 409; map p.811. Chow down on simple, cheap and hearty vegetarian food at this matchbox-sized restaurant where wheat soups and butter-bean stews make up the S/5 lunch menu. There's an extensive selection of vegetarian takes on Peruvian classics (such as *lomo saltado* and *lomo a lo pobre*) on the larger menu. Mon–Thurs 8am–2pm & 5–8pm, Fri 8am–2pm.

★ **Noventainueve Sushi Lounge** Jr Silva Santisteban 157 ☎076 362 928; map p.811. An incongruously sleek and stylish sushi bar with Japanese decoration and a wide selection of Peruvian-style sashimi and sushi: think prawns, avocado and lashings of cream cheese. Sushi from S/20. Daily 6–11pm.

Salas Jr Amalia Puga 637 ☎076 362 867; map p.811. *Salas* has been around since 1947 and is a local institution with a repertoire of regional dishes that's hard to fault. There's *cuy* with potato and rice stew (S/30), dish-of-the-day specials at S/10, and sandwiches and light bites too. Daily 7am–10pm.

Sanguchon.com Jr Junín 1137 ☎076 343 066, ⓦsanguchon.com.pe; map p.811. This lively hole-in-the-wall-cum-bar specializes in huge sandwiches. Choose from overflowing burgers, grilled chicken sandwiches (the "Californichicken" stands out) or really push the boat out with "Vito Corleone" – an epic creation comprising steak, double cheese, eggs and more. S/9–15. Mon–Sat 6–11.30pm.

Vicafe Jr Amalia Puga 746 ☎976 034 919; map p.811. Just off the plaza, this does a great line in cheap breakfasts: from traditional Andean feasts of *chicharrón* or chicken dishes to simple sandwich (S/4) and coffee (S/3) combinations, plus large fruit juices. Daily 8am–noon & 5–11pm.

DRINKING AND NIGHTLIFE

Peña Tisné Jr San Martín 265; map p.811. This is neither a real *peña* nor a real bar, but a one-of-a-kind Peruvian experience that should not be missed. Knock on the unmarked door and Don Victor will lead you through his house to his bohemian back garden, full of cosy tables and memorabilia soaked in Cajamarcan history. Try the home-made *macerado* – a delicious liquor made from fermenting tomatillo (an exotic fruit) and sugar (pitcher S/16). Daily 9am–midnight.

★ **Peña Usha Usha** Amalia Puga 142; map p.811. This is the best venue in town for live Peruvian music, especially *criolla* music, as well as Cuban troubador-style performances. A small space particularly busy at weekends but also entertaining during the week when owner Jaime Valera entertains locals and tourists alike with his incredibly talented and versatile guitar playing and singing. Often lit only by candle, this bar has a cosy and inviting atmosphere. Entry S/5. Thurs–Sat 9m–2am.

SHOPPING

Cajamarca is known for its high-quality pottery, and the general standard in some of the small shops here is excellent – there is some unique craftwork you'll not find elsewhere.

Cajamarca Colors & Creations Jr Belén 628 ⓦcajamarcacyc.com; map p.811. Wonderfully imaginative jewellery, ceramics, shawls and gifts for children.

Quinde Ex Jr 2 de Mayo 264 ☎976 495 319; map p.811. Colourful textiles, cushion covers and handbags made of Andean woven belts. Daily 9.30am–1.3pm & 3–6.30pm.

9

DIRECTORY

Banks and exchange BCP, Jr Del Comercio 675; Banco de La Nación, Jr Tarapaca 647; Scotiabank, Jr Amazonas 750. *Moneychangers* are on Jr Amalia Puga on the main plaza.
Hospital Clínica Limatambo, Jr Puno 263 (☎076 362 241). Private, high-standard 24hr care.
Post office SERPOST, Jr Apurimac 626.
Tourist police Jr Del Comercio 1013 (☎076 354 515).

DAY-TRIPS FROM CAJAMARCA

There are several sites of interest easily accessible from Cajamarca. One is the aqueduct of **Cumbe Mayo**, thought to be one of the oldest man-made structures in South America. From the parking area, a 2km trail loops past the Bosque de Piedras (Forest of Stones), where huge clumps of eroded limestone taper into some fanciful shapes. A little further on, you'll see the well-preserved and skilfully constructed **canal**, built almost 1200 years BC. Dotted along the canal there are some interesting **petroglyphs** attributed to the early Cajamarca culture. The easiest way to visit is with a half-day tour (around S/20–25).

Another interesting half-day excursion is to the **Ventanillas de Otuzco** (daily 9am–6pm; S/5), a hillside necropolis 8km away whose graves resemble little alcoves or windows (*ventanillas*). *Combis* go here from the corner of Jr Gladiolos and Calle Tayabamba in Cajamarca (20min; S/1); you can take an organized tour or do a two-hour walk from the Baños del Inca. Twelve kilometres further east from the Ventanillas de Otuzco are the **Ventanillas de Combayo**, an even bigger necropolis; *combis* from block one of Jr Pérez (S/5) pass nearby but you have to ask the driver to drop you off in the right place.

On the road towards Celendín, the spectacular mosaics of **the Santuario de la Virgen de Polloc** (daily 8am–6pm; donations welcome) demonstrate hours of patient work by a brigade of local children housed in the *albergue* here, with magnificent religious-themed friezes wrapping the external walls of the school and continuing inside the church. *Combis* leave from Av Atahualapa (opposite the entrance to C Uchuracy; 40min; S/3).

CHACHAPOYAS

The thriving market town of **CHACHAPOYAS**, high up in the Andes at

Huancas

CHACHAPOYAS

DRINKING
Licores La Reina — 1

EATING
Amazonas 632 — 3
El Batán del Tayta — 5
Café Fusiones — 2
El Tejado — 1
Terra Mia — 4

ACCOMMODATION
Aventura Backpackers Lodge — 2
Chacha International — 4
Chachapoyas Backpackers — 3
Hostal Revash — 1

Cajamarca via Chiclayo

2334m, is first and foremost a springboard for a wealth of nearby pre-Columbian remains that litter the Utcubamba valley. The city itself is a colonial delight and its citizens are known for their friendliness. But what "Chachas" really offers is the chance to see some extraordinary sights, not least the marvellous remains of the **Kuélap** fortress, that easily rival those of significantly younger archeological sites in the south.

WHAT TO SEE AND DO

The town is centred on the tranquil **Plaza de Armas**, surrounded by the cathedral and municipal buildings and with a colonial bronze fountain, a monument to Toribio Rodríguez de Mendoza, as its centrepiece. Born here in 1750, he is considered the main ideological inspiration for Peru's independence from Spain. The town's main church of interest, **Iglesia de Santa Ana**, Jr Santa Ana 1056, was built in 1569. The **Museo el Reino de las Nubes**, on the plaza at Jr Ayacucho 904 (Mon 3–5.30pm, Tues–Fri 9am–1pm & 3–5pm; free), has an assorted collection of local artefacts, including 1000-year-old textiles, a reconstruction of a Kuélap dwelling and a collection of mummies.

ARRIVAL AND DEPARTURE

By bus The best of the bus companies, the comfortable Móvil Tours at Libertad 464 (☎041 478 545) have various departures for Lima, Chiclayo and Trujillo, while Civa at Jr Ortiz Arrieta 279 (☎041 478 048) also run to Lima and Chiclayo.
Destinations Chiclayo (4 daily; 9hr); Lima (3 daily; 22hr); Trujillo (1 daily; 12hr).

By colectivo and combi *Combis* and *colectivos* to regional destinations depart from the Terminal Terrestre, around ten blocks from Plaza de Armas. Vírgen del Carmen (☎976 015 594) has daily minibuses to Cajamarca via Leymebamba; Turismo Selva (☎961 659 443) has four daily services to Tarapoto, from where you can catch a bus to Yurimaguas for boats to Iquitos (see page 820).
Destinations Cajamarca (1 daily at 7.30pm; 10–12hr); Lamud (several daily; 2hr); Tarapoto (4 daily; 8hr).

INFORMATION AND TOURS

Tourist information Jr Ortiz Arrieta 582 (Mon–Sat 9am–6pm, Sun 9am–1pm; ☎041 477 292). Run by iPerú; some English spoken.
Tour operators There are numerous tour operators dotted around the Plaza de Armas, all of which offer standard

day-trips to Kuélap (S/90); Karajía, combined with either Pueblo de Los Muertos or the Quiocta Cave (S/90); and Gocta waterfall (S/60). Turismo Explorer, at Jr Grau 509 on the plaza (☎041 478 162, ⓦturismoexplorerperu.com), is highly recommended and the guides speak excellent English. Amazon Expeditions, at Jr Ortiz Arietta 508 (☎041 798 718, ⓦamazonexpedition.com.pe), is a very professional outfit that also runs four-day treks to Gran Vilaya combined with Kuélap and Karajía (S/650), three-day treks to Laguna de Los Cóndores (S/850), and the more adventurous day trek to the Gocta waterfall.

ACCOMMODATION

Aventura Backpackers Lodge Jr Amazonas 1416 ☎041 477 407 ⓔaventurachachapoyas@gmail.com; map p.814. Basic rooms, a small kitchen and a handful of bathrooms make up Chachapoyas' cheapest hostel. No breakfast and no lockers; it's possible to bargain over the price of the room. Dorms **S/18**, doubles **S/40**
★ **Chachapoyas Backpackers** Jr 2 de Mayo 639 ☎041 478 879, ⓦchachapoyasbackpackers.com; map p.814. Run by an effusive, English-speaking host, this central hostel is a great budget choice. The simple rooms (some with own bathrooms) come with cool lamps in the shape of Karajía sarcophagi, guests congregate in the kitchen, and laundry service is a welcome perk. Dorms **S/20**, doubles **S/45**
Chacha International Jr Triunfo 1098 ☎948 757 586, ⓔchacha17international@gmail.com; map p.814. Clean rooms and beds with the added luxury of an actual duvet cover. Lacking a bit in atmosphere, but has a decent shared kitchen and an attached language school. Dorms **S/18**, doubles **S/40**
Hostal Revash Jr Grau 517, Plaza de Armas ☎041 477 391; map p.814. Centred around a greenery-filled courtyard featuring a replica Karajía sarcophagus, this guesthouse is renowned for having the best hot showers in town, and the spacious rooms (the cheapest singles are S/50) come with comfortable beds. There's a buffet breakfast and a rather persistent in-house tour agency. **S/120**

EATING

The Mercado Central, one block north of Plaza de Armas between Grau and Ortiz Arrieta, sells fresh produce and cheap meals.
Amazonas 632 Jr Amazonas 632; map p.814. Tremendously friendly service and an owl obsession make this charming café an excellent pitstop for coffee and cake, although the three generously portioned breakfasts –including one veggie option – are also hard to beat (S/6.90–8.90). Mon–Fri 7.30am–12.30pm & 5–11pm, Sat & Sun 5–11pm.
El Batán del Tayta Jr La Merced 604 ☎982 777 219; map p.814. A corridor inscribed with messages from

9

TWO ROADS BETWEEN CHACHAPOYAS AND CAJAMARCA

There are two routes between Chachapoyas and Cajamarca. The far longer and less exciting route is the road that passes through Chiclayo (changing buses at Pedro Ruíz); this route has fewer and lower passes but is more prone to landslides during the rainy season.

A fascinating **alternative route to Chachapoyas** is the direct scenic route taken by the Virgen del Carmen bus company – a paved yet precarious one-lane highway from Cajamarca that passes through the village of **Leymebamba**, winding its way up and down several massive valleys and passes. There's a reason why they hand out sick bags: the curves can be nausea-inducing and it's best if you have a head for heights, given the sheer drop to one side (which is stunning or terrifying, depending on your outlook). This scenic route also runs overnight, although it's advisable to only travel during the day due to the real possibility of a drunk bus driver; unfortunately, the return service to Cajamarca only travels this route at night. It's well worth stopping in Leymebamba to visit the fantastic Museo de Leymebamba (5km from town), home to 219 remarkably well-preserved Chachapoyas mummies, found in 1996 at the Laguna de Los Condores – itself reachable via a very scenic three-day guided trek either from Leymebamba proper or from Chachapoyas (see page 814).

happy customers greets you as you enter, and the menu is as eclectic as the decor, including steak flambéed in pisco, rice with duck and wonderful, imaginative salads. Wash it down with pineapple sangria or one of their signature sours. Mains from S/22. Daily noon–11pm.

★ **Café Fusiones** Jr Ayacucho 952 ☎ 960 119 965, ⦿ caféfusiones.com; map p.814. This bohemian hangout specializes in largely organic "slow food". Come here for spicy lentil burgers, fresh juices, chunky sandwiches, ample breakfasts and great teas and coffees. A book exchange makes it even more linger-worthy. Mains from S/12. 7am–10.30pm; closed Wed.

El Tejado Santo Domingo 424 ☎ 041 477 592; map p.814. Really good traditional Peruvian and local cuisine served in a warm and friendly place set around a patio. The speciality here is several takes on *tacu tacu*, a rice-and-beans dish. Lunch from S/10. Daily noon–4pm.

★ **Terra Mia** Jr Chincha Alta 557 ☎ 041 477 217; map p.814. A cultured hangout with an artistic air – walls are painted a deep red hue and there are colourful Andean cushions. But what marks this place out are the breakfasts (from S/13.50) – a welcome change from bread, juice and coffee. Try the spinach and cheese omelette or waffles. Daily 7.30am–12.30pm & 3.30–10pm.

DRINKING

Licores La Reina Jr Ayacucho 544; map p.814. Set around a wide patio, this is the locals' favourite bar for a drink of the boisterously potent, locally made *macerado* (cane sugar *aguardiente*, infused with fruit), which is guaranteed to put hairs on your chest at only S/3 a small glass. Daily 9am–1am.

DIRECTORY

Banks and exchange BCP is on Triunfo, seven blocks from the Plaza de Armas and next to the hospital. Banco de la Nación is at block eight of Ayacucho where you can change money.

Hospital The hospital (open 24hr) is on Jr Ortiz Arrieta, at Plaza de Armas (☎ 041 477 052).

Post office Jr Salamanca 956.

DAY-TRIPS FROM CHACHAPOYAS

There are many remote ruins dotted around the stunning countryside, all easily reachable by day tour. West of Chachapoyas lie the **Pueblo de los Muertos** and **Karajía**, two impressive cliff-face burial centres for the elite of the Chachapoyas peoples; southeast are the marvellous remains of the **Kuélap** citadel, second only to Machu Picchu in terms of location and magnificence, while northeast are **Gocta**, and **Yumbilla**, two of Peru's tallest waterfalls.

Kuélap

If you only see one sight in the northern highlands, make it **KUÉLAP** (daily 8am–5pm; S/20). This impressive pre-Inca fortress, 3100m up in the clouds, 700m long and with 20m-tall walls, was built around 500 AD and would have housed around four thousand people in 500 circular thatched huts. Some of these houses, or what's left of them, are decorated with characteristic Chachapoyas diamond and zigzag patterns. Elsewhere, you may spot small, carved animal heads, condor designs and intricate serpent figures. The site is atmospherically overgrown with trees, bromeliads and mosses. One of the most interesting buildings is the temple, containing *El Tintero* ("the ink well"), a large, bottle-shaped cavity, possibly a place of sacrifice, since archeologists have found human bones there, accessed via a hole in the roof.

You can get to Kuélap by day tour using the new *teleférico* that brings you straight to the ticket office in twenty minutes, via the colectivos that still shuttle along the winding, precipitous road past the villages of Choctamal and Malca to the ticket office at Kuélap (and add an extra hour to your journey), or as part of a four-day trek that passes by the collection of ruins known as **Gran Vilaya** – some tour companies in Chachapoyas run excursions (around S/650 per person and includes food, accommodation and transport).

Cateratas de Gocta

There's some debate about the global ranking of the waterfalls at **GOCTA** (771m), about a two-hour drive from Chachapoyas, but whatever their placing they're certainly impressive. Getting to a good viewpoint – from where you can make out the main two tiers of the falls (231m above and another 540m below) – requires a two-hour hike through the cloudforest either from the village of San Pablo or from Cocachimba. It's easy enough to visit without a guide; take a colectivo to Cochuayco followed by a *mototaxi* to Cocachima or San Pablo (S/10) and pay your S/10 entrance at the office at the main square. There are

various budget lodgings available in Cocachimba.

Caterata Yumbilla

Another forty minutes beyond the turn-off for Cocachimba, the equally magnificent, but lesser-known **Caterata Yumbilla is** accessed by a one-and-a-half-hour trek through dense cloud forest. At 896m, it's considered by some rankings to be the fifth tallest in the world, although you may find yourself disappointed out of rainy season when it's known to run dry. Take a *colectivo* to Pedro de Ruíz (1hr; S/5) then a *mototaxi* to the main square in Quispes (S/10); pay S/10 at the office and ask the *mototaxi* to drop you at the trailhead.

Karajía and the Pueblo de los Muertos

Two cliffside mausoleums, Karajía and the Pueblo de los Muertos ("town of the dead"), are both easiest reached by day tour, as it can take a long time to get here using public transport. From the plaza in the village of Cruz Pata, it's a 1km (20min) descent via dirt road to **KARAJÍA**. Thirty metres above the walkway is a row of six sarcophagi, elaborately painted clay coffins moulded around a cone made of wooden poles, with heads reminiscent of Easter Island's *moai*. Up to 2m in height, they house the mummies of the most important individuals, such as chieftains, warriors and shamans, as well as their most prized belongings. The two skulls above them are thought to be trophy skulls. From the far end of the walkway you can see another five sarcophagi to the left of the main group – these are far less elaborate and have been thoroughly desecrated

The **PUEBLO DE LOS MUERTOS** is similarly interesting, with more sarcophagi and also burial houses, again perched precariously on a ledge with a huge drop into the valley below. It's a 45-minute walk downhill from Lamud, and one hour thirty minutes back up.

During the rainy season, the walk to the Pueblo de Los Muertos becomes a mud bath and tour companies visit **CAVERNA DE QUIOCTA** (10km northwest of Lamud; 2hr walk each way) instead. It's an impressive (and extremely muddy) cave

9

with jaw-dropping stalagmites and stalactites, also the site of some

Chachapoyas human remains; tour companies supply rubber boots.

The Northern Amazon

Over half of Peru is covered by rainforest, with its eastern regions offering easy access to the world's largest and most famous jungle, the **Amazon**. Of the Amazon's original area, around six million square kilometres (about eighty percent) remains intact, fifteen percent of which lies in Peru. It's the most biodiverse region on earth, and much that lies beyond the main waterways remains relatively untouched and unexplored.

Although far easier to access by air from Lima, you can get to the northern jungle from the northern Peruvian coast via an adventurous three-day boat journey down the Río Marañon from Yurimaguas to

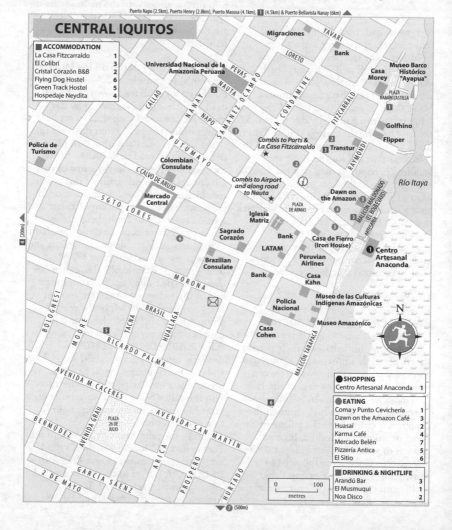

Puerto Napo (2.5km), Puerto Henry (2.8km), Puerto Masusa (4.1km), 🚤 (4.5km) & Puerto Bellavista Nanay (6km) ▲

CENTRAL IQUITOS

■ **ACCOMMODATION**
La Casa Fitzcarraldo	1
El Colibrí	3
Cristal Corazón B&B	2
Flying Dog Hostel	6
Green Track Hostel	5
Hospedaje Neydita	4

Migraciones

Universidad Nacional de la Amazonía Peruana

YAVARÍ

LORETO

Bank

Casa Morey

Museo Barco Histórico "Ayapua"

PEVAS

NAUTA

SAMANEZ OCAMPO

NANAY

NAPO

CALLAO

LA CONDAMINE

FITZCARRALDO

PLAZA RAMÓN CASTILLA

PUTUMAYO

Policía de Turismo

Colombian Consulate

C CALVO DE ARUJO

Combis to Ports & La Casa Fitzcarraldo ★

Transtur

RAYMONDI

Golfhino

Flipper

SGTO LORES

Mercado Central

Combis to Airport and along road to Nauta ★

PLAZA DE ARMAS

ℹ

Dawn on the Amazon

MALECÓN MALDONADO (EL BOULEVARD)

ARTESANÍA

Río Itaya

4 (200m)

Iglesia Matriz

Sagrado Corazón

Bank

Casa de Fierro (Iron House)

Centro Artesanal Anaconda

LATAM

Peruvian Airlines

Brazilian Consulate

MORONA

Bank

Casa Kahn

BOLOGNESI

MOORE

TACNA

BRASIL

HUALLAGA

Policía Nacional

Museo de las Culturas Indígenas Amazónicas

Museo Amazónico

Casa Cohen

MALECÓN TARAPACÁ

N

RICARDO PALMA

AVENIDA M CACERES

AVENIDA SAN MARTIN

BERMÚDEZ

AVENIDA GRAU

PLAZA 26 DE JULIO

ARICA

PROSPERO

HURTADO

2 DE MAYO

GARCÍA SAENZ

0   100
metres

7 (500m)

■ **SHOPPING**
Centro Artesanal Anaconda	1

■ **EATING**
Coma y Punto Cevichería	1
Dawn on the Amazon Café	3
Huasaí	2
Karma Café	4
Mercado Belén	7
Pizzería Antica	5
El Sitio	6

■ **DRINKING & NIGHTLIFE**
Arandú Bar	3
El Musmuqui	1
Noa Disco	2

Iquitos. This will take you close to an animal-rich national reserve the size of many European countries, **Pacaya Samiria**; budget travellers should consider accessing this astonishing wetland from the small town of **Lagunas,** which lies between Yurimaguas and Iquitos.

IQUITOS

The largest city in the world not accessible by road, **IQUITOS** began life in 1739 when the Jesuits established settlements on the Río Mazán. By the end of the nineteenth century, it was, along with Manaus in Brazil, one of the great rubber towns – as depicted in Werner Herzog's 1982 film *Fitzcarraldo* – but during the last century has oscillated between prosperity and depression. Yet its role as Peru's busiest river port and the nearby three-way frontier with Colombia and Brazil (see page 828) has ensured both its economic and strategic importance.

Iquitos is a busy, cosmopolitan town of about 500,000 and growing (people from smaller Amazon villages flock here looking for a better life), with elegant architectural reminders of the rubber boom years, eccentric expats and the atmospheric *barrio* of **Puerto Belén**.

WHAT TO SEE AND DO

Iquitos is easily overlooked in favour of the surrounding rainforest, but don't be too quick to dismiss this steamy metropolis. It has a few sights, more than its fair share of quirks, surprisingly good food and a lively nightlife.

Plaza de Armas
The only real sight on **Plaza de Armas** is the unusual **Casa de Fierro** (Iron House). Originally created by Eiffel for the 1889 Paris exhibition, it was shipped out to Iquitos in pieces by one of the rubber barons and erected here in the 1890s.

Along the river
The two best sections of the **old riverfront** run parallel to the Plaza de Armas. Malecón Maldonado, locally known as **El Boulevard**, is the busier of the two, especially at night, as it's full of bars and

WHEN TO VISIT
The city of Iquitos is good to visit year-round. There is no rainy season as such; instead, the year is divided into "high water" (Dec–May) and "low water" (June–Nov) seasons. The weather is always hot and humid, with temperatures averaging 23–30°C and an annual rainfall of about 2600mm. Most visitors come between June and August, but the high-water months can be the best time for **wildlife**, because the animals are crowded into smaller areas of dry land and more rivers can be navigated.

restaurants and there's a small dugout amphitheatre hosting street performers. The other section, **Malecón Tarapaca**, has fine old mansions with Portuguese *azulejos* (painted tiles), brilliantly extravagant in their Moorish inspiration. The impressive **Museo de las Culturas Indígenas Amazónicas** (Malecón Tarapacá 332; daily 8am–7.30pm; S/15) showcases the culture and rituals of the fourteen different indigenous peoples of the Amazon Basin, including pre-Columbian funerary urns, splendid ceremonial feathered headgear of the Wayana-Apari and the Kaiapo and a totem-pole-like mask of the Tikuna. You can also check out a trophy shrunken head of the Jivaro and learn about the Matses poison frog ceremony.

The nearby municipal **Museo Amazónico** (Malecón Tarapacá 386; Mon–Fri 9am–12.30pm & 2–5pm; S/3) is less impressive, and essentially a collection of life-size fibreglass statues modelled on people from various Amazonian indigenous groups. The statues are arranged around the cloistered courtyard of Iquitos' original Casa del Gobierno, which now houses the Ministerio de la Cultura.

Museo Barco Histórico "Ayapua"
Docked by the waterfront across the little Plaza Ramón Castilla from Casa Morey is this triple-decked 1906 **steamer**, the *Ayapua* (daily 9am–5pm; S/10), dating back to the height of the rubber boom. Inside the beautifully restored cabins are displays that cover the European

9

exploration of the Amazon, missionaries, the rubber boom and the notorious rubber barons who got rich from it, such as Carlos Fermín Fitzcarrald and Luis Morey, and the merciless exploitation of the indigenous populations because of it.

Próspero and around

Strolling along Calle Próspero, you'll see many fine examples of *azulejo*-covered buildings; a useful one is the 1905 **Casa Cohen**, the biggest supermarket in the centre. The name serves as a reminder that the rubber boom drew a mostly Moroccan, Sephardic Jewish community to Iquitos in the 1870s. There is a small Jewish cemetery within the main Peruvian **cemetery** (Av Alfonso Ugarte, at Av Fanning; daily 8am–7pm); both cemeteries are worth a visit, the former for its elegant tiled and Art Deco graves and the latter for wildly colourful and unusual ones – don't miss the tug boat or the castle.

Puerto Belén

Simply follow Próspero south for nine blocks from Plaza de Armas or take a *mototaxi*, turn left towards the river and you'll see the most memorable *barrio* in Iquitos, **Puerto Belén**. It consists almost entirely of wooden huts raised on stilts and houses constructed on floating platforms, which rise and fall to accommodate the changing water levels. When the tide is high enough, get a canoe to take you out on the flooded streets. Puerto Belén has changed little over its hundred years or so of life.

The **Mercado Belén** (best in the mornings around 7am–1pm, before the vultures –the winged-variety– take over the streetsis one of Peru's most atmospheric markets – ask for directions to Pasaje Paquito, the busy herbalist alley, which synthesizes the rich flavour of the place. This is one of the poorest areas of the city, so leave valuables at home and do not buy any animals or animal products from the market – it encourages illegal poaching, and setting them free may introduce disease into the forest. Do sample some of the more exotic edible offerings, though (see page 821).

ARRIVAL AND DEPARTURE

BY PLANE

Flights land at the Aeropuerto Internacional Francisco Secada Vignetta, 6km southwest of town. LATAM, Peruvian Airlines and Star Perú all have daily flights to Lima; Star Perú also flies to Tarapoto and Pucallpa, while Peruvian Airlines serves Pucallpa. At the time of going to press LATAM was about to start direct flights between Cusco and Iquitos. Taxis (S/20) and *mototaxis* (S/10–15) from the airport run to central Iquitos.

BY BOAT

Slow boats from Yurimaguas, Leticia or Tabatinga arrive at Puerto Masusa (Av 4.5km northeast of the Plaza de Armas. Motonaves Henry boats from Pucallpa arrive at their own Puerto Henry (Av La Marina and 28 de Julio). However, if you're travelling downriver from either Pucallpa or Yurimaguas, you will probably disembark at Nauta – the small river port at the end of the isolated 100km strip of tarred road that runs southwest from Iquitos; by transferring to a minibus here, you'll avoid several extra hours extra travel round a large meander in the Río Amazonas in favour of a two-hour short-cut by road. The new ferry *Amazonas* from Santa Rosa and the Colombian and Brazilian borders arrives at Puerto Napo (Av la Marina, at 28 de Julio), 3km north of the centre, as do the speedboats.

Local boats go from Puerto Bellavista Nanay (see page 823). If you plan to travel by boat, your basic choices are *rápidos* (speedboats) or *lanchas* (slow cargo boats), the former being more reliable and a lot faster, and the latter calmer and cheaper, with a less predictable departure time. Tickets for *lanchas* can only be bought from the ports on, or the day before, the day of travel (buy from the boat captain or from the designated office by the dock); speedboat companies have offices in town. On the Yurimaguas–Iquitos route, it's possible to stop off in Lagunas to find guides and inexpensive tours to Reserva Nacional Pacaya Samiria (see page 824). Prices on both types of boat include meals but the food is not great, so consider bringing your own. If you take a cargo boat, your best option is to swing your own hammock – easily purchased in a market; cabins tend to be airless boxes (though useful for storing your luggage). You will need to bring your own plate, mug and cutlery too.

To Lagunas and Yurimaguas Motonaves Eduardo, Puerto Masusa, (2–3 days; Mon, Wed & Fri at 6pm from S/100; ☎ 065 351 270). Flipper (see below) operates a *rápido* from Nauta (Mon, Wed & Fri, returning from Yurimaguas Tues, Thurs & Sat; 12hr; S/160); other speedboat operators have offices in Nauta.

To Pucallpa Motonaves Henry, Puerto Henry (4 days; Mon, Wed & Fri at 6pm; from S/100 ☎ 065 263 948).

To Santa Rosa (three-way border): departing from either Puerto Pesquero or Puerto Masusa (2.5–3 days; daily at 6pm except Sun; from S/80; ☎ 065 250 440). Golfinho, Jr Raimondi 378 (☎ 065 225 118), Flipper, Raimondi 350

AMAZON FIESTA

At the end of June (supposedly June 24, but actually spread over three or four days), the main **Fiesta de San Juan** takes place across the Peruvian jungle. It is believed that, on this date, Saint John blesses all local rivers; locals flock to bathe in them to bring good luck for the year to come. In Iquitos, dancing, parades and a feast mark the festival.

(☎065 766 303) and Transtur, Raimondii 384 (☎065 233188) have *rápidos* to the border (9–10hr; daily except Mon at 5am; S/150–170), leaving 5am(ish) from Puerto Napo. Ferry Amazonas, Jr Pevas 197 (☎065 233188, ⓦferryamazonias.com) runs a comfortable ferry service (12–15hr; Tues, Thurs & Sat at 5am; 12–15hr; S/160).

GETTING AROUND

By boat For any local journey on the river, head to Puerto Bellavista Nanay, in the suburb of Bellavista, by *mototaxi* (10min; S/4). Canoes can be rented and you can catch river *colectivos* to islands and other villages nearby.
By combi The majority of *combis* in Iquitos generally go one-way back and forth out of the city to the airport (S/1).
By mototaxi *Mototaxis* are ubiquitous and can be taken everywhere. Short hops are S/3.

INFORMATION

Tourist information The main iPerú tourist office is at Jr Napo 161 (Mon–Sat 9am–6pm, Sun 9am–1pm; ☎065 236 144). The staff provide free advocacy should you run into any problems with tour companies. There's also a helpful tourist information kiosk at the airport (daily 8am–9pm; ☎065 260 251).
Tourist permits If you are planning a trip into the jungle with just a guide (as opposed to a group) or to Pacaya Samiria National Reserve, then talk to SERNANP (☎065 223 555), located at C Chávez 930–942 (behind the military base).

ACCOMMODATION

El Colibrí Jr Nauta 172 ☎065 241 737, ⓔhostalelcolibri@hotmail.com; map p.818. A modern, clean and secure guesthouse stacked up on four floors right in the centre. Double or triple rooms have cable TV, private bath with hot water, a/c (S/20 extra) or fan There's also a decent breakfast (S/8). A good deal. **S/50**
Cristal Corazón B&B C Nanay 130 ☎065 222 070, ⓦcristalcorazon.com; map p.818. A cosy B&B with orthopaedic beds, healthy breakfasts, a large communal kitchen and a patio. Mosquito nets and repellent can be provided. Host Miguel Pizango can organize expeditions, lodge stays and *ayahuasca* ceremonies. Dorms **S/25**, doubles **S/50**

Flying Dog Hostel Malecón Tarapacá 592 ☎065 223 755, ⓦflyingdogperu.com; map p.818. The city's best hostel in a perfect location, complete with colourful rooms (some en suite), spacious guest lounge with graffitied testimony from happy guests, shared kitchen and plenty of *buena onda* (good vibes). Dorms **S/28**, doubles **S/99**
Green Track Hostel Jr Palma 516 ☎065 600 805, ⓦgreentrack-jungle.com; map p.818. Popular backpacker haunt a short distance from the plaza with all facilities that travellers expect, as well as an appealing courtyard filled with greenery, and a rooftop terrace. Rooms are small, and bare, with no lock; dorms are better value though mattresses can be squidgy. *Green Track* also has its own jungle lodge (see page 818) in the Reserva Tapiche and the owner is renowned for his efforts to protect the local wildlife. Dorms **S/26**, doubles **S/65**
Hospedaje Neydita Morona 979 Parque Sargento Lores ☎948 635 900, ⓦhospedajeneydita.com; map p.818. You'll get a warm welcome from your hosts in this spotless guesthouse, a 15min walk from the waterfront. Rooms have fans, tiled floors and more furniture than usual for these bargain rates; a clean guests' kitchen provides filtered water and hot drinks. **S/60**

EATING

Coma y Punto Cevichería Jr Napo 488 ☎065 225 268; map p.818. A popular lunchtime place that serves some of Iquitos' best *ceviche*, made from different types of river fish (from S/16). Other dishes include portions of *arroz con mariscos* (seafood rice) and *chicharrón de pescado* (chunks of fried, battered fish). Mains from S/20. Tues–Sun 11am–4pm.
★ **Dawn on the Amazon Café** Malecón Maldonado 185 ☎065 234 921, ⓦdawnontheamazoncafe. com; map p.818. Hugely popular, relaxed spot on the

★ TREAT YOURSELF

La Casa Fitzcarraldo Av La Marina 2153, Punchana ☎065 601 138, ⓦcasafitzcarraldo. com; map p.818. For your own slice of Amazonian and movie history, stay in this luxurious B&B where the cast and crew of *Fitzcarraldo* lodged during the filming (Mick Jagger stayed in the Blue Room – S/386) before he quit to tour with the Stones). The owner, Walter, was the producer on the film and speaks five languages. It's slightly out of the centre (5min by *motokar*; S/4), so you'll feel you've stumbled out of the city and into an orchid-rich jungle oasis. If you can't afford the stay, S/10 will get you in to use their pool (9am–6pm) and treehouse or to eat in their excellent restaurant. Book ahead as there are only seven rooms, individually priced; airport pick-up included. **S/258**

9

waterfront that runs the gamut from American-style all-day breakfasts and ample salads (S/10) to spicy Mexican fajitas, falafel burgers and grilled fish. Owner Bill is a mine of local information. Mains from around S/20. Mon–Sat 7.30am–10pm.

Huasaí Jr Fizcarrald 131 ⓣ065 242 222; map p.818. Family-run traditional Peruvian restaurant serving regional dishes – plenty of rice, beans and plantain – always heaving with locals. Serves an excellent and huge S/16 lunch *menú* including starter, main and a jug of juice and has a vast array of breakfast combos (S/10–13). Simply delicious. Mon–Sat 7am–4pm

★ **Karma Café** Napo 138 ⓣ065 223 663; map p.818. All psychedelic wall hangings, incense and bright colours, with plenty to please vegetarians (falafel burgers, veggie curry) and spice lovers (Thai curries; S/27). Also huge fruit juices and salads (S/20), and in the evening the place gets so packed with travellers that you'll be lucky to find a spare beanbag to sprawl on. Live music Thurs–Sun, plus dance classes, yoga and other activities. Daily 9am–late.

Mercado Belén Puerto Belén; map p.818. The chaotic Mercado Belén is a great spot for cheap eats, particularly generous helpings of fresh fruit juices (try the *jugo especial* – jungle juice), and real rainforest staples of juicy Amazon grubs on a stick, *sikisapa*, fried leafcutter ants, rice-studded *morcilla* (black pudding) and more. From S/3. Daily 7am–5pm.

Pizzería Antica Jr Napo, between the plaza and the Malecón ⓣ065 241 988; map p.818. A large space with ceiling fans and driftwood decor, this Italian joint has an extensive menu of wood-fired pizzas (from S/22), pasta and immense calzones, including good veggie options and some dishes incorporating jungle ingredients. Daily noon–midnight.

El Sitio Sargento Lores 404; map p.818. Recognisable by the graffiti from their many satisfied customers in lieu of wall decoration, this hole-in-the wall café specializes in *anticuchos* (kebabs) – from cheese, chicken and apricot to an all-veggie skewer (S/5–8). Choose from the chill cabinet and sip a beer, while waiting for them to be char-grilled. Mon–Sat 8.30am–1.30pm & 6.30–11pm.

DRINKING AND NIGHTLIFE

Arandú Bar Malecón Maldonado 113; map p.818. With a prime location on the Boulevard, this bar is often packed in the evenings, with seating spilling outside. Serves a range of drinks (pisco sour S/16, large beer S/8) and a few snacks. Daily 4pm until late.

★ **El Musmuqui** Raymondi 382; map p.818. A specialist in exotic cocktails, this tiny but lively bar is packed with locals every night. Come here to try traditional jungle liquors, many of which are said to have strong aphrodisiac properties (S/6–8), hence the raunchy names and crimson lighting. Try the house speciality charapita ardiente. Also serves snack food. Mon–Thurs & Sun 5pm–midnight, Fri & Sat 5pm–3am.

Noa Disco Fitzcarrald 298 ⓣ065 222 555, ⓦnoadisco.com; map p.818. Easily identified after midnight by the huge number of flashy motorbikes lined up outside, this is the most popular and lively of the clubs in Iquitos, though drinks are expensive. It has five bars and DJs pump out Latino music at high volume, with occasional live bands. S/15 entry. Thurs–Sat 10pm–6am.

SHOPPING

Craft stalls Malecón Maldonado s/n. The Centro Artesanal Anaconda (map p.818) and surrounding craft stalls on the waterfront sell a really good selection of psychedelic Shipibo embroidery, the designs allegedly inspired by *ayahuasca* visions.

Mercado Artesanal San Juan Some 2km east of the airport along the main road. Popular souvenir market where you can pick up Shipibo embroidery and jewellery.

ANIMAL RESCUE CENTRES

Visiting an **animal rescue centre** is often a core activity of the most popular day trips tour operators offer from Iquitos. However, many are insalubrious animal encounters in the form of visits to self-proclaimed "animal rescue centres" where you're offered the opportunity to wrap an anaconda or python around yourself or hold a sloth or monkey for that exotic holiday snap. These are nothing more than decrepit zoos and are best avoided, since visiting them perpetuates the **illegal animal trade** in endangered species and dooms the unhappy monkeys, sloths, macaws and snakes to a short life in a cage. Even in the more reputable animal sanctuaries that give refuge to injured or trafficked animals rescued by the authorities, animals are rarely rehabilitated and released back into the wild. Although these animals generally live in better conditions than in the places from where they were rescued, visiting tour guides – keen to increase their chance of a tip – may rattle cages or disturb animals to coax them into showing their face for their clients to photograph. Since all such centres are heavily reliant on the tourist dollar, it is hard for the centres to regulate such behaviour.

The exception to the above is the **Centro de Rescate Amazónico** (see page 823), which rehabilitates orphaned manatees.

Other items not to miss are the vases carved out of beautiful tropical hardwoods, some of them true works of art.

DIRECTORY

Banks and exchange Banco de Crédito, Jr Putumayo 201; Banco de la Nación, Jr Condamine, cuadra 4; Banco Continental, Jr Próspero, cuadra 4; and Interbank, Jr Próspero, cuadra 1, all have global ATMs (the moneychangers on Próspero can't always be trusted).

Consulates Brazil, Jr Lores 363 (☎ 065 235 151); Colombia, C Calvo de Araujo 431 (☎ 065 231 461).

Health Clínica Ana Stahl, Av La Marina 285 (☎ 065 252 535) is a good 24hr private clinic. TrámazonDoctor, Jr Bolívar 222 (☎ 959 464 131, ⓦ tramazondoctor.com), provides a 24hr emergency callout service.

Immigration You can extend or renew your Peruvian tourist card or visa at Migraciónes, Cáceres, block 18, Morona Cocha ☎ 065 235 371 (Mon–Fri 8am–4pm, Sat 8am–noon).

Laundry Lavandería Imperial, Jr Nauta, cuadra 1 (Mon–Sat 8am–8pm).

Post office SERPOST, C Arica 402 (Mon–Fri 8am–5pm, Sat 8am–2pm).

Tourist police Sargento Lores 834 (☎ 065 242 081).

DAY-TRIPS FROM IQUITOS

For an inexpensive boat trip on the Amazon, and one of the best chances of spotting **pink river dolphins,** head for the confluence of the ríos Amazonas and Nanay. Take a river *colectivo* from Puerto Bellavista Nanay in Iquitos to Padre Cocha, on the Río Nanay (S/5; 20min), and keep a look out on the way there – and back. To encounter a different aquatic mammal, travel 2km past the airport, to the Centro de Rescate Amazónico (daily 9am–3pm; S/20; show passport on entry). The centre specializes principally in the rehabilitation of orphaned baby **manatees** whose mothers

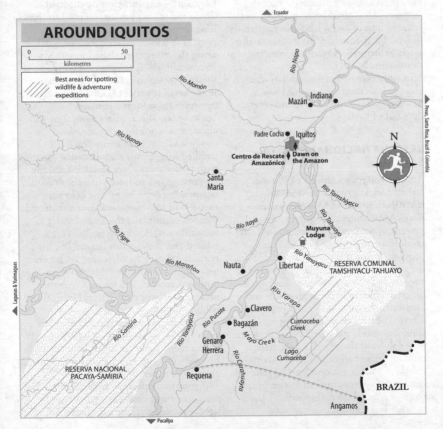

AROUND IQUITOS

0 — 50
kilometres

Best areas for spotting wildlife & adventure expeditions

Ecuador

Río Napo

Río Momón

Mazán Indiana

Río Nanay

Padre Cocha Iquitos

Centro de Rescate Dawn on
Amazónico the Amazon

Santa
María

N

Río Tamshiyacu

Río Tahuayo

Río Itaya

Muyuna
Lodge

Río Tigre

Río Yanayacu

RESERVA COMUNAL
TAMSHIYACU-TAHUAYO

Río Marañon Nauta Libertad

Río Yarapa

Clavero

Río Pucate Bagazán Cumaceba
Creek

Río Yanayacu Mayo Creek

Genaro
Herrera Lago
Cumaceba

Río Samiria Río Carahuata

RESERVA NACIONAL
PACAYA-SAMIRIA Requena

BRAZIL

Angamos

Pucallpa

Lagunas & Yurimaguas

Pevas, Santa Rosa, Brazil & Colombia

9

SHAMANS AND AYAHUASCA SESSIONS

Ayahuasca retreats have long been a booming business in Iquitos, and account for a third of its tourism industry. A jungle vine (*Banisteriopsis caapi*) that grows in the Western Amazon region, *ayahuasca* has been used for thousands of years as a "teacher plant", gaining a worldwide reputation for divination, inspiration and healing of physical, emotional and spiritual ailments. The vine is generally mixed with other rainforest plants to transform it into a bitter-tasting hallucinogenic brew, usually taken in a public session with a shaman, following a period of preparation – in terms of diet, for example.

While each indigenous community in the area has a shaman, not all practitioners who offer *ayahuasca* sessions in and around Iquitos are qualified to do so. If mixed with a particular plant, or if you have an allergic reaction, *ayahuasca* can lead to dangerously high blood pressure and even death, though this is rare. Since the plant is a powerful hallucinogen, participants may undergo hours of intense visions, along with intense purging (vomiting). The business is currently not regulated at all; ⓦ ayaadvisor.org is a good starting point if you want to read about the experiences of others and decide what's right for you.

There are dozens of *ayahuasca* retreats around Iquitos, some of them very upmarket, with plush accommodation and a cleansing superfood diet, and while it's difficult to give specific recommendations, the **Temple of the Way of Light** (ⓦ templeofthewayoflight.org) has many female Shipibo shamans – and some female-only retreats –as well as a good reputation for combining *ayahuasca* ceremonies with charitable and environmental work.

have been killed by poachers. The manatees are nursed back to health and released into the wild when they are ready to fend for themselves. Tours are usually given in Spanish. A *mototaxi* from the city centre costs S/10–12.

To truly experience Amazonian wildlife and the lush rainforest round Iquitos, however, you will need to spend several days out of Iquitos.

RESERVA NACIONAL PACAYA SAMIRIA

Around 130km southwest of Iquitos, several hours upriver, the **RESERVA NACIONAL PACAYA SAMIRIA** comprises over 20,000 square kilometres (about 1.5 percent of the landmass of Peru) of lush rainforest and is home to the Cocama peoples. The area is a swampland during the rainy season (Dec–March), when the streams and rivers all rise; as such you'll see different wildlife in the high-water and low-water seasons (both good in different ways). The reserve is famous for its abundance of fauna, particularly pink and grey dolphins, river turtles, manatees, caimans, giant otters, numerous species of monkeys and an astounding 450-plus bird species. Away from human settlement, there's a good chance of spotting a jaguar or other big mammal.

Lagunas – exploration by dugout
To do the reserve justice you need to spend time here. The cheapest and most rewarding way to explore the rich wildlife along the mangrove-tangled waterways of Pacaya Samiria, is to do a tour with one of the four **community tourism** organizations in the small town of **LAGUNAS**, two days upstream from Iquitos towards Yurimaguas. This requires more time and effort, and is not for everyone, since conditions are challenging: you'll be paddled in a narrow **dugout canoe** (often with no seat back) by a Spanish-speaking Cocama guide, and sleep in a combination of rustic huts over water and on a thin mattress or in a hammock over a sheltered wooden platform in the forest (under a mosquito net). Catering facilities are limited and the menu is limited but the rewards for such an adventure are superb: total immersion in the rainforest – no outboard motors, few tourists, a chance to get to know your guide(s), and exceptional wildlife-spotting opportunities. Come prepared from Iquitos/Yurimaguas with extra snacks, water (or the means to purify it), repellent, sunscreen, hat, hammock, first aid kit, torch, biodegradable toiletries, extra toilet paper and so on.

All four **tour operators** have offices on the main street and charge the same rates for similar packages. Three days is the

IQUITOS TOURS AND JUNGLE LODGES

The massive river system around Iquitos offers some of the best access to indigenous villages, lodges and primary rainforest in the entire Amazon. While it's often easier to travel with a tour company, when it comes to visiting indigenous villages, you are better off making contact with villagers themselves. A good place to start is to ask iPerú for a list of contacts for indigenous communities engaged in *turismo vivencial* (community-based tourism), and of indigenous certified guides, who will have links with their home village. Some lodge tours include a visit to the nearby Bora and Yagua communities where the locals put on traditional costume and a song and dance for visitors; the experience is contrived, and although it's arguably a way to preserve what's left of their culture, most of the money stays with the tour operator.

If you've come to Iquitos to see Amazonian wildlife in the wild, staying at a jungle lodge is generally the best option. Cheapest of all is to access the Reserva Nacional Pacaya Samiria from Lagunas (see page 824).

When choosing a lodge, consider the location (its distance from Iquitos and whether it's on the Amazon, or up a tributary, where wildlife sightings are likely to be better), the company's commitment to conservation, involvement with local communities, the level of comfort you want and what's included in the price. Most lodge itineraries will include dolphin-watching, fishing for piranha, visiting an indigenous village, jungle walks and caiman-spotting on the river by night.

In general, the best companies should be booked in advance, have fixed prices and never tout for business in the street. Prices below are based on a three-day/two-night stay per person sharing, and the addresses included are for the Iquitos-based booking offices.

TOUR OPERATORS AND LODGES

San Pedro Lodge 1hr north of Iquitos by car and boat ☎ 955 628 164, ⓦ sanpedrolodge.com. Excellent value, this small community-managed lodge 1hr north of Iquitos on the Río Yarapa, lies close to the Bora community of Padre Cocha. Accommodation for twelve is in very basic wood-and-thatch cabañas (no electricity) with shared and private cold-water ablutions – or you can choose to sleep in a tent. **S/950**

★ **Muyuna Lodge** Putumayo 163 ☎ 065 242 858, ⓦ muyuna.com. Overlooking the narrow Río Yanayacu, in the Reserva Comunal Tamshiyacu-Tahuayo, *Muyuna* offers attractive, en-suite, mosquito-proof thatched cabins and activities such as forest walks and dolphin-spotting river safaris, and even a little kayaking. The lodge works hard to distinguish itself as a protector of wild animals and most of their guides come from nearby indigenous communities. **S/1230**

minimum tour worth taking – five is better, but a couple of the guides have taken tourists for up to twenty days, finishing up at the far end of the park, close to Nauta.

Costs are an affordable S/50/person per day, including all meals, accommodation, transport and guiding (in Spanish); in addition, bring sufficient cash to cover a night either side of your tour in one of the town's sparse lodgings (doubles around S/60), your onward transport, tip for the guide and the park fee (S/60 for two to three days; S/150 four days or more) payable to SERNANP at the park entrance before you start paddling.

ARRIVAL AND DEPARTURE

By boat The slow *lanchas* between Iquitos and Yurimaguas all stop at Lagunas though their timings are unpredictable. Daily *rápidos* from Nauta (11–12hr; S/110) and Yurimaguas (5hr; S/50) also stop at Lagunas.

INFORMATION AND TOURS

Tour operators Two recommended operators are: ACATUPEL (ⓦ facebook.com/acatupel) the community-run organization, a 20min walk up the main drag from the dock, or S/1 by mototaxi; and Huayruro Tours (ⓦ peruselva.com), which can also sometimes be contacted in Yurimaguas as well as on the main street in Lagunas.

The Southern Amazon

Part of the Peruvian Amazon basin – a large, forested region with a searingly hot and humid climate, punctuated with sudden cold spells (*friajes*) between June and August – the **southern Amazon** regions of Peru have only been

9

systematically explored since the 1950s and were largely unknown to Europeans until the twentieth century, when rubber began to leave Peru through Bolivia and Brazil, eastwards along the rivers. Cusco (see page 750) is the best base for trips into the jungles of the southern selva, with road access to the frontier town of **Puerto Maldonado**, itself a good base for budget travellers. The nearby forests of Madre de Dios are rich in flora and fauna, especially in the R**eserva Biósfera del Manu**, though the **Reserva Nacional de Tambopata** is more readily accessible to budget travellers.

MADRE DE DIOS

Named after the broad river that flows through the heart of the southern jungle, the still relatively wild *departamento* of **MADRE DE DIOS** is changing rapidly, with agribusinesses moving in to clear mahogany trees and set up brazil-nut plantations, and prospectors panning for gold dust along the riverbanks. Much of this activity is illegal, resulting in increasing pressures on the environment and on the indigenous communities that live there. Nearly half of Madre de Dios *departamento*'s 78,000 square kilometres are theoretically protected in national parks and protected areas such as **La Reserva Biosfera del Manu, La Reserva Nacional Tambopata** and the **Parque Nacional Bahuaja-Sonene**, between them containing some of the richest flora and fauna in the world.

Madre de Dios still feels very much like a frontier zone, centred on the rapidly growing river town of **Puerto Maldonado**, supposedly founded by legendary explorer and rubber baron Fitzcarrald.

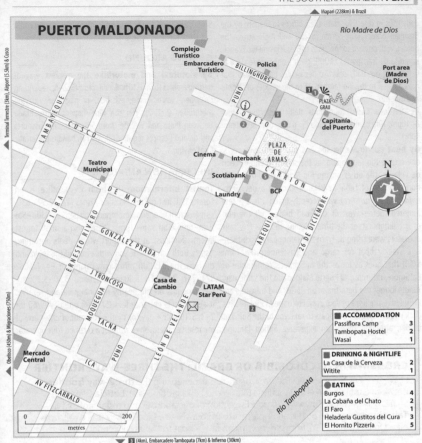

PUERTO MALDONADO

ACCOMMODATION
Passiflora Camp	3
Tambopata Hostel	2
Wasai	1

DRINKING & NIGHTLIFE
La Casa de la Cerveza	2
Witite	1

EATING
Burgos	4
La Cabaña del Chato	2
El Faro	3
Heladería Gustitos del Cura	1
El Hornito Pizzería	5

Puerto Maldonado

Despite its position firmly on the Carretera Interoceánica, connecting the Peruvian and Brazilian coasts, the jungle town of **PUERTO MALDONADO** still has a raw feel to it, its *mototaxi*-clogged streets often culminating in pitted dirt tracks. With an economy based on gold panning, logging, cattle ranching and brazil-nut gathering, it has grown enormously over the last twenty years, becoming the thriving capital of a region that feels very much on the threshold of major upheavals.

The town is centred on a pleasant **Plaza de Armas**. Ten blocks from the plaza is the large, bustling **market**, which covers an entire block, and if you follow Avenida Fitzcarrald beyond it, you'll reach the **Obelisco** (generally 8am–8pm but Wed am only & Sun pm only; S/3), a phallic tower offering an expansive panorama of the entire city and the jungle beyond, though the view from the roof terrace of the *Hotel Centenario* is even better – and free.

ARRIVAL AND DEPARTURE

By plane Puerto Maldonado International Airport is 4km from the centre of town. *Mototaxis* cost around S/7 for the ride. LATAM and Star Perú have daily flights to Cusco (50min) and Lima (1hr 40min).

By bus All buses arrive at the Terminal Terrestre, located 4km away from the airport and 3.5km from the town centre, along Carretera Tambopata. A dozen bus companies run overnight services to Cusco (Cruz del Sur and Movil Tours are the most comfortable); there are also direct departures to Juliaca, with connections to Puno and Arequipa. Transportes Turismo Iñapari (Jr Ica 547; ☎ 948 000 515) and Turismo Real Dorado, corner of Ica and Ribera, make

9

daily trips in colectivos from their offices to Iñapari, by the Brazilian border (3hr 30min; S/25), and Assis across the border, with onward connections to Brasiléia and Río Branco. Empresa de Transportes FAQUIP, on Jr Lambayeque close to Cajamarca, has daily *colectivo* departures up the road that runs parallel to the Río Tambopata to the villages of Chonta and Infierno.

Destinations Cusco (numerous daily, departing either 8–10pm; 10hr); Juliaca, for Puno (5–6 daily 6pm & 6.30pm; 10hr).

By boat Puerto Maldonado has two main river ports: one on the Río Tambopata, at the southern end of León de Velarde, the other on the Río Madre de Dios, at the northern end of León de Velarde, though a new jetty (*embarcadero turístico*) was recently inaugurated a few hundred metres west of the road bridge, off the end of Jr Billinghurst; at the time of going to press few tour operators were using it. From the Tambopata dock there is a weekly boat for cargo and passengers (Fri 7am; S/50) that goes as far as the indigenous community of Baltimore, returning to Puerto Maldonado the same day. Jungle lodges use both the main docks, and transfers are included in the price of your stay. From the Madre de Dios dock you can hire private boats to take you to the Bolivian border, although this is an expensive option (around S/600; 6hr), and traffic beyond is infrequent, so you could get stuck for several days.

GETTING AROUND

By mototaxi and motorbike The quickest way of getting around town is to hail a *mototaxi* (S/2–6, depending on where you're going; ask first) or passenger-carrying motorbikes (S/1–2). You can rent mopeds along Prada between Puno and Velarde (from S/5 per hour; passports and driving licences required) if you can handle the erratic local driving.

INFORMATION AND TOURS

Tourist information The main iPerú office is on Loreto 390, just off the Plaza de Armas (☎082 571 830, ✉iperuptomaldonado@promperu.gob.pe; Mon–Sat 9am–6pm, Sun 9am–1pm). There's also a small tourist information kiosk at the airport which meets oncoming flights. Both can provide you with a map of the town and the area. The SERNANP office at Av Cajamarca, 943 (☎082 571 247; Mon–Fri 8.30am–12.30pm, 3.30–5.30pm), has handouts on the nearby national park and reserve. It also collects entrance fees (S/30 for one day; S/60 for 2–3; S/150 for 4 days or more). You cannot enter any of the reserves themselves without a certified tour operator

---

CROSSING INTO COLOMBIA OR BRAZIL: THE THREE-WAY FRONTIER

Leaving or entering Peru via the Amazon means experiencing the **three-way frontier** between Santa Rosa (Peru), Tabatinga (Brazil) and Leticia (Colombia). **Leticia** (see page 560) is a lively jungle town with a good selection of guesthouses and restaurants, while **Tabatinga** (see page 561) is an unpretty urban sprawl a few blocks away (the two towns blend into one another), from where you can take a boat to Manaus if continuing on in Brazil.

The route by river from Iquitos to **Santa Rosa** takes some 9–10hr by *rápido* (speedboat; S/160 one-way, including meals) or 2.5–3 days in a standard cargo boat (from S/100 hammock one-way; cabin from S/160). Bring or buy (S/12) your own hammock, and a plate, mug and cutlery is a good idea too. In 2017 a new, larger ferry started operating three times a week between Iquitos and Santa Rosa (❿ferryamazonia.com; 12–15hr; S/160), with plans to extend service up to Yurimaguas and Pucallpa later in 2018.

Boats drop you off at immigration in Santa Rosa (daily 7.30am–5pm) where you must obtain an **exit stamp** from Peru if you're leaving (show your tourist card to do this), or get an **entry stamp and tourist card** if arriving. Larger boats may take you all the way to Tabatinga (Brazil) or Leticia (Colombia), in which case an immigration official may board the vessel and do the paperwork there and then. If not, Brazilian entry and exit formalities are processed at the Policía Federal's office, Av da Amizade (daily 7am–noon & 2–6pm; ☎097 3412 2180) in Tabatinga. US citizens need a visa to enter Brazil, which must be obtained in advance. To officially enter Colombia, take a short *mototaxi* ride to Leticia's airport and get a Colombian tourist card from the immigration office there (daily 8am–5pm). Motorized canoes connect Santa Rosa with Tabatinga and Leticia (15–20min).

Heading up the Río Napo to Ecuador from Iquitos (3–4 days) involves several boats: first to Mazán (2hr), then, after crossing the neck of the peninsula by *mototaxi* to the Napo port in Mazán, another (infrequent) boat to Pantoja (2 days), where you need to get your Peruvian exit stamp, before catching another speedboat to Nuevo Rocafuerte on the border, where you will get an Ecuadorian entry stamp.

PUERTO MALDONADO JUNGLE LODGES

Although it's a lot more expensive compared with independent travel, a stay at a jungle lodge saves time and adds varying degrees of comfort. It also ensures that you're exploring the jungle with someone who knows the area, who probably speaks English and can introduce you to the flora, fauna, culture and regions. It's best to book through the lodge offices before travelling to Puerto Maldonado, though in low season, you can usually negotiate the price and organize something on the spot for the following day. The cheapest option with jungle lodges is a two-day and one-night tour, but then you will spend most of your time travelling and sleeping, so it's best to allow at least three to four days.

A stay at one of the many lodges around Puerto Maldonado, mainly on the ríos Madre de Dios and Tambopata, offers a good taste of the rainforest, and the cost typically includes full board (though not tips for guides or drinks), transfers, some activities and bilingual guides. The quality of wildlife sightings depends on the location; the further you travel from Puerto Maldonado, the more likely you are to see large mammals, particularly along the Río Tambopata, as there's considerably less in the way of human settlement.

The prices given below are for three days/two nights per person sharing.

JUNGLE LODGES

Explorer's Inn Puerto Maldonado ☎082 572 078, ⓦexplorersinn.com. Over two hours upriver in the Reserva Tambopata and featuring en-suite rustic doubles and triples. It offers 38km of forest trails and sits in an area of staggering biodiversity, with 620 species of bird spotted in the surrounding forest. Activities include canoeing on the oxbow lake of Cococoha (inhabited by giant otters), and visits to a macaw clay lick, accompanied by experienced naturalist guides. Activities limited on the final day. English, French and German spoken. U̲S̲$̲2̲9̲9̲

Hospedaje El Gato Jr Junín cuadra 1 s/n ☎941223676, ⓦbaltimore.org.pe. Community-run association involving homestays in rustic accommodation for those who want to immerse themselves more in local culture as well as experiencing the surrounding rainforest. Even cheaper if you get there

on your own steam via combi plus a 15km hike to the village. U̲S̲$̲2̲0̲6̲

Las Tres Chimbadas Puerto Maldonado ☎999605519, ⓦtreschimbadaslakelodge.com. On an oxbow lake an hour up the Río Tambopata, this budget lodge has a long, thatched dorm as well as private cabins. Activities include a farming tour with local villagers as well as excursions on the lake – inhabited by giant river otters – and rainforest walks. Dorms U̲S̲$̲2̲2̲9̲, doubles U̲S̲$̲2̲4̲0̲

Wasai Tambopata Lodge Parque Grau on Jr Billinghurst ☎082 572 290, ⓦwasai.com. Run by *Wasai* in Puerto Maldonado, this lodge lies a 3hr boat ride up the Río Tambopata (though slightly cheaper three-day tours prefer to take the overland route). Highlights include visiting the famous "El Chuncho" macaw claylick, kayaking and fishing, with optional adventure activities thrown in. U̲S̲$̲3̲9̲2̲

or independent guide (iPerú has a list); if you follow the latter route, or intend to enter with an indigenous guide from a *comunidad nativa*, make sure that they or you have paid for the entry permit from SERNANP before you set out.

Visas Migraciones is at Av 28 de Julio 467 (Mon–Fri 8am–1pm; ☎082 571 069). Get your passport stamped here if leaving for Bolivia by river.

Tour operators *Tambopata Hostel* (☎082 574 201; see page 829), run by a former Rainforest Expeditions guide, offers authentic backpacker jungle tours (1–5 days), including trips to lagos Valencia and Sandoval, where you stay overnight with a local family; they also head up the Río Tambopata to their own lodge, taking in clay licks, a little kayaking, fishing and various wildlife-viewing activities. Green House Tambopata (☎082 637 636, ⓦgreenhousetambopata.com) also offers a variety of affordable tours from wildlife-watching and biking

to fishing, kayaking or joining in community activities; they also possess an inexpensive guesthouse.

ACCOMMODATION

Passiflora Camp Km 4.8 on the Corridor Turístico Tambopata ☎966 382 139, ⓦcorredortambopataaootam.org; map p.827. Set among fruit trees and pleasantly wooded grounds are three rooms (including a two-bed dorm) in two delightful rustic cabins on stilts with shared bathrooms, and shaded hammock space. There's rewarding birdwatching but boat trips, mountain biking and other activities can easily be added to the menu (for relatively little cost) by the congenial hosts. Breakfast is included but other meals can be prepared on request. No wi-fi. Dorms S̲/̲8̲0̲,̲ doubles S̲/̲9̲7̲

★ **Tambopata Hostel** 234 ☎082 574 201, ⓦtambopatahostel.com; map p.827. Owned by a

9

professional local guide, this great-value pad has stark, high-ceilinged dorms and private rooms (some en suite) – though with limited privacy. Rooms are screened and there's a communal kitchen and laundry but the star attraction is the refreshing pool area at the back (complete with hammocks), plus the affordable jungle tours. Dorms S/30, doubles S/70

★ **Wasai** Parque Grau on Jr Billinghurst ☎082 572 290, ⓦwasai.com; map p.827. The best of the higher-end options, offering fine views over the Río Madre de Dios, and an apple-shaped swimming pool with a waterfall and bar set among trees. All rooms are cabin-style with TV and shower, and staff here also organize local tours and run the *Wasai Lodge* (see page 829). A new hostel section comprises two small wooden dorms sharing a balcony with river views and bathroom facilities (bed only) and a simple private room with breakfast included. Dorms S/39, doubles S/111, cabins S/242

EATING

★ **Burgos** Av 26 de Diciembre, Cuadra 1 ☎082 502 373; map p.827. This open-fronted restaurant with woven prickly-pear lamps and dangling clay pots serves a range of regional dishes heavily influenced by Amazonian ingredients (*juanes* with wild pig and *criollo* salad, grilled fish with star-fruit sauce) and an evening buffet for S/24 (pick a main and then help yourself to fried yuca, sweet potato, salads and more) – get there early for it to be fresh. The exotic cocktails (starfruit sour, for example) pack a punch. Mains S/22–32. Daily noon–3pm & 6–10pm.

La Cabaña del Chato Loreto 385; map p.827. Hands down the town's best *cevichería*, this cheery wooden cabaña is a bit of a squeeze, with only a handful of tables. There are several *ceviches* on offer (S/10–15): one with a serious kick, "el classico", and a fiery *ceviche Amazónico* with cocomo. Daily 9am–2pm.

El Faro At Wasai Parque Grau on Jr Billinghurst ☎082 572 290; map p.827. Under a breezy rancho with views of the river, you can feast on a good-value buffet breakfast (S/15) and an executive *menú del día* for lunch (S/10); evening dishes are moderately priced (S/20–26), à la carte and well prepared – try the steak in cocoma sauce. Daily 7–9am, noon–2pm & 6–9pm.

Heladería Gustitos del Cura Jr Loreto 286; map p.827. The profits at this pleasant café, run by a Swiss priest, help fund a local orphanage. Try one of their seventeen exotic flavours of home-made ice cream (S/3/scoop), as well as sweet cakes (S/6) and light bites. Daily 8am–8pm.

El Hornito Pizzería Jr Carrión 271, 1st floor ☎082 572 082; map p.827. This is arguably Puerto Maldonado's best pizzeria, with ample portions of wood-fired pizza, calzones and an array of pasta dishes. Six-piece pizzas from S/22 to S/68 for a twenty-piece "Terminator" size. Daily 6–10pm.

DRINKING AND NIGHTLIFE

Weekends round the main plaza are often heaving as folk flock here from as far away as Brazil and even Cusco to party. Watch for the places with live cumbia bands and dancers.

La Casa de la Cerveza Jr Velarde, at Jr Carrión; map p.827. Popular two-storey watering hole right on the Plaza, with a good range of beers and some stronger options if you feel like courting oblivion. Live music on Saturday nights after 9pm. Daily 6pm–late.

Witite Jr Velarde 151 map p.827. This popular club packs with 20-somethings for some pop, rock and salsa tunes on Friday and Saturday nights and keeps going until the early hours of the morning. Entry is sometimes S/10. Fri & Sat 11pm–6am.

Wildlife reserves around Puerto Maldonado

Madre de Dios boasts spectacular virgin lowland rainforest and exceptional wildlife. Brazil-nut-tree trails, a range of lodges, some excellent local guides and ecologists plus indigenous and colonist cultures are all within a few hours of Puerto Maldonado. There are two main ways to explore: either by arranging your own boat and boatman, or by taking an excursion up to one of the lodges, which is more expensive but also more convenient.

Less than one hour downriver from Puerto Maldonado (1hr 30min return) is **Lago Sandoval**, a large oxbow lake, home to caimans, giant otters and a host of birds. It's best to stay here overnight and do a boat ride on the lake in the early morning – the best time for wildlife-spotting, though it's also possible to do the lake as a day-trip. Take one of the recommended tours (see page 829) or hire a boat (around S/160 for up to five people) to drop you off at the start of the trail (1hr walk to the lake) and to pick you up later. A guide is compulsory (ask IPerú for contact details names). You'll also need to pay the reserve entry fee: S/30 or S/60 if you're staying overnight. Bring your own food and water.

Further along the river, 60km from Puerto Maldonado, lies the huge **Lago Valencia**. It's easiest to visit it from one of the lodges along Río Madre de Dios; its remoteness increases your chances of seeing wildlife and the lake is also good for fishing.

MANU ON A BUDGET

Tours to Manu are much more expensive than to Tambopata, and since you've to travel from Cusco, they involve a whole day of travelling (on a dirt road for some of the way) to get to and from the nearest action. For adventurous budget travellers, the best option is to sample some of the **cloudforest** in the Zona Cultural; take a bus to the small town of Pillcopata (8hr from the San Jerónimo bus stop in Cusco; buses leave when full, so go early in the morning) and Atalaya – a further 40min by *colectivo*. In this area, there are a few local *hospedajes* and basic lodges favoured by birdwatchers. The lodges are generally owned by tour companies, and visited by tour groups, but provided there is space you may be able to negotiate a deal on the spot. Alternatively, local hospedajes may be able to set you up with a local guide to explore some of the surrounding forest, or take you out on the water; you would not, however, be allowed into the Zona Reservada.

Indigenous community tourism associations get you into the forest, for relatively little cost, as well as offering opportunities to learn about their cultures (though you'll need some Spanish): The Machiguenga community in Shipetiari runs a lodge (☏084 225595, ⊛alberguepankotsi.com; S/196/day); also contact the Turismo Comunitario Wanamei (26 de Diciembre 276 ☏082 572 539 in Puerto Maldonado, and Av Sol 814 ☏084 234608 in Cusco); they run multi-day tours into their reserve.

South of Puerto Maldonado, Río Tambopata flows into the heart of the Reserva Nacional Tambopata, where you'll find several excellent lodges, as well as the indigenous communities of Infierno and Batimore. The remote Parque Nacional Bahuaja-Sonene is even further upstream (6hr minimum) – though also accessible from Río Madre de Dios by the Bolivian border – and features some of the best wildlife in the Peruvian Amazon as well as the Tambopata Research Centre, located next to the Colpa de Guacamayos – one of the largest **macaw clay licks** in the Amazon. To visit the reserve and the national park, book a guided tour at one of the lodges; alternatively, enquire at the Iperú office about communities engaged in turismo vivencial (community-based tourism), whom you can deal with directly, and reach through a combination of bus and local river transport.

RESERVA BIÓSFERA DEL MANU

Encompassing almost 20,000 square kilometres (about half the size of Switzerland) on the foothills of the eastern Andes, **MANU**, declared a Biosphere Reserve by UNESCO in 1977, features a uniquely varied environment of pristine rainforest, from crystalline cloudforest streams and waterfalls down to slow-moving rivers in the dense lowland rainforest populated with towering trees. Manu is one of the most biologically diverse places in South America; rich in macaw clay licks and otter lagoons, it's also home to thirteen species of monkey and seven species of macaw. Sometimes big mammals such as **capybara** or **white-lipped peccaries** can be spotted lurking in the undergrowth, and the fortunate have been known to see a jaguar.

Manu is reachable via an eight-hour bus journey from Cusco along a partially paved road, followed by several hours along Río Madre de Dios, making it a destination for serious jungle enthusiasts with at least a week to spare. The reserve is divided into three parts: the **Zona Cultural**, encompassing the bus route and several

WHEN TO VISIT

The Manu region experiences a **rainy season** from December to March, when the road into the park is particularly susceptible to landslides, so is best visited between May and August when it's much drier, although at that time the temperatures often exceed 30°C. Bring a jacket just in case, as roughly once a month the jungle experiences several days of *friaje* – a cold spell that can bring the temperature down as low as 12°C.

9

villages within the cloudforest; the **Zona Reservada**, with the jungle lodges and oxbow lakes, located along Río Madre de Dios and Río Manu, accessible only as part of a guided tour with only a handful of licensed operators (see page 831); and the **Zona Restringida** (Restricted Zone), consisting of pristine jungle, home to several uncontacted indigenous peoples, and completely off-limits to visitors.

MONTEVIDEO

Uruguay

❶ Montevideo Eclectic architecture, sweeping beaches and hip nightlife. See page 839

❷ Colonia del Sacramento Picturesque and historical town with excellent food. See page 846

❸ Carmelo Sleepy town, home to vineyards and riverside beaches. See page 850

❹ Minas Ride with gauchos through Uruguay's vast interior. See page 851

❺ Punta del Este Flashy beach resort with surf and celebrities. See page 853

❻ Cabo Polonio Laidback hippie vibes at the electricity-free beach, the antithesis of Punta. See page 856

HIGHLIGHTS ARE MARKED ON THE MAP ON PAGE 836

ROUGH COSTS

Daily budget Basic US$60, occasional treat US$80

Drink Pilsen beer (1 litre) US$3.50

Food *Asado de tira* steak US$13

Hostel/budget hotel US$18–55

Travel Montevideo–Colonia del Sacramento (150km) by bus: 2hr 45min, US$14

FACT FILE

Population 3.4 million
Language Spanish
Currency Peso uruguayo (UR$)
Capital Montevideo (population: 1.3 million)
International phone code ☎ 598
Time zone GMT -3hr

Introduction

If, as the saying goes, countries get the government they deserve, then Uruguay's most popular former president José "Pepe" Mujica was a great fit for Uruguay – modest, but sure of himself, progressive, but totally laidback; Uruguayans are certainly the most relaxed South Americans. With a plethora of sandy riverside and ocean-facing beaches, unspoiled open countryside, historical towns that verge on retro and kindly locals who usually clasp a flask and mate under one arm, you can expect a warm welcome as you traverse their land.

Through misfortune and good times, Uruguayans maintain their traditionally cheerful attitude, and it's not hard to see why. From the secluded **surfing beaches** of the Atlantic coast, to the rolling pastoral land of the interior tended by **gauchos**, or the picturesque streets of **Colonia del Sacramento** and the buzzing nightlife of **Montevideo**, theirs is a gem of a nation set between the South American giants of Brazil and Argentina. "*Tranquilo*" (peaceful) could be Uruguay's national motto, and, after witnessing the beauty of the land and the relaxed kindness of its people, you are unlikely to be in any hurry to leave.

CHRONOLOGY

Pre-1600 Uruguay is home to the Charrúa, a hunter-gatherer people hostile to the European invaders.
Early 1600s Spanish settlers introduce cattle to Uruguay and the gaucho lifestyle of cattle-ranching develops.
1680 The Portuguese establish Colonia del Sacramento as the first major colony in Uruguay.
1726 The Spanish retaliate by founding Montevideo in an attempt to cement their power in the region. Their wars with the Portuguese continue for the next century.
1811 José Artigas begins an independence campaign against the Spanish, who finally leave Uruguay in 1815, only for Brazil and Argentina to fight over control of the territory.

1820 Artigas, defeated by the Portuguese, is exiled to Paraguay, where he stays until his death.
1825 Juan Lavalleja leads the legendary Treinta y Tres Orientales (a group of 33 revolutionaries) to victory over the Brazilians. Uruguay gains its independence a year later.
1831 Uruguay's 500 remaining Charrúa are massacred by the government.
1834–51 Uruguay plunged into civil war pitting the Colorados against the Blancos, names that have survived as political parties to this day.
1903–15 President José Batlle y Ordoñez of the Colorado Party makes sweeping social reforms, effectively making Uruguay South America's first welfare state.
1950–60s Inflation and political corruption leads to the stagnation of Uruguay's industries, and social unrest ensues.
1973 The Congress is dissolved and the army takes control of the government. Twelve years of military dictatorship ensue.
1984 The military allows free elections to take place. Colorado wins, Dr Julio Sanguinetti becomes president and holds office until 1989, returning to power from 1995 until 2000.
2000 Personal possession and use of marijuana is legalized.
2001 The economic crisis in Argentina leads to a collapse in the value of the Uruguayan peso; inflation and wide-spread unemployment ensues.
2009 José Mujica, a former militant leftist taken prisoner and tortured during the military regime, easily wins the presidency.
2012 Uruguay becomes the second Latin American country, after Cuba, to legalize abortion.
2013 A year later, it becomes the first country in the world to legalize marijuana sales.
2014 Mujica's successor Tabaré Vázquez wins the November election.

ARRIVAL AND DEPARTURE

FROM ARGENTINA

Many visitors arrive via **ferry** from Buenos Aires to Colonia del Sacramento or to

---

WHEN TO VISIT

One of Uruguay's main draws is its beaches, so it's best to visit from **November to February** when it's warm, although bear in mind that prices in beach towns soar. Winters in Uruguay can be downright frigid, with cold wet air blowing in from the ocean, but you should still get some sunny days.

Montevideo as an easy day-trip (see page 46). Those coming by long-distance bus will be dropped at Tres Cruces bus terminal (⊕trescruces.com.uy) in downtown Montevideo.

FROM BRAZIL

Coaches pass through border town Chuy to Tres Cruces.

Those **flying** into Uruguay usually arrive at Montevideo's **Aeropuerto de Carrasco** (see page 843); check online for the full list of airlines flying here (⊕aeropuertodecarrasco.com.uy).

VISAS

Citizens of the EU, US, UK, Australia, New Zealand, South Africa and Canada, among others, do not need a visa to visit Uruguay. Check the *Preguntas Frecuentes* (FAQ) section of ⊕mrree.gub.uy for a full list of countries.

GETTING AROUND

BY BUS

The most convenient and cheapest means of transport in Uruguay are **intercity buses**, which operate from the bus terminal (*terminal de ómnibus*) in most towns. Montevideo's main terminal Tres Cruces has an excellent website (⊕trescruces.com.uy) with details of all the companies and timetables operating there. Long-distance buses are comfortable and many have wi-fi.

BY CAR

Uruguay is an easy country to drive around; all the major routes are asphalted, well signposted, and, outside of summer along the coast, there are few drivers on the roads. Non-paved roads off the numbered routes tend to be in pretty good shape, except after rain when they may become too muddy without a 4WD. Even Montevideo is fairly straightforward to get in and out of, thanks to the coastal road (the *ramblas*) linking the airport with the centre and old town. In low season, you can find **rental cars** for as little as UR$1700/day, and from UR$2000 in

high season (all the major international car rental companies have offices), but petrol costs are equivalent to European prices. Fines for speeding are high (from US$220), so be sure to adhere to the national speed limits of 45km/hr in inner cities and 90km/hr on the main roads between towns. Note that Uruguay operates a zero-alcohol tolerance for drivers. **Taxis** tend to be safe as long as they're licensed, but look out for *remises* (minicabs), which sometimes offer better rates for fixed distances as they are booked in advance – ask at your hostel for reliable companies.

BY BIKE

With a predominantly flat landscape and good-quality roads, Uruguay is a tempting place for cyclists.

Accommodation is never more than 50km apart along the coast (although in the interior and north facilities are sparser) and there are repair shops in many cities. As with elsewhere in South America, however, you must beware of the recklessness of local drivers.

ACCOMMODATION

Uruguay's coastal towns house plenty of **youth hostels** and other towns will offer basic hotels for those on a budget. Off the main tourist routes, however, places to stay can be few and far between; it's also worth checking if your trip coincides with a public holiday as accommodation can book up fast. Tourist information offices are usually happy to help find accommodation. During the summer holidays from December to February you need to book ahead, and prices soar, so a dorm bed can be as expensive as sharing a double room in a basic hotel. Hotels and hostels often have a set dollar exchange rate, rather than going by the daily rate, which can mean you'll be slightly better off paying in dollars than pesos.

FOOD AND DRINK

Uruguay may not provide the most cosmopolitan of culinary experiences, but if you enjoy **beef** or most kinds of

10

seafood, you will not go hungry. Uruguayan steakhouses (*parrillas*) serve steaks that are larger and (as the locals insist) more tender than their Argentine counterparts, with the most popular cuts being the ribs (*asado de tira*) and tenderloin (*bife de chorizo*).

The best dining option for **vegetarians** tends to be the ubiquitous pizza and pasta restaurants. **Desserts** (*postres*) also bear an Italian influence and Uruguay's *confiterías* (patisseries) and *heladerías* (ice-cream parlours) are bursting with delicious treats. *Dulce de leche* is an irresistible type of caramel that you'll find in almost any form on dessert menus (and as part of your hostel breakfast to spread on toast). The national snack is the **chivito**, essentially a whopping burger stacked with fried egg, ham, cheese

and bacon, but with a whole steak instead of ground beef, best bought from a street food truck (UR$150) and slathered in sauces for an authentic experience.

Uruguayans don't really do breakfast – most cafés open around 10am, but most hotels and hostels provide a basic breakfast for tourists. Lunch is eaten early, between noon and 1pm, making time for the *merienda* or *té*: a sumptuous afternoon tea – usually advertised for two – full of sweet and savoury snacks along with tea or coffee, which is taken around 5pm. Thanks to this tradition, dinner is always late; you'll normally be eating on your own if you arrive at a restaurant before 9pm.

Restaurant **prices** are fairly high for South America: the average price for a lunch set menu is around UR$300–400 in

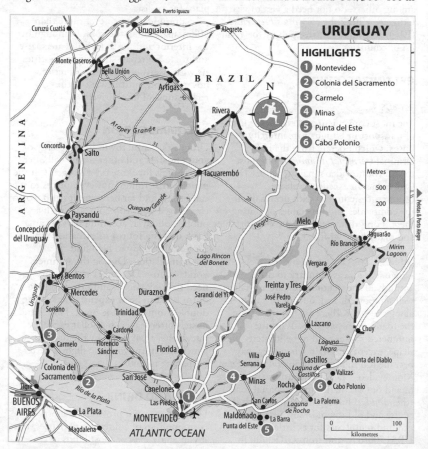

10

THE ART OF DRINKING MATE

You are unlikely to walk down a single street in Uruguay without seeing someone carrying the thermos, pots and metal straw (*bombilla*) required for **mate**. In a tradition that goes back to the earliest gauchos, Uruguayans are said to drink even more of the grassy tea than Argentines, and a whole set of social rituals surrounds it. Whenever it's drunk, *mate* is meticulously prepared before being passed round in a circle; the drinker makes a small sucking noise when the pot needs to be refilled, but if this is your position, beware making three such noises: this is considered rude.

Montevideo, and *à la carte* prices can be much higher.

DRINK

Mate (pronounced mah-tey) is the national drink and involves a whole set of paraphernalia to partake in drinking it. Coffee is the other non-alcoholic drink of choice here, and teas and bottled water are always available, along with fresh juices and smoothies (*licuados*).

When not clutching their thermos, Uruguayans enjoy the local beers – especially the ubiquitous **Pilsen** – which come in one-litre bottles (UR$100) fit for sharing. Uruguayan wine is becoming more prominent, especially the Tannat grape which makes a fine red (*tinto*). You may also see wine offered as *medio y medio* which is a blend of sparkling and slightly sweet white wine. **Tap water** is fine to drink.

CULTURE AND ETIQUETTE

Uruguayans of all ages tend to be warm, relaxed people, fond of lively conversation over a beer or barbecue (*asado*). As a nation in which the overwhelming majority of people are descended from Italian and Spanish immigrants, Uruguay also maintains some conservative **Catholic** religious and social practices, especially in the countryside, although the coastal towns are liberal by South American standards. Uruguayans display a rugged sense of independence that recalls the romantic figure of the **gaucho**, the cowboys who still roam the grassy plains of the interior. Women and men alike greet each other with one kiss on the cheek. It's usual to leave a ten percent **tip** anywhere with table service.

SPORTS AND OUTDOOR ACTIVITIES

Ever since the first football World Cup, in 1930, was held in Uruguay and won by the national team, **football** has been the sport to raise the passions of the normally laidback Uruguayans. In the countryside, **horseriding** (*cabalgata*) is more a part of working life than a sport, but there are many opportunities for tourists to go riding – many hostels and most *estancias* (see page 849) offer horseriding. **Cycling** is a popular way of seeing the cities (many hostels provide free or cheap bikes), while **fishing** is another favoured afternoon pursuit.

Surfing is increasing in popularity, thanks to fantastic Atlantic waves, and many beach hostels will rent out boards or advertise lessons.

A widely accepted translation of the Guaraní word *uruguay* is "river of painted birds", so it's no surprise that the country offers fantastic **birdwatching** opportunities, including flamingos, vultures, hawks, rheas and Magellanic penguins. Tourist information offices have excellent leaflets about twitching in Uruguay.

COMMUNICATIONS

Internet cafés charge UR$20–30/hr and are present in all towns. Antel run the **public phone** service and you'll find street phones and *cabinas telefónicas* (booths inside shops) wherever you go. You can buy phone cards (*tarjeta telefónica*), available wherever you see the Antel signs,

---

EMERGENCY NUMBERS

Police and fire services ☎911
Ambulance ☎105
Tourist police ☎08008226

10

or use change. The **national post office**, *Correo Uruguayo* (ⓦcorreo.com.uy), provides an expensive and sometimes unreliable service for international mail; for urgent deliveries, you are much better using a private mailing company like FedEx, at Juncal 1321 in Montevideo's old town. There are no postboxes on the street; you either need to go to a post office branch, or in Montevideo most museums have *buzones* (boxes) in their foyers.

CRIME AND SAFETY

Uruguayans pride themselves on how safe their country is, although statistically crime is on the rise. **Thefts** from dorms, as well as pickpocketing, do occur, especially in Montevideo and the beach resorts during the summer months. Store your valuables in lockers whenever possible, but you shouldn't feel worried carrying valuables around with you during the day. The Uruguayan police are courteous, but unlikely to speak English.

While some visitors may head to Uruguay to take advantage of the 2103 law that allows **marijuana** grown by certified producers to be purchased – the first country in the world to do so – remember that it's illegal for **tourists** to buy or consume the local product.

HEALTH

Uruguay's public healthcare system is in pretty good shape; there are adequate public **hospitals** in the major cities. Contact your embassy, or ask locals, for advice on the best facilities, and check that they will accept your insurance.

INFORMATION AND MAPS

The national **tourist board**, run by the Ministerio de Turismo y Deporte (Minitur; ☏1885, ⓦturismo.gub.uy) is branded as **Uruguay Natural**, and it runs offices in all of Uruguay's major towns, alongside local tourist offices run by the municipality. Uruguay Natural in Montevideo (see page 843) can give you free maps of every department, or you can buy high-quality road maps in petrol

stations and bookshops. Uruguayans often write addresses using the abbreviations "esq.", meaning "at the corner with", and "c/", meaning "almost at", or "nearby".

MONEY AND BANKS

The Uruguayan currency is the **peso uruguayo** (UR$). Coins come as 50 centimos and 1, 2, 5 and 10 pesos; notes as 10, 20, 50, 100, 200, 500 and 1000 pesos. At the time of writing, the **exchange rate** was £1 = UR$40, €1 = UR$35 and US$1 = UR$28.

Money changing is stress-free as everyone has to buy at the same rate, which varies slightly day to day (you can always find it displayed on the front of the daily newspapers). Breaking large banknotes is less of a problem than in most South American countries, though you are still advised to carry smaller notes in the countryside.

While major **credit cards** are widely accepted, and **ATMs** are common in cities (look out for the Banred and RedBrou ATMs that accept international cards), you should always carry a relatively large supply of **cash** for places where this is not the case. This applies especially to the beach villages of Eastern Uruguay, such as Punta del Diablo, which don't have ATMs. ATMs charge around UR$85 per withdrawal. Paying by foreign credit or debit card benefits from an instant tax refund in high season: 22 percent for hotels, restaurants and car rental; two percent in supermarkets.

OPENING HOURS AND HOLIDAYS

Most **shops and post offices** open on weekdays from 8am until noon, before closing for lunch, reopening around 4pm until 7 pm. Most businesses work at least a half-day on Saturday, but most close on Sundays. Banks are usually open Monday to Friday 1 to 5pm and closed at weekends. The exception to this is many shops in Montevideo, the main coastal tourist centres, and **supermarkets** in general; the latter are often open as late as 11pm during the week.

Most **museums and historic monuments** are open daily, though times vary, and tend to close once a week for maintenance.

PUBLIC HOLIDAYS

Jan 1 New Year's Day (*Año Nuevo*)

Jan 6 Epiphany (*Día de Magos*)

Easter (*Semana Santa* or *Pascuas*) is celebrated on Maunday Thursday and Good Friday

April 19 Landing of the 33 Patriots (*Desembarco de los 33 Orientales*)

May 1 Labour Day

May 18 Battle of Las Piedras (Batalla de Las Piedras)

June 19 Birth of José Artigas

July 18 Constitution Day (Jura de la Constitución)

Aug 25 Independence Day (*Declaratoria de la independencia*)

Oct 15 Columbus Day (*Día de la Raza*)

Nov 2 All Souls Day (*Día de los Difuntos*)

Dec 25 Christmas Day (*Navidad*)

FESTIVALS

Jan/Feb–March Carnaval. Montevideo hosts South America's longest Carnaval celebrations – a full forty days' worth. Unmissable.

10

Montevideo

With a population of around 1.6 million, over fifteen times larger than the second city of Paysandú, **Montevideo** is Uruguay's political, economic and transport hub. Founded in 1726 as a fortress against Portuguese encroachment on the northern shore of the **Río de la Plata**, it had an excellent trading position and, following a turbulent and often violent early history, its growth was rapid. The nineteenth century saw mass immigration from Europe – mostly Italy and Spain – that has resulted in a vibrant mix of architectural styles and a cosmopolitan atmosphere.

More relaxed, but less affluent than its Argentine neighbour, the Uruguayan capital has nevertheless seen an economic improvement in recent years, and wisely invested in its culture, infrastructure and beaches. Montevideo may appear humble at first, but this is a seriously cool, confident city.

WHAT TO SEE AND DO

Montevideo can sometimes be overshadowed by its snazzy neighbour Buenos Aires, but this, Uruguayans will tell you, is the true home of the **tango**, with plenty of free classes and *milongas* – bars playing traditional music – not to mention the best place to experience South America's longest **Carnaval** season (see page 841). There are tons of quirky **museums**, especially in the charming **Ciudad Vieja** and east to the **Centro**, based around Avenida 18 de Julio. Close to here, **Calle Tristan Narvaja** is filled with independent bookshops and cultural spaces, and holds a huge weekly flea market (see page 842). You may well stay in **Barrio Sur** – the traditional Afro-Uruguayan neighbourhood where **candombe** drumming was cultivated – or affluent areas **Punta Carretas** or **Pocitos**, where you'll find some of the best food and nightlife.

Ciudad Vieja

If you've ever seen a fictionalized version of Havana on TV or film, it's quite possible it was actually shot in Montevideo's **Ciudad Vieja**, so reminiscent are its streets of those in the Cuban capital. Dotted among the crumbling houses and cobbled streets are endearingly bizarre (and mostly free) **museums** and galleries, while the highlight is the glorious **Mercado del Puerto.**

Plaza Independencia and around

A good place to start a walking tour of the Ciudad Vieja is the **Puerta de la Ciudadela**, dating to 1746, marking the original site of the Citadel of Montevideo on the **Plaza Independencia**. This square commemorates the emergence of Uruguay as a sovereign nation, and a 17m-high statue and mausoleum (under the statue; Mon noon–6pm, Tues–Sun 10am–6pm) of **José Artigas**, the man credited with kick-starting Uruguay's independence campaign against Spain and Portugal, stands aptly in the centre.

The area around the plaza contains eclectic architectural styles, from the rather ugly **Torre Ejecutiva** where the president performs his duties, to the bulbous tower of the **Palacio Salvo**, built on the reported

10

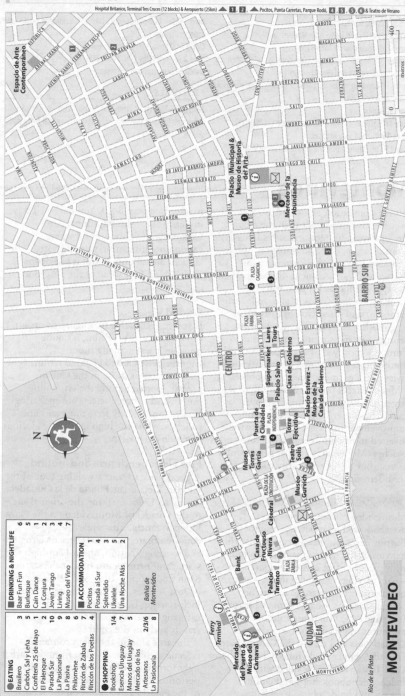

● EATING	
Brasilero	3
Carbón, Sal y Leña	5
Confitería 25 de Mayo	1
El Palenque	2
Parada Sur	10
La Pasionaria	9
La Pasiva	8
Philomène	6
Rincón de Zabala	7
Rincón de los Poetas	4

■ DRINKING & NIGHTLIFE	
Baar Fun Fun	6
Burlesque	5
Caín Dance	1
La Conjura	2
Joven Tango	3
Living	4
Museo del Vino	7

▲ ACCOMMODATION	
Pocitos	4
Posada al Sur	1
Splendido	3
Ukelele	5
Una Noche Más	2

● SHOPPING	
Bookshop	1/4
Esencia Uruguay	7
Manos del Uruguay	5
Mercado de los Artesanos	2/3/6
La Pasionaria	8

Espacio de Arte Contemporáneo

Palacio Municipal & Museo de Historia del Arte

Mercado de la Abundancia

PLAZA CAGANCHA

PLAZA FABINI

Supermarket Lares Tours

Casa de Gobierno

Palacio Salvo

Palacio Estévez – Museo de la Casa de Gobierno

Puerta de la Ciudadela

PLAZA INDEPENDENCIA

Torre Ejecutiva

Teatro Solís

Museo Torres García

Museo Gurvich

PLAZA DE LA CONSTITUCIÓN

Catedral

Bank

Casa de Fructuoso Rivera

Palacio Taranco

PLAZA ZABALA

Ferry Terminal

Mercado del Puerto & Museo del Carnaval

Bahía de Montevideo

Río de la Plata

MONTEVIDEO

CIUDAD VIEJA

CENTRO

BARRIO SUR

N

0   400   metres

CARNAVAL

You will not truly understand the lure of Montevideo unless you experience **Carnaval**. It's a three-month celebration of Uruguayan culture with parades, neighbourhood stages known as *tablados* which host *murgas* (street bands where singing groups are accompanied by wild drumming – *candombe* – originating in the African rhythms brought over by slaves), plays, parodists and comedians, all wildly dressed and there to entertain. The spectacular opening and closing parades take place on Avenida 18 de Julio and the biggest competitions are held at the **Teatro de Verano** (see page 845). If you plan to be in Montevideo during Carnaval, email the tourist office to find out key dates and book accommodation well ahead.

10

---

site of the first ever performance of tango.

Tucked behind the plaza's southwestern corner is the celebrated **Teatro Solís** (see page 845), the most prestigious theatre in the country, completed in 1856 and remodelled a few times thereafter. The guided tours (Tues & Thurs 4pm, Wed & Fri–Sun 11am, noon & 4pm; UR$90 in English; tours in all available languages are free on Wed; ☎1950 3323, ⍟teatrosolis. org.uy) are a fun way to see behind the scenes, but to experience its full splendour, you really have to watch a performance.

On the south side of the plaza, the old Presidential palace, a Neoclassical building from 1873, now houses the intriguing **Palacio Estévez – Museo de la Casa de Gobierno** (Mon–Fri 10am–5pm; free; ☎02 1505902), which charts the history of the country via its often-eccentric presidents.

Plaza de la Constitución and around

Lively pedestrian boulevard **Sarandí** cuts through the centre of the old city – starting at the Puerta de la Ciudadela – with its street-sellers, artisans, buskers and frequent parades, to the **Plaza de la Constitución**. Also referred to as the Plaza Matríz, this is Uruguay's oldest square, dating back to 1726. It's dominated by the **Catedral Metropolitana** (also known as Iglesia Matríz), which, despite dating back to 1790, is underwhelming by Latin American standards.

Museo Torres García and Museo Gurvich

Two of Uruguay's finest art galleries are near Plaza de la Constitución. **Museo Torres García**, at Sarandí 683 (Mon–Sat 10am–6pm; UR$120; ☎29162663, ⍟torresgarcia.org.uy), is devoted to the work of Uruguay's visionary artist Joaquín Torres García, who championed the creation of a Latin American art form and created the upside-down image of South America that is so prevalent in *artesanía* in Uruguay. Torres García's most famous pupil is honoured on the Plaza Matríz around the corner at the excellent **Museo Gurvich** (Sarandí 524; Mon–Fri 10am–6pm, Sat 11am–3pm; UR$180; ☎29157826, ⍟museogurvich.org). Lithuanian Jewish immigrant José Gurvich gained fame in his own right with elaborate murals and sculptures, reminiscent of Chagall and Miró.

Around Plaza Zabala

Named for the founder of Montevideo, leafy **Plaza Zabala** might be overlooked if it weren't for **Palacio Taranco** on the north side. An opulent private home that was designed by Charles Louis Girault and Jules Leon Chifflot – the same French team who created the Arc de Triomphe – it now holds the **Museo de Artes Decorativas** (entry at 25 de Mayo 376; Mon–Fri 12.30–5.30pm; free; ☎29151101, ⍟cultura.mec.gub.uy). The beautifully displayed collection includes Uruguayan art and an expansive world pottery collection.

Also worth a look, two blocks east of Plaza Zabala at Rincón 437, is the **Casa de Fructuoso Rivera** (Wed–Sun noon–6pm; free; ☎2915 1051, ⍟museohistorico.gub. uy), which traces Uruguay's history from prehistoric to modern times through art and artefacts, with a focus on the life of Artigas.

Mercado del Puerto

A foodie's dream and an architectural gem, the **Mercado del Puerto**, at the end of pedestrian street Pérez Castellano by the port (daily for lunch, some restaurants also

10

open for dinner; ⓦmercadodelpuerto.com.
uy), is one of Montevideo's highlights. It's
so popular, in fact, that the restaurants
cash in by charging extortionately;
however, it's well worth soaking up the
atmosphere and seeing the wandering
minstrels, even if you don't stay to eat (see
page 845). The **port** (*puerto*) and ferry
terminal are on the northern edge, along
with both the municipal and national
tourist information offices (see page 843).

Set into the Mercado del Puerto, with its
entrance on the Rambla, is the **Museo del
Carnaval** (April–Nov Wed–Sun 11am–
5pm; Dec–March daily 11am–5pm;
UR$100, includes a coffee in the café;
ⓣ29165493, ⓦmuseodelcarnaval.org),
filled with colourful exhibits from the
city's Carnaval celebrations (see page
841).

Avenida 18 de Julio and around

Extending from the eastern end of Plaza
Independencia, **Avenida 18 de Julio** is
central Montevideo's main shopping
thoroughfare and the most important
stopping point for the majority of the
city's buses.

Try to pass **Plaza Fabini**, a verdant square
on the avenue, on a Saturday, when you'll
come across people of all ages dancing
tango (from 4pm) for a supportive
audience. The **Plaza Cagancha** (also known
as Plaza Libertad) is the next grand square
on 18 de Julio; pass through it on your
way to the huge **Palacio Municipal** building
a little further east. Ask at the tourist
information office at its base for a ticket to
enter, as the **mirador panorámico** on the
22nd floor offers far-reaching views over
the city (daily 10am–4pm; guided tours at
11.15am on weekdays; free; ⓔvisitas@
imm.gub.uy).

Museo de Historia del Arte

Underneath the Palacio Municipal the
underrated **Museo de Historia del Arte**
(Ejido 1326; Tues–Sun: mid-March to
mid-Dec noon–5.30pm; mid-Dec to
mid-March 1.30–7pm; free; ⓦmuhar.
montevideo.gub.uy) is a treasure-trove of
pre-Columbian, colonial and
international items, beautifully laid out,
but you'll soon notice that much of what
is displayed are copies, designed to
demonstrate the evolution of art; look out
for the items with red dots telling you
they're authentic. It has a particularly
strong collection of original pre-Hispanic
pieces, including Peruvian and
Mesoamerican ceramics, some huge urns
from Argentina's Santa María culture, and
Guatemalan textiles.

Tristan Narvaja

A street synonymous with Montevideo's
largest **street market** (Sun 10am–3pm),
Tristan Narvaja is a few blocks east from
the Palacio Municipal. Spanning six
blocks, this is a real flea market selling
everything from fruit and veg to antiques
to pets. On other days, it's a pleasant
neighbourhood to wander around as the
streets are lined with eclectic independent
shops and cafés.

Espacio de Arte Contemporáneo

Three blocks northeast from the top of
Tristan Narvaja, in a partly refurbished
prison dating to 1888, you'll find the
Espacio de Arte Contemporáneo (Arenal
Grande 1930; Wed–Sat 2–8pm, Sun
11am–5pm, guided visits Sat 5pm, Sun
3pm; free; ⓦeac.gub.uy), exhibiting
beautifully curated, world-class
contemporary art. You can see resident
artists at work in the old cells.

CROSSING THE RÍO DE LA PLATA

Every day, two Buquebus **ferries** leave from Montevideo (morning and late afternoon) to
Buenos Aires (2hr 12min; UR$800–1500 one-way). For a more frequent service, both Buquebus
and Seacat Colonia offer a combined bus and ferry ticket to Colonia del Sacramento (see
page 846); ferries depart every couple of hours and take just one hour (often cheaper) to the
Argentine capital. Although less convenient, the most picturesque ferry crossing is operated
by Cacciola between Tigre, a northern suburb of Buenos Aires, and Carmelo, a one-hour bus
ride to the west of Colonia (2 daily; 2hr 30min; UR$900 one-way; ⓣ24079657 ⓦcacciolaviajes.
com). They also run bus connections to Montevideo.

TOUR URUGAY

Uruguay's large countryside makes it difficult to tackle without a car, but there are some excellent tour operators who can get you out in the sticks.

TOUR OPERATORS

Biking Uruguay (Gabriel Pereira 3297 ☏ 27090636, ⓦ bikinguruguay.com); & **Bike Tours Uruguay** (☏ 099592709, ⓦ biketoursuruguay.com). Both companies run cycling tours in Montevideo and Punta del Este.

Caballos de Luz ☏ 099400446, ⓦ caballosdeluz. com. Recommended, good-value horseriding tours in Rocha department.

Lares W. Ferreira Aldunate 1322, office 14, Montevideo ☏ 29019120, ⓦ larestours.com. A popular nationwide tour operator, specializing in outdoor activities and nature.

The Wine Experience ☏ 097348445, ⓦ thewine-experience.com. South African Ryan runs raved-about gourmet food and vineyard tours from both Montevideo and Colonia; prices depend on number of people in tour.

10

ARRIVAL AND DEPARTURE

By plane The Aeropuerto de Carrasco (ⓦ aeropuertodecarrasco.com.uy) is 25km east of the city centre. Eschew the extortionately priced taxis (30min; UR$1400) and take a bus (every 15min; 24hr, reduced service overnight and at weekends; 25min; UR$140) run by COT (ⓦ cot.com.uy) and COPSA (ⓦ copsa.com.uy) to Tres Cruces bus station. Passengers in transit must pay a US$44 tax on international flights (US$20 to Buenos Aires), and US$2 on internal flights, payable at the airport.

Destinations There are several daily flights with Aerolíneas Argentinas (ⓦ aerolineas.com.ar) and Amazonas (ⓦ amazonas.com) to Buenos Aires' Aeroparque and Ezeiza airports (the former is better for central BA). Buquebus (ⓦ flybqb.com.uy) run the only domestic flights. International flights to: Asunción (2 daily; 3hr); Lima (2 daily; 5hr); Miami (daily; 9hr); Madrid (9 weekly); Panama City (daily; 7hr 30min); Rio de Janeiro (daily; 2hr 40min); Santiago de Chile (4 daily; 2hr 40min); São Paulo (8 daily; 2hr 30min).

By bus All intercity buses operate out of Tres Cruces bus station (ⓦ trescruces.com.uy), 2km northeast of the centre. From here bus CA1 (every 15min; 15min; UR$36, UR$29 with STM card) goes to the centre, down Av 18 de Julio to the Plaza Independencia, loops around the Ciudad Vieja, then returns via the same route. The #183 runs to Pocitos. Obtain a free STM travel card from the Cutscsa office in the basement of Tres Cruces then top it up for cheaper fares.

Destinations International: Asunción, Paraguay (2 weekly; 22hr); Buenos Aires, Argentina (3 daily; 8–10hr); Córdoba, Argentina (daily; 15hr); Porto Alegre, Brazil (3 daily; 12hr); Rosario, Argentina (5 weekly; 9); Santiago, Chile (weekly; 28hr). National: Cabo Polonio (8 daily; 4hr); Carmelo (9 daily; 3hr 30min); Colonia del Sacramento (hourly; 2hr 45min); Minas (hourly; 1hr 40min–2hr 30min); Punta del Diablo (hourly; 4–5hr); Punta del Este (every 30min–every 2hr, 24hr a day; 2hr); Valizas (5 daily; 4–5hr).

Backpacker bus Summer Bus (☏ 42775781, ⓦ summerbus.com) is a beach-hopping backpacker bus which conveniently picks you up from your hostel during summer months (Nov–April; hop-on-hop-off ticket to twelve beaches US$95).

By ferry See page 842.

GETTING AROUND

Most points of interest are within walking distance of Plaza Independencia, while Pocitos and Punta Carretas are easily reached by bus. Note that the roads crossing Av 18 de Julio north–south change names either side of the main road.

By bus There are no route maps available, but there is a bus journey planner at ⓦ montevideo.gub.uy/aplicacion/como-ir and a list of inner-city route numbers with destinations at ⓦ cutcsa.com.uy. You can catch buses to most parts of the city from outside the Teatro Solís. Buses heading for the centre are marked "Aduana" or "Ciudad Vieja". Ask for a "centrico" ticket (UR$36) if you're only going within the *centro*, or a "común" (UR$40), cheaper with STM card. Buses run regularly from 6am until midnight, when services thin out dramatically.

By bike Renting a bike is a popular way to see the city, and the lovely Ramblas hugging the estuary beaches makes it easy. Most hostels rent bikes cheaply. If you're staying for a while, it might be worth signing up to the free (after a one-off UR$140 fee) bike scheme. ⓦ movete.montevideo. gub.uy (Spanish only).

By taxi Journeys within the city rarely amount to more than UR$200 in hailed street taxis or *remises* (minicabs). The meter does not give the fare but rather the distance, which corresponds to a pre-fixed rate (taxis should always have the rates displayed).

INFORMATION AND TOURS

Tourist information The Minitur office on Rambla 25 de Agosto de 1825 at the end of Yacaré (daily 8am–5pm; ☏ 1885, ⓦ turismo.gub.uy) has the best range of maps, leaflets and information in English in Uruguay. There are also information kiosks at the airport (daily 8am–9pm; ☏ 26040386), and at Tres Cruces bus station (daily 8am–9pm; ☏ 24097399). There are municipal tourist offices (daily: April–Nov 9am–5.30pm; Dec–March 11am–5pm;

10

☎ 29168434) on the port side of the Mercado del Puerto, as well as outside the Palacio Municipal (☎ 19508363).

City tours LB Tour (Carlos Quijano 1333, office 905, ☎ 29007159, ⊚ lbtour.com.uy) run some of the most popular city tours in Montevideo, also available in Colonia; Tip-based Free Walking Tour (⊚ freewalkingtour.com.uy) does what it says on the tin. Soccer fans won't do better than Fanaticos Fútbol Tours (☎ 099862325, ⊚ futboltours. com.uy), who live and breathe the beautiful game (from US$50). *Hostel Posada al Sur* (see page 844) has responsible tourism in mind with tours that benefit locals.

Websites The website ⊚ descubrimontevideo.uy has comprehensive tourist information, including an excellent downloadable guide in English (under Montevideo – *Guía Práctica – Guía en Inglés*). Look out for the *Friendly Map Magazine* (⊚ friendlymap.com.uy) at tourist information offices for LGBTQ listings. The ciudad y cultura section on government site ⊚ montevideo.gub.uy (Spanish only) is great for cultural listings.

ACCOMMODATION

Although the Ciudad Vieja is dotted with cheap hotels and hostels, away from the pedestrianized Sarandí it can be unsafe at night. Barrio Sur is a good bet for character and excellently placed for the old town and nightlife, while Punta Carretas and Pocitos are best for safety, shopping, beaches and partying. Hostels usually offer bikes for rent and tango classes, and you can assume breakfast, internet and wi-fi, a/c and heat are provided unless otherwise mentioned. Prices are given for the cheapest bed or double room in high season, which starts in mid-Nov and ends after Carnaval.

BARRIO VIEJO AND CENTRO

★ **Posada al Sur** Pérez Castellano 1424 ☎ 29165287, ⊚ posadaalsur.com.uy; map p.840. The most ethically conscious choice in Montevideo, with organic breakfasts and community-oriented tours. Light common areas enhance the *buena onda* ("good vibes"). Its location close to the port is great during the day, but you might want to take a taxi back at night. Dorms US$510, doubles US$1300, en-suite apartment US$2100

★ **Splendido** Bartolomé Mitre 1314 ☎ 29164900, ⊚ splendidohotel.com.uy; map p.840. This budget hotel with retro styling is truly splendid. All twenty rooms overlook Teatro Solís, and each has a different shabby-chic personality. There's a kitchen you can use and the breakfast is good; the only downside is that it's above the most popular bars in the Ciudad Vieja, so bring earplugs. Rooms sleep 1–5 people. Singles US$1300, doubles US$1600

Ukelele Maldonado 1183 between Michelini and Ruíz ☎ 29027844, ⊚ ukelelehostel.com; map p.840. You can relax in what was the family home of owner Patricia. This enormous house with soaring ceilings eschews the institutional feel and, unusually for Montevideo, has a large

pool and pretty patio garden. Breakfast is simple, and, with no central heating, the place becomes fridge-like in winter. Dorms US$511, doubles US$1700

POCITOS AND PUNTA CARRETAS

Pocitos Sarmiento 2641 ☎ 27118780, ⊚ pocitoshostel. com; map p.840. Let the good times roll in one of the city's most likeable – if cramped – backpacker joints, with a lovely garden and good rates on private rooms. The young owners also have a hostel in Colonia. Dorms US$511, doubles US$1420

Una Noche Mas Patria 712, Punta Carretas ☎ 96227406, ⊚ unanochemas.com.uy; map p.840. Delightful B&B in Carla and Eduardo's home. Cosy rooms, a lovely roof terrace and an abundant breakfast with free coffee and tea 24/7. Doubles US$4550

EATING

Café culture is big in Montevideo, with several galleries and design stores doubling as cafés and small restaurants, and there are some truly great eating experiences.

BARRIO VIEJO AND CENTRO

★ **Brasilero** Ituzaingó 1447 ⊚ cafebrasilero.com.uy; map p.840. Established in 1877, this is Montevideo's most classic café, with cosy dark wooden walls and furniture. With its good, fresh food and huge selection of tea and coffee, it's no wonder it has been favoured by Uruguayan literary giants such Mario Benedetti and Eduardo Galeano. Coffee and cake US$100. Mon–Fri 9am–8pm, Sat 9am–6pm.

Confitería 25 de Mayo 25 de Mayo 655, at Bartolomé Mitre; map p.840. A patisserie/bakery with an unbeatable selection of snacks and takeaway lunches, known for mouth-watering pastries, sold by weight, adorning the windows. Mon–Sat 7am–9pm.

Parada Sur Paraguay 1049, at Gardel ☎ 29082327; map p.840. A neighbourhood *parrilla* with friendly service, and whose walls and food are infused with gaucho tradition. For the less carnivorous there's fish, pasta and salads too. Steak from US$250. Mon & Sat 8pm–1am, Tues–Sun noon–4pm & 8pm–1am.

★ **La Pasionaria** Reconquista 587 ⊚ lapasionaria.com. uy; map p.840. This gourmet café, beloved among the city's arty crowd, serves fresh, seasonal and inventive dishes and is tucked away in La Pasionaria art complex. Mains US$280. Mon–Thurs 10am–6pm, Fri 8–11pm, Sat 11am–5pm.

La Pasiva Sarandí 600, at Plaza de la Constitución ☎ 29157988; map p.840. A national institution for one thing and one thing only; *panchos* (hot dogs) and beer at the bar. This one is the original, but it is now a nationwide chain. Mon–Thurs 8am–1am, Fri 8am–2am, Sat 8am–3am.

Rincón de los Poetas San José 1312, at Yaguarón; ☎ 29015102; map p.840. For big, cheap plates of comfort food, try this popular lunch and dinner spot above the artisan market in the beautiful old Mercado

★ TREAT YOURSELF

El Palenque ☎ 29170190, ⓦ elpalenque.com.uy; map p.840. The atmospheric Mercado del Puerto (see page 841) has become a victim of its own success with most restaurants offering overpriced and distinctly average food. While *El Palenque* is a little overpriced (the UR$130 cover charge could buy you a whole meal elsewhere), it bucks the trend by serving truly excellent food. You'll spend at least UR$600 for the fresh seafood and meat, cooked on the grill in front of you, but it's worth it. Mon, Sat & Sun noon–5pm (last reservation) Tues–Fri noon–9pm. There's also a branch in Punta del Este.

de la Abundancia. *Menú del día* UR$240–270. Mon–Sat 11.30am–11.30pm.

Rincón de Zabala Zabala 387, Ciudad Vieja and also at Buxareo 1321, Pocitos ⓦ rdz.com.uy; map p.840. Those really on a budget cannot do better than this *empanada* joint where everything is made to order and arrives piping hot. There are twenty fillings to choose from, both savoury and sweet. The molten *dulce de leche* filling is divine. *Empanadas* UR$30–50. Lunch only. Mon–Fri 11.30am–2.30pm.

POCITOS AND PUNTA CARRETAS

Carbón, Sal y Leña España 2688, at Fco. Aguilar, Pocitos ☎ 27113422; map p.840. A highly recommended *parrilla* run by a friendly husband and wife who cook the best steak in the city on their wood-fired grill. Imaginative sides, stir-fries and home-made pasta too. Mains UR$250–450. Tues–Sat from 8pm.

Philomène Solano García 2455, at Miñones ☎ 27111770 ⓦ philomenecafe.com; map p.840. An elegant, but cosy, French-style café serving some great light bites – including gourmet soups, sandwiches and salads (UR$240) – as well as the finest real tea in the city. Mon–Fri 9am–8.30pm, Sat 11am–8.30pm.

DRINKING AND NIGHTLIFE

There are several good bars in the Ciudad Vieja, mainly along Bartolomé Mitre and Ciudadela. The area known as the "World Trade Centre" in Pocitos (Av Dr Luís A. de Herrera leading up from the Rambla República del Perú) has a huge number of bars and clubs, but they tend to be more expensive than in the centre. Bars open in the early evening and close in the early hours, when, at weekends, clubs will open.

BARS AND CLUBS

Baar Fun Fun Soriano 922 ☎ 29044859 ⓦ barfunfun.com. uy; map p.840. Open since 1895, *Fun Fun* has been visited by the likes of the Chilean president to Bryan Adams. You can watch some top tango singers and dancers while you try the house speciality drink, *uvita* (similar to grappa), for just UR$130.

Burlesque Av Dr Luís A. de Herrera 1136 ☎ 29044859; map p.840. One of the most popular bars in Pocitos, this Americana-themed place has a massive range of whiskies (more than 40), good Tex-Mex food and is a great place to start – or finish – on this buzzing nightlife boulevard. Mon–Fri 6pm–1am, Sat & Sun 7pm–2am.

Caín Dance Cerro Largo 1833 ⓦ caindance.com; map p.840. Uruguay is one of the most gay-friendly countries in South America and *Caín* is the friendliest gay club in town, getting its groove on every Friday and Saturday night. Opens at midnight, though no one goes before 3am.

Living Paullier 1044; map p.840. A chilled-out grungy bar, between the centre and Pocitos, that will make you feel at home in Montevideo. The staff will join you for a shot of the house Grappamiel (UR$80), and DJs might take over the downstairs room. Wed–Sun 9pm–3/6am.

★ Museo del Vino Maldonado 1150 ☎ 29083430, ⓦ museodelvino.com.uy; map p.840. Despite its name, this is no museum but a wine (only national wines are sold) and tango bar. Live music covers are UR$250, but the ambience is worth it. There are free *milongas* (community tango dances) every week. Tues–Sat from 9pm; tango classes Wed 8pm.

LIVE MUSIC AND DANCE

★ La Conjura Tristán Narvaja 1634, at Uruguay ☎ 091684957; map p.840. A second-hand bookstore that also sells locally made clothes and has a cheap café (daily noon–8pm; *menú del día* UR$500), plus live *Candombe*, tango and Afro-Uruguayan beats (Fri & Sat 10.15pm–4am).

Joven Tango Mercado de la Abundancia, San José 1312 ☎ 29015561, ⓦ joventango.org; map p.840. If you are a tango enthusiast, head to the food court of this market, which is converted into a dance-floor for classes followed by dancing. Mon–Fri 5–10pm.

ENTERTAINMENT

Teatro Solís Reconquista s/n, corner of Mitre ☎ 19503323, ⓦ teatrosolis.org.uy. Uruguayans are justly proud of their historic theatre. Shows the best of Uruguayan opera, music and theatre at subsidized prices. Tickets start at around UR$150.

Teatro de Verano Rambla Wilson, at Cachón ☎ 27124972, ⓦ www.teatrodeverano.org.uy. For some of the biggest moments during Carnaval and to see international music stars, try this outdoor amphitheatre in Parque Rodó.

Cinemas Most films are shown in their original language with Spanish subtitles. The best selection is at Life Cinemas (ex Casablanca, Ellauri 350, at 21 de Septiembre; ☎ 27073037, ⓦ lifecinemas.com.uy) in Punta Carretas, and the enormous Movicenter in Montevideo Shopping (Luis Alberto de Herrera 1290; ☎ 29003900, ⓦ movie.com.uy) in Pocitos. Tickets cost UR$290.

10

10

SHOPPING

Av 18 de Julio is Montevideo's main commercial street, while there are some large malls located in Pocitos and Punta Carretas.

Bookshop Central shops at Sarandí 640 and at 18 de Julio 1296 with Yaguarón (shops 4–5); map p.840. See ⓦ bookshop.com.uy for locations (surcursales). Stocks a good range of English-language novels.

Esencia Uruguay Sarandí 359 ⓦ esenciauruguay.com. uy; map p.840. If you can't get out to the *bodegas* in the countryside, sampling Uruguay's fine wine selection at this pleasant shop may well be the next best thing.

Manos del Uruguay San José 1111; map p.840. Stocks a range of high-quality woollen clothes, all of which are handmade using traditional methods in Uruguay by women working in co-operatives. Open Mon–Fri 10.30am–6.30pm, Sat 10am–2pm.

Mercado de los Artesanos Mercado de la Abundancia, San José 1312; map p.840; Mercado de la Plaza, Plaza Cagancha; Espacio Cultural Barradas, Piedras 258, at Pérez Castellano, ⓦ mercadodelosartesanos.com.uy. Three excellent indoor artisan markets where you can find original, high-quality souvenirs.

La Pasionaria Reconquista 587 ⓦ lapasionaria.com. uy; map p.840. A sophisticated multipurpose art complex housing a design store, boutique clothing shop, small gallery, and the excellent café *Doméstico*.

DIRECTORY

Banks and exchange You'll find ATMs in Tres Cruces Terminal, and branches of all the major banks along Av 18 de Julio in the centre, or at the World Trade Centre in Pocitos.

Embassies and consulates Argentina, Cuareim 1470 (☎ 29028623); Australia, Cerro Largo 1000 (☎ 29010743); Brazil, Artigas 1394 (☎ 27072119); Canada, Plaza Independencia 749, office number 102 (☎ 29022030); South Africa, Dr Gabriel Otero 6337 (☎ 26017591); UK, Marco Bruto 1073 (☎ 26223630); US, Lauro Muller 1776 (☎ 17702000).

Hospital Hospital Británico, near Tres Cruces Bus Station on Italia 2400 (☎ 24871020), offers good private healthcare.

Internet and phone Cyber Fast, Treinta y Tres 1375, at Sarandí, is open Mon–Fri 9am–7pm.

Laundry Most of the hostels have cheap laundry services. There are no self-service laundrettes but Lavadero Mis Niños, at Andes 1333 in Ciudad Vieja, charges UR$240 to wash and dry a backpack full of clothes.

Post office Misiones 1328 (Ciudad Vieja), at Ejido; between San José and Soriano (central).

Tourist police Uruguay 1667, at Minas (☎ 08008226).

Western Uruguay

Although Western Uruguay is often neglected by visitors heading for the eastern beaches, **Colonia del Sacramento**, just one hour away from Buenos Aires, is the most common point of entry for tourists – especially Argentine day-trippers – as well as being one of the most beautiful and intriguing towns on the whole continent. The even sleeper **Carmelo** is small Uruguayan town personified, where you can get out into the vineyards or relax at the quiet riverside beaches.

COLONIA DEL SACRAMENTO

Originally a seventeenth-century Portuguese smuggling port designed to disrupt the Spanish base of Buenos Aires across the Río de la Plata, **COLONIA DEL SACRAMENTO** (often referred to simply as "Colonia") is a picturesque town with charming little museums, plenty of outdoor activities and some of the best foodie culture in Uruguay. Despite an increasing number of tourists visiting, the town retains a sleepy indifference to the outside world and merits more than just a day-trip to get to know it.

WHAT TO SEE AND DO

Start your trip at **BIT**, the "Uruguay experience", the country's flagship tourist information centre (Odriozola 434; daily 10am–7pm; ☎ 45221072, ⓦ bitcolonia.com; free), two blocks from both the bus terminal and ferry port. It's architecturally interesting – built in a modernist glass box at the old railway station, beautifully integrated with the disused tracks – and is also a fantastic source of information for both Colonia and the whole country. From there it's an easy stroll around the atmospheric **Barrio Histórico** (old quarter), or there's an easy half-day excursion on foot or by bus to the eerie abandoned resort of **Real de San Carlos**.

Plaza Mayor and around

At the southwestern corner of the plaza is the 1857-constructed **lighthouse** (daily 10am–1pm & 2.30pm–sunset; UR$25),

COLONIA DEL SACRAMENTO

ACCOMMODATION
El Capullo	4
El Nido	1
Rivera	5
Sur	6
El Viajero B&B Posada	2
El Viajero Hostel & Suites	3

SHOPPING
El Abrazo	1
Colonia Shopping	2

EATING
La Bodeguita	3
Buen Suspiro	5
Lentas Maravillas	2
Mi Carrito	1
Viejo Barrio	4

DRINKING & NIGHTLIFE
Barbot	2
Tr3s Cu4tro	1

Río de la Plata

10

which affords great views from the cupola, while at the southeastern corner lie the remains of the old (if heavily restored) city gateway, the **Portón de Campo**. Once charged with protecting the important trade centre from invading forces, now they permanently separate old Colonia from the "new" city.

A few blocks north of the plaza, along Vasconcellos, the **Iglesia Matríz** claims to be the oldest church in Uruguay, with some columns from the original Portuguese building constructed in 1730.

The central museums

Dotted around the Barrio Histórico, a UNESCO World Heritage Site, is a series of nine modest **museums** (all 11.15am–4.45pm, each closed one day a week on different days; joint ticket for all nine UR$50; ⓦ museoscolonia.com.uy). The **Museo Municipal** (closed Tues), on the west side of Plaza Mayor, is the only place you can buy the joint ticket. It houses town treasures and a small natural history museum and is worth a peek around. A few of the other museums deserve a look if you have time, especially the restored **Casa**

Nacarello (closed Tues), next to the Museo Municipal, whose tiny rooms, with period furnishings, give you a taste of colonial life. The **Museo del Período Histórico Portugés** (between De Solís and De los Suspiros on the Plaza; closed Wed & Fri) is also worth a visit; you'll find some fine *azulejos (tiles)* here, and the internal walls are constructed in rectangular and diagonal brick patterns, dating back to around 1720.

The similarly named **Museo del Período Histórico Español** (De España, at De San José; closed Wed), at the north end of the Barrio Histórico, also exhibits colonial items, but, most interestingly, has seven evocative oil paintings by Uruguay's most famous contemporary painter, Carlos Páez Vilaró, creator of Casapueblo (see page 853), depicting important moments in Colonia's history.

Bastión del Carmen

If you wander along the piers on the northern edge of the Barrio Histórico, you'll notice the striking red-brick **Bastión del Carmen** (Rivadavia 223; Tues–Sun 1–8pm; free; ☎45227201), with walls

10

dating from the time of Governor Vasconcellos (1722–49). Once a fortress, it was converted into a factory producing soap and gelatine products in the 1880s, and a chimney from that period still stands. Today it operates as a cultural centre, with a theatre, gallery and a small museum dedicated to its history.

Real de San Carlos

Outside of Colonia's centre, the only other attraction is the **Real de San Carlos**. The brainchild of millionaire Nicolas Mihanovic, who conceived it as an exclusive tourist complex for rich Argentines, it now lies largely deserted. Between 1903 and 1912, he constructed a magnificent bullring, which was used only eight times in two years, a *frontón* (Basque pelota) court which now lies decaying, and a racecourse, which is the only part of the resort still operational.

Regular **horse races** take place, and the horses can frequently be seen exercising along the nearby beach. If you fancy a ride yourself, the *Hostel Colonial* organizes **horseriding** trips for up to two hours (UR$850) to forests and wineries outside town. To get there either walk the 5km north along the *rambla*, or catch a bus (10min) from the bottom end of Avenida General Flores.

ARRIVAL AND DEPARTURE

By bus and ferry The terminal and port are located next to each other three blocks to the south of Av General Flores (the main street). The town centre is a 10min walk to the west along Manuel Lobo. Ferries run by Buquebus, Colonia Express and Seacat run to Buenos Aires every couple of hours (1–3hr; UR$600–1500 one-way).

Destinations by bus Carmelo (every 2hr Mon–Sat, 5 daily Sun; 45min–1hr 30min); Montevideo (every 1–2hr; 2hr 45min).

INFORMATION AND TOURS

Tourist information Colonia has no shortage of tourist information centres. BIT is the main one (see page 846); there's another branch on Manuel Lobo by the Portón de Campo, run by the Intendencia (daily 9am–6pm; ☎ 45228506, ⊛ coloniaturismo.com), and smaller offices in the bus and ferry terminals.

Tour operators Local operator Borra Vino Wine Tours (☎ 093724893, ⊛ borravinowinetours.com) can take you on vineyard tours around Colonia and Carmelo around US$100/person for a half-day tour. City walks with professional guides start at the tourist information office on Lobo daily at 11am and 3pm (UR$150; ☎ 099379167).

Bus Turístico Colonia (⊛ busturistico.com.uy) runs a bus tour (US$25) and walking tour (US$20).

ACCOMMODATION

The standard of budget accommodation in Colonia is dire and prices are higher than elsewhere, though most are central. It's worth investigating the out-of-town *Estancia El Galope* (see page 849) or splashing out more for a nicer place such as *El Nido*. Breakfast is included unless otherwise stated. For a comprehensive list of hotels and hostels by star rating, try ⊛ hotelesencolonia.com.

HOSTELS

★ **Sur** Rivadavia 448, at Mendez ☎ 45220553, ⊛ surhostel.com; map p.847. The lovely lads who run this and *Pocitos Hostel* in Montevideo have made it their mission to spread *buena onda* ("good vibes") among their guests, and the staff are always on hand to give a local perspective. Dorms UR$450, doubles UR$1200

El Viajero Hostel & Suites/B&B Posada W. Barbot 164 ☎ 45222683; Odriozola 269 ☎ 45228645, ⊛ elviajerohostels.com; map p.847. Success has made this Uruguayan chain of HI hostels feel a little formulaic and institutional, but it is a reliable choice. In Colonia, there is a hostel with some "suites" (private rooms), and around the corner is a "B&B Posada" offering nice private rooms with TV, some with river views. Dorms UR$570, suites UR$900, B&B Posada doubles UR$2250

HOTELS AND B&BS

These hotels provide rooms with TV, private bathrooms and a free breakfast.

★ **El Capullo** 18 de Julio 219 ☎ 45230135, ⊛ elcapullo. com; map p.847. This boutique hotel is stylish yet cosy, with a gorgeous garden, swimming pool and a great breakfast buffet. Not cheap, but head and shoulders above other places which charge only a couple of hundred pesos less. UR$3900

El Nido Tula Suárez de Cutinella s/n, Paraje El Caño ☎ 45203223, ⊛ facebook.com/elnidocolonia; map p.847. Two adorable treehouses with well-equipped kitchens overlooking vineyards a true really laidback

★ TREAT YOURSELF

No visit to the countryside would be complete without a stay or at least a daytime visit to an *estancia* – a working ranch; note that *estancias turísticas* are essentially rural hotels (download a list from ⓦ turismo.gub.uy).

El Galope 50km west of Colonia near Colonia Suiza, ⓦ elgalope.com.uy. One of the few *estancias* run with backpackers in mind, English-speaking owners Miguel and Mónica aim to provide "a holiday from your holiday", offering R'n'R, Uruguayan style. With horseriding, a sauna and great food all priced separately, you can choose how much or how little you do (meals UR$200–300, horseriding UR$850). Dorms UR$710, doubles UR$1930

experience 8km from downtown Colonia. There is also a country cottage for rent. Bring provisions. UR$2700
Rivera Rivera 131 ☎ 45220807, ⓦ hotelrivera.com.uy; map p.847. A comfy hotel with an Alpine feel, conveniently located a block from the bus terminal and port with rooms for up to five. UR$2465

EATING

Although restaurants in the Barrio Histórico are pricey, the quality on the whole is excellent and the ambience is hard to beat.

La Bodeguita Del Comercio 167 ☎ 45225329, ⓦ labodeguita.net; map p.847. Buzzing, stylish place whose three terraces overlooking the river get crowded with people who've heard rumours of the best pizzas in town (UR$190). Tues–Sun from 8pm, Sat & Sun 12.30–3.30pm.
Buen Suspiro Calle de los Suspiros 90 ☎ 45226160; map p.847. On the most photographed street in Uruguay, only recognizable by a discreet sign, this intimate foodie heaven specializes in fine wines, cheeses, charcuterie and preserves attractively served on platters for sharing (as a main for two UR$360–650). Reservations recommended. Mon & Thurs–Sun 11am–midnight.
★ **Lentas Maravillas** Santa Rita 61, ☎ 45220636; map p.847. If you've got an afternoon to relax you won't find a cosier way to do it than perusing owner Maggie's English-language books in front of the fire or on the riverside deck. Inventive baked goods with a superb carrot cake, gourmet sandwiches (UR$320) and hot drinks. Mon–Thurs & Sun 1–8pm, weekends only April–Nov.
★ **Mi Carrito** Rivadavia 302, at Lavalleja; map p.847. There is nowhere locals rave about for budget food more than this food truck selling the best bad food you'll ever eat. Try the epic *milanesa* for two with every topping imaginable (UR$190), or the *pancho* wrapped in bacon with mozzarella

(UR$100). Mon–Sat 11.30am–4pm & 8.30pm–1am, Sun 11.30am–4pm
Viejo Barrio Vasconcellos 169 ☎ 45225339; map p.847. This otherwise decent Italian restaurant serves the best veal *milanesas* (schnitzel) this side of Vienna, including one stuffed with ham and cheese (UR$380). Mon & Thurs–Sun 10am–4pm & 6–11pm, Tues 10am–4pm.

DRINKING AND NIGHTLIFE

Barbot Washington Barbot 160; map p.847. Notable for being the first craft brewer in town, *Barbot* is buzzy, friendly and pulls a mean pint of IPA. Its central location in a revamped colonial house means there are plenty of corners to kick back in. Also serves up decent pizza and Tex-Mex (UR$200–450). Wed–Sun from 6pm.
Tr3s Cu4tro Alberto Mendez 295; map p.847. Their slogan says it all: "One building, two courtyards, three dancefloors, four bars, steaming hot". A great Uruguayan *boliche* (bar/nightclub), good for a few drinks, or for staying up all night. There is an entry fee (UR$100–200), but once you get in, food and drinks are reasonably priced. There's often live music too. Wed–Sat from 11pm.

SHOPPING

The Barrio Histórico is littered with fashionable, pricey boutiques selling locally made as well as more generic leather goods, but the best deals for handicrafts are to be found at either the *fería* or the artisans' market (Dr Daniel Fosalba; daily 10am–6pm).
El Abrazo Flores 272; map p.847. A commendable little shop selling Uruguay-specific books, including English translations of national authors Benedetti and Galeano, music, and locally made gifts and clothes. Daily 10am–7pm.
Colonia Shopping Roosevelt 458 ⓦ coloniashopping.com.uy; map p.847. Mall with all the expected facilities, including a cinema.

DIRECTORY

Banks and exchange Av General Flores is the main commercial street and has many banks, casas de cambio and ATMs.
Hospital 18 de Julio between Rivera and Mendez.
Internet Free wi-fi in the Plaza 25 de Agosto, computers either at the main Antel office, or there's an internet café at Flores 172, open until 9pm every night.
Laundry Arco Iris on Suárez between Flores and 28 de Julio.
Post office and telephone Correo Uruguayo and Antel have offices next to each other on Lavalleja on Plaza 25 de Agosto, and share an office in the ferry terminal.
Taxi A 24hr service is run from the corner of Flores with Mendez (☎ 45222920).
Tourist Police At the main *comisaría* on Flores opposite Plaza 25 de Mayo (☎ 21527100).

10

10

WINERIES NEAR CARMELO

Bodega Familia Irurtia Ing. Quim. Dante Irurtia & Paraje Curupi ☎98874281, ⊚irurtia.com.uy. Founded in 1913 by Don Lorenzo Irurtia, this winery remains in the family's capable hands. Book ahead for a guided visit of the vineyards and *bodega* before tasting some Tannat, Pinot Noir and Malbec in a cellar steeped in history. Daily 10am–4pm.

Narbona Wine Lodge Av Ruta 21, Km268 ☎45446831, ⊚narbona.com.uy. If staying at this stunning complex is way out of your budget at URS9400 for a double, at least a wine tasting is within reach. Comprising the old cellar dating back to 1909 and a more contemporary one, sample a variety of Narbona's wares at a tasting or at the country cottage-style restaurant.

CARMELO

Despite being the only town founded by Uruguayan hero General Artigas in 1816, **CARMELO** isn't as historically rich as nearby Colonia del Sacramento. However, it does offer a good supply of natural resources, from quiet and pristine riverside beaches to rolling hills and boutique wineries. Carmelo is slowly picking up speed as a popular, if pricey, destination for those in the know. The town is also a good base from which to visit legendary meat-extraction town Fray Bentos, 136km up river.

WHAT TO SEE AND DO

Local **wineries** (see page 850) welcome visitors to wine and olive-oil tastings; once the hard work is out the way, kick back on one of the sandy beaches. **Playa Sere**, at Av Grito de Asencio and Avenida Del Exodo, a fifteen-minute walk from downtown, is a shady and peaceful part of the coastline, with uninterrupted expanses of white sand.

Fray Bentos

When the Anglo meat-packing factory opened in Fray Bentos in 1858, it proved the industrial revolution had arrived on the shores of the River Plate. The plant-turned-museum **Museo de la Revolución Industrial**, Rambla Andrés Montaño, Fray Bentos (daily 9.30am–5.30pm; guided visits 2pm Tues, Fri & Sat UR$50, 3pm Fri & Sun UR$90; ☎1935, ⊜museo.anglo@rionegro. gub.uy), showcases the beginnings of Uruguay's beef industry – as well as offering a trip down foodie memory lane for Brits of a certain age. Agencia Central buses leave Carmelo twice a day for Fray Bentos (18 de Julio 811; ☎45422987).

ARRIVAL AND INFORMATION

By plane Carmelo has a small international airport, Zagarzazú, with small charter flights and private planes arriving from San Fernando in Argentina.

By bus Although plans are afoot for a central bus station, buses arrive and depart at their own office. Berrutti (from Colonia) is located at Uruguay 337 (☎45422504), while Agencia Central (Sabelin and Chardre lines from Montevideo) is at 18 de Julio 411 (☎454222987).

Destinations Colonia (hourly; 1hr 30min); Montevideo (8 daily; 3hr).

By boat The *Cacciola* arrives twice daily to Carmelo from Tigre in Argentina.

Tourist information 19 de Abril 246, Casa de la Cultura (daily 9am–6pm, ☎45423840).

ACCOMMODATION

If it's time to splash out, the delightful *Narbona Wine Lodge* (see page 850) is a real treat.

Camping Naútico Carmelo Rambla de Carmelo, south of the stream ☎45422058, ⊜dnhcarmelo@adinet. com.uy. Well-sized campsite close to Playa Sere beach catering for up to 300 people. Clean bathrooms are a bonus, while *asadores* in the making can make use of the grills. Two-person tent UR$250

CampoTinto Camino de los Peragrinos, Colonia Estrella ☎45427744, ⊚posadacampotinto.com. Treat yourself to one of the four rooms at this lovely posada set among Tannat vineyards 5km out of town. Breakfast is abundant, service professional, and there's an on-site restaurant, swimming pool and bikes for borrowing. UR$4400

Posada del Navegante Rodó 383 ☎45423973, ⊚posadadelnavegante.com. A stone's throw from the beach, this simple eight-room hotel comes with most mod cons. UR$2500

EATING

El Horno 19 de Abril 101, at Ignacio Barros ☎45422555. Locals rave about the wood-oven pizzas and *chivito* at this place. Great service helps tip the balance at this joint. UR$250–350. Wed–Mon & Wed–Sun noon–midnight, Tues 8pm–midnight.

Piccolino 19 de Abril, at Roosevelt ☎ 45424850. More of the same fodder at this decent diner opposite the main square serving up well-priced Uruguayan staples (UR$300–UR$400. Daily except Tues 10.30am–1am.

The interior

Some of South America's most undiscovered natural beauty awaits you in Uruguay's interior. This is real **gaucho country** and it's easily accessible, if little known about. While most of the interior is unknown to tourists, largely because it's mostly covered in vast ranches, some of Uruguay's finest and least explored pastoral landscapes are within reach of **Minas**, a small town with a big history.

MINAS AND AROUND

Just 120km from Montevideo, but far from the usual backpacker trail, **MINAS**, the capital of the Lavalleja department, is an excellent base for exploring the rolling hills and romantic traditions of Uruguay's interior – you won't have to go far before you see a genuine mounted gaucho wearing a poncho and clutching his *mate*. Delving into this region's history can give you a deeper understanding of the Uruguayan mentality and the nation's history.

WHAT TO SEE AND DO

In Minas, there are some interesting **museums** worth visiting, as well as pleasant parks, but around Minas is where the real fun lies. **Parque del Salto Penitente**, in craggy moor-like countryside, offers outdoor adventures aplenty, while **Villa Serrana** is a copse of isolated houses offering complete rest and relaxation in pretty surroundings.

Central Minas

Most of the region's draw lies in the rolling hills surrounding the town, but there are some cultural surprises here that warrant a pause before heading out into the countryside. The city is easily navigated; the main shopping street, 18 de Julio, is parallel with Avenida Treinta y Tres which runs along the north side of the main square, **Plaza Libertad**, and onwards to the bus terminal. Full of palm trees and with a horseback statue of the national hero Juan Lavalleja, who lends his name to the department, Plaza Libertad is a pleasant place to sit and enjoy a pastry from one of the country's most renowned patisseries.

Casa de la Cultura

One block south of the main plaza is the excellent series of museums housed in the **Casa de la Cultura** (Lavalleja 572, at Rodó; daily 8am–6pm; free), including rooms displaying gaucho artefacts from the nineteenth century and a room dedicated to Uruguayan composer Eduardo Fabini. Independence leader Lavalleja's childhood house sits in the central courtyard; one of the forty original houses from the town's foundation, it has been restored, but its original ceiling beams made from palm trees are intact.

Teatro Lavalleja

The city's most surprising building is the grand old **Teatro Lavalleja** (Batlle y Ordóñez between Florencio Sánchez and Sarandí), a magnificent brick construction finished in 1909, with regular productions and also housing the odd **Museo del Humor y la Historieta** (Mon–Fri 8am–6pm, Sat & Sun 1–6pm; free), dedicated to caricatures.

Cerro Artigas

The city is surrounded by some very pleasant parks. **Cerro Artigas** is worth visiting for its great views of the city and surrounding hills, as well as its imposing 10m-high concrete statue of the liberator Artigas on his horse, said to be one of the largest equine statues in the world. Avenida Varela goes all the way to Cerro Artigas from central Minas – around a 45-minute walk – or a taxi costs UR$200.

Parque del Salto Penitente

At the heart of this private natural reserve is a delicate waterfall, the eponymous **Salto del Penitente**, which falls some 60m before following its course. Here there is a restaurant (open daily for lunch), precariously cantilevered off the hillside

10

over the falls, as well as a hostel and terrace affording graceful views across the park, all under the same management (☎44403096, ⊛saltodelpenitente.com). Sleeping is in shared wood cabins (UR$1500), or you can camp, and there's a rustic common room with an open fire. Activities include horseriding, rock-climbing, zip-wiring and abseiling (all UR$350–500), as well as hiking and birdwatching. It's tricky to get to without a car, but the management can collect you from Minas or a taxi is around UR$1000.

Villa Serrana

With zero amenities, other than a handful of places to stay, it's hard to even award **Villa Serrana** village status; it's more a cluster of houses 25km from Minas. However, its location is Elysian, perching on top of a horseshoe string of hills around a lake, with splendid walking, fishing and horseriding opportunities – not to mention magical sunsets. Its other major attraction is a remarkable historic hotel, the **Ventorrillo de la Buena Vista**, designed by Uruguayan architect Julio Vilamajó, which attracts architecture fans from across the world. Built in 1946, its brilliance lies in its synthesis with its surroundings, and it has been tastefully restored to run as a splendid restaurant and inn (see page 852). There are just two **buses** a week to and from Minas to Villa Serrana (Tues & Thurs 9am & 5.30pm, returning shortly after that; 30min), but if you're staying there you'll probably be able to arrange a lift with your hosts. Taxis cost UR$1300.

ARRIVAL AND INFORMATION

By bus Intercity and local buses arrive and depart from the Terminal de Omnibuses (☎44429791), three blocks west of Plaza Libertad on Treinta y Tres between Claudio Williman and Sarandí.
Destinations Montevideo (hourly; 1hr 40min–2hr 30min); Punta del Este (10 daily; 2hr); Villa Serrana (4 weekly; 30min).
Taxi 24hr service from the Plaza Libertad (☎095749380). Set prices to surrounding areas.
Tourist information At the bus station (daily 8am–7pm; ☎44429796, ⊛lavalleja.gub.uy).

ACCOMMODATION

It's worth booking ahead; accommodation is limited and fills up fast, especially during Minas' large festivals over nine days in October and on April 9.

Camping Arequita 10km north of town on Ruta 12 ☎44402503, ⊛lavalleja.gub.uy/web/lavalleja/campingarequita. Set in pleasant grounds at the foot of Cerro Verdún (a grand rocky peak with caves to explore), each plot has electricity and a barbecue. Horseriding can be arranged, but there's no internet. 12km from town; buses from Minas run Dec–Feb. Self-catering cabins UR$1600, mini-cabins (beds only) UR$800, camping/person UR$160

Posada Verdún Dr Washington Beltrán 715, at Beltrán ☎44424563, ⊛hotelposadaverdun.com. The same family has run this posada, the best-value place in town, for more than two decades. The rooms are clean with private bathrooms and TV; there's also a recommended restaurant. Doubles (includes breakfast) UR$1700

★ **Villa Serrana B&B** The green thatched house in Villa Serrana ☎098280811. Owned by the exuberant Zen López, who speaks fluent English, the house has three spacious rooms and is decorated with flea-market finds and bright colours. There is also an adjacent self-catering bungalow for groups. Horseriding and other day-trips in the country can be arranged. Doubles UR$1900, bungalow (up to 8 people, breakfast not included) UR$2600

EATING

★ **Confitería Irisarri** Treinta y Tres 618, Plaza Libertad ☎44422038 ⊛confiteriairisarri.com.uy. A family business originating in 1898, this confectionery shop and tearoom is one of the great treats in the region. Try their speciality – yemas – bonbons designed to look like egg yolks. Selection of pastries with coffee UR$100. Daily 9am–9pm.

Ki-Joia Domingo Pérez 489, Plaza Libertad ☎4442 5884. A surprisingly modern, decent-value parrilla with quick and friendly service and alfresco tables overlooking the plaza. The meat is good and the home-made pasta is excellent. Mains UR$220–500. Daily 6pm–1am; parrilla open from 8pm.

★ **Ventorrillo de la Buena Vista** Villa Serrana ☎44402036, ⊛ventorrillodelabuenavista.com.uy. The name means "Good View Inn", and if you can't afford the UR$2000 for a double designer room (each has a living room with working fireplace as well as bed and bath), at least eat at the restaurant and enjoy one of the best views and meals in Uruguay (mains UR$250–450). Try the borego confitado – lamb, date and walnuts with beetroot pasta. Mon–Fri 10am–9pm, or 11.30pm at weekends for dinner.

DIRECTORY

Banks and exchange Av 18 de Julio is the main commercial street and has many banks, casas de cambio and ATMs.

Hospital On Av Pedro Varela between Maldonado and Dighiero ☏ 44422058.
Internet Cyber Peatonal on 25 de Mayo charges UR$20/hr.

Police Off Plaza Libertad down Vidal, at Fuentes.
Post office Wáshington Beltrán, at 25 de Mayo.

The eastern beaches

Uruguay's biggest draw is its vast, and largely unspoilt, coastline. Humans have made their mark with *balnearios* (coastal resorts or villages), each with very personalities. Between Maldonado and Rocha departments you can choose between the hedonistic party life in **Punta del Este**, the isolated and rugged **Cabo Polonio**, the blissful beaches and dunes of **Valizas** or wild surfing and nightlife in **Punta del Diablo**, all with shimmering **lagoons** full of birdlife in between.

The towns are easy to hop between, especially in the summer; but they change drastically off-season; in winter, everything shuts down and they can feel completely deserted. Other than in luxurious Punta del Este, be sure to come with enough **cash** to fuel your stay; there are no banks or ATMs in the smaller villages.

PUNTA DEL ESTE

Situated on a narrow peninsula 140km east of Montevideo, **PUNTA DEL ESTE** – simply called Punta – is a jungle of high-rise hotels, expensive restaurants, casinos and designer stores bordered by some of the finest beaches on the coast. Exclusive, luxurious and often prohibitively expensive, between this and the nearby towns of **La Barra** and **José Ignacio**, this is *the* place to be seen for many South American celebrities in summer.

WHAT TO SEE AND DO

The best thing to do in Punta is what everyone else does: hit the beach during the day and go drinking at night. Within striking distance and well worth the trip is the whitewashed **Casapueblo**, a remarkable villa and art gallery.

The beaches

These are what attract most visitors to Punta del Este, and two of the best are on either side of the neck of the peninsula.

Playa Mansa on the bay side is a huge, arcing stretch of sand, with plenty of space for sunbathing and gentle waves, while **Playa Brava** on the eastern side is where you go if you're serious about **surfing**, or simply to compare your height to the fingers of the uncanny **Hand in the Sand** sculpture, one of Uruguay's most famous sights. Both sides are commonly referred to by these names, although there are actually many beaches with their own names.

Off the coast

From Playa Mansa, there are excellent views out to the wooded **Isla de Gorriti**, once visited by Sir Francis Drake (boats daily in high season if sufficient demand; UR$400/person). Slightly further off the coast lies the **Isla de Lobos**, home to one of the largest **sea-lion colonies** in the world. Calypso (opposite *La Galerna* at the entrance to the harbour; ☏ 424461521, ☏ calypso.com.uy) offer expensive tours, though if you just want to see sea lions, it's worth heading down to the port itself in the early morning: they are often out sunbathing as the fishermen set sail.

On the peninsula

Life on the peninsula offers a glimpse of what the town must have been like when it was a modest holiday village a few decades back – the **port** area up to **Plaza el Faro** is charmingly old-world and the houses represent a host of architectural styles not present in the identikit luxury developments that have sprung up all along the adjacent coastal roads.

Casapueblo

The area's best sight is the vision of Uruguayan artist Carlos Páez Vilaró – **Casapueblo** (daily 10am–sunset; UR$240 for entry to museum; upwards of UR$6000 for a room out of high season; ☏ 42578041, ☏ carlospaezvilaro.com.uy & ☏ clubhotelcasapueblo.com). He started the

10

10

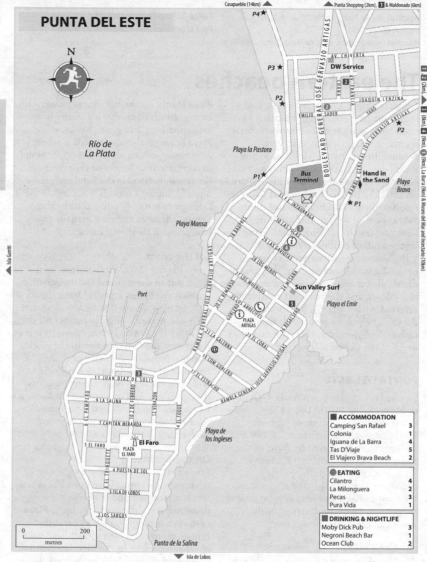

PUNTA DEL ESTE

Casapueblo (14km) ▲   ▲ Punta Shopping (2km), **1** & Maldonado (6km)

P4 ★

Río de
La Plata

Isla Gorriti ◄

Playa la Pastora

AV. CHIVERTA
DW Service
AV. FRANCIA
EMILIO
JOAQUÍN LENZINA
VARO

P3 ★
P2
BOULEVARD GENERAL JOSÉ GERVASIO ARTIGAS
RAMBLA GENERAL JOSÉ GERVASIO ARTIGAS
P2 ★

Bus
Terminal
★ P1
Hand in
the Sand
Playa
Brava

P1 ★
11 F.E. INZAURRAGA
30 LAS FOCAS
Playa Mansa
28 LAS GAVIOTAS
24 LOS MEROS
25 LOS MURGOS
Sun Valley Surf
Playa el Emir
Port
26 LOS ARRECIFES
27 LOS MELUZAS
PLAZA
ARTIGAS
23 EL CORAL
21 LA GALERNA
19 CON GORLERO
17 EL ESTRACHO
13 JUAN DÍAZ DE SOLÍS
10 2 DE FEBRERO
12 VIRAZÓN
14 EL ROQUE
RAMBLA GENERAL JOSÉ GERVASIO ARTIGAS
9 LA SALINA
8 EL CAMPERO
7 CAPITÁN MIRANDA
5 EL FARO
El Faro
PLAZA
EL FARO
6 EL TRINQUETE
4 PUESTA DE SOL
3 ISLA DE LOBOS
2 LOS SARGOS
Playa de
los Ingleses

0   200
metres

Punta de la Salina

▼ Isla de Lobos

■ ACCOMMODATION	
Camping San Rafael	3
Colonia	1
Iguana de La Barra	4
Tas D'Viaje	5
El Viajero Brava Beach	2

● EATING	
Cilantro	4
La Milonguera	2
Pecas	3
Pura Vida	1

■ DRINKING & NIGHTLIFE	
Moby Dick Pub	3
Negroni Beach Bar	1
Ocean Club	2

construction himself in the late 1950s, and today it's an unwieldy yet strangely beautiful villa, restaurant, hotel and art gallery clinging to the side of a craggy peninsula 15km west of Punta. Bright white and lacking any right angles, it's well worth a visit to see Vilaró's artwork and have a cocktail in the bar at sunset. To get there, take any bus from the terminal towards Montevideo and ask to be dropped at the

entrance to Punta Ballena, from where you'll have a thirty-minute walk up along the peninsula. A taxi will cost UR$700–800.

La Barra

Sandwiched between forested hills on one side and golden beaches on the other, **La Barra** took over as the fashionable place to stay for those tired of the Punta crowds, and its characterful houses are set along tree-lined dirt tracks which preserve its rustic feel. With gentrification, hippy cafés have been replaced with designer clothing stores, but it's still the place for summer nightlife, with new "it" clubs, bars and restaurants springing up each year. One kilometre from the famous **undulating bridge** connecting Punta with La Barra, you'll find the frankly bizarre **Museo del Mar & Insectario** (well signposted; daily 10.30am–5.30pm/8.30pm; UR$160; ☎ 42771817, ⓦ museodelmar.com.uy), whose intriguing collection of marine artefacts includes a mind-boggling array of seashells, insects, and a 19m whale skeleton.

ARRIVAL AND DEPARTURE

Addresses are often given by their *parada* – or bus stop number – which you'll see on poles in the middle of the large dual carriageway – the Costanera – which hugs the coast either side of PdE. The streets in the peninsula have names and numbers, but addresses usually give their numbers.

By bus Punta del Este's bus station lies at the top end of Av Gorlero, just past the roundabout, at the neck of the peninsula. It's a 10min walk to the port along Av Gorlero, or a 5min walk to Playas Mansa or Brava. To reach the beaches further east, you need to get back to the main Ruta 9 by catching the #1 or #2 bus from Punta del Este to San Carlos (every 15min–1hr; 50min) from C 20 (winter), or C 26 (summer). From there most buses with Chuy as the destination will stop in Punta del Diablo (2hr 30min), or get off at Castillos for connecting buses to Cabo Polonio or Valizas. Alternatively, there are two buses direct to Castillos each day (11am & 5pm) from Punta's terminal.

Destinations Minas (4–7 daily; 2hr); Montevideo (every 30min; 2hr).

GETTING AROUND

Local buses #9, #12, #17, #19 and #24 go from C 20 (winter), or C 26 (summer) to Maldonado via Punta Shopping (every 30min; daily 6am–11pm; 20min). Codesa buses go from the terminal to La Barra, Manantiales and José Ignacio (Mon–Sat hourly 5.20am–midnight; Sun 6am–9pm; more buses in summer). See ⓦ codesa.com.uy for timetables (*horarios*).

Taxis Taxi stands by the beaches, on Gorlero and at the bus terminal. Minicabs are sometimes cheaper than metered cabs – Punta can get snarled up with traffic. Try Conrad Remises at Artigas, at Chiverta (☎ 42490302), or driver José Techera (☎ 098447000).

INFORMATION, TOURS AND ACTIVITIES

Tourist information National tourist office at Gorlero 942, at C 30 (high season: daily 10am–1.30pm & 2.30–6pm; low season: Mon–Sat 10am–5pm, Sun noon–4pm). Local tourist office in Plaza Artigas (daily 8am–5pm or later in high season; ☎ 42446510), and in the bus terminal. The website ⓦ welcomeuruguay.com has good information in English.

Tour operators Most tour companies offer city tours (usually including Casapueblo), boat trips, vineyard and ranch tours, as well as organizing motorized transport such as Segways and quad bikes, or renting cars or bikes. Hostels generally provide the most backpacker-friendly tours, but try A.G.T. (☎ 42490570, ⓦ agtviajesyturismo.com) in the bus terminal, or DW Service (Artigas, at Chiverta; ☎ 94440812, ⓦ dwservice.net; see p853). Nationwide tour operators covering Punta are also worth checking out (see page 843).

Surfing Sunvalley Surf (☎ 42481388, ⓦ sunvalleysurf.com) has two stores in Punta, one at Playa El Emir (C 28, at Rambla Artigas) on the peninsula and the other at Playa Brava, between *paradas* 3 and 4 (daily 11am–7pm all year), and another opposite the Nike shop in La Barra (daily 11am–11pm all year).

ACCOMMODATION

In the summer months (Dec–Feb) accommodation is wildly overpriced (you may pay upwards of US$40 for a dorm bed), yet this does not put people off; book at least a month in advance. In winter you won't need to book and prices will be affordable again, but most hostels close down completely. Options listed here are open year-round (except the campsite). If you're stuck, try the tourist information offices, who can help with accommodation.

CAMPING

San Rafael Aparicio Saravia s/n 800m from Parada 30 ☎ 42486715, ⓦ campingsanrafael.com.uy; map p.854. Set in pleasant woods, this campsite has a minimart and wi-fi, and lies just 1km from La Barra. It's 15 percent cheaper off season and there are other discounts for longer stays; closed April–Oct. Camping/person **UR$360**, self-catering cabin (sleeps four) **UR$3500**

HOSTELS

Several buses run every hour (and throughout the night in high season) to La Barra and Manantiales (10min). Dorm beds in January can cost upwards of UR$1000, but quickly fall back to normal prices after that. Prices are given for the cheapest dorm beds and doubles in Jan, breakfast included.

Iguana de La Barra C 8, at Ruta 10, La Barra ☎ 42772947, ⓦ iguanadelabarra.hostel.com; map p.854. The friendly owners have made their home welcoming and relaxing, with built-in beds instead of bunks in private rooms, and a fireplace downstairs. Dorms **UR$450**, doubles **US$1140**

Tas d'Viaje C 25, at 27 & 28 ☎ 42448789, ⓦ tasdviaje.com; map p.854. A good choice in the hostel scene in Punta, which can be grotty. This place feels like home and is probably the best located of all the hostels, right in the centre of the peninsula. Dorms **UR$1200**, doubles **UR$1800**

10

El Viajero Brava Beach Salazar, at Charrúa ☎ 42480331, ⓦ elviajerohostels.com; map p.854. Part of the successful Uruguayan chain, this house on the edge of the peninsula has a large common room with a pool table and fireplace. In high season a second hostel opens at Manantiales beach (Ruta 10 Km164, just past La Barra), 11km away from Punta, which, outside of Dec–Jan, can be around half the cost. Dorms UR$750, en-suite twins UR$5300

HOTELS

Hotel rates are typically more reasonable in Maldonado, 20min by bus from Punta (take the #10 from C 20).
Colonia 18 de Julio 884, Maldonado ☎ 42223346, ⓦ colonialhotel.com.uy; see map p.854. An old-fashioned hotel with modern touches. Located opposite San Fernando church, and Playa Mansa is 1.5km away. Price includes breakfast. Doubles UR$2860, apartment UR$5300

EATING

The peninsula is packed with expensive restaurants, and even the best-value places are pricey, though there are bargains if you look around. Restaurants usually go by standard Uruguayan opening hours out of season, but in summer you can eat until about 2am. For very cheap fast food, head to Av Gorlero, where places are open 24hr in high season. Cheap seafood is not available in restaurants, so try the stalls below the port for the freshest hauls and cook at your hostel.
Cilantro C 29, at Gorlero; map p.854. Vegetarians can tuck into abundant fresh salads at this central spot, which also serves decent sandwiches and veggie burgers for under UR$500. Tues–Sun 9am–4pm & 7pm–1am.
La Milonguera Joaquín Lenzina, at Blvd Artigas; map p.854. The big wagon wheel outside characterizes this rustic *parrilla*, popular with locals, which serves tasty grilled meat such as *vacío* and pastas at fair prices. Mains UR$450–500. Daily noon–4pm, 8pm–midnight.
Pecas Gorlero, at Las Focas, ⓦ heladeriapecas.com.uy; map p.854. Better than its rivals across the street, and slightly cheaper (ice cream: two flavours and two toppings UR$120), *Pecas* also serves breakfasts. Daily 9am–late.
★ **Pura Vida** Ruta 10 Km160, behind the petrol station in La Barra, ☎ 4277 2938 ⓦ puravidaresto.com; map p.854. Informal but elegant restaurant with a slow food ethos and a huge range of interesting dishes, including plenty for vegetarians. Worth the trip to La Barra (mains UR$350–600). Summer daily 10–12.30am; winter Mon, Wed, Thurs & Sun 11am–5pm, Fri & Sat 11am–11.45pm.

DRINKING AND NIGHTLIFE

Punta is home to a wild nightlife scene; most bars serve drinks from midday, but the real parties start at around 2am and rarely end before sunrise. The top clubs change every season; check ⓦ ilovepunta.com.

Moby Dick Pub Artigas 650, ☎ 42441240 ⓦ mobydick.com.uy; map p.854. The only reliable and down-to-earth watering hole in town, albeit with inflated prices. There's a good range of cocktails (UR$350) to sip outside as you watch the ships go by, and there's also live music and food. Daily from noon; low season daily from 5pm.
Negroni Beach Bar Ruta 10, Km164.5, ☎ 094363400, ⓦ negronibistrobar.com; map p.854. This Buenos Aires fixture pops up each summer, offering a great if pricey range of cocktails designed by celebrity bartenders (UR$450). In the thick of things in Manantiales, burgers are one of the menu highlights (UR$450). Daily from noon; high season only.
Ocean Club Parada 12, Playa Brava; map p.854. A multi-room venue right on the beach, and one of just two clubs that are open year-round (women free before 2am, men around UR$400), this place is flashy and loud, playing pop, rock and house. Dress to impress. Opens 1am Fri & Sat.

SHOPPING

Between Gorlero and the huge mall Punta Shopping (Roosevelt between Los Alpes and Gattas; ⓦ puntashopping.com.uy), you'll find most services, including a supermarket, cinema and bowling. There's a pleasant artisan market (daily in summer, weekends only in low season, 10am–6pm) in Plaza Artigas.

DIRECTORY

Banks ATMs are located along Gorlero, and at Punta Shopping.
Hospital Hospital de Maldonado, in Maldonado (Continuación Ventura Alegre; ☎ 42559137, ⓦ hospitaldemaldonado.com).
Laundry Espumas del Virrey, C 28, at 18.
Police 2 de Febrero, at Artigas (☎ 21525221).
Post office Gorlero 1035.

CABO POLONIO

Moving east from brash Punta del Este can be a shock to the system – the *balnearios* thin out and become increasingly rustic – but even the hardiest rural-dweller would find the lack of infrastructure in **CABO POLONIO** surprising. Originally no more than a few fishermen's huts, the settlement consists of 95 permanent residents who live in rustic dwellings; the cape with its dunes and forests is protected as a national park and camping is not allowed.

There's little to see or do other than soak up the beauty of the cape, spot **sea lions** near the 135-year-old **lighthouse**, climb it (daily 10am–1pm & 3pm–sunset; UR$25) or hike (you can walk unobstructed both ways along the coast to Valizas 10km to the east, or as far as La Pedrera 43km to the west). Ask around to arrange horseriding, or trips to the **Laguna de Castillos** with its strange *ombú* trees. Although in high season it can be inundated with tourists during the day, it still exudes a dreamy, other-worldly isolation, thanks to its lack of roads and electricity, best experienced by staying overnight.

ARRIVAL AND DEPARTURE

To reach the cape from Valizas it's possible to hike, ride or pay someone with a rowing boat, but most guests arrive via the visitor centre (☎095643217, ⊛turismorocha.gub.uy) at the entrance to the national park at Km264.5 of Ruta 10. This is where buses from Montevideo (5 daily) or Castillos (at least 3 daily; more during summer) to Cabo Polonio will drop you (the car park costs UR$190/24hr). From here walk the final 7km (over sand), or take a truck-bus (30min drive; daily, hourly 7am–10pm Dec–Feb, less frequent March–Nov; UR$230 round trip).

ACCOMMODATION AND EATING

Cabo Polonio Hostel ☎099445943, ⊛cabopoloniohostel.com. A rustic place with solar-powered electricity and a pedal-powered washing machine. Meals can be pricey in the village, so bring supplies and use the kitchen. Dorms UR$850, doubles UR$2450
Lo de Dany Camino Posadas s/n ☎099875584. Sweet wooden and tin roof place close to the main square serving up *chivitos*, pizza, fresh fish and *milanesas*. Dishes from UR$250. Open all year round.

BARRA DE VALIZAS

In the summer, Cabo Polonio's slightly more grown-up next-door neighbour, **VALIZAS** (as it's more commonly known), feels like you're at one big festival. You'll either love or hate the hazy, dreadlocked, guitar-strumming vibes, with people practically living on the enormous and ancient sand dunes from Christmas until Carnaval in February, but it's worth staying both for its beauty and because in January, when prices along the coast soar, you'll find better value here. Out of season you'll have the sweeping sun-bleached beaches to yourself.

ARRIVAL AND DEPARTURE

By bus There are local buses from Castillos (every 2–3hr; 30min) and Montevideo (7 daily; 4–5hr).

ACCOMMODATION AND EATING

Lucky Valizas Tomás Cambre 115 (stroll across the football pitch one block to the right of where the bus will drop you) ☎44754070, ⊛luckyvalizas. blogspot. com. Stay with Lucky in her home-turned-eco-hostel; she knows everyone in town and can arrange horseriding or boats to Cabo Polonio. Prices include breakfast and are halved, or more, off-season. Dorms UR$580, cabins for two UR$1470, camping/pitch UR$600
El Rabuk By the lake. At the only restaurant open year-round for lunch and dinner, this husband-and-wife team serves excellent fresh fish at bargain prices. Grilled fish with salad UR$250.

PUNTA DEL DIABLO

For a similar mix of remoteness and natural beauty to Cabo Polonio but within reach of a supermarket, electricity and heady nightlife, **PUNTA DEL DIABLO** is the place to go. Stay in a hostel or beach cabin; relax in a hammock or go out and hit the waves.

WHAT TO SEE AND DO

During the summer months, the population swells from some 1500 inhabitants to over 20,000 and you'll find pop-up businesses, hostels and internet facilities appear – they even wheel in an ATM. The rest of the year you're stuck with a handful of restaurants by the **Playa Pescadores**, the main beach strewn with fishing boats (a tourist information office springs up here during summer months).

The **surfing** is excellent all year, and the hostels are the best place to rent gear out of season. There are other beaches either side of Pescadores: northeast the **Playa Grande** is vast and will lead you to the **Parque Santa Teresa** 10km away (around a 3hr walk), a small national park with some easy forest treks and an impressive fort. Along the southwest edge of town, the **Playa de la Viuda** tends to get the biggest waves, although all are good for surfing and the abundance of wide beaches means it never gets unbearably crowded.

Don't miss the twenty-minute walk up Avenida Central (starts at the northern end of the Playa de los Pescadores) until the houses start to thin out. Keep looking to your right, and soon you'll come across **La Casa Mágica** – the Magic House. Built by a

10

10

CROSSING THE BRAZILIAN BORDER

Crossing the border is straightforward if you catch an international **bus** from Montevideo or any major town (the last of which is San Carlos) on the Ruta 9 heading north: the bus driver will take your passport details at the start of the journey and get all the required stamps for you en route. If you want to stop in Chuy itself (a haven for duty-free and electrical shops and not much else), or are planning to cross the border from any of the beach towns on the northern coast, it becomes more complicated. It is essential that you have all the correct visas in place, and receive all necessary **entrance and exit stamps** from both the Uruguayan and Brazilian border controls before entering Brazil.

All local buses heading north stop at the Brazilian border, 2km to the north of Chuy, but Uruguayan bus drivers do not routinely stop at the Uruguayan border control, so you'll have to ask to get off. The **tourist office at customs** (daily 9am–5pm; ☎44742003, ⊛turismorocha. gub.uy) can assist with information regarding crossings.

---

local woodworker, it's in the shape of a head, the steps leading up to the door form the tongue, and it's made entirely from carved wood and found objects. When someone's in, you'll be welcomed inside to admire the workmanship and artwork.

ARRIVAL AND DEPARTURE

By bus In high season, buses stop at the new terminal on Bulevar Santa Teresa, about 3km from the centre. In low season, they all go into town to Av de los Pescadores, the street that leads to the main beach, from where you'll be able to spot the hostels off to the right when you look back. Offices for the three bus companies which serve the town are located at the terminal; however, you can pay on board, though you might lose your seat to a pre-paid traveller. Destinations Chuy (hourly; 1hr 30min); Montevideo (10-plus daily; 4hr); Rocha (hourly; 1hr 30min); San Carlos (for Punta del Este; 6 daily; 3hr 30min). Check ⊛turismorocha. gub.uy for timetables.

ACCOMMODATION

Hostels have sprung up in the last few years; check online before you go for hostels which open seasonally. Locals throughout the town also rent out their cabañas for tourists – look out for the signs saying *se alquila*, but these are generally only cheaper if you're in a group. Expect the prices to be more than halved outside of Dec–April.

Botella al Mar ⊛marosierras.blogspot.com. Two sweet white cabins just 150m from the Playa Pescadores right in the centre of town; one sleeps two and the other four. They come fully equipped (apart from sheets and towels), and have sea views. Cabin for two per day, minimum stay seven days UR$1720

★ **La Casa de las Boyas** C 5 s/n, also access from Av Central ☎44772074, ⊛lacasadelasboyas.com. This well-equipped hostel – the oldest in town – sprawls over several buildings all connected with wooden walkways.

Kitchenettes in the dorms furthest away from the house, lots of bathrooms and a swimming pool elevate this from the rest. Dorms UR$700, lofts (sleeps up to six) with kitchenette UR$1000

★ **El Diablo Tranquilo Hostel & Br** Hostel on Av Central, Suites opposite on beach ☎44772647, ⊛eldiablotranquilo.com. Bright red hostel with open-plan common areas and a fun terrace kitchen with sea views, which compensate for the rather cramped dorms. There are boutique en-suite rooms and dorms in both locations; the newer building is on the beach with a funky bar for guests. Dorms UR$800, doubles UR$3100

EATING AND DRINKING

The best place to start for food or drink is the Av de los Pescadores, leading down to Playa de los Pescadores. In high season bars and clubs open down by Playa de la Viuda and at the top of Av Central (there are huge parties held near the old bus station). Everywhere runs on less than reliable opening hours out of season. In summer everything opens late and closes late.

Cero Stress Close to the police station, Av de los Pescadores ☎094711377. Suitably nautical and also nice, this space is one of the better dining options in Punta del Diablo, plus it boasts a deck with a sea view. Tuck into the catch of the day dressed up in a hearty stew (UR$460), or one of the many beef cuts (UR$300). Friendly staff is a bonus. Open all year round daily for lunch and dinner.

Lo de Olga Av de los Pescadores ☎099919822. Olga has more than thirty years' experience serving up the freshest fish in town with an excellent range of seafood, fish, pastas and Uruguayan staples like *chivitos*, all under UR$400. Service can be haphazard. Ask for the *menú túristico*, which will be much cheaper than *à la carte*.

Mirjo Av de los Pescadores ☎099874478. A classy joint serving fine food and Italian coffee right by the beach. Grilled fish with side dish UR$400.

ORINOCO DELTA

Venezuela

❶ **Mérida** A high-altitude adventure sports paradise. See page 889

❷ **Los Llanos** Endless horizons, stunning wildlife, and cowboys. See page 895

❸ **The Amazon** Tropical rainforest and otherworldly geography. See page 897

❹ **Angel Falls** The world's tallest waterfall. See page 902

❺ **Orinoco Delta** A vast region of waterways and indigenous tribes. See page 905

❻ **Parque Nacional Mochima** Deserted beaches, luminescent plankton and fantastic seafood. See page 908

HIGHLIGHTS ARE MARKED ON THE MAP ON PAGE 861

ROUGH COSTS

Daily budget Basic US$15, occasional treat US$25 (see page 869)
Drink Polar beer (300ml) US$0.04
Food *Arepa* US$0.80
Budget hotel US$5
Travel Caracas–Ciudad Bolívar (596km) by bus, US$8.75

FACT FILE

Population 31.3 million
Language Spanish
Currency Bolívar Soberano (BsS). See page 869
Capital Caracas (population: 2.9 million)
International phone code ☎58
Time zone GMT -4hr

Introduction

Currently in a state of crisis, with chronic shortages of food, medicines and other necessities, Venezuela is not an easy nor especially a safe place to visit at present, although the plummeting currency and black market exchange rates do make it very cheap, and it remains one of the most underrated destinations in South America. Unfortunately, the desperate situation in which most Venezuelans now find themselves has led many into crime, with much of the country barely under any kind of police control, and opportunistic robberies are common. On top of this, the authorities are blaming the situation on foreigners, so foreign travellers in the country may be seen as suspect. Western governments including the US State Department and the UK Foreign Office advise against all but essential travel, and in particular warn against travel anywhere near the Colombian border, where armed smuggling gangs may operate. These warnings may also invalidate your travel insurance if you do go there, so be sure to check that in advance. Of course we hope the situation in Venezuela will improve, and soon, but in the meantime, you should keep your ear to the ground and think twice before deciding to visit.

Venezuela's prime attractions lie outside its major urban areas, with 43 **national parks** preserving the country's natural beauty. The capital, **Caracas**, a lively city of petrol-financed concrete, is towered over by the jungled **Ávila**, a stunning mountain range separating the city from the Caribbean coast – a geographical feature which affords the capital one of the planet's most agreeable year-round climates. Venezuela also has a stunning 2600km-long Caribbean **coast**. Several hours east of the capital, **Parque Nacional Mochima** boasts red-sand beaches, fishing villages, fantastic seafood and playful dolphins, while **Parque Nacional Henri Pittier**, about three hours west, offers wildlife-spotting opportunities, crystal-clear lagoons and a lively social life. Further west is **Parque Nacional Morrocoy**, which features picturesque white-sand cays. More exclusive, the **Los Roques Archipelago** in the Caribbean contains the country's most pristine beaches with fewer crowds, given the off-mainland transport issues.

Mérida, in the northern extent of the continent-spanning Andes range, is the best place to arrange trips to **Los Llanos**, the extensive plains that provide some of

the best wildlife and birdwatching opportunities on the continent. The enormous region of **Guayana** encompasses most of the south and east portions of the country and boasts a number of adventure-based attractions. Here you'll find the **Orinoco Delta**, a labyrinth of jungle waterways formed as the enormous river reaches the Atlantic Ocean. Further up the Orinoco, the historic town of **Ciudad Bolívar** is the most economical base from which to explore **Parque Nacional Canaima**, where **Angel Falls**, the world's highest waterfall, plunges a vertical kilometre into the jungle below.

CHRONOLOGY

C.13,000 BC–1498 AD Roughly 500,000 indigenous people live in the area today covered by Venezuela, belonging to three principal ethno-linguistic groups: Carib, Arawak and Chibcha.

1498 Christopher Columbus arrives August 4 at the eastern tip of the Paria Peninsula and continues south to the Orinoco Delta.

1502 Italian Amerigo Vespucci sees the Arawak houses on wooden stilts in Lake Maracaibo and calls the place Venezuela, or "little Venice". Enslavement of the indigenous population for pearl harvesting begins.

WHEN TO VISIT

Venezuela can be visited year-round, but you are most likely to get the best out of visiting during the November-to-May **dry season**. On **the coast**, there is less rain and fewer mosquitoes, although humidity is an issue year-round. Wildlife spotting in **Los Llanos** is much better in the dry season, when animals congregate at the few watering holes, while the abundance of mosquitoes during the wet season makes walking very unpleasant. Travel in the **Guayana** region is more comfortable during the dry season, though Angel Falls tends to be fuller and therefore more spectacular during the wet season.

If you are after beach time, it is best to come outside the national holiday periods of Easter, Carnaval (which begins at the end of Feb or beginning of March), Christmas (Dec 15–Jan 15) and the summer holidays (July 15–Sept 15). Venezuelans generally spend their holidays at the beach and the hordes drive prices up and the tranquillity down.

1521 The first European settlement is established at Cumaná, on the northeast coast, serving as a base for Catholic missionaries and further exploration.

Late 1500s The Creoles, Spanish descendants born in the New World, accumulate slaves, agricultural wealth and a large degree of autonomy.

1819–21 Simón Bolívar, a wealthy Creole landowner from Caracas, wins several naval battles against the Spanish and liberates the territory of Colombia. Bolívar proclaims the new Republic of Gran Colombia, an independent nation made up of modern-day Venezuela, Colombia and Ecuador.

1829 Gran Colombia disbands in the face of irreconcilable internal disputes, and Bolívar, bitterly disappointed by the dissolution of his dream, succumbs to tuberculosis.

1859–63 A power struggle between Liberals and Conservatives, known as the Federal War, results in Liberal control of Venezuela for forty years.

11

11

1908–35 General Juan Vicente Gómez rules the country and becomes one of Venezuela's most brutal dictators. Press and public freedoms are curtailed and political dissidents murdered.

1918 Oil is discovered in Venezuela along the Caribbean coastline, and ten years later the country is the largest producer in the world. Gómez pays off foreign debts and invests in infrastructure.

1973 Carlos Andrés Pérez is elected and governs Venezuela through one of its most prosperous periods, during which the petroleum industry is nationalized.

Late 1970s–80s Increased oil production in other countries sends prices spiralling downwards. Inflation and unemployment increase and Venezuela sells much of its precious oil reserves to pay its debts.

1992 A mid-level military officer named Hugo Chávez launches an unsuccessful coup attempt against Pérez and is imprisoned; soon after, Pérez is found guilty of corruption charges.

1994 Chávez is pardoned for his coup attempt and continues gathering support around the country.

1998 In a landslide victory over former Miss Universe Irene Sáez, Chávez is elected president and, through a referendum, establishes a new constitution that dismantles the Senate, increases state control over the oil industry and grants the military greater autonomy.

2000 Chávez wins a new election.

2002 Government officials and the middle class, angered by Chávez's reform laws and a weakening economy, incite massive, violent protests on April 11; the next day, Chávez is taken into military custody. Two days later the interim government collapses and Chávez regains control.

2007 Chávez attempts to pass, by national referendum, a constitutional reform that would facilitate federal expropriation of private property and, most controversially, allow him to be re-elected indefinitely. He is narrowly defeated. Shortly after, Chávez turns the clocks back a half-hour, claiming it will increase the country's productivity.

2010 The opposition overturns Chávez's two-thirds majority in Parliament, reducing the president's sway on the National Assembly.

2012 Hugo Chávez wins his third presidential election, defeating his closest challenger yet, Henrique Capriles. The victory extends Chávez's term as president until 2018, although he misses his January inauguration due to ill health.

2013 Hugo Chávez's death to cancer is announced by the Venezuelan government. Following a closely fought emergency presidential election, former foreign minister and Chavez's anointed heir, Nicolás Maduro, wins the presidency by less than one percent. Over 25,000 murders are committed in Venezuela during the year.

2014–15 Global oil prices hit a fifty-year low, decimating the economy. Inflation hits sixty percent. Shortages throughout the country, with long queues for basic foodstuffs.

2016 Supreme Court bans four legislators, National Assembly swears them in anyway, so the court suspends it and rules its decisions null. Protests and food riots erupt nationwide.

2018 Inflation hits six thousand percent by the end of February. In May a controversial election sees Nicolás Maduro wins a second term in office.

ARRIVAL AND DEPARTURE

Venezuela can be reached by land from neighbouring Colombia and Brazil, but not directly from Guyana to the east. In January 2018, the Venezuelan government banned direct travel to or from Curaçao, Bonaire and Aruba, but private firms are still running ferries between Güiria and Trinidad.

BY AIR

Nearly all international flights land at Simón Bolívar International Airport in Maiquetía, often known simply as **Maiquetía Airport**, between 45 minutes and an hour from central Caracas (see page 870). Lately, a number of airlines have suspended flights to Venezuela, often citing fears for the safety of their staff, but also because of the sharp drop in tourism during the current crisis. From many places, therefore, you may have to fly via Panama.

BY LAND

The Venezuelan government has banned direct road transport across the border with Colombia and Brazil. You can still cross on foot, however. In typical South American style, Venezuela claims two thirds of Guyana, and does not allow direct access across the (actual as opposed to imaginary) border, although travel to Guyana is easy enough via Boa Vista in Brazil. The border situation is complicated by huge numbers of Venezuelans trying to leave the country, and by periodic border closures. When crossing, you must get an exit stamp before leaving the country you're coming from and an entry stamp from the country you're going to – omitting to do either of those will almost certainly result in you being sent back, and could incur fines and cause you trouble with the authorities. You may be asked for a yellow fever vaccination certificate when crossing in either direction by land.

PASSPORTS AND VISAS

Citizens of Canada, Australia, New Zealand, South Africa, Ireland, the UK and other EU countries do not need a **visa** to enter Venezuela, but US citizens do need one, and this should be arranged as far ahead as possible as it may take weeks to issue. Upon arrival from Brazil you may be asked for a certificate of yellow fever vaccination. You will need to present a passport valid for at least six more months and they will often ask to see an onward ticket.

Always keep multiple photocopies of your passport to hand as Venezuelan officials can be fastidious. Make sure you have your passport number memorized, as you will be asked to supply it for nearly every transaction you make in the country.

To extend your stay for an additional ninety days, go to SAIME, the country's immigration agency, in Caracas (see page 879). Bring your passport, two photos and your return or onward ticket. The process takes a maximum of 72 hours (although it is usually issued the same day) and costs roughly US$50.

GETTING AROUND

The public transport system of buses and *por puestos* is convenient and inexpensive. Internal flights are not always reliable, but are by far the safest way to travel between cities. Nighttime road travel is not recommended.

BY AIR

Flying within Venezuela is a stressful experience, made more difficult for international travellers subject to the whims of uncompromising airline staff. Booking domestic flights online yourself is best avoided as you need a Venezuelan *cédula* (national identity card). You can reserve flights in person through airline offices in major cities and at airports, or – the least stressful option – have a Venezuelan travel agency do it for you. Flights are often booked up many weeks in advance during the high season.

Always call to confirm flight times, and arrive at airports up to two hours in advance, as queues can be formidable. Bring your passport and two photocopies. Domestic flights are usually subject to a local airport tax.

BY BUS

Buses are the primary mode of transport throughout Venezuela and invariably the cheapest. Tickets go on sale on the day of departure and are bought from the various private company ticket booths in the bus terminals. In smaller towns your hotel can reserve your ticket ahead of time.

Venezuelans book all bus travel with their national identification numbers (*cédula*), for which you should use your passport number. You'll usually have to pay a *tasa*, or tax, on top of the bus fare, bought from the dedicated terminal booth and presented when you board the bus or depart the terminal. Most regional bus services end at around 6pm or 7pm.

Local buses, or *busetas*, are minibuses, recognizable by the myriad destination cards stuck to the inside of the windscreens, which can be hailed from roadsides along their routes. Payment is either collected when the bus is in motion or when you alight. If you want to get off at a specific point, shout "*parada!*" (meaning "stop") at the driver, who will let you off at the nearest possible place. Economical buses, or *servicio normal*, are common for shorter distances. These are often cramped, with no toilet or air conditioning; when choosing your seat, try to select one away from the sound system as music is blasted at deafening volumes. More comfortable executive buses, or *servicio ejecutivo*, run longer distances and have toilets. Air conditioning, however, is so intense that you'll need a blanket or sleeping bag. If you're travelling overnight, be sure to take a *bus-cama*, with almost fully reclining seats.

In Venezuela's current state of insecurity it is inadvisable to take overnight bus services. Even though everyone has to show ID, hold-ups occur (even in daylight), usually with on-board accomplices, and killings of passengers who don't co-operate are not unknown.

11

VENEZUELA TOURS

Venezuela's government formerly took the attitude that, "We don't need tourism, we have oil." Now, despite its tanking economy caused by dropping oil prices, the country has yet to develop any passable infrastructure for budget holidaymakers. This means that independent travellers often turn to **agencies** for assistance in arranging trips and activities to the country's top attractions. Booking tours is always cheapest in the closest town to the attraction itself, but if your time is limited, or if you're looking for a multi-destination tour, the following Caracas- and Mérida-based companies can arrange trips anywhere. Companies will require payment either in cash or to an international bank account (see page 869), allowing you to pay at *mercado paralelo* rates. Don't pay with credit cards within Venezuela.

TOUR OPERATORS

Akanán C Bolívar, Ed Grano de Oro, Ground Floor, Chacao ☎ 212 264 0080, ⊛ akanan.com. Akanán offer various hikes, river trips and wildlife expeditions, and their office has plenty of material for researching trips.

Andes Tropicales Av 2 con C 41, Urbanización El Encanto, Mérida ☎ 0274 263 8633, ⊛ andestropicales.org. A Mérida-based company devoted to helping local communities protect the natural environment while promoting tourism in remote areas.

Angel Eco-Tours Edificio Guarimba, 9th floor, Suite 94, Av Francisco de Miranda, Dos Caminos, Caracas ☎ 0414 201 7077, ⊛ angel-ecotours.com. British expat Paul Stanley runs this excellent agency specializing in slightly more luxurious travel than affiliate Osprey.

The company also does a huge amount of community work wherever its tours go, and is particularly active with the indigenous Pemón community of Parque Nacional Canaima (see page 901).

Club Aventurismo Av Andres Bello and 2nd Transversal, Los Palos Grandes ☎ 0212 285 8541, ⊛ aventurismo.com. A tour company covering the entire country, Club Aventurismo offers complete packages ranging from Los Roques beach breaks to exploring the heart of Venezuela's Amazon. Pricing in Bolívars make this a very economical option.

Osprey Expeditions Same office as Angel Eco-Tours ☎ 0414 310 4491, ⊛ ospreyexpeditions.com. The most economical option for backpacker-friendly, nationwide trips, with exceptionally friendly staff. They can also organize pick-ups from Caracas airport.

BY POR PUESTO OR TAXI

Another economical option is the ubiquitous **por puesto** or **carrito**. Essentially shared taxis, *por puestos* are gas-guzzling American sedans in which you pay for one of four or five places and depart when the car is full. They are generally twice the price of a bus ride, but take half the time and are sometimes the only available option. "*¿Cuantos faltan?*" is a useful expression to ask how many places are still to be filled before the car can depart. At black-market rates, taking a **taxi** between cities can be surprisingly affordable, even if there is no *por puesto* service.

BY TAXI

Taxis never have meters, so you should agree on a price before your journey. In towns where public buses are rare, taxis are the established way of getting around. In these cases, fares within the town are set; ask a local beforehand. Don't get into the car until you've agreed upon the price.

ACCOMMODATION

Naturally enough, you'll find Venezuela's best low-end **accommodation** in the towns that attract the most backpackers. Consequently Mérida (see page 889), Choroní (see page 882) and Ciudad Bolívar (see page 899) have excellent budget options. Cheap accommodation is generally poor in larger cities such as Caracas and Puerto La Cruz. It's not uncommon for budget hotels in larger towns to rent out rooms by the hour, and although this is no cause for safety concern, it may offer a clue as to how backpacker-friendly your hotel is. Nevertheless, you can always expect clean sheets and towels. Hot water is rare outside Mérida and other Andean towns.

Dormitories are not common, while youth hostels are virtually non-existent; solo travellers are often stuck paying for a *matrimonial* (double), cheaper than a twin but more expensive than a single. Quality is much higher beyond the big cities and usually appears in the form of **posadas**, affordable family-owned guesthouses, often with lots of individual character. Many posadas and backpacker spots are run by French and German expats. Because of the dearth of tourism during the country's current political and economic situation, many budget hotels in what would ordinarily be tourist destinations are now given over to long-term boarders.

Camping hasn't caught on among Venezuelans, and in general is not recommended because of the risk of robberies, even on isolated beaches and cays.

FOOD AND DRINK

Venezuelan cuisine centres around **meat**, with the most common accompaniments being rice, black beans and *tajadas* (fried plantain strips). Corn flour is the carbohydrate staple of all Venezuelan cooking, the base (and often sole) ingredient in **arepas** (fried cornbread disks), **empanadas** (fried savoury turnovers), **bollos** (boiled corn dough) and the **cachapa** (a sweet-meal pancake folded over a slab of cheese). The **arepa**, the quintessential Venezuelan food, is ubiquitous and given variety by the endless number of fillings which are available. Among the most common are *carne mechada* (shredded beef), *queso amarillo* (yellow cheese) and *reina pepeada* (shredded chicken, mayonnaise and avocado). *Arepa* can be very thick, and those with smaller appetites should tell the restaurant to "*saca la masa*" (scoop out the uncooked interior) before inserting the filling. *Areperas*, restaurants serving up the staple, are generally open 24 hours.

Though rather difficult to find, **vegetarian food** (*comida vegetariana*) and health food (*comida dietética*) are usually available in larger cities, often in restaurants dedicated to these cuisines.

Breakfasts are generally small, usually little more than an *empanada* or *arepa*, and always accompanied by a thimble-sized cup of scalding-hot coffee. Lunch is generally lighter – a good economic choice is the *menú ejecutivo* (soup, main dish and a drink) which many restaurants offer. Common dinner options include fried fish, rotisserie chicken and southern-fried chicken. Italian, Portuguese, Spanish and Arabic food are popular international dishes, thanks to large immigrant communities.

The Venezuelan national dish is **pabellón criollo**, which consists of shredded beef, plantain, cheese, rice and beans; a breakfast version of this is the *desayuno criollo*. *Pabellón*-stuffed *empanadas* are particularly good and should be sampled if stumbled upon.

The ocean, abundant rivers and mountain lakes afford plenty of fresh **fish**, the most common varieties being *mero* (grouper), *dorado* (dolphin fish), *pargo* (red snapper), *trucha* (trout), *corvina* (sea bass) and *corocoro* (grunt).

Common **desserts** are strawberries and cream, *dulce de leche* (milk caramel) and sweets made from guava or plantains. Venezuelan *cacao* (cocoa) is considered among the best in the world, but, as nearly all of it is exported to Europe, Venezuelan chocolate is difficult to find. Two particularly good products are the *CriCri* bars and the *Pirulin* chocolate-filled wafer rolls.

Restaurants tend to open around 6am for breakfast and stay open for dinner, which ends around 8pm. Although restaurants close early, burger and condiment-heavy hotdog stands keep serving until around midnight on main streets. Ask a local for the best in the area as quality varies tremendously.

In most restaurants, it's customary to leave a tip of around ten percent. Restaurants may also add the 13.5 percent tax to the bill.

DRINK

Fruit juices, or *jugos* (also known as *batidos*), are delicious, inexpensive and safe to drink; combined with milk and whipped, they become *merengadas*. The most common flavours are *lechosa* (papaya), *parchita* (passion fruit), mango, *piña* (pineapple), *guayaba* (guava), *guanábana* (soursop) and *tamarindo* (tamarind). Another sweet, refreshing drink is *papelón con limón* (lemonade made with unrefined brown sugar). Bottled water is inexpensive and available everywhere.

Coffee in Venezuela is served very strong, black, sweetened and in small amounts. The tiny red straws that come with the drink are

11

for stirring rather than drinking through. If you want it with milk, ask for *marrón* (brown).

Although you can always depend on being served an ice-cold one, Venezuelan **beer** is bad compared to what you'll drink elsewhere. The major brand is Polar, with several varieties, distinguished informally by colour: the watery Solera comes in *verde* (green) and the weaker azul (blue) varieties, negra (black) refers to the pilsener, and blanca (white) denotes either the light or "ice" varieties.

Dark rum is generally the liquor of choice – try the Santa Teresa 1796 – mixed with cola, lime and plenty of ice to produce the "Cuba Libre", the nation's most popular cocktail. Whisky is popular among the more affluent set (particularly Buchanan's 12 Year and Old Parr).

SELF-CATERING

Given Venezuela's immense **shortages** of every staple from milk to shampoo, those who prefer to self-cater may find serious challenges. Many supermarkets in the country now resort to rationing in order to provide for everyone who braves the six-hour queues, and foreign tourists may not be allowed to buy certain basic items if they are particularly in demand. A good option for those who are determined not to eat out are the road-side bus stops, which sell groceries at an inflated rate compared with the government-controlled supermarket prices, but where prices are nevertheless far cheaper than anywhere else on the continent.

CULTURE AND ETIQUETTE

Thanks to its location at the crown of South America, Venezuela combines distinctive elements of Caribbean and Latin American **culture**. Visitors familiar with these regions won't be surprised to find the country a fairly relaxed place, whose warm, cheerful nationals place a high value on socializing, recreation, food and (loud) music. By the same token, **machismo** is an inescapable aspect of Venezuelan society, and women will experience cat-calling throughout the day. However, Venezuelan law places a high price on female integrity, and should harassment persist past casual flirtation the individual should be reported to the authorities.

Venezuelans are a passionate people, and while a conversation between family members may seem to verge on violence, conversation on any topic invariably leads to raised voices and aggressive gestures. Do not be offended if a Venezuelan interrupts you in the middle of a sentence; simply continue speaking at a higher volume.

Understandably, given their government's notoriety, Venezuelans are **politically aware** and eager to discuss their thoughts about their country. Even in death, President Hugo Chávez excites both zealous fervour and fearful hatred. Venezuelans will listen with good grace to anything you may have to say on the subject of politics, but it's best to be asked before sharing. Don't share any negative opinions about the current government unless you are sure of your company. Anyone dressed in a red T-shirt should be regarded with caution.

SPORTS AND OUTDOOR ACTIVITIES

Close to Caribbean nations such as Cuba and the Dominican Republic, Venezuela's primary sporting obsession is **baseball**. You'll see fans across the country wearing gear from both Venezuelan and American Major League Baseball teams. There is a long history of players heading to the major leagues in the US; the Detroit Tigers are particularly favoured due to Venezuela's large representation on the team. The LVBP (Liga Venezolana de Beisbol Profesional) consists of eight teams, the most prominent being the Caracas Leones and Valencia's Navegantes del Magallanes. The regular season runs from October until December, and attending a game (see page 878) is an excellent experience.

Despite baseball's dominance, **football** has a large following, particularly when the national side, nicknamed the *Vinotinto* (red wine) because of the colour of their strip, plays.

The country is also an **outdoor** enthusiast's paradise, with a variety of landscapes and climates offering the ideal conditions for hiking, paragliding, kite-surfing, snorkelling, scuba diving, white-water rafting and more. Most outdoor activities are concentrated in the few backpacker-friendly destinations, namely Mérida (see page 889), Caripe (see page 909), Ciudad Bolívar (see page 899) and Santa Elena de Uairén (see page 903).

COMMUNICATIONS

Venezuela is relatively technologically savvy, and call centres and internet cafés are found in all major towns; except in the most remote outposts, you should have no trouble finding a reasonable **internet** connection.

Movistar and CANTV (and its cellphone subsidiary Movilnet) are the most visible **telecommunications** providers. All have call centres and outlets in most towns and cities. Pre-paid SIM cards can be topped up by street vendors or in your provider's store. Calls are inexpensive, and data plans are available on every network, including texts, local and international calls. To place an international call, first dial 00 and then the code of the country you are calling.

Ipostel, the Venezuelan national **postal service**, is fairly unreliable. If you have an important letter or package to send, do so through an international carrier like MRW or DHL, which have offices in most major cities. Ipostel branches are typically open weekdays from 8am to 4pm.

CRIME AND SAFETY

Venezuela is not currently a particularly **safe** place to travel in. Certain regions such as the Colombian borderlands – which the UK Foreign Office and US State Department currently recommend avoiding altogether – and areas of Caracas are tense and uninviting, while a corrupt police force sees backpackers as easy targets for extortion.

Opportunistic crime is common in Venezuela, and travellers should always keep an eye on their belongings while using public transport. Do not walk down poorly lit streets after dark and leave your valuables in the hotel (but carry a photocopy of your passport and entry stamp). Don't take things like phones and cameras out in urban areas, always take taxis in cities after dark rather than walking, and don't travel by road at night. If you are unlucky enough to be robbed, calmly accede to the criminal's demands.

Police corruption is a fact of life in Venezuela: police officers earn very little, and see bribery as a legitimate subsidy to their wages. Bribes should never be openly offered to police officers, and never suggested at all to anyone in plain clothes. If stuck with a police officer who refuses to let you go, the suggestion of a "*propinita*" (a tip) for a few hundred Bolívars may be what he is waiting for. Bribery is not condoned, but can make for an easier travel experience in the country.

Illegal drugs are common in Venezuela, most notably *creepy* (a potent strain of cannabis), cocaine and *base* (a crude crack cocaine). Although it's unlikely that you will be offered any, illicit substances should be avoided due to unpredictable police searches and serious penalties for possession.

HEALTH

The main illnesses in Venezuela are dengue fever, yellow fever, hepatitis A, hepatitis B and malaria. Make sure you consult a doctor before travelling; they will be able to recommend which vaccinations to get pre-trip. If entering the country from Brazil you may be asked for a certificate of **yellow-fever** vaccination. The vaccination should be procured four weeks in advance to ensure effectiveness. **Malaria** is a risk in rural parts of the country, particularly Amazonas and the Orinoco Delta.

11

11

Prevention is the best cure with malaria, and the only protection against other mosquito-borne viruses such as dengue, Zika and chikungunya, so take plenty of high-DEET or PMD repellent and long-sleeved clothing. If you plan on a longer stay, consider a course of anti-malarials.

Good **medical care** is available in Venezuela, although this tends to be of a higher standard in Caracas than in the rest of the country. It may be very hard to find a hospital with good facilities, let alone good doctors, in remote areas. Foreigners tend to rely on private clinics, which offer high-quality service.

INFORMATION AND MAPS

What Venezuela's tourism officials – all overseen by the national body Mintur (Wwww.mintur.gob.ve) – lack in useful knowledge for budget travellers, they make up for with charm and enthusiasm. Unfortunately, many offices don't abide by any logical schedule. Additionally, most states have their own tourism entity located in its capital city. Though information provided by private tour agencies is rarely unbiased, independent travellers will find them useful, as they are more in touch with current public transport schedules and black market exchange rates.

A variety of country and regional **maps** is available in Venezuela, the best being

Miro Popic's *Guia Vial de Venezuela/Atlas de Carreteras* and individual city maps. Elizabeth Klein's guidebooks to Venezuela are also an excellent source of information, and these, along with maps, are available in most bookshops.

MONEY AND BANKS

Money – and how to get the most value from it – is likely to be your biggest concern while in Venezuela (see page 869). The country's economy – entirely dependent on oil exports – has the world's highest inflation and a black market with runaway prices. Consequently, Venezuelans and foreigners alike resort to foreign currency transactions through the **black market**, or *mercado paralelo*. This is both a blessing and a curse for international travellers: it makes Venezuela the cheapest country on the continent to travel in with black market rates upwards of twenty times the official, but also means having to keep all one's money in the form of cash, unless you can find someone willing to do you a deal for use of their Venezuelan debit card. The exchange rate varies by the day, with latest information at W dolartoday.com.

Bank hours vary hugely, but are generally open Monday to Friday, 8am to 4pm. Two reliable banks are BBVA Provincial (W provincial.com) and Banco Mercantíl (W mercantilbanco.com), both found in most sizeable towns.

VENEZUELA ONLINE

W **www.mintur.gob.ve** Official site of the government's tourism arm, with current, tourism-related news and links to similar federal agencies.

W **inparques.gob.ve** Official site of the national parks agency, with contact info and descriptions of parks and reserves.

W **miropopic.com** Website for the publisher of Venezuelan maps and reference books, with an online "gastronomic guide".

W **venezuelatuya.com** Decent overview of travel and accommodation in Venezuela, with a smattering of country facts.

W **valentinaquintero.com.ve** An extensive and detailed guide covering all parts of the country, particularly useful for out-of-the-way towns away from the tourist trail.

OPENING HOURS AND HOLIDAYS

Most **shops** are open from 8am until 7pm on weekdays, often closing for lunch from around 12.30pm until 2 or 3pm. **Shopping centres**, however, generally stay open until 9 or 10pm. In addition to their regular business hours, **pharmacies** operate on a "*turno*" system, with a rotating duty to stay open all night; the designated pharmacy will advertise *turno* in neon. All **banks** take a bank holiday on one Monday each month, although these off-days have no fixed timings since they are often scheduled to coincide with other public holidays. Businesses are generally closed on Sunday, while hours are unpredictable if they do open – don't expect to get much done.

MUCH ADO ABOUT MONEY

Visitors to Venezuela should not use ATMs, pay with bank cards or use any form of electronic payment which will incur charges at the official exchange rate, a rate which will have you paying US$30 for a simple *arepa*. Instead, travellers should sell international currency (either in the form of cash or international bank transfers) at **black market rates**. This is due to the country's current economic situation.

Venezuela's government sets an official "DICOM" rate for its currency (BsS49.4775 to US$1 at time of writing) rather than floating it on the international market. At the same time the state controls which citizens are allowed to exchange their Bolívars for other currencies, so ordinary Venezuelans without political connections cannot get hold of international currency, and are desperate to exchange a currency whose inflation rate tops 6000 percent. In March 2018, the government announced a new currency (BsS), knocking three zeros off the old one (BsF), but this cosmetic measure is unlikely to change the situation much.

Changing money informally – on what is known as the *mercado negro, oscuro* or *paralelo* – is technically illegal for Venezuelans, but not for international travellers, who will not incur punishments for doing so. Dollars are easily exchanged with Venezuelans (every hotel listed in this guide will exchange at *paralelo* rates), and the only issue you will encounter will be at what price to sell.

The website **dolartoday** (🌐 dolartoday.com) gives the daily value of the Bolívar against the dollar (the number represents how many BsS you can expect per single dollar exchanged). The website is constantly being shut down by the government, although an internet search will direct you to its latest location. Don't accept anything less than five points off the dolartoday price for bank transfers, or ten points less for cash. If your hotel is offering you less, any independent business may offer more favourable rates.

Do not change money in the airport or border towns. If unavoidable, change only enough to reach a hotel where you can get a more favourable rate. Unfortunately, carrying large amounts of cash is often unavoidable, as it is often better to change large amounts whenever a favourable rate becomes available. Ensure that your stash is divided between different locations in your luggage.

As a result of **massive inflation** in Venezuela it is unlikely that, although correct at the time of research, hotel and restaurant prices listed in this guide will be current.

You do not have to declare carrying cash up to the value of US$10,000 when entering the country.

PUBLIC HOLIDAYS

January 1 New Year's Day (*Año Nuevo*).

January 6 Epiphany (*Día de los Reyes Magos*). Banks close but many businesses stay open.

February Carnaval (seven weeks before Easter). Shrove Monday and Tuesday are public holidays. The most famous celebrations are in Carupano and El Callao.

March or April *Semana Santa* (Holy Week). Due to the pressure of economic crisis, the whole week running up to Easter is now a public holiday.

April 19 *Decleración de Independencia* (Independence Declaration Day). Celebrates the declaration of independence under a local *junta* in Caracas in 1810.

May 1 *Día del Trabajo*. International Labour Day.

May Ascension Day (seven weeks after Maundy Thursday, the Thursday of Holy Week). Banks close but many businesses stay open.

May/June Corpus Christi (ten weeks after Maundy Thursday). Banks close but many businesses stay open.

June 24 St John's Day (*Día de San Juan Bautista*). Choroní, El Higuerote and Ocumare del Tuy. Venezuelans celebrate with drumming and dancing on the streets.

June 24 St Peter and St Paul (*Día de San Pedro y San Paulo*).

July 5 *Día de la Independencia* (Independence Day). Anniversary of the declaration of independence in 1811.

July 24 *Cumpleaños de Simón Bolívar*. Simón Bolívar's birthday.

August 15 *Día de la Asunción*. Religious celebration of the Virgin Mary's Assumption to Heaven.

November 1 *Día de Todos los Santos* (All Saints' Day). The day after Hallowe'en.

December 8 *Inmaculada Condepción* (Immaculate Conception Day). Banks close but many businesses stay open.

December 25 Christmas (*Navidad*). Only Christmas Eve, Christmas Day and New Year's Day are official holidays, but in in practice the entire country shuts down for a week.

FESTVALS

Festivals, most with a religious basis, seem to occur constantly. Some are national, while others are local, as each town celebrates its patron saint. Many overlap with the public holidays listed above. Of particular note is the **Festival de los Diablos Danzantes** in San Francisco de Yare in late May/early June (see page 879).

Caracas

The Venezuelan capital gets something of a bad rap, and while expensive living costs, poor budget accommodation and high crime rates have tended to deter visitors, this cosmopolitan capital nevertheless has some diverting attractions. *Caraqueños* are proud of their vibrant city with its excellent artistic, culinary and social scenes; you'll be surprised at how readily and enthusiastically they are willing to help a foreign traveller.

Caracas's most famous native, **Simón Bolívar**, was born to an influential Creole (Spanish descendant) family in 1783. After several years abroad he returned in 1813 and captured the city from the Spanish. He had to abandon it a year later, but Bolívar had already earned the epithet "El Libertador". When Venezuela became fully independent in 1830, Caracas was made the capital of the new nation. Since then, various political eras have left their mark on the city's architecture, though the predominant aesthetic is the mid-twentieth-century concrete high-rise.

WHAT TO SEE AND DO

The bustling and attractive district of **El Centro** has some excellent museums and budget restaurants, perfect for getting an authentic taste of Venezuela if Caracas is your first port of call in the country. Street vendors and heavy traffic along the wider arteries can be an irritation, but the area is interesting enough for a day's wandering. Sightseeing around this area is best kept to daylight hours as it has a reputation for street crime after dark. Away from El Centro, visitors can take in the gritty street life of **Sabana Grande**, enjoy the business end of town in **Altamira**, immerse themselves in the restaurant scene around residential **Los Palos Grandes**, or party with the beautiful people until the morning in **Las Mercedes**. Slow the pace slightly with a trip to the arty suburb of **El Hatillo**, or treat your lungs to some fresh air with an excursion to **Parque Nacional El Ávila**.

Plaza Bolívar

As with all Venezuelan towns, the **Plaza Bolívar** is the main square, and Caracas's version, a leafy hub northeast of the Capitolio/El Silencio metro station, is a good starting spot for a walking tour. The south side of the square features the **Consejo Municipal** (City Hall), which doubles as the **Museo Caracas** (Tues–Sat 8am–4pm; free), containing artefacts from the city's history as well as seasonal art exhibitions.

Built in 1575, the colonial-style **Catedral de Caracas** on the east side of the plaza houses Bolívar's parents and wife, who are buried in a chapel on the right-hand side. Next door at the **Museo Sacro de Caracas**

CARACAS METROPOLITAN AREA

LA PASTORA

Airport (26km)

Teleférico

Parque Nacional El Ávila

SAN BERNARDINO

AVENIDA BOYACA

LOS PALOS GRANDES

LA FLORIDA

N

AVENIDA ANDRÉS BELLO

AVENIDA BARALT

AVENIDA ARMADA

CENTRO

LA CASTELLANA

AVENIDA LIBERTADOR

SEE 'SABANA GRANDE' MAP

ALTAMIRA

SEE 'EL CENTRO/PARQUE CENTRAL' MAP

SABANA GRANDE

AV. RÓMULO GALLEGOS

AV. FRANCISCO DE MIRANDA

Jardín Botánico

Parque del Este

AV. NUEVA GRANADA

AVENIDA LOS ILUSTRES

EL ROSAL

LA CARLOTA

Terminal La Bandera

BELLO MONTE

SEE 'EASTERN CARACAS' MAP

CHUAO

SANTA MÓNICA

0   2

kilometres

VALLE ARRIBA

● **SHOPPING**

Librería Tecni-Ciencias/ Centro Comercial Lider   1

El Hatillo (6km)

11

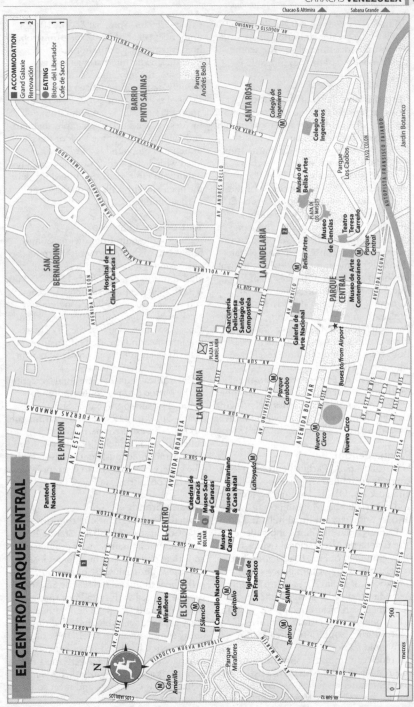

EL CENTRO/PARQUE CENTRAL

ACCOMMODATION
Grand Galaxie   1
Renovación   2

EATING
Bistro del Libertador   1
Cafe de Sacro   1

(Mon–Fri 9am–4pm; ☎0212 861 6562) you'll find a greater collection of artwork with summaries in English. The serene *Café del Sacro* (see page 876) inside is well worth a visit.

Museo Bolivariano and around

If you're interested in learning more about the man who lends his name to seemingly every aspect of Venezuelan life, visit the **Museo Bolivariano** (Mon–Fri 9am–4pm, Sat & Sun 10am–4pm; free), with its entrance on the western side of Plaza Venezolano, one block southeast of the Plaza Bolívar. It contains portraits of El Libertador and his family, carefully preserved relics from his life, and gangs of children on school trips. Next door is the painstakingly reconstructed **Casa Natal** (Mon–Fri 8am–4pm; free), where Bolívar was born and lived until the age of 9. There are portraits and some original furniture, but little in the way of explanation. At his final resting place, the **Panteón Nacional**, five blocks north of Plaza Bolívar, soldiers stand guard over Bolívar's tomb and the more recent addition of Hugo Chávez.

The **Iglesia de San Francisco**, on the south side of Avenida Universidad, is one of Venezuela's oldest churches. Its principal claim to fame is as the place where Bolívar was proclaimed "El Libertador" in 1813.

Parque Central

Not really a park, **Parque Central** is a long concrete strip filled with vendors selling pirated CDs, DVDs, hammocks, jewellery and miracle herbs. More importantly, the district is the city's cultural hub, and home to Caracas's best museums and galleries. The **Galería de Arte Nacional** (Mon–Fri 9am–5pm, Sat & Sun 10am–5pm; free; ☎0212 576 8707, ⊕fmn.gob.ve) is one block west of Bellas Artes metro station on Avenida México. Its primary offering is a permanent exhibition tracing Venezuelan art throughout the last five centuries, while visiting exhibitions often feature household names.

A block east from the same metro stop, the oval Plaza de los Museos has two excellent museums facing one another. On the northern side, the **Museo de Bellas Artes** (Mon–Fri 9am–5pm, Sat & Sun 10am–5pm; free; ☎0212 578 0275, ⊕fmn.gob.ve) houses temporary exhibitions by Venezuelan and international artists. Opposite, the more modern and child-friendly design of the **Museo de Ciencias** (Mon–Fri 9am–5pm, Sat & Sun 10am–5pm; free; ☎0212 573 4398, ⊕fmn.gob.ve) focuses on Venezuelan geography, habitats and wildlife. Around the back of the museums' compound is a leafy walkway lined with coffee stalls and wine bars, a rare opportunity in Caracas to enjoy a drink in the open air. The stalls are open from noon until around 9pm.

Teatro Teresa Carreño

A quick walk south from the museums brings you to the **Teatro Teresa Carreño** (box office Mon–Fri 9am–1pm & 2–5pm; guided tours Mon–Sat 9am–4pm, BsS0.60; ☎0212 574 9034, ⊕teatroteresacarreno. gob.ve), whose compelling concrete and black-glass design contributes to excellent acoustics within. Some of the city's best music, dance and theatre performances take place here; enquire by phone or in person for details of what's on.

The ironically un-contemporary exterior of the **Museo de Arte Contemporáneo** (Mon–Fri 9am–5pm, Sat & Sun 10am–5pm; ☎0212 573 8289, ⊕fmn.gob. ve) belies an excellent permanent collection inside, including Picasso, Miró, Moore and infectiously enthusiastic staff. The gallery is across Teatro Carreño's concrete pedestrian walkway.

Sabana Grande

Named after its 1.5km-long commercial artery, the district of **Sabana Grande** is filled with cheap restaurants, locals promenading and street performers who offer an insight into the Venezuelan sense of humour.

The pedestrianized **Bulevar de Sabana Grande** is lined with numerous specialist shopping malls (see page 878), as well as every other conceivable trade, legitimate or otherwise, on street level. The callejón, a graffiti-rich bar-lined street between the Sabana Grande and Plaza Venezuela metro stations, is a fun, if slightly sketchy, place to have a few cold beers and meet some characters.

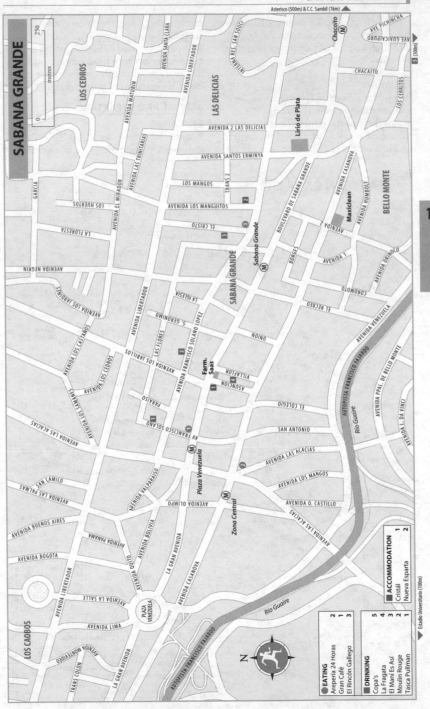

SABANA GRANDE

Asterisco (500m) & C.C. Sambil (1km)

LOS CEDROS

LAS DELICIAS

BELLO MONTE

LOS CAOBOS

AVENIDA SANTA CLARA
AVENIDA LIBERTADOR
INTERNA RES. SAN SOUCI
Chacaíto Ⓜ
AVE PICHINCHA
AVE GUAICAIPURO
S [300m]
CHACAÍTO
LOS CERRITOS

AVENIDA MATURIN
AVENIDA EL MIRADOR
AVENIDA LAS TRINITARIAS
AVENIDA 2 LAS DELICIAS
AVENIDA SANTOS ERMINYA
Lirio de Plata

GARCIA
LA FLORESTA
LOS HUERTOS
AVENIDA EL MIRADOR
LOS MANGOS
TRANS 2
AVENIDA LOS MANGUITOS
EL CRISTO
BOULEVARD DE SABANA GRANDE
AVENIDA CASANOVA
Maxiclean
AVENIDA HUMBOLT
AVENIDA ORINOCO

AVENIDA NEGRIN
AVENIDA LOS JARDINES
AVENIDA LIBERTADOR
LA IGLESIA
S. GERONIMO
Sabana Grande Ⓜ
SABANA GRANDE
BORGES
AVENIDA 1
AVENIDA 2
COROMOTO
AVENIDA VENEZUELA

AVENIDA LOS CASTAÑOS
AVENIDA LOS CEDROS
AVENIDA LOS JABILLOS
LAS FLORES
AVENIDA FRANCISCO SOLANO LOPEZ
UNION
EL RECREO

AVENIDA LAS ACACIAS
AVENIDA LOS SAMANES
PARAISO
Farm. Saas
VILLAFLOR
ASUNCION
EL COLEGIO
AVENIDA FRANCISCO FAJARDO
Río Guaire

SAN CAMILO
AVENIDA LAS PALMAS
AVENIDA VENEZUELA
AV FRANCISCO SOLANO
Ⓜ Plaza Venezuela
SAN ANTONIO
AVENIDA LAS ACACIAS
AVENIDA PPAL. DE BELLO MONTE
AVENIDA L. DA VINCI

AVENIDA BUENOS AIRES
AVENIDA VALPARAISO
Ⓜ
AVENIDA LOS MANGOS
Río Guaire

AVENIDA BOGOTA
AVENIDA PANAMA
AVENIDA BOLIVIA
Ⓜ Zona Central
AVENIDA OLIMPO
AVENIDA O. CASTILLO

AVENIDA LIBERTADOR
AVENIDA QUITO
LA GRAN AVENIDA
AVENIDA CASANOVA
AVENIDA LAS ACACIAS

AVENIDA LA SALLE
LA GRAN AVENIDA
PLAZA VENEZUELA
AVENIDA LIMA
TRANS COLON
AVENIDA MONTEVIDEO

Río Guaire
AUTOPISTA FRANCISCO FAJARDO
Estadio Universitario (100m)

metros
0   250

11

N

11

A heightened police presence has done much to improve security in the area, although you should keep to where there are crowds.

El Hatillo

The pretty suburb of **El Hatillo** provides a welcome respite from the intense atmosphere of the centre. The only street noise here is gallery and boutique owners chatting on the pavement or faint salsa music wafting out of café doorways. There are good eating (see page 877) and shopping (see page 878) options here. The best way to **get here** from central Caracas is by cab, especially as the metrobús service from Altamira has been suspended.

ARRIVAL AND DEPARTURE

BY PLANE

Maiquetía International Airport (☎0212 303 1014, ⊛aeropuerto-maiquetia.com.ve), 26km northwest of

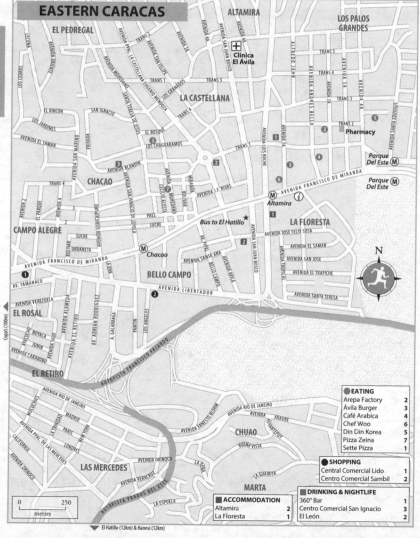

EASTERN CARACAS

ALTAMIRA
LOS PALOS GRANDES
EL PEDREGAL
Clinica El Ávila
LA CASTELLANA
EL RINCON
LOS JARDINES
LOS CHAGUARAMOS
Pharmacy
Parque Del Este Ⓜ
Parque Del Este Ⓜ
CHACAO
AVENIDA FRANCISCO DE MIRANDA
Altamira (ⓘ)
Bus to El Hatillo ★
LA FLORESTA
CAMPO ALEGRE
Ⓜ Chacao
BELLO CAMPO
CAMPO ALEGRE
AVENIDA FRANCISCO DE MIRANDA
AVENIDA LIBERTADOR
AV. TAMANACO
EL ROSAL
Copa's (100m)
AUTOPISTA FRANCISCO FAJARDO
EL RETIRO
AVENIDA RIO DE JANEIRO
AVENIDA RIO DE JANEIRO
AVENIDA
ARAURE
CHUAO
BUENA VISTA
LAS MERCEDES
AVENIDA ORINOCO
LA PEÑA
LA GUAIRITA
MARTA
AUTOPISTA PRADOS DEL ESTE
LA ESPUELA
LA ESPUELA

0 — 250 metres

N

▼ El Hatillo (12km) & Hannsi (12km)

● EATING	
Arepa Factory	2
Ávila Burger	3
Café Arabica	4
Chef Woo	6
Din Din Korea	5
Pizza Zeina	7
Sette Pizza	1

● SHOPPING	
Central Comercial Lido	1
Centro Comercial Sambil	2

■ ACCOMMODATION	
Altamira	2
La Floresta	1

■ DRINKING & NIGHTLIFE	
360° Bar	1
Centro Comercial San Ignacio	3
El León	2

SAFETY IN CARACAS

While Caracas is not as dangerous as its dreadful international reputation would have you believe, **crime rates** in the capital are the country's highest and **robberies** are not uncommon. Simple common sense is the best policy: don't carry around excessive cash or anything you can't afford to lose. Don't venture up deserted side streets and stick to where there are crowds after dark, especially in and around El Centro and Sabana Grande. Try to look like a local, and not a rich one; wearing overtly touristy clothes will earn you odd looks even from those who don't pose a threat, though grimy backpacker-chic is best saved for towns more accustomed to budget travellers. Change money calmly, in a secure place, and only once you've had a chance to gauge current *paralelo* rates (see page 869). Don't change money in the street; you'll be an easy target for passing opportunists and could also get landed with fake notes.

The Caracas **police** are a constant presence. Street-level officers are usually helpful, while the bored staff manning the red or blue police gazebos in pedestrianized areas (particularly common in Sabana Grande) are best avoided; giving them a wide berth is usually enough to avoid unwanted interaction. Spot searches are rare, but if you are unlucky enough to be pulled into a gazebo for an inspection, insist that you unpack your things yourself, one item at a time – things are less likely to go missing if you don't allow yourself to be rushed. Never offer bribes. If you are asked to pay a fine, always ask for the official paperwork.

All that said, there is no reason for paranoia and Caracas is one of South America's friendlier capital cities; exercise your common sense, don't take unnecessary risks, stay alert to your surroundings at all times and you should have an incident-free stay.

11

Caracas, is the country's primary hub for international flights, and also serves domestic destinations across the country. The airport has two terminals, one for domestic and another for international, although they are in the same building.

From the airport into town Buses to Parque Central (daily 5am–10pm; 1hr; ☎0212 352 4140) leave every 20min from in front of the international terminal. From the bus stop, it's best to continue to your accommodation by taxi. Red Sitssa buses (hourly 7.30am–8.30pm; ☎0212 572 1609, ⊚ sitssa.gob.ve) also connect the airport to *Hotel Alba* in Parque Central, from where Bellas Artes metro station is two blocks away. Official taxis to and from the airport take about an hour, depending on the time of day. Taxis waiting at arrivals are 4WD *camionetas*; buy a prepaid ride at one of the clearly marked counters inside the terminal upon arrival. Many hotels and tour agencies will arrange private pick-ups from the airport. Under no circumstances accept a ride from the touts who approach you in the terminal.

Tickets International flights are impossible to buy in advance using Venezuelan currency; any international travel must be booked through airline websites. It is possible to fly domestically extremely cheaply paying in Bolívars by going on standby for a flight at Maiquetía, although it requires showing up at least three hours in advance, bringing lots of cash and making it known to the airline staff that you are willing to offer tips for their help in putting you on the flight.

Destinations (international) Bogotá (6 weekly; 1hr 50min); Buenos Aires (3 weekly; 6hr 30min); Lima (6 weekly; 4hr 30min); Panama City (3–4 daily; 2hr 25min); Santiago de Chile (1 weekly; 6hr 35min).

Destinations (domestic) Barquisimeto (4 weekly; 50min); Maracaibo (4 weekly; 1hr); Porlamar (1–2 daily; 1hr). There are currently no flights to Mérida: visitors must fly to nearby El Vigía (4 weekly; 1hr) and take a bus.

BY BUS

Caracas has two major bus terminals, La Bandera and Oriente. Bus tickets can only be bought on the day of departure. It is advisable to buy your ticket early (to book, you'll need to know your passport number or have it to hand), and even then, buses may not turn up. Tickets are often bought up at official prices by speculators who then resell them at inflated rates. Aeroexpresos Ejecutivos, with services to Ciudad Bolívar, Maracaibo, Valencia, Puerto La Cruz and other cities has a terminal on Av Principal de Bello Campo in Chacao.

Terminal La Bandera Av Nueva Granada, two blocks uphill from the metro station of the same name (on line 3). Serves destinations south and west of the capital.

Destinations Barinas (3 daily; 9hr); Coro (several daily; 7hr); Maracaibo (4 daily; 12hr); Mérida (3 daily; 13hr); Puerto Ayacucho (1 daily; 15hr); San Antonio del Táchira (2 daily; 13hr 30min); San Fernando de Apure (3 daily; 8hr). Buses for Maracay and Valencia leave when full (usually every 15min); simply take a seat and wait for departure.

Terminal de Oriente Km1, Autopista Petare–Guarenas (take the metro to Petare station, where you can take a 15min *buseta* to the terminal). Serves destinations to the east, southeast and (when operating) international routes.

Destinations Barcelona (several daily; 5hr); Carúpano (several daily; 9hr); Ciudad Bolívar (5 daily; 9hr); Cumaná (5 daily; 7hr); Puerto La Cruz (several daily; 5hr 30min); Puerto Ordaz (5 daily; 10hr).

11

GETTING AROUND

By bus Olive-green metrobuses, running 5.30am–11pm, connect metro stations with outlying destinations. There is also a virtually infinite number of unofficial *busetas* running their own routes, with stops listed on their windshields.

By metro Operates from 5.30am to 11pm daily and is cheap, efficient and safe – by far the best way to get around the city, although it can be extremely crowded during peak times. Line 1, the most useful, runs east to west. Lines 2 and 3 run south from the line 1 transfer stations of Capitolio/El Silencio and Plaza Venezuela respectively. Multi-ride tickets can save you time. Beware at peak hours as pickpockets intentionally cause jams between boarding and alighting passengers to create a distraction.

By taxi Official taxis are white with yellow licence plates; take these rather than their unmarked *pirata* ("pirate") counterparts. Taxis do not have meters and fares should be agreed before you get in. Ask a local what the price should be before bartering with a *taxista*. A cheaper and quicker option is the two-wheeled *mototaxi*, on which helmets come provided. Look for the riders wearing hi-vis orange jackets (who are hailed like a regular taxi) advertising the service.

INFORMATION AND TOURS

Tourist information There are Mintur desks in the airport's international and domestic terminals. There's also an office on the first floor of the Edificio Mintur, on Av Francisco de Miranda in Altamira (Mon–Fri 8.30am–4pm; ☎0212 208 7918), though this is more administrative and they'll be surprised to see you.

Travel agents Candes (☎0212 953 1632, ⊛candesturismo.com) in Edificio Roraima Av Francisco de Miranda; Club del Trotamundo (☎0212 740 3072) in Torre Libertador, Nucleo A, 5th floor, suite A-53, Av Libertador, Chacao. Caracas also has a number of reputable tour operators (see page 864).

ACCOMMODATION

Budget accommodation in Caracas is underwhelming. For your safety and comfort after dark you should look for accommodation in the Chacao/Altamira district.

EL CENTRO/PARQUE CENTRAL

Grand Galaxie Av Baralt Truco, at Caja de Agua ☎0212 864 9011; map p.871. This basic hostel has a bustling lobby and a good bakery next door; the rooms themselves have a/c and hot water. BsS420

Renovación Av Este 2, 154 ☎0212 571 0133; map p.871. The upside is the proximity to the city museums, the downside is putting up with the sour-faced staff. Some of the rooms (all en suite) have comically ostentatious bathtubs and there's a great place to eat on the nearby corner. BsS500

SABANA GRANDE

Cristál Pasaje Asunción, at Bulevar Sabana Grande ☎0212 761 9131; map p.873. A good option for sampling the Caracas nightlife as the location on the graffiti-strewn *callejón* is a popular and friendly spot with numerous bars, although you should avoid it if getting an early night is a higher priority. Avoid the drug dealers who loiter about the entrance. Expect adequate service and clean rooms, all with a/c, en suite and TV. BsS300

Nueva Esparta Av Los Manguitos, between Libertador and Solano ☎0212 761 5732; map p.873. The ostentatious entrance sets this pristine lodging back from a bustling side street. Rooms are all en suite, with a/c and TV, but otherwise basic. The hotel also has a decent pizzeria opposite the tiny reception booth. BsS300

ALTAMIRA

Caracas's business district, Altamira is safer than other areas of the city.

★**Altamira** Av José Félix Sosa, at Av Altamira Sur ☎0212 267 4255; map p.874. Secure, stylish and relaxed, this friendly place on a quiet side street has homely rooms with hot showers, a/c and TV. A short walk from Altamira metro station, the rates are a bargain given the high-end nature of accommodation in the area. BsS880

La Floresta Av Ávila Sur below Plaza Altamira ☎0212 263 1955; map p.874. Perfectly decent rooms all have a/c and en suite, while some have balconies. Don't expect quality service; the shifty and disinterested staff can be comically rude. BsS1021

EATING

In addition to established cafés and restaurants, there is no shortage of street vendors hawking burgers and hot dogs. Street food, including fresh fruit juice, is generally safe when prepared in front of you.

EL CENTRO/PARQUE CENTRAL

Bistro del Libertador Av del Sur at Plaza Bolívar (by Museo Sacro); map p.871. Attractive little place where you can get breakfasts, lunches, *arepas*, salads, coffees, even fried mozarella fingers with salsa to dip. Mon–Sat 8am–6pm.

Café de Sacro Inside Museo Sacro; map p.871. A haven of serenity on the raucous Plaza Bolívar. Grab a coffee and cake and sit back to admire the pretty surroundings. You'll have to pay the museum entry fee whether you're interested in the art gallery or not, although the peace and quiet are well worth it. Mon–Fri noon–3.30pm.

SABANA GRANDE

★**Arepería 24 Horas** Av Casanova, at Av Las Acacias ☎0212 793 7961; map p.873. Open 24hr for when you need your *arepa* fix, this open-fronted diner brims with colourful characters. Look behind the glass counters to select your fillings, which include octopus, tuna and roast pork. For more leisurely dining, the table service area has slick waiters and sports channels rolling on the numerous TVs, although the other patrons are far more interesting. Also does excellent *batidos*. Daily 24hr.

Gran Café Blvd de Sabana Grande, at C Pascual Navarro; map p.873. Founded by *Papillon* author Henri Charrière and patronized in its day by writers and intellectuals such as Carlos Fuentes and Gabriel García Márquez, this popular lunch destination serves potent coffee, sandwiches, ice cream, pastries and more. Daily 7am–10pm.

El Rincón Gallego Av Francisco Solano López, at C Los Manguitos; map p.873. The unstoppably chatty owner Lola emigrated from Spain over fifty years ago and the restaurant, when open, dishes out traditional favourites from her homeland. It was closed at last check but should reopen in the future.

ALTAMIRA/LOS PALOS GRANDES

Arepa Factory Transversal 2, at Av 2, Los Palos Grandes; map p.874. They've fixed what isn't broken with artesanal, slim or wholemeal *arepa* options, although the staff admit nothing beats the original. The fillings menu is extensive. Bag a seat first and order at the counter. Tues–Fri 7.30am–8pm, Sat 8am–1pm, Sun 8.30am–1pm.

Ávila Burger C Chaguaramo, behind Centro Comercial San Ignacio, Chacao ⓦavilaburger.com; map p.874. Massive and juicy burgers served with enormous sides of fried *yuca*, bacon-cheese fries and washed down with ice-cold beer. Who said Creole-Americana wasn't a wonderful fusion? The service is also excellent by Venezuelan standards. Daily noon–9pm.

Café Arabica Av Andres Bello, at Transversal 1, Los Palos Grandes; map p.874. A famous opposition hangout in Caracas, so expect to get kicked to the kerb for expounding the merits of petro-socialism. Good food (get the jam-packed *empanadas*), excellent coffee and beers later on, although don't expect much from the service. DOC restaurant next door does a great steak. Daily 6.30am–11pm.

Chef Woo Av 1, above Av Francisco de Miranda, Los Palos Grandes; map p.874. Students and businessmen alike flock to this Chinese restaurant for cheap beers, lively conversation and sometimes even Chinese food, though this is usually lower down the list of priorities. Daily 11.30am–10pm.

★**Din Din Korea** Av 1, at Transversal 1, Los Palos Grandes; map p.874. Bored with Venezuelan food? Head to this restaurant run by a Korean family. All the kimchi-munching delights of Korean cuisine, authentically prepared. Ask the English-speaking staff for that day's off-menu items. Mon–Sat noon–3pm & 6–9pm.

Pizza Zeina Av Mohedano beside Plaza Chacao; map p.874. Not a pizzeria as the name suggests, but rather an informal lunch spot serving up authentic Lebanese food, prepared fresh daily. The *Plato Mixto* gives a rounded taste of the kitchen's delights, washed down with refreshing yoghurt drinks. Gets very busy at lunchtime. Mon–Sat 9am–5pm.

Sette Pizza Av 4 between Transversals 2 & 3, Los Palos Grandes; map p.874. Down a side street, this over-staffed pizza joint stone-bakes tasty artisan pizzas to compensate for underwhelming service. The pasta menu operates on a "choose your shape, choose your sauce" basis. Daily noon–11pm.

EL HATILLO

Dulces Criollos C La Paz on Plaza Bolívar. Come in for a gawp at the sweets and pastries that run three rows deep at this rustically contemporary (or contemporarily rustic) cake shop. The coffee is excellent and the cakes are delicous. Scoff them down at a bar stool or enjoy them outside in the leafy Plaza Bolívar. Daily 8am–11pm.

DRINKING AND NIGHTLIFE

Caracas has bars and clubs for virtually anyone, and at any time – many establishments stay open until the last patron leaves. Being a large and cosmopolitan city, it also has a decent selection of LGBTQ nightclubs. Check ⓦrumbacaracas.com for a variety of club and event listings. Especially in the western districts, most streets empty out after dark, and you should always take taxis to and from your destination then.

SABANA GRANDE

★**El Maní Es Así** C El Cristo; map p.873. This self-proclaimed "temple of salsa" is a Caracas legend where they relish gringos getting involved. Thursday to Saturday sees live bands fill the wide dancefloor from 9pm, while the enormous sound system thumps out salsa the rest of the time. Tues–Sat 7pm–3am; arrive early for occasional salsa lessons.

Moulin Rouge Av Francisco Solano; map p.873. With a giant, two-dimensional windmill for a facade, you can't miss this ever-popular dive bar, where the city's rockers, ravers and gutter-punks convene for live alternative music. See their Facebook page (ⓦfacebook.com/elmolinoccs) for who's performing soon. Thurs–Sat 9pm–6am.

ALTAMIRA/LOS PALOS GRANDES

★**360° Bar** Hotel Altamira Suites, 19th floor, Av 1 at Transversal 1; map p.874. The coolest bar in Caracas, right above the Plaza Altamira, this rooftop bar affords stunning views of the city in all directions as well as of the beautiful clientele within. Throw yourself into a hammock, order a cocktail and feel yourself a world apart from the intensity of Caracas life below. Daily 10pm–late.

11

11

TAKE ME OUT TO THE BALL GAME

It won't take you long to notice Venezuela's **baseball** obsession, with what seems like every fifth person sporting club gear. If you're in town during the October-to-December season, attending an **LVBP** (Liga Venezolana de Beisbol Profesional) game in the capital is a good way to see what all the fuss is about. The two local teams, the Leones and Tiburones (Lions and Sharks), share the **Estadio Universitario** in Sabana Grande, and there are games on most days of the week. The biggest fixture of the year pits the Caracas Leones against their fiercest rivals, Valencia's Navegantes del Magallanes.

Tickets can be bought online at ⓦ leones.com, although you'll need a local friend to reserve them, as the site doesn't accept international credit cards. Alternatively, you can buy tickets from the stadium box office from 9am on game days. Arrive early as service at the four ticket windows is slow. Tickets for the *tribuna* (main stand) start at BsS37.50; unreserved-seating tickets for the *grada* (terrace) around the outfield are cheaper and you can jump the queue to buy them. If you can't get tickets in advance, show up to the *grada* gate beside the ticket office and slip the attendant US$5 to let you through.

The stadium is a ten-minute walk south of Plaza Venezuela metro station. Walk to Arepería 24 Horas and you'll see the floodlights. Check ⓦ lvbp.com for upcoming fixtures.

Centro Comercial San Ignacio Av Blandín ⓦ centrosanignacio.com; map p.874. An upmarket shopping centre with a wide selection of bars and clubs where wealthy *Caraqueños* come to show off their latest moves and fashionable purchases. Try *Suka*, which gets particularly busy on Wednesday nights, and hosts regular DJs, or neighbouring *Pi'Sko*, the building's *merengue* dancing spot. Also nearby is *Samoa* with its wacky South Pacific theme. There are plenty of eating options here too. Suka Wed–Fri 5.30pm–3am, Sat 6pm–3am; Pi'Sko Tues–Sat noon–5am; Samoa Mon–Thurs & Sun noon–2am, Fri & Sat noon–3am.

El León Transversal de la Castellana 2; map p.874. A popular bar (and pizzeria) where the waiters keep the drinks coming. Grab a seat at the wide outdoor patio, relax and watch the Venezuelan motorists crossing the poorly designed roundabout nearby. Keep note of how many beers you've had, as the waiters have been known to add a couple to the bill. Mon–Sat 7am–3am, Sun 11am–2am.

LBGTQ CARACAS

Copa's C Guaicaipuro, close to Chacaíto metro station; map p.873. Caracas's best (and possibly only) lesbian spot, where the overzealous security is worth putting up with for the friendly crowd, which has become very mixed of late. Wed–Sat 10.30pm–4am.

La Fragata C Villa Flor, Sabana Grande; map p.873. This popular club brings in a friendly, mostly male clientele, although the good location and party-hard reputation are beginning to attract a fun-loving non-LGBTQ crowd as well. Excuse the cheesy, neon-heavy decor and focus instead on the cheap drinks and crowded dancefloor. Mon–Sat 6pm–3.30am, Sun 6pm–midnight.

Tasca Pullman Edificio Ovidio, Av Francisco Solano, Sabana Grande; map p.873. One of Caracas's oldest gay bars, and still sporting a distinctly 1980s vibe, this dimly lit place draws a friendly, working-class crowd and the occasional drag queen. Mostly male, though women are welcome. Daily 5pm–3am.

SHOPPING

Shopping culture in Caracas is dominated by mega-malls, where your chances of finding unique, inexpensive crafts are virtually nonexistent. Street shopping is a bit more promising, at least in terms of prices, and the Hannsi crafts outlet in El Hatillo (see below) is your best source for souvenirs.

Centro Comercial Lido Av Francisco de Miranda, Chacao; map p.874. A good place to get things done; services include airline offices and major phone network outlets. Among the mall's actual shops, *South Beach* is a good spot to stock up on women's beachwear before a trip to the coast. Libreria Tecni-Ciencias (see below) also has a branch here. Mon–Sat 6.30am–8pm, Sun 7am–6pm.

Centro Comercial Sambil Av Libertador, at C los Ángeles, Chacao; ⓦ tusambil.com/caracas; map p.874. The most famous of the city's malls, this mind-bogglingly enormous complex hosts every conceivable amenity, including top international brands. Mon–Sat 10am–8pm, Sun & holidays noon–8pm.

Hannsi C Bolívar No 12, El Hatillo ⓦ hannsi.com.ve. This enormous craft shop sprawls through several buildings, filled throughout with astonishing amounts of chintzy junk, although the occasional gem is buried beneath it all. You can choose your own coffee beans to grind at the café, which also has pastries and savoury snacks. Daily 10am–1pm & 2.30–7pm.

Libreria Tecni-Ciencias Centro Comercial Lider, Av Francisco de Miranda, Los Cortijos ⓦ tecniciencia.com; map p.870. The prices are a bit high, but this chain is one of the best options for books in Caracas, with ten outlets citywide, including branches in Centro Comercial Lido (see above) and Centro Comercial San Ignacio (see above). Mon–Sat 9.30am–7pm, Sun 10am–6pm.

DIRECTORY

Banks and exchange There are plenty of banks, not that you should ever consider using their ATMs (see page 869). The international airport terminal has exchange desks. Italcambio has five branches in the capital (at ⓦwww. italcambio.com, click on "Nuestras Sucursales" for locations).

Embassies and consulates Brazil, Av Mohedano, at C Los Chaguaramos in La Castellana (ⓣ0212 918 6000, ⓦcaracas. itamaraty.gov.br); Canada, Av Francisco de Miranda at Av Sur, Altamira (ⓣ0212 600 3000, ⓦcanadainternational. gc.ca/venezuela); Colombia, 2a Av de Campo Alegre at Av Francisco de Miranda, Torre Credival (ⓣ0212 216 9596, ⓦcancilleria.gov.co/embajada-colombia-venezuela); Guyana, Quinta Los Tutis, Segunda Avenida, Entre 9 y 10 Transversales, Altamira, Chacao 212 267-7095; UK, Av Principal de la Castellana, Torre La Castellana 11th Floor (ⓣ0212 319 5800, ⓦgov.uk/world/venezuela); USA, Colinas de Valle Arriba, C F at C Suapure (ⓣ0212 975 6411, ⓦve.usembassy.gov/embassy).

Hospitals Two recommended clinics are Hospital de Clínicas Caracas, on Av Panteón at Av Alameda, five blocks north of Metro Bellas Artes (ⓣ0212 508 6111, ⓦclinicaracas.com), and Clinica El Ávila, on Av San Juan Bosco, at 6ta Transversal in Altamira (ⓣ0212 276 1111, ⓦclinicaelavila.com).

Immigration office SAIME (El Servicio Administrativo de Identificación, Migración y Extranjería) at Av Baralt in front of Plaza Miranda opposite Teatros metro station (ⓣ0800 724 6300, ⓦsaime.gob.ve).

Internet There are numerous internet cafés in Caracas, especially in pedestrian-heavy Sabana Grande. Two reliable options are MSX Cybershop, at C San Antonio above Bulevar de Sabana Grande, and Ciberplace, at C Villaflor below Bulevar de Sabana Grande.

Laundry Many hotels will do your laundry. Otherwise, try Maxiclean, which has branches around the city including on Av Casanova at Av 2 in Sabana Grande.

Pharmacy Pharmacies are as ubiquitous as banks. On Bulevar de Sabana Grande, Farmacia Saas is at C Villaflor. In Altamira, Farmacia San Andrés is on Av 3 at Transversal 2, or there's a large Farmatodo on Av Andres Bello and Transversal 3 in Los Palos Grandes.

Phones CANTV and Movistar have shops throughout the city for buying SIM cards and credit, and outlets around Plaza Bolívar and Centro Plaza in Altamira

Post office Ipostel beside the cathedral in Plaza la Candelaria (ⓦipostel.gob.ve). There are other branches around town, often in *Puntos de Gestión* (administration offices). For packages, better, private alternatives such as MRW (ⓦmrw.com.ve) and DHL (ⓦdhl.com.ve) have numerous offices around the city.

DAY-TRIPS FROM CARACAS

For a quick escape from the hustle and bustle of Caracas, ride the cable car that ascends the slopes of **Parque Nacional El Ávila**, with its spectacular views and hiking trails. If you've got more time, consider visiting **Colonia Tovar**, a Black Forest-style village built by nineteenth-century German immigrants. On the other side of the coastal range, Caracas boasts some fabulous beaches, particularly popular with surfers from the capital.

Parque Nacional El Ávila

The lush mountain ridge that separates Caracas from the coast, **PARQUE NACIONAL EL ÁVILA** (ⓦel-avila.com) is a popular escape from the urban mayhem for *Caraqueños*. On clear days there are

---

FESTIVAL DE LOS DIABLOS DANZANTES

The otherwise nondescript town of **San Francisco de Yare**, 60km southeast of Caracas, is the site of one of Venezuela's most famous spectacles, the **Festival de los Diablos Danzantes** ("dancing devils"). In observance of the Catholic holy day Corpus Christi (a Thursday in late May or early June, nine and a half weeks after Easter Sunday), townspeople don elaborate devil costumes and engage in highly ritualized performances. While similar festivals occur in other parts of Venezuela, including Ocumare de la Costa, Chuao, Naiguatá and Cuyagua, Yare's is considered the definitive.

To get here from Caracas, take the **metro** to the Nuevo Circo station and walk one block to the bus terminal of the same name. From here, **buses** (every 15min until 9pm; 1hr 30min) leave for Ocumare del Tuy from the designated stand. From the Ocumare terminal, frequent *busetas* to Santa Teresa drop passengers at Yare's Plaza Bolívar (20min). To return to Caracas, Ocumare-bound *busetas* pass one block northeast of the Plaza Bolívar. Buses from Ocumare to Caracas leave every 15min until 9pm.

11

stunning views of the city to the south and the Caribbean to the north.

There are several ways to explore the park. For those who want to explore on foot there are four well-marked hiking trails accessible via Avenida Boyacá – best accessed via taxi/*mototaxi*, although infrequent *busetas* do go from points along the Avenida Liberator. The most popular trail is **Sabas Nieves**, a fairly strenuous hour-long trail, packed with posing fitness buffs. From here the trail continues up the mountain to the **Silla de Caracas** (4hr) and the spectacular summit at the **Pico Oriental** (6hr). All routes are well signposted and the trails well trodden. For similarly stunning views with less exertion, the **Cotamil** is a 5km path that traverses the Ávila at a height of 1000m above sea level, from Altamira to Plaza Venezuela. Access points at both ends are guarded by Inparques checkpoints.

However, the most popular option is the **teleférico** (box office Tues & Sun noon–6pm, Wed–Sat 10.30am–6pm, closed Mon; last return 9pm), a high-speed cable car. To get to the base station, go to Colegio de Ingenieros metro station and take a bus or a taxi from outside the entrance. There's an ice-rink at the top as well as some more predictable attractions, while a steep trail leads down to the pretty village of **Galipán**. Jeeps wait at either end to ferry passengers up and down the trail. Numerous roadside stands sell strawberries and cream and local honey, while restaurants in the village have superb views.

To explore the park further, contact Akanán Tours (see page 864). Alternatively, take a taxi to Avenida Peñalver between Cotiza and San Bernadín, at the foot of the hill, where *colectivos* leave for Galipán when full.

The northern coast

The coast of Vargas state, separated from Caracas by Parque Nacional El Ávila, provides a good sample of Venezuela's **beaches** if you don't have time to venture further afield. The surfing here is particularly good, with some of the best breaks at Anare, Los Caracas and Playa Pantaleta. To **get here** under your own steam, catch the bus from Parque Central to the airport and continue 35km by taxi to La Guaira or Macuto, where you can flag down one of the numerous *busetas* that ply the seaside highway in both directions; hop off and on wherever you choose.

Colonia Tovar

Founded by German immigrants in 1843, the small mountain village of **COLONIA TOVAR**, 60km west of Caracas, is still

---

★ TREAT YOURSELF: LOS ROQUES

An underwater extension of the Andes range, the **Los Roques** archipelago is Venezuela's closest thing to desert-island paradise. Populated mostly by posada owners and boatmen, the high cost of flying to Los Roques has helped keep them both exclusive and unspoilt. Most Caracas travel agencies (see page 876) and tour operators (see page 864) offer package trips, but you'll save a lot of money organizing things yourself.

Trips are cheaper during the week, when the major carrier for the archipelago, Aereotuy (W tuy.com), offers return flights with a night's accommodation. Chapi Air (☎ 0414 311 1117, W chapiair.com) serves Los Roques from Maiquetia and Higuerote.

Good **posadas** include *El Botuto* (☎ 0416 622 0061, W posadaelbotuto.com; generally part of a package with plane or US$35/person with breakfast), which has great service and lovely outside showers.

Camping is a safer option than on the mainland, although you'll need a permit from the Inparques office (at the far end of town from the landing strip). Camping is restricted to a designated area on Gran Roque and a few of the smaller, uninhabited islands, for a maximum of eight days.

A boatmen's cooperative for transport around the islands operates out of Oscar Shop next to the landing strip, which also rents snorkelling gear. Arrecife Divers, near Inparques, runs **scuba-diving** trips and courses. Tourist numbers and prices rise substantially in the June-to-September high season.

inhabited by their descendants. Most of the houses have been built in traditional Black Forest style, and restaurants selling German-style bratwurst line the main roads of the village. "Colonia" is a popular weekend destination, when it becomes packed with bemused *Caraqueños*, who turn the whole place into a Deutsch Disneyland. The **Museo de Historia y Artesanía** (Sat, Sun & festivals 9am–6pm) features a small collection of documents, clothes, tools, guns and other relics of the village's early days.

ARRIVAL AND DEPARTURE

By metro and buseta To get here from Caracas, take the metro to La Yaguara station. Join the queue around the corner for a *buseta* to El Junquito (every 15min; 1hr), and then change at the same spot for an onward bus to Colonia Tovar (every 15min; 1hr). To return to Caracas, *busetas* leaving Colonia Tovar depart 300m outside the village on the road to El Junquito; many of them go directly to Caracas. The last *buseta* leaves Colonia at 6pm. If you want to move on to the western coast, take a *buseta* to La Victoria from the other end of town. From La Victoria buses leave regularly for Maracay, the access point for Parque Nacional Henri Pittier (see page 881).

TOUR OPERATORS

Douglas Pridham ☎ 0416 743 8939, ⓦ vivatrek.com. An expert paraglider who can get you airborne from the steep hillsides around Colonia Tovar. His outfit also offers guided excursions into Parque Nacional Henri Pittier.

The northwest coast

Some of Venezuela, and indeed the Caribbean's, finest beaches stretch along the country's **northwest coast**, where pretty colonial towns, two fine national parks and spectacular landscapes inland also bid for visitors' attention.

Parque Nacional Henri Pittier, roughly 150km from Caracas, has palm-lined sands, striking mountain ranges and four vegetation zones, which are home to a tremendous array of birds and plant life. If taking a speedboat to the beach appeals, then make for popular **Parque Nacional Morrocoy**, a few hours to the west, for its offshore cays surrounded by crystalline water. Three hours closer to Colombia from Morrocoy, the well-preserved colonial town of **Coro** serves as a good breather between the coast and the Andes, while a short hop across a land bridge to the **Paraguana Peninsula** will reward visitors with some of the country's finest aquatic sports. For those heading directly to Colombia, Coro is the most backpacker-friendly spot en route to the border (see page 887) 360km away.

PARQUE NACIONAL HENRI PITTIER

Venezuela's first national park, created in 1937, **PARQUE NACIONAL HENRI PITTIER** was named after the Swiss geographer and botanist who classified more than thirty thousand plants in the region. Despite the park's great biodiversity, the vast majority of visitors come for its **beaches**, which can be overrun at weekends but are generally quiet the rest of the time.

Pittier's wide array of **flora and fauna** is a result of the relatively short space in which it climbs from sea level to 2430m, producing distinct vegetation zones. The park's wildlife is best experienced from the Universidad Central de Venezuela's **Estación Biológica**. The area is renowned among birdwatchers, having one of the highest densities of birds in the world, with at least 582 species including the stunning red ibis. The park also has large reptile and mammal populations; noteworthy residents include sea turtles, jaguars, pumas, spider monkeys and rattlesnakes.

Entry to the park is free, and most people access the beach communities of **Choroní** and **Ocumare de la Costa** by bus from the terminal in uninspiring **Maracay**. Choroní, on the eastern side of the park, is the nicer of the two, with lots of places to stay and a lively atmosphere. Ocumare, named after the indigenous Cumarí people, is only worth visiting in order to reach the stunning La Ciénaga lagoon around the coast. Guided tours of the park are organized from Choroní or Ocumare, rather than Maracay.

Estación Biológica Rancho Grande

The park can be explored along hiking trails from Choroní or the extensive

11

mangroves around La Ciénaga, but the best base for serious wildlife-spotting is the atmospheric **Estación Biológica Rancho Grande**, a complex which has sadly fallen out of regular use by the Universidad Central de Venezuela. Visits must be arranged in advance – contact Oskar Padilla (see page 882) on ☎0412 892 5308 or ✉oskarpadilla@hotmail.com – and visitors are likely to see an incredible variety of fauna, including sloths, anteaters and howler monkeys. The station has a dormitory, although guests must bring their own sheets or a sleeping bag and food.

ARRIVAL AND DEPARTURE

By bus Maracay is the access point for Henri Pittier and has a busy terminal serving countrywide locations. The Estación Biológica's entrance is a nondescript gate beside a bus stop on the road between Maracay and Ocumare de la Costa; to get there, board a bus heading in either direction and ask the bus driver to let you off at Rancho Grande. To get away, hail a passing bus from beside the entrance. Buses for Choroní and Ocumare de la Costa depart from the terminal when full (roughly every 30min) until 9pm.

Destinations from Maracay Caracas (roughly every 20min; 2hr); Maracaibo (2 daily; 10hr); San Cristóbal (3 daily; 11hr); Puerto la Cruz (2 daily; 8hr); Puerto Ordaz (1 daily; 12hr); San Fernando de Apure (3 daily; 6hr); Valencia (25 daily; 45min).

INFORMATION AND TOURS

Tourist information Don't show up at the Estación Biológica unannounced, as it's likely that you'll find the gates locked and the building unoccupied. You should advise Inparques in Maracay if you plan to walk the trails, although you're better off getting in touch with Oskar Padilla.

Tour operators Oskar Padilla, a helpful, experienced and English-speaking guide (☎0412 892 5308, ✉oskarpadilla@hotmail.com), offers hiking and birdwatching around Rancho Grande, works with local firm Explocación (✇explocation.net) and will happily do your permit administration for you. Casa Luna Espinoza in Choroní (see page 883) can also arrange stays and activities at the research centre.

Choroní

Choroní actually consists of two parts: the colonial town of **CHORONÍ** and **PUERTO COLOMBIA**, a beach town 2km away where the action is concentrated. Puerto Colombia's beating heart is its lively **malecón** (seafront) where the fishing boats dock, revellers congregate and on weekends it's common to see *tambores*, a coastal tradition of African drum-playing, singing and energetic dancing.

WHAT TO SEE AND DO

The **Mirador de Cristo** on the eastern headland (named *Papelón*, or Sugar Loaf) offers a view over the tiny town and stunning relief surrounding it. A path weaves towards it from the Playa Grande side of the bridge.

The one beach easily reached on foot is **Playa Grande**, a sheltered bay of jungled hills and a curving sandbar, which consequently attracts the most visitors.

About the same distance to the west, but harder to reach, **Playa El Diario** is a 45-minute walk from the village. To get

PUERTO COLOMBIA (CHORONÍ)

■ ACCOMMODATION
Casa Nova	1
Hostal Nuevo Colonial	2
Posada Los Guanches	3

CARIBBEAN SEA

Playa Grande

Police station

Mirador del Cristo

lanchas

MALECÓN

Pharmacy

CONCEPCIÓN

Coop. Alcatours

JOSE MATTIN

Pc Accion @

LOS COCOS

MORILLO

UNION

TRINO RANGEL

TRINO RANGEL

TRINO RANGEL

PUERTO COLOMBIA

COLEGIO

CALLE PRINCIPAL DE CHORONÍ

N

(200m)

● EATING
Brisas del Mar	1
Madera Fina	4
Paco's Pizza	3
Restaurant Araguaneyes	2

■ DRINKING
| Bar La Playa | 1 |
| Jalio Surf Bar | 2 |

Bus Terminal

0   100
metres

Playa El Diario (1.5km)

here from the midpoint of the main Choroní–Puerto Colombia road, follow Calle Cementerio past the cemetery, bear left at the split and follow it around the headland to the sea.

To access the other nearby beaches you will need to take a *lancha*, which can be arranged at the malecón. To the east, the closest beach is **Playa Valle Seco**, which has some coral reefs and decent snorkelling. Farther east, **Playa Chuao** offers postcard good looks and a path that runs inland to Chuao town. Some of the world's best cocoa is grown here. If you don't visit, you can still stock up on their fantastic chocolate from Sabor A Cacao (see page 884) in Puerto Colombia. Still farther east is equally nice **Playa Cepe**, which is generally the least crowded.

To combine these beaches in a single trip, negotiate a price with the *lanchero*. Pack a lunch.

ARRIVAL AND DEPARTURE

By bus The only road to Choroní is from Maracay. Buses leave when full until 8pm, taking 2hr. Puerto Colombia is a safe 15min stroll from the bus terminal. Take a left out of the entrance and follow the other passengers.

By boat If you're coming from or going to Ocumare de la Costa, a rapid and scenic alternative is to negotiate a ride with a *lanchero* from either end (1hr). It's also possible to get to and from Caracas (via Catia el Mar or La Guaira) by sea, a 2hr speedboat trip which takes in the stunning northern coast of the continent. Ask the boatmen hawking beach trips at either end of the journey before noon, and haggle hard on price.

By taxi Taxis from Maracay take half the time of the bus journey. Alternatively, take a seat in a *por puesto* (shared taxi). Both depart regularly from the Maracay terminal.

INFORMATION AND TOURS

Claudia, the owner of *Casa Luna Espinoza*, can organize tours of the park, the chocolate plantations in Chuao and speedboat trips to various beaches along the coast.

ACCOMMODATION

Camping isn't especially worthwhile as there is a good selection of budget accommodation in Puerto Colombia – the location of all those listed below. Reservations are recommended in the high season.

Casa Nova C Morillo 37 ☎ 0412 779 8935, ⍟jungletrip. de; map p.882. Knowledgeable German *dueña* Claudia speaks English (though staff may not). This hostel is a good choice with a pool and eight en-suite rooms, all with

mountain views and a hammock out front, and there's a communal kitchen. **€16**

★ **Hostal Nuevo Colonial** C Morillo ☎0243 951 5321, ⍟jungletrip.de; map p.882. This friendly, good-value guesthouse with fountains, a pool and a good restaurant is run by the same owner as the *Casa Nova* next door. The spacious rooms (some with en suite and a/c) are fan-cooled and thankfully set back from the noisy main road. **€12**

Posada Los Guanches C Colón, Transversal 1, Casa 5 ☎0243 991 1209, ⍟choroni.info/losguanches; map p.882. The only noise you'll be disturbed by in this mercifully cool building is your own echo. Run by the welcoming family that lives on the opposite side of the flowery backstreet, rooms are fan-cooled, en suite and basic. Have a browse of the bamboo jewellery on sale. **BsS500**

EATING

A small courtyard opposite the malecón in Puerto Colombia opens in the evenings to serve hamburgers and hotdogs. There are numerous shacks lining the path to Playa Grande that sell plates of fish, rice and salad until the foot traffic coming back from the beach slows down.

Brisas del Mar Av los Cocos 2 ☎0243 991 1268; map p.882. Not the most peaceful place in town to eat, being next to *Bar La Playa*, and usually offers squid dishes or pasta, but lately has been selling mainly beer. Daily 8.30am–11pm.

Hostal Nuevo Colonial C Morillo; map p.882. The restaurant at this hotel (see page 883) serves up economical local dishes, and also offers vegetarian options. Daily 8am–9pm.

Madera Fina Sector la Bokaina, west of Puerto Colombia ☎0243 991 1043; map p.882. The poshest restaurant in Choroní, with a terrace overlooking the sea. Fri–Sun noon–10.30pm.

Paco's Pizza C Trino Rangel; map p.882. The best pizzas in town, a little bit pricey by local standards, but made with fresh ingredients, and they also do fish and chicken dishes, and breakfasts. Daily 8am–10pm.

Restaurant Araguaneyes Av Los Cocos ☎0243 991 1166; map p.882. Enjoy huge portions of fresh fish and seafood on the large upstairs terrace while listening to music that for once isn't salsa. Also open for breakfast. Daily 8am–11pm.

DRINKING

Nightlife, if you can call it that, is very casual – most people just buy a few beers and drink them on the malecón.

Bar La Playa At the beach end of Av Los Cocos; map p.882. By day, holidaymakers laze about in the plastic chairs on the covered patio, sipping beers and watching the fishermen come and go. At night, the focus is on rum, high-volume salsa and getting flirty. Daily until late.

11

Jalio Surf Bar C Concepción; map p.882. The most upscale option in town, promising tapas by day and cocktails by night. Thurs–Sat, if the owners feel like it.

SHOPPING

For food to cook in your posada's kitchen, you can buy fish directly from the fishermen on the malecón or go to Pescadería Choroní down the side of *Bar La Playa*. There are numerous fruit and veg stands at the sea-end of Av Los Cocos.
Sabor A Cacao C Morillo, at C Unión; map p.882. Excellent chocolate products, including cocoa butter lip-salve from nearby Chuao. Daily 9am–1pm & 3–7pm.

DIRECTORY

Internet There's a cybercafé on C Morillo, a block north of *Hostal Nuevo Colonia*.
Pharmacy There's a small pharmacy next door to *Brisas del Mar*.
Phones Ask at your accommodation or head for the malecón, where there will usually be someone with a phone on a plastic table to rent by the minute.
Post office C Bolívar 2.

Ocumare de la Costa

The main reason to visit **OCUMARE DE LA COSTA** is for the stunning lagoon around the coast, where sea turtles, red ibis and barracuda abound. Only accessible by *lancha*, **La Ciénaga** used to be a safe haven for pirates while today it's a peaceful spot where day-trippers come to sunbathe, snorkel, kayak and swim.

Around 5km east of the town is **Playa Cata**, which is one of the country's finest beaches hidden between bulky headlands, accessible via an hour-long hike or short boat ride. Farther east, surfing beach **Playa Cuyagua** can get fairly large waves, so swimmers should exercise caution.

ARRIVAL AND DEPARTURE

By bus Buses run to and from Maracay (hourly; 90min). The ride is a rough one, so if there are enough of you, share a taxi.
By taxi Taxis from Maracay depart from the gas station outside the terminal entrance (*por puestos* don't operate this route).

GETTING AROUND

By bus All buses stop at Ocumare de la Costa's main plaza. Buses depart regularly to Playa Cata (30min) and Playa Cuyagua (40min).
By boat *Lanchas* to the various destinations around the Ocumare hub depart from La Boca at the eastern end of

---

★ **TREAT YOURSELF**

Coral Lagoon Lodge La Ciénaga ⓦ angel-ecotours.com/coral_lagoon. Located right on the shores of La Ciénaga lagoon, *Coral Lagoon Lodge* might just be the most relaxing place on Venezuela's northwest coast. An all-inclusive overnight package here includes boat transfers, kayaks and snorkelling equipment, and fantastic meals involving plenty of fresh fish and drinks. For two days, life won't get any more taxing than deciding between a swim, early morning turtle-spotting or that hammock under a tree. During the week, particularly outside the July–September school holiday season, you'll probably have the whole magical lagoon almost to yourself. If your budget won't stretch to an overnight stay, Ocumare's *Eco-Lodge* organize day-trips to La Ciénaga. All-Inclusive package/person US$150

Ocumare's malecón (negotiate a price for where you want to go). The staff at *Eco-Lodge* can arrange trips for you.

ACCOMMODATION

Eco-Lodge ☏ 0243 993 1986, ⓦ ecovenezuela.com. The best accommodation in El Playón (Ocumare's main beach area) is the luxurious *Eco-Lodge* at the western end of the malecón. This posada also runs *Coral Lagoon Lodge* (see page 884). Breakfast included. US$70

PARQUE NACIONAL MORROCOY

Gorgeous white-sand cays surrounded by azure water are the highlights of **PARQUE NACIONAL MORROCOY**, one of the most popular national parks in Venezuela. The 300-square-kilometre reserve, spread primarily over water, was created in 1974, but today it doesn't feel much like a national park. Hordes of eco-unfriendly Venezuelans are a weekend presence year-round, although some of the more remote cays still have that remote desert island feel. The park is home to nearly four-fifths of Venezuela's aquatic **bird species**, as well as several types of mammal.

Chichiriviche and **Tucacas** both serve as bases for forays into the park. Neither is particularly attractive, although the profusion of decent budget accommodation options and restaurants in Chichiriviche makes it a better base for further exploration.

WHAT TO SEE AND DO

There is a total of 22 **cays**, or cayos, in the park, most differing only in size and facilities. Day-trips can be arranged by most posadas for no extra charge, while *lancheros* hawk return trips from the malecón end of Calle Zamora in the mornings. If you want snorkelling gear it should come included in the journey price for no extra charge. Prices are negotiable, and a jokey attitude will be a great help when bargaining.

Dotted with shade-giving palms, **Cayo Sombrero**, halfway between Chichiriviche and Tucacas, is the most popular of the cays, although with beaches on all sides you can still find uncrowded parts. There are numerous food stands as well as *lancha*-restaurants, boats with rudimentary kitchens that bring the meal directly to your sun lounger. Food is expensive, however, so it's a good idea to pack a lunch. There are some good snorkelling spots, although it's generally better around **Cayo Sal**. *Lanchas* also make trips to cayos Muerto, Pelón, Peraza and Varadero. You can combine multiple spots on either a short or long day tour, which includes visiting the 200-year-old shipwrecked *Barco Hundido*, the questionably romantic "tunnel of love" through thick mangroves and Piscina Los Juanes, sapphire-blue shallows where you can hunt for clams.

Chichiriviche

Chichiriviche's spread-out format, numerous *liquorerías* and gritty street style render it an unexceptional town. It nevertheless attracts plenty of tourists who come for its useful proximity to the cays.

Calle Zamora, the town's main artery, dead-ends at the malecón, where most activity is centred. By day it's bustling with *lancha* passengers headed to the cays; by night hippie street vendors descend to sell handmade jewellery, strum guitars and watch the fishing boats rocking beside the sea wall.

ARRIVAL AND INFORMATION

By bus Of destinations served from Chichiriviche, Valencia has the most onward connections, serving Caracas, Mérida, Coro and other major cities. Buses arrive and depart 500m inland on C Zamora from 5.30am. To travel between Coro and Chichiriviche, ask your driver to let you off at Sanare, a junction where a road to Chichiriviche meets the Coro–Maracay highway; move to the corresponding bus stop, where you shouldn't have to wait too long for a passing bus in either direction. In high season (July–Sept), especially at weekends, there can be long traffic lines in and out of Chichiriviche.

Destinations Barquisimeto (4–12 daily; 3hr); Valencia (roughly hourly; 2hr). All pass through Sanare.

ACCOMMODATION

Most accommodation is within a couple of blocks of the malecón, a generally safe part of town with lots of foot traffic. Camping in the national park is banned.

Posada La Negra C Mariño ☎ 0259 815 0476. The place to come if you need a bed or a haircut, *La Negra* is the only posada-hairdressers you're likely to encounter on your trip. Friendly, brightly coloured rooms around a communal kitchen come with a/c, en suite and TVs. There's a five-person apartment for BsS300. BsS400

EATING AND DRINKING

Chichiriviche's nightlife amounts to hanging around the liquor stores while they're open, and drinking on the malecón when they're closed. Your best bet for a drink in more relaxed settings is *Txalupa* and its neighbouring seafront restaurants.

Panadería El Centro C Zamora ☎ 0259 818 6906. Now on the corner next to the old shop, impressively moustachioed José serves up good coffee and inexpensive bread. The mini cinnamon rolls, enormous bags of crisps and bottled juices will be all you need for a trip to the cays. Rooms available upstairs. Shop open daily 7am–5pm. BsS500

Txalupa Av Principal, at C Zamora ☎ 0259 818 6425. The portions are big and not outrageously expensive at this first-floor balcony restaurant overlooking the malecón. The speciality is seafood – try the fish fillet in seafood sauce, accompanied by a cold beer. Daily noon–10pm.

CORO

CORO, Venezuela's prettiest colonial town, was named a national monument in 1950 and a World Heritage Site in 1993. A pleasant stopover between the coast and the mountains, Coro contains some of the country's best backpacker accommodation. The town is at its prettiest in the **casco histórico**, where a number of colonial mansions have opened their doors to the public as museums. The nearby **Parque Nacional Médanos de Coro** lies on the edge of town, a mini-desert of golden sand dunes and wild goats.

11

WHAT TO SEE AND DO

You only need wander the sleepy streets of central Coro to get a flavour of the town's Spanish imperial heritage. If you're in town on a Tuesday, head over to the Museo de Arte de Coro at 7pm, when **Cine en la Calle** hosts a weekly showing of classic movies in a makeshift street cinema.

Churches

The centre of the *casco histórico* is the Plaza Bolívar, on the east end of which stands Venezuela's oldest **Cathedral**, begun in 1583 and finished in 1634. Two blocks north on Plaza San Clemente, the **Iglesia San Clemente** was originally built in 1538 by the town's founder, Juan de Ampíes. Totally rebuilt in the eighteenth century, San Clemente is one of three churches in the country built in the shape of a cross. Beside it, a small monument contains the **Cruz de San Clemente**, the wooden cross used in the first Mass after the town was founded.

Colonial mansions

El Balcón de los Arcaya (daily 9am–7pm; free), at the western edge of the Plaza San Clemente on Calle Zamora, is a mansion once owned by the affluent Arcaya family; it houses impressive mastodon excavations and some less-than-scientific diagrams. Further down the road, the **Casa de las Ventanas de Hierro** (Tues–Sun 9am–5pm; free) is a colonial museum where the staff are kitted out in period dress. The work of local artists is displayed at the **Casa del Tesoro** (Tues–Sun 9am–5pm; free), another stately mansion next door. A block and a half to the northeast of Plaza Bolívar on Avenida Talavera, the **Museo de Arte de Coro** (Mon–Fri 9am–5pm, Sat & Sun 10am–5pm; free) has temporary exhibits featuring international names in a beautifully restored eighteenth-century townhouse.

Parque Nacional Médanos de Coro

A short taxi ride will take you to the entrance of the eighty-square-kilometre

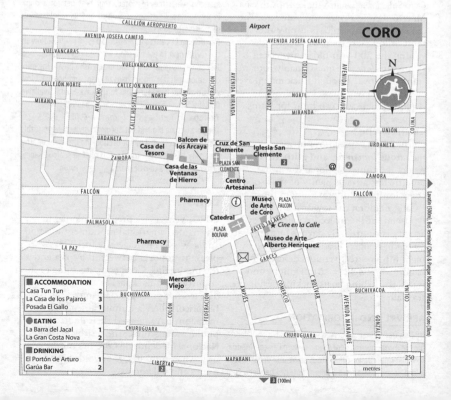

CORO

INTO COLOMBIA

There are three main **border crossings** between Venezuela and Colombia. The northernmost, at Paraguachón, offers the best connections to coastal cities like Cartagena; Cúcuta has onward services to Bogotá. Before leaving Venezuela you must pay the **exit tax** (BsS0.45 at time of research, but check in advance) and get your passport stamped by the SAIME emigration office. Across the border, visit the Colombian immigration office for an entry stamp. Don't forget to do this or you will be sent back and possibly fined. Colombian time is one hour behind Venezuela.

Relations between Venezuela and Colombia are volatile, and can deteriorate at short notice. It is wise to seek up-to-date advice on the current political situation, and on **security**, before using any of the three crossings. At present, no motor traffic is allowed across the border, so you can only cross on foot. Note also that the border area is regarded as particularly unsafe due to the presence of smuggling gangs, so exercise extra caution.

PARAGUACHÓN (MARACAIBO–MAICAO)

It is still possible to take a *por puesto* from the **Maracaibo** terminal to **Maicao**, Colombia, where you can switch to a bus for Santa Marta (4hr), Cartagena (8hr) and other destinations. Expect numerous police checks on the way to the border and don't be surprised if they decide to search you. The Venezuelan and Colombian passport stamping points are 200m apart on the border itself. However, the point for paying the Venezuelan exit tax is 2km before the border, so make sure you ask your driver to stop briefly so you can buy it. Set off in the morning to ensure that you arrive in Maicao with plenty of time to catch an onward bus. The border is open 6am–9pm.

CÚCUTA

Open 7am–8pm (Venezuelan time). Access is via **San Cristóbal**, which is served from numerous destinations including Mérida and Caracas. From there get a bus or taxi to the border town of San Antonio del Táchira, where immigration and customs are 400m before the border itself. On the Colombian side there are regular buses into Cúcuta, which has regular bus connections to Bucaramanga (5hr) and Bogotá (15hr).

PUERTO CARREÑO

This crossing is the most remote, with few transport connections on the Colombian side. Check in advance that the border is open, as it has a habit of closing unexpectedly. Go to the SAIME office on Avenida Aguerrevere in Puerto Ayacucho to get your Venezuelan exit stamp before crossing. Then catch a *por puesto* from the Puerto Ayacucho bus terminal to El Burro (45min) for a *lancha* across the Orinoco to the Colombian city of Puerto Carreño (10min), where you can get your Colombian stamp. The onward journey by road from Puerto Carreño to Bogotá is long, and feasible only in the December–March dry season. Otherwise, there are Satena flights (🌐satena.com) six times weekly for Bogotá and once for Villaviciencio, sometimes supplemented by cargo flights.

11

Parque Nacional Médanos de Coro, a mini-desert where you can stroll the sand dunes, spy on wild goats or go sandboarding with the staff of *Posada El Gallo* (see page 888). To get back to town try hitching a ride with any of the numerous visitors at the entrance, otherwise it's a 500m stroll to the main road where you can hail a taxi. Robberies have occurred here, so don't linger long after dark and be discreet with any valuables.

ARRIVAL AND DEPARTURE

By bus The bus terminal is 2km east of town on Av Los Médanos. There's no luggage storage. *Por puestos* run regularly from the terminal until around 5pm for closer destinations like Punto Fijo and Maracaibo.

Destinations Caracas (several daily; 7hr); Puerto La Cruz (1 daily; 12hr); San Cristóbal (1 daily; 10hr).

INFORMATION AND TOURS

Tourist information Corfaltur is on Paseo Alameda (a continuation of Av Miranda) at C Falcón (☎0268 253 0260).
Tour operators Araguato Expeditions (☎0426 560 0924, 🌐araguato.org), in *Casa Tun Tun* does day-trips to the Paraguaná Peninsula, San Luís mountains (including the "Spanish trail", a jungle path once used by European explorers) and the eerie Catatumbo lightning (see page 891), as well as safaris in the Llanos and visits to reserves in Canaima (see page 901), Roraima (see page 904), Los

Roques (see page 880) and the Orinoco Delta (see page 905). *Posada El Gallo* and *Casa de los Pajaros* can take you sandboarding on the Parque Médanos de Coro dunes.

ACCOMMODATION

Casa Tun Tun C Zamora ✉ casatuntun@hotmail.com; map p.886. A relaxed atmosphere generated by Parisian owner Damien and his wife Norka, *Tun Tun* has everything you could want from a posada: hammocks, kitchen, barbecue, clean rooms with a/c (some en suite) and a good selection of board games. Bs$500

La Casa de los Pajaros C Monzon 74 (between calles Ampiés and Comercio) ☎ 0268 252 8215; map p.886. A warm welcome at this beautiful posada, with lovely rooms and great hosts, who also offer tours and sandboarding. US$4

★ **Posada El Gallo** C Federación 26 ☎ 0268 252 9481, ✉ posadaelgallo@gmail.com; map p.886. This beautiful French-run colonial townhouse is a popular spot for backpackers (including non-guests) to hang out in. Beer is on the honour system and there is an abundance of hammocks to swing in. Two dorm rooms are useful for solo travellers, while the intimate doubles are fan cooled, some with en suite. The friendly owners organize sandboarding and other trips throughout the area. US$10

EATING

There are a number of inexpensive restaurants in Coro, many doubling as bars in the evening, although opening hours are generally lax. Be sure to try *chivo* (goat), the regional speciality.

La Barra del Jacal C Unión, at Av Manaure; map p.886. *Al fresco* dining, decent pizzas, good chicken *chicharrón*, cold beers – all in all, a cool place to hang out of an evening. Daily 5pm–midnight.

La Gran Costa Nova Av Manaure opposite Hotel Intercaribe; map p.886. This *panadería* makes good coffee and bakes great bread, *pastelitos* and cakes. It's also a good spot to stock up on provisions for your posada's kitchen. If you're eating in, pay at the till first and give your receipt to the staff behind the counter. Daily 8am–9pm.

DRINKING

El Portón de Arturo C Falcón, at Toledo; map p.886. A big saloon serving up great seafood and meat, as well as Creole classics. There's an ample and friendly bar where Coro natives of all generations will happily join you for a few drinks. Mon–Sat 8am–8pm.

Garúa Bar C Manzo, at Colón; map p.886. Claiming the title of Coro's oldest bar, this working man's saloon is a safe place to sit and talk rubbish with barman and owner Luis. Beers are at socialist prices and the patrons will be happy to act as taxi drivers for your return to the hotel when you're finished. Wed–Sat 6pm–midnight, Sun noon–6pm.

SHOPPING

Artesanía There are a few places selling *artesanía* in Coro, though none of it is very compelling. Local potters sell their wares in Plaza Falcón, and the Centro Artesanal next to Plaza San Clemente has a momentarily diverting array of paintings, dioramas, and *dulce de leche* made from goat's milk. Officially, it's open daily 9am–6pm, though the vendors tend to operate on their own schedules.

Market There's a small food market, the Mercado Viejo, on C Garcés at Colón (daily until about 7pm), where you can pick up supplies for self-catering.

DIRECTORY

Banks and exchange Banco de Venezuela on Paseo Talavera at Ciencias and on C Comercio at Buchivaco; Banco Mercantil on C Falcón at Colina.

Internet *Hotel Intercaribe* opposite La Gran Costa Nova on Av Manaure has a popular internet café next door.

Pharmacy Farmacia Santa Catalina, C Federación, at Falcón; Farmacia Catedral, C Colón, at La Paz.

Phones Movistar c/o Go Cellular, ground floor, Ferial mall, C Falcón, at Hernández.

Post office Ipostel, Casa de las 100 Ventanas, C Ampiés.

PARAGUANÁ PENINSULA

A Caribbean island connected to mainland South America by a thin land bridge, the **PARAGUANÁ PENINSULA** is a tax-free watersports haven. It's also the site of Venezuela's last functioning oil refinery, though this is nowhere near its tourist centres.

The island's only city is on its western shores, **Punto Fijo**, a shopping haven where government-enforced "fair prices" allow international visitors to buy designer goods for astonishingly low prices. On the breezier eastern edge, the sleepy town of **Adícora** offers surf enthusiasts the country's best kite- and windsurfing, while backpackers can catch an island-feel breather from the intensity of the mainland on their way to or from Colombia.

WHAT TO SEE AND DO

Crossing the land bridge from Coro to Paraguaná is like a scene out of Mario Kart. Belting the motor along at breakneck speeds, your battered bus or shared taxi will dodge around wandering goats and encroaching sand dunes in order to get to **Adícora**, the best town to base yourself as a budget traveller. The sleepy town is a peninsula on a peninsula, jutting out east into the Caribbean, with beaches five blocks apart on both north and south sides. It's on the wide and windswept **Playa Sur** that the wind- and kitesurfing takes place, while **Playa Norte** is the social hub, with a posada- and restaurant-lined seafront and more shelter from the elements.

Across the peninsula is **Punto Fijo**, an ugly city and the island's administrative hub, where you will have to go if you want either to take advantage of the island's tax-free shopping, or journey directly to anywhere further afield than Coro.

ARRIVAL AND DEPARTURE

By shared taxi The only way to get directly to Adícora from the mainland is via shared taxi from Coro. Cars arrive and depart from the Coro bus terminal and the Adícora bus shelter on the main road. If coming from further afield, you should go to Punto Fijo before catching an onward bus to Adícora from the same terminal.

By bus The Punto Fijo bus terminal is an airport-like structure serving nationwide destinations as well as towns along Colombia's northern coast.

Destinations Adícora (roughly every 15min; 1hr); Caracas (several daily; 8hr); Maracaibo (roughly every 30min; 5hr 30min); Maracay (several daily; 6hr 30min); Mérida (3 daily; 15hr); Puerto La Cruz (1 daily; 14hr).

INFORMATION AND ACTIVITIES

Tourist information There's a tourist information desk inside the Punto Fijo bus terminal, but you'll be lucky to find

it staffed. Hotel operators in Adícora are more on the ball, and can organize tours.

Watersports Chicho's School (☎0414 583 3156, ✉chichcoskitecamp@gmail.com), Playa Sur, or at *Chicho's Posada*, one of the watersports institutions along the beach, is one of the few to offer both wind- and kitesurfing in the same place. Rents equipment and offers 8hr courses. North Shore Windsurf (☎0424 627 0359), located next to the police station on Playa Norte; friendly windsurf champion Carlos and his crew offer 8hr courses spread over two days and rentals.

ACCOMMODATION

La Casa Rosada Blvd de Adícora ☎0269 988 8004, ⓦposadalacasarosada.com. A lovely colonial building in a great position on the pedestrian seafront. All rooms have a/c and there's a good restaurant specializing in seafood. BsS1000

Chicho's Posada C La Pastora ☎0414 583 3156, ✉chichcosposada@gmail.com. Italian Francesco, known as Chicho, runs this chilled-out spot in the centre of town alongside his surf school. It boasts pool tables, a lively bar and local kids hanging out. The place to stay if you're in town for the watersports. BsS2600

EATING AND DRINKING

A lot of restaurants don't open on weekdays, so you may have to resort to the various burger stands on the north beach malecón, which operate nightly until late.

Los Sartenes C Comercio, at La Matina ☎0269 988 8064. Fresh fish, cold beer, the best grub in town. Try the grouper (*mero*) fillet with fries and tartar sauce. Daily 10.30am–1pm.

Mérida and the Andes

Occupying the northernmost limit of the Andes range, the mountainous state of **Mérida** is a region of lofty peaks and raw natural beauty. The region has long been Venezuela's most popular backpacker destination, and facilities for budget travellers are among the best in the country. The state capital, also called Mérida, has a sizeable student population, resulting in some of the country's most entertaining nightlife, an excellent place to blow off steam after the various adventure sports the region is known for. To the city's south and east, the **Parque Nacional Sierra Nevada**, dominated by the famed Pico Bolívar (5007m) and Pico Humboldt (4920m), offers some of the finest hiking

opportunities in the region. To the north, the Carretera Transandina, or the Trans-Andean Highway, passes several charming mountain towns on its weaving way to Barinas, including **Apartaderos**, which has one of the world's highest observatories, the **Observatorio Astronómico Nacional**.

MÉRIDA

From the bottom of a deep valley, the city of **MÉRIDA** enjoys stunning views of the surrounding mountains. Based in Mérida, **La Universidad de los Andes** is one of the country's most prestigious universities and runs numerous international exchange programmes, adding undergraduates of all backgrounds to its already sizeable student population. Despite its cosmopolitan sensibilities, Mérida offers reasonable prices, safe streets and a block numbering system that makes the town easily navigable.

Owing to its natural endowment as well as the efforts of several excellent tour operators, Mérida's chief attraction is **adventure sports** (see page 891). However, if you've got some down time, or if you're allergic to adrenaline, the city offers a couple of sights, as well as some diverting **day-trips**.

WHAT TO SEE AND DO

The old town around Plaza Bolívar makes for a pleasant half-day's wandering. The town has a small old-fashioned zoo at its northern limit with some impressive species on show.

The Old Town

Walking the streets of the **old town** to admire its colonial houses, pretty parks and inordinate number of shoe shops will only take a few hours. Right on the Plaza Bolívar,

the impressive **Catedral** was only completed in 1958, after over 150 years of stalled construction. Of the several decent museums in the area, the most interesting is the **Museo Arqueológico** (Tues–Fri 8.30–11.30am & 2–3.30pm; BsS1) on Avenida 3 at the Plaza Bolívar. It presents pre-Columbian artefacts from the region, augmented by thorough historical descriptions.

Parque Zoológico

The zoo (daily 8am–5pm, closed Mon in low season) at the northeastern limit of the town has a good selection of native and foreign animals including a tiger, a lion, a condor brought down from the refuge above Apartaderos (see page 894), and a spectacled bear. To get here take a bus bound for Los Chorros from the intersection of Avenida 5 and Calle 23.

The Mukumbarí cable car

Mérida's greatest attraction, the world's highest and longest **cable car** (*teleférico*)

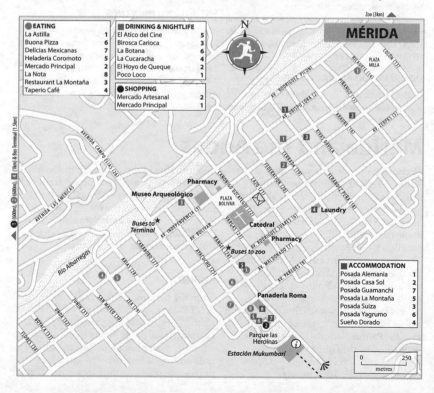

EATING

La Astilla	1
Buona Pizza	6
Delicias Mexicanas	7
Heladería Coromoto	5
Mercado Principal	8
La Nota	8
Restaurant La Montaña	3
Taperio Café	4

DRINKING & NIGHTLIFE

El Ático del Cine	5
Birosca Carioca	3
La Botana	6
La Cucaracha	4
El Hoyo de Queque	2
Poco Loco	1

SHOPPING

Mercado Artesanal	2
Mercado Principal	1

MÉRIDA

Zoo (3km)

Pharmacy
Museo Arqueológico
PLAZA BOLÍVAR
Laundry
Buses to Terminal
Catedral
Pharmacy
Buses to zoo
Río Albarregas
Panadería Roma
Parque las Heroínas
Estación Mukumbarí

ACCOMMODATION

Posada Alemania	1
Posada Casa Sol	2
Posada Guamanchi	7
Posada La Montaña	5
Posada Suiza	3
Posada Yagrumo	6
Sueño Dorado	4

0 — 250 metres

ADVENTURE SPORTS AND TOURS

Mérida's surroundings provide the perfect conditions for an astounding range of **adventure sports**. There's an array of tour companies in town, so it's a good idea not to jump at the first tour offered (usually by your accommodation). Companies compete particularly hard for business outside of the July–September high season, and the more you shop around, the more likely you are to find an itinerary, group or price that suits you.

Tour prices generally decrease as more customers register, so ask your company about joining an existing group. Many trips require a minimum number of customers, so it's a good move to check availability before you arrive in town, easily done through the companies' websites. Paying in cash is the most cost-efficient option, but bank transfers can be arranged for better rates than you would pay on a credit card. Except on one-day trips, all meals and accommodation are included in tour prices.

Due to Venezuela's volatile economy and fierce competition among companies, **prices** listed here are approximate. For the latest rates, contact the tour operators directly. Most operators offer all of the following activities, though some claim individual specialities.

ACTIVITIES

Canyoning A combination of abseiling, scrambling and climbing around and under waterfalls, typically taking a day, with a two-person minimum.

Climbing and trekking There are numerous less challenging treks than the popular Pico Humboldt (see page 895) and Pico Bolívar (see page 895) routes. These include Pico Pan de Azúcar or Los Nevados; both routes take three to four days to complete.

It is possible for experienced hikers to trek independently, although they should notify Inparques at the cable-car base station beforehand.

Mountain biking Many companies rent out good bikes, and will happily indicate where to head for the best routes. It is also possible to engage a guide, with prices depending on whether you want a jeep to access the more remote trails. Some companies also offer horseriding.

Paragliding The slopes above Mérida are the jumping-off point for a thrilling thirty-minute descent by paraglider. Be sure to bring a jacket and don't eat before going if you're prone to motion sickness. Some agencies also offer paragliding courses.

Rafting Rivers in Mérida and Barinas states have Class III to V rapids. Rafting season is from June to November; it's possible in December but companies don't generally take advance bookings due to unpredictable water levels. Some agencies have private camps in Barinas where you'll spend the night.

Los Llanos and Catatumbo Mérida is the main staging point for guided trips to Los Llanos, the wildlife-filled wetlands east of the Andes. The natural phenomenon of the **Catatumbo lightning** (Relámpago del Catatumbo) – the highest concentration of lightning flashes in the world, often for hours at a time – occurs where the Catatumbo River meets Lake Maracaibo, on average three out of every four nights of the year, most intensely at the height of the wet season in October, when you can see an average of 28 flashes per minute, with rather less during the January–February dry season. Most companies go for only one night, but if you want to double your chances of seeing it, Alan Highton (see below) goes for two nights.

TOUR OPERATORS

Colibrí In Posada Suiza ☎0274 252 4961, ⓦcolibri-tours. com. This expert outfit is one of Mérida's oldest and can sort out every activity including tailor-made trips. Ask about the owner's signature Jají day-trip and he'll draw you a map.

Fanny Tours C 24 between Av 8 and Parque Las Heroínas ☎0274 252 2952, ⓦfanny-tours.com. Specializes in mountaineering; also offers trips to Los Llanos. Multiple languages spoken, including English.

Gravity Tours C 24 between Av 7 and 8 ☎0274 251 1279, ⓦgravity-tours.com. Offers a popular two-day combo of mountain biking and rafting, as well as trips throughout the country. Very helpful, English-speaking staff.

Guamanchí Expeditions C 24 between Av 8 and Parque Las Heroínas ☎0274 252 2080, ⓦguamanchi.com. With more than 20 years of experience in the Andes and Los Llanos, this company supplies quality equipment for its specialities of climbing and trekking. Also offers day-trips to Laguna Negra (see page 894) and birdwatching tours.

Alan Highton ☎0414 756 2575, ⓦcocolight.com. Local community worker who runs the best available tour to the Catatumbo lightning, a three-day/two-night expedition for groups of six or more. Alan's also a butterfly expert and will share his passion with you: he's even had a species named after him.

11

11

rising to 4893m above sea level (daily 11am–8pm). The base station (☎0274 252 5080) is situated at the newly refurbished Parque Las Heroínas, from where the car climbs 3000m vertically and 12.5km horizontally across three intermediate stations to the **Pico Espejo** (4865m). It is a good idea to pause for acclimatization at the penultimate, Loma Redonda (4045m), as the rapid changes in height can cause mild altitude sickness.

From Loma Redonda, you can also follow various hiking trails (4hr) to the small Andean town of **Los Nevados** 13km away, which contains several posadas and places to eat. You can do this walk on your own, but should notify Inparques beforehand, whose main office is at the base station.

ARRIVAL AND INFORMATION

By plane The closest functioning airport to Mérida is El Vigía two hours away, where dedicated shared taxis and buses wait to ferry visitors up to the mountain town. Buses arrive into the terminal, while shared and private cars will drop you off at your destination. Conviasa (W conviasa.aero) and Laser (W laser.com.ve) are the main operators to El Vigía.
Destinations Caracas (4 weekly; 1hr); Porlamar (1 weekly; 1hr 20min).
By bus The bus terminal is 2km outside the city centre. Take a bus into town from the stop on the opposite side of the main road to the terminal. Buses back to the terminal pass via Av 2 beside the bridge.
Destinations Caracas (19 daily; 12hr); Coro (3 nightly; 12hr); Maracaibo (3 nightly; to go by day take a *por puesto*; 8hr); Puerto La Cruz (daily at midnight; 20hr); San Cristóbal (roughly every 20min; 5hr 30min). For Ciudad Bolívar you have to change at Puerto La Cruz or Barinas, with the most reliable onward connections from the first of those.
Tourist information Cormetur (☎0800 637 4300) has an office at the base station of the cable car.

ACCOMMODATION

Mérida has a good selection of budget hostels and posadas. Most of the cheapest options are conveniently found near Parque Las Heroínas, where nearly all the tour agencies have their offices. Mid-range options can be much cheaper during the Nov–June low season, although the posadas tend to remain the same price year-round. Unlike the rest of the country, hot water is taken as given in Mérida. To camp in the surrounding national parks, contact the Inparques office at the cable car base station.
Posada Alemania Av 2 between calles 17 and 18 ☎0274 252 4067, W posadaalemania.com; map p.890. A hangout at the back with communal kitchen, hammocks

and chunky furniture gives this otherwise basic posada a friendly feel. Spacious dorm beds, and a computer. Dorms BsS240, doubles BsS552
★ **Posada Guamanchi** C 24 between Av 8 and Parque las Heroínas ☎0274 252 2080, W guamanchi.com; map p.890. This three-floor building has a nice location beside Parque las Heroínas. The wi-fi reaches to the top-floor terrace, which contains some of the hammocks that are slung throughout. Also has a posada in Los Nevados. BsS800
Posada La Montaña C 24 no. 6–47 ☎0274 252 5977, e posadalamontanamerida@gmail.com; map p.890. *La Montaña* looks rather like a posada that set up shop in a botanical garden; bursting with greenery, its upper-balcony rooms have stunning views of the even lusher scenery outside. BsS600
Posada Suiza Av 3 between calles 17 and 18 ☎0274 252 4961, W colibri-tours.com; map p.890. Professional and friendly staff run the Colibrí tours company from the large reception, while a courtyard at the back is ringed by dorms and pleasant rooms, all with colourful tartan blankets and en suite. A short walk back from the bars. Breakfast included. BsS2100
Posada Yagrumo C 24, at Av 8, next door to Posada Guamanchi ☎0274 252 9539, W posadayagrumo.com; map p.890. Good-value en-suite doubles, although not all with natural light. They have cable TV, and there's a communal kitchen, laundry service and internet booths. BsS500
Sueño Dorado Av 6 between calles 19 and 20 ☎0274 251 1192, W hotelsuenodorado.com.ve; map p.890. A smart hotel with steel banisters and plate glass cleverly designed into more rustic architecture. Rooms upstairs have great views of the mountains as well as safes and cable TV. The restaurant downstairs is a good place for a coffee break while wandering the hilly backstreets. BsS550

EATING

The cuisine from Mérida and the Andes is famous throughout the country. Some specialities include *arepas de trigo* (made

---

★ TREAT YOURSELF

Posada Casa Sol Av 4 between calles 15 and 16 ☎0274 252 4164, W posadacasasol.com; map p.890. Mérida's best attempt at the boutique hotel, this haven of serenity has an excellent restaurant, balconies suited to Shakespearean soliloquy and an interesting water feature full of carp. Rooms are elegant, the beds are super-soft and showers are excellent – the perfect spot to reward yourself after an arduous trek or bus journey. Breakfast included. BsS725

from wheat flour), *queso ahumado* (smoked cheese) and *trucha* (trout). *Vino de mora* is wine made from blackberries.

★ **La Astilla** C 14, between avenidas 2 and 3; map p.890. They eventually decided on every colour when they chose the paint scheme for this place. Positioned on the leafy Plaza Milla, much of the vegetation has made its way inside. Friendly staff, tiled tabletops, local specialities like trout, plus pizza and the best *batidos* in town. Across the way, *El Andino* is another good option in a less colourful setting. Daily 9–10.30pm.

Buona Pizza Av 7 between calles 24 and 25; map p.890. Chunks of gooey mozzarella on crunchy-crusted pizzas follow Nonna's original recipe. This long-standing restaurant dresses itself up for the holidays and offers some quirky toppings; who knew guava was good on a pizza? Daily 11am–10pm.

Delicias Mexicanas Ground floor of Hotel Altamira, C 25 between Av 7 and 8; map p.890. Pricey, but if you need your taco fix this stylish eatery is the place to come. Does the Tex-Mex classics alongside a few interesting attempts at Andean-fusion, mainly involving trout. Wed–Sun noon–11pm.

★ **Heladería Coromoto** Av 3 between calles 28 and 29; map p.890. This Mérida institution holds the Guinness World Record for the most ice-cream flavours (863!), although with a menu including sardines-in-brandy, *pabellón criollo* and beer, the importance of the record clearly got a bit out of hand. A quintessential Mérida experience, only around sixty flavours are available daily. Tues–Sat 2.15–8pm.

Mercado Principal Av Las Américas, at Viaducto Miranda; map p.890. Shop for blackberry wine and magic herbs then head up to the fun food court on the second floor, which has competitive outlets serving up good set menus. The area becomes rammed at lunchtime. Mon–Sat 7am–5pm, Sun 7am–1.30pm.

La Nota Av 8 by Parque las Heroínas, beside the bus terminal and several other locations about town; map p.890. Popular local chain which *Mérideños* promote as "how McDonald's should be" (although the excellent street-level burger stands do just as good a job). There are also subs, teriyaki and steaks. Daily 8am–6pm.

★ **Restaurant La Montaña** In Posada La Montaña, C 24 no. 6–47; map p.890. Roses on the tables, an open-fronted kitchen and an excellent lunchtime *menú del día* make this modest trattoria-style place a fine-dining choice for relative peanuts. The menu changes daily, scrawled on the blackboard out front. Daily 8am–9.30pm.

Taperio Café Av 3, at C 29; map p.890. An atmospheric street-corner joint with iron-grille walls and a café-culture crowd. A very chilled spot for a beer in the evening; there's live music on the weekends and tasty food, while the *merengadas* are big and bad in a good way. Mon–Sat 11am–9.45pm.

DRINKING AND NIGHTLIFE

In large part because of the immense student population, Mérida enjoys an active nightlife, particularly between Wednesday and Saturday.

El Atico del Cine C 25 next to La Nota; map p.890. Beer comes in coffee mugs and the cocktails are named after classic movies (see if you can translate them all) in this trendy little café-bar. Plays a wide range of music and is a popular starting point for students on a night out. Tues–Sat 11am–midnight.

Birosca Carioca Av 2, at C 24; map p.890. Pounding samba and students define this friendly, ever-popular club, as do the red buckets of "La Bomba", a rum-and-beer concoction for sharing. Open until the crowd goes home – it's situated on a shady street so be careful outside when leaving. Mon–Sat 8.30pm–3am.

La Botana Parque las Heroínas, beside the Mercado Artesanal; map p.890. A rasta-themed bar popular for its pizza, which they keep producing even when it's rammed. A good bar to spend the evening at if you can secure one of the few tables. Tues–Sat 10am–1am, Sun 10am–midnight.

La Cucaracha In Centro Comercial Las Tapias on Av Urdaneta; map p.890. One of Mérida's oldest nightspots, this large but always crowded disco has two floors, one with techno and the other with salsa and *merengue*. It's part of a small chain that caters to various budgets and clienteles around town. Daily until late.

★ **El Hoyo de Queque** Av 4, at C 19; map p.890. You can't miss Mérida's most popular student bar a few blocks up from the Plaza Bolívar; for starters it's painted bright purple. DJs pack the place from 8pm, while the draught beer and *menú ejecutivo* make it a good spot for an easy afternoon. After hours numerous burger stands accumulate outside. Mon–Sat 2pm–1am.

Poco Loco Av 3 between calles 18 and 19; map p.890. Although it's a little odd for a bar in Andean Venezuela to be staunchly FC Barcelona, this is Mérida's best alternative venue, with cheap draught beer and a friendly crowd, and all Barça games televised in HD. Dare you to show up in a Real Madrid shirt. Mon–Sat 1pm–1am, DJs from 8pm.

SHOPPING

Mérida is a decent place to buy souvenirs or stock up on travel essentials.

Antiques You can find a number of antique shops along the road to Apartaderos, which specialize particularly in wooden furniture, as well as preserves and fruit liquors.

Markets The most renowned destination among bargain-hunters is the green-and-yellow-striped Mercado Principal. This three-storey, tourist-oriented market (Mon–Sat 7am–6pm, Sun until 1.30pm) on the other side of the river sells quality Andean produce and there's a good food court on the second floor for lunch. More *artesanía* can be found

11

at the much smaller Mercado Artesanal in front of Parque Las Heroínas, where a permanent installation of stalls sells ceramics, jewellery, blackberry wine, leather goods and woodcarvings.

DIRECTORY

Banks and exchange Banco de Venezuela, Av 4 between calles 23 and 24. Various agencies and hotels around town offer international bank transfers for vastly superior rates.

Camping equipment Cumbre Azul, C 24 opposite Parque Las Heroínas, is a good place to rent or buy camping and hiking equipment.

Internet and phones Several useful *centros de conexiones* offer internet, phone services and photo-copying. There's a CANTV centre beside *Posada Guamanchi*, another *centro* in the bus terminal, and a handful of internet cafés around the cable car base.

Medical care A reputable clinic with some English-speaking doctors is Clínica Mérida (☎0274 263 9011) on Av Urdaneta next to the airport.

Pharmacy Farmacía Central on Av 3, at Plaza Bolívar; Farmacía 6ta Avenida on Av 6, at C 22.

Police The main station is on Av Urdaneta, adjacent to Parque Gloria Patrias (☎ 0800 765 4637).

Post office Ipostel, C 21 between Av 4 and 5, and in the bus terminal.

APARTADEROS AND AROUND

Most of the quaint Andean towns northeast of Mérida are set alongside the Carretera Transandina (Trans-Andean Highway), with beautiful views of the Sierra Nevada range to the south and the Sierra Culata range to the north. Two hours up the valley, the mountain town of **APARTADEROS** makes a diverting day-trip from Mérida, although you should head out early as it tends to rain in the afternoons. The strip of houses here looks a lot like a town in the Scottish Highlands; there are fabulous views of the valley below when it's clear, although, like bonny Scotland, it's utterly dismal when the rain comes down.

The nearby **Refugio del Cóndor**, best accessed by hailing a passing cab from the main road (daily 7am–5pm; no phone, contact Inparques in Mérida for more details), is home to the Andean condor conservation and research project. If you want to see a condor without making the trip, visit Mérida Zoo (see page 890), which is home to a condor from this project. Visitors are shown an instructional

five-minute video in English or Spanish.

Two kilometres away, the **Observatorio Astronómico Nacional** (Aug & Sept daily 5–11pm; ☎0274 245 0106, ⍟cida.gob.ve) opens its doors to the public during August and September to showcase its work in one of the world's highest observatories.

The Carretera Transandina highway eventually crosses the highest driveable summit in Venezuela, at Pico El Águila, and begins the spectacular descent to Barinas and Los Llanos (see page 895).

ARRIVAL AND DEPARTURE

By bus Buses for Apartaderos (2hr) depart from the Mérida terminal every 20min or so. To get back to Mérida, flag down one of the buses that pass along the route until around 6.30pm.

By taxi From Apartaderos taxis will take tourists to the condor refuge or the observatory. Getting back is as simple as walking the kilometre (or paying anyone with a car to drive you) back to the bus route.

PARQUE NACIONAL SIERRA NEVADA

Looming above Mérida to the south and east, the Sierra Nevada runs northeast along the Carretera Transandina and through the 2760-square-kilometre **PARQUE NACIONAL SIERRA NEVADA**. There is great diversity in flora and fauna here, but the park's most famous inhabitant, the threatened spectacled bear, is a shy creature that you'll be lucky to see, although Mérida's zoo (see page 890) has one. The park features the country's highest mountains, which reach over 5000m, as well as its best **adventure activities**. You can easily explore the lower reaches on your own, but guides (see page 891) are recommended for the two higher peaks unless you are an experienced mountaineer.

Just inside the northern entrance to the park, a few kilometres along the highway from Apartaderos, is **Laguna Mucubají**. Camping is allowed here; you will need permission from the Inparques office near the entrance. A good hiking trail connects Laguna Mucubají with **Laguna Negra**, a trout-filled lake with dark water. The beautiful hike takes two hours, and you can continue another one hour thirty minutes to the pretty **Laguna Los Patos**. In

LOS LLANOS

Taking up nearly a third of the country, the immense plains and wetlands of **Los Llanos** are one of the continent's premier wildlife-viewing areas. Some of the most abundant species are alligators, anacondas and capybaras, the world's largest rodent. Other common species are river dolphins, jaguars, pumas, howler and capuchin monkeys and anteaters. However, the livelihood of the region's human inhabitants, the **Llaneros**, is most closely linked with domesticated animals. Llaneros are extremely skilled horsemen and work in secluded groups on **hatos**, enormous ranches with cattle often numbering in the tens of thousands. Many comparisons have been drawn between the Llaneros and the cowboys of the American West. Known for being tough and independent, both are portrayed as embodying the spirit of their countries.

Los Llanos has two very pronounced **seasons**. During the wet season, from May to November, much of the land becomes flooded and extremely verdant. In the dry season the land becomes parched and dusty, and vegetation changes colour to match the dry surroundings. The best wildlife viewing comes when water is scarce, when animals congregate at the few watering holes.

Unless you have a wad of cash to spend on a stay at one of the *hatos*, you'll most likely visit Los Llanos as part of a **multi-day tour** from Mérida (see page 891).

11

the wet season, it's best to leave early to avoid rain and fog that could limit visibility considerably.

Pico Bolívar

At 5007m, **Pico Bolívar** is the country's highest and most hiked peak. There are multiple routes up, varying in difficulty and length of ascent. Many walkers get off at the last Mukumbarí cable car station, Pico Espejo, and make the five-hour ascent along the Ruta Weiss. This is not very technical in the dry season (Dec–May). The Ruta Sur Este and North Flank are two more challenging routes, which involve ice-climbing and require ice axes and crampons. Views from the top are spectacular – on a clear day, you can see the city of Mérida, the Colombian Andes and the vast expanse of Los Llanos.

Pico Humboldt

Another renowned peak, **Pico Humboldt** can be combined with a climb of Pico Bolívar or tackled on its own. Starting at the entrance of Parque Nacional La Mucuy, about 10km to the northeast of Mérida,

the first day's ascent is 1000m; after the six-hour, 9km walk, most people camp around the picturesque Laguna Coromoto. The ascent on the second day is shorter but steeper as you get into the rocky terrain above the tree line. The final day's ascent to the peak and return to the campsite usually takes at least eight hours, depending upon your ice-climbing ability. The fourth day is for the descent back to La Mucuy.

ARRIVAL AND DEPARTURE

By bus The park entrance is on the Apartaderos route from Mérida; simply stay on the bus for a few kilometres after Apartaderos. To get back to Mérida or onwards to Barinas, flag down a passing bus in either direction.

INFORMATION AND TOURS

Tourist information As well as the Inparques offices in Mérida at the cable car base station (see page 890), there is one near the park entrance that can issue camping permits and dispense advice (Spanish only).

Tour operators Companies (see page 891) organize groups on a one-guide-to-two-clients ratio. Routes (Weiss, Sur Este, North Flank) can be selected depending on experience and generally take six days, a time which can be cut to four with higher levels of expertise.

Guayana

Covering the southern and southeastern half of Venezuela, the **Guayana** region (not to be confused with the country Guyana) covers three of Venezuela's largest states

– Amazonas, Bolívar and Delta Amacuro. The region contains the vast majority of Venezuela's natural resources such as gold, iron ore, bauxite and diamonds. It also

11

supplies hydroelectricity for large swathes of the country. Despite the immensity of Guayana, there are only two real cities, **Puerto Ordaz** and **Ciudad Bolívar**, whose residents are vastly outnumbered by those of indigenous communities belonging to the Yanomami, Pemón, Warao and Piaroa peoples, all of whom have retained many of their traditional customs.

The region is estimated to have been above sea level for three billion years; the resulting landscape is the area's biggest tourist draw, although its size means the individual sights are spread far apart. Attractions include the **tropical rainforests** of the Amazon, the mighty **Orinoco Delta**, the breathtaking **Angel Falls** and the magnificent *tepuis*, or flat-topped mountains. *Tepuis* means "Houses of the Gods" in the indigenous Pemón language, and the two most popular are the beautiful and isolated **Autana**, deep in the heart of thick jungle, and the immense **Mount Roraima** – the inspiration for Sir Arthur Conan Doyle's *The Lost World*.

PUERTO AYACUCHO

A sleepy town that's home to half the inhabitants of Amazonas, **PUERTO AYACUCHO** is the state's only major municipality, founded in 1924 as a port for shipping timber downriver. Across the Orinoco from Colombia, it is the access point for the most southerly of the three Colombian border crossings (see page 887), although the difficulty of onward transport makes it the least convenient. Puerto Ayacucho is also the principal entry point for the Amazon region.

WHAT TO SEE AND DO

Like many other Venezuelan municipalities, Puerto Ayacucho itself has almost no intrinsic appeal, but there are several nearby attractions, the most popular of which is the immense **Autana**, a sole *tepui* which towers above the jungle around it.

In town, the **Museo Etnológico de Amazonas** (Tues–Fri 8.30am–noon &

Border at Casuarito (1km)

PUERTO AYACUCHO

Río Orinoco

Mercado Municipal

AVENIDA ORINOCO

CALLE AYACUCHO

AYARICO

EVELIA ROA

Pharmacy

AVENIDA AGUERREVERE

PIAR

BOLIVAR

AVENIDA RÍO NEGRO

CALLE AMAZONAS

Centro Cultural Amazonas

LA GUARDIA

Museo Etnológico de Amazonas

PLAZA DE LOS INDIOS

SAIME Office

Coyote Expediciones

AVENIDA AGUERREVERE

Pharmacy

AVENIDA 23 DE ENERO

UNION

Banesco

Cerro Perico

Banco de Venezuela

AVENIDA ORINOCO

El Mercadito

LUISA CACERES

CARABOBO

N

■ ACCOMMODATION
Gran Hotel Apure   2
Hotel Mawari   1

Hospital (2km), Bus Terminal (4km) & Eco-Destinos

● EATING
Café Rey David   3
El Guariqueño   1
El Mercadito   2

0   200
metres

Mercatradona (300m), El Mirador (700m), Airport (6km) & Tourist Info

AMAZON TOURS

Squeezing all of the Amazon's wonders into a three-day tour is impossible, but a few companies in Ayacucho do their best. The classic tour is a three-day/two-night trip up the Sipapo and Autana rivers to **Cerro Autana**, a 1200m-high *tepui* seen from an adjacent vantage point. You'll spend the nights in hammocks with an indigenous community, explore waterways in small boats and fish for exotic species which you can eat for dinner if successful. More in-depth and expensive options include the ten- to twelve-day **Ruta Humboldt**, following in the footsteps of the famous explorer, and even longer journeys to meet the Yanomami and other isolated indigenous peoples. Tour operators should provide any necessary jungle access permits and can often help you plan a journey into Brazil.

Finally, a **disclaimer**: many people expect to see amazing wildlife in the Amazon, but in reality the density of the jungle and the reclusiveness of the animals make this quite difficult. If you're set on wildlife-watching, save your money for a trip to Los Llanos (see page 895).

TOUR OPERATORS

Eco-Destinos Ent. Urbanización Bolivariana, Quinta Los Abuelos ☎ 0248 521 3964 or ☎ 0416 448 6394, ✉ henryamazonas@hotmiail.com. Lets customers fully customize trips, for instance by suggesting they bring and prepare their own food to mitigate expenses.

2.30–5.45pm, Sat 8.30am–noon), on Avenida Río Negro, showcases the culture and history of the region's indigenous tribes. In front of the museum is **Plaza de los Indios**, a market selling local handicrafts including *catara*, a delicious hot sauce made from leafcutter ants; like peanut butter, it comes either crunchy or smooth.

One block east of the plaza on Avenida Amazonas is the **Centro Cultural Amazonas** or *Casa Azul* (Mon–Sat 8am–6pm; free), where the art gallery has an indigenous-themed permanent exhibit. Styles range from classical to quasi-pornographic absurdism. Ask the friendly staff for what's on at the amphitheatre next door.

The town's most popular attraction lies 30km away at the **Parque Tobogán de la Selva**, where a natural waterslide has been dammed at the bottom to create a rustic infinity pool. If you take a taxi to the park, make sure you arrange for pick-up.

ARRIVAL AND DEPARTURE

You can cross into Colombia (see page 887) or Brazil (see page 905) from this region.

By plane Puerto Ayacucho Airport is 6km southeast of town. Avior (⊕ aviorair.com) operates flights to and from Caracas (2 weekly; 1hr 5min). Buses from the airport into town are rare; it's much easier to take a taxi.

By bus The bus terminal is 4km east of the centre and has nowhere to leave luggage. Taxis into town are hailed from the road outside the main entrance.

Destinations Caracas (daily at 7pm; 15hr); Ciudad Bolívar (several daily; 12hr); San Fernando de Apure (daily at 7pm; 6hr 30min).

GETTING AROUND

By taxi Although Puerto Ayacucho does have city buses, you rarely see them and schedules are unpredictable. Most locals take taxis; look for the "taxi" window-stickers rather than the rooftop signs. *Mototaxis* are a good option for when traffic clogs the city streets at peak hours.

ACCOMMODATION

Gran Hotel Apure Centro Comercial Apure, Av Orinoco ☎ 0248 521 4443, ✉ granhotelapure2014@gmail.com; map p.896. Quite a posh establishment with a/c, en-suite rooms – all bright, cosy and spick and span – made affordable by black market currency rates. **Bs5500**

Hotel Mawari C Evelio Roa 35 ☎ 0248 521 3189; map p.896. You may find yourself showering out of a bucket, since the plumbing occasionally gives out at this otherwise peaceful posada. Rooms (some with a/c) are very basic and set around a courtyard that's more concrete than greenery. **Bs5200**

EATING

In addition to the range of inexpensive restaurants about town, there is a string of food stalls along Av Aguerrevere, west of Av Orinoco, hawking *empanadas*, burgers, fried chicken and fish each evening.

Café Rey David Av Orinoco, south of the mercadito; map p.896. Self-titled "King David" is something of a silver fox, and regally presides over his popular open-fronted place positioned right in the thick of it. Tasty *pollo asado*, sandwiches, *empanadas* and *arepas*. Mon–Sat 8am–7pm.

El Guariqueño Av 23 de Enero; map p.896. A popular place with *Ayacuchans* thanks to its big portions of *pollo* *al ajillo* or *pollo a la plancha*. Numerous ceiling fans make this an excellent spot to duck out of the heat and grab a refresher from the long list of juices. Mon–Sat 8am–4pm.

El Mercadito Between Av Orinoco and Av Amazonas, south of Av 23 de Enero; map p.896. The destination of choice for workers on a lunch break. Various indoor restaurants at the east end of the market serve inexpensive *comida criolla*, but for the real deal slurp down a steaming bowl of *sopa de gallina* surrounded by market sellers.

DIRECTORY

Banks and exchange Banesco and Banco de Venezuela, both on Av Orinoco south of Av 23 de Enero.

Consulates Brazil, Av Rômulo Gallegos, Edifivio Tierra Magica, 3rd floor, Bairro Aramare (☎0248 521 5208); Colombia, C Yapacana 5, Quinta Beatriz (☎0248 521 0789, ⓦ puertoayacucho.consulado.gov.co).

Hospital Clínica Amazonas, Av Rómulo Gallegos (☎0248 521 2491); Clínica Zerpa, Av 23 de Enero (☎0248 521 2815).

Immigration SAIME, Av Aguerrevere 60 (Mon–Fri 8am–4.30pm; ☎0248 521 4188). .

Internet Connections in Puerto Ayacucho are slow. Inversiones Friends, Av Orinoco 31, at Av Aguerrevere; Servinet, C Ayachuco, at Evelio Roa.

Pharmacy Farmacia Autana, Av Río Negro, at C Evelio Roa; FarmaLlanos, Av Orinoco south of Av Aguerrevere.

Phones CANTV and Movilnet, Edificio Maniglia, Av Orinoco, at Av Aguerrevere.

Post office Ipostel, C Evelia Roa at Av Amazonas.

Shopping For local artisan jewellery head to Plaza de los Indios (Mon–Sat 8am–6pm, Sun until noon).

PUERTO ORDAZ

Most of the visitors who pass through **PUERTO ORDAZ** are on their way to Ciudad Bolívar, a much better jumping-off point for the main attractions in the state. The town is the base for Venezuela's aluminium, steel and iron industries, as well as a large producer of hydroelectric power from various dams in the area. It is consequently of little interest to the backpacker and is more of a transport hub. Nearby **San Félix**, an indecorous and seedy town, is best avoided entirely.

WHAT TO SEE AND DO

Built on an industrial scale, Puerto Ordaz's few sights are spread kilometres apart. Taxis are the easiest and safest way to look around; public transport is not advised.

The **Ecomuseo de Caroní** (Tues–Sun 9am–5pm; free; ☎0286 960 4464), next to

the 23 de Enero dam, has temporary exhibitions, all with a conservational theme, as well as a large window through which you can see the dam's gargantuan generators. **Parque Llovizna**, just across from the museum, and **Parque Cachamay** feature expanses of life-affirming greenery and some nice waterfalls.

ARRIVAL AND INFORMATION

By plane Manuel Carlos Piar Guayana Airport is located along the road to Ciudad Bolívar, best reached by taxi; bus routes are inconvenient. Avior (ⓦ avioairlines.com) runs flights to Barcelona (4 weekly; 55min), where you'll need to change for points beyond.

By bus Puerto Ordaz's terminal is on Av Guayana, a 10min taxi ride into town; *taxistas* wait at the entrance. There is nowhere to leave luggage in the terminal. Some buses arrive in nearby San Félix (keep a close eye on your belongings), from where it's a 15min taxi ride to Puerto Ordaz.

Destinations Caracas (hourly; 12hr); Ciudad Bolívar (every 30min; 1hr 30min); Cumaná (4 daily; 5hr); Maracay/Valencia (several daily; 12hr 30min); Puerto La Cruz (4 daily; 6hr); Santa Elena de Uairén (4 daily; 9hr).

ACCOMMODATION

La Casa del Lobo Villa Africana, Manzana 39, Casa 2 ☎0286 961 6286, ⓦ lobo-tours.de. Friendly German owner Wolfgang, who goes by the name of Lobo, runs the only backpacker-friendly place in town and has a travel story or two to tell of his own. The house he built himself has three rooms, all en suite, in a separate part of the house for guests. His tour company Lobo Tours organizes trips to his excellent *campamento* in the Orinoco Delta (see page 905). BsS250

EATING

The Orinokia Mall has plenty of restaurants.

Chiquito's Av Las Américas, Local 8 and 9, Centro Comercial Anto. Local café and bakery serving a range of sweet and savoury pastries as well as coffees. Mon–Sat 7am–7pm, Sun 7am–1pm.

El Rincón del Chivo Av Loefling, Sector La Esperancita. An excellent barbecue house with long benches and a party atmosphere fuelled by the mouth-watering smells of the open grill-pit area. Enormous hunks of meat, *cachapas* and a big selection of sides keep the ravenous and friendly crowd happy. Tues–Sun noon–5pm.

DIRECTORY

Banks BBVA, Carrera Upata, at Av Ciudad Bolívar. Banco Caroní, Vía Venezuela at Carrera España.

Internet There are plenty of internet cafés in the Centro Comercial Trebol I, II and III on C Upata (Mon–Sat 9am–6pm).

Phones Movistar, c/o TEL KA-PA, Santo Tomé III mall, ground floor, Av Atlantico, Los Olivos.

Post office Ipostel, on Av Bolivia, at C Popayán in Sector Villa Colombia.

Shopping For a dose of commercialist perversity (and US-style fast food), check out the massive Orinokia Mall, bordered by Av Las Américas and Av Guayana (daily 10am–8pm).

CIUDAD BOLÍVAR

Sitting on the south bank of the Orinoco at one of its widest points, state capital **CIUDAD BOLÍVAR** is the jumping-off point for the region's numerous attractions, and is one of Venezuela's most backpacker-friendly places. The city is attractive, easily walkable, and its various highlights can be seen in a single day. To the city's south lie the endless expanses of **Parque Nacional Canaima** (see page 901) and the **Gran Sabana** (see page 904).

WHAT TO SEE AND DO

Ciudad Bolívar's cobbled streets, well-preserved colonial buildings and compact size make it a pleasant place to explore on foot. There are a couple of historic sites to bone up on Venezuelan history, while nature-lovers will want to visit the botanical gardens. While you'll see the town at its prettiest in the historic centre, its lifeblood flows alongside Venezuela's mightiest river on the **Paseo Orinoco**. This noisy riverside boulevard has shopping centres, food stalls and jewellery vendors spilling out onto the busy road.

Casco histórico

Most of the city's colonial architecture is in the **casco histórico**, a ten-block area built on a mound on the Orinoco's southern bank, centred on the **Plaza Bolívar**. On the east side of the plaza, the bright yellow 1840 **Catedral** has an interior which, while not particularly ornate, offers a cool escape

11

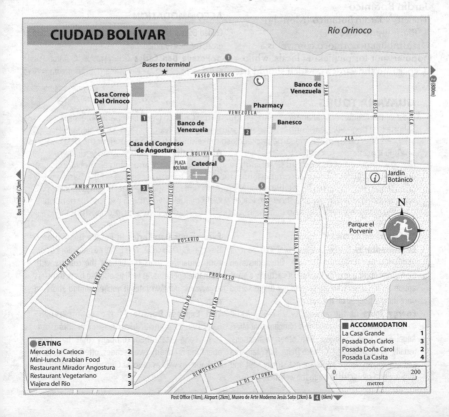

CIUDAD BOLÍVAR

Río Orinoco

Buses to terminal

PASEO ORINOCO

Casa Correo
Del Orinoco

Banco de
Venezuela

Pharmacy

VENEZUELA

Banco de
Venezuela

Banesco

Casa del Congreso
de Angostura

C. BOLÍVAR

PLAZA
BOLÍVAR

Catedral

Jardín
Botánico

AMOR PATRIA

Parque el
Porvenir

N

ROSARIO

PROGRESO

EATING
Mercado la Carioca	2
Mini-lunch Arabian Food	4
Restaurant Mirador Angostura	1
Restaurant Vegetariano	5
Viajera del Rio	3

ACCOMMODATION
La Casa Grande	1
Posada Don Carlos	3
Posada Doña Carol	2
Posada La Casita	4

0   200
metres

from the intense year-round heat that Bolívar is known for.

To the west of the plaza, the **Casa del Congreso de Angostura** (Tues–Sun 8am–5pm; free) is the site where Bolívar and the Angostura Congress founded Gran Colombia, the post-imperialist super-state that encompassed modern-day Venezuela, Colombia and Ecuador.

Museo de Arte Moderno Jesús Soto

The works of Jesús Soto, Venezuela's most famous contemporary artist and a Ciudad Bolívar native, are displayed in the excellent **Museo de Arte Moderno Jesús Soto** (Tues–Fri 9am–5pm, Sat & Sun 10am–4pm; free), south of the centre. Many of his paintings and sculptures make use of optical illusions, and you can ask to be accompanied by one of the guides who will point out the visual tricks. To return, catch a bus from the *McDonald's* across the street.

Jardín Botánico

The city's **Jardín Botánico** (Mon–Fri 8.30am–4pm; free; ⓦjardinbotanicoorinoco.com.ve) is a popular spot for picnicking locals, while deeper into the gardens, which should be toured with a guide (free, but a tip is appreciated), is an impressive array of plants from around the world. The park's main entrance is on Avenida Bolívar at the intersection with Calle Caracas.

ARRIVAL AND DEPARTURE

By plane Tomás de Heres Airport is at the southeastern edge of town, on Av Táchira, at Av Aeropuerto. Buses displaying Ruta 1 or Ruta 2 in the windscreen go via the airport; hail one from the shopping side of the Paseo Orinoco. Tickets for Canaima can be bought in advance at the airport or organized by your hotel.

By bus The terminal lies southwest of the centre on Av República, at Av Sucre. Buses heading to the terminal can be hailed from the river side of Paseo Orinoco. Tickets can only be bought on the day of departure; for less-served destinations (particularly Santa Elena and Barinas) you should buy your night bus ticket in the morning.

Destinations Barinas (2 daily; 15hr); Caracas (several daily; 9hr); Puerto Ayacucho (several daily; 12hr); Puerto Ordaz (every 30min; 1hr); Santa Elena de Uairén (6 daily, mostly night buses; 12hr); Valencia (several daily; 10hr 30min).

ACCOMMODATION

Ciudad Bolívar is rivalled only by Mérida in its selection of great, cheap accommodation.

★ **Posada Don Carlos** C Boyacá, at C Amor Patrio ☎0285 632 6017, ⓦposada-doncarlos.com; map

---

GUAYANA TOURS

Most of the Ciudad Bolívar agencies also sell tours of the Orinoco Delta (see page 905) and Gran Sabana (see page 905), although for the latter you'll find better tour prices in Santa Elena. All agencies offer pretty much the same packages, so make sure you shop around for the best deal.

While it's possible to cobble together a trip to **Angel Falls** (see page 902) on your own, the small amount of money you save hardly warrants the effort of arranging all the various components (flights, boats, accommodation, food). Local tourism operates on the basis of package tours arranged elsewhere (usually Ciudad Bolívar), and the needs of maverick travellers are generally an afterthought. Prices should include everything except the national park fee payable when you land in Canaima, and the Ciudad Bolívar airport departure tax.

TOUR OPERATORS

Eco-Adventures In the bus terminal ☎0285 651 9546, ⓦadventurevenezuela.com. Often mistaken for a pirate outfit due to its location, it's actually a great option for travellers who are keen to get things sorted once they've hopped off the bus.

Energy Tours At the airport ☎0285 654 8418, ⓦenergytour.com. Italian-owned company that offers Angel Falls trips combined with other destinations, usually the Gran Sabana, Orinoco Delta, Isla Margarita and Los Roques. Office hours are not strictly kept and they are best contacted through the website.

Excursiones Don Carlos In Posada Don Carlos, C Boyacá ☎0285 632 6017, ⓦposada-doncarlos.com. Organizes tours throughout the country with reputable operators, as well as offering bank transfers at *mercado paralelo* rates if you're running short on cash.

Turi Express Dorado At the airport ☎0285 6327089, ⓦagenciaturiexpressdorado.blogspot.com. Long-established company that has been operating for nearly two decades, offering the usual packages as well as tours of Ciudad Bolívar itself.

p.899. You can just picture Venezuelan gentry sipping on some dark rum at the bar of this characterful posada. Rooms are off the large colonial courtyard, dotted with all sorts of nineteenth-century knick-knacks. There's a dormitory/balcony area with bunk beds and hammocks for BsS300. Also runs a reputable tour agency. **BsS600**

Posada Doña Carol C Libertad 28 ☎0285 634 0989, ✉jmaury2008@hotmail.com; map p.899. Wacky grandma Doña Carol welcomes you into her oddly decorated house with a friendly smile. There's a bright colour scheme, five spotless rooms (some with a/c) and a balcony upstairs that overlooks the surrounding roofs. **BsS750**

Posada la Casita Av Ligia Pulido, Urbanización Asentamiento Turistico 24 de Julio (6km southeast of the city centre) ☎0285 617 0832, ✪posada-la-casita. com; map p.899. It's a bit of a way out of town, but this charming little posada with a restaurant and pool offers free pick-ups from the airport or bus station. **BsS1700**

EATING

Ciudad Bolívar is not particularly noted for its food, but a few decent options exist. Local fish such as *dorado*, *palometa* and *sapoara* are fresh and tasty.

Mercado la Carioca Paseo Orinoco, at Av 19 de Abril; map p.899. Lots of good and inexpensive food options at this busy market east of town on the way to Laguna del Medio, with fresh river fish the speciality. Daily 8am–5pm.

Mini-lunch Arabian Food C Amor Patrio, at C Igualdad ☎0285 632 7208; map p.899. A little corner café that provides a fix of Middle Eastern fare for when you can't handle beans and rice any more. There's *shawarma*, falafel, *kibbe*, tabbouleh and hummus, and you can get a big mixed plate with a bit of everything. Daily 7am–7pm.

Restaurant Mirador Angostura Paseo Orinoco, between calles Igualdad and Liberdad; map p.899. Dine out with a great river view. Serves fish dishes and food from Venezuela's Caribbean zone. The area gets a bit deserted after dark, so it's wise to leave before then. Tues–Sun 9am–6.30pm.

Restaurant Vegetariano C Amor Patrio, at C Dalla Costa ☎0285 632 6381; map p.899. Four-course vegetarian meals and daily yoga classes. An oasis of patrician calm. Grab a few guavas from the tree in the courtyard on your way in or out. Mon–Fri noon–3pm.

Viajera del Rio C Bolívar, between calles Igualdad and Liberdad; map p.899. Great coffee, cakes and pastries at this cool little city-centre café, named after a popular tune ("river traveller", a reference to the floating water hyacinth) by local composer Manuel Yánez. Daily 9am–7.30pm.

DIRECTORY

Banks and exchange Banco de Venezuela, Paseo Orinoco, at C Pilar, and C Venezuela, at C Constitución; Banesco, C Dalla Costa, at C Venezuela.

★ TREAT YOURSELF

La Casa Grande C Venezolana, at C Boyacá ☎0414 851 2295, ✪hotel-casagrande-ciudadbolivar.com.ve; map p.899. Utterly peerless in Ciudad Bolívar, if not in Venezuela, this luxurious boutique hotel seamlessly blends graceful modern flair with charming imperial decadence in the former headquarters of the Red Cross. A skylit atrium contains plants and a fountain, and a rooftop pool has expansive views of the Orinoco. En-suite rooms have a/c, flat-screen TVs, exposed original stonework and safes. The staff provide free transport to and from the bus terminal and airport. **BsS1150**

Hospital Hospital Ruiz y Páez, Av Germania (☎0426 181 3357).

Pharmacy Numerous around town, *por turno* (only one open at a time) on Sun. Farmacia Unión, C Venezuela, at C Libertad (Mon–Sat 7.30am–5.30pm); Hospifárma, C Independencia at Av Sucre (Mon–Sat noon–midnight).

Phones Movistar c/o Cedecon DVD, Edificio Don Jorge, ground floor, Paseo Meneses at Av Guayana.

Post office Ipostel, Av Táchira at C Guasipati, 1km south of the *casco histórico*.

Shopping For groceries there's a fruit/veg market along C Venezuela until 4pm daily; numerous stands and shops along the Paseo Orinoco sell *artesanía*, cheap clothing and electronics.

PARQUE NACIONAL CANAIMA

One of the world's largest national parks, **PARQUE NACIONAL CANAIMA** is Venezuela's number one tourist attraction, due entirely to the world's tallest waterfall, the astonishing Salto Ángel, or **Angel Falls**. The park is inhabited by roughly twenty thousand Pemón, made up of three major tribes: Kamakoto, Arekuna and Taurepan. Most live in small villages of between 100 and 200 people. At the centre of it all is **Canaima Village**, originally a small Pemón settlement that is now the hub of a tourism industry vastly superior to those you are likely to witness elsewhere in Venezuela. The falls are a world-class attraction without the accompanying crowds – perhaps due in part to a reliance on local guides and agencies that have garnered reputations for unprofessionalism.

Canaima Village

The most visited village in the park, **Canaima** is the principal base for trips to

11

11

Angel Falls. On the other side of **Laguna de Canaima** from the lodges are four postcard-worthy waterfalls – **Salto Ucaima, Salto Golondrina, Salto Guadima** and **Salto Hacha** – the latter being the largest, discharging enough water to fill an Olympic-sized swimming pool in a single second. The lagoon has a sandy beach and palm trees jutting out of the water, at the end of which is the hydroelectric power station that supplies the village and surrounding area with electricity. It can be visited at all hours, but is usually seen on the way to the jetty above the falls from where the boats depart upriver.

Tour packages (see page 900) include a short excursion to another nearby waterfall, **Salto El Sapo**, which you can actually walk right behind (make sure you protect your camera properly, as you will get soaked).

Angel Falls

At nearly a vertical kilometre (980m), **ANGEL FALLS** (Salto Ángel in Spanish) is the world's tallest waterfall – around sixteen times the height of Niagara Falls and twelve times the height of Iguazú Falls. It is created by the Churún River, which makes a dramatic plunge from the edge of the enormous Auyantepui and into the verdant jungle below.

Seeing the falls is one of the highlights of a trip to Venezuela, and you can arrange a visit through tour agencies in Ciudad Bolívar (see page 899) and even Caracas (see page 870). The first leg of the trip is a three-hour, 70km and very wet boat ride up the Caroní and Carrao rivers from Canaima Village; the second leg is an hour's hike through the jungle, ending at the falls' principal vantage point. The falls themselves are generally fuller, and therefore more spectacular, during the rainy season; the trade-off is less visibility, as the top of the falls can be covered in clouds during those months.

In the **dry season** (Jan–May), low water levels in the access rivers can complicate the journey, sometimes requiring passengers to unload and push the boat. Tour agencies are usually diligent about warning customers of such conditions, but it's a good idea to ask anyway.

ARRIVAL AND TOURS

By plane Canaima is primarily accessed by small planes, and in most cases moving on is simply a matter of boarding your pre-arranged return flight from Ciudad Bolívar (1hr 30min) or Puerto Ordaz (2hr). The airstrip is on the village's main road. The main airline is Serami (☏ 0286 952 0424, ⊛ serami.com. ve). Tickets can be purchased at the airline desks in Ciudad Bolívar airport, or online. In theory you can charter a plane from Santa Elena, but you'd need a group of at least five, and it's usually more viable to take the bus to Ciudad Bolívar and fly from there. There are not usually direct flights to Caracas.

Tour operators Angel Eco-Tours in Caracas (see page 864) is one of the best operators here, and several firms in Ciudad Bolívar offer tours (see page 899).

ACCOMMODATION

Like transport, accommodation in Canaima is included in pre-arranged tour packages. All lodgings, save the exclusive luxury ones, are *campamentos* of varying simplicity (the cheapest are listed here; they charge per person rather than per room). On the excursion to Angel Falls you'll spend the night in one of the various camps built close to the falls, usually around an hour's walk to the viewing point. Note that tour prices from Canaima exclude flights.

Campamento Morichal ☏ 0289 416 1928, ✉ morichalcanaima@gmail.com. Just 50m from the lagoon and right near the airport, with good food and comfy beds, this place also offers tour packages (US$280 per person for three days and two nights with all meals and excursions thrown in), and can organize and add flights from Ciudad Bolívar or Puerto Ordaz on request. Full board **US$220**

Tiuna ☏ 0414 864 0033, ✉ tiunatours@hotmail.com. By far the most receptive option (as well as the cheapest) for independent travellers, *Tiuna* has a serene location at the edge of Canaima Lagoon but they were closed for repairs on our last check and did not know when they would reopen.

EATING AND DRINKING

Food is included in tour prices; vegetarians should notify the agency when purchasing a tour. Prices for groceries are outrageous since all stock is flown in, so consider bringing your own supplies. As a tourist hub, Canaima has a fairly decent social life, with locals, tourists and guides always up for a party.

Bar Morichal At Campamento Morichal. A beach bar popular with the locals, guides and tourists alike. The dancefloor has disco lights, an impressive sound system and DJs. If your salsa isn't up to scratch, grab a few unsurprisingly expensive beers from the bar, take a seat in one of the parked boats and watch the waterfalls across the lagoon. Daily noon until the last patron leaves.

Venetur Campamento Canaima Occupying the best spot on the lagoon, the state-owned resort has a restaurant and bar with unreal views of Canaima's waterfalls across the water. Come to watch the sunset from the specially designed viewing terrace, order a cocktail and soak it all in. Daily 6am–midnight.

SANTA ELENA DE UAIRÉN

SANTA ELENA DE UAIRÉN grew significantly when the paved road connecting it with the rest of the country was completed, but, with a population of only eighteen thousand, it's still a quiet town. Many of its inhabitants are originally from Brazil, whose border is just 15km away. The town serves as a good base for exploring the awe-inspiring *tepuis*, as well as being a **good access point for Brazil** (see page 905), where Manaus is the closest major city, and it's also the way to get from Venezuela to Guyana (via Brazil, as you cannot cross from Venezuela directly). Although there's little to do, Santa Elena is a very backpacker-friendly town, with reasonably priced accommodation and restaurants. Two blocks southeast of the Plaza Bolívar a **baseball field** hosts local matches in the evenings, where the party atmosphere is fun, beers are cheap and gringos are warmly welcomed whether or not they can follow what's going on. The town is the best place to book tours to the **Gran Sabana** and up **Mount Roraima** (see page 904).

ARRIVAL AND DEPARTURE

By plane The airport, 6km south of town on the way to the Brazilian border, currently has no scheduled services, but there are sometimes flights on small planes to Canaima, Porlamar, Ciudad Bolívar or Puerto Ordaz.

By bus The bus terminal is 3km from the town centre; there are no city buses. From Ciudad Bolívar there are two checkpoints on the way to Santa Elena as well as a full baggage search when you arrive at the terminal, so keep your passport handy.

Destinations Caracas (daily; 22hr); Ciudad Bolívar (6 daily; 12hr), Puerto Ordaz (4 daily; 9hr); Puerto la Cruz (2 daily; 16hr).

ACCOMMODATION

The best places, along with most other backpacker services, are on C Urdaneta between C Icarabú and Av Perimetral.

Lucrecia Av Perimetral ☎0289 995 1105; map p.904. Spacious plot, popular with Brazilians and Venezuelans. The rooms are pleasant, and there's a good-sized swimming pool out back. BsS2000

★ **Posada Los Pinos** ☎0289 995 1430 or ☎0414 886 7227, ⌨posadapinos.com; map p.904. Under the same management as Backpacker Tours (see page 905), this option is a 10min walk from town and has nineteen rooms, each inspired by indigenous communities and Venezuelan plants. There's also a fun Flintstones-esque pool with a slide. US$29

EATING

Santa Elena has some good eating options, particularly if you want to sample authentic Brazilian fare. After dark, numerous burger stands set up along C Icabarú between calles Urdaneta and Zea and serve up tasty grub until around midnight.

Churrasquería Careca Av Perimetral, at C Urdaneta; map p.904. You'll know you're not far from Brazil when the mouthwatering aroma of the wood-fired oven reaches you. Load up with sides from the buffet trolley, but leave room for the skewers – staff slice pork, chicken, beef, fish and whatever else they might have directly onto your plate. Tues–Sun 8am–6pm.

Servi Kilo Av Perimetral, at C Raúl Leoni; map p.904. Don't expect the same quality of food that you'd get in a Brazilian

11

EXCHANGING BRAZILIAN REAIS FOR BOLÍVARES

The Brazilian town of Pacaraima's designation as "**puerto libre**" – permitting visitors across the border without immigration formalities if they return the same day – allows you to replenish funds without resorting to Venezuela's unfavourable official exchange rate at an ATM or bank.

Grab your passport and bankcard and head to the intersection of calles Icabaru and Roscio, where *por puestos* leave regularly for the border (20min). In the unlikely event that you're stopped when crossing, explain to officials that you're returning to Venezuela the same day; make sure they **do not stamp** your passport (if they do, you'll have to wait a day to return to Venezuela). Once you're over, visit one of several available ATMs and withdraw Brazilian reais (current exchange rate US$1 = R$3.30. Note however that some ATMs may have low cash withdrawal limits; those of Bradesco and Banco do Brasil are your best bet.

Back in Santa Elena, head to the intersection of calles Urdaneta and Bolívar, where unofficial moneychangers congregate. You can change cash on the street, although they often have better rates at the open-fronted offices where you can sit and take your time over the transaction.

11

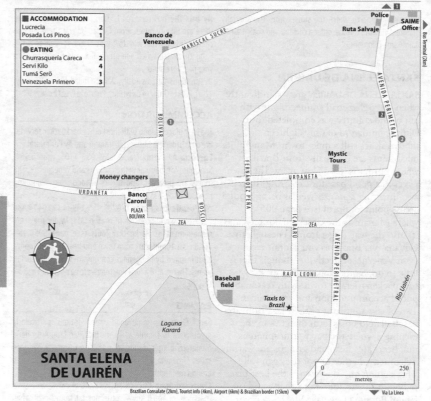

ACCOMMODATION
Lucrecia	2
Posada Los Pinos	1

EATING
Churrasquería Careca	2
Servi Kilo	4
Tumá Serö	1
Venezuela Primero	3

Police
SAIME Office
Ruta Salvaje
Bus Terminal (2km)

Banco de Venezuela
MARISCAL SUCRE
AVENIDA PERIMETRAL

Mystic Tours
URDANETA

Money changers
URDANETA
Banco Caroní
PLAZA BOLÍVAR
ZEA
FERNANDEZ PEÑA
ROSCIO
ICABARU
ZEA
AVENIDA PERIMETRAL
Río Uairén

N

Baseball field
RAÚL LEONI

Taxis to Brazil

Laguna Karará

SANTA ELENA DE UAIRÉN

0   250
metres

Brazilian Consulate (2km), Tourist info (4km), Airport (6km) & Brazilian border (15km)   Via La Línea

"*por kilo*" restaurant, but do expect all sorts of meats, rice, beans, *farofa*, flan and even *guaraná*. Food runs out quickly so make sure you get there early. Mon–Sat 11am–3pm.

★ **Tumá Serö** Between calles Roscio and Bolívar; map p.904. An indoor food-alley, with numerous restaurants and their pushy representatives hollering for your business. A good choice for a quick bite or a slap-up meal. If you're adventurous and like spicy food, ask your kitchen owner for *catara*, a delicious hot sauce made from ants. Daily 6am–10pm, although it's rare that more than half the stalls will be open at any one time.

Venezuela Primero Av Perimetral, at C Urdaneta; map p.904. Ironically, paella is a speciality at this restaurant. The smartly dressed staff are lackadaisical although the food covers a wide range of cuisines. Mon–Sat 11am–3pm & 6–10pm, Sun 11am–2pm.

DIRECTORY

Banks and exchange Banco de Venezuela, C Mariscal Sucre, at C Bolívar; Banco Caroní on the east side of the Plaza Bolívar. Unofficial moneychangers at the intersection of calles Urdaneta and Bolívar take dollars, euros and Brazilian reais.

Hospital Hospital Rosario, Av Perimetral ☏ 0289 995 1155.
Police The police station (open 24hr; ☏ 0289 995 1556) is on C Akarabisis, a colourful building facing *Ruta Salvaje*.

LA GRAN SABANA AND RORAIMA

While few Venezuelans have ever visited the vast region of lush grassland, deep primary rainforest and mighty *tepuis* that is the **GRAN SABANA**, it is nevertheless one of the grandest natural spectacles their country has to offer. At the triple frontier of Venezuela, Brazil and Guyana lies the area's principal attraction: the beautiful and climbable **MOUNT RORAIMA**, a flat-topped mountain with 400m-high cliffs protecting its summit, which is renowned for its otherworldly landscape and was the inspiration for Sir Arthur Conan Doyle's *The Lost World*. The entire region is filled with other magnificent *tepuis* and waterfalls, separated by vast expanses of grasslands.

INTO BRAZIL

The main border crossing between Venezuela and Brazil is at **Santa Elena de Uairén** (see page 903), a simple affair where the Brazilian side has good onward connections to Manaus and Guyana.

Visitors crossing this border in either direction should have a valid yellow fever vaccination certificate, although it may not always be demanded.

The Brazilian Consulate in Santa Elena, on C Los Castaños (Mon–Fri 8am–2pm; T 0289 995 1256), supplies visas within 72hr, although they usually process them the same day. You must provide a passport photo and give the address for your first port of call in Brazil. If you have a problem, there's a SAIME office behind the police station in Santa Elena.

From within Brazil regular buses run to Manaus from Boa Vista, the terminal of which you can get to from the border in a taxi for R$40 (there's also one bus a day). LATAM (W latam.com; 2 weekly) and Azul (W voeazul.com.br; 6 weekly) also fly from Boa Vista to Manaus (1hr 20min).

You can cross the border without a stamp if going only to the border town of Pacaraima and back, for example to change money (see page 903).

One of the most famous waterfalls is **Quebrada de Jaspe**, noted for its bright red jasper rock. Other well-known waterfalls in the region include the 105m-high **Salto Aponguao**, where you can swim in the nearby **Pozo Escondido**, and **Quebrada Pacheco**, two pretty falls with natural waterslides.

THE ORINOCO DELTA

A unique phenomenon, the enormous **Orinoco Delta** is formed as Venezuela's mightiest river reaches the Atlantic below Trinidad, finishing its 2736km course through the country. It is here that it divides and seeps through a 44,000-square-kilometre area of jungle, forming a network of navigable waterways (known as *caños*) on which the Warao communities have lived for millennia. Trips to the Orinoco Delta go to tourist *campamentos* built on the riverbanks, although all are very basically equipped.

The northeast coast and islands

The **northeast coast** is home to some of the country's most ruggedly beautiful coastline, where sleepy fishing villages lie unperturbed by the proximity of some of the country's most energetic cities. **Puerto La Cruz**, a high-rise fast-food paradise, is

GRAN SABANA AND RORAIMA TOURS

The classic six-day trek to the top of **Mount Roraima**, considered by many to be one of the best hikes in South America, is now also one of the cheapest if you book using Bolívars, thanks to the state of Venezuela's economy. Since the price is based on distance rather than time, agencies are usually willing to add or subtract a day to fit your schedule. Multi-day **Gran Sabana** tours typically take a minimum of five people and include all meals. One- or two-day trips to **El Paují**, **El Abismo**, **Salto Aponguao** and other sites can also be added. The following are operators in Santa Elena:

TOUR OPERATORS

Backpacker Tours C Urdaneta T 0289 995 1430, W backpacker-tours.com. The most expensive, but has a permanent guide staff, sells air tickets and supplies its own equipment, including high-quality tents, bicycles and trucks. Offers shorter alternatives (Mantopai and Chiricayén) to the six-day Roraima trek.

Ruta Salvaje Av Mariscal Sucre, at C Akarabisis T 0289 995 1134 or T 0416 490 7832, E rutasalvaje@gmail.com. From a hut beside the police station, Ruta Salvaje sells art painted by the owner's family and organizes excursions and activities around the Gran Sabana including abseiling. You may need a minimum number of participants, and rates go down the larger the group gets.

11

ORINOCO DELTA TOURS

There are various lodges within the delta, which you can contact directly, as well as agencies throughout the country that organize trips in the region. The region is generally accessed from the cities of Ciudad Bolívar and Puerto Ordaz, from which boats are taken down the mighty Orinoco before it reaches the delta. Activities generally include visiting indigenous Warao villages, canoeing through the small *caños*, fishing for piranha and observing local flora and fauna on jungle walks.

TOUR OPERATORS

Orinoco Queen ☎0414 871 9339, ⊚lobo-tours.de. Built and run by the owner of *Casa del Lobo* in Puerto Ordaz, the *Orinoco Queen* is the smallest and most personal of the numerous camps in the area. A three-night stay, one of them spent in the hammocks at a nearby Warao village, includes all food and activities; piranha fishing, jungle walks and expeditions in dugout canoes. Can also organize customized tours throughout the country.

Tucupita Expeditions Cano El Guamal, Estado Delta Amacuro ☎0287 808 5697 or ☎0414 789 8343,

⊚orinocodelta.net. Ecologically responsible company operating trips to the Orinoco, with stays in their well-designed lodge deep in the jungle. English-speaking guides available. The firm aims for low-impact tourism and funds a local education project.

Waro Waro Lodge ☎0424 162 1960, ⊚orinocodeltatours.com. Named after the Warao word for the electric-blue butterflies that flutter around the region, this intimate rustic French-Argentine owned lodge is located on the Jaropuna channel northwest of the delta. The lodge arranges transport from Maturín on the northeast coast or from Ciudad Bolívar.

the coastline's main hub, and makes for a diverting afternoon's people-watching on the seafront. A short ferry ride away is **Isla Margarita**, Venezuela's largest island, whose mega-resorts and island vibe are a huge magnet for Venezuelans taking a break from the mainland.

Between Puerto La Cruz and Cumaná (the continent's first European settlement, although there's little to see) is **Parque Nacional Mochima**, loved for its uninhabited cays and under-the-radar charm. Still further east, **Caripe** is a pretty mountain town nestled away at chillier altitudes, where mountain sports, volunteer work and the astonishing Cueva del Guácharo are excellent diversions.

PUERTO LA CRUZ

The bustling collection of high-rises that calls itself **PUERTO LA CRUZ** isn't that long removed from being a fishing village. Not that you'll notice much to give away its rural past; it acts primarily as a hub for tourists heading to Parque Nacional Mochima (see page 908) or taking the ferry to Isla Margarita (see page 906). There's little reason to spend long here, although the wide seafront promenade makes for an enjoyable afternoon of

strolling and people-watching, especially when there's a cool breeze rolling in off the Caribbean.

WHAT TO SEE AND DO

There's really nothing much to see in Puerto La Cruz itself – most **activities** take place outside the urban limits. For beaches and boat rides in Parque Nacional Mochima, you're better off organizing excursions from Santa Fe or Mochima within the park.

Los Altos de Sucre

A do-it-yourself diversion is to head to the bus terminal for the frequent shared jeeps to **Los Altos de Sucre**, a small community hidden in the hills above Puerto La Cruz, near the border of Anzoátegui State. The lush, rural roads couldn't be further in spirit from the city's mayhem, and are known for their numerous pastry and *artesanía* shops and spectacular views of the bay below. Shout "*¡parada!*" at the bus driver wherever you want to get off along the Via Principal de los Altos.

ARRIVAL AND INFORMATION

By plane The nearest airport is in Barcelona, roughly 20km southwest of Puerto La Cruz and served by frequent buses. From the Barcelona terminal, numerous local bus routes

PUERTO LA CRUZ

■ ACCOMMODATION
Neptuno — 2
Posada Turística Diana — 1
Posada Turística Montecarlo — 3

● EATING
El Bufalo — 3
La Colmena — 2
Tio Pepe — 1

11

cover the airport. All scheduled flights here are with Avior (ⓦaviorair.com).

Destinations Caracas (1 daily; 50min); Miami (1 daily; 3hr 40min); Porlamar (1 daily; 35min); Puerto Ordaz (4 weekly; 55min); Valencia (1 daily; 1hr).

By bus The bus terminal on C Democracia at C Concordia is an easy walk from most accommodation. Playa Colorada, Santa Fe and Mochima are all served along the same route. *Busetas* depart (6am–8pm) when full from C Democracia outside the terminal.

Destinations Barquisimeto (4 daily; 10hr); Caracas (hourly; 5hr); Ciudad Bolívar (8 daily; 5hr); Coro (1 daily; 11hr); Cumaná (half-hourly; 1hr 30min); Mérida (4 daily; 17hr); Puerto Ordaz (8 daily; 6hr); Santa Elena de Uairén (1 daily; 15hr); Valencia (several daily; 7hr).

By ferry The port terminal is about 3km west of the town centre. Ferries arrive and depart daily from Isla Margarita with Conferry (T0281 267 7847), Gran Cacique (ⓣ0281 267 7286, ⓦgrancacique.com.ve) and Navibus (ⓣ0295 500 6284, ⓦnavibus.com.ve).

ACCOMMODATION

Most of the centre's budget accommodation is strung along Paseo Colón, in the centre.

Neptuno Paseo Colón south of C Juncal ⓣ0281 265 5790; map p.907. Rooms are clean, all with a/c and en suite, while the furniture is on its last legs. The hotel lobby has an internet café and is, bizarrely, football themed. **Bs$650**

Posada Turística Diana Paseo Colón, just north of C Sucre ⓣ0281 265 3517; map p.907. Rooms in this sparsely decorated posada all lack natural light, but are otherwise clean with en suite, a/c and TV. **Bs$350**

Posada Turística Montecarlo Paseo Colón 119 ⓣ0281 268 5677; map p.907. The chirping canaries in the lobby do little to drown out the thundering a/c in this rather brown posada. Rooms are perfectly decent, all en suite, although showers amount to little more than a cold dribble. **Bs$400**

EATING

Curiously, Paseo Colón is lined with numerous, nearly identical, Lebanese restaurants serving good-value shawarma, *kibbe* and *tabbouleh*. These tend to stay open very late.

El Bufalo Paseo Colón 49; map p.907. You can't miss *El Bufalo*, due in part to the massive angry bovine stuccoed above the wide entrance. They import some of their more gourmet cuts from Argentina, while the outside terrace is a popular evening spot for cheap beers, sea views and live music on the weekends. Daily 11am–midnight.

La Colmena Paseo Colón, west of C Miranda; map p.907. A little health-food shop serving up vegetarian food in the back at lunchtime only. Mon–Fri 11.30am–2.30pm.

Tio Pepe Paseo Colón, at Plaza Colón; map p.907. Great Spanish-style seafood including paella and *zarzuela* (fish stew). It's named after a Spanish *fino* (dry) sherry, of which they should have a bottle somewhere in case you want to try a glass or two as an apéritif. Daily 11am–11.30pm.

DIRECTORY

Banks and exchange Banco de Venezuela, C Libertad, at C Miranda; Banco Banesco, C Freites, at C Libertad.

Hospital Policlínica Puerto La Cruz, Av 5 de Julio at C Arismendi, open 24hr (☎0281 268 5332).

Internet Sky Intern@tional, C Maneiro, at Paseo Colón.

Pharmacy Meditotal, C Bolívar 38.

Police Av Municipal by Centro Comercial Regina (☎0281 266 1414).

Post office Ipostel, C Freites, at C Honduras.

Shopping There are numerous souvenir shops on the road to Los Altos de Sucre.

PARQUE NACIONAL MOCHIMA

The 950-square-kilometre **PARQUE NACIONAL MOCHIMA** was created in 1973 to protect 36 uninhabited cays and the surrounding coastal area. Teeming with coral, dolphins and pelicans, and with laidback locals providing a genial social life, this area is one of Venezuela's most undervalued. While the beaches, some of which are deep red in colour, aren't as postcard-perfect as those you'll find in Morrocoy and Henri Pittier, the snorkelling and scuba diving are far superior.

There are limited services and no banks or ATMs in Playa Colorada, Santa Fe or Mochima – stock up on cash in Puerto La Cruz (see page 906) or Cumaná.

Playa Colorada

In a protected cove lined with swaying palm trees, **PLAYA COLORADA** is rather winding down from the glory days of Venezuelan tourism, but nevertheless offers a welcome retreat from the more intense coastal towns. Deriving its name from the stretch of terracotta sand, few day-trippers ever venture to the other side of the highway where the town's numerous posadas and single restaurant are to be found. The sandbar's visitors triple at the weekends, but during the week you'll be left pretty much alone.

ARRIVAL AND DEPARTURE

By bus Buses operating the coastal highway between Puerto La Cruz, Santa Fe and Cumaná all pass through Playa Colorada. Shout *"¡parada!"* at the driver to alight when you see the red sand. Buses from Puerto La Cruz depart from beside the liquor store on C Demoncracia outside the terminal. To get out of town, simply hail a passing bus in the direction you need.

Santa Fe

One of the best spots along Venezuela's coastline, **SANTA FE**'s thin strip of sand is lined with good-value accommodation, crystal-clear water and hordes of pelicans whose signature fishing style is very entertaining to watch. The atmosphere is a little sketchier away from the well-populated seafront, and you should stick to the beach and road behind it (Calle Cochaima) after dark. At the far end of the beach, Santa Fe's bright-blue **market** makes for entertaining wandering, as well as a good spot to shop for fresh produce for your posada's kitchen.

The area's best activity is a day's island-hopping in which you'll cruise alongside dolphins, snorkel in coral reefs, visit island fishing outposts and barbecue your lunch on a secluded beach. You can also hop across to popular individual destinations such as **Isla Arapo** and **La Piscina** from the *lancheros* outside the market.

ARRIVAL AND TOURS

By bus The terminal is a 500m walk from the beach on C La Plata. *Busetas* come and go regularly (5am–7pm).

Destinations Cumaná (every 30min; 1hr) via Mochima (30min); Puerto La Cruz (every 30min; 50min) via Playa Colorada (10min).

Tour operators You can arrange island-hopping through your posada. One excellent local guide is Johnny López (☎0412 487 9063, ✉johnnychilopez@hotmail.com).

ACCOMMODATION

Camping on the beach is unsafe.

Café del Mar Far end of Cochaima beach ☎0293 231 0009. Formerly a beach restaurant with rooms, now just the rooms, but still on the beach, with fourteen rooms, but not the warmest welcome in town. BsS300

Hotel Cochaima C Cochaima ☎0293 642 0728. Matriarch Margot runs the town's first posada, which has cheap rooms and a family atmosphere. Numerous white-tiled rooms (a/c, en suite) are faded but spotless, while the upper floor has excellent sea views. Discounts negotiable for multiple nights and guests. BsS400

★ **Posada Bahía del Mar** C Cochaima ☎0293 231 0073, ⊚capvenezuela.fr. Charming French couple Mado and Jean (and their friendly pets) run this delightful posada with its entrance right on the beach. Rooms are nicely decorated, clean and spacious; ask for no. 7 or no. 8, open-fronted doubles with fantastic views. Delicious smells from the outdoor kitchen. BsS680

Posada Sierra Inn C Cochaima ☎0293 231 0042, ⊝posadasdeamigos@gmail.com. The family atmosphere is infectious in this colourful beach posada where chunky rocking chairs are favoured. There's a communal kitchen below an outpost-like beach lookout, decent rooms with a/c and TV, and hot water when the electricity permits. Bs500

EATING

Seafood-lovers are in for a treat in Santa Fe, where the produce is freshly caught daily.

El Mercado On Cochaima beach past Café del Mar. An excellent breakfast option, as well as a place to stock up on supplies (you can buy fish directly from the fishermen outside in the mornings). Numerous stands where *empanadas* and *arepas* are made to order while you sit back and watch the pelicans sneaking up on the fishermen. Daily breakfast & lunch.

Mochima

The village after which the national park is named occupies a pretty inlet 3km from the main coastal road. Originally a fishing village, **MOCHIMA** has a lively malecón, though no beach, and is tricky to get to.

The main activity in Mochima is, once again, **boat trips** to the cays of the national park, all of which depart from the Terminal de Lanchas in the town centre. Prices for each destination are written on a board above the booth where you buy your tickets. If there's a group of you, you may want to rent a *lancha* (speedboat) for the day.

ARRIVAL AND DEPARTURE

By bus and jeep The road to Mochima breaks off from the main coastal highway (heading towards Puerto La Cruz or Cumaná) beside various food stands; shout "¡parada!" at the bus driver to let you off, or hail a bus from the roadside to get on. Walking the road to Mochima is not recommended as robberies have occurred. Intermittent jeeps and *busetas*) shuttle back and forth along the road daily until 8pm.

EATING

Restaurant Puerto Viejo Right next to the jetty (you'll get splashed at your table if a boat roars away quickly enough). The three-in-one platter at this jolly little fish restaurant combines fresh octopus, squid and shrimp, and they also mix up an excellent *piña colada*. Daily 8am–6pm.

CARIPE

Tucked away in the mountainous state of Monagas, the rounded limestone hills and lush forest around **CARIPE** offer respite from the heat of the coast. The town is famous for the **Cueva del Guácharo**, a 10km-long cave home to screeching nocturnal birds that add an unearthly atmosphere to an astonishing natural phenomenon.

WHAT TO SEE AND DO

The pretty town centre is easily walkable and safe at all times of day. The region is renowned across the country for its fruit; make sure you sample the strawberries and cream on offer from vendors around town.

Venezuela's first national monument, the **Cueva del Guácharo** is a cave set deep in the limestone mountainside inhabited by oilbirds. You can take a tour (Tues–Sun 8am–2pm; ☎0291 641 7543) through the first 1200m of the cave, during which gas-lamp-toting guides point out distinctively shaped rock formations. At the entrance there's a museum dedicated to Alexander Von Humboldt, who first made oilbirds known to science. Taxis will take you to the entrance of Parque Nacional El Guácharo from the centre.

Hiking opportunities abound in Monagas and a popular walk is the **Cerro Turumiquire**, the region's highest point at 2600m.

11

ARRIVAL AND DEPARTURE

By bus The bus terminal is behind the municipal market. Buses run to state capital Maturín (1hr 30min), which has connections nationwide. Direct *por puestos* depart intermittently from the terminal to Puerto Ordaz or Cumaná. To get here from the coast, take a morning bus from Cumaná (3hr); if you miss the direct morning buses, *por puestos* leave irregularly from Cumaná bus terminal, or you can take a bus to Maturín and change there.

ACCOMMODATION

Campamento Kenya Sector El Guácharo ☎ 0416 396 8376. Friendly tour guide and local legend Carlos Kenya runs his "Lost Boys"-style homestay close to the Guácharo cave. There's a dormitory and four cosy en-suite doubles. Carlos also runs tours and volunteering projects throughout the region. BsS200

Posada Dios es Amor las Malvinas San Agustín ☎ 0414 841 4994, ✉ posadadiosesamor@gmail.com. All the creature comforts – hot water, cable TV, communal kitchen. – plus a nice garden and lush scenery, all make this a good option at the northern end of Caripe towards San Agustín. BsS900

DIRECTORY

Bank Banco Caroní in the Bolívar Plaza mall on Av Bolívar.
Internet Centro de Conexiones, C Bolívar.
Pharmacy Farmacia El Cristo, Av Enrique Chaumer 158.
Police Av Guzman Blanco.
Shopping You can buy artisan jewellery in the pedestrian park in the middle of C Bolívar beside the Plaza Bolívar most evenings.

ISLA DE MARGARITA

The 940-square-kilometre island of **ISLA DE MARGARITA** mainly attracts well-to-do Venezuelan holidaymakers. While the island's rampant commercialism means that prices are inflated, Margarita can still provide an entertaining taste of mainstream Venezuelan-style tourism.

WHAT TO SEE AND DO

Isla de Margarita has many beach communities and just a few developed urban centres, **PORLAMAR** being the largest and containing the lion's share of inexpensive services. It's therefore best to base yourself here and take day-trips to the island's other attractions.

Ten kilometres north of Porlamar lies the more peaceful town of **Pampatar**. Founded in 1530, it was one of the first settlements in Venezuela, and even today it retains some of

its former charm, with the remains of a Spanish fortress, Castillo de San Carlos Borromeo, completed in 1684 (daily 8am–5pm; free).

Margarita's most famous beach, **Playa El Agua** (1hr from Porlamar by bus), is 3km of white sand, palm trees and plenty of tourists. Less rammed beaches around the island include playas Manzanillo, El Yaque, Caribe, Guayacán, Puerto Abajo and Cardón.

ARRIVAL AND INFORMATION

By plane Santiago Mariño Airport is about 27km southwest of Porlamar.
Destinations Barcelona (1 daily; 35min); Caracas (1–2 daily; 45min–1hr); Valencia (2 weekly; 1hr).
By ferry The cheapest way to get to and from Isla de Margarita is by ferry (see page 906). Buses to the ferry dock at Punta de Piedras (which stop at the top of the jetties) come and go from the bus terminal in Porlamar five blocks west of the Plaza Bolívar between calles Velasquez and Igualdad until 7pm. Keep in mind that ferry companies leave from different jetties at Punta de Piedras, so ensure you tell your bus or taxi driver which company you are travelling with.
Tourist information Corpotur, Centro Artesanal Gilberto Menchini in Los Robles (☎ 0295 262 2322 or ☎ 0295 268 2514, ⊕ facebook.com/CorpoturMargarita), roughly 3km from the centre.

GETTING AROUND

By bus Buses (daily 6am–9pm) are the cheapest way to explore the island. The primary bus terminal is five blocks west of the Plaza Bolívar, serving Punta de Piedras and various locations in the north of the island. Otherwise, bus stops throughout Porlamar's centre correspond to the island's more popular locales.

ACCOMMODATION

PORLAMAR

Porlamar is the undisputed commercial centre of the island and rocks a distinctly more Caribbean vibe than the mainland. It's also the best spot for reasonably priced accommodation and dining options. Make sure to ask for low-season discounts outside the island's peak periods of Dec–Jan, Carnaval and Easter.

Casa Lutecia C Campo Sur, at Marcano ☎ 0295 263 8526, ⊕ margarita.travel/lutecia; map p.911. There's a choice of economy rooms and suites – not to mention a pool, and poolside restaurant service – at this lovely little fourteen-room posada scrupulously run by French *dueña* Madame Colette. BsS100

España C Mariño, at Av La Marina ☎ 0295 261 2479; map p.911. An alarm clock is unnecessary in this friendly

EATING
Gaia	1
La Casa del Mero	2
La Casa de Rubén	4
Punto Criollo	3

DRINKING & NIGHTLIFE
Beach Bar	1
British Bulldog	2

ACCOMMODATION
Casa Lutecia	1
España	3
Posada Bahía del Rey	2

establishment as the frisky canaries (and one mad parrot) don't shut up after their covers come off. The rooms are decent enough, with fan, TV and en suite. **BsS200**

★ **Posada Bahía del Rey** C Fermín, at Av Raúl Leoni ☎0414 310 6334, ✉posadabahiadelrey@gmail.com; map p.911. Bright-yellow posada away from the chaos of the city, and only five steps from the seashore. Catch some rays on their lounge chairs on the beach before heading back to the warm and welcoming rooms (en suite, TV). **BsS450**

EATING

PORLAMAR

Gaia C Campo Sur, at Maria Patiño; map p.911. This long-running Italian trattoria is reliable for all the favourites – *spaghetti alle vongole* (with clams), tiramisú, good antipasti – maybe not the cheapest eat in town, but it certainly won't break the bank. Tues & Wed noon–5pm, Thurs–Sat noon–5pm & 7–10pm.

La Casa del Mero Av Raul Leoni; map p.911. Right on the beach, this tiki-themed restaurant serves up huge plates of the freshest fish and seafood from its open-front kitchen. The service is also efficient and friendly, making the place something of a diamond in the rough. Mon–Sat 11am–10pm.

La Casa de Rubén C Santiago Mariño; map p.911. Rubén, whose smiling countenance grins at you from all over his establishment, is the author of several traditional Venezuelan cookbooks. Meat is served, but the emphasis is on locally sourced seafood. Mon–Sat noon–6pm.

★ **Punto Criollo** C Igualdad, at Fraternidad; map p.911. Towering plates of mixed seafood and *comida criolla* at every table of this constantly packed local joint. Meat dishes feature heavily, including a juicy *filet mignon*, and great service too. Daily 10.30am–7pm.

DRINKING AND NIGHTLIFE

Night owls are in for a treat on the island. Most action takes place in Pampatar or in the Centro Comercial Costa Azul, on Av Bolivar a kilometre east of town. Most clubs have no cover charge.

11

BOAT TRANSPORT TO AND FROM ISLA DE MARGARITA

Ferries to Isla de Margarita depart from either Puerto La Cruz or Cumaná, the towns at either end of Parque Mochima. They dock on the island at **Punta de Piedras**, an hour's bus ride from Porlamar. Two companies operate the ferries: Navibus and Naviarca/Gran Cacique (see below for contact details). You're asked to arrive 1hr 30min prior to departure to "confirm" your ticket at a company booth. As with intercity buses, you'll need your passport number to book a ticket. Irregular *lanchas* from Chacopata are cheaper, but not tremendously safe.

FROM PUERTO LA CRUZ

Puerto La Cruz's port is roughly 3km west of the centre. From here, Naviarca/Gran Cacique run one boat a day, Navibus run two, with extra boats around Christmas, New Year, Carnaval and Semana Santa.

FROM CUMANÁ

Cumaná's terminal is 1km from the town's centre. At present only Naviarca/Gran Cacique are running crossings from here.

FROM ISLA DE MARGARITA

If you didn't buy a return ticket on the mainland, make sure you visit a ferry office in Porlamar a day before you wish to leave. Naviarca/Gran Cacique have boats to Puerto La Cruz and Cumaná, Navibus at present to Puerto La Cruz only.

There may also be *lanchas* (speedboats) from the El Faro dock in Porlamar, which act like *por puestos*, departing when full between Porlamar and Chacopata on the mainland. Note that, although cheaper, these are informal and may not follow basic safety procedures. If you do use them despite this, check with other passengers how much they are paying, as drivers have been known to hike prices for foreigners. *Por puestos* serve Chacopata from Maturín and Cumaná bus terminals.

OPERATORS

Naviarca/Gran Cacique (ⓦ grancacique.com.ve) C Colón, opposite the church, Punta de Piedras ☎0295 297 6408; Edificio Sucre, Via Terminal de Ferrys, Cumaná ☎0293 432 0011; ferry terminal, Av Prolongación Paseo Colón, Puerto La Cruz ☎0281 263 0935; Edificio Blue Sky, suite 3, Av Santiago Mariño, Porlamar ☎0295 264 2945.

Navibus (☎0295 500 6250 or ☎0295 500 6284, ⓦ navibus.com.ve) Av Juan Bautista Arismendi, Faro de Aves, Punta de Piedras; ferry terminal, Av el Islote, Cumaná; ferry terminal, Av Prolongación Paseo Colón, Puerto La Cruz; Centro Comercial Sigo la Proveeduría, Av Juan Bautista Arismendi, Porlamar.

Beach Bar C El Cristo, La Caranta, Pampatar; map p.911. Have a few refreshing cocktails *après-plage* at this laidback bar with bamboo gazebos facing the beach. Tues–Sun 7pm–3am.

British Bulldog Centro Comercial Costa Azul, Av Bolívar; map p.911. You've got to give the place credit for trying so hard with the pub theme – with memorabilia, advertisements for drinks they don't serve and an enormous Union Jack. At weekends, local bands play amazingly accurate renditions of European and American hard-rock classics. Thurs–Sat 9pm–4am.

DIRECTORY

Banks and exchange Banesco, Av 4 Mayo, at C Milano; Banco de Venezuela, Bd Guevara, at C Zanora.

Hospital Clínica Margarita, C Marcano, at Díaz (☎0295 261 4611).

Internet Cyber Tipirijillo, Centro Comercial Real, shop 4B, Av 4 de Mayo.

Laundry Lavandería Ediko's, C Marcano, at Fermín.

Pharmacy FarmaSigo, C Marcano, at Díaz.

Post office Ipostel, C Maneiro between C Fraternidad and Bulevar Gómez.

Shopping Margarita is famed for its duty-free shopping. Two pedestrianized streets, Bulevar Gómez and Bulevar Guevara, are lined with vendors selling mostly knock-off items and pirated CDs – though the occasional used-book vendor may be holding some treasures.

Museos
Museums

Terminal de Transportes
Bus Station

Language

Spanish

Although there are dozens of indigenous tongues scattered throughout South America – some thirty in the Peruvian Amazon alone – this is, in general, a Spanish-speaking continent. The Spanish you will hear in South America does not always conform to what you learned in the classroom, and even competent speakers of peninsular Spanish will find it takes a bit of getting used to. In addition to the odd differences in pronunciation – discussed in detail below – words from native languages as well as various European tongues have infiltrated the different dialects of South American Spanish, giving them each their own unique character.

For the most part, the language itself is the same throughout the continent, while the pronunciation varies slightly. In parts of Argentina, for example, the *ll* and *y* sound like a *zh* (the English equivalent is the *s* in "treasure"), while the final *s* of a word is often not pronounced.

Spanish itself is not a difficult language to pick up and there are numerous learning products on the market. You'll be further helped by the fact that most South Americans, with the notable exception of fast-talking Chileans, speak relatively slowly (at least compared with Spaniards) and that there's no need to get your tongue round the lisping pronunciation. *Spanish: The Rough Guide Phrasebook* is a concise and handy **phrasebook**.

Pronunciation

The rules of Spanish **pronunciation** are pretty straightforward. All syllables are pronounced. Unless there's an accent, words ending in d, l, r and z are **stressed** on the last syllable, all others on the second last. All **vowels** are pure and short.

A somewhere between the "A" sound of b**a**ck and that of f**a**ther.

E as in get.

I as in police.

O as in hot.

U as in rule.

C is soft before E and I, hard otherwise: cerca is pronounced "serka".

G works the same way: a guttural **H** sound (like the ch in loch) before E or I, a hard G elsewhere – gigante becomes "higante".

H is always silent.

J is the same sound as a guttural **G**: jamón is pronounced "hamón".

LL sounds like an English **Y**: tortilla is pronounced "torteeya".

N is as in English unless it has a tilde (accent) over it, when it becomes NY: mañana sounds like "manyana".

QU is pronounced like an English **K**.

R is rolled, RR doubly so.

V sounds more like **B**, vino becoming "beano".

X is slightly softer than in English – sometimes almost SH – except between vowels in place names where it has an "H" sound – for example México (Meh-Hee-Ko) or Oaxaca.

Z is the same as a soft **C**, so cerveza becomes "servesa".

WORDS AND PHRASES

The following will help you with your most basic day-to-day language needs.

BASIC EXPRESSIONS

Yes, No Sí, No

Please, Thank you Por favor, Gracias

Where, When? ¿Dónde, Cuándo?

What, How much? ¿Qué, Cuánto?

Here, There Aquí, Allí

This, That Este, Eso

Now, Later Ahora, Más tarde/Luego

Open, Closed Abierto/a, Cerrado/a

Pull, Push Tire, Empuje

Entrance, Exit Entrada, Salida

With, Without Con, Sin
For Para/Por
Good, Bad Buen(o)/a, Mal(o)/a
Big, Small Gran(de), Pequeño/a
A little, A lot Poco/a, Mucho/a
More, Less Más, Menos
Another Otro/a
Today, Tomorrow Hoy, Mañana
Yesterday Ayer
But Pero
And Y
Nothing, Never Nada, Nunca

GREETINGS AND RESPONSES

Hello, Goodbye Hola, Adios
Good morning Buenos días
Good afternoon/night Buenas tardes/noches
See you later Hasta luego
Sorry Lo siento/Discúlpeme
Excuse me Con permiso/Perdón
How are you? ¿Como está (usted)?
What's up? ¿Qué pasa?
I (don't) understand (No) Entiendo
Not at all/You're welcome De nada
Do you speak English? ¿Habla (usted) inglés?
I (don't) speak Spanish (No) Hablo español
My name is ... Me llamo ...
What's your name? ¿Como se llama usted?
I am English/American Soy inglés(a)/ americano(a)
Cheers Salud

ASKING DIRECTIONS, GETTING AROUND

Where is...? ¿Dónde está...?
...the bus station ...la estación de auto-buses
...the train station ...la estación de ferro-carriles
...the nearest bank ...el banco más cercano
...the post office ...el correo
...the toilet ...el baño/sanitario
Is there a hotel nearby? ¿Hay un hotel aquí cerca?
Left, right, straight on Izquierda, derecha, derecho
Where does the bus to ¿De dónde sale el ... leave
   from? autobús para...?
How do I get to...? ¿Por dónde se va a...?
I'd like a (return) Quiero un boleto (de ticket to... ida
   y vuelta) para...
What time does it leave? ¿A qué hora sale?

ACCOMMODATION

Private bathroom Baño privado
Shared bathroom Baño compartido
Hot water (all day) Agua caliente (todo el día)
Cold water Agua fría
Fan Ventilador
Air-conditioned Aire-acondicionado

Mosquito net Mosquitero
Key Llave
Check-out time Hora de salida
Do you have...? ¿Tiene ...?
... a room ... ...una habitación
... with two beds/ ...con dos camas/double bed ...
   cama matrimonial...
It's for one person Es para una persona(two people)
   (dos personas)
...for one night ... ...para una noche...
...one week ...una semana
It's fine, how much is it? ¿Está bien, cuánto es?
It's too expensive Es demasiado caro
Don't you have anything ¿No tiene algo más cheaper?
   barato?

NUMBERS AND DAYS

1 un/uno/una
2 dos
3 tres
4 cuatro
5 cinco
6 seis
7 siete
8 ocho
9 nueve
10 diez
11 once
12 doce
13 trece
14 catorce
15 quince
16 dieciséis
20 veinte
21 veintiuno
30 treinta
40 cuarenta
50 cincuenta
60 sesenta
70 setenta
80 ochenta
90 noventa
100 cien(to)
200 doscientos
500 quinientos
1000 mil
Monday lunes
Tuesday martes
Wednesday miércoles
Thursday jueves
Friday viernes
Saturday sábado
Sunday domingo

USEFUL WORDS

Barrio Suburb, or sometimes shantytown
Carretera Route or highway
Cerro Hill, mountain peak
Colectivo Shared taxi/bus
Combi Small minibus that runs urban routes
Cordillera Mountain range
Criollo "Creole". a person of Spanish blood born In the American colonies
Entrada Ticket (for theatre, football match, etc)
Estancia Ranch, or large estate
Farmacia Chemist
Gaucho The typical Argentine "cowboy", or rural *estancia* worker
Gringo Foreigner, Westerner (not necessarily a derogatory term)
Hacienda Large estate
Mestizo Person of mixed Spanish and indigenous blood
Micro City bus
Mirador Viewpoint
Peña Venue with live music
Soroche Altitude sickness

A SPANISH MENU READER

While menus vary by country and region, these words and terms will help negotiate most of them.

BASIC DINING VOCABULARY

Almuerzo Lunch
Asada Barbecue
Carta (la)/Lista (la) Menu
Cena Dinner
Comida típica Typical cuisine
Cuchara Spoon
Cuchillo Knife
Desayuno Breakfast
La cuenta, por favor The bill, please
Merienda Set menu
Plato fuerte Main course
Plato vegetariano Vegetarian dish
Tenedor Fork

FRUIT (FRUTAS)

Cereza Cherry
Chirimoya Custard apple
Ciruela Plum
Fresa/frutilla Strawberry
Guayaba Guava
Guineo Banana
Higo Fig
Limón Lemon or lime
Manzana Apple
Maracuyá Passion fruit
Melocotón/durazno Peach
Mora Blackberry
Naranja Orange
Pera Pear
Piña Pineapple
Plátano Plantain
Pomelo/toronja Grapefruit
Sandía Watermelon

VEGETABLES (LEGUMBRES/VERDURAS)

Aguacate Avocado
Alcachofa Artichoke
Cebolla Onion
Champiñón Mushroom
Choclo Maize/sweetcorn
Coliflor Cauliflower
Espinaca Spinach
Frijoles Beans
Guisantes/arvejas Peas
Hongo Mushroom
Lechuga Lettuce
Lentejas Lentil
Menestra Bean/lentil stew
Palmito Palm heart
Patata Potato
Papas fritas French fries
Pepinillo Gherkin
Pepino Cucumber
Tomate Tomato
Zanahoria Carrot

MEAT (CARNE) AND POULTRY (AVES)

Carne de chancho Pork
Cerdo Pork
Chicharrones Pork scratchings, crackling
Chuleta Pork chop
Churrasco Grilled meat with sides
Conejo Rabbit
Cordero Lamb
Cuero Pork crackling
Cuy Guinea pig
Jamón Ham
Lechón Suckling pig
Lomo Steak
Pato Duck
Pavo Turkey
Pollo Chicken
Res Beef
Ternera Veal
Tocino Bacon
Venado Venison

OFFAL (MENUDOS)
Chunchules Intestines
Guatita Tripe
Hígado Liver
Lengua Tongue
Mondongo Tripe
Patas Trotters

SHELLFISH (MARISCOS) AND FISH (PESCADO)
Anchoa Anchovy
Atún Tuna
Calamares Squid
Camarón Prawn
Cangrejo Crab
Ceviche Seafood marinated in lime juice with onions
Corvina Sea bass
Erizo Sea urchin
Langosta Lobster
Langostina King prawn
Lenguado Sole
Mejillón Mussel
Ostra Oyster
Trucha Trout

COOKING TERMS
A la parrilla Barbecued
A la plancha Lightly fried
Ahumado Smoked
Al ajillo In garlic sauce
Al horno Oven-baked
Al vapor Steamed
Apanado Breaded
Asado Roast
Asado al palo Spit roast
Crudo Raw
Duro Hard boiled
Encebollado Cooked with onions
Encocado In coconut sauce
Frito Fried
Picant Spicy hot
Puré Mashed
Revuelto Scrambled
Saltado Sautéed
Secado Dried

DRINKS (BEBIDAS)
Agua (mineral) Mineral water
Con gas Sparkling
Sin gas Still
Sin hielo Without ice
Aguardiente Sugar-cane spirit
Aromática Herbal tea
Manzanilla Camomile

Menta Mint
Batido Milkshake
Café (con leche) Coffee (with milk)
Caipirinha Cocktail of rum, lime, sugar and ice
Cerveza Beer
Chicha Fermented corn drink
Gaseosa Fizzy drink
Jugo Juice
Leche Milk
Limonada Fresh lemonade
Mate de coca Coca leaf tea
Ron Rum
Té Tea
Vino blanco White wine
Vino tinto Red wine
Yerba (hierba) mate Herbal infusion with *mate*

FOOD GLOSSARY
Aceite Oil
Ají Chilli
Ajo Garlic
Arroz Rice
Azúcar Sugar
Galletas Biscuits
Hielo Ice
Huevos Eggs
Mantequilla Butter
Mermeleda Jam
Miel Honey
Mixto Mixed seafood/meats
Mostaza Mustard
Pan (integral) Bread (wholemeal)
Pimienta Pepper
Queso Cheese
Sal Salt
Salsa de tomate Tomato sauce

SOUPS
Caldosa Broth
Caldo de gallina Chicken broth
Caldo de patas Cattle-hoof broth
Crema de espárragos Cream of asparagus
Locro Cheese and potato soup
Sopa de bolas de verde Plantain dumpling soup
Sopa del día Soup of the day
Yaguarlocro Blood sausage (black pudding) soup

SNACKS (BOCADILLOS)
Bolón de verde Baked cheese and potato dumpling
Chifles Banana chips/crisps
Empanada Cheese/meat pasty
Hamburguesa Hamburger
Humitas Ground corn and cheese
Omelet Omelette

Palomitas Popcorn
Patacones Thick-cut dried banana/ plantain
Salchipapas Sausage, fries and sauces
Sanwiche Sandwich
Tamale Ground maize with meat/ cheese wrapped
in leaf
Tortilla de huevos Firm omelette
Tostada Toast
Tostado Toasted maize

DESSERT (POSTRES)
Cocados Coconut candy
Ensalada de frutas Fruit salad
Flan Crème caramel
Helado Ice cream
Manjar de leche Very sweet caramel made from
condensed milk
Pastas Pastries
Pastel Cake
Torta Tart

Portuguese

The great exception to the Spanish-speaking rule in South America is, of course, Portuguese-speaking Brazil (that is, putting the Guianas to the side). Unfortunately, far too many people – especially Spanish-speakers – are put off going to Brazil solely because of the language, while this should actually be one of your main reasons for going. Brazilian Portuguese is a colourful, sensual language full of wonderfully rude and exotic vowel sounds, swooping intonation and hilarious idiomatic expressions.

The best **dictionary** currently available is *Collins Portuguese Dictionary*, which has a pocket edition. For a **phrasebook**, look no further than *Portuguese: The Rough Guide Phrasebook*, with useful two-way glossaries and a brief and simple grammar section.

Pronunciation

Although its complex pronunciation is far too difficult to be described in detail here, for the most part, Brazilian Portuguese is spoken more slowly and clearly than its European counterpart. The neutral vowels so characteristic of European Portuguese tend to be sounded out in full; in much of Brazil outside Rio the slushy "sh" sound doesn't exist; and the "de" and "te" endings of words like *cidade* and *diferente* are palatalized so they end up sounding like "sidadgee" and "djiferentchee".

WORDS AND PHRASES

You'll also find that Brazilians will greatly appreciate even your most rudimentary efforts, and every small improvement in your Portuguese will make your stay in Brazil much more enjoyable.

BASIC EXPRESSIONS

Yes, No Sim, Não
Please Por favor
Thank you Obrigado (men)/ Obrigada (women)
Where, When? Onde, Quando?
What, How much? Que, Quanto?
This, That Este, Esse, Aquele
Now, Later Agora, Mais tarde
Open, Closed Aberto/a, Fechado/a
Pull, Push Puxe, Empurre
Entrance, Exit Entrada, Saída
With, Without Com, Sem
For Para/Por
Good, Bad Bom, Ruim
Big, Small Grande, Pequeno
A little, A lot Um pouco, Muito
More, Less Mais, Menos
Another Outro/a
Today, Tomorrow Hoje, Amanhã
Yesterday Ontem
But Mas (pronounced like "mice")
And E (pronounced like "ee" in "seek")

Something, Nothing Alguma coisa, Nada
Sometimes Às vezes

GREETINGS AND RESPONSES

Hello, Goodbye Oi, Tchau (like the Italian "ciao")
Good morning Bom dia
Good afternoon/night Boa tarde/Boa noite
Sorry Desculpa
Excuse me Com licença
How are you? Como vai?
Fine Bem
I don't understand Não entendo
Do you speak English? Você fala inglês?
I don't speak Portuguese Não falo português
My name is … Meu nome é …
What's your name? Como se chama?
I am English/American Sou inglês/americano
Cheers Saúde

ASKING DIRECTIONS, GETTING AROUND

Where is…? Onde fica…?**…the bus station** …a rodoviária**…the bus stop** …a parada de ônibus**…the nearest hotel** …o hotel mais próximo**…the toilet** …o banheiro/sanitário
Left, right, straight on Esquerda, direita, direto
Where does the bus to De onde sai o ônibus … **leave from?** para…?

Is this the bus to Rio? É esse o ônibus para Rio?
Do you go to…? Você vai para…?
I'd like a (return) ticket to… Quero uma passagem **ticket to…** (ida e volta) para…
What time does it leave? Que horas sai?

ACCOMMODATION

Do you have a room? Você tem um quarto?**…with two beds** …com duas**…with double bed** …camas/cama de casal
It's for one person/two people É para uma pessoa/**two people** duas pessoas
It's fine, how much is it? Está bom, quanto é?
It's too expensive É caro demais
Do you have anything cheaper? Tem algo mais barato?**cheaper?**
Is there a hotel/campsite nearby? Tem um hotel/**campsite nearby?** camping por aqui?

NUMBERS AND DAYS

1 um, uma
2 dois, duas
3 três
4 quatro
5 cinco
6 seis
7 sete
8 oito
9 nove
10 dez
11 onze
12 doze
13 treze
14 quatorze
15 quinze
16 dezesseis
17 diecisiete
18 dieciocho
19 diecinueve
20 vinte
21 vinte e um
30 trinta
40 quarenta
50 cinquenta
60 sesenta
70 setenta

80 oitenta
90 noventa
100 cem
200 duzentos
300 trezentos
500 quinhentos
1000 mil

Monday segunda-feira (or segunda)
Tuesday terça-feira (or terça)
Wednesday quarta-feira (or quarta)
Thursday quinta-feira (or quinta)
Friday sexta-feira (or sexta)
Saturday sábado
Sunday domingo

USEFUL WORDS

Azulejo Decorative glazed tiling
Boîte Club or bar with dancing
Candomblé African-Brazilian religion
Capoeira African-Brazilian martial art/dance form
Carimbó Music and dance style from the north
Carioca Someone or something from Rio de Janeiro
Dancetaria Night spot where the emphasis is on dancing
Favela Shantytown, slum
Fazenda Country estate, ranch house
Feira Country market
Ferroviária Train station
Forró Dance and type of music from the Northeast
Frevo Frenetic musical style and dance from Recife
Gaúcho Person or thing from Rio Grande do Sul; also southern cowboy
Gringo/a Foreigner, Westerner (not necessarily derogatory)
Latifúndios Large agricultural estates
Leito Luxury express bus
Louro/a Fair-haired/blonde – Westerners in general
Maconha Marijuana
Mirante Viewing point
Paulista Person or thing from São Paulo state
Rodovia Highway
Rodoviária Bus station
Visto/visa Visa

A BRAZILIAN MENU READER

BASIC DINING VOCABULARY

Almoço/lonche Lunch
Café de manhã Breakfast
Cardápio Menu
Colher Spoon
Conta/nota Bill

Copo Glass
Entrada Hors d'oeuvre
Faca Knife
Garçon Waiter
Garfo Fork
Jantar Dinner, to have dinner

Prato Plate
Sobremesa Dessert
Sopa/Caldo Soup
Taxa de serviço Service charge

FRUIT (FRUTAS)
Abacate Avocado
Abacaxi Pineapple
Ameixa Plum, prune
Caju Cashew fruit
Carambola Star fruit
Cerejas Cherries
Côco Coconut
Fruta do conde Custard apple (also *ata*)
Goiaba Guava
Laranja Orange
Limão Lime
Maçã Apple
Mamão Papaya
Maracujá Passion fruit
Melancia Watermelon
Melão Melon
Morango Strawberry
Pera Pear
Pêssego Peach
Uvas Grapes

VEGETABLES (LEGUMES)
Alface Lettuce
Arroz e feijão Rice and beans
Azeitonas Olives
Batatas Potatoes
Cebola Onion
Cenoura Carrot
Dendê Palm oil
Ervilhas Peas
Espinafre Spinach
Macaxeira Roasted manioc
Mandioca Manioc/cassava/yucca
Milho Corn
Palmito Palm heart
Pepinho Cucumber
Repolho Cabbage
Tomate Tomato

MEAT (CARNE) AND POULTRY (AVES)
Bife Steak
Bife a cavalo Steak with egg and *farinha*
Cabrito Kid (goat)
Carne de porco Pork
Carneiro Lamb
Costela Ribs
Costeleta Chop
Feijoada Black bean, pork and sausage stew

Fígado Liver
Frango Chicken
Leitão Suckling pig
Lingüiça Sausage
Pato Duck
Peito Breast
Perna Leg
Peru Turkey
Picadinha Stew
Salsicha Hot dog
Veado Venison
Vitela Veal

SEAFOOD (FRUTOS DO MAR)
Acarajé Fried bean cake stuffed with *vatapá*
Agulha Needle fish
Atum Tuna
Camarão Prawn, shrimp
Caranguejo Large crab
Filhote Amazon river fish
Lagosta Lobster
Lula Squid
Mariscos Mussels
Moqueca Seafood stewed in palm oil and coconut
sauce
Ostra Oyster
Pescada Seafood stew, or hake
Pirarucu Amazon river fish
Pitu Crayfish
Polvo Octopus
Siri Small crab
Sururu A type of mussel
Vatapá Bahian shrimp dish, cooked with palm oil,
skinned tomato and coconut milk, served with fresh
coriander and hot peppers

COOKING TERMS
Assado Roasted
Bem gelado Well chilled
Churrasco Barbecue
Cozido Boiled, steamed
Cozinhar To cook
Grelhado Grilled
Mal passado/Bem passado Rare/well done (meat)
Médio Medium-grilled
Milanesa Breaded
Na chapa/Na brasa Charcoal-grilled

SPICES (TEMPEROS)
Alho Garlic
Canela Cinnamon
Cheiro verde Fresh coriander
Coentro Parsley
Cravo Clove

Malagueta Very hot pepper, looks like red or yellow cherry

DRINKS (BEBIDAS)

Água mineral Mineral water
Batida Fresh fruit juice (sometimes with *cachaça*)
Cachaça Sugar-cane rum
Café com leite Coffee with hot milk
Cafézinho Small black coffee
Caipirinha Rum and lime cocktail
Cerveja Bottled beer
Chopp Draught beer
Com gás/sem gás Sparkling/still
Suco Fruit juice
Vinho Wine
Vitamina Fruit juice made with milk

FOOD GLOSSARY

Açúcar Sugar
Alho e óleo Garlic and olive oil sauce
Arroz Rice
Azeite Olive oil
Farinha Dried manioc flour beans
Manteiga Butter
Molho Sauce
Ovos Eggs
Pão Bread
Pimenta Pepper
Queijo Cheese
Sal Salt
Sorvete Ice cream

Small print and index

A ROUGH GUIDE TO ROUGH GUIDES

Published in 1982, the first Rough Guide – to Greece – was a student scheme that became a publishing phenomenon. Mark Ellingham, a recent graduate in English from Bristol University, had been travelling in Greece the previous summer and couldn't find the right guidebook. With a small group of friends he wrote his own guide, combining a contemporary, journalistic style with a thoroughly practical approach to travellers' needs.

The immediate success of the book spawned a series that rapidly covered dozens of destinations. And, in addition to impecunious backpackers, Rough Guides soon acquired a much broader readership that relished the guides' wit and inquisitiveness as much as their enthusiastic, critical approach and value-for-money ethos. These days, Rough Guides include recommendations from budget to luxury and cover more than 120 destinations around the globe, from Amsterdam to Zanzibar, all regularly updated by our team of roaming writers.

Browse all our latest guides, read inspirational features and book your trip at **roughguides.com**.

Rough Guide credits

Editors: Rebecca Hallett, Ann-Marie Shaw, Aimee White
Cartography: Carte, Katie Bennett
Managing editor: Rachel Lawrence
Picture editor: Aude Vauconsant

Cover photo research: Richard Czapnik
Senior DTP coordinator: Dan May
Head of DTP and Pre-Press: Rebeka Davies

Publishing information

Fifth edition 2019

Distribution

UK, Ireland and Europe
Apa Publications (UK) Ltd; sales@roughguides.com
United States and Canada
Ingram Publisher Services; ips@ingramcontent.com
Australia and New Zealand
Woodslane; info@woodslane.com.au
Southeast Asia
Apa Publications (SN) Pte; sales@roughguides.com
Worldwide
Apa Publications (UK) Ltd; sales@roughguides.com
Special Sales, Content Licensing and CoPublishing
Rough Guides can be purchased in bulk quantities
at discounted prices. We can create special editions,
personalised jackets and corporate imprints tailored to
your needs. sales@roughguides.com.

roughguides.com
Printed in China by CTPS
All rights reserved
A catalogue record for this book is available from the
British Library
The publishers and authors have done their best to ensure
the accuracy and currency of all the information in **The
Rough Guide to South America on a Budget**, however,
they can accept no responsibility for any loss, injury, or
inconvenience sustained by any traveller as a result of
information or advice contained in the guide.

Help us update

We've gone to a lot of effort to ensure that the fifth edition
of **The Rough Guide to South America on a Budget** is
accurate and up-to-date. However, things change – places
get "discovered", opening hours are notoriously fickle,
restaurants and rooms raise prices or lower standards. If
you feel we've got it wrong or left something out, we'd like
to know, and if you can remember the address, the price,
the hours, the phone number, so much the better.

Please send your comments with the subject line
"Rough Guide South America on a Budget Update" to
mail@uk.roughguides.com. We'll credit all contributions
and send a copy of the next edition (or any other Rough
Guide if you prefer) for the very best emails.

Reader's updates

Thanks to all the readers who have taken the time to write in with comments and suggestions (and apologies if we've
inadvertently omitted or misspelt anyone's name):
Dave Bain; Charlotte de Beule; Andrew Coulthurst; Chris Dehondt; etwn123; Nikki Frick; Ariel Harroche; Ery Hughes;
Megan Kenna; Bryan Kingsfield; Tim Laslevic; Anna Letts; Marc and Mich; Jeremy Marx; Erika Massoud; Tom McCormick-
Cox; Corrie Moxon; Emma Maev O'Connell; Leena Pandit; Koos Reitsma; Howard Shallard-Brown; Adam Scherling; and
Tiffany Woods-Shepherd.

Acknowledgements

Steph Dyson All of the local people I met who offered me their time, wisdom and a pisco sour pick-me-up where
necessary; Lucho Hurtado at Incas del Perú; Nuevos Caminos Travel in Chachapoyas; Sara Humphreys for her invaluable
help and advice; the motley crew at El Jardin in Asunción; John Gimlette, who started it all; Olivia Richards, for her
unwavering optimism and enthusiasm; and Gonzalo Benavides, for his love, support and everything in between.
Nick Edwards would like to thank the following people for invaluable help and hospitality along the way: Naomi McKee,
Rio Amazonas in Santiago, Hostal Sonchek in San Pedro, Backpackers Hostel Iquique, and Ross of Sunny Days & Charlie of
Latinorizons in Arica. Thanks to Annie for silky smooth editing. Love as always to Maria and Gandalf at base camp.
Sara Humphreys Appreciation is due to the very helpful iPerú offices throughout the country and to various officials
from SERNANP. Thanks also to Ann-Marie Shaw for being such an understanding editor and to Adrian for constant home
support.
Daniel Jacobs Bolivia: Eduardo Zeballos, Claudio Vera Loza, Mauricio Vera Loza (Rosario), Derren Patterson (Gravity Bolivia)
and Jeff Sandifort (Climbing South America), Remo Baptista and Claudia Arteaga and Leticia Sandi (Adventure Brew),
Jasmin Caballero and Teresa Flores (America Tours Bolivia), Ani at the Green House in Oruro, Koala Tours & Koala Café in
Potosí, Alex Cruz Mamani and David Mamani Chambi (Vertical Bolivia, Uyuni), Fabiola Mitru (Hotel Mitru, Tupiza), Ana
Gabriela Sánchez (Villazón), Fatima Belmonte (Café Bistrot, Copacabana), Charlotte De Beule and Emma Maev O'Connell.
Brazil: Bob Nadkarni and everyone at The Maze in Rio, Patrick, Shane, Edge, Marcelo Armstrong (Favela Tour, Rio),
Liliana Ferrarese (Oasis, São Paulo), and special thanks to Teri Oliveira and Ernesto Klotzel. Colombia: Salome Aramburo
Calle, Martha Belcasas, Estebano Jordan and Simone Heinke (Hostal la Jangada, Leticia), Oscar Gilède (Colombian
Highlands, Villa de Leyva), Wilson Torres (Cocuy), José Navarro (Guadalupe), Shaun Clohesy (Macondo Hostel, San Gil),

Tim Woodhouse and Milo Butterick (KGB, Bucaramanga), Tim Harbour (Plantation House, Salento), Isabel Cristina Giraldo and Felipe Echevery (Paramo Trek, Salento), Greg Hillen (Lake View Hostel, Guatapé), Nick Martin (Enso Hostel, Medellín). Venezuela: Alasdair Baverstock and Claudia Beckmann (Casa Nova and Hostal Nuevo Colonial, Choroní).

Anna Kaminski I would like to thank Mani and Ed, my fellow authors and Annie the editor, as well as the Erratic Rock team, Patagonia Camp and EcoCamp Patagonia, Rob & Monica, Sarina, Carolyn, Kevin, the drivers who fished my car out of the mud in Hornopiren, Kris Tompkins, Amory & Fernando, Marie & Fernando, Daniel, Silvie, Mariano, Zoe & Leo, Maison Nomade, Patagonia House and everyone else who helped me along the way.

Shafik Megjhi Thanks to the many travellers and locals who helped out along the way. A special muchas gracias to: Ann-Marie Shaw; Mani Ramaswamy, Ed Aves and Becca Hallett; Kati Taylor; Janette Simbron; everyone at Chalalan Ecolodge; Lyliam Gonzalez; Miriam and Efrem Hinojosa; Gabriela Aranibar and Stephen Taranto; Frank Reinkens; Daniela Röthlisberger; Sylvain Truchot; Naomi McKee at Senderos; Simon Evans at Chimu Adventures; Carolina Gutierrez Prado at Accor; Kristina Shreck of Azure PR; Janak Jani in Valpo; Iain Hardy in Valpo; Cyril Christensen of Chiloé Natural; James Grant-Peterkin of Easter Island Spirit; Lanny Grossman; John Rees in Punta Arenas; Yamila Giserman of Destino Argentina; Alberto Serrano in Puerto Williams; Jean, Nizar and Nina Meghji; and Sioned Jones.

Sorrel Moseley-Williams With thanks to Richard Townley for the company, Juani of Bio Conexión in Jujuy, El Porvenir de Cafayate for the wine, Lucia Romero, Dolores Lavaque and Alicia Lanfranconi of Finca Quara, Juliana Estevez of Destino Argentina and Allan Kelin.

Todd Obolsky Many, many thanks to Paulo, Suzanne, Beatrice, Emilie(!), and especially my Dad, who always encourages my efforts in travel and in life. Also I'm very appreciative of the support of Aaron Paiva Leyton of TourGuidePeru and Rex Broekman of The Huaraz Telegraph.

Daniel Schechter Heartfelt thanks to the following fellow travellers, expats, lodge holders and tourism experts for providing their time, knowledge, insights and more: in Guyana, Colin Edwards, Raquel Thomas, Candace Phillips, Tom Martin and Patrick van de Velde; in Suriname Marcel Chandoesing, Gijs Haanschoten & Annemarie Voerman, Thais Wilson, Randy Ngaliman, Jason Cressey, Eline Dirkzwager, Eury Dest, Joris Bens and Fabienne; in French Guiana, Nadia Polemone, Elsa Mora, Jörn Harland and Vanessa Van de Walle. Special mention is merited by Surinamer German Blank for saving my skin in Parbo.

Iain Stewart Thanks to my expert editor Ann-Marie Shaw and all the Rough Guides team. In Ecuador I was helped by Ecuador Freedom Bikes, staff at iTur throughout the country and Royal Galapagos.

Madelaine Triebe Many thanks to Edward Aves for the initial commission, Ann-Marie Shaw for being a pleasure to work with and to my family and friends. A very special thanks to Larissa and her invaluable guidance in Pantanal and Cuiabá and to Tatiana, Vagner, Diego and Matheus for showing me the best (and sometimes worst!) of Campo Grande and Corumbá. Muitosbeijos!

Chris Wallace Thanks to Claudio Chena at Mãe Natureza Ecoturismo, Antonio Gomes at Amazon Antonio Jungle Tours, Gil Serique of Gil Serique tours in Alter do Chao, and the great Jono from Hostel Galeria 13, in Salvador.

Photo credits

(Key: T-top; C-centre; B-bottom; L-left; R-right)

Index

Q

R

Map symbols

The symbols below are used on maps throughout the book

▬▬▬	International boundary	Ⓜ▶	Metro stop	🎿	Ski area	⚓	Swimming pool
─────	Province boundary	@	Internet access	🏛	Monument	/l\	Volcano
▓▓▓▓	Highway	✉	Post office	♠	Museum	▲	Mountain peak
═══════	Main road	ⓘ	Tourist office	🍇	Vineyard	⌃⌃	Mountain range
┅┅┅┅	Minor road	☏	Telephone office	⊤	Gardens	✡	Synagogue
▪▪▪▪	Pedestrian road	$	Bank/ATM	⛽	Petrol station	☪	Mosque
┉┉┉┉┉	Steps	⊞	Hospital	⚓	Harbour/port	✝	Church
┄┄┄┄	Unpaved road	◆	Place of interest	⛵	Boat	▓▓	Building
━╍━	Railway	◆	National park	⛳	Golf course	🏪	Market
─ ─ ─ ─	Path	◠	Cave	∩	Arch	⬭	Stadium
────────	Ferry route	∴	Ruin	🗼	Lighthouse	▢	Park/national park
▬▬▬	Wall	♜	Fortress	⛺	Mountain refuge	🏖	Beach
┈┈┈┈	Funicular	▮	Tower	🏛	Park HQ	▢	Christian cemetery
●–●–●	Cable car	🔀	Viewpoint	⚓	Border crossing	▢	Marsh/swamp
✈	International airport	⊠	Gate	╲╱	Spring	▨	Glacier
✈	Domestic airport/airstrip	⚐	Campsite	🎆	Waterfall	▢	Salt flats
★	Transport stop	⊙	Statue				

Listings key

■ Accommodation

● Eating

■ Drinking/nightlife

● Shopping

ESCAPE THE EVERYDAY

ADVENTURE BECKONS
YOU JUST NEED TO KNOW WHERE TO LOOK

roughguides.com